DRAMA

Classical to Contemporary

John C. Coldewey
University of Washington

W. R. Streitberger
University of Washington

Prentice Hall   Upper Saddle River, NJ 07458

Library of Congress Cataloging-in-Publication Data
Drama : classical to contemporary / John C. Coldewey, W. R.
Streitberger.—1st/ ed.
  p. cm.
  Includes bibliographical references.
  ISBN 0–13–359647–8
  1. Plays. I. Coldewey, John C. II. Streitberger, W. R.
PN6111.D67 1998
808.82—dc20   96—30972 CIP

Editorial Director : Charlyce Jones Owen
Acquisitions Editor: Carrie Brandon
Director of Production and Manufacturing: Barbara Kittle
Senior Managing Editor: Bonnie Biller
Production Editor: Randy Pettit
Manufacturing Manager: Nick Sklitsis
Prepress and Manufacturing Buyer: Mary Ann Gloriande
Marketing Director: Gina Sluss
Marketing Manager: Rob Mejia
Interior Design: Lisa Jones
Art Director: Jayne Conte
Cover Design: Bruce Kenselaar
Cover Art: Edward Hopper, American (1882–1967) "Two on the Aisle" (1935 .49), oil on
    canvas, 40 1/8 × 48 1/4 in. (101.9 × 122.5 cm). The Toledo Museum of Art, Toledo,
    Ohio; Purchased with Funds from the Libbey Endownment, gift of Edward
    Drummond Libbey.
Page Formatting: Kerry Reardon, David Tay
Photo Researcher: Rona Tucillo

This book was set in 10/12 Palatino,
and printed and bound by Courier Westford.
The cover was printed by Phoenix Color Corp.

 © 1998 by Prentice-Hall Inc.
Simon & Schuster / A Viacom Company
Upper Saddle River, New Jersey 07458

For permission to use copyrighted material, grateful
acknowledgement is made to the copyright holders
listed on page 1378, which is considered an extension
of this copyright page.

Printed in the United States of America
10 9 8 7 6 5 4 3 2 1

ISBN 0-13-359647-8

Prentice-Hall International (UK) Limited, *London*
Prentice-Hall of Australia Pty. Limited, *Sydney*
Prentice-Hall Canada Inc., *Toronto*
Prentice-Hall Hispanoamerica, S.A., *Mexico*
Prentice-Hall of India Private Limited, *New Delhi*
Prentice-Hall of Japan, Inc., *Tokyo*
Simon & Schuster Asia Pte., Ltd., *Singapore*
Editora Prentice-Hall do Brasil, Ltda., *Rio de Janeiro*

Contents

iii

PART VII: CONTEMPORARY DRAMA AND THEATER *1039*

Preface

Drama: *Classical to Contemporary* brings together a collection of thirty-eight important plays from the classical period to the present day, making it one of the most comprehensive anthologies of drama available anywhere. It includes generous selections of Greek drama (four plays), of medieval drama (two plays), of Renaissance drama (four plays), of neoclassical and Restoration drama (three plays), of early modern European drama (seven plays), of later modern European and American drama (seven plays), and a rich and varied selection of contemporary drama (twelve plays). The earliest play included was written around 458 B.C., the latest in 1994.

Drama: Classical to Contemporary is divided into parts that focus on important periods in the history of Western drama and theater: the classical drama of ancient Greece; the medieval, Renaissance, neoclassical, and modern drama of Europe; and contemporary drama from Europe, Africa, South America, and North America. The plays have been selected to serve the needs of both beginning and intermediate students, and the anthology can be used in literature, drama, and humanities departments in a variety of courses, such as introductions to drama, general surveys of drama and theater, studies of tragedy and/or comedy, and studies of tradition and/or innovation in drama since the late nineteenth century. The anthology contains a sound selection of historically important plays, but proportionately the emphasis is on modern and contemporary plays.

The study of drama has undergone tremendous change during the late twentieth century. *Drama: Classical to Contemporary* reflects that change by providing substantial selections from critical essays that illustrate different approaches to the experience of reading drama. Each part of *Drama: Classical to Contemporary* begins with an introduction that situates drama in the context of cultural and theatrical practices of the period, describing contemporary production practices, audience expectations, and performance. Illustrations of theater architecture, costuming, and other conventions are also included in each section to help the reader develop an understanding of staging possibilities. Each play is prefaced by a brief biography of the playwright and a short introduction that reviews the critical reception of the play and discusses interpretative possibilities. Each part of the book concludes with excerpts from critical readings as well as documents or essays that reflect aesthetic and cultural concerns in the period. This material has been selected to complement our contemporary interest in situating drama and theater within the contexts of literary history, theater history, and social history, and in discussing drama in terms of its representation of gender, race, ethnicity, sexuality, economics, and politics.

Drama: Classical to Contemporary includes traditionally important statements on the drama and theater by Aristotle, Sir Philip Sidney, Ben Jonson, Madame de Staël, Henri Bergson, Émile Zola, Bertolt Brecht, Antonin Artaud, Martin Esslin, and many others. It also includes recent criticism by Victor Turner, Elaine Showalter, Eldred Durosimi Jones, David Mamet, Howard Barker, and others. These critical perspectives underscore the ways in which drama and theater have contributed to shaping the culture of different periods.

Drama: Classical to Contemporary is designed as a resource for students of drama and theater. In addition to an ample and representative selection of plays and commentaries, it includes four appendices. Appendix 1, "Writing About Drama," offers suggestions to help beginning students in the process of writing essays on dramatic and theatrical subjects. Appendix 2 is a glossary with definitions of dramatic, theatrical, and literary concepts and terms. Appendix 3, "Suggestions for Further Reading," provides an up-to-date selected bibliography of theoretical studies and criticism on the major periods of drama and theater. It also includes biographies, critical studies, and theoretical essays on all of the playwrights and their plays. Appendix 4, "Film and Video Productions," offers a handy guide to film and video productions of the plays included in this volume.

All of these resources combine in *Drama: Classical to Contemporary* to help students grasp the traditional issues in understanding and interpreting drama, to encourage them to investigate drama in wider theatrical and cultural contexts, and to help them shape informed responses to the plays.

ACKNOWLEDGMENTS

In the preparation of this anthology we have accrued many debts, and it is a pleasure to acknowledge them. We would like first of all to thank the team of professionals at Prentice Hall, who initially approached us with the idea of such a text and who have been unfailingly supportive throughout its preparation. These include: Alison Reeves, D. Anthony English, Joan Polk, Nancy Perry, Michael Kramer, Randy Pettit, Kathy Graehl, and Fred Rothwell.

In addition, we are especially grateful for the help and guidance we received from the many teachers of theater and drama who offered their unvarnished advice and suggestions regarding the selection of plays and accompanying materials in this book. Their enthusiasm, caveats, and criticism regarding our early typescript draft of the work helped provide its current. They are :

Mary M. Dunlap, *Appalacian State University*
JoAnna S. Mink, *Mankato State University*

D.C. Payne, *American University*
Sally Burke, *University of Rhode Island*
Sanford Sternlicht, *Syracuse University*
Norma Jenckes, *University of Cincinnati*
Robert D. Hume, *Pennsylvania State University*
Jenny S. Spencer, *University of Massachusetts*
Richard Barr, *Rutgers University*
Anne Marie Drew, *United States Naval Academy*
George L. Meshke, *Yakima Valley Community College*
Morgan Y. Himelstein, *Adelphi University*
Allan Lefcowitz, *United States Naval Academy*
Don Kunz, *University of Rhode Island*
Franklin Case, *Eastern Michigan University*
Alexis Levitin, *SUNY Plattsburgh*
Ina Rae Hark, *University of South Carolina*
Howard L. McMillen, *Indiana State University*
Gene Barnett, *Fairleigh Dickinson University*
Evelyn S. Newlyn, *SUNY Brockport*
Mildred Kuner, *CUNY Hunter College*
Robert Grimes, *California University of Pennsylvania*

JOHN C. COLDEWEY
W.R. STREITBERGER

Introduction

More than two thousand years ago, the Greek philosopher Aristotle offered a succinct but powerfully apt definition of drama: Drama, to translate his original words, is the "imitation of an action." Action is fundamental to our conception of drama; in fact, the word *drama* is derived from a Greek verb meaning "to do" or "to act." The action of drama, however, is not "real" action, but action imitated or represented; note that in their most specific usage, the words *act* and *actor* refer not to real-life actions, but to play-acting before an audience or camera. Defining drama as the "imitation of an action" also distinguishes the genre from other literary forms. A novel or other narrative work may be made up of actions, but these are described, not imitated. A lyric poem may imitate an internal state of mind or observation but it is not embodied in action. In its fusion of narrative and poetry, early drama—such as that on which Aristotle based his definition—also brought together action and imitation.

The action of drama can be highly physical, of course. *Hamlet*, like Shakespeare's other tragedies, includes considerable onstage violence and sword-play. The action of drama can also be internal or psychological, however. In fact, many would argue that the real action of *Hamlet* is its depiction of its protagonist's internal struggle, a struggle that is manifested in the external action of the play. Nothing much happens physically in *Oedipus Rex*, other than characters entering and exiting the stage. Nonetheless, a complex action of inquiry and discovery is played out as the Theban king Oedipus seeks to find the source of his country's sufferings. The action of a drama is the sum of everything that happens in the course of the play.

It should also be noted that the imitation of action in drama is not a straight-forward imitation of life. Rather, it is a highly structured, even stylized, imitation that often includes unrealistic elements, such as characters speaking in verse, and is always marked by the shape of a plot, a pattern of exposition, anticipation, climax, and ultimate resolution that we do not find in life. So if we think of drama as the "imitation of action," we must do so in a flexible, imaginative way.

The history of dramatic activity extends far back, beyond historical or literary records, and virtually every culture in every period has produced spectacles or shows of one sort or another. All of these are of some interest to students of drama, history, and anthropology because such shows provide insights into the cultures that produced them. But a few important periods in Western history produced drama and theater of remarkable durability—plays that are still performed, playing spaces that are still used, and theatrical conventions that continue to influence not only the way we think about drama and theater, but the way playwrights still write their plays as well. These periods—classical, medieval, Renaissance, neoclassical and Restoration, modern, and, of course, contemporary—are the focus of this drama anthology. Reading plays from all these periods requires a sensitivity to how radically cultures have differed and continue to differ from each other, and it will be important to keep in mind the cultural contexts discussed in each of the section introductions. In addition, the following general guidelines should make it easier to read plays effectively from the start.

Reading Drama

By their very nature, plays are intended to be performed and to be seen and heard. We attend the performance of a play in a theater—a word that derives from the Greek "seeing place"—and there we form part of an audience—a word that derives from the Latin "to hear." In a theater we experience the sights and sounds of the production of a play script by a director, designers, and actors. Each setting or stage property we see, each sound we hear, each change of lighting we experience, as well as each of the actors' movements, gestures, facial expressions, and vocal intonations is the result of an artistic conception of how best to communicate the action of the play. Directors, designers, and actors base these artistic conceptions on their own reading of the play script. In order to read effectively, we too must give attention to some of the same features of the play that these theater artists have.

Literate audiences have been reading plays since the sixteenth century, when drama began to be staged in commercial theaters and plays were first printed for private reading. By the late nineteenth century, reading plays had become so much a part of ordinary literary culture that playwrights often published their plays before they were performed in theaters. This development in turn affected the way playwrights composed plays. Henrik Ibsen and other playwrights included detailed stage directions, and George Bernard Shaw wrote long prefaces, some almost as long as the plays themselves. Increasingly, such features were directed toward a reading audience. Now, in the late twentieth century, plays are expected to be read as well as performed.

Reading a play is a different experience from attending a theatrical performance. Attending a theatrical production is a social experience; reading is a private matter. We must follow a performance at its own pace and according to its own interpretation; reading can be a leisurely and open-ended activity. As readers we can take time to examine each line carefully and to pause over words or images. We can refer to earlier scenes to trace clues or connections or image patterns, and we can appreciate ever more complicated and sophisticated implications and ranges of meaning. We can balance several interpretative possibilities of a play in our imaginations at the same time, never having to choose one over another.

Reading a play is also a different experience from reading prose fiction. When we read a novel or story, we encounter a plot, characters, and a setting just as we do in reading a play. As mentioned earlier, however, novels and stories do not imitate an action; they describe or represent action, often in a way that can seem more real than life around us. When we read plays or witness theatrical performances, on the other hand, we are aware of the imitation or the pretense of characters coming to life on a stage set before an audience, making entrances and exits into an offstage void. When reading plays, we interpret them not as an imaginative reality, but in performance. Consequently, reading plays depends on certain basic skills.

Play scripts, with their directions and notations, can be compared to written musical compositions; both are notations for performance. Reading music requires not only the knowledge of the measures, keys, and notes—the various symbols represented on the page—but also the ability to hear in our imaginations how the music might sound in performance. So too in reading a play we need not only the ability to read the words on the page, but also the ability to imagine how the play might look and sound in performance

At the outset we need to understand that all of the information contained in a play script is important and that giving sufficient attention to this information will enhance our reading experience. We should begin reading by examining the very first things we see, the list of characters and whatever descriptions of them the playwright might provide. This is our introduction to the play's characters and will help us sort them out as we read their dialogue. Next, we should pay careful attention to whatever description of the set the playwright provides. We should try not only to envision the physical details of the set but also to imagine the atmosphere or feeling it evokes. As we read through the play, we should try to picture where and how the action takes place within the set. Stage directions can help us here, but not always; sometimes we have to infer action from the dialogue. In any case, where the actors stand and how they move within the set often communicates important information. Finally, when we read the dialogue we should try to understand what the characters hope to accomplish when they speak. Not only what the characters say but how they say it is important, and on some occasions even what a character does not say can communicate valuable information. As we imagine the tone of the dialogue, we should try also to imagine what body language or gestures the characters might use to reveal themselves.

When we stage a play in our imaginations, it is only natural that we draw on the conventions of the theaters most familiar to us. But not all the plays in this anthology were written with the conventions of modern theater in mind. Over the more than two thousand years of history covered by the plays in this anthology, different kinds of playing spaces have come and gone. The physical features of a theater have a tremendous effect on the relationship between the audience and the action onstage, and this relationship influences the way playwrights conceive and write their plays. The large outdoor public theaters in Shakespeare's time, for example, were physically very different from the smaller indoor theaters with proscenium stages in Chekhov's time. Plays in the public theaters of

Shakespeare's time were staged during the afternoon on thrust stages surrounded by the audience on at least three sides. No changeable scenery and few properties were used. Shakespeare's theater, like many earlier theaters, was not representational; it depended on an active imaginative agreement, a kind of understood contract between audience and actors that the same stage set could represent any location from midnight in a forest to high noon in a sumptuous palace. Not surprisingly, the characters in Shakespeare's plays frequently describe the time or setting or atmosphere in their speeches, and on occasion they urge the audience to draw on their own imaginative powers to fully appreciate the action.

By contrast, plays performed in the indoor theaters of Chekhov's time were usually staged in the evening with artificial lighting on proscenium stages faced by a silent audience sitting in a darkened auditorium. This theater, like many modern theaters, was representational, but it too depended on an imaginative agreement between audience and actors. The stage behind the proscenium arch represented an entire "real" world, one that the audience could see into through its missing fourth wall. Thus theaters of different cultures and different historical periods vary greatly from one another, and it may prove helpful to look at the illustrations of theaters provided in the introductions to each part of this anthology. They can help a reader, sometimes distant in space and time, to imagine the physical conditions of performance for actors and audiences, and they can help a reader to imaginatively stage the plays written especially for those spaces.

In the following section we examine Susan Glaspell's *Trifles*, one of the most widely anthologized one-act plays written in America, as an example of how to go about reading a play.

Reading Susan Glaspell's *Trifles*

Written and first performed in 1916, *Trifles* is a taut, compact drama portraying a murder investigation at an isolated Midwestern farmhouse in the dead of winter. Admired for its attention to realistic physical detail and its naturalistic dialogue, the play is also notable for the way it explores tense differences between male and female perceptions and values.

Glaspell (1882–1948) was born in Iowa and later worked as a reporter and writer there, in Chicago, and in New York's Greenwich Village. She and her husband formed the Provincetown Players to present experimental and unconventional plays by writers who could not get backing in commercial theaters. *Trifles* was Glaspell's first play, written for the company's opening season. Based on a murder trial she had covered as a reporter, it was conceived, Glaspell later said, as she sat in a theater, imagining the action coming to life as she looked at the bare stage. She later wrote a short story based on the play, titled "A Jury of Her Peers."

Trifles

SUSAN GLASPELL

CHARACTERS

GEORGE HENDERSON, *County Attorney*
HENRY PETERS, *Sheriff*
LEWIS HALE, *A Neighboring Farmer*

MRS. PETERS
MRS. HALE

SCENE: *The kitchen in the now abandoned farmhouse of* JOHN WRIGHT, *a gloomy kitchen, and left without having been put in order—unwashed pans under the sink, a loaf of bread outside the bread-box, a dish-towel on the table—other signs of incompleted work. At the rear the outer door opens and the* SHERIFF *comes in followed by the* COUNTY ATTORNEY *and* HALE. *The* SHERIFF *and* HALE *are men in middle life, the* COUNTY ATTORNEY *is a young man; all are much bundled up and go at once to the stove. They are followed by the two women—the* SHERIFF'S *wife first; she is a slight wiry woman, a thin nervous face.* MRS. HALE *is larger and would ordinarily be called more comfortable look-ing, but she is disturbed now and looks fearfully about as she enters. The women have come in slowly, and stand close together near the door.*

COUNTY ATTORNEY: (*Rubbing his hands.*) This feels good. Come up to the fire, ladies.

MRS. PETERS: (*After taking a step forward.*) I'm not—cold.

SHERIFF: (*Unbuttoning his overcoat and stepping away from the stove as if to mark the beginning of official business.*) Now, Mr. Hale, before we move things about, you explain to Mr. Henderson just what you saw when you came here yester-day morning.

COUNTY ATTORNEY: By the way, has anything been moved? Are things just as you left them yester-day?

SHERIFF: (*Looking about.*) It's just the same. When it dropped below zero last night I thought I'd better send Frank out this morning to make a fire for us—no use getting pneumonia with a big case on, but I told him not to touch any-thing except the stove—and you know Frank.

COUNTY ATTORNEY: Somebody should have been left here yesterday.

SHERIFF: Oh—yesterday. When I had to send Frank to Morris Center for that man who went crazy—I want you to know I had my hands full yester-day. I knew you could get back from Omaha by today and as long as I went over everything here myself—

COUNTY ATTORNEY: Well, Mr. Hale, tell just what hap-pened when you came here yesterday morning.

HALE: Harry and I had started to town with a load of potatoes. We came along the road from my place and as I got here I said, "I'm going to see if I can't get John Wright to go in with me on a party telephone." I spoke to Wright about it once before and he put me off, saying folks talked too much anyway, and all he asked was peace and quiet—I guess you know about how much he talked himself; but I thought maybe if I went to the house and talked about it before his wife, though I said to Harry that I didn't know as what his wife wanted made much dif-ference to John—

COUNTY ATTORNEY: Let's talk about that later, Mr. Hale. I do want to talk about that, but tell now just what happened when you got to the house.

HALE: I didn't hear or see anything; I knocked at the door, and still it was all quiet inside. I knew they must be up, it was past eight o'clock. So I knocked again, and I thought I heard some-body say, "Come in." I wasn't sure, I'm not sure yet, but I opened the door—this door (*indicating the door by which the two women are still standing*) and there in that rocker—(*point-ing to it*) sat Mrs. Wright.

[*They all look at the rocker.*]

COUNTY ATTORNEY: What—was she doing?

HALE: She was rockin' back and forth. She had her apron in her hand and was kind of—pleating it.

COUNTY ATTORNEY: And how did she—look?

HALE: Well, she looked queer.

COUNTY ATTORNEY: How do you mean—queer?

HALE: Well, as if she didn't know what she was going to do next. And kind of done up.

COUNTY ATTORNEY: How did she seem to feel about your coming?

HALE: Why, I don't think she minded—one way or other. She didn't pay much attention. I said, "How do, Mrs. Wright, it's cold, ain't it?" And she said, "Is it?"—and went on kind of pleating at her apron. Well, I was surprised; she didn't ask me to come up to the stove, or to sit down, but just sat there, not even looking at me, so I said, "I want to see John." And then she—laughed. I guess you would call it a laugh. I thought of Harry and the team outside, so I said a little sharp: "Can't I see John?" "No," she says, kind o' dull like. "Ain't he home?" says I. "Yes," says she, "he's home." "Then why can't I see him?" I asked her, out of patience. "'Cause he's dead," says she. *"Dead?"* says I. She just nodded her head, not getting a bit excited, but rockin' back and forth. "Why—where is he?" says I, not knowing what to say. She just pointed upstairs—like that (*himself pointing to the room above*). I got up, with the idea of going up there. I walked from there to here—then I says, "Why, what did he die of?" "He died of a rope round his neck," says she, and just went on pleatin' at her apron. Well, I went out and called Harry. I thought I might—need help. We went upstairs and there he was lyin'—

COUNTY ATTORNEY: I think I'd rather have you go into that upstairs, where you can point it all out. Just go on now with the rest of the story.

HALE: Well, my first thought was to get that rope off. It looked …(*Stops, his face twitches*)…but Harry, he went up to him, and he said, "No, he's dead all right, and we'd better not touch anything." So we went back down stairs. She was still sitting that same way. "Has anybody been notified?" I asked. "No," says she, unconcerned. "Who did this, Mrs. Wright?" said Harry. He said it business-like—and she stopped pleatin' of her apron. "I don't know," she says. "You don't *know?*" says Harry. "No," says she. "Weren't you sleepin' in the bed with him?" says Harry. "Yes," says she, "but I was on the inside." "Somebody slipped a rope round his neck and strangled him and you didn't wake up?" says Harry. "I didn't wake up," she said after him. We must 'a looked as

if we didn't see how that could be, for after a minute she said, "I sleep sound." Harry was going to ask her more questions but I said maybe we ought to let her tell her story first to the coroner, or the sheriff, so Harry went fast as he could to Rivers' place, where there's a telephone.

COUNTY ATTORNEY: And what did Mrs. Wright do when she knew that you had gone for the coroner?

HALE: She moved from that chair to this one over here (*Pointing to a small chair in the corner*) and just sat there with her hands held together and looking down. I got a feeling that I ought to make some conversation, so I said I had come in to see if John wanted to put in a telephone, and at that she started to laugh, and then she stopped and looked at me—scared. (*The County Sheriff, who has had his notebook out, makes a note.*) I dunno, maybe it wasn't scared. I wouldn't like to say it was. Soon Harry got back, and then Dr. Lloyd came, and you, Mr. Peters, and so I guess that's all I know that you don't.

COUNTY ATTORNEY: (*Looking around.*) I guess we'll go upstairs first—and then out to the barn and around there. (*To the* SHERIFF.) You're convinced that there was nothing important here—nothing that would point to any motive.

SHERIFF: Nothing here but kitchen things.

[*The* COUNTY ATTORNEY, *after again looking around the kitchen, opens the door of a cupboard closet. He gets up on a chair and looks on a shelf. Pulls his hand away, sticky.*]

COUNTY ATTORNEY: Here's a nice mess.

[*The women draw nearer.*]

MRS. PETERS: (*To the other woman.*) Oh, her fruit; it did freeze. (*To the* LAWYER.) She worried about that when it turned so cold. She said the fire'd go out and her jars would break.

SHERIFF: Well, can you beat the women! Held for murder and worryin' about her preserves.

COUNTY ATTORNEY: I guess before we're through she may have something more serious than preserves to worry about.

HALE: Well, women are used to worrying over trifles.

[*The two women move a little closer together.*]

COUNTY ATTORNEY: (*With the gallantry of a young politician.*) And yet, for all their worries, what would we do without the ladies? (*The women do not unbend. He goes to the sink, takes a dipperful of water from the pail and pouring it into a* basin, *washes his hands. Starts to wipe them on the roller-towel, turns it for a cleaner place.*) Dirty towels! (*Kicks his foot against the pans under the sink.*) Not much of a housekeeper, would you say, ladies?

MRS. HALE: (*Stiffly.*) There's a great deal of work to be done on a farm.

COUNTY ATTORNEY: To be sure. And yet (*With a little bow to her*) I know there are some Dickson county farmhouses which do not have such roller towels.

[*He gives it a pull to expose its full length again.*]

MRS. HALE: Those towels get dirty awful quick. Men's hands aren't always as clean as they might be.

COUNTY ATTORNEY: Ah, loyal to your sex, I see. But you and Mrs. Wright were neighbors. I suppose you were friends, too.

MRS. HALE: (*Shaking her head.*) I've not seen much of her of late years. I've not been in this house— it's more than a year.

COUNTY ATTORNEY: And why was that? You didn't like her?

MRS. HALE: I liked her all well enough. Farmers' wives have their hands full, Mr. Henderson. And then—

COUNTY ATTORNEY: Yes—?

MRS. HALE: (*Looking about.*) It never seemed a very cheerful place.

COUNTY ATTORNEY: No—it's not cheerful. I shouldn't say she had the homemaking instinct.

MRS. HALE: Well, I don't know as Wright had, either.

COUNTY ATTORNEY: You mean that they didn't get on very well?

MRS. HALE: No, I don't mean anything. But I don't think a place'd be any cheerfuller for John Wright's being in it.

COUNTY ATTORNEY: I'd like to talk more of that a little later. I want to get the lay of things upstairs now.

[*He goes to the left, where three steps lead to a stair door.*]

SHERIFF: I suppose anything Mrs. Peters does'll be all right. She was to take in some clothes for her, you know, and a few little things. We left in such a hurry yesterday.

COUNTY ATTORNEY: Yes, but I would like to see what you take, Mrs. Peters, and keep an eye out for anything that might be of use to us.

MRS. PETERS: Yes, Mr. Henderson.

[*The women listen to the men's steps on the stairs, then look about the kitchen.*]

MRS. HALE: I'd hate to have men coming into my kitchen, snooping around and criticising.

[*She arranges the pans under sink which the* LAWYER *had shoved out of place.*]

MRS. PETERS: Of course it's no more than their duty.

MRS. HALE: Duty's all right, but I guess that deputy sheriff that came out to make the fire might have got a little of this on. (*Gives the roller towel a pull.*) Wish I'd thought of that sooner. Seems mean to talk about her for not having things slicked up when she had to come away in such a hurry.

MRS. PETERS: (*Who has gone to a small table in the left rear corner of the room, and lifted one end of a towel that covers a pan.*) She had bread set.

[*Stands still.*]

MRS. HALE: (*Eyes fixed on a loaf of bread beside the bread-box, which is on a low shelf at the other side of the room. Moves slowly toward it.*) She was going to put this in there. (*Picks up loaf, then abruptly drops it. In a manner of returning to familiar things.*) It's a shame about her fruit. I wonder if it's all gone. (*Gets up on the chair and looks.*) I think there's some here that's all right, Mrs. Peters. Yes—here; (*Holding it toward the window*) this is cherries, too. (*Looking again.*) I declare I believe that's the only one. (*Gets down, bottle in her hand. Goes to the sink and wipes it off on the outside.*) She'll feel awful bad after all her hard work in the hot weather. I remember the afternoon I put up my cherries last summer.

[*She puts the bottle on the big kitchen table, center of the room. With a sigh, is about to sit down in the rocking-chair. Before she is seated realizes what chair it is; with a slow look at it, steps back. The chair which she has touched rocks back and forth.*]

MRS. PETERS: Well, I must get those things from the front room closet. (*She goes to the door at the right, but after looking into the other room, steps back.*) You coming with me, Mrs. Hale? You could help me carry them.

[*They go in the other room; reappear,* MRS. PETERS *carrying a dress and skirt,* MRS. HALE *following with a pair of shoes.*]

MRS. PETERS: My, it's cold in there.

[*She puts the clothes on the big table, and hurries to the stove.*]

MRS. HALE: (*Examining the skirt.*) Wright was close. I think maybe that's why she kept so much to herself. She didn't even belong to the Ladies Aid. I suppose she felt she couldn't do her part, and then you don't enjoy things when you feel shabby. She used to wear pretty clothes and be lively, when she was Minnie Foster, one of the town girls singing in the choir. But that—oh, that was thirty years ago. This all you was to taken in?

MRS. PETERS: She said she wanted an apron. Funny thing to want, for there wasn't much to get you dirty in jail, goodness knows. But I suppose just to make her feel more natural. She said they was in the top drawer in this cupboard. Yes, here. And then her little shawl that always hung behind the door. (*Opens stair door and looks.*) Yes, here it is.

[*Quickly shuts door leading upstairs.*]

MRS. HALE: (*Abruptly moving toward her.*) Mrs. Peters?

MRS. PETERS: Yes, Mrs. Hale?

MRS. HALE: Do you think she did it?

MRS. PETERS: (*In a frightened voice.*) Oh, I don't know.

MRS. HALE: Well, I don't think she did. Asking for an apron and her little shawl. Worrying about her fruit.

MRS. PETERS: (*Starts to speak, glances up, where footsteps are heard in the room above. In a low voice.*) Mr. Peters says it looks bad for her. Mr. Henderson is awful sarcastic in a speech and he'll make fun of her sayin' she didn't wake up.

MRS. HALE: Well, I guess John Wright didn't wake when they was slipping that rope under his neck.

MRS. PETERS: No, it's strange. It must have been done awful crafty and still. They say it was such a—funny way to kill a man, rigging it all up like that.

MRS. HALE: That's just what Mr. Hale said. There was a gun in the house. He says that's what he can't understand.

MRS. PETERS: Mr. Henderson said coming out that what was needed for the case was a motive; something to show anger, or—sudden feeling.

MRS. HALE: (*Who is standing by the table.*) Well, I don't see any signs of anger around here. (*She puts her hand on the dish towel which lies on the table, stands looking down at table, one half of which is clean, the other half messy.*) It's wiped to here. (*Makes a move as if to finish work, then turns and looks at loaf of bread outside the breadbox. Drops towel. In that voice of coming back to familiar things.*) Wonder how they are finding things upstairs. I hope she had it a little more red-up up there. You know, it seems kind of *sneaking*. Locking her up in town and then coming out here and trying to get her own house to turn against her!

MRS. PETERS: But Mrs. Hale, the law is the law.

MRS. HALE: I s'pose 'tis. (*Unbuttoning her coat.*) Better loosen up your things, Mrs. Peters. You won't feel them when you go out.

[MRS. PETERS *takes off her fur tippet, goes to hang it on hook at back of room, stands looking at the under part of the small corner table.*]

MRS. PETERS: She was piecing a quilt.

[*She brings the large sewing basket and they look at the bright pieces.*]

MRS. HALE: It's log cabin pattern. Pretty, isn't it? I wonder if she was goin' to quilt it or just knot it?

[*Footsteps have been heard coming down the stairs. The* SHERIFF *enters followed by* HALE *and the* COUNTY ATTORNEY.]

SHERIFF: They wonder if she was going to quilt or just knot it!

[*The men laugh, the women look abashed.*]

COUNTY ATTORNEY: (*Rubbing his hands over the store.*) Frank's fire didn't do much up there, did it? Well, let's go out to the barn and get that cleared up.

[*The men go outside.*]

MRS. HALE: (*Resentfully.*) I don't know as there's anything so strange, our takin' up our time with little things while we're waiting for them to get the evidence. (*She sits down at the big table smoothing out a block with decision.*) I don't see as it's anything to laugh about.

MRS. PETERS: (*Apologetically.*) Of course they've got awful important things on their minds.

[*Pulls up a chair and joins* MRS. HALE *at the table.*]

MRS. HALE: (*Examining another block.*) Mrs. Peters, look at this one. Here, this is the one she was working on, and look at the sewing! All the rest of it has been so nice and even. And look at this! It's all over the place! Why, it looks as if she didn't know what she was about!

[*After she has said this they look at each other, then start to glance back at the door. After an instant* MRS. HALE *has pulled at a knot and ripped the sewing.*]

MRS. PETERS: Oh, what are you doing, Mrs. Hale?

MRS. HALE: (*Mildly.*) Just pulling out a stitch or two that's not sewed very good. (*Threading a needle.*) Bad sewing always made me fidgety.

MRS. PETERS: (*Nervously.*) I don't think we ought to touch things.

MRS. HALE: I'll just finish up this end. (*Suddenly stopping and leaning forward.*) Mrs. Peters?

MRS. PETERS: Yes, Mrs. Hale?

MRS. HALE: What do you suppose she was so nervous about?

MRS. PETERS: Oh—I don't know. I don't know as she was nervous. I sometimes sew awful queer when I'm just tired. (MRS. HALE *starts to say something, looks at* MRS. PETERS, *then goes on sewing.*) Well I must get these things wrapped up. They may be through sooner than we think. (*Putting apron and other things together.*) I wonder where I can find a piece of paper, and string.

MRS. HALE: In that cupboard, maybe.

MRS. PETERS: (*Looking in cupboard.*) Why, here's a birdcage. (*Holds it up.*) Did she have a bird, Mrs. Hale?

MRS. HALE: Why, I don't know whether she did or not—I've not been here for so long. There was a man around last year selling canaries cheap, but I don't know as she took one; maybe she did. She used to sing real pretty herself.

MRS. PETERS: (*Glancing around.*) Seems funny to think of a bird here. But she must have had one, or why would she have a cage? I wonder what happened to it.

MRS. HALE: I s'pose maybe the cat got it.

MRS. PETERS: No, she didn't have a cat. She's got that feeling some people have about cats—being afraid of them. My cat got in her room and she was real upset and asked me to take it out.

MRS. HALE: My sister Bessie was like that. Queer, ain't it?

MRS. PETERS: (*Examining the cage.*) Why, look at this door. It's broke. One hinge is pulled apart.

MRS. HALE: (*Looking too.*) Looks as if someone must have been rough with it.

MRS. PETERS: Why, yes.

[*She brings the cage forward and puts it on the table.*]

MRS. HALE: I wish if they're going to find any evidence they'd be about it. I don't like this place.

MRS. PETERS: But I'm awful glad you came with me, Mrs. Hale. It would be lonesome for me sitting here alone.

MRS. HALE: It would, wouldn't it? (*Dropping her sewing.*) But I tell you what I do wish, Mrs. Peters. I wish I had come over sometimes when *she* was here. I—(*Looking around the room.*)—wish I had.

MRS. PETERS: But of course you were awful busy, Mrs. Hale—your house and your children.

MRS. HALE: I could've come. I stayed away because it weren't cheerful—and that's why I ought to have come. I—I've never liked this place. Maybe because it's down in a hollow and you don't see the road. I dunno what it is, but it's a lonesome place and always was. I wish I had come over to see Minnie Foster sometimes. I can see now—

[*Shakes her head.*]

MRS. PETERS: Well, you mustn't reproach yourself, Mrs. Hale. Somehow we just don't see how it is with other folks until—something comes up.

MRS. HALE: Not having children makes less work—but it makes a quiet house, and Wright out to work all day, and no company when he did come in. Did you know John Wright, Mrs. Peters?

MRS. PETERS: Not to know him; I've seen him in town. They say he was a good man.

MRS. HALE: Yes—good; he didn't drink, and kept his word as well as most, I guess, and paid his debts. But he was a hard man, Mrs. Peters. Just to pass the time of day with him—(*Shivers.*) Like a raw wind that gets to the bone. (*Pauses, her eye falling on the cage.*) I should think she would 'a wanted a bird. But what do you suppose went with it?

MRS. PETERS: I don't know, unless it got sick and died.

[*She reaches over and swings the broken door, swings it again, both women watch it.*]

MRS. HALE: You weren't raised round here, were you? (MRS. PETERS *shakes her head.*) You didn't know—her?

MRS. PETERS: Not till they brought her yesterday.

MRS. HALE: She—come to think of it, she was kind of like a bird herself—real sweet and pretty, but kind of timid and—fluttery. How—she—did—change. (*Silence; then as if struck by a happy thought and relieved to get back to everyday things.*) Tell you what, Mrs. Peters, why don't you take the quilt in with you? It might take up her mind.

MRS. PETERS: Why, I think that's a real nice idea, Mrs. Hale. There couldn't possibly be any objection to it, could there? Now, just what would I take? I wonder if her patches are in here—and her things.

[*They look in the sewing basket.*]

MRS. HALE: Here's some red. I expect this has got sewing things in it. (*Brings out a fancy box.*) What a pretty box. Looks like something somebody would give you. Maybe her scissors are in here. (*Opens box. Suddenly puts her hand to her nose.*) Why—(Mrs. Peters *bends nearer, then turns her face away.*) There's something wrapped up in this piece of silk.

MRS. PETERS: Why, this isn't her scissors.

MRS. HALE: (*Lifting the silk.*) Oh, Mrs. Peters—it's—

[Mrs. Peters *bends closer.*]

MRS. PETERS: It's the bird.

MRS. HALE: (*Jumping up.*) But, Mrs. Peters—look at it! Its neck! Look at its neck! It's all—other side *to.*

MRS. PETERS: Somebody—wrung—its—neck.

[*Their eyes meet. A look of growing comprehension, of horror. Steps are heard outside.* MRS. HALE *slips box under quilt pieces, and sinks into her chair. Enter* SHERIFF *and* COUNTY ATTORNEY. MRS. PETERS *rises.*]

COUNTY ATTORNEY: (*As one turning from serious things to little pleasantries.*) Well, ladies, have you decided whether she was going to quilt it or knot it?

MRS. PETERS: We think she was going to—knot it.

COUNTY ATTORNEY: Well, that's interesting, I'm sure. (*Seeing the birdcage.*) Has the bird flown?

MRS. HALE: (*Putting more quilt pieces over the box.*) We think the—cat got it.

COUNTY ATTORNEY: (*Preoccupied.*) Is there a cat?

[MRS. HALE *glances in a quick covert way at* MRS. PETERS.]

MRS. PETERS: Well, not *now.* They're superstitious, you know. They leave.

COUNTY ATTORNEY: (*To* SHERIFF PETERS, *continuing an interrupted conversation.*) No sign at all of anyone having come from the outside. Their own rope. Now let's go up again and go over it piece by piece. (*They start upstairs.*) It would have to have been someone who knew just the—

[MRS. PETERS *sits down. The two women sit there not looking at one another, but as if peering into something and at the same time holding back. When they talk now it is in the manner of feeling their way over strange ground, as if afraid of what they are saying, but as if they can not help saying it.*]

MRS. HALE: She liked the bird. She was going to bury it in that pretty box.

MRS. PETERS: (*In a whisper.*) When I was a girl—my kitten—there was a boy who took a hatchet, and before my eyes—and before I could get there—(*Covers her face an instant.*) If they hadn't held me back I would have—(*Catches herself, looks upstairs where steps are heard, falters weakly*)—hurt him.

MRS. HALE: (*With a slow look around her.*) I wonder how it would seem never to have had any children around. (*Pause.*) No, Wright wouldn't like the bird—a thing that sang. She used to sing. He killed that, too.

MRS. PETERS: (*Moving uneasily.*) We don't know who killed the bird.

MRS. HALE: I knew John Wright.

MRS. PETERS: It was an awful thing was done in this house that night, Mrs. Hale. Killing a man while he slept; slipping a rope around his neck that choked the life out of him.

MRS. HALE: His neck. Choked the life out of him.

[*Her hand goes out and rests on the bird-cage.*]

MRS. PETERS: (*With rising voice.*) We don't know who killed him. We don't know.

MRS. HALE: (*Her own feeling not interrupted.*) If there'd been years and years of nothing, then a bird to sing to you, it would be awful—still, after the bird was still.

MRS. PETERS: (*Something within her speaking.*) I know what stillness is. When we homesteaded in Dakota, and my first baby died—after he was two years old, and me with no other then—

MRS. HALE: (*Moving.*) How soon do you suppose they'll be through, looking for the evidence?

MRS. PETERS: I know what stillness is. (*Pulling herself back.*) The law has got to punish crime, Mrs. Hale.

MRS. HALE: (*Not as if answering that.*) I wish you'd seen Minnie Foster when she wore a white dress with blue ribbons and stood up there in the choir and sang. (*A look around the room.*) Oh, I *wish* I'd come over here once in a while! That was a crime! That was a crime! Who's going to punish that?

MRS. PETERS: (*Looking upstairs.*) We mustn't—take on.

MRS. HALE: I might have known she needed help! I know how things can be—for women. I tell you, it's queer, Mrs. Peters. We live close together and we live far apart. We all go through the same things—it's all just a different kind of the same thing. (*Brushes her eyes, noticing the bottle of fruit, reaches out for it.*) If I was you I wouldn't tell her her fruit was gone. Tell her it *ain't.* Tell her it's all right. Take this in to prove it to her. She—she may never know whether it was broke or not.

MRS. PETERS: (*Takes the bottle, looks about for something to wrap it in; takes petticoat from the clothes brought from the other room, very nervously begins winding this around the bottle. In a false voice.*) My, it's a good thing the men couldn't hear us. Wouldn't they just laugh! Getting all stirred up over a little thing like a—dead canary. As if that could have anything to do with—with—wouldn't they *laugh*!

[*The men are heard coming down stairs.*]

MRS. HALE: (*Under her breath.*) Maybe they would—maybe they wouldn't.

COUNTY ATTORNEY: No, Peters, it's all perfectly clear except a reason for doing it. But you know juries when it comes to women. If there was some definite thing. Something to show—something to make a story about—a thing that would connect up with this strange way of doing it—

[*The women's eyes meet for an instant. Enter* HALE *from outer door.*]

HALE: Well, I've got the team around. Pretty cold out there.

COUNTY ATTORNEY: I'm going to stay here a while by myself. (*To the* SHERIFF.) You can send Frank out for me, can't you? I want to go over everything. I'm not satisfied that we can't do better.

SHERIFF: Do you want to see what Mrs. Peters is going to take in?

[*The* LAWYER *goes to the table, picks up the apron, laughs.*]

COUNTY ATTORNEY: Oh, I guess they're not very dangerous things the ladies have picked out. (*Moves a few things about, disturbing the quilt pieces which cover the box. Steps back.*) No, Mrs. Peters doesn't need supervising. For that matter, a sheriff's wife is married to the law. Ever think of it that way, Mrs. Peters?

MRS. PETERS: Not—just that way.

SHERIFF: (*Chuckling.*) Married to the law. (*Moves toward the other room.*) I just want you to come in here a minute, George. We ought to take a look at these windows.

COUNTY ATTORNEY: (*Scoffingly.*) Oh, windows!

SHERIFF: We'll be right out, Mr. Hale.

[HALE *goes outside. The* SHERIFF *follows the* COUNTY ATTORNEY *into the other room. Then* MRS. HALE *rises, hands tight together, looking intensely at* MRS. PETERS, *whose eyes make a slow turn, finally meeting* MRS. HALE'S. *A moment* MRS. HALE *holds her, then her own eyes point the way to where the box is concealed. Suddenly* MRS. PETERS *throws back quilt pieces and tries to put the box in the bag she is wearing. It is too big. She opens box, starts to take bird out, cannot touch it, goes to pieces, stands there helpless. Sound of a knob turning in the other room.* MRS. HALE *snatches the box and puts it in the pocket of her big coat. Enter* COUNTY ATTORNEY *and* SHERIFF.]

COUNTY ATTORNEY: (*Facetiously.*) Well, Henry, at least we found out that she was not going to quilt it. She was going to—what is it you call it, ladies?

MRS. HALE: (*Her hand against her pocket.*) We call it—knot it, Mr. Henderson.

Curtain

Before we begin to stage *Trifles* imaginatively, we should consider the conventions of drama and theater that Glaspell employed. In 1916, realism was till a fairly new movement in the theater. Henrik Ibsen's *Hedda Gabler*, August Strindberg's *Miss Julie*, and Anton Chekhov's *The Cherry Orchard* were pioneering examples of realism, as were many of the plays of Eugene O'Neill, also closely associated with the Provincetown Players. Realistic plays depend on an imaginative agreement between playwright and audiences that the set, properties, and action onstage represent the world outside the theater with some degree of accuracy. We should observe that in *Trifles* Glaspell carefully supplies natural dialogue to capture the culture of the American Midwest, and she supplies precise details for the setting and properties. The play's stark realism was noted early in its performance history. One English reviewer who saw a production of the play in New York remarked on Glaspell's ability to evoke the cold, bleak landscape of the Midwest and its closed culture. He thought that the play was so purely American that the parts of Mrs. Hale and Mrs. Peters probably could not be played effectively by English actresses.

In her short story "A Jury of Her Peers," based on the play, Glaspell gives a wealth of detail about the characters, about their relationships, and some insights into their values; but there is no narrator in *Trifles*, and for this information we have to rely not only on the dialogue but also on the stage directions and whatever explanations Glaspell provides in her script.

We can begin our reading by imagining the **setting.** Glaspell opens the play with a detailed description of what we might see in a theater: the kitchen of John and Minnie Wright's farmhouse. Her stage direction goes further to establish the atmosphere, explaining that it is "a gloomy kitchen, and left without having been put in order—unwashed pots under the sink, a loaf of bread outside the breadbox, a dish-towel on the table—other signs of incompleted work." These details tell us something about the people who live here. We may suspect perhaps that something has occurred to upset their rather bleak existence. Later, when we learn more about them, our initial impression is confirmed. Plays, of course, can use more than one set, sometimes to suggest startling contrasts, as in William Shakespeare's *A Midsummer Night's Dream*. The single set of *Trifles* expresses something about the oppressive relationship between John and Minnie Wright. By the end of the play, Mrs. Hale and Mrs. Peters have come to a similar conclusion; they implicitly recognize the connection between this depressing environment and the terrible event that took place here.

In addition to set, playwrights often employ **properties** to convey meaning. August Strindberg, for example, uses the count's boot in his play *Miss Julie* to evoke the authoritarian presence of Miss Julie's father, even though the count himself never appears in the play. In *Volpone* Ben Jonson uses Volpone's hoard of gold at the opening of that play to reveal his values. Instead of saying morning prayers, Volpone "prays" to his fortune. In *Trifles* the bird cage contributes a great deal to our understanding of the action. When Mrs. Peters discovers a broken bird cage, Mrs. Hale remembers Minnie as "kind of like a bird herself—real sweet and pretty, but kind of timid and—fluttery. How—she—did—change." Glaspell's dialogue makes explicit the connection between Minnie's life in this isolated and depressing farmhouse and that of a caged bird. The pieces of the quilt that Mrs. Peters accidentally discovers in Minnie's sewing basket are also meaningful. The discovery not only serves to bring the women closer together in sympathy for

Minnie, but also serves to represent how Mrs. Hale and Mrs. Peters are themselves piecing together the details of Minnie's life. At the conclusion of the play, that box containing the dead bird is a particularly crucial property, the hiding of which serves as the play's dramatic climax.

Sometimes the connection between properties and action is not so explicit, as with the jars of preserves in *Trifles*. When Henderson puts his hand on the sticky shelf where Minnie had kept her preserves, he withdraws it in disgust and washes at the sink. Left alone, Mrs. Hale and Mrs. Peters find only one jar of preserves unbroken; with no heat in the farmhouse, all but one of the glass jars had frozen and burst. Knowing the labor involved in canning and the concern Minnie had shown about the jars, Mrs. Hale and Mrs. Peters commiserate over the loss. The entire incident may seem puzzling at first. Why should a woman being held on suspicion of murdering her husband be concerned with jars of preserves? Glaspell may have wanted to suggest that the disheveled state of Minnie's kitchen is not an accurate reflection of her housekeeping habits; moreover, the burst jars act as an emblem of Minnie's recent tragedy, a life bursting under pressure in an emotionally frozen climate. Most importantly, the preserves call attention to the bond uniting the women characters. All of the women regard these preserves as important, while the men regard them as trifles, things "women are used to worrying over." By the end of the play this difference between the men and the women in their concern for such trifles becomes crucial to the resolution.

So, even in a realistic play like this one, a playwright can use setting and properties to communicate information and emotion. Even an empty stage or one that uses a simplified setting can communicate a great deal. Samuel Beckett's *Endgame*, for example, included in this anthology, is a famous example of a minimalist approach, to setting, properties, characters, and action; Beckett's minimalist approach, paradoxically, generates an extraordinary wealth of information about the play's world.

Actors' movements and **groupings** on stage also communicate important information in plays. In *Trifles*, for example, Peters, Henderson, and Hale all move to the stove to warm themselves when they first enter the stage. It is bitterly cold even inside the farmhouse. But the men are also seeking a place of warmth or comfort to counteract the chilling investigation they are conducting. The stage directions specify that the men be grouped around the stove but that the women stand together near the door, still in the cold, apart from the men. Groupings like this can set up relationships among characters, and here in these opening few moments Glaspell underscores the male and female polarities that she intends to explore in the play. A little later these polarities intensify with another grouping movement. With the first disparaging remarks from the men about Minnie's housekeeping, the stage directions call for the women to "draw nearer" to one another. The physical movement of the actors coming closer together suggests, or course, a movement on a deeper level, extremely important information not communicated in the dialogue. Mrs. Peters and Mrs. Hale remain very formal in their interactions, never addressing one another by their first names. Yet by the end of the play they have developed a close relationship.

Gestures can be important in a play, often conveying a character's state of mind. For example, in *Trifles*, when Mrs. Hale first enters the stage, the direction calls for her to communicate her agitation in body language and facial expression: "She is disturbed now and looks fearfully around as she enters." Or we might consider the moment when the two women examine the sewing on the last piece Minnie added to the quilt. They discover the stitches are "all over the place," and here the stage directions indicate that "they look at each other, then start to glance back at the door." Their gestures and body language indicate that both women recognize the significance of the discovery and at the same time instinctively want to conceal it from the men.

Sound effects, too, are important. One of the most famous sound effects in any play is the snapping string in Anton Chekhov's *The Cherry Orchard*, a sound that signals the end of the old aristocratic way of life. Eugene O'Neill uses sound effects in *The Emperor Jones* to communicate important information about Brutus Jones' deteriorating state of mind. In *Trifles* sound effects come into play when Henderson and the other men enter and exit in the course of investigating the upper level of the farmhouse and the barn outside. In the men's absence Mrs. Hale and Mrs. Peters begin to discover the most meaningful clues about the murder. Each time the men return, the sound of their footsteps on the stairs or the porch gives the women's activities a conspiratorial air.

Dialogue in a play continually provides insights into character while also developing the plot. In *Trifles*, for example, we might consider the reaction of Mrs. Hale to the men's criticism of Minnie's housekeeping. Mrs. Hale is unsettled by the men trying "to get [Minnie's] own house to turn against her," and when Henderson tries to get the women to admit that Minnie was a bad housekeeper, Mrs. Hale points out that "there's a great deal of work to be done on a farm." She notes, pointedly, that men's "hands are not always as clean as they might be." In defending Minnie, Mrs. Hale is also (perhaps unconsciously at this point) defending herself against the implication that women alone are responsible for the state of a household, and as the play proceeds she takes the matter to heart. When she arranges the pans that Henderson has disturbed, Mrs. Hale remarks that she would "hate to have men coming into my kitchen, snooping around and criticising." So, the more criticism is leveled at Minnie and the more the men joke at the expense of women, the more personally Mrs. Hale takes it. Dialogue also reveals the bond that develops between Mrs. Hale and Mrs. Peters, which will affect their ultimate relationship with the men.

In addition, dialogue helps us understand two important characters in *Trifles* who never appear on stage: John and Minnie Wright. Like Miss Julie's father, the count, in Strindberg's *Miss Julie*, whom we learn about only from stage properties and from the dialogue between Miss Julie and the valet Jean, we learn about Minnie and John Wright from the dialogue between Mrs. Peters and Mrs. Hale. The women do not regard themselves as detectives, as the men do, though they turn out to be better at piecing together clues. They do not object to doing what the men regard as women's work, and they do not object to the men doing their work. They simply gather items for Minnie, and as they do so, their conversation leads them—and us—to a more complete understanding of Minnie, of her relationship with John, and of her possible motive for murder.

Dialogue also can create **dramatic irony**—the difference between what we know as readers or audience members and what some or all of the characters know. The Greek tragedians Aeschylus and Sophocles employed dramatic irony at the very beginning of Western drama. Aeschylus's audience knew the fate of

Agamemnon just as we know what Oedipus does not—that the criminal he searches for is himself. Glaspell uses dramatic irony effectively in her presentation of the men's investigation of the murder scene. Near the end of the play, Henderson implies that because juries are more sympathetic to women defendants, it is important for his case that he be able to prove Minnie's "reason for doing it," that he have something to show "that would connect up with this strange way of doing it." In their official search, however, he and the other men turn up no such evidence because they ignore the "kitchen things," the trifles through which the real story can be told. Dismissed by the men, it is the women, ironically, who are able to piece together Minnie's reason for killing her husband as she did. At the conclusion of the play, they choose to hide the crucial evidence— the broken-necked bird—and in so doing contribute to Minnie Wright's possible acquittal. In the ironic final exchange of dialogue, Henderson returns to an earlier disparagement of the women and jokingly suggests the men did at least discover one thing in their search—that Minnie "was not going to quilt it." He can't, remember the term the ladies used for what she was going to do with the pieces of cloth. "We call it—knot it, Mr. Henderson," Mrs. Hale replies, turning around the earlier joke. We understand what she means, but the men do not.

Through dialogue playwrights also create patterns of **imagery** that add complexity to the drama's fabric. In *Trifles*, for example, the word *knot* reverberates with meaning by the close of the play. It is the knot that Minnie might have used to make the quilt. It is the knot that Minnie probably tied to strangle John. It is the "knot" that Mrs. Hale and Mrs. Peters have untied by discovering the probable motive for the murder. We could even continue further and imagine that it is a denial of the more obvious clues to a motive that the men have been searching for: "Not it." We could also see it as the "knot" or bond that develops between Mrs. Hale and Mrs. Peters. Interpreting such recurring imagery in dialogue can deepen our understanding of a play.

Plays are often organized around one or more central ideas or **themes**, although themes are not written into play scripts. Discussion of themes can make our reading experience more coherent, but we should be aware that such discussions are conditioned by the historical period we live in, the culture we come from, our economic status, and our beliefs and values. All the plays included in this anthology raise questions of enduring interest and concern, but each age has responded to such questions with different answers. In *Trifles* one of the central ideas or thematic concerns is gender roles and conflicts. Some readers have suggested that the play is an early twentieth-century feminist statement about the subversive tactics women must take in order to function in a world dominated by men. Glaspell was herself concerned about women's rights, but we should notice that *Trifles* raises other complicated and disturbing questions; some social, some legal, and some moral. Are Mrs. Hale and Mrs. Peters legally in the right to conceal evidence in a murder investigation? Are they morally right to do so? What causes the tension between men and women as portrayed in this play? Is the tension culturally determined, a product of socialized gender roles, or is it something even deeper than that? If Glaspell were writing an essay on the subject, she might have tried to answer those questions for us; because she is writing a play, however, she gives no clear answers. Instead, she raises these important questions to encourage us to resist pronouncements based on abstract notions of legality, justice, morality, and gender. The play prompts us to think and to talk about these questions, but the answers we give will say at least as much about our values as they will say about Glaspell's play.

Like Glaspell's *Trifles*, each of the plays included in this anthology presents unique reading and interpretive challenges. However, each play will respond to the general reading and critical skills we have already begun to develop here. Practicing these skills with each new play will replay the effort with increasing dividends, as each reading experience will help develop more imaginative and more sophisticated responses to drama. As the dramatic imagination develops, the enjoyment of reading plays—and, when possible, seeing them—grows. As confidence builds, the rewards of reading and seeing drama can continue to instruct and entertain well beyond the pages of this anthology.

PART I

Greek Drama and Theater

An artist's reconstruction of the Stage of the Theatre of Dionysus, Athens. Note the double doors in the center of the building leading to an enclosed central corridor and the flat roof over that corridor; this provided for the possibility of an upper acting area for use by gods.

The tradition of Western drama began with the ancient Greeks about twenty-five hundred years ago. They built the first theaters; they originated concepts of character, of dialogue, and of acting; they developed forms of drama that are still practiced; they worked out original theories of the relationship between actor and audience; and they pioneered self-conscious dramatic criticism. The Greeks left a significant legacy to Western theater, a legacy that includes many plays that are still regularly performed today.

DRAMA AND SOCIETY

Important achievements in drama occur when the theater occupies a central place in society, as it did in Athens in the fifth century B.C., a century in which Greek military and commercial expansion in the Mediterranean region had reached its height. From the eighth to the fifth century B.C., Greek culture spread west to Sicily and Italy and northeast as far as the Ukraine. At the beginning of the fifth century, with the victory over the Persians in 492 B.C., Greek civilization approached its zenith, and Athens became the most powerful city in the Mediterranean. The fifth and fourth centuries B.C. are known as the classical period in Athens and in Greece, an age that produced some of the most important architecture, sculpture, and drama in Western history.

Spectacles and all kinds of performances were produced in many Greek cities, but drama as we know it developed in Athens. Musical performances and dramatic recitations both were part of the four religious festivals associated with the annual grape harvest held between December and March. The festivals honored Dionysus, the god of wine and revelry. Beginning in the sixth century B.C., three of the festivals featured public competitions in drama, but the most important of them was the Great or City Dionysia, held for about five days in late March or early April. Several days of animal sacrifices and parades preceded the dramatic contests, in which playwrights, actors, and choruses competed for prizes. Held in an outdoor amphitheater located near the temple of Dionysus, the festival involved all of the major social groups or "tribes" in the city. Noncitizens also attended the City Dionysia, and thus the festival was entwined in the religious, social, and political life of the whole city-state. While honoring Dionysus, the festival also acted as a showpiece for Athenian culture, wealth, and power.

For many years, the festival included several days of dithyramb contests—competitions involving hymns or narrative lyrics sung by a large chorus. For these contests, each of the tribes of Athens sponsored two choruses, one of men and one of boys. The dithyramb contests were followed by the main competition between dramatists, who were sponsored by wealthy individuals. Each playwright produced a trilogy of tragedies and one satyr play over the period of three days. The three tragedies might focus on a single subject or on unrelated subjects, while the satyr play ordinarily consisted of a farce on an erotic subject and a Dionysian theme, with actors costumed as satyrs, half-man and half-goat. Overseeing the contests were important citizens who served as judges and awarded prizes to playwrights, actors, and sponsors.

Apparent in the drama of this period are the social customs of Athenian society. Only men had full citizenship; slaves had no rights; and women had only certain privileges defined by marriage. Women did not participate in the dramatic competitions, either as playwrights or as actors, although it is likely they were spectators. The plays were written by men, and men also performed female roles onstage. The concerns of the Greek plays from this period, however, often transcend class and gender stereotyping; the comedies question pat social assumptions, and the tragedies use stereotypes as a fulcrum for more universal meditations.

THEATER

By the fifth century B.C. the Greek theater had acquired its basic design, and amphitheaters became established features of Greek communities all around the Aegean and Mediterranean world. They were marvels of design. At the heart of the semicircular amphitheater, and at its lowest level, stood the round orchestra, the "dancing place" where the chorus performed. It contained the altar of Dionysus, where festival sacrifices were performed and where much of the action of the plays took place. The orchestra was ringed on three sides by rising tiers of seats, often carved out of hillsides; the seats were crafted originally of wood and later of stone. The scale was immense. The stage alone of the Theater of Dionysus in Athens (which still can be seen on the south slope of the Acropolis) measures about 150 feet across—the width of a modern football field. The whole enormous edifice originally accommodated some fifteen thousand to seventeen thousand spectators.

Behind the orchestra was a rectangular building called the skene, made of wood or stone with a roof supported by large pillars. This skene, decorated with backdrops of painted scenery or props, was used as a space for actors to change masks or costumes and as a permanent background for the plays. Some theaters employed mechanisms with winches and a boom that could raise and lower props or characters on and off the stage. Later called the deus ex machina ("god from the machine"), it allowed an actor playing a god to be lowered into the action to intervene in the plot. Aristotle thought that the deus ex machina should be used only if such an intervention followed naturally from the construction of the plot. The term *deus ex machina* is still used in modern criticism to refer to an unlikely or unexpected turn of events that artificially resolves a plot.

Many ancient Greek amphitheaters still survive—for example, the Theater of Dionysus in Athens or the equally impressive ones at Olympia and Epidaurus. These theaters were originally designed to accommodate musical performances as easily as plays, and they have excellent acoustics. A small coin dropped on the floor of the orchestra can be heard clearly in the audience and even whispers carry to the farthest seat in the theater.

PERFORMANCE

According to Aristotle, Greek drama originated in the singing of dithyrambs by choruses. By the sixth century B.C., a masked actor was introduced into the dithyrambs, and he entered into a dialogue with the chorus. This innovation is credited to Thespis (from which the word *thespian*, a synonym for *actor*, is derived), a playwright about whom little else is known. Aeschylus (ca. 525–456 B.C.) was the first dramatist to use two characters, and Sophocles (ca. 496–406 B.C.)

introduced a third. Sophocles' *Oedipus Rex*, in fact, can be performed with only three actors and a chorus, if the actors double roles by taking more than one part. The same is true of all other classical Greek tragedies.

The actors, musicians, and chorus members were all male citizens of Athens. The chorus in tragedies was composed of ten to twelve young men who sang and danced, wearing long flowing robes and identical masks. The actors wore more elaborate and individualized costumes and distinctive masks. The actors also wore platform shoes, called *kothornoi*, which gave them physical dominance, and they wore gowns decorated to indicate the social status of the character they were playing. The actors' masks in comedy were also individualized, and in the satyr plays the most distinctive feature of the costumes was the huge leather phalluses worn by actors. Every kind of play employed striking visual effects.

Because the performance of Greek tragedy was tied from earliest times to the singing and dancing of the chorus, the chorus became, in effect, a significant "character." Most plays begin with a prologue, followed by the parodos, the entrance of the chorus singing and dancing. Episodes follow in which the characters engage one another and the chorus in dialogue. The chorus sings and dances to several odes written in poetic meter different from that spoken by the characters. The purpose of the odes is to enlarge the issues and to comment on the dialogue of the episodes. The catastrophe registers a change in the protagonist's status, and this is followed by the departure of the characters from the stage. The exodos, or departure of the chorus while singing and dancing, marks the conclusion of the performance. Even comedy was structured very much like this, judging from the surviving plays. The comedies of Aristophanes also contained a parabasis, a choral ode that treats political issues, and a kommos, a choral dance.

GENRE

Greek tragedy took its plots and themes from a variety of sources. Warlike exploits from the recent and distant past, familiar Homeric epics, and religious mythology were all mined for material. From these larger-than-life sources came stories of how the gods treated humankind and each other. The stories often highlighted raw displays of power, trickery and deceit, and the crushing of human hope and resources. In these stories, only one mistake or misapprehension about the gods can lead to serious consequences, not only for the hero but often for the entire family line, from generation to generation, all of whom suffer for the crimes or mistakes of the father. Behind everything lay the power of fate, and tragedies showed human beings as subject to a fate which they could only partly understand and could not escape. Contemplation of the human suffering brought about by fate fueled the Greek tragic vision.

The subject of drama, the impact of theatricality, and the nature of tragedy were all explored in the *Poetics* by Aristotle (384–322 B.C.), one of the most important philosophers in the history of Western thought. Aristotle's was the first formal work of dramatic criticism, and his observations are still considered important in discussing these topics today. Plato (428–348 B.C.), Aristotle's mentor, had spoken out against literary invention. In contrast, Aristotle based his observations about dramatic art on the concept of mimesis, or imitation, the process by which an artist seeks truthful representation. Aristotle claimed that plot was the most important element in drama, for it is from plot—the arrangement of incidents—that all the other elements followed. Aristotle discussed a range of possible tragic actions, but he felt strongly that the best tragedy shows a man of high social station fall from prosperity to misery because of *hamartia*, an error or mistake in judgment. In the course of the tragic action, the protagonist is led to a *peripeteia*, or reversal, at which point his fortunes change. This, in turn, leads to the *anagnorisis*, or recognition. Such a spectacle, according to Aristotle, is capable of awakening emotions of pity and fear in the spectator and then of effecting a catharsis, or purging, of these emotions. Aristotle frequently used the example of *Oedipus Rex* to illustrate the workings of the best kind of tragedy. Oedipus fulfills Aristotle's criteria: he is a man of high social station brought to misery through the workings of fate and through his own mistakes. For all of the suffering portrayed in tragedy, violent events themselves were not represented onstage. Such events were simply reported, and the tragic action focused on the horrified responses of the characters or the poetic musings of the chorus.

Greek comedy grew up alongside tragedy. The first recorded comedy was acted in 486 B.C., and the earliest surviving comic play dates from 425 B.C.. The two great Greek comedians whose works have survived were Aristophanes (ca. 450–385 B.C.) and Menander (342–292 B.C.). Aristophanes practiced a form we now call Old Comedy, which was characterized by political and social satire of the Athenian state and by bawdy humor. Aristophanes' late plays are seen as the best representatives of Greek Middle Comedy, which turned to parodies of literary and philosophical fashions. The influence of Aristophanes' brand of Old Comedy is still alive in satiric comedy today. Menander, writing a hundred years later, is considered master of what we now call New Comedy, which is characterized by a concern with manners and by more refined humor. Menander was more interested in satirizing the failings of a class of people than those of individuals. His comedies depict the struggle between parents or guardians and their children over the issue of love or marriage. This outline of comic action is often used in romantic comedies and comedies of manners today.

ROMAN DRAMA AND THEATER

Classical Greek drama came to an end as it had begun, amid larger economic, political, and cultural circumstances. During the course of the fifth century B.C. the balance that had been maintained by trade agreements and alliances unraveled as the Greek city-states grew in power and began to rival one another. Athens and Sparta, in particular, developed bitter antagonisms, which broke into open hostilities that escalated into the Peloponnesian War (431–404 B.C.) eventually won by Sparta. Less than a hundred years later, prolonged political and military struggles brought about the breakup of the loose confederation of city-states. In 338 B.C. the Macedonian general Philip II conquered Greece, and his son Alexander the Great created an empire that stretched to Persia. During the Hellenistic Age, the period between the death of Alexander in 323 B.C. and the formation of the Roman Empire in 30 B.C., Greek language and culture spread throughout the eastern Mediterranean. When Rome conquered the Mediterranean world, the Empire became heir to Greek culture and traditions.

Although many of their traditions were derived from Greece, the Romans developed a distinctive kind of theater. Roman plays, usually farces, became associated with games or *ludi* held in April, July, September, and November. Unlike the Greek festivals, these games did not officially include dramatic competitions, but dramatists and actors were hired to put on plays for the entertainment of spectators, who were also busy watching acrobatic acts, gladiatorial combats, chariot races, athletic events, and animal baiting. Greek drama was first introduced at these games in 240 B.C., and by 179 B.C. it was being performed at the games throughout the year; but it shared its audiences with native Roman drama, which seems to have consisted of improvised plots with stock characters.

Before the first century A.D. Roman theaters made of wood were erected and taken down for each festival. Later, permanent theaters were constructed, modeled on Greek amphitheaters but with important differences. Roman theaters were built on level ground rather than on hillsides. Semicircular seating rose in steep tiers from a semicircular orchestra. Behind the orchestra was a stage house or *scaena*, like the Greek *skene*, but many of the Roman *scaena* were three stories high. Their facades were decorated with columns.

All of the Roman plays that have survived show the influence of Greek drama, but they were not merely imitations. In many ways the Romans paid Greek drama its highest compliment: they emulated its forms, copied its characters and plots, and used its costumes, while reworking the plays and adapting them to their own culture. The greatest Roman comic dramatist was Plautus (254–184 B.C.). His plots follow Greek New Comedy in that they are often based on mistaken identity or romantic love and are characterized by witty dialogue. The young almost always triumph in their struggles with their parents, sometimes with the help of a witty slave who provides humor. Plautus is thought to have written over a hundred plays, although only about twenty have survived, the most famous of which are *Amphitryon, The Braggart Soldier,* and *The Twin Menaechmi.* Terence (ca. 190–159 B.C.), a freed slave who wrote only six comedies, was keenly interested in adapting Greek comedy. His most famous plays are *Phormio* and *The Brothers.* Plautus and Terence were to have an enormous impact on the forms of comedy in the European tradition over a thousand years later, for their plays were used to teach Latin in the humanist schools of the late Middle Ages and the Renaissance. Some of the greatest playwrights in Western history, including Shakespeare and Molière, imitated their work unashamedly.

The only Roman tragedies that survived the classical era are those of Seneca (B.C.–65 A.D.). His plays were derived from Greek originals but added a new sensationalism. Interested in the violent themes of murder, revenge, and incest, Seneca was also concerned with the inner workings of the mind, and many of his protagonists have long, self-revealing soliloquies. Ghosts and the supernatural also figure prominently in his work. His plays are written in such a highly rhetorical style that there is some question whether they were ever intended for performance. Only nine of them survive, the most famous of which are *Medea, Phaedra,* and *Thyestes.* Whether or not his plays were originally performed, Seneca's work also had an important influence on later European drama, particularly in the English Renaissance, when his themes, characters, and rhetorical style were widely imitated.

AESCHYLUS (CA. 525–456 B.C.)

Aeschylus was born during the last quarter of the sixth century B.C. and died in the middle of the fifth century B.C., when Athens was still at the height of its power. We know from his epitaph that he was the son of Euphorion and that he was proud of his military career. He fought in the battle of Marathon, in which his brother was killed, and probably in several other battles as well. He is said to have begun writing tragedies at an early age, but his first victory at City Dionysia was in 484 B.C. His reputation as a dramatist was so secure that after his death his plays were put on in competition with living playwrights. In these competitions Aeschylus' plays continued to win prizes. Altogether, he is said to have won thirteen prizes in his lifetime and to have written more than seventy plays. The exact number is uncertain, and only seven of his plays have survived: *The Suppliants, The Persians, The Seven Against Thebes, Prometheus Bound,* and the *Oresteia* trilogy (*Agamemnon, The Libation Bearers,* and *The Eumenides*).

He visited Sicily in 476 B.C. and produced *The Women of Etna* in the new city, which Hieron of Syracuse had founded, and in 472 B.C. he produced *The Persians* at Athens with Pericles himself as his official sponsor. The play was produced in the following year at Syracuse. In 468 B.C. he was defeated by Sophocles in the competition at City Dionysia. Some have speculated that Aeschylus left Athens because of this defeat. Others have suggested that he left because he was defeated by the lyric poet Simonides in a competition for writing the epitaph for those who died at Marathon. Still others argue that he left because he disliked the direction of Athenian politics after the death of Pericles. We know, however, that Aeschylus remained in Athens for some time after his defeat by Sophocles and that he won the competition in the following year with a set of plays that included *The Seven Against Thebes.* He was still in Athens in 458 B.C. when he presented his greatest work, the *Oresteia* trilogy. Sicily was the great western frontier of the Greek colonies in the Mediterranean, presenting much in the way of opportunities. Aeschylus returned to Sicily at the end of his life and died in Gela, Sicily, in 456 or 455 B.C.

Agamemnon

The *Oresteia* (composed of *Agamemnon, The Libation Bearers,* and *The Eumenides*) is the only complete trilogy to survive from the great age of Greek drama. The trilogy is thought to be the last work Aeschylus composed before his death. It won the prize at City Dionysia in 458 P.C.

Each play of the trilogy is a part of a larger project in which Aeschylus traces the working out of the curse on the house of Atreus. The basic story was known in several versions, like most of the myths and legends known to the Athenians. In Aeschylus' version, Atreus and Thyestes, the sons of Pelops, became enemies because Thyestes had seduced his brother's wife and challenged the throne of Argos. Thyestes was defeated by his brother and driven out of Argos, but he returned along with his children to make peace with Atreus. Atreus invited them to a feast where he killed all of his brother's children except one and served them for dinner to their father. When Thyestes discovered what had happened, he cursed the house of Atreus and fled with his surviving son, Aegisthus.

Agamemnon and Menelaus, the sons of Atreus, succeeded to the kingdom of Argos, and married the sisters Clytemnestra and Helen. When Paris, the son of king Priam, seduced Helen and took her to Troy, Agamemnon and Menelaus organized a great expeditionary force of Greek warriors to win her back and take revenge. Gathered at Aulis, the expeditionary force was stalled because of high winds and by dissention among the soldiers. Calchas the seer construed this situation to be caused by the anger of Artemis, which could be appeased only by the human sacrifice of Agamemnon's daughter Iphigenia. Agamemnon agonized about the sacrifice, but pressured by Calchas and public opinion and by his sense of responsibility to the army, agreed to sacrifice Iphigenia. After a ten-year siege, Troy fell to the Greeks, and Agamemnon returned home.

Aeschylus opens *Agamemnon* at this point. The scene is Argos, and Clytemnestra, grief-stricken over the death of her daughter, has taken Aegisthus, the sole surviving son of Thyestes, as her lover. She has sent her son, Orestes, out of the country, and is preparing to take her revenge on Agamemnon. Agamemnon enters with all the pomp of a great conquering hero and is accompanied by Cassandra, princess and prophetess of Troy, whom he has taken as his concubine. But the spectacle of the great purple tapestry spread for the king to walk on into the palace is a chilling reminder of the doom waiting within. Clytemnestra pinions him and stabs him to death. The calm exterior masking the tense psychological strain under which Clytemnestra labors during the play is released only through her exaltation when she murders her husband. She also kills Cassandra and then, exhausted, defends her actions to the people of Argos.

In the *Oresteia* trilogy Aeschylus investigates the effects of a curse passed from one generation to the next. The pattern of crime and revenge, which was established in the generation of Atreus and Thyestes, is repeated again in the generation of Menealaus and Agamemnon, and yet again in the generation of Iphigenia, Orestes, and Electra. Orestes returns from exile, and in *The Libation Bearers* he and Electra avenge the murder of their father. They kill Aegisthus, and then Orestes kills his mother. He is pursued by the furies, demons who torment him with guilt and remorse. In the final play of the trilogy, *The Eumenides*, Aeschylus explores the idea of submitting such cases to the judgment of a court. Athena convenes the Areopagus to hear and judge Orestes' case. The trilogy is not only a story of a curse working its way through generations but a story about the development of human consciousness itself and about the cost of such development. Whatever progress may be gained at the end of the trilogy is dearly bought with generations of hatred, crime, violence, and suffering.

Agamemnon

AESCHYLUS

TRANSLATED BY HUGH LLOYD-JONES

CHARACTERS

AEGISTHUS, cousin of AGAMEMNON
AGAMEMNON, king of ARGOS
CASSANDRA, Trojan captive
CHORUS, Argive elders

CLYTEMNESTRA, queen of Argos
HERALD
WATCHMAN

The play opens with the Watchman lying on the roof of Agamemnon's palace at Argos and gazing out into the night.

1   WATCHMAN: The gods I beg for deliverance from these toils,
    From my watch a year long, through which, sleeping
    upon the house of the Atreidae, like a dog,°
    I have learned to know the assembly of the stars of night
5   and those who bring winter and summer to mortals,
    the bright potentates,° shining in the sky,
    the stars, when they set and at their rising.
    And now I am watching for the signal of the torch,
    the gleam of fire bringing news from Troy
10   and the tidings of her capture; for such is the rule
    of a woman's man-counseling, ever hopeful, heart.
    And when I keep my couch that sends me wandering by night, my couch wet with dew,
    this couch of mine that no dreams visit°—
    for Fear instead of Sleep stands by it,
15   so that I may not close my eyes fast in sleep—
    and when I have a mind to sing or hum,
    incising this remedy of song° against sleep,
    then I weep, lamenting the misfortune of this house,
    not now, as in time past, excellently kept in order.
    But now may there come a happy deliverance
20   from toil,
    as the fire that brings good news shines through the darkness!

[He sees the beacon.]

    Hail, lamp that shows by night the light of day,
    and ordains the setting-up of many dances
    in Argos for the sake of this event!
    Hurrah, hurrah!   25
    To Agamemnon's wife I give clear signal,
    that she may rise from her bed in all speed
    and raise a jubilant cry of thanksgiving at this torch,
    if truly the city of Ilium
    is taken, as the beacon's light announces.   30
    And I myself shall dance a prelude,
    for my masters' throw has been lucky, and I will turn it to my advantage,
    now that this beacon-watching has thrown triple six for me.
    Well, may it come to pass that the lord of the house
    comes back, and that I clasp his well-loved hand in mine.   35
    But for the rest I am silent; a great ox stands
    upon my tongue;° but the house itself, if it could find a voice,
    could tell the tale most truly; for I of my choice
    speak to those who know; but for those who do not know I forget.

[EXIT THE WATCHMAN. The CHORUS, consisting of old men of Argos, who as members of the Council help the queen to govern in the king's absence, enter and march around the orchestra until they take up their positions for the first ode.]

NB: The line numbers in the margins are those of the original greek text.   **3** In the Middle East watchdogs still sometimes spend the night on the roof.   **6** The stars are called "potentates" because they "bring winter and summer to mortals"; in Aeschylus' time the Greeks knew nothing of astrology.   **13** The words used suggest the metaphor of a sickbed not visited by the proper doctor.   **17** The two methods of ancient surgery were cautery and incision; here the remedy of song is described by a metaphor taken from the latter.

---

37 **a great ox stands upon my tongue** a proverbial way of saying, "I am inhibited from speaking out." Later in the play the house of the Atreidae (*At rye' dee*) will find a voice, which will be understood only by the captive Trojan prophetess CASSANDRA (*Kass and' ra*).

40   It is now the tenth year since Priam's
       great adversary at law,
       King Menelaus and Agamemnon,
       the pair of sons of Atreus mighty in honor,
       put out with an Argive armament of a thousand
45   ships
       from this land,
       to aid their cause in battle,
       uttering from their hearts a great cry for war
       like vultures, who in grief
50   extreme for their children high above their beds
       circle around,
       rowed on the oarage of their wings,
       having seen go for nothing the labor of guarding
       the bed that held their chicks.
55   And on high Apollo, it may be, hears,
       or Pan, or Zeus, the bird-voiced
       shrill cry of these fellow dwellers in the sky
       and sends on the transgressors her who brings
           punishment,
       though late, the Erinys.°
60   And thus are the sons of Atreus sent
       against Alexander by him whose power is greater,
       Zeus, guardian of host and guest; for the sake of a
           woman of many men,
       many wrestlings that wear down the limbs,
       while the knee is brought low in the dust
       and the spearshaft is snapped in the action before
65   the sacrifice,°
       shall he ordain for the Danaans
       and Trojans alike. The matter stands where now
       it stands; and it shall be accomplished to its des-
           tined end.
       Not by the persuasion of burnt offerings nor of
           libations,
70   of sacrifices that know no fire
       shall he cajole aside unflinching wrath.
       But we, who have not yet paid the debt due to
           our aged flesh,
       we who were left behind from that expedition,
       remain here; we guide with staves°
75   our strength no greater than a child's.

For the fresh stuff of life that within
the breast holds sway
is like an old man's, and the war-god is not at his
    post;
and great age with the leaf already
withering on three feet   80
walks, and with strength no greater than a child's
like a dream seen by day wanders.

[The Chorus *turns to face the palace.]*

But you, Tyndareus'°
daughter, Queen Clytemnestra,
what is the matter, what the news, what have you
    learned,   85
what message
has prevailed on you, that you send messengers
    around and sacrifice?
The altars of all the gods that guide the city,
gods on high and gods below the earth, gods of
    the doors   90
and of the market-place,
blaze with offerings;
and from this side and that as high as heaven
torches send up their light,
charmed by the hallowed unguent's
soft guileless coaxing,   95
the royal offering from the inmost store.
Of these matters tell us what you can and may,
and become the healer
of this anxiety.
Now it carries thoughts of ill,   100
and now from the sacrifices you reveal
springs hope that gives protection, so that worry
    insufferable
[cannot grieve my heart].

STROPHE 1

I have power to tell of the auspicious command
    of the expedition, the command of men
in authority; for still from the gods am I inspired   105
with persuasive power, my strength in song, by
    the life that has grown up with me:
to tell how the two-throned command of the
    Achaeans, of the youth of Hellas
the concordant leadership,
was sped with avenging spear and arm   110
by the warlike bird of omen to the Teucrian° land,
the king of birds appearing to the kings of the
    ships,

---

59 The hearer is kept waiting until the end of the sentence and the period for the sinister last word—Erinys (*Ee rine' iss*). The Erinyes, originally the personified curses of the dead, are the supernatural beings who are supposed to punish murderers of their own kin; they will play an important part in the *Oresteia*, and in its last play, *The Eumenides* (*Yū' men ih dēz*), they form the chorus.   **65** The destruction of Troy is metaphorically compared to a sacrifice, in that a word that denotes the preliminaries to a sacrifice is used of the battles that preceded the destruction.   **74** Old men in Greece commonly walked with the aid of sticks; such sticks seem to have been a regular property of tragic choruses that represented old men.

---

83 Tyndareus, (*Tin' dar yuse*), king of Sparta, was the husband of Leda and father of Castor and CLYTEMNESTRA; Helen and Polydeuces (Pollux) were Leda's children by Zeus.   **112** **Teucrian** (*Tyuke' ri an*) "Trojan."

115　the black eagle and behind it the white one,
　　appearing near the palace on the hand in which
　　　　the spear is brandished,
　　in seats conspicuous,
　　feeding upon the hare, her womb teeming with
　　　　young,
120　checked from running her final course.
　　Sing sorrow, sorrow, but may the good prevail!

ANTISTROPHE 1

　　And when the trusty prophet of the army° saw it,
　　　　he knew
　　the warlike tearers of the hare for the two
　　　　Atreidae, two in temper,
　　the chiefs who launched the expedition; and thus
125　　he spoke, interpreting the portent:
　　"In time does this expedition capture Priam's city,
　　and all the abundant herds
　　of the people before the walls
　　shall Fate violently ravage.
　　Only let no envy from the gods cast into darkness,
　　struck beforehand, the great bit for Troy's mouth
　　that is the army encamped. For in pity holy
135　　Artemis is angry
　　with the swift hounds of her father
　　that sacrifice the wretched hare with all her
　　　　young before the birth;
　　she loathes the feast of the eagles.
　　Sing sorrow, sorrow, but may the good prevail!

EPODE

140　Kindly as is the Fair One
　　to the helpless young of savage lions
　　and delightful to the breast-loving whelps
　　of all beasts that roam the wild,
145　she begs that these portents be made valid;
　　favorable, but not faultless, are the signs.
　　I call upon the blessed Healer,°
　　that Artemis may not bring to pass delay in port
150　　through adverse
　　winds, long lasting, holding fast the ships,
　　working to bring about another sacrifice, one
　　　　without song or feast,
　　an architect of quarrels grown up with the family,
　　with no fear of the husband. For there abides, ter-
　　　　rible, ever again arising,
　　a keeper of the house guileful, unforgetting,
155　　Wrath child-avenging."
　　Such were the fateful words that Calchas
　　　　shrieked, together with great good,

as he read the omen of the birds by the way for
　　the royal house;
and in harmony with these
sing sorrow, sorrow, but may the good prevail!

STROPHE 2

Whoever Zeus may be, if this name　　　　　　　160
is pleasing to him,
by this name I address him.
I can compare with him,
measuring all things against him,
none but Zeus, if from my mind the vain burden　165
may be cast in sincerity.

ANTISTROPHE 2

Not even he° who in time past was great,
abounding in boldness irresistible,
he shall not even be counted, since he was of the
　　past;　　　　　　　　　　　　　　　　　　170
and he who then came into being
is gone, having met his victor in three falls.
But he who gladly sings the triumph of Zeus
shall hit full on the target of understanding:　　175

STROPHE 3

of Zeus who put men on the way to wisdom
by making it a valid law
that by suffering they shall learn.
There drips before the heart instead of sleep
pain that reminds them of their wounds;　　　　180
and against their will there comes discretion.
There is, I think, a grace that comes by violence
　　from the gods
seated upon the dread bench of the helmsman.

ANTISTROPHE 3

And then the senior chieftain
of the Achaean ships,　　　　　　　　　　　　185
blaming no prophet,
letting his spirit go with the sudden blasts of for-
　　tune
when a delay in port that kept their stomachs
　　empty

---

[122] Calchas (*Kall' khas*), the son of Thestor, in the *Iliad* is the prophet of the Greek army. [146] Paian, "The Healer," is a title of Apollo, who is implored to intercede with his sister Artemis.

[167] The first ruler of the universe was Ouranos; he was defeated and deposed by his son Krōnos (*Kro' nōs*); Kronos in his turn was defeated and deposed by his son Zeus (Hesiod, *Theogony* 453f.). The words used to describe the struggles for the lordship of the universe suggest the wrestling matches that were an important feature of the Greek athletic festivals at Olympia, Delphi, and elsewhere. The victorious wrestler had to throw his adversary in three bouts; his victory would in all likelihood be celebrated in a hymn of triumph, such as the hymns of Pindar.

190 pressed hard the host of the Achaeans,
as they held the shore opposite Chalcis
in the region of Aulis where the seas roar to and fro,

STROPHE 4

and the winds coming from the Strymon
causing a cruel delay, bringing starvation, evil for
    ships at anchor,
making men wander,
unsparing of ships and cables,
195 doubling the length of passing time,
with wasting wore away the flower of the Argives;
and when another remedy
against the cruel storm
more grievous for the chiefs,
200 was shrieked out by the prophet,
putting forward Artemis as cause, so that the
    Atreidae
beat the ground with their staves
and could not hold back a tear,

ANTISTROPHE 4

205 then the senior prince gave tongue and said,
"A grievous doom is disobedience,
and a grievous doom it is
if I massacre my daughter, the pride of my house,
polluting with streams of slaughtered maiden's
    blood
210 a father's hands hard by the altar.
Which of these courses is free from evil?
How am I to become a deserter of my ships,
losing my allies?
For that they should long
for a sacrifice to still the winds and for a maiden's
    blood
215 with passion exceeding passion
is right in the eyes of heaven. May all be for the
    best!"

STROPHE 5

And when he had put on the yoke-strap of com-
    pulsion,
his spirit's wind veering to an impious blast,
220 impure, unholy, from that moment
his mind changed to a temper of utter ruthlessness.
For mortals are made reckless by the evil counsels
of merciless Infatuation, beginner of disaster.
And so he steeled himself to become the sacrificer
225 of his daughter, to aid a war
fought to avenge a woman's loss
and to pay beforehand for his ships.

ANTISTROPHE 5

And her prayers and cries of "Father!"
and her maiden years they let go for nothing,

230 those arbiters eager for battle;
and her father told his servants after a prayer
to lift her face downwards like a goat above the
    altar,
as she fell about his robes to implore him with all
    her heart,
235 and by gagging her lovely mouth
to stifle a cry
that would have brought a curse upon his house;
using violence, and the bridle's stifling power.

STROPHE 6

And with her robe of saffron dye streaming
    downwards
240 she shot each of the sacrificers
with a piteous dart from her eye
standing out as in a picture, wishing
to address each by name, since often
in her father's hospitable halls
245 she had sung, and virginal with pure voice
had lovingly honored the paean
of felicity at the third libation
of her loving father.

ANTISTROPHE 6

And what came next I did not see, nor do I relate
    it;
but the arts of Calchas do not fail of fulfilment,
and Justice sways the balance,
bringing to some learning by suffering. The
    future
250 you may learn when it comes. Rejoice in it before
    it comes!
But all is one if we lament before;
for it will come clear with the rays of dawn.
Well, in what follows may achievement turn out
    prosperous,
255 as is the will of this nearest
sole bulwark of the Apian land!°

[Enter CLYTEMNESTRA.*]*

CHORUS: I have come, Clytemnestra, in reverence for
    your power;
260 for it is right to honor the wife of a king
when the throne has been made empty of the male.
And whether you have heard good news or have
    not,
but sacrifice in the hope of happy tidings,
I would in loyalty learn; nor shall I resent your
    silence.
CLYTEMNESTRA: Happy tidings, as the proverb has it,

---

²⁵⁷ **the Apian** (*Ape′ i an*) **land** an ancient designation of the
Peloponnese, at this time under the rule of AGAMEMNON.

265 may the dawn bring as she comes from night her
mother.
But greater than hope is the joy you shall hear of;
for Priam's city is taken by the Argives.
CHORUS: How do you say? Your words have escaped
me, since they were beyond belief.
CLYTEMNESTRA: That Troy is in the hands of the
Achaeans; do I speak clearly?
270 CHORUS: Delight steals over me, calling forth a tear.
CLYTEMNESTRA: Yes, your eye proclaims your loyalty.
CHORUS: What sign do you trust? Have you any
proof of this?
CLYTEMNESTRA: I have; of course I have, if a god has
not deceived me.
CHORUS: But do you respect as persuasive the visions
seen in dreams?
275 CLYTEMNESTRA: I would not accept the fancy of a
slumbering mind.
CHORUS: But has some wingless rumor encouraged
you to believe this?
CLYTEMNESTRA: You greatly scorn my intelligence, as
though it were a young girl's.
CHORUS: But within what space of time has the city
been taken?
CLYTEMNESTRA: I say, during the night that lately
gave birth to the light we see.
CHORUS: And what kind of messenger could arrive
280 with such speed as this?
CLYTEMNESTRA: Hephaestus,° sending from Ida a
bright flame.
And beacon began to send beacon this way by
means of the courier fire;
Ida° sent it to the rock of Hermes
in Lemnos, and as the mighty torch came from
the island
285 Zeus's crag of Athos° was third to receive it.
And rising aloft to skim the surface of the sea
the might of the traveling torch . . . . . .°
the pine, like another sun, passing on
the golden light of its flame to the watchers of
Macistus.°
And he delayed not, nor was he in heedlessness
290 overcome
by sleep, so as to neglect the duty of a messenger;

but far off the beacon's light
signaled to the guards upon Messapion its coming over the waters of Euripus.°
And they shone an answering light and passed
far on the message,
kindling fire in a heap of gray brushwood. 295
And in strength the torch and not yet growing dim,
leaping over the plain of the Asopus,°
like a radiant moon, to Cithaeron's rock
awoke another succession of convoying fire.
And the light sent from afar was not rejected 300
by the watch; it burned more than was appointed;
and the light plunged beyond the lake of the
Gorgon face,
and reaching the mountain of the wandering goats
urged that the covenant of the fire be not [neglected?].
And kindling the fire with unstinting strength
the men sent ahead 305
the great beard of flame, so that it passed far beyond
the headland that looks upon the crossing point
of Saron,°
blazing as it went. Then it plunged downwards,
and reached
to the peak of Arachne,° the watch close by the city.
And then it plunged down upon this house of the
Atreidae. 310
this light not without an ancestor in the fire of Ida.
Such are the laws that govern my torch-bearers;
each is supplied in relays from another;°
and victory belongs both to the first and to the
last to run the course.
Such is the proof and token that I tell you of, 315
since my husband has sent the news from Troy to
me.
CHORUS: To the gods, lady, I shall address my prayer
later;°

---

281 Hephaestus (*He feest' us*), as the fire-god, is identified with
the fire of the chain of beacons lit on heights that has brought
the news across the Aegean and all the way to Argos. 283 Ida
(*Eye' da*) is the great mountain behind Troy; Lemnos (*Lemm'
nos*) is an island off the coast of Asia Minor. 285 Mount Athos
(*Aye' thos*) on the Thracian coast, like many mountains, was
sacred to Zeus. 287 A line seems to have been dropped out
after 287. 289 According to an ancient grammarian's note
here, Macistus (*May sis' tus*) was the name of a mountain in
Euboea; but there is no other evidence for this, and it may be
nothing better than a guess. If it is the name of a place, then
in 290 that place is personified.

293 The Euripus is the strait between Euboea and the mainland, and Messapion (*Mess aye' py on*) is a mountain on its
western side, in Boeotia. 297 The Asopus (*Aye sō' pus*) is the
main river of Boeotia; Cithaeron (*Sith ee' ron*) is the great
mountain range that separates Boeotia from Attica to the
south. 307 The Saronic Gulf. 309 **Arachne** pronounced *Ar
akh' nē*: Mount Arachnaion, now called Arna, stands north of
the highway from Argos to Epidaurus. 312 Torch-races were
held each year at Athens in honor of Prometheus (*Pro mē' thē
us*), Athene (*A thē' nē*), and Hephaestus, and later in honor of
the Thracian goddess Bendis. The race was a relay race in
which the torch was passed from one member of each team to
the next. It is these torch-races that the beacon system is compared to in this passage. 317 It would be normal for the
CHORUS to render immediate thanks to the gods for the
reported victory; but before doing so it demands that
CLYTEMNESTRA repeat her announcement. The imaginative
picture she now paints of the fall of Troy (330 f.) in no way
amounts to the "sure proof" that the Coryphaeus calls it
(352); but for the time being the CHORUS is convinced.

but for this tale of yours, I would hear it to the end
again and exhaust my wonder at it.
320 CLYTEMNESTRA: Troy is this day in the hands of the
      Achaeans.
    Cries, I think, that will not blend ring out in the
      city.
    If you pour vinegar and oil into the same vessel,
    you may say they stand apart in no friendly fash-
      ion;
    so also one may hear apart from one another the
      voices
325   of conquered and conquerors, voices of their
      different fortunes.
    For the conquered, falling about the bodies
    of men, brothers and fathers,
    of children and aged men, from a throat no longer
      free
    lament the end of their dear ones.
330   As for the conquerors, the toil that sends them
      wandering in the night after the battle
    assigns them, starving, to places where they
      breakfast off what the city holds,
    not by means of any duly allotted billet,
    but as each has drawn the lot of chance.
    In the Trojan houses captured by their spears
    they dwell already, from the frosts and dews
335   beneath the open sky
    released; and as men favored by the gods
    they shall sleep all night long without a watch!
    If they reverence the city-keeping gods
    of the conquered land and the divinities' abodes,
    then the conquerors shall not be conquered in their
340   turn.
    But may no longing first come on the army
    to ravage what they should not ravage, van-
      quished by love of gain!
    For they still need to win their way safe home,
    to round in due course the second bend of the
      racecourse.
    And even if the army should return without
345   offense against the gods,
    the agony of the dead might awaken;
    may it wreak no sudden havoc!
    Such is the tale you hear from me, a woman;
    but may the good prevail, in no uncertain fashion;
    for many are the blessings whose enjoyment I now
350   pray for.
CHORUS: Lady, you speak wisely, like a prudent man.
    And now that I have heard from you sure proofs,
    I make ready to address in praise the gods;
    for not unworthy of our labors is the return they
      have accomplished.
355 O Zeus the King and kindly Night,
    possessor of great glories,
    you who hurled upon the towers of Troy
    a net without holes, so that none full grown
    nor any of the young could overleap

slavery's mighty   360
dragnet, of all-capturing destruction.
It is the mighty Zeus, lord of host and guest, that
  I revere,
he that has accomplished this; against Alexander
long since he has been bending his bow
so that neither short of the mark nor beyond it   365
should the bolt of the stars° fall vainly.

STROPHE 1

They may speak of a stroke from Zeus;
that at least can be traced out.
He has accomplished it as he ordained. Men have
  said
that the gods did not deign to attend to mortals   370
by whom the grace of things inviolable
was trampled; but such men are impious.
And the penalty for daring what may not be
  dared has been revealed
to the descendants of those whose pride is greater
  than is right,   375
when their house abounds with wealth in excess,
beyond what is best. May it be granted me
to have good sense, so that the gods
are content to leave me free from harm!   380
For there is no defense
for a man who in the surfeit of his wealth
has kicked the great altar
of Justice out of sight.

ANTISTROPHE 1

He is overborne by relentless Persuasion,   385
child irresistible of forecounseling Destruction.
And every remedy is vain; not hidden,
but conspicuous, a lurid-shining light, is the plague. 390
And like bad bronze°
when rubbed and battered
he is stained with a black indelible;
for he is like a boy that pursues a flying bird.°   395
Unbearable the affliction he has brought upon his
  city.
His prayers none among the gods will hear,
and him that has dealings with such men
Justice brings down.
Such a one was Paris, who went   400
to the house of the Atreidae
and shamed the hospitable board
by the theft of a wife.

---

366 the bolt of the stars the thunderbolt; *asterope* or *astrape*
(lightning) was derived from *aster* or *astron* (star).   **391 bad
bronze** bronze that has been adulterated with lead; when
such bronze suffers wear and contusion, it turns black.   **395**
"To chase something that has wings" is a proverbial way of
describing the quest of the impossible.

STROPHE 2

And she, leaving for her fellow citizens the din
of shields, the forming of companies
405   and fitting out of ships,
and bringing to Ilium as her dower destruction,
sped swiftly through
the gates, daring a deed beyond daring; many
     were the groans
of the prophets of the house as they spoke these
     words:
"Alas, alas for the house, for the house and for
410   the princes!
alas for the bed she shared with her husband!
we may see the dishonored silence of one
sitting apart, not reviling, not beseeching.
And as he longs for her that is beyond the sea
415   a ghost shall seem to rule the house.
And the charm of her beautiful statues
is hateful to her husband;
and in the absence of her eyes
gone is all the power of love.°

ANTISTROPHE 2

420   And visions seen in dreams, persuasive,
are there, bringing a pleasure that is deceitful.
For deceitfully, when he thinks he sees his beloved
slipping through his arms
425   the vision is gone, never afterwards
on its wings following the paths of sleep."
The sorrows in the house, at the hearth,
are these and worse than these;
and everywhere for them that went forth from the
     land of Hellas
430   a mourning woman, one that suffered much,
is found in each one's house;
yes, there is much to cut to the very heart.
For those they sent away
they know, but instead of men
435   to each one's home
there come back urns and ashes.

STROPHE 3

And Ares, the gold-changer of bodies
and holder of the scales in the battle of the spear
from Ilium sends to their dear ones
440   heavy gold dust that has felt the fire,
dust bitterly bewailed; with ashes
that were once men he loads the urns, easily stowed.

---

418 The Greeks believed that love was implanted in the lover
by a ray from the eyes of the beloved. Hence the absence of
the beloved's eyes is singled out for mention. Other scholars
find here a reference to the emptiness of Menelaus' eyes in
Helen's absence.

And they lament them, praising this man 445
as skilled in battle,
and that as having died a noble death amid the
     slaughter—
"for the sake of another's wife."
These are the words they mutter low;
and over them comes grief with resentment 450
against the champions of justice, the Atreidae.
But the men where they fell about the wall
in all their beauty occupy
their tombs in Ilium's earth;
and the enemy land covers its occupiers. 455

ANTISTROPHE 3

Grievous is the talk of the citizens when they are
     angry;
The curse the people has pronounced ordains that
     a penalty must be paid.
My anxious thought waits to hear
a thing shrouded in darkness. 460
For the killers of many do not go
unwatched by the gods; and the black
Erinyes in time consign to darkness
him who is fortunate without justice,
wearing away his life while his fortune is reversed, 465
and among the vanished
he has no protection.
The burden of excessive praise
is heavy; for by the eyes of Zeus
the thunderbolt is hurled. 470
My choice is prosperity that brings no envy.
May I not be a sacker of cities,
nor yet, myself the captive of others
eat away my life!

EPODE

At the bidding of the fire that brought good news 475
through the city runs the swift
message; but if it is true
who knows, or if it is some lie sent by the gods?
Who is so childish or so far shaken out of his senses
as to let his heart take fire 480
at the new message of the beacon
and then to suffer when the story is changed?
It is like a woman's rule
to join in approving thanksgiving before the thing
     is manifest.
Too persuasive, a woman's ordinance spreads far, 485
traveling fast; but dying fast
a rumor voiced by a woman comes to nothing.

[Enter CLYTEMNESTRA.*]*

CLYTEMNESTRA: Soon shall we know about the
     beacon-watchings
and the fire-transmissions of the light-bearing
     torches, 490

whether they tell the truth or, as is the way of dreams,

this light that brought joy in its coming has beguiled us.

I see here a herald from the shore, his brow shaded with twigs of olive; and mud's brother

495 and neighbor, thirsty dust, attests this much,

that he is not voiceless, nor will you find him kindling

the flame of mountain brushwood to make signals with a fire that is illusion.

But either he will speak out, so that we rejoice the more . . .

but the opposite news is less to my liking.

May we have good besides the appearance of

500 good!

CHORUS: May whoever prays otherwise for our city reap in his own person the fruit of his mind's evil!

[Enter the HERALD.*]*

HERALD: Hail, earth of my fathers, earth of the Argive land!

In the light of this tenth year have I come home to you;

many hopes were shattered, but this one have I

505 had fulfilled.

Yes, never did I think that in this land of Argos I should die and have right of burial in soil most dear.

Now I say hail to my country, and hail to the sun's light,

and to you, supreme Zeus of the land, and you, Pythian° king,

with your bow no longer darting your shafts

510 against us.

The enmity you showed us by Scamander's° banks was enough;

but now be once more our preserver and healer, lord Apollo! and I address all the gods

in their assembly, and the guardian of my privilege,

515 Hermes, beloved herald, whom heralds revere,

and the heroes who were our escort; in kindness once again

may they receive the army that the spear has spared!

Hail, palace of our kings, beloved house,

and seats revered, and gods that face the sun!

520 Long ago, I think, with gladness in those eyes

did you wish us farewell; and now with . . . . . .

honor welcome the king after long lapse of time.

For he is come, bringing light in darkness to you

and to all present here together, the lord Agamemnon.°

Come, give him good greeting, for it is proper,

him who has uprooted Troy with the mattock of

525 Zeus who does justice

with which the soil has been worked over.

And the altars and the seats of the gods are vanished,

and the seed is perishing from all that land.

Such is the yoke that he has cast about the neck of Troy,

the senior chief born of Atreus, a man dear to the gods,

530

he that is come, worthiest of honor among men now living! for neither Paris nor Paris' confederate city

boasts that what they did was more than what they suffered.

For cast in a suit for rapine and for theft

he lost his booty, and in utter destruction

535

brought down the house of his fathers with his land.

Double was the atonement paid by the sons of Priam.

CHORUS: Herald of the Achaeans from the army, I wish you joy!

HERALD: I rejoice; and if the gods wish my death, I shall no longer say no.

CHORUS: Is it longing for this your native land that has afflicted you?

540

HERALD: Yes, so that my eyes fill with tears of joy.

CHORUS: Then this was an agreeable malady that was upon you.

HERALD: How so? if you instruct me I shall be master of this saying.

CHORUS: Because they for whom you were smitten with desire returned your longing.

HERALD: Do you mean that this land longed for the army that longed for it?

545

CHORUS: Yes, so that I sighed often from a darkened spirit.

HERALD: From where came this dejection? It was on the army that this oppression lay.

CHORUS: Long since silence has been my remedy against harm.

HERALD: How so? in the absence of the princes, were there some you feared?

---

[507] It was a great sorrow for a Greek to think that he would be buried abroad, with no kindred near to perform rituals at his tomb (cf. 452f. above). [509] **Pythian** pronounced *Pie' thi an:* Apollo, so called from Pytho, a name of his oracle at Delphi. The HERALD remembers the plague sent upon the Greeks by Apollo with his arrows and described in the first book of the *Iliad*. [511] **Scamander:** pronounced *Ska man' der*. [524] A line from some lost epic runs, "If he were to be done by as he did, then would true justice have been done." The expression "to be done by as one did" is proverbial and is used of the Persians, who invaded Greece with Xerxes, soon after the mention of their destruction of the temples in the passage just alluded to (*The Persians*, 813 f.).

CHORUS: So that, in your words, even death would
550   be a great joy.
HERALD: Yes, for success has been achieved; and of
these things in all the length of time
a part, one may say, has fallen out well
and part, again, may be faulted; but who except
the gods
is without pain for his whole lifetime's length?
555 For if I were to tell of our labors and hard bivouacs,
the narrow gangways, with their wretched bedding . . . and what groans
did we not utter, when we did not receive our
daily portion?
And other things, again, happened on land, and
these were yet more hateful;
for our beds were up against the walls of the
enemy;
560 and from the sky and from the meadowland
dews drizzled down upon us, to the constant ruin
of our clothing, filling our hair with creatures.
And if one were to tell of the winter, killer of birds,
intolerable as the snow of Ida made it,
565 or of the heat, when the sea in its noonday
repose without a wind lay where it had fallen
with no wave. . . .
Why should I lament for this? Our toil is past,
past so that the dead, for their part, care not even
to rise again.
570 Why must I tell the tale of those who perished,
and why must the living groan again over malignant fortune?
I hold that what has happened warrants us even
to feel great joy.
And for us who are left from the Argive army
gain prevails, and sorrow does not countervail it:
575 so that we may rightly boast to this sun's light,
as our fame flies over sea and land:
"After taking Troy once did the Argive host
nail up these spoils to the gods of Greece,
an ancient glory for their shrines."
When men hear such words, they must praise the
580   city
and her generals; and the grace of Zeus,
that accomplished these deeds, shall be honored.
You have heard all I have to say.
CHORUS: Your words prevail on me, and I do not
reject them;
for eagerness to learn is always a renewal of
youth for the old.
But it is proper that this should concern the house
585   and Clytemnestra
most, and that I should share the wealth it brings.
CLYTEMNESTRA: I raised the cry of triumph long since,
when there came the first message of the fire,
telling of the taking and the razing of Ilium.
And there were some who rebuked me, and said,
590   "Persuaded by

the beacons, do you think Troy has been sacked?
Indeed it is like a woman to let her feelings carry
her away."
By such words as these I was made to seem to
wander in my wits;
but nonetheless I sacrificed, and as is women's
custom
one here, one there in the city uttered   595
the jubilant cry, giving praise in the gods' abodes,
lulling the fragrant flame that feeds on incense.
And now, for the full story, what need have you
to tell it me?
From the king himself I shall hear all the tale.   600
But that I may make best haste to receive my honored husband
on his return—for what day's light
dawns sweeter for a woman than this,
when a god has brought her man safe home from
a campaign
and she unbars the door? . . . —take this message
to my husband!
May he come as soon as possible, the city's darling, 605
and may he find his wife faithful in his house,
just as he left her, the watchdog of the palace,
loyal to him, an enemy to his ill-wishers,
one alike in all things; in the length of time
she has destroyed no seal set there by him.
I know no more of delight—nor of censorious
rumor—   610
coming from another man, than I know how
bronze is dipped.
Such is my boast, a boast replete with truth,
not shameful for a noble lady to utter.
CHORUS: Thus has she spoken; if you understand   615
through clear interpreters, her speech looks fair.
But you speak, Herald! It is of Menelaus that I ask,
whether safely returned once more
he will come with you, a power dear to this land.
HERALD: It cannot be that I speak what is false as fair, 620
so that my friends harvest it for the long time
ahead.
CHORUS: If only you can tell good news and still
speak truth!
When good news and true news are severed, it is
not easy to conceal.
HERALD: The man is vanished from the Achaean host,
he and his ship; what I say is no lie.   625
CHORUS: Did he put out in your sight from Ilium,
or did a storm, a sorrow to all alike, snatch him
from the army?
HERALD: You have hit the mark, like a master archer;
and a long tale of woe you have briefly voiced.
CHORUS: Was it as living or as dead   630
that rumor on the other voyagers' lips told of him?
HERALD: No one knows so as to give clear report,
except the Sun that nurtures life upon the earth.

CHORUS: Then how do you say the storm came upon
    the fleet,
635   and how did it end, by the anger of the gods?
HERALD: It is not fitting to mar the day of good news
    with the tongue of ill report; apart is the honor
      paid to the gods.
    But when a messenger brings to a city news of
      calamity to be prayed against,
    with gloomy countenance, news of its army's fall—
    telling how one wound afflicting the whole people
640   has befallen the city,
    and how many men have been hounded forth
      from many homes,
    by the double scourge that Ares loves,
    a two-tipped spear of ruin, a bloody pair of yoke-
      fellows:
    when a messenger is loaded with such woes as
      these,
645   then it is proper to utter this paean of the Erinyes.°
    But when with good news of events bringing sal-
      vation
    he comes to a city rejoicing in prosperity . . .
    how shall I mix good with the bad, telling
    of the storm that afflicted the Achaeans, not with-
      out the wrath of heaven?
650   For a covenant was sworn by those former enemies,
    fire and sea, and they gave earnest of their friend-
      ship
    by destroying the unhappy host of the Argives;
    and in darkness evil arose from the stormy waves.
    The ships were dashed against each other by the
      winds of Thrace;
655   and they, butting against each other of necessity
    beneath the storm of the hurricane and the spray
      of beating rain,
    vanished out of sight, like sheep scattered by an
      evil shepherd.
    And when the sun's bright light arose,
660   we saw the Aegean sea flower with the corpses
    of Achaean men and with the wrecks of ships.
    But we and our ship, its hull unscathed,
    were stolen away or else begged off
    by some god who set his hand to the tiller.
    And preserving fortune graciously took her seat
      upon our vessel,
    so that we had not to stay at anchor and fear the
665   welter of the waves,
    nor did we run aground upon a rocky shore.
    And then, having escaped a watery Hades,
    in the bright light of day, not believing in our fortune,

we let our thoughts seek remedy for our new reverse,
for the host had suffered and been sorely pounded.   670
And now, if any of them yet breathes,
they speak of us as dead, of course;
and we suppose their fate to be the same.
May it turn out as well as possible! As for
    Menelaus,
first and chiefly, expect that he will come.   675
Well, if some ray of the sun finds him out
still flourishing in life, by the contrivance of a Zeus
who does not yet wish to exterminate his house,
there is some hope that he may come back home.
Know that in hearing so much you have heard
    the truth!   680

STROPHE 1

CHORUS: Who can have named her
with such utter truth?
Was it perhaps some unseen one
who in foreknowledge of what was fated
guided his tongue rightly?   685
Her, the bride of the spear, the object of contention,
Helen? For in a manner fitting to her name
destroyer of ships, destroyer of men, destroyer
of cities from the delicate tissues   690
of her bower she sailed,
sped by the breeze of Zephyrus° the giant.
And many huntsmen that bore shields
were gone in the wake of the oars   695
when they had put in to Simois'
leafy shores
through the work of bloody strife.

ANTISTROPHE 1

And for Ilium was a kedos° true to its name
accomplished by a wrath that fulfilled its purpose;   700
for the dishonoring of the guest-table
and of hospitable Zeus in later time
it exacted vengeance from those who loudly
celebrated the song in the bride's honor,   705
the song which then fell to the bridegroom's kin
    to sing.
And learning a different tune
Priam's aged city,   710
a tune of many sorrows,
loudly, I think, laments, calling upon
Paris of the disastrous marriage.
She has endured a life of ruin
and of lamentation through her citizens'
piteous slaughter.   715

---

645 The paean was originally a song in honor of Apollo, and
therefore joyful; the Erinyes (see note on 59), like other gods
of the underworld, had no place in any joyful form of worship, so that the notion of a paean of the Erinyes carries an
effect of powerful paradox.

---

692 Zephyrus pronounced *Zeff' ir us*: Zephyrus was the west
wind, not normally called a giant.   **699 Kedos**: this word can
mean either "A connection by marriage" or "mourning."

STROPHE 2

A man reared a lion's offspring
in his house, unsuckled, just as it was,
720 in the beginnings of its life
gentle, dear to children
and a delight to the aged.
And often he took it in his arms
like a new-born child
bright-eyed, and fawning on the hand
725 as its belly's needs compelled it.

ANTISTROPHE 2

But in time it showed the temper
it had from its parents; for returning
kindness to those that reared it
730 with horrid slaughter of their cattle
it made a feast unbidden,
and the house was befouled with blood,
woe irresistible to the servants,
a vast havoc of much slaughter.
735 And by the act of a god a priest of Ruin
had been reared within the house.

STROPHE 3

And at first I would say there came to Ilium's city
740 a temper of windless calm,
and a delicate adornment of wealth,
a soft dart of the eyes,
the flower of love that stings the heart.
And after bedding them together she° brought
about
745 a bitter end of the marriage,
evil in her sojourn, evil in her company
sped to the sons of Priam
by the guidance of the hospitable Zeus,
she that brings tears to brides, the Erinys.

ANTISTROPHE 3

And long has there been current among men an
750   ancient saying,
that a man's great prosperity, brought to completion,
has offspring, and does not perish childless;
755 and that from good fortune for a family
there is born insatiable woe.
And I am apart from others, alone in thought;
for the impious act
begets more after it,
760 like to the stock from whence they come.

---

744 The matron who presides over the nuptials is in this case
none other than the avenger of Zeus Xenios, the Erinys; the
audience is kept waiting until the end of the sentence and
stanza for the awful name (cf. 55–59).

For the fate of houses that walk straight in the
paths of justice
is a fair offspring of their former fate.

STROPHE 4

But ancient insolence is used
to beget an insolence that has its youth
among the woes of mortals, soon or late, when
the appointed time   765
of birth is come, and a spirit
irresistible, unconquerable, is brought forth,
the recklessness that is Ruin, black for the house,   770
like to its parents.

ANTISTROPHE 4

Justice shines
beneath smoky rafters
and honors the righteous life;   775
but the gold-bespangled halls where there are
hands unclean
she quits with eyes averted
and goes to what is holy, having no respect for
the power of wealth made counterfeit with praise.   780
And she guides all things to their appointed end.

[*Enter* AGAMEMNON *in his chariot, accompanied by*
CASSANDRA.]

CHORUS: Come, king, sacker of Troy,
offspring of Atreus,
how am I to address you? How am I to revere you,   785
neither overshooting nor falling short of
the right measure of my gratitude?
Many among mortals give preference to seeming,
transgressing against justice.
To echo the groans of the unfortunate   790
each one is ready; but the sting of pain
does not reach their hearts.
And seeming as though they share his joy,
constraining their mirthless faces
. . . . . .
But whoever is a good judge of his flock   795
cannot fail to know that look in a man's eyes
which seems to come from a loyal mind
but which fawns on him with watery friendship.
And of you long ago when you launched your
expedition
for the sake of Helen—I will not conceal it—   800
I painted a most unskillful picture
. . . . . .
and as not wielding well the tiller of your mind,
trying by sacrifices to bring back
courage to dying men [?].
But now not from the mind's edge nor without
friendship   805
I say, "Sweet is toil to them who have accomplished."

And in time shall you learn by inquiry
which of the citizens has guarded the city justly
and which has failed to keep the proper limit.
810 AGAMEMNON: First Argos and the gods of the land,
It is right that I address,
they that have a share in
my safe return and in the satisfaction exacted
from Priam's city. For by no spoken word the gods
815 heard the parties' pleas, and in no uncertain fashion
their votes for the death of men and ruin of Ilium
they put into the urn of blood;° and to the opposite vessel
hope of a hand approached, but the vessel was
  not filled.
And even now the smoke marks out the conquered city.
Destruction's storms have life; and dying with the
  city
820 the embers waft forth rich breaths of wealth.
For this must the gods with very mindful gratitude
be paid, since their arrogant rapine
has been avenged, and for a woman's sake
their city was ground to dust by the Argive monster,°
825 the offspring of a horse, the shield-bearing army,
which launched its leap as the Pleiads set.
And the ravening lion leaped over the wall,
and licked his fill of the blood of kings.
To the gods I have drawn out this prelude.
But as for what you think, I have listened and
830   remember,
and I too say the same and you have me as a fellow advocate.
For in few among men it is inbred
to pay respect without envy to a friend in his
  prosperity.
For the poison of hatred lodged near the heart
835 doubles the burden for him who has the malady;
he is burdened with his own sorrows,
and he groans as he looks upon another's happiness.
I can speak from knowledge—well I know
the mirror of society, the image of a shadow,
840 those who seem most kindly towards me.
But only Odysseus, who sailed against his will,
once yoked proved a ready trace-horse for me;
whether he is alive or dead, I say
this of him. But for the rest, in the sight of the city
  and the gods
845 we shall hold general conclave in full assembly

and shall take counsel. As for that which is well,
we must plan that it continue well.
But as for that which has need of healing remedies,
either by burning or by the kindly knife
we shall try to turn back the pain of the disease. 850
But now I shall come to my halls and to the house
  where lies my hearth,
and my first greeting shall be for the gods
who sped me far and have brought me back;
and since victory has attended me, may she abide!
CLYTEMNESTRA: Men of the city, honored lords of
  Argos here, 855
I shall feel no shame to speak to you
of the love I bear my husband; for in time timidity
dies away for human kind. It is not from others
that I have learned; I shall speak of my own life
  of sorrow
so long as this man was beneath Ilium. 860
First, for a woman far from her husband
to sit in her house alone is a fearful grief,
hearing many a malignant rumor;
as one messenger follows another
bringing yet worse tidings, uttering sorrow for the
  house. 865
And if this man has endured as many wounds
as rumor channeled to our house
made him, he is riddled with more holes than a net.
And if he had been dead, as many stories reported,
then with three bodies, like a second Geryon,° 870
he could have claimed to receive a threefold cloak
  of earth
—much earth above, I do not speak of that below!—
perishing once under each aspect.
Because of such malignant rumors as these
many nooses were knotted for my neck and hung
  on high, 875
untied by others by force after they had seized me
  against my will.
This, I say, is why our son does not stand here,
the warrant of your pledges and of mine,
as he should have stood, Orestes°; do not be surprised at this.
For he is the guest of a kindly ally, 880
Strophius the Phocian°, who warned me of trouble
on two accounts, of your peril
before Ilium, and of how the people's lawless clamor
might overthrow the council, since it is inbred
in mortals to kick the man who has fallen. 885

---

817 In a fifth-century Athenian law-court there was an urn of condemnation and an urn of acquittal; the juror received one pebble, which he put into one or the other of them. He may have taken care to preserve the secrecy of the ballot by approaching the other urn also and pretending to put his pebble into it; but we do not have to suppose this in order to understand the text.   824 The Wooden Horse.

870 Geryon (*Gee' ry on*; hard "*g*"), or Geryones, was a monster with three bodies and three heads who lived near Tartessos in Spain (in the neighborhood of Cadiz) and was killed by Heracles.   879 One story was that Orestes was rescued, either by Electra or by a faithful nurse, at the time of the murder. 881 Strophius (*Stroff' i us*), king of Phocis, was the father of Pylades, Orestes' (*Or' est' ēs*) great friend.

Such a pretext carries no deceit.
For me the gushing fountains of my tears
have run dry, and no drop is left in them;
and my late-watching eyes are sore
890 with weeping for the beacon-fires for you
left ever unattended. And in my dreams
the light sounds of a gnat's trumpeting
would wake me, since I saw more sufferings concerning you
than the time through which I slept had room for.
Now, having endured all this, with a heart free
895 from mourning
I can call my husband here the watchdog of the fold,
the forestay that preserves the ship, the firmly
grounded pillar
of the lofty roofs, only-begotten child to a father,
land appearing to sailors beyond hope,
900 fair weather seen after the storm,
for the thirsty traveler the water of a fountain;
it is a joy to escape any manner of constraint.
Such are the appellations of which I hold him
worthy.
But let envy be absent; for many are the sufferings
905 which I bore in time past; and now, dear one,
descend from this your chariot, not setting upon
the ground
your foot, O king, the foot that conquered Troy!
Handmaids, why do you delay, you who have
assigned to you the task
of strewing the ground he walks on with tapestries?
910 At once let his path be spread with purple,
that Justice may lead him to the home he never
hoped to see!
And for the rest, may forethought not overcome
by sleep
accomplish all justly with the gods' aid as it is fated!
AGAMEMNON: Offspring of Leda, guardian of my house,
915 your speech matches my absence;
for you have drawn it out at length. But to give me
fitting praise, that is an honor that should come
from others.
And for the rest do not in woman's fashion
pamper me; do not as if I were a barbarian
920 gape at me with prostrations and loud cries;
do not by strewing my path with raiment make it
exposed
to envy. It is the gods you should honor with
such things;
and to walk, being a mortal, on embroidered
splendors
is impossible for me without fear.
925 I tell you to honor me with honors human, not
divine.
Apart from footwipers and embroideries
the voice of fame resounds; and good sense
is the god's greatest gift. We must pronounce him
fortunate

who has ended his life in the prosperity he cherishes;°
and if in all things I may fare so, I do not lack
confidence. 930
CLYTEMNESTRA: Come, tell me this, not against your
judgment.
AGAMEMNON: My judgment, be assured, I shall not
suppress.
CLYTEMNESTRA: Would you have vowed to the gods,
in a moment of fear, that you would act after
this fashion?
AGAMEMNON: Yes, if any with sure knowledge had
prescribed this ritual.
CLYTEMNESTRA: What do you think Priam would have
done, had he accomplished this? 935
AGAMEMNON: Indeed he would have walked upon
embroideries, I think.
CLYTEMNESTRA: Then feel no scruple for the reproach
of men.
AGAMEMNON: Yet talk in the mouths of the people
has great power.
CLYTEMNESTRA: But he of whom none is jealous is not
envied.
AGAMEMNON: It is not a woman's part to desire
contention. 940
CLYTEMNESTRA: But for the fortunate even to yield up
victory is becoming.
AGAMEMNON: Do you in truth value victory in this
contest?
CLYTEMNESTRA: Be persuaded; you are the winner, if
willingly you leave all to me.
AGAMEMNON: Well, if this is your pleasure, let someone swiftly loose
my boots, which serve my feet as slaves; 945
and as I tread upon these purples of the gods,
let no eye's envy strike me from afar.
For I feel much reluctance to waste the house's
substance with my feet,
ruining wealth and tissues bought with silver.
For this, so much; but in kindly fashion 950
bring in this stranger; on him who is gentle in the
use of power
the god from afar looks favorably;
for none of his own will bows to the yoke of slavery.
And she came with me as the chosen flower
out of much wealth, the army's gift.° 955
But since I am constrained to defer to you in this,

---

928 It is a commonplace of Greek popular thought that a man can only be pronounced fortunate after his death.   **955** It was a common practice in the heroic age for an army that had sacked a city to bestow upon its chiefs female captives as a token of regard. These women enjoyed the status of a secondary wife, and sometimes had children by their captors who themselves attained heroic status, although inferior in position to the children of the chief wife.

I will go into the halls of the palace, treading
  upon purple.
CLYTEMNESTRA: There is a sea—and who shall dry it
  up?—
  that breeds a gush of much purple, precious as
    silver,
960 ever renewed, for the dyeing of garments.
  And a store of such stuffs by the gods' grace, king,
  is here for us to have; the palace does not know
    poverty.
  And I would have vowed the trampling of much
    raiment,
  had it been prescribed at the seat of an oracle,
965 in contriving the homecoming of this man's life.
  For while the root survives, the leaves return to
    the house,
  stretching their shade over against the dogstar;
  and with your return to the hearth of the palace,
  you signal warmth in winter by your coming.
970 And when Zeus makes from the unripe grape
  wine, then at once is there coolness in the house,
  while a man of power walks about the palace.
  Zeus, Zeus with power to accomplish, accomplish
    my prayer;
  and may what you are about to accomplish be
    your care!

STROPHE 1

975 CHORUS: Why, ever constant, does this
  terror, set before my divining heart°
  hover,
  and prophecy speaks in a song unbidden, unpaid
    for,°
980 nor does trustful confidence
  sit on my mind's throne
  so that I can spurn it away
  like a dream hard to interpret?
  Time has passed its youth
985 since the cables were thrown
  onto the sandy shore,
  when to Ilium
  the army came in its ships.

ANTISTROPHE 1

And I learn with my own eyes

of his return, myself my witness;
but nonetheless the dirge without a lyre   990
is chanted,
the dirge of the Erinys is chanted by my mind,
  self-taught
within me, altogether lacking
the cherished confidence of hope.
And my inward parts do not speak vainly,   995
while near a mind instinct with justice
my heart swirls in eddies
that bring fulfillment.
Yet I pray that from my
expectation these things may fall
so that they fail to be fulfilled.   1000

STROPHE 2

Indeed great good health
is never content with its limits. For sickness,
a neighbor that shares a wall, presses it hard;
and a man's fortune, steering a straight course 1005
strikes a hidden reef.
But if beforehand any part of the possessions
that he owns is hurled by apprehension
from the derrick° of moderation—   1010
then the house entire does not sink,
overfull of abundance,
nor does the hull plunge beneath the waves.
Great and abundant is the gift that comes from
  Zeus,
which from the furrows of each year's harvest   1015
destroys the plague of famine.

ANTISTROPHE 2

But the black blood that has once
poured to the ground in front of a man
in death who could call back   1020
with incantations?
Even him° that knew well
how to raise men up from the dead
Zeus checked in no gentle fashion.
And did not one portion appointed   1025
by the gods restrain another
from going beyond its due,
then my heart would outstrip
my tongue and would be pouring this forth.

---

976 The early Greeks believed the seat of the intelligence to be the heart; the importance of the brain was realized by the fifth-century medical writer, Alcmaeon of Croton.   **979** The minstrels who sing in the halls of kings in the Homeric poems perform only at the bidding of their patrons, who later reward them for their performances. The CHORUS compares its presentiment of evil with a song of a different nature; the comparison is made easier because the presentiment is called a prophecy, and prophets often put their predictions into verse.

1010 A derrick is an apparatus for slinging off cargo which is to be jettisoned.   **1022** The reference is to Asclepius, son of Apollo by the mortal woman Coronis, who was so great a physician that he could restore the dead to life. According to the early legend, he restored Hippolytus to please Artemis, and for doing so he was killed by Zeus with the thunderbolt. This legend became less prominent in later times, when the cult of Asclepius had attained great importance and his shrines at Epidaurus, Cos, and Pergamum had become places of pilgrimage.

1030　But as things are it murmurs in darkness
　　　full of sad thoughts and having no hope
　　　of accomplishing any timely purpose,
　　　while fire is kindled in my mind.

[Enter CLYTEMNESTRA.]

　　　CLYTEMNESTRA: Bring yourself in, you too, I mean
1035　　　Cassandra!
　　　Since without anger Zeus has made you with our
　　　　house
　　　a sharer in lustral water, with many slaves
　　　taking your stand near the altar of Zeus, god of
　　　　possessions,
　　　descend from the chariot here, and do not be proud.
　　　Why, they say that even the son of Alcmene° once
1040　　endured to be sold. . . . . .
　　　At least, if the constraint of this lot befalls one,
　　　one should feel much gratitude at having lords
　　　　whose wealth is ancient;
　　　for those who have reaped a fair harvest which
　　　　they never hoped for
1045　　are cruel to slaves in all things, and according to
　　　　strict rule
　　　　. . . . . .
　　　I have told you the nature of our custom.
　　　CHORUS: It is to you she speaks, a clear speech,
　　　　and now she pauses.
　　　Caught as you are in the toils of fate,
　　　obey her if you will; but perhaps you will not.
1050　CLYTEMNESTRA: Why, if she is not, like a swallow,°
　　　possessed of an unintelligible barbarian tongue,
　　　I speak within the compass of her wits [?], and try
　　　　to prevail on her with my words.
　　　CHORUS(to CASSANDRA): Go with her; what she
　　　　orders is best as things now are.
　　　Obey, leaving your seat here on the wagon.
　　　CLYTEMNESTRA: I have no time to linger here by the
1055　　door;
　　　for the cattle of Hestia of the central navel-stone
　　　stand there already, sacrifices to reward the fire,
　　　for us who never hoped to have this joy.
　　　And you, if you have a mind to obey any of my
　　　　orders, make no delay;
　　　but if you lack understanding and do not take in
1060　　my words,

1040 **Alcmene**: pronounce *Alk meen' ē* (mother of Heracles): Heracles was punished for his treacherous murder of Iphitus by being taken to Lydia by Hermes and there sold to the queen Omphale, whom he served for a period (see Sophocles, *The Women of Trachis* 248f.).　　1050 The Greeks called foreigners, particularly the Orientals, by the contemptuous name *"barbaroi"* ("barbarians"), originally descriptive of what they thought to be their incoherent speech, which was sometimes compared to the twittering of swallows.

then instead of speech make indication with bar-
　　barian hand.
CHORUS: The stranger seems to need a clear inter-
　　preter;
and her manner is that of a newly captured beast.
CLYTEMNESTRA: Indeed she is crazy and obeys the
　　prompting of a mischievous mind,
she who has come leaving a city newly conquered 1065
and does not know how to bear the bridle
till she has spent her strength in bloody foam.
I say I will not waste more words to be insulted.

[Exit CLYTEMNESTRA.]

CHORUS: But I will not be angry, for I pity her.
　　Come, unhappy one, desert this carriage, 1070
　　and bowing to constraint submit to the unaccus-
　　tomed yoke.

[CASSANDRA utters a cry of distress.]

CASSANDRA: Apollo, Apollo!°
CHORUS: Why do you utter cries of woe, invoking
　　Loxias?
　　He is not such that a singer of dirges should come
　　his way. 1075

[CASSANDRA utters another cry.]

CASSANDRA: Apollo, Apollo!
CHORUS: Once more she calls with voice ill-omened
　　on the god,
　　one in no way suited to stand by when tears are
　　shed.
CASSANDRA: Apollo, Apollo! 1080
　　You of the roadside, my destroyer.
　　For you have a second time easily destroyed me.
CHORUS: She will prophesy about her own sorrows;
　　the god's gift remains in her mind, even in servitude.
CASSANDRA: Apollo, Apollo! 1085
　　You of the roadside, my destroyer!
　　Ah, where have you brought me? To what house?
CHORUS: To that of the Atreidae; if you do not
　　understand this,
　　I tell it you; and you shall not say that it is false.
CASSANDRA: No, to a house that hates the gods, one 1090
　　that knows
　　many sad tales of kindred murder . . . ,
　　a slaughter-place for men, a place where the
　　ground is sprinkled.
CHORUS: The stranger seems to have keen scent, like
　　a hound,

1073 The Olympian gods, and Apollo in particular, can have no part in scenes of mourning. *Loxias (Lox' i as)* is a title of Apollo, especially associated with his aspect as a god of prophecy.

and she is on the track of those whose blood she
  will discover.
1095 CASSANDRA(*pointing to the door of the palace*): Yes, for
  here are the witnesses that I believe.
  These are children weeping for their slaughter,
  and for the roasted flesh their father ate.
  CHORUS: Indeed we had heard of your prophetic fame;
  but we seek no interpreters of the gods.
1100 CASSANDRA: O horror, what plot is this?
  What is this great new agony?
  A great evil is being plotted in this house,
  unbearable for its friends, hard to remedy;
  and protection stands far off.
1105 CHORUS: These prophecies I know not;
  but the others I recognized; for it is the talk of all
    the city.
  CASSANDRA: Ah, wretched one, will you accomplish
    this?
  The husband who shares your bed
  you have washed in the bath, and . . . how shall I
    tell the end?
1110 For soon this shall be; and she stretches forth hand
  after hand, reaching out.
  CHORUS: I do not yet understand; for now her riddles
  leave me perplexed at her obscure oracles.
  CASSANDRA: Ah, ah! Alas, alas, what is this that
    comes into view?
1115 Indeed it is some net of Hades.
  But it is the net that shares his bed, that shares the
    guilt
  of murder. And let that company whom the fami-
    ly can never sate
  raise a shout over the sacrifice that stoning must
    avenge!
  CHORUS: What Erinys do you bid raise her cry
1120 over the house? Your words give me no joy.
  And to my heart runs a drop of saffron dye,
  the drop that for men who fall by the spear
  accompanies the rays of life's sun as it sets;
  and swiftly comes destruction.
1125 CASSANDRA: Ah, ah! Look, look! Keep away the bull
  from the cow! In the robe
  she has caught him with the contrivance of her
    black horn,
  and she strikes; and he falls in the vessel of water.
  It is the stroke struck by the cauldron of cunning
    murder that I speak of.
  CHORUS: I would not boast of being a master judge
1130 of oracles,
  but this seems to me like some evil thing.
  But from oracles what good message
  is sent to men? For through evil
  the wordy arts of soothsayers
1135 bring fear to their listeners.
  CASSANDRA: Oh, oh! The unhappy fate of me in my
    misery!

For I speak of my own agony; another cup has
  been poured out.
Where have you brought me, one unfortunate?
For nothing but to share your death? Why else?
CHORUS: Your wits are crazed and a god carries you
  away,   1140
and over yourself you chant
a song unmusical, like that tawny one,
who, never tired of crying, cries, alas, with sad
  heart
lamenting for Itys, for Itys throughout a life
with sorrow beset on both sides, a nightingale.°
CASSANDRA: Oh, oh! The end of the songful
  nightingale!   1145
For about her the gods cast a winged body
and give her a happy ordeal, free from cries of pain.
But for me there waits a rending with the two-
  edged spear.
CHORUS: From where have you the rushing pangs of
  possession by a god,   1150
pangs that are in vain
and you shape your song of fear with ill-omened
  shriek
and in piercing notes alike?
From where have you the boundaries of your
  prophetic way
that tell of evil?   1155
CASSANDRA: O the marriage of Paris, deadly to those
  he loved!
O my native stream of Scamander!
Then I was reared and grew
about your banks, ah me!
But about the shores of Cocytus and of Acheron°   1160
I am likely soon to prophesy.
CHORUS: Why have you voiced this saying, all too
  clear?
A child might hear and understand.
And I am struck once more by a deadly pang,
by your grievous fate, listening to your shrill
  plaintive notes   1165
shattering for me to hear.
CASSANDRA: O the sorrows, the sorrows of my city
  that perished utterly!

1144 The nightingale was originally Procne, daughter of
Pandion, king of Athens and wife of Tereus, king of Thrace.
Her sister Philomela was ravished by Tereus, who cut her
tongue out to keep his crime secret, but Philomela by depicting the story on a tapestry informed her sister. Together they
took revenge on Tereus by killing Itys (*Eye' tis*), his infant son
by Procne; then the gods changed Procne into the nightingale,
Philomela into the swallow. Philomela becomes the nightingale, as far as we know, only in Roman poetry.   1160 Cocytus
(*Kō kye' tus*), which means "the river of weeping," and
Acheron, which was popularly derived from a word meaning
"sorrow" (cf. 1557), were two of the rivers of Hades.

O my father's sacrifices before the walls,
prodigal in slaughter of cattle that cropped the
1170   grass!
But they did not suffice for a remedy
to save the city from suffering as was fated.
And I whose mind is all aflame shall soon fall to
the ground. [?]
CHORUS: These utterances follow on those before;
and some malignant spirit falls
1175   grievously upon you and makes you
sing of sorrows full of tears and charged with death.
And the end I do not know.
CASSANDRA: Now shall my oracle be no longer one
that looks forth
from a veil, like a newly wedded bride,
1180   but as a bright, clear wind it shall rush
toward the sunrise, so that like a wave
there shall surge toward the light a woe far greater
than this; no more in riddles shall I instruct you.
You bear me witness, running beside me as I
scent out
1185   the track of the ills accomplished long ago!
For this house is never left by a choir°
that sings in unison, yet with no pleasant sound;
for not pleasant are its words.
Yes, and it has drunk—so that it grows all the
bolder—
of human blood, and stays in the house, a band of
revelers
not easily sent away, composed of the Erinyes
1190   bred with the family.
And the song they sing as they beset the rooms
is one of destruction that began it all; and each in
turn they spit
on a brother's marriage-bed that brought harm to
its violator.°
Have I missed the mark, or do I like an archer
make a hit?
Or am I a false prophet who knocks at doors, a
1195   babbler?
Speak out in witness, taking oath that I know

1186 After a *symposion* (drinking party), the guests would often take part in a *kōmos* (a word sometimes translated "revel" and sometimes "serenade," according to the context; Milton's Comus derives his name from it). Carrying torches, they would set forth to serenade one house after another in their more or less drunken state; such scenes are sometimes depicted on Greek vases. The members of this *kōmos* have drunk deep, not of wine but of blood, and instead of going from house to house, they remain at the house of the Atreidae. 1193 Thyestes first seduced Aerope, the wife of his brother Atreus, and had her hand over to him the golden lamb that was the token of Atreus' sovereignty, a story perhaps glanced at at 1585. Atreus took vengeance by killing all his brother's children except one (he killed a dozen, if the text at 1605 is sound) and serving them to him at a banquet.

---

the crimes of the house, old in story!°
CHORUS: And how could the plighting of an oath,
though truly plighted,
avail for remedy? But I marvel at you,
that though bred beyond the seas you speak truly   1200
of a foreign city, as though you had been present.
CASSANDRA: It was the prophet Apollo who set me in
this office.
CHORUS: Struck with desire, god though he is?
CASSANDRA: Earlier, modesty made me not speak of
this.
CHORUS: Yes, we are all fastidious when we have
great good fortune.   1205
CASSANDRA: Well, he was a wrestler who mightily
breathed his grace upon me.
CHORUS: Did you come to the act of getting children,
as is the way?
CASSANDRA: I consented, and then played Loxias false.
CHORUS: Being already seized by the prophetic arts?
CASSANDRA: Already I was foretelling to the citizens
all their sufferings.   1210
CHORUS: How then were you unscathed by the
wrath of Loxias?
CASSANDRA: I could make none in anything believe
me, once I had committed this offense.
CHORUS: Yet to us your divinations seem worthy of
belief.
CASSANDRA: Ah, ah! O misery!
Once more the dread pain of true prophecy
whirls me round,   1215
troubling me with sinister preludes.
Do you see here sitting near the house
these young ones, like to the shapes we see in
dreams?
Children slain, as it were, by the hands of their
kindred,
their hands full of the meat of their own flesh;   1220
the vitals with the entrails I see them holding,
a pitiful load, of which their father ate.
For these, so I declare, there is one who plots
revenge
a cowardly lion, tumbling in the bed,
watching at home, alas, for the master on his return, 1225
my master—for I must bear the yoke of slavery.
And the commander of the fleet, the destroyer of
Ilium
does not know what kind of hateful bitch's tongue,
uttering and drawing out at length, with welcoming smile, its plea,
shall hit, with an evil hitting, upon the target of
crafty destruction.   1230
Such is her daring; the female is the murderer of
the male.

1196 A Greek prophet was supposed to know not only the future but also the present and the past.

She is—what is the proper name for me to give
the hateful monster?—an amphisbaena°, or a Scylla
living in the rocks, a bane to sailors,
1235   a raging hell-mother, breathing truceless war
against her own! And how she cried out in joy,
she who dares all things, as though at the turning
point of battle!
And she seems to revel in his safe homecoming.
And if I fail to convince you of this, all is one;
how can it be otherwise?
1240   The future will come; and soon you shall stand here
to pronounce me, in pity, a prophet who spoke all
too true.
CHORUS: Thyestes' feast upon his children's flesh
I understand and shudder at, and fear possesses me
as I hear it truly told and not in images.
But when I hear the rest I lose the track and run
1245   off the path.
CASSANDRA: I say that you shall look on
Agamemnon's end.
CHORUS: Unhappy one, lull your voice to utter no ill-
omened word!
CASSANDRA: But no healer stands by while this word
is uttered.
CHORUS: No, if indeed it must be so; but may it not
happen!
CASSANDRA: You utter prayers, but others are about
1250   the business of killing.
CHORUS: Who is the man by whom this woeful deed
is being brought about!
CASSANDRA: Far, indeed, you have been thrown from
the track of my oracles.
CHORUS: Yes, for I do not understand the scheme of
him who will accomplish it.
CASSANDRA: And yet I know the Greek tongue all
too well.
CHORUS: So do the oracles of Pytho; yet they are hard
1255   to understand no less.
CASSANDRA: Ah, ah! It is like fire, and it comes over me!
Oh, Lycean Apollo, woe is me!
This two-footed lioness that beds
with the wolf in the noble lion's absence
1260   will kill me, poor wretch; and as though brewing
a potion she will put in the cup a wage for me also.
She boasts, as she sharpens the sword for the man,
that he shall pay with murder for his bringing of me.
Why do I preserve these things to mock myself,
this staff and these fillets of prophecy about my
1265   neck?
You I shall destroy before my death!
Go you to ruin! As you fall, so I pay you back!
Make rich with destruction some other instead of
me!

But see, Apollo himself stripping me
of my prophetic raiment, he who has watched me   1270
mightily mocked even with these ornaments
upon me
by friends turned enemies,° mocked without
doubt in vain.
And like a wandering mendicant
I bore with being called beggar, wretch,
starveling;
and now the prophet has undone me, his
prophetess,   1275
and has hailed me off to such a deadly fate as this.
Instead of my father's altar,° a chopping-block
awaits me,
soon to be red with my hot blood when I am
struck before the sacrifice.
Yet shall my death not go without vengeance
from the gods!
For there shall come another to avenge us in turn,   1280
a son that slays his mother, an atoner for his father;
an exile and a wanderer, estranged from this land
he shall return to put the coping-stone on this
destruction for his kin.
For a great oath has been sworn by the gods,
that the stroke that laid his father low shall fetch
him home.   1285
Why do I make this pitiful lament,
now that I have seen Ilium's city
faring as it fared, and those that took the city
have come off like this in the judgment of the gods?
I shall go and act; I shall endure to die;
and I call on these gates as gates of Hades.   1290
I pray I may receive a mortal stroke,
that without a struggle my blood may gush forth
in easy death, and I may close these eyes of mine.
CHORUS: Woman much to be pitied and very wise,   1295
your speech has been long. But if truly
you know your fate, why like a cow whom the god
impels, do you go fearlessly to the altar?°
CASSANDRA: There is no escape, strangers, for any
further length of time.
CHORUS: But the last of one's time is valued most.   1300
CASSANDRA: This day is come; little shall I gain by
flight.
CHORUS: Well, know that your endurance comes
from a valiant heart.
CASSANDRA: None among the fortunate hears such
words.
CHORUS: But a glorious death is happiness for a mortal.

1272 **friends turned enemies** CASSANDRA's own family, who
under the influence of Apollo's curse mocked at her prophecies.   1277 Priam was cut down by Neoptolemus, son of
Achilles, at the altar of Zeus, at which he had taken refuge as
a suppliant.   1298 If a sacrificial victim seemed to go willingly to the altar, it was considered a good omen.

1233 **amphisbaena:** a mythical monster, a snake with a head at
both ends. **Scylla** a many headed monster.

CASSANDRA: Alas for you, father, and for your noble
1305   children!

[CASSANDRA *starts to advance toward the door of the palace, but starts back.*]

CHORUS: What is the matter? What fear turns you
        back?
CASSANDRA: Ah, ah!
CHORUS: Why do you cry, "Ah"?—unless it is some
        repulsion in your mind.
CASSANDRA: The house breathes slaughter, dripping
        blood.
CHORUS: How so? This is the smell of the sacrifice at
1310   the hearth.
CASSANDRA: The same scent as from a tomb assails me.
CHORUS: It is no Syrian incense, giving splendor to
        the house, of which you speak.
CASSANDRA: See, I go and in the house to lament my
        fate
        and Agamemnon's. Enough of life!
1315   Ah, my hosts!
        I cry not out in terror, like a bird before a bush,
        but in death bear me witness to this,
        when a woman shall die in return for me, a
        woman,
        and a man for a man unfortunate in his wife.
        And I call on you thus, my hosts, as one about
1320   to die.
CHORUS: Poor lady, I pity you for the end you have
        foretold.
CASSANDRA: I wish to make one speech more, or sing
        a dirge
        over myself: I pray to the sun's
        last light that to my avengers
1325   my enemies may pay for my murder also,
        for the death of a slave, an easy overthrow.
        Alas for the affairs of men! When they are fortu-
        nate,
        one may liken them to a shadow; and if they are
        unfortunate
        a wet sponge with one dash blots out the picture.
1330   And I pity this far more than that.

[CASSANDRA *goes into the house.*]

CHORUS: Of prosperity all mortals can never
        have too much; and from the halls
        to which men's fingers point none bars it
        and turns it away with these words:
        "Enter no more."
1335   To this man the blessed ones granted
        That he should take Priam's city,
        and honored by the gods he returns home.
        But now if he is to atone for the blood of some
        who are of the past
        and by dying for the dead is to ordain
1340   a penalty that consists in other deaths,

who, who among mortals may boast himself born
with a fortune beyond reach of harm?
AGAMEMNON (*offstage*): Oh, I am struck deep with a
        mortal blow!
CHORUS: Silence! Who tells of a blow, mortally
        wounded?
AGAMEMNON: Oh! Yet again, a second time I am
1345   struck!
CHORUS: I think the deed is done, from the king's
        cries of pain.
        But let us take counsel together, in the hope that
        there is some
        safe plan.
CHORUS 1: I for my part tell you my opinion;
        we should sound a summons to the citizens to
        bring help here to the palace.
CHORUS 2: But I think we had best break in at once,   1350
        and prove the deed while the sword is newly
        streaming.
CHORUS 3: I too join in such a proposal,
        and vote for action; it is no time for delay.
CHORUS 4: It is clear; their prelude is that of people
        whose acts betoken tyranny for the city.   1355
CHORUS 5: Yes, for we loiter; but they tread under-
        foot
        the fair fame of the goddess Delay, and show
        themselves awake with actions.
CHORUS 6: I do not know what plan I can hit on and
        put forward;
        it is to the doer that deliberation too belongs.
CHORUS 7: I too am of like mind, for I am at a loss   1360
        for how to raise up the dead again with words.
CHORUS 8: Are we even to protract our lives while
        yielding thus
        to these defilers of the house as leaders?
CHORUS 9: Why, it cannot be borne, but death is bet-
        ter;
        for that is a gentler fate than to have tyranny.   1365
CHORUS 10: Must we truly, inferring from his cries of
        pain,
        guess that the man has perished?
CHORUS 11: We should know for sure before we dis-
        cuss this matter;
        for guessing is different from sure knowledge.
CHORUS 12: All my votes go for approving this
        opinion,   1370
        that we should know for certain how it is with
        the son of Atreus.

[CLYTEMNESTRA *comes into view, standing over the dead bodies of* AGAMEMNON *and* CASSANDRA.]

CLYTEMNESTRA: Before I said much to suit the time,
        but I shall feel no shame to say the opposite.
        For if one has in hand acts of enmity against enemies
        who seem to be friends, how else can one fence up
        the nets   1375

of harm to a height beyond overleaping?
For me this contest, sprung from an ancient quarrel,
has been matter for thought long since; but in
time it has come;
and I stand where I struck, with the deed done.
1380   And I so acted—and I will not deny it—
that he could neither escape nor ward off death.
A covering inextricable, like a net for fish,
I threw around him, an evil wealth of raiment;
I struck him twice; and while uttering two cries
he let go, where he was, his legs; and after he had
1385   fallen
I added a third stroke, a votive offering
for the Zeus below the earth, the savior of
corpses.
So did he fall and quickly breathed away his life,
and spouting out a sharp jet of blood
1390   he struck me with a dark shower of gory dew,
while I rejoiced no less than the crop rejoices
in the Zeus-given moisture at the birth of the bud.
So stands the case, my honored lords of Argos
here;
rejoice, if you will rejoice, but I exult in it.
And if one could pour over a corpse libation of a
1395   fitting liquid,
would it be just to pour this, no, more than just!
Such a mixing bowl of evils, sprung from the
curse, did he
fill up in the house and return himself to drain!
CHORUS: We wonder at your tongue, at its audacity,
1400   that you utter such a speech over your husband.
CLYTEMNESTRA: You make trial of me as though of a
foolish woman;
but I with fearless heart speak to those who
know—
and whether you wish to praise or blame me,
all is one—this is Agamemnon, my husband,
1405   and a corpse, the work of this right hand,
a just workman. So stands the case.
CHORUS: Woman, what evil
food nurtured by the earth or what drink
sprung from the flowing sea have you tasted,
that you have put on yourself this murder, and
1410   incurred the people's curses?
You have cast away, you have cut away; and
away from the city shall you go,
an object of grievous hate to the citizens.
CLYTEMNESTRA: Now you pass judgment on me of
exile from the city
and declare that the citizens' hate and the people's curse shall be mine,
though then you raised no opposition to this
man,
who holding it of no special account, as though it
1415   were the death of a beast,
where sheep in their fleecy flocks abound,

sacrificed his own child, a travail
most dear to me, to charm the winds of Thrace?
Was it not he whom you should have driven from
this land,
as penalty for his polluting act? But when you take
cognizance   1420
of my actions, you are a harsh judge. But I bid
you
utter such threats, being prepared
that if in fight on equal terms you vanquish me
you shall rule; but if a god ordains the opposite,
you shall have a lesson, and shall learn, though
late, discretion.   1425
CHORUS: Great is your daring,
arrogant your words; just as your mind
is maddened by the bloody deed,
the blood-fleck in your eyes° is clear to see.
In requital yet you must, deprived of friends,
pay with blow for blow.   1430
CLYTEMNESTRA: This too you are hearing, the solemn
power of my oath!
I swear by the justice accomplished for my child,
and by Ruin and the Erinys, to whom I sacrificed
this man,
for me no expectation walks the hall of fear,
so long as the fire upon my hearth is kindled by   1435
Aegisthus, as in time past loyal to me;
for in him I have no slight shield of confidence.
Low he lies, he who did outrage against me his
wife,
the darling of each Chryseis° beneath Ilium!
And this woman here, the captive and soothsayer 1440
and bedfellow for him, the trusty prophetess
who shared his couch, the public harlot
of the sailors' benches! They have not failed to get
the honor due them.
For he lies as I have described, and she after
singing
like a swan° her last lament in death   1445
lies beside him, his lover; when he brought in
a side-dish for his bed, he pandered to my
delight!

1428 Bloodshot eyes were thought to be a symptom of madness. The idea that CLYTEMNESTRA's eyes are actually stained
with blood is wholly foreign to the conventions of Greek
tragedy, which disdained this kind of realism.   **1439** In the
first book of the *Iliad*, AGAMEMNON quarrels with Achilles
because of having had to give up Chryseis, daughter of
Chryses, priest of Apollo, a captive who has been handed
over to him. In open council AGAMEMNON declares that he
prefers Chryseis to CLYTEMNESTRA, whose equal she is in all
respects (*Iliad* 1. 113f.).   **1445** This is the earliest allusion to the
belief that swans sing before they are to die. The swan is often
said to be sacred to Apollo.

STROPHE 1

CHORUS: Alas! If only swiftly, without grievous pain,
and with no watching of the sick-bed,
1450   some Fate would come bringing to us
the sleep that never ends, now that he is slain,
the kindest of guardians!
He suffered much for a woman's sake; and at a
woman's
hand has he lost his life.

REFRAIN 1

1455   Ah, ah, mad Helen,
you who alone destroyed the many, the very
many
lives beneath Troy,
now you have put on yourself the last, the perfect
garland,
through the blood not washed away. Truly there
1460   was then in the house
a strife strong to conquer, a sorrow for the husband.
CLYTEMNESTRA: Do not pray for the fate of death,
grieved by this event!
Do not turn your wrath against Helen,
1465   calling her a destroyer of men, one who alone
took the lives of many Danaan men
and accomplished a woe none might resist!

ANTISTROPHE 1

CHORUS: Spirit that falls upon the house and the two
sons of Tantalus,°
1470   and through women holds an evil sway,
a sway grievous to my heart,
over the body like an evil crow
you stand and glory in singing with discordant note
a song of evil!
CLYTEMNESTRA: Now have you set right the opinion
you pronounce,
1475   calling on the thrice glutted
spirit of this race!
For by his will a lust to lick blood
is nurtured in its belly; before the old agony
1480   ceases, there flows fresh pus.

STROPHE 2

CHORUS: Mighty for this house
is the spirit you tell of, heavy his wrath.
Alas, alas, evil is your tale,

never satiate of baneful fortune.
Woe, woe, through the act of Zeus,   1485
cause of all, doer of all;
for what is accomplished for mortals without
Zeus?
Which of these things is not god-ordained?

REFRAIN 2

O my king, my king,
how shall I weep for you?   1490
What word shall I utter from a loving heart?
And you lie in this spider's web,
gasping out your life in an impious death—
alas, on this shameful bed,
brought low by a guileful death,   1495
by a two-edged weapon sped by [your wife's]
hand.
CLYTEMNESTRA: You aver that this deed is mine.
But do not consider
that I am Agamemnon's consort!
But in the likeness of this dead man's wife   1500
the ancient savage avenger°
of Atreus, the cruel banqueter,
slew him in requital,
sacrificing a grown man after children.

ANTISTROPHE 2

CHORUS: That you have no guilt   1505
for this murder, who shall bear witness?
How, how can it be so? But the avenger
from his father's time may have been your helper.
And amid streams
of kindred blood black Ares°   1510
forces his way to where he shall pay atonement
to the gore congealed of the children that were
devoured.

REFRAIN 2

O my king, my king,
how shall I weep for you?
What word shall I utter from a loving heart?   1515
And you lie in this spider's web,
gasping out your life in an impious death—
alas, on this shameful bed,
brought low by a guileful death,
by a two-edged weapon sped by [your wife's] hand. 1520
CLYTEMNESTRA: Neither, I think, was this man's death
shameful. . . . . .
For did not he accomplish guileful
destruction in the house?

1469 Tantalus was father of Pelops, who in the usual genealo-
gy was father of Atreus. "Daimon" can mean a god, a minor
divinity, or a spirit; here it is the personified curse upon the
family.

1501 ancient savage avenger identical with the Daimon (see
n. 1469).   **1510** The name of the war-god stands for violence.

1525   But my child raised up from him,
Iphigeneia, much bewailed,—
unworthy was what he did to her, worthy was
   what he suffered!
Let him utter no loud boast in Hades,
now that he has paid with death for what he began.

STROPHE 3

1530   CHORUS: I do not know, deprived of meditation's
   resourceful thought,
which way to turn, while the house falls.
I fear the beating of the rain that brings the house
   low,
the rain of blood; and the drizzle ceases.
1535   Justice is sharpened for another deed of harm
on other whetstones by the hand of Fate.
O earth, earth, would you had received me,
before I saw him occupy the lowly bed
1540   of the bath with silver walls!
Who shall bury him? Who shall lament him?
Shall you dare to do this, to slay
your husband and then lament him,
1545   and for his soul decree thanks that are no thanks
in return for his mighty deeds?
Who shall pronounce with tears
praise at the tomb over the godlike man,
1550   laboring in sincerity of heart?
   CLYTEMNESTRA: It does not fall to you to take thought
   for this
duty; by my hand
he fell, by my hand he died, and my hand shall
   bury him,
to the accompaniment of no weeping from the
   house.
1555   But gladly Iphigeneia,
his daughter, as is fitting,
shall meet her father at the swift
ferry of sorrows
and cast her arm round him and kiss him.

ANTISTROPHE 3

1560   CHORUS: Taunt is now met with taunt,
and it is hard to judge;
the plunderer is plundered and the slayer slain.
But it abides, while Zeus abides upon his throne,
that he who does shall suffer; for it is the law.
Who shall cast out the brood of curses from the
1565   house?
The race is fastened to destruction.
   CLYTEMNESTRA: With truth you have come upon
   this oracle. But I for my part
am willing to swear a covenant with the demon
of the Pleisthenids so that I bear all this,
1570   hard though it is to endure; and he may go for the
   future
from this house and wear away some other family

through deaths at the hands of kindred.
Even if my share of possessions
is small, I shall be content with all things,   1575
if I have rid our halls
of the frenzies in which we shed each other's
   blood.

[Enter AEGISTHUS.*]*

AEGISTHUS: O kindly light of the day that has
   brought justice,
now I can say that as guardians of the rights of
   men
the gods from above look upon the woes of earth,
now that I have seen this man lie here   1580
in the woven robes of the Erinyes, to my delight,
paying for the deed his father's hand contrived.
For Atreus, ruler of this land and this man's
   father,
drove my father, Thyestes—to put the matter
   clearly—
his brother, since his power was challenged,   1585
away from the city and his home.
And when he returned as a suppliant at his
   hearth,
poor Thyestes found a safety,
in that he did not in death stain with his blood his
   native earth
himself; but by way of hospitable entertainment
   the godless father of this man here,   1590
even Atreus, more a willing than a kindly host,
seeming to keep the day of meat-eating with
   good cheer,
served to my father a feast of his children's flesh.
The footparts and the ends of the hands
he chopped up small above . . . . sitting
   each by himself.   1595
And taking at once in ignorance a part that could
   not be recognized,
he ate, a meal bringing ruin to his family, as you
   see.
And then he understood the monstrous act
and cried out, and fell back, spewing out the
   butchery,
and called down on the Pelopids a fate unbearable, 1600
kicking over the table to mark the justice of his
   curse,
that so might perish all the race of Pleisthenes.
So it has come about that you can see this man
   fallen here;
and I am the just schemer of this murder.
For he left me, the thirteenth child, and with my
   wretched father   1605
he drove me out, an infant in swaddling clothes.
But when I had been reared up, Justice brought
   me back,
and from far off I laid my finger on this man,

stitching together the whole scheme of the fatal
    plan.
1610 So even death is agreeable to me,
    now that I have seen this man in the toils of
    Justice.
CHORUS: Aegisthus, insolence over others' misfor-
    tune is a thing I care not to practice.
    And do you say that you deliberately slew this man,
    and that you alone planned this piteous murder?
    I say that on the day of reckoning your head shall
1615   not escape,
    know it for certain, the curses that bring stoning
    at the people's hands.
AEGISTHUS: Do you speak thus, seated at the oar
    below
    when those upon the bench are masters of the
    ship?
    Old as you are, you shall learn that a lesson
    comes hard
1620 to one of your years, when discretion is enjoined.
    Bonds and whips and the pangs of hunger
    are excellent prophet-doctors
    for the wits. Have you eyes, and do you not see
    this?°
    Do not kick against the pricks, so that you do not
    strike them and feel pain.°
CHORUS: Woman, do you do this to those newly
1625   returned from battle—
    keeping the house and shaming the husband's
    bed
    did you plot this death for the general?
AEGISTHUS: These words too are the breeders of a
    race of tears.
    But you have a tongue the opposite of that of
    Orpheus.
    For he led all things with his voice° by means of
1630   the delight he gave;
    but you stir up anger by your foolish barkings,
    and shall be led; once mastered you shall show
    yourself more tame.
CHORUS: So you are to be tyrant of the Argives,
    you who when you had plotted death against
    him,
1635 did not dare to do this deed with your own hand!
AEGISTHUS: Yes, for the deception was clearly the
    woman's part,

and I, an ancient enemy of the house, was sus-
    pect.
    And with his possessions I shall try
    to rule the citizens; and him that will not obey
    I shall yoke with a heavy yoke; no trace-horse   1640
    fed on barley,° he! But the hateful housemate
    of darkness, hunger, shall see him grow soft.
CHORUS: Why with your cowardly heart did you not
    kill this man yourself, but with you a woman
    —polluting the land and its gods—   1645
    killed him? Does Orestes somewhere see the light,
    that he may return here with favoring fortune
    and become the all-prevailing slayer of both these
    two?
AEGISTHUS: Well, since you wish to act and speak
    thus, you shall soon learn!
CHORUS: Come now, dear comrades, the work to be
    done is near at hand!   1650
AEGISTHUS: Come now, let each make ready his
    sword with hand on hilt!
CHORUS: I too have hand on hilt and do not refuse
    death.
AEGISTHUS: We accept the omen when you speak of
    death; and we choose to take what will come
    to pass.
CLYTEMNESTRA: By no means, dearest of men, let us
    do further harm;
    but even this is much to reap, a sad harvest.   1655
    There is enough of ruin; let us shed no blood.
    Go . . . . . . , elders to the house, yielding
    to Fate before you suffer; you must acquiesce in
    this as we have done it.
    If we could have had enough of these troubles,
    we should be content,
    grievously struck as we have been by the spirit's
    hoof.   1660
    Such is the saying of a woman, if any condescend
    to hear it.
AEGISTHUS: But are these men to pelt me with the
    flowers of a random tongue,
    and to fling out such words as these, making trial
    of their fortune,
    and miss the target of good sense, rejecting the
    man in power?
CHORUS: This would not be the way of Argives, to
    fawn upon an evil fellow.   1665
AEGISTHUS: Well, in days to come I shall still pursue
    you.
CHORUS: Not if the spirit guide Orestes to return
    here.
AEGISTHUS: I know that men in exile feed on hope.

1623 For the proverb, cf. Mark 8:18 (Matthew 13:13); the proverb
is common in classical literature.   1624 The proverb occurs at
Apostles 26:14; this proverb too was well known during the
classical period. AEGISTHUS' constant use of the tritest cant sayings seems to be one of the features meant to characterize him
as a mean and contemptible person.   1629 Rocks and trees were
alleged to have followed Orpheus (*Orfe yuse*) in order to hear
his song. The feeble comparison is one more mark of the contemptible character of AEGISTHUS.

1641 The trace-horse, which ran to the right of the pair pulling a
chariot or wagon in order to lend assistance when a special
effort was required, was better fed than other horses.

CHORUS: Act, grow fat, polluting justice, since you
    have the power!

AEGISTHUS: Know that you shall pay me the penalty

1670   for this foolishness in time!

CHORUS: Boast in confidence, like a cock beside his
    hen!

CLYTEMNESTRA: Do not care for these idle barkings;
    you and I,
    ruling this house, shall order all things for good.

SOPHOCLES (CA. 496–406 B.C.)

Sophocles' life spanned the fifth century B.C., a time when Athens reached the pinnacle of its political, military, and cultural power. By the midpoint of the century, the stunning military successes of Pericles against the Persians brought Athenian dominance to the entire eastern Mediterranean. The economic prosperity that followed was complemented by great civic and artistic achievements.

Sophocles was a prominent citizen. He held several public offices, served as treasurer of the Athenian league, and acted as a priest in some sacred cults. Like that of Aeschylus before him, Sophocles' career as a public figure complemented rather than competed with his career as a playwright. In 441 B.C. he was appointed one of the twelve generals under Pericles in the war against Samos. Tradition has it that he received this appointment because of the success of his play *Antigone*, which had been produced the previous year. Finally, he was appointed to the committee that examined the failed military campaign in Sicily.

Sophocles is credited with a number of innovations in drama. In contrast to the practice of his predecessors, he did not act in his own plays, reportedly because his voice was not strong enough. He did make some appearances, however, as a member of the chorus and as a musician. Aristotle credits Sophocles with adding the third actor to tragedy and with using a chorus composed of fifteen. But his main accomplishment was his fine control of the tragic action itself, and Aristotle often turns to the plays of Sophocles to illustrate the best means of structuring a tragic play.

Sophocles won the annual competition at City Dionysia twenty-four times, the first time against Aeschylus in 468 B.C. He is credited with over one hundred twenty plays, but only seven have survived: *Ajax, Trachiniae, Electra, Philoctetes, Oedipus Rex, Oedipus at Colonus,* and *Antigone*. The most famous of his surviving plays, *Oedipus Rex* (429–425 B.C.), *Oedipus at Colonus* (401 B.C.), and *Antigone* (402–401 B.C.), are often performed together to form what is known as the Oedipus cycle, though they were not conceived or written by Sophocles as a trilogy or cycle.

Oedipus Rex

Oedipus Rex was originally staged before an enormous audience of fifteen thousand people gathered in an outdoor amphitheater with about the same sense of intimacy as a modern football stadium. The actors and the chorus wore more or less elaborate masks to indicate the distinguishing features of the characters they played. They also wore long, decorated robes indicating social class, and probably the large elevated shoes called *kothornoi* which increased their stature. They declaimed their lines and moved about the stage in a formal dancelike manner.

It would be hard to imagine anything more foreign to the experience of modern audiences, yet one of the remarkable features of *Oedipus Rex* is that the play remains powerful and moving in virtually any theatrical space. It has been performed on many different kinds of stages and in an astonishing variety of styles. Its action and poetry have inspired, challenged, and haunted audiences for nearly twenty-five hundred years. Aristotle used this play in his *Poetics* as an example of the best kind of tragedy. Why? Where does the play draw its power? Why is it still taught and read over a hundred generations after its composition? If there were easy answers to these questions, perhaps this play would never have achieved such fame or withstood such scrutiny. It may help to know that the Oedipus story haunted Sophocles' imagination, too, for thirty years, and he wrote three plays on the subject—*Oedipus Rex, Oedipus at Colonus,* and *Antigone.*

Sophocles could count on his audience to know something of the legend of Oedipus. In Sophocles' version, it has been revealed to King Laios and Queen Iocaste of Thebes that the son to be born to them would murder his father and marry his mother. To avoid this horror, they exposed the baby with his feet pinned together (*Oedipus* means "swollen foot") to die on a mountain-side. He was rescued by a shepherd and brought to Corinth, where he was raised by Polybus and Merope, whom he believed to be his parents, as a prince. Oedipus learned his terrible fate—that he would kill his father and marry his mother—from the oracle, and so he fled Corinth. Eventually, his wandering brought him to Thebes, though on the way he killed an old man (his father) in an angry roadside confrontation. He found Thebes in the grip of the Sphinx, who killed anyone who could not solve her riddle. Oedipus solved the riddle, thereby liberating Thebes, and his reward was the throne and the queen (his mother) in marriage. He ruled Thebes for years, and then, mysteriously, the city became subject to a plague that could be removed only by finding the murderer of Laios. Sophocles opens the play at this point in the story.

Oedipus Rex is concerned with the unpredictability, the power, and the relentlessness of fate. Oedipus tries earnestly to circumvent the terrible prophecy of the oracle of Apollo, which foretells patricide and incest, two of the most heinous crimes. Leaving his home in order to avoid any possibility of wrongdo-ing, he attempts to alter his destiny but instead runs headlong into it. At the end of the play, Oedipus' self-imposed exile restores fertility to plague-ridden Thebes. The connection Sophocles makes between the health and well-being of the king and the health and well-being of the state is a commonplace Greek notion, but one which opens a consideration of the interdependence of the indi-vidual, the state, and fate itself.

From a structural point of view, the play is virtually unrivaled in drama. Beginning the plot near the end of the story, Sophocles exploits the dramatic irony of the situation—the difference between what his audience knows and what his characters know. Oedipus becomes acquainted step by step with the facts of his past. Though drawn in broad strokes, the principal characters are masterful creations. Creon serves as a balance to Oedipus; he shows reserve and restraint in contrast to Oedipus' hastiness and rashness. Iocaste, a loyal wife to

Oedipus, exudes just enough maternal judgment to make the realities of their relationship believable. Oedipus of course dominates the play. Sophocles connects the qualities of greatness in Oedipus' character—his attempt to circumvent the oracle, his solving of the riddle of the Sphinx, his relentless pursuit of the truth—to the rash and prideful qualities that lead him to his catastrophe. His character is by turns brilliant and astoundingly obtuse, unable to see more than one thing at a time. Indeed, Sophocles plays with the opposition of sight and blindness in the play. By dismissing the advice of the blind Teiresias not to pursue the truth, Oedipus chooses his own fate. The physically blind Teiresias has true knowledge; the sighted Oedipus is blind. At the end of the play, when he at last sees the truth, Oedipus deprives himself of the organs which he has allowed to deceive him. Blinded, he now sees clearly.

One main source of brilliance in *Oedipus Rex* is the insight Sophocles provides about the relation between individual choices and fate. Oedipus' character traits lead him both to greatness and to his catastrophe. The gods may condemn a man like Oedipus to a horrible fate, but his struggle against it speaks for a human grandeur that gives him unmistakably heroic as well as tragic dimensions.

Oedipus Rex

SOPHOCLES

TRANSLATED BY DUDLEY FITTS AND ROBERT FITZGERALD

CHARACTERS

OEDIPUS
A PRIEST
CREON
TEIRESIAS
IOCASTE

MESSENGER
SHEPHERD OF LAÏOS
SECOND MESSENGER
CHORUS OF THEBAN ELDERS

THE SCENE. Before the palace of Oedipus, King of Thebes. A central door and two lateral doors open onto a platform which runs the length of the façade. On the platform, right and left, are altars; and three steps lead down into the 'orchestra', or chorus-ground. At the beginning of the action these steps are crowded by suppliants who have brought branches and chaplets of olive leaves and who lie in various attitudes of despair. OEDIPUS enters.

PROLOGUE

OEDIPUS: My children, generations of the living
   In the line of Kadmos,° nursed at his ancient
      hearth:
   Why have you strewn yourselves before these
      altars

In supplication, with your boughs and garlands?
The breath of incense rises from the city   5
With a sound of prayer and lamentation.
                                             Children,
I would not have you speak through messengers,
And therefore I have come myself to hear you—
I, Oedipus, who bear the famous name.

---

² **Kadmos** founder of Thebes and great-grandfather of Laios.

[To a PRIEST:]

10   You, there, since you are eldest in the company,
         Speak for them all, tell me what preys upon you,
         Whether you come in dread, or crave some bless-
           ing:
         Tell me, and never doubt that I will help you
         In every way I can; I should be heartless
15   Were I not moved to find you suppliant here.
    PRIEST: Great Oepidus, O powerful King of Thebes!
         You see how all the ages of our people
         Cling to your altar steps: here are boys
         Who can barely stand alone, and here are priests
20   By weight of age, as I am a priest of God,
         And young men chosen from those yet unmarried;
         As for the others, all that multitude,
         They wait with olive chaplets in the squares,
         At the two shrines of Pallas, and where Apollo°
         Speaks in the glowing embers.
25   Your own eyes
         Must tell you: Thebes is in her extremity
         And can not lift her head from the surge of death.
         A rust consumes the buds and fruits of the earth;
         The herds are sick; children die unborn,
30   And labour is vain. The god of plague and pyre
         Raids like detestable lightning through the city,
         And all the house of Kadmos is laid waste,
         All emptied, and all darkened: Death alone
         Battens upon the misery of Thebes.
35   You are not one of the immortal gods, we know;
         Yet we have come to you to make our prayer
         As to the man of all men best in adversity
         And wisest in the ways of God. You saved us
         From the Sphinx,° that flinty singer, and the tribute
40   We paid to her so long; yet you were never
         Better informed than we, nor could we teach you:
         It was some god breathed in you to set us free.
         Therefore, O mighty King, we turn to you:
         Find us our safety, find us a remedy,
45   Whether by counsel of the gods or men.
         A king of wisdom tested in the past
         Can act in a time of troubles, and act well.
         Noblest of men, restore
         Life to your city! Think how all men call you
50   Liberator for your triumph long ago;
         Ah, when your years of kingship are remembered,
         Let them not say *We rose, but later fell*—
         Keep the State from going down in the storm!
         Once, years ago, with happy augury,
55   You brought us fortune; be the same again!

         No man questions your power to rule the land:
         But rule over men, not over a dead city!
         Ships are only hulls, citadels are nothing,
         When no life moves in the empty passageways.
    OEDIPUS: Poor children! You may be sure I know   60
         All that you longed for in your coming here.
         I know that you are deathly sick; and yet,
         Sick as you are, not one is as sick as I.
         Each of you suffers in himself alone
         His anguish, not another's; but my spirit   65
         Groans for the city, for myself, for you.
         I was not sleeping, you are not waking me.
         No, I have been in tears for a long while
         And in my restless thought walked many ways.
         In all my search, I found one helpful course,   70
         And that I have taken: I have sent Creon,
         Son of Menoikeus, brother of the Queen,
         To Delphi, Apollo's place of revelation,
         To learn there, if he can,
         What act or pledge of mine may save the city.   75
         I have counted the days, and now, this very day,
         I am troubled, for he has overstayed his time.
         What is he doing? He has been gone too long.
         Yet whenever he comes back, I should do ill
         To scant whatever hint the god may give.   80
    PRIEST: It is a timely promise. At this instant
         They tell me Creon is here.
    OEDIPUS: O Lord Apollo!
         May his news be fair as his face is radiant!
    PRIEST: It could not be otherwise: he is crowned with
           bay,
         The chaplet is thick with berries.°
    OEDIPUS: We shall soon know;   85
         He is near enough to hear us now.

[Enter CREON.]

                                        O Prince.
         Brother: son of Menoikeus:
         What answer do you bring us from the god?
    CREON: It is favourable. I can tell you, great afflictions
         Will turn out well, if they are taken well.   90
    OEDIPUS: What was the oracle? These vague words
         Leave me still hanging between hope and fear.
    CREON: Is it your pleasure to hear me with all these
         Gathered around us? I am prepared to speak,
         But should we not go in?
    OEDIPUS: Let them all hear it.   95
         It is for them I suffer, more than for myself.
    CREON: Then I will tell you what I heard at Delphi.
         In plain words
         The god commands us to expel from the land of
           Thebes

---

²⁴ **Pallas** Athena, daughter of Zeus; goddess of wisdom.
Apollo son of Zeus; god of light, music, poetry; patron of
Teiresias and of the oracle at Delphi.   ³⁹ **Sphinx** winged
monster with the body of a lion and the face of a woman. The
sphinx killed those who could not solve her riddle.

---

⁸⁴ **crowned . . . berries** the laurel, sacred to Apollo, worn in a
chaplet or wreath around the head as a symbol of victory.

100 An old defilement that it seems we shelter.
    It is a deathly thing, beyond expiation.
    We must not let it feed upon us longer.
OEDIPUS: What defilement? How shall we rid our-
    selves of it?
105 CREON: By exile or death, blood for blood. It was
    Murder that brought the plague-wind on the city.
OEDIPUS: Murder of whom? Surely the god has
    named him?
CREON: My lord: long ago Laïos was our king,
    Before you came to govern us.
OEDIPUS: I know;
    I learned of him from others; I never saw him.
CREON: He was murdered; and Apollo commands us
110 now
    To take revenge upon whoever killed him.
OEDIPUS: Upon whom? Where are they? Where shall
    we find a clue
    To solve that crime, after so many years?
CREON: Here in this land, he said.
                              If we make enquiry,
115 We may touch things that otherwise escape us.
OEDIPUS: Tell me: Was Laïos murdered in his house,
    Or in the fields, or in some foreign country?
CREON: He said he planned to make a pilgrimage.
    He did not come home again.
OEDIPUS: And was there no one,
120 No witness, no companion, to tell what happened?
CREON: They were all killed but one, and he got away
    So frightened that he could remember one thing
    only.
OEDIPUS: What was that one thing? One may be the
    key
    To everything, if we resolve to use it.
CREON: He said that a band of highwaymen attacked
125 them,
    Outnumbered them, and overwhelmed the King.
OEDIPUS: Strange, that a highwayman should be so
    daring—
    Unless some faction here bribed him to do it.
CREON: We thought of that. But after Laïos' death
130 New troubles arose and we had no avenger.
OEDIPUS: What troubles could prevent your hunting
    down the killers?
CREON: The riddling Sphinx's song
    Made us deaf to all mysteries but her own.
OEDIPUS: Then once more I must bring what is dark
    to light.
135 It is most fitting that Apollo shows,
    As you do, this compunction for the dead.
    You shall see how I stand by you, as I should,
    To avenge the city and the city's god,
    And not as though it were for some distant friend,
140 But for my own sake, to be rid of evil.
    Whoever killed King Laïos might—who knows?—
    Decide at any moment to kill me as well.
    By avenging the murdered king I protect myself.

Come, then, my children: leave the altar steps,
Lift up your olive boughs!
    One of you go   145
And summon the people of Kadmos to gather here.
I will do all that I can; you may tell them that.

[Exit a PAGE.*]*

So, with the help of God,
    We shall be saved—or else indeed we are lost.
PRIEST: Let us rise, children. It was for this we came,   150
    And now the King has promised it himself.
    Phoibos° has sent us an oracle; may he descend
    Himself to save us and drive out the plague.

[Exeunt OEDIPUS *and* CREON *into the palace by the
central door. The* PRIEST *and the* SUPPLIANTS *disperse
R and L. After a short pause the* CHORUS *enters the
orchestra.]*

PÁRODOS

STROPHE I

CHORUS: What is the god° singing in his profound
    Delphi of gold and shadow?   155
    What oracle for Thebes, the sunwhipped city?
    Fear unjoints me, the roots of my heart tremble.
    Now I remember, O Healer, your power, and
        wonder:
    Will you send doom like a sudden cloud, or
        weave it
    Like nightfall of the past?   160
    Ah no: be merciful, issue of holy sound:
    Dearest to our expectancy: be tender!

ANTISTROPHE I

Let me pray to Athenê, the immortal daughter of
    Zeus,
And to Artemis° her sister
Who keeps her famous throne in the market ring,   165
And to Apollo, bowman at the far butts of heaven—
O gods, descend! Like three streams leap against
The fires of our grief, the fires of darkness;
Be swift to bring us rest!
As in the old time from the brilliant house   170
Of air you stepped to save us, come again!

STROPHE 2

Now our afflictions have no end,
Now all our stricken host lies down
And no man fights off death with his mind;
The noble plowland bears no grain,   175
And groaning mothers can not bear—

---

[152] **Phoibos** Apollo   [154] **god** Apollo   [164] **Artemis** twin sister of Apollo

See, how our lives like birds take wing,
Like sparks that fly when a fire soars,
To the shore of the god of evening.

ANTISTROPHE 2

180 The plague burns on, it is pitiless,
Though pallid children laden with death
Lie unwept in the stony ways,
And old grey women by every path
Flock to the strand about the altars
185 There to strike their breasts and cry
Worship of Zeus in wailing prayers:
Be kind, God's golden child!

STROPHE 3

There are no swords in this attack by fire,
No shields, but we are ringed with cries.
190 Send the besieger plunging from our homes
Into the vast sea-room of the Atlantic
Or into the waves that foam eastward of Thrace—
For the day ravages what the night spares—
Destroy our enemy, lord of the thunder!
195 Let him be riven by lightning from heaven!

ANTISTROPHE 3

Phoibos Apollo, stretch the sun's bowstring,
That golden cord, until it sing for us,
Flashing arrows in heaven!
                    Artemis, Huntress,
Race with flaring lights upon our mountains!
200 O scarlet god, O golden-banded brow,
O Theban Bacchos in a storm of Maenads,°

[Enter OEDIPUS, *C.]*

Whirl upon Death, that all the Undying hate!
Come with blinding cressets, come in joy!

Scene 1

OEDIPUS: Is this your prayer? It may be answered.
    Come,
205 Listen to me, act as the crisis demands,
And you shall have relief from all these evils.
Until now I was a stranger to this tale,
As I had been a stranger to the crime.
Could I track down the murderer without a clue?
210 But now, friends,
As one who became a citizen after the murder,
I make this proclamation to all Thebans:
If any man knows by whose hand Laïos, son of
    Labdakos,
Met his death, I direct that man to tell me everything,

No matter what he fears for having so long
    withheld it.   215
Let it stand as promised that no further trouble
Will come to him, but he may leave the land in
    safety.
Moreover: If anyone knows the murderer to be
    foreign,
Let him not keep silent: he shall have his reward
    from me.
However, if he does conceal it; if any man   220
Fearing for his friend or for himself disobeys this
    edict,
Hear what I propose to do:
I solemnly forbid the people of this country,
Where power and throne are mine, ever to receive
    that man
Or speak to him, no matter who he is, or let him   225
Join in sacrifice, lustration, or in prayer.
I decree that he be driven from every house,
Being, as he is, corruption itself to us: the Delphic
Voice of Zeus has pronounced this revelation.
Thus I associate myself with the oracle   230
And take the side of the murdered king.
As for the criminal, I pray to God—
Whether it be a lurking thief, or one of a number—
I pray that that man's life be consumed in evil
    and wretchedness.
And as for me, this curse applies no less   235
If it should turn out that the culprit is my guest here,
Sharing my hearth.
                    You have heard the penalty.
I lay it on you now to attend to this
For my sake, for Apollo's, for the sick
Sterile city that heaven has abandoned.   240
Suppose the oracle had given you no command:
Should this defilement go uncleansed for ever?
You should have found the murderer: your king,
A noble king, had been destroyed!
                                    Now I,
Having the power that he held before me,   245
Having his bed, begetting children there
Upon his wife, as he would have, had he lived—
Their son would have been my children's brother,
If Laïos had had luck in fatherhood!
(But surely ill luck rushed upon his reign)—   250
I say I take the son's part, just as though
I were his son, to press the fight for him
And see it won! I'll find the hand that brought
Death to Labdakos' and Polydoros' child,
Heir of Kadmos' and Agenor's line.°   255
And as for those who fail me,
May the gods deny them the fruit of the earth,

---

201 **Maenads** ecstatic women in the train of Dionysus, god of
wine.

255 **Labdakos' . . . line** The child is Laïos; his father was
Labdakos, his grandfather Polydoros, his great-grandfather
Kadmos, and his great-great-grandfather Agenor.

Fruit of the womb, and may they rot utterly!
Let them be wretched as we are wretched, and worse!
260 For you, for loyal Thebans, and for all
Who find my actions right, I pray the favour
Of justice, and of all the immortal gods.
CHORAGOS: Since I am under oath, my lord, I swear
I did not do the murder, I can not name
265 The murderer. Might not the oracle
That has ordained the search tell where to find him?
OEDIPUS: An honest question. But no man in the world
Can make the gods do more than the gods will.
CHORAGOS: There is one last expedient—
OEDIPUS: Tell me what it is.
270 Though it seem slight, you must not hold it back.
CHORAGOS: A lord clairvoyant to the lord Apollo,
As we all know, is the skilled Teiresias.
One might learn much about this from him,
Oedipus.
OEDIPUS: I am not wasting time:
275 Creon spoke of this, and I have sent for him—
Twice, in fact; it is strange that he is not here.
CHORAGOS: The other matter— that old report—
seems useless.
OEDIPUS: Tell me. I am interested in all reports.
CHORAGOS: The King was said to have been killed
by highwaymen.
280 OEDIPUS: I know. But we have no witnesses to that.
CHORAGOS: If the killer can feel a particle of dread,
Your curse will bring him out of hiding!
OEDIPUS: No.
The man who dared that act will fear no curse.

[Enter the blind seer TEIRESIAS, *led by a* PAGE.]

CHORAGOS: But there is one man who may detect the
criminal.
285 This is Teiresias, this is the holy prophet
In whom, alone of all men, truth was born.
OEDIPUS: Teiresias: seer: student of mysteries,
Of all that's taught and all than no man tells,
Secrets of Heaven and secrets of the earth:
290 Blind though you are, you know the city lies
Sick with plague; and from this plague, my lord,
We find that you alone can guard or save us.
Possibly you did not hear the messengers?
Apollo, when we sent to him,
295 Sent us back word that this great pestilence
Would lift, but only if we established clearly
The identity of those who murdered Laïos.
They must be killed or exiled.
                                          Can you use
Birdflight° or any art of divination
300 To purify yourself, and Thebes, and me
From this contagion? We are in your hands.

---
²⁹⁹ **Birdflight** Seers could prophesy from the flight of birds.

There is no fairer duty
Than that of helping others in distress.
TEIRESIAS: How dreadful knowledge of the truth can be
When there's no help in truth! I knew this well,   305
But did not act on it: else I should not have come.
OEDIPUS: What is troubling you? Why are your eyes
so cold?
TEIRESIAS: Let me go home. Bear your own fate, and I'll
Bear mine. It is better so: trust what I say.
OEDIPUS: What you say is ungracious and unhelpful   310
To your native country. Do not refuse to speak.
TEIRESIAS: When it comes to speech, your own is nei-
ther temperate
Nor opportune. I wish to be more prudent.
OEDIPUS: In God's name, we all beg you—
TEIRESIAS: You are all ignorant.
No; I will never tell you what I know.   315
Now it is my misery; then, it would be yours.
OEDIPUS: What! You do know something, and will
not tell us?
You would betray us all and wreck the State?
TEIRESIAS: I do not intend to torture myself, or you.
Why persist in asking? You will not persuade me.   320
OEDIPUS: What a wicked old man you are! You'd try
a stone's
Patience! Out with it! Have you no feeling at all?
TEIRESIAS: You call me unfeeling. If you could only see
The nature of your own feelings . . .
OEDIPUS: Why,
Who would not feel as I do? Who could endure   325
Your arrogance toward the city?
TEIRESIAS: What does it matter!
Whether I speak or not, it is bound to come.
OEDIPUS: Then, if 'it' is bound to come, you are
bound to tell me.
TEIRESIAS: No, I will not go on. Rage as you please.
OEDIPUS: Rage? Why not!
                              And I'll tell you what I think: 330
You planned it, you had it done, you all but
Killed him with your own hands: if you had eyes,
I'd say the crime was yours, and yours alone.
TEIRESIAS: So? I charge you, then,
Abide by the proclamation you have made: 335
From this day forth
Never speak again to these men or to me;
You yourself are the pollution of this country.
OEDIPUS: You dare say that! Can you possibly think
you have
Some way of going free, after such insolence?   340
TEIRESIAS: I have gone free. It is the truth sustains me.
OEDIPUS: Who taught you shamelessness? It was not
your craft.
TEIRESIAS: You did. You made me speak. I did not
want to.
OEDIPUS: Speak what? Let me hear it again more clearly.
TEIRESIAS: Was it not clear before? Are you tempting
me?   345

OEDIPUS: I did not understand it. Say it again.

TEIRESIAS: I say that you are the murderer whom you
seek.

OEDIPUS: Now twice you have spat out infamy.
You'll pay for it!

TEIRESIAS: Would you care for more? Do you wish to
be really angry?

OEDIPUS: Say what you will. Whatever you say is
worthless.

350 TEIRESIAS: I say that you live in hideous love with her
Who is nearest you in blood. You are blind to the
evil.

OEDIPUS: It seems you can go on mouthing like this
for ever.

TEIRESIAS: I can, if there is power in truth.

OEDIPUS: There is:
But not for you, not for you,

355   You sightless, witless, senseless, mad old man!

TEIRESIAS: You are the madman. There is no one here
Who will not curse you soon, as you curse me.

OEDIPUS: You child of endless night! You can not
hurt me
Or any other man who sees the sun.

360 TEIRESIAS: True: it is not from me your fate will come.
That lies within Apollo's competence,
As it is his concern.

OEDIPUS: Tell me:
Are you speaking for Creon, or for yourself?

TEIRESIAS: Creon is no threat. You weave your own
doom.

365 OEDIPUS: Wealth, power, craft of statesmanship!
Kingly position, everywhere admired!
What savage envy is stored up against these,
If Creon, whom I trusted, Creon my friend,
For this great office which the city once

370   Put in my hands unsought—if for this power
Creon desires in secret to destroy me!
He has bought this decrepit fortune-teller, this
Collector of dirty pennies, this prophet fraud—
Why, he is no more clairvoyant than I am!

                                                    Tell us:
Has your mystic mummery ever approached the

375   truth?
When that hellcat the Sphinx was performing here,
What help were you to these people?
Her magic was not for the first man who came along:
It demanded a real exorcist. Your birds—
What good were they? or the gods, for the matter

380   of that?
But I came by,
Oedipus, the simple man, who knows nothing—
I thought it out for myself, no birds helped me!
And this is the man you think you can destroy,

385   That you may be close to Creon when he's king!
Well, you and your friend Creon, it seems to me,
Will suffer most. If you were not an old man,
You would have paid already for your plot.

CHORAGOS: We can not see that his words or yours
Have been spoken except in anger, Oedipus,   390
And of anger we have no need. How can God's will
Be accomplished best? That is what most concerns us.

TEIRESIAS: You are a king. But where argument's con-
cerned
I am your man, as much a king as you.
I am not your servant, but Apollo's   395
I have no need of Creon to speak for me.
Listen to me. You mock my blindness, do you?
But I say that you, with both your eyes, are blind:
You can not see the wretchedness of your life,
Nor in whose house you live, no, nor with whom.   400
Who are your father and mother? Can you tell me?
You do not even know the blind wrongs
That you have done them, on earth and in the
world below.
But the double lash of your parents' curse will
whip you
Out of this land some day, with only night   405
Upon your precious eyes.
Your cries then—where will they not be heard?
What fastness of Kithairon° will not echo them?
And that bridal-descant of yours—you'll know it
then,
The song they sang when you came here to Thebes   410
And found your misguided berthing.
All this, and more, that you can not guess at now,
Will bring you to yourself among your children.
Be angry, then. Curse Creon. Curse my words.
I tell you, no man that walks upon the earth   415
Shall be rooted out more horribly than you.

OEDIPUS: Am I to bear this from him?—Damnation
Take you! Out of this place! Out of my sight!

TEIRESIAS: I would not have come at all if you had
not asked me.

OEDIPUS: Could I have told that you'd talk nonsense,
that   420
You'd come here to make a fool of yourself, and
of me?

TEIRESIAS: A fool? Your parents thought me sane
enough.

OEDIPUS: My parents again!—Wait: who were my
parents?

TEIRESIAS: This day will give you a father, and break
your heart.

OEDIPUS: Your infantile riddles! Your damned
abracadabra!   425

TEIRESIAS: You were a great man once at solving riddles.

OEDIPUS: Mock me with that if you like; you will
find it true.

TEIRESIAS: It was true enough. It brought about your
ruin.

---

[408] **Kithairon** a mountain near Thebes where Oedipus was
abandoned as an infant

OEDIPUS: But if it saved this town?

[To the PAGE:]

TEIRESIAS: Boy, give me your hand.
OEDIPUS: Yes, boy; lead him away.
430   —While you are here
  We can do nothing. Go; leave us in peace.
TEIRESIAS: I will go when I have said what I have to say.
  How can you hurt me? And I tell you again:
  The man you have been looking for all this time,
435 The damned man, the murderer of Laïos,
  That man is in Thebes. To your mind he is foreign-
        born,
  But it will soon be shown that he is a Theban,
  A revelation that will fail to please.
                                    A blind man,
  Who has his eyes now; a penniless man, who is
        rich now;
  And he will go tapping the strange earth with his
440   staff.
  To the children with whom he lives now he will be
  Brother and father—the very same; to her
  Who bore him, son and husband—the very same
  Who came to his father's bed, wet with his
        father's blood.
445 Enough. Go think that over.
  If later you find error in what I have said,
  You may say that I have no skill in prophecy.

[Exit TEIRESIAS, led by his PAGE. OEDIPUS goes into the palace.]

STROPHE I

CHORUS: The Delphic stone of prophecies
  Remembers ancient regicide
450 And a still bloody hand.
  That killer's hour of flight has come.
  He must be stronger than riderless
  Coursers of untiring wind,
  For the son of Zeus° armed with his father's thunder
455 Leaps in lightning after him;
  And the Furies° follow him, the sad Furies.

ANTISTROPHE I

  Holy Parnassos'° peak of snow
  Flashes and blinds that secret man,
  That all shall hunt him down:
460 Though he may roam the forest shade
  Like a bull gone wild from pasture
  To rage through glooms of stone.
  Doom comes down on him; flight will not avail him;

  For the world's heart calls him desolate,
  And the immortal Furies follow, for ever follow.   465

STROPHE 2

  But now a wilder thing is heard
  From the old man skilled at hearing Fate in the
        wing-beat of a bird.
  Bewildered as a blown bird, my soul hovers and
        can not find
  Foothold in this debate, or any reason or rest of
        mind.
  But no man ever brought—none can bring   470
  Proof of strife between Thebes' royal house,
  Labdakos' line, and the son of Polybos;°
  And never until now has any man brought word
  Of Laïos' dark death staining Oedipus the King.

ANTISTROPHE 2

  Divine Zeus and Apollo hold   475
  Perfect intelligence alone of all tales ever told;
  And well though this diviner works, he works in
        his own night;
  No man can judge that rough unknown or trust
        in second sight,
  For wisdom changes hands among the wise.
  Shall I believe my great lord criminal   480
  At a raging word that a blind old man let fall?
  I saw him, when the carrion woman° faced him
        of old,
  Prove his heroic mind! These evil words are lies.

Scene 2

[Enter CREON]

CREON: Men of Thebes:
  I am told that heavy accusations
  Have been brought against me by King Oedipus.   485
  I am not the kind of man to bear this tamely.
  If in these present difficulties
  He holds me accountable for any harm to him
  Through anything I have said or done—why, then,
  I do not value life in this dishonour.   490
  It is not as though this rumour touched upon
  Some private indiscretion. The matter is grave.
  The fact is that I am being called disloyal
  To the State, to my fellow citizens, to my friends.
CHORAGOS: He may have spoken in anger, not from
        his mind.   495
CREON: But did you not hear him say I was the one
  Who seduced the old prophet into lying?
CHORAGOS: The thing was said; I do not know how
        seriously.

---

454 **son of Zeus** Apollo   456 **Furies** deities associated with retribution   457 **Parnassos** mountain sacred to Apollo

472 **son of Polybos** Oedipus was adopted by Polybos
482 **carrion woman** the Sphinx

CREON: But you were watching him! Were his eyes
        steady?
     Did he look like a man in his right mind?
500 CHORAGOS: I do not know.
     I can not judge the behaviour of great men.
     But here is the King himself.

[Enter OEDIPUS*]*

OEDIPUS: So you dared come back.
     Why? How brazen of you to come to my house,
     You murderer!
                         Do you think I do not know
     That you plotted to kill me, plotted to steal my
505   throne?
     Tell me, in God's name: am I coward, a fool,
     That you should dream you could accomplish this?
     A fool who could not see your slippery game?
     A coward, not to fight back when I saw it?
510 You are the fool, Creon, are you not? hoping
     Without support or friends to get a throne?
     Thrones may be won or bought: you could do
        neither.
CREON: Now listen to me. You have talked; let me
        talk, too.
     You can not judge unless you know the facts.
OEDIPUS: You speak well: there is one fact; but I find
515   it hard
     To learn from the deadliest enemy I have.
CREON: That above all I must dispute with you.
OEDIPUS: That above all I will not hear you deny.
CREON: If you think there is anything good in being
        stubborn
520 Against all reason, then I say you are wrong.
OEDIPUS: If you think a man can sin against his own
        kind
     And not be punished for it, I say you are mad.
CREON: I agree. But tell me: what have I done to you?
OEDIPUS: You advised me to send for that wizard,
        did you not?
CREON: I did. I should do it again.
525 OEDIPUS: Very well. Now tell me:
     How long has it been since Laïos—
CREON: What of Laïos?
OEDIPUS: Since he vanished in that onset by the road?
CREON: It was long ago, a long time.
OEDIPUS: And this prophet,
     Was he practicing here then?
530 CREON: He was; and with honour, as now.
OEDIPUS: Did he speak of me at that time?
CREON: He never did;
     At least, not when I was present.
OEDIPUS: But . . . the enquiry?
     I suppose you held one?
CREON: We did, but we learned nothing.
OEDIPUS: Why did the prophet not speak against me
535   then?

CREON: I do not know; and I am the kind of man
     Who holds his tongue when he has no facts to go on.
OEDIPUS: There's one fact that you know, and you
        could tell it.
CREON: What fact is that? If I know it, you shall have it.
OEDIPUS: If he were not involved with you, he could
        not say   540
     That it was I who murdered Laïos.
CREON: If he says that, you are the one that knows it!—
     But now it is my turn to question you.
OEDIPUS: Put your questions. I am no murderer.
CREON: First, then: You married my sister?
OEDIPUS: I married your sister.   545
CREON: And you rule the kingdom equally with her?
OEDIPUS: Everything that she wants she has from me.
CREON: And I am the third, equal to both of you?
OEDIPUS: That is why I call you a bad friend.
CREON: No. Reason it out, as I have done.   550
     Think of this first: Would any sane man prefer
     Power, with all a king's anxieties,
     To that same power and the grace of sleep?
     Certainly not I.
     I have never longed for the king's power—only
        his rights.   555
     Would any wise man differ from me in this?
     As matters stand, I have my way in everything
     With your consent, and no responsibilities.
     If I were king, I should be a slave to policy.
     How could I desire a sceptre more   560
     Than what is now mine—untroubled influence?
     No, I have not gone mad; I need no honours,
     Except those with the perquisites I have now.
     I am welcome everywhere; every man salutes me,
     And those who want your favour seek my ear,   565
     Since I know how to manage what they ask.
     Should I exchange this case for that anxiety?
     Besides, no sober mind is treasonable.
     I hate anarchy
     And never would deal with any man who likes it. 570
     Test what I have said. Go to the priestess
     At Delphi, ask if I quoted her correctly.
     And as for this other thing: if I am found
     Guilty of treason with Teiresias,
     Then sentence me to death! You have my word   575
     It is a sentence I should cast my vote for—
     But not without evidence!
                         You do wrong
     When you take good men for bad, bad men for
        good.
     A true friend thrown aside—why, life itself
     Is not more precious!
                    In time you will know this well: 580
     For time, and time alone, will show the just man,
     Though scoundrels are discovered in a day.
CHORAGOS: This is well said, and a prudent man
        would ponder it.
     Judgments too quickly formed are dangerous.

585 OEDIPUS: But is he not quick in his duplicity?
        And shall I not be quick to parry him?
        Would you have me stand still, hold my peace,
            and let
        This man win everything, through my inaction?
    CREON: And you want—what is it, then? To banish me?
590 OEDIPUS: No, not exile. It is your death I want,
        So that all the world may see what treason means.
    CREON: You will persist, then? You will not believe me?
    OEDIPUS: How can I believe you?
    CREON: Then you are a fool.
    OEDIPUS: To save myself?
    CREON: In justice, think of me.
    OEDIPUS: You are evil incarnate.
595 CREON: But suppose that you are wrong?
    OEDIPUS: Still I must rule.
    CREON: But not if you rule badly.
    OEDIPUS: O city, city!
    CREON: It is my city, too!
    CHORAGOS: Now, my lords, be still. I see the Queen,
        Iocastê, coming from her palace chambers;
600   And it is time she came, for the sake of you both.
        This dreadful quarrel can be resolved through her.

[Enter IOCASTE]

IOCASTE: Poor foolish men, what wicked din is this?
        With Thebes sick to death, is it not shameful
        That you should rake some private quarrel up?

[To OEDIPUS:*]*

        Come into the house.
605   —And you, Creon, go now:
        Let us have no more of this tumult over nothing.
    CREON: Nothing? No, sister: what your husband
            plans for me
        Is one of two great evils: exile or death.
    OEDIPUS: He is right.
                    Why, woman I have caught him squarely
        Plotting against my life.
610 CREON: No! Let me die
        Accurst if ever I have wished you harm!
    IOCASTE: Ah, believe it, Oedipus!
        In the name of the gods, respect this oath of his
        For my sake, for the sake of these people here!

STROPHE 1

    CHORAGOS: Open your mind to her, my lord. Be
615   ruled by her, I beg you!
    OEDIPUS: What would you have me do?
    CHORAGOS: Respect Creon's word. He has never spo-
        ken like a fool,
        And now he has sworn an oath.
    OEDIPUS: You know what you ask?
    CHORAGOS: I do.
    OEDIPUS: Speak on, then.

CHORAGOS: A friend so sworn should not be baited so,
    In blind malice, and without final proof.   620
OEDIPUS: You are aware, I hope, that what you say
    Means death for me, or exile at the least.

STROPHE 2

CHORAGOS: No, I swear by Helios, first in Heaven!
    May I die friendless and accurst,
    The worst of deaths, if ever I meant that!   625
    It is the withering fields
        That hurt my sick heart:
    Must we bear all these ills,
    And now your bad blood as well?
OEDIPUS: Then let him go. And let me die, if I must, 630
    Or be driven by him in shame from the land of
        Thebes.
    It is your unhappiness, and not his talk,
    That touches me.
                                As for him—
    Wherever he is, I will hate him as long as I live.
CREON: Ugly in yielding, as you were ugly in rage!
    Natures like yours chiefly torment themselves.   635
OEDIPUS: Can you not go? Can you not leave me?
CREON: I can.
    You do not know me; but the city knows me,
    And in its eyes I am just, if not in yours.

[Exit CREON]

ANTISTROPHE 1

CHORAGOS: Lady Iocastê, did you not ask the King to
        go to his chambers?
IOCASTE: First tell me what has happened.   640
CHORAGOS: There was suspicion without evidence;
        yet it rankled
    As even false charges will.
IOCASTE: On both sides?
CHORAGOS: On both.
IOCASTE: But what was said?
CHORAGOS: Oh let it rest, let it be done with!
    Have we not suffered enough?   645
OEDIPUS: You see to what your decency has brought
        you:
    You have made difficulties where my heart saw
        none.

ANTISTROPHE 2

CHORAGOS: Oedipus, it is not once only I have told
        you—
    You must know I should count myself unwise
    To the point of madness, should I now forsake
        you—   650
        You, under whose hand,
            In the storm of another time,
        Our dear land sailed out free.
        But now stand fast at the helm!

IOCASTE: In God's name, Oedipus, inform your wife
655   as well:
     Why are you so set in this hard anger?
OEDIPUS: I will tell you, for none of these men
     deserves
     My confidence as you do. It is Creon's work,
     His treachery, his plotting against me.
660 IOCASTE: Go on, if you can make this clear to me.
OEDIPUS: He charges me with the murder of Laïos.
IOCASTE: Has he some knowledge? Or does he speak
     from hearsay?
OEDIPUS: He would not commit himself to such a
     charge,
     But he has brought in that damnable soothsayer
     To tell his story.
665 IOCASTE: Set your mind at rest.
     If it is a question of soothsayers, I tell you
     That you will find no man whose craft gives
     knowledge
     Of the unknowable.
            Here is my proof:
     An oracle was reported to Laïos once
670   (I will not say from Phoibos himself, but from
     His appointed ministers, at any rate)
     That his doom would be death at the hands of his
     own son—
     His son, born of his flesh and of mine!
     Now, you remember the story: Laïos was killed
     By marauding strangers where three highways
675   meet;
     But his child had not been three days in this
     world
     Before the King had pierced the baby's ankles
     And had him left to die on a lonely mountain.
     Thus, Apollo never caused that child
680   To kill his father, and it was not Laïos' fate
     To die at the hands of his son, as he had feared.
     This is what prophets and prophecies are worth!
     Have no dread of them.
           It is God himself
     Who can show us what he wills, in his own way.
OEDIPUS: How strange a shadowy memory crossed
685   my mind,
     Just now while you were speaking; it chilled my
     heart.
IOCASTE: What do you mean? What memory do you
     speak of?
OEDIPUS: If I understand you, Laïos was killed
     At a place where three roads meet.
IOCASTE: So it was said;
     We have no later story.
690 OEDIPUS: Where did it happen?
IOCASTE: Phokis, it is called: at a place where the
     Theban Way
     Divides into the roads toward Delphi and Daulia.
OEDIPUS: When?
IOCASTE: We had the news not long before you came

     And proved the right to your succession here.
OEDIPUS: Ah, what net has God been weaving for
     me?   695
IOCASTE: Oedipus! Why does this trouble you?
OEDIPUS: Do not ask me yet.
     First, tell me how Laïos looked, and tell me
     How old he was.
IOCASTE: He was tall, his hair just touched
     With white; his form was not unlike your own.
OEDIPUS: I think that I myself may be accurst   700
     By my own ignorant edict.
IOCASTE: You speak strangely.
     It makes me tremble to look at you, my King.
OEDIPUS: I am not sure that the blind man can not
     see.
     But I should know better if you were to tell me—
IOCASTE: Anything—though I dread to hear you ask
     it.   705
OEDIPUS: Was the King lightly escorted, or did he
     ride
     With a large company, as a ruler should?
IOCASTE: There were five men with him in all: one
     was a herald;
     And a single chariot, which he was driving.
OEDIPUS: Alas, that makes it plain enough!
              But who—   710
     Who told you how it happened?
IOCASTE: A household servant,
     The only one to escape.
OEDIPUS: And is he still
     A servant of ours?
IOCASTE: No; for when he came back at last
     And found you enthroned in the place of the
     dead king,
     He came to me, touched my hand with his, and
     begged   715
     That I would send him away to the frontier dis-
     trict
     Where only the shepherds go—
     As far away from the city as I could send him.
     I granted his prayer; for although the man was a
     slave,
     He had earned more than this favour at my hands.   720
OEDIPUS: Can he be called back quickly?
IOCASTE: Easily.
     But why?
OEDIPUS: I have taken too much upon myself
     Without enquiry; therefore I wish to consult him.
IOCASTE: Then he shall come.
            But am I not one also   725
     To whom you might confide these fears of yours?
OEDIPUS: That is your right; it will not be denied
     you,
     Now least of all; for I have reached a pitch
     Of wild foreboding. Is there anyone
     To whom I should sooner speak?   730
     Polybos of Corinth is my father.

My mother is a Dorian: Meropê.
I grew up chief among the men of Corinth
Until a strange thing happened—
735   Not worth my passion, it may be, but strange.
At a feast, a drunken man maundering in his cups
Cries out that I am not my father's son!
I contained myself that night, though I felt anger
And a sinking heart. The next day I visited
My father and mother, and questioned them.
740   They stormed,
Calling it all the slanderous rant of a fool;
And this relieved me. Yet the suspicion
Remained always aching in my mind;
I knew there was talk; I could not rest;
And finally, saying nothing to my parents,
745   I went to the shrine at Delphi.
The god dismissed my question without reply;
He spoke of other things.
            Some were clear,
Full of wretchedness, dreadful, unbearable:
750   As, that I should lie with my own mother, breed
Children from whom all men would turn their eyes;
And that I should be my father's murderer.
I heard all this, and fled. And from that day
Corinth to me was only in the stars
755   Descending in that quarter of the sky,
As I wandered farther and farther on my way
To a land where I should never see the evil
Sung by the oracle. And I came to this country
Where, so you say, King Laïos was killed.
760   I will tell you all that happened there, my lady.
There were three highways
Coming together at a place I passed;
And there a herald came towards me, and a
     chariot
Drawn by horses, with a man such as you describe
765   Seated in it. The groom leading the horses
Forced me off the road at his lord's command;
But as this charioteer lurched over towards me
I struck him in my rage. The old man saw me
And brought his double goad down upon my head
As I came abreast.
770   He was paid back, and more!
Swinging my club in this right hand I knocked him
Out of his car, and he rolled on the ground.
                    I killed him.
I killed them all.
Now if that stranger and Laïos were—kin,
775   Where is a man more miserable than I?
More hated by the gods? Citizen and alien alike
Must never shelter me or speak to me—
I must be shunned by all.
           And I myself
Pronounced this malediction upon myself!
780   Think of it: I have touched you with these hands,
These hands that killed your husband. What
     defilement!

Am I all evil, then? It must be so,
Since I must flee from Thebes, yet never again
See my own countrymen, my own country,
For fear of joining my mother in marriage   785
And killing Polybos, my father.
          Ah,
If I was created so, born to this fate,
Who could deny the savagery of God?
O holy majesty of heavenly powers!
May I never see that day! Never!   790
Rather let me vanish from the race of men
Than know the abomination destined me!
CHORAGOS: We too, my lord, have felt dismay at this.
     But there is hope: you have yet to hear the shep-
        herd.
OEDIPUS: Indeed, I fear no other hope is left me.   795
IOCASTE: What do you hope from him when he comes?
OEDIPUS: This much:
     If his account of the murder tallies with yours,
     Then I am cleared.
IOCASTE: What was it that I said
     Of such importance?
OEDIPUS: Why, 'marauders', you said,
     Killed the King, according to this man's story.   800
     If he maintains that still, if there were several,
     Clearly the guilt is not mine: I was alone.
     But if he says one man, singlehanded, did it,
     Then the evidence all points to me.
IOCASTE: You may be sure that he said there were
       several;   805
     And can he call back that story now? He cán not.
     The whole city heard it as plainly as I.
     But suppose he alters some detail of it:
     He can not ever show that Laïos' death
     Fulfilled the oracle: for Apollo said   810
     My child was doomed to kill him; and my child—
     Poor baby!—it was my child that died first.
     No. From now on, where oracles are concerned,
     I would not waste a second thought on any.
OEDIPUS: You may be right.   815
                    But come: let someone go
     For the shepherd at once. This matter must be settled.
IOCASTE: I will send for him.
     I would not wish to cross you in anything,
     And surely not in this.—Let us go in.   820

[Exeunt into the palace]

ODE 2

STROPHE I

CHORUS: Let me be reverent in the ways of right,
     Lowly the paths I journey on;
     Let all my words and actions keep
     The laws of the pure universe
     From highest Heaven handed down.   825

For Heaven is their bright nurse,
Those generations of the realms of light;
Ah, never of mortal kind were they begot,
Nor are they slaves of memory, lost in sleep:
830   Their Father is greater than Time, and ages not.

ANTISTROPHE 1

The tyrant is a child of Pride
Who drinks from his great sickening cup
Recklessness and vanity,
Until from his high crest headlong
835   He plummets to the dust of hope.
That strong man is not strong.
But let no fair ambition be denied;
May God protect the wrestler for the State
In government, in comely policy,
840   Who will fear God, and on His ordinance wait.

STROPHE 2

Haughtiness and the high hand of disdain
Tempt and outrage God's holy law;
And any mortal who dares hold
No immortal Power in awe
845   Will be caught up in a net of pain:
The price for which his levity is sold.
Let each man take due earnings, then,
And keep his hands from holy things,
And from blasphemy stand apart—
850   Else the crackling blast of heaven
Blows on his head, and on his desperate heart;
Though fools will honour impious men,
In their cities no tragic poet sings.

ANTISTROPHE 2

Shall we lose faith in Delphi's obscurities,
855   We who have heard the world's core
Discredited, and the sacred wood
Of Zeus at Elis praised no more?
The deeds and the strange prophecies
Must make a pattern yet to be understood.
860   Zeus, if indeed you are lord of all,
Throned in light over night and day,
Mirror this in your endless mind:
Our masters call the oracle
Words on the wind, and the Delphic vision blind!
865   Their hearts no longer know Apollo,
And reverence for the gods has died away.

Scene 3

[Enter IOCASTE]

IOCASTE: Princes of Thebes, it has occurred to me
To visit the altars of the gods, bearing
These branches as a suppliant, and this incense.
870   Our King is not himself: his noble soul
Is overwrought with fantasies of dread,

Else he would consider
The new prophecies in the light of the old.
He will listen to any voice that speaks disaster,
And my advice goes for nothing.

[She approaches the altar, right.]

To you, then, Apollo,   875
Lycean lord°, since you are nearest, I turn in prayer.
Receive these offerings, and grant us deliverance
From defilement. Our hearts are heavy with fear
When we see our leader distracted, as helpless
   sailors
Are terrified by the confusion of their helmsman.   880

[Enter MESSENGER]

MESSENGER: Friends, no doubt you can direct me:
Where shall I find the house of Oedipus,
Or, better still, where is the King himself?
CHORAGOS: It is this very place, stranger; he is inside.
This is his wife and mother of his children.   885
MESSENGER: I wish her happiness in a happy house,
Blest in all the fulfillment of her marriage.
IOCASTE: I wish as much for you: your courtesy
Deserves a like good fortune. But now, tell me:
Why have you come? What have you to say to us?   890
MESSENGER: Good news, my lady, for your house
   and your husband.
IOCASTE: What news? Who sent you here?
MESSENGER: I am from Corinth.
The news I bring ought to mean joy for you,
Though it may be you will find some grief in it.
IOCASTE: What is it? How can it touch us in both
   ways?   895
MESSENGER: The people of Corinth, they say,
Intend to call Oedipus to be their king.
IOCASTE: But old Polybos—is he not reigning still?
MESSENGER: No. Death holds him in his sepulchre.
IOCASTE: What are you saying? Polybos is dead?   900
MESSENGER: If I am not telling the truth, may I die
   myself.

[To a MAIDSERVANT:]

IOCASTE: Go in, go quickly; tell this to your master.
O riddlers of God's will, where are you now!
This was the man whom Oedipus, long ago,
Feared so, fled so, in dread of destroying him—   905
But it was another fate by which he died.

[Enter OEDIPUS, center]

OEDIPUS: Dearest Iocastê, why have you sent for me?
IOCASTE: Listen to what this man says, and then tell
   me

---

[876] **Lycean lord** Apollo

What has become of the solemn prophecies.

910 OEDIPUS: Who is this man? What is his news for me?

IOCASTE: He has come from Corinth to announce
    your father's death!

OEDIPUS: Is it true, stranger? Tell me in your own
    words.

MESSENGER: I can not say it more clearly: the King is
    dead.

OEDIPUS: Was it by treason? Or by an attack of illness?

915 MESSENGER: A little thing brings old men to their rest.

OEDIPUS: It was sickness, then?

MESSENGER: Yes, and his many years.

OEDIPUS: Ah!
    Why should a man respect the Pythian hearth°, or
    Give heed to the birds that jangle above his head?

920 They prophesied that I should kill Polybos,
    Kill my own father; but he is dead and buried,
    And I am here—I never touched him, never,
    Unless he died of grief for my departure,
    And thus, in a sense, through me. No. Polybos

925 Has packed the oracles off with him underground.
    They are empty words.

IOCASTE: Had I not told you so?

OEDIPUS: You had; it was my faint heart that
    betrayed me.

IOCASTE: From now on never think of those things
    again.

OEDIPUS: And yet—must I not fear my mother's bed?

930 IOCASTE: Why should anyone in this world be afraid,
    Since Fate rules us and nothing can be foreseen?
    A man should live only for the present day.
    Have no more fear of sleeping with your mother:
    How many men, in dreams, have lain with their
    mothers!

935 No reasonable man is troubled by such things.

OEDIPUS: That is true; only—
    If only my mother were not still alive!
    But she is alive. I can not help my dread.

IOCASTE: Yet this news of your father's death is won-
    derful.

940 OEDIPUS: Wonderful. But I fear the living woman.

MESSENGER: Tell me, who is this woman that you fear?

OEDIPUS: It is Meropê, man; the wife of King Polybos.

MESSENGER: Meropê? Why should you be afraid of
    her?

OEDIPUS: An oracle of the gods, a dreadful saying.

MESSENGER: Can you tell me about it? or are you

945 sworn to silence?

OEDIPUS: I can tell you, and I will.
    Apollo said through his prophet that I was the man
    Who should marry his own mother, shed his
    father's blood

---

918 Pythian hearth A reference to the Delphic oracle. Apollo
killed the serpent python on the spot where he established his
oracle.

With his own hands. And so, for all these years
    I have kept clear of Corinth, and no harm has
    come—   950
    Though it would have been sweet to see my par-
    ents again.

MESSENGER: And is this the fear that drove you out
    of Corinth?

OEDIPUS: Would you have me kill my father?

MESSENGER: As for that
    You must be reassured by the news I gave you.

OEDIPUS: If you could reassure me, I would reward
    you.   955

MESSENGER: I had that in mind, I will confess: I thought
    I could count on you when you returned to
    Corinth.

OEDIPUS: No: I will never go near my parents again.

MESSENGER: Ah, son, you still do not know what you
    are doing—

OEDIPUS: What do you mean? In the name of God
    tell me!   960

MESSENGER: —If these are your reasons for not going
    home.

OEDIPUS: I tell you, I fear the oracle may come true.

MESSENGER: And guilt may come upon you through
    your parents?

OEDIPUS: That is the dread that is always in my heart.

MESSENGER: Can you not see that all your fears are
    groundless?   965

OEDIPUS: How can you say that? They are my par-
    ents, surely?

MESSENGER: Polybos was not your father.

OEDIPUS: Not my father?

MESSENGER: No more your father than the man
    speaking to you.

OEDIPUS: But you are nothing to me!

MESSENGER: Neither was he.

OEDIPUS: Then why did he call me son?

MESSENGER: I will tell you: 970
    Long ago he had you from my hands, as a gift.

OEDIPUS: Then how could he love me so, if I was not
    his?

MESSENGER: He had no children, and his heart
    turned to you.

OEDIPUS: What of you? Did you buy me? Did you
    find me by chance?

MESSENGER: I came upon you in the crooked pass of
    Kithairon.   975

OEDIPUS: And what were you doing there?

MESSENGER: Tending my flocks.

OEDIPUS: A wandering shepherd?

MESSENGER: But your saviour, son, that day.

OEDIPUS: From what did you save me?

MESSENGER: Your ankles should tell you that.

OEDIPUS: Ah, stranger, why do you speak of that
    childhood pain?   980

MESSENGER: I cut the bonds that tied your ankles
    together.

OEDIPUS: I have had the mark as long as I can
      remember.
MESSENGER: That was why you were given the name
      you bear.°
OEDIPUS: God! Was it my father or my mother who
      did it?
      Tell me!
MESSENGER: I do not know. The man who gave you
985   to me
      Can tell you better than I.
OEDIPUS: It was not you that found me, but another?
MESSENGER: It was another shepherd gave you to me.
OEDIPUS: Who was he? Can you tell me who he was?
MESSENGER: I think he was said to be one of Laïos'
990   people.
OEDIPUS: You mean the Laïos who was king here
      years ago?
MESSENGER: Yes; King Laïos; and the man was one of
      his herdsmen.
OEDIPUS: Is he still alive? Can I see him?
MESSENGER: These men here
      Know best about such things.
OEDIPUS: Does anyone here
995   Know this shepherd that he is talking about?
      Have you seen him in the fields, or in the town?
      If you have, tell me. It is time things were made
      plain.
CHORAGOS: I think the man he means is that same
      shepherd
      You have already asked to see. Iocastê perhaps
      Could tell you something.
1000 OEDIPUS: Do you know anything
      About him, Lady? Is he the man we have sum-
      moned?
      Is that the man this shepherd means?
IOCASTE: Why think of him?
      Forget this herdsman. Forget it all.
      This talk is a waste of time.
OEDIPUS: How can you say that,
1005   When the clues to my true birth are in my hands?
IOCASTE: For God's love, let us have no more ques-
      tioning!
      Is your life nothing to you?
      My own is pain enough for me to bear.
OEDIPUS: You need not worry. Suppose my mother a
      slave,
1010   And born of slaves: no baseness can touch you.
IOCASTE: Listen to me, I beg you: do not do this thing!
OEDIPUS: I will not listen; the truth must be made
      known.
IOCASTE: Everything that I say is for your own good!
OEDIPUS: My own good
      Snaps my patience, then; I want none of it.

IOCASTE: You are fatally wrong! May you never learn
      who you are!   1015
OEDIPUS: Go, one of you, and bring the shepherd here.
      Let us leave this woman to brag of her royal name.
IOCASTE: Ah, miserable!
      That is the only word I have for you now.
      That is the only word I can ever have.   1020

[Exit into the palace]

CHORAGOS: Why has she left us, Oedipus? Why has
      she gone
      In such a passion of sorrow? I fear this silence:
      Something dreadful may come of it.
OEDIPUS: Let it come!
      However base my birth, I must know about it.
      The Queen, like a woman, is perhaps ashamed   1025
      To think of my low origin. But I
      Am a child of Luck; I can not be dishonoured.
      Luck is my mother; the passing months, my
      brothers,
      Have seen me rich and poor.
                            If this is so,
      How could I wish that I were someone else?   1030
      How could I not be glad to know my birth?

ODE III

STROPHE

CHORUS: If ever the coming time were known
      To my heart's pondering,
      Kithairon, now by Heaven I see the torches
      At the festival of the next full moon,   1035
      And see the dance, and hear the choir sing
      A grace to your gentle shade:
      Mountain where Oedipus was found,
      O mountain guard of a noble race!
      May the god who heals° us lend his aid,   1040
      And let that glory come to pass
      For our king's cradling-ground.

ANTISTROPHE

      Of the nymphs that flower beyond the years,
      Who bore you, royal child,
      To Pan of the hills or the timberline Apollo,   1045
      Cold in delight where the upland clears,
      Or Hermês for whom Kyllenê's° heights are piled?
      Or flushed as evening cloud,°
      Great Dionysos, roamer of mountains,
      He—was it he who found you there,   1050
      And caught you up in his own proud

1040 god who heals Apollo   **1047 Kyllenê** mountain sacred to
Hermes, messenger of Zeus   **1048 flushed . . . cloud**
Dionysus, the god of wine, flushed from drinking

---

983 name you bear *Oedipus* means "swollen foot"

Arms from the sweet god-ravisher°
Who laughed by the Muses' fountains?°

Scene 4

OEDIPUS: Sirs: though I do not know the man,
1055   I think I see him coming, this shepherd we want:
        He is old, like our friend here, and the men
        Bringing him seem to be servants of my house.
        But you can tell, if you have ever seen him.

[Enter SHEPHERD *escorted by servants]*

CHORAGOS: I know him, he was Laïos' man. You can
        trust him.
OEDIPUS: Tell me first, you from Corinth: is this the
1060   shepherd
        We were discussing?
MESSENGER: This is the very man.

[To SHEPHERD:*]*

OEDIPUS:
        Come here. No, look at me. You must answer
        Everything I ask.—You belonged to Laïos?
SHEPHERD: Yes: born his slave, brought up in his house.
OEDIPUS: Tell me: what kind of work did you do for
1065   him?
SHEPHERD: I was a shepherd of his, most of my life.
OEDIPUS: Where mainly did you go for pasturage?
SHEPHERD: Sometimes Kithairon, sometimes the hills
        near-by.
OEDIPUS: Do you remember ever seeing this man out
        there?
1070 SHEPHERD: What would he be doing there? This man?
OEDIPUS: This man standing here. Have you ever
        seen him before?
SHEPHERD: No. At least, not to my recollection.
MESSENGER: And that is not strange, my lord. But I'll
        refresh
        His memory: he must remember when we two
        Spent three whole seasons together, March to
1075   September,
        On Kithairon or thereabouts. He had two flocks;
        I had one. Each autumn I'd drive mine home
        And he would go back with his to Laïos' sheep-
        fold.—
        Is this not true, just as I have described it?
1080 SHEPHERD: True, yes; but it was all so long ago.
MESSENGER: Well, then: do you remember, back in
        those days,

That you gave me a baby boy to bring up as my
        own?
SHEPHERD: What if I did? What are you trying to say?
MESSENGER: King Oedipus was once that little child.
SHEPHERD: Damn you, hold your tongue!
OEDIPUS: No more of that! 1085
        It is your tongue needs watching, not this man's.
SHEPHERD: My King, my Master, what is it I have
        done wrong?
OEDIPUS: You have not answered his question about
        the boy.
SHEPHERD: He does not know . . . He is only making
        trouble . . .
OEDIPUS: Come, speak plainly, or it will go hard
        with you.   1090
SHEPHERD: In God's name, do not torture an old man!
OEDIPUS: Come here, one of you; bind his arms
        behind him.
SHEPHERD: Unhappy king! What more do you wish
        to learn?
OEDIPUS: Did you give this man the child he speaks of?
SHEPHERD: I did.
        And I would to God I had died that very day. 1095
OEDIPUS: You will die now unless you speak the truth.
SHEPHERD: Yet if I speak the truth, I am worse than
        dead.
OEDIPUS: Very well; since you insist upon delaying—
SHEPHERD: No! I have told you already that I gave
        him the boy.
OEDIPUS: Where did you get him? From your house?
        From somewhere else?   1100
SHEPHERD: Not from mine, no. A man gave him to me.
OEDIPUS: Is that man here? Do you know whose
        slave he was?
SHEPHERD: For God's love, my King, do not ask me
        any more!
OEDIPUS: You are a dead man if I have to ask you
        again.
SHEPHERD: Then . . . Then the child was from the
        palace of Laïos.   1105
OEDIPUS: A slave child? or a child of his own line?
SHEPHERD: Ah, I am on the brink of dreadful speech!
OEDIPUS: And I of dreadful hearing. Yet I must hear.
SHEPHERD: If you must be told, then . . .
                              They said it was Laïos' child;
        But it is your wife who can tell you about that. 1110
OEDIPUS: My wife!—Did she give it to you?
SHEPHERD: My lord, she did.
OEDIPUS: Do you know why?
SHEPHERD: I was told to get rid of it.
OEDIPUS: An unspeakable mother!
SHEPHERD: There had been prophecies . . .
OEDIPUS: Tell me.
SHEPHERD: It was said that the boy would kill his
        own father.
OEDIPUS: Then why did you give him over to this
        old man?   1115

1052 **god-ravisher** The chorus wonders whether Oedipus is
the son of a nymph and a god (Pan or Apollo or Hermes or
Dionysus).   1053 **Muses' fountains** Helicon, springs sacred
to Apollo and to the muses

SHEPHERD: I pitied the baby, my King,
   And I thought that this man would take him far
      away
   To his own country.
                     He saved him—but for what a fate!
   For if you are what this man says you are,
1120   No man living is more wretched than Oedipus.
OEDIPUS: Ah God!
   It was true!
                  All the prophecies!
                              —Now,
   O Light, may I look on you for the last time!
   I, Oedipus,
   Oedipus, damned in his birth, in his marriage
1125   damned,
   Damned in the blood he shed with his own hand!

[*He rushes into the palace*]

Ode IV

STROPHE I

CHORUS: Alas for the seed of men.
   What measure shall I give these generations
   That breathe on the void and are void
1130   And exist and do not exist?
   Who bears more weight of joy
   Than mass of sunlight shifting in images,
   Or who shall make his thought stay on
   That down time drifts away?
1135   Your splendour is all fallen.
   O naked brow of wrath and tears,
   O change of Oedipus!
   I who saw your days call no man blest—
   Your great days like ghósts góne.

ANTISTROPHE I

1140   That mind was a strong bow.
   Deep, how deep you drew it then, hard archer,
   At a dim fearful range,
   And brought dear glory down!
   You overcame the stranger—
1145   The virgin with her hooking lion claws—
   And though death sang, stood like a tower
   To make pale Thebes take heart.
   Fortress against our sorrow!
   Divine king, giver of laws,
1150   Majestic Oedipus!
   No prince in Thebes had ever such renown,
   No prince won such grace of power.

STROPHE 2

   And now of all men ever known
   Most pitiful is this man's story:
1155   His fortunes are most changed, his state
   Fallen to a low slave's

Ground under bitter fate.
   O Oedipus, most royal one!
   The great door that expelled you to the light
   Gave at night—ah, gave night to your glory: 1160
   As to the father, to the fathering son.
   All understood too late.
   How could that queen whom Laïos won,
   The garden that he harrowed at his height,
   Be silent when that act was done?   1165

ANTISTROPHE 2

   But all eyes fail before time's eye,
   All actions come to justice there.
   Though never willed, though far down the deep
      past,
   Your bed, your dread sirings,
   Are brought to book at last.   1170
   Child by Laïos doomed to die,
   Then doomed to lose that fortunate little death,
   Would God you never took breath in this air
   That with my wailing lips I take to cry:
   For I weep the world's outcast.   1175
   Blind I was, and can not tell why;
   Asleep, for you had given ease of breath;
   A fool, while the false years went by.

ÉXODOS

[*Enter, from the palace,* SECOND MESSENGER]

SECOND MESSENGER: Elders of Thebes, most hon-
      oured in this land,
   What horrors are yours to see and hear, what
      weight   1180
   Of sorrow to be endured, if, true to your birth,
   You venerate the line of Labdakos!
   I think neither Istros nor Phasis, those great
      rivers,
   Could purify this place of the corruption
   It shelters now, or soon must bring to light—   1185
   Evil not done unconsciously, but willed.
   The greatest griefs are those we cause ourselves.
CHORAGOS: Surely, friend, we have grief enough
      already;
   What new sorrow do you mean?
SECOND MESSENGER: The Queen is dead.
CHORAGOS: Iocastê? Dead? But at whose hand?
SECOND MESSENGER: Her own.   1190
   The full horror of what happened you can not
      know,
   For you did not see it; but I, who did, will tell you
   As clearly as I can how she met her death.
   When she had left us,
   In passionate silence, passing through the court, 1195
   She ran to her apartment in the house,
   Her hair clutched by the fingers of both hands.
   She closed the doors behind her; then, by that bed

Where long ago the fatal son was conceived—
1200 That son who should bring about his father's
        death—
We heard her call upon Laïos, dead so many years,
And heard her wail for the double fruit of her
        marriage,
A husband by her husband, children by her child.
Exactly how she died I do not know:
1205 For Oedipus burst in moaning and would not let us
Keep vigil to the end: it was by him
As he stormed about the room that our eyes were
        caught.
From one to another of us he went, begging a
        sword,
Cursing the wife who was not his wife, the mother
Whose womb had carried his own children and
1210   himself.
I do not know: it was none of us aided him,
But surely one of the gods was in control!
For with a dreadful cry
He hurled his weight, as though wrenched out of
        himself,
1215 At the twin doors: the bolts gave, and he rushed in.
And there we saw her hanging, her body swaying
From the cruel cord she had noosed about her
        neck.
A great sob broke from him, heartbreaking to hear,
As he loosed the rope and lowered her to the
        ground.
I would blot out from my mind what happened
1220   next!
For the King ripped from her gown the golden
        brooches
That were her ornament, and raised them, and
        plunged them down
Straight into his own eyeballs, crying, 'No more,
'No more shall you look on the misery about me,
'The horrors of my own doing! Too long you have
        known
'The faces of those whom I should never have seen,
'Too long been blind to those for whom I was
        searching!
'From this hour, go in darkness!' And as he spoke,
He struck at his eyes—not once, but many times;
1230 And the blood spattered his beard,
Bursting from his ruined sockets like red hail.
So from the unhappiness of two this evil has
        sprung,
A curse on the man and woman alike. The old
Happiness of the house of Labdakos
1235 Was happiness enough: where is it today?
It is all wailing and ruin, disgrace, death—all
The misery of mankind that has a name—
And it is wholly and for ever theirs.
CHORAGOS: Is he in agony still? Is there no rest for him?
SECOND MESSENGER: He is calling for someone to lead
1240   him to the gates

So that all the children of Kadmos may look upon
His father's murderer, his mother's—no,
I can not say it!
                        And then he will leave Thebes,
Self-exiled, in order that the curse
Which he himself pronounced may depart from
        the house.   1245
He is weak, and there is none to lead him,
So terrible is his suffering.
                        But you will see:
Look, the doors are opening; in a moment
You will see a thing that would crush a heart of
        stone.

[*The central door is opened;* OEDIPUS, *blinded, is led in*]

CHORAGOS: Dreadful indeed for men to see.   1250
    Never have my own eyes
    Looked on a sight so full of fear.
    Oedipus!
    What madness came upon you, what daemon
    Leaped on your life with heavier   1255
    Punishment than a mortal man can bear?
    No: I can not even
    Look at you, poor ruined one.
    And I would speak, question, ponder,
    If I were able. No.   1260
    You make me shudder.
OEDIPUS: God. God.
    Is there a sorrow greater?
    Where shall I find harbour in this world?
    My voice is hurled far on a dark wind.   1265
    What has God done to me?
CHORAGOS: Too terrible to think of, or to see.

STROPHE I

OEDIPUS: O cloud of night,
    Never to be turned away: night coming on,
    I can not tell how: night like a shroud!   1270
    My fair winds brought me here.
                        O God. Again
    The pain of the spikes where I had sight,
    The flooding pain
    Of memory, never to be gouged out.
CHORAGOS: This is not strange.   1275
    You suffer it all twice over, remorse in pain,
    Pain in remorse.

ANTISTROPHE I

OEDIPUS: Ah dear friend
    Are you faithful even yet, you alone?
    Are you still standing near me, will you stay here, 1280
Patient, to care for the blind?
                        The blind man!
    Yet even blind I know who it is attends me,
    By the voice's tone—
    Though my new darkness hide the comforter.

1285 CHORAGOS: Oh fearful act!
        What god was it drove you to rake black
        Night across your eyes?

STROPHE 2

OEDIPUS: Apollo. Apollo. Dear
        Children, the god was Apollo.
1290   He brought my sick, sick fate upon me.
        But the blinding hand was my own!
        How could I bear to see
        When all my sight was horror everywhere?
CHORAGOS: Everywhere; that is true.
1295 OEDIPUS: And now what is left?
        Images? Love? A greeting even,
        Sweet to the senses? Is there anything?
        Ah, no, friends: lead me away.
        Lead me away from Thebes.
                        Lead the great wreck
1300   And hell of Oedipus, whom the gods hate.
CHORAGOS: Your fate is clear, you are not blind to that.
        Would God you had never found it out!

ANTISTROPHE 2

OEDIPUS: Death take the man who unbound
        My feet on that hillside
1305   And delivered me from death to life! What life?
        If only I had died,
        This weight of monstrous doom
        Could not have dragged me and my darlings down.
CHORAGOS: I would have wished the same.
1310 OEDIPUS: Oh never to have come here
        With my father's blood upon me! Never
        To have been the man they call his mother's hus-
            band!
        Oh accurst! Oh child of evil,
        To have entered that wretched bed—
                        the selfsame one!
1315   More primal than sin itself, this fell to me.
CHORAGOS: I do not know how I can answer you.
        You were better dead than alive and blind.
OEDIPUS: Do not counsel me any more. This punishment
        That I have laid upon myself is just.
1320   If I had eyes,
        I do not know how I could bear the sight
        Of my father, when I came to the house of Death,
        Or my mother: for I have sinned against them both
        So vilely that I could not make my peace
        By strangling my own life.
                        Or do you think my children,
1325   Born as they were born, would be sweet to my eyes?
        Ah never, never! Nor this town with its high walls,
        Nor the holy images of the gods.
                        For I,
        Thrice miserable!—Oedipus, noblest of all the line
1330   Of Kadmos, have condemned myself to enjoy
        These things no more, by my own malediction

Expelling that man whom the gods declared
To be a defilement in the house of Laïos.
After exposing the rankness of my own guilt,
How could I look men frankly in the eyes?   1335
No, I swear it,
If I could have stifled my hearing at its source,
I would have done it and made all this body
A tight cell of misery, blank to light and sound:
So I should have been safe in a dark agony   1340
Beyond all recollection.
                        Ah Kithairon!
Why did you shelter me? When I was cast upon you,
Why did I not die? Then I should never
Have shown the world my execrable birth.
Ah Polybos! Corinth, city that I believed   1345
The ancient seat of my ancestors: how fair
I seemed, your child! And all the while this evil
Was cancerous within me!
                        For I am sick
In my daily life, sick in my origin.   1350
O three roads, dark ravine, woodland and way
Where three roads met: you, drinking my father's
    blood,
My own blood, spilled by my own hand: can you
    remember
The unspeakable things I did there, and the things
I went on from there to do?
                        O marriage, marriage!
The act that engendered me, and again the act   1355
Performed by the son in the same bed—
                        Ah, the net
Of incest, mingling fathers, brothers, sons,
With brides, wives, mothers: the last evil
That can be known by men: no tongue can say
How evil!
                No. For the love of God, conceal me   1360
Somewhere far from Thebes; or kill me; or hurl me
Into the sea, away from men's eyes for ever.
Come, lead me. You need not fear to touch me.
Of all men, I alone can bear this guilt.

[Enter CREON*]*

CHORAGOS: We are not the ones to decide; but Creon
    here   1365
    May fitly judge of what you ask. He only
    Is left to protect the city in your place.
OEDIPUS: Alas, how can I speak to him? What right
    have I
    To beg his courtesy whom I have deeply wronged?   1370
CREON: I have not come to mock you, Oedipus,
    Or to reproach you, either.

[To ATTENDANTS:*]*

                —You, standing there:
    If you have lost all respect for man's dignity,

1375 At least respect the flame of Lord Helios:
Do not allow this pollution to show itself
Openly here, an affront to the earth
And Heaven's rain and the light of day. No, take him
Into the house as quickly as you can.
For it is proper
1380 That only the close kindred see his grief.
OEDIPUS: I pray you in God's name, since your courtesy
Ignores my dark expectation, visiting
With mercy this man of all men most execrable:
Give me what I ask—for your good, not for mine.
1385 CREON: And what is it that you would have me do?
OEDIPUS: Drive me out of this country as quickly as may be
To a place where no human voice can ever greet me.
CREON: I should have done that before now—only,
God's will had not been wholly revealed to me.
1390 OEDIPUS: But his command is plain: the parricide
Must be destroyed. I am that evil man.
CREON: That is the sense of it, yes; but as things are,
We had best discover clearly what is to be done.
OEDIPUS: You would learn more about a man like me?
1395 CREON: You are ready now to listen to the god.
OEDIPUS: I will listen. But it is to you
That I must turn for help. I beg you, hear me.
The woman in there—
Give her whatever funeral you think proper:
She is your sister.
1400 —But let me go, Creon!
Let me purge my father's Thebes of the pollution
Of my living here, and go out to the wild hills,
To Kithairon, that has won such fame with me,
The tomb my mother and father appointed for me,
1405 And let me die there, as they willed I should.
And yet I know
Death will not ever come to me through sickness
Or in any natural way: I have been preserved
For some unthinkable fate. But let that be.
1410 As for my sons, you need not care for them.
They are men, they will find some way to live.
But my poor daughters, who have shared my table,
Who never before have been parted from their father—
Take care of them, Creon; do this for me.
1415 And will you let me touch them with my hands
A last time, and let us weep together?
Be kind, my lord,
Great prince, be kind!
Could I but touch them,
They would be mine again, as when I had my eyes.

[*Enter* ANTIGONE *and* ISMENE, *attended*]

1420 Ah, God!
Is it my dearest children I hear weeping?

Has Creon pitied me and sent my daughters?
CREON: Yes, Oedipus: I knew that they were dear to you
In the old days, and know you must love them still.
OEDIPUS: May God bless you for this—and be a friendlier 1425
Guardian to you than he has been to me!
Children, where are you?
Come quickly to my hands: they are your brother's—
Hands that have brought your father's once clear eyes
To this way of seeing—
Ah dearest ones, 1430
I had neither sight nor knowledge then, your father
By the woman who was the source of his own life!
And I weep for you—having no strength to see you—,
I weep for you when I think of the bitterness
That men will visit upon you all your lives. 1435
What homes, what festivals can you attend
Without being forced to depart again in tears?
And when you come to marriageable age,
Where is the man, my daughters, who would dare
Risk the bane that lies on all my children? 1440
Is there any evil wanting? Your father killed
His father; sowed the womb of her who bore him;
Engendered you at the fount of his own existence!
That is what they will say of you.
Then, whom
Can you ever marry? There are no bridegrooms for you, 1445
And your lives must wither away in sterile dreaming.
O Creon, son of Menoikeus!
You are the only father my daughters have,
Since we, their parents, are both of us gone for ever.
They are your own blood: you will not let them 1450
Fall into beggary and loneliness;
You will keep them from the miseries that are mine!
Take pity on them; see, they are only children,
Friendless except for you. Promise me this,
Great Prince, and give me your hand in token of it. 1455

[CREON *clasps his right hand*]

Children:
I could say much, if you could understand me,
But as it is, I have only this prayer for you:
Live where you can, be as happy as you can—
Happier, please God, than God has made your father! 1460
CREON:
Enough. You have wept enough. Now go within.
OEDIPUS: I must; but it is hard.
CREON:
Time eases all things.

OEDIPUS: But you must promise—
CREON: Say what you desire.
OEDIPUS: Send me from Thebes!
CREON: God grant that I may!
OEDIPUS: But since God hates me . . .
1465 CREON: No, he will grant your wish.
OEDIPUS: You promise?
CREON: I can not speak beyond my knowledge.
OEDIPUS: Then lead me in.
CREON: Come now, and leave your children.
OEDIPUS: No! Do not take them from me!
CREON: Think no longer
    That you are in command here, but rather think
    How, when you were, you served your own
1470   destruction.

[Exeunt into the house all but the CHORUS; *the*
CHORAGOS *chants directly to the audience:]*

CHORAGOS: Men of Thebes: look upon Oedipus.
    This is the king who solved the famous riddle
    And towered up, most powerful of men.
    No mortal eyes but looked on him with envy,
1475   Yet in the end ruin swept over him.
    Let every man in mankind's frailty
    Consider his last day; and let none
    Presume on his good fortune until he find
    Life, at his death, a memory without pain.

EURIPIDES (CA. 484–406 B.C.)

Euripides came from Salamis, an island in the Saronic Gulf where the Greeks had defeated the Persians. Toward the end of the fifth century B.C., the thirty-year-long Peloponnesian War led to the exhaustion of the Athenian treasury, and finally Sparta won dominance over Athens, in the first stage of the breakup of the Greek city-states. The period coincided with Euripides' dramatic career, and he often took a critical view of the decline of Athens.

Euripides introduced significant innovations in the Greek theater. He used the skene—traditionally used to represent a palace—to represent a variety of common locations. He used machines to achieve theatrical effects, and he often resorted to the deus ex machina—the crane that lifted actors into or out of the dramatic action—to resolve his plays. His choral odes, too, are unique in that they are not intricately connected to the action of his plays. Finally, his dialogue is more colloquial than that of any of his predecessors. These innovations tend to emphasize human characters and human issues. Euripides is credited with approximately ninety plays. Eighteen of them have survived, more than for any other Greek tragedian: *Alcestis, Medea, Heracleidae, Hippolytus, Cyclops, Heracles, Iphigenia in Tauris, Helen, Hecuba, Andromache, The Trojan Women, Ion, The Suppliant Women, Orestes, Electra,* and *The Phoenician Women*. Three other plays (*Iphigenia in Aulis, The Bacchae,* and the now-lost *Alcmadon at Corinth*) were written at the court of Archileus of Macedon, where Euripides moved in 408 B.C. His son brought this trilogy to Athens after Euripides died, and it won the prize at City Dionysia.

Euripides was not as successful in his own lifetime as Aeschylus and Sophocles had been. Of the twenty plays he produced for the City Dionysia, only five were awarded prizes, and one of these was a posthumous award. History, however, has treated him more kindly than his contemporaries: fully one-fifth of his dramatic output has been preserved, and many of his plays are regarded as innovative masterpieces.

Medea

Many of Euripides' plays center on women—certainly an innovation at the time. Medea, for example, is the first developed female character in Greek theater. She is not defined by her relationship to her husband or her father; rather, she is an individual in her own right. Such a ploy may well have been startling in a culture in which women had a distinctly inferior status. *Medea* won third prize at the City Dionysia in 431 B.C.

Like his predecessors in the Greek theater, Euripides counts on his audience's knowledge of the legend that forms the background to his play. At the order of his usurper uncle, Pelias, king of Iolcus, Jason sailed to capture the Golden Fleece, carefully guarded by Aeetes, king of Colchis. He enlisted a group of heroes and demigods in the project and built the *Argo*, the first ship. Only with the help of the princess Medea's sorcery did Jason succeed in getting the fleece. Medea deceived her father and killed her brother for Jason's sake, and they returned together to the court of King Pelias. Jason held the rightful title to the crown of Iolcus, and Medea once again helped him. She convinced Pelias' daughters that they could restore their father's lost youth by cutting him into pieces and then boiling the remains with special herbs. The daughters did so, but Medea intentionally supplied them with the wrong herbs, and Pelias died. However, they were unable to seize power, and Jason and Medea, along with their two sons, escaped to Corinth.

Euripides begins his play with Jason and Medea in Corinth. At this point Jason has deserted Medea to marry the daughter of King Creon. He claims that he did so in order to guarantee the welfare of his and Medea's children, since his marriage will make them members of the nobility. The chorus sings of the legitimate right Jason has to enter into this marriage and to take a younger woman as his wife. At the same time, Euripides creates Jason as an egotist who has difficulty accepting the fact that he owes so much to Medea. Meanwhile, Medea, whose single passion is Jason, justifiably feels betrayed.

The theme of *Medea* is fully accessible to modern audiences in ways that the tragedies of Agamemnon or of Oedipus, for example, are not. Medea has been betrayed, and her powerful love for Jason is converted into a hatred so strong as to preclude all human sympathy. She intentionally sets out to kill Jason's new wife and Creon with the gifts of the poisoned robe and chaplet. More horrifying still, she intends to kill those whom she knows Jason loves best, their own children.

Euripides takes a startling perspective on the story of Jason and Medea. He focuses on Medea's powerful feelings about the relationship and on her awareness of her actions and their consequences. In contrast to other handlings of the story, Euripides uses a deus ex machina—a dragon chariot—to save Medea at the end of the play from the wrath of Jason and the outrage of the people of Corinth. But Jason and Medea both are devastated by the action of this tragedy, and the play remains unrivaled in its portrayal of the psychological and emotional extremities of betrayal and revenge.

Medea

EURIPIDES

TRANSLATED BY PAUL ROCHE

CHARACTERS

NURSE
TUTOR to Medea's sons
MEDEA, Asiatic princess
CHORUS of Corinthian women
CREON, king of Corinth
JASON, husband of Medea

AEGEUS, king of Athens
MESSENGER
TWO BOYS, sons of Medea
HANDMAIDS of Medea
ATTENDANTS AND GUARDS for Creon and Aegeus

TIME AND SETTING: *It is midmorning outside Jason's house in Corinth. Ten years have passed since the Argonauts sailed home after finding the Golden Fleece. During that time, Jason and Medea [the Asian bride he brought back with him] have been living modestly in Corinth: models of an unassailable married life of devotion to each other and their children. But the news has just broken that Jason is to marry the daughter of the king of Corinth. [The exit on stage left leads to the town and royal palace, that on the right to the country].*

[Enter the NURSE *from the house. She is an old woman who has looked after* MEDEA *from babyhood. Her face, the only part of her showing from the dark, heavy clothes that envelop her, is puckered with age and distress]*

PROLOGUE

NURSE: Why did the winged oars of the Argo°
  ever weave between those gnashing blue
  fjords towards the land of Colchis?
   Why did the pines in the dells of Pelion°
  ever fall to the axe and fill
5 the rowing hands of heroes sent by Pelias°
  to fetch the Golden Fleece?
   My mistress, Medea, then
  never would have sailed to Iolcus with its towers
  or been struck to the heart with love of Jason.
   She never would have baited Pelias' daughters
10 to the murder of their father°

and be living here in Corinth° now
with her husband and her children . . .
  Ah, she has merited this city's good opinion,
exile though she came,
and was in everything Jason's perfect foil,
being in marriage that saving thing:
a wife who does not go against her man.   15

[With a despairing glance toward the house]

  Now everything has turned to hate,
her passion to a plague.
  Jason has betrayed his sons and her,
takes to bed a royal bride,
Creon's daughter—the king of Corinth's.
  Medea, spurned and desolate,   20
breaks out in oaths,
invokes the solemnest vows,
calls the gods to witness
how Jason has rewarded her.
  She does not eat,
lies prostrate, slumped in anguish,
wastes away in day-long tears.   25
  Ever since she heard of Jason's perfidy
she has not raised her eyes
or looked up from the floor.
  She might be a rock or wave of the sea,
for all she heeds of sympathy from friends,

N.B. The line numbers in the margins are those of the original Greek text. ¹ **Argo** the ship in which Jason and his companions sailed on the quest for the Golden Fleece   ⁴ **Pelion** a mountain in northern Greece   ⁵ **Pelias** When Jason came to claim the kingdom of Iolcus, from which Pelias had expelled Jason's father, Pelias sent him to get the Golden Fleece.   ⁹ **She never . . . murder of their father** Medea, a sorceress by reputation, tricked Pelias' daughters into cutting their father into pieces and boiling them, on the pretext that this would magically restore him to youth. Her revenge on Pelias, who had murdered Jason's father Aeson during Jason's absence on the quest for the Golden Fleece, was successful.

---

¹¹ Jason and Medea were expelled from the kingdom, and they took refuge in Corinth, a wealthy city and rival of Athens, located on the isthmus between the Péloponnese and Attica.

30   except sometimes to tilt her pale head away
and moan to herself about her father—
whom she loved—
and her country and the home she sacrificed°
to journey here
with a man—oh—who so disdains her now.
    Yes, now she knows
at a terrible first hand
35   what it is to miss one's native land.

[She pauses; almost whispers the next words]

    She hates her sons.
    Takes no pleasure in their sight.
    I dread to think
of what is hatching in her mind.
    She is a fierce spirit:
takes no insult lying down.
39   I know her well. She frightens me:°
a dangerous woman, and
anyone who crosses her
45   will not easily sing a song of triumph.
    But here come the boys after their run:
suspecting nothing of a mother's tragedy . . .
    Oh, it is true—
unhappy thoughts and youth never go together.

[Enter TUTOR *with* TWO BOYS, *aged about eight and
ten.* TUTOR *is an old man, dressed loosely in an ocher-
colored cloak. The boys are squeezed into shorts and
have close-fitting woolen caps on their heads. They
hang about in the background, laughing and talking,
while the old man advances]*

TUTOR: *[With a half-teasing familiarity]* Ah, Nurse!
    Faithful old appendage of my Lady's home,
what are you doing here all forlorn,
50   standing moaning to yourself outside the gates?
    Does Medea really want to be left alone?
NURSE: Ah, dogged old pedagogue of Jason's sons,
when a master's fortunes are struck down
55   the heart of a faithful slave is stricken too.
    I am plunged in such a depth of grief
I came out here to tell the earth and sky
Medea's catastrophe.
TUTOR: What! Has the poor woman not stopped her
    crying yet?
NURSE: Stopped! You amaze me.
60   Her ordeal, far from halfway done,

---

32 Home she sacrificed Medea had helped Jason take the
Golden Fleece away from her own father's kingdom.   **39**
Lines 40–43 are bracketed by many editors as doubtful.
Dramatically they are certainly a mistake: *I am frightened she
will slip / into the palace unawares, / and in the nuptial bedroom /
ram a sharp knife into Jason's side, / or even kill the King as well as
bridegroom / and get herself a far worse doom.*

hardly has begun.
TUTOR: Poor innocent fool—to be quite frank about
    our mistress—
she knows little of the latest blow.
NURSE: Latest? What's that, old man?
    Don't keep it from me.
TUTOR: Nothing, nothing . . . I'm sorry I even spoke.
NURSE: Come now, we're both slaves here, are we not?
    By your own gray beard, do not hold it back . . .   65
I can keep a secret if I must.
TUTOR: Well, I'd gone to where the old dice-players sit,
    near Pirene's sacred fountain,
and there I overheard (pretending not to listen)
someone say:
    "Creon, this country's king,
is making plans to drive these boys from Corinth—   70
their mother too"—
I don't know if the story's true.
    I hope that it is not.
NURSE: No, surely no?
    Jason would not let his sons be treated so,
however far he's parted from their mother.   75
TUTOR: *[Grimly]* Old loves are left behind by new.
    That man is not this house's friend.
NURSE: We're all finished, then—
    if we ship this second wave
before we've bailed the first.
TUTOR: Now listen—
    this is not the time to let our mistress know.   80
Just keep quiet about it—not a word.
NURSE: *[With an anguished glance over her shoulder, in a
whisper]* Poor little boys,
    do you hear how much your father's worth to you?
    I wish he were . . .

[Checks herself]

    no, not dead, he is my master still . . .
but, oh, what an enemy he's proved
to those he should have loved!
TUTOR: What human being is not?   85
    Is this news to you,
that every person's dearest neighbor is himself:
some rightly so, some out of greed and selfishness.
    This father does not love his sons, but—
his new wedding bed.
NURSE: Come along, boys, into the house.
    Everything is going to be all right.

[Dropping her voice]

    Keep them away as much as you can.   90
    Do not let them near their mother.
so long as she is in this deadly mood.
    Already I have caught her eyes on them:
the eyes of a mad bull.
    There's something she is plotting

and her fury won't lie down—this I know—
until the lightning strikes and someone's felled.
95   Let us hope it's enemies, not friends.

*[A long-drawn-out sob—*MEDEA'*s—is heard from the house]°*

MEDEA: I am so unhappy—oh!
the misery of it! I wish I were dead.
NURSE: [*Hustling the children toward the door*]
Listen—there . . . poor children, your mother,
Raking her heart up, raking her rage.
100   Quick, inside: into the house.
Don't come anywhere near her sight.
Don't approach. Beware, watch out
For her savage mood, destructive spleen:
Yes and her implacable will.
105   Off with you now; hurry inside.
Soon, I know, her fury will flare
Out from the slowly gathering cloud
What will she perpetrate then, I fear—
Proud, importunate willful soul—
110   So bitterly spurned.

[Exeunt TUTOR *and* BOYS]

[A long-suppressed shout is heard from inside: MEDEA'*s voice]*

MEDEA: Oh, what misery! Oh, what pain!
Cursed sons, and a mother for cursing!
Death take you all—you and your father:
The whole house wither.
115 NURSE: [*Sobbing*] Oh, how it grieves me!
Why make the sons
share in their father's
Guilt? Oh, why
should *they* be hated?
Poor young children, your danger appals me.
Ruthless is the temper of royalty:
120   Often commanding, seldom commanded;
Terribly slow to forgive and forget.
How much better to live among equals.
I want no part of greatness and glory:
Let me decline in a safe old age.
125   The very name of the "middle way"
Has health in it: is best for man.
Good never comes from overreaching,
And when it provokes the gods, it destroys
130   All the more thoroughly.

PARADOS OR ENTRY SONG

[The CHORUS *of Corinthian women enters, full of*

apprehension and concern for MEDEA]

CHORUS: I heard her voice, I heard her shout,
It was the most unhappy
Woman from Colchis—far from calm yet—
But tell me, old Nurse.
From the porch of the house, it moaned outside.   135
O women, I cannot delight
In the pain of Jason's house:
A house I have loved very well.
NURSE: House there is none: life of it gone.
The master is had . . . by a princess's bed.   140
The mistress in her boudoir pines.
There are no words her friends can find
To touch her disconsolate heart.
MEDEA: [*In another spasm*] Ahhh!
Cleave my brain with a flash from the sky.
What good is left for me in living?   145
Alas! Alas! Come Death, unloose
My life from a life I loathe.

STROPHE

CHORUS: Listen, O Zeus and Earth and Light
To the stricken tune of this plangent° wife.   150
And you, loveless lady,
What yearning for love on a bed of delight
Could make you hurry to death, the night?
Pray not for that.
If your husband has gone to adore   155
A new bride in his bed, why, this
Has often happened before.
Do not harrow your soul. For Zeus
Will succor your cause. What use
To lessen your life with grief
For a lost lord?
MEDEA: [*From inside*] O mighty Themis°, and
Artemis, Queen,°   160
For all the fine vows I bound him with,
See what my hated husband has done.
Grant me to watch him, at last, with his bride,
Palace and all, crumble in ruin.
How dare they do to me what they have done!   165
O Father, my country, the land I abandoned,
Flagrantly killing my brother.°
NURSE: Hear what she says
with her cry from the heart
To Themis and Zeus:
(goddess of rights
And he whom mankind

---

95 The next 116 lines in the Greek are cast in a different meter, transposed into the nearest English equivalent.

150 **Plangent** lamenting   160 **Themis** justice   **Artemis** guardian of women. Called Diana by the Latins.   167 **Killing my brother** Medea slew her brother Absyrtus when she escaped with Jason, and tossed him piecemeal over the side of the ship, knowing that their pursuers would stop to pick the pieces up.

170 makes keeper of vows.)
Certainly soon
in no small way
Her fury will play itself out.

ANTISTROPHE

CHORUS: If she would come out and, face to face,
175   Listen to what we have to say,
She might let go
This rampant anger, spite of soul.
I hope I never fail my friends.
180 So go, Nurse, entice her to come:
Say we are *with* her: we are her friends.
Hurry, before she does any harm
To those inside . . .
Grief can swell to enormity.
NURSE: [*walking to the door*] I'll do my best, but am
185   afraid
May *not* be able to persuade
My Lady; and yet
I am glad to shoulder the burden;
Although she glares with a bull-mad gaze
(Or is it a lioness with her whelps)
When anyone comes or speaks or helps.

[She turns at the door]

190   Oh, botchers and blunderers! Yes,
That's what they were, those artists of old:
Makers of music for life and joy,
For grand celebrations and groaning boards;
195 But, oh, nothing for sorrow and pain:
No music or song on hand-plucked lyre
For the thing that brings death
And terrible endings to many a home.
Oh, what a blessing is missed
200   by having no music for this!
What a waste of it, then
by singing in vain,
When fullness at feasts
is its own joy and gain.

[Exit NURSE into the house]

CHORUS: Deep is her sobbing from depths of pain:
205   Shrill the news her suffering brings
Of marriage betrayed, a love gone wrong.
Outraged, she
importunate prays
To Themis, the daughter of Zeus:
Keeper of vows, who sailed her through
Those dangerous straits and the night
210 To Hellas° across the salt of the sea.

---

²¹⁰ **Hellas** Greece

FIRST EPISODE

[MEDEA enters from the house, colorfully, even opulent-ly, dressed. She is wan and her eyes red with weeping, but she is surprisingly calm and in control]

MEDEA: Women of Corinth, be indulgent, please: 215
I have obeyed you and come out.
The charge of aloofness—as I know too well—
is something often leveled
at both the retiring and the busy man.
He who chooses a quiet life
has this alleged against him too:
laziness and lack of spirit.
Yes, public opinion has most shallow eyes.   220
People hate at sight
a harmless human being,
knowing nothing of the real man.
I agree, of course,
that a foreigner should conform,
adapt to his society . . .
and a citizen is censurable no less
when too self-centered or uncouth
to avoid offending his companions.
Nevertheless, I . . .

[She breaks off with a pang]

I . . . out of a clear sky
have been struck a blow that breaks my heart.   225
My friends, it is over.
I want to die.
Life has lost all point.
The man who was my life
—and he knows it too—
has become for me beneath contempt.

[She surveys the women]

Of all the creatures that can feel and think,   230
we women are the worst-treated things alive.
To begin with,
we bid the highest price in dowries
just to buy some man
to be dictator of our bodies . . .
How that compounds the wrong!
Then there is the terrifying risk: 235
Shall we get a good man or a bad?
Divorce is a disgrace
(at least for women),
to repudiate the man, not possible.
So, plunged into habits new to her,
conventions she has never known at home,
she has to guess like some clairvoyant
how to handle the man who shares her bed.   240
And if we learn our lesson well
in this exacting role,

and our husband does not kick against the mar-
      riage yoke,
   oh, ours is an enviable life!
      Otherwise, we are better dead.
      When a man gets bored with wife and home,
245 he simply roams abroad,
   relieves the tedium of his spirit:
   turns to a friend or finds his cronies.
      We women, on the other hand,
   turn only to a single man.
      We live safe at home, they say.
      They do battle with the spear.
250   How superficial!
   I had rather stand my ground three times among
      the shields
   than face a childbirth once.
      Anyway,
   your case and mine are not the same.
      You have your city.
      You have your father's home.
      Life offers you the sweet fellowship of friends.
255   I am alone,
   without a city, wronged by a husband,
   uprooted from a foreign land.
      I have no mother, brother, cousin;
   am without a haven from this storm.
      So, please, I ask you this:
260 if I can find a way to pay my husband back—
   your silence.
      Woman, on the whole, is a timid thing:
   the din of war, the flash of steel, unnerves her;
265 but, wronged in love,
   there is no heart more murderous.
LEADER: As you wish, Medea.
      You have a score to settle with your lord.
      I do not wonder that you smart . . .
      But, look, I see Creon coming:
   this country's king—
270 bristling, I dare say, with new decisions.

[Enter CREON *with attendants. He is a bearded man of
about sixty, royally but modestly dressed. His face
wears a look of troubled resolution.]*

CREON: Go, Medea. Remove yourself.
      Get packing from this land.
      I order you—
   you with your black-faced fury
   lowering against your lord.
      And take your brace of offspring with you;
   no dallying either.
      I am here to see this order done,
   and until I've pushed you out and over the bor-
      der,
275 I'll not go home.
MEDEA: So.
      I am lost—crushed utterly.

My enemies let out the sail,
while I have no place to disembark from doom.
      Nevertheless, hard-pressed as I am,   280
I ask you this:
      For what reason, Creon, do you drive me out?
CREON: Fear:
   no need to camouflage the fact;
   I am afraid you'll deal my child some lethal blow
      . . .
   and many things conspire to make me fear.
      You are a woman of some knowledge,   285
   versed in many an unsavory skill.
      Your husband's gone:
   your soul is raw with loss of love . . .
   and now it is reported that you threaten me:
   mean to hurt the father of the bride
   and of course the bride and groom.
      That is what I want to guard against—
   an accident.
      Madam, better to be hated now by you   290
   than soften and pay later with regrets.
MEDEA: [Exchanging a look with the CHORUS]
   Heaven help me!
      My reputation is a curse:
   This is not the only time it has done me lasting
      harm.
      Oh, let the perspicacious man
   keep his children from enlightenment—   295
   above the general run.
      It will earn them only
   the sneer of uselessness
   and the spiteful jealousy of fellow men.
      Bring education to the dolt
   and, far from being accounted wise,
   you will yourself be cast as dolt.
      Outshine a pundit of established fame   300
      and you become a byword of distaste.
      This precisely
   is what I have to face.
      Because I have a little knowledge,
   some are filled with jealousy,
   others think me secretive, and crazy.
      In point of fact, my knowledge
   does not amount to much.   305

[She turns upon CREON *eyes pathetic with innocence]*

      But now I frighten *you:*
   do you think I'll strike some death-knell on your
      house?
      No, no: I am not like that.
      Creon, forget your fear:
   I have no criminal intent against a king.
      For how have *you* wronged me?
      You simply gave your virgin child
   to a suitor of your bent.   310
      No, it is my husband that I hate.

You, I think, have acted prudently
and even now I don't begrudge your enterprise
    success.
    Marry them both and blessings on you,
only let me go on living in this land.
    Ill-used though I am, I shall keep quiet:
315   I am overruled.
    CREON: Reassuring talk,
    but it chills me to the marrow.
        What are you really hatching in your mind?
    I trust you, Madam,
    less even than I did before.
    The impassioned woman,
320   like the impassioned man,
    is easier to watch than the crafty and the quiet.
        So, leave, I say, at once,
    and no speeches, please.
        My mind's made up.
        You are dangerous.
        All your cleverness
    shall not keep you here.
    MEDEA: Please, I beg you—on my knees—
    by your fresh young daughter-bride . . .
    CREON: You waste your words.
325   I am adamant.
    MEDEA: Will you expel me—
    heedless of my prayers?
    CREON: I will. For I love you less
    than I love my home.
    MEDEA: Ah, home! My own beloved country.
    What memories crowd upon me now!
    CREON: Exactly: next to my own children,
    my country is *my* dearest love as well.
330 MEDEA: Love, did you say?
    It is a mighty curse.
    CREON: In my opinion . . . that depends . . .
    MEDEA: O Zeus, remember
    the author of this crime.
    CREON: Go away—you poor deluded thing—
    rid me of my troubles.
    MEDEA: The troubles are all mine:
    I have a glut of them.
    CREON: [*Turning on his heel*] I'll call the servants:
335   They'll put you out by force.
    MEDEA: [*Clinging to him*] No, not that . . . Creon,
    I have something else . . .
    CREON: You seem determined, Madam,
    to make a nuisance of yourself.
    MEDEA: No, I'll go into banishment . . .
    That is not what I beg you now.
    CREON: Then, why not *go*, and let this land be rid of
        you?
340 MEDEA: Just let me stay this single day
    to arrange my exodus from here
    and make provision for my little sons—
    whose father cannot bring himself to care.
    Be kind to them.

You are a father too: 345
you know what kindly feelings are.
    As for me,
it means nothing to me
whether I stay or go.
    It's them I shed my tears for:
their lot is hard.
CREON: [*After a tussle with himself*]
    My soul is not tyrannical enough.
    My heart has often let me down . . .
    So now, Medea,
though I know I take a false step: 350
have it your own way.
    But let me warn you solemnly,
if tomorrow's holy light
sees you and your two children
still inside the borders of this realm,
you die.
    Every word of this I mean.
    Now, stay if you must; but one day only . . .   355
not long enough for you to perpetrate anything I
    dread.

[*Exit* CREON]

CHORUS: Ill-starred woman,
    Oh, what a nightmare of anguish is on you!
    Whom will you turn to? Where will you turn?
    What country, what stranger, what home for a
        haven?   360
        Who will receive you?
    God has certainly steered you—
    Oh, my poor Medea—
    Into a sea-race of sorrows.
MEDEA: [*Turning on them with the gleam of revenge*]
    In the center of disasters, yes,
but all is far from lost—make no mistake—   365
a test awaits the newlyweds,
no little ordeal for the happy pair.

[*With a laugh of derision*]

    Do you think I ever would have toadied to this
        man
if nothing could be got from it, no gain, no tool?
No, not one syllable,
not a touch with my little finger.   370
    The fool!
    He could have scotched me with one stroke,
flung me out;
instead he lets me stay one extra day,
to make three enemies three corpses:
ha! father, daughter, and my husband.   375

[*She leans toward the* CHORUS]

    Friends,
I can think of several ways to bring their death about.

Which one shall I choose?
Shall I set their house of honeymoon alight,
or creep into the nuptial bower
380 and plunge a sharp knife through their vitals?
One thing makes me pause:
if I am caught entering the palace, or red-handed,
I die . . . and give my enemies the last laugh.
No, there is a surer way,
one more direct;
for which I have a natural bent:
385 death by poison.
Yes, that is it.

[She walks, thinking]

Well, suppose they are dead:
will any city take me in,
will any man afford me home in a country safe
for living
and shield me from reprisals?
No, there is none.
I must postpone it, therefore, for a while
390 until some tower of strength appears for me;
then, through trickery and stealth,
I shall proceed with death by poison
What if I'm forced to go before it's done?
Ah, then I shall seize a sword,
face certain death,
and with my own hands run them through.
395 I shall not shrink from such a step,
by Hecate,° no: the goddess who abides
in the shrine of my inner hearth—
the one I reverence most of all the gods
and have chosen to abet me.
Nobody breaks my heart—
with impunity.
Their wedding I'll reduce
to agony and grief:
agony for having met and married,
400 and grief for having banished me.
Good!
Use your magic to the hilt.
Plot, Medea, devise your recipes:
advance to the deadly act that tests your courage.
See your present plight:
laughed at by the seed of Sisyphus°
405 because of Jason's match?
Never.
Your father was a king:
his father, Helios the Sun . . .
be aware of *that*.

Besides, you are a born woman:
feeble when it comes to the sublime,
marvelously inventive over crime.

First Choral Ode

[The Chorus sings an ode about the topsy-turvy changing standards of the world. Out of the turmoil will come a new importance for women, and a new reverence. Meanwhile, Medea is a harbinger of female independence and vitality]

Strophe 1

Back to their fountains   410
the sacred rivers are falling;
The cosmos and all morality
turning to chaos.
The mind of a man is nothing but fraud
and his faith in the gods a delusion.   415
One day the story will change:
then shall the glory
of women resound,
And reverence will come to the race of woman,
Reversing at last the sad
reputation of ladies.   420

Antistrophe 1

The ballads of ages gone by
that harped on the falseness
Of women, will cease to be sung . . .
If only Apollo,
Prince of the lyric, had put
in *our* hearts the invention
Of music and songs for the lyre,   425
Wouldn't I then have raised
up a feminine paean
To answer the epic of men?
Time in the roll of the ages has much to unfold
Of the fortunes of women no less
than the fortunes of men.   430

Strophe 2

So you, Medea, sailing away
from your father's house,
Threading a passage with heart on fire
through the jowls of the Euxine
Cliffs° to inhabit a strange
land where your bed is empty of man   435
(The lover you lost, O heartbroken lady!)
Now are chased from the realm,
shamed and banned.

Antistrophe 2

The joy of a bond is gone;

---

396 Hecate Identified with Artemis, and sometimes called Persephone (Roman name: Proserpine), she was supposed to preside over magic and witchcraft. **404 Sisyphus** To be a descendant of Sisyphus was considered disgraceful by the ancients.

---

434 Euxine Cliffs on the Black Sea

440   and wide of the world of Hellas,
All shame has flown—
    high in the sky and away.
Bereft of a fatherly home,
Where can you sail for a haven against
The storm, unfortunate woman—
    Your bed
Royally quelled by another
445   who queens it in your home?

SECOND EPISODE

[JASON *enters from the road that leads to the palace.
He is a young-looking man, dressed in the swashbuck-
ling cloak and plumed helmet of a captain in the
King's Guards*]

JASON: [*Embarrassed and exasperated*]
    So . . . this is not the first time
I have seen irrevocable damage done
by a barbarous rage.
    You could have stayed here,
in this land, in this house,
had you submitted quietly to your ruler's plans.
450   Instead, you ranted like a lunatic . . .
so now are banished.
    To me your tirade does not mean a thing:
go on declaiming what a monster Jason is.
    But when it comes to royalty,
the princess and the king,
count yourself lucky to be only banished.
455   I have tried continuously to calm things down;
for I should like you to remain.
    But you, Madam,
obstinate in folly,
have continuously reviled our royalty,
    And so you are banished.
    Yet, in spite of everything, I come, Medea,
patient to the last with someone I am fond of,
460   to do what I can to help.
    You and the children
need not leave the country penniless
and unprovided for . . .
exile drags with it a chain of troubles.
    And hate me though you may,
I cannot bring myself to wish you harm.
465 MEDEA: You criminal—
an epithet too good for you... such inhumanity...
so you come to me, do you,
you byword of aversion both in heaven and on
    earth,°
to me your own worst enemy?
    This is not courage.
    This is not being brave:

---

468 Editors bracket this line as doubtful.

to look a victim in the eyes whom you've
    betrayed—   470
somebody you loved—
    This is a disease,
and the foulest that a man can have:
you are shameless.

[*With the thinnest of smiles*]

    But you have done well to come:
I can unload some venom from my heart
and you can smart to hear it.
    To begin at the beginning,   475
yes, first things first:
    I saved your life—
as every son of Greece who stepped on board the
    Argo knows.
    You were sent to yoke
the fire-breathing bulls
and sow the plot of death.
    Yes, I saved you, lit up life for you,
when I slew the guardian of the Golden Fleece,
that giant snake which hugged it, sleepless,   480
coil on coil.
    I deserted my own father and my home
to come away with you to Iolcus by Mount
    Pelion,
full of zeal and very little sense.   485
    King Pelias, I killed,
a most horrid death—
perpetrated through his daughters—
and overturned their home.
    All this for you,
I even bore you sons—you most reprobate man—
just to be discarded for a new bride.
    Had you been childless,   490
this craving for another bedmate
might have been forgiven.
    But no: all faith in vows is shattered.
    I am baffled:
    Do you suppose the gods of old no longer rule?
    Or is it that mankind
now has different principles—
because your every vow to me, I'm sure you know,   495
is null and void.
    Curse this right hand of mine,
so often held by yours;
and these knees of mine—
sullied to no purpose
by the grasp of a rotten man.
    You turned my hopes to lies.
    Come now, tell me frankly—
as if we were two friends,
as if you really were prepared to help   500
(and I hope the question makes you feel
    ashamed)—
where do I go from here?

[With a bitter laugh]

> Home to my father, perhaps,
> and my native land,
> both of whom I sacrificed for *you*?
> Or to the poor deprived daughters of Pelias?
> 505 They would be overjoyed to entertain
> their father's murderer.
> Yes: this is how things stand.
> Among my own friends
> I am an execrated woman.
> There was no call for me to hurt *them*,
> but now I have a death-feud on my hands—
> and all for you.
> What a reward!
> What a heroine you have made me
> 510 among the daughters of Hellas!
> Lucky Medea, having *you*:
> such a wonderful husband . . . and so loyal!
> I leave this land displaced, expelled,
> deprived of friends,
> only my children with me, and alone.
> What a charming record for our new bride-
> groom this:
> 515 "His own sons and the wife who saved him
> are wayside beggars."

[She breaks off and looks upward]

> O Zeus, what made you give us
> clear signs for telling
> mere glitter from true gold,
> but when we need to know
> the base metal of a man
> no stamp upon his flesh for telling counterfeit?

520 LEADER: How frightening is resentment
> how difficult to cure,
> When lovers hurl past love
> at one another's hate.

JASON: I'll have to choose my words
> with no uncommon skill, it seems . . .
> like a good sailor riding out a storm,
> if I am to sail close-sheeted, Madam,
> 525 through your lashing, dangerous tongue.

[Folding his arms]

> So, you pile up what you did for me
> into pinnacles of grace.
> Well, as far as I am concerned,
> it was Aphrodite° and no one else in heaven or earth
> who saved me on my voyage.
> Your cleverness played a part, of course,
> but I could underline, if I wanted to be ungenerous,
> 530 how it was infatuation, sheer shooting passion,

---

527 **Aphrodite** goddess of love, called by the Latins *Venus*

> that drove you to save my life.
> I shall not stress the point.
> After all, your service did no harm.
> But this I shall maintain:
> that what you gained by saving me
> was far more than you gave. 535

[Holds up a hand to stop MEDEA from interrupting]

> In the first place,
> you have a home in Hellas
> instead of some barbarian land.
> You have known justice:
> the benefit of laws which never yield to might;
> have had your talents recognized all over Greece
> and won renown.
> For, were you living at the world's ends, 540
> your name would not be known . . .
> Oh, to me, houses crammed with gold,
> and a sweeter song than Orpheus sang,
> are nothing with no name.
> But, enough discussion of my dangerous voyage: 545
> an argument which *you* provoked.
> Now to your vindictive challenge
> of my royal marriage.
> I'll show you, first, it was an act of common sense,
> secondly, unselfish,
> and, finally, a mark of my devotion
> to you and all my family. 550

[MEDEA gives a gasp of incredulity]

> No, be still.
> When I came here from the land of Iolcus,
> frustrations crowding on my trail,
> could I, a wretched fugitive,
> have hit upon a greater stroke of luck
> than marriage to the daughter of the king?
> It was not—which cuts you to the quick—
> that I was tired of your attractions 555
> and smitten with a longing for a new wife;
> still less that I was out to multiply my offspring,
> (I am quite satisfied with the sons we have);
> no, it was simply that I wanted above all
> to let us live in comfort, not be poor . . . 560
> I know too well
> how the pauper is avoided by his friends.
> I wanted our children to be reared
> in a manner worthy of my ancestry,
> and, begetting others, brothers for your sons,
> knit them all together
> into one close and happy family.
> What point was there for you to have more
> children? 565
> My intention was—and it seemed real gain—
> to help the ones I have,
> through those I hope to have.
> Was this such a wicked plan?

You would not say so,
except through jealousy—that stinging jealousy of
    bed.
You women are all the same.
570   If your love life goes all right,
everything is fine;
but once crossed in bed,
the liveliest and best that life can offer
might as well be wormwood.
    What we poor males really need
is a way of having babies on our own—
no females, please.
    Then the world would be
575   completely trouble-free.
LEADER: [*Sternly*] Jason, this speech of yours is plausible,
But say what you like, it is not right
To sacrifice your wife.
MEDEA: [*With cold disdain*]
My outlook must be very different, then, from others.
580   To my mind a hypocrite who is too glib
only multiplies the danger that it puts him in:
the more he glozes° falsehood with his tongue,
the more confident and rash he grows.
    He ends by not being very clever.
    So, you, toward me—
585   you'd better drop your specious pleading.
    One simple observation
lays the whole thing flat:
were you not a coward, it was your duty
to convince *me*; not go sneaking off to marry.
JASON: And you would have welcomed the sugges-
    tion, I am sure.
590   Why, even now you can't contain your blazing rage.
MEDEA: *That* was not what governed you:
    you felt your glory tarnished by an aging oriental
    wife.
JASON: Please, please believe me:
    it was nothing to do with women—
    my desire to make this match—
595   but as I have already said
    to safeguard you and rear young princes
    to be brothers to my sons . . .
    so make our family solid.
MEDEA: [*With a bitter laugh*]
Haha! Solid happiness on the grave of love;
Prosperity with a secret sting . . .
O you gods—not for me—ever.
JASON: [*Earnestly*] Please change your prayer to this
600   and make it reasonable:
    "May success not seem to me sad failure,
    nor good fortune ever a disaster."
MEDEA: You go on mocking me: *you* have roof and
    shelter.
I am deserted, flying for my life, alone.

JASON: *You* chose it. Blame no one else.   605
MEDEA: Did I? I was the one who wed and then
    betrayed?
JASON: No: you just swore a heap of filthy curses on
    the king.
MEDEA: Yes, and you shall find that *I* am the curse
    that Fate has made to haunt you.
JASON: There's no point in talking any more with
    you.   610

[*Preparing to go*]

    Anything that you or the children want in exile,
let me know; I'd gladly furnish it,
or send letters of introduction for you
to friends abroad who will be kind.
    To turn this offer down, Medea,
is nothing short of madness.
    Forget your feelings of resentment: 615
let yourself be helped.
MEDEA: [*Spitting out the words*]
Not your friends, not your things:
I would not touch anything of yours—
how dare you offer it!
    The presents of the wicked are pure poison.
JASON: [*Flinging his cloak about him*]
In that case, heaven be my witness:
all my design to help you and your sons   620
is thwarted by your preference for evil.
    Your self-will cuts you off.
    Suffer then accordingly.

[*He begins to go*]

MEDEA: Go then. Don't waste your passion here:
go to the fresh young virgin you can't wait for . . .
    Have her.

[*As* JASON *exits, furious and embarrassed*]

    And God grant   625
the match you make, you'll long to have unmade.

SECOND CHORAL ODE

[*The women of the Chorus, appalled by what has
happened to* MEDEA, *speak of the dangers of love and
the sufferings of exile*]

STROPHE 1

Love is a dangerous thing:
Loving without any limit.
Discredit and loss it can bring . . .
But, oh, if the goddess should visit   630
A love that is modest and right,
No god is so exquisite.
Great lady, aim not at me

---

582 **glozes** Glosses over

Your gold and infallibly
Passion-tipped, poisoned delight.

ANTISTROPHE 1

635 Stay me with innocent living:
Most beautiful gift of the gods.
Never let Cypris° the fierce
Queen of desire propel
My heart to a dissolute lust
From old to a new and another
Bed and a dissonant longing,
640 But test with a sweet eye for peace
The love-bonds of reverent women.

STROPHE 2

O my country, my home, never let
Me lose my state and my city—
Living that desperate loss
645 so helpless and hard, without pity.
Death: I would bargain with death,
To die such a day to a finish.
For nothing is like the sorrow
650 Or supersedes the sadness
Of losing your native land.

ANTISTROPHE 2

LEADER: The thing is before my eyes.
Learned from no rumor or lies:
Medea without city or friends
655 Nowhere where pity extends—
Oh, how you must suffer!. . .
Let a man rot in a charmless lot
If he never unshutters his heart
660 To the cleansing esteem of another.
He'll not be my friend: no, never.

THIRD EPISODE

[Enter AEGEUS *from the country. He is a man in his early middle years and dressed in traveling clothes. His open features—kindly but unimaginative—seem preoccupied. In his retinue are* NOBLEMEN *and* SERVANTS*]*

AEGEUS: [*Stretching out his hands*]
Medea, all health and happiness. . .
and one can say a fairer thing when greeting friends?
MEDEA: [*Wanly*] Health and happiness to you, good
665 Aegeus,
wise Panidon's son . . . But where do you stem from?
AEGEUS: I have just left Apollo's ancient oracle at
Delphi.
MEDEA: What—a pilgrim there—the nub of the
world of prophecy?
AEGEUS: I went to ask for progeny—for a fruitful seed.

MEDEA: [*Suddenly interested*]
In the name of heaven! Have you been childless   670
all this time.
AEGEUS: Childless, yes—by some design of heaven.
MEDEA: But with a wife. . . or have you never married?
AEGEUS: I am married. Yes, I have a wife who shares
my bed.
MEDEA: And what did Apollo say about your having
children?
AEGEUS: Something far too deep for me, a mere
mortal, to unravel.
MEDEA: Am I allowed to know the god's reply?
AEGEUS: Certainly. It would take a mind like yours
to fathom.
MEDEA: Tell me . . . what did he say . . . since you are
allowed?
AEGEUS: Why, just this:
"Do not unstopper the wine-skin till . . ."°
MEDEA: Till you've done something—been
somewhere—special?   680
AEGEUS: [*Baffled*] Until I'm back at home again.
MEDEA: Then why did you sail in here?
AEGEUS: There is a man called Pittheus, king of
Troezen . . .
MEDEA: Yes, a son of Pelops: a very pious man, they
say.
AEGEUS: I want to ask his help about this oracle.   685
MEDEA: Yes, a clever man, and an expert in such
things.
AEGEUS: And of all my old battle cronies, my favorite.
MEDEA: Well, I hope that all your dreams come true.
AEGEUS: Medea, you look so pale, so sad. What is it?
MEDEA: My husband, Aegeus: he is the world's most
wicked man.   690
AEGEUS: You don't say? . . . Come, tell me all about
your troubles.
MEDEA: He's set up a mistress to queen it in my home.
AEGEUS: Dear me! Would he really do a thing like
that?   695
MEDEA: Yes, yes . . . And I am deposed—the one he
loved.
AEGEUS: Did he fall in love . . . or is he just tired of *you*?
MEDEA: In love—Ha—head over heels . . . flinging
all fidelity to the winds.
AEGEUS: Let him get on with it . . . since he's as
wicked as you say he is.
MEDEA: But it was with royalty he fell in love: 700
a king's daughter.
AEGEUS: Eh? What king's daughter? Please go on.
MEDEA: Creon's, king of Corinth.
AEGEUS: In that case, Madam, it *is* serious.
You have my sympathies.
MEDEA: It is the end. What is more, I am being banished.

---

636 **Cypris** Aphrodite, goddess of love. Roman Venus

679 **"Do not . . . wine-skin"** probably, "Do not have sexual intercourse."

705 AEGEUS: Banished? This is indeed a crowning blow—
    but by whom?
MEDEA: Creon: he wants to banish me from Corinth.
AEGEUS: And Jason agrees? I find that monstrous.
MEDEA: [*With fierce irony*] Oh, he says he doesn't—
    but he'll bear it bravely.

[*On her knees*]

        Aegeus, I beg you,
    by your beard,
710 by these knees of yours I clasp,
    pity me, pity my unhappiness.
        Do not see me banished and alone,
    let me come to Athens, shelter me,
    accept me in your home.
        The gods will pay you back,
    give you the children you so long to have,
715 surround your death with happiness.
        You do not guess how Providence has blessed
        you, meeting
    me.
        I mean to end your childlessness
    and make your seed bear sons.

[*Almost in a whisper*]

        I promise it. I know the drugs.
AEGEUS: [*Impressed*] Medea, many reasons make me
    ready
    to acquiesce in your request,
720 not least of all the gods;
    then because you've given me—a promise:
    promise of children . . .
    oh, left to myself, I had all but given up.

[*Gently raising her*]

        My proposition, then is this:
    get yourself to Athens
    and there, as is incumbent on me,
    I shall do my utmost to protect you.
725   However, I must tell you clearly,
    I cannot take you with me out of Corinth,
    but if you reach my palace on your own,
    there you shall have full sanctuary
    and to no one shall I give you up.
        So, by your own means you must leave this land:
    I cannot risk offending the Corinthians—
730 who are also friends of mine.
MEDEA: As you say . . . but . . .
    if only you could promise it on oath,
    it would make it all so . . . settled between us.
AEGEUS: Do you not trust me? What is the matter now?
MEDEA: [*Glancing nervously over her shoulders*]
        I do trust you . . . but . . .
    but I have my enemies.
735   It isn't only Creon,

there is the house of Pelias too:
They'll want to prize me from your territories.
    If you are bound by oath
you will not give me up.
    But if you have only made a promise,
not sworn it to the gods,
there is always the chance that sheer diplomacy
will win you to their wishes.
    I have no weapons on my side,
on theirs is wealth and all the weight of royalty. 740
AEGEUS: You are very provident, Medea.
    However, if that is what you want,
    I shall not go against it.
    In point of fact,
    to swear an oath protects me too:
    I can counter those who wish you ill
    with a clear excuse;
    and you of course, are well secured.
        So, name your deities. 745
MEDEA: [*In crystal-cold syllables*]
    Swear by the Earth on which you tread.
    Swear by the Sun, my father's father dread.
    Swear by every god and godhead.
AEGEUS: Yes, but what to do or not to do? Please say.
MEDEA: Never yourself to drive me from your land,
    and if an enemy of mine tries to drag me off, 750
    never while you live to let me go.
AEGEUS: I swear by the Earth and sacred light of the
    Sun
    to abide by the words you have just pronounced.
MEDEA: [*Relentlessly*]
    Good . . . but if you break your word—what
    penalty?
AEGEUS: The penalty for sacrilege. 755

[*They clasp hands in silence*]

MEDEA: Go now and be glad. All is well.
    I shall come to Athens as quickly as I can,
    but first I have some work to do, to carry out a
    plan.

[*As AEGEUS is leaving*]

LEADER: We hope that Hermes, master of journeys,
    Will hasten you home safely to Athens: 760
    Home to the hope of your heart's desire,
        For Aegeus, you are
        A most magnanimous man.
MEDEA: [*Wheels round and faces the CHORUS*]
    O Zeus and lady daughter, Justice,
    O resplendent Sun!
    And you my friends, 765
        At last we are on the road to vengeance
    and to our song of triumph. At last there is hope:
    we shall see my enemies put down.
        At the very point my plot could founder,

770 this man opens up a port, an anchorage.
So to Athens I shall go
and moor to her fast towers.

[She beckons the women closer]

Now I can unfold to you my whole design:
there is nothing sweet in it, as you will see.
I send a servant of my house to Jason
775 asking him to come to me.
He arrives
I tell him in the softest accents;
how I now agree;
how it all seems for the best:
his royal marriage, his sacrifice of me;
everything that he has planned is for the best.
780 But I ask him to let my children stay . . .
with no intention—you understand—
of leaving any child of mine in a hostile place
for those who hate me to maltreat.
No, this is just a device
for murdering the daughter of the king.
I send them there with presents in their hands,
785 presents for the bride—as a kind of plea
against their banishment—
yes, a gown of gossamer and a diadem made of
beaten gold.
If she takes this finery and puts it on,
the girl will die in agony
and anyone who touches her;
so deadly are the poisons I shall steep the presents
in.
790 But now my whole tone changes:
a sob of pain for the next thing I must do.
I kill my sons—my own—
no one shall snatch them from me.
And when I have desolated Jason's house
beyond recall,
I shall escape from here:
795 fly from the murder of my little ones,
my mission done.
People that one hates, my friends,
must never have the last laugh.
Well, so be it.
What good is life to me?
I have no father, home, defense from danger.
800 Oh, the mistake I made was when I left his house,
trusting the word of a man from Greece . . .
but he is going to pay the price.
Never again alive
shall he see the sons he had by me,
nor any child by this new bride of his—
805 poor girl, who has to die a wretched death,
poisoned by me.
Let no man think me insignificant or weak:
I am no meek martyr, no—quite the contrary—
relentless an enemy I make;

though kind enough to friends.
Such is the genius of my life.
LEADER: [Imploringly]
Though you have shared all this in confidence
with us, Medea,
and though I long to be of help,
we must uphold the laws of life:
and so I say to you: "You must not do it."
MEDEA: There is no other way.
And though I understand your sentiments,
you have not been through my agony. 815
LEADER: But, my lady, to kill your own two sons . . .?
MEDEA: It is the supreme way to hurt my husband.
LEADER: And it makes you the most desolate of
women.
MEDEA: Be that as it may.
Argument is now superfluous.

*[She turns to the NURSE, who has entered during the
previous dialogue]*

Nurse, when I need real loyalty
you are the one I always turn to.
Go now and fetch Jason here. 820
But as you are a woman
and a faithful servant of this house,
whisper no syllable of what I plan.

[Exit NURSE, dragging her feet]

THIRD CHORAL ODE

*[The WOMEN of Corinth desperately try to move MEDEA
from her purpose. Does she imagine Athens, that blessed
land, will welcome a murderess? Surely, she herself will
flinch from the cold-blooded killing of her sons?]*

STROPHE 1

The people of Athens are blest through the ages, 825
Seeds of the all-hallowed gods,
Born on a soil unravaged and holy,
They feed on the wide
Bright pastures of knowledge.
Lightly they walk through the crystal air 830
In a land where Harmonia,
Goldenly fair,
Once gave birth, they say, to the nine
Muses, the pure
Maids of Pieria.°

---

834 Where Harmonia . . . Maids of Pieria Harmonia, the balance of nature, and the genius of the people resulted in the cultivation of the arts. Pieria was a holy fountain in Boetia where the nine Muses were supposed to live.

ANTISTROPHE 1

835 And out of the sweetly flowing currents
Of Cephisus,° they declare,
Aphrodite sprinkles the land
And fragrantly breathes
Delicate breezes.
840 Forever she sheds from the stream of her hair,
Plaited with roses,
Scented petals; and sends the Loves—the
Erotes—
To preside with Wisdom over the heart
And together prepare
845 The glories of art.

STROPHE 2

How then shall a glorious city,
City of sacred rivers,
Host of the salutary guest,
Kindly take to the killer of children,
850 Harbor among them a murderess?
Think of how you are stabbing your sons.
Think, too, of the blood you assume.
Do not, please, we beg by your knees,
By everything and every means—
855 Murder your children.

ANTISTROPHE 2

Where, when, will you find the mind,
The hand or the callous heart
Hardened enough to strike
These, yours—oh, heartless enough?—
860 How then will you see through your gaze
Swollen with tears as you sight your aim?
No, no, when your little ones kneel
Crying for mercy, you will not
Find the nerve, never be able,
865 To bloody your hands.

FOURTH EPISODE

[JASON *enters with the* NURSE *behind him. On his face is written apprehension mixed with hope; on hers, despair*]

JASON: I have come, Medea, because you asked me.
I put myself at your disposal
even though you are against me.
What, Madam, can I do for you?
MEDEA: [*In a small, contrite voice*]
870 Jason please forgive me for all the things I said.
Bear lightly with my outbursts, will you,
if only in remembrance of our great love together.
I have been arguing with myself,
have taxed myself severely.
"You raving fool," I said,

---

836 **Cephisus** an Athenian river

"To antagonize those who want to do you good,
setting yourself against your rulers and your
husband.   875
His royal marriage
and his design to bring up brothers for your sons
does you the greatest service that he could.
Why not calm yourself?
Are *you* suffering because the gods are good?
Have you no children of your own?   880
And are you not aware
you came as fugitive with not too many friends?"
Such reflections made me realize
I have been out of my mind, hysterical.
Now I thank you.
Now I am convinced
that in securing us this benefit   885
you are the wise one, *I* the fool—
I who should have been your ally
and encouraged you.
Yes, I should have been at hand to help,
decked the bed, dressed the bride—
and been glad to do it . . .
But we women—
well, we are what we are: let's leave it at that!
Do not copy us in our perverseness   890
or try to get your own back, giving tit for tat.
I ask your pardon.
I admit to being wrong.
I've thought better of it now.

[*With an upsurge of put-on happiness*]

Children, children, come out here,
out of the house.

[*The two* BOYS *appear with their* TUTOR]

Come greet your father, hug him, join with me   895
in loving, not resenting him.
Your mother's rancor's over.
There's peace between us: the fighting's done.
Come, take his hand.

[*As the children run into their father's arms*]

O God, what a presentiment!
What an image looming in the dark!   900
JASON: My sons, my sons,°
if only you could go on living, go on loving,
with your arms stretched out like that to me forever
. . .

MEDEA: [*Choking*] It breaks my heart;

---

901 No doubt this line and half the next (in the Greek) go to Jason, and not Medea. Otherwise, Medea's remark in 930 makes no sense.

I am far too prone to tears, too full of tears . . .
it is the sudden ending of my quarrel with your
    father
which makes them flow.
A sight so touching . . .
905   it overflows.
LEADER: My eyes, too, are stinging,
    but may this be the worst that is to come.
JASON: [*Gently releasing the* BOYS] I praise you now,
    Medea,
    and I did not blame you then.
    It is natural for a woman to be enraged
    when her husband goes off making second
910   marriages.
    But now
      you are in a better frame of mind
    and, even if it took a little time,
    realize the good points of this plan . . .
    the decision is a level-headed woman's.

[*Turning to the children*]

    As for you, my boys,
    your father has been far from idle
    and, heaven willing, he has made
915   good settlements for you.
    In time I shouldn't wonder
    if you were not first citizens in Corinth—
    along with your new brothers.

[*Laying his hands on their shoulders*]

    Grow up now fine fellows.
    Your father and a kindly providence
920   have the rest in hand.
    How I look toward the time
    when you will be two strapping grown young men,
    trampling down my enemies.

[MEDEA *has averted her head and is sobbing. Her feelings, though genuine, are being used by her to further
her next move*]

    But, Medea, what is this—
    these dewy eyes, these tears;
    your white face turned away
925   as if my words struck pain, not joy?
MEDEA: It is nothing.
    I was just thinking of our sons.
JASON: Well, be of good heart now:
    I shall see them through.
MEDEA: I will do my best . . . it isn't that I don't
    believe you,
    but you know how women weep.
JASON: I know, but don't be said for *them* . . . why
    should you?
MEDEA: [*Watching the tender look on* JASON'*s face*]
    I am their mother.

When you prayed just now   930
for a long life for your sons,
a sudden sadness whispered: "Will this be?"
    Well, that's one item only
of what I had to say.
    The other thing is this:
    Since the king has set his mind
on sending me away from Corinth,
and since I've come to recognize that this is best   935
(for I'd only be an obstacle to you,
living with the royal family here—
who think I am a menace to their house),
I shall take myself away, go into banishment.
    But the children, please, I should like *them*
to grow up under your own hand.
    Persuade Creon to let them stay.   940
JASON: [*Taken off his guard, but flattered*]
    I—I am not certain that I can:
    it'll take a little trying.
MEDEA: But you could ask your wife to beg her
    father
    to let the two boys stay.
JASON: [*Reflecting*] Why not? I think I can get her to
    agree.
MEDEA: Of course you can:
    if she's the slightest bit like any woman.   945
    And here *I* can play a useful part.
    I shall send her a present
    more ravishingly beautiful, believe me,
    than anything this age has seen:
    a gown of gossamer and a diadem of beaten gold.
    These the boys shall carry them to her.   950

[*She claps her hands and two* MAIDS *appear*]

    Go quickly, one of you,
    and bring the gorgeous presents here.

[*One of the* MAIDS *hurries into the house*]

    What a double delight
    What a shower of happiness for her
    to have you for a hero husband
    and how these treasures which were handed down
    by my father's father—the glorious Sun.   955

[*The* MAID *comes back with two boxes.* MEDEA *turns to
the* BOYS]

    Boys, take hold of this wedding gift.
    Carry it to the happy princess-bride.
    Place it in her hands.
    It is not the kind of present she'll despise.
JASON: [*As the* BOYS *step forward*]
    You foolish woman—why empty your hands?
    Do you think a royal wardrobe is in want,   960
or a palace short of gold?
    Keep these things. Don't give them up.

If my wife values me at all,
my mere wish will have more weight than *things*,
I'm sure of that.
MEDEA: [*With an onrush of conviction*] Do not deny me.
Even the gods, they say, succumb to gifts,
965   and gold is stronger than the strongest wits.
She is lucky, *she* is blessed, *she* increases.
This exile I would barter for my babies
not just with gold but with my life.

[*Forcing the boxes into the* BOYS' *hands*]

Go, my sons, into the halls of wealth;
down on your knees and beg her—
970   this new wife of your father's, and my mistress—
to let you stay in Corinth.
Most important of all,
see that she takes the precious things
into her own hands.

[*Packing them off*]

Quick, now, go. Success be yours.
975   Come and tell me the good news.
Your mother waits with all ears.

[*Exeunt the* BOYS *with their* TUTOR, *followed by* JASON]

FOURTH CHORAL ODE

[*The* CHORUS *deplores the multimurders*]

STROPHE 1

Now has the last hope gone of the children living,
Gone and forever: they walk already to murder.
The bride is taking the golden diadem,
    Is taking the poison and doom.
Over her yellow hair her hands are fitting
980   The decorated dying.

ANTISTROPHE 1

The gorgeousness of the gossamer gown will win,
And the beaten gold of the diadem embrace her.
985   The bride is decked and ready to meet the dead.
    The trap is lethally set:
Doomed miserable woman, doomed to fall in—
    Ineluctably caught by Fate.

STROPHE 2

990   And you who are groomed for a murder:
        Son-in-law of a king,
        Jason unsuspecting—
Are to bring on your sons a demise, and a death
On your bride of a hideous kind.
    Unhappy man, how far
995   You are falling.

ANTISTROPHE 2

And you the unenviable mother,
    How I weep for your pain!
    Killer of children for
A vengeance of love that has gone, betrayed   1000
    By your man for another
    Bride whom he sleeps beside
        In his wrong.

FIFTH EPISODE

[*The* TUTOR *hurries in from the palace with the two* BOYS]

TUTOR: [*Breathless with excitement*] My lady, your
    boys—
they won't be banished.
    And the princess, the bride—
with her own hands—
she took your presents, oh, so gladly . . .
    Now the children's danger is over!   1005

[*Baffled by* MEDEA's *grim reaction*]

Well I never! Isn't this good news?
What so transfixes you?

[MEDEA *draws in her breath in a muffled cry of pain*]

TUTOR: What I hear is out of tune with what I say.

[MEDEA *sighs deeply*]

TUTOR: I thought I brought good news.   1010
    What kind of news, I wonder, have I brought?
MEDEA: What you have brought, you have brought:
    the fault is not with you.
TUTOR: Why, my Lady, these shuttered eyes:
    these tears falling?
MEDEA: Oh, I am pressed, old friend—hard pressed:
    the gods and my own evil counsels.
TUTOR: Courage, dear mistress: 1015
    Your sons will always bring you home.
MEDEA: [*In a kind of trance*]
    Home? . . . First I must send others there . . .
        Mercy!
TUTOR: You are not the only mother to be severed
    from her sons.
We have to bear our own humanity—humanely.
MEDEA: [*Pressing his hand*]
    I shall try . . . Now go inside
and see to what the children need today.   1020

[*Exit* TUTOR, *worried*]

MEDEA: [*Throwing out her arms toward the two* BOYS]
    My sons, my sons,
you will have a city and a home
far from me.

I shall be left lonely,
and you will live without your mother always.
    For I must go in exile to another land:
never have my joy in you,
1025   or see your bright young progress;
never deck your brides, your marriage beds,
or light you radiant to your wedding day.

[The BOYS *are now in her arms]*

Oh, what a blight my ruthlessness has been!
    How useless, little ones,
my nursing all your growing up!
1030   How useless all the cares endured:
the wearying solicitudes,
the shooting agony of giving you your lives.
    And now, how miserably have dwindled
my innumerable dreams of you:
your loving comfort when I'm old,
your own hands dressing me when I am dead—
1035   a passing every person might desire.
    Such sweet fancy vanishes
and, wrenched from you instead,
I shall drag my sad life out alone.

[She cups their faces in her hands in turn]

Your own dear eyes shall miss forever
your poor mother's face—
your way of life and hers utterly apart.
    Oh, children,
1040   do you let those eyes now stare their fill,
and your last smiles linger to the last?

[She turns to the CHORUS, *panting]*

O–h! What shall I do?
My heart dissolves
when I gaze into their bright irises . . .
    No, I cannot do it.
Goodbye to my determination.
1045   I shall take my boys away with me.
Why damage *them* in trying to hurt their father,
and only hurt myself twice over?
    No, I cannot.
Goodbye to my decisions.

[A pause, then she suddenly breaks away from the BOYS]

What—what undermines me now?
1050   Do I really mean to let my enemies go,
to laugh at me?
    Steel yourself, Medea:
away with this cowardice, these arguments that melt.

[Almost pushing them]

Go, Boys, into the house.

[She turns to the CHORUS *grimly]*

Anyone whose conscience will not let him stay
let him look to it: avoid my sacrifice . . .
this hand of mine shall never falter.   1055

*[Another spasm of emotion grips her, and she runs to
the* BOYS *as they reach the door]*

No, no! Stop me, my heart:
we must not do this thing.
    Let them go, you stricken woman,
spare your sons.
    Let them live with you in Athens:
they will be your joy.

[Throwing her arms round them again]

Ah! Not by all the haunting spirits of the
    underworld,
shall I leave my children for my enemies to
    trample down.
No, never.°   1060

[With a sharp realization]

But—they have to die—
the whole thing is settled anyway . . .
    Yes . . . the diadem is on her head . . .   1065
the royal bride at this moment rots,
dying in her gown—I know it.

[She turns to the CHORUS *as if to explain her second
impulsive embrace]*

You see: the path I have to tread
is unutterably sad,
but the one I set these children on
is sadder still . . .
    Therefore I desire to speak with them.

[Seizing their hands]

Give me your right hands to kiss,
each of you, my little ones—
give them to your mother.   1070

[Covering their hands, their faces, their bodies, in kisses]

How adorable—this hand—and this . . .
These lips—how very much adored!
And this face and form of childhood's
ingenuous nobility . . . how I bless you both . . .
not here—beyond . . .

1060 Some editors omit lines 1062 and 1063 as a melodramatic
interpolation: "But they have to die, and since they must, / let
it be by the hands of her who gave them life."

1075
every blessing here your father has despoiled.
    So sweet . . . the mere touch of you:
the bloom of children's skin—so soft . . .
their breath—a perfect balm.

*[Gently releasing them; then almost savagely turning
her back]*

    Go, go . . . I cannot look at you.
I am in an agony, and lost.

[The two Boys, *weeping, hurry into the house]*

    The evil that I do, I understand full well,
But a passion drives me greater than my will.
        Passion is the curse of man:
1080
        It wreaks the greatest ill.

FIFTH CHORAL ODE

[The CHORUS *wonders if there can be a feminine
philosophy of parenthood, is its honest judgment
likely to be that children are worth it after all?]*

    So often before
Have I gone toward concepts far too tenuous
And come upon questions far too deep
For the race of woman to try to unravel.
Nevertheless, even we women
1085
Have a muse of our own, that ushers us in.
(Though, alas, not all) to the world of wisdom.
Perhaps you might find it one in a thousand.
It serves to inspire the talent of ladies,
1090
And makes me able now to proclaim
That people without the function of parent
Are happier than begetters of offspring.
The childless man has no way of telling
1095
Whether he misses a curse or a blessing.
Nevertheless, the childless person
Certainly misses many a burden.
I mark how the man with children growing
1100
Sweetly at home is worn with worrying:
How to make sure they are properly fed,
How to leave them a livelihood.
And then after all to be in the dark:
1105
Were all the worries worth it or not?
Were they a worthy or worthless lot?
    But now let me tell
Of the worst and saddest trait of all.
Suppose the children have quite a good life,
1110
Reach their teenhood honest and fine,
What if a fate like Death the cruel
Carries them downward body and soul?
What is the use if after all
(On top of all those other ones)
1115
The gods let loose this grief as well . . .
Just for the joy of having sons?

SIXTH EPISODE

*[*MEDEA *has been sitting during the Chorus. Now she
leaps up as she catches sight of a man lunging breathlessly toward them from the street: the* MESSENGER*]*

MEDEA: Somebody with news at last, my friends,
    And from the right direction.
        Yes, I see him:
one of Jason's men—panting as he hurries—
With some tremendous news of bad.   1120

[The MESSENGER—*an official of the Bride's house—
bursts in: hardly able to get his words out]*

MESSENGER: Run, Medea, run!
    What—you have done... is... too unthinkable...
too awful . . .
    Seize whatever means you can . . .
sailing boat or chariot . . . Escape!
MEDEA: Run? Escape? Is it then so vital?
MESSENGER: Dead . . . They are this minute dead . . .
the princess royal with her father—
and through your poisons.   1125
MEDEA: What a pretty word you bring—
my benefactor, my friend forever!
MESSENGER: *[Recoiling]* What are you saying,
    Madam?
    Are you in your right mind—not unhinged?
A king's home a charnel house—   1130
and you rejoice? . . . Are you not afraid?
MEDEA: I have my ready answer too,
so don't be hasty, friend,
but tell me how they perished.
An appalling death
would give me double joy.   1135
MESSENGER: *[Supports himself against a pillar as he
    begins to recollect an agonizing experience]*
    We were so pleased to see your brace of boys
come hand in hand to the bride's house with their
    father:
for your ordeal had upset us servants greatly.
    The rumor went racing through the house
that all was well again between your husband
    and yourself.   1140
    Some of us kissed the children's hands,
kissed their golden tops;
and I in my enthusiasm even followed them
to the women's wing.
    There, the mistress—
I mean the one we have to honor now—
had eyes so taken up with Jason
she did not even see at first   1145
the two boys hand in hand.
    But when she did,
a veil of scorn dropped over her eyes,
she turned her lovely face away,

bristling at your sons' intrusion.
    Your husband then began to woo her
1150   from her petulance and girlish tantrums, saying:
    "You must not hate your friends.
    Stop being hurt and turn your head around.
    Consider yours your husband's loved ones.
    Come, won't you take their presents
    and beseech your father
1155   to let these boys off banishment—just for me?"

[Pauses and sits down hopelessly on a step]

    When she saw how exquisite the presents were,
far from holding out on him,
there was nothing she withheld:
but gave in completely to her groom.
    And hardly had your husband and your children
left the house
when she took the gorgeous robe and put it on,
1160   and placed the golden circlet on her curls,
arranging the ringlets in the brightness of a mir-
    ror
and smiling at her own dead image there.
    Then rising from her stool
she minced off through the halls
on dainty milk white toes,
1165   wildly pleased with what she had received,
over and over again
running her eyes down the clear sweep to her
    heels.
    But all at once
a hideous spectacle took place.
    Her color changed. She tottered back;
shuddered in every limb; was able just in time
1170   to fall into a chair and not upon the floor.
    An old woman there, attending her
thinking that perhaps the fierce possession of
    Pan°
or some other power was on her,
broke into a chant of wonder,
then saw the white froth spuming at her lips,
her eyeballs bulging all askew,
1175   her skin quite leached of blood,
and changed her chanting to a yelp:
a wail of horror.
    A maid went dashing to the palace for her father,
another went to tell the fresh-wed groom
what was happening to his bride.
1180   The whole house rang with footsteps running.
    It took no longer than a sprinter takes
to go the hundred yards,
before the poor girl lay unconscious with her eye-
    lids shut.

Then suddenly she rallied
and gave a curdling shriek,
fighting off a double nightmare.   1185

[He pauses, gulps, takes a deep breath]

    The golden diadem that clasped her head
burst into a voracious and uncanny flow of fire,
while the robe of gossamer your children gave her
began to eat her tender flesh away.
    Streaming with flame,
she leapt up from her chair and fled,   1190
tossing her mane of hair from side to side,
in a frantic bid to shake the diadem off.
    But its grip was adamant
and the golden circlet held.
    The more she tossed,
the more the fire flowed,
till, overwhelmed with pain,   1195
she sank down to the floor—
unrecognizable to all except her father—
her calm regard grotesquely twisted,
her sweet symmetry all shattered;
and from the crown of her head in molten clots
fire and blood dripped down together.
    The flesh curdled off her bones   1200
like the teardrops congealing out of pines,
inexplicably dissolved by those ravening venoms.
    It was curious and horrible to see.
    No one dared to touch her body:
the warning was too obvious.
    But her father, unawares, poor man,
rushed headlong through the room,   1205
flung himself lamenting on the body,
hugged and kissed it, sobbing out:
    "My stricken darling,
what evil power has done this to you,
who has made you dead
and left me, like some ancient tombstone,
    derelict?
O gods! . . . let me die with you, my daughter."   1210
    But . . . but when he stopped . . .
from these outpourings—
these melancholy sobs . . .
and tried to lift his aged carcass up,
he found himself stuck fast—
clamped to the flimsy robe
like ivy to a laurel bole.
    A ghastly wrestling match ensued.
    He would try to raise a knee,   1215
she would drag him back;
and when he took to force,
his own decrepit flesh
pulled off from the bone.
    At last, exhausted,
pathetically unable
to lift himself above the shambles,

1171 Pan, the god of wild nature, who was supposed to be the
cause of seizures and sudden madness. Hence, "panic."

1220
 he gave his spirit up.
  There they lie, corpse by corpse,
 father and young daughter—
 fit objects for our tears.

[He rises, swaying]

  To you, Medea . . . from me . . .
 there are no words to say.
  Retribution? You yourself will know
 the best escape . . .
 though in my esteem—and not just for today—
1225
 the whole of life is shadow,
 and I would even say:
 the people who know best or seem to know,
 the subtlest professors,
 are the very ones who pay the dearest price.

[Flinging his cloak about him]

  A happy human being? Ha, there's no such
   thing . . .
 more prosperity, more success in one maybe:
1230
 but happier? . . . It does not make one happy.

[Exit MESSENGER*]*

LEADER: Justice personified this day
 has brought on Jason's head
 —oh, we have seen it!—
 the richest retribution.
  But it is you we weep for,
 poor blighted child of Creon,
 walking through the gates of death
1235
 because you married Jason.
MEDEA: *[In clear, cold tones]*
  Now, friends, to complete this mission with dispatch:
 to slay my children and hurry from this land.
 I must not dawdle and betray my sons
 to much more savage hands than mine to kill.
1240
  There's no way out. They have to die.
  And since they must,
 let me be the one to cut them down:
 the very one who gave them life!

*[She begins her walk to the door, almost like a sleep-
walker, talking to herself]*

  Yes, heart, be steel.
  Why vacillate?
  The act is . . .
 necessary as it is cruel and hard.
  Come, reluctant hand,
 grip the sword—grip it, Medea:
1245
 cross your borderline of lifelong pain.
  Away this flinching!
  Away this longing:

 consign to oblivion the love you had for them—
 the children of your flesh.
  Even when you kill them they are dear . . .
 oh, my sons! . . . I am in despair, despair.
1250

*[*MEDEA, *with the* NURSE *mutely following in tears,
passes into the house]*

SIXTH CHORAL ODE

[The CHORUS *of women pray desperately for something
to stop the imminent murder]*

STROPHE

Come Earth, come sunshafts of the Sun,
Behold this woman and withhold her
From her laying scarlet fingers
On the children of her blood.
Gold of your gold are they begotten:
1255
Heinous is to spill this holy
Ichor in the blood of mortals.
Curb her, stop her, godborn Light, oh,
Keep this house from murder! Keep it
Never haunted by the Furies.°
1260

ANTISTROPHE

Were those birth pangs wasted bearing:
Children's birth pangs wasted birth?
You, my lady, after sailing
Safe between the dark blue clashing
Gorges, will you hug a rankling
1265
Hatred to your heart, a loathsome
Rage for murder and revenge?
Those that spill the blood of family
Stain themselves with heaven's anger,
Haunt their homes with doom forever.
1270

SEVENTH EPISODE OR DENOUEMENT

[Cries are heard from inside the house]

FIRST WOMAN: A shout—listen—a shout from the boys.
FIRST BOY: O–h! What can we do? . . .
 Our mother is on us!
SECOND BOY: Brother, brother! . . . We're going to be
 killed.
SECOND WOMAN: That murderous relentless woman!
THIRD WOMAN: Shall we break in, snatch them from
 death?
1275
FIRST BOY: Yes, by heaven . . . save us . . . help!
SECOND BOY: We're trapped, cornered . . . now . . . by
 her sword.

1260 Furies ministers of the vengeance of the gods, employed
in punishing the guilty on earth as well as in the underworld

[*As the* CHORUS *beat on the barred doors, there are groans and cries, and presently a trickle of blood oozes from under the doors. The women watch it, fascinated*]

CHORUS: Woman of stone, heart of iron,
1280   Disconsolate woman, ready to kill
    The seed of your hands with the hand that tilled.
    One other only, one have I known
    Murderously handle the fruit of her womb:
    Ino the maniac, god-driven one,
    Whom Zeus's wife drove out to roam—°
1285   Desperate woman goaded to slaughter
    The sons of her flesh, clean against nature.
    She pitched from the precipice into the sea,
    Fell where her foot fell into the ocean,
1290   Dashing two infants to death with her own.
    What ghastlier thing is left to be known?
    Women, O women, in love and in pangs,
    What ruin you've brought on us human beings!

[JASON, *breathless, his face twisted with hatred, bursts in with a troop of servants*]

JASON: You women standing here outside this house,
1295   is that she-ravager, Medea, still at home,
    or has she fled?

[*He waits for a reply, but the women cower before the door*]

       Deep down in the earth let that woman hide,
    or wing into the highest alcoves of the sky,
    before she ever saves herself from justice by this
       royal house.
       Does she think that she can kill
    a princess and a country's king
1300   and vanish with impunity?

[*He strides toward the door*]

       But it is my sons, not her, I fear for.
       She, she shall be repaid
    through her victims.
       I have come to save my children's lives
    from some enormous retribution by the family of
       the dead
1305   for those enormities their mother did.
LEADER: Jason, you poor optimistic man,
    you still don't know the evils that have come—
    or you would not say what you have said.
JASON: What? Does she mean to kill me too?

LEADER: Your sons are dead: murdered by their
    mother.
JASON: [*Reeling*] What—did—you—say?
    Oh, woman—my own wife—you kill me too.   1310
LEADER: [*As the women form an avenue to the door, and*
    JASON *sees for the first time the blood beginning to*
    trickle down the steps]
    Yes. Your children.
    You cannot think of them as being alive.
JASON: [*Limply*]
    Where did she kill them . . . here . . . outside,
    or was it in the house?
LEADER: Force these doors
    and you will see your children in their blood.
JASON: [*Drawing his sword in a frenzy*] Servants, on
    the double,
    break these bolts,
    force the hinges: let me see   1315
    the double homicide,
    the murdered dead . . . and the murderess to die.

[*There is a rumbling sound, and out of a cloud above the house* MEDEA *appears in a chariot drawn by dragons. By her side are the dead bodies of the two* BOYS]°

MEDEA: [*In triumphant disdain*]
    Why this battering, this beating at the doors?
    Are you looking for their bodies—
    and for me who did this thing?
    Save yourself the trouble.
    If there's anything you want, then ask.   1320
    But me you shall not lay a hand upon.
    This chariot, the Sun
    —my father's father—gave me
    to keep me safe against my enemies.
JASON: [*Hissing with revulsion*]
    You miserable, mephitic woman!
    Beyond abhorrence—
    by me, the gods, the rest of men—
    you could put your own sons to the sword,   1325
    the sons you bore,
    and kill me too with childlessness . . .
    Yet still look upon the sun, see the earth . . .
    Be damned! . . .
    At last I understand
    what I never understood before,
    when I took you from your foreign home to live
       in Greece,   1330
    the sheer wickedness of you,
    the treachery to your father and the land that
       reared you.
    You are possessed
    and the gods have unleashed the fiend in you on *me*;

1284 Ino the maniac . . . out to roam Ino, a daughter of Cadmus and Harmonia, tried to destroy her two stepchildren so that her own two children might ascend the throne. Pursued, in turn, by their father, her husband Athamas, she leapt into the sea with her two boys. This is Euripides' version.

1316 Euripides was a past master at theatrical effects. He loved *ex machina* contrivances.

on your own brother, too, cut down in his home
1335   before you came aboard the sweet ship *Argo*'s hull.
　　　Your work already had begun.
　　　You married me, bore my sons,
　　and murdered them through jealousy of love.
　　No woman in the whole of Hellas
1340   would have dared so much;
　　yet you were the one I married,
　　not a girl from Greece.
　　　Oh, I married a tigress,
　　not a woman, not a wife,
　　and yoked myself to a hater and destroyer:
　　to a viciousness more fierce than any Tuscan Scylla.°

[Turning away from the door in a gesture of helplessness]

　　　But why go on?
　　A million accusations would not make you wince:
1345   you are shameless through and through . . .
　　you—you bloodstained ogress, infanticide . . .
　　　Hell take you!
　　Leave me to mourn my destiny of pain:
　　my fresh young wedding without joy,
　　my sons begot and reared and lost—
1350   never to be seen alive again.
MEDEA: *[With acid imperiousness from the chariot]*
　　　How tediously
　　I could rebut you point by point!
　　　Zeus the Father knows
　　exactly what you got from me
　　and how you then behaved.
　　　I would not let you or your royal princess
　　set our wedded life aside,
　　make me cheap,
1355   so that you could live in bliss;
　　or let that match-arranger, Creon,
　　dismiss me from the land without a fight.
　　　So, call me a tigress if you like,
　　or a Scylla haunting the Tyrrhenian shore,
　　I have done what I ought:
1360   broken your own heart to the core.
JASON: *[Wheeling round to face her]*
　　You are in agony too:
　　you share my broken life.
MEDEA: It is worth the suffering
　　　since *you* cannot scoff.
JASON: Poor children, what a monster
　　　fate gave you for a mother!
MEDEA: Poor sons, what a disaster
　　　your selfish father was!
JASON: It was not *his* right hand
1365   　that killed and struck them down.

MEDEA: No, it was his pride:
　　　the lust of his new love.
JASON: You think it right to murder
　　　just for a thwarted bed.
MEDEA: And do you think that a thwarted bed
　　　is trifling to a woman?
JASON: A modest woman, yes:
　　　to you the world's worst crime.
MEDEA: *[Pointing at the dead children]*
　　See, they are no more:
　　　I can hurt you too.   1370
JASON: They'll live, I think,
　　　in your tormented brain.
MEDEA: The gods know who began
　　　this whole calamity.
JASON: Yes, the gods know well
　　　your pernicious heart.
MEDEA: Hate then: I spurn
　　　the wormwood from your lips.
JASON: As I do yours; so let us
　　　be rid of one another.   1375
MEDEA: Yes, but on what terms?
　　　That's also what *I* want.
JASON: Let me have the boys—
　　　to mourn and bury them.
MEDEA: Never!
　　My own hands shall bury them, they shall be carried
　　to the sanctuary of Hera on the Cape,
　　where no enemy shall ever do them harm   1380
　　or violate their sepulchre.
　　　Here in Corinth, the land of Sisyphus,
　　I shall inaugurate a solemn festival°
　　with rites in perpetuity
　　to exorcise this murder.
　　　I myself shall go to Athens, land of Erechtheus,
　　to live with Aegeus, Pandion's son . . .   1385
　　you to a paltry death that fits you well:
　　your skull smashed by a fragment of the *Argo*'s
　　　hull:
　　ironic ending to the saga of your love for me.

THE EXODOS

[As the CHORUS *begin to form for the exodos march,
the meter changes to anapests and dactyls.* JASON
strides into the middle of the arena]

JASON: Murder is punished, and you'll be destroyed
　　by the avenging phantoms of your children.   1390
MEDEA: What power or divine one is ready to hear
　　　you:
　　perjurer, liar, treacherous guest?
JASON: Vile, vile, murderess of little ones!

1343 Tuscan Scylla a monster that inhabited the straits between Italy and Sicily and snatched sailors off passing ships and devoured them

1382 Solemn festival similar ceremonies were still performed at Corinth in Euripides' time.

MEDEA: Go—go and bury your bride.
1395   JASON: Broken I go: bereft of two sons.
MEDEA: You bemoan too soon: wait till you're old.
JASON: Dearest children!
MEDEA: Dear to their mother.
JASON: And so she slew them.
MEDEA: To get at your heart.
JASON: You did! You did! How I long to press
1400   my little children's lips to mine!
MEDEA: Now you are longing, now you call;
you utterly turned from them before.
JASON: For the love of the gods, allow me this:
to stroke my children's tender skin.
MEDEA: No, you shall not: you waste your words.
JASON: [Flinging out his arms] Zeus, do you hear
1405   how I'm at bay,
Dismissed by this ogress, odious woman,
Tigress besmirched with the blood of her young?
So I mourn and call on the gods while I may,
1410   On the powers to witness how you have slain
My children, and now prevent my hands
From touching them, dead, interring their clay.
I'd rather they'd never been born to me
Than have lived to see you destroy them this day.

[Before the end of these words, MEDEA, *with a cold,
vindictive smile, has moved off in the chariot.* JASON
staggers out of the arena]

ENVOI

1415   CHORUS: Wide is the range of Zeus on Olympus.
Wide the surprise which the gods can bring:
What was expected is never perfected,
What was not, finds a way opened up . . .
So ended this terrible thing.

ARISTOPHANES (CA. 450–CA.385 B.C.)

Aristophanes' dramatic career spanned the most turbulent period in the history of Athens. The economic and political stability of the Periclean age had been replaced by the debilitating Peloponnesian Wars and the ceaseless internal political struggles between democratic and oligarchic power factions.

Aristophanes' plays belong to the genre of Old Comedy, an irreverent and satirical form that ridiculed prominent individuals and institutions in Athens or criticized social and political policies. Some of his plays, including *The Birds, Lysistrata*, and *The Assembly of Women*, criticize the wars. Others take a more personal approach. His first victory at City Dionysia in 426 B.C. was for a now-lost play which we know satirized the policies and character of the military leader Cleon. *The Frogs*, which features a chorus in frog costumes, satirizes Athenian heroes of the stage. In this play, a pompous Aeschylus and a bitter Euripides come from Hades to compete with one another. In *The Clouds*, Aristophanes ridicules sophists—Socrates in particular—for their ability to argue any side of an issue. In fact, in Plato's *Apology*, Socrates blames Aristophanes' play for turning Athenian popular opinion against him.

Aristophanes wrote more than thirty plays, but only eleven have survived: *The Acharnians, The Knights, The Clouds, Wasps, Peace, The Birds, Lysistrata, Women Celebrating the Thesmophoria, The Frogs, Assembly of Women*, and *Plutus*. Aristophanes was as innovative as his more famous predecessors in Greek drama. His later plays, in which he virtually abandons the idea of the chorus as a character in the action, point to the development of newer forms of comedy.

Lysistrata

Lysistrata is an antiwar play. It shared the theme with two other plays by Aristophanes, *The Acharnians* and *Peace*, but the antiwar theme is treated differently in this play. When Aristophanes brought *Lysistrata* to the stage, Athens had been at war for more than twenty years. The costly and ill-fated Sicilian invasion, about which Aristophanes had already written *The Birds* (414 B.C.), led to another phase of the Peloponnesian War. The city-states of Peloponnesus had contributed money to support Pericles and the Athenian defeat of the Persians. After that war Pericles had demanded that the support continue in the form of tribute, all of which went to projects to enhance the grandeur of Athens. The Peloponnesian War, which began in 431 B.C., lasted nearly thirty years. These two wars proved costly and debilitating, and Athens was eventually defeated by

Sparta. When Aristophanes wrote *Lysistrata* in 411 B.C., Athens was already in a desperate position.

Lysistrata is a play clearly accessible to modern audiences. In the play the men who manage finance and policy at home in Athens are old, while all the young men are away at war, and as soon as one war is concluded another begins. Lysistrata is fed up, and she has gathered a band of women to negotiate a settlement and bring peace. She puts forward the plan that women withhold sex from their husbands until the men agree to negotiate a peace treaty. She argues that the women will surely have the sympathy of women in other states, who must also feel as they do. The women form commando groups to occupy the Acropolis and seize the treasury.

Out of this outrageous situation, Aristophanes generates a number of amusing scenes that satirize both sexes mercilessly. Lysistrata has not counted on the kind of objections she gets from the women themselves, who do not want to do without sex. Aristophanes plays on double meanings in virtually all of their conversations, and he also uses visual humor in costuming. The men in the play all carry gigantic erect phalluses that protrude beneath their gowns. The unashamed jokes about sexuality and the references to homosexuality—in the threat that the women may have to satisfy their own needs and in the offer by Kleisthenes to take over if the wives do not relent—is typical of Old Comedy. Aristophanes uses two choruses in this play—one of men and one of women—to argue and express opposing views of the male and female characters in the play. *Lysistrata* is the first play by Aristophanes in which woman characters form the chorus or assume important roles. The play openly challenges Athenian social codes that prevented women from participation in government, leveling political criticism—however hilarious—at the governors of Athens. In this play it is the women who have the viable political vision, but they find it difficult to come by the will to make that vision a reality.

Lysistrata

ARISTOPHANES

TRANSLATED BY DUDLEY FITTS

CHARACTERS

LYSISTRATA
KALONIKE
MYRRHINE
LAMPITO
CHORUS
MAGISTRATE

KINESIAS
SPARTAN HERALD
SPARTAN AMBASSADOR
A SENTRY
ATHENIAN DRUNKARD

SCENE: *Athens. First, a public square; later, beneath the walls of the Akropolis; later, a courtyard within the Akropolis. Time: early in 411 B.C.*

Until the éxodos, the CHORUS *is divided into two hemichori: the first, of Old Men; the second, of Old Women. Each of these has its* CHORAGOS. *In the éxodos, the hemichori return as Athenians and Spartans.*

The supernumeraries include the BABY SON *of Kinesias;* STRATYLLIS, *a member of the hemichorus of Old Women; various individual speakers, both Spartan and Athenian.*

PROLOGUE

[Athens; a public square; early morning; LYSISTRATA *alone]*

LYSISTRATA: If someone had invited them to a festival—
    Bacchos's, say, or Pan's,° or Aphroditê's, or
    that Genetyllis business—, you couldn't get
       through the streets,
    what with the drums and the dancing. But now,
    not a woman in sight!

5
                    Except–oh, yes!

[Enter KALONIKE*]*

    Here's one, at last. Good
    morning, Kalonikê.
KALONIKE: Good morning, Lysistrata.
                      Darling,
    don't frown so! You'll ruin your face!
LYSISTRATA: Never mind my face.
    Kalonikê,
    the way we women behave! Really, I don't blame
10   the men
    for what they say about us.
KALONIKE: No; I imagine they're right.

LYSISTRATA: For example: I call a meeting
    to think out a most important matter—and what
     happens?
    The women all stay in bed!
KALONIKE: Oh, they'll be along.
    It's hard to get away, you know: a husband, a cook, 15
    a child… Home life can be *so* demanding!
LYSISTRATA: What I have in mind is even more
    demanding.
KALONIKE: Tell me: what is it?
LYSISTRATA: Something big.
KALONIKE: Goodness! *How* big?
LYSISTRATA: Big enough for all of us.
KALONIKE: But we're not all here!
LYSISTRATA: We would be, if *that's* what was up!
                   No, Kalonikê, 20
    this is something I've been turning over for nights;
    and, I may say, sleepless nights.
KALONIKE: Can't be so hard, then,
    if you've spent so much time on it.
LYSISTRATA: Hard or not,
    it comes to this: Only we women can save Greece!
KALONIKE: Only we women? Poor Greece!
LYSISTRATA: Just the same, 25
    it's up to us. First, we must liquidate
    the Peloponnesians—

---

² **Bacchos's . . . business** Both Bacchos and Pan are gods associated with wine festivals; Aphrodite is the goddess of love; Genetyllis is a name applied to Aphrodite as goddess of procreation and to the minor deities attendant on her.

²⁷ **Boiotians** Boiotia, a country north of Greece, was famous for its seafood, especially its eels.

KALONIKE: Fun, fun!

LYSISTRATA: —and then the Boiotians.°

KALONIKE: Oh! But not those heavenly eels!

LYSISTRATA: You needn't worry.
    Athens shall have her sea food. —But here's the
      point:

30   If we can get the women from those places
    to join us women here, why, we can save
    all Greece!

KALONIKE: But dearest Lysistrata!
    How can women do a thing so austere, so
    political? We belong at home. Our only armor's

35   our transparent saffron dresses and
    our pretty little shoes!

LYSISTRATA: That's it exactly.
    Those transparent saffron dresses, those little
      shoes—
    well, there we are!

KALONIKE: Oh?

LYSISTRATA: Not a single man would lift
    his spear—

KALONIKE: I'll get my dress from the dyer's tomorrow!

LYSISTRATA: —or need a shield—

40 KALONIKE: The sweetest little negligée—

LYSISTRATA: —or bring out his sword.

KALONIKE: I know where I can buy
    the dreamiest sandals!

LYSISTRATA: Well, so you see. Now, shouldn't
    the women have come?

KALONIKE: Come? They should have *flown*!

LYSISTRATA: Athenians are always late.

45   But imagine!
    There's no one here from the South Shore.

KALONIKE: They go to work early,
    I can swear to that.

LYSISTRATA: And nobody from Acharnai.
    They should have been here hours ago!

KALONIKE: Well, you'll get
    that awful Theagenês woman: she's been having
    her fortune told at Hekatê's shrine.

50   But look!
    Someone at last! Can you see who they are?

[Enter MYRRHINE *and other women]*

LYSISTRATA: People from the suburbs.

KALONIKE: Yes! The entire
    membership of the Suburban League!

MYRRHINE: Sorry to be late, Lysistrata.
              Oh come,

55   don't scowl so! Say something!

LYSISTRATA: My dear Myrrhinê,
    what is there to say? After all,
    you've been pretty casual about the whole thing.

MYRRHINE: Couldn't find
    my girdle in the dark, that's all.
              But what *is*

'the whole thing'?

LYSISTRATA: Wait for the rest of them.   60

KALONIKE: I suppose so. But, look!
    Here's Lampitô!

[Enter LAMPITO *with women from Sparta]*

LYSISTRATA: Darling Lampitô,
    how pretty you are today! What a nice color!
    Goodness, you look as though you could strangle
    a bull!

LAMPITO: Ah think Ah could! It's the work-out   65
    in the gym every day; and, of co'se that dance° of
    ahs
    where y' kick yo' own tail.

LYSISTRATA: What lovely breasts!

LAMPITO: Lawdy, when y' touch me lahk that,
    Ah feel lahk a heifer at the altar!

LYSISTRATA: And this young lady?
    Where is she from?   70

LAMPITO: Boiotia. Social-Register type.

LYSISTRATA: Good morning, Boiotian. You're as pretty
    as green grass.

KALONIKE: And if you look,
    you'll find that the lawn has just been cut.

LYSISTRATA: And this lady?

LAMPITO: From Korinth. But a good woman.

LYSISTRATA: Well, in Korinth   75
    anything's possible.

LAMPITO: But let's get to work. Which one of you
    called this meeting, and why?

LYSISTRATA: *I* did.

LAMPITO: Well, then:
    what's up?

MYRRHINE: Yes, what *is* 'the whole thing,' after all?

LYSISTRATA: I'll tell you.—But first, one question.

MYRRHINE: Ask away!

LYSISTRATA: It's your husbands. Fathers of your
    children. Doesn't it bother you   80
    that they're always off with the Army? I'll stake
      my life,
    not one of you has a man in the house this minute!

KALONIKE: Mine's been in Thrace the last five
    months, keeping an eye
    on that General.°

MYRRHINE: Mine's been in Pylos for seven.

LAMPITO: And mahn,
    whenever he gets a *dis*charge, he goes raht back   85
    with that li'l ole speah of his, and enlists again!

LYSISTRATA: And not the ghost of a lover to be found!
    From the very day the war began—
               those Milesians!

---

[66] **dance** a dance (the *bibasis*) performed in Sparta, in which
girls kicked their buttocks with their heels   [82] **that General**
Eukrates

I could skin them alive!
           —I've not seen so much, even,
90   as one of those devices they call Widow's Delight.
       But there! What's important is: If I've found a way
       to end the war, are you with me?
       MYRRHINE: I should *say* so!
       Even if I have to pawn my best dress and
       drink up the proceeds.°
       KALONIKE: Me, too! Even if they split me
       right up the middle, like a flounder.
95   LAMPITO: Ah'm shorely with you.
       Ah'd crawl up Taÿgetos on mah knees
       if that'd bring peace.
       LYSISTRATA: Then here it is.
       Women! Sisters!
100   If we really want our men to make an armistice,
       we must be ready to give up—
       MYRRHINE: Give up what?
       Quick, tell us!
       LYSISTRATA: But *will* you?
       MYRRHINE: We will, even if it kills us.
       LYSISTRATA: Then we must give up sleeping with our
       men.

[Long silence]

       Oh? So now you're sorry? Won't look at me?
       Doubtful? Pale? All teary-eyed?
105   But come: be frank with me,
       as I've certainly been with you. Will you do it?
       MYRRHINE: I couldn't. No.
       Let the war go on.
       KALONIKE: Nor I. Let the war go on.
       LYSISTRATA: You, you little flounder,
       ready to be split up the middle?
       KALONIKE: Lysistrata, no!
       I'd walk through fire for you—you *know* I
110   would!—, but don't
       ask us to give up *that*! Why, there's nothing like it!
       LYSISTRATA: And you?
       BOIOTIAN: No. I must say I'*d* rather walk through fire.
       LYSISTRATA: You little salamanders!
       No wonder poets write tragedies about women.
       All we want's a quick tumble!
115   But you from Sparta:
       if you stand by me, we may win yet! Will you?
       It means so much!
       LAMPITO: Ah sweah, it means *too* much!
       By the Two Goddesses, it does! Asking a girl
       to sleep—Heaven knows how long!—in a great
         big bed
       with nobody there but herself! But Ah'll stay with
120   you!

Peace comes first!
       LYSISTRATA: Spoken like a true Spartan!
       KALONIKE: But if—
             oh dear!
             —if we give up what you tell us to,
       will there *be* any peace?
       LYSISTRATA: Why, mercy, of course there will!
       We'll just sit snug in our very thinnest gowns,
       perfumed and powdered from top to bottom, and
         those men   125
       simply won't stand still! And when we say No,
       they'll go out of their minds! And there's your
         peace.
       You can take my word for it.
       LAMPITO: Ah seem to remember
       that Colonel Menelaos threw his sword away
       when he saw Helen's breast° all bare.
       KALONIKE: But, goodness me! 130
       What if they just get up and leave us?
       LYSISTRATA: Well,
       we'd have to fall back on ourselves, of course.
       But they won't.
       KALONIKE: What if they drag us into the bedroom?
       LYSISTRATA: Hang on to the door.
       KALONIKE: What if they slap us?
       LYSISTRATA: If they do, you'd better give in. 135
       But be sulky about it. Do I have to teach you how?
       You know there's no fun for men when they have
         to force you.
       There are millions of ways of getting them to see
         reason.
       Don't you worry: a man
       doesn't like it unless the girl co-operates. 140
       KALONIKE: I suppose so. Oh, all right! We'll go along!
       LAMPITO: Ah imagine us Spahtans can arrange a
         peace. But you
       Athenians! Why, you're just war-mongerers!
       LYSISTRATA: Leave that to me.
       I know how to make them listen.
       LAMPITO: Ah don't see how.
       After all, they've got their boats; and there's lots
         of money   145
       piled up in the Akropolis.°
       LYSISTRATA: The Akropolis? Darling,
       we're taking over the Akropolis today!
       That's the older women's job. All the rest of us
       are going to the Citadel to sacrifice—you under-
         stand me?
       And once there, we're in for good!
       LAMPITO: Whee! Up the rebels! 150
       Ah can see you're a good strat*ee*gist.

---

⁹⁴ **drink up the proceeds** Athenian women were reputed to be heavy drinkers.

¹³⁰ **Helen's breast** an allusion to Euripides' *Andromache*, in which Menelaus, about to stab his wife, is overcome by her beauty and drops his sword   ¹⁴⁶ **Akropolis** Pericles had stored emergency funds in the Acropolis.

LYSISTRATA: Well, then, Lampitô,
  let's take the oath.
LAMPITO: Say it. We'll sweah.
LYSISTRATA: This is it.
  —But Lord! Where's our Inner Guard? Never mind.
                             —You see this
  shield? Put it down there. Now bring me the vic-
    tim's entrails.
KALONIKE: But the oath?
155 LYSISTRATA: You remember how in Aischylos' *Seven*
  they killed a sheep and swore on a shield? Well,
  then?
KALONIKE: But I don't see how you can swear for
  peace on a shield.
LYSISTRATA: What else do you suggest?
KALONIKE: Why not a white horse?
  We could swear by that.
LYSISTRATA: And where will you get a white horse?
KALONIKE: I never thought of that. *What* can we do?
160 MYRRHINE: I have it!
  Let's set this big black wine-bowl on the ground
  and pour in a gallon or so of Thasian, and swear
  not to add one drop of water.
LAMPITO: Ah lahk *that* oath!
LYSISTRATA: Bring the bowl and the wine-jug.
KALONIKE: Oh, what a simply *huge* one!
LYSISTRATA: Set it down; and, women, place your
165   hands on the gift-offering.
  O Goddess of Persuasion! And thou, O Loving-cup!
  Look upon this our sacrifice, and
  be gracious!
KALONIKE: It spills out like blood. How red and pret-
  ty it is!
LAMPITO: And Ah must say it smells good.
170 MYRRHINE: Let me swear first!
KALONIKE: No, by Aphroditê, let's toss for it!
LYSISTRATA: Lampitô: all of you women: come, touch
  the bowl,
  and repeat after me:
  I WILL HAVE NOTHING TO DO WITH MY HUSBAND OR
    MY LOVER
KALONIKE: *I will have nothing to do with my husband or*
175   *my lover*
LYSISTRATA: THOUGH HE COME TO ME IN PITIABLE CONDI-
  TION
KALONIKE: *Though he come to me in pitiable condition*
  (Oh Lysistrata! This is killing me!)
LYSISTRATA: I WILL STAY IN MY HOUSE UNTOUCHABLE
180 KALONIKE: *I will stay in my house untouchable*
LYSISTRATA: IN MY THINNEST SAFFRON SILK
KALONIKE: *In my thinnest saffron silk*
LYSISTRATA: AND MAKE HIM LONG FOR ME.
KALONIKE: *And make him long for me.*
185 LYSISTRATA: I WILL NOT GIVE MYSELF
KALONIKE: *I will not give myself*
LYSISTRATA: AND IF HE CONSTRAINS ME
KALONIKE: *And if he constrains me*

LYSISTRATA: I WILL BE AS COLD AS ICE AND NEVER MOVE
KALONIKE: *I will be as cold as ice and never move*   190
LYSISTRATA: I WILL NOT LIFT MY SLIPPERS TOWARD THE
  CEILING
KALONIKE: *I will not lift my slippers toward the ceiling*
LYSISTRATA: OR CROUCH ON ALL FOURS LIKE THE LIONESS
  IN THE CARVING
KALONIKE: *Or crouch on all fours like the lioness in the*
  carving
LYSISTRATA: AND IF I KEEP THIS OATH LET ME DRINK FROM
  THIS BOWL   195
KALONIKE: *And if I keep this oath let me drink from this*
  bowl
LYSISTRATA: IF NOT, LET MY OWN BOWL BE FILLED WITH
  WATER
KALONIKE: *If not, let my own bowl be filled with water.*
LYSISTRATA: You have all sworn?
MYRRHINE: We have.
LYSISTRATA: Then thus
  I sacrifice the victim.

[Drinks largely]

KALONIKE: Save some for us!   200
  Here's to you, darling, and to you, and to you!
    It's all
  for us women.

[Loud cries off-stage]

LAMPITO: What's all *that* whoozy-goozy?
LYSISTRATA: Just what I told you.
  The older women have taken the Akropolis. Now
    you, Lampitô,
  rush back to Sparta. We'll take care of things here.
    And   205
  be sure you get organized!
                      The rest of you girls,
  up to the Citadel: and mind you push in the bolts.
KALONIKE: But the men? Won't they be after us?
LYSISTRATA: Just you leave
  the men to me. There's not fire enough in the world
  to make me open *my* door.
KALONIKE: I hope so, by Aphroditê!   210
  At any rate,
  let's remember the League's reputation for hang-
    ing on!

[Exeunt]

PÁRODOS: CHORAL EPISODE

[The hillside just under the Akropolis. Enter CHORUS
OF OLD MEN *with burning torches and braziers; much
puffing and coughing]*

CHORAGOS [m]: Easy, Drakês, old friend! Don't skin
  your shoulders

with those damnable big olive-branches. What a
job!

STROPHE I

215 CHORUS ^m: Forward, forward, comrades! Whew!
The things that old age does to you!
Neighbor Strymodoros, would you have thought
it?
We've caught it—
And from women, too!
Women that used to board with us, bed with us—
220 Now, by the gods, they've got ahead of us,
Taken the Akropolis (Heaven knows why!),
Profanèd the sacred statuar-y,°
And barred the doors,
The aggravating whores!
CHORAGOS ^m: Come, Philourgos, quick, pile your
225 brushwood
next to the wall there.
These traitors to Athens and to us,
we'll fry each last one of them! And the very first
will be old Lykôn's wife.

ANTISTROPHE I

CHORUS ^m: By Deméter I swear it—(ouch!),
230 I'll not perform the Kleomenês-crouch!
How he looked—and a good soldier, too—
When out he flew,
that filthy pouch
Of a body of his all stinking and shaggy,
Bare as an eel, except for the bag he
235 Covered his rear with. Lord, what a mess!
Never a bath in six years, I'd guess!
Unhappy Sparta,
With such a martyr!
CHORAGOS ^m: What a siege, friends! Seventeen ranks
strong
240 we stood at the Gate, and never a chance for a nap.
And all because of women, whom the gods hate
(and so does Euripidês).
It's enough to make a veteran
turn in his medals from Marathon!

STROPHE 2

CHORUS ^m: Forward, men! Just up the hillside,
245 And we're there!
Keep to the path! A yoke of oxen
Wouldn't care
To haul this lumber. Mind the fire,
Or it'll die before we're higher!
250 Puff! Puff!
This smoke will strangle me, sure enough!

---

²²² **sacred statuary** the statue of Pallas Athena, which was
said to have fallen from heaven to the Acropolis

ANTISTROPHE 2

Holy Heraklês, I'm blinded,
Sure as fate!
It's Lemnos-fire we've been toting;
And isn't it great   255
To be singed by this infernal flame?
(Lachês, remember the Goddess: for shame!)
Woof! Woof!
A few steps more, and we're under the roof!
CHORAGOS ^m: It catches! It's blazing!   260
Down with your loads!
We'll sizzle 'em now,
By all the gods!
Vine-branches here, quick!
Light 'em up,   265
And in through the gate with 'em!
If that doesn't stop
Their nonsense—well,
We'll smoke 'em to Hell.
Ker*shoo*!   270
(What we really need
Is a grad-u-ate,
Top of his class,
From Samos Military State.
Achoo!)   275
Come, do
Your duty, you!
Pour out your braziers,
Embers ablaze!
But first, Gentlemen, allow me to raise   280
The paian:
Lady
Victory, now
Assist thine adherents
Here below!
Down with women!   285
Up with men!
Iô triumphe!
CHORUS ^m: Amen!

*[Enter CHORUS OF OLD WOMEN on the walls of the
Akropolis, carrying jars of water to extinguish the fire
set by the CHORUS OF OLD MEN]*

CHORAGOS ^w: Fire, fire!
Quickly, quickly, women, if we're to save our-
selves!   290

STROPHE

CHORUS ^w: Nikodikê, run!
Or Kalykê's done
To a turn, and poor Kratylla's
Smoked like a ham.
Damn
These men and their wars,   295
Their hateful ways!

I nearly died before I got to the place
Where we fill our jars:
    Slaves pushing and jostling—
300   Such a hustling
I never saw in all my days!

ANTISTROPHE

But here's water at last.
Sisters, make haste
And slosh it down on them,
The silly old wrecks!
305   Sex
Almighty! What they want's
A hot bath? Send it down!
And thou, Athenê of Athens town,
Assist us in drowning their wheezy taunts!
310   O Trito-born!° Helmet of Gold!
      Help us to cripple their backs, the old
Fools with their semi-incendiary brawn!

[The OLD MEN *capture a woman,* STRATYLLIS*]*

STRATYLLIS: Let me go! Let me go!
CHORAGOS ᵂ: You walking corpses,
    have you no shame?
CHORAGOS ᵐ: I wouldn't have believed it!
315   An army of women in the Akropolis!
CHORAGOS ᵂ: So we scare you, do we? Grandpa,
    you've seen
    only our pickets yet!
CHORAGOS ᵐ: Hey, Phaidrias!
    Help me with the necks of these jabbering hens!
CHORAGOS ᵂ: Down with your pots, girls! We'll need
      both hands
    if these antiques attack us.
320 CHORAGOS ᵐ: Want your face kicked in?
CHORAGOS ᵂ: Want to try my teeth?
CHORAGOS ᵐ: Look out! I've got a stick!
CHORAGOS ᵂ: You lay a half-inch of your stick on
      Stratyllis,
    and you'll never stick again!
CHORAGOS ᵐ: Fall apart!
CHORAGOS ᵂ: I'll chew your guts!
CHORAGOS ᵐ: Euripidês! Master!
    How well you knew women!
325 CHORAGOS ᵂ: Listen to him! Rhodippê,
    up with the pots!
CHORAGOS ᵐ: Demolition of God,
    what good are your pots?
CHORAGOS ᵂ: You refugee from the tomb,
    what good is your fire?
CHORAGOS ᵐ: Good enough to make a pyre
    to barbecue you!

---

310 **Trito-born** name for Athena, who according to some
accounts was born near Lake Tritonis in Libya

CHORAGOS ᵂ: We'll squizzle your kindling!
CHORAGOS ᵐ: You think so?
CHORAGOS ᵂ: Yah! Just hang around a while! 330
CHORAGOS ᵐ: Want a touch of my torch?
CHORAGOS ᵂ: Your torch needs a bath.
CHORAGOS ᵐ: How about you?
CHORAGOS ᵂ: Soap for a senile bridegroom!
CHORAGOS ᵐ: Senile? Hold your trap!
CHORAGOS ᵂ: Just *you* try to hold it!
CHORAGOS ᵐ: The yammer of women!
CHORAGOS ᵂ: The yatter of men! 335
    But you'll never sit in the jury-box again.
CHORAGOS ᵐ: Gentlemen, I beg you, burn off that
      woman's hair!
CHORAGOS ᵂ: Let it come down!

[They empty their pots on the men]

CHORAGOS ᵐ: What a way to drown!
CHORAGOS ᵂ: Hot, hey?
CHORAGOS ᵐ: Say,
    enough!
CHORAGOS ᵂ: Dandruff 340
    needs watering. I'll make you
    nice and fresh.
CHORAGOS ᵐ: For God's sake, you
    sluts, hold off!

Scene 1

[Enter a MAGISTRATE *accompanied by four constables]*

MAGISTRATE: These degenerate women! What a rack-
    et of little drums,
    what a yapping for Adonis on every house-top! 345
    It's like the time in the Assembly when I was lis-
    tening
    to a speech—out of order, as usual—by that fool
    Demostratos,°all about troops for Sicily,°
    that kind of nonsense—
               and there was his wife
    trotting around in circles howling 350
    Alas for Adonis!°—
           and Demostratos insisting
    we must draft every last Zakynthian that can
      walk—
    and his wife up there on the roof,
    drunk as an owl, yowling
    Oh weep for Adonis!—

---

348 **Demostratos** Athenian politician **troops for Sicily** a
reference to the Sicilian expedition of 416 B.C., in which
Athens was defeated   351 **Adonis** a fertility god whose
death and resurrection was celebrated by women in an annual two-day festival

355 and that damned ox Demostratos
mooing away through the rumpus. That's what
we get
for putting up with this wretched woman-business!
CHORAGOS ᵐ: Sir, you haven't heard the half of it.
They laughed at us!
Insulted us! They took pitchers of water
and nearly drowned us! We're still wringing out
360 our clothes,
for all the world like unhousebroken brats.
MAGISTRATE: And a good thing, by Poseidon!
Whose fault is it if these women-folk of ours
get out of hand? We coddle them,
we teach them to be wasteful and loose. You'll see
365 a husband
go into a jeweler's. 'Look,' he'll say,
'jeweler,' he'll say, 'you remember that gold choker
'you made for my wife? Well, she went to a dance
last night
'and broke the clasp. Now, I've got to go to Salamis,
'and can't be bothered. Run over to my house
370 tonight,
'will you, and see if you can put it together for her.'
Or another one
goes to a cobbler—a good strong workman, too,
with an awl that was never meant for child's play.
'Here,'
375 he'll tell him, 'one of my wife's shoes is pinching
'her little toe. Could you come up about noon
'and stretch it out for her?'
Well, what do you expect?
Look at me, for example. I'm a Public Officer,
and it's one of my duties to pay off the sailors.
380 And where's the money? Up there in the Akropolis!
And those blasted women slam the door in my
face!
But what are we waiting for?
—Look here, constable,
stop sniffing around for a tavern, and get us
some crowbars. We'll force their gates! As a matter of fact,
I'll do a little forcing myself.

[Enter LYSISTRATA, *above, with* MYRRHINE, KALONIKE,
and the BOIOTIAN]

385 LYSISTRATA: No need of forcing.
Here I am, of my own accord. And all this talk
about locked doors—! We don't need locked
doors,
but just the least bit of common sense.
MAGISTRATE: Is that so, ma'am!
—Where's my constable?
—Constable,
390 arrest that woman, and tie her hands behind her.
LYSISTRATA: If he touches me, I swear by Artemis
there'll be one scamp dropped from the public

pay-roll tomorrow!
MAGISTRATE: Well, constable? You're not afraid, I
suppose? Grab her,
two of you, around the middle!
KALONIKE: No, by Pándrosos!
Lay a hand on her, and I'll jump on you so hard 395
your guts will come out the back door!
MAGISTRATE: That's what *you* think!
Where's the sergeant?—Here, you: tie up that
trollop first,
the one with the pretty talk!
MYRRHINE: By the Moon-Goddess!
Just you try it, and you'd better call a surgeon!
MAGISTRATE: Another one!
Officer, seize that woman!
I swear 400
I'll put an end to this riot!
BOIOTIAN: By the Taurian,
one inch closer and you won't have a hair on
your head!
MAGISTRATE: Lord, what a mess! And my constables
seem to have left me.
But—women get the best of us? By God, no!
—Skythians!
Close ranks and forward march!
LYSISTRATA: 'Forward,' indeed! 405
By the Two Goddesses, what's the sense in *that*?
They're up against four companies of women
armed from top to bottom.
MAGISTRATE: Forward, my Skythians!
LYSISTRATA: Forward, yourselves, dear comrades!
You grainlettucebeanseedmarket girls! 410
You garlicandonionbreadbakery girls!
Give it to 'em! Knock 'em down! Scratch 'em!
Tell 'em what you think of 'em!

[General mêlée; the Skythians yield]

—Ah, that's enough!
Sound a retreat: good soldiers don't rob the dead!
MAGISTRATE: A nice day *this* has been for the police! 415
LYSISTRATA: Well, there you are.—Did you really
think we women
would be driven like slaves? Maybe now you'll
admit
that a woman knows something about glory.
MAGISTRATE: Glory enough,
especially glory in bottles! Dear Lord Apollo!
CHORAGOS ᵐ: Your Honor, there's no use talking to
them. Words 420
mean nothing whatever to wild animals like these.
Think of the sousing they gave us! and the water
was not, I believe, of the purest.
CHORAGOS ʷ: You shouldn't have come after us. And
if you try it again,
you'll be one eye short!—Although, as a matter of
fact, 425

what I like best is just to stay at home and read,
like a sweet little bride: never hurting a soul, no,
never going out. But if you *must* shake hornets'
    nests,
look out for the hornets!

STROPHE

CHORUS ᵐ: Good God, what can we do?
430   What are we coming to?
These women! Who could bear it? But, for that
    matter, who
                    Will find
            What they had in mind
        When they seized Kranaos' city
435   And held it (more's the pity!)
Against us men of Athens, and our police force, too?
CHORAGOS ᵐ: We might question them, I suppose.
        But I warn you, sir,
    don't believe anything you hear! It would be un-
        Athenian
    not to get to the bottom of this plot.
MAGISTRATE: Very well.
440   My first question is this: Why, so help you God,
    did you bar the gates of the Akropolis?
LYSISTRATA: Why?
    To keep the money, of course. No money, no war.
MAGISTRATE: You think that money's the cause of war?
LYSISTRATA: I do.
    Money brought about that Peisandros° business
    and all the other attacks on the State. Well and
445   good!
    They'll not get another cent here!
MAGISTRATE: And what will you do?
LYSISTRATA: What a question! From now on, we intend
    to control the Treasury.
MAGISTRATE: Control the Treasury!
LYSISTRATA: Why not? Does that seem strange? After all,
    we control our household budgets.
450   MAGISTRATE: But that's different!
LYSISTRATA: 'Different'? What do you mean?
MAGISTRATE: I mean simply this:
    it's the Treasury that pays for National Defense.
LYSISTRATA: Unnecessary. We propose to abolish war!
MAGISTRATE: Good God.—And National Security?
LYSISTRATA: Leave that to us.
MAGISTRATE: You?
LYSISTRATA: Us.
MAGISTRATE: We're done for, then!
455   LYSISTRATA: Never mind.
    We women will save you in spite of yourselves.
MAGISTRATE: What nonsense!
LYSISTRATA: If you like. But you must accept it, like it
        or not.
MAGISTRATE: Why, this is downright subversion!

---

⁴⁴⁴ **Peisandros** a plotter against Athenian democracy

LYSISTRATA: Maybe it is.
    But we're going to save you, Judge.
MAGISTRATE: I don't *want* to be saved!
LYSISTRATA: Tut. The death-wish. All the more reason.
MAGISTRATE: But the idea   460
    of women bothering themselves about peace and
        war!
LYSISTRATA: Will you listen to me?
MAGISTRATE: Yes. But be brief, or I'll—
LYSISTRATA: This is no time for stupid threats.
MAGISTRATE: By the gods,
    I'm losing my mind!
AN OLD WOMAN: That's nice. If you do, remember
    you've less to lose than *we* have.
MAGISTRATE: Quiet, you old buzzard!   465
    Now, Lysistrata: tell me what you're thinking.
LYSISTRATA: Glad to.
                    Ever since this war began
    we women have been watching you men, agree-
        ing with you,
    keeping our thoughts to ourselves. That doesn't
        mean
    we were happy: we weren't, for we saw how
        things were going;   470
    but we'd listen to you at dinner
    arguing this way and that.
                    —Oh you, and your big
    Top Secrets!—
                    And then we'd grin like little patriots
    (though goodness knows we didn't feel like grin-
        ning) and ask you:
    'Dear, did the Armistice come up in Assembly
        today?'   475
    And you'd say, 'None of your business! Pipe
        down!', you'd say.
    And so we would.
AN OLD WOMAN: *I* wouldn't have, by God!
MAGISTRATE: You'd have taken a beating, then!
                                    —Please go on.
LYSISTRATA: Well, we'd be quiet. But then, you know,
        all at once
    you men would think up something worse than
        ever.   480
    Even *I* could see it was fatal. And, 'Darling,' I'd say,
    'have you gone completely mad?' And my hus-
        band would look at me
    and say, 'Wife, you've got your weaving to attend
        to.
    Mind your tongue, if you don't want a slap.
        "War's a man's affair!"°
MAGISTRATE: Good words, and well pronounced!   485
LYSISTRATA: You're a fool if you think so.

---

⁴⁸⁵ **War's a man's affair** Hector's line to his wife,
Andromache, in Homer, *Iliad*, VI: 492

It was hard enough
to put up with all this banquet-hall strategy.
But then we'd hear you out in the public square:
'Nobody left for the draft-quota here in Athens?'
you'd say; and, 'No,' someone else would say,
'not a man!'
490 And so we women decided to rescue Greece.
You might as well listen to us now: you'll have to,
later.
MAGISTRATE: *You* rescue Greece? Absurd!
LYSISTRATA: You're the absurd one!
MAGISTRATE: You expect me to take orders from a
woman?
LYSISTRATA: Heavens, if that's what's bothering you,
495 take my veil,
here, and my girdle, and my market-basket. Go
home
to your weaving and your cooking! I tell you, "War's
a woman's affair!"
CHORAGOS ᵂ: Down with your pitchers, comrades,
but keep them close at hand. It's time for a rally!

ANTISTROPHE

500 CHORUS ᵂ: Dance, girls, dance for peace!
                 Who cares if our knees
Wobble and creak? Shall we not dance for such
allies as these?
          Their wit! their grace! their beauty!
                 It's a municipal duty
To dance them luck and happiness who risk their
505 all for Greece!
CHORAGOS ᵂ: Women, remember your grandmoth-
ers! Remember, you were born
among brambles and nettles! Dance for victory!
LYSISTRATA: O Erôs, god of delight! O Aphroditê!
Kyprian!
Drench us now with the savor of love!
510 Let these men, getting wind of us, dream such joy
that they'll tail us through all the provinces of
Hellas!
MAGISTRATE: And if we do?
LYSISTRATA: Well, for one thing, we shan't have to
watch you
going to market, a spear in one hand, and heaven
knows
what in the other.
CHORAGOS ᵂ: Nicely said, by Aphroditê!
LYSISTRATA: As things stand now, you're neither men
515 nor women.
Armor clanking with kitchen pans and pots—
you sound like a pack of Korybantês!
MAGISTRATE: A man must do what a man must do.
LYSISTRATA: So I'm told.
But to see a General, complete with Gorgon-
shield,
520 jingling along the dock to buy a couple of herrings!

CHORAGOS ᵂ: *I* saw a Captain the other day—lovely
fellow he was,
nice curly hair—sitting on his horse; and—can
you believe it?—
he'd just bought some soup, and was pouring it
into his helmet!
And there was a soldier from Thrace
swishing his lance like something out of
Euripidês,   525
and the poor fruit-store woman got so scared
that she ran away and let him have his figs free!
MAGISTRATE: All this is beside the point.
                     Will you be so kind
as to tell me how you mean to save Greece?
LYSISTRATA: Of course!
Nothing could be simpler.
MAGISTRATE: I assure you, I'm all ears. 530
LYSISTRATA: Do you know anything about weaving?
Say the yarn gets tangled: we thread it
this way and that through the skein, up and
down,
until it's free. And it's like that with war.
We'll send our envoys   535
up and down, this way and that, all over Greece,
until it's finished.
MAGISTRATE: Yarn? Thread? Skein?
Are you out of your mind? I tell you,
war is a serious business.
LYSISTRATA: So serious
that I'd like to go on talking about weaving.   540
MAGISTRATE: All right. Go ahead.
LYSISTRATA: The first thing we have to do
is to wash our yarn, get the dirt out of it.
You see? Isn't there too much dirt here in Athens?
You must wash those men away.
                     Then our spoiled wool—
that's like your job-hunters, out for a life   545
of no work and big pay. Back to the basket,
citizens or not, allies or not,
or friendly immigrants!
                     And your colonies?
Hanks of wool lost in various places. Pull them
together, weave them into one great whole,   550
and our voters are clothed for ever.
MAGISTRATE: It would take a woman
to reduce state questions to a matter of carding
and weaving!
LYSISTRATA: You fool! Who were the mothers whose
sons sailed off
to fight for Athens in Sicily?
MAGISTRATE: Enough!
I beg you, do not call back those memories.
LYSISTRATA: And then, 555
instead of the love that every woman needs,
we have only our single beds, where we can
dream

of our husbands off with the Army.
                    Bad enough for wives!
But what about our girls, getting older every day,
and older, and no kisses?
560 MAGISTRATE: Men get older, too.
LYSISTRATA: Not in the same sense.
                   A soldier's discharged,
and he may be bald and toothless, yet he'll find
a pretty young thing to go to bed with.
                   But a woman!
Her beauty is gone with the first grey hair.
565 She can spend her time
consulting the oracles and the fortune-tellers,
but they'll never send her a husband.
MAGISTRATE: Still, if a man can rise to the occasion—
LYSISTRATA: Rise? Rise, yourself!

[Furiously]

Go invest in a coffin!
             You've money enough.
570   I'll bake you
a cake for the Underworld.
              And here's your funeral
wreath!

[She pours water upon him]

MYRRHINE: And here's another!

[More water]

KALONIKE: And here's
my contribution!

[More water]

LYSISTRATA: What are you waiting for?
All aboard Styx Ferry!
               Charôn's° calling for you!
575 It's sailing-time: don't disrupt the schedule!
MAGISTRATE: The insolence of women! And to me!
No, by God, I'll go back to court and show
the rest of the Bench the things that might happen
to them!

[Exit MAGISTRATE*]*

LYSISTRATA: Really, I suppose we should have laid
    out his corpse
on the doorstep, in the usual way.
580   But never mind!
We'll give him the rites of the dead tomorrow
    morning!

---

⁵⁷⁴ **Charon** the god who ferried the souls of the dead across the river styx to Hades

[Exit LYSISTRATA *with* MYRRHINE *and* KALONIKE*]*

CHORAL EPISODE

STROPHE I

CHORUS ᵐ: Sons of Liberty, strip off your clothes for
    action! Men, arise!
Shall we stand here limp and useless while old
    Kleisthenês' ° allies
Prod a herd of furious grandmas to attempt to
    bring to pass
A female restoration of the Reign of Hippias?°   585
           Forbid it, gods misogynist!
            Return our Treasury, at least!
We must clothe ourselves and feed ourselves to
    face these civic
rages,
And who can do a single thing if they cut off our
    wages?
CHORAGOS ᵐ: Gentlemen, we are disgraced forever
    if we allow   590
these madwomen to jabber about spears and
    shields
and make friends with the Spartans. What's a
    Spartan? a wild
wolf's a safer companion any day! No; their
    plan's
to bring back Dictatorship; and we won't stand
    for that!
From now on, let's go armed, each one of us   595
a new Aristogeiton!
                And to begin with,
I propose to poke a number of teeth
down the gullet of that harridan over there.

ANTISTROPHE I

CHORUS ʷ: Hold your tongues, you senile bravoes,
    or, I swear, when you get home
Your own mothers wouldn't know you! Strip for
    action, ladies, come!   600
I bore the holy vessels° in my eighth year, and at
    ten
I was pounding out the barley for Athenê
    Goddess; then
           They elected me Little Bear
           For Artemis at Brauron Fair;°

---

⁵⁸³ **Kleisthenes** a bisexual Athenian   ⁵⁸⁵ **Hippias** Athenian tyrant (d. 490 B.C.)   ⁶⁰¹ **bore the holy vessels** Four girls of high social standing were chosen each year as acolytes to Athena in the Akropolis.   ⁶⁰⁴ **Little Bear. . . Fair** Brauron was a town on the eastern coast of Greece where every five years a festival of Artemis was celebrated; its symbol was the bear, an animal sacred to Artemis.

605 I'd been made a Basket-Carrier by the time I came
       of age:
    So trust me to advise you in this feminist rampage!
    CHORAGOS ᵂ: As a woman, I pay my taxes to the
       State,
    though I pay them in baby boys. What do you
       contribute,
    you impotent horrors? Nothing but waste:
610 our treasury,° the so-called Glory of the Persian
       Wars,
    gone! rifled! parceled out for privilege! And you
    have the insolence to control public policy,
    leading us all to disaster!
                                   No, don't answer back
    unless you want the heel of my slipper
615 slap against that ugly jaw of yours!

STROPHE 2

CHORUS ᵐ:

                   What impudence!
                   What malevolence!
                   Comrades, make haste,
    All those of you who still are sensitive below the
       waist!
620   Off with your clothes, men!
                   Nobody knows when
                   We'll put them back on.
                   Remember Leipsydrion!°
                   We may be old,
625   But let's be bold!
    CHORAGOS ᵐ: Give them an inch, and we're done for!
       We'll have them
    launching boats next and planning naval strategy.
    Or perhaps they fancy themselves as cavalry!
    That's fair enough: women know how to ride,
    they're good in the saddle. Just think of Mikôn's
630   paintings,
    all those Amazons wrestling with men! No, it's time
    to bridle these wild mares!

ANTISTROPHE 2

CHORUS ᵂ: Hold on, or
                   You *are* done for,
635   By the Two Goddesses above!
    Strip, strip, my women: we've got the veterans on
       the move!
                   Tangle with me, Gramps,
                   And you'll have cramps
                   For the rest of your days!

---

⁶¹⁰ **treasury** Funded by money originally contributed by
Athens and her allies to finance the war against the Persians,
contributions fell off after the disaster of the Sicilian war; the
fund was now being raided by Athenian politicians.
⁶²³ **Leipsydrion** a fortified town defended by the Patriots
after their expulsion from Athens

No more beans! No more cheese!   640
                   My two legs
                   Will scramble your eggs!
CHORAGOS ᵂ: If Lampitô stands by me, and that ele-
   gant
Theban girl, Ismenia—what good are *you*?
                                   Pass your laws!
Laws upon laws, you decrepit legislators!   645
At the worst you're just a nuisance, rationing
   Boiotian eels
on the Feast of Hekatê, making our girls go without!
That was statesmanship! And we'll have to put up
   with it
until some patriot slits your silly old gizzards!

[Exeunt omnes]

Scene 2

*[The scene shifts to a court within the Akropolis. Re-
enter LYSISTRATA]*

CHORAGOS ᵂ: But Lysistrata! Leader! Why such a
   grim face?   650
LYSISTRATA: Oh the behavior of these idiotic women!
   There's something about the female temperament
   that I can't bear!
CHORAGOS ᵂ: What in the world do you mean?
LYSISTRATA: Exactly what I say.
CHORAGOS ᵂ: What dreadful thing has happened?
   Come, tell us: we're all your friends.
LYSISTRATA: It isn't easy   655
   to say it; yet, God knows, we can't hush it up.
CHORAGOS ᵂ: Well, then? Out with it!
LYSISTRATA: To put it bluntly,
   we're desperate for men.
CHORAGOS ᵂ: Almighty God!
LYSISTRATA: Why bring God into it?—No, it's just as I
   say.
   I can't manage them any longer: they've gone
      man-crazy,   660
   they're all trying to get out.
                                   Why, look:
   one of them was sneaking out the back door
   over there by Pan's cave; another
   was sliding down the walls with rope and tackle;
   another was climbing aboard a sparrow, ready to
      take off   665
   for the nearest brothel—I dragged *her* back by the
      hair!
   They're all finding some reason to leave.
                                   Look there!
   There goes another one.
                                   —Just a minute, you!
   Where are you off to so fast?
FIRST WOMAN: I've got to get home!

670   I've a lot of Milesian wool, and the worms are
      spoiling it.
LYSISTRATA: Oh bother you and your worms! Get
    back inside!
FIRST WOMAN: I'll be back right away, I swear I will!
    I just want to get it stretched out on my bed.
LYSISTRATA: You'll do no such thing. You'll stay right
    here.
FIRST WOMAN: And my wool?
    You want it ruined?
675 LYSISTRATA: Yes, for all I care.
SECOND WOMAN: Oh dear! My lovely new flax from
    Amorgos—
    I left it at home, all uncarded!
LYSISTRATA: Another one!
    And all she wants is someone to card her flax.
    Get back in there!
SECOND WOMAN: But I swear by the Moon-Goddess,
    the minute I get it done, I'll be back!
680 LYSISTRATA: I say No!
    If you, why not all the other women as well?
THIRD WOMAN: O Lady Eileithyia!° Radiant goddess!
    Thou
    intercessor for women in childbirth! Stay, I pray
    thee,
    oh stay this parturition! Shall I pollute
    a sacred spot?
685 LYSISTRATA: And what's the matter with *you*?
THIRD WOMAN: I'm having a baby—any minute now!
LYSISTRATA: But you weren't pregnant yesterday.
THIRD WOMAN: Well, I am today!
    Let me go home for a midwife, Lysistrata:
    there's not much time.
LYSISTRATA: I never heard such nonsense.
    What's that bulging under your cloak?
690 THIRD WOMAN: A little baby boy.
LYSISTRATA: It certainly isn't. But it's something hollow,
    like a basin or—Why, it's the helmet of Athenê!
    And you said you were having a baby!
THIRD WOMAN: Well, I am! So there!
LYSISTRATA: Then why the helmet?
THIRD WOMAN: I was afraid that my pains
695   might begin here in the Akropolis; and I wanted
    to drop my chick into it, just as the dear doves do.
LYSISTRATA: Lies! Evasions!—But at least one thing's
    clear:
    you can't leave the place before your purification.
THIRD WOMAN: But I can't stay here in the Akropolis!
    Last night I dreamed
    of a snake.
FIRST WOMAN: And those horrible owls, the noise
700   they make!
    I can't get a bit of sleep; I'm just about dead.
LYSISTRATA: You useless girls, that's enough: Let's

have no more lying.
Of course you want your men. But don't you
    imagine
that they want you just as much? I'll give you my
    word,
their nights must be pretty hard.
                      Just stick it out! 705
A little patience, that's all, and our battle's won.
I have heard an Oracle. Should you like to hear it?
FIRST WOMAN: An Oracle? Yes, tell us!
LYSISTRATA: Quiet, then.—Here
    is what it said:
IF EVER THE SWALLOWS, ESCHEWING HOOPOE-
    BIRDS,   710
SHALL CONSPIRE TOGETHER TO DENY THEM ALL
    ACCESS,
THEIR GRIEF IS FOREVER OVER.
                   These are the words
from the Shrine itself.
              AYE, AND ZEUS WILL REDRESS
    THEIR WRONGS, AND SET THE LOWER ABOVE
    THE HIGHER.
FIRST WOMAN: Does that mean we'll be on top?
LYSISTRATA: BUT IF THEY RETIRE, 715
    EACH SWALLOW HER OWN WAY, FROM THIS
      HOLY PLACE,
    LET THE WORLD PROCLAIM NO BIRD OF SORRIER
      GRACE
    THAN THE SWALLOW.
FIRST WOMAN: I swear, *that* Oracle makes sense!
LYSISTRATA: Now, then, by all the gods,
    let's show that we're bigger than these annoyances. 720
    Back to your places! Let's not disgrace the Oracle.

[Exeunt LYSISTRATA *and the dissident women; the*
CHORUSES *renew their conflict.]*

CHORAL EPISODE

STROPHE

CHORUS ᵐ: I know a little story that I learned way
    back in school
Goes like this:
Once upon a time there was a young man—and
    no fool—
Named Melanion; and his   725
One aversi-on was marriage. He loathed the very
    thought!
So he ran off to the hills, and in a special grot
Raised a dog, and spent his days
Hunting rabbits. And it says
That he never never never did come home.   730
It might be called a refuge *from* the womb.
All right,
           all right,
                      all right!

---

682 Eileithyia goddess of childbirth

We're as pure as young Melanion, and we hate the very sight
Of you sluts!

735 A MAN: How about a kiss, old woman?
A WOMAN: Here's an onion in your eye!
A MAN: A kick in the guts, then?
A WOMAN: Try, old bristle-tail, just try!
A MAN: Yet they say Myronidês
740 On hands and knees
Looked just as shaggy fore and aft as I!

ANTISTROPHE

CHORUS ᵂ: Well, *I* know a little story, and it's just as good as yours.
Goes like this:
Once there was a man named Timon—a rough diamond, of course,
745 And that whiskery face of his
Looked like murder in the shrubbery. By God, he was a son
Of the Furies, let me tell you! And what did he do but run
From the world and all its ways,
Cursing mankind! And it says
750 That his choicest execrations as of then
Were leveled almost wholly at *old* men.
All right,
            all right,
                        all right!
But there's one thing about Timon: he could always stand the sight
Of us 'sluts'!

755 A WOMAN: How about a crack in the jaw, Pop?
A MAN: I can take it, Ma—no fear!
A WOMAN: How about a kick in the face?
A MAN: You'd show your venerable rear.
A WOMAN: I may be old;
760 But I've been told
That I've nothing to worry about down there!

Scene 3

[Re-enter LYSISTRATA]

LYSISTRATA: Oh, quick, girls, quick! Come here!
CHORAGOS ᵂ: What is it?
LYSISTRATA: A man!
A man simply bulging with love!
O Kyprian Queen,°
O Paphian, O Kythereian! Hear us and aid us!
CHORAGOS ᵂ: Where is this enemy?
765 LYSISTRATA: Over there, by Deméter's shrine.
CHORAGOS ᵂ: Damned if he isn't. But who *is* he?

---

⁷⁶³ Kyprian Queen Aphrodite

MYRRHINE: My husband.
Kinesias.
LYSISTRATA: Oh then, get busy! Tease him!
Undermine him!
Wreck him! Give him everything—kissing, tickling, nudging,
whatever you generally torture him with—: give him everything
except what we swore on the wine we would not give. 770
MYRRHINE: Trust me!
LYSISTRATA: I do. But I'll help you get him started.
The rest of you women, stay back.

[Enter KINESIAS]

KINESIAS: Oh God! Oh my God!
I'm stiff for lack of exercise. All I can do to stand up!
LYSISTRATA: Halt! Who are you, approaching our lines?
KINESIAS: Me? I.
LYSISTRATA: A man?
KINESIAS: You have eyes, haven't you?
LYSISTRATA: Go away. 775
KINESIAS: Who says so?
LYSISTRATA: Officer of the Day.
KINESIAS: Officer, I beg you,
by all the gods at once, bring Myrrhinê out!
LYSISTRATA: Myrrhinê? And who, my good sir, are you?
KINESIAS: Kinesias. Last name's Pennison. Her husband.
LYSISTRATA: Oh, of course. I beg your pardon. We're glad to see you. 780
We've heard so much about you. Dearest Myrrhinê
is always talking about 'Kinesias'—never nibbles an egg
or an apple without saying
'Here's to Kinesias!'
KINESIAS: Do you really mean it?
LYSISTRATA: I do.
When we're discussing men, she always says, 785
'Well, after all, there's nobody like Kinesias!'
KINESIAS: Good God.—Well, then, please send her down here.
LYSISTRATA: And what do *I* get out of it?
KINESIAS: A standing promise.
LYSISTRATA: I'll take it up with her.

[Exit LYSISTRATA]

KINESIAS: But be quick about it!
Lord, what's life without a wife? Can't eat. Can't sleep. 790

Every time I go home, the place is so empty, so
insufferably sad! Love's killing me! Oh,
hurry!

[Enter MANES, *a slave, with* KINESIAS' *baby; the voice
of* MYRRHINE *is heard off-stage.]*

MYRRHINE:
    But of course I love him! Adore him!—But no,
he hates love. No. I won't go down.

[Enter MYRRHINE, *above]*

KINESIAS: Myrrhinê!
795   Darlingest little Myrrhinê! Come down quick!
MYRRHINE: Certainly not.
KINESIAS: Not? But why, Myrrhinê?
MYRRHINE: Why? You don't need me.
KINESIAS: Need you? My God, *look* at me!
MYRRHINE: So long!

[Turns to go]

KINESIAS: Myrrhinê, Myrrhinê, Myrrhinê!
    If not for my sake, for our child!

[Pinches BABY*]*

              —All right, you: pipe up!
BABY: Mummie! Mummie! Mummie!
800 KINESIAS: You hear that?
    Pitiful, I call it. Six days now
    with never a bath; no food; enough to break your
      heart!
MYRRHINE: My darlingest child! What a father *you*
    acquired!
KINESIAS: At least come down for his sake!
MYRRHINE: I suppose I must.
    Oh, this mother business!

[Exit.]

805 KINESIAS: How pretty she is! And younger!
    She's so much nicer when she's bothered!

*[*MYRRHINE *enters, below]*

MYRRHINE: Dearest child,
    you're as sweet as your father's horrid. Give me a
    kiss.
KINESIAS: Now you see how wrong it was to get
    involved
    in this scheming League of women. All this agony
    for nothing!
MYRRHINE: Keep your hands to yourself!
810 KINESIAS: But our house
    going to rack and ruin?
MYRRHINE: *I* don't care.
KINESIAS: And your knitting

all torn to pieces by the chickens? Don't you care?
MYRRHINE: Not at all.
KINESIAS: And our vows to Aphroditê?
    Oh, *won't* you come back?
MYRRHINE: No.—At least, not until you men
    make a treaty to end the war.
KINESIAS: Why, if that's all you want, 815
    by God, we'll make your treaty!
MYRRHINE: Oh? Very well.
    When you've done that, I'll come home. But
      meanwhile,
    I've sworn an oath.
KINESIAS: Don't worry.—Now, let's have fun.
MYRRHINE: No! Stop it! I said no!
              —Although, of course,
    I *do* love you.
KINESIAS: I know you do. Darling Myrrhinê: 820
    come, shall we?
MYRRHINE: Are you out of your mind?
                In front of the child?
KINESIAS:
    Take him home, Manês.

[Exit MANES *with baby]*

           There. He's gone.
                      Come on!
    There's nothing to stop us now.
MYRRHINE: You devil! But where?
KINESIAS: In Pan's cave. What could be snugger than
    that?
MYRRHINE: But my purification before I go back to
    the Citadel? 825
KINESIAS: There's always the Klepsydra.°
MYRRHINE: And my oath?
KINESIAS: Leave the oath to me.
    After all, I'm the man.
MYRRHINE: Well . . . if you say so!
                I'll go find a bed.
KINESIAS: Oh, bother a bed! The ground's good
    enough for me!
MYRRHINE: No. You're a bad man, but you deserve
    something better than dirt.

[Exit MYRRHINE*]*

KINESIAS: What a love she is! And how thoughtful!

[Re-enter MYRRHINE*]*

MYRRHINE: Here's your bed. 830
    Now let me get my clothes off.
                But, good horrors!
    We haven't a mattress!

---

[826] **klepsydra** a sacred spring beneath the walls of the
Acropolis. The suggestion has overtones of blasphemy.

KINESIAS: Oh, forget the mattress!
MYRRHINE: No.
    Just lying on blankets? Too sordid!
KINESIAS: Give me a kiss.
MYRRHINE: Just a second.

[Exit MYRRHINE*]*

KINESIAS: I swear, I'll explode!

[Re-enter MYRRHINE*]*

MYRRHINE: Here's your mattress.
    Go to bed now. I'll just take my dress off.
835   But look—
    where's our pillow?
KINESIAS: I don't need a pillow!
MYRRHINE: Well, *I* do.

[Exit MYRRHINE*]*

KINESIAS:
    I don't suppose even Heraklês
    would stand for this!

[Re-enter MYRRHINE*]*

MYRRHINE: There we are. Ups-a-daisy!
KINESIAS: So we are. Well, come to bed.
MYRRHINE: But I wonder:
    is everything ready now?
840   KINESIAS: I can swear to that. Come, darling!
MYRRHINE: Just getting out of my girdle.
                        But remember, now,
    what you promised about the treaty!
KINESIAS: I'll remember.
MYRRHINE: But no coverlet!
KINESIAS: Damn it, I'll be
    your coverlet!
MYRRHINE: Be right back.

[Exit MYRRHINE*]*

KINESIAS: This girl and her coverlets
    will be the death of me.

[Re-enter MYRRHINE*]*

845   MYRRHINE: Here we are. Up you go!
KINESIAS: Up? I've been up for ages!
MYRRHINE: Some perfume?
KINESIAS: No, by Apollo!
MYRRHINE: Yes, by Aphroditê!
    I don't care whether you want it or not.

[Exit MYRRHINE*]*

KINESIAS: For love's sake, hurry!

[Re-enter MYRRHINE*]*

MYRRHINE: Here, in your hand. Rub it right in.
KINESIAS: Never cared for perfume.   850
    And this is particularly strong. Still, here goes!
MYRRHINE: What a nitwit I am! I brought you the
    Rhodian bottle!
KINESIAS: Forget it.
MYRRHINE: No trouble at all. You just wait here.

[Exit MYRRHINE*]*

KINESIAS: God damn the man who invented per-
    fume!

[Re-enter MYRRHINE*]*

MYRRHINE: At last! The right bottle!
KINESIAS: I've got the rightest   855
    bottle of all, and it's right here waiting for you.
    Darling, forget everything else. Do come to bed!
MYRRHINE: Just let me get my shoes off.
                    —And, by the way,
    you'll vote for the treaty?
KINESIAS: I'll think about it.

*[*MYRRHINE *runs away]*

    There! That's done it! Off she runs,   860
    with never a thought for the way I'm feeling. I
        must
    have *some*one, or I'll go mad! Myrrhinê
    has just about ruined me.
                    And you, strutting little soldier:
    what about you? There's nothing for it, I guess,
    but an expedition to old Dog-fox's bordello.   865
CHORUS ᵐ: She's left you in a sorry state:
            You have my sympathy.
        What upright citizen could bear
            Your pain? I swear, not I!
Just the look of you, with never a woman   870
    To come to your aid! It isn't human!
KINESIAS: The agony!
CHORAGOS ᵐ: Well, why not?
        She has you on the spot!
CHORAGOS ʷ: A lovelier girl never breathed, you old
        sot!
KINESIAS: A lovelier girl? Zeus! Zeus!   875
            Produce a hurricane
        To hoist these lovely girls aloft
            And drop them down again
    Bump on our lances! Then they'd know
    What they do that makes men suffer so.   880

[Exit KINESIAS*]*

Scene 4

[Enter a SPARTAN HERALD*]*

HERALD: Gentlemen, Ah beg you will be so kind
    as to direct me to the Central Committee.
    Ah have a communication.

[Re-enter MAGISTRATE*]*

MAGISTRATE: Are you a man,
    or a fertility symbol?
HERALD: Ah refuse to answer that question!
    Ah'm a certified herald from Spahta, and Ah've
885   come
    to talk about an ahmistice.
MAGISTRATE: Then why
    that spear under your cloak?
HERALD: Ah have no speah!
MAGISTRATE: You don't walk naturally, with your
    tunic
    poked out so. You have a tumor, maybe,
    or a hernia?
HERALD: No, by Kastor!
890 MAGISTRATE: Well,
    something's wrong, I can see that. And I don't
    like it.
HERALD: Colonel, Ah resent this.
MAGISTRATE: So I see. But what *is* it?
HERALD: A scroll
    with a message from Spahta.
MAGISTRATE: Oh. I've heard about these scrolls.
    Well, then, man, speak out: How are things in
    Sparta?
895 HERALD: Hard, Colonel, hard! We're at a standstill.
    Can't seem to think of anything but women.
MAGISTRATE: How curious! Tell me, do you Spartans
    think
    that maybe Pan's to blame?
HERALD: Pan? No. Lampitô and her little naked friends.
900   They won't let a man come near them.
MAGISTRATE: How are you handling it?
HERALD: Losing our minds,
    if you want to know, and walking around
      hunched over
    like men carrying candles in a gale.
    The women have sworn they'll have nothing to
      do with us
    until we get a treaty.
905 MAGISTRATE: Yes. I know.
    It's a general uprising, sir, in all parts of Greece.
    But as for the answer—
                Sir: go back to Sparta
    and have them send us your Armistice
      Commission.
    I'll arrange things in Athens.
                And I may say
    that my standing is good enough to make them
910   listen.
HERALD: A man after mah own heart! Sir, Ah thank
    you!

[Exit HERALD*]*

CHORAL EPISODE

STROPHE

CHORUS ᵐ: Oh these women! Where will you find
    A slavering beast that's more unkind?
      Where a hotter fire?
    Give me a panther, any day!   915
    He's not so merciless as they,
      And panthers don't conspire!

ANTISTROPHE

CHORUS ʷ: We may be hard, you silly old ass,
    But who brought you to this stupid pass?
      You're the ones to blame.   920
    Fighting with us, your oldest friends,
    Simply to serve your selfish ends—
      Really, you have no shame!
CHORAGOS ᵐ: No, I'm through with women for ever!
CHORAGOS ʷ: If you say so.
    Still, you might put some clothes on. You look
      too absurd   925
    standing around naked. Come, get into this cloak.
CHORAGOS ᵐ: Thank you; you're right. I merely took
    it off
    because I was in such a temper.
CHORAGOS ʷ: That's much better
    Now you resemble a man again.
                Why have you been so horrid?
    And look: there's some sort of insect in your eye! 930
    Shall I take it out?
CHORAGOS ᵐ: An insect, is it? So that's
    what's been bothering me! Lord, yes: take it out!
CHORAGOS ʷ: You might be more polite.
                —But, heavens!
    What an enormous gnat!
CHORAGOS ᵐ: You've saved my life.
    That gnat was drilling an artesian well   935
    in my left eye.
CHORAGOS ʷ: Let me wipe
    those tears away!—And now: one little kiss?
CHORAGOS ᵐ: Over my dead body!
CHORAGOS ʷ: You're so difficult!
CHORAGOS ᵐ: These impossible women! How they
    do get around us!
    The poet was right: Can't live with them, or
      without them!   940
    But let's be friends.
    And to celebrate, you might lead off with an Ode.

STROPHE

CHORUS ʷ: Let it never be said
      That my tongue is malicious:
      Both by word and by deed   945

I would set an example that's noble and gracious.
We've had sorrow and care
Till we're sick of the tune.
Is there anyone here
950 Who would like a small loan?
My purse is crammed,
As you'll soon find;
And you needn't pay me back if the Peace gets
signed!
I've invited to lunch
955 Some Karystian rips—
An esurient bunch,
But I've ordered a menu to water their lips!
I can still make soup
And slaughter a pig.
960 You're all coming, I hope?
But a bath first, I beg!
Walk right up
As though you owned the place,
And you'll get the front door slammed to in your
face!

Scene 5

[Enter SPARTAN AMBASSADOR, with entourage]

CHORAGOS ᵐ: The Commission has arrived from
Sparta.
965   How oddly
they're walking!
                         Gentlemen, welcome to Athens!
How is life in Lakonia?
AMBASSADOR: Need we discuss that?
Simply use your eyes.
CHORUS ᵐ: The poor man's right:
                   What a sight!
AMBASSADOR: Words fail me.
970 But come, gentlemen, call in your Commissioners,
and let's get down to a Peace.
CHORAGOS ᵐ: The state we're in! Can't bear
a stitch below the waist. It's a kind of pelvic
paralysis.
AN ATHENIAN:
                    Won't somebody call Lysistrata?
She has the answer.
A SPARTAN: Yes, there, look at him.
Same thing.
975   Seh, do y'all feel a certain strain
early in the morning?
ATHENIAN: I do, sir. It's worse than a strain.
A few more days, and there's nothing for us but
Kleisthenês,
that broken blossom!
CHORAGOS ᵐ: But you'd better get dressed again.
You know these prudes who go around Athens
with chisels,

looking for prominent statues.°
ATHENIAN: Sir, you are right.   980
SPARTAN: He certainly is! Ah'll put mah own clothes
back on.

[Enter ATHENIAN COMMISSIONERS]

AN ATHENIAN: They're no better off than we are!
            —Greetings, Lakonians!
SPARTAN: [*To one of his own group:*] Colonel, we got
dressed just in time. Ah sweah,
if they'd seen us the way we were, there'd have
been a new war
between the states.   985
ATHENIAN:
Call the meeting to order.
                    Now, Lakonians,
what's your proposal?
AMBASSADOR: We'd lahk to consider peace.
ATHENIAN: Good. That's on our minds, too.
                    —Summon Lysistrata.
We'll never get anywhere without her.
AMBASSADOR: Lysistrata?
Summon Lysis-*any*body! Only, summon!
CHORAGOS ᵐ: No need to summon: 990
here she is, herself.

[Enter LYSISTRATA]

                    Lysistrata! Lion of women!
This is your hour to be
hard and yielding, outspoken and sly, austere and
gentle. You see here
the best brains of Hellas (confused, I admit,   995
by your devious charming) met as one man
to turn the future over to you.
LYSISTRATA:
                    That's fair enough,
unless you men take it into your heads
to turn to each other instead of to me. But I'd
know
soon enough if you did!
            —Where is that goddess of Peace?   1000
Go, some of you: bring her here.

[Exeunt two SERVANTS]

                    And now,   1005
summon the Spartan Commission. Treat them
courteously:
our husbands have been lax in that respect.
Take them by the hand, women,

---

⁹⁷⁹ **prominent statues** Shortly before the Sicilian invasion,
vandals chiseled off the heads and the phalluses of these statues of Hermes. The vandalism was regarded as a foreboding
sign.

or by anything else, if they seem unwilling.
1005   —Spartans:
you stand here. Athenians: on this side. Now listen to me.

[Re-enter SERVANTS, *staggering under the weight of a more than life-size statue of a naked woman: this is* PEACE.*]*

I'm only a woman, I know; but I've a mind,
and I can distinguish between sense and foolishness.
I owe the first to my father; the rest
1010 to the local politicians. So much for that.
Now, then.
What I have to say concerns both sides in this war.
We are all Greeks.
Must I remind you of Thermopylai?°of Olympia?
1015 of Delphoi? names deep in all our hearts?
And yet you men go raiding through the country,
Greek killing Greek, storming down Greek cities—
and all the time the Barbarian across the sea
is waiting for his chance.—That's my first point.
AN ATHENIAN: Lord! I can hardly contain myself!
1020 LYSISTRATA: And you Spartans:
Was it so long ago that Perikleidês°
came here to beg our help? I can see him still,
his white face, his sombre gown. And what did he want?
An army from Athens! Messenia
1025 was at your heels, and the sea-god splitting your shores.
Well, Kimôn and his men,
four thousand infantry, marched out of here to save you.
What thanks do we get? You come back to murder us.
ATHENIAN: Can't trust a Spartan, Lysistrata!
A SPARTAN: Ah admit it.
When Ah look at those legs, Ah sweah Ah can't
1030 trust mahself!
LYSISTRATA: And you, men of Athens:
you might remember that bad time when we were down,
and an army came from Sparta
and sent Hippias and the Thessalians
1035 whimpering back to the hills. That was Sparta,
and only Sparta; without Sparta, we'd now be
cringing helots, not walking about like free men!

1014 **Thermopylai** the narrow pass where in 480 B.C. an army of 300 Spartans held off a vastly superior Persian army   1021 **Perikleidês** Spartan ambassador to Athens who successfully urged Athenian aid to Sparta to put down a revolt

[From this point, the male responses are less to LYSISTRATA *than to the statue of* PEACE.*]*

A SPARTAN: An eloquent speech!
AN ATHENIAN: An elegant construction!
LYSISTRATA: Why are we fighting each other? Why not make peace?
AMBASSADOR: Spahta is ready, ma'am,   1040
so long as we get that place back.
LYSISTRATA: Place? What place?
AMBASSADOR: Ah refer to Pylos.
MAGISTRATE: Not while I'm alive, by God!
LYSISTRATA: You'd better give in.
MAGISTRATE: But—what were we fighting about?
LYSISTRATA: Lots of places left.
MAGISTRATE: All right. Well, then:
Hog Island first, and that gulf behind there, and the land between   1045
the Legs of Megara.
AMBASSADOR: Mah government objects.
LYSISTRATA: Over-ruled. Why fuss about a pair of legs?

[General assent; the statue of PEACE *is removed]*

AN ATHENIAN: Let's take off our clothes and plow our fields.
A SPARTAN: Ah'll fertilize mahn first, by the Heavenly Twins!
LYSISTRATA: And so you shall,   1050
once we have peace. If you are serious,
go, both of you, and talk with your allies.
ATHENIAN: Too much talk already. We'll stand together!
We've only one end in view. All that we want
is our women: and I speak for our allies.   1055
AMBASSADOR: Mah government concurs.
ATHENIAN: So does Karystos.
LYSISTRATA: Good.—But before you come inside
to join your wives at supper, you must perform
the usual lustration. Then we'll open
our baskets for you, and all that we have is yours. 1060
But you must promise upright good behavior
from this day on. Then each man home with his woman!
ATHENIAN: Let's get it over with!
SPARTAN: Lead on: Ah follow!
ATHENIAN: Quick as a cat can wink!

[Exeunt all but the CHORUSES*]*

ANTISTROPHE

CHORUS ᵂ: Embroideries ánd   1065
        Twinkling ornaments ánd
        Pretty dresses—I hand
Them all over to you, and with never a qualm.
        They'll be nice for your daughters
        On festival days   1070
        When the girls bring the Goddess

The ritual prize.
Come in, one and all:
Take what you will.
I've nothing here so tightly corked that you can't
1075   make it spill!
You may search my house,
But you'll not find
The least thing of use,
Unless your two eyes are keener than mine.
1080   Your numberless brats
Are half starved? and your slaves?
Courage, grandpa! I've lots
Of grain left, and big loaves.
I'll fill your guts,
1085   I'll go the whole hog;
But if you come too close to me, remember: 'ware
the dog!

[Exeunt CHORUSES*]*

ÉXODOS

[An ATHENIAN DRUNKARD *approaches the gate and is
halted by a* SENTRY*]*

DRUNKARD: Open. The. Door.
SENTRY: Now, friend, just shove along!
So you want to sit down! If it weren't such an old
joke,
I'd tickle your tail with this torch. Just the sort of
thing
that this kind of audience appreciates.
1090   DRUNKARD: I. Stay. Right. Here.
SENTRY: Oh, all right. But you'll see some funny sights!
DRUNKARD: Bring. Them. On.
SENTRY: No, what am I thinking of?
The gentlemen from Sparta are just coming back
from supper.
Get out of here, or I'll scalp you!

[Exit DRUNKARD; *the general company re-enters; the
two* CHORUSES *now represent* SPARTANS *and*
ATHENIANS.*]*

MAGISTRATE: I must say,
I've never tasted a better meal. And those
1095   Lakonians!
They're gentlemen, by the Lord! Just goes to
show:
a drink to the wise is sufficient. And why not?
A sober man's an ass.
Men of Athens, mark my words: the only efficient
1100   Ambassador's a drunk Ambassador. Is that clear?
Look: we go to Sparta,
and when we get there we're dead sober. The
result?

Everyone cackling at everyone else. They make
speeches;
and even if we understand, we get it all wrong
when we file our reports in Athens. But today—!   1105
Everybody's happy. Couldn't tell the difference
between *Drink to Me Only* and
the *Star Spangled Athens.*
                    What's a few lies,
washed down in good strong drink?

[Re-enter DRUNKARD*]*

SENTRY:
                    God almighty,
he's back again!
DRUNKARD:
                    I. Resume. My. Place.   1110
A SPARTAN: [*To an* ATHENIAN:] I beg you, seh,
take your instrument in your hand and play for us.
Ah'm told
you understand the in*tri*cacies of the floot?
Ah'd lahk to execute a song and dance   1115
in honor of Athens,
                    and, of course, of Spahta.
DRUNKARD: Toot. On. Your. Flute.

*[The following song is a solo—an aria—accompanied by
the flute. The* CHORUS OF SPARTANS *begins a slow dance.]*

CHORAGOS [s]: Mnemosynê,
Inspire once more the Grecian Muse
To sing of glory glory glory without end.   1120
Sing Artemesion's shore,
Where Athens fluttered the Persian fleet—
Alalaí, that great
Victory! Sing Leonidas and his men,
Those wild boars, sweat and blood   1125
Down in a red drench. Then, then
The barbarians broke, though they had stood
A myriad strong before!
                    O Artemis,
Virgin Goddess, whose darts
Flash in our forests: approve   1130
This pact of peace, and join our hearts,
From this day on, in love.
Huntress, descend!
LYSISTRATA: All that will come in time.
                    But now, Lakonians,
take home your wives. Athenians, take yours.   1135
Each man be kind to his woman; and you,
women,
be equally kind. Never again, pray God,
shall we lose our way in such madness.
                    —And now
let's dance our joy!

[From this point the dance becomes general]

CHORUS OF ATHENIANS:
    Dance!
                    Dance!
1140   Dance, you Graces!
        Artemis, dance!
                        Dance, Phoibos, Lord of dancing!
        Dance, Dionysos, in a scurry of Maenads!°
                                Dance, Zeus Thunderer!
                    Dance, Lady Herê,°
        Queen of the Sky!
                                Dance, dance, all you gods!
1145   Dance for the dearest, the bringer of peace,
        Deathless Aphroditê!
LYSISTRATA:
    Now let us have another song from Sparta.
CHORUS OF SPARTANS:
            From Taÿgetos'° skyey summit,
            Lakonian Muse, come down!
1150   Sing the glories of Apollo,
                Regent of Amyklai° Town.
                Sing of Leda's Twins,°
                Those gallant sons,
                On the banks of Eurotas—
1155   *Alalaí Evohé*!
        Here's to our girls
            With their tangling curls,
                Lets a-wriggle,
                Bellies a-jiggle,
1160   A riot of hair,
                A fury of feet,
        Evohé! Evohaí! Evohé!
                            as they pass
            Dancing,
                    dancing,
                            dancing,
                                to greet
        Athenê of the House of Brass!

1142 Maenads ecstatic women in the train of Dionysus, god of wine   **1143 Herê** wife of Zeus   **1148 Taÿgetos** a mountain range in Lakonia, near Sparta   **1151 Amyklai** a town in Lakonia, the center of the cult of Phoebus Apollo   **1152 Leda's Twins** Raped by Zeus in the form of a swan, Leda gave birth to quadruplets: Helen and Klytainestra and two sons, Kastor and Polydeukes.   **1164 Athenê of the House of Brass** a temple standing on the Akropolis of Sparta

CONTEXTS AND COMMENTARIES

Aristotle (384–322 B.C.)

Aristotle was born in Macedonia and studied with Plato in Athens. After Plato's death Aristotle became tutor to the young Alexander the Great in Macedonia. When he returned to Athens he founded his school, the Lyceum, in 355 B.C. Aristotle lectured extensively on a wide range of topics from rhetoric to politics, from natural history to art, from metaphysics to ethics. The *Poetics*, one of the most important documents on aesthetics in Western tradition, was a lecture written sometime after 355 B.C., about a century after the theater in Athens had reached it zenith. Aristotle looks back as what playwrights actually did in order to formulate his ideas about drama.

THE POETICS OF ARISTOTLE

TRANSLATED BY S. H. BUTCHER

Comedy is, as we have said, an imitation of characters of a lower type—not, however, in the full sense of the word bad, the Ludicrous being merely a subdivision of the ugly. It consists in some defect or ugliness which is not painful or destructive. To take an obvious example, the comic mask is ugly and distorted, but does not imply pain.

The successive changes through which Tragedy passed, and the authors of these changes, are well known, whereas Comedy has had no history, because it was not at first treated seriously. It was late before the Archon granted a comic chorus to a poet; the performers were till then voluntary. Comedy had already taken definite shape when comic poets, distinctively so called, are heard of. Who furnished it with masks, or prologues, or increased the number of actors—these and other similar details remain unknown. As for the plot, it came originally from Sicily; but of Athenian writers Crates was the first who, abandoning the 'iambic' or lampooning form, generalised his themes and plots.

Epic poetry agrees with Tragedy in so far as it is an imitation in verse of characters of a higher type. They differ, in that Epic poetry admits but one kind of metre, and is narrative in form. They differ, again, in their length: for Tragedy endeavours, as far as possible, to confine itself to a single revolution of the sun, or but slightly to exceed this limit; whereas the Epic action has no limits of time. This, then, is a second point of difference; though at first the same freedom was admitted in Tragedy as in Epic poetry.

118

4   Of their constituent parts some are common to both, some peculiar to Tragedy: whoever, therefore, knows what is good or bad Tragedy, knows also about Epic poetry. All the elements of an Epic poem are found in Tragedy, but the elements of a Tragedy are not all found in the Epic poem.

5   Of the poetry which imitates in hexameter verse, and of Comedy, we will speak hereafter. Let us now discuss Tragedy, resuming its formal definition, as resulting from what has been already said.

Tragedy, then, is an imitation of an action that is serious, complete, and of a certain magnitude; in language embellished with each kind of artistic ornament, the several kinds being found in separate parts of the play; in the form of action, not of narrative; through pity and fear effecting the proper purgation of these emotions. By 'language embellished,' I mean language into which rhythm, 'harmony,' and song enter. By 'the several kinds in separate parts,' I mean, that some parts are rendered through the medium of verse alone, others again with the aid of song.

Now as tragic imitation implies persons acting, it necessarily follows, in the first place, that Spectacular equipment will be a part of Tragedy. Next, Song and Diction, for these are the medium of imitation. By 'Diction' I mean the mere metrical arrangement of the words: as for 'Song,' it is a term whose sense every one understands.

Again, Tragedy is the imitation of an action; and an action implies personal agents, who necessarily possess certain distinctive qualities both of character and thought; for it is by these that we qualify actions themselves, and these—thought and character—are the two natural causes from which actions spring, and on actions again all success or failure depends. Hence, the Plot is the imitation of the action:—for by plot I here mean the arrangement of the incidents. By Character I mean that in virtue of which we ascribe certain qualities to the agents. Thought is required wherever a statement is proved, or, it may be, a general truth enunciated. Every Tragedy, therefore, must have six parts, which parts determine its quality—namely, Plot, Character, Diction, Thought, Spectacle, Song. Two of the parts constitute the medium of imitation, one the manner, and three the objects of imitation. And these complete the list. These elements have been employed, we may say, by the poets to a man; in fact, every play contains Spectacular elements as well as Character, Plot, Diction, Song, and Thought.

But most important of all is the structure of the incidents. For Tragedy is an imitation, not of men, but of an action and of life, and life consists in action, and its end is a mode of action, not a quality. Now character determines men's qualities, but it is by their actions that they are happy or the reverse. Dramatic action, therefore, is not with a view to the representation of character: character comes in as subsidiary to the actions. Hence the incidents and the plot are the end of a tragedy; and the end is the chief thing of all. Again, without action there cannot be a tragedy; there may be without character. The tragedies of most of our modern poets fail in the rendering of character; and of poets in general this is often true. It is the same in painting; and here lies the difference between Zeuxis and Polygnotus. Polygnotus delineates character well: the style of Zeuxis is devoid of ethical quality. Again, if you string together a set of speeches expressive of character, and well finished in point of diction and thought, you will not produce the essential tragic effect nearly so well as with a play which, however deficient in these respects, yet has a plot and artistically constructed incidents. Besides which, the most powerful elements of emotional interest in Tragedy—Peripeteia or Reversal of the Situation, and Recognition scenes—are parts of the plot. A further proof is, that novices in the art attain to finish of diction and precision of portraiture before they can construct the plot. It is the same with almost all the early poets.

The Plot, then, is the first principle, and, as it were, the soul of a tragedy: Character holds the second place. A similar fact is seen in painting. The most beautiful colours, laid on confusedly, will not give as much pleasure as the chalk outline of a portrait. Thus Tragedy is the imitation of an action, and of the agents mainly with a view to the action.

Third in order is Thought—that is, the faculty of saying what is possible and pertinent in given circumstances. In the case of oratory, this is the function of the political art and of the art of rhetoric: and so indeed the older poets make their characters speak the language of civic life; the poets of our time, the language of the rhetoricians. Character is that which reveals moral purpose, showing what kind of things a man chooses or avoids. Speeches, therefore, which do not make this manifest, or in which the speaker does not choose or avoid anything whatever, are not expressive of character. Thought, on the other hand, is found where something is proved to be or not to be, or a general maxim is enunciated.

Fourth among the elements enumerated comes Diction; by which I mean, as has been already said, the expression of the meaning in words; and its essence is the same both in verse and prose.

Of the remaining elements Song holds the chief place among the embellishments.

The Spectacle has, indeed, an emotional attraction of its own, but, of all the parts, it is the least artistic, and connected least with the art of poetry. For the power of Tragedy, we may be sure, is felt even apart from representation and actors. Besides, the production of spectacular effects depends more on the art of the stage machinist than on that of the poet.

These principles being established, let us now discuss the proper structure of the Plot, since this is the first and most important thing in Tragedy.

Now, according to our definition, Tragedy is an imitation of an action that is complete, and whole, and of a certain magnitude; for there may be a whole that is wanting in magnitude. A whole is that which has a beginning, a middle, and an end. A beginning is that which does not itself follow anything by causal necessity, but after which something naturally is or comes to be. An end, on the contrary, is that which itself naturally follows some other thing, either by necessity, or as a rule, but has nothing following it. A middle is that which follows something as some other thing follows it. A well constructed plot, therefore, must neither begin nor end at haphazard, but conform to these principles.

Again, a beautiful object, whether it be a living organism or any whole composed of parts, must not only have an orderly arrangement of parts, but must also be of a certain magnitude; for beauty depends on magnitude and order. Hence a very small animal organism cannot be beautiful; for the view of it is confused, the object being seen in an almost imperceptible moment of time. Nor, again, can one of vast size be beautiful; for as the eye cannot take it all in at once, the unity and sense of the whole is lost for the spectator; as for instance if there were one a thousand miles long. As, therefore, in the case of animate bodies and organisms a certain magnitude is necessary, and a magnitude which may be easily embraced in one view; so in the plot, a certain length is necessary, and a length which can be easily embraced by the memory. The limit of length in relation to dramatic competition and sensuous presentment, is no part of artistic theory. For had it been the rule for a hundred tragedies to compete together, the performance would have been regulated by the water-clock—as indeed we are told was formerly done. But the limit as fixed by the nature of the drama itself is this:—the greater the length, the more beautiful will the piece be by reason of its size, provided that the whole be perspicuous. And to define the matter roughly, we may say that the proper magnitude is comprised within such limits, that the sequence of events, according to the law of probability or necessity, will admit of a change from bad fortune to good, or from good fortune to bad.

Unity of plot does not, as some persons think, consist in the unity of the hero. For infinitely various are the incidents in one man's life which cannot be reduced to unity; and so, too, there are many actions of one man out of which we cannot make one action. Hence the error, as it appears, of all poets who have composed a Heracleid, a Theseid, or other poems of the kind. They imagine that as Heracles was one man, the story of Heracles must also be a unity. But Homer, as in all else he is of surpassing merit, here too—whether from art or natural genius—seems to have happily discerned the truth. In composing the Odyssey he did not include all the adventures of Odysseus—such as his wound on Parnassus, or his feigned madness at the mustering of the host—incidents between which there was no necessary or probable connexion: but he made the Odyssey, and likewise the Iliad, to centre round an action that in our sense of the word is one. As therefore, in the other imitative arts, the imitation is one when the object imitated is one, so the plot, being an imitation of an action, must imitate one action and that a whole, the structural union of the parts being such that, if any one of them is displaced or removed, the whole will be disjointed and disturbed. For a thing whose presence or absence makes no visible difference, is not an organic part of the whole.

It is, moreover, evident from what has been said, that it is not the function of the poet to relate what has happened, but what may happen—what is possible according to the law of probability or necessity. The poet and the historian differ not by writing in verse or in prose. The work of Herodotus might be put into verse, and it would still be a species of history, with metre no less than without it. The true difference is that one relates what has happened, the other what may happen. Poetry, therefore, is a more philosophical and a higher thing than history: for poetry tends to express the universal, history the particular. By the universal I mean how a person of a certain type will on occasion speak or act, according to the law of probability or necessity; and it is this universality at which poetry aims in the names she attaches to the personages. The particular is—for example—what Alcibiades did or suffered. In Comedy this is already apparent: for here the poet first constructs the plot on the lines of probability, and then inserts characteristic names;—unlike the lampooners who write about particular individuals. But tragedians still keep to real names, the reason being that what is possible is credible: what has not happened we do not at once feel sure to be possible: but what has happened is manifestly possible: otherwise it would not have happened. Still there are even some tragedies in which there are only one or two well known names, the rest being fictitious. In others, none are well known—as in Agathon's Antheus, where incidents and names alike are fictitious, and yet they give none the less pleasure. We must not, therefore, at all costs keep to the received legends, which are the usual subjects of Tragedy. Indeed, it would be absurd to attempt it; for even subjects that are known are known only to a few, and yet give pleasure to all. It clearly follows that the poet or 'maker' should be the maker of plots rather than of verses; since he is a poet because he imitates, and what he imitates are actions. And even if he chances to take an historical subject, he is none the less a poet; for there is no reason why some events that have actually happened should not conform to the law of the probable and possible, and in virtue of that quality in them he is their poet or maker.

Of all plots and actions the epeisodic are the worst. I call a plot 'epeisodic' in which the episodes or acts succeed one another without probable or necessary sequence. Bad poets compose such pieces by their own fault, good poets, to please the players; for, as they write show pieces for competition, they stretch the plot beyond its capacity, and are often forced to break the natural continuity.

But again, Tragedy is an imitation not only of a complete action, but of events inspiring fear or pity. Such an effect is best produced when the events come on us by surprise; and the effect is heightened when, at the same time, they follow as cause and effect. The tragic wonder will then be greater than if they happened of themselves or by accident; for even coincidences are most striking when they have an air of design. We may instance the statue of Mitys at Argos, which fell upon his murderer while he was a spectator at a festival, and killed him. Such events seem not to be due to mere chance. Plots, therefore, constructed on these principles are necessarily the best.

Plots are either Simple or Complex, for the actions in real life, of which the plots are an imitation, obviously show a similar distinction. An action which is one and continuous in the sense above defined, I call Simple, when the change of fortune takes place without Reversal of the Situation and without Recognition.

A Complex action is one in which the change is accompanied by such Reversal, or by Recognition, or by both. These last should arise from the internal structure of the plot, so that what follows should be the necessary or probable result of the preceding action. It makes all the difference whether any given event is a case of *propter hoc* or *post hoc*.

Reversal of the Situation is a change by which the action veers round to its opposite, subject always to our rule of probability or necessity. Thus in the Oedipus, the messenger comes to cheer Oedipus and free him from his alarms about his mother, but by revealing who he is, he produces the opposite effect. Again in the Lynceus, Lynceus is being led away to his death, and Danaus goes with him, meaning to slay him; but the outcome of the preceding incidents is that Danaus is killed and Lynceus saved.

Recognition, as the name indicates, is a change from ignorance to knowledge, producing love or hate between the persons destined by the poet for good or bad fortune. The best form of recognition is coincident with a Reversal of the

Situation, as in the Oedipus. There are indeed other forms. Even inanimate things of the most trivial kind may in a sense be objects of recognition. Again, we may recognise or discover whether a person has done a thing or not. But the recognition which is most intimately connected with the plot and action is, as we have said, the recognition of persons. This recognition, combined with Reversal, will produce either pity or fear; and actions producing these effects are those which, by our definition, Tragedy represents. Moreover, it is upon such situations that the issues of good or bad fortune will depend. Recognition, then, being between persons, it may happen that one person only is recognised by the other—when the latter is already known—or it may be necessary that the recognition should be on both sides. Thus Iphigenia is revealed to Orestes by the sending of the letter; but another act of recognition is required to make Orestes known to Iphigenia.

Two parts, then, of the Plot—Reversal of the Situation and Recognition—turn upon surprises. A third part is the Scene of Suffering. The Scene of Suffering is a destructive or painful action, such as death on the stage, bodily agony, wounds and the like.

[The parts of Tragedy which must be treated as elements of the whole have been already mentioned. We now come to the quantitative parts—the separate parts into which Tragedy is divided—namely, Prologue, Episode, Exode, Choric song; this last being divided into Parode and Stasimon. These are common to all plays: peculiar to some are the songs of actors from the stage and the Commoi.

The Prologue is that entire part of a tragedy which precedes the Parode of the Chorus. The Episode is that entire part of a tragedy which is between complete choric songs. The Exode is that entire part of a tragedy which has no choric song after it. Of the Choric part the Parode is the first undivided utterance of the Chorus: the Stasimon is a Choric ode without anapaests or trochaic tetrameters: the Commos is a joint lamentation of Chorus and actors. The parts of Tragedy which must be treated as elements of the whole have been already mentioned. The quantitative parts—the separate parts into which it is divided—are here enumerated.][1]

As the sequel to what has already been said, we must proceed to consider what the poet should aim at, and what he should avoid, in constructing his plots; and by what means the specific effect of Tragedy will be produced.

A perfect tragedy should, as we have seen, be arranged not on the simple but on the complex plan. It should, moreover, imitate actions which excite pity and fear, this being the distinctive mark of tragic imitation. It follows plainly, in the first place, that the change of fortune presented must not be the spectacle of a virtuous man brought from prosperity to adversity: for this moves neither pity nor fear; it merely shocks us. Nor, again, that of a bad man passing from adversity to prosperity: for nothing can be more alien to the spirit of Tragedy; it possesses no single tragic quality; it neither satisfies the moral sense nor calls forth pity or fear. Nor, again, should the downfall of the utter villain be exhibited. A plot of this kind would, doubtless, satisfy the moral sense, but it would inspire neither pity nor fear; for pity is aroused by unmerited misfortune, fear by the misfortune of a man like ourselves. Such an event, therefore, will be neither piti-

---

[1] This section is defective in the Greek text.

ful nor terrible. There remains, then, the character between these two extremes—that of a man who is not eminently good and just, yet whose misfortune is brought about not by vice or depravity, but by some error or frailty. He must be one who is highly renowned and prosperous—a personage like Oedipus, Thyestes, or other illustrious men of such families.

A well constructed plot should, therefore, be single in its issue, rather than double as some maintain. The change of fortune should be not from bad to good, but, reversely, from good to bad. It should come about as the result not of vice, but of some great error or frailty, in a character either such as we have described, or better rather than worse. The practice of the stage bears out our view. At first the poets recounted any legend that came in their way. Now, the best tragedies are founded on the story of a few houses—on the fortunes of Alcmaeon, Oedipus, Orestes, Meleager, Thyestes, Telephus, and those others who have done or suffered something terrible. A tragedy, then, to be perfect according to the rules of art should be of this construction. Hence they are in error who censure Euripides just because he follows this principle in his plays, many of which end unhappily. It is, as we have said, the right ending. The best proof is that on the stage and in dramatic competition, such plays, if well worked out, are the most tragic in effect; and Euripides, faulty though he may be in the general management of his subject, yet is felt to be the most tragic of the poets.

In the second rank comes the kind of tragedy which some place first. Like the Odyssey, it has a double thread of plot, and also an opposite catastrophe for the good and for the bad. It is accounted the best because of the weakness of the spectators; for the poet is guided in what he writes by the wishes of his audience. The pleasure, however, thence derived is not the true tragic pleasure. It is proper rather to Comedy, where those who, in the piece, are the deadliest enemies—like Orestes and Aegisthus—quit the stage as friends at the close, and no one slays or is slain.

Fear and pity may be aroused by spectacular means; but they may also result from the inner structure of the piece, which is the better way, and indicates a superior poet. For the plot ought to be so constructed that, even without the aid of the eye, he who hears the tale told will thrill with horror and melt to pity at what takes place. This is the impression we should receive from hearing the story of the Oedipus. But to produce this effect by the mere spectacle is a less artistic method, and dependent on extraneous aids. Those who employ spectacular means to create a sense not of the terrible but only of the monstrous, are strangers to the purpose of Tragedy; for we must not demand of Tragedy any and every kind of pleasure, but only that which is proper to it. And since the pleasure which the poet should afford is that which comes from pity and fear through imitation, it is evident that this quality must be impressed upon the incidents.

Let us then determine what are the circumstances which strike us as terrible or pitiful.

Actions capable of this effect must happen between persons who are either friends or enemies or indifferent to one another. If an enemy kills an enemy, there is nothing to excite pity either in the act or the intention—except so far as the suffering in itself is pitiful. So again with indifferent persons. But when the tragic incident occurs between those who are near or dear to one another—if, for example, a brother kills, or intends to kill, a brother, a son his father, a mother her son, a son his mother, or any other deed of the kind is done—these are the situations to be looked for by the poet. He may not indeed destroy the framework of the received legends—the fact, for instance, that Clytemnestra was slain by Orestes and Eriphyle by Alcmaeon—but he ought to show invention of his own, and skilfully handle the traditional material. Let us explain more clearly what is meant by skilful handling.

The action may be done consciously and with knowledge of the persons, in the manner of the older poets. It is thus too that Euripides makes Medea slay her children. Or, again, the deed of horror may be done, but done in ignorance, and the tie of kinship or friendship be discovered afterwards. The Oedipus of Sophocles is an example. Here, indeed, the incident is outside the drama proper; but cases occur where it falls within the action of the play: one may cite the Alcmaeon of Astydamas, or Telegonus in the Wounded Odysseus. Again, there is a third case—‹to be about to act with knowledge of the persons and then not to act. The fourth case is›[2] when some one is about to do an irreparable deed through ignorance, and makes the discovery before it is done. These are the only possible ways. For the deed must either be done or not done—and that wittingly or unwittingly. But of all these ways, to be about to act knowing the persons, and then not to act, is the worst. It is shocking without being tragic, for no disaster follows. It is, therefore, never, or very rarely, found in poetry. One instance, however, is in the Antigone, where Haemon threatens to kill Creon. The next and better way is that the deed should be perpetrated. Still better, that it should be perpetrated in ignorance, and the discovery made afterwards. There is then nothing to shock us, while the discovery produces a startling effect. The last case is the best, as when in the Cresphontes Merope is about to slay her son, but, recognising who he is, spares his life. So in the Iphigenia, the sister recognises the brother just in time. Again in the Helle, the son recognises the mother when on the point of giving her up. This, then, is why a few families only, as has been already observed, furnish the subjects of tragedy. It was not art, but happy chance, that led the poets in search of subjects to impress the tragic quality upon their plots. They are compelled, therefore, to have recourse to those houses whose history contains moving incidents like these.

Enough has now been said concerning the structure of the incidents, and the right kind of plot.

In respect of Character there are four things to be aimed at. First, and most important, it must be good. Now any speech or action that manifests moral purpose of any kind will be expressive of character: the character will be good if the purpose is good. This rule is relative to each class. Even a woman may be good, and also a slave; though the woman may be said to be an inferior being, and the slave quite worthless. The second thing to aim at is propriety. There is a type of manly valour; but valour in a woman, or unscrupulous cleverness, is inappropriate. Thirdly, character must be true to life: for this is a distinct thing from goodness and propriety, as here described. The fourth point is consistency: for though the subject of the imitation, who suggested the type, be inconsistent, still

---

[2] ‹to be . . . is› possibly a glossary note supplied by a later scribe.

he must be consistently inconsistent. As an example of motiveless degradation of character, we have Menelaus in the Orestes: of character indecorous and inappropriate, the lament of Odysseus in the Scylla, and the speech of Melanippe: of inconsistency, the Iphigenia at Aulis—for Iphigenia the suppliant in no way resembles her later self.

As in the structure of the plot, so too in the portraiture of character, the poet should always aim either at the necessary or the probable. Thus a person of a given character should speak or act in a given way, by the rule either of necessity or of probability; just as this event should follow that by necessary or probable sequence. It is therefore evident that the unravelling of the plot, no less than the complication, must arise out of the plot itself, it must not be brought about by the *Deus ex Machina*—as in the Medea, or in the Return of the Greeks in the Iliad. The *Deus ex Machina* should be employed only for events external to the drama—for antecedent or subsequent events, which lie beyond the range of human knowledge, and which require to be reported or foretold; for to the gods we ascribe the power of seeing all things. Within the action there must be nothing irrational. If the irrational cannot be excluded, it should be outside the scope of the tragedy. Such is the irrational element in the Oedipus of Sophocles.

Again, since Tragedy is an imitation of persons who are above the common level, the example of good portrait-painters should be followed. They, while reproducing the distinctive form of the original, make a likeness which is true to life and yet more beautiful. So too the poet, in representing men who are irascible or indolent, or have other defects of character, should preserve the type and yet ennoble it. In this way Achilles is portrayed by Agathon and Homer.

These then are rules the poet should observe. Nor should he neglect those appeals to the senses, which, though not among the essentials, are the concomitants of poetry; for here too there is much room for error. But of this enough has been said in our published treatises.

What Recognition is has been already explained. We will now enumerate its kinds.

First, the least artistic form, which, from poverty of wit, is most commonly employed—recognition by signs. Of these some are congenital—such as 'the spear which the earth-born race bear on their bodies,' or the stars introduced by Carcinus in his Thyestes. Others are acquired after birth; and of these some are bodily marks, as scars; some external tokens, as necklaces, or the little ark in the Tyro by which the discovery is effected. Even these admit of more or less skilful treatment. Thus in the recognition of Odysseus by his scar, the discovery is made in one way by the nurse, in another by the swineherds. The use of tokens for the express purpose of proof—and, indeed, any formal proof with or without tokens—is a less artistic mode of recognition. A better kind is that which comes about by a turn of incident, as in the Bath Scene in the Odyssey.

Next come the recognitions invented at will by the poet, and on that account wanting in art. For example, Orestes in the Iphigenia reveals the fact that he is Orestes. She, indeed, makes herself known by the letter; but he, by speaking himself, and saying what the poet, not what the plot requires. This, therefore, is nearly allied to the fault above mentioned:—for Orestes might as well have brought tokens with him. Another similar instance is the 'voice of the shuttle' in the Tereus of Sophocles.

The third kind depends on memory when the sight of some object awakens a feeling: as in the Cyprians of Dicaeogenes, where the hero breaks into tears on seeing the picture; or again in the 'Lay of Alcinous,' where Odysseus, hearing the minstrel play the lyre, recalls the past and weeps; and hence the recognition.

The fourth kind is by process of reasoning. Thus in the Choëphori:—'Some one resembling me has come: no one resembles me but Orestes: therefore Orestes has come.' Such too is the discovery made by Iphigenia in the play of Polyidus the Sophist. It was a natural reflexion for Orestes to make, 'So I too must die at the altar like my sister.' So, again, in the Tydeus of Theodectes, the father says, 'I came to find my son, and I lose my own life.' So too in the Phineidae: the women, on seeing the place, inferred their fate:—'Here we are doomed to die, for here we were cast forth.' Again, there is a composite kind of recognition involving false inference on the part of one of the characters, as in the Odysseus Disguised as a Messenger. A said ⟨that no one else was able to bend the bow; . . . hence B (the disguised Odysseus) imagined that A would⟩[3] recognise the bow which, in fact, he had not seen; and to bring about a recognition by this means—the expectation that A would recognise the bow—is false inference.

But, of all recognitions, the best is that which arises from the incidents themselves, where the startling discovery is made by natural means. Such is that in the Oedipus of Sophocles, and in the Iphigenia; for it was natural that Iphigenia should wish to dispatch a letter. These recognitions alone dispense with the artificial aid of tokens or amulets. Next come the recognitions by process of reasoning.

Oliver Taplin (b. 1943)

Scholar Oliver Taplin finds Gorgias' comments on the emotions aroused by drama helpful in illuminating some of Aristotle's observations. Taplin here gives attention to the notion that the emotional experience of the audience is essential to tragedy.

EMOTION AND MEANING IN GREEK TRAGEDY (1983)

. . . Gorgias'[1] own views are, I suggest, worth pursuing; and the following passage, which comes from his virtuoso apologia for Helen, surely has tragedy in mind. 'All poetry I consider and define as discourse in metre. There comes over the audience of poetry a fearful horror and tearful pity and doleful yearning. By

---

[3] ⟨that ... would⟩ possibly a glossary note supplied by a later scribe   [1] **Gorgias** Greek orator and rhetorician (ca. 483–376 B.C.).

means of the discourse their spirit feels a personal emotion on account of the good and bad fortune of others.' This passage alone should be enough to rescue Gorgias from the common slander that he was merely a word-juggler. Above all he sees that *emotions* are at the heart of tragic poetry. And what is more he has put his finger on one of the most vital and remarkable features of this experience: that the emotions are generous—altruistic almost—that we feel disturbed personally for *other* people, for people who have no direct connection with us and indeed belong to another world from ours. (What's Hecuba to us?) This outgoing emotion, as opposed to introverted self-absorption, is characteristic of Greek tragedy, and of most (perhaps all) great tragedy. This point is well brought home by the anecdote in Herodotus about Phrynichus, a contemporary of Aeschylus, who produced a tragedy about the sack of Miletus, a recent outrage on a city closely connected with Athens. Phrynichus, was prosecuted and fined for reminding the Athenians of their *own* troubles; this is not the playwright's function.

Can we characterize these tragic emotions? Gorgias' list is, I think, extraordinarily apt, and far more evocative than Aristotle's terse and derivative 'pity and fear' (*eleos kai phobos*). Literally Gorgias writes 'ultra-fearful shuddering and much-weeping pity and grief-loving longing'. The greatest of these is surely pity, however much Plato and Nietzsche may protest (how deluded Nietzsche was in claiming the Greeks as his authority for denouncing pity). We feel an overwhelming *compassion* for these other people who undergo the tribulations, pain and waste which are the stuff of tragedy. Yet this compassion is seldom if ever separable from other emotions. We pity Agamemnon, Oedipus, Agaue; yet at the same time we feel horror, alarm (*phrīkē*); and at the same time we *want* Agamemnon to be murdered, Oedipus to find out the truth, Agaue to recognize her son's head. We have a longing (*pothos*) which wants grief (*philopenthēs*): it is such sweet sorrow. I shall return to the paradoxical pleasure of these doleful feelings; the important new point for now is that the emotions of the tragic experience are *complex*, and they are of course ever-shifting. Perhaps, indeed, the better the tragedy, the more complex and labile the emotions it arouses. This may be why there are certain strong emotions which Greek tragedy does not as a rule subject us to, notably hatred and lust. These are domineering and single-minded obsessions which do not permit mental companions.

It seems to me, then, that Gorgias is right that tragedy is essentially the *emotional experience of its audience*. Whatever it tells us about the world is conveyed by means of these emotions. Plato agreed with Gorgias in this, but he disapproved of the process and regarded it as harmful. Aristotle agreed with him too, but, contrary to Plato, regarded it as beneficial and salutary. Plato's objection was that such emotions are not the province of the highest part of the soul, the intellectual part. This is the forefather of the error made by so many later critics who have not acknowledged the centrality of emotion in the communication of tragedy. They think that if tragedy is essentially an emotional experience, it must be *solely* that; and they think this because they assume that strong emotion is necessarily in opposition to thought, that the psychic activities are mutually exclusive. But is this right? Understanding, reason, learning, moral discrimination—these things are not, in my experience, incompatible with emotion (nor presumably in the experience of Gorgias and Aristotle): what is incompatible is cold insensibility. Whether or not emotion is inimical to such intellectual processes depends on the *circumstances in which it is aroused*.

The characteristic tragic emotions—pity, horror, fascination, indignation, and so forth—are felt in many other situations besides in the theatre. Above all we suffer them in the face of the misfortunes of real life, of course. What distinguishes the experience of a great tragedy? For one thing, as already remarked, we feel for the fortunes of people who have no direct personal relation to us: while this does not decrease the intensity of the emotion, it affords us some distance and perspective. We can feel and at the same time observe from outside. But does this distinguish tragedy from other 'contrived' emotional experiences (most of them tending to the anti-intellectual) for example an animal hunt, a football match, an encounter group, reading a thriller, or watching a horror movie? Well, the experience of tragedy is by no means a random series of sensations. Our emotional involvement has perspective and context at the same time, and not just in retrospect. Thus the events of the tragedy are in an ordered *sequence*, a sequence which gives shape and comprehensibility to what we feel. And, most important of all, the affairs of the characters which move us are given a moral setting which is argued and explored in the play. They act and suffer within situations of moral conflict, of social, intellectual and theological conflict. The quality of the tragedy depends *both* on its power to arouse our emotions *and* on the setting of those emotions in a sequence of moral and intellectual complications which is set out and examined. Tragedy evokes our feelings for others, like much else; but it is distinguished by the order and significance it imparts to suffering. So if the audience is not moved, then the tragedy, however intellectual, is a total failure: if its passions are aroused, but in a thoughtless, amorphous way, then it is merely a bad tragedy, sensational, melodramatic.

Thus it is that our emotions in the theatre, far from driving out thought and meaning, are indivisible from them: they are simultaneous and mutually dependent. The experience of tragedy can achieve this coherence in a way that the emotional experiences of real life generally cannot because they are too close, too cluttered with detail and partiality, to be seen in perspective. Tragedy makes us feel that we understand life in its tragic aspects. We have the sense that we can better sympathize with and cope with suffering, misfortune and waste. It is this sense of understanding (not isolated pearls of wisdom) that is the 'message' of a tragedy, that the great playwright imparts. This is well put in T. S. Eliot's[2] essay 'Shakespeare and the Stoicism of Seneca', where he argues that it is the quality of the emotional expression rather than the quality of the philosophy which makes literature great, which makes it 'strong, true and informative . . . useful and beneficial in the sense in which poetry is useful and beneficial'. 'All great poetry' Eliot writes 'gives the illusion of a view of life . . . for every precise emotion tends towards intellectual formulation' . . .

---

[2] **T. S. Eliot** poet and critic (1888–1965)

Brooks Otis (B. 1908)

In his essay "The Guilt of Agamemnon" scholar Brooks Otis examines the differences between the tragedies of Aeschylus and those of Sophocles.

THE GUILT OF AGAMEMNON

. . . One cannot get a "tragic" effect from the destruction of the villain or the saint, but only from that of the good hero with some sort of flaw, a fatal readiness to blunder at the pivotal moment. A vast amount of discussion has been devoted to the flaw—the *hamarti*—and to the desiderated tragic effect, the purging (*catharsis*) of pity and fear by their dramatic presentation in the theater. This has obscured the quite limited and descriptive purpose of Aristotle's account. Assuming that one wants this sort of tragic effect, the *Oedipus Rex* is, as Aristotle insisted, the perfect model. The audience is "shocked" by the fate of a good man it can sympathize with. Because he is "good" he is not really to blame. Oedipus falls into a trap designed for him by the gods and especially by Apollo. If he had been a saint or a meticulously cautious person, he might have avoided it. He is not represented as a guilty sinner or a man with a real moral problem. The initial mistake or crime of Laius (letting Oedipus be born at all)—in other words the Aeschylean problem of inherited sin or the chain of crimes and vengeances—is taken as a datum, not a problem. The actual crimes of Oedipus (patricide and incest) are committed in ignorance and so without real moral responsibility. The justifiability of Oedipus' slaying of his father Laius (from the standpoint of Oedipus at the time of the slaying) is perhaps doubtful, but the slaying *per se* is not the cause of Oedipus' real trouble, which is his misapprehension of his paternity. That Oedipus thinks he knows, when he is actually ignorant (in this sense, blind) is a leitmotiv of the play and underlines his tragic human condition. His ignorance or blindness precludes the clear fixing of moral responsibility. The tragic effect depends upon reducing his responsibility to the smallest possible compass.

The *Oedipus Rex* is an extreme instance, but it is hard not to agree with Aristotle that it is the classic tragedy if tragedy is conceived as the deliberate excitation of pity and fear. This is what we might be if we had been in Oedipus' shoes, for are we not also ignorant of our actual condition? Is this not the very stuff of fear and sympathy? Sophocles knew that other outcomes are possible—we have the *Philoctetes* and *Oedipus Coloneus*—and none of his other heroes (Heracles or Antigone, for example) is quite like Oedipus. The moral responsibility of Heracles, Antigone, or Oedipus can never be pushed to the point of real desert or equivalence with their fates. Theodicy is, after all, not the stuff of Sophoclean tragedy.

Aeschylus stands at the opposite extreme. The main reason why the *Agamemnon* is some six hundred lines longer than each of the two other plays of the *Oresteia* trilogy, is that it includes very long choral passages concerned primarily with the guilt or moral responsibility of Agamemnon for the fate that overtakes him. His tragedy—his murder by his wife Clytemnestra—is conceived as punishment for his own misdeeds or for the nature (*ethos*) from which the misdeeds came. But Agamemnon's murder also belongs to a chain of crimes and vengeances that perpetuate each other without end. This chain is conceived as a divine necessity, the work of an ancestral spirit—*daimon*, Erinys, Moira, or Ara (curse)—whose relation to the high god, Zeus, is full of ambiguity and contradiction. The murder of Agamemnon triggers a new process by which the ambiguity is cleared up, the contradiction overcome. Everybody recognizes this fact: the last play of the trilogy—the *Eumenides*—has a "happy ending" that eliminates the possibility of similar tragedies. What is not yet clear is what the optimistic theodicy does to the actual tragedy of Agamemnon. How is the relation between moral responsibility and divine causation in Agamemnon's case different from that of Sophocles' *Oedipus*? How does this difference affect our conception or definition of tragedy? . . .

Let us consider the much-disputed question of Agamemnon's guilt. In the long parodos, or first choral passage, Agamemnon is said to have been sent by Zeus Xenios (Zeus as the god of hospitality) to avenge on Troy the adultery and wife-abduction of Paris (60–62). Agamemnon and Menelaus are vultures crying for punishment against the robbers of their empty nest. But they become, in the next section of the parados (104–20), the birds of an omen, twin eagles rending a defenseless, pregnant hare. This omen is said not only to predict the destruction of Troy but also to provoke the anger of Artemis, who resents the wanton killing of the hare and its young. Thus the hare episode is treated as much more than an omen: it is an active cause of the sacrifice of Iphigenia, the human victim that Artemis demands in requital for the hare. The sacrifice itself is said to mark a decisive change in Agamemnon's character. Faced by the terrible necessity of either abandoning his army or killing his daughter, he chooses the latter. The one entailed both disobedience of Zeus and abrogation of all his civil and military responsibilities; the other entailed a horrible inversion of his paternal feelings and responsibilities. The necessity of making such a choice is said to have hardened and coarsened his whole nature. He becomes a cruel and ruthless general, at time reckless of gods and men, the unfeeling and haughty figure who finally appears before his palace and walks the purple carpet to his death.

The whole sequence teems with difficulties. How can an omen of Troy's destruction and Agamemnon's action at Troy (as destroying eagle) cause Artemis' anger, when it is actually precedent to his going to Troy and is not literally conceived as his own act at all, but that of the two eagles? None of the answers to this question have I think been very satisfactory.[1] Scholars have been much more successful in refuting each other than in their constructive efforts at a solution. Eduard Fraenkel has pointed out that the eagle-hare omen is a much more effective cause of Artemis' wrath than the accidental killing of the stag which Sophocles used in the *Electra* and which was originally set forth in a Cyclic epic, the *Cypria*.[2] The omen is a symbol of the destruction of Troy and gives a moral dimension to Agamemnon's guilt that the stag episode could not supply. But one can hardly stop there as Fraenkel does and consign the difficul-

---

[1] For recent thoughts on this and full bibliography to 1977, see Mark W. Edwards, "Agamemnon's Decision: Freedom and Folly in Aeschylus," *California Studies in Classical Philology* 10 (1977) 18–38.
[2] *Aeschylus "Agamemnon,"* VOL. 2 (Oxford, 1950) 96–99.

ties of the hare omen to Aeschylus' "poetical" mode of statement. His great—
even dominating—concern with Agamemnon's guilt excludes any such easy
solution. Nor can we say that Agamemnon could or should have simply refused
to make the sacrifice and therefore abandoned the army and the war. The war
may be invested with ominous connotations, but its connection with Zeus' will,
as well as its moral justification (the punishment of Paris' crime), are both made
clear. Nor can one agree with H. D. F. Kitto that the human and divine motives
(or motives of Artemis and Agamemnon) are distinct in such a way that the one
does not determine the other.[3] The text makes this impossible: Agamemnon
knows and even agonizes over the divine command. It seems evident that such
writers as Albin Lesky and Jacqueline de Romilly have correctly seen that the
divine and human responsibilities are inextricably connected.[4] The moral error is
committed under a necessity imposed by the gods. Agamemnon changes at the
moment of enforced decision, so that he takes on an internal, moral responsibility for his act and becomes a sinner who must eventually suffer for his sin. This
does not mean that the objective act of sacrifice is itself converted into a sin. The
text says that at this point (when confronted by the necessity) Agamemnon's
nature changed and that he in consequence became something like the destroying eagle of the omen. There is ambiguity in the description of the war (first and
second stasima) so that we are in doubt as to whether the war as such (or even
any war as such) or only Agamemnon's conduct of the war is most reprehended.
But there is little doubt that Agamemnon's conduct itself had changed. The man
who returns, confronts Clytemnestra and walks the carpet is not represented as
a simple innocent: he is both a successful and a harsh and prideful general. He is
both responsible for and indifferent to the suffering he has caused.

Nevertheless, Agamemnon was subjected to a harsh necessity. The question whether he could have avoided the fatal change of character can only be
hypothetical. What we feel is the coincidence of the necessity and the sin. So the
timing of the omen (before the events it signified) and the consequent inversion
of cause and effect, as well as the ambiguity of the omen itself, are disturbing
only on the most narrowly logical interpretation. Agamemnon was envisaged as
a man whose whole career was determined, so that the time sequence made little difference. The omen rightly depicted how he would change and act: his sacrifice of Iphigenia and his harshness as a general at Troy are part of the same
character. The fact of decision, of change, of sin, is the important thing, not its
date or logically sequential position.

Agamemnon is caught up by a necessity that he did not create and in fact
abhorred. The initial necessity which changed his character was imposed from
without by the gods. He could be punished for being the kind of man who
would change under such a necessity—he is represented as responsible for the
change—but he certainly did not enjoy, much less initiate, the necessity himself.
We can perhaps say that Artemis anticipated his action at Troy and proleptically

---

[3] *Form and Meaning in Drama* (London, 1956) 1–8. [4] Lesky, "Decision and Responsibility in the Tragedy of Aeschylus," *Journal of Hellenic Studies* 86 (1966) 78–85, and de Romilly, "Vengeance humaine et vengeance divine: remarques sur l'*Orestes* d'Eschyle," *Das Altertum*, Festschrift W. Schadewaldt (Stuttgart, 1970) 65–77.

punished him for it, because she already recognized in him an *ethos* which would change under pressure. But we cannot avoid the *external* pressure of the necessity. He is not represented as simply bad or sinful. His sin is in part involuntary. Thyestes and Atreus were sinners in a different sense, as were later Clytemnestra and Aegisthus, though these two were also involved in some sort of necessity. Each had a crime to avenge and each was driven by a supernatural power, the *daimon* or Erinys of the house. But the distinction between them and Agamemnon is clear: the guilt of Agamemnon is far less deliberate, far less absolute. He is also a great general and king who did not in the least deserve his terrible and disgraceful death. The very ambiguity of his conduct poses a new question. What was the justification of the necessity and how could it be overcome? In what way could the justice of Zeus be realized? The very doubtfulness of Agamemnon's guilt marked the beginning of a new question, a new stage or kind of justice.

From this standpoint the tragedy of Agamemnon, compared to Atreus, Thyestes, Aegisthus, or Clytemnestra, is almost Sophoclean or Aristotelian. He is a good man with a *hamartia*, or moral flaw, brought out by a divinely imposed necessity, a fatal trap or dilemma that he could not foresee or avoid. But Aeschylus is very un-Sophoclean in his treatment of Agamemnon's murder. Instead of terminating a self-contained tragedy concerned with the awful futility and blindness of human existence, he raises the demand for more justice and enlightenment. The play breaks the ambiguity and ignorance of the past and forces a decision, a new relationship of gods and men. The murder is a great cosmic event as well as a decisive event in the house of Atreus and the history of the *polis.*

The true importance of Agamemnon's guilt is defined by its ambiguity. The guilt is too great to be exorcised by anything short of his death. The guilt of Clytemnestra is much greater and not at all ambiguous. By the next play, the *Choephoroe,* the balance between guilt and innocence is changed. Orestes is no Agamemnon, but a man whose guilt is only a minor accompaniment of the divine necessity by which he is bound. The problem changes from one of guilt to one of necessity itself and of the divine orders behind it. The murder of Clytemnestra finally raises the level of dramatic action from the human to the divine sphere with which the last play, the *Eumenides,* deals.

The ambiguous nature of the connection between divine necessity and human responsibility is crucial. In Sophocles this is taken for granted. His sort of tragedy depends on the fact that no one can be called happy until his life is completed, or removed from the ambiguity—the ignorance—which up to the very last moment conceals the possibility of a most frightful reversal of his prior life-pattern. Sophoclean tragedy maintains and magnifies this ambiguity, regards it as an unalterable, inevitable part of the human condition. This is why human life is so "tragic." Aeschylus stresses the ambiguity because it cannot be permanent; it must be cleared up. He is concerned not with one human condition but with two—with the old, Sophoclean ignorance or confusion of divine and human wills and with a new, Aeschylean enlightenment in which the relation of the divine and human is clarified and made intelligible.

Bernard Knox (B. 1933)

Bernard Knox, director of the Center for Hellenic Studies in Washington, D.C., discusses the power of Sophocles' *Oedipus* to touch some of the deepest fears that have plagued Western civilization up to the present moment.

THE FREEDOM OF OEDIPUS

'Oedipus the King'is universally recognized as the dramatic masterpiece of the Greek theater. Aristotle cites it as the most brilliant example of theatrical plot, the model for all to follow, and all the generations since who have seen it staged—no matter how inadequate the production or how poor the translation—have agreed with his assessment as they found themselves moved to pity and fear by the swift development of its ferociously logical plot. The story of Oedipus, the myth, was of course very old in Sophocles's time and very well known to his audience. It was his use of the well-known material that made the play new. He chose to concentrate attention not on the actions of Oedipus that had made his name a byword—his violation of the two most formidable taboos observed by almost every human society—but on the moment of his discovery of the truth. And Sophocles engineered this discovery not by divine agency (as Homer did) and not by chance, but through the persistent, courageous action of Oedipus himself. The hero of the play is thus his own destroyer; he is the detective who tracks down and identifies the criminal—who turns out to be himself.

The play has also been almost universally regarded as the classic example of the "tragedy of fate." To the rationalist critics of the eighteenth century and still more to the firm believers in human progress of the nineteenth, this aspect of the play was a historical curiosity, to be discounted, but our own more anxious age has seen in the situation of Oedipus an image of its own fears. In the very first year of our century Sigmund Freud in his *Interpretation of Dreams* offered a famous and influential interpretation of the destiny of Oedipus the King:

> There must be something which makes a voice within us ready to recognize the compelling force of destiny in the *Oedipus*, while we can dismiss as merely arbitrary such dispositions as are laid down in . . . modern tragedies of destiny. And a factor of this kind is in fact involved in the story of King Oedipus. His destiny moves us only because it might have been ours . . . . It is the fate of all of us, perhaps, to direct our first sexual impulse towards our mother and our first hatred and . . . murderous wish against our father. Our dreams convince us that this is so.

This passage is of course a landmark in the history of modern thought, and it is fascinating to observe that this idea, which, valid or not, has had enormous influence, stems from an attempt to answer a literary problem—why does the play have this overpowering effect on modern audiences?—and that this problem is raised by an ancient Greek tragedy. As a piece of literary criticism, however, it leaves much to be desired. If the effect of the play did indeed depend on the "particular nature of the material," then one would expect modern audiences to be just as deeply moved by a performance of Voltaire's *Edipe*, whereas, in fact, the play is rarely produced, and then only as a museum piece. At any rate, though the primordial urges and fears that are Freud's concern are perhaps inherent in the myths, they are not exploited in the Sophoclean play. And indeed Freud himself, in a later passage in the same work, admits as much: "the further modification of the legend," he says, "originates . . . in a misconceived secondary revision of the material, which has sought to exploit it for theological purposes." This "further modification" is the Sophoclean play.

Sophocles's play has served modern man and his haunted sense of being caught in a trap not only as a base for a psychoanalytic theory that dooms the male infant to guilt and anxiety from his mother's breast, but also as the model for a modern drama that presents to us, using the ancient figures, our own terror of the unknown future that we fear we cannot control—our deep fear that every step we take forward on what we think is the road of progress may really be a step toward a foreordained rendezvous with disaster. The greatest of these modern versions is undoubtedly Jean Cocteau's *Machine Infernale*; the title alone is, as the French say, a whole program. Cocteau also worked with Stravinsky on an operatic version of the Sophoclean play (the text in liturgical Latin), and for a recording of this work he wrote a prologue that sums up his compelling vision of man's place in a strange and haunted universe. "*Spectateurs*," says the author in his forceful, rather nasal voice, "*sans le savoir* . . . without knowing it, Oedipus is at grips with the powers that watch us from the other side of death. They have spread for him, since the day of his birth, a trap and you are going to watch it snap shut." This is of course much more explicit (and much more despairing) than the Sophoclean play; it stems, like the beautiful and terrifying second act of the *Machine Infernale*, in which the Sphinx and Anubis play their fiendish game with Oedipus, out of a modern vision of a death-haunted universe, from the obsessed imagination that gives us also, in the film *Orphée*, the unforgettable images of Death at work: her black-uniformed motorcyclists, enigmatic radio messages, and rubber gloves.

Parallel with this modern adaptation of the Oedipus story, serving new psychologies and mythologies of the irrational, goes a reinterpretation of the Sophoclean play itself by scholars and critics. Yeats, who translated the play for production at the Abbey Theatre in Dublin, described his reaction to a rehearsal in the words, "I had but one overwhelming emotion, a sense as of the actual presence in a terrible sacrament of the god." Taking his cue from the work of Frazer and Harrison, who emphasize the religious, tribal, and primitive aspects of the Greek tradition, Francis Fergusson, in his brilliant book *The Idea of a Theater*, gives us a vision of the Sophoclean masterpiece as an Athenian mystery play, a solemn rite of sacrifice that purges the community of its collective guilt by punishing a scapegoat, one man who perishes for the good of the people.

All this is a reaction, predictable and perhaps even necessary, against the nineteenth-century worship of the Greek rational "enlightenment"—a vision of ancient Greece dear to the hearts of optimistic Victorians who found in Greece, as each successive generation in the West has done since the Renaissance, their own image. But the reaction toward the mysterious, the irrational has gone too far. For Sophocles's play, read without preconceptions of any kind, gives an entirely different impression. There is not one supernatural event in it, no gods (as there are in so many other Greek plays), no monsters—nothing that is not, given the mythical situation, inexorably logical and human. Destiny, fate, and the will of the gods do indeed loom ominously behind the human action, but that action, far from suggesting primeval rituals and satanic divinities, reflects, at every point, contemporary realities familiar to the audience that first saw the play.

The voice of destiny in the play is the oracle of Apollo. Through his priests at Delphi, Apollo told Laius that he would be killed by his own son, and later told Oedipus that he would kill his father and marry his mother. At the beginning of the play Apollo tells Creon that Thebes will be saved from the plague only when the murderer of Laius is found and expelled. This Delphic oracle, which for modern poets—Yeats, for example—can conjure up mystic romantic visions, was, for Sophocles and his audience, a fact of life, an institution as present and solid, as uncompromising (and sometimes infuriating) as the Vatican is for us. States and individuals alike consulted it as a matter of course about important decisions. Sparta asked Apollo if it should declare war on Athens in 431 B.C. (it was told to go ahead and was promised victory). The oracle promoted revolutions, upheld dynasties, guided the foundation of colonies. Its wealth and political influence were immense.

Its power was based on a widespread, indeed in early times universal, belief in the efficacy of divine prophecy. The gods knew everything, including what was going to happen, and so their advice was precious; the most famous dispenser of such advice was Apollo, son of Zeus. Private individuals and official representatives of state had for centuries made the journey by land and sea to Apollo's temple in its magnificent setting on a high plateau below Mount Parnassus; in gratitude for the god's advice, kings and cities had lavished gifts on the sanctuary and even built treasuries on the site to house their precious offerings.

But in the second half of the fifth century B.C., particularly in Athens, this belief in prophecy and with it belief in the religious tradition as a whole was under attack. Philosophers and sophists (the new professional teachers of rhetoric, political theory, and a host of allied subjects) were examining all accepted ideas with a critical eye: the fifth century in Athens was an age of intellectual revolution. Among the younger intellectuals, prophecies, especially those peddled by self-appointed professional seers (a class of operator common in ancient Greece but not unknown in modern America), were viewed with skepticism if not scorn; inevitably some of the skepticism spread to embrace the more respectable oracular establishments that claimed to transmit divine instructions. Thucydides, the historian of the Peloponnesian War, dismissed prophecy contemptuously in a couple of cynical sentences, and Euripides attacked it, sometimes lightheartedly, sometimes bitterly, in one play after another. The philosophical attack on it was more radical; the dictum of the sophist Protagoras—

"the individual man is the measure of all things, of the existence of what exists and the nonexistence of what does not"—subjected prophecy, and for that matter the gods themselves, to a harsh criterion that found them wanting.

When he chose as the subject of his tragedy a story about a man who tried to avoid the fulfillment of a prophecy of Apollo, believed he had succeeded and cast scorn on all the oracles, only to find that he had fulfilled that prophecy long ago, Sophocles was dealing with matters that had urgent contemporary significance; prophecy was one of the great controversial questions of the day. It was in fact the key question, for the rationalist critique of the whole archaic religious tradition had concentrated its fire on this particular sector. Far more than prophecy was involved. For if the case for divine foreknowledge could be successfully demolished, the whole traditional religious edifice went down with it. If the gods did not know the future, they did not know any more than man. These are in fact the terms of the Sophoclean play. When the chorus hears Jocasta dismiss divine prophecy and Oedipus agree with her, they actually pray to Zeus to fulfill the dreadful prophecies they have just heard Jocasta and Oedipus report. They identify prophecy with the very existence of the gods. Never again, they say, will they go reverent to Delphi or to any oracular shrine of the gods

> unless these prophecies all come true
> for all mankind to point toward in
> wonder. . . .
> They are dying, the old oracles sent to
> Laius,
> now our masters strike them off the rolls.
> Nowhere Apollo's golden glory now—
> the gods, the gods go down.

By this emphasis Sophocles gave the age-old story contemporary and controversial significance, and he had other ways besides to make his audience see themselves in the ancient figures he brought to such disturbing life on stage. The play opens, for example, with a citizen delegation begging a ruler for relief from plague. The Athenians were all too familiar with plague; in the second summer of the war, in a city overcrowded with refugees from the Spartan invasion of Attica, plague had raged in the city, and it had recurred over the next three or four years.

But more important for the play's impact on the audience than this grim setting is the characterization of the play's central figure, Oedipus the King. The poet's language presents him to the audience not as a figure of the mythical past but as one fully contemporary; in fact he is easily recognizable as an epitome of the Athenian character as they themselves conceived it and as their enemies saw it too. One trait after another in the character of Sophocles's Oedipus corresponds to Athenian qualities praised by Pericles in his Funeral Speech or denounced by the Corinthians in their attack on Athenian imperialism at the congress in Sparta before the war.

Oedipus is quick to decide and to act; he anticipates advice and suggestion. When the priest hints that he should send to Delphi for help, he has already done so; when the chorus suggests sending for Tiresias, the prophet has already been summoned and is on the way. This swiftness in action is a well-known Athenian quality, one their enemies are well aware of. "They are the only people," say the Corinthians, "who simultaneously hope for and have what they plan, because of their quick fulfillment of decisions." But this action is not rash, it is based on reflection; Oedipus reached the decision to apply to Delphi "groping, laboring over many paths of thought." This too is typically Athenian. "We are unique," says Pericles, "in our combination of the most courageous action and rational discussion of our plans." The Athenians also spoke with pride of the intelligence that informed such discussion: Pericles attributes the Athenian victories over the Persians "not to luck, but to intelligence." And this is the claim of Oedipus, too. "The flight of my own intelligence hit the mark," he says, as he recalls his solution of the riddle of the Sphinx. The riddle has sinister verbal connections with his fate (his name in Greek is *Oidipous*, and *dipous* is the Greek word for "two-footed" in the riddle, not to mention the later prophecy of Tiresias that he would leave Thebes as a blind man, "a stick tapping before him step by step"), but the answer he proposed to the riddle—"Man"—is appropriate for the optimistic picture of man's achievement and potential that the figure of Oedipus represents.

Above all, as we see from the priest's speech in the prologue and the prompt, energetic action Oedipus takes to rescue his subjects from the plague, he is a man dedicated to the interests and the needs of the city. It is this public spirit that drives him on to the discovery of the truth—to reject Creon's hint that the matter should be kept under wraps, to send for Tiresias, to pronounce the curse and sentence of banishment on the murderer of Laius. This spirit was the great civic virtue that Pericles preached—"I would have you fix your eyes every day on the greatness of Athens until you fall in love with her"—and which the enemies of Athens knew they had to reckon with—"In the city's service," say the Corinthians, "they use their bodies as if they did not belong to them."

All this does not necessarily mean that Sophocles's audience drew a conscious parallel between Oedipus and Athens (or even that Sophocles himself did); what is important is that they could have seen in Oedipus a man endowed with the temperament and talents they prized most highly in their own democratic leaders and in their ideal vision of themselves. Oedipus the King is a dramatic embodiment of the creative vigor and intellectual daring of the fifth-century Athenian spirit.

But there is an even greater dimension to this extraordinary dramatic figure. The fifth century in Athens saw the birth of the historical spirit. The past came to be seen no longer as a golden age from which there had been a decline if not a fall, but as a steady progress from primitive barbarism to the high civilization of the city-state. One of the new teachers, the sophist Protagoras, was particularly associated with this idea; and there is a particularly clear reflection of his ideas in that chorus of *Antigone* that sings the praise of man the resourceful. "Man the master, ingenious past all measure . . ./he forges on. . . ." Three of the most important achievements of man celebrated in that ode are his conquest of the earth, the sea, and the animals. And Oedipus, in the images of the play, is presented to us as hunter, sailor, and plowman. He is the hunter who follows "the trail of the ancient guilt"; the sailor who, in the chorus's words, "set our beloved land—storm-tossed, shattered—straight on course"; and he is also the plowman—"How," sings the chorus when the truth is out at last,

> *how could the furrows your father*
> *plowed bear you, your agony,*
>   *harrowing*
> *on in silence O so long?*

But Oedipus speaks too in terms that connect him with more advanced stages of human progress. Among these—the culmination of the *Antigone* ode—was the creation of the city-state, "the mood and mind for law that rules the city." Oedipus is a ruling statesman; he is a self-made man who has won and kept control of the state, a master of the political art, and he is conscious of his achievement and its value. And, as head of the state, Oedipus is the enforcer of the law. He is, in the play, the investigator, prosecutor, and judge of a murderer. In all these aspects he represents the social and intellectual progress that had resulted in the establishment of Athenian democracy and its courts of law, a triumph of human progress celebrated in the last play of Aeschylus's *Oresteia*.

The figure of Oedipus represents not only the techniques of the transition from savagery to civilization and the political achievements of the newly settled society, but also the temper and methods of the fifth-century intellectual revolution. His speeches are full of words, phrases, and attitudes that link him with the "enlightenment" of Sophocles's own Athens. "I'll bring it all to light," he says; he is like some Protagoras or Democritus dispelling the darkness of ignorance and superstition. He is a questioner, a researcher, a discoverer—the Greek words are those of the sophistic vocabulary. Above all Oedipus is presented to the audience as a symbol of two of the greatest scientific achievements of the age—mathematics and medicine. Mathematical language recurs incessantly in the imagery of the play—such terms as "measure" (*metrein*), "equate" (*isoun*), "define" (*diorizein*)—and at one climactic moment Oedipus expresses his hope as a mathematical axiom that a discrepancy in the evidence will clear him of the charge of Laius's murder: "One can't equal many." This obsessive image, Oedipus the calculator, is one more means of investing the mythical figure with the salient characteristics of the fifth-century achievement, but it is also magnificently functional. For, in his search for truth, he is engaged in a great calculation to determine the measure of man, whom Protagoras called "the measure of all things."

Functional too is the richly developed image of Oedipus as a physician. Hippocrates of Cos and his school of physicians had in this same century founded Western medicine; their treatises and casebooks are still extant, and in them we can see the new methods at work: detailed observations of hundreds of cases, classification of symptoms, plotting of the regular course of individual diseases and then diagnosis, prognosis (these are Greek words, their words). In the play the city suffers from a disease and Oedipus is the physician to whom all turn for a cure.

And all these images, like the plot, like the hero, have what Aristotle called their *peripeteia*, their reversal. The hunter catches a dreadful prey, the seaman steers his ship into an unspeakable harbor—"one and the same wide harbor served you/son and father both"—the plowman sows and reaps a fearful harvest, the investigator finds the criminal, and the judge convicts him—they are all the same man—the revealer turns into the thing revealed, the finder into the thing found, the calculator finds he is himself the solution of the equation, and the physician discovers that he is the disease. The catastrophe of the tragic hero thus becomes the catastrophe of fifth-century man; all his furious energy and intellectual daring drive him on to this terrible discovery of his fundamental ignorance. He is not the measure of all things but the thing measured and found wanting.

The reversal of the tragic hero is singled out for praise by Aristotle because it comes about through recognition, in this case Oedipus's recognition of his own identity. But he recognizes also that the prophecies given to his father and to him by Apollo were true prophecies, that they had been fulfilled long ago, that every step taken to evade them, from the exposure of the child to the decision never to go back to Corinth, was part of the pattern of their fulfillment. And this poses, for the modern reader as for the ancient spectator, the question of fate and, though those spectators could not have expressed the idea in abstract terms, of free will and human freedom.

This basic theme has often been discounted on the grounds that the opposition of fate and free will, providence and chance, determined and open universe, was not explicitly formulated until much later than Sophocles's time, in the philosophical discussions of the late fourth and third centuries. This is true, but it does not necessarily follow that because a problem had not yet been given philosophical expression, it could not be conceived. The myth of Oedipus itself—like the stories of attempts to escape a predicted fate so frequent in the *Histories* of Sophocles's friend Herodotus—poses the problem in poetic form, and one of the functions of myth in preliterate societies, as Levi-Strauss has so brilliantly demonstrated, is to raise deeply disturbing problems that will later demand more precise formulation.

Even though what remains of early Greek literature shows no verbal consciousness of the ideas we associate with freedom of the will, there is abundant evidence, from the earliest times, for a related concept that is in fact almost inseparable from it: individual responsibility. No one can be held fully responsible for actions committed under some kind of external constraint, and in early Greek belief such constraint might be exerted by a host of nonhuman powers. When Agamemnon, in Homer's *Iliad*, makes his apologies to Achilles for the harsh treatment that led to the death of so many heroes, he tries to evade responsibility: he is claiming, in other words, that he did not act freely: "I am not responsible/but Zeus is, and Destiny. . . ." The context suggests that this is merely an excuse. But the negative implication of this is clear: that a man *is* responsible for those actions that are not performed under constraint, which are the expression of his free will. The question of Oedipus's responsibility for what happens (and what has happened) is, as we shall see, posed in the play; it is also discussed much later, in *Oedipus at Colonus*, which deals with Oedipus's old age and death.

It is interesting to note that in those later centuries, when the stoic philosophers do pose the problem in abstract form, they start from this same mythical base, the oracle given to Laius. Chrysippus uses this oracle to illustrate his almost completely determinist position (the only freedom he allows man is that of a dog tied to a moving cart); Carneades reinterprets the oracle to allow man a little more freedom; Alexander of Aphrodisias takes up the challenge on the same ground, and Cicero debates the meaning of this same oracular prophecy. As long as Greek philosophy lasts, the discussion of Oedipus's freedom or his subjection to fate goes on—even in the commentaries on Plato by Albinus in the second and Calcidus in the sixth century A.D.

The end of Greek philosophy and the triumph of Christianity brought no end to the argument, only new terms in which to phrase it. St. Augustine wrote his book *On Freedom of the Will (De Libero Arbitrio)* just as Cicero had written his *On Fate (De Fato)*; Augustine is no longer concerned with the oracle given to Laius, but he is just as tormented (as he claims all humanity is) by the contradiction between our free will and God's foreknowledge that we will sin. It was of course an argument that was to go further; Bergson, Croce, and Friedrich Engels, to name only a few, continue it into modern times. It has become much more complicated and sophisticated with the years; the terms of the opposition can be, and have been, continually redefined in philosophically elegant formulas that are designed, and may even seem, to abolish it; and of course modern analytical philosophers can dismiss the problem as a mere verbal misunderstanding. But to the ordinary man, now as in Sophocles's day, there is a problem in the coexistence of predictable pattern and free will, whether that pattern be thought of as divine providence, the will of history, or the influence of the stars.

There are two obvious ways of avoiding the contradiction, both of them extreme positions and at opposite poles; one might call them, to use a political metaphor, the right and the left. The right is all for order and pattern; it escapes the dilemma by dispensing with freedom altogether. It sees history, individual and general, as a rigidly determined succession of events in time. If you take such a view, whether Christian with St. Augustine—that all history is God's providential preparation of two cities, one of God, one of Satan, and that certain souls are predestined for salvation (or with Calvin, that other souls are destined for damnation); or materialist and atheist with Marx and Engels, denying the freedom of history to all classes but the proletariat—"Freedom," wrote Engels: "is the recognition of necessity" (which is a German version of Chrysippus's dog tied to a cart)—if you take either of these determinist views, you have no antinomy, no contradiction. But you have no freedom, and unless you happen to be one of the Christian or the Marxist elect, you have no future either.

What we have called the left, on the other hand, is all for freedom. To the devil with pattern and order; they are for anarchy, the human will is absolutely free and nothing is predictable; there is no pattern of order in the universe, which is merely the operation of blind chance. If you deny the possibility of prediction and the existence of order, whether as an "atomic" theorist like Democritus, or out of sheer desperation, as Jocasta does in the play—"What should a man fear? It's all chance, chance rules our lives"—you have abolished the logical contradiction. But you accept a blind, pointless, meaningless universe—the universe of the absurd.

Both of these extremes are of course repugnant to the human spirit and especially to that of the West, which is that of the Greeks. We want both the freedom of our will and the assurance of order and meaning; we want to have our cake and eat it too, and in this non-Christian and Christian are alike. But no matter what subtle distinctions we invent and refine, the basic contradiction remains. Insofar as any meaningful pattern or divine providence exists, it must encroach to some extent on human freedom; if human freedom is unlimited, the possibility of pattern or order is denied.

As a logical proposition, the two concepts are irreconcilable. The only way to believe in the pattern and the freedom at once is not as a logical proposition but as a mystery; the medium of exploration is not philosophy but religion—or art. We can say, as Tertullian is supposed to have said (but almost certainly didn't), "I believe it precisely because it is absurd," or we can express the contradiction in poetic terms that transcend logic. It is significant that Plato's main discussion of the problem is not phrased in the cut and thrust of dialectic, but in the great myths, as in the myth of Er, where Socrates is no longer subject to questioning. Only a mood of religious humility or a work of art can hold in precarious coexistence the irreconcilable concepts. But for one form of art, the drama, this is a particularly dangerous subject. For the power of drama depends on our feeling that the actors are free, that their choice of action is significant. The dramatist who, like Sophocles, dares to base his drama on a story that seems to question if not rule out freedom of action is walking a perilous tightrope.

The soul of drama, as Aristotle says, is plot—the action that demands and succeeds in engaging our attention so that we are no longer detached spectators but are involved in the progress of the stage events. Its outcome is important for us; in the greatest plots (and the plot of this play by Sophocles is perhaps the greatest) it is for the moment the most important thing in the world. But this engagement of the audience proceeds from an identification with the figures on stage, and this is not possible if we are made to feel that the action of the characters is not free, not effective. We expect to be made to feel that there is a meaningful relation between the hero's action and his suffering, and this is possible only if that action is free, so that he is responsible for the consequences.

The hero's will must be free, but something else is needed: it must have some causal connection with his suffering. It is the function of great art to give meaning to human suffering, and so we expect that if the hero is crushed by a bulldozer in Act II, there will be some reason for it, and not just some reason but a good one, one that makes sense in terms of the hero's personality and action. In fact, we expect to be shown that he is in some way *responsible* for what happens to him.

If so, the hero obviously cannot be "fated," predestined or determined to act as he does. And Oedipus in Sophocles's play *is* a free agent, and he is responsible for the catastrophe. For the plot of the play consists not of the actions that Oedipus was "fated" to perform, or rather, that were predicted—the plot of the play consists of his discovery that he has already fulfilled the prediction. And this discovery is entirely due to his action.

He dismisses Creon's politic advice to discuss the Delphic response in private; he undertakes a public and vigorous inquiry into the murder of Laius. He is the driving force that, against the reluctance of Tiresias, the dissuasion of Jocasta, and the final supplication of the shepherd, pushes on triumphantly and disastrously to the discovery of the truth. If it had not been for Oedipus, the play persuades us, the truth would never have been discovered, or at least it would not have been discovered *now*. This presentation of the hero's freedom and responsibility, in the context of the dreadful prophecy already unwittingly and unwillingly fulfilled, is an artistic juxtaposition, a momentary illusion of full reconciliation between the two mighty opposites, freedom and destiny. It is an illusion because of course the question of responsibility for what happened *before* the play, of Oedipus's freedom in the context of divine prophecies fulfilled, is evaded. But it makes the play a triumphant tour de force. Oedipus is the free agent who, by his own self-willed action, discovers that his own predicted destiny has already been fulfilled. This is why the play moves us as a spectacle of heroic action and why the figure of Oedipus, dominating the stage, arouses our admiration as well as our sympathy. It is noticeable that in Cocteau's masterpiece, where Oedipus is deliberately portrayed as a marionette in the hands of demonic powers, the greatest dramatic excitement is generated by the action and speech not of Oedipus but of those divine powers, Anubis and the Sphinx.

Oedipus's heroic achievement is the discovery of the truth, and that discovery is the most thoroughgoing and dreadful catastrophe the stage has ever presented. The hero who, in his vigor, courage, and intelligence stands as a representative of all that is creative in man, discovers a truth so dreadful that the chorus that sums up the results of the great calculation sees in his fall the reduction of man to nothing:

> *O the generations of men*
> *the dying generations—adding the total*
> *of all your lives I find they come to*
> > *nothing*

The existence of human freedom, dramatically represented in the *action* of Oedipus in the play, seems to be a mockery. The discovery to which it led is a catastrophe out of all proportion to the situation. Critics have tried, with contradictory results, to find some flaw in Oedipus's character that will justify his reversal. But there is nothing in his actions that can make it acceptable to us. The chorus's despairing summation, "come to nothing," echoes our own feelings as we watch Oedipus rush into the palace.

But this estimate of the situation is not the last word; in fact, it is contradicted by the final scene of the play. Oedipus's first thought, we are told by the messenger, was to kill himself—he asked for a sword—but he blinds himself instead. This action is one that the audience must have expected; it was mentioned in the earlier *Antigone*, for example, and Oedipus as the blind, exiled wanderer seems to have been one of the invariable elements in fifth-century versions of the myth. But, though the blindness was foreseen by Tiresias, Oedipus's action did not figure in the prophecies made to and about him by Apollo. When the messenger comes from inside the palace to describe the catastrophe, he uses words that emphasize the independence of this action: "terrible things, and none done blindly now, all done with a will." And as Oedipus, wearing a mask with blood running from the eye sockets, stumbles on stage, he makes the same distinction when the chorus asks him what power impelled him to attack his eyes:

> *Apollo, friends, Apollo—*
> *he ordained by agonies—*
> *these, my pains on pains!*
> *But the hand that struck my eyes was mine,*
> *mine alone—no one else—*

These two passages suggest that in his decision to blind himself Oedipus is acting freely, that the intricate pattern of his destiny was complete when he knew the truth. To that terrible revelation some violent reaction was inevitable; the choice was left to him. He resisted the first suicidal impulse perhaps (though Sophocles is silent on the point) because of a latent conviction, fully and openly expounded in the last play (*Oedipus at Colonus*), that he was not to blame. He chose to blind himself, he tells the chorus, because he could not bear to see the faces of his children and his fellow citizens. But his action has, in the context of this play, an impressive rightness; the man who, proud of his far-seeing intelligence, taunted Tiresias with his blindness, now realizes that all his life long he has himself been blind to the dreadful realities of his identity and action.

The messenger's description of the horrors that took place inside the palace has prepared the audience for the spectacle of a broken man. So Oedipus seems to be at first, but very soon this bloodstained, sightless figure begins to reassert that magnificent imperious personality that was his from the beginning. He reproaches the chorus for wishing him dead rather than blind, defends his decision to blind himself, issues instructions to Creon, and finally has to be reminded that he is no longer master in Thebes. The despairing summation based on the fate of Oedipus—the great example (as the chorus calls him) that man is equal to nothing—is corrected by the reemergence of Oedipus as his old forceful self. Formidable as of old he may be, but with a difference. The confident tone in which the blind man speaks so regally is based on knowledge, knowledge of his own identity and of the truth of divine prophecy. This new knowledge, won at such a terrible price, makes clear what it was in the hero that brought about the disaster. It was ignorance.

In spite of his name *Oidipous*, with its resemblance to the Greek word *oida* ("I know")—a theme that Sophocles hammers home with continual word-play—Oedipus, who thought he knew so much, did not even know who his mother and father were. But ignorance can be remedied, the ignorant can learn, and the force with which Oedipus now reasserts his presence springs from the truth he now understands: that the universe is not a field for the play of blind chance, and that man is not its measure. This knowledge gives him a new strength that sustains him in his misery and gives him the courage needed to go on living, though he is now an outcast, a man from whom his fellow men recoil in horror.

The play, then, is a tremendous reassertion of the traditional religious view that man is ignorant, that knowledge belongs only to the gods—Freud's "theological purpose." And it seems to present at first sight a view of the universe as rigid on the side of order as Jocasta's was anarchic on the side of freedom. Jocasta thought that there was no order or design in the world, that dreams and prophecies had no validity; that man had complete freedom because it made no difference what he did—nothing made any sense. Jocasta was wrong; the design was there, and when she saw what it was she hanged herself. But the play now seems to give us a view of man's position that is just as comfortless as her acceptance of a meaningless universe. What place is there in it for human freedom and meaningful action?

Oedipus did have one freedom: he was free to find out or not find out the truth. This was the element of Sophoclean sleight of hand that enabled him to make a drama out of the situation which the philosophers used as the classic demonstration of man's subjection to fate. But it is more than a solution to an apparently insoluble dramatic problem; it is the key to the play's tragic theme and the protagonist's heroic stature. One freedom is allowed him: the freedom to search for the truth, the truth about the prophecies, about the gods, about himself. And of this freedom he makes full use. Against the advice and appeals of others, he pushes on, searching for the truth, the whole truth, and nothing but the truth. And in this search he shows all those great qualities that we admire in him—courage, intelligence, perseverance—the qualities that make human beings great. This freedom to search, and the heroic way Oedipus uses it, makes the play not a picture of man's feebleness caught in the toils of fate, but on the contrary, a heroic example of man's dedication to the search for truth, the truth about himself. This is perhaps the only human freedom, the play seems to say, but there could be none more noble.

Margaret Visser (B. 1940)

On the basis of her study of myths about women's roles in Greek and Roman family and society, Margaret Visser illustrates the aesthetic and social context for Aeschylus' Clytemnestra and Medea.

MEDEA: DAUGHTER, SISTER, WIFE AND MOTHER. NATAL FAMILY *VERSUS* CONJUGAL FAMILY IN GREEK AND ROMAN MYTHS ABOUT WOMEN

. . . The myth of the Rape of the Sabine Women and the meaning attached to it in historical times is the exact opposite of the myth of Medea. Both stories are about marriage as an institution whose purpose is to knit society together. Medea, in her destructiveness, is just as revealing about what normal marriage is supposed to achieve as the Sabine Women are exemplary and therefore edifying.

Married women, in ancient Athens as in ancient Rome, were indispensable for linking families and creating alliances. Antiphon lamented the marriage tie from a man's point of view, much as Euripides' Medea complained about the hard lot of married women (*Med.* 230–251). Antiphon is especially bitter because even if a marriage is unhappy "it may be a real blow to end it, since this means *the enmity of your wife's family*." These are people you get on with and know to be worthy, or you would not have married your wife.

Every woman brings her father and her brothers into relationship with the family of her husband. To this end, it is essential that a woman should keep the close bonds she has with her original family, as well as entering wholly into her husband's house. As a link, she is necessarily pulled in two directions at once; she is the point of contact between her natal family and her conjugal family.[1] The problem for her was that Greek society was patrilocal; when a new household was set up the hearth and home was an expression of the husband's, not the wife's, lineage.

Vernant has described the mythic world of Greek marriage in terms of motion and stillness, and in terms of space.[2] A woman's position in the home was represented by the stationary and interior hearth, and by the virgin goddess Hestia. A man's role was that of the "mover", Hermes, whose place was external to the home, and who in geographical terms represented the boundary of the property. A woman, however, left her house on marriage and entered a new one. In her husband's *oikos* she took up a position as guardian of the Hestia, the central and unmoving *focus* of the house. Therefore, every man's wife, the "unmoving" principle and centre of his home, was a foreigner. More, she had displaced herself from another man's hearth and home to join him. It was marriage which produced this paradox and played havoc with the ancient, hallowed categories. To fit them, a woman would have never to marry.

Vernant shows how the "unbedded" maiden Electra "expresses Hestia". She is the unwavering upholder of her father's rights. A woman who marries must leave her father: the initiation for a woman into sex and marriage is a source of anxiety which underlies girls' folktales the world over. Electra is the "double and opposite" of Clytemnestra. Neither is contained by marriage: Electra is a virgin, Clytemnestra an adulteress. Clytemnestra's relationship with Aegisthus avoids the contradiction entailed by the marriage contract, because Aegisthus *comes to her* as her lover. Clytemnestra stays at home—as a woman should, but as any married woman (once) has not.

Aeschylus made Clytemnestra a "man-woman" and the murderer of her husband; in Homer, it was Aegisthus who killed Agamemnon, and the accomplice Clytemnestra has nothing like the fearsome stature of Aeschylus' tragic Queen. Aegisthus "took her home with him" when he seduced her (*Od.* 3.272), and part of the horror of Agamemnon's death in the *Odyssey* is that a host slaughters his guest at dinner. At 3.234–5. Agamemnon is described as having been murdered ἐφέστιοζ, presumably at his (and the Queen's) own hearth. But it is possible that Homer conceived of Clytemnestra as living in Aegisthus' house until the killing, after which they both moved to the palace of the Atreidae (3.256–7). Aeschylus' Clytemnestra, on the other hand, summoned Aegisthus to live with her, and this appears to have contributed in no small measure to the confusion which the tragic Clytemnestra creates in the sphere of sexual roles. But "staying at home", as Clytemnestra does in the *Oresteia*, is woman's proper role, a proper role which of necessity she violates when she marries. Clytemnestra is being diabolically logical in making Aegisthus join her, and this serves to multi-

---

[1] I prefer these two terms to what seem to be the more common ones in anthropological and sociological literature: "the family of orientation" and "the family of procreation".   [2] "Hestia-Hermès. Sur l'expression religieuse de l'espace et du mouvement chez les Grecs", *Mythe et pensée chez les Grecs* I (Paris 1974) 124–170. Vernant does not apply his findings to Medea.

ply the discomfiture of the audience and increase the power of Clytemnestra.

Hardly anyone today would insist that we should explain the actions of Euripides' Medea as entirely those of a barbarian witch. Medea now has many supporters, and few people pretend that they do not understand her. Nor do we exclaim, with Jason, that "no Greek wife would dare" to do what she has done, that she is a beast and a monster, not a woman.[3] Nevertheless it is important to the plot that she is a barbarian, and Medea herself tells us one reason why that is so. A woman, when she marries, "arrives among different kinds of manners and laws" and suddenly has to cope with these as well as with her new husband. In marriage, a woman is a foreigner, who has left her home and every person she has ever cared for. And once she is in the new house there is no going back (236–240). Medea's expression of a woman's crossing over from one house to another, the "betrayal" of her father and her brother, was achieved by means of robbery and murder. Her initiation into the married state was a passage between the Clashing Rocks, "sailing away from her father's home" (*Med.* 2, 431–33, 1262–64).

However, at lines 252–3 Medea says to the Chorus: "Yet my case and yours are not the same. This city is your home and these houses belong to your families." Medea comes from another country, not just another house. The legend of Medea in Colchis was the story of her choice of marriage over virginity, the rejection of her natal home for Jason. She betrayed her country and her father by handing over the Golden Fleece. With the fleece went Medea herself, as the *sine qua non* for success in the hero's quest: in a sense the theft of the Fleece was also the carrying-off of Medea by the foreigner, Jason. Men are foreigners before marriage, coming to take the bride away; women are foreigners afterwards. Next, she cut herself off further by murdering her brother. In Euripides' play we do not hear the grisly tale that Apsyrtos was chopped in pieces to delay his father in the chase; rather, Medea murders her brother παοέστιον (1334)—at the hearth, the sacred symbol of her natal home. Kin murder at the hearth, by or with the connivance of its supposed guardian, is especially virulent, as in the murder of Agamemnon ἐφέστιον at *Od.* 3.234–5.

Euripides takes the tale of Medea at Colchis, a mythic statement of a woman's break with the natal family for the sake of marriage, and by dramatizing what happened later forces us to look at women and at marriage in a savage new light. He shows us a real woman on the stage, and so makes her "initiation" myth no longer symbolic but a catalogue of real crimes. Euripides makes the consequences of a myth about getting married into the starting point for a play about marriage breaking down. In real life, the "rejection" of the natal family was followed by acceptance of the conjugal household, the woman bringing her husband friendship with her natal family to increase his status and serve her

---

[3] For an excellent articulation of the view that Medea was conceived as a typical barbarian, see Page's introduction. *Euripides: Medea* (Oxford 1938) xviii–xxi. More recent criticism has a greater tendency to see the Eternal Woman in Medea: B. Knox, "The *Medea* of Euripides", in *Word and Action* (Baltimore 1980) 295–322; P. Pucci, *The Violence of Pity in Euripides' Medea* (Ithaca 1980); P. E. Easterling, "The Infanticide in Euripides' *Medea*", *YCS* 25 (1977) 177–191; M. Shaw, "The Female Intruder: Women in 5th Century Drama", *CP* 70 (1975) 255–266; A. P. Burnett, "Medea and the Tragedy of Revenge", *CP* 68 (1973) 1–24; K. J. Reckford, "Medea's First Exit", *TAPA* 99 (1968) 329–359; D. J. Conacher, *Euripidean Drama: Myth, Theme and Structure* (Toronto 1967) 183–198.

own. Finally, children sealed the link for ever. If marriage broke down, the wife's father and brothers would support her (Eur. *Alc*. 730–3). Medea, being literally foreign and having literally betrayed her father and killed her brother, ought to be utterly helpless and weak when Jason leaves her. But she is in fact strong, for in place of the support of her natal family the plot provides Medea with magic ointments and a god-given chariot. Medea does have a member of her natal family whom she can still call upon: her grandfather, who happens to be the Sun. Euripides' Medea is a barbarian with incalculable power; she is also an archetypal Married Wife, and as such an isolated foreigner. This second aspect of Medea, together with the relentlessly recognizable portrayal of her as a woman wronged, is designed to prevent every man in the audience from comfortably dissociating her from his own Greek spouse.

The Sabine Women linked conjugal and natal families. Medea ruined one family for the other, and then destroyed the second family also. The opposition between natal and conjugal families, common in Greek and Roman myths about women and their double role in marriage, means that one family can be preferred to the other. . . .

Euripides made Medea kill her children as well as Creon and his daughter because she had been dishonoured by Jason. A late source makes Medea cause the Lemnian women to repel their husbands by their odour in jealousy over Jason's amour with Hypsipyle. In Ovid's *Heroides* Hypsipyle is jealous of Jason's barbarian mistress, Medea. The theme of jealousy has attached itself to Medea, and the idea of murdering all the men must have brought to mind the woman who, in Euripides' celebrated play, had destroyed all her male kin as well as her husband. But Medea does not kill Jason; for the purpose of revenge she prefers the "female" method of laying waste her husband's life. *Medea* is not a play about simple sexual hatred, about "men versus women", so much as a treatment of the theme of marriage. Medea does not, as the Lemnian Women do, destroy only the men, and she does not commit all her crimes in one swoop. She really loved Jason in the beginning or "first half" of her story, betraying her natal family for him; only when he broke oath and abandoned her did she turn on her conjugal family.

The Sabine Women, upholding loyalties to their new family as well as to their old, managed to restrain their angry fathers and brothers because they had borne children. This, they said, gave the two sets of men a sacred kinship link: now they could not kill each other, even in vengeance, or pollution would ensue. Marriage, of course, resulted in children, who were the most perfect bond between husband and wife (*Med*. 490–1), and between their respective natal families. Having children was a married woman's main duty, and success in this earned her honour and respect. But women went to live with their husbands when they married, and it was in their husband's houses that they brought up their babies. The conjugal family is the "family of procreation" in a patrilocal system.

The mother's bond with her baby is of course of primal importance; once a woman became a mother she was committed fully to her new family, which she now helped to create. Deliberate infanticide by the child's mother is very rare in Greek mythology. Mothers nearly kill their children by mistake, but are stopped in the nick of time, in Euripides' *Ion* and *Cresphontes*. Mothers may kill their children in error (as Themisto did in Euripides' *Ino*), or in a Bacchic frenzy: they would never do it in their right minds (Agave, the Minyads, the Proitids). The Chorus in Euripides' *Medea* say they can think of only one woman besides Medea who could bring herself to do this thing: Ino, and she had been sent out of her home, struck with insanity by Hera (1282–5).

The Lemnian Women's hatred for all men led them to kill their children, but only their male children. With the sole exception of this case and of Medea, women in Greek mythology find only one reason grave enough to warrant the killing of their own children in cold blood, and that is vengeance on behalf of their natal family. From a woman's point of view, positioned as she is between two families, her children are classified with her husband, just as her brothers and sisters are linked with her parents. Althaea destroys Meleager to avenge her brother, Procne or Aedon butchers her sons to avenge a sister, Iliona protects her brother with her son's life. Tyro murders her sons by Sisyphus so that they will not grow up to kill her father (Hyginus 60, 239, 254). In most cases we are told that the woman weeps forever for her lost infant (cf. *Medea* 1047, 1361).

Euripides chose between two conflicting traditions when he made Medea kill her children. His is the first source we have for Medea's committing infanticide on purpose, and Euripides may well have invented this feature. He used Medea's barbarian origin to make her both an archetypal wife and a weird and savage sorceress. She is all the more terrifying for having intimate knowledge of her husband's weaknesses and access to the most private and vulnerable place in his house (380, 41). Medea was one of Euripides' many famous "Bad Women", yet she was not a villain always and in all traditions, and in the play Medea has been "pleasing" to the Corinthians (11–12); Aegeus admires her; and the Chorus is loyal to her. For the first half of the play we sympathize with Medea.

Medea was part of the Thessalian saga of the Argonauts; but she was also part of the history of Corinth. E. Will believed that there were in fact two Medeas, one a Corinthian and one a Thessalian; certainly his conclusion fits the fact that there are two entirely different sets of myths concerning her. She was a legendary witch in a story whose hero was Jason; and she was a primeval Mother Goddess with the power to grant immortality, but whose cult had been replaced and then misremembered: by historical times her solemn sacrificial rites had degenerated into tales of revivifying cauldrons and child murder. In Corinth Medea killed her children, the King and the Princess and ruined her husband. In Colchis she destroyed her natal family. Euripides lets the first part of the story provide the circumstances and the background for the second. The early kin murders and the death of Pelias are not just female initiation myths: in the play they are the past of a real woman's life, and they impinge on the present, prefigure it, and explain it. In Euripides' hands, *Medea* has become the negation of the ancient picture of marriage as it is drawn in a story like "The Sabine Women"; instead of providing a fruitful and profitable link between two families and keeping a loving relationship alive in both households at once, Medea destroys first one family and then the other. She is a Lemnian in her ferocity, but a destroyer of the pattern of marriage and not a simple man-hater.

However we consider Medea, we are forced to see her as a combination of opposite aspects. She is a "demon mistress", a fairy lover who (as often in folklore) kills her rival with a magic, treacherous gift; Medea is also a very human woman abandoned, who causes the death of her husband's children. She is the granddaughter of Helios the Sun god, brightness itself; but she is also an Erinys, a dark and bloody curse in the house of Jason. Jason broke his oath when he abandoned Medea, which means that she will get away with her dreadful deed because she is both under the protection of the Sun (god of oaths) and she is a Curse (the punishment of those who break oaths). At last Jason understands: "When I brought you to a Greek home from your barbarous house and country, you betrayer of your father and your native land, you murderer of your brother by your hearth, the gods sent your Alastor upon *me*" (1330–3). Medea is not to pay; Jason instead is to receive all the punishment from the gods, and the Corinthians, not she, will have to propitiate her children for the revolting crime (1383, 1371–2).

She is last seen at the top of the *skênê* where gods traditionally appear. Jason orders his attendants to unlock the great doors to the palace. Behind those doors the children have been heard screaming as they were stabbed, and the audience expects the traditional *ekkyklêma* scene after the murder. Medea arrives, carrying with her the corpses of her children, above. The chariot she rides in is the gift of the fiery Sun god himself; yet it is drawn by serpents, the symbol of the chthonic, female Erinyes. Its position, aloft, marks it as divine and Olympian: "up" as opposed to "down" was ever bright and celestial and "male".

Medea the Married Woman, who came into Corinth as Jason's bride, is now leaving. Built into every Greek's idea of marriage was the thought that a woman, once she had made the dramatic, difficult and paradoxical crossing from her father's to her husband's house, would now stay: her marriage, her children would make her stay; her place was henceforth in her new home. Plutarch tells us that in the marriage ritual of Boeotia the axle of the carriage in which a woman arrived at her new home was ceremonially burned, "signifying that the bride must remain, since her means of departure has been destroyed". Women, men said, did not want to go away from their conjugal families. Woe to the man rash enough to try and make a woman leave, for the Erinyes would get him (*Odyssey* 2.130–37; cf. *Medea* 431–8). "Leaving", Medea said, "is not well thought of, for a woman" (*Medea* 236–7). Yet Medea left: in fact, she flew away. Medea, the married woman, is given the quintessentially masculine power of Hermes, Hestia's opposite.

Medea is passionate, as females are, but she has a male intelligence. She is a mother, but to her mind honour, the kind of honour that males most admire, is greater than mother love. Medea, the wife of Jason, knows all about heroism, heroic honour, and heroic quests: it was only with her help that Jason had completed his own famous deeds. Medea knows how countless heroes had set off on dangerous journeys to find a magic token and bring it home. Medea did things differently, because Medea was a woman, and she did not bring life and hope to Corinth, but death and destruction. Medea did not set out from home and later return: she came into the city, destroyed both the city's king and her husband's house, and then left—a sickening reversal of the heroic pattern. Medea could give Aegeus children, and she had borne children to Jason—but Medea destroyed those very children for the sake of vengeance; and this gave her a hideous freedom. She did not choose, when she killed her children, her traditionally "female" methods of poison, cookery, and deceit, but instead committed a "male", straightforward and violent butchery with the sword.

The Sabine women were everything women should be: virginal but ready to accept men when it became clear that duty lay in acceptance; agreeing to be mothers, wives, sisters and daughters simultaneously; peace-makers and creators of political alliance; devoted to the family but in such a way that the city benefited. *Medea* is an extravaganza on the theme of marriage, and it turns "The Sabine Women" upside down—or rather, inside out. Medea relentlessly inverts, manipulates, but always presupposes all the conventional wisdom about married men and women, their obligations and rights, their spheres of competence and authority, their societal roles, and even their cosmic connotations. Medea's last appearance sums up all this, in a *coup de théâtre* which ought to leave any audience gasping.

PART II

Medieval Drama and Theater in England

The Martyrdom of St. Appolonia, ca. 1452–56, (a manuscript illustration by Jean Fouquet to the Book of Hours of Etienne Chevalier, Musée Condé, Chantilly, France). Note the five scaffold stages in the background, including Hellmouth with devils (far right), a minstrel's gallery (far left), and a Heaven stage with access ladder (second from left). The foreground depicts the saint's death by torture.

DRAMA AND SOCIETY

During the many centuries it flourished, the Roman Empire established an extraordinary culture and an elaborate network of institutions, not only military, but social, political, economic, legal, religious—and theatrical. Around 430 A.D., after a long history of struggles, Rome fell to barbarian invaders. By 463 A.D., the city had been sacked twice, and the vast civilization that had stretched from northern Europe to the Middle East collapsed.

Nearly a thousand years elapsed between the fall of Rome and the rise of Italian city-states, birthplaces of the Renaissance, in the thirteenth and fourteenth centuries. During this millennium, the so-called Middle Ages, the roads, aqueducts, and other material systems that had unified the Roman Empire decayed. Transportation, communication, and commerce became more difficult. Law and order broke down. It took nearly five hundred years—from about the fifth until the tenth centuries—for European society to shake off the continuing catastrophic raids from the north, and another five hundred to consolidate its cultural identity. During this long era a series of narrow cultures emerged in place of the vast Roman Empire, and the Roman system of civil order was gradually replaced by two forces: the rule of Christian conduct promulgated by the Catholic Church, with its hierarchy of pope, bishops, and priests; and the social rule of feudalism, a code built on the concept of loyalty to a liege lord whose power protected the men who served him. The Church built monasteries, parish churches, and cathedrals as sites of spiritual and temporal power, while feudal lords staked out territories protected by fortified castles and manors. The three social classes of the Middle Ages emerged from this new order: the warrior class, the priestly class, and the peasant class. All three were to be implicated in the emergence of new kinds of drama.

In the latter days of the Roman Empire, public spectacles and blood sports, such as chariot races and gladiatorial contests in coliseums, came to dominate the world of entertainment. A few late survivals of Roman drama are recorded in the fourth and fifth centuries, along with occasional plays and performances by traveling troupes of mimes, jugglers, and actors who roamed the land. But by the sixth century the Roman amphitheaters were gone forever, and the Church vigorously opposed any reestablishment of secular theatrical practices. It was once believed that no drama or theater survived the collapse of the Empire at all. In fact, a dramatic tradition did survive in the Eastern Empire (in what is now modern Turkey), though this drama did not influence developments in western Europe.

The first signs of theatrical activity in the west occurred in the tenth century. Hrotswitha, a noblewoman and nun attached to the Benedictine monastery near Gandersheim in modern Germany, wrote seven plays based on the comedies of the Roman playwright Terence, indicating some knowledge of Roman plays in the Middle Ages. Hrotswitha's plays endorsed contemporary Christian morality and may have been closet dramas (intended only to be read). In any case, her work appears to have grown and died on its own, and there is no known connection between Hrotswitha's startling achievement and what was to follow in the Middle Ages, or between it and the neoclassical drama that would develop several centuries later. Curiously enough, the principal impetus to revive theater in western Europe came gradually from within the Church itself, and drama's development

This artist's reconstruction of the ground plan for the stage for the morality play, *The Castle of Perserverance*, shows five scaffolds surrounding a playing area with a castle in the center. The ditch surrounding the castle may have kept spectators at a distance from the play.

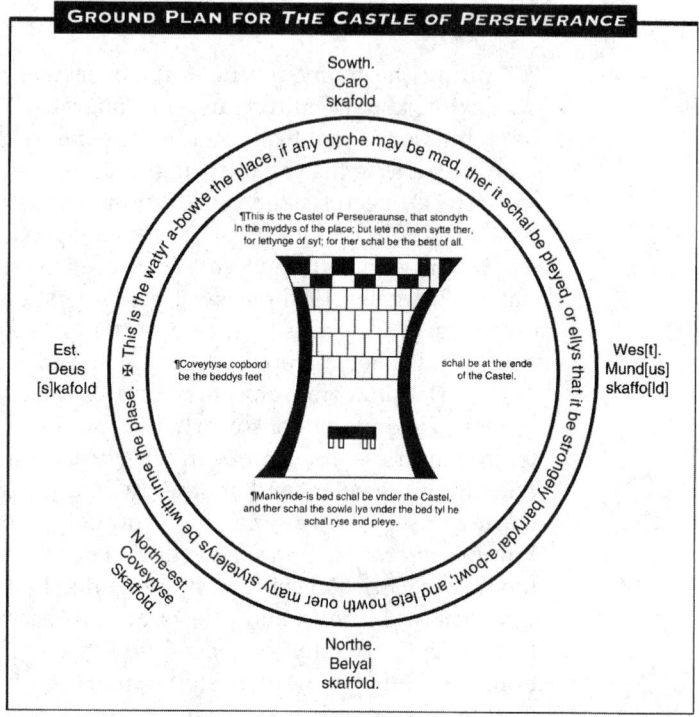

GROUND PLAN FOR *THE CASTLE OF PERSEVERANCE*

Sowth.
Caro
skafold

This is the watyr a-bowte the place, if any dyche may be mad, ther it schal be pleyed, or ellys that it be strongly barryd al a-bowt; and lete nowth over many stytelerys be with-inne the place. ✠ This is the watyr a-bowte the plase.

¶This is the Castel of Perseueraunse, that stondyth in the myddys of the place; but lete no men sytte ther, for lettynge of syt; for ther schal be the best of all.

¶Coveytyse copbord be the beddys feet

schal be at the ende of the Castel.

¶Mankynde-is bed schal be vnder the Castel, and ther schal the sowle lye vnder the bed tyl he schal ryse and pleye.

Est.
Deus
[s]kafold

Wes[t].
Mund[us]
skaffo[ld]

Northe-est.
Coveytyse
Skaffold.

Northe.
Belyal
skaffold.

from the tenth to the fifteenth centuries was intimately connected with the Church's rituals, its doctrine, and its liturgical observances.

By the ninth century the Church was effectively the only religion in western Europe, and it wielded immense spiritual and temporal power. Its political aspirations came to rival those of feudal kings. In the year 800 A.D. Charlemagne was crowned by the Pope in Rome, and the Holy Roman Empire came into existence, uniting church and state and marrying religion to politics for centuries to come. With a monopoly on literacy and learning, the Church preserved the shreds of classical knowledge that had survived the fall of the Roman Empire, and it shaped scholastic goals to conform to Christian teaching. The Church achieved a pervasive cultural presence in this period in politics, in education, and in the daily lives of ordinary people.

However vast and geographically dispersed the congregation of the Catholic Church, it was unified by the ritual expression of its liturgy. This Latin liturgy, written in the universal language of the literate in western Europe, provided an ordering principle for passing the entire year in the service of God, season by season, week by week, feast day by feast day, canonical hour by canonical hour. Included in the liturgy were prayers for every occasion and event, with specific directions for sacred rites and sacramental practices, including incantations, dialogue, music, and dress. Out of the liturgy of the Church a new kind of drama arose.

As early as the ninth century, musical elaborations of significant Latin phrases in the liturgy began to appear. Called *tropes*, they developed as part of devotions at certain feasts during the year. The purpose of the tropes was to heighten and enhance the religious experience of worshippers. In monasteries and abbeys tropes seem to have developed into rudimentary theatrical practice. The best-known example, the so-called *quem quaeritis* trope of the tenth century, dramatizes the Easter morning biblical episode in which the three Marys approach the sepulcher where Jesus was buried, and they are asked by the angel guarding the tomb, "*Quem quaeritis?*" ("Whom do you seek?"). They respond that they are seeking Jesus, and the angel tells them that he has risen. In the *Regularis Concordia* (965–975 A.D.), a Benedictine monastic handbook written by Ethelwold, Bishop of Winchester, elaborate directions for performing this trope are given. In it, clerics are instructed to dress for the parts and to sing the dialogue antiphonally (in two parts, answering each other).

Tropes were initially conceived as ways to enhance meditation. The dramatic sequences that developed out of them are not plays in any modern sense of the word. However, they have all the basic elements of drama: progressive plots, brief development of character, conflict, resolution, and, as Ethelwold's directions suggest, a sense of visual spectacle. They were also tied intimately to musical performances.

Such an arrangement was characteristic of the liturgical drama as it developed into more elaborate performances over the hundreds of years it was to be practiced. From small tropes these performances developed into more complicated ones. The subjects of most of them were biblical, but some depicted stories such as the life of the Virgin or the raising of Lazarus. Liturgical plays were enacted in monasteries and in churches by the clergy, by choirboys and monks, and they were chanted or sung in Latin rather than in native languages. The actors were almost always males. Because the audience consisted almost entirely of those living in monastic communities, the influence of this liturgical drama was limited, though real, on the vernacular plays that developed about the same time.

Perhaps the most momentous event of the later Middle Ages was the spread of bubonic plague. This disease, transmitted by fleas carried by rats, swept across Europe as an epidemic beginning in 1348. For the next three hundred years it continued to erupt without warning, bringing hideous suffering and often grotesque disfigurement before death. Fully one-third, probably more, of the population of Europe died from it. Survivors of the plague faced an altered world. Labor was now scarce and expensive, translating into economic opportunity for the poorer ranks. Many people left the countryside for the cities, which grew into important economic and cultural centers during the late fourteenth century. Craft guilds were formed, functioning as a combination of labor unions and fraternal organizations, giving workers a stake in the new economic prosperity. Meanwhile, the suffering and devastation of the Black Death shattered earlier spiritual and philosophical certainties and gave rise to new religious sects and practices. Society itself was altered in the wake of the plague's destruction, signaling the beginning of the end of the feudal order. The growth of towns, the founding of guilds, and the new prosperity provided motive and opportunity for a second kind of medieval drama.

THE *QUEM QUÆRITIS* TROPE OF THE LORD'S RESURRECTION

Question [of the angels]:
Whom seen ye in the sepulchre, O followers of Christ?
Answer [of the Marys]:
Jesus of Nazareth, which was crucified, O celestial ones.
5   [The angels:]
He is not here; he is risen, just as he foretold.
Go, announce that he is risen from the sepulchre.
After this [the third responsory] let two boys, in albs,[1] one at the right of the altar, the other at the left, sing:
10   *Whom seek ye in the sepulchre, O followers of Christ?*
Let three chaplains, garbed in white dalmatics,[2] with covered heads,[3] standing before the altar, reply:
Jesus of Nazareth, which was crucified, O celestial ones.
Then the boys:
15   *He is not here; he is risen, just as he foretold.*
Go, announce that he is risen from the dead.
Then those three, approaching the altar and looking within, turning towards the choir, say in a loud voice:
Alleluia, the Lord is risen!
20   After this the cantor[4] begins:
We praise thee, O God.
While the third lesson is being chanted, let four brethren vest themselves; of whom let one, vested in an alb, enter as if to take part in the service, and let him without being observed approach the place of the sepulchre, and there, holding a palm in his hand, let him sit down quietly. While
25   the third responsory is being sung, let the remaining three follow, all of them vested in copes, and carrying in their hands censers filled with incense; and slowly, in the manner of seeking something, let them come before the place of the sepulchre. These things are done in imitation of the angel seated in the monument, and of the women coming with spices to
30   anoint the body of Jesus. When therefore that one seated shall see the three, as if straying about and seeking something, approach him, let him begin in a dulcet voice of medium pitch to sing:
Whom seek ye in the sepulchre, O followers of Christ?
When he has sung this to the end, let the three respond in unison:
35   *Jesus of Nazareth, which was crucified, O celestial one.*
To whom that one:
He is not here; he is risen, just as he foretold.
Go, announce that he is risen from the dead.
At the word of this command let those three turn themselves to the choir,
40   saying:
Alleluia! The Lord is risen to-day,
The strong lion, the Christ, the Son of God. Give thanks to God, huzza!

---

[1] A full-length vestment of white linen.   [2] A vestment resembling the alb, but with slits in the side.   [3] Probably in order that they might the better represent women.
[4] The leader of the choir, who regularly sang the *Te Deum* marking the end of the Matin service.

Types of Medieval Drama

This best-known kind of medieval drama, the so-called cycle or mystery plays, arose not in churches or monasteries but in prosperous towns and cities throughout Europe beginning in the late fourteenth century. Mystery plays (from the French *mystère*, "craft") was were sanctioned by the Church, but produced by guilds. They are also known as cycle plays, because they portray the cycle of Christian history from the Creation of the world until the Last Judgment. Their purpose was to teach Christian history in a memorable and entertaining form. The cycle plays were vast productions, and they stood as visible testimony to the piety and wealth of the prosperous civic corporations that sponsored them. They were performed not by clerics and priests but by crowds of laypeople, and they were watched not in monasteries but in the streets of cities and towns, often as part of special feast day celebrations, such as Corpus Christi or Whitsunday, near the middle of the year.

In the cycle plays the long biblical history from Creation to Judgment was broken into short pageants (dramatized episodes) and assigned to individual guilds. Pageants were often assigned to a guild with expertise in the central topic of the play. The Shipwrights Guild might produce the Noah play, for example, the Goldsmiths Guild the Visit of the Magi, the Carpenters Guild the Crucifixion, and so on. The town council decided on the venue, but each guild had to finance its pageant, assemble the cast, secure properties and costumes, erect and decorate stages or pageant wagons (carts with decorated superstructures to accommodate the action), arrange for rehearsals, and perform the play. Few towns performed their cycle plays every year, but the plays were performed often enough for the guilds to establish routines. The cycle plays included a large number of pageants—the York Cycle contains forty-eight of them—and they could take whole days to perform, often as part of larger civic festival. In one way or another a sizable number of citizens participated in the productions, as managers, actors, supporting cast, or stage crew. The audience, too, was large and diverse, made up of virtually every level of provincial society in towns and villages within traveling distance of the sponsoring community. Practically speaking, it would have been very difficult for any single spectator to see an entire cycle in any given year, but over the course of a lifetime repeated exposures might well familiarize one with all of the pageants.

Because individual pageants were performed by separate guilds, each pageant was to some degree approached as an independent dramatic entity. But in conception and in performance the cycle plays were constructed as a unified sequence of episodes whose pious intent dictated the form, the content, and the mode of production. Some techniques—such as the anachronistic mixing of historical and contemporary characters and events—are common to many of the cycle plays, producing surprising and delightful ironies. But each of the cycles has a unique character, derived from their use of differing characters and themes, carried through from pageant to pageant. These mystery cycles flourished from the last quarter of the fourteenth century to the late sixteenth century, when they fell victim to Reformation sensibilities, which insisted upon stricter biblical standards, less ostentation, and altogether more sober public ceremonies.

Despite the number and importance of the cycle plays, the most common form of medieval dramatic experience relied on other kinds of plays. Most towns and vil-

DESCRIPTION OF THE CHESTER CYCLE

In 1623 a local Chester antiquarian named John Rogers described the nature and background of the Chester cycle, which had not been played for nearly 50 years. He based this description in part on the recollections of this father.

Now of the playes of Chester
Called the whitson playes:

	The maker and first Inuenter of them was one Rondoll a monke	The author of them:
5	in the Abbaye of Chester whoe did transelate the same, into	
	Englishe, & made them into partes and pagiantes, as they then	
	weare played: The matter of them was the historye of the bible,	The matter of them:
	mixed with some other matter: The time they weare firste sett	
	forthe, and played was in an*no* :1339: S*ir* Iohn, 'Arnewaye'	The first time played:
10	beinge mayor of Chester: The actors and players, weare the	
	occupations & Companies of this Cittie, the Charges and costes	The players &
	'thereof' *which* weare greate, was theires also: The time of the	charges thereof:
	yeare they weare played was on monday, tuesday & wenseday in	
	whitson weeke: The maner of these playes weare, euery Company	The manner of them:
15	had his pagiant or p*arte* w*hich* pagiants, weare a high scafolde	
	with 2. rowmes ahiger & alower, vpon 4 wheeles In the lower	
	they apparelled them selues, And In the higher rowme they	
	played beinge all open on the tope that all behoulders mighte	
	heare & see them,: The places where the played them was in	The places where ye
20	euery streete, They begane first at the Abay gates, and when the	played them:
	firste pagiante was played, it was wheeled to the |highe Crosse	
	before the mayor, and so to euery streete, and soe euery streete	
	had a pagiant playinge before them at one time tell ‸'all' the	
	pagiantes for the daye appoynted weare played, and when one	
25	pagiant was neere ended worde was broughte from streete to	
	streete that soe the might‸ 'come' in place thereof, excedinge	
	orderlye and all the streetes haue theire pagiantes afore them	
	all at one time playeinge togeather to se w*hich* playes was greate	
	resorte, and also scafoldes and stages made in the streetes ‸'in'	
30	those places where they determined to playe theire pagiantes:	

(The list of companies and their parts follow.)
...

	... the laste time these playes weare played in Chester was an*no* do*mini*
35	:1574: S*ir* Iohn Sauage beinge mayor of Chester Iohn Allen & william
	Goodman sheriffes thus in briefe of the playes of Chester:

lages shared their governance between parish church and appointed officials, and so most communities were simply too small to have in place the necessary governing, commercial, and social structures to produce the elaborate cycle plays. The drama produced in these smaller towns is referred to as non-cycle plays. In number, frequency of performance, and geographical distribution, they were the rule rather than the exception for hundreds of communities during the later Middle Ages.

Generally speaking, the non-cycle plays fall into three categories: saint plays, morality plays, and biblical or secular history plays. Saint plays dramatized the lives, the conversions, the miracles, and sometimes the martyrdom of saints. They were often performed in parishes, perhaps to celebrate the feast days of patron saints. Biblical or secular history plays depict strange, violent, or otherwise compelling stories. One of the most famous of these plays, the Digby *Killing of the Children*, dramatizes the biblical story of the slaughter of innocent babes ordered by King Herod. Another, the Croxton *Play of the Sacrament*, traces the violent history of a consecrated host that is stolen and desecrated by unbelievers. Although these plays were more or less pious, many late medieval town or parish records indicate that the purpose of such plays was more economic: to raise money to support serious town or church projects.

The most famous and influential of the non-cycle plays are the moralities, which flourished from the fourteenth century through the sixteenth century. These plays typically dramatize an allegory of each Christian's journey through life toward salvation. The chief characters in morality plays are allegorical figures with names like Mankind or Everyman, who are beset by abstract vices such as Covetousness and aided by abstract virtues such as Good Deeds or Penance. All show the spiritual struggle for salvation. The plots of early morality plays revolve around temptation (*Mankind*); or around the summoning to death (*Everyman*); or around other religious themes, including the actual Judgment in heaven (*The Castle of Perseverance*). These plots and characters proved to be extraordinarily flexible. Many of their dramatic devices were adapted to secular purposes in the sixteenth century. The temptation plot and the vice characters proved especially adaptable. Marlowe used them in *Dr. Faustus*, which portrays a character who is alternately counseled by good and bad angels. The morality play's structure was also used to dramatize the problems of political rather than moral choice, as John Skelton did with *Magnificence*. Vice characters appear often in secular plays throughout the century, and vestiges of the vice's dramatic heritage lie behind the creation of such famous characters such as Shakespeare's Richard III, who declares that he is "like the vice, Iniquity," or Falstaff, who is described as a misleader of youth, "a reverend vice."

STAGING MEDIEVAL DRAMA

Whether staged in churches and monasteries or in the streets of cities and towns, certain basic principles applied to the staging of medieval plays. The playing place, indoors or outdoors, could represent several different locations at the same time, and the meaning of the action was enhanced by visual symbols understood by the audience.

Liturgical drama was performed in churches and monasteries, where existing church architecture could be used. The altar might represent the tomb of Christ; the crypt might represent hell, the choir heaven. For more elaborate plays, mansions (small scenic structures) might be built, some large enough to contain several actors. Costumes were ordinary church vestments to which symbolic elements might be added. Sometimes special effects required machinery capable of flying actors in and out of the playing space: angels might descend, the Magi might follow the star of Bethlehem, or Christ might rise.

Mystery plays were performed out of doors in cities and towns. Many throughout Europe were performed on fixed stages, while others in England and in parts of Spain were performed on movable stages. In fixed staging, mansions were set up in the shape of a circle, square, or rectangle, and the playing space and audience area were established accordingly. Two types of movable staging were used in England. In some cycles the audience remained stationary while the pageants and their plays went in a procession through the main streets of the town; the pageants might also be arranged in an area for the performance. The audience could then move from one pageant to another. Sometimes, as seems to have happened at York and Chester, pageant wagons followed a set course through the town, stopping at several stations to perform before different audiences.

Song and spectacle were common features of many pageants, and town musicians frequently accompanied the performances. Staging was calculated to produce a close and powerful relationship between performance and audience. Herod's ranting—as in the Coventry *Play of the Magi*, in which Herod actually leaps from the pageant wagon and rages in the midst of the audience—was so well known that Shakespeare could refer to it in *Hamlet* as an illustration of over-acting. This interaction between actor and audience, which carried over into the drama of the age of Shakespeare, makes clear that the place of the action in medieval drama was not localized to the stage. Herod could move from the fictional Jerusalem onstage into the audience and back again. Even onstage places were easily transformed. This kind of simultaneous staging permitted playwrights to treat stage space symbolically or emblematically. Non-cycle plays, particularly moralities, followed similar conventions.

DESCRIPTION OF A NORWICH PAGEANT WAGON AND THEATRICAL PROPERTIES

The 1565 accounts of the Grocer's Guild in Norwich describe the properties needed for their plays "Creation of the World" and "Adam and Eve" and the fate of their pageant wagon.

Grocers' Guild Records

Inventory. of ye *p*articulars appartaynyng to ye Company of ye Grocers. Ad, 1565.

A Pageant. *y*at is to saye a Howsse of Waynskott. paynted & buylded on a Carte w*itth* fowre whelys.

a square toppe to sett over ye sayde Howsse.

a Gryffon gylte w*ith* a fane to sett on ye sayde Toppe.

a bygger Iron fane to sett on ye ende of ye Pageante.

IIIJ^{XX}. iij. small Fanes belongyng to ye same Pageante

5   A Rybbe Colleryd Redd.

a Cote & hosen w*ith* a bagg & capp for dolor stayned

2 Cotes & a payre hosen for Eve stayned

a Cote & Hosen for Adam stayned.

a Cote w*ith* hosen & tayle for ye cerpente stayned

10   w*ith* a w*hitte* heare.

a Cote of yellow buckram w*ith* ye Grocers arms for ye Pendon bearer.

an Angell*es* Cote & over hoses of apis Skynns

3 paynted clothes to hange abowte ye Pageante.

15   a face & heare for ye Father.

2 hearys for Adam & Eve

4 headstallis of brode Inkle with knopps & tassell*es*

6 Horsse Clothes stayned w*ith* knops & tassells.

Item. Weights. &c.

20   Item yt is to be noted, that for asmuch as for ye space of 8 yeris, ther was neyther Semblye nor metynge in ye meane season ye Pageant remaynynge 6. yeris in ye Gate house of M*r* John Sotherton of London, vntyll ye ferme came to 20 s. and bycaus ye Surveiors in M*r* Sothertons tyme, wold not dysburs ani moni

25   therfor, ye Pageaunt was sett owte in ye strete & so remayned at ye Blak fryers brydge in open strete when both yt was so <.> weather beaten, *y*at ye cheife *p*arte was rotton wherupon. M*r* John Aldrich then Maior ye yer 1570, together w*ith* M*r* Tho*mas* Whall Alderman offred. yt to teCompani to sell for ye some of 20 s.

30   and when no *p*erson wold buy yt for *y*at price, and *y*at yt styll remayned, & nowe one pece therof rent off & nowe another as was lyke to come to nothinge. Nicholas Sotherton then offycer to M*r* Maior was requested to take yt in peces for ye dept dewe to hym for ye seyd Housse ferme therof for 6 yeris

35   aforesayde at 3 s. 4 d. a yere. who accordinglye dyd take downe ye same & howsed yt accordinglye.

THE WAKEFIELD MASTER

The Wakefield Cycle originated in the late fourteenth century, and additions to the original plays and revisions of older plays continued to be made until the sixteenth century. Like the other surviving cycles, the Wakefield Cycle consists of plays written and rewritten by a number of authors working at different periods in its history. New plays might be added as guilds became larger or more prosperous. Older plays might be dropped or combined with others if a guild could no longer afford to produce them. Revisions could also be made to satisfy the objections of the church or town officials or to respond to the interests of the community.

The anonymous author of the Wakefield *Second Shepherds' Play* (so called because it is the second of two shepherd's plays in this cycle) is known as the Wakefield Master, and we know almost nothing about him. He is thought to have written in the mid-fifteenth century. From his knowledge of biblical literature and Latin liturgy, it appears that he may have been a member of the clergy. However, he does not appear to have been a cloistered monk, for the plays he contributed to the Wakefield Cycle display familiarity with a wide range of characters and situations in society at large. The work of the Wakefield Master, which includes many whole pageants and pieces of others, stands out as the most distinctive contribution in all medieval drama. His *Second Shepherds' Play* is perhaps the best known and best loved play to have survived from this period.

The Wakefield Master's work can be identified by his verse form—a nine-line stanza that he uses throughout his plays and in his revisions to others. The form appears nowhere else in the Wakefield Cycle. The first four lines have four beats, the fifth has one, the sixth through the eighth have three, and the ninth line two beats. The first four lines of his stanza have identical end rhymes and identical internal rhymes. The last five lines have a different rhyme scheme.

The Second Shepherds' Play

In addition to his metrical skill, the Wakefield Master is admired for his play structure and vivid characterization. The longest of his works, *The Second Shepherds' Play*, has only 754 lines, yet the Wakefield Master manages to create a fully realized world of shepherds and a Christmas scene, all of which combine to appeal both as farce and as a significant religious play. The first three shepherds are presented as individualized characters: Coll is a social critic, obsessed by his poverty and incensed by the gentry's exploitation of the poor; Gib is preoccupied with the problems of married life; and Daw is disgusted with his position, having to tend others' sheep. These different characters are united by their concerns with exploitation, and they gather onstage in ferocious winter weather. Their social and physical suffering presents a picture of a world in need of help.

 The sheep-stealing episode with Mak is a fine example of the Wakefield Master's skill at turning a simple idea into a meaningful drama that can brilliantly illuminate the Christmas story. He takes the story of the birth of Christ from the Gospel of Luke, transports it to England, and makes these shepherds the very ones who attend the nativity on Christmas day. As the farcical part of the play unfolds, it becomes clear that the story of Mak, Gyll, and the sheep in swaddling clothes is a parody of the nativity of Christ. When Mak's crime is exposed, he is in fact liable to severe punishment. He can be executed for stealing sheep, and Daw wants to carry out that penalty. Coll suggests a lesser penalty, and in the spirit of the meaning of Christmas, the shepherds find it in them to show mercy, tossing Mak in a blanket. Their suffering and compassion, in the logic of the play, brings about God's gift of his son to humanity.

The Second Shepherds' Play
THE WAKEFIELD MASTER

EDITED BY JOHN C. COLDEWAY

CHARACTERS
COLL (*Shepherd 1*)
GIB (*Shepherd 2*)
DAW (*Shepherd 3*)
MAK, *a Sheep-stealer*

GYLL, Mak's Wife
ANGEL
MARY (*with baby Jesus*)

SCENE: Open fields; bad weather

[*Enter* COLL]

COLL: Lord! What these weathers are cold! And I am ill wrapped.
 I am near-hand° numb, so long have I napped;   *nearly*
 My legs they fold,° my fingers are chapped.   *collapse*
 It is not as I would, for I am all lapped°   *wrapped*
5 In sorrow.
 In storms and tempest,
 Now in the east, now in the west,
 Woe is him has never rest
  Midday nor morrow!

10 But we simple husbands° that walk on the moor,   *husbandmen*
 In faith we are near-hands out of the door.°   *homeless*
 No wonder, as it stands, if we be poor,
 For the tilth of our lands lies fallow as the floor,°   *ground*
  As ye ken.°   *know*
15 We are so hammed,°   *hemmed in*
 Fortaxed° and rammed,°   *overtaxed / beaten down*
 We are made hand-tamed
  By these gentlery-men.

	Thus they reave° us our rest, our Lady them curse!	*rob*
20	These men that are lord-fast,° they cause the plow tarry.	*bound to a lord*
	That men say is for the best, we find it contrary.	
	Thus are husbands° oppressed, in point to miscarry	*husbandmen*
	In life;	
	Thus hold they us under,	
25	Thus they bring us in blunder;°	*trouble*
	It were great wonder	
	If ever should we thrive.	

	For may he get a paint sleeve° or a brooch° nowadays,	*livery / badge*
	Woe is him that him grieves or one word gainsays!	
30	No man dares him reprove, whatever power he has;	
	And yet may no man believe one word that he says,	
	No° letter.	*not a*
	He can make purveyance°	*demand*
	With boast and bragance,°	*bragging*
35	And all is through maintenance°	*support by a lord*
	Of men that are greater.	

	There shall come a swain as proud as a peacock;	
	He must borrow my wagon, my plow also;	
	Then I am full fain° to grant ere he go.	*ready*
40	Thus live we in pain, anger, and woe,	
	By night and day.	
	He must have, if he longs° it,	*wants*
	If I should forgang° it;	*do without*
	I were better be hanged	
45	Then once say him nay.	

	It does me good, as I walk thus by mine own,	
	Of this world for to talk in manner of moan.	
	To my sheep will I stalk, and hearken anon,	
	There abide on a balk,° or sit on a stone	*unplowed strip of land*
50	Full soon;	
	For I trow, pardie,°	*trust, by God*
	True men if they be,	
	We get more company	
	Ere it be noon.	

[*Enter* GIB]

55	GIB: Bensté, and Dominus,° what may this bemean?	*bless us, and Lord*
	Why fares this world thus? Oft have we not seen?	
	Lord, these weathers are spiteful, and the winds full keen	
	And the frosts so hideous they water mine eyne—	
	No lie.	
60	Now in dry, now in wet,	
	Now in snow, now in sleet,	
	When my shoes freeze to my feet	
	It is not all easy.	

	But as far as I ken,° or yet as I go,	*know*
65	We simple husbands endure much woe:	
	We have sorrow then and then;° it falls oft so.	*again and again*
	Silly Copple, our hen, both to and fro	
	She cackles;	

But begins she to croak,
To groan or to cluck,
Woe to him is our cock,
   For he is in the shackles.°   *under her spell*

These men that are wed have not all their will;
When they are full hard bestead,° they sigh full still.   *very hard put*
God knows they are led full hard and full ill;
In bower nor in bed they say naught theretill.
   This tide
My part have I found,
I know my lesson:
Woe is him that is bound,
   For he must abide.

But now late in our lives—a marvel to me,
That I think my heart rives,° such wonders to see;   *breaks*
Whatever destiny drives, it should so be—
Some men will have two wives, and some men three
   In store;
Some are woe that have any.
But so far know I:
Woe is him that has many,
   For he feels sore.

[*To the audience*]

But, young men, of wooing, for God that you bought,°   *redeemed*
Be well wary of wedding, and think in your thought:
"Had-I-wist"° is a thing that serves of nought   *known*
Mickle still mourning° has wedding home brought,   *great unhappiness*
   And griefs,
With many a sharp shower;
For thou may catch in an hour
That shall sow° thee full sorrow   *bring*
   As long as thou lives.

For, as ever read I epistle,° I have one to my fere°   *read the Bible / mate*
As sharp as thistle, as rough as a brier;
She is browed like a bristle, with a sour-laden cheer;
Had she once wet her whistle, she could sing full clear
   Her Paternoster.°   *Our Father*
She is as great as a whale,
She has a gallon of gall;
By Him that died for us all,
   I would I had run til I had lost her!

COLL: God look over the row!° Full deafly ye stand.   *Bless this company!*
GIB: Yea, the devil in thy maw,° so tarrying!   *stomach*
   Saw thou anything of Daw?
COLL: Yea, on a lea-land°   *pasture land*
   Heard I him blow. He comes here at hand,
      Not far.
   Stand still.
GIB: Why?
COLL: For he comes, hope I.

Line numbers: 70, 75, 80, 85, 90, 95, 100, 105, 110, 115

GIB: He will make us both a lie
   But if we beware.

[*Enter* DAW]

DAW: Christ's cross me speed,° and Saint Nicholas!   *help me*
   Thereof had I need; it is worse than it was.
120   Whoso could, take heed and let the world pass,
   It is ever in dread and brickle° as glass,   *brittle*
      And slides.
   This world fared never so,
   With marvels more and more—
125   Now in weal, now in woe,
      And all things writhes.°   *everything changes*

   Was never since Noah's flood such floods seen,
   Winds and rains so rude, and storms so keen—
   Some stammered, some stood in doubt, as I ween.°   *think*
130   Now God turn all to good! I say as I mean,
      For ponder:
   These floods so they drown,
   Both in fields and in town,
   And bears all down;
135   And that is a wonder.

   We that walk on the nights, our cattle to keep,
   We see sudden sights when other men sleep.
   Yet me think my heart lights; I see shrews peep.°   *rascals peeping*
   Ye are two allwights°—I will give my sheep   *ghosts*
140   A turn.
   But full ill have I meant;
   As I walk on this land,
   I may lightly repent,
      My toes if I spurne.°   *stumble*

[*He recognizes his friends*]

145   A, sir, God you save, and master mine!
   A drink fain° would I have, and somewhat to dine.   *gladly*
COLL: Christ's curse, my knave, thou art a evil swine!
GIB: What, the boy list° rave! Abide unto syne;°   *does / later*
      We have made it.
150   Ill thrift on thy pate!
   Though the rogue came late,
   Yet is he in state
      To dine—if he had it.

DAW: Such servants as I, that sweats and swinks,°   *works*
155   Eat our bread full dry, and that me forthinks.°   *I regret*
   We are oft wet and weary when master-men winks;
   Yet comes full late both dinners and drinks.
      But neatly
   Both our dame and our sire,
160   When we have run in the mire,
   They can nip at our hire,°   *cut our wages*
      And pay us full lately.

  But hear my truth, master: for the fare° that ye make,   *wages*
  I shall do, hereafter—work as I take.
165 I shall do a little, sir, and in between play,
  For yet lay my supper never on my stomach
   In fields.
  Whereto should I threap°?   *haggle*
  With my staff can I leap;
170 And men say, "Light cheap   *"A cheap bargain*
   Lightly foryields."°   *pays back badly."*

COLL: Thou were an ill lad, to ride a-wooing
  With a man that had but little of spending.
GIB: Peace, boy, I bade. No more jangling,
175 Or I shall make thee full afeared, by the heavens king!
   With thy gawds°—   *tricks*
  Where are our sheep, boy?—we scorn.
DAW: Sir, this same day at morn
  I them left in the corn,
180   When they rang lauds.°   *i.e., at dawn*

  They have pasture good, they cannot go wrong.
COLL: That is right. By the rood°, these nights are long!   *cross*
  Yet I would, ere we go, one gave us a song.
GIB: So I thought as I stood, to mirth us among.
185 DAW: I grant.
COLL: Let me sing the tenory.°   *tenor*
GIB: And I the treble so high.
DAW: Then the mean falls to me.
   Let see how ye chant.

[*They sing*]

Tunc intrat MAK, in clamide   *Then Mak enters with a cloak*
se super togam vestitus   *draped over his tunic*

190 MAK: Now, Lord, for thy names seven, that made both moon and stars
   Well more then I can name, thy will, Lord, of me tharns.°   *is lacking*
  I am all uneven;° that moves oft my brains.   *upset*
  Now would God I were in heaven, for there weep no bairns°   *children*
   So still.
195 COLL: Who is that pipes so poor?
MAK: Would God ye knew how I fare!
  Lo, a man that walks on the moor,
   And has not all his will.

GIB: Mak, where has thou gone? Tell us tidings.
200 DAW: Is he come? Then everyone take heed to his thing.

Et accipit clamidem ab ipso   *He removes Mak's cloak*

MAK: What! ich be a yeoman,° I tell you, of the king,   *I am a yeoman (Mak*
  The self and the same, sent from a great lording,   *adopts a Southern dialect)*
   And such.
  Fie on you! Go hence
205 Out of my presence!
  I must have reverence.
   Why, who be ich?°   *Who do you think I am?*

COLL: Why make ye it° so quaint Mak, ye do wrong.   *your speech*
GIB: But, Mak, list ye saint?° I trow that ye long.   *Playing saint?*
210 DAW: I trow° the shrew can paint, the devil might him hang!   *think*
MAK: Ich shall make complaint, and get you all a thwang°   *flogging*
    At a word,
    And tell even how ye doth.°   *do wrong*
COLL: But, Mak, is that sooth?°   *true*
215   Now take out that Southern tooth,°   *accent*
      And set in a turd!

GIB: Mak, the devil in your eye! A stroke would I lend you.
DAW: Mak, know ye not me? By God, I could tend° you.   *hurt*
MAK: God look you all three! Me thought I had seen you.

[*Admitting he knows them*]

220   Ye are a fair company.
COLL: Can ye now mean you?°   *identify yourself*
GIB: Shrew, peep!°   *Troublemaker, look out!*
    Thus late as thou goes,°   *When you go out late*
    What will men suppose?
    And thou has an ill noise°   *bad reputation*
225   Of stealing of sheep.

MAK: And I am true as steel, all men wot;°   *know*
    But a sickness I feel that holds me full hot:
    My belly fares not well; it is out of astate.°   *shape*
DAW: Seldom lies the devil dead by the gate.
230 MAK: Therefore
    Full sore am I and ill,
    If I stand stone-still.
    I eat not an needle
      This month and more.

235 COLL: How fares thy wife? By thy hood, how fares she?
MAK: Lies waltering°—by the rood°—by the fire, lo!   *lounging / cross*
    And a house full of brood. She drinks well, too
    Ill speed other good that she will do!
      But she
240   Eats as fast as she can,
    And ilk° year that comes to man   *every*
    She brings forth a lakan°—   *baby*
      And, some years, two.

    But were I now more gracious and richer by far,
245   I were eaten out of house and of harbor.°   *garden*
    Yet is she a foul dowse,° if ye come near;   *slut*
    There is none that trows nor knows a worse
      Then ken I.
    Now will ye see what I proffer?
250   To give all in my coffer
    Tomorrow at next to offer
      Her head-masspenny.°   *funeral donation*

GIB: I wot° so forwaked° is none in this shire;   *think / tired*
    I would sleep, if I taked less to my hire.
255 DAW: I am cold and naked, and would have a fire.

COLL: I am weary, forwracked,° and run in the mire— *wretched*
    Wake thou!
GIB: Nay, I will lie down by,
    For I must sleep, truly,
260 DAW: As good a man's son was I
    As any of you.

    But, Mak, come hither! Between shalt thou lie down.
MAK: Then might I hinder you of that ye would rown,° *whisper*
    No dread.° *doubt*
265 From my top to my toe,
    Manus tuas commendo,° *Into your hands I commend*
    Pontio Pilato;° *Pontius Pilate*
    Christ cross me speed!

Tunc surgit, pastoribus dormientibus, et dicit° *Then he rises while the shepherds are sleeping and says*

    Now were time for a man that lacks what he would
270 To stalk prively then unto a fold,
    And nimbly to work then, and be not too bold,
    For he might pay for the bargain, if it were told
    At the ending.
    Now were time for to move;
275 But he needs good counsel
    That fain would fare well,
    And has but little spending.° *money*

    But about you a circle, as round as a moon,
    To I have done that I will,° till that it be noon, *do what I want*
280 That ye lie stone-still to that I have done;
    And I shall say thereto of good words a foyne:° *few*
    "On height,
    Over your heads, my hand I lift.
    Out go your eyes! Foredo° your sight!" *Perish*
285 But yet I must make better shift
    If it be right.

    Lord, but they sleep hard! That may ye all hear.
    Was I never a shepherd, but now will I learn.
    If the flock be scared, yet shall I nip near.
290 How! draws hitherward! Now mends our cheer
    From sorrow
    A fat sheep, I dare say,
    A good fleece, dare I lay.
    Eft-whyte° when I may, *Pay back*
295 But this will I borrow.

[MAK *steals a sheep and brings it home*]

    How, Gyll, art thou in? Get us some light.
GYLL: Who makes such din this time of the night?
    I am set for to spin; I hope that I might
    Raise° a penny to win, I curse them on height! *earn*
300 So fares
    A housewife that has been
    To be raised thus between.° *interrupted*
    Here may no notice be seen

For such small chores.

305   MAK: Good wife, open the hek!° Seest thou not what I bring?   *door*
      GYLL: I may let thee draw the snek.° A, come in, my sweeting!   *bolt*
      MAK: Yea, thou there not reckon° of my long standing.   *care*
      GYLL: By the naked neck art thou like for to hang.
      MAK: Go way!
310   I am worthy of my meat,°   *food*
          For in a pinch can I get
          More than they that swink° and sweat   *work*
            All the long day.

          Thus it fell to my lot, Gyll; I had such grace.
315   GYLL: It were a foul blot to be hanged for the case.
      MAK: I have escaped, Gylott, often as hard a place.
      GYLL: "But so long goes the pot to the water," men says,
            "At last
          Comes it home broken."
320   MAK: Well know I the token,°   *saying*
          But let it never be spoken!
            But come and help fast.

          I would he were slain; I'd like well to eat.
          This twelvemonth was I not so fain° of one sheep's meat.   *glad*
325   GYLL: Should they come ere he be slain, and hear the sheep bleat—
      MAK: Then might I be taken. That were a cold sweat!
            Go bar
          The gate door.
      GYLL: Yes, Mak,
          For if they come at thy back—
330   MAK: Then might I buy° from all the pack   *get*
          The devil of a war!

      GYLL: A good trick have I spied, since thou ken° none: *know*
          Here shall we him hide till they be gone,
          In my cradle. Abide! Let me alone,
335   And I shall lie beside in childbed, and groan.
      MAK: Get ready,
          And I shall say thou was lightened°   *delivered*
          Of a knave° child this night.   *boy*
      GYLL: Now well is the day bright
340   That ever was I bred!

          This is a good guise° and a far cast;   *clever device*
          Yet a woman's advice helps at the last.
          I wot never° who spies; again go thou fast.   *don't know*
      MAK: Unless I come ere they rise, then blows a cold blast!
345   I will go sleep.

      [MAK *returns to the circle of shepherds*]

          Yet sleeps all this company;
          And I shall go stalk prively,°   *secretly*
          As it had never been I
            That carried their sheep.

350   COLL: *Resurrex a mortuus*°! Have hold of my hand.   *Rise from the dead*

Judas carnas dominus!° I may not well stand;　　　　　　*Judas, lord of the flesh*
My foot sleeps, by Jesus, and I water fasted.°　　　　　　　　　　　*need*
I thought° that we laid us full near England.　　　　　　　　　　　*dreamt*

GIB: Ah, yea?
355　　Lord, but I have slept well!
　　　As fresh as an eel,
　　　As light I me feel
　　　　As leaf on a tree.

DAW: Bensté° be herein! So my body shakes,　　　　　　　　　*Blessings*
360　　My heart is out of skin, but so it quakes.
　　　Who makes all this din? As my brows are black,
　　　To the door will I win.° Hark, fellows, wake!　　　　　　　　*go*
　　　　We were four—
　　　See ye aught of Mak now?
365 COLL: We were up ere thou.
　　GIB: Man, I give God a vow,
　　　　That he went nowhere.

DAW: Me thought he was lapped in a wolf skin.
COLL: So are many wrapped now, namely within.
370 DAW: When we had long napped, me thought with a gin°　　　*trap*
　　　A fat sheep he trapped; but he made no din.
GIB: Be still!
　　　Thy dream makes thee wood;°　　　　　　　　　　　　　　*angry*
　　　It is but phantom, by the rood.°　　　　　　　　　　　　　　*cross*
375 COLL: Now God turn all to good,
　　　　If it be his will.

GIB: Rise, Mak, for shame! Thou lies right long.
MAK: Now Christ's holy name be us among!
　　　What is this? For Saint James, I may not well gang!°　　　*go well*
380　　I think I be the same. Ah! my neck has lain wrong
　　　　Enough.
　　　Mickle° thank! Since yester-even,　　　　　　　　　　　　*Many*
　　　Now by Saint Steven,
　　　I was flayed° with a dream—　　　　　　　　　　　　　　*tortured*
385　　　My heart out of slew!°　　　　　　　　　　　　　*killed my heart*

　　　I thought Gyll began to croak° and travail full sad,　　　　*moan*
　　　Well-near at the first cock, of a young lad
　　　For to mend° our flock. Then be I never glad;　　　　　　*increase*
　　　I have two on my rock° more than ever I had.　　　　　　　*trouble*
390　　Ah, my head!
　　　A house full of young bellies,
　　　The devil knock out their brains!
　　　Woe is him has many bairns,°　　　　　　　　　　　　　*children*
　　　　And thereto little bread.

395　　I must go home, by your leave, to Gyll, as I thought.
　　　I pray you look my sleeve, that I steal nought;
　　　I am loath you to grieve, or from you take aught.

[*Goes toward home*]

DAW: Go forth, ill might thou achieve! Now would I we sought,
　　　This morn,

400   That we had all our store.°   *sheep*
     COLL: But I will go before;
       Let us meet.
     GIB: Where?
     DAW: At the crooked thorn.

[*The* SHEPHERDS *search for their sheep;* MAK *arrives at his home*]

     MAK: Undo this door! Who is here? How long shall I stand?
405   GYLL: Who makes such a stir? Now walk in the waning!°   *waning moon*
     MAK: Ah, Gyll, what cheer? It is I, Mak, your husband.
     GYLL: Then may we see here the devil in a band,°   *noose (i.e., Mak hanged)*
       Sir Guile!
     Lo, he comes with a lote,°   *noise*
410   As he were holden in the throat.
     I may not sit at my note°   *work*
       A handlong° while.   *short*

     MAK: Will ye hear what lengths° she makes to get her a gloss? *excuse*
     And does nought but plays, and scratches her toes.
415   GYLL: Why, who wanders, who wakes? Who comes, who goes?
     Who brews, who bakes? What makes me thus hoarse?
       And then
     It is ruth° to behold—   *sad*
     Now in hot, now in cold,
420   Full woeful is the household
       That wants a woman.

     But what end has thou made with the shepherds, Mak?
     MAK: The last word that they said, when I turned my back,
     They would look that they had their sheep, all the pack.
425   I hope they will not be well paid when they their sheep lack,
       Pardie!°   *By God*
     But however the game goes,
     To me they will suppose,
     And make a foul noise,
430   And cry out upon me.

     But thou must do as thou hight.°   *promised*
     GYLL: I accord me theretill;°   *consent to that*
     I shall swaddle him right in my cradle.
     If it were a greater slight,° yet could I help till.   *trick*
     I will lie down straight. Come cover me.
     MAK: I will.
435   GYLL: Behind!
     Come Coll and his marroo,°   *friend*
     They will nip° us full narrow.°   *trap / tightly*
     MAK: But I may cry "out, harrow!"°   *help!*
       The sheep if they find.

440   GYLL: Hearken aye when they call; they will come anon.
     Come and make ready all, and sing by thine own;
     Sing "lullaby" thou shall, for I must groan,
     And cry out by the wall on Mary and John,
       For sore.°   *pain*
445   Sing "lullaby" fast
     When thou hears at the last;

Unless I play a false cast,°   *trick*
Trust me no more.

[*The* SHEPHERDS *meet*]

DAW: Ah, Coll, good morn! Why sleeps thou not?
450 COLL: Alas, that ever was I borne! We have a foul blot—
A fat wether° have we lorn.°   *sheep / lost*
DAW: Marry, God's forbid!
GIB: Who should do us that scorn? That were a foul spot.
COLL: Some shrew.°   *wretch*
I have sought with my dogs
455 All Horbery shrugs°   *thickets*
And of fifteen hogs°   *sheep*
Found I but one ewe.

DAW: Now trust me, if ye will—by Saint Thomas of Kent,
Either Mak or Gyll was at that assent.
460 COLL: Peace, man, be still! I saw when he went.
Thou slanders him ill; thou ought to repent
Good speed.
GIB: Now as ever might I thrive,
If I should even here die,
465 I would say it were he
That did that same deed.

DAW: Go we thither, I rede,° and run on our feet.   *advise*
Shall I never eat bread, the sooth to I wit.°   *until I know the truth*
COLL: Nor drink in my head,° with him till I meet.   *mouth*
470 GIB: I will rest in no stead till that I him greet,
My brother.
One thing I will plight:°   *pledge*
Till I see him in sight,
Shall I never sleep one night
475   Where I do another.

[*They approach* MAK's *house;* MAK *sings while* GYLL *moans as if in labor*]

DAW: Will ye hear how they hack°? Our sire list croon.°   *sing / likes crooning*
COLL: Heard I never none crack so clear out of tune.
Call on him.
GIB: Mak, undo your door soon!
MAK: Who is that spake, as it were noon,
480   On loft?
Who is that, I say?
DAW: Good fellows, were it day.
MAK: As far as ye may,
Good, speak soft,

485 Over a sick woman's head that is at malaise;
I had rather be dead than that she had any disease.
GYLL: Go to another place! I may not well wheeze;°   *breathe*
Each foot that ye tread goes through my nose
So high.
490 COLL: Tell us, Mak, if ye may,
How fare ye, I say?

MAK: But are ye in this town today?
    Now how fare ye?

    Ye have run in the mire, and are wet yet;
495   I shall make you a fire, if ye will sit.
    A nurse would I hire. Think ye on yet?
    Well paid is my hire—my dream, this is it—
      In season.
    I have bairns,° if ye knew,   *children*
500   Well more than enough;
    But we must drink as we brew,
      And that is but reason.

    I would have ye dined ere ye go. Me think that ye sweat.
GIB: Nay, neither mends our mood, drink nor meat.
505 MAK: Why, sir, ails you aught but good?
DAW: Yea, our sheep that we get°   *tend*
    Are stolen as they go. Our loss is great.
MAK: Sirs, drink!
    Had I been there,
    Some should have bought it full sore.
510 COLL: Mary, some men think that ye were,
      And that's what we think.

GIB: Mak, some men believe that it should be ye.
DAW: Either ye or your spouse, so say we.
MAK: Now if ye have suspicions of Gyll or of me,
515   Come and rip our house, and then may ye see
      Who had her.
    If I any sheep got,
    Either cow or stott°—   *livestock*
    And Gyll, my wife, rose not
520   Since here she laid her—

    As I am true and leal,° to God here I pray   *honest*
    That this be the first meal that I shall eat this day.
COLL: Mak, as have I sele,° advise thee, I say: *As I hope for salvation*
    He learned timely to steal that could not say nay.
525 GYLL: I swelt!°   *swoon*
    Out, thieves, from my house!
    Ye come to rob us for the nonce.
MAK: Here ye not how she groans?
      Your hearts should melt.

530 GYLL: Out, thieves, from my bairn!° Approach him not there!   *child*
MAK: Wist ye how° she had borne, your hearts would be sore.   *If you knew*
    Ye do wrong, I you warn, that thus comes before
    To a woman that has borne°—but I say no more.   *has been in labor*
GYLL: Ah, my middle!
535   I pray to God so mild,
    If ever I you beguiled,
    That I eat this child
      That lies in this cradle.

MAK: Peace, woman, for God's pain, and cry not so!
540   Thou hurts thy brain, and makes me full woe.
GIB: I think our sheep be slain. What find ye two?

DAW: All work we in vain; as well may we go.

    But hatters!°   *Bother!*

I can find no flesh,

545   Hard nor nesh,°   *Firm or soft*

Salt nor fresh—

    But two empty platters.

    No cattle but this,° tame nor wild,   *i.e., the baby*

    None, as have I bliss, as lewd° as he smelled.   *awful*

550 GYLL: No, so God me bliss, and give me joy of my child!

COLL: We have marked amiss,° I hold us beguiled.   *made a mistake*

GIB: Sir, done.

    Sir—our Lady him save!

    Is your child a knave?°   *boy*

555 MAK: Any lord might him have,

    This child, as his son.

    When he wakens he kips,° that joy is to see.   *grabs*

DAW: In good time to his hips,° and in glee!   *keeps time by kicking*

    But who were his godparents, so soon ready?

560 MAK: So fair fall their lips!°   *Only good can be said*

COLL: [*Aside*]   Hark now, a lie.

MAK: So God them thank,

    Parkyn, and Gibbon Waller, I say,

    And gentle John Horne,° in good faith—   *character in the First Shepherds' Play*

    He made all the garray°—   *commotion*

565   With his great shank.°   *long legs*

GIB: Mak, friends will we be, for we are all one.

MAK: We? Now I hold for me, for amends get I none.

    Farewell, all three! All glad were ye gone.

[*The* SHEPHERDS *leave*]

DAW: Fair words may there be, but love is there none

570   This year.

COLL: Gave ye the child anything?

GIB: I believe not one farthing.

DAW: Fast back will I fling;

    Abide ye me there.

[*He returns*]

575   Mak, take it to no grief if I come to thy bairn.°   *child*

MAK: Nay, thou does me great reproof, and foul has thou fared.

DAW: The child will it not grieve, that little day-star.

    Mak, with your leave, let me give your bairn

    But sixpence.

580 MAK: Nay, go way! He sleeps.

DAW: Me think he peeps.°   *looks about*

MAK: When he wakens he weeps.

    I pray you, go hence!

DAW: Give me leave him to kiss, and lift up the clout.°   *cloth*

[*Sees the sheep*]

585   What the devil is this? He has a long snout!   *deformed / do ill to pry*
COLL: He is marked amiss.° We wait ill about.°   *proverb: Ill-spun weaving*
GIB: "Ill-spun weft," iwis, "ay comes foul out"°   *comes out badly*
    Aye, so!

[He recognizes the sheep]

    He is like to our sheep!
590 DAW: How, Gib, may I peep?
COLL: I think nature will creep°   *proverb: Evil will creep*
    Where it may not go.°   *where it cannot walk*

GIB: This was a quaint gawd° and a far-cast.°   *prank / clever trick*
    It was a high fraud.
DAW: Yea, sirs, was't.
595   Let's burn this bawd and bind her fast.
    A false scold will hang at last;
      So shall thou.
    Will ye see how they swaddle
    His four feet in the middle?
600   Saw I never in a cradle
      A horned lad ere now.

MAK: Peace, bid I! What! Let be your fare!
    I am he that him begot, and yond woman him bare.
COLL: What devil shall he be called, Mak? Lo, God, Mak's heir!
605 GIB: Let be all that! Now God give him care;
      I saw!°   *i.e., the sheep*
GYLL: A pretty child is he
    As sits on a woman's knee;
    A dillydown,° pardie,°   *darling / by God*
610   To make a man laugh.

DAW: I know him by the ear-mark; that is a good token.
MAK: I tell you, sirs, hark! His nose was broken.
    Later a clerk told me that he was forspoken.°   *spooked*
COLL: This is a false work; I would fain be wroken.°   *revenged*
615   Get a weapon!
GYLL: He was taken by an elf,
    I saw it myself;
    When the clock stroke twelve
      Was he misshapen.°   *transformed*

620 GIB: Ye two are well suited, the same in a stead.
COLL: Since they maintain their theft, let do them to death.
MAK: If I trespass eft, gird off my head.
    With you will I be left.°   *At your mercy*
DAW: Sirs, take my lead:°   *advice*
    For this trespass
625   We will neither curse nor fight,
    Quarrel nor chide,
    But have done as tight,°   *quickly*
      And cast him in canvas.

[They toss MAK in a canvas sheet]

COLL: Lord, how I am sore, in point for to burst!

630   In faith, I may no more; therefore will I rest.
GIB: As a sheep of seven score he weighed in my fist.
For to sleep anywhere methinks that I list.° .... *like*
DAW: Now I pray you
Lie down on this green.
635 COLL: On these thieves yet I mind.° .... *think*
DAW: Whereto should ye strain?° .... *be angry*
Do as I say you.

[*They sleep*]

ANGELUS cantat "Gloria in excelsis,"   *An Angel sings "Glory to God in*
postea dicat: *the highest," afterwards let him say*

ANGEL: Rise, herd-men hend!° For now is he born .... *gentle shepherds*
That shall take from the fiend what Adam had lorn;° .... *lost*
640 That warlock to shend,° this night is he born. .... *destroy*
God is made your friend now at this morn,
He behests.° .... *promises*
At Bethlehem go see
Where lies that Free° .... *Noble one*
645 In a crib full poorly,
Betwixt two beasts.

COLL: This was the strangest voice that ever yet I heard.
It is a marvel to name, thus to be scared.
GIB: Of God's son of heaven he spoke upward.° .... *from on high*
650 All the wood in a levin° methought that he made .... *light*
To appear.
DAW: He spake of a bairn° .... *babe*
In Bethlehem, I you warn.
COLL: That betokens yond star;
655   Let us seek him there.

GIB: Say, what was his song? Heard ye not how he cracked° it, ... *sang*
Three briefs° to a long? .... *short notes*
DAW: Yea, Marry, he hacked° it: .... *trilled*
Was no crochet° wrong, nor nothing that lacked it. .... *note*
COLL: For to sing us among, right as he knacked° it, ... *sang*
660   I can.
GIB: Let see how ye croon!
Can ye bark at the moon?
DAW: Hold your tongues! Have done!
COLL: Hark after, then.

[*They sing*]

665 GIB: To Bethlehem he bade that we should gang;° .... *go*
I am full adread that we tarry too lang.° .... *long*
DAW: Be merry and not sad—of mirth is our song!
Everlasting joy as reward may we fang,° .... *get*
Without noise.° .... *fuss*
670 COLL: Therefore thither hie we,
If we be wet and weary,
To that child and that lady;
We have it not to lose.

GIB: We find by the prophecy—let be your din!—
675   Of David and Isaiah and more than I mind°—   *can remember*
    They prophesied by clergy—that in a virgin
    Should he alight and lie, to slacken° our sin,   *redeem*
      And slake it,
    Save our race from woe;
680   For Isaiah said so:
        " *Ecce virgo*°   *Behold a virgin*
        Concipiet"° a child that is naked.   *will conceive*

DAW: Full glad may we be, and abide that day
    That lovely to see, that all mights° may.   *can do all*
685   Lord, well were me, for once and for aye,°   *forever*
    Might I kneel on my knee, some word for to say
      To that child.
    But the angel said
    In a crib was he laid;
690   He was poorly arrayed,
      Both humble and mild.

COLL: Patriarchs that have been, and prophets before,
    They desired to have seen this child that is born.
    They are gone full clean;° that have they lorn.°   *are dead / lost that (hope)*
695   We shall see him, I ween,° ere it be morn,   *believe*
      To token.°   *sign*
    When I see him and feel,°   *touch him*
    Then know I full well
    It is true as steel
700   That prophets have spoken:

    To such poor as we are that he would appear,
    First find,° and declare by his messenger.   *to find us*
GIB: Go we now, let us fare; the place is us near.
DAW: I am ready, prepared; go we in together
705   To that bright.
    Lord, if thy will be—
    We are simple all three—
    Grant us some kind of glee
      To comfort thy wight.°   *child*

710 COLL: Hail, comely and clean! Hail, young child!
    Hail, maker, as I mean, of a maiden so mild!
    Thou has cursed, I ween,° the warlock so wild: *believe*
    The false guiler of teen,° now goes he beguiled.   *harm*
      Lo, he merry is,
715   Lo, he laughs, my sweeting!
    A welfare° meeting!   *happy*
    I have holden my heting:°   *promise*
      Have a bob° of cherries.   *bunch*

GIB: Hail, sovereign savior, for thou has us sought!
720   Hail, noble child and flower, that all things has wrought!
    Hail, full of favor, that made all of nought!
    Hail! I kneel and I cower. A bird have I brought
      To my bairn.°   *babe*
    Hail, little tiny mop!°   *child*

725 Of our creed thou art crop;°   *head*
    I would drink of thy cup,
        Little day-star.

DAW: Hail, darling dear, full of Godhead!
    I pray thee be near when that I have need.
730 Hail, sweet is thy cheer! My heart would bleed
    To see thee sit here in so poor weed,°   *clothing*
        With no pennies.
    Hail! Put forth thy dall!°   *hand*
    I bring thee but a ball:
735 Have and play thee withal,
        And go to the tennis.°   *lawn*

MARY: The father of heaven, God omnipotent,
    That set all in seven days, his son has he sent.
    My name could he neven,° and alighted° ere he went.   *name / descended*
740 I conceived him full even through might,° as he meant;   *i.e., by God's power*
        And now is he born.
    May he keep you from woe!
    I shall pray him so.
    Tell it forth as ye go,
745   And mind on this morn.

COLL: Fare well, lady, so fair to behold,
    With thy child on thy knee.
GIB: But he lies full cold.
    Lord, well is me! Now we go, thou behold.
DAW: Forsooth, already it seems to be told
750   Full oft.
COLL: What grace we have found!
GIB: Come forth; now are we won!°   *redeemed*
DAW: To sing are we bound—
    Let's take aloft!°   *begin on a high note*

[*They exit, singing*]

                Explicit pagina Pastorum   *The end of the Shepherds' play*

Everyman

Anonymous

EDITED BY JOHN C. COLDEWAY

CHARACTERS

GOD	COUSIN	STRENGTH
MESSENGER	GOODS	DISCRETION
DEATH	GOOD DEEDS	FIVE WITS
EVERYMAN	CONFESSION	ANGEL
FELLOWSHIP	KNOWLEDGE	DOCTOR
KINDRED	BEAUTY	

*Here beginneth a treatise how the high Father of heaven sendeth Death
to summon every creature to come and give account of their lives in
this world, and is in manner of a moral play*

MESSENGER: I pray you all give your audience,
    And hear this matter° with reverence,   *form*
    By figure° a moral play.
    The Summoning of Everyman called it is,
5   That of our lives and ending shows
    How transitory we be all day.
    This matter is wondrous precious;
    But the intent of it is more gracious,
    And sweet to bear away.°   *take with you*
10   The story saith: Man, in the beginning
    Look well, and take good heed to the ending,
    Be you never so gay!
    Ye think sin in the beginning full sweet,
    Which in the end causeth the soul to weep,
15   When the body lyeth in clay.
    Here shall you see how Fellowship and Jollity,
    Both Strength, Pleasure and Beauty,
    Will fade from thee as flower in May;
    For ye shall hear how our Heaven King
20   Calleth Everyman to a general reckoning.
    Give audience, and hear what he doth say.

[*Exit* MESSENGER]

GOD *speketh*

GOD: I perceive, here in my majesty,
    How that all creatures be to me unkind,°   *unnatural*
    Living without dread in worldly prosperity.
25   Of ghostly sight° the people be so blind,   *spiritual vision*
    Drowned in sin, they know me not for their God.
    In worldly riches is all their mind;
    They fear not my righteousness, the sharp rod.
    My law that I showed, when I for them died,
30   They forget clean, and shedding of my blood red.
    I hanged between two thieves, it can not be denied;
    To get them life I suffered to be dead;

I healed° their feet, with thorns hurt was my head.   *washed [John 13:1-20]*
I could do no more than I did, truly;
35   And now I see the people do clean forsake me.
They use the seven deadly sins damnable,
As pride, covetise, wrath, and lechery°   *gluttony, sloth, and*
Now in the world be made commendable;   *envy are the other three*
And thus they leave of angels the heavenly company.
40   Every man liveth so after his own pleasure,
And yet of their life they be nothing sure.
I see the more that I them forbear
The worse they be from year to year.
All that liveth appaireth° fast;   *degenerates*
45   Therefore I will, in all the haste,
Have a reckoning° of every man's person;   *final accounting*
For, and° I leave the people thus alone   *if*
In their life and wicked tempests,
Verily they will become much worse than beasts,
50   For now one would by envy another up eat;
Charity they do all clean forget.
I hoped well that every man
In my glory should make his mansion,°   *take his place [John 14:2]*
And thereto I had them all elect;
55   But now I see, like traitors deject,°   *abject*
They thank me not for the pleasure° that I to them meant,   *goodness*
Nor yet for their being that I them have lent.
I proffered the people great multitude of mercy,
And few there be that asketh it heartily.
60   They be so encumbered with worldly riches
That needs on them I must do justice,
On every man living without fear.
Where art thou, Death, thou mighty messenger?

[*Enter* DEATH]

DEATH: Almighty God, I am here at your will,
65   Your commandment to fulfill.
GOD: Go thou to Everyman
And show him, in my name,
A pilgrimage he must on him take,
Which he in no wise may escape;
70   And that he bring with him a sure reckoning
Without delay or any tarrying.
DEATH: Lord, I will in the world go run over-all°   *everywhere*
And cruelly out-search both great and small.°   *all classes*
Every man will I beset that liveth beastly°   *like a beast*
75   Out of God's laws, and dreadeth not folly.
He that loveth riches I will strike with my dart,
His sight to blind, and from heaven to depart°—   *cut off from*
Except that alms be his good friend—
In hell for to dwell, world without end.

[*Exit* GOD; *Enter* EVERYMAN]

80   Lo, yonder I see Everyman walking.
Full lightly he thinketh on my coming;
His mind is on fleshly lusts° and his treasure,   *sensual pleasures*
And great pain it shall cause him to endure

Before the Lord, Heaven King.
85   Everyman, stand still! Whither art thou going
Thus gaily? Hast thou thy Maker forget?
EVERYMAN: Why askest thou?
Wouldest thou wit?°   *know*
DEATH: Yea, sir. I will show you:
90   In great haste I am sent to thee
From God out of his majesty.
EVERYMAN: What, sent to me?
DEATH: Yea, certainly.
Though thou have forget him here,
95   He thinketh on thee in the heavenly sphere,
As, ere we depart, thou shalt know.
EVERYMAN: What desireth God of me?
DEATH: That shall I show thee:
A reckoning he will needs have
100   Without any longer respite.
EVERYMAN: To give a reckoning longer leisure I crave;
This blind° matter troubleth my wit.   *dark*
DEATH: On thee thou must take a long journey;
Therefore thy book of count° with thee thou bring,   *accounts*
105   For turn again thou can not by no way.
And look thou be sure of thy reckoning,
For before God thou shalt answer, and show
Thy many bad deeds, and good but a few;
How thou hast spent thy life, and in what wise,
110   Before the chief Lord of paradise.
Have ado that thou were in that way,°   *prepare to go*
For wit thou well° thou shalt make none° attorney.   *know well / have no*
EVERYMAN: Full unready I am such reckoning to give.
I know thee not. What messenger art thou?
115 DEATH: I am Death that no man dreadeth—
For every man I rest°—and no man spareth;   *arrest*
For it is God's commandment
That all to me should be obedient.
EVERYMAN: O Death, thou comest when I had thee least in mind!
120   In thy power it lieth me to save;
Yet of my good will I give thee, if thou will be kind—
Yea, a thousand pound shalt thou have—
And defer this matter till an other day.
DEATH: Everyman, it may not be by no way.
125   I set not by gold, silver, nor riches,
Nor by pope, emperor, king, duke, nor princes;
For, and° I would receive gifts great,   *if*
All the world I might get;
But my custom is clean contrary.
130   I give thee no respite. Come hence, and not tarry!
EVERYMAN: Alas, shall I have no longer respite?
I may say Death giveth no warning!
To think on thee, it maketh my heart sick,
For all unready is my book of reckoning.
135   But twelve year and° I might have abiding,   *if*
My counting-book I would make so clear
That my reckoning I should not need to fear.
Wherefore, Death, I pray thee, for God's mercy,
Spare me till I be provided of remedy.

140 DEATH: Thee availeth not to cry, weep, and pray;
But haste thee lightly° that thou were gone that journey,   *quickly*
And prove° thy friends if thou can.   *test*
For wit° thou well the tide abideth no man,   *know*
And in the world each living creature
145 For Adam's sin must die of nature.
EVERYMAN: Death, if I should this pilgrimage take,
And my reckoning surely make,
Show me, for saint° charity,   *holy*
Should I not come again shortly?
150 DEATH: No, Everyman; and thou be once there,
Thou mayst never more come here,
Trust me verily.
EVERYMAN: O gracious God in the high seat celestial,
Have mercy on me in this most need!
155 Shall I have no company from this vale terrestrial°   *world*
Of mine acquaintance, that way me to lead?
DEATH: Yea, if any be so hardy
That would go with thee and bear thee company.
Hie° thee that thou were gone to God's magnificence,   *Hurry*
160 Thy reckoning to give before his presence.
What, weenest thou° thy life is given thee,   *do you think*
And thy worldly goods also?
EVERYMAN: I had weened so, verily.
DEATH: Nay, nay, it was but lent thee;
165 For as soon as thou art go,°   *gone*
Another a while shall have it, and then go therefro,
Even as thou hast done.
Everyman, thou art mad! Thou hast thy wits five,
And here on earth will not amend thy life;
170 For suddenly I do come.
EVERYMAN: O wretched caitiff,° whither shall I flee,   *villain*
That I might escape this endless sorrow?
Now, gentle Death, spare me till tomorrow,
That I may amend me
175 With good advisement°   *advice*
DEATH: Nay, thereto I will not consent,
Nor no man will I respite;
But to the heart suddenly I shall smite
Without any advisement.
180 And now out of thy sight I will me hie.°   *hurry*
See thou make thee ready shortly,
For thou mayst say this is the day
That no man living may scape away.

[*Exit* DEATH]

EVERYMAN: Alas, I may well weep with sighs deep!
185 Now have I no manner of company
To help me in my journey, and me to keep;°   *protect*
And also my writing° is full unready.   *accounting*
How shall I do now for to excuse me?
I would to God I had never be get°   *been begotten*
190 To my soul a full great profit it had be,
For now I fear pains huge and great.
The time passeth. Lord, help, that all wrought!°   *created everything*

For though I mourn, it availeth nought.
The day passeth and is almost ago;°   *gone*
195 I wot° not well what for to do.   *know*
To whom were I best my complaint to make?
What and° I to Fellowship thereof spake,   *if*
And showed him of this sudden chance?
For in him is all mine affiance;°   *trust*
200 We have in the world so many a day
Be good friends in sport and play.
I see him yonder, certainly.
I trust that he will bear me company;
Therefore to him will I speak to ease my sorrow.
205 Well met, good Fellowship, and good morrow!

[*Enter* FELLOWSHIP]

FELLOWSHIP: Everyman, good morrow, by this day!
Sir, why lookest thou so piteously?
If any thing be amiss, I pray thee me say,
That I may help to remedy.
210 EVERYMAN: Yea, good Fellowship, yea,
I am in great jeopardy.
FELLOWSHIP: My true friend, show to me your mind.
I will not forsake thee to my life's end,
In the way of good company.
215 EVERYMAN: That was well spoken and lovingly.
FELLOWSHIP: Sir, I must needs know your heaviness;
I have pity to see you in any distress.
If any have you wronged, ye shall revenged be,
Though I on the ground be slain for thee,
220 Though that I know before that I should die.
EVERYMAN: Verily, Fellowship, gramercy.°   *great thanks*
FELLOWSHIP: Tush! by thy thanks I set not a straw.°   *care nothing*
Show me your grief, and say no more.
EVERYMAN: If I my heart should to you break,°   *open*
225 And then you to turn your mind from me
And would not me comfort when ye hear me speak,
Then should I ten time sorrier be.
FELLOWSHIP: Sir, I say as I will do in deed.
EVERYMAN: Then be you a good friend at° need.   *in*
230 I have found you true herebefore.
FELLOWSHIP: And so ye shall evermore;
For, in faith, and° thou go to hell,   *even if*
I will not forsake thee by the way.
EVERYMAN: Ye speak like a good friend; I believe you well.
235 I shall deserve it, and° I may.   *if*
FELLOWSHIP: I speak of no deserving, by this day!
For he that will say, and nothing do,
Is not worthy with good company to go;
Therefore show me the grief of your mind,
240 As to your friend most loving and kind.
EVERYMAN: I shall show you how it is:
Commanded I am to go a journey,
A long way hard and dangerous,
And give a straight° account, without delay,   *strict*
245 Before the high Judge, Adonai.°   *God*

Wherefore, I pray you, bear me company,
As ye have promised, in this journey.
FELLOWSHIP: That is matter indeed! Promise is duty;
But, and° I should take such a voyage on me,   *if*
250   I know it well, it should be to my pain;
Also it maketh me afeared, certain.
But let us take counsel here as well as we can,
For your words would fear° a strong man.   *frighten*
EVERYMAN: Why, ye said if I had need
255   Ye would me never forsake, quick° nor dead,   *alive*
Though it were to hell, truly.
FELLOWSHIP: So I said, certainly,
But such pleasures be set aside, the sooth° to say;   *truth*
And also, if we took such a journey,
260   When should we again come?
EVERYMAN: Nay, never again till the day of doom.
FELLOWSHIP: In faith, then will not I come there!
Who hath you these tidings brought?
EVERYMAN: Indeed, Death was with me here.
265 FELLOWSHIP: Now, by God that all hath bought,°   *redeemed*
If Death were the messenger,
For no man that is living today
I will not go that loath journey—
Not for the father that begot me!
270 EVERYMAN: Ye promised otherwise, pardie.°   *by God*
FELLOWSHIP: I wot° well I said so, truly;   *know*
And yet, if thou wilt eat and drink and make good cheer,
Or haunt° to women the lusty company,   *frequent*
I would not forsake you while the day is clear,°   *all day*
275   Trust me verily.
EVERYMAN: Yea, thereto ye would be ready!
To go to mirth, solace, and play
Your mind will sooner apply,
Than to bear me company in my long journey.
280 FELLOWSHIP: Now, in good faith, I will not that way;
But and° thou will murder, or any man kill,   *If*
In that I will help thee with a good will.
EVERYMAN: O, that is a simple advice° indeed.   *matter*
Gentle fellow, help me in my necessity!
285   We have loved long, and now I need;
And now, gentle Fellowship, remember me.
FELLOWSHIP: Whether ye have loved me or no,
By Saint John I will not with thee go!
EVERYMAN: Yet, I pray thee, take the labor and do so much for me
290   To bring me forward,° for saint charity,   *escort me*
And comfort me till I come without° the town.   *outside of*
FELLOWSHIP: Nay, and thou would give me a new gown,
I will not a foot with thee go;
But, and thou had tarried, I would not have left thee so.
295   And as now God speed thee in thy journey,
For from thee I will depart as fast as I may.
EVERYMAN: Whither away, Fellowship? Will thou forsake me?
FELLOWSHIP: Yea, by my fay°! To God I betake° thee.   *faith / commend*
EVERYMAN: Farewell, good Fellowship! For thee my heart is sore.
300   Adieu for ever! I shall see thee no more.
FELLOWSHIP: In faith, Everyman, fare well now at the ending!

For you I will remember that parting is mourning.

[*Exit* FELLOWSHIP]

EVERYMAN: Alack, shall we thus depart° indeed—   *part*
    Lady,° help!—without any more comfort?   *(Blessed) Lady*
305   Lo, Fellowship forsaketh me in my most need.
    For help in this world whither shall I resort?
    Fellowship herebefore with me would merry make,
    And now little sorrow for me doth he take.
    It is said, "In prosperity men friends may find,
310   Which in adversity be full unkind."
    Now whither for succor shall I flee,
    Since that Fellowship hath forsaken me?
    To my kinsmen I will, truly,
    Praying them to help me in my necessity.
315   I believe that they will do so,
    For "kind° will creep where it may not go."°   *kinship / walk*
    I will go say,° for yonder I see them.   *try*
    Where be ye now, my friends and kinsmen?

[*Enter* KINDRED *and* COUSIN]

KINDRED: Here be we now at your commandment.
320   Cousin, I pray you show us your intent
    In any wise,° and not spare.°   *in everything / do not hesitate*
COUSIN: Yea, Everyman, and to us declare
    If ye be disposed to go anywhither;
    For, wit° you well, we will live and die together.   *know*
325 KINDRED: In wealth and woe we will with you hold,
    For over° his kin a man may be bold.°   *with / straightforward*
EVERYMAN: Gramercy,° my friends and kinsmen kind.   *Great thanks*
    Now shall I show you the grief of my mind:
    I was commanded by a messenger,
330   That is a high king's chief officer.
    He bade me go a pilgrimage, to my pain,
    And I know well I shall never come again.
    Also I must give a reckoning straight,°   *strict accounting*
    For I have a great enemy that hath me in wait,
335   Which intendeth me for to hinder.
KINDRED: What account is that which ye must render?
    That would I know.
EVERYMAN: Of all my works I must show
    How I have lived and my days spent;
340   Also of ill deeds that I have used°   *done*
    In my time, since life was me lent;
    And of all virtues that I have refused.
    Therefore, I pray you, go thither with me
    To help to make mine account, for saint charity.
345 COUSIN: What, to go thither? Is that the matter?
    Nay, Everyman, I had lever° fast bread and water   *rather*
    All this five year and more.
EVERYMAN: Alas, that ever I was bore!°   *born*
    For now shall I never be merry,
350   If that you forsake me.
KINDRED: Ay, sir, what ye be a merry man!
    Take good heart to you, and make no moan.

But one thing I warn you, by Saint Anne—
As for me, ye shall go alone.
355 EVERYMAN: My Cousin, will you not with me go?
COUSIN: No, by our Lady! I have the cramp in my toe.
Trust not to me; for, so God me speed,°   *God help me*
I will deceive you in your most need.
KINDRED: It availeth not us to tice.°   *entice*
360 Ye shall have my maid with all my heart;
She loveth to go to feasts, there to be nice,°   *wanton*
And to dance, and abroad to start.°   *go*
I will give her leave to help you in that journey,
If that you and she may agree.
365 EVERYMAN: Now show me the very effect of your mind:
Will you go with me, or abide behind?
KINDRED: Abide behind? Yea, that will I, and I may!
Therefore farewell till another day.

[*Exit* KINDRED]

EVERYMAN: How should I be merry or glad?
370 For fair promises men to me make,
But when I have most need they me forsake.
I am deceived; that maketh me sad.
COUSIN: Cousin Everyman, farewell now,
For verily I will not go with you.
375 Also of mine own an unready reckoning
I have to account; therefore I make tarrying.°   *must stay behind*
Now God keep thee, for now I go.

[*Exit* COUSIN]

EVERYMAN: Ah, Jesus, is all come hereto?°   *has it come to this*
Lo, fair words maketh fools fain,°   *glad*
380 They promise, and nothing will do, certain.
My kinsmen promised me faithfully
For to abide with me steadfastly,
And now fast away do they flee.
Even so Fellowship promised me.
385 What friend were best me of to provide?
I lose my time here longer to abide.
Yet in my mind a thing there is:
All my life I have loved riches;
If that my Good° now help me might,   *Goods*
390 He would make my heart full light.
I will speak to him in this distress.
Where art thou, my Goods and riches?

[GOODS *speaks*]

GOODS: Who calleth me? Everyman? What, hast thou haste?
I lie here in corners, trussed and piled so high,
395 And in chests I am locked so fast,
Also sacked in bags. Thou mayst see with thine eye
I can not stir; in packs, low I lie.
What would ye have? Lightly me say.°   *quickly tell me*
EVERYMAN: Come hither, Goods, in all the haste thou may,
400 For of counsel I must desire thee.

GOODS: Sir, and° ye in the world have sorrow or adversity,   *if*
    That can I help you to remedy shortly.
EVERYMAN: It is another disease° that grieveth me;   *problem*
    In this world it is not, I tell thee so.
405   I am sent for, another way to go,
    To give a straight account general
    Before thy highest Jupiter of all.
    And all my life I have had joy and pleasure in thee,
    Therefore, I pray thee, go with me;
410   For, peradventure,° thou mayst before God Almighty   *perhaps*
    My reckoning help to clean and purify,
    For it is said ever among
    That "money maketh all right that is wrong."
GOODS: Nay, Everyman, I sing another song.
415   I follow no man in such voyages;
    For and° I went with thee,   *if*
    Thou shouldst fare much the worse for me.
    For because on me thou did set thy mind,
    Thy reckoning I have made blotted and blind,°   *uncertain and dark*
420   That thine account thou cannot make truly—
    And that hast thou for the love of me!
EVERYMAN: That would grieve me full sore,
    When I should come to that fearful answer.°   *final reckoning*
    Up, let us go thither together.
425 GOODS: Nay, not so! I am too brittle, I may not endure.
    I will follow no man one foot, be ye sure.
EVERYMAN: Alas, I have thee loved, and had great pleasure
    All my life-days on good and treasure.
GOODS: That is to thy damnation, without leasing,°   *lying*
430   For my love is contrary to the love everlasting.
    But if thou had me loved moderately during,°   *during life*
    As to the poor give part of me,
    Than shouldst thou not in this dolor be,
    Nor in this great sorrow and care.
435 EVERYMAN: Lo, now was I deceived ere I was ware;
    And all I may wite° misspending of time.   *blame on*
GOODS: What, weenest thou° that I am thine?   *do you think*
EVERYMAN: I had weened so.
GOODS: Nay, Everyman, I say no.
440   As for a while I was lent thee;
    A season thou hast had me in prosperity.
    My condition is man's soul to kill;
    If I save one, a thousand I do spill.
    Weenest thou that I will follow thee?
445   Nay, from this world not, verily.
EVERYMAN: I had weened otherwise.
GOODS: Therefore to thy soul Good is a thief;
    For when thou art dead, this is my guise°—   *trick*
    Another to deceive in this same wise
450   As I have done thee, and all to his soul's reprief.°   *shame*
EVERYMAN: O false Good, cursed thou be,
    Thou traitor to God, that has hast deceived me
    And caught me in thy snare!
GOODS: Marry, thou brought thy self in care,°   *got yourself into trouble*
455   Whereof I am glad.
    I must needs laugh; I can not be sad.

EVERYMAN: Ah, Good, thou hast had long my heartly love;
　　　I gave thee that which should be the Lord's above.
　　　But wilt thou not go with me indeed?
460　　I pray thee truth to say.
　　GOODS: No, so God me speed!°   *God help me*
　　　Therefore farewell, and have good day.

[*Exit* GOODS]

EVERYMAN: O, to whom shall I make my moan
　　　For to go with me in that heavy journey?
465　　First Fellowship said he would with me gone;
　　　His words were very pleasant and gay,
　　　But afterward he left me alone.
　　　Than spake I to my kinsmen, all in despair,
　　　And also they gave me words fair;
470　　They lacked no fair speaking,
　　　But all forsake me in the ending.
　　　Then went I to my Goods that I loved best,
　　　In hope to have comfort; but there had I least,
　　　For my Goods sharply did me tell
475　　That he bringeth many into hell.
　　　Then of myself I was ashamed,
　　　And so I am worthy to be blamed;
　　　Thus may I well myself hate.
　　　Of whom shall I now counsel take?
480　　I think that I shall never speed
　　　Till that I go to my Good Deed.
　　　But, alas, she is so weak
　　　That she can neither go° nor speak;   *walk*
　　　Yet will I venture on her now.
485　　My Good Deeds, where be you?

[GOOD DEEDS *speaks while lying on the ground*]

GOOD DEEDS: Here I lie, cold in the ground.
　　　Thy sins hath me sore bound,
　　　That I can not stir.
　　EVERYMAN: O Good Deeds, I stand in fear!
490　　I must you pray of counsel,
　　　For help now should come right well.
　　GOOD DEEDS: Everyman, I have understanding
　　　That ye be summoned, account to make
　　　Before Messias,° of Jerusalem king;   *Messiah*
495　　And you do by me,° that journey with you will I take.   *If you do as I say*
　　EVERYMAN: Therefore I come to you my moan to make.
　　　I pray you that ye will go with me.
　　GOOD DEEDS: I would full fain,° but I can not stand, verily.   *very gladly*
　　EVERYMAN: Why, is there anything on you fall?
500　　GOOD DEEDS: Yea, sir, I may thank you of all.
　　　If ye had perfectly cheered me,°   *treated me better*
　　　Your book of accounts full ready had be.

[*Shows book*]

　　　Look, the books of your works and deeds eke°   *also*
　　　As how they lie under the feet,

505   To your soul's heaviness.
        EVERYMAN: Our Lord Jesus help me!
          For one letter here I can not see.
        GOOD DEEDS: There is a blind° reckoning in time of distress.   *dark*
        EVERYMAN: Good Deeds, I pray you help me in this need,
510   Or else I am for ever damned indeed;
          Therefore help me to make reckoning
          Before the Redeemer of all thing,
          That King is, and was, and ever shall.
        GOOD DEEDS: Everyman, I am sorry of your fall,
515   And fain° would I help you, and° I were able.   *gladly / if*
        EVERYMAN: Good Deeds, your counsel I pray you give me.
        GOOD DEEDS.: That shall I do verily.
          Though that on my feet I may not go,
          I have a sister that shall with you also,
520   Called Knowledge,° which shall with you abide,   *acknowledgment*
          To help you to make that dreadful reckoning.

        [*Enter* KNOWLEDGE]

        KNOWLEDGE: Everyman, I will go with thee and be thy guide,
          In thy most need to go by thy side.
        EVERYMAN: In good condition I am now in everything,
525   And am wholly content with this good thing,
          Thanked be God my creator.
        GOOD DEEDS: And when she hath brought you there
          Where thou shalt heal thee of thy smart,°   *pain*
          Then go you with your reckoning and your Good Deeds together,
530   For to make you joyful at heart
          Before the Blessed Trinity.
        EVERYMAN: My Good Deeds, gramercy!°   *great thanks*
          I am well content, certainly,
          With your words sweet.
535   KNOWLEDGE: Now go we together lovingly
          To Confession, that cleansing river.
        EVERYMAN: For joy I weep; I would we were there!
          But, I pray you, give me cognition
          Where dwelleth that holy man, Confession.
540   KNOWLEDGE: In the house of salvation;
          We shall find him in that place,
          That shall us comfort, by God's grace.

        [KNOWLEDGE *leads* EVERYMAN *to* CONFESSION]

          Lo, this is Confession. Kneel down and ask mercy,
          For he is in good conceit° with God Almighty.   *good grace*
545   EVERYMAN: O glorious fountain, that all uncleanness doth clarify,°   *purify*
          Wash from me the spots of vice unclean,
          That on me no sin may be seen.
          I come with Knowledge for my redemption,
          Redeemed with heart and full contrition;
550   For I am commanded a pilgrimage to take,
          And great accounts before God to make.
          Now I pray you, Shrift,° mother of salvation,   *Confession*
          Help my Good Deeds for my piteous exclamation.
        CONFESSION: I know your sorrow well, Everyman.
555   Because with Knowledge ye come to me,

I will you comfort as well as I can.
And a precious jewel I will give thee,
Called penance, voider of adversity;
Therewith shall your body chastised be,
560   With abstinence and perseverance in God's service.
Here shall you receive that scourge° of me,   *lash*
Which is penance strong that ye must endure,
To remember thy Saviour was scourged for thee
With sharp scourges, and suffered it patiently;
565   So must thou or° thou scape that painful pilgrimage.   *before*
Knowledge, keep him in this voyage,
And by that time Good Deeds will be with thee.
But in any wise be seker° of mercy,   *certain*
For your time draweth fast;° and ye will saved be,   *time is running out*
570   Ask God mercy, and he will grant truly.
When with the scourge of penance man doth him bind,°   *punish*
The oil of forgiveness then shall he find.
EVERYMAN: Thanked be God for his gracious work!
For now I will my penance begin.
575   This hath rejoiced and lighted my heart,
Though the knots be painful and hard within.
KNOWLEDGE: Everyman, look your penance that ye fulfill,
What pain that ever it to you be;
And Knowledge shall give you counsel at will
580   How your account ye shall make clearly.
EVERYMAN: O eternal God, O heavenly figure,
O way of righteousness, O goodly vision,
Which descended down in a virgin pure
Because he would every man redeem,
585   Which Adam forfeited by his disobedience:
O blessed Godhead, elect and high divine,
Forgive me my grievous offence!
Here I cry thee mercy in this presence.
O ghostly treasure, O ransomer and redeemer,
590   Of all the world hope and conductor,
Mirror of joy, founder of mercy,
Which enlumineth heaven and earth thereby,
Hear my clamorous complaint, though it late be,
Receive my prayers unworthy in this heavy life!
595   Though I be a sinner most abominable,
Yet let my name be written in Moses' table.°   *tablet of the elect*
O Mary, pray to the Maker of all thing,
Me for to help at my ending;
And save me from the power of my enemy,
600   For Death assaileth me strongly.
And, Lady, that I may by mean of thy prayer
Of your Son's glory to be partner,
By the means of his passion, I it crave;
I beseech you help my soul to save.
605   Knowledge, give me the scourge of penance;
My flesh therewith shall give acquaintance.°   *satisfaction*
I will now begin if God give me grace.
KNOWLEDGE: Everyman, God give you time and space!
Thus I bequeath you in the hands of our Saviour;
610   Now may you make your reckoning sure.
EVERYMAN: In the name of the Holy Trinity,

My body sore punished shall be:

[*Flogs himself*]

<table>
<tr><td></td><td>Take this, body, for the sin of the flesh!</td><td></td></tr>
<tr><td></td><td>Also thou delights° to go gay and fresh,</td><td>*as*</td></tr>
<tr><td>615</td><td>And in the way of damnation thou did me bring;</td><td></td></tr>
<tr><td></td><td>Therefore suffer now strokes of punishing.</td><td></td></tr>
<tr><td></td><td>Now of penance I will wade the water clear,</td><td></td></tr>
<tr><td></td><td>To save me from Purgatory, that sharp fire.</td><td></td></tr>
</table>

[GOOD DEEDS *rises from the ground*]

GOOD DEEDS: I thank God, now I can walk and go,
620   And am delivered of my sickness and woe.
        Therefore with Everyman I will go, and not spare;
        His good works I will help him to declare.
KNOWLEDGE: Now, Everyman, be merry and glad!
        Your Good Deeds cometh now; ye may not be sad.
625   Now is your Good Deeds whole and sound,
        Going upright upon the ground.
EVERYMAN: My heart is light, and shall be evermore;
        Now will I smite° faster than I did before.   *strike*
GOOD DEEDS: Everyman, pilgrim, my special friend,
630   Blessed be thou without end!
        For thee is prepared the eternal glory.
        Ye have me made whole and sound,
        Therefor I will bide by thee in every stound.°   *trial*
EVERYMAN: Welcome, my Good Deeds! Now I hear thy voice
635   I weep for very sweetness of love.
KNOWLEDGE: Be no more sad, but ever rejoice;
        God seeth thy living in his throne above.
        Put on this garment to thy behove,°   *benefit*
        Which is wet with your tears,
640   Or else before God you may it miss,
        When ye to your journey's end come shall.
EVERYMAN: Gentle Knowledge, what do ye it call?
KNOWLEDGE: It is a garment of sorrow;
        From pain it will you borrow°   *release*
645   Contrition it is
        That getteth forgiveness;
        He pleaseth God passing well.
GOOD DEEDS: Everyman, will you wear it for your heal°?   *spiritual health*
EVERYMAN: Now blessed be Jesu, Mary's son,
650   For now have I on true contrition;
        And let us go now without tarrying.
        Good Deeds, have we clear our reckoning?
GOOD DEEDS: Yea, indeed, I have it here.
EVERYMAN: Then I trust we need not fear.
655   Now, friends, let us not part in twain.
KNOWLEDGE: Nay, Everyman, that will we not, certain.
GOOD DEEDS: Yet must thou lead with thee
        Three persons of great might.
EVERYMAN: Who should they be?
660 GOOD DEEDS: Discretion and Strength they hight,°   *are called*
        And thy Beauty may not abide behind.
KNOWLEDGE: Also ye must call to mind

Your Five Wits as for your counsellors.
GOOD DEEDS: You must have them ready at all hours.
665 EVERYMAN: How shall I get them hither
KNOWLEDGE: You must call them all together,
And they will hear you incontinent.°   *immediately*
EVERYMAN: My friends, come hither and be present,
Discretion, Strength, my Five Wits, and Beauty.

[*Enter* BEAUTY, STRENGTH, DISCRETION, FIVE WITS]

670 BEAUTY: Here at your will we be all ready.
What would ye that we should do?
GOOD DEEDS: That ye would with Everyman go,
And help him in his pilgrimage.
Advise you, will ye with him or not in that voyage?
675 STRENGTH: We will bring him all thither,
To his help and comfort, ye may believe me.
DISCRETION: So will we go with him all together.
EVERYMAN: Almighty God, loved may thou be!
I give thee laud that I have hither brought
680 Strength, Discretion, Beauty, and Five Wits. Lack I nought.
And my Good Deeds, with Knowledge clear,
All be in company at my will here.
I desire no more to my business.
STRENGTH: And I, Strength, will by you stand in distress,
685 Though thou would in battle fight on the ground.
FIVE WITS: And though it were through the world round,
We will not depart for sweet nor sour.
BEAUTY: No more will I unto death's hour,
Whatsoever thereof befall.
690 DISCRETION: Everyman, advise you first of all;
Go with a good advisement and deliberation.
We all give you virtuous monition°   *advice*
That all shall be well.
EVERYMAN: My friends, harken what I will tell:
695 I pray God reward you in his heavenly sphere.
Now hearken, all that be here,
For I will make my testament
Here before you all present:
In alms, half my good I will give with my hands twain
700 In the way of charity with good intent,
And the other half still shall remain
In queth,° to be returned there it ought to be.   *bequest*
This I do in despite of the fiend of hell,
To go quite out of his peril°   *power*
705 Ever after and this day.°   *today and always*
KNOWLEDGE: Everyman, hearken what I say:
Go to Priesthood, I you advise,
And receive of him in any wise°   *however possible*
The holy sacrament° and ointment together.   *Extreme Unction*
710 Then shortly see ye turn again hither;
We will all abide you here.
FIVE WITS: Yea, Everyman, hie you that ye ready were.
There is no emperor, king, duke, nor baron,
That of God hath commission
715 As hath the least priest in the world being;

For of the blessed sacraments pure and benign
He beareth the keys, and thereof hath the cure
For man's redemption—it is ever sure—
Which God for our soul's medicine
720 Gave us out of his heart with great pine.° *pain*
Here in this transitory life, for thee and me,
The blessed sacraments seven there be:
Baptism, confirmation, with priesthood good,° *Holy Orders*
And the sacrament of God's precious flesh and blood,° *Communion*
725 Marriage, the holy extreme unction, and penance.
These seven be good to have in remembrance.
Gracious sacraments of high divinity.
EVERYMAN: Fain would I receive that holy body,° *Communion*
And meekly to my ghostly° father I will go. *spiritual*
730 FIVE WITS: Everyman, that is the best that ye can do.
God will you to salvation bring,
For priesthood exceedeth all other thing:
To us Holy Scripture they do teach,
And converteth man from sin, heaven to reach;
735 God hath to them more power given
Than to any angel that is in heaven.
With five words° he may consecrate, *Hoc est enim corpus meum, "This is my*
God's body in flesh and blood to make, *body." [Matthew 26:26]*
And handleth his Maker between his hands.
740 The priest bindeth and unbindeth all bands,° *of sin*
Both in earth and in heaven.
Thou ministers° all the sacraments seven; *administer*
Though we kiss thy feet, thou were worthy.
Thou art surgeon that cureth sin deadly;
745 No remedy we find under God
But all only° priesthood. *only through the*
Everyman, God gave priest that dignity,
And setteth them in his stead among us to be;
Thus be they above angels in degree.

[EVERYMAN *exits to receive Communion and Extreme Unction*]

750 KNOWLEDGE: If priests be good, it is so, surely.
But when Jesus hanged on the cross with great smart,° *pain*
There he gave out of his blessed heart
The seven sacraments in great torment;
He sold them not to us, that Lord omnipotent.
755 Therefore Saint Peter the apostle doth say
That Jesus curse hath all they° *those priests*
Which God their Saviour do buy or sell,
Or they for any money do take or tell.° *who commit simony*
Sinful priests giveth the sinners example bad:
760 Their children sitteth by other men's fires, I have heard;
And some haunteth women's company
With unclean life, as lusts of lechery.
These be with sin made blind.
FIVE WITS: I trust to God no such may we find;
765 Therefore let us priesthood honor,
And follow their doctrine for our souls' succor.° *comfort*
We be their sheep, and they shepherds be
By whom we all be kept in surety.

Peace! For yonder I see Everyman come,
770   Which hath made true satisfaction.
GOOD DEEDS: Me think it is he indeed.

[EVERYMAN *reenters*]

EVERYMAN: Now Jesu be your alder speed!°   *great helper*
    I have received the sacrament for my redemption,
    And then mine extreme unction.
775   Blessed be all they that counselled me to take it!
    And now, friends, let us go without longer respite.
    I thank God that ye have tarried so long.
    Now set each of you on this rood° your hand,   *cross*
    And shortly follow me.
780   I go before there I would be.° God be our guide!   *where I wish to be*
STRENGTH: Everyman, we will not from you go
    Till ye have done this voyage long.
DISCRETION: I, Discretion, will bide by you also.
KNOWLEDGE: And though this pilgrimage be never so strong,°   *difficult*
785   I will never part you fro.
    Everyman, I will be as sure by thee   *who thought that strength came*
    As ever I did by Judas Maccabee.°   *from heaven [1 Maccabees 3:19]*
EVERYMAN: Alas, I am so faint I may not stand;
    My limbs under me do fold.
790   Friends, let us not turn again to this land,
    Not for all the world's gold;
    For into this cave° must I creep   *grave*
    And turn to earth, and there to sleep.
BEAUTY: What, in to this grave? Alas!
795 EVERYMAN: Yea, there shall ye consume,° more and less.   *be consumed*
BEAUTY: And what, should I smother here?
EVERYMAN: Yea, by my faith, and never more appear.
    In this world live no more we shall,
    But in heaven before the highest Lord of all.
800 BEAUTY: I cross out all this!° adieu, by Saint John!   *Count me out*
    I take my cap in my lap and am gone.
EVERYMAN: What, Beauty, whither will ye?
BEAUTY: Peace! I am deaf. I look not behind me,
    Not and thou would give me all the gold in thy chest.

[*Exit* BEAUTY]

805 EVERYMAN: Alas, whereto may I trust?
    Beauty goeth fast away from me.
    She promised with me to live and die.
STRENGTH: Everyman, I will thee also forsake and deny;
    Thy game liketh° me not at all.   *pleases*
810 EVERYMAN: Why, then, ye will forsake me all?
    Sweet Strength, tarry a little space.
STRENGTH: Nay, sir, by the rood° of grace!   *cross*
    I will hie me from thee fast,
    Though thou weep to thy heart tobrast.°   *breaks*
815 EVERYMAN: Ye would ever bide by me, ye said.
STRENGTH: Yea, I have you far enough conveyed.
    Ye be old enough, I understand,
    Your pilgrimage to take on hand.
    I repent me that I hither came.

820 EVERYMAN: Strength, you to displease I am to blame.
Yet promise is debt, that ye well wot°   *know*
STRENGTH: In faith, I care not.
Thou art but a fool to complain;
You spend your speech and waste your brain.
825 Go thrust thee into the ground.

[*Exit* STRENGTH]

EVERYMAN: I had weened° sure I should you have found.   *thought*
He that trusteth in his Strength,
She him deceiveth at the length.
Both Strength and Beauty forsaketh me;
830 Yet they promised me fair and lovingly.
DISCRETION: Everyman, I will after Strength be gone.
As for me, I will leave you alone.
EVERYMAN: Why, Discretion, will ye forsake me?
DISCRETION: Yea, in faith, I will go from thee,
835 For when Strength goeth before
I follow after ever more.
EVERYMAN: Yet, I pray thee, for the love of the Trinity,
Look in my grave once piteously.
DISCRETION: Nay, so near will I not come.
840 Farewell, everyone!

[*Exit* DISCRETION]

EVERYMAN: O, all thing faileth, save God alone—
Beauty, Strength, and Discretion;
For when Death bloweth his blast,
They all run from me full fast.
845 FIVE WITS: Everyman, my leave now of thee I take.
I will follow the other, for here I thee forsake.
EVERYMAN: Alas, then may I wail and weep,
For I took you for my best friend.
FIVE WITS: I will no longer thee keep.
850 Now farewell, and there an end.

[*Exit* FIVE WITS]

EVERYMAN: O Jesu, help! All hath forsaken me.
GOOD DEEDS: Nay, Everyman, I will bide with thee.
I will not forsake thee in deed;
Thou shalt find me a good friend at need.
855 EVERYMAN: Gramercy°, Good Deeds! Now may I true friends see.   *great thanks*
They have forsaken me, everyone;
I loved them better than my Good Deeds alone.
Knowledge, will ye forsake me also?
KNOWLEDGE: Yea, Everyman, when ye to Death shall go;
860 But not yet, for no manner of danger.
EVERYMAN: Gramercy, Knowledge, with all my heart,
KNOWLEDGE: Nay, yet I will not from hence depart
Till I see where ye shall become.
EVERYMAN: Methink, alas, that I must be gone
865 To make my reckoning and my debts pay,
For I see my time is nigh spent away.
Take example, all ye that this do hear or see,

How they that I loved best do forsake me,
Except my Good Deeds that bideth truly.
870 GOOD DEEDS: All earthly things is but vanity:°   *[Ecclesiastes 12:8]*
Beauty, Strength and Discretion do man forsake,
Foolish friends and kinsmen that fair spake—
All fleeth save Good Deeds, and that am I.
EVERYMAN: Have mercy on me, God most mighty,
875 And stand by me, thou mother and maid, Holy Mary!
GOOD DEEDS: Fear not; I will speak for thee.
EVERYMAN: Hear, I cry God mercy.
GOOD DEEDS: Short° our end and minish° our pain;   *shorten / diminish*
Let us go and never come again.
880 EVERYMAN: In to thy hands, Lord, my soul I commend;
Receive it, Lord, that it be not lost.
As thou me boughtest,° so me defend,   *redeemed*
And save me from the fiend's boast,
That I may appear with that blessed host
885 That shall be saved at the day of doom.
In manus tuas,° of mights most   *Into your hands*
For ever, *commendo spiritum meum.*°   *I commend my spirit*

[*He descends into the grave*]

KNOWLEDGE: Now hath he suffered that we all shall endure;
The Good Deeds shall make all sure.
890 Now hath he made ending;
Methinketh that I hear angels sing
And make great joy and melody
Where Everyman's soul received shall be.

[*Enter* ANGEL]

ANGEL: Come, excellent elect spouse, to Jesu!
895 Here above thou shalt go
Because of thy singular virtue.
Now thy soul is taken thy body fro,
Thy reckoning is crystal clear.
Now shalt thou into the heavenly sphere,
900 Unto the which all ye shall come
That liveth well before the day of doom.

[*Exit* ANGEL; *Enter* DOCTOR]

DOCTOR: This moral men may have in mind.
Ye hearers, take it of worth, old and young,
And forsake Pride, for he deceiveth you in the end;
905 And remember Beauty, Five Wits, Strength, and Discretion,
They all at the last do Everyman forsake,
Save his Good Deeds there doth he take.
But beware, for and° they be small,   *if*
Before God he hath no help at all:
910 None excuse may be there for Everyman.
Alas, how shall he do than?
For after death amends may no man make,
For then mercy and pity doth him forsake.
If his reckoning be not clear when he doth come,
915 God will say, "*Ite, maledicti, in ignem eternum!*"°   *"Depart, ye cursed into ever-*
And he that hath his account whole and sound,   *lasting fire!" [Matthew 25:41]*

High in heaven he shall be crowned.
Unto which place God bring us all thither,
That we may live body and soul together.
920   Thereto help the Trinity!
Amen, say ye, for saint charity.

FINIS

Thus endeth this moral play of Everyman
Imprinted at London in Poule's church yard by me
Johan Skot

Contexts and Commentaries

David Mills

Scholar, critic, and editor of The Chester Cycle, *David Mills is a Professor of English at Liverpool University. The essay from which this is taken appeared in 1969. In it, Mills discusses the larger contexts of the* Second Shepherds' Play.

Approaches to Medieval Drama

... The main "problem-play" is surely the Towneley *Secunda Pastorum.* From a purely literary standpoint the success of the play should lie in the balance of comic and serious scenes; but the comic element, particularly the character of Mak, seems to acquire so much weight and importance that it obscures the Nativity section. Doctrinally, a unity can be postulated for the play. It presents a theme of disorder—the chaos of a realm under a disordered ruler (Herod) and characteristic of a sinful world with no redeeming Saviour. The disorder at the top of the social ladder, in Herod and his knights, is manifested also in the misery of the shepherds lower down the scale. At this level, Mak is the agent of disorder, a magician casting a spell on the shepherds to steal their lamb. The forgiveness of Mak is a necessary prelude to the Nativity scene, and the lamb as baby is a thematic reversal of the Christ-child as sacrificial Lamb. So the first part of the play is the thematic reversal and type of the second, important, not only as secular comedy but also as the prefiguration of a central episode, the Nativity. Mak's lamb produces disorder, but the Lamb of God will restore harmony.

Evidently this co-existence of naturalism and doctrine is inseparable from the nature of the Corpus Christi plays themselves. The thematic significance of a play depends upon the relation of the play to the wider context of medieval religious thought, especially in relation to Biblical exegesis, which might be familiar to the audience. Structurally, it depends not upon the individual episode but upon the connexion between the episodes, upon the total framework of the cycle which exists to serve doctrinal ends. By this approach, we are much closer to a modern concept of a play than in the liturgical drama, but the dramatic effect is still secondary. The prophets and the plays of Moses have a secondary importance in cyclical structure, according to Kolve, because they do not have doctrinal centrality in conformity to his twin principles of selection, not because they are incapable of satisfactory dramatic development or presentation (which they are). At best, we respond on two levels—to the immediate emotional impact of the presentation and to its wider analogical significance in the cyclical structure. Structural unity is not necessarily the same as thematic unity, although the

199

attraction of Kolve's approach is that it indicates a means of relating the two, although neither necessarily produces dramatic unity.

To counteract any tendency to regard the cyclical framework as providing an adequate structural and thematic unity, I would emphasize not only the tension between tone and doctrine in, say, the plays of the Flood and of Abraham and Isaac, but also the effect produced by passing from one to the other. Doctrinally, the picture of God's wrath gives way to the picture of God's love, but the dramatic transition is from comedy to tragedy. Such variations in emphasis and tone run throughout the cycles and leave the impression not of a unified structure but rather of a sequence of distinct dramatic episodes, each separately conceived.

This impression is strengthened when we examine the production of the cycles in the Middle Ages. Were the postulated civic registers collections of plays independently commissioned by individual guilds, or were the guild-texts individual copies from a centrally written register? Notes in the York plays suggest that some guilds were performing plays of which no record was officially made, and at Chester, during the revision of 1575, the Smiths submitted two versions of their play for approval. If we believe that revisions of plays were the responsibility of the guilds, it is easy to see how the individual episode could develop at the expense of overall structure. This problem can be exemplified from the manuscript of the Towneley Plays which is clearly a compilation. At some time, it is postulated, this cycle borrowed a number of plays, with minor variations, from the York Cycle, and at another time some six plays, it is claimed, were rewritten by a single author, distinguished by his own stanza-form and dramatic style, and usually called "The Wakefield Master." There are two ways of regarding these theories. Perhaps Wakefield borrowed its cyclical base from York and employed one man to redraft certain plays and modify the total thematic structure. Or perhaps the Wakefield authorities decided to stage a cycle but left the responsibility for texts to the guilds. The poorer guilds took plays from York, but the richer ones could afford to employ their own writer, a man who produced powerful and entertaining work which enhanced the status of the guild that performed it; nor need this last development have taken place when the cycle was originally formed.

Robert A. Potter (b. 1934)

Playwright, scholar, and critic Robert Potter teaches at the University of California, Santa Barbara. In this selection from The English Morality Play *(1975), Professor Potter discusses Everyman's death.*

From THE ENGLISH MORALITY PLAY: ORIGINS, HISTORY, AND INFLUENCE OF A DRAMATIC TRADITION

Everyman, the most artistically successful of the moralities, is also the most imaginative and philosophical in dramatizing repentance in human terms. Here the consciousness of approaching death, which plays a part in the repentance scenes of *Perseverance, Wisdom*, and the other moralities, is expanded into a controlling metaphor for the human situation. Within this metaphor damnation and salvation are present possibilities; behind the grim aspect of death (as in other treatises on the "art of dying") lies the exemplary atoning death of Christ. The problem which *Everyman* presents with such daring and subtlety is the effort of dying mankind to find a solution for death. The solution, as it is systematically discovered in the action of the play, is not to be found in either external relationships (Fellowship, Kindred, Cousin, and Goods) or internal attributes (Discretion, Strength, Beauty, Five Wits). Nevertheless, substantiated by external good deeds and informed by internal knowledge, it is possible for mankind to discover the theological answer to the dilemma. The solution leads, by way of repentance, toward putting the sequence of one's life and death in consonance with the redeeming life and death of Christ, and hence with the pattern of salvation.

The crucial transformation of Everyman is from a state of sin to a state of grace. This transformation is accomplished, in the central sequence of the play (II. 463–654), by a closely detailed act of repentance. Everyman's repentance begins with contrition as a result of his estrangement from the external attributes upon which he had always depended—Fellowship, Kindred and Cousin, and Goods. With their departure he feels remorse:

> Than of my selfe I was ashamed,
> And so I am worthy to be blamed
> Thus may I well my selfe hate.
> (II. 476–8)

Because of this remorse he is able to recognize the perilous weakness of his Good Deeds and to be directed thereby to seek Knowledge. Having achieved this consciousness of his own spiritual illness, Everyman is ready to receive the specific doctrine of repentance. Knowledge leads to a higher state,

> Where thou shalte hele thee of thy smarte . . .
> . . . .
> Now go we togyder louyngly
>   To Confessyon, that clensynge ryvere.
> (ll. 528, 535–6)

In the 'house of Salvation' Everyman finds Confession, a 'holy man' who accepts his contrition and prescribes a remedy for his illness in the form of penance. Everyman is to scourge himself, in remembrance of Christ's sacrifice and in petition for God's mercy. In a lengthy prayer Everyman acknowledges Christ as his redeemer and asks the intercession of Mary.

> that I may be meane of thy prayer
> Of your Sones glory to be partynere,
> By the meanes of his passyon, I it craue.
> (ll. 601–3)

Everyman completes the penance by scourging his body, in satisfaction of the sacrament. In doing so he makes the transition from a state of sin to a state of grace. The reality of this change is verified by three visible facts: first, Good Deeds, who has been hobbled by Everyman's sins, rises before the eyes of all to accompany Everyman on his journey; second, Knowledge provides Everyman with a penitent's garment in token of his contrition, which Everyman willingly puts on; third, Everyman's book of reckoning, which previously had been rendered illegible by his sins, is now seen to be clear.

In full view of his audience, Everyman completes and demonstrates his repentance. The tension of the rest of the play lies in whether he will persevere in his state of grace or fall back into sin under the strain of approaching death. Everyman's inner attributes (Discretion, Strength, Beauty, and Five Wits) are revealed to him and as quickly taken from him. Even the counsel of Knowledge is ultimately lost to him. Everyman, denied (like Christ) by all, yet sustained by his good deeds, and bound (with Christ) in the sacraments, dies in a state of grace. His last thoughts are of Christ's redeeming death, and his last words (from the sacrament of extreme unction) are Christ's last words:

> *In manus tuas*, of myghtes moost
> For euer, *Commendo spiritum meum*.
> (ll. 886–7)

Victor W. Turner (1920–1983)

Distinguished anthropologist Victor Turner was known for his groundbreaking studies, including Essays in the Ritual of Social Relations *(1963),* The Forest of Symbols: Essays on African Religion *(1966), an edition of* Political Anthropology *(1966) with M. Swartz and A. Tulden, and* Ritual Process *(1969). In* From Ritual to Theater *(1982), Turner discusses the theater as an outgrowth of jural and ritual processes.*

From Ritual to Theatre: The Human Seriousness of Play

In large-scale modern societies, social dramas may escalate from the local level to national revolutions, or from the very beginning may take the form of war between nations. In all cases, from the familial and village level to international conflict, social dramas reveal "subcutaneous" levels of the social structure, for every "social system," from tribe to nation, to fields of international relations, is composed of many "groups," social categories," statuses and roles, arranged in hierarchies and divided into segments. In small-scale societies there are oppositions among clans, sub-clans, lineages, families, age-sets, religious and political associations, and many more. In our own industrial societies, we are familiar with oppositions between classes, sub-classes, ethnic groups, sects and cults, regions, political parties, and associations based on gender, division of labor, and relative age. Other societies are internally divided by caste and traditional craft. Social dramas have a habit of activating these "classifactory" *oppositions* and many more: *factions* (which may cut across traditional caste, class, or lineage *divisions* in pursuit of immediate, contemporary interests), *religious "revitalization" movements* which may mobilize former "tribal" enemies in joint opposition to foreign, colonizing overlords with superior military technology, international *alliances* and *coalitions* of ideologically disparate groups who see themselves as having a common enemy (often equally heterogeneous in national, religious, class, ideological, economic make-up), and common immediate interests—and turning them into *conflicts.*

Social life, then, even its apparently quietest moments, is characteristically "pregnant" with social dramas. It is as though each of us has a "peace" face and a "war" face, that we are programmed for cooperation, but prepared for conflict. The primordial and perennial agonistic mode is the social drama. But as our species has moved through time and become more dexterous in the use and manipulation of symbols, as our technological mastery of nature and our powers of self-destruction have grown exponentially in the past few thousand years, in similar measure we have become somewhat more adept in devising cultural modes of confronting, understanding, assigning meaning to, and sometimes coping with crisis—the second stage of the ineradicable social drama that besets us at all times, all places, and all levels of sociocultural organization. The third stage, modes of redress, which always contained at least the germ of self-reflexivity, a public way of assessing our social behavior, has moved out of the domains of law and religion into those of the various arts. The growing complexity of the social and economic division of labor, giving specialization and professionalization their opportunity to escape from embedment in the total ongoing social process, has also provided complex sociocultural systems with effective instruments for scrutinizing themselves. By means of such genres as theatre, including puppetry and shadow theatre, dance drama, and professional story-telling, performances are presented which probe a community's weaknesses, call its leaders to account, desacralize its most cherished values and beliefs, portray its characteristic conflicts and suggest remedies for them, and generally take stock of its current situation in the known "world."

Thus the roots of theatre are in social drama, and social drama accords well with Aristotle's abstraction of dramatic form from the works of the Greek playwrights. But theatre in complex, urbanized societies on the scale of "civilizations" has become a specialized domain, where it has become legitimate to experiment with modes of presentation, many of which depart radically (and, indeed, consciously) from Aristotle's model. But these sophisticated departures are themselves implicit in the fact that theatre owes its specific genesis to the third phase of social drama, a phase which is essentially an attempt to ascribe meaning to "social dramatic" events by the process which Richard Schechner has recently described as "restoring the past." Theatre is, indeed, a hypertrophy, an exaggeration, of jural and ritual processes; it is not a simple replication of the "natural" total processual pattern of the social drama. There is, therefore, in theatre something of the investigative, judgmental, and even punitive character of law-in-action, and something of the sacred, mythic, numinous, even "supernatural" character of religious action—sometimes to the point of sacrifice. ...

PART III

Renaissance Drama
and Theater in England

An artist's reconstruction of a design for a theatre by Inigo Jones shows the interior arrangement of an English hall or indoor theatre of the seventeenth century.

DRAMA AND SOCIETY

The period between 1576—when the first licensed public theater was built in London—and 1642—when the theaters were closed at the outbreak of the civil war—is often called the Golden Age of English drama, although the age was not especially golden for those who lived through it. For nearly a century, farm laborers had been displaced by the enclosure of agricultural land for pastures. Unemployment in the countryside was high, and the situation was made worse by unchecked inflation. Meanwhile, crop failures, threats of war abroad, and brutal religious strife had shaken English society by the time Elizabeth I came to the throne in 1558. Although the so-called Elizabethan settlement produced a period of relative calm, toward the end of the century the queen's refusal to name a successor brought about widespread discontent and threatened civil war even before her death in 1603. The accession of James I in 1603 was initially greeted with enthusiasm, but during the following years, religious, class, and political divisions intensified. Despite these changes, or perhaps because of them, this turbulent era produced the most important drama in Western history.

Rural unemployment drove many to London, whose population grew to around 200,000, twice its size at mid-century, making it the largest city in Europe. Not surprisingly, this astounding growth was accompanied by a general collapse of established social order. The city had became the center of English political, social, and economic life, offering opportunities for almost anyone to rise to prominence. But many hopefuls found themselves victimized instead by the radical shift from a dying feudal and agrarian social order to a capitalist economy.

The crumbling values were not only social. Religious struggles had dominated English politics from the 1520s to the 1560s, when enforced professions of faith shifted from Protestant to Catholic and back again. These shifts, zealously enforced by repressive regimes with torture and execution, offered evidence to some that there was little value in any version of Christianity. Because of the traditional view that order in society was connected to order in the universe, faith in any notion of order was undermined. And everywhere old ideas were under attack. Protestants, beginning with Martin Luther in 1517, had insisted that every individual bore responsibility directly to God rather than to the established church hierarchy. Political theorists, beginning with Machiavelli in 1513, had asserted the notion that political power did not emanate from God. And intellectuals, beginning with Montaigne in 1580, posited the idea that "truth" was culturally determined, while questioning the notion of a stable, coherent "self." From the recently discovered New World, explorers brought back tales of people, social systems, beliefs, and customs unimaginably different from those in Europe. In the early sixteenth century, Copernicus and, later, Galileo devised new astronomical theories and instruments, confirming that the earth was not in fact the center of the universe. The dissemination of such information was made relatively cheap and easy by the astonishing spread of printing from the late fifteenth century onward, dramatically increasing literacy, and circulating ideas through western Europe faster than had ever been possible before.

Writers grappled with this flood of new discoveries, ideas, and technologies. Some saw the changes as signs that the end of the world was near; others saw

Johannes de Witt's drawing (ca. 1596) of a play at the Swan Theatre in London shows a raised thrust stage projecting into the middle of a pit or standing area. The whole is surrounded by galleries for spectators. Note that the galleries have roofs while the middle of the structure is open to the elements.

them positively and hailed the birth of the age of the individual. The contradictions in every arena are registered in the experiences in the protagonists of the drama of the age. Humanity is no longer represented in the experience of abstract types like Everyman or Mankind, but rather in towering, fully realized figures like Faustus, Hamlet, and King Lear, characters who face the insolvable mysteries of their age and whose pain is unique. The new emphasis on individual thought, action, and responsibility can be found in all forms of endeavor during these times, from religion, where individuals now read scripture for themselves, to science, where individuals sifted through evidence for their own results rather than turning to authorities for answers.

PROFESSIONAL THEATER

Playwrights thought of themselves as poets, and most were, but they were not regarded as serious artists in the Renaissance. The modern analogy would be to screenwriters in film and television. Like them, Renaissance playwrights turned out a commercial product, often in collaboration. Serious literary aspirations like those of Ben Jonson were the exception rather than the rule. Once sold, plays became the property of the acting companies that bought them, and title pages of plays published in the period were more likely to bear the name of the company that owned them than the author. The view that drama was simply entertainment did not change until the seventeenth century. In 1616 Jonson published his works in an expensive folio edition, and in 1623 John Heminges and Henry Condell did the same for Shakespeare's works, clearly indicating that plays by some writers were thought to have literary merit and were worth preserving.

Precisely because drama was not generally considered serious literature, playwrights were free to treat virtually any subject that might interest and appeal to a broad spectrum of people, from the monarch to the lowliest person who could afford the price of admission to a public theater. In contrast to serious literature, the drama of the period was relatively free to respond to social issues and concerns of the age, inspired rather than hampered by tradition.

Not everyone was pleased. As Puritans gained in numbers and influence, they came to view the drama as downright depraved, and they said so repeatedly in treatises directed against it. For their part, playwrights responded with open mockery, with stage parodies that heaped abuse on Puritans, and few in the theatergoing public took the charges seriously. Most plays, in fact, were as provocative as the Puritans claimed, and the majority of theater patrons appear to have liked it that way.

Drama was certainly taken seriously by the authorities. Throughout the sixteenth century, proclamations were issued with regularity to prevent the performance of plays treating religious and political issues. In 1581 Queen Elizabeth I issued a commission to her Master of the Revels to censor drama throughout the country and to license plays and theaters. He in turn sometimes demanded changes in play texts before they were licensed and on occasion suppressed them altogether. The anonymous *Sir Thomas More* (ca. 1595) was never produced after the Master of the Revels censored it, and the deposition scene in Shakespeare's *Richard II* (1595) was never printed during Elizabeth's lifetime. The Master of the Revels was not the only overseer. The Privy Council, which also kept an eye on the drama, summoned Ben Jonson on a charge of treason for dramatizing political corruption at the court of Tiberius in *Sejanus* (1603). Thomas Middleton's *A Game at Chess* (1616) was closed down for its obvious allegory of the diplomatic relations between England and Spain, and other evidence confirms that the sovereigns and their governments continued to be concerned about offensive matter in plays.

Despite such regulation, the theater could not have survived without the support of the court. By the end of the fifteenth century, the king, members of the royal family, many powerful members of the aristocracy, and a number of cities and towns patronized actors who performed at court or in the great houses during the holidays between Christmas and Ash Wednesday and who toured in the counties during the rest of the year. They were given low-level positions in great households and wore livery, or uniforms, to identify their allegiance. This practice continued well into the period, and Shakespeare himself was appointed to a position in the royal household in 1603 when James I took over patronage of his playing company. Statutes had been enacted throughout the century to regulate the activities of these traveling troupes, subjecting actors to arrest and imprisonment along with vagrants. Actors needed patrons for political protection. But in the mid-1570s some companies began to receive patents (or licenses) which recognized them as legal entities and which specified their rights and restrictions at the very same time that public theaters began to be built and licensed in London. The first such building, erected in 1576, was called simply the Theater, and it soon became apparent to civic authorities that as plays brought large numbers of people together, they provided opportunities for the spread of crime and disease. They distracted people from their trades and encouraged them to disregard traditional values. City officials in London and elsewhere sided with Puritan objections, although principally for reasons of keeping public order.

While legally servants of a nobleman, theatrical companies after 1576 were also business enterprises in the modern sense: their incomes depended on their box office success. Sharers (or investors) in theater companies were involved in all facets of the operation and were paid a percentage of the profits. Shakespeare's company, the Lord Chamberlain's Men, was patronized by Henry and George Carey, Queen Elizabeth's cousins and Lords Chamberlain of the royal household. After Elizabeth's death in 1603, King James I took over patronage of the company and it became known as the King's Men. The sharers in the King's Men included Shakespeare, who was the company's chief playwright; Richard Burbage, the company's star actor; the actors John Heminges and Henry Condell; and a number of others. Sharers acted together to rent or build theaters, to commission or buy scripts, and to hire actors and apprentices, and together they assumed legal liability for the company. Some did very well. Shakespeare and Burbage, for example, profited. But many did not: the most famous playwright of the age, Ben Jonson, died in debt.

By the end of the sixteenth century, London had come to dominate in every kind of business, and the city led the way in theatrical activity as well. Now the cultural and economic center of the country, London became the preferred site for high-profile professional theater, a reputation it has maintained to this day.

PUBLIC THEATERS

Three kinds of theaters existed in and around London from 1576 to 1642. First, a number of large outdoor public theaters were built. Shakespeare's reference to "this wooden O" in *Henry V* suggests a circular structure, but in fact their size and shape varied: the Boar's Head was a converted innyard shaped like a *U*; the Fortune was rectangular; and others, like the Globe and the Rose, were eight- to twelve-sided structures. The Globe, the most famous of these, had a covered three-story gallery surrounding a pit that was open to the sky for natural lighting during afternoon performances. In shape, some public theaters resembled the bearbaiting rings that competed for audiences with the theaters. In these rings, bears were chained to a stake and set upon by large mastiffs that were trained to fight. The Hope theater, in fact, was used for both plays and for bearbaiting. The foundation for the Rose, discovered in London in 1988 near the site of the Globe, revealed it to have been a twelve-sided structure, about seventy feet wide, with a thrust stage measuring approximately twenty-five by fifteen feet and projecting into the pit. On one level above the stage, rooms were used for musicians and for scenes needing to be played "above," like the balcony scene in *Romeo and Juliet*. The main stage had a trapdoor and, in the roof above, a pulley to raise and lower properties and actors.

Patrons paid a penny admission for standing room in the pit, or higher prices for seats in the galleries. Estimates of the size of the largest of these theaters vary. The Globe and the Fortune are thought to have held from two thousand to three thousand spectators. Other theaters, like the Rose and the Boar's Head, which could seat approximately one thousand spectators, were smaller.

PRIVATE THEATERS

By 1610, for the obvious reasons of comfort and scenic control, indoor private theaters became more popular than the public theaters. The best-known of these theaters was the Blackfriars playhouse, located within a fifty-acre precinct once owned by the Dominicans, who were known as the Black Friars. Blackfriars was a liberty, quasi-independent of London and so not subject to the strict laws of the city. The theater had been used by boy playing companies since 1576 and eventually was acquired by Shakespeare's company to become their winter home. The success of their venture led other companies to open private theaters as well. Performances were lighted by torches, chandeliers, and standing candelabra; a raised stage was set at one end of the hall. Benches were placed in front of the stage and to its side in galleries. Some seating could also be had onstage. In contrast to the low entrance price to public theaters, private theaters were more expensive.

THEATRICAL PRODUCTIONS AT COURT

Performances of plays took place at court during the holidays from Christmas to Shrovetide as part of a series of entertainments known as the revels. The period was gradually extended to run from late September to June. A government office, the Office of the Revels, was given the job of producing a full series of entertainments, which consisted of masques, plays, and other shows. Elizabeth I saw an average of eight plays a year, all performed during the holidays; James I and Charles I saw considerably more. The most important and expensive entertainments at court were masques, elaborate shows featuring amateur aristocratic performers. Masques employed visual spectacle in scenery, costumes, properties, music, dance, song, and poetry (in descending order of importance), and they often celebrated some current fashion or event at court. They were tremendously expensive: a single masque performed at the court of James I cost over four thousand pounds to mount, and this in an age when a hundred pounds (the estimated annual income of an artisan) was an adequate annual income. The most famous masques were written and produced at James I's court by Ben Jonson and Inigo Jones. Jonson became the most famous dramatist of his time and Jones the best-known architect. Jones had studied in Italy, where experiments in using perspective scenery to revive classical plays had been going on for over a century. Jones used staggered wings and backdrop staging to convey a sense of perspective, and he developed triangular flats that could be turned to reveal three separate backdrops. His designs set the pattern for changeable scenery for over a century after his death.

In contrast to the public and private theaters, where scenery was kept to a minimum, performances at Elizabeth's court were marked by elaborate scenic effects. "Houses" were constructed of timber frames with canvas stretched over them and painted in perspective. During the decade of the 1570s these structures included battlements, towns, cities, forests, and castles. Such scenic properties continued to be used at James I's court.

PERFORMANCE

The same plays were often performed in the public theaters, in private theaters, and at court, but under widely differing conditions and with widely different stage effects. Understandably, plays created to meet the demands of these theaters ranged in subject matter. Shakespeare's writing career acts as a convenient register of how fashions changed. Before 1600 he wrote a good number of history plays on English subjects, such as *Richard II* and *I Henry IV*, and on Roman subjects, such as *Julius Caesar*. He also wrote romantic comedies, including *A Midsummer Night's Dream* and *As You Like It*, at this time. Beginning in 1600 he began writing his most successful tragedies—*Hamlet, Othello, King Lear*, and *Macbeth*. Even his comedies written at this time, such as *Measure for Measure*, explore serious social and moral problems. Toward the end of his career he wrote what his contemporary John Fletcher referred to as tragicomedies—the late romances such as *The Winter's Tale* and *The Tempest*, plays dealing with forgiveness and hope.

A long run of performances of a single play was unknown on the Renaissance stage. Companies kept a number of plays in repertory, performing several different plays each week. The repertory of acting companies was large, and actors had to keep a number of parts in memory, learning new ones every few weeks. The actor-audience relationship was conditioned by the physical arrangement of the theaters themselves. In the public theaters plays were ordinarily performed against an unchanging facade, varied only by use of portable scenic elements or other special effects. As on the medieval stage, playing spaces could be used to represent different locations at the same time. The close proximity of actor to audience, and the reliance chiefly on language instead of realistic scenery, made attending plays a much more self-conscious experience than it is today. Audiences went to "hear" a play, and they were often urged in the plays themselves to use their imaginations to supply the lack of spectacle and to develop sympathetic relationships to the action.

Women's parts in late Elizabethan plays, some of the most demanding roles in the drama, were performed by boys and by men. Cross-dressing was standard practice, and it occasionally was used to highlight political and sexual intrigue. Self-conscious attention to boys playing women shows up in some of Shakespeare's comedies, as in *As You Like It* and *Twelfth Night*. This attention clearly interrogated or confirmed the role of gender in society.

Like social customs, theatrical conventions derive from the values of the culture that produces them. Renaissance plays were written in response to social and cultural tensions peculiar to their age, and they were performed under theatrical conditions very difficult to reproduce today. But the problems they treat are still recognizable. The public and private qualities of the characters in these plays have become familiar to all of us who live in the post-Renaissance world. They easily carry past cultural and social barriers to speak to us with amazing directness.

CHRISTOPHER MARLOWE

(1564–1593)

Christopher Marlowe was born in the same year as Shakespeare, but the two men followed different paths to the theater. Son of a cobbler, Marlowe was educated at the King's grammar school in Canterbury. He was awarded an Archbishop Matthew Parker scholarship to Corpus Christi college, Cambridge, indicating that he was expected to take holy orders. But Marlowe clearly changed his mind, for when he left Cambridge in 1587 he turned to playwriting in London, where parts I and II of his *Tamburlane* were performed to great acclaim in that year. Meanwhile, upset by his lack of attendance during terms, university authorities attempted to deprive Marlowe of his degree. The Privy Council intervened, stating that Marlowe had been in the queen's service, and it now seems likely that he was involved in espionage at the Jesuit school at Reims. The queen's secretary Francis Walsingham headed the English secret service, and in 1593 Marlowe was living with Walsingham's brother Thomas. We know few other details of his personal life. In 1589 he was arrested after a street fight in which a man was killed, and in 1592 he was bound to keep the peace after threatening the lives of two London constables. He was summoned to appear before the Council in 1593, but before that meeting he was stabbed to death in a tavern brawl in Deptford. He was twenty-eight years old. Shortly afterward, an informant named Richard Baines submitted a report accusing Marlowe of heresy, atheism, and homosexuality, among other things, stating that some "great men" might be implicated in Marlowe's scandalous life-style.

The chronology of Marlowe's plays is not certain, partly because his dramatic career was so short, spanning only about six years. During that time he wrote some of the most brilliant plays of the era. Besides *Tamburlane* he wrote *The Jew of Malta, The Massacre of Paris, Edward II*, and *Doctor Faustus*. All were exceptionally popular, and the leading roles were performed by Edward Alleyne, chief player of the Lord Admiral's company and one of the greatest tragedians of the day. Marlowe's career ended just as Shakespeare's was beginning, and by any reckoning his literary and dramatic achievements were extraordinary. He developed what Ben Jonson rightly called the "mighty line," an iambic pentameter blank verse line that Shakespeare would later perfect. Many of Marlowe's plays are dominated by a towering central character or by a character opposed by a foil, a pattern imitated by Shakespeare and others in the early 1590s. Despite Marlowe's brief career, the power and depth of his principal characters, with their profound psychological complexity and self-involvement, lighted the way for his successors on the English stage.

Doctor Faustus

Marlowe based *Doctor Faustus* on a German original that was translated into English in 1592 as *The Damnable Life and Deserved Death of Doctor Johann Faustus*. Its Lutheran bias, and specifically anti-Catholic point of view, shows up in Marlowe's play, most obviously in the scenes at the papal court.

In the play's spectacular conclusion, Faustus is dragged screaming to hell, but his fall is complicated by Marlowe's powerfully attractive account of Faustus's pride and aspirations. The Faust story illustrates the inevitable fate of the soul that yields itself to the temptation to forbidden knowledge. Such attraction was a theme of great interest in Marlowe's age. The lines between allowable and damnable knowledge is defined differently by different ages. In the 1590s, conservative Christian sects held that any knowledge that did not contribute to salvation was wrong. Faustus is attracted to everything the soul must reject in its path to salvation: vain knowledge, wealth, sensuality, power. The God Faustus serves, by his own admission, is his appetite. For this he sells his soul, though he gets little in return. Mephistophilis is able to tell him no more than he already knows, and Faustus gains none of the knowledge he seeks. In the end, wealth, power, and sensuality become desperate means to distract his mind from despair.

Within the play's world, an absolute power validates itself by crushing Faustus, revealing Marlowe's familiarity with the pattern of classical tragedy. But other features show Marlowe's reliance on elements from the morality play: the temptation plot, the good and evil angels, the pageant of the seven deadly sins, and the reality of a judgment by a Christian God. Marlowe opposes the Christian structure by making Faustus into a kind of humanist Everyman. Unlike the classical tragic protagonists, Faustus comes from a low social station. Base-born but brilliant, he presents something of an image of Marlowe himself. Faustus speaks in blank verse, alludes to classical literature and mythology, and is driven to fulfill the promise of his own mind. The result is an irreconcilable tension between the Christian scheme of salvation and Faustus's willed resistance to it, an echo of the classical struggle against an impersonal and implacable fate. Ordinary human beings never transcend these bounds, but Faustus is driven by his own brilliance, by his fascination for knowledge and experiences beyond the pale of the ordinary. He is perhaps one of the finest expressions of Renaissance aspirations in the drama of the period. In *Doctor Faustus*, Marlowe charts a collision course between the comforting certainties of the medieval world and the anxieties of the modern world. Faustus is torn between these alternatives, and his tragedy is, to an extent, the tragedy of the age in which he lives.

The greatness of the play lies not in its adherence to a traditional Christian scheme—the depiction of a limiting absolute that confirms itself by destroying the protagonist—but in Faustus's resistance to it. Like all tragic protagonists, Faustus struggles and suffers beyond the limits imposed on ordinary people. At the beginning of the play Faustus's pride in his abilities leads him to reject human learning except magic. Despite all the warnings he sets out on a self-destructive course—"A sound magician is a demi-god." Toward the end of the play, when he has almost been persuaded by the Old Man to repent, Faustus instead embraces the demon Helen of Troy. He once again alienates himself from salvation through his own choice, as he has done throughout the play. But his doomed resistance to the law, and the nobility of the language he uses to do it, transform him into an archetype of modern man. His folly, like his blasphemy, has a wilful poetic splendor. Even during his last hour of agony, his speeches are balanced between the sensuousness of Ovid's poetry on the one hand and the terrifying apocalyptic images of John's Revelation on the other. The most striking of these images is that of Christ's blood streaming in the firmament, signifying both the mercy of redemption and the justice of damnation.

Doctor Faustus is a play that makes passivity impossible. Marlowe involves us in Faustus's moments of self-doubt and yearning for the safety and peace of salvation as well as in his rejection of this for the excitement of the unknown. His tragedy speaks directly to us as the tragedy of modern humanity.

Doctor Faustus

Christopher Marlowe

EDITED BY RUSSELL A. FRASER AND NORMAN RABKIN

CHARACTERS

THE CHORUS	MARTINO ⎫	A CARTER
DOCTOR FAUSTUS	FREDERICK ⎬ Gentlemen of his	HOSTESS
WAGNER, his servant	BENVOLIO ⎭ Court	GOOD ANGEL
VALDES ⎫	A KNIGHT	BAD ANGEL
CORNELIUS ⎭ friends to Faustus	DUKE OF SAXONY	EVIL ANGEL
THREE SCHOLARS	DUKE OF ANHOLT	MEPHISTOPHILIS
AN OLD MAN	DUCHESS OF ANHOLT	LUCIFER
THE POPE	BISHOPS, MONKS, FRIARS, SOLDIERS,	BELZEBUB
RAYMOND, King of Hungary	and ATTENDANTS	DEVILS
BRUNO	CLOWN	THE SEVEN DEADLY SINS
TWO CARDINALS	ROBIN, an ostler	ALEXANDER THE GREAT ⎫
ARCHBISHOP OF RHEIMS	DICK	PARAMOUR OF ALEXANDER ⎪
CARDINAL OF LORRAINE	RALPH	DARIUS ⎬ Spirits
CHARLES, Emperor of Germany	A VINTNER	HELEN ⎪
	A HORSE-COURSER	TWO CUPIDS ⎭

ACT I

PROLOGUE

[Enter Chorus.]

CHORUS: Not marching in fields of Thrasimen,°
    Where Mars did mate the warlike Carthagens;°
    Nor sporting in the dalliance of love,
    In courts of kings, where state is overturned;
5   Nor in the pomp of proud audacious deeds,
    Intends our Muse to vaunt his heavenly verse:
    Only this, Gentles—we must now perform
    The form of Faustus' fortunes, good or bad:
    And now to patient judgments we appeal,
10   And speak for Faustus in his infancy.
    Now is he born, of parents base of stock,
    In Germany, within a town called Rhodes.°
    At riper years, to Wittenberg he went,
    Whereas° his kinsmen chiefly brought him up.
15   So much he profits in divinity,
    The fruitful plot of scholarism graced,°
    That shortly he was graced° with Doctor's name,
    Excelling all and sweetly can dispute

    In the heavenly matters of theology;
    Till swoln with cunning,° of a self-conceit,   20
    His waxen wings° did mount above his reach,
    And melting, heavens conspired his overthrow;
    For, falling to a devilish exercise,
    And glutted now with learning's golden gifts,
    He surfeits upon cursed necromancy;   25
    Nothing so sweet as magic is to him,
    Which he prefers before his chiefest bliss:
    And this the man that in his study sits.

[Exit.]

Scene 1

[Enter FAUSTUS in his study.]

FAUSTUS: Settle thy studies, Faustus, and begin
    To sound the depth of that thou wilt profess:°
    Having commenced,° be a divine in show,°
    Yet level° at the end of every art,
    And live and die in Aristotle's works.°   5

---

[1] **Thrasimen** Lake Trasimene was the site of a great victory over the Romans by Hannibal in 217 B.C.   [2] **mate... Carthagens** ally himself with the Carthaginians (Hannibal's party)(?)   [12] **Rhodes** perhaps Roda in the Duchy of Saxe-Altenburg   [14] **Whereas** where   [16] **plot...graced** garden adorned (by him)   [17] **graced** technical term from Marlowe's Cambridge and signifying the right of a candidate to proceed to his degree

[20] **cunning** knowledge   [21] **waxen wings** like those which betrayed Icarus to his death

SCENE 1:   [2] **profess** be an adept in   [3] **commenced** another technical term from Cambridge—proceeded to a degree (in theology)   [3] **in show** in appearance   [4] **level** aim   [5] **Aristotle's works** which dominated the study of logic in sixteenth-century universities

Sweet Analytics, 'tis thou has ravished me!
Bene disserere est finis logices.°
Is, to dispute° well, logic's chiefest end?
Affords this art no greater miracle?
10 Then read no more; thou hast attained that end.
A greater subject fitteth Faustus' wit:
Bid *ὄν χαὶ μὴ ὄν*° farewell; and Galen °come;
Seeing, *Ubi desinit philosophus ibi incipit medicus,*°
Be a physician, Faustus; heap up gold,
15 And be eternized for some wondrous cure!
Summum bonum medicinae sanitas,
The end of physic is our body's health.
Why, Faustus, hast thou not attained that end?
Is not thy common talk sound aphorisms?°
20 Are not thy bills° hung up as monuments,
Whereby whole cities have escaped the plague,
And thousand desperate maladies been cured?
Yet art thou still but Faustus, and a man.
Couldst thou make men to live eternally,
25 Or, being dead, raise them to life again,
Then this profession were to be esteemed.
Physic, farewell! Where is Justinian?
[*Reads*] "*Si una eademque res legatur duobus
Alter rem, alter valorem rei,*" *etc.*°
30 A petty case of paltry legacies!
[*Reads*] "*Exhaereditare filium non potest pater nisi*"°
Such is the subject of the Institute,
And universal body of the law.
This study fits a mercenary drudge,
35 Who aims at nothing but external trash;
Too servile and illiberal for me.
When all is done, divinity is best:
Jeromè's Bible,° Faustus; view it well.
[*Reads*] "*Stipendium peccati mors est.*"°—Ha!
"*Stipendium,*" *etc.*
40 The reward of sin is death: that's hard.
[*Reads*] "*Si peccasse negamus, fallimur
Et nulla est in nobis veritas.*"°—
If we say that we have no sin,
We deceive ourselves, and there is no truth in us.
45 Why, then, belike we must sin,

And so consequently die:
Ay, we must die an everlasting death.
What doctrine call you this, *Che sera, sera*:
What will be, shall be? Divinity, adieu!
50 These metaphysics of magicians
And necromantic books are heavenly;
Lines, circles, letters, and characters;
Ay, these are those that Faustus most desires.
Oh, what a world of profit and delight,
55 Of power, of honor, and omnipotence,
Is promised to the studious artisan!°
All things that move between the quiet poles
Shall be at my command: emperors and kings
Are but obeyed in their several° provinces,
60 Nor can they raise the wind, or rend the clouds;
But his dominion that exceeds in this
Stretcheth as far as doth the mind of man;
A sound magician is a demi-god:
Here, tire my brains to get° a deity!

[*Enter* WAGNER.]

Wagner, commend me to my dearest friends, 65
The German Valdes and Cornelius;
Request them earnestly to visit me.
WAGNER: I will, sir.

[*Exit.*]

FAUSTUS: Their conference° will be a greater help to me
Than all my labors, plod I ne'er so fast. 70

[*Enter the* GOOD ANGEL *and* BAD ANGEL.]

GOOD ANGEL: O Faustus, lay that damnèd book aside,
And gaze not on it, lest it tempt thy soul,
And heap God's heavy wrath upon thy head!
Read, read the Scriptures:—that is blasphemy.
BAD ANGEL: Go forward, Faustus, in that famous art 75
Wherein all Nature's treasure is contained:
Be thou on earth as Jove is in the sky,
Lord and commander of these elements.

[*Exeunt Angels.*]

FAUSTUS: How am I glutted with conceit° of this!
Shall I make spirits fetch me what I please, 80
Resolve me of° all ambiguities,
Perform what desperate enterprise I will?
I'll have them fly to India° for gold,
Ransack the ocean for orient° pearl,
And search all corners of the new found world 85
For pleasant fruits and princely delicates;°
I'll have them read me strange philosophy,

---

7 L. This axiom, translated in the next line, reflects not Aristotle but his chief opponent in Marlowe's time, Peter Ramus. **8 dispute** engage in a disputation according to the principles of logic **12 Gk.** Aristotle's "being and not being" (emended from the garbled transliterating of Q1604—"Oncaymaeon") **Galen** chief authority on medicine to the Middle Ages **13 L.** adapting Aristotle (as the next quotation does, also)—"Where the philosopher leaves off, the physician begins." **18 aphorisms** like those of the Greek physician Hippocrates (fifth century B.C.); medical memoranda **20 bills** prescriptions **29 L.** garbling Justinian's *Institutes* on Roman law (as the next quotation does)—"If the same thing is willed to two persons, let one have the thing and the other the value of the thing." **31 L.** a father is not able to disinherit his son unless **38 Jerome's Bible** the so-called Vulgate **39 L.** Epistle to the Romans 6:23 **42 L.** I Epistle of St. John 1:8

---

56 artisan practitioner of the higher arts **59 several** particular **20 get** beget **64 conference** talk, conferring **79 conceit** imagination (of achieving) **81 Resolve me of** satisfy me regarding **83 India** presumably the West Indies **84 orient** lustrous **86 delicates** delicacies

And tell the secrets of all foreign kings;
I'll have them wall all Germany with brass,°
90   And make swift Rhine circle fair Wittenberg.
I'll have them fill the public schools° with skill,°
Wherewith the students shall be bravely clad;
I'll levy soldiers with the coin they bring,
And chase the Prince of Parma° from our land,
95   And reign sole king of all the Provinces;°
Yea, stranger engines for the brunt of war,
Than was the fiery keel at Antwerp bridge,°
I'll make my servile spirits to invent.

[Enter VALDES *and* CORNELIUS.]

Come, German Valdes and Cornelius,
100   And make me blest with your sage conference!
Valdes, sweet Valdes, and Cornelius,
Know that your words have won me at the last
To to practise magic and concealèd arts:
Yet not your words only, but mine own fantasy,
105   That will receive no object; for my head
But ruminates on necromantic skill.°
Philosophy is odious and obscure;
Both law and physics are for petty wits;
Divinity is basest of the three,
110   Unpleasant, harsh, contemptible, and vile:
'Tis magic, magic, that hath ravished me.
Then, gentle friends, aid me in this attempt,
And I, that have with subtle syllogisms
Gravelled° the pastors of the German church,
115   And made the flowering pride of Wittenberg
Swarm to my problems° as the infernal spirits
On sweet Musaeus° when he came to hell,
Will be as cunning as Agrippa° was,

Whose shadows made all Europe honor him.
VALDES: Faustus, these books, thy wit, and our
   experience   120
Shall make all nations to canònize us.
As Indian Moors° obey their Spanish lords,
So shall the spirits of every element
Be always serviceable to us three;
Like lions shall they guard us when we please;   125
Like Almaine rutters° with their horsemen's
   staves,
Or Lapland giants, trotting by our sides;
Sometimes like women, or unwedded maids,
Shadowing° more beauty in their airy° brows
Than has the white breasts of the queen of love: 130
From Venice shall they drag huge argosies,°
And from America the golden fleece°
That yearly stuffs old Philip's° treasury;
If learned Faustus will be resolute.
FAUSTUS: Valdes, as resolute am I in this   135
As thou to live: therefore object it not.°
CORNELIUS: The miracles that magic will perform
Will make thee vow to study nothing else.
He that is grounded in astrology,
Enriched with tongues,° well seen in° minerals,   140
Hath all the principles magic doth require;
Then doubt not, Faustus, but to be renowned,
And more frequented for this mystery
Than heretofore the Delphian oracle.
The spirits tell me they can dry the sea,   145
And fetch the treasure of all foreign wrecks,
Yea, all the wealth that our forefathers hid
Within the massy entrails of the earth:
Then tell me, Faustus, what shall we three want?°
FAUSTUS: Nothing, Cornelius. Oh, this cheers my soul! 150
Come, show me some demonstrations magical,
That I may conjure in some bushy grove,
And have these joys in full possession.
VALDES: Then haste thee to some solitary grove,
And bear wise Bacon's and Albanus'° works,   155
The Hebrew Psalter, and New Testament;°
And whatsoever else is requisite

---

[89] **wall...brass** Friar Bacon, the "white" magician in Robert Greene's play, intended to do the same for England.   [91] **public schools** lecture rooms of the University   **skill** often emended to "silk" (affluence, not characteristic of scholars)   [94] **Parma** Governor General of the Spanish Netherlands from 1579 to 1592, and hence one of the topical references involved (not very helpfully) in dating the play   [95] **Provinces** i.e., of the Netherlands   [97] **fiery...bridge** On April 4, 1585 the Netherlands employed a fireship to demolish the bridge Parma had built across the river Scheldt to complete his blockade of Antwerp.   [106] **Yet...skill** It is not simply the persuasion of his friends that has won Faustus to magic but his own wayward "fantasy" (the part of the mind that receives sense impressions and synthesizes them), which declines to work on any sense impression, so preoccupied is he with necromancy.   [114] **Gravelled** disconcerted   [116] **problems** intellectual demonstrations   [117] **Musaeus** Virgil locates this semimythological Greek poet in the Underworld in *Aeneid*, VI. 666*ff*. But it is worth recalling also that another Musaeus (fifth century A.D.) wrote a poem on Hero and Leander.   [118] **Agrippa** Henry Cornelius Agrippa of Nettlesheim, a sixteenth-century physician, was part propagandist of science (hence in the popular imagination a mage who could call up the shades of the dead, "shadows") and part hysterical moralist.

[122] **Moors** generically, dark-skinned persons; here, American Indians   [126] **Almaine rutters** German horsemen   [129] **Shadowing** harboring   **airy** ethereal, heavenly   [131] **argosies** large merchant vessels   [132] **golden fleece** the fabulous prize of Jason, the leader of the Argonauts, and hence emblematic of riches   [133] **Philip's** King Philip of Spain died in 1598; hence Q1614 revises Q1604 and gives the verb in the past tense, "stuffed."   [136] **object is not** don't make that a condition   [140] **tongues** languages   **seen in** versed in (the properties of)   [149] **want** lack   [155] **Bacon's and Albanus'** Roger Bacon, the thirteenth-century Franciscan, was a celebrated scientist (hence magician); Albanus (frequently emended to "Albertus" for the thirteenth-century Dominican philosopher, Albertus Magnus) may signify Pietro d'Albano, an alchemist of the thirteenth century, or a German saint (Alban) venerated at Cologne.   [156] **Psalter Testament** each used in conjuring spirits

We will inform thee ere our conference cease.

CORNELIUS: Valdes, first let him know the words of art;
160   And then, all other ceremonies learned,
Faustus may try his cunning by himself.

VALDES: First I'll instruct thee in the rudiments,
And then wilt thou be perfecter than I.

FAUSTUS: Then come and dine with me, and, after meat,
165   We'll canvass every quiddity° thereof;
For, ere I sleep, I'll try what I can do:
This night I'll conjure, though I die therefore.

[Exeunt omnes.]

Scene 2

[Enter TWO SCHOLARS.*]*

1 SCHOLAR: I wonder what's become of Faustus,
that was wont to make our schools ring
with *sic probo.*°

[Enter WAGNER.*]*

2 SCHOLAR: That shall we presently° know; here
5   comes his boy.

1 SCHOLAR: How now, sirrah! where's thy master?

WAGNER: God in heaven knows.

2 SCHOLAR: Why, dost not thou know, then?

WAGNER: Yes, I know; but that follows not.

10   1 SCHOLAR: Go to, sirrah! leave your jesting,
and tell° us where he is.

WAGNER: That follows not by force of argument,
which you, being Licentiates,° should stand
upon; therefore, acknowledge your error, and
15   be attentive.°

2 SCHOLAR: Then you will not tell us?

WAGNER: You are deceived, for I will tell you: yet, if
you were not dunces, you would never ask me
such a question; for is he not *corpus naturale*
20   And is not that *mobile?*° Then wherefore should
you ask me such a question? But that I am by
nature phlegmatic, slow to wrath, and prone to
lechery (to love, I would say), it were not for

you to come within forty foot of the place of
execution,° although I do not doubt but to see   25
you both hanged the next sessions.° Thus having triumphed over you, I will set my countenance like a precisian,° and begin to speak
thus:—Truly, my dear brethren, my master is
within at dinner,° with Valdes and Cornelius, as   30
this wine, if it could speak, would inform your
worships: and so, the Lord bless you, preserve
you, and keep you, my dear brethren.

[Exit.]

1 SCHOLAR: O Faustus. Then I fear that which I have
long suspected,
That thou art fallen into that damnèd art   35
For which they two are infamous through the
world.

2 SCHOLAR: Were he a stranger, not allied to me,
The danger of his soul would make me mourn.
But, come, let us go and inform the Rector,°
It may be his grave counsel may reclaim him.   40

1 SCHOLAR: I fear me nothing will reclaim him now!

2 SCHOLAR: Yet let us see what we can do.

[Exeunt.]

Scene 3

[Thunder. Enter LUCIFER *and four* DEVILS, FAUSTUS *to them with this speech.]*

FAUSTUS: Now that the gloomy shadow of the night,
Longing to view Orion's drizzling look,°
Leaps from the antarctic world unto the sky,
And dims the welkin° with her pitchy° breath,
Faustus, begin thine incantations,   5
And try if devils will obey thy hest,°
Seeing thou has prayed and sacrificed to them.
Within this circle is Jehovah's name,
Forward and backward anagrammatized;°
Th' abbreviated names of holy saints,   10
Figures of every adjunct° to the heavens,
And characters° of signs° and erring° stars,

---

¹⁶⁵ **canvass every quiddity** examine every essential element (a Scholastic term)

SCENE 2:   ² **L.** thus I prove (a term from Scholastic debate)   ⁴ **presently** immediately   ¹³ **Licentiates** scholars licensed to proceed to a Master's or a Doctor's degree   ¹⁵ **attentive** At this point there follows in Q1604 only a four-line exchange among Wagner and the Scholars. It is a good illustration of what most editors take to be the interpolations in 1602 of Birde and Rowley.   ²⁰ **L.** The scholastic term for the subject matter of physics is *"Corpus naturale seu mobile"*; Wagner is parading his learning.

²⁵ **place of execution** dining room   ²⁶ **sessions** when the court sits   ²⁸ **precisian** Puritan   ³⁰ **within at dinner** With these words, Wagner gives the scene; we are before Faustus' house.   ³⁹ **Rector** head of the university

SCENE 3:   ² **Orion's drizzling look** Echoing Virgil, *Aeneid,* I. 535. When the constellation Orion set at the beginning of November, storm and rain ensued.   ⁴ **welkin** heaven   **pitchy** black   ⁶ **hest** command   ⁹ **anagrammatized** transposed to form another word   ¹¹ **adjunct** The heavenly bodies are represented as being joined to the solid firmament of the sky   ¹² **characters** symbols   **signs** the figures of the zodiac   **erring** wandering: not fixed

By which the spirits are enforced to rise:
Then fear not, Faustus, to be resolute,
15   And try the utmost magic can perform.

[Thunder.]

Sint mihi Dii Acherontis propitii! Valeat
numen triplex Jehovae! Ignis, aeris, aquae,
terrae spiritus, salvete! Orientis princeps,
Belzebub, inferni ardentis monarcha, et
20   *Demogorgon, propitiamus vos, ut appareat*
et surgat Mephistophilis.° [Enter] Dragon
[above.] Quod tumeraris;° per Jehovam
Gehennam, et consecratam aquam quam nunc
spargo, signum crucis quod nunc facio,
25   *et per vota nostra, ipse nunc surgat nobis*
dicatus Mephistophilis!°

[Enter a DEVIL.*]*

I charge thee to return, and change thy shape;
Thou art too ugly to attend on me:
Go, and return an old Franciscan friar;
30   That holy shape becomes a devil best.

[Exit Devil.]

I see there's virtue in my heavenly words:°
Who would not be proficient in this art?
How pliant is this Mephistophilis,
Full of obedience and humility!
35   Such is the force of magic and my spells:
Now, Faustus, thou art conjuror laureate,°
That canst command great Mephistophilis.
Quin regis, Mephistophilis, fratris imagine!°

[Enter MEPHISTOPHILIS.*]*

MEPHISTOPHILIS: Now, Faustus, what would'st thou
        have me do?
40   FAUSTUS: I charge thee wait upon me whilst I live,
        To do whatever Faustus shall command,

Be it to make the moon drop from her sphere
Or the ocean to overwhelm the world.
MEPHISTOPHILIS: I am a servant to great Lucifer,
        And may not follow thee without his leave;   45
        No more than he commands must we perform.
FAUSTUS: Did not he charge thee to appear to me?
MEPHISTOPHILIS: No, I came now hither of mine own
        accord.
FAUSTUS: Did not my conjuring raise thee? Speak.
MEPHISTOPHILIS: That was the cause, but yet *per acci-*
        dens,°   50
        For, when we hear one rack° the name of God,
        Abjure the Scriptures and his Savior Christ,
        We fly, in hope to get his glorious soul;
        Nor will we come, unless he use such means
        Whereby he is in danger to be damned.   55
        Therefore the shortest cut for conjuring
        Is stoutly to abjure the Trinity,
        And pray devoutly to the prince of hell.
FAUSTUS: So Faustus hath
        Already done; and holds this principle,   60
        There is no chief but only Belzebub;
        To whom Faustus doth dedicate himself.
        This word "damnation" terrifies not me,
        For I confound hell in Elysium:°
        My ghost be with the old° philosophers!   65
        But, leaving these vain trifles of men's souls,
        Tell me what is that Lucifer thy lord?
MEPHISTOPHILIS: Arch-regent and commander of all
        spirits.
FAUSTUS: Was not that Lucifer an angel once?
MEPHISTOPHILIS: Yes, Faustus, and most dearly loved
        of God.   70
FAUSTUS: How comes it then that he is prince of dev-
        ils?
MEPHISTOPHILIS: Oh, by aspiring pride and insolence;
        For which God threw him from the face of heaven.
FAUSTUS: And what are you that live with Lucifer?
MEPHISTOPHILIS: Unhappy spirits that fell with Lucifer,   75
        Conspired against our God with Lucifer,
        And are forever damned with Lucifer.
FAUSTUS: Where are you damned?
MEPHISTOPHILIS: In hell.
FAUSTUS: How comes it then thou art out of hell?
MEPHISTOPHILIS: Why this is hell, nor am I out of it: 80
        Think'st thou that I, that saw the face of God,
        And tasted the eternal joys of heaven,
        Am not tormented with ten thousand hells,
        In being deprived of everlasting bliss?
        O Faustus, leave these frivolous demands,   85
        Which strikes a terror to my fainting soul!

---

21 L. May the gods of Acheron be favorable to me! Away with
the triple deity (? i.e., Trinity) of Jehovah! Hail, spirits of fire,
air, water, earth! Prince of the East, Belzebub, monarch of burning hell, and Demogorgon, we ask you that Mephistophilis
may appear and rise.   **22 L.** Not intelligible as it stands, and
perhaps representing a corruption of a phrase beginning
"Quod tu me . . ." Editors often emend to *"Quid tu moraris?"*
("Why do you linger?"), which makes good sense.   **26 L.** By
Jehovah, hell, and the holy water that I now sprinkle, and by
the sign of the Cross that I now make, and by our vows, may
Mephistophilis himself now rise to serve us.   **31 heavenly**
words scriptural invocations used in conjuring   **36 conjuror**
laureate like "poet laureate"   **37 L.** Nay but you rule,
Mephistophilis, in the likeness of a friar. Editors often emend
"regis" to *"redis"* ("you return").

---

50 L. incidentally (another formulaic term from scholasticism)
51 rack torture, as by anagrammatizing or transposing letters
64 confound . . . Elysium make no distinction between hell
and heaven.   **65 old** i.e., pre-Christian

FAUSTUS: What, is great Mephistophilis so passionate°
For being deprived of the joys of heaven?
Learn thou of Faustus manly fortitude,
90 And scorn those joys thou never shalt possess.
Go bear these tidings to great Lucifer:
Seeing Faustus hath incurred eternal death
By desperate thoughts against Jove's deity,
Say, he surrenders up to him his soul,
95 So he will spare him four-and-twenty years,
Letting him live in all voluptuousness;
Having thee ever to attend on me,
To give me whatsoever I shall ask,
To tell me whatsoever I demand,
100 To slay mine enemies, and to aid my friends,
And always be obedient to my will.
Go, and return to mighty Lucifer,
And meet me in my study at midnight,
And then resolve me of thy master's mind.
105 MEPHISTOPHILIS: I will, Faustus.

[Exit.]

FAUSTUS: Had I as many souls as there be stars,
I'd give them all for Mephistophilis.
By him I'll be great emperor of the world.
And make a bridge thorough° the moving air,
110 To pass the ocean with a band of men;
I'll join the hills that bind° the Afric shore,
And make that country continent to° Spain,
And both contributory to my crown:
The Emperor shall not live but by my leave,
115 Nor any potentate of Germany.
Now that I have obtained what I desired,
I'll live in speculation° of this art,
Till Mephistophilis return again.

[Exit.]

Scene 4

[Enter WAGNER *and the* CLOWN.*]*

WAGNER: Come hither, sirrah boy.
CLOWN: Boy! Oh, disgrace to my person. Zounds, boy
in your face! You have seen many boys with
beards, I am sure.
5 WAGNER: Sirrah, hast thou no comings in?°
CLOWN: Yes, and goings out too, you may see, sir.
WAGNER: Alas, poor slave! see how poverty jests in his
nakedness! I know the villain's out of service,
and so hungry that I know he would give his

soul to the devil for a shoulder of mutton, 10
though it were blood-raw.
CLOWN: Not so, neither. By'r lady, I had need to have
it well roasted, and good sauce to it, if I pay so
dear, I can tell you.
WAGNER: Sirrah, wilt thou be my man and wait on me, 15
and I will make thee go like *Qui mihi discipulus?*°
CLOWN: What, in verse?
WAGNER: No, salve; in beaten° silk and staves-acre.°
CLOWN: Staves-acre! that's good to kill vermin. Then,
belike, if I serve you, I shall be lousy. 20
WAGNER: Why, so thou shalt be, whether thou do'st it
or no. For sirrah, if thou dost not presently bind
thyself to me for seven years, I'll turn all the lice
about thee into familiars,° and make them tear
thee in pieces. 25
CLOWN: Nay, sir, you may save yourself a labor, for
they are as familiar with me as if they had paid
for their meat and drink, I can tell you.
WAGNER: Well, sirrah, leave your jesting and take these
guilders.° 30
CLOWN: Yes, marry, sir, and I thank you too.
WAGNER: So, now thou art to be at an hour's warning,
whensoever and wheresoever the devil shall
fetch thee.
CLOWN: Here, take your guilders again, I'll none of 'em. 35
WAGNER: Not I, thou art pressed,° for I will presently
raise up two devils to carry thee away—Banio,
Belcher!
CLOWN: Belcher! and° Belcher come here, I'll belch
him. I am not afraid of a devil. 40

[Enter two DEVILS.*]*

WAGNER: How now, sir, will you serve me now?
CLOWN: Ay, good Wagner, take away the devil then.
WAGNER: Spirits, away! Now, sirrah, follow me.

[Exeunt Devils.]

CLOWN: I will, sir, but hark you, master, will you teach
me this conjuring occupation? 45
WAGNER: Ay, sirrah, I'll teach thee to turn thyself to a
dog, or a cat, or a mouse, or° a rat, or anything.
CLOWN: A dog, or a cat, or a mouse, or a rat, O brave
Wagner!
WAGNER: Villain, call me Master Wagner, and see that 50
you walk attentively and let your right eye be
always diametrally° fixed upon my left heel,
that thou may'st *quasi vestigias nostras insistere.*°

CLOWN: Well, sir, I warrant you.

[Exeunt.]

ACT II

Scene 1

[Enter FAUSTUS *in his study.]*

FAUSTUS: Now, Faustus, must
    Thou needs be damned, and canst thou not be
      saved.
    What boots it, then, to think on God or heaven?
    Away with such vain fancies, and despair;
5   Despair in God, and trust in Belzebub:
    Now go not backward; Faustus, be resolute:
    Why waver'st thou? Oh, something soundeth in
      mine ear,
    "Abjure this magic, turn to God again!"
    Ay, and Faustus will turn to God again.
10   To God? He loves thee not;
    The God thou serv'st is thine own appetite,
    Wherein is fixed the love of Belzebub:
    To him I'll build an altar and a church,
    And offer lukewarm blood of new-born babes.

[Enter GOOD ANGEL *and* EVIL [ANGEL].*]*

15 BAD ANGEL: Go forward, Faustus, in that famous art.
    GOOD ANGEL: Sweet Faustus, leave that execrable art.
    FAUSTUS: Contrition, prayer, repentance—what of these?
    GOOD ANGEL: Oh, they are means to bring thee unto
      heaven!
    BAD ANGEL: Rather illusions, fruits of lunacy,
20   That make them foolish that do use them most.
    GOOD ANGEL: Sweet Faustus, think of heaven and
      heavenly things.
    BAD ANGEL: No, Faustus; think of honor and of wealth.

[Exeunt (Angels).]

FAUSTUS: Wealth! why, the signiory of Embden° shall
    be mine.
    When Mephistophilis shall stand by me,
25   What God can hurt me? Faustus, thou art safe:
    Cast no more doubts—Mephistophilis, come!
    And bring glad tidings from great Lucifer;
    Is't not midnight?—come, Mephistophilis,
    Veni,° veni, Mephistophile!

[Enter MEPHISTOPHILIS.*]*

    Now tell me what saith Lucifer, thy lord?   30
MEMPHISTOPHILIS: That I shall wait on Faustus while
    he lives,
    So he will buy my service with his soul.
FAUSTUS: Already Faustus hath hazarded that for thee.
MEPHISTOPHILIS:But now thou must bequeath it
    solemnly,
    And write a deed of gift with thine own blood;   35
    For that security craves Lucifer.
    If thou deny it, I must back to hell.
FAUSTUS: Stay, Mephistophilis, tell me what good
    Will my soul do thy lord?
MEPHISTOPHILIS: Enlarge his kingdom.
FAUSTUS: Is that the reason why he tempts us thus?   40
MEPHISTOPHILIS: *Solamen miseris socios habuisse doloris.°*
FAUSTUS: Why, have you any pain that torture others?
MEPHISTOPHILIS: As great as have the human souls of
    men.
    But tell me, Faustus, shall I have thy soul?
    And I will be thy slave, and wait on thee,   45
    And give thee more then thou hast wit to ask.
FAUSTUS: Ay, Mephistophilis, I'll give it him.°
MEPHISTOPHILIS: Then, Faustus, stab thy arm coura-
    geously,
    And bind° thy soul, that at some certain day
    Great Lucifer may claim it as his own;   50
    And then be thou as great as Lucifer.

*[*FAUSTUS *stabs his arm.]*

FAUSTUS: Lo, Mephistophilis, for love of thee,
    I cut mine arm, and with my proper° blood
    Assure° my soul to be great Lucifer's,
    Chief lord and regent of perpetual night!   55
    View here this blood that trickles from mine arm,
    And let it be propitious for my wish.
MEPHISTOPHILIS: But, Faustus,
    Write it in manner of a deed of gift.
FAUSTUS: Ay, so I do. [*Writes*] But, Mephistophilis,   60
    My blood congeals, and I can write no more.
MEPHISTOPHILIS: I'll fetch thee fire to dissolve it straight.

[Exit.]

FAUSTUS: What might the staying° of my blood
    portend?
    Is it unwilling I should write this bill?
    Why streams it not, that I may write afresh?   65
    Faustus gives to thee his soul: oh, there it stayed!
    Why shouldst thou not? Is not thy soul thine own?
    Then write again, *Faustus gives to thee his soul.*

[Enter MEPHISTOPHILIS *with the chafer° of fire.]*

ACT II, SCENE 1: **23 signiory of Embden** The important mer-
cantile town of Emden in East Friesland had considerable
trade relations with England in Marlowe's time. **29 L.** Come.

41 L. Misery loves company. **47 him** Lucifer **49 bind** give
a bond for **53 proper** own **54 Assure** Pledge **63 staying**
failing to flow (congealing)

MEPHISTOPHILIS: See, Faustus, here is fire, set it° on.
70 FAUSTUS: So, now the blood begins to clear again;
     Now will I make an end immediately.

[Writes.]

MEPHISTOPHILIS: *[Aside]* What will not I do to obtain
     his soul?
FAUSTUS: *Consummatum est,°* this bill is ended,
     And Faustus hath bequeathed his soul to Lucifer.
75 But what is this inscription on mine arm?
     Homo, fuge!° whither should I fly?
     If unto God, he'll throw me down to hell.
     My senses are deceived; here's nothing writ:
     Oh, yes, I see it plain; even here is writ,
80 *Homo, fuge!* yet shall not Faustus fly.
MEPHISTOPHILIS: *[Aside]* I'll fetch him somewhat to
     delight his mind.

[Exit.]

[Enter DEVILS, *giving crowns and rich apparel to*
FAUSTUS. *They dance, and then depart.]*

[Enter MEPHISTOPHILIS.*]*

85 FAUSTUS: What means this show? Speak, Mephistophilis.
MEPHISTOPHILIS: Nothing, Faustus, but to delight thy
     mind,
     And let thee see what magic can perform.
FAUSTUS: But may I raise such spirits when I please?
MEPHISTOPHILIS: Ay, Faustus, and do greater things
     than these.
FAUSTUS: Then there's enough for a thousand souls.
     Here, Mephistophilis, receive this scroll,
     A deed of gift of body and of soul:
90 But yet conditionally that thou perform
     All articles prescribed between us both.
MEPHISTOPHILIS: Faustus, I swear by hell and Lucifer
     To effect all promises between us both.
FAUSTUS: Then hear me read it, Mephistophilis.

95 On these conditions following.
     First, that Faustus may be a spirit in form and
     substance.
     Secondly, that Mephistophilis shall be his servant,
     and be by him commanded.
100 Thirdly, that Mephistophilis shall do for him, and
     bring him whatsoever.
     Fourthly, that he shall be in his chamber or house
     invisible.
     Lastly, that he shall appear to the said John Faustus at

all times, in what form or shape soever he please.   105
     I, John Faustus, of Wittenberg, Doctor, by these
     presents, do give both body and soul to Lucifer
     Prince of the East, and his minister Mephisto-
     philis: and furthermore grant unto them that,
     four and twenty years being expired, and these   110
     articles above written being inviolate, full power
     to fetch or carry the said John Faustus, body and
     soul, flesh, blood, or goods, into their habitation
     whersoever.
     By me, John Faustus.   115

MEPHISTOPHILIS: Speak, Faustus, do you deliver this
     as your deed?
FAUSTUS: Ay, take it, and the devil give thee good of it!
MEPHISTOPHILIS: So, now, Faustus, ask me what thou
     wilt.
FAUSTUS: First I will question with thee about hell.
     Tell me, where is the place that men call hell?   120
MEPHISTOPHILIS: Under the heavens.
FAUSTUS: Ay, so are all things else, but whereabouts?
MEPHISTOPHILIS: Within the bowels of these elements,
     Where we are tortured and remain forever:
     Hell hath no limits, nor is circumscribed   125
     In one self° place; but where we are is hell,
     And where hell is, there must we ever be:
     And, to be short, when all the world dissolves,
     And every creature shall be purified,
     All places shall be hell that is not heaven.   130
FAUSTUS: I think hell's a fable.
MEPHISTOPHILIS: Ay, think so, till experience change
     thy mind.
FAUSTUS: Why, dost thou think that Faustus shall be
     damned?
MEPHISTOPHILIS: Ay, of necessity, for here's the scroll
     In which thou hast given thy soul to Lucifer.   135
FAUSTUS: Ay, and body too: but what of that?
     Think'st thou that Faustus is so fond° to imagine
     That, after this life, there is any pain?
     No, these are trifles and mere old wives' tales.
MEPHISTOPHILIS: But I am an instance to prove the
     contrary;   140
     For I tell thee I am damned, and now in hell.
FAUSTUS: Nay, and this be hell, I'll willingly be damned:
     What! sleeping, eating, walking, and disputing!
     But, leaving off this, let me have a wife,
     The fairest maid in Germany, for I   145
     Am wanton and lascivious
     And cannot live without a wife.
MEPHISTOPHILIS: Well, Faustus, thou shalt have a wife.

[He fetches in a WOMAN DEVIL.*]*

FAUSTUS: What sight is this?
MEPHISTOPHILIS: Now, Faustus, wilt thou have a wife?   150

---

68 S.d. **chafer** vessel (used for heating)   69 **it** the blood   73 **L.**
It is finished (echoing Christ on the Cross: John 29:30).   76 **L.**
Man, fly.

126 **self** same   137 **fond** foolish

FAUSTUS: Here's a hot whore indeed! No, I'll no wife.
MEPHISTOPHILIS: Marriage is but a ceremonial toy:
    And if thou lovest me, think no more of it.
    I'll cut thee out the fairest courtesans,°
155   And bring them every morning to thy bed:
    She whom thine eye shall like, thy heart shall have,
    Were she as chaste as was Penelope,°
    As wise as Saba,° or as beautiful
    As was bright Lucifer before his fall.
160   Here, take this book, and peruse it well:
    The iterating° of these lines brings gold;
    The framing of this circle on the ground
    Brings thunder, whirlwinds, storm, and lightning;
    Pronounce this thrice devoutly to thyself,
165   And men in harness° shall appear to thee,
    Ready to execute what thou command'st.
FAUSTUS: Thanks, Mephistophilis, for this sweet book.
    This will I keep as chary° as my life.

[Exeunt°]

Scene 2

[Enter FAUSTUS in his study and MEPHISTOPHILIS.]

FAUSTUS: When I behold the heavens, then I repent,
    And curse thee, wicked Mephistophilis,
    Because thou hast deprived me of those joys.
MEPHISTOPHILIS: 'Twas thine own seeking, Faustus,
    thank thyself.
5   But think'st thou heaven is such a glorious thing?
    I tell thee, Faustus, it is not half so fair
    As thou, or any man that breathes on earth.
FAUSTUS: How provest thou that?
MEPHISTOPHILIS: 'Twas made for man; then he's more
    excellent.
FAUSTUS: If heaven was made for man, 'twas made
10   for me:
    I will renounce this magic and repent.

[Enter the two ANGELS.]

GOOD ANGEL: Faustus, repent; yet° God will pity thee.

BAD ANGEL: Thou art a spirit;° God cannot pity thee.
FAUSTUS: Who buzzeth in mine ears, I am a spirit?
    Be I a devil, yet God may pity me;   15
    Yea, God will pity me, if I repent.
BAD ANGEL: Ay, but Faustus never shall repent.

[Exeunt Angels.]

FAUSTUS: My heart is hardened, I cannot repent:
    Scarce can I name salvation, faith, or heaven,
    But fearful echoes thunders in mine ears,   20
    "Faustus, thou art damned!" Then swords, and
      knives
    Poison, guns, halters, and envenomed° steel
    Are laid before me to dispatch myself;
    And long ere this I should have done the deed,
    Had not sweet pleasure conquered deep despair.   25
    Have not I made blind Homer sing to me
    Of Alexander's° love and Oenon's death?
    And hath not he,° that built the walls of Thebes,
    With ravishing sound of his melodious harp,
    Made music with my Mephistophilis?   30
    Why should I die, then, or basely despair?
    I am resolved; Faustus shall not repent.
    Come, Mephistophilis, let us dispute again,
    And reason of° divine astrology.
    Speak, are there many heavens above the moon?   35
    Are all celestial bodies but one globe,
    As is the substance of this centric earth?°
MEPHISTOPHILIS: As are the elements, such are the
    heavens,
    Even from the moon unto the imperial orb,
    Mutually folded in each other's spheres,   40
    And jointly move upon one axletree,
    Whose terminè is termed the world's wide pole;
    Nor are the names of Saturn, Mars, or Jupiter
    Feigned, but are erring stars.°
FAUSTUS: But have they all
    One motion, both *situ et tempore?*°   45

SCENE 2:   [12] **yet** even now   [13] **spirit** devil   [22] **envenomed** tipped with poison   [27] **Alexander's** Paris's (the lover of Oenone, who committed suicide after his death)   [28] **he** Amphion   [34] **reason of** discourse about   [37] **Are...earth** Is the universe really constituted of layers of spheres (nine is the number subsequently assigned), one above another? Do all the apparently separate heavenly bodies actually compose a single globe, like the earth (which in the old astronomy is understood to be at the center of the universe)?   [44] **As...stars** Just as the four elements are distinct and yet combine with one another, so the various spheres, ascending from the moon to the heaven imperial (highest of all), are distinct. In this they are like the heavenly bodies, also distinct and yet connected to the axletree or pole (described as a boundary or farthest limit) on which the universe turns, and moving or wandering (hence "erring stars") in each other's spheres. We are right, then, to give the planets individual names.   [45] **L.** in position and in time (in the direction in which they move and in the duration of their movement around the earth)

---

[154] **courtesans** elegant prostitutes   [157] **Penelope** whose long faithfulness to her absent husband, Ulysses, made her the type of the chaste wife   [158] **Saba** Sheba, Solomon's queen, was proverbial for her wisdom.   [161] **iterating** repeating   [165] **harness** armor   [168] **chary** carefully   **Exeunt** Q1604 carries the scene forward with further talk between Faustus and Mephistophilis. Q1616 follows the stage direction with a brief appearance on stage of Wagner, "solus." Because what Wagner says abridges the speech of the Chorus that functions as Prologue to Act III, his lines are omitted here. Editors conjecture that he figured at this point in a lost comic scene, especially because, when the action begins again, we meet Faustus and Mephistophilis in the same setting. Evidently time has passed and some action has ensued.

MEPHISTOPHILIS: All move from east to west in
   four and twenty hours upon the poles of the
   world; but differ in their motions upon
   the poles of the zodiac.°
50 FAUSTUS: These slender questions Wagner can decide:
   Hath Mephistophilis no greater skill?
   Who knows not the double motion of the planets?
   That the first is finished in a natural day;
   The second thus: Saturn in 30 years;
55 Jupiter in 12; Mars in 4; the Sun, Venus,
   and Mercury in a year; the Moon in 28
   days.° These are freshmen's questions. But,
   tell me, hath every sphere a dominion
   or intelligentia?°
60 MEPHISTOPHILIS: Ay.
   FAUSTUS: How many heavens or spheres are there?
   MEPHISTOPHILIS: Nine; the seven planets, the
   firmament,° and the imperial heaven.
   FAUSTUS: But is there not *coelum igneum, et cristallinum?*°
65 MEPHISTOPHILIS: No, Faustus, they be but fables.
   FAUSTUS: Resolve° me then in this one question:
   why are not conjunctions, oppositions,
   aspects,° eclipses, all at one time, but in
   some years we have more, in some less?
70 MEPHISTOPHILIS: *Per inaequalum motum respectu
   totius.*°
   FAUSTUS: Well, I am answered. Now tell me who
   made the world.
   MEPHISTOPHILIS: I will not.
75 FAUSTUS: Sweet Mephistophilis, tell me.
   MEPHISTOPHILIS: Move me not, Faustus.
   FAUSTUS: Villain, have not I bound thee to tell
   me any thing?
   MEPHISTOPHILIS: Ay, that is not against our kingdom.
80 This is: thou art damned; think thou of hell.
   FAUSTUS: Think, Faustus, upon God that made the
   world.

---

⁴⁹ **All. . . zodiac** The duration of their movement around the earth is the same for each planet (twenty-four hours), but the time it takes them to revolve around the common axle-tree is different in each case. (Their movement, as Faustus goes on to say, is "double.")   ⁵⁷ **Saturn. . . days** Faustus has got it right for Saturn and Jupiter (in their revolution not around the earth but the sun); he overestimates in the case of Mars, Venus, and Mercury.   ⁵⁹ **dominion or intelligentia** ruling spirit or angel   ⁶³ **firmament** abode of the fixed (as opposed to "erring") stars   ⁶⁴ **L.** Sphere of fire and the crystalline sphere. The latter, in the Ptolemaic system, is above the firmament; the former is conceived as a belt or "element" encircling the earth (which was bounded also by elements of air and water).   ⁶⁶ **Resolve** Enlighten   ⁶⁸ **conjunctions, oppositions, aspects** The first denotes the apparent proximity of two heavenly bodies, the second their extreme divergence, the third any other relative position for the two.   ⁷⁰ **L.** Because of their unequal motion with respect to the whole. In other words, the heavenly bodies move at different speeds within the universe.

MEPHISTOPHILIS: Remember this.

[Exit.]

FAUSTUS: Ay, go, accursèd spirit, to ugly hell!
   'Tis thou hast damned distressèd Faustus' soul.   85
   Is't not too late?

[Enter the two ANGELS.*]*

BAD ANGEL: Too late.
GOOD ANGEL: Never too late, if Faustus will repent.
BAD ANGEL: If thou repent, devils will tear thee in
   pieces.   90
GOOD ANGEL: Repent, and they shall never raze° thy
   skin.

[Exeunt Angels.]

FAUSTUS: O Christ, my Savior, my Savior,
   Help to save distressèd Faustus' soul!

[Enter LUCIFER, BELZEBUB, *and* MEPHISTOPHILIS.*]*

LUCIFER: Christ cannot save thy soul, for he is just:
   There's none but I have interest in° the same.   95
FAUSTUS: Oh, what art thou that looks't so terribly?
LUCIFER: I am Lucifer,
   And this is my companion prince in hell.
FAUSTUS: O Faustus, they are come to fetch thy soul!
BELZEBUB: We are come to tell thee thou dost injure us.   100
LUCIFER: Thou call'st on Christ, contrary to thy
   promise.
BELZEBUB: Thou shouldst not think on God.
LUCIFER: Think on the devil.
BELZEBUB: And his dam too.
FAUSTUS: Nor° will I henceforth: pardon me in this,   105
   And Faustus vows never to look to heaven,
   Never to name God, or to pray to him,
   To burn his Scriptures, slay his ministers,
   And make my spirits pull his churches down.
LUCIFER: So shalt thou show thyself an obedient ser-
   vant,   110
   And we will highly gratify thee for it.
BELZEBUB: Faustus, we are come from hell in
   person to show thee some pastime: sit down,
   and thou shalt behold the Seven Deadly Sins
   appear to thee in their own proper shapes   115
   and likeness.
FAUSTUS: That sight will be as pleasing unto me
   As Paradise was to Adam, the first day
   Of his creation.
LUCIFER: Talk not of paradise or creation; but   120
   mark the show. Go, Mephistophilis, fetch
   them in.

---

⁹¹ **raze** graze, touch the surface of   ⁹⁵ **interest in** a legal claim on   ¹⁰⁵ **Nor** responding to the injunction not to think on God

[Enter the SEVEN DEADLY SINS.*]*

BELZEBUB: Now, Faustus, question them of their
    names and dispositions.
FAUSTUS: That shall I soon. What are thou,
125   the first?
PRIDE: I am Pride. I disdain to have any parents. I am
    like to Ovid's flea;° I can creep into every corner
    of a wench; sometimes, like a periwig,° I sit upon
    her brow; next, like a necklace, I hang about her
130   neck; then, like a fan of feathers, I kiss her lips,
    and then, turning myself to a wrought smock°
    do what I list. But, fie, what a smell is here! I'll
    not speak another word, unless the ground be
    perfumed, and covered with cloth of arras.°
FAUSTUS: Thou art a proud knave, indeed! what are
135   thou, the second?
COVETOUSNESS: I am Covetousness, begotten of an old
    churl in a leather bag: and might I now obtain
    my wish, this house, you and all, should turn to
    gold, that I might lock you safe into my chest.
140   Oh, my sweet gold!
FAUSTUS: And what art thou, the third?
ENVY: I am Envy, begotten of a chimney-sweeper and
    an oyster-wife.° I cannot read, and therefore
    wish all books burned. I am lean with seeing
145   others eat. Oh, that there would come a famine
    over all the world, that all might die and I live
    alone! then thou should'st see how fat I'd be.
    But must thou sit, and I stand? Come down,
    with a vengeance!
FAUSTUS: Out, envious wretch!—But what art thou,
150   the fourth?
WRATH: I am Wrath, I had neither father nor mother: I
    leaped out of a lion's mouth when I was scarce
    an hour old; and ever since have run up and
    down the world with these case of rapiers,
155   wounding myself when I could get none to
    fight withal.° I was born in hell; and look to it,
    for some° of you shall° be my father.
FAUSTUS: And what are thou, the fifth?
GLUTTONY: I am Gluttony, My parents are all dead, and
    the devil a penny they have left me, but° a small
160   pension, and that buys me thirty meals a day and
    ten bevers°—a small trifle to suffice nature. I
    come of a royal pedigree! my father was a
    Gammon of Bacon, and my mother was a
    Hogshead of Claret wine; my godfathers were

these, Peter Pickled-herring° and Martin
165
Martlemas-beef.° But my godmother, oh, she was
an ancient gentlewoman, her name was Margery
March-beer.° Now, Faustus, thou hast heard all
my progeny;° wilt thou bid me to supper?
FAUSTUS: Not I.
170
GLUTTONY: Then the devil choke thee.
FAUSTUS: Choke thyself, glutton!—What art thou, the
sixth?
SLOTH: Heigh ho! I am Sloth. I was begotten on a
sunny bank, where I have lain ever since; and
you have done me great injury to bring me from
175
thence: let me be carried thither again by
Gluttony and Lechery. Heigh ho! I'll not speak
a word more for a king's ransom.
FAUSTUS: And what are you, Mistress Minx, the seventh and last.
LECHERY: Who, I, sir? I am one that loves an inch of
180
raw mutton° better than an ell° of fried stockfish,° and the first letter of my name begins
with Lechery.
LUCIFER: Away, to hell, away, on Piper!°

[Exeunt the SEVEN SINS.*]*

FAUSTUS: Oh, how this sight doth delight my soul!
185
LUCIFER: But, Faustus, in hell is all manner of delight.
FAUSTUS: Oh, might I see hell, and return again safe,
how happy were I then!
LUCIFER: Faustus, thou shalt. At midnight I will send
for thee.
Meanwhile peruse this book and view it throughly°
190
And thou shalt turn thyself into what shape thou
wilt.
FAUSTUS: Thanks, mighty Lucifer!
This will I keep as chary as my life.
LUCIFER: Now, Faustus, farewell.
FAUSTUS: Farewell, great Lucifer. Come,
Mephistophilis.
195 ·

[Exeunt omnes several ways.°]

Scene 3

[Enter the CLOWN ROBIN *with a book.]*

---

127 **Ovid's flea** A Latin "Song of the Flea," probably written
in the Middle Ages, was attributed to Ovid.   128 **periwig** wig
131 **wrought smock** embroidered undergarment   134 **cloth of
arras** tapestry, from Arras in Flanders   143 **chimney-sweeper.
. . oyster-wife** suggesting dirt and fishy smells   156 **withal**
with   157 **some** one (of the devils on stage)   **shall** must
159 **but** only   161 **bevers** snacks

165 **Pickled-herring** cant   for   "buffoon"   166 **Martin
Martlemas-beef** November 11 (Martinmas) was the time for
hanging up beef that had been salted for the winter.
168 **March-beer** choice ale made in March   169 **progeny**
ancestry   181 **mutton** cant for "prostitute"   **ell** i.e., more
than a yard   182 **fried stockfish** dried codfish   184 **Piper**
addressing a musician on stage, who leads off the procession
of the Sins   190 **throughly** thoroughly   s.d. **Exeunt. . . ways**
What follows in Q1616 is omitted in Q1604, which offers a
different version later in the play.

ROBIN: What, Dick, look to the horses there,° till I come again. I have gotten one of Doctor Faustus' conjuring books, and now we'll have such knavery, as't passes.°

[Enter DICK.]

5 DICK: What, Robin, you must come away and walk the horses.

ROBIN: I walk the horses? I scorn't, faith', I have other matters in hand, let the horses walk themselves and° they will. *[Reads]* A per se; a, t. h. e. the; o per
10 se; o deny orgon, gorgon.° Keep further from me, O thou illiterate and unlearned hostler.

DICK: 'Snails,° what hast thou got there? A book? Why, thou canst not tell ne'er a word on't.

ROBIN: That thou shalt see presently. Keep out of the
15 circle, I say, lest I send you into the ostry° with a vengeance.

DICK: That's like, 'faith: you had best leave your foolery, for an° any master come, he'll conjure you, 'faith.

ROBIN: My master conjure me? I'll tell thee what, an
20 my master come here, I'll clap as fair a pair of horns on's head as e'er thou sawest in thy life.

DICK: Thou need'st not do that, for my mistress hath done it.

ROBIN: Ay, there be of us here that have waded as deep
25 into matters° as other men, if they were disposed to talk.

DICK: A plague take you, I thought you did not sneak up and down after her for nothing. But I prithee tell me in good sadness,° Robin, is that a con-
30 juring book?

ROBIN: Do but speak what thou't have me to do, and I'll do't: If thou't dance naked, put off thy clothes, and I'll conjure thee about presently: or if thou't go but to the tavern with me, I'll give
35 thee white wine, red wine, claret wine, sack, muscadine, malmesey, and whippincrust,° hold belly, hold, and we'll not pay one penny for it.

DICK: Oh, brave, prithee let's to it presently, for I am as dry as a dog.

40 ROBIN: Come then, let's away.

[Exeunt.]

SCENE 3: ¹ **look...there** The reference to horses places the scene; we are in an innyard. ⁴ **as't passes** as beats everything. ⁹ **and** if **A per se** A by itself; i.e., a unique thing (Robin's mock attempt at conjuring) ¹⁰ **o gorgon** for Demogorgon, whom Faustus had invoked ¹² **Snails** God's nails ¹⁸ **ostry** inn ¹⁸ **an** and; i.e., if ²⁵ **matters** a euphemism for sexual business; here, the woman herself ²⁹ **sadness** seriousness ³⁶ **muscadine, malmesey, and whippincrust** The first and second are strong sweet wines, the third perhaps a corruption for "hippocras," a spice-flavored wine.

ACT III

Prologue

[Enter the CHORUS.]

CHORUS: Learned Faustus,
  To find the secrets of astronomy
  Graven in the book of Jove's high firmament,
  Did mount him up to scale Olympus' top,
  Where sitting in a chariot burning bright,   5
  Drawn by the strength of yokèd dragons' necks,
  He views the clouds, the planets, and the stars,
  The tropic zones, and quarters of the sky,
  From the bright circle of the hornèd moon,
  E'en to the height of *Primum Mobile:*°   10
  And whirling round with this circumference,
  Within the concave compass of the pole;
  From east to west his dragons swiftly glide,
  And in eight days did bring him home again.
  Not long he stayed within his quiet house,   15
  To rest his bones after his weary toil,
  But new exploits do hale him out again,
  And mounted then upon a dragon's back,
  That with his wings did part the subtle° air,
  He now is gone to prove cosmography,   20
  That measures coasts, and kingdoms of the earth:
  And, as I guess, will first arrive at Rome,
  To see the Pope and manner of his court,
  And take some part of holy Peter's feast,
  The which this day is highly solemnized.   25

[Exit.]

Scene 1

[Enter FAUSTUS and MEPHISTOPHILIS.]

FAUSTUS: Having now, my good Mephistophilis,
  Passed with delight the stately town of Trier,°
  Environed round with airy mountain tops,
  With walls of flint, and deep entrenchèd lakes,°
  Not to be won by our conquering prince;   5
  From Paris next, coasting° the realm of France,
  We saw the river Maine fall into Rhine,
  Whose banks are set with groves of fruitful vines;
  Then up to Naples, rich Campania,
  Whose buildings fair and gorgeous to the eye,   10
  The streets straight forth,° and paved with finest
    brick,

ACT III. PROLOGUE: ¹⁰ **Primum Mobile** The axle of the heavens, by which God moves all the concentric spheres ¹⁹ **subtle** rarefied

SCENE 1: ² **Trier** Treves, on the river Mosel ⁴ **entrenchèd lakes** i.e., a moat ⁶ **coasting** passing along the side of ¹¹ **straight forth** running from one end of the town to another in a straight line

Quarters the town in four equivalents;°
There saw we learned Maro's° golden tomb
The way he cut, an English mile in length

15 Thorough a rock of stone, in one night's space;°
From thence to Venice, Padua, and the East,
In one of which a sumptuous temple° stands,
That threats the stars with her aspiring top,
Whose frame is paved with sundry colored stones,

20 And roofed aloft with curious° work in gold.
Thus hitherto hath Faustus spent his time:
But tell me now, what resting place is this?
Hast thou, as erst° I did command,
Conducted me within the walls of Rome?

MEPHISTOPHILIS: I have, my Faustus, and for proof
25   thereof
This is the goodly palace of the Pope;
And cause we are no common guests
I choose his privy-chamber° for our use.

FAUSTUS: I hope his Holiness will bid us welcome.

MEPHISTOPHILIS: All's one,° for we'll be bold with his
30   venison.
But now, my Faustus, that thou may'st perceive
What Rome contains for to delight thine eyes,
Know that this city stands upon seven hills
That underprop the groundwork of the same:

35 Just through the midst runs flowing Tiber's stream,
With winding banks that cut it in two parts;
Over the which four stately bridges lean,°
That make safe passage to each part of Rome:
Upon the bridge called Ponte Angelo

40 Erected is a castle° passing strong,
Where thou shalt see such store of ordinance,
As that the double cannons, forged of brass,
Do match the number of the days contained
Within the compass of one complete year:

45 Beside the gates, and high pyramides,°
That Julius Caesar brought from Africa.

FAUSTUS: Now, by the kingdoms of infernal rule,
Of Styx, of Acheron, and the fiery lake
Of ever-burning Phlegethon,° I swear

50 That I do long to see the mounuments
And situation of bright splendent° Rome:
Come therefore, let's away.

MEPHISTOPHILIS: Nay, stay, my Faustus; I know you'd
see the Pope
And take some part of holy Peter's feast,
The which, in state and high solemnity,   55
This day is held through Rome and Italy,
In honor of the Pope's triumphant victory.

FAUSTUS: Sweet Mephistophilis, thou pleasest me.
Whilst I am here on earth, let me be cloyed°
With all things that delight the heart of man.   60
My four-and-twenty years of liberty
I'll spend in pleasure and in dalliance,
That Faustus' name, whilst this bright frame doth
stand,
May be admired through the furthest land.

MEPHISTOPHILIS: 'Tis well said, Faustus; come then,
stand by me   65
And thou shalt see them come immediately.

FAUSTUS: Nay, stay, my gentle Mephistophilis,
And grant me my request, and then I go.
Thou know'st within the compass of eight days
We viewed the face of heaven, of earth and hell.   70
So high our dragons soared into the air,
That looking down, the earth appeared to me
No bigger than my hand in quantity.
There did we view the kingdom of the world,
And what might please mine eye, I there beheld.   75
Then in this show let me an actor be,
That this proud Pope may Faustus' cunning see.

MEPHISTOPHILIS: Let it be so, my Faustus, but first stay,
And view their triumphs,° as they pass this way.
And then devise what best contents thy mind   80
By cunning in thine art to cross the Pope,
Or dash the pride of this solemnity;
To make his monks and abbots stand like apes,
And point like antics° at his triple crown:
To beat the beads about the friars' pates,   85
Or clap huge horns upon the Cardinals' heads;
Or any villainy thou canst devise,
And I'll perform it, Faustus: Hark! they come:
This day shall make thee be admired° in Rome.

[Enter the CARDINALS *and* BISHOPS, *some bearing
crosiers,°some the pillars,°* MONKS *and* FRIARS *singing
their procession.° Then the* POPE, *and* RAYMOND, KING
OF HUNGARY *with* BRUNO° *led in chains.]*

---

12 Quarters. . . equivalents Divides in four equal parts. This line, occurring in Q1604 but not in Q1616, is an instance in which the earlier edition is more ample than the later for reasons that have nothing to do with the interposing of the censor. **13 Maro's** Virgil's (buried at Naples in 19 B.C.) **15 The... space** This prodigious feat reflects Virgil's reputation in the Middle Ages as a necromancer. **17 temple** St. Mark's in Venice **20 curious** intricate **23 erst** formerly **28 privy-chamber** another instance in which dialogue sets the scene **30 All's one** It doesn't matter. **37 lean** arch **40 castle** The Castello di Sant' Angelo, built A.D. 135 by Emperor Hadrian as his mausoleum but not, despite Mephistophilis, on the bridge itself **45 pyramides** obelisks **49 Styx... Acheron... Phlegethon** rivers of the underworld

---

51 bright splendent resplendent **59 cloyed** sated, stuffed **79 triumphs** spectacular entertainments **84 antics** fools, madmen **89 admired** wondered at **S.d crosiers** bishops' staffs, shaped like shepherds' crooks **89 pillars** emblems of office, perhaps (as in medieval painting) figuring the pillar against which Christ was scourged, and used in England in the sixteenth century in lieu of the mace **89 procession** processional chant, litany **89 Raymond. . . Bruno** Neither has been identified. It is plausible to see Marlowe as capitalizing on the fame of the Italian philosopher Giordano Bruno, who had traveled in England and who was burned in Rome a few years after the writing of the play.

POPE: Cast down our footstool.
90 RAYMOND: Saxon Bruno, stoop,
    Whilst on thy back his Holiness ascends
    Saint Peter's chair and state° pontifical.
BRUNO: Proud Lucifer, that state belongs to me:
    But thus I fall to Peter, not to thee.
95 POPE: To me and Peter shalt thou grovelling lie,
    And crouch before the Papal dignity;
    Sound trumpets, then, for thus Saint Peter's heir,
    From Bruno's back, ascends Saint Peter's chair.

[A flourish° while he ascends.]

    Thus, as the gods creep on with feet of wool,
100   Long ere with iron hands they punish men,
    So shall our sleeping vengeance now arise,
    And smite with death thy hated enterprise.
    Lord Cardinals of France and Padua,
    Go forthwith to our holy Consistory,°
105   And read amongst the Statutes Decretal,°
    What, by the holy Council held at Trent,°
    The sacred synod° hath decreed for him
    That doth assume the Papal government
    Without election, and a true consent:
110   Away, and bring us word with speed.
I CARDINAL: We go, my lord.

[Exeunt CARDINALS.]

POPE: Lord Raymond.
FAUSTUS: Go, haste thee, gentle Mephistophilis,
    Follow the Cardinals to the Consistory;
115   And as they turn their superstitious books,
    Strike them with sloth, and drowsy idleness;
    And make them sleep so sound, that in their
      shapes
    Thyself and I may parley with this Pope,
    This proud confronter of the Emperor:
120   And in despite of all his Holiness
    Restore this Bruno to his liberty,
    And bear him to the States of Germany.
MEPHISTOPHILIS: Faustus, I go.
FAUSTUS: Dispatch it soon,
125   The Pope shall curse that Faustus came to Rome.

[Exeunt FAUSTUS and MEPHISTOPHILIS.]

BRUNO: Pope Adrian,° let me have right of law,
    I was elected by the Emperor.

POPE: We will depose the Emperor for that deed,
    And curse the people that submit to him;
    Both he and thou shalt stand excommunicate, 130
    And interdict from Church's privilege
    And all society of holy men:
    He grows too proud in his authority,
    Lifting his lofty head above the clouds,
    And like a steeple over-peers the Church: 135
    But we'll pull down his haughty insolence.
    And as Pope Alexander, our progenitor,°
    Trod on the neck of German Frederick,°
    Adding this golden sentence to our praise:—
    "That Peter's heirs should tread on Emperors, 140
    And walk upon the dreadful adder's back,
    Treading the lion and the dragon down,
    And fearless spurn the killing basilisk:°
    So will we quell that haughty schismatic;°
    And by authority apostolical° 145
    Depose him from his regal government.
BRUNO: Pope Julius swore to princely Sigismond,°
    For him, and the succeeding Popes of Rome,
    To hold the Emperors their lawful lords.
POPE: Pope Julius did abuse the Church's rites, 150
    And therefore none of his decrees can stand.
    Is not all power on earth bestowed on us?
    And therefore, though we would, we cannot err.
    Behold this silver belt, whereto is fixed
    Seven golden keys° fast sealed with seven seals 155
    In token of our sevenfold power from Heaven,
    To bind or loose, lock fast, condemn, or judge,
    Resign,° or seal, or whatso pleaseath us.
    Then he and thou, and all the world shall stoop,
    Or be assured of our dreadful curse, 160
    To light as heavy as the pains of hell.

[Enter FAUSTUS and MEPHISTOPHILIS like the CARDINALS.]

MEPHISTOPHILIS: Now tell me, Faustus, are we not fitted°
    well?
FAUSTUS: Yes, Mephistophilis, and two such
    Cardinals
    Ne'er served a holy Pope as we shall do.
    But whilst they sleep within the Consistory, 165

---

92 **state** estate, office   s.d. **flourish** fanfare of trumpets   104 **Consistory** Ecclesiastical Senate   105 **Statutes Decretal** which incorporated Papal rulings on doctrine and church law   106 **Trent** The Council of Trent, 1545–63, was called in response to the Protestant Reformation.   107 **synod** ecclesiastical council   126 **Adrian** Pope Adrian VI (1522–23) was contemporary with the historical Faustus.

137 **progenitor** ancestor   138 **Alexander. . . Frederick** Pope Alexander III (1159–81) forced the German Emperor Frederick Barbarossa to stoop before him.   143 **basilisk** a monster supposedly able to kill with a look   144 **schismatic** maker of schisms or divisions in the Church   145 **apostolical** derived from the Apostles   147 **Julius. . . Sigismond** sonorous names more than historical sense here; the Pope and Emperor do not overlap in time   155 **keys** In token of the sevenfold power bestowed from heaven and enumerated below. Original reads "seals"—a careless printer's anticipation of what follows.   157 **Resign** Unseal(?)   162 **fitted** dressed

Let us salute his reverend Fatherhood.
RAYMOND: Behold, my Lord, the Cardinals are returned.
POPE: Welcome, grave Fathers, answer presently,
   What have our holy Council there decreed,
170   Concerning Bruno and the Emperor,
   In quittance of° of their late conspiracy
   Against our state and Papal dignity?
FAUSTUS: Most sacred Patron of the Church of Rome,
   By full consent of all the synod
175   Of priests and prelates, it is thus decreed:
   That Bruno and the German Emperor
   Be held as Lollards° and bold schismatics
   And proud disturbers of the Church's peace.
   And if that Bruno, by his own assent,
180   Without enforcement of° the German peers,
   Did seek to wear the triple diadem,
   And by your death to climb Saint Peter's chair,
   The Statutes Decretal have thus decreed,
   He shall be straight condemned of heresy,
185   And on a pile of fagots burned to death.
POPE: It is enough: Here, take him to your charge,
   And bear him straight to Ponte Angelo,
   And in the strongest tower enclose him fast;
   Tomorrow, sitting in our Consistory,
190   With all our College of grave Cardinals,
   We will determine of his life or death.
   Here, take his triple crown along with you,
   And leave it in the Church's treasury.
   Make haste again, my good Lord Cardinals,
195   And take our blessing apostolical.
MEPHISTOPHILIS: So, so; was never devil thus blessed
   before.
FAUSTUS: Away, sweet Mephistophilis, be gone,
   The Cardinals will be plagued for this anon.

[Exeunt FAUSTUS and MEPHISTOPHILIS (with BRUNO).]

POPE: Go presently and bring a banquet forth,
200   That we may solemnize Saint Peter's feast,
   And with Lord Raymond, King of Hungary,
   Drink to our late and happy victory.

[Exeunt.]

Scene 2

[A SENNET° *while the banquet is brought in; and then enter* FAUSTUS *and* MEPHISTOPHILIS *in their own shapes.]*

MEPHISTOPHILIS: Now, Faustus, come, prepare thyself
   for mirth:
   The sleepy Cardinals are hard at hand
   To censure° Bruno, that is posted hence,
   And on a proud-paced steed, as swift as thought,
   Flies o'er the Alps to fruitful Germany,   5
   There to salute the woeful Emperor.
FAUSTUS: The Pope will curse them for their sloth
   today,
   That slept both Bruno and his crown away:
   But now, that Faustus may delight his mind,
   And by their folly make some merriment,   10
   Sweet Mephistophilis, so charm me here
   That I may walk invisible to all,
   And do whate'er I please, unseen of any.
MEPHISTOPHILIS: Faustus, thou shalt, then kneel down
   presently:
   Whilst on thy head I lay my hand,   15
   And charm thee with this magic wand.
   First wear this girdle,° then appear
   Invisible to all are here:
   The Planets seven, the gloomy air,
   Hell and the Furies' forkèd hair,   20
   Pluto's blue fire, and Hecate's tree,°
   With magic spells so compass thee.
   That no eye may thy body see.
   So, Faustus, now for all their holiness,
   Do what thou wilt, thou shalt not be discerned.   25
FAUSTUS: Thanks, Mephistophilis; now, friars, take
   heed,
   Lest Faustus make your shaven crowns to bleed.
MEPHISTOPHILIS: Faustus, no more: see where the
   Cardinals come.

[Enter POPE *and all the* LORDS. *Enter the* CARDINALS *with a book.]*

POPE: Welcome, Lord Cardinals: come, sit down.
   Lord Raymond, take your seat. Friars, attend,   30
   And see that all things be in readiness,
   As best beseems this solemn festival.
I CARDINAL: First, may it please your sacred Holiness
   To view the sentence of the reverend synod,
   Concerning Bruno and the Emperor?   35
POPE: What needs this question? Did I not tell you,
   Tomorrow we would sit i' the Consistory,
   And there determine of his punishment?
   You brought us word even now, it was decreed
   That Bruno and the cursèd Emperor   40
   Were by the holy Council both condemned
   For loathèd Lollards and base schismatics:
   Then wherefore would you have me view that book?

I CARDINAL: Your Grace mistakes, you gave us no
    such charge.

45 RAYMOND: Deny it not, we all are witnesses
    That Bruno here was late delivered° you,
    With his rich triple crown to be reserved°
    And put into the Church's treasury.

BOTH CARDINALS: By holy Paul, we saw them not.

50 POPE: By Peter, you shall die,
    Unless you bring them forth immediately:
    Hale them to prison, lade their limbs with gyves:°
    False prelates, for this hateful treachery,
    Cursed be your souls to hellish misery.

[Exeunt ATTENDANTS with the two CARDINALS.]

55 FAUSTUS: So, they are safe: now, Faustus, to the feast,
    The Pope had never such a frolic° guest.

POPE: Lord Archbishop of Rheims,° sit down with us.

ARCHBISHOP: I thank your Holiness.

FAUSTUS: Fall to, the devil choke you an you spare.

POPE: How now? Who's that which spake?—Friars,
60   look about.

FRIAR: Here's nobody, if it like° your Holiness.

POPE: Lord Raymond, pray fall to, I am beholding
    To the Bishop of Milan for this so rare a present.

FAUSTUS: I thank you, sir.

[Snatches the dish.]

POPE: How now? who's that which snatched the
65   meat from me?
    Villains, why speak you not?—
    My good Lord Archbishop, here's a most dainty
    dish,
    Was sent me from a Cardinal in France.

FAUSTUS: I'll have that too.

[Snatches the dish.]

70 POPE: What Lollards do attend our Holiness,
    That we receive such great indignity?
    Fetch me some wine.

FAUSTUS: Ay, pray do, for Faustus is a-dry.

POPE: Lord Raymond, I drink unto your grace.

75 FAUSTUS: I pledge your grace.

[Snatches the cup.]

POPE: My wine gone too?—Ye lubbers,° look about
    And find the man that doth this villainy,
    Or by our sanctitude, you all shall die.

I pray, my lords, have patience at this
    Troublesome banquet.   80

ARCHBISHOP: Please it your Holiness, I think it be
    Some ghost crept out of Purgatory, and now
    Is come unto your Holiness for his pardon.

POPE: It may be so:
    Go then command our priests to sing a dirge.   85
    To lay the fury of this same troublesome ghost.

[Exit an ATTENDANT.]

Once again, my lord, fall to.

[The POPE crosseth himself.]

FAUSTUS: How now?
    Must every bit be spiced with a cross?
    Nay then, take that.   90

[Strikes the POPE.°]

POPE: Oh, I am slain, help me, my lords;
    Oh, come and help to bear my body hence:
    Damned be his soul forever for this deed!

[Exeunt the POPE and his train.]

MEPHISTOPHILIS: Now, Faustus, what will you do now,
    for I can tell you you'll be cursed with bell,   95
    book, and candle.°

FAUSTUS: Bell, book, and candle—candle, book, and
    bell,—
    Forward and backward, to curse Faustus to hell!
    Anon you shall hear a hog grunt, a calf bleat, and
    an ass bray,
    Because it is St. Peter's holy day.   100

[Enter the FRIARS with bell, book, and candle for the Dirge.]

I FRIAR: Come, brethren, let's about our business
    with good devotion.
    Sing this.
    Cursed be he that stole his Holiness' meat from the
    table!   105
      Maledicat Dominus!°
    Cursed be he that struck his Holiness a blow on the face!
      Maledicat Dominus!
    Cursed be he that took° Fair Sandelo a blow on the pate!
      Maledicat Dominus!   110

---

⁴⁶ **delivered** delivered to   ⁴⁷ **reserved** preserved   ⁵² **lade gyves** load fetters   ⁵⁶ **frolic** frolicsome   ⁵⁷ **Archbishop of Rheims** The title had been held in the sixteenth century by three members of the House of Guise, which furnished the infamous hero of Marlowe's play *The Massacre at Paris*.   ⁶¹ **like** please   ⁷⁶ **lubbers** louts

⁹⁰ **Strikes the Pope** The stage direction from Q1604 is worth preserving: "Cross again, and Faustus hits him a box of the ear, and they all run away."   ⁹⁶ **bell, book, and candle** The office of excommunication concludes with the tolling of the bell, closing of the book, and snuffing of the candle.   ¹⁰⁶ **L.** Let God curse him.   ¹⁰⁹ **took** struck (the reading of Q1616, which is inadvertently repeating "struck" from the line before)

Cursed be he that disturbeth our holy dirge!
   Maledicat Dominus!
Cursed be he that took away his Holiness' wine!
   Maledicat Dominus!
115 *Et omnes Sancti° Amen!*

*[(*MEPHISTOPHILIS *and* FAUSTUS) *beat the* FRIARS, *fling fireworks among them; and exeunt.]*

Scene 3

[Enter CLOWN (ROBIN) *and* DICK, *with a cup.]*

DICK: Sirrah Robin, we were best look that your devil
    can answer the stealing of this same cup, for the
    vintner's boy follows us at the hard° heels.
ROBIN: 'Tis no matter! let him come; an he follow us
5   I'll so conjure him as he was never conjured in
    his life, I warrant him. Let me see the cup.

[Enter VINTNER.]

DICK: Here 'tis. Yonder he comes. Now, Robin, now or
    never show thy cunning.
VINTNER: Oh, are you here? I am glad I have found
10   you, you are a couple of fine companions;° pray,
    where's the cup you stole from the tavern?
ROBIN: How, how? We steal a cup? Take heed what you
    say; we look not like cup-stealers, I can tell you.
VINTNER: Never deny 't, for I know you have it, and
15   I'll search you.
ROBIN: Search me? Ay, and spare not. *[Aside to* DICK]
    Hold the cup, Dick. Come, come, search me,
    search me!

*[*VINTNER *searches him.]*

VINTNER: *[To* DICK] Come on, sirrah, let me search you
20   now!
DICK: Ay, ay, do! *[Aside to* ROBIN] Hold the cup,
    Robin—I fear not your searching; we scorn to
    steal your cups, I can tell you.

*[*VINTNER *searches him.]*

VINTNER: Never outface me for the matter,° for, sure,
25   the cup is between you two.
ROBIN: Nay, there you lie, 'tis beyond us both.°
VINTNER: A plague take you! I thought 'twas your
    knavery to take it away; come, give it me again.
ROBIN: Ay, much; when? Can you tell?° Dick, make me

a circle, and stand close at my back, and stir not   30
for thy life. Vintner, you shall have your cup
anon. Say nothing,
DICK. *[Reads]* O per se, o Demogorgon, Belcher and
    Mephistophilis!

[Enter MEPHISTOPHILIS.]

MEPHISTOPHILIS: You princely legions of infernal rule,   35
    How am I vexèd by these villains'° charms!
    From Constantinople have they brought me
    now Only for pleasure of these damnèd slaves.

[Exit VINTNER.]

ROBIN: By Lady, sir, you have had a shrewd° journey
    of it. Will it please you to take a shoulder of   40
    mutton to° supper, and a tester° in your purse,
    and go back again?
DICK: Ay, ay. I pray you heartily, sir, for we called you
    but in jest, I promise you.
MEPHISTOPHILIS: To purge the rashness of this cursèd   45
    deed, First be thou turnèd to this ugly shape,
    For apish deeds transformèd to an ape.
ROBIN: Oh, brave! an ape! I pray, sir, let me have the
    carrying of him about to show some tricks.
MEPHISTOPHILIS: And so thou shalt: be thou trans-   50
    formed to a dog, and carry him upon thy back.
    Away, be gone!
ROBIN: A dog! that's excellent; let the maids look well
    to their porridge-pots, for I'll into the kitchen
    presently. Come, Dick, come.   55

[Exeunt the TWO CLOWNS.]

MEPHISTOPHILIS: Now with° the flames of ever-burning
    fire, I'll wing myself, and forthwith fly amain°
    Unto my Faustus, to the Great Turk's Court.

[Exit.]

ACT IV

[PROLOGUE]

[Enter CHORUS.°]

---

[36] **villains'** peasants'   [39] **shrewd** hard   [41] **to** for   **tester** sixpence   [56] **with** the aid of   [57] **amain** at full speed

ACT IV. PROLOGUE: [s.d.] **Chorus** This speech, omitted in Q1616, occurs in Q1604 after the excommunication ceremony (in this text, the close of III.ii). That it ought to follow the scene between the Clowns and the Vintner (III.iii) is suggested by the reference Mephistophilis makes in that scene to his traveling with Faustus. Now, as IV opens, these particular travels have been concluded and Faustus is said to have returned home.

---

[115] **L.** And all the saints (i.e., curse him)

SCENE 3:   [3] **hard** very (intensive)   [10] **companions** base fellows   [24] **outface matter** try to brave the matter out with me   [26] **beyond us both** out of our hands   [29] **Ay. . . tell** an impudent rejoinder—"That'll be the day!"

CHORUS: When Faustus had with pleasure ta'en the
            view
        Of rarest things, and royal courts of kings,
        He stayed his course, and so returnèd home;
        Where such as bear his absence but with grief,
5   I mean his friends and near'st companions,
        Did gratulate° his safety with kind words,
        And in their conference° of what befell,
        Touching his journey through the world and air,
        They put forth questions of astrology,
10   Which Faustus answered with such learned skill
        As they admired and wondered at his wit.
        Now is his fame spread forth in every land:
        Amongst the rest the Emperor is one,
        Carolus the Fifth,° at whose palace now
15   Faustus is feasted 'mongst his noblemen.
        What there he did, in trial of° his art,
        I leave untold; your eyes shall see performed.

[Exit.]

Scene 1

The Emperor's Court at Innsbruck.

[Enter MARTINO, and FREDERICK at several° doors.]

MARTINO: What ho, officers, gentlemen,
        Hie to the presence° to attend the Emperor,°
        Good Frederick, see the rooms be voided
            straight,°
        His majesty is coming to the hall;
5   Go back, and see the state° in readiness.
FREDERICK: But where is Bruno, our elected Pope,
        That on a fury's back came post° from Rome?
        Will not his grace consort° the Emperor?
MARTINO: Oh, yes, and with him comes the German
            conjuror,
10   The learned Faustus, fame of Wittenberg,
        The wonder of the world for magic art;
        And he intends to show great Carolus
        The race of all his stout° progenitors;
        And bring in presence of his majesty
15   The royal shapes and warlike semblances
        Of Alexander and his beauteous paramour.

FREDERICK: Where is Benvolio?
MARTINO: Fast asleep, I warrant you,
        He took his rouse° with stoups° of Rhenish wine
        So kindly yesternight to Bruno's health,   20
        That all this day the sluggard keeps his bed.
FREDERICK: See, see, his window's ope, we'll call to
            him.
MARTINO: What ho, Benvolio!

[Enter BENVOLIO above, at a window, in his nightcap;
buttoning.°]

BENVOLIO: What a° devil ail you two?
MARTINO: Speak softly, sir, lest the devil hear you: 25
        For Faustus at the court is late arrived,
        And at his heels a thousand furies wait,
        To accomplish whatsoever the Doctor please,
BENVOLIO: What of this?
MARTINO: Come, leave thy chamber first, and thou
            shalt see   30
        This conjuror perform such rare exploits,
        Before the Pope° and royal Emperor,
        As never yet was seen in Germany.
BENVOLIO: Has not the Pope enough of conjuring yet?
        He was upon the devil's back late enough;   35
        And if he be so far in love with him,
        I would he would post with him to Rome again.
FREDERICK: Speak, wilt thou come and see this sport?
BENVOLIO: Not I.
MARTINO: Wilt thou stand in thy window, and see it
            then?   40
BENVOLIO: Ay, an I fall not asleep i' th' meantime.
MARTINO: The Emperor is at hand, who comes to see
        What wonders by black spells may compassed° be.
BENVOLIO: Well, go you attend the Emperor: I am con-
        tent for this once to thrust my head out at a win- 45
        dow; for they say, if a man be drunk overnight
        the devil cannot hurt him in the morning; if that
        be true, I have a charm in my head shall control
        him as well as the conjuror, I warrant you.

[Exit.]

A Sennet. CHARLES, *the* GERMAN EMPEROR, BRUNO,
SAXONY, FAUSTUS, MEPHISTOPHILIS, FREDERICK,
MARTINO, *and* ATTENDANTS.

EMPEROR: Wonder of men, renowned magician,   50
        Thrice-learnèd Faustus, welcome to our court.
        This deed of thine, in setting Bruno free
        From his and our professèd° enemy,

---

⁶ **gratulate** express joy at ⁷ **conference** discussion ¹⁴
Carolus the Fifth King of Spain and Holy Roman Emperor
from 1519 to 1556 ¹⁶ **in trial of** by way of experiment in

SCENE 1: ˢ·ᵈ· **several** separate ² **presence** royal chamber ²
Emperor The scene has shifted to the Emperor's court in
Germany. ³ **voided straight** emptied immediately ⁵ **see
the state** see that the throne is ⁷ **post** with speed ⁹ **consort**
accompany ¹³ **stout** brave, hardy

---

¹⁹ **took his rouse** drank deep **stoups** tankards ²³ **buttoning** i.e., himself up ²⁴ **a** the ³² **Pope** Bruno ⁴³ **compassed** achieved ⁵⁴ **professèd** Avowed

55 Shall add more excellence unto thine art,
Than if by powerful necromantic spells,
Thou couldst command the world's obedience:
For ever be beloved of Carolus,
And if this Bruno thou hast late redeemed°
60 In peace possess the triple diadem,
And sit in Peter's chair, despite of chance,
Thou shalt be famous through all Italy,
And honored of the German Emperor.
FAUSTUS: These gracious words, most royal Carolus,
Shall make poor Faustus to his utmost power,
65 Both love and serve the German Emperor,
And lay his life at holy Bruno's feet.
For proof whereof, if so your grace be pleased,
The Doctor stands prepared by power of art
To cast his magic charms, that shall pierce through
70 The ebon° gates of ever-burning hell,
And hale the stubborn Furies from their caves,
To compass whatsoe'er your grace commands.
BENVOLIO: [*Above*] 'Blood, he speaks terribly: but for
all that I do not greatly believe him: he looks as
75 like a conjuror as the Pope° to a costermonger.°
EMPEROR: Then, Faustus, as thou late didst promise us,
We would behold that famous conqueror,
Great Alexander, and his paramour°
In their true shapes and state majestical,
80 That we may wonder at their excellence.
FAUSTUS: Your majesty shall see them presently.
Mephistophilis away.
And with a solemn noise of trumpets' sound
Present before this royal Emperor
85 Great Alexander and his beauteous paramour.
MEPHISTOPHILIS: Faustus, I will.
BENVOLIO: Well, Master Doctor, an your devils come
not away quickly, you shall have me asleep
presently: zounds, I could eat myself for anger,
90 to think I have been such an ass all this while to
stand gaping after the devil's governor, and can
see nothing.
FAUSTUS: I'll make you feel something anon, if
my art fail me not.—
95 My lord, I must forewarn your majesty,
That when my spirits present the royal shapes
Of Alexander and his paramour,
Your grace demand no questions of the King,
But in dumb silence let them come and go.
100 EMPEROR: Be it as Faustus please, we are content.
BENVOLIO: Ay, ay, and I am content too; and thou bring
Alexander and his paramour before the Emperor,
I'll be Actaeon° and turn myself to a stag.

FAUSTUS: And I'll play Diana, and send you the
horns presently.   105

Sennet. Enter at one door the EMPEROR ALEXANDER, *at
the other* DARIUS; *they meet,* DARIUS *is thrown down,*
ALEXANDER *kills him; takes off his crown, and offering
to go out, his paramour meets him, he embraceth her,
and sets* DARIUS' *crown upon her head; and coming
back, both salute the* EMPEROR, *who, leaving his state,
offers to embrace them, which,* FAUSTUS *seeing, suddenly stays him. Then trumpets cease, and music
sounds.*

My gracious lord, you do forget yourself,
These are but shadows, not substantial.
EMPEROR: Oh, pardon me, my thoughts are so ravished
With sight of this renownèd Emperor,
That in mine arms I would have compassed° him.   110
But, Faustus, since I may not speak to them,
To satisfy my longing thoughts at full,
Let me tell thee: I have heard it said,
That this fair lady whilst she lived on earth,
Had on her neck a little wart, or mole;   115
How may I prove that saying to be true?
FAUSTUS: Your majesty may boldly go and see.
EMPEROR: Faustus, I see it plain,
And in this sight thou better pleasest me,
Than if I gained another monarchy.   120
FAUSTUS: Away, be gone!

[Exit show.]

See, see, my gracious lord, what strange beast is
yon, that thrusts his head out at window?
EMPEROR: Oh, wondrous sight: see, Duke of Saxony,
Two spreading horns most strangely fastened   125
Upon the head of young Benvolio.
SAXONY: What, is he asleep, or dead?
FAUSTUS: He sleeps, my lord, but dreams not of his
horns.
EMPEROR: This sport is excellent; we'll call and wake
him.
What ho, Benvolio.   130
BENVOLIO: A plague upon you, let me sleep awhile.
EMPEROR: I blame thee not to sleep much, having
such a head of thine own.
SAXONY: Look up, Benvolio, 'tis the Emperor calls.
BENVOLIO: The Emperor? Where?—Oh, zounds,
my head!   135
EMPEROR: Nay, and thy horns hold, 'tis no matter
for thy head, for that's armed sufficiently.
FAUSTUS: Why, how now, Sir Knight, what, hanged by
the horns? This is most horrible: fie, fie, pull in
your head for shame, let not all the world wonder 140
at you.

---

⁵⁸ **redeemed** freed   ⁷⁰ **ebon** black   ⁷⁵ **Pope** i.e.,   Bruno
costermonger literally, appleseller (term of abuse)   ⁷⁸ **paramour** in this context, "consort," "queen"   ¹⁰³ **Actaeon**
famous hunter who, for looking on Diana naked, was transformed to a stag and torn to pieces by his own hounds

¹¹⁰ **compassed** enfolded

BENVOLIO: Zounds, Doctor, is this your villainy?
FAUSTUS: Oh, say not so, sir: the Doctor has no skill,
No art, no cunning, to present these lords,
145 Or bring before this royal Emperor
The mighty monarch, warlike Alexander.
If Faustus do it, you are straight resolved
In bold Actaeon's shape to turn a stag.
And therefore, my lord, so please your majesty,
150 I'll raise a kennel of hounds, shall hunt him so,
As all his footmanship shall scarce prevail
To keep his carcass from their bloody fangs.
Ho, Belimote, Argiron, Asterote,
BENVOLIO: Hold, hold! Zounds, he'll raise up a kennel
155 of devils, I think, anon: good, my lord, entreat
for me: 'sblood, I am never° able to endure
these torments.
EMPEROR: Then, good Master Doctor,
Let me entreat you to remove his horns,
160 He has done penance now sufficiently.
FAUSTUS: My gracious lord, not so much for injury
done to me, as to delight your majesty with
some mirth, hath Faustus justly requited this
injurious° knight, which being all I desire, I am
165 content to remove his horns. Mephistophilis,
transform him.

[MEPHISTOPHILIS removes the horns.]

and hereafter, sir, look you speak well of scholars.
BENVOLIO: Speak well of ye? 'Sblood, and scholars be
such cuckold-makers to clap horns of° honest
170 men's heads o' this order,° I'll ne'er trust smooth
faces and small ruffs,° more. But an I be not
revenged for this, would I might be turned to a
gaping oyster, and drink nothing but salt water.
EMPEROR: Come, Faustus, while the Emperor lives,
175 In recompense of this thy high desert,
Thou shalt command the state of Germany,
And live beloved of mighty Carolus.

[Exeunt omnes.°]

---

156 **am never** shall never be 164 **injurious** insulting 169 **of** on **o' this order** in this way 171 **smooth. . . ruffs** beardless scholars in academic attire s.d. **Exeunt omnes** In Q1604, after the exit of the Emperor, Faustus speaks six lines that "sound" authentic. That is not sufficient reason to include them in the text; but it is sufficient reason, perhaps, to give them in a footnote:

> Now, Mephistophilis, the restless course
> That time doth run, with calm and silent foot
> Shortening my days and thread of vital life,
> Calls for the payment of my latest years:
> Therefore, sweet Mephistophilis, let us
> Make haste to Wittenberg.

Scene 2

[Enter BENVOLIO, MARTINO, FREDERICK, and SOLDIERS.]

MARTINO: Nay, sweet Benvolio, let us sway thy
thoughts
From this attempt against the conjuror.
BENVOLIO: Away, you love me not, to urge me thus.
Shall I let slip so great an injury,
When every servile groom° jests at my wrongs,   5
And in their rustic gambols° proudly say,
"Benvolio's head was graced with horns today?"
Oh, may these eyelids never close again,
Till with my sword I have that conjuror slain.
If you will aid me in this enterprise,   10
Then draw your weapons, and be resolute:
If not, depart: here will Benvolio die,
But Faustus' death shall quit° my infamy.
FREDERICK: Nay, we will stay with thee, betide° what
may,
And kill that Doctor if he comes this way.   15
BENVOLIO: Then, gentle Frederick, hie thee to the
grove,°
And place our servants and our followers
Close° in an ambush there behind the trees.
By this (I know) the conjuror is near;
I saw him kneel and kiss the Emperor's hand,   20
And take his leave laden with rich rewards.
Then, soldiers, boldly fight; if Faustus die,
Take you the wealth, leave us the victory.
FREDERICK: Come, soldiers, follow me unto the grove;
Who kills him shall have gold and endless love.   25

[Exit FREDERICK with the SOLDIERS.]

BENVOLIO: My head is lighter than it was by° th'
horns,
But yet my heart's more ponderous than my head,
And pants until I see that conjuror dead.
MARTINO: Where shall we place ourselves, Benvolio?
BENVOLIO: Here will we stay to bide the first assault. 30
Oh, were that damnèd hell-hound but in place,°
Thou soon shouldst see me quit my foul disgrace.

[Enter FREDERICK.]

FREDERICK: Close, close, the conjuror is at hand,
And all alone comes walking in his gown;
Be ready then, and strike the peasant down.   35
BENVOLIO: Mine be that honor then: now, sword,
strike home,
For horns he gave I'll have his head anon.

SCENE 2: 5 **groom** base fellow 6 **gambols** frolics 13 **quit** requite 14 **betide** happen 16 **grove** The scene, then, is near a grove outside the city. 18 **Close** Hidden 26 **by** for the absence of 31 **in place** at hand

[Enter FAUSTUS *with the false head.]*

MARTINO: See, see, he comes.
BENVOLIO:　　　　　　No words: this blow ends all,
　　Hell take his soul, his body thus must fall.

[Stabs FAUSTUS, *who falls.]*

40　FAUSTUS: Oh!
FREDERICK: Groan you, Master Doctor?
BENVOLIO: Break may his heart with groans: dear
　　　　Frederick, see,
　　Thus will I end his griefs immediately.
MARTINO: Strike with a willing hand.

*[*BENVOLIO *strikes off* FAUSTUS' *false head.]*

　　　　　　　　　　　　　　His head is off.
BENVOLIO: The devil's dead, the Furies° now may
45　　　laugh.
FREDERICK: Was this that stern aspèct, that awful
　　　　frown,
　　Made° the grim monarch° of infernal spirits
　　Tremble and quake at his commanding charms?
MARTINO: Was this that damnèd head, whose heart°
　　　　conspired°
50　　Benvolio's shame before the Emperor?
BENVOLIO: Ay, that's the head, and here the body lies,
　　Justly rewarded for his villainies.
FREDERICK: Come let's devise how we may add more
　　　　shame
　　To the black scandal of his hated name.
BENVOLIO: First, on his head, in quittance of my
55　　　wrongs,
　　I'll nail huge forkèd horns, and let them hang
　　Within the window where he yoked° me first,
　　That all the world may see my just revenge.
MARTINO: What use shall we put his beard to?
60　BENVOLIO: We'll sell it to a chimney-sweeper; it will
　　　　wear out ten birchen brooms, I warrant you.
FREDERICK: What shall his eyes do?
BENVOLIO: We'll put out his eyes, and they shall serve
　　　　for buttons to his lips, to keep his tongue from
65　　　catching cold.
MARTINO: An excellent policy: and now, sirs, having
　　　　divided him, what shall the body do?

*[*FAUSTUS *rises.]*

BENVOLIO: Zounds, the devil's alive again.
FREDERICK: Give him his head, for God's sake.

FAUSTUS: Nay, keep it: Faustus will have heads and
　　　　hands,　　　　　　　　　　　　　　　　　70
　　Ay, all your hearts to recompense this deed.
　　Knew you not, traitors, I was limited°
　　For four-and-twenty years to breathe on earth?
　　And had you cut my body with your swords,
　　Or hewed this flesh and bones as small as sand,　　75
　　Yet in a minute had my spirit returned,
　　And I had breathed a° man made free from harm.
　　But wherefore do I dally my revenge?
　　Asteroth, Belimoth, Mephistophilis,

[Enter MEPHISTOPHILIS *and other* DEVILS.]*

　　Go, horse these traitors on your fiery backs,　　　80
　　And mount aloft with them as high as heaven,
　　Thence pitch them headlong to the lowest hell:
　　Yet, stay, the world shall see their misery,
　　And hell shall after plague their treachery.
　　Go, Belimoth, and take this caitiff hence,　　　　85
　　And hurl him in some lake of mud and dirt:
　　Take thou this other, drag him through the
　　　　woods,
　　Amongst the pricking thorns, and sharpest briers,
　　Whilst with my gentle Mephistophilis,
　　This traitor flies unto some steepy° rock,　　　　90
　　That, rolling down, may break the villain's bones,
　　As he intended to dismember me.
　　Fly hence, dispatch° my charge immediately.
FREDERICK: Pity us, gentle Faustus, save our lives!
FAUSTUS: Away!　　　　　　　　　　　　　　　　　95
FREDERICK: He must needs go that the devil drives.°

[*Exeunt* SPIRITS *with the* KNIGHTS.]

[Enter the ambushed° SOLDIERS.]*

I SOLDIER: Come, sirs, prepare yourselves in readi-
　　　　ness,
　　Make haste to help these noble gentlemen,
　　I heard them parley with the conjuror.
2 SOLDIER: See where he comes, dispatch, and kill the
　　　　slave.　　　　　　　　　　　　　　　　　100
FAUSTUS: What's here? An ambush to betray my life:
　　Then, Faustus, try thy skill: base peasants, stand:
　　For lo! these trees remove° at my command,
　　And stand as bulwarks 'twixt yourselves and me,
　　To shield me from your hated treachery:　　　　105
　　Yet to encounter this your weak attempt,
　　Behold an army comes incontinent.°

---

43 **Furies** Tisiphone, Alecto, and Megaera, avenging deities who punished criminality in this world and after death.
47 **Made** That made　**monarch** Pluto, god of the Underworld
49 **heart** frequently emended to "art"　**conspired** plotted
57 **yoked** held fast, as with a yoke

72 **limited** given a fixed period　77 **a** as a　90 **steepy** precipitous　93 **dispatch** carry out　96 **He drives** proverbial—"There's nothing for it."　S.d. **ambushed** i.e., hidden in ambush　103 **remove** uproot themselves and move to another place　107 **incontinent** hastily

[FAUSTUS *strikes the door,° and enter a devil playing on a drum, after him another bearing an ensign;° and divers° with weapons,* MEPHISTOPHILIS *with fireworks; they set upon the* SOLDIERS, *and drive them out.*]

[Exit FAUSTUS.]

[*Enter at several° doors* BENVOLIO, FREDERICK, *and* MARTINO, *their heads and faces bloody, and besmeared with mud and dirt, all having horns on their heads.*]

MARTINO: What ho, Benvolio!

BENVOLIO: Here, what, Frederick, ho!

FREDERICK: Oh, help me, gentle friend; where is
110   Martino?

MARTINO: Dear Frederick, here,
    Half smothered in a lake of mud and dirt,
    Through which the furies dragged me by the heels.

FREDERICK: Martino, see Benvolio's horns again.

115 MARTINO: Oh, misery, how now, Benvolio?

BENVOLIO: Defend me, heaven, shall I be haunted still?

MARTINO: Nay, fear not, man; we have no power to
    kill.°

BENVOLIO: My friends transformèd thus! Oh, hellish
    spite,
    Your heads are all set with horns.

FREDERICK: You hit it right:
120   It is your own you mean, feel on your head.

BENVOLIO: 'Zounds, horns again!

MARTINO: Nay, chafe not, man, we all are sped.°

BENVOLIO: What devil attends this damned magician,
    That, spite of spite, our wrongs are doubled?

FREDERICK: What may we do, that we may hide our
125   shames?

BENVOLIO: If we should follow him to work revenge,
    He'd join long asses' ears to these huge horns,
    And make us laughing-stocks to all the world.

MARTINO: What shall we then do, dear Benvolio?

130 BENVOLIO: I have a castle joining° near these woods,
    And thither we'll repair and live obscure,°
    Till time shall alter these our brutish shapes:
    Sith° black disgrace hath thus eclipsed our fame,
    We'll rather die with grief than live with shame.

[Exeunt omnes.]

Scene 3

[*Enter* FAUSTUS *and the* HORSE-COURSER,° *and* MEPHISTOPHILIS.°]

HORSE-COURSER: I beseech your worship, accept of these forty dollars.

FAUSTUS: Friend, thou canst not buy so good a horse for so small a price. I have no great need to sell him, but if thou likest him for ten dollars more take   5
him, because I see thou hast a good mind to him.

HORSE-COURSER: I beseech you, sir, accept of this; I am a very poor man and have lost very much of late by horseflesh, and this bargain will set me   10
up again.

FAUSTUS: Well, I will not stand with° thee, give me the money.

[HORSE-COURSER *gives* FAUSTUS *the money.*]

    Now, sirrah, I must tell you that you may ride him o'er hedge and ditch, and spare him not;   15
    but, do you hear? In any case ride him not into the water.

HORSE-COURSER: How, sir, not into the water? Why, will he not drink of all waters?°

FAUSTUS: Yes, he will drink of all waters, but ride him   20
    not into the water; o'er hedge and ditch, or where thou wilt, but not into the water. Go, bid the ostler deliver him unto you, and remember what I say.

HORSE-COURSER: I warrant you, sir. Oh, joyful day,   25
now am I a made man for ever.

[Exit.]

FAUSTUS: What art thou, Faustus, but a man condemned to die?
    Thy fatal° time draws to a final end, Despair
    doth drive distrust into my thoughts.
    Confound° these passions with a quiet sleep.   30
    Tush! Christ did call the thief upon the Cross;
    Then rest thee, Faustus, quiet in conceit.°

[*He sits to sleep.*]

[*Enter the* HORSE-COURSER *wet.*]

HORSE-COURSER: Oh, what a cozening° Doctor was this? I was riding my horse into the water,

---

S.d. **door** stage door, which Faustus strikes to cue those who are about to come on   **ensign** flag   **divers** several others   **several** separate   117 **we . . . kill** We are not hunters (playing on "haunted" above) who will kill you because of your horns.   122 **sped** done for.   130 **joining** adjoining   131 **obscure** obscurely   133 **Sith** Since

SCENE 3:   S.d **Horse-courser** Horse-dealer   **Mephistophilis** Because he does not speak during the scene, most editors dispense with his presence. One can see him, however, as observing the proceedings with a speaking silence.   12 **stand with** Haggle   19 **will . . . waters** Will he not be ready for anything?   28 **fatal** allotted   30 **Confound** Allay   32 **conceit** thought   33 **cozening** cheating

35 thinking some hidden mystery had been in the
horse. I had nothing under me but a little straw,
and had much ado to escape drowning. Well,
I'll go rouse him and make him give me my
forty dollars again. Ho, sirrah Doctor, you coz-
40 ening scab!° Master Doctor, awake and rise, and
give me my money again, for your horse is
turned to a bottle° of hay, Master Doctor.

[He pulls off his leg.]

Alas! I am undone, what shall I do? I have
pulled off his leg.
FAUSTUS: Oh, help, help, the villain hath murdered
45 me.
HORSE-COURSER: Murder, or not murder, now he has
but one leg, I'll outrun him, and cast this leg
into some ditch or other.

[Runs out.]

FAUSTUS: Stop him, stop him, stop him!—ha, ha, ha.
50 Faustus hath his leg again, and the horse-courser a bundle of hay for his forty dollars.

[Enter WAGNER.*]*

How now, Wagner, what news with thee?
WAGNER: If it please you, the Duke of Anholt doth
earnestly entreat your company, and hath sent
55 some of his men to attend you with provision fit
for your journey.
FAUSTUS: The Duke of Anholt's an honorable gentleman, and one to whom I must be no niggard° of
my cunning. Come away!

[Exeunt.]

Scene 4

[Enter CLOWN [ROBIN], DICK, HORSE-COURSER, *and a*
CARTER.*]*

CARTER: Come, my masters, I'll bring you to the best
beer in Europe. What ho, hostess!—where be
these whores?°

[Enter HOSTESS.*]*

HOSTESS: How now, what lack you? What, my old
5   guesse,° welcome.

ROBIN: Sirrah Dick, dost thou know why I stand so
mute?
DICK: No, Robin, why is't?
ROBIN: I am eighteenpence on the score,° but say noth-
ing, see if she have forgotten me.   10
HOSTESS: Who's this, that stands so solemnly by him-
self? what, my old guest?
ROBIN: O hostess, how do you? I hope my score stands
still.°
HOSTESS: Ay, there's no doubt of that, for methinks   15
you make no haste to wipe it out.
DICK: Why, hostess, I say, fetch us some beer.
HOSTESS: You shall presently:° look up into th' hall
there, ho!°

[Exit.]

DICK: Come sirs, what shall we do now till mine host-   20
ess comes?
CARTER: Marry, sir, I'll tell you the bravest tale how a
conjuror served me; you know Doctor Fauster?
HORSE-COURSER: Ay, a plague take him, here's some
on's° have cause to know him; did he conjure   25
thee too?
CARTER: I'll tell you how he served me: As I was going
to Wittenberg t'other day, with a load of hay, he
met me, and asked me what he should give me
for as much hay as he could eat; now, sir, I,   30
thinking that a little would serve his turn, bade
him take as much as he would for three farthings; so he presently gave me my money, and
fell to eating; and, as I am a cursen° man, he
never left eating, till he had eat up all my load   35
of hay.
ALL: Oh, monstrous, eat a whole load of hay!
ROBIN: Yes, yes, that may be; for I have heard of one
that has eat a load of logs.
HORSE-COURSER: Now, sirs, you shall hear how vil-   40
lainously he served° me: I went to him yesterday to buy a horse of him, and he would by no
means sell him under forty dollars; so, sir,
because I knew him to be such a horse as would
run over hedge and ditch and never tire, I gave   45
him his money. So when I had my horse, Doctor
Fauster bade me ride him night and day, and
spare him no time; but, quoth he, in any case,
ride him not into the water. Now, sir, I, thinking
the horse had had some rare quality that he   50
would not have me know of, what did I but rid
him into a great river, and when I came just in
the midst, my horse vanished away, and I sat

---

⁴⁰ **scab** scurvy fellow   ⁴² **bottle** bundle   ⁵⁸ **be. . . niggard**
not be sparing

SCENE 4:   ³ **where. . . whores** Addressed to the company; the
Hostess and her staff are whores. The scene, it is clear, is an inn.
⁵ **guesse** guests

⁹ **on the score** on the tick: in debt to the Hostess   ¹⁴ **stands still**
doesn't increase; is permitted to stand or remain   ¹⁸ **shall
presently** shall have it at once   ¹⁹ **look. . . ho** be lively (spoken
to the servants)   ²⁵ **on's** of us   ³⁴ **cursen** Christian
⁴¹ **served** dealt with

straddling upon a bottle of hay.

55 ALL: Oh, brave Doctor!

HORSE-COURSER: But you shall hear how bravely I served him for it; I went me° home to his house, and there I found him asleep; I kept a hallooing and whooping in his ears, but all could not
60 wake him: I seeing that, took him by the leg, and never rested pulling, till I had pulled me his leg quite off, and now 'tis at home in mine hostry.°

ROBIN:° And has the Doctor but one leg then? That's excellent, for one of his devils turned me into
65 the likeness of an ape's face.

CARTER: Some more drinks, hostess.

ROBIN: Hark you, we'll into another room and drink a while, and then we'll go seek out the Doctor.

[Exeunt omnes.]

Scene 5

[Enter the DUKE OF ANHOLT, *his* DUCHESS, FAUSTUS, *and* MEPHISTOPHILIS.*]*

DUKE: Thanks, Master Doctor, for these pleasant sights. Nor know I how sufficiently to recompense your great deserts in erecting that enchanted castle in the air, the sight whereof so
5 delighted me, As nothing in the world could please me more.

FAUSTUS: I do think myself, my good lord, highly recompensed in that it pleaseth yourgrace to think but well of that which Faustus hath performed.
10 But gracious lady, it may be that you have taken no pleasure in those sights; therefore, I pray you tell me, what is the thing you most desire to have; be it in the world, it shall be yours. I have heard that great-bellied women do long for
15 things are° rare and dainty.

DUCHESS: True, Master Doctor, and since I find you so kind, I will make known unto you what my heart desires to have; and were it now summer, as it is January, a dead time of the winter, I would
20 request no better meat than a dish of ripe grapes.

FAUSTUS: This is but a small matter. Go, Mephistophilis, away!

[Exit MEPHISTOPHILIS.]

Madam, I will do more than this for your content.

[Enter MEPHISTOPHILIS *again with the grapes.]*

Here now taste ye these; they should be good,
For they come from a far country, I can tell you.   25

DUKE: This makes me wonder more than all the rest
That at this time of the year, when every tree
Is barren of his fruit, from whence you had
These ripe grapes.

FAUSTUS: Please it your grace the year is divided into   30
two circles over the whole world, so that when
it is winter with us, in the contrary circle it is
likewise summer with them, as in India, Saba°
and such countries that lie far east, where they
have fruit twice a year. From whence, by means   35
of a swift spirit that I have, I had these grapes
brought, as you see.

DUCHESS: And trust me, they are the sweetest grapes
that e'er I tasted.

[The CLOWNS *bounce° at the gate within.]*

DUKE: What rude disturbers have we at the gate?   40
Go pacify their fury, set it ope,
And then demand of them what they would have.

[They knock again, and call out to talk with FAUSTUS.*]*

SERVANT: Why, how now, masters, what a coil° is there?
What is the reason you disturb the Duke?

DICK: We have no reason for it, therefore a fig for   45
him.°

SERVANT: Why, saucy varlets, dare you be so bold?

HORSE-COURSER: I hope, sir, we have wit enough to be
more bold than welcome.

SERVANT: It appears so, pray be bold elsewhere,   50
And trouble not the Duke.

DUKE: What would they have?

SERVANT: They all cry out to speak with Doctor
Faustus.

CARTER: Ay, and we will speak with him.   55

DUKE: Will you sir? Commit° the rascals.

DICK: Commit with us! he were as good commit with
his father as commit with us.

FAUSTUS: I do beseech your grace let them come in,
They are good subject for a merriment.   60

DUKE: Do as thou wilt, Faustus, I give thee leave.

FAUSTUS: I thank your grace.

[Enter the CLOWN [ROBIN], DICK, CARTER, *and* HORSE-COURSER.*]*

---

⁵⁷ **me** The reflexive (here and below) is common in Elizabethan English and gratuitous.   ⁶² **hostry** hostelry   ⁶³ **Robin** Editors often give this speech to Dick, who had been so transformed, rather than to "Clown" (i.e., Robin) as in the original.

SCENE 5:   ¹⁵ **are** that are

³³ **Saba** Sheba   ˢ·ᵈ· **bounce** bang   ⁴³ **coil** commotion   ⁴⁶ **fig for him** Dick makes a contemptuous gesture, biting his thumb or thrusting it between two of his fingers.   ⁵⁶ **Commit** Imprison; and giving rise to the pun on sexual intercourse in the next line

Why, how now, my good friends?
'Faith you are too outrageous,° but come near,
65   I have procured your pardons: welcome all.
ROBIN: Nay, sir, we will be welcome for our money,
and we will pay for what we take. What ho,
give's half a dozen of beer here, and be hanged.
FAUSTUS: Nay, hark you, can you tell me where you
70   are?°
CARTER: Ay, marry can I; we are under heaven.
SERVANT: Ay, but, sir sauce-box,° know you in what
place?
HORSE-COURSER: Ay, ay, the house is good enough to
75   drink in: Zouns, fill us some beer, or we'll break
all the barrels in the house, and dash out all
your brains with your bottles.
FAUSTUS: Be not so furious: come, you shall have beer.
My lord, beseech you give me leave a while,
80   I'll gage° my credit, 'twill content your grace.
DUKE: With all my heart, kind Doctor, please thyself;
Our servants and our court's at thy command.
FAUSTUS: I humbly thank your grace: then fetch some
beer.
85   HORSE-COURSER: Ay, marry, there spake a Doctor
indeed, and, 'faith, I'll drink a health to thy
wooden leg for that word.
FAUSTUS: My wooden leg! what dost thou mean by
that?
90   CARTER: Ha, ha, ha, dost hear him, Dick? He has forgot his leg.
HORSE-COURSER: Ay, ay, he does not stand much upon°
that.
FAUSTUS: No, 'faith not much upon a wooden leg.
95   CARTER: Good Lord, that flesh and blood should be so
frail with your worship. Do not you remember
a horse-courser you sold a horse to?
FAUSTUS: Yes, I remember I sold one a horse.
CARTER: And do you remember you bid he should not
100   ride him into the water?
FAUSTUS: Yes, I do very well remember that.
CARTER: And do you remember nothing of your leg?
FAUSTUS: No, in good sooth.
CARTER: Then, I pray, remember your courtesy.
105   FAUSTUS: I thank you, sir.
CARTER: 'Tis not so much worth; I pray you tell me one
thing.
FAUSTUS: What's that?
CARTER: Be both your legs bedfellows every night
110   together?
FAUSTUS: Wouldst thou make a Colossus° of me, that
thou askest me such questions?

CARTER: No, truly, sir: I would make nothing° of you,
but I would fain know that.

[Enter HOSTESS *with drink.]*

FAUSTUS: Then I assure thee certainly they are.   115
CARTER: I thank you, I am fully satisfied.
FAUSTUS: But wherefore dost thou ask?
CARTER: For nothing, sir: but methinks you should
have a wooden bedfellow of one of 'em.
HORSE-COURSER: Why, do you hear, sir, did not I pull   120
off one of your legs when you were asleep?
FAUSTUS: But I have it again, now I am awake: look
you here, sir.
ALL: Oh, horrible, had the Doctor three legs?
CARTER: Do you remember, sir, how you cozened   125
me and ate up my load of—

*[*FAUSTUS *charms him dumb.]*

DICK: Do you remember how you made me wear an
ape's—
HORSE-COURSER: You whoreson conjuring scab, do you
remember how you cozened me with a ho—   130
ROBIN: Ha' you forgotten me? You think to carry it
away° with your *hey-pass* and *re-pass,*° do you
remember the dogs' fa—

[Exeunt CLOWNS.*]*

HOSTESS: Who pays for the ale? Hear you, Master
Doctor, now you have sent away my guesse, I   135
pray who shall pay me for my a—

[Exit HOSTESS.*]*

LADY: My lord,
We are much beholding to this learned man.
DUKE: So are we, madam, which we will recompense
With all the love and kindness that we may.   140
His artful sport drives all sad thoughts away.

[Exeunt.]

ACT V

Scene 1

[Thunder and lightning. Enter DEVILS *with covered
dishes.* MEPHISTOPHILIS *leads them into* FAUSTUS' *study.
Then enter* WAGNER.*]*

WAGNER: I think my master means to die shortly,
He has made his will, and given me his wealth,
His house, his goods, and store of golden plate,

---

[64] **outrageous** violent   [70] **where you are** i.e., in the ducal court
[72] **sauce-box** impudence   [80] **gage** pledge as security   [92] **stand
much upon** in the obvious sense; but meaning also "make
much of."   [111] **Colossus** which stood with legs astride (hence
not "bedfellows") at the entrance to the harbor of Rhodes

[113] **make nothing** in the obvious sense, and also "make light"
[132] **away** off   **hey-pass. . . re-pass** exclamations used by
conjurors and jugglers

Besides two thousand ducats ready coined.
5   I wonder what he means; if death were nigh
He would not frolic thus. He's now at supper
With the scholars, where there's such belly-cheer
As Wagner in his life ne'er saw the like.
And see where they come, belike the feast is done.

[Exit.]

[Enter FAUSTUS, MEPHISTOPHILIS, *and two or three*
SCHOLARS.*]*

10   1 SCHOLAR: Master Faustus, since our conference°
about fair ladies, which was the beautifullest in
all the world, we have determined with ourselves that Helen of Greece was the admirablest
lady that ever lived: therefore, Master Doctor, if
15   you will do us so much favor as to let us see that
peerless dame of Greece, whom all the world
admires for majesty, we should think ourselves
much beholding unto you.
FAUSTUS: Gentlemen,
20   For that° I know your friendship is unfeigned,
It is not Faustus' custom to deny
The just request of those that wish him well,
You shall behold that peerless dame of Greece,
No otherwise for pomp or majesty
25   Than when Sir Paris crossed the seas with her,
And brought the spoils° to rich Dardania.°
Be silent, then, for danger is in words.

[Music sound, MEPHISTOPHILIS *brings in* HELEN, *she*
passeth over the stage.]

2 SCHOLAR: Was this fair Helen, whose admired worth
Made Greece with ten years' wars afflict poor Troy?
30   Too simple is my wit to tell her praise,
Whom all the world admires for majesty.
3 SCHOLAR: No marvel though the angry Greeks pur-
sued°
With ten years' war the rape of such a queen,
Whose heavenly beauty passeth all compare.
1 SCHOLAR: Now we have seen the pride of nature's
35   work,
And only paragon of excellence,
We'll take our leaves; and for this blessèd sight
Happy and blessed be Faustus evermore!
FAUSTUS: Gentlemen, farewell: the same wish I to you.

[Exeunt SCHOLARS.*]*

[Enter an OLD MAN.*]*

OLD MAN: O gentle Faustus, leave this damnèd art,   40
This magic, that will charm thy soul to hell,
And quite bereave thee of salvation.
Though thou hast now offended like a man,
Do not persèver in it like a devil;
Yet, yet, thou hast an amiable° soul,   45
If sin by custom grow not into nature:
Then, Faustus, will repentance come too late,
Then thou art banished from the sight of heaven;
No mortal can express the pains of hell.
It may be this my exhortation   50
Seems harsh and all unpleasant; let it not,
For gentle son, I speak it not in wrath,
Or envy of° thee, but in tender love,
And pity of thy future misery.
And so have hope, that this my kind rebuke,   55
Checking° thy body, may amend thy soul.
Break heart, drop blood, and mingle it with tears,
Tears falling from repentant heaviness
Of thy most vile and loathsome filthiness,
The stench whereof corrupts the inward soul   60
With such flagitious crimes of heinous° sins
As no commiseration may expel,
But mercy, Faustus, of thy Savior sweet,
Whose blood alone must wash away thy guilt.
FAUSTUS: Where art thou, Faustus? Wretch, what hast
thou done?   65
Damned art thou, Faustus, damned; despair and
die!

*[*MEPHISTOPHILIS *gives him a dagger.]*

Hell claims his right, and with a roaring voice
Says, "Faustus, come; thine hour is almost come,"
And Faustus now will come to do thee right.
OLD MAN: Oh, stay, good Faustus, stay thy desperate
steps!   70
I see an angel hover o'er thy head,
And, with a vial full of precious grace,
Offers to pour the same into thy soul:
Then call for mercy, and avoid despair.
FAUSTUS: O friend, I feel   75
Thy words to comfort my distressèd soul!
Leave me a while to ponder on my sins.
OLD MAN: Faustus, I leave thee; but with grief of
heart,
Fearing the enemy of thy hapless soul.

[Exit.]

ACT V, SCENE 1: ¹⁰ **conference** discussion ²⁰ **For that**
Because ²⁷ **spoils** destruction **Dardania** Troy ³² **pursued** revenged. (The dialogue and assigning of speeches in
this scene conflate the editions of 1604 and 1616.)

⁴⁵ **amiable** worthy of (divine) love ⁵³ **envy of** animosity
toward ⁵⁶ **Checking** Reproving ⁶¹ **flagitious. . . heinous**
flagrant/hateful

80   FAUSTUS: Accursèd Faustus, where is mercy now?
        I do repent; and yet I do despair:
        Hell strives with grace for conquest in my breast:
        What shall I do to shun the snares of death?
      MEPHISTOPHILIS: Thou traitor, Faustus, I arrest thy
          soul
85   For disobedience to my sovereign lord:
        Revolt,° or I'll in piecemeal tear thy flesh.
      FAUSTUS: I do repent I e'er offended him.
        Sweet Mephistophilis, entreat thy lord
        To pardon my unjust presumption,
90   And with my blood again I will confirm
        The former vow I made to Lucifer.
      MEPHISTOPHILIS: Do it, then, Faustus, with unfeignèd
          heart,
        Lest greater dangers do attend thy drift.°

*[FAUSTUS stabs his arm, and writes on a paper with
his blood.]*

      FAUSTUS: Torment, sweet friend, that base and agèd man,
95   That durst dissuade me from thy Lucifer,
        With greatest torments that our hell affords.
      MEPHISTOPHILIS: His faith is great; I cannot touch his
          soul;
        But what I may afflict his body with
        I will attempt, which is but little worth.
      FAUSTUS: One thing, good servant, let me crave of
100   thee,
        To glut the longing of my heart's desire,—
        That I may have unto my paramour
        That heavenly Helen which I saw of late,
        Whose sweet embraces may extinguish clean
105   Those thoughts that do dissuade me from my vow,
        And keep my oath I made to Lucifer.
      MEPHISTOPHILIS: This, or what else, my Faustus shall
          desire,
        Shall be performed in twinkling of an eye.

*[Enter HELEN again, passing over between two
Cupids.]*

      FAUSTUS: Was this the face that launched a thousand
          ships,
110   And burnt the topless° towers of Ilium?—
        Sweet Helen, make me immortal with a kiss.—

[Kisses her.]

        Her lips suck forth my soul: see where it flies!—
        Come, Helen, come, give me my soul again.
        Here will I dwell, for heaven is in these lips,
115   And all is dross that is not Helena.

[Enter OLD MAN.]

        I will be Paris, and for love of thee,
        Instead of Troy, shall Wittenberg be sacked;
        And will combat with weak Menelaus,°
        And wear thy colors on my plumèd crest:
        Yea, I will wound Achilles in the heel,°   120
        And then return to Helen for a kiss.
        Oh, thou art fairer than the evening's air
        Clad in the beauty of a thousand stars;
        Brighter art thou than flaming Jupiter
        When he appeared to hapless Semele;°   125
        More lovely than the monarch of the sky
        In wanton Arethusa's azured arms;°
        And none but thou shalt be my paramour!

[Exeunt (FAUSTUS, HELEN, and Cupids).]

      OLD MAN: Accursèd Faustus, miserable man,
        That from thy soul exclud'st the grace of heaven,   130
        And fliest the throne of His tribunal-seat!

[Enter the DEVILS.]

        Satan begins to sift° me with his pride:°
        As in this furnace God shall try my faith,
        My faith, vile hell, shall triumph over thee.
        Ambitious fiends, see how the heavens smiles   135
        At your repulse, and laughs your state° to scorn!
        Hence, hell! for hence I fly unto my God.

[Exeunt.]

*[Thunder. Enter LUCIFER, BELZEBUB, and
MEPHISTOPHILIS.]*

      LUCIFER: Thus from infernal Dis° do we ascend
        To view the subject of our monarchy,
        Those souls which sin seals° the black sons of hell,   140
        'Mong which as chief, Faustus, we come to thee,
        Bringing with us lasting damnation
        To wait upon thy soul: the time is come
        Which makes it forfeit.
      MEPHISTOPHILIS: And this gloomy night,
        Here in this room will wretched Faustus be.   145
      BELZEBUB: And here we'll stay,

---

¹¹⁸ **Menelaus** husband of Helen and type of the cuckold;
hence, "weak."   ¹²⁰ **wound. . . heel** as Paris, the lover of
Helen, did   ¹²⁵ **Semele** to whom her lover Jupiter appeared
as the god of thunder, consuming her with his flames
¹²⁷ **Arethusa's azured arms** The arms of this Nereid are sky
blue in token of the fountain in which she dwelt. Her relation
to the "monarch of the sky" is not recorded elsewhere.
¹³² **sift** try (a reminiscence of Luke 22:31) **pride** power
¹³⁶ **state** dignity, power   ¹³⁸ **Dis** properly, the ruler of the
Underworld; here, the region   ¹⁴⁰ **seals** marks irrevocably

---

⁸⁶ **Revolt** i.e., from God.   ⁹³ **drift** purpose   ¹¹⁰ **topless** lofty
(the tops being too high to be visible)

To mark° him how he doth demean° himself.
MEPHISTOPHILIS: How should he, but in desperate
  lunacy?
  Fond° worldling, now his heart-blood dries with
    grief,
His conscience kills it, and his laboring brain
Begets a world of idle fantasies
To over-reach the Devil; but all in vain,
His store of pleasures must be sauced° with pain.
He and his servant, Wagner, are at hand.
Both come from drawing° Faustus' latest° will.
See where they come!

[Enter FAUSTUS *and* WAGNER.]

FAUSTUS: Say, Wagner, thou hast perused my will,
  How dost thou like it?
WAGNER: Sir, so wondrous well,
  As in all humble duty, I do yield
My life and lasting service for your love.

[Enter the SCHOLARS.]

FAUSTUS: Gramercies,° Wagner. Welcome, gentlemen.

[Exit WAGNER.]

1 SCHOLAR: Now, worthy Faustus, methinks your
  looks are changed.
FAUSTUS: Oh, gentlemen!
2 SCHOLAR: What ails Faustus?
FAUSTUS: Ah, my sweet chamber-fellow,° had I lived
  with thee, then had I lived still! but now must
  die eternally. Look, sirs, comes he not? Comes
  he not?
I SCHOLAR: O my dear Faustus, what imports this
  fear?
2 SCHOLAR: Is all our pleasure turned to
  melancholy?
3 SCHOLAR: He is not well with being over-
  solitary.
2 SCHOLAR: If it be so, we'll have physicians
  And Faustus shall be cured.
3 SCHOLAR: 'Tis but a surfeit,° sir; fear nothing.
FAUSTUS: A surfeit of deadly sin, that hath damned both
  body and soul.
2 SCHOLAR: Yet, Faustus, look up to heaven;
  remember God's mercies are infinite.
FAUSTUS: But Faustus' offense can ne'er be pardoned:
  the serpent that tempted Eve may be saved, but

not Faustus. Oh, gentlemen, hear me with
patience, and tremble not at my speeches!
Though my heart pant and quiver to remember
that I have been a student here these thirty
years, oh, would I had never seen Wittenberg,
never read book! and what wonders I have
done, all Germany can witness, yea, all the
world; for which Faustus hath lost both
Germany and the world; yea, heaven itself,
heaven, the seat of God, the throne of the
blessed, the kingdom of joy; and must remain in
hell for ever—hell, oh, hell for ever!
Sweet friends, what shall become of Faustus,
being in hell for ever?
2 SCHOLAR: Yet, Faustus, call on God.
FAUSTUS: On God, whom Faustus hath abjured! on God,
  whom Faustus hath blasphemed! Oh, my God, I
  would weep! but the devil draws in my tears.
  Gush forth blood, instead of tears! yea, life and
  soul—Oh, he stays my tongue! I would lift up my
  hands; but see, they hold 'em, they hold 'em!
ALL: Who, Faustus?
FAUSTUS: Why, Lucifer and Mephistophilis. Oh, gentlemen, I gave them my soul for my cunning!
ALL: Oh, God forbid!
FAUSTUS: God forbade it, indeed; but Faustus hath
  done it: for the vain pleasure of four and twenty
  years hath Faustus lost eternal joy and felicity. I
  writ them a bill with mine own blood: the date
  is expired; this is the time, and he will fetch me.
I SCHOLAR: Why did not Faustus tell us of this before,
  that divines might have prayed for thee?
FAUSTUS: Oft have I thought to have done so; but the
  Devil threatened to tear me in pieces, if I named
  God; to fetch me, body and soul, if I once gave
  ear to divinity: and now 'tis too late.
  Gentlemen, away, lest you perish with me.
2 SCHOLAR: Oh, what may we do to save Faustus?
FAUSTUS: Talk not of me, but save yourselves, and
  depart.
3 SCHOLAR: God will strengthen me; I will stay with
  Faustus.
1 SCHOLAR: Tempt not God, sweet friend; but let us
  into the next room, and pray for him.
FAUSTUS: Ay, pray for me, pray for me; and what noise
  soever you hear, come not unto me, for nothing
  can rescue me.
2 SCHOLAR: Pray thou, and we will pray that God may
  have mercy upon thee.
FAUSTUS: Gentlemen, farewell: if I live till morning, I'll
  visit you; if not, Faustus is gone to hell.
ALL: Faustus, farewell.

[Exeunt SCHOLARS.]

MEPHISTOPHILIS: Ay, Faustus, now thou hast no hope
  of heaven;

---

¹⁴⁷ **mark** note   **demean** conduct   ¹⁴⁹ **Fond** Foolish
¹⁵³ **sauced** paid for (and also in our sense of mixed with something   sharp)   ¹⁵⁵ **drawing** drawing   up   **latest** last
¹⁶¹ **Gramercies** Thanks   ¹⁶⁵ **chamber-fellow** student with
whom one shared the same room   ¹⁷⁴ **surfeit** disorder as
from too much eating

Therefore despair, think only upon hell,
For that must be thy mansion, there to dwell.
FAUSTUS: O thou bewitching fiend, 'twas thy tempta-
    tion
235   Hath robbed me of eternal happiness.
MEPHISTOPHILIS: I do confess it, Faustus, and rejoice;
    'Twas I, that when thou wert i' the way to heaven,
    Dammed up thy passage; when thou took'st the
      book,
    To view the Scriptures, then I turned the leaves,
240   And led thine eye.—
    What, weep'st thou? 'Tis too late, despair,
      farewell!
    Fools that will laugh on earth must weep in hell.

[Exit.]

[Enter the GOOD ANGEL *and the* BAD ANGEL *at several doors.]*

GOOD ANGEL: Oh, Faustus, if thou hadst given ear to
    me,
    Innumerable joys had followed thee.
    But thou didst love the world.
245 BAD ANGEL: Gave ear to me,
    And now must taste hell's pains perpetually.
GOOD ANGEL: Oh, what will all thy riches, pleasures,
      pomps,
    Avail thee now?
BAD ANGEL: Nothing but vex thee more,
    To want in hell, that had on earth such store.

[Music while the throne° descends.]

250 GOOD ANGEL: Oh, thou hast lost celestial happiness,
    Pleasures unspeakable, bliss without end.
    Hadst thou affected° sweet divinity,
    Hell, or the devil, had had no power on thee.
    Hadst thou kept on that way, Faustus, behold
255   In what replendent glory thou hadst sat
    In yonder throne, like those bright shining saints,°
    And triumphed over hell: that hast thou lost:
    And now, poor soul, must thy good angel leave
      thee,

[The throne ascends.]

The jaws of hell are open to receive thee.

[Exit.]

[Hell is discovered.°]

BAD ANGEL: Now, Faustus, let thine eyes with horror
    stare   260
    Into that vast perpetual torture-house.
    There are the Furies tossing damnèd souls
    On burning forks; their bodies boil in lead:
    There are live quarters broiling on the coals,
    That ne'er can die: this ever-burning chair   265
    Is for o'er-tortured souls to rest them in;
    These that are fed with sops of flaming fire,
    Were gluttons and loved only delicates,°
    And laughed to see the poor starve at their gates:
    But yet all these are nothing; thou shalt see 270
    Ten thousand tortures that more horrid be.
FAUSTUS: Oh, I have seen enough to torture me.
BAD ANGEL: Nay, thou must feel them, taste the
    smart of all:
    He that loves pleasure, must for pleasure fall:
    And so I leave thee, Faustus, till anon;   275
    Then wilt thou tumble in confusion.

[Exit.]

[The clock strikes eleven.]

FAUSTUS: Oh, Faustus,
    Now hast thou but one bare hour to live,
    And then thou must be damned perpetually!
    Stand still, you ever moving spheres of heaven, 280
    That time may cease, and midnight never come;
    Fair nature's eye, rise, rise, again, and make
    Perpetual day; or let this hour be but
    A year, a month, a week, a natural day,
    That Faustus may repent and save his soul! 285
    O lente, lente currite, noctis equi!°
    The stars move still, time runs, the clock will strike,
    The devil will come, and Faustus must be
      damned.
    Oh, I'll leap up to my God!—Who pulls me down?—
    See, see, where Christ's blood streams in the fir-
      mament!   290
    One drop would save my soul, half a drop: oh,
      my Christ!—
    Ah, rend not my heart for naming of my Christ!
    Yet will I call on him: Oh, spare me, Lucifer!—
    Where is it° now? 'Tis gone: and see, where God
    Stretcheth out his arm, and bends his ireful brows! 295
    Mountains and hills, come, come, and fall on me,
    And hide me from the heavy wrath of God!
    No, no!

---

[231] **Mephistophilis** Who at this point comes forward
[S.d.] **throne** let down from the "heavens" above the stage by
cords and pulleys [252] **affected** cultivated [256] **saints** presumably brightly dressed actors occupied the throne

[S.d.] **discovered** as by drawing back a curtain to reveal a "Hellmouth" or, less ambitiously, a painted cloth [268] **delicates** delicacies [286] **L.** Adapting Ovid's *Amores*, I. xiii. 40: "O run
slowly, slowly, horses of the night!" [294] **it** Christ's blood

Then will I headlong run into the earth:
300   Earth, gape! Oh, no, it will not harbor me!
You stars that reigned at my nativity,
Whose influence° hath allotted death and hell,
Now draw up Faustus, like a foggy mist,
Into the entrails of yon laboring° cloud
305   That, when you° vomit forth into the air,
My limbs may issue from your smoky mouths,
So that my soul may but ascend to heaven!

[The watch strikes.]

Oh, half the hour is past! 'twill all be passed anon.
O God,
310   If Thou wilt not have mercy on my soul,
Yet for Christ's sake, whose blood hath ransomed
me,
Impose some end to my incessant pain;
Let Faustus live in hell a thousand years,
A hundred thousand, and at last be saved!
315   No end is limited° to damnèd souls!
Why wert thou not a creature wanting soul?
Or why is this immortal that thou hast?
Ah, Pythagoras' *metempsychosis*,° were that true,
This soul should fly from me, and I be changed
320   Unto some brutish beast! all beasts are happy,
For, when they die,
Their souls are soon dissolved in° elements;
But mine must live still to be plagued in hell.
Cursed be the parents that engendered me!
325   No, Faustus, curse thyself, curse Lucifer
That hath deprived thee of the joys of heaven.

[The clock strikes twelve.]

It strikes, it strikes! Now, body, turn to air,
Or Lucifer will bear thee quick° to hell!
O soul, be changed into small water-drops,
330   And fall into the ocean, ne'er be found!

[Thunder and enter the DEVILS.*]*

My God, my God, look not so fierce on me!
Adders and serpents, let me breathe a while!
Ugly hell, gape not! come not, Lucifer!
I'll burn my books!—Oh, Mephistophilis!

[Exeunt with him.]

[Enter the SCHOLARS.*]*

I SCHOLAR: Come, gentlemen, let us go visit Faustus,   335
For such a dreadful night was never seen,
Since first the world's creation did begin,
Such fearful shrieks and cries were never heard:
Pray heaven the Doctor have escaped the danger.
2 SCHOLAR: Oh, help us heaven! see, here are
Faustus' limbs,   340
All torn asunder by the hand of death.
3 SCHOLAR: The devils whom Faustus served have
torn him thus:
For 'twixt the hours of twelve and one,
methought
I heard him shriek and call aloud for help:
At which self° time the house seemed all on fire,   345
With dreadful horror of these damnèd fiends.
2 SCHOLAR: Well, gentlemen, though Faustus' end be
such
As every Christian heart laments to think on,
Yet for° he was a scholar, once admired
For wondrous knowledge in our German schools,   350
We'll give his mangled limbs due burial;
And all the students, clothed in mourning black,
Shall wait upon° his heavy° funeral.

[Exeunt.]

Epilogue

Enter CHORUS.

CHORUS: Cut is the branch that might have grown
full straight,
And burnèd is Apollo's° laurel bough,
That sometime grew within this learned man.
Faustus is gone: regard° his hellish fall,
Whose fiendful° fortune may exhort the wise,   5
Only to wonder° at unlawful things,
Whose deepness doth entice such forward wits
To practice more than heavenly power permits.

[Exit.]

Terminat hora diem; terminat Author opus.°

FINIS

---

302 influence the decisive power over men imputed by astrology to the stars   **304 laboring** working; contorted, contracting and expanding as with pain in the entrails   **305 you** the cloud   **315 limited** appointed   **318 Pythagoras' metempsychosis** alluding to the belief of the Greek philosopher in the transmigration of souls   **322 in** into   **328 quick** alive

345 self same   **349 for** because   **353 wait upon** attend   **heavy** sorrowful

EPILOGUE: **2 Apollo's** alluding to his patronage of learning   **4 regard** The injunction that follows is often denied to Marlowe on the grounds that it is too positive.   **3 fiendful** devilish   **6 Only to wonder** To be satisfied with wondering   **9 L.** The hour ends the day; the author ends his work.

WILLIAM SHAKESPEARE

(1564–1616)

Perhaps the first notion to dispel about Shakespeare is that someone else wrote his plays. Francis Bacon, Francis Walsingham, Edward de Vere (the earl of Oxford), and others have been put forward as possible candidates. Such suggestions are based on conspiracy theories and a rather free use of historical evidence. In fact, we have more solid historical evidence about the life of William Shakespeare than about any other dramatist of the Elizabethan period with the exception of Ben Jonson. Shakespeare was born in Stratford-upon-Avon, a small market town about 150 miles northwest of London. He was baptized on 26 April 1564, indicating that he was probably born a few days before that date. The traditional date of his birth is given as April 23, the date on which he also died, and the feast also of England's patron, St. George. Shakespeare's mother came from a fairly wealthy farming family, and his father was a tanner and glover, successful enough in the 1560s to be elected to the local office of bailiff—equivalent to a modern mayor. His fortunes declined in the 1570s, however. There is no evidence that Shakespeare had a university education, but universities of that period focused on professional, not literary, training. In all likelihood Shakespeare attended the king's new grammar school in Stratford from the time he was six or seven years old. The school was free to citizens of the town, and like others in England at the time, it taught Latin grammar and Roman culture—philosophy, oratory, literature, drama, law, and other social institutions. Graduating at fourteen to sixteen years of age, a student of such a grammar school would have had a command of the Latin language and literature equal perhaps to that of a modern classics major. Like many of his fellow dramatists of the period, Shakespeare later drew on his knowledge of the Roman writers that were taught in the schools—Plautus, Terence, Seneca, Ovid, Virgil, Livy, and Caesar.

In 1582 he married Anne Hathaway from nearby Shottery. He was eighteen and she twenty-six. In 1583 their first child, Susanna, was born and in 1585 the twins, Hamnet (who died at eleven years of age) and Judith. They had no more children, so Shakespeare's family was complete by the time he was twenty-one, and they remained in Stratford throughout his career in London. We have no certain evidence of his activities between 1585 and about 1592. He may have joined one of the acting companies that traveled through Stratford, but by 1592 he was established in London. He had already written several plays, and when the theaters were closed because of an outbreak of plague between 1592 and 1594 he wrote two narrative poems, *Venus and Adonis* and *The Rape of Lucrece*, dedicated to the young earl of Southampton. Like all self-respecting Elizabethan poets he wrote sonnets, which circulated in manuscript before they were finally

245

published without his permission in 1609. In 1594 he became a shareholder in the Lord Chamberlain's Men, which was to become one of the most highly esteemed playing companies of the period. Shakespeare was one of the principal investors in the company, sharing with other investors both its debts and profits. His duties in the company would have ranged from handling publicity to hiring actors, to renting theaters, to acting parts in plays, to buying or writing play scripts. We know that Shakespeare acted in Ben Jonson's *Every Man In His Humour* and *Sejanus*, and he probably played parts in his own plays, but most of his energy went into writing. As chief playwright for the Lord Chamberlain's Men, he produced an average of two new plays a year, a pace he maintained throughout his active career. One of his colleagues, Richard Burbage, the principal actor in the company, was the son of a theatrical entrepreneur, James Burbage, who had financed and built the first professional English theater, the Theater, in Shoreditch in 1576. When the elder Burbage died, he left the Theater to his sons, so in 1598 the Lord Chamberlain's Men tore down the structure and moved the timbers south of the Thames to erect the Globe Theater. This would be the company's main "public" theater during Shakespeare's career, though they also performed at court and in indoor halls or private theaters.

The range of Shakespeare's accomplishment is truly astonishing. Of the thirty-seven or so plays he wrote, about one-third are history plays, another third comedies, and a third tragedies. He was a highly experimental dramatist whose work in each genre again and again pushed the limits of contemporary practice. Some of his history plays—*Richard III, Richard II, Henry IV* Parts I and II, *Henry V*—some of his comedies—*A Midsummer Night's Dream, As You Like It, Twelfth Night, The Tempest*—and some of his tragedies—*Hamlet, Othello, King Lear, Macbeth*—are regarded as the best plays of their kind ever written. Throughout the world today, his plays are revived more often than those of any other dramatist in history.

A Midsummer Night's Dream

A Midsummer Night's Dream was probably written about 1595, early in Shakespeare's career, when he was writing primarily comedies and histories. It may have been written as part of the wedding celebration of the Duchess of Southampton, the mother of Shakespeare's patron. In the play, two sets of virtually indistinguishable lovers embark on a journey from the harsh rule of law in Athens into the dreamlike woods nearby, where they are transformed by their experiences. Within its contrasting realms of law, authority, and order on the one hand and imaginative escape from these constraints into nature on the other, the play interweaves four distinct plots: the wedding of Theseus and Hippolyta, the journey of the four lovers, the story of the fairies, and the story of Bottom and his friends. Each of these plots contains one or more pairs of lovers whose happiness has been frustrated by conflict, jealousy, misunderstanding, or authority. Theseus and Hippolyta, whose wedding plans and celebration open and close the play, were formerly enemies. The other plots are contained by theirs. Theseus is called on to support Athenian law and parental authority, forcing the young lovers to flee into the woods. Titania and Oberon, King and Queen of the fairies, have come to Athens specifically to celebrate the wedding, but they remain at odds because of Oberon's earlier affection for Hippolyta and Titania's for Theseus. Meanwhile, Bottom and his friends are in the forest to practice a play they hope to perform at the wedding.

All of the characters who enter the forest undergo a transformation. Puck's mistake with the love juice in carrying out Oberon's command puts the young lovers through a series of romantic pairings until they are all properly sorted out and united. Although Puck plays a role similar to that of Cupid, he is clearly a bumbling English folk spirit. His detached amusement—and the fact that all works well in the end—highlight Shakespeare's doubled-edged view of love in the play. Love is a universal power that subdues and transforms, but it also has a sinister side that provokes idiocy, illness, self-disgust, or violence.

In the woods irrational forces rule, the dimly understood forces of nature that sometimes frustrate the hopes of human beings to control their own lives. The fairy spirits in the play are not merely benevolent representations of nature; they are also associated with apparitions, with witchcraft and demonology, with birth defects, and with death. Without Oberon's oversight, Puck's mistakes are as likely to produce disaster as amusement. Magic in the play is related to irrational forces that are capable of doing great good as well as great harm.

Oberon and Titania seem more clearly tied than Puck to classical mythology. They are the immortal sovereigns of the fairies, and the disharmony in their relationship is reflected in nature; their quarrel is responsible for the disordered seasons in the play. The trick Oberon plays on Titania with the love juice leads to the cruel but funny interlude with Bottom, who has been transformed with the head of an ass. The darker implications of this love scene are ameliorated by Bottom's innocence and foolishness.

The affair between Bottom and Titania flirts humorously with classical ideas about relationships between the gods and mortals. The affair specifically raises questions about the relationship between illusion and reality, questions that intensify when Bottom and his friends act out the classical story of Pyramus and Thisbe at the end of the play. Their production makes an attempt to communicate an imaginative experience realistically, literally, with representations of moonshine; personifications of the man in the moon, his dog, and his thornbush; an apologetic lion; and a talking wall. In the process they transform a tragedy into a comedy, eliciting supercilious comments from the courtly audience. Because this audience is contained within Shakespeare's play, we understand their responses to be as partial and restrictive as those of Bottom and his friends. Bottom and his friends are awed by the power of art while Theseus's skepticism seeks to contain and to dismiss its irrationality. Shakespeare has the final word, and all of the marriages are blessed by the very spirits that rationality would deny.

Over all these events shines the moon, which comes to suggest both the darker and brighter sides of the plays' irrational forces. It is associated both with the threatening fears which Puck sweeps behind the door for the moment and the benevolent lunacy which Shakespeare allows to pervade the play. In the end,

A Midsummer Night's Dream offers a rich and playful excursion into the double-edged comic forces that ultimately transform society and make it fruitful. Shakespeare's final word about the relationship between imagination and reality is delivered in the epilogue, in which Puck invites applause and suggests that anyone who dislikes the play should imagine it as a dream.

A Midsummer Night's Dream

WILLIAM SHAKESPEARE

EDITED BY OSCAR CAMPBELL

CHARACTERS

THESEUS, Duke of Athens
EGEUS, father to Hermia
LYSANDER,
DEMETRIUS, } Both in love with Hermia
PHILOSTRATE, Master of the Revels to Theseus
QUINCE, a carpenter; Prologue in the play
SNUG, a joiner; Lion in the play
BOTTOM, a weaver; Pyramus in the play
FLUTE, a bellows-mender; Thisby in the play
SNOUT, a tinker; Wall in the play
STARVELING, a tailor; Moonshine in the play
HIPPOLYTA, queen of the Amazons, betrothed to Theseus

HERMIA, daughter to Egeus, in love with Lysander
HELENA, in love with Demetrius
OBERON, king of the fairies
TITANIA, queen of the fairies
PUCK, or ROBIN GOODFELLOW
PEASEBLOSSOM
COBWEB
MOTH } fairies
MUSTARDSEED
Other FAIRIES attending their KING and QUEEN
ATTENDANTS on THESEUS and HIPPOLYTA

SCENE: Athens, and a wood nearby.

ACT I

Scene 1.

Athens. The palace of THESEUS.

[*Enter* THESEUS, HIPPOLYTA, PHILOSTRATE, *and* ATTENDANTS.]

THESEUS: Now, fair Hippolyta, our nuptial hour
    Draws on apace; four happy days bring in
    Another moon: but, O, methinks, how slow
    This old moon wanes! she lingers° my desires
5   Like to a step-dame or a dowager°

    Long withering out° a young man's revenue.
HIPPOLYTA: Four days will quickly steep themselves
        in night;
    Four nights will quickly dream away the time;
    And then the moon, like to a silver bow
    New-bent in heaven, shall behold the night   10
    Of our solemnities.
THESEUS: Go, Philostrate,
    Stir up the Athenian youth to merriments;
    Awake the pert° and nimble spirit of mirth:
    Turn melancholy forth to funerals;
    The pale companion is not for our pomp.   15

    [Exit Philostrate.]

    Hippolyta, I woo'd thee with my sword,
    And won thy love, doing thee injuries;
    But I will wed thee in another key,
    With pomp, with triumph° and with revelling.

Characters: The name of each artisan suggests his craft: Quince, or quoins, wedges of wood; Snug, tight-fitting; Bottom, core of a ball of yarn and the ball itself; Flute, the pipes or flutes of an organ.

ACT I, SCENE 1:   ⁴ **lingers** delays the fulfillment of ⁵ **dowager** a widow with property inherited from her husband.

⁶ **withering out** making dwindle   ¹³ **pert** lively   ¹⁹ **triumph** public show

[Enter EGEUS, HERMIA, LYSANDER, *and* DEMETRIUS.*]*

20 EGEUS: Happy be Theseus, our renownèd duke!
THESEUS: Thanks, good Egeus: what's the news with
    thee?
EGEUS: Full of vexation come I, with complaint
    Against my child, my daughter Hermia.
    Stand forth, Demetrius. My noble lord,
25   This man hath my consent to marry her.
    Stand forth, Lysander: and, my gracious duke,
    This man hath bewitch'd the bosom° of my child:
    Thou, thou, Lysander, thou hast given her rhymes
    And interchanged love-tokens with my child:
30   Thou hast by moonlight at her window sung
    With feigning° voice verses of feigning° love,
    And stolen the impression of her fantasy°
    With bracelets of thy hair, rings, gawds,° con-
    ceits,°
    Knacks,° trifles, nosegays, sweetmeats,° messen-
    gers
35   Of strong prevailment° in unharden'd youth:
    With cunning hast thou filch'd my daughter's
    heart,
    Turn'd her obedience, which is due to me,
    To stubborn harshness: and, my gracious duke,
    Be it so she will not here before your grace
40   Consent to marry with Demetrius,
    I beg the ancient privilege of Athens,
    As she is mine, I may dispose of her:
    Which shall be either to this gentleman
    Or to her death, according to our law
45   Immediately° provided in that case.
THESEUS: What say you, Hermia? be advised, fair
    maid;
    To you your father should be as a god;
    One that composed your beauties, yea, and one
    To whom you are but as a form in wax
50   By him imprinted and within his power
    To leave the figure or disfigure° it.
    Demetrius is a worthy gentleman.
HERMIA: So is Lysander.
THESEUS: In himself he is;
    But in this kind,° wanting° your father's voice,°
55   The other must be held the worthier.
HERMIA: I would my father look'd but with my eyes.
THESEUS: Rather your eyes must with his judgement
    look.
HERMIA: I do entreat your grace to pardon me.

    I know not by what power I am made bold,
    Nor how it may concern° my modesty,   60
    In such a presence here to plead my thoughts;
    But I beseech your grace that I may know
    The worst that may befall me in this case,
    If I refuse to wed Demetrius.
THESEUS: Either to die the death or to abjure   65
    For ever the society of men.
    Therefore, fair Hermia, question your desires;
    Know of your youth, examine well your blood,
    Whether, if you yield not to your father's choice,
    You can endure the livery of a nun,   70
    For aye to be in shady cloister mew'd,°
    To live a barren sister all your life,
    Chanting faint hymns to the cold fruitless moon.
    Thrice-blessèd they that master so their blood,°
    To undergo such maiden pilgrimage;   75
    But earthlier happy° is the rose distill'd,
    Than that which withering on the virgin thorn
    Grows, lives and dies in single blessedness.
HERMIA: So will I grow, so live, so die, my lord,
    Ere I will yield my virgin patent° up   80
    Unto his lordship, whose unwishèd yoke
    My soul consents not to give sovereignty.
THESEUS: Take time to pause; and, by the next new
    moon—
    The sealing-day betwixt my love and me,
    For everlasting bond of fellowship—   85
    Upon that day either prepare to die
    For disobedience to your father's will,
    Or else to wed Demetrius, as he would;
    Or on Diana's altar to protest°
    For aye austerity and single life.   90
DEMETRIUS: Relent, sweet Hermia: and Lysander,
    yield
    Thy crazèd° title to my certain right.
LYSANDER: You have her father's love, Demetrius;
    Let me have Hermia's: do you marry him.
EGEUS: Scornful Lysander! true, he hath my love,   95
    And what is mine my love shall render him.
    And she is mine, and all my right of her
    I do estate unto° Demetrius.
LYSANDER: I am, my lord, as well derived° as he,
    As well possess'd;° my love is more than his;   100
    My fortunes every way as fairly rank'd,
    If not with vantage, as Demetrius';
    And, which is more than all these boasts can be,
    I am beloved of beauteous Hermia:
    Why should not I then prosecute my right?   105

---

[27] **bosom** i.e., the seat of the emotions   [31] **feigning** decep-
tive; **feigning** feigned   [32] **and . . . fantasy** captured her
imagination by impressing your image upon it   [33] **gawds**
pieces of jewelry; conceits, showy trinkets   [34] **knacks** knickknacks; sweetmeats, candy   [35] **strong prevailment** great
influence   [45] **immediately** expressly   [51] **disfigure** obliterate   [54] **kind** instance; wanting lacking; voice, approval

[60] **concern** befit   [71] **mew'd** shut up   [74] **blood** passion   [76]
earthlies happy happier on earth   [80] **patent** phrase formed
on the analogy of "letters patent," here, identification mark,
i.e., maidenhead   [89] **protest** vow   [92] **crazed** unsound   [98]
estate unto settle upon   [99] **well-derived** of as good birth
[100] **as well possess'd** as well off

Demetrius, I'll avouch it to his head,°
Made love to Nedar's daughter, Helena,
And won her soul; and she, sweet lady, dotes,
Devoutly dotes, dotes in idolatry,
110 Upon this spotted and inconstant man.
THESEUS: I must confess that I have heard so much,
And with Demetrius thought to have spoke there-
of;
But, being over-full of self-affairs,
My mind did lose it. But, Demetrius, come;
115 And come, Egeus; you shall go with me,
I have some private schooling for you both.
For you, fair Hermia, look you arm yourself
To fit your fancies to your father's will;
Or else the law of Athens yields you up—
120 Which by no means we may extenuate°—
To death, or to a vow of single life.
Come, my Hippolyta: what cheer, my love?
Demetrius and Egeus, go along:
I must employ you in some business
125 Against° our nuptial and confer with you
Of something nearly that° concerns yourselves.
EGEUS: With duty and desire we follow you.

[Exeunt all but LYSANDER and HERMIA.]

LYSANDER: How now, my love! why is your cheek so
pale?
How chance the roses there do fade so fast?
130 HERMIA: Belike° for want of rain, which I could well
Beteem them° from the tempest of my eyes.
LYSANDER: Ay me! for aught that I could ever read,
Could ever hear by tale or history,
The course of true love never did run smooth;
135 But, either it was different in blood—
HERMIA: O cross!° too high to be enthrall'd to low.°
LYSANDER: Or else misgraffèd° in respect of years—
HERMIA: O spite! too old to be engaged to young.
LYSANDER: Or else it stood upon° the choice of
friends—
140 HERMIA: O hell! to choose love by another's eyes.
LYSANDER: Or, if there were a sympathy in choice,
War, death, or sickness did lay siege to it,
Making it momentany° as a sound,
Swift as a shadow, short as any dream;
145 Brief as the lightning in the collied° night,
That, in a spleen,° unfolds both heaven and earth,
And ere a man hath power to say "Behold!"
The jaws of darkness do devour it up:

So quick bright things come to confusion.°
HERMIA: If then true lovers have been ever cross'd, 150
It stands as an edict in destiny:
Then let us teach our trial patience,°
Because it is a customary cross,
As due to love as thoughts and dreams and sighs,
Wishes and tears, poor fancy's° followers. 155
LYSANDER: A good persuasion: therefore, hear me,
Hermia.
I have a widow aunt, a dowager
Of great revénue, and she hath no child:
From Athens is her house remote seven leagues;
And she respects° me as her only son. 160
There, gentle Hermia, may I marry thee;
And to that place the sharp Athenian law
Cannot pursue us. If thou lovest me then,
Steal forth thy father's house to-morrow night;
And in the wood, a league without the town, 165
Where I did meet thee once with Helena,
To do observance to a morn of May,°
There will I stay for thee.
HERMIA: My good Lysander!
I swear to thee, by Cupid's strongest bow,
By his best arrow with the golden head, 170
By the simplicity of Venus' doves,
By that which knitteth souls and prospers loves,°
And by that fire which burn'd the Carthage
queen,°
When the false Troyan under sail was seen,
By all the vows that ever men have broke, 175
In number more than ever women spoke,
In that same place thou hast appointed me,
To-morrow truly will I meet with thee.
LYSANDER: Keep promise, love. Look, here comes
Helena.

[Enter HELENA.]

HERMIA: God speed fair Helena! whither away? 180
HELENA: Call you me fair? that fair again unsay.
Demetrius loves your fair:° O happy fair!
Your eyes are lode-stars;° and your tongue's
sweet air
More tuneable° than lark to shepherd's ear,
When wheat is green, when hawthorn buds
appear. 185
Sickness is catching: O, were favour° so,
Yours would I catch, fair Hermia, ere I go;

---

106 **avouch . . . head** affirm it to his face 120 **extenuate** mitigate, alleviate 125 **against** in anticipation of 126 **nearly that** that intimately 130 **belike** probably 131 **Beteem them** bring forth for them 136 **cross** perversity; enthrall'd to low made servant to one of low birth 137 **misgraffed** badly matched 139 **stood upon** concerned 143 **momentany** momentary 145 **collied** coal-black 146 **spleen** fit of anger

149 **confusion** ruin 152 **teach . . . patience** teach ourselves patience to endure the trial 155 **fancy's** love's 160 **respects** regards 167 **do . . . May** celebrate May Day 172 **that . . . loves** i.e., the girdle of Venus 173 **And . . . Queen** according to Vergil's Aeneid [Book IV], Dido, deserted by Aeneas, burned herself to death on a funeral pyre. 182 **your fair** your beauty 183 **lode-stars** guiding stars 184 **tuneable** musical 186 **favour** (1) physical appearance, (2) affection

My ear should catch your voice, my eye your eye,
My tongue should catch your tongue's sweet
   melody.
190 Were the world mine, Demetrius being bated,°
The rest I'ld give to be to you translated°
O, teach me how you look, and with what art
You sway the motion° of Demetrius' heart.
HERMIA: I frown upon him, yet he loves me still.
HELENA: O that your frowns would teach my smiles
195   such skill!
HERMIA: I give him curses, yet he gives me love.
HELENA: O that my prayers could such affection move!
HERMIA: The more I hate, the more he follows me.
HELENA: The more I love, the more he hateth me.
200 HERMIA: His folly, Helena, is no fault of mine.
HELENA: None, but your beauty: would that fault
   were mine!
HERMIA: Take comfort: he no more shall see my face;
Lysander and myself will fly this place.
Before the time I did Lysander see,
205 Seem'd Athens as a paradise to me:
O, then, what graces in my love do dwell,
That he hath turn'd a heaven unto a hell!
LYSANDER: Helen, to you our minds we will unfold:
To-morrow night, when Phœbe° doth behold
210 Her silvery visage in the watery glass,
Decking with liquid pearl the bladed grass,
A time that lovers' flights doth still conceal,
Through Athens' gates have we devised to steal.
HERMIA: And in the wood, where often you and I
215 Upon faint° primrose beds were wont to lie,
Emptying our bosoms of their counsel sweet,
There my Lysander and myself shall meet;
And thence from Athens turn away our eyes,
To seek new friends and stranger companies.
220 Farewell, sweet playfellow: pray thou for us;
And good luck grant thee thy Demetrius!
Keep word, Lysander: we must starve our sight
From lovers' food till morrow deep midnight.
LYSANDER: I will, my Hermia.

[Exit HERMIA.]

Helena, adieu:
225 As you on him, Demetrius dote on you!

[Exit.]

HELENA: How happy some o'er other some can be!
Through Athens I am thought as fair as she.
But what of that? Demetrius thinks not so;
He will not know what all but he do know:
230 And as he errs, doting on Hermia's eyes,

So I, admiring of his qualities:
Things base and vile, holding no quantity,
Love can transpose to form and dignity:
Love looks not with the eyes, but with the mind;
And therefore is wing'd Cupid painted blind: 235
Nor hath Love's mind of any judgement taste;
Wings and no eyes figure° unheedy haste:
And therefore is Love said to be a child,
Because in choice he is so oft beguiled.
As waggish boys in game themselves forswear, 240
So the boy Love is perjured every where:
For ere Demetrius look'd on Hermia's eyne,°
He hail'd down oaths that he was only mine;
And when this hail some heat from Hermia felt,
So he dissolved, and showers of oaths did melt. 245
I will go tell him of fair Hermia's flight:
Then to the wood will he to-morrow night
Pursue her; and for this intelligence°
If I have thanks, it is a dear expense:°
But herein mean I to enrich my pain,   250
To have his sight thither and back again.

[Exit.]

Scene 2

Athens. QUINCE*'s house.*

[Enter QUINCE, SNUG, BOTTOM, FLUTE, SNOUT, *and*
STARVELING.*]*

QUINCE: Is all our company here?
BOTTOM: You were best to call them generally° man by
   man, according to the scrip.°
QUINCE: Here is the scroll of every man's name, which
   is thought fit, through all Athens, to play in our 5
   interlude before the duke and the duchess, on
   his wedding-day at night.
BOTTOM: First, good Peter Quince, say what the play
   treats on, then read the names of the actors, and
   so grow to° a point.   10
QUINCE: Marry, our play is, The most lamentable comedy, and most cruel death of Pyramus and Thisby.
BOTTOM: A very good piece of work, I assure you, and
   a merry. Now, good Peter Quince, call forth your
   actors by the scroll. Masters, spread yourselves. 15
QUINCE: Answer as I call you. Nick Bottom, the weaver.
BOTTOM: Ready. Name what part I am for, and proceed.

---

237 **figure** are a symbol of 240 **waggish** playful 242 **eyne**
eyes 248 **intelligence** news 249 **dear expense** a thing that
will cost me dear

SCENE 2: 2 **generally** severally, the first of Bottom's many
malapropisms 3 **scrip** written list 10 **grow to** come to

---

190 **bated** excepted 191 **translated** transformed 193 **notion**
inclination 209 **Phœbe** Diana, the moon 215 **faint** pale

QUINCE: You, Nick Bottom, are set down for Pyramus.

BOTTOM: What is Pyramus? a lover, or a tyrant?

20 QUINCE: A lover, that kills himself most gallant for love.

BOTTOM: That will ask some tears in the true performing of it: if I do it, let the audience look to their
eyes; I will move storms, I will condole° in
25   some measure. To the rest: yet my chief humour
is for a tyrant: I could play Ercles° rarely, or a
part to tear a cat in to make all split.°

> The raging rocks
> And shivering shocks
30 > Shall break the locks
> Of prison gates;
> And Phibbus'° car
> Shall shine from far
> And make and mar
35 > The foolish Fates.

This was lofty! Now name the rest of the players. This is Ercles' vein, a tyrant's vein; a lover
is more condoling.

QUINCE: Francis Flute, the bellows-mender.

40 FLUTE: Here, Peter Quince.

QUINCE: Flute, you must take Thisby on you.

FLUTE: What is Thisby? a wandering knight?

QUINCE: It is the lady that Pyramus must love.

FLUTE: Nay, faith, let not me play a woman; I have a
45   beard coming.

QUINCE: That's all one: you shall play it in a mask, and
you may speak as small° as you will.

BOTTOM: An° I may hide my face, let me play Thisby
too, I'll speak in a monstrous little voice,
50   "Thisne, Thisne;" "Ah Pyramus, my lover dear!
thy Thisby dear, and lady dear!"

QUINCE: No, no; you must play Pyramus: and, Flute,
you Thisby.

BOTTOM: Well, proceed.

55 QUINCE: Robin Starveling, the tailor.

STARVELING: Here, Peter Quince.

QUINCE: Robin Starveling, you must play Thisby's
mother. Tom Snout, the tinker.

SNOUT: Here, Peter Quince.

60 QUINCE: You, Pyramus' father: myself, Thisby's father.
Snug, the joiner; you, the lion's part: and, I
hope, here is a play fitted.°

SNUG: Have you the lion's part written? pray you, if it
be, give it to me, for I am slow of study.

QUINCE: You may do it extempore, for it is nothing but 65
roaring.

BOTTOM: Let me play the lion too: I will roar, that I will
do any man's heart good to hear me; I will roar,
and that I will make the duke say "Let him roar
again, let him roar again." 70

QUINCE: An you should do it too terribly, you would
fright the duchess and the ladies, that they
would shriek; and that were enough to hang us
all.

ALL: That would hang us, every mother's son. 75

BOTTOM: I grant you, friends, if that you should fright
the ladies out of their wits, they would have no
more discretion but to hang us: but I will aggra-
vate° my voice so that I will roar you as gently
as any sucking° dove; I will roar you as 'twere 80
any nightingale.

QUINCE: You can play no part but Pyramus; for
Pyramus is a sweet-faced man; a proper man, as
one shall see in a summer's day; a most lovely
gentleman-like man: therefore you must needs 85
play Pyramus.

BOTTOM: Well, I will undertake it. What beard were I
best to play it in?

QUINCE: Why, what you will.

BOTTOM: I will discharge° it in either your straw 90
colour beard, your orange-tawny beard, your
purple-in-grain° beard, or your French-crown
colour° beard, your perfect yellow.

QUINCE: Some of your French crowns have no hair at
all, and then you will play barefaced. But, mas- 95
ters, here are your parts: and I am to entreat
you, request you and desire you, to con° them
by to-morrow night; and meet me in the palace
wood, a mile without the town, by moonlight;
there will we rehearse, for if we meet in the city, 100
we shall be dogged with company, and our
devices° known. In the meantime I will draw a
bill of properties, such as our play wants. I pray
you, fail me not.

BOTTOM: We will meet; and there we may rehearse 105
most obscenely° and courageously. Take pains;
be perfect: adieu.

QUINCE: At the duke's oak we meet.

BOTTOM: Enough; hold or cut bow-strings.°

[Exeunt.]

---

²⁴ **condole** lament   ²⁶ **Ercles** Hercules was a ranting character in the earlier drama; tear a cat, proverbial for "rant."
²⁷ **make all split** proverbial for "cause an uproar"
³² **Phibbus'** Phoebus'   ⁴² **wandering knight** knight errant
⁴⁷ **small** shrilly   ⁴⁸ **an** if   ⁶² **fitted** i.e., cast

⁷⁹ **aggravate** he means "moderate"   ⁸⁰ **sucking** i.e., not full-
fledged   ⁸³ **proper** handsome   ⁹⁰ **discharge** perform
⁹² **purple-in-grain** deep red   ⁹³ **French crown-colour** i.e.,
golden   ⁹⁷ **con** learn by heart   ¹⁰² **devices** i.e., dramatic
plans   ¹⁰⁶ **obscenely** mistake for "obscurely," i.e., privately
¹⁰⁹ **hold . . . strings** i.e., be on hand or give up the play.

ACT II

Scene 1

A wood near Athens.

[Enter, from opposite sides, a FAIRY, and PUCK.]

PUCK: How now, spirit! whither wander you?
FAIRY: Over hill, over dale,

    Thorough bush, thorough brier,
  Over park, over pale,°
5   Thorough flood, thorough fire,
  I do wander every where,
  Swifter than the moon's sphere;
  And I serve the fairy queen,
  To dew her orbs° upon the green.
10   The cowslips tall her pensioners° be:
  In their gold coats spots you see;
  Those be rubies, fairy favours,
  In those freckles live their savours:

  I must go seek some dewdrops here
15   And hang a pearl in every cowslip's ear.
  Farewell, thou lob° of spirits; I'll be gone:
  Our queen and all her elves come here anon.
PUCK: The king doth keep his revels here to-night:
  Take heed the queen come not within his sight;
20   For Oberon is passing fell° and wrath,
  Because that she as her attendant hath
  A lovely boy, stolen from an Indian king;
  She never had so sweet a changeling;°
  And jealous Oberon would have the child
25   Knight of his train, to trace the forests wild;
  But she perforce withholds the lovèd boy,
  Crowns him with flowers and makes him all her
    joy:
  And now they never meet in grove or green,
  By fountain clear, or spangled starlight sheen,
30   But they do square,° that all their elves for fear
  Creep into acorn-cups and hide them there.
FAIRY: Either I mistake your shape and making quite,
  Or else you are that shrewd° and knavish sprite
  Call'd Robin Goodfellow: are not you he
35   That frights the maidens of the villagery;
  Skim milk, and sometimes labour in the quern°
  And bootless° make the breathless housewife churn;

And sometime make the drink to bear no barm;°
Mislead night-wanderers, laughing at their harm?
Those that Hobgoblin call you and sweet Puck, 40
You do their work, and they shall have good luck:
Are not you he?
PUCK: Thou speak'st aright;
I am that merry wanderer of the night.
I jest to Oberon and make him smile
When I a fat and bean-fed horse beguile, 45
Neighing in likeness of a filly foal:
And sometime lurk I in a gossip's bowl,°
In very likeness of a roasted crab,°
And when she drinks, against her lips I bob
And on her wither'd dewlap° pour the ale. 50
The wisest aunt,° telling the saddest tale,
Sometime for three-foot stool mistaketh me;
Then slip I from her bum, down topples she,
And "tailor"° cries, and falls into a cough;
And then the whole quire° hold their hips and
  laugh, 55
And waxen in their mirth and neeze° and swear
A merrier hour was never wasted there.
But, room, fairy! here comes Oberon.
FAIRY: And here my mistress. Would that he were
  gone!

*[Enter, from one side, OBERON, with his train; from the
other, TITANIA, with hers.]*

OBERON: Ill met by moonlight, proud Titania. 60
TITANIA: What, jealous Oberon! Fairies, skip hence:
  I have forsworn his bed and company.
OBERON: Tarry, rash wanton: am not I thy lord?
TITANIA: Then I must be thy lady: but I know
  When thou hast stolen away from fairy land, 65
  And in the shape of Corin sat all day,
  Playing on pipes of corn° and versing love
  To amorous Phillida.° Why art thou here,
  Come from the farthest steppe° of India?
  But that, forsooth, the bouncing° Amazon,° 70
  Your buskin'd° mistress and your warrior love,
  To Theseus must be wedded, and you come
  To give their bed joy and prosperity.
OBERON: How canst thou thus for shame, Titania,
  Glance at° my credit° with Hippolyta, 75

---

38 **barm** yeast formed on brewing liquors   47 **bowl** i.e., of liquor   48 **crab** crabapple, often put in drink   50 **dewlap** loose skin about the throat   51 **aunt** old woman   54 **"tailor"** allusion obscure, probably a play on the word "tail."   55 **quire** company   56 **neeze** sneeze   66–8 **corin . . . Phillida** conventional names of shepherds in pastoral literature   67 **pipes of corn** pipes made out of oaten straws   69 **steppe** mountain range   70 **bouncing** big and lusty; Amazon Hippolyta, Queen of the Amazons   71 **buskin'd** wearing half-boots   75 **glance at** allude to contemptuously   **credit** reputation

---

ACT II, SCENE I: 4 **pale** fence   9 **orbs** fairy rings   10 **pensioners** royal bodyguard   16 **lob** lout   20 **passing fell** extremely angry   23 **changeling** a child left by the fairies in the place of one they have stolen. Here merely "stolen child."   30 **square** quarrel; that, so that   33 **shrewd** mischievous, vexatious   36 **quern** hand mill for grinding wheat   37 **bootless** vainly

Knowing I know thy love to Theseus?
Didst thou not lead him through the glimmering
 night
From Perigenia, whom he ravished?
And make him with fair Ægle break his faith,
80 With Ariadne and Antiopa?°
 TITANIA: These are the forgeries of jealousy:
And never, since the middle summer's spring,°
Met we on hill, in dale, forest or mead,
By payèd fountain or by rushy brook,
85 Or in° the beached margent of the sea,
To dance our ringlets° to the whistling wind,
But with thy brawls thou hast disturb'd our sport.
Therefore the winds, piping to us in vain,
As in revenge, have suck'd up from the sea
90 Contagious fogs; which falling in the land
Have every pelting° river made so proud
That they have overborne their continents:°
The ox hath therefore stretch'd his yoke in vain,
The ploughman lost his sweat, and the green corn
95 Hath rotted ere his youth attain'd a beard;
The fold stands empty in the drownèd field,
And crows are fatted with the murrion° flock;
The nine men's morris° is fill'd up with mud,
And the quaint mazes° in the wanton green
100 For lack of tread are undistinguishable:
The human mortals want° their winter here;
No night is now with hymn or carol blest:
Therefore the moon, the governess of floods,
Pale in her anger, washes all the air,
105 That rheumatic diseases do abound:
And thorough° this distemperature° we see
The seasons alter: hoary-headed frosts
Fall in the fresh lap of the crimson rose,
And on old Hiems'° thin and icy crown
110 An odorous chaplet of sweet summer buds
Is, as in mockery, set: the spring, the summer,
The childing° autumn, angry winter, change
Their wonted liveries, and the mazed° world,
By their increase, now knows not which is which:
115 And this same progeny of evils comes
From our debate, from our dissension;
We are their parents and original.°

OBERON: Do you amend it then; it lies in you:
Why should Titania cross her Oberon?
I do but beg a little changeling boy,   120
To be my henchman.°
TITANIA: Set your heart at rest:
The fairy land buys not the child of me.
His mother was a votaress of my order:
And, in the spicèd Indian air, by night,
Full often hath she gossip'd by my side,   125
And sat with me on Neptune's yellow sands,
Marking the embarkèd traders° on the flood,
When we have laugh'd to see the sails conceive
And grow big-bellied with the wanton wind;
Which she, with pretty and with swimming gait 130
Following,—her womb then rich with my young
 squire,—
Would imitate, and sail upon the land,
To fetch me trifles, and return again,
As from a voyage, rich with merchandise.
But she, being mortal, of that boy did die; 135
And for her sake do I rear up her boy,
And for her sake I will not part with him.
OBERON: How long within this wood intend you stay?
TITANIA: Perchance till after Theseus' weddingday.
If you will patiently dance in our round° 140
And see our moonlight revels, go with us;
If not, shun me, and I will spare° your haunts.
OBERON: Give me that boy, and I will go with thee.
TITANIA: Not for thy fairy kingdom. Fairies, away!
We shall chide downright, if I longer stay. 145

[Exit TITANIA with her train.]

OBERON: Well, go thy way: thou shalt not from this
 grove
Till I torment thee for this injury.
My gentle Puck, come hither. Thou rememberest
Since° once I sat upon a promontory,
And heard a mermaid on a dolphin's back 150
Uttering such dulcet and harmonious breath
That the rude sea grew civil at her song
And certain stars shot madly from their spheres,°
To hear the sea-maid's music.
PUCK: I remember.
OBERON: That very time I saw, but thou couldst not,
Flying between the cold moon and the earth, 155
Cupid all arm'd: a certain aim he took
At a fair vestal° thronèd by the west,
And loosed his love-shaft smartly from his bow,

78–80 **Perigenia . . . Antiopa** These are the women whom, according to Plutarch (Life of Theseus), Theseus had loved. 82 **middle summer's spring** the beginning of midsummer 85 **in** on 86 **ringlets** round dances 91 **pelting** paltry 92 **continents** banks 97 **murrion** diseased 98 **nine men's morris** squares on the village green, marked out by nine stones, on which a kind of bowling game was played 99 **quaint mazes** intricate figures marked out on the green **wanton green** luxuriant grass 101 **want** lack 106 **thorough** through **distemperature** bad weather 109 **Hiems'** God of Winter 000 **childing** fruitful 113 **mazed** bewildered 117 **original** source

---

121 **henchman** attendant page 127 **embarked traders** merchant ships 140 **round** i.e., round dance 142 **spare** avoid 149 **since** when 148–168 **Thou . . . love-in-idleness** for the occasion to which this probably refers, see the Introduction. 151 **breath** voice 153 **And . . . spheres** i.e., skyrockets and other forms of fireworks 158 **vestal** vestal virgin, hence virgin

160   As it should pierce a hundred thousand hearts;
       But I might see young Cupid's fiery shaft
       Quench'd in the chaste beams of the watery
          moon,
       And the imperial votaress° passèd on,
       In maiden meditation, fancy-free.°
165   Yet mark'd I where the bolt° of Cupid fell:
       It fell upon a little western flower,
       Before milk-white, now purple with love's
          wound,
       And maidens call it love-in-idleness.°
       Fetch me that flower; the herb I shew'd thee once:
170   The juice of it on sleeping eye-lids laid
       Will make or man or woman madly dote
       Upon the next live creature that it sees.
       Fetch me this herb; and be thou here again
       Ere the leviathan° can swim a league.
175 PUCK: I'll put a girdle round about the earth°
       In forty minutes.

[Exit.]

OBERON: Having once this juice,
       I'll watch Titania when she is asleep,
       And drop the liquor of it in her eyes.
       The next thing then she waking looks upon,
180   Be it on lion, bear, or wolf, or bull,
       On meddling monkey, or on busy ape,
       She shall pursue it with the soul of love:
       And ere I take this charm from off her sight,
       As I can take it with another herb,
185   I'll make her render up her page to me.
       But who comes here? I am invisible;
       And I will overhear their conference.

[Enter DEMETRIUS, HELENA *following him.]*

DEMETRIUS: I love thee not, therefore pursue me not.
       Where is Lysander and fair Hermia?
190   The one I'll slay, the other slayeth me.
       Thou told'st me they were stolen unto this wood;
       And here am I, and wode° within this wood,
       Because I cannot meet my Hermia.
       Hence, get thee gone, and follow me no more.
195 HELENA: You draw me, you hard-hearted adamant;°
       But yet you draw not iron, for my heart
       Is true as steel: leave° you your power to draw,
       And I shall have no power to follow you.
DEMETRIUS: Do I entice you? do I speak you fair?°
200   Or, rather, do I not in plainest truth
       Tell you, I do not, nor I cannot love you?

HELENA: And even for that do I love you the more.
       I am your spaniel; and, Demetrius,
       The more you beat me, I will fawn on you:
       Use me but as your spaniel, spurn me, strike me,   205
       Neglect me, lose me; only give me leave,
       Unworthy as I am, to follow you.
       What worser place can I beg in your love,—
       And yet a place of high respect with me,—
       Than to be usèd as you use your dog?   210
DEMETRIUS: Tempt not too much the hatred of my
         spirit,
       For I am sick when I do look on thee.
HELENA: And I am sick when I look not on you.
DEMETRIUS: You do impeach° your modesty too much,
       To leave the city and commit yourself   215
       Into the hands of one that loves you not;
       To trust the opportunity of night
       And the ill counsel of a desert place
       With the rich worth of your virginity.
HELENA: Your virtue is my privilege:° for that   220
       It is not night when I do see your face,
       Therefore I think I am not in the night;
       Nor doth this wood lack worlds of company,
       For you in my respect° are all the world:
       Then how can it be said I am alone,   225
       When all the world is here to look on me?
DEMETRIUS: I'll run from thee and hide me in the
         brakes,°
       And leave thee to the mercy of wild beasts.
HELENA: The wildest hath not such a heart as you.
       Run when you will, the story shall be changed: 230
       Apollo flies, and Daphne holds the chase;°
       The dove pursues the griffin;° the mild hind°
       Makes speed to catch the tiger; bootless speed,
       When cowardice pursues and valour flies.
DEMETRIUS: I will not stay thy questions;° let me go: 235
       Or, if thou follow me, do not believe
       But I shall do thee mischief in the wood.
HELENA: Ay, in the temple, in the town, the field,
       You do me mischief. Fie, Demetrius!
       Your wrongs do set a scandal on my sex: 240
       We cannot fight for love, as men may do;
       We should be woo'd and were not made to woo.

[Exit DEMETRIUS.]

I'll follow thee and make a heaven of hell,
       To die upon° the hand I love so well.

[Exit.]

---

163 imperial votaress i.e., Queen Elizabeth **164 fancy-free** intouched by love **165 bolt** arrow **168 love-in-idleness** pansy **174 leviathan** whale **175 I'll... earth** I fly around the earth **192 wode** mad **195 adamant** loadstone **197 leave** give up **199 speak you fair** speak to you in a friendly manner

214 impeach discredit **220 privilege** protection **224 in my respect** as far as I am concerned **227 brakes** thickets **231 holds the chase** In Ovid, Apollo pursues Daphne; here the rôles are reversed **232 griffin** fabulous beast with an eagle's head attached to a lion's body; hind; doe **235 stay thy questions** listen to your talk **244 upon** by

OBERON: Fare thee well, nymph: ere he do leave this
245   grove,
        Thou shalt fly him and he shall seek thy love.

[Re-enter PUCK.]

Hast thou the flower there? Welcome, wanderer.
PUCK: Ay, there it is.
OBERON: I pray thee, give it me.
        I know a bank where the wild thyme blows,°
250   Where oxlips° and the nodding violet grows,
        Quite over-canopied with luscious woodbine,°
        With sweet musk-roses and with eglantine:°
        There sleeps Titania sometime of the night,
        Lull'd in these flowers with dances and delight;
255   And there the snake throws her enamell'd skin,
        Weed° wide enough to wrap a fairy in:
        And with the juice of this I'll streak her eyes,°
        And make her full of hateful fantasies.
        Take thou some of it, and seek through this grove:
260   A sweet Athenian lady is in love
        With a disdainful youth: anoint his eyes;
        But do it when the next thing he espies
        May be the lady: thou shalt know the man
        By the Athenian garments he hath on.
265   Effect it with some care that he may prove
        More fond° on her than she upon her love:
        And look thou meet me ere the first cock crow.
PUCK: Fear not, my lord, your servant shall do so.

[Exeunt.]

Scene 2

Another part of the wood.

[Enter TITANIA, with her train.]

TITANIA: Come, now a roundel° and a fairy song;
        Then, for the third part of a minute, hence;
        Some to kill cankers° in the musk-rose buds,
        Some war with rere-mice° for their leathern wings,
5   To make my small elves coats, and some keep back
        The clamorous owl that nightly hoots and wonders
        At our quaint° spirits. Sing me now asleep;
        Then to your offices° and let me rest.

THE FAIRIES *sing.*

        You spotted snakes with double tongue,

Thorny hedgehogs, be not seen;   10
Newts and blind-worms,° do no wrong,
    Come not near our fairy queen.
    Philomel,° with melody
    Sing in our sweet lullaby;
Lulla, lulla, lullaby, lulla, lulla, lullaby: 15
    Never harm,
    Nor spell nor charm,
Come our lovely lady nigh;
So, good night, with lullaby.

Weaving spiders, come not here;   20
    Hence, you long-legg'd spinners, hence!
Beetles black, approach not near;
    Worm nor snail, do no offence.
    Philomel, with melody, &c.

A FAIRY. Hence, away! now all is well: 25
        One aloof stand sentinel.

[Exeunt FAIRIES. TITANIA sleeps.]

*[Enter OBERON, and squeezes the flower on TITANIA's
eyelids.]*

OBERON:

What thou seest when thou dost wake,
Do it for thy true-love take,
Love and languish for his sake:
Be it ounce,° or cat, or bear,   30
Pard° or boar with bristled hair,
In thy eye that shall appear
When thou wakest, it is thy dear:
Wake when some vile thing is near.

[Exit.]

[Enter LYSANDER and HERMIA.]

LYSANDER: Fair love, you faint with wandering in the
        wood;   35
        And to speak troth,° I have forgot our way:
        We'll rest us, Hermia, if you think it good,
        And tarry for the comfort of the day.
HERMIA: Be it so, Lysander: find you out a bed;
        For I upon this bank will rest my head.   40
LYSANDER: One turf shall serve as pillow for us both;
        One heart, one bed, two bosoms and one troth.
HERMIA: Nay, good Lysander; for my sake, my dear,

---

²⁴⁹ **blows** blossoms   ²⁵⁰ **oxlips** hybrid primroses   ²⁵¹ **woodbine** honeysuckle, Virginia creeper   ²⁵² **eglantine** the sweet-
brier   ²⁵⁶ **weed** garment   ²⁵⁷ **streak her eyes** rub her eyelids
²⁶⁶ **fond** doting

SCENE 2:   ¹ **roundel** dance in a ring   ³ **cankers** canker-
worms   ⁴ **rere-mice** bats   ⁷ **quaint** dainty   ⁸ **offices** duties

---

¹¹ **blind-worms** legless lizards, small snakelike animals   ¹³
Philomel i.e., the nightingale   ³⁰ **ounce** lynx; cat, wildcat
³¹ **Pard** leopard   ³⁶ **troth** truth

Lie further off yet, do not lie so near.

45 LYSANDER: O, take the sense, sweet, of my innocence!
Love takes the meaning in love's conference.
I mean, that my heart unto yours is knit
So that but one heart we can make of it;
Two bosoms interchainèd with an oath;
50 So then two bosoms and a single troth.°
Then by your side no bed-room me deny;
For lying so, Hermia, I do not lie.
HERMIA: Lysander riddles very prettily:
Now much beshrew° my manners and my pride,
55 If Hermia meant to say Lysander lied.
But, gentle friend, for love and courtesy
Lie further off; in human° modesty,
Such separation as may well be said
Becomes a virtuous bachelor and a maid,
60 So far be distant; and, good night, sweet friend:
Thy love ne'er alter till thy sweet life end!
LYSANDER: Amen, amen, to that fair prayer, say I;
And then end life when I end loyalty!
Here is my bed: sleep give thee all his rest!
HERMIA: With half that wish the wisher's eyes be
65   press'd!

[They sleep.]

[Enter PUCK.*]*

PUCK: Through the forest have I gone,
But Athenian found I none,
On whose eyes I might approve°
This flower's force in stirring love.
70 Night and silence.—Who is here?
Weeds of Athens he doth wear:
This is he, my master said,
Despisèd the Athenian maid;
And here the maiden, sleeping sound,
75 On the dank and dirty ground.
Pretty soul! she durst not lie
Near this lack-love, this kill-courtesy.
Churl, upon thy eyes I throw
All the power this charm doth owe.°
80 When thou wakest, let love forbid
Sleep his seat on thy eyelid:
So awake when I am gone;
For I must now to Oberon.

[Exit.]

[Enter DEMETRIUS *and* HELENA, *running.]*

HELENA: Stay, though thou kill me, sweet Demetrius.

DEMETRIUS: I charge thee, hence, and do not haunt
me thus.   85
HELENA: O, wilt thou darkling° leave me? do not so.
DEMETRIUS: Stay, on thy peril: I alone will go.

[Exit.]

HELENA: O, I am out of breath in this fond° chase!
The more my prayer, the lesser is my grace.°
Happy is Hermia, wheresoe'er she lies;   90
For she hath blessèd and attractive eyes.
How came her eyes so bright? Not with salt tears:
If so, my eyes are oftener wash'd than hers.
No, no, I am as ugly as a bear;
For beasts that meet me run away for fear: 95
Therefore no marvel though Demetrius
Do, as a monster, fly my presence thus.
What wicked and dissembling° glass of mine
Made me compare with Hermia's sphery eyne?°
But who is here? Lysander! on the ground!   100
Dead? or asleep? I see no blood, no wound.
Lysander, if you live, good sir, awake.
LYSANDER: *[Awaking]* And run through fire I will for
thy sweet sake.
Transparent Helena! Nature shows art,
That through thy bosom makes me see thy heart.   105
Where is Demetrius? O, how fit a word
Is that vile name to perish on my sword!
HELENA: Do not say so, Lysander; say not so.
What though he love your Hermia? Lord, what
though?
Yet Hermia still loves you: then be content.   110
LYSANDER: Content with Hermia! No; I do repent
The tedious minutes I with her have spent.
Not Hermia but Helena I love:
Who will not change a raven for a dove?
The will of man is by his reason sway'd;   115
And reason says you are the worthier maid.
Things growing are not ripe until their season:
So I, being young, till now ripe° not to reason;
And touching now the point° of human skill,
Reason becomes the marshal to my will°   120
And leads me to your eyes, where I o'erlook
Love's stories written in love's richest book.
HELENA: Wherefore was I to this keen mockery born?
When at your hands did I deserve this scorn?
It's not enough, is't not enough, young man,   125
That I did never, no, nor never can,
Deserve a sweet look from Demetrius' eye,
But you must flout° my insufficiency?
Good troth, you do me wrong, good sooth, you do,

---

⁸⁶ **darkling** in the dark   ⁸⁸ **fond** foolish   ⁸⁹ **grace** good fortune   ⁹⁸ **dissembling** deceiving   ⁹⁹ **sphery eyne** starry eyes
¹¹⁸ **ripe** grown ripe   ¹¹⁹ **point** apex   ¹²⁰ **will** passion   ¹²⁸
flout make fun of, insult

---

⁵⁰ **troth** troth-plight   ⁵⁴ **beshrew** curse (a mild oath).
⁵⁷ **human** courteous   ⁶⁸ **approve** test   ⁷⁹ **owe** possess

130 In such disdainful manner me to woo.
But fare you well: perforce I must confess
I thought you lord of more true gentleness.
O, that a lady, of one man refused,
Should of another therefore be abused!

[Exit.]

LYSANDER: She sees not Hermia. Hermia, sleep thou
135   there:
And never mayst thou come Lysander near!
For as a surfeit of the sweetest things
The deepest loathing to the stomach brings,
Or as the heresies that men do leave
140 Are hated most of those they did deceive,
So thou, my surfeit and my heresy,
Of all be hated, but the most of me!
And, all my powers, address your love and might
To honour Helen and to be her knight!

[Exit.]

145 HERMIA: [*Awaking*] Help me, Lysander, help me! do
thy best
To pluck this crawling serpent from my breast!
Ay me, for pity! what a dream was here!
Lysander, look how I do quake with fear:
Methought a serpent eat my heart away,
150 And you sat smiling at his cruel prey.°
Lysander! what, removed? Lysander! lord!
What, out of hearing? gone? no sound, no word?
Alack, where are you? speak, an if you hear;
Speak, of all loves!° I swoon almost with fear.
155 No? then I well perceive you are not nigh:
Either death or you I'll find immediately.

[Exit.]

ACT III

Scene 1

The wood. TITANIA *lying asleep.*

[*Enter* QUINCE, SNUG, BOTTOM, FLUTE, SNOUT, *and*
STARVELING.]

BOTTOM: Are we all met?
QUINCE: Pat, pat; and here's a marvellous convenient
place for our rehearsal. This green plot shall be
our stage, this hawthorn-brake our tiring-

house;° and we will do it in action as we will do   5
it before the duke.
BOTTOM: Peter Quince,—
QUINCE: What sayest thou, bully Bottom?°
BOTTOM: There are things in this comedy of Pyramus
and Thisby that will never please. First, Pyramus   10
must draw a sword to kill himself; which the
ladies cannot abide. How answer you that?
SNOUT: By'r lakin,° a parlous° fear.
STARVELING: I believe we must leave the killing out,
when all is done.   15
BOTTOM: Not a whit: I have a device to make all well.
Write me a prologue; and let the prologue seem
to say, we will do no harm with our swords and
that Pyramus is not killed indeed; and, for the
more better assurance, tell them that I Pyramus   20
am not Pyramus, but Bottom the weaver: this
will put them out of fear.
QUINCE: Well, we will have such a prologue; and it
shall be written in eight and six.°
BOTTOM: No, make it two more; let it be written in   25
eight and eight.
SNOUT: Will not the ladies be afeard of the lion?
STARVELING: I fear it, I promise you.
BOTTOM: Masters, you ought to consider with yourselves: to bring in—God shield us!—a lion   30
among ladies, is a most dreadful thing; for there
is not a more fearful wild-fowl than your lion
living; and we ought to look to't.
SNOUT: Therefore another prologue must tell he is not
a lion.   35
BOTTOM: Nay, you must name his name, and half his
face must be seen through the lion's neck: and he
himself must speak through, saying thus, or to
the same defect,°—"Ladies,"—or "Fair ladies,—
I would wish you,"—or "I would request   40
you,"—or "I would entreat you,—not to fear, not
to tremble: my life for yours. If you think I come
hither as a lion, it were pity of my life:° no, I am
no such thing; I am a man as other men are;" and
there indeed let him name his name, and tell   45
them plainly he is Snug the joiner.
QUINCE: Well, it shall be so. But there is two hard
things; that is, to bring the moonlight into a
chamber; for, you know, Pyramus and Thisby
meet by moonlight.   50
SNOUT: Doth the moon shine that night we play our
play?
BOTTOM: A calendar, a calendar! look in the almanac;
find out moonshine, find out moonshine.

---

150 **prey** preying [on me]   154 **of all loves** for the sake of all
love

ACT III, SCENE 1:   5 **tiring-house** dressing room   8 **bully
Bottom** "good old" Bottom   13 **By'r lakin** by our ladykin,
i.e., Virgin Mary;   **parlous** dangerous, risky   24 **eight and
six** alternate lines of eight and six syllables   39 **defect** mistake for "effect."   43 **pity of my life** sad thing for me

55 QUINCE: Yes, it doth shine that night.
BOTTOM: Why, then may you leave a casement of the
great chamber° window, where we play, open,
and the moon may shine in at the casement.
QUINCE: Ay; or else one must come in with a bush of
60 thorns and a lanthorn, and say he comes to disfigure,° or to present, the person of Moonshine.
Then, there is another thing: we must have a
wall in the great chamber; for Pyramus and
Thisby, says the story, did talk through the
65 chink of a wall.
SNOUT: You can never bring in a wall. What say you,
Bottom?
BOTTOM: Some man or other must present Wall: and
let him have some plaster, or some loam, or
70 some rough-cast° about him, to signify wall;
and let him hold his fingers thus, and through
that cranny shall Pyramus and Thisby whisper.
QUINCE: If that may be, then all is well. Come, sit
down, every mother's son, and rehearse your
75 parts. Pyramus, you begin: when you have spoken your speech, enter into that brake;: and so
every one according to his cue.

[Enter PUCK *behind.]*

PUCK: What hempen home-spuns have we swagger-
ing here,
80 So near the cradle of the fairy queen?
What, a play toward!° I'll be an auditor;
An actor too perhaps, if I see cause.
QUINCE: Speak, Pyramus. Thisby, stand forth.
BOTTOM: Thisby, the flowers of odious savours sweet,—
85 QUINCE: Odours, odours.
BOTTOM: —odours savours sweet:
So hath thy breath, my dearest Thisby dear.
But hark, a voice! stay thou but here awhile,
And by and by I will to thee appear.

[Exit.]

90 PUCK: A stranger Pyramus than e'er played here.

[Exit.]

FLUTE: Must I speak now?
QUINCE: Ay, marry, must you; for you must understand he goes but to see a noise that he heard,
and is to come again.
95 FLUTE: Most radiant Pyramus, most lily-white of hue,
Of colour like the red rose on triumphant brier,
Most brisky juvenal° and eke most lovely Jew,°

As true as truest horse that yet would never tire
I'll meet thee, Pyramus, at Ninny's tomb.
QUINCE: "Ninus'° tomb," man: why, you must not speak 100
that yet; that you answer to Pyramus: you speak
all your part at once, cues and all. Pyramus enter:
your cue is past; it is, "never tire."
FLUTE: O,—As true as truest horse, that yet would never
tire.   105

[Re-enter PUCK, *and* BOTTOM *with an ass's head.]*

BOTTOM: If I were fair, Thisby, I were only thine.
QUINCE: O monstrous! O strange! we are haunted.
Pray, masters! fly, masters! Help!

[Exeunt QUINCE, SNUG, FLUTE,
SNOUT, *and* STARVELING.]*

PUCK: I'll follow you, I'll lead you about a round,°
Through bog, through bush, through brake,
through brier: 110
Sometime a horse I'll be, sometime a hound,
A hog, a headless bear, sometime a fire;
And neigh, and bark, and grunt, and roar, and burn,
Like horse, hound, hog, bear, fire, at every turn.

[Exit.]

BOTTOM: Why do they run away? this is a knavery of 115
them to make me afeard.

[Re-enter SNOUT.]*

SNOUT: O Bottom, thou art changed! what do I see on
thee?
BOTTOM: What do you see? you see an ass-head of your
own, do you?   120

[Exit SNOUT.]*

[Re-enter QUINCE.]*

QUINCE: Bless thee, Bottom! bless thee! thou art
translated.°

[Exit.]

BOTTOM: I see their knavery: this is to make an ass of
me; to fright me, if they could. But I will not stir
from this place, do what they can: I will walk up 125
and down here, and I will sing, that they shall
hear I am not afraid.

[Sings.]

---

57 great chamber hall of a great house **61 disfigure** mistake for "prefigure" **70 rough-cast** coarse plaster
81 toward about to begin **97 brisky juvenal** brisk youth;
Jew nonsensical repetition of the first syllable of juvenal

100 Ninus, founder of Babylon, at whose tomb in Ovid's story
the lovers used to meet **103 about a round** round about
122 translated transformed

The ousel° cock so black of hue,
  With orange-tawny bill,
130 The throstle° with his note so true,
  The wren with little quill,°—

TITANIA: [Awakening] What angel wakes me from
  my flowery bed?

BOTTOM: [Sings.]
  The finch, the sparrow and the lark,
  The plain-song° cuckoo gray,
135 Whose note full many a man doth mark,
  And dares not answer nay;—

  for, indeed, who would set his wit to so foolish a
  bird? who would give a bird the lie, though he
  cry "cuckoo"° never so?

140 TITANIA: I pray thee, gentle mortal, sing again:
  Mine ear is much enamour'd of thy note;
  So is mine eye enthrallèd to thy shape;
  And thy fair virtue's force° perforce doth move me
  On the first view to say, to swear, I love thee.

145 BOTTOM: Methinks, mistress, you should have little
  reason for that: and yet, to say the truth, reason
  and love keep little company together now-a-
  days; the more the pity that some honest neighbours will not make them friends. Nay, I can
150 gleek° upon occasion.

TITANIA: Thou art as wise as thou art beautiful.

BOTTOM: Not so, neither: but if I had wit enough to get
  out of this wood, I have enough to serve mine
  own turn.

155 TITANIA: Out of this wood do not desire to go:
  Thou shalt remain here, whether thou wilt or no.
  I am a spirit of no common rate:°
  The summer still doth tend upon° my state;°
  And I do love thee: therefore, go with me;
160 I'll give thee fairies to attend on thee,
  And they shall fetch thee jewels from the deep,
  And sing while thou on pressèd flowers dost sleep:
  And I will purge thy mortal grossness so
  That thou shalt like an airy spirit go.
165 Peaseblossom! Cobweb! Moth! and Mustardseed!

[Enter PEASEBLOSSOM, COBWEB, MOTH, *and*
MUSTARDSEED.*]*

PEASEBLOSSOM: Ready.
COBWEB: And I.
MOTH: And I.
MUSTARDSEED: And I.

ALL: Where shall we go?

TITANIA: Be kind and courteous to this gentleman;
  Hop in his walks and gambol° in his eyes;
  Feed him with apricocks and dewberries,
  With purple grapes, green figs, and mulberries; 170
  The honey-bags steal from the humble-bees,
  And for night-tapers crop° their waxen thighs
  And light them at the fiery glow-worm's eyes,
  To have my love to bed and to arise;
  And pluck the wings from painted butterflies 175
  To fan the moonbeams from his sleeping eyes:
  Nod to him, elves, and do him courtesies.

PEASEBLOSSOM: Hail, mortal!
COBWEB: Hail!
MOTH: Hail! 180
MUSTARDSEED: Hail!

BOTTOM: I cry your worships mercy,° heartily:
  I beseech your worship's name.

COBWEB: Cobweb.

BOTTOM: I shall desire you of more acquaintance, good 185
  Master Cobweb: if I cut my finger, I shall make
  bold with you. Your name, honest gentleman?

PEASEBLOSSOM: Peaseblossom.

BOTTOM: I pray you, commend me to Mistress
  Squash,° your mother, and to Master Peascod, 190
  your father. Good Master Peaseblossom, I shall
  desire you of more acquaintance too. Your
  name, I beseech you, sir?

MUSTARDSEED: Mustardseed.

BOTTOM: Good Master Mustardseed, I know your 195
  patience° well: that same cowardly, giant-like
  ox-beef hath devoured many a gentleman of
  your house: I promise you your kindred hath
  made my eyes water ere now. I desire your
  more acquaintance, good Master Mustardseed. 200

TITANIA: Come, wait upon him; lead him to my bower.
  The moon methinks looks with a watery eye;
  And when she weeps, weeps every little flower,
  Lamenting some enforcèd° chastity.
  Tie up my love's tongue, bring him silently. 205

[Exeunt.]

Scene 2

Another part of the wood.

[Enter OBERON.*]*

OBERON: I wonder if Titania be awaked;
  Then, what it was that next° came in her eye,

---

¹²⁸ **ousel** blackbird   ¹³⁰ **throstle** thrush   ¹³¹ **quill** pipe
¹³⁴ **plain song** singing a simple air   ¹³⁹ **"cuckoo"** The word
sounded like "cuckold," which meant a deceived husband.
What married man dare contradict the bird's accusation?
¹⁴³ **fair virtue's force** the power of your beauty.   ¹⁵⁰ **gleek**
scoff   ¹⁵⁷ **rate** value, estimation   ¹⁵⁸ **still,** always; **tend upon**
serve as an attendant

---

¹⁶⁸ **gambol** caper   ¹⁷² **crop** snip off   ¹⁸² **I … mercy** I beg your
worship's pardon   ¹⁹⁰ **squash** unripe peaspod   ¹⁹⁶ **patience**
sufferings   ²⁰⁴ **enforced** violated.

SCENE 2:   ² **next** first

Which she must dote on in extremity.°

[Enter PUCK.]

　Here comes my messenger.
　　　　　　　　　　　　How now, mad spirit!
　What night-rule° now about this haunted grove?

5　PUCK: My mistress with a monster is in love.
　Near to her close and consecrated bower,
　While she was in her dull and sleeping hour,
　A crew of patches,° rude mechanicals,°
10　That work for bread upon Athenian stalls,°
　Were met together to rehearse a play
　Intended for great Theseus' nuptial-day.
　The shallowest thick-skin of that barren sort,°
　Who Pyramus presented, in their sport
15　Forsook his scene and enter'd in a brake:°
　When I did him at this advantage take,
　An ass's nole° I fixèd on his head:
　Anon his Thisby must be answerèd,
　And forth my mimic° comes. When they him spy,
20　As wild geese that the creeping fowler eye,
　Or russet-pated choughs,° many in sort,°
　Rising and cawing at the gun's report,
　Sever themselves and madly sweep the sky,
　So, at his sight, away his fellows fly;
25　And, at our stamp, here o'er and o'er one falls;
　He murder cries and help from Athens calls.
　Their sense thus weak, lost with their fears thus
　　　strong,
　Made senseless things begin to do them wrong;
　For briers and thorns at their apparel snatch;
　Some sleeves, some hats, from yielders all things
30　　catch.
　I led them on in this distracted fear,
　And left sweet Pyramus translated there:
　When in that moment, so it came to pass,
　Titania waked and straightway loved an ass.
35　OBERON: This falls out better than I could devise.
　But hast thou yet latch'd° the Athenian's eyes
　With the love-juice, as I did bid thee do?
　PUCK: I took him sleeping,—that is finish'd too,—
　And the Athenian woman by his side;
40　That, when he waked, of force° she must be eyed.

[Enter HERMIA and DEMETRIUS.]

OBERON: Stand close:° this is the same Athenian.
PUCK: This is the woman, but not this the man.

DEMETRIUS: O, why rebuke you him that loves you
　　so?
　Lay breath so bitter on your bitter foe.
HERMIA: Now I but chide; but I should use thee
　　worse,　　　　　　　　　　　　　　　　　　45
　For thou, I fear, hast given me cause to curse.
　If thou hast slain Lysander in his sleep,
　Being o'er shoes in blood, plunge in the deep,
　And kill me too.
　The sun was not so true unto the day　　　　　50
　As he to me: would he have stolen away
　From sleeping Hermia? I'll believe as soon
　The whole earth may be bored and that the moon
　May through the centre° creep and so displease
　Her brother's noontide with the Antipodes.　　55
　It cannot be but thou hast murder'd him;
　So should a murderer look, so dead,° so grim.
DEMETRIUS: So should the murder'd look, and so
　　should I,
　Pierced through the heart with your stern cruelty:
　Yet you, the murderer, look as bright, as clear,　60
　As yonder Venus in her glimmering sphere.
HERMIA: What's this to my Lysander? where is he?
　Ah, good Demetrius, wilt thou give him me?
DEMETRIUS: I had rather give his carcass to my
　　hounds.
HERMIA: Out, dog! out, cur! thou drivest me past the
　　bounds　　　　　　　　　　　　　　　　　65
　Of maiden's patience. Hast thou slain him, then?
　Henceforth be never number'd among men!
　O, once tell true, tell true, even for my sake!
　Durst thou have look'd upon him being awake,
　And hast thou kill'd him sleeping? O brave touch°　70
　Could not a worm,° an adder, do so much?
　An adder did it; for with doubler tongue
　Than thine, thou serpent, never adder stung.
DEMETRIUS: You spend your passion on a misprised
　　mood:°
　I am not guilty of Lysander's blood;　　　　　75
　Nor is he dead, for aught that I can tell.
HERMIA: I pray thee, tell me then that he is well.
DEMETRIUS: And if I could, what should I get there-
　　fore?
HERMIA: A privilege never to see me more.
　And from thy hated presence part I so:　　　　80
　See me no more, whether he be dead or no.

[Exit.]

DEMETRIUS: There is no following her in this fierce
　　vein:°

---

³ **in extremity** extremely　⁵ **night-rule** mischief　⁹ **patch-es** clowns, dolts　**mechanicals** laborers　¹⁰ **upon Athenian stalls** in Athenian shops　¹³ **barren sort** stupid crowd　¹⁵ **brake** thicket　¹⁷ **nole** head　¹⁹ **mimic** buffoon　²¹ **rus-set-pated choughs** gray-headed grackles　**in sort** together　³⁶ **latch'd** charmed　⁴⁰ **of force** of necessity　⁴¹ **close** hid-den

⁵⁴ **center** i.e., of the earth　⁵⁷ **dead** deadly　⁷⁰ **brave touch** splendid exploit　⁷¹ **worm** snake　⁷⁴ **on a misprised mood** in mistaken anger　⁸² **in . . . vein** while she is in this fierce mood

Here therefore for a while I will remain.
So sorrow's heaviness doth heavier grow
85   For debt that bankrupt sleep doth sorrow owe;
Which now in some slight measure it will pay,
If for his tender here I make some stay.°

[Lies down and sleeps.]

OBERON: What has thou done? thou hast mistaken
quite
And laid the love-juice on some true-love's sight:
90   Of thy misprision° must perforce ensue
Some true love turn'd and not a false turn'd true.
PUCK: Then fate o'er-rules, that, one man holding
troth,
A million fail, confounding oath on oath.
OBERON: About the wood go swifter than the wind,
95   And Helena of Athens look thou find:
All fancy-sick° she is and pale of cheer,°
With sighs of love,° that costs the fresh blood
dear:
By some illusion° see thou bring her here:
I'll charm his eyes against° she do appear.
100   PUCK: I go, I go; look how I go,
Swifter than arrow from the Tartar's bow.

[Exit.]

OBERON: Flower of this purple dye,
Hit with Cupid's archery,
Sink in apple of his eye.
105   When his love he doth espy,
Let her shine as gloriously
As the Venus of the sky.
When thou wakest, if she be by,
Beg of her for remedy.

[Re-enter PUCK.*]*

110   PUCK: Captain of our fairy band,
Helena is here at hand;
And the youth, mistook by me,
Pleading for a lover's fee.
Shall we their fond pageant° see?
115   Lord, what fools these mortals be!
OBERON: Stand aside: the noise they make
Will cause Demetrius to awake.
PUCK: Then will two at once woo one;
That must needs be sport alone;
120   And those things do best please me

That befall preposterously.°

[Enter LYSANDER *and* HELENA.*]*

LYSANDER: Why should you think that I should woo
in scorn?
Scorn and derision never come in tears:
Look, when I vow, I weep; and vows so born,
In their nativity all truth appears.°   125
How can these things in me seem scorn to you,
Bearing the badge of faith, to prove them true?
HELENA: You do advance your cunning more and
more.
When truth kills truth, O devilish-holy fray!
These vows are Hermia's: will you give her o'er?   130
Weigh oath with oath, and you will nothing
weigh:
Your vows to her and me, put in two scales,
Will even weigh, and both as light as tales.
LYSANDER: I had no judgement when to her I swore.
HELENA: Nor none, in my mind, now you give her
o'er.   135
LYSANDER: Demetrius loves her, and he loves not
you.
DEMETRIUS: [*Awaking*] O Helen, goddess, nymph, per-
fect, divine!
To what, my love, shall I compare thine eyne?
Crystal is muddy. O, how ripe in show
Thy lips, those kissing cherries, tempting grow!   140
That pure congealèd white, high Taurus° snow,
Fann'd with the eastern wind, turns to a crow
When thou hold'st up thy hand: O, let me kiss
This princess of pure white, this seal° of bliss!
HELENA: O spite! O hell! I see you all are bent   145
To set against me for your merriment:
If you were civil and knew courtesy,
You would not do me thus much injury.
Can you not hate me, as I know you do,
But you must join in souls to mock me too?   150
If you were men, as men you are in show,
You would not use a gentle lady so;
To vow, and swear, and superpraise° my parts,
When I am sure you hate me with your hearts.
You both are rivals, and love Hermia;   155
And now both rivals, to mock Helena:
A trim° exploit, a manly enterprise,
To conjure tears up in a poor maid's eyes
With your derision! none of noble sort
Would so offend a virgin and extort°   160

---

87 **If . . . stay** if I wait for sleep's offer [of himself]   50 **mispri-
sion** mistake   96 **fancy-sick** love-sick **cheer** face   97 **sighs
of love** allusion to the belief that each sigh costs the heart a
drop of blood   98 **illusion** deception   99 **against** by the time
that   114 **fond pageant** silly spectacle

121 **preposterously** contrary to reason   124 **vows . . . appears**
i.e., vows born in tears seem at their birth to be wholly true.
141 **Taurus** a mountain range in Asia Minor   144 **seal**
pledge, ratification   153 **superpraise** overpraise   157 **trim**
fine (used ironically)   160 **extort** torture

A poor soul's patience, all to make you sport.
LYSANDER: You are unkind, Demetrius; be not so;
     For you love Hermia; this you know I know:
     And here, with all good will, with all my heart,
165   In Hermia's love I yield you up my part;
     And yours of Helena to me bequeath,
     Whom I do love and will do till my death.
HELENA: Never did mockers waste more idle breath.
DEMETRIUS: Lysander, keep thy Hermia; I will none:°
170   If e'er I loved her, all that love is gone.
     My heart to her but as guest-wise sojourn'd,°
     And now to Helen is it home return'd,
     There to remain.
LYSANDER: Helen, it is not so.
DEMETRIUS: Disparage not the faith thou dost not
     know,
175   Lest, to thy peril, thou aby° it dear.
     Look, where thy love comes; yonder is thy dear.

[Re-enter HERMIA.*]*

HERMIA: Dark night, that from the eye his° function
     takes,
     The ear more quick of apprehension makes;
     Wherein it doth impair the seeing sense,
180   It pays the hearing double recompense.
     Thou art not by mine eye, Lysander, found;
     Mine ear, I thank it, brought me to thy sound
     But why unkindly didst thou leave me so?
LYSANDER: Why should he stay, whom love doth
     press to go?
HERMIA: What love could press Lysander from my
185   side?
LYSANDER: Lysander's love, that would not let him
     bide,
     Fair Helena, who more engilds the night
     Than all yon fiery oes° and eyes of light.
     Why seek'st thou me? could not this make thee
     know,
190   The hate I bear thee made me leave thee so?
HERMIA: You speak not as you think: it cannot be.
HELENA: Lo, she is one of this confederacy!
     Now I perceive they have conjoin'd all three
     To fashion this false sport, in spite of me.
195   Injurious° Hermia! most ungrateful maid!
     Have you conspired, have you with these con-
     trived
     To bait me with this foul derision?
     Is all the counsel that we two have shared,
     The sisters' vows, the hours that we have spent,
200   When we have chid the hasty-footed time
     For parting us,—O, is it all forgot?

All school-days' friendship, childhood innocence?
We, Hermia, like two artificial° gods,
Have with our needles created both one flower,
Both on one sampler,° sitting on one cushion,   205
Both warbling of one song, both in one key,
As if our hands, our sides, voices and minds,
Had been incorporate.° So we grew together,
Like to a double cherry, seeming parted,
But yet an union in partition;   210
Two lovely berries moulded on one stem;
So, with two seeming bodies, but one heart;
Two of the first, like coats in heraldry,
Due but to one and crownèd with one crest.°
And will you rent our ancient love asunder,   215
To join with men in scorning your poor friend?
It is not friendly, 'tis not maidenly:
Our sex, as well as I, may chide you for it,
Though I alone do feel the injury.
HERMIA: I am amazèd at your passionate words.   220
     I scorn you not: it seems that you scorn me.
HELENA: Have you not set Lysander, as in scorn,
     To follow me and praise my eyes and face?
     And made your other love, Demetrius,
     Who even but now did spurn me with his foot,   225
     To call me goddess, nymph, divine and rare,
     Precious, celestial? Wherefore speaks he this
     To her he hates? and wherefore doth Lysander
     Deny your love, so rich within his soul,
     And tender me, forsooth, affection,   230
     But by your setting on, by your consent?
     What though I be not so in grace as you,
     So hung upon with love, so fortunate,
     But miserable most, to love unloved?
     This you should pity rather than despise.   235
HERMIA: I understand not what you mean by this.
HELENA: Ay, do, persèver,° counterfeit sad° looks,
     Make mouths upon° me when I turn my back;
     Wink each at other; hold the sweet jest up:
     This sport, well carried, shall be chronicled.   240
     If you have any pity, grace, or manners,
     You would not make me such an argument.°
     But fare ye well: 'tis partly my own fault;
     Which death or absence soon shall remedy.
LYSANDER: Stay, gentle Helena; hear my excuse: 245
     My love, my life, my soul, fair Helena!
HELENA: O excellent!
HERMIA: Sweet, do not scorn her so.
DEMETRIUS: If she cannot entreat, I can compel.

---

169 **will none** i.e., none of her   171 **as guest-sojourned** has made a short stay   175 **aby** atone for   177 **his** its   188 **oes** circles, i.e., stars   195 **injurious** insulting

203 **artificial** skilled in art   205 **sampler** a piece of embroidery   208 **incorporate** parts of the same body   213–4 **Two . . . one crest** i.e., the two bodies are like the double coats of arms which belong to husband and wife, yet have but one crest, as we have but one heart.   237 **persèver** persevere; sad, serious   238 **make mouths upon** make faces at   242 **argument** plot for a story

LYSANDER: Thou canst compel no more than she
    entreat:
      Thy threats have no more strength than her weak
250   prayers.
      Helen, I love thee; by my life, I do:
      I swear by that which I will lose for thee,
      To prove him false that says I love thee not.
DEMETRIUS: I say I love thee more than he can do.
255 LYSANDER: If thou say so, withdraw, and prove it too.
DEMETRIUS: Quick, come!
HERMIA: Lysander, whereto tends all this?
LYSANDER: Away, you Ethiope!
DEMETRIUS: No, no; he'll . . .
      Seem to break loose; take on as you would follow,
      But yet come not: you are a tame man, go!
LYSANDER: Hang off,° thou cat, thou burr! vile thing,
260   let loose,
      Or I will shake thee from me like a serpent!
HERMIA: Why are you grown so rude? what change
    is this?
      Sweet love,—
LYSANDER: Thy love! out, tawny Tartar, out!
      Out, loathèd medicine! hated potion, hence!
HERMIA: Do you not jest?
265 HELENA: Yes, sooth; and so do you.
LYSANDER: Demetrius, I will keep my word with
    thee.
DEMETRIUS: I would I had your bond,° for I perceive
      A weak bond holds you: I'll not trust your word.
LYSANDER: What, should I hurt her, strike her, kill her
    dead?
270   Although I hate her, I'll not harm her so.
HERMIA: What, can you do me greater harm than
    hate?
      Hate me! wherefore? O me! what news,° my love!
      Am not I Hermia? are not you Lysander?
      I am as fair now as I was erewhile.°
      Since night you loved me; yet since night you left
275   me:
      Why, then you left me—O, the gods forbid!—
      In earnest, shall I say?
LYSANDER: Ay, by my life;
      And never did desire to see thee more.
      Therefore be out of hope, of question, of doubt;
280   Be certain, nothing truer; 'tis no jest
      That I do hate thee and love Helena.
HERMIA: O me! you juggler!° you canker-blossom!°
      You thief of love! what, have you come by night
      And stolen my love's heart from him?
HELENA: Fine, i' faith!
285   Have you no modesty, no maiden shame,

No touch of bashfulness? What, will you tear
      Impatient answers from my gentle tongue?
      Fie, fie! you counterfeit, you puppet,° you!
HERMIA: Puppet? why so? ay, that way goes the
    game.
      Now I perceive that she hath made compare   290
      Between our statures; she hath urged her height;
      And with her personage, her tall personage,
      Her height, forsooth, she hath prevail'd with him.
      And are you grown so high in his esteem,
      Because I am so dwarfish and so low?   295
      How low am I, thou painted maypole? speak;
      How low am I? I am not yet so low
      But that my nails can reach unto thine eyes.
HELENA: I pray you, though you mock me, gentle-
    men,
      Let her not hurt me: I was never curst;°   300
      I have no gift at all in shrewishness;
      I am a right maid for my cowardice:°
      Let her not strike me. You perhaps may think,
      Because she is something lower than myself,
      That I can match her.
HERMIA: Lower! hark, again.   305
HELENA: Good Hermia, do not be so bitter with me.
      I evermore did love you, Hermia,
      Did ever keep your counsels, never wrong'd you;
      Save that, in love unto Demetrius,
      I told him of your stealth° unto this wood.   310
      He follow'd you; for love I follow'd him;
      But he hath chid me hence and threaten'd me
      To strike me, spurn° me, nay, to kill me too:
      And now, so you will let me quiet go,
      To Athens will I bear my folly back   315
      And follow you no further: let me go:
      You see how simple and how fond I am.
HERMIA: Why, get you gone: who is't that hinders you?
HELENA: A foolish heart, that I leave here behind.
HERMIA: What, with Lysander?   320
HELENA: With Demetrius.
LYSANDER: Be not afraid; she shall not harm thee,
    Helena.
DEMETRIUS: No, sir, she shall not, though you take
    her part.
HELENA: O, when she's angry, she is keen and
    shrewd!°
      She was a vixen when she went to school;
      And though she be but little, she is fierce.   325
HERMIA: "Little" again! nothing but "low" and "little"!
      Why will you suffer her to flout me thus?

---

²⁶⁰ **hang off** let go   ²⁶⁷ **bond** written agreement   ²⁷² **what
news** i.e., what's the matter   ²⁷⁴ **erewhile** a little while ago
²⁸² **juggler** deceiver; **canker-blossom** canker worm

²⁸⁸ **puppet** doll-like person; the epithet suggests that she was
very small. Cf. dwarfish, line 295   ³⁰⁰ **curst** shrewish   ³⁰² **I .
. . cowardice** in my lack of courage I am a true woman   ³¹⁰
stealth stealing away   ³¹³ **spurn** kick   ³²³ **shrewd,** sharp-
tongued

Let me come to her.
LYSANDER: Get you gone, you dwarf;
   You minimus,° of hindering knot-grass° made;
   You bead, you acorn.
330   DEMETRIUS: You are too officious
   In her behalf that scorns your services.
   Let her alone: speak not of Helena;
   Take not her part; for, if thou dost intend°
   Never so little show of love to her,
335   Thou shalt aby° it.
LYSANDER: Now she holds me not;
   Now follow, if thou darest, to try whose right,
   Of thine or mine, is most in Helena.
DEMETRIUS: Follow! nay, I'll go with thee, cheek by
      jole.° [*Exeunt* LYSANDER *and* DEMETRIUS.]
HERMIA: You, mistress, all this coil° is 'long of you:
340   Nay, go not back.
HELENA: I will not trust you, I,
   Nor longer stay in your curst company.
   Your hands than mine are quicker for a fray,
   My legs are longer though, to run away.

[*Exit.*]

HERMIA: I am amazed, and know not what to say.

[*Exit.*]

345   OBERON: This is thy negligence:° still thou mistakest,
   Or else committ'st thy knaveries wilfully.
PUCK: Believe me, king of shadows, I mistook.
   Did not you tell me I should know the man
   By the Athenian garments he had on?
350   And so far blameless proves my enterprise,
   That I have 'nointed an Athenian's eyes;
   And so far am I glad it so did sort°
   As this their jangling° I esteem a sport.
OBERON: Thou see'st these lovers seek a place to fight:
355   Hie therefore, Robin, overcast the night;
   The starry welkin cover thou anon
   With drooping fog as black as Acheron,°
   And lead these testy rivals so astray
   As° one come not within another's way.
360   Like to Lysander sometime frame thy tongue,
   Then stir Demetrius up with bitter wrong;°
   And sometime rail thou like Demetrius;
   And from each other look thou lead them thus,
   Till o'er their brows death-counterfeiting sleep
365   With leaden legs and batty wings doth creep:
   Then crush this herb into Lysander's eye;

Whose liquor hath this virtuous° property,
To take from thence all error with his might,°
And make his eyeballs roll with wonted sight.
When they next wake, all this derision   370
Shall seem a dream and fruitless vision,
And back to Athens shall the lovers wend,
With league whose date till death shall never end.
Whiles I in this affair do thee employ,
I'll to my queen and beg her Indian boy: 375
And then I will her charmèd eye release
From monster's view, and all things shall be peace.
PUCK: My fairy lord, this must be done with haste,
   For night's swift dragons° cut the clouds full fast,
   And yonder shines Aurora's harbinger;°   380
   At whose approach, ghosts, wandering here and
      there,
   Troop home to churchyards: damnèd spirits all,
   That in crossways° and floods have burial,
   Already to their wormy beds are gone;
   For fear lest day should look their shames upon,   385
   They wilfully themselves exile from light
   And must for aye consort with black-brow'd
      night.
OBERON: But we are spirits of another sort:°
   I with the morning's love° have oft made sport,
   And, like a forester, the groves may tread,   390
   Even till the eastern gate, all fiery-red,
   Opening on Neptune with fair blessèd beams,
   Turns into yellow gold his salt green streams.
   But, notwithstanding, haste; make no delay:
   We may effect this business yet ere day.   395

[*Exit.*]

PUCK: Up and down, up and down,
   I will lead them up and down:
   I am fear'd in field and town:
   Goblin, lead them up and down.

   Here comes one.   400

[*Re-enter* LYSANDER.]

LYSANDER: Where art thou, proud Demetrius?
   speak thou now.

PUCK: Here, villain; drawn° and ready.
    Where art thou?
LYSANDER: I will be with thee straight.
PUCK: Follow me, then,
    To plainer° ground.

[Exit LYSANDER, as following the voice.]

[Re-enter DEMETRIUS.]

DEMETRIUS: Lysander! speak again:
405   Thou runaway, thou coward, art thou fled?
    Speak! In some bush? Where dost thou hide thy
        head?
PUCK: Thou coward, art thou bragging to the stars,
    Telling the bushes that thou look'st for wars,
    And wilt not come? Come, recreant;° come, thou
        child,
410   I'll whip thee with a rod: he is defiled
    That draws a sword on thee.
DEMETRIUS: Yea, art thou there?
PUCK: Follow my voice: we'll try no manhood here.

[Exeunt.]

[Re-enter LYSANDER.]

LYSANDER: He goes before me and still dares me on:
    When I come where he calls, then he is gone.
415   The villain is much lighter-heel'd than I:
    I follow'd fast, but faster he did fly;
    That fallen am I in dark uneven way,
    And here will rest me. *[Lies down.]* Come, thou
        gentle day!
    For if but once thou show me thy grey light,
420   I'll find Demetrius and revenge this spite.

[Sleeps.]

[Re-enter PUCK and DEMETRIUS.]

PUCK: Ho, ho, ho! Coward, why comest thou not?
DEMETRIUS: Abide me, if thou darest; for well I wot°
    Thou runn'st before me, shifting every place.
    And darest not stand, nor look me in the face.
    Where art thou now?
425   PUCK: Come hither: I am here.
DEMETRIUS: Nay, then, thou mock'st me. Thou shalt
        buy this dear,
    If ever I thy face by daylight see:
    Now, go thy way. Faintness constraineth me
    To measure out my length on this cold bed.
430   By day's approach look to be visited.

[Lies down and sleeps.]

[Re-enter HELENA.]

HELENA: O weary night, O long and tedious night,
    Abate° thy hours! Shine comforts from the east,
    That I may back to Athens by daylight,
    From these that my poor company detest:
    And sleep, that sometimes shuts up sorrow's eye,   435
    Steal me awhile from mine own company.

[Lies down and sleeps.]

PUCK: Yet but three? Come one more;
    Two of both kinds makes up four.
    Here she comes, curse° and sad:
    Cupid is a knavish lad,   440
    Thus to make poor females mad.

[Re-enter HERMIA.]

HERMIA: Never so weary, never so in woe,
    Bedabbled with the dew and torn with briers,
    I can no further crawl, no further go;
    My legs can keep no pace with my desires.   445
    Here will I rest me till the break of day.
    Heavens shield Lysander, if they mean a fray!

[Lies down and sleeps.]

PUCK: On the ground
                            Sleep sound:
                                I'll apply
                            To your eye,
    Gentle lover, remedy.   450

[Squeezing the juice on LYSANDER's eyes.]

                    When thou wakest,
                        Thou takest
                        True delight   455
                        In the sight
                    Of thy former lady's eye:
    And the country proverb known,
    That every man should take his own,
    In your waking shall be shown: 460
                        Jack shall have Jill;
                        Nought shall go ill;
    The man shall have his mare again, and all shall
        be well.

[Exit.]

---

402 **drawn** with sword drawn   404 **plainer** more level
409 **recreant** coward   422 **wot** know

432 **abate** shorten   439 **curst** shrewish

ACT IV

Scene 1

The same. LYSANDER, DEMETRIUS, HELENA, *and* HERMIA
lying asleep.

[*Enter* TITANIA *and* BOTTOM; PEASEBLOSSOM. COBWEB,
MOTH, MUSTARDSEED, *and other* FAIRIES *attending;*
OBERON *behind unseen.*]

TITANIA: Come, sit thee down upon this flowery bed,
    While I thy amiable cheeks do coy,°
  And stick musk-roses in thy sleek smooth head,
    And kiss thy fair large ears, my gentle joy.
5 BOTTOM: Where's Peaseblossom?
PEASEBLOSSOM: Ready.
BOTTOM: Scratch my head, Peaseblossom. Where's
  Mounsieur Cobweb?
COBWEB: Ready.
10 BOTTOM: Mounsieur Cobweb, good mounsieur, get
  you your weapons in your hand, and kill me a
  red-hipped humble-bee on the top of a thistle;
  and, good mounsieur, bring me the honey-bag.
  Do not fret yourself too much in the action,
15   mounsieur; and, good mounsieur, have a care
  the honey-bag break not; I would be loath to
  have you overflown with a honey-bag, signior.
  Where's Mounsieur Mustardseed?
MUSTARDSEED: Ready.
20 BOTTOM: Give me your neaf,° Mounsieur Mustardseed.
  Pray you, leave your courtesy,° good mounsieur.
MUSTARDSEED: What's your will?
BOTTOM: Nothing, good mounsieur, but to help
  Cavalery Cobweb to scratch. I must to the bar-
25   ber's, mounsieur; for methinks I am marvellous
  hairy about the face; and I am such a tender ass,
  if my hair do but tickle me, I must scratch.
TITANIA: What, wilt thou hear some music, my sweet
  love?
BOTTOM: I have a reasonable good ear in music. Let's
30   have the tongs and the bones.°
TITANIA: Or say, sweet love, what thou desirest to eat.
BOTTOM: Truly, a peck of provender: I could munch
  your good dry oats. Methinks I have a great
  desire to a bottle° of hay: good hay, sweet hay,
35   hath no fellow.
TITANIA: I have a venturous fairy that shall seek
  The squirrel's hoard, and fetch thee new nuts.

BOTTOM: I had rather have a handful or two
  of dried peas. But, I pray you, let none of
  your people stir me: I have an exposition of   40
  sleep come upon me.
TITANIA: Sleep thou, and I will wind thee in my
  arms.
  Fairies, be gone, and be all ways° away.

        [*Exeunt* FAIRIES.]

So doth the woodbine the sweet honeysuckle
  Gentle entwist; the female ivy so   45
  Enrings the barky fingers of the elm.
  O, how I love thee! how I dote on thee!

[*They sleep.*]

[*Enter* PUCK.]

OBERON: [*Advancing*] Welcome, good Robin.
  See'st thou this sweet sight?
  Her dotage now I do begin to pity: 50
  For, meeting her of late behind the wood,
  Seeking sweet favours° for this hateful fool,
  I did upbraid her and fall out with her;
  For she his hairy temples then had rounded
  With coronet of fresh and fragrant flowers;   55
  And that same dew, which sometime on the buds
  Was wont to swell like round and orient° pearls,
  Stood now within the pretty flowerets' eyes
  Like tears that did their own disgrace bewail.
  When I had at my pleasure taunted her   60
  And she in mild terms begg'd my patience,
  I then did ask of her changeling child;
  Which straight she gave me, and her fairy sent
  To bear him to my bower in fairy land.
  And now I have the boy, I will undo   65
  This hateful imperfection of her eyes:
  And, gentle Puck, take this transformèd scalp
  From off the head of this Athenian swain;
  That, he awaking when the other° do,
  May all to Athens back again repair   70
  And think no more of this night's accidents
  But as the fierce° vexation of a dream.
  But first I will release the fairy queen.
    Be as thou wast wont to be;
    See as thou wast wont to see: 75
    Dian's bud° o'er Cupid's flower
    Hath such force and blessèd power.
  Now, my Titania; wake you, my sweet queen.

ACT IV, SCENE 1: ² **coy** stroke, caress ²⁰ **neaf** fist ²¹ **leave
your courtesy** i.e., put on your hat ²⁴ **Cavalery,** cavaliero,
i.e., gentleman. ³¹ **tongs and bones** crude musical instruments: tongs—a kind of triangle; bones—clappers ³⁴ **bottle**
bundle (of hay)

⁴⁰ **exposition of** Bottom means "disposition to." ⁴³ **all
ways** in every direction ⁵³ **favours** nosegays ⁵⁷ **orient**
lustrous, because the most beautiful pearls were supposed to
come from the Orient ⁶⁹ **other** others ⁷² **fierce** violent
⁷⁶ **Dian's bud** a plant, agnus castus, which was supposed to
preserve chastity

TITANIA: My Oberon! what visions have I seen!
    Methought I was enamour'd of an ass.
80 OBERON: There lies your love.
TITANIA: How came these things to pass?
    O, how mine eyes do loathe his visage now!
OBERON: Silence awhile. Robin, take off this head.
    Titania, music call; and strike more dead
    Than common sleep° of all these five° the sense.
TITANIA: Music, ho! music, such as charmeth sleep!

[Music, still.°]

PUCK: Now, when thou wakest, with thine own fool's
    eyes peep.°
OBERON: Sound, music! Come, my queen, take hands
    with me,
90   And rock the ground whereon these sleepers be.
    Now thou and I are new in amity
    And will to-morrow midnight solemnly
    Dance in Duke Theseus' house triumphantly
    And bless it to all fair prosperity:
95   There shall the pair of faithful lovers be
    Wedded, with Theseus, all in jollity.

PUCK: Fairy king, attend, and mark:
    I do hear the morning lark.
OBERON: Then, my queen, in silence sad,°
100 Trip we after night's shade:
    We the globe can compass soon,
    Swifter than the wandering moon.
TITANIA: Come, my lord, and in our flight
    Tell me how it came this night
105 That I sleeping here was found
    With these mortals on the ground.

[Exeunt.]

[Horns winded within.]

[Enter THESEUS, HIPPOLYTA, EGEUS, *and train.]*

THESEUS: Go, one of you, find out the forester;
    For now our observation° is perform'd;
    And since we have the vaward° of the day,
110 My love shall hear the music of my hounds.
    Uncouple in the western valley; let them go:
    Dispatch,° I say, and find the forester.

[Exit an ATTENDANT.*]*

We will, fair queen, up to the mountain's top
And mark the musical confusion

Of hounds and echo in conjunction.   115
HIPPOLYTA: I was with Hercules and Cadmus once,
    When in a wood of Crete they bay'd the bear
    With hounds of Sparta: never did I hear
    Such gallant chiding;° for, besides the groves,
    The skies, the fountains, every region near   120
    Seem'd all one mutual cry: I never heard
    So musical a discord, such sweet thunder.
THESEUS: My hounds are bred out of the Spartan kind,
    So flew'd,° so sanded,° and their heads are hung
    With ears that sweep away the morning dew;   125
    Crook-knee'd, and dew-lapp'd like Thessalian bulls;
    Slow in pursuit, but match'd in mouth° like bells,
    Each under each.° A cry° more tuneable
    Was never holla'd to, nor cheer'd with horn,
    In Crete, in Sparta, nor in Thessaly: 130
    Judge when you hear. But, soft! what nymphs are
    these?
EGEUS: My lord, this is my daughter here asleep;
    And this, Lysander; this Demetrius is;
    This Helena, old Nedar's Helena:
    I wonder of their being here together.   135
THESEUS: No doubt they rose up early to observe
    The rite of May, and, hearing our intent,
    Came here in grace of our solemnity.°
    But speak, Egeus; is not this the day
    That Hermia should give answer of her choice?   140
EGEUS: It is, my lord.
THESEUS: Go, bid the huntsmen wake them with their
    horns.

[Horns and shout within.° LYSANDER, DEMETRIUS,
HELENA, *and* HERMIA, *wake and start up.]*

Good morrow, friends. Saint Valentine is past:
    Begin these wood-birds but to couple now?°
LYSANDER: Pardon, my lord.
THESEUS: I pray you all, stand up.   145
    I know you two are rival enemies:
    How comes this gentle concord in the world,
    That hatred is so far from jealousy,
    To sleep by hate, and fear no enmity?
LYSANDER: My lord, I shall reply amazedly,   150
    Half sleep, half waking: but as yet, I swear,
    I cannot truly say how I came here;
    But, as I think,—for truly would I speak,
    And now I do bethink me, so it is,—
    I came with Hermia hither: our intent   155

---

85 **strike . . . sleep** make them sleep more soundly than normal   **these five** Bottom and the two pair of lovers   87 **s.d. Music, still** continuous music   88 **peep** take a look   99 **sad** serious   108 **observation** May Day rites   109 **vaward** vanguard, i.e., early part   112 **Dispatch** hurry   119 **chiding** clamor   124 **flew'd** with large hanging chaps **sanded** of a sandy color   127 **mouth** voice. Elizabethan huntsmen chose hounds whose baying would make harmony.   128 **Each under each** each harmonious with the rest; **cry** pack of hounds   138 **in grace of our solemnity** to do honor to our wedding ceremony   142 **s.d. within** offstage   144 **Begin . . . couple now** birds were supposed to choose their mates on St. Valentine's Day.

Was to be gone from Athens, where° we might,
Without° the peril of the Athenian law.
EGEUS: Enough, enough, my lord; you have enough:°
I beg the law, the law, upon his head.
They would have stolen away: they would,
160   Demetrius,
Thereby to have defeated you and me,
You of your wife and me of my consent,
Of my consent that she should be your wife.
DEMETRIUS: My lord, fair Helen told me of their stealth,
165   Of this their purpose hither to this wood;
And I in fury hither follow'd them,
Fair Helena in fancy° following me.
But, my good lord, I wot not by what power,—
But by some power it is,—my love to Hermia,
170   Melted as the snow, seems to me now
As the remembrance of an idle gawd°
Which in my childhood I did dote upon;
And all the faith, the virtue of my heart,
The object and the pleasure of mine eye,
175   Is only Helena. To her, my lord,
Was I betroth'd ere I saw Hermia:
But, like in sickness, did I loathe this food;
But, as in health, come to my natural taste,
Now I do wish it, love it, long for it,
180   And will for evermore be true to it.
THESEUS: Fair lovers, you are fortunately met:
Of this discourse we more will hear anon.
Egeus, I will overbear your will;
For in the temple, by and by,° with us
185   These couples shall eternally be knit:
And, for the morning now is something worn,
Our purposed hunting shall be set aside.
Away with us to Athens; three and three,
We'll hold a feast in great solemnity.
190   Come, Hippolyta.

[Exeunt THESEUS, HIPPOLYTA, EGEUS, and train.]

DEMETRIUS: These things seem small and undistin-
guishable,
Like far-off mountains turned into clouds.
HERMIA: Methinks I see these things with parted eye,°
When every thing seems double.
HELENA: So methinks:
195   And I have found Demetrius like a jewel,
Mine own, and not mine own.
DEMETRIUS: Are you sure
That we are awake? It seems to me
That yet we sleep, we dream. Do not you think
The duke was here, and bid us follow him?

HERMIA: Yea; and my father.   200
HELENA: And Hippolyta.
LYSANDER: And he did bid us follow to the temple.
DEMETRIUS: Why, then, we are awake: let's follow him;
And by the way let us recount our dreams.

[Exeunt.]

BOTTOM: [*Awaking*] When my cue comes, call me, and
I will answer: my next is, "Most fair Pyramus." 205
Heigh-ho! Peter Quince! Flute, the bellows-
mender! Snout, the tinker! Starveling! God's my
life, stolen hence, and left me asleep! I have had
a most rare vision I have had a dream, past the
wit of man to say what dream it was: man is but 210
an ass, if he go about° to expound this dream.
Methought I was—there is no man can tell
what. Methought I was,—and methought I
had,—but man is but a patched° fool, if he will
offer to say what methought I had. The eye of 215
man hath not heard, the ear of man hath not
seen, man's hand is not able to taste, his tongue
to conceive, nor his heart to report, what my
dream was. I will get Peter Quince to write a
ballad of this dream: it shall be called Bottom's 220
Dream, because it hath no bottom; and I will
sing it in the latter end of a play, before the
duke: peradventure, to make it the more gracious, I shall sing it at her death.

[Exit.]

Scene 2

Athens. QUINCE*'s house.*

[Enter QUINCE, FLUTE, SNOUT, *and* STARVELING.*]*

QUINCE: Have you sent to Bottom's house? is he come
home yet?
STARVELING: He cannot be heard of. Out of doubt he is
transported.°
FLUTE: If he come not, then the play is marred: it goes 5
not forward, doth it?
QUINCE: It is not possible: you have not a man in all
Athens able to discharge Pyramus but he.
FLUTE: No, he hath simply the best wit of any handi-
craft man in Athens. 10
QUINCE: Yea, and the best person too; and he is a very
paramour for a sweet voice.
FLUTE: You must say 'paragon:' a paramour is, God
bless us, a thing of naught.° 15

---

156 **where** whereever 157 **without** beyond the reach of
158 **enough** i.e., enough to convict him 167 **in fancy** out of
love 171 **idle gawd** worthless trifle 184 **by and by** immediately 193 **parted eye** unfocused eyes

211 **go about** attempt 214 **patched** dressed in motley

SCENE 2:   4 **transported** carried off 15 **a thing of naught**
wicked things

[Enter SNUG.*]*

SNUG: Masters, the duke is coming from the temple,
and there is two or three lords and ladies more
married: if our sport had gone forward, we had
all been made men.

20 FLUTE: O sweet bully Bottom! Thus hath he lost sixpence a day during his life; he could not have
'scaped sixpence a day:° an the duke had not
given him sixpence a day for playing Pyramus,
I'll be hanged; he would have deserved it: six-
25 pence a day in Pyramus, or nothing.

[Enter BOTTOM.*]*

BOTTOM: Where are these lads? where are these
hearts?°
QUINCE: Bottom! O most courageous day! O most
happy hour!
30 BOTTOM: Masters, I am to discourse wonders: but ask
me not what; for if I tell you, I am no true
Athenian. I will tell you every thing, right as it
fell out.
QUINCE: Let us hear, sweet Bottom.
35 BOTTOM: Not a word of me. All that I will tell you is,
that the duke hath dined. Get your apparel
together, good strings to your beards, new ribbons to your pumps; meet presently° at the
palace; every man look o'er his part; for the
40 short and the long is, our play is preferred.° In
any case, let Thisby have clean linen; and let not
him that plays the lion pare his nails, for they
shall hang out for the lion's claws. And, most
dear actors, eat no onions nor garlic, for we are
45 to utter sweet breath; and I do not doubt but to
hear them say, it is a sweet comedy. No more
words: away! go, away!

[Exeunt.]

ACT V

Scene 1

Athens. The palace of THESEUS.

[Enter THESEUS, HIPPOLYTA, PHILOSTRATE, LORDS, *and*
ATTENDANTS.*]*

HIPPOLYTA: 'Tis strange, my Theseus, that these
lovers speak of.

THESEUS: More strange than true: I never may°
believe
These antique° fables, nor these fairy toys.°
Lovers and madmen have such seething brains,
Such shaping fantasies, that apprehend   5
More than cool reason ever comprehends.
The lunatic, the lover and the poet
Are of imagination all compact:°
One sees more devils than vast hell can hold,
That is, the madman: the lover, all as frantic,   10
Sees Helen's beauty in a brow of Egypt:°
The poet's eye, in a fine frenzy rolling,
Doth glance from heaven to earth, from earth to
heaven;
And as imagination bodies forth
The forms of things unknown, the poet's pen   15
Turns them to shapes and gives to airy nothing
A local habitation and a name.
Such tricks hath strong imagination,
That, if it would but apprehend some joy,
It comprehends some bringer of that joy;   20
Or in the night, imagining some fear,
How easy is a bush supposed a bear!
HIPPOLYTA: But all the story of the night told over,
And all their minds transfigured so together,
More witnesseth than fancy's images°   25
And grows to something of great constancy;°
But, howsoever, strange and admirable.
THESEUS: Here come the lovers, full of joy and mirth.

[Enter LYSANDER, DEMETRIUS, HERMIA, *and* HELENA.*]*

Joy, gentle friends! joy and fresh days of love
Accompany your hearts!   30
LYSANDER: More than to us
Wait in your royal walks, your board, your bed!
THESEUS: Come now; what masques, what dances
shall we have,
To wear away this long age of three hours
Between our after-supper and bed-time?
Where is our usual manager of mirth?   35
What revels are in hand? Is there no play,
To ease the anguish of a torturing hour?
Call Philostrate.
PHILOSTRATE: Here, mighty Theseus.
THESEUS: Say, what abridgement° have you for this
evening?
What masque? what music? How shall we beguile   40
The lazy time, if not with some delight?

---

21 **sixpence a day** i.e., as a royal pension   27 **hearts** good
fellows   38 **presently** at once   40 **preferred** chosen over its
rivals for presentation

ACT V, SCENE 1:   2 **may** can   3 **antique** strange; toys trifles
8 **Are . . . compact** are wholly composed of the power of seeing things   11 **Sees Helen's . . . Egypt** sees in the face of a
dusky gypsy the beauty of Helen of Troy   25 **More . . .
images** is evidence of more than just imagination   26 **constancy** certainty   39 **abridgement** pastime

PHILOSTRATE: There is a brief° how many sports are
    ripe:
    Make choice of which your highness will see first.

[Giving a paper.]

THESEUS: [*Reads*] "The battle with the Centaurs,° to be
    sung
45   By an Athenian eunuch to the harp."
    We'll none of that: that have I told my love,
    In glory of my kinsman Hercules.
    [*Reads*] "The riot of the tipsy Bacchanals,
    Tearing the Thracian singer in their rage."°
50   That is an old device; and it was play'd
    When I from Thebes came last a conqueror.
    [*Reads*] "The thrice three Muses mourning for the
    death
    Of Learning, late deceased in beggary."
    That is some satire, keen and critical,
55   Not sorting with° a nuptial ceremony.
    [*Reads*] "A tedious brief scene of young Pyramus
    And his love Thisby; very tragical mirth."
    Merry and tragical! tedious and brief!
    That is, hot ice and wondrous strange snow.
60   How shall we find the concord of this discord?
PHILOSTRATE: A play there is, my lord, some ten
    words long,
    Which is as brief as I have known a play;
    But by ten words, my lord, it is too long,
    Which makes it tedious; for in all the play
65   There is not one word apt, one player fitted:
    And tragical, my noble lord, it is;
    For Pyramus therein doth kill himself.
    Which, when I saw rehearsed, I must confess,
    Made mine eyes water; but more merry tears
70   The passion of loud laughter never shed.
THESEUS: What are they that do play it?
PHILOSTRATE: Hard-handed men that work in Athens
    here,
    Which never labour'd in their minds till now,
    And now have toil'd their unbreathed° memories
75   With this same play, against° your nuptial.
THESEUS: And we will hear it.
PHILOSTRATE: No, my noble lord;
    It is not for you: I have heard it over,
    And it is nothing, nothing in the world;
    Unless you can find sport in their intents,
80   Extremely stretch'd° and conn'd° with cruel pain,
    To do you service.

THESEUS: I will hear that play;
    For never anything can be amiss,
    When simpleness and duty tender it.
    Go, bring them in: and take your places, ladies.

[Exit PHILOSTRATE.]

HIPPOLYTA: I love not to see wretchedness o'er-charged° 85
    And duty in his service perishing.°
THESEUS: Why, gentle sweet, you shall see no such
    thing.
HIPPOLYTA: He says they can do nothing in this kind.
THESEUS: The kinder we, to give them thanks for
    nothing.
    Our sport shall be to take what they mistake: 90
    And what poor duty cannot do, noble respect
    Takes it in might, not merit.°
    Where I have come, great clerks° have purposed
    To greet me with premeditated welcomes;
    Where I have seen them shiver and look pale,   95
    Make periods° in the midst of sentences,
    Throttle their practised accent in their fears
    And in conclusion dumbly have broke off,
    Not paying me a welcome. Trust me, sweet,
    Out of this silence yet I pick'd a welcome;   100
    And in the modesty of fearful duty
    I read as much as from the rattling tongue
    Of saucy and audacious eloquence.
    Love, therefore, and tongue-tied simplicity
    In least speak most, to my capacity.°   105

[Re-enter PHILOSTRATE.]

PHILOSTRATE: So please your grace, the Prologue is
    address'd.°
THESEUS: Let him approach.

[Flourish of trumpets.]

[Enter QUINCE for the PROLOGUE.]

PROLOGUE°: If we offend, it is with our good will
    That you should think, we come not to offend,
    But with good will. To show our simple skill,   110
    That is the true beginning of our end.
    Consider then we come but in despite.
    We do not come as minding to content you,
    Our true intent is. All for your delight
    We are not here. That you should here repent you, 115
    The actors are at hand and by their show

---

42 **brief** list 44 **The battle . . . Centaurs** Ovid tells of a battle between the Centaurs and Lapithae 48 **The riot . . . rage** Orpheus was torn limb from limb by the maenads, female priests of Bacchus. 55 **not sorting with** not fitting for 74 **unbreathed** unexercised 75 **against,** in preparation for 80 **stretch'd** strained **conn'd** learned by heart

85 **o'ercharged** oppressed 86 **perishing** ruining itself 92 **Takes . . . merit** i.e., takes the will for the deed 93 **clerks** learned men 96 **periods** long stops 105 **capacity** sympathetic comprehension 106 **Prologue is address'd** the speaker of the prologue is ready

You shall know all that you are like to know.
THESEUS: This fellow doth not stand upon points.°
LYSANDER: He hath rid his prologue like a rough colt;
120   he knows not the stop.° A good moral, my lord:
it is not enough to speak, but to speak true.
HIPPOLYTA: Indeed he hath played on his prologue like
a child on a recorder;° a sound, but not in government.°
125 THESEUS: His speech was like a tangled chain; nothing
impaired, but all disordered. Who is next?

[Enter PYRAMUS *and* THISBE, WALL, MOONSHINE, *and*
LION.]

PROLOGUE: Gentles, perchance you wonder at this
show;
But wonder on, till truth make all things plain.
This man is Pyramus, if you would know;
130   This beauteous lady Thisby is certain.
This man, with lime and rough-cast, doth present
Wall, that vile Wall which did these lovers sun-
der;
And through Wall's chink, poor souls, they are
content
To whisper. At the which let no man wonder.
135 This man, with lanthorn, dog, and bush of thorn,
Presenteth Moonshine; for, if you will know,
By moonshine did these lovers think no scorn
To meet at Ninus' tomb, there, there to woo.
This grisly beast, which Lion hight° by name,
140 The trusty Thisby, coming first by night,
Did scare away, or rather did affright;
And, as she fled, her mantle she did fall,°
Which Lion vile with bloody mouth did stain.
Anon comes Pyramus, sweet youth and tall,°
145   And finds his trusty Thisby's mantle slain:
Whereat, with blade, with bloody blameful blade,
He bravely broach'd° his boiling bloody breast;
And Thisby, tarrying in mulberry shade,
His dagger drew, and died. For all the rest,
150 Let Lion, Moonshine, Wall, and lovers twain
At large discourse, while here they do remain.

[Exeunt PROLOGUE, PYRAMUS, THISBE, LION, *and*
MOONSHINE.]

THESEUS: I wonder if the lion be to speak.°

---
[117] Quince perverts the sense of his speech by blundering punctuation.   [118] **stand upon points** "pays no attention to punctuation," also "does not care about trifles"   [120] **the stop** quibble
on (1) period or end of a sentence, (2) signal to halt, e.g.,
"whoa."   [123] **recorder** a wind instrument something like a
flute   [124] **in government** under control   [139] **hight** is called
[142] **fall** let fall   [144] **tall** brave   [147] **broach'd** opened, i.e.,
stabbed   [152] **be to speak** is going to speak

DEMETRIUS: No wonder, my lord: one lion may, when
many asses do.
WALL: In this same interlude it doth befall   155
That I, one Snout by name, present a wall;
And such a wall, as I would have you think,
That had in it a crannied hole or chink,
Through which the lovers, Pyramus and Thisby,
Did whisper often very secretly.   160
This loam, this rough-cast and this stone doth show
That I am that same wall; the truth is so:
And this the cranny° is, right and sinister,°
Through which the fearful lovers are to whisper.
THESEUS: Would you desire lime and hair to speak bet-
ter?   165
DEMETRIUS: It is the wittiest partition° that ever I heard
discourse, my lord.

[Re-enter PYRAMUS.]

THESEUS: Pyramus draws near the wall: silence!
PYRAMUS: O grim-look'd° night! O night with hue so
black!
O night, which ever art when day is not!   170
O night, O night! alack, alack, alack,
I fear my Thisby's promise is forgot!
And thou, O wall, O sweet, O lovely wall,
That stand'st between her father's ground and
mine!
Thou wall, O wall, O sweet and lovely wall,   175
Show me thy chink, to blink through with mine
eyne! [*Wall holds up his fingers.*]
Thanks, courteous wall: Jove shield thee well for
this!
But what see I? No Thisby do I see.
O wicked wall, through whom I see no bliss!
Cursed be thy stones for thus deceiving me!   180
THESEUS: The wall, methinks, being sensible,° should
curse again.
PYRAMUS: No, in truth, sir, he should not. "Deceiving
me" is Thisby's cue: she is to enter now, and I
am to spy her through the wall. You shall see, it   185
will fall pat as I told you. Yonder she comes.

[Re-enter THISBE.]

THISBE: O wall, full often hast thou heard my moans,
For parting my fair Pyramus and me!
My cherry lips have often kiss'd thy stones,
Thy stones with lime and hair knit up in thee.   190
PYRAMUS: I see a voice: now will I to the chink,
To spy an I can hear my Thisby's face.
Thisby!

---
[163] **cranny** chink; sinister left   [166] **partition** quibble on (1)
wall, (2) a section of a book   [169] **grim-look'd** grim-faced
[181] **sensible** capable of feeling

THISBE: My love thou art, my love I think.
PYRAMUS: Think what thou wilt, I am thy lover's
                   grace;
195   And, like Limander,° am I trusty still.
THISBE: And I like Helen,° till the Fates me kill.
PYRAMUS: Not Shafalus to Procrus° was so true.
THISBE: As Shafalus to Procrus, I to you.
PYRAMUS: O, kiss me through the hole of this vile
                   wall!
200   THISBE: I kiss the wall's hole, not your lips at all.
PYRAMUS: Wilt thou at Ninny's tomb meet me
                   straightway?
THISBE: 'Tide life, 'tide death,° I come without delay.

[Exeunt PYRAMUS and THISBE.]

WALL: Thus have I, Wall, my part discharged so;
          And, being done, thus Wall away doth go.

[Exit.]

205   THESEUS: Now is the mural° down between the two
                   neighbours.
DEMETRIUS: No remedy, my lord, when walls are so
                   wilful to hear without warning.
HIPPOLYTA: This is the silliest stuff that ever I heard.
210   THESEUS: The best in this kind are but shadows; and the
                   worst are no worse, if imagination amend them.
HIPPOLYTA: It must be your imagination then, and not
                   theirs.
THESEUS: If we imagine no worse of them than they of
215   themselves, they may pass for excellent men.
          Here come two noble beasts in, a man and a lion.

[Re-enter LION and MOONSHINE.]

LION: You, ladies, you, whose gentle hearts do fear
          The smallest monstrous mouse that creeps on
                   floor,
          May now perchance both quake and tremble here,
220   When lion rough in wildest rage doth roar
          Then know that I, one Snug the joiner, am
          A lion-fell,° nor else no lion's dam;
          For, if I should as lion come in strife
          Into this place, 'twere pity on my life.°
225   THESEUS: A very gentle beast, and of a good conscience.
DEMETRIUS: The very best at a beast, my lord, that e'er
                   I saw.
LYSANDER: This lion is a very fox for his valour.
THESEUS: True; and a goose for his discretion.

DEMETRIUS: Not so, my lord; for his valour cannot carry   230
          his discretion; and the fox carries the goose.
THESEUS: His discretion, I am sure, cannot carry his
          valour; for the goose carries not the fox. It is
          well: leave it to his discretion, and let us listen
          to the moon.   235
MOON: This lanthorn doth the hornèd moon present;—
DEMETRIUS: He should have worn the horns on his
          head.°
THESEUS: He is no crescent, and his horns are invisible
          within the circumference.   240
MOON: This lanthorn doth the horned moon present;
          Myself the man i' the moon do seem to be.
THESEUS: This is the greatest error of all the rest: the
          man should be put into the lanthorn. How is it
          else the man i' the moon?   245
DEMETRIUS: He dares not come there for° the candle;
          for, you see, it is already in snuff.°
HIPPOLYTA: I am aweary of this moon: would he would
          change!
THESEUS: It appears, by his small light of discretion,   250
          that he is in the wane; but yet, in courtesy, in all
          reason, we must stay the time.°
LYSANDER: Proceed, Moon.
MOON: All that I have to say, is, to tell you that the lan-
          thorn is the moon; I, the man in the moon; this   255
          thorn-bush, my thorn-bush; and this dog, my dog.
DEMETRIUS: Why, all these should be in the lanthorn;
          for all these are in the moon. But, silence! here
          comes Thisby.

[Re-enter THISBE.]

THISBE: This is old Ninny's tomb. Where is my love?   260
LION: *[Roaring] Oh—[THISBE runs off.]*
DEMETRIUS: Well roared, Lion.
THESEUS: Well run, Thisby.
HIPPOLYTA: Well shone, Moon. Truly, the moon shines
          with a good grace.   265

[The LION shakes THISBE's mantle, and exit.]

THESEUS: Well moused,° Lion.
LYSANDER: And so the lion vanished.
DEMETRIUS: And then came Pyramus.

[Re-enter PYRAMUS.]

PYRAMUS: Sweet Moon, I thank thee for thy sunny
          beams;
          I thank thee, Moon, for shining now so bright;   270
          For, by thy gracious, golden, glittering gleams,

---

195 **Limander** blunder for Leander   196 **Helen** he means
Hero   197 **Shafalus to Procrus** blunder for "Cephalus to
Procris."   202 **Tide . . . death** whether life or death betide
[happens]   205 **mural** wall   222 **lion-fell** lion skin, i.e., he is
a lion only in that he is cased in a lion skin   224 **'twere . . . life**
i.e., I should be in danger of hanging

237–8 **He . . . head** the ancient joke about the horns of a cuckold   246 **for** because of   247 **in snuff** quibble (1) in need of
snuffing, (2) offended   252 **stay . . . time** see it through
266 **moused** shaken (as a cat shakes a mouse)

I trust to take of truest Thisby sight.
But stay, O spite!
But mark, poor knight,
275 What dreadful dole° is here!
Eyes, do you see?
How can it be?
O dainty duck! O dear!
Thy mantle good,
280 What, stain'd with blood!
Approach, ye Furies fell!°
O Fates, come, come,
Cut thread and thrum;°
Quail,° crush, conclude, and quell!°

285 THESEUS: This passion, and the death of a dear friend,
would go near to make a man look sad.
HIPPOLYTA: Beshrew my heart, but I pity the man.
PYRAMUS: O wherefore, Nature, didst thou lions frame?
Since lion vile hath here deflower'd my dear:
290 Which is—no, no—which was the fairest dame
That lived, that loved, that liked, that look'd
with cheer.°

Come, tears, confound;
Out, sword, and wound
295 The pap of Pyramus;
Ay, that left pap,
Where heart doth hop: [*Stabs himself.*]
Thus die I, thus, thus, thus.
Now am I dead,
300 Now am I fled;
My soul is in the sky:
Tongue, lose thy light;
Moon, take thy flight:

[*Exit MOONSHINE.*]

Now die, die, die, die, die.

[*Dies.*]

305 DEMETRIUS: No die, but an ace,° for him; for he is but one.
LYSANDER: Less than an ace, man; for he is dead; he is
nothing.
THESEUS: With the help of a surgeon he might yet recover, and prove an ass.
310 HIPPOLYTA: How chance Moonshine is gone before
Thisby comes back and finds her lover?
THESEUS: She will find him by starlight. Here she
comes; and her passion ends the play.

[*Re-enter THISBE.*]

HIPPOLYTA: Methinks she should not use a long one for
such a Pyramus: I hope she will be brief. 315
DEMETRIUS: A mote will turn the balance, which
Pyramus, which Thisby, is the better; he for a man,
God warrant us; she for a woman, God bless us.
LYSANDER: She hath spied him already with those sweet
eyes. 320
DEMETRIUS: And thus she means,° videlicet:—
THISBE: Asleep, my love?
What, dead, my dove?
O Pyramus, arise!
Speak, speak. Quite dumb? 325
Dead, dead? A tomb
Must cover thy sweet eyes.
These lily lips,
This cherry nose,
These yellow cowslip cheeks, 330
Are gone, are gone:
Lovers, make moan:
His eyes were green as leeks.
O Sisters Three,°
Come, come to me, 335
With hands as pale as milk;
Lay them in gore,
Since you have shore
With shears his thread of silk.
Tongue, not a word: 340
Come, trusty sword;
Come, blade, my breast imbrue:°

[*Stabs herself.*]

And, farewell, friends;
Thus Thisby ends:
Adieu, adieu, adieu. 345

[*Dies.*]

THESEUS: Moonshine and Lion are left to bury the dead.
DEMETRIUS: Ay, and Wall too.
BOTTOM: [*Starting up*] No, I assure you; the wall is
down that parted their fathers. Will it please
you to see the epilogue, or to hear a Bergomask° 350
dance between two of our company?
THESEUS: No epilogue, I pray you; for your play needs
no excuse. Never excuse; for when the players
are all dead, there need none to be blamed.
Marry, if he that writ it had played Pyramus and 355

---

²⁷⁵ **dole** grief ²⁸¹ **fell** fierce ²⁸³ **thread and thrum** the
warp of a piece of cloth and the fringe-like threads at the end
²⁸⁴ **quail** subdue; quell; kill ²⁹² **with cheer** with a face ³⁰⁵
No . . . ace pun (1) die=perish, (2) die=the singular of dice

---

³²¹ **means** moans ³³⁴ **Sisters Three** the Fates ³⁴² **imbrue**
wet with gore ³⁵⁰ **Bergomask dance** a grotesque rustic
dance (named from the Italian town Bergamo)

hanged himself in Thisby's garter, it would have
been a fine tragedy: and so it is, truly; and very
notably discharged. But, come, your Bergomask;
let your epilogue alone.

[A dance.]

360 The iron tongue of midnight hath told twelve:
Lovers, to bed; 'tis almost fairy time.
I fear we shall out-sleep the coming morn
As much as we this night have overwatch'd.
This palpable-gross° play hath well beguiled
365 The heavy gait of night. Sweet friends, to bed.
A fortnight hold we this solemnity,
In nightly revels and new jollity.

[Exeunt.]

[Enter PUCK.*]*

PUCK: Now the hungry lion roars,
      And the wolf behowls the moon;
370 Whilst the heavy ploughman snores,
      All with weary task fordone.°
Now the wasted brands do glow,
      Whilst the screech-owl, screeching loud,
Puts the wretch that lies in woe
375   In remembrance of a shroud.
Now it is the time of night
      That the graves all gaping wide,
Every one lets forth his sprite,
      In the church-way paths to glide:
380 And we fairies, that do run
      By the triple Hecate's° team,
From the presence of the sun,
      Following darkness like a dream,
Now are frolic:° not a mouse
385 Shall disturb this hallow'd house:
I am sent with broom before,
To sweep the dust behind the door.°

[Enter OBERON *and* TITANIA *with their train.]*

OBERON: Through the house give glimmering light,
      By the dead and drowsy fire:
390 Every elf and fairy sprite
      Hop as light as bird from brier;
And this ditty, after me,
      Sing, and dance it trippingly.
TITANIA: First, rehearse your song by rote,

To each word a warbling note: 395
Hand in hand, with fairy grace,
Will we sing, and bless this place.

[Song and dance.]

OBERON: Now, until the break of day,
      Through this house each fairy stray.
To the best bride-bed will we,   400
Which by us shall blessèd be;
And the issue there create°
Ever shall be fortunate.
So shall all the couples three
Ever true in loving be;   405
And the blots of Nature's hand
Shall not in their issue stand;
Never mole, hare lip, nor scar,
Nor mark prodigious,° such as are
Despisèd in nativity,   410
Shall upon their children be.
With this field-dew consecrate,°
Every fairy take his gait;
And each several° chamber bless,
Through this palace, with sweet peace;   415
And the owner of it blest
Ever shall in safety rest.
Trip away; make no stay;
Meet me all by break of day.

[Exeunt OBERON, TITANIA, and train.]

PUCK: If we shadows have offended,   420
Think but this, and all is mended,
That you have but slumber'd here
While these visions did appear.
And this weak and idle theme,
No more yielding but a dream,   425
Gentles, do not reprehend:
If you pardon, we will mend:
And, as I am an honest Puck,
If we have unearnèd luck
Now to 'scape the serpent's tongue,°   430
We will make amends ere long;
Else the Puck a liar call:
So, good night unto you all.
Give me your hands,° if we be friends,
And Robin shall restore amends.   435

[Exit.]

---

³⁶⁴ **palpable-gross** palpably crude ³⁷¹ **fordone** worn out
³⁸¹ **triple Hecate** Diana was three-formed; she was called
Cynthia in heaven, Diana on earth, Hecate in hell. ³⁸⁴ **frolic**
gay ³⁸⁷ **To . . . door** Robin Goodfellow was a domestic
sprite, who could be induced to do the housework by night.

⁴⁰² **create** created ⁴⁰⁹ **prodigious** unnatural ⁴¹² **consecrate** consecrated ⁴¹⁴ **several** separate ⁴³⁰ **serpent's
tongue** i.e., hissing ⁴³⁴ **Give . . . hands** applaud

Hamlet, Prince of Denmark

Hamlet is the world's most famous play. More has been written about it than about any other literary or dramatic work, and each age has seen its own concerns and ideals reflected in the play. In the late eighteenth century critics began to pose questions about the play's consistency. Was Hamlet a bold and heroic character, or was he sensitive and irresolute? Coleridge in the early nineteenth century thought that Hamlet was a man of great intellect, but because the prince thought too much he could not bring himself to act. The speculative qualities of Hamlet's speeches were admired because they inspired readers and viewers to think about the great questions of human existence. As William Hazlitt once said, "It is we who are Hamlet." In the later nineteenth century, under the influence of the literary movements of naturalism and realism, more questions were posed about the play: Why does Hamlet delay? Is his madness real or feigned?

Many of the concerns of the realists were summed up in A. C. Bradley's *Shakespearean Tragedy* (1904) and so became the standard against which twentieth-century critics defined themselves. Concerned with realistic motivation and character analysis, Bradley claimed that Hamlet's psychology must be imaged as completely as that of any living person. His own reconstruction of that psychology finds Hamlet suffering from abnormal melancholy, a sickness which produced a mental condition that Hamlet did not fully understand. The cause was the shock of the sudden discovery of his mother's shallowness and coarse sensuality. At nearly the same time as Bradley was writing, Freud was using the Oedipus and Hamlet stories in his own psychoanalytical practice and studies. Freud hypothesized that rather than grief for his dead father, it was a primal and forbidden attraction for his mother that caused Hamlet's problems. For both Freud and Bradley, Hamlet has an unacknowledged emotion that criticism must explain. Ernest Jones, a disciple of Freud, wrote psychoanalytic studies of Hamlet that influenced Laurence Olivier's 1947 film version of the play. The sexualized treatment of the relationship between Hamlet and Gertrude there set a pattern for many subsequent productions.

The interrogative mood of *Hamlet* is introduced in the first line with Barnardo's question, "Who's there?" It is an anxious question, and Francisco speaks for virtually all of the characters in the play when he says, "'Tis bitter cold,/And I am sick at heart." Many of the characters are disturbed by a sense of something sinister beneath external appearances, and many of them, like Hamlet, are concerned to dig beneath the surface to find the truth. All of the major and many of the minor characters become involved in spying; in Polonius's terms, they use "indirections to find directions out."

On the most literal level, what is concealed is Claudius's crime. He has killed his brother in order to marry his sister-in-law and assume the crown of Denmark. Claudius compares his crime to the archetypal killing of Abel by Cain—the first story in the Bible after the fall from the Garden of Eden. This concealed crime is what is "rotten in the state of Denmark." At the heart of the kingdom, the king's guilt spreads like poison through the state, much as the poison of the "cursed hebona" literally spread through the veins of old King Hamlet.

The poison shows up again in the play-within-the-play and in the conclusion, when Laertes and Claudius use poison to try to kill Hamlet.

When he returns to Denmark, Hamlet is grieved by his father's sudden death and revolted by his mother's overhasty marriage to his uncle. But when he hears the story of betrayal and murder from his father's ghost, he is overwhelmed by a revulsion for the depths to which human nature can stoop and burdened by the need to do something about the murder. *Hamlet* is thus a revenge play, a subgenre of tragedy that flourished in the late sixteenth and early seventeenth centuries in England. The first play of this kind was *The Spanish Tragedy* (ca. 1587) by Thomas Kyd. Like Kyd, Shakespeare includes a ghost, a play-within-the-play, the motif of madness associated with a frustrated attempt to find justice, and a gory conclusion with piles of bodies left onstage. Unlike Kyd, Shakespeare interrogates the revenge genre by having Hamlet delay his revenge and articulate his feelings and ideas about some of the central questions of his experience. Part of the reason for the delay is Hamlet's suspicions about the role of revenger itself, which has been imposed on him by his father's ghost. Certainly, the fate of Laertes, who goes straight to the task of revenge for his father's murder only to become a pawn in Claudius's plot, suggests that Hamlet may be right to be cautious. But there is no exit from the entrapment of revenge in this play. Does Hamlet finally take revenge through his own plan, or does he simply respond to circumstances in which he has become Claudius's victim? Virtually any course of action in this play and any train of thought leads ultimately to fascinating and disquieting paradox.

T. S. Eliot wrote that *Hamlet* was an aesthetic failure because it did not provide an adequate "objective correlative" to Hamlet's emotion. In Eliot's view, Gertrude is simply not evil enough to evoke Hamlet's excessive emotions. Many critics responded by discovering motives to justify Hamlet's emotion: that Gertrude has committed adultery or that she is fundamentally corrupt. Concerns about Gertrude's function in the play were eventually taken up by feminist critics who see her sexualized femininity as a scapegoat. For these critics the heart of the play is Act III, in Hamlet's confrontations with Ophelia and with Gertrude.

Philosophical responses to the play became fashionable after World War II under the influence of existential philosophy. The puzzles or inconsistencies identified by earlier critics were now considered mysteries. Hamlet's problems were not personal and individual but rather universal because they reflected the human position in the universe. Corruption was not specific to Denmark or Hamlet but to human nature itself, and the interrogative mood of the play poses anguished and unanswerable questions on the nature of existence. For these critics, the heart of the play is the ghost walking the ramparts in Act I and the graveyard scene in Act V.

Still later, metatheatrical (theater about theater) critics relying on Brecht's theories emphasized the self-consciousness and theatricality of the play, which parallels Hamlet's self-consciousness and theatricality. Much of this kind of criticism became focused on how interpretation has shaped culture and on the cultural function of art. For these critics the heart of the play is the "mouse-trap" in Act III.

As a detective story of sorts, the play teases us into speculations—in somewhat the same way it does Hamlet. But there are no definitive answers to the problems or mysteries the play poses. As Hamlet suggests to Rosencrantz and Guildenstern, it is not possible "to pluck out the heart" of the mystery. Rather like many great works of art, *Hamlet* touches every reader or viewer in every age precisely because it takes them near to what they have all considered important questions that lie beyond the range of full explication.

Hamlet, Prince of Denmark

WILLIAM SHAKESPEARE

EDITED BY OSCAR CAMPBELL

CHARACTERS

CLAUDIUS, king of Denmark
HAMLET, son to the late, and nephew to the present king
POLONIUS, lord chamberlain
HORATIO, friend to Hamlet
LAERTES, son to Polonius
VOLTIMAND ⎫
CORNELIUS   ⎪
ROSENCRANTZ ⎬ courtiers
GUILDENSTERN ⎪
OSRIC   ⎭
A GENTLEMAN,
A PRIEST.

MARCELLUS, ⎫ officers
BERNARDO, ⎭
FRANCISCO, a soldier
REYNALDO, servant to Polonius
PLAYERS
TWO CLOWNS, grave-diggers
FORTINBRAS, prince of Norway
A CAPTAIN
ENGLISH AMBASSADORS
GERTRUDE, queen of Denmark, and mother to Hamlet
OPHELIA, daughter to Polonius
LORDS, LADIES, OFFICERS, SOLDIERS, SAILORS, MESSENGERS, and other ATTENDANTS. GHOST of Hamlet's father

SCENE: Denmark

ACT I

Scene 1

Elsinore. A platform before the castle.

[FRANCISCO at his post. Enter to him BERNARDO.]

BERNARDO: Who's there?
FRANCISCO: Nay, answer me:° stand, and unfold yourself.°
BERNARDO: Long live the king!°
FRANCISCO: Bernardo?
5   BERNARDO: He.

FRANCISCO: You come most carefully upon your hour.°
BERNARDO: 'Tis now struck twelve; get thee to bed, Francisco.
FRANCISCO: For this relief much thanks: 'tis bitter cold, And I am sick at heart.
BERNARDO: Have you had quiet guard?
FRANCISCO: Not a mouse stirring.   10
BERNARDO: Well, good night.
   If you do meet Horatio and Marcellus,
   The rivals° of my watch, bid them make haste.
FRANCISCO: I think I hear them. Stand, ho! Who's there?

[Enter HORATIO and MARCELLUS.]

HORATIO: Friends to this ground.

ACT I, SCENE 1:   ² **answer me** i.e., give the countersign; **unfold yourself** tell who you are and what you want   ³ **long . . . king** the password, or countersign

⁶ **carefully . . . hour** i.e., on the dot   ¹³ **rivals** companions

15   MARCELLUS: And liegemen to the Dane°.
     FRANCISCO: Give you° good night.
     MARCELLUS: O, farewell, honest soldier:
     Who hath relieved you?
     FRANCISCO: Bernardo has my place.
     Give you good night.

[Exit.]

     MARCELLUS: Holla! Bernardo!
     BERNARDO: Say,°
     What,° is Horatio there?
     HORATIO: A piece of him.
20   BERNARDO: Welcome, Horatio: welcome, good Marcellus.
     MARCELLUS: What, has this thing appear'd again to-night?
     BERNARDO: I have seen nothing.
     MARCELLUS: Horatio says 'tis but our fantasy,°
     And will not let belief take hold of him
25   Touching this dreaded sight, twice seen of us:
     Therefore I have entreated him along
     With us to watch the minutes of this night;
     That if again this apparition come,
     He may approve our eyes° and speak to it.
     HORATIO: Tush, tush, 'twill not appear.
30   BERNARDO: Sit down awhile;
     And let us once again assail your ears,
     That are so fortified against our story
     What we have two nights seen.
     HORATIO: Well, sit we down,
     And let us hear Bernardo speak of this.
35   BERNARDO: Last night of all,°
     When yond same star that's westward from the pole°
     Had made his course to illume that part of heaven
     Where now it burns, Marcellus and myself,
     The bell then beating one—

[Enter GHOST.]

     MARCELLUS: Peace, break thee off;° look, where it comes
40   again!
     BERNARDO: In the same figure, like the king that's dead.
     MARCELLUS: Thou art a scholar;° speak to it, Horatio.
     BERNARDO: Looks it not like the king? mark it, Horatio.
     HORATIO: Most like: it harrows° me with fear and
     wonder.
     BERNARDO: It would be spoke to.
45   MARCELLUS: Question it, Horatio.
     HORATIO: What art thou that usurp'st° this time of night,

Together with° that fair and warlike form°
In which the majesty of buried Denmark
Did sometimes° march? by heaven I charge thee,
     speak!
MARCELLUS: It is offended.   50
BERNARDO: See, it stalks away!
HORATIO: Stay! speak, speak! I charge thee, speak!

[Exit GHOST.]

MARCELLUS: 'Tis gone, and will not answer.
BERNARDO: How now, Horatio! you tremble and look
     pale:
     Is not this something more than fantasy?
     What think you on 't?   55
HORATIO: Before my God, I might not this believe
     Without the sensible and true avouch°
     Of mine own eyes.
MARCELLUS: Is it not like the king?
HORATIO: As thou art to thyself:
     Such was the very armour he had on   60
     When he the ambitious Norway° combated;
     So frown'd he once, when, in an angry parle,°
     He smote the sledded° Polacks on the ice.
     'Tis strange.
MARCELLUS: Thus twice before, and jump° at this
     dead hour,   65
     With martial stalk hath he gone by our watch.
HORATIO: In what particular thought to work I know
     not;°
     But in the gross and scope° of my opinion,
     This bodes° some strange eruption° to our state.
MARCELLUS: Good now,° sit down, and tell me, he
     that knows,   70
     Why this same strict and most observant watch
     So nightly toils the subject° of the land,
     And why such daily cast° of brazen cannon,
     And foreign mart for° implements of war;
     Why such impress° of shipwrights, whose sore°
     task   75
     Does not divide the Sunday from the week;
     What might be toward,° that this sweaty haste
     Doth make the night joint-labourer with the day:
     Who is't that can inform me?
HORATIO: That can I;
     At least, the whisper goes so. Our last king,   80

---

15 liegemen . . . Dane loyal subjects of the Danish King   **16 Give you** may God give you   **19 Say** say on   **What** i.e., tell me   **23 fantasy** imagination   **29 approve our eyes** verify what we have seen   **35 Last . . . all** only last night   **36 pole** north star   **40 Peace . . . off** keep still, stop talking   **42 scholar** i.e., you know Latin. The set phrases which exorcised an evil spirit were in Latin.   **44 harrows** plows up, torments   **46 usurp'st** wrongfully take possession of

47 Together with i.e., wrongfully assume warlike form, i.e., the King as he looked in battle array   **49 sometimes** formerly   **57 sensible . . . avouch** true testimony of the senses   **61 Norway** King of Norway   **62 parle** encounter   **63 sledded** who ride in sledges   **65 jump** exactly   **67 In . . . not** i.e., I do not know just what to think about it   **68 gross and scope** main drift   **69 bodes** forebodes **eruption** i.e., calamity   **70 Good now** come then   **72 toils the subject** makes the subjects toil   **73 cast** casting   **74 mart for** trade in   **75 impress** drafting **sore** difficult   **77 toward** in preparation

Whose image even but now appear'd to us,
Was, as you know, by Fortinbras of Norway,°
Thereto prick'd on by a most emulate° pride,
Dared to the combat; in which our valiant
    Hamlet°—
85   For so° this side of our known world esteem'd
    him—
Did slay this Fortinbras; who, by a seal'd compact,°
Well ratified by law and heraldry,°
Did forfeit, with his life, all those his lands
Which he stood seized of,° to the conqueror:
90   Against the which, a moiety competent°
Was gagèd° by our king; which had return'd°
To the inheritance of Fortinbras,
Had he been vanquisher; as, by the same covenant,
And carriage of the article design'd,°
95   His fell to Hamlet. Now, sir, young Fortinbras,
Of unimprovèd mettle° hot and full,
Hath in the skirts° of Norway here and there
Shark'd up° a list of lawless resolutes,°
For food and diet, to some enterprise
100 That hath a stomach in 't;° which° is no other—
As it doth well appear unto our state—
But to recover of us, by strong hand
And terms compulsatory,° those foresaid lands
So by his father lost: and this, I take it,
105 Is the main motive of our preparations,
The source of this our watch and the chief head°
Of this post-haste and romage° in the land.
BERNARDO: I think it be no other but e'en so:
Well may it sort° that this portentous figure
110 Comes armed through our watch; so like the king
That was and is the question° of these wars.
HORATIO: A mote it is to trouble the mind's eye.
In the most high and palmy° state of Rome,
A little ere the mightiest Julius fell,
115 The graves stood tenantless and the sheeted° dead°
Did squeak and gibber° in the Roman streets:

As stars with trains of fire° and dews of blood,
Disasters° in the sun; and the moist star°
Upon whose influence Neptune's empire stands
Was sick almost to doomsday° with eclipse: 120
And even the like precurse° of fierce events,
As harbingers° preceding still° the fates
And prologue to the omen° coming on,
Have heaven and earth together demonstrated
Unto our climatures° and countrymen.—   125
But soft, behold! lo, where it comes again!

[Re-enter GHOST.*]*

I'll cross° it, though it blast me.° Stay, illusion.
If thou hast any sound, or use of voice,
Speak to me:
If there be any good thing to be done,   130
That may to thee do ease and grace° to me,
Speak to me:

[Cock crows.]

If thou art privy to° thy country's fate,
Which, happily,° foreknowing may avoid,
O, speak!   135
Or if thou has uphoarded° in thy life
Extorted treasure° in the womb of earth,
For which, they say, you spirits oft walk in death,
Speak of it: stay, and speak! Stop it, Marcellus.
MARCELLUS: Shall I strike at it with my partisan?°   140
HORATIO: Do, if it will not stand.
BERNARDO: 'Tis here!
HORATIO: 'Tis here!
MARCELLUS: 'Tis gone!

[Exit GHOST.*]*

We do it wrong, being so majestical,
To offer it the show of violence;
For it is, as the air, invulnerable,   145
And our vain° blows malicious mockery.°
BERNARDO: It was about to speak, when the cock crew.
HORATIO: And then it started like a guilty thing

---

82 of Norway King of Norway, father of young Fortinbras
83 emulate jealous **84 Hamlet** i.e., "our last king," of line
80 **85 so** i.e., as valiant **86 sealed compact** formal agreement **87 Well . . . heraldry** i.e., in accordance with both law
and the usages of chivalry **89 stood . . . of** had in his possession **90 moiety competent** an equal portion (of land) **91
gaged** pledged had return'd would have reverted to **94
carriage . . . design'd** terms of the agreement as drawn up
96 unimproved mettle untried courage **97 skirts** remote
districts **98 Shark'd up** collected through trickery **resolutes** reckless men **100 hath . . . in 't** requires courage;
which i.e., the purpose of the enterprise **103 compulsatory**
dictated by force **106 head** origin **107 post-haste and
romage** great haste and bustle **109 Well . . . sort** i.e., this
may well be the reason **111 question** cause **113 palmy**
flourishing **115 sheeted** in their shrouds **116** A line seems
to have dropped out between ll. 11. 116 and 117. **116 gibber**
make inarticulate sounds

117 As . . . fire meteors **118 Disasters** unlucky omens; **moist
star** the moon, because it influences the tides **120 sick . . .
doomsday** turned almost completely dark. In Matthew XIV,
29, it is prophesied that on doomsday the sun "shall be darkened and the moon not give her light." **121 precurse** warning **122 harbingers** advance agents; **still** always **123 omen**
fatal event **125 climatures** regions **127 cross** i.e., cross his
path, supposed to be an invitation to misfortune **blast me**
cause me to wither away **131 grace** blessedness **133 art
privy to** to know the secret of **124 happily** by good fortune
136 uphoarded stored up **137 Extorted treasure** wealth
wrung by force (from its rightful owner) **140 partisan** long-shafted spear **146 vain** ineffective **malicious mockery**
futile gestures of hatred

150
Upon a fearful summons. I have heard,
The cock, that is the trumpet to the morn,
Doth with his lofty° and shrill-sounding throat
Awake the god of day; and, at his warning,
Whether in sea or fire, in earth or air,
The extravagant° and erring° spirit hies
155
To his confine:° and of the truth herein
This present object made probation.°
MARCELLUS: It faded on the crowing of the cock.
Some say that ever 'gainst that season comes°
Wherein our Saviour's birth is celebrated,
160
The bird of dawning° singeth all night long:
And then, they say, no spirit° dare stir abroad;
The nights are wholesome; then no planets strike,
No fairy takes,° nor witch hath power to charm,
So hallow'd and so gracious° is the time.
165
HORATIO: So have I heard and do in part believe it.
But, look, the morn, in russet mantle clad,
Walks o'er the dew of yon high eastward hill:
Break we our watch up; and by my advice,
Let us impart what we have seen to-night
170
Unto young Hamlet; for, upon my life,
This spirit, dumb to us, will speak to him.
Do you consent we shall acquaint him with it,
As needful in our loves,° fitting our duty?
MARCELLUS: Let's do 't, I pray; and I this morning
know
175
Where we shall find him most conveniently.

[Exeunt.]

Scene 2

A room of state in the castle.

[Enter the KING, QUEEN, HAMLET, POLONIUS, LAERTES,
VOLTIMAND, CORNELIUS, LORDS, *and* ATTENDANTS.*]*

KING: Though yet of Hamlet our dear brother's death
The memory be green, and that° it us befitted
To bear our hearts in grief and our whole kingdom
To be contracted in one brow of woe,
5
Yet so far hath discretion° fought with nature°
That we with wisest sorrow think on him,
Together with remembrance of ourselves.°

Therefore our sometime° sister, now our queen,
The imperial jointress to° this warlike state,
Have we, as 'twere with a defeated° joy,—   10
With an auspicious° and a dropping° eye,
With mirth in funeral and with dirge in marriage,
In equal scale weighing delight and dole,°—
Taken to wife: nor have we herein barr'd
Your better wisdoms,° which have freely gone   15
With this affair along. For all, our thanks.
Now follows, that° you know, young Fortinbras,
Holding a weak supposal° of our worth,
Or thinking by our late dear brother's death
Our state to be disjoint and out of frame,°   20
Colleagued with° the dream of his advantage,°
He hath not fail'd to pester us with message,
Importing° the surrender of those lands
Lost by his father, with all bonds of law,°
To our most valiant brother. So much for him.   25
Now for ourself and for this time of meeting:
Thus much the business° is: we have here writ
To Norway, uncle of young Fortinbras,—
Who, impotent and bed-rid, scarcely hears
Of this his nephew's purpose,—to suppress   30
His further gait° herein; in that the levies,
The lists and full proportions,° are all made
Out of his subject:° and we here dispatch
You, good Cornelius, and you, Voltimand,
For bearers of this greeting to old Norway;   35
Giving to you no further personal power
To business° with the king, more than the scope
Of these delated articles° allow.
Farewell, and let your haste commend your
duty.°
CORNELIUS: } In that and all things will we show
VOLTIMAND: } our duty.   40
KING: We doubt it nothing: heartily farewell.

[Exeunt VOLTIMAND *and* CORNELIUS.]*

And now, Laertes, what's the news with you?
You told us of some suit, what is 't, Laertes?
You cannot speak of reason to the Dane,

---

151 **lofty** high-pitched 154 **extravagant** straying **erring**
wandering 155 **confine** habitation 156 **made probation**
give proof 158 **'gainst . . . comes** at the approach of that season 160 **bird of dawning** the cock 162 **strike** exert a bale-
ful influence 163 **takes** bewitches 164 **gracious** blessed
173 **As . . . loves** as something our love dictates

SCENE 2: 2 **that** though 5 **discretion** common sense;
nature natural impulse (to excessive grief) 7 **remembrance
of ourselves** consideration of our duties (as living men)

---

8 **our sometime** my former 9 **imperial jointress to** royal
inheritor of 10 **defeated** impaired 11 **auspicious** joyful;
dropping weeping 13 **dole** grief 14-15 **barr'd . . . wisdoms**
ignored your wiser opinions (as to my proper course of
action) 17 **that** that which 18 **weak supposal** disparaging
opinion 20 **out of frame** in disorder 21 **Colleagued with**
supported by **advantage** good chance 23 **Importing** urging 24 **with . . . law** together with all legal claim to them 27
business present state of affairs 31 **gait** action 32 **proportions** quotas 33 **Out . . . subject** i.e., from the King of
Norway's subjects 37 **To business** to transact business 38
delated articles detailed instructions 39 **let . . . duty** Let
prompt action take the place of a ceremonious farewell.

And lose your voice:° what wouldst thou beg,
45   Laertes,
That shall not be my offer,° not thy asking?
The head is not more native° to the heart,
The hand more instrumental° to the mouth,
Than is the throne of Denmark to thy father.
What wouldst thou have, Laertes?
50 LAERTES: My dread° lord,
Your leave and favour° to return to France;
From whence though willingly I came to
       Denmark,
To show my duty° in your coronation,
Yet now, I must confess, that duty done,
55 My thoughts and wishes bend again toward
       France
And bow them to° your gracious leave and par-
       don.°
KING: Have you your father's leave? What says
       Polonius?
POLONIUS: He hath, my lord, wrung from me my
       slow leave°
By laboursome petition, and at last
60 Upon his will° I seal'd my hard consent:°
I do beseech you, give him leave to go.
KING: Take thy fair hour,° Laertes; time be thine.°
And thy best graces spend it at thy will!°
But now, my cousin° Hamlet, and my son,—
HAMLET: [*Aside*] A little more than kin, and less than
65   kind.°
KING: How is it that the clouds still hang on you?
HAMLET: Not so, my lord; I am too much i' the sun.°
QUEEN: Good Hamlet, cast thy nighted colour off,
And let thine eye look like a friend on Denmark.
70 Do not forever with thy vailèd° lids
Seek for thy noble father in the dust:
Thou know'st 'tis common; all that lives must die,
Passing through nature to eternity.
HAMLET: Ay, madam, it is common.
QUEEN: If it be,
75 Why seems it so particular with thee?
HAMLET: Seems, madam! nay, it is; I know not
       "seems."

'Tis not alone my inky cloak, good mother,
Nor customary suits of solemn black,
Nor windy suspiration of forced breath,°
No, nor the fruitful° river in the eye,   80
Nor the dejected 'haviour° of the visage,
Together with all forms, moods, shapes of grief,
That can denote me truly: these indeed seem,
For they are actions that a man might play:
But I have that within which passeth show;°   85
These but the trappings° and the suits of woe.
KING: 'Tis sweet and commendable in your nature,
       Hamlet,
To give these mourning duties to your father:
But, you must know, your father lost a father;
That father lost, lost his, and the survivor bound   90
In filial obligation for some term
To do obsequious sorrow;° but to perséver
In obstinate condolement° is a course
Of impious stubbornness; 'tis unmanly grief;
It shows a will most incorrect° to heaven,   95
A heart unfortified,° a mind impatient,
An understanding simple and unschool'd:
For what we know must be and is as common
As any the most vulgar thing to sense,°
Why should we in our peevish opposition   100
Take it to heart? Fie! 'tis a fault to heaven,
A fault against the dead, a fault to nature,
To reason most absurd; whose° common theme
Is death of fathers, and who still hath cried,
From the first corse till he that died to-day,   105
"This must be so." We pray you, throw to earth
This unprevailing° woe, and think of us
As of a father: for let the world take note,
You are the most immediate° to our throne;
And with no less nobility of love   110
Than that which dearest father bears his son,
Do I impart toward you.° For your intent
In going back to school in Wittenberg,
It is most retrograde° to our desire:
And we beseech you, bend you° to remain   115
Here, in the cheer and comfort of our eye,
Our chiefest courtier, cousin, and our son.
QUEEN: Let not thy mother lose her prayers, Hamlet:
I pray thee, stay with us; go not to Wittenberg.

---

⁴⁵ **lose your voice** fail to have your wish granted   ⁴⁶ **shall...
offer** that I shall not freely offer   ⁴⁷ **native** related by nature
⁴⁸ **instrumental** serviceable   ⁵⁰ **dread** respected   ⁵¹ **leave
and favour** kind permission   ⁵³ **show my duty** pay my
respects   ⁵⁶ **bow them to** beg; **leave and pardon** permission to go   ⁵⁸ **slow leave** grudging consent   ⁶⁰ **will** desire
sealed . . . consent given with reluctance   ⁶² **Take... hour**
enjoy the happiness of youth;   **time be thine** pass the time
as you wish   ⁶³ **thy . . . will** may you wish to spend it as
your best qualities dictate   ⁶⁴ **cousin** used for any relationship outside the immediate family   ⁶⁵ **less than kind** lower
in moral nature than our family (kind)   ⁶⁷ **the sun** (1) glory
of the court, (2) of a son   ⁷⁰ **vailed** lowered

---

⁷⁹ **windy . . . breath** forced sighs   ⁸⁰ **fruitful** full   ⁸¹ **'haviour** expression   ⁸⁵ **passeth show** is too strong to be
expressed by outward manifestations (of grief)   ⁸⁶ **trappings**
outward signs   ⁹² **obsequious sorrow** sorrow suitable for a
funeral   ⁹³ **condolement** mourning   ⁹⁵ **incorrect** unsub-
missive   ⁹⁶ **unfortified** i.e., by religion   ⁹⁹ **As any... sense**
as any of the most ordinary sense impressions   ¹⁰³ **whose**
antecedent is "nature"   ¹⁰⁷ **unprevailing** useless   ¹⁰⁹ **most
immediate** closest, i.e., next heir   ¹¹² **Do . . . you** do I
express myself to you   ¹¹⁴ **retrograde** contrary   ¹¹⁵ **bend
you** show an inclination

120 HAMLET: I shall in all my best° obey you, madam.
KING: Why, 'tis a loving and a fair reply:
     Be as ourself in Denmark. Madam, come;
     This gentle and unforced accord° of Hamlet
     Sits smiling to my heart: in grace whereof,°
125 No jocund health that Denmark drinks today,
     But the great cannon to the clouds shall tell,
     And the king's rouse° the heavens shall bruit
        again,°
     Re-speaking earthly thunder. Come away.

[Exeunt all but HAMLET.]

     HAMLET: O, that this too too solid flesh would melt,
130 Thaw and resolve itself into a dew!
     Or that the Everlasting had not fix'd
     His canon° 'gainst self-slaughter! O God! God!
     How weary, stale, flat and unprofitable,
     Seem to me all the uses of this world!°
135 Fie on 't! ah fie! 'tis an unweeded garden,
     That grows to seed; things rank and gross in
        nature
     Possess it merely.° That it should come to this!
     But two months dead: nay, not so much, not two:
     So excellent a king; that was, to this,
140 Hyperion° to a satyr;° so loving to my mother
     That he might not beteem° the winds of heaven
     Visit her face too roughly. Heaven and earth!
     Must I remember? why, she would hang on him,
     As if increase of appetite had grown
145 By what it fed on: and yet, within a month—
     Let me not think on 't—Frailty, thy name is
        woman!—
     A little month, or ere those shoes were old
     With which she follow'd my poor father's body,
     Like Niobe,° all tears:—why she, even she—
150 O God! a beast, that wants discourse° of reason,
     Would have mourn'd longer—married with my
        uncle,
     My father's brother, but no more like my father
     Than I to Hercules: within a month:
     Ere yet the salt of most unrighteous° tears
155 Had left the flushing in her gallèd eyes,°
     She married. O, most wicked speed, to post°

     With such dexterity° to incestuous sheets!
     It is not nor it cannot come to good:
     But break, my heart; for I must hold my tongue.

[Enter HORATIO, MARCELLUS, *and* BERNARDO.]

HORATIO: Hail to your lordship!
HAMLET: I am glad to see you well: 160
     Horatio,—or I do forget myself.
HORATIO: The same, my lord, and your poor servant
        ever.
HAMLET: Sir, my good friend; I'll change° that name
        with you:
     And what make you from° Wittenberg, Horatio?
     Marcellus?   165
MARCELLUS: My good lord—
HAMLET: I am very glad to see you. Good even, sir.
     But what, in faith, make you from Wittenberg?
HORATIO: A truant disposition,° good my lord.
HAMLET: I would not hear your enemy say so,   170
     Nor shall you do mine ear that violence,
     To make it truster° of your own report
     Against yourself: I know you are no truant.
     But what is your affair° in Elsinore?
     We'll teach you to drink deep ere you depart.   175
HORATIO: My lord, I came to see your father's funeral.
HAMLET: I pray thee, do not mock me, fellow-stu-
        dent;
     I think it was to see my mother's wedding.
HORATIO: Indeed, my lord, it follow'd hard upon.°
HAMLET: Thrift, thrift, Horatio! the funeral baked
        meats°   180
     Did coldly furnish forth° the marriage tables.
     Would I had met my dearest° foe in heaven
     Or ever I had seen that day, Horatio!
     My father!—methinks I see my father.
HORATIO: Where, my lord?
HAMLET: In my mind's eye, Horatio.   185
HORATIO: I saw him once; he was a goodly° king.
HAMLET: He was a man, take him for all in all,
     I shall not look upon his like again.
HORATIO: My lord, I think I saw him yesternight.
HAMLET: Saw? who?   190
HORATIO: My lord, the king your father.
HAMLET: The king my father!
HORATIO: Season your admiration° for a while
     With an attent° ear, till I may deliver,°

---

120 **in . . . best** to the best of my ability   123 **accord** consent
124 **in grace whereof** in thanksgiving for which   127 **rouse**
deep draught, here, a toast   **bruit** again **re-echo**   132 **canon**
law   134 **uses . . . world** human experience   137 **merely** completely   140 **Hyperion** the Greek sun god, the most beautiful
of all gods;   **Satyr** an ugly, lascivious beast, half goat and half
man   141 **beteem** allow   149 **Niobe** a character in Greek
mythology. The gods, angered at her boasting of her children,
slew them all and turned Niobe into a mass of rock from which
her tears flowed in a never-ending stream.   150 **discourse** faculty   154 **unrighteous** i.e., because insincere   155 **left . . . eyes**
ceased to flow in her reddened eyes   156 **post** hurry

---

157 **dexterity** speed   163 **change** exchange   164 **what . . .
from?** what are you doing away from   169 **truant disposition** a whim to play the truant   172 **truster** believer   174
affair actual business   179 **hard upon** close after   180
baked meats meat pies   181 **Did coldly furnish forth** were
served up cold at   182 **dearest** worst-hated   186 **goodly**
handsome and regal   192 **Season your admiration** restrain
your astonishment   193 **attent** attentive **deliver** report

Upon the witness of these gentlemen,
This marvel to you.
195 HAMLET: For God's love, let me hear.
HORATIO: Two nights together had these gentlemen,
Marcellus and Bernardo, on their watch,
In the dead vast° and middle of the night,
Been thus encounter'd. A figure like your father,
200 Armed at point° exactly, cap-a-pe,°
Appears before them, and with solemn march
Goes slow and stately by them: thrice he walk'd
By their oppress'd° and fear-surprised eyes,
Within his truncheon's° length; whilst they, distil-
l'd°
205 Almost to jelly with the act° of fear,
Stand dumb and speak not to him. This to me
In dreadful secrecy° impart they did;
And I with them the third night kept the watch:
Where, as they had deliver'd, both in time,
Form of the thing, each word made true and
210   good,
The apparition comes: I knew your father;
These hands are not more like.
HAMLET: But where was this?
MARCELLUS: My lord, upon the platform° where we
    watch'd.
HAMLET: Did you not speak to it?
HORATIO: My lord, I did;
215 But answer made it none: yet once methought
It lifted up it head and did address
Itself to motion,° like as it would speak;
But even then the morning cock crew loud,
And at the sound it shrunk in haste away,
And vanish'd from our sight.
220 HAMLET: 'Tis very strange.
HORATIO: As I do live, my honour'd lord, 'tis true;
And we did think it writ down in our duty
To let you know of it.
HAMLET: Indeed, indeed, sirs, but this troubles me.
Hold you the watch to-night?
225 MARCELLUS: ⎫
BERNARDO: ⎬ We do, my lord.
HAMLET: Arm'd, say you?
MARCELLUS: ⎫
BERNARDO: ⎬ Arm'd, my lord.
HAMLET: From top to toe?
MARCELLUS: ⎫
BERNARDO: ⎬ My lord, from head to foot.
HAMLET: Then saw you not his face?

HORATIO: O, yes, my lord; he wore his beaver° up.   230
HAMLET: What, look'd he frowningly?
HORATIO: A countenance more in sorrow than in
    anger.
HAMLET: Pale or red?
HORATIO: Nay, very pale.
HAMLET: And fix'd his eyes upon you?
HORATIO: Most constantly.
HAMLET: I would I had been there.   235
HORATIO: It would have much amazèd° you.
HAMLET: Very like, very like. Stay'd it long?
HORATIO: While one with moderate haste might tell°
    a hundred.
MARCELLUS: ⎫
BERNARDO: ⎬ Longer, longer.
HORATIO: Not when I saw 't.
HAMLET: His beard was grizzled,°—no?   240
HORATIO: It was, as I have seen it in his life,
    A sable silver'd.°
HAMLET: I will watch to-night;
Perchance 'twill walk again.
HORATIO: I warrant it will.
HAMLET: If it assume my noble father's person,
I'll speak to it, though hell itself should gape   245
And bid me hold my peace. I pray you all,
If you have hitherto conceal'd° this sight,
Let it be tenable° in your silence still;
And whatsoever else shall hap to-night,
Give it an understanding, but no tongue: 250
I will requite your loves.° So, fare you well:
Upon the platform, 'twixt eleven and twelve,
I'll visit you.
ALL: Our duty to your honour.
HAMLET: Your loves, as mine to you:° farewell.

[Exeunt all but HAMLET.]

My father's spirit in arms! all is not well;   255
I doubt° some foul play: would the night were
    come!
Till then sit still, my soul: foul deeds will rise,
Though all the earth o'erwhelm them, to men's
    eyes.

[Exit.]

Scene 3

A room in POLONIUS' house.

---

[198] **vast** great emptiness   [200] **at point** completely **cap-a-pe** from head to foot   [203] **oppress'd** overwhelmed (by dread)   [204] **truncheon** an officer's short staff **distill'd** dissolved, i.e., quaking with fear like jelly   [206] **with the act** through the action   [207] **In . . . secrecy** as a terrifying secret   [213] **platform,** i.e., level walk along the ramparts   [216-7] **address . . . motion** began to make movements

[230] **beaver** visor (of a helmet)   [236] **amazed** utterly bewildered   [238] **tell** count   [240] **grizzled** gray   [242] **Sable silver'd** i.e., black flecked with white   [247] **conceal'd** kept secret   [248] **tenable** held fast   [251] **requite your loves** repay your kindness   [254] **Your loves . . . you** i.e., offer me the affection of a friend and I will do the same   [256] **doubt** suspect

[Enter LAERTES *and* OPHELIA.*]*

LAERTES: My necessaries° are embark'd: farewell:
    And, sister, as° the winds give benefit
    And convoy is assistant,° do not sleep,
    But let me hear from you.
OPHELIA: Do you doubt that?
5   LAERTES: For° Hamlet and the trifling of his favour,
    Hold it a fashion° and a toy in blood,°
    A violet in the youth of primy nature,°
    Forward,° not permanent, sweet, not lasting,
    The perfume and suppliance° of a minute;
    No more.
OPHELIA: No more but so?
10 LAERTES: Think it no more:
    For nature, crescent,° does not grow alone
    In thews° and bulk, but as this temple° waxes,
    The inward service of° the mind and soul
    Grows wide withal.° Perhaps he loves you now,
15   And now no soil nor cautel° doth besmirch
    The virtue of his will:° but you must fear,
    His greatness weigh'd,° his will is not his own;
    For he himself is subject to his birth:
    He may not, as unvalued persons° do,
20   Carve° for himself; for on his choice depends
    The safety and health of this whole state;
    And therefore must his choice be circumscribed
    Unto the voice and yielding° of that body
    Whereof he is the head. Then if he says he loves you,
25   It fits your wisdom so far to believe it
    As he in his particular act and place
    May give his saying deed;° which is no further
    Than the main voice° of Denmark goes withal.°
    Then weigh what loss your honour may sustain,
30   If with too credent° ear you list his songs,
    Or lose your heart, or your chaste treasure open
    To his unmaster'd importunity.°
    Fear it, Ophelia, fear it, my dear sister,
    And keep you in the rear of your affection,°

Out of the shot and danger of desire.   35
    The chariest° maid is prodigal enough,°
    If she unmask her beauty to the moon:
    Virtue itself 'scapes not calumnious° strokes:
    The canker° galls the infants of the spring,
    Too oft before their buttons° be disclosed,   40
    And in the morn and liquid dew of youth
    Contagious blastments° are most imminent.
    Be wary then; best safety lies in fear:
    Youth to itself rebels, though none else near.°
OPHELIA: I shall the effect° of this good lesson keep, 45
    As watchman to my heart. But, good my brother,
    Do not, as some ungracious° pastors do,
    Show me the steep and thorny way to heaven;
    Whiles, like a puff'd° and reckless libertine,
    Himself the primrose path of dalliance° treads, 50
    And recks° not his own rede.°
LAERTES: O, fear me not.°
    I stay too long: but here my father comes.

[Enter POLONIUS.*]*

A double blessing is a double grace;
    Occasion smiles upon a second leave.°
POLONIUS: Yet here, Laertes! aboard, aboard, for
      shame!   55
    The wind sits in the shoulder of your sail,°
    And you are stay'd for. There; my blessing with
      thee!
    And these few precepts in thy memory
    See thou character.° Give thy thoughts no tongue,
    Nor any unproportion'd° thought his act. 60
    Be thou familiar,° but by no means vulgar.°
    Those friends thou hast, and their adoption
      tried,°
    Grapple them to thy soul with hoops of steel;
    But do not dull thy palm with entertainment°
    Of each new-hatch'd, unfledged comrade.
    Beware   65
    Of entrance to a quarrel, but being in,
    Bear 't° that the opposèd may beware of thee.

SCENE 3:   [1] **necessaries** baggage [2] **as** according as [3] **convey is assistant** means of conveyance is at hand [5] **For** as for [6] **fashion** whim; **toy in blood** an idle fancy of passion [7] **primy nature** i.e., spring [8] **Forward** premature [9] **suppliance of** diversion to fill [11] **nature** crescent, the nature of a human being, as it grows [12] **thews** sinews, i.e., strength **temple**, i.e., body [13] **inward service of** service conducted inside by [14] **Grows wide withal** expands at the same time [15] **cautel** deceit [16] **virtue of his will** his virtuous intentions [17] **His . . . weigh'd** when you consider his high rank [19] **unvalued persons** i.e., commoners [20] **Carve** choose [23] **voice and yielding** approval and assent [26-7] **in his . . . saying deed** acting as his peculiar circumstances and rank allow, may keep his promises [28] **main voice** public approval; **goes withal**, permits [30] **credent** credulous [32] **unmaster'd importunity** unrestrained persistence [34] **keep . . . affection** i.e., keep your love out of danger of being wounded

[36] **chariest** most scrupulous **prodigal enough** generous enough with her favors [38] **calumnious** slanderous [39] **canker** cankerworm [40] **buttons** buds [42] **blastments** blights [44] **Youth . . . else near** youth of its very nature is rebellious, even though subject to no outward temptation [45] **effect** purport [47] **ungracious** worldly [49] **puff'd** bloated [50] **dalliance** self-indulgence [51] **recks** heeds **rede** advice; **fear me not** don't worry about me [54] **Occasion . . . leave** i.e., it is good luck to say farewell twice [56] **The . . . sail** i.e., you have a favorable wind [59] **character** write down [60] **unproportion'd** unbalanced, ill-considered [61] **familiar** approachable **vulgar** too familiar [62] **adoption tried** loyalty tested [64] **dull . . . entertainment** callous your palm by giving a welcome to everyone [67] **Bear't** act in such a way

Give every man thy ear, but few thy voice;
Take each man's censure,° but reserve thy judge-
 ment.
70   Costly thy habit° as thy purse can buy,
But not express'd in fancy;° rich, not gaudy;
For the apparel oft proclaims the man,
And they in France of the best rank and station
Are of a most select and generous chief in that.°
75   Neither a borrower nor a lender be;
For loan oft loses both itself and friend,
And borrowing dulls the edge of husbandry.°
This above all: to thine own self be true,
And it must follow, as the night the day,
80   Thou canst not then be false to any man.
Farewell: my blessing season this° in thee!
LAERTES: Most humbly do I take my leave, my lord.
POLONIUS: The time invites you; go; your servants
  tend.
LAERTES: Farewell, Ophelia; and remember well
  What I have said to you.
85 OPHELIA: 'Tis in my memory lock'd,
And you yourself shall keep the key of it.
LAERTES: Farewell.

[Exit.]

POLONIUS: What is 't, Ophelia, he hath said to you?
OPHELIA: So please you, something touching the
  Lord Hamlet.
90 POLONIUS: Marry, well bethought:°
'Tis told me, he hath very oft of late
Given private time to you;° and you yourself
Have of your audience° been most free and boun-
  teous:
If it be so, as so 't is put on me,°
95   And that in way of caution, I must tell you,
You do not understand yourself so clearly
As it behooves my daughter and your honour.
What is between you? give me up the truth.
OPHELIA: He hath, my lord, of late made many ten-
  ders°
100   Of his affection to me.
POLONIUS: Affection! pooh! you speak like a green girl.
Unsifted° in such perilous circumstance.
Do you believe his tenders, as you call them?
OPHELIA: I do not know, my lord, what I should
  think.

POLONIUS: Marry, I'll teach you: think yourself a baby;   105
That you have ta'en these tenders for true pay,
Which are not sterling.° Tender° yourself more
  dearly;°
Or—not to crack the wind° of the poor phrase,
Running it thus—you'll tender me° a fool.
OPHELIA: My lord, he hath impórtuned me with love   110
In honourable fashion.
POLONIUS: Ay, fashion° you may call it; go to,° go to.
OPHELIA: And hath given countenance° to his speech,
  my lord,
With almost all the holy vows of heaven.
POLONIUS: Ay, springes° to catch woodcocks.° I do
  know,   115
When the blood° burns, how prodigal° the soul
Lends the tongue vows: these blazes, daughter,
Giving more light than heat, extinct in both.°
Even in their promise,° as it is a-making,
You must not take for fire. From this time   120
Be somewhat scanter of your maiden presence;
Set your entreatments° at a higher rate
Than a command to parley.° For Lord Hamlet,
Believe so much in him,° that he is young,
And with a larger tether may he walk   125
Than may be given you: in few,° Ophelia,
Do not believe his vows; for they are brokers,°
Not of that dye which their investments° show,
But mere implorators of unholy suits,°
Breathing° like sanctified° and pious bawds,   130
The better to beguile. This is for all:°
I would not, in plain terms, from this time forth,
Have you so slander° any moment leisure,
As to give words or talk with the Lord Hamlet.
Look to 't, I charge you: come your ways.°   135
OPHELIA: I shall obey, my lord.

[Exeunt.]

---

107 **sterling** real money **Tender** regard; **more dearly** of higher value   108 **crack the wind** i.e., make the phrase pant (as though it were a wounded horse)   109 **tender me** present me with (i.e., a fool for a daughter)   112 **fashion** mere form **go to** nonsense!   113 **given countenance to** confirmed   115 **springes** traps; **woodcocks** stupid birds, hence simpletons   116 **blood** passion; **prodigal** lavishly   118 **extinct in both** i.e., both show and substance of this love   119 **Even . . . promise** even while the lover is promising   122 **entreatments** favors entreated   123 **command to parley** request for conference (to discuss terms of surrender)   124 **so much in him** only so much about him as   126 **few** brief   127 **brokers** procurers; **investments** garments   129 **implorators . . . suits** i.e., tempters to vice   130 **Breathing** soliciting in whispers **sanctified** hypocritical   131 **This . . . all** the sum of my advice is this   133 **slander** disgrace   135 **your ways** along

---

69 **Take . . . censure** listen to everyone's opinion   70 **habit** clothing   71 **express'd in fancy** bizarre in design   74 **Are... chief in that** show their best aristocratic and discriminating taste in (the choice of clothes)   77 **husbandry** thrift   81 **season this** make this (advice) bear fruit   83 **invites** summons **tend** wait for you   90 **Marry** well bethought by the Virgin Mary; well remembered   92 **Given . . . you** seen you alone   93 **audience** company   94 **'t is . . . me** I have been informed   99 **tenders** offers of pay   102 **Unsifted** untried

Scene 4

The platform.

[Enter HAMLET, HORATIO, *and* MARCELLUS.*]*

HAMLET: The air bites shrewdly;° it is very cold.
HORATIO: It is a nipping and an eager° air.
HAMLET: What hour now?
HORATIO: I think it lacks of twelve.
MARCELLUS: No, it is struck.
HORATIO: Indeed? I heard it not: then it draws near
5   the season
      Wherein the spirit held his wont° to walk.

[A flourish of trumpets, and ordnance shot off, within.]

What does this mean, my lord?
HAMLET: The king doth wake° to-night and takes his
      rouse,°
      Keeps wassail,° and the swaggering up-spring°
      reels;
10   And, as he drains his draughts of Rhenish° down,
      The kettle-drum and trumpet thus bray out
      The triumph of his pledge.°
HORATIO: Is it a custom?
HAMLET: Ay, marry,° is 't:
      But to my mind, though I am native here
15   And to the manner born,° it is a custom
      More honour'd in the breach than the observance.
      This heavy-headed revel east and west°
      Makes us traduced and tax'd° of other nations:
      They clepe° us drunkards, and with swinish
      phrase
20   Soil our addition;° and indeed it takes
      From our achievements, though perform'd at
      height,°
      The pith and marrow of our attribute.°
      So, oft it chances in particular men,
      That for some vicious mole of nature° in them,
25   As, in their birth—wherein they are not guilty,
      Since nature cannot choose his origin—
      By the o'ergrowth of some complexion,°
      Oft breaking down the pales° and forts of reason,

Or by some habit that too much o'er-leavens°
      The form of plausive° manners, that these men,   30
      Carrying, I say, the stamp of one defect,
      Being nature's livery,° or fortune's star,°—
      Their virtues else—be they as pure as grace,
      As infinite as man may undergo°—
      Shall in the general censure° take corruption   35
      From that particular fault: the dram of eale°
      Doth all the noble substance often dout°
      To his own scandal.°
HORATIO: Look, my lord, it comes!

[Enter GHOST.]*

HAMLET: Angels and ministers of grace defend us!
      Be thou a spirit of health° or goblin damn'd,°   40
      Bring with thee airs from heaven or blasts from
      hell,
      Be thy intents wicked or charitable,
      Thou comest in such a questionable° shape
      That I will speak to thee: I'll call thee Hamlet,
      King, father, royal Dane: O, answer me!   45
      Let me not burst in ignorance; but tell
      Why thy canónized° bones, hearsèd in death,
      Have burst their cerements;° why the sepulchre,
      Wherein we saw thee quietly interr'd,
      Hath oped his ponderous and marble jaws,   50
      To cast thee up again. What may this mean,
      That thou, dead corse, again in cómplete steel
      Revisit'st thus the glimpses of the moon,
      Making night hideous; and we fools° of nature
      So horridly to shake our disposition°   55
      With thoughts beyond the reaches of our souls?
      Say, why is this? wherefore? what should we do?

*[*GHOST *beckons* HAMLET.]*

HORATIO: It beckons you to go away with it,
      As if it some impartment° did desire
      To you alone.
MARCELLUS: Look, with what courteous action   60
      It waves you to a more removèd° ground:
      But do not go with it.
HORATIO: No, by no means.

SCENE 4:   ¹ **shrewdly** keenly   ² **eager** sharp   ⁶ **held his wont** was accustomed   ⁸ **wake** revel;   **takes his rouse** is drinking heavily   ⁹ **Keeps wassail** holds a drinking bout; **up-spring** upstart   ¹⁰ **Rhenish** Rhine wine   ¹² **pledge** toast   ¹³ **marry** i.e., by the Virgin Mary, a mild oath   ¹⁵ **to . . . born** used to the custom from birth   ¹⁷ **east and west** far and wide   ¹⁸ **traduced and tax'd** censured and reproached   ¹⁹ **clepe** call   ¹⁹⁻²⁰ **with . . . addition** smirch our good name by calling us swine   ²¹ **perform'd at height** the best of which we are capable   ²² **attribute** reputation   ²⁴ **mole of nature** natural blemish   ²⁷ **complexion** natural quality   ²⁸ **pales** defenses

²⁹ **o'er-leavens** spoils (by overdevelopment of some quality, good in itself)   ³⁰ **plausive** pleasing   ³² **nature's livery** mark of nature, i.e., inborn;   **fortune's star** i.e., the result of chance   ³⁴ **As . . . undergo** as boundless as a man is capable of   ³⁵ **general censure** popular opinion   ³⁶ **eale** evil   ³⁷ **doubt** do out, banish   ³⁸ **scandal** disgrace   ⁴⁰ **spirit of health** blessed spirit; **goblin damn'd** devil from Hell   ⁴³ **questionable** inviting question   ⁴⁷ **canonized** consecrat' i.e., buried with all the rites of the church   ⁴⁸ **cereme** winding sheet   ⁵⁴ **fools** weak children   ⁵⁵ **shake . . . di** **sition** upset our mental equilibrium   ⁵⁹ **impartment** munication   ⁶¹ **removed** distant

HAMLET: It will not speak; then I will follow it.

HORATIO: Do not, my lord.

HAMLET: Why, what should be the fear?

65   I do not set my life at a pin's fee;°

And for my soul, what can it do to that,

Being a thing immortal as itself?

It waves me forth again: I'll follow it.

HORATIO: What if it tempt you toward the flood,° my

lord,

70   Or to the dreadful summit of the cliff

That beetles° o'er his base into the sea,

And there assume some other horrible form,

Which might deprive your sovereignty of° reason

And draw you into madness? think of it:

75   The very place puts toys of desperation,°

Without more motive, into every brain

That looks so many fathoms to the sea

And hears it roar beneath.

HAMLET: It waves me still.°

Go on; I'll follow thee.

MARCELLUS: You shall not go, my lord.

80   HAMLET: Hold off your hands.

HORATIO: Be ruled; you shall not go.

HAMLET: My fate cries out,°

And makes each petty artery in this body

As hardy as the Nemean lion's° nerve.°

Still am I call'd. Unhand me, gentleman.

85   By heaven, I'll make a ghost of him that lets° me!

I say, away! Go on; I'll follow thee.

[Exeunt GHOST and HAMLET.]

HORATIO: He waxes desperate with imagination.°

MARCELLUS: Let's follow; 'tis not fit thus to obey him.

HORATIO: Have after.° To what issue° will this come?

MARCELLUS: Something is rotten in the state of

90   Denmark.

HORATIO: Heaven will direct it.°

MARCELLUS: Nay, let's follow him.

[Exeunt.]

Scene 5

Another part of the platform.

[Enter GHOST and HAMLET.]

HAMLET: Where wilt thou lead me? speak; I'll go no

further.

GHOST: Mark me.

HAMLET: I will.

GHOST: My hour° is almost come,

When I to sulphurous and tormenting flames

Must render up myself.

HAMLET: Alas, poor ghost!

GHOST: Pity me not, but lend thy serious hearing   5

To what I shall unfold.

HAMLET: Speak; I am bound° to hear.

GHOST: So art thou to revenge, when thou shalt hear.

HAMLET: What?

GHOST: I am thy father's spirit,

Doom'd for a certain term to walk the night,   10

And for the day confined to fast° in fires,

Till the foul crimes° done in my days of nature°

Are burnt and purged away. But that I am forbid

To tell the secrets of my prison-house,

I could a tale unfold whose lightest word   15

Would harrow up thy soul, freeze thy young blood,

Make thy two eyes, like stars, start from their

spheres,°

Thy knotted and combinèd locks to part

And each particular hair to stand an end,°

Like quills upon the fretful porpentine:°   20

But this eternal blazon° must not be

To ears of flesh and blood. List, list, O, list!

If thou didst ever thy dear father love—

HAMLET: O God!

GHOST: Revenge his foul and most unnatural murder.   25

HAMLET: Murder!

GHOST: Murder most foul, as in the best° it is;

But this most foul, strange and unnatural.

HAMLET: Haste me to know't, that I, with wings as

swift

As meditation or the thoughts of love,   30

May sweep to my revenge.

GHOST: I find thee apt;°

And duller shouldst thou be than the fat° weed

That roots itself in ease on Lethe wharf,°

Wouldst thou not stir in this. Now, Hamlet, hear:

'Tis given out that, sleeping in my orchard,°   35

A serpent stung me; so the whole ear of Denmark

Is by a forgèd process° of my death

Rankly abused:° but know, thou noble youth,

---

65 **fee** value   69 **flood** i.e., the sea (which washed the castle's walls)   71 **beetles** juts out   73 **deprive . . . of** i.e.,
dethrone   75 **toys of desperation** desperate notions   78
waves me still keeps beckoning to me   81 **cries out** i.e.,
commands me   83 **Nemean lion** a monster slain by
Hercules **nerve** sinews   85 **lets** prevents   87 **imagination**
false conception, illusion   89 **Have after** follow him; **issue**
result   91 **it** i.e., the result

SCENE 5:   2 **hour** i.e., the dawn   6 **bound** duty bound   11
fast do penance   12 **foul crimes** ugly sins (those which
every mortal man commits);   **days of nature** mortal life   17
spheres orbits   19 **an end** on end   20 **porpentine** porcu-
pine   21 **eternal blazon** disclosure of matters concerning
eternal life   27 **in the best** at best, i.e., when committed for a
good reason   31 **apt** responsive   32 **fat** slimy   33 **wharf**
bank   35 **orchard** garden   37 **process** official account   38
abused deceived

The serpent that did sting thy father's life
Now wears his crown.

40 HAMLET: O my prophetic soul!
My uncle!
GHOST: Ay, that incestuous, that adulterate° beast,
With witchcraft of his wit, with traitorous gifts,—
O wicked wit and gifts, that have the power
45 So to seduce!—won to his shameful lust
The will of my most seeming-virtuous queen.
O Hamlet, what a falling-off was there
From me, whose love was of that dignity
That it went hand in hand even with the vow
50 I made to her in marriage, and to decline
Upon a wretch whose natural gifts were poor
To those of mine!
But virtue, as it never will be moved,
Though lewdness court it in a shape of heaven,°
55 So lust, though to a radiant angel link'd,
Will sate itself in a celestial bed,
And prey on garbage.
But, soft! methinks I scent the morning air;
Brief let me be. Sleeping within my orchard,
60 My custom always of the afternoon,
Upon my secure° hour thy uncle stole,
With juice of cursèd hebenon° in a vial,
And in the porches° of my ears did pour
The leperous distillment;° whose effect
65 Holds such an enmity with blood of man
That swift as quicksilver it courses through
The natural gates and alleys of the body,
And with a sudden vigour it doth posset°
And curd,° like eager° droppings into milk,
70 The thin and wholesome blood: so did it mine;
And a most instant tetter bark'd about,°
Most lazar-like,° with vile and loathsome crust,
All my smooth body.
Thus was I, sleeping, by a brother's hand
75 Of life, of crown, of queen, at once dispatch'd:°
Cut off even in the blossoms of my sin,
Unhousel'd, disappointed, unaneled,°
No reckoning° made, but sent to my account°
With all my imperfections on my head:
80 O, horrible! O, horrible! most horrible!
If thou hast nature in thee,° bear it not;

Let not the royal bed of Denmark be
A couch for luxury° and damned incest.
But, howsoever thou pursuest° this act,
Taint not° thy mind, nor let thy soul contrive   85
Against thy mother aught: leave her to heaven
And to those thorns that in her bosom lodge,
To prick and sting her. Fare thee well at once!
The glow-worm shows the matin° to be near,
And 'gins to pale his uneffectual° fire: 90
Adieu, adieu! Hamlet, remember me.

[Exit.]

HAMLET: O all you host of heaven! O earth! what else?
And shall I couple hell? O, fie! Hold, hold, my
     heart;
And you, my sinews, grow not instant old,
But bear me stiffly up. Remember thee!   95
Ay, thou poor ghost, while memory holds a seat
In this distracted globe.° Remember thee!
Yea, from the table° of my memory
I'll wipe away all trivial fond° records,
All saws° of books, all forms,° all pressures past,°   100
That youth and observation copied there;
And thy commandment all alone shall live
Within the book and volume of my brain,
Unmix'd with baser matter: yes, by heaven!
O most pernicious woman!   105
O villain, villain, smiling, damned villain!
My tables,—meet it is I set it down,
That one may smile, and smile, and be a villain;
At least I'm sure it may be so in Denmark:

[Writing.]

So, uncle, there you are. Now to my word;°   110
It is "Adieu, adieu! remember me."
I have sworn 't.
MARCELLUS: ⎫ [*Within*] My lord, my lord,—
HORATIO: ⎭
MARCELLUS: [*Within*]   Lord Hamlet,—
HORATIO: [*Within*]   Heaven secure° him!
HAMLET: So be it!
HORATIO: [*Within*] Hillo, ho, ho, my lord!   115
HAMLET: Hillo, ho, ho, boy! come, bird, come°

[Enter HORATIO *and* MARCELLUS.*]*

MARCELLUS: How is 't, my noble lord?

---

⁴² **adulterate** adulterous ⁵⁴ **shape of heaven** i.e., angel's
form ⁶¹ **secure** unsuspecting ⁶² **hebenon** henbane ⁶³
porches entrances ⁶⁴ **leperous distillment** liquid causing
leprosy ⁶⁸ **posset** curdle ⁶⁹ **curd** thicken; **eager** sour
⁷¹ **tetter...about** eruption broke out ⁷² **lazar-like** like leprosy ⁷⁵ **at once dispatch'd** suddenly deprived of all together ⁷⁷ **Unhousel'd ... unaneled** without having received
the sacrament, unprepared (through confession), without
final ceremony of anointing with holy oil ⁷⁸ **reckoning** i.e.,
of his sins through confession; **account** i.e., payment for
my sins ⁸¹ **thou ... thee** you have a son's natural feeling

---

⁸³ **luxury** lust ⁸⁴ **pursuest** seek to avenge ⁸⁵ **Taint not**
i.e., with suspicions of your mother ⁸⁹ **matin** dawn ⁹⁰
uneffectual i.e., ineffectual because of daylight ⁹⁷ **globe**
head of mine ⁹⁸ **table** notebook ⁹⁹ **fond** foolish ¹⁰⁰
saws wise sayings; **forms** ideas; **pressures past** impressions from the past ¹¹⁰ **word** cue ¹¹³ **secure** protect ¹¹⁶
Hillo ... come call used by falconer to call back his hawk

HORATIO: What news, my lord?

HAMLET: O, wonderful!

HORATIO: Good my lord, tell it.

HAMLET: No; you'll reveal it.

HORATIO: Not I, my lord, by heaven.

120 MARCELLUS: Nor I, my lord.

HAMLET: How say you,° then; would heart of man
    once think° it?
    But you'll be secret?

HORATIO: ⎫
MARCELLUS: ⎬ Ay, by heaven, my lord.

HAMLET: There's ne'er a villain dwelling in all
    Denmark
    But he's an arrant° knave.

HORATIO: There needs no ghost, my lord, come from
125   the grave
    To tell us this.

HAMLET: Why, right; you are i' the right;
    And so, without more circumstance° at all,
    I hold it fit that we shake hands and part:
    You, as your business and desire shall point° you;
130   For every man has business and desire,
    Such as it is; and for mine own poor part,
    Look you, I'll go pray.

HORATIO: These are but wild and whirling° words,
    my lord.

HAMLET: I'm sorry they offend you, heartily;
    Yes 'faith, heartily.

135 HORATIO: There's no offence, my lord.

HAMLET: Yes, by Saint Patrick,° but there is, Horatio,
    And much offence too. Touching this vision here,
    It is an honest° ghost, that let me tell you:
    For your desire to know what is between us,
140   O'ermaster 't° as you may. And now, good friends,
    As you are friends, scholars and soldiers,
    Give me one poor request.

HORATIO: What is 't, my lord? we will.

HAMLET: Never make known what you have seen to-
    night.

HORATIO: ⎫
MARCELLUS: ⎬ My lord, we will not.

HAMLET: Nay, but swear't.

145 HORATIO: In faith,
    My lord, not I.

MARCELLUS: Nor I, my lord, in faith.

HAMLET: Upon my sword.°

MARCELLUS: We have sworn, my lord, already.

HAMLET: Indeed, upon my sword, indeed.

GHOST: [*Beneath*] Swear.

HAMLET: Ah, ha, boy! say'st thou so? art thou there,
    truepenny?°   150
    Come on—you hear this fellow in the cellarage—
    Consent to swear.

HORATIO: Propose the oath, my lord.

HAMLET: Never to speak of this that you have seen,
    Swear by my sword.

GHOST: [*Beneath*] Swear.   155

HAMLET: Hic et ubique?° then we'll shift our ground.
    Come hither, gentlemen,
    And lay your hands again upon my sword:
    Never to speak of this that you have heard,
    Swear by my sword.   160

GHOST: [*Beneath*] Swear.

HAMLET: Well said, old mole! canst work i' the earth
    so fast?
    A worthy pioner!° Once more remove,° good
    friends.

HORATIO: O day and night, but this is wondrous
    strange!

HAMLET: And therefore as a stranger give it welcome.   165
    There are more things in heaven and earth,
    Horatio,
    Than are dreamt of in your philosophy.°
    But come;
    Here, as before, never, so help you mercy,
    How° strange or odd soe'er I bear myself,   170
    As° I perchance hereafter shall think meet
    To put an antic disposition on,°
    That you, at such times seeing me, never shall,
    With arms encumber'd° thus, or this headshake,
    Or by pronouncing of some doubtful phrase,   175
    As "Well, well, we know," or "We could, an if we
    would,"
    Or "If we list to speak,"° or "There be, an if they
    might,"
    Or such ambiguous giving out,° to note
    That you know aught of me: this not to do,
    So grace and mercy at your most need help you,   180
    Swear.

GHOST: [*Beneath*] Swear.

HAMLET: Rest, rest, perturbèd spirit! [*They swear.*] So,
    gentlemen,
    With all my love I do commend me to you:°
    And what so poor a man as Hamlet is   185
    May do, to express his love and friending° to you,

---

121 How say you? What do you think about this? **once think** ever believe **124 arrant** out and out **127 circumstance** ceremony **129 point** direct **131 whirling** incoherent **136 Saint Patrick** possibly because he was supposed to be the keeper of Purgatory **138 honest** real (and not a demon) **140 O'ermaster't** control it **147 Upon my sword** because the hilt of the sword formed a cross

150 truepenny trusty old fellow **156 Hic et ubique?** Here and everywhere? **163 pioner** sapper, military engineer (who used to dig tunnels); **remove** shift your position **167 philosophy** science **170 How** however **171 As** whenever **172 put . . . on** adopt grotesque behavior **174 encumber'd** folded **177 list to speak** cared to talk **178 giving out** pronouncement **184 commend . . . you** put myself in your hands **186 friending** good will

God willing, shall not lack.° Let us go in together;°
And still your fingers on your lips, I pray.
The time is out of joint:° O cursèd spite,°
190 That ever I was born to set it right!
Nay, come, let's go together.

[Exeunt.]

ACT II

Scene 1

A room in POLONIUS' *house.*

[Enter POLONIUS *and* REYNALDO.*]*

POLONIUS: Give him this money and these notes,
      Reynaldo.
REYNALDO: I will, my lord.
POLONIUS: You shall do marvellous wisely, good
      Reynaldo,
      Before you visit him, to make inquire
      Of his behaviour.
5 REYNALDO: My lord, I did intend it.
POLONIUS: Marry, well said; very well said. Look you,
      sir,
      Inquire me° first what Danskers° are in Paris;
      And how, and who, what means,° and where
      they keep,°
      What company,° at what expense; and finding
10   By this encompassment° and drift° of question
      That they do know my son, come you more nearer
      Than your particular demands° will touch it:
      Take you,° as 'twere, some distant knowledge of
      him;
      As thus, "I know his father and his friends,
15   And in part him:" do you mark this, Reynaldo?
REYNALDO: Ay, very well, my lord.
POLONIUS: "And in part him; but" you may say "not
      well:
      But, if 't be he I mean, he's very wild;
      Addicted so and so:" and there put on° him
20   What forgeries° you please; marry, none so rank°

As may dishonour him; take heed of that;
But, sir, such wanton,° wild and usual slips
As are companions noted° and most known
To youth and liberty.
REYNALDO: As gaming, my lord.
POLONIUS: Ay, or drinking, fencing, swearing,
      quarrelling,   25
      Drabbing:° you may go so far.
REYNALDO: My lord, that would dishonour him.
POLONIUS: 'Faith, no; as you may season it in the
      charge.°
      You must not put another scandal on him,
      That° he is open to incontinency;°   30
      That's not my meaning: but breathe his faults so
      quaintly°
      That they may seem the taints of liberty,°
      The flash and outbreak of a fiery mind,
      A savageness in unreclaimèd blood,°
      Of general assault.°
REYNALDO: But, my good lord,—   35
POLONIUS: Wherefore should you do this?
REYNALDO: Ay, my lord,
      I would know that.
POLONIUS: Marry, sir, here's my drift;°
      And, I believe, it is a fetch of warrant:°
      You laying° these slight sullies° on my son,
      As 'twere° a thing a little soil'd i' the working,° 40
      Mark you,
      Your party in converse, him you would sound,
      Having ever seen in the prenominate° crimes
      The youth you breathe of guilty, be assured
      He closes° with you in this consequence;°   45
      "Good sir," or so, or "friend," or "gentleman,"
      According to the phrase or the addition°
      Of man and country.
REYNALDO: Very good, my lord.
POLONIUS: And then, sir, does he this—he does—what
      was I about to say? By the mass, I was about to 50
      say something: where did I leave?°
REYNALDO: At "closes in the consequence," at
      "friend or so," and "gentleman."
POLONIUS: At "closes in the consequence," ay, marry;
      He closes thus: "I know the gentleman;   55

---

187 **lack** be lacking; **together** i.e., as equals 189 **time . . .
joint** the world is in a state of confusion; **spite** affliction

ACT II, SCENE 1: 7 **Inquire me** ask for me; **Danskers** Danes
8 **means** money [they have], **keep** live 9 **What company**
i.e., they keep 10 **encompassment** roundabout approach;
drift gradual approach 12 **particular demands** specific questions 13 **Take you** pretend 19 **put on** ascribe to 20 **forgeries** invented stories; **rank** gross

22 **wanton** gay 23 **companions noted** observed to be companions 28 **season . . . charge** tone down the accusation
even while you are making it 26 **Drabbing** whoring 30
That namely that; **open to incontinency** given to **habitual licentiousness** 31 **quaintly** artfully 32 **liberty** lack of
self-control 34 **unreclaimèd blood** untamed passion 35
general assault common to all [young men] 37 **drift**
scheme 38 **fetch of warrant** device that is sure to work 39
You laying when you lay; **sullies** aspersions 40 **'twere**
i.e., he were; **working** making 43 **prenominate** already
mentioned 45 **closes** agrees; **in this consequence** as follows 47 **addition** mode of address 51 **leave** leave off

I saw him yesterday, or t'other day,
Or then, or then; with such, or such; and, as you say,
There was a' gaming; there o'ertook in 's rouse;°
There falling out at tennis:" or perchance,
60   "I saw him enter such a house of sale,"
Videlicet,° a brothel, or so forth.
See you now;
Your bait of falsehood takes this carp of truth:
And thus do we of wisdom and of reach,°
65   With windlasses° and with assays of bias,°
By indirections find directions out:°
So by my former lecture and advice,
Shall you my son.° You have° me, have you not?
REYNALDO: My lord, I have.
POLONIUS: God be wi' you; fare you well.
70   REYNALDO: Good my lord!
POLONIUS: Observe his inclination in yourself.°
REYNALDO: I shall, my lord.
POLONIUS: And let him play his music.
REYNALDO: Well,° my lord.
POLONIUS: Farewell!

[Exit REYNALDO.]

[Enter OPHELIA.*]*

How now, Ophelia! what's the matter?
75   OPHELIA: O, my lord, my lord, I have been so affrighted!
POLONIUS: With what, i' the name of God?
OPHELIA: My lord, as I was sewing in my closet,°
    Lord Hamlet, with his doublet° all unbraced,°
    No hat upon his head; his stockings foul'd,°
80   Ungarter'd, and down-gyvèd° to his ancle;
    Pale as his shirt; his knees knocking each other;
    And with a look so piteous in purport
    As if he had been loosèd out of hell
    To speak of horrors—he comes before me.
POLONIUS: Mad for thy love?°
85   OPHELIA: My lord, I do not know;
    But truly, I do fear it.
POLONIUS: What said he?
OPHELIA: He took me by the wrist and held me hard;
    Then goes he to the length of all his arm;°
    And, with his other hand thus o'er his brow,

He falls to such perusal of my face   90
As he would draw it. Long stay'd he so;
At last, a little shaking of mine arm
And thrice his head thus waving up and down,
He raised a sigh so piteous and profound
As it did seem to shatter all his bulk   95
And end his being: that done, he lets me go:
And, with his head over his shoulder turn'd;
He seem'd to find his way without his eyes;
For out o' doors he went without their helps,
And, to the last, bended their light on me.   100
POLONIUS: Come, go with me: I will go seek the king.
This is the very ecstasy° of love,
Whose violent property° fordoes itself°
And leads the will to desperate undertakings
As oft as any passion under heaven   105
That does afflict our natures. I am sorry.
What, have you given him any hard words of late?
OPHELIA: No, my good lord, but, as you did command,
I did repel his letters and denied
His access to me.
POLONIUS: That hath made him mad.   110
I am sorry that with better heed and judgement
I had not quoted° him: I fear'd he did but trifle,
And meant to wreck thee; but, beshrew my jeal-
    ousy!°
By heaven, it is as proper° to our age°
To cast beyond° ourselves in our opinions   115
As it is common for the younger sort
To lack discretion. Come, go we to the king:
This must be known; which, being kept close,°
    might move
More grief to hide than hate to utter love.°

[Exeunt.]

Scene 2

A room in the castle.

[Enter KING, QUEEN, ROSENCRANTZ, GUILDENSTERN, *and*
ATTENDANTS.]*

KING: Welcome, dear Rosencrantz and Guildenstern!
    Moreover that° we much did long to see you,

---

⁵⁸ **o'ertook in 's rouse** overcome by drink   ⁶¹ **Videlicet** that is to say   ⁶⁴ **of reach** of vision   ⁶⁵ **windlasses** roundabout approaches;   **assays of bias** indirect ways. Bias was the curve a bowler put on his ball.   ⁶⁶ **find directions out** i.e., discover the truth   ⁶⁸ **you my son** i.e., find out the truth about my son;   **have** understand   ⁷¹ **in yourself** by your own inclinations   ⁷³ **Well** very well   ⁷⁷ **closet** private sitting room   ⁷⁸ **doublet** sleeveless jacket;   **unbraced** unfastened   ⁷⁹ **foul'd** muddy   ⁸⁰ **down-gyved** hanging down like fetters   ⁸⁵ **for thy love** because of his love for you   ⁸⁸ **goes . . . arm** i.e., he holds me at arm's length

¹⁰² **ecstasy** insanity   ¹⁰³ **property** nature;   **fordoes itself** destroys the person afflicted   ¹¹² **quoted** observed   ¹¹³ **jealousy** suspicion   ¹¹⁴ **proper** natural;   **our age** i.e., old age   ¹¹⁵ **cast beyond** lovershoot   ¹¹⁸ **being kept close** if it were concealed   ¹¹⁸⁻⁹ **might move . . . utter love** might cause more grief through its concealment than it would arouse hatred (on the part of Hamlet and/or his parents) through telling it.

SCENE 2:   ² **Moreover that** besides the fact that

The need we have to use you did provoke
Our hasty sending. Something have you heard
5   Of Hamlet's transformation; so call it,
Sith nor the exterior nor the inward man
Resembles that° it was. What it should be,
More than his father's death, that thus hath put him
So much from° the understanding of himself,°
10   I cannot dream of: I entreat you both,
That, being of so young days° brought up with him,
And sith so neighbour'd to his youth and haviour,
That you vouchsafe your rest° here in our court
Some little time: so° by your companies
15   To draw him on to pleasures, and to gather,
So much as from occasion° you may glean,
Whether aught, to us unknown, afflicts him thus,
That, open'd,° lies within our remedy.
QUEEN: Good gentlemen, he hath much talk'd of you;
20   And sure I am two men there are not living
To whom he more adheres.° If it will please you
To show us so much gentry° and good will
As to expend your time with us awhile,
For the supply and profit° of our hope,
25   Your visitation shall receive such thanks
As fits° a king's remembrance.
ROSENCRANTZ: Both your majesties
Might, by the sovereign power you have of° us,
Put your dread pleasures° more into command
Than to entreaty.
GUILDENSTERN: But we both obey,
30   And here give up ourselves, in the full bent°
To lay our service freely at your feet,
To be commanded.
KING: Thanks, Rosencrantz and gentle Guildenstern.
QUEEN: Thanks, Guildenstern and gentle
Rosencrantz:
35   And I beseech you instantly to visit
My too much changèd son. Go, some of you,
And bring these gentlemen where Hamlet is.
GUILDENSTERN: Heavens make our presence and our
practices°
Pleasant and helpful to him!
QUEEN: Ay, amen!

[Exeunt ROSENCRANTZ, GUILDENSTERN, *and some*
ATTENDANTS.*]*

[Enter POLONIUS.*]*

POLONIUS: The ambassadors from Norway, my good
lord,   40
Are joyfully return'd.
KING: Thou still° hast been the father of good news.
POLONIUS: Have I, my lord? I assure my good liege,
I hold my duty, as I hold my soul,
Both to my God and to my gracious king:°   45
And I do think, or else this brain of mine
Hunts not the trail of policy° so sure
As it hath used to do, that I have found
The very cause of Hamlet's lunacy.
KING: O, speak of that; that do I long to hear.   50
POLONIUS: Give first admittance to the ambassadors;
My news shall be the fruit° to that great feast.
KING: Thyself do grace to them,° and bring them in.

[Exit POLONIUS.*]*

He tells me, my dear Gertrude, he hath found
The head and source of all your son's distemper.°   55
QUEEN: I doubt it is no other but the main;°
His father's death, and our o'erhasty marriage.
KING: Well, we shall sift him.

[Re-enter POLONIUS, *with* VOLTIMAND *and* CORNELIUS.*]*

Welcome, my good friends!
Say, Voltimand, what from our brother Norway?
VOLTIMAND: Most fair return of greetings and desires. 60
Upon our first,° he sent out to suppress
His nephew's levies; which to him appear'd
To be a preparation 'gainst the Polack;
But, better look'd into, he truly found
It was against your highness: whereat grieved,   65
That so his sickness, age and impotence
Was falsely borne in hand,° sends out arrests°
On Fortinbras; which he, in brief, obeys;
Receives rebuke from Norway, and in fine°
Makes vow before his uncle never more   70
To give the assay of arms° against your majesty.
Whereon old Norway, overcome with joy,
Gives him three thousand crowns in annual fee,°
And his commission to employ those soldiers,
So levied as before, against the Polack: 75
With an entreaty, herein further shown,

---

7 **that** what   8-9 **put him . . . from** robbed him of   9 **the . . .
of himself** i.e., of his self-control   11 **of so . . . days** from
such an early age   13 **vouchsafe your rest** agree to stay   14
so so as   16 **from occasion** i.e., when opportunity offers   18
open'd disclosed   21 **more adheres** is more attached   22
gentry courtesy   24 **supply and profit** advancement and
fulfillment   26 **fits** befits   27 **of** over   28 **dread pleasures**
revered wishes   30 **in . . . bent** as much as we can—a figure
from archery, i.e., stretched to the uttermost   38 **practices**
actions

---

42 **still** always   44-5 **I hold . . . king** i.e., I regard my duty to
my gracious King [as sacred] as my soul's duty to my God
47 **policy** statecraft   52 **fruit** dessert   53 **do . . . them** welcome them   55 **distemper** illness, i.e., melancholy   56 **main**
chief cause   61 **first** i.e., representations   67 **falsely . . . hand**
dishonestly taken advantage of; **arrests** a royal summons
69 **in fine** finally   71 **give . . . arms** i.e., attack   73 **three . . .
fee** yielding an annual income of three thousand crowns. A
crown was worth five shillings.

[Giving a paper.]

That it might please you to give quiet pass°
Through your dominions for this enterprise,
On such regards of safety and allowance°
As therein are set down.

80   KING: It likes us well;°
And at our more consider'd time° we'll read,
Answer, and think upon this business.
Meantime we thank you for your well-took labour:
Go to your rest; at night we'll feast together:
Most welcome home!

[Exeunt VOLTIMAND and CORNELIUS.]

POLONIUS: This business is well ended.
85   My liege, and madam, to expostulate°
What majesty should be, what duty is,
Why day is day, night night, and time is time,
Were nothing but to waste night, day and time.
90   Therefore, since brevity is the soul of wit,°
And tediousness the limbs and outward flourishes,°
I will be brief: your noble son is mad:
Mad call I it; for, to define true madness,
What is 't but to be nothing else but mad?
But let that go.
95   QUEEN: More matter,° with less art.°
POLONIUS: Madam, I swear I use no art at all.
That he is mad, 'tis true: 'tis true 'tis pity;
And pity 'tis 'tis true: a foolish figure;°
But farewell° it, for I will use no art.
100   Mad let us grant him, then: and now remains
That we find out the cause of this effect,
Or rather say, the cause of this defect,
For this effect defective comes by cause:
Thus it remains, and the remainder thus,.
105   Perpend.°
I have a daughter—have while she is mine—
Who, in her duty and obedience, mark,
Hath given me this: now gather, and surmise.

[Reads]

"To the celestial and my soul's idol, the most
110   beautified° Ophelia,"

That's an ill phrase, a vile phrase; "beautified" is a
vile phrase: but you shall hear. Thus:

[Reads]

"In her excellent white bosom, these° etc."
QUEEN: Came this from Hamlet to her?
POLONIUS: Good madam, stay awhile;° I will be faithful.° 115

[Reads]

"Doubt thou the stars are fire;
Doubt that the sun doth move;
Doubt truth to be a liar;
But never doubt I love.
"O dear Ophelia, I am ill° at these numbers;° 120
I have not art to reckon° my groans: but that
I love thee best, O most best, believe it.
Adieu.
"Thine evermore, most dear lady,
whilst this machine° is to him,

HAMLET."

This, in obedience, hath my daughter shown me, 125
And more above,° hath his solicitings,°
As they fell out by time, by means and place,
All given to mine ear.
KING: But how hath she
Received his love?
POLONIUS: What do you think of me?
KING: As of a man faithful and honourable. 130
POLONIUS: I would fain prove so.° But what might
      you think,
When I had seen this hot love on the wing—
As I perceived it, I must tell you that,
Before my daughter told me—what might you,
Or my dear majesty your queen here, think, 135
If I had play'd the desk or table-book,°
Or given my heart a winking,° mute and dumb,
Or look'd upon this love with idle sight;°
What might you think? No, I went round° to
      work,
And my young mistress thus I did bespeak:° 140
"Lord Hamlet is a prince, out of thy star;°
This must not be:" and then I prescripts° gave her,
That she should lock herself from his resort,°

---

⁷⁷ **quiet pass** peaceful passage   ⁷⁹ **On . . . allowance** i.e., on such pledges to permit and to safeguard the passage (of the troops)   ⁸⁰ **It likes us well** it meets our approval   ⁸¹ **at . . . time** at a time more suitable for deliberation   ⁸⁶ **expostulate** his grandiloquent way of saying "expound."   ⁹⁰ **wit** good sense   ⁹¹ **outward flourishes** rhetorical ornaments   ⁹⁵ **matter** substance; **art** elaboration   ⁹⁸ **figure** figure of speech   ⁹⁹ **farewell** it good-bye to my foolish figure   ¹⁰⁵ **Perpend** consider   ¹¹⁰ **beautified** an emphatic but not uncommon synonym for beautiful. Polonius thinks it affected, suggesting the use of make-up.

¹¹³ **these** these lines, a conventional beginning of an Elizabethan letter   ¹¹⁵ **stay awhile** i.e., don't interrupt; **be faithful** to the text of the letter   ¹²⁰ **ill** unskillful; **these numbers** this verse-making   ¹²¹ **reckon** i.e., put into verse   ¹²⁴ **machine** body   ¹²⁶ **above** besides; **solicitings** wooing   ¹³¹ **prove so** show that I am   ¹³⁶ **play'd . . . table-book** i.e., shut the knowledge up as in a desk or notebook   ¹³⁷ **given . . . a winking** made my heart shut its eyes (on what was happening)   ¹³⁸ **idle sight** unseeing eyes   ¹³⁹ **round** directly   ¹⁴⁰ **bespeak** address   ¹⁴¹ **star** i.e., in a sphere above yours   ¹⁴² **prescripts** instructions   ¹⁴³ **resort** company

Admit no messengers, receive no tokens.
145 Which done, she took the fruits of my advice;
And he, repulsed—a short tale to make—
Fell into a sadness, then into a fast,
Thence to a watch,° thence into a weakness,
Thence to a lightness,° and, by this declension,°
150 Into the madness wherein now he raves,
And all we mourn for.
KING: Do you think 'tis this?
QUEEN: It may be, very likely.
POLONIUS: Hath there been such a time—I'd fain
        know that—
That I have positively said "'Tis so,"
When it proved otherwise?
155 KING: Not that I know.
POLONIUS: [*Pointing to his head and shoulder*] Take this
        from this, if this be otherwise:°
If circumstances lead me, I will find
Where truth is hid, though it were hid indeed
Within the centre.°
KING: How may we try° it further?
POLONIUS: You know, sometimes he walks four hours
160   together
Here in the lobby.°
QUEEN: So he does indeed.
POLONIUS: At such a time I'll loose my daughter to
        him:
Be you and I behind an arras° then;
Mark the encounter:° if he love her not
165 And be not from his reason fall'n thereon,
Let me be no assistant for a state,°
But keep a farm and carters.
KING: We will try it.
QUEEN: But, look, where sadly the poor wretch
        comes reading.
POLONIUS: Away, I do beseech you, both away:
I'll board him presently.°

[*Exeunt KING, QUEEN, and ATTENDANTS.*]

[*Enter HAMLET, reading.*]

170   O, give me leave:°
How does my good Lord Hamlet?
HAMLET: Well, God-a-mercy.°
POLONIUS: Do you know me, my lord?

HAMLET: Excellent well; you are a fishmonger.°
POLONIUS: Not I, my lord.   175
HAMLET: Then I would you were so honest a man.
POLONIUS: Honest, my lord!
HAMLET: Ay, sir; to be honest, as this world goes, is to
        be one man picked out of ten thousand.
POLONIUS: That's very true, my lord.   180
HAMLET: For if the sun breed maggots in a dead dog,
        being a god kissing carrion,°—Have you a
        daughter?
POLONIUS: I have, my lord.
HAMLET: Let her not walk i' the sun:° conception° is a   185
        blessing: but not as your daughter may con-
        ceive. Friend, look to 't.
POLONIUS: [*Aside*] How say you by that?° Still harping
        on my daughter: yet he knew me not at first; he
        said I was a fishmonger: he is far gone, far gone: 190
        and truly in my youth I suffered much extremi-
        ty for love; very near this. I'll speak to him
        again. What do you read, my lord?
HAMLET: Words, words, words.
POLONIUS: What is the matter,° my lord?   195
HAMLET: Between who?
POLONIUS: I mean, the matter that you read, my lord.
HAMLET: Slanders, sir: for the satirical rogue says here
        that old men have grey beards, that their faces
        are wrinkled, their eyes purging thick amber
        and plum-tree gum and that they have a plenti-   200
        ful lack of wit, together with most weak hams:
        all which, sir, though I most powerfully and
        potently believe, yet I hold it not honesty° to
        have it thus set down, for yourself, sir, should
        be old as I am, if like a crab you could go back-   205
        ward.
POLONIUS: [*Aside*] Though this be madness, yet there is
        method in 't. Will you walk out of the air, my
        lord?
HAMLET: Into my grave.
POLONIUS: Indeed, that is out o' the air. [*Aside*] How   210
        pregnant sometimes his replies are! a happi-
        ness° that often madness hits on, which reason
        and sanity could not so prosperously be deliv-
        ered of. I will leave him, and suddenly° con-
        trive the means of meeting between him and   215
        my daughter.—My honourable lord, I will most

---

148 **watch** state of insomnia   149 **lightness** mental instability; **declension** i.e., progress from bad to worse   156 **this be
otherwise** i.e., if I be wrong   159 **centre** center of the earth;
try test   160 **four** cant for "several"   161 **lobby** porch or
cloister   163 **arras** tapestry hanging loose against the wall
164 **encounter** behavior   166 **assistant . . . state** public official   170 **board him presently** accost him at once; **give me
leave** I beg your pardon (for the interruption)   172 **God-a-
mercy** I thank you

174 **fishmonger** probably a peddler of fish, whose trade was
humble and foul-smelling. It was also a cant term for "bawd."
182 **god kissing carrion** the sun god by touching a dead dog
with its rays breeds maggots in the rotting flesh   185 **i' the
sun** i.e., out of doors where temptation lurks   185–6 **conception** (1) understanding, (2) state of pregnancy   188 **How . . .
that?** What do you think of that?   194 **matter** (1) subject matter, (2) cause of a dispute   203 **honesty** decency   213 **happiness** pointedness   213 **prosperously** successfully   214 **suddenly** immediately

humbly take my leave of you.

HAMLET: You cannot, sir, take from me any thing that
I will more willingly part withal: except my life,
220 except my life, except my life.

POLONIUS: Fare you well, my lord.

HAMLET: These tedious old fools!

[Enter ROSENCRANTZ *and* GUILDENSTERN.*]*

POLONIUS: You go to seek the Lord Hamlet; there he is.

ROSENCRANTZ: *[To* POLONIUS*]* God save you, sir!

225 GUILDENSTERN: My honoured lord!

ROSENCRANTZ: My most dear lord!

HAMLET: My excellent good friends! How dost thou,
Guildenstern? Ah, Rosencrantz! Good lads,
how do ye both?

230 ROSENCRANTZ: As the indifferent° children of the
earth.

GUILDENSTERN: Happy, in that we are not overhappy;
On fortune's cap we are not the very button.

HAMLET: Nor the soles of her shoe?

235 ROSENCRANTZ: Neither,° my lord.

HAMLET: Then you live about her waist, or in the middle of her favours?

GUILDENSTERN: 'Faith, her privates we.

HAMLET: In the secret parts of fortune? O, most true;
240 she is a strumpet. What's the news?

ROSENCRANTZ: None, my lord, but that the world's
grown honest.

HAMLET: Then is doomsday near: 'but your news is
not true. Let me question more in particular:
245 what have you, my good friends, deserved at
the hands of fortune, that she sends you to
prison hither?

GUILDENSTERN: Prison, my lord!

HAMLET: Denmark's a prison.

250 ROSENCRANTZ: Then is the world one.

HAMLET: A goodly° one; in which there are many confines,° wards° and dungeons, Denmark being
one o' the worst.

ROSENCRANTZ: We think not so, my lord.

255 HAMLET: Why, then, 'tis none to you; for there is nothing either good or bad, but thinking makes it so:
to me it is a prison.

ROSENCRANTZ: Why then, your ambition makes it one;
'tis too narrow for your mind.

260 HAMLET: O God, I could be bounded in a nutshell and
count myself a king of infinite space, were it not
that I have bad dreams.

GUILDENSTERN: Which dreams indeed are ambition,
for the very substance of the ambitious is mere-
265 ly the shadow of a dream.

HAMLET: A dream itself is but a shadow.

ROSENCRANTZ: Truly, and I hold ambition of so airy
and light a quality that it is but a shadow's
shadow.

HAMLET: Then are our beggars bodies, and our mon- 270
archs and outstretched° heroes the beggars'
shadows. Shall we to the court? for, by my fay,°
I cannot reason.°

ROSENCRANTZ: ⎱
GUILDENSTERN: ⎰ We'll wait upon° you.

HAMLET: No such matter: I will not sort° you with the 275
rest of my servants, for, to speak to you like an
honest man, I am most dreadfully attended.°
But, in the beaten way° of friendship, what
make you° at Elsinore?

ROSENCRANTZ: To visit you, my lord; no other occasion. 280

HAMLET: Beggar that I am, I am even poor in thanks; but
I thank you: and sure, dear friends, my thanks are
too dear a° halfpenny. Were you not sent for? Is it
your own inclining? Is it a free visitation?° Come,
deal justly with me: come, come; nay, speak. 285

GUILDENSTERN: What should we say, my lord?

HAMLET: Why, any thing, but to the purpose. You
were sent for; and there is a kind of confession
in your looks which your modesties have not
craft enough to colour:° I know the good king 290
and queen have sent for you.

ROSENCRANTZ: To what end, my lord?

HAMLET: That you must teach me. But let me conjure°
you, by the rights of our fellowship, by the con-
sonancy° of our youth, by the obligation of our 295
ever-preserved love, and by what° more dear a
better proposer° could charge you withal,° be
even° and direct with me, whether you were
sent for, or no?

ROSENCRANTZ: *[Aside to* GUILDENSTERN*]* What say you? 300

HAMLET: *[Aside]* Nay, then, I have an eye of you.°—If
you love me, hold not off.

GUILDENSTERN: My lord, we were sent for.

HAMLET: I will tell you why; so shall my anticipation
prevent your discovery,° and your secrecy to the 305

---

²⁷¹ **outstretched** elongated (like a shadow) The passage
means: Beggars who lack ambition are the only substantial
beings. Hence monarchs and heroes who become puffed up
with ambition must be mere elongated shadows of the beggars. ²⁷² **fay** faith; ²⁷³ **reason** argue ²⁷⁴ **wait upon** accompany ²⁷⁵ **sort** classify ²⁷⁷ **dreadfully attended** i.e., I have
companions who fill me with dread ²⁷⁸ **beaten way** the
traveled road ²⁷⁹ **make you** are you doing ²⁸³ **a** by a
²⁸⁴ **free visitation** voluntary visit ²⁸⁹ **modesties** sense of
decency ²⁹⁰ **colour** disguise ²⁹³ **conjure** solemnly urge
²⁹⁵ **consonancy** congeniality ²⁹⁶ **what** whatever else; **pro-**
poser speaker ²⁹⁷ **charge you withal** urge upon you;
even straightforward ³⁰¹ **have . . . you** see through you
³⁰⁵ **prevent your discovery** anticipate your disclosure

---

²³⁰ **indifferent** ordinary ²³⁵ **Neither** not that either ²⁵¹
goodly extensive ²⁵² **confines** places of confinement;
wards prison cells

king and queen moult no feather.° I have of late—
but wherefore I know not—lost all my mirth, for-
gone° all custom of exercises; and indeed it goes
so heavily with my disposition that this goodly

310 frame,° the earth, seems to me a sterile promontory, this most excellent canopy, the air, look you,
this brave° o'erhanging firmament, this majestical roof fretted° with golden fire,° why, it appears
no other thing to me than a foul and pestilent

315 congregation of vapours. What a piece of work°
is a man! how noble in reason! how infinite in faculty!° in form and moving how express° and
admirable! in action how like an angel! in apprehension how like a god! the beauty of the world!

320 the paragon of animals! And yet, to me, what is
this quintessence° of dust? man delights not me:
no, nor woman neither, though by your smiling
you seem to say so.

ROSENCRANTZ: My lord, there was no such stuff in my
325   thoughts.

HAMLET: Why did you laugh then, when I said "man
    delights not me"?

ROSENCRANTZ: To think, my lord, if you delight not in
    man, what lenten entertainment° the players
330   shall receive from you: we coted° them on the
    way; and hither are they coming, to offer you
    service.

HAMLET: He that plays the king shall be welcome; his
    majesty shall have tribute of me; the adventurous
335   knight shall use his foil and target;° the lover
    shall not sigh gratis; the humorous man° shall
    end his part in peace;° the clown shall make those
    laugh whose lungs are tickle o' the sere;° and the
    lady shall say her mind freely, or the blank verse
340   shall halt for 't.° What players are they?

ROSENCRANTZ: Even those you were wont to take
    delight in, the tragedians of the city.

HAMLET: How chances it they travel? their residence,°
    both in reputation and profit, was better both
345   ways.°

ROSENCRANTZ: I think their inhibition° comes by the
    means of the late innovation.°

HAMLET: Do they hold the same estimation they did
    when I was in the city? are they so followed?°

ROSENCRANTZ: No, indeed, are they not.   350

HAMLET: How comes it? do they grow rusty?

ROSENCRANTZ: Nay, their endeavour keeps in the
    wonted pace: but there is, sir, an aery° of chil-
    dren, little eyases,° that cry out on the top of
    question,° and are most tyrannically° clapped   355
    for 't: these are now the fashion, and so berattle°
    the common stages—so they call them—that
    many wearing rapiers are afraid of goose-
    quills° and dare scarce come thither.

HAMLET: What, are they children? who maintains   360
    'em? how are they escoted?° Will they pursue
    the quality° no longer than they can sing?° will
    they not say afterwards, if they should grow
    themselves to common° players—as it is most
    like,° if their means are no better°—their writers   365
    do them wrong, to make them exclaim against°
    their own successsion?°

ROSENCRANTZ: 'Faith, there has been much to do° on
    both sides;° and the nation holds it no sin to tarre°
    them to controversy: there was, for a while, no   370
    money bid for argument,° unless the poet and the
    player went to cuffs° in the question.°

HAMLET: Is 't possible?

GUILDENSTERN: O, there has been much throwing
    about of brains.   375

HAMLET: Do the boys carry it away?°

ROSENCRANTZ: Ay, that they do, my lord; Hercules and
    his load° too.

HAMLET: It is not very strange; for mine uncle is king
    of Denmark, and those that would make mows°   380
    at him while my father lived, give twenty, forty,

---

306 moult no feather i.e., remain intact   **308 forgone** given up   **310 frame** structure   **312 brave** beautiful   **313 fretted** adorned   **golden fire** the stars   **315 piece of work** master-piece   **317 faculty** capacity   **express** well adapted to its purpose   **321 quintessence** the fifth or purest essence of which the heavenly bodies were supposed to be composed   **329 lenten entertainment** meagre (i.e., inhospitable) reception   **330 coted** overtook and passed   **335 foil and target** rapier and shield   **336 humorous man** the actor playing the humor character, i.e., the one ruled by a single folly   **337 in peace** i.e., without interruption from the audience   **338 tickle o' the sere** quick on the trigger   **340 or . . . for't** even though the blank verse has to limp to permit her to do it   **343 residence** i.e., in one of the London theatres   **345 both ways** i.e., both for their reputation and for their profit

346 inhibition formal prohibition from acting   **347 late innovation** recent novelty, probably the acting of the Children of the Revels in the Blackfriars' Theatre   **349 so followed** i.e., as popular as they were   **353 aery** nest (of a hawk or eagle)   **354 eyases** young hawks   **355 on. . . question** at a pitch higher and shriller than that of ordinary conversation   **tyrannically** violently   **356 berattle** run down   **358 wearing rapiers** i.e., gentlemen of fashion   **359 goose-quills** pens and so dramatists who satirize them   **361 escoted** supported   **362 pursue the quality** continue in their profession   **than . . . sing** i.e., until their voices change   **364 common** regular (i.e., professional)   **365 like** likely   **means are no better** if no better opportunity offers   **366 exclaim against** run down   **succession** future profession   **368 to do** commotion   **369 both sides** i.e., the children and the adult companies   **tarre** egg on   **371 argument** plot for a play   **372 went to cuffs** came to blows   **question** controversy   **376 carry it away** win out   **378 Hercules . . . load** the Globe Theatre; its sign was Hercules carrying a globe on his shoulders   **381 mows** faces fifty, an hundred ducats a-piece for his picture in little.° 'Sblood,° there is something in this more than natural, if philosophy° could find it out.

[Flourish of trumpets within.]

385 GUILDENSTERN: There are the players.

HAMLET: Gentlemen, you are welcome to Elsinore. Your hands, come then: the appurtenance° of welcome is fashion and ceremony:° let me comply° with you in this garb,° lest my extent° to
390 the players, which, I tell you, must show fairly outward,° should more appear like entertainment than yours.° You are welcome: but my uncle-father and aunt-mother are deceived.

GUILDENSTERN: In what, my dear lord?

395 HAMLET: I am but mad north-north-west: when the wind is southerly I know a hawk from a handsaw.°

[Re-enter POLONIUS.]

POLONIUS: Well be with you, gentlemen!

HAMLET: Hark you, Guildenstern; and you too: at each
400 ear a hearer: that great baby you see there is not yet out of his swaddling-clouts.°

ROSENCRANTZ: Happily° he's the second time come to them; for they say an old man is twice a child.

HAMLET: I will prophesy he comes to tell me of the
405 players; mark it. You say right, sir: o' Monday morning; 'twas so indeed.

POLONIUS: My lord, I have news to tell you.

HAMLET: My lord, I have news to tell you. When Roscius° was an actor in Rome,—

410 POLONIUS: The actors are come hither, my lord.

HAMLET: Buz, buz!°

POLONIUS: Upon mine honour,—

HAMLET: Then came each actor on his ass,—

POLONIUS: The best actors in the world, either for
415 tragedy, comedy, history, pastoral, pastoral-comical, historical-pastoral, tragical-historical,

tragical-comical-historical-pastoral, scene individable,° or poem unlimited:° Seneca cannot be too heavy, nor Plautus too light. For the law of writ and the liberty,° these are the only men.   420

HAMLET: O Jephthah,° judge of Israel, what a treasure hadst thou!

POLONIUS: What a treasure had he, my lord?

HAMLET: Why, "One fair daughter, and no more, The which he loved passing° well."   425

POLONIUS: *[Aside]* Still on my daughter.

HAMLET: Am I not i' the right, old Jephthah?

POLONIUS: If you call me Jephthah, my lord, I have a daughter that I love passing well.

HAMLET: Nay, that follows not.   430

POLONIUS: What follows, then, my lord?

HAMLET: Why,

      "As by lot, God wot,"

and then, you know,

   "It came to pass, as most like it was," —the first row° of the pious chanson° will show you more;° for look, where my abridgement° comes.   435

[Enter four or five PLAYERS.]

You are welcome, masters; welcome, all. I am glad to see thee well. Welcome, good friends. O, my old friend! thy face is valanced° since I saw thee last: comest thou to beard me in Denmark?   440 What, my young lady and mistress! By'r lady, your ladyship is nearer to heaven than when I saw you last, by the altitude of a chopine.° Pray God, your voice, like a piece of uncurrent gold, be not cracked within the ring.° Masters, you   445 are all welcome. We'll e'en to 't like French falconers, fly at any thing we see: we'll have a speech straight:° come, give us a taste of your quality;° come, a passionate speech.

FIRST PLAYER: What speech, my lord?   450

HAMLET: I heard thee speak me a speech once, but it was never acted; or, if it was, not above once; for the play, I remember, pleased not the million; 'twas caviare to the general:° but it was—

---

382 **picture in little** miniature   383 **'Sblood** God's blood, a violent oath   384 **philosophy** human knowledge   387 **appurtenance** proper accompaniment   388 **fashion and ceremony** fashionable ceremony   389 **comply** show formal courtesy **garb** fashion **extent** expression of welcome   391 **show . . . outward** be clearly manifested   392 **more . . . yours** seems more cordial than that which I have shown you   395 **north-north-west** only when the wind comes from a little west of north   397 **hawk . . . handsaw** i.e., I can distinguish between two objects having no resemblance to each other   401 **swaddling-clouts** linen bandages wrapped around newborn babies   403 **Happily** perhaps   409 **Roscius** a famous Roman actor, also nickname of Alleyn, the principal actor in the rival Admiral's Men   411 **Buz, buz** contemptuous exclamation meaning his news was stale

418 **scene individable** play observing unity of place **poem unlimited** a play failing to observe the foregoing unity   420 **law . . . liberty** written or extemporal plays   421 **Jephthah...Israel** title of a popular ballad on the subject of Jephthah and his daughter. The story of his sacrifice of his daughter is in Judges, II:30–40.   425 **passing** surpassingly   435 **row** stanza **pious chanson** sacred ballad   436 **more** i.e., of the story **abridgement** i.e., the person who will force me to curtail my quotation from the ballad   439 **valanced** fringed (with a beard)   443 **chopine** thick-soled shoe   445 **cracked . . . ring** A crack in a gold coin within a ring enclosing the sovereign's head in the center of the coin made it unfit for legal tender.   448 **straight** at once   449 **quality** professional skill   454 **caviare to the general** like caviar, not relished by the crowd

455 as I received it, and others, whose judgements
in such matters cried in the top of mine°—an
excellent play, well digested in the scenes, set
down with as much modesty as cunning.° I
remember, one said there were no sallets° in the
460 lines to make the matter savoury, nor no matter
in the phrase that might indict° the author of
affectation; but called it an honest° method, as
wholesome as sweet, and by very much more
handsome than fine.° One speech in it I chiefly
470 loved: 'twas Æneas' tale to Dido; and there-
about of it especially, where he speaks of
Priam's slaughter: if it live in your memory,
begin at this line: let me see, let me see—
"The rugged Pyrrhus,° like the Hyrcanian
beast,"—
475 it is not so:—it begins with Pyrrhus:—
"The rugged Pyrrhus, he whose sable arms°
Black as his purpose, did the night resemble
When he lay couched in the ominous horse,°
Hath now this dread and black complexion
smear'd
480 With heraldry° more dismal; head to foot
Now is he total gules;° horridly trick'd
With blood of fathers, mothers, daughters, sons,
Baked and impasted° with the parching° streets,
That lend a tyrannous° and damned light
485 To their lord's murder: roasted in wrath and fire,
And thus o'er-sized° with coagulate gore,
With eyes like carbuncles, the hellish Pyrrhus
Old grandsire Priam seeks."
So, proceed you.°
490 POLONIUS: 'Fore God, my lord, well spoken, with
good accent and good discretion.°
FIRST PLAYER: "Anon° he finds him
Striking too short at Greeks; his antique° sword,
Rebellious to his arm, lies where it falls,
Repugnant to° command: unequal match'd,

Pyrrhus at Priam drives; in rage strikes wide;   495
But with the whiff and wind of his fell sword
The unnerved° father falls. Then senseless Ilium,°
Seeming to feel this blow, with flaming top
Stoops to his° base, and with a hideous crash
Takes prisoner° Pyrrhus' ear: for, lo! his sword,   500
Which was declining on the milky head
Of reverend Priam, seem'd i' the air to stick:
So, as a painted tyrant,° Pyrrhus stood,
And like a neutral° to his will and matter,°
Did nothing.   505
But, as we often see, against° some storm,
A silence in the heavens, the rack° stand still,
The bold winds speechless and the orb below°
As hush as death, anon the dreadful thunder
Doth rend the region,° so, after Pyrrhus' pause,   510
Aroused vengeance sets him new awork;
And never did the Cyclops' hammers fall
On Mars's armour forged for proof eterne°
With less remorse than Pyrrhus' bleeding sword
Now falls on Priam.   515
Out, out, thou strumpet,° Fortune! All you gods,
In general synod,° take away her power;
Break all the spokes and fellies° from her wheel,
And bowl the round nave° down the hill of heaven,
As low as to the fiends!"   520
POLONIUS: This is too long.
HAMLET: It shall to the barber's, with your beard.
Prithee, say on: he's for a jig° or a tale of bawdry,
or he sleeps: say on: come to Hecuba.
FIRST PLAYER: "But who, O, who had seen
the mobled° queen—"   525
HAMLET: "The mobled queen?"
POLONIUS: That's good; "mobled queen" is good.
FIRST PLAYER: "Run barefoot up and down, threaten-
ing the flames
With bisson rheum;° a clout upon that head
Where late the diadem stood, and for a robe,   530
About her lank and all o'er-teemèd° loins,
A blanket, in the alarm of fear caught up;

---

456 **cried . . . mine** were of stronger (more authoritative) voice
than mine   458 **modesty as cunning** restraint as skill   459**sal-
lets** tasty bits, i.e., spicy jests   461 **indict** convict   462 **honest** in good taste   469 **handsome than fine** well propor-
tioned than ornate   474 **Pyrrhus** the son of Achilles and one
of the best of the Greek heroes in the Trojan War   **Hyrcanian
beast** the tiger of Hyrcania, a wild district north of the
Caspian Sea   476 **sable arms** i.e., with a black design on his
shield   478 **ominous horse** the hollow wooden horse at the
siege of Troy   480 **heraldry** i.e., the symbolic decoration on a
coat of arms   481 **gules** heraldic term for red; tricked,
heraldic term for "decorated"   483 **impasted** made into a
paste, i.e., clotted   **parching** because of the fire raging in the
city   484 **tyrannous** fierce   486 **o'ersized** smeared over;
size glue   489 **So . . . you** go on from this point   491 **discretion** interpretation   **Anon** immediately after   492 **antique**
used long before   494 **Repugnant to** resisting

497 **unnerved** weak in his sinews   **senseless Ilium** the
citadel of Troy, incapable of feeling   499 **his** its   500 **Takes
prisoner** that is, deafens   503 **painted tyrant** a tyrant as
depicted on the painted cloths which adorned the walls of
great halls, usually with uplifted arm   504 **neutral** person
indifferent   **will and matter** purpose and its fulfilment
506 **against** just before   507 **rack** mass of cloud   508 **orb
below** the round earth   510 **region** upper air   513 **for proof
eterne** i.e., to wear forever   516 **strumpet** harlot   517 **general synod** full assembly   518 **fellies** rims   519 **nave** hub   523
jig a musical farce usually presented as an afterpiece to the
main drama   525 **mobled** muffled, i.e., with a scarf wrapped
round her head; the unusual and homely word prompts
Hamlet's interruption   529 **bisson rheum** blinding tears   531
o'er-teemed worn out from childbearing

Who this had seen, with tongue in venom steep'd,
'Gainst Fortune's state° would treason have pro-
        nounced:

535 But if the gods themselves did see her then
When she saw Pyrrhus make malicious sport
In mincing with his sword her husband's limbs,
The instant burst of clamour that she made,
Unless things mortal move them not at all,
Would have made milch° the burning eyes of

540   heaven,°
And passion in the gods."
POLONIUS: Look, whether he has not turned° his colour
        and has tears in 's eyes. Pray you, no more.
HAMLET: 'Tis well;° I'll have thee speak out the rest

545   soon. Good my lord, will you see the players
        well bestowed?° Do you hear, let them be well
        used; for they are the abstract° and brief chron-
        icles of the time:° after your death you were bet-
        ter have a bad epitaph than their ill report while

550   you live.
POLONIUS: My lord, I will use them according to their
        desert.
HAMLET: God's bodykins,° man, much better: use every
        man after° his desert, and who should 'scape

555   whipping? Use them after your own honour and
        dignity: the less they deserve, the more merit is
        in your bounty. Take them in.
POLONIUS: Come, sirs.
HAMLET: Follow him, friends: we'll hear a play to-

560   morrow. [*Exit* POLONIUS *with all the* PLAYERS *but
        the* FIRST.] Dost thou hear me, old friend; can
        you play the Murder of Gonzago?
FIRST PLAYER: Ay, my lord.
HAMLET: We'll ha't to-morrow night. You could, for a

565   need,° study a speech of some dozen or sixteen
        lines, which I would set down and insert in 't,
        could you not?
FIRST PLAYER: Ay, my lord.
HAMLET: Very well. Follow that lord; and look you

570   mock him not. [*Exit* FIRST PLAYER.] My good
        friends, I'll leave you till night: you are wel-
        come to Elsinore.
ROSENCRANTZ: Good my lord!
HAMLET: Ay, so, God be wi' ye; [*Exeunt*
        ROSENCRANTZ *and* GUILDENSTERN.] Now I am
        alone.

575 O, what a rogue and peasant° slave am I!

Is it not monstrous that this player here,
But in a fiction, in a dream of passion,°
Could force his soul so to his own conceit°
That from her working all his visage wann'd,°
Tears in his eyes, distraction in 's aspect,   580
A broken voice, and his whole function suiting
With forms to his conceit?° and all for nothing!
For Hecuba!
What's Hecuba to him, or he to Hecuba,
That he should weep for her? What would he do,   585
Had he the motive and the cue for passion
That I have? He would drown the stage with tears
And cleave the general ear° with horrid speech,
Make mad the guilty and appal the free,°
Confound the ignorant, and amaze° indeed   590
The very faculties of eyes and ears.
Yet I,
A dull and muddy-mettled° rascal, peak,
Like John-a-dreams,° unpregnant of° my cause,
And can say nothing; no, not for a king,   595
Upon whose property° and most dear life
A damn'd defeat° was made. Am I a coward?
Who calls me villain? breaks my pate across?
Plucks off my beard, and blows it in my face?
Tweaks me by the nose? gives me the lie i' the throat, 600
As deep as to the lungs? who does me this?
Ha!
'Swounds, I should take it: for it cannot be
But I am pigeon-liver'd° and lack gall
To make oppression bitter, or ere this   605
I should have fatted all the region° kites
With this slave's offal:° bloody, bawdy villain!
Remorseless, treacherous, lecherous, kindless vil-
        lain!
O, vengeance!
Why, what an ass am I! This is most brave,°   610
That I, the son of a dear father murder'd,
Prompted to my revenge by heaven and hell,
Must, like a whore, unpack my heart with words,
And fall a-cursing, like a very drab,°
A scullion!°   615

---

577 **dream of passion** imaginary emotion   578 **to his own conceit** i.e., should so accept the conception (of the part he acts)
579 **wann'd** grew pale   582 **whole function . . . conceit** all his
physical powers acting in harmony with his conception   588
cleave . . . ear penetrate the ears of everyone (in the audience)   589 **free** innocent   590 **amaze** stun   593 **muddy-met-
tled** dull-spirited   594 **peak . . . dreams** mope like day-
dreamer   595 **unpregnant of** i.e., barren of plans for revenge
596 **property** personality   597 **defeat** destruction   598 **breaks...
across** strikes me over the head   604 **pigeon-liver'd** the
pigeon's liver was supposed to secrete no gall, the source of
bitterness   606 **region** of the upper air   607 **offal** rotting flesh
608 **kindless** unnatural   610 **most brave** makes a fine display
614 **drab** prostitute   615 **scullion** a menial kitchen servant

---

534 **state** governance of the world   540 **milch** milky or moist
eyes of heaven the stars   542 **turned** changed   544 **'Tis well**
i.e., that will do   546 **bestowed** lodged   547 **abstract** summary   548 **time** i.e., events   553 **God's bodykins** a vulgar and
outlandish oath. Bodykins = little body and refers to the bread
or holy wafer in the Communion service.   554 **after** according
to   565 **for a need** if there were need   575 **peasant** base

Fie upon 't! foh! About,° my brain! I have heard
That guilty creatures sitting at a play
Have by the very cunning of the scene
Been struck so to the soul that presently°
620 They have proclaim'd their malefactions;
For murder, though it have no tongue, will speak
With most miraculous organ. I'll have these players
Play something like the murder of my father
Before mine uncle: I'll observe his looks;
625 I'll tent° him to the quick: if he but blench,°
I know my course. The spirit that I have seen
May be the devil: and the devil hath power
To assume a pleasing shape; yea, and perhaps
Out of my weakness and my melancholy,
630 As he is very potent with such spirits,
Abuses me to damn me: I'll have grounds
More relative than this: the play's the thing
Wherein I'll catch the conscience of the king.

[Exit.]

ACT III

Scene 1

A room in the castle.

[Enter KING, QUEEN, POLONIUS, OPHELIA, ROSENCRANTZ, *and* GUILDENSTERN.]

KING: And can you, by no drift of circumstance,°
Get from him why he puts on this confusion,°
Grating° so harshly all his days of quiet
With turbulent and dangerous lunacy?
ROSENCRANTZ: He does confess he feels himself
5   distracted;
But from what cause he will by no means speak.
GUILDENSTERN: Nor do we find him forward° to be
      sounded,°
But, with a crafty madness, keeps aloof,
When we would bring him on to some confession
Of his true state.
10 QUEEN: Did he receive you well?
ROSENCRANTZ: Most like a gentleman.

GUILDENSTERN: But with much forcing of his disposi-
      tion.°
ROSENCRANTZ: Niggard of question;° but, of our
      demands,
Most free in his reply.
QUEEN: Did you assay him
To any pastime?°   15
ROSENCRANTZ: Madam, it so fell out, that certain players
We o'er-raught° on the way: of these we told him;
And there did seem in him a kind of joy
To hear of it: they are about the court,
And, as I think, they have already order   20
This night to play before him.
POLONIUS: 'Tis most true:
And he beseech'd me to entreat your majesties
To hear and see the matter.°
KING: With all my heart; and it doth much content me
To hear him so inclined.   25
Good gentlemen, give him a further edge,°
And drive his purpose on to these delights.
ROSENCRANTZ: We shall, my lord.

[Exeunt ROSENCRANTZ and GUILDENSTERN.]

KING: Sweet Gertrude, leave us too;
For we have closely° sent for Hamlet hither,
That he, as 'twere by accident, may here   30
Affront° Ophelia:
Her father and myself, lawful espials,°
Will so bestow° ourselves that, seeing, unseen,
We may of their encounter frankly° judge,
And gather by him, as he is behaved,   35
If 't be the affliction of his love or no
That thus he suffers for.
QUEEN: I shall obey you.
And for your part, Ophelia, I do wish
That your good beauties be the happy cause
Of Hamlet's wildness:° so shall I hope your virtues 40
Will bring him to his wonted way° again,
To both your honours.
OPHELIA: Madam, I wish it may.

[Exit QUEEN.]

POLONIUS: Ophelia, walk you here. Gracious, so
      please you,
We will bestow ourselves. [*To* OPHELIA] Read on
      this book;

---

616 About get to work **619 presently** immediately **625 tent**
probe **blench** flinch **630 spirits** humors (of melancholy)
631 abuses deceives **632 relative** i.e., more related (to the
facts) **this** i.e., the ghost's testimony **633 catch . . . king**
make the king betray the consciousness of his guilt.

ACT III, SCENE 1:   **1 drift of circumstance** manipulation of
the conversation **2 puts on . . . confusion** shows this distraction **3 Grating** vexing **4 forward** willing **sounded**
questioned

11 forcing . . . disposition against his will **12 Niggard of question** unwilling to open conversation **16 assay . . . pastime** try
to interest him in any sort of amusement? **18 o'er-raught** overtook and passed **9 matter** i.e., performance **24 edge** incitement (to this interest) **29 closely** secretly **31 Affront** meet
face to face **32 lawful espials** legitimate spies **33 bestow** station **34 frankly** easily **40 wildness** madness **41 way**
frame of mind

45   That show of such an exercise° may colour°
     Your loneliness. We are oft to blame in this,—
     'Tis too much proved°—that with devotion's visage°
     And pious action we do sugar o'er
     The devil himself.
     KING: [Aside] O, 'tis too true!
     How smart a lash that speech doth give my con-
50   science!
     The harlot's cheek, beautied with plastering art,
     Is not more ugly to° the thing° that helps it
     Than is my deed to my most painted word:
     O heavy burthen!
55   POLONIUS: I hear him coming: let's withdraw, my lord.

          [Exeunt KING and POLONIUS.]

     [Enter HAMLET.]

     HAMLET: To be, or not to be: that is the question:
     Whether 'tis nobler in the mind to suffer
     The slings° and arrows of outrageous fortune,
     Or to take arms against a sea of troubles,
60   And by opposing end them? To die: to sleep;
     No more; and by a sleep to say° we end
     The heart-ache and the thousand natural shocks
     That flesh is heir to, 'tis a consummation
     Devoutly to be wish'd. To die, to sleep;
65   To sleep: perchance to dream: ay, there's the rub;°
     For in that sleep of death what dreams may come
     When we have shuffled° off this mortal coil,°
     Must give us pause: there's the respect°
     That makes calamity of so long life;
70   For who would bear the whips and scorns of time,°
     The oppressor's wrong, the proud man's contumely,
     The pangs of déspised° love, the law's delay,
     The insolence of office° and the spurns
     That patient merit of° the unworthy takes,
75   When he himself might his quietus° make
     With a bare bodkin?° who would fardels° bear,
     To grunt and sweat under a weary life,
     But that the dread of something after death,
     The undiscover'd° country from whose bourn°
80   No traveller returns, puzzles° the will

     And makes us rather bear those ills we have
     Than fly to others that we know not of?
     Thus conscience° does make cowards of us all;
     And thus the native hue° of resolution
     Is sicklied o'er° with the pale cast of thought,°   85
     And enterprises of great pitch° and moment
     With this regard° their currents turn awry,
     And lose the name of action.—Soft you now!°
     The fair Ophelia! Nymph,° in thy orisons°
     Be all my sins remember'd.
     OPHELIA: Good my lord,   90
     How does your honour for this many a day?
     HAMLET: I humbly thank you; well, well, well.
     OPHELIA: My lord, I have remembrances of yours,
     That I have longed long to re-deliver;
     I pray you, now receive them.
     HAMLET: No, not I;   95
     I never gave you aught.
     OPHELIA: My honour'd lord, you know right well
          you did;
     And, with them, words of so sweet breath° com-
          posed
     As made the things more rich: their perfume lost,
     Take these again; for to the noble mind   100
     Rich gifts wax poor when givers prove unkind.
     There, my lord.
     HAMLET: Ha, ha! are you honest?°
     OPHELIA: My lord?
     HAMLET: Are you fair?   105
     OPHELIA: What means your lordship?
     HAMLET: That if you be honest and fair, your honesty
          should admit no discourse to° your beauty.
     OPHELIA: Could beauty, my lord, have better commerce°
          than with honesty?   110
     HAMLET: Ay, truly; for the power of beauty will soon-
          er transform honesty from what it is to a bawd°
          than the force of honesty can translate beauty into
          his likeness: this was sometime a paradox, but now
          the time° gives it proof. I did love you once.   115
     OPHELIA: Indeed, my lord, you made me believe so.
     HAMLET: You should not have believed me; for virtue
          cannot so inoculate° our old stock but we shall rel-
          ish° of it: I loved you not.
     OPHELIA: I was the more deceived.   120
     HAMLET: Get thee to a nunnery: why wouldst thou be
          a breeder of sinners? I am myself indifferent hon-

---

⁴⁵ **exercise** religious devotion **colour** seem to explain
⁴⁷ **'Tis . . . proved** i.e., as experience has made only too evident
devotion's visage the appearance of devoutness   ⁵² **to** compared to   **the thing** i.e., the paint   ⁵⁸ **slings** the missiles
sent from a sling   ⁶¹ **to say** let us say   ⁶⁵ **rub** hindrance (an
unevenness of the ground in the game of bowls)   ⁶⁷ **shuffled**
cast   **coil** (1) turmoil, (2) a ring of rope wound round an
object (as the flesh encircles the soul)   ⁶⁸ **respect** consideration   ⁷⁰ **time** the world   ⁷² **despised** rejected   ⁷³ **office** officials   ⁷⁴ **of** from   ⁷⁵ **quietus** full discharge (of a debt), here =
death   ⁷⁶ **bare bodkin** mere stiletto   **fardels** burdens   ⁷⁹
undiscover'd unexplored   **bourn** boundary   ⁸⁰ **puzzles** renders helpless, paralyzes

---

⁸³ **conscience** reflection   ⁸⁴ **native hue** natural healthy color
⁸⁵ **sicklied o'er** given a sickly tinge   **cast of thought** shade
which thought gives it   ⁸⁶ **pitch** height, a term in falconry
⁸⁷ **With this regard** because of this consideration   ⁸⁸ **Soft you
now** But wait!   ⁸⁹ **Nymph** (1) fair maiden, (2) in Elizabethan
times = harlot   **orisons** prayers   ⁹⁸ **breath** i.e., meaning
¹⁰³ **honest** chaste   ¹⁰⁸ **admit . . . to** allow no communication
with   ¹¹⁰ **commerce** intercourse   ¹¹² **bawd** procurer   ¹¹⁵ **the
time** present age   ¹¹⁸ **inoculate** graft   ¹¹⁹ **relish of** taste

est;° but yet I could accuse me of such things that
it were better my mother had not borne me: I am

125   very proud, revengeful, ambitious, with more
offences at my beck° than I have thoughts to put
them in, imagination to give them shape, or time to
act them in. What should such fellows as I do
crawling between earth and heaven? We are

130   arrant° knaves, all; believe none of us. Go thy ways
to a nunnery. Where's your father?

OPHELIA: At home, my lord.

HAMLET: Let the doors be shut upon him, that he may
play the fool no where but in's own house.

135   Farewell.

OPHELIA: O, help him, you sweet heavens!

HAMLET: If thou dost marry, I'll give thee this plague
for thy dowry: be thou as chaste as ice, as pure as
snow, thou shalt not escape calumny. Get thee to a

140   nunnery, go: farewell. Or, if thou wilt needs marry,
marry a fool; for wise men know well enough
what monsters° you make of them. To a nunnery,°
go, and quickly too. Farewell.

OPHELIA: O heavenly powers, restore him!

145   HAMLET: I have heard of your paintings too, well
enough; God has given you one face, and you
make yourselves another: you jig,° you amble, and
you lisp,° and nick-name God's creatures.° Go to, I'll

150   no more on 't; it hath made me mad. I say, we will
have no more marriages: those that are married
already, all but one, shall live; the rest shall keep as
they are. To a nunnery, go.

[Exit.]

OPHELIA: O, what a noble mind is here o'er-thrown!
The courtier's, soldier's, scholar's, eye, tongue,

155   sword;°
The expectancy and rose of the fair° state,
The glass° of fashion and the mould of form,°
The observed of all observers, quite, quite down!
And I, of ladies most deject and wretched,

160   That suck'd the honey of his music vows,
Now see that noble and most sovereign reason,
Like sweet bells jangled, out of tune and harsh;

That unmatch'd form and feature of blown° youth
Blasted with ecstasy:° O, woe is me,
To have seen what I have seen, see what I see!   165

[Re-enter KING and POLONIUS.]

KING: Love! his affections do not that way tend;
Nor what he spake, though it lack'd form a little,
Was not like madness. There's something in his soul,
O'er which his melancholy sits on brood;°
And I do doubt the hatch and the disclose°   170
Will be some danger: which for to prevent,
I have in quick determination
Thus set it down: he shall with speed to England,
For the demand of our neglected tribute:
Haply the seas and countries different   175
With variable objects° shall expel
This something-settled matter° in his heart,
Whereon his brains still beating° puts him thus
From fashion of himself.° What think you on 't?

POLONIUS: It shall do well:° but yet do I believe   180
The origin and commencement of his grief
Sprung from neglected° love. How now, Ophelia!
You need not tell us what Lord Hamlet said;
We heard it all. My lord, do as you please;
But, if you hold it fit, after the play   185
Let his queen mother all alone entreat him
To show his grief:° let her be round° with him;
And I'll be placed, so please you, in the ear
Of all their conference. If she find him° not,
To England send him, or confine him where   190
Your wisdom best shall think.

KING: It shall be so:
Madness in great ones must not unwatch'd go.

[Exeunt.]

Scene 2

A hall in the castle.

[Enter HAMLET and PLAYERS.]

HAMLET: Speak the speech, I pray you, as I pronounced it to you, trippingly° on the tongue: but if

---

123 indifferent honest fairly virtuous   **126 beck** bidding   **130
arrant** downright   **142 monsters** cuckolds (husbands with
faithless wives) were said to wear horns   **nunnery** besides
the usual meaning, in Elizabethan days = house of prostitution
147 jig walk with affected provocative movements   **148 lisp**
talk affectedly   **nick-name ... creatures** give indecent names
to   **149 make ... ignorance** pretend you are too innocent to
understand what you are saying   **155 The ... sword** i.e., the
courtier's eye, the scholar's tongue, the soldier's sword   **156
fair** because he adorned it   **157 glass** mirror   **mould of form**
model of polite behavior

163 feature of blown bodily shape of fully matured   **164 ecstasy** madness   **169 sits on brood** broods   **170 disclose** disclosure   **176 variable objects** unfamiliar sights   **177 something-
settled matter** i.e., obsession   **178 still beating** constantly
going over and over again   **179 From ... himself** i.e., makes
him unlike himself   **180 It ... well** i.e., your plan is good   **182
neglected** unreturned   **187 show his grief** reveal the cause of
his grief   **round** plain and direct   **189 find him** i.e., find him
out, get at his secret

SCENE 2:   **2 trippingly** without exaggerated emphasis

you mouth it, as many of your players° do, I had as lief the town-crier spoke my lines. Nor do not saw the air too much with your hand, thus, but use all gently; for in the very torrent, tempest, and, as I may say, the whirlwind of passion, you must acquire and beget a temperance° that may give it smoothness. O, it offends me to the soul to hear a robustious° periwig-pated° fellow tear a passion to tatters, to very rags, to split the ears of the groundlings,° who for the most part are capable of° nothing but inexplicable° dumb-shows and noise: I would have such a fellow whipped for o'er-doing Termagant;° it out-herods Herod:° pray you, avoid it.

FIRST PLAYER: I warrant your honour.°

HAMLET: Be not too tame neither, but let your own discretion° be your tutor: suit the action to the word, the word to the action; with this special observance, that you o'er-step not the modesty° of nature: for any thing so overdone is from° the purpose of playing,° whose end, both at the first° and now, was and is, to hold, as 't were, the mirror up to nature; to show virtue her own feature,° scorn her own image, and the very age and body of the time° his form and pressure. Now this overdone, or come tardy off,° though it make the unskillful° laugh, cannot but make the judicious grieve; the censure of the which one° must in your allowance° o'erweigh a whole theatre of others. O, there be players that I have seen play, and heard others praise, and that highly, not to speak it profanely, that, neither having the accent of Christians nor the gait of Christian, pagan, nor man, have so strutted and bellowed that I have thought some of nature's journeymen° had made men and not made them well, they imitated humanity so abominably.

FIRST PLAYER: I hope we have reformed that indifferently° with us, sir.

HAMLET: O, reform it altogether. And let those that play your clowns peak no more than is set down for them;° for there be of them° that will themselves laugh, to set on some quantity of barren° spectators to laugh too; though, in the mean time, some necessary question° of the play be then to be considered: that's villanous,° and shows a most pitiful° ambition in the fool that uses it. Go, make you ready.

[Exeunt players.]

[Enter POLONIUS, ROSENCRANTZ, *and* GUILDENSTERN.*]*

How now, my lord! will the king hear this piece of work?°

POLONIUS: And the queen too, and that presently.°

HAMLET: Bid the players make haste.

[Exit POLONIUS.*]*

Will you two help to hasten them?

ROSENCRANTZ:
GUILDENSTERN: } We will, my lord.

[Exeunt ROSENCRANTZ *and* GUILDENSTERN.*]*

HAMLET: What ho! Horatio!

[Enter HORATIO.*]*

HORATIO: Here, sweet lord, at your service.

HAMLET: Horatio, thou art e'en as just° a man
As e'er my conversation coped withal.°

HORATIO: O, my dear lord,—

HAMLET: Nay, do not think I flatter;
For what advancement may I hope from thee
That no revénue hast but thy good spirits,
To feed and clothe thee? Why should the poor be
    flatter'd?
No, let the candied° tongue lick absurd pomp,°
And crook the pregnant hinges° of the knee
Where thrift° may follow fawning. Dost thou
    hear?

---

³ **your players** actors in general   ⁸ **temperance** moderation   ¹⁰ **robustious** boisterous   **periwig-pated** wearing a wig   ¹² **groundlings** those who stood on the ground in an Elizabethan theatre and so the least intelligent part of the audience   ¹³ **capable of** can appreciate   **inexplicable** meaningless   **dumb-shows** scenes acted in pantomime   ¹⁵ **Termagant** a violent and noisy character in the mystery plays, supposed to be a god of the Saracens   **Herod** the Jewish King who ordered the slaughter of the children. In the mystery plays he was a ranting tyrant.   ¹⁷ **I warrant your honour** your lordship is quite right   ¹⁹ **discretion** judgment   ²¹ **modesty** moderation   ²² **from** contrary to   ²³ **playing** acting   **at the first** in earlier times   ²⁵ **feature** form   ²⁷ **age and body of the time** accurate picture of the age   **form and pressure** their appearance in general and in detail   ²⁸ **come tardy off** done half-heartedly   **unskilful** uncritical   ³⁰ **the which one** i.e., a single judicious person   ³¹ **allowance** estimation   ³⁷ **journeymen** those not yet become masters of their trade

---

⁴¹ **indifferently** fairly well   ⁴⁴ **there . . . them** there are some clowns   ⁴⁵ **barren** i.e., of intelligence   ⁴⁷ **necessary question** essential subject matter   ⁴⁸ **villainous** cheap   ⁴⁹ **pitiful** contemptible   ⁵² **piece of work** masterpiece   ⁵³ **presently** at once   ⁵⁸ **just** well balanced   ⁵⁹ **conversation coped withal** my experience has had to do with   ⁶⁴ **candied** sugared, hence flattering   **lick absurd pomp** fawn upon absurdly pompous persons   ⁶⁵ **pregnant hinges** ready-to-act (supple) joints   ⁶⁶ **thrift** worldly advantage. The phrase means, "where flattery pays."

Since my dear soul was mistress of her choice
And could of men° distinguish, her election°
Hath seal'd thee for herself; for thou hast been
70   As one, in suffering all, that suffers nothing,
A man that fortune's buffets and rewards
Hast ta'en with equal thanks: and blest are those
Whose blood and judgement° are so well com-
   mingled,
That they are not a pipe for fortune's finger
75   To sound what stop she please. Give me that man
That is not passion's slave, and I will wear him
In my heart's core, ay, in my heart of heart,
As I do thee.—Something too much of this.—
There is a play to-night before the king;
80   One scene of it comes near the circumstance
Which I have told thee of my father's death:
I prithee, when thou seest that act afoot,°
Even with the very comment of thy soul°
Observe mine uncle: if his occulted° guilt
85   Do not itself unkennel in one speech,
It is a damnèd ghost° that we have seen,
And my imaginations° are as foul
As Vulcan's stithy.° Give him heedful note;°
For I mine eyes will rivet to his face,
90   And after we will both our judgements join
In censure of his seeming.°
HORATIO: Well, my lord:
If he steal aught the whilst this play is playing,
And 'scape detecting, I will pay the theft.
HAMLET: They are coming to the play; I must be idle:°
95   Get you a place.

[Danish march. A flourish. Enter KING, QUEEN, POLONIUS,
OPHELIA, ROSENCRANTZ, GUILDENSTERN, *and others.]*

KING: How fares our cousin Hamlet?
HAMLET: Excellent, i' faith; of the chameleon's dish:° I
   eat the air, promise-crammed: you cannot feed
   capons so.
100   KING: I have nothing with° this answer, Hamlet; these
   words are not mine.°
HAMLET: No, nor mine now. [*To* POLONIUS] My lord,
   you played once i' the university, you say?
POLONIUS: That did I, my lord; and was accounted a
105   good actor.
HAMLET: What did you enact?

POLONIUS: I did enact Julius Cæsar: I was killed i' the
   Capitol; Brutus killed me.
HAMLET: It was a brute part° of him to kill so capital a
   calf there. Be the players ready?   110
ROSENCRANTZ: Ay, my lord; they stay upon your
   patience.°
QUEEN: Come hither, my dear Hamlet, sit by me.
HAMLET: No, good mother, here's metal more attrac-
   tive.
POLONIUS: [*To the* KING] O, ho! do you mark that?   115
HAMLET: Lady, shall I lie in your lap?

[Lying down at OPHELIA'*s feet.]*

OPHELIA: No, my lord.
HAMLET: I mean, my head upon your lap?
OPHELIA: Ay, my lord.
HAMLET: Do you think I meant country matters?   120
OPHELIA: I think nothing, my lord.
HAMLET: That's a fair thought to lie between maids'
   legs.
OPHELIA: What is, my lord?
HAMLET: Nothing.   125
OPHELIA: You are merry, my lord.
HAMLET: Who, I?
OPHELIA: Ay, my lord.
HAMLET: O God, your only jig-maker.° What should a
   man do but be merry? for, look you, how cheerful- 130
   ly my mother looks, and my father died within
   these two hours.
OPHELIA: Nay, 'tis twice two months, my lord.
HAMLET: So long? Nay then, let the devil wear black,
   for I'll have a suit of sables.° O heavens! died two 135
   months ago, and not forgotten yet? Then there's
   hope a great man's memory may outlive his life
   half a year: but by'r lady, he must build churches,
   then; or else shall he suffer not thinking on, with°
   the hobby-horse whose epitaph is "For, O, for, O,   140
   the hobby-horse is forgot."°

[Hautboys play. The dumb-show° enters.]

[Enter a KING *and a* QUEEN *very lovingly; the* QUEEN
*embracing him, and he her. She kneels, and makes
show of protestation° unto him. He takes her up, and*

---

[68] **of men** among men   **election** choice   [73] **blood and judge-ment** emotion and reason   [82] **afoot** being enacted   [83] **com-ment . . . soul** concentration of your entire attention   [84] **occult-ed** concealed   [86] **damned ghost** a devil   [87] **imaginations** suspicions   [88] **stithy** blacksmith's forge   **Give . . . note** pay close attention to him   [91] **censure . . . seeming** judgment of his behavior   [94] **be idle** seem crazy   [97] **chameleon's dish** the air, so the Elizabethans believed   [100] **I . . . with** I can make nothing of   [101] **not mine** no answer to my question

[109] **part** act   [111] **stay . . . patience** wait until you are ready   [129] **jig-maker** man to write a jig, a song and dance afterpiece   [135] **sables** black fur, i.e., mourning. The phrase means I'll wear mourning even if the Devil does, too.   [139] **suffer . . . with** endure not being remembered along with   [141] **hobby-horse is forgot** the hobby-horse had been a popular figure in the May Day celebrations. It had gone out of style in Shakespeare's day, partly because the Puritans thought it a relic of heathen rites. The word was also a cant term for harlot.   [sd] **s.d. dumb-show** a play presented in pantomime   [sd] **makes . . . protesta-tion** acts out a formal declaration (of affection)

declines his head upon her neck: lays him down upon a bank of flowers: she, seeing him asleep, leaves him. Anon° comes in a fellow, takes off his crown, kisses it, and pours poison in the KING's ears, and exit. The QUEEN returns; finds the KING dead, and makes passionate action. The POISONER, with some two or three MUTES, comes in again, seeming to lament with her. The dead body is carried away. The POISONER wooes the QUEEN with gifts: she seems loath and unwilling awhile, but in the end accepts his love.] [Exeunt.

OPHELIA: What means this, my lord?

HAMLET: Marry, this is miching mallecho;° it means mischief.

145   OPHELIA: Belike° this show imports the argument° of the play.

[Enter PROLOGUE.]

HAMLET: We shall know by this fellow: the players cannot keep counsel;° they'll tell all.

OPHELIA: Will he tell us what this show meant?

150   HAMLET: Ay, or any show that you'll show him: be not you ashamed to show, he'll not shame to tell you what it means.

OPHELIA: You are naught,° you are naught: I'll mark the play.

155   PROLOGUE: For us, and for our tragedy,
Here stooping to your clemency,
We beg your hearing patiently.

[Exit.]

HAMLET: Is this a prologue, or the posy of a ring?°

OPHELIA: 'Tis brief, my lord.

160   HAMLET: As woman's love.

[Enter two PLAYERS, KING and QUEEN.]

PLAYER KING: Full thirty times hath Phœbus' cart gone round
Neptune's salt wash and Tellus' orbèd ground,°
And thirty dozen moons with borrow'd sheen
About the world have times twelve thirties been,
165   Since love our hearts and Hymen did our hands
Unite commutual° in most sacred bands.

PLAYER QUEEN: So many journeys may the sun and moon
Make us again count o'er ere love be done!
But, woe is me, you are so sick of late,
170   So far from cheer and from your former state,

That I distrust° you. Yet, though I distrust,
Discomfort° you, my lord, it nothing must:
For women's fear and love holds quantity;
In neither aught, or in extremity.°
Now, what my love is, proof° hath made you know; 175
And as my love is sized, my fear is so:
Where love is great, the littlest doubts are fear;°
Where little fears grow great, great love grows there.

PLAYER KING: 'Faith, I must leave thee, love, and shortly too;
My operant powers their functions leave to do:° 180
And thou shalt live in this fair world behind,°
Honour'd, beloved; and haply one as kind
For husband shalt thou—

PLAYER QUEEN: O, confound the rest!°
Such love must needs be treason in my breast: 185
In second husband let me be accurst!
None wed the second but who kill'd the first.

HAMLET: [Aside] Wormwood, wormwood.

PLAYER QUEEN: The instances° that second marriage move°
Are base respects° of thrift, but none of love: 190
A second time I kill my husband dead,
When second husband kisses me in bed.

PLAYER KING: I do believe you think what now you speak;
But what we do determine oft we break.
Purpose is but the slave to memory, 195
Of violent birth, but poor validity:°
Which now, like fruit unripe, sticks on the tree;
But fall, unshaken, when they mellow be.
Most necessary 'tis that we forget
To pay ourselves what to ourselves is debt:° 200
What to ourselves in passion we propose,
The passion ending, doth the purpose lose.
The violence of either grief or joy
Their own enactures° with themselves destroy:
Where° joy most revels, grief doth most lament; 205
Grief joys, joy grieves, on slender accident.°
This world is not for aye, nor 'tis not strange
That even our loves° should with our fortunes change;

---

171 **distrust** am worried about you   172 **Discomfort** worry
174 **For . . . extremity** In women anxiety for a person's welfare is proportionate to the love. They feel neither love nor fear, or a great deal of both.   175 **proof** experience   177 **the littlest . . . fear** the slightest cause for anxiety produces fear   180 **My . . . do** My physical powers cease to function.   181 **behind** i.e., after my death   184 **confound the rest** strike dumb the rest [that you were going to say]   189 **instances** motives **move** induce   190 **respects** considerations   197 **validity** strength   200 **Most necessary . . . debt** i.e., it is inevitable that we should find it easy to break a promise (pay a debt) made to ourselves   204 **enactures** impulses to action   205 **Where** in persons in whom   206 **on slender accident** because of trifling incidents   208 **our loves** love others have for us

---

s.d. **Anon** presently   144 **miching mallecho** a sneaking (cowardly) crime   145 **Belike** perhaps   **imports the argument** reveals the plot   148 **counsel** a secret   153 **naught** indecent 158 **posy of a ring** a short rime (usually sentimental) engraved on the inside of a ring   162 **Tellus' . . . ground** the round earth. Shakespeare made the verse of this play bombastic. 166 **commutual** in mutual love

For 'tis a question left us yet to prove,
210 Whether love lead fortune, or else fortune love.°
The great man down, you mark his favourite flies;
The poor advanced makes friends of enemies.
And hitherto° doth love on fortune tend;
For who not needs shall never lack a friend,
215 And who in want a hollow friend doth try,
Directly seasons him his enemy.°
But, orderly° to end where° I begun,
Our wills and fates do so contrary run
That our devices still° are overthrown;
Our thoughts are ours, their ends none of our
220   own:
So think thou° wilt no second husband wed;
But die thy thoughts° when thy first lord is dead.
PLAYER QUEEN: Nor earth to me give food,° nor heav-
    en light!
Sport and repose lock from me day and night!
225 To desperation turn my trust and hope!
An anchor's° cheer° in prison be my scope!
Each opposite that blanks° the face of joy
Meet what I would have well° and it destroy!
Both here and hence° pursue me lasting strife,
230 If, once a widow, ever I be wife!
HAMLET: If° she should break it now!
PLAYER KING: 'Tis deeply sworn. Sweet, leave me
    here awhile;
My spirits grow dull, and fain I would beguile°
The tedious day with sleep.

[Sleeps.]

235 PLAYER QUEEN: Sleep rock thy brain;
And never come mischance between us twain!

[Exit.]

HAMLET: Madam, how like you this play?
QUEEN: The lady doth protest too much, methinks.
HAMLET: O, but she'll keep her word.
240 KING: Have you heard the argument?° Is there no
    offence in 't?
HAMLET: No, no, they do but jest, poison in jest; no
    offence i' the world.
KING: What do you call the play?

HAMLET: The Mouse-trap. Marry, how? Tropically.°   245
This play is the image° of a murder done in Vienna:
Gonzago is the duke's name; his wife, Baptista: you
shall see anon;° 't is a knavish piece of work: but
what o' that? your majesty and we that have free°
souls, it touches us not: let the galled jade° wince,   250
our withers° are unwrung.°

[Enter LUCIANUS.]

This is one Lucianus, nephew to the king.
OPHELIA: You are as good as a chorus, my lord.
HAMLET: I could interpret° between you and your
    love, if I could see the puppets dallying.   255
OPHELIA: You are keen,° my lord, you are keen.
HAMLET: It would cost you a groaning to take off my
    edge.
OPHELIA: Still better, and worse.
HAMLET: So you must take your husbands. Begin,   260
    murderer; pox,° leave thy damnable faces, and
    begin. Come: "the croaking raven doth bellow for
    revenge."
LUCIANUS: Thoughts black, hands apt, drugs fit, and
    time agreeing;
Confederate season,° else no creature° seeing;   265
Thou mixture rank, of midnight weeds collected,
With Hecate's° ban° thrice blasted, thrice infected,
Thy natural magic and dire property,°
On wholesome life usurp° immediately.

[Pours the poison into the sleeper's ears.]

HAMLET: He poisons him i' the garden for 's estate.   270
    His° name's Gonzago: the story is extant, and writ
    in choice Italian: you shall see anon how the mur-
    derer gets the love of Gonzago's wife.
OPHELIA: The king rises.
HAMLET: What, frighted with false fire!°   275
QUEEN: How fares my lord?
POLONIUS: Give o'er° the play.
KING: Give me some light: away!
ALL: Lights, lights, lights!

[Exeunt all but HAMLET and HORATIO.]

---

210 **Whether ... love** whether the regard of our fellows brings worldly success or vice versa   213 **hitherto** up to now   216 **seasons ... enemy** ripens him into an enemy   217 **orderly** properly   **where** with the point with which   219 **devices still** our plans always   221 **think thou** though you think   222 **die thy thoughts** your resolution will die   223 **Nor . . . food** may earth give me no food   226 **anchor's** anchorite's, hermit's **cheer** fare   227 **opposite that blanks** adverse event that blots out   228 **would have well** should like   229 **here and hence** this world and the next   231 **If** what if   233 **beguile** while away   240 **argument** plot

245 **Tropically** figuratively   246 **image** representation   248 **anon** presently   249 **free** i.e., from guilt   250 **galled jade** old broken down horse covered with sores from saddle or harness   251 **withers** shoulder bones of a horse   **unwrung** unchafed   254 **interpret** like an actor who explained the action of puppets   256 **keen** bitter, also "sexually aroused"   261 **pox** plague take it   265 **Confederate season** the time cooperating (with the murderer)   **else no creature** i.e., except time   267 **Hecate** goddess of witchcraft   **ban** curse   268 **dire property** harmful quality   265 **usurp** take harmful effect   271 **His** i.e., the murdered man's   275 **false fire** discharge of a blank cartridge   277 **Give o'er** stop

280 HAMLET: Why, let the stricken deer go weep,°
     The hart ungallèd play;
     For some must watch,° while some must sleep:
     So runs the world away.
     Would not this,° sir, and a forest of feathers°—if
285   the rest of my fortunes turn Turk° with me—
     with two Provincial roses° on my razed° shoes,
     get me a fellowship in a cry° of players, sir?
HORATIO: Half a share.°
HAMLET: A whole one, I.
290 For thou dost know, O Damon° dear,
     This realm dismantled° was
     Of Jove° himself; and now reigns here
     A very, very—pajock.°
HORATIO: You might have rhymed.
295 HAMLET: O good Horatio, I'll take the ghost's
     word for a thousand pound. Didst perceive?
HORATIO: Very well, my lord.
HAMLET: Upon the talk of the poisoning?
HORATIO: I did very well note him.
300 HAMLET: Ah, ha! Come, some music! come,
     the recorders!°
     For if the king like not the comedy,
     Why then, belike,° he likes it not, perdy.°
     Come, some music!

[Re-enter ROSENCRANTZ *and* GUILDENSTERN.*]*

305 GUILDENSTERN: Good my lord, vouchsafe me a word
     with you.
HAMLET: Sir, a whole history.
GUILDENSTERN: The king, sir,—
HAMLET: Ay, sir, what of him?
310 GUILDENSTERN: Is in his retirement marvellous dis-
     tempered.°
HAMLET: With drink, sir?
GUILDENSTERN: No, my lord, rather with choler.°
HAMLET: Your wisdom should° show itself more rich-

er to signify° this to his doctor; for, for me to put   315
him to his purgation would perhaps plunge him
into far more choler.
GUILDENSTERN: Good my lord, put your discourse
into some frame° and start not so wildly from my
affair.   320
HAMLET: I am tame, sir: pronounce.
GUILDENSTERN: The queen, your mother, in most great
affliction of spirit, hath sent me to you.
HAMLET: You are welcome.
GUILDENSTERN: Nay, good my lord, this courtesy is not   325
of the right breed. If it shall please you to make me
a wholesome° answer, I will do your mother's
commandment: if not, your pardon and my return
shall be the end of my business.
HAMLET: Sir, I cannot.   330
GUILDENSTERN: What, my lord?
HAMLET: Make you a wholesome answer; my wit's°
diseased: but, sir, such answer as I can make, you
shall command; or, rather, as you say, my mother:
therefore no more, but to the matter: my mother,   335
you say,—
ROSENCRANTZ: Then thus she says; your behaviour
hath struck her into amazement and admira- tion.°
HAMLET: O wonderful son, that can so astonish a
mother! But is there no sequel at the heels of this   340
mother's admiration. Impart.
ROSENCRANTZ: She desires to speak with you in her
closet,° ere you go to bed.
HAMLET: We shall obey, were she ten times our mother. Have you any further trade with us?   345
ROSENCRANTZ: My lord, you once did love me.
HAMLET: So do I still, by these pickers and stealers.°
ROSENCRANTZ: Good my lord, what is your cause of
distemper? you do, surely, bar the door upon your
own liberty, if you deny° your griefs to your   350
friend.
HAMLET: Sir, I lack advancement.
ROSENCRANTZ: How can that be, when you have the
voice° of the king himself for your succession in
Denmark?   355
HAMLET: Ay, sir, but "While the grass grows,"°—the
proverb is something musty.

[Re-enter PLAYERS *with recorders.]*

O, the recorders! let me see one. To withdraw° with

---

²⁸⁰ **stricken . . . weep** an allusion to the notion that a wounded deer goes off to weep and die alone   ²⁸² **watch** stay
awake, i.e., those whose sense of guilt keeps them awake
²⁸⁴ **this** i.e., manner of declamation   **feathers** i.e., that often
decorated an actor's hat   ²⁸⁵ **turn Turk** prove false, like a
Christian who turns Mohammedan   ²⁸⁶ **Provincial roses**
i.e., a variety of large rose, here the rosettes on an actor's
shoes   **razed** ornamented by open work   ²⁸⁷ **cry** pack (of
hounds)   ²⁸⁸ **Half a share** Shakespeare's company divided
the ownership among the actors, the less important receiving
only half a share.   ²⁹⁰ **Damon** the Greeks Damon and
Pythias were ideally faithful friends.   ²⁹¹ **dismantled** shorn
of adornment   ²⁹² **Jove** i.e., his father   ²⁹³ **pajock** peacock,
thought to be cruel and lustful   ³⁰¹ **recorders** musical
instruments resembling clarinets   ³⁰³ **belike** evidently
perdy corruption of "per dieu," a mild oath about = in truth
³¹¹ **distempered** ill   ³¹³ **choler** a bilious attack with a play on
the meaning "anger"   ³¹⁴ **should** would

³¹⁵ **to signify** by reporting   ³¹⁹ **frame** logical form   ³²⁷
wholesome sensible   ³³² **wit** intelligence   ³³⁸ **admiration**
astonishment   ³⁴³ **closet** private sitting room   ³⁴⁷ **pickers
and stealers** hands, referring to the phrase in the catechism
of the English Church, "To keep my hands from picking and
stealing"   ³⁵⁰ **deny** refuse to impart   ³⁵⁴ **voice** vote, promise
³⁵⁶ **"While . . . grows"** the last part of this proverb is, "the silly
horse starves."   ³⁵⁸ **withdraw** speak in private

you:—why do you go about to recover the wind of
360　me,° as if you would drive me into a toil?°
GUILDENSTERN: O, my lord, if my duty be too bold, my
　love is too unmannerly.°
HAMLET: I do not well understand that. Will you play
　upon this pipe?
365　GUILDENSTERN: My lord, I cannot.
HAMLET: I pray you.
GUILDENSTERN: Believe me, I cannot.
HAMLET: I do beseech you.
GUILDENSTERN: I know no touch° of it, my lord.
370　HAMLET: 'Tis as easy as lying: govern these ventages°
　with your fingers and thumb, give it breath with
　your mouth, and it will discourse most eloquent
　music. Look you, these are the stops.
GUILDENSTERN: But these cannot I command to any
375　utterance of harmony; I have not the skill.
HAMLET: Why, look you now, how unworthy a thing
　you make of me! You would play upon me; you
　would seem to know my stops, you would pluck
　out the heart of my mystery; you would sound me
380　from my lowest note to the top of my compass:°
　and there is much music, excellent voice, in this
　little organ;° yet cannot you make it speak.
　'Sblood, do you think I am easier to be played on
　than a pipe? Call me what instrument you will,
385　though you can fret° me, yet you cannot play
　upon me.

[Enter POLONIUS.]

God bless you, sir!
POLONIUS: My lord, the queen would speak with you,
　and presently.°
390　HAMLET: Do you see yonder cloud that's almost in
　shape of a camel?
POLONIUS: By the mass, and 'tis like a camel, indeed.
HAMLET: Methinks it is like a weasel.
POLONIUS: It is backed like a weasel.
395　HAMLET: Or like a whale?
POLONIUS: Very like a whale.
HAMLET: Then I will come to my mother by and by.
　They fool° me to the top of my bent. I will come by
　and by.

POLONIUS: I will say so.　　　　　　　　　　　　　400
HAMLET: By and by is easily said.

[Exit POLONIUS.]

Leave me, friends.

[Exeunt all but HAMLET.]

'Tis now the very witching time° of night,
When churchyards yawn and hell itself breathes
　out
Contagion to this world: now could I drink hot
　blood,　　　　　　　　　　　　　　　　　　405
And do such bitter business as the day
Would quake to look on. Soft! now to my mother.
O heart, lose not thy nature; let not ever
The soul of Nero° enter this firm bosom:
Let me be cruel, not unnatural:　　　　　　　410
I will speak daggers to her, but use none;
My tongue and soul in this be hypocrites;°
How in my words soever she be shent,°
To give them seals° never, my soul, consent!

[Exit.]

Scene 3

A room in the castle.

[Enter KING, ROSENCRANTZ, and GUILDENSTERN.]

KING: I like him° not, nor stands it safe with us
　To let his madness range.° Therefore prepare you;
　I your commission will forthwith dispatch,°
　And he to England shall along with you:
　The terms of our estate° may not endure　　　5
　Hazard so near us as doth hourly grow
　Out of his lunacies.
GUILDENSTERN:　　　　　We will ourselves provide:°
　Most holy and religious fear it is
　To keep those many many bodies safe
　That live and feed upon your majesty.　　　　10
ROSENCRANTZ: The single and peculiar° life is bound,
　With all the strength and armour of the mind,
　To keep itself from noyance;° but much more

---

360 **recover . . . me** get me to windward, a hunting phrase
meaning to get the prey between the hunter and the wind,
and so avoid giving it the scent of the pursuer　**toil** net　362
if . . . unmannerly if I have been officious in doing my duty
by you it is my love for you that is to blame.　369 **touch** any
act of the hands in playing an instrument　370 **ventages** stops
on the recorder　380 **compass** the range of a voice　382 **organ**
musical instrument, here the recorder　385 **fret** pun (1) irritate, (2) finger the frets on a stringed instrument　389 **presently** at once　398 **fool** treat me as though I were a fool (madman)　**top of my bent** limit of my endurance, i.e., extent to
which a bow can be bent

---

403 **witching time** time when witches are most about, i.e.,
midnight　409 **Nero** the Roman Emperor who murdered his
mother　412 **be hypocrites** give a false impression (of my real
feelings)　413 **shent** rebuked　414 **To . . . seals** i.e., confirm
them with action.

SCENE 3:　1 **him** i.e., his actions　2 **range** be at large　3 **dispatch**
draw up　5 **terms . . . estate** circumstances surrounding my
office [of King]　7 **provide** make ready　11 **single and peculiar**
individual and private　13 **noyance** harm

That spirit upon whose weal depend and rest
15 The lives of many. The cease° of majesty°
Dies not alone; but, like a gulf,° doth draw
What's near it with it: it is a massy wheel,
Fix'd on the summit of the highest mount,
To whose huge spokes ten thousand lesser things
20 Are mortised° and adjoin'd; which, when it falls,
Each small annexment, petty consequence,
Attends the boisterous ruin.° Never alone
Did the king sigh, but with a general° groan.
KING: Arm° you, I pray you, to this speedy voyage;
25 For we will fetters put upon this fear,
Which now goes too free-footed.

ROSENCRANTZ: }
GUILDENSTERN: } We will haste us.

[Exeunt ROSENCRANTZ and GUILDENSTERN.

[Enter POLONIUS.]

POLONIUS: My lord, he's going to his mother's closet:
Behind the arras I'll convey° myself,
To hear the process;° I'll warrant she'll tax him
    home:°
30 And, as you said, and wisely was it said,
'Tis meet° that some more audience than a mother,
Since nature make them partial, should o'er-hear
The speech, of vantage.° Fare you well, my liege:
I'll call upon you ere you go to bed,
And tell you what I know.
35 KING: Thanks, dear my lord.

[Exit POLONIUS.]

O, my offence is rank, it smells to heaven;
It hath the primal eldest curse° upon 't,
A brother's murder. Pray can I not,
Though inclination be as sharp as will:°
40 My stronger guilt defeats my strong intent;
And, like a man to double business bound,°
I stand in pause where° I shall first begin,
And both neglect. What if this cursèd hand
Were thicker than itself with brother's blood,
45 Is there not rain enough in the sweet heavens
To wash it white as snow? Whereto serves mercy

But to confront° the visage of offence?
And what's in prayer but this two-fold force,
To be forestallèd° ere we come to fall,
Or pardon'd being down? Then I'll look up;   50
My fault is past. But, O, what form of prayer
Can serve my turn? "Forgive me my foul murder"?
That cannot be: since I am still possess'd
Of those effects° for which I did the murder,
My crown, mine own ambition and my queen.   55
May one be pardon'd and retain the offence?
In the corrupted currents of this world
Offence's gilded° hand may shove by° justice,
And oft 'tis seen the wicked prize itself
Buys out the law:° but 'tis not so above;   60
There is no shuffling,° there the action lies°
In his° true nature; and we ourselves compell'd,
Even to the teeth and forehead of our faults,°
To give in evidence. What then? what rests?°
Try what repentance can: what can it not?   65
Yet what can it when one can not repent?
O wretched state! O bosom black as death!
O limèd° soul, that, struggling to be free,
Art more engaged! Help, angels! Make assay!°
Bow, stubborn knees; and, heart with strings of
    steel,   70
Be soft as sinews of the new-born babe!
All may be well.

[Retires and kneels.]

[Enter HAMLET.]

HAMLET: Now might I do it pat, now he is praying;
And now I'll do 't. And so he goes to heaven;
And so am I revenged. That would be scann'd:°   75
A villain kills my father; and for that,
I, his sole son, do this same villain send
To heaven.
O, this is hire and salary,° not revenge.
He took my father grossly,° full of bread;°   80
With all his crimes broad blown,° as flush° as May;

---

¹⁵ **cease** death **majesty** a king ¹⁶ **gulf** whirlpool ²⁰ **mortised** firmly attached ²² **boisterous ruin** thunderous downfall ²³ **general** i.e., of all society ²⁴ **Arm** prepare ²⁸ **convey** place secretly ²⁹ **process** course of events, what is going on **tax him home** censure him severely ³¹ **meet** fitting ³³ **of vantage** besides ³⁷ **primal . . . curse** the curse put upon Cain, the first fratricide ³⁹ **inclination . . . will** desire [to pray] be as strong as my determination [to do so] ⁴¹ **double . . . bound** under obligation to do two things at the same time ⁴² **stand . . . where** pause to consider which

---

⁴⁷ **confront** oppose face to face ⁴⁹ **forestalled** prevented ⁵⁴ **effects** intended results ⁵⁸ **gilded** i.e., lined with gold **shove by** push aside ⁶⁰ **wicked . . . the law** the money gained through crime may be used to corrupt the judge ⁶¹ **shuffling** trickery **action lies** a plea is made in accordance with ⁶² **his** its ⁶³ **teeth . . . faults** i.e., face to face with our sins (which will appear in court against us) ⁶⁴ **rests** remains [for me to do] ⁶⁸ **limed** caught as a bird with birdlime ⁶⁹ **Make assay** i.e., I will make the attempt ⁷⁵ **would be scann'd** should be looked into ⁷⁹ **hire and salary** i.e., like paying him for the deed ⁸⁰ **grossly** unpurified by repentance **full of bread** cf. Ezekiel XVI, "This was the iniquity . . . of Sodom, pride, fullness of bread." ⁸¹ **crimes broad blown** sins in full flower **flush** lusty

And how his audit° stands who knows save
   heaven?
But in our circumstance and course of thought,°
'Tis heavy with him:° and am I then revenged,
85 To take° him in the purging of his soul,
When he is fit and season'd° for his passage?
No!
Up, sword; and know thou a more horrid hent:°
When he is drunk asleep, or in his rage,°
90 Or in the incestuous pleasure of his bed;
At gaming, swearing, or about some act
That has no relish° of salvation in 't;
Then trip him, that his heels may kick at heaven,°
And that his soul may be as damn'd and black
95 As hell, whereto it goes. My mother stays:°
This physic° but prolongs thy sickly° days.

KING: [*Rising*] My words fly up, my thoughts remain
   below:
Words without thoughts never to heaven go.

[*Exit.*]

Scene 4

The QUEEN'*s closet.*

[*Enter* QUEEN *and* POLONIUS.]

POLONIUS: He will come straight.° Look you lay
   home° to him:
Tell him his pranks have been too broad° to bear
   with,
And that your grace hath screen'd and stood
   between
Much heat° and him. I'll sconce° me even here.
5 Pray you, be round° with him.
HAMLET: [*Within*] Mother, mother, mother!
QUEEN: I'll warrant you,°
Fear me not: withdraw, I hear him coming.

[POLONIUS *hides behind the arras.*]

[*Enter* HAMLET.]

HAMLET: Now, mother, what's the matter?
QUEEN: Hamlet, thou hast thy father much offended.
HAMLET: Mother, you have my father much offended. 10
QUEEN: Come, come, you answer with an idle° tongue.
HAMLET: Go, go, you question with a wicked tongue.
QUEEN: Why, how now, Hamlet!
HAMLET: What's the matter now?
QUEEN: Have you forgot me?°
HAMLET: No, by the rood,° not so:
You are the queen, your husband's brother's wife; 15
And—would it were not so!—you are my mother.
QUEEN: Nay, then, I'll set those to you that can speak.°
HAMLET: Come, come, and sit you down; you shall
   not budge;
You go not till I set you up a glass
Where you may see the inmost part of you. 20
QUEEN: What wilt thou do? thou wilt not murder me?
   Help, help, ho!
POLONIUS: [*Behind*] What, ho! help, help, help!
HAMLET: [*Drawing*] How now! a rat? Dead, for a
   ducat,° dead!

[*Makes a pass through the arras.*]

POLONIUS: [*Behind*] O, I am slain!

[*Falls and dies.*]

QUEEN: O me, what hast thou done?
HAMLET: Nay, I know not: 25
Is it the king?
QUEEN: O, what a rash and bloody deed is this!
HAMLET: A bloody deed! almost as bad, good mother,
As kill a king, and marry with his brother.
QUEEN: As kill a king!
HAMLET: Ay, lady, 'twas my word. 30

[*Lifts up the arras and discovers* POLONIUS.]

Thou wretched, rash, intruding fool, farewell!
I took thee for thy better: take thy fortune;
Thou find'st to be too busy° is some danger.
Leave wringing of your hands: peace! sit you down,
And let me wring your heart; for so I shall,
If it be made of penetrable stuff, 35
If damnèd custom have not brass'd° it so
That it be proof° and bulwark against sense.°
QUEEN: What have I done, that thou darest wag thy
   tongue
In noise so rude against me?

---

40   HAMLET: Such an act
       That blurs the grace and blush of modesty,
       Calls virtue hypocrite, takes off the rose°
       From the fair forehead of an innocent love
       And sets a blister° there, makes marriage-vows
45   As false as dicers' oaths: O, such a deed
       As from the body of contraction° plucks
       The very soul, and sweet religion makes
       A rhapsody° of words: heaven's face doth glow;°
       Yea, this solidity° and compound mass,
50   With tristful° visage, as against the doom,°
       Is thought-sick at the act.
    QUEEN: Ay me, what act,
       That roars so loud, and thunders in the index?°
    HAMLET: Look here, upon this picture, and on this.
       The counterfeit presentment° of two brothers.
55   See, what a grace was seated on this brow;
       Hyperion's° curls; the front° of Jove himself;
       An eye like Mars, to threaten and command;
       A station° like the herald Mercury
       New-lighted° on a heaven-kissing hill;
60   A combination and a form indeed,
       Where every god did seem to set his seal,
       To give the world assurance of a man:°
       This was your husband. Look you now, what fol-
         lows:
       Here is your husband; like a mildew'd ear,
65   Blasting his wholesome brother.° Have you eyes?
       Could you on this fair mountain leave to feed,°
       And batten° on this moor? Ha! have you eyes?
       You cannot call it love; for at your age
       The hey-day in the blood° is tame,° it's humble,
       And waits upon° the judgement: and what
70   judgement
       Would step from this to this? Sense,° sure, you have,
       Else could you not have motion;° but sure, that
        sense
       Is apoplex'd;° for madness would not err,°
       Nor sense to ecstasy° was ne'er so thrall'd°

       But it reserved some quantity of choice,°   75
       To serve in such a difference. What devil was 't
       That thus hath cozen'd° you at hoodmanblind?°
       Eyes without feeling, feeling without sight,
       Ears without hands or eyes, smelling sans all,°
       Or but a sickly part of one true sense   80
       Could not so mope.°
       O shame! where is thy blush? Rebellious hell,
       If thou canst mutine° in a matron's bones,
       To flaming youth let virtue be as wax,
       And melt in her° own fire: proclaim no shame   85
       When the compulsive° ardour gives the charge,°
       Since frost itself as actively doth burn
       And reason pandars will.°
    QUEEN: O Hamlet, speak no more:
       Thou turn'st mine eyes into my very soul;
       And there I see such black and grainèd° spots   90
       As will not leave their tinct.°
    HAMLET: Nay, but to live
       In the rank sweat of an enseamèd° bed,
       Stew'd in corruption, honeying and making love
       Over the nasty sty,—
    QUEEN: O, speak to me no more;
       These words, like daggers, enter in mine ears;   95
       No more, sweet Hamlet!
    HAMLET: A murderer and a villain;
       A slave that is not° twentieth part the tithe°
       Of your precedent lord;° a vice of° kings;
       A cutpurse° of the empire and the rule,
       That from a shelf the precious diadem stole,   100
       And put it in his pocket!
    QUEEN: No more!
    HAMLET: A king of shreds and patches,°—

[Enter GHOST.*]*

       Save me, and hover o'er me with your wings,
       You heavenly guards! What would your gracious
         figure?
    QUEEN: Alas, he's mad!   105
    HAMLET: Do you not come your tardy son to chide,
       That, lapsed in time and passion,° lets go by
       The important acting of your dread command?
       O, say!   110

---

⁴² **rose** i.e., the adornment, beauty   ⁴⁴ **blister** women guilty of adultery were branded on the forehead   ⁴⁶ **body of contraction** the contents of the marriage contract   ⁴⁸ **rhapsody** jumble **glow** blush (with shame)   ⁴⁹ **solidity . . . mass** i.e., this solid earth compounded of various elements   ⁵⁰ **tristful** sorrowful **against the doom** ready for doomsday   ⁵³ **index** table of contents   ⁵⁴ **counterfeit presentment** painted portrait   ⁵⁶ **Hyperion** a Greek sun god **front** forehead   ⁵⁸ **station** standing position, i.e., carriage   ⁵⁹ **New-lighted** just alighted   ⁶² **assurance of a man** guarantee that this is a man   ⁶⁵ **Blasting . . . brother** blighting the healthy ear next it   ⁶⁶ **leave to feed** stop feeding   ⁶⁷ **batten** stuff yourself gluttonously   ⁶⁹ **hey-day . . . blood** youthful passion **tame** under control   ⁷⁰ **waits upon** is subject to   ⁷¹ **Sense** the five senses **motion** impulse   ⁷³ **apoplex'd** paralyzed **err** lead you to make this mistake   ⁷⁴ **ecstasy** insanity **thrall'd** enslaved

⁷⁵ **quantity of choice** ability to choose   ⁷⁷ **cozen'd** cheated **hoodman-blind** blindman's buff   ⁷⁹ **sans all** without any of the other senses   ⁸¹ **so mope** be so dull   ⁸³ **mutine** rebel   ⁸⁵ **her** i.e., youth's   ⁸⁶ **compulsive** compelling **gives the charge** makes the attack   ⁸⁸ **will** desire   ⁹⁰ **grained** dyed in unfailing colors   ⁹¹ **leave their tinct** lose their color   ⁹² **enseamed** covered with grease   ⁹⁷ **is not** i.e., is not worth **tithe** tenth   ⁹⁸ **precedent lord** i.e., former husband **vice of** clown among. The Vice was the clown of the morality plays.   ⁹⁹ **cutpurse** thief   ¹⁰² **shreds and patches** the conventional costume of the Vice   ¹⁰⁷ **lapsed . . . passion** having let time and the strength of his resolution slip away

GHOST: Do not forget: this visitation
   Is but to whet thy almost blunted purpose.
   But, look, amazement° on thy mother sits:
   O, step between her and her fighting soul:°
   Conceit° in weakest bodies strongest works:
   Speak to her, Hamlet.
115 HAMLET: How is it with you, lady?
QUEEN: Alas, how is 't with you,
   That you do bend your eye on vacancy
   And with the incorporal air do hold discourse?
   Forth at your eyes your spirits wildly peep;
120   And, as the sleeping soldiers in the alarm,°
   Your bedded° hairs, like life in excrements,°
   Start up, and stand an end. O gentle son,
   Upon the heat and flame of thy distemper°
   Sprinkle cool patience. Whereon do you look?
HAMLET: On him, on him! Look you, how pale he
125   glares!
   His form and cause conjoin'd, preaching to
    stones,
   Would make them capable.° Do not look upon
    me;
   Lest with this piteous action you convert
   My stern effects:° then what I have to do
130   Will want true colour;° tears perchance for blood.
QUEEN: To whom do you speak this?
HAMLET: Do you see nothing there?
QUEEN: Nothing at all; yet all that is I see.
HAMLET: Nor did you nothing hear?
QUEEN: No, nothing but ourselves.
HAMLET: Why, look you there! look, how it steals
    away!
135   My father, in his habit as he lived!°
   Look, where he goes, even now, out at the portal!

[*Exit* GHOST.]

QUEEN: This is the very coinage of your brain:
   This bodiless creation ecstasy
   Is very cunning in.°
HAMLET: Ecstasy!
140   My pulse, as yours, doth temperately keep time,°
   And makes as healthful music: it is not madness
   That I have utter'd: bring me to the test,
   And I the matter will re-word, which madness
   Would gambol from. Mother, for love of grace,

Lay not that flattering unction° to your soul,   145
   That not your trespass, but my madness speaks:
   It will but skin and film the ulcerous place,
   Whiles rank corruption, mining all within,
   Infects unseen. Confess yourself to heaven;
   Repent what's past; avoid what is to come;°   150
   And do not spread the compost on the weeds,
   To make them ranker. Forgive me this my virtue;
   For in the fatness° of these pursy° times
   Virtue itself of vice must pardon beg,
   Yea, curb° and woo for leave to do him good.   155
QUEEN: O Hamlet, thou hast cleft my heart in twain.
HAMLET: O, throw away the worser part of it,
   And live the purer with the other half.
   Good night: but go not to mine uncle's bed;
   Assume a virtue, if you have it not.   160
   That monster, custom, who all sense doth eat,°
   Of habits devil,° is angel yet in this,
   That to the use of actions fair and good
   He likewise gives a frock or livery,
   That aptly is put on.° Refrain to-night,   165
   And that shall° lend a kind of easiness
   To the next abstinence: the next more easy;
   For use° almost can change the stamp of nature,
   And either curb the devil, or throw him out
   With wondrous potency. Once more, good night: 170
   And when you are desirous to be bless'd,°
   I'll blessing beg of you. For this same lord,

[Pointing to POLONIUS.*]*

I do repent: but heaven hath pleased it so,
   To punish me with this° and this with me,
   That I must be their° scourge and minister.   175
   I will bestow° him, and will answer well°
   The death I gave him. So, again, good night.
   I must be cruel, only to be kind:
   Thus bad begins and worse remains behind.
   One word more, good lady.
QUEEN: What shall I do?
HAMLET: Not this, by no means, that I bid you do:°
   Let the bloat° king tempt you again to bed;
   Pinch wanton on your cheek; call you his mouse;
   And let him, for a pair of reechy° kisses,
   Or paddling in your neck with his damn'd fingers,   185

---

112 **amazement** distraction   113 **fighting soul** i.e., the conflict in her soul   114 **Conceit** imagination   120 **in the alarm** i.e., when called to arms   121 **bedded** laid smooth and flat **excrements** outgrowths   123 **distemper** perturbation   127 **capable** i.e., of emotion   129 **convert . . . effects** turn me from my stern course of action   130 **want true colour** lose its proper character   135 **in . . . lived** in the clothes he wore when alive   139 **bodiless . . . cunning in** the cunning which characterizes madness is very skilful in creating something out of nothing   140 **temperately keep time** beat calmly

145 **flattering unction** soothing salve   150 **avoid . . . come** avoid doing wrong in the future   153 **fatness** grossness **pursy** disgustingly corpulent   155 **curb** bow the knee   161 **all sense doth eat** destroys all sense of right and wrong   162 **Of habits devil** the wicked attendant on habits   165 **aptly is put on** is easily donned   166 **shall** is certain to   168 **use** habit   171 **bless'd** i.e., by Heaven, repentant   174 **this** the dead man, i.e., the murder   175 **their** i.e., Heaven's   176 **bestow** dispose of **answer well** willingly be held responsible for   181 **Not. . . do** i.e., at least avoid doing the things I bid you not to do, namely   182 **bloat** bloated (with debauchery)   184 **reechy** filthy

Make you to ravel all this matter out,°
That I essentially° am not in madness,
But mad in craft. 'Twere good you let him know;
For who, that's but° a queen, fair, sober, wise,
190 Would from a paddock,° from a bat, a gib,°
Such dear concernings° hide? who would do so?
No, in despite of sense and secrecy,
Unpeg the basket on the house's top,
Let the birds fly, and, like the famous ape°
195 To try conclusions,° in the basket creep,
And break your own neck down.
QUEEN: Be thou assured, if words be made of breath,
And breath of life, I have no life to breathe
What thou hast said to me.
HAMLET: I must to England; you know that?
200 QUEEN: Alack,
I had forgot: 'tis so concluded on.°
HAMLET: There's letters seal'd: and my two schoolfel-
lows,
Whom I will trust as I will adders fang'd,
They bear the mandate;° they must sweep my way,°
205 And marshal me to knavery.° Let it work,
For 'tis the sport° to have the enginer°
Hoist° with his own petar:° and 't shall go hard
But° I will delve one yard below their mines,
And blow them at the moon: O, 'tis most sweet,
210 When in one line two crafts° directly meet.
This man shall set me packing:°
I'll lug the guts into the neighbour° room.
Mother, good night. Indeed this counsellor
Is now most still, most secret and most grave,
215 Who was in life a foolish prating knave.
Come, sir, to draw toward an end with you.
Good night, mother.

[Exeunt severally; HAMLET
dragging in Polonius.]

---

186 **ravel. . . out** unravel, give away   187 **essentially** in my
real nature   189 **that's but** except   190 **paddock** toad **gib**
tomcat   191 **dear concernings** matters of such deep importance   194 **Unpeg. . . ape** The reference is to the story of an
ape who opened a basket of birds on the house top and, after
watching them fly away one by one, tried to imitate them and
jumped to his death.   195 **try conclusions** repeat the experiment   201 **concluded on** decided   204 **bear the mandate**
have the instructions **sweep my way** clear my path   205
knavery the evil to be done to Hamlet   206 **'tis the sport** it
will be my game **enginer** inventor   207 **Hoist** blown up
petar bomb   208 **'t shall go hard But** about = I miss my guess
if I do not   210 **crafts** crafty schemes   211 **packing** a quibble
on three meanings: (1) loading, (2) plotting, (3) hurrying off
212 **neighbour** next

ACT IV

Scene 1: A room in the castle.

[Enter KING, QUEEN, ROSENCRANTZ, *and* GUILDENSTERN.*]*

KING: There's matter° in these sighs, these profound
    heaves:
    You must translate:° 'tis fit we understand them.
    Where is your son?
QUEEN: Bestow this place on us° a little while.

[Exeunt ROSENCRANTZ and GUILDENSTERN.]

    Ah, mine own lord, what have I seen tonight!   5
KING: What, Gertrude? How does Hamlet?
QUEEN: Mad as the sea and wind, when both con-
    tend
    Which is the mightier: in his lawless fit,
    Behind the arras hearing something stir,
    Whips out his rapier, cries, "A rat, a rat!"   10
    And, in this brainish apprehension,° kills
    The unseen good old man.
KING: O heavy° deed!
    It had been so with us,° had we been there:
    His liberty° is full of threats to all;
    To you yourself, to us,° to every one.   15
    Alas, how shall this bloody deed be answer'd?
    It will be laid to us, whose providence°
    Should have kept short,° restrain'd and out of
      haunt,°
    This mad young man: but so much was our love,
    We would not understand what was most fit;   20
    But, like the owner of a foul disease,
    To keep it from divulging,° let it feed
    Even on the pith of life. Where is he gone?
QUEEN: To draw apart° the body he hath kill'd:
    O'er whom his very madness, like some ore   25
    Among a mineral° of metals base,
    Shows itself pure; he weeps for what is done.
KING: O Gertrude, come away!
    The sun no sooner shall the mountains touch,
    But we will ship him hence: and this vile deed   30
    We must, with all our majesty and skill,
    Both countenance and excuse. Ho, Guildenstern!

[Re-enter ROSENCRANTZ *and* GUILDENSTERN.*]*

ACT IV, SCENE 1:   1 **matter** serious meaning   2 **translate**
explain   3 **Bestow. . . us** i.e., leave us   11 **brainish apprehension** brainsick delusion   12 **heavy** hard to bear   13 **us** i.e., me,
the King   14 **His liberty** his being at liberty   16 **answer'd**
explained away   17 **providence** foresight   18 **short** on short
tether **haunt** contact with other people   22 **divulging** coming
to light   24 **draw apart** take away   26 **mineral** mine

Friends both, go join you with° some further aid:
Hamlet in madness hath Polonius slain,
35　And from his mother's closet hath he dragg'd him:
Go seek him out; speak fair,° and bring the body
Into the chapel. I pray you, haste in this.

[Exeunt ROSENCRANTZ and GUILDENSTERN.]

Come, Gertrude, we'll call up our wisest friends;
And let them know, both what we mean to do,
40　And what's untimely done so, haply, slander
Whose whisper o'er the world's diameter,
As level° as the cannon to his blank,°
Transports his poison'd shot, may miss our name,
And hit the woundless° air. O, come away!
45　My soul is full of discord and dismay.

[Exeunt.]

Scene 2

Another room in the castle.

[Enter HAMLET.]

HAMLET: Safely stowed.°
ROSENCRANTZ: ⎱ *[Within]* Hamlet! Lord Hamlet!
GUILDENSTERN: ⎰
HAMLET: But soft, what noise? who calls on Hamlet?
　　O, here they come.

[Enter ROSENCRANTZ and GUILDENSTERN.]

ROSENCRANTZ: What have you done, my lord, with
5　　the dead body?
HAMLET: Compounded° it with dust, whereto 'tis kin.
ROSENCRANTZ: Tell us where 'tis, that we may take it
　　thence
　　And bear it to the chapel.
HAMLET: Do not believe it.
10　ROSENCRANTZ: Believe what?
HAMLET: That I can keep your counsel° and not mine
　　own. Besides, to be demanded of° a sponge! what
　　replication° should be made by the son of a king?
ROSENCRANTZ: Take you me for a sponge, my lord?
15　HAMLET: Ay, sir, that soaks up the king's counte-
　　nance,° his rewards, his authorities. But such
　　officers do the king best service in the end: he
　　keeps them, like an ape, in the corner of his jaw;

first mouthed,° to be last swallowed: when he
needs what you have gleaned, it is but squeez-　20
ing you, and, sponge, you shall be dry again.
ROSENCRANTZ: I understand you not, my lord.
HAMLET: I am glad of it: a knavish° speech sleeps in a
foolish ear.
ROSENCRANTZ: My lord, you must tell us where the　25
body is, and go with us to the king.
HAMLET: The body is with the king, but the king is not
with the body. The king is a thing—
GUILDENSTERN: A thing, my lord!
HAMLET: Of nothing: bring me to him. Hide fox,° and　30
all after.

[Exeunt.]

Scene 3

Another room in the castle.

[Enter KING, attended.]

KING: I have sent to seek him, and to find the body.
How dangerous is it that this man goes loose!
Yet must not we put the strong law on him:
He's loved of the distracted° multitude,
Who like not in° their judgement, but their eyes;　5
And where 'tis so, the offender's scourge° is
　　weigh'd,°
But never the offence. To bear all° smooth and even,
This sudden sending him away must seem
Deliberate pause:° diseases desperate grown
By desperate appliance° are relieved,　10
Or not at all.

[Enter ROSENCRANTZ]

　　　　　　　　How now! what hath befall'n?
ROSENCRANTZ: Where the dead body is bestow'd, my
　　lord,
We cannot get from him.
KING:　　　　　　　　　But where is he?
ROSENCRANTZ: Without,° my lord; guarded, to know
　　your pleasure.
KING: Bring him before us.　15
ROSENCRANTZ: Ho, Guildenstern! bring in my lord.

[Enter HAMLET and GUILDENSTERN]

KING: Now, Hamlet, where's Polonius?

---

³³ **join you with** procure　³⁶ **fair** civilly, tactfully　⁴² **level** straight　**blank** the center of the target　⁴⁴ **woundless** invulnerable

SCENE 2:　¹ **stowed** disposed of　⁶ **Compounded** mixed　¹¹ **counsel** secrets, i.e., that you are spying on me　¹² **demanded of** questioned by　¹³ **replication** formal reply　¹⁶ **countenance** favor

¹⁹ **mouthed** rolled about in the mouth　²³ **knavish** sinister
³⁰ **Hide fox** the cry used in hide and seek

SCENE 3:　⁴ **distracted** confused　⁵ **in** in accordance with　⁶ **scourge** punishment　**weigh'd** taken into consideration　⁷ **bear all** keep everything running　⁹ **Deliberate pause** a carefully planned rest (or vacation)　¹⁰ **appliance** remedy　¹⁴ **Without** outside

HAMLET: At supper.

KING: At supper! where?

20 HAMLET: Not where he eats, but where he is eaten: a certain convocation of politic° worms are e'en° at him. Your worm is your only emperor for diet: we fat all creatures else to fat us, and we fat ourselves for maggots: your fat king and your lean beggar is 25 but variable service,° two dishes, but to one table: that's the end.

KING: Alas, alas!

HAMLET: A man may fish with the worm that hath eat of a king, and eat of the fish that hath fed of that 30 worm.

KING: What dost thou mean by this?

HAMLET: Nothing but to show you how a king may go a progress° through the guts of a beggar.

KING: Where is Polonius?

35 HAMLET: In heaven; send thither to see: if your messenger find him not there, seek him i' the other place yourself. But indeed, if you find him not within this month, you shall nose him as you go up the stairs into the lobby.°

40 KING: Go seek him there.

[To some ATTENDANTS]

HAMLET: He will stay till you come.

[Exeunt ATTENDANTS.]

KING: Hamlet, this deed, for thine especial safety,— Which we do tender, as we dearly grieve° For that which thou hast done,—must send thee hence 45 With fiery quickness: therefore prepare thyself; The bark is ready, and the wind at help,° The associates° tend,° and everything is bent° For England.

HAMLET: For England!

KING: Ay, Hamlet.

HAMLET: Good.

KING: So is it, if thou knew'st our purposes.

50 HAMLET: I see a cherub° that sees them. But, come; for England! Farewell, dear mother.

KING: Thy loving father, Hamlet.

HAMLET: My mother: father and mother is man and wife; man and wife is one flesh; and so, my moth-55 er. Come, for England!

[Exit.]

KING: Follow him at foot;° tempt° him with speed aboard;

Delay it not; I'll have him hence to-night: Away! for every thing is seal'd and done That else leans on the affair:° pray you, make haste.

[Exeunt ROSENCRANTZ and GUILDENSTERN.]

And, England,° if my love thou hold'st at aught— 60 As my great power thereof may give thee sense,° Since yet° thy cicatrice° looks raw and red After the Danish sword, and thy free° awe Pays homage to us—thou mayst not coldly set° Our sovereign process;° which imports at full,° 65 By letters congruing to that effect, The present death of Hamlet. Do it, England; For like the hectic° in my blood he rages, And thou must cure me: till I know 'tis done, Howe'er my haps,° my joys were ne'er begun.° 70

[Exit.]

Scene 4

A plain in Denmark.

[Enter FORTINBRAS, a CAPTAIN, and SOLDIERS, marching.]

FORTINBRAS: Go, captain, from me greet the Danish king; Tell him that, by his license, Fortinbras Craves the conveyance° of a promised march Over his kingdom. You know the rendezvous. If that his majesty would aught with us, 5 We shall express our duty in his eye;° And let him know so.

CAPTAIN: I will do 't, my lord.

FORTINBRAS: Go softly° on.

[Exeunt FORTINBRAS and SOLDIERS.]

[Enter HAMLET, ROSENCRANTZ, GUILDENSTERN, and others.]

HAMLET: Good sir, whose powers are these?

CAPTAIN: They are of Norway, sir.

HAMLET: How purposed,° sir, I pray you? 10

---

²¹ **politic** statesman-like **e'en** right now ²⁵ **variable service** choice of alternatives ³³ **go a progress** make a royal journey ³⁹ **lobby** anteroom ⁴³ **Which. . . grieve** which we hold as dearly as we grieve ⁴⁶ **at help** favorable ⁴⁷ **associates** companions **tend** wait for you **bent** ready ⁵⁰ **cherub** one of the angels, hence one who sees everything

⁵⁶ **at foot** at his heels **tempt** coax ⁵⁹ **else. . .affair** has anything else to do with the business ⁶⁰ **England** the King of England ⁶¹ **As. . . sense** in accordance with the sense of it (my value) which my great power may give you ⁶² **yet** still **cicatrice** scar ⁶³ **free** i.e., not now compelled by Danish rule ⁶⁴ **coldly set** estimate lightly the importance of ⁶⁵ **process** beliest **imports at full** fully implies ⁶⁸ **hectic** fever ⁷⁰ **Howe'er my haps** whatever my lot **my joys . . . begun** I shall never begin to enjoy it

SCENE 4: ³ **conveyance** official escort ⁶ **in his eye** i.e., by appearing before him ⁸ **softly** slowly ¹¹ **How purposed?** what is their business?

CAPTAIN: Against some part of Poland.
HAMLET: Who commands them, sir?
CAPTAIN: The nephew to old Norway, Fortinbras.
15 HAMLET: Goes it against the main° of Poland, sir,
　　Or for some frontier?
CAPTAIN: Truly to speak, and with no addition,
　　We go to gain a little patch of ground
　　That hath in it no profit but the name.°
20　To pay five ducats,° five, I would not farm it;
　　Nor will it yield to Norway or the pole
　　A ranker° rate, should it be sold in fee.°
HAMLET: Why, then the Polack never will defend it.
CAPTAIN: Yes, it is already garrison'd.
HAMLET: Two thousand souls and twenty thousand
25　　ducats
　　Will not debate° the question of this straw:°
　　This is the imposthume° of much wealth and peace,
　　That inward breaks, and shows no cause without°
　　Why the man dies. I humbly thank you, sir.
CAPTAIN: God be wi' you, sir.

[Exit.]

30 ROSENCRANTZ: Will 't please you go, my lord?
HAMLET: I'll be with you straight. Go a little before.

[Exeunt all except HAMLET.]

How all occasions do inform° against me,
And spur my dull revenge! What is a man,
If his chief good and market of his time°
35 Be but to sleep and feed? a beast, no more.
Sure, he that made us with such large discourse,°
Looking before and after, gave us not
That capability and° god-like reason
To fust° in us unused. Now, whether it be
40 Bestial oblivion,° or some craven scruple
Of thinking too precisely on the event,°
A thought which, quarter'd, hath but one part
　　wisdom
And ever three parts coward, I do not know
Why yet I live to say "This thing's to do;"
45 Sith I have cause and will and strength and means
To do 't. Examples gross° as earth exhort me:
Witness this army of such mass and charge°
Led by a delicate and tender° prince,

Whose spirit with divine ambition puff'd
Makes mouths at the invisible event,°　　　　　50
Exposing what is mortal and unsure
To all that fortune, death and danger dare,
Even for an egg-shell. Rightly to be great
Is not to stir without great argument,°
But greatly to find quarrel in a straw　　　　　55
When honour's at the stake. How stand I then,
That have a father kill'd, a mother stain'd,
Excitements° of my reason and my blood,°
And let all sleep? while, to my shame, I see
The imminent death of twenty thousand men,　　60
That, for a fantasy and trick° of fame,
Go to their graves like beds, fight for a plot
Whereon the numbers cannot try the cause,°
Which is not tomb enough and continent°
To hide the slain? O, from this time forth,　　　65
My thoughts be bloody, or be nothing worth!

[Exit.]

Scene 5

Elsinore. A room in the castle.

[Enter QUEEN, HORATIO, and a GENTLEMAN]

QUEEN: I will not speak with her.
GENTLEMAN: She is importunate, indeed distract:
　　Her mood will needs be pitied.
QUEEN:　　　　　　　　　　What would she have?
GENTLEMAN: She speaks much of her father; says she
　　hears
　　There's tricks i' the world; and hems, and beats
　　　her heart;　　　　　　　　　　　　　　　　5
　　Spurns enviously at straws;° speaks things in doubt,°
　　That carry but half sense: her speech is nothing,°
　　Yet the unshaped use of it° doth move
　　The hearers to collection;° they aim° at it,
　　And botch° the words up fit° to their own thoughts;　10
　　Which, as her winks, and nods, and gestures
　　　yield° them,
　　Indeed would make one think there might be
　　　thought,°

---

⁵⁰ **invisible event** unknown outcome　⁵⁴ **argument** cause　⁵⁸
Excitements incitements　**blood** passion　⁶¹ **fantasy and
trick** illusion and whim　⁶³ **try the cause** i.e., fight the battle
(for possession of it)　⁶⁴ **continent** receptacle

SCENE 5:　³ **will needs** should be　⁴ **tricks** deceptions　⁵
heart breast　⁶ **Spurns . . . straws** kicks angrily at trifles
speaks . . . doubt talks incoherently　⁷ **is nothing** makes no
sense　⁸ **unshaped use of it** i.e., disconnected utterances　⁹
collection inference　**aim** guess　¹⁰ **botch** patch　**fit . . .
thoughts** harmonize with their own suspicions　¹¹ **yield**
accompany　¹² **thought** sense (behind them)

¹⁵ **the main** the whole　¹⁹ **the name** i.e., its name as one of
Norway's possessions　²⁰ **five ducats** i.e., as an annual rental
²² **ranker** larger　**sold in fee** sold outright (and the proceeds
invested)　²⁶　**debate** settle　**straw** trifling　matter　²⁷
imposthume hidden abscess　²⁸ **without** outwardly　³²
inform bear witness　³⁴ **market . . . time** that for which he
markets (uses) his time　³⁶ **discourse** power of reasoning　³⁸
and of　³⁹ **fust** grow moldy　⁴⁰ **Bestial oblivion** the forgetfulness of an animal　⁴¹ **event** outcome　⁴⁶ **gross** obvious　⁴⁷
such . . . charge so large and so expensive　⁴⁸ **delicate and tender** gentle and refined

Though nothing sure, yet much unhappily.°
HORATIO: 'Twere good she were spoken with: for she
    may strew
15   Dangerous conjectures in ill-breeding° minds.
QUEEN: Let her come in.

        [Exit HORATIO.]

To my sick soul, as sin's true nature is,°
Each toy seems prologue to some great amiss:°
So full of artless jealousy° is guilt,
20   It spills itself° in fearing to be spilt.

    [Re-enter HORATIO, with OPHELIA.]

OPHELIA: Where is the beauteous majesty of Denmark?
QUEEN: How now, Ophelia!
OPHELIA: [*Sings*] How should I your true love know
        From another one?
25   By his cockle hat° and staff,
      And his sandal shoon.

QUEEN: Alas, sweet lady, what imports this song?
OPHELIA: Say you?° nay, pray you, mark.

     [*Sings*] He is dead and gone, lady,
30   He is dead and gone;
      At his head a grass-green turf,
      At his heels a stone.

QUEEN: Nay, but, Ophelia,—
OPHELIA: Pray you, mark
35   [*Sings*] White his shroud as the mountain snow,—

    [Enter KING.]

QUEEN: Alas, look here, my lord.
OPHELIA: [*Sings*] Larded° with sweet flowers;
      Which bewept to the grave did go
      With true-love showers.
40 KING: How do you, pretty lady?
OPHELIA: Well, God 'ild° you! They say the owl was a
    baker's daughter.° Lord, we know what we are,
    but know not what we may be. God be at your
    table!

KING: Conceit upon° her father.   45
OPHELIA: Pray you, let's have no words of this;° but
    when they ask you what it means, say you this:
    [*Sings*] To-morrow is Saint Valentine's day,
      All in the morning° betime,°
    And I a maid at your window,   50
      To be your Valentine.
    Then up he rose, and donn'd his clothes,
      And dupp'd° the chamber-door;
    Let in the maid, that out a maid
      Never departed more.   55

KING: Pretty Ophelia!
OPHELIA: Indeed, la, without an oath, I'll make an
    end on 't:
    [*Sings*] By Gis° and by Saint Charity,
      Alack, and fie for shame!   60
    Young men will do 't, if they come to 't;
      By cock,° they are to blame.
    Quoth she, before you tumbled me,
      You promised me to wed.
    So would I ha' done, by yonder sun,   65
      An thou hadst not come to my bed.

KING: How long hath she been thus?
OPHELIA: I hope all will be well. We must be patient:
    but I cannot choose but weep, to think they
    should lay him i' the cold ground. My brother 70
    shall know of it: and so I thank you for your good
    counsel. Come, my coach! Good night, ladies;
    good night, sweet ladies; good night, good night.

        [Exit.]

KING: Follow her close; give her good watch,
    I pray you.   75

        [Exit HORATIO.]

O, this is the poison of deep grief; it springs
All from her father's death. O Gertrude, Gertrude,
When sorrows come, they come not° single spies,
But in battalions. First, her father slain:
Next, your son gone; and he most violent author 80
Of his own just remove:° the people muddied,°
Thick and unwholesome in their thoughts and
    whispers,
For good Polonius' death; and we have done but
    greenly,°

---

¹³**unhappily** suggesting mischief ¹⁵**ill-breeding** that breed
evil ¹⁷**as . . . is** i.e., as must always be the case when one has
a feeling of guilt ¹⁸**amiss** disaster ¹⁹**jealousy** suspicion
²⁰**spills itself** gives itself away ²⁵**cockle hat** a hat with a
cockle shell stuck in it as a sign its owner has been on a pilgrimage to a remote shrine. A lover was often referred to as a
pilgrim and his lady as the saint whose shrine he visited.
²⁸**Say you?** Is that what you want to know? ³⁷**Larded** decorated ⁴¹**'ild** yield or reward ⁴²**owl! . . . daughter** reference to a folk tale that a baker's daughter was turned into an
owl for trying to skimp the bread her mother baked for Christ.

---

⁴⁵**Conceit upon** thinking about ⁴⁶**let's . . . this** don't mention this to anyone ⁴⁹**in the morning** because it was
believed that the first girl a man saw on Valentine's day
would be his true love **betime** early ⁵³**dupp'd** opened
⁵⁹**Gis** Jesus ⁶²**cock** distortion of "God" ⁷⁸**come not** come
not like ⁸¹**remove** removal **muddied** stirred up (like a
muddy pool) ⁸³**greenly** foolishly

In hugger-mugger° to inter him: poor Ophelia
85 Divided from herself and her fair judgement,
Without the which we are pictures,° or mere
    beasts:
Last, and as much containing° as all these,
Her brother is in secret come from France;
Feeds on his wonder,° keeps himself in clouds,°
90 And wants not buzzers° to infect his ear
With pestilent speeches of his father's death;
Wherein necessity, of matter beggar'd,°
Will nothing stick° our person to arraign
In ear and ear.° O my dear Gertrude, this,
95 Like to a murdering-piece,° in many places
Gives me superfluous death. [*A noise within.*]
QUEEN: Alack, what noise is this?
KING: Where are my Switzers?° Let them guard the
    door.

[*Enter another* GENTLEMAN.]

What is the matter?
GENTLEMAN: Save yourself, my lord:
The ocean, overpeering of his list,°
100 Eats not the flats° with more impetuous haste
Than young Laertes, in a riotous head,°
O'erbears° your officers. The rabble call him lord;
And, as the world were now but to begin,
Antiquity forgot, custom not known,
105 The ratifiers and props of every word,°
They cry "Choose we:° Laertes shall be king:"
Caps, hands, and tongues, applaud it to the clouds:
"Laertes shall be king, Laertes king!"
QUEEN: How cheerfully on the false trail they cry!
110 O, this is counter,° you false Danish dogs!
KING: The doors are broke.

[*Noise within.*]

[*Enter* LAERTES, *armed*; DANES *following.*]

LAERTES: Where is this king? Sirs, stand you all without.
DANES: No, let's come in.

LAERTES: I pray you, give me leave.°
DANES: We will, we will.

[*They retire without the door.*]

LAERTES: I thank you: keep the door. O thou vile king, 115
    Give me my father!
QUEEN: Calmly, good Laertes.
LAERTES: That drop of blood that's calm proclaims
    me bastard,
    Cries cuckold to my father, brands the harlot
    Even here, between the chaste unsmirchèd brows
    Of my true mother.
KING: What is the cause, Laertes, 120
    That thy rebellion looks so giant-like?
    Let him go, Gertrude; do not fear° our person:
    There's such divinity° doth hedge° a king,
    That treason can but peep to° what it would,
    Acts little of his° will. Tell me, Laertes, 125
    Why thou art thus incensed. Let him go, Gertrude.
    Speak, man.
LAERTES: Where is my father?
KING: Dead.
QUEEN: But not by him.
KING: Let him demand his fill.
LAERTES: How came he dead? I'll not be juggled with: 130
    To hell, allegiance! vows,° to the blackest devil!
    Conscience and grace,° to the profoundest pit!
    I dare damnation. To this point I stand,°
    That both the worlds I give to negligence,°
    Let come what comes; only I'll be revenged 135
    Most throughly for my father.
KING: Who shall stay you?
LAERTES: My will, not all the world:°
    And for my means,° I'll husband them so well,
    They shall go far with little.
KING: Good Laertes,
    If you desire to know the certainty 140
    Of your dear father's death, is 't writ in your
    revenge,
    That, swoopstake,° you will draw both friend and
    foe,
    Winner and loser?
LAERTES: None but his enemies.
KING: Will you know them then?
LAERTES: To his good friends thus wide I'll ope my arms; 145

And like the kind life-rendering pelican,°
Repast° them with my blood.
KING: Why, now you speak
   Like a good child and a true gentleman.
   That I am guiltless of your father's death,
150   And am most sensibly in grief° for it,
   It shall as level° to your judgement pierce
   As day° does to your eye.
DANES: [*Within*] Let her come in.
LAERTES: How now! what noise is that?

[*Re-enter* OPHELIA.]

   O heat,° dry up my brains! tears seven times salt,
155   Burn out the sense and virtue° of mine eye.
   By heaven, thy madness shall be paid with
      weight,°
   Till our scale turn the beam.° O rose of May!
   Dear maid, kind sister, sweet Ophelia!
   O heavens! is't possible, a young maid's wits
160   Should be as mortal as an old man's life?
   Nature is fine in love,° and where 'tis fine,
   It sends some precious instance° of itself
   And the thing it loves.
OPHELIA: [*Sings*]
   They bore him barefaced on the bier;
165   Hey non nonny, nonny, hey nonny;
   And in his grave rain'd many a tear:—

      Fare you well, my dove!
LAERTES: Hadst thou thy wits, and didst persuade°
      revenge,
   It could not move thus.
OPHELIA: [*Sings*]
170   You must sing a-down a-down,
         An you call him a-down-a.
      O, how the wheel becomes it!° It is the false
      steward, that stole his master's daughter.
LAERTES: This nothing 's more than matter.°
175 OPHELIA: There's rosemary, that's for remembrance; pray,
      love, remember: and there is pansies,° that 's for
      thoughts.
LAERTES: A document in° madness, thoughts and
      remembrance fitted.

OPHELIA: There's fennel for you,° and columbines:°   180
   there's rue for you; and here's some for me: we
   may call it herb-grace° o' Sundays: O, you must
   wear your rue° with a difference.° There's a
   daisy:° I would give you some violets, but they
   withered all when my father died: they say he   185
   made a good end,—[*Sings*] For bonny sweet
   Robin is all my joy.
LAERTES: Thought° and affliction, passion, hell itself,
   She turns to favour° and to prettiness.
OPHELIA: [*Sings*]

   And will he not come again?   190
   And will he not come again?
      No, no, he is dead:
      Go to thy death-bed:
   He never will come again.
   His beard was as white as snow,   195
   All flaxen was his poll:°
      He is gone, he is gone,
      And we cast away° moan:
   God ha' mercy on his soul!
And of° all Christian souls, I pray God. God be
   wi' ye.   200

[Exit.]

LAERTES: Do you see this, O God?
KING: Laertes, I must commune with your grief,
   Or you deny me right. Go but apart,°
   Make choice of whom your wisest friends you
      will,
   And they shall hear and judge 'twixt you and me: 205
   If by direct or by collateral° hand
   They find us touch'd,° we will our kingdom give,
   Our crown, our life, and all that we call ours,
   To you in satisfaction; but if not,
   Be you content to lend your patience to us,   210
   And we shall jointly labour with your soul
   To give it due content.°
LAERTES: Let this be so;
   His means of death, his obscure° funeral—
   No trophy,° sword, nor hatchment° o'er his bones,
   No noble rite nor formal ostentation°—   215

---

146 **life-rendering pelican** the female pelican was supposed to feed her young with her own blood   147 **repast** feed   150 **most . . . grief** grieve most deeply   151 **level** with as straight an aim   152 **day** the rising run   154 **heat** i.e., generated by anger   155 **sense and virtue** sensation and power   155 **with weight** according to an even balance   156 **scale . . . beam** with vengeance outweigh the offense   161 **fine in love** refined by love   162 **instance** sample; in this case, her wits   168 **persuade** urge me to   172 **O . . . becomes it** how well the refrain suits the title of the song   174 **This . . . matter** this nonsense is more revealing than sensible talk   176 **pansies** pensées for "thoughts"   178 **document in** lessons conveyed through

180 **fennel for you** emblem of flattery for the Queen **columbines** emblem of ingratitude   182 **herb-grace** rue when mixed with holy water   183 **rue** emblem of sorrow and repentance   **difference** a heraldic term describing the distinction between two coats of arms belonging to different members of the same family   184 **daisy** for faithlessness   187 **Thought** sorrow   188 **favor** charm   196 **poll** head   198 **cast away** who are forsaken   200 **of** on   201 **commune with** share   203 **apart** away   206 **collateral** indirect   207 **touch'd** i.e., with guilt   212 **give . . . content** convince you of the truth (i.e., of my allegation)   213 **obscure** secret   214 **trophy** memorial **hatchment** tablet, bearing the coat of arms of the deceased   215 **ostentation** ceremony

Cry to be heard, as 'twere from heaven to earth,
That I must call 't in question.°
KING: So you shall;
And where the offence is let the great axe fall.
I pray you, go with me.

[Exeunt.]

Scene 6

Another room in the castle.

[Enter HORATIO and a SERVANT.]

HORATIO: What are they that would speak with me?
SERVANT: Sailors, sir: they say they have letters for you.
HORATIO: Let them come in.

[Exit SERVANT.]

I do not know from what part of the world I should
5   be greeted, if not from lord Hamlet.

[Enter SAILORS.]

FIRST SAILOR: God bless you, sir.
HORATIO: Let him bless thee too.
FIRST SAILOR: He shall, sir, an 't° please him. There's a
letter for you, sir; it comes from the ambassador
10   that was bound for England; if your name be
Horatio, as I am let to know° it is.
HORATIO: [*Reads*] "Horatio, when thou shalt have
overlooked° this, give these fellows some means°
to the king: they have letters for him. Ere we were
15   two days old at sea, a pirate of very warlike
appointment° gave us chase. Finding ourselves too
slow of sail, we put on a compelled valour,° and in
the grapple° I boarded them: on the instant they
got clear of our ship; so I alone became their pris-
20   oner. They have dealt with me like thieves of
mercy:° but they knew what they did; I am to do a
good turn for them. Let the king have the letters I
have sent; and repair° thou to me with as much
speed as thou wouldst fly death. I have words to
25   speak in thine ear will make thee dumb; yet are
they much too light for the bore° of the matter.
These good fellows will bring thee where I am.
Rozencrantz and Guildenstern hold their course
for° England: of them I have much to tell thee.
30   Farewell.

---

217 **call't in question** look into it

SCENE 6: 8 **an't** if it   11 **let to know** informed   13 **overlooked**
looked over   **means** means of access   16 **appointment** equipment   17 **put . . . valour** perforce acted bravely   18 **in the grapple** when the ships were grappled together   21 **thieves of
mercy** merciful thieves   23 **repair** return   26 **bore** calibre,
importance   29 **hold . . . for** continue on their way to

"He that thou knowest thine, HAMLET."
Come, I will make you way for° these your letters;
And do 't the speedier, that you may direct me
To him from whom you brought them.

[Exeunt.]

Scene 7

Another room in the castle.

[Enter KING and LAERTES.]

KING: Now must your conscience my acquittance seal,°
And you must put me in your heart for friend,
Sith you have heard, and with a knowing ear,
That he which hath your noble father slain
Pursued° my life.
LAERTES: It well appears: but tell me   5
Why you proceeded not° against these feats,°
So crimeful and so capital° in nature,
As by your safety, wisdom, all things else,
You mainly were stirr'd up.°
KING: O, for two special reasons;
Which may to you, perhaps, seem much unsinew'd,°   10
But yet to me they are strong. The queen his mother
Lives almost by his looks;° and for myself—
My virtue or my plague, be it either which°—
She's so conjunctive° to my life and soul,
That, as the star moves not but in his sphere,°   15
I could not but by her. The other motive,°
Why to a public count° I might not go,
Is the great love the general gender° bear him;
Who, dipping all his faults in their affection,
Would, like the spring° that turneth wood to stone,   20
Convert his gyves° to graces; so that my arrows,
Too slightly timber'd° for so loud° a wind,
Would have reverted to my bow again,
And not where I had aim'd them.
LAERTES: And so have I a noble father lost;   25
A sister driven into desperate terms,°
Whose worth, if praises may go back again,°

---

32 **make . . . for** gain you access to

SCENE 7: 1 **conscience . . . seal** Your knowledge of the facts
must acquit me of any guilt.   5 **Pursued** sought   6 **proceeded
not** took no legal action   **feats** deeds   7 **capital** punishable
by death   9 **As . . . stirr'd up** as anxiety for your safety, wisdom, and every other consideration strongly urged you   10
unsinew'd weak   12 **Lives . . . looks** acts as though her life
depended on his mere glance   13 **be . . . which** whichever you
choose to call it   14 **conjunctive** closely joined   15 **sphere**
orbit   16 **motive** reason   17 **count** reckoning   18 **general gender** common people   20 **the spring** reference to a famous
spring in Yorkshire   21 **gyves** fetters, turns his limitations to
virtues   22 **slightly timber'd** i.e., light-shafted   **loud** violent
26 **terms** conditions   27 **if praises . . . again** if I may praise her
for what she was before she became mad

Stood challenger on mount of all the age
For her perfections:° but my revenge will come.
KING: Break not your sleeps for that: you must not
30   think
That we are made of stuff so flat and dull
That we can let our beard be shook with danger°
And think it pastime. You shortly shall hear more:
I loved your father, and we love ourself;
35   And that, I hope, will teach you to imagine—

[Enter a MESSENGER.*]*

How now! what news?
MESSENGER: Letters, my lord, from Hamlet:
This to your majesty; this to the queen.
KING: From Hamlet! who brought them?
MESSENGER: Sailors, my lord, they say; I saw them not:
40   They were given me by Claudio; he received them
Of him that brought them.
KING: Laertes, you shall hear them.
Leave us.

[Exit MESSENGER.*]*

[Reads] "High and mighty, You shall know I am set
naked° on your kingdom. To-morrow shall I beg
45   leave to see your kingly eyes: when I shall, first
asking your pardon there unto, recount the
occasion of my sudden and more strange return.
                                        "HAMLET."
What should this mean? Are all the rest come
back?
50   Or is it some abuse,° and no such thing?
LAERTES: Know you the hand?
KING: 'Tis Hamlet's character.° "Naked!"
And in a postscript here, he says "alone."
Can you advise me?
55   LAERTES: I'm lost in it,° my lord. But let him come;
It warms the very sickness in my heart,
That I shall live and tell him to his teeth,
"Thus didst thou."
KING: If it be so, Laertes—
As how should it be so? how otherwise?°—
Will you be ruled by me?
60   LAERTES: Ay, my lord;
So you will not o'errule me to a peace.
KING: To thine own peace. If he be now return'd,
As checking° at his voyage, and that he means
No more to undertake it, I will work him

To an exploit, now ripe in my device,°   65
Under the which he shall not choose but fall:
And for his death no wind of blame shall breathe,
But even his mother shall uncharge the practice°
And call it accident.
LAERTES: My lord, I will be ruled;
The rather, if you could devise it so   70
That I might be the organ.°
KING: It falls right.
You have been talk'd of since your travel much,
And that in Hamlet's hearing, for a quality
Wherein, they say, you shine: your sum of parts°
Did not together pluck such envy from him   75
As did that one, and that, in my regard,
Of the unworthiest siege.°
LAERTES: What part is that, my lord?
KING: A very riband° in the cap of youth,
Yet needful too; for youth no less becomes
The light and careless livery that it wears   80
Than settled age his sables° and his weeds,°
Importing health and graveness.° Two months
since,
Here was a gentleman of Normandy:—
I've seen myself, and served against, the French,
And they can well° on horseback: but this gallant   85
Had witchcraft in 't; he grew unto his seat;
And to such wondrous doing brought his horse,
As had he been incorpsed and demi-natured°
With the brave beast: so far he topp'd° my
thought,°
That I, in forgery° of shapes and tricks,   90
Come short of what he did.
LAERTES: A Norman was 't?
KING: A Norman.
LAERTES: Upon my life, Lamond.°
KING: The very same.
LAERTES: I know him well: he is the brooch indeed
And gem of all the nation.   95
KING: He made confession° of you,
And gave you such a masterly report°
For art and exercise° in your defence
And for your rapier most especial,

---

⁶⁵ **ripe in my device** i.e., completely planned   ⁶⁸ **uncharge the
practice** acquit the plan of treachery   ⁷¹ **organ** instrument,
agent (of his death)   ⁷⁴ **your . . . parts** all your talents   ⁷⁷ **siege**
rank   ⁷⁸ **very riband** mere ornament   ⁸¹ **sables** rich furs
weeds garments   ⁸² **Importing . . . graveness** suiting the
gravity (of settled age) and protecting its health (because of
their warmth)   ⁸⁵ **can well** are skillful   ⁸⁸ **incorpsed and
demi-natured** made one body with and half shared the nature
of   ⁸⁹ **topp'd** surpassed   **thought** expectations   ⁹⁰ **in forgery**
in imagining   ⁹³ **Lamond** perhaps Pietro Monte (La Mont) a
famous French horseman   ⁹⁶ **confession** full report   ⁹⁷ **you . . .
report** reported you to be such a master   ⁹⁸ **For art and exercise** in the theory and practice

---

²⁹ **Stood . . . perfections** challenged from horseback the age to
dispute the claim that she surpassed all others in perfection
³² **our . . . danger** Let danger threaten us to our face   ⁴⁴ **naked**
destitute   ⁵⁰ **abuse** deception   ⁵² **character** handwriting
⁵⁵ **lost in it** at a loss to explain it   ⁵⁹ **otherwise** than true
⁶³ **checking** balking. A falcon "checked" when she stopped
her flight to dart at some unsuitable object.

100 That he cried out, 'twould be a sight indeed,
If one could match you: the scrimers° of their
    nation,
He swore, had neither motion, guard, nor eye,
If you opposed them. Sir, this report of his
Did Hamlet so envenom with his envy
105 That he could nothing do but wish and beg
Your sudden coming o'er,° to play° with him.
Now, out of this,—

LAERTES: What out of this, my lord?

KING: Laertes, was your father dear to you?
Or are you like the painting of a sorrow,
A face without a heart?

110 LAERTES: Why ask you this?

KING: Not that I think you did not love your father;
But that I know love is begun by time;
And that I see, in passages of proof,°
Time qualifies° the spark and fire of it.
115 There lives within the very flame of love
A kind of wick or snuff° that will abate it;
And nothing is at° a like goodness still;°
For goodness, growing to a plurisy,°
Dies in his own too much: that° we would do,
We should do when we would; for this "would"°
120   changes
And hath abatements and delays as many
As there are tongues, are hands, are accidents;
And then this "should" is like a spendthrift sigh,
That hurts by easing.° But, to the quick° o' the
    ulcer:—
125 Hamlet comes back: what would you undertake,
To show yourself your father's son in deed
More than in words?

LAERTES: To cut his throat i' the church.

KING: No place, indeed, should murder sanctuarize;°
Revenge should have no bounds. But, good Laertes,
130 Will you do this, keep close within your chamber.
Hamlet return'd shall know you are come home:
We'll put on° those shall praise your excellence
And set a double varnish on the fame
The Frenchman gave you, bring you in fine°
    together
135 And wager on your heads: he, being remiss,°

Most generous° and free from all contriving,°
Will not peruse° the foils; so that, with ease,
Or with a little shuffling, you may choose
A sword unbated,° and in a pass of practice°
Requite him for your father.

LAERTES: I will do 't: 140
And, for that purpose, I'll anoint my sword.
I bought an unction° of a mountebank,°
So mortal that, but dip a knife in it,
Where it draws blood no cataplasm° so rare,
Collected from all simples° that have virtue°   145
Under the moon, can save the thing from death
That is but scratch'd withal: I'll touch my point
With this contagion, that, if I gall° him slightly,
It may be death.

KING: Let's further think of this;
Weigh what convenience both of time and means 150
May fit us to our shape:° if this should fail,
And that our drift look through our bad perfor-
    mance,°
'Twere better not assay'd: therefore this project
Should have a back or second, that might hold,
If this should blast in proof. Soft! let me see: 155
We'll make a solemn° wager on your cunnings:°
I ha 't:
When in your motion° you are hot and dry—
As° make your bouts more violent to that end—
And that° he calls for drink, I'll have prepared him 160
A chalice for the nonce,° whereon but sipping,
If he by chance escape your venom'd stuck,°
Our purpose may hold there.°

[Enter QUEEN.]

                              How now, sweet queen!

QUEEN: One woe doth tread upon another's heel,
So fast they follow: your sister's drown'd, Laertes. 165

LAERTES: Drown'd! O, where?

QUEEN: There is a willow grows aslant a brook,
That shows his hoar° leaves in the glassy stream;
There with fantastic garlands did she come
Of crow-flowers,° nettles, daisies, and long purples° 170

---

101 **scrimers** fencers   106 **sudden coming o'er** your immediate
return **play** fence   113 **passages of proof** well-authenticat-
ed examples   114 **qualifies** diminishes   116 **wick or snuff** a
charred wick (of a candle)   117 **at** of**still** always   118 **plurisy**
excess   119 **that** what   120 **"would"** i.e., impulse to action
124 **like . . . easing** i.e., evaporates like a sigh (which was supposed by drawing blood from the heart to weaken it even
while relieving it)   **quick** most sensitive part; so the heart of
the difficulty   128 **sanctuarize** afford sanctuary and so offer
protection to a man from being murdered.   132 **put on those**
incite persons who   134 **in fine** finally   135 **remiss** gentle, i.e.,
gentlemanly

136 **generous** free from suspicion **contriving** plotting
137 **peruse** examine carefully   139 **unbated** unblunted **pass
of practice** a lunge with a treacherously prepared sword
142 **unction** salve **mountebank** quack doctor   144 **cataplasm**
poultice   145 **simples** herbs **virtue** medicinal property
148 **gall** scratch   151 **fit . . . shape** adapt us to our plan
152 **drift . . . performance** intention were disclosed by bungling
156 **solemn** formal **cunnings** skills   158 **motion** exercise
159 **As** i.e., as you must make   160 **that** when   161 **nonce** special occasion   162 **struck** thrust   163 **hold there** be accomplished in that way   168 **hoar** gray, refers to the color of the
under surface   170 **crow-flowers** buttercups **long purples** a
kind of orchid, "orchis mascula," a popular phallic symbol

That liberal° shepherds give a grosser name,
But our cold maids do dead men's fingers call them:
There, on the pendent boughs her coronet weeds°
Clambering to hang, an envious sliver° broke;
175 When down her weedy trophies° and herself
Fell in the weeping brook. Her clothes spread wide;
And, mermaid-like, awhile they bore her up:
Which time she chanted snatches of old tunes;
As one incapable of her own distress,
180 Or like a creature native and indued°
Unto that element: but long it could not be
Till that her garments, heavy with their drink,
Pull'd the poor wretch from her melodious lay
To muddy death.
LAERTES: Alas, then, she is drown'd?
185 QUEEN: Drown'd, drown'd.
LAERTES: Too much of water hast thou, poor Ophelia,
And therefore I forbid my tears: but yet
It is our trick;° nature her custom holds,
Let shame say what it will: when these° are gone,
190 The woman will be out.° Adieu, my lord:
I have a speech of fire, that fain would blaze,
But that this folly douts it.°

[Exit.]

KING: Let's follow, Gertrude:
How much I had to do to calm his rage!
Now fear I this will give it start again;
195 Therefore let's follow.

[Exeunt.]

ACT V

Scene 1

A churchyard.

[Enter two CLOWNS,° *with spades, etc.]*

FIRST CLOWN: Is she to be buried in Christian burial°
that willfully seeks her own salvation?
SECOND CLOWN: I tell thee she is; and therefore make
her grave straight:° the crowner hath sat on her,°

and finds it Christian burial.   5
FIRST CLOWN: How can that be, unless she drowned
herself in her own defence?
SECOND CLOWN: Why, 'tis found so.
FIRST CLOWN: It must be "se offendendo,"° it cannot be
else. For here lies the point: if I drown myself wit-   10
tingly, it argues an act: and an act hath three
branches; it is, to act, to do, and to perform: argal,°
she drowned herself wittingly.°
SECOND CLOWN: Nay, but hear you, goodman delver,°—
FIRST CLOWN: Give me leave.° Here lies the water;   15
good: here stands the man; good: if the man go to
this water, and drown himself, it is, will he, nill he,
he goes,—mark you that; but if the water come to
him and drown him, he drowns not himself: argal,
he that is not guilty of his own death shortens not   20
his own life.
SECOND CLOWN: But is this law?
FIRST CLOWN: Ay, marry, is 't; crowner's quest° law.
SECOND CLOWN: Will you ha' the truth on 't? If this
had not been a gentlewoman, she should have   25
been buried out o' Christian burial.°
FIRST CLOWN: Why, there thou say'st:° and the more
pity that great folk should have countance° in
this world to drown or hang themselves, more
than their even° Christian. Come, my spade. There   30
is no ancient gentlemen but gardeners, ditchers,
and grave-makers: they hold up Adam's profession.
SECOND CLOWN: Was he a gentleman?
FIRST CLOWN: A' was the first that ever bore arms.   35
SECOND CLOWN: Why, he had none.
FIRST CLOWN: What, art a heathen? How dost thou
understand the Scripture? The Scripture says
"Adam digged:" could he dig without arms? I'll
put another question to thee: if thou answerest me   40
not to the purpose, confess thyself—
SECOND CLOWN: Go to.°
FIRST CLOWN: What is he that builds stronger than either
the mason, the shipwright, or the carpenter?
SECOND CLOWN: The gallows-maker; for that frame   45
outlives a thousand tenants.
FIRST CLOWN: I like thy wit well, in good faith: the gallows does well;° but how does it well? it does well to
those that do ill: now thou dost ill to say the gallows
is built stronger than the church: argal, the gallows   50
may do well to thee. To 't again, come.

---

171 **liberal** licentious   173 **coronet weeds** garland made of
wildflowers   174 **envious sliver** spiteful branch   175 **weedy
trophies** memorials (to put on her father's grave) made of
wild flowers   180 **indued** adapted by nature   188 **trick** way
189 **these** i.e., tears   190 **The . . . out** i.e., all my gentler impulses will be gone   192 **this . . . douts it** i.e., this weakness (the
tears) puts it out (i.e., the speech of fire)

ACT V, SCENE 1:   **s.d., Clowns** country louts   1 **Christian burial**
i.e., within the churchyard; suicides were not allowed to be
buried in consecrated ground   4 **straight** at once   **crowner . . .
her** the coroner has rendered his decision about her

---

9 **"se offendendo"** He means "se defendendo," i.e., in self-
defense   12 **argal** ergo, therefore   13 **wittingly** on purpose
14 **delver** digger   15 **Give me leave** listen to me   23 **quest**
inquest   26 **out . . . burial** outside the churchyard   27 **there . . .
say'st** now you are talking   28 **countance** permission
30 **even** fellow   41 **confess thyself** "And be hanged" is the
rest of the proverb.   42 **Go to** Come, come.   48 **does well** is a
good enough answer

SECOND CLOWN: "Who builds stronger than a mason, a shipwright, or a carpenter?"
FIRST CLOWN: Ay, tell me that, and unyoke.°
55 SECOND CLOWN: Marry, now I can tell.
FIRST CLOWN: To 't.
SECOND CLOWN: Mass, I cannot tell.

[*Enter* HAMLET *and* HORATIO, *at a distance.*]

FIRST CLOWN: Cudgel thy brains no more about it, for your dull ass will not mend his pace with beating;
60 and, when you are asked this question next, say "a grave-maker:" the houses that he makes last till doomsday. Go, get thee to Yaughan:° fetch me a stoup° of liquor.

[***Exit* SECOND CLOWN.**]

[*He digs, and sings.*]

In youth, when I did love, did love,
65   Methought it was very sweet,
To contract, Oh, the time,° for, ah,° my behoove,°
Oh, methought, there was nothing meet.

HAMLET: Has this fellow no feeling of his business, that he sings at grave-making?
70 HORATIO: Custom hath made it in him a property of easiness.°
HAMLET: 'Tis e'en so: the hand of little employment hath the daintier sense.°

FIRST CLOWN: [*Sings*]
But age, with his stealing steps,
75   Hath claw'd me in his clutch,
And hath shipped me intil the land,°
   As if I had never been such.

[*Throws up a skull.*]

HAMLET: That skull had a tongue in it, and could sing once: how the knave jowls° it to the ground, as if it
80 were Cain's jaw-bone,° that did the first murder! It might be the pate of a politician,° which this ass now o'er-reaches,° one that would circumvent God, might it not?

HORATIO: It might, my lord.   85
HAMLET: Or of a courtier; which could say "Good morrow, sweet lord! How dost thou, good lord?" This might be my lord such-a-one, that praised my lord such-a-one's horse, when he meant to beg it; might it not?   90
HORATIO: Ay, my lord.
HAMLET: Why, e'en so: and now my Lady Worm's; chapless,° and knocked about the mazzard° with a sexton's spade: here's fine revolution, an we had the trick° to see 't. Did these bones cost no more the breeding, but to play at loggats° with 'em? mine 95
ache to think on 't.
FIRST CLOWN: [*Sings*]
A pick-axe, and a spade, a spade,
   For and a shrouding sheet:
O, a pit of clay for to be made
   For such a guest is meet.   100

[*Throws up another skull.*]

HAMLET: There's another: why may not that be the skull of a lawyer? Where be his quiddities° now, his quillets,° his cases, his tenures,° and his tricks? why does he suffer this rude knave now to knock him about the sconce° with a dirty shovel, and will 105
not tell him of his action of battery?° Hum! This fellow might be in 's time a great buyer of land, with his statutes,° his recognizances,° his fines, his double vouchers, his recoveries:° is this the fine° of his fines, and the recovery of his recoveries, to 110
have his fine pate full of fine dirt? will his vouchers vouch him no more of his purchases, and double ones too, than the length and breadth of a pair of indentures?° The very conveyances° of his lands will hardly lie in this box; and must the inheritor° 115
himself have no more, ha?
HORATIO: Not a jot more, my lord.
HAMLET: Is not parchment made of sheepskins?
HORATIO: Ay, my lord, and of calf-skins too.
HAMLET: They are sheep and calves which seek out 120
assurance in that.° I will speak to this fellow. Whose grave's this, sirrah?°

---

54 **unyoke** i.e., your team—your job is done 62 **Yaughan** probably the name of an alehouse keeper well-known to Shakespeare's audience 63**stoup** a large mug 66 **contract… the time** make the time pass quickly **ah** He grunts as he wields his pick-axe. **behoove** advantage 71 **property of uneasiness** an untroubled peculiarity or occupation 73 **hand . . . sense** The hand unused to work is more sensitive (i.e., not calloused). 76 **intil the land** ashore 79 **jowls** hurls 80**jaw-bone** The tradition was that Cain killed Abel with the jawbone of an ass. 81 **politician** plotter 82 **o'erreaches** (1) gets the better of, (2) reaches over

92 **chapless** jawless **mazzard** head 94 **trick** knack 95 **play at loggats** game in which skull-shaped pieces of wood (loggats) were thrown at stakes fixed in the ground, like quoits 102 **quiddities** quibbles 103 **quillets** evasions of the real issue by hair-splitting distinctions in the meaning of words **tenures** leases 105 **sconce** head 106 **battery** assault and battery 108 **statutes** mortgages **recognizances** promissory notes 109 **fines, recoveries** terms formerly used in transfer of real estate **fine** play on the meaning "end" 114 **pair of indentures** contracts issued in duplicate **conveyances** deeds 115 **inheritor** owner, with a pun on the more usual meaning 121 **assurance in that** safety in legal documents 122 **sirrah** form of address used to a social inferior

FIRST CLOWN: Mine sir.

[*Sings*] O, a pit of clay for to be made

125   For such a guest is meet.

HAMLET: I think it be thine, indeed; for thou liest in 't.

FIRST CLOWN: You lie out on 't, sir, and there for it is not yours: for my part, I do not lie in 't, and yet it is mine.

130   HAMLET: Thou dost lie in 't, to be in 't and say it is thine: 'tis for the dead, not for the quick;° therefore thou liest.

FIRST CLOWN: 'Tis a quick° lie, sir; 'twill away again, from me to you.

135   HAMLET: What man dost thou dig it for?

FIRST CLOWN: For no man, sir.

HAMLET: What woman, then?

FIRST CLOWN: For none, neither.

HAMLET: Who is to be buried in 't?

140   FIRST CLOWN: One that was a woman, sir; but, rest her soul, she's dead.

HAMLET: How absolute° the knave is! we must speak by the card,° or equivocation° will undo us. By the Lord, Horatio, these three years I have taken note

145   of it; the age is grown so picked° that the toe of the peasant comes so near the heel of the courtier, he galls his kibe.° How long hast thou been a grave-maker?

FIRST CLOWN: Of all the days i' the year, I came to 't

150   that day that our last king Hamlet overcame Fortinbras.

HAMLET: How long is that since?

FIRST CLOWN: Cannot you tell that? every fool can tell that: it was the very day that young Hamlet was

155   born; he that is mad, and sent into England.

HAMLET: Ay, marry, why was he sent into England?

FIRST CLOWN: Why, because he was mad: he shall recover his wits there; or, if he do not, it 's no great matter° there.

160   HAMLET: Why?

FIRST CLOWN: 'Twill not be seen in him there; there the men are as mad as he.

HAMLET: How came he mad?

FIRST CLOWN: Very strangely, they say.

165   HAMLET: How strangely?

FIRST CLOWN: Faith, e'en with losing his wits.

HAMLET: Upon what ground?

FIRST CLOWN: Why, here in Denmark: I have been sexton here, man and boy, thirty years.

170   HAMLET: How long will a man lie i' the earth ere he rot?

FIRST CLOWN: I' faith, if he be not rotten before he die—as we have many pocky° corses now-a-days, that will scarce hold the laying in—he will last you some eight year or nine year: a tanner will last you 175
nine year.

HAMLET: Why he more than another?

FIRST CLOWN: Why, sir, his hide is so tanned with his trade, that he will keep out water a great while; and your water is a sore° decayer of your whore- 180
son° dead body. Here's a skull now; this skull has lain in the earth three and twenty years.

HAMLET: Whose was it?

FIRST CLOWN: A whoreson mad fellow's it was: whose do you think it was? 185

HAMLET: Nay, I know not.

FIRST CLOWN: A pestilence on him for a mad rogue! a' poured a flagon of Rhenish° on my head once. This same skull, sir, was Yorick's skull, the king's jester.

HAMLET: This? 190

FIRST CLOWN: E'en that.

HAMLET: Let me see. [*Takes the skull.*] Alas, poor Yorick! I knew him, Horatio: a fellow of infinite jest,° of most excellent fancy: he hath borne me on his back a thousand times; and now, how abhorred 195
in my imagination it is! my gorge rises at it. Here hung those lips that I have kissed I know not how oft. Where be your gibes now? your gambols? your songs? your flashes of merriment, that were wont to set the table on a roar?° Not one now, to mock 200
your own grinning? quite chap-fallen?° Now get you to my lady's chamber, and tell her, let her paint an inch thick, to this favour° she must come; make her laugh at that. Prithee, Horatio, tell me one thing. 205

HORATIO: What's that, my lord?

HAMLET: Dost thou think Alexander looked o' this fashion i' the earth?

HORATIO: E'en so.°

HAMLET: And smelt so? pah! 210

[*Puts down the skull.*]

HORATIO: E'en so, my lord.

HAMLET: To what base° uses we may return, Horatio! Why may not imagination trace the noble dust of Alexander, till he find it stopping a bung-hole?

HORATIO: 'Twere to consider too curiously,° to consid- 215
er so.

---

131 **quick** living   133 **quick** swift because the joke is tossed swiftly back and forth   142 **absolute** meticulously accurate   143 **card** compass, so considering every point   **equivocation** ambiguity   145 **picked** refined, fastidious   147 **galls his kibe** chafes his chilblain   159 **no great matter** doesn't make much difference

173 **pocky** rotten with venereal disease   180 **sore** grievous   184 **whoreson** bastardly   188 **Rhenish** Rhine wine   194 **of infinite jest** with an endless number of jokes   200 **on a roar** roaring with laughter   201 **chap-fallen** a pun (1) down in the mouth, (2) having no lower jaw   203 **favour** appearance   209 **E'en so** just like that   212 **base** vile   215 **consider too curiously** think about it too minutely

HAMLET: No, faith, not a jot; but to follow him thither
    with modesty° enough, and likelihood to lead it: as
    thus: Alexander died, Alexander was buried,
220   Alexander returneth into dust; the dust is earth; of
    earth we make loam,° and why of that loam,
    whereto° he was converted, might they not stop a
    beer-barrel?
    Imperious° Cæsar, dead and turn'd to clay,
225   Might stop a hole to keep the wind away:
    O, that that earth, which kept the world in awe,
    Should patch a wall to expel the winter's flaw!°
    But soft! but soft! aside:° here comes the king,

[Enter PRIESTS, *etc., in procession; the Corpse of*
OPHELIA; LAERTES *and* MOURNERS, *following;* KING,
QUEEN, *their trains, etc.]*

    The queen, the courtiers: who is this they follow?
230   And with such maimèd° rites? This doth betoken
    The corse they follow did with desperate hand
    Fordo it° own life: 'twas of some estate.°
    Couch° we awhile, and mark.

[Retiring with HORATIO.]

LAERTES: What ceremony else?°
HAMLET: That is Laertes,
235   A very noble youth: mark.
LAERTES: What ceremony else?
FIRST PRIEST: Her obsequies have been as far enlarged
    As we have warranty:° her death was doubtful;°
    And, but that great command o'ersways the order,
240   She should in ground unsanctified have lodged
    Till the last trumpet; for charitable prayers,
    Shards,° flints and pebbles should be thrown on her:
    Yet here she is allow'd her virgin crants,°
    Her maiden strewments° and the bringing home°
245   Of bell and burial.
LAERTES: Must there no more be done?
FIRST PRIEST: No more be done:
    We should profane the service of the dead
    To sing a requiem° and such rest to her
    As to peace-parted souls.°
250 LAERTES: Lay her i' the earth:
    And from her fair and unpolluted flesh

May violets spring! I tell thee, churlish priest,
A ministering angel shall my sister be,
When thou liest howling.
HAMLET: What, the fair Ophelia!
QUEEN: Sweets to the sweet: farewell!   255

[Scattering flowers.]

I hoped thou shouldst have been my Hamlet's wife;
    I thought thy bride-bed to have deck'd, sweet maid,
    And not have strew'd thy grave.
LAERTES: O, treble woe
    Fall ten times treble° on that cursèd head,
    Whose wicked deed thy most ingenious sense°   260
    Deprived thee of! Hold off the earth awhile,
    Till I have caught her once more in mine arms:

[Leaps into the grave.]

    Now pile your dust upon the quick° and dead,
    Till of this flat a mountain you have made,
    To o'ertop° old Pelion,° or the skyish head   265
    Of blue Olympus.
HAMLET: *[Advancing]*   What is he whose grief
    Bears such an emphasis? whose phrase of sorrow
    Conjures the wandering stars,° and makes them
    stand
    Like wonder-wounded hearers? This is I,
    Hamlet the Dane.

[Leaps into the grave.]

LAERTES: The devil take thy soul! 270

[Grappling with him.]

HAMLET: Thou pray'st not well.
    I prithee, take thy fingers from my throat;
    For, though I am not splenitive° and rash,
    Yet have I something in me dangerous,
    Which let thy wiseness fear: hold off thy hand. 275
KING: Pluck them asunder.
QUEEN: Hamlet, Hamlet!
ALL: Gentlemen,—
HORATIO: Good my lord, be quiet.

[The ATTENDANTS *part them, and they come out of the
grave.*

HAMLET: Why, I will fight with him upon this theme
    Until my eyelids will no longer wag.°

---

²¹⁸ **with modesty** without exaggeration ²²¹ **loam** clay
²²² **whereto** into which ²²⁴ **Imperious** imperial ²²⁷ **flaw**
gust of wind ²²⁸ **aside** stand aside ²³⁰ **maimed** incomplete
²³² **Fordo it** destroy its **estate** high rank ²³³ **Couch** hide
What ceremony else? Are there to be no further ceremonies?
²³⁸ **warranty** permission **doubtful** suspicious ²⁴² **Shards**
pieces of broken pottery ²⁴³ **crants** garland ²⁴⁴ **strewments**
the strewing of flowers **bringing home** (1) bringing home a
bride after a wedding, (2) bringing Ophelia to her eternal
home ²⁴⁹ **requiem** i.e., mass for the dead ²⁵⁰ **peace-parted
souls** souls that died in peace

²⁵⁹ **treble** triple ²⁶⁰ **most ingenious sense** i.e., reason
²⁶³ **quick** living ²⁶⁵ **o'ertop** rise higher than **Pelion** the
mountain that the giants, in their war with the gods, piled up
on Mt. Ossa, so as to reach Olympus ²⁶⁸ **wandering stars**
planets ²⁷³ **splenitive** hot-tempered ²⁷⁹ **wag** move (with no
ludicrous connotation)

280 QUEEN: O my son, what theme?
  HAMLET: I loved Ophelia: forty thousand brothers
    Could not, with all their quantity of love,
    Make up my sum. What wilt thou do for her?
  KING: O, he is mad, Laertes.
285 QUEEN: For love of God, forbear° him.
  HAMLET: 'Swounds, show me what thou'lt do:
    Woo 't° weep? woo 't fight? woo 't fast? woo 't
      tear thyself?
    Woo 't drink up eisel?° eat a crocodile?
    I'll do 't. Dost thou come here to whine?
290   To outface me with leaping in her grave?
    Be buried quick with her, and so will I:
    And, if thou prate of mountains, let them throw
    Millions of acres on us, till our ground
    Singeing his pate against the burning zone,°
295   Make Ossa like a wart! Nay, an thou'lt mouth,°
    I'll rant as well as thou.
  QUEEN: This is mere° madness:
    And thus awhile the fit will work on him;
    Anon, as patient as the female dove,
    When that her golden couplets° are disclosed,
    His silence will sit drooping.
300 HAMLET: Hear you, sir;
    What is the reason that you use me thus?
    I loved you ever: but it is no matter;
    Let Hercules himself do what he may,
    The cat will mew and dog will have his day.

[Exit.]

305 KING: I pray you, good Horatio, wait upon him.

[Exit HORATIO.]

[*To* LAERTES] Strengthen your patience in° our last
    night's speech;°
  We'll put the matter to the present push.°
  Good Gertrude, set some watch over your son.
  This grave shall have a living° monument:
310 An hour of quiet shortly shall we see;
  Till then, in patience our proceeding be.

[Exeunt.]

Scene 2

A hall in the castle.

[*Enter* HAMLET *and* HORATIO.]

HAMLET: So much for this,° sir: now shall you see the
    other;
  You do remember all the circumstance?°
HORATIO: Remember it, my lord!
HAMLET: Sir, in my heart there was a kind of fighting,
  That would not let me sleep: methought I lay   5
  Worse than the mutines° in the bilboes.° Rashly,
  And praised be rashness for it, let us know,
  Our indiscretion sometimes serves us well,
  When our deep plots do pall:° and that should
    teach us
  There's a divinity that shapes our ends,   10
  Rough-hew them how we will,°—
HORATIO: That is most certain.
HAMLET: Up from my cabin,
  My sea-gown° scarf'd° about me, in the dark
  Groped I to find out° them; had my desire,
  Finger'd° their packet, and in fine° withdrew   15
  To mine own room again; making so bold,
  My fears forgetting manners, to unseal
  Their grand commission; where I found, Horatio,—
  O royal knavery!—an exact command,
  Larded° with many several sorts of reasons   20
  Importing° Denmark's health° and England's too,
  With, ho! such bugs° and goblins in my life,°
  That, on the supervise,° no leisure bated,°
  No, not to stay° the grinding of the axe,
  My head should be struck off.
HORATIO: Is 't possible?   25
HAMLET: Here's the commission: read it at more
    leisure.
  But wilt thou hear me how I did proceed?
HORATIO: I beseech you.
HAMLET: Being thus be-netted round with villanies,—
  Ere I could make a prologue to my brains,°   30
  They had begun the play—I sat me down,
  Devised a new commission, wrote it fair:°
  I once did hold it, as our statists° do,
  A baseness° to write fair and labour'd much
  How to forget that learning, but, sir, now   35
  It did me yeoman's° service: wilt thou know
  The effect° of what I wrote?
HORATIO: Ay, good my lord.

---

285 **forbear** have patience with   287 **Woo't** wilt, a form used only by illiterates and so insulting   288 **eisel** vinegar, a supposed antidote to anger   294 **burning zone** the sun's orbit **mouth** i.e., use extravagant language   296 **mere** complete   299 **golden couplets** the two newly hatched young of a dove are covered with golden down   306 **in** by remembering **last night's speech** i.e., what we said last night   307 **present push** immediate test   309 **living** lasting

---

SCENE 2:   1 **this** this part of the story   2 **circumstances** details   6 **mutines** mutineers **bilboes** fetters   9 **pall** fail   11 **Rough . . . will** shape them as roughly as we please   13 **sea-gown** short-sleeved gown reaching to the knee **scarf'd** thrown like a scarf   14 **find out** discover   15 **Finger'd** stole **in fine** finally   20 **Larded** dressed up   21 **Importing** bearing upon **health** welfare   22 **such . . . life** i.e., with exclamations about the evils I had done **bugs** bugbears   23 **on the supervise** upon looking it over **leisure bated** delay allowed   24 **stay** wait for   30 **make . . . brains** begin to think (how to act)   32 **fair** legibly   33 **statists** statesmen   34 **baseness** mark of low social position   36 **yeoman's** substantial   37 **effect** gist

HAMLET: An earnest conjuration° from the king,
    As England was his faithful tributary,
40   As love between them like the palm might flourish,
    As peace should still her wheaten garland wear
    And stand a comma° 'tween their amities,
    And many such-like "As"es° of great charge,°
    That, on the view and knowing of these contents,
45   Without debatement° further, more or less,
    He should the bearers put to sudden° death,
    Not shriving-time° allow'd.
HORATIO: How was this seal'd?
HAMLET: Why, even in that was heaven ordinant.°
    I had my father's signet in my purse,
50   Which was the model of that Danish seal;
    Folded the writ up in form of the other,
    Subscribed° it, gave 't the impression,° placed it
      safely,
    The changeling° never known. Now, the next day
    Was our sea-fight; and what to this was sequent°
55   Thou know'st already.
HORATIO: So Guildenstern and Rosencrantz go to 't.°
HAMLET: Why, man, they did make love to this
      employment;°
    They are not near° my conscience; their defeat°
    Does by their own insinuation° grow:
60   'Tis dangerous when the baser° nature comes
    Between the pass° and fell° incensèd points
    Of mighty opposites.°
HORATIO: Why, what a king is this!
HAMLET: Does it not, thinks't thee, stand me now
      upon°—
    He that hath kill'd my king and whored my mother,
65   Popp'd in between the election° and my hopes,
    Thrown out his angle° for my proper° life,
    And with such cozenage°—is't not perfect con-
      science,
    To quit° him with this arm? and is 't not to be
      damn'd,
    To let this canker of our nature° come
70   In° further evil?

HORATIO: It must be shortly known to him from
    England
    What is the issue of the business there.
HAMLET: It will be short: the interim is mine;
    And a man's life's no more than to say "One."°
    But I am very sorry, good Horatio,   75
    That to Laertes I forgot myself;
    For, by the image of my cause,° I see
    The portraiture of his: I'll court his favours:
    But, sure, the bravery° of his grief did put me
    Into a towering passion.
HORATIO: Peace! who comes here?   80

[Enter OSRIC.]

OSRIC: Your lordship is right welcome back
    to Denmark.
HAMLET: I humbly thank you, sir. Dost know
    this water-fly?
HORATIO: No, my good lord.   85
HAMLET: Thy state° is the more gracious;° for 'tis a
    vice to know him. He hath much land, and fertile:
    let a beast be lord of beasts, and his crib shall stand
    at the king's mess:° 'tis a chough;° but, as I say,
    spacious in the possession of dirt.   90
OSRIC: Sweet lord, if your lordship were at leisure, I
    should impart a thing to you from his majesty.
HAMLET: I will receive it, sir, with all diligence of spir-
    it. Put your bonnet° to his right use; 'tis for the
    head.   95
OSRIC: I thank your lordship, it is very hot.
HAMLET: No, believe me, 'tis very cold; the wind is
    northerly.
OSRIC: It is indifferent° cold, my lord, indeed.
HAMLET: But yet methinks it is very sultry and hot for   100
    my complexion.°
OSRIC: Exceedingly, my lord; it is very sultry,—as
    'twere,—I cannot tell how. But, my lord, his
    majesty bade me signify to you that he has laid a
    great wager on your head: sir, this is the matter,— 105
HAMLET: I beseech you, remember—

*[*HAMLET *moves him to put on his hat.]*

OSRIC: Nay, good my lord; for mine ease, in good
    faith. Sir, here is newly come to court Laertes;
    believe me, an absolute° gentleman, full of most
    excellent differences,° of very soft° society and   110

---

38 conjuration entreaty   **42 comma** here = connecting link
43 "As"es pun on "asses" **charge** weight   **45 debatement**
discussion **46 sudden** immediate **47 shriving-time** time for
confession and absolution **48 ordinant** ordering events
52 Subscribed signed **gave . . . impression** i.e., stamped it
with the King's seal **53 changeling . . . known** substitution
never detected **54 sequent** subsequent **56 to 't** i.e., to their
doom **57 make . . . employment** fairly begged to be treated in
this way **58 near** on **defeat** destruction **59 insinuation**
meddling **60 baser** lower in rank **61 pass** thrust **fell** cruel
62 opposites opponents **63 stand . . . upon** become my duty
65 election The Danish monarch was elective. **66 Thrown . . .
angle** angled for **proper** very **67 cozenage** deceit **68 quit**
get even with **69 canker of our nature** ulcer of humanity
70 come In wreak

74 to say "One" i.e., to get one good hit (in fencing) **77 image
. . . cause** reflection of my situation **79 bravery** ostentation
86 state situation **gracious** favorable **89 let . . . mess** Let a
man be rich enough and he can get into courtly society.
chough a crow; i.e., a chatterer **94 bonnet** cap **99 indifferent** rather **101 complexion** temperament **109 absolute** perfect **110 differences** distinguishing qualities, accomplishments **soft** refined

great showing:° indeed, to speak feelingly° of him, he is the card° or calendar of gentry, for you shall find in him the continent° of what part a gentleman would see.°

115 HAMLET: Sir, his definement° suffers no perdition in you; though, I know, to divide him inventorially would dizzy the arithmetic of memory,° and yet but yaw° neither, in respect of his quick sail.° But, in the verity of extolment, I take him to be a soul

120 of great article;° and his infusion of such dearth° and rareness,° as, to make true diction of him, his semblable° in his mirror; and who else would trace° him, his umbrage,° nothing more.

OSRIC: Your lordship speaks most infallibly of him.

125 HAMLET: The conernancy,° sir? why do we wrap the gentleman in our more rawer breath?

OSRIC: Sir?

HORATIO: Is 't not possible to understand in another tongue?° You will do't, sir, really.

130 HAMLET: What imports the nomination° of this gentleman?

OSRIC: Of Laertes?

HORATIO: His purse is empty already; all's golden words are spent.

135 HAMLET: Of him, sir.

OSRIC: I know you are not ignorant—

HAMLET: I would you did, sir; yet, in faith, if you did, it would not much approve° me. Well, sir?

OSRIC: You are not ignorant of what excellence Laertes

140 is—

HAMLET: I dare not confess that, lest I should compare with him in excellence; but, to know a man well, were to know himself.°

OSRIC: I mean, sir, for his weapon;° but in the imputa-

145 tion° laid on him by them, in his meed° he's unfellowed.°

HAMLET: What's his weapon?

OSRIC: Rapier and dagger.

HAMLET: That's two of his weapons: but, well.

OSRIC: The king, sir, hath wagered with him six 150 Barbary horses: against the which he has imponed,° as I take it, six French rapiers and poniards,° with their assigns,° as girdle, hangers,° and so: three of the carriages, in faith, are very dear to fancy, very responsive° to the hilts, most delicate 155 carriages,° and of very liberal conceit.°

HAMLET: What call you the carriages?

HORATIO: I knew you must be edified by the margent° ere you had done.

OSRIC: The carriages, sir, are the hangers. 160

HAMLET: The phrase would be more german° to the matter, if we could carry cannon by our sides: I would it might be hangers till then. But, on: six Barbary horses against six French swords, their assigns, and three liberal-conceited carriages; 165 that's the French bet against the Danish. Why is this "imponed," as you call it?

OSRIC: The king, sir, hath laid,° that in a dozen passes between yourself and him, he shall not exceed you three hits: he hath laid on twelve for nine;° and it 170 would come to immediate trial, if your lordship would vouchsafe the answer.°

HAMLET: How if I answer "no"?

OSRIC: I mean, my lord, the opposition of your person in trial. 175

HAMLET: Sir, I will walk here in the hall: if it please his majesty, 't is the breathing time° of day with me; let the foils be brought, the gentleman willing, and the king hold his purpose, I will win for him an I can; if not, I will gain nothing but my shame and the 180 odd hits.

OSRIC: Shall I re-deliver you° e'en so?

HAMLET: To this effect, sir; after what flourish your nature will.

OSRIC: I commend my duty to your lordship. 185

HAMLET: Yours, yours. [Exit OSRIC.] He does well to commend it himself; there are no tongues else for's turn.

HORATIO: This lapwing runs away with the shell on his head.° 190

---

111 **great showing** fine appearance **feelingly** justly
112 **card** compass 113 **continent** summary 114 **the . . . see** all the qualities of a perfect gentleman 115 **his definement** the description of him 117 **arithmetic of memory** the power of reckoning 118 **yaw . . . sail** i.e., the enumeration of Laertes' virtues is but a zig-zag-moving boat in trying to overtake the quick sailing of his attainments **yaw** move zigzag 120 **article** importance **of such dearth** so exceptional 121 **rareness** rarity 122 **semblable** image, i.e., no one is like him but his image in the mirrors 123 **trace** follow, imitate **umbrage** shadow 125 **The concernancy?** i.e., What has that to do with the matter? 129 **Is't . . . tongue?** i.e., Can't you understand your own jargon in another man's mouth? 130 **nomination** naming 138 **approve** command 143 **know himself** i.e., a man can really know no one well but himself 144 **for his weapon** in the use of his weapon (in dueling) 145 **imputation** reputation **meed** merits 146 **unfellowed** without equal

---

152 **imponed** wagered 153 **poniards** daggers **assigns** appendages **hangers** straps attaching the sword to a belt 155 **very responsive** corresponding exactly 156 **delicate carriages** i.e., hangers of delicate workmanship **liberal conceit** elaborate design 158 **margent** marginal comment 161 **german** germane, appropriate 168 **laid** bet 170 **he . . . twelve for nine** i.e., that in a dozen bouts Laertes cannot beat Hamlet by more than three up (to use a golf term) 172 **vouchsafe the answer** accept the challenge 177 **breathing time** time for exercise 182 **re-deliver you** take back your message 190 **lapwing . . . head** the lapwing (a kind of English sandpiper) was supposed to be so precocious that it ran away from its nest before completely hatched

HAMLET: He did commply with his dug,° before he
　　sucked it. Thus has he—and many more of the
　　same breed that I know the drossy° age dotes on—
　　only got the tune of the time and outward habit of
195　encounter;° a kind of yesty collection,° which car-
　　ries them through and through the most fond and
　　winnowed opinions;° and do but blow them to
　　their trial,° the bubbles are out.°

[Enter a LORD.*]*

LORD: My lord, his majesty commended him to you
200　by young Osric, who brings back to him,° that you
　　attend him in the hall: he sends to know if your
　　pleasure hold to play with Laertes, or that you will
　　take longer time.
HAMLET: I am constant to my purposes; they follow
205　the king's pleasure: if his fitness speaks° mine is
　　ready; now or whensoever, provided I be so able as
　　now.
LORD: The king and queen and all are coming down.
HAMLET: In happy time.°
210　LORD: The queen desires you to use some gentle enter-
　　tainment° to Laertes before you fall to play.
HAMLET: She well instructs me.

[Exit LORD.]

HORATIO: You will lose this wager, my lord.
HAMLET: I do not think so; since he went into France,
215　I have been in continual practice; I shall win at the
　　odds. But thou wouldst not think how ill all's here
　　about my heart: but it is no matter.
HORATIO: Nay, good my lord,—
HAMLET: It is but foolery;° but it is such a kind of gain-
220　giving,° as would perhaps trouble a woman.
HORATIO: If your mind dislike any thing, obey it: I will
　　forestall their repair hither, and say you are not fit.
HAMLET: Not a whit, we defy augury:° there's a spe-
　　cial providence in the fall of a sparrow. If it be now,
225　'tis not to come; if it be not to come, it will be now;
　　if it be not now, yet it will come: the readiness is all:
　　since no man has aught of what he leaves, what is't
　　to leave betimes? Let be.°

[Enter KING, QUEEN, LAERTES, LORDS, OSRIC, *and*
ATTENDANTS *with foils.]*

KING: Come, Hamlet, come, and take this hand from
　　me.

[The KING *puts* LAERTES' *hand into* HAMLET'*s.]*

HAMLET: Give me your pardon sir: I've done you
　　　　wrong;　　　　　　　　　　　　　　　　　　230
　　But pardon 't as you are a gentleman.
　　This presence° knows,
　　And you must needs have heard, how I am pun-
　　　　ish'd
　　With sore distraction.° What I have done,
　　That might your nature, honour and exception°　235
　　Roughly awake,° I here proclaim was madness.
　　Was 't Hamlet wrong'd Laertes? Never Hamlet:
　　If Hamlet from himself be ta'en away,
　　And when he's not himself does wrong Laertes,
　　Then Hamlet does it not, Hamlet denies it.　　240
　　Who does it, then? His madness: if 't be so,
　　Hamlet is of the faction that is wrong'd;
　　His madness is poor Hamlet's enemy.
　　Sir, in this audience,°
　　Let my disclaiming from a purposed evil　　　245
　　Free me so far in your most generous thoughts,
　　That I have shot mine arrow o'er the house,
　　And hurt my brother.
LAERTES:　　　　　　　　I am satisfied in nature,°
　　Whose motive,° in this case, should stir me most
　　To my revenge: but in my terms of honour°　　250
　　I stand aloof; and will no° reconcilement,
　　Till by some elder masters,° of known honour,
　　I have a voice and precedent° of peace,°
　　To keep my name ungored.° But till that time,
　　I do receive your offer'd love like love,　　　255
　　And will not wrong it.
HAMLET:　　　　　　　　I embrace it freely;
　　And will this brother's wager frankly play.°
　　Give us the foils.° Come on.
LAERTES:　　　　　　　　Come, one for me.
HAMLET: I'll be your foil, Laertes: in mine ignorance
　　Your skill shall, like a star i' the darkest night,　260
　　Stick fiery off° indeed.

---

191 **comply . . . dug** bowed to his mother's breast　193 **drossy**
worthless　195 **outward . . . encounter** superficial social manners　**yesty collection** frothy anthology (of phrases)
197 **which . . . opinions** which permeates (and contaminates)
the most trivial and the most refined judgments (of social
manners)　198 **blow . . . trial** test them by blowing on them
are out disappear　200 **that . . . him** the news that you are to
await him　205 **his fitness speaks** it meets his convenience
209 **In happy time** that's good　211 **use . . . entertainment** give
a friendly welcome　219 **follery** an absurd thing　220 **gain-
giving** misgiving　222 **repair** coming　223 **defy augury**
despite the superstitious belief in omens　228 **Let be** i.e.,
cease trying to dissuade me

232 **presence** royal assembly　234 **sore distraction** grievous
mental confusion (madness)　235 **exception** disapproval
236 **Roughly awake** arouse by my rough (crude) conduct
244 **audience** royal presence　248 **nature** my natural feelings
249 **Whose motive** the promptings of which　250 **in . . . honour**
as I understand the code of honor　251 **will no** will agree to
no　252 **masters** experts　253 **voice and precedent** decision
based on precedent　**of peace** for making up the quarrel
254 **name ungored** reputation unsullied　257 **frankly play**
fence without bitterness　258 **foil** (1) a blunted sword, (2) a
background to set off the brilliance of a jewel　261 **Stick fiery
off** shine in brilliant contrast

LAERTES: You mock me, sir.
HAMLET: No, by this hand.
KING: Give them the foils, young Osric. Cousin
     Hamlet,
     You know the wager?
HAMLET: Very well, my lord;
265   Your grace hath laid the odds o' the weaker side.
KING: I do not fear it; I have seen you both:
     But since he is better'd,° we have therefore odds.
LAERTES: This is too heavy, let me see another.
HAMLET: This likes° me well. These foils have all a
     length?

[They prepare to play.]

270   OSRIC: Ay, my good lord.
KING: Set me the stoups° of wine upon that table.
     If Hamlet give the first or second hit,
     Or quit in answer of° the third exchange,
     Let all the battlements their ordnance fire;
275   The king shall drink to Hamlet's better breath;
     And in the cup an union° shall he throw,
     Richer than that which four successive kings
     In Denmark's crown have worn. Give me the
         cups;
     And let the kettle° to the trumpet speak,
280   The trumpet to the cannoneer without,
     The cannons to the heavens, the heavens to earth,
     "Now the king drinks to Hamlet." Come, begin:
     And you, the judges, bear a wary eye.°
HAMLET: Come on, sir.
LAERTES: Come, my lord. *[They play]*
HAMLET: One.
LAERTES: No.
HAMLET: Judgement.
OSRIC: A hit, a very palpable hit.
285   LAERTES: Well; again.
KING: Stay; give me drink. Hamlet, this pearl is thine;
     Here's to thy health.

[Trumpets sound, and cannon shot off within.]

                              Give him the cup.
HAMLET: I'll play this bout first; set it by awhile.
     Come. *[They play.]* Another hit; what say you?
290   LAERTES: A touch, a touch, I do confess.
KING: Our son shall° win.
QUEEN: He's fat,° and scant of breath.
     Here, Hamlet, take my napkin,° rub thy brows:
     The queen carouses° to thy fortune, Hamlet.

HAMLET: Good madam!   295
KING: Gertrude, do not drink.
QUEEN: I will, my lord; I pray you, pardon me.
KING: [*Aside*] It is the poison'd cup: it is too late.
HAMLET: I dare not drink yet, madam; by and by.
QUEEN: Come, let me wipe thy face.
LAERTES: My lord, I'll hit him now.
KING: I do not think 't.   300
LAERTES: [*Aside*] And yet 'tis almost 'gainst my con-
     science.
HAMLET: Come, for the third, Laertes: you but dally,
     I pray you, pass° with your best violence;
     I am afeard you make a wanton of me.°
LAERTES: Say you so? come on. [*They play.*]   305
OSRIC: Nothing, neither way.°
LAERTES: Have at you now!

*[*LAERTES *wounds* HAMLET; *then, in scuffling, they
change rapiers, and* HAMLET *wounds* LAERTES.]*

KING: Part them; they are incensed.
HAMLET: Nay, come, again. [The QUEEN falls.]
OSRIC: Look to° the queen there, ho!   310
HORATIO: They bleed on both sides. How is it, my
     lord?
OSRIC: How is 't, Laertes?
LAERTES: Why, as a woodcock to mine own springe,°
     Osric;
     I am justly kill'd with mine own treachery.
HAMLET: How does the queen?
KING: She swounds to see them bleed.   315
QUEEN: No, no, the drink, the drink,—O my dear
     Hamlet,—
     The drink, the drink! I am poison'd. [*Dies.*]
HAMLET: O villany! Ho! let the door be lock'd:
     Treachery! Seek it out.
LAERTES: It is here,° Hamlet: Hamlet, thou art slain;   320
     No medicine in the world can do thee good;
     In thee there is not half an hour of life;
     The treacherous instrument is in thy hand,
     Unbated° and envenom'd: the foul practice°
     Hath turn'd itself on me; lo, here I lie,   325
     Never to rise again: thy mother's poison'd:
     I can° no more: the king, the king's to blame.
HAMLET: The point envenom'd too!
     Then, venom, to thy work. [*Stabs the* KING.
ALL: Treason! treason!   330
KING: O, yet defend me, friends; I am but hurt.°
HAMLET: Here, thou incestuous, murderous, damnèd

267 is better'd considered you superior   **269 likes** suits   **271 stoups** goblets   **273 quit . . . of** scores a draw in   **276 union** large pearl   **279 kettle** kettle drum   **283 bear . . . eye** watch very carefully   **291 shall** will surely   **293 napkin** handkerchief   **294 carouses** drinks a full goblet

303 pass thrust   **304 make . . . me** treat me as though I were a child   **306 Nothing, neither way** i.e., neither has scored a hit   **310 Look to** take care of   **313 springe** trap, i.e., a foolish victim of my own plot   **320 It is here** i.e., I am the inventor of the treachery   **324 Unbated** not blunted   **practice** plot   **327 can** can say   **331 hurt** slightly wounded

Dane,
Drink of this potion. Is thy union here?
Follow my mother.

[KING dies.]

LAERTES: He is justly served;°
335   It is a poison temper'd° by himself.
Exchange forgiveness with me, noble Hamlet:
Mine and my father's death come not upon thee,°
Nor thine on me!

[Dies.]

HAMLET: Heaven make thee free of it! I follow thee.
340   I am dead, Horatio. Wretched queen, adieu!
You that look pale and tremble at this chance,
That are but mutes° or audience to this act,
Had I but time—as this fell sergeant,° death,
Is strict in his arrest—O, I could tell you—
345   But let it be. Horatio, I am dead;
Thou livest; report me and my cause aright
To the unsatisfied.°
HORATIO: Never believe it:
I am more an antique Roman than a Dane:
Here's yet some liquor left.
HAMLET: As thou'rt a man,
350   Give me the cup: let go; by heaven, I'll have't.
O good Horatio, what a wounded name,
Things standing thus unknown, shall live behind
me!
If thou didst ever hold me in thy heart,
Absent thee from felicity awhile,
355   And in this harsh world draw thy breath in pain,
To tell my story.

[March afar off, and shot within.]

What warlike noise is this?
OSRIC: Young Fortinbras, with conquest come from
Poland,
To the ambassadors of England gives
This warlike volley.
HAMLET: O, I die, Horatio;
360   The potent poison quite o'er-crows my spirit:°
I cannot live to hear the news from England;
But I do prophesy the election lights
On Fortinbras: he has my dying voice;°
So tell him, with the occurrents,° more and less,
365   Which have solicited.° The rest is silence.

[Dies.]

HORATIO: Now cracks a noble heart. Good night,
sweet prince;
And flights of angels sing thee to thy rest!
Why does the drum come hither?

[March within.]

*[Enter FORTINBRAS, the ENGLISH AMBASSADORS, and
others.]*

FORTINBRAS: Where is this sight?
HORATIO: What is it ye would see?
If aught of woe or wonder, cease your search.   370
FORTINBRAS: This quarry° cries on havoc.° O proud
death,
What feast is toward° in thine eternal cell,
That thou so many princes at a shot
So bloodily hast struck?
FIRST AMBASSADOR: The sight is dismal;
And our affairs° from England come too late: 375
The ears are senseless that should give us hear-
ing,
To tell him his commandment is fulfill'd,
That Rosencrantz and Guildenstern are dead:
Where should we have our thanks?
HORATIO: Not from his° mouth,
Had it the ability of life° to thank you: 380
He never gave commandment for their death.
But since, so jump upon° this bloody question,°
You from the Polack wars, and you from England,
Are here arrived, give order that these bodies
High on a stage° be placed to the view;   385
And let me speak to the yet unknowing world
How these things came about: so shall you hear
Of carnal,° bloody, and unnatural acts,
Of accidental judgements,° casual° slaughters,
Of deaths put on° by cunning and forced cause,°   390
And, in this upshot,° purposes mistook°
Fall'n on the inventors' heads: all this can I
Truly deliver.
HORATIO: Let us haste to hear it,
And call the noblest to the audience.
For me, with sorrow I embrace my fortune: 395

---

371 quarry heap of dead bodies   **cries on havoc** proclaims
there has been a general slaughter here   **372 toward** in preparation   **375 affairs** reports of affairs   **376 senseless** deaf
379 his i.e., the King's   **380 ability of life** power of a living
person   **382 so jump upon** following so close upon
question quarrel   **385 stage** platform   **388 carnal** sensual
389 accidental judgements punishments inflicted by accident
casual accidental   **390 put on** brought about   **forced cause**
i.e., necessitated by self-defense   **391 upshot** conclusion (of
the tragedy)   **purposes mistook** intentions miscarried

---

334 served treated   **335 temper'd** concocted   **337 come . . . thee**
are not to be laid at your door   **342 mutes** actors without
speaking parts—"supers."   **343 fell sergeant** cruel police officer   **347 unsatisfied** uninformed   **360 o'er-crows my spirit**
triumphs over my vital energy   **363 voice** vote   **364 occurrents** events   **365 solicited** brought about

I have some rights of memory° in this kingdom,
Which now to claim my vantage doth invite me.°
HORATIO: Of that I shall have also cause to speak,
And from his mouth whose voice will draw on
     more:°
400   But let this same° be presently perform'd,°
Even while men's minds are wild;° lest more mis-
     chance,
On° plots and errors, happen.
FORTINBRAS: Let four captains
Bear Hamlet, like a soldier, to the stage;
For he was likely, had he been put on,°
405   To have proved most royally: and, for his passage,°
The soldiers' music and the rites of war
Speak° loudly for him.
Take up the bodies: such a sight as this
Becomes the field,° but here shows much amiss.°
410   Go, bid the soldiers shoot.

*[A dead march. Exeunt, bearing off the dead bodies;
after which a peal of ordnance is shot off.]*

---

396 rights of memory remembered claims   **397 my vantage...
invite me** my rights invite me (to seize)   **399 voice . . . more**
vote will influence more [votes]   **400 this same** i.e., arrangements for telling the story   **presently perform'd** done at
once   **401 wild** greatly excited   **402 On** as a result of   **404 put
on** promoted (to the throne)   **405 for his passage** to mark his
passing   **407 Speak** let speak   **409 field** battlefield   **shows
much amiss** is very inappropriate

BEN JONSON (1572–1637)

Ben Jonson was born eight years later than Shakespeare and outlived him by more than twenty years. He was one of the most learned and well-known playwrights of his time. Jonson received an early education at Westminster grammar school under the great humanist scholar William Camden. Following graduation in 1589, his stepfather forced him to become an apprentice bricklayer, but in the following year he left the profession to fight with the Dutch against the Spanish. By 1597 he was back in London, earning a living by acting and by writing and revising plays for Philip Henslowe, a wealthy theatrical broker. That same year Jonson was arrested for his part as actor and writer in the satiric comedy *The Isle of Dogs*. In the following year years, he was arrested again, this time for killing the actor Gabriel Spencer in a duel. Jonson escaped execution by pleading benefit of clergy, an exclusion from civil jurisdiction based on one's ability to read Latin. His dramatic career, too, was filled with controversy. Two of his plays for boy companies, *Cynthia's Revels* (1600) and *The Poetaster* (1601), sparked a satiric war among London's theatrical companies, and *Eastward Ho!* (1605), a play that contains a sarcastic remark about King James, got him imprisoned once again.

In the prologue to one of his early works—a satiric comedy in which Shakespeare acted, *Everyman in His Humour*—Jonson tells us that his drama is realistic in method and satiric in purpose. He thus sets himself in opposition to the romantic comedies that dominated the theater of the time. His portraits of Elizabethan character types in this play were so successful onstage that in the following year he wrote *Everyman out of His Humour*. In the prologue to that play Jonson explains his theory of dramatic satire further. Human behavior, he suggests, resulted from psychological states produced by physiological causes that the Elizabethans called humours. But individuals might affect a humour to mask their natural humour, and Jonson attempted to expose these affectations satirically. Using this theory, Jonson produced a series of plays that made him the preeminent satirist in English drama: *Volpone* (1606), *Epicoene* (1609), *The Alchemist* (1610), and *Bartholomew Fair* (1614). His comedies not only produced imitators among his contemporaries but also influenced the development of comedy of manners, the most popular form of comedy during the Restoration and the eighteenth century. At court, Jonson achieved his greatest reputation as a writer of masques. He wrote thirty-three of these extraordinarily elaborate and expensive aristocratic entertainments, most of them in collaboration with the famous architect and designer Inigo Jones.

In 1616 Jonson published his *Works* in a sumptuous and carefully edited folio. The volume included not only his poetry, which was considered serious literature, but his plays as well. Jonson lived long enough to become what Shakespeare never was, a revered literary figure in his own time. He received a royal pension from King James I and was granted honorary degrees by Cambridge and Oxford. But his last years were difficult. He quarreled with Jones, and his later work was not as highly regarded as his brilliant early plays. Nevertheless, at the time of his death in 1637, his reputation was so firmly established that his funeral was attended by virtually all of the nobility and gentry in London at the time, and he was buried at Westminster Abbey alongside other famous literary figures.

Volpone

In his epistle to *Volpone* Jonson allies himself with humanist theorists such as Sir Philip Sidney, claiming that comedy is satiric and didactic, intended to reform society. *Volpone* is a satire on human greed in which the main characters have animal names symbolic of their natures—Voltore (the vulture), Corvino (the crow), Corbaccio (the raven), Mosca (the fly), and Volpone (the fox). The setting is Venice, the commercial capitol of Renaissance Europe, the same setting Shakespeare used in *The Merchant of Venice* for Shylock and Antonio. Venice suggested all of the greed, viciousness, and corruption that the English popular mind had come to associate with Italy.

Volpone's values are inverted, as his morning "prayer" made to his treasure clearly indicates. In his world, gold has assumed the rightful place of God, as it has for the legacy hunters as well. Volpone can deceive them only because they also worship gold. As one of the *avocatori* or judges mentions near the end of the play, "These possess wealth, as sick men possess fevers, / Which trulier may be said to possess them" (V.7.101–2). All of these characters are "actors" insofar as they hide their real intentions and motives behind masks of one sort or another. The clever Mosca plays two roles at the same time: agent of the various legacy hunters, and honest servant to Volpone. But Volpone is by far the most skillful of the play's actors. He once performed the role of Antinous at the Valois court; he plays the role of the mountebank Scoto of Mantua; he proposes to act out his sexual fantasies with Celia; he plays the part of an officer of the court; and his role as a terminally ill man underscores the morally sick and degenerate condition of all of the characters whose main concern is wealth. The legacy hunters, cynically acting their parts as concerned friends, will go to any lengths to get Volpone's money, including disinheriting a son, prostituting a wife, and betraying an oath of office.

Volpone and Mosca are infatuated by the power that their acting ability confers on them, especially the ease with which they can deceive others and inflict pain on them. Their avarice and their inability to control their fascination with acting finally leads to their exposure. Acting becomes a metaphor for deceit in this play, and the exposure in the last court scene unmasks the characters for what they truly are. Jonson has no faith in human ability to get to the bottom of such greed and deceit. As one of the *avocatori* puts it, "Mischiefs feed like beasts / till they be fat and then they bleed."

Jonson's temperament and the tenor of his play are vastly different from what we find in Shakespeare. Shakespeare tends to be generous and forgiving; Jonson remains unmoved to pity. *Volpone* ends looking forward to severe punishments. Volpone himself will be chained in the hospital for the incurable until he dies; Mosca will die as a galley slave in Venetian ships. Devastating sentences are meted out to the legacy hunters as well. Only Sir Politic Would-be and Lady Would-be are spared severe punishment. This pair seems somewhat out of place in this sardonic play, and that too is by design. They are satirical portraits of dull-witted English travelers, in over their heads among the sophisticated and corrupt Italians. In the play's catalog of animals, they are parrots, repeating what they hear without understanding. As outsiders, they provide examples of a softer kind of Jonsonian humor, mere mockery, and many amusing moments. Sir Pol delights with his bland stupidity and ludicrous "politic" devices. His inability to deceive anyone contrasts with Volpone's brilliance and consummate acting skill, as do the punishments they both receive. Sir Pol is simply humiliated and sent home—no doubt for his own good. Because Sir Pol and his wife are not central to the plot, their parts are sometimes cut in productions, but such cuts can make the play more harsh than even Jonson would have it.

Volpone; or, The Fox

BEN JONSON

EDITED BY RUSSELL A. FRASER AND NORMAN RABKIN

[DEDICATION]
TO THE
MOST NOBLE AND MOST EQUAL SISTERS
THE TWO FAMOUS UNIVERSITIES
FOR THEIR
LOVE AND ACCEPTANCE SHOWN TO HIS POEM
IN THE PRESENTATION
BEN JONSON
THE GRATEFUL ACKNOWLEDGER
DEDICATES BOTH IT AND HIMSELF.

CHARACTERS

VOLPONE, a magnifico
MOSCA, his parasite
VOLTORE, an advocate
CORBACCIO, an old gentleman
CORVINO, a merchant
BONARIO, a young gentleman, [son to Corbaccio]
[SIR] POLITIC WOULD-BE, a Knight
PEREGRINE, a gentleman traveler
NANO, a dwarf
CASTRONE, a eunuch

ANDROGYNO, a hermaphrodite
GREGE [i.e., mob]
COMMANDADORI, officers [of justice]
MERCATORI, three merchants
AVOCATORI, four magistrates
NOTARIO, the register
FINE MADAM WOULD-BE, The Knight's wife
CELIA, The Merchant's wife
SERVITORI, servants
[TWO WAITING-] WOMEN

THE SCENE: Venice

The Argument

V OLPONE, *childless, rich, feigns sick, despairs,*
O ffers his state to hopes of several heirs,
L ies languishing; his parasite receives
P resents of all, assures, deludes; then weaves
O ther cross plots, which ope themselves, are told.
N ew tricks for safety are sought; they thrive: when bold,
E ach tempts the other again, and all are sold.

Prologue

Now, luck yet send us, and a little wit
Will serve to make our play hit;
According to the palates° of the season
Here is rhyme, not empty of reason.
5   This we were bid to credit from our poet,
Whose true scope, if you would know it,
In all his poems still° hath been his measure,
To mix profit with your pleasure;
And not as some, whose throats their envy failing,
10   Cry hoarsely, All he writes is railing;
And when his plays come forth, think they can
    flout them,
With saying, He was a year about them.
To to this there needs no lie, but this his creature,
Which was two months since no feature:
And though through he dares give them five lives
15   to mend it,
'Tis known, five weeks fully penned it,
From his own hand, without a coadjutor,°
Novice, journeyman, or tutor.
Yet thus much I can give you as a token
20   Of his play's worth, no eggs are broken,
Nor quaking custards° with fierce teeth affrighted,
Where with Wherewith your rout° are so delighted;
Nor hales he in a gull° old ends° reciting,
To stop gaps in his loose writing;
25   With such a deal of monstrous and forced action,
As might make Bethlem a faction:°
Nor made he his play for jests stolen from each table,°
But makes jests to fit his fable;
And so presents quick° comedy refined,
30   As best critics have designed.
The laws of time, place, persons° he observeth,

PROLOGUE: ³ **palates** taste   ⁷ **still** continually   ¹⁷ **coadjutor**
collaborator   ²¹ **custards** like those set on the lord mayor's
table at city feasts for the fool to jump into   ²² **rout** mob
²³ **gull** fool   **old ends** stale saws and sayings   ²⁶ **make . . .
faction** turn the inhabitants of Bedlam, the London mad-
house, into supporters   ²⁷ **jests . . . table** plagiarized from
other authors   ²⁹ **quick** lively   ³¹ **laws . . . persons** unities,
prescribing a single day for the entire action, which must
occur in a single setting, and which must feature characters
who are decorous: faithful to the type they embody.

From no needful rule he swerveth.
    All gall and copperas° from his ink he draineth,
Only a little salt remaineth,
    Where with Wherewith he'll rub your cheeks,
        till red with laughter,   35
They shall look fresh a week after.

ACT I

Scene 1

[Enter VOLPONE *and* MOSCA.°*]*

VOLPONE: Good morning to the day; and next, my
        gold!
    Open the shrine, that I may see my saint.

*[*MOSCA *draws the curtain and discovers piles of gold,
plate, jewels, etc.]*

Hail the world's soul, and mine! more glad than is
The teeming earth to see the longed-for sun
Peep through the horns of the celestial Ram,°   5
Am I, to view thy splendor darkening his;
That lying here, amongst my other hoards,
Show'st like a flame by night, or like the day
Struck out of chaos, when all darkness fled
Unto the center. O thou son of Sol,°   10
But brighter than thy father, let me kiss,
With adoration, thee, and every relic
Of sacred treasure in this blessèd room.
Well did wise poets, by thy the glorious name,
Title that age° which they would have the best;   15
Thou being the best of things, and far transcending
All style tyle of joy, in children, parents, friends,
Or any other waking dream on earth:
Thy looks when they to Venus° did ascribe,
They should have given her twenty thousand
        Cupids;   20
Such are thy beauties and our loves! Dear saint,
Riches, the dumb god, that giv'st all men tongues,
That canst do naught, and yet mak'st men do all
        things;
The price of souls; even hell, with thee to boot,
Is made worth heaven. Thou art virtue, fame,   25
Honor, and all things else. Who can get thee,
He shall be noble, valiant, honest, wise—

---

³⁴ **copperas** vitriol, i.e., bitterness

ACT I, SCENE 1:   ˢ·ᵈ **Mosca** the fly   ⁵ **Ram** zodiacal sign of
Aries   ¹⁰ **Sol** the sun   ¹⁵ **age** Golden Age   ¹⁹ **Venus**
described as "golden" by classical poets

Mosca: And what he will, sir. Riches are in fortune
    A greater good than wisdom is in nautre nature.
30 Volpone: True, my beloved Mosca. Yet I glory
    More in the cunning purchase° of my wealth
    Than in the glad possession, since I gain
    No common way. I use no trade, no venture;°
    I wound no earth with ploughshares, fat no
      beasts
35   To feed the shambles; have no mills for iron,°
    Oil, corn, or men, to grind 'hem into powder;
    I blow no subtle glass,° expose no ships
    To threat'nings of the furrow-facèd sea;
    I turn no monies in the public bank,
                       Nor usure private.
40 Mosca: No sir, nor devour
    Soft prodigals. You shall ha' some will swallow
    A melting heir as glibly as your Dutch°
    Will pills of butter, and ne'er purge for it;
    Tear forth the fathers of poor families
45   Out of their beds, and coffin them alive
    In some kind clasping prison, where their bones
    May be forthcoming, when the flesh is rotten.
    But your sweet nature doth abhor these courses;
    You loathe the widow's or the orphan's tears
    Should wash your pavements, or their piteous
50   cries
    Ring in your roofs, and beat the air for vengeance.
  Volpone: Right, Mosca; I do loathe it.
  Mosca: And, besides, sir,
    You are not like the thresher that doth stand
    With a huge flail, watching a heap of corn,
55   And, hungry, dares not taste the smallest grain,
    But feeds on mallows, and such bitter herbs;
    Nor like the merchant, who hath filled his vaults
    With Romagnia,° and rich Candian° wines,
    Yet drinks the lees of Lombard's vinegar:
60   You will not lie in straw, whilst moths and worms
    Feed on your sumptuous hangings and soft beds;
    You know the use of riches, and dare give now
    From that bright heap, to me, your poor observer,°
    Or to your dwarf, or your hermaphrodite,
65   Your eunuch, or what other household trifle°
    Your pleasure allows maintenance—
  Volpone: Hold thee, Mosca,
    Take of my hand; thou strik'st on truth in all,
    And they are envious° term thee parasite.
    Call forth my dwarf, my eunuch, and my fool,
    And let 'hem make me sport.

[Exit Mosca.]

                        What should I do,   70
But cocker up my genius,° and live free
To all delights my fortune calls me to?
I have no wife, no parent, child, ally,
To give my substance to: but whom I make
Must be my heir; and this makes men observe° me: 75
This draws new clients daily to my house,
Women and men of every sex and age,
That bring me presents, send me plate, coin, jewels
With hope that when I die (which they expect
Each greedy minute) it shall then return   80
Tenfold upon them; whilst some, covetous
Above the rest, seek to engross° me whole,
And counter-work the one unto the other,
Contend in gifts, as they would seem in love.
All which I suffer,° playing with their hopes,   85
And am content to coin 'hem into profit,
And look upon their kindness, and take more,
And look on that; still bearing them in hand,°
Letting the cherry knock against their lips,°
And draw it by their mouths, and back again.— 90
How now!

[Re-enter Mosca *with* Nano, Androgyno, *and*
Castrone.*]*

Nano: Now, room for fresh gamesters, who do will
    you to know,
They do bring you neither play nor university show;
And therefore do intreat you that whatsoever
    they rehearse,
May not fare a whit the worse, for the false pace
    of the verse.°   95
If you wonder at this, you will wonder more ere
    we pass,
For know, here° is enclosed the soul of
    Pythagoras,
That juggler divine, as hereafter shall follow;
Which soul, fast and loose, sir, came first from
    Apollo,
And was breathed into Aethalides,° Mercurius his
    son,   100
Where it had the gift to remember all that ever
    was done.
From thence it fled forth, and made quick trans-
    migration

---

31 cunning purchase ingenious acquisition **33 venture** speculation **35 no . . . iron** Volpone does not waste timber **37 glass**
for which Venice and its environs were famous **42 Dutch** supposed to be fond of butter **58 Romagnia** sweet Greek wine;
accent on next-to-last syllable **Candian** Malmsey wine from
Greece and Crete (Candy) **63 observer** follower **65 trifle**
hanger-on **68 envious** "who" is understood to follow

71 cocker . . . genius indulge my disposition **75 observe** dote
on **82 engross** appropriate **85 suffer** endure **88 bearing . . .**
hand beguiling them **89 Letting . . . lips** as in the game of
bob-cherry, in which one tries to bite the suspended fruit **95**
false . . . verse loose four-stressed verse, familiar from the
medieval moralities **97 here** pointing to Androgyno **100**
Aethalides herald of the Argonauts, who inherited perfect
memory from his father Mercury

To goldy-locked Euphorbus,° who was killed in
  good fashion,
At the siege of old Troy by the cuckold of Sparta.
105 Hermotimus° was next (I find it in my charta),
To whom it did pass, where no sooner it was
  missing,
But with one Pyrrhus of Delos it learned to go a-
  fishing;
And thence did it enter the sophist of Greece.°
From Pythagore, she went into a beautiful piece,
Hight Aspasia,° the meretrix;° and the next toss
110 of her
Was again of a whore, she became a philosopher,
Crates the cynic,° as itself° doth relate it:
Since kings, knights, and beggars, knaves, lords
  and fools gat it,
Besides ox and ass, camel, mule, goat, and brock;°
115 In all which it hath spoke , as in the cobbler's cock.
But I come not here to discourse of that matter,
Or his one, two, or three,° or his great oath, "By
  Quater!"°
His musics, his trigon, his golden thigh,°
Or his telling how elements shift; but I
120 Would ask, how of late thou hast suffered
  translation,
And shifted thy coat in these days of reformation.°
ANDROGYNO: Like one of the reformed, a fool, as you
  see,
  Counting all old doctrine° heresy.
NANO: But not on thine own forbid meats hast thou
  ventured?
125 ANDROGYNO: On fish, when first a Carthusian° I entered.
NANO: Why, then thy dogmatical silence hath left thee?
ANDROGYNO: Of that an obstreperous lawyer bereft me.
NANO: O wonderful change, when sir lawyer forsook
  thee!

For Pythagore's sake, what body then took thee?
ANDROGYNO: A good dull mule.
NANO: And how! by that means 130
  Thou wert brought to allow of the eating of beans?°
ANDROGYNO: Yes.
NANO: But from the mule into whom didst thou
  pass?
ANDROGYNO: Into a very strange beast, by some writ-
  ers called an ass;
  By others a precise, pure, illuminate brother°
  Of those devour flesh, and sometimes one another; 135
  And will drop you forth a libel, or a sanctified lie,
  Betwixt every spoonful of a nativity-pie.°
NANO: Now quit thee, for heaven, of that profane
  nation,
  And gently° report thy next transmigration.
ANDROGYNO: To the same that I am.
NANO: A creature of delight, 140
  And, what is more than a fool, a hermaphrodite!
  Now, pray thee, sweet soul, in all thy variation,
  Which body wouldst thou choose to take up thy
  station?
ANDROGYNO: Troth, this I am in: even here would I
  tarry.
NANO: 'Cause here the delight of each sex thou canst
  vary! 145
ANDROGYNO: Alas, those pleasures be stale and for-
  saken.
  No, 'tis your fool wherewith I am so taken,
  The only one creature that I can call blessèd;
  For all other forms I have proved most distressèd.
NANO: Spoke true, as thou wert in Pythagoras still, 150
  This learnèd opinion we celebrate will,
  Fellow eunuch, as behoves us, with our wit and art,
  To dignify that whereof ourselves are so great and
  special a part.
VOLPONE: Now, very, very pretty. Mosca, this
  Was thy invention?
MOSCA: If it please my patron, 155
  Not else.
VOLPONE: It doth, good Mosca.
MOSCA: Then it was, sir.

SONG

Fools, they are the only nation
Worth men's envy or admiration;
Free from care or sorrow-taking,
Selves and others merry making: 160
All they speak or do is sterling.
Your fool he is your great man's darling,

---

[103] **Euphorbus** Trojan hero, slain by Menelaus, "the cuckold of Sparta"   [105] **Hermotimus** mentioned with Pyrrhus of Delos in Diogenes Laertius. (What Jonson is after in this catalogue of those who harbor the soul of Pythagoras is sonority more than sense.)   [108] **sophist of Greece** Pythagoras   [110] **Highest Hight Aspasia** Called Aspasia, the mistress of Pericles   **meretrix** whore, as in *Cambyses*   [112] **Crates the cynic** philosopher of Thebes   **itself** Gallus, the "cobbler's cock" in Lucian's dialogue, is host to the soul of Pythagoras, who relates his transmigrations to his master.   [114] **brock** badger   [117] **one . . . three** Number is the principle of harmony and morality in the Pythagorean system   **Quater** The *quaternio* represented the number ten or decade as a four-tiered triangle (Trigon) of dots   [118] **golden thigh** this ancient tradition is glanced at in *The Alchemist*, and remembered by Yeats in "Among School Children"   [121] **reformation** i.e., the Protestant Reformation   [122] **old doctrine** Roman Catholic   [125] **Carthusian** This severe order prescribed fish instead of meat; the Pythagoreans disallowed even fish, as also speaking for a five-year period.

[131] **beans** forbidden by Pythagoras   [134] **illuminate brother** "inspired" Puritan   [136] **nativity-pie** Christmas-pie (the "precise" Puritans were averse to the suffix "mass")   [139] **gently** civilly

And your ladies' sport and pleasure;
Tongue and babble are his treasure.
165 E'en his face begetteth laughter,
And he speaks truth free from slaughter.°
He's the grace of every feast,
And sometimes the chiefest guest;
Hath his trencher° and his stool,
170 When wit waits upon the fool.
Oh, who would not be
He, he, he?

[One knocks without.]

VOLPONE: Who's that? Away! Look, Mosca.
MOSCA: Fool, begone!

[Exeunt NANO, CASTRONE, and ANDROGYNO.]

'Tis Signior Voltore, the advocate.
I know him by his knock.
175 VOLPONE: Fetch me my gown,
My furs, and night-caps; say my couch is changing.
And let him entertain himself awhile
Without i' the gallery.

[Exit MOSCA.]

                    Now, now my clients
Begin their visitation! Vulture, kite,°
180 Raven, and gorcrow,° all my birds of prey,
That think me turning carcass, now they come:
I am not for 'hem yet.

[Re-enter MOSCA.]

                    How now! the news?
MOSCA: A piece of plate, sir.
VOLPONE: Of what bigness?
MOSCA: Huge,
Massy, and antique, with your name inscribed,
And arms engraven.
185 VOLPONE: Good! and not a fox
Stretched on the earth, with fine delusive sleights,
Mocking a gaping crow? ha, Mosca!
MOSCA: Sharp, sir.
VOLPONE: Give me my furs. Why dost thou laugh so,
    man?
MOSCA: I cannot choose, sir, when I apprehend
190 What thoughts he has without now, as he walks:
That this might be the last gift he should give;
That this would fetch you; if you died today,
And gave him all, what he should be tomorrow;

What large return would come of all his ventures
How he should worshipped be, and reverenced;   195
Ride with his furs, and foot-cloths, waited on
By herds of fools and clients, have clear way
Made for his him mule,° as lettered as himself,
Be called the great and learnèd advocate;
And then concludes, there's nought impossible.   200
VOLPONE: Yes yes, to be learnèd, Mosca.
MOSCA: Oh, no: rich
Implies it. Hood an ass with reverend purple,
So you can hide his two ambitious° ears,
And he shall pass for a cathedral doctor.°
VOLPONE: My caps, my caps, good Mosca. Fetch him
    in.   205
MOSCA: Stay, sir; your ointment for your eyes.
VOLPONE: That's true;
Dispatch, dispatch: I long to have possession
Of my new present.
MOSCA: That, and thousands more,
I hope to see you lord of.
VOLPONE: Thanks, kind Mosca.
MOSCA ANO: And that, when I am lost in blended dust,   210
And hundreds such as I am, in succession—
VOLPONE: Nay, that were too much, Mosca.
MOSCA: You shall live
Still to delude these harpies.
VOLPONE: Loving Mosca!
'Tis well: my pillow now, and let him enter.

[Exit MOSCA.]

Now, my feignèd cough, my phthisic,° and my gout,   215
My apoplexy, palsy, and catarrhs,
Help, with your forcèd functions, this my posture,
Wherein, this three year, I have milked their hopes.
He comes; I hear him—Uh *[Coughing]* uh, uh! uh!
Oh—

[Re-enter MOSCA with VOLTORE.]

MOSCA: You still are what you were, sir. Only you,   220
Of all the rest, are he commands his love,
And you do wisely to preserve it thus,
With early visitation, and kind notes°
Of your good meaning to him, which, I know,
Cannot but come most grateful. Patron! sir!   225
Here's Signior Voltore is come—
VOLPONE: *[Faintly]*   What say you?
MOSCA: Sir, Signior Voltore is come this morning
To visit you.
VOLPONE: I thank him.
MOSCA: And hath brought

---

166 **free from slaughter** with impunity ("slaughter" and "laughter" are understood to rhyme)   169 **trencher** wooden plate   179 **kite** Lady Would-be, who is called subsequently a she-wolf   180 **gorcrow** carrion crow

198 **mule** appropriate to an advocate   203 **ambitious** prominent   204 **cathedral doctor** one who holds a professorial chair   215 **phthisic** consumption   223 **notes** tokens, i.e., the piece of plate

A piece of antique plate, bought of St. Mark,°
With which he here presents you.

230 VOLPONE: He is welcome.
Pray him to come more often.

MOSCA: Yes.

VOLTORE: What says he?

MOSCA: He thanks you, and desires you see him
often.

VOLPONE: Mosca.

MOSCA: My patron!

VOLPONE: Bring him near, where is he?
I long to feel his hand.

MOSCA: The plate is here, sir.

VOLTORE: How fare you, sir?

235 VOLPONE: I thank you, Signior Voltore;
Where is the plate? Mine eyes are bad.

VOLTORE: I'm sorry
To to see you still thus weak.

MOSCA: [Aside]   That he is not weaker.

VOLPONE: You are too munificent.

VOLTORE: No, sir; would to heaven,
I could as well give health to you, as that plate!

VOLPONE: You give, sir, what you can; I thank you.

240   Your love
Hath taste in this, and shall not be unanswered.
I pray you see me often.

VOLTORE: Yes, I shall, sir.

VOLPONE: Be not far from me.

MOSCA: Do you observe that, sir?

VOLPONE: Hearken unto me still;° it will concern you.

245 MOSCA: You are a happy man, sir; know your good.

VOLPONE: I cannot now last long—

MOSCA: You are his heir, sir.

VOLTORE: Am I?

VOLPONE: I feel me going. Uh! uh! uh! uh!
I'm sailing to my port, uh! uh! uh! uh!
And I am glad I am so near my haven.

250 MOSCA: Alas, kind gentleman! well, we must all go—

VOLPONE: But, Mosca—

MOSCA: Age will conquer.

VOLTORE: Pray thee, hear me.
Am I inscribed his heir for certain?

MOSCA: Are you!
I do beseech you, sir, you will vouchsafe
To write me i' your family.° All my hopes

255   Depend upon your worship. I am lost
Except the rising sun do shine on me.

VOLTORE: It shall both shine, and warm thee, Mosca.

MOSCA: Sir,
I am a man that have not done your love
All all the worst offices: here I wear your keys,

See all your coffers and your caskets locked,   260
Keep the poor inventory of your jewels,
Your plate, and monies; am your steward, sir,
Husband your goods here.

VOLTORE: But but am I sole Isole heir?

MOSCA: Without a partner, sir: confirmed this morning.
The wax is warm yet, and the ink scarce dry   265
Upon the parchment.

VOLTORE: Happy, happy me!
By what good chance, sweet Mosca?

MOSCA: Your desert, sir;
I know no second cause.

VOLTORE: Thy modesty
Is loath to know it; well, we shall requite it.

MOSCA: He ever liked your course, sir; that first took
him.   270
I oft have heard him say how he admired
Men of your large° profession, that could speak
To every cause, and the things mere° contraries,
Till they were hoarse again, yet all be law;
That, with most quick agility, could turn,   275
And return; make knots, and undo them;°
Give forked counsel; take provoking° gold
On either hand, and put it up;° these men,
He knew, would thrive with their humility.
And, for his part, he thought he should be blest   280
To have his heir of such a suffering spirit,
So wise, so grave, of so perplexed° a tongue,
And loud withal, that would not wag, nor scarce
Lie still without a fee; when every word
Your worship but lets fall is a cecchine!°   285

[Another knocks.]

Who's that? One knocks. I would not have you
seen sir.
And yet—pretend you came, came and went in
haste;
I'll fashion an excuse—and, gentle sir,
When you do come to swim in golden lard,
Up to the arms in honey, that your chin   290
Is borne up stiff with fatness of the flood,
Think on your vassal, but remember me:
I ha' not been your worst of clients.

VOLTORE: Mosca!—

MOSCA: When will you have your inventory brought,
sir?
Or see a copy of the will?—Anon!°   295

---

228 **of St. Mark** from a goldsmith in the Piazza San Marco   **244**
still continually   **254 write . . . family** make me a member of
your household

272 large generous   **273 mere** absolute   **276 And . . . them** The
voice pause after "return" counts as a syllable in the making
of the iambic pentameter line   **277 provoking** engendering;
money that works to a purpose, as by bribery brilbery   **278**
put . . . up pocket it   **282 perplexed** ambiguous   **285 cecchine**
chequin, Venetian gold coin   **295 Anon** Right away (to
Corbaccio)

I'll bring 'hem to you, sir. Away, begone,
Put business i' your face.

[Exit VOLTORE.*]*

VOLPONE: Excellent Mosca!
   Come hither, let me kiss thee.
MOSCA: Keep you still, sir.
   Here is Corbaccio.
VOLPONE: Set the plate away.
300   The vulture's gone, and the old raven's come.°
MOSCA: Betake you to your silence, and your sleep.
   Stand there and multiply.°

[Putting the plate with the rest of the treasure.]

                                   Now we shall see
   A wretch who is indeed more impotent
   Than this can feign to be; yet hopes to hop
   Over his grave.

[Enter CORBACCIO.*]*

305   Signior Corbaccio!
   You're very welcome, sir.
CORBACCIO: How does your patron?
MOSCA: Troth, as he did, sir; no amends.
CORBACCIO: What! mends he?
MOSCA: No, sir, he is rather worse.
CORBACCIO: That's well. Where is he?
MOSCA: Upon his couch, sir, newly fall'n asleep.
CORBACCIO: Does he sleep well?
310   MOSCA: No wink, sir, all this night,
   Nor yesterday; but slumbers.°
CORBACCIO: Good! he should take
   Some counsel of physicians. I have brought him
   An opiate here, from mine own doctor.
MOSCA: He will not hear of drugs.
CORBACCIO: Why? I myself
315   Stood by while it was made, saw all the ingredients,
   And know it cannot but most gently work.
   My life for his, 'tis but to make him sleep.
VOLPONE: *[Aside]* Ay, his last sleep, if he would take it.
MOSCA: Sir,
   He has no faith in physic.°
CORBACCIO: Say you, say you?
320   MOSCA: He has no faith in physic. He does think
   Most of your doctors are the greater danger,
   And worse disease, to escape. I often have
   Heard him protest that your physician
   Should never be his heir.
CORBACCIO: Not I his heir?
MOSCA: Not your physician, sir.
325   CORBACCIO: Oh, no, no, no.

I do not mean it.
MOSCA: No, sir, nor their fees
   He cannot brook. He says they flay a man
   Before they kill him.
CORBACCIO: Right, I do conceive° you.
MOSCA: And then they do it by experiment,°
   For which the law not only doth absolve 'hem   330
   But gives them great reward: and he is loath
   To hire his death so.
CORBACCIO: It is true, they kill
   With as much license as a judge.
MOSCA: Nay, more;
   For he but kills, sir, where the law condemns,
   And these can kill him too.
CORBACCIO: Ay, or me,   335
   Or any man. How does his apoplex?
   Is that strong on him still?
MOSCA: Most violent.
   His speech is broken, and his eyes are set,
   His face drawn longer than 'twas wont—
CORBACCIO: How! how!
   Stronger than he was wont?
MOSCA: No, sir, his face   340
   Drawn longer than 'twas wont.
CORBACCIO: Oh, good!
MOSCA: His mouth
   Is ever gaping, and his eyelids hang.
CORBACCIO: Good.
MOSCA: A freezing numbness stiffens all his joints,
   And make the color of his flesh like lead.
CORBACCIO: 'Tis good.
MOSCA: His pulse beats slow, and dull.
CORBACCIO: Good good symptoms still.   345
MOSCA: And from his brain—
CORBACCIO: Ha! how! not from his brain?
MOSCA: Yes, sir, and from his brain.
CORBACCIO: I conceive you; good.
MOSCA: Flows a cold sweat, with a continual rheum,°
   Forth the resolvèd° corners of his eyes.
CORBACCIO: Is't possible? Yet I am better, ha!   350
   How does he with the swimming of his head?
MOSCA: Oh, sir, 'tis past the scotomy;° he now
   Hath lost his feeling, and hath left° to snort.
   You hardly can perceive him, that he breathes.
CORBACCIO: Excellent, excellent! sure I shall outlast him.   355
   This makes me young again, a score of years.
MOSCA: I was a-coming for you, sir.
CORBACCIO: Has he made his will?
   What has he given me?
MOSCA: No, sir.
CORBACCIO: Nothing! ha?

°°°**vulture, raven** Voltore and Corbaccio   °°¹**Stand . . . multi-**
ply to the plate   ³¹¹**slumbers** dozes   ³¹⁹**physics** medicine

³²⁸**conceive** understand   ³²⁹**by experiment** as an experiment
³⁴⁸**rheum** flowing   ³⁴⁹**Forth . . . resolvèd** From the dissolving
³⁵²**scotomy** dizziness   ³⁵³**left** left off; stopped snoring

MOSCA: He has not made his will, sir.
CORBACCIO: Oh, oh, oh!
360   What then did Voltore, the lawyer, here?
MOSCA: He smelt a carcass, sir, when he but heard
       My master was about his testament;
       As I did urge him to it for your good—
CORBACCIO: He came unto him, did he? I thought so.
365 MOSCA: Yes, and presented him this piece of plate.
CORBACCIO: To be his heir?
MOSCA: I do not know, sir.
CORBACCIO: True:
       I know it too.
MOSCA: By your own scale, sir.
CORBACCIO: [Aside]   Well,
       I shall prevent° him yet.—See, Mosca, look,
       Here I have brought a bag of bright cecchines,
       Will quite weigh down his plate.
370 MOSCA: Yea, marry,° sir.
       This is true physic, this your sacred medicine;°
       No talk of opiates to this great elixir!
CORBACCIO: 'Tis *aurum palpabile, if not* potabile.°
MOSCA: It shall be ministered to him in his bowl.
CORBACCIO: Ay, do, do, do.
375 MOSCA: Most blessèd cordial!
       This will recover him.
CORBACCIO: Yes, do, do, do.
MOSCA: I think it were not best, sir.
CORBACCIO: What?
MOSCA: To recover him.
CORBACCIO: Oh, no, no, no; by no means.
MOSCA: Why, sir, this
       Will work some strange effect, if he but feel it.
CORBACCIO: 'Tis true, therefore forbear; I'll take my
380   venture:°
       Give me it again.
MOSCA: At no hand;° pardon me.
       You shall not do yourself that wrong, sir. I
       Will so advise you, you shall have it all.
CORBACCIO: How?
MOSCA: All, sir; 'tis your right, your own; no man
385   Can claim a part: 'tis yours without a rival,
       Decreed by destiny.
CORBACCIO: How, how, good Mosca?
MOSCA: I'll tell you sir. This fit he shall recover.
CORBACCIO: I do conceive you.
MOSCA: And on first advantage
       Of his gained° sense, will I re-importune him
390   Unto the making of his testament:
       And show him this.

[*Pointing to the money.*]

CORBACCIO: Good, good.
MOSCA: 'Tis better yet,
       If you will hear, sir,
CORBACCIO: Yes, with all my heart.
MOSCA: Now would I counsel you, make home with
       speed.
       There, frame a will, whereto you shall inscribe
       My master your sole heir.
CORBACCIO: And disinherit   395
       My son!
MOSCA: Oh, sir, the better: for that color°
       Shall make it much more taking.°
CORBACCIO: Oh, but° color?
MOSCA: This will, sir, you shall send it unto me.
       Now, when I come to enforce,° as I will do,
       Your cares, your watchings, and your many prayers,   400
       Your more than many gifts, your this day's pre-
       sent,
       And last, produce your will; where, without
       thought,
       Or least regard, unto your proper issue,°
       A son so brave,° and highly meriting,
       The stream of your diverted° love hath thrown you   405
       Upon my master, and made him your heir:
       He cannot be so stupid, or stone-dead,
       But out of conscience and mere gratitude—
CORBACCIO: He must pronounce me his?
MOSCA: 'Tis true.
CORBACCIO: This plot
       Did I think on before.
MOSCA: I do believe it.   410
CORBACCIO: Do you not believe it?
MOSCA: Yes, sir.
CORBACCIO: Mine own project.
MOSCA: Which, when he hath done, sir—
CORBACCIO: Published me his heir?
MOSCA: And you so certain to survive him—
CORBACCIO: Ay.
MOSCA: Being so lusty° a man—
CORBACCIO: 'Tis true.
MOSCA: Yes, sir—
CORBACCIO: I thought on that too. See, how he
       should be   415
       The very organ to express my thoughts!
MOSCA: You have not only done yourself a good—
CORBACCIO: But multiplied it on my son.
MOSCA: 'Tis right, sir.
CORBACCIO: Still, my invention.
MOSCA: 'Las, sir! heaven knows,
       It hath been all my study, all my care   420
       (I e'en grow gray withal), how to work things—

---

³⁶⁷ **prevent** forestall   ³⁷⁰ **marry** an interjection—"indeed!"
³⁷¹ **medicine** disyllabic   ³⁷³ **'Tis . . . potabile** The sovereign
remedy is gold that can be felt if not drunk.   ³⁸⁰ **venture** gift
³⁸¹ **at . . . hand** by no means   ³⁸⁹ **gained** regained

³⁹⁶ **color** appearance   ³⁹⁷ **taking** persuasive   **but** only   ³⁹⁹
enforce urge   ⁴⁰³ **proper issue** own child   ⁴⁰⁴ **brave** fine
⁴⁰⁵ **diverted** turned (from your son)   ⁴¹⁴ **lusty** vigorous

CORBACCIO: I do conceive, sweet Mosca.
MOSCA: You are he
  For whom I labor here.
CORBACCIO: Ay, do, do, do:
  I'll straight about it.
MOSCA: [*Aside*]   Rook go with you,° raven!
CORBACCIO: I know thee honest.
MOSCA: [*Aside*]   You do lie, sir!
425 CORBACCIO:
MOSCA: [*Aside*] Your knowledge is no better than
      your ears, sir.
CORBACCIO: I do not doubt to be a father to thee.
MOSCA: [*Aside*] Nor I to gull° my brother of his bless-
      ing.
CORBACCIO: I may ha' my youth restored to me, why
      not?
MOSCA: [*Aside*] Your worship is a precious ass!
430 CORBACCIO: What sayest thou?
MOSCA: I do desire your worship to make haste, sir.
CORBACCIO: 'Tis done, 'tis done; I go.

[*Exit; VOLPONE leaps from his couch.*]

VOLPONE: Oh, I shall burst!
  Let out my sides, let out my sides—
MOSCA: Contain
  Your flux° of laughter, sir: you know this hope
435 Is such a bait, it covers any hook.
VOLPONE: Oh, but thy working, and thy placing it!
  I cannot hold; good rascal, let me kiss thee:
  I never knew thee in so rare a humor.
MOSCA: Alas, sir, I but do as I am taught;
440 Follow your grave instructions; give 'hem words;
  Pour oil into their ears, and send them hence.
VOLPONE: 'Tis true, 'tis true. What a rare punishment
  Is avarice to itself!
MOSCA: Ay, with our help, sir.
VOLPONE: So many cares, so many maladies,
445 So many fears attending on old age.
  Yea, death so often called on, as no wish
  Can be more frequent with 'hem, their limbs faint,
  Their senses dull, their seeing, hearing, going,°
  All dead before them; yea, their very teeth,
450 Their instruments of eating, failing them:
  Yet this is reckoned life! Nay, here was one,
  Is not now gone home, that wishes to live longer!
  Feels not his gout, nor palsy; feigns himself
  Younger by scores of years, flatters his age
455 With confident belying it, hopes he may
  With charms like Aeson,° have his youth restored;
  And with these thoughts so battens, as if fate

Would be as easily cheated on° as he,
And all turns air!

[*Another knocks.*]

                          Who's that there, now? A third!
MOSCA: Close, to your couch again; I hear his voice.   460
  It is Corvino,° our spruce merchant.

And—[*VOLPONE lies down as before.*]

VOLPONE: Dead.
MOSCA: Another, bout, sir, with your eyes.° Who's
  there?

[*Enter CORVINO.*]

Signior Corvino! Come most wished for! Oh,
  How happy were you, if you knew it, now!
CORVINO: Why? What? Wherein?
MOSCA: The tardy hour is come, sir.   465
CORVINO: He is not dead?
MOSCA: Not dead, sir, but as good;
  He knows no man.
CORVINO: How shall I do then?
MOSCA: Why, sir?
CORVINO: I have brought him here a pearl.
MOSCA: Perhaps he has
  So much remembrance left as to know you, sir.
  He still calls on you: nothing but your name   470
  Is in his mouth. Is your pearl orient,° sir?
CORVINO: Venice was never owner of the like.
VOLPONE: [*Faintly*] Signior Corvino!
MOSCA: Hark.
VOLPONE: Signior Corvino.
MOSCA: He calls you; step and give it him. He's here,
    sir.
  And he has brought you a rich pearl.
CORVINO: How do you, sir?   475
  Tell him it doubles the twelve caract.°
MOSCA: Sir,
  He cannot understand, his hearing's gone;
  And yet it comforts him to see you—
CORVINO: Say
  I have a diamond for him, too.
MOSCA: Best show it, sir:
  Put it into his hand; 'tis only there   480
  He apprehends. He has his feeling yet.
  See how he grasps it!
CORVINO: 'Las, good gentleman!
  How pitiful the sight is!
MOSCA: Tut, forget, sir.

---

⁴²⁴ **Rook . . . you** May you be rooked, cheated; with a pun on
"rook" = "crow," Latin *corvus* ("raven") ⁴²⁸ **gull** cheat ⁴³⁴
flux outburst ⁴⁴⁸ **going** ability to walk ⁴⁵⁶ **Aeson** whom
Medea restored to youth

⁴⁵⁸ **cheated on** cheated ⁴⁶⁰ **Corvino** crow ⁴⁶² **Another... eyes**
Mosca anoints Volpone's eyes, to make them clear ⁴⁷¹ **orient**
especially lustrous ⁴⁷⁶ **caract** carat

The weeping of an heir should still be laughter
Under a visor.°
485 CORVINO: Why, am I his heir?
MOSCA: Sir, I am sworn, I may not show the will
    Till he be dead; but here has been Corbaccio,
    Here has been Voltore, here were others too,
    I cannot number 'hem, they were so many;
490 All gaping here for legacies. But I,
    Taking the vantage of his naming you,
    "Signior Corvino, Signior Corvino," took
    Paper, and pen, and ink, and there I asked him
    Whom he would have his heir! "Corvino." Who
495 Should be executor? "Corvino." And
    To any question he was silent to,
    I still interpreted the nods he made,
    Through weakness, for consent: and sent home
        th' others,
    Nothing bequeathed them, but to cry and curse.
CORVINO: Oh, my dear Mosca.

[They embrace]

500   Does he not perceive us?
MOSCA: No more than a blind harper. He knows no
        man,
    No face of friend, nor name of any servant,
    Who 'twas that fed him last, or gave him drink:
    Not those he had begotten, or brought up,
    Can he remember.
CORVINO: Has he the children?
505 MOSCA: Bastards,
    Some dozen, or more, that he begot on beggars,
    Gypsies, and Jews, and black-moors, when he
        was drunk.
    Knew you not that, sir? 'Tis the common fable.
    The dwarf, the fool, the eunuch, are all his.
510 He's the true father of his family,°
    In all save° me:—but he has given 'hem nothing.
CORVINO: That's well, that's well! Art sure he does
        not hear us?
MOSCA: Sure, sir! why, look you, credit your own sense.
    [Shouts in VOLPONE'S *'sear.]* The pox° approach,
        and add to your diseases,
515 If it would send you hence the sooner, sir,
    For your incontinence, it hath deserved it
    Throughly and throughly, and the plague to boot!—
    You may come near, sir.—Would you would once
        close
    Those filthy eyes of yours, that flow with slime,
520 Like two frog-pits; and those same hanging cheeks,
    Covered with hide instead of skin—Nay, help,° sir—
    That look like frozen dish-clouts set on end!

CORVINO: Or like an old smoked wall, on which the rain
    Ran down in streaks!
MOSCA: Excellent, sir! Speak out:
    You may be louder yet; a culverin°   525
    Dischargèd in his ear would hardly bore it.
CORVINO: His nose is like a common sewer, still run-
    ning.
MOSCA: 'Tis good! and what his mouth!
CORVINO: A very draught.
MOSCA: Oh, stop it up—
CORVINO: By no means.
MOSCA: Pray you, let me.
    Faith I could stifle him rarely with a pillow   530
    As well as any woman that should keep° him.
CORVINO: Do as you will; but I'll begone.
MOSCA: Be so;
    It is your presence makes him last so long.
CORVINO: I pray you use no violence.
MOSCA: No, sir! why?
    Why should you be thus scrupulous, pray you, sir?   535
CORVINO: Nay, at your discretion.
MOSCA: Well, good sir, be gone.
CORVINO: I will not trouble him now to take my pearl.°
MOSCA: Puh! nor your diamond. What a needless care.
    Is this afflicts you? Is not all here yours?
    Am not I here, whom you have made your creature?   540
    That owe my being to you?
CORVINO: Grateful Mosca!
    Thou art my friend, my fellow, my companion,
    My partner, and shalt share in all my fortunes.
MOSCA: Excepting one.
CORVINO: What's that?
MOSCA: Your gallant wife, sir.

[Exit CORVINO.*]*

    Now is he gone. We had no other means   545
    To shoot him hence but this.
VOLPONE: My divine Mosca!
    Thou hast today outgone thyself.

[Another knocks.]

                                        Who's there?
    I will be troubled with no more. Prepare
    Me music, dances, banquets, all delights.
    The Turk is not more sensual in his pleasures   550
    Than will Volpone. Let me see; a pearl!
    A diamond! plate! cecchines! good morning's pur-
        chase.°
    Why, this is better than rob churches, yet;
    Or fat,° by eating, once a month, a man—
    Who is 't?

---

⁴⁸⁴ **visor** mask (of pretended grief)   ⁵¹⁰ **family** household of
servants   ⁵¹¹ **save** except   ⁵¹⁴ **pox** veneral venereal disease
⁵²¹ **help** i.e., to abuse Volpone

⁵²⁵ **culverin** small cannon   ⁵³¹ **keep** care for (sardonically)
⁵³⁷ **pearl** which Volpone is holding   ⁵⁵² **purchase** loot   ⁵⁵⁴ **fat**
grow fat

555 MOSCA: The beauteous Lady Would-be, sir,
        Wife to the English knight, Sir Politic° Would-be,
        (This is the style, sir, is directed me,)
        Hath sent to know how you have slept tonight,
        And if you would be visited?
     VOLPONE: Not now:
        Some three hours hence.
560 MOSCA: I told the squire° so much.
     VOLPONE: When I am high with mirth and wine;
            then, then.
        'Fore heaven, I wonder at the desperate valor
        Of the bold English, that they dare let loose
        Their wives to all encounters!
     MOSCA: Sir, this knight
565   Had not his name for nothing, he is politic,
        And knows, howe'er his wife affect strange airs,
        She hath not yet the face° to be dishonest.°
        But had she Signior Corvino's wife's face—
     VOLPONE: Has she so rare a face?
     MOSCA: Oh, sir, the wonder,
570   The blazing star of Italy! a wench
        O' the first year,° a beauty ripe as harvest!
        Whose skin is whiter than a swan all over,
        Than silver, snow, or lilies; a soft lip,
        Would tempt you to eternity of kissing!
575   And flesh that melteth in the touch to blood!°
        Bright as your gold, and lovely as your gold!
     VOLPONE: Why had not I known this before?
     MOSCA: Alas, sir,
        Myself but yesterday discovered it.
     VOLPONE: How might I see her?
     MOSCA: Oh, not possible;
580   She's kept as warily as is your gold;
        Never does come abroad, never takes air
        But at a window.° All her looks are sweet,
        As the first grapes or cherries, and are watched
        As near° as they are.
     VOLPONE: I must see her.
     MOSCA: Sir,
585   There is a guard of ten spies thick upon her,
        All his whole household; each of which is set
        Upon his fellow, and have all their charge,
        When he goes out, when he comes in, examined.
     VOLPONE: I will go see her, though but at her window.
     MOSCA: In some disguise then.
590 VOLPONE: That is true; I must
        Maintain mine own shape still the same. We'll
            think.

[Exeunt.]

---

556 **Politic** Crafty   560 **squire** gentleman, with the scornful
implication of "pander"   567 **face** (1) beauty, (2) impudence
dishonest unchaste   571 **o' . . . year** Without blemish   575
blood passion   582 **window** here and hereafter, for "win-
dore" in original   584 **near** closely

ACT II

Scene 1

[Enter SIR POLITIC WOULD-BE *and* PEREGRINE.°*]*

SIR POLITIC: Sir, to a wise man, all the world's his soil.°
    It is not Italy, nor France, nor Europe,
    That must bound me, if my fates call me forth.
    Yet I protest, it is no salt° desire
    Of seeing countries, shifting a religion,   5
    Nor any disaffection to the state
    Where I was bred, and unto which I owe
    My dearest plots, hath brought me out; much less
    That idle, antique, stale, gray-headed project
    Of knowing men's minds and manners, with
        Ulysses!   10
    But a peculiar humor of my wife's
    Laid for this height° of Venice, to observe,
    To quote,° to learn the language, and so forth—
    I hope you travel, sir, with license?°
PEREGRINE: Yes.
SIR POLITIC: I dare the safelier converse—How long,
    sir,   15
    Since you left England?
PEREGRINE: Seven weeks.
SIR POLITIC: So lately!°
    You ha' not been with my lord ambassador?
PEREGRINE: Not yet sir.
SIR POLITIC: Pray you, what news, sir, vents° our climate?
    I heard last night a most strange thing reported
    By some of my lord's followers, and I long   20
    To hear how 'twill be seconded.°
PEREGRINE: What was't, sir?
SIR POLITIC: Marry, sir, of a raven° that should build°
    In a ship royal of the King's
PEREGRINE: *[Aside]*   This fellow,
    Does he gull me,° trow?° Or is gulled? Your name
    sir?
SIR POLITIC: My name is Politic Would-be.
PEREGRINE: *[Aside]*   Oh, that speaks him.   25
    A knight, sir?
SIR POLITIC: A poor knight, sir.
PEREGRINE: Your lady
    Lies° here in Venice, for intelligence°
    Of tires,° and fashions, and behavior,

ACT II. SCENE 1: s.d. **Peregrine** Traveler   1 **soil** native country   4 **salt** wanton   12 **Laid . . . height** Directed toward this
latitude   13 **quote** take note of   14 **license** permission from
the King   16 **lately** recently   18 **vents** publishes   21 **second-
ed** confirmed   22 **raven** bird of ill omen   **should build** is
said to have built   24 **gull me** make a fool of me   **trow**
expletive—"in faith"   27 **Lies** Sojourna Sojourns   **intelligence** information   28 **tires** attire

Among the courtesans? The fine Lady Would-be?

30 SIR POLITIC: Yes, sir; the spider and the bee oftimes
Suck from one flower.

PEREGRINE: Good Sir Politic.,
I cry you mercy;° I have heard much of you,
'Tis true, sir, of your raven.

SIR POLITIC: On your knowledge?

PEREGRINE: Yes, and your lion's whelping in the Tower.°

SIR POLITIC: Another whelp?

PEREGRINE: Another, sir.

35 SIR POLITIC: Now heaven!
What prodigies be these? The fires at Berwick!°
And the new star!° these things concurring,
    strange,
And full of omen! Saw you those meteors?

PEREGRINE: I did, sir.

SIR POLITIC: Fearful! Pray you, sir, confirm me,

40 Were there three porpoises° seen above the bridge
As they give out?

PEREGRINE: Six, and a sturgeon, sir.

SIR POLITIC: I am astonished.

PEREGRINE: Nay, sir, be not so;
I'll tell you a greater prodigy than these.

SIR POLITIC: What should these things portend?

PEREGRINE: The very day

45 (Let me be sure) that I put forth from London,
There was a whale discovered in the river,
As high as Woolwich, that had waited there,
Few know how many months, for the subversion
Of the Stode° fleet.

SIR POLITIC: Is't possible? Believe it,

50 'Twas either sent from Spain, or the archduke's:°
Spinola's whale,° upon my life, my credit!
Will they not leave these projects? Worthy sir,
Some other news.

PEREGRINE: Faith, Stone the fool is dead,
And they do lack a tavern fool extremely.

SIR POLITIC: Is Mass'° Stone dead?

55 PEREGRINE: He's dead, sir; why, I hope
You thought him not immortal? [*Aside*] Oh, this
    knight,
Were he well known, would be a precious thing
To fit our English stage. He that should write

But such a fellow, should be thought to feign
Extremely, if not maliciously.

SIR POLITIC: Stone dead!   60

PEREGRINE: Dead.—Lord! how deeply, sir, you appre-
    hend it!°
He was no kinsman to you?

SIR POLITIC: That° I know of.
Well! that same fellow was as an unknown° fool.

PEREGRINE: And yet you knew him, it seems?

SIR POLITIC: I did so, Sir.
I knew him one of the most dangerous heads   65
Living within the state, and so I held him.

PEREGRINE: Indeed, sir?

SIR POLITIC: While he lived, in action.
He has received weekly intelligence,
Upon my knowledge, out of the Low Countries,
For all parts of the world, in cabbages;°   70
And those dispensed again to ambassadors,
In oranges, musk-melons, apricots,
Lemons, pome-citrons, and such like; sometimes
In Colchester oysters, and your Selsey cockles.

PEREGRINE: You make me wonder.

SIR POLITIC: Sir, upon my knowledge.   75
Nay, I've observed him, at your public ordinary,°
Take his advertisement° from a traveler,
A concealed° statesman, in a trencher of meat;
And instantly, before the meal was done,
Convey an answer in a tooth-pick.

PEREGRINE: Strange!   80
How could this be, sir?

SIR POLITIC: Why, the meat was cut
So like his character,° and so laid as he
Must easily read the cipher.

PEREGRINE: I have heard
He could not read, sir.

SIR POLITIC: So 'twas given out,
In polity,° by those that did employ him.   85
But he could read, and had your languages.°
And to 't, as sound a noddle°—

PEREGRINE: I have heard, sir,
That your baboons were spies, and that they were
A kind of subtle nation near to China.

SIR POLITIC: Ay, ay, your Mamuluchi.° Faith, they had   90
Their hand in a French plot or two; but they
Were so extremely given to women, as°
They made discovery of all. Yet I

---

³²**I ... mercy** I beg your pardon   ³⁴**Tower** Tower of London,
where lion cubs were born just before the play was written
³⁶**Berwick** on the Scottish border, where ghostly armies were
reported in 1605   ³⁷**new star** discovered by Kepler in 1604
⁴⁰**porpoises** The annalist Stow mentions the appearance near
London   of   a   porpoise   and   whale   in   1606.
⁴⁹**Stode** Stade, port city near Hamburg, Germany   ⁵⁰**archduke's** governor of the Spanish Netherlands   ⁵¹**Spinola's
whale** The Marquis of Spinola, who commanded the Spanish
army in the Netherlands, was credited with having sent a
whale to drown London by spouting water on the city.
⁵⁴**Mass'** a vulgar shortening of Master

---

⁶¹**apprehend it** take it to heart   ⁶²**That** i.e., Not that   ⁶³
unknown inexpressible, without bottom   ⁷⁰**cabbages**
imported from Holland   ⁷⁶**ordinary** tavern   ⁷⁷**advertisement** "intelligence" (information)   ⁷⁸**concealed** disguised
⁸²**character** cipher or code, which the shape of the meat
spelled out   ⁸⁵**in polity** for political reasons   ⁸⁶**had ... languages** knew languages   ⁸⁷**noddle** head   ⁹⁰**Mamuluchi**
Mamelukes   ⁹²**as** that

Had my advices° here, on Wednesday last,
95   From one of their own coat,° they were returned,
Made their relations,° as the fashion is,
And now stand fair for fresh employment.
PEREGRINE: [*Aside*]
This Sir Pol will be ignorant of nothing.—
It seems, sir, you know all.
SIR POLITIC: Not all, sir; but
100   I have some general notions, I do love
To note and to observe: though I live out,
Free from the active torrent, yet I'd mark
The currents and the passages of things.
For mine own private use; and know the ebbs
And flows of state.
105   PEREGRINE: Believe it, sir, I hold
Myself in no small tie° unto my fortunes,
For casting me thus luckily upon you,
Whose knowledge, if your bounty equal it,
May do me great assistance, in instruction
110   For my behavior, and my bearing, which
Is yet so rude and raw.
SIR POLITIC: Why? Came you forth
Empty of rules for travel?
PEREGRINE: Faith, I had
Some common ones, from out that vulgar° grammar,
Which he that cried° Italian to me taught me.
SIR POLITIC: Why, this it is that spoils all our brave
115   bloods,°
Trusting our hopeful gentry unto pedants,
Fellows of outside, and mere bark. You seem
To be a gentleman of ingenuous° race—
I not profess it,° but my fate hath been
120   To be, where I have been consulted with,
In this high kind,° touching some great men's sons,
Persons of blood and honor—

[*Enter* MOSCA *and* NANO *disguised, followed by workmen.*]

PEREGRINE: Who be these, sir?
MOSCA: Under that window, there 't must be. The same.
SIR POLITIC: Fellows, to mount a bank. Did your
        instructor
125   In the dear tongues° never discourse to you
Of the Italian mountebanks?
PEREGRINE: Yes, sir.
SIR POLITIC: Why,
Here shall you see one.
PEREGRINE: They are quacksalvers,°

Fellows that live by venting° oils and drugs.
SIR POLITIC: Was that the character he gave you of them?
PEREGRINE: As I remember.
SIR POLITIC: Pity his ignorance.   130
They are the only knowing men of Europe!
Great scholars, excellent physicians,
Most admired statesmen, professed favorites,
And cabinet counselors to the greatest princes;
The only languaged men of all the world!   135
PEREGRINE: And, I have heard, they are most lewd°
        impostors;
Made all of terms and shreds;° no less beliers
Of great men's favors, than their own vile
        med'cines;
Which they will utter° upon monstrous oaths;
Selling the drug for twopence, ere they part,   140
Which they have valued at twelve crowns before.
SIR POLITIC: Sir, calumnies are answered best with
        silence.
Yourself shall judge.—Who is it mounts, my friends?
MOSCA: Scoto of Mantua,° sir.
SIR POLITIC: Is't he? Nay, then
I'll proudly promise, sir, you shall behold   145
Another man than has been phant'sied° to you.
I wonder yet, that he should mount his bank
Here in this nook, that has been wont t' appear
In face of the Piazza!—here he comes.

[*Enter* VOLPONE, *disguised as a mountebank doctor,
and followed by a crowd (i.e.,* GREGE) *of people.*]

VOLPONE: [*To Nano.*] Mount, Zany.°   150
GREGE: Follow, follow, follow, follow, follow!
SIR POLITIC: See how the people follow him! he's a man
May write ten thousand crowns in bank here. Note,
Mark but his gesture:—I do use° to observe
The state° he keeps in getting up.
PEREGRINE: 'Tis worth it, sir.   155
VOLPONE: Most noble gentlemen, and my worthy
patrons! It may seem strange that I, your Scoto
Mantuano, who was ever wont to fix my bank in
face of the public Piazza, near the shelter of the
Portico to the Procuratia,° should now, after eight   160
month's absence from this illustrious city of
Venice, humbly retire myself into an obscure nook
of the Piazza.
SIR POLITIC: Did not I now object the same?°
PEREGRINE: Peace, sir.

---

⁹⁴ **advices** dispatches (as from a diplomatic pouch)   ⁹⁵ **coat** kind   ⁹⁶ **relations** reports   ¹⁰⁶ **tie** debt   ¹¹³ **vulgar** common   ¹¹⁴ **cried** taught (an affectation)   ¹¹⁵ **brave bloods** gallant youth   ¹¹⁸ **ingenuous** noble   ¹¹⁹ **I . . . it** I do not boast about it.   ¹²¹ **high kind** important matter   ¹²⁵ **dear tongues** valued languages   ¹²⁷ **quacksalvers** charlatans

¹²⁸ **venting** selling   ¹³⁶ **lewd** ignorant   ¹³⁷ **terms and shreds** technical jargon   ¹³⁹ **utter** sell, vend   ¹⁴⁴ **Scoto of Mantua** Italian juggler who visited England   ¹⁴⁶ **phant'sied** fancied, falsely described   ¹⁵⁰ **Zany** Clown   ¹⁵⁴ **I . . . use** It is my custom.   ¹⁵⁵ **state** ceremony   ¹⁶⁰ **Procuratia** residence of the procurators (leading officials) of San Marco   ¹⁶⁴ **object . . . same** make the same point

165   VOLPONE: Let me tell you: I am not, as your Lombard proverb saith, cold on my feet;° or content to part with my commodities at a cheaper rate than I accustomed; look not for it. Nor that the calumnious reports of that impudent detractor, and

170   shame to our profession (Alessandro Buttone,° I mean), who gave out, in public, I was condemned *a'sforzato*° to the galleys, for poisoning the Cardinal Bembo's—cook,° hath at all attached,° much less dejected me. No, no, worthy gentlemen; to tell you

175   true, I cannot endure to see the rabble of these ground *cialitani*° that spread their cloaks on the pavement, as if they meant to do feats of activity° and then come in lamely, with their moldy tales out of Boccacio, like stale Tabarine° the faulist:°

180   some of them discoursing their travels, and of their tedious captivity in the Turk's galleys, when indeed, were the truth known, they were the Christian's galleys, where very temperately they eat° bread, and drunk water, as a wholesome

185   penance enjoined them by their confessors, for base pilferies.

SIR POLITIC: Note but his bearing, and contempt of these.

VOLPONE: These turdy-facy-nasty-paty-lousy-fartical

190   rogues, with one poor groat's-worth of unprepared antimony, finely wrapped up in several *scartoccios*,° are able, very well, to kill their twenty a week, and play; yet these meager, starved spirits, who have half stopped the organs of their minds

195   with earthly appilations,° want not their favorers among your shriveled salad-eating artisans, who are overjoyed that they may have their half-per'th° of physic; though it purge 'hem into another world, it makes no matter.

200   SIR POLITIC: Excellent! ha' you heard better language, sir?

VOLPONE: Well, let 'hem go. And, gentlemen, honorable gentlemen, know, that for this time, our bank, being thus removed from the clamors of the

205   *canaglia*,° shall be the scene of pleasure and delight; for I have nothing to sell, little or nothing to sell.

SIR POLITIC: I told you, sir, his end.

PEREGRINE: You did so, sir.

VOLPONE: I protest, I, and my six servants, are not able to make of this precious liquor, so fast as it is fetched away from my lodging by gentlemen of 210 your city; strangers of the *Terra-firma*;° worshipful merchants; ay, and senators too, who, ever since my arrival,° have detained me to their uses, by their splendidous liberalities. And worthily; for, what avails your rich man to have his magazines° 215 stuffed with *moscadelli*,° or of the purest grape, when his physicians prescribe him, on pain of death, to drink nothing but water cocted° with aniseeds? O health, health! the blessing of the rich! the riches of the poor! who can buy thee at too dear 220 a rate, since there is no enjoying this world without thee? Be not so sparing of your purses, honorable gentlemen, as to abridge the natural course of life—

PEREGRINE: You see his end.

SIR POLITIC: Ay, is't ay, is 't not good?   225

VOLPONE: For when a humid flux, or catarrh, by the mutability of air, falls from your head into an arm or shoulder, or any other part, take you a ducat, or your cecchine of gold, and apply to the place affected; see what good effect it can work. No, no, 230 'tis this blessed *unguento ungento*,° this rare extraction, that hath only power to disperse all malignant humors, that proceed either of hot, cold, moist, or windy causes—

PEREGRINE: I would he had put in dry too.

SIR POLITIC: Pray you observe.   235

VOLPONE: "To fortify the most indigest and crude° stomach, ay, were it of one that, through extreme weakness, vomited blood, applying only a warm napkin to the place, after the unction and fricace;°—for the *vertigine*° in the head, putting but 240 a drop into your nostrils, likewise behind the ears; a most sovereign and approved remedy; the *mal caduco*,° cramps, convulsions, paralysies, epilepsies, *tremor cordis*,° retired nerves,° ill vapors of the spleen, stoppings of the liver, the stone, the stran- 245 gury,° *hernia ventosa*,° *iliaca passio*;° stops a *dysenteria* immediately; easeth the torsion° of the small guts; and cures *melancholia hypondriaca*, being taken and applied, according to my printed receipt.   250

[Pointing to his bill and his glass.]

---

[166] **cold . . . feet** i.e., poor   [170] **Buttone** apparently a fellow mountebank   [172] **It** to forced labor   [173] **cook** The dash preceding suggests that the audience is being prepared for a less prosaic word, like "mistress" (the Cardinal being a notorious voluptuary).   [173] **attached** arrested   [176] **ground cialitani (It.)** common imposters   [177] **feats . . . activity** acrobatics, juggling tricks   [179] **Tabarine** Italian comedian prominent in Jonson's lifetime   [179] **fabulist** teller of tall stories   [184] **eat** ate   [192] **It.** paper containers container as used by apothecaries   [195] **appilations** obstructions   [197] **half-per'th** half   pennyworth   [205] **It.** "canaille," rabble

---

[211] **L.** Venetian possessions on the mainland   [215] **magazines** storehouses   [216] **It.** muscatel wines   [218] **cocted** boiled   [231] **It.** ointment   [236] **crude** lacking power to digest   [240] **fricace** chafing   [240] **L.** vertigo   [243] **L.** epilepsy   [244] **L.** palpitation of the heart   **retired nerves** shrunken sinews   [246] **strangury** condition of painful urination   **L.** gaseous tumor   **L.** colic   [247] **torsion** cramps

For this is the physician, this the medicine; this counsels, this cures; this gives the direction, this works the effect; and in sum, both together may be termed an abstract of the theoric and practice in the Aesculapian° art. 'Twill cost you eight crowns. And,—Zan Fritada,° pray thee sing a verse extempore in honor of it.

SIR POLITIC: How do you like him, sir?

PEREGRINE: Most strangely, I!

SIR POLITIC: Is not his language rare?

PEREGRINE: But° alchemy,
     I never heard the like; or Broughton's° books.

[NANO *sings.*]

                          Song
     Had old Hippocrates, or Galen,°
     That to their books put med'cines all in,
     But known this secret, they had never
     (Of which they will be guilty ever)
     Been murderers of so much paper,
     Or wasted many a hurtless taper;
     No Indian drug had e'er been famed,
     Tobacco, sassfras° not named;
     Ne° yet of guacum° one small stick, sir,
     Nor Raymund Lully's° great elixir.
     Ne had been known the Danish Gonswart°
     Or Paracelsus,° with his long sword.

PEREGRINE: All this, yet, will not do; either eight
     crowns is high.

VOLPONE: No more.—Gentlemen, if I had but time to
     discourse to you the miraculous effects of this my
     oil, surnamed *oglio del Scoto*; with the countless cat-
     alogue of those I have cured of the aforesaid, and
     many more diseases; the patents and privileges of
     all the princes and commonwealths of
     Christendom; or but the depositions of° those that
     appeared on my part, before the signiory of the
     Sanità° and most learned College of Physicians;

where I was authorized, upon notice taken of the admirable virtues of my medicaments, and mine own excellency in matter of rare and unknown secrets, not only to disperse them publicly in this famous city, but in all the territories that happily joy under the government of the most pious and magnificent states of Italy. But may some other gallant fellow say, oh, there be divers° that make profession to have as good, and as experimented receipts° as yours: indeed, very many have assayed,° like apes, in imitation of that, which is really and essentially in me, to make of this oil; bestowed great cost in furnaces, stills, alembics,° continual fires, and preparation of the ingredients (as indeed there goes to it six hundred several simples,° besides some quantity of human fat, for the conglutination, which we buy of the anatomists), but when these practitioners come to the last decoction, blow, blow, puff, puff, and all flies in *fumo.*° Ha, ha, ha! Poor wretches! I rather pity their folly and indiscretion than their loss of time and money; for those may be recovered by industry, but to be a fool born is a disease incurable. For myself, I always from my youth have endeavored to get the rarest secrets, and book them, either in exchange or for money. I spared nor cost nor labor where anything was worthy to be learned. And, gentlemen, honorable gentlemen, I will undertake, by virtue of chemical art, out of the honorable hat that covers your head, to extract the four elements; that is to say, the fire, air, water, and earth, and return you your felt without burn or stain. For, whilst others have been at the Balloo,° I have been at my book; and am now past the craggy paths of study, and come to the flowery plains of honor and reputation.

SIR POLITIC: I do assure you, sir, that is his aim.

VOLPONE: But to our price—

PEREGRINE: And that withal,° Sir Pol.

VOLPONE: You all know, honorable gentlemen, I never valued this *ampulla*, or vial, at less than eight crowns; but for this time, I am content to be deprived of it for six; six crowns is the price, and less in courtesy I know you cannot offer me; take it or leave it, howsoever, both it and I am at your service. I ask you not as the value of the thing, for then I should demand of you a thousand crowns, so the Cardinals Montalto, Fernese, the great Duke of Tuscany, my gossip,° with divers other princes, have given me; but I despise money. Only to show

---

255, 256, 259, 260, 261, 268, 269, 270, 271, 272, 282 (line numbers in margin)

285, 290, 295, 300, 305, 310, 315, 320, 325, 330 (line numbers in margin)

²⁵⁵ **Aesculapian** i.e., medical.   ²⁵⁶ **Zan Fritada** a real zany of the time; here, the name given to Nano   ²⁵⁹ **But** Except for   ²⁶⁰ **Broughton's** Hugh Broughton, a contemporary and highly abstruse Puritan, whom Jonson lampoons in *The Alchemist*   ²⁶¹ **Hippocrates . . . Galen** the most celebrated medical names of antiquity   ²⁶⁸ **Tobacco, sassafras** to which medicinal properties were attributed   ²⁶⁹ **Ne** Nor   **guacum** drug obtained from the bark of a tree   ²⁷⁰ **Raymond Lully** fourteenth-century Majorcan mystic and "scientist," reputed to have discovered the elixir of life   ²⁷¹ **Danish Gonswart** perhaps a certain Berthold Schwarz (="swart"), identified as a Dane said to have invented guns   ²⁷² **Paracelsus** sixteenth-century German physician who kept his wonderworking devil in the pommel of his sword   ²⁸² **signiory . . . Sanità** directors of the Venetian hospital

²⁹⁰ **divers** many   ²⁹² **experimented receipts** tested remedies   ²⁹³ **assayed** attempted   ²⁹⁵ **alembics** retorts   ²⁹⁸ **simples** herbs   ³⁰² **It.** smoke   ³¹⁵ **Balloo** Ballon (Venetian ball game)   ³²⁰ **withal** in addition   ³³⁰ **gossip** familiar friend

my affection to you, honorable gentlemen, and
your illustrious state here, I have neglected the
messages of these princes, mine own offices,
335 framed my journey° hither, only to present you
with the fruits of my travels. Tune your voices once
more to the touch of your instruments, and give
the honorable assembly some delightful recre-
ation."°

340 PEREGRINE: What monstrous and most painful circumstance Is here, to get some three or four
gazets,° Some threepence i' the whole! for that
'twill come to.

[NANO *sings.*]

Song
You that would last long, list to my song,
345 Make no more coil,° but buy of this oil.
Would you be ever fair and young?
Stout of teeth, and strong of tongue?
Tart of palate? Quick of ear?
Sharp of sight? Of nostril clear?
350 Moist of hand?° And light of foot?
Or, I will come nearer to't,
Would you live free from all diseases?
Do the act your mistress pleases,
Yet fright all aches° from your bones?
355 Here's a med'cine for the nones."°

VOLPONE: Well, I am in a humor at this time to make
a present of the small quantity my coffer contains,
to the rich in courtesy, and to the poor for God's
sake. Wherefore now mark: I asked you six
360 crowns, and six crowns, at other times, you have
paid me; you shall not give me six crowns, nor
five, nor four, nor three, nor two, nor one; nor half
a ducat; no, nor a *moccinigo.*° Sixpence it will cost
you, or six hundred pound—expect no lower
365 price, for, by the banner of my front,° I will not
bate a *bagatine,*°—that I will have, only, a pledge of
your loves, to carry something from amongst you,
to show I am not contemned° by you. Therefore,
now, toss your handkerchiefs, cheerfully, cheerful-
370 ly; and be advertised that the first heroic spirit
that deigns to grace me with a handkerchief, I will
give it a little remembrance of something,° beside,
shall please it better than if I had presented it with
a double pistolet.°

PEREGRINE: Will you be that heroic spark, Sir Pol?   375

[CELIA, *at the window, throws down her handkerchief.*]

Oh, see! the window has prevented° you.
VOLPONE: Lady, I kiss your bounty; and for this timely grace you have done your poor Scoto of
Mantua, I will return you, over and above my
oil, a secret of that high and inestimable nature,   380
shall make you for ever enamored on that
minute, wherein your eye first descended on so
mean, yet not altogether to be despised, an
object. Here is a powder concealed in this paper,
of which, if I should speak to the worth, nine   385
thousand volumes were but as one page, that
page as a line, that line as a word; so short is this
pilgrimage of man (which some call life) to the
expressing of it. Would I reflect on the price?
Why, the whole world were but as an empire,   390
that empire as a province, that province as a
bank, that bank as a private purse to the purchase of it. I will only tell you it is the powder
that, made Venus a goddess (given her by
Apollo), that kept her perpetually young,   395
cleared her wrinkles firmed her gums, filled her
skin, colored her hair; from her derived° to
Helen, and at the sack of Troy unfortunately
lost—till now, in this our age, it was as happily
recovered, by a studious antiquary, out of some   400
ruins of Asia, who sent a moiety° of it to the
court of France (but much sophisticated°),
wherewith the ladies there now color their hair.
The rest, at this present, remains with me,
extracted to a quintessence, so that, wherever it   405
but touches, in youth it perpetually preserves,
in age restores the complexion, seats your teeth,
did they dance like virginal jacks,° firm as a
wall: makes them white as ivory, that were
black as—   410

[*Enter* CORVINO.]

CORVINO: Spite o' the devil, and my shame! come
down here;
Come down—No house but mine to make your
scene?°
Signior Flaminio,° will you down, sir? Down?
What, is my wife your Franciscina,° sir?

---

³⁴² **gazets** small Venetian coins   ³⁴⁵ **coil** fuss   ³⁵⁰ **Moist . . . hand** denoting fruitfulness   ³⁵⁴ **aches** pronounced "aitch-es."   ³⁵⁵ **nones** nonce, occasion   ³⁶³ **It.** small Venetian coin   ³⁶⁵ **the . . . front** the flag that advertises his act   ³⁶⁶ **It.** anoth-er trivial coin   ³⁶⁸ **contemned** rejected   ³⁷⁴ **pistolet** Spanish gold coin

³⁷⁶ **prevented** forestalled   ³⁹⁷ **derived** imparted   ⁴⁰¹ **moiety** part   ⁴⁰² **sophisticated** adulterated   ⁴⁰⁸ **virginal jacks** pieces of wood fitted with quills that plucked the strings of the vir-ginal. In fact, the reference is, erroneously, to the keys.   ⁴¹² **scene** the stage Volpone has erected   ⁴¹³ **Flaminio** Italian actor; here used generically   ⁴¹⁴ **Franciscina** the serving-maid or Columbine of the *Commedia dell' Arte*

415   No windows on the whole Piazza, here,
      To make your properties, but mine? But mine?

[He beats away the mountebank, etc.]

      Heart! ere tomorrow I shall be new christened,
      And called the *Pantalone di Besogniosi,*°
      About the town.
PEREGRINE: What should this mean, Sir Pol?
SIR POLITIC: Some trick of state, believe it. I will
420   home.
PEREGRINE: It may be some design on you.
SIR POLITIC: I know not.
      I'll stand upon my guard.
PEREGRINE: It is your best, sir.
SIR POLITIC: This three weeks, all my advices, all my
         letters,
      They have been intercepted.
PEREGRINE: Indeed, sir!
      Best have a care.
SIR POLITIC: Nay, so I will.
425 PEREGRINE: This knight,
      I may not lose him, for my mirth, till night.

                   [Exeunt.]

Scene 2

[Enter VOLPONE *and* MOSCA.*]*

VOLPONE: Oh, I am wounded!
MOSCA: Where, sir?
VOLPONE: Not without;
      Those blows were nothing. I could bear them
         ever.
      But angry Cupid, bolting° from her eyes,
      Hath shot himself into me like a flame;
5   Where now he flings about his burning heat,
      As in a furnace an ambitious° fire,
      Whose vent is stopped. The fight is all within me.
      I cannot live, except thou help me, Mosca;
      My liver° melts, and I, without the hope
10   Of some soft air, from her refreshing breath,
      Am but a heap of cinders.
MOSCA: 'Las, good sir,
      Would you had never seen her!
VOLPONE: Nay, would thou
      Hadst never told me of her!
MOSCA: Sir, 'tis true;
      I do confess I was unfortunate,

And you unhappy; but I'm bound in conscience,   15
      No less than duty, to effect my best
      To to your release of torment, and I will, sir.
VOLPONE: Dear Mosca, shall I hope?
MOSCA: Sir, more than dear,
      I will not bid you to despair of aught
      Within a human compass.
VOLPONE: Oh, there spoke   20
      My better angel. Mosca, take my keys,
      Gold, plate, and jewels, all's at thy devotion.°
      Employ them how thou wilt, nay, coin me too,
      So thou in this but crown my longings, Mosca.
MOSCA: Use but your patience.
VOLPONE: So I have.
MOSCA: I doubt not   25
      To bring success to your desires.
VOLPONE: Nay, then,
      I not repent me of my late disguise.
MOSCA: If you can horn him,° sir, you need not.
VOLPONE: True:
      Besides, I never meant him for my heir.
      Is not the color o' my beard and eyebrows   30
      To make me known?
MOSCA: No jot.
VOLPONE: I did it well.
MOSCA: So well, would I could follow you in mine,
      With half the happiness! and yet I would
         Escape your epilogue.°
VOLPONE: But were they gulled
      With a belief that I was Scoto?
MOSCA: Sir,   35
      Scoto himself could hardly have distinguished!
      I have not time to flatter you now, we'll part;
      And as I prosper, so applaud my art.

                   [Exeunt.]

Scene 3

[Enter CORVINO, *dragging in* CELIA.*]*

CORVINO: Death of mine honor, with the city's fool!
      A juggling, tooth-drawing, prating mountebank!
      And at a public window! Where, whilst he,
      With his strained action, and his dole of faces,°
      To his drug-lecture, draws your itching ears,   5
      A crew of old, unmarried, noted lechers,
      Stood leering up like satyrs, and you smile
      Most graciously, and fan your favors forth,

---

²² **devotion** disposing   ²⁸ **horn him** make him a cuckold   ³⁴
epilogue the beating; or perhaps Mosca is speaking aside
and meditating already his plot against Volpone

SCENE 3: ⁴ **dole . . . faces** lot (range) of grimaces

To give your hot spectators satisfaction!
What, was your mountebank their call? Their
10 whistle?
Or were you enamored on his copper rings,°
His saffron jewel, with the toad-stone° in't,
Or his embroidered suit, with the cope-stitch,°
Made of a hearse cloth? Or his old tilt-feather?°
15 Or his starched° beard! Well you shall have him, yes!
He shall come home, and minister unto you
The fricace for the mother.° Or, let me see,
I think you'd rather mount; would you not
    mount?
Why, if you'll mount, you may; yes, truly, you may!
20 And so you may be seen, down to the foot.
Get you a cittern,° Lady Vanity,°
And be a dealer° with the virtuous man.
Make one. I'll but protest myself a cuckold,
And save your dowry. I am a Dutchman, I!
25 For if you thought me an Italian,
You would be damned ere you did this, you whore!
Thou'dst tremble, to imagine, that the murder
Of father, mother, brother, all thy race,
Should follow, as the subject of my justice.
CELIA: Good sir, have patience.
30 CORVINO: What couldst coulst thou propose
Less to thyself, than in this heat of wrath,
And stung with my dishonor, I should strike
This steel into thee, with as many stabs
As thou wert gazed upon with goatish eyes?
35 CELIA: Alas, sir, be appeased! I could not think
My being at the window should more now
Move your impatience than at other times.
CORVINO: No! not to seek and entertain a parley
With a known knave, before a multitude!
40 You were an actor with your handkerchief,
Which he most sweetly kissed in the receipt,
And might, no doubt, return it with a letter,
And point the place where you might meet; your
    sister's,
Your mother's, or your aunt's might serve the turn.
45 CELIA: Why, dear sir, when do I make these excuses
Or even ever stir abroad, but to the church?
And that so seldom—
CORVINO: Well, it shall be less;
And thy restraint before was liberty
To what I now decree. And therefore mark me.
50 First, I will have this bawdy light dammed up;
And till't be done, some two or three yards off,

I'll chalk a line, o'er which if thou but chance
To set thy desperate foot, more hell, more horror,
More wild remorseless rage shall seize on thee,
Than on a conjurer that had heedless left   55
His circle's safety ere his devil was laid.
Then here's a lock° which I will hang upon thee,
And, now I think on't, I will keep thee backwards;
Thy lodging shall be backwards; thy walks back-
    wards;
Thy prospect, all be backwards; and no pleasure,   60
That thou shalt know but backwards. Nay, since
    you force
My honest nature, know, it is your own,
Being too open, makes me use you thus:
Since you will not contain your subtle nostrils
In a sweet room, but they must snuff the air   65
Of rank and sweaty passengers.°

[Knock within.]

One kocks.
    Away, and be not seen, pain of thy life;
Not look toward the window; if thou dost—
Nay, stay, hear this—let me not prosper, whore,
But I will make thee an anatomy,°   70
Dissect thee mine own self, and read a lecture
Upon thee to the city, and in public.
Away!—

    [Exit CELIA.]

[Enter SERVITORE.]

          Who's there?
SERVITORE: 'Tis Signior Mosca, sir.
CORVINO: Let him come in.

    [Exit SERVITORE.]

          His master's dead; there's yet
Some good to help the bad.—

[Enter MOSCA.]

          My Mosca, welcome!   75
    I guess your news.
MOSCA: I fear you cannot, sir.
CORVINO: Is't not his death?
MOSCA: Rather the contrary.
CORVINO: Not his recovery?
MOSCA: Yes, sir.
CORVINO: I am cursed,
    I am bewitched, my crosses meet to vex me.
How? How? How? How?

---

11 **rings** appropriate to jugglers 12 **toad-stone** supposed jewel with fabulous properties found in the head of a toad 13 **cope-stitch** embroidery 14 **tilt-feathers** worn at a tournament or tilting 15 **starched** contemporary fashion 17 **fricace . . . mother** massage for hysteria 21 **cittern** zither **Lady Vanity** Assume that stock role in the old morality plays, and join Volpone's troupe. 22 **dealer** suggestion of "prostitute"

---

57 **lock** chastity girdle 66 **passengers** passers-by 70 **anatomy** cadaver for a surgeon to demonstrate on

80   MOSCA: Why, sir, with Scoto's oil.
       Corbaccio and Voltore brought of it,
       Whilst I was busy in an inner room—
       CORVINO: Death! that damned mountebank! But for
          the law
       Now, I could kill the rascal; it cannot be
85   His oil should have that virtue.° Ha' not I
       Known him a common rogue, come fiddling in
       To the *osteria*,° with a tumbling° whore,
       And, when he has done all his forced tricks, been
          glad
       Of a poor spoonful of dead wine, with flies in't?
90   It cannot be. All his ingredients
       Are a sheep's gall, a roasted bitch's marrow,
       Some few sod° earwigs, pounded caterpillars,
       A little capon's grease, and fasting spittle.°
       I know 'hem to a dram.
       MOSCA: I know not, sir.
95   But some on't, there, they poured into his ears,
       Some in his nostrils, and recovered him;
       Applying but the fricace.
       CORVINO: Pox o' that fricace!
       MOSCA: And since, to seem the more officious°
       And flatt'ring of his health, there, they have had,
100 At extreme fees, the college of physicians
       Consulting on him, how they might restore him;
       Where one would have a cataplasm° of spices,
       Another a flayed ape clapped to his breast,
       A third would ha' it a dog, a fourth an oil,
105 With wild cats' skins: at last, they all resolved
       That to preserve him, was no other means
       But some young woman must be straight sought
          out,
       Lusty, and full of juice juoice, to sleep by him;
       And to this service most unhappily,
110 And most unwillingly, am I now employed,
       Which here I thought to pre-acquaint you with,
       For your advice, since it concerns you most;
       Because I would not do that thing might cross
       Your ends, on whom I have my sole dependence,
          sir.
115 Yet, if I do it not, they may delate°
       My slackness to my patron, work me out
       Of his opinion; and there all your hopes,
       Ventures, or whatsoever, are all frustrate!
       I do but tell you, sir. Besides, they are all
       Now striving who shall first present him;
120   therefore—
       I could entreat you, briefly conclude somewhat;
       Prevent 'hem if you can.

CORVINO: Death to my hopes,
       This is my villainous fortunes! Best to hire
       Some common courtesan.
       MOSCA: Ay, I thought on that, sir;
       But they are all so subtle, full of art—   125
       And age again doting and flexible,°
       So as—I cannot tell—we may, perchance,
       Light on a quean° may cheat us all.
       CORVINO: 'Tis true.
       MOSCA: No, no: it must be one that has no tricks, sir,
       Some simple thing, a creature made unto it;   130
       Some wench you may command. Ha' you no
          kinswoman?
       Godso—Think, think, think, think, think, think,
          think, sir.
       One o' the doctors offered there his daughter.
       CORVINO: How!
       MOSCA: Yes, Signior Lupo,° the physician.
       CORVINO: His daughter!
       MOSCA: And a virgin, sir, Why, alas,   135
       He knows the state of's body, what it is;
       That naught can warm his blood, sir, but a fever;
       Nor any incantation raise his spirit.
       A long forgetfulness hath seized that part.
       Besides, sir, who shall know it? Some one or two— 140
       CORVINO: I pray thee give me leave. If any man
       But I had had this luck—The thing in't self,
       I know, is nothing—Wherefore should not I
       As well command my blood and my affections
       As this dull doctor? In the point of honor,   145
       The cases are all one of wife and daughter.
       MOSCA: [*Aside*] I hear him coming.°
       CORVINO: She shall do't: 'tis done.
       Slight!° if this doctor, who is not engaged,
       Unless 't be for his counsel, which is nothing,
       Offer his daughter, what should I, that am   150
       So deeply in? I will prevent° him: Wretch!
       Covetous wretch!—Mosca, I have determined.
       MOSCA: How, sir?
       CORVINO: We'll make all sure. The party you wot° of
       Shall be mine own wife, Mosca.
       MOSCA: Sir, the thing,
       But that I would not seem to counsel you,   155
       I should have motioned° to you, at the first.
       And make your count, you have cut all their throats.
       Why, 'tis directly taking a possession!
       And in his next fit, we may let him go.
       'Tis but to pull the pillow from his head,   160
       And he is throttled. It had been done before
       But for your scrupulous doubts.
       CORVINO: Ay, a plague on't,

My conscience fools my wit! Well, I'll be brief,
And so be thou, lest they should be before us.
165   Go home, prepare him, tell him with what zeal
And willingness I do it. Swear it was
On the first hearing, as thou mayst do, truly,
Mine own free motion.
MOSCA: Sir, I warrant you,
I'll so possess him with it, that the rest
170   Of his starved clients shall be banished all,
And only you received. But come not, sir,
Until I send, for I have something else
To ripen for your good, you must not know't.
CORVINO: But do not you forget to send now.
MOSCA: Fear not.

[Exit.]

CORVINO: Where are you, wife? My Celia! wife!

[Re-enter CELIA.]

                                                    —What,
175   blubbering?
Come, dry those tears. I think thou thought'st me
     in earnest.
Ha! by this light I talked so but to try thee.
Methinks, the lightness of the occasion
Should ha' confirmed thee. Come, I am not jealous.
CELIA: No!
180   CORVINO: Faith I am not, I, nor never was;
It is a poor unprofitable humor.
Do not I know, if women have a will,
They'll do° 'gainst all the watches o' the world,
And that the fiercest spies are tamed with gold?
185   Tut, I am confident in thee, thou shalt see't;
And see I'll give thee cause too, to believe it.
Come kiss me. Go go, and make thee ready straight,
In all thy best attire, thy choicest jewels,
Put 'hem all on, and, with 'hem, thy best looks.
190   We are invited to a solemn feast,
At old Volpone's, where it shall appear
How far I am free from jealousy or fear.

[Exeunt.]

ACT III

Scene 1

[Enter MOSCA.]

MOSCA: I fear I shall begin to grow in love
With my dear self, and my most prosperous parts,
They do so spring and burgeon. I can feel

---

183 **do** commit adultery

A whimsy° i' my blood: I know not how,
Success hath made me wanton. I could skip   5
Out of my skin now, like a subtle snake,
I am so limber. Oh! your parasite
Is a most precious thing, dropped from above,
Not bred 'mongst clods and clotpoles, here on earth.
I muse, the mystery° was not made a science,   10
It is so liberally° professed! Almost
All the wise world is little else, in nature,
But parasites or sub-parasites. And yet
I mean not those that have your bare town-art,
To know who's fit to feed 'hem; have no house,   15
No family, no care, and therefore mold
Tales for men's ears, to bait that sense; or get
Kitchen-invention,° and some stale receipts°
To please the belly, and the groin; nor those,
With their court dog-tricks, that can fawn and fleer, 20
Make their revenue° out of legs° and faces,
Echo my lord, and lick away a moth.
But your fine elegant rascal, that can rise
And stoop, almost together, like an arrow;
Shoot through the air as nimbly as a star;   25
Turn short as doth a swallow; and be here,
And there, and here, and yonder, all at once;
Present to any humor, all occasion;
And change a visor° swifter than a thought!
This is the creature had the art born with him;   30
Toils not to learn it, but doth practice it
Out of most excellent nature: and such sparks
Are the true parasites, others but their zanies.°

[Enter BONARIO.]

Who's this? Bonario, old Corbaccio's son?
The the person I was bound to seek. Fair sir,   35
You are happily met.
BONARIO: That cannot be by thee.
MOSCA: Why, sir?
BONARIO: Nay, pray thee know thy way, and leave me.
I would be loath to interchange discourse
With such a mate° as thou art.
MOSCA: Courteous sir,
Scorn not my poverty proverty.
BONARIO: Not I, by heaven;   40
But thou shalt give me leave to hate thy baseness
     basness.
MOSCA: Baseness!
BONARIO: Ay; answer me, is not thy sloth
Sufficient argument? Thy flattery?
Thy means of feeding?

ACT III, SCENE 1: ⁴**whimsy** whim ¹⁰**mystery** profession of
parasite ¹¹**liberally** widely ¹⁸**Kitchen-invention** Skill in
cookery **receipts** recipes ²¹**revenue** accent on second syllable **legs** bows ²⁹**visor** expression ³³**zanies** imitators
³⁹**mate** base follow fellow

MOSCA: Heaven be good to me!
45   These imputations are too common, sir,
     And easily stuck on virtue when she's poor.
     You are unequal° to me, and however
     Your sentence may be righteous, yet you are not,
     That, ere you know me, thus proceed in censure.
50   St. Mark bear witness 'gainst you, 'tis inhuman.

[Weeps.]

BONARIO: *[Aside]* What! does he weep? The sign is
        soft and good:
     I do repent me that I was so harsh.
MOSCA: 'Tis true, that, swayed by strong necessity,
     I am enforced to eat my careful° bread
55   With too much obsequy;° 'tis true, beside,
     That I am fain to spin mine own poor raiment
     Out of my mere observance,° being not born
     To a free fortune. But that I have done
     Base offices, in rending friends asunder,
60   Dividing families, betraying counsels,
     Whispering false lies, or mining° men with praises,
     Trained° their credulity with perjuries,
     Corrupted chastity chasity, or am in love
     With mine own tender ease, but would not rather
65   Prove° the most rugged and laborious course,
     That might redeem my present estimation,°
     Let me here perish, in all hope of goodness.
BONARIO: *[Aside.]* This cannot be a personated° pas-
        sion.
     I was to blame so to mistake thy nature;
70   Pray thee forgive me and speak out thy business.
MOSCA: Sir, it concerns you; and though I may seem
     At first to make a main° offense in manners,
     And in my gratitude unto my master;
     Yet for the pure love which I bear° all right,
75   And hatred of the wrong, I must reveal it.
     This very hour your father is in purpose
     To disinherit you—
BONARIO: How!
MOSCA: And thrust you forth
     As a mere stranger to his blood. 'Tis true, sir.
     The work no way engageth me, but, as
80   I claim an interest in the general state
     Of goodness and true virtue, which I hear
     To abound in you; and for which mere respect,°
     Without a second aim, sir, I have done it.
BONARIO: This tale hath lost thee much of the late trust
85   Thou hadst with me; it is impossible.
     I know not how to lend it any thought,

My father should be so unnatural.
MOSCA: It is a confidence that well becomes
     Your piety;° and formed, no doubt, it is
     From your own simple innocence, which makes   90
     Your wrong° more monstrous and abhorred. But, sir,
     I now will tell you more. This very minute,
     It is, or will be doing; and if you
     Shall be but pleased to go with me, I'll bring you,
     I dare not say where you shall see, but where   95
     Your ear shall be a witness of the deed;
     Hear yourself written bastard, and professed
     The common issue of the earth.°
BONARIO: I'm mazed!
MOSCA: Sir, if I do it not, draw your just jsut sword,
     And score your vengeance on my front and face;   100
     Mark me your villain: you have too much wrong,
     And I do suffer for you, sir. My heart
     Weeps blood in anguish—
BONARIO: Lead; I follow thee.

[Exeunt.]

Scene 2

[Enter VOLPONE.*]*

VOLPONE: Mosca stays long, methinks.—Bring forth
        your sports,
     And help to make the wretched time more sweet.

[Enter NANO, ANDROGYNO, *and* CASTRONE.*]*

NANO: Dwarf, fool, and eunuch, well met here we be.
     A question it were now, whether° of us three,
     Being all the known delicates°of a rich man,   5
     In pleasing him, claim the precedency can?
CASTRONE: I claim for myself.
ANDROGYNO: And so doth the fool.
NANO: 'Tis foolish indeed. Let me set you both to
        school.
     First for your dwarf, he's little and witty,
     And everything, as it is little, is pretty;   10
     Else why do men say to a creature of my shape,
     So soon as they see him, It's a pretty little ape?
     And why a pretty ape, but for pleasing imitation
     Of greater men's actions, in a ridiculous fashion?
     Beside, this feat° body of mine doth not crave   15
     Half the meat, drink, and cloth, one of your bulks
        will have.
     Admit your fool's face be the mother of laughter,
     Yet, for his brain, it must always come after;

---

⁴⁷ **unequal** unjust ⁵⁴ **careful** earned in sorrow ⁵⁵ **obsequy**
obsequiousness ⁵⁷ **observance** service ⁶¹ **mining** undermining ⁶² **Trained** Deceived ⁶⁵ **Prove** Attempt ⁶⁶ **estimation** reputation ⁶⁸ **personated** put on ⁷² **main** great ⁷⁴
bear i.e., bear to ⁸² **for . . . respect** on this consideration alone

⁸⁹ **piety** filial piety ⁹¹ **wrong** injury ⁹⁸ **professed . . . earth**
proclaimed a nobody

SCENE 2: ⁴ **whether** which ⁵ **known delicates** established
delights ¹⁵ **feat** delicate

And though that do feed him, it's a pitiful case,
20   His body is beholding to such a bad face.

[One knocks.]

VOLPONE: Who's there? My couch; away! look! Nano,
      see

[Exeunt ANDROGYNO *and* CASTRONE.]

Give me my caps first—go, inquire.

[Exit NANO.]

                                        Now, Cupid
      Send° it be Mosca, and with fair return!
NANO: *[Within]* It is the beauteous madam—
VOLPONE: Would-be—is it?
NANO: The same.
25   VOLPONE: Now torment on me! Squire her in;
      For she will enter, or dwell here for ever.
      Nay, quickly. I fear that my fit were past!
      A second hell too, that my loathing this
      Will quite expel my appetite to the other.°
30   Would she were taking now her tedious leave.
      Lord, how it threats me what I am to suffer!

[Re-enter NANO *with* LADY POLITIC WOULD-BE.]

LADY POLITIC: I thank you, good sir. Pray you signify
      Unto your patron I am here.—This band°
      Shows not my neck enough.—I trouble you, sir;
35   Let me request you bid one of my women
      Come hither to me. In good faith, I am dressed
      Most favorably today! It is no matter:
      'Tis well enough.

[Enter FIRST WAITING-WOMAN.]

                            Look, see these petulant things,
      How they have done this!
VOLPONE: *[Aside]*   I do feel the fever
40   Entering in at mine ears. Oh, for a charm,
      To fright it hence!
LADY POLITIC: Come nearer. Is this curl
      In his° right place, or this? Why is this higher
      Than all the rest? You ha' not washed° your eyes
            yet!
      Or do they not stand even i' your head?
      Where is your fellow? Call her.

[Exit WOMAN.]

45   NANO: Now, St. Mark
      Deliver us! anon she'll beat her women,
      Because her nose is red.

[Re-enter FIRST *with* SECOND WOMAN.]

LADY POLITIC: I pray you view
      This tire,° forsooth: are all things apt, or no?
1 WOMAN: One hair a little here sticks out, forsooth.
LADY POLITIC: Does't so, forsooth, and where was
            your dear° sight,   50
      When it did so, forsooth! What now! bird-eyed?°
      And you, too? Pray you, both approach and mend it.
      Now, by that light I muse° you are not ashamed!
      I, that have preached these things so oft unto you.
      Read you the principles, argued all the grounds,   55
      Disputed every fitness, every grace,
      Called you to counsel of so frequent dressings.
NANO: *[Aside]* More carefully than of your fame or
      honor.
LADY POLITIC: Made you acquainted what an ample
      dowry
      The knowledge of these things would be unto you,   60
      Able alone to get you noble husbands
      At your return: and you thus to neglect it!
      Besides, you seeing what a curious° nation
      The Italians are, what will they say of me?
      "The English lady cannot dress herself."   65
      Here's a fine imputation to our country!
      Well, go your ways, and stay i' the next room.
      This fucus° was too coarse too; it's no matter.—
      Good sir, you'll give 'hem entertainment?°

[Exeunt NANO *and* WAITING-WOMEN.]

VOLPONE: The storm comes toward me.
LADY POLITIC: How does my Volpone?   70
VOLPONE: Troubled with noise, I cannot sleep. I dreamt
      That a strange fury entered now my house,
      And, with the dreadful tempest of her breath,
      Did cleave my roof asunder.
LADY POLITIC: Believe me, and I
      Had the most fearful dream, could I remember't—   75
VOLPONE: *[Aside]* Out on my fate! I ha' given her the
      occasion
      How to torment me: she will tell me hers.
LADY POLITIC: Methought the golden mediocrity,°
      Polite, and delicate—
VOLPONE: Oh, if you do love me,
      No more: I sweat and suffer at the mention   80
      Of any dream; feel how I tremble yet.
LADY POLITIC: Alas, good soul! the passion of the heart.°
      Seed-pearl° were good now, boiled with syrup of
            apples,

---

48 **tire** headdress   50 **dear** precious (sarcastically)   51 **bird-
eyed** eagle-eyed (sarcastically)   53 **muse** wonder   63 **curious**
fastidious   68 **fucus** cosmetic   69 **give . . . entertainment** take
care of them   78 **golden mediocrity** golden mean (*auream
mediocritam*)   82 **passion . . . heart** heartburn   83 **Seed-pearl**
Here Lady Would-be begins a list of popular remedies

Tincture of gold, and coral, citron-pills,
85   Your elicampane root, myrobalanes—
VOLPONE: [*Aside*] Ah, me, I have ta'en a grasshopper°
      by the wing!
LADY POLITIC: Burnt silk and amber. You have muscadel
      Good i' the house—
VOLPONE: You will not drink, and part?
LADY POLITIC: No, fear not that. I doubt we shall not
      get
90   Some English saffron, half a dram would serve;
      Your sixteen cloves, a little musk, dried mints;
      Bugloss, and barley-meal—
VOLPONE: [*Aside*]   She's in again!
      Before I feigned disease, now I have one.
LADY POLITIC: And these applied with a right scarlet
      cloth.
95 VOLPONE: [*Aside*] Another flood of words! a very torrent!
LADY POLITIC: Shall I, sir, make you a poultice?
VOLPONE: No, no, no.
      I'm very well, you need prescribe no more.
LADY POLITIC: I have a little studied physic; but now
      I'm all for music, save, i' the forenoons,
100   An hour or two for painting. I would have
      A lady, indeed, to have all letters and arts,
      Be able to discourse, to write, to paint,
      But principal, as Plato holds, your music,
      And so does wise Pythagoras. I take it,
105   Is your true rapture; when there is concent°
      In face, in voice, and clothes: and is, indeed,
      Our sex's chiefest ornament.
VOLPONE: The poet
      As old in time as Plato, and as knowing,
      Says that your highest female grace is silence.
LADY POLITIC: Which o' your poets? Petrarch,° or
110   Tasso, or Dante?
        Guarini? Ariosto? Aretine?
        Cieco di Hadria? I have read them all.
VOLPONE: [*Aside*] Is everything a cause to my
      destruction?
LADY POLITIC: I think I ha' two or three of 'hem about
      me.
VOLPONE: [*Aside*] The sun, the sea, will sooner both
115   stand still
      Than her eternal tongue! nothing can'scape it.
LADY POLITIC: Here's *Pastor Fido*°—
VOLPONE: [*Aside*]   Profess obstinate silence;
      That's now my safest.°
LADY POLITIC: All our English writers,
      I mean such as are happy° in the Italian,
120   Will deign to steal out of this author, mainly;

Almost as much as from Montagnie:°
He has so modern and facile a vein,
Fitting the time, and catching the court-ear!
Your Petrarch is more passionate, yet he,
In days of sonnetting, trusted 'hem with much;°   125
Dante is hard, and few can understand him.
But for a desperate wit, there's Aretine;
Only his pictures° are a little obscene—
You mark me not.
VOLPONE: Alas, my mind's perturbed.
LADY POLITIC: Why, in such cases, we must cure
      ourselves.   130
   Make use of our philosophy—
VOLPONE: Oy, me!
LADY POLITIC: And as we find our passions do rebel,
      Encounter 'hem with treason, or divert 'hem,
      By giving scope unto some other humor
      Of lesser danger: as, in politic bodies,   135
      There's nothing more doth overwhelm the judgment
      And cloud the understanding, than too much
      Settling and fixing, and, as 'twere, subsiding
      Upon one object. For the incorporating
      Of these same outward things, into that part,   140
      Which we call mental, leaves some certain fæces
      That stop the organs, and, as Plato says,
      Assassinate our knowledge.
VOLPONE: [*Aside*]   Now, the spirit
      Of patience help me!
LADY POLITIC: Come, in faith, I must
      Visit you more a days, and make you well: 145
      Laugh and be lusty.
VOLPONE: [*Aside*]   My good angel save me!
LADY POLITIC: There was but one sole man in all the
      world
      With whom I e'er could sympathize; and he
      Would lie you, often, three, four hours together
      To hear me speak; and be sometime so rapt,   150
      As he would answer me quite from the purpose,
      Like you, and you are like him, just. I'll discourse,
      An't be but only, sir, to bring you asleep,
      How we did spend our time and loves together,
      For some six years.
VOLPONE: Oh, oh, oh, oh, oh, oh!   155
LADY POLITIC: For we were *coætanei*,° and brought up—
VOLPONE: Some power, some fate, some fortune rescue
      me!

[Enter MOSCA.]

MOSCA: God save you, madam!

---

86 grasshopper alluding to the noise it makes   **105 concent**
harmony   **110 Petrarch** Except for Cieco (literally, the blind
one of Adria, whose real name is Luigi Groto), these are all
famous Renaissance writers.   **117 Pastor Fido** *The Faithful
Shepherd* by Guarini   **118 safest** safest way   **119 happy** fluent

121 Montagnie Montaigne, the French essayist (pronounced
as four syllables)   **125 trusted . . . much** i.e., English poets
borrowed widely from Petrarch's love sonnets   **128 pictures**
Aretino's lascivious sonnets were written to illustrate
obscene engravings.   **156 coaetanei** of equal age

LADY POLITIC: Good sir.
VOLPONE: Mosca! welcome,
    Welcome to my redemption.
MOSCA: Why, sir?
VOLPONE: Oh,
160   Rid me of this my torture, quickly, there.
    My madam with the everlasting voice:
    The bells° in time of pestilence ne'er made
    Like noise, or were in that perpetual motion!
    The cock-pit comes not near it. All my house,
165   But now, steamed like a bath with her thick breath,
    A lawyer could not have been heard; nor scarce
    Another woman, such a hail of words
    She has let fall. For hell's sake, rid her hence.
MOSCA: Has she presented?°
VOLPONE: Oh, I do not care!
170   I'll take her absence upon any price,
    With any loss.
MOSCA: Madam—
LADY POLITIC: I ha' brought your patron
    A toy, a cap here, of mine own work.
MOSCA: 'Tis well.
    I had forgot to tell you I saw your knight,
    Where you would little think it.—
LADY POLITIC: Where?
MOSCA: Marry,
    Where yet, if you make haste, you may apprehend
175   him,
    Rowing upon the water in a *gondole*,
    With the most cunning courtesan of Venice.
LADY POLITIC: Is't true?
MOSCA: Pursue 'hem, and believe your eyes:
    Leave me to make your gift.

                    [Exit LADY POLITIC.]

                          I knew 'twould take:
180   For, lightly,° they that use themselves most license,
    Are still most jealous.
VOLPONE: Mosca, hearty thanks,
    For thy quick fiction, and delivery of me.
    Now to my hopes, what sayst thou?

[Re-enter LADY POLITIC WOULD-BE.]

LADY POLITIC: But do you hear, sir?—
VOLPONE: Again! I fear a paroxysm.
LADY POLITIC: Which way
    Rowed they together?
185 MOSCA: Toward the Rialto.°
LADY POLITIC: I pray you lend me your dwarf.
MOSCA: I pray you take him.

                    [Exit LADY POLITIC.]

Your hopes, sir, are like happy blossoms, fair,
And promise timely fruit, if you will stay
But the maturing; keep you at your couch,
Corbaccio will arrive straight, with the will.   190
When he is gone, I'll tell you more.

                    [Exit.]

VOLPONE: My blood,
    My spirits are returned; I am alive;
    And, like your wanton° gamester at primero,°
    Whose thought had whispered to him, not go° less,   195
    Methinks I lie, and draw—for an encounter.°

Scene 3

[Enter MOSCA and BONARIO.]

MOSCA: Sir, here concealed° you may hear all. But,
    pray you,
    Have patience, sir.

[One knocks.]

                          The same's your father knocks.
    I am compelled to leave you.

                    [Exit.]

BONARIO: Do so.—Yet.
    Cannot my thought imagine this a truth.

[Re-enter MOSCA and CORVINO, CELIA following.]

MOSCA: Death on me! you are come too soon, what
    meant you?   5
    Did not I say I would send?
CORVINO: Yes, but I feared
    You might forget it, and then they° prevent us.
MOSCA: [*Aside*] Prevent! Did e'er man haste so for his
    horns?
    A courtier would not ply it so for a place.—
    Well, now there's no helping it, stay here;   10
    I'll presently° return.

                    [Exit.]

CORVINO: Where are you, Celia?
    You know not wherefore I have brought you hither?

---
194 wanton lively **primero** card game **195 go** bid **196 encounter** like "go" and "draw," a term from the card game. Volpone, punning, draws the curtains of the inner stage, and looks forward to his encounter with Celia.

SCENE 3 **1 concealed** Bonario hides, perhaps behind a pillar supporting the "heavens" over the stage. **7 they** the supposed panders who are rivals to Corvino **11 presently** at once

162 bells which tolled constantly in time of plague **169 presented** made you a present **180 lightly** often **185 Rialto** bridge over the Grand Canal

CELIA: Not well, except you told me.
CORVINO: Now I will:
  Hark hither.°

[Re-enter MOSCA.*]*

[*To Bonario.*]
MOSCA: Sir, your father hath sent word,
15   It will be half an hour ere he come;
  And therefore, if you please to walk the while
  Into that gallery—at the upper end,
  There are some books to entertain the time.
  And I'll take care no man shall come unto you, sir.
BONARIO: Yes, I will stay there.—[*Aside*] I do doubt
20   this fellow.

[*Exit.*]

MOSCA: There; he is far enough; he can hear nothing:
  And for his father, I can keep him off.°
CORVINO: Nay, now, there is no starting back, and
      therefore,
  Resolve upon it: I have so decreed.
25   It must be done. Nor would I move't° afore,
  Because I would avoid all shifts and tricks,
  That might deny me.
CELIA: Sir, let me beseech you,
  Affect not these strange trials; if you doubt
  My chastity, why, lock me up for ever;
30   Make me the heir of darkness. Let me live
  Where I may please your fears, if not your trust.
CORVINO: Believe it, I have no such humor, I.
  All that I speak I mean; yet I'm not mad;
  Not horn-mad,° see you? Go to, show yourself
  Obedient, and a wife.
CELIA: O heaven!
35   CORVINO: I say it,
  Do so.
CELIA: Was this the train?°
CORVINO: I've told you reasons;
  What the physicians have set down; how much
  It may concern me; what my engagements are;
  My means, and the necessity of those means
40   For my recovery. Wherefore, if you be
  Loyal, and mine, be won, respect my venture.
CELIA: Before your honor?
CORVINO: Honor! tut, a breath.
  There's no such thing in nature; a mere term
  Invented to awe fools. What is my gold
45   The worse for touching, clothes for being looked on?
  Why, this 's no more. An old decrepit wretch,

That has no sense, no sinew; takes his meat
With other's fingers: only knows to gape
When you do scald his gums; a voice, a shadow;
And what can this man hurt you?
CELIA: [*Aside*]   Lord! what spirit   50
  Is this hath entered him?
CORVINO: And for your fame,
  That's such a jig;° as if I would go tell it,
  Cry it on the Piazza! Who shall know it
  But he that cannot speak it, and this fellow,
  Whose lips are i' my pocket? Save yourself.   55
  If you'll proclaim't, you may; I know no other
  Should come to know it.
CELIA: Are heaven and saints then nothing?
  Will they be blind or stupid?
CORVINO: How!
CELIA: Good sir,
  Be jealous still, emulate them; and think
  What hate they burn with toward every sin.   60
CORVINO: I grant you: if I thought it were a sin
  I would not urge you. Should I offer this
  To some young Frenchman, or hot Tuscan blood
  That had read Aretine, conned all his prints,
  Knew every quirk° within lust's labyrinth,   65
  And were professed critic° in lechery;
  And I would look upon him, and applaud him,
  This were a sin: but here, 'tis contrary,
  A pious work, mere charity for physic,
  And honest polity, to assure mine own.   70
CELIA: O heaven! canst thou suffer such a change?
VOLPONE: Thou art mine honor, Mosca, and my pride
  My joy, my tickling, my delight! Go bring 'hem.
MOSCA: Please you draw near, sir.
CORVINO: Come on, what—
  You will not be rebellious? By that light—
MOSCA: Sir,   75
  Signior Corvino, here, is come to see you.
VOLPONE: Oh!
MOSCA: And hearing of the consultation had,
  So lately, for your health, is come to offer,
  Or rather, sir, to prostitute—
CORVINO: Thanks, sweet Mosca.
MOSCA: Freely, unasked, or unintreated—
CORVINO: Well.   80
MOSCA: As the true fervent instance of his love,
  His own most fair and proper wife; the beauty
  Only of price° in Venice—
CORVINO: 'Tis well urged.
MOSCA: To be your comfortress, and to preserve you.
VOLPONE: Alas, I am past, already! pray you, thank him   85
  For his good care and promptness; but for that,
  'Tis a vain labor e'en to fight 'gainst heaven;

---

¹⁴**hither** Corvino and Celia presumably move away from center stage.   ²²**off** Mosca presumably opens the curtains on the
inner stage and confers with Volpone. Now Corvino and Celia
come forward again.   ²⁵**move't** suggest it   ³⁴**horn-mad** (1)
like a beast, (2) cuckold.   ³⁶**train** stratagem

---

⁵²**jig** farce   ⁶⁵**quirk** twist   ⁶⁶**critic** expert   ⁸³**Only . . .**
price Most precious

Applying fire to stone—[*Coughing*] uh, uh, uh, uh!
Making a dead leaf grow again. I take
His wishes gently, though; and you may tell him

90

What I have done for him. Marry, my state is
    hopeless.
Will him to pray for me, and to use his fortune
With reverence when he comes to 't.
MOSCA: Do you hear, sir?
    Go to him with your wife.
CORVINO: Heart of my father!

95

    Wilt thou persist thus? Come, I pray thee, come.
    Thou seest 'tis nothing, Celia. By this hand
    I shall grow violent. Come, do't, I say.
CELIA: Sir, kill me, rather. I will take down poison,
    Eat burning coals, do anything—
CORVINO: Be damned!

100

    Heart, I will drag thee hence home by the hair;
    Cry thee a strumpet through the streets; rip up
    Thy mouth unto thine ears; and slit thy nose,
    Like a raw rochet!°—Do not tempt me: come,
    Yield, I am loath—Death! I will buy some slave

105

    Whom I will kill, and bind thee to him alive!
    And at my window hang you forth, devising
    Some monstrous crime, which I, in capital letters,
    Will eat into thy flesh with *aquafortis*,°
    And burning corsives,° on this stubborn breast.

110

    Now, by the blood thou hast incensed, I'll do it!
CELIA: Sir, what you please, you may, I am your martyr.
CORVINO: Be not thus obstinate, I ha' not deserved it.
    Think who it is intreats you. Pray thee, sweet—
    Good faith, thou shalt have jewels, gowns, attires,
    What thou wilt think, and ask. Do but go kiss

115

    him.
    Or touch him but. For my sake. At my suit—
    This once. No! not! I shall remember this.
    Will you disgrace me thus? Do you thirst° my
      undoing?
MOSCA: Nay, gentle lady, be advised.
CORVINO: No, no.
    She has watched her time. God's precious, this is

120

      scurvy,
    'Tis very scurvy; and you are—
MOSCA: Nay, good sir.
CORVINO: An arrant locust°—by heaven, a locust!—
    Whore, crocodile, that hast thy tears prepared,
    Expecting how thou'lt bid 'hem flow—
MOSCA: Nay, pray you, sir!
    She will consider.

125

CELIA: Would my life would serve
    To satisfy—
CORVINO: 'Sdeath! if she would but speak to him,
    And save my reputation, 'twere somewhat;

But spitefully to affect my utter ruin!
MOSCA: Ay, now you have put your fortune in her hands.
    Why i'faith, it is her modesty, I must quit° her.   130
    If you were absent, she would be more coming;°
    I know it: and dare undertake for her.
    What woman can before her husband? Pray you,
    Let us depart, and leave her here.
CORVINO: Sweet Celia,
    Thou mayst redeem all yet. I'll say no more: 135
    If not, esteem yourself as lost. Nay, stay there.

[*Exit with* MOSCA.]

CELIA: O God, and his good angels! whither, whither,
    Is shame fled human breasts? That with such ease,
    Men dare put off your honors, and their own?
    Is that, which ever was a cause of life,   140
    Now placed beneath the basest circumstance,
    And modesty an exile made, for money?
VOLPONE: Ay, in Corvino, and such° earth-fed minds,

[He leaps off from his couch.]

    That never tasted the true heaven of love.
    Assure thee, Celia, he that would sell thee,   145
    Only for hope of gain, and that uncertain,
    He would have sold his part of paradise
    For ready money, had he met a cope-man.°
    Why art thou mazed to see me thus revived?
    Rather applaud thy beauty's miracle;   150
    'Tis thy great work that hath, not now alone,
    But sundry times raised me, in several shapes,
    And, but this morning, like a mountebank,
    To see thee at thy window, ay, before
    I would have left my practice,° for thy love,   155
    In varying figures,° I would have contended
    With the blue Proteus,° or the hornèd flood.°
    Now art thou welcome.
CELIA: Sir!
VOLPONE: Nay, fly me not.
    Nor let thy false imagination
    That I was bed-rid, make thee think I am so.   160
    Thou shalt not find it. I am now as fresh,
    As hot, as high, and in as jovial plight
    As, when, in that so celebrated scene,
    At recitation of our comedy,
    For entertainment of the great Valois,°   165
    I acted young Antinous° and attracted
    The eyes and ears of all the ladies present,

To admire each graceful gesture, note, and footing.

[Sings.]

Song°

Come, my Celia, let us prove
170 While we can, the sports of love,
Time will not be ours for ever,
He, at length, our good will sever;
Spend not then his gifts in vain:
Suns that set may rise again;
175 But if once we lose this light,
'Tis with us perpetual night.
Why should we defer our joys?
Fame and rumor are but toys.°
Cannot we delude the eyes
180 Of a few poor household spies?
Or his easier ears beguile,
Thus removèd by our wile?
'Tis no sin love's fruits to steal;
But the sweet thefts to reveal:
185 To be taken, to be seen,
These have crimes accounted been.

CELIA: Some serene° blast me, or dire lightning strike
    This my offending face.
VOLPONE: Why droops my Celia?
    Thou hast, in the place of a base husband, found
190 A worthy lover: use thy fortune well,
    With secrecy and pleasure. See, behold,
    What thou art queen of; not in expectation,
    As I feed others: but possessed and crowned.
    See, here, a rope of pearl; and each more orient°
195 Than that the brave Egyptian queen caroused.°
    Dissolve and drink them. See, a carbuncle,
    May put out both the eyes of our St. Mark;
    A diamond would have bought Lollia Paulina,°
    When she came in like star-light, hid with jewels,
200 That were the spoils of provinces. Take these
    And wear, and lose 'hem; yet remains an earring
    To purchase them again, and this whole state.
    A gem but worth a private patrimony.
    Is nothing; we will eat such at a meal.
205 The heads of parrots, tongues of nightingales,
    The brains of peacocks, and of estriches,
    Shall be our food, and, could we get the phoenix,°
    Though nature lost her kind, she were our dish.
CELIA: Good sir, these things might move a mind
    affected

With such delights; but I, whose innocence   210
Is all I can think wealthy, or worth th' enjoying,
And which, once lost, I have nought to lose
    beyond it,
Cannot be taken with these sensual baits.
If you have conscience—
VOLPONE: 'Tis the beggar's virtue;
    If thou hast wisdom, hear me, Celia.   215
    Thy baths shall be the juice of July-flowers,
    Spirit of roses, and of violets,
    The milk of unicorns, and panthers' breath
    Gathered in bags, and mixed with Cretan wines.
    Our drink shall be prepared gold and amber;   220
    Which we will take until my roof whirl round
    With the vertigo: and my dwarf shall dance,
    My eunuch sing, my fool make up the antic,°
    Whilst we, in changèd shapes, act Ovid's tales,°
    Thou, like Europa now, and I like Jove,°   225
    Then I like Mars, and thou like Erycine.°
    So of the rest, till we have quite run through,
    And wearied all the fables of the gods.
    Then will I have thee in more modern forms,
    Attired like some sprightly dame of France,   230
    Brave Tuscan lady, or proud Spanish beauty;
    Sometimes unto the Persian sophy's° wife;
    Or the grand signior's° mistress; and for change,
    To one of our most artful courtesans,
    Or some quick° Negro, or cold Russian;   235
    And I will meet thee in as many shapes:
    Where we may so transfuse our wandering souls
    Out at our lips, and score up sums of pleasures,

[Sings.]

That the curious shall not know
How to tell° them as they flow;   240
And the envious, when they find
What their number is, be pined.

CELIA: If you have ears that will be pierced—or eyes
    That can be opened—a heart that may be touched—
    Or any part that yet sounds man about you—   245
    If you have touch of holy saints—or heaven—
    Do me the grace to let me 'scape—if not,
    Be bountiful and kill me. You do know,
    I am a creature, hither ill betrayed,
    By one whose shame I would forget it were.   250
    If you will deign me neither of these graces,
    Yet feed your wrath, sir, rather than your lust
    (It is a vice comes nearer manliness),

Song adapted from Catullus [178] **toys** trifles [187] **serene** noxious dew or mist [194] **orient** lustrous, like the sun rising in the east [195] **queen caroused** Cleopatra, who drank dissolved pearls [198] **Lollia Paulina** extravagant wife of the Roman Emperor Caligula [247] **phoenix** unique bird that lived forever

[223] **antic** dance [224] **Ovid's tales** *Metamorphoses* [225] **Jove** who in the shape of a bull made love to Europa [226] **Erycine** Venus [232] **sophy's** shah's [233] **grand signior's** Turkish sultan's [235] **quick** lively [240] **tell** count

And punish that unhappy crime of nature,
255 Which you miscall my beauty. Flay my face,
Or poison it with ointment for seducing
Your blood to this rebellion. Rub these hands
With what may cause an eating leprosy,
E'en to my bones and marrow: anything
260 That may disfavor° me, save in my honor—
And I will kneel to you, pray for you, pay down
A thousand hourly vows, sir, for your health;
Report, and think you virtuous—
VOLPONE: Think me cold,
Frozen, and impotent, and so report me?
265 That I had Nestor's hernia,° thou wouldst think.
I do degenerate, and abuse my nation,
To play with opportunity thus long;
I should have done the act, and then have
    parleyed.
Yield, or I'll force thee.
CELIA: Oh, just God!
VOLPONE: In vain—
270 BONARIO: Forbear, foul ravisher! libidinous swine!

[He leaps out from where MOSCA *had placed him.]*

Free the forced lady, or thou diest, impostor.
But that I am loath to snatch thy punishment
Out of the hand of justice, thou shouldst yet
Be made the timely sacrifice of vengeance,
275 Before this altar and this dross, thy idol.—
Lady, let's quit the place, it is the den
Of villainy; fear nought, you have a guard:
And he ere long shall meet his just reward.

[Exeunt BONARIO and CELIA.]

VOLPONE: Fall on me, roof, and bury me in ruin!
280 Become my grave, that wert my shelter! oh!
I am unmasked, unspirited,° undone,
Betrayed to beggary, to infamy—

[Enter MOSCA.]

MOSCA: Where shall I run, most wretched shame of
    men,
To beat out my unlucky brains?
VOLPONE: Here, here.
What! dost thou bleed?
285 MOSCA: Oh, that his well-driven sword
Had been so courteous to have cleft me down
Unto the navel, ere I lived to see
My life, my hopes, my spirits, my patron, all
Thus desperately engagèd° by my error!
VOLPONE: Woe on thy fortune!

MOSCA: And my follies, sir.   290
VOLPONE: Thou hast made me miserable.
MOSCA: And myself, sir,
Who would have thought he would have hear-
    kened so?
VOLPONE: What shall we do?
MOSCA: I know not; if my heart
Could expiate the mischance, I'd pluck it out.
Will you be pleased to hang me, or cut my throat?   295
And I'll requite you,° sir. Let's die like Romans,°
Since we have lived like Grecians.°

[They knock without.]

VOLPONE: Hark! who's there?
I hear some footing; officers, the Saffi,°
Come to apprehend us! I do feel the brand
Hissing already at my forehead; now   300
Mine ears are boring.°
MOSCA: To your couch, sir, you.
Make that place good, however.°

[VOLPONE lies down as before.]

                                    Guilty men
Suspect what they deserve still.

[Enter CORBACCIO.]

                                    Signior Corbaccio!
CORBACCIO: Why, how now, Mosca?
MOSCA: Oh, undone, amazed, sir.
Your son, I know not by what accident,   305
Acquainted with your purpose to my patron,
Touching your will, and making him your heir,
Entered our house with violence, his sword
    drawn,
Sought for you, called you wretch, unnatural,
Vowed he would kill you.
CORBACCIO: Me!
MOSCA: Yes, and my patron.   310
CORBACCIO: This act shall disinherit him indeed.
Here is the will.
MOSCA: 'Tis well sir.
CORBACCIO: Right and well.
Be you as careful° now for me.

[Enter VOLTORE behind.]

MOSCA: My life, sir,
Is not more tendered.° I am only yours.

---

²⁶⁰ **disfavor** disfigure   ²⁶⁵ **Nestor's hernia** impotence, appropriate to the aged Greek counselor   ²⁸¹ **unspirited** dispirited
²⁸⁹ **engagèd** entrapped

²⁹⁶ **requite you** do the same   **die ... Romans** commit suicide
²⁹⁷ **Grecians** proverbially merry   ²⁹⁸ **Saffi** Venetian police
³⁰¹ **boring** being pierced, in token of his crime   ³⁰² **however**
in any case   ³¹³ **careful** provident   ³¹⁴ **tendered** carefully
provided for

CORBACCIO: How does he? Will he die shortly,
    think'st thou?
315 MOSCA: I fear
    He'll outlast May.
CORBACCIO: Today?
MOSCA: No, last out May, sir.
CORBACCIO: Couldst thou not give a dram?
MOSCA: Oh, by no means, sir.
CORBACCIO: Nay, I'll not bid you.

[VOLTORE *comes forward.*]

VOLTORE: This is a knave, I see.
MOSCA: [*Aside*] How! Signior Voltore! did he hear me?
VOLTORE: Parasite!
MOSCA: Who's that?—Oh, sir, most timely welcome—
320 VOLTORE: Scarce,
    To the discovery of your tricks, I fear.
    You are his, only? And mine also, are you not?
MOSCA: Who? I, sir!
VOLTORE: You sir. What device is this
    About a will?
MOSCA: A plot for you, sir.
VOLTORE: Come,
325 Put not your foists° upon me; I shall scent 'hem.
MOSCA: Did you not hear it?
VOLTORE: Yes, I hear Corbaccio
    Hath made your patron there his heir.
MOSCA: 'Tis true,
    By my device, drawn to it by my plot,
    With hope—
VOLTORE: Your patron should reciprocate?
    And you have promised?
330 MOSCA: For your good I did, sir.
    Nay more, I told his son, brought, hid him here,
    Where he might hear his father pass the deed;
    Being persuaded to it by this thought, sir,
    That the unnaturalness, first, of the act,
335 And then his father's oft disclaiming° in him
    (Which I did mean t' help on), would sure enrage
      him
    To do some violence upon his parent,
    On which the law should take sufficient hold,
    And you be stated° in a double hope.
340 Truth be my comfort, and my conscience,
    My only aim was to dig you a fortune
    Out of these two old rotten sepulchers—
VOLTORE: I cry thee mercy, Mosca.
MOSCA: Worth your patience,
    And your great merit, sir. And see the change!
VOLTORE: Why, what success?°
345 MOSCA: Most hapless! you must help, sir.
    Whilst we expected the old raven, in comes

Corvino's wife, sent hither by her husband—
VOLTORE: What, with a present?
MOSCA: No, sir, on visitation
    (I'll tell you how anon); and staying long,
    The youth he grows impatient, rushes forth,   350
    Seizeth the lady, wounds me, makes her swear
    (Or he would murder her, that was his vow)
    To affirm my patron to have done her rape:
    Which how unlike it is, you see! And hence,
    With that pretext he's gone, to accuse his father,   355
    Defame my patron, defeat you—
VOLTORE: Where is her husband?
    Let him be sent for straight.
MOSCA: Sir, I'll go fetch him.
VOLTORE: Bring him to the *Scrutineo*.°
MOSCA: Sir, I will.
VOLTORE: This must be stopped.
MOSCA: Oh, you do nobly, sir.
    Alas, 'twas labored all, sir, for your good;   360
    Nor was there want of counsel in the plot.
    But fortune can, at any time, o'erthrow
    The project of a hundred learnèd clerks,° sir.
CORBACCIO: What's that?
VOLTORE: Wilt please you, sir, to go along?

[Exit VOLTORE and CORBACCIO.]

MOSCA: Patron, go in, and pray for our success.   365
VOLPONE: Need makes devotion.° Heaven your labor
    bless!

[Exeunt.]

ACT IV

Scene 1

[*Enter* SIR POLITIC WOULD-BE *and* PEREGRINE.]

SIR POLITIC: I told you sir, it° was a plot. You see
    What observation is! You mentioned° me
    For some instructions. I will tell you, sir
    (Since we are met here in this height of Venice),
    Some few particulars I have set down,
    Only for this meridian, fit to be known   5
    Of your crude traveler; and they are these.
    I will not touch, sir, at your phrase, or clothes,
    For they are old.
PEREGRINE: Sir, I have better.

---

³⁵⁸ **Scrutineo** Senate-house ³⁶³ **clerks** scholars   ³⁶⁶ **Need...
devotion** Necessity makes us pious

ACT IV, SCENE 1: ¹ **it** presumably the driving out of Volpone
by Corvino ² **mentioned** applied to

---

³²⁵ **foists** tricks ³³⁵ **disclaiming** repudiating paternity ³³⁹
stated placed ³⁴⁵ **success** result

SIR POLITIC: Pardon,
    I meant, as they are themes.°
10 PEREGRINE: Oh, sir, proceed:
    I'll slander you no more of wit, good sir.
SIR POLITIC: First, for your garb,° it must be grave
    and serious,
    Very reserved and locked; not tell a secret
    On any terms, not to your father: scarce
15 A fable, but with caution: make sure choice
    Both of your company and discourse; beware
    You never speak a truth—
PEREGRINE: How!
SIR POLITIC: Not to strangers,
    For those be they you must converse with most;
    Others I would not know,° sir, but at distance.
20 So as I still might be a saver in 'hem:°
    You shall have tricks else passed upon you hourly.
    And then, for your religion, profess none,
    But wonder at the diversity of all;
    And, for your part, protest, were there no other
    But simply the laws o'the land, you could content
25   you.
    Nic. Machiavel and Monsieur Bodin,° both
    Were of this mind. Then must you learn the use
    And handling of your silver fork° at meals,
    The metal° of your glass (these are main matters
30 With your Italian), and to know the hour
    When you must eat your melons and your figs.
PEREGRINE: Is that a point of state too?
SIR POLITIC: Here it is.
    For your Venetian, if he see a man
    Preposterous° in the least, he has him straight;
35 He has; he strips him. I'll acquaint you, sir,
    I now have lived here 'tis some fourteen months.
    Within the first week of my landing here,
    All took me for a citizen of Venice,
    I knew the forms so well—
PEREGRINE: [*Aside*]   And nothing else.
40 SIR POLITIC: I had read Contarene,° took me a house,
    Dealt with my Jews to furnish it with movables.°
    Well, if I could but find one man, one man
    To mine own heart, whom I durst trust, I would—
PEREGRINE: What, what, sir?
SIR POLITIC: Make him rich; make him a fortune.

He should not think again. I would command it.   45
PEREGRINE: As how?
SIR POLITIC: With certain projects that I have,
    Which I may not discover.°
PEREGRINE: [*Aside*]   If I had
    But one to wager with, I would lay odds now,
    He tells me instantly.
SIR POLITIC: One is, and that
    I care not greatly who knows, to serve the state   50
    Of Venice with red herrings for three years,
    And at a certain rate, from Rotterdam,
    Where I have correspondence. There's a letter,
    Sent me from one o' the States,° and to that purpose.
    He cannot write his name, but that's his mark.   55
PEREGRINE: He is a chandler?°
SIR POLITIC: No, a cheesemonger.
    There are some others too with whom I treat
    About the same negotiation,
    And I will undertake it: for 'tis thus.
    I'll do't with ease, I have cast° it all. Your hoy°   60
    Carries but three men in her, and a boy;
    And she shall make me three returns a year:
    So if there come but one of three, I save;
    If two, I can defalk.° But this is now,
    If my main project fail.
PEREGRINE: Then you have others?   65
SIR POLITIC: I should be loath to draw the subtle air
    Of such a place, without my thousand aims.
    I'll not dissemble, sir; where'er I come,
    I love to be considerative;° and 'tis true,
    I have at my free hours thought upon   70
    Some certain goods unto the state of Venice,
    Which I do call my cautions;° and, sir, which
    I mean, in hope of pension, to propound
    To the Great Council, then unto the Forty,
    So to the Ten. My means are made already—   75
PEREGRINE: By whom?
SIR POLITIC: Sir, one that though his place be obscure,
    Yet he can sway, and they will hear him. He's
    A *commandadore.*
PEREGRINE: What! a common sergeant?
SIR POLITIC: Sir, such as they are, put it in their mouths,
    What they should say, sometimes; as well as greater.   80
    I think I have my notes to show you—
PEREGRINE: Good sir.
SIR POLITIC: But you shall swear unto me, on your
    gentry,
    Not to anticipate—
PEREGRINE: I, sir!

---

9 themes It is not Peregrine's language or clothing that is old, but the subject—"we have already discussed it." **12 garb** demeanor **19 know** great **20 as . . . 'hem** that I might keep up acquaintance with them **26 Machiavel . . . Bodin** Machiavelli is cited because of his reputation for godlessness and hypocrisy; Jean Bodin, the sixteenth-century French political writer, for his purely expedient advocacy of religious toleration. **28 fork** not much used in the early seventeenth century **29 metal** material **34 Preposterous** Unconventional **40 Contarene** Cardinal Gasparo Contarini, late sixteenth-century political writer **41 movables** furniture

---

47 discover reveal **54 one . . . States** someone in the States-General of Holland **56 chandler** candle maker (evidently the letter is greasy) **60 cast** calculated **hoy** small boat **63 defalk** defalcate, reduce the expense **69 considerative** thoughtful **72 cautions** precautions

SIR POLITIC: Nor reveal
    A circumstance—My paper is not with me.
PEREGRINE: Oh, but you remember, sir.
85 SIR POLITIC: My first is
    Concerning tinder-boxes. You must know,
    No family is here without its box.
    Now, sir, it being so portable a thing,
    Put case,° that you or I were ill affected
90 Unto the state, sir; with it in our pockets,
    Might not I go into the Arsenal,
    Or you come out again, and none the wiser?
PEREGRINE: Except yourself, sir.
SIR POLITIC: Go to, then. I therefore
    Advertise to the state, how fit it were
95 That none but such as were known patriots,
    Sound lovers of their country, should be suffered
    To enjoy them in their houses; and even those
    Sealed at some office, and at such a bigness
    As might not lurk in pockets.
PEREGRINE: Admirable!
SIR POLITIC: My next is, how to inquire, and be
100   resolved,
    By present demonstration, whether a ship,
    Newly arrived from Soria,° or from
    Any suspected part of all the Levant,
    Be guilty of the plague: and where they use
105 To lie out forty, fifty days, sometimes,
    About the Lazaretto,° for their trial;
    I'll save that charge and loss unto the merchant,
    And in an hour clear the doubt.
PEREGRINE: Indeed, sir!
SIR POLITIC: Or—I will lose my labor.
PEREGRINE: My faith, that's much.
SIR POLITIC: Nay, sir, conceive me. 'T will cost me in
110   onions,°
    Some thirty livres—
PEREGRINE: Which is one pound sterling.
SIR POLITIC: Beside my waterworks: for this I do, sir.
    First, I bring in your ship 'twixt two brick walls;
    But those the state shall venture. On the one
115 I strain° me a fair tarpaulin, and in that
    I stick my onions, cut in halves; the other
    Is full of loopholes, out of which I thrust
    The noses of my bellows; and those bellows
    I keep, with waterworks, in perpetual motion,
120 Which is the easiest matter of a hundred.
    Now, sir, your onion, which doth naturally
    Attract the infection, and your bellows blowing
    The air upon him,° will show instantly,
    By his changed color, if there be contagion;

Or else remain as fair as at the first.   125
    Now 'tis known, 'tis nothing.
PEREGRINE: You are right, sir.
SIR POLITIC: I would I had my note.
PEREGRINE: Faith, so would I.
    But you ha' done well for once, sir.
SIR POLITIC: Were I false,
    Or would be made so, I could show you reasons
    How I could sell this state now to the Turk,   130
    Spite of their galleys, or their—
PEREGRINE: Pray you, Sir Pol.
SIR POLITIC: I have 'hem not about me.
PEREGRINE: That I feared.
    They are there, sir.
SIR POLITIC: No, this is my diary,
    Wherein I note my actions of the day.
PEREGRINE: Pray you let's see, sir. What is here?
        "Notandum,   135
    A rat had gnawn my spur-leathers: notwithstanding,
    I put on new, and did go forth; but first
    I threw three beans over the threshold. Item,
    I went and bought two toothpicks, whereof one
    I burst immediately, in a discourse   140
    With a Dutch merchant, 'bout *ragion' del stato.*°
    From him I went and paid a *moccinigo*
    For piecing° my silk stockings; by the way
    I cheapened sprats;° and at St. Mark's I urined."
    Faith, these are politic notes!
SIR POLITIC: Sir, I do slip°   145
    No action of my life, thus I quote° it.
PEREGRINE: Believe me, it is wise!
SIR POLITIC: Nay, sir, read forth.

[Enter LADY POLITIC WOULD-BE, NANO, *and two*
WAITING-WOMEN.*]*

LADY POLITIC: Where should this loose knight be, trow?
    Sure he's housed.
NANO: Why, then, he's fast.°
LADY POLITIC: Ay, he plays both° with me.   150
    I pray you stay. This heat will do more harm
    To my complexion than his heart is worth.
    (I do not care to hinder, but to take him.)
    How it° comes off!
1 WOMAN: My master's yonder.
LADY POLITIC: Where?
2 WOMAN: With a young gentleman.
LADY POLITIC: That same's the party,   155
    In man's apparel! Pray you, sir, jog my knight.°
    I will be tender to his reputation,
    However he demerit.°

---

89 **Put case** Suppose   102 **Soria** Syria   106 **Lazaretto** pest-
house, where victims of the plague were quarantined
110 **onions** supposedly a remedy for the plague   115 **strain**
stretch   123 **him** it

141 **It.** affairs of state   142 **piecing** mending   143 **cheapened
sprats** bargained for fish   145 **slip** omit   146 **quote** record   149
fast secure   150 **both** i.e., fast and loose   154 **it** i.e., her cosmetics   156 **jog . . . knight** get his attention   158 **demerit** is at fault

SIR POLITIC: My lady!
PEREGRINE: Where?
SIR POLITIC: 'Tis she indeed, sir; you shall know her.
160   She is,
       Were she not mine, a lady of that merit,
       For fashion and behavior; and for beauty
       I durst compare—
PEREGRINE: It seems you are not jealous,
       That dare commend her.
SIR POLITIC: Nay, and for discourse—
PEREGRINE: Being your wife, she cannot miss that.
165 SIR POLITIC: Madam,
       Here is a gentleman, pray you, use him fairly;
       He seems a youth, but he is—
LADY POLITIC: None.
SIR POLITIC: Yes, one
       Has put his face as soon into the world—
LADY POLITIC: You mean, as early? But today?
SIR POLITIC: How's this?
LADY POLITIC: Why, in this habit, sir; you apprehend
170   me.
       Well, Master Would-be, this doth not become you;
       I had thought the odor, sir, of your good name
       Had been more precious to you; that you would
       not
       Have done this dire massàcre on your honor;
175   One of your gravity, and rank besides!
       But knights, I see, care little for the oath
       They make to ladies; chiefly their own ladies.
SIR POLITIC: Now, by my spurs, the symbol of my
       knighthood—
PEREGRINE: [*Aside*] Lord, how his brain is humbled
       for an oath!
SIR POLITIC: I reach° you not.
180 LADY POLITIC: Right, sir, your polity
       May bear it through thus. [*To* PEREGRINE] Sir, a
       word with you.
       I would be loath to contest publicly
       With any gentlewoman, or to seem
       Froward, or violent, as the courtier° says;
185   It comes too near rusticity in a lady,
       Which I would shun by all means: and however
       I may deserve from Master Would-be, yet
       T' have one fair gentlewoman thus be made
       The unkind instrument to wrong another,
190   And one she knows not, ay, and to persever:
       In my poor judgment, it not warranted°
       From being a solecism° in our sex,
       If not in manners.
PEREGRINE: How is this!
SIR POLITIC: Sweet madam,
       Come nearer to your aim.

LADY POLITIC: Marry, and will, sir.   195
       Since you provoke me with your impudence,
       And laughter of your light land-siren here,
       Your Sporus,° your hermaphrodite—
PEREGRINE: What's here?
       Poetic fury and historic storms!
SIR POLITIC: The gentleman, believe it, is of worth
       And of our nation.
LADY POLITIC: Ay, your Whitefriars nation.°   200
       Come, I blush for you, Master Would-be, I;
       And am ashamed you should ha' no more fore-
       head,°
       Than thus to be the patron, or St. George,
       To a lewd harlot, a base fricatrice,°
       A female devil, in a male outside.
SIR POLITIC: Nay,   205
       And° you be such a one, I must bid adieu
       To your delights. The case appears too liquid.°

                    [Exit.]

LADY POLITIC: Ay, you may carry't clear, with your
       state-face!°
       But for your carnival concupiscence,°
       Who here is fled for liberty of conscience,   210
       From furious persecution of the marshal,
       Her will I disc'ple.°
PEREGRINE: This is fine, i' faith!
       And do you use this often? Is this part
       Of your wit's exercise, 'gainst you have occasion?
       Madam—
LADY POLITIC: Go to, sir,
PEREGRINE: Do you hear me, lady?   215
       Why, if your knight have set you to beg shirts,
       Or to invite me home, you might have done it
       A nearer way by far.
LADY POLITIC: This cannot work you
       Out of my snare.
PEREGRINE: Why, am I in it, then?
       Indeed your husband told me you were fair,   220
       And so you are; only your nose inclines,
       That side that's next the sun, to the queen-apple.°
LADY POLITIC: This cannot be endured by any patience.

[Enter MOSCA.*]*

MOSCA: What's the matter, madam?
LADY POLITIC: If the senate

---

180 **reach** understand   184 **courtier** perhaps Castiglione's celebrated treatise on manners   191 **warranted** immune   192 **sole-
cism** impropriety

198 **Sporus** eunuch whom the Emperor Nero dressed as a
woman and married   200 **Whitefriars nation** unsavory London
district where criminals enjoyed the immunity once accorded to
the church of the Carmelites or Whitefriars   202 **forehead**
shame   204 **fricatrice** prostitute   206 **And** If   207 **liquid** clear
208 **state-face** as of a grave counselor   209 **carnival concupis-
cence** wench for whom you lust   212 **disc'ple** discipline
222 **your . . . queen-apple** you have a red nose, like a cider apple

225   Right not my quest in this, I will protest 'hem
    To all the world no aristocracy.
MOSCA: What is the injury, lady?
LADY POLITIC: Why, the callet°
    You told me of, here I have ta'en disguised.
MOSCA: Who? This! What means your ladyship? The
    creature
230   I mentioned to you is apprehended now,
    Before the senate; you shall see her—
LADY POLITIC: Where?
MOSCA: I'll bring you to her. This young gentleman,
    I saw him land this morning at the port.
LADY POLITIC: Is't possible! How has my judgment
    wandered?
235   Sir, I must, blushing, say to you, I have erred;
    And plead your pardon.
PEREGRINE: What, more changes yet!
LADY POLITIC: I hope you ha' not the malice to remember
    A gentlewoman's passion. If you stay
    In Venice here, please you to use me, sir—
MOSCA: Will you go, madam?
240 LADY POLITIC: Pray you, sir, use me; in faith,
    The more you see me the more I shall conceive
    You have forgot our quarrel.

[Exeunt LADY WOULD-BE, MOSCA, NANO, *and* WAITING-
WOMEN.*]*

PEREGRINE: This is rare!
    Sir Politic Would-be? No, Sir Politic Bawd,°
    To bring me thus acquainted with his wife!
245   Well, wise Sir Pol, since you have practiced thus
    Upon my freshman-ship, I'll try your salt-head,°
    What proof it is against a counter-plot.

[Exit.]

Scene 2

[Enter VOLTORE, CORBACCIO, CORVINO, *and* MOSCA.*]*

VOLTORE: Well, now you know the carriage of the
    business,
    Your constancy is all that is required
    Unto the safety of it.
MOSCA: Is the lie
    Safely conveyed amongst us? Is that sure?
    Knows every man his burden?
CORVINO: Yes.
5 MOSCA: Then shrink not.
CORVINO: But knows the advocate the truth?

MOSCA: Oh, sir,
    By no means. I devised a formal tale,
    That salved your reputation. But be valiant, sir.
CORVINO: I fear no one but him that this his pleading
    Should make him stand for a co-heir—
MOSCA: Co-halter!   10
    Hang him; we will but use his tongue, his noise,
    As we do croaker's° here.
CORVINO: Ay, what shall he do?
MOSCA: When we ha' done, you mean?
CORVINO: Yes.
MOSCA: Why, we'll think:
    Sell him for mummia.° He's half dust already.

[To VOLTORE.*]*

    Do you not smile, to see this buffalo,°   15
    How he doth sport it with his head? I should,
    If all were well and past.—Sir, only you

[To CORBACCIO.*]*

    Are he that shall enjoy the crop of all,
    And these not know for whom they toil.
CORBACCIO: Ay, peace.
MOSCA: But you shall eat it. *[Aside]* Much!—
    Worshipful sir,   20

[To CORVINO, *then to* VOLTORE *again.]*

    Mercury° sit upon your thundering tongue,
    Or the French Hercules,° and make your language
    As conquering as his club, to beat along,
    As with a tempest, flat, our adversaries;
    But much more yours, sir.
VOLTORE: Here they come, ha' done.   25
MOSCA: I have another witness, if you need, sir,
    I can produce.
VOLTORE: Who is it?
MOSCA: Sir, I have her.

[Enter AVOCATORI, *and take their seats,* BONARIO,
CELIA, NOTARIO, COMMANDADORI, SAFFI, *etc.]*

1 ADVOCATE: The like of this the senate never heard of.
2 ADVOCATE: 'Twill come most strange to them when
    we report it.
4 ADVOCATE: The gentlewoman has been ever held   30
    Of unreprovèd name.
3 ADVOCATE: So the young man.
4 ADVOCATE: The more unnatural part that of his father.
2 ADVOCATE: More of the husband.
1 ADVOCATE: I not know to give

---

227 callet whore   **243 Bawd** Pander. Peregrine takes Lady
Would-be's "use me" and "conceive" as a sexual invitation.
246 salt-head as opposed to fresh; also, lascivious

SCENE 2: **12 croaker's** Corbaccio's **14 mummia** Egyptian
mummy, valued as a medicine **15 buffalo** cuckold **21 Mercury**
god of eloquence **22 French Hercules** symbol of eloquence

His act a name, it is so monstrous!°
35 4 ADVOCATE: But the impostor, he's a thing created
To exceed example!
1 ADVOCATE: And all after-times!
2 ADVOCATE: I never heard a true voluptuary
Described but him.
3 ADVOCATE: Appear yet those were cited?
NOTARIO: All but the old magnifico, Volpone.
1 ADVOCATE: Why is not he here?
40 MOSCA: Please your fatherhoods,
Here is his advocate: himself's so weak,
So feeble—
4 ADVOCATE: What are you?
BONARIO: His parasite,
His knave, his pander. I beseech the court
45 He may be forced to come, that your grave eyes
May bear strong witness of his strange impostures.
VOLTORE: Upon my faith and credit with your virtues,
He is not able to endure the air.
2 ADVOCATE: Bring him, however.
3 ADVOCATE: We will see him.
4 ADVOCATE: Fetch him.

[Exeunt OFFICERS.]

VOLTORE: Your fatherhoods' fit pleasures be obeyed;
50 But sure, the sight will rather move your pities
Than indignation. May it please the court,
In the meantime, he may be heard in me.
I know this place most void of prejudice,
And therefore crave it, since we have no reason
To fear our truth should hurt our cause.
55 3 ADVOCATE: Speak free.
VOLTORE: Then know, most honored fathers, I must now
Discover to your strangely abusèd ears,
The most prodigious and most frontless° piece
Of solid impudence, and treachery,
60 That ever vicious nature yet brought forth
To shame the state of Venice. This lewd woman,
That wants no artificial looks or tears
To help the visor° she has now put on,
Hath long been known a close° adulteress
65 To that lascivious youth there; not suspected,
I say, but known, and taken in the act
With him; and by this man, the easy husband,
Pardoned; whose timeless° bounty makes him now
Stand here, the most unhappy, innocent person,
70 That ever man's own goodness made accused.
For these not knowing how to owe° a gift
Of that dear grace, but with their shame; being
placed
So above all powers of their gratitude,

Began to hate the benefit; and in place
Of thanks, devise t' extirpe° the memory   75
Of such an act: wherein I pray your fatherhoods
To observe the malice, yea, the rage of creatures.
Discovered in their evils: and what heart
Such take, even from their crimes—but that anon
Will more appear.—This gentleman, the father, 80
Hearing of this foul fact, with many others,
Which daily struck at his too tender ears,
And grieved in nothing more than that he could not
Preserve himself a parent (his son's ills
Growing to that strange flood), at last decreed 85
To disinherit him.
1 ADVOCATE: These be strange turns!
2 ADVOCATE: The young man's fame was ever fair
and honest.
VOLTORE: So much more full of danger is his vice,
That can beguile so under shade of virtue.
But, as I said, my honored sires, his father   90
Having this settled purpose, by what means
To him betrayed, we know not, and this day
Appointed for the deed; that parricide,
I cannot style him better, by confederacy
Preparing this his paramour to be there,   95
Entered Volpone's house (who was the man,
Your fatherhoods must understand, designed
For the inheritance), there sought his father—
But with what purpose sought he him, my lords?
I tremble to pronounce it, that a son   100
Unto a father, and to such a father,
Should have so foul, felonious intent!
It was to murder him: when being prevented
By his more happy absence, what then did he?
Not check his wicked thoughts; no, now new deeds 105
(Mischief doth ever end where it begins)—
An act of horror, fathers! he dragged forth
The agèd gentleman that had there lain bed-rid
Three years and more, out of his innocent couch,
Naked upon the floor, there left him; wounded   110
His servant in the face; and with this strumpet,
The stale° to his forged practice, who was glad
To be so active—(I shall here desire
Your fatherhoods to note but my collections,°
As most remarkable—) thought at once to stop   115
His father's ends, discredit his free choice
In the old gentleman, redeem themselves,
By laying infamy upon this man,
To whom, with blushing, they should owe their
lives.
1 ADVOCATE: What proofs have you of this?
BONARIO: Most honored fathers,   120
I humbly crave there be no credit given

---

³⁴ **monstrous** trisyllabic   ⁵⁸ **frontless** shameless   ⁶³ **visor**
mask   ⁶⁴ **close** secret   ⁶⁸ **timeless** ill-timed   ⁷¹ **owe** acknowledge

To this man's mercenary tongue.
2 ADVOCATE: Forbear.
BONARIO: His soul moves in his fee.
3 ADVOCATE: Oh, sir.
BONARIO: This fellow,
    For six sols° more would plead against his Maker.
1 ADVOCATE: You do forget yourself.
125   VOLTORE: Nay, nay, grave fathers,
    Let him have scope. Can any man imagine
    That he will spare his accuser, that would not
    Have spared his parent?
1 ADVOCATE: Well, produce your proofs.
CELIA: I would I could forget I were a creature.
VOLTORE: Signior Corbaccio!
4 ADVOCATE: What is he?
130   VOLTORE: The father.
2 ADVOCATE: Has he had an oath?
NOTARIO: Yes.
CORBACCIO: What must I do now?
NOTARIO: Your testimony's craved.
CORBACCIO: Speak to the knave?
    I'll ha' my mouth first stopped with earth; my
      heart
    Abhors his knowledge. I disclaim in him.
1 ADVOCATE: But for what cause?
135   CORBACCIO: The mere portent° of nature!
    He is an utter stranger to my loins.
BONARIO: Have they made° you to this?
CORBACCIO: I will not hear thee,
    Monster of men, swine, goat, wolf, parricide!
    Speak not, thou viper.
BONARIO: Sir, I will sit down,
140   And rather wish my innocence should suffer
    Than I resist the authority of a father.
VOLTORE: Signior Corvino!
2 ADVOCATE: This is strange.
1 ADVOCATE: Who's this?
NOTARIO: The husband.
4 ADVOCATE: Is he sworn?
NOTARIO: He is.
3 ADVOCATE: Speak then.
CORVINO: This woman, please your fatherhoods, is a
     whore,
145   Of most hot exercise, more than a partrich,°
    Upon record—
1 ADVOCATE: No more.
CORVINO: Neighs like a jennet.°
NOTARIO: Preserve the honor of the court.
CORVINO: I shall,
    And modesty of your most reverend ears.
    And yet I hope that I may say these eyes

Have seen her glued unto that piece of cedar,   150
That fine well timbered gallant: and that here°
The letters may be read, thorough the horn,°
That makes the story perfect.°
MOSCA: Excellent! Sir.
CORVINO: [*Aside to* MOSCA] There is no shame in this
    now, is there?
MOSCA: None.
CORVINO: Or if I said, I hope that she were onward   155
    To her damnation, if there be a hell
    Greater than whore and woman; a good Catholic
    May make the doubt.
3 ADVOCATE: His grief hath made him frantic.
1 ADVOCATE: Remove him hence.
2 ADVOCATE: Look to the woman.

[*She swoons.*]

CORVINO: Rare!
    Prettily feigned again!
4 ADVOCATE: Stand from about her.   160
1 ADVOCATE: Give her the air.
3 ADVOCATE: What can you say?
MOSCA: My wound,
    May it please your wisdom, speaks for me, received
    In aid of my good patron, when he missed
    His sought-for father, when that well-taught
     dame
    Had her cue given her to cry out a rape.   165
BONARIO: O most laid° impudence! fathers—
3 ADVOCATE: Sir, be silent.
    You had your hearing free, so must they theirs.
2 ADVOCATE: I do begin to doubt° the imposture here.
4 ADVOCATE: This woman has too many moods.
VOLTORE: Grave fathers,
    She is a creature of a most professed   170
    And prostituted lewdness.
CORVINO: Most impetuous,
    Unsatisfied, grave fathers!
VOLTORE: May her feignings
    Not take your wisdoms. But this day she baited
    A stranger, a grave knight, with her loose eyes,
    And more lascivious kisses. This man saw 'hem   175
    Together on the water, in a gondola.
MOSCA: Here is the lady herself, that saw 'hem too,
    Without; who then had in the open streets
    Pursued them, but for saving her knight's honor.
1 ADVOCATE: Produce that lady.
2 ADVOCATE: Let her come.

[*Exit* MOSCA.]

---

¹²³ **sols** halfpennies   ¹³⁵ **portent** prodigy, monster   ¹³⁷ **made** worked, manipulated   ¹⁴⁵ **partrich** partridge, proverbially libidinous   ¹⁴⁶ **jennet** horse

¹⁵¹ **here** i.e., on my forehead, where the horns of the cuckold are evident   ¹⁵² **horn** The alphabet ("letters") studied in school was covered by transparent horn.   ¹⁵³ **perfect** complete   ¹⁶⁵ **laid** plotted   ¹⁶⁸ **doubt** suspect

180 4 ADVOCATE: These things,
     They strike with wonder.
     3 ADVOCATE: I am turned a stone.

[Re-enter MOSCA *with* LADY WOULD-BE.*]*

MOSCA: Be resolute, madam.
LADY POLITIC: Ay, this same is she.

[Pointing to CELIA.*]*

        Out, thou chameleon° harlot! now thine eyes
        Vie tears with the hyena.° Dar'st thou look
185   Upon my wrongèd face? I cry your pardons,
        I fear I have forgettingly transgressed
        Against the dignity of the court—
     2 ADVOCATE: No, madam.
     LADY POLITIC: And been exorbitant—
     2 ADVOCATE: You have not, lady.
     4 ADVOCATE: These proofs are strong.
     LADY POLITIC: Surely, I had no purpose
        To scandalize your honors, or my sex's.
190 3 ADVOCATE: We do believe it.
     LADY POLITIC: Surely you may believe it.
     2 ADVOCATE: Madam, we do.
     LADY POLITIC: Indeed you may; my breeding
        Is not so coarse—
     4 ADVOCATE: We know it.
     LADY POLITIC: To offend
        With pertinancy°—
     3 ADVOCATE: Lady—
     LADY POLITIC: Such a presence!
        No surely.
     1 ADVOCATE: We well think it.
195 LADY POLITIC: You may think it.
     1 ADVOCATE: Let her o'er come. What witnesses have
           you,
        To make good your report?
     BONARIO: Our consciences.
     CELIA: And heaven, that never fails the innocent.
     4 ADVOCATE: These are no testimonies.
     BONARIO: Not in your courts,
200   Where multitude and clamor overcomes.
     1 ADVOCATE: Nay, then you do wax insolent.

*[*VOLPONE *is brought in, as impotent.]*

VOLTORE: Here, here,
        The testimony comes that will convince,
        And put to utter dumbness their bold tongues!
        See here, grave fathers, here's the ravisher,
205   The rider on men's wives, the great impostor,
        The grand voluptuary! Do you not think
        These limbs should affect venery? Or these eyes

Covet a concubine? Pray you mark these hands;
        Are they not fit to stroke a lady's breasts?
        Perhaps he doth dissemble!
BONARIO: So he does. 210
VOLTORE: Would you ha' him tortured?
BONARIO: I would have him proved.
VOLTORE: Best try him then with goads, or burning irons;
        Put him to the strappado.° I have heard
        The rack hath cured the gout. Faith, give it him,
        And help him of a malady; be courteous. 215
        I'll undertake, before these honored fathers,
        He shall have yet as many left diseases,
        As she has known adulterers, or thou strumpets.
        Oh, my most equal° hearers, if these deeds,
        Acts of this bold and most exorbitant strain, 220
        May pass with sufferance, what one citizen
        But owes the forfeit of his life, yea, fame,
        To him that dares traduce him? Which of you
        Are safe, my honored fathers? I would ask,
        With leave of your grave fatherhoods, if their plot 225
        Have any face or color like to truth?
        Or if, unto the dullest nostril here,
        It smell not rank, and most abhorrèd slander?
        I crave your care of this good gentleman,
        Whose life is much endangered by their fable. 230
        And as for them, I will conclude with this,
        That vicious persons, when they are hot, and fleshed°
        In impious acts, their constancy abounds.
        Damned deeds are done with greatest confidence.
1 ADVOCATE: Take 'hem to custody, and sever them. 235
2 ADVOCATE: 'Tis pity two such prodigies should live.
1 ADVOCATE: Let the old gentleman be returned with
        care.

[Exeunt OFFICERS *with* VOLPONE.*]*

        I'm sorry our credulity wronged him.
4 ADVOCATE: These are two creatures!
3 ADVOCATE: I have an earthquake in me.
2 ADVOCATE: Their shame, even in their cradles, fled
        their faces. 240
4 ADVOCATE: You have done a worthy service to the
        state, sir,
        In their discovery.
1 ADVOCATE: *[To* VOLTORE]   You shall hear, ere night,
        What punishment the court decrees upon 'hem.

[Exeunt AVOCATORI, NOTARIO, *and*
OFFICERS *with* BONARIO *and* CELIA.*]*

VOLTORE: We thank your fatherhoods. How like you it?
MOSCA: Rare.
        I'd ha' your tongue, sir, tipped with gold for this. 245
        I'd ha' you be the heir to the whole city.

The earth I'd have want° men ere you want living.
They're bound to erect your statue in St. Mark's.
Signior Corvino, I would have you go
And show yourself that you have conquered.
250 CORVINO: Yes.
MOSCA: It was much better that you should profess
  Yourself a cuckold thus, than that the other
  Should have been proved.
CORVINO: Nay, I considered that.
  Now it is her fault.
MOSCA: Then it had been yours.
CORVINO: True; I do doubt this advocate still.
255 MOSCA: I' faith,
  You need not, I dare ease you of that care.
CORVINO: I trust thee, Mosca.

[Exit.]

MOSCA: As your own soul, sir.
CORBACCIO: Mosca!
MOSCA: Now for your business, sir.
CORBACCIO: How! hav' you business?
MOSCA: Yes, yours, sir.
CORBACCIO: Oh, none else.
MOSCA: None else, not I.
CORBACCIO: Be careful then.
260 MOSCA: Rest you with both your eyes, sir.
CORBACCIO: Dispatch it.
MOSCA: Instantly.
CORBACCIO: And look that all,
  Whatever, be put in, jewels, plate, moneys,
  Household stuff, bedding, curtains.
MOSCA: Curtain-rings, sir—
  Only, the advocate's fee must be deducted.
265 CORBACCIO: I'll pay him now; you'll be too prodigal.
MOSCA: Sir, I must tender it.
CORBACCIO: Two cecchines is well?
MOSCA: No, six, sir.
CORBACCIO: 'Tis too much.
MOSCA: He talked a great while.
  You must consider that, sir.
CORBACCIO: Well, there's three—
MOSCA: I'll give it him.
CORBACCIO: Do so, and there's for thee.

[Exit.]

270 MOSCA: Bountiful bones! What horrid strange offense
  Did he commit 'gainst nature, in his youth,
  Worthy this age?—[*To* VOLTORE] You see, sir, how
    I work
  Unto your ends. Take you no notice.
VOLTORE: No,
  I'll leave you.

[Exit.]

MOSCA: All is yours, the devil and all.
  Good advocate!—Madam, I'll bring you home.   275
LADY POLITIC: No, I'll go see your patron.
MOSCA: That you shall not.
  I'll tell you why. My purpose is to urge
  My patron to reform his will, and for
  The zeal you have shown today, whereas before
  You were but third or fourth, you shall be now   280
  Put in the first—which would appear as begged
  If you were present. Therefore—
LADY POLITIC: You shall sway me.

[Exeunt.]

ACT V

Scene 1

[Enter VOLPONE.*]*

VOLPONE: Well, I am here, and all this brunt is past.
  I ne'er was in dislike with my disguise
  Till this fled moment. Here 'twas good, in private;
  But in your public,—*Cavè*° whilst I breathe.
  'Fore God, my left leg, 'gan to have the cramp,   5
  And I apprehended straight some power had
    struck me
  With a dead palsy. Well! I must be merry,
  And shake it off. A many of these fears
  Would out me into some villainous disease,
  Should they come thick upon me. I'll prevent
    'hem.   10
  Give me a bowl of lusty wine, to fright
  This humor from my heart.

[He drinks.]

                              Hum, hum, hum!
  'Tis almost gone already. I shall conquer.
  Any device now of rare ingenious knavery,
  That would possess me with a violent laughter,   15
  Would make me up again. So, so, so, so!

[Drinks again.]

This heat is life; 'tis blood by this time—Mosca!

[Enter MOSCA.*]*

MOSCA: How now, sir? Does the day look clear again?
  Are we recovered, and wrought out of error,
  Into our way, to see our path before us?
  Is our trade free once more?   20
VOLPONE: Exquisite Mosca!

ACT V, SCENE 1:   ⁴ **Cavè** Beware

MOSCA: Was it not carried learnedly?
VOLPONE: And stoutly.
    Good wits are greatest in extremities.
MOSCA: It were folly beyond thought to trust
25   Any grand act unto a cowardly spirit.
    You are not taken with it enough, methinks.
VOLPONE: Oh, more than if I had enjoyed the wench.
    The pleasure of all woman-kind's not like it.
MOSCA: Why, now you speak, sir. We must here be
        fixed;
30   Here we must rest; this is our masterpiece;
    We cannot think to go beyond this.
VOLPONE: True,
    Thou hast played thy prize, my precious Mosca.
MOSCA: Nay, sir,
    To gull the court—
VOLPONE: And quite divert the torrent
    Upon the innocent.
MOSCA: Yes, and to make
    So rare a music out of discords—
35   VOLPONE: Right.
    That yet to me's the strangest, how th' hast borne
        it!
    That these, being so divided 'mongst themselves,
    Should not scent somewhat, or in me or thee,
    Or doubt their own side.
MOSCA: True, they will not see't,
40   Too much light blinds 'hem, I think. Each of 'hem
    Is so possessed and stuffed with his own hopes
    That anything unto the contrary,
    Never so true, or never so apparent,
    Never so palpable, they will resist it—
VOLPONE: Like a temptation of the devil.
45   MOSCA: Right, sir.
    Merchants may talk of trade, and your great
        signiors
    Of land that yields well; but if Italy
    Have any glebe° more fruitful than these fellows,
    I am deceived. Did not your advocate rare?°
VOLPONE: Oh—"My most honored fathers, my
50   grave fathers,
    Under correction of your fatherhoods,
    What face of truth is here? If these strange deeds
    May pass, most honored fathers"—I had much
        ado
    To forbear laughing.
MOSCA: It seemed to me, you sweat, sir.
VOLPONE: In troth, I did a little.
55   MOSCA: But confess, sir,
    Were you not daunted?
VOLPONE: In good faith, I was
    A little in a mist, but not dejected;
    Never but still myself.
MOSCA: I think it, sir.

Now, so truth help me, I must needs say this, sir,
    And out of conscience for your advocate,   60
    He has taken pains, in faith, sir, and deserved,
    In my poor judgement, I speak it under favor,
    Not to contrary you, sir, very richly—
    Well—to be cozened.°
VOLPONE: Troth and I think so too,
    By that I heard him in the latter end.   65
MOSCA: Oh, but before, sir: had you heard him first
    Draw it to certain heads, then aggravate,°
    Then use his vehement figures°—I looked still
    When he would shift a shirt;° and doing this
    Out of pure love, no hope of gain—
VOLPONE: 'Tis right.   70
    I cannot answer him Mosca, as I would,
    Not yet; but for thy sake, at thy entreaty,
    I will begin, even now—to vex 'hem all,
    This very instant.
MOSCA: Good sir.
VOLPONE: Call the dwarf
    And eunuch forth.
MOSCA: Castrone, Nano!

[Enter CASTRONE *and* NANO.*]*

NANO: Here.   75
VOLPONE: Shall we have a jig now?
MOSCA: What you please, sir.
VOLPONE: Go,
    Straight give out about the streets, you two,
    That I am dead. Do it with constancy,
    Sadly,° do you hear? Impute it to the grief
    Of this late slander.

[Exeunt CASTRONE and NANO.]

MOSCA: What do you mean, sir?
VOLPONE: Oh,   80
    I shall have instantly my Vulture, Crow,
    Raven, come flying hither, on the news,
    To peck for carrion, my she-wolf, and all,
    Greedy, and full of expectation—
MOSCA: And then to have it ravished from their mouths!   85
VOLPONE: 'Tis true. I will ha' thee put on a gown,
    And take upon thee, as thou wert mine heir;
    Show 'hem a will. Open that chest, and reach
    Forth one of those that has the blanks; I'll straight
    Put in thy name.
MOSCA: It will be rare, sir.
VOLPONE: Ay,   90

---

48 **glebe** soil   49 **rare** rarely

64 **cozened** cheated   67 **Draw . . . aggravate** Order his argument and then make it more emphatic.   68 **figures** rhetorical figures, to persuade   69 **shift . . . shirt** change his clothing, given the violence of his address. Presumably Voltore has worked himself into a sweat   79 **Sadly** Seriously

When they ev'n gape, and find themselves delud-
    ed—
MOSCA: Yes.
VOLPONE: And thou use them scurvily! Dispatch,
    Get on thy gown.
MOSCA: But what, sir, if they ask
    After the body?
VOLPONE: Say, it was corrupted.
95 MOSCA: I'll say it stunk, sir; and was fain to have it
    Coffined up instantly, and sent away.
VOLPONE: Anything; what thou wilt. Hold, here's my
    will.
    Get thee a cap, a count-book,° pen and ink,
    Papers afore thee; sit as thou wert taking
100   An inventory of parcels. I'll get up
    Behind the curtain, on a stool, and hearken:
    Sometime peep over, see how they do look,
    With what degrees their blood doth leave their faces.
    Oh, 'twill afford me a rare meal of laughter!
105 MOSCA: Your advocate will turn stark dull upon it.
VOLPONE: It will take off his oratory's edge.
MOSCA: But your clarissimo,° old roundback, he
    Will crump° you like a hog-louse, with the touch.
VOLPONE: And what Corvino?
MOSCA: Oh, sir, look for him,
110   Tomorrow morning, with a rope and dagger,
    To visit all the streets. He must run mad,
    My lady too, that came into the court,
    To bear false witness for your worship—
VOLPONE: Yes,
    And kissed me 'fore the fathers, when my face
    Flowed all with oils—
115 MOSCA: And sweat, sir. Why, your gold
    Is such another med'cine, it dries up
    All those offensive savors: it transforms
    The most deformed, and restores 'hem lovely,
    As 'twere the strange poetical girdle.° Jove
120   Could not invent t' himself a shroud more subtle
    To pass Acrisius' guards.° It is the thing
    Makes all the world her grace, her youth, her beauty.
VOLPONE: I think she loves me.
MOSCA: Who? The lady, sir?
    She's jealous of you.
VOLPONE: Dost thou say so?

[Knocking within.]

MOSCA: Hark,
    There's some already.
VOLPONE: Look.

MOSCA: It is the Vulture;   125
    He has the quickest scent.
VOLPONE: I'll to my place,
    Thou to thy posture.
MOSCA: I am set.
VOLPONE: But, Mosca,
    Play the artificer° now, torture 'hem rarely.

[Enter VOLTORE.*]*

VOLTORE: How now, my Mosca?
MOSCA: *[Writing]*   "Turkey carpets, nine—"
VOLTORE: Taking an inventory! that is well.   130
MOSCA: "Two suits of bedding, tissue—"
VOLTORE: Where's the will?
    Let me read that, the while.

[Enter SERVANTS *with* CORBACCIO *in a chair.]*

CORBACCIO: So, set me down,
    And get you home.

[Exeunt SERVANTS.*]*

VOLTORE: Is he come now, to trouble us!
MOSCA: "Of cloth of gold, two more—"
CORBACCIO: Is it done, Mosca?
MOSCA: "Of several vellets,° eight—"
VOLTORE: I like his care.   135
CORBACCIO: Dost thou not hear?

[Enter CORVINO.*]*

CORVINO: Ha! is the hour come, Mosca?
VOLPONE: Ay, now they muster.

*[*VOLPONE *peeps from behind a traverse.°]*

CORVINO: What does the advocate here,
    Or this Corbaccio?
CORBACCIO: What do these here?

[Enter LADY POLITIC WOULD-BE.*]*

LADY POLITIC: Mosca!
    Is his thread spun?
MOSCA: "Eight chests of linen—"
VOLPONE: Oh,
    My fine Dame Would-be, too!
CORVINO: Mosca, the will,   140
    That I may show it these, and rid 'hem hence.
MOSCA: "Six chests of diaper,° four of damask,"—
    There

---

⁹⁸ **count-book** account book   ¹⁰⁷**clarissimo** Venetian grandee
¹⁰⁸ **crump** curl up (himself; "you" is an ethical dative, not
objective)   ¹¹⁹ **girdle** worn by Venus   ¹²¹ **Jove . . . guards** By
changing himself to a shower of gold, Jove got access to the
chamber of Danaë, the daughter of Acrisius.

---

¹²⁷ **artificer** craftsman in trickery   ¹³⁴ **vellets** velvets   ˢ·ᵈ· **traverse** perhaps a curtain closing off the inner stage; or a movable screen   ¹⁴² **diaper** linen

[Gives them the will carelessly, over his shoulder.]

CORBACCIO: Is that the will?
MOSCA: "Down-beds, and bolsters—"
VOLPONE: Rare!
    Be busy still. Now they begin to flutter.
145 They never think of me. Look, see, see, see!
    How their swift eyes run over the long deed,
    Unto the name, and to the legacies,
    What is bequeathed them there—
MOSCA: "Ten suits of hangings—"
VOLPONE: Ay i' their garters,° Mosca. Now their hopes
    Are at the gasp.
VOLTORE: Mosca the heir!
150 CORBACCIO: What's that?
VOLPONE: My advocate is dumb. Look to my merchant,
    He has heard of some strange storm, a ship is lost,
    He faints. My lady will swoon. Old glazen-eyes,
    He hath not reached his despair yet.
CORBACCIO: All these
155 Are out of hope. I am, sure, the man.
CORVINO: But, Mosca—
MOSCA: "Two cabinets—"
CORVINO: Is this in earnest?
MOSCA: "One
    Of ebony—"
CORVINO: Or do you but delude me?
MOSCA: "The other, mother of pearl"—I am very busy.
    Good faith, it is a fortune thrown upon me—
160 "Item, one salt° of agate"—not my seeking.
LADY POLITIC: Do you hear, sir?
MOSCA: "A perfumed box"—Pray you forbear,
    You see I am troubled—"made of an onyx—"
LADY POLITIC: How!
MOSCA: Tomorrow or next day, I shall be at leisure
    To talk with you all.
CORVINO: Is this my large hope's issue?
LADY POLITIC: Sir, I must have a fairer answer.
165 MOSCA: Madam!
    Marry, and shall. Pray you, fairly quit my house.
    Nay, raise no tempest with your looks; but hark
      you
    Remember what your ladyship offered° me
    To put you in an heir. Go to, think on it:
170 And what you said e'en your best madams did
    For maintenance; and why not you? Enough.
    Go home, and use the poor Sir Pol, your knight,
      well,
    For fear I tell some riddles; go, be melancholy.

[Exit LADY WOULD-BE.]

VOLPONE: Oh, my fine devil!
CORVINO: Mosca, pray you a word.
MOSCA: Lord! Will not you take your dispatch hence
    yet?   175
    Methinks, of all, you should have been the example.
    Why should you stay here? With what thought,
      what promise?
    Hear you; do you not know, I know you an ass,
    And that you would most fain have been a wittol°
    If fortune would have let you? That you are   180
    A declared cuckold, on good terms? This pearl,
    You'll say, was yours? Right: this diamond?
    I'll not deny't, but thank you. Much here else?
    It may be so. Why, think that these good works
    May help to hide your bad. I'll not betray you;   185
    Although you be but extraordinary,
    And have it° only in title, it sufficeth.
    Go home, be melancholic too, or mad.

[Exit CORVINO.]

VOLPONE: Rare Mosca! how his villainy becomes
    him!
VOLTORE: Certain he doth delude all these for me.   190
CORBACCIO: Mosca the heir!
VOLPONE: Oh, his four eyes° have found it.
CORBACCIO: I am cozened, cheated, by a parasite slave.
    Harlot,° thou hast gulled me.
MOSCA: Yes, sir. Stop your mouth
    Or I shall draw the only tooth is left.
    Are not you he, that filthy covetous wretch,   195
    With the three legs,° that here, in hope of prey,
    Have, any time this three years, snuffed about,
    With your most groveling nose, and would have
      hired
    Me to the poisoning of my patron, sir.
    Are not you he that have today in court   200
    Professed the disinheriting of your son?
    Perjured yourself? Go home, and die, and stink.
    If you but croak a syllable, all comes out.
    Away, and call your porters!

[Exit CORBACCIO.]

                    Go, go, stink.
VOLPONE: Excellent varlet!
VOLTORE: Now, my faithful Mosca,   205
    I find thy constancy—
MOSCA: Sir!
VOLTORE: Sincere.
MOSCA: *[Writing]*   "A table

---

149 **garters** with which they may hang themselves   160 **salt** saltcellar   168 **offered** i.e., herself

179 **wittol** deliberate cuckold   187 **it** name of cuckold   191 **four eyes** Corbaccio wears glasses   193 **Harlot** used originally of men and women indifferently—scoundrel   196 **three legs** his own and the cane that supports him

Of porphyry"—I mar'le° you'll be thus troublesome.
VOLTORE: Nay, leave off now, they are gone.
MOSCA: Why, who are you?
What! who did send for you? Oh, cry you mercy,
210   Reverend sir! good faith, I am grieved for you,
That any chance of mine should thus defeat
Your (I must needs say) most deserving travails.°
But I protest, sir, it was cast upon me,
And I could almost wish to be without it,
215   But that the will o' the dead must be observed.
Marry, my joy is that you need it not.
You have a gift, sir (thank your education),
Will never let you want, while there are men,
And malice, to breed causes.° Would I had
220   But half the like, for all my fortune, sir!
If I have any suits, as I do hope,
Things being so easy and direct, I shall not,
I will make bold with your obstreperous aid,
Conceive me—for your fee, sir. In mean time,
You that have so much law, I know ha' the
225   conscience
Not to be covetous of what is mine.
Good sir, I thank you for my plate; 'twill help
To set up a young man. Good faith, you look
As you were costive.° Best go home and purge, sir.

[Exit VOLTORE.]

[VOLPONE comes from behind the traverse.]

230   VOLPONE: Bid him eat lettuce° well. My witty mischief,
Let me embrace thee. O that I could now
Transform thee to a Venus—Mosca, go,
Straight take my habit of clarissimo,°
And walk the streets. Be seen, torment 'hem more.
235   We must pursue, as well as plot. Who would
Have lost this feast?
MOSCA: I doubt it will lose them.
VOLPONE: Oh, my recovery shall recover all.
That I could now but think on some disguise
To meet 'hem in, and ask 'hem questions.
240   How I would vex 'hem still at every turn!
MOSCA: Sir, I can fit you.
VOLPONE: Canst thou?
MOSCA: Yes, I know
One o' the commandadori, sir, so like you;°
Him will I straight make drunk, and bring you
his habit.
VOLPONE: A rare disguise, and answering thy brain!
245   Oh, I will be a sharp disease unto 'hem.

MOSCA: Sir, you must look for curses—
VOLPONE: Till they burst.
The Fox fares ever best when he is curst.°

[Exeunt.]

Scene 2

[Enter PEREGRINE disguised, and three MERCHANTS.]

PEREGRINE: Am I enough disguised?
1 MERCHANT: I warrant you.
PEREGRINE: All my ambition is to fright him only.
2 MERCHANT: If you could ship him away, 'twere
excellent.
3 MERCHANT: To Zant, or to Aleppo!
PEREGRINE: Yes, and ha' his
Adventures put i' the Book of Voyages,°   5
And his gulled story° registered for truth.
Well, gentlemen, when I am in a while,
And that you think us warm in our discourse,
Know your approaches.
1 MERCHANT: Trust it to our care.

[Exeunt MERCHANTS.]

[Enter WAITING-WOMAN.]

PEREGRINE: Save you, fair lady! Is Sir Pol within?   10
WOMAN: I do not know, sir.
PEREGRINE: Pray you say unto him
Here is a merchant, upon urgent business,
Desires to speak with him.
WOMAN: I will see, sir.

[Exit.]

PEREGRINE: Pray you.
I see the family is all female here.

[Re-enter WAITING-WOMAN.]

WOMAN: He says, sir, he has weighty affairs of state,   15
That now require him whole. Some other time
You may possess him.
PEREGRINE: Pray you say again,
If those require him whole, these will exact him,°
Whereof I bring him tidings.

[Exit WOMAN.]

---

207 **mar'le** marvel   212 **travails** labors, sufferings   219 **causes** lawsuits   229 **costive** constipated   230 **lettuce** remedy for constipation   233 **habit . . . clarissimo** costume of a grandee   242 **so . . . you** if it please you

247 **curst** for escaping—proverbial

SCENE 2:   5 **Book of Voyages** like Hakluyt's great collections of English and foreign voyages and travels   6 **gulled story** story of his gulling   18 **exact him** insist on his presence

What might be
20 His grave affair of state now! how to make
Bolognian sausages here in Venice, sparing
One o' the ingredients?

[Re-enter WAITING-WOMAN.]

WOMAN: Sir, he says, he knows
By your word "tidings"° that you are no states-
man,
And therefore wills you stay.
PEREGRINE: Sweet, pray you return him.
25 I have not read so many proclamations,
And studied them for words, as he has done—
But—here he deigns to come.

[Exit WOMAN.]

[Enter SIR POLITIC.]

SIR POLITIC: Sir, I must crave
Your courteous pardon. There hath chanced today
Unkind disaster 'twixt my lady and me;
30 And I was penning my apology,
To give her satisfaction, as you came now.
PEREGRINE: Sir, I am grieved I bring you worse disaster.
The gentleman you met at the port today,
That told you he was newly arrived—
SIR POLITIC: Ay, was
A fugitive punk?°
35 PEREGRINE: No, sir, a spy set on you.
And he has made relation to the Senate,
That you professed to him to have a plot
To sell the State of Venice to the Turk.
SIR POLITIC: Oh, me!
PEREGRINE: For which warrants are signed by this time,
40 To apprehend you, and to search your study
For papers—
SIR POLITIC: Alas, sir, I have none, but notes
Drawn out of play-books—
PEREGRINE: All the better, sir.
SIR POLITIC: And some essays. What shall I do?
PEREGRINE: Sir, best
Convey yourself into a sugar-chest:
45 Or, if you could lie round, a frail° were rare.
And I could send you aboard.
SIR POLITIC: Sir, I but talked so,
For discourse sake merely.
PEREGRINE: Hark! they are there.

[They knock without.]

SIR POLITIC: I am a wretch, a wretch!
PEREGRINE: What will you do, sir?
Ha' you ne'er a currant-butt° to leap into?
They'll put you to the rack; you must be sudden.   50
SIR POLITIC: Sir, I have an ingine°—
3 MERCHANT: Sir Politic Would-be!
2 MERCHANT: Where is he?
SIR POLITIC: That I have thought upon before time.
PEREGRINE: What is it?
SIR POLITIC: I shall ne'er endure the torture.
Marry, it is, sir, of a tortoise-shell,
Fitted for these extremities. Pray you sir, help me.   55
Here I've a place, sir, to put back my legs,
Please you to lay it on, sir, with this cap,
And my black gloves. I'll lie, sir, like a tortoise,
Till they are gone.
PEREGRINE: And call you this an ingine?
SIR POLITIC: Mine own device—Good sir, bid my
wife's women.   60
To burn my papers.

[They (the three MERCHANTS) rush in.]

1 MERCHANT: Where is he hid?
3 MERCHANT: We must,
And will sure find him.
2 MERCHANT: Which is his study?
1 MERCHANT: What
Are you, sir?
PEREGRINE: I am a merchant, that came here
To look upon this tortoise.
3 MERCHANT: How!
1 MERCHANT: St. Mark!
What beast is this?
PEREGRINE: It is a fish.
2 MERCHANT: Come out here!   65
PEREGRINE: Nay, you may strike him, sir, and tread
upon him.
He'll bear a cart.
1 MERCHANT: What, to run over him?
PEREGRINE: Yes.
3 MERCHANT: Let's jump upon him.
2 MERCHANT: Can he not go?
PEREGRINE: He creeps, sir.
1 MERCHANT: Let's see him creep.
PEREGRINE: No, good sir, you will hurt him.
2 MERCHANT: Heart, I will see him creep, or prick his
guts.   70
3 MERCHANT: Come out here!
PEREGRINE: Pray you, sir.
        [Aside to SIR POLITIC] Creep a little.
1 MERCHANT: Forth.
2 MERCHANT: Yet farther.

---

²³ **tidings** A statesman would have said, more pretentiously,
"intelligence." ³⁴ **punk** prostitute. Sir Pol has evidently
accepted his wife's erroneous impression. ⁴⁵ **frail** rush basket for packing fruit

---

⁴⁹ **currant-butt** cask for storing currants ⁵¹ **ingine** contrivance

PEREGRINE: Good sir! [*Aside*] Creep.
2 MERCHANT: We'll see his legs.

[*They pull off the shell and discover him.*]

3 MERCHANT: Ods so, he has garters!
1 MERCHANT: Ay, and gloves!
2 MERCHANT: Is this
    Your fearful tortoise?
PEREGRINE: Now, Sir Pol, we are even.
75   For your next project I shall be prepared.
    I am sorry for the funeral of your notes, sir.
1 MERCHANT: 'Twere a rare motion° to be seen in
    Fleet street.
2 MERCHANT: Ay i' the Term.
1 MERCHANT: Or Smithfield, in the fair.°
3 MERCHANT: Methinks 'tis but a melancholic sight.
PEREGRINE: Farewell, most politic tortoise!

[*Exeunt* PEREGRINE *and* MERCHANTS.]

[*Re-enter* WAITING-WOMAN.]

80 SIR POLITIC: Where's my lady?
    Knows she of this?
WOMAN: I know not, sir.
SIR POLITIC: Inquire—

[*Exit* WOMAN.]

Oh, I shall be the fable of all feasts,
    The freight of the gazetti,° ship-boys' tale;
    And, which is worst, even talk for ordinaries.°

[*Re-enter* WAITING-WOMAN.]

85 WOMAN: My lady's come most melancholic home,
    And says, sir, she will straight to sea, for physic.
SIR POLITIC: And I, to shun this place and clime for
    ever,
    Creeping with house on back, and think it well
    To shrink my poor head in my politic shell.

[*Exeunt.*]

Scene 3

[*Enter* VOLPONE *in the habit of a commandadore, and*
MOSCA *in that of a clarissimo.*]

VOLPONE: Am I then like him?
MOSCA: Oh, sir, you are he:
    No man can sever° you.
VOLPONE: Good.
MOSCA: But what am I?
VOLPONE: 'Fore heaven, a brave clarissimo; thou
    becom'st it!
    Pity thou wert not born one.
MOSCA: [*Aside*]   If I hold
    My made one,° 'twill be well.
VOLPONE: I'll go and see 5
    What news first at the court.

[*Exit.*]

MOSCA: Do so. My Fox
    Is out on° his hole, and ere he shall re-enter,
    I'll make him languish in his borrowed case,°
    Except° he come to composition° with me.
    Androgyno, Castrone, Nano!

[*Enter* ANDROGYNO, CASTRONE, *and* NANO.]

ALL: Here 10
MOSCA: Go, recreate yourselves abroad; go, sport—

[*Exeunt.*]

So, now I have the keys, and am possessed.
Since he will needs be dead afore his time,
I'll bury him, or gain by him: I am his heir,
And so will keep me, till he share at least. 15
To cozen him of all, were but a cheat
Well placed. No man would construe it a sin.
Let his sport pay for 't. This is called the Fox-trap.

[*Exit.*]

Scene 4

[*Enter* CORBACCIO *and* CORVINO.]

CORBACCIO: They say the court is set.
CORVINO: We must maintain
    Our first tale good, for both our reputations.
CORBACCIO: Why, mine's no tale. My son would there
    have killed me.
CORVINO: That's true, I had forgot. [*Aside*] Mine is, I
    am sure.
    But for your will, sir.
CORBACCIO: Ay, I'll come upon him 5
    For that hereafter, now his patron's dead.

---

[77] **motion** puppet show   [79] **Fleet-street . . . fair** Variously,
places and occasions proper to sideshows: freaks were shown
in Fleet Street and at Bartholomew Fair, and were especially
popular during the academic term of the law courts, when
London was full of visitors.   [83] **freight . . . gazetti** subject of
the newspapers   [84] **ordinaries** taverns

SCENE 3: [3] **sever** distinguish [5] **made one** as opposed to
"born one"—assumed character [7] **on** of [8] **case** disguise [9]
Except Unless **composition** agreement

[Enter VOLPONE.*]*

VOLPONE: Signior Corvino! and Corbaccio! sir,
    Much joy unto you.
CORVINO: Of what?
VOLPONE: The sudden good
    Dropped down upon you—
CORBACCIO: Where?
VOLPONE: And none knows how,
    From old Volpone, sir.
10 CORBACCIO: Out, arrant knave!
VOLPONE: Let not your too much wealth, sir, make
    you furious.
CORBACCIO: Away, thou varlet.
VOLPONE: Why, sir?
CORBACCIO: Dost thou mock me?
VOLPONE: You mock the world, sir. Did you not
    change wills?
CORBACCIO: Out, harlot!
VOLPONE: Oh, belike° you are the man,
15   Signior Corvino? Faith, you carry it well;
    You grow not mad withal; I love your spirit;
    You are not over-leavened° with your fortune.
    You should ha' some would swell now, like a
    wine-fat,°
    With such an autumn—Did he give you all, sir?
CORVINO: Avoid,° you rascal!
20 VOLPONE: Troth, your wife has shown
    Herself, a very° woman; but you are well,
    You need not care, you have a good estate,
    To bear it out, sir, better by this chance:
    Except Corbaccio have a share.
CORBACCIO: Hence, varlet.
VOLPONE: You will not be a 'known,° sir; why, 'tis
25   wise.
    Thus do all gamesters, at all games, dissemble.
    No man will seem to win.

[Exeunt CORVINO and CORBACCIO.]

                  Here comes my vulture,
    Heaving his beak up i' the air, and snuffing.

[Enter VOLTORE.*]*

VOLTORE: Outstripped thus, by a parasite! a slave,
30   Would run on errands, and make legs for crumbs.
    Well, what I'll do—
VOLPONE: The court stays for your worship.
    I e'en rejoice, sir, at your worship's happiness,
    And that it fell into so learnèd hands,
    That understand the fingering—
VOLTORE: What do you mean?

VOLPONE: I mean to be a suitor to your worship,   35
    For the small tenement, out of reparations,°
    That, at the end of your long row of houses,
    By the Piscaria.° It was, in Volpone's time,
    Your predecessor, ere he grew diseased,
    A handsome, pretty, customed° bawdy-house   40
    As any was in Venice, none dispraised:
    But fell with him: his body and that house
    Decayed together.
VOLTORE: Come, sir, leave your prating.
VOLPONE: Why, if your worship give me but your
    hand,°
    That I may ha' the refusal, I have done.   45
    'Tis a mere toy to you, sir; candle-rents;°
    As your learned worship knows—
VOLTORE: What do I know?
VOLPONE: Marry, no end of your wealth, sir; God
    decrease it!
VOLTORE: Mistaking knave! what, mock'st thou my
    misfortune?

[Exit.]

VOLPONE: His blessing on your heart, sir; would
    'twere more!—   50
    Now to my first again, at the next corner.

[Exit.]

[Enter CORBACCIO *and* CORVINO; MOSCA *passing over
the stage.]*

CORBACCIO: See, in our habit! see the impudent varlet!
CORVINO: That I could shoot mine eyes at him, like
    gun-stones!°

[Enter VOLPONE.*]*

VOLPONE: But is this true, sir, of the parasite?
CORBACCIO: Again, to afflict us! monster!
VOLPONE: In good faith, sir,   55
    I'm heartily grieved, a beard of your grave length
    Should be so over-reached,° I never brooked°
    That parasite's hair; methought his nose should
    cozen.
    There still was somewhat in his look, did promise
    The bane of a clarissimo.
CORBACCIO: Knave—
VOLPONE: Methinks   60
    Yet you, that are so traded° i' the world,
    A witty merchant, the fine bird, Corvino,

SCENE 4: **¹⁴ belike** perhaps **¹⁷ over-leavened** swelled up
¹⁸ fat vat **²⁰ Avoid** Be gone **²¹ very** true **²⁵ a'known** recognized

³⁶ reparations repair **³⁸ Piscaria** fish market **⁴⁰ customed**
well-patronized **⁴⁴ hand** agreement **⁴⁶ candle-rents**
income from deteriorating property **⁵³ gun-stones** cannonballs **⁵⁷ over-reached** outwitted **brooked** could endure
⁶¹ traded experienced

That have such moral emblems on your name,°
  Should not have sung your shame, and dropped
    your cheese,°
65 To let the Fox laugh at your emptiness.
  CORVINO: Sirrah, you think the privilege of the place,
    And your red saucy cap, that seems to me
    Nailed to your jolt-head° with those two
      cecchines,°
    Can warrant your abuses. Come you hither:
70   You shall perceive, sir, I dare beat you; approach.
  VOLPONE: No haste, sir, I do know your valor well,
    Since you durst publish what you are, sir.
  CORVINO: Tarry,
    I'd speak with you.
  VOLPONE: Sir, sir, another time—
  CORVINO: Nay, now.
  VOLPONE: O God, sir! I were a wise man,
75   Would stand the fury of a distracted cuckold.

[MOSCA walks by them.]

  CORBACCIO: What, come again!
  VOLPONE: Upon 'em, Mosca; save me.
  CORBACCIO: The air's infected where he breathes.
  CORVINO: Let's fly him.

[Exeunt CORVINO and CORBACCIO.]

  VOLPONE: Excellent basilisk!° Turn upon the vulture.

[Enter VOLTORE.]

  VOLTORE: Well, flesh-fly, it is summer with you now;
    Your winter will come on.
80 MOSCA: Good advocate,
    Pray thee not rail, nor threaten out of place thus;
    Thou'lt make a solecism, as madam says.
    Get you a biggen° more; your brain breaks loose.

[Exit.]

  VOLTORE: Well, sir.
  VOLPONE: Would you ha' me beat the insolent slave,
    Throw dirt upon his first good clothes?
85 VOLTORE: This same
    Is doubtless some familiar.°
  VOLPONE: Sir, the court,
    In troth, stays for you. I am mad, a mule
    That never read Justinian,° should get up,
    And ride an advocate. Had you no quirk

To avoid gullage, sir, by such a creature?   90
  I hope you do but jest; he has not done it.
  This's but confederacy to blind the rest.
  You are the heir?
  VOLTORE: A strange, officious,
  Troublesome knave! Thou dost torment me.
  VOLPONE: I know—
    It cannot be, sir, that you should be cozened;   95
    'Tis not within the wit of man to do it.
    You are so wise, so prudent; and 'tis fit
    That wealth and wisdom still should go together.

[Exeunt.]

Scene 5

*[Enter four AVOCATORI, NOTARIO, BONARIO, CELIA,
CORBACCIO, CORVINO, COMMANDADORI, SAFFI, etc.]*

1 ADVOCATE: Are all the parties here?
  NOTARIO: All but the advocate.
2 ADVOCATE: And here he comes.

[Enter VOLTORE and VOLPONE.]

1 ADVOCATE: Then bring 'hem forth to sentence.
  VOLTORE: O my most honored fathers, let your mercy
    Once win upon your justice, to forgive—
    I am distracted—
  VOLPONE: *[Aside]*   What will he do now?
  VOLTORE: Oh,   5
    I know not which to address myself to first;
    Whether your fatherhoods, or these innocents—
  CORVINO: *[Aside]* Will he betray himself?
  VOLTORE: Whom equally
    I have abused, out of most covetous ends—
  CORVINO: The man is mad!
  CORBACCIO: What's that?
  CORVINO: He is possessed.°   10
  VOLTORE: For which, now struck in conscience, here I
      prostrate
    Myself at your offended feet, for pardon.
1, 2 ADVOCATE: Arise.
  CELIA: O heaven, how just thou art!
  VOLPONE: *[Aside]*   I am caught
    I' mine own noose—
  CORVINO: *[To CORBACCIO]*
                            Be constant, sir; naught now
    Can help but impudence.
1 ADVOCATE: Speak forward.
  COMMANDADORI: Silence!   15
  VOLTORE: It is not passion in me, reverend fathers,
    But only conscience, conscience, my good sires,
    That makes me now tell truth. That parasite,

---

[63] **name** of "crow," to which contemporary emblem books assigned particular qualities   [64] **sung . . . cheese** In Aesop's fable, the crow opens its mouth to reply to the crafty fox and lets fall the cheese.   [68] **jolt-head** blockhead   **cecchines** gilt buttons   [78] **basilisk** fabled serpent, to look on which was fatal   [83] **biggen** cap   [86] **familiar** spirit, devil   [88] **Justinian** Roman emperor famous for his codifying of the law

---

SCENE 5:   [10] **possessed** as by a devil

That knave, hath been the instrument of all.
1 ADVOCATE: Where is that knave? Fetch him.
VOLPONE: I go.

[Exit.]

20 CORVINO: Grave fathers,
   This man's distracted; he confessed it now:
   For, hoping to be old Volpone's heir,
   Who now is dead—
3 ADVOCATE: How!
2 ADVOCATE: Is Volpone dead?
CORVINO: Dead since, grave fathers.
BONARIO: O sure vengeance!
1 ADVOCATE: Stay,
   Then he was no deceiver.
25 VOLTORE: Oh, no, none:
   This parasite, grave fathers.
CORVINO: He does speak
   Out of mere envy 'cause the servant's made
   The thing he gaped for. Please your fatherhoods,
   This is the truth, though I'll not justify
30 The other, but he may be some-deal° faulty.
VOLTORE: Ay, to your hopes, as well as mine,
   Corvino.
   But I'll use modesty. Pleaseth your wisdoms,
   To view these certain° notes, and but confer° them;
   And as I hope favor, they shall speak clear truth.
CORVINO: The devil has entered him!
35 BONARIO: Or bides in you.
4 ADVOCATE: We have done ill, by a public officer
   To send for him, if he be heir.
2 ADVOCATE: For whom?
4 ADVOCATE: Him that they call the parasite.
3 ADVOCATE: 'Tis true,
   He is a man of great estate, now left.
4 ADVOCATE: Go you, and learn his name, and say
40 the court
   Entreats his presence here, but to the clearing
   Of some few doubts.

[Exit NOTARIO.]

2 ADVOCATE: This same's a labyrinth!
1 ADVOCATE: Stand you unto your first report?
CORVINO: My state,
   My life, my fame—
BONARIO: Where is it?
CORVINO: Are at the stake.
1 ADVOCATE: Is yours so too?
45 CORBACCIO: The advocate's a knave,
   And has a forkèd tongue—
2 ADVOCATE: Speak to the point.
CORBACCIO: So is the parasite too.

1 ADVOCATE: This is confusion.
VOLTORE: I do beseech your fatherhoods, read but
   those—
CORVINO: And credit nothing the false spirit hath writ.
   It cannot be but he's possessed, grave fathers.   50

[Exeunt.]

Scene 6

[Enter VOLPONE.*]*

VOLPONE: To make a snare for mine own neck! and
   run
   My head into it, willfully! with laughter!
   When I had newly 'scaped, was free and clear!
   Out of mere wantonness! Oh, the dull devil
   Was in this brain of mine when I devised it,   5
   And Mosca gave it second; he must now
   Help to sear up° this vein, or we bleed dead.

[Enter NANO, ANDROGYNO, *and* CASTRONE.*]*

   How now! who let you loose? Whither go you
   now?
   What, to buy gingerbread, or to drown kitlings?°
NANO: Sir, Master Mosca called us out of doors,   10
   And bid us all go play, and took the keys.
ANDROGYNO: Yes.
VOLPONE: Did Master Mosca take the keys? Why, so!
   I'm farther in. These are my fine conceits!°
   I must be merry, with a mischief to me!
   What a vile wretch was I, that could not bear   15
   My fortune soberly? I must ha' my crochets,
   And my conundrums! Well, go you, and seek him.
   His meaning may be truer than my fear.
   Bid him, he straight come to me to the court;
   Thither will I, and, if't be possible,   20
   Unscrew my advocate, upon new hopes.
   When I provoked him, then I lost myself.

[Exeunt.]

Scene 7

[Four AVOCATORI, BONARIO, CELIA, CORBACCIO, CORVINO,
COMMANDADORI, SAFFI, *etc., as before.]*

1 ADVOCATE: These things can ne'er be reconciled. He
   here
   Professeth that the gentleman was wronged,
   And that the gentlewoman was brought thither,

SCENE 6:   ⁷ **sear up** cauterize   ⁹ **kitlings** kittens   ¹³ **conceits** imaginings, stratagems

Forced by her husband, and there left.
VOLTORE: Most true.
CELIA: How ready is heaven to those that pray!
5 1 ADVOCATE: But that
Volpone would have ravished her, he holds
Utterly false, knowing his impotence.
CORVINO: Grave fathers, he is possessed; again, I say,
Possessed. Nay, if there be possession and
Obsession° he has both.
10 3 ADVOCATE: Here comes our officer.

[Enter VOLPONE.*]*

VOLPONE: The parasite will straight be here, grave
fathers.
4 ADVOCATE: You might invent some other name, sir
varlet.
3 ADVOCATE: Did not the notary meet him?
VOLPONE: Not that I know.
4 ADVOCATE: His coming will clear all.
2 ADVOCATE: Yet it is misty.
VOLTORE: May't please your fatherhoods—

*[*VOLPONE *whispers the Advocate.]*

15 VOLPONE: Sir, the parasite
Willed me to tell you that his master lives;
That you are still the man; your hopes the same;
And this was only a jest—
VOLTORE: How?
VOLPONE: Sir, to try
If you were firm, and how you stood affected.
VOLTORE: Art sure he lives?
VOLPONE: Do I live, sir?
20 VOLTORE: Oh, me!
I was too violent.
VOLPONE: Sir, you may redeem it.
They said you were possessed. Fall down, and
seem so.
I'll help to make it good.

*[*VOLTORE *falls.]*

                                    God bless the man
Stop your wind hard, and swell—See, see, see,
see!
25   He vomits crooked pins!° His eyes are set,
Like a dead hare's hung in a poulter's shop!
His mouth's running away!° Do you see, signior?
Now it is in his belly.
CORVINO: Ay, the devil!

VOLPONE: Now in his throat.
CORVINO: Ay, I perceive it plain.
VOLTORE: 'Twill out, 'twill out! stand clear. See where
it flies,   30
In shape of a blue toad, with a bat's wings!
Do you not see it, sir?
CORBACCIO: What? I think I do.
CORVINO: 'Tis too manifest.
VOLTORE: Look! He comes to himself!
VOLTORE: Where am I?
VOLPONE: Take good heart, the worst is past, sir.
You are possessed.
1 ADVOCATE: What accident is this!   35
2 ADVOCATE: Sudden, and full of wonder!
3 ADVOCATE: If he were
Possessed, as it appears, all this is nothing.
CORVINO: He has been often subject to these fits.
1 ADVOCATE: Show him that writing:—do you know
it, sir?
VOLPONE: *[Whispers* VOLTORE.*]* Deny it, sir, forswear it;
know it not.   40
VOLTORE: Yes, I do know it well, it is my hand;
But all that it contains is false.
BONARIO: O practice!
2 ADVOCATE: What maze is this!
1 ADVOCATE: Is he not guilty then,
Whom you there name the parasite?
VOLTORE: Grave fathers,
No more than his good patron, old Volpone.   45
4 ADVOCATE: Why, he is dead.
VOLTORE: Oh, no, my honored fathers,
He lives—
1 ADVOCATE: How! lives?
VOLTORE: Lives.
2 ADVOCATE: This is subtler yet!
3 ADVOCATE: You said he was dead.
VOLTORE: Never.
3 ADVOCATE: You said so.
CORVINO: I heard so.
4 ADVOCATE: Here comes the gentleman; make him
way.

[Enter MOSCA.*]*

3 ADVOCATE: A stool.
4 ADVOCATE: *[Aside]* A proper° man; and were
Volpone dead,   50
A fit match for my daughter.
3 ADVOCATE: Give him way.
VOLPONE: *[Aside to* MOSCA*]* Mosca, I was almost lost;
the advocate
Had betrayed all; but now it is recovered.
All's on the hinge again—Say I am living.

SCENE 7:   [10] **possession . . . Obsession** the evil spirit controlling from within; and attacking from without   [25] **He . . . pins**
as bewitched persons were supposed to do   [27] **running away**
contorted

---

[50] **proper** handsome

MOSCA: What busy knave is this!—Most reverend
55   fathers,
    I sooner had attended your grave pleasures,
    But that my order for the funeral
    Of my dear patron did require me—
VOLPONE: [*Aside*]   Mosca!
MOSCA: Whom I intend to bury like a gentleman.
VOLPONE: [*Aside*] Ay, quick,° and cozen me of all.
60 2 ADVOCATE: Still stranger!
    More intricate!
1 ADVOCATE: And come about again!
4 ADVOCATE: [*Aside*] It is a match, my daughter is
    bestowed.
MOSCA: [*Aside to* VOLPONE] Will you give me half?
VOLPONE: First I'll be hanged.
MOSCA: I know
    Your voice is good, cry not so loud.
1 ADVOCATE: Demand°
65 The advocate.—Sir, did not you affirm
    Volpone was alive?
VOLPONE: Yes, and he is;
    This gentleman told me so. [*Aside to* MOSCA] Thou
    shalt have half.
MOSCA: Whose drunkard is this same? Speak, some
    that know him.
    I never saw his face. [*Aside to* VOLPONE] I cannot
    now
    Afford it you so cheap.
VOLPONE: No!
70 1 ADVOCATE: What say you?
VOLTORE: The officer told me.
VOLPONE: I did, grave fathers,
    And will maintain he lives, with mine own life,
    And that this creature told me. [*Aside*] I was born
    With all good stars my enemies.
MOSCA: Most grave fathers,
75 If such an insolence as this must pass
    Upon me, I am silent; 'twas not this
    For which you sent, I hope.
2 ADVOCATE: Take him away.
VOLPONE: Mosca!
3 ADVOCATE: Let him be whipped.
VOLPONE: Wilt thou betray me?
    Cozen me?
3 ADVOCATE: And taught to bear himself
    Toward a person of his rank.
80 4 ADVOCATE: Away

[*The* OFFICERS *seize* VOLPONE.]

MOSCA: I humbly thank your fatherhoods.
VOLPONE: [*Aside*]   Soft, soft: whipped!
    And lose all that I have! If I confess,

It cannot be much more.
4 ADVOCATE: Sir, are you married?
VOLPONE: They'll be allied anon: I must be resolute.

[*He puts off his disguise.*]

    The Fox shall here uncase.
MOSCA: Patron!
VOLPONE: Nay, now   85
    My ruin shall not come alone; your match
    I'll hinder sure. My substance shall not glue you,
    Nor screw you into a family.
MOSCA: Why, patron!
VOLPONE: I am Volpone, and this is my knave;
    This [*Pointing to* VOLTORE], his own knave; this
    [*To* CORBACCIO], avarice's fool;   90
    This [*To* CORVINO], a chimera° of wittol, fool, and
    knave.
    And, reverend fathers, since we all can hope.
    Nought but a sentence, let's not now despair it.
    You hear me brief.
CORVINO: May it please your fatherhoods—
COMMANDADOR: Silence.
1 ADVOCATE: The knot is now undone by miracle.   95
2 ADVOCATE: Nothing can be more clear.
3 ADVOCATE: Or can more prove
    These innocent.
1 ADVOCATE: Give 'hem their liberty.
BONARIO: Heaven could not long let such gross
    crimes be hid.
2 ADVOCATE: If this be held the highway to get riches,
    May I be poor!
3 ADVOCATE: This is not the gain, but torment.   100
1 ADVOCATE: These possess wealth, as sick men pos-
    sess fevers,
    Which trulier may be said to possess them.
2 ADVOCATE: Disrobe that parasite.
CORVINO, MOSCA: Most honored fathers—
1 ADVOCATE: Can you plead aught to stay the course
    of justice?
    If you can, speak.
CORVINO, VOLTORE: We beg favor.
CELIA: And mercy.   105
1 ADVOCATE: You hurt your innocence, suing for the
    guilty.
    Stand forth; and first the parasite. You appear
    T'have been the chiefest minister, if not plotter,
    In all these lewd impostures, and now, lastly,
    Have with your impudence abused the court,   110
    And habit of a gentleman of Venice,
    Being a fellow of no birth or blood.
    For which our sentence is, first, thou be whipped;
    Then live a perpetual prisoner in our galleys.

---

⁶⁰**quick** alive   ⁶⁴**Demand** Question   ⁹¹**chimera** fabled monster

VOLPONE: I thank you for him.
115 MOSCA: Bane to thy wolfish nature!
1 ADVOCATE: Deliver him to the Saffi.

[MOSCA is carried out.]

                                        Thou, Volpone,
    By blood and rank a gentleman, canst not fall
    Under like censure; but our judgment on thee
    Is, that thy substance° all be straight confiscate
120 To the hospital of the Incurabili.
    And since the most was gotten by imposture,
    By feigning lame, gout, palsy, and such diseases,
    Thou art to lie in prison, cramped with irons,
    Till thou be'st sick and lame indeed. Remove him.
125 VOLPONE: This is called mortifying° of a Fox.

[VOLPONE is taken away.]

1 ADVOCATE: Thou, Voltore, to take away the scandal,
    Thou hast given all worthy men of thy profession,
    Art banished from their fellowship, and our state.
    Corbaccio!—bring him near. We here possess
130 Thy son of all thy state, and confine thee
    To the monastery of San Spirito;
    Where, since thou knew'st not how to live well here,
    Thou shalt be learned to die well.
CORBACCIO: Ha! what said he?
COMMANDADOR: You shall know anon, sir.
1 ADVOCATE: Thou, Corvino, shalt
Be straight embarked from thine own house, and
135   rowed
    Round about Venice, through the Grand Canal,
    Wearing a cap, with fair long ass's ears,
    Instead of horns! and so to mount, a paper
    Pinned on thy breast, to the berlina.°
CORVINO: Yes,
140 And have mine eyes beat out with stinking fish,
    Bruised fruit, and rotten eggs—'tis well. I am glad
    I shall not see my shame yet.
1 ADVOCATE: And to expiate
    Thy wrongs done to thy wife, thou art to send her
    Home to her father, with her dowry trebled.
    And these are all your judgments.
145 ALL: Honored fathers—
1 ADVOCATE: Which may not be revoked. Now you
        begin,
    When crimes are done, and past, and to be punished,
    To think what your crimes are. Away with them.
    Let all that see these vices thus rewarded,
150 Take heart, and love to study 'hem. Mischiefs feed
    Like beasts, till they be fat, and then they bleed.

                    [Exeunt.]

VOLPONE*[comes forward]*:

    The seasoning of a play is the applause.
    Now, though the Fox be punished by the laws,
    He yet doth hope, there is no suffering due,
    For any fact° which he hath done 'gainst you.
    If there be, censure him; here he doubtful stands.
    If not, fare jovially, and clap your hands.

                    [Exit.]

                    FINIS

---

¹¹⁹ **substance** goods   ¹²⁵ **mortifying** pun; fowl are "mortified" or made tender by hanging them up for some time after
they have been killed   ¹³⁹ **berlina** pillory

¹¹ **fact** crime

Contexts and Commentaries

Sir Philip Sidney (1554–1586)

During his short life Sir Philip Sidney (1554–1586) achieved a significant literary reputation, one which continues to this day. A member of an influential family, Sidney aspired to succeed at court, but Elizabeth I was suspicious of his political and religious idealism and kept him at bay. His public career was thus filled with frustration, and he died—nobly, by all accounts—at the battle of Zutphen in the Netherlands in 1586. His *Astrophel and Stella* pioneered the late-century inventiveness of the sonnet sequence, a form that many others were to try, including Shakespeare. His prose romance, *Arcadia*, a precursor of the English novel, was read for over a century after his death. His literary taste, critical sensibilities, and theoretical sophistication are recorded in *An Apology for Poetry*, which remains the most original and admired critical treatise from sixteenth-century England. In it, Sidney puts forward a socially responsible view of literature and drama, defending poets on the grounds that they reform the manner and morals of society.

from AN APOLOGY FOR POETRY

. . . Nature never set forth the earth in so rich tapestry as divers poets have done, neither with so pleasant rivers, fruitful trees, sweet smelling flowers, nor whatsoever else may make the too much loved earth more lovely. Her world is brazen, the poets only deliver a golden. But let those things alone and go to man, for whom as the other things are, so it seemeth in him her uttermost cunning is employed, and know whether she have brought forth so true a lover as Theagenes,[1] so constant a friend as Pylades,[2] so valiant a man as Orlando,[3] so right a prince as Xenophon's Cyrus,[4] so excellent a man every way as Virgil's Aeneas.[5] Neither let this be jestingly conceived because the works of the one be essential, the other in imitation or fiction; for any understanding knoweth the skill of the artificer standeth in that idea or fore-conceit of the work, and not in the work itself. And that the poet hath that idea is manifest, by delivering them

---

[1] **Theagenes** Theagenes of Thessaly from Heliodorus's *Aethiopica*   [2] **Pylades** the faithful friend of Orestes   [3] **Orlando** the hero of Ariosto's epic poem *Orlando Furioso*   [4] **Cyrus** (d. 529 B.C), founder of the Persian empire, whose story is told in Xenophon's *Cyropaedia*   [5] **Aeneas** the hero of Virgil's *Aeneid*

forth in such excellency as he had imagined them. Which delivering forth also is not wholly imaginative, as we are wont to say by them that build castles in the air; but so far substantially it worketh, not only to make a Cyrus, which had been but a particular excellency as nature might have done, but to bestow a Cyrus upon the world to make many Cyruses, if they will learn aright why and how that maker made him.

Neither let it be deemed too saucy a comparison to balance the highest point of man's wit with the efficacy of nature; but rather give right honor to the heavenly Maker of that maker, who having made man to His own likeness, set him beyond and over all the works of that second nature: which in nothing he showeth so much as in poetry, when with the force of a divine breath he bringeth things forth far surpassing her doings, with no small argument to the incredulous of that first accursed fall of Adam, since our erected wit maketh us know what perfection is, and yet our infected will keepeth us from reaching unto it. But these arguments will by few be understood, and by fewer granted. This much I hope will be given me, that the Greeks with some probability of reason gave him[6] the name above all names of learning. Now let us go to a more ordinary opening of him, that the truth may be the more palpable: and so I hope, though we get not so unmatched a praise as the etymology of his names will grant, yet his very description, which no man will deny, shall not justly be barred from a principal commendation.

Poesy therefore is an art of imitation, for so Aristotle termeth it in the word *mimesis*, that is to say, a representing, counterfeiting, or figuring forth, to speak metaphorically, a speaking picture: with this end, to teach and delight . . .

Our tragedies and comedies (not without cause cried out against) observing rules neither of honest civility nor of skilful poetry, excepting *Gorboduc*[7] (again I say, of those that I have seen), which notwithstanding as it is full of stately speeches and well sounding phrases, climbing to the height of Seneca his style, and as full of notable morality, which it doth most delightfully teach, and so obtain the very end of poesy; yet in truth it is very defectuous in the circumstances, which grieveth me, because it might not remain as an exact model of all tragedies. For it is faulty both in place and time, the two necessary companions of all corporal actions. For where the stage should always represent but one place, and the uttermost time presupposed in it should be, both by Aristotle's precept and common reason, but one day, there is both many days, and many places, inartificially imagined.

But if it be so in *Gorboduc*, how much more in all the rest, where you shall have Asia of the one side, and Afric of the other, and so many other under-kingdomes, that the player when he cometh in, must ever begin with telling where he is, or else the tale will not be conceived? Now you shall have three ladies walk to gather flowers, and then we must believe the stage to be a garden. By and by we hear news of a shipwreck in the same place, and then we are to blame if we accept it not for a rock. Upon the back of that comes out a hideous

---

[6] **him** i.e., the poet   [7] **Gorboduc** the tragedy of Ferrex and Porrex, written in blank verse by Thomas Norton and Thomas Sackville and first performed at court before Elizabeth I in 1561

monster with fire and smoke, and then the miserable beholders are bound to take it for a cave. While in the meantime two armies fly in, represented with four swords and bucklers, and then what hard heart will not receive it for a pitched field?

Now, of time they are much more liberal, for ordinary it is that two young princes fall in love; after many traverses, she is got with child, delivered of a fair boy; he is lost, groweth a man, falls in love, and is ready to get another child; and all this in two hours' space: which how absurd it is in sense, even sense may imagine, and art hath taught, and all ancient examples justified—and at this day, the ordinary players in Italy will not err in. Yet will some bring in an example of *Eunuchus* in Terence, that containeth matter of two days, yet far short of twenty years. True it is, and so was it to be played in two days, and so fitted to the time it set forth. And though Plautus have in one place done amiss, let us hit with him, and not miss with him.

But they will say: How then shall we set forth a story which containeth both many places and many times? And do they not know that a tragedy is tied to the laws of poesy, and not of history; not bound to follow the story, but having liberty either to feign a quite new matter or to frame the history to the most tragical convenience? Again, many things may be told which cannot be showed, if they know the difference betwixt reporting and representing. As, for example, I may speak (though I am here) of Peru, and in speech digress from that to the description of Calicut; but in action I cannot represent it without Pacolet's horse;[8] and so was the manner the ancients took, by some Nuntius to recount things done in former time or other place. Lastly, if they will represent a history, they must not (as Horace saith) begin *ab ovo*,[9] but they must come to the principal point of that one action which they will represent.

By example this will be best expressed. I have a story of young Polydorus, delivered for safety's sake, with great riches, by his father Priam to Polymestor, king of Thrace, in the Trojan war time; he, after some years, hearing the overthrow of Priam, for to make the treasure his own, murdereth the child; the body of the child is taken up by Hecuba; she, the same day, findeth a sleight to be revenged most cruelly of the tyrant.[10] Where now would one of our tragedy writers begin, but with the delivery of that child? Then should he sail over into Thrace, and so spend I know not how many years, and travel numbers of places. But where doth Euripides? Even with the finding of the body, leaving the rest to be told by the spirit of Polydorus. This need no further be enlarged; the dullest wit may conceive it.

But besides these gross absurdities, how all their plays be neither right tragedies, nor right comedies, mingling kings and clowns, not because the matter so carrieth it, but thrust in clowns by head and shoulders to play a part in majestical matters with neither decency nor discretion, so as neither the admiration and commiseration, nor the right sportfulness, is by their mongrel tragicomedy obtained. I know Apuleius[11] did somewhat so, but that is a thing recounted

---

[8] **Pacolet's horse** the magic horse of the magician Pacolet in the French romance *Valentine and Orson*   [9] **ab ovo** Horace, *De Arte Poetica*: "from the egg"   [10] The story is that of Euripides' *Hecuba*.   [11] **Apuleius** second century A.D. author of *Golden Ass*

with space of time, not represented in one moment; and I know the ancients have one or two examples of tragi-comedies, as Plautus hath *Amphitryon*; but, if we mark them well, we shall find that they never, or very daintily, match horn-pipes and funerals. So falleth it out that, having indeed no right comedy, in that comical part of our tragedy, we have nothing but scurrility, unworthy of any chaste ears, or some extreme show of doltishness, indeed fit to lift up a loud laughter, and nothing else: where the whole tract of a comedy should be full of delight, as the tragedy should be still maintained in a well-raised admiration.

But our comedians think there is no delight without laughter; which is very wrong, for though laughter may come with delight, yet cometh it not of delight, as though delight should be the cause of laughter; but well may one thing breed both together. Nay, rather in themselves they have, as it were, a kind of contrariety: for delight we scarcely do but in things that have a conveniency to ourselves or to the general nature; laughter almost ever cometh of things most disporportioned to ourselves and nature. Delight hath a joy in it, either perma-nent or present. Laughter hath only a scornful tickling.

For example, we are ravished with delight to see a fair woman, and yet are far from being moved to laughter; we laugh at deformed creatures, wherein cer-tainly we cannot delight. We delight in good chances, we laught at mischances; we delight to hear the happiness of our friends, or country, at which he were worthy to be laughed at that would laugh; we shall contrarily, laugh sometimes to find a matter quite mistaken and go down the hill against the bias in the mouth of some such men, as for the respect of them one shall be heartily sorry, he cannot choose but laugh, and so is rather pained than delighted with laughter.

Yet deny I not but that they may go well together. For as in Alexander's pic-ture well set out we delight without laughter, and in twenty mad antics we laugh without delight; so in Hercules, painted with his great beard and furious counte-nance, in a woman's attire, spinning at Omphale's commandment, it breedeth both delight and laughter. For the representing of so strange a power in love pro-cureth delight, and the scornfulness of the action stirreth laughter. But speak I to this purpose, that all the end of the comical part be not upon such scornful mat-ters as stirreth laughter only, but mixed with it, that delightful teaching which is the end of poesy. And the great fault even in that point of laughter, and forbidden plainly by Aristotle, is that they stir laughter in sinful things, which are rather execrable than ridiculous, or in miserable, which are rather to be pitied than scorned. For what is it to make fools gape at a wretched beggar or a beggarly clown; or, against law of hospitality, to jest at strangers, because they speak not English so well as we do? What do we learn, since it is certain

> Nil habet infelix paupertas durius in se,
> Quam quod ridiculos homines facit?[12]

But rather, a busy loving courtier and a heartless threatening Thraso;[13] a self-wise-seeming schoolmaster; an awry-transformed traveller. These if we saw

---

[12] **Nihil . . . facit** from Juvenal, *Satires*, III, 152–153: "unfortunate poverty contains no more painful misery than that it exposes men to ridicule"   [13] **Thraso** a boaster

walk in stage names, which we play naturally, therein were delightful laughter, and teaching delightfulness, as in the other, the tragedies of Buchanan[14] do justly bring forth a divine admiration.

But I have lavished out too many words of this play matter. I do it because, as they are excelling parts of poesy, so is there none so much used in England, and none can be more pitifully abused; which, like an unmannerly daughter showing a bad education, causeth her mother Poesy's honesty to be called into question . . . .

Ben Jonson (1572–1637)

In his Epistle to Volpone, *addressed "to the most noble and most equal Sisters, the two famous universities" at Cambridge and Oxford, Jonson discusses his view of the contemporary state of dramatic poetry, gives his theory of comedy, and defends the ending of* Volpone.

EPISTLE TO *VOLPONE*

Never, most equal Sisters, had any man a wit so presently excellent as that it could raise itself; but there must come both matter, occasion, commenders, and favorers to it. If this be true, and that the fortune of all writers doth daily prove it, it behooves the careful to provide well toward these accidents, and, having acquired them, to preserve that part of reputation most tenderly wherein the benefit of a friend is also defended. Hence is it that I now render myself grateful and am studious to justify the bounty of your act, to which, though your mere authority were satisfying, yet, it being an age wherein poetry and the professors[1] of it hear so ill on all sides, there will a reason be looked for in the subject. It is certain, nor can it with any forehead be opposed, that the too much license of poetasters in this time hath much deformed their mistress,[2] that, every day, their manifold and manifest ignorance doth stick unnatural reproaches upon her; but for their petulancy it were an act of the greatest injustice either to let the learned suffer, or so divine a skill (which indeed should not be attempted with unclean hands) to fall under the least contempt. For, if men will impartially, and not asquint, look toward the offices and function of a poet, they will easily conclude to themselves the impossibility of any man's being the good poet without first being a good man. He that is said to be able to inform young men to all good disciplines, inflame grown men to all great virtues, keep old men in their best and supreme state, or, as they decline to childhood, recover them to their first

---

[14] **Buchanan** George Buchanan (1506–1582), Scottish humanist and poet

[1] **professors** i.e., poets   [2] **mistress** poetry

strength; that comes forth the interpreter and arbiter of nature, a teacher of things divine no less than human, a master in manners; and can alone, or with a few, effect the business of mankind; this, I take him, is no subject for pride and ignorance to exercise their railing rhetoric upon. But it will here be hastily answered that the writers of these days are other things: that not only their manners, but their natures, are inverted, and nothing remaining with them of the dignity of poet but the abused name, which every scribe usurps; that now, especially in dramatic, or as they term it, stage poetry, nothing but ribaldry, profanation, blasphemy, all license of offence to God and man is practiced. I dare not deny a great part of this, and am sorry I dare not, because in some men's abortive features (and would they had never boasted the light) it is over true; but that all are embarked in this bold adventure for hell is a most uncharitable thought, and, uttered, a more malicious slander. For my particular, I can, and from a most clear conscience, affirm that I have ever trembled to think toward the least profaneness, have loathed the use of such foul and unwashed bawdry as is now made the food of the scene.[3] And, howsoever I cannot escape, from some, the imputation of sharpness, but that they will say I have taken a pride, or lust, to be bitter, and not my youngest infant but hath come into the world with all his teeth; I would ask of these supercilious politics, what nation, society, or general order, or state I have provoked? what public person? whether I have not in all these preserved their dignity, as mine own person, safe? My works are read, allowed (I speak of those that are entirely mine); look into them. What broad reproofs have I used? where have I been particular? where personal? except to a minim, cheater, bawd, or buffoon, creatures for their insolencies worthy to be taxed? . . . the present trade of the stage, in all their misc'line[4], interludes, what learned or liberal soul doth not already abhor? where nothing but the filth of the time is uttered, and that with such impropriety of phrase, such plenty of solecisms, such as dearth of sense, so bold prolepses,[5] so racked metaphors, with brotherly able to violate the ear of a pagan, and blasphemy to turn the blood of a Christian to water. I cannot but be serious in a cause of this nature, wherein my fame and the reputations of divers honest and learned are the question: when a name[6], so full of authority, antiquity, and all great mark is, through their insolence, become the lowest scorn of the age; and those men subject to the petulancy of every vernaculous[7] orator that were wont to be the care of kings and happiest monarchs. This it is that hath not only rapt me to present indignation, but made me studious heretofore, and by all my actions to stand off from them; which may most appear in this my latest work, which you, most learned Arbitresses,[8] have seen, judged, and, to my crown, approved—wherein I have labored, for their instruction and amendment, to reduce not only the ancient forms, but manners of the scene: the easiness, the propriety, the innocence, and last, the doctrine, which is the principal end of poesie, to inform men in the best reason of living. And though my catastrophe[9] may in the strict rigor

---

[3] **food of the scene** i.e., the subject matter of plays   [4] **misc'line** mixed   [5] **prolepses** plural form of prolepsis, a rhetorical term referring to anticipation, especially describing an event as taking place before it could have, treating a future event as if it had already happened, or answering an argument before it has been advanced.   [6] **name** i.e., of a poet   [7] **vernaculous** low   [8] **Arbitresses** the two universities   [9] **catastrophe** the ending of *Volpone*

of comic law meet with censure, as turning back to my promise, I desire the learned and charitable critic to have so much faith in me to think it was done of industry: for with what ease I could have varied it nearer his scale (but that I fear to boast my own faculty) I could here insert. But my special aim being to put the snaffle in their mouths that cry out: We never punish vice in our interludes, and etc., I took the more liberty, though not without some lines of example drawn even in the ancients themselves, the goings-out[10] of whose comedies are not always joyful, but oft-times the bawds, the servants, the rivals, yea, and the masters are mulcted, and fitly, it being the office of a comic poet to imitate justice, and instruct to life, as well as purity of language, or stir up gentle affections. . . .

From my house in the Blackfriars, this 11th day of February 1607.

Jonathan Dollimore (B. 1948)

Jonathan Dollimore is a member of the faculty of the School of English and American Studies at the University of Sussex. Some of his well-known studies include Sexual Dissidence: Augustine to Wilde, Freud to Foucault *(1991) and* Political Shakespeare: Essays in Cultural Materialism *(1994). In* Radical Tragedy: Religion, Ideology, and Power in the Drama of Shakespeare and his Contemporaries *(1984, 1989), Dollimore suggests that the contradictions in Faustus' position provoke subversive questioning of the limiting structure of the play's world.*

from RADICAL TRAGEDY; *DR FAUSTUS* (C. 1589–92): SUBVERSION THROUGH TRANSGRESSION

One problem in particular has exercised critics of *Dr Faustus*: its structure, inherited from the morality form, apparently negates what the play experientially affirms—the heroic aspiration of 'Renaissance man.' Behind this discrepancy some have discerned a tension between, on the one hand, the moral and theological imperatives of a severe Christian orthodoxy and, on the other, an affirmation of Faustus as 'the epitome of Renaissance aspiration . . . all the divine discontent, the unwearied and unsatisfied striving after knowledge that marked the age in which Marlowe wrote'.[1]

Critical opinion has tended to see the tension resolved one way or anoth-

---

[10] **goings-out** endings

[1] Christopher Marlowe, *Doctor Faustus*, ed. Roma Gill (London: Benn, 1965), p. xix.

er—that is, to read the play as ultimately vindicating either Faustus or the morality structure. But such resolution is what *Dr Faustus* as interrogative text resists. It seems always to represent paradox—religious and tragic—as insecurely and provocatively ambiguous or, worse, as openly contradictory. Not surprisingly Max Bluestone, after surveying some eighty recent studies of *Dr Faustus*, as well as the play itself, remains unconvinced of their more or less equally divided attempts to find in it an orthodox or heterodox principle of resolution. On the contrary: 'conflict and contradiction inhere everywhere in the world of this play'.[2] If this is correct then we might see it as an integral aspect of what *Dr Faustus* is best understood as: not an affirmation of Divine Law, or conversely of Renaissance Man, but an exploration of subversion through transgression.

LIMIT AND TRANSGRESSION

Raymond Williams has observed how, in Victorian literature, individuals encounter limits of crucially different kinds. In *Felix Holt* there is the discovery of limits which, in the terms of the novel, are enabling: they vindicate a conservative identification of what it is to be human. In complete contrast *Jude the Obscure* shows its protagonist destroyed in the process—and ultimately because—of encountering limits. This is offered not as punishment for hubris but as 'profoundly subversive of the limiting structure'.[3] *Dr Faustus*, I want to argue, falls into this second category: a discovery of limits which ostensibly forecloses subversive questioning in fact provokes it.

What Erasmus had said many years before against Luther indicates the parameters of *Dr Faustus'* limiting structure:

> Suppose for a moment that it were true in a certain sense, as Augustine says somewhere, that 'God works in us good and evil, and rewards his own good works in us, and punishes his evil works in us' . . . Who will be able to bring himself to love God with all his heart when He created hell seething with eternal torments in order to punish His own misdeeds in His victims as though He took delight in human torments?[4]

But Faustus is not *identified* independently of this limiting structure and any attempt to interpret the play as Renaissance man breaking out of medieval chains always founders on this point: Faustus is constituted by the very limiting structure which he transgresses and his transgression is both despite and because of that fact.

Faustus is situated at the centre of a violently divided universe. To the extent that conflict and contradiction are represented as actually of its essence, it appears to be Manichean; thus Faustus asks 'where is the place that men call hell?', and Mephostophilis replies 'Within the bowels of these elements', adding:

> when all the world dissolves

---

[2] Max Bluestone, "*Libido Speculandi*: Doctrine and Dramaturgy in Contemporary Interpretations of Marlowe's *Doctor Faustus*," in Norman Rabkin, ed. *Reinterpretations of Renaissance Drama* (New York: Columbia University Press, 1969), p. 55. [3] Raymond Williams, "Forms of English Fiction in 1848," from *1848: The Forms of English Literature*, ed. F. Barker (Colchester: University of Essex, 1977), p. 287. [4] Stevie Davies, *Renaissance Views of Man* (Manchester: Manchester University Press, 1978), p. 92.

> And every creature shall be purify'd,
> All places shall be hell that is not heaven.
>> (v. 117, 120, 125–7)

If Greg is correct, and 'purified' means 'no longer mixed, but of one essence, either wholly good or wholly evil',[5] then the division suggested is indeed Manichean.[3] But more important than the question of precise origins is the fact that not only heaven and hell but God and Lucifer, the Good Angel and the Bad Angel, are polar opposites whose axes pass through and constitute human consciousness. Somewhat similarly, for Mephostophilis hell is not a place but a state of consciousness:

> Hell hath no limits, nor is circumscrib'd
> In one self place, but where we are is hell,
> And where hell is, there must we ever be.
>> (v. 122–4)

From Faustus' point of view—one never free-ranging but always coterminous with his position—God and Lucifer seem equally responsible in his final destruction, two supreme agents of power deeply antagonistic to each other yet temporarily co-operating in his demise. Faustus is indeed their subject, the site of their power struggle. For his part God is possessed of tyrannical power—'heavy wrath' (i. 71 and xix. 153), while at the beginning of scene xix Lucifer, Beelzebub and Mephostophilis enter syndicate-like 'To view the *subjects* of our monarchy'. Earlier Faustus had asked why Lucifer wanted his soul; it will, replies Mephostophilis, 'Enlarge his kingdom' (v. 40). In Faustus' final soliloquy both God and Lucifer are spatially located as the opposites which, *between them*, destroy him:

> O, I'll leap up to my God! Who pulls me down?
> see where God
> Stretcheth out his arm and bends his ireful brows
> My God, my God! Look not so fierce on me!
> Ugly hell, gape not! Come not, Lucifer.
>> (ll. 145, 150–1, 187, 189)

Before this the representatives of God and Lucifer have bombarded Faustus with conflicting accounts of his identity, position and destiny. Again, the question of whether in principle Faustus can repent, what is the point of no return, is less important than the fact that he is located on the axes of contradictions which cripple and finally destroy him.

By contrast, when, in Marlowe's earlier play, Tamburlaine speaks of the 'four elements/Warring within our breasts for regiment' he is speaking of a dynamic conflict conducive to the will to power—one which 'Doth teach us all to have aspiring minds' (1. II. vii. 18–20)—not the stultifying contradiction which constitutes Faustus and his universe. On this point alone *Tamburlaine* presents a

---

[5] Christopher Marlowe, *Dr. Faustus 1604–16: Parallel Texts*, ed. W. W. Greg (Oxford: Clarendon Press, 1950), p. 330.

fascinating contrast with *Dr Faustus*. With his indomitable will to power and warrior prowess, Tamburlaine really does approximate to the self-determining hero bent on transcendent autonomy—a kind of fantasy on Pico's theme of aspiring man. But like all fantasies this one excites as much by what it excludes as what it exaggerates. Indeed exclusion may be the basis not just of Tamburlaine as fantasy projection but *Tamburlaine* as transgressive text: it liberates from its Christian and ethical framework the humanist conception of man as essentially free, dynamic and aspiring; more contentiously, this conception of man is not only liberated from a Christian framework but reestablished in open defiance of it. But however interpreted, the objective of Tamburlaine's aspiration is very different from Pico's; the secular power in which Tamburlaine revels is part of what Pico wants to transcend in the name of a more ultimate and legitimate power. Tamburlaine defies origin, Pico aspires to it:

> A certain sacred striving should seize the soul so that, not content with the indifferent and middling, we may pant after the highest and so (for we can if we want to) force our way up to it with all our might. Let us despise the terrestrial, be unafraid of the heavenly, and then, neglecting the things of the world, fly towards that court beyond the world nearest to God the Most High.[6]

With *Dr Faustus* almost the reverse is true: transgression is born not of a liberating sense of freedom to deny or retrieve origin, nor from an excess of life breaking repressive bounds. It is rather a transgression rooted in an *impasse* of despair.

Even before he abjures God, Faustus expresses a sense of being isolated and trapped; an insecurity verging on despair pre-exists a damnation which, by a perverse act of free will, he 'chooses'. Arrogant he certainly is, but it is wrong to see Faustus at the outset as secure in the knowledge that existing forms of knowledge are inadequate. Rather, his search for a more complete knowledge is itself a search for security. For Faustus, 'born, of parents base of stock', and now both socially and geographically displaced (Prologue, II. 11, 13–19), no teleological integration of identity, self-consciousness and purpose obtains. In the opening scene he attempts to convince himself of the worth of several professions— divinity, medicine, law, and then divinity again—only to reject each in turn; in this he is almost schizoid:

> Having commenc'd, be a divine in show,
> Yet level at the end of every art,
> And live and die in Aristotle's works.
> Sweet Analytics, 'tis thou hast ravish'd me!
> When all is done, divinity is best.
> Philosophy is odious and obscure,
> Both law and physic are for petty wits,
> Divinity is basest of the three,
> Unpleasant, harsh, contemptible, and vile.
>
> (i. 3–6, 37, 105–8)

---

[6] Stevie Davies, *Renaissance Views of Man* (Manchester: Manchester University Press, 1978), pp. 69–70.

As he shakes free of spurious orthodoxy and the role of the conventional scholar, Faustus' insecurity intensifies. A determination to be 'resolved' of all ambiguities, to be 'resolute' and show fortitude (i. 32; iii. 14; v. 6; vi. 32, 64) is only a recurring struggle to escape agonised irresolution.

This initial desperation and insecurity, just as much as a subsequent fear of impending damnation, suggests why his search for knowledge so easily lapses into hedonistic recklessness and fatuous, self-forgetful 'delight' (i. 52; v. 82; vi. 170; viii. 59–60). Wagner cannot comprehend this psychology of despair:

> I think my master means to die shortly:
> He has made his will and given me his wealth
> I wonder what he means. If death were nigh,
> He would not banquet and carouse and swill
> Amongst the students.
>   (xviii. 1–2, 5–7)

Faustus knew from the outset what he would eventually incur. He willingly 'surrenders up . . . his soul' for twenty-four years of 'voluptuousness' in the knowledge that 'eternal death' will be the result (iii. 90–4). At the end of the first scene he exits declaring 'This night I'll conjure though I die therefor'. Later he reflects: 'long ere this I should have done the deed [i.e. suicide]/Had not sweet pleasure conquer'd deep despair' (vi. 24–5). This is a despairing hedonism rooted in the fatalism of his opening soliloquy: 'If we say that we have no sin, we deceive ourselves, and there's no truth in us. Why, then, belike we must sin, and so consequently die' (i. 41–4). Half-serious, half-facetious, Faustus registers a sense of human-kind as miscreated.

Tamburlaine's will to power leads to liberation through transgression. Faustus' pact with the devil, because an act of transgression without hope of liberation, is at once rebellious, masochistic and despairing. The protestant God—'an arbitrary and wilful, omnipotent and universal tyrant' (Walzer, p. 151)—demanded of each subject that s/he submit personally and without mediation. The modes of power formerly incorporated in mediating institutions and practices now devolve on Him and, to some extent and unintentionally, on His subject: abject before God, the subject takes on a new importance in virtue of just this direct relation.[5] Further, although God is remote and inscrutable he is also intimately conceived: 'The principal worship of God hath two parts. One is to yield subjection to him, the other to draw near to him and to cleave unto him'.[7] Such perhaps are the conditions for masochistic transgression: intimacy becomes the means of a defiance of power, the new-found importance of the subject the impetus of that defiance, the abjectness of the subject its self-sacrificial nature. (We may even see here the origins of sub-cultural transgression: the identity conferred upon the deviant by the dominant culture enables resistance as well as oppression.)

Foucault has written: 'limit and transgression depend on each other for whatever density of being they possess: a limit could not exist if it were absolutely uncrossable and, reciprocally, transgression would be pointless if it

---

[7] William Perkins, *Works*, ed. I. Breward (Abingdon: Sutton Courtenay Press, 1970), p. 313.

merely crossed a limit composed of illusions and shadows'.[8] It is a phenomenon of which the antiessentialist writers of the Renaissance were aware: 'Superiority and inferiority, maistry and subjection, are joyntly tied unto a naturall kinde of envy and contestation; they must perpetually enter-spoile one another'.[9]

In the morality plays sin tended to involve blindness to the rightness of God's law, while repentance and redemption involved a renewed apprehension of it. In *Dr Faustus* however sin is not the error of fallen judgement but a conscious and deliberate transgression of limit. It is a limit which, among other things, renders God remote and inscrutable yet subjects the individual to constant surveillance and correction; which holds the individual subject terrifyingly responsible for the fallen human condition while disallowing him or her any subjective power of redemption. Out of such conditions is born a mode of transgression identifiably protestant in origin: despairing yet defiant, masochistic yet wilful. Faustus is abject yet his is an abjectness which is strangely inseparable from arrogance, which reproaches the authority which demands it, which is not so much subdued as incited by that same authority:

> *Faustus:* I gave . . . my soul for my cunning.
> *All:* God forbid!
> *Faustus:* God forbade it indeed; but Faustus hath done it.
>
> (xix. 61–4)

Mephostophilis well understands transgressive desire; it is why he does not deceive Faustus about the reality of hell. It suggests too why he conceives of hell in the way he does; although his sense of it as a state of being and consciousness can be seen as a powerful recuperation of hell at a time when its material existence as a *place* of future punishment was being questioned, it is also an arrogant appropriation of hell, an incorporating of it into the consciousness of the subject.

A ritual pact advances a desire which cancels fear long enough to pass the point of no return:

> Lo, Mephostophilis, for love of thee
> Faustus hath cut his arm, and with his proper blood
> Assures his soul to be great Lucifer's,
> Chief lord and regent of perpetual night.
> View here this blood that trickles from mine arm,
> And let it be propitious for my wish.
>
> (v. 54–8)

But his blood congeals, preventing him from signing the pact. Mephostophilis exits to fetch 'fire to dissolve it'. It is a simple yet brilliant moment of dramatic suspense, one which invites us to dwell on the full extent of the violation about to be enacted. Faustus finally signs but only after the most daring blasphemy of all: 'Now will I make an end immediately/ . . . *Consummatum est*: this bill is ended' (v. 72–4). In transgressing utterly and desperately God's law, he appro-

---

[8] Michel Foucault, *Language, Counter-Memory, Practice* (Ithaca: Cornell, 1977), p. 34.   [9] Michel Montaigne, *Essays*, trans. John Florio (London: Dent, 1965), vol. III, p. 153.

priates Christianity's supreme image of masochistic sacrifice:[6] Christ dying on the cross—and his dying words (cf. John xix. 30). Faustus is not liberating himself, he is ending himself: 'it is finished'. Stephen Greenblatt is surely right to find in Marlowe's work 'a subversive identification with the alien', one which 'flaunts society's cherished orthodoxies, embraces what the culture finds loathsome or frightening'.[10] But what is also worth remarking about this particular moment is the way that a subversive identification with the alien is achieved and heightened through travesty of one such cherished orthodoxy.

Northrop Frye (1912–1991)

Northrop Frye was a literary theorist and critic whose most influential work was Anatomy of Criticism *(1957), a study of the basic structures and themes of Western literature. In this selection he discusses comic character-types in literature and indicates how they were adapted from the comedies of Plautus and Terence.*

THE MYTHOS OF SPRING: COMEDY

Dramatic comedy, from which fictional comedy is mainly descended, has been remarkably tenacious of its structural principles and character types. Bernard Shaw remarked that a comic dramatist could get a reputation for daring originality by stealing his method from Molière and his characters from Dickens: if we were to read Menander and Aristophanes for Molière and Dickens the statement would be hardly less true, at least as a general principle. The earliest extant European comedy, Aristophanes' *The Acharnians*, contains the *miles gloriosus* or military braggart who is still going strong in Chaplin's *Great Dictator*; the Joxer Daly of O'Casey's *Juno and the Paycock* has the same character and dramatic function as the parasites of twenty-five hundred years ago, and the audiences of vaudeville, comic strips, and television programs still laugh at the jokes that were declared to be outworn at the opening of *The Frogs*.

The plot structure of Greek New Comedy, as transmitted by Plautus and Terence, in itself less a form than a formula, has become the basis for most comedy, especially in its more highly conventionalized dramatic form, down to our own day. It will be most convenient to work out the theory of comic construction from drama, using illustrations from fiction only incidentally. What normally happens is that a young man wants a young woman, that his desire is resisted by some opposition, usually paternal, and that near the end of the play some twist in the plot enables the hero to have his will. In this simple pattern there are several complex elements. In the first place, the movement of comedy is usually

---

[10] Stephen Greenblatt, *Renaissance Self-Fashioning* (Chicago: University of Chicago Press, 1980), pp. 203, 220.

a movement from one kind of society to another. At the beginning of the play the obstructing characters are in charge of the play's society, and the audience recognizes that they are usurpers. At the end of the play the device in the plot that brings hero and heroine together causes a new society to crystallize around the hero, and the moment when this crystallization occurs is the point of resolution in the action, the comic discovery, *anagnorisis* or *cognitio*.

The appearance of this new society is frequently signalized by some kind of party or festive ritual, which either appears at the end of the play or is assumed to take place immediately afterward. Weddings are most common, and sometimes so many of them occur, as in the quadruple wedding at the end of *As You Like It*, that they suggest also the wholesale pairing off that takes place in a dance, which is another common conclusion, and the normal one for the masque. The banquet at the end of *The Taming of the Shrew* has an ancestry that goes back to Greek Middle Comedy; in Plautus the audience is sometimes jocosely invited to an imaginary banquet afterwards; Old Comedy, like the modern Christmas pantomime, was more generous, and occasionally threw bits of food to the audience. As the final society reached by comedy is the one that the audience has recognized all along to be the proper and desirable state of affairs, an act of communion with the audience is in order. Tragic actors expect to be applauded as well as comic ones, but nevertheless the word "plaudite" at the end of a Roman comedy, the invitation to the audience to form part of the comic society, would seem rather out of place at the end of a tragedy. The resolution of comedy comes, so to speak, from the audience's side of the stage; in a tragedy it comes from some mysterious world on the opposite side. In the movie, where darkness permits a more erotically oriented audience, the plot usually moves toward an act which, like death in Greek tragedy, takes place offstage, and is symbolized by a closing embrace.

The obstacles to the hero's desire, then, form the action of the comedy, and the overcoming of them the comic resolution. The obstacles are usually parental, hence comedy often turns on a clash between a son's and a father's will. Thus the comic dramatist as a rule writes for the younger men in his audience, and the older members of almost any society are apt to feel that comedy has something subversive about it. This is certainly one element in the social persecution of drama, which is not peculiar to Puritans or even Christians, as Terence in pagan Rome met much the same kind of social opposition that Ben Jonson did. There is one scene in Plautus where a son and father are making love to the same courtesan, and the son asks his father pointedly if he really does love mother. One has to see this scene against the background of Roman family life to understand its importance as psychological release. Even in Shakespeare there are startling outbreaks of baiting older men, and in contemporary movies the triumph of youth is so relentless that the moviemakers find some difficulty in getting anyone over the age of seventeen into their audiences.

The opponent to the hero's wishes, when not the father, is generally someone who partakes of the father's closer relation to established society: that is, a rival with less youth and more money. In Plautus and Terence he is usually either the pimp who owns the girl, or a wandering soldier with a supply of ready cash. The fury with which these characters are baited and exploded from the stage shows that they are father-surrogates, and even if they were not, they would still be usurpers, and their claim to possess the girl must be shown up as somehow fraudulent. They are, in short, impostors, and the extent to which they have real power implies some criticism of the society that allows them their power. In Plautus and Terence this criticism seldom goes beyond the immorality of brothels and professional harlots, but in Renaissance dramatists, including Jonson, there is some sharp observation of the rising power of money and the sort of ruling class it is building up.

The tendency of comedy is to include as many people as possible in its final society: the blocking characters are more often reconciled or converted than simply repudiated. Comedy often includes a scapegoat ritual of expulsion which gets rid of some irreconcilable character, but exposure and disgrace make for pathos, or even tragedy. *The Merchant of Venice* seems almost an experiment in coming as close as possible to upsetting the comic balance. If the dramatic role of Shylock is ever so slightly exaggerated, as it generally is when the leading actor of the company takes the part, it is upset, and the play becomes the tragedy of the Jew of Venice with a comic epilogue. *Volpone* ends with a great bustle of sentences to penal servitude and the galleys, and one feels that the deliverance of society hardly needs so much hard labor; but then *Volpone* is exceptional in being a kind of comic imitation of a tragedy, with the point of Volpone's hybris carefully marked.

The principle of conversion becomes clearer with characters whose chief function is the amusing of the audience. The original *miles gloriosus* in Plautus is a son of Jove and Venus who has killed an elephant with his fist and seven thousand men in one day's fighting. In other words, he is trying to put on a good show: the exuberance of his boasting helps to put the play over. The convention says that the braggart must be exposed, ridiculed, swindled, and beaten. But why should a professional dramatist, of all people, want so to harry a character who is putting on a good show—*his* show at that? When we find Falstaff invited to the final feast in *The Merry Wives*, Caliban reprieved, attempts made to mollify Malvolio, and Angelo and Parolles allowed to live down their disgrace, we are seeing a fundamental principle of comedy at work. The tendency of the comic society to include rather than exclude is the reason for the traditional importance of the parasite, who has no business to be at the final festival but is nevertheless there. The word "grace," with all its Renaissance overtones from the graceful courtier of Castiglione to the gracious God of Christianity, is a most important thematic word in Shakespearean comedy.

The action of comedy in moving from one social center to another is not unlike the action of a lawsuit, in which plaintiff and defendant construct different versions of the same situation, one finally being judged as real and the other as illusory. This resemblance of the rhetoric of comedy to the rhetoric of jurisprudence has been recognized from earliest times. A little pamphlet called the *Tractatus Coislinianus*, closely related to Aristotle's *Poetics*, which sets down all the essential facts about comedy in about a page and a half, divides the *dianoia* of comedy into two parts, opinion (*pistis*) and proof (*gnosis*). These correspond roughly to the usurping and the desirable societies respectively. Proofs (i.e., the means of bringing about the happier society) are subdivided into oaths, compacts, witnesses, ordeals (or tortures), and laws—in other words the five forms of material proof in law cases listed in the *Rhetoric*. We notice how often the action of a Shakespearean comedy begins with some absurd, cruel, or irrational law: the law of killing Syracusans in the *Comedy of Errors*, the law of compulsory marriage in *A Midsummer Night's Dream*, the law that confirms Shylock's bond, the attempts of Angelo to legislate people into righteousness, and the like, which the action of the comedy then evades or breaks. Compacts are as a rule the conspiracies formed by the hero's society; witnesses, such as overhearers of conversations or people with special knowledge (like the hero's old nurse with her retentive memory for birthmarks), are the commonest devices for bringing about the comic discovery. Ordeals (*basanoi*) are usually tests or touchstones of the hero's character: the Greek word also means touchstones, and seems to be echoed in Shakespeare's Bassanio whose ordeal it is to make a judgement on the worth of metals.

There are two ways of developing the form of comedy: one is to throw the main emphasis on the blocking characters; the other is to throw it forward on the scenes of discovery and reconciliation. One is the general tendency of comic irony, satire, realism, and studies of manners; the other is the tendency of Shakespearean and other types of romantic comedy. In the comedy of manners the main ethical interest falls as a rule on the blocking characters. The technical hero and heroine are not often very interesting people: the *adulescentes* of Plautus and Terence are all alike, as hard to tell apart in the dark as Demetrius and Lysander, who may be parodies of them. Generally the hero's character has the neutrality that enables him to represent a wish-fulfilment. It is very different with the miserly or ferocious parent, the boastful or foppish rival, or the other characters who stand in the way of the action. In Molière we have a simple but fully tested formula in which the ethical interest is focussed on a single blocking character, a heavy father, a miser, a misanthrope, a hypocrite, or a hypochondriac. These are the figures that we remember, and the plays are usually named after them, but we can seldom remember all the Valentins and Angeliques who wriggle out of their clutches. In *The Merry Wives* the technical hero, a man named Fenton, has only a bit part, and this play has picked up a hint or two from Plautus's *Casina*, where the hero and heroine are not even brought on the stage at all. Fictional comedy, especially Dickens, often follows the same practice of grouping its interesting characters around a somewhat dullish pair of technical leads. Even Tom Jones, though far more fully realized, is still deliberately associated, as his commonplace name indicates, with the conventional and typical.

Comedy usually moves toward a happy ending, and the normal response of the audience to a happy ending is "this should be," which sounds like a moral judgement. So it is, except that it is not moral in the restricted sense, but social. Its opposite is not the villainous but the absurd, and comedy finds the virtues of Malvolio as absurd as the vices of Angelo. Molière's misanthrope, being committed to sincerity, which is a virtue, is morally in a strong position, but the audience soon realizes that his friend Philinte, who is ready to lie quite cheerfully in order to enable other people to preserve their self-respect, is the more genuinely sincere of the two. It is of course quite possible to have a moral comedy, but the result is often the kind of melodrama that we have described as comedy without humor, and which achieves its happy ending with a self-right-eous tone that most comedy avoids. It is hardly possible to imagine a drama without conflict, and it is hardly possible to imagine a conflict without some kind of enmity. But just as love, including sexual love, is a very different thing from lust, so enmity is a very different thing from hatred. In tragedy, of course, enmity almost always includes hatred; comedy is different, and one feels that the social judgement against the absurd is closer to the comic norm than the moral judgement against the wicked.

The question then arises of what makes the blocking character absurd. Ben Jonson explained this by his theory of the "humor," the character dominated by what Pope calls a ruling passion. The humor's dramatic function is to express a state of what might be called ritual bondage. He is obsessed by his humor, and his function in the play is primarily to repeat his obsession. A sick man is not a humor, but a hypochondriac is, because, *qua* hypochondriac, he can never admit to good health, and can never do anything inconsistent with the role that he has prescribed for himself. A miser can do and say nothing that is not connected with the hiding of gold or saving of money. In *The Silent Woman*, Jonson's near-est approach to Molière's type of construction, the whole action recedes from the humor of Morose, whose determination to eliminate noise from his life produces so loquacious a comic action.

The principle of the humor is the principle that unincremental repetition, the literary imitation of ritual bondage, is funny. In a tragedy—*Oedipus Tyrannus* is the stock example—repetition leads logically to catastrophe. Repetition over-done or not going anywhere belongs to comedy, for laughter is partly a reflex, and like other reflexes it can be conditioned by a simple repeated pattern. In Synge's *Riders to the Sea* a mother, after losing her husband and five sons at sea, finally loses her last son, and the result is a very beautiful and moving play. But if it had been a full-length tragedy plodding glumly through the seven drown-ings one after another, the audience would have been helpless with unsympa-thetic laughter long before it was over. The principle of repetition as the basis of humor both in Jonson's sense and in ours is well known to the creators of comic strips, in which a character is established as a parasite, a glutton (often confined to one dish), or a shrew, and who begins to be funny after the point has been made every day for several months. Continuous comic radio programs, too, are much more amusing to habitués than to neophytes. The girth of Falstaff and the hallucinations of Quixote are based on much the same comic laws. Mr. E. M. Forster speaks with disdain of Dickens's Mrs. Micawber, who never says any-thing except that she will never desert Mr. Micawber: a strong contrast is marked here between the refined writer too finicky for popular formulas, and the major one who exploits them ruthlessly.

The humor in comedy is usually someone with a good deal of social pres-tige and power, who is able to force much of the play's society into line with his obsession. Thus the humor is intimately connected with the theme of the absurd or irrational law that the action of comedy moves toward breaking. It is signifi-cant that the central character of our earliest humor comedy, *The Wasps*, is obsessed by law cases: Shylock, too, unites a craving for the law with the humor of revenge. Often the absurd law appears as a whim of a bemused tyrant whose will is law, like Leontes or the humorous Duke Frederick in Shakespeare, who makes some arbitrary decision or rash promise: here law is replaced by "oath," also mentioned in the *Tractatus*. Or it may take the form of a sham Utopia, a society of ritual bondage constructed by an act of humorous or pedantic will, like the academic retreat in *Love's Labor's Lost*. This theme is also as old as Aristophanes, whose parodies of Platonic social schemes in *The Birds* and *Ecclesiazusae* deal with it.

The society emerging at the conclusion of comedy represents, by contrast, a kind of moral norm, or pragmatically free society. Its ideals are seldom defined or formulated: definition and formulation belong to the humors, who want predictable activity. We are simply given to understand that the newly-married couple will live happily ever after, or that at any rate they will get along in a relatively unhumorous and clear-sighted manner. That is one reason why the character of the successful hero is so often left undeveloped: his real life begins at the end of the play, and we have to believe him to be potentially a more interesting character than he appears to be. In Terence's *Adelphoi*, Demea, a harsh father, is contrasted with his brother Micio, who is indulgent. Micio being more liberal, he leads the way to the comic resolution, and converts Demea, but then Demea points out the indolence inspiring a good deal of Micio's liberality, and releases him from a complementary humorous bondage.

Thus the movement from *pistis* to *gnosis*, from a society controlled by habit, ritual bondage, arbitrary law and the older characters to a society controlled by youth and pragmatic freedom is fundamentally, as the Greek words suggest, a movement from illusion to reality. Illusion is whatever is fixed or definable, and reality is best understood as its negation: whatever reality is, it's not *that*. Hence the importance of the theme of creating and dispelling illusion in comedy: the illusions caused by disguise, obsession, hypocrisy, or unknown parentage.

The comic ending is generally manipulated by a twist in the plot. In Roman comedy the heroine, who is usually a slave or courtesan, turns out to be the daughter of somebody respectable, so that the hero can marry her without loss of face. The *cognitio* in comedy, in which the characters find out who their relatives are, and who is left of the opposite sex not a relative, and hence available for marriage, is one of the features of comedy that have never changed much: *The Confidential Clerk* indicates that it still holds the attention of dramatists. There is a brilliant parody of a *cognitio* at the end of *Major Barbara* (the fact that the hero of this play is a professor of Greek perhaps indicates an unusual affinity to the conventions of Euripides and Menander), where Undershaft is enabled to break the rule that he cannot appoint his son-in-law as successor by the fact that the son-in-law's own father married his deceased wife's sister in Australia, so that the son-in-law is his own first cousin as well as himself. It sounds complicated, but the plots of comedy often are complicated because there is something inherently absurd about complications. As the main character interest in comedy is so often focussed on the defeated characters, comedy regularly illustrates a victory of arbitrary plot over consistency of character. Thus, in striking contrast to tragedy, there can hardly be such a thing as inevitable comedy, as far as the action of the individual play is concerned. That is, we may know that the convention of comedy will make some kind of happy ending inevitable, but still for each play the dramatist must produce a distinctive "gimmick" or "weenie," to use two disrespectful Hollywood synonyms for *anagnorisis*. Happy endings do not impress us as true, but as desirable, and they are brought about by manipulation. The watcher of death and tragedy has nothing to do but sit and wait for the inevitable end; but something gets born at the end of comedy, and the watcher of birth is a member of a busy society.

The manipulation of plot does not always involve metamorphosis of character, but there is no violation of comic decorum when it does. Unlikely conversions, miraculous transformations, and providential assistance are inseparable from comedy. Further, whatever emerges is supposed to be there for good: if the curmudgeon becomes lovable, we understand that he will not immediately relapse again into his ritual habit. Civilizations which stress the desirable rather than the real, and the religious as opposed to the scientific perspective, think of drama almost entirely in terms of comedy. In the classical drama of India, we are told, the tragic ending was regarded as bad taste, much as the manipulated endings of comedy are regarded as bad taste by novelists interested in ironic realism.

The total *mythos* of comedy, only a small part of which is ordinarily presented, has regularly what in music is called a ternary form: the hero's society rebels against the society of the *senex* and triumphs, but the hero's society is a Saturnalia, a reversal of social standards which recalls a golden age in the past before the main action of the play begins. Thus we have a stable and harmonious order disrupted by folly, obsession, forgetfulness, "pride and prejudice," or events not understood by the characters themselves, and then restored. Often there is a benevolent grandfather, so to speak, who overrules the action set up by the blocking humor and so links the first and third parts. An example is Mr. Burchell, the disguised uncle of the wicked squire, in *The Vicar of Wakefield*. A very long play, such as the Indian *Sakuntala*, may present all three phases; a very intricate one, such as many of Menander's evidently were, may indicate their outlines. But of course very often the first phase is not given at all: the audience simply understands an ideal state of affairs which it knows to be better than what is revealed in the play, and which it recognizes as like that to which the action leads. This ternary action is, ritually, like a contest of summer and winter in which winter occupies the middle action; psychologically, it is like the removal of a neurosis or blocking point and the restoring of an unbroken current of energy and memory. The Jonsonian masque, with the antimasque in the middle, gives a highly conventionalized or "abstract" version of it.

We pass now to the typical characters of comedy. In drama, characterization depends on function; what a character is follows from what he has to do in the play. Dramatic function in its turn depends on the structure of the play; the character has certain things to do because the play has such and such a shape. The structure of the play in its turn depends on the category of the play; if it is a comedy, its structure will require a comic resolution and a prevailing comic mood. Hence when we speak of typical characters, we are not trying to reduce lifelike characters to stock types, though we certainly are suggesting that the sentimental notion of an antithesis between the lifelike character and the stock type is a vulgar error. All lifelike characters, whether in drama or fiction, owe their consistency to the appropriateness of the stock type which belongs to their dramatic function. That stock type is not the character but it is as necessary to the character as a skeleton is to the actor who plays it.

With regard to the characterization of comedy, the *Tractatus* lists three types of comic characters: the *alazons* or impostors, the *eirons* or self-deprecators, and the buffoons (*bomolochoi*). This list is closely related to a passage in the *Ethics* which contrasts the first two, and then goes on to contrast the buffoon with a character whom Aristotle calls *agroikos* or churlish, literally rustic. We may reasonably accept the churl as a fourth character type, and so we have two opposed pairs. The contest of *eiron* and *alazon* forms the basis of the comic action, and the buffoon and the churl polarize the comic mood.

We have previously dealt with the terms *eiron* and *alazon*. The humorous blocking characters of comedy are nearly always impostors, though it is more frequently a lack of self-knowledge than simple hypocrisy that characterizes them. The multitudes of comic scenes in which one character complacently soliloquizes while another makes sarcastic asides to the audience show the contest of *eiron* and *alazon* in its purest form, and show too that the audience is sympathetic to the *eiron* side. Central to the *alazon* group is the *senex iratus* or heavy father, who with his rages and threats, his obsessions and his gullibility, seems closely related to some of the demonic characters of romance, such as Polyphemus. Occasionally a character may have the dramatic function of such a figure without his characteristics: an example is Squire Allworthy in *Tom Jones*, who as far as the plot is concerned behaves almost as stupidly as Squire Western. Of heavy-father surrogates, the *miles gloriosus* has been mentioned: his popularity is largely due to the fact that he is a man of words rather than deeds, and is consequently far more useful to a practising dramatist than any tight-lipped hero could ever be. The pedant, in Renaissance comedy often a student of the occult sciences, the fop or coxcomb, and similar humors, require no comment. The female *alazon* is rare: Katharina the shrew represents to some extent a female *miles gloriosus*, and the *précieuse ridicule* a female pedant, but the "menace" or siren who gets in the way of the true heroine is more often found as a sinister figure of melodrama or romance than as a ridiculous figure in comedy.

The *eiron* figures need a little more attention. Central to this group is the hero, who is an *eiron* figure because, as explained, the dramatist tends to play him down and make him rather neutral and unformed in character. Next in importance is the heroine, also often played down: in Old Comedy, when a girl accompanies a male hero in his triumph, she is generally a stage prop, a *muta persona* not previously introduced. A more difficult form of *cognitio* is achieved when the heroine disguises herself or through some other device brings about the comic resolution, so that the person whom the hero is seeking turns out to be the person who has sought him. The fondness of Shakespeare for this "she stoops to conquer" theme needs only to be mentioned here, as it belongs more naturally to the *mythos* of romance.

Another central *eiron* figure is the type entrusted with hatching the schemes which bring about the hero's victory. This character in Roman comedy is almost always a tricky slave (*dolosus servus*), and in Renaissance comedy he becomes the scheming valet who is so frequent in Continental plays, and in Spanish drama is called the *gracioso*. Modern audiences are most familiar with him in Figaro and in the Leporello of *Don Giovanni*. Through such intermediate nineteenth-century figures as Micawber and the Touchwood of Scott's *St. Ronan's Well*, who, like the gracioso, have buffoon affiliations, he evolves into the amateur detective of modern fiction. The Jeeves of P. G. Wodehouse is a more direct descendant. Female confidantes of the same general family are often brought in to oil the machinery of the well-made play. Elizabethan comedy had another type of trickster, represented by the Matthew Merrygreek of *Ralph Roister Doister*, who is generally said to be developed from the vice or iniquity of the morality plays: as usual, the analogy is sound enough, whatever historians decide about origins. The vice, to give him that name, is very useful to a comic dramatist because he acts from pure love of mischief, and can set a comic action going with the minimum of motivation. The vice may be as light-hearted as Puck or as malignant as Don John in *Much Ado*, but as a rule the vice's activity is, in spite of his name, benevolent. One of the tricky slaves in Plautus, in a soliloquy, boasts that he is the *architectus* of the comic action: such a character carries out the will of the author to reach a happy ending. He is in fact the spirit of comedy, and the two clearest examples of the type in Shakespeare, Puck and Ariel, are both spiritual beings. The tricky slave often has his own freedom in mind as the reward of his exertions: Ariel's longing for release is in the same tradition.

The role of the vice includes a great deal of disguising, and the type may often be recognized by disguise. A good example is the Brainworm of Jonson's *Every Man in His Humour*, who calls the action of the play the day of his metamorphoses. Similarly Ariel has to surmount the difficult stage direction of "Enter invisible." The vice is combined with the hero whenever the latter is a cheeky, improvident young man who hatches his own schemes and cheats his rich father or uncle into giving him his patrimony along with the girl.

Another *eiron* type has not been much noticed. This is a character, generally an older man, who begins the action of the play by withdrawing from it, and ends the play by returning. He is often a father with the motive of seeing what his son will do. The action of *Every Man in His Humour* is set going in this way by Knowell Senior. The disappearance and return of Lovewit, the owner of the house which is the scene of *The Alchemist*, has the same dramatic function, though the characterization is different. The clearest Shakespearean example is the Duke in *Measure for Measure*, but Shakespeare is more addicted to the type than might appear at first glance. In Shakespeare the vice is rarely the real *architectus*: Puck and Ariel both act under orders from an older man, if one may call Oberon a man for the moment. In *The Tempest* Shakespeare returns to a comic action established by Aristophanes, in which an older man, instead of retiring from the action, builds it up on the stage. When the heroine takes the vice role in Shakespeare, she is often significantly related to her father, even when the father is not in the play at all, like the father of Helena, who gives her his medical knowledge, or the father of Portia, who arranges the scheme of the caskets. A more conventionally treated example of the same benevolent Prospero figure turned up recently in the psychiatrist of *The Cocktail Party*, and one may compare the mysterious alchemist who is the father of the heroine of *The Lady's Not for Burning*. The formula is not confined to comedy: Polonius, who shows so many of the disadvantages of a literary education, attempts the role of a retreating paternal *eiron* three times, once too often.

Hamlet and *King Lear* contain subplots which are ironic versions of stock comic themes, Gloucester's story being the regular comedy theme of the gullible *senex* swindled by a clever and unprincipled son.

We pass now to the buffoon types, those whose function it is to increase the mood of festivity rather than to contribute to the plot. Renaissance comedy, unlike Roman comedy, had a great variety of such characters, professional fools, clowns, pages, singers, and incidental characters with established comic habits like malapropism or foreign accents. The oldest buffoon of this incidental nature is the parasite, who may be given something to do, as Jonson gives Mosca the role of a vice in *Volpone*, but who *qua* parasite, does nothing but entertain the audience by talking about his appetite. He derives chiefly from Greek Middle Comedy, which appears to have been very full of food, and where he was, not unnaturally, closely associated with another established buffoon type, the cook, a conventional figure who breaks into comedies to bustle and order about and make long speeches about the mysteries of cooking. In the role of cook the buffoon or entertainer appears, not simply as a gratuitous addition like the parasite, but as something more like a master of ceremonies, a center for the comic mood. There is no cook in Shakespeare, though there is a superb description of one in the *Comedy of Errors*, but a similar role is often attached to a jovial and loquacious host, like the "mad host" of *The Merry Wives* or the Simon Eyre of *The Shoemakers Holiday*. In Middleton's *A Trick to Catch the Old One* the mad host type is combined with the vice. In Falstaff and Sir Toby Belch we can see the affinities of the buffoon or entertainer type both with the parasite and with the master of revels. If we study this entertainer or host role carefully we shall soon realize that it is a development of what in Aristophanic comedy is represented by the chorus, and which in its turn goes back to the *komos* or revel from which comedy is said to be descended.

Finally, there is a fourth group to which we have assigned the word *agroikos*, and which usually means either churlish or rustic, depending on the context. This type may also be extended to cover the Elizabethan gull and what in vaudeville used to be called the straight man, the solemn or inarticulate character who allows the humor to bounce off him, so to speak. We find churls in the miserly, snobbish, or priggish characters whose role is that of the refuser of festivity, the killjoy who tries to stop the fun, or, like Malvolio, locks up the food and drink instead of dispensing it. The melancholy Jaques of *As You Like It*, who walks out on the final festivities, is closely related. In the sulky and self-centered Bertram of *All's Well* there is a most unusual and ingenious combination of this type with the hero. More often, however, the churl belongs to the *alazon* group, all miserly old men in comedies, including Shylock, being churls. In *The Tempest* Caliban has much the same relation to the churlish type that Ariel has to the vice or tricky slave. But often, where the mood is more light-hearted, we may translate *agroikos* simply by rustic, as with the innumerable country squires and similar characters who provide amusement in the urban setting of drama. Such types do not refuse the mood of festivity, but they mark the extent of its range. In a pastoral comedy the idealized virtues of rural life may be represented by a simple man who speaks for the pastoral ideal, like Corin in *As You Like It*. Corin has the same *agroikos* role as the "rube" or "hayseed" of more citified comedies, but the moral attitude to the role is reversed. Again we notice the principle that dramatic structure is a permanent and moral attitude a variable factor in literature.

In a very ironic comedy a different type of character may play the role of the refuser of festivity. The more ironic the comedy, the more absurd the society, and an absurd society may be condemned by, or at least contrasted with, a character that we may call the plain dealer, an outspoken advocate of a kind of moral norm who has the sympathy of the audience. Wycherley's Manly, though he provides the name for the type, is not a particularly good example of it: a much better one is the Cleante of *Tartuffe*. Such a character is appropriate when the tone is ironic enough to get the audience confused about its sense of the social norm: he corresponds roughly to the chorus in a tragedy, which is there for a similar reason. When the tone deepens from the ironic to the bitter, the plain dealer may become a malcontent or railer, who may be morally superior to his society.

HAMLET

Every age since the Renaissance has seen its concerns reflected in Shakespeare's *Hamlet*. The following selection of criticism illustrates some of those concerns during our own century.

Writing just after the turn of the century and under the influence of the late nineteenth century realist movement in drama, A. C. Bradley summed up the Victorian preoccupation with character analysis in his influential book, *Shakespearean Tragedy* (1904). It is only a short step from Bradley's position to that taken by Ernest Jones, a disciple of Freud, in his *Hamlet and Oedipus* (1949). For Jones, as it was for Freud, the object of criticism of the play is something like the object of psychoanalysis, to discover the malady that lies behind Hamlet's delay and to elucidate its effects.

T. S. Eliot's essay, *Hamlet* (1919), singles out the character of Gertrude to articulate his famous aesthetic theory of the "objective correlative." Eliot insisted that "a set of objects, a situation, a chain of events" must be the formula for any "particular emotion." He finds that *Hamlet* does not entirely measure up to this test because Gertrude is not really evil enough to provoke the emotions Hamlet displays. Like Bradley's before him, Eliot's essay provoked an enormous number of essays and studies on the play.

Elaine Showalter's essay, "Representing Ophelia," expresses more contemporary views about the play, but like Bradley, Eliot, and Jones she is concerned with the problem of the feminine in general in the play and in particular with the sexualized female body.

A. C. Bradley (1851–1935)

from *SHAKESPEAREAN TRAGEDY*

Let us first ask ourselves what we can gather from the play, immediately or by inference, concerning Hamlet as he was just before his father's death. And I begin by observing that the text does not bear out the idea that he was one-sidedly reflective and indisposed to action. Nobody who knew him seems to have noticed this weakness. Nobody regards him as a mere scholar who has 'never formed a resolution or executed a deed.' In a court which certainly would not much admire such a person he is the observed of all observers. Though he has been disappointed of the throne everyone shows him respect; and he is the favourite of the people, who are not given to worship philosophers. Fortinbras, a sufficiently practical man, considered that he was likely, had he been put on, to have proved most royally. He has Hamlet borne by four captains 'like a soldier' to his grave; and Ophelia says that Hamlet *was* a soldier. If he was fond of acting, an aesthetic pursuit, he was equally fond of fencing, an athletic one: he practised it assiduously even in his worst days. So far as we can conjecture from what we see of him in those bad days, he must normally have been charmingly frank, courteous and kindly to everyone, of whatever rank, whom he liked or respected, but by no means timid or deferential to others; indeed, one would gather that he was rather the reverse, and also that he was apt to be decided and even imperious if thwarted or interfered with. He must always have been fearless,—in the play he appears insensible to fear of any ordinary kind. And, finally, he must have been quick and impetuous in action; for it is downright impossible that the man we see rushing after the Ghost, killing Polonius, dealing with the King's commission on the ship, boarding the pirate, leaping into the grave, executing his final vengeance, could *ever* have been shrinking or slow in an emergency. Imagine Coleridge doing any of these things!

If we consider all this, how can we accept the notion that Hamlet's was a weak and one-sided character? 'Oh, but he spent ten or twelve years at a University!' Well, even if he did, it is possible to do that without becoming the victim of excessive thought. But the statement that he did rests upon a most insecure foundation.

Where then are we to look for the seeds of danger?

1. Trying to reconstruct from the Hamlet of the play, one would not judge that his temperament was melancholy in the present sense of the word; there seems nothing to show that; but one would judge that by temperament he was inclined to nervous instability, to rapid and perhaps extreme changes of feeling and mood, and that he was disposed to be, for the time, absorbed in the feeling or mood that possessed him, whether it were joyous or depressed. This temperament the Elizabethans would have called melancholic; and Hamlet seems to be an example of it, as Lear is of a temperament mixedly choleric and sanguine. And the doctrine of temperaments was so familiar in Shakespeare's time—as

Burton, and earlier prose-writers, and many of the dramatists show—that Shakespeare may quite well have given this temperament to Hamlet consciously and deliberately. Of melancholy in its developed form, a habit, not a mere temperament, he often speaks. He more than once laughs at the passing and half-fictitious melancholy of youth and love; in Don John in *Much Ado* he had sketched the sour and surly melancholy of discontent; in Jaques a whimsical self-pleasing melancholy; in Antonio in the *Merchant of Venice* a quiet but deep melancholy, for which neither the victim nor his friends can assign any cause.[1] He gives to Hamlet a temperament which would not develop into melancholy unless under some exceptional strain, but which still involved a danger. In the play we see the danger realised, and find a melancholy quite unlike any that Shakespeare had as yet depicted, because the temperament of Hamlet is quite different.

2. Next, we cannot be mistaken in attributing to the Hamlet of earlier days an exquisite sensibility, to which we may give the name 'moral,' if that word is taken in the wide meaning it ought to bear. This, though it suffers cruelly in later days, as we saw in criticising the sentimental view of Hamlet, never deserts him; it makes all his cynicism, grossness and hardness appear to us morbidities, and has an inexpressibly attractive and pathetic effect. He had the soul of the youthful poet as Shelley and Tennyson have described it, an unbounded delight and faith in everything good and beautiful. We know this from himself. The world for him was *herrlich wie am ersten Tag*—'this goodly frame the earth, this most excellent canopy the air, this brave o'erhanging firmament, this majestical roof fretted with golden fire.' And not nature only: 'What a piece of work is a man! how noble in reason! how infinite in faculty! in form and moving how express and admirable! in action how like an angel! in apprehension how like a god!' This is no commonplace to Hamlet; it is the language of a heart thrilled with wonder and swelling into ecstasy.

Doubtless it was with the same eager enthusiasm he turned to those around him. Where else in Shakespeare is there anything like Hamlet's adoration of his father? The words melt into music whenever he speaks of him. And, if there are no signs of any such feeling towards his mother, though many signs of love, it is characteristic that he evidently never entertained a suspicion of anything unworthy in her,—characteristic, and significant of his tendency to see only what is good unless he is forced to see the reverse. For we find this tendency elsewhere, and find it going so far that we must call it a disposition to idealise, to see something better than what is there, or at least to ignore deficiencies. He says to Laertes, 'I loved you ever,' and he describes Laertes as a 'very noble youth,' which he was far from being. In his first greeting of Rosencrantz and Guildenstern, where his old self revives, we trace the same affectionateness and readiness to take men at their best. His love for Ophelia, too, which seems strange to some, is surely the most natural thing in the world. He saw her innocence, simplicity and sweetness, and it was like him to ask no more; and it is

---

[1] The critics have laboured to find a cause, but it seems to me Shakespeare simply meant to portray a pathological condition; and a very touching picture he draws. Antonio's sadness, which he describes in the opening lines of the play, would never drive him to suicide, but it makes him indifferent to the issue of the trial, as all his speeches in the trial-scene show.

noticeable that Horatio, though entirely worthy of his friendship, is, like Ophelia, intellectually not remarkable. To the very end, however clouded, this generous disposition, this 'free and open nature,' this unsuspiciousness survive. They cost him his life; for the King knew them, and was sure that he was too 'generous and free from all contriving' to 'peruse the foils.' To the very end, his soul, however sick and tortured it may be, answers instantaneously when good and evil are presented to it, loving the one and hating the other. He is called a sceptic who has no firm belief in anything, but he is never sceptical about *them*.

And the negative side of his idealism, the aversion to evil, is perhaps even more developed in the hero of the tragedy than in the Hamlet of earlier days. It is intensely characteristic. Nothing, I believe, is to be found elsewhere in Shakespeare (unless in the rage of the disillusioned idealist Timon) of quite the same kind as Hamlet's disgust at his uncle's drunkenness, his loathing of his mother's sensuality, his astonishment and horror at her shallowness, his contempt for everything pretentious or false, his indifference to everything merely external. This last characteristic appears in his choice of the friend of his heart, and in a certain impatience of distinctions of rank or wealth. When Horatio calls his father 'a goodly king,' he answers, surely with an emphasis on 'man,'

> He was a man, take him for all in all,
> I shall not look upon his like again.

He will not listen to talk of Horatio being his 'servant.' When the others speak of their 'duty' to him, he answers, 'Your love, as mine to you.' He speaks to the actor precisely as he does to an honest courtier. He is not in the least a revolutionary, but still, in effect, a king and a beggar are all one to him. He cares for nothing but human worth, and his pitilessness towards Polonius and Osric and his 'school-fellows' is not wholly due to morbidity, but belongs in part to his original character.

Now, in Hamlet's moral sensibility there undoubtedly lay a danger. Any great shock that life might inflict on it would be felt with extreme intensity. Such a shock might even produce tragic results. And, in fact, *Hamlet* deserves the title 'tragedy of moral idealism' quite as much as the title 'tragedy of reflection.'

3. With this temperament and this sensibility we find, lastly, in the Hamlet of earlier days, as of later, intellectual genius. It is chiefly this that makes him so different from all those about him, good and bad alike, and hardly less different from most of Shakespeare's other heroes. And this, though on the whole the most important trait in his nature, is also so obvious and so famous that I need not dwell on it at length. But against one prevalent misconception I must say a word of warning. Hamlet's intellectual power is not a specific gift, like a genius for music or mathematics or philosophy. It shows itself, fitfully, in the affairs of life as unusual quickness of perception, great agility in shifting the mental attitude, a striking rapidity and fertility in resource; so that, when his natural belief in others does not make him unwary, Hamlet easily sees through them and masters them, and no one can be much less like the typical helpless dreamer. It shows itself in conversation chiefly in the form of wit or humour; and, alike in conversation and in soliloquy, it shows itself in the form of imagination quite as

much as in that of thought in the stricter sense. Further, where it takes the latter shape, as it very often does, it is not philosophic in the technical meaning of the word. There is really nothing in the play to show that Hamlet ever was 'a student of philosophies,' unless it be the famous lines which, comically enough, exhibit this supposed victim of philosophy as its critic:

> There are more things in heaven and earth, Horatio,
> Than are dreamt of in your philosophy.

His philosophy, if the word is to be used, was, like Shakespeare's own, the immediate product of the wondering and meditating mind; and such thoughts as that celebrated one, 'There is nothing either good or bad but thinking makes it so,' surely needed no special training to produce them. Or does Portia's remark, 'Nothing is good without respect,' *i.e.*, out of relation, prove that she had studied metaphysics?

Still Hamlet had speculative genius without being a philosopher, just as he had imaginative genius without being a poet. Doubtless in happier days he was a close and constant observer of men and manners, noting his results in those tables which he afterwards snatched from his breast to make in wild irony his last note of all, that one may smile and smile and be a villain. Again and again we remark that passion for generalisation which so occupied him, for instance, in reflections suggested by the King's drunkenness that he quite forgot what it was he was waiting to meet upon the battlements. Doubtless, too, he was always considering things, as Horatio thought, too curiously. There was a necessity in his soul driving him to penetrate below the surface and to question what others took for granted. That fixed habitual look which the world wears for most men did not exist for him. He was for ever unmaking his world and rebuilding it in thought, dissolving what to others were solid facts, and discovering what to others were old truths. There were no old truths for Hamlet. It is for Horatio a thing of course that there's a divinity that shapes our ends, but for Hamlet it is a discovery hardly won. And throughout this kingdom of the mind, where he felt that man, who in action is only like an angel, is in apprehension like a god, he moved (we must imagine) more than content, so that even in his dark days he declares he could be bounded in a nutshell and yet count himself a king of infinite space, were it not that he had bad dreams.

If now we ask whether any special danger lurked *here*, how shall we answer? We must answer, it seems to me, 'Some danger, no doubt, but, granted the ordinary chances of life, not much.' For, in the first place, that idea which so many critics quietly take for granted—the idea that the gift and the habit of meditative and speculative thought tend to produce irresolution in the affairs of life—would be found by no means easy to verify. Can you verify it, for example, in the lives of the philosophers, or again in the lives of men whom you have personally known to be addicted to such speculation? I cannot. Of course, individual peculiarities being set apart, absorption in *any* intellectual interest, together with withdrawal from affairs, may make a man slow and unskilful in affairs; and doubtless, individual peculiarities being again set apart, a mere student is likely to be more at a loss in a sudden and great practical emergency than a soldier or a lawyer. But in all this there is no difference between a physicist, a historian, and a philosopher; and again, slowness, want of skill, and even helplessness are something totally different from the peculiar kind of irresolution that Hamlet shows. The notion that speculative thinking specially tends to produce *this* is really a mere illusion.

In the second place, even if this notion were true, it has appeared that Hamlet did *not* live the life of a mere student, much less of a mere dreamer, and that his nature was by no means simply or even one-sidedly intellectual, but was healthily active. Hence, granted the ordinary chances of life, there would seem to be no great danger in his intellectual tendency and his habit of speculation; and I would go further and say that there was nothing in them, taken alone, to unfit him even for the extraordinary call that was made upon him. In fact, if the message of the Ghost had come to him within a week of his father's death, I see no reason to doubt that he would have acted on it as decisively as Othello himself, though probably after a longer and more anxious deliberation. And therefore the Schlegel-Coleridge view (apart from its descriptive value) seems to me fatally untrue, for it implies that Hamlet's procrastination was the normal response of an over-speculative nature confronted with a difficult practical problem.

On the other hand, under conditions of a peculiar kind, Hamlet's reflectiveness certainly might prove dangerous to him, and his genius might even (to exaggerate a little) become his doom. Suppose that violent shock to his moral being of which I spoke; and suppose that under this shock, any possible action being denied to him, he began to sink into melancholy; then, no doubt, his imaginative and generalising habit of mind might extend the effects of this shock through his whole being and mental world. And if, the state of melancholy being thus deepened and fixed, a sudden demand for difficult and decisive action in a matter connected with the melancholy arose, this state might well have for one of its symptoms an endless and futile mental dissection of the required deed. And, finally, the futility of this process, and the shame of his delay, would further weaken him and enslave him to his melancholy still more. Thus the speculative habit would be *one* indirect cause of the morbid state which hindered action; and it would also reappear in a degenerate form as one of the *symptoms* of this morbid state.

Now this is what actually happens in the play. Turn to the first words Hamlet utters when he is alone; turn, that is to say, to the place where the author is likely to indicate his meaning most plainly. What do you hear?

> O, that this too too solid flesh would melt,
> Thaw and resolve itself into a dew!
> Or that the Everlasting had not fix'd
> His canon 'gainst self-slaughter! O God! God!
> How weary, stale, flat and unprofitable,
> Seem to me all the uses of this world!
> Fie on't! ah fie! 'tis an unweeded garden,
> That grows to seed; things rank and gross in nature
> Possess it merely.

Here are a sickness of life, and even a longing for death, so intense that nothing stands between Hamlet and suicide except religious awe. And what has caused them? The rest of the soliloquy so thrusts the answer upon us that it might seem impossible to miss it. It was not his father's death; that doubtless brought deep grief, but mere grief for some one loved and lost does not make a noble spirit loathe the world as a place full only of things rank and gross. It was not the vague suspicion that we know Hamlet felt. Still less was it the loss of the crown; for though the subserviency of the electors might well disgust him, there is not a reference to the subject in the soliloquy, nor any sign elsewhere that it greatly occupied his mind. It was the moral shock of the sudden ghastly disclosure of his mother's true nature, falling on him when his heart was aching with love, and his body doubtless was weakened by sorrow. And it is essential, however disagreeable, to realise the nature of this shock. It matters little here whether Hamlet's age was twenty or thirty: in either case his mother was a matron of mature years. All his life he had believed in her, we may be sure, as such a son would. He had seen her not merely devoted to his father, but hanging on him like a newly-wedded bride, hanging on him

> As if increase of appetite had grown
> By what it fed on.

He had seen her following his body 'like Niobe, all tears.' And then within a month—'O God! a beast would have mourned longer'—she married again, and married Hamlet's uncle, a man utterly contemptible and loathsome in his eyes; married him in what to Hamlet was incestuous wedlock;[2] married him not for any reason of state, nor even out of old family affection, but in such a way that her son was forced to see in her action not only an astounding shallowness of feeling but an eruption of coarse sensuality, 'rank and gross,'[3] speeding post-haste to its horrible delight.

Is it possible to conceive an experience more desolating to a man such as we have seen Hamlet to be; and is its result anything but perfectly natural? It brings bewildered horror, then loathing, then despair of human nature. His whole mind is poisoned. He can never see Ophelia in the same light again: she is a woman, and his mother is a woman: if she mentions the word 'brief' to him, the answer drops from his lips like venom, 'as woman's love.' The last words of the soliloquy, which is *wholly* concerned with this subject, are,

> But break, my heart, for I must hold my tongue!

---

[2] This aspect of the matter leaves *us* comparatively unaffected, but Shakespeare evidently means it to be of importance. The Ghost speaks of it twice, and Hamlet thrice (once in his last furious words to the King). If, as we must suppose, the marriage was universally admitted to be incestuous, the corrupt acquiescence of the court and the electors to the crown would naturally have a strong effect on Hamlet's mind.   [3] It is most significant that the metaphor of this soliloquy reappears in Hamlet's adjuration to his mother (III. iv. 150):

> Repent what's past; avoid what is to come;
> And do not spread the compost on the weeds
> To make them ranker.

He can do nothing. He must lock in his heart, not any suspicion of his uncle that moves obscurely there, but that horror and loathing; and if his heart ever found relief, it was when those feelings, mingled with the love that never died out in him, poured themselves forth in a flood as he stood in his mother's chamber beside his father's marriage-bed.[4]

If we still wonder, and ask why the effect of this shock should be so tremendous, let us observe that *now* the conditions have arisen under which Hamlet's highest endowments, his moral sensibility and his genius, become his enemies. A nature morally blunter would have felt even so dreadful a revelation less keenly. A slower and more limited and positive mind might not have extended so widely through its world the disgust and disbelief that have entered it. But Hamlet has the imagination which, for evil as well as good, feels and sees all things in one. Thought is the element of his life, and his thought is infected. He cannot prevent himself from probing and lacerating the wound in his soul. One idea, full of peril, holds him fast, and he cries out in agony at it, but is impotent to free himself ('Must I remember?' 'Let me not think on't'). And when, with the fading of his passion, the vividness of this idea abates, it does so only to leave behind a boundless weariness and a sick longing for death.

And this is the time which his fate chooses. In this hour of uttermost weakness, this sinking of his whole being towards annihilation, there comes on him, bursting the bounds of the natural world with a shock of astonishment and terror, the revelation of his mother's adultery and his father's murder, and, with this, the demand on him, in the name of everything dearest and most sacred, to arise and act. And for a moment, though his brain reels and totters, his soul leaps up in passion to answer this demand. But it comes too late. It does but strike home the last rivet in the melancholy which holds him bound.

> The time is out of joint! O cursed spite
> That ever I was born to set it right,—

so he mutters within an hour of the moment when he vowed to give his life to the duty of revenge; and the rest of the story exhibits his vain efforts to fulfil this duty, his unconscious self-excuses and unavailing self-reproaches, and the tragic results of his delay.

---

[4] If the reader will now look at the only speech of Hamlet's that precedes the soliloquy, and is more than one line in length—the speech beginning 'Seems, madam! nay, it *is*'—he will understand what, surely, when first we come to it, sounds very strange and almost boastful. It is not, in effect, about Hamlet himself at all; it is about his mother (I do not mean that it is intentionally and consciously so; and still less that she understood it so).

T. S. Eliot (1888–1965)

Hamlet

Few critics have even admitted that *Hamlet* the play is the primary problem, and Hamlet the character only secondary. And Hamlet the character has had an especial temptation for that most dangerous type of critic: the critic with a mind which is naturally of the creative order, but which through some weakness in creative power exercises itself in criticism instead. These minds often find in Hamlet a vicarious existence for their own artistic realization. Such a mind had Goethe, who made of Hamlet a Werther; and such had Coleridge, who made of Hamlet a Coleridge; and probably neither of these men in writing about Hamlet remembered that his first business was to study a work of art. The kind of criticism that Goethe and Coleridge produced, in writing of Hamlet, is the most misleading kind possible. For they both possessed unquestionable critical insight, and both make their critical aberrations the more plausible by the substitution—of their own Hamlet for Shakespeare's—which their creative gift effects. We should be thankful that Walter Pater did not fix his attention on this play.

Two writers of our own time, Mr. J. M. Robertson and Professor Stoll of the University of Minnesota, have issued small books which can be praised for moving in the other direction. Mr. Stoll performs a service in recalling to our attention the labours of the critics of the seventeenth and eighteenth centuries,° observing that

> "they knew less about psychology than more recent Hamlet
> critics, but they were nearer in spirit to Shakespeare's art; and
> as they insisted on the importance of the effect of the whole
> rather than on the importance of the leading character, they
> were nearer, in their old-fashioned way, to the secret of dra-
> matic art in general."

Qua work of art, the work of art cannot be interpreted; there is nothing to interpret; we can only criticise it according to standards, in comparison to other works of art; and for "interpretation" the chief task is the presentation of relevant historical facts which the reader is not assumed to know. Mr. Robertson points out, very pertinently, how critics have failed in their "interpretation" of *Hamlet* by ignoring what ought to be very obvious; that *Hamlet* is a stratification, that it represents the efforts of a series of men, each making what he could out of the work of his predecessors. The *Hamlet* of Shakespeare will appear to us very differently if, instead of treating the whole action of the play as due to Shakespeare's design, we perceive his *Hamlet* to be superposed upon much cruder material which persists even in the final form.

We know that there was an older play by Thomas Kyd, that extraordinary dramatic (if not poetic) genius who was in all probability the author of two plays so dissimilar as *The Spanish Tragedy* and *Arden of Feversham*; and what this play was like we can guess from three clues: from *The Spanish Tragedy* itself, from the tale of Belleforest upon which Kyd's *Hamlet* must have been based, and from a version acted in Germany in Shakespeare's lifetime which bears strong evidence of having been adapted from the earlier, not from the later, play. From these three sources it is clear that in the earlier play the motive was a revenge-motive simply; that the action or delay is caused, as in *The Spanish Tragedy*, solely by the difficulty of assassinating a monarch surrounded by guards; and that the "madness" of Hamlet was feigned in order to escape suspicion, and successfully. In the final play of Shakespeare, on the other hand, there is a motive which is more important than that of revenge, and which explicitly "blunts" the latter; the delay in revenge is unexplained on grounds of necessity or expediency; and the effect of the "madness" is not to lull but to arouse the king's suspicion. The alteration is not complete enough, however, to be convincing. Furthermore, there are verbal parallels so close to *The Spanish Tragedy* as to leave no doubt that in places Shakespeare was merely *revising* the text of Kyd. And finally there are unexplained scenes—the Polonius-Laertes and the Polonius-Reynaldo scenes—for which there is little excuse; these scenes are not in the verse style of Kyd, and not beyond doubt in the style of Shakespeare. These Mr. Robertson believes to be scenes in the original play of Kyd reworked by a third hand, perhaps Chapman, before Shakespeare touched the play. And he concludes, with very strong show of reason, that the original play of Kyd was, like certain other revenge plays, in two parts of five acts each. The upshot of Mr. Robertson's examination is, we believe, irrefragable: that Shakespeare's *Hamlet*, so far as it is Shakespeare's, is a play dealing with the effect of a mother's guilt upon her son, and that Shakespeare was unable to impose this motive successfully upon the "intractable" material of the old play.

Of the intractability there can be no doubt. So far from being Shakespeare's masterpiece, the play is most certainly an artistic failure. In several ways the play is puzzling, and disquieting as is none of the others. Of all the plays it is the longest and is possibly the one on which Shakespeare spent most pains; and yet he has left in it superfluous and inconsistent scenes which even hasty revision should have noticed. The versification is variable. Lines like

> Look, the morn, in russet mantle clad,
> Walks o'er the dew of yon high eastern hill,

are of the Shakespeare of *Romeo and Juliet*. The lines in Act v, sc. ii,

> Sir, in my heart there was a kind of fighting
> That would not let me sleep . . .
> Up from my cabin,
> My sea-gown scarf'd about me, in the dark
> Grop'd I to find out them: had my desire;
> Finger'd their packet;

are of his quite mature. Both workmanship and thought are in an unstable position. We are surely justified in attributing the play, with that other profoundly interesting play of "intractable" material and astonishing versification, *Measure for Measure*, to a period of crisis, after which follow the tragic successes which culminate in *Coriolanus. Coriolanus* may be not as "interesting" as *Hamlet*, but it is, with *Antony and Cleopatra*, Shakespeare's most assured artistic success. And probably more people have thought *Hamlet* a work of art because they found it interesting, than have found it interesting because it is a work of art. It is the "Mona Lisa" of literature.

The grounds of *Hamlet's* failure are not immediately obvious. Mr. Robertson is undoubtedly correct in concluding that the essential emotion of the play is the feeling of a son towards a guilty mother:

"[Hamlet's] tone is that of one who has suffered tortures on the score of his mother's degradation. . . . The guilt of a mother is an almost intolerable motive for drama, but it had to be maintained and emphasized to supply a psychological solution, or rather a hint of one."

This, however, is by no means the whole story. It is not merely the "guilt of a mother" that cannot be handled as Shakespeare handled the suspicion of Othello, the infatuation of Antony, or the pride of Coriolanus. The subject might conceivably have expanded into a tragedy like these, intelligible, self-complete, in the sunlight. *Hamlet*, like the sonnets, is full of some stuff that the writer could not drag to light, contemplate, or manipulate into art. And when we search for this feeling, we find it, as in the sonnets, very difficult to localize. You cannot point to it in the speeches; indeed, if you examine the two famous soliloquies you see the versification of Shakespeare, but a content which might be claimed by another, perhaps by the author of the *Revenge of Bussy d'Ambois*, Act v, sc. i. We find Shakespeare's Hamlet not in the action, not in any quotations that we might select, so much as in an unmistakable tone which is unmistakably not in the earlier play.

The only way of expressing emotion in the form of art is by finding an "objective correlative"; in other words, a set of objects, a situation, a chain of events which shall be the formula of that *particular* emotion; such that when the external facts, which must terminate in sensory experience, are given, the emotion is immediately evoked. If you examine any of Shakespeare's more successful tragedies, you will find this exact equivalence; you will find that the state of mind of Lady Macbeth walking in her sleep has been communicated to you by a skilful accumulation of imagined sensory impressions; the words of Macbeth on hearing of his wife's death strike us as if, given the sequence of events, these words were automatically released by the last event in the series. The artistic "inevitability" lies in this complete adequacy of the external to the emotion; and this is precisely what is deficient in *Hamlet*. Hamlet (the man) is dominated by an emotion which is inexpressible, because it is in *excess* of the facts as they appear. And the supposed identity of Hamlet with his author is genuine to this point: that Hamlet's bafflement at the absence of objective equivalent to his feelings is a prolongation of the bafflement of his creator in the face of his artistic problem. Hamlet is up against the difficulty that his disgust is occasioned by his mother, but that his mother is not an adequate equivalent for it; his disgust envelops and exceeds her. It is thus a feeling which he cannot understand; he cannot objectify it, and it therefore remains to poison life and obstruct action.

None of the possible actions can satisfy it; and nothing that Shakespeare can do with the plot can express Hamlet for him. And it must be noticed that the very nature of the *données* of the problem precludes objective equivalence. To have heightened the criminality of Gertrude would have been to provide the formula for a totally different emotion in Hamlet; it is just *because* her character is so negative and insignificant that she arouses in Hamlet the feeling which she is incapable of representing.

The "madness" of Hamlet lay to Shakespeare's hand; in the earlier play a simple ruse, and to the end, we may presume, understood as a ruse by the audience. For Shakespeare it is less than madness and more than feigned. The levity of Hamlet, his repetition of phrase, his puns, are not part of a deliberate plan of dissimulation, but a form of emotional relief. In the character Hamlet it is the buffoonery of an emotion which can find no outlet in action; in the dramatist it is the buffoonery of an emotion which he cannot express in art. The intense feeling, ecstatic or terrible, without an object or exceeding its object, is something which every person of sensibility has known; it is doubtless a subject of study for pathologists. It often occurs in adolescence: the ordinary person puts these feelings to sleep, or trims down his feelings to fit the business world; the artist keeps them alive by his ability to intensify the world to his emotions. The Hamlet of Laforgue is an adolescent; the Hamlet of Shakespeare is not, he has not that explanation and excuse. We must simply admit that here Shakespeare tackled a problem which proved too much for him. Why he attempted it at all is an insoluble puzzle; under compulsion of what experience he attempted to express the inexpressibly horrible, we cannot ever know. We need a great many facts in his biography; and we should like to know whether, and when, and after or at the same time as what personal experience, he read Montaigne, II. xii, *Apologie de Raimond Sebond*. We should have, finally, to know something which is by hypothesis unknowable, for we assume it to be an experience which, in the manner indicated, exceeded the facts. We should have to understand things which Shakespeare did not understand himself.

Ernest Jones (1879–1958)

from HAMLET AND OEDIPUS

Now, in trying to define Hamlet's attitude towards his uncle we have to guard against assuming off-hand that this is a simple one of mere execration, for there is a possibility of complexity arising in the following way: The uncle has not merely committed *each* crime, he has committed *both* crimes, a distinction of considerable importance, since the *combination* of crimes allows the admittance of a new factor, produced by the possible inter-relation of the two, which may prevent the result from being simply one of summation. In addition, it has to be borne in mind that the perpetrator of the crimes is a relative, and an exceedingly near relative. The possible inter-relationship of the crimes, and the fact that the author of them is an actual member of the family, give scope for a confusion in their influence on Hamlet's mind which may be the cause of the very obscurity we are seeking to clarify.

Let us first pursue further the effect on Hamlet of his mother's misconduct. Before he even knows with any certitude, however much he may suspect it, that his father has been murdered he is in the deepest depression, and evidently on account of this misconduct. The connection between the two is unmistakable in the monologue in Act I, Sc. 2, in reference to which Furnivall writes: "One must insist on this, that before any revelation of his father's murder is made to Hamlet, before any burden of revenging that murder is laid upon him, he thinks of suicide as a welcome means of escape from this fair world of God's, made abominable to his diseased and weak imagination by his mother's lust, and the dishonour done by her to his father's memory".

> O that this too too solid[1] flesh would melt,
> Thaw and resolve itself into a dew,
> Or that the Everlasting had not fix'd
> His canon 'gainst self-slaughter, O God, God,
> How weary, stale, flat, and unprofitable
> Seem to me all the uses of this world!
> Fie on 't, O fie, 'tis an unweeded garden
> That grows to seed, things rank and gross in nature
> Possess it merely, that it should come to this,
> But two months dead, nay, not so much, not two,
> So excellent a king; that was to this
> Hyperion to a satyr, so loving to my mother,
> That he might not beteem the winds of heaven
> Visit her face too roughly—heaven and earth
> Must I remember? why, she would hang on him
> As if increase of appetite had grown
> By what it fed on, and yet within a month,

---

[1] Dover Wilson (*Times Literary Supplement*, May 16, 1918) brings forward excellent reasons for thinking that this word is a misprint for "sullied". I use the Shakespearean punctuation he has restored.

Let me not think on 't; frailty thy name is woman!
A little month or ere those shoes were old
With which she follow'd my poor father's body
Like Niobe all tears, why she, even she—
O God, a beast that wants discourse of reason
Would have mourn'd longer—married with my uncle,
My father's brother, but no more like my father
Than I to Hercules, within a month,
Ere yet the salt of most unrighteous tears
Had left the flushing in her galled eyes,
She married. O most wicked speed . . . to post
With such dexterity to incestuous sheets!
It is not, nor it cannot come to good,
But break my heart, for I must hold my tongue.

According to Bradley, Hamlet's melancholic disgust at life was the cause of his aversion from "any kind of decided action". His explanation of the whole problem of Hamlet is "the moral shock of the sudden ghastly disclosure of his mother's true nature", and he regards the effect of this shock, as depicted in the play, as fully comprehensible. He says: 'Is it possible to conceive an experience more desolating to a man such as we have seen Hamlet to be; and is its result anything but perfectly natural? It brings bewildered horror, then loathing, then despair of human nature. His whole mind is poisoned . . . A nature morally blunter would have felt even so dreadful a revelation less keenly. A slower and more limited and positive mind might not have extended so widely through the world the disgust and disbelief that have entered it."

But we can rest satisfied with this seemingly adequate explanation of Hamlet's weariness of life only if we accept unquestioningly the conventional standards of the causes of deep emotion. Many years ago Connolly, a well-known psychiatrist, pointed out the disproportion here existing between cause and effect, and gave as his opinion that Hamlet's reaction to his mother's marriage indicated in itself a mental instability, "a predisposition to actual unsoundness"; he writes: "The circumstances are not such as would at once turn a healthy mind to the contemplation of suicide, the last resource of those whose reason has been overwhelmed by calamity and despair." In T. S. Eliot's opinion, also, Hamlet's emotion is in *excess* of the facts as they appear, and he specially contrasts it with Gertrude's negative and insignificant personality. Wihan attributes the exaggerated effect of his misfortunes to Hamlet's "Masslosigkeit" (lack of moderation), which is displayed in every direction. We have unveiled only the exciting cause, not the predisposing cause. The very fact that Hamlet is apparently content with the explanation arouses our misgiving, for, as will presently be expounded, from the very nature of the emotion he cannot be aware of the true cause of it. If we ask, not what ought to produce such soul-paralysing grief and distaste for life, but what in actual fact does produce it, we are compelled to go beyond this explanation and seek for some deeper cause. In real life speedy second marriages occur commonly enough without leading to any such result as is here depicted, and when we see them followed by this result we invariably find, if the opportunity for an analysis of the subject's mind presents itself, that there is some other and more hidden reason why the event is followed by this inordinately great effect. The reason always is that the event has awakened to increased activity mental processes that have been "repressed" from the subject's consciousness. His mind has been specially prepared for the catastrophe by previous mental processes with which those directly resulting from the event have entered into association. This is perhaps what Furnivall means when he speaks of the world being made abominable to Hamlet's "diseased imagination". In short, the special nature of the reaction presupposes some special feature in the mental predisposition. Bradley himself has to qualify his hypothesis by inserting the words "to a man such as we have seen Hamlet to be".

We come at this point to the vexed question of Hamlet's sanity, about which so many controversies have raged. Dover Wilson authoritatively writes: "I agree with Loening, Bradley and others that Shakespeare meant us to imagine Hamlet as suffering from some kind of mental disorder throughout the play". The question is what kind of mental disorder and what is its significance dramatically and psychologically. The matter is complicated by Hamlet's frequently displaying simulation (the Antic Disposition), and it has been asked whether this is to conceal his real mental disturbance or cunningly to conceal his purposes in coping with the practical problems of this task? This is a topic that presently will be considered at some length, but there can be few who regard it as a comprehensive statement of Hamlet's mental state. As T. S. Eliot has neatly expressed it, "Hamlet's 'madness' is less than madness and more than feigned". . . .

More to the point is the actual account given in the play by the King, the Queen, Ophelia, and above all, Polonius. In his description, for example, we note—if the Elizabethan language is translated into modern English—the symptoms of dejection, refusal of food, insomnia, crazy behaviour, fits of delirium, and finally of raving madness; Hamlet's poignant parting words to Polonius ("except my life", etc.) cannot mean other than a craving for death. These are undoubtedly suggestive of certain forms of melancholia, and the likeness to manic-depressive insanity, of which melancholia is now known to be but a part, is completed by the occurrence of attacks of great excitement that would nowadays be called "hypomanic", of which Dover Wilson counts no fewer than eight. Nevertheless, the rapid and startling oscillations between intense excitement and profound depression do not accord with the accepted picture of this disorder, and if I had to describe such a condition as Hamlet's in clinical terms—which I am not particularly inclined to—it would have to be as a severe case of hysteria on a cyclothymic basis.

All this, however, is of academic interest only. What we are essentially concerned with is the psychological understanding of the dramatic effect produced by Hamlet's personality and behaviour. That effect would be quite other were the central figure in the play to represent merely a "case of insanity". When that happens, as with Ophelia, such a person passes beyond our ken, is in a sense no more human, whereas Hamlet successfully claims our interest and sympathy to the very end. Shakespeare certainly never intended us to regard Hamlet as insane, so that the "mind o'erthrown" must have some other meaning than its literal one. Robert Bridges has described the matter with exquisite delicacy:

Hamlet himself would never have been aught to us, or we
To Hamlet, wer't not for the artful balance whereby
Shakespeare so gingerly put his sanity in doubt
Without the while confounding his Reason.

I would suggest that in this Shakespeare's extraordinary powers of observation and penetration granted him a degree of insight that it has taken the world three subsequent centuries to reach. Until our generation (and even now in the juristic sphere) a dividing line separated the sane and responsible from the irresponsible insane. It is now becoming more and more widely recognized that much of mankind lives in an intermediate and unhappy state charged with what Dover Wilson well calls "that sense of frustration, futility and human inadequacy which is the burden of the whole symphony" and of which Hamlet is the supreme example in literature. This intermediate plight, in the toils of which perhaps the greater part of mankind struggles and suffers, is given the name of psychoneurosis, and long ago the genius of Shakespeare depicted it for us with faultless insight.

Extensive studies of the past half century, inspired by Freud, have taught us that a psychoneurosis means a state of mind where the person is unduly, and often painfully, driven or thwarted by the "unconscious" part of his mind, that buried part that was once the infant's mind and still lives on side by side with the adult mentality that has developed out of it and should have taken its place. It signifies *internal* mental conflict. We have here the reason why it is impossible to discuss intelligently the state of mind of anyone suffering from a psychoneurosis, whether the description is of a living person or an imagined one, without correlating the manifestations with what must have operated in his infancy and is *still operating*. That is what I propose to attempt here.

For some deep-seated reason, which is to him unacceptable, Hamlet is plunged into anguish at the thought of his father being replaced in his mother's affections by someone else. It is as if his devotion to his mother had made him so jealous for her affection that he had found it hard enough to share this even with his father and could not endure to share it with still another man. Against this thought, however, suggestive as it is, may be urged three objections. First, if it were in itself a full statement of the matter, Hamlet would have been aware of the jealousy, whereas we have concluded that the mental process we are seeking is hidden from him. Secondly, we see in it no evidence of the arousing of an old and forgotten memory. And, thirdly, Hamlet is being deprived by Claudius of no greater share in the Queen's affection than he had been by his own father, for the two brothers made exactly similar claims in this respect—namely, those of a loved husband. The last-named objection, however, leads us to the heart of the situation. How if, in fact, Hamlet had in years gone by, as a child, bitterly resented having had to share his mother's affection even with his own father, had regarded him as a rival, and had secretly wished him out of the way so that he might enjoy undisputed and undisturbed the monopoly of that affection? If such thoughts had been present in his mind in childhood days they evidently would have been "repressed", and all traces of them obliterated, by filial piety and other educative influences. The actual realization of his early wish in the death of his father at the hands of a jealous rival would then have stimulated into activity these "repressed" memories, which would have produced, in the form of depression and other suffering, an obscure aftermath of his childhood's conflict. This is at all events the mechanism that is actually found in the real Hamlets who are investigated psychologically.

The explanation, therefore, of the delay and self-frustration exhibited in the endeavour to fulfil his father's demand for vengeance is that to Hamlet the thought of incest and parricide combined is too intolerable to be borne. One part of him tries to carry out the task, the other flinches inexorably from the thought of it. How fain would he blot it out in that "bestial oblivion" which unfortunately for him his conscience contemns. He is torn and tortured in an insoluble inner conflict.

Elaine Showalter

from "Representing Ophelia: Women, Madness, and the Responsibilities of Feminist Criticism"

. . . I would like to propose instead that Ophelia *does* have a story of her own that feminist criticism can tell; it is neither her life story, nor her love story, nor Lacan's story, but rather the *history* of her representation. This essay tries to bring together some of the categories of French feminist thought about the "feminine" with the empirical energies of American historical and critical research: to yoke French theory and Yankee know-how.

Tracing the iconography of Ophelia in English and French painting, photography, psychiatry, and literature, as well as in theatrical production, I will be showing first of all the representational bonds between female insanity and female sexuality. Second, I want to demonstrate the two-way transaction between psychiatric theory and cultural representation. As one medical historian has observed, we could provide a manual of female insanity by chronicling the illustrations of Ophelia; this is so because the illustrations of Ophelia have played a major role in the theoretical construction of female insanity. Finally, I want to suggest that the feminist revision of Ophelia comes as much from the actress's freedom as from the critic's interpretation. When Shakespeare's heroines began to be played by women instead of boys, the presence of the female body and female voice, quite apart from details of interpretation, created new meanings and subversive tensions in these roles, and perhaps most importantly with Ophelia. Looking at Ophelia's history on and off the stage, I will point out the contest between male and female representations of Ophelia, cycles of critical repression and feminist reclamation of which contemporary feminist criticism is only the most recent phase. By beginning with these data from cultural history, instead of moving from the grid of literary theory, I hope to conclude with a fuller sense of the responsibilities of feminist criticism, as well as a new perspective on Ophelia.

"Of all the characters in *Hamlet*,"Bridget Lyons has pointed out, "Ophelia is most persistently presented in terms of symbolic meanings." Her behavior, her appearance, her gestures, her costume, her props, are freighted with emblematic significance, and for many generations of Shakespearean critics her part in the play has seemed to be primarily iconographic. Ophelia's symbolic meanings, moreover, are specifically feminine. Whereas for Hamlet madness is metaphysical, linked with culture, for Ophelia it is a product of the female body and female nature, perhaps that nature's purest form. On the Elizabethan stage, the conventions of female insanity were sharply defined. Ophelia dresses in white, decks herself with "fantastical garlands" of wildflowers, and enters, according to the stage directions of the "Bad" Quarto, "distracted" playing on a lute with her "hair down singing." Her speeches are marked by extravagant metaphors, lyrical free associations, and "explosive sexual imagery." She sings wistful and bawdy ballads and ends her life by drowning.

All of these conventions carry specific messages about femininity and sexuality. Ophelia's virginal and vacant white is contrasted with Hamlet's scholar's garb, his "suits of solemn black." Her flowers suggest the discordant double images of female sexuality as both innocent blossoming and whorish contamination; she is the "green girl" of pastoral, the virginal "Rose of May," and the sexually explicit madwoman who, in giving away her wildflowers and herbs, is symbolically deflowering herself. The "weedy trophies" and phallic "long purples" which she wears to her death intimate an improper and discordant sexuality that Gertrude's lovely elegy cannot quite obscure. In Elizabethan and Jacobean drama, the stage direction that a woman enters with disheveled hair indicates that she might either be mad or the victim of a rape; the disordered hair, her offense against decorum, suggests sensuality in each case. The mad Ophelia's bawdy songs and verbal license, while they give her access to "an entirely different range of experience" from what she is allowed as the dutiful daughter, seem to be her one sanctioned form of self-assertion as a woman, quickly followed, as if in retribution, by her death.

Drowning too was associated with the feminine, with female fluidity as opposed to masculine aridity. In his discussion of the "Ophelia complex," the phenomenologist Gaston Bachelard traces the symbolic connections between women, water, and death. Drowning, he suggests, becomes the truly feminine death in the dramas of literature and life, one which is a beautiful immersion and submersion in the female element. Water is the profound and organic symbol of the liquid woman whose eyes are so easily drowned in tears, as her body is the repository of blood, amniotic fluid, and milk. A man contemplating this feminine suicide understands it by reaching for what is feminine in himself, like Laertes, by a temporary surrender to his own fluidity—that is, his tears; and he becomes a man again in becoming once more dry—when his tears are stopped.

Clinically speaking, Ophelia's behavior and appearance are characteristic of the malady the Elizabethans would have diagnosed as female love-melancholy, or erotomania. From about 1580, melancholy had become a fashionable disease among young men, especially in London, and Hamlet himself is a prototype of the melancholy hero. Yet the epidemic of melancholy associated with intellectual and imaginative genius "curiously bypassed women." Women's melancholy was seen instead as biological and emotional in origins.

On the stage, Ophelia's madness was presented as the predictable outcome of erotomania. From 1660, when women first appeared on the public stage, to the beginnings of the eighteenth century, the most celebrated of the actresses who played Ophelia were those whom rumor credited with disappointments in love. The greatest triumph was reserved for Susan Mountfort, a former actress at Lincoln's Inn Fields who had gone mad after her lover's betrayal. One night in 1720 she escaped from her keeper, rushed to the theater, and just as the Ophelia of the evening was to enter for her mad scene, "sprang forward in her place . . . with wild eyes and wavering motion." As a contemporary reported, "she was in truth *Ophelia herself*, to the amazement of the performers as well as of the audience—nature having made this last effort, her vital powers failed her and she died soon after." These theatrical legends reinforced the belief of the age that female madness was a part of female nature, less to be imitated by an actress than demonstrated by a deranged woman in a performance of her emotions.

The subversive or violent possibilities of the mad scene were nearly eliminated, however, on the eighteenth-century stage. Late Augustan stereotypes of female love-melancholy were sentimentalized versions which minimized the force of female sexuality and made female insanity a pretty stimulant to male sensibility. Actresses such as Mrs. Lessingham in 1772, and Mary Bolton in 1811, played Ophelia in this decorous style, relying on the familiar images of the white dress, loose hair, and wildflowers to convey a polite feminine distraction, highly suitable for pictorial reproduction, and appropriate for Samuel Johnson's description of Ophelia as young, beautiful, harmless, and pious. Even Mrs. Siddons in 1785 played the mad scene with stately and classical dignity. . . . For much of the period, in fact, Augustan objections to the levity and indecency of Ophelia's language and behavior led to censorship of the part. Her lines were frequently cut, and the role was often assigned to a singer instead of an actress, making the mode of representation musical rather than visual or verbal.

But whereas the Augustan response to madness was a denial, the Romantic response was an embrace. The figure of the madwoman permeates Romantic literature, from the Gothic novelists to Wordsworth and Scott in such texts as "The Thorn" and *The Heart of Midlothian*, where she stands for sexual victimization, bereavement, and thrilling emotional extremity. Romantic artists such as Thomas Barker and George Shepheard painted pathetically abandoned Crazy Kates and Crazy Anns, while Henry Fuseli's "Mad Kate" is almost demonically possessed, an orphan of the Romantic storm. . . . By the turn of the century, there was both a male and a female discourse on Ophelia. A. C. Bradley spoke for the Victorian male tradition when he noted in *Shakespearean Tragedy* (1906) that "a large number of readers feel a kind of personal irritation against Ophelia; they seem unable to forgive her for not having been a heroine". The feminist counterview was represented by actresses in such works as Helena Faucit [Martin]'s study of

Shakespeare's female characters, and *The True Ophelia*, written by an anonymous actress in 1914, which protested against the "insipid little creature" of criticism and advocated a strong and intelligent woman destroyed by the heartlessness of men. In women's paintings of the fin de siècle as well, Ophelia is depicted as an inspiring, even sanctified emblem of righteousness.[1]

While the widely read and influential essays of Mary Cowden Clarke are now mocked as the epitome of naive criticism, these Victorian studies of the girlhood of Shakespeare's heroines are of course alive and well as psychoanalytic criticism, which has imagined its own prehistories of oedipal conflict and neurotic fixation; and I say this not to mock psychoanalytic criticism, but to suggest that Clarke's musings on Ophelia are a pre-Freudian speculation on the traumatic sources of a female sexual identity. The Freudian interpretation of *Hamlet* concentrated on the hero but also had much to do with the resexualization of Ophelia. As early as 1900, Freud had traced Hamlet's irresolution to an Oedipus complex, and Ernest Jones, his leading British disciple, developed this view, influencing the performances of John Gielgud and Alec Guinness in the 1930s. In his final version of the study, *Hamlet and Oedipus*, published in 1949, Jones argued that "Ophelia should be unmistakably sensual, as she seldom is on stage. She may be 'innocent' and docile, but she is very aware of her body".

In the theater and in criticism, this Freudian edict has produced such extreme readings as that Shakespeare intends us to see Ophelia as a loose woman and that she had been sleeping with Hamlet. Rebecca West has argued that Ophelia was not "a correct and timid virgin of exquisite sensibilities," a view she attributes to the popularity of the Millais painting; but rather "a disreputable young woman." In his delightful autobiography, Laurence Olivier, who made a special pilgrimage to Ernest Jones when he was preparing his *Hamlet* in the 1930s, recalls that one of his predecessors as actor-manager had said in response to the earnest question, "Did Hamlet sleep with Ophelia?"—"In my company, always."

The most extreme Freudian interpretation reads *Hamlet* as two parallel male and female psychodramas, the counterpointed stories of the incestuous attachments of Hamlet and Ophelia. As Theodor Lidz presents this view, while Hamlet is neurotically attached to his mother, Ophelia has an unresolved oedipal attachment to her father. She has fantasies of a lover who will abduct her from or even kill her father, and when this actually happens, her reason is destroyed by guilt as well as by lingering incestuous feelings. According to Lidz, Ophelia breaks down because she fails in the female developmental task of shifting her sexual attachment from her father "to a man who can bring her fulfillment as a woman." We see the effects of this Freudian Ophelia on stage productions since the 1950s, where directors have hinted at an incestuous link between Ophelia and her father, or more recently, because this staging conflicts with the usual ironic treatment of Polonius, between Ophelia and Laertes. Trevor Nunn's production with Helen Mirren in 1970, for example, made Ophelia and Laertes flirtatious doubles, almost twins in their matching fur-trimmed doublets, play-

---

[1] Among these paintings are the Ophelias of Henrietta Rae and Mrs. F. Littler. Sarah Bernhardt sculpted a bas-relief of Ophelia for the Women's Pavilion at the Chicago World's Fair in 1893.

ing duets on the lute with Polonius looking on, like Peter, Paul, and Mary. In other productions of the same period, Marianne Faithfull was a haggard Ophelia equally attracted to Hamlet and Laertes, and, in one of the few performances directed by a woman, Yvonne Nicholson sat on Laertes' lap in the advice scene and played the part with "rough sexual bravado."[2]

Since the 1960s, the Freudian representation of Ophelia has been supplemented by an antipsychiatry that represents Ophelia's madness in more contemporary terms. In contrast to the psychoanalytic representation of Ophelia's sexual unconscious that connected her essential femininity to Freud's essays on female sexuality and hysteria, her madness is now seen in medical and biochemical terms, as schizophrenia. This is so in part because the schizophrenic woman has become the cultural icon of dualistic femininity in the mid-twentieth century as the erotomaniac was in the seventeenth and the hysteric in the nineteenth. It might also be traced to the work of R. D. Laing on female schizophrenia in the 1960s. Laing argued that schizophrenia was an intelligible response to the experience of invalidation within the family network, especially to the conflicting emotional messages and mystifying double binds experienced by daughters. Ophelia, he noted in *The Divided Self*, is an empty space. "In her madness there is no one there. . . . There is no integral selfhood expressed through her actions or utterances. Incomprehensible statements are said by nothing. She has already died. There is now only a vacuum where there was once a person."

Despite his sympathy for Ophelia, Laing's readings silence her, equate her with "nothing," more completely than any since the Augustans; and they have been translated into performances which only make Ophelia a graphic study of mental pathology. The sickest Ophelias on the contemporary stage have been those in the productions of the pathologist-director Jonathan Miller. In 1974 at the Greenwich Theatre his Ophelia sucked her thumb; by 1981, at the Warehouse in London, she was played by an actress much taller and heavier than the Hamlet (perhaps punningly cast as the young actor Anton Lesser). She began the play with a set of nervous tics and tuggings of hair which by the mad scene had become a full set of schizophrenic routines—head banging, twitching, wincing, grimacing, and drooling.[3]

But since the 1970s too we have had a feminist discourse which has offered a new perspective on Ophelia's madness as protest and rebellion. For many feminist theorists, the madwoman is a heroine, a powerful figure who rebels against the family and the social order; and the hysteric who refuses to speak the language of the patriarchal order, who speaks otherwise, is a sister. In terms of effect on the theater, the most radical application of these ideas was probably realized in Melissa Murray's agitprop play *Ophelia*, written in 1979 for the English women's theater group "Hormone Imbalance." In this blank-verse retelling of the Hamlet story, Ophelia becomes a lesbian and runs off with a woman servant to join a guerrilla commune.

While I've always regretted that I missed this production, I can't proclaim

---

[2] This was the production directed by Buzz Goodbody, a brilliant young feminist radical who killed herself that year.   [3] Thanks to Marianne DeKoven, Rutgers University, for the description of the 1981 Warehouse production.

that this defiant ideological gesture, however effective politically or theatrically, is all that feminist criticism desires or all to which it should aspire. When feminist criticism chooses to deal with representation, rather than with women's writing, it must aim for a maximum interdisciplinary contextualism, in which the complexity of attitudes toward the feminine can be analyzed in their fullest cultural and historical frame. The alternation of strong and weak Ophelias on the stage, virginal and seductive Ophelias in art, inadequate or oppressed Ophelias in criticism, tells us how these representations have overflowed the text and how they have reflected the ideological character of their times, erupting as debates between dominant and feminist views in periods of gender crisis and redefinition. The representation of Ophelia changes independently of theories of the meaning of the play or the Prince, for it depends on attitudes toward women and madness. The decorous and pious Ophelia of the Augustan age and the postmodern schizophrenic heroine who might have stepped from the pages of Laing can be derived from the same figure; they are both contradictory and complementary images of female sexuality in which madness seems to act as the "switching-point, the concept which allows the coexistence of both sides of the representation." There is no "true" Ophelia for whom feminist criticism must unambiguously speak, but perhaps only a Cubist Ophelia of multiple perspectives, more than the sum of all her parts.

But in exposing the ideology of representation, feminist critics have also the responsibility to acknowledge and to examine the boundaries of our own ideological positions as products of our gender and our time. A degree of humility in an age of critical hubris can be our greatest strength, for it is by occupying this position of historical self-consciousness in both feminism and criticism that we maintain our credibility in representing Ophelia, and that, unlike Lacan, when we promise to speak about her, we make good our word.

PART IV

French Neoclassical and English Restoration Drama and Theater

An artist sketch shows the interior and exterior arrangement of William Davennant's The Duke's Theatre in Lincoln's Inn Field, one of only two patent theatres in London in the Restoration period.

From the mid-seventeenth century until the nineteenth century in Paris and London, the primary social force affecting the composition and performance of plays was the court, which both patronized and regulated them. Playwriting was influenced by the principles of neoclassicism, which eventually hardened into formulas, while staging was influenced by Italian practices in theater architecture and set design. Theaters were built in a form that would remain virtually unchanged for nearly two hundred years.

FRENCH DRAMA AND SOCIETY IN THE AGE OF LOUIS XIV

By the 1640s the French, like the English, had developed a sophisticated drama that could reflect social practices and tensions, and which openly displayed the artistic ideals of the time. Authoritarian policies during the reigns of King Louis XIII (1610–1643) and King Louis XIV (1643–1715) centralized control at court over every phase of French society and everyday life. The power of the aristocracy to oppose the king was checked by the Crown's chief ministers, Cardinal Richelieu (1585–1642) and his successor Cardinal Mazarin (1602–1661). Between them, king and Church created an elaborate new government bureaucracy, staffed by the clergy and the laity loyal to the Crown. These new bureaucrats were allowed to purchase aristocratic titles, bringing a good deal of profit to the Crown and further weakening the position of the aristocracy. Meanwhile, tax collectors were commissioned to channel the wealth of the aristocracy into Crown coffers in order to finance grand projects like the building of the magnificent palace at Versailles. Such taxes also supported the court's lavish life-style. Rebellions led by aristocrats in the 1640s failed, and the nobles were obligated to serve their turn as courtiers at Versailles. When Louis XIV came to the throne he cultivated the image of the Sun King, a monarch whose power was validated by God rather than by a political process. Indeed, he played the role of Sun King in a court ballet in 1653. But the reality of French society and politics was a different matter entirely. Crop failure, economic stagnation, and taxation drove peasants into open revolt, while legislation had to be enacted to deal with increasingly volatile religious dissent. The ostentatious wealth and lavish expenditures of the court, combined with the decline of aristocratic wealth and the crushing poverty of the lower classes, became the seeds that would grow into the French Revolution of 1798, less than 100 years after the death of Louis XIV.

For over 150 years before that time, however, the court dominated politics, patronizing and regulating the arts, particularly the public arts of drama and theater. At Versailles, the brilliance of the palace and court was illuminated by the arts. Here Louis XIV sponsored a wide array of entertainments, and he personally participated in many of them. To produce and promote the arts and sciences, whole institutions and organizations were created, of which the Académie Française was the most prestigious. Chartered in 1637, its aim was the purification of the French language and literature and the advancement of culture. Louis XIV had already sponsored a number of academies and patronized theater companies, and in 1672 he became protector of the Académie.

An artist's projection shows the interior arrangement of the Comédie Française, Paris, in 1689. Notice the wings and backdrops at the sides and top of the stage.

To perform a play in Paris, a theatrical company needed the king's license. Louis XIV licensed several companies, including Molière's, which became known as the King's Troupe. In 1680 the merger of several French companies created the Comédie Française, which held a monopoly on the production of all spoken French drama. The Comédie Française was the first national theater in Europe; it still performs plays today more than three centuries later.

Neoclassicism

Neoclassicism ("new classicism") refers to the revival of the classical style of Greece and Rome in the arts. Interest in classical literature was revived as early as the fourteenth century, and from the fifteenth century until the seventeenth century under the influence of the Christian Humanism movement, new school curricula sprang up throughout western Europe for the study of classical languages and literature. These courses of study produced a sense of artistic appreciation that came to regard classical form and style as the highest achievements in art.

The aesthetic tenets of neoclassicism were furthered by Cardinal Richelieu in

SUMMARY OF A POETIC OF THE DRAMA

Jean Chapelain; Translated by Barrett H. Clark

The object of representative as well as of narrative poetry is the imitation of human action; their necessary condition is truth to life [*le vraysemblable*]; in its perfection it strives for the marvelous.

From the judicious union of the verisimilar and the marvelous springs the excellence of works of this sort. Both these elements belong to invention.

In Tragedy, which is the noblest form of drama, the poet imitates the actions of the great; in Comedy, those of people in middle or low condition. The ending of Comedy is happy.

Tragi-comedy was known to the Ancients only as tragedy with a happy ending. Witness the *Iphigenia in Tauris*. The modern French have made the form very popular, and as a result of the characters and the action have put it into a class nearer to tragedy than to comedy.

The Pastoral was invented and introduced by the Italians less than a hundred years after the Eclogue; it is a sort of Tragi-comedy, imitating the actions of shepherds, but in a more elevated manner and with higher sentiments than can be employed in the Eclogue.

In plays, poets depict, besides action, the various manners, customs, and passions of human beings.

They take particular care to make each personage speak according to his condition, age, and sex; and by propriety they mean not only that which is descent, but what is fitting and appropriate to the characters—be they good or evil—as they are at first set forth in the play.

In their tragedies and comedies a good plot never had more than one principal action, to which the others are related. This is what is termed Unity of Action.

They have allowed to the development of the action of a play the space of a single natural day. This is what is termed the Twenty-four-hour rule.

They have set the physical limit of their action to a single place. This is what is termed the Unity of Place.

All this is a necessary corollary to the verisimilar, without which the mind is neither moved nor persuaded.

The action of the play consists in exposition of the story, its complication [*embrouillement*] and its development.

The most worthy and agreeable effect that can be produced by a play, is that as a result of the artful conduct of the story the spectator is left suspended and puzzled to know the outcome, and cannot decide what the end of the adventure will be.

The Latins divided plays into five acts, while the Greeks divided them only into scenes.

Each act has several scenes. It will seem too short if it have only four, and too long if more than seven.

In the first act the principal points of the story are made clear; in the second, complications arise; in the third, the trouble deepens; in the fourth, matters look desperate; in the fifth, the knot is loosed—in a natural way, however, but in an unforeseen manner—and from this results the Marvelous.

There are some who insist that no more than three characters should appear on the stage at the same time in the same scene, in order to avoid confusion. I approve of this, except when it applies to the last scenes of the last act, where everything ought to point toward the end and where confusion only renders the unraveling more noble and more beautiful.

Others insist that each scene be intimately bound to the other. This, it is true, produces a more agreeable effect; but the practice of the Ancients proves how unnecessary it is.

What seems most necessary to me is that no character should enter or leave without apparent reason.

response to a critical controversy sparked by Pierre Corneille's play *The Cid*. The play was based on a Spanish original that Corneille attempted to revise according to neoclassical practice. Corneille's critics objected to the play, and Richelieu directed the Académie Française to determine if the play could be regarded as a successful tragedy on neoclassical principles. The distinguished academy ruled in an official report that although the play succeeded in some of its parts, it was deficient in others because it did not adhere to strict neoclassical rules. Those rules are set out in a posthumously published summary by Jean Chapelain (1595–1674), a well-known member of the literary establishment in Paris, founding member of the Académie Française, and chief author of the critique of Corneille's *The Cid*.

Several principles are fundamental to neoclassicism: verisimilitude (the appearance of truth), decorum, the purity of genres, the unities, a five-act structure, and a serious moral purpose. Verisimilitude meant representing the general or typical rather than the particular or individual. The aim of verisimilitude was modified by the requirement that drama should teach moral lessons. Rather than treat specific details, dramatists were to reveal the moral pattern of life by finding the general truth, or norm, that governed a whole class of cases, and to show how the moral pattern operated. The purpose of drama was to teach such truths by delighting and entertaining audiences. The principle of decorum, like that of verisimilitude, required that characters in drama embody the traits normally held by any members of their class. So, for instance, a play that portrayed a physician as a typical social type might be praised while one that detailed the individual difficulties of a particular physician—as the later nineteenth-century realists were to do—might not be highly regarded.

Rigid interpretations of Horace's *Ars Poetica* and Aristotle's *Poetics*, neoclassicism's main theoretical texts, produced ideas about the so-called unities of time, place, and action and a five-act structure. Theorists wanted plays to observe the unity of time so that verisimilitude would not be strained. Such straining occurred when the action onstage took significantly longer than it might in life. Similarly, verisimilitude would be strained when different places were represented in the same play, so the unity of place was held to be important. Finally, verisimilitude might be strained when incomplete, scattered, or conflicting actions were represented, so the unity of action became important. On the basis of Horace's discussion, theorists believed that the standard length of a play should be five acts.

A belief that human nature was subject to unchanging governing norms made neoclassical drama unconcerned with individualizing details. Instead, dramatists were preoccupied with universal aspects of character and circumstance. Assuming a close relationship between experience and art, theorists concluded that art could in fact discover important insights into real experience and so have a positive social effect. Insisting on the purity of genres meant that tragedy and comedy each had their own normative patterns and that these patterns should not be mixed. No element belonging to one should appear in the other. Characters in tragedy, for example, were to be of high social station; its stories about affairs of state or the downfall of rulers; its style lofty and poetic; its endings unhappy. By contrast, comedy's characters were to be from the middle and lower classes; its stories about domestic and private affairs; its style direct and unadorned; its endings happy.

Drama in France was supported by a court that sponsored efforts to classicize the theater, and so tragic drama from this period was principally modeled on classical practice. The most famous and enduring tragedians of the period, Pierre Corneille (1606–1684) and Jean Racine (1639–1699), capitalized on the tradition while invigorating it with their experimentation. Racine's *Phaedra* marks the high point of French neoclassical tragedy, focusing on universal psychological conflicts.

French comedy was influenced by the techniques and characters of the Italian commedia del l'arte, a popular, professional improvisational theater that spread throughout Europe in the sixteenth century. Commedia companies traveled the countryside and played wherever they could find an audience. They consisted of ten to twelve male and female actors specializing in stock characters that have become famous. Actors playing the *innamorato* and the *innamorata* (young lovers), the *capitano* (braggart solider), the *pantalone* (old man), and the *zanni* (a tricky servant like Harlequin) relied on the traits of their characters and on stock stage business to improvise plots and dialogue. The energy, wit, and conventions of the commedia had an enormous influence on the greatest French comic playwright and actor, Jean Baptiste Poquelin, who assumed the name of Molière (1622–1673). A favorite of Louis XIV, Molière was influenced by the classical dramatic conventions of Plautus and Terence, and his plays represent the highest achievement of French comedy in the period.

By 1680, however, with the passing of Corneille, Racine, and Molière, the great age of French playwriting came to an end. Neoclassical drama became rigid and undistinguished; insistence on observing the letter of neoclassical standards led to the stifling of originality and talent, and, ironically, to the deterioration of the forms themselves.

ENGLISH DRAMA AND SOCIETY: THE RESTORATION

After Shakespeare's death in 1616, the English stage was supplied with memorable plays by powerful and accomplished playwrights: Ben Jonson (1572–1637); John Webster (ca. 1580?–1634?); Francis Beaumont (1584–1616); Philip Massinger (1583–1640); Thomas Middleton (ca. 1580–1627); John Ford (1586–1639); James Shirley (1596–1666); and John Fletcher (1579–1625), who had succeeded Shakespeare as principal playwright for the King's Men. By 1642, however, religious and political differences that had been growing between King Charles I and a Puritan-dominated Parliament exploded into civil war and brought the theater to a standstill.

Puritans were "purists" in religion and politics. They associated theater with the extravagance and wastefulness of the aristocracy and with the unruly and immoral behavior of the lower classes. After several years of bloody civil strife, Charles I was defeated by parliamentary forces. In 1649 he was executed, the only English king ever to be sentenced to death by his subjects. Now under the Puritan Commonwealth government, theaters in England were officially closed for nearly twenty years. The king's son, Charles II, escaped to the Continent, to France, where he was educated in the sophisticated French achievements in comedy and in classical tragedy.

In 1660 the parliamentary government in England collapsed, and Charles II returned from exile to be "restored" to the throne of England. The Restoration period that followed lasted for nearly thirty years, to 1688. It was characterized by a struggle for power and prerogatives between the Crown and Parliament, which in turn acted as a focal point for wider tensions between ideas of authoritarian and representative government. Parliament won the struggle once again. It succeeded in deposing Charles II's Catholic brother James II in favor of Mary II, James II's daughter who was Protestant and thus acceptable to rule jointly with her husband, William III of Orange, also a Protestant and James II's nephew. By gaining the power to approve the royal succession by this Act of Settlement in 1701, Parliament not only succeeded in ensuring a Protestant succession but also succeeded in establishing a constitutional monarchy, one that persists to this day.

The Restoration of Charles II in 1660 inaugurated a period of significant dramatic activity. After twenty years of Puritan dominance, audiences were now interested in exciting and heroic tragedies, and—more pointedly—in comedies that ridiculed rigid morals and outmoded social institutions. Plays written for the stage now had an entirely different flavor than those written before the English civil war. Because Charles II had become familiar with French culture, English tragedy of the period was influenced not only by the plays of Shakespeare and his successors but also by the heroic tragedies written in France and Spain. Likewise, English Restoration comedy shows the influence of the earlier satirical comedies of Ben Jonson and also that of the more nearly contemporary Molière. Restoration comedy developed a unique voice and style, and its high-water mark was reached with the work of William Wycherley (1640–1716), and William Congreve (1670–1729), especially in *The Way of the World*. Restoration comedy appealed to a fairly small circle of upper-class theatergoers. It used wit to satirize the foppishness of the age. Its plots often involve aristocrats, city dwellers, and the fortunes of country ladies and gentlemen who are implicated in sexual intrigue. The style of Restoration comedy is elegant, witty, and polished. Its principal concerns are class, privilege, manners, and sex. Concerned almost entirely with contemporary social behavior, it became the first true comedy of manners.

Under increasing political pressure from organizations like the Society for the Reformation of Manners and zealots like Jeremy Collier, the theater reformed itself beginning in the 1690s, turning in the early eighteenth century to softer genres like domestic tragedy and sentimental comedies. Licensing laws were enacted in 1737, formalizing the procedure for subjecting plays to censorship, which had been done in various ways since the early sixteenth century, and limiting performances to licensed theaters. The licensing provision was not repealed until 1968, but the limitation on patent theaters was repealed in 1843 after having been increasingly disregarded for a generation.

Restoration theater had responded to the tastes of the court and concerned itself with the amusement of fashionable people. By the second quarter of the eighteenth century, this theater of wit had alienated the growing middle classes. The prosperous middle class that now patronized the theater had much less interest in courtly manners and style and in the subject of sexual license. A few playwrights, like George Farquhar (1678–1707), continued the Restoration tradition but softened it to please a less sophisticated public. Later in the eighteenth century, two Irishmen, Oliver Goldsmith (1728–1774), author of *She Stoops to Conquer*, and Richard Brinsley Sheridan (1751–1816), purchaser of the Drury Lane Theater and author of *The School for Scandal*, wrote plays that are still revived on occasion.

THEATERS IN ENGLAND AND FRANCE

Like neoclassicism itself, the techniques of Italianate staging had developed as a combination of ideas from both the classical period and contemporary practice. In the sixteenth century the publication of Vitruvius' *De Architetura* (15 B.C.), a book dealing with architecture and scenery, sparked interest in classical staging techniques. Sebastiano Serlio (1475–1554) wrote a detailed study of the subject, (*Architettura*) which became the most influential book on staging in Europe for over a century. Serlio elaborated Vitruvius' sketchy descriptions into detailed directions and illustrations, drawn in perspective, of tragic, comic, and satiric scenes: classical architecture for tragedy; urban architecture for comedy; and natural landscapes for satiric plays. These staging concepts, which had been pioneered in Italy, significantly influenced the practice of theater architecture and staging in England and especially in France, where it continued well into the late seventeenth and eighteenth centuries, when neoclassicism came to dominate aesthetic theory.

Although details differ in each country that adopted Italianate scenic conventions, there are some common features. The stage was raked (sloped) to enhance its sense of depth. A set of wings (constructed of wooden frames covered with fabric and then painted) were located on each side of the stage and arranged so as to suggest a long perspective. At the rear of the stage hung a backdrop constructed of a wooden frame covered with fabric and painted in perspective. All this stage scenery was placed behind a proscenium arch so that the entire set formed a background for the action. The players performed on the apron of the stage in front of the proscenium. Overhead machinery, hidden from view by borders (short curtains), was arranged to complement perspective. Indeed, the proscenium arch framing the entire set suggested the illusion of a painting in perspective.

In France, theaters were renovated or built to accommodate neoclassical drama and Italianate scenery. In 1641 Cardinal Richelieu built a theater of the Italian type in his palace; this was the first permanent proscenium arch in France. Named the Palais-Royal after Richelieu's death, the theater eventually became the home of Molière's acting company. The Hôtel (or hall) de Bourgogne—perhaps the first permanent theater building in Europe when it was built in 1545—was remodeled in 1647 with a proscenium arch. It served as a model for other theaters, also equipped with proscenium arches and raked stages facing an open pit where spectators stood. The auditorium of the Hôtel de Bourgogne was equipped with box seats on three sides and a balcony above the boxes; initially it could accommodate 1,600 people.

The same sets of wings and backdrop could be used for many different plays. On the continent setting often represented a single place, with little emphasis on particular detail because of the neoclassical ideal of verisimilitude. Spectators could sit onstage, and the acting area was confined. Actors performed in the midst of spectators, and dramatic illusion was deemphasized.

Under the direction of Racine and Molière, two Parisian acting companies were organized into sharing companies. Each consisted of ten to fifteen members, or sharers, much like those in Shakespeare's London. These sharers divided the costs of productions and the profits from them, and they hired additional actors and stagehands when needed. Each sharer had a vote in the operation of the company, including women members, who had equal rights and equal pay. Although actors might perform in both comedies and tragedies, they usually specialized in one or the other, as Molière did in comedy. Women ordinarily played women's roles, but in comedy older women were often played by men. Molière's brother-in-law, Louis Béjart, specialized in these roles.

In England, too, new theaters were built to accommodate Italianate staging. Upon his restoration King Charles II granted Thomas Killigrew (1612–1683) a royal patent to form an acting company, the King's Servants, while Sir William Davenant (1606–1668) received a patent to form the Duke's Company. Despite changes introduced later, these patented companies held a monopoly on the legitimate theater in England until the nineteenth century. They built theaters to accommodate their plays. William Davenant built his first one in 1661, calling it Lincoln's Inn theater; two years later, Thomas Killigrew built the Theatre Royal. When that burned down in 1672 he built the Theatre Royal in Drury Lane, which initially accommodated about 700 spectators. From that time to the present day a theater has stood on this site. As in France, these English theaters used proscenium stages with movable painted wings and a backdrop to create the illusion of perspective. One setting was used for comedy and another for tragedy. Footlights illuminated the stage, and the auditorium itself was illuminated with chandeliers, making the audience at these plays fully aware of itself. In English theaters, however, the pit was arranged differently than in France: instead of standing room, the pit was raked and equipped with benches for seating. Other parts of the theaters were similar to those in France. There were box seats on the sides and at the rear and a balcony above. Audiences consisted mainly of the nobility and the more affluent members of the middle class. Distinctions in the seating were intended to underscore wealth and class, with the most expensive seats in the lower boxes and the least expensive in the upper balcony.

Professional women actors appeared onstage in England for the first time during the Restoration. The novelty made the witty actresses of the period an important box office attraction. Nell Gwynn, one of the best-known of them, was also the mistress of Charles II; she remains one of the legends of the English stage. In part because Restoration comedies were often about sexual intrigue, the new actresses developed a reputation for immorality. The age inaugurated the entrance of women in England not only as actors but also as playwrights. Aphra Behn (1640–1689), the first professional woman English playwright, wrote seventeen plays for the stage.

MOLIÈRE (1622–1673)

Molière was born Jean Baptiste Poquelin, the second son in a prosperous family with connections to the court. His father received an annual pension as court *tapissier* (or upholsterer), an income which Jean Baptiste inherited in 1660 after his older brother's death. Educated in Jesuit schools and at the College de Clermont, where he studied the humanities and philosophy, Jean Baptiste went on to study law at Orleans in 1641, although he never took up the practice. In 1643 he joined the Illustre Théâtre, an acting company headed by the Béjart family, and took the stage name of Molière. After a disastrous period in Paris, during which time he was imprisoned for debt, Molière toured with the company in the provinces, learning the techniques of commedia del l'arte. Eventually he became director of the company and attracted some of the best actors and actresses of the day to join. In 1658, now patronized by the Duke of Anjou, the company was invited to perform in Paris. Here it attracted the attention of Louis XIV, and Molière's company was granted permission to perform at one of the few licensed theaters in the city. In 1661 he was performing at the Palais-Royal, and in 1665 his company was designated the King's Company. Beginning in 1659 he wrote and performed a series of plays that satirized the manners of polite society. Their success led to his being invited to perform at court. Now, in addition to plays, Molière prepared other entertainments for the king, including royal pageants and ballets, and he even staged plays devised by the king himself. One of Molière's plays, for example, *The Would-be Gentleman* (1670), was originally a comic ballet, written and prepared at the king's command; it included a musical segment based on a Turkish theme.

Many of Molière's plays for the stage were considered scandalous by members of polite society, who thought that he was attacking specific people. But Molière claimed he satirized types, not individuals. And in fact he ordinarily did write plays that focused on the absurd behavior of a single individual dominated by an obsession. In his first controversial play, *The School for Wives* (1662), Arnolphe is so horrified by the unfaithful wives he sees in Paris that he decides to raise his own wife, a girl of six, in a convent for thirteen years to train her properly. In response to charges that the play was immoral and scandalous, Molière wrote *Criticism of the School for Wives* (1663). In *Tartuffe* (1664), a religious hypocrite is thought to be a saint; he insinuates himself into a noble household and attempts to seduce the mistress of the house. The powerful Society of the Holy Sacrament found the subject and treatment so offensive that it blocked production of the play. Molière appealed to the king and attempted to revise the play, but that version too was suppressed by the Society. Not until 1669, when the Society itself was dissolved, was *Tartuffe* produced in Paris.

Despite the status Molière enjoyed at court, the profession of acting was not regarded as respectable, and the controversies surrounding his plays had not helped matters. When he died in 1673, shortly after performing the title role in his play *The Imaginary Invalid*, the clergy refused to bury him in consecrated ground. Once again the king intervened, but he succeeded only in getting Molière buried in a parish cemetery at night with no funeral ceremony. Today Molière is regarded as the most important comic dramatist in the history of French theater, and his plays are frequently revived.

The Misanthrope

Like all of Molière's plays, *The Misanthrope* (1666) pays careful attention to French society and manners. It was not Molière's most successful play in his own day, possibly because it does not end with a marriage—or, for that matter, even happily—and so does not conform to neoclassical expectations for comedy. Today it is the most popular of his plays. The romance between Alceste and Célimène is modeled on that between Molière and his wife, and when Molière played the role he emphasized the comedy. By the late eighteenth century, however, actors began to play the role seriously, and the tradition continues today.

In the play, the protagonist, Alceste, is repulsed by the hypocrisy he sees in polite French society, his friends tell lies and then talk behind each other's backs. He attempts to live a life of integrity, telling only the truth, a course that proves both admirable and absurd at the same time. Alceste's dedication to truth and honesty seems admirable, particularly when compared to the cruel social lies and backbiting that surround him. But it is absurd as well, because Alceste mechanically insists on honesty in all situations, regardless of the consequences. That such rigidity is out of harmony with the way social life actually works becomes painfully and comically obvious in Alceste's love for Célimène. She is his opposite in personality, young, vivacious, a born coquette who almost never says what she thinks—and she is unwilling to commit herself to a single relationship. She loves the attention she gets from her suitors. At the play's conclusion Célimène agrees to commit to a relationship with Alceste and to curb her hypocrisy, but she cannot bring herself to leave the sophistication of French society. Alceste, rigid as ever, is incapable of compromise, and the play concludes with his determination to find a place where he can live with a clear conscience and a sense of honor.

Although in this play Molière employs the structure of new comedy as discussed by Northrop Frye, he frustrates the traditional ending. By shattering the comic frame, he pushes the play to the border regions of comedy, perhaps even into tragicomedy. Our frustrated hopes for an ending in which the central couple marry—the standard ending of such comedy—has implications for the way we view the society Molière has depicted in the play. At the end of the play nothing has changed. Society remains as hypocritical as ever, and Alceste as rigid as ever, while we vacillate between these competing claims. Honesty and integrity are important personal values, but so is social compromise, and the two do not coexist easily; this universal dilemma lies at the heart of the play's strong appeal.

The Misanthrope

MOLIÈRE

TRANSLATED BY RICHARD WILBUR

CHARACTERS

ALCESTE, in love with Célimène
PHILINTE, Alceste's friend
ORONTE, in love with Célimène
CÉLIMÈNE, Alceste's beloved
ELIANTE, Célimène's cousin
ARSINOÉ, a friend of Célimène's

ACASTE }
CLITANDRE } marquesses
BASQUE, Célimène's servant
A GUARD of the Marshalsea
DUBOIS, Alceste's valet

The scene throughout is in Célimène's house at Paris.

ACT I

Scene 1

[PHILINTE, ALCESTE]

PHILINTE: Now, what's got into you?
ALCESTE (*seated*):   Kindly leave me alone.
PHILINTE: Come, come, what is it? This lugubrious
    tone…
ALCESTE: Leave me, I said; you spoil my solitude.
PHILINTE: Oh, listen to me, now, and don't be rude.
5 ALCESTE: I choose to be rude, Sir, and to be hard of
        hearing.
PHILINTE: These ugly moods of yours are not endearing;
    Friends though we are, I really must insist…
ALCESTE (*abruptly rising*): Friends? Friends, you say?
                        Well, cross me off your list.
    I've been your friend till now, as you well know;
10   But after what I saw a moment ago
    I tell you flatly that our ways must part.
    I wish no place in a dishonest heart.
PHILINTE: Why, what have I done, Alceste? Is this
        quite just?
ALCESTE: My God, you ought to die of self-disgust.
15   I call your conduct inexcusable, Sir,
    And every man of honor will concur.
    I see you almost hug a man to death,
    Exclaim for joy until you're out of breath,
    And supplement these loving demonstrations
20   With endless offers, vows, and protestations;
    Then when I ask you "Who was that?", I find
    That you can barely bring his name to mind!
    Once the man's back is turned, you cease to love
        him,
    And speak with absolute indifference of him!
25   By God, I say it's base and scandalous
    To falsify the heart's affections thus;
    If I caught myself behaving in such a way,
    I'd hang myself for shame, without delay.
PHILINTE: It hardly seems a hanging matter to me;
    I hope that you will take it graciously   30
    If I extend myself a slight reprieve,
    And live a little longer, by your leave.
ALCESTE: How dare you joke about a crime so grave?
PHILINTE: What crime? How else are people to
        behave?
ALCESTE: I'd have them be sincere, and never part   35
    With any word that isn't from the heart.
PHILINTE: When someone greets us with a show of
        pleasure,
    It's but polite to give him equal measure,
    Return his love the best that we know how,
    And trade him offer for offer, vow for vow.   40
ALCESTE: No, no, this formula you'd have me follow,
    However fashionable, is false and hollow,
    And I despise the frenzied operations
    Of all these barterers of protestations,
    These lavishers of meaningless embraces,   45
    These utterers of obliging commonplaces,
    Who court and flatter everyone on earth
    And praise the fool no less than the man of worth.
    Should you rejoice that someone fondles you,
    Offers his love and service, swears to be true,   50
    And fills your ears with praises of your name,
    When to the first damned fop he'll say the same?
    No, no: no self-respecting heart would dream
    Of prizing so promiscuous an esteem;
    However high the praise, there's nothing worse   55
    Than sharing honors with the universe.
    Esteem is founded on comparison:
    To honor all men is to honor none.
    Since you embrace this indiscriminate vice,
    Your friendship comes at far too cheap a price;   60
    I spurn the easy tribute of a heart
    Which will not set the worthy man apart:
    I choose, Sir, to be chosen; and in fine,
    The friend of mankind is no friend of mine.

65 PHILINTE: But in polite society, custom decrees
        That we show certain outward courtesies....
    ALCESTE: Ah, no! we should condemn with all our
        force
        Such false and artificial intercourse.
        Let men behave like men; let them display
70   Their inmost hearts in everything they say;
        Let the heart speak, and let our sentiments
        Not mask themselves in silly compliments.
    PHILINTE: In certain cases it would be uncouth
        And most absurd to speak the naked truth;
75   With all respect for your exalted notions,
        It's often best to veil one's true emotions.
        Wouldn't the social fabric come undone
        If we were wholly frank with everyone?
        Suppose you met with someone you couldn't
            bear;
80   Would you inform him of it then and there?
    ALCESTE: Yes.
    PHILINTE: Then you'd tell old Emilie it's pathetic
        The way she daubs her features with cosmetic
        And plays the gay coquette at sixty-four?
    ALCESTE: I would.
    PHILINTE: And you'd call Dorilas a bore,
85   And tell him every ear at court is lame
        From hearing him brag about his noble name?
    ALCESTE: Precisely.,
    PHILINTE: Ah, you're joking.
    ALCESTE: Au contraire:
        In this regard there's none I'd choose to spare.
        All are corrupt; there's nothing to be seen
90   In court or town but aggravates my spleen.
        I fall into deep gloom and melancholy
        When I survey the scene of human folly,
        Finding on every hand base flattery,
        Injustice, fraud, self-interest, treachery....
95   Ah, it's too much; mankind has grown so base,
        I mean to break with the whole human race.
    PHILINTE: This philosophic rage is a bit extreme;
        You've no idea how comical you seem;
        Indeed, we're like those brothers in the play
100   Called *School for Husbands*, one of whom was
            prey...
    ALCESTE: Enough, now! None of your stupid similes.
    PHILINTE: Then let's have no more tirades, if you
        please.
        The world won't change, whatever you say or do;
        And since plain speaking means so much to you,
105   I'll tell you plainly that by being frank
        You've earned the reputation of a crank,
        And that you're thought ridiculous when you rage
        And rant against the manners of the age.
    ALCESTE: So much the better; just what I wish to hear.
110   No news could be more grateful to my ear.
        All men are so detestable in my eyes,
        I should be sorry if they thought me wise.
    PHILINTE: Your hatred's very sweeping, is it not?

    ALCESTE: Quite right: I hate the whole degraded lot.
    PHILINTE: Must all poor human creatures be embraced,   115
        Without distinction, by your vast distaste?
        Even in these bad times, there are surely a few...
    ALCESTE: No, I include all men in one dim view:
        Some men I hate for being rogues; the others
        I hate because they treat the rogues like brothers,   120
        And, lacking a virtuous scorn for what is vile,
        Receive the villain with a complaisant smile.
        Notice how tolerant people choose to be
        Toward that bold rascal who's at law with me.
        His social polish can't conceal his nature;   125
        One sees at once that he's a treacherous creature;
        No one could possibly be taken in
        By those soft speeches and that sugary grin.
        The whole world knows the shady means by
            which
        The low-brow's grown so powerful and rich,   130
        And risen to a rank so bright and high
        That virtue can but blush, and merit sigh.
        Whenever his name comes up in conversation,
        None will defend his wretched reputation;
        Call him knave, liar, scoundrel, and all the rest,   135
        Each head will nod, and no one will protest.
        And yet his smirk is seen in every house,
        He's greeted everywhere with smiles and bows,
        And when there's any honor that can be got
        By pulling strings, he'll get it, like as not.   140
        My God! It chills my heart to see the ways
        Men come to terms with evil nowadays;
        Sometimes, I swear, I'm moved to flee and find
        Some desert land unfouled by humankind.
    PHILINTE: Come, let's forget the follies of the times   145
        And pardon mankind for its petty crimes;
        Let's have an end of rantings and of railings,
        And show some leniency toward human failings.
        This world requires a pliant rectitude;
        Too stern a virtue makes one stiff and rude;   150
        Good sense views all extremes with detestation,
        And bids us to be noble in moderation.
        The rigid virtues of the ancient days
        Are not for us; they jar with all our ways
        And ask of us too lofty a perfection.   155
        Wise men accept their times without objection,
        And there's no greater folly, if you ask me,
        Than trying to reform society.
        Like you, I see each day a hundred and one
        Unhandsome deeds that might be better done,   160
        But still, for all the faults that meet my view,
        I'm never known to storm and rave like you.
        I take men as they are, or let them be,
        And teach my soul to bear their frailty;
        And whether in court or town, whatever the scene,   165
        My phlegm's as philosophic as your spleen.
    ALCESTE: This phlegm which you so eloquently com-
        mend,
        Does nothing ever rile it up, my friend?

170 Suppose some man you trust should treacherously
Conspire to rob you of your property,
And do his best to wreck your reputation?
Wouldn't you feel a certain indignation?
PHILINTE: Why, no. These faults of which you so complain
175 Are part of human nature, I maintain,
And it's no more a matter for disgust
That men are knavish, selfish and unjust,
Than that the vulture dines upon the dead,
And wolves are furious, and apes ill-bred.
ALCESTE: Shall I see myself betrayed, robbed, torn to bits,
180 And not... Oh, let's be still and rest our wits.
Enough of reasoning, now. I've had my fill.
PHILINTE: Indeed, you would do well, Sir, to be still.
Rage less at your opponent, and give some thought
To how you'll win this lawsuit that he's brought.
185 ALCESTE: I assure you I'll do nothing of the sort.
PHILINTE: Then who will plead your case before the court?
ALCESTE: Reason and right and justice will plead for me.
PHILINTE: Oh, Lord. What judges do you plan to see?
ALCESTE: Why, none. The justice of my cause is clear.
190 PHILINTE: Of course, man; but there's politics to fear....
ALCESTE: No, I refuse to lift a hand. That's flat.
I'm either right, or wrong.
PHILINTE: Don't count on that.
ALCESTE: No, I'll do nothing.
PHILINTE: Your enemy's influence
Is great, you know...
ALCESTE: That makes no difference.
195 PHILINTE: It will; you'll see.
ALCESTE: Must honor bow to guile?
If so, I shall be proud to lose the trial.
PHILINTE: Oh, really...
ALCESTE: I'll discover by this case
Whether or not men are sufficiently base
And impudent and villainous and perverse
200 To do me wrong before the universe.
PHILINTE: What a man!
ALCESTE: Oh, I could wish, whatever the cost,
Just for the beauty of it, that my trial were lost.
PHILINTE: If people heard you talking so, Alceste,
They'd split their sides. Your name would be a jest.
205 ALCESTE: So much the worse for jesters.
PHILINTE: May I enquire
Whether this rectitude you so admire,
And these hard virtues you're enamored of
Are qualities of the lady whom you love?
It much surprises me that you, who seem
210 To view mankind with furious disesteem,
Have yet found something to enchant your eyes
Amidst a species which you so despise.
And what is more amazing, I'm afraid,
Is the most curious choice your heart has made.

The honest Eliante is fond of you,   215
Arsinoé, the prude, admires you too;
And yet your spirit's been perversely led
To choose the flighty Célimène instead,
Whose brittle malice and coquettish ways
So typify the manners of our days.   220
How is it that the traits you most abhor
Are bearable in this lady you adore?
Are you so blind with love that you can't find them?
Or do you contrive, in her case, not to mind them?
ALCESTE: My love for that young widow's not the kind   225
That can't perceive defects; no, I'm not blind.
I see her faults, despite my ardent love,
And all I see I fervently reprove.
And yet I'm weak; for all her falsity,
That woman knows the art of pleasing me,   230
And though I never cease complaining of her,
I swear I cannot manage not to love her.
Her charm outweighs her faults; I can but aim
To cleanse her spirit in my love's pure flame.
PHILINTE: That's no small task; I wish you all success. 235
You think then that she loves you?
ALCESTE: Heavens, yes!
I wouldn't love her did she not love me.
PHILINTE: Well, if her taste for you is plain to see,
Why do these rivals cause you such despair?
ALCESTE: True love, Sir, is possessive, and cannot bear   240
To share with all the world. I'm here today
To tell her she must send that mob away.
PHILINTE: If I were you, and had your choice to make,
Eliante, her cousin, would be the one I'd take;
That honest heart, which cares for you alone,   245
Would harmonize far better with your own.
ALCESTE: True, true: each day my reason tells me so;
But reason doesn't rule in love, you know.
PHILINTE: I fear some bitter sorrow is in store;
This love...   250

Scene 2

[ORONTE, ALCESTE, PHILINTE]

ORONTE (to Alceste): The servants told me at the door
That Eliante and Célimène were out,
But when I heard, dear Sir, that you were about,
I came to say, without exaggeration,
That I hold you in the vastest admiration,   5
And that it's always been my dearest desire
To be the friend of one I so admire.
I hope to see my love of merit requited,
And you and me in friendship's bond united.
I'm sure you won't refuse—if I may be frank—   10
A friend of my devotedness—and rank.

[*During this speech of Oronte's, Alceste is abstracted, and seems unaware that he is being spoken to. He only breaks off his reverie when Oronte says:*]

It was for you, if you please, that my words were
    intended.
ALCESTE: For me, Sir?
ORONTE: Yes, for you. You're not offended?
ALCESTE: By no means. But this much surprises me....
15   The honor comes most unexpectedly....
ORONTE: My high regard should not astonish you;
    The whole world feels the same. It is your due.
ALCESTE: Sir...
ORONTE: Why, in all the State there isn't one
    Can match your merits; they shine, Sir, like the sun.
20 ALCESTE: Sir...
ORONTE: You are higher in my estimation
    Than all that's most illustrious in the nation.
ALCESTE: Sir...
ORONTE: If I lie, may heaven strike me dead!
    To show you that I mean what I have said,
    Permit me, Sir, to embrace you most sincerely,
25   And swear that I will prize our friendship dearly.
    Give me your hand. And now, Sir, if you choose,
    We'll make our vows.
ALCESTE: Sir...
ORONTE: What! You refuse?
ALCESTE: Sir, it's a very great honor you extend:
    But friendship is a sacred thing, my friend;
30   It would be profanation to bestow
    The name of friend on one you hardly know.
    All parts are better played when well-rehearsed;
    Let's put off friendship, and get acquainted first.
    We may discover it would be unwise
35   To try to make our natures harmonize.
ORONTE: By heaven! You're sagacious to the core;
    This speech has made me admire you even more.
    Let time, then, bring us closer day by day;
    Meanwhile, I shall be yours in every way.
40   If, for example, there should be anything
    You wish at court, I'll mention it to the King.
    I have his ear, of course; it's quite well known
    That I am much in favor with the throne.
    In short, I am your servant. And now, dear friend,
45   Since you have such fine judgment, I intend
    To please you, if I can, with a small sonnet
    I wrote not long ago. Please comment on it,
    And tell me whether I ought to publish it.
ALCESTE: You must excuse me, Sir; I'm hardly fit
50   To judge such matters.
ORONTE: Why not?
ALCESTE: I am, I fear,
    Inclined to be unfashionably sincere.
ORONTE: Just what I ask; I'd take no satisfaction
    In anything but your sincere reaction.
    I beg you not to dream of being kind.

ALCESTE: Since you desire it, Sir, I'll speak my mind.   55
ORONTE: *Sonnet.* It's a sonnet.... *Hope...* The poem's
    addressed
    To a lady who wakened hopes within my breast.
    Hope... this is not the pompous sort of thing,
    Just modest little verses, with a tender ring.
ALCESTE: Well, we shall see.
ORONTE: *Hope...* I'm anxious to hear   60
    Whether the style seems properly smooth and
    clear,
    And whether the choice of words is good or bad.
ALCESTE: We'll see, we'll see.
ORONTE: Perhaps I ought to add
    That it took me only a quarter-hour to write it.
ALCESTE: The time's irrelevant, Sir: kindly recite it.   65
ORONTE (*reading*): Hope comforts us awhile, 'tis true,
    Lulling our cares with careless laughter,
    And yet such joy is full of rue,
    My Phyllis, if nothing follows after.
PHILINTE: I'm charmed by this already; the style's
    delightful.   70
ALCESTE (*sotto voce, to Philinte*): How can you say
    that? Why, the thing is frightful.
ORONTE: Your fair face smiled on me awhile,
    But was it kindness so to enchant me?
    'Twould have been fairer not to smile,
    If hope was all you meant to grant me.   75
PHILINTE: What a clever thought! How handsomely
    you phrase it!
ALCESTE (*sotto voce, to Philinte*): You know the thing is
    trash. How dare you praise it?
ORONTE: If it's to be my passion's fate
    Thus everlastingly to wait,
    Then death will come to set me free: 80
    For death is fairer than the fair;
    Phyllis, to hope is to despair
    When one must hope eternally.
PHILINTE: The close is exquisite—full of feeling and
    grace.
ALCESTE (*sotto voce, aside*): Oh, blast the close; you'd
    better close your face   85
    Before you send your lying soul to hell.
PHILINTE: I can't remember a poem I've liked so well.
ALCESTE (*sotto voce, aside*): Good Lord!
ORONTE (*to Philinte*): I fear you're flattering me a bit.
PHILINTE: Oh, no!
ALCESTE (*sotto voce, aside*): What else d'you call it, you
    hypocrite?
ORONTE (*to Alceste*): But you, Sir, keep your promise
    now: don't shrink   90
    From telling me sincerely what you think.
ALCESTE: Sir, these are delicate matters; we all desire
    To be told that we've the true poetic fire.
    But once, to one whose name I shall not mention,
    I said, regarding some verse of his invention,   95
    That gentlemen should rigorously control

That itch to write which often afflicts the soul;
That one should curb the heady inclination
To publicize one's little avocation;
100   And that in showing off one's works of art
One often plays a very clownish part.
  ORONTE: Are you suggesting in a devious way
   That I ought not...
  ALCESTE: Oh, that I do not say.
   Further, I told him that no fault is worse
105 Than that of writing frigid, lifeless verse,
   And that the merest whisper of such a shame
   Suffices to destroy a man's good name.
  ORONTE: D'you mean to say my sonnet's dull and
   trite?
  ALCESTE: I don't say that. But I went on to cite
110 Numerous cases of once-respected men
   Who came to grief by taking up the pen.
  ORONTE: And am I like them? Do I write so poorly?
  ALCESTE: I don't say that. But I told this person,
   "Surely
   You're under no necessity to compose;
115 Why you should wish to publish, heaven knows.
   There's no excuse for printing tedious rot
   Unless one writes for bread, as you do not.
   Resist temptation, then, I beg of you;
   Conceal your pastimes from the public view;
120 And don't give up, on any provocation,
   Your present high and courtly reputation,
   To purchase at a greedy printer's shop
   The name of silly author and scribbling fop."
   These were the points I tried to make him see.
125 ORONTE: I sense that they are also aimed at me;
   But now—about my sonnet—I'd like to be told...
  ALCESTE: Frankly, that sonnet should be pigeonholed.
   You've chosen the worst models to imitate.
   The style's unnatural. Let me illustrate:
130   For example, Your fair face smiled on me
       awhile,
     Followed by, 'Twould have been fairer not to
       smile!
     Or this: such joy is full of rue;
     Or this: For death is fairer than the fair;
     Or, Phyllis, to hope is to despair
135   When one must hope eternally!
   This artificial style, that's all the fashion,
   Has neither taste, nor honesty, nor passion;
   It's nothing but a sort of wordy play,
   And nature never spoke in such a way.
140 What, in this shallow age, is not debased?
   Our fathers, though less refined, had better taste;
   I'd barter all that men admire today
     For one old love-song I shall try to say:
       If the King had given me for my own
145   Paris, his citadel,
     And I for that must leave alone
     Her whom I love so well,

     I'd say then to the Crown,
     Take back your glittering town;
     My darling is more fair, I swear,   150
     My darling is more fair.
   The rhyme's not rich, the style is rough and old,
   But don't you see that it's the purest gold
   Beside the tinsel nonsense now preferred,
   And that there's passion in its every word?   155
     If the King had given me for my own
     Paris, his citadel,
     And I for that must leave alone
     Her whom I love so well,
     I'd say then to the Crown,   160
     Take back your glittering town;
     My darling is more fair, I swear,
     My darling is more fair.
   There speaks a loving heart. (*To Philinte*) You're
     laughing, eh?
   Laugh on, my precious wit. Whatever you say, 165
   I hold that song's worth all the bibelots
   That people hail today with ah's and oh's.
  ORONTE: And I maintain my sonnet's very good.
  ALCESTE: It's not at all surprising that you should.
     You have your reasons; permit me to have mine 170
     For thinking that you cannot write a line.
  ORONTE: Others have praised my sonnet to the skies.
  ALCESTE: I lack their art of telling pleasant lies.
  ORONTE: You seem to think you've got no end of wit.
  ALCESTE: To praise your verse, I'd need still more of it. 175
  ORONTE: I'm not in need of your approval, Sir.
  ALCESTE: That's good; you couldn't have it if you
     were.
  ORONTE: Come now, I'll lend you the subject of my
     sonnet;
     I'd like to see you try to improve upon it.
  ALCESTE: I might, by chance, write something just as
     shoddy;   180
     But then I wouldn't show it to everybody.
  ORONTE: You're most opinionated and conceited.
  ALCESTE: Go find your flatterers, and be better treat-
     ed.
  ORONTE: Look here, my little fellow, pray watch your
     tone.
  ALCESTE: My great big fellow, you'd better watch
     your own.   185
  PHILINTE (*stepping between them*): Oh, please, please,
     gentlemen! This will never do.
  ORONTE: The fault is mine, and I leave the field to
     you.
     I am your servant, Sir, in every way.
  ALCESTE: And I, Sir, am your most abject valet.

Scene 3

[*PHILINTE, ALCESTE*]

PHILINTE: Well, as you see, sincerity in excess
 Can get you into a very pretty mess;
 Oronte was hungry for appreciation....
ALCESTE: Don't speak to me.
PHILINTE: What?
ALCESTE: No more conversation.
5 PHILINTE: Really, now...
ALCESTE: Leave me alone.
PHILINTE: If I...
ALCESTE: Out of my sight!
PHILINTE: But what...
ALCESTE: I won't listen.
PHILINTE: But...
ALCESTE: Silence!
PHILINTE: Now, is it polite...
ALCESTE: By heaven, I've had enough. Don't follow
 me.
PHILINTE: Ah, you're just joking. I'll keep you compa-
 ny.

ACT II

Scene 1

[ALCESTE, CÉLIMÈNE]

ALCESTE: Shall I speak plainly, Madam? I confess
 Your conduct gives me infinite distress,
 And my resentment's grown too hot to smother.
 Soon, I foresee, we'll break with one another.
5 If I said otherwise, I should deceive you;
 Sooner or later, I shall be forced to leave you,
 And if I swore that we shall never part,
 I should misread the omens of my heart.
CÉLIMÈNE: You kindly saw me home, it would
  appear,
10 So as to pour invectives in my ear.
ALCESTE: I've no desire to quarrel. But I deplore
 Your inability to shut the door
 On all these suitors who beset you so.
 There's what annoys me, if you care to know.
15 CÉLIMÈNE: Is it my fault that all these men pursue me?
 Am I to blame if they're attracted to me?
 And when they gently beg an audience,
 Ought I to take a stick and drive them hence?
ALCESTE: Madam, there's no necessity for a stick;
20 A less responsive heart would do the trick.
 Of your attractiveness I don't complain;
 But those your charms attract, you then detain
 By a most melting and receptive manner,
 And so enlist their hearts beneath your banner.
25 It's the agreeable hopes which you excite
 That keep these lovers round you day and night;
 Were they less liberally smiled upon,
 That sighing troop would very soon be gone.

But tell me, Madam, why it is that lately
This man Clitandre interests you so greatly? 30
Because of what high merits do you deem
Him worthy of the honor of your esteem?
Is it that your admiring glances linger
On the splendidly long nail of his little finger?
Or do you share the general deep respect 35
For the blond wig he chooses to affect?
Are you in love with his embroidered hose?
Do you adore his ribbons and his bows?
Or is it that this paragon bewitches
Your tasteful eye with his vast German breeches? 40
Perhaps his giggle, or his falsetto voice,
Makes him the latest gallant of your choice?
CÉLIMÈNE: You're much mistaken to resent him so.
 Why I put up with him you surely know:
 My lawsuit's very shortly to be tried, 45
 And I must have his influence on my side.
ALCESTE: Then lose your lawsuit, Madam, or let it
  drop;
 Don't torture me by humoring such a fop.
CÉLIMÈNE: You're jealous of the whole world, Sir.
ALCESTE: That's true,
 Since the whole world is well-received by you. 50
CÉLIMÈNE: That my good nature is so unconfined
 Should serve to pacify your jealous mind;
 Were I to smile on one, and scorn the rest,
 Then you might have some cause to be distressed.
ALCESTE: Well, if I mustn't be jealous, tell me, then, 55
 Just how I'm better treated than other men.
CÉLIMÈNE: You know you have my love. Will that not
  do?
ALCESTE: What proof have I that what you say is
  true?
CÉLIMÈNE: I would expect, Sir, that my having said it
 Might give the statement a sufficient credit. 60
ALCESTE: But how can I be sure that you don't tell
 The selfsame thing to other men as well?
CÉLIMÈNE: What a gallant speech! How flattering to
  me!
 What a sweet creature you make me out to be!
 Well then, to save you from the pangs of doubt, 65
 All that I've said I hereby cancel out;
 Now, none but yourself shall make a monkey of
  you:
 Are you content?
ALCESTE: Why, why am I doomed to love you?
 I swear that I shall bless the blissful hour
 When this poor heart's no longer in your power! 70
 I make no secret of it: I've done my best
 To exorcise this passion from my breast;
 But thus far all in vain; it will not go;
 It's for my sins that I must love you so.
CÉLIMÈNE: Your love for me is matchless, Sir; that's
  clear. 75
ALCESTE: Indeed, in all the world it has no peer;

Words can't describe the nature of my passion,
And no man ever loved in such a fashion.
CÉLIMÈNE: Yes, it's a brand-new fashion, I agree:
80   You show your love by castigating me,
  And all your speeches are enraged and rude.
  I've never been so furiously wooed.
ALCESTE: Yet you could calm that fury, if you chose.
  Come, shall we bring our quarrels to a close?
85   Let's speak with open hearts, then, and begin…

Scene 2

[CÉLIMÈNE, ALCESTE, BASQUE]

CÉLIMÈNE: What is it?
BASQUE: Acaste is here.
CÉLIMÈNE: Well, send him in.

Scene 3

[CÉLIMÈNE, ALCESTE]

ALCESTE: What! Shall we never be alone at all?
  You're always ready to receive a call,
  And you can't bear, for ten ticks of the clock,
  Not to keep open house for all who knock.
5 CÉLIMÈNE: I couldn't refuse him: he'd be most put
    out.
ALCESTE: Surely that's not worth worrying about.
CÉLIMÈNE: Acaste would never forgive me if he
    guessed
  That I consider him a dreadful pest.
ALCESTE: If he's a pest, why bother with him then?
10 CÉLIMÈNE: Heavens! One can't antagonize such men;
  Why, they're the chartered gossips of the court,
  And have a say in things of every sort.
  One must receive them, and be full of charm;
  They're no great help, but they can do you harm,
15   And though your influence be ever so great,
  They're hardly the best people to alienate.
ALCESTE: I see, dear lady, that you could make a case
  For putting up with the whole human race;
  These friendships that you calculate so nicely…

Scene 4

[ALCESTE, CÉLIMÈNE, BASQUE]

BASQUE: Madam, Clitandre is here as well.
ALCESTE: Precisely.
CÉLIMÈNE: Where are you going?
ALCESTE: Elsewhere.
CÉLIMÈNE: Stay.
ALCESTE: No, no.
CÉLIMÈNE: Stay, Sir.

ALCESTE: I can't.
CÉLIMÈNE: I wish it.
ALCESTE: No, I must go.
  I beg you, Madam, not to press the matter;
  You know I have no taste for idle chatter.   5
CÉLIMÈNE: Stay: I command you.
ALCESTE: No, I cannot stay.
CÉLIMÈNE: Very well; you have my leave to go away.

Scene 5

[ELIANTE, PHILINTE, ACASTE, CLITANDRE, ALCESTE,
CÉLIMÈNE, BASQUE]

ELIANTE (*to Célimène*): The Marquesses have kindly
    come to call.
  Were they announced?
CÉLIMÈNE: Yes. Basque, bring chairs for all.

[Basque provides the chairs, and exits]

  [To Alceste] You haven't gone?
ALCESTE: No; and I shan't depart
  Till you decide who's foremost in your heart.
CÉLIMÈNE: Oh, hush.
ALCESTE: It's time to choose; take them, or me.   5
CÉLIMÈNE: You're mad.
ALCESTE: I'm not, as you shall shortly see.
CÉLIMÈNE: Oh?
ALCESTE: You'll decide.
CÉLIMÈNE: You're joking now, dear friend.
ALCESTE: No, no; you'll choose; my patience is at an
    end.
CLITANDRE: Madam, I come from court, where poor
    Cléonte
  Behaved like a perfect fool, as is his wont.   10
  Has he no friend to counsel him, I wonder,
  And teach him less unerringly to blunder?
CÉLIMÈNE: It's true, the man's a most accomplished
    dunce;
  His gauche behavior charms the eye at once;
  And every time one sees him, on my word,   15
  His manner's grown a trifle more absurd.
ACASTE: Speaking of dunces, I've just now conversed
  With old Damon, who's one of the very worst;
  I stood a lifetime in the broiling sun
  Before his dreary monologue was done.   20
CÉLIMÈNE: Oh, he's a wondrous talker, and has the
    power
  To tell you nothing hour after hour:
  If, by mistake, he ever came to the point,
  The shock would put his jawbone out of joint.
ELIANTE (*to Philinte*): The conversation takes its usual
    turn,   25
  And all our dear friends' ears will shortly burn.

CLITANDRE: Timante's a character, Madam.

CÉLIMÈNE: Isn't he, though?
   A man of mystery from top to toe,
   Who moves about in a romantic mist
30   On secret missions which do not exist.
   His talk is full of eyebrows and grimaces;
   How tired one gets of his momentous faces;
   He's always whispering something confidential
   Which turns out to be quite inconsequential;
35   Nothing's too slight for him to mystify;
   He even whispers when he says "good-by."

ACASTE: Tell us about Géralde.

CÉLIMÈNE: That tiresome ass.
   He mixes only with the titled class,
   And fawns on dukes and princes, and is bored
40   With anyone who's not at least a lord.
   The man's obsessed with rank, and his discourses
   Are all of hounds and carriages and horses;
   He uses Christian names with all the great,
   And the word Milord, with him, is out of date.

45 CLITANDRE: He's very taken with Bélise, I hear.

CÉLIMÈNE: She is the dreariest company, poor dear.
   Whenever she comes to call, I grope about
   To find some topic which will draw her out,
   But, owing to her dry and faint replies,
50   The conversation wilts, and droops, and dies.
   In vain one hopes to animate her face
   By mentioning the ultimate commonplace;
   But sun or shower, even hail or frost
   Are matters she can instantly exhaust.
55   Meanwhile her visit, painful though it is,
   Drags on and on through mute eternities,
   And though you ask the time, and yawn, and
     yawn,
   She sits there like a stone and won't be gone.

ACASTE: Now for Adraste.

CÉLIMÈNE: Oh, that conceited elf
60   Has a gigantic passion for himself;
   He rails against the court, and cannot bear it
   That none will recognize his hidden merit;
   All honors given to others give offense
   To his imaginary excellence.

65 CLITANDRE: What about young Cléon? His house,
     they say,
   Is full of the best society, night and day.

CÉLIMÈNE: His cook has made him popular, not he:
   It's Cléon's table that people come to see.

ELIANTE: He gives a splendid dinner, you must
     admit.

70 CÉLIMÈNE: But must he serve himself along with it?
   For my taste, he's a most insipid dish
   Whose presence sours the wine and spoils the
     fish.

PHILINTE: Damis, his uncle, is admired no end.
   What's your opinion, Madam?

CÉLIMÈNE: Why, he's my friend.

PHILINTE: He seems a decent fellow, and rather clever.   75

CÉLIMÈNE: He works too hard at cleverness, however.
   I hate to see him sweat and struggle so
   To fill his conversation with bons mots.
   Since he's decided to become a wit
   His taste's so pure that nothing pleases it;   80
   He scolds at all the latest books and plays,
   Thinking that wit must never stoop to praise,
   That finding fault's a sign of intellect,
   That all appreciation is abject,
   And that by damning everything in sight   85
   One shows oneself in a distinguished light.
   He's scornful even of our conversations:
   Their trivial nature sorely tries his patience;
   He folds his arms, and stands above the battle,
   And listens sadly to our childish prattle.   90

ACASTE: Wonderful, Madam! You've hit him off pre-
     cisely.

CLITANDRE: No one can sketch a character so nicely.

ALCESTE: How bravely, Sirs, you cut and thrust at all
   These absent fools, till one by one they fall:
   But let one come in sight, and you'll at once   95
   Embrace the man you lately called a dunce,
   Telling him in a tone sincere and fervent
   How proud you are to be his humble servant.

CLITANDRE: Why pick on us? Madame's been speak-
     ing, Sir,
   And you should quarrel, if you must, with her.   100

ALCESTE: No, no, by God, the fault is yours, because
   You lead her on with laughter and applause,
   And make her think that she's the more delightful
   The more her talk is scandalous and spiteful.
   Oh, she would stoop to malice far, far less   105
   If no such claque approved her cleverness.
   It's flatterers like you whose foolish praise
   Nourishes all the vices of these days.

PHILINTE: But why protest when someone ridicules
   Those you'd condemn, yourself, as knaves or
     fools?   110

CÉLIMÈNE: Why, Sir? Because he loves to make a fuss.
   You don't expect him to agree with us,
   When there's an opportunity to express
   His heaven-sent spirit of contrariness?
   What other people think, he can't abide;   115
   Whatever they say, he's on the other side;
   He lives in deadly terror of agreeing;
   'Twould make him seem an ordinary being.
   Indeed, he's so in love with contradiction,
   He'll turn against his most profound conviction   120
   And with a furious eloquence deplore it
   If only someone else is speaking for it.

ALCESTE: Go on, dear lady, mock me as you please;
   You have your audience in ecstasies.

PHILINTE: But what she says is true: you have a way   125
   Of bridling at whatever people say;
   Whether they praise or blame, your angry spirit

Is equally unsatisfied to hear it.

ALCESTE: Men, Sir, are always wrong, and that's the
    reason
130 That righteous anger's never out of season;
    All that I hear in all their conversation
    Is flattering praise or reckless condemnation.

CÉLIMÈNE: But…

ALCESTE: No, no, Madam, I am forced to state
    That you have pleasures which I deprecate,
135 And that these others, here, are much to blame
    For nourishing the faults which are your shame.

CLITANDRE: I shan't defend myself, Sir; but I vow
    I'd thought this lady faultless until now.

ACASTE: I see her charms and graces, which are many;
140 But as for faults, I've never noticed any.

ALCESTE: I see them, Sir; and rather than ignore
    them,
    I strenuously criticize her for them.
    The more one loves, the more one should object
    To every blemish, every least defect.
145 Were I this lady, I would soon get rid
    Of lovers who approved of all I did,
    And by their slack indulgence and applause
    Endorsed my follies and excused my flaws.

CÉLIMÈNE: If all hearts beat according to your measure,
150 The dawn of love would be the end of pleasure;
    And love would find its perfect consummation
    In ecstasies of rage and reprobation.

ELIANTE: Love, as a rule, affects men otherwise,
    And lovers rarely love to criticize.
155 They see their lady as a charming blur,
    And find all things commendable in her.
    If she has any blemish, fault, or shame,
    They will redeem it by a pleasing name.
    The pale-faced lady's lily-white, perforce;
160 The swarthy one's a sweet brunette, of course;
    The spindly lady has a slender grace;
    The fat one has a most majestic pace;
    The plain one, with her dress in disarray,
    They classify as *beauté négligée;*
165 The hulking one's a goddess in their eyes,
    The dwarf, a concentrate of Paradise;
    The haughty lady has a noble mind;
    The mean one's witty, and the dull one's kind;
    The chatterbox has liveliness and verve,
170 The mute one has a virtuous reserve.
    So lovers manage, in their passion's cause,
    To love their ladies even for their flaws.

ALCESTE: But I still say…

CÉLIMÈNE: I think it would be nice
    To stroll around the gallery once or twice.
175 What! You're not going, Sirs?

CLITANDRE AND ACASTE: No, Madam, no.

ALCESTE: You seem to be in terror lest they go.,
    Do what you will, Sirs; leave, or linger on,
    But I shan't go till after you are gone.

ACASTE: I'm free to linger, unless I should perceive
    Madame is tired, and wishes me to leave.   180

CLITANDRE: And as for me, I needn't go today
    Until the hour of the King's *coucher.*

CÉLIMÈNE (*to Alceste*): You're joking, surely?

ALCESTE: Not in the least; we'll see
    Whether you'd rather part with them, or me.

Scene 6

[ALCESTE, CÉLIMÈNE, ELIANTE, ACASTE, PHILINTE,
CLITANDRE, BASQUE]

BASQUE (*to Alceste*): Sir, there's a fellow here who bids
    me state
    That he must see you, and that it can't wait.

ALCESTE: Tell him that I have no such pressing
    affairs.

BASQUE: It's a long tailcoat that this fellow wears,
    With gold all over.

CÉLIMÈNE (*to Alceste*):   You'd best go down and see.   5
    Or—have him enter.

Scene 7

[ALCESTE, CÉLIMÈNE, ELIANTE, ACASTE, PHILINTE,
CLITANDRE, A GUARD of the Marshalsea]

ALCESTE (*confronting the guard*): Well, what do you
    want with me?
    Come in, Sir.

GUARD: I've a word, Sir, for your ear.

ALCESTE: Speak it aloud, Sir; I shall strive to hear.

GUARD: The Marshals have instructed me to say
    You must report to them without delay.   5

ALCESTE: Who? Me, Sir?

GUARD: Yes, Sir; you.

ALCESTE: But what do they want?

PHILINTE (*to Alceste*): To scotch your silly quarrel with
    Oronte.

CÉLIMÈNE: (*to Philinte*): What quarrel?

PHILINTE: Oronte and he have fallen out
    Over some verse he spoke his mind about;
    The Marshals wish to arbitrate the matter.   10

ALCESTE: Never shall I equivocate or flatter!

PHILINTE: You'd best obey their summons; come, let's
    go.

ALCESTE: How can they mend our quarrel, I'd like to
    know?
    Am I to make a cowardly retraction,
    And praise those jingles to his satisfaction?   15
    I'll not recant; I've judged that sonnet rightly.
    It's bad.

PHILINTE: But you might say so more politely….

ALCESTE: I'll not back down; his verses make me sick.

PHILINTE: If only you could be more politic!
20   But come, let's go.
ALCESTE: I'll go, but I won't unsay
      A single word.
PHILINTE: Well, let's be on our way.
ALCESTE: Till I am ordered by my lord the King
      To praise that poem, I shall say the thing
      Is scandalous, by God, and that the poet
25   Ought to be hanged for having the nerve to show it.

[To Clitandre and Acaste, who are laughing]

      By heaven, Sirs, I really didn't know
      That I was being humorous.
CÉLIMÈNE: Go, Sir, go;
      Settle your business.
ALCESTE: I shall, and when I'm through,
      I shall return to settle things with you.

ACT III

Scene 1

[CLITANDRE, ACASTE]

CLITANDRE: Dear Marquess, how contented you appear;
      All things delight you, nothing mars your cheer.
      Can you, in perfect honesty, declare
      That you've a right to be so debonair?
5 ACASTE: By Jove, when I survey myself, I find
      No cause whatever for distress of mind.
      I'm young and rich; I can in modesty
      Lay claim to an exalted pedigree;
      And owing to my name and my condition
10   I shall not want for honors and position.
      Then as to courage, that most precious trait,
      I seem to have it, as was proved of late
      Upon the field of honor, where my bearing,
      They say, was very cool and rather daring.
15   I've wit, of course; and taste in such perfection
      That I can judge without the least reflection,
      And at the theater, which is my delight,
      Can make or break a play on opening night,
      And lead the crowd in hisses or bravos,
20   And generally be known as one who knows.
      I'm clever, handsome, gracefully polite;
      My waist is small, my teeth are strong and white;
      As for my dress, the world's astonished eyes
      Assure me that I bear away the prize.
25   I find myself in favor everywhere,
      Honored by men, and worshiped by the fair;
      And since these things are so, it seems to me
      I'm justified in my complacency.
CLITANDRE: Well, if so many ladies hold you dear,
30   Why do you press a hopeless courtship here?
ACASTE: Hopeless, you say? I'm not the sort of fool

      That likes his ladies difficult and cool.
      Men who are awkward, shy, and peasantish
      May pine for heartless beauties, if they wish,
      Grovel before them, bear their cruelties,   35
      Woo them with tears and sighs and bended knees,
      And hope by dogged faithfulness to gain
      What their poor merits never could obtain.
      For men like me, however, it makes no sense
      To love on trust, and foot the whole expense.   40
      Whatever any lady's merits be,
      I think, thank God, that I'm as choice as she;
      That if my heart is kind enough to burn
      For her, she owes me something in return;
      And that in any proper love affair   45
      The partners must invest an equal share.
CLITANDRE: You think, then, that our hostess favors
      you?
ACASTE: I've reason to believe that that is true.
CLITANDRE: How did you come to such a mad con-
      clusion?
      You're blind, dear fellow. This is sheer delusion. 50
ACASTE: All right, then: I'm deluded and I'm blind.
CLITANDRE: Whatever put the notion in your mind?
ACASTE: Delusion.
CLITANDRE: What persuades you that you're right?
ACASTE: I'm blind.
CLITANDRE: But have you any proofs to cite?
ACASTE: I tell you I'm deluded.
CLITANDRE: Have you, then,   55
      Received some secret pledge from Célimène?
ACASTE: Oh, no: she scorns me.
CLITANDRE: Tell me the truth, I beg.
ACASTE: She just can't bear me.
CLITANDRE: Ah, don't pull my leg.
      Tell me what hope she's given you, I pray.
ACASTE: I'm hopeless, and it's you who win the day.   60
      She hates me thoroughly, and I'm so vexed
      I mean to hang myself on Tuesday next.
CLITANDRE: Dear Marquess, let us have an armistice
      And make a treaty. What do you say to this?
      If ever one of us can plainly prove   65
      That Célimène encourages his love,
      The other must abandon hope, and yield,
      And leave him in possession of the field.
ACASTE: Now, there's a bargain that appeals to me;
      With all my heart, dear Marquess, I agree.   70
      But hush.

Scene 2

[CÉLIMÈNE, ACASTE, CLITANDRE]

CÉLIMÈNE: Still here?
CLITANDRE: T'was love that stayed our feet.
CÉLIMÈNE: I think I heard a carriage in the street.
      Whose is it? D'you know?

Scene 3

[CÉLIMÈNE, ACASTE, CLITANDRE, BASQUE]

BASQUE: Arsinoé is here,
   Madame.
CÉLIMÈNE: Arsinoé, you say? Oh, dear.
BASQUE: Eliante is entertaining her below.
CÉLIMÈNE: What brings the creature here, I'd like to
      know?
5 ACASTE: They say she's dreadfully prudish, but in
      fact
      I think her piety…
CÉLIMÈNE: It's all an act.
      At heart she's worldly, and her poor success
      In snaring men explains her prudishness.
      It breaks her heart to see the beaux and gallants
10   Engrossed by other women's charms and talents,
      And so she's always in a jealous rage.
      Against the faulty standards of the age.
      She lets the world believe that she's a prude
      To justify her loveless solitude,
15   And strives to put a brand of moral shame
      On all the graces that she cannot claim.
      But still she'd love a lover; and Alceste
      Appears to be the one she'd love the best.
      His visits here are poison to her pride;
20   She seems to think I've lured him from her side;
      And everywhere, at court or in the town,
      The spiteful, envious woman runs me down.
      In short, she's just as stupid as can be,
      Vicious and arrogant in the last degree,
25   And…

Scene 4

[ARSINOÉ, CÉLIMÈNE, CLITANDRE, ACASTE]

CÉLIMÈNE: Ah! What happy chance has brought you
      here?
      I've thought about you ever so much, my dear.
ARSINOÉ: I've come to tell you something you should
      know.
CÉLIMÈNE: How good of you to think of doing so!

[Clitandre and Alcaste go out, laughing]

Scene 5

[ARSINOÉ, CÉLIMÈNE]

ARSINOÉ: It's just as well those gentlemen didn't
      tarry.
CÉLIMÈNE: Shall we sit down?
ARSINOÉ: That won't be necessary.

Madam, the flame of friendship ought to burn
Brightest in matters of the most concern,
And as there's nothing which concerns us more   5
Than honor, I have hastened to your door
To bring you, as your friend, some information
About the status of your reputation.
I visited, last night, some virtuous folk,
And, quite by chance, it was of you they spoke;   10
There was, I fear, no tendency to praise
Your light behavior and your dashing ways.
The quantity of gentlemen you see
And your by now notorious coquetry
Were both so vehemently criticized   15
By everyone, that I was much surprised.
Of course, I needn't tell you where I stood;
I came to your defense as best I could,
Assured them you were harmless, and declared
Your soul was absolutely unimpaired.   20
But there are some things, you must realize,
One can't excuse, however hard one tries,
And I was forced at last into conceding
That your behavior, Madam, is misleading,
That it makes a bad impression, giving rise   25
To ugly gossip and obscene surmise,
And that if you were more *overtly* good,
You wouldn't be so much misunderstood.
Not that I think you've been unchaste—no! no!
The saints preserve me from a thought so low!   30
But mere good conscience never did suffice:
One must avoid the outward show of vice.
Madam, you're too intelligent, I'm sure,
To think my motives anything but pure
In offering you this counsel—which I do   35
Out of a zealous interest in you.
CÉLIMÈNE: Madam, I haven't taken you amiss;
      I'm very much obliged to you for this;
      And I'll at once discharge the obligation
      By telling you about *your* reputation.   40
      You've been so friendly as to let me know
      What certain people say of me, and so
      I mean to follow your benign example
      By offering you a somewhat similar sample.
      The other day, I went to an affair   45
      And found some most distinguished people there
      Discussing piety, both false and true.
      The conversation soon came round to you.
      Alas! Your prudery and bustling zeal
      Appeared to have a very slight appeal.   50
      Your affectation of a grave demeanor,
      Your endless talk of virtue and of honor,
      The aptitude of your suspicious mind
      For finding sin where there is none to find,
      Your towering self-esteem, that pitying face   55
      With which you contemplate the human race,
      Your sermonizings and your sharp aspersions
      On people's pure and innocent diversions—
      All these were mentioned, Madam, and, in fact,

60   Were roundly and concertedly attacked.
"What good," they said, "are all these outward
     shows,
When everything belies her pious pose?
She prays incessantly; but then, they say,
She beats her maids and cheats them of their pay;
65   She shows her zeal in every holy place,
But still she's vain enough to paint her face;
She holds that naked statues are immoral,
But with a naked *man* she'd have no quarrel."
Of course, I said to everybody there
70   That they were being viciously unfair;
But still they were disposed to criticize you,
And all agreed that someone should advise you
To leave the morals of the world alone,
And worry rather more about your own.
75   They felt that one's self-knowledge should be great
Before one thinks of setting others straight;
That one should learn the art of living well
Before one threatens other men with hell,
And that the Church is best equipped, no doubt,
80   To guide our souls and root our vices out.
Madam, you're too intelligent, I'm sure,
To think my motives anything but pure
In offering you this counsel—which I do
Out of a zealous interest in you.
85   ARSINOÉ: I dared not hope for gratitude, but I
Did not expect so acid a reply;
I judge, since you've been so extremely tart,
That my good counsel pierced you to the heart.
CÉLIMÈNE: Far from it, Madam. Indeed, it seems to me
90   We ought to trade advice more frequently.
One's vision of oneself is so defective
That it would be an excellent corrective.
If you are willing, Madam, let's arrange
Shortly to have another frank exchange
95   In which we'll tell each other, *entre nous,*
What you've heard tell of me, and I of you.
ARSINOÉ: Oh, people never censure you, my dear;
It's me they criticize. Or so I hear.
CÉLIMÈNE: Madam, I think we either blame or praise
100   According to our taste and length of days.
There is a time of life for coquetry,
And there's a season, too, for prudery.
When all one's charms are gone, it is, I'm sure,
Good strategy to be devout and pure:
105   It makes one seem a little less forsaken.
Some day, perhaps, I'll take the road you've
     taken:
Time brings all things. But I have time aplenty,
And see no cause to be a prude at twenty.
ARSINOÉ: You give your age in such a gloating tone
110   That one would think I was an ancient crone;
We're not so far apart, in sober truth,
That you can mock me with a boast of youth!
Madam, you baffle me. I wish I knew
What moves you to provoke me as you do.

CÉLIMÈNE: For my part, Madam, I should like to know   115
Why you abuse me everywhere you go.
Is it my fault, dear lady, that your hand
Is not, alas, in very great demand?
If men admire me, if they pay me court
And daily make me offers of the sort   120
You'd dearly love to have them make to you,
How can I help it? What would you have me do?
If what you want is lovers, please feel free
To take as many as you can from me.
ARSINOÉ: Oh, come. D'you think the world is losing
     sleep   125
Over that flock of lovers which you keep,
Or that we find it difficult to guess
What price you pay for their devotedness?
Surely you don't expect us to suppose
Mere merit could attract so many beaux?   130
It's not your virtue that they're dazzled by;
Nor is it virtuous love for which they sigh.
You're fooling no one, Madam; the world's not blind;
There's many a lady heaven has designed
To call men's noblest, tenderest feelings out,   135
Who has no lovers dogging her about;
From which it's plain that lovers nowadays
Must be acquired in bold and shameless ways,
And only pay one court for such reward
As modesty and virtue can't afford.   140
Then don't be quite so puffed up, if you please,
About your tawdry little victories;
Try, if you can, to be a shade less vain,
And treat the world with somewhat less disdain.
If one were envious of your amours,   145
One soon could have a following like yours;
Lovers are no great trouble to collect
If one prefers them to one's self-respect.
CÉLIMÈNE: Collect them then, my dear; I'd love to see
You demonstrate that charming theory;   150
Who knows, you might...
ARSINOÉ: Now, Madam, that will do;
It's time to end this trying interview.
My coach is late in coming to your door,
Or I'd have taken leave of you before.
CÉLIMÈNE: Oh, please don't feel that you must rush
     away;   155
I'd be delighted, Madam, if you'd stay.
However, lest my conversation bore you,
Let me provide some better company for you;
This gentleman, who comes most apropos,
Will please you more than I could do, I know.   160

Scene 6

[ALCESTE, CÉLIMÈNE, ARSINOÉ]

CÉLIMÈNE: Alceste, I have a little note to write
Which simply must go out before tonight;

Please entertain *Madame*; I'm sure that she
Will overlook my incivility.

Scene 7

[*ALCESTE, ARSINOÉ*]

ARSINOÉ: Well, Sir, our hostess graciously contrives
  For us to chat until my coach arrives;
  And I shall be forever in her debt
  For granting me this little tête-à-tête.
5 We women very rightly give our hearts
  To men of noble character and parts,
  And your especial merits, dear Alceste,
  Have roused the deepest sympathy in my breast.
  Oh, how I wish they had sufficient sense
10 At court, to recognize your excellence!
  They wrong you greatly, Sir. How it must hurt you
  Never to be rewarded for your virtue!
ALCESTE: Why, Madam, what cause have I to feel
    aggrieved?
  What great and brilliant thing have I achieved?
15 What service have I rendered to the King
  That I should look to him for anything?
ARSINOÉ: Not everyone who's honored by the State
  Has done great services. A man must wait
  Till time and fortune offer him the chance.
20 Your merit, Sir, is obvious at a glance,
  And…
ALCESTE: Ah, forget my merit; I'm not neglected.
  The court, I think, can hardly be expected
  To mine men's souls for merit, and unearth
  Our hidden virtues and our secret worth.
25 ARSINOÉ: *Some* virtues, though, are far too bright
    to hide;
  Yours are acknowledged, Sir, on every side.
  Indeed, I've heard you warmly praised of late
  By persons of considerable weight.
ALCESTE: This fawning age has praise for everyone,
30 And all distinctions, Madam, are undone.
  All things have equal honor nowadays,
  And no one should be gratified by praise.
  To be admired, one only need exist,
  And every lackey's on the honors list.
35 ARSINOÉ: I only wish, Sir, that you had your eye
  On some position at court, however high;
  You'd only have to hint at such a notion
  For me to set the proper wheels in motion;
  I've certain friendships I'd be glad to use
40 To get you any office you might choose.
ALCESTE: Madam, I fear that any such ambition
  Is wholly foreign to my disposition.
  The soul God gave me isn't of the sort
  That prospers in the weather of a court.
45 It's all too obvious that I don't possess
  The virtues necessary for success.

My one great talent is for speaking plain;
I've never learned to flatter or to feign;
And anyone so stupidly sincere
Had best not seek a courtier's career.   50
Outside the court, I know, one must dispense
With honors, privilege, and influence;
But still one gains the right, foregoing these,
Not to be tortured by the wish to please.
One needn't live in dread of snubs and slights,   55
Nor praise the verse that every idiot writes,
Nor humor silly Marquesses, nor bestow
Politic sighs on Madam So-and-So.
ARSINOÉ: Forget the court, then; let the matter rest.
  But I've another cause to be distressed   60
  About your present situation, Sir.
  It's to your love affair that I refer.
  She whom you love, and who pretends to love you,
  Is, I regret to say, unworthy of you.
ALCESTE: Why, Madam! Can you seriously intend   65
  To make so grave a charge against your friend?
ARSINOÉ: Alas, I must. I've stood aside too long
  And let that lady do you grievous wrong;
  But now my debt to conscience shall be paid:
  I tell you that your love has been betrayed.   70
ALCESTE: I thank you, Madam; you're extremely kind.
  Such words are soothing to a lover's mind.
ARSINOÉ: Yes, though she *is* my friend, I say again
  You're very much too good for Célimène.
  She's wantonly misled you from the start.   75
ALCESTE: You may be right; who knows another's heart?
  But ask yourself if it's the part of charity
  To shake my soul with doubts of her sincerity.
ARSINOÉ: Well, if you'd rather be a dupe than doubt
    her,
  That's your affair. I'll say no more about her.   80
ALCESTE: Madam, you know that doubt and vague
    suspicion
  Are painful to a man in my position;
  It's most unkind to worry me this way
  Unless you've some real proof of what you say.
ARSINOÉ: Sir, say no more: all doubt shall be removed, 85
  And all that I've been saying shall be proved.
  You've only to escort me home, and there
  We'll look into the heart of this affair.
  I've ocular evidence which will persuade you
  Beyond a doubt, that Célimène's betrayed you.   90
  Then, if you're saddened by that revelation,
  Perhaps I can provide some consolation.

Act IV

Scene 1

[*ELIANTE, PHILINTE*]

PHILINTE: Madam, he acted like a stubborn child;

I thought they never would be reconciled;
In vain we reasoned, threatened, and appealed;
He stood his ground and simply would not yield.
The Marshals, I feel sure, have never heard   5
An argument so splendidly absurd.
"No, gentlemen," said he, "I'll not retract.
His verse is bad: extremely bad, in fact.
Surely it does the man no harm to know it.
Does it disgrace him, not to be a poet?   10
A gentleman may be respected still,
Whether he writes a sonnet well or ill.
That I dislike his verse should not offend him;
In all that touches honor, I commend him;
He's noble, brave, and virtuous—but I fear   15
He can't in truth be called a sonneteer.
I'll gladly praise his wardrobe; I'll endorse
His dancing, or the way he sits a horse;
But, gentlemen, I cannot praise his rhyme.
In fact, it ought to be a capital crime   20
For anyone so sadly unendowed
To write a sonnet, and read the thing aloud."
At length he fell into a gentler mood
And, striking a concessive attitude,
He paid Oronte the following courtesies: 25
"Sir, I regret that I'm so hard to please,
And I'm profoundly sorry that your lyric
Failed to provoke me to a panegyric."
After these curious words, the two embraced,
And then the hearing was adjourned—in haste.   30
ELIANTE: His conduct has been very singular lately;
Still, I confess that I respect him greatly;
The honesty in which he takes such pride
Has—to my mind—its noble, heroic side.
In this false age, such candor seems outrageous;   35
But I could wish that it were more contagious.
PHILINTE: What most intrigues me in our friend Alceste
Is the grand passion that rages in his breast.
The sullen humors he's compounded of
Should not, I think, dispose his heart to love;   40
But since they do, it puzzles me still more
That he should choose your cousin to adore.
ELIANTE: It does, indeed, belie the theory
That love is born of gentle sympathy,
And that the tender passion must be based   45
On sweet accords of temper and of taste.
PHILINTE: Does she return his love, do you suppose?
ELIANTE: Ah, that's a difficult question, Sir. Who
knows?
How can we judge the truth of her devotion?
Her heart's a stranger to its own emotion.   50
Sometimes it thinks it loves, when no love's there;
At other times it loves quite unaware.
PHILINTE: I rather think Alceste is in for more
Distress and sorrow than he's bargained for;
Were he of my mind, Madam, his affection   55
Would turn in quite a different direction,
And we would see him more responsive to

The kind regard which he receives from you.
ELIANTE: Sir, I believe in frankness, and I'm inclined,
In matters of the heart, to speak my mind,   60
I don't oppose his love for her; indeed,
I hope with all my heart that he'll succeed,
And were it in my power, I'd rejoice
In giving him the lady of his choice.
But if, as happens frequently enough   65
In love affairs, he meets with a rebuff—
If Célimène should grant some rival's suit—
I'd gladly play the role of substitute;
Nor would his tender speeches please me less
Because they'd once been made without success.   70
PHILINTE: Well, Madam, as for me, I don't oppose
Your hopes in this affair; and heaven knows
That in my conversations with the man
I plead your cause as often as I can.
But if those two should marry, and so remove   75
All chance that he will offer you his love,
Then I'll declare my own, and hope to see
Your gracious favor pass from him to me.
In short, should you be cheated of Alceste,
I'd be most happy to be second best.   80
ELIANTE: Philinte, you're teasing.
PHILINTE: Ah, Madam, never fear;
No words of mine were ever so sincere,
And I shall live in fretful expectation
Till I can make a fuller declaration.

Scene 2

[ALCESTE, ELIANTE, PHILINTE]

ALCESTE: Avenge me, Madam! I must have satisfac-
tion,
Or this great wrong will drive me to distraction!
ELIANTE: Why, what's the matter? What's upset you
so?
ALCESTE: Madam, I've had a mortal, mortal blow.
If Chaos repossessed the universe,   5
I swear I'd not be shaken any worse.
I'm ruined.... I can say no more.... My soul...
ELIANTE: Do try, Sir, to regain your self-control.
ALCESTE: Just heaven! Why were so much beauty and
grace
Bestowed on one so vicious and so base?   10
ELIANTE: Once more, Sir, tell us....
ALCESTE: My world has gone to wrack;
I'm—I'm betrayed; she's stabbed me in the back:
Yes, Célimène (who would have thought it of her?)
Is false to me, and has another lover.
ELIANTE: Are you quite certain? Can you prove these
things?   15
PHILINTE: Lovers are prey to wild imaginings
And jealous fancies. No doubt there's some mis-
take....

ALCESTE: Mind your own business, Sir, for heaven's
 sake.

[To Eliante]

 Madam, I have the proof that you demand
20 Here in my pocket, penned by her own hand.
 Yes, all the shameful evidence one could want
 Lies in this letter written to Oronte—
 Oronte! whom I felt sure she couldn't love,
 And hardly bothered to be jealous of.
25 PHILINTE: Still, in a letter, appearances may deceive;
 This may not be so bad as you believe.
 ALCESTE: Once more I beg you, Sir, to let me be;
 Tend to your own affairs; leave mine to me.
 ELIANTE: Compose yourself; this anguish that you
 feel…
30 ALCESTE: Is something, Madam, you alone can heal.
 My outraged heart, beside itself with grief,
 Appeals to you for comfort and relief.
 Avenge me on your cousin, whose unjust
 And faithless nature has deceived my trust;
35 Avenge a crime your pure soul must detest.
 ELIANTE: But how, Sir?
 ALCESTE: Madam, this heart within my breast
 Is yours; pray take it; redeem my heart from her,
 And so avenge me on my torturer.
 Let her be punished by the fond emotion,
40 The ardent love, the bottomless devotion,
 The faithful worship which this heart of mine
 Will offer up to yours as to a shrine.
 ELIANTE: You have my sympathy, Sir, in all you
 suffer;
 Nor do I scorn the noble heart you offer;
45 But, I suspect you'll soon be mollified,
 And this desire for vengeance will subside.
 When some beloved hand has done us wrong
 We thirst for retribution—but not for long;
 However dark the deed that she's committed,
50 A lovely culprit's very soon acquitted.
 Nothing's so stormy as an injured lover,
 And yet no storm so quickly passes over.
 ALCESTE: No, Madam, no—this is no lovers' spat;
 I'll not forgive her; it's gone too far for that;
55 My mind's made up; I'll kill myself before
 I waste my hopes upon her any more.
 Ah, here she is. My wrath intensifies.
 I shall confront her with her tricks and lies,
 And crush her utterly, and bring you then
60 A heart no longer slave to Célimène.

Scene 3

[CÉLIMÈNE, ALCESTE]

ALCESTE: *(aside)* Sweet heaven, help me to control my
 passion.

CÉLIMÈNE: *(Aside to Alceste)*
 Oh, Lord. Why stand there staring in that fash-
 ion?
 And what d'you mean by those dramatic sighs,
 And that malignant glitter in your eyes?
ALCESTE: I mean that sins which cause the blood to
 freeze   5
 Look innocent beside your treacheries;
 That nothing Hell's or Heaven's wrath could do
 Ever produced so bad a thing as you.
CÉLIMÈNE: Your compliments were always sweet and
 pretty.
ALCESTE: Madam, it's not the moment to be witty. 10
 No, blush and hang your head; you've ample rea-
 son,
 Since I've the fullest evidence of your treason.
 Ah, this is what my sad heart prophesied;
 Now all my anxious fears are verified;
 My dark suspicion and my gloomy doubt 15
 Divined the truth, and now the truth is out.
 For all your trickery, I was not deceived;
 It was my bitter stars that I believed.
 But don't imagine that you'll go scot-free;
 You shan't misuse me with impunity. 20
 I know that love's irrational and blind;
 I know the heart's not subject to the mind,
 And can't be reasoned into beating faster;
 I know each soul is free to choose its master;
 Therefore had you but spoken from the heart, 25
 Rejecting my attentions from the start,
 I'd have no grievance, or at any rate
 I could complain of nothing but my fate.
 Ah, but so falsely to encourage me—
 That was a treason and a treachery 30
 For which you cannot suffer too severely,
 And you shall pay for that behavior dearly.
 Yes, now I have no pity, not a shred;
 My temper's out of hand; I've lost my head;
 Shocked by the knowledge of your double-
 dealings,   35
 My reason can't restrain my savage feelings;
 A righteous wrath deprives me of my senses,
 And I won't answer for the consequences.
CÉLIMÈNE: What does this outburst mean? Will you
 please explain?
 Have you, by any chance, gone quite insane? 40
ALCESTE: Yes, yes, I went insane the day I fell
 A victim to your black and fatal spell,
 Thinking to meet with some sincerity
 Among the treacherous charms that beckoned
 me.
CÉLIMÈNE: Pooh. Of what treachery can you
 complain?   45
ALCESTE: How sly you are, how cleverly you feign!
 But you'll not victimize me any more.
 Look: here's a document you've seen before.
 This evidence, which I acquired today,

50   Leaves you, I think, without a thing to say.
        CÉLIMÈNE: Is this what sent you into such a fit?
        ALCESTE: You should be blushing at the sight of it.
        CÉLIMÈNE: Ought I to blush? I truly don't see why.
        ALCESTE: Ah, now you're being bold as well as sly;
55   Since there's no signature, perhaps you'll claim…
        CÉLIMÈNE: I wrote it, whether or not it bears my
            name.
        ALCESTE: And you can view with equanimity
            This proof of your disloyalty to me!
        CÉLIMÈNE: Oh, don't be so outrageous and extreme.
60   ALCESTE: You take this matter lightly, it would seem.
            Was it no wrong to me, no shame to you,
            That you should send Oronte this billet-doux?
        CÉLIMÈNE: Oronte! Who said it was for him?
        ALCESTE: Why, those
            Who brought me this example of your prose.
65   But what's the difference? If you wrote the letter
            To someone else, it pleases me no better.
            My grievance and your guilt remain the same.
        CÉLIMÈNE: But need you rage, and need I blush for
            shame,
            If this was written to a *woman* friend?
70   ALCESTE: Ah! Most ingenious. I'm impressed no end;
            And after that incredible evasion
            Your guilt is clear. I need no more persuasion.
            How dare you try so clumsy a deception?
            D'you think I'm wholly wanting in perception?
75   Come, come, let's see how brazenly you'll try
            To bolster up so palpable a lie:
            Kindly construe this ardent closing section
            As nothing more than sisterly affection!
            Here, let me read it. Tell me, if you dare to,
80   That this is for a woman…
        CÉLIMÈNE: I don't care to.
            What right have you to badger and berate me,
            And so highhandedly interrogate me?
        ALCESTE: Now, don't be angry; all I ask of you
            Is that you justify a phrase or two…
85   CÉLIMÈNE: No, I shall not. I utterly refuse,
            And you may take those phrases as you choose.
        ALCESTE: Just show me how this letter could be
            meant
            For a woman's eyes, and I shall be content.
        CÉLIMÈNE: No, no, it's for Oronte; you're perfectly
            right.
90   I welcome his attentions with delight,
            I prize his character and his intellect,
            And everything is just as you suspect.
            Come, do your worst now; give your rage free rein;
            But kindly cease to bicker and complain.
95   ALCESTE (*aside*): Good God! Could anything be
            more inhuman?
            Was ever a heart so mangled by a woman?
            When I complain of how she has betrayed me,
            She bridles, and commences to upbraid me!
            She tries my tortured patience to the limit;

        She won't deny her guilt; she glories in it!   100
            And yet my heart's too faint and cowardly
            To break these chains of passion, and be free,
            To scorn her as it should, and rise above
            This unrewarded, mad, and bitter love.
        [*To Célimène*]
            Ah, traitress, in how confident a fashion   105
            You take advantage of my helpless passion,
            And use my weakness for your faithless charms
            To make me once again throw down my arms!
            But do at least deny this black transgression;
            Take back that mocking and perverse confession; 110
            Defend this letter and your innocence,
            And I, poor fool, will aid in your defense.
            Pretend, pretend, that you are just and true,
            And I shall make myself believe in you.
        CÉLIMÈNE: Oh, stop it. Don't be such a jealous dunce, 115
            Or I shall leave off loving you at once.
            Just why should I *pretend*? What could impel me
            To stoop so low as that? And kindly tell me
            Why, if I loved another, I shouldn't merely
            Inform you of it, simply and sincerely!   120
            I've told you where you stand, and that admis-
            sion
            Should altogether clear me of suspicion;
            After so generous a guarantee,
            What right have you to harbor doubts of me?
            Since women are (from natural reticence)   125
            Reluctant to declare their sentiments,
            And since the honor of our sex requires
            That we conceal our amorous desires,
            Ought any man for whom such laws are broken
            To question what the oracle has spoken?   130
            Should he not rather feel an obligation
            To trust that most obliging declaration?
            Enough, now. Your suspicions quite disgust me;
            Why should I love a man who doesn't trust me?
            I cannot understand why I continue,   135
            Fool that I am, to take an interest in you.
            I ought to choose a man less prone to doubt,
            And give you something to be vexed about.
        ALCESTE: Ah, what a poor enchanted fool I am;
            These gentle words, no doubt, were all a sham;   140
            But destiny requires me to entrust
            My happiness to you, and so I must.
            I'll love you to the bitter end, and see
            How false and treacherous you dare to be.
        CÉLIMÈNE: No, you don't really love me as you ought.   145
        ALCESTE: I love you more than can be said or thought;
            Indeed, I wish you were in such distress
            That I might show my deep devotedness.
            Yes, I could wish that you were wretchedly poor,
            Unloved, uncherished, utterly obscure;   150
            That fate had set you down upon the earth
            Without possessions, rank, or gentle birth;
            Then, by the offer of my heart, I might
            Repair the great injustice of your plight;

155   I'd raise you from the dust, and proudly prove
      The purity and vastness of my love.
   CÉLIMÈNE: This is a strange benevolence indeed!
      God grant that I may never be in need....
      Ah, here's Monsieur Dubois, in quaint disguise.

Scene 4

[CÉLIMÈNE, ALCESTE, DUBOIS]

   ALCESTE: Well, why this costume? Why those fright-
         ened eyes?
      What ails you?
   DUBOIS: Well, Sir, things are most mysterious.
   ALCESTE: What do you mean?
   DUBOIS: I fear they're very serious.
   ALCESTE: What?
   DUBOIS: Shall I speak more loudly?
   ALCESTE: Yes; speak out.
 5 DUBOIS: Isn't there someone here, Sir?
   ALCESTE: Speak, you lout!
      Stop wasting time.
   DUBOIS: Sir, we must slip away.
   ALCESTE: How's that?
   DUBOIS: We must decamp without delay.
   ALCESTE: Explain yourself.
   DUBOIS: I tell you we must fly.
   ALCESTE: What for?
   DUBOIS: We mustn't pause to say good-by.
10 ALCESTE: Now what d'you mean by all of this, you
         clown?
   DUBOIS: I mean, Sir, that we've got to leave this town.
   ALCESTE: I'll tear you limb from limb and joint from
         joint
      If you don't come more quickly to the point.
   DUBOIS: Well, Sir, today a man in a black suit,
15   Who wore a black and ugly scowl to boot,
      Left us a document scrawled in such a hand
      As even Satan couldn't understand.
      It bears upon your lawsuit, I don't doubt;
      But all hell's devils couldn't make it out.
20 ALCESTE: Well, well, go on. What then? I fail to see
      How this event obliges us to flee.
   DUBOIS: Well, Sir: an hour later, hardly more,
      A gentleman who's often called before
      Came looking for you in an anxious way.
25   Not finding you, he asked me to convey
      (Knowing I could be trusted with the same)
      The following message.... Now, what *was* his name?
   ALCESTE: Forget his name, you idiot. What did he say?
   DUBOIS: Well, it was one of your friends, Sir, anyway.
30   He warned you to begone, and he suggested
      That if you stay, you may well be arrested.
   ALCESTE: What? Nothing more specific? Think, man,
         think!
   DUBOIS: No, Sir. He had me bring him pen and ink,

      And dashed you off a letter which, I'm sure,
      Will render things distinctly less obscure.   35
   ALCESTE: Well—let me have it!
   CÉLIMÈNE: What *is* this all about?
   ALCESTE: God knows; but I have hopes of finding
         out.
      How long am I to wait, you blitherer?
   DUBOIS (*after a protracted search for the letter*): I must
         have left it on your table, Sir.
   ALCESTE: I ought to...
   CÉLIMÈNE: No, no, keep your self-control;   40
      Go find out what's behind his rigmarole.
   ALCESTE: It seems that fate, no matter what I do,
      Has sworn that I may not converse with you;
      But, Madam, pray permit your faithful lover
      To try once more before the day is over.   45

ACT V

Scene 1

[ALCESTE, PHILINTE]

   ALCESTE: No, it's too much. My mind's made up, I
         tell you.
   PHILINTE: Why should this blow, however hard, com-
         pel you...
   ALCESTE: No, no, don't waste your breath in argument;
      Nothing you say will alter my intent;
      This age is vile, and I've made up my mind   5
      To have no further commerce with mankind.
      Did not truth, honor, decency, and the laws
      Oppose my enemy and approve my cause?
      My claims were justified in all men's sight;
      I put my trust in equity and right;   10
      Yet, to my horror and the world's disgrace,
      Justice is mocked, and I have lost my case!
      A scoundrel whose dishonesty is notorious
      Emerges from another lie victorious!
      Honor and right condone his brazen fraud,   15
      While rectitude and decency applaud!
      Before his smirking face, the truth stands charmed,
      And virtue conquered, and the law disarmed!
      His crime is sanctioned by a court decree!
      And not content with what he's done to me,   20
      The dog now seeks to ruin me by stating
      That I composed a book now circulating,
      A book so wholly criminal and vicious
      That even to speak its title is seditious!
      Meanwhile Oronte, my rival, lends his credit   25
      To the same libelous tale, and helps to spread it!
      Oronte! a man of honor and of rank,
      With whom I've been entirely fair and frank;
      Who sought me out and forced me, willy-nilly,
      To judge some verse I found extremely silly;   30

And who, because I properly refused
To flatter him, or see the truth abused,
Abets my enemy in a rotten slander!
There's the reward of honesty and candor!
35 The man will hate me to the end of time
For failing to commend his wretched rhyme!
And not this man alone, but all humanity
Do what they do from interest and vanity;
They prate of honor, truth, and righteousness,
40 But lie, betray, and swindle nonetheless.
Come then: man's villainy is too much to bear;
Let's leave this jungle and this jackal's lair.
Yes! treacherous and savage race of men,
You shall not look upon my face again.
45 PHILINTE: Oh, don't rush into exile prematurely;
Things aren't as dreadful as you make them, surely.
It's rather obvious, since you're still at large,
That people don't believe your enemy's charge.
Indeed, his tale's so patently untrue
50 That it may do more harm to him than you.
ALCESTE: Nothing could do that scoundrel any harm:
His frank corruption is his greatest charm,
And, far from hurting him, a further shame
Would only serve to magnify his name.
55 PHILINTE: In any case, his bald prevarication
Has done no injury to your reputation,
And you may feel secure in that regard.
As for your lawsuit, it should not be hard
To have the case reopened, and contest
60 This judgment…
ALCESTE: No, no, let the verdict rest.
Whatever cruel penalty it may bring,
I wouldn't have it changed for anything.
It shows the times' injustice with such clarity
That I shall pass it down to our posterity
65 As a great proof and signal demonstration
Of the black wickedness of this generation.
It may cost twenty thousand francs; but I
Shall pay their twenty thousand, and gain thereby
The right to storm and rage at human evil,
70 And send the race of mankind to the devil.
PHILINTE: Listen to me….
ALCESTE: Why? What can you possibly say?
Don't argue, Sir; your labor's thrown away.
Do you propose to offer lame excuses
For men's behavior and the times' abuses?
75 PHILINTE: No, all you say I'll readily concede:
This is a low, dishonest age indeed;
Nothing but trickery prospers nowadays,
And people ought to mend their shabby ways.
Yes, man's a beastly creature; but must we then
80 Abandon the society of men?
Here in the world, each human frailty
Provides occasion for philosophy,
And that is virtue's noblest exercise;
If honesty shone forth from all men's eyes,
85 If every heart were frank and kind and just,

What could our virtues do but gather dust
(Since their employment is to help us bear
The villainies of men without despair)?
A heart well-armed with virtue can endure….
ALCESTE: Sir, you're a matchless reasoner, to be sure;   90
Your words are fine and full of cogency;
But don't waste time and eloquence on me.
My reason bids me go, for my own good.
My tongue won't lie and flatter as it should;
God knows what frankness it might next commit,   95
And what I'd suffer on account of it.
Pray let me wait for Célimène's return
In peace and quiet. I shall shortly learn,
By her response to what I have in view,
Whether her love for me is feigned or true.   100
PHILINTE: Till then, let's visit Eliante upstairs.
ALCESTE: No, I am too weighed down with somber
cares.
Go to her, do; and leave me with my gloom
Here in the darkened corner of this room.
PHILINTE: Why, that's no sort of company, my friend;   105
I'll see if Eliante will not descend.

Scene 2

[CÉLIMÈNE, ORONTE, ALCESTE]

ORONTE: Yes, Madam, if you wish me to remain
Your true and ardent lover, you must deign
To give me some more positive assurance.
All this suspense is quite beyond endurance.
If your heart shares the sweet desires of mine,   5
Show me as much by some convincing sign;
And here's the sign I urgently suggest:
That you no longer tolerate Alceste,
But sacrifice him to my love, and sever
All your relations with the man forever.   10
CÉLIMÈNE: Why do you suddenly dislike him so?
You praised him to the skies not long ago.
ORONTE: Madam, that's not the point. I'm here to find
Which way your tender feelings are inclined.
Choose, if you please, between Alceste and me,   15
And I shall stay or go accordingly.
ALCESTE (*emerging from the corner*): Yes, Madam,
    choose; this gentleman's demand
Is wholly just, and I support his stand.
I too am true and ardent; I too am here
To ask you that you make your feelings clear.   20
No more delays, now; no equivocation;
The time has come to make your declaration.
ORONTE: Sir, I've no wish in any way to be
An obstacle to your felicity.
ALCESTE: Sir, I've no wish to share her heart with you;   25
That may sound jealous, but at least it's true.
ORONTE: If, weighing us, she leans in your direction…
ALCESTE: If she regards you with the least affection…

ORONTE: I swear I'll yield her to you there and then.
30 ALCESTE: I swear I'll never see her face again.
ORONTE: Now, Madam, tell us what we've come to
   hear.
ALCESTE: Madam, speak openly and have no fear.
ORONTE: Just say which one is to remain your lover.
ALCESTE: Just name one name, and it will all be over.
35 ORONTE: What! Is it possible that you're undecided?
ALCESTE: What! Can your feelings possibly be divided?
CÉLIMÈNE: Enough: this inquisition's gone too far:
   How utterly unreasonable you are!
   Not that I couldn't make the choice with ease;
40   My heart has no conflicting sympathies;
   I know full well which one of you I favor,
   And you'd not see me hesitate or waver.
   But how can you expect me to reveal
   So cruelly and bluntly what I feel?
45   I think it altogether too unpleasant
   To choose between two men when both are present;
   One's heart has means more subtle and more kind
   Of letting its affections be divined,
   Nor need one be uncharitably plain
50   To let a lover know he loves in vain.
ORONTE: No, no, speak plainly; I for one can stand it.
   I beg you to be frank.
ALCESTE: And I demand it.
   The simple truth is what I wish to know,
   And there's no need for softening the blow.
55   You've made an art of pleasing everyone,
   But now your days of coquetry are done:
   You have no choice now, Madam, but to choose,
   For I'll know what to think if you refuse;
   I'll take your silence for a clear admission
60   That I'm entitled to my worst suspicion.
ORONTE: I thank you for this ultimatum, Sir,
   And I may say I heartily concur.
CÉLIMÈNE: Really, this foolishness is very wearing:
   Must you be so unjust and overbearing?
65   Haven't I told you why I must demur?
   Ah, here's Eliante; I'll put the case to her.

Scene 3

[ELIANTE, PHILINTE, CÉLIMÈNE, ORONTE, ALCESTE]

CÉLIMÈNE: Cousin, I'm being persecuted here
   By these two persons, who, it would appear,
   Will not be satisfied till I confess
   Which one I love the more, and which the less,
5   And tell the latter to his face that he
   Is henceforth banished from my company.
   Tell me, has ever such a thing been done?
ELIANTE: You'd best not turn to me; I'm not the one
   To back you in a matter of this kind:
10   I'm all for those who frankly speak their mind.
ORONTE: Madam, you'll search in vain for a defender.

ALCESTE: You're beaten, Madam, and may as well
   surrender.
ORONTE: Speak, speak, you must; and end this awful
   strain.
ALCESTE: Or don't, and your position will be plain.
ORONTE: A single word will close this painful scene. 15
ALCESTE: But if you're silent, I'll know what you
   mean.

Scene 4

*[ARSINOÉ, CÉLIMÈNE, ELIANTE, ALCESTE, PHILINTE,
ACASTE, CLITANDRE, ORONTE]*

ACASTE (*to Célimène*): Madam, with all due deference,
   we two
   Have come to pick a little bone with you.
CLITANDRE (*to Oronte and Alceste*): I'm glad you're
   present, Sirs; as you'll soon learn,
   Our business here is also your concern.
ARSINOÉ (*to Célimène*): Madam, I visit you so soon
   again   5
   Only because of these two gentlemen,
   Who came to me indignant and aggrieved
   About a crime too base to be believed.
   Knowing your virtue, having such confidence in it,
   I couldn't think you guilty for a minute,   10
   In spite of all their telling evidence;
   And, rising above our little difference,
   I've hastened here in friendship's name to see
   You clear yourself of this great calumny.
ACASTE: Yes, Madam, let us see with what composure   15
   You'll manage to respond to this disclosure.
   You lately sent Clitandre this tender note.
CLITANDRE: And this one, for Acaste, you also wrote.
ACASTE (*to Oronte and Alceste*): You'll recognize this
   writing, Sirs, I think;
   The lady is so free with pen and ink   20
   That you must know it all too well, I fear.
   But listen: this is something you should hear.
   "How absurd you are to condemn my lightheart-
   edness in society, and to accuse me of being
   happiest in the company of others. Nothing   25
   could be more unjust; and if you do not come to
   me instantly and beg pardon for saying such a
   thing, I shall never forgive you as long as I live.
   Our big bumbling friend the Viscount…"
   What a shame that he's not here.   30
   "Our big bumbling friend the Viscount, whose
   name stands first in your complaint, is hardly a
   man to my taste; and ever since the day I
   watched him spend three-quarters of an hour
   spitting into a well, so as to make circles in the 35
   water, I have been unable to think highly of
   him. As for the little Marquess…"
   In all modesty, gentlemen, that is I.

40 "As for the little Marquess, who sat squeezing my
hand for such a long while yesterday, I find him
in all respects the most trifling creature alive;
and the only things of value about him are his
cape and his sword. As for the man with the
green ribbons…"

45 *[To Alceste]* It's your turn now, Sir.
"As for the man with the green ribbons, he amuses me now and then with his bluntness and his
bearish ill-humor; but there are many times
indeed when I think him the greatest bore in the
50 world. And as for the sonneteer…"
[To Oronte] Here's your helping.
"And as for the sonneteer, who has taken it into his
head to be witty, and insists on being an author
in the teeth of opinion, I simply cannot be both-
55 ered to listen to him, and his prose wearies me
quite as much as his poetry. Be assured that I
am not always so well-entertained as you suppose; that I long for your company, more than I
dare to say, at all these entertainments to which
60 people drag me; and that the presence of those
one loves is the true and perfect seasoning to all
one's pleasures."
CLITANDRE: And now for me.
"Clitandre, whom you mention, and who so
65 pesters me with his saccharine speeches, is the
last man on earth for whom I could feel any
affection. He is quite mad to suppose that I love
him, and so are you, to doubt that you are
loved. Do come to your senses; exchange your
70 suppositions for his; and visit me as often as
possible, to help me bear the annoyance of his
unwelcome attentions."
It's a sweet character that these letters show,
And what to call it, Madam, you well know.
75 Enough. We're off to make the world acquainted
With this sublime self-portrait that you've painted.
ACASTE: Madam, I'll make you no farewell oration;
No, you're not worthy of my indignation.
Far choicer hearts than yours, as you'll discover,
80 Would like this little Marquess for a lover.

Scene 5

[CÉLIMÈNE, ELIANTE, ARSINÓE, ALCESTE, ORONTE, PHILINTE]

ORONTE: So! After all those loving letters you wrote,
You turn on me like this, and cut my throat!
And your dissembling, faithless heart, I find,
Has pledged itself by turns to all mankind!
5 How blind I've been! But now I clearly see;
I thank you, Madam, for enlightening me.
My heart is mine once more, and I'm content;
The loss of it shall be your punishment.

[To Alceste] Sir, she is yours; I'll seek no more to stand
Between your wishes and this lady's hand.

Scene 6

[CÉLIMÈNE, ELIANTE, ARSINÓE, ALCESTE, PHILINTE]

ARSINÓE (*to Célimène*): Madam, I'm forced to speak. I'm far too stirred
To keep my counsel, after what I've heard.
I'm shocked and staggered by your want of morals.
It's not my way to mix in others' quarrels;
But really, when this fine and noble spirit,   5
This man of honor and surpassing merit,
Laid down the offering of his heart before you,
How *could* you…
ALCESTE: Madam, permit me, I implore you,
To represent myself in this debate.
Don't bother, please, to be my advocate.   10
My heart, in any case, could not afford
To give your services their due reward;
And if I chose, for consolation's sake,
Some other lady, t'would not be you I'd take.
ARSINÓE: What makes you think you could, Sir? And how dare you   15
Imply that I've been trying to ensnare you?
If you can for a moment entertain
Such flattering fancies, you're extremely vain.
I'm not so interested as you suppose
In Célimène's discarded gigolos.   20
Get rid of that absurd illusion, do.
Women like me are not for such as you.
Stay with this creature, to whom you're so attached;
I've never seen two people better matched.

Scene 7

[CÉLIMÈNE, ELIANTE, ALCESTE, PHILINTE]

ALCESTE (*to Célimène*): Well, I've been still throughout this exposé,
Till everyone but me has said his say.
Come, have I shown sufficient self-restraint?
And may I now…
CÉLIMÈNE: Yes, make your just complaint.
Reproach me freely, call me what you will;   5
You've every right to say I've used you ill.
I've wronged you, I confess it; and in my shame
I'll make no effort to escape the blame.
The anger of those others I could despise;
My guilt toward you I sadly recognize.   10
Your wrath is wholly justified, I fear;
I know how culpable I must appear,

I know all things bespeak my treachery,
And that, in short, you've grounds for hating me.
15   Do so; I give you leave.
    ALCESTE: Ah, traitress—how,
How should I cease to love you, even now?
Though mind and will were passionately bent
On hating you, my heart would not consent.

[To Eliante and Philinte]

Be witness to my madness, both of you;
20   See what infatuation drives one to;
But wait; my folly's only just begun,
And I shall prove to you before I'm done
How strange the human heart is, and how far
From rational we sorry creatures are.

[To Célimène]

25   Woman, I'm willing to forget your shame,
And clothe your treacheries in a sweeter name;
I'll call them youthful errors, instead of crimes,
And lay the blame on these corrupting times.
My one condition is that you agree
30   To share my chosen fate, and fly with me
To that wild, trackless, solitary place
In which I shall forget the human race.
Only by such a course can you atone
For those atrocious letters; by that alone
35   Can you remove my present horror of you,
And make it possible for me to love you.
    CÉLIMÈNE: What! *I* renounce the world at my young
        age,
And die of boredom in some hermitage?
    ALCESTE: Ah, if you really loved me as you ought,
40   You wouldn't give the world a moment's
        thought;
Must you have me, and all the world beside?
    CÉLIMÈNE: Alas, at twenty one is terrified
Of solitude. I fear I lack the force
And depth of soul to take so stern a course.
45   But if my hand in marriage will content you,
Why, there's a plan which I might well consent to,
And…
    ALCESTE: No, I detest you now. I could excuse
Everything else, but since you thus refuse
To love me wholly, as a wife should do,
50   And see the world in me, as I in you,
Go! I reject your hand, and disenthrall
My heart from your enchantments, once for all.

Scene 8

[ELIANTE, ALCESTE, PHILINTE]

ALCESTE (*to Eliante*): Madam, your virtuous beauty
        has no peer;

Of all this world, you only are sincere;
I've long esteemed you highly, as you know;
Permit me ever to esteem you so,
And if I do not now request your hand,   5
Forgive me, Madam, and try to understand.
I feel unworthy of it; I sense that fate
Does not intend me for the married state,
That I should do you wrong by offering you
My shattered heart's unhappy residue,   10
And that in short…
    ELIANTE: Your argument's well taken:
Nor need you fear that I shall feel forsaken.
Were I to offer him this hand of mine,
Your friend Philinte, I think, would not decline.
    PHILINTE: Ah, Madam, that's my heart's most
        cherished goal,   15
For which I'd gladly give my life and soul.
    ALCESTE (*to Eliante and Philinte*): May you be true to
        all you now profess,
And so deserve unending happiness.
Meanwhile, betrayed and wronged in everything,
I'll flee this bitter world where vice is king,   20
And seek some spot unpeopled and apart
Where I'll be free to have an honest heart.
    PHILINTE: Come, Madam, let's do everything we can
To change the mind of this unhappy man.

JEAN RACINE (1639–1699)

Racine's parents died while he was still a child, and they left him to be brought up by his grandparents, who in turn sent him to school at the abbey at Port-Royal. It is now generally agreed that the education he received there profoundly influenced his drama. The abbey at Port-Royal was run by the Jansenists, a sect of the Catholic Church which was later suppressed. Its founder, Cornelius Jansen (1585–1638), held that human beings were essentially corrupt, and he recommended withdrawal from the world of action into monastic contemplation. The Jansenist promotion of a contemplative clergy independent of Rome ran counter to the Church's essentially active political and social role in France. Racine never dealt directly with Jansenist issues in his plays, but his plots and characters clearly embody the fundamentals of Jansenist belief, including the inevitability of sin, the importance of introspection, the futility of action, and the unavoidability of guilt. Throughout his life Racine maintained contact with the school and abbey at Port-Royal, which had clearly served him in place of a family. He responded to any criticism of his plays that emanated from the school, and he later wrote a history of the abbey.

While at school Racine studied the classics. At one point he considered taking holy orders, but eventually he aspired to a public life. His poetry about Louis XIV brought him to the attention of court writers, including Molière, and his first play, *La Thebaïde*, was performed by Molière's company in 1664. In the following year he wrote *Alexandre*, but he was disappointed with Molière's production of it, and so he presented it to a rival company at the Hôtel de Bourgogne. Molière was so incensed that he stopped production of his version of the play immediately. Hostility between the two playwrights intensified over the next two years, culminating in 1667, when Molière's leading lady left his company to play the title role in Racine's *Andromaque*. This play initiated the series of Racine's great plays: *Britannicus* (1669), *Bérénice* (1670), *Bajazet* (1672), *Mithridate* (1673), *Iphigénie* (1674), and *Phaedra* (1677).

After finishing *Phaedra*, Racine married, and he was appointed to the position of court historiographer to Louis XIV. In 1684, he wrote a history of Louis XIV's wars, and between 1688 and 1690 he wrote two religious plays, *Esther* and *Athalie*, for Louis's wife, Madame de Maintenon, both of which were performed privately at St. Cyr academy for girls. Racine retired to Port-Royal after his success with *Phaedra*, and he died there in 1699. He was buried at Port-Royal, though his grave was removed when the abbey was destroyed.

Phaedra

Racine's most celebrated and most controversial play, originally entitled *Phaedra and Hippolytus*, opened on 1 January 1667 at the Hôtel de Bourgogne. Racine's enemies at court encouraged Jacques Pradon (1632–1698), a minor playwright, to open his own version of *Phaedra* at another theater. The similar plays invited comparison and criticism, and the mounting rancor between the two playwrights grew so conspicuous that it had to be arbitrated by the king's brother two months later.

In his preface Racine mentions that *Phaedra* was inspired by Euripides' *Hippolytus*, which dramatizes the conflict between Artemis and Aphrodite. In it, Hippolytus is the hero and Phaedra only a secondary character. Racine, however, places Phaedra at the center of the action, insisting in his preface that she fulfills Aristotle's requirements for a tragic protagonist because she inspires pity and terror. He also insists on the moral nature of the subject. Phaedra is dominated by an all-consuming adulterous and incestuous passion. Racine's Jansenist education had taught him that sin is unavoidable and that action can lead only to further degradation, and this view provides a context for his tragic vision in the play. Phaedra is a victim, but the forces that victimize her come from within her nature, and she eventually accepts responsibility for her flaws as well as for the consequences of her actions. Like the other major characters in the play, Phaedra defines herself by her aspiration to an unattainable ideal that is subverted by her passions. Her love for her stepson destroys her honor, in turn destroying her and all the rest of the major characters.

Racine manages to displace the wrongness of Phaedra's desire onto the wrongness of her actions. Victimized by passions, Phaedra seems a sympathetic character, but the lie she condones, which leads Hippolytus to his death, cannot be excused. To fall in love is one thing; to lie is another. In the action, Racine materializes the tragedy of Phaedra's desire through this lie. Phaedra must then bear responsibility for what happens to Hippolytus, and this is the price that must be paid for the release of her destructive passion.

Jean Racine's Preface to Phaedra

Here is another tragedy on a subject taken from Euripides. The action follows a somewhat different course, but I have enriched my play with everything in his that I considered most strikingly beautiful. Had I borrowed no more than the conception of Phaedra's character, I might say I owe him the most reasonable thing, perhaps, that I have given to the theatre. I am not surprised that this character was so successful in Euripides' time, and now again in our own, considering that it has every quality required by Aristotle in the tragic hero, and proper to arouse compassion and terror. For Phaedra is not altogether guilty, and not altogether innocent. She is drawn by her destiny, and the anger of the Gods, into an unlawful passion which she is the first to hold in horror. She makes every endeavour to overcome it. She chooses death rather than disclose it to anyone. And when forced to reveal it, she speaks of it with such shame and confusion as leave no doubt that her crime is rather a punishment from the Gods, than an impulse of her own will.

I have even taken pains to make her a little less odious than she is in the tragedies of antiquity, where she brings herself, unprompted, to accuse Hippolytus. I felt that a false testimony was something too base, too black, to put into the mouth of a Princess possessed otherwise of sentiments so noble and virtuous. Such baseness seemed to me more fitting to a Nurse, who might have more slave-like propensities; though even she only enters upon the lying accusation to save the life and honour of her mistress. If Phaedra acquiesces, it is because she is beside herself in the agitation of her thoughts, and the next moment she comes on with the intention of vindicating the guiltless and publishing the truth.

Hippolytus is accused, in Euripides and in Seneca, of actually violating his step-mother—*vim corpus tulit*; here, of no more than the intention. I desired to spare Theseus a sense of outrage which might have made him less acceptable to my audience.

As for the figure of Hippolytus, I had read in ancient authors that Euripides was blamed for depicting him as a philosopher free of all imperfection—so that the death of the youthful Prince gave rise to far more indignation than pity. I felt I should give him a failing that might render him somewhat guilty towards his father, without detracting at all from that magnanimity which makes him spare Phaedra's honour and go to his doom without accusing her. By failing I mean his involuntary passion for Aricia, the daughter and the sister of his father's mortal enemies.

This Aricia is not a child of my invention. Vergil relates that Hippolytus married her, and she bore him a son, after Aesculapius had brought him back to life. And I have read too, in certain authors, that Hippolytus had married and brought into Italy an Athenian maiden of high birth, named Aricia, who had given her name to an Italian township.

I adduce these authorities, because I have most scrupulously endeavoured to keep close to the legend. I have even taken the history of Theseus just as it is in Plutarch.

It is this historian who mentions that the belief in Theseus' descent to the underworld to abduct Proserpine, was occasioned by a journey he made into Epirus towards the source of the Acheron, where a King, whose wife Pirithous sought to carry off, held Theseus prisoner after putting Pirithous to death. Thus I have tried to retain the verisimilitude of history, and yet to lose none of the embellishments of fable, so rich in the stuff of poetry. And the rumour of Theseus' death, based on the legendary journey, gives rise to that declaration of Phaedra's love which proves one of the principal causes of her unhappy plight, and which she would never have dared utter while she believed her husband to be alive.

For the rest, I dare not yet assert this play to be in truth the best of my tragedies. I leave my readers, and time, to set its rightful price upon it. What I can assert is that I have composed none where virtue is shown to more advantage than here. The slightest faults are severely punished. The bare thought of crime is regarded with no less horror than crime itself. The failings of love are treated as real failings. The passions are offered to view only to show all the ravage they create. And vice is everywhere painted in such hues, that its hideous face may be recognized and loathed. Here is the proper aim for every man to keep in sight who works for the public. And this, above all, was the purpose of the earliest tragic poets. Their stage was a school where virtue was taught no less well than in the schools of the philosophers. Thus Aristotle consented to draw up rules for the dramatic poem; Socrates, the sagest of the philosophers, thought it no shame to set his hand to the tragedies of Euripides. It were much to be desired that our works should be found as serious and as full of useful instruction as the pages of those poets. It might bring about a reconciliation between the tragic art and a number of persons, noted for their religion and learning, who have denounced it of late, but might well look upon it with less disfavour if authors cared as much to instruct as to entertain their audience, and carried out thereby the true purpose of tragedy.

Phaedra

JEAN RACINE

TRANSLATED BY R. C. KNIGHT

CHARACTERS

THESEUS, son of Aegeus, King of Athens
PHAEDRA, wife of Theseus, and daughter of King
    Minos of Crete and Pasiphaë
HIPPOLYTUS, son of Theseus by Antiope Queen of the
    Amazons
ARICIA, daughter of Pallas, descended from the
    ancient Kings of Athens

OENONE, formerly Nurse of Phaedra
THERAMENES, preceptor and attendant to Hippolytus
ISMENE, confidant of Aricia
PANOPE, one of Phaedra's women
GUARDS

The scene is in the royal residence at Trozen, a depen-
dency of Athens in the Peloponnese.

ACT I

[HIPPOLYTUS, THERAMENES]

HIPPOLYTUS: I have made up my mind, Theramenes.
 No more for me the tranquil days of Trozen,
 For in the mortal tempest of my doubts
 I am dishonoured if I linger here.
5 Six months ago my father sailed and left me
 Ignorant what befalls a head so cherished,
 Ignorant even where he may be hidden—
THERAMENES: So where will you go to look for him,
 my lord?
 Already, to relieve a fear I shared,
10 I have scoured the two seas that Corinth holds
 asunder,
 Demanded Theseus of the tribes that live
 Where Acheron drives down headlong into Hell,
 Searched Elis, skirted Taenarum, and even
 Traversed the waves where Icarus fell and perished.
15 What hope new-risen or what happier skies
 Will light you to his footsteps? Why, perhaps,
 Who knows, perhaps the King your father wishes
 Not to unveil the mystery of his venture,
 And while his peril fills your thought and ours,
20 Serene, weaving the latest of his loves,
 The hero waits to seize the unguarded moment—
HIPPOLYTUS: Stop, good Theramenes. You slander
 Theseus;
 There is a nobler cause for these delays;
 After the follies of forgotten youth
25 The wanderings of his inconstant heart
 Are fixed at length, and Phaedra fears no rival.
 So once more—I shall go where duty points
 And leave a land I cannot bear to see.
THERAMENES: But my lord, how long have you
 despised the presence

Of these calm fields, the pleasure of your childhood 30
 Whose solitude was dearer to you than
 The splendid stir of Athens and the Court?
 What fear has banished you, or else what
 heartache?
HIPPOLYTUS: Those days are past. Pleasure and peace
 have vanished
 Since first the Gods directed to our shore 35
 The child of Minos and Pasiphaë.
THERAMENES: I see: there is the cause, the hated pres-
 ence—
 Phaedra, who came, your father's dangerous bride,
 Looked on you once, and by your prompt exile
 Gave the first measure of her new-won power. 40
 But all that dogged hate and old aversion
 Has passed with time, passed or at least abated;
 And after all what danger lies in her,
 A woman dying, crying out for death?
 Stricken by ills that none can make her utter, 45
 Tired of her life, tired of the day that lights her
 What can she do to you?
HIPPOLYTUS: I do not fear
 Anything her aversion could devise.
 I go to escape another enemy,
 I do admit: I fly Aricia, 50
 The youngest and the last of all that house
 In fatal league against ours.
THERAMENES: You, my lord,
 Are turned against her too? But Pallas' daughter
 Surely had no part in her brothers' treason,
 And must you hate that unoffending grace? 55
HIPPOLYTUS: I'd not avoid her if I hated her.
THERAMENES: My lord, have I permission to interpret
 Your leaving? Must I think that you are not
 The old implacable Hippolytus,
 The outlaw of Love's empire, he that vowed 60
 Never to wear the yoke his father wore?

Can it be that a slighted and a smarting Goddess
Will press you to the service of her shrine,
Reduce you to the rank of common men
65 And vindicate that father by your fate?
Can it be love, my lord?
HIPPOLYTUS: How can you say it,
My friend, that knew the childhood of my heart
And all its growth in pride and fierce resolve?
Shall I dishonour it, disown myself?
70 First, as a babe, at an Amazonian breast
I drank the resolution that astounds you,
But once of age to look upon myself
I wished to be no other than I was.
Then, in the faithful service of your kindness
75 As you rehearsed for me my father's story,
Do you remember how my soul blazed up
At each particular in the noble toils
Of the intrepid hero, as you showed him
Turning the world from thoughts of lost Alcides
80 By monsters strangled and by brigands slain—
Procrustes, Sinnis, Sciro, Cercyon
And Epidaurus scattered with the limbs
Of her gigantic tyrant, and the gore
Reeking from all Crete, of the Minotaur?
85 But when you told other ignobler feats—
A faith so cheaply pledged, and ever new,
Helen torn from a mother's arms in Sparta;
In Salamis the sighs of Periboea;
So many more than he can even name,
90 Victims too credulous of a lover's tongue;
What empty shores heard Ariadne's sorrows;
How Phaedra, last and under happier auspice,
Followed him—then I wished the tale untold;
Often I urged you hasten and be done;
95 And would my wishes had redeemed from fame
That darker half of such a fair renown!
And now, by the spite of Heaven, shall I be
Degraded to the same indignity?
—Baseness beyond excuse, for those were frailties
100 Unseen amid a multitude of honours,
While not one trophy of a monster slain
Entitles me to fail as he has failed.
Even if I lost my freedom and my pride
How could I yield them to Aricia?
105 How could my disobedient sense forget
That which divides us irremovably?
The King denies her, denies her fallen brothers,
By violent laws, continuance of their line;
Their name must die for ever in her death,
110 Their guilty branch must bear no other fruit,
And till the tomb, submissive and sequestered,
No gleam of the Hymeneal torch must find her.
Am I to oppose my father and his wrath?
Embrace her claims? and give a precedent
115 To treason? and embark my youth—
THERAMENES: My lord,
If the marked hour draws on, our arguments

Escape the notice of the incurious Heavens.
No. Theseus wished you blind, and gave you eyes;
His hate inflames the passion he forbids you,
And adds enchantment to his prisoner's charms.   120
But come, why look askance at honest love?
Why not make trial where its sweetness lies?
Why be enchained by vain and foolish scruples?
Who fears to stray that follows Hercules?
Many a stubborn heart has Venus bent—   125
Where would you be yourself and your defiance
Had chaste Antiope been as chaste as you
And never warmed to Theseus' flame? But why
Face out a falsehood with the pride of words?
Confess how things have changed: not now as once,   130
Aloof, intractable, we see you guide
A skimming chariot along the beaches
Or, adept in the mystery Neptune taught,
Break an unmastered courser to the curb;
Less often our halloos awake the forests;   135
Your eyes droop, weighted with a secret fire…
The case is clear—you are in love, in flame,
In torment, and you will not show your wound.
Is it Aricia?
HIPPOLYTUS: Theramenes,
I leave to-day, and go to find my father.   140
THERAMENES: Without an audience of Phaedra?
HIPPOLYTUS: No.
I will see her; I cannot well do less.
You may send word.—But what is the fresh mis-
fortune
Disturbs her favourite Oenone so?

[Enter OENONE]

OENONE: Ah, good my lord, what grief can equal mine?   145
The Queen is near her utmost bourne of fate;
She that I watch by night and day unsleeping
Dies in my arms, and will not tell her sickness.
Her thought is all at variance with itself;
Her sick disquiet drives her from her bed   150
To see the light of day. But by her orders
No eye of man may see her suffering.
—Here she is.
HIPPOLYTUS: Very well; then I retire
Not to offend with this unwelcome face.

[Exeunt HIPPOLYTUS and THERAMENES]

[Enter PHAEDRA]

PHAEDRA: No more, for I can move no more, Oenone.   155
Let me rest; I am faint, my strength has left me.
My darkened eyes are dazzled by the light,
My wavering knees are weak beneath my weight.
Ah me!

[Sits]

OENONE: High Gods, relent and see our tears!

160 PHAEDRA: These fripperies, these veils, they hang so
         heavy!
     Whose was the unkind hand that piled and bound
     These clustering locks that weigh upon my brow?
     So feeble and so weary, all these things
     Grieve me and weary me.
     OENONE: How can we please you?
165   Yourself, repentant of your wicked thoughts,
     You called in haste for clothes and ornaments;
     Yourself you rallied your forgotten vigour,
     You wanted to be out and see the sunlight.
     Now here it is, my lady, and it seems
170   You loathe the very light that you desired.
     PHAEDRA: Splendid begetter of a seed afflicted,
     Father from whom my mother claimed her birth,
     O blushing Sun ashamed of my despair,
     Now, for the last time, I salute thy face.
175 OENONE: What, still possessed of such a fearful
         purpose?
     Shall I for ever see you, turned from life,
     Enact the mournful ritual of your death?
     PHAEDRA: Oh give me the shadow of the forest glades!
     Or let my eye piercing the glorious dust
180   Follow the wheeling chariot in the course!
     OENONE: My lady?
     PHAEDRA: Oh, I am mad. What have I said?
     Where am I, where are my thoughts, my wander-
         ing mind?
     Lost, for the Gods have taken it away.
     My face is hot, Oenone, with my shame;
185   I cannot hide my guilty sufferings
     And tears descend that I cannot restrain.
     OENONE: Blush if you must, but blush to keep a silence
     That doubles all the misery you suffer.
     Rebellious to all tending, deaf to all pleas,
190   Will you unpitying allow your life
     To flow away? What madness cuts it short?
     What spell, what poison stanches up its course?
     Thrice has the sky been muffled up in shade
     And sleep is still a stranger to your eyes;
195   Thrice has the day displaced the gloom of night
     And still you fast, and still your body wastes.
     What dark temptation leads you on? What right
     Invests you with the power to take your life—
     Wronging the Gods from whom you draw your
         being,
200   Failing the husband who received your promise,
     Failing still more your helpless children, doomed
     To bitter lives of bondage: for reflect,
     The very day that takes their mother from them
     Rebuilds the hope of that Barbarian's child,
205   That arrogant enemy of you and yours,
     The boy the Amazonian stranger bore
     Hippolytus—
     PHAEDRA: O Gods!
     OENONE: That charge strikes home!
     PHAEDRA: Woman, how dare you name that name to me?

OENONE: Why, now your anger is most justly roused.
     It heartens me that you should shrink to hear   210
     That fatal name. Then live. For love, for duty,
     Live; if you would not have the Scythian's son,
     Bending your children to his hated yoke,
     Lord it over the fairest blood of Greece
     And of the Gods. But do not wait, each moment   215
     You die. Rally, betimes, your prostrate vigour
     While yet your almost spent and guttering life
     Still glows, and may be kindled once again.
PHAEDRA: I have outlived the right to live already.
OENONE: Why, is there some remorse that feeds upon
         you?   220
     What have you done that drives you so distraught?
     your hands have never dipped in guiltless blood?
PHAEDRA: I thank the Gods my hands are free of evil.
     Would that my heart were innocent as they!
OENONE: What resolution, then, have you conceived   225
     To terrify your heart before the time?
PHAEDRA: I have said enough. Ask me no more, have
         pity;
     For if I die it is to keep within me
     This dreadful secret.
OENONE: Keep it then, and die;
     But other hands, not mine, will close your eyes.   230
     Yours is a weak and flickering fire, but I
     Will lose my spirit first among the dead;
     There are many avenues and all unbarred;
     An injured heart will soon perceive the best.—
     Ungrateful mistress, when did I betray you?   235
     Have you forgotten that these hands received you
     When you were born? My children and my home,
     I have left all for you: and all for this.
PHAEDRA: What do you think to gain by this beseech-
         ing?
     You will shrink with horror if I break my silence.   240
OENONE: What can you tell me then more horrible
     Than thus to see you die before my face?
PHAEDRA: And when you know my destiny and my
         weakness
     Still I shall die, and only die more guilty.
OENONE: My lady, by the tears I shed for you,   245
     By these your trembling knees I hold entwined,
     Deliver me from deadly fear and doubt.
PHAEDRA: You wish it. Rise.
OENONE: Speak on, and I will listen.
PHAEDRA: How shall I tell, ye Gods, or where begin?
OENONE: Your fears are insults to my loyalty.   250
PHAEDRA: O deathless hate of Venus, fatal vengeance!
     O heavy doom of love upon my mother!
OENONE: Forget, my lady. Hide that memory
     And keep it from the ears of later times.
PHAEDRA: Love left thee dying, sweet sister Ariadne,   255
     Lying forsaken by the alien waters.
OENONE: Let be, my lady. Must your mortal grief
     Be vented on the dearest of your blood?
PHAEDRA: Of this doomed blood, I, by the will of Venus,

260   I perish now the last and most accursed.
OENONE: You love!
PHAEDRA: To madness and to ecstasy.
OENONE: Whom?
PHAEDRA: There's the horror that surpasses horror:
     I love… at the fatal name I blench and tremble—
     I love…
OENONE: But whom?
PHAEDRA: You know the Amazon's son,
265   The young Prince who endured so much, through
         me…
OENONE: O Gods! Hippolytus!
PHAEDRA: You spoke the name!
OENONE: Sweet Heavens! You have chilled my very
       blood.
    O race polluted, hopeless, lamentable!
    Woe worth the day that brought us to these
       shores!
270   Why did we venture?
PHAEDRA: It was long ago
    And far from here. When first the rite of Hymen
    Bound my obedience to the son of Aegeus—
    My happiness, my peace then seemed so plain—
    Careless in Athens stood my conqueror.
275   I saw and gazed, I blushed and paled again,
    A blind amazement rose and blurred my mind;
    My eyes were dim, my lips forgot to speak,
    This, I knew, was the awful flame of Venus,
    The fated torment of her chosen victims.
280   I tried to ward it off with prayers, with vows
    And offerings, a temple built and decked,
    And in the midst of endless sacrifices
    I searched the entrails for my erring wisdom.
    Weak drugs for irremediable love!
285   Even as my hand split incense at the shrine,
    Even as my lips invoked the name of Venus
    I prayed Hippolytus, my eyes beheld
    Hippolytus, and while the altars steamed
    I offered all to him I dared not name.
290   I fled him everywhere., O bitterness,
    He looked upon me in his father's features.
    At last, I turned upon myself. I forced
    Myself to play the torturer against
    The dreaded enemy I loved too well,
295   Put on the bride's abhorrence of the stepson,
    Pleaded and pressed until I banished him
    Out of his father's arms, his father's heart.
    Once more I breathed; and after this, Oenone,
    My life, serener, flowed in blameless ways,
300   Pleasing my husband, covering my pain,
    Tending the fruits of his unhappy bed:
    Foolish expedients! and inexorable
    Hardness of destiny!—My lord himself
    Brought me to Trozen and my banished foe.
305   The ancient wound gaped deep, and bled again.
    No longer is it a secret flame that flickers
    About my veins: headlong in onset Venus

Hangs on her quarry! I abhorred my guilt,
Life was a curse, my love a misery;
I looked for death to save my name, and bury   310
Far from the day the darkness of these fires.
I could not face your strivings and your tears.
Now you know all; and it is well, if you
Stand but aside from my advancing death,
Abstain at last from undeserved reproaches,   315
And leave your useless effort to revive
The embers of a fast-expiring fire.

[Enter PANOPE]

PANOPE: I wish that I could hide the news, my lady,
    That I am forced to bring you. Death has taken
    Your lord, our most indomitable King;   320
    And you alone are ignorant of your loss.
OENONE: What is this, Panope?
PANOPE: My lady's prayers
    Will never now bring Theseus back to Athens,
    And mariners that landed here to-day
    Have told Hippolytus that he is dead.   325
PHAEDRA: Gods!
PANOPE: Athens wavers in the choice of masters.
    One boasts allegiance to the Prince your son;
    One, reckless of the statutes of the land,
    Presumes to favour the Barbarian's child,
    My lady; and they say a rank sedition   330
    Proclaims Aricia and the blood of Pallas.
    I knew it was my duty to report
    Such perils. Even now Hippolytus
    Embarks, and many fear if he arrives
    In this tempestuous season, he will sway   335
    A shifting multitude.
OENONE: Panope, thank you:
    Your news was precious, and the Queen has
       heard.

[Exit PANOPE]

OENONE: My lady, I had thrown away all pleadings,
    All hope to move you, and my only thought
    Was to attend you past the gates of the tomb.   340
    But new disaster points new purposes,
    An altered fortune, and an altered duty.
    Theseus is dead, and you are his successor,
    My lady, with a son that looks to you—
    A slave alone, and if you live, a King.   345
    No other will uphold his friendless quarrel,
    No other wipe away his orphan tears;
    Only in Heaven will his hearers be
    The Gods, your judges and his ancestors.
    Live then, in liberty from all misgiving;   350
    Your love is now as unremarkable
    As any love, for death disjoins the bond
    That made its foulness and its infamy.
    Henceforth the image of Hippolytus

355 Is not so terrible, and you may see him
    With perfect guiltlessness. But what if now,
    Despairing of a better understanding,
    He takes command of these rebellious throngs?
    Open his eyes, soften that stubborn heart.
360 Prince of these smiling coasts, his patrimony
    Is here in Trozen, but he knows the laws;
    He knows that they deliver to your son
    The queenly ramparts that Minerva reared.
    Your rightful enemy is also his:
365 Unite your forces to defeat Aricia.
    PHAEDRA: So be it. I commit my way to you.
    I will live, if I still have strength to live
    And if a mother's love can even now
    Revive in my wasted flesh the seeds of life.

ACT II

[ARICIA, ISMENE]

ARICIA: He asked to see me here? Hippolytus
    Wanted to see me and to say farewell?
    Are you quite certain? Is this true, Ismene?
ISMENE: Much more than this, now that the King is
    dead.
5   Prepare yourself, my lady; all the hearts
    He kept at bay will cluster at your feet.
    All Greece will bring its tribute to Aricia,
    Enfranchised now and sovereign of her fortunes.
ARICIA: So then, Ismene, it is no idle talk
10 And I have no oppressor and no foe?
ISMENE: My lady, none. The Heavens have relented
    And Theseus walks among your fathers' shades.
ARICIA: What enterprise has brought him to his
    death?
    Do they say?
ISMENE: Rumours wild and past belief:
15 Some say that in a lover's last adventure
    The seas have claimed this ever-wandering hus-
    band;
    Some say, and everywhere the news is sown,
    That with Pirithous he went down to Hell,
    Saw the Cocytus and the coasts of darkness
20 And stood alive amid a world of shadows,
    But could not scale the gloomy track again
    Nor pass the bourne men never pass but once.
ARICIA: Shall mortal men, before the last leave-taking,
    Fathom those sullen deeps of the Departed?
25 What sorcery lured him to their awful shore?
ISMENE: My lady, he is dead, and you alone
    Doubt it. All Athens grieves for him, all Trozen
    Knows, and salutes Hippolytus for Prince.
    And in these walls, despairing for her son,
30 Phaedra takes counsel of her trembling friends.
ARICIA: And you suppose that, kinder than his father,
    Hippolytus will make my bondage sweeter

    And pity me?
ISMENE: My lady, yes, I do.
ARICIA: But do you know the hard Hippolytus?
    What makes you fancy he could feel compassion   35
    For me alone, who never felt for woman?
    He never joins our customary paths
    And hides himself wherever we are not.
ISMENE: Oh, I know all the legend of his coldness;
    But when you met the proud Hippolytus   40
    I own the strangeness of his reputation
    Sharpened the edge of my curiosity.
    I saw a face at variance with the fable;
    At once your eyes disturbed that hard assurance
    And his, avoiding you but all in vain,   45
    Melted at once, and could not turn away.
    His pride may yet refuse the name of lover
    But I'll believe his looks, and not his tongue.
ARICIA: Ah, sweet Ismene, how my heart devours
    The unhoped-for comfort of a mere perhaps!   50
    You that have known me, did you once imagine
    This heart, the plaything of unpitying Fate,
    Starved of all sustenance except despair,
    Would learn of love and the wild woes of love?
    Child of Earth's child, last of a royal lineage,   55
    Sole remnant spared by battlefield and hatred,
    I lost the last proud blossoms of our tree,
    Six brothers, in the springtime of their year.
    The steel reaped all, and Earth's unwilling furrows
    Drank her own blood, the blood of her
    Erechtheus.   60
    Since then you know what rigorous decree
    Defies all Greeks to lift their eyes to mine—
    For a mutinous ardour in the sister's breast
    Might wake the embers in her brothers' urns—
    And you remember how I laughed to scorn   65
    Those calculations of the victor's fear;
    I held that love itself was slavery
    And even thanked the King for a constraint
    So fit and favourable to my distaste—
    Then, yes; but then I had not seen his son.   70
    Not that subservient to the eye's seduction
    I love him for that beauty, that demeanour,
    Graces of partial Nature, gifts that he
    Ignores, if ever he has noticed them;
    I see richer and dearer treasures in him—   75
    His father's parts, and not his father's failings;
    For I confess I love the manly pride
    That never bent under the yoke of love.
    Phaedra was flattered by the doubtful glory
    Of Theseus' courtly sighs: but I am prouder   80
    And will not stoop to share an easy prize
    Or occupy an undefended heart.
    No, but to shape a will as yet unbending,
    To waken pain in a proof-armoured bosom,
    To lead a slave that never thought to serve,   85
    Vainly at war against the pleasing chain—
    There's a reward worthy of my ambition;

Hercules was an easier adversary
Who readily disarmed and quick to yield
90   Lent no such lustre to his overthrow.
But dear Ismene, these are reckless dreams:
Resistance there will be, and all too stubborn,
And you shall hear me soon in humbler strain
Lament the coldness that I praise to-day.
95   He love, Hippolytus? What height of fortune
Could ever bring him—

ISMENE: Only let him speak;
He is coming now.

[Enter HIPPOLYTUS*]*

HIPPOLYTUS: My lady, before I go
I owe you some account of my intentions.
My father's dead: and well enough my fears
100   Foretold the causes of his late home-coming—
Death only, and the closure of his toils
Could hold him from the world so long. His Gods
At last abandon to the fatal Spinners
Alcides' friend, his fellow, his successor.
105   —I know your enmity will not forbid
His son to assert these titles he has earned.—
One hope alleviates my deepest sorrow,
For I can end a harsh and long subjection:
I here revoke laws that have caused me grief—
110   The full bestowal of your life and hand
Is yours alone, and in my patrimony,
This Trozen, seat of Pittheus my grandfather,
Which willingly defers his crown to me
I leave you free—, and freer than its Prince.
115   ARICIA: Show me less kindness, I could bear it better.
So much regard for me in my abjection
Binds me, my lord, more even than you know,
To that constraint you would have put away.
HIPPOLYTUS: Doubtful who stands the next in title,
      Athens
120   Canvasses you, and me, and Phaedra's son.
ARICIA: Me, my lord?
HIPPOLYTUS: I have never shut my eyes
To arrogant laws that seem to bar my claim:
The Greeks reject me for my mother's race.
But if my only rival were my brother
125   I can appeal to certain natural laws
And make them good against the law's caprice.
I have a better reason to refrain—
To you I yield, say rather I restore,
The seat, the sceptre, that your fathers held
130   Of the illustrious mortal, son of Earth.
It only passed to Aegeus by adoption;
And next my father, Athens' second founder,
Was hailed and crowned for all his benefits
While your unhappy brothers lay forgot.
135   Now, Athens calls you home within her ramparts.
Too long the ancient quarrel lives in pain,
Too long your blood, shed on the Attic soil,

Reeks from the furrows where it found its birth.—
Trozen I hold. As for the son of Phaedra
The Cretan acres yield him rich retirement.   140
Attica falls to you. I sail, to join
Your partisans with mine, to serve your cause.
ARICIA: At every word more troubled and bewildered,
Can I, or dare I, think I heard you rightly?
Have I my senses, is this your intent?   145
What God, my lord, what God inspired your mind?
Rightly your glory sounds in every climate
But reputation falls behind the truth.
What, will you cheat yourself on my behalf?
It was enough indeed to think that you   150
Hated me not, and held a mind untainted
By this long enmity—
HIPPOLYTUS: How could I hate you?
Men may deride this proud unconquered heart
But do they think a monster gave me birth?
What brutishness or what inveterate malice   155
Could see your face and not forget its fury?
And how should I withstand the subtle spell—
ARICIA: My lord!…
HIPPOLYTUS: My tongue has carried me too far;
But wisdom fails and yields to the compulsion…
Now that my silence has been partly broken,   160
My lady, I must needs go on, and speak
The secret that my soul cannot contain.—
Here stands a Prince of all men most unhappy,
A monument of overthrown presumption;
I, long a truant from the law of love   165
And long a mocker of its votaries,
That stayed ashore watching the luckless sailor
And never thought myself to fight the tempest,
Levelled at last beneath the common fate
By strange tides I am borne far from myself.   170
My wanton liberty has learnt to yield
And in an instant this bold heart was tamed.
Six months or nearly, in despair and shame,
I've borne the arrow burning in my side;
Vainly I pit my strength against myself   175
And you. I fly you where you are, and find you
Where you are not; deep in the forest glade
Your picture chases me; sunlight and dark
Alike retrace your features and alike
Betray the fugitive that would be free,   180
And I, for all my fruitless pains, look round
To find Hippolytus, and know him not.
My bow, my hounds, my spear, my chariot,
Weary me, Neptune's lessons are forgotten;
Only my lamentations fill the groves,   185
My stabled coursers know my voice no more.
Perhaps this tale I tell of uncouth passion
Will make you blush to own your handiwork:
Wild terms, indeed, to offer up a heart!
And chains too fair for such a slave to claim!   190
And yet my tribute therefore ranks the higher;
Consider that I speak an unknown language

And do not spurn these faltered words of love
That you alone could teach Hippolytus.

[Enter THERAMENES]

195 THERAMENES: Close on my heels, my lord, the Queen
          approaches
        Asking for you.
     HIPPOLYTUS: For me?
     THERAMENES: In what intention
        I do not know, but messengers have come
        Bidding you wait on her before you sail.
     HIPPOLYTUS: The Queen? What should I say to her?
        Or she…
200 ARICIA: You cannot disappoint her wish, my lord.
        Even to such an enemy is due
        Some sign of formal pity for her grief.
     HIPPOLYTUS: So you go. And I sail. And still I know not
        Whether my worship has incensed my goddess,
205   Whether this heart I leave in your two hands…
     ARICIA: Sail, Prince. Pursue your noble purposes;
        Bring me the realm of Athens for dominion;
        Whatever gift you make shall be accepted,
        But that imperial and unhoped-for state
210   Is not the dearest of your offerings.

[Exit ARICIA]

     HIPPOLYTUS: Good friend, are all things ready?—But I
          hear
        The Queen.—Have all things ordered for our
          leaving.
        Send out the signal. Haste, command, return
        And free me from the burden of this meeting.

[Exit THERAMENES]

[Enter PHAEDRA and OENONE]

215 PHAEDRA (*to Oenone*): He is here. My blood retreats
          toward my heart.
        I see him, and forget what I should speak.
     OENONE: Be mindful of the son that trusts in you!
     PHAEDRA: They say that you are leaving us at once,
        My lord. I came to join my grief with yours,
220   And with the story of a mother's terrors—
        My child is fatherless, and soon the day
        Will dawn that brings him to another deathbed;
        So fiercely even now assailed and threatened,
        Your strength alone can champion his weak-
          ness.—
225   But deep within me throbs the preying thought
        That his complaint will never reach your ear,
        That through my child your angry justice soon
        Will strike a hated memory.
     HIPPOLYTUS: My lady,
        So infamous a wish was never mine.
230 PHAEDRA: But you have seen me unremittingly

Pursue your hate, my lord; and how could you
Explore the bottom of my soul and read
My secret there? I threw myself upon
Your just resentment; I would not suffer you
Within the self-same frontiers; privily   235
And openly I waged my war, and set
The width of the sea between your path and mine.
I even gave explicit orders not
To breathe your name before my presence. Yet,
If by the wrong the penalty were measured,   240
If only hatred could achieve your hatred,
Never did woman more deserve your tears,
My lord, and less your enmity.
HIPPOLYTUS: No mother
  That watches for her children's interest
  Forgives the other children of her house;   245
  I know, my lady. Untoward mistrust
  Is always near when men have married twice.
  Another in your place would have conceived
  No less suspicion, and I might have suffered
  Deeper indignities.
PHAEDRA: Ah but, my lord,   250
  The Gods—as now they stand my witnesses—
  Deigned to release me from this general law.
  How different are the thoughts that ravage me!
HIPPOLYTUS: It is too soon, my lady, for such
          thoughts;
  The sunshine may still light your husband's eye,   255
  And Heaven still may yield him to our prayers;
  For he will supplicate, and not in vain,
  The love and the high patronage of Neptune.
PHAEDRA: No man has twice explored the coasts of
          Death,
  My lord. If Theseus touched the sullen shores   260
  Vainly we look for Gods to send him home:
  Harsh Acheron is grasping and holds fast
  His prey. But did I say that he is dead?
  He breathes again in you; I see the King,
  See him, speak to him, thrill… My mind is
          wandering,   265
  My lord, my madness speaks the thing it should
          not.
HIPPOLYTUS: This is a prodigy of loyal love:
  Theseus is gone, yet lives within your mind
  And fires the ardour of your loving heart.
PHAEDRA: Yes, Prince, for him indeed I yearn, I
          languish;   270
  I love him—not the man that Hell has claimed,
  The butterfly that every beauty lured,
  The adulterous ravisher that would have stained
  The God of Hell's own bed; but faithful, fine,
  Sometimes aloof, and pure, gallant and gay,   275
  Young, stealing every heart upon his road—
  So do they character our Gods, and so
  I see you now; those eyes, that voice, were his,
  That generous red of virtue in your cheek,
  When first he drove across the Cretan foam,   280

Meet meditation for the virgin dreams
Of Minos' daughters. You, where were you then
Among the flower and chivalry of Greece?
Where was Hippolytus—alas, too young—
285 The day his vessel grounded on our shore?
You would have slain the terror of the island,
The monster lapped in labyrinthine wiles;
Into your hand my sister would have thrust,
To unweave those riddling and deceitful ways,
290 The thread of life and death. But no, she would
      not—
Love would have found a readier wit in me,
And I, Prince, I, devoted and assured,
Could have resolved the devious Labyrinth;
What would I not have done for that sweet head?
295 How should a thread content your fearful lover?
Half-claimant in the peril that you claimed
I would have walked before you in the way,
And Phaedra, steadfast in the Labyrinth,
Would have returned again with you, or else
Fallen with you.
300 HIPPOLYTUS: Great Gods, what have you said?
My lady, can it be that you forget
That you are Theseus' wife, and I his son?
PHAEDRA: And why do you suppose I had forgotten,
Prince? Do I appear so careless of my honour?
305 HIPPOLYTUS: Forgive, my lady. I own, I blush to own
How blameless are the words that I reproved.
My shame can face it out no more before you,
So let me go…
PHAEDRA: Ah, leave your heartless lying.
You understand and you have heard enough.
310 Very well then, you shall learn what Phaedra is
And all her frenzy. Yes: I am in love.
But never think that even while I love you
I can absolve myself, or hide my face
From my own guiltiness. And never think
315 The wanton love that blurs my better mind
Grew with the treachery of my consent.
I, singled out for a celestial vengeance,
Unpitied victim, I abhor myself
More than you hate me. Let the Gods bear wit-
      ness,
320 Those Gods that set the fire within my breast,
The fatal fire of my accursed line;
Those Gods whose majesty and might exulted
In the beguiling of a mortal's weakness.
Turn back the past yourself: how I have laboured
325 To seem malignant, savage, how I fostered
Your hatred as my ally in the fight.
Did I escape you? No, I banished you.
What fruit repaid these unavailing cares?
You loathed me more, I could not love you less;
330 Your suffering doubled the spell that binds me,
The withering ravage of my flames, my tears.
Your eyes can testify that this is true—
If for one moment they could bear my sight.

Why, this confession of my bitter secret,
My shameful secret, do you think that I   335
Have made it willingly? I came in fear
For one defenceless that I dare not fail:
I came to pray you not to hate my child.
Precarious resolution of a mind
Too full of what it loves! I came, and spoke   340
Of nothing but yourself.—So now, do justice.
Punish me for this execrable passion.
Approve yourself a hero's son indeed
And sweep this monster from the universe.
Dare Theseus' widow love Hippolytus?   345
Truly so vile a monster must not live.
My heart is here, and here is where you strike.
Eager to make atonement for its fault
I feel it swell and bound to meet your hand:
Strike. Or am I unworthy of your steel,   350
Or will your hate refuse so sweet a doom,
Or would ignoble blood sully your fingers?
Then hold your hand and let me have your sword.
Give me it.
OENONE: Stop, my lady. Heavenly powers!
What would you do? But somebody is coming: 355
Escape their sight, be quick, come back, or face
Inevitable shame.

[Exeunt PHAEDRA and OENONE]

[Enter THERAMENES]

THERAMENES: Was that the Queen
Half dragged, half rushing out? What, my lord,
      what
Are all these marks of grief? You stand disarmed,
Dumb, pale…
HIPPOLYTUS: Come, let us go, Theramenes.   360
I cannot think of what I have heard and witnessed;
I cannot see myself without disgust.
Phaedra…. No more, great Gods! Oblivion
Must shroud away that secret with its shame.
THERAMENES: If you would leave, my lord, the sail
      hangs ready;   365
But Athens is beforehand with her answer:
Her chiefs have counted votes among the tribes;
Your brother has their suffrage, Phaedra wins.
HIPPOLYTUS: Phaedra!
THERAMENES: A herald of the will of Athens
Will bring the reins of state into her hands.   370
Her son is King.
HIPPOLYTUS: Ye Gods that know her heart,
Is it her righteousness you would repay?
THERAMENES: And now dark rumours speak again of
      Theseus:
Some tell that men have seen him in Epirus
Alive; though I, who went to seek him there,   375
I know full well, my lord…
HIPPOLYTUS: It may be so.

But I would hear whatever rumour tells,
Consult this public cry, divine its sources.
If it be worthless to delay our journey
380   Then forward! Cost the venture what it will
I'll save the sceptre for a worthy hand.

ACT III

[PHAEDRA, OENONE]

PHAEDRA: Send them away, these heralds and these
          honours.
      Have they a balm to ease a tortured mind?
      Be kind: is Phaedra fit for public show?
      Rather conceal me, for my secret's out:
5   Intemperate desire has seen the light,
      And what these lips had never thought to utter
      He heard. Immortal Gods! and how he listened,
      How long he parried, how deviously he turned
      To baffle the approaches of my speech!
10   How visibly he yearned to leave my presence!
      How painfully his blush revived my shame!
      Why did you disappoint me of my death?
      Ah, when his weapon pointed at my breast
      Did he blench? Did he stir to snatch it back?
15   Enough for him my fingers at the hilt
      And in his heartless reckoning it was vile,
      Profaned, a blade that would defile his hand.
OENONE: And so complaining, dwelling on your sorrow,
      You feed a fire that wisdom would have quenched.
20   Should not a worthy child of Minos' blood
      Look for serenity in nobler tasks,
      Fly from a struggle that you cannot win,
      Learn to assume the guidance of a kingdom
      And be a Queen?
PHAEDRA: Queen, I? And hold command,
25   When my own senses rage in mutiny,
      When in my soul wisdom has lost dominion,
      When shame and slavery have bowed my head,
      And death is waiting?
OENONE: Fly.
PHAEDRA: I cannot leave him.
OENONE: You drove him away, and cannot go yourself?
30 PHAEDRA: I cannot now. He has seen my raging soul,
      Seen me transgress the rigid pale of virtue;
      Before those stony eyes I have poured out
      My shame, and now, unbidden, secret hope
      Has slipped into my breast. Ay, you yourself,
35   Rallying the wasted forces of my life,
      The parting spirit ready on my lips,
      Wooed me from death with false and soothing
          words;
      You half persuaded me that I might love.
OENONE: Ah, call me guilty, or call me innocent,
40   I would do worse if anything could save you.
      But, if resentment ever stung your mind,

Can you forget the blow of his rebuff,
The insolence, the icy cruelty
That eyed you all but prostrate at his feet,
The arrogant disdain?—how odious   45
Had Phaedra only seen him as I saw!
PHAEDRA: What if he lost this arrogance, Oenone?
    He has the harshness of his forest ways,
    And in his hardy life Hippolytus
    Has never heard of love until to-day.   50
    What if surprise had robbed him of his speech?
    What if we blamed him more than he deserved?
OENONE: He was conceived in a Barbarian's womb.
PHAEDRA: Barbarian, Scythian, still she learned to love.
OENONE: He hates our sex with firm and deadly hate.   55
PHAEDRA: So I shall never fear another woman.
    Enough: such counsels had their season once;
    My passion now commands you, and not my rea-
        son.
    Though hard and inaccessible to love,
    Another side lies weaker to attack—   60
    The sweets of empire tempted him, I think;
    Athens allured him more than he could hide.
    His ships already turned their prows to sea
    With canvas rigged and offered to the breeze.
    Find him, Oenone, find this ambitious boy,   65
    Show him the glitter of the Athenian crown,
    Bid him assume the diadem and the glory;
    I only ask to lay it on his brow.
    Into his hand descends authority
    I cannot grasp, and he shall teach my son   70
    The science of command—even he might
    Look as a father on him. In his power
    I now resign the orphan and the mother.
    Incline his heart by any means you know,
    Use—do not blush—the voice of supplication,   75
    I sanction all. I have no other hope;
    Go, till you come again I cannot tell
    What else I have to do.

[Exit OENONE]

[PHAEDRA alone]

                                O Thou, that knowest
How deep in shame my soul is overwhelmed,
Venus, O Venus unappeasable,   80
This is the consummation of thy hatred.
These must be the limits of thy cruelty.
Thy triumph is entire, each shot has told.
Art thou not sated yet with victory?
Find tougher quarry then: Hippolytus   85
Rejects thy deity, derides thy wrath,
He never bent the knee before thy altar;
Thy name seems hideous in his stubborn ears.
Goddess, avenge; and vengeance will be mine!
Teach him to love... Oenone, here so soon?   90
I am rejected then, you were not heard.

[Enter OENONE]

OENONE: Stifle the memory of a hopeless passion,
    My lady; summon up your earlier virtue.
    The King's not dead, and you will see him soon.
95   Theseus has landed. He is coming here.
    The populace are rushing to salute him,
    And as I passed obedient to your mission
    Unending cheers rose up on every hand—
PHAEDRA: He is not dead. Nothing else signifies,
100   Oenone. I revealed a lawless love
    That wounds him in his honour. And he lives.
    What needs there more?
OENONE: But yet—
PHAEDRA: I told you so;
    And you would not. Foreboding and remorse
    Have yielded to your tears. Only this morning
105   My death was not unworthy to be pitied:
    I took your counsel, and I die disgraced.
OENONE: Die?
PHAEDRA: Righteous Gods! The things this day has
        seen!
    And now, as I meet my husband and his son
    I know this witness of adulterous passion
110   Studies my countenance before his father—
    My heart heavy with sighs he would not hear,
    My eyelids drenched with tears that he despised.
    Do you think his tenderness for Theseus' honour
    Would hide away the memory of my falsehood,
115   My treason to a father and a King?
    Will he repress the loathing I inspire?
    What if he did? I know my treachery,
    Oenone. And if there are intrepid women
    Who taste a flawless quietude in crime
120   And force their countenance to show no shame,
    I am not such. My misdeeds rise before me;
    And even now these over-arching walls
    Seem full of tongues, impatient to accuse me
    Before my husband, and proclaim his wrong.
125   Oh for a death, and surcease from my anguish!
    Is life so precious and so hard to leave?
    Need the tormented hesitate to die?
    Only I fear the name I leave behind—
    The legacy of horror for my children,
130   Whose blood, the very blood of Jupiter,
    Should swell their hearts with pride: now they
        must lift
    The burden of a mother's infamy.
    My soul foretells that malice, soon or late,
    Will throw my black reproach into their faces,
135   And crushed so cruelly they may never dare
    To look with level eyes upon their kind.
OENONE: It is most true. They both are to be pitied,
    And never sorrow was foretold more surely.
    But why abandon them to the ordeal?
140   Why be the witness that betrays your cause?
    For all is lost; and all the world will judge

That Phaedra knows her guilt, and dare not wait
The awful presence of an outraged husband.
Hippolytus should thank you for a deed
Stronger than all his words on his behalf;   145
And what can I respond to your accuser?
Confounded, tongue-tied, I must live to see
Him taste a hideous triumph undisturbed
And chronicle your shame to all mankind.
May fire from Heaven fall upon me sooner!   150
But tell me this, and tell without dissembling:
Do you still love him, this presumptuous Prince?
How does he now appear… ?
PHAEDRA: I see him now
    Grim as a monster and as terrible.
OENONE: Then why concede him victory unresisted? 155
    Do you fear him? Attack before he strikes
    And use the imputation he prepares
    For you. What can refute you? Every sign
    Informs against him—first his sword that Fortune
    Leaves in your hands, and then this day's distress, 160
    And those disconsolate months of misery,
    And long ago his father's mind prepared
    When long ago you claimed his banishment.
PHAEDRA: Shall I defame and murder innocence?
OENONE: Lend me but silence and my zeal suffices. 165
    Like you I shudder at my remedy
    And dread it deeper than a thousand deaths.
    But either this, or else I lose my mistress,
    And in your loss all other values fade.
    So I will speak. Theseus will rage, but still   170
    He'll take no more revenge than banishment.
    A father punishing is still a father
    Whose love is louder than the voice of justice;
    But guiltless blood is nothing in the scales
    Against the imperilled honour of your name. 175
    That is a jewel far too dear to hazard;
    It is a law we dare not disobey;
    And when our honour stands at such a cost
    Virtue itself must go for sacrifice.
    —Here they are. I see Theseus.
PHAEDRA: And I see 180
    Hippolytus, and his unflinching eyes
    Spell my dishonour. Do what you will, Oenone.
    I am in your hands. In this tormented hour
    To save myself is more than I can do.

[Enter THESEUS, HIPPOLYTUS, and THERAMENES]

THESEUS: Fortune has smiled again, my dearest lady, 185
    And now your sweet embrace—
PHAEDRA: No, Theseus; stop,
    Do not pollute this love and this delight.
    No longer I deserve this tenderness.
    You have been wronged. The jealousy of Fortune
    Has not respected her you left behind you; 190
    And now, unworthy to approach your love,
    My sole desire must be for solitude.

[Exit PHAEDRA]

THESEUS: What is this cheerless welcome that I find
          here,
     My son?
HIPPOLYTUS: A riddle Phaedra must interpret,
195   No one else can. But now if prayers can move
     I ask but this, my lord, never to see
     Her face again, but to live out my life
     Safe, far away, forgotten by the Queen.
THESEUS: And now my son forsakes me!
HIPPOLYTUS: For you know
200   I never sought her, but you brought her here
     At your departure; and the coasts of Trozen
     Became the dwelling of Aricia
     And of the Queen. I was to be their guardian.
     But now what duty keeps me from my life?
205   Inglorious victories among the forests
     Weary my idle youth, my wasted skill.
     I long to waken from obscurity
     And dip my hunter's spear in a nobler red.
     Before you had spent the years that I have count-
          ed
210   What robbers, what oppressors, and what
          monsters
     Had known the weight of that revengeful arm
     Victor and scourge of wanton insolence!
     While on the quiet shores of either sea
     The traveller learnt to take his road in peace;
215   Hercules heard your prowess and drew breath,
     Leaving his triumphs and his toils to you—
     And I, the unknown son of such a father,
     Have much to do to reach my mother's footsteps.
     Now let my unfledged valour learn to dare;
220   Let me, if anywhere some monster yet
     Escapes you, drag its trophy to your feet,
     Or by the record of a glorious failure
     Find life for ever in a fitting death
     And show posterity I was your son.
225 THESEUS: What is it? What invading blast of fear
     Empties my very home at my approach?
     Why, O ye Gods, to face these shrinking looks,
     This lack of love, did ye deliver me?
     I had one friend. His unregarding passion
230   Conspired to carry back from far Epirus
     The tyrant's Queen. I helped, against my will,
     But Fate was pitiless, and we were blind.
     The villain caught me all unarmed, unwatching,
     And these two eyes—that weep him yet—beheld
235   Pirithous under the fangs of beasts
     Fatted on human slaughter; and I spent
     Deep in the sightless silence of his dungeons
     Down near the horrible empire of the Dead,
     Six months. Then Heaven thought on me again.
240   I tricked the watchful eyes. I purged creation
     Of one perfidious enemy, and his blood
     Glutted his own fell monsters. Now at length

Free, and restored to all that's left to love,
Now that my soul aspires to nothing more
Than the enjoyment of their blessed sight,   245
Grief and lament is all my salutation,
None will abide to suffer my embraces;
And, chilled by the contagion of the fears
That breathe about my path, I'd rather be
A prisoner again and in Epirus.   250
Speak out. Phaedra declares I've been betrayed.
Who wronged me? Why is not the wrong
     avenged?
Has Greece, so long beholden to this arm,
Offered a refuge to the criminal?
—You will not answer? Is my son, my son,   255
A shield and ally of my enemies?
I will go in, for this suspense unmans me.
I will find out the culprit and the offence.
Phaedra must tell me what her sorrow is.

[Exit THESEUS]

HIPPOLYTUS: What did her words portend? They
          froze my blood.   260
     Would Phaedra in her ecstasy of frenzy
     Denounce her guilt and give her case away?
     Gods, when the King is told! Death-dealing Love,
     What blighting mists thou hast wrapped around
          his house!
     And I with my secret of disloyal passion,   265
     What was I once, what will he think me now!
     My mind is dark with unaccomplished shapes
     Of evil: but should innocence be afraid?
     I must look for better times and better ways
     To move my father's heart, and then reveal   270
     Love he may doom to parting and to tears
     But fixed beyond his force to overthrow.

ACT IV

[THESEUS, OENONE]

THESEUS: Ah! What have you said? The rebel, the
          betrayer
     Conceived this outrage on his father's honour?
     How unrelenting is thy hand upon me,
     O Destiny! I know not where I go,
     I know not what I do. All my long kindness   5
     Wasted, paid with this hideous wanton plot!
     And with the argument and threat of steel
     To enforce his dark design! I know that sword,
     I gave it him, I strapped it to his side—
     For nobler work than this. Not all the bonds   10
     Of blood itself could hold him back; and she
     Could hesitate to punish, and her silence
     Showed mercy to the wrongdoer!
OENONE: Say rather

Showed mercy to a father's suffering.
15 Shamed by a lover's frenzy, and ashamed
That her chaste eyes could kindle such a fire,
She would have died, my lord, and dimmed for
       ever
Herself the innocent lustre of those eyes.
The arm was raised. I hastened, I preserved
20 Her life for the embraces of her lord,
And pitying your fears and her confusion
Became the unwilling spokesman of her tears.
THESEUS: The perfidy! Yes, for all his craft, he paled;
He quaked with fear, I saw it as he came;
25 I marvelled then to feel his joylessness
And froze against the chill of his embrace.
—Did you not say, the love that burns in him
Had shown itself in Athens long before?
OENONE: My lord, remember how the Queen
       abhorred him;
30 It was unhallowed love that caused her hatred.
THESEUS: And now, in Trozen, it has flared again?
OENONE: I have told you all, my lord; but I have left
My lady too long now with her deadly sorrow,
And, by your leave, my place is at her side.

[Exit OENONE]

[Enter HIPPOLYTUS]

35 THESEUS: So, here he comes. Great Gods, that noble
       carriage
Would it not blind another's eye, as mine?
Then sacrilegious and adulterous heads
May flaunt the sacred emblem of the pure?
Why is there no infallible badge to blazon
40 The minds of our dissembling race of men?
HIPPOLYTUS: May I not know, my lord, why such a
       weight
Of cloud darkens the majesty of your brow?
Must this be secret from my loyalty?
THESEUS: Dissembler! Dare you come so near to me?
45 Monster the thunderbolts reprieve too long,
Corrupted straggler of the brigand race
I cleansed the earth of once, how dare you still
Parade that odious face, here where your frenzy
Clutched at a father's bed? How dare you pace
50 These halls where all things tell of your dishonour?
Why are you not far hence, where skies unknown
Illumine coasts that never knew my name?
Be gone, you traitor. Lingering you taunt too long
A hate, an anger hardly to be stayed.
55 Enough for me the indelible reproach
Of fathering you, without the soil of murder
To smother my bright deeds from memory.
—Be gone. And if you would not share the sen-
       tence
Of malefactors doomed by this swift hand
60 Take care that never again the sun that lights us

Finds your rebellious feet upon this shore.
Be gone I tell you, out of my dominions
And cleanse them for ever of your loathsome
       presence.
And now hear, Neptune, hear. If once my courage
Scoured off a scum of bandits from thy coasts   65
Remember thou hast sworn in recompense
To grant one prayer. In long and stern confinement
I called not thy undying power; I saved thee,
Thrifty of all the aid I hoped for, till
A greater need. To-day I pray: avenge   70
A mourning father. To thy wrath I entrust
This profligate. Stifle his lust in blood.
Let Theseus read thy kindness in thy rage.
HIPPOLYTUS: With such a love Hippolytus is charged
By Phaedra! Weight of horror crushes me;   75
So many assaults unlooked-for, stroke on stroke,
Leave me no words.
THESEUS: And so you judged that Phaedra's
Compliant silence would have muffled up
Your savage insolence. You might have waited
To gather up the sword that now, in her hands,   80
Helps to convict you. Or why not, better still,
Heap up the measure of your infamy
With one good blow to finish breath and life?
HIPPOLYTUS: In anger at a calumny so monstrous,
My lord, I should speak out, but for a secret   85
That partly touches you. I beg you sanction
Respect that silences what I might say;
Labour no more to probe into your pain,
Look on my life, consider what I am:
The greatest crimes have lesser crimes before them;   90
The rest is easy when the way is known;
Like virtue, vice is gradual. No one day
Made any good man vile, murderous, incestuous,
And innocence is slow to dare, and slow
To push beyond the boundaries of law.   95
I had a mother, as chaste as she was valiant,
Nor have I derogated from her blood;
Pittheus, wise among men, took up my nurture
After her hands. I would not praise myself,
But, if one virtue was allotted mine,   100
May I not claim, my lord, to loathe that act
My enemies presume to speak of? This
Has made Hippolytus his name in Greece—
Unstudied honour rude in its excess,
Rugged, intractable austerity.   105
The daylight is no cleaner than the deeps
Of this my heart. What, sacrilegious lust
Could stain Hippolytus?
THESEUS: And this condemns you:
That was the foul source fed your vaunted cold-
       ness—
No other woman's love was worth your interest   110
Unless it offered pleasures more than lawful.
HIPPOLYTUS: No, father, you shall hear the truth. This
       heart

Has not refused an honourable yoke.
Here at your feet I will confess—I love,
115 And love in disobedience to your will.
Aricia's beauty holds my heart enslaved
And Pallas' daughter has subdued your son.
I worship her, forgetful of my duty
And have no room to feel another passion.
120 THESEUS: You love her! No—a pitiful pretence;
You feign that crime to clear yourself of this.
HIPPOLYTUS: These six months I have hid from love,
   and loved,
My lord; I came here to confess to you
In trembling. But is it so? Will nothing move you?
125 What fearful oath will win you to believe?
Witness the Earth, the Heavens, and all Nature…
THESEUS: What felon ever feared a perjury?
Peace, peace. Waste no more time on idle stories
If that fine virtue rests on aids like these.
130 HIPPOLYTUS: You see it as a mockery, a lie:
But Phaedra in her heart of hearts knows better.
THESEUS: Shall I endure so much effrontery?
HIPPOLYTUS: What place of exile, and how long a time
Do you appoint?
THESEUS: Past the Pillars of Hercules
135 A traitor's presence is too close for me.
HIPPOLYTUS: What friendship shall I find to comfort me
When you have cast me out, dishonoured thus?
THESEUS: Find yourself friends whose dangerous
   regard
Goes to adultery and honours incest,
140 Deceivers, ingrates, free of law and shame,
Fit to protect a suppliant like you.
HIPPOLYTUS: And still you taunt me with adultery
And incest. How can I reply? But Phaedra
Came of a mother, Phaedra's is a blood,
145 My lord, you do not need me to recall it,
More laden with their awful taint than mine.
THESEUS: How dare you go so far before my face?
For the last time, villain, avoid my sight,
Leave me; or force a father in his rage
150 To have you flung with infamy from the place.

[Exit HIPPOLYTUS]

THESEUS (*alone*): And now you go towards your wait-
   ing doom
Irrevocably. For by that River's name
Terrible even to the immortal Gods,
Neptune has sworn his oath, and will perform it.
155 Yes, and I loved you, and in spite of all,
Before the hour is come, my bowels yearn
For pity of you. But I have too much cause—
Did ever a deeper injury wound a father?
Ye righteous Gods, that see me thus prostrated,
160 Did I give being to a son like this?

[Enter PHAEDRA]

PHAEDRA: My lord, you see me here impelled by ter-
   ror:
Just now, when that terrible voice assailed my
   ears,
I thought the threat might come to a fulfilment.
Let me beg you, if there still is time, have pity
On your own race, save your own flesh; spare me, 165
My lord, the dreadful cry of murdered blood,
Spare me the endless misery of laying
That horrible stain on a paternal hand.
THESEUS: My lady, I have kept my hand unstained
And still the unnatural boy has not escaped;   170
Immortal hands will undertake his doom,
Neptune's my debtor; you shall be avenged.
PHAEDRA: Your debtor, Neptune! Then your prayer of
   hate…
THESEUS: Are you afraid it might be heard too soon?
No, join your own entreaty with my curses,   175
Paint me his crimes once more in all their blackness
Inflame my faint and still-too-sluggish rage—
He has added guilt more than the guilt you knew:
His frenzy spends itself in railing on you,
He swears that all your words are perjuries,   180
He says Aricia claims his heart, his love,
His loyalty.
PHAEDRA: No, my lord!
THESEUS: That is what he told me;
Not that a flimsy lie could impose on me.
I hope to hear that Neptune's justice falls
Swiftly, and till that hour I'll ply his altars   185
And keep him mindful of his undying word.

[Exit THESEUS]

[PHAEDRA alone]

PHAEDRA: He leaves me, with this dreadful news,
   alone.
Ah Gods, the fire that I dreamed was safely stifled
To wake no more! Dreadful, unlooked-for news!
All trepidation and remorse, all speed   190
Out of Oenone's clinging arms of fear
I came to save his son. And who can tell
What might have been had conscience had its
   way?
Whether I might have spoken of my guilt,
Might have let slip, had he but left me time,   195
The entire and awful truth?—He has felt love,
Hippolytus, who never felt for me;
Aricia claims his loyalty, his love…
Gods! while I pleaded, while my prayer beat
On those rigid eyes, that unrelenting brow,   200
I thought he bore impenetrable armour
Always the same and closed to all alike.
And now another has overthrown his pride,
Another finds favour in the tyrant's eyes;
Perhaps his heart is easy to entreat   205

And condescends to any plea but mine.
And I am fool enough to be his friend!

[Enter OENONE*]*

—Oenone, do you know what I have heard?
OENONE: No; I have tried to find you in alarm,
210   Wondering what sudden impulse drove you here
And how it may imperil you…
PHAEDRA: Oenone,
Who would have thought there was another
        woman?
OENONE: You say—
PHAEDRA: Hippolytus, I tell you, loves—
215   The adversary I could never shake,
Vexed by submission, impatient of complaining,
The ogre that I never could encounter
Undaunted; he is tamed and brought to heel,
Aricia has forced the access to his heart.
OENONE: Aricia!
PHAEDRA: Oh, I never thought of these,
220   These newest tortures that I live to taste:
All the old despairs, the ecstasies, the broodings,
Raging of flame, and horror of remorse,
And that slight of unendurable denial
Were barely foretastes of my torment here.
225   They, lovers! Did they bewitch these watchful eyes?
What time did they find to meet? Since when?
        What place?
What furtive means? You knew. Why was I left
To treasure foolish dreams? You might have told me
Of their stolen pleasure. Were they often seen
230   Speaking, or lingering? Was it the forest shades
That sheltered them? Ah, but they had liberty
To see the face they sought. The Heavens smiled
On the innocence of their embrace, no fear
Restrained their eager steps, and each fair day
235   Rose clear and candid on their love. And I
Disowned, dishonoured in the whole creation
I fled the sun, I could not face the daylight,
Death was the only godhead I could pray;
Gall on my tongue, and tears my only drink;
240   Happy, if any privacy of grief
Had left me this one pitiable solace,
To taste a last precarious luxury;
But the forced travesty of a smiling face
Deprived me even of the right to weep.
245   OENONE: They reap no harvest of their vain desires:
They'll meet no more.
PHAEDRA: They'll love for evermore.
Now as I speak—the poison of the thought!—
Mocking the fury of a rival wronged,
Forgetful of the exile that divides them,
250   They swear a thousand times never to part.
No, I will not yield to the insult of their joy,
Oenone. Help me, pity my jealousy.
Aricia must be crushed. I must stir up

My husband's wrath against that hated house—
No feeble sentence serves, the sister's crime   255
Is more than all her brothers'. I'll entreat him
In rage and jealousy.
                                        What am I doing?
Where is reason in my wandering mind? I, jealous?
I, entreat Theseus? He, my husband, lives
And still I love—and whom? Still yearn—for whom?   260
At every word each separate hair lifts up
Upon my head. My guilt has filled the measure—
I crave for incest, dream of calumny,
My murderous hands, avid for vengeance, burn
To bathe in the blood of innocence. Misery!   265
And dare I live, and dare I face the sight
Of that sacred Sun, the giver of my life,
I, grandchild of the high Father of the Gods,
My forbears crowding Heaven and all creation?
Where may I hide? Flee to the night of Hell?   270
No, no, not there; for there my father's hands
Inexorable lift the doomsday urn,
They say, and Minos stands in deathly justice
Over the pallid multitudes of men.
Will that great shade not start in ghastly anger   275
When I in shame before his awful gaze,
His daughter, plead my guilt, and deeds perhaps
Unheard in all the calendar of Hell?
Father, what will you say to these? I see
The tremendous urn roll thundering at your feet;   280
I see you ponder unknown penalties
To execute yourself upon your own…
Forgive. A cruel God detests your seed,
A heavenly vengeance breathed in me the frenzy
You see. Alas, and still of all the guilt   285
And all the shame that never will release me
My fearful heart has never reaped the sweets.
Pursued while yet I breathe by ceaseless evils
I wait to yield a bruised and broken life.
OENONE: My lady, come, dismiss a causeless terror, 290
Be more indulgent to a venial failing—
You love; but driven by a fatal charm.
It is not ours to challenge Destiny.
Was this a wonder never seen till now?
Were you the first that Love has overthrown?   295
Weakness was always part of man's inheritance;
So, mortal, bow to a mortal's destiny.
You struggle against an immemorial yoke:
Even the Gods that live in high Olympus
Whose judgements hold a guilty world in fear   300
Have loved, and sometimes loved against the law.
PHAEDRA: Still you dare speak? And this is your
        advice,
And till the end you mean to drug my mind?
I hate you. All your help has been my downfall.
You dragged me back to the unbearable sunshine;   305
Your prayers were louder than the voice of right;
The man that I had shunned, you made me see.
Was it your business? And now have all the lies

Of those false lips dared blacken such a life?
310　You may have killed him. His father's impious
　　　　vows
　　And blind revenge perhaps are gratified
　　Already. I'll hear no more. Leave me alone,
　　Loathly inhuman temptress; leave my sight,
　　Leave me alone to shape my bitter future.
315　On you I pray the justice of the Gods;
　　And may they make you the eternal warning
　　Of all cringing cunning sycophants that nourish
　　Their masters' dearest weakness, urge the way
　　Their cravings tend, and smooth the slope of
　　　　crime,
320　Accursed courtiers, deadliest gift of all
　　That angry Heaven inflicts upon a King!

[Exit PHAEDRA]

OENONE: O ye Gods! To have borne so much for her,
　　　　forgone
　　So much!—This is my pay. And it is just.

ACT V

[HIPPOLYTUS, ARICIA]

ARICIA: And in this extremity you will not speak
　　And will not undeceive a loving father?
　　Cruel, if you can disregard my tears
　　And lightly say good-bye to me for ever,
5　Then go, and leave Aricia with her grief;
　　But do not go in certainty of death.
　　Fight the foul imputation on your honour,
　　Constrain your father to unsay his curses.
　　There is time yet. What reason, or what folly
10　Makes you leave all the advantage to the accuser?
　　Tell Theseus what you know.
HIPPOLYTUS:　　　　　　　　Have I not told
　　What may be told? Would you have me reveal
　　To light the shameful mystery of his bed
　　Or by too scrupulous report bring down
15　Confusion on a father's honoured head?
　　Alone you know this horror. You, and the Gods,
　　Alone receive the outpourings of my heart.
　　See if I love you: I have shown to you
　　What I would fain have veiled from my own
　　　　thoughts.
20　But under what a seal, you know. Forget,
　　My lady, if you can, that I have spoken;
　　Let me believe this hideous affair
　　Will never be breathed between those blameless
　　　　lips.
　　We set our trust upon the righteous heavens.
25　My cause is theirs; and Phaedra, whether soon
　　Or in the slow procedure of their justice,
　　Will not elude disgrace. This deference

I ask of you; and all the rest I sweep
Before the liberty of my wrath. I bid you
No longer be a slave. I bid you dare　　　　　　30
To come with me, dare to be banned with me.
Break from a poisoned house where Virtue
　　breathes
A deathly and a desecrated air;
Turn into profit for a headlong flight
All the disorder following on my fall.　　　　　　35
The means I offer: you have still no guard
But my own men. Most powerful patrons wait
　　us—
Argos extends her arms, and Sparta welcomes;
Let common friends receive our just laments,
Otherwise Phaedra rakes our wreckage up,　　　　40
Evicts us both from a throne our fathers left us,
And strips us both for spoils to deck her son.
The moment beckons, grasp it. But what fear
Restrains you? What suspends your doubtful
　　mind?
Only for your sake have I dared so far.　　　　　45
When I am all on fire, why are you ice?
Are you unwilling to adventure on
An outlaw's path?
ARICIA:　　　　　　　Oh, but how happily,
　　My lord, I'd taste of exile so; how eagerly
　　Embrace a life forgotten of all beside　　　　50
　　And linked with yours! But lacking that sweet
　　　　bond
　　Can I in honour join your wanderings?
　　I know the sternest laws do not forbid me
　　To fly your father's power: he is not mine,
　　I owe him no obedience; and to fly　　　　　55
　　From an oppressor is the right of all.
　　But you, my lord, love me. And anxious honour…
HIPPOLYTUS: And can you think I rate that honour
　　　　cheaply?
　　No, no. I came with worthier designs—
　　Escape your foes, and follow as my bride.　　　60
　　Free in adversity, since Fate has freed us,
　　Our pledges need no words but ours, and Hymen
　　Robbed of his torchlit rites is Hymen still.
　　By Trozen's gates, among those sepulchres,
　　Antique memorials of my fathers' pride,　　　65
　　A wayside temple holy and renowned
　　Stands grim protector of the plighted word;
　　There falsehood dare not raise her voice, or falls
　　Blasted at once, and certitude of death
　　Lays chains invincible on perjury.　　　　　70
　　May we not there with solemn mutual oath
　　Give and receive our hearts' enduring faith
　　Before the shrine, and pray the Deity
　　For his protection and paternal love?
　　I will invoke each mighty God to hear me—　　75
　　Maiden Diana, Juno's majesty,
　　And every name whose present patronage
　　Shall seal and sanctify my true intent.

ARICIA: The King is here. Go, Prince, depart at once.
80   I shall remain awhile to hide my purpose.
     Away—but send me back a trusty servant
     To guide my footsteps safely to your side.

[Exit HIPPOLYTUS]

[Enter THESEUS]

THESEUS: Lighten the mists, ye Gods, and show my
       eyes
     The truth they seek for here!
ARICIA: Now, sweet Ismene,
85   See everything is done. Be ready quickly.

[Exit ISMÉNE]

THESEUS: You seem disturbed, your colour fails, my
       lady.
     What was Hippolytus doing in this place?
ARICIA: Taking an everlasting leave, my lord.
THESEUS: And so your eyes have tamed that rebel
       heart
90   And brought him to his earliest thoughts of love.
ARICIA: I must not hide the truth from you, my lord.
     You have not given him your unjust hatred;
     He did not treat me like a criminal.
THESEUS: You mean he vowed you everlasting pas-
       sion.
95   I should not build on that unsettled heart.
     He swore as deep to others!
ARICIA: He, my lord?
THESEUS: I wish you could have taught him constancy.
     How could you bear that loathsome competition?
ARICIA: And how can you bear loathsome calumnies
100   To blacken all the lustre of his fame?
     Have you so little knowledge of his nature?
     Can you not tell the guiltless from the guilty?
     Only your eyes are darkened by a cloud
     That lets his goodness gleam on all the world.
105   Oh stop, relent. He must not be the victim
     Of false accusers. Repent your murderous curses.
     Tremble, my lord, tremble, lest frowning Heaven
     Hate you enough to take you at your word—
     Gods may accept our offerings in anger
110   And punish with the presents we entreated.
THESEUS: No, blind as you are with ill-requited love
     You will not blind me to his villainy;
     For I have witnesses, beyond reproach,
     Beyond suspicion—I have seen tears flow,
115   Tears that were true.
ARICIA: Look to yourself, my lord:
     Your matchless weight of arm redeemed mankind
     From monsters past all counting—but not all,
     The breed is not destroyed, and you have saved
     One.... I must say no more; your son forbids me.
120   Knowing what deference his heart still holds
     I should increase his suffering too much

Dared I continue. Let me imitate
His generous scruple, and excuse myself
While nothing forces me to break my silence.

[Exit ARICIA]

THESEUS (*alone*): But what is in her mind? What lurks
       below   125
     A tale so often broached, and never told?
     Is it a stratagem without a meaning?
     Is it conspiracy to bind me on
     A rack of doubt? And secret in my heart
     Steeled to be cruel, what is the still voice   130
     That pleads for mercy, and unmans my wrath,
     Perplexes me and tears me?—I must see
     Her woman once again; I know too little.
     —Guard! Fetch Oenone, send her in alone.

[Enter PANOPE]

PANOPE: I cannot say what thoughts are in her
       bosom,   135
     But the distracted motions of the Queen
     Fill me with fear, my lord. Death and despair
     Are painted on her face, and the deathly tint
     Sits even now upon her cheeks. Already
     Pursued with scorn and chiding from her side,   140
     Oenone has plunged to death among the waves.
     None knows what wild will drove her, but the tide
     Has covered her for ever from our sight.
THESEUS: What have you said?
PANOPE: Her going gave no peace;
     Distraction gains in the Queen's divided soul: 145
     One moment, soothing her mysterious grief,
     She takes her children, bathes them in her tears;
     And suddenly, her motherhood dismissed,
     She drives them from her with a look of loathing.
     Her restless steps come and go purposeless   150
     And we are strangers in her fevered eyes.
     Thrice she has written, only to repent,
     And thrice destroyed the message uncompleted.
     My lord, be gracious: see her, comfort her.
THESEUS: Is it so? The one is dead, the other waits   155
     For death. Call for my son, let him plead his cause,
     Let him speak to me, and I will listen.—Neptune,
     Delay thy deadly gift, be not too sudden,
     Rather refuse it utterly. What if
     I was seduced too soon by worthless words?   160
     What if my cruel hands were raised too rashly?
     What wretchedness would follow from that vow!

[Enter THERAMENES. Exit PANOPE]

THESEUS: Is it you, Theramenes? Where is my son?
     What have you done with him? His careful tending
     Has been your charge from earliest infancy.   165
     But why the tears I see upon your cheeks?
     What of my son?

THERAMENES: O late, O vain regret,
    O useless love! The Prince's life is done.
THESEUS: Oh Gods!
THERAMENES: I saw him die, the best and sweetest
170   Of human kind—and, let me say, my lord,
    The purest also.
THESEUS: Is my son dead? Now,
    Now that these arms reached out for him, the Gods
    Impatient urged his execution on?
    How did I lose him? What immortal stroke… ?
175 THERAMENES: Still close behind us lay the gates of
          Trozen.
    He drove his chariot, his grieving guard
    Matching his silence, marched on either hand.
    Sunk in his thought, the loose reins lying free,
    He brought us on the causeway to Mycenae;
180   And the noble beasts, so eager once to leap
    At the least inflexion of a master's voice,
    Now bent dull eyes to earth and drooping crests
    As if communing with his bitter mood.
    —Suddenly from the sea an awful cry
185   Shattered the silence of the air. And then
    A second voice wailed answer from the landward.
    Our blood was frozen in our inmost hearts.
    Stiffly uprose the listening horses' manes.
    And now from the level deep immense there heaves
190   A boiling mount of brine, and still it swells,
    Bears wavelike foaming down on us and breaks
    To belch a ravening monster at our feet
    Whose threatening brow is broadened with huge
        horns,
    Whose body, cased in golden glint of scales,
195   Thrashes a train of sinuous writhing whorls.
    Indomitable bull, malignant dragon,
    Its long-drawn bellows rumble down the shore;
    Heaven quails, earth shudders at the portent, air
    Reeks with its pestilential breath. The wave
200   Withdraws again, aghast at what it bore.
    We fly to the nearby temple; not one lingers
    Or wraps himself in unavailing valour.
    Hippolytus, honouring his hero blood,
    Hippolytus alone checks, wheels his team,
205   Snatches the spears, charges upon the creature,
    Aims, and unerring flings. A gaping slash
    Fair in the monster's flank drives it in bounds
    Of pain and fury to the horses' feet
    To roar and wallow and gnash with flaming jaws
210   And spatter them with blood and cloud and fire.
    They plunge reckless aside. They hear no more,
    Answer no more to bridle or to voice.
    The charioteer spends all his strength in strivings
    While they redden the bits with spume that is
        bright with blood.
215   Even, men say, some more than mortal shape
    Borne on the horrible confusion plied
    Their dusty flanks with goads. Where terror leads
        them

Stand rocks. The axle screeches, snaps. The car
Crashes in fragments; and my fearless master
Drops tangled in the reins…—Forgive my
    weakness.   220
In that tormenting image lives a source
Of quenchless tears.—I watched, my lord, I
    watched
Your helpless son dragging behind the steeds
His hands had fed. He tries to call to them,
In vain: his cries startle them. So they gallop   225
And make one wound of all his living flesh.
Now as the plain is pealing with our grief
The violent fit is spent. They slacken speed,
And stop, where close at hand his fathers' tombs
And ancient sculptures hold the chill remains   230
And memories of Kings. I run, behind me
Run all his guard, reading the traces painted
By his gallant blood, past the empurpled crags,
Past dripping brambles hung about with spoils
Of bloody hair. I reach him, I speak; he gives me   235
A hand and greets me with a dying gaze
That quickly closes. And I hear these words:
'My guiltless days are forfeit to the Gods.
Do you after my death be watchful over
The sad Aricia; and, sweet friend, if ever   240
My father undeceived should come to mourn
The misadventure of a slandered son,
To lay in peace my blood and wailing shade
Bid him be gentle to the captive maid,
Render her—'On the word the lifeless youth   245
Fell back into my arms a ravaged corpse,
The dreadful triumph of an angry Heaven,
Where not a father's eye could undertake
To know his child.
THESEUS: O child! O dearest hope
    I cast away! Gods, ye unswerving Gods,   250
    Too faithfully ye served me! Now must life
    Henceforward be a death of long-drawn sorrow.
THERAMENES: And now in fear and haste Aricia,
    Stealing, my lord, from your capitivity
    To hear his nuptial vow before the Gods,   255
    Approached. There are the red and steaming
        grasses,
    And there—what welcome for a bride's regard!—
    The hero of her love, but motionless,
    Featureless, bloodless. First she seeks to question
    Her misery, and, seeing, still demands   260
    Hippolytus. Then, too pitifully assured,
    After one glance reproachful to the skies
    Cold, with one cry, lifeless upon the dead
    She falls. Ismene, weeping, is beside her
    And draws her back to life and life's despair;   265
    And I, still subject to the hostile daylight,
    Return to speak a hero's last desires
    And so fulfil the grievous ministry
    His dying heart committed to my love.
    —But here I see the deadliest of his foes.   270

[Enter PHAEDRA, PANOPE, and GUARDS]

THESEUS: Well, victory is yours: my son is gone.
    Much, much I could suspect; deep rankling doubt
    Acquits him in my heart and troubled mind—
    But he is dead: your sacrifice, my lady;
275   Take it, find satisfaction in the forfeit
    Unmerited or just. It matters little
    That evermore my eyes be blindfolded;
    Let him be criminal if you accuse.
    His loss alone is theme enough for sorrow,
280   No need to look for new and fearful knowledge
    That, impotent to bring the dead again,
    Could pile at most new suffering on the old.
    Let me escape, leave you and leave these shores,
    Flying the bloody image of a son
285   Mangled—before that harrying memory
    I could long for exile from the world of men.
    All things upbraid me, all increase my anguish—
    My very name (for nameless, I could hide),
    The very honours that the Gods bestowed,
290   Whose murderous grace I'll mourn, and not again
    Importune them with fruitless prayers of mine;
    Do what they might, their fatal condescension
    Could not console for what they took away.
PHAEDRA: Theseus, I have repented of my silence.
295   Your son requires his innocence from my lips;
    Yes, he was guiltless.
THESEUS: This to me, his father!
    And on your solemn faith I sentenced him.
    Can any pretext for that cruel act—
PHAEDRA: My time is measured. Listen to me,
    Theseus.
300   I, on your dutiful and temperate son,
    Looked with profaning and incestuous eyes—
    The flame of Heaven lighted in my bosom
    A fatal fire. Oenone did the rest;
    She feared Hippolytus, my passion known
305   Would publish all the madness that he loathed;
    Presuming on my feebleness, she came
    With that base story of my victim's guilt.
    Self-chosen, easy death among the waves
    Punished her perfidy and foiled my anger,
310   And by now the knife would have cleft my destiny,
    But goodness still cried out for vindication.
    I chose the slower path. I chose to pour
    Into your ears before I joined the dead
    The chronicle of my remorse. I have drained
315   And mingled with my burning blood a draught
    Medea left in Athens. Now already
    Her poison makes its progress toward my heart
    Striking that heart with cold it never knew;
    Faintly already I perceive the daylight
320   And you I wound by my unworthy presence;
    And death, blurring the sunbeams from these eyes
    Whose glance polluted them, restores the light
    To perfect purity.

PANOPE: My lord, she is dying.
THESEUS: And would the dark remembrance too
    might die
    Of what she has done! Come, all is now too plain.   325
    I must enfold what still remains to touch
    Of my dear son, and weeping expiate
    The blind curse I shall evermore bewail
    With dear-bought honours rendered at his tomb;
    And, better to placate his injured spirit,   330
    I will forget the voice of ancient vengeance
    And look upon his lover as my child.

WILLIAM CONGREVE (1670–1729)

William Congreve was born in England but grew up in Ireland, where his father commanded a garrison. He studied at Kilkenny School and at Trinity College, Dublin. Here he met Jonathan Swift; the two were to become influential figures in London literary circles later in their lives. Congreve returned to London to study law at the Middle Temple.

Congreve's first literary effort, the novel *Incognita or Love and Duty* (1691), impressed John Dryden, as did virtually all of Congreve's work. His first play, *The Old Bachelor* (1693), established his reputation as a playwright immediately. His second play, *The Double Dealer* (1693), though highly praised by Dryden, received only a lukewarm reception until Queen Mary requested a special performance. His next play, *Love for Love* (1695), was his most popular both in its own time and in twentieth-century London revivals. His one tragedy, *The Mourning Bride* (1697), though successful in its own time, has not been revived. Shortly after the production of the tragedy, Congreve wrote a rejoinder to Jeremy Collier's famous attack on the theater, titling it *Amendments of Mr. Collier's False and Imperfect Citations*. Congreve's seventh and last play, *The Way of the World*, appeared in 1700. The play did not meet with success when it first appeared, and Congreve retired from the stage, perhaps because he thought *The Way of the World* did not receive the critical acclaim it deserved. He may also have retired because of the Jeremy Collier controversy or for reasons of ill health. Congreve had suffered terribly from gout, and by 1710 he became blind. He spent the rest of his life in the company of the Duchess of Marlborough (to whom he left £10,000 on his death) and continued to write poetry and libretti for several operas. In his own time as well as in succeeding centuries, Congreve's plays were considered the best examples of late-seventeenth-century English comedy. *The Way of the World* is now generally regarded as his masterpiece.

The Way of the World

The Way of the World is a comedy of manners. In it Congreve makes use of stock characters whose names often indicate their chief traits. These characters exhibit the behavior and values of their various types, but Congreve was especially adept at pushing his characters beyond the limits of stock types, primarily with witty dialogue. Conversation in Congreve's plays shows an extraordinary intelligence and sensitivity to language. His main characters display true wit—the quality of quick minds that allows them to make sharp juxtapositions and illuminating turns of ideas and phrases. *The Way of the World*, like other plays of the period, was written for a sophisticated theater audience that appreciated and valued such dazzling displays. But the technique has a larger function for Congreve, who uses implication and irony to develop a critical and satirical view of his characters and of society.

Characteristic of Congreve—and representative of the values of the audience—are the central plot issues of the play: inheritance, marriage, and adultery. Mrs. Millamant, the female protagonist, has inherited £6,000 and will inherit another £6,000 if she marries in accordance with the wishes of her aunt, Lady Wishfort. Mirabell, the male protagonist—a rake with a long series of sexual conquests—wishes to marry Mrs. Millamant. Lady Wishfort, one of his former conquests, feels that she has merely been used by him to get close to Mrs. Millamant. Lady Wishfort favors the suit of Sir Wilfull Witwoud, whose name indicates the level of his intelligence. The disguise, deceptions, and misunderstandings that occupy much of the plot result from Mirabell's attempt to change Lady Wishfort's mind about his suit. Like Beatrice and Benedick in Shakespeare's *Much Ado About Nothing*, Mirabell and Mrs. Millamant derive much of their charm from their engaging battles of wit. Mirabell is a calculating manipulator, but he is not finally vicious. While he appreciates her money, he also respects Mrs. Millamant. Mrs. Millamant, who is not attracted to the idea of becoming a subservient wife, manages to negotiate a marriage contract with Mirabell which guarantees her independence. She is every bit a match for him.

As the play's epilogue makes clear, Congreve intended the play to be a satire of manners, and he uses the complicated relationships among the characters to point up the foibles of this callous and self-seeking society. The case of Lady Wishfort's daughter makes the point: formerly married to Mr. Languish (now dead), she is married to the cad Fainall. But before marrying Fainall, she was Mirabell's mistress, and she married Fainall only because she thought she was pregnant. The marriage, arranged by Mrs. Mirabell, was acceptable to all— to her for the sake of respectability, to Fainall for her money, and to Mirabell for his freedom. As it turns out, Mrs. Fainall was not pregnant after all, and she now regrets her marriage. Fainall, meantime, is having an affair with Mrs. Marwood. When he discovers that she is attracted to Mirabell, Fainall is no longer interested in Mrs. Marwood. However, because she could expose him as an adulterer to his wife, he continues his relationship with her. Fainall is the villain of the play because he wants to control Mrs. Millamant's fortune for his own purposes, but as Congreve makes clear, Fainall is not much different from the rest of the characters in this play, all of whom are self-seeking.

The play does not end happily for everyone, but deceptions are exposed, complications are unraveled, and Mirabell and Mrs. Millamant look forward to marriage and the future. Other less witty characters remain caught in the web of their own deceit. There is no clear good here, no clear bad, only better and worse. It is Congreve's view of the way of the world.

The Way of the World

WILLIAM CONGREVE

EDITED BY LOUIS KRONENBERGER

CHARACTERS

FAINALL, in love with MRS. MARWOOD
MIRABELL, in love with MRS. MILLAMANT
WITWOUD, } Followers of MRS. MILLAMANT
PETULANT,
SIR WILFULL WITWOUD, Half brother to WITWOUD, and
  Nephew to LADY WISHFORT
WAITWELL, Servant to MIRABELL
LADY WISHFORT, Enemy to MIRABELL, for having
  falsely pretended love to her
MRS. MILLAMANT, a fine Lady, Niece to LADY
  WISHFORT, and loves MIRABELL

MRS. MARWOOD, Friend to MR. FAINALL, and likes
  MIRABELL
MRS. FAINALL, Daughter to LADY WISHFORT, and Wife
  to FAINALL, formerly Friend to MIRABELL
FOIBLE, Woman to LADY WISHFORT
MINCING, Woman to MRS. MILLAMANT
BETTY, Waiting-maid at a Chocolate-house
PEG, Maid to LADY WISHFORT
COACHMEN, DANCERS, FOOTMEN, and ATTENDANTS

THE SCENE: London

PROLOGUE

Of those few fools who with ill stars are curst,
Sure scribbling fools, called poets, fare the worst:
For they're a sort of fools which Fortune makes,
And after she has made 'em fools, forsakes.
5   With Nature's oafs 'tis quite a different case,
For Fortune favours all her idiot-race.
In her own nest the cuckoo-eggs we find,
O'er which she broods to hatch the changeling-kind.
No portion for her own she has to spare,
10   So much she dotes on her adopted care.
Poets are bubbles, by the town drawn in,
Suffered at first some trifling stakes to win;
But what unequal hazards do they run!
Each time they write they venture all they've won:
15   The squire that's buttered° still, is sure to be undone.
This author heretofore has found your favour;
But pleads no merit from his past behaviour.
To build on that might prove a vain presumption,
Should grants, to poets made, admit resumption:
20   And in Parnassus he must lose his seat.
If that be found a forfeited estate.
He owns with toil he wrought the following scenes;
But, if they're naught, ne'er spare him for his pains:
Damn him the more; have no commiseration
25   For dulness on mature deliberation,
He swears he'll not resent one hissed-off scene,
Nor, like those peevish wits, his play maintain,
Who, to assert their sense, your taste arraign.
Some plot we think he has, and some new
  thought;

Some humour too, no farce; but that's a fault.   30
Satire, he thinks, you ought not to expect;
For so reformed a town who dares correct?
To please, this time, has been his sole pretence,
He'll not instruct, lest it should give offence.
Should he by chance a knave or fool expose,   35
That hurts none here, sure here are none of those:
In short, our play shall (with your leave to show it)
Give you one instance of a passive poet,
Who to your judgments yields all resignation;
So save or damn, after your own discretion.   40

ACT I

Scene 1

A Chocolate House

[MIRABELL and FAINALL, *rising from cards,* BETTY
waiting]

MIRABELL: You are a fortunate man, Mr. Fainall!
FAINALL: Have we done?
MIRABELL: What you please: I'll play on to entertain
  you.
FAINALL: No, I'll give you your revenge another time,   5
  when you are not so indifferent; you are thinking of something else now, and play too negli-
  gently; the coldness of a losing gamester lessens
  the pleasure of the winner. I'd no more play
  with a man that slighted his ill fortune than I'd   10
  make love to a woman who undervalued the
  loss of her reputation.

---

¹⁵ **buttered** flattered

MIRABELL: You have a taste extremely delicate, and are for refining on your pleasures.

15 FAINALL: Prithee, why so reserved? Something has put you out of humour.

MIRABELL: Not at all: I happen to be grave to day, and you are gay; that's all.

FAINALL: Confess, Millamant and you quarrelled last

20 night after I left you; my fair cousin has some humours that would tempt the patience of a Stoic. What, some coxcomb came in, and was well received by her, while you were by?

MIRABELL: Witwoud and Petulant; and what was

25 worse, her aunt, your wife's mother, my evil genius: or to sum up all in her own name, my old Lady Wishfort came in.

FAINALL: O there it is then! She has a lasting passion for you, and with reason.—What, then my wife

30 was there?

MIRABELL: Yes, and Mrs. Marwood, and three or four more, whom I never saw before. Seeing me, they all put on their grave faces, whispered one another; then complained aloud of the vapours,

35 and after fell into a profound silence.

FAINALL: They had a mind to be rid of you.

MIRABELL: For which reason I resolved not to stir. At last the good old lady broke through her painful taciturnity with an invective against

40 long visits. I would not have understood her, but Millamant joining in the argument, I rose, and, with a constrained smile, told her, I thought nothing was so easy as to know when a visit began to be troublesome. She reddened,

45 and I withdrew, without expecting her reply.

FAINALL: You were to blame to resent what she spoke only in compliance with her aunt.

MIRABELL: She is more mistress of herself than to be under the necessity of such a resignation.

50 FAINALL: What! though half her fortune depends upon her marrying with my lady's approbation?

MIRABELL: I was then in such a humour, that I should have been better pleased if she had been less

55 discreet.

FAINALL: Now, I remember, I wonder not they were weary of you; last night was one of their cabal nights; they have 'em three times a-week, and meet by turns at one another's apartments,

60 where they come together like the coroner's inquest, to sit upon the murdered reputations of the week. You and I are excluded; and it was once proposed that all the male sex should be excepted; but somebody moved that, to avoid

65 scandal, there might be one man of the community; upon which motion Witwoud and Petulant were enrolled members.

MIRABELL: And who may have been the foundress of this sect? My Lady Wishfort, I warrant, who

publishes her detestation of mankind; and full 70 of the vigour of fifty-five, declares for a friend and ratafia° and let posterity shift for itself, she'll breed no more.

FAINALL: The discovery of your sham addresses to her, to conceal your love to her niece, has provoked 75 this separation; had you dissembled better, things might have continued in the state of nature.

MIRABELL: I did as much as man could, with any reasonable conscience; I proceeded to the very last 80 act of flattery with her, and was guilty of a song in her commendation. Nay, I got a friend to put her into a lampoon, and compliment her with the imputation of an affair with a young fellow, which I carried so far, that I told her the mali- 85 cious town took notice that she was grown fat of a sudden; and when she lay in of a dropsy, persuaded her she was reported to be in labour. The devil's in't, if an old woman is to be flattered further, unless a man should endeavour 90 downright personally to debauch her; and that my virtue forbade me. But for the discovery of this amour I am indebted to your friend, or your wife's friend, Mrs. Marwood.

FAINALL: What should provoke her to be your enemy, 95 unless she has made you advances which you have slighted? Women do not easily forgive omissions of that nature.

MIRABELL: She was always civil to me till of late.—I confess I am not one of those coxcombs who are 100 apt to interpret a woman's good manners to her prejudice, and think that she who does not refuse 'em everything, can refuse 'em nothing.

FAINALL: You are a gallant man, Mirabell; and though you may have cruelty enough not to satisfy a 105 lady's longing, you have too much generosity not to be tender of her honour. Yet you speak with an indifference which seems to be affected, and confesses you are conscious of a negligence. 110

MIRABELL: You pursue the argument with a distrust that seems to be unaffected, and confesses you are conscious of a concern for which the lady is more indebted to you than is your wife.

FAINALL: Fy, fy, friend! if you grow censorious I must 115 leave you.—I'll look upon the gamesters in the next room.

MIRABELL: Who are they?

FAINALL: Petulant and Witwoud.—[*To* Betty] Bring me some chocolate. 120

[Exit]

---

⁷² **ratafia** fruit-flavored brandy

MIRABELL: Betty, what says your clock?
BETTY: Turned of the last canonical hour,° sir.

[Exit]

125 MIRABELL: How pertinently the jade answers me!—[*Looking at his watch*]—Ha! almost one o'clock!—O, y'are come!

[Enter FOOTMAN]

Well, is the grand affair over? You have been something tedious.
FOOTMAN: Sir, there's such coupling at Pancras,° that they stand behind one another, as 'twere in a
130 country dance. Ours was the last couple to lead up; and no hopes appearing of despatch: besides, the parson growing hoarse, we were afraid his lungs would have failed before it came to our turn; so we drove round to Duke's-
135 place;° and there they were rivetted in a trice.°
MIRABELL: So, so, you are sure they are married.
FOOTMAN: Married and bedded, sir; I am witness.
MIRABELL: Have you the certificate?
FOOTMAN: Here it is, sir.
140 MIRABELL: Has the tailor brought Waitwell's clothes home, and the new liveries?
FOOTMAN: Yes, sir.
MIRABELL: That's well. Do you go home again, d'ye hear, and adjourn the consummation till further
145 orders. Bid Waitwell shake his ears, and Dame Partlet° rustle up her feathers, and meet me at one o'clock by Rosamond's Pond,° that I may see her before she returns to her lady; and as you tender your ears be secret.

[Exeunt]

Scene 2

The same

MIRABELL, FAINALL, and BETTY

FAINALL: Joy of your success, Mirabell; you look pleased.
MIRABELL: Ay; I have been engaged in a matter of some sort of mirth, which is not yet ripe for dis-

covery. I am glad this is not a cabal night. I won- 5
der, Fainall, that you who are married, and of consequence should be discreet, will suffer your wife to be of such a party.
FAINALL: Faith, I am not jealous. Besides, most who are engaged are women and relations; and for 10 the men, they are of a kind too contemptible to give scandal.
MIRABELL: I am of another opinion. The greater the coxcomb, always the more the scandal: for a woman, who is not a fool, can have but one rea- 15 son for associating with a man who is one.
FAINALL: Are you jealous as often as you see Witwoud entertained by Millamant?
MIRABELL: Of her understanding I am, if not of her person. 20
FAINALL: You do her wrong; for, to give her her due, she has wit.
MIRABELL: She has beauty enough to make any man think so; and complaisance enough not to contradict him who shall tell her so. 25
FAINALL: For a passionate lover, methinks you are a man somewhat too discerning in the failings of your mistress.
MIRABELL: And for a discerning man, somewhat too passionate a lover; for I like her with all her 30 faults; nay, like her for her faults. Her follies are so natural, or so artful, that they become her; and those affectations which in another woman would be odious, serve but to make her more agreeable. I'll tell thee, Fainall, she once used 35 me with that insolence, that in revenge I took her to pieces; sifted° her, and separated her failings; I studied 'em, and got 'em by rote. The catalogue was so large, that I was not without hopes one day or other to hate her heartily: to 40 which end I so used myself to think of 'em, that at length, contrary to my design and expectation, they gave me every hour less and less disturbance; till in a few days it became habitual to me to remember 'em without being displeased. 45 They are now grown as familiar to me as my own frailties; and in all probability, in a little time longer, I shall like 'em as well.
FAINALL: Marry her, marry her! be half as well acquainted with her charms, as you are with 50 her defects, and my life on't, you are your own man again.
MIRABELL: Say you so?
FAINALL: Ay, ay, I have experience: I have a wife, and so forth. 55

[Enter MESSENGER]

---

¹²² **last canonical hour** noon; during the canonical hours, 8 A.M. until noon, marriages could legally be performed
¹²⁸ **Pancras** St. Pancras Church and St. James in Duke's Place were two of several places where marriages were performed without special license or publication of banns   ¹³⁵ **Duke's-place** See previous note.   ⁶ **rivetted in a trice** married quickly   ¹⁴⁶ **Dame Partlet** the hen in Chaucer's "Nun's Priest's Tale"   ¹⁴⁷ **Rosamond's Pond** in St. James's Park

³⁷ **sifted** questioned

MESSENGER: Is one Squire Witwoud here?

BETTY: Yes, what's your business?

MESSENGER: I have a letter for him, from his brother Sir Wilfull, which I am charged to deliver into his own hands.

BETTY: He's in the next room, friend—that way.

[Exit MESSENGER]

MIRABELL: What, is the chief of that noble family in town, Sir Wilfull Witwoud?

FAINALL: He is expected to-day. Do you know him?

MIRABELL: I have seen him. He promises to be an extraordinary person; I think you have the honour to be related to him.

FAINALL: Yes; he is half brother to this Witwoud by a former wife, who was sister to my Lady Wishfort, my wife's mother. If you marry Millamant, you must call cousins too.

MIRABELL: I had rather be his relation than his acquaintance.

FAINALL: He comes to town in order to equip himself for travel.

MIRABELL: For travel! why, the man that I mean is above forty.

FAINALL: No matter for that; 'tis for the honour of England, that all Europe should know we have blockheads of all ages.

MIRABELL: I wonder there is not an act of parliament to save the credit of the nation, and prohibit the exportation of fools.

FAINALL: By no means; 'tis better as 'tis. 'Tis better to trade with a little loss, than to be quite eaten up with being overstocked.

MIRABELL: Pray, are the follies of this knight-errant, and those of the squire his brother, anything related?

FAINALL: Not at all; Witwoud grows by the knight, like a medlar grafted on a crab.° One will melt in your mouth, and t'other set your teeth on edge; one is all pulp, and the other all core.

MIRABELL: So one will be rotten before he be ripe, and the other will be rotten without ever being ripe at all.

FAINALL: Sir Wilfull is an odd mixture of bashfulness and obstinacy.—But when he's drunk he's as loving as the monster in the Tempest,° and much after the same manner. To give t'other his due, he has something of good-nature, and does not always want wit.

MIRABELL: Not always: but as often as his memory fails him, and his common-place of comparisons. He is a fool with a good memory, and some few scraps of other folks' wit. He is one whose conversation can never be approved, yet it is now and then to be endured. He has indeed one good quality, he is not exceptious; for he so passionately affects the reputation of understanding raillery, that he will construe an affront into a jest; and call downright rudeness and ill language, satire and fire.

FAINALL: If you have a mind to finish his picture, you have an opportunity to do it at full length. Behold the original!

[Enter WITWOUD]

WITWOUD: Afford me your compassion, my dears! pity me, Fainall! Mirabell, pity me!

MIRABELL: I do from my soul.

FAINALL: Why, what's the matter?

WITWOUD: No letters for me, Betty?

BETTY: Did not a messenger bring you one but now, sir?

WITWOUD: Ay, but no other?

BETTY: No, sir.

WITWOUD: That's hard, that's very hard.—A messenger! a mule, a beast of burden! he has brought me a letter from the fool my brother, as heavy as a panegyric in a funeral sermon, or a copy of commendatory verses from one poet to another: and what's worse, 'tis as sure a forerunner of the author, as an epistle dedicatory.

MIRABELL: A fool, and your brother, Witwoud!

WITWOUD: Ay, ay, my half brother. My half brother he is, no nearer upon honour.

MIRABELL: Then 'tis possible he may be but half a fool.

WITWOUD: Good, good, Mirabell, *le drôle!°* good, good; hang him, don't let's talk of him.—Fainall, how does your lady? Gad, I say anything in the world to get this fellow out of my head. I beg pardon that I should ask a man of pleasure, and the town, a question at once so foreign and domestic. But I talk like an old maid at a marriage; I don't know what I say: but she's the best woman in the world.

FAINALL: 'Tis well you don't know what you say, or else your commendation would go near to make me either vain or jealous.

WITWOUD: No man in town lives well with a wife but Fainall.—Your judgment, Mirabell.

MIRABELL: You had better step and ask his wife, if you would be credibly informed.

WITWOUD: Mirabell?

MIRABELL: Ay.

---

¹¹¹ **medlar grafted on a crab** The medlar is a fruit eaten when soft and sweet; the crab apple is sour and hard.   ¹¹⁹ **monster in the Tempest** Caliban from the 1667 version of Shakespeare's play *The Tempest* by John Dryden and William Davenant

---

¹⁵⁶ *le drôle* witty individual

WITWOUD: My dear, I ask ten thousand pardons;—gad,
175   I have forgot what I was going to say to you!
MIRABELL: I thank you heartily, heartily.
WITWOUD: No, but prithee excuse me:—my memory is
    such a memory.
MIRABELL: Have a care of such apologies, Witwoud;
180   for I never knew a fool but he affected to com-
    plain, either of the spleen or his memory.
FAINALL: What have you done with Petulant?
WITWOUD: He's reckoning his money—my money it
    was.—I have no luck to-day.
185 FAINALL: You may allow him to win of you at play: for
    you are sure to be too hard for him at repartee;
    since you monopolise the wit that is between
    you, the fortune must be his of course.
MIRABELL: I don't find that Petulant confesses the
190   superiority of wit to be your talent, Witwoud.
WITWOUD: Come, come, you are malicious now, and
    would breed debates.—Petulant's my friend,
    and a very honest fellow, and a very pretty fel-
    low, and has a smattering—faith and troth, a
195   pretty deal of an odd sort of a small wit: nay, I'll
    do him justice. I'm his friend, I won't wrong
    him neither.—And if he had any judgment in
    the world, he would not be altogether con-
    temptible. Come, come, don't detract from the
200   merits of my friend.
FAINALL: You don't take your friend to be over-nicely
    bred?
WITWOUD: No, no, hang him, the rogue has no man-
    ners at all, that I must own:—no more breeding
205   than a bum-bailiff,° that I grant you:—'tis pity,
    faith; the fellow has fire and life.
MIRABELL: What, courage?
WITWOUD: Hum, faith I don't know as to that, I can't
    say as to that—Yes, faith, in a controversy, he'll
210   contradict anybody.
MIRABELL: Though 'twere a man whom he feared, or a
    woman whom he loved.
WITWOUD: Well, well, he does not always think before
    he speaks;—we have all our failings: you are too
215   hard upon him, you are, faith. Let me excuse
    him—I can defend most of his faults, except one
    or two: one he has, that's the truth on't; if he were
    my brother, I could not acquit him:—that, indeed,
    I could wish were otherwise.
220 MIRABELL: Ay, marry, what's that, Witwoud?
WITWOUD: O pardon me!—expose the infirmities of
    my friend!—No, my dear, excuse me there.
FAINALL: What, I warrant he's unsincere, or 'tis some
    such trifle.
225 WITWOUD: No, no; what if he be? 'tis no matter for
    that, his wit will excuse that: a wit should no

more be sincere, than a woman constant; one
    argues a decay of parts, as t'other of beauty.
MIRABELL: Maybe you think him too positive?
WITWOUD: No, no, his being positive is an incentive to 230
    argument, and keeps up conversation.
FAINALL: Too illiterate?
WITWOUD: That! that's his happiness:—his want of
    learning gives him the more opportunities to
    show his natural parts. 235
MIRABELL: He wants words?
WITWOUD: Ay: but I like him for that now; for his want
    of words gives me the pleasure very often to
    explain his meaning.
FAINALL: He's impudent? 240
WITWOUD: No, that's not it.
MIRABELL: Vain?
WITWOUD: No.
MIRABELL: What! he speaks unseasonable truths some-
    times, because he has not wit enough to invent 245
    an evasion?
WITWOUD: Truths! ha! ha! ha! no, no; since you will
    have it,—I mean, he never speaks truth at all,—
    that's all. He will lie like a chambermaid, or a
    woman of quality's porter. Now that is a fault. 250

[Enter COACHMAN]

COACHMAN: Is Master Petulant here, mistress?
BETTY: Yes.
COACHMAN: Three gentlewomen in a coach would
    speak with him.
FAINALL: O brave Petulant! three! 255
BETTY: I'll tell him.
COACHMAN: You must bring two dishes of chocolate
    and a glass of cinnamon-water.

[Exeunt BETTY and COACHMAN]

WITWOUD: That should be for two fasting strumpets,
    and a bawd troubled with the wind. Now you 260
    may know what the three are.
MIRABELL: You are very free with your friend's
    acquaintance.
WITWOUD: Ay, ay, friendship without freedom is as
    dull as love without enjoyment, or wine with- 265
    out toasting. But to tell you a secret, these are
    trulls whom he allows coach-hire, and some-
    thing more, by the week, to call on him once a-
    day at public places.
MIRABELL: How! 270
WITWOUD: You shall see he won't go to 'em, because
    there's no more company here to take notice of
    him.—Why this is nothing to what he used to
    do:—before he found out this way, I have
    known him call for himself. 275
FAINALL: Call for himself! what dost thou mean?
WITWOUD: Mean! why he would slip you out of this
    chocolate-house, just when you had been talk-

---

²⁰⁵ **bum-bailiff** minor court officer

280   ing to him—as soon as your back was turned—whip he was gone!—then trip to his lodging, clap on a hood and scarf, and a mask, slap into a hackney-coach, and drive hither to the door again in a trice, where he would send in for himself; that I mean, call for himself, wait for

285   himself; nay, and what's more, not finding himself, sometimes leave a letter for himself.

MIRABELL: I confess this is something extraordinary.—I believe he waits for himself now, he is so long a-coming: Oh! I ask his pardon.

[Enter PETULANT and BETTY]

290   BETTY: Sir, the coach stays.

PETULANT: Well, well;—I come.—'Sbud,° a man had as good be a professed midwife, as a professed whoremaster, at this rate! to be knocked up and raised at all hours, and in all places. Pox

295   on 'em, I won't come!—D'ye hear, tell 'em I won't come:—let 'em snivel and cry their hearts out.

FAINALL: You are very cruel, Petulant.

PETULANT: All's one, let it pass:—I have a humour to

300   be cruel.

MIRABELL: I hope they are not persons of condition that you use at this rate.

PETULANT: Condition! condition's a dried fig, if I am not in humour!—By this hand, if they were

305   your—a—a—your what d'ye-call-'ems themselves, they must wait or rub off,° if I want appetite.

MIRABELL: What d'ye-call-'ems! what are they, Witwoud?

310   WITWOUD: Empresses, my dear:—by your what-d'ye-call-'ems he means sultana queens.

PETULANT: Ay, Roxolanas.°

MIRABELL: Cry you mercy!

FAINALL: Witwoud says they are—

315   PETULANT: What does he say th'are?

WITWOUD: I? fine ladies, I say.

PETULANT: Pass on, Witwoud.—Hark'ee, by this light his relations:—two co-heiresses his cousins, and an old aunt, who loves caterwauling better than

320   a conventicle.

WITWOUD: Ha! ha! ha! I had a mind to see how the rogue would come off.—Ha! ha! ha! gad, I can't be angry with him, if he had said they were my mother and my sisters.

325   MIRABELL: No!

WITWOUD: No; the rogue's wit and readiness of invention charm me. Dear Petulant.

---

291 **'Sbud** contraction for "by God's body"   306 **rub off** go away   312 **Roxolanas** Roxolana is the wife of the Sultan in Davenant's *The Siege of Rhodes*

BETTY: They are gone, sir, in great anger.

PETULANT: Enough, let 'em trundle. Anger helps complexion, saves paint.   330

FAINALL: This continence is all dissembled; this is in order to have something to brag of the next time he makes court to Millamant, and swear he has abandoned the whole sex for her sake.

MIRABELL: Have you not left off your impudent pretensions there yet? I shall cut your throat some time or other, Petulant, about that business.   335

PETULANT: Ay, ay, let that pass—there are other throats to be cut.

MIRABELL: Meaning mine, sir?   340

PETULANT: Not I—I mean nobody—I know nothing:—but there are uncles and nephews in the world—and they may be rivals—what then! all's one for that.

MIRABELL: How! hark'ee, Petulant, come hither:—explain, or I shall call your interpreter.   345

PETULANT: Explain! I know nothing.—Why, you have an uncle, have you not, lately come to town, and lodges by my Lady Wishfort's?

MIRABELL: True.   350

PETULANT: Why, that's enough—you and he are not friends; and if he should marry and have a child, you may be disinherited, ha?

MIRABELL: Where hast thou stumbled upon all this truth?   355

PETULANT: All's one for that; why then say I know something.

MIRABELL: Come, thou art an honest fellow, Petulant, and shalt make love to my mistress, thou sha't, faith. What hast thou heard of my uncle?   360

PETULANT: I? nothing I. If throats are to be cut, let swords clash! snug's the word, I shrug and am silent.

MIRABELL: Oh, raillery, raillery! Come, I know thou art in the women's secrets.—What, you're a cabalist; I know you stayed at Millamant's last night, after I went. Was there any mention made of my uncle or me? tell me. If thou hadst but good-nature equal to thy wit, Petulant, Tony Witwoud, who is now thy competitor in fame,   370 would show as dim by thee as a dead whiting's eye by a pearl of orient; he would no more be seen by thee, than Mercury is by the sun. Come, I'm sure thou wo't tell me.   365

PETULANT: If I do, will you grant me common sense   375 then for the future?

MIRABELL: Faith, I'll do what I can for thee, and I'll pray that Heaven may grant it thee in the meantime.

PETULANT: Well, hark'ee.

[MIRABELL and PETULANT talk apart]

FAINALL: Petulant and you both will find Mirabell as   380 warm a rival as a lover.

WITWOUD: Pshaw! pshaw! that she laughs at Petulant is plain. And for my part, but that it is almost a fashion to admire her, I should—hark'ee—to
385 tell you a secret, but let it go no further—between friends, I shall never break my heart for her.

FAINALL: How!

WITWOUD: She's handsome; but she's a sort of an
390 uncertain woman.

FAINALL: I thought you had died for her.

WITWOUD: Umh—no—

FAINALL: She has wit.

WITWOUD: 'Tis what she will hardly allow anybody
395 else:—now, demme, I should hate that, if she were as handsome as Cleopatra. Mirabell is not so sure of her as he thinks for.

FAINALL: Why do you think so?

WITWOUD: We stayed pretty late there last night, and
400 heard something of an uncle to Mirabell, who is lately come to town—and is between him and the best part of his estate. Mirabell and he are at some distance, as my Lady Wishfort has been told; and you know she hates Mirabell worse
405 than a quaker hates a parrot, or than a fishmonger hates a hard frost. Whether this uncle has seen Mrs. Millamant or not, I cannot say, but there were items of such a treaty being in embryo; and if it should come to life, poor
410 Mirabell would be in some sort unfortunately fobbed, i'faith.

FAINALL: 'Tis impossible Millamant should hearken to it.

WITWOUD: Faith, my dear, I can't tell; she's a woman,
415 and a kind of humourist.

MIRABELL: And this is the sum of what you could collect last night?

PETULANT: The quintessence. Maybe Witwoud knows more, he staid longer:—besides, they never
420 mind him; they say anything before him.

MIRABELL: I thought you had been the greatest favourite.

PETULANT: Ay, *tête-à-tête*, but not in public, because I make remarks.

425 MIRABELL: You do?

PETULANT: Ay, ay; pox, I'm malicious, man! Now he's soft you know; they are not in awe of him—the fellow's well-bred; he's what you call a—what-d'ye-call-'em, a fine gentleman; but he's silly
430 withal.

MIRABELL: I thank you, I know as much as my curiosity requires.—Fainall, are you for the Mall?°

FAINALL: Ay, I'll take a turn before dinner.

WITWOUD: Ay, we'll all walk in the Park; the ladies
435 talked of being there.

---

432 **Mall** in St. James Park

MIRABELL: I thought you were obliged to watch for your brother Sir Wilfull's arrival.

WITWOUD: No, no; he comes to his aunt's, my Lady Wishfort. Pox on him! I shall be troubled with him too; what shall I do with the fool?   440

PETULANT: Beg him for his estate, that I may beg you afterwards: and so have but one trouble with you both.

WITWOUD: O rare Petulant! thou art as quick as fire in a frosty morning; thou shalt to the Mall with us,   445
and we'll be very severe.

PETULANT: Enough, I'm in a humour to be severe.

MIRABELL: Are you? pray then walk by yourselves: let not us be accessory to your putting the ladies out of countenance with your senseless rib-   450
aldry, which you roar out aloud as often as they pass by you; and when you have made a handsome woman blush, then you think you have been severe.

PETULANT: What, what! then let 'em either show their   455
innocence by not understanding what they hear, or else show their discretion by not hearing what they would not be thought to understand.

MIRABELL: But hast not thou then sense enough to   460
know that thou oughtest to be most ashamed thyself, when thou hast put another out of countenance?

PETULANT: Not I, by this hand!—I always take blushing either for a sign of guilt, or ill-breeding.   465

MIRABELL: I confess you ought to think so. You are in the right, that you may plead the error of your judgment in defence of your practice.
Where modesty's ill-manners, 'tis but fit
That impudence and malice pass for wit.   470

[Exeunt]

ACT II

Scene 1

St. James's Park

MRS. FAINALL *and* MRS. MARWOOD

MRS. FAINALL: Ay, ay, dear Marwood, if we will be happy, we must find the means in ourselves, and among ourselves. Men are ever in extremes; either doating or averse. While they are lovers, if they have fire and sense, their jeal-   5
ousies are insupportable; and when they cease to love (we ought to think at least) they loathe; they look upon us with horror and distaste; they meet us like the ghosts of what we were,

10 and as such, fly from us.

MRS. MARWOOD: True, 'tis an unhappy circumstance of life, that love should ever die before us; and that the man so often should outlive the lover. But say what you will, 'tis better to be left, than

15 never to have been loved. To pass our youth in dull indifference, to refuse the sweets of life because they once must leave us, is as preposterous as to wish to have been born old, because we one day must be old. For my part, my youth

20 may wear and waste, but it shall never rust in my possession.

MRS. FAINALL: Then it seems you dissemble an aversion to mankind, only in compliance to my mother's humour?

25 MRS. MARWOOD: Certainly. To be free; I have no taste of those insipid dry discourses, with which our sex of force must entertain themselves, apart from men. We may affect endearments to each other, profess eternal friendships, and seem to

30 doat like lovers; but 'tis not in our natures long to persevere. Love will resume his empire in our breasts; and every heart, or soon or late, receive and readmit him as its lawful tyrant.

MRS. FAINALL: Bless me, how have I been deceived!

35 why you profess a libertine.

MRS. MARWOOD: You see my friendship by my freedom. Come, be as sincere, acknowledge that your sentiments agree with mine.

MRS. FAINALL: Never!

40 MRS. MARWOOD: You hate mankind?

MRS. FAINALL: Heartily, inveterately.

MRS. MARWOOD: Your husband?

MRS. FAINALL: Most transcendently; ay, though I say it, meritoriously.

45 MRS. MARWOOD: Give me your hand upon it.

MRS. FAINALL: There.

MRS. MARWOOD: I join with you; what I have said has been to try you.

MRS. FAINALL: Is it possible? dost thou hate those

50 vipers, men?

MRS. MARWOOD: I have done hating 'em, and am now come to despise 'em; the next thing I have to do, is eternally to forget 'em.

MRS. FAINALL: There spoke the spirit of an Amazon, a

55 Penthesilea!°

MRS. MARWOOD: And yet I am thinking sometimes to carry my aversion further.

MRS. FAINALL: How?

MRS. MARWOOD: Faith, by marrying; if I could but find

60 one that loved me very well, and would be thoroughly sensible of ill usage, I think I should

do myself the violence of undergoing the ceremony.

MRS. FAINALL: You would not make him a cuckold?

MRS. MARWOOD: No; but I'd make him believe I did,   65
and that's as bad.

MRS. FAINALL: Why, had not you as good do it?

MRS. MARWOOD: Oh! if he should ever discover it, he would then know the worst, and be out of his pain; but I would have him ever to continue   70
upon the rack of fear and jealousy.

MRS. FAINALL: Ingenious mischief! would thou wert married to Mirabell.

MRS. MARWOOD: Would I were!

MRS. FAINALL: You change colour.   75

MRS. MARWOOD: Because I hate him.

MRS. FAINALL: So do I; but I can hear him named. But what reason have you to hate him in particular?

MRS. MARWOOD: I never loved him; he is, and always was, insufferably proud.   80

MRS. FAINALL: By the reason you give for your aversion, one would think it dissembled; for you have laid a fault to his charge, of which his enemies must acquit him.

MRS. MARWOOD: Oh then, it seems, you are one of his   85
favourable enemies! Methinks you look a little pale, and now you flush again.

MRS. FAINALL: Do I? I think I am a little sick o' the sudden.

MRS. MARWOOD: What ails you?   90

MRS. FAINALL: My husband. Don't you see him? He turned short upon me unawares, and has almost overcome me.

[Enter FAINALL and MIRABELL]

MRS. MARWOOD: Ha! ha! ha! he comes opportunely for you.   95

MRS. FAINALL: For you, for he has brought Mirabell with him.

FAINALL: My dear!

MRS. FAINALL: My soul!

FAINALL: You don't look well to-day, child.   100

MRS. FAINALL: D'ye think so?

MIRABELL: He is the only man that does, madam.

MRS. FAINALL: The only man that would tell me so at least; and the only man from whom I could hear it without mortification.   105

FAINALL: O my dear, I am satisfied of your tenderness; I know you cannot resent anything from me; especially what is an effect of my concern.

MRS. FAINALL: Mr. Mirabell, my mother interrupted you in a pleasant relation last night; I would   110
fain hear it out.

MIRABELL: The persons concerned in that affair have yet a tolerable reputation.—I am afraid Mr. Fainall will be censorious.

MRS. FAINALL: He has a humour more prevailing than   115

---

⁵⁵ **Penthesilea** Queen of the Amazons, the race of women warriors, in the Trojan War

his curiosity, and will willingly dispense with
the hearing of one scandalous story, to avoid
giving an occasion to make another by being
seen to walk with his wife. This way, Mr.
120 Mirabell, and I dare promise you will oblige us
both.

[Exeunt Mrs. FAINALL *and* MIRABELL*]*

FAINALL: Excellent creature! Well, sure if I should live to
be rid of my wife, I should be a miserable man.
MRS. MARWOOD: Ay!
125 FAINALL: For having only that one hope, the accomplishment of it, of consequence, must put an
end to all my hopes; and what a wretch is he
who must survive his hopes! Nothing remains
when that day comes, but to sit down and weep
130 like Alexander,° when he wanted other worlds
to conquer.
MRS. MARWOOD: Will you not follow 'em?
FAINALL: Faith, I think not.
MRS. MARWOOD: Pray let us; I have a reason.
135 FAINALL: You are not jealous?
MRS. MARWOOD: Of whom?
FAINALL: Of Mirabell.
MRS. MARWOOD: If I am, is it inconsistent with my love
to you that I am tender of your honour?
140 FAINALL: You would intimate, then, as if there were a
fellow-feeling between my wife and him.
MRS. MARWOOD: I think she does not hate him to that
degree she would be thought.
FAINALL: But he, I fear, is too insensible.
145 MRS. MARWOOD: It may be you are deceived.
FAINALL: It may be so. I do now begin to apprehend it.
MRS. MARWOOD: What?
FAINALL: That I have been deceived, madam, and you
are false.
150 MRS. MARWOOD: That I am false! what mean you?
FAINALL: To let you know I see through all your little
arts.—Come, you both love him; and both have
equally dissembled your aversion. Your mutual
jealousies of one another have made you clash
155 till you have both struck fire. I have seen the
warm confession reddening on your cheeks,
and sparkling from your eyes.
MRS. MARWOOD: You do me wrong.
FAINALL: I do not. 'Twas for my ease to oversee and
160 wilfully neglect the gross advances made him
by my wife; that by permitting her to be
engaged, I might continue unsuspected in my
pleasures; and take you oftener to my arms in
full security. But could you think, because the
165 nodding husband would not wake, that e'er the
watchful lover slept?

MRS. MARWOOD: And wherewithal can you reproach
me?
FAINALL: With infidelity, with loving another, with
love of Mirabell.   170
MRS. MARWOOD: 'Tis false! I challenge you to show an
instance that can confirm your groundless accusation. I hate him.
FAINALL: And wherefore do you hate him? he is insensible, and your resentment follows his neglect.   175
An instance! the injuries you have done him are
a proof: your interposing in his love. What
cause had you to make discoveries of his pretended passion? to undeceive the credulous
aunt, and be the officious obstacle of his match   180
with Millamant?
MRS. MARWOOD: My obligations to my lady urged me;
I had professed a friendship to her; and could
not see her easy nature so abused by that dissembler.   185
FAINALL: What, was it conscience then? Professed a
friendship! O the pious friendships of the
female sex!
MRS. MARWOOD: More tender, more sincere, and more
enduring, than all the vain and empty vows of   190
men, whether professing love to us, or mutual
faith to one another.
FAINALL: Ha! ha! ha! you are my wife's friend too.
MRS. MARWOOD: Shame and ingratitude! do you
reproach me? you, you upbraid me? Have I   195
been false to her, through strict fidelity to you,
and sacrificed my friendship to keep my love
inviolate? And have you the baseness to charge
me with the guilt, unmindful of the merit? To
you it should be meritorious, that I have been   200
vicious: and do you reflect that guilt upon me,
which should lie buried in your bosom?
FAINALL: You misinterpret my reproof. I meant but to
remind you of the slight account you once
could make of strictest ties, when set in compe- 205
tition with your love to me.
MRS. MARWOOD: 'Tis false, you urged it with deliberate malice! 'twas spoken in scorn, and I never
will forgive it.
FAINALL: Your guilt, not your resentment, begets your 210
rage. If yet you loved, you could forgive a jealousy: but you are stung to find you are discovered.
MRS. MARWOOD: It shall be all discovered. You too
shall be discovered; be sure you shall. I can but 215
be exposed.—If I do it myself I shall prevent°
your baseness.
FAINALL: Why, what will you do?
MRS. MARWOOD: Disclose it to your wife; own what
has passed between us.   220

---

¹³⁰ **Alexander** Alexander the Great

²¹⁶ **prevent** anticipate

FAINALL: Frenzy!

MRS. MARWOOD: By all my wrongs I'll do't!—I'll publish to the world the injuries you have done me,
both in my fame and fortune! With both I trust-
225   ed you, you bankrupt in honour, as indigent of
wealth.

FAINALL: Your fame I have preserved: your fortune
has been bestowed as the prodigality of your
love would have it, in pleasures which we both
230   have shared. Yet, had not you been false, I had
ere this repaid it—'tis true—had you permitted
Mirabell with Millamant to have stolen their
marriage, my lady had been incensed beyond
all means of reconcilement: Millamant had for-
235   feited the moiety of her fortune; which then
would have descended to my wife;—and
wherefore did I marry, but to make lawful prize
of a rich widow's wealth, and squander it on
love and you?

240   MRS. MARWOOD: Deceit and frivolous pretence!

FAINALL: Death, am I not married? What's pretence?
Am I not imprisoned, fettered? Have I not a
wife? nay a wife that was a widow, a young
widow, a handsome widow; and would be
245   again a widow, but that I have a heart of proof,
and something of a constitution to bustle
through the ways of wedlock and this world!
Will you yet be reconciled to truth and me?

MRS. MARWOOD: Impossible. Truth and you are incon-
250   sistent: I hate you, and shall for ever.

FAINALL: For loving you?

MRS. MARWOOD: I loathe the name of love after such
usage; and next to the guilt with which you
would asperse me, I scorn you most. Farewell!

255   FAINALL: Nay, we must not part thus.

MRS. MARWOOD: Let me go.

FAINALL: Come, I'm sorry.

MRS. MARWOOD: I care not—let me go—break my
hands, do—I'd leave 'em to get loose.

260   FAINALL: I would not hurt you for the world. Have I
no other hold to keep you here?

MRS. MARWOOD: Well, I have deserved it all.

FAINALL: You know I love you.

MRS. MARWOOD: Poor dissembling!—O that—well, it
265   is not yet—

FAINALL: What? what is it not? what is it not yet? It is
not yet too late—

MRS. MARWOOD: No, it is not yet too late;—I have that
comfort.

270   FAINALL: It is, to love another.

MRS. MARWOOD: But not to loathe, detest, abhor
mankind, myself, and the whole treacherous
world.

FAINALL: Nay, this is extravagance.—Come, I ask your
275   pardon—no tears—I was to blame, I could not
love you and be easy in my doubts. Pray forbear—I believe you; I'm convinced I've done

you wrong; and any way, every way will make
amends. I'll hate my wife yet more, damn her!
I'll part with her, rob her of all she's worth, and   280
we'll retire somewhere, anywhere, to another
world. I'll marry thee—be pacified.—'Sdeath,°
they come, hide your face, your tears;—you
have a mask, wear it a moment. This way, this
way—be persuaded.   285

[Exeunt]

Scene 2

The same

MIRABELL *and* MRS. FAINALL

MRS. FAINALL: They are here yet.

MIRABELL: They are turning into the other walk.

MRS. FAINALL: While I only hated my husband, I could
bear to see him; but since I have despised him,
he's too offensive.   5

MIRABELL: O you should hate with prudence.

MRS. FAINALL: Yes, for I have loved with indiscretion.

MIRABELL: You should have just so much disgust for
your husband, as may be sufficient to make you
relish your lover.   10

MRS. FAINALL: You have been the cause that I have
loved without bounds, and would you set limits to that aversion of which you have been the
occasion? why did you make me marry this
man?   15

MIRABELL: Why do we daily commit disagreeable and
dangerous actions? to save that idol, reputation.
If the familiarities of our loves had produced
that consequence of which you were apprehensive, where could you have fixed a father's   20
name with credit, but on a husband?° I knew
Fainall to be a man lavish of his morals, an
interested and professing friend, a false and a
designing lover; yet one whose wit and outward fair behaviour have gained a reputation   25
with the town enough to make that woman
stand excused who has suffered herself to be
won by his addresses. A better man ought not
to have been sacrificed to the occasion; a worse
had not answered to the purpose. When you are   30
weary of him you know your remedy.

MRS. FAINALL: I ought to stand in some degree of credit with you, Mirabell.

---

²⁸² **'Sdeath** contraction for "by God's death"   ¹⁸⁻²¹ **If the
familiarities... husband** Mirabell refers to his affair with
Mrs. Fainall, which occurred between the death of her first
husband, Mr. Languish, and her marriage to Fainall.

MIRABELL: In justice to you, I have made you privy to
35   my whole design, and put it in your power to
    ruin or advance my fortune.

MRS. FAINALL: Whom have you instructed to represent
    your pretended uncle?

MIRABELL: Waitwell, my servant.

40   MRS. FAINALL: He is an humble servant to Foible my
    mother's woman, and may win her to your
    interest.

MIRABELL: Care is taken for that—she is won and
    worn by this time. They were married this
45   morning.

MRS. FAINALL: Who?

MIRABELL: Waitwell and Foible. I would not tempt my
    servant to betray me by trusting him too far. If
    your mother, in hopes to ruin me, should con-
50   sent to marry my pretended uncle, he might,
    like Mosca in the Fox,° stand upon terms; so I
    made him sure beforehand.

MRS. FAINALL: So if my poor mother is caught in a con-
    tract, you will discover the imposture betimes;
55   and release her by producing a certificate of her
    gallant's former marriage?

MIRABELL: Yes, upon condition that she consent to my
    marriage with her niece, and surrender the moi-
    ety of her fortune in her possession.

60   MRS. FAINALL: She talked last night of endeavouring
    at a match between Millamant and your uncle.

MIRABELL: That was by Foible's direction, and my
    instruction, that she might seem to carry it more
    privately.

65   MRS. FAINALL: Well, I have an opinion of your success;
    for I believe my lady will do anything to get a
    husband; and when she has this, which you
    have provided for her, I suppose she will sub-
    mit to anything to get rid of him.

70   MIRABELL: Yes, I think the good lady would marry
    anything that resembled a man, though 'twere
    no more than what a butler could pinch out of a
    napkin.°

MRS. FAINALL: Female frailty! we must all come to it, if
75   we live to be old, and feel the craving of a false
    appetite when the true is decayed.

MIRABELL: An old woman's appetite is depraved like
    that of a girl—'tis the green sickness of a second
    childhood; and, like the faint offer of a latter
80   spring, serves but to usher in the fall, and with-
    ers in an affected bloom.

MRS. FAINALL: Here's your mistress.

[Enter Mrs. MILLAMANT, WITWOUD, and MINCING]

MIRABELL: Here she comes, i'faith, full sail, with her
    fan spread and her streamers out, and a shoal of
    fools for tenders; ha, no, I cry her mercy!   85

MRS. FAINALL: I see but one poor empty sculler; and he
    tows her woman after him.

MIRABELL: [*To MRS. MILLAMANT*] You seem to be unat-
    tended, madam—you used to have the *beau
    monde°* throng after you; and a flock of gay fine   90
    perukes° hovering round you.

WITWOUD: Like moths about a candle.—I had like to
    have lost my comparison for want of breath.

MRS. MILLAMANT: O I have denied myself airs today, I
    have walked as fast through the crowd.   95

WITWOUD: As a favourite just disgraced; and with as
    few followers.

MRS. MILLAMANT: Dear Mr. Witwoud, truce with your
    similitudes; for I'm as sick of 'em—

WITWOUD: As a physician of a good air.—I cannot help   100
    it, madam, though 'tis against myself.

MRS. MILLAMANT: Yet, again! Mincing, stand between
    me and his wit.

WITWOUD: Do, Mrs. Mincing, like a screen before a
    great fire.—I confess I do blaze to-day, I am too   105
    bright.

MRS. FAINALL: But, dear Millamant, why were you so
    long?

MRS. MILLAMANT: Long! Lord, have I not made violent
    haste; I have asked every living thing I met for   110
    you; I have inquired after you, as after a new
    fashion.

WITWOUD: Madam, truce with your similitudes.—No,
    you met her husband, and did not ask him for
    her.   115

MRS. MILLAMANT: By your leave, Witwoud, that were
    like inquiring after an old fashion, to ask a hus-
    band for his wife.

WITWOUD: Hum, a hit! a hit! a palpable hit! I confess it.

MRS. FAINALL: You were dressed before I came abroad.   120

MRS. MILLAMANT: Ay, that's true.—O but then I had—
    Mincing, what had I? why was I so long?

MINCING: O mem, your la'ship stayed to peruse a
    packet of letters.

MRS. MILLAMANT: O ay, letters—I had letters—I am   125
    persecuted with letters—I hate letters—
    Nobody knows how to write letters, and yet
    one has 'em, one does not know why. They
    serve one to pin up one's hair.

WITWOUD: Is that the way? Pray, madam, do you pin   130
    up your hair with all your letters? I find I must
    keep copies.

MRS. MILLAMANT: Only with those in verse, Mr.
    Witwoud, I never pin up my hair with prose.—

---

⁵¹ **Mosca in the Fox** In Ben Jonson's *Volpone*, Mosca tries to
blackmail Volpone by threatening to expose him as a fraud.
⁷²⁻³ **pinch... napkin** table napkins can be folded into fancy
shapes.

⁸⁹⁻⁹⁰ *beau monde* fashionable world   ⁹¹ **perukes** wigs worn
by fashionable gentlemen

135   I think I tried once, Mincing.

MINCING: O mem, I shall never forget it.

MRS. MILLAMANT: Ay, poor Mincing tift and tift all the morning.

140   MINCING: Till I had the cramp in my fingers, I'll vow, mem: and all to no purpose. But when your la'-ship pins it up with poetry, it sits so pleasant the next day as anything, and is so pure and so crips.°

WITWOUD: Indeed, so crips?

145   MINCING: You're such a critic, Mr. Witwoud.

MRS. MILLAMANT: Mirabell, did you take exceptions last night? O ay, and went away.—Now I think on't I'm angry—no, now I think on't I'm pleased—for I believe I gave you some pain.

150   MIRABELL: Does that please you?

MRS. MILLAMANT: Infinitely; I love to give pain.

MIRABELL: You would affect a cruelty which is not in your nature; your true vanity is in the power of pleasing.

155   MRS. MILLAMANT: Oh I ask you pardon for that—one's cruelty is one's power; and when one parts with one's cruelty, one parts with one's power; and when one has parted with that, I fancy one's old and ugly.

160   MIRABELL: Ay, ay, suffer your cruelty to ruin the object of your power, to destroy your lover—and then how vain, how lost a thing you'll be! Nay, 'tis true: you are no longer handsome when you've lost your lover; your beauty dies upon the

165   instant; for beauty is the lover's gift; 'tis he bestows your charms—your glass is all a cheat. The ugly and the old, whom the looking-glass mortifies, yet after commendation can be flattered by it, and discover beauties in it; for that

170   reflects our praises, rather than your face.

MRS. MILLAMANT: O the vanity of these men!—Fainall, d'ye hear him? If they did not commend us, we were not handsome! Now you must know they could not commend one, if one was not hand-

175   some. Beauty the lover's gift!—Lord, what is a lover, that it can give? Why, one makes lovers as fast as one pleases, and they live as long as one pleases, and they die as soon as one pleases; and then, if one pleases, one makes more.

180   WITWOUD: Very pretty. Why, you make no more of making of lovers, madam, than of making so many card-matches.°

MRS. MILLAMANT: No more owes one's beauty to a lover, than one's wit to an echo. They can but

185   reflect what we look and say; vain empty things if we are silent or unseen, and want a being.

MIRABELL: Yet to those two vain empty things you owe the two greatest pleasures of your life.

MRS. MILLAMANT: How so?

190   MIRABELL: To your lover you owe the pleasure of hearing yourselves praised; and to an echo the pleasure of hearing yourselves talk.

WITWOUD: But I know a lady that loves talking so incessantly, she won't give an echo fair play;

195   she has that everlasting rotation of tongue, that an echo must wait till she dies, before it can catch her last words.

MRS. MILLAMANT: O fiction!—Fainall, let us leave these men.

200   MIRABELL: [Aside to MRS. FAINALL] Draw off Witwoud.

MRS. FAINALL: Immediately.—I have a word or two for Mr. Witwoud.

[Exeunt MRS. FAINALL and WITWOUD]

MIRABELL: I would beg a little private audience too.— You had the tyranny to deny me last night;

205   though you knew I came to impart a secret to you that concerned my love.

MRS. MILLAMANT: You saw I was engaged.

MIRABELL: Unkind! You had the leisure to entertain a herd of fools; things who visit you from their

210   excessive idleness; bestowing on your easiness that time which is the incumbrance of their lives. How can you find delight in such society? It is impossible they should admire you, they are not capable: or if they were, it should be to

215   you as a mortification; for sure to please a fool is some degree of folly.

MRS. MILLAMANT: I please myself:—besides, sometimes to converse with fools is for my health.

MIRABELL: Your health! is there a worse disease than

220   the conversation of fools?

MRS. MILLAMANT: Yes, the vapours; fools are physic for it, next to asafœtida.°

MIRABELL: You are not in a course of fools?

MRS. MILLAMANT: Mirabell, if you persist in this offen-

225   sive freedom, you'll displease me.—I think I must resolve, after all, not to have you:—we shan't agree.

MIRABELL: Not in our physic, it may be.

MRS. MILLAMANT: And yet our distemper, in all likeli-

230   hood, will be the same; for we shall be sick of one another. I shan't endure to be reprimanded nor instructed: 'tis so dull to act always by advice, and so tedious to be told of one's faults—I can't bear it. Well, I won't have you,

235   Mirabell—I'm resolved—I think—you may go.—Ha! ha! ha! what would you give, that you could help loving me?

---

¹⁴³ **crips** crisp   ¹⁸¹ **card-matches** matches made of heavy paper, the tips of which were dipped in sulphur

---

²²² **asafoetida** an antidote for the "vapors"

MIRABELL: I would give something that you did not
    know I could not help it.

40 MRS. MILLAMANT: Come, don't look grave then. Well,
    what do you say to me?

MIRABELL: I say that a man may as soon make a friend
    by his wit, or a fortune by his honesty, as win a
    woman by plain-dealing and sincerity.

45 MRS. MILLAMANT: Sententious Mirabell!—Prithee,
    don't look with that violent and inflexible wise
    face, like Solomon° at the dividing of the child
    in an old tapestry hanging.

MIRABELL: You are merry, madam, but I would per-
50   suade you for a moment to be serious.

MRS. MILLAMANT: What, with that face? no, if you
    keep your countenance, 'tis impossible I should
    hold mine. Well, after all, there is something
    very moving in a love-sick face. Ha! ha! ha!—
55   well, I won't laugh, don't be peevish—Heigho!
    now I'll be melancholy, as melancholy as a
    watch-light. Well, Mirabell, if ever you will win
    me woo me now.—Nay, if you are so tedious,
    fare you well;—I see they are walking away.

60 MIRABELL: Can you not find in the variety of your dis-
    position one moment—

MRS. MILLAMANT: To hear you tell me Foible's mar-
    ried, and your plot like to speed;—no.

MIRABELL: But how come you to know it?

65 MRS. MILLAMANT: Without the help of the devil, you
    can't imagine; unless she should tell me herself.
    Which of the two it may have been I will leave
    you to consider; and when you have done
    thinking of that, think, of me.

[Exit]

70 MIRABELL: I have something more.—Gone!—Think of
    you? to think of a whirlwind, though't were in
    a whirlwind, were a case of more steady con-
    templation; a very tranquillity of mind and
    mansion. A fellow that lives in a windmill, has
75   not a more whimsical dwelling than the heart of
    a man that is lodged in a woman. There is no
    point of the compass to which they cannot turn,
    and by which they are not turned; and by one as
    well as another; for motion, not method, is their
80   occupation. To know this, and yet continue to
    be in love, is to be made wise from the dictates
    of reason, and yet persevere to play the fool by
    the force of instinct.—Oh, here come my pair of
    turtles!°—What, billing so sweetly! is not
85   Valentine's day over with you yet?

[Enter WAITWELL and FOIBLE]

Sirrah, Waitwell, why sure you think you were
    married for your own recreation, and not for
    my conveniency.

WAITWELL: Your pardon, sir. With submission, we
    have indeed been solacing in lawful delights;   290
    but still with an eye to business, sir. I have
    instructed her as well as I could. If she can take
    your directions as readily as my instructions,
    sir, your affairs are in a prosperous way.

MIRABELL: Give you joy, Mrs. Foible.   295

FOIBLE: O las, sir, I'm so ashamed!—I'm afraid my
    lady has been in a thousand inquietudes for me.
    But I protest, sir, I made as much haste as I
    could.

WAITWELL: That she did indeed, sir. It was my fault   300
    that she did not make more.

MIRABELL: That I believe.

FOIBLE: But I told my lady as you instructed me, sir,
    that I had a prospect of seeing Sir Rowland
    your uncle; and that I would put her ladyship's   305
    picture in my pocket to show him; which I'll be
    sure to say has made him so enamoured of her
    beauty, that he burns with impatience to lie at
    her ladyship's feet, and worship the original.

MIRABELL: Excellent Foible! matrimony has made you   310
    eloquent in love.

WAITWELL: I think she has profited, sir, I think so.

FOIBLE: You have seen Madam Millamant, sir?

MIRABELL: Yes.

FOIBLE: I told her, sir, because I did not know that you   315
    might find an opportunity; she had so much
    company last night.

MIRABELL: Your diligence will merit more—in the
    mean time—

[Gives money]

FOIBLE: O dear sir, your humble servant!   320

WAITWELL: Spouse.

MIRABELL: Stand off, sir, not a penny!—Go on and
    prosper, Foible:—the lease shall be made good,
    and the farm stocked, if we succeed.

FOIBLE: I don't question your generosity, sir: and you   325
    need not doubt of success. If you have no more
    commands, sir, I'll be gone; I'm sure my lady is
    at her toilet, and can't dress till I come.—O dear,
    I'm sure that *[Looking out]* was Mrs. Marwood
    that went by in a mask! If she has seen me with   330
    you I'm sure she'll tell my lady. I'll make haste
    home and prevent her. Your servant, sir.—
    B'w'y,° Waitwell.

[Exit]

WAITWELL: Sir Rowland, if you please.—The jade's so

---

²⁴⁷ **Solomon** See I Kings 3:16–28.   ²⁸⁴ **turtles** turtle doves;
lovebirds

³³³ **B'w'y** contraction for "God be with you"

335   pert upon her preferment she forgets herself.
MIRABELL: Come, sir, will you endeavour to forget yourself, and transform into Sir Rowland?
WAITWELL: Why, sir, it will be impossible I should remember myself.—Married, knighted, and
340   attended all in one day! 'tis enough to make any man forget himself. The difficulty will be how to recover my acquaintance and familiarity with my former self, and fall from my transformation to a reformation into Waitwell. Nay, I shan't be quite the same Waitwell neither; for now, I remember me, I'm married, and can't be my own man again.
Ay there's my grief; that's the sad change of life,
To lose my title, and yet keep my wife.

[Exeunt]

ACT III

Scene 1

A Room in LADY WISHFORT's *House.* LADY WISHFORT *at her toilet,* PEG *waiting*

LADY WISHFORT: Merciful! no news of Foible yet?
PEG: No, madam.
LADY WISHFORT: I have no more patience.—If I have not fretted myself till I am pale again, there's no
5   veracity in me! Fetch me the red—the red, do you hear, sweetheart?—An arrant ash-colour, as I am a person! Look you how this wench stirs! Why dost thou not fetch me a little red? didst thou not hear me, Mopus?°
10   PEG: The red ratafia° does your ladyship mean, or the cherry-brandy?
LADY WISHFORT: Ratafia, fool! no, fool. Not the ratafia, fool—grant me patience!—I mean the Spanish paper,° idiot—complexion, darling. Paint,
15   paint, paint, dost thou understand that, changeling, dangling thy hands like bobbins° before thee? Why dost thou not stir, puppet? thou wooden thing upon wires!
PEG: Lord, madam, your ladyship is so impatient!—I
20   cannot come at the paint, madam; Mrs. Foible has locked it up, and carried the key with her.
LADY WISHFORT: A pox take you both!—fetch me the cherry-brandy then. [*Exit* Peg] I'm as pale and as faint, I look like Mrs. Qualmsick, the curate's
25   wife, that's always breeding.—Wench, come, come, wench, what art thou doing? sipping, tasting?—Save thee, dost thou not know the bottle?

[Re-enter PEG *with a bottle and china cup]*

PEG: Madam, I was looking for a cup.
LADY WISHFORT: A cup, save thee! and what a cup hast   30 thou brought!—Dost thou take me for a fairy, to drink out of an acorn? Why didst thou not bring thy thimble? Hast thou ne'er a brass thimble clinking in thy pocket with a bit of nutmeg?—I warrant thee. Come, fill, fill!—So—again.—   35 [*Knocking at the door*]—See who that is.—Set down the bottle first—here, here, under the table.—What, wouldst thou go with the bottle in thy hand, like a tapster? As I am a person, this wench has lived in an inn upon the road,   10 before she came to me, like Maritornes the Asturian in Don Quixote!°—No Foible yet?
PEG: No, madam; Mrs. Marwood.
LADY WISHFORT: Oh, Marwood; let her come in.— Come in, good Marwood.   15

[Enter MRS. MARWOOD*]*

MRS. MARWOOD: I'm surprised to find your ladyship in dishabille° at this time of day.
LADY WISHFORT: Foible's a lost thing; has been abroad since morning, and never heard of since.
MRS. MARWOOD: I saw her but now, as I came masked   20 through the park, in conference with Mirabell.
LADY WISHFORT: With Mirabell!—You call my blood into my face, with mentioning that traitor. She durst not have the confidence! I sent her to negotiate an affair, in which, if I'm detected, I'm   25 undone. If that wheedling villain has wrought upon Foible to detect me, I'm ruined. O my dear friend, I'm a wretch of wretches if I'm detected.
MRS. MARWOOD: O madam, you cannot suspect Mrs.   30 Foible's integrity!
LADY WISHFORT: Oh, he carries poison in his tongue that would corrupt integrity itself! If she has given him an opportunity, she has as good as put her integrity into his hands. Ah, dear   35 Marwood, what's integrity to an opportunity?—Hark! I hear her!—dear friend, retire into my closet, that I may examine her with more freedom.—You'll pardon me, dear friend; I can make bold with you.—There are books over the   40

---

⁹ **Mopus** a dull-witted girl   ¹⁰ **ratafia** See note 2 to Act I.
¹³⁻¹⁴ **Spanish paper** cosmetic rouge imported from Spain
¹⁶ **bobbins** spools of yarn

¹¹⁻¹² **Maritornes... Quixote** Don Quixote imagines himself in love with Maritornes, an Austrian chambermaid, in Cervantes, *Don Quixote*, pt. 1, ch. 16.   ¹⁷ **dishabille** i.e., *déshabille*, casual attire

chimney.—Quarles° and Prynne,° and "The
Short View of the Stage,"° with Bunyan's
works,° to entertain you.—[*To* PEG]—Go, you
thing, and send her in.

[Exeunt MRS. MARWOOD *and* PEG]

[Enter FOIBLE]

45 LADY WISHFORT: O Foible, where hast thou been? what
hast thou been doing?
FOIBLE: Madam, I have seen the party.
LADY WISHFORT: But what hast thou done?
FOIBLE: Nay, 'tis your ladyship has done, and are to
50 do; I have only promised. But a man so enam-
oured—so transported!—Well, here it is, all that
is left; all that is not kissed away.—Well, if wor-
shipping of pictures be a sin—poor Sir
Rowland, I say.
55 LADY WISHFORT: The miniature has been counted
like;—but hast thou not betrayed me, Foible?
hast thou not detected me to that faithless
Mirabell?—What hadst thou to do with him in
the Park? Answer me, has he got nothing out of
60 thee?
FOIBLE (*aside*): So the devil has been beforehand with
me. What shall I say?—[*Aloud*]—Alas, madam,
could I help it, if I met that confident thing? was
I in fault? If you had heard how he used me,
65 and all upon your ladyship's account, I'm sure
you would not suspect my fidelity. Nay, if that
had been the worst, I could have borne; but he
had a fling at your ladyship too; and then I
could not hold; but i'faith I gave him his own.
70 LADY WISHFORT: Me? what did the filthy fellow say?
FOIBLE: O madam! 'tis a shame to say what he said—
with his taunts and his fleers, tossing up his
nose. Humph! (says he) what, you are a hatching some plot (says he), you are so early abroad,
75 or catering (says he), ferreting for some dis-
banded officer, I warrant.—Half-pay is but thin
subsistence (says he);—well, what pension does
your lady propose? Let me see (says he), what,
she must come down pretty deep now, she's
80 superannuated (says he) and—
LADY WISHFORT: Odds° my life, I'll have him, I'll have

him murdered! I'll have him poisoned! Where
does he eat?—I'll marry a drawer to have him
poisoned in his wine. I'll send for Robin from
Locket's° immediately.   85
FOIBLE: Poison him! poisoning's too good for him.
Starve him, madam, starve him; marry Sir
Rowland, and get him disinherited. Oh you
would bless yourself to hear what he said!
LADY WISHFORT: A villain! superannuated!   90
FOIBLE: Humph (says he), I hear you are laying
designs against me too (says he), and Mrs.
Millamant is to marry my uncle (he does not
suspect a word of your ladyship); but (says he)
I'll fit you for that. I warrant you (says he) I'll   95
hamper you for that (says he); you and your old
frippery too (says he); I'll handle you—
LADY WISHFORT: Audacious villain! handle me; would
he durst!—Frippery! old frippery! was there
ever such a foul-mouthed fellow? I'll be mar-   100
ried to-morrow, I'll be contracted to-night.
FOIBLE: The sooner the better, madam.
LADY WISHFORT: Will Sir Rowland be here, sayest
thou? when, Foible?
FOIBLE: Incontinently, madam. No new sheriff's wife   105
expects the return of her husband after knighthood with that impatience in which Sir
Rowland burns for the dear hour of kissing
your ladyship's hand after dinner.
LADY WISHFORT: Frippery! superannuated frippery!   110
I'll frippery the villain; I'll reduce him to frippery and rags! a tatterdemalion!° I hope to see
him hung with tatters, like a Long-lane pent-
house° or a gibbet thief. A slander-mouthed
railer! I warrant the spendthrift prodigal's in   115
debt as much as the million lottery° or the
whole court upon a birthday.° I'll spoil his credit with his tailor. Yes, he shall have my niece
with her fortune, he shall.
FOIBLE: He! I hope to see him lodge in Ludgate° first,   120
and angle into Blackfriars for brass farthings
with an old mitten.
LADY WISHFORT: Ay, dear Foible; thank thee for that,
dear Foible. He has put me out of all patience. I
shall never recompose my features to receive   125

---

41 Quarles Francis Quarles (1592–1644), author of *Emblems, Divine and Moral* (1635) and other religious writings; **Prynne** William Prynne (1600–1669), author of *Histriomastix* (1633)—a Puritan attack on the stage—and other pamphlets; **"The Short View of the Stage"** Jeremy Collier's 1698 attack on the stage was specifically aimed at Congreve's earlier comedies; **Bunyan's works** John Bunyan was a great Puritan writer and preacher; his works were issued in one volume in 1692.   **81 Odds** God's

84-85 Robin from Locket's Robin was a common name for a waiter; Locket's was a fashionable tavern in Charing Cross. **112 tatterdemalion** ragamuffin   **114 Long-lane pent-house** a stall in Long Lane, famous for shops selling secondhand clothing   **116 million lottery** In 1694 the government raised a million pounds by means of a lottery.   **117 the whole court... birthday** Courtiers were expected to attend the sovereign's birthday celebration wearing new and expensive clothing.   **120 Ludgate** The Fleet in Ludgate, in the district of Blackfriars, was a debtor's prison where inmates begged money from passersby in the manner suggested by Foible.

Sir Rowland with any economy of face.° This wretch has fretted me that I am absolutely decayed. Look, Foible.

FOIBLE: Your ladyship has frowned a little too rashly,
130 indeed, madam. There are some cracks discernible in the white varnish.

LADY WISHFORT: Let me see the glass.—Cracks, sayest thou?—why, I am errantly flayed—I look like an old peeled wall. Thou must repair me,
135 Foible, before Sir Rowland comes, or I shall never keep up to my picture.

FOIBLE: I warrant you, madam, a little art once made your picture like you; and now a little of the same art must make you like your picture. Your
140 picture must sit for you, madam.

LADY WISHFORT: But art thou sure Sir Rowland will not fail to come? or will he not fail when he does come? Will he be importunate, Foible, and push? For if he should not be importunate, I
145 shall never break decorums:—I shall die with confusion, if I am forced to advance.—Oh no, I can never advance!—I shall swoon if he should expect advances. No, I hope Sir Rowland is better bred than to put a lady to the necessity of
150 breaking her forms. I won't be too coy, neither.— I won't give him despair—but a little disdain is not amiss; a little scorn is alluring.

FOIBLE: A little scorn becomes your ladyship.

LADY WISHFORT: Yes, but tenderness becomes me
155 best—a sort of dyingness—you see that picture has a sort of a—ha, Foible! a swimmingness in the eye—yes, I'll look so—my niece affects it; but she wants features. Is Sir Rowland handsome? Let my toilet be removed—I'll dress
160 above. I'll receive Sir Rowland here. Is he handsome? Don't answer me. I won't know: I'll be surprised, I'll be taken by surprise.

FOIBLE: By storm, madam, Sir Rowland's a brisk man.

LADY WISHFORT: Is he! O then he'll importune, if he's
165 a brisk man. I shall save decorums if Sir Rowland importunes. I have a mortal terror at the apprehension of offending against decorums. O, I'm glad he's a brisk man. Let my things be removed, good Foible.

[Exit]

170 *[Enter MRS. FAINALL]*

MRS. FAINALL: O Foible, I have been in a fright, lest I should come too late! That devil Marwood saw you in the Park with Mirabell, and I'm afraid will discover it to my lady.

FOIBLE: Discover what, madam!

MRS. FAINALL: Nay, nay, put not on that strange face, I 175 am privy to the whole design, and know that Waitwell, to whom thou wert this morning married, is to personate Mirabell's uncle, and as such, winning my lady, to involve her in those difficulties from which Mirabell only must 180 release her, by his making his conditions to have my cousin and her fortune left to her own disposal.

FOIBLE: O dear madam, I beg your pardon. It was not my confidence in your ladyship that was defi- 185 cient; but I thought the former good correspondence between your ladyship and Mr. Mirabell might have hindered his communicating this secret.

MRS. FAINALL: Dear Foible, forget that. 190

FOIBLE: O dear madam, Mr. Mirabell is such a sweet, winning gentleman—but your ladyship is the pattern of generosity.—Sweet lady, to be so good! Mr. Mirabell cannot choose but be grateful. I find your ladyship has his heart still. Now, 195 madam, I can safely tell your ladyship our success; Mrs. Marwood had told my lady; but I warrant I managed myself; I turned it all for the better. I told my lady that Mr. Mirabell railed at her; I laid horrid things to his charge, I'll vow; 200 and my lady is so incensed that she'll be contracted to Sir Rowland to-night, she says; I warrant I worked her up, that he may have her for asking for, as they say of a Welsh maidenhead.

MRS. FAINALL: O rare Foible! 205

FOIBLE: Madam, I beg your ladyship to acquaint Mr. Mirabell of his success. I would be seen as little as possible to speak to him:—besides, I believe Madam Marwood watches me.—She has a month's mind;° but I know Mr. Mirabell can't 210 abide her.—John!—*[Calls]* remove my lady's toilet.—Madam, your servant: my lady is so impatient, I fear she'll come for me if I stay.

MRS. FAINALL: I'll go with you up the back-stairs, lest I should meet her. 215

[Exeunt]

Scene 2

LADY WISHFORT's Closet. MRS. MARWOOD

MRS. MARWOOD: Indeed, Mrs. Engine,° is it thus with you? are you become a go-between of this importance? yes, I shall watch you. Why this

---

wench is the *passe-partout*, a very master-key to everybody's strong-box. My friend Fainall,° have you carried it so swimmingly? I thought there was something in it; but it seems 'tis over with you. Your loathing is not from a want of appetite, then, but from a surfeit. Else you could never be so cool to fall from a principal to be an assistant; to procure for him! a pattern of generosity that, I confess. Well, Mr. Fainall, you have met with your match.—O man, man! woman, woman! the devil's an ass: if I were a painter, I would draw him like an idiot, a driveller with a bib and bells: man should have his head and horns,° and woman the rest of him. Poor simple fiend!—"Madam Marwood has a month's mind, but he can't abide her."—'Twere better for him you had not been his confessor in that affair, without you could have kept his counsel closer. I shall not prove another pattern of generosity: he has not obliged me to that with those excesses of himself! and now I'll have none of him. Here comes the good lady, panting ripe; with a heart full of hope, and a head full of care, like any chemist upon the day of projection.°

[Enter LADY WISHFORT]

LADY WISHFORT: O dear, Marwood, what shall I say for this rude forgetfulness?—but my dear friend is all goodness.

MRS. MARWOOD: No apologies, dear madam, I have been very well entertained.

LADY WISHFORT: As I'm a person, I am in a very chaos to think I should so forget myself:—but I have such an olio° of affairs, really I know not what to do.—Foible!—[*Calls*] I expect my nephew, Sir Wilfull, every moment too.—Why, Foible!—He means to travel for improvement.

MRS. MARWOOD: Methinks Sir Wilfull should rather think of marrying than travelling at his years. I hear he is turned of forty.

LADY WISHFORT: O he's in less danger of being spoiled by his travels—I am against my nephew's marrying too young. It will be time enough when he comes back, and has acquired discretion to choose for himself.

MRS. MARWOOD: Methinks Mrs. Millamant and he would make a very fit match. He may travel afterwards. 'Tis a thing very usual with young gentlemen.

LADY WISHFORT: I promise you I have thought on't—and since 'tis your judgment, I'll think on't again. I assure you I will; I value your judgment extremely. On my word, I'll propose it.

[Enter FOIBLE]

LADY WISHFORT: Come, come, Foible—I had forgot my nephew will be here before dinner:—I must make haste.

FOIBLE: Mr. Witwoud and Mr. Petulant are come to dine with your ladyship.

LADY WISHFORT: O dear, I can't appear till I'm dressed—Dear Marwood, shall I be free with you again, and beg you to entertain 'em? I'll make all imaginable haste. Dear friend, excuse me.

[Exeunt]

Scene 3

A Room in LADY WISHFORT's House. MRS. MARWOOD, MRS. MILLAMANT and MINCING

MRS. MILLAMANT: Sure never anything was so unbred as that odious man!—Marwood, your servant.

MRS. MARWOOD: You have a colour; what's the matter?

MRS. MILLAMANT: That horrid fellow, Petulant, has provoked me into a flame:—I have broken my fan.—Mincing, lend me yours; is not all the powder out of my hair?

MRS. MARWOOD: No. What has he done?

MRS. MILLAMANT: Nay, he has done nothing; he has only talked—nay, he has said nothing neither; but he has contradicted everything that has been said. For my part, I thought Witwoud and he would have quarrelled.

MINCING: I vow, mem, I thought once they would have fit.°

MRS. MILLAMANT: Well, 'tis a lamentable thing, I swear, that one has not the liberty of choosing one's acquaintance as one does one's clothes.

MRS. MARWOOD: If we had that liberty, we should be as weary of one set of acquaintance, though never so good, as we are of one suit though never so fine. A fool and a doily stuff° would now and then find days of grace, and be worn for variety.

MRS. MILLAMANT: I could consent to wear 'em, if they would wear alike; but fools never wear out—they are such *drap de Berri*° things! without one could give 'em to one's chambermaid after a day or two.

---

⁵ **Fainall** i.e., Mrs. Fainall   ¹⁷ **horns** the traditional symbol of the cuckold, a husband whose wife is unfaithful   ²⁸ **like... projection** Projection is the last step of an alchemical experiment to transmute base metal into gold.   ³⁶ **olio** variety

¹⁵ **fit** fought   ²² **doily stuff** cheap woolen cloth   ²⁶ *drap de Berri* woolen cloth from Berry in France

MRS. MARWOOD: 'Twere better so indeed. Or what think you of the playhouse? A fine gay glossy fool should be given there, like a new masking habit, after the masquerade is over, and we have done with the disguise. For a fool's visit is always a disguise; and never admitted by a woman of wit, but to blind° her affair with a lover of sense. If you would but appear barefaced now, and own Mirabell, you might as easily put off Petulant and Witwoud as your hood and scarf. And indeed, 'tis time, for the town has found it; the secret is grown too big for the pretence. 'Tis like Mrs. Primly's great belly; she may lace it down before, but it burnishes° on her hips. Indeed, Millamant, you can no more conceal it, than my Lady Strammel can her face; that goodly face, which in defiance of her Rhenish wine tea, will not be comprehended in a mask.°

MRS. MILLAMANT: I'll take my death, Marwood, you are more censorious than a decayed beauty, or a discarded toast.—Mincing, tell the men they may come up.—My aunt is not dressing here; their folly is less provoking than your malice. [*Exit* Mincing] The town has found it! what has it found? That Mirabell loves me is no more a secret, than it were a secret that you discovered it to my aunt, or than the reason why you discovered it is a secret.

MRS. MARWOOD: You are nettled.°

MRS. MILLAMANT: You're mistaken. Ridiculous!

MRS. MARWOOD: Indeed, my dear, you'll tear another fan, if you don't mitigate those violent airs.

MRS. MILLAMANT: O silly! ha! ha! ha! I could laugh immoderately. Poor Mirabell! his constancy to me has quite destroyed his complaisance for all the world beside. I swear, I never enjoined it him to be so coy—If I had the vanity to think he would obey me, I would command him to show more gallantry—'tis hardly well-bred to be so particular° on one hand, and so insensible on the other. But I despair to prevail, and so let him follow his own way. Ha! ha! ha! pardon me, dear creature, I must laugh, ha! ha! ha! though I grant you 'tis a little barbarous, ha! ha! ha!

MRS. MARWOOD: What pity 'tis so much fine raillery, and delivered with so significant gesture, should be so unhappily directed to miscarry!

MRS. MILLAMANT: Ha! dear creature, I ask your pardon—I swear I did not mind you.

MRS. MARWOOD: Mr. Mirabell and you both may think it a thing impossible, when I shall tell him by telling you—

MRS. MILLAMANT: O dear, what? for it is the same thing if I hear it—ha! ha! ha!

MRS. MARWOOD: That I detest him, hate him, madam.

MRS. MILLAMANT: O madam, why so do I—and yet the creature loves me, ha! ha! ha! how can one forbear laughing to think of it.—I am a sibyl° if I am not amazed to think what he can see in me. I'll take my death, I think you are handsomer—and within a year or two as young—if you could but stay for me, I should overtake you—but that cannot be.—Well, that thought makes me melancholic.—Now, I'll be sad.

MRS. MARWOOD: Your merry note may be changed sooner than you think.

MRS. MILLAMANT: D'ye say so? Then I'm resolved I'll have a song to keep up my spirits.

[Re-enter MINCING]

MINCING: The gentlemen stay but to comb,° madam, and will wait on you.

MRS. MILLAMANT: Desire Mrs.—that is in the next room to sing the song I would have learned yesterday.—You shall hear it, madam—not that there's any great matter in it—but 'tis agreeable to my humour.

SONG

> Love's but the frailty of the mind,
>   When 'tis not with ambition joined;
> A sickly flame, which, if not fed, expires,
> And feeding, wastes in self-consuming fires.
> 'Tis not to wound a wanton boy
>   Or amorous youth, that gives the joy;
> But 'tis the glory to have pierced a swain,
> For whom inferior beauties sighed in vain.
>   Then I alone the conquest prize,
>   When I insult a rival's eyes:
> If there's delight in love, 'tis when I see
> That heart, which others bleed for, bleed for me.

[Enter PETULANT and WITWOUD]

MRS. MILLAMANT: Is your animosity composed, gentlemen?

WITWOUD: Raillery, raillery, madam; we have no animosity—we hit off a little wit now and then, but no animosity.—The falling-out of wits is like the falling-out of lovers:—we agree in the main, like treble and bass.—Ha, Petulant?

PETULANT: Ay, in the main—but when I have a

---

[35] **blind** conceal   [42-3] **burnishes** spreads out   [45-7] **goodly face… mask** i.e., her face is so fat that a mask could not hide it. Rhenish wine was thought beneficial for the figure. [58] **nettled** annoyed   [69] **particular** focused on one woman, i.e., Millamant

[87] **sibyl** prophetess   [98] **comb** i.e., comb their wigs

125 humour to contradict—
WITWOUD: Ay, when he has a humour to contradict, then I contradict too. What, I know my cue. Then we contradict one another like two battledores; for contradictions beget one another like Jews.
130 PETULANT: If he says black's black—if I have a humour to say 'tis blue—let that pass—all's one for that. If I have a humour to prove it, it must be granted.
WITWOUD: Not positively must—but it may—it may.
PETULANT: Yes, it positively must, upon proof positive.
135 WITWOUD: Ay, upon proof positive it must; but upon proof presumptive it only may.—That's a logical distinction now, madam.
MRS. MARWOOD: I perceive your debates are of importance, and very learnedly handled.
140 PETULANT: Importance is one thing, and learning's another, but a debate's a debate, that I assert.
WITWOUD: Petulant's an enemy to learning; he relies altogether on his parts.
PETULANT: No, I'm no enemy to learning; it hurts not
145 me.
MRS. MARWOOD: That's a sign indeed it's no enemy to you.
PETULANT: No, no, it's no enemy to anybody but them that have it.
150 MRS. MILLAMANT: Well, an illiterate man's my aversion: I wonder at the impudence of any illiterate man to offer to make love.
WITWOUD: That I confess I wonder at too.
MRS. MILLAMANT: Ah! to marry an ignorant that can
155 hardly read or write!
PETULANT: Why should a man be any further from being married, though he can't read, than he is from being hanged? The ordinary's° paid for setting the psalm, and the parish-priest for
160 reading the ceremony. And for the rest which is to follow in both cases, a man may do it without book—so all's one for that.
MRS. MILLAMANT: D'ye hear the creature?—Lord, here's company, I'll be gone.

[Exit]

[Enter SIR WILFULL WITWOUD in a riding dress, followed by FOOTMAN]

165 WITWOUD: In the name of Bartlemew and his fair,° what have we here?
MRS. MARWOOD: 'Tis your brother, I fancy. Don't you know him?
WITWOUD: Not I.—Yes, I think it is he—I've almost

170 forgot him; I have not seen him since the Revolution.°
FOOTMAN: [*To* SIR WILFULL] Sir, my lady's dressing. Here's company; if you please to walk in, in the mean time.
175 SIR WILFULL: Dressing! what, it's but morning here, I warrant, with you in London; we should count it towards afternoon in our parts, down in Shropshire.—Why then, belike, my aunt han't dined yet, ha, friend?
180 FOOTMAN: Your aunt, sir?
SIR WILFULL: My aunt, sir! yes, my aunt, sir, and your lady, sir; your lady is my aunt, sir.—Why, what dost thou not know me, friend? why then send somebody hither that does. How long hast thou
185 lived with thy lady, fellow, ha?
FOOTMAN: A week, sir; longer than anybody in the house, except my lady's woman.
SIR WILFULL: Why then belike thou dost not know thy lady, if thou seest her, ha, friend?
190 FOOTMAN: Why, truly, sir, I cannot safely swear to her face in a morning, before she is dressed. 'Tis like I may give a shrewd guess at her by this time.
SIR WILFULL: Well, prithee try what thou canst do; if thou canst not guess, inquire her out, dost hear,
195 fellow? and tell her, her nephew, Sir Wilfull Witwoud, is in the house.
FOOTMAN: I shall, sir.
SIR WILFULL: Hold ye, hear me, friend; a word with you in your ear; prithee who are these gallants?
200 FOOTMAN: Really, sir, I can't tell; here come so many here, 'tis hard to know 'em all.

[Exit]

SIR WILFULL: Oons,° this fellow knows less than a starling; I don't think a' knows his own name.
MRS. MARWOOD: Mr. Witwoud, your brother is not behindhand in forgetfulness—I fancy he has
205 forgot you too.
WITWOUD: I hope so—the devil take him that remembers first, I say.
SIR WILFULL: Save you, gentlemen and lady!
MRS. MARWOOD: For shame, Mr. Witwoud; why don't
210 you speak to him?—And you, sir.
WITWOUD: Petulant, speak.
PETULANT: And you, sir.
SIR WILFULL: No offence, I hope.

[Salutes MRS. MARWOOD]

MRS. MARWOOD: No sure, sir.   215
WITWOUD: This is a vile dog, I see that already. No

---

158 ordinary's The ordinary, or prison chaplain, read a psalm before the execution of a prisoner.   **165 Bartlemew... fair** a popular fair held in Smithfield around St. Bartholomew's Day (24 August)

171 Revolution i.e., the Glorious Revolution of 1688, which dethroned James II and crowned William and Mary   **202 Oons** contraction for "By God's wounds" offence! ha! ha! ha! To him; to him, Petulant, smoke him.

PETULANT: It seems as if you had come a journey, sir; hem, hem.

[Surveying him round]

SIR WILFULL: Very likely, sir, that it may seem so.

PETULANT: No offence, I hope, sir.

WITWOUD: Smoke the boots, the boots; Petulant, the boots; ha! ha! ha!

SIR WILFULL: May be not, sir; thereafter, as 'tis meant, sir.

PETULANT: Sir, I presume upon the information of your boots.

SIR WILFULL: Why, 'tis like you may, sir: if you are not satisfied with the information of my boots, sir, if you will step to the stable, you may inquire further of my horse, sir.

PETULANT: Your horse, sir! your horse is an ass, sir!

SIR WILFULL: Do you speak by way of offence, sir?

MRS. MARWOOD: The gentleman's merry, that's all sir.—*[Aside]* S'life, we shall have a quarrel betwixt an horse and an ass before they find one another out.—*[Aloud]* You must not take anything amiss from your friends, sir. You are among your friends here, though it may be you don't know it.—If I am not mistaken, you are Sir Wilfull Witwoud.

SIR WILFULL: Right, lady; I am Sir Wilfull Witwoud, so I write myself; no offence to anybody, I hope; and nephew to the Lady Wishfort of this mansion.

MRS. MARWOOD: Don't you know this gentleman, sir?

SIR WILFULL: Hum! what, sure 'tis not—yea by'r Lady, but 'tis—s'heart,° I know not whether 'tis or no—yea, but 'tis, by the Wrekin.° Brother Anthony! what Tony, i'faith! what, dost thou not know me? By'r Lady, nor I thee, thou art so becravated, and so beperiwigged.—S'heart, why dost not speak? art thou overjoyed?

WITWOUD: Odso,° brother, is it you? your servant, brother.

SIR WILFULL: Your servant! why yours, sir. Your servant again—s'heart, and your friend and servant to that—and a—flap-dragon° for your service, sir! and a hare's foot and a hare's scut° for your service, sir! an you be so cold and so courtly.

WITWOUD: No offence, I hope, brother.

SIR WILFULL: S'heart, sir, but there is, and much

offence!—A pox, is this your inns o' court° breeding, not to know your friends and your relations, your elders and your betters?

WITWOUD: Why, brother Wilfull of Salop,° you may be as short as a Shrewsbury-cake,° if you please. But I tell you 'tis not modish to know relations in town: you think you're in the country, where great lubberly brothers slabber and kiss one another when they meet, like a call of serjeants°—'tis not the fashion here; 'tis not indeed, dear brother.

SIR WILFULL: The fashion's a fool; and you're a fop, dear brother. S'heart, I've suspected this—by'r Lady, I conjectured you were a fop, since you began to change the style of your letters, and write on a scrap of paper gilt round the edges, no bigger than a *subpœna*. I might expect this when you left off, "Honoured brother;" and "hoping you are in good health," and so forth—to begin with a "Rat me,° knight, I'm so sick of a last night's debauch"—'ods heart, and then tell a familiar tale of a cock and a bull, and a whore and a bottle, and so conclude.—You could write news before you were out of your time, when you lived with honest Pimple Nose the attorney of Furnival's Inn°—you could entreat to be remembered then to your friends round the Wrekin. We could have gazettes, then, and Dawks's Letter, and the Weekly Bill,° till of late days.

PETULANT: S'life, Witwoud, were you ever an attorney's clerk? of the family of the Furnival? Ha! ha! ha!

WITWOUD: Ay, ay, but that was but for a while: not long, not long. Pshaw! I was not in my own power then;—an orphan, and this fellow was my guardian; ay, ay, I was glad to consent to that, man, to come to London: he had the disposal of me then. If I had not agreed to that, I might have been bound 'prentice to a feltmaker in Shrewsbury; this fellow would have bound me to a maker of fells.

SIR WILFULL: S'heart, and better than to be bound to a maker of fops; where, I suppose, you have served your time; and now you may set up for yourself.

---

²⁴⁹ **s'heart** contraction for "By God's heart"   ²⁵⁰ **Wrekin** a hill in Shropshire   ²⁵⁵ **Odso** contraction for "Godso," an exclamation   ²⁵⁹ **flap-dragon** the Christmas game of catching a raisin; here used to suggest something of small value   ²⁶⁰ **scut** tail

²⁶⁴ **inns o' court** The Inns of Court are the societies in which lawyers are trained in London.   ²⁶⁷ **Salop** i.e., Shropshire   ²⁶⁸ **Shrewsbury-cake** shortbread   ²⁷²⁻³ **a call of serjeants** a group of lawyers who have all been raised to the rank of sergeant-at-law at the same time   ²⁸³ **Rat me** i.e., "God rot me"   ²⁸⁹ **Furnival's Inn** one of the Inns of Court   ²⁹² **Dawks's Letter... Weekly Bill** *Dawks's News-Letter* was a weekly summary of the news; the Weekly Bill contained notices of deaths in London.

310 MRS. MARWOOD: You intend to travel, sir, as I'm
       informed.
     SIR WILFULL: Belike I may, madam. I may chance to
       sail upon the salt seas, if my mind hold.
     PETULANT: And the wind serve.
315 SIR WILFULL: Serve or not serve, I shan't ask licence of
       you, sir; nor the weathercock your companion:
       I direct my discourse to the lady, sir.—'Tis like
       my aunt may have told you, madam—yes, I
       have settled my concerns, I may say now, and
320   am minded to see foreign parts. If an how that
       the peace° holds, whereby that is, taxes abate.
     MRS. MARWOOD: I thought you had designed for
       France at all adventures.
     SIR WILFULL: I can't tell that; 'tis like I may, and 'tis like
325   I may not. I am somewhat dainty in making a
       resolution—because when I make it I keep it. I
       don't stand shill I, shall I,° then; if I say't, I'll
       do't; but I have thoughts to tarry a small matter
       in town, to learn somewhat of your lingo first,
330   before I cross the seas. I'd gladly have a spice of
       your French as they say, whereby to hold dis-
       course in foreign countries.
     MRS. MARWOOD: Here's an academy in town for that
       use.
335 SIR WILFULL: There is? 'Tis like there may.
     MRS. MARWOOD: No doubt you will return very much
       improved.
     WITWOUD: Yes, refined, like a Dutch skipper from a
       whale fishing.°

     [Enter LADY WISHFORT *and* FAINALL*]*

340 LADY WISHFORT: Nephew, you are welcome.
     SIR WILFULL: Aunt, your servant.
     FAINALL: Sir Wilfull, your most faithful servant.
     SIR WILFULL: Cousin Fainall, give me your hand.
     LADY WISHFORT: Cousin Witwoud, your servant; Mr.
345   Petulant, your servant—nephew, you are wel-
       come again. Will you drink anything after your
       journey, nephew; before you eat? dinner's
       almost ready.
     SIR WILFULL: I'm very well, I thank you, aunt—howev-
350   er, I thank you for your courteous offer. S'heart I
       was afraid you would have been in the fashion
       too, and have remembered to have forgot your
       relations. Here's your cousin Tony, belike, I
       mayn't call him brother for fear of offence.
355 LADY WISHFORT: O, he's a railleur, nephew—my
       cousin's a wit: and your great wits always rally
       their best friends to choose. When you have been

abroad, nephew, you'll understand raillery better.

*[*FAINALL *and* MRS. MARWOOD *talk apart]*

SIR WILFULL: Why then let him hold his tongue in the
  mean time; and rail when that day comes.   360

[Enter MINCING*]*

MINCING: Mem, I am come to acquaint your la'ship
  that dinner is impatient.
SIR WILFULL: Impatient! why then belike it won't stay
  till I pull off my boots.—Sweetheart, can you
  help me to a pair of slippers?—My man's with   365
  his horses, I warrant.
LADY WISHFORT: Fy, fy, nephew! you would not pull off
  your boots here?—Go down into the hall—dinner
  shall stay for you.—My nephew's a little unbred,
  you'll pardon him, madam.—Gentlemen, will   370
  you walk?—Marwood—
MRS. MARWOOD: I'll follow you, madam—before Sir
  Wilfull is ready.

[Exeunt all but MRS. MARWOOD *and* FAINALL*]*

FAINALL: Why then, Foible's a bawd, an arrant, rank,
  match-making bawd: and I, it seems, am a hus-   375
  band, a rank husband; and my wife a very
  arrant, rank wife—all in the way of the world.
  'Sdeath, to be a cuckold by anticipation, a cuckold in embryo! sure I was born with budding
  antlers, like a young satyr, or a citizen's child.°   380
  'Sdeath! to be out-witted—to be out-jilted—out-
  matrimony'd!—If I had kept my speed like a
  stag, 'twere somewhat,—but to crawl after, with
  my horns, like a snail, and be outstripped by
  my wife—'tis scurvy wedlock.   385
MRS. MARWOOD: Then shake it off; you have often
  wished for an opportunity to part—and now
  you have it. But first prevent their plot—the
  half of Millamant's fortune is too considerable
  to be parted with, to a foe, to Mirabell.   390
FAINALL: Damn him! that had been mine—had you
  not made that fond discovery—that had been
  forfeited, had they been married. My wife had
  added lustre to my horns by that increase of fortune; I could have worn 'em tipped with gold,   395
  though my forehead had been furnished like a
  deputy-lieutenant's hall.°

---

321 peace The Peace of Ryswick (1697) had temporarily halted the war with France, causing a rise in taxes. **327 shill I,
shall I** shilly-shally **339 whale fishing** Refining whale oil
left a distinctive odor on the whalers.

378-80 cuckold… citizen's child Fainall combines two jokes,
one about cuckolds (husbands with unfaithful wives), who
are supposed to have horns grow on their foreheads, and
another about the seduction of citizens' wives by gentlemen.
396-7 forehead… hall i.e., though his forehead were covered
with antlers, like the walls of the country house of a deputy
lieutenant

MRS. MARWOOD: They may prove a cap of mainte-
nance° to you still, if you can away with your
400   wife. And she's no worse than when you had
her—I dare swear she had given up her game
before she was married.

FAINALL: Hum! that may be.

MRS. MARWOOD: You married her to keep you; and if
405   you can contrive to have her keep you better
than you expected, why should you not keep
her longer than you intended?

FAINALL: The means, the means.

MRS. MARWOOD: Discover to my lady your wife's con-
410   duct; threaten to part with her!—my lady loves
her, and will come to any composition to save
her reputation. Take the opportunity of breaking it, just upon the discovery of this imposture.
My lady will be enraged beyond bounds, and
415   sacrifice niece, and fortune, and all, at that con-
juncture. And let me alone to keep her warm; if
she should flag in her part, I will not fail to
prompt her.

FAINALL: Faith, this has an appearance.

420   MRS. MARWOOD: I'm sorry I hinted to my lady to
endeavour a match between Millamant and Sir
Wilfull: that may be an obstacle.

FAINALL: Oh, for that matter, leave me to manage him;
I'll disable him for that; he will drink like a
425   Dane;° after dinner, I'll set his hand in.

MRS. MARWOOD: Well, how do you stand affected
towards your lady?

FAINALL: Why, faith, I'm thinking of it.—Let me see—I
am married already, so that's over:—my wife
430   has played the jade with me—well, that's over
too:—I never loved her, or if I had, why that
would have been over too by this time:—jealous
of her I cannot be, for I am certain; so there's an
end of jealousy:—weary of her I am, and shall
435   be—no, there's no end of that—no, no, that were
too much to hope. Thus far concerning my
repose; now for my reputation. As to my own, I
married not for it, so that's out of the question;—and as to my part in my wife's—why, she
440   had parted with hers before; so bringing none to
me, she can take none from me; 'tis against all
rule of play, that I should lose to one who has
not wherewithal to stake.

MRS. MARWOOD: Besides, you forget, marriage is hon-
445   ourable.

FAINALL: Hum, faith, and that's well thought on; marriage is honourable as you say; and if so, where-

fore should cuckoldom be a discredit, being
derived from so honourable a root?

MRS. MARWOOD: Nay, I know not; if the root be hon-   450
ourable, why not the branches?°

FAINALL: So, so, why this point's clear—well, how do
we proceed?

MRS. MARWOOD: I will contrive a letter which shall be
delivered to my lady at the time when that ras-   455
cal who is to act Sir Rowland is with her. It shall
come as from an unknown hand—for the less I
appear to know of the truth, the better I can
play the incendiary. Besides, I would not have
Foible provoked if I could help it—because you   460
know she knows some passages°—nay, I expect
all will come out—but let the mine be by
sprung first, and then I care not if I am discovered.

FAINALL: If the worst come to the worst—I'll turn my   465
wife to grass°—I have already a deed of settlement of the best part of her estate; which I
wheedled out of her; and that you shall partake
at least.

MRS. MARWOOD: I hope you are convinced that I hate   470
Mirabell now; you'll be no more jealous?

FAINALL: Jealous! no—by this kiss—let husbands be
jealous; but let the lover still believe; or if he
doubt, let it be only to endear his pleasure, and
prepare the joy that follows, when he proves his   475
mistress true. But let husbands' doubts convert
to endless jealousy; or if they have belief, let it
corrupt to superstition and blind credulity. I am
single, and will herd no more with 'em. True, I
wear the badge, but I'll disown the order. And   480
since I take my leave of 'em, I care not if I leave
'em a common motto to their common crest:—
All husbands must or pain or shame endure;
The wise too jealous are, fools too secure.

[Exeunt]

ACT IV

Scene 1

A Room in LADY WISHFORT's *House.* LADY WISHFORT *and*
FOIBLE

LADY WISHFORT: Is Sir Rowland coming, sayest thou,
Foible? and are things in order?

FOIBLE: Yes, madam, I have put wax lights in the
sconces, and placed the footmen in a row in the

398-99 **cap of maintenance** a heraldic term referring to the cap
carried before a high official. Mrs. Marwood plays on the
word *maintenance* to suggest that Fainall may be able to blackmail Lady Wishfort.   424-5 **drink like a Dane** Danes had a
reputation for heavy drinking.

451 **branches** cuckold's horns   461 **knows some passages**
Foible knows of Mrs. Marwood's affair with Mr. Fainall.
465-6 **turn... grass** i.e., put my wife out to pasture

5 hall, in their best liveries, with the coachman and postillion to fill up the equipage.

LADY WISHFORT: Have you pulvilled° the coachman and postillion, that they may not stink of the stable when Sir Rowland comes by.

10 FOIBLE: Yes, madam.

LADY WISHFORT: And are the dancers and the music ready, that he may be entertained in all points with correspondence to his passion?

FOIBLE: All is ready, madam.

15 LADY WISHFORT: And—well—and how do I look, Foible?

FOIBLE: Most killing well, madam.

LADY WISHFORT: Well, and how shall I receive him? In what figure shall I give his heart the first impression? there is a great deal in the first impression.

20 Shall I sit?—no, I won't sit—I'll walk—ay, I'll walk from the door upon his entrance; and then turn full upon him—no, that will be too sudden. I'll lie—ay, I'll lie down—I'll receive him in my little dressing-room, there's a couch—yes, yes, I'll

25 give the first impression on a couch.—I won't lie neither, but loll and lean upon one elbow: with one foot a little dangling off, jogging in a thoughtful way—yes—and then as soon as he appears, start, ay, start and be surprised, and rise to meet

30 him in a pretty disorder—yes—O, nothing is more alluring than a levee from a couch, in some confusion:—it shows the foot to advantage, and furnishes with blushes, and recomposing airs beyond comparison. Hark! there's a coach.

35 FOIBLE: 'Tis he, madam.

LADY WISHFORT: O dear!—Has my nephew made his addresses to Millamant? I ordered him.

FOIBLE: Sir Wilfull is set in to drinking, madam, in the parlour.

40 LADY WISHFORT: Odds my life, I'll send him to her. Call her down, Foible; bring her hither. I'll send him as I go—when they are together, then come to me, Foible, that I may not be too long alone with Sir Rowland.

[Exit]

[Enter Mrs. MILLAMANT and Mrs. FAINALL]

45 FOIBLE: Madam, I stayed here, to tell your ladyship that Mr. Mirabell has waited this half hour for an opportunity to talk with you: though my lady's orders were to leave you and Sir Wilfull together. Shall I tell Mr. Mirabell that you are at

50 leisure?

MRS. MILLAMANT: No,—what would the dear man have? I am thoughtful, and would amuse myself—bid him come another time.

"There never yet was woman made   55
Nor shall but to be cursed."°

[Repeating, and walking about]

That's hard.

MRS. FAINALL: You are very fond of Sir John Suckling to-day, Millamant, and the poets.

MRS. MILLAMANT: He? Ay, and filthy verses—so I am.

FOIBLE: Sir Wilfull is coming, madam. Shall I send Mr.   60
Mirabell away.

MRS. MILLAMANT: Ay, if you please, Foible, send him away—or send him hither—just as you will, dear Foible.—I think. I'll see him—shall I? ay, let the wretch come.   65

[Exit Foible]

"Thyrsis, a youth of the inspirèd train."°

[Repeating]

Dear Fainall, entertain Sir Wilfull—thou hast philosophy to undergo a fool, thou art married and hast patience—I would confer with my own thoughts.   70

MRS. FAINALL: I am obliged to you, that you would make me your proxy in this affair; but I have business of my own.

[Enter SIR WILFULL]

MRS. FAINALL: O Sir Wilfull, you are come at the critical instant. There's your mistress up to the ears   75
in love and contemplation; pursue your point now or never.

SIR WILFULL: Yes; my aunt will have it so—I would gladly have been encouraged with a bottle or two, because I'm somewhat wary at first before   80
I am acquainted.—*[This while MILLAMANT walks about repeating to herself]*—But I hope, after a time, I shall break my mind—that is, upon further acquaintance—so for the present, cousin, I'll take my leave—if so be you'll be so kind to   85
make my excuse, I'll return to my company—

MRS. FAINALL: O fy, Sir Wilfull! what, you must not be daunted.

SIR WILFULL: Daunted! no, that's not it, it is not so much for that—for if so be that I set on't, I'll   90
do't. But only for the present, 'tis sufficient till further acquaintance, that's all—your servant.

MRS. FAINALL: Nay, I'll swear you shall never lose so

---

7 **pulvilled** scented with powder

55 **"There... cursed"** the opening lines of a poem by Sir John Suckling (1609–1642)   66 **"Thyrsis... train"** The first line of *The Story of Phoebus and Daphne, Applied* by Edmund Waller (1606–1687)

95   favourable an opportunity, if I can help it. I'll leave you together, and lock the door.

[Exit]

SIR WILFULL: Nay, nay, cousin—I have forgot my gloves—what d'ye do?—S'heart, a'has locked the door indeed, I think—nay, Cousin Fainall, open the door—pshaw, what a vixen trick is this?—Nay, now a'has seen me too.—Cousin, I made bold to pass through as it were—I think this door's enchanted!

100

MRS. MILLAMANT: *[Repeating]*

"I prithee spare me, gentle boy,
Press me no more for that slight toy."

105   SIR WILFULL: Anan?° Cousin, your servant.

MRS. MILLAMANT: *[Repeating]*

"That foolish trifle of a heart."
Sir Wilfull!

SIR WILFULL: Yes—your servant. No offence, I hope, cousin.

MRS. MILLAMANT: *[Repeating]*

110   *"I swear it will not do its part,*
Though thou dost thine, employest thy power and art."

Natural, easy Suckling!°

SIR WILFULL: Anan?° Suckling! no such suckling neither, cousin, nor stripling: I thank Heaven, I'm no minor.

115

MRS. MILLAMANT: Ah, rustic, ruder than Gothic!

SIR WILFULL: Well, well, I shall understand your lingo one of these days, cousin; in the meanwhile I must answer in plain English.

120   MRS. MILLAMANT: Have you any business with me, Sir Wilfull?

SIR WILFULL: Not at present, cousin—yes I make bold to see, to come and know if that how you were disposed to fetch a walk this evening, if so be that I might not be troublesome, I would have sought a walk with you.

125

MRS. MILLAMANT: A walk! what then?

SIR WILFULL: Nay, nothing—only for the walk's sake, that's all.

130   MRS. MILLAMANT: I nauseate walking; 'tis a country diversion; I loathe the country, and everything that relates to it.

SIR WILFULL: Indeed! ha! look ye, look ye, you do? Nay, 'tis like you may—here are choice of pastimes here in town, as plays and the like; that must be confessed indeed.   135

MRS. MILLAMANT: *Ah l'étourdi!°* I hate the town too.

SIR WILFULL: Dear heart, that's much—ha! that you should hate 'em both! ha! 'tis like you may; there are some can't relish the town, and others can't away with the country—'tis like you may be one of those, cousin.   140

MRS. MILLAMANT: Ha! ha! ha! yes, 'tis like I may.—You have nothing further to say to me?

SIR WILFULL: Not at present, cousin.—'Tis like when I have an opportunity to be more private—I may break my mind in some measure—I conjecture you partly guess—however, that's as time shall try—but spare to speak and spare to speed, as they say.   145

150

MRS. MILLAMANT: If it is of no great importance, Sir Wilfull, you will oblige me to leave me; I have just now a little business—

SIR WILFULL: Enough, enough, cousin: yes, yes, all a case—when you're disposed: now's as well as another time; and another time as well as now. All's one for that—yes, yes, if your concerns call you, there's no haste; it will keep cold, as they say.—Cousin, your servant—I think this door's locked.   155

160

MRS. MILLAMANT: You may go this way, sir.

SIR WILFULL: Your servant; then with your leave I'll return to my company.

[Exit]

MRS. MILLAMANT: Ay, ay; ha! ha! ha!

"Like Phœbus sung the no less amorous boy."   165

[Enter MIRABELL]

MIRABELL: *"Like Daphne she, as lovely and as coy."°* Do you lock yourself up from me, to make my search more curious? or is this pretty artifice contrived to signify that here the chase must end, and my pursuits be crowned? For you can fly no further.   170

MRS. MILLAMANT: Vanity! no—I'll fly, and be followed to the last moment. Though I am upon the very verge of matrimony, I expect you should solicit me as much as if I were wavering at the grate of a monastery, with one foot over the threshold. I'll be solicited to the very last, nay, and afterwards.   175

---

[112] **"I prithee... Suckling"** The first stanza of a song by Sir John Suckling   [105], [113] **Anan** an interjection equivalent to "pardon me"

[137] *Ah l'étourdi* Ah, the fool   [165-6] **"Like Phoebus sung... coy"** Millamant and Mirabell speak a couplet from Waller's poem; see note 3.

MIRABELL: What, after the last?

MRS. MILLAMANT: Oh, I should think I was poor and
180   had nothing to bestow, if I were reduced to an
       inglorious ease, and freed from the agreeable
       fatigues of solicitation.

MIRABELL: But do not you know, that when favours
       are conferred upon instant and tedious solicita-
185   tion, that they diminish in their value, and that
       both the giver loses the grace, and the receiver
       lessens his pleasure?

MRS. MILLAMANT: It may be in things of common
       application; but never sure in love. Oh, I hate a
190   lover that can dare to think he draws a
       moment's air, independent of the bounty of his
       mistress. There is not so impudent a thing in
       nature, as the saucy look of an assured man,
       confident of success. The pedantic arrogance of
195   a very husband has not so pragmatical an air.
       Ah! I'll never marry, unless I am first made sure
       of my will and pleasure.

MIRABELL: Would you have 'em both before marriage?
       or will you be contented with the first now, and
200   stay for the other till after grace?

MRS. MILLAMANT: Ah! don't be impertinent.—My dear
       liberty, shall I leave thee? my faithful solitude,
       my darling contemplation, must I bid you then
       adieu? Ay-h adieu—my morning thoughts,
205   agreeable wakings, indolent slumbers, all ye
       douceurs, ye *sommeils du matin*, adieu?°—I can't
       do't, 'tis more than impossible—positively,
       Mirabell, I'll lie abed in a morning as long as I
       please.

210 MIRABELL: Then I'll get up in a morning as early as I
       please.

MRS. MILLAMANT: Ah! idle creature, get up when you
       will—and d'ye hear, I won't be called names after
       I'm married; positively I won't be called names.

215 MIRABELL: Names!

MRS. MILLAMANT: Ay, as wife, spouse, my dear, joy,
       jewel, love, sweetheart, and the rest of that nau-
       seous cant, in which men and their wives are so
       fulsomely familiar—I shall never bear that—
220   good Mirabell, don't let us be familiar or fond,
       nor kiss before folks, like my Lady Fadler and
       Sir Francis: nor go to Hyde-park together the
       first Sunday in a new chariot, to provoke eyes
       and whispers, and then never to be seen there
225   together again; as if we were proud of one
       another the first week, and ashamed of one
       another ever after. Let us never visit together,
       nor go to a play together; but let us be very
       strange and well-bred: let us be as strange as if

we had been married a great while; and as well   230
bred as if we were not married at all.

MIRABELL: Have you any more conditions to offer?
       Hitherto your demands are pretty reasonable.

MRS. MILLAMANT: Trifles!—As liberty to pay and
       receive visits to and from whom I please; to
       write and receive letters, without interrogato-   235
       ries or wry faces on your part; to wear what I
       please; and choose conversation with regard
       only to my own taste; to have no obligation
       upon me to converse with wits that I don't like,
       because they are your acquaintance: or to be   240
       intimate with fools, because they may be your
       relations. Come to dinner when I please; dine in
       my dressing-room when I'm out of humour,
       without giving a reason. To have my closet invi-
       olate; to be sole empress of my tea-table, which   245
       you must never presume to approach without
       first asking leave. And lastly, wherever I am,
       you shall always knock at the door before you
       come in. These articles subscribed, if I continue
       to endure you a little longer, I may by degrees   250
       dwindle into a wife.

MIRABELL: Your bill of fare is something advanced in
       this latter account.—Well, have I liberty to offer
       conditions—that when you are dwindled into a
       wife, I may not be beyond measure enlarged   255
       into a husband?

MRS. MILLAMANT: You have free leave; propose your
       utmost, speak and spare not.

MIRABELL: I thank you.—*Imprimis*° then, I covenant,
       that your acquaintance be general; that you   260
       admit no sworn confidant, or intimate of your
       own sex; no she friend to screen her affairs
       under your countenance, and tempt you to
       make trial of a mutual secrecy. No decoy duck
       to wheedle you a fop-scrambling to the play in   265
       a mask—then bring you home in a pretended
       fright, when you think you shall be found out—
       and rail at me for missing the play, and disap-
       pointing the frolic which you had to pick me
       up, and prove my constancy.   270

MRS. MILLAMANT: Detestable *imprimis*! I go to the play
       in a mask!

MIRABELL: *Item*, I article,° that you continue to like
       your own face, as long as I shall: and while it
       passes current with me, that you endeavour not   275
       to new-coin it. To which end, together with all
       vizards for the day, I prohibit all masks for the
       night, made of oiled-skins, and I know not
       what—hogs' bones, hares' gall, pig-water, and
       the marrow of a roasted cat.° In short, I forbid   280

---

²⁰⁶ *ye douceurs... adieu* you sweet pleasures, you morning
slumbers, good-bye

²⁷¹ *Imprimis* first   ²⁷³ **article** stipulate   ²⁷⁹⁻⁸⁰ **hogs'... cat**
ingredients in cosmetics

all commerce with the gentlewoman in what d'ye call it court. *Item,* I shut my doors against all bawds with baskets, and pennyworths of muslin, china, fans, atlasses,° etc.—*Item,* when
285 you shall be breeding—

MRS. MILLAMANT: Ah! name it not.

MIRABELL: Which may be presumed with a blessing on our endeavours.

MRS. MILLAMANT: Odious endeavours!

290 MIRABELL: I denounce against all strait lacing, squeezing for a shape, till you mould my boy's head like a sugar-loaf, and instead of a man child, make me father to a crooked billet. Lastly, to the dominion of the tea-table I submit—but with
295 proviso, that you exceed not in your province; but restrain yourself to native and simple tea-table drinks, as tea, chocolate, and coffee: as likewise to genuine and authorised tea-table talk—such as mending of fashions, spoiling
300 reputations, railing at absent friends, and so forth—but that on no account you encroach upon the men's prerogative, and presume to drink healths, or toast fellows; for prevention of which I banish all foreign forces, all auxiliaries
305 to the tea-table, as orange-brandy, all aniseed, cinnamon, citron, and Barbadoes waters, together with ratafia, and the most noble spirit of clary°—but for cowslip wine, poppy water, and all dormitives,° those I allow.—These pro-
310 visos admitted, in other things I may prove a tractable and complying husband.

MRS. MILLAMANT: O horrid provisos! filthy strong-waters! I toast fellows! odious men! I hate your odious provisos.

315 MIRABELL: Then we are agreed! shall I kiss your hand upon the contract? And here comes one to be a witness to the sealing of the deed.

[Enter MRS. FAINALL]

MRS. MILLAMANT: Fainall, what shall I do? shall I have him? I think I must have him.

320 MRS. FAINALL: Ay, ay, take him, take him, what should you do?

MRS. MILLAMANT: Well then—I'll take my death I'm in a horrid fright—Fainall, I shall never say it—well—I think—I'll endure you.

325 MRS. FAINALL: Fy! fy! have him, have him, and tell him so in plain terms: for I am sure you have a mind to him.

MRS. MILLAMANT: Are you? I think I have—and the horrid man looks as if he thought so too—well,
330 you ridiculous thing you, I'll have you—I won't

be kissed, nor I won't be thanked—here kiss my hand though.—So, hold your tongue now, don't say a word.

MRS. FAINALL: Mirabell, there's a necessity for your obedience;—you have neither time to talk nor 335 stay. My mother is coming; and in my conscience if she should see you, would fall into fits, and maybe not recover time enough to return to Sir Rowland, who, as Foible tells me, is in a fair way to succeed. Therefore spare your ecstacies 340 for another occasion, and slip down the back-stairs, where Foible waits to consult you.

MRS. MILLAMANT: Ay, go, go. In the mean time I suppose you have said something to please me.

MIRABELL: I am all obedience. 345

[Exit]

MRS. FAINALL: Yonder Sir Wilfull's drunk, and so noisy that my mother has been forced to leave Sir Rowland to appease him; but he answers her only with singing and drinking—what they may have done by this time I know not; but Petulant 350 and he were upon quarrelling as I came by.

MRS. MILLAMANT: Well, if Mirabell should not make a good husband, I am a lost thing,—for I find I love him violently.

MRS. FAINALL: So it seems; for you mind not what's 355 said to you.—If you doubt him, you had best take up with Sir Wilfull.

MRS. MILLAMANT: How can you name that superannuated lubber? foh!

[Enter WITWOUD]

MRS. FAINALL: So, is the fray made up, that you have 360 left 'em?

WITWOUD: Left 'em? I could stay no longer—I have laughed like ten christnings—I am tipsy with laughing—if I had stayed any longer I should have burst,—I must have been let out and pieced 365 in the sides like an unsized camlet.°—Yes, yes, the fray is composed; my lady came in like a *noli prosequi,*° and stopped the proceedings.

MRS. MILLAMANT: What was the dispute?

WITWOUD: That's the jest; there was no dispute. They 370 could neither of 'em speak for rage, and so fell a sputtering at one another like two roasting apples.

[Enter PETULANT, drunk]

WITWOUD: Now, Petulant, all's over, all's well. Gad, my head begins to whim it about—why dost thou 375

---

not speak? thou art both as drunk and as mute as a fish.

PETULANT: Look you, Mrs. Millamant—if you can love me, dear nymph—say it—and that's the conclu-
380   sion—pass on, or pass off—that's all.

WITWOUD: Thou hast uttered volumes, folios, in less than *decimo sexto*,° my dear Lacedemonian.° Sirrah, Petulant, thou art an epitomiser of words.

PETULANT: Witwoud—you are an annihilator of sense.

385 WITWOUD: Thou art a retailer of phrases; and dost deal in remnants of remnants, like a maker of pin-cushions—thou art in truth (metaphorically speaking) a speaker of shorthand.

PETULANT: Thou art (without a figure) just one half of
390   an ass, and Baldwin° yonder, thy half-brother, is the rest.—A Gemini° of asses split would make just four of you.

WITWOUD: Thou dost bite, my dear mustard-seed; kiss me for that.

395 PETULANT: Stand off!—I'll kiss no more males—I have kissed your twin yonder in a humour of recon-ciliation, till he [*Hiccups*] rises upon my stom-ach like a radish.

MRS. MILLAMANT: Eh! filthy creature! what was the
400   quarrel?

PETULANT: There was no quarrel—there might have been a quarrel.

WITWOUD: If there had been words enow between 'em to have expressed provocation, they had gone
405   together by the ears like a pair of castanets.

PETULANT: You were the quarrel.

MRS. MILLAMANT: Me!

PETULANT: If I have a humour to quarrel, I can make less matters conclude premises.—If you are not
410   handsome, what then, if I have a humour to prove it? If I shall have my reward, say so; if not, fight for your face the next time yourself—I'll go sleep.

WITWOUD: Do, wrap thyself up like a wood-louse, and
415   dream revenge—and hear me, if thou canst learn to write by to-morrow morning, pen me a challenge.—I'll carry it for thee.

PETULANT: Carry your mistress's monkey a spider!—Go flea dogs, and read romances!—I'll go to bed
420   to my maid.

[Exit]

MRS. FAINALL: He's horridly drunk.—How came you all in this pickle?

WITWOUD: A plot! a plot! to get rid of the night—your husband's advice; but he sneaked off.

Scene 2

The Dining-room in LADY WISHFORT'*s House.* SIR WILFULL *drunk,* LADY WISHFORT, WITWOUD, MRS. MILLAMANT, *and* MRS. FAINALL

LADY WISHFORT: Out upon't, out upon't! At years of discretion, and comport yourself at this rantipole° rate!

SIR WILFULL: No offence, aunt.

LADY WISHFORT: Offence! as I'm a person, I'm   5 ashamed of you—foh! how you stink of wine! D'ye think my niece will ever endure such a Borachio!° you're an absolute Borachio.

SIR WILFULL: Borachio?

LADY WISHFORT: At a time when you should commence   10 an amour, and put your best foot foremost—

SIR WILFULL: S'heart, an you grutch me your liquor, make a bill—give me more drink, and take my purse—

[*Sings*]

"*Prithee fill me the glass,*   15
Till it laugh in my face,
With ale that is potent and mellow;
   He that whines for a lass,
   Is an ignorant ass,
For a bumper has not its fellow."   20

But if you would have me marry my cousin—say the word, and I'll do't—Wilfull will do't, that's the word—Wilfull will do't, that's my crest—my motto I have forgot.

LADY WISHFORT: My nephew's a little overtaken,   25 cousin—but 'tis with drinking your health—O' my word you are obliged to him.

SIR WILFULL: *In vino veritas*,° aunt.—If I drunk your health to-day, cousin—I am a Borachio. But if you have a mind to be married, say the word,   30 and send for the piper; Wilfull will do't. If not, dust it away, and let's have t'other round.—Tony!—Odds heart, where's Tony!—Tony's an honest fellow; but he spits after a bumper, and that's a fault.—   35

[*Sings*]

"*We'll drink, and we'll never ha' done, boys,*
Put the glass then around with the sun, boys,

---

382 *decimo sexto* a small book format; i.e., tiny
382 **Lacedemonian** Spartan   390 **Baldwin** the name of the ass in the medieval tale *Reynard the Fox*   391 **A Gemini** i.e., twins

3 **rantipole** wild   8 **Borachio** from the Spanish word for *drunkard*; a reference to the character in Shakespeare's *Much Ado About Nothing*   28 *In vino veritas* "In wine there is truth"; i.e., drunkards speak the truth.

Let Apollo's example invite us;
*   For he's drunk every night,*
40 *   And that makes him so bright,*
That he's able next morning to light us."

The sun's a good pimple,° an honest soaker; he
has a cellar at your Antipodes. If I travel, aunt, I
touch at your Antipodes.—Your Antipodes are a
45 good, rascally sort of topsy-turvy fellows: if I had
a bumper, I'd stand upon my head and drink a
health to 'em.—A match or no match, cousin
with the hard name?—Aunt, Wilfull will do't. If
she has her maidenhead, let her look to't; if she
50 has not, let her keep her own counsel in the
meantime, and cry out at the nine months' end.

MRS. MILLAMANT: Your pardon, madam, I can stay no
longer—Sir Wilfull grows very powerful. Eh!
how he smells! I shall be overcome, if I stay.—
55 Come, cousin.

[Exeunt MRS. MILLAMANT, and MRS. FAINALL]

LADY WISHFORT: Smells! he would poison a tallow-chan-
dler° and his family! Beastly creature, I know not
what to do with him!—Travel, quotha! ay, travel,
travel, get thee gone, get thee gone, get thee but
60 far enough, to the Saracens, or the Tartars, or the
Turks!—for thou art not fit to live in a Christian
commonwealth, thou beastly Pagan!

SIR WILFULL: Turks, no; no Turks, aunt: your Turks are
infidels, and believe not in the grape. Your
65 Mahometan, your Mussulman, is a dry
stinkard°—no offence, aunt. My map says that
your Turk is not so honest a man as your
Christian. I cannot find by the map that your
Mufti° is orthodox—whereby it is a plain case,
70 that orthodox is a hard word, aunt, and
[Hiccups] Greek for claret.—

[Sings]

"To drink is a Christian diversion,
Unknown to the Turk or the Persian:
*   Let Mahometan fools*
75 *   Live by heathenish rules,*
And be damned over tea-cups and coffee.
*   But let British lads sing,*
*   Crown a health to the king,*
And a fig for your sultan and sophy!"°

80 Ah Tony!

[Enter FOIBLE, who whispers to LADY WISHFORT]

LADY WISHFORT: [Aside to Foible]—Sir Rowland impatient? Good lack! what shall I do with this beastly tumbril?°—[Aloud] Go lie down and sleep, you
sot!—or, as I'm a person, I'll have you bastina-
doed with broomsticks.—Call up the wenches. 85
SIR WILFULL: Ahey! wenches, where are the wenches?
LADY WISHFORT: Dear Cousin Witwoud, get him away,
and you will bind me to you inviolably. I have
an affair of moment that invades me with some
precipitation—you will oblige me to all futurity. 90
WITWOUD: Come, knight.—Pox on him, I don't know
what to say to him.—Will you go to a cockmatch?
SIR WILFULL: With a wench, Tony! Is she a shakebag,°
sirrah? Let me bite your cheek° for that.
WITWOUD: Horrible! he has a breath like a bag-pipe!— 95
Ay, ay; come, will you march, my Salopian?°
SIR WILFULL: Lead on, little Tony—I'll follow thee, my
Anthony, my Tantony, sirrah, thou shalt be my
Tantony, and I'll be thy pig.°

[Sings]

"And a fig for your sultan and sophy." 100

[Exeunt SIR WILFULL and WITWOUD]

LADY WISHFORT: This will never do. It will never make
a match—at least before he has been abroad.

[Enter WAITWELL, disguised as SIR ROWLAND]

LADY WISHFORT: Dear Sir Rowland, I am confounded
with confusion at the retrospection of my own
rudeness!—I have more pardons to ask than the 105
pope distributes in the year of jubilee.° But I
hope where there is likely to be so near an
alliance, we may unbend the severity of decorums, and dispense with a little ceremony.
WAITWELL: My impatience, madam, is the effect of my 110
transport; and till I have the possession of your
adorable person, I am tantalised on the rack;
and do but hang, madam, on the tenter° of
expectation.
LADY WISHFORT: You have excess of gallantry, Sir 115
Rowland, and press things to a conclusion with
a most prevailing vehemence.—But a day or
two for decency of marriage—

---

⁸³ **tumbril** cart ⁹³ **shakebag** a fighting cock ⁹⁴ **bite your cheek** give you a kiss ⁹⁶ **Salopian** from Shropshire ⁹⁸⁻⁹ **Anthony... pig** St. Anthony, or Tanthony, patron of swineherds, was represented in art accompanied by a pig. ¹⁰⁶ **jubilee** the year in which the Pope grants a general remission of sins; about every twenty-five years ¹¹³ **tenter** tenterhook

⁴² **pimple** companion ⁵⁶⁻⁷ **tallow-chandler** candlemaker ⁶⁵⁻⁶ **dry stinkard** Muslims do not drink alcohol. ⁶⁹ **Mufti** the Grand Mufti, the religious leader of Turkey ⁷⁹ **sophy** a title for the Shah of Persia

WAITWELL: For decency of funeral, madam! The delay
120   will break my heart—or, if that should fail, I
   shall be poisoned. My nephew will get an
   inkling of my designs, and poison me—and I
   would willingly starve him before I die—I
   would gladly go out of the world with that sat-
125   isfaction.—That would be some comfort to me,
   if I could but live so long as to be revenged on
   that unnatural viper!
LADY WISHFORT: Is he so unnatural, say you? Truly I
130   would contribute much both to the saving of
   your life, and the accomplishment of your
   revenge.—Not that I respect myself, though he
   has been a perfidious wretch to me.
WAITWELL: Perfidious to you!
LADY WISHFORT: O Sir Rowland, the hours that he has
135   died away at my feet, the tears that he has shed,
   the oaths that he has sworn, the palpitations that
   he has felt, the trances and the tremblings, the
   ardours and the ecstacies, the kneelings and the
   risings, the heart-heavings and the hand-grip-
140   ings, the pangs and the pathetic regards of his
   protesting eyes!—Oh, no memory can register!
WAITWELL: What, my rival! is the rebel my rival?—a'
   dies.
LADY WISHFORT: No, don't kill him at once, Sir
145   Rowland, starve him gradually, inch by inch.
WAITWELL: I'll do't. In three weeks he shall be barefoot;
   in a month out at knees with begging an alms.—
   He shall starve upward and upward, till he has
   nothing living but his head, and then go out in a
150   stink like a candle's end upon a save-all.°
LADY WISHFORT: Well, Sir Rowland, you have the
   way—you are no novice in the labyrinth of
   love—you have the clue.—But as I am a person,
   Sir Rowland, you must not attribute my yield-
155   ing to any sinister appetite, or indigestion of
   widowhood; nor impute my complacency to
   any lethargy of continence—I hope you do not
   think me prone to any iteration of nuptials—
WAITWELL: Far be it from me—
160 LADY WISHFORT: If you do, I protest I must recede—or
   think that I have made a prostitution of decorums; but in the vehemence of compassion, and
   to save the life of a person of so much importance—
165 WAITWELL: I esteem it so.
LADY WISHFORT: Or else you wrong my condescension.
WAITWELL: I do not, I do not!
LADY WISHFORT: Indeed you do.
WAITWELL: I do not, fair shrine of virtue!
170 LADY WISHFORT: If you think the least scruple of car-

nality was an ingredient—
WAITWELL: Dear madam, no. You are all camphor°
   and frankincense, all chastity and odour.
LADY WISHFORT: Or that—

[Enter FOIBLE]

FOIBLE: Madam, the dancers are ready; and there's one   175
   with a letter, who must deliver it into your own
   hands.
LADY WISHFORT: Sir Rowland, will you give me leave?
   Think favourably, judge candidly, and conclude
   you have found a person who would suffer   180
   racks in honour's cause, dear Sir Rowland, and
   will wait on you incessantly.

[Exit]

WAITWELL: Fy, fy!—What a slavery have I undergone!
   Spouse, hast thou any cordial; I want spirits.
FOIBLE: What a washy rogue art thou, to pant thus for   185
   a quarter of an hour's lying and swearing to a
   fine lady!
WAITWELL: Oh, she is the antidote to desire! Spouse,
   thou wilt fare the worse for't—I shall have no
   appetite to iteration of nuptials this eight-and-   190
   forty hours.—By this hand I'd rather be a chairman in the dog-days°—than act Sir Rowland till
   this time to-morrow!

[Re-enter LADY WISHFORT, with a letter]

LADY WISHFORT: Call in the dancers.—Sir Rowland,
   we'll sit, if you please, and see the entertainment.   195
   [A Dance] Now, with your permission, Sir
   Rowland, I will peruse my letter.—I would open
   it in your presence, because I would not make
   you uneasy. If it should make you uneasy, I
   would burn it.—Speak, if it does—but you may   200
   see the superscription is like a woman's hand.
FOIBLE: *[Aside to WAITWELL]* By Heaven! Mrs.
   Marwood's, I know it.—My heart aches—get it
   from her.
WAITWELL: A woman's hand! no, madam, that's no   205
   woman's hand, I see that already. That's somebody whose throat must be cut.
LADY WISHFORT: Nay, Sir Rowland, since you give me
   a proof of your passion by your jealousy, I
   promise you I'll make a return, by a frank com-   210
   munication.—You shall see it—we'll open it
   together—look you here.—*[Reads]* "Madam,
   though unknown to you"—Look you there, 'tis
   from nobody that I know—"I have that honour

---

[150] **save-all** the device in a candle holder that ensures that
the candle burns completely

[172] **camphor** a substance believed to suppress sexual desire
[191-2] **chairman... dog-days** i.e., a sedan chair carrier in the
hottest days of July and August

215 for your character, that I think myself obliged to let you know you are abused. He who pretends to be Sir Rowland, is a cheat and a rascal."—Oh Heavens! what's this?

FOIBLE: [*Aside*] Unfortunate! all's ruined!

220 WAITWELL: How, how, let me see, let me see!—[*Reads*] "A rascal, and disguised and suborned for that imposture,"—O villainy! O villainy!—"by the contrivance of—"

LADY WISHFORT: I shall faint, I shall die, oh!

225 FOIBLE: [*Aside to* WAITWELL] Say 'tis your nephew's hand—quickly, his plot, swear it, swear it!

WAITWELL: Here's a villain! madam, don't you perceive it, don't you see it?

LADY WISHFORT: Too well, too well! I have seen too 230 much.

WAITWELL: I told you at first I knew the hand.—A woman's hand! The rascal writes a sort of a large hand; your Roman hand;—I saw there was a throat to be cut presently. If he were my son,
235 as he is my nephew, I'd pistol him!

FOIBLE: O treachery!—But are you sure, Sir Rowland, it is his writing?

WAITWELL: Sure! am I here? do I live? do I love this pearl of India? I have twenty letters in my pock-
240 et from him in the same character.

LADY WISHFORT: How!

FOIBLE: O what luck it is, Sir Rowland, that you were present at this juncture!—This was the business that brought Mr. Mirabell disguised to Madam
245 Millamant this afternoon. I thought something was contriving, when he stole by me and would have hid his face.

LADY WISHFORT: How, how!—I heard the villain was in the house indeed; and now I remember, my
250 niece went away abruptly, when Sir Wilfull was to have made his addresses.

FOIBLE: Then, then, madam, Mr. Mirabell waited for her in her chamber! but I would not tell your ladyship to discompose you when you were to
255 receive Sir Rowland.

WAITWELL: Enough, his date is short.

FOIBLE: No, good Sir Rowland, don't incur the law.

WAITWELL: Law! I care not for law. I can but die, and 'tis in a good cause.—My lady shall be satisfied
260 of my truth and innocence, though it cost me my life.

LADY WISHFORT: No, dear Sir Rowland, don't fight; if you should be killed I must never show my face; or hanged—O, consider my reputation, Sir
265 Rowland!—No, you shan't fight—I'll go in and examine my niece; I'll make her confess. I conjure you, Sir Rowland, by all your love, not to fight.

WAITWELL: I am charmed, madam, I obey. But some proof you must let me give you; I'll go for a black
270 box, which contains the writings of my whole estate, and deliver them into your hands.

LADY WISHFORT: Ay, dear Sir Rowland, that will be some comfort, bring the black box.

WAITWELL: And may I presume to bring a contract to be signed this night? may I hope so far? 275

LADY WISHFORT: Bring what you will; but come alive, pray come alive. Oh, this is a happy discovery!

WAITWELL: Dead or alive I'll come—and married we will be in spite of treachery; ay, and get an heir that shall defeat the last remaining glimpse of 280 hope in my abandoned nephew. Come, my buxom widow:—

Ere long you shall substantial proofs receive,
That I'm an errant knight°—

FOIBLE: [*Aside*]   Or arrant knave.° 285

[Exeunt]

ACT V

Scene 1

LADY WISHFORT and FOIBLE. *A Room in* LADY WISHFORT'S *House.*

LADY WISHFORT: Out of my house, out of my house, thou viper! thou serpent, that I have fostered! thou bosom traitress, that I raised from nothing!—Begone! begone! begone!—go! go!—That I took from washing of old gauze and weaving 5 of dead hair, with a bleak blue nose over a chafing-dish of starved embers, and dining behind a traverse rag,° in a shop no bigger than a birdcage!—Go, go! starve again, do, do!

FOIBLE: Dear madam, I'll beg pardon on my knees. 10

LADY WISHFORT: Away! out! out!—Go, set up for yourself again!—Do, drive a trade, do, with your threepennyworth of small ware, flaunting upon a packthread, under a brandy-seller's bulk,° or against a dead wall by a ballad-monger! Go, 15 hang out an old Frisoneer gorget,° with a yard of yellow colberteen° again. Do; an old gnawed mask, two rows of pins, and a child's fiddle; a glass necklace with the beads broken, and a quilted nightcap with one ear. Go, go, drive a 20 trade!—These were your commodities, you treacherous trull! this was the merchandise you dealt in when I took you into my house, placed you next myself, and made you governante of my whole family! You have forgot this, have you, 25 now you have feathered your nest?

---

²⁸⁴ **arrant knight** i.e., a "wandering" knight   ²⁸⁵ **arrant knave** i.e., an arrant, "downright" villain

⁸ **traverse rag** a curtain   ¹⁴ **bulk** stall   ¹⁶ **Frisoneer gorget** neck scarf   ¹⁷ **colberteen** a kind of lace

FOIBLE: No, no, dear madam. Do but hear me, have but a moment's patience, I'll confess all. Mr. Mirabell seduced me; I am not the first that he has wheedled with his dissembling tongue; your ladyship's own wisdom has been deluded by him; then how should I, a poor ignorant, defend myself? O madam, if you knew but what he promised me, and how he assured me your ladyship should come to no damage!—Or else the wealth of the Indies should not have bribed me to conspire against so good, so sweet, so kind a lady as you have been to me.

LADY WISHFORT: No damage! What, to betray me, and marry me to a cast-servingman!° to make me a receptacle, an hospital for a decayed pimp! No damage! O thou frontless impudence, more than a big-bellied actress!

FOIBLE: Pray, do but hear me, madam; he could not marry your ladyship, madam.—No, indeed, his marriage was to have been void in law, for he was married to me first, to secure your ladyship. He could not have bedded your ladyship; for if he had consummated with your ladyship, he must have run the risk of the law, and been put upon his clergy.°—Yes, indeed, I inquired of the law in that ease before I would meddle or make.

LADY WISHFORT: What then, I have been your property, have I? I have been convenient to you, it seems!—While you were catering for Mirabell, I have been broker for you! What, have you made a passive bawd of me?—This exceeds all precedent; I am brought to fine uses, to become a botcher of second-hand marriages between Abigails and Andrews!—I'll couple you!—Yes, I'll baste you together, you and your Philander!° I'll Duke's-place you, as I am a person! Your turtle is in custody already: you shall coo in the same cage, if there be a constable or warrant in the parish.

[Exit]

FOIBLE: Oh that ever I was born! Oh that I was ever married!—A bride!—ay, I shall be a Bridewell-bride°—Oh!

[Enter MRS. FAINALL]

MRS. FAINALL: Poor Foible, what's the matter?

FOIBLE: O madam, my lady's gone for a constable. I shall

---

be had to a justice, and put to Bridewell to beat hemp. Poor Waitwell's gone to prison already.

MRS. FAINALL: Have a good heart, Foible; Mirabell's gone to give security for him. This is all Marwood's and my husband's doing.

FOIBLE: Yes, yes; I know it, madam: she was in my lady's closet, and overheard all that you said to me before dinner. She sent the letter to my lady; and that missing effect, Mr. Fainall laid this plot to arrest Waitwell, when he pretended to go for the papers; and in the meantime Mrs. Marwood declared all to my lady.

MRS. FAINALL: Was there no mention made of me in the letter? My mother does not suspect my being in the confederacy? I fancy Marwood has not told her, though she has told my husband.

FOIBLE: Yes, madam; but my lady did not see that part; we stifled the letter before she read so far,—Has that mischievous devil told Mr. Fainall of your ladyship then?

MRS. FAINALL: Ay, all's out—my affair with Mirabell—everything discovered. This is the last day of our living together, that's my comfort.

FOIBLE: Indeed, madam; and so 'tis a comfort if you knew all;—he has been even with your ladyship, which I could have told you long enough since, but I love to keep peace and quietness by my goodwill. I had rather bring friends together, than set 'em at distance: but Mrs. Marwood and he are nearer related than ever their parents thought for.

MRS. FAINALL: Sayest thou so, Foible? canst thou prove this?

FOIBLE: I can take my oath of it, madam; so can Mrs. Mincing. We have had many a fair word from Madam Marwood, to conceal something that passed in our chamber one evening when you were at Hyde-park; and we were thought to have gone a-walking, but we went up unawares;—though we were sworn to secrecy too. Madam Marwood took a book and swore us upon it, but it was but a book of poems. So long as it was not a bible-oath, we may break it with a safe conscience.

MRS. FAINALL: This discovery is the most opportune thing I could wish.—Now, Mincing!

[Enter MINCING]

MINCING: My lady would speak with Mrs. Foible, mem. Mr. Mirabell is with her; he has set your spouse at liberty, Mrs. Foible, and would have you hide yourself in my lady's closet till my old lady's anger is abated. Oh, my old lady is in a perilous passion at something Mr. Fainall has said; he swears, and my old lady cries. There's a fearful hurricane, I vow. He says, mem, how

---

40 **cast-servingman** a servant who has been discharged 51 **put upon his clergy** Members of the clergy as well as people who could read could plead "benefit of clergy" to escape a death sentence. 62 **Philander** the lover in Beaumont and Fletcher's *The Laws of Candy* 68 **Bridewell-bride** Bridewell was a house of correction.

125   that he'll have my lady's fortune made over to
       him, or he'll be divorced.
MRS. FAINALL: Does your lady or Mirabell know that?
MINCING: Yes, mem; they have sent me to see if Sir
       Wilfull be sober, and to bring him to them. My
130   lady is resolved to have him, I think, rather than
       lose such a vast sum as six thousand pounds.—O
       come, Mrs. Foible, I hear my old lady.
MRS. FAINALL: Foible, you must tell Mincing that she
       must prepare to vouch when I call her.
135 FOIBLE: Yes, yes, madam.
MINCING: O yes, mem, I'll vouch anything for your
       ladyship's service, be what it will.

Scene 2

Another Room in LADY WISHFORT'*s House.* MRS. FAINALL,
LADY WISHFORT, *and* MRS. MARWOOD

LADY WISHFORT: O my dear friend, how can I enumer-
       ate the benefits that I have received from your
       goodness! To you I owe the timely discovery of
       the false vows of Mirabell; to you I owe the detec-
5   tion of the impostor Sir Rowland. And now you
       are become an intercessor with my son-in-law, to
       save the honour of my house, and compound for
       the frailties of my daughter. Well, friend, you are
       enough to reconcile me to the bad world, or else
10   I would retire to deserts and solitudes, and feed
       harmless sheep by groves and purling streams.
       Dear Marwood, let us leave the world, and retire
       by ourselves and be shepherdesses.
MRS. MARWOOD: Let us first despatch the affair in
15   hand, madam. We shall have leisure to think of
       retirement afterwards. Here is one who is con-
       cerned in the treaty.
LADY WISHFORT: Oh daughter, daughter! is it possible
       thou shouldst be my child, bone of my bone, and
20   flesh of my flesh, and, as I may say, another me,
       and yet transgress the most minute particle of
       severe virtue? Is it possible you should lean
       aside to iniquity, who have been cast in the direct
       mould of virtue? I have not only been a mould
25   but a pattern for you, and a model for you, after
       you were brought into the world.
MRS. FAINALL: I don't understand your ladyship.
LADY WISHFUL: Not understand! Why, have you not
       been naught?° have you not been sophisticated?°
       Not understand! here I am ruined to compound°
       for your caprices and your cuckoldoms. I must
30   pawn my plate and my jewels, and ruin my
       niece, and all little enough—

MRS. FAINALL: I am wronged and abused, and so are
       you. 'Tis a false accusation, as false as hell, as   35
       false as your friend there, ay, or your friend's
       friend, my false husband.
MRS. MARWOOD: My friend, Mrs. Fainall! your hus-
       band my friend! what do you mean?
MRS. FAINALL: I know what I mean, madam, and so do   40
       you; and so shall the world at a time convenient.
MRS. MARWOOD: I am sorry to see you so passionate,
       madam. More temper would look more like
       innocence. But I have done. I am sorry my zeal
       to serve your ladyship and family should admit   45
       of misconstruction, or make me liable to
       affronts. You will pardon me, madam, if I med-
       dle no more with an affair in which I am not
       personally concerned.
LADY WISHFORT: O dear friend, I am so ashamed that   50
       you should meet with such returns!—[*To* Mrs.
       Fainall] You ought to ask pardon on your knees,
       ungrateful creature! she deserves more from you
       than all your life can accomplish.—[*To* Mrs.
       Marwood] Oh, don't leave me destitute in this   55
       perplexity!—no, stick to me, my good genius.
MRS. FAINALL: I tell you, madam, you are abused.—
       Stick to you! ay, like a leech, to suck your best
       blood—she'll drop off when she's full. Madam,
       you shan't pawn a bodkin,° nor part with a   60
       brass counter,° in composition for me. I defy
       'em all. Let 'em prove their aspersions; I know
       my own innocence, and dare stand a trial.

[*Exit*]

LADY WISHFORT: Why, if she should be innocent, if she
       should be wronged after all, ha?—I don't know   65
       what to think;—and I promise you her educa-
       tion has been unexceptionable—I may say it; for
       I chiefly made it my own care to initiate her
       very infancy in the rudiments of virtue, and to
       impress upon her tender years a young odium   70
       and aversion to the very sight of men:—ay,
       friend, she would ha' shrieked if she had but
       seen a man, till she was in her teens. As I am a
       person 'tis true;—she was never suffered to
       play with a male child, though but in coats; nay,   75
       her very babies° were of the feminine gender.
       Oh, she never looked a man in the face but her
       own father, or the chaplain, and him we made a
       shift to put upon her for a woman, by the help
       of his long garments, and his sleek face, till she   80
       was going in her fifteen.
MRS. MARWOOD: 'Twas much she should be deceived
       so long.

---

²⁹ **naught** naughty, immoral   ²⁹ **sophisticated** corrupted
³⁰ **compound** compensate

⁶⁰ **bodkin** hairpin   ⁶¹ **brass counter** farthing   ⁷⁶ **babies**
dolls

85 LADY WISHFORT: I warrant you, or she would never have borne to have been catechised by him; and have heard his long lectures against singing and dancing, and such debaucheries; and going to filthy plays, and profane music-meetings, where the lewd trebles squeak nothing but bawdy, and

90 the basses roar blasphemy. Oh, she would have swooned at the sight or name of an obscene play-book!—and can I think, after all this, that my daughter can be naught? What, a whore? and thought it excommunication to set her foot with-

95 in the door of a playhouse! O dear friend, I can't believe it, no, no! as she says, let him prove it, let him prove it.

MRS. MARWOOD: Prove it, madam! What, and have your name prostituted in a public court! yours and

100 your daughter's reputation worried at the bar by a pack of bawling lawyers! To be ushered in with an Oyez° of scandal; and have your case opened by an old fumbling lecher in a quoif° like a man-midwife; to bring your daughter's infamy to

105 light; to be a theme for legal punsters and quibblers by the statute; and become a jest against a rule of court, where there is no precedent for a jest in any record—not even in doomsday-book;° to discompose the gravity of the bench, and pro-

110 voke naughty interrogatories in more naughty law Latin; while the good judge, tickled with the proceeding, simpers under a grey beard, and fidgets off and on his cushion as if he had swallowed cantharides,° or sat upon cow-itch!°—

115 LADY WISHFORT: Oh, 'tis very hard!

MRS. MARWOOD: And then to have my young revellers of the Temple° take notes, like 'prentices at a conventicle;° and after talk it over again in commons;° or before drawers in an eating-house.

120 LADY WISHFORT: Worse and worse!

MRS. MARWOOD: Nay, this is nothing; if it would end here 'twere well. But it must, after this, be consigned by the short-hand writers to the public press; and from thence be transferred to the

125 hands, nay into the throats and lungs of hawkers, with voices more licentious than the loud flounderman's:° and this you must hear till you are stunned; nay, you must hear nothing else for

some days.

130 LADY WISHFORT: Oh, 'tis insupportable! No, no, dear friend, make it up, make it up; ay, ay, I'll compound. I'll give up all, myself and my all, my niece and her all—anything, everything for composition.

135 MRS. MARWOOD: Nay, madam, I advise nothing. I only lay before you, as a friend, the inconveniences which perhaps you have overseen. Here comes Mr. Fainall; if he will be satisfied to huddle up all in silence, I shall be glad. You must think I would

140 rather congratulate than condole with you.

[Enter FAINALL]

LADY WISHFORT: Ay, ay, I do not doubt it, dear Marwood; no, no, I do not doubt it.

FAINALL: Well, madam; I have suffered myself to be overcome by the importunity of this lady your

145 friend; and am content you shall enjoy your own proper estate during life, on condition you oblige yourself never to marry, under such penalty as I think convenient.

LADY WISHFUL: Never to marry!

150 FAINALL: No more Sir Rowlands;—the next imposture may not be so timely detected.

MRS. MARWOOD: That condition, I dare answer, my lady will consent to without difficulty; she has already but too much experienced the perfidi-

155 ousness of men.—Besides, madam, when we retire to our pastoral solitude we shall bid adieu to all other thoughts.

LADY WISHFORT: Ay, that's true; but in case of necessity, as of health, or some such emergency—

160 FAINALL: Oh, if you are prescribed marriage, you shall be considered; I will only reserve to myself the power to choose for you. If your physic be wholesome, it matters not who is your apothecary. Next, my wife shall settle on me the

165 remainder of her fortune, not made over already; and for her maintenance depend entirely on my discretion.

LADY WISHFORT: This is most inhumanly savage; exceeding the barbarity of a Muscovite husband.

170 FAINALL: I learned it from his Czarish majesty's retinue,° in a winter evening's conference over brandy and pepper, amongst other secrets of matrimony and policy, as they are at present practised in the northern hemisphere. But this

175 must be agreed unto, and that positively. Lastly, I will be endowed, in right of my wife, with that six thousand pounds, which is the moiety of Mrs. Millamant's fortune in your possession;

---

102 Oyez a call for silence and attention by a public crier or court officer   **103 quoif** coif, the white headdress of a lawyer   **108 doomsday-book** the book recording William the Conqueror's survey of England   **114 cantharides** an aphrodisiac   **114 cow-itch** cowage, a plant that causes itching   **117 Temple** one of the Inns of Court in London   **117-18 'prentices at a conventicle** Puritans often required their apprentices to take notes on the weekly sermon in the meetinghouse (conventicle).   **119 commons** dining hall   **127 flounderman's** fishmonger's

170-71 Czarish majesty's retinue Peter the Great had visited England in 1698.

180 and which she has forfeited (as will appear by the last will and testament of your deceased husband, Sir Jonathan Wishfort) by her disobedience in contracting herself against your consent or knowledge; and by refusing the offered

185 match with Sir Wilfull Witwoud, which you, like a careful aunt, had provided for her.

LADY WISHFORT: My nephew was *non compos*,° and could not make his addresses.

FAINALL: I come to make demands—I'll hear no objections.

190 LADY WISHFORT: You will grant me time to consider?

FAINALL: Yes, while the instrument° is drawing, to which you must set your hand till more sufficient deeds can be perfected: which I will take care shall be done with all possible speed. In the

195 meantime I'll go for the said instrument, and till my return you may balance this matter in your own discretion.

[Exit]

LADY WISHFORT: This insolence is beyond all precedent, all parallel; must I be subject to this mer-

200 ciless villain?

MRS. MARWOOD: 'Tis severe indeed, madam, that you should smart for your daughter's wantonness.

LADY WISHFORT: 'Twas against my consent that she married this barbarian, but she would have

205 him, though her year° was not out.—Ah! her first husband, my son Languish, would not have carried it thus. Well, that was my choice, this is hers: she is matched now with a witness.°—I shall be mad!—Dear friend, is there no

210 comfort for me? must I live to be confiscated at this rebel-rate?°—Here come two more of my Egyptian plagues° too.

[Enter MRS. MILLAMANT, and SIR WILFULL WITWOUD]

SIR WILFULL: Aunt, your servant.

LADY WISHFORT: Out, caterpillar, call not me aunt! I

215 know thee not!

SIR WILFULL: I confess I have been a little in disguise,° as they say.—S'heart! and I'm sorry for't. What would you have? I hope I have committed no offence, aunt—and if I did I am willing to make

220 satisfaction; and what can a man say fairer? If I have broke anything I'll pay for't, an it cost a

pound. And so let that content for what's past, and make no more words. For what's to come, to pleasure you I'm willing to marry my cousin. So pray let's all be friends, she and I are agreed 225 upon the matter before a witness.

LADY WISHFORT: How's this, dear niece? have I any comfort? can this be true?

MRS. MILLAMANT: I am content to be a sacrifice to your repose, madam; and to convince you that I had 230 no hand in the plot, as you were misinformed, I have laid my commands on Mirabell to come in person, and be a witness that I give my hand to this flower of knighthood: and for the contract that passed between Mirabell and me, I have 235 obliged him to make a resignation of it in your ladyship's presence;—he is without, and waits your leave for admittance.

LADY WISHFORT: Well, I'll swear I am something revived at this testimony of your obedience; but 240 I cannot admit that traitor.—I fear I cannot fortify myself to support his appearance. He is as terrible to me as a gorgon;° if I see him I fear I shall turn to stone, and petrify incessantly.

MRS. MILLAMANT: If you disoblige him, he may resent 245 your refusal, and insist upon the contract still. Then 'tis the last time he will be offensive to you.

LADY WISHFORT: Are you sure it will be the last time?—If I were sure of that—shall I never see him again? 250

MRS. MILLAMANT: Sir Wilfull, you and he are to travel together, are you not?

SIR WILFULL: S'heart, the gentleman's a civil gentleman, aunt, let him come in; why, we are sworn brothers and fellow-travellers.—We are to be 255 Pylades and Orestes,° he and I.—He is to be my interpreter in foreign parts. He has been overseas once already; and with proviso that I marry my cousin, will cross 'em once again, only to bear me company.—S'heart, I'll call him 260 in,—an I set on't once, he shall come in; and see who'll hinder him.

[Goes to the door and hems]

MRS. MARWOOD: This is precious fooling, if it would pass; but I'll know the bottom of it.

LADY WISHFORT: O dear Marwood, you are not going. 265

MRS. MARWOOD: Not far, madam; I'll return immediately.

[Exit]

---

186 ***non compos*** i.e., *non compos mentis*, not in his right mind
191 **instrument** agreement   205 **her year** formal period of mourning for her first husband   208-9 **with a witness** without a doubt   211 **rebel-rate** The property of a rebel was confiscated by the Crown.   212 **Egyptian plagues** Lady Wishfort compares Mrs. Millamant and Sir Wilfull Witwoud to the biblical plagues described in Exodus.   216 **disguise** drunk

---

243 **gorgon** mythological female creature with snakes instead of hair, whose gaze could turn beholders into stone
356 **Pylades and Orestes** In Greek mythology, Pylades was the friend of Orestes, son of Agamemnon; i.e., exemplary friends.

[Enter MIRABELL]

SIR WILFULL: Look up, man, I'll stand by you; 'sbud an she do frown, she can't kill you;—besides—har-
270　kee, she dare not frown desperately, because her face is none of her own. S'heart, an she should, her forehead would wrinkle like the coat of a cream-cheese; but mum for that, fel-low-traveller.

275　MIRABELL: If a deep sense of the many injuries I have offered to so good a lady, with a sincere remorse, and a hearty contrition, can but obtain the least glance of compassion, I am too happy.—Ah, madam, there was a time!—but let
280　it be forgotten—I confess I have deservedly for-feited the high place I once held of sighing at your feet. Nay, kill me not, by turning from me in disdain.—I come not to plead for favour;—nay, not for pardon; I am a suppliant only for
285　pity—I am going where I never shall behold you more—

SIR WILFULL: How, fellow-traveller! you shall go by yourself then.

MIRABELL: Let me be pitied first, and afterwards for-
290　gotten.—I ask no more.

SIR WILFULL: By'r lady, a very reasonable request, and will cost you nothing, aunt! Come, come, for-give and forget, aunt; why you must, an you are a Christian.

295　MIRABELL: Consider, madam, in reality, you could not receive much prejudice; it was an innocent device; though I confess it had a face of guilti-ness,—it was at most an artifice which love con-trived;—and errors which love produces have
300　ever been accounted venial. At least think it is punishment enough, that I have lost what in my heart I hold most dear, that to your cruel indig-nation I have offered up this beauty, and with her my peace and quiet; nay, all my hopes of
305　future comfort.

SIR WILFULL: An he does not move me, would I may never be o' the quorum!°—an it were not as good a deed as to drink, to give her to him again, I would I might never take shipping!—
310　Aunt, if you don't forgive quickly, I shall melt, I can tell you that. My contract went no farther than a little mouth-glue, and that's hardly dry;—one doleful sigh more from my fellow-traveller, and 'tis dissolved.

315　LADY WISHFORT: Well, nephew, upon your account— Ah, he has a false insinuating tongue!—Well, sir, I will stifle my just resentment at my nephew's request.—I will endeavour what I can to forget,—but on proviso that you resign the

contract with my niece immediately.
MIRABELL: It is in writing, and with papers of concern; but I have sent my servant for it, and will deliv-er it to you, with all acknowledgments for your transcendent goodness.
LADY WISHFORT: *[Aside]* Oh, he has witchcraft in his　325 eyes and tongue!—When I did not see him, I could have bribed a villain to his assassination; but his appearance rakes the embers which have so long lain smothered in my breast.

Scene 3

The same. LADY WISHFORT, MRS. MILLAMANT, SIR WILFULL, MIRABELL, FAINALL, and MRS. MARWOOD

FAINALL: Your date of deliberation, madam, is expired. Here is the instrument; are you pre-pared to sign?
LADY WISHFORT: If I were prepared, I am not impow-ered. My niece exerts a lawful claim, having　5 matched herself by my direction to Sir Wilfull.
FAINALL: That sham is too gross to pass on me—though 'tis imposed on you, madam.
MRS. MILLAMANT: Sir, I have given my consent.
MIRABELL: And, sir, I have resigned my pretensions.　10
SIR WILFULL: And, sir, I assert my right; and will main-tain it in defiance of you, sir, and of your instru-ment. S'heart, an you talk of an instrument, sir, I have an old fox° by my thigh that shall hack your instrument of ram vellum° to shreds,　15 sir!—it shall not be sufficient for a mittimus° or a tailor's measure. Therefore withdraw your instrument, sir, or by'r lady, I shall draw mine.
LADY WISHFORT: Hold, nephew, hold!
MRS. MILLAMANT: Good Sir Wilfull, respite your valour.　20
FAINALL: Indeed! Are you provided of your guard, with your single beef-eater° there? but I'm pre-pared for you, and insist upon my first propos-al. You shall submit your own estate to my management, and absolutely make over my　25 wife's to my sole use, as pursuant to the pur-port and tenor of this other covenant.—I sup-pose, madam, your consent is not requisite in this case; nor, Mr. Mirabell, your resignation; nor, Sir Wilfull, your right.—You may draw　30 your fox if you please, sir, and make a bear-gar-den° flourish somewhere else; for here it will

---

307　**quorum** a member of the bench of magistrates

14 **fox** sword　15 **ram vellum** sheepskin, commonly used for legal documents　16 **mittimus** warrant for arrest　22 **beef-eater** guard at the Tower of London　31-2 **bear-garden** Bearbaiting was still a popular spectacle in London, and the bear gardens in which they took place were known for unruly behavior.

not avail. This, my Lady Wishfort, must be subscribed, or your darling daughter's turned
adrift, like a leaky hulk, to sink or swim, as she
and the current of this lewd town can agree.

LADY WISHFORT: Is there no means, no remedy to stop
my ruin? Ungrateful wretch! dost thou not owe
thy being, thy subsistence, to my daughter's
fortune?

FAINALL: I'll answer you when I have the rest of it in
my possession.

MIRABELL: But that you would not accept of a remedy
from my hands—I own I have not deserved you
should owe any obligation to me; or else perhaps I could advise—

LADY WISHFORT: O what? what? to save me and my
child from ruin, from want, I'll forgive all that's
past; nay, I'll consent to anything to come, to be
delivered from this tyranny.

MIRABELL: Ay, madam; but that is too late, my reward
is intercepted. You have disposed of her who
only could have made me a compensation for
all my services; but be it as it may, I am resolved
I'll serve you! you shall not be wronged in this
savage manner.

LADY WISHFORT: How! dear Mr. Mirabell, can you be so
generous at last! But it is not possible. Harkee, I'll
break my nephew's match; you shall have my
niece yet, and all her fortune, if you can but save
me from this imminent danger.

MIRABELL: Will you? I'll take you at your word. I ask
no more. I must have leave for two criminals to
appear.

LADY WISHFORT: Ay, ay, anybody, anybody!

MIRABELL: Foible is one, and a penitent.

[Enter MRS. FAINALL, FOIBLE, and MINCING]

MRS. MARWOOD: O my shame! [Mirabell *and* Lady
Wishfort *go to* Mrs. Fainall *and* Foible] These corrupt things are brought hither to expose me.

[To FAINALL]

FAINALL: If it must all come out, why let 'em know it;
'tis but the way of the world. That shall not urge
me to relinquish or abate one tittle of my terms;
no, I will insist the more.

FOIBLE: Yes, indeed, madam, I'll take my Bible oath of it.

MINCING: And so will I, mem.

LADY WISHFORT: O Marwood, Marwood, art thou
false? my friend deceive me! hast thou been a
wicked accomplice with that profligate man?

MRS. MARWOOD: Have you so much ingratitude and
injustice to give credit against your friend, to
the aspersions of two such mercenary trulls.

MINCING: Mercenary, mem? I scorn your words. 'Tis
true we found you and Mr. Fainall in the blue

garret; by the same token, you swore us to
secrecy upon Messalina's poems.° Mercenary!
No, if we would have been mercenary, we
should have held our tongues; you would have
bribed us sufficiently.

FAINALL: Go, you are an insignificant thing!—Well, what
are you the better for this; is this Mr. Mirabell's
expedient? I'll be put off no longer.—You thing,
that was a wife, shall smart for this! I will not
leave thee wherewithall to hide thy shame; your
body shall be naked as your reputation.

MRS. FAINALL: I despise you, and defy your malice!—
you have aspersed me wrongfully—I have
proved your falsehood—go you and your
treacherous—I will not name it, but starve
together—perish!

FAINALL: Not while you are worth a groat,° indeed,
my dear.—Madam, I'll be fooled no longer.

LADY WISHFORT: Ah, Mr. Mirabell, this is small comfort, the detection of this affair.

MIRABELL: Oh, in good time—your leave for the other
offender and penitent to appear, madam.

[Enter WAITWELL with a box of writings]

LADY WISHFORT: O Sir Rowland!—Well, rascal!

WAITWELL: What your ladyship pleases. I have
brought the black box at last, madam.

MIRABELL: Give it me.—Madam, you remember your
promise.

LADY WISHFORT: Ay, dear sir.

MIRABELL: Where are the gentlemen?

WAITWELL: At hand, sir, rubbing their eyes—just risen
from sleep.

FAINALL: 'Sdeath, what's this to me? I'll not wait your
private concerns.

[Enter PETULANT and WITWOUD]

PETULANT: How now? What's the matter? whose
hand's out?

WITWOUD: Heyday! what, are you all got together, like
players at the end of the last act?

MIRABELL: You may remember, gentlemen, I once
requested your hands as witnesses to a certain
parchment.

WITWOUD: Ay, I do, my hand I remember—Petulant
set his mark.

MIRABELL: You wrong him, his name is fairly written, as
shall appear.—You do not remember, gentlemen,
anything of what that parchment contains?—

[Undoing the box]

---

⁸⁵ **Messalina** a malapropism for "miscellaneous" poems.
Messalina was the notoriously profligate wife of the Roman
emperor Claudius.   ¹⁰⁰ **groat** an old silver coin

WITWOUD: No.

130 PETULANT: Not I; I writ, I read nothing.

MIRABELL: Very well, now you shall know.—Madam, your promise.

LADY WISHFORT: Ay, ay, sir, upon my honour.

MIRABELL: Mr. Fainall, it is now time that you should
135 know, that your lady, while she was at her own disposal, and before you had by your insinuations wheedled her out of a pretended settlement of the greatest part of her fortune—

FAINALL: Sir! pretended!

140 MIRABELL: Yes, sir. I say that this lady while a widow, having it seems received some cautions respecting your inconstancy and tyranny of temper, which from her own partial opinion and fondness of you she could never have suspected—
145 she did, I say, by the wholesome advice of friends, and of sages learned in the laws of this land, deliver this same as her act and deed to me in trust, and to the uses within mentioned. You may read if you please—[*Holding out the*
150 *parchment*] though perhaps what is written on the back may serve your occasions.

FAINALL: Very likely, sir. What's here?—Damnation! [*Reads*] "A deed of conveyance of the whole estate real of Arabella Languish, widow, in trust
155 to Edward Mirabell."—Confusion!

MIRABELL: Even so, sir; 'tis the Way of the World, sir, of the widows of the world. I suppose this deed may bear an elder date than what you have obtained from your lady.

160 FAINALL: Perfidious fiend! then thus I'll be revenged.

[*Offers to run at* MRS. FAINALL]

SIR WILFULL: Hold, sir! now you may make your bear-garden flourish somewhere else, sir.

FAINALL: Mirabell, you shall hear of this, sir, be sure you shall.—Let me pass, oaf!

[*Exit*]

165 MRS. FAINALL: Madam, you seem to stifle your resentment; you had better give it vent.

MRS. MARWOOD: Yes, it shall have vent—and to your confusion; or I'll perish in the attempt.

[*Exit*]

LADY WISHFORT: O daughter, daughter! 'tis plain thou
170 hast inherited thy mother's prudence.

MRS. FAINALL: Thank Mr. Mirabell, a cautious friend, to whose advice all is owing.

LADY WISHFORT: Well, Mr. Mirabell, you have kept your promise—and I must perform mine.—
175 First, I pardon, for your sake, Sir Rowland there, and Foible; the next thing is to break the matter to my nephew—and how to do that—

MIRABELL: For that, madam, give yourself no trouble; let me have your consent. Sir Wilfull is my friend; he has had compassion upon lovers, and generous-
180 ly engaged a volunteer in this action, for our service; and now designs to prosecute his travels.

SIR WILFULL: S'heart, aunt, I have no mind to marry. My cousin's a fine lady, and the gentleman loves her, and she loves him, and they deserve
185 one another; my resolution is to see foreign parts—I have set on't—and when I'm set on't I must do't. And if these two gentlemen would travel too, I think they may be spared.

PETULANT: For my part, I say little—I think things are
190 best off or on.

WITWOUD: I'gad, I understand nothing of the matter; I'm in a maze yet, like a dog in a dancing-school.

LADY WISHFORT: Well, sir, take her, and with her all the
195 joy I can give you.

MRS. MILLAMANT: Why does not the man take me? would you have me give myself to you over again?

MIRABELL: Ay, and over and over again; [*Kisses her
200 hand*] I would have you as often as possibly I can. Well, Heaven grant I love you not too well, that's all my fear.

SIR WILFULL: S'heart, you'll have time enough to toy after you're married; or if you will toy now, let
205 us have a dance in the mean time, that we who are not lovers may have some other employment besides looking on.

MIRABELL: With all my heart, dear Sir Wilfull. What shall we do for music?
210

FOIBLE: O sir, some that were provided for Sir Rowland's entertainment are yet within call. [*A Dance*]

LADY WISHFORT: As I am a person, I can hold out no longer;—I have wasted my spirits so to-day already, that I am ready to sink under the
215 fatigue; and I cannot but have some fears upon me yet, that my son Fainall will pursue some desperate course.

MIRABELL: Madam, disquiet not yourself on that account; to my knowledge his circumstances
220 are such he must of force comply. For my part, I will contribute all that in me lies to a reunion; in the mean time, madam,—[*To* MRS. FAINALL] let me before these witnesses restore to you this deed of trust; it may be a means, well-managed,
225 to make you live easily together.

From hence let those be warned who mean to wed;
  Lest mutual falsehood stain the bridal bed;
For each deceiver to his cost may find,
  That marriage-frauds too oft are paid in kind.
230

[*Exeunt omnes*]

EPILOGUE

After our Epilogue this crowd dismisses,
I'm thinking how this play'll be pulled to pieces.
But pray consider, ere you doom its fall,
How hard a thing 'twould be to please you all.
5   There are some critics so with spleen diseased,
They scarcely come inclining to be pleased:
And sure he must have more than mortal skill,
Who pleases any one against his will.
Then all bad poets we are sure are foes,
And how their number's swelled, the town well
10   knows:
In shoals I've marked 'em judging in the pit;
Though they're, on no pretence, for judgment fit,
But that they have been damned for want of wit.
Since when, they by their own offences taught,
15   Set up for spies on plays, and finding fault.
Others there are whose malice we'd prevent;
Such who watch plays with scurrilous intent
To mark out who by characters are meant.
And though no perfect likeness they can trace,
20   Yet each pretends to know the copied face.
These with false glosses° feed their own ill nature,
And turn to libel what was meant a satire.
May such malicious fops this fortune find,
To think themselves alone the fools designed:
25   If any are so arrogantly vain,
To think they singly can support a scene,
And furnish fool enough to entertain.
For well the learned and the judicious know
That satire scorns to stoop so meanly low,
30   As any one abstracted° fop to show.
For, as when painters form a matchless face,
They from each fair one catch some different
      grace;
And shining features in one portrait blend,
To which no single beauty must pretend;
35   So poets oft do in one piece expose
Whole belles-assemblées° of coquettes and beaux.

---

[21] **glosses** marginal notes   [30] **abstracted** particular   [36] **belles-assemblées** beautiful gatherings

CONTEXTS AND COMMENTARIES

William Congreve (1670–1729)

CONCERNING HUMOR IN COMEDY

. . . To define humor perhaps were as difficult as to define wit; for, like that, it is of infinite variety. To enumerate the several humors of men were a work as endless as to sum up their several opinions. And, in my mind, *Quot homines tot sententiae*, might have been more properly interpreted of humor; since there are many men of the same opinion in many things, who are yet quite different in humors. But though we cannot certainly tell what wit is, or what humor is, yet we may go near to show something which is not wit or not humor, and yet often mistaken for both. And since I have mentioned wit and humor together, let me make the first distinction between them, and observe to you that *wit is often mistaken for humor*.

I have observed that when a few things have been wittily and pleasantly spoken by any character in a comedy, it has been very usual for those who make their remarks on a play while it is acting, to say, *Such a thing is very humorously spoken; There is a great deal of humor in that part*. Thus the character of the person speaking, may be, surprisingly and pleasantly is mistaken for a character of humor, which indeed is a character of wit. But there is a great difference between a comedy wherein there are many things *humorously*, as they call it, which is *pleasantly*, spoken, and one where there are several characters of humor, distinguished by the particular and different humors appropriated to the several persons represented, and which naturally arise from the different constitutions, complexions, and dispositions of men. The saying of humorous things does not distinguish characters; for every person in a comedy may be allowed to speak them. From a witty man they are expected; and even a fool may be permitted to stumble on 'em by chance. Though I make a difference betwixt wit and humor, yet I do think that humorous characters exclude wit: no, but the manner of wit should be adapted to the humor. As, for instance, a character of a splenetic and peevish humor should have a satirical wit. A jolly and sanguine humor should have a facetious wit. The former should speak positively; the latter, carelessly: for the former observes and shows things as they are; the latter rather overlooks nature, and speaks things as he would have them, and wit and humor have both of them less alloy of judgment than the others.

523

As wit, so its opposite, *folly, is sometimes mistaken for humor*.

When a poet brings a character on the stage committing a thousand absurdities, and talking impertinencies, roaring aloud, and laughing immoderately on every or rather upon no occasion, this is a character of humor.

Is anything more common than to have a pretended comedy stuffed with such grotesques, figures and farce fools? Things that either are not in nature, or, if they are, are monsters and births of mischance, and consequently, as such, should be stifled and huddled out of the way, like *Sooterkins*. That mankind may not be shocked with an appearing possibility of the degeneration of a godlike species. For my part, I am as willing to laugh as anybody, and as easily diverted with an object truly ridiculous; but at the same time, I can never care for seeing things that force me to entertain low thoughts of any nature. I don't know how it is with others, but I confess freely to you, I could never look long upon a monkey without very mortifying reflections, though I never heard anything to the contrary why that creature is not originally of a distinct species. As I don't think humor exclusive of wit, neither do I think it inconsistent with folly; but I think the follies should be only such as men's humors may incline 'em to, and not follies entirely abstracted from both humor and nature.

Sometimes *personal defects are misrepresented for humors*.

I mean, sometimes characters are barbarously exposed on the stage, ridiculing natural deformities, casual defects in the senses, and infirmities of age. Sure the poet must be very ill-natured himself, and think his audience so, when he proposes by showing a man deformed, or deaf, or blind, to give them an agreeable entertainment, and hopes to raise their mirth by what is truly an object of compassion....

External habit of body is often mistaken for humor.

By *external habit* I do not mean the ridiculous dress or clothing of a character, though that goes a good way in some received characters. (But undoubtedly, a man's humor may incline him to dress differently from other people.) But I mean a singularity of manners, speech, and behavior, peculiar to all or most of the same country, trade, profession, or education. I cannot think that a humor which is only a habit or disposition contracted by use or custom; for by a disuse, or compliance with other customs, it may be worn off or diversified.

Affectation is generally mistaken for humor.

These are indeed so much alike that at a distance they may be mistaken one for the other. For what is humor in one may be affectation in another; and nothing is more common than for some to affect particular ways of saying and doing things, peculiar to others whom they admire and would imitate. Humor is the life, affectation the picture. He that draws a character of affectation shows humor at the second hand; he at best but publishes a translation, and his pictures are but copies.

But as these two last distinctions are the nicest, so it may be most proper to explain them by particular instances from some author of reputation. Humor I take either to be born with us, and so of a natural growth, or else to be grafted into us by some accidental change in the constitution, or revolution of the internal habit of body, by which it becomes, if I may so call it, naturalized.

Humor is from nature, habit from custom, and affectation from industry.

Humor shows us as we are.

Habit shows us as we appear under a forcible impression.

Affectation shows what we would be under a voluntary disguise.

Though here I would observe by the way that a continued affectation may in time become a habit....

I should be unwilling to venture even on a bare description of humor, much more to make a definition of it, but now my hand is in, I'll tell you what serves one instead of either. I take it to be *A singular and unavoidable manner of doing or saying anything, peculiar and natural to one man only, by which his speech and actions are distinguished from those of other men.*

Our humor has relation to us and to what proceeds from us, as the accidents have to a substance; it is a color, taste, and smell, diffused through all; though our actions are never so many and different in form, they are all splinters of the same wood, and have naturally one complexion, which, though it may be disguised by art, yet cannot be wholly changed: we may paint it with other colors, but we cannot change the grain. So the natural sound of an instrument will be distinguished, though the notes expressed by it are never so various, and the divisions never so many. Dissimulation may by degrees become more easy to our practice; but it can never absolutely transubstantiate us into what we would seem: it will always be in some proportion a violence upon nature.

A man may change his opinion but I believe he will find it a difficulty to part with his humor, and there is nothing more provoking than the being made sensible of that difference. Sometimes one shall meet with those who perhaps innocently enough, but at the same time impertinently, will ask the question, *Why are you not merry? Why are you not gay, pleasant, and cheerful?* then, instead of answering, could I ask such a one, *Why are you not handsome? Why have you not black eyes and a better complexion?* Nature abhors to be forced.

The two famous philosophers of Ephesus and Abdera have their different sects at this day. Some weep and others laugh, at one and the same thing.

I don't doubt but you have observed several men laugh when they are angry, others who are silent, some that are loud; yet I cannot suppose that it is the passion of anger which is in itself different, or more or less in one than in t'other, but that it is in the humor of the man that is predominant, and urges him to expect it in that manner. Demonstrations of pleasure are as various: one man has a humor of retiring from all company, when anything has happened to please him beyond expectation; he hugs himself alone, and thinks it an addition to the pleasure to keep it secret. Another is upon thorns till he has made proclamation of it, and must make other people sensible of his happiness before he can be so himself. So it is in grief and other passions. Demonstrations of love and the effects of that passion upon several humors are infinitely different; but here the ladies who abound in servants are the best judges. Talking of the ladies, methinks something should be observed of the humor of the fair sex, since they are sometimes so kind as to furnish out a character for comedy. But I must confess I have never made any observation of what I apprehend to be true humor in women. Perhaps passions are too powerful in that sex to let humor have its course; or may be by reason of their natural coldness, humor cannot exert itself to that extravagant degree which it often does in the male sex. For if ever anything does appear comical or ridiculous in a woman, I think it is little more than an acquired folly or an affectation. We may call them the weaker sex, but I think the true reason is because our follies are stronger and our faults are more prevailing.

One might think that the diversity of humor, which must be allowed to be diffused throughout mankind, might afford endless matter for the support of comedies. But when we come closely to consider that point, and nicely to distinguish the differences of humors, I believe we shall find the contrary. For though we allow every man something of his own, and a peculiar humor, yet every man has it not in quantity to become remarkable by it; or, if many do become remarkable by their humors, yet all those humors may not be diverting. Nor is it only requisite to distinguish what humor will be diverting, but also how much of it, what part of it to show in light, and what to cast in shades, how to set it off by preparatory scenes, and by opposing other humors to it in the same scene. Through a wrong judgment, sometimes, men's humors may be opposed when there is really no specific difference between them, only a greater proportion of the same in one than in t'other, occasioned by his having more phlegm, or choler, or whatever the constitution is from whence their humors derive their source....

I will make but one observation to you more, and have done; and that is grounded upon an observation of your own, and which I mentioned at the beginning of my letter, viz., that there is more of humor in our English comic writers than in any others. I do not at all wonder at it, for I look upon humor to be almost of English growth; at least, it does not seem to have found such increase on any other soil. And what appears to me to be the reason of it is the greater freedom, privilege, and liberty which the common people of England enjoy. Any man that has a humor is under no restraint or fear of giving it vent; they have a proverb among them, which, may be, will show the bent and genius of the people as well as a longer discourse: "He that will have a may-pole, shall have a may-pole." This is a maxim with them, and their practice is agreeable to it. I believe something considerable too may be ascribed to their feeding so much on flesh, and the grossness of their diet in general.

Madame de Staël (1766–1817)

Madame de Staël was one of the most influential and controversial writers of her time. Her writing on the subject of literature had an impact on the development of romanticism. She argues that a nation's literature arises from its political structures. These in turn are influenced by a country's social structure and by inherited patterns of consciousness that interact with the environment.

from LITERATURE CONSIDERED IN RELATION TO SOCIAL INSTITUTIONS

TRANSLATED BY PAUL LAUTER

One can discern different kinds of joking[1] in the literature of all countries, and nothing better serves to reveal the customs of a nation than the character of the mirth generally adopted by its writers. Alone, one is serious; one is merry for others—above all in one's writing. And laughter can be produced only by notions that are so familiar to those hearing them that they strike them instantly and do not require their careful attention.

Although joking cannot do without national success as easily as a philosophical work, it is subject, like anything related to wit, to the judgment of universal good taste. It takes great subtlety to give an account of the causes of the comic effect; but it is nonetheless true that general agreement must be obtained to determine the masterpieces of this, like any other, genre.

The mirth which is owed, so to speak, to the inspiration of taste and genius, the mirth produced by combinations of wit, and the mirth which the English call "humor" have almost no connection with one another. And none of these designations includes the mirth occasioned by character, because a great number of examples prove that it has nothing to do with the talent for writing merry works. Witty mirth is easy for all witty men; but only the genius of one man and the good taste of several others can inspire genuine comedy.

In one of the following chapters I will examine why the French alone were able to achieve that perfection of taste, grace, subtlety, and insight to the human heart which has yielded us the masterpieces of Molière. We now wish to discover why the customs of the English stand in the way of the true genius of mirth.

In England most men, absorbed by business, only seek pleasure as a diversion. And just as hard toil, while exciting hunger, makes it easy to satisfy, so continuous work and reflection dispose one to be content with any sort of distraction. Their domestic life, their rather stern religion, their serious occupa-

---

[1] Mme. de Staël's word here and in the chapter title is *plaisanterie*. It might better be translated as "humor" except that she uses the special sense of that English word later in the chapter. I therefore use "joking" for her *plaisanterie* as well as "mirth" for her *gaieté*. The latter may also be taken to mean words or actions of a playful, frolicsome, or sprightly character.

tions, a muggy climate make the English particularly susceptible to the distemper of boredom; and it is for this very reason that the nice entertainments of wit do not suffice them. Strong jolts are necessary for that sort of low spirits; and their authors share the taste of the spectators in this respect, or conform to it.

The mirth which participates in making a true comedy presumes a very acute observation of character. In order for the comic genius to develop, he must live much in society, attach great importance to social success, and be a connoisseur, be brought up close to that multitude of vain interests which occasions all the ridiculousness and all the contrivances of self-love. The English live withdrawn among their families or collect in public assemblies for discussion of national issues. The intermediate situation which is called society hardly exists at all among them; and it is in that interval of life, however frivolous, that one develops acuteness and taste.

The political relations among their men effaces subtleties while producing strongly decided characters. The greatness of goals, the power of means make everything which does not have a useful result drop from their sight. In monarchical states, where one depends on the character and will of a single man or on a small number of his deputies, everyone makes it his study to know the most secret thoughts of others, the most volatile gradations of feeling and the foibles of individuals.[2] But when public opinion and popular reputation are the primary influences, ambition forsakes what ambition does not need, and the mind does not exert itself to grasp what is fleeting when it has absolutely no interest in fathoming it.

The English haven't any comic writer like Molière; and if they had one, they would not appreciate all his acuteness. Even in such works as *The Miser, Tartuffe, The Misanthrope*, which portray human nature everywhere, the English would simply not notice the humorous subtleties, the nuances of self-love; they would not recognize themselves there, however true to nature they might be drawn. They do not learn about themselves in such detail; their deep passions and important occupations have made them take life more in a heap.

There is sometimes in Congreve subtle wit and skillful humor, but not any representation of natural feeling. By a singular contrast, the more simple and pure the private morals of the English, the more they exaggerate, in their comedies, the portrait of all vices. The indecency of Congreve's works would never have been tolerated in the French theater; one finds in the dialogue ingenious notions, but the morals which these comedies represent are imitated from bad French novels, which never themselves portrayed the morals of France. Nothing less resembles the English than their comedies.

One would think that, wishing to be gay, they believed it necessary to be as different as possible from what they really are; or that, profoundly respecting the sentiments which produce the happiness of their domestic life, they have not permitted them to be squandered in their theater.

Congreve and many of his imitators heaped up, with as little measure as probability, immoralities of all kinds. Such scenes are without consequence to

---

[2] England is governed by a king; but all its institutions carefully preserve civil liberty and political guarantees.

such a nation as the English; it amuses itself with them as with fairy tales, as with fantastic images of a world which is not its own. But in France, comedy, portraying customs truly, can influence them; and it then becomes more important to impose severe rules on it.

In English comedy one rarely finds truly English characters: perhaps the dignity of a free people, in England as in Rome, stands in the way of their permitting a representation of their own customs on the stage. The French voluntarily amuse themselves with themselves. Shakespeare and a few others have represented in their pieces some popular caricatures, like Falstaff, Pistol, etc.; but the effort almost entirely excludes probability. People of all nations are amused by gross jokes; but it is only in France that the most biting mirth is at once the most delicate.

Mr. Sheridan has composed in English some comedies in which the most brilliant and original wit appears in almost every scene. But, aside from the fact that one exception does not change a general rule, it is still necessary to distinguish the mirth of the talented wit, of which Molière is the model. In all countries, a writer capable of conceiving so many ideas is certain to acquire the art of opposing them to one another in a pungent manner. But as antitheses do not alone constitute eloquence, contrasts are not the only secrets of mirth; and there is in the mirth of some French authors something more natural and more inexplicable—thought can analyze it, but thought alone does not produce it. It is a sort of electricity communicated by the general *esprit* of the nation.

Mirth and eloquence are connected only in that it is involuntary inspiration which permits a man to achieve in writing or speaking perfection in one or the other. The spirit of those who surround you, of the nation in which you live, develops in you the power of persuasion or of joking much more certainly than reflection or study. Sensations come from without, and all the talents which depend immediately on sensations need the impetus given by others. Mirth and eloquence are not at all the simple results of combinations of wit; it is necessary to be shaken, altered by the emotion which gives birth to one or the other, to achieve a successful talent in those two forms. But, the common disposition of most of the English in no way stimulates their writers to mirth.

Swift, in *Gulliver* and *The Tale of a Tub*, like Voltaire in his philosophical writings, draws the happiest jokes from the opposition which exists between received error and proscribed truth, between institutions and the nature of things. Innuendos, allegories, all the fictions of the imagination, all the disguises which it borrows are combinations with which one produces mirth; and, in all the genres, although the efforts of the intellect go a long way, they are not able to achieve the versatility, the easiness of custom, the unexpected success of spontaneous impressions.

There exists, nevertheless, a kind of mirth in some English writing which has an original and natural quality. The English language has created a word, "humor," in order to express that mirth which is a disposition of the blood almost as much as of the spirit. It comes from the nature of the climate and of the national manners and customs; it would be altogether inimitable where the same causes have not developed. Some works of Fielding and of Swift, *Peregrine Pickle, Roderick Random*, but above all the works of Sterne, give a complete idea of the genre called "humor."

There is a moroseness, I could almost say a sadness, in this mirth; he who makes you laugh does not experience the pleasure he causes. One sees that he writes in a somber mood, and that he would almost be irritated at you because he amuses you. As blunt forms sometimes give more spice to praise, the mirth of "humor" is thrown into relief by the gravity of its author. The English have very rarely admitted on the stage the kind of wit they call "humor"; its effect would in no way be theatrical.

There is some misanthropy in English joking itself, and of sociability in that of the French; the one should be read when one is alone, the other is striking in proportion to the size of the audience. What the English have of mirth almost always leads to a philosophic or moral result; French mirth often has only pleasure itself as an end.

What the English draw with great talent are bizarre characters, because there are many among them. Society effaces oddities; life in the country preserves them all.

Imitation becomes the English especially badly; their attempts in the forms of elegance and mirth characteristic of French literature mostly lack delicacy and charm. They expound upon all the ideas, they exaggerate all the nuances, they believe themselves heard only when they shout and understood only when they tell all. A singular note is that leisured people find it much more difficult to utilize the time they give to their pleasure than do working men. Men devoted to business are accustomed to long expositions; men devoted to pleasure are much sooner fatigued, and the much-practiced taste experiences the most rapid satiety.

One rarely finds delicacy in minds which always apply themselves to positive results—what is truly useful and very easy to understand, and which one does not have to look at keenly to perceive. A country which stretches toward equality is also less conscious of violations of decorum. The nation being more of a unit, the writer gets used to addressing himself in his work to the judgment and feelings of all classes. In short, free countries are, and should be, serious.

When the government is based on force, one does not fear the inclination of the nation to humor; but when authority depends upon general confidence, when the public spirit is the main strength, the talent and the mirth which uncover the ridiculous and take delight in mockery are excessively dangerous to political liberty and equality. We have spoken of the misfortunes which happened to the Athenians as a result of their immoderate taste for humor. And the French would have furnished us with a fine example to corroborate the last idea, if the force of events in the revolution had permitted personalities to take their natural development.

Henri Bergson (1859–1941)

Henri Bergson began as a mathematician but eventually emerged as the preeminent philosopher of intuition. His later philosophical works, *Time and Free Will, Creative Evolution,* and *The Two Sources of Morality and Religion,* influenced the novels of Marcel Proust. Bergson's famous essay "Laughter" began to take shape as early as 1884 in his academic lectures on the subject, but Bergson continued to work on it until its publication in 1900.

LAUGHTER

TRANSLATED BY CLOUDESLEY BRERETON AND FRED ROTHWELL

What does laughter mean? What is the basal element in the laughable? What common ground can we find between the grimace of a merry-andrew, a play upon words, an equivocal situation in a burlesque and a scene of high comedy? What method of distillation will yield us invariably the same essence from which so many different products borrow either their obtrusive odour or their delicate perfume? The greatest of thinkers, from Aristotle downwards, have tackled this little problem, which has a knack of baffling every effort, of slipping away and escaping only to bob up again, a pert challenge flung at philosophic speculation.

Our excuse for attacking the problem in our turn must lie in the fact that we shall not aim at imprisoning the comic spirit within a definition. We regard it, above all, as a living thing. However trivial it may be, we shall treat it with the respect due to life. We shall confine ourselves to watching it grow and expand. Passing by imperceptible gradations from one form to another, it will be seen to achieve the strangest metamorphoses. We shall disdain nothing we have seen. Maybe we may gain from this prolonged contact, for the matter of that, something more flexible than an abstract definition—a practical, intimate acquaintance, such as springs from a long companionship. And maybe we may also find that, unintentionally, we have made an acquaintance that is useful. For the comic spirit has a logic of its own, even in its wildest eccentricities. It has a method in its madness. It dreams, I admit, but it conjures up in its dreams visions that are at once accepted and understood by the whole of a social group. Can it then fail to throw light for us on the way that human imagination works, and more particularly social, collective, and popular imagination? Begotten of real life and akin to art, should it not also have something of its own to tell us about art and life?

At the outset we shall put forward three observations which we look upon as fundamental. They have less bearing on the actually comic than on the field within which it must be sought.

The first point to which attention should be called is that the comic does not exist outside the pale of what is strictly *human.* A landscape may be beautiful, charming and sublime, or insignificant and ugly; it will never be laughable. You may laugh at an animal, but only because you have detected in it some human attitude or expression. You may laugh at a hat, but what you are making fun of, in this case, is not the piece of felt or straw, but the shape that men have given it—the human caprice whose mould it has assumed. It is strange that so important a fact, and such a simple one too, has not attracted to a greater degree the attention of philosophers. Several have defined man as "an animal which laughs." They might equally well have defined him as an animal which is laughed at; for if any other animal, or some lifeless object, produces the same effect, it is always because of some resemblance to man, of the stamp he gives it or the use he puts it to.

Here I would point out, as a symptom equally worthy of notice, the *absence of feeling* which usually accompanies laughter. It seems as though the comic could not produce its disturbing effect unless it fell, so to say, on the surface of a soul that is thoroughly calm and unruffled. Indifference is its natural environment, for laughter has no greater foe than emotion. I do not mean that we could not laugh at a person who inspires us with pity, for instance, or even with affection, but in such a case we must, for the moment, put our affection out of court and impose silence upon our pity. In a society composed of pure intelligences there would probably be no more tears, though perhaps there would still be laughter; whereas highly emotional souls, in tune and unison with life, in whom every event would be sentimentally prolonged and re-echoed, would neither know nor understand laughter. Try, for a moment, to become interested in everything that is being said and done; act, in imagination, with those who act, and feel with those who feel; in a word, give your sympathy its widest expansion: as though at the touch of a fairy wand you will see the flimsiest of objects assume importance, and a gloomy hue spread over everything. Now step aside, look upon life as a disinterested spectator: many a drama will turn into a comedy. It is enough for us to stop our ears to the sound of music in a room, where dancing is going on, for the dancers at once to appear ridiculous. How many human actions would stand a similar test? Should we not see many of them suddenly pass from grave to gay, on isolating them from the accompanying music of sentiment? To produce the whole of its effect, then, the comic demands something like a momentary anesthesia of the heart. Its appeal is to intelligence, pure and simple.

This intelligence, however, must always remain in touch with other intelligences. And here is the third fact to which attention should be drawn. You would hardly appreciate the comic if you felt yourself isolated from others. Laughter appears to stand in need of an echo. Listen to it carefully: it is not an articulate, clear, well-defined sound; it is something which would fain be prolonged by reverberating from one to another, something beginning with a crash, to continue in successive rumblings, like thunder in a mountain. Still, this reverberation cannot go on for ever. It can travel within as wide a circle as you please: the circle remains, none the less, a closed one. Our laughter is always the laughter of a group. It may, perchance, have happened to you, when seated in a railway carriage or at *table d'hôte*, to hear travellers relating to one another stories which must have been comic to them, for they laughed heartily. Had you been one of their company, you would have laughed like them, but, as you were not, you had no desire whatever to do so. A man who was once asked why he did not weep at a sermon when everybody else was shedding tears replied: "I don't belong to the parish!" What that man thought of tears would be still more true of laughter. However spontaneous it seems, laughter always implies a kind of secret freemasonry, or even complicity, with other laughers, real or imaginary. How often has it been said that the fuller the theatre, the more uncontrolled the laughter of the audience! On the other hand, how often has the remark been made that many comic effects are incapable of translation from one language to another, because they refer to the customs and ideas of a particular social group! It is through not understanding the importance of this double fact that the comic has been looked upon as a mere curiosity in which the mind finds amusement, and laughter itself as a strange, isolated phenomenon, without any bearing on the rest of human activity. Hence those definitions which tend to make the comic into an abstract relation between ideas: "an intellectual contrast," "a patent absurdity," etc., definitions which, even were they really suitable to every form of the comic, would not in the least explain why the comic makes us laugh. How, indeed, should it come about that this particular logical relation, as soon as it is perceived, contracts, expands and shakes our limbs, whilst all other relations leave the body unaffected? It is not from this point of view that we shall approach the problem. To understand laughter, we must put it back into its natural environment, which is society, and above all must we determine the utility of its function, which is a social one. Such, let us say at once, will be the leading idea of all our investigations. Laughter must answer to certain requirements of life in common. It must have a *social* signification.

Let us clearly mark the point towards which our three preliminary observations are converging. The comic will come into being, it appears, whenever a group of men concentrate their attention on one of their number, imposing silence on their emotions and calling into play nothing but their intelligence....

Before going further, let us halt a moment and glance around. As we hinted at the outset of this study, it would be idle to attempt to derive every comic effect from one simple formula. The formula exists well enough in a certain sense, but its development does not follow a straightforward course. What I mean is that the process of deduction ought from time to time to stop and study certain culminating effects, and that these effects each appear as models round which new effects resembling them take their places in a circle. These latter are not deductions from the formula, but are comic through their relationship with those that are. To quote Pascal again, I see no objection, at this stage, to defining the process by the curve which that geometrician studied under the name of *roulette* or cycloid—the curve traced by a point in the circumference of a wheel when the carriage is advancing in a straight line: this point turns like the wheel, though it advances like the carriage. Or else we might think of an immense avenue such as are to be seen in the forest of Fontainebleau, with *crosses* at intervals to indicate the crossways: at each of these we shall walk round the cross, explore for a while the paths that open out before us, and then return to our original course. Now, we have just reached one of these mental crossways. *Something mechanical encrusted on the living* will represent a cross at which we must halt, a central image from which the imagination branches off in different directions. What are these directions? There appear to be three main ones. We will follow them one after the other, and then continue our onward course.

1. In the first place, this view of the mechanical and the living dovetailed into each other makes us incline towards the vaguer image of *some rigidity or other* applied to the mobility of life, in an awkward attempt to follow its lines and counterfeit its suppleness. Here we perceive how easy it is for a garment to become ridiculous. It might almost be said that every fashion is laughable in some respect. Only, when we are dealing with the fashion of the day, we are so accustomed to it that the garment seems, in our mind, to form one with the individual wearing it. We do not separate them in imagination. The idea no longer occurs to us to contrast the inert rigidity of the covering with the living suppleness of the object covered: consequently, the comic here remains in a latent condition. It will only succeed in emerging when the natural incompatibility is so deep-seated between the covering and the covered that even an immemorial association fails to cement this union: a case in point is our head and top hat. Suppose, however, some eccentric individual dresses himself in the fashion of former times our attention is immediately drawn to the clothes themselves; we absolutely distinguish them from the individual, we say that the latter *is disguising himself*—as though every article of clothing were not a disguise!—and the laughable aspect of fashion comes out of the shadow into the light.

Here we are beginning to catch a faint glimpse of the highly intricate difficulties raised by this problem of the comic. One of the reasons that must have given rise to many erroneous or unsatisfactory theories of laughter is that many things are comic *de jure* without being comic *de facto*, the continuity of custom having deadened within them the comic quality. A sudden dissolution of continuity is needed, a break with fashion, for this quality to revive. Hence the impression that this dissolution of continuity is the parent of the comic, whereas all it does is to bring it to our notice. Hence, again, the explanation of laughter by *surprise, contrast*, etc., definitions which would equally apply to a host of cases in which we have no inclination whatever to laugh. The truth of the matter is far from being so simple....

2. Our starting-point is again "something mechanical encrusted upon the living." Where did the comic come from in this case? It came from the fact that the living body became rigid, like a machine. Accordingly, it seemed to us that the living body ought to be the perfection of suppleness, the ever-alert activity of a principle always at work. But this activity would really belong to the soul rather than to the body. It would be the very flame of life, kindled within us by a higher principle and perceived through the body, as though through a glass. When we see only gracefulness and suppleness in the living body, it is because we disregard in it the elements of weight, of resistance, and, in a word, of matter; we forget its materiality and think only of its vitality, a vitality which we regard as derived from the very principle of intellectual and moral life. Let us suppose, however, that our attention is drawn to this material side of the body; that, so far from sharing in the lightness and subtlety of the principle with which it is animated, the body is no more in our eyes than a heavy and cumbersome vesture, a kind of irksome ballast which holds down to earth a soul eager to rise aloft. Then the body will become to the soul what, as we have just seen, the garment was to the body itself—inert matter dumped down upon living energy. The impression of the comic will be produced as soon as we have a clear appre-

hension of this putting the one on the other. And we shall experience it most strongly when we are shown the soul *tantalised* by the needs of the body: on the one hand, the moral personality with its intelligently varied energy, and, on the other, the stupidly monotonous body, perpetually obstructing everything with its machine-like obstinacy. The more paltry and uniformly repeated these claims of the body, the more striking will be the result. But that is only a matter of degree, and the general law of these phenomena may be formulated as follows: *Any incident is comic that calls our attention to the physical in a person, when it is the moral side that is concerned....*

3. Let us then return, for the last time, to our central image—something mechanical encrusted on something living. Here, the living being under discussion was a human being, a person. A mechanical arrangement, on the other hand, is a thing. What, therefore, incited laughter, was the momentary transformation of a person into a thing, if one considers the image from this standpoint. Let us then pass from the exact idea of a machine to the vaguer one of a thing in general. We shall have a fresh series of laughable images which will be obtained by taking a blurred impression, so to speak, of the outlines of the former and will bring us to this new law: *We laugh every time a person gives us the impression of being a thing....*

Every small society that forms within the larger is thus impelled, by a vague kind of instinct, to devise some method of discipline or "breaking in," so as to deal with the rigidity of habits that have been formed elsewhere and have now to undergo a partial modification. Society, properly so called, proceeds in exactly the same way. Each member must be ever attentive to his social surroundings; he must model himself on his environment; in short, he must avoid shutting himself up in his own peculiar character as a philosopher in his ivory tower. Therefore society holds suspended over each individual member, if not the threat of correction, at all events the prospect of a snubbing, which, although it is slight, is none the less dreaded. Such must be the function of laughter. Always rather humiliating for the one against whom it is directed, laughter is really and truly a kind of social "ragging."

Hence the equivocal nature of the comic. It belongs neither altogether to art nor altogether to life. On the one hand, characters in real life would never make us laugh were we not capable of watching their vagaries in the same way as we look down at a play from our seat in a box; they are only comic in our eyes because they perform a kind of comedy before us. But, on the other hand, the pleasure caused by laughter, even on the stage, is not an unadulterated enjoyment; it is not a pleasure that is exclusively esthetic or altogether disinterested. It always implies a secret or unconscious intent, if not of each one of us, at all events of society as a whole. In laughter we always find an unavowed intention to humiliate, and consequently to correct our neighbour, if not in his will, at least in his deed. This is the reason a comedy is far more like real life than a drama is. The more sublime the drama, the more profound the analysis to which the poet has had to subject the raw materials of daily life in order to obtain the tragic element in its unadulterated form. On the contrary, it is only in its lower aspects, in light comedy and farce, that comedy is in striking contrast to reality: the higher it rises, the more it approximates to life; in fact, there are scenes in real life so closely bordering on high-class comedy that the stage might adopt them without changing a single word.

Hence it follows that the elements of comic character on the stage and in actual life will be the same. What are these elements? We shall find no difficulty in deducing them.

It has often been said that it is the *trifling* faults of our fellow-men that make us laugh. Evidently there is a considerable amount of truth in this opinion; still, it cannot be regarded as altogether correct. First, as regards faults, it is no easy matter to draw the line between the trifling and the serious; maybe it is not because a fault is trifling, that it makes us laugh, but rather because it makes us laugh that we regard it as trifling; for there is nothing disarms us like laughter. But we may go even farther, and maintain that there are faults at which we laugh, even though fully aware that they are serious—Harpagon's avarice, for instance. And then, we may as well confess—though somewhat reluctantly—that we laugh not only at the faults of our fellow-men, but also, at times, at their good qualities. We laugh at Alceste. The objection may be urged that it is not the earnestness of Alceste that is ludicrous, but rather the special aspect which earnestness assumes in his case; and, in short, a certain eccentricity that mars it in our eyes. Agreed; but it is none the less true that this eccentricity in Alceste, at which we laugh, *makes his earnestness laughable*, and that is the main point. So we may conclude that the comic is not always an indication of a fault, in the moral meaning of the word, and if critics insist on seeing a fault, even though a trifling one, in the ludicrous, they must point out what it is here that exactly distinguishes the trifling from the serious.

The truth is, the comic character may, strictly speaking, be quite in accord with stern morality. All it has to do is to bring itself into accord with society. The character of Alceste is that of a thoroughly honest man. But then he is unsociable, and, on that very account, ludicrous. A flexible vice may not be so easy to ridicule as a rigid virtue. It is *rigidity* that society eyes with suspicion. Consequently, it is the rigidity of Alceste that makes us laugh, though here rigidity stands for honesty. The man who withdraws into himself is liable to ridicule, because the comic is largely made up of this very withdrawal. This accounts for the comic being so frequently dependent on the manners or ideas, or, to put it bluntly, on the prejudices, of a society.

Roland Barthes (1915–1980)

Roland Barthes studied at the University of Paris and taught in Egypt and Romania before joining the faculty of the Centre National de la Recherche Scientifique in Paris. Barthes' interests were in the fields of sociology and linguistics, particularly in the relationship between the structure of language and the structure of other systems of signification. His "structuralism" was widely adapted in a number of fields between the 1950s and 1970s. The following is an excerpt from his discussion of *Phaedra* from his book *On Racine*.

ON RACINE

TRANSLATED BY RICHARD HOWARD

To name or not to name, that is the question. In *Phèdre* it is language's very being that is put on the stage: the profoundest of Racine's tragedies is also the most formal; for the tragic stake here is less the meaning of language than its manifestation, less Phaedra's love than her avowal. Or more exactly: to name Evil is to exhaust it entirely. Evil is a tautology, *Phèdre* a nominalist tragedy.

From the outset, Phaedra knows she is guilty, and it is not her guilt that constitutes a problem, it is her silence: that is where her freedom is. Phaedra breaks this silence three times: before Oenone (I, 3), before Hippolytus (II, 5), before Theseus (V, 7). These three outbursts have a mounting gravity; from one to the next, Phaedra approaches an increasingly pure state of language. The first confession is still narcissistic, Oenone is merely her maternal double: Phaedra disburdens herself to herself, seeks her identity, makes her own history; her confession is an epic one. The second time, Phaedra binds herself magically to Hippolytus by a performance: she *represents* her love, her avowal is dramatic. The third time, she confesses publicly before the person who by his mere being has instituted the transgression; her confession is literal, purified of all theatre; her language is totally coincident with the fact, it is a *correction:* Phaedra can die, the tragedy is exhausted. We are dealing, then, with a silence tormented by the notion of its own destruction. Phaedra *is* her silence: to break this silence is to die, but also to die can only mean *having spoken.* Before the tragedy begins, Phaedra already wants to die, but this death is suspended: only speech will release this motionless death, restore to the world its movement.

Phaedra, moreover, is not the only figure of secrecy; not only is her secret contagious, Hippolytus and Aricia also refusing to give any name to Phaedra's disease, but further, Phaedra has a double who is also constrained by the terror of language: Hippolytus. For Hippolytus as for Phaedra, to love is to be guilty before that same Theseus who forbids his son to marry as a consequence of the vendettal law, and who never dies. Further, to love and to speak that love is, for Hippolytus, the same scandal; once again the guilt of the emotion is not distinguished from its nomination. Theramenes speaks to Hippolytus exactly as Oenone speaks to Phaedra. Yet as Phaedra's double, Hippolytus represents a much more archaic state of mutism, he is a regressive double; for Hippolytus' constriction is one of essence, Phaedra's is one of situation. Hippolytus' oral constraint is openly given as a sexual constraint: Hippolytus is mute *because* he is sterile; despite Racine's worldly precautions, Hippolytus is the rejection of sex, anti-Nature; his confidant, by his very curiosity, attests to the monstrous character of Hippolytus, whose virginity is a spectacle. Doubtless Hippolytus' sterility is directed against the Father; it is a reproach to the Father for the anarchic profusion with which he squanders life. But the Racinian world is an immediate world. Hippolytus hates the flesh as a literal disease. Eros is contagious, one must disinfect oneself, avoid contact with the objects it has touched: Phaedra's mere glance at Hippolytus corrupts him, his sword becomes loathsome once Phaedra has touched it. Aricia, in this regard, is merely the homologue of Hippolytus: her vocation is sterility, not only by Theseus' decree, but by her very being.

Constriction is thus the form that accounts for shame, for guilt, and for sterility, and *Phèdre* is on all levels a tragedy of the imprisoned word, of life repressed. For speech is a substitute for life: to speak is to lose life, and all effusive behavior is experienced initially as a gesture of dilapidation: by the avowal, the flood of words released, it is the very principle of life that seems to be leaving the body; to speak is to spill oneself, that is, to castrate oneself, so that the tragedy is subject to the economy of an enormous avarice. But at the same time, of course, this blocked speech is fascinated by its own expansion: it is at the moment Phaedra guards her silence most intensely that by a compensatory gesture she flings off the garments which envelop her and tries to reveal her nakedness. We realize then that *Phèdre* is also a tragedy of accouchement. Oenone is truly the nurse, the midwife, who seeks to liberate Phaedra from her words at any price, who "delivers" language from the deep cavity in which it is confined. This intolerable confinement of the self, which is both mutism and sterility , in the same impulse, is also, as we know, the essence of Hippolytus: Aricia will thus be Hippolytus' midwife as Oenone is Phaedra's; if Aricia is interested in Hippolytus, it is precisely in order to pierce him, to make his words flow at last. Further, in fantasy it is this midwife's role that Phaedra would play for Hippolytus; like her sister Ariadne, untangler of the Labyrinth, she wants to unravel the skein, reel off the thread, lead Hippolytus out of the cavern into daylight.

Then what is it that makes speech so terrible? First of all, it is because it is an act that the word is so powerful. But chiefly it is because it is irreversible: no speech can be taken back. Surrendered to the *logos*, time cannot be reversed, its creation is definitive. Thus by avoiding speech, one avoids action, shifting the responsibility for it to others; and if one has begun to speak out of an "involuntary distraction," it is no use breaking off, one must go on to the end. And Oenone's ruse consists not in *retracting* Phaedra's confession, in annulling it, which is impossible, but in *reversing* it: Phaedra will accuse Hippolytus of the very crime she herself is guilty of; speech will remain intact, simply transferred from one character to the other. For language is indestructible: the hidden divinity of *Phèdre* is neither Venus nor the Sun. It is that god "terrible to perjurers" whose temple stands at the gates of Troezen, surrounded by ancestral tombs, and before which Hippolytus will die. Theseus himself is the true victim of this god: though he has been able to *return* from the Underworld, to recover the irrecoverable, he is the one who speaks too soon. Semidivine, powerful enough to dominate the contradiction of death, he nonetheless cannot unsay what he had said: the gods send back the word he has uttered, in the form of a dragon that devours him in his son.

Of course, as the panic drama of defenestration, of opening, *Phèdre* employs an abundant thematics of concealment. Its central image is the Earth; Theseus, Hippolytus, Aricia and her brothers are all descended from the Earth. Theseus is a strictly chthonian hero, a familiar of the underworld whose asphyxiating concavity his palace reproduces; a labyrinthian hero, he has been able to triumph over the cavern, to pass back and forth between darkness and light, to know the unknowable and yet to return, while the site natural to Hippolytus is the shadowy forest, where he nourishes his own sterility. Confronting this telluric bloc, Phaedra is divided: through her father, Minos, she participates in the order of the buried, of the deep; through her mother, Pasiphaë, she is descended from the Sun. Her principle is a troubled vacillation between these terms. She ceaselessly suppresses her secret, returns to the interior cavern, but ceaselessly, too, a force drives her to leave it, to expose herself, to join the Sun; and ceaselessly she testifies to the ambiguity of her nature: she fears the light, yet invokes it; she thirsts for the day, yet taints it. In a word, her principle is the paradox of a *black light*, that is, of a contradiction of essences.

Now this contradiction has, in *Phèdre*, an absolute form: the monster. At first, the monstrous threatens all the characters; they are all monsters to each other, and all monster-seekers as well. But above all, it is a monster, this time a real one, which intervenes to resolve the tragedy. And this monster is the very essence of the monstrous—in other words, it epitomizes in its biological structure the fundamental paradox of *Phèdre*. It is the force that bursts out of the depths of the sea, it is what pounces upon the secret, breaks it open, ravishes it, tears it apart, scatters and disperses it. To Hippolytus' principle of enclosure corresponds tragically—that is, ironically—his death by the dismemberment, the pulverization, broadly *extended* by the narrative, of a body hitherto essentially compact. Theramenes' narrative constitutes, then, the critical point where the tragedy is resolved, that is, where the previous retention of all the characters is undone by a total catastrophe. So it is actually Hippolytus who is the exemplary character in *Phèdre* (though not the principal one); he is truly the propitiatory victim, in whom the secret and its explosion achieve their most gratuitous form. And in relation to this great mythic function of the broken secret, Phaedra herself is an impure character. Her secret, whose outcome is in a sense *tried out* twice, is finally released through an extended confession. In Phaedra, language recovers *in extremis* a positive function: she has time to die, there is finally an agreement between her language and her death, both have the same measure (whereas even the last word is stolen from Hippolytus). Like a sheet of water, a slow death creeps into her, and like a sheet of water too, a pure, even language emerges from her; tragic time, that dreadful time which separates the spoken order from the real order, is purified, nature's unity is restored.

Phèdre thus proposes an identification of interiority with guilt; in *Phèdre* things are not hidden because they are culpable (that would be a prosaic view, Oenone's, for example, to whom Phaedra's transgression is merely contingent, linked to the life of Theseus); things are culpable from the very moment that they are hidden: the Racinian being does not release himself, and that is his sickness: nothing better attests the *formal* character of the transgression than its explicit identification with a disease. Phaedra's objective guilt (adultery, incest) is actually an artificial construction, intended to naturalize the suffering of the secret, to change form into content usefully. This inversion coincides with a more general movement, which establishes the entire Racinian edifice: Evil is terrible to the very degree that it is empty, man suffers from a *form*. This is what Racine expresses so well apropos of Phaedra when he says that for her, crime itself is a punishment. Phaedra's entire effort consists in *fulfilling* her transgression, that is, in absolving God.

PART V

Modern Drama and Theater: Backgrounds and Beginnings

An artist's sketch of the interior of the English Opera House (formerly the Lyceum), Strand, London, in 1817. Note the imposing effect of the proscenium arch.

REALISM AND NATURALISM

Realism and naturalism arose partly as theatrical innovations and partly as extensions of new social, scientific, and philosophical conditions that emerged in the middle of the nineteenth century. Philosophically, realists were materialists in that they began with the physical world as their base; they were objectivists in that they thought everything knowable could be discovered through the scientific method; and they were positivists in that they believed in the progress of human knowledge and the betterment of society through these means. For realists, the goals and means of science became the goals and means of art. Realist and naturalist playwrights adopted a disinterested scrutiny of social and behavioral problems, setting their plays in ordinary parlors in the present rather than in exotic remote locations or in the past. Following the lead of science, playwrights now regarded the forces of heredity and environment as chief determiners of individual and social life.

The chief representative of naturalism was Émile Zola (1840–1902), who urged playwrights to analyze and report real conditions in society and real problems of ordinary people. Zola advocated a drama based on "real life"—plays about characters taken from the middle or lower classes, who spoke realistic dialogue. Realist playwrights extended the techniques first explored by Zola and his generation of writers. Realist directors and actors not only used dialogue modeled on actual speech patterns but inserted self-conscious patterns of "real" actions filled with meaning. Frequently in realist plays, middle- and lower-class characters are enmeshed in plots involving the discovery of a secret hidden in the past. Realist set designers created three-dimensional stage sets that appeared "real" and often ordinary, like parlors or other domestic interiors. The proscenium arch achieved absolute status as an invisible fourth wall, so that now audiences perceived the stage as a separate living picture, one that accurately reflected their own world. It is no coincidence that the rise of realism followed closely on the heels of the invention of photography.

FROM ROMANTICISM TO MODERNISM

Realism and naturalism were reactions to what came to be regarded as the excessively literary and essentially unrealistic drama of the romantic period. Romanticism itself began in the late eighteenth century as a reaction to neoclassicism. Although it took many forms and manifested itself differently throughout Europe and America, there are some common threads in romanticism's social, political, and aesthetic outlook. First of all, the romantics were interested in nature. Neoclassical gardens had followed formal patterns and shapes, while romantic gardens showcased naturally occurring forms. The neoclassical standard of judgment was educated opinion, while the romantic standard was instinct—a product of nature rather than of civilization. The romantic celebration of nature echoed and reflected social ideals as well. Native Americans, Africans, and Pacific Islanders were admired as natural people, uncontaminated by civilization. For similar reasons, the ordinary attitudes of common people in western Europe, especially rural peasants, were championed. Primitivism, the belief in the superi-

An artist's projection of the interior arrangement of The Little Theater, New York, in 1912 showing a stage and auditorium design that emphasizes sight lines in response to realistic set design.

ority of a life closer to nature, led to widespread study of ancient societies and of the Middle Ages.

Generally speaking, the romantics tended to believe in social equality. To them, class structure seemed the artificial creation of corrupt "civilized" societies. The romantic age spawned upheaval and revolutions in working out this ideal: the American Revolution (1776), the French Revolution (1791), the European revolutions of 1830 and 1848, and the American Civil War (1861) are all associated with romantic political visions. Reactionary forces supporting monarchy, or slavery, or even the male vote sooner or later clashed with romantic revolutionaries who supported democracy, or abolition, or women's suffrage.

While neoclassical art relied upon the notion of generality, the romantics placed a premium on particular detail. Because all parts of the universe were thought to be related and interconnected, it seemed natural that a focus on unique details could lead to a better understanding of the whole. The function of art was to lead the way in producing insights into this interconnectedness, because perception depended on intuition. Unlike neoclassical art, which was judged by its adherence to rules, romantic art turned to the subjective and introspective. For the first time in Western history, artists were regarded as gifted visionaries misunderstood by the great majority of people. Just as the creation of art was a personal and intuitive process, so was its appreciation. No set of external criteria could be applied to judgment. Art stimulated the perceiver's intuitions, and intuition formed opinions, but because one person's opinion was considered as good as another's, criticism became democratized.

Romantic artists were fascinated by remote and exotic locations and by "primitive" characters such as children, commoners, and natural people. Romantic theater appealed more to the emotions than to the intellect. The subject matter of romantic plays, along with their great concern with special effects, appealed to the middle and lower classes. Revivals of Shakespeare, now regarded as a great natural genius, were frequent in the romantic theater, but they tended to emphasize elaborate sets and to stress exotic qualities.

The romantic ideal was first fully articulated in Germany, where the most influential philosophers, poets, and dramatists of the period flourished. Out of the German movement known as *Sturm and Drang* (storm and stress)—which flourished from around 1770 to 1790—emerged two particularly significant dramatists: Johann Christoph Friedrich von Schiller (1759–1805) and Johann Wolfgang von Goethe (1749–1832), the so-called German Shakespeare. Goethe's most famous play, *Faust*, a reworking of the same material Christopher Marlowe had used for *Doctor Faustus*, is considered one of the greatest literary works in the German language. Meanwhile, in England a number of romantic playwrights flourished, though few are revived today.

MELODRAMA

Melodrama (melody or music drama) was the most popular form of drama in the nineteenth century. While many of the characteristics of melodrama appear in plays of all periods, the form came into its own fully during this era. Melodramas observe strict moral justice: good and evil are clearly embodied in stock characters, in predictable action, and often in an explicit moral. Typically, a virtuous hero and heroine undergo superhuman trials at the hands of a villain, often in repetitive episodes. Acting as a kind of counterpoint, comic characters provide relief from the moral tension. At first melodramas were accompanied by music that underscored the emotions of the play, as in many movies and television shows today. Music also helped to identify characters; in fact, "signature music" ordinarily was played when a character was about to enter or leave the stage. In addition, incidental songs and dance found their way into these plays, along with a wide variety of special effects. Some quite popular melodramas featured animals, particularly horses and dogs, to entertain the audience.

In Germany, the development of melodrama is associated with the work of August Friedrich Ferdinand von Kotzebue (1761–1819), one the most popular playwrights of the period. Kotzebue wrote more than two hundred plays, many of them translated into French and English. He lent dignified treatment to the lives of ordinary people in his domestic melodramas, which commonly featured repentant wives and forgiving husbands, and he intrigued audiences, treating controversial subjects without offending theatergoers' sensibilities. Meanwhile, in France, René Charles Guilbert de Pixérécourt (1773–1844) wrote over one hundred melodramas. Famous for his disaster and canine plays, Pixérécourt often used highly spectacular effects, such as floods or volcanos, which he insisted on directing himself to ensure that they worked as he intended. In the history of drama, melodrama is of more than passing interest because for the first time in nearly two centuries the theater was able to attract a mass audience and to appeal to middle- and lower-class patrons.

THE WELL-MADE PLAY

Following on the heels of melodrama's popularity, a new form of drama made its debut in France: the well-made play. These two forms were the mainstay of the nineteenth-century theater. The popularity of the well-made play can be attributed to Augustin Eugène Scribe (1791–1861), a French playwright who wrote over three hundred of them. Scribe was easily the most popular playwright of the period. Many of his works were translated into English and German, and their frequent production abroad made French comedy a standard worldwide. Scribe's strength was the plotting of his plays, which relied on tight-knit action, on cause and effect, on act and consequence. Virtually every one of Scribe's plays exhibits the following characteristics: a careful exposition of the situation, careful preparation for future events, mounting suspense, unexpected reversals, and a logical resolution. The term *well-made play* was originally used as a compliment to describe the tightly knit plots for which Scribe became famous. Later critics, however, deplored the predictability and superficiality of Scribe's work, and the term came to be used derisively. Still, Scribe pioneered a formula still used in many popular plays, films, and television scripts. His focus on tightly knit cause-and-effect plots was appropriated for powerful purposes by the next generation of dramatists, the naturalists and realists.

NINETEENTH-CENTURY THEATERS

Although few plays from the early nineteenth century remain popular today, the theater as an institution enjoyed enormous success. Large new theaters were built or renovated to increase seating capacity for eager audiences and to provide greater capabilities for spectacle. At the beginning of the nineteenth century, for example, audience capacity at the Covent Garden Theatre in London was expanded to seat 3,000 people, and at the Drury Lane Theatre to seat 3,600. By the middle of the century in Germany, over sixty-five new permanent theaters had been built, most with the technology to effect rapid scene changes.

By this time, sitting onstage was no longer permitted in England and France. Such seating took up too much valuable space, which was now necessary for scenic effects and a broad acting area. Designers produced elaborate sets, sometimes closely reproducing actual places. The standard wing-and-background scenery of the neoclassical period became wing-and-drop scenery. Unchanging backgrounds were replaced by drops (pieces of fabric suspended from the ceiling and reaching down to the floor of the stage), by borders (short curtains above the stage), and ground rows (freestanding flats set on the stage floor). The various scenic pieces were coordinated to achieve the illusion of reality. Some stage properties, such as bridges, were constructed in three dimensions, but most of the scenery was two-dimensional, painted on flats. In general, historical and geographical accuracy of detail was sought in stage design, and details particularized sets. Scenes formerly lit by candles or oil lamps now glowed with the use of newly invented gas lamps and limelights, placed as footlights and onstage behind the wings. The new limelight could produce the realistic illusion of sunlight or moonlight. The audience area in the new theaters still included box seats, the pit (later called the orchestra after the ancient Greek model), and balconies. In the neoclassical period, boxes had been the most expensive seats, but spectacle rather than language had now become paramount, and good sight lines rather than hearing distance took precedence. Pit or orchestra seats replaced box seats as the most desirable and expensive in the house. Cheap seats, then as now, were in the upper balconies.

Richard Wagner (1813–1883), known principally for his music and operas, built an experimental theater in 1876, the Bayreuth Festspielhaus. It differed from other theaters in providing a "classless" seating arrangement. Box, pit, and balcony were eliminated in favor of a fan arrangement in which every seat had good sight lines. Although the experiment had little immediate impact, the arrangement strongly influenced twentieth-century theater design. Wagner also made the director of a play all-powerful for the first time, with every aspect of theatrical production under his control. This development had a profound impact on late-nineteenth-century and twentieth-century practices. Starting at this time the director came to be regarded as the central artist in the theater.

BEGINNINGS OF MODERN DRAMA AND THEATER

The realists and naturalists, influenced by developments earlier in the nineteenth century, transformed these influences into plays, performances, and staging techniques that have reshaped our idea of theater. Like the romantics, realists were interested in characters from the lower and middle classes, but instead of idealizing these individuals the realists subjected the lives of ordinary people and their social conditions to scrutiny. Realist playwrights paid careful attention to constructing their plays, as Eugène Scribe had done, with action moving progressively from one event to another. Instead of the expected, reassuring conclusion, however, the realists provided surprising or shocking perspectives.

As the modern theater began to develop, new ideas about drama were buttressed with new ideas about acting. George II, Duke of Saxe-Meiningen (fl. 1870s–1880s), influenced early realist designers and actors by pioneering changes in acting and production. His troupe unified all the elements of production—dialogue, acting, costume, and setting—onstage to conform to a particular point of view. The unified style rejected drama as a vehicle for star players, emphasizing instead the importance of all the actors in contributing to a total effect. Even minor characters were given specific actions or lines, and stage groupings were carefully arranged in diagonal rather than parallel lines, with every actor assuming a different stance. Together these tactics created an impression of the variety of life onstage. Historical accuracy in scenery and costuming, three-dimensional scenery, and platforms to vary the level of the stage were also hallmarks of his productions. André Antoine (1858–1943) and Konstantin Stanislavsky (1863–1938) pushed these ideas to their logical conclusion. European tours by the Duke of Saxe-Meiningen's company in the late 1870s and 1880s inspired Antoine to adapt naturalistic behavior to acting and inspired Stanislavsky to develop his famous method style of acting, which he described in a series of books starting in 1924. It was Stanislavsky's experience in directing Chekhov's plays that led him to approach acting by focusing on psychological verisimilitude and, like the Duke of Saxe-Meiningen, to do away with the idea of typecasting. Stanislavsky trained his actors to use their own psychological histories as a means of interpreting stage characters. The technique allowed actors to be emotionally spontaneous and hence more convincing.

Set design was also anticipated by the Duke of Saxe-Meiningen, but the realists carried the idea of naturalistic staging to its logical conclusion by constructing an apparently real world on stage. The apparent reflection of the audience and the world they lived in, along with the daring content of realist plays that treated serious social issues, shocked original audiences deeply. Rather than supporting traditional social values, realist playwrights treated time-honored social customs and traditional morality as the *cause* of problems. The very values and social support systems of traditional theater patrons were attacked in plays such as Henrik Ibsen's *Hedda Gabler*, August Strindberg's *Miss Julie*, George Bernard Shaw's *Major Barbara*, and Anton Chekhov's *Cherry Orchard*. Middle-class patrons of the theater were treated to plays on such sensational subjects as incest, marital unhappiness, betrayal, desertion, class conflict and hostility, despair, suicide, and sexual license. Women often appeared as central characters in realist plays, perhaps because the position of women in the late nineteenth century readily lent itself to an exploration of social problems. Realism thus registered as an avant-garde reaction to the heroic, sentimental, melodramatic, and spectacular plays that mainstream audiences had favored for several generations.

The commercial risk of producing realist plays on controversial subjects was taken on by small, independent theaters, formed outside the commercial mainstream. The first of these, the Théâtre Libre (Free Theater), was founded in 1887 by André Antoine in Paris and dedicated as a "machine of war" in the struggle to promote realism. Other such theaters were established in Germany and England—the Freie Bühne (Free Stage) in 1889 in Berlin and the Independent Theatre in 1891 in London. But the most important was the Moscow Art Theatre, founded in 1898 by Konstantin Stanislavsky and Vladimir Nemirovich-Danchenko. Famous at first for its realistic set design, the Moscow Art Theater became even more famous for Stanislavsky's method of psychological realism in acting. The first experimental American theater of this kind was the Wharf Theater, founded in 1915 in Provincetown, Massachusetts, by Susan Glaspell and George Cram Cook to produce nonmainstream plays. The best-known plays to be produced there included those of Susan Glaspell herself and of Eugene O'Neill.

HENRIK IBSEN (1828–1906)

Henrik Ibsen was born in Skien, a small provincial town in Norway. When Ibsen was eight years old, his father's bankruptcy forced the family to live in an attic apartment. Ibsen never forgot this reversal of economic fortune and the psychological hardships it brought to the family, and the theme of financial ruin looms large in his work. In his twenties he turned his attention to writing, and from 1850 to 1864 he was associated with the Norwegian National Theater in Bergen and the Mollergate Theater in Oslo, where he worked as literary manager, stage manager, and assistant director. He wrote a series of romantic history plays in prose and verse which were popular in Norway, but his fame now rests on the work of his later career.

In 1864 Ibsen settled in Rome, where he wrote *Brand* (1866) and *Peer Gynt* (1867), which established his reputation in Europe. *Brand* concerns an idealistic minister who sacrifices his child, his wife, and finally himself to the cause of his ministry. This theme—the cost of moral idealism in the modern world—would remain one of Ibsen's central concerns. *Peer Gynt* concerns a man who is the opposite of Brand. Peer Gynt devotes his life to satisfying his selfish desires through deceit, and not until his death does he realize the shallowness of his character and hollowness of his life.

Ibsen turned from writing plays about history and myth to writing about contemporary social problems; his style changed from romantic to realistic; his medium switched from verse to prose. In 1877 he wrote *Pillars of Society*, a play that exposes the hypocritical behavior of a socially respectable businessman. This work began a remarkable series of plays on modern life. In *A Doll's House* (1879), *Ghosts* (1881), and *An Enemy of the People* (1882), Ibsen explored the tragic conflict between personal freedom and the social and moral restrictions of middle-class society. In *A Doll's House*, the knowledge that she has remained a helpless child prompts Nora to leave her husband. The play shocked audiences, but Ibsen continued in this vein with *Ghosts*, in which he shows the consequences of not leaving: Mrs. Alving denies her love for a minister and at his advice stays with an unfaithful husband who has fathered a child by a household maid and has also bequeathed congenital syphilis to his son. Seen as a vicious attack on social and religious values, the play so outraged audiences that it was banned in Norway. In *An Enemy of the People*, Ibsen portrays the difficulties of an outsider who brings unflattering and unpleasant truths to the attention of the community.

Ibsen achieved success by adapting the conventions of the well-made play, popularized throughout the world by Eugène Scribe, to scrutinize and criticize middle-class society and values. In his later plays—*The Wild Duck* (1885), *Rosmersholm* (1887), *Hedda Gabler* (1890), and *The Master Builder* (1892)—Ibsen continued to concern himself with the conflict between personal vitality and social convention. Increasingly, however, he abandoned the form of the well-made play as he became more concerned with the psychological exploration of destructive relationships than with social problems.

Ibsen's plays were translated into all major European languages, and they had a profound effect not only on his contemporaries but on the course of modern drama. Partly because his plays were so often the subject of controversy, the desire to stage them throughout Europe and the United States did much to inspire the independent theater movement. In his own day Ibsen's plays were often thought of in terms of their shocking content, and even today they are often approached as social criticism. He brought new social issues to the stage, but it was his artistic vision as a playwright that was truly revolutionary. He adapted fourth-wall realism, a concern with the burden of past secrets, and the idea of a determining social order to his plays, and he also created the first modern characters—contradictory individuals driven by a desire for something they cannot quite articulate. In 1901 Ibsen suffered a paralyzing stroke that made it impossible for him to write. He died in 1906.

Hedda Gabler

Ibsen's plays owe a great deal to the conventions of Eugène Scribe's well-made play, which by Ibsen's time had become associated with banal social chatter. Most of Ibsen's plays hinge upon a secret in the past that insists on being revealed in the present, often with explosive force, triggering a conflict between deadening social conventions and inner vitality. The force of social convention usually wins, extinguishing the vitality of many of his central characters. In his later, mature plays, Ibsen raises more shocking social issues than he did in earlier plays—a wife leaving her husband (in *A Doll's House*), for example, or the ravages of syphilis on an innocent generation (in *Ghosts*).

By 1890, when Ibsen wrote *Hedda Gabler*, he was already regarded as a playwright concerned with social and moral reform. Some of his plays had scandalized audiences or provoked irritation and hostility from critics, but his plays were also expected to provoke serious thought about social and moral issues. The response to *Hedda Gabler*, however, when the play was first performed in Munich in January 1891—and for at least three decades afterward—was generally contemptuous, hostile, or puzzled. And certainly, when compared with Ibsen's earlier realist works, this play presents a number of puzzles. Is it simply another study of the crushing effects of familial and social expectations, or does it present a true tragic figure? Is Hedda victimized by bourgeois morality and conventions, or is she stymied by decadence? Is the play a case study in abnormal psychology or an illustration of pathetic exhaustion? Does Hedda embody a new kind of Nora (from *A Doll's House*), now gone berserk? Do the contradictory strains in Hedda's manner keep her from being a sympathetic character? Chekhov, in a characteristic insight, found Hedda realistic enough, but he thought the play melodramatic rather than tragic because in real life women like

Hedda do *not* commit suicide. Critical opinion continues to be fascinated and divided by the contradictory traits in Hedda's character, and today, only slightly less than at the turn of the century, the most easily scandalized critics are shocked by the "sewer" of Ibsen's imagination.

Focusing on the title character rather than on her complicated and confining situation in the play itself may do a disservice to Ibsen's conception. In Hedda he created a distinctly modern character, in many ways a case study of a fragmented and alienated identity. Rather than a psychological type plugged into a drawing-room play, Hedda is a character who transcends the limits of confining critical categories. Driven by a desire for something grander, for something with a larger sense of purpose, Hedda is barely recognizable by the end of the play, even to herself. Like a modern-day Medea, she is incomprehensible in her depth of passion.

Hedda's character is defined and dominated by the memory of her aristocratic and powerful father, the General, whose pistols she has inherited. Her marriage to Tesman, whom she despises, was supposed to bring her influence and comfort because of his apparent prospects for a professorship. But it becomes clear through the series of visits that Hedda hosts during the course of the play that she is forcing and being forced into a future completely beyond her control—ironically, because her own past is entirely compromised.

In the Act I Aunt Julle and Berte give us a glimpse of the young Hedda on horseback. That vision of the aristocratic girl's freedom and movement contrasts with her present situation; she is bored and irritated by the whining and trivial burgher mentality and the well-meaning banalities associated with Tesman and his relatives, and the play underscores Hedda's entrapment in a home that she in fact dominates. The people who visit her enclosed world come from different strata of outside society, and they seem to offer escape, or at least a momentary sense of purpose to her life. Judge Brack offers a world of elegant sophistication, of wit and grace and charm, and of completely cynical manipulation. Tesman's two aunts—decent people with genuine virtues—have narrow horizons that they share with the unimaginative pedant Tesman. Løvborg seems to present brilliant intellect and passion in their most positive and negative forms. That he needs to be rehabilitated from his debaucheries makes him powerfully attractive to Hedda, who believes she can at last control him. In fact, Hedda remains at the center of all of these characters, attempting to find a stable identity in a shifting world. Finally she falls prey to impulses she neither comprehends nor controls. Attempting to live vicariously through Løvborg, who echoes her temperament, Hedda succeeds only in bringing about his squalid death. Her aristocratic "dueling" with Judge Brack, who shares her social pretensions, only puts him in total control. Her marriage to Tesman, with the hint of a baby on the way, offers the most brutal suffocation of her being. Hedda's attempts to control these different worlds by manipulating the men who inhabit them remains a sign of her own desperation and emptiness. Her two decisive actions involve infanticide: one—of Løvborg's manuscript—is symbolic, and the other one—associated with her own suicide—real.

The rivalry between Hedda and Thea frames the entire play and is its ironic center. Hedda takes Løvborg away from Thea, but the sordid manner of his

death undermines her triumph. She "kills their baby" by burning the manuscript, but Thea and Tesman are busy "resurrecting" it by the last act. Tesman's
pedantry, the very quality Hedda finds so despicable in him, now becomes the
means to "father" Thea and Løvborg's book child. Hedda comes to be neither
needed nor wanted in the marriage. Unlike Hedda, Thea can take on the roles of
both mother and inspiring soulmate, and one of the paradoxes Ibsen builds into
the play is that Thea, though an almost perfectly "feminine" woman, is childless
while Hedda, who hates sex and fears pregnancy and birth or even the very idea
of children, is pregnant.

Totally defeated, Hedda returns to the back room, where the General's portrait hangs over the sofa, an icon to inspire a deed of violent courage. After a
final frenzied piece on the piano, surely playing out her frustrated passion for
life in dance and music, she uses the General's second pistol to exit the ugly
world she has helped engineer.

Hedda Gabler

Henrik Ibsen

Translated by Otto Reinert

CHARACTERS

Jorgen Tesman, University Research Fellow in the
  History of Civilization
Hedda, his wife
Miss Juliane Tesman, his aunt

Mre. Elvsted
Judge Brack
Eilert Løvborg
Berte, the Tesmans' maid

SCENE: *The Tesmans' villa in a fashionable residential
section of the town.*

A note on pronunciation

*The approximate Norwegian pronunciation of names
likely to be difficult to a speaker of English is suggested
below (the syllable in capitals is accented; the unac-
cented e is close to English e in quiet).*

  Jørgen yur-gen (g as in bargain)
  Julle yool-le (short oo)
  Eilert Løvborg ay-lert luv-borg[1]
  Berte bair-te

---

[1] Løvborg means, literally, "leaf-castle,"—a fact of possible
bearing on the play's symbolism.

ACT I

A spacious, handsome, tastefully furnished room. Dark décor. In the rear, a wide doorway with open portieres. Beyond is a smaller room, furnished in the same style as the front room, from which a double door, right, leads to the front hall. Left, French doors, with portieres drawn aside, through which can be seen a part of a roofed verandah and trees with autumn foliage. Front center, an oval table covered with a cloth. Chairs around it. Front right, a wide, dark, porcelain stove, a high-backed easy chair, a footstool with a pillow, and two ottomans. In the corner far right, a sofa and a small, round table. Front left, a sofa, set out from the wall. Far left, beyond the French doors, an upright piano. On both sides of the doorway, rear center, whatnots with knickknacks. Against the rear wall of the inner room, a sofa, and in front of it a table and two chairs. Above the sofa, a portrait of a handsome, elderly man in general's uniform. Over the table hangs a lamp with milky, white glass. Bouquets of flowers, in vases and glasses are everywhere in the front room. Others are lying on the tables. Thick carpets on the floors of both rooms. The morning sun is shining through the French doors.

MISS JULIANE TESMAN, with hat and parasol, enters right, followed by BERTE, who carries a bouquet of flowers wrapped in paper. MISS TESMAN is a nice-looking woman of 65, of pleasant mien, neatly but not expensively dressed in a gray suit. BERTE is a middle-aged servant girl, of rather plain and countrified appearance.

MISS TESMAN (*stops inside the door, listens, says in a low voice*): On my word—I don't think they are even up yet!

BERTE (*also softly*): That's what I told you, miss. When you think how late the steamer got in last night. And afterwards—! Goodness!—all the stuff she wanted unpacked before she turned in.

MISS TESMAN: Well—just let them sleep. But fresh morning air—that they'll have when they get up. (*Goes and opens the French doors wide.*)

BERTE (*by the table, lost, still holding the flowers*): Please, miss—I just don't see a bit of space anywhere! I think I'd better put these over here. (*Puts the flowers down on the piano.*)

MISS TESMAN: Well, well, my dear Berte. So you've got yourself a new mistress now. The good Lord knows it was hard for me to let you go.

BERTE (*near tears*): What about me, then, miss! What shall *I* say? I who have served you and Miss Rina all these blessed years.

MISS TESMAN: We shall just have to make the best of

it, Berte. That's all. Jørgen can't do without you, you know. He just can't. You've looked after him ever since he was a little boy.

BERTE: Yes, but miss—I'm ever so worried about leaving Miss Rina. The poor dear lying there all helpless. With that new girl and all! She'll never learn how to make things nice and comfortable for an invalid.

MISS TESMAN: Oh yes, you'll see. I'll teach her. And of course, you know, I'll do most of it myself. So don't you worry yourself about my poor sister, Berte.

BERTE: Yes, but there's another thing, too, miss. I'm scared I won't be able to suit young Mrs. Tesman.

MISS TESMAN: Oh, well. Good heavens. So there is a thing or two—Right at first—

BERTE: For I believe she's ever so particular.

MISS TESMAN: Can you wonder? General Gabler's daughter? Just think of the kind of life she was used to when the General was alive. Do you remember when she rode by with her father? That long black riding habit she wore? And the feather in her hat?

BERTE: Oh, I remember, all right. But I'll be blessed if I ever thought she and the young master would make a pair of it.

MISS TESMAN: Nor did I. By the way, while I think of it, Berte. Jørgen has a new title now. From now on you should call him "the Doctor."

BERTE: Yes, the young mistress said something about that, too, last night. Soon as they were inside the door. Then it's really so, miss?

MISS TESMAN: It certainly is. Just think, Berte—they have made him a doctor abroad. During the trip, you know. I hadn't heard a thing about it till last night on the pier.

BERTE: Well, I daresay he could be anything he put his mind to, *he* could—smart as *he* is. But I must say I'd never thought he'd turn to doctoring people, too.

MISS TESMAN: Oh, that's not the kind of doctor he is. (*Nods significantly.*) And as far as that is concerned, there is no telling but pretty soon you may have to call him something grander yet.

BERTE: You don't say! What might that be, miss?

MISS TESMAN (*smiles*): Wouldn't you like to know! (*Moved.*) Ah yes, indeed—! If only dear Jochum could see from his grave what has become of his little boy! (*Looking around.*) But look, Berte—what's this for? Why have you taken off all the slip covers?

BERTE: She told me to. Said she can't stand slip covers on chairs.

MISS TESMAN: Do you think they mean to make this their everyday living room, then?

BERTE: It sure sounded that way. Mrs. Tesman did, I

mean. For he—the doctor—he didn't say anything.

[*JØRGEN TESMAN enters from the right side of the inner
room. He is humming to himself. He carries an open,
empty suitcase. He is of medium height, youthful-
looking, thirty-three years old; somewhat plump.
Round, open, cheerful face. Blond hair and beard. He
wears glasses and is dressed in a comfortable, rather
casual suit.*]

MISS TESMAN: Good morning, good morning, Jørgen!
TESMAN (*in the doorway*): Auntie! Dearest Aunt Julle!
(*Comes forward and shakes her hand.*) All the way
out here—as early as this! Hm?
MISS TESMAN: Well—I just had to drop in for a
moment. To see how you are getting along, you
know.
TESMAN: Even though you haven't had a good
night's sleep.
MISS TESMAN: Oh, that doesn't matter at all.
TESMAN: But you did get home from the pier all
right, I hope. Hm?
MISS TESMAN: Oh yes, I certainly did, thank you. The
Judge was kind enough to see me all the way to
my door.
TESMAN: We were so sorry we couldn't give you a
ride in our carriage. But you saw for yourself—all
the boxes Hedda had.
MISS TESMAN: Yes, she certainly brought quite a col-
lection.
BERTE (*to TESMAN*): Should I go and ask Mrs. Tesman
if there's anything I can help her with?
TESMAN: No, thank you, Berte—you'd better not. She
said she'll ring if she wants you.
BERTE (*going right*): Well, all right.
TESMAN: But, look—you might take this suitcase with
you.
BERTE (*takes it*): I'll put it in the attic. (*Exits right.*)
TESMAN: Just think, Auntie—that whole suitcase was
brimful of copies of old documents. You wouldn't
believe me if I told you all the things I have collected from libraries and archives all over. Quaint
old items nobody has known anything about.
MISS TESMAN: Well, no, Jørgen. I'm sure you haven't
wasted your time on your honeymoon.
TESMAN: No, I think I may say I have not. But take
your hat off, Auntie—for goodness' sake. Here!
Let me untie the ribbon for you. Hm?
MISS TESMAN (*while he does so*): Ah, God forgive me, if
this isn't just as if you were still at home with us!
TESMAN (*inspecting the hat*): My, what a fine-looking
hat you've got yourself!
MISS TESMAN: I bought it for Hedda's sake.
TESMAN: For Hedda's sake? Hm?
MISS TESMAN: So she won't need to feel ashamed of
me if we ever go out together.

TESMAN (*patting her cheek*): If you don't think of
everything, Auntie! (*Puts the hat down on a chair by
the table.*) And now—over here to the sofa—we'll
just sit and chat for a while till Hedda comes.

[*They seat themselves. She places her parasol in the
corner by the sofa.*]

MISS TESMAN (*takes both his hands in hers and gazes at
him*): What a blessing it is to have you back again,
Jørgen, big as life! You—Jochum's little boy!
TESMAN: For me, too, Aunt Julle. Seeing you again.
For you have been both father and mother to me.
MISS TESMAN: Ah, yes—don't you think I know you'll
always keep a spot in your heart for these two
old aunts of yours!
TESMAN: So Aunt Rina isn't any better, hm?
MISS TESMAN: Oh no. We mustn't look for improvement in her case, poor dear. She is lying there just
as she has been all these years. Just the same, may
the good Lord keep her for me a long time yet!
For else I just wouldn't know what to do with
myself, Jørgen. Especially now, when I don't have
you to look after any more.
TESMAN (*pats her back*): There, there, now!
MISS TESMAN (*changing tone*): And to think that you
are a married man, Jørgen! And that you were the
one to walk off with Hedda Gabler. The lovely
Hedda Gabler. Just think! As many admirers as
she had!
TESMAN (*hums a little, smiles complacently*): Yes, I daresay I have quite a few good friends here in town
who'd gladly be in my shoes, hm?
MISS TESMAN: And such a long honeymoon you had!
More than five—almost six months!
TESMAN: Well, you know—for me it has been a kind
of study tour as well. All the collections I had to
go through. And the books I had to read!
MISS TESMAN: Yes, I suppose. (*More confidentially, her
voice lowered a little.*) But listen, Jørgen—haven't
you got something—something special to tell me?
TESMAN: About the trip?
MISS TESMAN: Yes.
TESMAN: No—I don't know of anything besides what
I wrote in my letters. They gave me a doctor's
degree down there—but I told you that last night;
I'm sure I did.
MISS TESMAN: Well, yes, that sort of thing—What I
mean is—don't you have certain—certain—expec-
tations?
TESMAN: Expectations?
MISS TESMAN: Ah for goodness' sake, Jørgen! I am
your old Auntie, after all!
TESMAN: Certainly I have expectations.
MISS TESMAN: Well!!
TESMAN: I fully expect to be made a professor one of
these days.

MISS TESMAN: Professor—oh yes—

TESMAN: I may even say I am quite certain of it. But dear Aunt Julle—you know this just as well as I do!

MISS TESMAN (*laughing a little*): Of course I do. You're quite right. (*Changing topic.*) But about the trip. It must have cost a great deal of money—hm, Jørgen?

TESMAN: Well, now; you know that large stipend went quite a long way.

MISS TESMAN: I just don't see how you made it do for both of you, though.

TESMAN: No, I suppose that's not so easy to understand, hm?

MISS TESMAN: Particularly with a lady along. For I have always heard that is ever so much more expensive.

TESMAN: Well, yes, naturally. That *is* rather more expensive. But Hedda had to have this trip, Auntie! She really had to. Nothing less would do.

MISS TESMAN: No, I daresay. For a wedding journey is quite the thing these days. But now tell me—have you had a chance to look around here yet?

TESMAN: I certainly have. I have been up and about ever since dawn.

MISS TESMAN: And what do you think of it all?

TESMAN: Delightful! Perfectly delightful! The only thing is I don't see what we are going to do with the two empty rooms between the second sitting room in there and Hedda's bedroom.

MISS TESMAN (*with a chuckle*): Oh my dear Jørgen—you may find them useful enough—when the time comes!

TESMAN: Of course, you're right, Auntie! As my library expands, hm?

MISS TESMAN: Quite so, my dear boy. It was your library I was thinking of.

TESMAN: But I'm really most happy on Hedda's behalf. For you know, before we were engaged she used to say she wouldn't care to live anywhere but in Secretary Falk's house.

MISS TESMAN: Yes, just think—wasn't that a lucky coincidence, that it was up for sale right after you had left?

TESMAN: Yes, Aunt Julle. We've certainly been lucky. Hm?

MISS TESMAN: But it will be expensive, my dear Jørgen. Terribly expensive—all this.

TESMAN (*looks at her, a bit crestfallen*): Yes, I daresay it will, Auntie.

MISS TESMAN: Heavens, yes!

TESMAN: How much, do you think? Roughly. Hm?

MISS TESMAN: No, I couldn't possibly say till all the bills arrive.

TESMAN: Well, anyway, Judge Brack managed to get very reasonable terms for us. He said so himself in a letter to Hedda.

MISS TESMAN: Yes, and I won't have you uneasy on that account, Jørgen. Besides, I have given security for the furniture and the carpets.

TESMAN: Security? You? But dear Aunt Julle—what kind of security could you give?

MISS TESMAN: The annuity.

TESMAN (*jumps up*): What! Your and Aunt Rina's annuity?

MISS TESMAN: Yes. I didn't know what else to do, you see.

TESMAN (*standing before her*): But are you clear out of your mind, Auntie! That annuity—that's all the two of you have to live on!

MISS TESMAN: Oh well, there's nothing to get so excited about, I'm sure. It's all just a matter of form, you know. That's what the Judge said, too. For he was kind enough to arrange the whole thing for me. Just a matter of form—those were his words.

TESMAN: That's all very well. Still—

MISS TESMAN: For now you'll have your own salary, you know. And, goodness—what if we do have a few expenses—Help out a bit right at first—? That would only be a joy for us—

TESMAN: Oh, Auntie! When will you ever stop making sacrifices for my sake!

MISS TESMAN (*gets up, puts her hands on his shoulders*): But what other happiness do I have in this world than being able to smooth your way a little, my own dear boy? Orphan as you were, with no one to lean on but us? And now the goal is in sight, Jørgen. Things may have looked black at times. But heaven be praised; now you've arrived!

TESMAN: Yes, it's really quite remarkable the way things have worked out.

MISS TESMAN: Yes—and those who were against you—who tried to block your way—now they are tasting defeat. They are down, Jørgen! He, the most dangerous of them all, his fall was the greatest! He made his bed, and now he is lying in it—poor, lost wretch that he is!

TESMAN: Have you had any news about Eilert? Since I went away, I mean?

MISS TESMAN: Just that he is supposed to have published a new book.

TESMAN: What? Eilert Løvborg? Recently? Hm?

MISS TESMAN: That's what they say. But I wonder if there can be much to it, you know? Ah—but when *your* new book comes, that will be something quite different, Jørgen! What is it going to be about?

TESMAN: It deals with the domestic industries of Brabant during the Middle Ages.

MISS TESMAN: Just think—being able to write about something like that!

TESMAN: But as far as that is concerned, it may be quite some time before it is ready. I have all these collections to put in order first, you see.

MISS TESMAN: Yes, collecting and putting things in order—you certainly know how to do that. In that you are your father's own son.

TESMAN: Well, I must say I am looking forward to getting started. Particularly now, that I've got my own delightful home to work in.

MISS TESMAN: And most of all now that you have the one your heart desired, dear Jørgen.

TESMAN (*embracing her*): Oh yes, yes, Aunt Julle! Hedda—she is the most wonderful part of it all! (*Looks toward the doorway.*) There—I think she is coming now, hm?

[*HEDDA enters from the left side of the inner room. She is twenty-nine years old. Both features and figure are noble and elegant. Pale, ivory complexion. Steel-gray eyes, expressive of cold, clear calm. Beautiful brown hair, though not particularly ample. She is dressed in a tasteful, rather loose-fitting morning costume.*]

MISS TESMAN (*going toward her*): Good morning, my dear Hedda! A very happy morning to you!

HEDDA (*giving her hand*): Good morning, dear Miss Tesman! So early a call? That is most kind.

MISS TESMAN (*seems slightly embarrassed*): And—has the little lady of the house slept well the first night in her new home?

HEDDA: Passably, thank you.

TESMAN (*laughs*): Passably! You are a good one, Hedda! You were sleeping like a log when I got up.

HEDDA: Fortunately. And then, of course, Miss Tesman, it always takes time to get used to new surroundings. That has to come gradually. (*Looks left.*) Oh dear. The maid has left the verandah doors wide open. There's a veritable flood of sunlight in here.

MISS TESMAN (*toward the doors*): Well, then, we'll just close them.

HEDDA: No, no, not that. Tesman, dear, please pull the curtains. That will give a softer light.

TESMAN (*over by the French doors*): Yes, dear. There, now! Now you have both shade and fresh air, Hedda.

HEDDA: We certainly can use some air in here. Such loads of flowers—But, Miss Tesman, please—won't you be seated?

MISS TESMAN: No thanks just the same. I just wanted to see if everything was all right—and so it is, thank goodness. I had better get back to Rina. I know she is waiting for me, poor thing.

TESMAN: Be sure to give her my love, Auntie. And tell her I'll be around to see her later today.

MISS TESMAN: I'll certainly do that!—Oh my! I almost forgot! (*Searches the pocket of her dress.*) I have something for you, Jørgen. Here.

TESMAN: What's that, Auntie? Hm?

MISS TESMAN (*pulls out a flat parcel wrapped in newspaper and gives it to him*): Here you are, dear.

TESMAN (*opens the parcel*): Well, well, well! So you took care of them for me, Aunt Julle! Hedda! Now, isn't that sweet, hm?

HEDDA (*by the whatnot, right*): If you'd tell me what it is—

TESMAN: My old slippers! *You* know!

HEDDA: Oh really? I remember you often talked about them on the trip.

TESMAN: Yes, for I missed them so. (*Walks over to her.*) Here—now you can see what they're like, Hedda.

HEDDA (*crosses toward stove*): Thanks. I don't know that I really care.

TESMAN (*following*): Just think—Aunt Rina embroidered these slippers for me. Ill as she was. You can't imagine how many memories they hold for me!

HEDDA (*by the table*): Hardly for me.

MISS TESMAN: That's true, you know, Jørgen.

TESMAN: Yes, but—I just thought that now that she's one of the family—

HEDDA (*interrupting*): I don't think we'll get on with that maid, Tesman.

MISS TESMAN: Not get on with Berte?

TESMAN: Whatever makes you say that, dear? Hm?

HEDDA (*points*): Look—she has left her old hat on the chair over there.

TESMAN (*appalled, drops the slippers*): But Hedda—!

HEDDA: What if somebody were to come and see it!

TESMAN: No, no, Hedda—that's Aunt Julle's hat!

HEDDA: Oh?

MISS TESMAN (*picking up the hat*): Yes, indeed it is. And it isn't old either, my dear young lady.

HEDDA: I really didn't look that closely—

MISS TESMAN (*tying the ribbons*): I want you to know that this is the first time I have had it on my head. On my word it is!

TESMAN: And very handsome it is, too. Really a splendid-looking hat!

MISS TESMAN: Oh, I don't know that it is anything so special, Jørgen. (*Looks around.*) My parasol—? Ah, here it is. (*Picks it up.*) For that is mine, too. (*Mutters.*) Not Berte's.

TESMAN: New hat and new parasol! What do you think of that, Hedda!

HEDDA: Nice and pretty indeed.

TESMAN: Yes, don't you think so? Hm? But, Auntie, take a good look at Hedda before you leave. She how nice and pretty *she* looks.

MISS TESMAN: Dear me, Jørgen; that's nothing new. Hedda has been lovely all her days. (*She nods and walks right.*)

TESMAN (*following*): Yes, but have you noticed how full-figured and healthy she looks after the trip? How she has filled out?

HEDDA (*crossing*): Oh—stop it!

MISS TESMAN (*halts, turns around*): Filled out?

TESMAN: Yes, Aunt Julle. You can't see it so well now when she wears that dress. But I, who have the opportunity—

HEDDA (*by the French doors, impatiently*): Oh, you haven't any opportunities at all!

TESMAN: It must be the mountain air in Tyrol.

HEDDA (*curtly interrupting*): I am just as I was when I left.

TESMAN: Yes, so you say. I just don't think you're right. What do you think, Auntie?

MISS TESMAN (*has folded her hands, gazes at* HEDDA): Lovely—lovely—lovely; that is what Hedda is. (*Goes over to her, inclines her head forward with both her hands, and kisses her hair.*) God bless and keep Hedda Tesman. For Jørgen's sake.

HEDDA (*gently freeing herself*): There, there. Now let me go.

MISS TESMAN (*in quiet emotion*): Every single day I'll be over and see you two.

TESMAN: Yes, please do, Auntie. Hm?

MISS TESMAN: Goodbye, goodbye!

[*She leaves through door, right.* TESMAN *sees her out. The door remains ajar.* TESMAN *is heard repeating his greetings for* AUNT RINA *and his thanks for the slippers. In the meantime,* HEDDA *paces up and down, raises her arms, clenching her fists, as in quiet rage. Opens the curtains by the French doors and stands looking out. In a few moments,* TESMAN *re-enters and closes the door behind him.*]

TESMAN (*picking up the slippers*): What are you looking at, Hedda?

HEDDA (*once again calm and controlled*): Just the leaves. They are so yellow. And withered.

TESMAN (*wrapping the slippers in their paper, putting the parcel down on the table*): Well, you know—we're in September now.

HEDDA (*again restless*): Yes—just think. It's already—September.

TESMAN: Don't you think Aunt Julle acted strange, Hedda? Almost solemn. I wonder why. Hm?

HEDDA: I hardly know her, you see. Isn't she often like that?

TESMAN: Not the way she was today.

HEDDA (*turning away from the French doors*): Do you think she minded that business with the hat?

TESMAN: Oh, I don't think so. Not much. Perhaps a little bit right at the moment—

HEDDA: Well, I'm sorry, but I must say it strikes me as very odd—putting her hat down here in the living room. One just doesn't do that.

TESMAN: Well, you may be sure Aunt Julle won't ever do it again.

HEDDA: Anyway, I'll make it up to her, somehow.

TESMAN: Oh yes, Hedda; if only you would!

HEDDA: When you go over there today, why don't you ask her over for tonight?

TESMAN: I'll certainly do that. And then there is one other thing you could do that she'd appreciate ever so much.

HEDDA: What?

TESMAN: If you could just bring yourself to call her Auntie. For my sake, Hedda, hm?

HEDDA: No, Tesman, no. You really mustn't ask me to do that. I have already told you I can't. I'll try to call her Aunt Juliane. That will have to do.

TESMAN: All right, if you say so. I just thought that now that you're part of the family—

HEDDA: Hmmm—I don't know about that—(*She walks toward the doorway.*)

TESMAN (*after a brief pause*): Anything the matter, Hedda? Hm?

HEDDA: I'm just looking at my old piano. It doesn't quite go with the other furniture in here.

TESMAN: As soon as I get my first pay check we'll have it traded in.

HEDDA: No—I don't want to do that. I want to keep it. But let's put it in this inner room and get another one for out here. Whenever it's convenient, I mean.

TESMAN (*a little taken back*): Well—yes—we could do that—

HEDDA (*picks up the bouquet from the piano*): These flowers weren't here last night.

TESMAN: I suppose Aunt Julle brought them for you.

HEDDA (*looking at the flowers*): There's a card here. (*Takes it out and reads.*) "Will be back later." Can you guess who it's from?

TESMAN: No. Who? Hm?

HEDDA: Thea Elvsted.

TESMAN: No, really? Mrs. Elvsted! Miss Rysing that was.

HEDDA: That's right. The one with that irritating head of hair she used to show off with. An old flame of yours, I understand.

TESMAN (*laughs*): Well, now—that didn't last long! Anyway, that was before I knew you, Hedda. Just think—her being in town.

HEDDA: Strange, that she'd call on us. I have hardly seen her since we went to school together.

TESMAN: As far as that goes, I haven't seen her either for—God knows how long. I don't see how she can stand living in that out-of-the-way place. Hm?

HEDDA (*suddenly struck by a thought*): Listen, Tesman—isn't it some place near there that he lives—what's his name—Eilert Løvborg?

TESMAN: Yes, that's right. He is up there, too.

[BERTE *enters right.*]

BERTE: Ma'am, she's here again, that lady who

brought those flowers a while back. (*Pointing.*)
The flowers you're holding in your hand, ma'am.

HEDDA: Ah, she is? Well, show her in, please.

[BERTE *opens the door for* MRS. ELVSTED *and exits.* MRS. ELVSTED *is of slight build, with a pretty, soft face. Her eyes are light blue, large, round, rather prominent, of a timid and querying expression. Her hair is strikingly light in color, almost whitish, and unusually rich and wavy. She is a couple of years younger than* HEDDA. *She is dressed in a dark visiting dress, tasteful, but not quite in the most recent fashion.*]

HEDDA (*walks toward her. Friendly*): Good morning, my dear Mrs. Elvsted. How very nice to see you again.

MRS. ELVSTED (*nervous, trying not to show it*): Well, yes, it is quite some time since we met.

TESMAN (*shaking hands*): And we, too. Hm?

HEDDA: Thank you for your lovely flowers—

MRS. ELVSTED: Please, don't—I would have come here yesterday afternoon. But I was told you were still traveling—

TESMAN: You've just arrived in town, hm?

MRS. ELVSTED: I got here yesterday, at noon. Oh, I was quite desperate when I learned you weren't home.

HEDDA: Desperate? But why?

TESMAN: But my dear Mrs. Rysing—I mean Mrs. Elvsted—

HEDDA: There is nothing wrong, I hope?

MRS. ELVSTED: Yes there is. And I don't know a single soul other than you that I can turn to here.

HEDDA (*putting the flowers down on the table*): Come— let's sit down here on the sofa.

MRS. ELVSTED: Oh, I'm in no mood to sit!

HEDDA: Of course you are. Come on. (*She pulls* MRS. ELVSTED *over to the sofa and sits down next to her.*)

TESMAN: Well, now, Mrs. —? Exactly what—?

HEDDA: Has something—special happened at home?

MRS. ELVSTED: Well, yes—and no. Oh, but I am so afraid you won't understand!

HEDDA: In that case, it seems to me you ought to tell us exactly what has happened, Mrs. Elvsted.

TESMAN: After all, that's why you are here. Hm?

MRS. ELVSTED: Yes, yes, of course. Well, then, maybe you already know—Eilert Løvborg is in town.

HEDDA: Is Løvborg—!

TESMAN: No! You don't say! Just think, Hedda— Løvborg's back!

HEDDA: All right. I can hear.

MRS. ELVSTED: He has been here a week already. Imagine—a whole week! In this dangerous place. Alone! With all that bad company around.

HEDDA: But my dear Mrs. Elvsted—why is he a concern of yours?

MRS. ELVSTED (*with an apprehensive look at her, says quickly*): He tutored the children.

HEDDA: Your children?

MRS. ELVSTED: My husband's. I don't have any.

HEDDA: In other words, your stepchildren.

MRS. ELVSTED: Yes.

TESMAN (*with some hesitation*): But was he—I don't quite know how to put this—was he sufficiently—regular—in his way of life to be thus employed? Hm?

MRS. ELVSTED: For the last two years, there hasn't been a thing to object to in his conduct.

TESMAN: No, really? Just think, Hedda!

HEDDA: I hear.

MRS. ELVSTED: Not the least little bit, I assure you! Not in any respect. And yet—knowing he's here—in the big city—And with all that money, too! I'm scared to death!

TESMAN: But in that case, why didn't he remain with you and your husband? Hm?

MRS. ELVSTED: After his book came out, he was too restless to stay.

TESMAN: Ah yes, that's right. Aunt Julle said he has published a new book.

MRS. ELVSTED: Yes, a big new book, about the course of civilization in general. It came out about two weeks ago. And since it has had such big sales and been discussed so much and made such a big splash—

TESMAN: It has, has it? I suppose this is something he has had lying around from better days?

MRS. ELVSTED: You mean from earlier?

TESMAN: Yes.

MRS. ELVSTED: No; it's all been written since he came to stay with us. During this last year.

TESMAN: Well, now! That's very good news, Hedda! Just think!

MRS. ELVSTED: Yes, if it only would last!

HEDDA: Have you seen him since you came to town?

MRS. ELVSTED: No, not yet. I had a great deal of trouble finding his address. But this morning I finally tracked him down.

HEDDA (*looks searchingly at her*): Isn't it rather odd that your husband—hm—

MRS. ELVSTED (*with a nervous start*): My husband! What about him?

HEDDA: That he sends you to town on such an errand? That he doesn't go and look after his friend himself?

MRS. ELVSTED: Oh, no, no—my husband doesn't have time for things like that. Besides, I have some— some shopping to do, anyway.

HEDDA (*with a slight smile*): Well, in that case, of course—

MRS. ELVSTED (*getting up, restlessly*): And now I beg of you, Mr. Tesman—won't you please receive Eilert Løvborg nicely if he calls on you? And I am sure he will. After all—Such good friends as you two used to be. And then you both do the same kind of work—the same field of study, as far as I know.

TESMAN: We used to, at any rate.

MRS. ELVSTED: Yes. And that's why I implore you to please, please, try to keep an eye on him—you too. You'll do that, Mr. Tesman, won't you? Promise?

TESMAN: With the greatest pleasure, Mrs. Rysing.

HEDDA: Elvsted.

TESMAN: I'll gladly do as much for Eilert as I possibly can. You may certainly count on that.

MRS. ELVSTED: Oh, how good and kind you are! (*Clasps his hands.*) Thank you, thank you, thank you! (*Nervously.*) You see, my husband is so very fond of him.

HEDDA (*getting up*): You ought to write him a note, Tesman. Maybe he won't come without an invitation.

TESMAN: Yes, I suppose that would be the right thing to do, Hedda. Hm?

HEDDA: The sooner the better. Right away, *I* think.

MRS. ELVSTED (*pleadingly*): If only you would!

TESMAN: I'll write this minute. Do you have his address, Mrs.—Mrs. Elvsted?

MRS. ELVSTED: Yes. (*Pulls a slip of paper from her bag and gives it to him.*) Here it is.

TESMAN: Very good. Well, then, if you'll excuse me— (*Looks around.*) By the way—the slippers? Ah, here we are. (*Leaving with the parcel.*)

HEDDA: Be sure you write a nice, warm, friendly letter, Tesman. And a long one, too.

TESMAN: Certainly, certainly.

MRS. ELVSTED: But not a word that it is I who—!

TESMAN: No, that goes without saying, I should think. Hm? (*Goes out right through inner room.*)

HEDDA (*goes over to* MRS. ELVSTED, *smiles, says in a low voice*): There! We just killed two birds with one stone.

MRS. ELVSTED: What do you mean?

HEDDA: Didn't you see I wanted him out of the room?

MRS. ELVSTED: Yes, to write that letter—

HEDDA: And to speak to you alone.

MRS. ELVSTED (*flustered*): About this same thing?

HEDDA: Exactly.

MRS. ELVSTED (*anxious*): But there *is* nothing more, Mrs. Tesman! Really, there isn't!

HEDDA: Oh yes, there is. There is considerably more. I can see that much. Over here—We are going to have a real, nice, confidential talk, you and I. (*She forces* MRS. ELVSTED *down in the easy chair and seats herself on one of the ottomans.*)

MRS. ELVSTED (*worried, looks at her watch*): But my dear Mrs. Tesman—I had really thought I would be on my way now.

HEDDA: Oh I am sure there is no rush. Now, then.

Tell me about yourself. How are things at home?

MRS. ELVSTED: That is just what I don't want to talk about.

HEDDA: But to me—! After all, we are old schoolmates.

MRS. ELVSTED: But you were a year ahead of me. And I used to be so scared of you!

HEDDA: Scared of me?

MRS. ELVSTED: Terribly. For when we met on the stairs, you always ruffled my hair.

HEDDA: Did I really?

MRS. ELVSTED: Yes. And once you said you were going to burn it off.

HEDDA: Oh, but you know—I wasn't serious!

MRS. ELVSTED: No, but I was such a silly, then. Anyway, afterwards we drifted far apart. Our circles are so very different, you know.

HEDDA: All the more reason for getting close again. Listen. In school we called each other by our first names.

MRS. ELVSTED: Oh I'm sure you're wrong—

HEDDA: I'm sure I'm not! I remember it quite clearly. And now we want to be open with one another, just the way we used to. (*Moves the ottoman closer.*) There, now! (*Kisses her cheek.*) You call me Hedda.

MRS. ELVSTED (*seizes her hands*): Oh, you are so good and kind! I'm not used to that.

HEDDA: There, there! And I'll call you my dear Thora, just as in the old days.

MRS. ELVSTED: My name is Thea.

HEDDA: So it is. Of course. I meant Thea. (*Looks at her with compassion.*) So you're not much used to goodness and kindness, Thea? Not in your own home?

MRS. ELVSTED: If I even had a home! But I don't. I never have had one.

HEDDA (*looks at her for a moment*): I thought there might be something like this.

MRS. ELVSTED (*helplessly, looking straight ahead*): Yes—yes—yes—

HEDDA: I am not sure if I quite remember—Didn't you first come to your husband as his housekeeper?

MRS. ELVSTED: I was really hired as governess. But his wife—his first wife—was ailing already then and practically bedridden. So I had to take charge of the household as well.

HEDDA: But in the end you became his wife.

MRS. ELVSTED (*dully*): So I did.

HEDDA: Let's see. How long ago is that?

MRS. ELVSTED: Since my marriage?

HEDDA: Yes.

MRS. ELVSTED: About five years.

HEDDA: Right. It must be that long.

MRS. ELVSTED: Oh, those five years! Or mostly the last two or three! Oh, Mrs. Tesman—if you could just imagine!

HEDDA (*slaps her hand lightly*): Mrs. Tesman? Shame on you!

MRS. ELVSTED: Oh yes; all right, I'll try. Yes—if you could just—conceive—understand—

HEDDA (*casually*): And Eilert Løvborg has been living near you for some three years or so, hasn't he?

MRS. ELVSTED (*looks at her uncertainly*): Eilert Løvborg? Yes—he has.

HEDDA: Did you know him before? Here in town?

MRS. ELVSTED: Hardly at all. That is, of course I did in a way. I mean, I knew *of* him.

HEDDA: But up there—You saw a good deal of him; did you?

MRS. ELVSTED: Yes, he came over to us every day. He was supposed to tutor the children, you see. For I just couldn't do it all by myself.

HEDDA: Of course not. And your husband—? I suppose he travels quite a bit.

MRS. ELVSTED: Well, yes, Mrs. Tes—Hedda—as a public magistrate, you know, he very often has to travel all over his district.

HEDDA (*leaning against the armrest on the easy chair*): Thea—poor, sweet Thea—now you have to tell me everything—just as it is.

MRS. ELVSTED: You'd better ask me, then.

HEDDA: How *is* your husband, Thea? I mean—you know—*really?* To be with. What kind of person is he? Is he good to you?

MRS. ELVSTED (*evasively*): I believe he thinks he does everything for the best.

HEDDA: But isn't he altogether too old for you? He is more than twenty years older, isn't he?

MRS. ELVSTED (*with irritation*): Yes, there is that, too. But there isn't just one thing. Every single little thing about him repels me! We don't have a thought in common, he and I. Not a thing in the world!

HEDDA: But isn't he fond of you all the same? I mean in his own way?

MRS. ELVSTED: I don't know. I think I am just useful to him. And I don't use much money. I am inexpensive.

HEDDA: That is foolish of you.

MRS. ELVSTED (*shakes her head*): Can't be changed. Not with him. I don't think he cares for anybody much except himself. Perhaps the children a little.

HEDDA: And Eilert Løvborg, Thea.

MRS. ELVSTED (*looks at her*): Eilert Løvborg? What makes you think that?

HEDDA: Well, it seems to me that when he sends you all the way to town to look after him—(*With an almost imperceptible smile.*) Besides, you said so yourself. To Tesman.

MRS. ELVSTED (*with a nervous twitch*): Did I? I suppose I did. (*With a muted outburst.*) No! I might as well tell you now as later. For it's bound to come out, anyway.

HEDDA: But my dear Thea—?

MRS. ELVSTED: All right. My husband doesn't know I've gone!

HEDDA: What! He doesn't know?

MRS. ELVSTED: Of course not. He wasn't even home. Away on another trip. Oh, I just couldn't take it any longer, Hedda! It had become utterly impossible. All alone as I was going to be.

HEDDA: So what did you do?

MRS. ELVSTED: I packed some of my things. Just the most necessary. Without telling anybody. And left.

HEDDA: Just like that?

MRS. ELVSTED: Yes. And took the next train to town.

HEDDA: But dearest Thea—how did you dare to do a thing like that!

MRS. ELVSTED (*rises, walks*): What else could I do?

HEDDA: But what do you think your husband will say when you go back?

MRS. ELVSTED (*by the table; looks at her*): Go back to him?

HEDDA: Yes!

MRS. ELVSTED: I'll never go back.

HEDDA (*rises, approaches her slowly*): So you have really, seriously—left everything?

MRS. ELVSTED: Yes. It seemed to me there was nothing else I could do.

HEDDA: And quite openly, too.

MRS. ELVSTED: You can't keep a thing like that secret, anyway.

HEDDA: But what do you think people will say, Thea?

MRS. ELVSTED: In God's name, let them say whatever they like. (*Sits down on the sofa, dully, tired.*) For I have only done what I had to do.

HEDDA (*after a brief silence*): And what do you plan to do with yourself? What sort of work will you do?

MRS. ELVSTED: I don't know yet. I only know I have to live where Eilert Løvborg is. If I am to live at all.

HEDDA (*moves a chair from the table closer to* MRS. ELVSTED, *sits down, strokes her hands*): Thea—tell me. How did this—this friendship between you and Eilert Løvborg—how did it begin?

MRS. ELVSTED: Oh, it grew little by little. I got some sort of power over him.

HEDDA: Oh?

MRS. ELVSTED: He dropped his old ways. Not because I asked him to. I never dared to do that. But I think he must have noticed how I felt about that kind of life. So he changed.

HEDDA (*quickly suppresses a cynical smile*): So you have—rehabilitated him, as they say. Haven't you, little Thea?

MRS. ELVSTED: At least, that's what *he* says. On the other hand, he has turned me into a real human being. Taught me to think—and understand—all sorts of things.

HEDDA: Maybe he tutored you, too?

MRS. ELVSTED: No, not tutored exactly. But he talked to me. About so many, many things. And then came that lovely, lovely time when I could share his work with him. He let me help him!

HEDDA: He did?

MRS. ELVSTED: Yes! Whatever he wrote, he wanted us to be together about it.

HEDDA: Just like two good comrades.

MRS. ELVSTED (*with animation*): Comrades!—that's it! Imagine, Hedda—that's just what he called it, too. Oh, I really ought to feel so happy. But I can't. For you see, I don't know if it will last.

HEDDA: You don't trust him any more than that?

MRS. ELVSTED (*heavily*): The shadow of a woman stands between Eilert Løvborg and me.

HEDDA (*tensely, looks at her*): Who?

MRS. ELVSTED: I don't know. Somebody or other from—his past. I don't think he has ever really forgotten her.

HEDDA: What has he told you about it?

MRS. ELVSTED: He has mentioned it only once—just casually.

HEDDA: And what did he say?

MRS. ELVSTED: He said that when they parted she was going to kill him with a gun.

HEDDA (*cold, controlled*): Oh, nonsense. People don't do that sort of thing here.

MRS. ELVSTED: No, I know. And that is why I think it must be that red-headed singer he used to—

HEDDA: Yes, I suppose so.

MRS. ELVSTED: For I remember people said she carried a loaded gun.

HEDDA: Well, then I'm sure it's she.

MRS. ELVSTED (*wringing her hands*): Yes, but just think, Hedda—now I hear that she—that singer—that she's here in town again, too! Oh, I'm just desperate—!

HEDDA (*with a glance toward the inner room*): Shhh! Here's Tesman. (*Rises and whispers.*) Not a word about all this to anybody, Thea!

MRS. ELVSTED (*jumps up*): No, no. For God's sake—!

[*TESMAN, carrying a letter, enters from the right side of the inner room.*]

TESMAN: There, now—here's the missive, all ready to go!

HEDDA: Good. But I believe Mrs. Elvsted wants to be on her way. Wait a moment. I'll see you to the garden gate.

TESMAN: Say, Hedda—do you think Berte could take care of this?

HEDDA (*takes the letter*): I'll tell her.

[*BERTE enters right.*]

BERTE: Judge Brack is here and wants to know if

you're receiving.

HEDDA: Yes, ask the Judge please to come in. And—here—drop this in a mailbox, will you?

BERTE (*takes the letter*): Yes, ma'am.

[*She opens the door for JUDGE BRACK and exits. The JUDGE is forty-five years of age. Rather thickset, but well-built and with brisk, athletic movements. Roundish face, aristocratic profile. His hair is short, still almost completely black, very neatly dressed. Lively, sparkling eyes. Thick eyebrows and mustache with cut-off points. He is dressed in an elegant suit, though a trifle youthful for his age. He wears a pince-nez, attached to a string, and lets it drop from time to time.*]

JUDGE BRACK (*hat in hand, salutes*): May one pay one's respects as early as this?

HEDDA: One certainly may.

TESMAN (*shaking his hand*): You are always welcome. (*Introducing.*) Judge Brack—Miss Rysing—

[*HEDDA groans.*]

BRACK (*bowing*): Delighted!

HEDDA (*looks at him, laughs*): How nice it is to see you in daylight, Judge!

BRACK: You find me changed, perhaps?

HEDDA: A bit younger, I think.

BRACK: Much obliged.

TESMAN: But what do you think of Hedda? Hm? Did you ever see her in such bloom? She positively—

HEDDA: Will you please leave me out of this? You had better thank the Judge for all the trouble he has taken.

BRACK: Oh, nonsense. It's been a pleasure.

HEDDA: Yes, you are indeed a faithful soul. But my friend here is dying to be off. Don't leave, Judge. I'll be back in a minute.

[*Mutual goodbyes. MRS. ELVSTED and HEDDA exit, right.*]

BRACK: Well, now—your wife—is she tolerably satisfied?

TESMAN: Yes, indeed, and we really can't thank you enough. That is, I understand there will have to be some slight changes made here and there. And there are still a few things—just a few trifles—we'll have to get.

BRACK: Oh? Really?

TESMAN: But we certainly don't want to bother you with that. Hedda said she's going to take care of it herself. But do sit down, hm?

BRACK: Thanks. Maybe just for a moment—(*Sits down by the table.*) There's one thing I'd like to talk to you about, my dear Tesman.

TESMAN: Oh? Ah, I see! (*Sits down.*) I suppose it's the

serious part of the festivities that's beginning now. Hm?

BRACK: Oh—there's no great rush yet as far as the money is concerned. Though I must say I wish we could have established ourselves a trifle more economically.

TESMAN: Out of the question, my dear fellow! Remember, it's all for Hedda! You, who know her so well—! After all, I couldn't put her up like any little middle-class housewife—

BRACK: No, I suppose—That's just it.

TESMAN: Besides—fortunately—it can't be long now before I receive my appointment.

BRACK: Well, you know—things like that have a way of hanging fire.

TESMAN: Perhaps you have heard something? Something definite? Hm?

BRACK: No, nothing certain—(*Interrupting himself.*) But that reminds me. I have some news for you.

TESMAN: Oh?

BRACK: Your old friend Eilert Løvborg is back in town.

TESMAN: I know that already.

BRACK: So? Who told you?

TESMAN: The lady who just left.

BRACK: I see. What did you say her name was again? I didn't quite catch—

TESMAN: Mrs. Elvsted.

BRACK: Ah yes—the Commissioner's wife. Yes, it's up in her part of the country that Løvborg has been staying, too.

TESMAN: And just think. I am so glad to hear it. He is quite respectable again.

BRACK: Yes, so they say.

TESMAN: And he has published a new book, hm?

BRACK: Oh yes.

TESMAN: Which is making quite a stir.

BRACK: Quite an unusual stir.

TESMAN: Just think! Isn't that just wonderful! He— with his remarkable gifts. And I was so sure he'd gone under for good.

BRACK: That seems to have been the general opinion.

TESMAN: What I don't understand, though, is what he is going to do with himself. What sort of living can he make? Hm?

[During the last remark HEDDA re-enters, right.]

HEDDA (*to BRACK, with a scornful little laugh*): Tesman is forever worrying about how people are going to make a living.

TESMAN: Well, you see, we are talking about poor Eilert Løvborg, Hedda.

HEDDA (*with a quick look at him*): You are? (*Sits down in the easy chair by the stove and asks casually.*) What is the matter with him?

TESMAN: Well, you see, I believe he's run through his

inheritance a long time ago. And I don't suppose he can write a new book every year. Hm? So I really must ask how he is going to make out.

BRACK: Maybe I could help you answer that.

TESMAN: Yes?

BRACK: Remember, he has relatives with considerable influence.

TESMAN: Ah—unfortunately, those relatives have washed their hands of him long ago.

BRACK: Just the same, they used to call him the hope of the family.

TESMAN: Yes, before! But he has ruined all that.

HEDDA: Who knows? (*With a little smile.*) I hear the Elvsteds have rehabilitated him.

BRACK: And then this book—

TESMAN: Well, I certainly hope they will help him to find something or other. I just wrote him a letter. Hedda, dear, I asked him to come out here tonight.

BRACK: Oh dear, I am sorry. Don't you remember— you're supposed to come to my little stag dinner tonight? You accepted last night on the pier, you know.

HEDDA: Had you forgotten, Tesman?

TESMAN: So I had.

BRACK: Oh well. I'm sure he won't come, so it doesn't really make any difference.

TESMAN: Why is that? Hm?

BRACK (*gets up somewhat hesitantly, rests his hands on the back of the chair*): Dear Tesman—and you, too, Mrs. Tesman—I cannot in good conscience let you remain in ignorance of something, which— which—

TESMAN: Something to do with Eilert?

BRACK: With both you and him.

TESMAN: But my dear Judge, do speak!

BRACK: You must be prepared to find that your appointment will not come through as soon as you hope and expect.

TESMAN (*jumps up, nervously*): Something's hap-pened? Hm?

BRACK: It may conceivably be made contingent upon the result of a competition.

TESMAN: Competition! Just think, Hedda!

HEDDA (*leaning farther back in her chair*): Ah—I see, I see—!

TESMAN: But with whom? Don't tell me with—?

BRACK: Precisely. With Eilert Løvborg.

TESMAN (*claps his hands together*): No, no! This can't be! It is unthinkable! Quite impossible! Hm?

BRACK: All the same, that's the way it may turn out.

TESMAN: No, but Judge, this would amount to the most incredible callousness toward me! (*Waving his arms.*) For just think—I'm a married man! We married on the strength of these prospects, Hedda and I. Got ourselves deep in debt. Borrowed money from Aunt Julle, too. After all, I had practically been promised the post, you know. Hm?

BRACK: Well, well. I daresay you'll get it in the end. If only after a competition.

HEDDA (*motionless in her chair*): Just think, Tesman. It will be like a kind of contest.

TESMAN: But dearest Hedda, how can you be so unconcerned!

HEDDA (*still without moving*): I'm not at all unconcerned. I'm dying to see who wins.

BRACK: In any case, Mrs. Tesman, I'm glad you know the situation as it is. I mean—before you proceed to make the little additional purchases I understand you threaten us with.

HEDDA: This makes no difference as far as that is concerned.

BRACK: Really? Well, in that case, of course— Goodbye! (*To* TESMAN.) I'll pick you up on my afternoon walk.

TESMAN: What? Oh yes, yes, of course. I'm sorry; I'm just all flustered.

HEDDA (*without getting up, gives her hand*): Goodbye, Judge. Come back soon.

BRACK: Thanks. Goodbye, goodbye.

TESMAN (*sees him to the door*): Goodbye, my dear Judge. You really must excuse me—

[*JUDGE BRACK exits, right.*]

TESMAN (*pacing the floor*): Oh, Hedda, Hedda! One should never venture into fairyland. Hm?

HEDDA (*looks at him, smiles*): Do *you* do that?

TESMAN: Well, yes—it can't be denied—it was most venturesome of me to rush into marriage and set up a home on the strength of mere prospects.

HEDDA: Well, maybe you're right.

TESMAN: Anyway—we do have our own nice, comfortable home, now. Just think, Hedda—the very home both of us dreamed about. Set our hearts on, I may almost say. Hm?

HEDDA (*rises, slowly, tired*): The agreement was that we were to maintain a certain position— entertain—

TESMAN: Don't I know it! Dearest Hedda—I have been so looking forward to seeing you as hostess in a select circle! Hm? Well, well, well! In the meantime, we'll just have to be content with one another. See Aunt Julle once in a while. Nothing more. And you were meant for such a different kind of life, altogether!

HEDDA: I suppose a footman is completely out of the question.

TESMAN: I'm afraid so. Under the circumstances, you see—we couldn't possibly—

HEDDA: And as for getting my own riding horse—

TESMAN (*aghast*): Riding horse!

HEDDA: I suppose I mustn't even think of that.

TESMAN: Good heavens, no! That goes without say-

ing, I hope!

HEDDA (*walking*): Well—at least I have one thing to amuse myself with in the meantime.

TESMAN (*overjoyed*): Oh thank goodness for that! And what *is* that, Hedda, Hm?

HEDDA (*in the doorway, looks at him with suppressed scorn*): My guns—Jørgen!

TESMAN (*in fear*): Your guns!

HEDDA (*with cold eyes*): General Gabler's guns. (*She exits left, through the inner room.*)

TESMAN (*runs up to the doorway, calls after her*): But Hedda! Good gracious! Hedda, dear! Please don't touch those dangerous things! For my sake, Hedda! Hm?

ACT II

The same room at the TESMANS'. *The piano has been moved out and replaced by an elegant little writing desk. A small table has been placed near the sofa, left. Most of the flowers have been removed.* MRS. ELVSTED'*s bouquet is on the big table front center. Afternoon.*

HEDDA, *dressed to receive callers, is alone. She is standing near the open French doors, loading a revolver. Its mate is lying in an open case on the desk.*

HEDDA (*looking down into the garden, calls*): Hello there, Judge! Welcome back!

JUDGE BRACK (*off stage*): Thanks, Mrs. Tesman!

HEDDA (*raises the gun, sights*): I am going to shoot you, Judge Brack!

BRACK (*calls off stage*): No—no—no! Don't point the gun at me like that!

HEDDA: That's what you get for sneaking in the back door! (*Fires.*)

BRACK (*closer*): Are you out of your mind—!

HEDDA: Oh dear—did I hit you?

BRACK (*still off stage*): Stop that nonsense!

HEDDA: Come on in, then.

[*JUDGE BRACK, dressed for dinner, enters, left. He carries a light overcoat over his arm.*]

BRACK: Dammit! Do you still fool around with that thing? What are you shooting at, anyway?

HEDDA: Oh—just firing off into blue air.

BRACK (*gently but firmly taking the gun away from her*): With your permission, Mrs. Tesman. (*Looks at it.*) Ah yes, I remember this gun very well. (*Looks around.*) Where is the case? Ah, here we are. (*Puts the gun in the case and closes it.*) That's enough of that silliness for today.

HEDDA: But in the name of heaven, what do you expect me to do with myself?

BRACK: No callers?

HEDDA (*closing the French doors*): Not a soul. All my close friends are still out of town, it seems.

BRACK: And Tesman is out, too, perhaps?

HEDDA (*by the desk, puts the gun case in a drawer*): Yes. He took off for the aunts' right after lunch. He didn't expect you so early.

BRACK: I should have thought of that. That was stupid of me.

HEDDA (*turns her head, looks at him*): Why stupid?

BRACK: I would have come a little—sooner.

HEDDA (*crossing*): If you had, you wouldn't have found anybody home. For I have been in my room ever since lunch, changing my clothes.

BRACK: And isn't there the tiniest little crack in the door for negotiations?

HEDDA: You forgot to provide one.

BRACK: Another stupidity.

HEDDA: So we'll have to stay in here. And wait. For I don't think Tesman will be back for some time.

BRACK: By all means. I'll be very patient.

[HEDDA *sits on the sofa in the corner.* BRACK *puts his overcoat over the back of the nearest chair and sits down, keeping his hat in his hand. Brief silence. They look at one another.*]

HEDDA: Well?

BRACK (*in the same tone*): Well?

HEDDA: I said it first.

BRACK (*leans forward a little*): All right. Let's have a nice little chat, Mrs. Tesman.

HEDDA (*leans back*): Don't you think it's an eternity since last time we talked! I don't count last night and this morning. That was nothing.

BRACK: You mean—just the two of us?

HEDDA: Mmm. If you like.

BRACK: There hasn't been a day I haven't wished you were back again.

HEDDA: My feelings, exactly.

BRACK: Yours? Really, Mrs. Tesman? And I have been assuming you were having such a wonderful time traveling.

HEDDA: I'd say!

BRACK: All Tesman's letters said so.

HEDDA: Oh yes, he! He's happy just poking through old collections of books. And copying old parchments—or whatever they are.

BRACK (*with a touch of malice*): Well, that's his calling, you know. Partly, anyway.

HEDDA: Yes, so it is. And in that case I suppose—But I! Oh, Judge! You've no idea how bored I've been.

BRACK (*with sympathy*): Really? You're serious?

HEDDA: Surely you can understand that? For a whole half year never to see anyone who knows even a little bit about our circle? And talks our language?

BRACK: Yes, I think I would find that trying, too.

HEDDA: And then the most unbearable thing of all—

BRACK: Well?

HEDDA: —everlastingly to be in the company of the same person—

BRACK (*nods in agreement*): Both early and late—yes. I can imagine—at all possible times—

HEDDA: I said everlastingly.

BRACK: All right. Still, it seems to me that with as excellent a person as our Tesman, it ought to be possible—

HEDDA: My dear Judge—Tesman is a specialist.

BRACK: Granted.

HEDDA: And specialists are not at all entertaining travel companions. Not in the long run, at any rate.

BRACK: Not even—the specialist—one happens to love?

HEDDA: Bah! That nauseating word!

BRACK (*puzzled*): Really, now, Mrs. Tesman—?

HEDDA (*half laughing, half annoyed*): *You* ought to try it some time! Listening to talk about the history of civilization, early and late—

BRACK: Everlastingly—

HEDDA: All right. And then this business about the domestic industry in the Middle Ages—! That's the ghastliest part of it all!

BRACK (*looking searchingly at her*): But in that case— tell me—how am I to explain—?

HEDDA: That Jørgen Tesman and I made a pair of it, you mean?

BRACK: If you want to put it that way—yes.

HEDDA: Come now. Do you really find that so strange?

BRACK: Both yes and no—Mrs. Tesman.

HEDDA: I had danced myself tired, my dear Judge. My season was over—(*Gives a slight start.*) No, no—I don't really mean that. Won't think it, either!

BRACK: Nor do you have the slightest reason to, I am sure.

HEDDA: Oh—as far as reasons are concerned—(*Looks at him as if trying to read his mind.*) And, after all, Jørgen Tesman must be said to be a most proper young man in all respects.

BRACK: Both proper and substantial. Most certainly.

HEDDA: And one can't say there is anything exactly comical about him. Do you think there is?

BRACK: Comical? No—o. I wouldn't say that—

HEDDA: All right, then. And he is a most assiduous collector. Nobody can deny that. I think it is perfectly possible he may go quite far, after all.

BRACK (*looks at her rather uncertainly*): I assumed that you, like everybody else, thought he'll in time become an exceptionally eminent man?

HEDDA (*with a weary expression*): Yes, I did. And then, you see—there he was, wanting so desperately to be allowed to provide for me—I don't know why I shouldn't have accepted?

BRACK: No, certainly. From that point of view—

HEDDA: For you know, my dear Judge, that was considerably more than my other admirers were willing to do.

BRACK (*laughs*): Well! Of course I can't answer for all the others. But as far as I am concerned, I have always had a certain degree of—respect for the bonds of matrimony. You know—as a general proposition, Mrs. Tesman.

HEDDA (*lightly*): Well, I never really counted very heavily on *you*—

BRACK: All I want is a nice, confidential circle, in which I can be of service, both in deed and in counsel. Be allowed to come and go like a true and tried friend—

HEDDA: You mean, of the master of the house—?

BRACK (*with a slight bow*): To be perfectly frank—rather of the mistress. But by all means—the master, too, of course. Do you know, that kind of—shall I say, triangular?—relationship can really be a great comfort to all parties involved.

HEDDA: Yes, many were the times I missed a second travel companion. To be twosome in the compartment—brrr!

BRACK: Fortunately, the wedding trip is over.

HEDDA (*shakes her head*): There's a long journey ahead. I've just arrived at a station on the way.

BRACK: Well, at the station one gets out and moves around a bit, Mrs. Tesman.

HEDDA: I never get out.

BRACK: Really?

HEDDA: No. For there's always someone around, who—

BRACK (*laughs*): —looks at one's legs; is that it?

HEDDA: Exactly.

BRACK: Oh well, really, now—

HEDDA (*with a silencing gesture*): I won't have it! Rather stay in my seat—once I'm seated. Twosome and all.

BRACK: I see. But what if a third party were to join the couple?

HEDDA: Well, now—*that* would be something altogether different!

BRACK: A proven, understanding friend—

HEDDA: —entertaining in all sorts of lively ways—

BRACK: —and not at all a specialist!

HEDDA (*with audible breath*): Yes, that would indeed be a comfort.

BRACK (*hearing the front door open, looking at her*): Triangle complete.

HEDDA (*half aloud*): And the train goes on.

[*TESMAN, in gray walking suit and soft hat, enters, right. He carries a pile of paperbound books under his arm. Others are stuffed in his pockets.*]

TESMAN (*as he walks up to the table in front of the corner sofa*): Puuhh—! Quite some load to carry, all this—and in this heat, too. (*Puts the books down.*) I am positively perspiring, Hedda. Well, well. So you're here already, my dear Judge. Hm? And Berte didn't tell me.

BRACK (*rises*): I came through the garden.

HEDDA: What are all those books?

TESMAN (*leafing through some of them*): Just some new publications in my special field.

HEDDA: Special field, hm?

BRACK: Ah yes—professional publications, Mrs. Tesman.

[*BRACK and HEDDA exchange knowing smiles.*]

HEDDA: Do you still need more books?

TESMAN: Yes, my dear. There is no such thing as having too many books in one's special field. One has to keep up with what is being written and published, you know.

HEDDA: I suppose.

TESMAN (*searching among the books*): And look. Here is Eilert Løvborg's new book, too. (*Offers it to her.*) Want to take a look at it, Hedda? Hm?

HEDDA: No—thanks just the same. Or perhaps later.

TESMAN: I glanced at it on my way home.

BRACK: And what do you think of it? As a specialist yourself?

TESMAN: It is remarkable for its sobriety. He never wrote like that before. (*Gathers up all the books.*) I just want to take these into my study. I am so much looking forward to cutting them open! And then I'll change. (*To* BRACK.) I assume there's no rush to be off, is there?

BRACK: Not at all. We have plenty of time.

TESMAN: In that case, I think I'll indulge myself a little. (*On his way out with the books he halts in the doorway and turns.*) By the way, Hedda—Aunt Julle won't be out to see you tonight, after all.

HEDDA: No? Is it that business with the hat, do you think?

TESMAN: Oh, no—not at all. How can you believe a thing like that about Aunt Julle! Just think! No, it's Aunt Rina. She's feeling very poorly.

HEDDA: Isn't she always?

TESMAN: Yes, but it's especially bad today, poor thing.

HEDDA: Well, in that case I suppose the other one ought to stay home. I shall have to put up with it; that's all.

TESMAN: And you have no idea how perfectly delighted Aunt Julle was, even so. Because of how splendid you look after the trip, Hedda!

HEDDA (*half aloud, rising*): Oh, these everlasting aunts!

TESMAN: Hm?

HEDDA (*walks over to the French doors*): Nothing.

TESMAN: No? All right. Well, excuse me. (*Exits right,*

through inner room.)

BRACK: What is this about a hat?

HEDDA: Oh, something with Miss Tesman this morning. She had put her hat down on the chair over there. (*Looks at him, smiles.*) So I pretended to think it was the maid's.

BRACK (*shakes his head*): But my dear Mrs. Tesman—how could you do a thing like that! And to that excellent old lady, too!

HEDDA (*nervously pacing the floor*): Well, you see—something just comes over me at times. And then I can't help myself—(*Throws herself down in the easy chair near the stove.*) Oh I can't explain it even to myself.

BRACK (*behind her chair*): You aren't really happy—that's the trouble.

HEDDA (*staring into space*): I don't know any reason why I should be—happy. Do you?

BRACK: Well, yes—partly because you've got the home you've always wanted.

HEDDA (*looks up at him and laughs*): So you too believe that story about my great desire?

BRACK: You mean, there is nothing to it?

HEDDA: Well, yes; there is *something* to it.

BRACK: Well?

HEDDA: There is this much to it, that last summer I used Tesman to see me home from evening parties.

BRACK: Unfortunately—my route was in quite a different direction.

HEDDA: True. You walked on other roads last summer.

BRACK (*laughs*): Shame on you, Mrs. Tesman! So, all right—you and Tesman—?

HEDDA: One evening we passed by here. And Tesman, poor thing, was practically turning himself into knots trying to find something to talk about. So I felt sorry for all that erudition—

BRACK (*with a doubting smile*): You did? Hm—

HEDDA: I really did. So, just to help him out of his misery, I said without thinking I'd like to live in this house.

BRACK: Just that?

HEDDA: That was all—*that* evening.

BRACK: But afterwards—?

HEDDA: Yes, my thoughtlessness had consequences, Judge.

BRACK: Unfortunately—that's often the way with our little thoughtlessness. It happens to all of us, Mrs. Tesman.

HEDDA: Thanks! So in our common enthusiasm for Mr. Secretary Falk's villa Tesman and I found each other, you see! The result was engagement and wedding and honeymoon abroad and all the rest of it. Well, yes, my dear Judge—I've made my bed—I almost said.

BRACK: But this is priceless! And you didn't really care for the house at all?

HEDDA: God knows, no!

BRACK: Not even now? After all, we've set up quite a comfortable home for you here, haven't we?

HEDDA: Oh—it seems to me I smell lavender and rose sachets in all the rooms. But maybe that's a smell Aunt Julle brought with her.

BRACK (*laughs*): My guess is rather the late lamented Secretary's wife.

HEDDA: It smells of mortality, whoever it is. Like corsages—the next day. (*Clasps her hands behind her neck, leans back, looks at him.*) Judge, you have no idea how dreadfully bored I'll be—out here.

BRACK: But don't you think life may hold some task for you, too, Mrs. Tesman?

HEDDA: A task? With any kind of appeal?

BRACK: Preferably that, of course.

HEDDA: Heaven knows what kind of task that might be. There are times when I wonder if—(*Interrupts herself.*) No; I'm sure that wouldn't work, either.

BRACK: Who knows? Tell me.

HEDDA: It has occurred to me that maybe I could get Tesman to enter politics.

BRACK (*laughs*): Tesman! No, really—I must confess that—politics doesn't strike me as being exactly Tesman's line.

HEDDA: I agree. But suppose I were to prevail on him, all the same?

BRACK: What satisfaction could you possibly find in that? If he can't succeed—why do you want him even to try?

HEDDA: Because I am bored, I tell you! (*After a brief pause.*) So you think it's quite out of the question that Tesman could ever become prime minister?

BRACK: Well, you see, Mrs. Tesman—to do that he'd first of all have to be a fairly wealthy man.

HEDDA (*getting up, impatiently*): Yes! There we are! These shabby circumstances I've married into! (*Crosses the floor.*) That's what makes life so mean. So—so—ridiculous! For that's what it is, you know.

BRACK: Personally I believe something else is to blame.

HEDDA: What?

BRACK: You've never been through anything that's really stirred you.

HEDDA: Something serious, you mean?

BRACK: If you like. But maybe it's coming now.

HEDDA (*with a toss of her head*): You are thinking of that silly old professorship! That's Tesman's business. I refuse to give it a thought.

BRACK: As you wish. But now—to put it in the grand style—now when a solemn challenge of responsibility is being posed? Demands made on you? (*Smiles.*) New demands, Mrs. Tesman.

HEDDA (*angry*): Quiet! You'll never see anything of the kind.

BRACK (*cautiously*): We'll talk about this a year from

now—on the outside.

HEDDA (*curtly*): I'm not made for that sort of thing, Judge! No demands for me!

BRACK: But surely you, like most women, are made for a duty, which—

HEDDA (*over by the French doors*): Oh, do be quiet! Often it seems to me there's only one thing in the world that I am made for.

BRACK (*coming close*): And may I ask what that is?

HEDDA (*looking out*): To be bored to death. Now you know. (*Turns, looks toward the inner room, laughs.*) Just as I thought. Here comes the professor.

BRACK (*warningly, in a low voice*): Steady, now, Mrs. Tesman!

[TESMAN, dressed for a party, carrying his hat and gloves, enters from the right in the inner room.]

TESMAN: Hedda, any word yet from Eilert Løvborg that he isn't coming, hm?

HEDDA: No.

TESMAN: In that case, I wouldn't be a bit surprised if we have him here in a few minutes.

BRACK: You really think he'll come?

TESMAN: I am almost certain he will. For I'm sure it's only idle gossip that you told me this morning.

BRACK: Oh?

TESMAN: Anyway, that's what Aunt Julle said. She doesn't for a moment believe he'll stand in my way. Just think!

BRACK: I'm very glad to hear that.

TESMAN (*puts his hat and his gloves down on a chair, right*): But you must let me wait for him as long as possible.

BRACK: By all means. We have plenty of time. Nobody will arrive at my place before seven—seven-thirty, or so.

TESMAN: And in the meantime we can keep Hedda company. Take our time. Hm?

HEDDA (*carrying BRACK's hat and coat over to the sofa in the corner*): And if worst comes to worst, Mr. Løvborg can stay here with me.

BRACK (*trying to take the things away from her*): Let me, Mrs. Tesman—What do you mean—"if worst comes to worst?"

HEDDA: If he doesn't want to go with you and Tesman.

TESMAN (*looks dubiously at her*): But, dearest Hedda—do you think that will quite do? He staying here with you? Hm? Remember, Aunt Julle won't be here.

HEDDA: No, but Mrs. Elvsted will. The three of us will have a cup of tea together.

TESMAN: Oh yes; *that* will be perfectly all right!

BRACK (*with a smile*): And perhaps the wiser course of action for him.

HEDDA: What do you mean?

BRACK: Begging your pardon, Mrs. Tesman—you've often enough looked askance at my little stag dinners. You've said that only men of the firmest principles ought to attend.

HEDDA: I should think Mr. Løvborg is firm-principled enough now. A reformed sinner—

[BERTE appears in door, right.]

BERTE: Ma'am—there's a gentleman here who asks if—

HEDDA: Show him in, please.

TESMAN (*softly*): I'm sure it's he! Just think!

[EILERT LØVBORG enters, right. He is slim, gaunt. Of TESMAN's age, but he looks older and somewhat dissipated. Brown hair and beard. Pale, longish face, reddish spots on the cheekbones. Dressed for visiting in elegant, black, brand-new suit. He carries a silk hat and dark gloves in his hand. He remains near the door, makes a quick bow. He appears a little embarrassed.]

TESMAN (*goes over to him, shakes his hand*): My dear Eilert—at last we meet again!

EILERT LØVBORG (*subdued voice*): Thanks for your note, Jørgen! (*Approaching HEDDA.*) Am I allowed to shake your hand, too, Mrs. Tesman?

HEDDA (*accepting his proffered hand*): I am very glad to see you, Mr. Løvborg. (*With a gesture.*) I don't know if you two gentlemen—

LØVBORG (*with a slight bow*): Judge Brack, I believe.

BRACK (*also bowing lightly*): Certainly. Some years ago—

TESMAN (*to LØVBORG, both hands on his shoulders*): And now I want you to feel quite at home here, Eilert! Isn't that right, Hedda? For you plan to stay here in town, I understand. Hm?

LØVBORG: Yes, I do.

TESMAN: Perfectly reasonable. Listen—I just got hold of your new book, but I haven't had a chance to read it yet.

LØVBORG: You may save yourself the trouble.

TESMAN: Why do you say that?

LØVBORG: There's not much to it.

TESMAN: Just think—you saying that!

BRACK: Nevertheless, people seem to have very good things to say about it.

LØVBORG: That's exactly why I wrote it—so everybody would like it.

BRACK: Very wise of you.

TESMAN: Yes, but Eilert—!

LØVBORG: For I am trying to rebuild my position. Start all over again.

TESMAN (*with some embarrassment*): Yes, I suppose you are, aren't you? Hm?

LØVBORG (*smiles, puts his hat down, pulls a parcel out of his pocket*): When *this* appears—Jørgen Tesman—

this you must read. For this is the real thing. This is me.

TESMAN: Oh really? And what is it?

LØVBORG: The continuation.

TESMAN: Continuation? Of what?

LØVBORG: Of the book.

TESMAN: Of the new book?

LØVBORG: Of course.

TESMAN: But Eilert—you've carried the story all the way up to the present!

LØVBORG: So I have. And this is about the future.

TESMAN: The future! But, heavens—we don't know a thing about the future!

LØVBORG: No, we don't. But there are a couple of things to be said about it all the same. (*Unwraps the parcel.*) Here, let me show you—

TESMAN: But that's not your handwriting.

LØVBORG: I have dictated it. (*Leafs through portions of the manuscript.*) It's in two parts. The first is about the forces that will shape the civilization of the future. And the second (*riffling through more pages*)—about the course which that future civilization will take.

TESMAN: How remarkable! It would never occur to me to write anything like that.

HEDDA (*over by the French doors, her fingers drumming the pane*): Hmm—I dare say—

LØVBORG (*replacing the manuscript in its wrappings and putting it down on the table*): I brought it along, for I thought maybe I'd read parts of it aloud to you this evening.

TESMAN: That's very good of you, Eilert. But this evening—? (*Looks at* BRACK.) I'm not quite sure how to arrange that—

LØVBORG: Some other time, then. There's no hurry.

BRACK: You see, Mr. Løvborg, there's a little get-together over at my house tonight. Mainly for Tesman, you know—

LØVBORG (*looking for his hat*): In that case, I certainly won't—

BRACK: No, listen. Won't you do me the pleasure to join us?

LØVBORG (*firmly*): No, I won't. But thanks all the same.

BRACK: Oh come on! Why don't you do that? We'll be a small, select circle. And I think I can promise you a fairly lively evening, as Hed—as Mrs. Tesman would say.

LØVBORG: I don't doubt that. Nevertheless—

BRACK: And you may bring your manuscript along and read aloud to Tesman over at my house. I have plenty of room.

TESMAN: Just think, Eilert! Wouldn't that be nice, hm?

HEDDA (*intervening*): But can't you see that Mr. Løvborg doesn't want to? I'm sure he would rather stay here and have supper with me.

LØVBORG (*looks at her*): With you, Mrs. Tesman?

HEDDA: And with Mrs. Elvsted.

LØVBORG: Ah—! (*Casually.*) I ran into her at noon today.

HEDDA: Oh? Well, she'll be here tonight. So you see your presence is really required, Mr. Løvborg. Otherwise she won't have anybody to see her home.

LØVBORG: True. All right, then, Mrs. Tesman—I'll stay, thank you.

HEDDA: Good. I'll just tell the maid. (*She rings for* BERTE *over by the door, right.*)

[BERTE *appears just off stage.* HEDDA *talks with her in a low voice, points toward the inner room.* BERTE *nods and exits.*]

TESMAN (*while* HEDDA *and* BERTE *are talking, to* LØVBORG): Tell me, Eilert—is it this subject—about the future—is that what you plan to lecture on?

LØVBORG: Yes.

TESMAN: For the bookseller told me you have announced a lecture series for this fall.

LØVBORG: Yes, I have. I hope you won't mind.

TESMAN: Of course not! But—

LØVBORG: For of course I realize it is rather awkward for you.

TESMAN (*unhappily*): Oh well—I certainly can't expect—that just for my sake—

LØVBORG: But I will wait till you receive your appointment.

TESMAN: Wait? But—but—but—you mean you aren't going to compete with me? Hm?

LØVBORG: No. Just triumph over you. In people's opinion.

TESMAN: Oh, for goodness' sake! Then Aunt Julle was right, after all! I knew it all the time. Hedda! Do you hear that! Just think—Eilert Løvborg isn't going to stand in our way after all.

HEDDA (*tersely*): Our? Please leave me out of this.

[HEDDA *walks into the inner room, where* BERTE *is bringing in a tray with decanters and glasses.* HEDDA *nods her approval and comes forward again.*]

TESMAN (*during the foregoing business*): How about that, Judge? What do you say to this? Hm?

BRACK: I say that moral victory and all that—hm—may be beautiful and all that—

TESMAN: Oh, I agree. All the same—

HEDDA (*looks at* TESMAN *with a cold smile*): You look thunderstruck.

TESMAN: Well, I am—pretty much—I really believe—

BRACK: After all, Mrs. Tesman, that was quite a thunderstorm that just passed over.

HEDDA (*points to the inner room*): How about a glass of cold punch, gentlemen?

BRACK (*looks at his watch*): A stirrup cup. Not a bad idea.

TESMAN: Splendid, Hedda. Perfectly splendid. In such a lighthearted mood as I am now—

HEDDA: Please. You, too, Mr. Løvborg.

LØVBORG (*with a gesture of refusal*): No, thanks. Really. Nothing for me.

BRACK: Good heavens, man! Cold punch isn't poison, you know!

LØVBORG: Perhaps not for everybody.

HEDDA: I'll keep Mr. Løvborg company in the meantime.

TESMAN: All right, Hedda. You do that.

[*He and BRACK go into the inner room, sit down, drink punch, smoke cigarettes, and engage in lively conversation during the next scene. EILERT LØVBORG remains standing near the stove. HEDDA walks over to the desk.*]

HEDDA (*her voice a little louder than usual*): I'll show you some pictures, if you like. You see—Tesman and I, we took a trip through Tyrol on our way back.

[*She brings an album over to the table by the sofa. She sits down in the far corner of the sofa. LØVBORG approaches, stops, looks at her. He takes a chair and sits down at her left, his back toward the inner room.*]

HEDDA (*opens the album*): Do you see these mountains, Mr. Løvborg? They are the Ortler group. Tesman has written their name below. Here it is: "The Ortler group near Meran."

LØVBORG (*has looked steadily at her all this time. Says slowly*): Hedda—Gabler!

HEDDA (*with a quick glance sideways*): Not that! Shhh!

LØVBORG (*again*): Hedda Gabler!

HEDDA (*looking at the album*): Yes, that used to be my name. When—when we two knew each other.

LØVBORG: And so from now on—for the whole rest of my life—I must get used to never again saying Hedda Gabler.

HEDDA (*still occupied with the album*): Yes, you must. And you might as well start right now. The sooner the better, I think.

LØVBORG (*with indignation*): Hedda Gabler married? And married to—Jørgen Tesman!

HEDDA: Yes—so it goes.

LØVBORG: Oh, Hedda, Hedda—how could you throw yourself away like that!

HEDDA (*with a fierce glance at him*): What's this? I won't have any of that!

LØVBORG: What do you mean?

[*TESMAN enters from the inner room.*]

HEDDA (*hears him coming and remarks casually*): And this here, Mr. Løvborg, this is from somewhere in the Ampezzo valley. Just look at those peaks over there. (*With a kindly look at TESMAN.*) What did you say those strange-looking peaks were called, dear?

TESMAN: Let me see. Oh, they—they are the Dolomites.

HEDDA: Right. Those are the Dolomites, Mr. Løvborg.

TESMAN: Hedda, I thought I'd just ask you if you don't want me to bring you some punch, after all? For you, anyway? Hm?

HEDDA: Well, yes; thanks. And a couple of cookies, maybe.

TESMAN: No cigarettes?

HEDDA: No.

TESMAN: All right.

[*He returns to the inner room, then turns right. BRACK keeps looking at HEDDA and LØVBERG from time to time.*]

LØVBORG (*still in a low voice*): Answer me, Hedda. How could you do a thing like that?

HEDDA (*apparently engrossed in the album*): If you keep on using my first name I won't talk to you.

LØVBORG: Not even when we're alone?

HEDDA: No. You may think it, but you must not say it.

LØVBORG: I see. If offends your love for—Jørgen Tesman.

HEDDA (*glances at him, smiles*): Love? That's a good one!

LØVBORG: Not love, then.

HEDDA: But no infidelities, either! I won't have it.

LØVBORG: Hedda—answer me just this one thing—

HEDDA: Shhh!

[*TESMAN enters with a tray from the inner room.*]

TESMAN: Here! Here are the goodies. (*Puts the tray down.*)

HEDDA: Why don't you get Berte to do it?

TESMAN (*pouring punch*): Because I think it's so much fun waiting on you, Hedda.

HEDDA: But you've filled both glasses. And Mr. Løvborg didn't want any—

TESMAN: I know, but Mrs. Elvsted will soon be here, won't she?

HEDDA: That's right. So she will.

TESMAN: Had you forgotten about her? Hm?

HEDDA: We've been so busy looking at this. (*Shows him a picture.*) Remember that little village?

TESMAN: That's the one just below the Brenner Pass, isn't it? We spent the night there—

HEDDA: —and ran into that lively crowd of summer guests.

TESMAN: Right! Just think—if we only could have had you with us, Eilert! Oh well.

[*Returns to the inner room, sits down, and resumes his conversation with BRACK.*]

LØVBORG: Just tell me this, Hedda—

HEDDA: What?

LØVBORG: Wasn't there love in your feelings for me, either? Not a touch—not a shimmer of love? Wasn't there?

HEDDA: I wonder. To me, we seemed to be simply two good comrades. Two close friends. (*Smiles.*) You, particularly, were very frank.

LØVBORG: You wanted it that way.

HEDDA: And yet—when I look back upon it now, there was something beautiful, something thrilling, something brave, I think, about the secret frankness—that comradeship that not a single soul so much as suspected.

LØVBORG: Yes, wasn't there, Hedda? Wasn't there? When I called on your father in the afternoons— And the General sat by the window with his newspapers—his back turned—

HEDDA: And we two in the sofa in the corner—

LØVBORG: —always with the same illustrated magazine—

HEDDA: —for want of an album, yes—

LØVBORG: Yes, Hedda—and then when I confessed to you—! Told you all about myself, things the others didn't know. Sat and told you about my debaucheries by day and night. Debauchery day in and day out! Oh, Hedda—what sort of power in you was it that forced me to tell you things like that?

HEDDA: You think there was some power in me?

LØVBORG: How else can I explain it? And all those veiled questions you asked—

HEDDA: —which you understood so perfectly well—

LØVBORG: That you could ask such questions! With such complete frankness!

HEDDA: *Veiled*, if you please.

LØVBORG: But frankly all the same. All about—that!

HEDDA: And to think that you answered, Mr. Løvborg!

LØVBORG: Yes, that's just what I can't understand— now, afterwards. But tell me, Hedda; wasn't love at the bottom of our whole relationship? Didn't you feel some kind of urge to—purify me—when I came to you in confession? Wasn't that it?

HEDDA: No, not quite.

LØVBORG: Then what made you do it?

HEDDA: Do you find it so very strange that a young girl—when she can do so, without anyone knowing—

LØVBORG: Yes—?

HEDDA: —That she wants to take a peek into a world which—

LØVBORG: —which—?

HEDDA: —she is not supposed to know anything about?

LØVBORG: So that was it!

HEDDA: That, too. That, too—I think—

LØVBORG: Companionship in the lust for life. But why couldn't *that* at least have continued?

HEDDA: That was your own fault.

LØVBORG: You were the one who broke off.

HEDDA: Yes, when reality threatened to enter our relationship. Shame on you, Eilert Løvborg! How could you want to do a thing like that to your frank and trusting comrade?

LØVBORG (*clenching his hands*): Oh, why didn't you do it! Why didn't you shoot me down, as you said you would!

HEDDA: Because I'm scared of scandal.

LØVBORG: Yes, Hedda. You are really a coward.

HEDDA: A terrible coward. (*Changing her tone.*) But that was your good luck, wasn't it? And now you've found such wonderful consolation with the Elvsteds.

LØVBORG: I know what Thea has told you.

HEDDA: Perhaps you have told her about us?

LØVBORG: Not a word. She is too stupid to understand.

HEDDA: Stupid?

LØVBORG: In things like that.

HEDDA: And I'm a coward. (*Leans forward, without looking in his eyes, whispers.*) But now I am going to confess something to you.

LØVBORG (*tense*): What?

HEDDA: That I didn't dare to shoot—

LØVBORG: Yes—?

HEDDA: —that was not the worst of my cowardice that night.

LØVBORG (*looks at her a moment, understands, whispers passionately*): Oh, Hedda! Hedda Gabler! Now I begin to see what was behind the companionship! You and I! So it *was* your lust for life—!

HEDDA (*in a low voice, with an angry glance*): Take care! Don't you believe it!

[*Darkness is falling. The door, right, is opened, by* BERTE.]

HEDDA (*closing the album, calls out, smiling*): At last! So there you are, dearest Thea! Come in!

[*MRS. ELVSTED enters. She is dressed for a party. The door is closed behind her.*]

HEDDA (*on the sofa, reaching out for* MRS. ELVSTED): Sweetest Thea, you have no idea how I've waited for you.

[*In passing, MRS. ELVSTED exchanges quick greetings with* TESMAN *and* BRACK *in the inner room. She walks up to the table and shakes* HEDDA's *hand.* EILERT LØVBORG *rises. He and* MRS. ELVSTED *greet one another with a silent nod.*]

MRS. ELVSTED: Shouldn't I go in and say hello to your husband?

HEDDA: No, never mind that. Leave them alone. They're soon leaving, anyway.

MRS. ELVSTED: Leaving?

HEDDA: They're going out to drink.

MRS. ELVSTED (*quickly, to* LØVBORG): Not you?

LØVBORG: No.

HEDDA: Mr. Løvborg stays here with us.

MRS. ELVSTED (*pulls up a chair, is about to sit down next to* LØVBORG): Oh, how wonderful it is to be here!

HEDDA: Oh no, little Thea. Not that. Not there. Over here by me, please. *I* want to be in the middle.

MRS. ELVSTED: Just as you like. (*She walks in front of the table and seats herself on the sofa, on* HEDDA's *right.* LØVBORG *sits down again on his chair.*)

LØVBORG (*after a brief pause, to* HEDDA): Isn't she lovely to look at?

HEDDA (*gently stroking her hair*): Just to look at?

LØVBORG: Yes. For you see—she and I—we are real comrades. We have absolute faith in one another. And we can talk together in full freedom.

HEDDA: Unveiled, Mr. Løvborg?

LØVBORG: Well—

MRS. ELVSTED (*in a low voice, clinging to* HEDDA): Oh, I am so happy, Hedda! For just think—he also says I have inspired him!

HEDDA (*looks at her with a smile*): No, really! He says that?

LØVBORG: And she has such courage, Mrs. Tesman! Such courage of action.

MRS. ELVSTED: Oh, my God—courage—! I!

LØVBORG: Infinite courage—when it concerns the comrade.

HEDDA: Yes, courage—if one only had that.

LØVBORG: What then?

HEDDA: Then maybe life would be tolerable, after all. (*Changing her tone.*) But now, dearest Thea, you want a glass of nice, cold punch.

MRS. ELVSTED: No, thanks. I never drink things like that.

HEDDA: Then what about you, Mr. Løvborg?

LØVBORG: Thanks. Nothing for me, either.

MRS. ELVSTED: No, nothing for him, either.

HEDDA (*looks firmly at him*): If I say so?

LØVBORG: Makes no difference.

HEDDA (*laughs*): Poor little me! So I have no power over you at all?

LØVBORG: Not about that.

HEDDA: Seriously, though; I really think you should. For your own sake.

MRS. ELVSTED: No, but Hedda—!

LØVBORG: Why so?

HEDDA: Or rather for people's sake.

LØVBORG: Oh?

HEDDA: For else they might think you don't really trust yourself—That you lack self-confidence—

MRS. ELVSTED (*softly*): Don't, Hedda!

LØVBORG: People may think whatever they like for all I care—for the time being.

MRS. ELVSTED (*happy*): Exactly!

HEDDA: I could easily tell from watching Judge Brack just now.

LØVBORG: Tell what?

HEDDA: He smiled so contemptuously when you didn't dare to join them in there.

LØVBORG: Didn't I dare to! It's just that I'd much rather stay here and talk with you!

MRS. ELVSTED: But that's only natural, Hedda.

HEDDA: The Judge had no way of knowing that. And I also noticed he smiled and looked at Tesman when you didn't dare to go to his silly old party.

LØVBORG: Didn't dare! Are you saying I didn't dare?

HEDDA: *I* am not. But that's how Judge Brack understood it.

LØVBORG: Let him.

HEDDA: So you're not going?

LØVBORG: I'm staying here with you and Thea.

MRS. ELVSTED: Of course, he is, Hedda!

HEDDA (*smiles, nods approvingly*): That's what I call firm foundations. Principled forever; that's the way a man ought to be! (*Turning to* MRS. ELVSTED, *stroking her cheek.*) What did I tell you this morning—when you came here, quite beside yourself—?

LØVBORG (*puzzled*): Beside herself?

MRS. ELVSTED (*in terror*): Hedda—Hedda—don't!

HEDDA: Now do you see? There was no need at all for that mortal fear of yours—(*Interrupting herself.*) There, now! Now we can all three relax and enjoy ourselves.

LØVBORG (*startled*): What's all this, Mrs. Tesman?

MRS. ELVSTED: Oh, God, Hedda—what are you saying? What are you doing?

HEDDA: Please be quiet. That horrible Judge is looking at you.

LØVBORG: In mortal fear? For my sake? So that's it.

MRS. ELVSTED (*softly, wailing*): Oh, Hedda—if you only knew how utterly miserable you have made me!

LØVBORG (*stares at her for a moment. His face is distorted.*): So that was the comrade's happy confidence in me!

MRS. ELVSTED: Oh, my dearest friend—listen to me first—!

LØVBORG (*picks up one of the glasses of punch, raises it, says hoarsely*): Here's to you, Thea! (*Empties the glass, puts it down, picks up the other one.*)

MRS. ELVSTED (*softly*): Hedda, Hedda—why did you want to do this?

HEDDA: Want to! I! Are you mad?

LØVBORG: And here's to you, too, Mrs. Tesman! Thanks for telling me the truth. Long live the truth! (*He drains the glass and is about to fill it again.*)

HEDDA (*restrains him*): That's enough for now. Remember you are going to a party.

MRS. ELVSTED: No, no, no!

HEDDA: Shhh! They are looking at you.

LØVBORG (*puts his glass down*): Listen, Thea—tell me the truth—

MRS. ELVSTED: I will, I will!

LØVBORG: Did the Commissioner know you were coming after me?

MRS. ELVSTED (*wringing her hands*): Oh, Hedda—do you hear what he's asking?

LØVBORG: Did the two of you agree that you were to come here and look after me? Maybe it was his idea, even? Did he send you? Ah, I know what it was—he missed me in the office, didn't he? Or was it at the card table?

MRS. ELVSTED (*softly, in agony*): Oh, Løvborg, Løvborg!

LØVBORG (*grabs a glass and is about to fill it*): Here's to the old Commissioner, too!

HEDDA (*stops him*): No more now. You're supposed to read aloud for Tesman tonight—remember?

LØVBORG (*calm again, puts the glass down*): This was silly of me, Thea. I'm sorry. Taking it this way. Please, don't be angry with me, dear, dear comrade. You'll see—both you and all those others—that even if I have been down—I've gotten up again. With your help, Thea.

MRS. ELVSTED (*beaming*): Oh, thank God—!

(*In the meantime, BRACK has looked at his watch. He and TESMAN get up and come forward.*)

BRACK (*picking up his coat and hat*): Well, Mrs. Tesman; our time is up.

HEDDA: I suppose it is.

LØVBORG (*rising*): Mine, too, Judge.

MRS. ELVSTED (*softly, pleadingly*): Oh, Løvborg—don't do it!

HEDDA (*pinches her arm*): They can hear you!

MRS. ELVSTED (*with a soft exclamation*): Ouch!

LØVBORG (*to BRACK*): You were good enough to ask me—

BRACK: So you're coming, after all?

LØVBORG: If I may.

BRACK: I'm delighted.

LØVBORG (*picks up his manuscript and says to TESMAN*): For there are a couple of things here I'd like to show you before I send it off.

TESMAN: Just think! Isn't that nice! But—dearest Hedda—? In that case, how are you going to get Mrs. Elvsted home? Hm?

HEDDA: We'll manage somehow.

LØVBORG (*looking at the two women*): Mrs. Elvsted? I'll be back to pick her up, of course. (*Coming closer.*) About ten o'clock, Mrs. Tesman? Is that convenient?

HEDDA: Certainly. That will be fine.

TESMAN: Then everything is nice and settled. But don't expect me that early, Hedda.

HEDDA: You just stay as long as—as long as you want to, dear.

MRS. ELVSTED (*in secret fear*): I'll be waiting for you here, then, Mr. Løvborg.

LØVBORG (*hat in hand*): Of course, Mrs. Elvsted.

BRACK: All aboard the pleasure train, gentlemen! I hope we'll have a lively evening—as a certain fair lady would say.

HEDDA: Ah—if only the fair lady could be present. Invisibly.

BRACK: Why invisibly?

HEDDA: To listen to some of your unadulterated liveliness, Judge.

BRACK (*laughs*): I shouldn't advise the fair lady to do that!

TESMAN (*also laughing*): You're a good one, Hedda! Just think!

BRACK: Well—good night, ladies!

LØVBORG (*with a bow*): Till about ten, then.

[*BRACK, LØVBORG, and TESMAN go out, right. At the same time BERTE enters from the inner room with a lighted lamp, which she places on the table, front center. She goes out the same way.*]

MRS. ELVSTED (*has risen and paces restlessly up and down*): Hedda, Hedda—how do you think all this will end?

HEDDA: At ten o'clock he'll be here. I see him already. With vine leaves in his hair. Flushed and confident.

MRS. ELVSTED: I only hope you're right.

HEDDA: For then, you see, he'll have mastered himself. And be a free man for all the days of his life.

MRS. ELVSTED: Dear God—how I hope you are right! That he'll come back like that.

HEDDA: That is the way he will come. No other way. (*She rises and goes closer to MRS. ELVSTED.*) *You* may doubt as long as you like. I believe in him. And now we'll see—

MRS. ELVSTED: There is something behind all this, Hedda. You've got some hidden purpose in mind.

HEDDA: Yes, I do! For once in my life I want to have power over a human destiny.

MRS. ELVSTED: But don't you already?

HEDDA: I don't and I never have.

MRS. ELVSTED: But your husband?

HEDDA: You think that's worth the trouble? Oh, if you knew how poor I am! And you got to be so rich! (*Embraces her passionately.*) I think I'll have to burn your hair off, after all!

MRS. ELVSTED: Let me go! Let me go! You scare me, Hedda!

BERTE (*in the doorway*): Supper is served, ma'am.

HEDDA: Good. We're coming.

MRS. ELVSTED: No, no, no! I'd rather go home by myself! Right now!

HEDDA: Nonsense! You'll have your cup of tea first, you little silly. And then—at ten o'clock—Eilert Løvborg comes—with vine leaves in his hair! (*She almost pulls* MRS. ELVSTED *toward the doorway.*)

ACT III

The same room at the TESMANS'. *The doorway and the French windows both have their portieres closed. The lamp, turned half down, is still on the table. The stove is open. Some dying embers can be seen.*

MRS. ELVSTED, *wrapped in a big shawl, is in the easy chair near the stove, her feet on a footstool.* HEDDA, *also dressed, is lying on the sofa, covered by a blanket.*

MRS. ELVSTED (*after a while suddenly sits up, listens anxiously; then she wearily sinks back in her chair, whimpers softly*): Oh my God, my God—not yet!

*[*BERTE *enters cautiously, right, carrying a letter.]*

MRS. ELVSTED (*turns and whispers tensely*): Well—has anybody been here?
BERTE (*in a low voice*): Yes. Just now there was a girl with this letter.
MRS. ELVSTED (*quickly, reaches for it*): A letter! Give it to me.
BERTE: No, ma'am. It's for the Doctor.
MRS. ELVSTED: I see.
BERTE: Miss Tesman's maid brought it. I'll leave it here on the table.
MRS. ELVSTED: All right.
BERTE (*puts the letter down*): I'd better put out the lamp. It just reeks.
MRS. ELVSTED: Yes, do that. It must be daylight soon, anyway.
BERTE (*putting out the lamp*): It's light already, ma'am.
MRS. ELVSTED: Light already! And still not back!
BERTE: No, so help us. Not that I didn't expect as much—
MRS. ELVSTED: You did?
BERTE: Yes, when I saw a certain character was back in town. Taking them off with him. We sure heard enough about him in the old days!
MRS. ELVSTED: Not so loud. You are waking up Mrs. Tesman.
BERTE (*looks toward the sofa, sighs*): God forbid—! Let her sleep, poor thing. Do you want me to get the fire going again?
MRS. ELVSTED: Not on my account, thank you.
BERTE: All right. (*Exits quietly, right.*)
HEDDA (*awakened by the closing door*): What's that?
MRS. ELVSTED: Just the maid.
HEDDA (*looks around*): Why in here—? Oh, I remember! (*Sits up, rubs her eyes, stretches.*) What time is it, Thea?

MRS. ELVSTED (*looks at her watch*): Past seven.
HEDDA: When did Tesman get home?
MRS. ELVSTED: He didn't.
HEDDA: Not home yet!
MRS. ELVSTED (*getting up*): Nobody's come.
HEDDA: And we waited till four!
MRS. ELVSTED (*wringing her hands*): And *how* we waited!
HEDDA (*her hand covering a yawn*): We—ll. We could have saved ourselves that trouble.
MRS. ELVSTED: Did you get any sleep at all?
HEDDA: Yes, I slept pretty well, I think. Didn't you?
MRS. ELVSTED: Not a wink. I just couldn't, Hedda! It was just impossible.
HEDDA (*rises, walks over to her*): Well, now! There's nothing to worry about, for heaven's sake. I know exactly what's happened.
MRS. ELVSTED: Then tell me please. Where do you think they are?
HEDDA: Well, first of all, I'm sure they were terribly late leaving the Judge's—
MRS. ELVSTED: Dear, yes. I'm sure you're right. Still—
HEDDA: —and so Tesman didn't want to wake us up in the middle of the night. (*Laughs.*) Maybe he didn't want us to see him, either—after a party like that.
MRS. ELVSTED: But where do you think he has gone?
HEDDA: To the aunts', of course. His old room is still there, all ready for him.
MRS. ELVSTED: No, he can't be there. Just a few minutes ago there came a letter for him from Miss Tesman. It's over there.
HEDDA: Oh? (*looks at the envelope.*) So it is—Auntie Julle herself. In that case, I suppose he's still at Brack's. And there's Eilert Løvborg, too—reading aloud, with vine leaves in his hair.
MRS. ELVSTED: Oh Hedda—you're only saying things you don't believe yourself.
HEDDA: My, what a little imbecile you really are, Thea!
MRS. ELVSTED: Yes, I suppose I am.
HEDDA: And you look dead tired, too.
MRS. ELVSTED: I *am* dead tired.
HEDDA: Why don't you do as I say. Go into my room and lie down.
MRS. ELVSTED: No, no—I wouldn't be able to go to sleep, anyway.
HEDDA: Of course, you would.
MRS. ELVSTED: And your husband is bound to be home any minute now. And I have to know right away.
HEDDA: I'll let you know as soon as he gets here.
MRS. ELVSTED: You promise me that, Hedda?
HEDDA: Count on it. You just go to sleep.
MRS. ELVSTED: Thanks. At least I'll try. (*Exits through inner room.*)

*[*HEDDA *goes to the French doors, opens the portieres.*

The room is now in full daylight. She picks up a little hand mirror from the desk, looks at herself, smooths her hair. Walks over to door, right, rings the bell for the maid. BERTE presently appears.]

BERTE: You want something, ma'am?

HEDDA: Yes. You'll have to start the fire again. I'm cold.

BERTE: Yes, ma'am! I'll get it warm in no time. (*Rakes the embers together and puts in another piece of wood. Stops. She suddenly listens.*) There's the doorbell, ma'am.

HEDDA: So see who it is. I'll take care of the stove myself.

BERTE: You'll have a nice blaze going in a minute. (*Exits right.*)

[*HEDDA kneels on the footstool and puts in more pieces of wood. Presently TESMAN enters, right. He looks tired and somber. He tiptoes toward the doorway and is about to disappear between the portieres.]*

HEDDA (*by the stove, without looking up*): Good morning.

TESMAN (*turning*): Hedda! (*Comes closer.*) For heaven's sake—you up already! Hm?

HEDDA: Yes, I got up very early this morning.

TESMAN: And I was so sure you'd still be sound asleep! Just think!

HEDDA: Not so loud. Mrs. Elvsted is asleep in my room.

TESMAN: Mrs. Elvsted stayed here all night?

HEDDA: Yes. Nobody came for her, you know.

TESMAN: No, I suppose—

HEDDA (*closes the stove, rises*): Well, did you have a good time at the Judge's?

TESMAN: Were you worried about me? Hm?

HEDDA: I'd never dream of worrying about you. I asked if you had a good time.

TESMAN: Yes, indeed. Nice for a change, anyway. But I think I liked it best early in the evening. For then Eilert read to me. Just think—we were more than an hour early! And Brack, of course, had things to see to. So Eilert read.

HEDDA (*sits down at the right side of the table*): So? Tell me all about it.

TESMAN (*sits down on an ottoman near the stove*): Oh Hedda, you'll never believe what a book that will be! It must be just the most remarkable thing ever written! Just think!

HEDDA: Yes, but I don't really care about that—

TESMAN: I must tell you, Hedda—I have a confession to make. As he was reading—something ugly came over me—

HEDDA: Ugly?

TESMAN: I sat there envying Eilert for being able to write like that! Just think, Hedda!

HEDDA: All right. I'm thinking!

TESMAN: And yet, with all his gifts—he's incorrigible, after all.

HEDDA: I suppose you mean he has more courage for life than the rest of you?

TESMAN: No, no—that's just it. You see, he's incapable of exercising moderation in his pleasures.

HEDDA: What happened—in the end?

TESMAN: Well—I would call it a bacchanal, Hedda.

HEDDA: Did he have vine leaves in his hair?

TESMAN: Vine leaves? No, I didn't notice any vine leaves. But he gave a long, muddled speech in honor of the woman who had inspired him in his work. Those were his words.

HEDDA: Did he mention her name?

TESMAN: No, he didn't. But I'm sure it must be Mrs. Elvsted. You just wait and see if I'm not right!

HEDDA: And where did you and he part company?

TESMAN: On the way back to town. We left—the last of us did—at the same time. And Brack came along, too, to get some fresh air. Then we decided we'd better see Eilert home. You see, he had had altogether too much to drink!

HEDDA: I can imagine.

TESMAN: But then the strangest thing of all happened, Hedda! Or maybe I should say the saddest. I'm almost ashamed—on Eilert's behalf—even talking about it.

HEDDA: Well—?

TESMAN: You see, on the way back I happened to be behind the others a little. Just for a minute or two—you know—

HEDDA: All right, all right—!

TESMAN: And when I hurried to catch up with them, can you guess what I found by the roadside? Hm?

HEDDA: How can I possibly—?

TESMAN: You mustn't tell this to a living soul, Hedda! Do you hear! Promise me that, for Eilert's sake. (*Pulls a parcel out of his coat pocket.*) Just think—I found this!

HEDDA: Isn't that what he had with him here yesterday?

TESMAN: Yes! It's his whole, precious, irreplaceable manuscript! And he had dropped it—just like that! Without even noticing! Just think , Hedda! Isn't that awfully sad?

HEDDA: But why didn't you give it back to him?

TESMAN: In the condition he was in! Dear—I just didn't dare to.

HEDDA: And you didn't tell any of the others that you had found it, either?

TESMAN: Of course not. I didn't want to, for Eilert's sake—don't you see?

HEDDA: So nobody knows that you have Eilert Løvborg's papers?

TESMAN: Nobody. And nobody must know, either.

HEDDA: And what did you and he talk about afterwards?

TESMAN: I didn't have a chance to talk to him at all after that. For when we came into town, he and a couple of the others simply vanished. Just think!

HEDDA: Oh? I expect they took him home.

TESMAN: I suppose that must be it. And Brack took off on his own, too.

HEDDA: And what have you been up to since then?

TESMAN: Well, you see, I and some of the others went home with one of the younger fellows and had a cup of early morning coffee. Or night coffee maybe, rather. Hm? And now, after I've rested a bit and poor Eilert's had some sleep, I'll take this back to him.

HEDDA (reaches for the parcel): No—don't do that! Not right away, I mean. Let me look at it first.

TESMAN: Dearest Hedda—honestly, I just don't dare to.

HEDDA: Don't you dare to?

TESMAN: No, for I'm sure you realize how utterly desperate he'll be when he wakes up and finds that the manuscript is gone. For he hasn't a copy, you know. He said so himself.

HEDDA (looks searchingly at him): But can't a thing like that be written over again?

TESMAN: Hardly. I really don't think so. For, you see—the inspiration—

HEDDA: Yes, I suppose. (Casually.) By the way, here's a letter for you.

TESMAN: Imagine!

HEDDA (gives it to him): It came early this morning.

TESMAN: It's from Aunt Julle, Hedda! I wonder what it can be. (Puts the manuscript down on the other ottoman, opens the letter, skims the content, jumps up.) Oh Hedda! She says here that poor Aunt Rina is dying!

HEDDA: You know we had to expect that.

TESMAN: And if I want to see her again I had better hurry. I'll rush over right away.

HEDDA (suppressing a smile): You'll rush?

TESMAN: Dearest Hedda of mine—if only you could bring yourself to come along! Hm?

HEDDA (rises, weary, with an air of refusal): No, no. You mustn't ask me that. I don't want to look at death and disease. I don't want anything to do with ugliness.

TESMAN: Well, all right—(Rushing around.) My hat? My coat? Oh—out here in the hall. I just hope I won't be too late, Hedda. Hm?

HEDDA: Oh I'm sure that if you rush—

[BERTE appears in the door, right.]

BERTE: Judge Brack is here and wants to know if he may see you.

TESMAN: At this hour! No, no. I can't possibly see him now!

HEDDA: But I can. (To BERTE.) Tell the Judge please to come in.

[BERTE exits.]

HEDDA (with a quick whisper): Tesman! The package! (She grabs it from the ottoman.)

TESMAN: Yes! Give it to me!

HEDDA: No, no. I'll hide it for you till later.

[She walks over to the desk and sticks the parcel in among the books on the shelf. In his hurry TESMAN is having difficulties getting his gloves on. JUDGE BRACK enters, right.]

HEDDA (nods to him): If you aren't an early bird—

BRACK: Yes, don't you think so? (To TESMAN.) You're going out, too?

TESMAN: Yes, I must go and see the aunts. Just think, the invalid—she's dying!

BRACK: Oh, I'm terribly sorry! In that case, don't let me keep you. At such a moment—

TESMAN: Yes, I really must run. Goodbye, goodbye! (Hurries out, right.)

HEDDA (approaching BRACK): It appears that things were quite lively last night over at your house.

BRACK: Indeed, Mrs. Tesman—I didn't get to bed at all.

HEDDA: You didn't either?

BRACK: As you see. But tell me—what has Tesman told you about the night's adventures?

HEDDA: Just some tiresome story about having coffee with somebody someplace.

BRACK: I know all about that coffee. Eilert Løvborg wasn't one of them, was he?

HEDDA: No, they had taken him home first.

BRACK: Tesman, too?

HEDDA: No. Some of the others, he said.

BRACK (smiles): Jørgen Tesman is really an ingenuous soul, you know.

HEDDA: He certainly is. But why do you say that? Is there something more to all this?

BRACK: I'm afraid there is.

HEDDA: Well! In that case, why don't we make ourselves comfortable, Judge. You'll tell your story better, too.

[She sits down at the left side of the table, BRACK at the long side of the table, near her.]

HEDDA: All right?

BRACK: For reasons of my own I wanted to keep track of my guests' movements last night. Or, rather—some of my guests.

HEDDA: Eilert Løvborg was one of them, perhaps?

BRACK: To tell the truth—he was.

HEDDA: Now you are really making me curious.

BRACK: Do you know where he and a couple of the

others spent the rest of the night, Mrs. Tesman?

HEDDA: No—tell me. If it can be told.

BRACK: Oh, certainly. They turned up at an exceptionally animated early morning gathering.

HEDDA: Of the lively kind?

BRACK: Of the liveliest.

HEDDA: A little more about this, Judge.

BRACK: Løvborg had been invited beforehand. I knew about that. But he had declined. He is a reformed character, you know.

HEDDA: As of his stay with the Elvsteds—yes. But he went after all?

BRACK: Well, yes, you see, Mrs. Tesman—unfortunately, the spirit moved him over at my house last evening.

HEDDA: Yes, I understand he became inspired.

BRACK: Quite violently inspired. And that, I gather, must have changed his mind. You know, we men don't always have as much integrity as we ought to have.

HEDDA: Oh, I'm sure you're an exception, Judge Brack. But about Løvborg—?

BRACK: To make a long story short—he ended up at Miss Diana's establishment.

HEDDA: Miss Diana's?

BRACK: She was the hostess at this gathering—a select circle of intimate friends, male and female.

HEDDA: Is she a redhead, by any chance?

BRACK: That's correct.

HEDDA: And a singer—of sorts?

BRACK: Yes—that, too. And a mighty huntress—of men, Mrs. Tesman. You seem to have heard of her. Eilert Løvborg used to be one of her most devoted protectors in his more affluent days.

HEDDA: And how did it all end?

BRACK: Not in a very friendly fashion, apparently. It seems that after the tenderest reception Miss Diana resorted to brute force—

HEDDA: Against Løvborg?

BRACK: Yes. He accused her or her women friends of having stolen something of his. Said his wallet was gone. And other things, too. In brief, he's supposed to have started a pretty wicked row.

HEDDA: And—?

BRACK: Well—there was a general free-for-all—men and women both. Fortunately, the police stepped in—

HEDDA: The police—!

BRACK: Yes. But I'm afraid this will be an expensive escapade for Eilert Løvborg, crazy fool that he is.

HEDDA: Well!

BRACK: It appears that he resisted quite violently—struck an officer in the ear and tore his coat. So they had to take him along.

HEDDA: How do you know all this?

BRACK: From the police.

HEDDA (*staring straight ahead*): So that's how it was.

No vine leaves in his hair.

BRACK: Vine leaves, Mrs. Tesman?

HEDDA (*changing her tone*): But tell me, Judge Brack—why did you keep such a close watch on Eilert Løvborg?

BRACK: Well—for one thing, it is obviously of some concern to me if he testifies that he came straight from my party.

HEDDA: So you think there will be an investigation?

BRACK: Naturally. But I suppose that doesn't really matter too much. However, as a friend of the house I considered it my duty to give you and Tesman a full account of his night-time exploits.

HEDDA: Yes, but why?

BRACK: Because I very strongly suspect that he intends to use you as a kind of screen.

HEDDA: Really! Why do you think that?

BRACK: Oh, come now, Mrs. Tesman! We can use our eyes, can't we? This Mrs. Elvsted—she isn't leaving town right away, you know.

HEDDA: Well, even if there should be something going on between those two, I'd think there would be plenty of other places they could meet.

BRACK: But no home. After last night, every respectable house will once again be closed to Eilert Løvborg.

HEDDA: And so should mine, you mean?

BRACK: Yes. I admit I would find it more than embarrassing if the gentleman were to become a daily guest here, Mrs. Tesman. If he, as an outsider—a highly dispensable outsider—if he were to intrude himself—

HEDDA: —into the triangle?

BRACK: Precisely. It would amount to homelessness for me.

HEDDA (*smiling*): Sole cock-o'-the-walk—so, that's your goal, is it, Judge?

BRACK (*nods slowly, lowers his voice*): Yes. That is my goal. And for that I will fight with every means at my disposal.

HEDDA (*her smile fading*): You're really a dangerous person, you know—when you come right down to it.

BRACK: You think so?

HEDDA: Yes. I am beginning to think so now. And I must say I am exceedingly glad you don't have any kind of hold on me.

BRACK (*with a noncommittal laugh*): Well, well, Mrs. Tesman! Maybe you're right, at that. Who knows what I might do if I did.

HEDDA: Really, now, Judge Brack! Are you threatening me?

BRACK (*rising*): —Nonsense! For the triangle, you see—is best maintained and protected on a voluntary basis.

HEDDA: My sentiments, exactly.

BRACK: Well, I have said what I came to say. And

now I should get back to town. Goodbye, Mrs.
Tesman! (*Walks toward the French doors.*)
HEDDA (*rises*): You're going through the garden?
BRACK: Yes. For me that's a short cut.
HEDDA: Yes, and then it's a back way.
BRACK: Quite true. I have nothing against back ways.
There are times when they are most titillating.
HEDDA: You mean when real ammunition is used?
BRACK (*in the doorway, laughs back at her*): Oh for
heavens sake! I don't suppose one shoots one's
tame roosters!
HEDDA (*laughs also*): No—not if one has only one—!

[*They nod to each other, both still laughing. He
leaves. She closes the door behind him. For a few
moments she remains by the door, quite serious now,
looking into the garden. Then she walks over to the
doorway and opens the portieres wide enough to look
into the inner room. Goes to the desk, pulls LØVBORG's
manuscript from the bookshelf and is about to read in
it when BERTE's voice, very loud, is heard from the
hall, right. HEDDA turns around, listens. She hurriedly
puts the manuscript into the drawer of the desk and
puts the key down on its top. EILERT LØVBORG, wearing
his coat and with his hat in his hand, flings open the
door, right. He looks somewhat confused and excited.*]

LØVBORG (*turned toward the invisible* BERTE *in the hall*):
—And I tell you I must! (*He closes the door, turns,
sees* HEDDA, *immediately controls himself, greets her.*)
HEDDA (*by the desk*): Well, well, Mr. Løvborg—aren't
you a trifle late coming for Thea?
LØVBORG: Or a trifle early for calling on you. I
apologize.
HEDDA: How do you know she is still here?
LØVBORG: The people she is staying with told me
she's been gone all night.
HEDDA (*walks over to the table*): Did they seem—
strange—when they said it?
LØVBORG (*puzzled*): Strange?
HEDDA: I mean, did they seem to find it a little—
unusual?
LØVBORG (*suddenly understands*): Ah, I see what you
mean! Of course! I'm dragging her down with
me. No, as a matter of fact, I didn't notice any-
thing. I suppose Tesman isn't up yet?
HEDDA: I—I don't think so—
LØVBORG: When did he get home?
HEDDA: Very late.
LØVBORG: Did he tell you anything?
HEDDA: Yes, he said you'd all had quite a time over
at Brack's.
LØVBORG: Just that?
HEDDA: I think so. But I was so awfully sleepy—

[MRS. ELVSTED *enters through portieres in the rear.*]

MRS. ELVSTED (*toward him*): Oh, Løvborg! At last!

LØVBORG: Yes, at last. And too late.
MRS. ELVSTED (*in fear*): What is too late?
LØVBORG: Everything is too late now. It's all over
with me.
MRS. ELVSTED: Oh no, no! Don't say things like that!
LØVBORG: You'll say the same yourself when you
hear—
MRS. ELVSTED: I don't want to hear—!
HEDDA: Maybe you'd rather talk with her alone? I'll
leave.
LØVBORG: No, stay—you, too. I beg you to.
MRS. ELVSTED: But I don't want to listen, do you hear?
LØVBORG: It isn't last night I want to talk about.
MRS. ELVSTED: What about, then?
LØVBORG: We'll have to part, Thea.
MRS. ELVSTED: Part!
HEDDA (*involuntarily*): I knew it!
LØVBORG: For I don't need you any more.
MRS. ELVSTED: And you can stand there and tell me a
thing like that! Don't need me! Why can't I help
you the way I did before? Aren't we going to
keep on working together?
LØVBORG: I don't intend to work any more.
MRS. ELVSTED (*desperately*): What am I going to do
with my life, then?
LØVBORG: You'll have to try to live your life as if
you'd never known me.
MRS. ELVSTED: But I can't do that!
LØVBORG: Try, Thea. Go back home.
MRS. ELVSTED (*agitated*): Never again! Where you are I
want to be! And you can't chase me away just like
that. I want to stay right here! Be with you when
the book appears.
HEDDA (*in a tense whisper*): Ah—yes—the book!
LØVBORG (*looks at her*): My book—and Thea's. For
that's what it is.
MRS. ELVSTED: That's what I feel, too. And that's why
I have the right to be with you when it comes out.
I want to see all the honor and all the fame you'll
get. And the joy—I want to share the joy, too.
LØVBORG: Thea, our book is never going to come out.
HEDDA: Ah!
MRS. ELVSTED: It won't!
LØVBORG: *Can't* ever appear.
MRS. ELVSTED (*with fearful suspicion*): Løvborg, what
have you done with the manuscript?
HEDDA (*watching him tensely*): Yes—what about the
manuscript?
MRS. ELVSTED: Where is it?
LØVBORG: Oh Thea—please, don't ask me about that!
MRS. ELVSTED: Yes, yes—I want to be told! I have the
right to know—right now!
LØVBORG: All right. I've torn it to pieces.
MRS. ELVSTED (*screams*): Oh, no! No!
HEDDA (*involuntarily*): But that's not—!
LØVBORG (*looks at her*): Not true, you think?
HEDDA (*composing herself*): Well, of course, if you say

so. You should know. It just sounds so—so unbelievable.

Løvborg: All the same, it's true.

Mrs. Elvsted (*hands clenched*): Oh God—oh God, Hedda. He has torn his own work to pieces!

Løvborg: I have torn my whole life to pieces, so why not my life's work as well?

Mrs. Elvsted: And that's what you did last night?

Løvborg: Yes, I tell you! In a thousand pieces. And scattered them in the fjord. Far out—where the water is clean and salty. Let them drift there, with wind and current. Then they'll sink. Deeper and deeper down. Like me, Thea.

Mrs. Elvsted: Do you know, Løvborg—this thing you've done to the book—all the rest of my life I'll think of it as killing a little child.

Løvborg: You are right. It is like murdering a child.

Mrs. Elvsted: But then, how could you? For the child was mine, too!

Hedda (*almost soundlessly*): The child—

Mrs. Elvsted (*with a deep sigh*): So it's all over. I'll go now, Hedda.

Hedda: But you aren't leaving town?

Mrs. Elvsted: Oh, I don't know myself what I'll do. There's only darkness before me. (*Exits, right.*)

Hedda (*waits for a moment*): Aren't you going to see her home, Mr. Løvborg?

Løvborg: I? Through the streets? Letting people see her with me?

Hedda: Of course, I don't know what else may have happened last night. But is it really so absolutely irreparable—?

Løvborg: Last night is not the end of it. That I know. And yet, I don't really care for that kind of life any more. Not again. She has broken all the courage for life and all the defiance that was in me.

Hedda (*staring ahead*): So that sweet little goose has had her hand in a human destiny. (*Looks at him.*) But that you could be so heartless, even so!

Løvborg: Don't tell me I was heartless!

Hedda: To ruin everything that's filled her soul for such a long time! You don't call that heartless!

Løvborg: Hedda—to you I can tell the truth.

Hedda: The truth?

Løvborg: But first promise me—give me your word you'll never let Thea know what I'm going to tell you now.

Hedda: You have it.

Løvborg: All right. It isn't true, what I just told her.

Hedda: About the manuscript?

Løvborg: Yes. I have not torn it up. Not thrown it in the sea, either.

Hedda: But then—where is it?

Løvborg: I've destroyed it just the same. Really, I have, Hedda!

Hedda: I don't understand.

Løvborg: Thea said that what I had done seemed to her like murdering a child.

Hedda: Yes—she did.

Løvborg: But killing a child, that's not the worst thing a father can do to it.

Hedda: No?

Løvborg: No. And the worst is what I don't want Thea to know.

Hedda: What *is* the worst?

Løvborg: Hedda—suppose a man, say, early in the morning, after a stupid, drunken night—suppose he comes home to his child's mother and says: Listen, I've been in such and such a place. I've been here—and I've been there. And I had our child with me. In all those places. And the child is lost. Gone. Vanished. I'll be damned if I know where it is. Who's got hold of it—

Hedda: Yes—but when all is said and done—it is only a book, you know.

Løvborg: Thea's pure soul was in that book.

Hedda: I realize that.

Løvborg: Then you surely also realize that she and I can have no future together.

Hedda: Where do you go from here?

Løvborg: Nowhere. Just finish everything off. The sooner the better.

Hedda (*a step closer*): Listen—Eilert Løvborg— Couldn't you make sure it's done beautifully?

Løvborg: Beautifully? (*Smiles.*) With vine leaves in the hair, as you used to say.

Hedda: Oh no. I don't believe in vine leaves any more. But still beautifully! For once. Goodbye. Go now. And don't come back.

Løvborg: Goodbye, Mrs. Tesman. Give my regards to Jørgen Tesman. (*He is about to leave.*)

Hedda: Wait! I want to give you something—a remembrance. (*Goes to the desk, opens the drawer, takes out the gun case. Returns to* Løvborg *with one of the revolvers.*)

Løvborg: The gun? That's the remembrance?

Hedda (*nods slowly*): Do you recognize it? It was pointed at you once.

Løvborg: You should have used it then.

Hedda: Take it! *You* use it.

Løvborg (*pockets the gun*): Thanks!

Hedda: And beautifully, Eilert Løvborg! That's all I ask!

Løvborg: Goodbye, Hedda Gabler. (*Exits, right.*)

[*Hedda listens by the door for a moment. Then she crosses to the desk, takes out the manuscript, glances inside the cover, pulls some of the pages halfway out and looks at them. Carries the whole manuscript over to the chair by the stove. She sits down with the parcel in her lap. After a moment she opens the stove and then the manuscript.*]

Hedda (*throws a bundle of sheets into the fire, whispers*):

Now I'm burning your child, Thea. You—curly-head! (*Throws more sheets in.*) Your and Eilert Løvborg's child. (*Throws all the rest of the manuscript into the stove.*) I am burning—I am burning your child.

ACT IV

The same rooms at the TESMANS'. *Evening. The front room is dark. The inner room is lighted by the ceiling lamp over the table. Portieres cover the French doors.*

HEDDA, in black, is walking up and down in the dark of the front room. She goes into the inner room, turning left in the doorway. She is heard playing a few bars on the piano. She reappears and comes forward again. BERTE enters from the right side of the inner room. She carries a lighted lamp, which she puts down on the table in front of the corner sofa. Her eyes show signs of weeping; she wears black ribbons on her uniform. She exits quietly, right. HEDDA goes over to the French windows, looks between the portieres into the dark. Presently MISS TESMAN, in mourning, with hat and veil, enters, right. HEDDA walks over to meet her, gives her her hand.

MISS TESMAN: Yes, my dearest Hedda—here you see me in my garb of grief. For now at last my poor sister has fought her fight to the end.

HEDDA: I already know—as you see. Tesman sent word.

MISS TESMAN: Yes, he promised he'd do that. But I thought that to you, Hedda—here in the house of life—I really ought to bring you the tidings of death myself.

HEDDA: That is very kind of you.

MISS TESMAN: Ah, but Rina shouldn't have died just now. There should be no mourning in Hedda's house at this time.

HEDDA (*changing the topic*): I understand she had a very quiet end.

MISS TESMAN: Oh so beautiful, so peaceful! She left us so quietly! And then the unspeakable happiness of seeing Jørgen one more time! To say goodbye to him to her heart's content! Isn't he back yet?

HEDDA: No. He wrote I mustn't expect him back very soon. But do sit down.

MISS TESMAN: No—no, thanks, my dear, blessed Hedda. Not that I wouldn't like to. But I don't have much time. I must go back and prepare her as best I can. I want her to look right pretty when she goes into her grave.

HEDDA: Is there anything I can help you with?

MISS TESMAN: I won't have you as much as think of it! That's not for Hedda Tesman to lend a hand to. Or lend thoughts to, either. Not now, of all times!

HEDDA: Oh—thoughts! We can't always control our thoughts—

MISS TESMAN (*still preoccupied*): Ah yes—such is life. At home we're making a shroud for Rina. And here, too, there'll be sewing to do soon, I expect. But of quite a different kind, thank God!

[MISS TESMAN enters, right.]

HEDDA: Finally!

TESMAN: You here, Aunt Julle? With Hedda? Just think!

MISS TESMAN: I am just about to leave, Jørgen dear. Well—did you do all the things you promised me you'd do?

TESMAN: No, I'm afraid I forgot half of them, Auntie. I'd better run in again tomorrow. I'm all confused today. I can't seem to keep my thoughts together.

MISS TESMAN: But dearest Jørgen—you mustn't take it this way!

TESMAN: Oh, I mustn't? How do you mean?

MISS TESMAN: You ought to be joyful in the midst of your sorrow. Glad for what's happened. The way I am.

TESMAN: Oh yes, of course. You're thinking of Aunt Rina.

HEDDA: You're going to feel lonely now, Miss Tesman.

MISS TESMAN: The first few days, yes. But I hope that won't last long. Dear Rina's little parlor won't be empty for long, if I can help it!

TESMAN: Oh? And who do you want to move in there. Hm?

MISS TESMAN: Ah—it's not very hard to find some poor soul who needs nursing and comfort.

HEDDA: And you really want to take on such a cross all over again?

MISS TESMAN: Heavens! God forgive you, child—cross? It has not been a cross to me.

HEDDA: Still—a stranger, who—

MISS TESMAN: Oh, it's easy to make friends with sick people. And I need somebody to live for, too. Well, the Lord be praised, maybe soon there'll be a thing or two an old aunt can turn her hand to here.

HEDDA: Oh, never mind us—

TESMAN: Yes, just think—how lovely it would be for the three of us, if only—

HEDDA: If only—?

TESMAN (*uneasy*): Oh, nothing. I daresay it will all work out. Let's hope it will, hm?

MISS TESMAN: Well, well. I can see that you two have something to talk about. (*With a smile.*) And perhaps Hedda has something to tell *you*, Jørgen! Goodbye! I'm going home to Rina, now. (*Turns around in the door.*) Dear, dear—how strange to think—Now Rina is both with me and with Jochum!

TESMAN: Yes, just think, Aunt Julle! Hm?

[MISS TESMAN *exits, right.*]

HEDDA (*coldly scrutinizing* TESMAN): I wouldn't be at all surprised if you aren't more affected by this death than she is.

TESMAN: Oh, it isn't just Aunt Rina's death, Hedda. It's Eilert I worry about.

HEDDA (*quickly*): Any news about him?

TESMAN: I went over to his room this afternoon to tell him the manuscript is safe.

HEDDA: Well? And didn't you see him?

TESMAN: No. He wasn't home. But then I ran into Mrs. Elvsted and she told me he'd been here early this morning.

HEDDA: Yes, right after you'd left.

TESMAN: And he said he'd torn up the manuscript? Did he really say that?

HEDDA: Yes. So he claimed.

TESMAN: But dear God—in that case he really must have been out of his mind! So I assume you didn't give it to him either, hm, Hedda?

HEDDA: No. He didn't get it.

TESMAN: But you told him we had it, of course?

HEDDA: No. (*Quickly.*) Did you tell Mrs. Elvsted?

TESMAN: No, I didn't want to. But you ought to have told him, Hedda. Just think—what if he does something rash—something to hurt himself! Give me the manuscript, Hedda! I want to rush down to him with it right this minute. Where is it?

HEDDA (*cold, motionless, one arm resting on the chair*): I haven't got it any more.

TESMAN: You haven't got it! What do you mean by that?

HEDDA: I burned it—the whole thing.

TESMAN (*jumps up*): Burned it! Burned Eilert's book!

HEDDA: Don't shout. The maid might hear you.

TESMAN: Burned it? But good God—no, no, no—! This can't be—!

HEDDA: It is, all the same.

TESMAN: But do you realize what you've done, Hedda? It's against the law! Willful destruction of lost property! You just ask Judge Brack! He'll tell you!

HEDDA: You'd better not talk about this to anyone—the Judge or anybody else.

TESMAN: But how could you do a thing like that! I never heard anything like it! What came over you? What can possibly have been going on in your head? Answer me! Hm?

HEDDA (*suppresses an almost imperceptible smile*): I did it for your sake, Jørgen.

TESMAN: For my sake!

HEDDA: When you came back this morning and told me he had read aloud to you—

TESMAN: Yes, yes! What then?

HEDDA: You admitted you were jealous of him for having written such a book.

TESMAN: But good gracious—! I didn't mean it as literally as all that!

HEDDA: All the same. I couldn't stand the thought that somebody else was to overshadow you.

TESMAN (*in an outburst of mingled doubt and joy*): Hedda—oh Hedda! Is it true what you're saying! But—but—but—I never knew you loved me like that! Just think!

HEDDA: In that case, I might as well tell you—that—just at this time—(*Breaks off, vehemently.*) No, no! You can ask Aunt Julle. She'll tell you.

TESMAN: I almost think I know what you mean, Hedda! (*Claps his hands.*) For goodness sake! Can that really be so! Hm?

HEDDA: Don't shout so! The maid can hear you.

TESMAN (*laughing with exuberant joy*): The maid! Well, if you don't take the prize, Hedda! The maid—but that's Berte! I'm going to tell Berte myself this very minute!

HEDDA (*her hands clenched in despair*): Oh I'll die—I'll die, in all this!

TESMAN: In what, Hedda? Hm?

HEDDA (*cold and composed*): In all this—ludicrousness, Jørgen.

TESMAN: Ludicrous? That I'm so happy? Still—maybe I oughtn't to tell Berte, after all.

HEDDA: Oh, go ahead. What difference does it make?

TESMAN: No, not yet. But on my word—Aunt Julle must be told. And that you've started to call me "Jørgen," too! Just think! She'll be ever so happy—Aunt Julle will!

HEDDA: Even when you tell her that I have burned Eilert Løvborg's papers?

TESMAN: No, oh no! That's true! That about the manuscript—nobody must know about that. But to think that you'd burn for me, Hedda—I certainly want to tell *that* to Aunt Julle! I wonder now—is that sort of thing usual with young wives, hm?

HEDDA: I think you should ask Aunt Julle about that, too.

TESMAN: I will—I certainly will, when I get the chance. (*Looks uneasy and disturbed again.*) But the manuscript! Good God—I don't dare to think what this is going to do to poor Eilert!

[MRS. ELVSTED, *dressed as on her first visit, wearing hat and coat, enters, right.*]

MRS. ELVSTED (*gives a hurried greeting, is obviously upset*): Oh Hedda, you must forgive me for coming here again!

HEDDA: What has happened, Thea?

TESMAN: Something to do with Eilert Løvborg again? Hm?

MRS. ELVSTED: Yes, yes—I'm so terribly afraid something's happened to him.

HEDDA (*seizing her arm*): Ah—you think so?

TESMAN: Oh dear—why do you think that, Mrs. Elvsted?

MRS. ELVSTED: I heard them talking about him in the boarding house, just as I came in. And people are saying the most incredible things about him today.

TESMAN: Yes, imagine! I heard that, too! And I can testify that he went straight home to bed! Just think!

HEDDA: And what did they say in the boarding house?

MRS. ELVSTED: Oh, I didn't find out anything. Either they didn't know any details or—They all became silent when they saw me. And I didn't dare to ask.

TESMAN (*pacing the floor uneasily*): We'll just have to hope—to hope that you heard wrong, Mrs. Elvsted!

MRS. ELVSTED: No, no. I'm sure it was he they were talking about. And somebody said something about the hospital or—

TESMAN: The hospital—!

HEDDA: Surely, that can't be so!

MRS. ELVSTED: I got so terribly frightened! So I went up to his room and asked for him there.

HEDDA: Could you bring yourself to do that, Thea?

MRS. ELVSTED: What else could I do? For I felt I just couldn't stand the uncertainty any longer.

TESMAN: But I suppose you didn't find him in, either, did you? Hm?

MRS. ELVSTED: No. And the people there didn't know anything about him. He hadn't been home since yesterday afternoon, they said.

TESMAN: Yesterday! Just think! How could they say that!

MRS. ELVSTED: I don't know what else *to* think—something bad must have happened to him!

TESMAN: Hedda, dear—? What if I were to walk downtown and ask around for him—?

HEDDA: No, no—don't you go and get mixed up in all this.

[*JUDGE BRACK, hat in hand, enters through the door, right, which BERTE opens and then closes. He looks serious and greets the others in silence.*]

TESMAN: So here you are, Judge, hm?

BRACK: Yes. I had to see you this evening.

TESMAN: I can see you have got Aunt Julle's message.

BRACK: That, too—yes.

TESMAN: Isn't it sad, though?

BRACK: Well, my dear Tesman—that depends on how you look at it.

TESMAN (*looks at him uncertainly*): Has something else happened?

BRACK: Yes.

HEDDA (*tense*): Something sad, Judge Brack?

BRACK: That, too, depends on how you look at it, Mrs. Tesman.

MRS. ELVSTED (*bursting out*): Oh, I'm sure it has something to do with Eilert Løvborg!

BRACK (*looks at her for a moment*): Why do you think that, Mrs. Elvsted? Maybe you already know something—?

MRS. ELVSTED (*confused*): No, no; not at all. It's just—

TESMAN: For heaven's sake, Brack, out with it!

BRACK (*shrugging his shoulders*): Well—unfortunately, Eilert Løvborg's in the hospital. Dying.

MRS. ELVSTED (*screams*): Oh God, oh God!

TESMAN: In the hospital! And dying!

HEDDA (*without thinking*): So soon—!

MRS. ELVSTED (*wailing*): And we didn't even part as friends, Hedda!

HEDDA (*whispers*): Thea, Thea—for heaven's sake—!

MRS. ELVSTED (*paying no attention to her*): I want to see him! I want to see him alive!

BRACK: Won't do you any good, Mrs. Elvsted. Nobody can see him.

MRS. ELVSTED: Then tell me what's happened to him! What?

TESMAN: For, surely, he hasn't himself—!

HEDDA: I'm sure he has.

TESMAN: Hedda! How can you—!

BRACK (*observing her all this time*): I am sorry to say that your guess is absolutely correct, Mrs. Tesman.

MRS. ELVSTED: Oh, how awful!

TESMAN: Did it himself! Just think!

HEDDA: Shot himself!

BRACK: Right again, Mrs. Tesman.

MRS. ELVSTED (*trying to pull herself together*): When did this happen, Judge?

BRACK: This afternoon. Between three and four.

TESMAN: But dear me—where can he have done a thing like that? Hm?

BRACK (*a little uncertain*): Where? Well—I suppose in his room. I don't really know—

MRS. ELVSTED: No, it can't have been there. For I was up there sometime between six and seven.

BRACK: Well, then, some other place. I really can't say. All I know is that he was found. He had shot himself—in the chest.

MRS. ELVSTED: Oh, how horrible to think! That he was to end like that!

HEDDA (*to BRACK*): In the chest?

BRACK: Yes—as I just told you.

HEDDA: Not the temple?

BRACK: In the chest, Mrs. Tesman.

HEDDA: Well, well—the chest is a good place, too.

BRACK: How is that, Mrs. Tesman?

HEDDA (*turning him aside*): Oh—nothing.

TESMAN: And you say the wound is fatal? Hm?

BRACK: No doubt about it—absolutely fatal. He's probably dead already.

MRS. ELVSTED: Yes, yes! I feel you're right! It's over! It's all over! Oh, Hedda!

TESMAN: But tell me—how do *you* know all this?

BRACK (*tersely*): A man on the force told me. One I had some business with.

HEDDA (*loudly*): At last a deed!

TESMAN (*appalled*): Oh dear—what are you saying, Hedda!

HEDDA: I am saying there is beauty in this.

BRACK: Well, now—Mrs. Tesman—

TESMAN: Beauty—! Just think!

MRS. ELVSTED: Oh, Hedda—how can you talk about beauty in a thing like this!

HEDDA: Eilert Løvborg has settled his account with himself. He has had the courage to do—what had to be done.

MRS. ELVSTED: But you mustn't believe it happened that way! He did it when he was not himself!

TESMAN: In despair! That's how!

HEDDA: He did not. I am certain of that.

MRS. ELVSTED: Yes he did! He was not himself! That's the way he tore up the book, too!

BRACK (*puzzled*): The book? You mean the manuscript? Has he torn it up?

MRS. ELVSTED: Yes, last night.

TESMAN (*whispers*): Oh, Hedda—we'll never get clear of all this!

BRACK: That is strange.

TESMAN (*walking the floor*): To think that this was to be the end of Eilert! Not to leave behind him anything that would have preserved his name—

MRS. ELVSTED: Oh, if only it could be put together again!

TESMAN: Yes, if only it could. I don't know what I wouldn't give—

MRS. ELVSTED: Maybe it can, Mr. Tesman.

TESMAN: What do you mean?

MRS. ELVSTED (*searching her dress pocket*): Look. I have kept these little slips he dictated from.

HEDDA (*a step closer*): Ah—!

TESMAN: You've kept them, Mrs. Elvsted? Hm?

MRS. ELVSTED: Yes. Here they are. I took them with me when I left. And I've had them in my pocket ever since—

TESMAN: Please, let me see—

MRS. ELVSTED (*gives him a pile of small paper slips*): But it's such a mess. Without any kind of system or order—!

TESMAN: But just think if we could make sense out of them, all the same! Perhaps if we helped each other—

MRS. ELVSTED: Oh yes! Let's try, anyway!

TESMAN: It will work! It *has* to work! I'll stake my whole life on this!

HEDDA: You, Jørgen? Your life?

TESMAN: Yes, or at any rate all the time I can set aside. My own collections can wait. Hedda, you understand—don't you? Hm? This is something I owe Eilert's memory.

HEDDA: Maybe so.

TESMAN: And now, my dear Mrs. Elvsted, we want to get to work. Good heavens, there's no point brooding over what's happened. Hm? We'll just have to acquire sufficient peace of mind to—

MRS. ELVSTED: All right, Mr. Tesman. I'll try my best.

TESMAN: Very well, then. Come over here. Let's look at these slips right away. Where can we sit? Here? No, it's better in the other room. If you'll excuse us, Judge! Come along, Mrs. Elvsted.

MRS. ELVSTED: Oh dear God—if only it were possible—!

[*TESMAN and MRS. ELVSTED go into the inner room. She takes off her hat and coat. Both sit down at the table under the hanging lamp and absorb themselves in the slips. HEDDA walks over toward the stove and sits down in the easy chair. After a while, BRACK walks over to her.*]

HEDDA (*in a low voice*): Ah, Judge—what a liberation there is in this thing with Eilert Løvborg!

BRACK: Liberation, Mrs. Tesman? Well, yes, for him perhaps one may say there was liberation of a kind—

HEDDA: I mean for me. There is liberation in knowing that there is such a thing in the world as an act of free courage. Something which becomes beautiful by its very nature.

BRACK (*smiles*): Well—dear Mrs. Tesman—

HEDDA: Oh I know what you're going to say! For you see—you really are a kind of specialist, too, like—oh never mind.

BRACK (*looks at her fixedly*): Eilert Løvborg has meant more to you than perhaps you're willing to admit, even to yourself. Or am I wrong?

HEDDA: I won't answer such questions. All I know is that Eilert Løvborg had the courage to live his own life. And then now—this—magnificence! The beauty of it! Having the strength and the will to get up and leave life's feast—so early—

BRACK: Believe me, Mrs. Tesman, this pains me, but I see it is necessary that I destroy a pretty illusion—

HEDDA: An illusion?

BRACK: Which could not have been maintained for very long, anyway.

HEDDA: And what is that?

BRACK: He didn't shoot himself—of his own free will.

HEDDA: Not of his own—!

BRACK: No. To tell the truth, the circumstances of Eilert Løvborg's death aren't exactly what I said they were.

HEDDA (*tense*): You've held something back? What?

BRACK: For the sake of poor Mrs. Elvsted I used a few euphemisms.

HEDDA: What?

BRACK: First—he is already dead.

HEDDA: In the hospital.

BRACK: Yes. And without regaining consciousness.

HEDDA: What else haven't you told?

BRACK: That fact that it didn't happen in his room.

HEDDA: Well, does that really make much difference?

BRACK: Some. You see—Eilert Løvborg was found shot in Miss Diana's bedroom.

HEDDA (*is about to jump up, but sinks back*): That's impossible, Judge Brack! He can't have been there again today!

BRACK: He was there this afternoon. He came to claim something he said they had taken from him. Spoke some gibberish about a lost child—

HEDDA: So that's why—!

BRACK: I thought maybe he meant his manuscript. But now I hear he has destroyed that himself. So I suppose it must have been something else.

HEDDA: I suppose. So it was there—so they found him there?

BRACK: Yes. With a fired gun in his pocket. Mortally wounded.

HEDDA: Yes—in the chest.

BRACK: No—in the gut.

HEDDA (*looks at him with an expression of disgust*): That, too! What is this curse that turns everything I touch into something ludicrous and low!

BRACK: There is something else, Mrs. Tesman. Something I'd call—nasty.

HEDDA: And what is that?

BRACK: The gun they found—

HEDDA (*breathless*): What about it?

BRACK: He must have stolen it.

HEDDA (*jumps up*): Stolen! That's not true! He didn't!

BRACK: Anything else is impossible. He *must* have stolen it.—Shhh!

[*TESMAN and MRS. ELVSTED have risen from the table and come forward into the front room.*]

TESMAN (*with papers in both hands*): D'you know, Hedda—you can hardly see in there with that lamp! Just think!

HEDDA: I am thinking.

TESMAN: I wonder if you'd let us use your desk, hm?

HEDDA: Certainly, if you like. (*Adds quickly.*) Wait a minute, though! Let me clear it off a bit first.

TESMAN: Ah, there's no need for that, Hedda. There's plenty of room.

HEDDA: No, no. I want to straighten it up. I'll carry all this in here. I'll put it on top of the piano for the time being.

[*She has pulled an object, covered by sheet music, out*

of the bookcase. She puts several other sheets of paper on top of it and carries the whole pile into the left part of the inner room. TESMAN puts the papers down on the desk and moves the lamp from the corner table over to the desk. He and MRS. ELVSTED sit down and resume their work. HEDDA returns.]

HEDDA (*behind* MRS. ELVSTED's *chair, softly ruffling her hair*): Well, little Thea—how is Eilert Løvborg's memorial coming along?

MRS. ELVSTED (*looks up at her, discouraged*): Oh God— I'm sure it's going to be terribly hard to make anything out of all this.

TESMAN: But we have to. We just don't have a choice. And putting other people's papers in order— that's just the thing for me.

[*HEDDA walks over to the stove and sits down on one of the ottomans. BRACK stands over her, leaning on the easy chair.*]

HEDDA (*whispers*): What were you saying about the gun?

BRACK (*also softly*): That he must have stolen it.

HEDDA: Why, necessarily?

BRACK: Because any other explanation ought to be out of the question, Mrs. Tesman.

HEDDA: Oh?

BRACK (*looks at her for a moment*): Eilert Løvborg was here this morning, of course. Isn't that so?

HEDDA: Yes.

BRACK: Were you alone with him?

HEDDA: Yes, for a while.

BRACK: You didn't leave the room while he was here?

HEDDA: No.

BRACK: Think. Not at all? Not even for a moment?

HEDDA: Well—maybe just for a moment—out in the hall.

BRACK: And where was the gun case?

HEDDA: In the—

BRACK: Mrs. Tesman?

HEDDA: On the desk.

BRACK: Have you looked to see if both guns are still there?

HEDDA: No.

BRACK: You needn't bother. I saw the gun they found on Løvborg, and I knew it immediately. From yesterday—and from earlier occasions, too.

HEDDA: Perhaps you have it?

BRACK: No, the police do.

HEDDA: What are the police going to do with it?

BRACK: Try to find the owner.

HEDDA: Do you think they will?

BRACK (*leans over her, whispers*): No, Hedda Gabler— not as long as I keep quiet.

HEDDA (*with a hunted look*): And if you don't?

BRACK (*shrugs his shoulders*): Of course, there's always

the chance that the gun was stolen.

HEDDA (*firmly*): Rather die!

BRACK (*smiles*): People *say* things like that. They don't *do* them.

HEDDA (*without answering*): And if the gun was not stolen—and if they find the owner—then what happens?

BRACK: Well, Hedda—then comes the scandal!

HEDDA: The scandal!

BRACK: Yes—the scandal. That you are so mortally afraid of. You will of course be required to testify. Both you and Miss Diana. Obviously, she'll have to explain how the whole thing happened. Whether it was accident or homicide. Did he try to pull the gun out of his pocket to threaten her? And did it fire accidentally? Or did she grab the gun away from him, shoot him, and put it back in his pocket? She might just possibly have done that. She's a pretty tough girl—Miss Diana.

HEDDA: But this whole disgusting mess has nothing to do with me.

BRACK: Quite so. But you'll have to answer the question: Why did you give Eilert Løvborg the gun? And what inferences will be drawn from the fact that you did?

HEDDA (*lowers her head*): That's true. I hadn't thought of that.

BRACK: Well—luckily, there's nothing to worry about as long as I don't say anything.

HEDDA (*looks up at him*): So then I'm in your power, Judge. From now on you can do anything you like with me.

BRACK (*in an even softer whisper*): Dearest Hedda— believe me, I'll not misuse my position.

HEDDA: In your power, all the same. Dependent on your will. Servant to your demands. Not free. Not free! (*Rises suddenly.*) No—I can't stand that thought! Never!

BRACK (*looks at her, half mockingly*): Most people submit to the inevitable.

HEDDA (*returning his glance*): Perhaps. (*Walks over to the desk. Suppresses a smile and mimics* TESMAN's *way of speaking.*) Well? Do you think you can do it, Jørgen? Hm?

TESMAN: Lord knows, Hedda. Anyway, I can already see it will take months.

HEDDA (*still mimicking*): Just think! (*Runs her hands lightly through* MRS. ELVSTED's *hair.*) Doesn't this seem strange to you, Thea? Sitting here with Tesman—just the way you used to with Eilert Løvborg?

MRS. ELVSTED: Oh God—if only I could inspire your husband, too!

HEDDA: Oh, I'm sure that will come—in time.

TESMAN: Well, yes—do you know, Hedda? I really think I begin to feel something of the kind. But why don't you go and talk to the Judge again.

HEDDA: Is there nothing you two can use me for?

TESMAN: No, not a thing, dear. (*Turns around.*) From now on, you must be good enough to keep Hedda company, my dear Judge!

BRACK (*glancing at* HEDDA): I'll be only too delighted.

HEDDA: Thank you. But I'm tired tonight. I think I'll go and lie down for a while.

TESMAN: Yes, you do that, dear; why don't you? Hm?

[HEDDA *goes into the inner room, closes the portieres behind her. Brief pause. Suddenly, she is heard playing a frenzied dance tune on the piano.*]

MRS. ELVSTED (*jumps up*): Oh God! What's that!

TESMAN (*running to the doorway*): But dearest Hedda—you mustn't play dance music tonight, for goodness' sake! Think of Aunt Rina! And Eilert, too!

HEDDA (*peeks in from between the portieres*): And Aunt Julle. And everybody. I'll be quiet. (*She pulls the portieres shut again.*)

TESMAN (*back at the desk*): I don't think it's good for her to see us at such a melancholy task. I'll tell you what, Mrs. Elvsted. You move in with Aunt Julle, and then I'll come over in the evenings. Then we can sit and work over there. Hm?

MRS. ELVSTED: Maybe that would be better—

HEDDA (*from the inner room*): I hear every word you're saying, Tesman. And how am I going to spend my evenings?

TESMAN (*busy with the papers*): Oh, I'm sure Judge Brack will be good enough to come out and see you, anyway.

BRACK (*in the easy chair, calls out gaily*): Every single night, as far as I'm concerned, Mrs. Tesman! I'm sure we're going to have a lovely time, you and I!

HEDDA (*loud and clear*): Yes, don't you think that would be nice, Judge Brack? You—sole cock-o'-the-walk—

[*A shot is heard from the inner room.* TESMAN, MRS. ELVSTED, *and* JUDGE BRACK *all jump up.*]

TESMAN: There she is, fooling with those guns again.

[*He pulls the portieres apart and runs inside.* MRS. ELVSTED *also.* HEDDA, *lifeless, is lying on the sofa. Cries and confusion.* BERTE, *flustered, enters, right.*]

TESMAN (*shouts to* BRACK): She's shot herself! In the temple! Just think!

BRACK (*half stunned in the easy chair*): But, merciful God—! One just doesn't *do* that!

AUGUST STRINDBERG

(1849–1912)

August Strindberg was born in Stockholm, the fourth of twelve children. His mother died when he was thirteen years old, and his father immediately married the family housekeeper. As a young man Strindberg worked at a number of jobs—telegraph clerk, actor, tutor, librarian—but when he met and married his first wife, the actress Siri von Essen in 1877, he devoted himself almost wholly to writing. They remained married until 1891, but the relationship was plagued by jealousy and quarrels. The marriage and resulting divorce—one of three marriages and divorces in Strindberg's life—left him with a bitter view of women and a curious hostility to his dramatic rival Ibsen, who he thought advocated domination by women. Strindberg wrote several autobiographical novels during the disintegration of his marriage, one of which details the relationship with Siri and her former husband, Baron von Essen, whom she had divorced to marry Strindberg. He also wrote a series of naturalistic plays dealing with sexual and psychological conflict. *The Father* (1887) was Strindberg's response to Ibsen's *Doll's House*, which he thought was as sick as he believed its author to be and which he despised as promoting a "Nora cult." *The Father* was intended as an experiment in naturalism. It concerns the struggle for domination in a relationship. Strindberg sent it to Zola, who thought it did not deal enough with social reality. Strindberg then wrote *Miss Julie* (1888) and in a preface explained in detail not only his use of naturalism but also his incorporation of earlier dramatic techniques, such as improvisational miming. In all of Strindberg's early plays the struggle for domination between men and women continued to be a principal theme.

In 1894, now in his second marriage, Strindberg suffered a psychological breakdown characterized by hallucinations. He believed at one point that his wife was driving him to insanity by sending rays through the walls of his room. Eventually he committed himself to the care of a doctor. During this period he read extensively in the works of Emanuel Swedenborg and experimented with alchemy. He wrote about his breakdown in an autobiographical novel, *Inferno* (1897), and beginning with his recovery in 1898 he went into another creative period that lasted until the end of his life. By the time of his death in 1912 he had written over fifty plays.

Strindberg composed a series of twenty-one chronicle plays on Swedish history from the thirteenth century to the eighteenth century, but his most famous plays from this period reflect his preoccupation with guilt, atonement, evil, and spiritual quests. In these later plays Strindberg abandoned the naturalism of his early period for expressionism and symbolism. *A Dream Play* (1902) gives

Strindberg's perspective on the lot of mankind. Brahman, the World Soul, has been asked by the World Mother, Maya, to propagate himself. As a result of this celestial "sin"—the mating of spirit and matter—the world is born and populated with characters who vainly aspire to free themselves from matter. Strindberg's conclusion is that "men are pitiable creatures." Strindberg explained in his note to the play that because the play is a dream, everything is possible and probable. Characters can split, double, multiply, or converge. In 1907 he founded the Intimate Theater, bringing the independent theater movement to Sweden, to produce his later plays. Among them was *The Ghost Sonata* (1907), a play in which the stage is peopled with ghost-like living human beings, dead men that suddenly come to life, and living persons who turn into mummies. The demonic landscape of the play conveys Strindberg's sense at this point in his career that life is evil. Strindberg was working on the landscape of dreams and the unconscious at about the time Freud was exploring the same territory in the field of psychology. Strindberg pioneered the theatrical uses of expressionism and symbolism, both of which were developed further during the twentieth century.

Miss Julie

The first production of *Miss Julie*, scheduled in 1889 in Copenhagen, was canceled by the state censors. It was still produced that year, privately, in the Copenhagen University Student Union. In 1893 André Antoine produced it in his Théâtre Libre in Paris in 1893, and Max Reinhardt, who eventually produced many of Strindberg's plays, put on a production of it in Berlin in 1904. Strindberg himself produced it in his Intimate Theater in Stockholm in 1906.

In his preface to the play, Strindberg describes Miss Julie as a modern "man-hating half-woman," who struggles to be equal to men. In this naturalistic theater, such a tendency is seen to run in the blood: her mother had betrayed her husband, the Count, by taking a lover, and later she burned down their house after the insurance expired. Her final humiliation of her husband was to have her lover loan him the money to rebuild. Like her mother, Miss Julie attempts to dominate and manipulate the men in her life. Before the opening of the play, her fiancé has left her, refusing to submit to her will. Her father, the Count, is away for a time, and we never see him in the play, but his dominating presence and authority is always felt onstage, represented by his boots. Miss Julie and her father's valet, Jean, vie for dominance over one another, and the battle progresses from social encounter to personal confession to sexual exploit to directed suicide.

Although *Miss Julie* seems a realist play, Strindberg has infused it with a dreamlike quality, turning it into a complex psychodrama that probes the power relations of gender and class. The play takes place on Midsummer Eve, traditionally a mysterious time associated with passion and with magical transformations. Indeed, this is the same dreamlike time that Shakespeare uses for *A Midsummer Night's Dream*, and similar contrasts are employed for different ends in the two plays. For Shakespeare the confining rigidity and tyrannical laws of Athens lead to the freedom and terrors of the wood outside as antidote; for Strindberg the suffocating social expectations of the aristocratic class come into conflict with the material temptations and sexual freedoms that lie outside society's norms. Miss Julie's position in society makes her into a kind of fairy princess and Jean into a discontented and disturbed version of Bottom the Weaver. Jean's childhood visions of the Count's garden are as Eden itself, guarded by angry angels to keep the boy out. His early vision of Julie in a pink dress and white stockings while he was covered in filth helps to set the fundamental contradictions in his psyche. At the time the play opens, his ambition in love has been limited to Kristine, the cook. Jean's slavish dedication to his master appears in his willingness to die for him if ordered, yet he has ambitions to break free of his social station to become the proprietor of a first-class hotel—a dream Miss Julie can hardly share with enthusiasm. During the play, the violence embedded in these contradictions is stunningly displayed in the decapitation of Miss Julie's pet bird.

Miss Julie's desperation comes from similar contradictions. Her privileged life, hedged by expectations that are supposed to sustain and to contain her, is also edged by the pattern of her mother's behavior. Miss Julie desperately wants and needs a change as much as Jean, but she is without a means to redirect her life except through men, who fail her precisely because of her desperation. Trapped, she sinks deeper and deeper into what she sees as the depravity of her rebellions—"can't repent, can't run away, can't stay, can't live—can't die." At the play's conclusion, helpless and broken, she leaves on Jean's orders to commit suicide.

AUTHOR'S PREFACE

The theatre has long seemed to me to be, like art in general, a *Biblia pauperum*, a Bible in pictures for those who can't read what is written or printed, and the playwright a lay preacher hawking the ideas of the day in popular form, so popular that the middle classes, the theatre's primary audience, can understand the basic questions without too much effort. And so the theatre has always been a public school for the young, the half-educated, and women, who still possess that primitive capacity for deceiving themselves or letting themselves be deceived, that is to say, are receptive to the illusion, to the playwright's power of suggestion. It seems to me, therefore, in our time, when rudimentary, undeveloped, and fanciful ways of thinking seem to be evolving toward reflection, investigation, and analysis, that the theatre, like religion, is dying out, a form for whose enjoyment we lack the necessary preconditions. Supporting this assertion is the serious theatre crisis now prevailing throughout Europe, especially in those bastions of culture that produced the greatest thinkers of the age, England and Germany, where the art of drama, like most of the other fine arts, is dead.

In other countries people have believed it possible to create a new drama by filling old forms with new contents. For a number of reasons, however, this has failed: in part because there has not been sufficient time to popularize the new ideas, so that the public does not understand the basic questions; in part because partisan politics has stirred up emotions, making dispassionate enjoyment impossible—how can people be objective when their innermost beliefs are offended or when they are subjected in the confines of a theatre to the public pressure of an applauding or hissing audience?; and in part because new forms have not been found for the new contents, so that the new wine has burst the old bottles.

In the following play, instead of trying to do anything new—which is impossible—I have simply modernized the form in accordance with demands I think contemporary audiences make upon this art. Toward this end, I have chosen, or let myself be moved by, a theme that can be said to lie outside partisan politics since the problem of social climbing or falling, of higher or lower, better or worse, man or woman, are, have been, and will be of lasting interest. When I took this theme from a true story I heard told some years ago, which made a strong impression on me, I found it appropriate for tragedy, for it still seems tragic to see someone favored by fortune go under, much more to see a family die out. Perhaps the time will come when we will be so advanced, so enlightened, that we can witness with indifference what now seem the coarse, cynical, heartless dramas life has to offer, when we have closed down those lower, unreliable mechanisms of thought called feelings, because better developed organs of judgment will have found them superfluous and harmful. The fact that the heroine arouses compassion is because we are too weak to resist the fear that the same fate could overtake us. A hypersensitive spectator may not be satisfied with compassion alone, while a man with faith in the future may demand some positive proposals to remedy the evil, in other words, a program of some kind. But for one thing there is no absolute evil. The fall of one family can mean a chance for another family to rise, and the alternation of rising and falling fortunes is one of life's greatest delights since happiness lies only in comparison. And to the man who wants a program to remedy the unpleasant fact that the bird of prey eats the dove and the louse eats the bird of prey I ask: why should it be remedied? Life is not so idiotically mathematical that only the great eat the small; it is just as common for a bee to kill a lion or at least drive it mad.

If my tragedy depresses many people, it is their own fault. When we become as strong as the first French revolutionaries, it will afford nothing but pleasure and relief to witness the thinning out in royal parks of overage, decaying trees that have long stood in the way of others equally entitled to their time in the sun, the kind of relief we feel when we see someone incurably ill die!

Recently, my tragedy *The Father* was criticized for being too sad, as if one should expect cheerful tragedies. People clamor pretentiously for "the joy of life," and theatre managers call for farces, as if the joy of life lay in being silly and depicting people as if they were all afflicted with St. Vitus's dance or imbecility. I find the joy of life in its cruel and powerful struggles, and my enjoyment comes from being able to know something, being able to learn something. That is why I have chosen an unusual case, but one from which we can learn much—in a word an exception, but an important exception which proves the rule—though this will probably offend those who love the conventional and predictable. What will next shock simple minds is that I have not motivated the action in a simple way, nor is there a single point of view. Every event in life—and this is a rather new discovery!—is ordinarily the result of a whole series of more or less deep-lying motives. The spectator, however, usually singles out the one that is either easiest for him to understand or is most advantageous to him personally. Take the case of a suicide. "Financial problems," says a businessman. "Unrequited love," says a woman. "Physical illness," says an invalid. "Dashed hopes," says a shipwrecked man. It might be that all or none of these were motives and that the deceased concealed the real motive by advancing a totally different one that would bring the most credit to his memory!

I have motivated Miss Julie's tragic fate by a great number of circumstances: her mother's primary instincts, her father raising her incorrectly, her own nature, and the influence of her fiancé on her weak and degenerate brain. Also, more particularly: the festive atmosphere of midsummer night, her father's absence, her monthly indisposition, her preoccupation with animals, the provocative effect of the dancing, the magical midsummer twilight, the powerfully aphrodisiac influence of flowers, and, finally, the chance that drives the couple together into a room alone—plus the boldness of the aroused man.

My treatment of the subject has thus been neither one-sidedly physiological nor exclusively psychological. I have not put the entire blame on what she inherited from her mother, nor on her monthly indisposition, nor on immorality. I have not even preached morality—this I left to the cook in the absence of a minister.

This multiplicity of motives, it pleases me to assert, is in keeping with the times. And if others have done it before me, then it pleases me that I have not been alone in my "paradoxes," as all discoveries are called.

As for characterization, I have made my people rather "characterless" for the following reasons:

The word *character* has come to mean many things over the course of time. Originally, it must have meant the dominant trait in the soul-complex and was confused with temperament. Later it became the middle-class expression for the automaton, one whose disposition was fixed once and for all or had adapted himself to a particular role in life. In a word, someone who had stopped growing was called a character. In contrast the person who continued to develop, the skillful navigator on the river of life, sailing not with sheets belayed, but veering before the wind to luff again, was called characterless—in a derogatory sense, of course—because he was so difficult to understand, classify, and keep track of. This bourgeois concept of the immobility of the soul was transferred to the stage, which the bourgeoisie has always dominated. There a character became a man who was ready-made; whenever he appeared, he was drunk or comical or sad. The only thing necessary to characterize him was to give him a physical defect—a clubfoot, a wooden leg, a red nose—or have him repeat an expression, such as "that was splendid" or "Barkis is willin'." This simplified view of human character still survives in the great Molière. Harpagon is nothing but a miser although he could have been not only a miser but an excellent financier, or splendid father and good citizen. What is worse is that his "defect" is very advantageous to his son-in-law and daughter, who are his heirs and therefore should not criticize him, even if they have to wait a bit before climbing into bed together. Therefore, I do not believe in simple theatrical characters. And an author's summary judgments of people—this one is stupid, that one brutal, this one jealous, that one stingy—should be challenged by naturalists, who know how rich the soul-complex is and realize that "vice" has a reverse side closely resembling virtue.

As modern characters living in an age of transition more compulsively hysterical than the one that preceded it at least, I have depicted my people as more vacillating and disintegrating than their predecessors, a mixture of the old and the new. If the valet belches something modern from the depths of his ancient slave's soul, it is because I think it not improbable that through newspapers and conversations modern ideas filter down even to the level a servant lives on. There are those who find it wrong in modern drama for characters to speak Darwinism. At the same time they hold up Shakespeare as a model. I would like to remind these critics that the gravedigger in *Hamlet* speaks the fashionable philosophy of the day—Giordano Bruno's (Bacon's)—which is more improbable since there were fewer means then for the spread of ideas than there are now. Besides, "Darwinism" has existed in every age, ever since the description in Genesis of the steps in creation from lower animals to man. It is just that only now have we discovered and formulated it.

My souls (characters) are conglomerates of past and present cultural phases, bits from books and newspapers, scraps of humanity, pieces torn from fine clothes and become rags, patched together as is the human soul. I have also added a little evolutionary history by having the weaker mind steal and repeat words from the stronger. Ideas are induced through the power of suggestion: from other people, from the surroundings (the blood of the greenfinch), and from attributes (the straight razor); and I have inanimate objects (the Count's boots, the bell) serve as agents for *Gedankenübertragung* ["thought transference"]. Finally, I have used "open suggestion," a variation of sleeplike hypnosis, which is now so well known and popularized that it cannot arouse the kind of ridicule or skepticism it would have done in Mesmer's time.

Miss Julie is a modern character. Not that the man-hating half-woman has not existed in all ages but because now that she has been discovered, she has come out in the open to make herself heard. The half-woman is a type who pushes her way ahead, selling herself nowadays for power, decorations, honors, and diplomas, as formerly she used to do for money. The type implies a retrogressive step in evolution, an inferior species who cannot endure. Unfortunately, they are able to pass on their wretchedness; degenerate men seem unconsciously to choose their mates from among them. And so they breed, producing an indeterminate sex for whom life is a torture. Fortunately, the offspring go under either because they are out of harmony with reality or because their repressed instincts break out uncontrollably or because their hopes of achieving equality with men are crushed. The type is tragic, revealing the drama of a desperate struggle against Nature, tragic as the romantic heritage now being dissipated by naturalism, which has a contrary aim: happiness, and happiness belongs only to the strong and skillful species.

But Miss Julie is also: a relic of the old warrior nobility now giving way to a new nobility of nerve and intellect, a victim of her own flawed constitution, a victim of the discord caused in a family by a mother's "crime," a victim of the delusions and conditions of her age—and together these are the equivalent of the concept of Destiny, or Universal Law, of antiquity. Guilt has been abolished by the naturalist, along with God, but the consequences of an action—punishment, imprisonment or the fear of it—that he cannot erase, for the simple reason that they remain, whether he pronounces acquittal or not. Those who have been injured are not as kind and understanding as an unscathed outsider can afford to be. Even if her father felt constrained not to seek revenge, his daughter would wreak vengeance upon herself, as she does here, out of an innate or acquired sense of honor, which the upper classes inherit—from where? From barbarism, from the ancient Aryan home of the race, from medieval chivalry. It is a beautiful thing, but nowadays a hindrance to the survival of the race. It is the nobleman's harikari, which compels him to slit open his own stomach when someone insults him and which survives in a modified form in the duel, that privilege of the nobility. That is why Jean, the servant, lives, while Miss Julie cannot live without honor. The slave's advantage over the nobleman is that he lacks this fatal preoccupation with honor. But in all of us Aryans there is something of the nobleman, or a Don Quixote. And so we sympathize with the suicide, whose act means a loss of honor. We are noblemen enough to be pained when we see the mighty fallen and as superfluous as a corpse, yes, even if the fallen should rise again and make amends through an honorable act. The servant Jean is a race-founder, someone in whom the process of differentiation can be detected. Born the son of a tenant farmer, he has educated himself in the things a gentleman should know. He has been quick to learn, has finely developed senses (smell, taste, sight) and a feeling for what is beautiful. He is already moving up in the world and is not embarrassed about using other people's help. He is alienated from his fellow servants, despising them as parts of a past he has already put behind him. He fears and flees them because they know his secrets, pry into his intentions, envy his rise, and look forward eagerly to his fall. Hence his dual, indecisive nature, vacillating between sympathy for people in high social positions and hatred for those who currently occupy those positions. He is an aristocrat, as he himself says, has learned the secrets of good society, is polished on the surface but coarse beneath, wears a frock coat tastefully but without any guarantee that his body is clean.

He has respect for Miss Julie, but is afraid of Kristine because she knows his dangerous secrets. He is sufficiently callous not to let the night's events disturb his plans for the future. With both a slave's brutality and a master's lack of squeamishness, he can see blood without fainting and shake off misfortune easily. Consequently, he comes through the struggle unscathed and will probably end up an innkeeper. And even if *he* does not become a Rumanian count, his son will become a university student and possibly a county police commissioner.

In any case he has important things to say about the lower classes' view of life—when he is telling the truth, that is, which he often does not do, for he is more interested in saying what is favorable to himself than in telling the truth. When Miss Julie says she assumes the lower classes feel oppressed from above, Jean naturally agrees since it is his intention to win sympathy, but he quickly changes his attitude when he realizes that it is more to his advantage to distance himself from the "rabble."

Apart from the fact that Jean is rising in the world, he is superior to Miss Julie because he is a man. Sexually, he is an aristocrat because of his masculine strength, his more keenly developed senses, and his capacity for taking the initiative. His sense of inferiority is mostly due to the social circumstances in which he happens to be living, and he can probably shed it along with his valet's jacket.

His slave mentality expresses itself in the fearful respect he has for the Count (the boots) and his religious superstition; but he respects the Count mainly as the occupant of the kind of high position to which he himself aspires; and the respect remains even after he has conquered the daughter of the house and seen how empty the lovely shell was.

I do not believe that love in any "higher" sense can exist between two people of such different natures, and so I have Miss Julie's love as something she fabricates in order to protect and excuse herself; and I have Jean suppose himself capable of loving her under other social circumstances. I think it is the same with love as with the hyacinth, which must take root in darkness *before* it can produce a sturdy flower. Here a flower shoots up, blooms, and goes to seed all at once, and that is why it dies so quickly.

Kristine, finally, is a female slave. Years standing over the stove have made her conventional and lethargic; instinctively hypocritical, she uses morality and religion as cloaks and scapegoats. A strong person would not need these because he can either bear his guilt or reason it away. Kristine goes to church as a quick and easy way to unload her household thefts on Jesus and to take on a new charge of innocence. Furthermore, she is a minor character, and I purposely simply sketched her in, as I did the minister and the doctor in *The Father*, because I wanted ordinary people, as country ministers and provincial doctors usually are. If my minor characters seem abstract to some people, it is because ordinary people are abstract to some extent in their occupations. As they carry out their duties, they lose their individuality, showing only one side of themselves, and as long as the spectator has no need to see them from several sides, my abstract depiction of them is probably correct.

As for the dialogue, I have broken with tradition somewhat by not making my characters catechists who ask stupid questions in order to elicit clever replies. I have avoided the symmetrical, mathematical, constructed dialogue of French drama and let characters' minds function irregularly, as they do in a real-life conversation, where no topic of discussion is exhausted entirely and one mind by chance finds a cog in another mind in which to engage. Consequently, the dialogue also wanders, presenting material in the opening scenes that is later taken up, reworked, repeated, expanded, and developed, like the theme in a musical composition.

The plot is serviceable enough, and since it really concerns only two people, I have concentrated on them, including only one minor character, the cook, and having the father's unhappy spirit hover over and behind the action. I have done this because I believe that people of today are most interested in the psychological process. Our inquisitive souls are not satisfied just to see something happen; we want to know how it happened. We want to see the strings, the machinery, examine the double-bottomed box, feel for the seam in the magic ring, look at the cards to see how they are marked.

In this regard I have kept in mind the monographic novels of the brothers Goncourt, which I find more appealing than anything else in contemporary literature.

As for the technical aspects of composition, I have experimented with eliminating act divisions. The reason is that I believe our dwindling capacity for accepting illusion is possibly further disturbed by intermissions, during which the spectator has time to reflect and thereby escape the suggestive influence of the author-hypnotist. My play will probably run an hour and a half, and since people can listen to a lecture, sermon, or conference discussion for just as long or longer, I imagine that a ninety-minute theatre piece will not be too tiring. I tested this concentrated form in 1872 in one of my first plays, *The Outlaw*, although with little success. The first draft was in five acts, and when I noticed the disjointed, restless effect it produced, I burned it. From the ashes rose a single, long, coherent act of fifty pages in print, with a playing time of one hour. And so the form is not new, and I seem to have a feel for it; changing tastes may make it timely. My hope for the future is to so educate audiences that they can sit through a one-act play that lasts an entire evening. But this will require experimentation. Meanwhile, in order to relax tension for the audience and the actors, without breaking the illusion for the audience, I have used three art forms traditionally associated with drama: monologue, mime, and ballet. The original association was with the tragedy of antiquity, monody having become monologue, and chorus, ballet.

Our realists today condemn the monologue as implausible, but if I motivate it, I can make it plausible and use it to advantage. It is perfectly plausible for an orator to pace the floor alone and practice his speech aloud, plausible for an actor to rehearse his lines aloud, for a servant girl to talk to her cat, a mother babble to her baby, an old maid jabber to her parrot, a sleeper talk in his sleep. And in order to give the actor a chance, for once, to work independently, free for a moment of the author's authority, I have sketched in the monologues rather than worked them out in detail. Since it is irrelevant what someone says in his sleep or to a parrot or to a cat, for this has no influence on the action, a talented actor, absorbed in the mood and the situation, perhaps can improvise the monologue more effectively than the author, who cannot determine in advance how much may be spoken, and for how long, before an audience senses that the illusion is broken.

As we know, some Italian theatres have returned to improvisation, producing actors who are creative in their own right, although in accordance with the author's intentions. This could be the beginning of a fertile new art form, something worthy of the name *creative*.

In places where a monologue would be implausible, I have resorted to mime, and here I leave the actor even greater freedom to be creative—and to win independent acclaim. But in order not to try the audience beyond its limits, I have let music—coming from the midsummer dance, and thus believably motivated—exercise its illusion-evoking power during the sections of dumb show. I beg the music director to consider carefully his choice of pieces; the wrong mood may be produced if there are familiar selections from popular dances or operettas, or unusual folk melodies, no matter how ethnographically correct.

The ballet I have indicated cannot be replaced by a so-called "crowd scene" because crowd scenes are always badly acted, with a mob of grimacing idiots trying to use the occasion to appear clever and so disturb the illusion. And since uneducated people do not improvise when they wish to poke fun maliciously but use ready-made material that can take on a double meaning, I did not compose the taunting song they sing. Instead, I used a little-known dance song[1] I discovered myself in the Stockholm area. The words are only approximately appropriate, but this is intentional, for the slyness (weakness) of the slave does not permit him to make a direct attack. And so the seriousness of the action forbids clowning; there must be no coarse sneering in a situation which closes the lid on a family coffin.

As for the scenery, I have borrowed from impressionist painting the device of making a setting appear cut off and asymmetrical, thus strengthening the illusion. When we see only part of a room and a portion of the furniture, we are left to conjecture, that is to say, our imagination goes to work and complements what is seen. I have also profited by doing away with those tiresome exits through doors because scenery doors, made of canvas, wobble at the slightest touch; they cannot even allow a father to express his anger after a bad dinner by going out and slamming the door behind him "so that the whole house shakes." (In the theatre it wobbles.) I have also confined the action to one setting, both to allow the characters more time to interact with their environment and to break with the tradition of expensive scenery. With only one setting we should be able to demand that it be realistic, but nothing is more difficult than to get a room on stage to look like a room, however easily the scene painter can produce flaming volcanoes and waterfalls. Even if the walls must be of canvas, it is surely time to stop painting shelves and kitchen utensils on them. We have so many other stage conventions in which we are asked to believe, we should not have to strain ourselves trying to believe in painted pots and pans.

I have placed the upstage wall and the table diagonally so that the actors can play facing the audience or in half-profile when they sit opposite each other at the table. I saw a diagonal backdrop in a production of *Aïda*; it led the eye out into unknown vistas and did not look simply like a defiant reaction to the boredom of straight lines.

Another perhaps necessary innovation is the removal of footlights. The purpose of this lighting from below is said to be to make the actors' faces fatter, but I ask: why must all actors have fat faces? Does not this lighting obliterate many subtleties in the lower part of the face, especially the jaws, distort the shape of the nose, and cast shadows up over the eyes? Even if this were not so, one thing is certain: actors find it so painful for their eyes that they are unable to use them with full expressiveness. Footlights strike the retina in places usually protected (except in the case of seamen, who have to look at the sun's reflection in the water), and so we seldom see anything but a crude rolling of the eyes, either to the side or up toward the balconies, exposing the whites. Perhaps this

---

[1] The version of the song as it appears in this translation of the play is a free interpretation of the playwright's intention rather than a literal rendering of the actual song he chose (translator).

also accounts for the tedious habit, especially common among actresses, of blinking eyelashes. And when anyone on stage wants to speak with his eyes, he must resort to staring straight out, thus breaking the wall of the curtain line and coming into direct contact with the audience. Justly or unjustly, this unfortunate practice is called "greeting your friends."

Would not sufficiently strong side lighting (using parabolic reflectors, for example) provide the actor with a new advantage: the strengthening of mime effects through the most expressive asset in his face—the play of his eyes?

I have no illusions about getting the actor to play for the audience rather than with it, although this would be desirable. I cannot hope to see an actor play with his back to the audience throughout an entire important scene, though I wish very much that crucial scenes were staged, not next to the prompter's box, like duets intended to evoke applause, but in places more appropriate to the action. In other words, I call for no revolution, just small modifications, for to really transform the stage into a room where the fourth wall is removed, and consequently a portion of the furniture faces away from the audience, would probably, for the present, produce a disturbing effect.

When it comes to makeup, I dare not hope to be listened to by the ladies, who would rather be beautiful than believable. But the actor might consider whether it is really to his advantage when putting on makeup to fix an abstract character, like a mask, on his face. Picture an actor who has put the sharp, charcoal lines of anger of an old man between his eyes and then, with that incensed look, has to smile in response to someone else's line. What a terrible grimace there would be as a result! And how would the false forehead attached to his wig, bald as a billiard ball, wrinkle when the old man got angry?

In a modern psychological drama, where the subtlest movements of the soul must be revealed more through the face than through gesture and sound, it would probably be best to experiment with strong side lighting on a small stage, and with actors wearing no makeup, or at least a minimum of it.

If, in addition, we could avoid having the orchestra visible, its lights disturbing, and the musicians' faces turned toward the audience; if the seating in the auditorium were raised so that eye level for the spectator was higher than the hollow of the actor's knee; if we could get rid of stage boxes (behind bull's-eye openings), with their grinning late arrivals from dinners and supper parties; if we could have complete darkness during performances; and, finally, and most importantly, a *small* stage and a *small* auditorium, then perhaps we might see a new drama arise, or at the very least a theatre that was once again a place of entertainment for educated people. While waiting for this theatre, we will just have to go on writing, preparing the repertoire that will one day be needed.

Here is an attempt! If it fails, there is surely time enough for another!

Miss Julie

AUGUST STRINDBERG

TRANSLATED BY EVERT SPRINCHORN

CHARACTERS
MISS JULIE, 25 years old
JEAN, her father's valet, 30 years old
KRISTINE, her father's cook, 35 years old

The action takes place in the count's kitchen on midsummer eve.

THE SETTING. A large kitchen, the ceiling and side walls of which are hidden by draperies. The rear wall runs diagonally from down left to up right. On the wall down left are two shelves with copper, iron, and pewter utensils; the shelves are lined with scalloped paper. Visible to the right is most of a set of large, arched glass doors, through which can be seen a fountain with a statue of Cupid, lilac bushes in bloom, and the tops of some Lombardy poplars. At down left is the corner of a large tiled stove; a portion of its hood is showing. At right, one end of the servants' white pine dining table juts out; several chairs stand around it. The stove is decorated with birch branches; juniper twigs are strewn on the floor. On the end of the table stands a large Japanese spice jar, filled with lilac blossoms. An ice-box, a sink, and a washstand. Above the door is an old-fashioned bell on a spring; to the left of the door, the mouthpiece of a speaking tube is visible.

KRISTINE is frying something on the stove. She is wearing a light-colored cotton dress and an apron. JEAN enters. He is wearing livery and carries a pair of high riding-boots with spurs, which he puts down on the floor where they can be seen by the audience.

JEAN: Miss Julie's crazy again tonight; absolutely crazy!

KRISTINE: So you finally came back?

JEAN: I took the Count to the station and when I returned past the barn I stopped in for a dance. Who do I see but Miss Julie leading off the dance with the gamekeeper! But as soon as she saw me she rushed over to ask me for the next waltz. And she's been waltzing ever since—I've never seen anything like it. She's crazy!

KRISTINE: She always has been, but never as bad as the last two weeks since her engagement was broken off.

JEAN: Yes, I wonder what the real story was there. He was a gentleman, even if he wasn't rich. Ah! These people have such romantic ideas. (*Sits at the end of the table.*) Still, it's strange, isn't it? I mean that she'd rather stay home with the servants on midsummer eve instead of going with her father to visit relatives?

KRISTINE: She's probably embarrassed after that row with her fiancé.

JEAN: Probably! He gave a good account of himself, though. Do you know how it happened, Kristine? I saw it, you know, though I didn't let on I had.

KRISTINE: No! You saw it?

JEAN: Yes, I did.——That evening they were out near the stable, and she was "training" him—as she called it. Do you know what she did? She made him jump over her riding crop, the way you'd teach a dog to jump. He jumped twice and she hit him each time. But the third time he grabbed the crop out of her hand, hit her with it across the cheek, and broke it in pieces. Then he left.

KRISTINE: So, that's what happened! I can't believe it!

JEAN: Yes, that's the way it went!——What have you got for me that's tasty, Kristine?

KRISTINE (*serving him from the pan*): Oh, it's only a piece of kidney I cut from the veal roast.

JEAN (*smelling the food*): Beautiful! That's my favorite *délice*. (*feeling the plate*) But you could have warmed the plate!

KRISTINE: You're fussier than the Count himself, once you start! (*She pulls his hair affectionately.*)

JEAN (*angry*): Stop it, leave my hair alone! You know I'm touchy about that.

KRISTINE: Now, now, it's only love, you know that. (*JEAN eats. KRISTINE opens a bottle of beer.*)

JEAN: Beer? On midsummer eve? No thank you! I can do better than that. (*opens a drawer in the table and takes out a bottle of red wine with yellow sealing wax*) See that? Yellow seal! Give me a glass! A wine glass! I'm drinking this *pur*.

KRISTINE (*returns to the stove and puts on a small saucepan*): God help the woman who gets you for a husband! What a fussbudget.

JEAN: Nonsense! You'd be damned lucky to get a man like me. It certainly hasn't done you any harm to have people call me your sweetheart. (*tastes the wine*) Good! Very good! Just needs a little warming. (*warms the glass between his hands*) We bought this in Dijon. Four francs a liter, not counting the cost of the bottle, or the customs duty. ——What are you cooking now? It stinks like hell!

KRISTINE: Oh, some slop Miss Julie wants to give Diana.

JEAN: Watch your language, Kristine. But why should you have to cook for that damn mutt on midsummer eve? Is she sick?

KRISTINE: Yes, she's sick! She sneaked out with the gatekeeper's dog—and now there's hell to pay. Miss Julie won't have it!

JEAN: Miss Julie has too much pride about some things and not enough about others, just like her mother was. The Countess was most at home in the kitchen and the cowsheds, but a *one*-horse carriage wasn't elegant enough for her. The cuffs of her blouse were dirty, but she had to have her coat of arms on her cufflinks. —— And Miss Julie won't take proper care of herself either. If you ask me, she just isn't refined. Just now, when she was dancing in the barn, she pulled the gamekeeper away from Anna and made him dance with her. *We* wouldn't behave like that, but that's what happens when aristocrats pretend they're common people—they get *common!* —— But she is quite a woman! Magnificent! What shoulders,

and what—et cetera!

KRISTINE: Oh, don't overdo it! I've heard what Clara says, and she dresses her.

JEAN: Ha, Clara! You're all jealous of each other! I've been out riding with her . . . And the way she dances!

KRISTINE: Listen, Jean! You've going to dance with me, when I'm finished here, aren't you?

JEAN: Of course I will.

KRISTINE: Promise?

JEAN: Promise? When I say I'll do something, I do it! By the way, the kidney was very good. (*corks the bottle*)

JULIE (*in the doorway to someone outside*): I'll be right back! You go ahead for now! (*JEAN sneaks the bottle back into the table drawer and gets up respectfully. MISS JULIE enters and crosses to KRISTINE by the stove.*) Well? Is it ready? (*KRISTINE indicates that JEAN is present.*)

JEAN (*gallantly*): Are you ladies up to something secret?

JULIE (*flicking her handerkchief in his face*): None of your business!

JEAN: Hmm! I like the smell of violets!

JULIE (*coquettishly*): Shame on you! So you know about perfumes, too? You certainly know how to dance. Ah, ah! No peeking! Go away.

JEAN (*boldly but respectfully*): Are you brewing up a magic potion for midsummer eve? Something to prophecy by under a lucky star, so you'll catch a glimpse of your future husband!

JULIE (*caustically*): You'd need sharp eyes to see him! *to* KRISTINE) Pour out half a bottle and cork it well. —— Come and dance a schottische with me, Jean . . .

JEAN (*hesitating*): I don't want to be impolite to anyone, and I've already promised this dance to Kristine . . .

JULIE: Oh, she can have another one—can't you Kristine? Won't you lend me Jean?

KRISTINE: It's not up to me, ma'am. (*to* JEAN) If the mistress is so generous, it wouldn't do for you to say no. Go on, Jean, and thank her for the honor.

JEAN: To be honest, and no offense intended, I wonder whether it's wise for you to dance twice running with the same partner, especially since these people are quick to jump to conclusions . . .

JULIE (*flaring up*): What's that? What sort of conclusions? What do you mean?

JEAN (*submissively*): If you don't understand, ma'am, I must speak more plainly. It doesn't look good to play favorites with your servants. . . .

JULIE: Play favorites! What an idea! I'm astonished! As mistress of the house, I honor your dance with my presence. And when I dance, I want to dance with someone who can lead, so I won't look ridiculous.

JEAN: As you order, ma'am! I'm at your service!

JULIE (*gently*): Don't take it as an order! On a night like this we're all just ordinary people having fun, so we'll forget about rank. Now, take my arm! —— Don't worry, Kristine! I won't steal your sweetheart! (JEAN *offers his arm and leads* MISS JULIE *out.*)

Mime

[The following should be played as if the actress playing KRISTINE *were really alone. When she has to, she turns her back to the audience. She does not look toward them, nor does she hurry as if she were afraid they would grow impatient. Schottische music played on a fiddle sounds in the distance.* KRISTINE *hums along with the music. She clears the table, washes the dishes, dries them, and puts them away. She takes off her apron. From a table drawer she removes a small mirror and leans it against the bowl of lilacs on the table. She lights a candle, heats a hairpin over the flame, and uses it to set a curl on her forehead. She crosses to the door and listens, then returns to the table. She finds the handkerchief* MISS JULIE *left behind, picks it up, and smells it. Then, preoccupied, she spreads it out, stretches it, smoothes out the wrinkles, and folds it into quarters, and so forth.]*

JEAN (*enters alone*): God, she really *is* crazy! What a way to dance! Everybody's laughing at her behind her back. What do you make of it, Kristine?

KRISTINE: Ah! It's that time of the month for her, and she always gets peculiar like that. Are you going to dance with me now?

JEAN: You're not mad at me, are you, for leaving . . .?

KRISTINE: Of course not! —— Why should I be, for a little thing like that? Besides, I know my place . . .

JEAN (*puts his arm around her waist*): You're a sensible girl, Kristine, and you'd make a good wife . . .

JULIE (*entering; uncomfortably surprised; with forced good humor*): What a charming escort—running away from his partner.

JEAN: On the contrary, Miss Julie. Don't you see how I rushed back to the partner I abandoned!

JULIE (*changing her tone*): You know, you're a superb dancer! ——But why are you wearing livery on a holiday? Take it off at once!

JEAN: Then I must ask you to go outside for a moment. You see, my black coat is hanging over here . . . (*gestures and crosses right*)

JULIE: Are you embarrassed about changing your coat in front of me? Well, go in your room then. Either that or stay and I'll turn my back.

JEAN: With your permission, ma'am! (*He crosses right. His arm is visible as he changes his jacket.*)

JULIE (*to* KRISTINE): Tell me, Kristine—you two are so

close——. Is Jean your fiancé?

KRISTINE: Fiancé? Yes, if you wish. We can call him that.

JULIE: What do you mean?

KRISTINE: You had a fiancé yourself, didn't you? So . . .

JULIE: Well, we were properly engaged . . .

KRISTINE: But nothing came of it, did it? (JEAN *returns dressed in a frock coat and bowler hat.*)

JULIE: *Très gentil, monsieur Jean! Très gentil!*

JEAN: *Vous voulez plaisanter, madame!*

JULIE: *Et vous voulez parler français!* Where did you learn that?

JEAN: In Switzerland, when I was wine steward in one of the biggest hotels in Lucerne!

JULIE: You look like a real gentleman in that coat! *Charmant!* (*sits at the table*)

JEAN: Oh, you're flattering me!

JULIE (*offended*): Flattering you?

JEAN: My natural modesty forbids me to believe that you would really compliment someone like me, and so I took the liberty of assuming that you were exaggerating, which polite people call flattering.

JULIE: Where did you learn to talk like that? You must have been to the theatre often.

JEAN: Of course. And I've done a lot of traveling.

JULIE: But you come from here, don't you?

JEAN: My father was a farm hand on the district attorney's estate nearby. I used to see you when you were little, but you never noticed me.

JULIE: No! Really?

JEAN: Sure. I remember one time especially . . . but I can't talk about that.

JULIE: Oh, come now! Why not? Just this once!

JEAN: No, I really couldn't, not now. Some other time, perhaps.

JULIE: Why some other time? What's so dangerous about now?

JEAN: It's not dangerous, but there are obstacles. —— Her, for example. (*indicating* KRISTINE, *who has fallen asleep in a chair by the stove*)

JULIE: What a pleasant wife she'll make! She probably snores, too.

JEAN: No, she doesn't, but she talks in her sleep.

JULIE (*cynically*): How do *you* know?

JEAN (*audaciously*): I've heard her! (*pause, during which they stare at each other*)

JULIE: Why don't you sit down?

JEAN: I couldn't do that in your presence.

JULIE: But if I order you to?

JEAN: Then I'd obey.

JULIE: Sit down, then. ——No , wait. Can you get me something to drink first?

JEAN: I don't know what we have in the ice box. I think there's only beer.

JULIE: Why do you say "only"? My tastes are so

simple I prefer beer to wine. (JEAN *takes a bottle of beer from the ice box and opens it. He looks for a glass and a plate in the cupboard and serves her.*)

JEAN: Here you are, ma'am.

JULIE: Thank you. Won't you have something yourself?

JEAN: I'm not partial to beer, but if it's an order . . .

JULIE: An order? ——Surely a gentleman can keep his lady company.

JEAN: You're right, of course. (*opens a bottle and gets a glass*)

JULIE: Now, drink to my health! (*He hesitates.*) What? A man of the world—and shy?

JEAN (*In mock romantic fashion, he kneels and raises his glass.*): Skål to my mistress!

JULIE: Bravo! ——Now kiss my shoe, to finish it properly. (JEAN *hesitates, then boldly seizes her foot and kisses it lightly.*) Perfect! You should have been an actor.

JEAN (*rising*): That's enough now, Miss Julie! Someone might come in and see us.

JULIE: What of it?

JEAN: People talk, that's what! If you knew how their tongues were wagging just now at the dance, you'd . . .

JULIE: What were they saying? Tell me! —— Sit down!

JEAN (*sits*): I don't want hurt you, but they were saying things ——suggestive things, that, that . . . well, you can figure it out for yourself! You're not a child. If a woman is seen drinking alone with a man—let alone a servant—at night—then . . .

JULIE: Then what? Besides, we're not alone. Kristine is here.

JEAN: Asleep!

JULIE: Then I'll wake her up. (*rising*) Kristine! Are you asleep? (KRISTINE *mumbles in her sleep.*)

JULIE: Kristine! ——She certainly can sleep!

KRISTINE (*in her sleep*): The Count's boots are brushed—put the coffee on—right away, right away—uh, huh—oh!

JULIE (*grabbing* KRISTINE's *nose*): Will you wake up!

JEAN (*severely*): Leave her alone—let her sleep!

JULIE (*sharply*): What?

JEAN: Someone who's been standing over a stove all day has a right to be tired by now. Sleep should be respected . . .

JULIE (*changing her tone*): What a considerate thought—it does you credit—thank you! (*offering her hand*) Come outside and pick some lilacs for me! (*During the following,* KRISTINE *awakens and shambles sleepily off right to bed.*)

JEAN: Go with you?

JULIE: With me!

JEAN: We couldn't do that! Absolutely not!

JULIE: I don't understand. Surely you don't imagine . . .

JEAN: No, I don't, but the others might.

JULIE: What? That I've fallen in love with a servant?

JEAN: I'm not a conceited man, but such things happen—and for these people, nothing is sacred.

JULIE: I do believe you're an aristocrat!

JEAN: Yes, I am.

JULIE: And I'm stepping down . . .

JEAN: Don't step down, Miss Julie, take my advice. No one'll believe you stepped down voluntarily. People will always say you fell.

JULIE: I have a higher opinion of people than you. Come and see! ——Come! (*She stares at him broodingly.*)

JEAN: You're very strange, do you know that?

JULIE: Perhaps! But so are you! ——For that matter, everything is strange. Life, people, everything. Like floating scum, drifting on and on across the water, until it sinks down and down! That reminds me of a dream I have now and then. I've climbed up on top of a pillar. I sit there and see no way of getting down. I get dizzy when I look down, and I must get down, but I don't have the courage to jump. I can't hold on firmly, and I long to be able to fall, but I don't fall. And yet I'll have no peace until I get down, no rest unless I get down, down on the ground! And if I did get down to the ground, I'd want to be under the earth . . . Have you ever felt anything like that?

JEAN: No. I dream that I'm lying under a high tree in a dark forest. I want to get up, up on top, and look out over the bright landscape, where the sun is shining, and plunder the bird's nest up there, where the golden eggs lie. And I climb and climb, but the trunk's so thick and smooth, and it's so far to the first branch. But I know if I just reached that first branch, I'd go right to the top, like up a ladder. I haven't reached it yet, but I will, even if it's only in a dream!

JULIE: Here I am chattering with you about dreams. Come, let's go out! Just into the park! (*She offers him her arm, and they start to leave.*)

JEAN: We'll have to sleep on nine midsummer flowers, Miss Julie, to make our dreams come true! (*They turn at the door.* JEAN *puts his hand to his eye.*)

JULIE: Did you get something in your eye?

JEAN: It's nothing—just a speck—it'll be gone in a minute.

JULIE: My sleeve must have brushed against you. Sit down and let me help you. (*She takes him by the arm and seats him. She tilts his head back and with the tip of a handkerchief tries to remove the speck.*) Sit still, absolutely still! (*She slaps his hand.*) Didn't you hear me? —— Why, you're trembling; the big, strong man is trembling! (*feels his biceps*) What muscles you have!

JEAN (*warning*): Miss Julie!

JULIE: Yes, *monsieur* Jean.

JEAN: *Attention! Je ne suis qu'un homme!*

JULIE: Will you sit still! —— There! Now it's gone! Kiss my hand and thank me.

JEAN (*rising*): Miss Julie, listen to me! —— Kristine has gone to bed! —— Will you listen to me!

JULIE: Kiss my hand first!

JEAN: Listen to me!

JULIE: Kiss my hand first!

JEAN: All right, but you've only yourself to blame!

JULIE: For what?

JEAN: For what? Are you still a child at twenty-five? Don't you know that's it's dangerous to play with fire?

JULIE: Not for me. I'm insured.

JEAN (*boldly*): No, you're not! But even if you were, there's combustible material close by.

JULIE: Meaning you?

JEAN: Yes! Not because it's me, but because I'm young ——

JULIE: And handsome—what incredible conceit! A Don Juan perhaps! Or a Joseph! Yes, that's it, I do believe you're a Joseph!

JEAN: Do you?

JULIE: I'm almost afraid so. (JEAN *boldly tries to put his arm around her waist and kiss her. She slaps his face.*) How dare you?

JEAN: Are you serious or joking?

JULIE: Serious.

JEAN: Then so was what just happened. You play games too seriously, and that's dangerous. Well, I'm tired of games. You'll excuse me if I get back to work. I haven't done the Count's boots yet and it's long past midnight.

JULIE: Put the boots down!

JEAN: No! It's the work I have to do. I never agreed to be your playmate, and never will. It's beneath me.

JULIE: You're proud.

JEAN: In certain ways, but not in others.

JULIE: Have you ever been in love?

JEAN: We don't use that word, but I've been fond of many girls, and once I was sick because I couldn't have the one I wanted. That's right, sick, like those princes in the Arabian Nights—who couldn't eat or drink because of love.

JULIE: Who was she? (JEAN *is silent.*) Who was she?

JEAN: You can't force me to tell you that.

JULIE: But if I ask you as an equal, as a—friend! Who was she?

JEAN: You!

JULIE (*sits*): How amusing . . .

JEAN: Yes, if you like! It was ridiculous! —— You see, that was the story I didn't want to tell you earlier. Maybe I will now. Do you know how the world looks from down below? —— Of course you don't. Neither do hawks and falcons, whose backs we can't see because they're usually soaring up there above us. I grew up in a shack with seven brothers and sisters and a pig, in the middle of a wasteland, where there wasn't a single tree. But from our window I could see the tops of apple trees above the wall of your father's garden. That was the Garden of Eden, guarded by angry angels with flaming swords. All the same, the other boys and I managed to find our way to the Tree of Life. —— Now you think I'm contemptible, I suppose.

JULIE: Oh, all boys steal apples.

JEAN: You say that, but you think I'm contemptible anyway. Oh well! One day I went into the Garden of Eden with my mother, to weed the onion beds. Near the vegetable garden was a small Turkish pavilion in the shadow of jasmine bushes and overgrown with honeysuckle. I had no idea what it was used for, but I'd never seen such a beautiful building. People went in and came out again, and one day the door was left open. I sneaked close and saw walls covered with pictures of kings and emperors, and red curtains with fringes at the windows—now you know the place I mean. I —— (*breaks off a sprig of lilac and holds it in front of* MISS JULIE's *nose*) —— I'd never been inside the manor house, never seen anything except the church—but this was more beautiful. From then on, no matter where my thoughts wandered, they returned—there. And gradually I got a longing to experience, just once, the full pleasure of—*enfin*, I sneaked in, saw, and marveled! But then I heard someone coming! There was only one exit for ladies and gentlemen, but for me there was another, and I had no choice but to take it! (MISS JULIE, *who has taken the lilac sprig, lets it fall on the table.*) Afterwards, I started running. I crashed through a raspberry bush, flew over a strawberry patch, and came up onto the rose terrace. There I caught sight of a pink dress and a pair of white stockings—it was you. I crawled under a pile of weeds, and I mean under—under thistles that pricked me and wet dirt that stank. And I looked at you as you walked among the roses, and I thought: if it's true that a thief can enter heaven and be with the angels, then why can't a farmhand's son here on God's earth enter the manor house garden and play with the Count's daughter?

JULIE (*romantically*): Do you think all poor children would have thought the way you did?

JEAN (*at first hesitant, then with conviction*): If *all* poor—yes—of course. Of course!

JULIE: It must be terrible to be poor!

JEAN (*with exaggerated suffering*): Oh, Miss Julie! Oh!

—— A dog can lie on the Countess's sofa, a horse can have his nose patted by a young lady's hand, but a servant —— (*changing his tone*) —— oh, I know—now and then you find one with enough stuff in him to get ahead in the world, but how often? —— Anyhow, do you know what I did then? —— I jumped in the millstream with my clothes on, was pulled out, and got a beating. But the following Sunday, when my father and all the others went to my grandmother's, I arranged to stay home. I scrubbed myself with soap and water, put on my best clothes, and went to church so that I could see you! I saw you and returned home, determined to die. But I wanted to die beautifully, and pleasantly, without pain. And then I remembered that it was dangerous to sleep under an elder bush. We had a big one, and it was in full flower. I plundered its treasures and bedded down under them in the oat bin. Have you ever noticed how smooth oats are? —and soft to the touch, like human skin . . . ! Well, I shut the lid and closed my eyes. I fell asleep and woke up feeling very sick. But I didn't die, as you can see. What was I after? —— I don't know. There was no hope of winning you, of course. —— You were a symbol of the hopelessness of ever rising out of the class in which I was born.

JULIE: You're a charming storyteller. Did you ever go to school?

JEAN: A bit, but I've read lots of novels and been to the theatre often. And then I've listened to people like you talk—that's where I learned most.

JULIE: Do you listen to what we say?

JEAN: Naturally! And I've heard plenty, too, driving the carriage or rowing the boat. Once I heard you and a friend . . .

JULIE: Oh? —— What did you hear?

JEAN: I'd better not say. But I was surprised a little. I couldn't imagine where you learned such words. Maybe at bottom there isn't such a great difference between people as we think.

JULIE: Shame on you! We don't act like you when we're engaged.

JEAN (*staring at her*): Is that true? —— You don't have to play innocent with me, Miss . . .

JULIE: The man I gave my love to was a swine.

JEAN: That's what you all say—afterwards.

JULIE: All?

JEAN: I think so. I know I've heard that phrase before, on similar occasions.

JULIE: What occasions?

JEAN: Like the one I'm talking about. The last time . . .

JULIE (*rising*): Quiet! I don't want to hear any more!

JEAN: That's interesting—that's what *she* said, too. Well, if you'll excuse me, I'm going to bed.

JULIE (*gently*): To bed? On midsummer eve?

JEAN: Yes! Dancing with the rabble out there doesn't amuse me much.

JULIE: Get the key to the boat and row me out on the lake. I want to see the sun come up.

JEAN: Is that wise?

JULIE: Are you worried about your reputation?

JEAN: Why not? Why should I risk looking ridiculous and getting fired without a reference, just when I'm trying to establish myself. Besides, I think I owe something to Kristine.

JULIE: So, now it's Kristine . . .

JEAN: Yes, but you, too. —— Take my advice, go up and go to bed!

JULIE: Am I to obey you?

JEAN: Just this once—for your own good! Please! It's very late. Drowsiness makes people giddy and liable to lose their heads! Go to bed! Besides—unless I'm mistaken—I hear the others coming to look for me. And if they find us together, you'll be lost!

[*The* CHORUS *approaches, singing:*]

> The swineherd found his true love
> a pretty girl so fair,
> The swineherd found his true love
> but let the girl beware.
>
> For then he saw the princess
> the princess on the golden hill,
> but then saw the princess,
> so much fairer still.
>
> So the swineherd and the princess
> they danced the whole night through,
> and he forgot his first love,
> to her he was untrue.
>
> And when the long night ended,
> and in the light of day, of day,
> the dancing too was ended,
> and the princess could not stay.
>
> Then the swineherd lost his true love,
> and the princess grieves him still,
> and never more she'll wander
> from atop the golden hill.

JULIE: I know all these people and I love them, just as they love me. Let them come in and you'll see.

JEAN: No, Miss Julie, they don't love you. They take your food, but they spit on it! Believe me! Listen to them, listen to what they're singing! —— No, don't listen to them!

JULIE (*listening*): What are they singing?

JEAN: It's a dirty song! About you and me!

JULIE: Disgusting! Oh! How deceitful! ——

JEAN: The rabble is always cowardly! And in a battle like this, you don't fight; you can only run away!

JULIE: Run away? But where? We can't go out—or into Kristine's room.

JEAN: True. But there's my room. Necessity knows no rules. Besides, you can trust me. I'm your friend and I respect you.

JULIE: But suppose—suppose they look for you in there?

JEAN: I'll bolt the door, and if anyone tries to break in, I'll shoot! —— Come! (*on his knees*) Come!

JULIE (*urgently*): Promise me . . .?

JEAN: I swear! (MISS JULIE *runs off right.* JEAN *hastens after her.*)

Ballet

[*Led by a fiddler, the servants and farm people enter, dressed festively, with flowers in their hats. On the table they place a small barrel of beer and a keg of schnapps, both garlanded. Glasses are brought out, and the drinking starts. A dance circle is formed and "The Swineherd and the Princess" is sung. When the dance is finished, everyone leaves, singing.*]

[MISS JULIE *enters alone. She notices the mess in the kitchen, wrings her hands, then takes out her powder puff and powders her nose.*]

JEAN (*enters, agitated*): There, you see? And you heard them. We can't possibly stay here now, you know that.

JULIE: Yes, I know. But what can we do?

JEAN: Leave, travel, far away from here.

JULIE: Travel? Yes, but where?

JEAN: To Switzerland, to the Italian lakes. Have you ever been there?

JULIE: No. Is it beautiful?

JEAN: Oh, an eternal summer—oranges growing everywhere, laurel trees, always green . . .

JULIE: But what'll we do there?

JEAN: I'll open a hotel—with first-class service for first-class people.

JULIE: Hotel?

JEAN: That's the life, you know. Always new faces, new languages. No time to worry or be nervous. No hunting for something to do—there's always work to be done: bells ringing night and day, train whistles blowing, carriages coming and going, and all the while gold rolling into the till! That's the life!

JULIE: Yes, it sounds wonderful. But what'll I do?

JEAN: You'll be mistress of the house: the jewel in our crown! With your looks . . . and your manner— oh—success is guaranteed! It'll be wonderful! You'll sit in your office like a queen and push an electric button to set your slaves in motion. The guests will file past your throne and timidly lay their treasures before you. ——You have no idea how people tremble when they get their bill. —— I'll salt the bills and you'll sweeten them with your prettiest smile. ——Let's get away from here —— (*takes a timetable out of his pocket*) —— Right away, on the next train! —— We'll be in Malmö six-thirty tomorrow morning, Hamburg at eight-forty; from Frankfort to Basel will take a day, then on to Como by way of the St. Gotthard Tunnel, in, let's see, three days. Three days!

JULIE: That's all very well! But Jean—you must give me courage! —— Tell me you love me! Put your arms around me!

JEAN (*hesitating*): I want to—but I don't dare. Not in this house, not again. I love you—never doubt that—you don't doubt it, do you, Miss Julie?

JULIE (*shy; very feminine*): "Miss!" —— Call me Julie! There are no barriers between us any more. Call me Julie!

JEAN (*tormented*): I can't! There'll always be barriers between us as long as we stay in this house. —— There's the past and there's the Count. I've never met anyone I had such respect for. —— When I see his gloves lying on a chair, I feel small. —— When I hear that bell up there ring, I jump like a skittish horse. —— And when I look at his boots standing there so stiff and proud, I feel like bowing! (*kicking the boots*) Superstitions and prejudices we learned as children—but they can easily be forgotten. If I can just get to another country, a republic, people will bow and scrape when they see my livery—*they'll* bow and scrape, you hear, not me! I wasn't born to cringe. I've got stuff in me, I've got character, and if I can only grab onto that first branch, you watch me climb! I'm a servant today, but next year I'll own my own hotel. In ten years I'll have enough to retire. Then I'll go to Rumania and be decorated. I could—mind you I said *could*—end up a count!

JULIE: Wonderful, wonderful!

JEAN: Ah, in Rumania you just buy your title, and so you'll be a countess after all. My countess!

JULIE: But I don't care about that—that's what I'm putting behind me! Show me you love me, other-wise—otherwise, what am I?

JEAN: I'll show you a thousand times—afterwards! Not here! And whatever you do, no emotional outbursts, or we'll both be lost! We must think this through coolly, like sensible people. (*He takes out a cigar, snips the end, and lights it.*) You sit there, and I'll sit here. We'll talk as if nothing happened.

JULIE (*desperately*): Oh, my God! Have you no

feelings?

JEAN: Me? No one has more feelings than I do, but I know how to control them.

JULIE: A little while ago you could kiss my shoe—and now!

JEAN (*harshly*): Yes, but that was before. Now we have other things to think about.

JULIE: Don't speak harshly to me!

JEAN: I'm not—just sensibly! We've already done one foolish thing, let's not have any more. The Count could return any minute, and by then we've got to decide what to do with our lives. What do you think of my plans for the future? Do you approve?

JULIE: They sound reasonable enough. I have only one question: for such a big undertaking you need capital—do you have it?

JEAN (*chewing on the cigar*): Me? Certainly! I have my professional expertise, my wide experience, and my knowledge of languages. That's capital enough, I should think!

JULIE: But all that won't even buy a train ticket.

JEAN: That's true. That's why I'm looking for a partner to advance me the money.

JULIE: Where will you find one quickly enough?

JEAN: That's up to you, if you want to come with me.

JULIE: But I can't; I have no money of my own. (*pause*)

JEAN: Then it's all off . . .

JULIE: And . . .

JEAN: Things stay as they are.

JULIE: Do you think I'm going to stay in this house as your lover? With all the servants pointing their fingers at me? Do you imagine I can face my father after this? No! Take me away from here, away from shame and dishonor —— Oh, what have I done! My God, my God! (*She cries.*)

JEAN: Now, don't start that old song! —— What have you done? The same as many others before you.

JULIE (*screaming convulsively*): And now you think I'm contemptible! ——I'm falling, I'm falling!

JEAN: Fall down to my level and I'll lift you up again.

JULIE: What terrible power drew me to you? The attraction of the weak to the strong? The falling to the rising? Or was it love? Was this love? Do you know what love is?

JEAN: Me? What do you take me for? You don't think this was my first time, do you?

JULIE: The things you say, the thoughts you think!

JEAN: That's the way I was taught, and that's the way I am! Now don't get excited and don't play the grand lady, because we're in the same boat now! —— Come on, Julie, I'll pour you a glass of something special! (*He opens a drawer in the table, takes out a wine bottle, and fills two glasses already used.*)

JULIE: Where did you get that wine?

JEAN: From the cellar.

JULIE: My father's burgundy!

JEAN: That'll do for his son-in-law, won't it?

JULIE: And I drink beer! Beer!

JEAN: That only shows I have better taste.

JULIE: Thief!

JEAN: Planning to tell?

JULIE: Oh, oh! Accomplice of a common thief! Was I drunk? Have I been walking in a dream the whole evening? Midsummer eve! A time of innocent fun!

JEAN: Innocent, eh?

JULIE (*pacing back and forth*): Is there anyone on earth more miserable than I am at this moment?

JEAN: Why should you be? After such a conquest? Think of Kristine in there. Don't you think she has feelings, too?

JULIE: I thought so awhile ago, but not any more. No, a servant is a servant . . .

JEAN: And a whore is a whore!

JULIE (*on her knees, her hands clasped*): Oh, God in Heaven, end my wretched life! Take me away from the filth I'm sinking into! Save me! Save me!

JEAN: I can't deny I feel sorry for you. When I lay in that onion bed and saw you in the rose garden, well . . . I'll be frank . . . I had the same dirty thoughts all boys have.

JULIE: And you wanted to die for me!

JEAN: In the oat bin? That was just talk.

JULIE: A lie, in other words!

JEAN (*beginning to feel sleepy*): More or less! I got the idea from a newspaper story about a chimney sweep who curled up in a firewood bin full of lilacs because he got a summons for not supporting his illegitimate child . . .

JULIE: So, that's what you're like . . .

JEAN: I had to think of something. And that's the kind of story women always go for.

JULIE: Swine!

JEAN: *Merde!*

JULIE: And now you've seen the hawk's back . . .

JEAN: Not exactly its *back* . . .

JULIE: And I was to be the first branch . . .

JEAN: But the branch was rotten . . .

JULIE: I was to be the sign on the hotel . . .

JEAN: And I the hotel . . .

JULIE: Sit at your desk, entice your customers, pad their bills . . .

JEAN: That I'd do myself . . .

JULIE: How can anyone be so thoroughly filthy?

JEAN: Better clean up then!

JULIE: You lackey, you menial, stand up, when I speak to you!

JEAN: Menial's strumpet, lackey's whore, shut up and get out of here! Who are you to lecture me on coarseness? None of my kind is ever as coarse as you were tonight. Do you think one of your maids would throw herself at a man the way you did? Have you ever seen any girl of my class offer herself like that? I've only seen it among animals and streetwalkers.

JULIE (*crushed*): You're right. Hit me, trample on me. I don't deserve any better. I'm worthless. But help me! If you see any way out of this, help me, Jean, please!

JEAN (*more gently*): I'd be lying if I didn't admit to a sense of triumph in all this, but do you think that a person like me would have dared even to look at someone like you if you hadn't invited it? I'm still amazed . . .

JULIE: And proud . . .

JEAN: Why not? Though I must say it was too easy to be really exciting.

JULIE: Go on, hit me, hit me harder!

JEAN (*rising*): No! Forgive me for what I've said! I don't hit a man when he's down, let alone a woman. I can't deny though, that I'm pleased to find out that what looked so dazzling to us from below was only tinsel, that the hawk's back was only gray, after all, that the lovely complexion was only powder, that those polished fingernails had black edges, and that a dirty handkerchief is still dirty, even if it smells of perfume . . .! On the other hand, it hurts me to find out that what I was striving for wasn't finer, more substantial. It hurts me to see you sunk so low that you're inferior to your own cook. It hurts like watching flowers beaten down by autumn rains and turned into mud.

JULIE: You talk as if you were already above me.

JEAN: I am. You see, I could make you a countess, but you could never make me a count.

JULIE: But I'm the child of a count—something you could never be!

JEAN: That's true. But I could be the father of counts—if . . .

JULIE: But you're a thief. I'm not.

JEAN: There are worse things than being a thief! Besides, when I'm working in a house, I consider myself sort of a member of the family, like one of the children. And you don't call it stealing when a child snatches a berry off a full bush. (*His passion is aroused again.*) Miss Julie, you're a glorious woman, much too good for someone like me! You were drinking and you lost your head. Now you want to cover up your mistake by telling yourself that you love me! You don't. Maybe there was a physical attraction—but then your love is no better than mine. —— I could never be satisfied to be no more than an animal to you, and I could never arouse real love in you.

JULIE: Are you sure of that?

JEAN: You're suggesting it's possible —— Oh, I could fall in love with you, no doubt about it. You're beautiful, you're refined —— (*approaching and taking her hand*) —— cultured, lovable when you want to be, and once you start a fire in a man, it never goes out. (*putting his arm around her waist*) You're like hot, spicy wine, and one kiss from you . . . (*He tries to lead her out, but she slowly frees herself.*)

JULIE: Let me go!? —— You'll never win me like that.

JEAN: *How* then? —— Not like that? Not with caresses and pretty speeches. Not with plans about the future or rescue from disgrace! *How* then?

JULIE: How? How? I don't know! —— I have no idea! —— I detest you as I detest rats, but I can't escape from you.

JEAN: Escape with me!

JULIE (*pulling herself together*): Escape? Yes, we must escape! —— But I'm so tired. Give me a glass of wine? (JEAN *pours the wine. She looks at her watch.*) But we must talk first. We still have a little time. (*She drains the glass, then holds it out for more.*)

JEAN: Don't drink so fast. It'll go to your head.

JULIE: What does it matter?

JEAN: What does it matter? It's vulgar to get drunk! What did you want to tell me?

JULIE: We must escape! But first we must talk, I mean I must talk. You've done all the talking up to now. You told about your life, now I want to tell about mine, so we'll know all about each other before we go off together.

JEAN: Just a minute! Forgive me! If you don't want to regret it afterwards, you'd better think twice before revealing any secrets about yourself.

JULIE: Aren't you my friend?

JEAN: Yes, sometimes! But don't rely on me.

JULIE: You're only saying that. —— Besides, everyone already knows my secrets. —— You see, my mother was a commoner—very humble background. She was brought up believing in social equality, women's rights, and all that. The idea of marriage repelled her. So, when my father proposed, she replied that she would never become his wife, but he could be her lover. He insisted that he didn't want the woman he loved to be less respected than he. But his passion ruled him, and when she explained that the world's respect meant nothing to her, he accepted her conditions.

But now his friends avoided him and his wife was restricted to taking care of the estate, which couldn't satisfy him. I came into the world—against my mother's wishes, as far as I can understand. She wanted to bring me up as a child of nature, and, what's more, to learn everything a boy had to learn, so that I might be an example of how a woman can be as good as a man. I had to wear boy's clothes and learn to take care of horses, but I was never allowed in the cowshed. I had to groom and harness the horses and go hunting—and even had to watch them slaughter animals—that was disgusting! On the estate men were put on women's jobs and women on men's jobs—with the result that the property became run down and we became the laughing stock of the district. Finally, my father must have awakened from his trance because he rebelled and changed everything his way. My parents were then married quietly. Mother became ill—I don't know what illness it was—but she often had convulsions, hid in the attic and in the garden, and sometimes stayed out all night. Then came the great fire, which you've heard about. The house, the stables, and the cowshed all burned down, under very curious circumstances, suggesting arson, because the accident happened the day after the insurance had expired. The quarterly premium my father sent in was delayed because of a messenger's carelessness and didn't arrive in time. (*She fills her glass and drinks.*)

JEAN: Don't drink any more!

JULIE: Oh, what does it matter. —— We were left penniless and had to sleep in the carriages. My father had no idea where to find money to rebuild the house because he had so slighted his old friends that they had forgotten him. Then my mother suggested that he borrow from a childhood friend of hers, a brick manufacturer who lived nearby. Father got the loan without having to pay interest, which surprised him. And that's how the estate was rebuilt. —— (*drinks again*) Do you know who started the fire?

JEAN: The Countess, your mother.

JULIE: Do you know who the brick manufacturer was?

JEAN: Your mother's lover?

JULIE: Do you know whose money it was?

JEAN: Wait a moment—no, I don't.

JULIE: It was my mother's.

JEAN: You mean the Count's, unless they didn't sign an agreement when they were married.

JULIE: They didn't. —— My mother had a small inheritance which she didn't want under my father's control, so she entrusted it to her—friend.

JEAN: Who stole it!

JULIE: Exactly! He kept it. —— All this my father found out, but he couldn't bring it to court, couldn't repay his wife's lover, couldn't prove it was his wife's money! It was my mother's revenge for being forced into marriage against her will. It nearly drove him to suicide—there was a rumor that he tried with a pistol, but failed. So, he managed to live through it and my mother

had to suffer for what she'd done. You can imagine that those were a terrible five years for me. I loved my father, but I sided with my mother because I didn't know the circumstances. I learned from her to hate men—you've heard how she hated the whole male sex—and I swore to her I'd never be a slave to any man.

JEAN: But you got engaged to that lawyer.

JULIE: In order to make him my slave.

JEAN: And he wasn't willing?

JULIE: He was willing, all right, but I wouldn't let him. I got tired of him.

JEAN: I saw it—out near the stable.

JULIE: What did you see?

JEAN: I saw—how he broke off the engagement.

JULIE: That's a lie! I was the one who broke it off. Has he said that he did? That swine . . .

JEAN: He was no swine, I'm sure. So, you hate men, Miss Julie?

JULIE: Yes! —— Most of the time! But sometimes—when the weakness comes, when passion burns! Oh, God, will the fire never die out?

JEAN: Do you hate me, too?

JULIE: Immeasurably! I'd like to have you put to death, like an animal . . .

JEAN: I see—the penalty for bestiality—the woman gets two years at hard labor and the animal is put to death. Right?

JULIE: Exactly!

JEAN: But there's no prosecutor here—and no animal. So, what'll we do?

JULIE: Go away!

JEAN: To torment each other to death?

JULIE: No! To be happy for—two days, a week, as long as we can be happy, and then—die . . .

JEAN: Die? That's stupid! It's better to open a hotel!

JULIE (*without listening*): —— on the shore of Lake Como, where the sun always shines, where the laurels are green at Christmas and the oranges glow.

JEAN: Lake Como is a rainy hole, and I never saw any oranges outside the stores. But tourists are attracted there because there are plenty of villas to be rented out to lovers, and that's a profitable business. —— Do you know why? Because they sign a lease for six months—and then leave after three weeks?

JULIE (*naively*): Why after three weeks?

JEAN: They quarrel, of course! But they still have to pay the rent in full! And so you rent the villas out again. And that's the way it goes, time after time. There's never a shortage of love—even if it doesn't last long!

JULIE: You don't want to die with me?

JEAN: I don't want to die at all! For one thing, I like living, and for another, I think suicide is a crime against the Providence which gave us life.

JULIE: You believe in God? *You?*

JEAN: Of course I do. And I go to church every other Sunday. —— To be honest, I'm tired of all this, and I'm going to bed.

JULIE: Are you? And do you think I can let it go at that? A man owes something to the woman he's shamed.

JEAN (*taking out his purse and throwing a silver coin on the table*): Here! I don't like owing anything to anybody.

JULIE (*pretending not to notice the insult*): Do you know what the law states . . .

JEAN: Unfortunately the law doesn't state any punishment for the woman who seduces a man!

JULIE (*as before*): Do you see any way out but to leave, get married, and then separate?

JEAN: Suppose I refuse such a *mésalliance*?

JULIE: *Mésalliance* . . .

JEAN: Yes, for me! You see, I come from better stock than you. There's no arsonist in my family.

JULIE: How do you know?

JEAN: You can't prove otherwise. We don't keep charts on our ancestors—there's just the police records! But I've read about your family. Do you know who the founder was? He was a miller who let the king sleep with his wife one night during the Danish War. I don't have any noble ancestors like that. I don't have any noble ancestors at all, but I could become one myself.

JULIE: This is what I get for opening my heart to someone unworthy, for giving my family's honor . . .

JEAN: Dishonor! —— Well, I told you so: when people drink, they talk, and talk is dangerous!

JULIE: Oh, how I regret it! —— How I regret it! —— If you at least loved me.

JEAN: For the last time—what do you want? Shall I cry; shall I jump over your riding crop? Shall I kiss you and lure you off to Lake Como for three weeks, and then God knows what . . . ? What shall I do? What do you want? This is getting painfully embarrassing! But that's what happens when you stick your nose in women's business. Miss Julie! I see that you're unhappy. I know you're suffering, but I can't understand you. We don't have such romantic ideas; there's not this kind of hate between us. Love is a game we play when we get time off from work, but we don't have all day and night, like you. I think you're sick, really sick. Your mother was crazy, and her ideas have poisoned your life.

JULIE: Be kind to me. At least now you're talking like a human being.

JEAN: Be human yourself, then. You spit on me, and you won't let me wipe myself off ——

JULIE: Help me! Help Me! Just tell me what to do, where to go!

JEAN: In God's name, if I only knew myself!

JULIE: I've been crazy, out of my mind, but isn't there any way out?

JEAN: Stay here and keep calm! No one knows anything!

JULIE: Impossible! The others know and Kristine knows.

JEAN: No they don't, and they'd never believe a thing like that!

JULIE (*hesitantly*): But—it could happen again!

JEAN: That's true!

JULIE: And then?

JEAN (*frightened*): Then? —— Why didn't I think about that? Yes, there is only one thing to do—get away from here! Right away! I can't come with you, then we'd be finished, so you'll have to go alone—away—anywhere!

JULIE: Alone? —— Where? —— I can't do that!

JEAN: You must! And before the Count gets back! If you stay, you know what'll happen. Once you make a mistake like this, you want to continue because the damage has already been done . . . Then you get bolder and bolder—until finally you're caught! So leave! Later you can write to the Count and confess everything—except that it was me! He'll never guess who it was, and he's not going to be eager to find out, anyway.

JULIE: I'll go if you come with me.

JEAN: Are you out of your head? Miss Julie runs away with her servant! In two days it would be in the newspapers, and that's something your father would never live through.

JULIE: I can't go and I can't stay! Help me! I'm so tired, so terribly tired. —— Order me! Set me in motion—I can't think or act on my own . . .

JEAN: What miserable creatures you people are! You strut around with your noses in the air as if you were the lords of creation! All right, I'll order you. Go upstairs and get dressed! Get some money for the trip, and then come back down!

JULIE (*in a half-whisper*): Come up with me!

JEAN: To your room? —— Now you're crazy again! (*hesitates for a moment*) No! Go, at once! (*takes her hand to lead her out*)

JULIE (*as she leaves*): Speak kindly to me, Jean!

JEAN: An order always sounds unkind—now you know how it feels. (JEAN, *alone, sighs with relief. He sits at the table, takes out a notebook and pencil, and begins adding up figures, counting aloud as he works. He continues in dumb show until* KRISTINE *enters, dressed for church. She is carrying a white tie and shirt front.*)

KRISTINE: Lord Jesus, what a mess! What have you been up to?

JEAN: Oh, Miss Julie dragged everybody in here. You mean you didn't hear anything? You must have been sleeping soundly.

KRISTINE: Like a log.

JEAN: And dressed for church already?

KRISTINE: Of course! You remember you promised to come with me to communion today!

JEAN: Oh, yes, that's right. —— And you brought my things. Come on, then! (*He sits down.* KRISTINE *starts to put on his shirt front and tie. Pause.* JEAN *begins sleepily*) What's the gospel text for today?

KRISTINE: On St. John's Day?—the beheading of John the Baptist., I should think!

JEAN: Ah, that'll be a long one, for sure. —— Hey, you're choking me! —— Oh, I'm sleepy, so sleepy!

KRISTINE: Yes, what have you been doing, up all night? Your face is absolutely green.

JEAN: I've been sitting here gabbing with Miss Julie.

KRISTINE: She has no idea what's proper, that one! (*pause*)

JEAN: You know, Kristine . . .

KRISTINE: What?

JEAN: It's really strange when you think about it. —— Her!

KRISTINE: What's so strange?

JEAN: Everything! (*pause*)

KRISTINE (*looking at the half-empty glasses standing on the table*): Have you been drinking together, too?

JEAN: Yes.

KRISTINE: Shame on you! —— Look me in the eye!

JEAN: Well?

KRISTINE: Is it possible? Is it possible?

JEAN (*thinking it over for a moment*): Yes, it is.

KRISTINE: Ugh! I never would have believed it! No, shame on you, shame!

JEAN: You're not jealous of her, are you?

KRISTINE: No, not of her! If it had been Clara or Sofie I'd have scratched your eyes out! —— I don't know why, but that's the way I feel. —— Oh, it's disgusting!

JEAN: Are you angry at her, then?

KRISTINE: No, at you! That was an awful thing to do, awful! Poor girl! —— No, I don't care who knows it—I won't stay in a house where we can't respect the people we work for.

JEAN: Why should we respect them?

KRISTINE: You're so clever, you tell me! Do you want to wait on people who can't behave decently? Do you? You disgrace yourself that way, if you ask me.

JEAN: But it's a comfort to know they aren't any better than us.

KRISTINE: Not for me. If they're no better, what do we have to strive for to better ourselves. —— And think of the Count! Think of him! As if he hasn't

had enough misery in his life! Lord Jesus! No, I won't stay in this house any longer! —— And it had to be with someone like you! If it had been that lawyer, if it had been a real gentleman . . .

JEAN: What do you mean?

KRISTINE: Oh, you're all right for what you are, but there are men and gentlemen, after all! —— No, this business with Miss Julie I can never forget. She was so proud, so arrogant with men, you wouldn't have believed she could just go and give herself—and to someone like you! And she was going to have poor Diana shot for running after the gatekeepers' mutt! —— Yes, I'm giving my notice, I mean it—I won't stay here any longer. On the twenty-fourth of October, I leave!

JEAN: And then?

KRISTINE: Well, since the subject has come up, it's about time you looked around for something since we're going to get married, in any case.

JEAN: Where am I going to look? I couldn't find a job like this if I was married.

KRISTINE: No, that's true. But you can find work as a porter or as a caretaker in some government office. The state doesn't pay much, I know, but it's secure, and there's a pension for the wife and children . . .

JEAN (*grimacing*): That's all very well, but it's a bit early for me to think about dying for a wife and children. My ambitions are a little higher than that.

KRISTINE: Your ambitions, yes! Well, you have obligations, too! Think about them!

JEAN: Don't start nagging me about obligations, I know what I have to do! (*listening for something outside*) Besides, this is something we have plenty of time to think over. Go and get ready for church.

KRISTINE: Who's that walking around up there?

JEAN: I don't know, unless it's Clara.

KRISTINE (*going*): You don't suppose it's the Count, who came home without us hearing him?

JEAN (*frightened*): The Count? No, I don't think so. He'd have rung.

KRISTINE (*going*): Well, God help us! I've never seen anything like this before. (*The sun has risen and shines through the treetops in the park. The light shifts gradually until it slants in through the windows.* JEAN *goes to the door and signals.* MISS JULIE *enters, dressed in travel clothes and carrying a small birdcage, covered with a cloth, which she places on a chair.*)

JULIE: I'm ready now.

JEAN: Shh! Kristine is awake.

JULIE (*very nervous during the following*): Does she suspect something?

JEAN: She doesn't know anything. But my God, you look awful!

JULIE: Why? How do I look?

JEAN: You're pale as a ghost and—excuse me, but your face is dirty.

JULIE: Let me wash up then. —— (*She goes to the basin and washes her hands and face.*) Give me a towel! —— Oh—the sun's coming up.

JEAN: Then the goblins will disappear.

JULIE: Yes, there must have been goblins out last night! —— Jean, listen, come with me! I have some money now.

JEAN (*hesitantly*): Enough?

JULIE: Enough to start with. Come with me! I just can't travel alone on a day like this—midsummer day on a stuffy train—jammed in among crowds of people staring at me. Eternal delays at every station, while I'd wish I had wings. No, I can't, I can't! And then there'll be memories, memories of midsummer days when I was little. The church—decorated with birch leaves and lilacs; dinner at the big table with relatives and friends; the afternoons in the park, dancing, music, flowers, and games. Oh, no matter how far we travel, the memories will follow in the baggage car, with remorse and guilt!

JEAN: I'll go with you—but right away, before it's too late. Right this minute!

JULIE: Get dressed, then! (*picking up the bird cage*)

JEAN: But no baggage! It would give us away!

JULIE: No, nothing! Only what we can have in the compartment with us.

JEAN (*has taken his hat*): What've you got there? What is it?

JULIE: It's only my greenfinch. I couldn't leave her behind.

JEAN: What? Bring a birdcage with us? You're out of your head! Put it down!

JULIE: It's the only thing I'm taking from my home—the only living being that loves me, since Diana was unfaithful. Don't be cruel! Let me take her!

JEAN: Put the cage down, I said! —— And don't talk so loudly—Kristine will hear us!

JULIE: No, I won't leave her in the hands of strangers! I'd rather you killed her.

JEAN: Bring the thing here, then, I'll cut its head off!

JULIE: Oh! But don't hurt her! Don't . . . no, I can't.

JEAN: Bring it here! I can!

JULIE (*taking the bird out of the cage and kissing it*): Oh, my little Serena, must you die and leave your mistress?

JEAN: Please don't make a scene! Your whole future is at stake! Hurry up! (*He snatches the bird from her, carries it over to the chopping block, and picks up a meat cleaver.* MISS JULIE *turns away.*) You should have learned how to slaughter chickens instead of how to fire pistols. (*He chops off the bird's head.*) Then you wouldn't feel faint at the sight of blood.

JULIE (*screaming*): Kill me, too! Kill me! You, who can slaughter an innocent animal without blinking an eye! Oh, how I hate, how I detest you! There's blood between us now! I curse the moment I set eyes on you! I curse the moment I was conceived in my mother's womb!

JEAN: What good does cursing do? Let's go!

JULIE (*approaching the chopping block, as if drawn against her will*): No, I don't want to go yet. I can't . . . until I see . . . Shh! I hear a carriage —— (*She listens, but her eyes never leave the cleaver and the chopping block.*) Do you think I can't stand the sight of blood? You think I'm so weak . . . Oh—I'd like to see your blood and your brains on a chopping block! —— I'd like to see your whole sex swimming in a sea of blood, like my little bird . . . I think I could drink from your skull! I'd like to bathe my feet in your open chest and eat your heart roasted whole! —— You think I'm weak. You think I love you because my womb craved your seed. You think I want to carry your spawn under my heart and nourish it with my blood—bear your child and take your name! By the way, what is your family name? I've never heard it. —— Do you have one? I was to be Mrs. Bootblack—or Madame Pigsty. —— You dog, who wears my collar, you lackey, who bears my coat of arms on your buttons—do I have to share you with my cook, compete with my own servant? Oh! Oh! Oh! —— You think I'm a coward who wants to run away! No, now I'm staying—and let the storm break! My father will come home . . . to find his desk broken open . . . and his money gone! Then he'll ring—that bell . . . twice for his valet—and then he'll send for the police . . . and then I'll tell everything! Everything! Oh, what a relief it'll be to have it all end—if only it will end! —— And then he'll have a stroke and die . . . That'll be the end of all of us—and there'll be peace . . . quiet . . . eternal rest! —— And then our coat of arms will be broken against his coffin—the family title extinct—but the valet's line will go on in an orphanage . . . win laurels in the gutter, and end in jail!

JEAN: There's the blue blood talking! Very good, Miss Julie! Just don't let that miller out of the closet! (KRISTINE *enters, dressed for church, with a psalmbook in her hand.*)

JULIE (*rushing to* KRISTINE *and falling into her arms, as if seeking protection*): Help, me Kristine! Help me against this man!

KRISTINE (*unmoved and cold*): What a fine way to behave on a Sunday morning! (*sees the chopping block*) And look at this mess! —— What does all this mean? Why all this screaming and carrying on?

JULIE: Kristine! You're a woman and my friend! Beware of this swine!

JEAN (*uncomfortable*): While you ladies discuss this, I'll go in and shave. (*slips off right*)

JULIE: You must listen to me so you'll understand!

KRISTINE: No, I could never understand such disgusting behavior! Where are you off to in your traveling clothes? —— And he had his hat on. —— Well? —— Well? ——

JULIE: Listen to me, Kristine! Listen, and I'll tell you everything ——

KRISTINE: I don't want to hear it . . .

JULIE: But you must listen to me . . .

KRISTINE: What about? If it's about this silliness with Jean, I'm not interested, because it's none of my business. But if you're thinking of tricking him into running out, we'll soon put a stop to that!

JULIE (*extremely nervous*): Try to be calm now, Kristine, and listen to me! I can't stay here, and neither can Jean—so we must go away . . .

KRISTINE: Hm, hm!

JULIE (*brightening*): You see, I just had an idea —— What if all three of us go—abroad—to Switzerland and start a hotel together? —— I have money, you see—and Jean and I could run it—and I thought you, you could take care of the kitchen . . . Wouldn't that be wonderful? —— Say yes! And come with us, and then everything will be settled! —— Oh, do say yes! (*embracing* KRISTINE *and patting her warmly*)

KRISTINE (*coolly, thoughtfully*): Hm, hm!

JULIE (*presto tempo*): You've never traveled, Kristine. —— You must get out and see the world. You can't imagine how much fun it is to travel by train—always new faces—new countries. —— And when we get to Hamburg, we'll stop off at the zoo—you'll like that. —— And then we'll go to the theatre and the opera—and when we get to Munich, dear, there we have museums, with Rubens and Raphael, th444e great painters, as you know. —— You've heard of Munich, where King Ludwig lived—the king who went mad. —— And then we'll see his castles—they're still there and they're like castles in fairy tales. —— And from there it isn't far to Switzerland—and the Alps. —— Imagine—the Alps have snow on them even in the middle of summer! —— And oranges grow there and laurel trees that are green all year round —— (JEAN *can be seen in the wings right, sharpening his razor on a strop which he holds with his teeth and his left hand. He listens to the conversation with satisfaction, nodding now and then in approval.* MISS JULIE *continues tempo prestissimo.*) And then we'll start a hotel—and I'll be at the desk, while Jean greets the guests . . . does the shopping . . . writes letters. —— You have no idea what a life it'll be—the train

whistles blowing and the carriages arriving and the bells ringing in the rooms and down in the restaurant. —— And I'll make out the bills—and I know how to salt them! . . . You'll never believe how timid travelers are when they have to pay their bills! —— And you—you'll be in charge of the kitchen. —— Naturally, you won't have to stand over the stove yourself. —— And since you're going to be seen by people, you'll have to wear beautiful clothes. —— And you, with your looks—no, I'm not flattering you—one fine day you'll grab yourself a husband! —— You'll see! —— A rich Englishman—they're so easy to —— (*slowing down*) —— catch—and then we'll get rich—and build ourselves a villa on Lake Como. —— It's true it rains there a little now and then, but —— (*dully*) —— the sun has to shine sometimes—although it looks dark—and then . . . of course we could always come back home again — — (*pause*) —— here—or somewhere else ——

KRISTINE: Listen, Miss Julie, do you believe all this?

JULIE (*crushed*): Do I believe it?

KRISTINE: Yes!

JULIE (*wearily*): I don't know. I don't believe in anything any more. (*She sinks down on the bench and cradles her head in her arms on the table.*) Nothing! Nothing at all!

KRISTINE (*turning right to where* JEAN *is standing*): So, you thought you'd run out!

JEAN (*embarrassed; puts the razor on the table*): Run out? That's no way to put it. You hear Miss Julie's plan, and even if she is tired after being up all night, it's still a practical plan.

KRISTINE: Now you listen to me! Did you think I'd work as a cook for that . . .

JEAN (*sharply*): You watch what you say in front of your mistress! Do you understand?

KRISTINE: Mistress!

JEAN: Yes!

KRISTINE: Listen to him! Listen to him!

JEAN: Yes, you listen! It'd do you good to listen more and talk less! Miss Julie is your mistress. If you despise her, you have to despise yourself for the same reason!

KRISTINE: I've always had enough self-respect ——

JEAN: —— to be able to despise other people!

KRISTINE: —— to stop me from doing anything that's beneath me. You can't say that the Count's cook has been up to something with the groom or the swineherd! Can you?

JEAN: No, you were lucky enough to get hold of a gentleman!

KRISTINE: Yes, a gentleman who sells the Count's oats from the stable.

JEAN: You should talk—taking a commission from the grocer and bribes from the butcher.

KRISTINE: What?

JEAN: And you say you can't respect your employers any longer. You, you, you!

KRISTINE: Are you coming to church with me, now? You could use a good sermon after your fine deed!

JEAN: No, I'm not going to church today. You'll have to go alone and confess what you've been up to.

KRISTINE: Yes, I'll do that, and I'll bring back enough forgiveness for you, too. The Savior suffered and died on the Cross for all our sins, and if we go to Him with faith and a penitent heart, He takes all our sins on Himself.

JEAN: Even grocery sins?

JULIE: And do you believe that, Kristine?

KRISTINE: It's my living faith, as sure as I stand here. It's the faith I learned as a child, Miss Julie, and kept ever since. "Where sin abounded, grace did much more abound!"

JULIE: Oh, if I only had your faith. If only . . .

KRISTINE: Well, you see, we can't have it without God's special grace, and that isn't given to everyone ——

JULIE: Who is it given to then?

KRISTINE: That's the great secret of the workings of grace, Miss Julie, and God is no respecter of persons, for the last shall be the first . . .

JULIE: Then He does respect the last.

KRISTINE (continuing): . . . and it is easier for a camel to go through the eye of a needle, than for a rich man to enter the Kingdom of God. That's how it is, Miss Julie! Anyhow, I'm going now—alone, and on the way I'm going to tell the groom not to let any horses out, in case anyone wants to leave before the Count gets back! —— Goodbye! (leaves)

JEAN: What a witch! —— And all this because of a greenfinch! ——

JULIE (dully): Never mind the greenfinch! —— Can you see any way out of this? Any end to it?

JEAN (thinking): No!

JULIE: What would you do in my place?

JEAN: In your place? Let's see—as a person of position, as a woman who had—fallen. I don't know—wait, now I know.

JULIE (taking the razor and making a gesture): You mean like this?

JEAN: Yes! But—understand—I wouldn't do it! That's the difference between us!

JULIE: Because you're a man and I'm a woman? What sort of difference is that?

JEAN: The usual difference—between a man and a woman.

JULIE (with the razor in her hand): I want to, but I can't! —— My father couldn't either, the time he should have done it.

JEAN: No, he shouldn't have! He had to revenge himself first.

JULIE: And now my mother is revenged again, through me.

JEAN: Didn't you ever love your father, Miss Julie?

JULIE: Oh yes, deeply, but I've hated him, too. I must have done so without realizing it! It was he who brought me up to despise my own sex, making me half woman, half man. Whose fault is what's happened? My father's, my mother's, my own? My own? I don't have anything that's my own. I don't have a single thought that I didn't get from my father, not an emotion that I didn't get from my mother, and this last idea—that all people are equal—I got that from my fiancé. —— That's why I called him a swine! How can it be my fault? Shall I let Jesus take on the blame, the way Kristine does? —— No, I'm too proud to do that and too sensible—thanks to my father's teachings. —— And as for someone rich not going to heaven, that's a lie. But Kristine won't get in—how will she explain the money she has in the savings bank? Whose fault is it? —— What does it matter whose fault it is? I'm still the one who has to bear the blame, face the consequences . . .

JEAN: Yes, but . . . (the bell rings sharply twice. MISS JULIE jumps up. JEAN changes his coat.) The Count is back! Do you suppose Kristine—(He goes to the speaking tube, taps the lid, and listens.)

JULIE: He's been to his desk!

JEAN: It's Jean, sir! (listening; the audience cannot hear the Count's voice.) Yes, sir! (listening) Yes, sir! Right away! (listening) At once, sir! (listening) I see, in half an hour!

JULIE (desperately frightened): What did he say? Dear Lord, what did he say?

JEAN: He wants his boots and his coffee in half an hour.

JULIE: So, in half an hour! Oh, I'm so tired. I'm not able to do anything. I can't repent, can't run away, can't stay, can't live—can't die! Help me now! Order me, and I'll obey like a dog! Do me this last service, save my honor, save his name! You know what I should do, but don't have the will to . . . You will it, you order me to do it!

JEAN: I don't know why —— but now I can't either —— I don't understand. —— It's as if this coat made it impossible for me to order you to do anything. —— And now, since the Count spoke to me—I—I can't really explain it—but—ah, it's the damn lackey in me! —— I think if the Count came down here now—and ordered me to cut my throat, I'd do it on the spot.

JULIE: Then pretend you're he, and I'm you! —— You gave such a good performance before when you knelt at my feet. —— You were a real nobleman.

—— Or—have you ever seen a hypnotist in the theatre? (JEAN *nods.*) He says to his subject: "Take the broom," and he takes it. He says: "Sweep," and he sweeps ——

JEAN: But the subject has to be asleep.

JULIE (*ecstatically*): I'm already asleep. —— The whole room is like smoke around me . . . and you look like an iron stove . . . shaped like a man in black, with a tall hat—and your eyes glow like coals when the fire is dying—and your face is a white patch, like ashes —— (*The sunlight has reached the floor and now shines on* JEAN.) —— it's so warm and good —— (*She rubs her hands as if warming them before a fire.*) —— and bright—and so peaceful!

JEAN (*taking the razor and putting it in her hand*): Here's the broom! Go now while it's bright—out to the barn—and . . . (*whispers in her ear*)

JULIE (*awake*): Thank you. I'm going now to rest! But just tell me—that those who are first can also receive the gift of grace. Say it, even if you don't believe it.

JEAN: The first? No, I can't! —— But wait—Miss Julie—now I know! You're no longer among the first—you're now among—the last!

JULIE: That's true. —— I'm among the very last. I'm the last one of all! Oh! —— But now I can't go! —— Tell me once more to go!

JEAN: No, now I can't either! I can't!

JULIE: And the first shall be the last!

JEAN: Don't think, don't think! You're taking all my strength from me, making me a coward. —— What was that? I thought the bell moved! —— No! Shall we stuff paper in it? —— To be so afraid of a bell! —— But it isn't just a bell. —— There's someone behind it—a hand sets it in motion—and something else sets the hand in motion. —— Maybe if you cover your ears—cover your ears! But then it rings even louder! rings until someone answers. —— And then it's too late! And then the police come—and—then —— (*The bell rings twice loudly .* JEAN *flinches, then straightens up.*) It's horrible! But there's no other way! —— Go! (MISS JULIE *walks firmly out through the door.*)

ANTON CHEKHOV (1860–1904)

A
nton Chekhov was born in the town of Taganrog, a resort in Crimea near Yalta. His father's business failed, forcing the family to move to Moscow, but Chekhov remained in Taganrog to complete his schooling. In 1880, now twenty, he rejoined the family in Moscow and entered medical school. At first he wrote short stories to help support himself. Eventually he did become a physician, but he continued to spend a great deal of his time writing. By 1888 Chekhov had published several hundred stories, and he now practiced medicine only during epidemics. During this time Chekhov began to write short plays. *The Boor* (1888), *The Proposal* (1889), and *The Wedding* (1890) were all well received. His first full-length plays, however—*Ivanov* (1887) and *The Wood Demon* (1889)—were failures. When *The Seagull* was produced at the Alexandrinsky Theater in St. Petersburg in 1896, actors and audiences alike were baffled. Its indirect plot, low-key characters, and seemingly aimless dialogue departed radically from the conventions of nineteenth-century drama. Actors had no experience in conveying the psychological complexity of the loneliness and frustration required to stage the play, and audiences familiar with the sensationalism of melodrama found the play pointless and dull.

The Seagull found its way into print in a literary magazine, where it came to the attention of Konstantin Stanislavsky and Vladimir Nemirovich-Danchenko, who were forming the Moscow Art Theatre. Like the Duke of Saxe-Meiningen, Stanislavsky and Nemirovich-Danchenko dispensed with the star system and used ensemble acting, in which all the members of the company gave close attention to portraying their parts. They were also developing a new style of realistic, psychologically motivated performance, one perfectly suited to the complexity of Chekhov's play *The Seagull*. In 1898 the play was produced at the Moscow Art Theatre, and it was greeted as a resounding success, making both the Theatre's and Chekhov's reputations. Three more of Chekhov's plays were produced there in the following years. *Uncle Vanya*, a revision of *The Wood Demon*, was produced in 1899. In this play the main character recognizes that the man to whom he has devoted his life is not the brilliant professor he had thought but merely a mediocre pedant. *The Three Sisters* was produced in 1901. In this play, the three sisters of the title never manage to fulfill any of their ambitions or desires, despite their comfortable inheritance. Even something as seemingly simple as a desire to go to Moscow proves impossible to realize. In *The Cherry Orchard*, produced in 1904, this sense of futility is investigated in terms of an entire culture. Here the aristocratic class is helpless to preserve itself, and the rising middle class cannot find meaning in anything beyond the acquisition of money and land.

Chekhov's plays, like his short stories, take a detached and clinical view of Russian life and an ironic attitude toward the characters. Chekhov believed that onstage everything should be portrayed as simple and at the same time as complex as it is in real life. People do ordinary things, like eat dinner, but during the course of dinner their lives may take a dramatic turn. Chekhov's own life changed in this way. In 1884, before he had reached the age of twenty-five, Chekhov discovered that he had contracted tuberculosis, a disease for which there was no known cure and which required long periods of convalescence. He died in 1904 in Yalta after twenty years of illness, a mere six months after *The Cherry Orchard* opened at the Moscow Art Theatre.

The Cherry Orchard

Stanislavsky directed the premiere of *The Cherry Orchard* at the Moscow Art Theatre in 1904. Although Chekhov and Stanislavsky had developed a close professional relationship, the two men often disagreed, and particularly about this play. Chekhov wanted Stanislavsky to play the part of Lopahin, but Stanislavsky chose to play Gaev. Chekhov thought of the play as a comedy, while Stanislavsky thought of it as a tragedy. Their conflict illustrates the appeal of Chekhov's work. His plays manage to evoke seemingly contradictory responses. How readers interpret the play will depend on how they view Madame Ranevsky and Lopahin. As a member of the old aristocracy she is replaced by the competent and aggressive capitalists from the new rising middle class. *The Cherry Orchard* is thus in part a play about the inevitable collapse of outmoded social and economic systems; less than fifteen years after the premiere came the success of the Russian Revolution, and the play was interpreted primarily in this way.

Yet Chekhov humanizes the collapse of the aristocracy. On the one hand the cherry orchard has been created and maintained by the exploitation of generations of serfs and servants. But on the other hand the old way of life was not simply exploitative. The very existence of the cherry orchard and its delicate beauty depended on the will and the ability of the aristocracy to preserve it. In this regard, Madame Ranevsky's generosity to everyone who asks for money—despite the fact that she is desperately in debt—reveals a complexity typical of Chekhov's vision. From an economic point of view her generosity is utterly foolish, and it reveals how incapable she is of dealing with the pressing realities of a changing world. On the other hand, these are gestures that reflect the profound human feeling embedded in social relationships in the old class-bound society. Her behavior embodies her natural tendency to try to preserve these relationships, just as she wishes to preserve the beauty of the cherry orchard. From this perspective, perhaps Stanislavsky was right to think of the play as tragic. In any case, the play makes Madame Ranevsky and the rest of her entourage victims of change as well as complicit in their own destruction.

The Cherry Orchard

ANTON CHEKHOV

TRANSLATED BY CONSTANCE GARNETT

CHARACTERS

MADAME RANEVSKY (LYUBOV ANDREYEVNA), the
owner of the Cherry Orchard
ANYA, her daughter, aged 17
VARYA, her adopted daughter, aged 24
GAEV (LEONID ANDREYEVITCH), brother of Madame
Ranevsky
LOPAHIN (YERMOLAY ALEXEYEVITCH), a Merchant
TROFIMOV (PYOTR SERGEYEVITCH), a Student
SEMYONOV-PISHTCHIK, a Landowner

CHARLOTTA IVANOVNA, a Governess
EPIHODOV (SEMYON PANTALEYEVITCH), a Clerk
DUNYASHA, a Maid
FIRS, an old Valet, aged 87
YASHA, a young Valet
A VAGRANT
THE STATION MASTER
A POST-OFFICE CLERK
VISITORS, SERVANTS

The action takes place on the estate of MADAME
RANEVSKY.

ACT I

*A room, which has always been called the nursery.
One of the doors leads into* ANYA's *room. Dawn, sun
rises during the scene. May, the cherry trees in
flower, but it is cold in the garden with the frost of
early morning. Windows closed.*

[Enter DUNYASHA *with a candle and* LOPAHIN *with a
book in his hand.]*

LOPAHIN: The train's in, thank God. What time is it?
DUNYASHA: Nearly two o'clock (*puts out the candle*).
 It's daylight already.
LOPAHIN: The train's late! Two hours, at least (*yawns
 and stretches*). I'm a pretty one; what a fool I've
 been. Came here on purpose to meet them at the
 station and dropped asleep.... Dozed off as I sat
 in the chair. It's annoying.... You might have
 waked me.
DUNYASHA: I thought you had gone (*listens*). There, I
 do believe they're coming!
LOPAHIN (*listens*): No, what with the luggage and one
 thing and another (*a pause*): Lyubov Andreyevna
 has been abroad five years; I don't know what
 she is like now.... She's a splendid woman. A
 good-natured, kind-hearted woman. I remember
 when I was a lad of fifteen, my poor father—he
 used to keep a little shop here in the village in
 those days—gave me a punch in the face with his
 fist and made my nose bleed. We were in the yard
 here, I forget what we'd come about—he had had

a drop. Lyubov Andreyevna—I can see her now—
she was a slim young girl then—took me to wash
my face, and then brought me into this very
room, into the nursery. "Don't cry, little peasant,"
says she, "it will be well in time for your wedding
day" ... (*a pause*). Little peasant.... My father
was a peasant, it's true, but here am I in a white
waistcoat and brown shoes, like a pig in a bun
shop. Yes, I'm a rich man, but for all my money,
come to think, a peasant I was, and a peasant I
am (*turns over the pages of the book*). I've been reading this book and I can't make head or tail of it. I
fell asleep over it (*a pause*).
DUNYASHA: The dogs have been awake all night, they
 feel that the mistress is coming.
LOPAHIN: Why, what's the matter with you,
 Dunyasha?
DUNYASHA: My hands are all of a tremble. I feel as
 though I should faint.
LOPAHIN: You're a spoilt soft creature, Dunyasha.
 And dressed like a lady too, and your hair done

up. That's not the thing. One must know one's place.

[Enter EPIHODOV with a nosegay; he wears a pea-jacket and highly polished creaking topboots; he drops the nosegay as he comes in.]

EPIHODOV (*picking up the nosegay*): Here! the gardener's sent this, says you're to put it in the dining-room (*gives DUNYASHA the nosegay*).

LOPAHIN: And bring me some kvass.

DUNYASHA: I will (*goes out*).

EPIHODOV: It's chilly this morning, three degrees of frost, though the cherries are all in flower. I can't say much for our climate (*sighs*). I can't. Our climate is not often propitious to the occasion. Yermolay Alexeyevitch, permit me to call your attention to the fact that I purchased myself a pair of boots the day before yesterday, and they creak, I venture to assure you, so that there's no tolerating them. What ought I to grease them with?

LOPAHIN: Oh, shut up! Don't bother me.

EPIHODOV: Every day some misfortune befalls me. I don't complain, I'm used to it, and I wear a smiling face.

[DUNYASHA comes in, hands LOPAHIN the kvass.]

EPIHODOV: I am going (*stumbles against a chair, which falls over*). There! (*as though triumphant*). There you see now, excuse the expression, an accident like that among others. . . . It's positively remarkable (*goes out*).

DUNYASHA: Do you know, Yermolay Alexeyevitch, I must confess, Epihodov has made me a proposal.

LOPAHIN: Ah!

DUNYASHA: I'm sure I don't know. . . . He's a harmless fellow, but sometimes when he begins talking, there's no making anything of it. It's all very fine and expressive, only there's no understanding it. I've a sort of liking for him too. He loves me to distraction. He's an unfortunate man; every day there's something. They tease him about it—two and twenty misfortunes they call him.

LOPAHIN (*listening*): There! I do believe they're coming.

DUNYASHA: They *are* coming! What's the matter with me? . . . I'm cold all over.

LOPAHIN: They really are coming. Let's go and meet them. Will she know me? It's five years since I saw her.

DUNYASHA (*in a flutter*): I shall drop this very minute. . . . Ah, I shall drop.

[There is a sound of two carriages driving up to the house. LOPAHIN and DUNYASHA go out quickly. The stage is left empty. A noise is heard in the adjoining

rooms. FIRS, *who has driven to meet MADAME RANEVSKY, crosses the stage hurriedly leaning on a stick. He is wearing old fashioned livery and a high hat. He says something to himself, but not a word can be distinguished. The noise behind the scenes goes on increasing. A voice: "Come, let's go in here." Enter LYUBOV ANDREYEVNA, ANYA, and CHARLOTTA IVANOVNA with a pet dog on a chain, all in travelling dresses, VARYA in an out-door coat with a kerchief over her head, GAEV, SEMYONOV-PISHTCHIK, LOPAHIN, DUNYASHA with bag and parasol, servants with other articles. All walk across the room.]*

ANYA: Let's come in here. Do you remember what room this is, mamma?

LYUBOV (*joyfully, through her tears*): The nursery!

VARYA: How cold it is, my hands are numb. (*To LYUBOV ANDREYEVNA*) Your rooms, the white room and the lavender one, are just the same as ever, mamma.

LYUBOV: My nursery, dear delightful room. . . . I used to sleep here when I was little . . . (*cries*). And here I am, like a little child . . . (*kisses her brother and VARYA, and then her brother again*). Varya's just the same as ever, like a nun. And I knew Dunyasha (*kisses DUNYASHA*).

GAEV: The train was two hours late. What do you think of that? Is that the way to do things?

CHARLOTTA (*to PISHTCHIK*): My dog eats nuts, too.

PISHTCHIK (*wonderingly*): Fancy that!

[They all go out except ANYA and DUNYASHA.]

DUNYASHA: We've been expecting you so long (*takes ANYA's hat and coat*).

ANYA: I haven't slept for four nights on the journey. I feel dreadfully cold.

DUNYASHA: You set out in Lent, there was snow and frost, and now? My darling! (*laughs and kisses her*). I *have* missed you, my precious, my joy. I must tell you . . . I can't put it off a minute. . . .

ANYA (*wearily*): What now?

DUNYASHA: Epihodov, the clerk, made me a proposal just after Easter.

ANYA: It's always the same thing with you . . . (*straightening her hair*). I've lost all my hairpins . . . (*she is staggering from exhaustion*).

DUNYASHA: I don't know what to think, really. He does love me, he does love me so!

ANYA (*looking towards her door, tenderly*): My own room, my windows just as though I had never gone away. I'm home! To-morrow morning I shall get up and run into the garden. . . . Oh, if I could get to sleep! I haven't slept all the journey, I was so anxious and worried.

DUNYASHA: Pyotr Sergeyevitch came the day before

yesterday.

ANYA (*joyfully*): Petya!

DUNYASHA: He's asleep in the bath house, he has settled in there. I'm afraid of being in their way, says he. (*Glancing at her watch*) I was to have waked him, but Varvara Mihalovna told me not to. Don't you wake him, says she.

[*Enter VARYA with a bunch of keys at her waist.*]

VARYA: Dunyasha, coffee and make haste. . . . Mamma's asking for coffee.

DUNYASHA: This very minute (*goes out*).

VARYA: Well, thank God, you've come. You're home again (*petting her*). My little darling has come back! My precious beauty has come back again!

ANYA: I have had a time of it!

VARYA: I can fancy!

ANYA: We set off in Holy Week—it was so cold then, and all the way Charlotta would talk and show off her tricks. What did you want to burden me with Charlotta for?

VARYA: You couldn't have travelled all alone, darling. At seventeen!

ANYA: We got to Paris at last, it was cold there—snow. I speak French shockingly. Mamma lives on the fifth floor, I went up to her, and there were a lot of French people, ladies, an old priest with a book. The place smelt of tobacco and so comfortless. I felt sorry, oh! so sorry for mamma all at once, I put my arms round her neck, and hugged her and wouldn't let her go. Mamma was as kind as she could be, and she cried. . . .

VARYA (*through her tears*): Don't speak of it, don't speak of it!

ANYA: She had sold her villa at Mentone, she had nothing left, nothing. I hadn't a farthing left either, we only just had enough to get here. And mamma doesn't understand! When we had dinner at the stations, she always ordered the most expensive things and gave the waiters a whole rouble. Charlotta's just the same. Yasha too must have the same as we do; it's simply awful. You know Yasha is mamma's valet now, we brought him here with us.

VARYA: Yes, I've seen the young rascal.

ANYA: Well, tell me—have you paid the arrears on the mortgage?

VARYA: How could we get the money?

ANYA: Oh, dear! Oh, dear!

VARYA: In August the place will be sold.

ANYA: My goodness!

LOPAHIN (*peeps in at the door and moo's like a cow*): Moo! (*disappears*).

VARYA (*weeping*): There, that's what I could do to him (*shakes her fist*).

ANYA (*embracing VARYA, softly*): Varya, has he made you an offer? (VARYA *shakes her head.*) Why, but he loves you. Why is it you don't come to an understanding? What are you waiting for?

VARYA: I believe that there never will be anything between us. He has a lot to do, he has no time for me . . . and takes no notice of me. Bless the man, it makes me miserable to see him. . . . Everyone's talking of our being married, everyone's congratulating me, and all the while there's really nothing in it; it's all like a dream. (*In another tone*) You have a new brooch like a bee.

ANYA (*mournfully*): Mamma bought it. (*Goes into her own room and in a light-hearted childish tone*) And you know, in Paris I went up in a balloon!

VARYA: My darling's home again! My pretty is home again!

[DUNYASHA *returns with the coffee-pot and is making the coffee.*]

VARYA (*standing at the door*): All day long, darling, as I go about looking after the house, I keep dreaming all the time. If only we could marry you to a rich man, then I should feel more at rest. Then I would go off by myself on a pilgrimage to Kiev, to Moscow . . . and so I would spend my life going from one holy place to another. . . . I would go on and on. . . . What bliss!

ANYA: The birds are singing in the garden. What time is it?

VARYA: It must be nearly three. It's time you were asleep, darling (*going into ANYA's room*). What bliss!

[YASHA *enters with a rug and a travelling bag.*]

YASHA (*crosses the stage, mincingly*): May one come in here, pray?

DUNYASHA: I shouldn't have known you, Yasha. How you have changed abroad.

YASHA: H'm! . . . And who are you?

DUNYASHA: When you went away, I was that high (*shows distance from floor*). Dunyasha, Fyodor's daughter. . . . You don't remember me!

YASHA: H'm! . . . You're a peach! (*looks round and embraces her: she shrieks and drops a saucer. YASHA goes out hastily*).

VARYA (*in the doorway, in a tone of vexation*): What now?

DUNYASHA (*through her tears*): I have broken a saucer.

VARYA: Well, that brings good luck.

ANYA (*coming out of her room*): We ought to prepare mamma: Petya is here.

VARYA: I told them not to wake him.

ANYA (*dreamily*): It's six years since father died. Then only a month later little brother Grisha was drowned in the river, such a pretty boy he was, only seven. It was more than mamma could bear, so she went away, went away without looking back (*shuddering*). . . . How well I understand her, if only she knew! (*a pause*) And Petya Trofimov was Grisha's tutor, he may remind her.

[Enter FIRS: he is wearing a pea-jacket and a white waistcoat.]

FIRS (*goes up to the coffee-pot, anxiously*): The mistress will be served here (*puts on white gloves*). Is the coffee ready? (*Sternly to* DUNYASHA) Girl! Where's the cream?

DUNYASHA: Ah, mercy on us! (*goes out quickly*).

FIRS (*fussing round the coffee-pot*): Ech! you good-for-nothing! (*muttering to himself*) Come back from Paris. And the old master used to go to Paris too . . . horses all the way (*laughs*).

VARYA: What is it, Firs?

FIRS: What is your pleasure? (*Gleefully*) My lady has come home! I have lived to see her again! Now I can die (*weeps with joy*).

[Enter LYUBOV ANDREYEVNA, GAEV and SEMYONOV-PISHTCHIK; the latter is in a short-waisted full coat of fine cloth, and full trousers. GAEV, as he comes in, makes a gesture with his arms and his whole body, as though he were playing billiards.]

LYUBOV: How does it go? Let me remember. Cannon off the red!

GAEV: That's it—in off the white! Why, once, sister, we used to sleep together in this very room, and now I'm fifty-one, strange as it seems.

LOPAHIN: Yes, time flies.

GAEV: What do you say?

LOPAHIN: Time, I say, flies.

GAEV: What a smell of patchouli!

ANYA: I'm going to bed. Good-night, mamma (*kisses her mother*).

LYUBOV: My precious darling (*kisses her hands*). Are you glad to be home? I can't believe it.

ANYA: Good-night, uncle.

GAEV (*kissing her face and hands*): God bless you! How like you are to your mother! (*To his sister*) At her age you were just the same, Lyuba.

[ANYA shakes hands with LOPAHIN and PISHTCHIK, then goes out, shutting the door after her.]

LYUBOV: She's quite worn out.

PISHTCHIK: Aye, it's a long journey, to be sure.

VARYA (*to LOPAHIN and PISHTCHIK*): Well, gentlemen? It's three o'clock and time to say good-bye.

LYUBOV (*laughs*): You're just the same as ever, Varya (*draws her to her and kisses her*). I'll just drink my coffee and then we will all go and rest. (FIRS *puts a cushion under her feet.*) Thanks, friend. I am so fond of coffee, I drink it day and night. Thanks, dear old man (*kisses* FIRS).

VARYA: I'll just see whether all the things have been brought in (*goes out*).

LYUBOV: Can it really be me sitting here? (*laughs*). I want to dance about and clap my hands. (*Covers her face with her hands*) And I could drop asleep in a moment! God knows I love my country, I love it tenderly; I couldn't look out of the window in the train, I kept crying so. (*Through her tears*) But I must drink my coffee, though. Thank you, Firs, thanks, dear old man. I'm so glad to find you still alive.

FIRS: The day before yesterday.

GAEV: He's rather deaf.

LOPAHIN: I have to set off for Harkov directly, at five o'clock. . . . It is annoying! I wanted to have a look at you, and a little talk. . . . You are just as splendid as ever.

PISHTCHIK (*breathing heavily*): Handsomer, indeed. . . . Dressed in Parisian style . . . completely bowled me over.

LOPAHIN: Your brother, Leonid Andreyevitch here, is always saying that I'm a low-born knave, that I'm a money-grubber, but I don't care one straw for that. Let him talk. Only I do want you to believe in me as you used to. I do want your wonderful tender eyes to look at me as they used to in the old days. Merciful God! My father was a serf of your father and of your grandfather, but you—you—did so much for me once, that I've forgotten all that; I love you as though you were my kin . . . more than my kin.

LYUBOV: I can't sit still, I simply can't . . . (*jumps up and walks about in violent agitation*). This happiness is too much for me. . . . You may laugh at me, I know I'm silly. . . . My own bookcase (*kisses the bookcase*). My little table.

GAEV: Nurse died while you were away.

LYUBOV (*sits down and drinks coffee*): Yes, the Kingdom of Heaven be hers! You wrote me of her death.

GAEV: And Anastasy is dead. Squinting Petrushka has left me and is in service now with the police captain in the town (*takes a box of caramels out of his pocket and sucks one*).

PISHTCHIK: My daughter, Dashenka, wishes to be remembered to you.

LOPAHIN: I want to tell you something very pleasant and cheering (*glancing at his watch*). I'm going directly . . . there's no time to say much . . . well, I can say it in a couple of words. I needn't tell you your cherry orchard is to be sold to pay your debts; the 22nd of August is the date fixed for the sale; but don't you worry, dearest lady, you may sleep in peace, there is a way of saving it. . . . This is what I propose. I beg your attention! Your estate is not twenty miles from the town, the railway runs close by it, and if the cherry orchard and the land along the river bank were cut up into building plots and then let on lease for summer villas, you would make an income of at least 25,000 roubles a year out of it.

GAEV: That's all rot, if you'll excuse me.

LYUBOV: I don't quite understand you, Yermolay Alexeyevitch.

LOPAHIN: You will get a rent of at least 25 roubles a year for a three-acre plot from summer visitors, and if you say the word now, I'll bet you what you like there won't be one square foot of ground vacant by the autumn, all the plots will be taken up. I congratulate you; in fact, you are saved. It's a perfect situation with that deep river. Only, of course, it must be cleared—all the old buildings, for example, must be removed, this house too, which is really good for nothing, and the old cherry orchard must be cut down.

LYUBOV: Cut down? My dear fellow, forgive me, but you don't know what you are talking about. If there is one thing interesting—remarkable indeed—in the whole province, it's just our cherry orchard.

LOPAHIN: The only thing remarkable about the orchard is that it's a very large one. There's a crop of cherries every alternate year, and then there's nothing to be done with them, no one buys them.

GAEV: This orchard is mentioned in the `Encyclopædia.'

LOPAHIN (*glancing at his watch*): If we don't decide on something and don't take some steps, on the 22nd of August the cherry orchard and the whole estate too will be sold by auction. Make up your minds! There is no other way of saving it, I'll take my oath on that. No, no!

FIRS: In old days, forty or fifty years ago, they used to dry the cherries, soak them, pickle them, make jam too, and they used—

GAEV: Be quiet, Firs.

FIRS: And they used to send the preserved cherries to Moscow and to Harkov by the waggon-load. That brought the money in! And the preserved cherries in those days were soft and juicy, sweet and fragrant. . . . They knew the way to do them then. . . .

LYUBOV: And where is the recipe now?

FIRS: It's forgotten. Nobody remembers it.

PISHTCHIK (*to* LYUBOV ANDREYEVNA): What's it like in Paris? Did you eat frogs there?

LYUBOV: Oh, I ate crocodiles.

PISHTCHIK: Fancy that now!

LOPAHIN: There used to be only the gentlefolks and the peasants in the country, but now there are these summer visitors. All the towns, even the small ones, are surrounded nowadays by these summer villas. And one may say for sure, that in another twenty years there'll be many more of these people and that they'll be everywhere. At present the summer visitor only drinks tea in his verandah, but maybe he'll take to working his bit of land too, and then your cherry orchard would become happy, rich and prosperous. . . .

GAEV (*indignant*): What rot!

[*Enter* VARYA *and* YASHA.]

VARYA: There are two telegrams for you, mamma (*takes out keys and opens an old-fashioned bookcase with a loud crack*). Here they are.

LYUBOV: From Paris (*tears the telegrams, without reading them*). I have done with Paris.

GAEV: Do you know, Lyuba, how old that bookcase is? Last week I pulled out the bottom drawer and there I found the date branded on it. The bookcase was made just a hundred years ago. What do you say to that? We might have celebrated its jubilee. Though it's an inanimate object, still it is a *book* case.

PISHTCHIK (*amazed*): A hundred years! Fancy that now.

GAEV: Yes. . . . It is a thing . . . (*feeling the bookcase*). Dear, honoured, bookcase! Hail to thee who for more than a hundred years hast served the pure ideals of good and justice; thy silent call to fruitful labour has never flagged in those hundred years, maintaining (*in tears*) in the generations of man, courage and faith in a brighter future and fostering in us ideals of good and social consciousness (*a pause*).

LOPAHIN: Yes. . . .

LYUBOV: You are just the same as ever, Leonid.

GAEV (*a little embarrassed*): Cannon off the right into the pocket!

LOPAHIN (*looking at his watch*): Well, it's time I was off.

YASHA (*handing* LYUBOV ANDREYEVNA *medicine*): Perhaps you will take your pills now.

PISHTCHIK: You shouldn't take medicines, my dear madam . . . they do no harm and no good. Give them here . . . honoured lady (*takes the pill-box, pours the pills into the hollow of his hand, blows on them, puts them in his mouth and drinks off some kvass*). There!

LYUBOV (*in alarm*): Why, you must be out of your mind!

PISHTCHIK: I have taken all the pills.

LOPAHIN: What a glutton! (*All laugh.*)

FIRS: His honour stayed with us in Easter week, ate a

gallon and a half of cucumbers . . . (*mutters*).

LYUBOV: What is he saying?

VARYA: He has taken to muttering like that for the last three years. We are used to it.

YASHA: His declining years!

[*CHARLOTTA IVANOVNA, a very thin, lanky figure in a white dress with a lorgnette in her belt, walks across the stage.*]

LOPAHIN: I beg your pardon, Charlotta Ivanovna, I have not had time to greet you (*tries to kiss her hand*).

CHARLOTTA (*pulling away her hand*): If I let you kiss my hand, you'll be wanting to kiss my elbow, and then my shoulder.

LOPAHIN: I've no luck to-day! (*All laugh.*) Charlotta Ivanovna, show us some tricks!

LYUBOV: Charlotta, do show us some tricks!

CHARLOTTA: I don't want to. I'm sleepy (*goes out*).

LOPAHIN: In three weeks' time we shall meet again (*kisses LYUBOV ANDREYEVNA's hand*). Good-bye till then—I must go. (*To GAEV*) Good-bye. (*Kisses PISHTCHIK*) Good-bye. (*Gives his hand to VARYA, then to FIRS and YASHA*) I don't want to go. (*To LYUBOV ANDREYEVNA*) If you think over my plan for the villas and make up your mind, then let me know; I will lend you 50,000 roubles. Think of it seriously.

VARYA (*angrily*): Well, do go, for goodness sake.

LOPAHIN: I'm going, I'm going (*goes out*).

GAEV: Low-born knave! I beg pardon, though . . . Varya is going to marry him, he's Varya's fiancé.

VARYA: Don't talk nonsense, uncle.

LYUBOV: Well, Varya, I shall be delighted. He's a good man.

PISHTCHIK: He is, one must acknowledge, a most worthy man. And my Dashenka . . . says too that . . . she says . . . various things (*snores, but at once wakes up*). But all the same, honoured lady, could you oblige me . . . with a loan of 240 roubles . . . to pay the interest on my mortgage to-morrow?

VARYA (*dismayed*): No, no.

LYUBOV: I really haven't any money.

PISHTCHIK: It will turn up (*laughs*). I never lose hope. I thought everything was over, I was a ruined man, and lo and behold—the railway passed through my land and . . . they paid me for it. And something else will turn up again, if not to-day, then to-morrow . . . Dashenka'll win two hundred thousand . . . she's got a lottery ticket.

LYUBOV: Well, we've finished our coffee, we can go to bed.

FIRS (*brushes GAEV, reprovingly*): You have got on the wrong trousers again! What am I to do with you?

VARYA (*softly*): Anya's asleep. (*Softly opens the window*) Now the sun's risen, it's not a bit cold. Look, mamma, what exquisite trees! My goodness! And the air! The starlings are singing!

GAEV (*opens another window*): The orchard is all white. You've not forgotten it, Lyuba? That long avenue that runs straight, straight as an arrow, how it shines on a moonlight night. You remember? You've not forgotten?

LYUBOV (*looking out of the window into the garden*): Oh, my childhood, my innocence! It was in this nursery I used to sleep, from here I looked out into the orchard, happiness waked with me every morning and in those days the orchard was just the same, nothing has changed (*laughs with delight*). All, all white! Oh, my orchard! After the dark gloomy autumn, and the cold winter; you are young again, and full of happiness, the heavenly angels have never left you. . . . If I could cast off the burden that weighs on my heart, if I could forget the past!

GAEV: H'm! and the orchard will be sold to pay our debts; it seems strange. . . .

LYUBOV: See, our mother walking . . . all in white, down the avenue! (*laughs with delight*). It is she!

GAEV: Where?

VARYA: Oh, don't, mamma!

LYUBOV: There is no one. It was my fancy. On the right there, by the path to the arbour, there is a white tree bending like a woman. . . .

[*Enter TROFIMOV wearing a shabby student's uniform and spectacles.*]

LYUBOV: What a ravishing orchard! White masses of blossom, blue sky. . . .

TROFIMOV: Lyubov Andreyevna! (*She looks round at him.*) I will just pay my respects to you and then leave you at once (*kisses her hand warmly*). I was told to wait until morning, but I hadn't the patience to wait any longer. . . .

[*LYUBOV ANDREYEVNA looks at him in perplexity.*]

VARYA (*through her tears*): This is Petya Trofimov.

TROFIMOV: Petya Trofimov, who was your Grisha's tutor. . . . Can I have changed so much?

[*LYUBOV ANDREYEVNA embraces him and weeps quietly.*]

GAEV (*in confusion*): There, there, Lyuba.

VARYA (*crying*): I told you, Petya, to wait till tomorrow.

LYUBOV: My Grisha . . . my boy . . . Grisha . . . my son!

VARYA: We can't help it, mamma, it is God's will.

TROFIMOV (*softly through his tears*): There . . . there.

LYUBOV (*weeping quietly*): My boy was lost . . .

drowned. Why? Oh, why, dear Petya? (*More quietly*) Anya is asleep in there, and I'm talking loudly . . . making this noise. . . . But, Petya. Why have you grown so ugly? Why do you look so old?

TROFIMOV: A peasant-woman in the train called me a mangy-looking gentleman.

LYUBOV: You were quite a boy then, a pretty little student, and now your hair's thin—and spectacles. Are you really a student still? (*goes towards the door*).

TROFIMOV: I seem likely to be a perpetual student.

LYUBOV (*kisses her brother, then* VARYA): Well, go to bed. . . . You are older too, Leonid.

PISHTCHIK (*follows her*): I suppose it's time we were asleep. . . . Ugh! my gout. I'm staying the night; Lyubov Andreyevna, my dear soul, if you could . . . to-morrow morning . . . 240 roubles.

GAEV: That's always his story.

PISHTCHIK: 240 roubles . . . to pay the interest on my mortgage.

LYUBOV: My dear man, I have no money.

PISHTCHIK: I'll pay it back, my dear . . . a trifling sum.

LYUBOV: Oh, well, Leonid will give it you. . . . You give him the money, Leonid.

GAEV: Me give it him! Let him wait till he gets it!

LYUBOV: It can't be helped, give it him. He needs it. He'll pay it back.

[*LYUBOV ANDREYEVNA, TROFIMOV, PISHTCHIK and FIRS go out. GAEV, VARYA and YASHA remain.*]

GAEV: Sister hasn't got out of the habit of flinging away her money. (*To* YASHA) Get away, my good fellow, you smell of the hen-house.

YASHA (*with a grin*): And you, Leonid Andreyevitch, are just the same as ever.

GAEV: What's that? (*To* VARYA) What did he say?

VARYA (*to* YASHA): Your mother has come from the village; she has been sitting in the servants' room since yesterday, waiting to see you.

YASHA: Oh, bother her!

VARYA: For shame!

YASHA: What's the hurry? She might just as well have come to-morrow (*goes out*).

VARYA: Mamma's just the same as ever, she hasn't changed a bit. If she had her own way, she'd give away everything.

GAEV: Yes (*a pause*). If a great many remedies are suggested for some disease, it means that the disease is incurable. I keep thinking and racking my brains; I have many schemes, a great many, and that really means none. If we could only come in for a legacy from somebody, or marry our Anya to a very rich man, or we might go to Yaroslavl and try our luck with our old aunt, the Countess. She's very, very rich, you know.

VARYA (*weeps*): If God would help us.

GAEV: Don't blubber. Aunt's very rich, but she doesn't like us. First, sister married a lawyer instead of a nobleman. . . .

[*ANYA appears in the doorway.*]

GAEV: And then her conduct, one can't call it virtuous. She is good, and kind, and nice, and I love her, but, however one allows for extenuating circumstances, there's no denying that she's an immoral woman. One feels it in her slightest gesture.

VARYA (*in a whisper*): Anya's in the doorway.

GAEV: What do you say? (*a pause*). It's queer, there seems to be something wrong with my right eye. I don't see as well as I did. And on Thursday when I was in the district Court . . .

[*Enter* ANYA.]

VARYA: Why aren't you asleep, Anya?

ANYA: I can't get to sleep.

GAEV: My pet (*kisses* ANYA's *face and hands*). My child (*weeps*). You are not my niece, you are my angel, you are everything to me. Believe me, believe . . .

ANYA: I believe you, uncle. Everyone loves you and respects you . . . but, uncle dear, you must be silent . . . simply be silent. What were you saying just now about my mother, about your own sister? What made you say that?

GAEV: Yes, yes . . . (*puts his hand over his face*). Really, that was awful! My God, save me! And to-day I made a speech to the bookcase . . . so stupid! And only when I had finished, I saw how stupid it was.

VARYA: It's true, uncle, you ought to keep quiet. Don't talk, that's all.

ANYA: If you could keep from talking, it would make things easier for you, too.

GAEV: I won't speak (*kisses* ANYA's *and* VARYA's *hands*). I'll be silent. Only this is about business. On Thursday I was in the district Court; well, there was a large party of us there and we began talking of one thing and another, and this and that, and do you know, I believe that it will be possible to raise a loan on an I.O.U. to pay the arrears on the mortgage.

VARYA: If the Lord would help us!

GAEV: I'm going on Tuesday; I'll talk of it again. (*To* VARYA) Don't blubber. (*To* ANYA) Your mamma will talk to Lopahin; of course, he won't refuse her. And as soon as you're rested you shall go to Yaroslavl to the Countess, your great-aunt. So we shall all set to work in three directions at once, and the business is done. We shall pay off arrears,

I'm convinced of it (*puts a caramel in his mouth*). I swear on my honour, I swear by anything you like, the estate shan't be sold (*excitedly*). By my own happiness, I swear it! Here's my hand on it, call me the basest, vilest of men, if I let it come to an auction! Upon my soul I swear it!

ANYA (*her equanimity has returned, she is quite happy*): How good you are, uncle, and how clever! (*embraces her uncle*). I'm at peace now! Quite at peace! I'm happy!

[*Enter* FIRS.]

FIRS (*reproachfully*): Leonid Andreyevitch, have you no fear of God? When are you going to bed?

GAEV: Directly, directly. You can go, Firs. I'll . . . yes, I will undress myself. Come, children, bye-bye. We'll go into details tomorrow, but now go to bed (*kisses* ANYA *and* VARYA). I'm a man of the eighties. They run down that period, but still I can say I have had to suffer not a little for my convictions in my life. It's not for nothing that the peasant loves me. One must know the peasant! One must know how . . .

ANYA: At it again, uncle!

VARYA: Uncle dear, you'd better be quiet!

FIRS (*angrily*): Leonid Andreyevitch!

GAEV: I'm coming. I'm coming. Go to bed. Potted the shot—there's a shot for you! A beauty! (*goes out,* FIRS *hobbling after him*).

ANYA: My mind's at rest now. I don't want to go to Yaroslavl, I don't like my great-aunt, but still my mind's at rest. Thanks to uncle (*sits down*).

VARYA: We must go to bed. I'm going. Something unpleasant happened while you were away. In the old servants' quarters there are only the old servants, as you know—Efimyushka, Polya and Yevstigney—and Karp too. They began letting stray people in to spend the night—I said nothing. But all at once I heard they had been spreading a report that I gave them nothing but pease pudding to eat. Out of stinginess, you know. . . . And it was all Yevstigney's doing. . . . Very well, I said to myself. . . . If that's how it is, I thought, wait a bit. I sent for Yevstigney . . . (*yawns*). He comes. . . . "How's this, Yevstigney," I said, "you could be such a fool as to? . . ." (*Looking at* ANYA) Anitchka! (*a pause*). She's asleep (*puts her arm round* ANYA). Come to bed . . . come along! (*leads her*). My darling has fallen asleep! Come . . . (*They go.*)

[*Far away beyond the orchard a shepherd plays on a pipe.* TROFIMOV *crosses the stage and, seeing* VARYA *and* ANYA, *stands still.*]

VARYA: 'Sh! She's asleep, asleep. Come, my own.

ANYA (*softly, half asleep*): I'm so tired. Still those bells. Uncle . . . dear . . . mamma and uncle. . . .

VARYA: Come, my own, come along.

[*They go into* ANYA *'s room.*]

TROFIMOV (*tenderly*): My sunshine! My spring.

Curtain.

ACT II

The open country. An old shrine, long abandoned and fallen out of the perpendicular; near it a well, large stones that have apparently once been tombstones, and an old garden seat. The road to GAEV'S *house is seen. On one side rise dark poplars; and there the cherry orchard begins. In the distance a row of telegraph poles and far, far away on the horizon there is faintly outlined a great town, only visible in very fine clear weather. It is near sunset.* CHARLOTTA, YASHA *and* DUNYASHA *are sitting on the seat. Epihodov is standing near, playing something mournful on a guitar. All sit plunged in thought.* CHARLOTTA *wears an old forage cap; she has taken a gun from her shoulder and is tightening the buckle on the strap.*

CHARLOTTA (*musingly*): I haven't a real passport of my own, and I don't know how old I am, and I always feel that I'm a young thing. When I was a little girl, my father and mother used to travel about to fairs and give performances—very good ones. And I used to dance *salto-mortale* and all sorts of things. And when papa and mamma died, a German lady took me and had me educated. And so I grew up and became a governess. But where I came from, and who I am, I don't know. . . . Who my parents were, very likely they weren't married . . . I don't know (*takes a cucumber out of her pocket and eats*). I know nothing at all (*a pause*). One wants to talk and has no one to talk to . . . I have nobody.

EPIHODOV (*plays on the guitar and sings*): "What care I for the noisy world! What care I for friends or foes!" How agreeable it is to play on the mandoline!

DUNYASHA: That's a guitar, not a mandoline (*looks in a hand-mirror and powders herself*).

EPIHODOV: To a man mad with love, it's a mandoline. (*Sings*) "Were her heart but aglow with love's mutual flame." (YASHA *joins in.*)

CHARLOTTA: How shockingly these people sing! Foo! Like jackals!

DUNYASHA (*to* YASHA): What happiness, though, to

visit foreign lands.

YASHA: Ah, yes! I rather agree with you there (*yawns, then lights a cigar*).

EPIHODOV: That's comprehensible. In foreign lands everything has long since reached full complexion.

YASHA: That's so, of course.

EPIHODOV: I'm a cultivated man, I read remarkable books of all sorts, but I can never make out the tendency I am myself precisely inclined for, whether to live or to shoot myself, speaking precisely, but nevertheless I always carry a revolver. Here it is . . . (*shows revolver*).

CHARLOTTA: I've had enough, and now I'm going (*puts on the gun*). Epihodov, you're a very clever fellow, and a very terrible one too, all the women must be wild about you. Br-r-r! (*goes*). These clever fellows are all so stupid; there's not a creature for me to speak to. . . . Always alone, alone, nobody belonging to me . . . and who I am, and why I'm on earth, I don't know (*walks away slowly*).

EPIHODOV: Speaking precisely, not touching upon other subjects, I'm bound to admit about myself, that destiny behaves mercilessly to me, as a storm to a little boat. If, let us suppose, I am mistaken, then why did I wake up this morning, to quote an example, and look round, and there on my chest was a spider of fearful magnitude . . . like this (*shows with both hands*). And then I take up a jug of kvass, to quench my thirst, and in it there is something in the highest degree unseemly of the nature of a cockroach (*a pause*). Have you read Buckle? (*a pause*). I am desirous of troubling you, Dunyasha, with a couple of words.

DUNYASHA: Well, speak.

EPIHODOV: I should be desirous to speak with you alone (*sighs*).

DUNYASHA (*embarrassed*): Well—only bring me my mantle first. It's by the cupboard. It's rather damp here.

EPIHODOV: Certainly. I will fetch it. Now I know what I must do with my revolver (*takes guitar and goes off playing on it*).

YASHA: Two and twenty misfortunes! Between ourselves, he's a fool (*yawns*).

DUNYASHA: God grant he doesn't shoot himself! (*a pause*). I am so nervous, I'm always in a flutter. I was a little girl when I was taken into our lady's house, and now I have quite grown out of peasant ways, and my hands are white, as white as a lady's. I'm such a delicate, sensitive creature, I'm afraid of everything. I'm so frightened. And if you deceive me, Yasha, I don't know what will become of my nerves.

YASHA (*kisses her*): You're a peach! Of course a girl must never forget herself; what I dislike more than anything is a girl being flighty in her behaviour.

DUNYASHA: I'm passionately in love with you, Yasha; you are a man of culture—you can give your opinion about anything (*a pause*).

YASHA (*yawns*): Yes, that's so. My opinion is this: if a girl loves anyone, that means that she has no principles (*a pause*). It's pleasant smoking a cigar in the open air (*listens*). Someone's coming this way . . . it's the gentlefolk (DUNYASHA *embraces him impulsively*). Go home, as though you had been to the river to bathe; go by that path, or else they'll meet you and suppose I have made an appointment with you here. That I can't endure.

DUNYASHA (*coughing softly*): The cigar has made my head ache . . . (*goes off*).

[YASHA remains sitting near the shrine. Enter LYUBOV ANDREYEVNA, GAEV and LOPAHIN.]

LOPAHIN: You must make up your mind once for all—there's no time to lose. It's quite a simple question, you know. Will you consent to letting the land for building or not? One word in answer: Yes or no? Only one word!

LYUBOV: Who is smoking such horrible cigars here? (*sits down*).

GAEV: Now the railway line has been brought near, it's made things very convenient (*sits down*). Here we have been over and lunched in town. Cannon off the white! I should like to go home and have a game.

LYUBOV: You have plenty of time.

LOPAHIN: Only one word! (*Beseechingly*) Give me an answer!

GAEV (*yawning*): What do you say?

LYUBOV (*looks in her purse*): I had quite a lot of money here yesterday, and there's scarcely any left to-day. My poor Varya feeds us all on milk soup for the sake of economy; the old folks in the kitchen get nothing but pease pudding, while I waste my money in a senseless way (*drops purse, scattering gold pieces*). There, they have all fallen out! (*annoyed*).

YASHA: Allow me, I'll soon pick them up (*collects the coins*).

LYUBOV: Pray do, Yasha. And what did I go off to the town to lunch for? Your restaurant's a wretched place with its music and the tablecloth smelling of soap. . . . Why drink so much, Leonid? And eat so much? And talk so much? To-day you talked a great deal again in the restaurant, and all so inappropriately. About the era of the 'seventies, about the decadents. And to whom? Talking to waiters about decadents!

LOPAHIN: Yes.

GAEV (*waving his hand*): I'm incorrigible; that's evident. (*Irritably to* YASHA) Why is it you keep fidgeting about in front of us!

YASHA (*laughs*): I can't help laughing when I hear your voice.

GAEV (*to his sister*): Either I or he . . .

LYUBOV: Get along! Go away, Yasha.

YASHA (*gives* LYUBOV ANDREYEVNA *her purse*): Directly (*hardly able to suppress his laughter*). This minute . . . (*goes off*).

LOPAHIN: Deriganov, the millionaire, means to buy your estate. They say he is coming to the sale himself.

LYUBOV: Where did you hear that?

LOPAHIN: That's what they say in town.

GAEV: Our aunt in Yaroslavl has promised to send help; but when, and how much she will send, we don't know.

LOPAHIN: How much will she send? A hundred thousand? Two hundred?

LYUBOV: Oh, well! . . . Ten or fifteen thousand, and we must be thankful to get that.

LOPAHIN: Forgive me, but such reckless people as you are—such queer, unbusiness-like people—I never met in my life. One tells you in plain Russian your estate is going to be sold, and you seem not to understand it.

LYUBOV: What are we to do? Tell us what to do.

LOPAHIN: I do tell you every day. Every day I say the same thing. You absolutely must let the cherry orchard and the land on building leases; and do it at once, as quick as may be—the auction's close upon us! Do understand! Once make up your mind to build villas, and you can raise as much money as you like, and then you are saved.

LYUBOV: Villas and summer visitors—forgive me saying so—it's so vulgar.

GAEV: There I perfectly agree with you.

LOPAHIN: I shall sob, or scream, or fall into a fit. I can't stand it! You drive me mad! (*To* GAEV) You're an old woman!

GAEV: What do you say?

LOPAHIN: An old woman! (*gets up to go*).

LYUBOV (*in dismay*): No, don't go! Do stay, my dear friend! Perhaps we shall think of something.

LOPAHIN: What is there to think of?

LYUBOV: Don't go, I entreat you! With you here it's more cheerful, anyway (*a pause*). I keep expecting something, as though the house were going to fall about our ears.

GAEV (*in profound dejection*): Potted the white! It fails —a kiss.

LYUBOV: We have been great sinners. . . .

LOPAHIN: You have no sins to repent of.

GAEV (*puts a caramel in his mouth*): They say I've eaten up my property in caramels (*laughs*).

LYUBOV: Oh, my sins! I've always thrown my money away recklessly like a lunatic. I married a man who made nothing but debts. My husband died of champagne—he drank dreadfully. To my misery I loved another man, and immediately—it was my first punishment—the blow fell upon me, here, in the river . . . my boy was drowned and I went abroad—went away for ever, never to return, not to see that river again . . . I shut my eyes, and fled, distracted, and *he* after me . . . pitilessly, brutally. I bought a villa at Mentone, for *he* fell ill there, and for three years I had no rest day or night. His illness wore me out, my soul was dried up. And last year, when my villa was sold to pay my debts, I went to Paris and there he robbed me of everything and abandoned me for another woman; and I tried to poison myself. . . . So stupid, so shameful! . . . And suddenly I felt a yearning for Russia, for my country, for my little girl . . . (*dries her tears*). Lord, Lord, be merciful! Forgive my sins! Do not chastise me more! (*Takes a telegram out of her pocket*) I got this to-day from Paris. He implores forgiveness, entreats me to return (*tears up the telegram*). I fancy there is music somewhere (*listens*).

GAEV: That's our famous Jewish orchestra. You remember, four violins, a flute and a double bass.

LYUBOV: That still in existence? We ought to send for them one evening, and give a dance.

LOPAHIN (*listens*): I can't hear . . . (*Hums softly*) "For money the Germans will turn a Russian into a Frenchman." (*Laughs*) I did see such a piece at the theatre yesterday! It was funny!

LYUBOV: And most likely there was nothing funny in it. You shouldn't look at plays, you should look at yourselves a little oftener. How grey your lives are! How much nonsense you talk.

LOPAHIN: That's true. One may say honestly, we live a fool's life (*pause*). My father was a peasant, an idiot; he knew nothing and taught me nothing, only beat me when he was drunk, and always with his stick. In reality I am just such another blockhead and idiot. I've learnt nothing properly. I write a wretched hand. I write so that I feel ashamed before folks, like a pig.

LYUBOV: You ought to get married, my dear fellow.

LOPARIN: Yes . . . that's true.

LYUBOV: You should marry our Varya, she's a good girl.

LOPAHIN: Yes.

LYUBOV: She's a good-natured girl, she's busy all day long, and what's more, she loves you. And you have liked her for ever so long.

LOPAHIN: Well? I'm not against it. . . . She's a good girl (*pause*).

GAEV: I've been offered a place in the bank: 6,000 roubles a year. Did you know?

LYUBOV: You would never do for that! You must stay as you are.

[Enter FIRS with overcoat.]

FIRS: Put it on, sir, it's damp.

GAEV (*putting it on*): You bother me, old fellow.

FIRS: You can't go on like this. You went away in the morning without leaving word (*looks him over*).

LYUBOV: You look older, Firs!

FIRS: What is your pleasure?

LOPAHIN: You look older, she said.

FIRS: I've had a long life. They were arranging my wedding before your papa was born . . . (*laughs*). I was the head footman before the emancipation came. I wouldn't consent to be set free then; I stayed on with the old master . . . (*a pause*). I remember what rejoicings they made and didn't know themselves what they were rejoicing over.

LOPAHIN: Those were fine old times. There was flogging anyway.

FIRS (*not hearing*): To be sure! The peasants knew their place, and the masters knew theirs; but now they're all at sixes and sevens, there's no making it out.

GAEV: Hold your tongue, Firs. I must go to town tomorrow. I have been promised an introduction to a general, who might let us have a loan.

LOPAHIN: You won't bring that off. And you won't pay your arrears, you may rest assured of that.

LYUBOV: That's all his nonsense. There is no such general.

[Enter TROFIMOV, ANYA and VARYA.]

GAEV: Here come our girls.

ANYA: There's mamma on the seat.

LYUBOV (*tenderly*): Come here, come along. My darlings! (*embraces ANYA and VARYA*). If you only knew how I love you both. Sit beside me, there, like that. (*All sit down.*)

LOPAHIN: Our perpetual student is always with the young ladies.

TROFIMOV: That's not your business.

LOPAHIN: He'll soon be fifty, and he's still a student.

TROFIMOV: Drop your idiotic jokes.

LOPAHIN: Why are you so cross, you queer fish?

TROFIMOV: Oh, don't persist!

LOPAHIN (*laughs*): Allow me to ask you what's your idea of me?

TROFIMOV: I'll tell you my idea of you, Yermolay Alexeyevitch: you are a rich man, you'll soon be a millionaire. Well, just as in the economy of nature a wild beast is of use, who devours everything that comes in his way, so you too have your use.

[All laugh.]

VARYA: Better tell us something about the planets, Petya.

LYUBOV: No, let us go on with the conversation we had yesterday.

TROFIMOV: What was it about?

GAEV: About pride.

TROFIMOV: We had a long conversation yesterday, but we came to no conclusion. In pride, in your sense of it, there is something mystical. Perhaps you are right from your point of view; but if one looks at it simply, without subtlety, what sort of pride can there be, what sense is there in it, if man in his physiological formation is very imperfect, if in the immense majority of cases he is coarse, dull-witted, profoundly unhappy? One must give up glorification of self. One should work, and nothing else.

GAEV: One must die in any case.

TROFIMOV: Who knows? And what does it mean—dying? Perhaps man has a hundred senses, and only the five we know are lost at death, while the other ninety-five remain alive.

LYUBOV: How clever you are, Petya!

LOPAHIN (*ironically*): Fearfully clever!

TROFIMOV: Humanity progresses, perfecting its powers. Everything that is beyond its ken now will one day become familiar and comprehensible; only we must work, we must with all our powers aid the seeker after truth. Here among us in Russia the workers are few in number as yet. The vast majority of the intellectual people I know, seek nothing, do nothing, are not fit as yet for work of any kind. They call themselves intellectual, but they treat their servants as inferiors, behave to the peasants as though they were animals, learn little, read nothing seriously, do practically nothing, only talk about science and know very little about art. They are all serious people, they all have severe faces, they all talk of weighty matters and air their theories, and yet the vast majority of us—ninety-nine per cent.—live like savages, at the least thing fly to blows and abuse, eat piggishly, sleep in filth and stuffiness, bugs everywhere, stench and damp and moral impurity. And it's clear all our fine talk is only to divert our attention and other people's. Show me where to find the crèches there's so much talk about, and the reading-rooms? They only exist in novels: in real life there are none of them. There is nothing but filth and vulgarity and Asiatic apathy. I fear and dislike very serious faces. I'm afraid of serious conversations. We should do better to be silent.

LOPAHIN: You know, I get up at five o'clock in the morning, and I work from morning to night; and I've money, my own and other people's, always passing through my hands, and I see what people are made of all round me. One has only to begin to do anything to see how few honest, decent people there are. Sometimes when I lie awake at night, I think: "Oh! Lord, thou hast given us immense forests, boundless plains, the widest horizons, and living here we ourselves ought really to be giants."

LYUBOV: You ask for giants! They are no good except in story-books; in real life they frighten us.

[EPIHODOV advances in the background, playing on the guitar.]

LYUBOV (*dreamily*): There goes Epihodov.
ANYA (*dreamily*): There goes Epihodov.
GAEV: The sun has set, my friends.
TROFIMOV: Yes.
GAEV (*not loudly, but, as it were, declaiming*): O nature, divine nature, thou art bright with eternal lustre, beautiful and indifferent! Thou whom we call mother, thou dost unite within thee life and death! Thou dost give life and dost destroy.
VARYA (*in a tone of supplication*): Uncle!
ANYA: Uncle, you are at it again!
TROFIMOV: You'd much better be cannoning off the red!
GAEV: I'll hold my tongue, I will.

[All sit plunged in thought. Perfect stillness. The only thing audible is the muttering of FIRS. Suddenly there is a sound in the distance, as it were from the sky— the sound of a breaking harp-string, mournfully dying away.]

LYUBOV: What is that?
LOPAHIN: I don't know. Somewhere far away a bucket fallen and broken in the pits. But somewhere very far away.
GAEV: It might be a bird of some sort—such as a heron.
TROFIMOV: Or an owl.
LYUBOV (*shudders*): I don't know why, but it's horrid (*a pause*).
FIRS: It was the same before the calamity—the owl hooted and the samovar hissed all the time.
GAEV: Before what calamity?
FIRS: Before the emancipation (*a pause*).
LYUBOV: Come, my friends, let us be going; evening is falling. (*To* ANYA) There are tears in your eyes. What is it, darling? (*embraces her*).
ANYA: Nothing, mamma; it's nothing.

TROFIMOV: There is somebody coming.

[The wayfarer appears in a shabby white forage cap and an overcoat; he is slightly drunk.]

WAYFARER: Allow me to inquire, can I get to the station this way?
GAEV: Yes. Go along that road.
WAYFARER: I thank you most feelingly (*coughing*). The weather is superb. (*Declaims*) My brother, my suffering brother! . . . Come out to the Volga! Whose groan do you hear? . . . (*To* VARYA) Mademoiselle, vouchsafe a hungry Russian thirty kopecks.

[VARYA utters a shriek of alarm.]

LOPAHIN (*angrily*): There's a right and a wrong way of doing everything!
LYUBOV (*hurriedly*): Here, take this (*looks in her purse*). I've no silver. No matter—here's gold for you.
WAYFARER: I thank you most feelingly! (*goes off*).

[Laughter.]

VARYA (*frightened*): I'm going home—I'm going . . . Oh, mamma, the servants have nothing to eat, and you gave him gold!
LYUBOV: There's no doing anything with me. I'm so silly! When we get home, I'll give you all I possess. Yermolay Alexeyevitch, you will lend me some more . . . !
LOPAHIN: I will.
LYUBOV: Come, friends, it's time to be going. And Varya, we have made a match of it for you. I congratulate you.
VARYA (*through her tears*): Mamma, that's not a joking matter.
LOPAHIN: "Ophelia, get thee to a nunnery!"
GAEV: My hands are trembling; it's a long while since I had a game of billiards.
LOPAHIN: "Ophelia! Nymph, in thy orisons be all my sins remember'd."
LYUBOV: Come, it will soon be supper-time.
VARYA: How he frightened me! My heart's simply throbbing.
LOPAHIN: Let me remind you, ladies and gentlemen: on the 22nd of August the cherry orchard will be sold. Think about that!   Think about it!

[All go off, except TROFIMOV and ANYA.]

ANYA (*laughing*): I'm grateful to the wayfarer! He frightened Varya and we are left alone.
TROFIMOV: Varya's afraid we shall fall in love with each other, and for days together she won't leave us. With her narrow brain she can't grasp that we are above love. To eliminate the petty and transi-

tory which hinders us from being free and happy—that is the aim and meaning of our life. Forward! We go forward irresistibly towards the bright star that shines yonder in the distance. Forward! Do not lag behind, friends.

ANYA (*claps her hands*): How well you speak! (*a pause*). It is divine her to-day.

TROFIMOV: Yes, it's glorious weather.

ANYA: Somehow, Petya, you've made me so that I don't love the cherry orchard as I used to. I used to love it so dearly. I used to think that there was no spot on earth like our garden.

TROFIMOV: All Russia is our garden. The earth is great and beautiful—there are many beautiful places in it (*a pause*). Think only, Anya, your grandfather, and great-grandfather, and all your ancestors were slave-owners—the owners of living souls—and from every cherry in the orchard, from every leaf, from every trunk there are human creatures looking at you. Cannot you hear their voices? Oh, it is awful! Your orchard is a fearful thing, and when in the evening or at night one walks about the orchard, the old bark on the trees glimmers dimly in the dusk, and the old cherry trees seem to be dreaming of centuries gone by and tortured by fearful visions. Yes! We are at least two hundred years behind, we have really gained nothing yet, we have no definite attitude to the past, we do nothing but theorise or complain of depression or drink vodka. It is clear that to begin to live in the present we must first expiate our past, we must break with it; and we can expiate it only by suffering, by extraordinary unceasing labour. Understand that, Anya.

ANYA: The house we live in has long ceased to be our own, and I shall leave it, I give you my word.

TROFIMOV: If you have the house keys, fling them into the well and go away. Be free as the wind.

ANYA (*in ecstasy*): How beautifully you said that!

TROFIMOV: Believe me, Anya, believe me! I am not thirty yet, I am young, I am still a student, but I have gone through so much already! As soon as winter comes I am hungry, sick, careworn, poor as a beggar, and what ups and downs of fortune have I not known! And my soul was always, every minute, day and night, full of inexplicable forebodings. I have a foreboding of happiness, Anya. I see glimpses of it already.

ANYA (*pensively*): The moon is rising.

[*EPIHODOV is heard playing still the same mournful song on the guitar. The moon rises. Somewhere near the poplars VARYA is looking for ANYA and calling "Anya! where are you?"*]

TROFIMOV: Yes, the moon is rising (*a pause*). Here is happiness—here it comes! It is coming nearer and nearer; already I can hear its footsteps. And if we never see it—if we may never know it—what does it matter? Others will see it after us.

VARYA'S VOICE: Anya! Where are you?

TROFIMOV: That Varya again! (*Angrily*) It's revolting!

ANYA: Well, let's go down to the river. It's lovely there.

TROFIMOV: Yes, let's go. (*They go.*)

VARYA'S VOICE: Anya! Anya!

Curtain.

ACT III

A drawing-room divided by an arch from a larger drawing-room. A chandelier burning. The Jewish orchestra, the same that was mentioned in Act II, is heard playing in the ante-room. It is evening. In the larger drawing-room they are dancing the grand chain. The voice of SEMYONOV-PISHTCHIK: "Promenade à une paire!" Then enter the drawing-room in couples, first PISHTCHIK and CHARLOTTA IVANOVNA, then TROFIMOV and LYUBOV ANDREYEVNA, thirdly ANYA with the Post-Office Clerk, fourthly VARYA with the Station Master, and other guests. VARYA is quietly weeping and wiping away her tears as she dances. In the last couple is DUNYASHA. They move across the drawing-room. PISHTCHIK shouts: "Grand rond, balancez~!" and "Les Cavaliers à genou et remerciez vos dames."

FIRS in a swallow-tail coat brings in seltzer water on a tray. PISHTCHIK and TROFIMOV enter the drawing-room.

PISHTCHIK: I am a full-blooded man; I have already had two strokes. Dancing's hard work for me, but as they say, if you're in the pack, you must bark with the rest. I'm as strong, I may say, as a horse. My parent, who would have his joke—may the Kingdom of Heaven be his!—used to say about our origin that the ancient stock of the Semyonov-Pishtchiks was derived from the very horse that Caligula made a member of the senate (*sits down*). But I've no money, that's where the mischief is. A hungry dog believes in nothing but meat . . . (*snores, but at once wakes up*). That's like me . . . I can think of nothing but money.

TROFIMOV: There really is something horsy about your appearance.

PISHTCHIK: Well . . . a horse is a fine beast . . . a horse can be sold.

[*There is the sound of billiards being played in an adjoining room. VARYA appears in the arch leading to the larger drawing-room.*]

TROFIMOV (*teasing*): Madame Lopahin! Madame Lopahin!

VARYA (*angrily*): Mangy-looking gentleman!

TROFIMOV: Yes, I am a mangy-looking gentleman, and I'm proud of it!

VARYA (*pondering bitterly*): Here we have hired musicians and nothing to pay them! (*goes out*).

TROFIMOV (*to* PISHTCHIK): If the energy you have wasted during your lifetime in trying to find the money to pay your interest, had gone to something else, you might in the end have turned the world upside down.

PISHTCHIK: Nietzsche, the philosopher, a very great and celebrated man . . . of enormous intellect . . . says in his works, that one can make forged bank-notes.

TROFIMOV: Why, have you read Nietzsche?

PISHTCHIK: What next . . . Dashenka told me. . . . And now I am in such a position, I might just as well forge bank-notes. The day after to-morrow I must pay 310 roubles—130 I have procured (*feels in his pockets, in alarm*). The money's gone! I have lost my money! (*Through his tears*) Where's the money? (*Gleefully*) Why here it is behind the lining. . . . It has made me hot all over.

[*Enter* LYUBOV ANDREYEVNA *and* CHARLOTTA IVANOVNA.]

LYUBOV (*hums the Lezginka*): Why is Leonid so long? What can he be doing in town? (*To* DUNYASHA) Offer the musicians some tea.

TROFIMOV: The sale hasn't taken place, most likely.

LYUBOV: It's the wrong time to have the orchestra, and the wrong time to give a dance. Well, never mind (*sits down and hums softly*).

CHARLOTTA (*gives* PISHTCHIK *a pack of cards*): Here's a pack of cards. Think of any card you like.

PISHTCHIK: I've thought of one.

CHARLOTTA: Shuffle the pack now. That's right. Give it here, my dear Mr. Pishtchik. Ein, zwei, drei—now look, it's in your breast pocket.

PISHTCHIK (*taking a card out of his breast pocket*): The eight of spades! Perfectly right! (*Wonderingly*) Fancy that now!

CHARLOTTA (*holding pack of cards in her hands, to* TROFIMOV): Tell me quickly which is the top card.

TROFIMOV: Well, the queen of spades.

CHARLOTTA: It is! (*To* PISHTCHIK) Well, which card is uppermost?

PISHTCHIK: The ace of hearts.

CHARLOTTA: It is! (*claps her hands, pack of cards disappears*). Ah! what lovely weather it is to-day!

[*A mysterious feminine voice which seems coming out of the floor answers her.* "*Oh, yes, it's magnificent weather, madam.*"]

CHARLOTTA: You are my perfect ideal.

VOICE: And I greatly admire you too, madam.

STATION MASTER (*applauding*): The lady ventriloquist—bravo!

PISHTCHIK (*wonderingly*): Fancy that now! Most enchanting Charlotta Ivanovna. I'm simply in love with you.

CHARLOTTA: In love? (*shrugging shoulders*). What do you know of love, guter Mensch, aber schlechter Musikant.

TROFIMOV (*pats* PISHTCHIK *on the shoulder*): You dear old horse. . . .

CHARLOTTA: Attention, please! Another trick! (*takes a travelling rug from a chair*). Here's a very good rug; I want to sell it (*shaking it out*). Doesn't anyone want to buy it?

PISHTCHIK (*wonderingly*): Fancy that!

CHARLOTTA: Ein, zwei, drei! (*quickly picks up rug she has dropped; behind the rug stands* ANYA; *she makes a curtsey, runs to her mother, embraces her and runs back into the larger drawing-room amidst general enthusiasm.*)

LYUBOV (*applauds*): Bravo! Bravo!

CHARLOTTA: Now again! Ein, zwei, drei! (*lifts up the rug; behind the rug stands* VARYA, *bowing*).

PISHTCHIK (*wonderingly*): Fancy that now!

CHARLOTTA: That's the end (*throws the rug at* PISHTCHIK, *makes a curtsey, runs into the larger drawing-room*).

PISHTCHIK (*hurries after her*): Mischievous creature! Fancy! (*goes out*).

LYUBOV: And still Leonid doesn't come. I can't understand what he's doing in the town so long! Why, everything must be over by now. The estate is sold, or the sale has not taken place. Why keep us so long in suspense?

VARYA (*trying to console her*): Uncle's bought it. I feel sure of that.

TROFIMOV (*ironically*): Oh, yes!

VARYA: Great-aunt sent him an authorisation to buy it in her name, and transfer the debt. She's doing it for Anya's sake, and I'm sure God will be merciful. Uncle will buy it.

LYUBOV: My aunt in Yaroslavl sent fifteen thousand to buy the estate in her name, she doesn't trust us—but that's not enough even to pay the arrears (*hides her face in her hands*). My fate is being sealed to-day, my fate . . .

TROFIMOV (*teasing* VARYA): Madame Lopahin.

VARYA (*angrily*): Perpetual student! Twice already you've been sent down from the University.

LYUBOV: Why are you angry, Varya? He's teasing you about Lopahin. Well, what of that? Marry Lopahin if you like, he's a good man, and interesting; if you don't want to, don't! Nobody compels you, darling.

VARYA: I must tell you plainly, mamma, I look at the matter seriously; he's a good man, I like him.

LYUBOV: Well, marry him. I can't see what you're waiting for.

VARYA: Mamma, I can't make him an offer myself. For the last two years, everyone's been talking to me about him. Everyone talks; but he says nothing or else makes a joke. I see what it means. He's growing rich, he's absorbed in business, he has no thoughts for me. If I had money, were it ever so little, if I had only a hundred roubles, I'd throw everything up and go far away. I would go into a nunnery.

TROFIMOV: What bliss!

VARYA (to TROFIMOV): A student ought to have sense! (In a soft tone with tears) How ugly you've grown, Petya! How old you look! (To LYUBOV ANDREYEVNA, no longer crying) But I can't do without work, mamma; I must have something to do every minute.

[Enter YASHA.]

YASHA (hardly restraining his laughter): Epihodov has broken a billiard cue! (goes out).

VARYA: What is Epihodov doing here? Who gave him leave to play billiards? I can't make these people out (goes out).

LYUBOV: Don't tease her, Petya. You see she has grief enough without that.

TROFIMOV: She is so very officious, meddling in what's not her business. All the summer she's given Anya and me no peace. She's afraid of a love affair between us. What's it to do with her? Besides, I have given no grounds for it. Such triviality is not in my line. We are above love!

LYUBOV: And I suppose I am beneath love. (Very uneasily) Why is it Leonid's not here? If only I could know whether the estate is sold or not! It seems such an incredible calamity that I really don't know what to think. I am distracted . . . I shall scream in a minute . . . I shall do something stupid. Save me, Petya, tell me something, talk to me!

TROFIMOV: What does it matter whether the estate is sold to-day or not? That's all done with long ago. There's no turning back, the path is overgrown. Don't worry yourself, dear Lyubov Andreyevna. You mustn't deceive yourself; for once in your life you must face the truth!

LYUBOV: What truth? You see where the truth lies, but I seem to have lost my sight, I see nothing. You settle every great problem so boldly, but tell me, my dear boy, isn't it because you're young—because you haven't yet understood one of your problems through suffering? You look forward boldly, and isn't it that you don't see and don't expect anything dreadful because life is still hidden from your young eyes? You're bolder, more honest, deeper than we are, but think, be just a little magnanimous, have pity on me. I was born here, you know, my father and mother lived here, my grandfather lived here, I love this house. I can't conceive of life without the cherry orchard, and if it really must be sold, then sell me with the orchard (embraces TROFIMOV, kisses him on the forehead). My boy was drowned here (weeps). Pity me, my dear kind fellow.

TROFIMOV: You know I feel for you with all my heart.

LYUBOV: But that should have been said differently, so differently (takes out her handkerchief, telegram falls on the floor). My heart is so heavy to-day. It's so noisy here, my soul is quivering at every sound, I'm shuddering all over, but I can't go away; I'm afraid to be quiet and alone. Don't be hard on me, Petya . . . I love you as though you were one of ourselves. I would gladly let you marry Anya—I swear I would—only, my dear boy, you must take your degree, you do nothing—you're simply tossed by fate from place to place. That's so strange. It is, isn't it? And you must do something with your beard to make it grow somehow (laughs). You look so funny!

TROFIMOV (picks up the telegram): I've no wish to be a beauty.

LYUBOV: That's a telegram from Paris. I get one every day. One yesterday and one to-day. That savage creature is ill again, he's in trouble again. He begs forgiveness, beseeches me to go, and really I ought to go to Paris to see him. You look shocked, Petya. What am I to do, my dear boy, what am I to do? He is ill, he is alone and unhappy, and who'll look after him, who'll keep him from doing the wrong thing, who'll give him his medicine at the right time? And why hide it or be silent? I love him, that's clear. I love him! I love him! He's a millstone about my neck, I'm going to the bottom with him, but I love that stone and can't live without it (presses TROFIMOV's hand). Don't think ill of me, Petya, don't tell me anything, don't tell me . . .

TROFIMOV (through his tears): For God's sake forgive my frankness: why, he robbed you!

LYUBOV: No! No! No! You mustn't speak like that (covers her ears).

TROFIMOV: He is a wretch! You're the only person that doesn't know it! He's a worthless creature! A despicable wretch!

LYUBOV (getting angry, but speaking with restraint): You're twenty-six or twenty-seven years old, but you're still a schoolboy.

TROFIMOV: Possibly.

LYUBOV: You should be a man at your age! You should understand what love means! And you ought to be in love yourself. You ought to fall in love! (*angrily*). Yes, yes, and it's not purity in you, you're simply a prude, a comic fool, a freak.

TROFIMOV (*in horror*): The things she's saying!

LYUBOV: I am above love! You're not above love, but simply as our Firs here says, "You are a good-for-nothing." At your age not to have a mistress!

TROFIMOV (*in horror*): This is awful! The things she is saying! (*goes rapidly into the larger drawing-room clutching his head*). This is awful! I can't stand it! I'm going! (*goes off, but at once returns*). All is over between us! (*goes off into the ante-room*).

LYUBOV (*shouts after him*): Petya! Wait a minute! You funny creature! I was joking! Petya! (*There is a sound of somebody running quickly downstairs and suddenly falling with a crash.* ANYA *and* VARYA *scream, but there is a sound of laughter at once.*)

LYUBOV: What has happened?

[ANYA *runs in.*]

ANYA (*laughing*): Petya's fallen downstairs! (*runs out*).

LYUBOV: What a queer fellow that Petya is!

[*The Station Master stands in the middle of the larger room and reads "The Magdalene," by Alexey Tolstoy. They listen to him, but before he has recited many lines strains of a waltz are heard from the ante-room and the reading is broken off. All dance.* TROFIMOV, ANYA, VARYA *and* LYUBOV ANDREYEVNA *come in from the ante-room.*]

LYUBOV: Come, Petya—come, pure heart! I beg your pardon. Let's have a dance! (*dances with* PETYA).

[ANYA *and* VARYA *dance.* FIRS *comes in, puts his stick down near the side door.* YASHA *also comes into the drawing-room and looks on at the dancing.*]

YASHA: What is it, old man?

FIRS: I don't feel well. In old days we used to have generals, barons and admirals dancing at our balls, and now we send for the post-office clerk and the station master and even they're not over anxious to come. I am getting feeble. The old master, the grandfather, used to give sealing-wax for all complaints. I have been taking sealing-wax for twenty years or more. Perhaps that's what's kept me alive.

YASHA: You bore me, old man! (*yawns*). It's time you were done with.

FIRS: Ach, you're a good-for-nothing! (*mutters*).

[TROFIMOV *and* LYUBOV ANDREYEVNA *dance in larger room and then on to the stage.*]

LYUBOV: Merci. I'll sit down a little (*sits down*). I'm tired.

[*Enter* ANYA.]

ANYA (*excitedly*): There's a man in the kitchen has been saying that the cherry orchard's been sold to-day.

LYUBOV: Sold to whom?

ANYA: He didn't say to whom. He's gone away.

[*She dances with* TROFIMOV, *and they go off into the larger room.*]

YASHA: There was an old man gossiping there, a stranger.

FIRS: Leonid Andreyevitch isn't here yet, he hasn't come back. He has his light overcoat on, *demi-saison*, he'll catch cold for sure. Ach! Foolish young things!!

LYUBOV: I feel as though I should die. Go, Yasha, find out to whom it has been sold.

YASHA: But he went away long ago, the old chap (*laughs*).

LYUBOV (*with slight vexation*): What are you laughing at? What are you pleased at?

YASHA: Epihodov is so funny. He's a silly fellow, two and twenty misfortunes.

LYUBOV: Firs, if the estate is sold, where will you go?

FIRS: Where you bid me, there I'll go.

LYUBOV: Why do you look like that? Are you ill? You ought to be in bed.

FIRS: Yes (*ironically*). Me go to bed and who's to wait here? Who's to see to things without me? I'm the only one in all the house.

YASHA (*to* LYUBOV ANDREYEVNA): Lyubov Andreyevna, permit me to make a request of you; if you go back to Paris again, be so kind as to take me with you. It's positively impossible for me to stay here. (*looking about him; in an undertone*) There's no need to say it, you see for yourself—an uncivilised country, the people have no morals, and then the dullness! The food in the kitchen's abominable, and then Firs runs after one muttering all sorts of unsuitable words. Take me with you, please do!

[*Enter* PISHTCHIK.]

PISHTCHIK: Allow me to ask you for a waltz, my dear lady. (LYUBOV ANDREYEVNA *goes with him.*) Enchanting lady, I really must borrow of you just 180 roubles (*dances*), only 180 roubles. (*They pass into the larger room.*)

YASHA (*hums softly*): "Knowest thou my soul's emotion."

[*In the larger drawing-room, a figure in a grey top hat and in check trousers is gesticulating and jumping about. Shouts of " Bravo, Charlotta Ivanovna."*]

DUNYASHA (*she has stopped to powder herself*): My young lady tells me to dance. There are plenty of gentlemen, and too few ladies, but dancing makes me giddy and makes my heart beat. Firs, the post-office clerk said something to me just now that quite took my breath away.

[*Music becomes more subdued.*]

FIRS: What did he say to you?
DUNYASHA: He said I was like a flower.
YASHA (*yawns*): What ignorance! (*goes out*).
DUNYASHA: Like a flower. I am a girl of such delicate feelings, I am awfully fond of soft speeches.
FIRS: Your head's being turned.

[*Enter EPIHODOV.*]

EPIHODOV: You have no desire to see me, Dunyasha. I might be an insect (*sighs*). Ah! life!
DUNYASHA: What is it you want?
EPIHODOV: Undoubtedly you may be right (*sighs*). But of course, if one looks at it from that point of view, if I may so express myself, you have, excuse my plain speaking, reduced me to a complete state of mind. I know my destiny. Every day some misfortune befalls me and I have long ago grown accustomed to it, so that I look upon my fate with a smile. You gave me your word, and though I—
DUNYASHA: Let us have a talk later, I entreat you, but now leave me in peace, for I am lost in reverie (*plays with her fan*).
EPIHODOV: I have a misfortune every day, and if I may venture to express myself, I merely smile at it, I even laugh.

[*VARYA enters from the larger drawing-room.*]

VARYA: You still have not gone, Epihodov. What a disrespectful creature you are, really! (*To* DUNYASHA) Go along, Dunyasha! (*To* EPIHODOV) First you play billiards and break the cue, then you go wandering about the drawing-room like a visitor!
EPIHODOV: You really cannot, if I may so express myself, call me to account like this.
VARYA: I'm not calling you to account, I'm speaking to you. You do nothing but wander from place to place and don't do your work. We keep you as a counting-house clerk, but what use you are I

can't say.
EPIHODOV (*offended*): Whether I work or whether I walk, whether I eat or whether I play billiards, is a matter to be judged by persons of understanding and my elders.
VARYA: You dare to tell me that! (*Firing up*) You dare! You mean to say I've no understanding. Begone from here! This minute!
EPIHODOV (*intimidated*): I beg you to express yourself with delicacy.
VARYA (*beside herself with anger*): This moment! get out! away! (*He goes towards the door, she following him*). Two and twenty misfortunes! Take yourself off! Don't let me set eyes on you! (EPIHODOV *has gone out, behind the door his voice, "I shall lodge a complaint against you"*). What! You're coming back? (*snatches up the stick* FIRS *has put down near the door*). Come! Come! Come! I'll show you! What! you're coming? Then take that! (*she swings the stick, at the very moment that* LOPAHIN *comes in*).
LOPAHIN: Very much obliged to you!
VARYA (*angrily and ironically*): I beg your pardon!
LOPAHIN: Not at all! I humbly thank you for your kind reception!
VARYA: No need of thanks for it (*moves away, then looks round and asks softly*) I haven't hurt you?
LOPAHIN: Oh, no! Not at all! There's an immense bump coming up, though!
VOICES FROM LARGER ROOM: Lopahin has come! Yermolay Alexeyevitch!
PISHTCHIK: What do I see and hear? (*kisses* LOPAHIN). There's a whiff of cognac about you, my dear soul, and we're making merry here too!

[*Enter LYUBOV ANDREYEVNA.*]

LYUBOV: Is it you, Yermolay Alexeveyitch? Why have you been so long? Where's Leonid?
LOPAHIN: Leonid Andreyevitch arrived with me. He is coming.
LYUBOV (*in agitation*): Well! Well! Was there a sale? Speak!
LOPAHIN (*embarrassed, afraid of betraying his joy*): The sale was over at four o'clock. We missed our train—had to wait till half-past nine. (*Sighing heavily*) Ugh! I feel a little giddy.

[*Enter GAEV. In his right hand he has purchases, with his left hand he is wiping away his tears.*]

LYUBOV: Well, Leonid? What news? (*Impatiently, with tears*) Make haste, for God's sake!
GAEV (*makes her no answer, simply waves his hand. To* FIRS,*weeping*): Here, take them; there's anchovies, Kertch herrings. I have eaten nothing all day. What I have been through! (*Door into the billiard*

room is open. *There is heard a knocking of balls and the voice of* YASHA *saying "Eighty-seven."* GAEV's *expression changes, he leaves off weeping*). I am fearfully tired. Firs, come and help me change my things (*goes to his own room across the larger drawing-room*).

PISHTCHIK: How about the sale? Tell us, do!

LYUBOV: Is the cherry orchard sold?

LOPAHIN: It is sold.

LYUBOV: Who has bought it?

LOPAHIN: I have bought it. (*A pause.* LYUBOV *is crushed; she would fall down if she were not standing near a chair and table.*)

*[*VARYA *takes keys from her waist-band, flings them on the floor in middle of drawing-room and goes out.]*

LOPAHIN: I have bought it! Wait a bit, ladies and gentlemen, pray. My head's a bit muddled, I can't speak (*laughs*). We came to the auction. Deriganov was there already. Leonid Andreyevitch only had 15,000 and Deriganov bid 30,000, besides the arrears, straight off. I saw how the land lay. I bid against him. I bid 40,000 , he bid 45,000, I said 55, and so he went on, adding 5 thousands and I adding 10. Well . . . So it ended. I bid 90, and it was knocked down to me. Now the cherry orchard's mine! Mine! (*chuckles*). My God, the cherry orchard's mine! Tell me that I'm drunk, that I'm out of my mind, that it's all a dream (*stamps with his feet*). Don't laugh at me! If my father and my grandfather could rise from their graves and see all that has happened! How their Yermolay, ignorant, beaten Yermolay, who used to run about barefoot in winter, how that very Yermolay has bought the finest estate in the world! I have bought the estate where my father and grandfather were slaves, where they weren't even admitted into the kitchen. I am asleep, I am dreaming! It is all fancy, it is the work of your imagination plunged in the darkness of ignorance (*picks up keys, smiling fondly*). She threw away the keys; she means to show she's not the housewife now (*jingles the keys*). Well, no matter. (*The orchestra is heard tuning up.*) Hey, musicians! Play! I want to hear you. Come, all of you, and look how Yermolay Lopahin will take the axe to the cherry orchard, how the trees will fall to the ground! We will build houses on it and our grandsons and great-grandsons will see a new life springing up there. Music! Play up!

[Music begins to play. LYUBOV ANDREYEVNA *has sunk into a chair and is weeping bitterly.]*

LOPAHIN (*reproachfully*): Why, why didn't you listen to me? My poor friend! Dear lady, there's no turning back now. (*With tears*) Oh, if all this could be over, oh, if our miserable disjointed life could somehow soon be changed!

PISHTCHIK (*takes him by the arm, in an undertone*): She's weeping, let us go and leave her alone. Come (*takes him by the arm and leads him into the larger drawing-room*).

LOPAHIN: What's that? Musicians, play up! All must be as I wish it. (*With irony*) Here comes the new master, the owner of the cherry orchard! (*accidentally tips over a little table, almost upsetting the candelabra*). I can pay for everything! (*goes out with* PISHTCHIK. *No one remains on the stage or in the larger drawing-room except* LYUBOV, *who sits huddled up, weeping bitterly. The music plays softly.* ANYA *and* TROFIMOV *come in quickly.* ANYA *goes up to her mother and falls on her knees before her.* TROFIMOV *stands at the entrance to the larger drawing-room*).

ANYA: Mamma! Mamma, you're crying, dear, kind, good mamma! My precious! I love you! I bless you! The cherry orchard is sold, it is gone, that's true, that's true! But don't weep, mamma! Life is still before you, you have still your good, pure heart! Let us go, let us go, darling, away from here! We will make a new garden, more splendid than this one; you will see it, you will understand. And joy, quiet, deep joy, will sink into your soul like the sun at evening! And you will smile, mamma! Come, darling, let us go!

Curtain.

ACT IV

SCENE: Same as in First Act. There are neither curtains on the windows nor pictures on the walls: only a little furniture remains piled up in a corner as if for sale. There is a sense of desolation; near the outer door and in the background of the scene are packed trunks, travelling bags, etc. On the left the door is open, and from here the voices of VARYA *and* ANYA *are audible.* LOPAHIN *is standing waiting.* YASHA *is holding a tray with glasses full of champagne. In front of the stage* EPIHODOV *is trying up a box. In the background behind the scene a hum of talk from the peasants who have come to say goodbye. The voice of* GAEV: *"Thanks, brothers, thanks!"*

YASHA: The peasants have come to say good-bye. In my opinion, Yermolay Alexeyevitch, the peasants are good-natured, but they don't know much about things.

[The hum of talk dies away. Enter across front of stage LYUBOV ANDREYEVNA *and* GAEV. *She is not weeping, but is pale; her face is quivering—she cannot speak.]*

GAEV: You gave them your purse, Lyuba. That won't do—that won't do!

LYUBOV: I couldn't help it! I couldn't help it!

[Both go out.]

LOPAHIN (*in the doorway, calls after them*): You will take a glass at parting? Please do. I didn't think to bring any from the town, and at the station I could only get one bottle. Please take a glass (*a pause*). What? You don't care for any? (*comes away from the door*). If I'd known, I wouldn't have bought it. Well, and I'm not going to drink it. (YASHA *carefully sets the tray down on a chair.*) You have a glass, Yasha, anyway.

YASHA: Good luck to the travellers, and luck to those that stay behind! (*drinks*). This champagne isn't the real thing, I can assure you.

LOPAHIN: It cost eight roubles the bottle (*a pause*). It's devilish cold here.

YASHA: They haven't heated the stove to-day—it's all the same since we're going (*laughs*).

LOPAHIN: What are you laughing for?

YASHA: For pleasure.

LOPAHIN: Though it's October, it's as still and sunny as though it were summer. It's just right for building! (*Looks at his watch; says in doorway*) Take note, ladies and gentlemen, the train goes in forty-seven minutes; so you ought to start for the station in twenty minutes. You must hurry up!

*[*TROFIMOV *comes in from out of doors wearing a greatcoat.]*

TROFIMOV: I think it must be time to start, the horses are ready. The devil only knows what's become of my goloshes; they're lost. (*In the doorway*) Anya! My goloshes aren't here. I can't find them.

LOPAHIN: And I'm getting off to Harkov. I am going in the same train with you. I'm spending all the winter at Harkov. I've been wasting all my time gossiping with you and fretting with no work to do. I can't get on without work. I don't know what to do with my hands, they flap about so queerly, as if they didn't belong to me.

TROFIMOV: Well, we're just going away, and you will take up your profitable labours again.

LOPAHIN: Do take a glass.

TROFIMOV: No, thanks.

LOPAHIN: Then you're going to Moscow now?

TROFIMOV: Yes. I shall see them as far as the town, and to-morrow I shall go on to Moscow.

LOPAHIN: Yes, I daresay, the professors aren't giving any lectures, they're waiting for your arrival.

TROFIMOV: That's not your business.

LOPAHIN: How many years have you been at the University?

TROFIMOV: Do think of something newer than that— that's stale and flat (*hunts for goloshes*). You know we shall most likely never see each other again, so let me give you one piece of advice at parting: don't wave your arms about—get out of the habit. And another thing, building villas, reckoning up that the summer visitors will in time become independent farmers—reckoning like that, that's not the thing to do either. After all, I am fond of you: you have fine delicate fingers like an artist, you've a fine delicate soul.

LOPAHIN (*embraces him*): Good-bye, my dear fellow. Thanks for everything. Let me give you money for the journey, if you need it.

TROFIMOV: What for? I don't need it.

LOPAHIN: Why, you haven't got a halfpenny.

TROFIMOV: Yes, I have, thank you. I got some money for a translation. Here it is in my pocket, (*anxiously*) but where can my goloshes be!

VARYA (*from the next room*): Take the nasty things! (*flings a pair of goloshes on to the stage*).

TROFIMOV: Why are you so cross, Varya? h'm! . . . but those aren't my goloshes.

LOPAHIN: I sowed three thousand acres with poppies in the spring, and now I have cleared forty thousand profit. And when my poppies were in flower, wasn't it a picture? So here, as I say, I made forty thousand, and I'm offering you a loan because I can afford to. Why turn up your nose? I am a peasant—I speak bluntly.

TROFIMOV: Your father was a peasant, mine was a chemist—and that proves absolutely nothing whatever. (LOPAHIN *takes out his pocket-book.*) Stop that—stop that. If you were to offer me two hundred thousand I wouldn't take it. I am an independent man, and everything that all of you, rich and poor alike, prize so highly and hold so dear, hasn't the slightest power over me—it's like so much fluff fluttering in the air. I can get on without you. I can pass by you. I am strong and proud. Humanity is advancing towards the highest truth, the highest happiness, which is possible on earth, and I am in the front ranks.

LOPAHIN: Will you get there?

TROFIMOV: I shall get there (*a pause*). I shall get there, or I shall show others the way to get there.

[In the distance is heard the stroke of an axe on a tree.]

LOPAHIN: Good-bye, my dear fellow; it's time to be

off. We turn up our noses at one another, but life is passing all the while. When I am working hard without resting, then my mind is more at ease, and it seems to me as though I too know what I exist for; but how many people there are in Russia, my dear boy, who exist, one doesn't know what for. Well, it doesn't matter. That's not what keeps things spinning. They tell me Leonid Andreyevitch has taken a situation. He is going to be a clerk at the bank—6,000 roubles a year. Only, of course, he won't stick to it—he's too lazy.

ANYA (*in the doorway*): Mamma begs you not to let them chop down the orchard until she's gone.

TROFIMOV: Yes, really, you might have the tact (*walks out across the front of the stage*).

LOPAHIN: I'll see to it! I'll see to it! Stupid fellows! (*goes out after him*).

ANYA: Has Firs been taken to the hospital?

YASHA: I told them this morning. No doubt they have taken him.

ANYA (*to* EPIHODOV, *who passes across the drawing-room*): Semyon Pantaleyevitch, inquire, please, if Firs has been taken to the hospital.

YASHA (*in a tone of offence*): I told Yegor this morning—why ask a dozen times?

EPIHODOV: Firs is advanced in years. It's my conclusive opinion no treatment would do him good; it's time he was gathered to his fathers. And I can only envy him (*puts a trunk down on a cardboard hat-box and crushes it*). There, now, of course—I knew it would be so.

YASHA (*jeeringly*): Two and twenty misfortunes!

VARYA (*through the door*): Has Firs been taken to the hospital?

ANYA: Yes.

VARYA: Why wasn't the note for the doctor taken too?

ANYA: Oh, then, we must send it after them (*goes out*).

VARYA (*from the adjoining room*): Where's Yasha? Tell him his mother's come to say good-bye to him.

YASHA (*waves his hand*): They put me out of all patience! (DUNYASHA *has all this time been busy about the luggage. Now, when* YASHA *is left alone, she goes up to him.*)

DUNYASHA: You might just give me one look, Yasha. You're going away. You're leaving me (*weeps and throws herself on his neck*).

YASHA: What are you crying for? (*drinks the champagne*). In six days I shall be in Paris again. Tomorrow we shall get into the express train and roll away in a flash. I can scarcely believe it! Vive la France! It doesn't suit me here—it's not the life for me; there's no doing anything. I have seen enough of the ignorance here. I have had enough of it (*drinks champagne*). What are you crying for?

Behave yourself properly, and then you won't cry.

DUNYASHA (*powders her face, looking in a pocket-mirror*): Do send me a letter from Paris. You know how I loved you, Yasha—how I loved you! I am a tender creature, Yasha.

YASHA: Here they are coming!

[*Busies himself about the trunks, humming softly. Enter* LYUBOV ANDREYEVNA, GAEV, ANYA *and* CHARLOTTA IVANOVNA.]

GAEV: We ought to be off. There's not much time now (*looking at* YASHA). What a smell of herrings!

LYUBOV: In ten minutes we must get into the carriage (*casts a look about the room*). Farewell, dear house, dear old home of our fathers! Winter will pass and spring will come, and then you will be no more; they will tear you down! How much those walls have seen! (*kisses her daughter passionately*). My treasure, how bright you look! Your eyes are sparkling like diamonds! Are you glad? Very glad?

ANYA: Very glad! A new life is beginning, mamma.

GAEV: Yes, really, everything is all right now. Before the cherry orchard was sold, we were all worried and wretched, but afterwards, when once the question was settled conclusively, irrevocably, we all felt calm and even cheerful. I am a bank clerk now—I am a financier—cannon off the red. And you, Lyuba, after all, you are looking better; there's no question of that.

LYUBOV: Yes. My nerves are better, that's true. (*Her hat and coat are handed to her*). I'm sleeping well. Carry out my things, Yasha. It's time. (*To* ANYA) My darling, we shall soon see each other again. I am going to Paris. I can live there on the money your Yaroslavl auntie sent us to buy the estate with—hurrah for auntie!—but that money won't last long.

ANYA: You'll come back soon, mamma, won't you? I'll be working up for my examination in the high school, and when I have passed that, I shall set to work and be a help to you. We will read all sorts of things together, mamma, won't we? (*kisses her mother's hands*). We will read in the autumn evenings. We'll read lots of books, and a new wonderful world will open out before us (*dreamily*). Mamma, come soon.

LYUBOV: I shall come, my precious treasure (*embraces her*).

[*Enter* LOPAHIN. CHARLOTTA *softly hums a song.*]

GAEV: Charlotta's happy: she's singing!

CHARLOTTA (*picks up a bundle like a swaddled baby*): Bye, bye, my baby. (*A baby is heard crying: "Ooah!*

ooah!"). Hush, hush, my pretty boy! (*Ooah! ooah!*). Poor little thing! (*throws the bundle back*). You must please find me a situation. I can't go on like this.

LOPAHIN: We'll find you one, Charlotta Ivanovna. Don't you worry yourself.

GAEV: Everyone's leaving us. Varya's going away. We have become of no use all at once.

CHARLOTTA: There's nowhere for me to be in the town. I must go away. (*Hums*) What care I . . .

[Enter PISHTCHIK.]

LOPAHIN: The freak of nature!

PISHTCHIK (*gasping*): Oh! . . . let me get my breath. . . . I'm worn out . . . my most honoured . . . Give me some water.

GAEV: Want some money, I suppose? Your humble servant! I'll go out of the way of temptation (*goes out*).

PISHTCHIK: It's a long while since I have been to see you . . . dearest lady. (*To* LOPAHIN) You are here . . . glad to see you . . . a man of immense intellect . . . take . . . here (*gives* LOPAHIN *money*) 400 roubles. That leaves me owing 840.

LOPAHIN (*shrugging his shoulders in amazement*): It's like a dream. Where did you get it?

PISHTCHIK: Wait a bit . . . I'm hot . . . a most extraordinary occurrence! Some Englishmen came along and found in my land some sort of white clay. (*To* LYUBOV ANDREYEVNA) And 400 for you . . . most lovely . . . wonderful (*gives money*). The rest later (*sips water*). A young man in the train was telling me just now that a great philosopher advises jumping off a house-top. "Jump!" says he; "the whole gist of the problem lies in that." (*Wonderingly*) Fancy that, now! Water, please!

LOPAHIN: What Englishmen?

PISHTCHIK: I have made over to them the rights to dig the clay for twenty-four years . . . and now, excuse me . . . I can't stay . . . I must be trotting on. I'm going to Znoikovo . . . to Kardamanovo. . . . I'm in debt all round (*sips*). . . . To your very good health! . . . I'll come in on Thursday.

LYUBOV: We are just off to the town, and to-morrow I start for abroad.

PISHTCHIK: What! (*in agitation*). Why to the town? Oh, I see the furniture . . . the boxes. No matter . . . (*through his tears*) . . . no matter . . . men of enormous intellect . . . these Englishmen. . . . Never mind . . . be happy. God will succour you . . . no matter . . . everything in this world must have an end (*kisses* LYUBOV ANDREYEVNA's *hand*). If the rumour reaches you that my end has come, think of this . . . old horse, and say: "There once was such a man in the world . . . Semyonov-Pishtchik . . . the kingdom of heaven be his!" . . . most extraordi-

nary weather . . . yes. (*Goes out in violent agitation, but at once returns and says in the doorway*) Dashenka wishes to be remembered to you (*goes out*).

LYUBOV: Now we can start. I leave with two cares in my heart. The first is leaving Firs ill. (*Looking at her watch*) We have still five minutes.

ANYA: Mamma, Firs has been taken to the hospital. Yasha sent him off this morning.

LYUBOV: My other anxiety is Varya. She is used to getting up early and working; and now, without work, she's like a fish out of water. She is thin and pale, and she's crying, poor dear! (*a pause*). You are well aware, Yermolay Alexeyevitch, I dreamed of marrying her to you, and everything seemed to show that you would get married (*whispers to* ANYA *and motions to* CHARLOTTA *and both go out*). She loves you—she suits you. And I don't know—I don't know why it is you seem, as it were, to avoid each other. I can't understand it!

LOPAHIN: I don't understand it myself, I confess. It's queer somehow, altogether. If there's still time, I'm ready now at once. Let's settle it straight off, and go ahead; but without you, I feel I shan't make her an offer.

LYUBOV: That's excellent. Why, a single moment's all that's necessary. I'll call her at once.

LOPAHIN: And there's champagne all ready too (*looking into the glasses*). Empty! Someone's emptied them already. (*YASHA coughs*.) I call that greedy.

LYUBOV (*eagerly*): Capital! We will go out. Yasha, *allez!* I'll call her in. (*At the door*) Varya, leave all that; come here. Come along! (*goes out with* YASHA).

LOPAHIN (*looking at his watch*): Yes.

[A pause. Behind the door, smothered laughter and whispering, and, at last, enter VARYA.]

VARYA (*looking a long while over the things*): It is strange, I can't find it anywhere.

LOPAHIN: What are you looking for?

VARYA: I packed it myself, and I can't remember (*a pause*).

LOPAHIN: Where are you going now, Varvara Mihailova?

VARYA: I? To the Ragulins. I have arranged to go to them to look after the house—as a housekeeper.

LOPAHIN: That's in Yashnovo? It'll be seventy miles away (*a pause*). So this is the end of life in this house!

VARYA (*looking among the things*): Where is it? Perhaps I put it in the trunk. Yes, life in this house is over—there will be no more of it.

LOPAHIN: And I'm just off to Harkov—by this next train. I've a lot of business there. I'm leaving Epihodov here, and I've taken him on.

VARYA: Really!

LOPAHIN: This time last year we had snow already, if you remember; but now it's so fine and sunny. Though it's cold, to be sure—three degrees of frost.

VARYA: I haven't looked (*a pause*). And besides, our thermometer's broken (*a pause*).

[Voice at the door from the yard: "Yermolay Alexeyevitch!"]

LOPAHIN (*as though he had long been expecting this summons*): This minute!

[LOPAHIN goes out quickly. VARYA sitting on the floor and laying her head on a bag full of clothes, sobs quietly. The door opens. LYUBOV ANDREYEVNA comes in cautiously.]

LYUBOV: Well? (*a pause*). We must be going.

VARYA (*has wiped her eyes and is no longer crying*): Yes, mamma, it's time to start. I shall have time to get to the Ragulins to-day, if only you're not late for the train.

LYUBOV (*in the doorway*): Anya, put your things on.

[Enter ANYA, then GAEV and CHARLOTTA IVANOVNA. GAEV has on a warm coat with a hood. Servants and cabmen come in. EPIHODOV bustles about the luggage.]

LYUBOV: Now we can start on our travels.

ANYA (*joyfully*): On our travels!

GAEV: My friends—my dear, my precious friends! Leaving this house for ever, can I be silent? Can I refrain from giving utterance at leave-taking to those emotions which now flood all my being?

ANYA (*supplicatingly*): Uncle!

VARYA: Uncle, you mustn't!

GAEV (*dejectedly*). Cannon and into the pocket . . . I'll be quiet. . . .

[Enter TROFIMOV and afterwards LOPAHIN.]

TROFIMOV: Well, ladies and gentlemen, we must start.

LOPAHIN: Epihodov, my coat!

LYUBOV: I'll stay just one minute. It seems as though I have never seen before what the walls, what the ceilings in this house were like, and now I look at them with greediness, with such tender love.

GAEV: I remember when I was six years old sitting in that window on Trinity Day watching my father going to church.

LYUBOV: Have all the things been taken?

LOPAHIN: I think all. (*Putting on overcoat, to EPIHODOV*) You, Epihodov, mind you see everything is right.

EPIHODOV (*in a husky voice*): Don't you trouble, Yermolay Alexeyevitch.

LOPAHIN: Why, what's wrong with your voice?

EPIHODOV: I've just had a drink of water, and I choked over something.

YASHA (*contemptuously*): The ignorance!

LYUBOV: We are going—and not a soul will be left here.

LOPAHIN: Not till the spring.

VARYA (*pulls a parasol out of a bundle, as though about to hit someone with it. LOPAHIN makes a gesture as though alarmed*): What is it? I didn't mean anything.

TROFIMOV: Ladies and gentlemen, let us get into the carriage. It's time. The train will be in directly.

VARYA: Petya, here they are, your goloshes, by that box. (*With tears*) And what dirty old things they are!

TROFIMOV (*putting on his goloshes*): Let us go, friends!

GAEV (*greatly agitated, afraid of weeping*): The train—the station! Double baulk, ah!

LYUBOV: Let us go!

LOPAHIN: Are we all here? (*locks the side-door on left*). The things are all here. We must lock up. Let us go!

ANYA: Good-bye, home! Good-bye to the old life!

TROFIMOV: Welcome to the new life!

[TROFIMOV goes out with ANYA. VARYA looks round the room and goes out slowly. YASHA and CHARLOTTA IVANOVNA, with her dog, go out.]

LOPAHIN: Till the spring, then! Come, friends, till we meet! (*goes out*).

[LYUBOV ANDREYEVNA and GAEV remain alone. As though they had been waiting for this, they throw themselves on each other's necks, and break into subdued smothered sobbing, afraid of being overheard.]

GAEV (*in despair*): Sister, my sister!

LYUBOV: Oh, my orchard!—my sweet, beautiful orchard! My life, my youth, my happiness, good-bye! good-bye!

VOICE OF ANYA (*calling gaily*): Mamma!

VOICE OF TROFIMOV (*gaily, excitedly*): Aa—oo!

LYUBOV: One last look at the walls, at the windows. My dear mother loved to walk about this room.

GAEV: Sister, sister!

VOICE OF ANYA: Mamma!

VOICE OF TROFIMOV: Aa—oo!

LYUBOV: We are coming. (*They go out.*)

[The stage is empty. There is the sound of the doors being locked up, then of the carriages driving away. There is silence. In the stillness there is the dull stroke of an axe in a tree, clanging with a mournful lonely sound. Footsteps are heard. FIRS appears in the door-

way on the right. He is dressed as always—in a pea-jacket and white waistcoat, with slippers on his feet. He is ill.]

FIRS (*goes up to the doors, and tries the handles*): Locked! They have gone . . . (*sits down on sofa*). They have forgotten me. . . . Never mind . . . I'll sit here a bit. . . . I'll be bound Leonid Andreyevitch hasn't put his fur coat on and has gone off in his thin overcoat (*sighs anxiously*). I didn't see after him. . . . These young people . . . (*mutters something that can't be distinguished*). Life has slipped by as though I hadn't lived. (*Lies down*) I'll lie down a bit. . . . There's no strength in you, nothing left you—all gone! Ech! I'm good for nothing (*lies motionless*).

[A sound is heard that seems to come from the sky, like a breaking harp-string, dying away mournfully. All is still again, and there is heard nothing but the strokes of the axe far away in the orchard.]

Curtain.

GEORGE BERNARD SHAW

(1856–1950)

George Bernard Shaw was born and raised in Dublin. His father was an unsuccessful businessman and an alcoholic; his mother was a talented musician who paid little attention to running the household. Early on she left for London and worked as a music teacher. At fifteen Shaw dropped out of school, and at nineteen he moved to London to live with his mother, who supported him while he developed his writing career. At this period in his life, Shaw read widely, and in 1883 he became involved in the Fabian Society, a political organization that worked for gradual social reform by electing party officials to office rather than through the violent revolution advocated by Marxists. This gradual scheme for social reform complemented Shaw's belief in the creative evolution of humanity; he rejected Darwin's biological model of evolution through natural selection. Shaw believed that enlightened societies could will themselves to evolve in positive directions. To achieve these goals, Shaw and the Fabians wrote leaflets, pamphlets, books, and newspaper articles, and they delivered lectures on the economic, political, and social issues of the time. By the late 1880s Shaw was also writing book reviews and music, theater, and art criticism for several London newspapers. As a theater critic, Shaw objected to the conventions of nineteenth-century melodrama, and in 1891 he wrote his famous *Quintessence of Ibsenism*, bringing serious attention to Ibsen's work from the English public for the first time.

Shaw's career as a playwright did not begin until he was in his late thirties. His earliest works, such as *Widowers' Houses* (1892) and *Mrs. Warren's Profession* (1893), were concerned with the social issues of poor housing and with prostitution. In contrast to the psychological depth of Ibsen's characters, Shaw's dramatic figures were witty spokespersons for his own social and political views. So strong was this quality of his work that the term *Shavian* was invented to describe any play in which the interest in ideas overshadows interest in character. But Shaw is often very funny and entertaining as well as intellectually interesting. Perhaps the best-known example of his comic wit is *Pygmalion* (1913), later remade as the musical *My Fair Lady* (1956), in which Professor Henry Higgins transforms the cockney Eliza Doolittle by teaching her to speak with an upper-class accent and then falls in love with her. Shaw manages to put across his point about class barriers and creative evolution while still managing to entertain. At heart Shaw was a philosophical playwright whose natural focus was on key social issues. In *Arms and the Man* (1894) Shaw ridicules romanticized views of love and war. In *Candida* (1894) he exposes the hypocrisy of conventional views of women and marriage. In *Caesar and Cleopatra* (1898) he rewrites Shakespeare's characters and view of history, making Cleopatra into a naive girl and Caesar into a portrait of politically astute greatness. Shaw's Caesar was the first of his "supermen," whose power to change history derived from an inner vitality and a rejection of confining social conventions.

Shaw's prefaces to his plays—often as long as the plays themselves—explain in detail his own views on his characters, plots, and themes. The preface to *Man and Superman* (1903), for example, explains Shaw's ideas of the "life force" and "creative evolution" and explores how genetic engineering and planning can create a race of supermen. The preface to *Major Barbara* (1905) explores the connection between conventional morality and poverty. Several of Shaw's plays were produced at the Court Theatre under the direction of his friend Harley Granville-Barker. Between 1904 and 1907 the Court Theatre became the most important theatre in London, and it made Shaw's dramatic reputation.

World War I undermined Shaw's confidence in the perfection of humanity, and his later plays are philosophically much more uncertain. *Heartbreak House* (1920), modeled on Chekhov's *Cherry Orchard*, presents an apocalyptic vision, and *Saint Joan* (1923) dramatizes the conflict between the life force in an individual genius and political institutions. Already professionally active in the late nineteenth century, Shaw continued to write throughout the first half of the twentieth century. One of the most prolific of all British dramatists, he lived to be ninety-six and wrote over fifty plays.

Major Barbara

When *Major Barbara* opened in London in 1905, critics found it lacking as drama but stimulating in its presentation of ideas. Like so much of Shaw's dramatic work, it is a thesis play, one that advances a particular view on a subject. The subject is poverty, which Shaw declares in his preface to be a modern social crime. The play explores both idealistic and realistic approaches to the subject. Andrew Undershaft, the millionaire munitions manufacturer, and his daughter, Major Barbara of the Salvation Army, represent these two extreme positions. Major Barbara is an idealist who believes that the manufacture of munitions is immoral, and she attempts to save lives and souls through social work. Her father is a pragmatic realist who regards his profession as the natural product of his society—and world. He sells munitions to those who can afford to pay; what the buyers do with the equipment is not his concern. His contempt for idealists stems from his understanding of the realities of capitalistic economies. He knows that market supply and demand, and the wealth that such market forces create, ultimately not only determine the way businesses operate but also profoundly affect the lives and ideals of everyone in society. The Salvation Army, for example, which seeks to save lives and souls, cannot operate without funding, and, as Undershaft demonstrates, its sources of funding in this play are tainted. The need for funding makes the Salvation Army dependent on people like Bodger, who sells alcohol to the desperately poor, and on Undershaft, who sells weapons of mass destruction. In *Major Barbara* Shaw is interested in fostering thought on the subject, not in offering simplistic solutions. After all, both Wilton Crescent, where the upper class thrives, and West Ham, where the Salvation Army tries to do its work, are alike dependent on men like Bodger and Undershaft.

According to tradition Undershaft must retire and pass the business on to a foundling. That turns out to be Adolphus Cusins, the professor of Greek who falls in love with Barbara. In the end Adolphus accepts the business and proposes to Barbara; she agrees to leave the Salvation Army to support him. Her idealistic position at the beginning of the play, now modified by her recognition of the interconnectedness of social and economic relations, must acknowledge that nothing in such a society is free from contamination. The third act of the play is often described as its weak point. Is Perivale St. Andrews and the utopian socialism it is founded upon a suitable solution to the problems Shaw has raised? Few have thought so, and some have suggested that Shaw may have constructed the act purposefully to encourage further thought on the issues he has brought before the audience.

Major Barbara is also a parody of the melodramatic parlor play, so popular in Victorian times, enlivening domestic scenes with lightweight humor and ending with an edifying moral. Shaw turns the old conventions on their head throughout the play. The penniless dowager widow has become Lady Britomart—wealthy because of her former husband's trade and scornful of it at the same time, despite her continuing dependence on it. The virtuous young "shrinking violet" figure has become Major Barbara, a formidable young woman for whom idealistic philosophical principles take precedence over her interest in love. The manly hero has become Adolphus Cusins, whose slight build and cerebral pursuits as a professor of Greek would seem to put him at a disadvantage. The villain has become Undershaft, who triumphs at the end of the play, having transformed Barbara's principles and Cusins's occupation. Shaw exulted in these kinds of delicious contradictions, which have endured far more gracefully than the social theses that originally lay at the heart of so many of his plays.

Major Barbara

GEORGE BERNARD SHAW

N.B. The Euripidean verses in the second act of Major Barbara are not by me, nor even directly by Euripides. They are by Professor Gilbert Murray, whose English version of The Bacchæ came into our dramatic literature with all the impulsive power of an original work shortly before Major Barbara was begun. The play, indeed, stands indebted to him in more ways than one.

G. B. S.

PREFACE TO *MAJOR BARBARA*

First Aid to Critics

Before dealing with the deeper aspects of Major Barbara, let me, for the credit of English literature, make a protest against an unpatriotic habit into which many of my critics have fallen. Whenever my view strikes them as being at all outside the range of, say, an ordinary suburban churchwarden, they conclude that I am echoing Schopenhauer, Nietzsche, Ibsen, Strindberg, Tolstoy, or some other heresiarch in northern or eastern Europe.

I confess there is something flattering in this simple faith in my accomplishment as a linguist and my erudition as a philosopher. But I cannot countenance the assumption that life and literature are so poor in these islands that we must go abroad for all dramatic material that is not common and all ideas that are not superficial. I therefore venture to put my critics in possession of certain facts concerning my contact with modern ideas.

About half a century ago, an Irish novelist, Charles Lever, wrote a story entitled A Day's Ride: A Life's Romance. It was published by Charles Dickens in Household Words, and proved so strange to the public taste that Dickens pressed Lever to make short work of it. I read scraps of this novel when I was a child; and it made an enduring impression on me. The hero was a very romantic hero, trying to live bravely, chivalrously, and powerfully by dint of mere romance-fed imagination, without courage, without means, without knowledge, without skill, without anything real except his bodily appetites. Even in my childhood I found in this poor devil's unsuccessful encounters with the facts of life, a poignant quality that romantic fiction lacked. The book, in spite of its first failure, is not dead: I saw its title the other day in the catalogue of Tauchnitz.

Now why is it that when I also deal in the tragi-comic irony of the conflict between real life and the romantic imagination, critics never affiliate me to my countryman and immediate forerunner, Charles Lever, whilst they confidently derive me from a Norwegian author of whose language I do not know three words, and of whom I knew nothing until years after the Shavian *Anschauung* was already unequivocally declared in books full of what came, ten years later, to be perfunctorily labelled Ibsenism? I was not Ibsenist even at second hand; for Lever, though he may have read Henri Beyle, *alias* Stendhal, certainly never read Ibsen. Of the books that made Lever popular, such as Charles O'Malley and Harry Lorrequer, I know nothing but the names and some of the illustrations. But the story of the day's ride and life's romance of Potts (claiming alliance with Pozzo di Borgo) caught me and fascinated me as something strange and significant, though I already knew all about Alnaschar and Don Quixote and Simon Tappertit and many another romantic hero mocked by reality. From the plays of Aristophanes to the tales of Stevenson that mockery has been made familiar to all who are properly saturated with letters.

Where, then, was the novelty in Lever's tale? Partly, I think, in a new seriousness in dealing with Potts's disease. Formerly, the contrast between madness and sanity was deemed comic: Hogarth shews us how fashionable people went in parties to Bedlam to laugh at the lunatics. I myself have had a village idiot exhibited to me as something irresistibly funny. On the stage the madman was once a regular comic figure: that was how Hamlet got his opportunity before Shakespear touched him. The originality of Shakespear's version lay in his taking the lunatic sympathetically and seriously, and thereby making an advance towards the eastern consciousness of the fact that lunacy may be inspiration in disguise, since a man who has more brains than his fellows necessarily appears as mad to them as one who has less. But Shakespear did not do for Pistol and Parolles what he did for Hamlet. The particular sort of madman they represented, the romantic make-believer, lay outside the pale of sympathy in literature: he was pitilessly despised and ridiculed here as he was in the east under the name of Alnaschar, and was doomed to be, centuries later, under the name of Simon Tappertit. When Cervantes relented over Don Quixote, and Dickens relented over Pickwick, they did not become impartial: they simply changed sides, and became friends and apologists where they had formerly been mockers.

In Lever's story there is a real change of attitude. There is no relenting towards Potts: he never gains our affections like Don Quixote and Pickwick: he has not even the infatuate courage of Tappertit. But we dare not laugh at him, because, somehow, we recognize ourselves in Potts. We may, some of us, have enough nerve, enough muscle, enough luck, enough tact or skill or address or knowledge to carry things off better than he did; to impose on the people who saw through him; to fascinate Katinka (who cut Potts so ruthlessly at the end of the story); but for all that, we know that Potts plays an enormous part in ourselves and in the world, and that the social problem is not a problem of storybook heroes of the older pattern, but a problem of Pottses, and of how to make men of them. To fall back on my old phrase, we have the feeling—one that Alnaschar, Pistol, Parolles, and Tappertit never gave us—that Potts is a piece of really scientific natural history as distinguished from funny story telling. His author is not throwing a stone at a creature of another and inferior order, but making a confession, with the effect that the stone hits each of us full in the conscience and causes our self-esteem to smart very sorely. Hence the failure of Lever's book to please the readers of Household Words. That pain in the self-esteem nowadays causes critics to raise a cry of Ibsenism. I therefore assure them that the sensation first came to me from Lever and may have come to him from Beyle, or at least out of the Stendhalian atmosphere. I exclude the hypothesis of complete originality on Lever's part, because a man can no more be completely original in that sense than a tree can grow out of air.

Another mistake as to my literary ancestry is made whenever I violate the romantic convention that all women are angels when they are not devils; that they are better looking than men; that their part in courtship is entirely passive; and that the human female form is the most beautiful object in nature. Schopenhauer wrote a splenetic essay which, as it is neither polite nor profound, was probably intended to knock this nonsense violently on the head. A sentence denouncing the idolized form as ugly has been largely quoted. The English critics have read that sentence; and I must here affirm, with as much gentleness as the implication will bear, that it has yet to be proved that they have dipped any deeper. At all events, whenever an English playwright represents a young and marriageable woman as being anything but a romantic heroine, he is disposed of without further thought as an echo of Schopenhauer. My own case is a specially hard one, because, when I implore the critics who are obsessed with the Schopenhauerian formula to remember that playwrights, like sculptors, study their figures from life, and not from philosophic essays, they reply passionately that I am not a playwright and that my stage figures do not live. But even so, I may and do ask them why, if they must give the credit of my plays to a philosopher, they do not give it to an English philosopher? Long before I ever read a word by Schopenhauer, or even knew whether he was a philosopher or a chemist, the Socialist revival of the eighteen-eighties brought me into contact, both literary and personal, with Ernest Belfort Bax, an English Socialist and philosophic essayist, whose handling of modern feminism would provoke romantic protests from Schopenhauer himself, or even Strindberg. As a matter of fact I hardly noticed Schopenhauer's disparagements of women when they came under my notice later on, so thoroughly had Bax familiarized me with the homoist attitude, and forced me to recognize the extent to which public opinion, and consequently legislation and jurisprudence, is corrupted by feminist sentiment.

Belfort Bax's essays were not confined to the Feminist question. He was a ruthless critic of current morality. Other writers have gained sympathy for dramatic criminals by eliciting the alleged "soul of goodness in things evil"; but Bax would propound some quite undramatic and apparently shabby violation of our commercial law and morality, and not merely defend it with the most disconcerting ingenuity, but actually prove it to be a positive duty that nothing but the certainty of police persecution should prevent every right-minded man from at once doing on principle. The Socialists were naturally shocked, being for the most part morbidly moral people; but at all events they were saved later on from the delusion that nobody but Nietzsche had ever challenged our mercanto-Christian morality. I first heard the name of Nietzsche from a German mathematician, Miss Borchardt, who had read my Quintessence of Ibsenism, and told me that she saw what I had been reading: namely, Nietzsche's Jenseits von Gut und Böse. Which I protest I had never seen, and could not have read with any comfort, for want of the necessary German, if I had seen it.

Nietzsche, like Schopenhauer, is the victim in England of a single much quoted sentence containing the phrase "big blonde beast." On the strength of this alliteration it is assumed that Nietzsche gained his European reputation by a senseless glorification of selfish bullying as the rule of life, just as it is assumed, on the strength of the single word Superman (Übermensch) borrowed by me from Nietzsche, that I look for the salvation of society to the despotism of a single Napoleonic Superman, in spite of my careful demonstration of the folly of that outworn infatuation. But even the less recklessly superficial critics seem to believe that the modern objection to Christianity as a pernicious slave-morality was first put forward by Nietzsche. It was familiar to me before I ever heard of Nietzsche. The late Captain Wilson, author of several queer pamphlets, propagandist of a metaphysical system called Comprehensionism, and inventor of the term "Crosstianity" to distinguish the retrograde element in Christendom, was wont thirty years ago, in the discussions of the Dialectical Society, to protest earnestly against the beatitudes of the Sermon on the Mount as excuses for cowardice and servility, as destructive of our will, and consequently of our honor and manhood. Now it is true that Captain Wilson's moral criticism of Christianity was not a historical theory of it, like Nietzsche's; but this objection cannot be made to Stuart-Glennie, the successor of Buckle as a philosophic historian, who devoted his life to the elaboration and propagation of his theory that Christianity is part of an epoch (or rather an aberration, since it began as recently as 6000 B.C. and is already collapsing) produced by the necessity in which the numerically inferior white races found themselves to impose their domination on the colored races by priestcraft, making a virtue and a popular religion of drudgery and submissiveness in this world not only as a means of achieving saintliness of character but of securing a reward in heaven. Here was the slave-morality view formulated by a Scotch philosopher of my acquaintance long before we all began chattering about Nietzsche.

As Stuart-Glennie traced the evolution of society to the conflict of races, his theory made some sensation among Socialists—that is, among the only people who were seriously thinking about historical evolution at all—by its collision with the class-conflict theory of Karl Marx. Nietzsche, as I gather, regarded the slave-morality as having been invented and imposed on the world by slaves making a virtue of necessity and a religion of their servitude. Stuart-Glennie regarded the slave-morality as an invention of the superior white race to subjugate the minds of the inferior races whom they wished to exploit, and who would have destroyed them by force of numbers if their minds had not been subjugated. As this process is in operation still, and can be studied at first hand not only in our Church schools and in the struggle between our modern proprietary classes and the proletariat, but in the part played by Christian missionaries in reconciling the black races of Africa to their subjugation by European Capitalism, we can judge for ourselves whether the initiative came from above or below. My object here is not to argue the historical point, but simply to make our theatre critics ashamed of their habit of treating Britain as an intellectual void, and assuming that every philosophical idea, every historic theory, every criticism of our moral, religious and juridical institutions, must necessarily be either a foreign import, or else a fantastic sally (in rather questionable taste) totally unrelated to the existing body of thought. I urge them to remember that this body of thought is the slowest of growths and the rarest of blossomings, and that if there be such a thing on the philosophic plane as a matter of course, it is that no individual can make more than a minute contribution to it. In fact, their conception of clever persons parthenogenetically bringing forth complete original cosmogonies by dint of sheer "brilliancy" is part of that ignorant credulity which is the despair of the honest philosopher, and the opportunity of the religious impostor.

The Gospel of St Andrew Undershaft

It is this credulity that drives me to help my critics out with Major Barbara by telling them what to say about it. In the millionaire Undershaft I have represented a man who has become intellectually and spiritually as well as practically conscious of the irresistible natural truth which we all abhor and repudiate: to wit, that the greatest of our evils and the worst of our crimes is poverty, and that our first duty, to which every other consideration should be sacrificed, is not to be poor. "Poor but honest," "the respectable poor," and such phrases are as intolerable and as immoral as "drunken but amiable," "fraudulent but a good after-dinner speaker," "splendidly criminal," or the like. Security, the chief pretence of civilization, cannot exist where the worst of dangers, the danger of poverty, hangs over everyone's head, and where the alleged protection of our persons from violence is only an accidental result of the existence of a police force whose real business is to force the poor man to see his children starve whilst idle people overfeed pet dogs with the money that might feed and clothe them.

It is exceedingly difficult to make people realize that an evil is an evil. For instance, we seize a man and deliberately do him a malicious injury: say, imprison him for years. One would not suppose that it needed any exceptional clearness of wit to recognize in this an act of diabolical cruelty. But in England such a recognition provokes a stare of surprise, followed by an explanation that the outrage is punishment or justice or something else that is all right, or perhaps by a heated attempt to argue that we should all be robbed and murdered in our beds if such stupid villainies as sentences of imprisonment were not committed daily. It is useless to argue that even if this were true, which it is not, the alternative to adding crimes of our own to the crimes from which we suffer is not helpless submission. Chickenpox is an evil; but if I were to declare that we must either submit to it or else repress it sternly by seizing everyone who suffers from it and punishing them by inoculation with smallpox, I should be laughed at; for though nobody could deny that the result would be to prevent chickenpox to some extent by making people avoid it much more carefully, and to effect a further apparent prevention by making them conceal it very anxiously, yet people would have sense enough to see that the deliberate propagation of smallpox was a creation of evil, and must therefore be ruled out in favor of purely humane and hygienic measures. Yet in the precisely parallel case of a man breaking into my house and stealing my wife's diamonds I am expected as a matter of course to steal ten years of his life, torturing him all the time. If he tries to defeat that monstrous retaliation by shooting me, my survivors hang him. The net result suggested by the police statistics is that we inflict atrocious injuries on the burglars we catch in order to make the rest take effectual precautions against detection; so that instead of saving our wives' diamonds from burglary we only greatly decrease our chances of ever getting them back, and increase our chances of being shot by the robber if we are unlucky enough to disturb him at his work.

But the thoughtless wickedness with which we scatter sentences of imprisonment, torture in the solitary cell and on the plank bed, and flogging, on moral invalids and energetic rebels, is as nothing compared to the silly levity with which we tolerate poverty as if it were either a wholesome tonic for lazy people or else a virtue to be embraced as St Francis embraced it. If a man is indolent, let him be poor. If he is drunken, let him be poor. If he is not a gentleman, let him be poor. If he is addicted to the fine arts or to pure science instead of to trade and finance, let him be poor. If he chooses to spend his urban eighteen shillings a week or his agricultural thirteen shillings a week on his beer and his family instead of saving it up for his old age, let him be poor. Let nothing be done for "the underserving": let him be poor. Serve him right! Also—somewhat inconsistently—blessed are the poor!

Now what does this Let Him Be Poor mean? It means let him be weak. Let him be ignorant. Let him become a nucleus of disease. Let him be a standing exhibition and example of ugliness and dirt. Let him have rickety children. Let him be cheap, and drag his fellows down to his own price by selling himself to do their work. Let his habitations turn our cities into poisonous congeries of slums. Let his daughters infect our young men with the diseases of the streets, and his sons revenge him by turning the nation's manhood into scrofula, cowardice, cruelty, hypocrisy, political imbecility, and all the other fruits of oppression and malnutrition. Let the undeserving become still less deserving; and let the deserving lay up for himself, not treasures in heaven, but horrors in hell upon earth. This being so, is it really wise to let him be poor? Would he not do ten times less harm as a prosperous burglar, incendiary, ravisher or murderer, to the utmost limits of humanity's comparatively negligible impulses in these directions? Suppose we were to abolish all penalties for such activities, and decide that poverty is the one thing we will not tolerate—that every adult with less than, say, £365 a year, shall be painlessly but inexorably killed, and every hungry half naked child forcibly fattened and clothed, would not that be an enormous improvement on our existing system, which has already destroyed so many civilizations, and is visibly destroying ours in the same way?

Is there any radicle of such legislation in our parliamentary system? Well, there are two measures just sprouting in the political soil, which may conceivably grow to something valuable. One is the institution of a Legal Minimum Wage. The other, Old Age Pensions. But there is a better plan than either of these. Some time ago I mentioned the subject of Universal Old Age Pensions to my fellow Socialist Cobden-Sanderson, famous as an artist-craftsman in bookbinding and printing. "Why not Universal Pensions for Life?" said Cobden-Sanderson. In saying this, he solved the industrial problem at a stroke. At present we say callously to each citizen "If you want money, earn it" as if his having or not having it were a matter that concerned himself alone. We do not even secure for him the opportunity of earning it: on the contrary, we allow our industry to be organized in open dependence on the maintenance of "a reserve army of unemployed" for the sake of "elasticity." The sensible course would be Cobden-Sanderson's: that is, to give every man enough to live well on, so as to guarantee the community against the possibility of a case of the malignant disease of poverty, and then (necessarily) to see that he earned it.

Undershaft, the hero of Major Barbara, is simply a man who, having grasped the fact that poverty is a crime, knows that when society offered him the alternative of poverty or a lucrative trade in death and destruction, it offered him, not a choice between opulent villainy and humble virtue, but between energetic enterprise and cowardly infamy. His conduct stands the Kantian test, which Peter Shirley's does not. Peter Shirley is what we call the honest poor man. Undershaft is what we call the wicked rich one: Shirley is Lazarus, Undershaft Dives. Well, the misery of the world is due to the fact that the great mass of men act and believe as Peter Shirley acts and believes. If they acted and believed as Undershaft acts and believes, the immediate result would be a revolution of incalculable beneficence. To be wealthy, says Undershaft, is with me a point of honor for which I am prepared to kill at the risk of my own life. This preparedness is, as he says, the final test of sincerity. Like Froissart's medieval hero, who saw that "to rob and pill was a good life" he is not the dupe of that public sentiment against killing which is propagated and endowed by people who would otherwise be killed themselves, or of the mouth-honor paid to poverty and obedience by rich and insubordinate do-nothings who want to rob the poor without courage and command them without superiority. Froissart's knight, in placing the achievement of a good life before all the other duties—which indeed are not duties at all when they conflict with it, but plain wickednesses—behaved bravely, admirably, and, in the final analysis, public-spiritedly. Medieval society, on the other hand, behaved very badly indeed in organizing itself so stupidly that a good life could be achieved by robbing and pilling. If the knight's contemporaries had been all as resolute as he, robbing and pilling would have been the shortest way to the gallows, just as, if we were all as resolute and clearsighted as Undershaft, an attempt to live by means of what is called "an independent income" would be the shortest way to the lethal chamber. But as, thanks to our political imbecility and personal cowardice (fruits of poverty, both), the best imitation of a good life now procurable is life on an independent income, all sensible people aim at securing such an income, and are, of course, careful to legalize and moralize both it and all the actions and sentiments which lead to it and support it as an institution. What else can they do? They know, of course, that they are rich because others are poor. But they cannot help that: it is for the poor to repudiate poverty when they have had enough of it. The thing can be done easily enough: the demonstrations to the contrary made by the economists, jurists, moralists, and sentimentalists hired by the rich to defend them, or even doing the work gratuitously out of sheer folly and abjectness, impose only on those who want to be imposed on.

The reason why the independent income-tax payers are not solid in defence of their position is that since we are not medieval rovers through a sparsely populated country, the poverty of those we rob prevents our having the good life for which we sacrifice them. Rich men or aristocrats with a developed sense of life—men like Ruskin and William Morris and Kropotkin—have enormous social appetites and very fastidious personal ones. They are not content with handsome houses; they want handsome cities. They are not content with bediamonded wives and blooming daughters: they complain because the charwoman is badly dressed, because the laundress smells of gin, because the sempstress is anemic, because every man they meet is not a friend and every woman not a romance. They turn up their noses at their neighbors' drains, and are made ill by the architecture of their neighbors' houses. Trade patterns made to suit vulgar people do not please them (and they can get nothing else): they cannot sleep nor sit at ease upon "slaughtered" cabinet makers' furniture. The very air is not good enough for them: there is too much factory smoke in it. They even demand abstract conditions: justice, honor, a noble moral atmosphere, a mystic nexus to replace the cash nexus. Finally they declare that though to rob and pill with your own hand on horseback and in steel coat may have been a good life, to rob and pill by the hands of the policeman, the bailiff, and the soldier, and to underpay them meanly for doing it, is not a good life, but rather fatal to all possibility of even a tolerable one. They call on the poor to revolt, and, finding the poor shocked at their ungentlemanliness, despairingly revile the proletariat for its "damned wantlessness" (*verdammte Bedürfnislosigkeit*).

So far, however, their attack on society has lacked simplicity. The poor do not share their taste nor understand their art-criticisms. They do not want the simple life, nor the esthetic life; on the contrary, they want very much to wallow in all the costly vulgarities from which the elect souls among the rich turn away with loathing. It is by surfeit and not by abstinence that they will be cured of their hankering after unwholesome sweets. What they do dislike and despise and are ashamed of is poverty. To ask them to fight for the difference between the Christmas number of the Illustrated London News and the Kelmscott Chaucer is silly: they prefer the News. The difference between a stockbroker's cheap and dirty starched white shirt and collar and the comparatively costly and carefully dyed blue shirt of William Morris is a difference so disgraceful to Morris in their eyes that if they fought on the subject at all, they would fight in defence of the starch. "Cease to be slaves, in order that you may become cranks" is not a very inspiring call to arms; nor is it really improved by substituting saints for cranks. Both terms denote men of genius; and the common man does not want to live the life of a man of genius: he would much rather live the life of a pet collie if that were the only alternative. But he does want more money. Whatever else he may be vague about, he is clear about that. He may or may not prefer Major Barbara to the Drury Lane pantomime; but he always prefers five hundred pounds to five hundred shillings.

Now to deplore this preference as sordid, and teach children that it is sinful to desire money, is to strain towards the extreme possible limit of impudence in lying and corruption in hypocrisy. The universal regard for money is the one hopeful fact in our civilization, the one sound spot in our social conscience. Money is the most important thing in the world. It represents health, strength, honor, generosity and beauty as conspicuously and undeniably as the want of it represents illness, weakness, disgrace, meanness and ugliness. Not the least of its virtues is that it destroys base people as certainly as it fortifies and dignifies noble people. It is only when it is cheapened to worthlessness for some, and made impossibly dear to others, that it becomes a curse. In short, it is a curse only in such foolish social conditions that life itself is a curse. For the two things are inseparable: money is the counter that enables life to be distributed socially: it *is* life as truly as sovereigns and bank notes are money. The first duty of every citizen is to insist on having money on reasonable terms; and this demand is not complied with by giving four men three shillings each for ten or twelve hours' drudgery and one man a thousand pounds for nothing. The crying need of the nation is not for better morals, cheaper bread, temperance, liberty, culture, redemption of fallen sisters and erring brothers, nor the grace, love and fellowship of the Trinity, but simply for enough money. And the evil to be attacked is not sin, suffering, greed, priestcraft, kingcraft, demagogy, monopoly, ignorance, drink, war, pestilence, nor any other of the scapegoats which reformers sacrifice, but simply poverty.

Once take your eyes from the ends of the earth and fix them on this truth just under your nose; and Andrew Undershaft's views will not perplex you in the least. Unless indeed his constant sense that he is only the instrument of a Will or Life Force which uses him for purposes wider than his own, may puzzle you. If so, that is because you are walking either in artificial Darwinian darkness, or in mere stupidity. All genuinely religious people have that consciousness. To them Undershaft the Mystic will be quite intelligible, and his perfect comprehension of his daughter the Salvationist and her lover the Euripidean republican natural and inevitable. That, however, is not new, even on the stage. What is new, as far as I know, is that article in Undershaft's religion which recognizes in Money the first need and in poverty the vilest sin of man and society.

This dramatic conception has not, of course, been attained *per saltum*. Nor has it been borrowed from Nietzsche or from any man born beyond the Channel. The late Samuel Butler, in his own department the greatest English writer of the latter half of the XIX century, steadily inculcated the necessity and morality of a conscientious Laodiceanism in religion and of an earnest and constant sense of the importance of money. It drives one almost to despair of English literature when one sees so extraordinary a study of English life as Butler's posthumous Way of All Flesh making so little impression that when, some years later, I produce plays in which Butler's extraordinarily fresh, free and future-piercing suggestions have an obvious share, I am met with nothing but vague cacklings about Ibsen and Nietzsche, and am only too thankful that they are not about Alfred de Musset and Georges Sand. Really, the English do not deserve to have great men. They allowed Butler to die practically unknown, whilst I, a comparatively insignificant Irish journalist, was leading them by the nose into an advertisement of me which has made my own life a burden. In Sicily there is a Via Samuele Butler. When an English tourist sees it, he either asks "Who the devil was Samuele Butler?" or wonders why the Sicilians should perpetuate the memory of the author of Hudibras.

Well, it cannot be denied that the English are only too anxious to recognize a man of genius if somebody will kindly point him out to them. Having pointed myself out in this manner with some success, I now point out Samuel Butler, and trust that in consequence I shall hear a little less in future of the novelty and foreign origin of the ideas which are now making their way into the English theatre through plays written by Socialists. There are living men whose originality and power are as obvious as Butler's; and when they die that fact will be discovered. Meanwhile I recommend them to insist on their own merits as an important part of their own business.

The Salvation Army

When Major Barbara was produced in London, the second act was reported in an important northern newspaper as a withering attack on the Salvation Army, and the despairing ejaculation of Barbara deplored by a London daily as a tasteless blasphemy. And they were set right, not by the professed critics of the theatre but by religious and philosophical publicists like Sir Oliver Lodge and Dr Stanton Coit, and strenuous Nonconformist journalists like William Stead, who not only understood the act as well as the Salvationists themselves, but also saw it in its relation to the religious life of the nation, a life which seems to lie not only outside the sympathy of many of our theatre critics, but actually outside their knowledge of society. Indeed nothing could be more ironically curious than the confrontation Major Barbara effected of the theatre enthusiasts with the religious enthusiasts. On the one hand was the playgoer, always seeking pleasure, paying exorbitantly for it, suffering unbearable discomforts for it, and hardly ever getting it. On the other hand was the Salvationist, repudiating gaiety and courting effort and sacrifice, yet always in the wildest spirits, laughing, joking, singing, rejoicing, drumming, and tambourining: his life flying by in a flash of excitement, and his death arriving as a climax of triumph. And, if you please, the playgoer despising the Salvationist as a joyless person, shut out from the heaven of the theatre, self-condemned to a life of hideous gloom; and the Salvationist mourning over the playgoer as over a prodigal with vine leaves in his hair, careering outrageously to hell amid the popping of champagne corks and the ribald laughter of sirens! Could misunderstanding be more complete, or sympathy worse misplaced?

Fortunately, the Salvationists are more accessible to the religious character of the drama than the playgoers to the gay energy and artistic fertility of religion. They can see, when it is pointed out to them, that a theatre, as a place where two or three are gathered together, takes from that divine presence an inalienable sanctity of which the grossest and profanest farce can no more deprive it than a hypocritical sermon by a snobbish bishop can desecrate Westminster Abbey. But in our professional playgoers this indispensable preliminary conception of sanctity seems wanting. They talk of actors as mimes and mummers, and, I fear, think of dramatic authors as liars and pandars, whose main business is the voluptuous soothing of the tired city speculator when what he calls the serious business of the day is over. Passion, the life of drama, means nothing to them but primitive sexual excitement: such phrases as "impassioned poetry" or "passionate love of truth" have fallen quite out of their vocabulary and been replaced by "passional crime" and the like. They assume, as far as I can gather, that people in whom passion has a larger scope are passionless and therefore uninteresting. Consequently they come to think of religious people as people who are not interesting and not amusing. And so, when Barbara cuts the regular Salvation Army jokes, and snatches a kiss from her lover across his drum, the devotees of the theatre think they ought to appear shocked, and conclude that the whole play is an elaborate mockery of the Army. And then either hypocritically rebuke me for mocking, or foolishly take part in the supposed mockery!

Even the handful of mentally competent critics got into difficulties over my demonstration of the economic deadlock in which the Salvation Army finds itself. Some of them thought that the Army would not have taken money from a distiller and a cannon founder: others thought it should not have taken it: all assumed more or less definitely that it reduced itself to absurdity or hypocrisy by taking it. On the first point the reply of the Army itself was prompt and conclusive. As one of its officers said, they would take money from the devil himself and be only too glad to get it out of his hands and into God's. They gratefully acknowledged that publicans not only give them money but allow them to collect it in the bar—sometimes even when there is a Salvation meeting outside preaching teetotalism. In fact, they questioned the verisimilitude of the play, not because Mrs Baines took the money, but because Barbara refused it.

On the point that the Army ought not to take such money, its justification is obvious. It must take the money because it cannot exist without money, and there is no other money to be had. Practically all the spare money in the country consists of a mass of rent, interest, and profit, every penny of which is bound up with crime, drink, prostitution, disease, and all the evil fruits of poverty, as inextricably as with enterprise, wealth, commercial probity, and national prosperity. The notion that you can earmark certain coins as tainted is an unpractical individualist superstition. None the less the fact that all our money is tainted gives a very severe shock to earnest young souls when some dramatic instance of the taint first makes them conscious of it. When an enthusiastic young clergyman of the Established Church first realizes that the Ecclesiastical Commissioners receive the rents of sporting public houses, brothels, and sweating dens; or that the most generous contributor at his last charity sermon was an employer trading in female labor cheapened by prostitution as unscrupulously as a hotel keeper trades in waiters' labor cheapened by tips, or commissionaires' labor cheapened by pensions; or that the only patron who can afford to rebuild his church or his schools or give his boys' brigade a gymnasium or a library is the son-in-law of a Chicago meat King, that young clergyman has, like Barbara, a very bad quarter hour. But he cannot help himself by refusing to accept money from anybody except sweet old ladies with independent incomes and gentle and lovely ways of life. He has only to follow up the income of the sweet ladies to its industrial source, and there he will find Mrs Warren's profession and the poisonous canned meat and all the rest of it. His own stipend has the same root. He must either share the world's guilt or go to another planet. He must save the world's honor if he is to save his own. This is what all the Churches find just as the Salvation Army and Barbara find it in the play. Her discovery that she is her father's accomplice; that the Salvation Army is the accomplice of the distiller and the dynamite maker: that they can no more escape one another than they can escape the air they breathe: that there is no salvation for them through personal righteousness, but only through the redemption of the whole nation from its vicious, lazy, competitive anarchy: this discovery has been made by everyone except the Pharisees and (apparently) the professional playgoers, who still wear their Tom Hood shirts and underpay their washerwomen without the slightest misgiving as to the elevation of their private characters, the purity of their private atmospheres, and their right to repudiate as foreign to themselves the coarse depravity of the garret and the slum. Not that they mean any harm: they only desire to be, in their little private way, what they call gentlemen. They do not understand Barbara's lesson because they have not, like her, learnt it by taking their part in the larger life of the nation.

Barbara's Return to the Colors

Barbara's return to the colors may yet provide a subject for the dramatic historian of the future. To go back to the Salvation Army with the knowledge that even the Salvationists themselves are not saved yet; that poverty is not blessed, but a most damnable sin; and that when General Booth chose Blood and Fire for the emblem of Salvation instead of the Cross, he was perhaps better inspired than he knew: such knowledge, for the daughter of Andrew Undershaft, will clearly lead to something hopefuller than distributing bread and treacle at the expense of Bodger.

It is a very significant thing, this instinctive choice of the military form of organization, this substitution of the drum for the organ, by the Salvation Army. Does it not suggest that the Salvationists divine that they must actually fight the devil instead of merely praying at him? At present, it is true, they have not quite ascertained his correct address. When they do, they may give a very rude shock to that sense of security which he has gained from his experience of the fact that hard words, even when uttered by eloquent essayists and lecturers, or carried unanimously at enthusiastic public meetings on the motion of eminent reformers, break no bones. It has been said that the French Revolution was the work of Voltaire, Rousseau and the Encyclopedists.

It seems to me to have been the work of men who had observed that virtuous indignation, caustic criticism, conclusive argument and instructive pamphleteering, even when done by the most earnest and witty literary geniuses, were as useless as praying, things going steadily from bad to worse whilst the Social Contract and the pamphlets of Voltaire were at the height of their vogue. Eventually, as we know, perfectly respectable citizens and earnest philanthropists connived at the September massacres because hard experience had convinced them that if they contented themselves with appeals to humanity and patriotism, the aristocracy, though it would read their appeals with the greatest enjoyment and appreciation, flattering and admiring the writers, would none the less continue to conspire with foreign monarchists to undo the revolution and restore the old system with every circumstance of savage vengeance and ruthless repression of popular liberties.

The nineteenth century saw the same lesson repeated in England. It had its Utilitarians, its Christian Socialists, its Fabians (still extant): it had Bentham, Mill, Dickens, Ruskin, Carlyle, Butler, Henry George, and Morris. And the end of all their efforts is the Chicago described by Mr Upton Sinclair, and the London in which the people who pay to be amused by my dramatic representation of Peter Shirley turned out to starve at forty because there are younger slaves to be had for his wages, do not take, and have not the slightest intention of taking, any effective step to organize society in such a way as to make that everyday infamy impossible. I, who have preached and pamphleteered like any Encyclopedist, have to confess that my methods are no use, and would be no use if I were Voltaire, Rousseau, Bentham, Marx, Mill, Dickens, Carlyle, Ruskin, Butler, and Morris all rolled into one, with Euripides, More, Montaigne, Molière, Beaumarchais, Swift, Goethe, Ibsen, Tolstoy, Jesus and the prophets all thrown in (as indeed in some sort I actually am, standing as I do on all their shoulders). The problem being to make heroes out of cowards, we paper apostles and artist-magicians have succeeded only in giving cowards all the sensations of heroes whilst they tolerate every abomination, accept every plunder, and submit to every oppression. Christianity, in making a merit of such submission, has marked only that depth in the abyss at which the very sense of shame is lost. The Christian has been like Dickens' doctor in the debtor's prison, who tells the newcomer of its ineffable peace and security: no duns; no tyrannical collectors of rates, taxes, and rent; no importunate hopes nor exacting duties; nothing but the rest and safety of having no farther to fall.

Yet in the poorest corner of this soul-destroying Christendom vitality suddenly begins to germinate again. Joyousness, a sacred gift long dethroned by the hellish laughter of derision and obscenity, rises like a flood miraculously out of the fetid dust and mud of the slums; rousing marches and impetuous dithyrambs rise to the heavens from people among whom the depressing noise called "sacred music" is a standing joke; a flag with Blood and Fire on it is unfurled, not in murderous rancor, but because fire is beautiful and blood a vital and splendid red; Fear, which we flatter by calling Self, vanishes; and transfigured men and women carry their gospel through a transfigured world, calling their leader General, themselves captains and brigadiers, and their whole body an Army: praying, but praying only for refreshment, for strength to fight, and for needful Money (a notable sign, that); preaching, but not preaching submission; daring ill-usage and abuse, but not putting up with more of it than is inevitable; and practising what the world will let them practise, including soap and water, color and music. There is danger in such activity; and where there is danger there is hope. Our present security is nothing, and can be nothing, but evil made irresistible.

Weaknesses of the Salvation Army

For the present, however, it is not my business to flatter the Salvation Army. Rather must I point out to it that it has almost as many weaknesses as the Church of England itself. It is building up a business organization which will compel it eventually to see that its present staff of enthusiast-commanders shall be succeeded by a bureaucracy of men of business who will be no better than bishops, and perhaps a good deal more unscrupulous. That has always happened sooner or later to great orders founded by saints; and the order founded by St William Booth is not exempt from the same danger. It is even more dependent than the Church on rich people who would cut off supplies at once if it began to preach that indispensable revolt against poverty which must also be a revolt against riches. It is hampered by a heavy contingent of pious elders who are not really Salvationists at all, but Evangelicals of the old school. It still, as Commissioner Howard affirms, "sticks to Moses," which is flat nonsense at this time of day if the Commissioner means, as I am afraid he does, that the Book of Genesis contains a trustworthy scientific account of the origin of species, and that the god to whom Jephthah sacrificed his daughter is any less obviously a tribal idol than Dagon or Chemosh.

Further, there is still too much other-worldliness about the Army. Like Frederick's grenadier, the Salvationist wants to live for ever (the most monstrous way of crying for the moon); and though it is evident to anyone who has ever heard General Booth and his best officers that they would work as hard for human salvation as they do at present if they believed that death would be the end of them individually, they and their followers have a bad habit of talking as if the Salvationists were heroically enduring a very bad time on earth as an investment which will bring them in dividends later on in the form, not of a better life to come for the whole world, but of an eternity spent by themselves personally in a sort of bliss which would bore any active person to a second death. Surely the truth is that the Salvationists are unusually happy people. And is it not the very diagnostic of true salvation that it shall overcome the fear of death? Now the man who has come to believe that there is no such thing as death, the change so called being merely the transition to an exquisitely happy and utterly careless life, has not overcome the fear of death at all: on the contrary, it has overcome him so completely that he refuses to die on any terms whatever. I do not call a Salvationist really saved until he is ready to lie down cheerfully on the scrap heap, having paid scot and lot and something over, and let his eternal life pass on to renew its youth in the battalions of the future.

Then there is the nasty lying habit called confession, which the Army encourages because it lends itself to dramatic oratory, with plenty of thrilling incident. For my part, when I hear a convert relating the violences and oaths and blasphemies he was guilty of before he was saved, making out that he was a very terrible fellow then and is the most contrite and chastened of Christians now, I believe him no more than I believe the millionaire who says he came up to London or Chicago as a boy with only three halfpence in his pocket. Salvationists have said to me that Barbara in my play would never have been taken in by so transparent a humbug as Snobby Price; and certainly I do not think Snobby could have taken in any experienced Salvationist on a point on which the Salvationist did not wish to be taken in. But on the point of conversion all Salvationists wish to be taken in; for the more obvious the sinner the more obvious the miracle of his conversion. When you advertize a converted burglar or reclaimed drunkard as one of the attractions at an experience meeting, your burglar can hardly have been too burglarious or your drunkard too drunken. As long as such attractions are relied on, you will have your Snobbies claiming to have beaten their mothers when they were as a matter of prosaic fact habitually beaten by them, and your Rummies of the tamest respectability pretending to a past of reckless and dazzling vice. Even when confessions are sincerely autobiographic we should beware of assuming that the impulse to make them was pious or that the interest of the hearers is wholesome. As well might we assume that the poor people who insist on shewing disgusting ulcers to district visitors are convinced hygienists, or that the curiosity which sometimes welcomes such exhibitions is a pleasant and creditable one. One is often tempted to suggest that those who pester our police superintendents with confessions of murder might very wisely be taken at their word and executed, except in the few cases in which a real murderer is seeking to be relieved of his guilt by confession and expiation. For though I am not, I hope, an unmerciful person, I do not think that the inexorability of the deed once done should be disguised by any ritual, whether in the confessional or on the scaffold.

And here my disagreement with the Salvation Army, and with all propagandists of the Cross (which I loathe as I loathe all gibbets) becomes deep indeed. Forgiveness, absolution, atonement, are figments: punishment is only a pretence of cancelling one crime by another; and you can no more have forgiveness without vindictiveness than you can have a cure without a disease. You will never get a high morality from people who conceive that their misdeeds are revocable and pardonable, or in a society where absolution and expiation are officially provided for us all. The demand may be very real; but the supply is spurious. Thus Bill Walker, in my play, having assaulted the Salvation Lass, presently finds himself overwhelmed with an intolerable conviction of sin under the skilled treatment of Barbara. Straightway he begins to try to unassault the lass and deruffianize his deed, first by getting punished for it in kind, and, when that relief is denied him, by fining himself a pound to compensate the girl. He is foiled both ways. He finds the Salvation Army as inexorable as fact itself. It will not punish him: it will not take his money. It will not tolerate a redeemed ruffian: it leaves him no means of salvation except ceasing to be a ruffian. In doing this, the Salvation Army instinctively grasps the central truth of Christianity and discards its central superstition: that central truth being the vanity of revenge and punishment, and that central superstition the salvation of the world by the gibbet.

For, be it noted, Bill has assaulted an old and starving woman also; and for this worse offence he feels no remorse whatever, because she makes it clear that her malice is as great as his own. "Let her have the law of me, as she said she would," says Bill: "what I done to her is no more on what you might call my conscience than sticking a pig." This shews a perfectly natural and wholesome state of mind on his part. The old woman, like the law she threatens him with, is perfectly ready to play the game of retaliation with him: to rob him if he steals, to flog him if he strikes, to murder him if he kills. By example and precept the law and public opinion teach him to impose his will on others by anger, violence, and cruelty, and to wipe off the moral score by punishment. That is sound Crosstianity. But this Crosstianity has got entangled with something which Barbara calls Christianity, and which unexpectedly causes her to refuse to play the hangman's game of Satan casting out Satan. She refuses to prosecute a drunken ruffian; she converses on equal terms with a blackguard to whom no lady should be seen speaking in the public street: in short, she imitates Christ. Bill's conscience reacts to this just as naturally as it does to the old woman's threats. He is placed in a position of unbearable moral inferiority, and strives by every means in his power to escape from it, whilst he is still quite ready to meet the abuse of the old woman by attempting to smash a mug on her face. And that is the triumphant justification of Barbara's Christianity as against our system of judicial punishment and the vindictive villain-thrashings and "poetic justice" of the romantic stage.

For the credit of literature it must be pointed out that the situation is only partly novel. Victor Hugo long ago gave us the epic of the convict and the bishop's candlesticks, of the Crosstian policeman annihilated by his encounter with the Christian Valjean. But Bill Walker is not, like Valjean, romantically changed from a demon into an angel. There are millions of Bill Walkers in all classes of society today; and the point which I, as a professor of natural psychology, desire to demonstrate, is that Bill, without any change in his character or circumstances whatsoever, will react one way to one sort of treatment and another way to another.

In proof I might point to the sensational object lesson provided by our commercial millionaires today. They begin as brigands: merciless, unscrupulous, dealing out ruin and death and slavery to their competitors and employees, and facing desperately the worst that their competitors can do to them. The history of the English factories, the American Trusts, the exploitation of African gold, diamonds, ivory and rubber, outdoes in villainy the worst that has ever been imagined of the buccaneers of the Spanish Main. Captain Kidd would have marooned a modern Trust magnate for conduct unworthy of a gentleman of fortune. The law every day seizes on unsuccessful scoundrels of this type and punishes them with a cruelty worse than their own, with the result that they come out of the torture house more dangerous than they went in, and renew their evil doing (nobody will employ them at anything else) until they are again seized, again tormented, and again let loose, with the same result.

But the successful scoundrel is dealt with very differently, and very Christianly. He is not only forgiven: he is idolized, respected, made much of, all but worshipped. Society returns him good for evil in the most extravagant overmeasure. And with what result? He begins to idolize himself, to respect himself, to live up to the treatment he receives. He preaches sermons; he writes books of the most edifying advice to young men, and actually persuades himself that he got on by taking his own advice: he endows educational institutions; he supports charities; he dies finally in the odor of sanctity, leaving a will which is a monument of public spirit and bounty. And all this without any change in his character. The spots of the leopard and the stripes of the tiger are as brilliant as ever; but the conduct of the world towards him has changed; and his conduct has changed accordingly. You have only to reverse your attitude towards him—to lay hands on his property, revile him, assault him, and he will be a brigand again in a moment, as ready to crush you as you are to crush him, and quite as full of pretentious moral reasons for doing it.

In short, when Major Barbara says that there are no scoundrels, she is right: there are no absolute scoundrels, though there are impracticable people of whom I shall treat presently. Every reasonable man (and woman) is a potential scoundrel and a potential good citizen. What a man is depends on his character; but what he does, and what we think of what he does, depends on his circumstances. The characteristics that ruin a man in one class make him eminent in another. The characters that behave differently in different circumstances behave alike in similar circumstances. Take a common English character like that of Bill Walker. We meet Bill everywhere: on the judicial bench, on the episcopal bench, in the Privy Council, at the War Office and Admiralty, as well as in the Old Bailey dock or in the ranks of casual unskilled labor. And the morality of Bill's characteristics varies with these various circumstances. The faults of the burglar are the qualities of the financier: the manners and habits of a duke would cost a city clerk his situation. In short, though character is independent of circumstances, conduct is not; and our moral judgments of character are not: both are circumstantial. Take any condition of life in which the circumstances are for a mass of men practically alike: felony, the House of Lords, the factory, the stables, the gipsy encampment or where you please! In spite of diversity of character and temperament, the conduct and morals of the individuals in each group are as predicable and as alike in the main as if they were a flock of sheep, morals being mostly only social habits and circumstantial necessities. Strong people know this and count upon it. In nothing have the master-minds of the world been distinguished from the ordinary suburban season-ticket holder more than in their straightforward perception of the fact that mankind is practically a single species, and not a menagerie of gentlemen and bounders, villains and heroes, cowards and daredevils, peers and peasants, grocers and aristocrats, artisans and laborers, washerwomen and duchesses, in which all the grades of income and caste represent distinct animals who must not be introduced to one another or intermarry. Napoleon constructing a galaxy of generals and courtiers, and even of monarchs, out of his collection of social nobodies; Julius Cæsar appointing as governor of Egypt the son of a freedman—one who but a short time before would have been legally disqualified for the post even of a private soldier in the Roman army; Louis XI. making his barber his privy councillor: all these had in their different ways a firm hold of the scientific fact of human equality, expressed by Barbara in the Christian formula that all men are children of one father. A man who believes that men are naturally divided into upper and lower and middle classes morally is making exactly the same mistake as the man who believes that they are naturally divided in the same way socially. And just as our persistent attempts to found political institutions on a basis of social inequality have always produced long periods of destructive friction relieved from time to time by violent explosions of revolution; so the attempt—will Americans please note—to found moral institutions on a basis of moral inequality can lead to nothing but unnatural Reigns of the Saints relieved by licentious Restorations; to Americans who have made divorce a public institution turning the face of Europe into one huge sardonic smile by refusing to stay in the same hotel with a Russian man of genius who has changed wives without the sanction of South Dakota; to grotesque hypocrisy, cruel persecution, and final utter confusion of conventions and compliances with benevolence and respectability. It is quite useless to declare that all men are born free if you deny that they are born good. Guarantee a man's goodness and his liberty will take care of itself. To guarantee his freedom on condition that you approve of his moral character is formally to abolish all freedom whatsoever, as every man's liberty is at the mercy of a moral indictment which any fool can trump up against everyone who violates custom, whether as a prophet or as a rascal. This is the lesson Democracy has to learn before it can become anything but the most oppressive of all the priesthoods.

Let us now return to Bill Walker and his case of conscience against the Salvation Army. Major Barbara, not being a modern Tetzel, or the treasurer of a hospital, refuses to sell absolution to Bill for a sovereign. Unfortunately, what the Army can afford to refuse in the case of Bill Walker, it cannot refuse in the case of Bodger. Bodger is master of the situation because he holds the purse strings. "Strive as you will," says Bodger, in effect: "me you cannot do without. You cannot save Bill Walker without my money." And the Army answers, quite rightly under the circumstances, "We will take money from the devil himself sooner than abandon the work of Salvation." So Bodger pays his conscience-money and gets the absolution that is refused to Bill. In real life Bill would perhaps never know this. But I, the dramatist whose business it is to shew the connexion between things that seem apart and unrelated in the haphazard order of events in real life, have contrived to make it known to Bill, with the result that the Salvation Army loses its hold of him at once.

But Bill may not be lost, for all that. He is still in the grip of the facts and of his own conscience, and may find his taste for blackguardism permanently spoiled. Still, I cannot guarantee that happy ending. Walk through the poorer quarters of our cities on Sunday when the men are not working, but resting and chewing the cud of their reflections. You will find one expression common to every mature face, the expression of cynicism. The discovery made by Bill Walker about the Salvation Army has been made by everyone there. They have found that every man has his price; and they have been foolishly or corruptly taught to mistrust and despise him for that necessary and salutary condition of social existence. When they learn that General Booth, too, has his price, they do not admire him because it is a high one, and admit the need of organizing society so that he shall get it in an honorable way: they conclude that his character is unsound and that all religious men are hypocrites and allies of their sweaters and oppressors. They know that the large subscriptions which help to support the Army are endowments, not of religion, but of the wicked doctrine of docility in poverty and humility under oppression; and they are rent by the most agonizing of all the doubts of the soul, the doubt whether their true salvation must not come from their most abhorrent passions, from murder, envy, greed, stubbornness, rage, and terrorism, rather than from public spirit, reasonableness, humanity, generosity, tenderness, delicacy, pity and kindness. The confirmation of that doubt, at which our newspapers have been working so hard for years past, is the morality of militarism; and the justification of militarism is that circumstances may at any time make it the true morality of the moment. It is by producing such moments that we produce violent and sanguinary revolutions, such as the one now in progress in Russia and the one which Capitalism in England and America is daily and diligently provoking.

At such moments it becomes the duty of the Churches to evoke all the powers of destruction against the existing order. But if they do this, the existing order must forcibly suppress them. Churches are suffered to exist only on condition that they preach submission to the State as at present capitalistically organized. The Church of England itself is compelled to add to the thirtysix articles in which it formulates its religious tenets, three more in which it apologetically protests that the moment any of these articles comes in conflict with the State it is to be entirely renounced, abjured, violated, abrogated and abhorred, the policeman being a much more important person than any of the Persons of the Trinity. And this is why no tolerated Church nor Salvation Army can ever win the entire confidence of the poor. It must be on the side of the police and the military, no matter what it believes or disbelieves; and as the police and the military are the instruments by which the rich rob and oppress the poor (on legal and moral principles made for the purpose), it is not possible to be on the side of the poor and of the police at the same time. Indeed the religious bodies, as the almoners of the rich, become a sort of auxiliary police, taking off the insurrectionary edge of poverty with coals and blankets, bread and treacle, and soothing and cheering the victims with hopes of immense and inexpensive happiness in another world when the process of working them to premature death in the service of the rich is complete in this.

Christianity and Anarchism

Such is the false position from which neither the Salvation Army nor the Church of England nor any other religious organization whatever can escape except through a reconstitution of society. Nor can they merely endure the State passively, washing their hands of its sins. The State is constantly forcing the consciences of men by violence and cruelty. Not content with exacting money from us for the maintenance of its soldiers and policemen, its gaolers and executioners, it forces us to take an active personal part in its proceedings on pain of becoming ourselves the victims of its violence. As I write these lines, a sensational example is given to the world. A royal marriage has been celebrated, first by sacrament in a cathedral, and then by a bullfight having for its main amusement the spectacle of horses gored and disembowelled by the bull, after which, when the bull is so exhausted as to be no longer dangerous, he is killed by a cautious matador. But the ironic contrast between the bullfight and the sacrament of marriage does not move anyone. Another contrast—that between the splendor, the happiness, the atmosphere of kindly admiration surrounding the young couple, and the price paid for it under our abominable social arrangements in the misery, squalor and degradation of millions of other young couples—is drawn at the same moment by a novelist, Mr Upton Sinclair, who chips a corner of the veneering from the huge meat packing industries of Chicago, and shews it to us as a sample of what is going on all over the world underneath the top layer of prosperous plutocracy. One man is sufficiently moved by that contrast to pay his own life as the price of one terrible blow at the responsible parties. His poverty has left him ignorant enough to be duped by the pretence that the innocent young bride and bridegroom, put forth and crowned by plutocracy as the heads of a State in which they have less personal power than any policeman, and less influence than any Chairman of a Trust, are responsible. At them accordingly he launches his sixpennorth of fulminate, missing his mark, but scattering the bowels of as many horses as any bull in the arena, and slaying twentythree persons, besides wounding ninetynine. And of all these, the horses alone are innocent of the guilt he is avenging: had he blown all Madrid to atoms with every adult person in it, not one could have escaped the charge of being an accessory, before, at, and after the fact, to poverty and prostitution, to such wholesale massacre of infants as Herod never dreamt of, to plague, pestilence and famine, battle, murder and lingering death—perhaps not one who had not helped, through example, precept, connivance, and even clamor, to teach the dynamiter his well-learnt gospel of hatred and vengeance, by approving every day of sentences of years of imprisonment so infernal in their unnatural stupidity and panic-stricken cruelty, that their advocates can disavow neither the dagger nor the bomb without stripping the mask of justice and humanity from themselves also.

Be it noted that at this very moment there appears the biography of one of our dukes, who, being a Scot, could argue about politics, and therefore stood out as a great brain among our aristocrats. And what, if you please, was his grace's favorite historical episode, which he declared he never read without intense satisfaction? Why, the young General Bonapart's pounding of the Paris mob to pieces in 1795, called in playful approval by our respectable classes "the whiff of grapeshot," though Napoleon, to do him justice, took a deeper view of it, and would fain have had it forgotten. And since the Duke of Argyll was not a demon, but a man of like passions with ourselves, by no means rancorous or cruel as men go, who can doubt that all over the world proletarians of the ducal kidney are now revelling in "the whiff of dynamite" (the flavor of the joke seems to evaporate a little, does it not?) because it was aimed at the class they hate even as our argute duke hated what he called the mob.

In such an atmosphere there can be only one sequel to the Madrid explosion. All Europe burns to emulate it. Vengeance! More blood! Tear "the Anarchist beast" to shreds. Drag him to the scaffold. Imprison him for life. Let all civilized States band together to drive his like off the face of the earth; and if any State refuses to join, make war on it. This time the leading London newspaper, anti-Liberal and therefore anti-Russian in politics, does not say "Serve you right" to the victims, as it did, in effect, when Bobrikoff, and De Plehve, and Grand Duke Sergius, were in the same manner unofficially fulminated into fragments. No: fulminate our rivals in Asia by all means, ye brave Russian revolutionaries; but to aim at an English princess! monstrous! hideous! hound down the wretch to his doom; and observe, please, that we are a civilized and merciful people, and, however much we may regret it, must not treat him as Ravaillac and Damiens were treated. And meanwhile, since we have not yet caught him, let us soothe our quivering nerves with the bullfight, and comment in a courtly way on the unfailing tact and good taste of the ladies of our royal houses, who, though presumably of full normal natural tenderness, have been so effectually broken in to fashionable routine that they can be taken to see the horses slaughtered as helplessly as they could no doubt be taken to a gladiator show, if that happened to be the mode just now.

Strangely enough, in the midst of this raging fire of malice, the one man who still has faith in the kindness and intelligence of human nature is the fulminator, now a hunted wretch, with nothing, apparently, to secure his triumph over all the prisons and scaffolds of infuriate Europe except the revolver in his pocket and his readiness to discharge it at a moment's notice into his own or any other head. Think of him setting out to find a gentleman and a Christian in the multitude of human wolves howling for his blood. Think also of this: that at the very first essay he finds what he seeks, a veritable grandee of Spain, a noble, high-thinking, unterrified, malice-void soul, in the guise—of all masquerades in the world!—of a modern editor. The Anarchist wolf, flying from the wolves of plutocracy, throws himself on the honor of the man. The man, not being a wolf (nor a London editor), and therefore not having enough sympathy with his exploit to be made bloodthirsty by it, does not throw him back to the pursuing wolves—gives him, instead, what help he can to escape, and sends him off acquainted at last with a force that goes deeper than dynamite, though you cannot buy so much of it for sixpence. That righteous and honorable high human deed is not wasted on Europe, let us hope, though it benefits the fugitive wolf only for a moment. The plutocratic wolves presently smell him out. The fugitive shoots the unlucky wolf whose nose is nearest; shoots himself; and then convinces the world, by his photograph, that he was no monstrous freak of reversion to the tiger, but a good looking young man with nothing abnormal about him except his appalling courage and resolution (that is why the terrified shriek Coward at him): one to whom murdering a happy young couple on their wedding morning would have been an unthinkably unnatural abomination under rational and kindly human circumstances.

Then comes the climax of irony and blind stupidity. The wolves, balked of their meal of fellow-wolf, turn on the man, and proceed to torture him, after their manner, by imprisonment, for refusing to fasten his teeth in the throat of the dynamiter and hold him down until they came to finish him.

Thus, you see, a man may not be a gentleman nowadays even if he wishes to. As to being a Christian, he is allowed some latitude in that matter, because, I repeat, Christianity has two faces. Popular Christianity has for its emblem a gibbet, for its chief sensation a sanguinary execution after torture, for its central mystery an insane vengeance bought off by a trumpery expiation. But there is a nobler and profounder Christianity which affirms the sacred mystery of Equality, and forbids the glaring futility and folly of vengeance, often politely called punishment or justice. The gibbet part of Christianity is tolerated. The other is criminal felony. Connoisseurs in irony are well aware of the fact that the only editor in England who denounces punishment as radically wrong, also repudiates Christianity; calls his paper The Freethinker; and has been imprisoned for "bad taste" under the law against blasphemy.

Sane Conclusions

And now I must ask the excited reader not to lose his head on one side or the other, but to draw a sane moral from these grim absurdities. It is not good sense to propose that laws against crime should apply to principals only and not to accessories whose consent, counsel, or silence may secure impunity to the principal. If you institute punishment as part of the law, you must punish people for refusing to punish. If you have a police, part of its duty must be to compel everybody to assist the police. No doubt if your laws are unjust, and your policemen agents of oppression, the result will be an unbearable violation of the private consciences of citizens. But that cannot be helped: the remedy is, not to license everybody to thwart the law if they please, but to make laws that will command the public assent, and not to deal cruelly and stupidly with law-breakers. Everybody disapproves of burglars; but the modern burglar, when caught and overpowered by a householder, usually appeals, and often, let us hope, with success, to his captor not to deliver him over to the useless horrors of penal servitude. In other cases the lawbreaker escapes because those who could give him up do not consider his breach of the law a guilty action. Sometimes, even, private tribunals are formed in opposition to the official tribunals; and these private tribunals employ assassins as executioners, as was done, for example, by Mahomet before he had established his power officially, and by the Ribbon lodges of Ireland in their long struggle with the landlords. Under such circumstances, the assassin goes free although everybody in the district knows who he is and what he has done. They do not betray him, partly because they justify him exactly as the regular Government justifies its official executioner, and partly because they would themselves be assassinated if they betrayed him: another method learnt from the official government. Given a tribunal, employing a slayer who has no personal quarrel with the slain; and there is clearly no moral difference between official and unofficial killing.

In short, all men are anarchists with regard to laws which are against their consciences, either in the preamble or in the penalty. In London our worst anarchists are the magistrates, because many of them are so old and ignorant that when they are called upon to administer any law that is based on ideas or knowledge less than half a century old, they disagree with it, and being mere ordinary homebred private Englishmen without any respect for law in the abstract, naïvely set the example of violating it. In this instance the man lags behind the law; but when the law lags behind the man, he becomes equally an anarchist. When some huge change in social conditions, such as the industrial revolution of the eighteenth and nineteenth centuries, throws our legal and industrial institutions out of date, Anarchism becomes almost a religion. The whole force of the most energetic geniuses of the time in philosophy, economics, and art, concentrates itself on demonstrations and reminders that morality and law are only conventions, fallible and continually obsolescing. Tragedies in which the heroes are bandits, and comedies in which law-abiding and conventionally moral folk are compelled to satirize themselves by outraging the conscience of the spectators every time they do their duty, appear simultaneously with economic treatises entitled "What is Property? Theft!" and with histories of "The Conflict between Religion and Science."

Now this is not a healthy state of things. The advantages of living in society are proportionate, not to the freedom of the individual from a code, but to the complexity and subtlety of the code he is prepared not only to accept but to uphold as a matter of such vital importance that a lawbreaker at large is hardly to be tolerated on any plea. Such an attitude becomes impossible when the only men who can make themselves heard and remembered throughout the world spend all their energy in raising our gorge against current law, current morality, current respectability, and legal property. The ordinary man, uneducated in social theory even when he is schooled in Latin verse, cannot be set against all the laws of his country and yet persuaded to regard law in the abstract as vitally necessary to society. Once he is brought to repudiate the laws and institutions he knows, he will repudiate the very conception of law and the very ground work of institutions, ridiculing human rights, extolling brainless methods as "historical," and tolerating nothing except pure empiricism in conduct, with dynamite as the basis of politics and vivisection as the basis of science. That is hideous; but what is to be done? Here am I, for instance, by class a respectable man, by common sense a hater of waste and disorder, by intellectual constitution legally minded to the verge of pedantry, and by temperament apprehensive and economically disposed to the limit of old-maidishness; yet I am, and have always been, and shall now always be, a revolutionary writer, because our laws make law impossible; our liberties destroy all freedom; our property is organized robbery; our morality is an impudent hypocrisy; our wisdom is administered by inexperienced or malexperienced dupes, our power wielded by cowards and weaklings, and our honor false in all its points. I am an enemy of the existing order for good reasons; but that does not make my attacks any less encouraging or helpful to people who are its enemies for bad reasons. The existing order may shriek that if I tell the truth about it, some foolish person may drive it to become still worse by trying to assassinate it. I cannot help that, even if I could see what worse it could do than it is already doing. And the disadvantage of that worst even from its own point of view is that society, with all its prisons and bayonets and whips and ostracisms and starvations, is powerless in the face of the Anarchist who is prepared to sacrifice his own life in the battle with it. Our natural safety from the cheap and devastating explosives which every Russian student can make, and every Russian grenadier has learnt to handle in Manchuria, lies in the fact that brave and resolute men, when they are rascals, will not risk their skins for the good of humanity, and, when they are not, are sympathetic enough to care for humanity, abhorring murder, and never committing it until their consciences are outraged beyond endurance. The remedy is, then, simply not to outrage their consciences.

Do not be afraid that they will not make allowances. All men make very large allowances indeed before they stake their own lives in a war to the death with society. Nobody demands or expects the millennium. But there are two things that must be set right, or we shall perish, like Rome, of soul atrophy disguised as empire.

The first is, that the daily ceremony of dividing the wealth of the country among its inhabitants shall be so conducted that no crumb shall, save as a criminal's ration, go to any able-bodied adults who are not producing by their personal exertions not only a full equivalent for what they take, but a surplus sufficient to provide for their superannuation and pay back the debt due for their nurture.

The second is that the deliberate infliction of malicious injuries which now goes on under the name of punishment be abandoned; so that the thief, the ruffian, the gambler, and the beggar, may without inhumanity be handed over to the law, and made to understand that a State which is too humane to punish will also be too thrifty to waste the life of honest men in watching or restraining dishonest ones. That is why we do not imprison dogs. We even take our chance of their first bite. But if a dog delights to bark and bite, it goes to the lethal chamber. That seems to me sensible. To allow the dog to expiate his bite by a period of torment, and then let him loose in a much more savage condition (for the chain makes a dog savage) to bite again and expiate again, having meanwhile spent a great deal of human life and happiness in the task of chaining and feeding and tormenting him, seems to me idiotic and superstitious. Yet that is what we do to men who bark and bite and steal. It would be far more sensible to put up with their vices, as we put up with their illnesses, until they give more trouble than they are worth, at which point we should, with many apologies and expressions of sympathy, and some generosity in complying with their last wishes, place them in the lethal chamber and get rid of them. Under no circumstances should they be allowed to expiate their misdeeds by a manufactured penalty, to subscribe to a charity, or to compensate the victims. If there is to be no punishment there can be no forgiveness. We shall never have real moral responsibility until everyone knows that his deeds are irrevocable, and that his life depends on his usefulness. Hitherto, alas! humanity has never dared face these hard facts. We frantically scatter conscience money and invent systems of conscience banking, with expiatory penalties, atonements, redemptions, salvations, hospital subscription lists and what not, to enable us to contract-out of the moral code. Not content with the old scapegoat and sacrificial lamb, we deify human saviors, and pray to miraculous virgin intercessors. We attribute mercy to the inexorable; soothe our consciences after committing murder by throwing ourselves on the bosom of divine love; and shrink even from our own gallows because we are forced to admit that it, at least, is irrevocable—as if one hour of imprisonment were not as irrevocable as any execution!

If a man cannot look evil in the face without illusion, he will never know what it really is, or combat it effectually. The few men who have been able (relatively) to do this have been called cynics, and have sometimes had an abnormal share of evil in themselves, corresponding to the abnormal strength of their minds; but they have never done mischief unless they intended to do it. That is why great scoundrels have been beneficent rulers whilst amiable and privately harmless monarchs have ruined their countries by trusting to the hocus-pocus of innocence and guilt, reward and punishment, virtuous indignation and pardon, instead of standing up to the facts without either malice or mercy. Major Barbara stands up to Bill Walker in that way, with the result that the ruffian who cannot get hated, has to hate himself. To relieve this agony he tries to get punished; but the Salvationist whom he tries to provoke is as merciless as Barbara, and only prays for him. Then he tries to pay, but can get nobody to take his money. His doom is the doom of Cain, who, failing to find either a savior, a policeman, or an almoner to help him to pretend that his brother's blood no longer cried from the ground, had to live and die a murderer. Cain took care not to commit another murder, unlike our railway shareholders (I am one) who kill and maim shunters by hundreds to save the cost of automatic couplings, and make atonement by annual subscriptions to deserving charities. Had Cain been allowed to pay off his score, he might possibly have killed Adam and Eve for the mere sake of a second luxurious reconciliation with God afterwards. Bodger, you may depend on it, will go on to the end of his life poisoning people with bad whisky, because he can always depend on the Salvation Army or the Church of England to negotiate a redemption for him in consideration of a trifling percentage of his profits.

There is a third condition too, which must be fulfilled before the great teachers of the world will cease to scoff at its religions. Creeds must become intellectually honest. At present there is not a single credible established religion in the world. That is perhaps the most stupendous fact in the whole world-situation. This play of mine, Major Barbara, is, I hope, both true and inspired; but whoever says that it all happened, and that faith in it and understanding of it consist in believing that it is a record of an actual occurrence, is, to speak according to Scripture, a fool and a liar, and is hereby solemnly denounced and cursed as such by me, the author, to all posterity.

London, June 1906.

ACT I

It is after dinner in January 1906, in the library in LADY BRITOMART UNDERSHAFT's house in Wilton Crescent. A large and comfortable settee is in the middle of the room, upholstered in dark leather. A person sitting on it (it is vacant at present) would have, on his right, LADY BRITOMART's writing table, with the lady herself busy at it; a smaller writing table behind him on his left; the door behind him on LADY BRITOMART's side; and a window with a window seat directly on his left. Near the window is an armchair.

LADY BRITOMART is a woman of fifty or thereabouts, well dressed and yet careless of her dress, well bred and quite reckless of her breeding, well mannered and yet appallingly outspoken and indifferent to the opinion of her interlocutors, amiable and yet peremptory, arbitrary, and high-tempered to the last bearable degree, and withal a very typical managing matron of the upper class, treated as a naughty child until she grew into a scolding mother, and finally settling down with plenty of practical ability and worldly experience, limited in the oddest way with domestic and class limitations, conceiving the universe exactly as if it were a large house in Wilton Crescent, though handling her corner of it very effectively on that assumption, and being quite enlightened and liberal as to the books in the library, the pictures on the walls, the music in the portfolios, and the articles in the papers.

Her son, STEPHEN, comes in. He is a gravely correct young man under 25, taking himself very seriously, but still in some awe of his mother, from childish habit and bachelor shyness rather than from any weakness of character.

STEPHEN: Whats the matter?
LADY BRITOMART: Presently, Stephen.

[STEPHEN submissively walks to the settee and sits down. He takes up a Liberal weekly called The Speaker.]

LADY BRITOMART: Dont begin to read, Stephen. I shall require all your attention.
STEPHEN: It was only while I was waiting—
LADY BRITOMART: Dont make excuses, Stephen. (*He puts down The Speaker*). Now! (*She finishes her writing; rises; and comes to the settee*). I have not kept you waiting very long, I think.
STEPHEN: Not at all, mother.
LADY BRITOMART: Bring me my cushion. (*He takes the cushion from the chair at the desk and arranges it for her as she sits down on the settee*). Sit down. (*He sits down and fingers his tie nervously*). Dont fiddle with your tie, Stephen: there is nothing the matter with it.
STEPHEN: I beg your pardon. (*He fiddles with his watch chain instead*).
LADY BRITOMART: Now are you attending to me, Stephen?
STEPHEN: Of course, mother.
LADY BRITOMART: No: it's not of course. I want something much more than your everyday matter-of-course attention. I am going to speak to you very seriously, Stephen. I wish you would let that chain alone.
STEPHEN (*hastily relinquishing the chain*): Have I done anything to annoy you, mother? If so, it was quite unintentional.
LADY BRITOMART (*astonished*): Nonsense! (*With some remorse*) My poor boy, did you think I was angry with you?
STEPHEN: What is it, then, mother? You are making me very uneasy.
LADY BRITOMART (*squaring herself at him rather aggressively*): Stephen: may I ask how soon you intend to realize that you are a grown-up man and that I am only a woman?
STEPHEN (*amazed*): Only a—
LADY BRITOMART: Dont repeat my words, please: it is a most aggravating habit. You must learn to face life seriously, Stephen. I really cannot bear the whole burden of our family affairs any longer. You must advise me: you must assume the responsibility.
STEPHEN: I!
LADY BRITOMART: Yes, you, of course. You were 24 last June. Youve been at Harrow and Cambridge. Youve been to India and Japan. You must know a lot of things, now; unless you have wasted your time most scandalously. Well, advise me.
STEPHEN (*much perplexed*): You know I have never interfered in the household—
LADY BRITOMART: No: I should think not. I dont want you to order the dinner.
STEPHEN: I mean in our family affairs.
LADY BRITOMART: Well, you must interfere now; for they are getting quite beyond me.
STEPHEN (*troubled*): I have thought sometimes that perhaps I ought; but really, mother, I know so little about them; and what I do know is so painful! it is so impossible to mention some things to you—(*he stops, ashamed*).
LADY BRITOMART: I suppose you mean your father.
STEPHEN (*almost inaudibly*): Yes.
LADY BRITOMART: My dear: we cant go on all our lives not mentioning him. Of course you were quite right not to open the subject until I asked you to; but you are old enough now to be taken into my confidence, and to help me to deal with him about the girls.
STEPHEN: But the girls are all right. They are engaged.
LADY BRITOMART (*complacently*): Yes: I have made a very good match for Sarah. Charles Lomax will be a millionaire at 35. But that is ten years ahead; and in the meantime his trustees cannot under the terms of his father's will allow him more than £800 a year.
STEPHEN: But the will says also that if he increases his

income by his own exertions, they may double the increase.

LADY BRITOMART: Charles Lomax's exertions are much more likely to decrease his income than to increase it. Sarah will have to find at least another £800 a year for the next ten years; and even then they will be as poor as church mice. And what about Barbara? I thought Barbara was going to make the most brilliant career of all of you. And what does she do? Joins the Salvation Army; discharges her maid; lives on a pound a week; and walks in one evening with a professor of Greek whom she has picked up in the street, and who pretends to be a Salvationist, and actually plays the big drum for her in public because he has fallen head over ears in love with her.

STEPHEN: I was certainly rather taken aback when I heard they were engaged. Cusins is a very nice fellow, certainly: nobody would ever guess that he was born in Australia; but—

LADY BRITOMART: Oh, Adolphus Cusins will make a very good husband. After all, nobody can say a word against Greek: it stamps a man at once as an educated gentleman. And my family, thank Heaven, is not a pig-headed Tory one. We are Whigs, and believe in liberty. Let snobbish people say what they please: Barbara shall marry, not the man they like, but the man *I* like.

STEPHEN: Of course I was thinking only of his income. However, he is not likely to be extravagant.

LADY BRITOMART: Dont be too sure of that, Stephen. I know your quiet, simple, refined, poetic people like Adolphus: quite content with the best of everything! They cost more than your extravagant people, who are always as mean as they are second rate. No: Barbara will need at least £2000 a year. You see it means two additional households. Besides, my dear, you must marry soon. I dont approve of the present fashion of philandering bachelors and late marriages; and I am trying to arrange something for you.

STEPHEN: It's very good of you, mother; but perhaps I had better arrange that for myself.

LADY BRITOMART: Nonsense! you are much too young to begin matchmaking: you would be taken in by some pretty little nobody. Of course I dont mean that you are not to be consulted: you know that as well as I do. (STEPHEN *closes his lips and is silent*). Now dont sulk, Stephen.

STEPHEN: I am not sulking, mother. What has all this got to do with—with—with my father?

LADY BRITOMART: My dear Stephen: where is the money to come from? It is easy enough for you and the other children to live on my income as long as we are in the same house; but I cant keep four families in four separate houses.

You know how poor my father is: he has barely seven thousand a year now; and really, if he were not the Earl of Stevenage, he would have to give up society. He can do nothing for us. He says, naturally enough, that it is absurd that he should be asked to provide for the children of a man who is rolling in money. You see, Stephen, your father must be fabulously wealthy, because there is always a war going on somewhere.

STEPHEN: You need not remind me of that, mother. I have hardly ever opened a newspaper in my life without seeing our name in it. The Undershaft torpedo! The Undershaft quick firers! The Undershaft ten inch! the Undershaft disappearing rampart gun! the Undershaft submarine! and now the Undershaft aerial battleship! At Harrow they called me the Woolwich Infant. At Cambridge it was the same. A little brute at King's who was always trying to get up revivals, spoilt my Bible— your first birthday present to me—by writing under my name, "Son and heir to Undershaft and Lazarus, Death and Destruction Dealers: address, Christendom and Judea." But that was not so bad as the way I was kowtowed to everywhere because my father was making millions by selling cannons.

LADY BRITOMART: It is not only the cannons, but the war loans that Lazarus arranges under cover of giving credit for the cannons. You know, Stephen, it's perfectly scandalous. Those two men, Andrew Undershaft and Lazarus, positively have Europe under their thumbs. That is why your father is able to behave as he does. He is above the law. Do you think Bismarck or Gladstone or Disraeli could have openly defied every social and moral obligation all their lives as your father has? They simply wouldnt have dared. I asked Gladstone to take it up. I asked The Times to take it up. I asked the Lord Chamberlain to take it up. But it was just like asking them to declare war on the Sultan. They wouldnt. They said they couldnt touch him. I believe they were afraid.

STEPHEN: What could they do? He does not actually break the law.

LADY BRITOMART: Not break the law! He is always breaking the law. He broke the law when he was born: his parents were not married.

STEPHEN: Mother! Is that true?

LADY BRITOMART: Of course it's true: that was why we separated.

STEPHEN: He married without letting you know this!

LADY BRITOMART (*rather taken aback by this inference*): Oh no. To do Andrew justice, that was not the sort of thing he did. Besides, you know the Undershaft motto: Unashamed. Everybody knew.

STEPHEN: But you said that was why you separated.

LADY BRITOMART: Yes, because he was not content

with being a foundling himself: he wanted to disinherit you for another foundling. That was what I couldnt stand.

STEPHEN (*ashamed*): Do you mean for—for—for—

LADY BRITOMART: Dont stammer, Stephen. Speak distinctly.

STEPHEN: But this is so frightful to me, mother. To have to speak to you about such things!

LADY BRITOMART: It's not pleasant for me, either, especially if you are still so childish that you must make it worse by a display of embarrassment. It is only in the middle classes, Stephen, that people get into a state of dumb helpless horror when they find that there are wicked people in the world. In our class, we have to decide what is to be done with wicked people; and nothing should disturb our self-possession. Now ask your question properly.

STEPHEN: Mother: have you no consideration for me? For Heaven's sake either treat me as a child, as you always do, and tell me nothing at all; or tell me everything and let me take it as best I can.

LADY BRITOMART: Treat you as a child! What do you mean? It is most unkind and ungrateful of you to say such a thing. You know I have never treated any of you as children. I have always made you my companions and friends, and allowed you perfect freedom to do and say whatever you liked, so long as you liked what I could approve of.

STEPHEN (*desperately*): I daresay we have been the very imperfect children of a very perfect mother; but I do beg you to let me alone for once, and tell me about this horrible business of my father wanting to set me aside for another son.

LADY BRITOMART (*amazed*): Another son! I never said anything of the kind. I never dreamt of such a thing. This is what comes of interrupting me.

STEPHEN: But you said—

LADY BRITOMART (*cutting him short*): Now be a good boy, Stephen, and listen to me patiently. The Undershafts are descended from a foundling in the parish of St Andrew Undershaft in the city. That was long ago, in the reign of James the First. Well, this foundling was adopted by an armorer and gun-maker. In the course of time the foundling succeeded to the business; and from some notion of gratitude, or some vow or something, he adopted another foundling, and left the business to him. And that foundling did the same. Ever since that, the cannon business has always been left to an adopted foundling named Andrew Undershaft.

STEPHEN: But did they never marry? Were there no legitimate sons?

LADY BRITOMART: Oh yes: they married just as your father did; and they were rich enough to buy land for their own children and leave them well provided for. But they always adopted and trained some foundling to succeed them in the business; and of course they always quarrelled with their wives furiously over it. Your father was adopted in that way; and he pretends to consider himself bound to keep up the tradition and adopt somebody to leave the business to. Of course I was not going to stand that. There may have been some reason for it when the Undershafts could only marry women in their own class, whose sons were not fit to govern great estates. But there could be no excuse for passing over my son.

STEPHEN (*dubiously*): I am afraid I should make a poor hand of managing a cannon foundry.

LADY BRITOMART: Nonsense! you could easily get a manager and pay him a salary.

STEPHEN: My father evidently had no great opinion of my capacity.

LADY BRITOMART: Stuff, child! you were only a baby: it had nothing to do with your capacity. Andrew did it on principle, just as he did every perverse and wicked thing on principle. When my father remonstrated, Andrew actually told him to his face that history tells us of only two successful institutions: one the Undershaft firm, and the other the Roman Empire under the Antonines. That was because the Antonine emperors all adopted their successors. Such rubbish! The Stevenages are as good as the Antonines, I hope; and you are a Stevenage. But that was Andrew all over. There you have the man! Always clever and unanswerable when he was defending nonsense and wickedness: always awkward and sullen when he had to behave sensibly and decently!

STEPHEN: Then it was on my account that your home life was broken up, mother. I am sorry.

LADY BRITOMART: Well, dear, there were other differences. I really cannot bear an immoral man. I am not a Pharisee, I hope; and I should not have minded his merely doing wrong things: we are none of us perfect. But your father didnt exactly do wrong things: he said them and thought them: that was what was so dreadful. He really had a sort of religion of wrongness. Just as one doesnt mind men practising immorality so long as they own that they are in the wrong by preaching morality; so I couldnt forgive Andrew for preaching immorality while he practised morality. You would all have grown up without principles, without any knowledge of right and wrong, if he had been in the house. You know, my dear, your father was a very attractive man in some ways. Children did not dislike him; and he took advantage of it to put the wickedest ideas into their heads, and make them quite unmanageable. I did not dislike him myself: very far from it; but nothing can bridge over moral disagreement.

STEPHEN: All this simply bewilders me, mother. People may differ about matters of opinion, or even about religion; but how can they differ about right and wrong? Right is right; and wrong is wrong; and if a man cannot distinguish them properly, he is either a fool or a rascal: thats all.

LADY BRITOMART (*touched*): Thats my own boy (*she pats his cheek*)! Your father never could answer that: he used to laugh and get out of it under cover of some affectionate nonsense. And now that you understand the situation, what do you advise me to do?

STEPHEN: Well, what can you do?

LADY BRITOMART: I must get the money somehow.

STEPHEN: We cannot take money from him. I had rather go and live in some cheap place like Bedford Square or even Hampstead than take a farthing of his money.

LADY BRITOMART: But after all, Stephen, our present income comes from Andrew.

STEPHEN (*shocked*): I never knew that.

LADY BRITOMART: Well, you surely didnt suppose your grandfather had anything to give me. The Stevenages could not do everything for you. We gave you social position. Andrew had to contribute something. He had a very good bargain, I think.

STEPHEN (*bitterly*): We are utterly dependent on him and his cannons, then?

LADY BRITOMART: Certainly not: the money is settled. But he provided it. So you see it is not a question of taking money from him or not: it is simply a question of how much. I dont want any more for myself.

STEPHEN: Nor do I.

LADY BRITOMART: But Sarah does; and Barbara does. That is, Charles Lomax and Adolphus Cusins will cost them more. So I must put my pride in my pocket and ask for it, I suppose. That is your advice, Stephen, is it not?

STEPHEN: No.

LADY BRITOMART (*sharply*): Stephen!

STEPHEN: Of course if you are determined—

LADY BRITOMART: I am not determined: I ask your advice; and I am waiting for it. I will not have all the responsibility thrown on my shoulders.

STEPHEN (*obstinately*): I would die sooner than ask him for another penny.

LADY BRITOMART (*resignedly*): You mean that I must ask him. Very well, Stephen: it shall be as you wish. You will be glad to know that your grandfather concurs. But he thinks I ought to ask Andrew to come here and see the girls. After all, he must have some natural affection for them.

STEPHEN: Ask him here!!!

LADY BRITOMART: Do not repeat my words, Stephen.

Where else can I ask him?

STEPHEN: I never expected you to ask him at all.

LADY BRITOMART: Now dont tease, Stephen. Come! you see that it is necessary that he should pay us a visit, dont you?

STEPHEN (*reluctantly*): I suppose so, if the girls cannot do without his money.

LADY BRITOMART: Thank you, Stephen: I knew you would give me the right advice when it was properly explained to you. I have asked your father to come this evening. (STEPHEN *bounds from his seat*) Dont jump, Stephen: it fidgets me.

STEPHEN (*in utter consternation*): Do you mean to say that my father is coming here tonight—that he may be here at any moment?

LADY BRITOMART (*looking at her watch*): I said nine. (*He gasps. She rises*). Ring the bell, please. (STEPHEN *goes to the smaller writing table; presses a button on it; and sits at it with his elbows on the table and his head in his hands, outwitted and overwhelmed*). It is ten minutes to nine yet; and I have to prepare the girls. I asked Charles Lomax and Adolphus to dinner on purpose that they might be here. Andrew had better see them in case he should cherish any delusions as to their being capable of supporting their wives. (*The butler enters:* LADY BRITOMART *goes behind the settee to speak to him*). Morrison: go up to the drawing room and tell everybody to come down here at once. (MORRISON *withdraws.* LADY BRITOMART *turns to* STEPHEN). Now remember, Stephen: I shall need all your countenance and authority. (*He rises and tries to recover some vestige of these attributes*). Give me a chair, dear. (*He pushes a chair forward from the wall to where she stands, near the smaller writing table. She sits down; and he goes to the armchair, into which he throws himself*). I dont know how Barbara will take it. Ever since they made her a major in the Salvation Army she has developed a propensity to have her own way and order people about which quite cows me sometimes. It's not ladylike: I'm sure I dont know where she picked it up. Anyhow, Barbara shant bully me; but still it's just as well that your father should be here before she has time to refuse to meet him or make a fuss. Dont look nervous, Stephen: it will only encourage Barbara to make difficulties. *I* am nervous enough, goodness knows; but I dont shew it.

[SARAH *and* BARBARA *come in with their respective young men,* CHARLES LOMAX *and* ADOLPHUS CUSINS, *SARAH is slender, bored, and mundane.* BARBARA *is robuster, jollier, much more energetic.* SARAH *is fashionably dressed:* BARBARA *is in Salvation Army uniform.* LOMAX, *a young man about town, is like many other young men about town. He is afflicted with a frivolous sense of humor which plunges him at the*

*most inopportune moments into paroxysms of imper-
fectly suppressed laughter. CUSINS is a spectacled student, slight, thin haired, and sweet voiced, with a
more complex form of LOMAX's complaint. His sense of
humor is intellectual and subtle, and is complicated
by an appalling temper. The lifelong struggle of a
benevolent temperament and a high conscience
against impulses of inhuman ridicule and fierce impatience has set up a chronic strain which has visibly
wrecked his constitution. He is a most implacable,
determined, tenacious, intolerant person who by mere
force of character presents himself as—and indeed
actually is—considerate, gentle, explanatory, even
mild and apologetic, capable possibly of murder, but
not of cruelty or coarseness. By the operation of some
instinct which is not merciful enough to blind him with
the illusions of love, he is obstinately bent on marrying
BARBARA. LOMAX likes SARAH and thinks it will be rather
a lark to marry her. Consequently he has not attempted to resist LADY BRITOMART's arrangements to that
end.*

*All four look as if they had been having a good
deal of fun in the drawing room. The girls enter first,
leaving the swains outside. Sarah comes to the settee.
Barbara comes in after her and stops at the door.]*

BARBARA: Are Cholly and Dolly to come in?

LADY BRITOMART (*forcibly*): Barbara: I will not have
Charles called Cholly: the vulgarity of it positively makes me ill.

BARBARA: It's all right, mother: Cholly is quite correct
nowadays. Are they to come in?

LADY BRITOMART: Yes, if they will behave themselves.

BARBARA (*through the door*): Come in, Dolly; and
behave yourself.

*[BARBARA comes to her mother's writing table. CUSINS
enters smiling, and wanders towards LADY BRITOMART.]*

SARAH (*calling*): Come in, Cholly. (*LOMAX enters, controlling his features very imperfectly, and places himself vaguely between SARAH and BARBARA*).

LADY BRITOMART (*peremptorily*): Sit down, all of you.
(*They sit. CUSINS crosses to the window and seats himself there. LOMAX takes a chair. BARBARA sits at the
writing table and SARAH on the settee*). I dont in the
least know what you are laughing at, Adolphus. I
am surprised at you, though I expected nothing
better from Charles Lomax.

CUSINS (*in a remarkably gentle voice*): Barbara has been
trying to teach me the West Ham Salvation
March.

LADY BRITOMART: I see nothing to laugh at in that;
nor should you if you are really converted.

CUSINS (*sweetly*): You were not present. It was really
funny, I believe.

LOMAX: Ripping.

LADY BRITOMART: Be quiet, Charles. Now listen to me,
children. Your father is coming here this evening.

*[General stupefaction. LOMAX, SARAH, and BARBARA rise:
SARAH scared, and BARBARA amused and expectant.]*

LOMAX (*remonstrating*): Oh I say!

LADY BRITOMART: You are not called on to say anything, Charles.

SARAH: Are you serious, mother?

LADY BRITOMART: Of course I am serious. It is on your
account, Sarah, and also on Charles's. (*Silence.
SARAH sits, with a shrug. CHARLES looks painfully
unworthy*). I hope you are not going to object,
Barbara.

BARBARA: I! why should I? My father has a soul to
be saved like anybody else. He's quite welcome
as far as I am concerned. (*She sits on the table, and
softly whistles 'Onward, Christian Soldiers'*).

LOMAX (*still remonstrant*): But really, dont you know!
Oh I say!

LADY BRITOMART (*frigidly*): What do you wish to convey, Charles?

LOMAX: Well, you must admit that this is a bit thick.

LADY BRITOMART (*turning with ominous suavity to
CUSINS*): Adolphus: you are a professor of Greek.
Can you translate Charles Lomax's remarks into
reputable English for us?

CUSINS (*cautiously*): If I may say so, Lady Brit, I think
Charles has rather happily expressed what we all
feel. Homer, speaking of Autolycus, uses the same
phrase. πνκινον δομον ελειν means a bit thick.

LOMAX (*handsomely*): Not that I mind, you know, if
Sarah dont. (*He sits*).

LADY BRITOMART (*crushingly*): Thank you. Have I
your permission, Adolphus, to invite my own
husband to my own house?

CUSINS (*gallantly*): You have my unhesitating support
in everything you do.

LADY BRITOMART: Tush! Sarah: have you nothing to
say?

SARAH: Do you mean that he is coming regularly to
live here?

LADY BRITOMART: Certainly not. The spare room is
ready for him if he likes to stay for a day or two
and see a little more of you; but there are limits.

SARAH: Well, he cant eat us, I suppose. *I* dont mind.

LOMAX (*chuckling*): I wonder how the old man will
take it.

LADY BRITOMART: Much as the old woman will, no
doubt, Charles.

LOMAX (*abashed*): I didnt mean—at least—

LADY BRITOMART: You didnt think, Charles. You never
do; and the result is, you never mean anything.
And now please attend to me, children. Your
father will be quite a stranger to us.

LOMAX: I suppose he hasnt seen Sarah since she was

a little kid.

LADY BRITOMART: Not since she was a little kid, Charles, as you express it with that elegance of diction and refinement of thought that seem never to desert you. Accordingly—er—(*impatiently*) Now I have forgotten what I was going to say. That comes of your provoking me to be sarcastic, Charles. Adolphus: will you kindly tell me where I was.

CUSINS (*sweetly*): You were saying that as Mr Undershaft has not seen his children since they were babies, he will form his opinion of the way you have brought them up from their behavior tonight, and that therefore you wish us all to be particularly careful to conduct ourselves well, especially Charles.

LADY BRITOMART (*with emphatic approval*): Precisely.

LOMAX: Look here, Dolly: Lady Brit didnt say that.

LADY BRITOMART (*vehemently*): I did, Charles. Adolphus's recollection is perfectly correct. It is most important that you should be good; and I do beg you for once not to pair off into opposite corners and giggle and whisper while I am speaking to your father.

BARBARA: All right, mother. We'll do you credit. (*She comes off the table, and sits in her chair with ladylike elegance*).

LADY BRITOMART: Remember, Charles, that Sarah will want to feel proud of you instead of ashamed of you.

LOMAX: Oh I say! theres nothing to be exactly proud of, dont you know.

LADY BRITOMART: Well, try and look as if there was.

[*MORRISON, pale and dismayed, breaks into the room in unconcealed disorder.*]

MORRISON: Might I speak a word to you, my lady?

LADY BRITOMART: Nonsense! Shew him up.

MORRISON: Yes, my lady. (*He goes*).

LOMAX: Does Morrison know who it is?

LADY BRITOMART: Of course. Morrison has always been with us.

LOMAX: It must be a regular corker for him, dont you know.

LADY BRITOMART: Is this a moment to get on my nerves, Charles, with your outrageous expressions?

LOMAX: But this is something out of the ordinary, really—

MORRISON (*at the door*): The—er—Mr Undershaft. (*He retreats in confusion*).

[*ANDREW UNDERSHAFT comes in. All rise. LADY BRITOMART meets him in the middle of the room behind the settee.*

Andrew is, on the surface, a stoutish, easygoing

elderly man, with kindly patient manners, and an engaging simplicity of character. But he has a watchful, deliberate, waiting, listening face, and formidable reserves of power, both bodily and mental, in his capacious chest and long head. His gentleness is partly that of a strong man who has learnt by experience that his natural grip hurts ordinary people unless he handles them very carefully, and partly the mellowness of age and success. He is also a little shy in his present very delicate situation.]

LADY BRITOMART: Good evening, Andrew.

UNDERSHAFT: How d'ye do, my dear.

LADY BRITOMART: You look a good deal older.

UNDERSHAFT (*apologetically*): I am somewhat older. (*Taking her hand with a touch of courtship*) Time has stood still with you.

LADY BRITOMART (*throwing away his hand*): Rubbish! This is your family.

UNDERSHAFT (*surprised*): Is it so large? I am sorry to say my memory is failing very badly in some things. (*He offers his hand with paternal kindness to* LOMAX).

LOMAX (*jerkily shaking his hand*): Ahdedoo.

UNDERSHAFT: I can see you are my eldest. I am very glad to meet you again, my boy.

LOMAX (*remonstrating*): No but look here dont you know—(*Overcome*) Oh I say!

LADY BRITOMART (*recovering from momentary speechlessness*): Andrew: do you mean to say that you dont remember how many children you have?

UNDERSHAFT: Well, I am afraid I—. They have grown so much—er. Am I making any ridiculous mistake? I may as well confess: I recollect only one son. But so many things have happened since, of course—er—

LADY BRITOMART (*decisively*): Andrew: you are talking nonsense. Of course you have only one son.

UNDERSHAFT: Perhaps you will be good enough to introduce me, my dear.

LADY BRITOMART: That is Charles Lomax, who is engaged to Sarah.

UNDERSHAFT: My dear sir, I beg your pardon.

LOMAX: Notatall. Delighted, I assure you.

LADY BRITOMART: This is Stephen.

UNDERSHAFT (*bowing*): Happy to make your acquaintance, Mr Stephen. Then (*going to* CUSINS) you must be my son. (*Taking* CUSINS' *hands in his*) How are you, my young friend? (*To* LADY BRITOMART) He is very like you, my love.

CUSINS: You flatter me, Mr Undershaft. My name is Cusins: engaged to Barbara. (*Very explicitly*) That is Major Barbara Undershaft, of the Salvation Army. That is Sarah, your second daughter. This is Stephen Undershaft, your son.

UNDERSHAFT: My dear Stephen, I beg your pardon.

STEPHEN: Not at all.

UNDERSHAFT: Mr Cusins: I am much indebted to you for explaining so precisely. (*Turning to* SARAH) Barbara, my dear—

SARAH (*prompting him*): Sarah.

UNDERSHAFT: Sarah, of course. (*They shake hands. He goes over to* BARBARA) Barbara—I am right this time, I hope?

BARBARA: Quite right. (*They shake hands*).

LADY BRITOMART (*resuming command*): Sit down, all of you. Sit down, Andrew. (*She comes forward and sits on the settee.* CUSINS *also brings his chair forward on her left.* BARBARA *and* STEPHEN *resume their seats.* LOMAX *gives his chair to* SARAH *and goes for another*).

UNDERSHAFT: Thank you, my love.

LOMAX (*conversationally, as he brings a chair forward between the writing table and the settee, and offers it to* UNDERSHAFT): Takes you some time to find out exactly where you are, dont it?

UNDERSHAFT (*accepting the chair, but remaining standing*): That is not what embarrasses me, Mr Lomax. My difficulty is that if I play the part of a father, I shall produce the effect of an intrusive stranger; and if I play the part of a discreet stranger, I may appear a callous father.

LADY BRITOMART: There is no need for you to play any part at all, Andrew. You had much better be sincere and natural.

UNDERSHAFT (*submissively*): Yes, my dear: I daresay that will be best. (*He sits down comfortably*). Well, here I am. Now what can I do for you all?

LADY BRITOMART: You need not do anything, Andrew. You are one of the family. You can sit with us and enjoy yourself.

[*A painfully conscious pause.* BARBARA *makes a face at* LOMAX, *whose too long suppressed mirth immediately explodes in agonized neighings.*]

LADY BRITOMART (*outraged*): Charles Lomax: if you can behave yourself, behave yourself. If not, leave the room.

LOMAX: I'm awfully sorry, Lady Brit; but really you know, upon my soul! (*He sits on the settee between* LADY BRITOMART *and* UNDERSHAFT, *quite overcome*).

BARBARA: Why dont you laugh if you want to, Cholly? It's good for your inside.

LADY BRITOMART: Barbara: you have had the education of a lady. Please let your father see that; and dont talk like a street girl.

UNDERSHAFT: Never mind me, my dear. As you know, I am not a gentleman; and I was never educated.

LOMAX (*encouragingly*): Nobody'd know it, I assure you. You look all right, you know.

CUSINS: Let me advise you to study Greek, Mr. Undershaft. Greek scholars are privileged men. Few of them know Greek; and none of them know anything else; but their position is unchallengeable. Other languages are the qualifications of waiters and commercial travellers: Greek is to a man of position what the hallmark is to silver.

BARBARA: Dolly: dont be insincere. Cholly: fetch your concertina and play something for us.

LOMAX (*jumps up eagerly, but checks himself to remark doubtfully to* UNDERSHAFT): Perhaps that sort of thing isnt in your line, eh?

UNDERSHAFT: I am particularly fond of music.

LOMAX (*delighted*): Are you? Then I'll get it. (*He goes upstairs for the instrument*).

UNDERSHAFT: Do you play, Barbara?

BARBARA: Only the tambourine. But Cholly's teaching me the concertina.

UNDERSHAFT: Is Cholly also a member of the Salvation Army?

BARBARA: No: he says it's bad form to be a dissenter. But I dont despair of Cholly. I made him come yesterday to a meeting at the dock gates, and take the collection in his hat.

UNDERSHAFT (*looks whimsically at his wife*)!!

LADY BRITOMART: It is not my doing, Andrew. Barbara is old enough to take her own way. She has no father to advise her.

BARBARA: Oh yes she has. There are no orphans in the Salvation Army.

UNDERSHAFT: Your father there has a great many children and plenty of experience, eh?

BARBARA (*looking at him with quick interest and nodding*): Just so. How did you come to understand that? (LOMAX *is heard at the door trying the concertina*).

LADY BRITOMART: Come in, Charles. Play us something at once.

LOMAX: Righto! (*He sits down in his former place, and preludes*).

UNDERSHAFT: One moment, Mr Lomax. I am rather interested in the Salvation Army. Its motto might be my own: Blood and Fire.

LOMAX (*shocked*): But not your sort of blood and fire, you know.

UNDERSHAFT: My sort of blood cleanses: my sort of fire purifies.

BARBARA: So do ours. Come down tomorrow to my shelter—the West Ham shelter—and see what we're doing. We're going to march to a great meeting in the Assembly Hall at Mile End. Come and see the shelter and then march with us: it will do you a lot of good. Can you play anything?

UNDERSHAFT: In my youth I earned pennies, and even shillings occasionally, in the streets and in public house parlors by my natural talent for stepdancing. Later on, I became a member of the Undershaft orchestral society, and performed passably on the tenor trombone.

LOMAX (*scandalized—putting down the concertina*): Oh I say!

BARBARA: Many a sinner has played himself into heaven on the trombone, thanks to the Army.

LOMAX (*to* BARBARA, *still rather shocked*): Yes; but what about the cannon business, dont you know? (*To* UNDERSHAFT) Getting into heaven is not exactly in your line is it?

LADY BRITOMART: Charles!!!

LOMAX: Well; but it stands to reason, dont it? The cannon business may be necessary and all that: we cant get on without cannons; but it isnt right, you know. On the other hand, there may be a certain amount of tosh about the Salvation Army—I belong to the Established Church myself—but still you cant deny that it's religion; and you cant go against religion, can you? At least unless youre downright immoral, dont you know.

UNDERSHAFT: You hardly appreciate my position, Mr Lomax—

LOMAX (*hastily*): I'm not saying anything against you personally—

UNDERSHAFT: Quite so, quite so. But consider for a moment. Here I am, a profiteer in mutilation and murder. I find myself in a specially amiable humor just now because, this morning, down at the foundry, we blew twenty-seven dummy soldiers into fragments with a gun which formerly destroyed only thirteen.

LOMAX (*leniently*): Well, the more destructive war becomes, the sooner it will be abolished, eh?

UNDERSHAFT: Not at all. The more destructive war becomes the more fascinating we find it. No, Mr Lomax: I am obliged to you for making the usual excuse for my trade; but I am not ashamed of it. I am not one of those men who keep their morals and their business in water-tight compartments. All the spare money my trade rivals spend on hospitals, cathedrals, and other receptacles for conscience money, I devote to experiments and researches in improved methods of destroying life and property. I have always done so; and I always shall. Therefore your Christmas card moralities of peace on earth and goodwill among men are of no use to me. Your Christianity, which enjoins you to resist not evil, and to turn the other cheek, would make me a bankrupt. My morality—my religion—must have a place for cannons and torpedoes in it.

STEPHEN (*coldly—almost sullenly*): You speak as if there were half a dozen moralities and religions to choose from, instead of one true morality and one true religion.

UNDERSHAFT: For me there is only one true morality; but it might not fit you, as you do not manufacture aerial battleships. There is only one true morality for every man; but every man has not the same true morality.

LOMAX (*overtaxed*): Would you mind saying that again? I didnt quite follow it.

CUSINS: It's quite simple. As Euripides says, one man's meat is another man's poison morally as well as physically.

UNDERSHAFT: Precisely.

LOMAX: Oh, that! Yes, yes, yes. True. True.

STEPHEN: In other words, some men are honest and some are scoundrels.

BARBARA: Bosh! There are no scoundrels.

UNDERSHAFT: Indeed? Are there any good men?

BARBARA: No. Not one. There are neither good men nor scoundrels: there are just children of one Father; and the sooner they stop calling one another names the better. You neednt talk to me: I know them. Ive had scores of them through my hands: scoundrels, criminals, infidels, philanthropists, missionaries, county councillors, all sorts. Theyre all just the same sort of sinner; and theres the same salvation ready for them all.

UNDERSHAFT: May I ask have you ever saved a maker of cannons?

BARBARA: No. Will you let me try?

UNDERSHAFT: Well, I will make a bargain with you. If I go to see you tomorrow in your Salvation Shelter, will you come the day after to see me in my cannon works?

BARBARA: Take care. It may end in your giving up the cannons for the sake of the Salvation Army.

UNDERSHAFT: Are you sure it will not end in your giving up the Salvation Army for the sake of the cannons?

BARBARA: I will take my chance of that.

UNDERSHAFT: And I will take my chance of the other. (*They shake hands on it*). Where is your shelter?

BARBARA: In West Ham. At the sign of the cross. Ask anybody in Canning Town. Where are your works?

UNDERSHAFT: In Perivale St Andrews. At the sign of the sword. Ask anybody in Europe.

LOMAX: Hadnt I better play something?

BARBARA: Yes. Give us Onward, Christian Soldiers.

LOMAX: Well, thats rather a strong order to begin with, dont you know. Suppose I sing Thou'rt passing hence, my brother. It's much the same tune.

BARBARA: It's too melancholy. You get saved, Cholly; and youll pass hence, my brother, without making such a fuss about it.

LADY BRITOMART: Really, Barbara, you go on as if religion were a pleasant subject. Do have some sense of propriety.

UNDERSHAFT: I do not find it an unpleasant subject, my dear. It is the only one that capable people really care for.

LADY BRITOMART (*looking at her watch*): Well, if you are determined to have it, I insist on having it in a proper and respectable way. Charles: ring for prayers.

[General amazement. STEPHEN rises in dismay.]

LOMAX (*rising*): Oh I say!

UNDERSHAFT (*rising*): I am afraid I must be going.

LADY BRITOMART: You cannot go now, Andrew: it would be most improper. Sit down. What will the servants think?

UNDERSHAFT: My dear: I have conscientious scruples. May I suggest a compromise? If Barbara will conduct a little service in the drawing room, with Mr Lomax as organist, I will attend it willingly. I will even take part, if a trombone can be procured.

LADY BRITOMART: Dont mock, Andrew.

UNDERSHAFT (*shocked—to BARBARA*): You dont think I am mocking, my love, I hope.

BARBARA: No, of course not; and it wouldnt matter if you were: half the Army came to their first meeting for a lark. (*Rising*) Come along. (*She throws her arm round her father and sweeps him out, calling to the others from the threshold*) Come, Dolly. Come, Cholly.

[CUSINS rises.]

LADY BRITOMART: I will not be disobeyed by everybody. Adolphus: sit down. (*He does not*). Charles: you may go. You are not fit for prayers: you cannot keep your countenance.

LOMAX: Oh I say! (*He goes out*).

LADY BRITOMART (*continuing*): But you, Adolphus, can behave yourself if you choose to. I insist on your staying.

CUSINS: My dear Lady Brit: there are things in the family prayer book that I couldnt bear to hear you say.

LADY BRITOMART: What things, pray?

CUSINS: Well, you would have to say before all the servants that we have done things we ought not to have done, and left undone things we ought to have done, and that there is no health in us. I cannot bear to hear you doing yourself such an injustice, and Barbara such an injustice. As for myself, I flatly deny it: I have done my best. I shouldnt dare to marry Barbara—I couldnt look you in the face—if it were true. So I must go to the drawing room.

LADY BRITOMART (*offended*): Well, go. (*He starts for the door*). And remember this, Adolphus (*he turns to listen*): I have a very strong suspicion that you went to the Salvation Army to worship Barbara and nothing else. And I quite appreciate the very clever way in which you systematically humbug me. I have found you out. Take care Barbara doesnt. Thats all.

CUSINS (*with unruffled sweetness*): Dont tell on me. (*He steals out*).

LADY BRITOMART: Sarah: if you want to go, go. Anything's better than to sit there as if you wished you were a thousand miles away.

SARAH (*languidly*): Very well, mamma. (*She goes*).

[LADY BRITOMART, with a sudden flounce, gives way to a little gust of tears.]

STEPHEN (*going to her*): Mother: whats the matter?

LADY BRITOMART (*swishing away her tears with her handkerchief*): Nothing. Foolishness. You can go with him, too, if you like, and leave me with the servants.

STEPHEN: Oh, you mustnt think that, mother. I—I dont like him.

LADY BRITOMART: The others do. That is the injustice of a woman a lot. A woman has to bring up her children; and that means to restrain them, to deny them things they want, to set them tasks, to punish them when they do wrong, to do all the unpleasant things. And then the father, who has nothing to do put pet them and spoil them, comes in when all her work is done and steals their affection from her.

STEPHEN: He has not stolen our affection from you. It is only curiosity.

LADY BRITOMART (*violently*): I wont be consoled, Stephen. There is nothing the matter with me. (*She rises and goes towards the door*).

STEPHEN: Where are you going, mother?

LADY BRITOMART: To the drawing room, of course (*She goes out. Onward, Christian Soldiers, on the concertina, with tambourine accompaniment, is heard when the door opens*). Are you coming, Stephen?

STEPHEN: No. Certainly not. (*She goes. He sits down on the settee, with compressed lips and an expression of strong dislike*).

ACT II

The yard of the West Ham shelter of the Salvation Army is a cold place on a January morning. The building itself, an old warehouse, is newly whitewashed. Its gabled end projects into the yard in the middle, with a door on the ground floor, and another in the loft above it without any balcony or ladder, but with a pulley rigged over it for hoisting sacks. Those who come from this central gable end into the yard have the gateway leading to the street on their left, with a stone horse trough just beyond it, and, on the right, a penthouse shielding a table from the weather. There are forms at the table; and on them are seated a man and a woman, both much down on their luck, finishing a meal of bread (one thick slice each, with margarine and golden syrup) and diluted milk.

The man, a workman out of employment, is young, agile, a talker, a poser, sharp enough to be capable of anything in reason except honesty or altruistic consider-ations of any kind. The woman is a commonplace old bundle of poverty and hard-worn humanity. She looks sixty and probably is forty-five. If they were rich people, gloved and muffed and well wrapped up in furs and overcoats, they would be numbed and miser-able; for it is a grindingly cold raw January day; and a glance at the background of grimy warehouses and leaden sky visible over the whitewashed walls of the yard would drive any idle rich person straight to the Mediterranean. But these two, being no more troubled with visions of the Mediterranean than of the moon, and being compelled to keep more of their clothes in the pawnshop, and less on their persons, in winter than in summer, are not depressed by the cold: rather are they stung into vivacity, to which their meal has just now given an almost jolly turn. The man takes a pull at his mug, and then gets up and moves about the yard with his hands deep in his pockets, occasionally breaking into a stepdance.

THE WOMAN: Feel better arter your meal, sir?

THE MAN: No. Call that a meal! Good enough for you, praps; but wot is it to me, an intelligent workin man.

THE WOMAN: Workin man! Wot are you?

THE MAN: Painter.

THE WOMAN (*sceptically*): Yus, I dessay.

THE MAN: Yus, you dessay! I know. Every loafer that cant do nothink calls isself a painter. Well, I'm a real painter: grainer, finisher, thirty-eight bob a week when I can get it.

THE WOMAN: Then why dont you go and get it?

THE MAN: I'll tell you why. Fust: I'm intelligent— fffff! it's rotten cold here (*he dances a step or two*)— yes: intelligent beyond the station o life into which it has pleased the capitalists to call me; and they dont like a man that sees through em. Second, an intelligent bein needs a doo share of appiness; so I drink somethink cruel when I get the chawnce. Third, I stand by my class and do as little as I can so's to leave arf the job for me fellow workers. Fourth, I'm fly enough to know wots inside the law and wots outside it; and inside it I do as the capitalists do: pinch wot I can lay me ands on. In a proper state of society I am sober, industrious and honest: in Rome, so to speak, I do as the Romans do. Wots the consequence? When trade is bad—and it's rotten bad just now—and the employers az to sack arf their men, they gen-erally start on me.

THE WOMAN: Whats your name?

THE MAN: Price. Bronterre O'Brien Price. Usually called Snobby Price, for short.

THE WOMAN: Snobby's a carpenter, aint it? You said you was a painter.

PRICE: Not that kind of snob, but the genteel sort. I'm too uppish, owing to my intelligence, and my father being a Chartist and a reading, thinking man: a stationer, too. I'm none of your common hewers of wood and drawers of water; and dont you forget it. (*He returns to his seat at the table, and takes up his mug*). Wots your name?

THE WOMAN: Rummy Mitchens, sir.

PRICE (*quaffing the remains of his milk to her*): Your elth, Miss Mitchens.

RUMMY (*correcting him*): Missis Mitchens.

PRICE: Wot! Oh Rummy, Rummy! Respectable mar-ried woman, Rummy, gittin rescued by the Salvation Army by pretendin to be a bad un. Same old game!

RUMMY: What am I to do? I cant starve. Them Salvation lasses is dear good girls; but the better you are, the worse they likes to think you were before they rescued you. Why shouldnt they av a bit o credit, poor loves? theyre worn to rags by their work. And where would they get the money to rescue us if we was to let on we're no worse than other people? You know what ladies and gentlemen are.

PRICE: Thievin swine! Wish I ad their job, Rummy, all the same. Wot does Rummy stand for? Pet name praps?

RUMMY: Short for Romola.

PRICE: For wot!?

RUMMY: Romola. It was out of a new book. Somebody me mother wanted me to grow up like.

PRICE: We're companions in misfortune, Rummy. Both on us got names that nobody cawnt pro-nounce. Consequently I'm Snobby and youre Rummy because Bill and Sally wasnt good enough for our parents. Such is life!

RUMMY: Who saved you, Mr Price? Was it Major Barbara?

PRICE: No: I come here on my own. I'm goin to be Broterre O'Brien Price, the converted painter. I know wot they like. I'll tell em how I blasphemed and gambled and wopped my poor old mother—

RUMMY (*shocked*): Used you to beat your mother?

PRICE: Not likely. She used to beat me. No matter: you come and listen to the converted painter, and youll hear how she was a pious woman that taught me me prayers at er knee, an how I used to come home drunk and drag her out o bed be er snow white airs, an lam into er with the poker.

RUMMY: Thats whats so unfair to us women. Your confessions is just as big lies as ours: you dont tell what you really done no more than us; but you men can tell your lies right out at the meetins and be made much of for it; while the sort o confes-sions we az to make az to be wispered to one lady at a time. It aint right, spite of all their piety.

PRICE: Right! Do you spose the Army 'd be allowed if it went and did right? Not much. It combs our air and makes us good little blokes to be robbed and put upon. But I'll play the game as good as any of em. I'll see somebody struck by lightnin, or hear a voice sayin "Snobby Price: where will you spend eternity?" I'll av a time of it, I tell you.

RUMMY: You wont be let drink, though.

PRICE: I'll take it out in gorspellin, then. I dont want to drink if I can get fun enough any other way.

[JENNY HILL, a pale, overwrought, pretty Salvation lass of 18, comes in through the yard gate, leading PETER SHIRLEY, a half hardened, half worn-out elderly man, weak with hunger.]

JENNY (*supporting him*): Come! pluck up. I'll get you something to eat. Youll be all right then.

PRICE (*rising and hurrying officiously to take the old man off JENNY's hands*): Poor old man! Cheer up, brother: youll find rest and peace and appiness ere. Hurry up with the food, miss: e's fair done. (*JENNY hurries into the shelter*). Ere, buck up, daddy! she's fetchin y'a thick slice o breadn treacle, an a mug o skyblue. (*He seats him at the corner of the table*).

RUMMY (*gaily*): Keep up your old art! Never say die!

SHIRLEY: I'm not an old man. I'm only 46. I'm as good as ever I was. The grey patch come in my hair before I was thirty. All it wants is three pennorth o hair dye: am I to be turned on the streets to starve for it? Holy God! Ive worked ten to twelve hours a day since I was thirteen, and paid my way all through; and now am I to be thrown into the gutter and my job given to a young man that can do it no better than me because Ive black hair that goes white at the first change?

PRICE (*cheerfully*): No good jawrin about it. Youre ony a jumped-up, jerked-off, orspittle-turned-out incurable of an ole workin man: who cares about you? Eh? Make the thievin swine give you a meal: theyve stole many a one from you. Get a bit o your own back. (*JENNY returns with the usual meal*). There you are, brother. Awsk a blessin an tuck that into you.

SHIRLEY (*looking at it ravenously but not touching it, and crying like a child*): I never took anything before.

JENNY (*petting him*): Come, come! the Lord sends it to you: he wasnt above taking bread from his friends; and why should you be? Besides, when we find you a job you can pay us for it if you like.

SHIRLEY (*eagerly*): Yes, yes: thats true. I can pay you back: it's only a loan. (*Shivering*) Oh Lord! oh Lord! (*He turns to the table and attacks the meal ravenously*).

JENNY: Well, Rummy, are you more comfortable now?

RUMMY: God bless you, lovey! youve fed my body and saved my soul, havnt you? (*JENNY, touched, kisses her*). Sit down and rest a bit: you must be ready to drop.

JENNY: Ive been going hard since morning. But theres more work than we can do. I mustnt stop.

RUMMY: Try a prayer for just two minutes. Youll work all the better after.

JENNY (*her eyes lighting up*): Oh isnt it wonderful how a few minutes prayer revives you! I was quite lightheaded at twelve o'clock, I was so tired; but Major Barbara just sent me to pray for five minutes; and I was able to go on as if I had only just begun. (*To PRICE*) Did you have a piece of bread?

PRICE (*with unction*): Yes, miss; but Ive got the piece that I value more; and thats the peace that passeth hall hanner-stennin.

RUMMY (*fervently*): Glory Hallelujah!

[BILL WALKER, a rough customer of about 25, appears at the yard gate and looks malevolently at JENNY.]

JENNY: That makes me so happy. When you say that, I feel wicked for loitering here. I must get to work again.

[She is hurrying to the shelter, when the new-comer moves quickly up to the door and intercepts her. His manner is so threatening that she retreats as he comes at her truculently, driving her down the yard.]

BILL: Aw knaow you. Youre the one that took awy maw girl. Youre the one that set er agen me. Well, I'm gowin to ev er aht. Not that Aw care a carse for er or you: see? Bat Aw'll let er knaow; and Aw'll let you knaow. Aw'm gowing to give her a doin thatll teach er to cat awy from me. Nah in wiv you and tell er to cam aht afore Aw cam in and kick er aht. Tell er Bill Walker wants er. She'll knaow wot thet means; and if she keeps me witin itll be worse. You stop to jawr beck at me; and Aw'll stawt on you: d'ye eah? Theres your wy. In you gow. (*He takes her by the arm and slings her towards the door of the shelter. She falls on her hand and knee. RUMMY helps her up again*).

PRICE (*rising, and venturing irresolutely towards BILL*): Easy there, mate. She aint doin you no arm.

BILL: Oo are you callin mite? (*Standing over him threateningly*): Youre gowin to stend ap for er, aw yer? Put ap your ends.

RUMMY (*running indignantly to him to scold him*): Oh, you great brute—(*He instantly swings his left hand back against her face. She screams and reels back to the trough, where she sits down, covering her bruised face with her hands and rocking herself and moaning with pain*).

JENNY (*going to her*): Oh, God forgive you! How could

you strike an old woman like that?

BILL (*seizing her by the hair so violently that she also screams, and tearing her away from the old woman*): You Gawd , forgimme again an Aw'll Gawd forgive you one on the jawr thetll stop you pryin for a week. (*Holding her and turning fiercely on* PRICE) Ev you ennything to sy agen it?

PRICE (*intimidated*): No, matey: she aint anything to do with me.

BILL: Good job for you! Aw'd pat two meals into you and fawt you with one finger arter, you stawved cur. (*To* JENNY) Nah are you gowin to fetch aht Mog Ebbijem; or em Aw to knock your fice off you and fetch her meself?

JENNY (*writhing in his grasp*): Oh please someone go in and tell Major Barbara—(*she screams again as he wrenches her head down; and* PRICE *and* RUMMY *flee into the shelter*).

BILL: You want to gow in and tell your Mijor of me, do you?

JENNY: Oh please dont drag my hair. Let me go.

BILL: Do you or downt you? (*She stifles a scream*). Yus or nao?

JENNY: God give me strength—

BILL (*striking her with his first in the face*): Gow an shaow her thet, and tell her if she wants one lawk it to cam and interfere with me. (JENNY, *crying with pain, goes into the shed. He goes to the form and addresses the old man*). Eah: finish your mess; an git aht o maw wy.

SHIRLEY (*springing up and facing him fiercely, with the mug in his hand*): You take a liberty with me, and I'll smash you over the face with the mug and cut your eye out. Aint you satisfied—young whelps like you—with takin the bread out o the mouths of your elders that have brought you up and slaved for you, but you must come shovin and cheekin and bullyin in here, where the bread o charity is sickenin in our stummicks?

BILL: (*contemptuously, but backing a little*): Wot good are you, you aold palsy mag? Wot good are you?

SHIRLEY: As good as you and better. I'll do a day's work agen you or any fat young soaker of your age. Go and take my job at Horrockses, where I worked for ten year. They want young men there: they cant afford to keep men over forty-five. Theyre very sorry—give you a character and happy to help you to get anything suited to your years—sure a steady man wont be long out of a job. Well, let em try you. Theyll find the differ. What do you know? Not as much as how to beeyave yourself—layin your dirty fist across the mouth of a respectable woman!

BILL: Downt provowk me to ly it across yours: d'ye eah?

SHIRLEY: (*with blighting contempt*): Yes: you like an old man to hit, dont you, when youve finished with the women. I aint seen you hit a young one yet.

BILL (*stung*): You loy, you aold soupkitchener, you. There was a yang menn eah. Did Aw offer to itt him or did Aw not?

SHIRLEY: Was he starvin or was he not? Was he a man or only a crosseyed thief an a loafer? Would you hit my son-in-law's brother?

BILL: Oo's ee?

SHIRLEY: Todger Fairmile o Balls Pond. Him that won £20 off the Japanese wrastler at the music hall by standin out 17 minutes 4 seconds agen him.

BILL (*sullenly*): Aw'm nao music awl wrastler. Ken he box?

SHIRLEY: Yes: an you cant.

BILL: Wot! Aw cawnt, cawnt Aw? Wots thet you sy (*threatening him*)?

SHIRLEY (*not budging an inch*): Will you box Todger Fairmile if I put him on to you? Say the word.

BILL (*subsiding with a slouch*): Aw'll stend ap to enny menn alawv, if he was ten Todger Fairmawls. But Aw downt set ap to be a perfeshnal.

SHIRLEY (*looking down on him with unfathomable disdain*): You box! Slap an old woman with the back o your hand! You hadnt even the sense to hit her where a magistrate couldnt see the mark of it, you silly young lump of conceit and ignorance. Hit a girl in the jaw and ony make her cry! If Todger Fairmile'd done it, she wouldnt a got up inside o ten minutes, no more than you would if he got on to you. Yah! I'd set about you myself if I had a week's feedin in me instead o two months starvation. (*He turns his back on him and sits down moodily at the table*).

BILL (*following him and stooping over him to drive the taunt in*): You loy! youve the bread and treacle in you that you cam eah to beg.

SHIRLEY (*bursting into tears*): Oh God! it's true: I'm only an old pauper on the scrap heap. (*Furiously*) But youll come to it yourself; and then youll know. Youll come to it sooner than a teetotaller like me, fillin yourself with gin at this hour o the mornin!

BILL: Aw'm nao gin drinker, you oald lawr; bat wen Aw want to give my girl a bloomin good awdin Aw lawk to ev a bit o devil in me: see? An eah Aw emm, talkin to a rotten aold blawter like you sted o givin her wot for. (*Working himself into a rage*) Aw'm gowin in there to fetch her aht. (*He makes vengefully for the shelter door*).

SHIRLEY: Youre goin to the station on a stretcher, more likely; and theyll take the gin and the devil out of you there when they get you inside. You mind what youre about: the major here is the Earl o Stevenage's granddaughter.

BILL (*checked*): Garn!

SHIRLEY: Youll see.

BILL (*his resolution oozing*): Well, Aw aint dan nathin to er.

SHIRLEY: Spose she said you did! who'd believe you?

BILL (*very uneasy, skulking back to the corner of the penthouse*): Gawd! theres no jastice in this cantry. To think wot them people can do! Aw'm as good as er.

SHIRLEY: Tell her so. It's just what a fool like you would do.

[BARBARA, *brisk and businesslike, comes from the shelter with a note book, and addresses herself to* SHIRLEY. BILL, *cowed, sits down in the corner on a form, and turns his back on them.*]

BARBARA: Good morning.

SHIRLEY (*standing up and taking off his hat*): Good morning, miss.

BARBARA: Sit down: make yourself at home. (*He hesitates; but she puts a friendly hand on his shoulder and makes him obey*). Now then! since youve made friends with us, we want to know all about you. Names and addresses and trades.

SHIRLEY: Peter Shirley. Fitter. Chucked out two months ago because I was too old.

BARBARA (*not at all surprised*): Youd pass still. Why didnt you dye your hair?

SHIRLEY: I did. Me age come out at a coroner's inquest on me daughter.

BARBARA: Steady?

SHIRLEY: Teetotaller. Never out of a job before. Good worker. And sent to the knackers like an old horse!

BARBARA: No matter: if you did your part God will do his.

SHIRLEY (*suddenly stubborn*): My religion's no concern of anybody but myself.

BARBARA (*guessing*): I know. Secularist?

SHIRLEY (*hotly*): Did I offer to deny it?

BARBARA: Why should you? My own father's a Secularist, I think. Our Father—yours and mine—fulfils himself in many ways; and I daresay he knew what he was about when he made a Secularist of you. So buck up, Peter! we can always find a job for a steady man like you. (SHIRLEY, *disarmed and a little bewildered, touches his hat. She turns from him to* BILL). Whats your name?

BILL (*insolently*): Wots thet to you?

BARBARA (*calmly making a note*): Afraid to give his name. Any trade?

BILL: Oo's afride to give is nime? (*Doggedly, with a sense of heroically defying the House of Lords in the person of Lord Stevenage*) If you want to bring a chawge agen me, bring it. (*She waits, unruffled*). Moy nime's Bill Walker.

BARBARA (*as if the name were familiar: trying to remember how*): Bill Walker? (*Recollecting*) Oh, I know: youre the man that Jenny Hill was praying for inside just now. (*She enters his name in her note book*).

BILL: Oo's Jenny Ill? And wot call as she to pry for me?

BARBARA: I don't know. Perhaps it was you that cut her lip.

BILL [*defiantly*]: Yus, it was me that cat her lip. Aw aint afride o you.

BARBARA: How could you be, since youre not afraid of God? Youre a brave man, Mr Walker. It takes some pluck to do our work here; but none of us dare lift our hand against a girl like that, for fear of her father in heaven.

BILL (*sullenly*): I want nan o your kentin jawr. I spowse you think Aw cam eah to beg from you, like this demmiged lot eah. Not me. Aw downt want your bread and scripe and ketlep. Aw dont blieve in your Gawd, no more than you do yourself.

BARBARA (*sunnily apologetic and ladylike, as on a new footing with him*): Oh, I beg your pardon for putting your name down, Mr Walker. I didnt understand. I'll strike it out.

BILL (*taking this as a slight, and deeply wounded by it*): Eah! you let maw nime alown. Aint it good enaff to be in your book?

BARBARA (*considering*): Well, you see, theres no use putting down your name unless I can do something for you, is there? Whats your trade?

BILL (*still smarting*): Thets nao concern o yours.

BARBARA: Just so. (*Very businesslike*) I'll put you down as (*writing*) the man who—struck—poor little Jenny Hill—in the mouth.

BILL (*rising threateningly*): See eah. Awve ed enaff o this.

BARBARA (*quite sunny and fearless*): What did you come to us for?

BILL: Aw cam for maw gel, see? Aw cam to tike her aht o this and to brike er jawr for er.

BARBARA (*complacently*): You see I was right about your trade. (BILL, *on the point of retorting furiously, finds himself, to his great shame and terror, in danger of crying instead. He sits down again suddenly*). Whats her name?

BILL (*dogged*): Er nime's Mog Ebbijem: thets wot her nime is.

BARBARA: Mog Habbijam! Oh, she's gone to Canning Town, to our barracks there.

BILL (*fortified by his resentment of* MOG's *perfidy*): Is she? (*Vindictively*) Then Aw'm gowin to Kennintahn arter her. (*He crosses to the gate; hesitates; finally comes back at* BARBARA). Are you loyin to me to git shat o me?

BARBARA: I dont want to get shut of you. I want to keep you here and save your soul. Youd better stay: youre going to have a bad time today, Bill.

BILL: Oo's gowin to give it to me? You, preps?

BARBARA: Someone you dont believe in. But youll be glad afterwards.

BILL (*slinking off*): Aw'll gow to Kennintahn to be aht o reach o your tangue. (*Suddenly turning on her with intense malice*) And if Aw downt fawnd Mog there, Aw'll cam beck and do two years for you, selp me Gawd if Aw downt!

BARBARA (*a shade kindlier, if possible*): It's no use, Bill. She's got another bloke.

BILL: Wot!

BARBARA: One of her own converts. He fell in love with her when he saw her with her soul saved, and her face clean, and her hair washed.

BILL (*surprised*): Wottud she wash it for, the carroty slat? It's red.

BARBARA: It's quite lovely now, because she wears a new look in her eyes with it. It's a pity youre too late. The new bloke has put your nose out of joint, Bill.

BILL: Aw'll put his nowse aht o joint for him. Not that Aw care a carse for er, mawnd thet. But Aw'll teach her to drop me as if Aw was dirt. And Aw'll teach him to meddle with maw judy Wots iz bleedin nime?

BARBARA: Sergeant Todger Fairmile.

SHIRLEY (*rising with grim joy*): I'll go with him, miss. I want to see them two meet. I'll take him to the infirmary when it's over.

BILL (*to SHIRLEY, with undissembled misgiving*): Is thet im you was speakin on?

SHIRLEY: Thats him.

BILL: Im that wrastled in the music awl?

SHIRLEY: The competitions at the National Sportin Club was worth nigh a hundred a year to him. He's gev em up now for religion; so he's a bit fresh for want of the exercise he was accustomed to. He'll be glad to see you. Come along.

BILL: Wots is wight?

SHIRLEY: Thirteen four. (*BILL's last hope expires*).

BARBARA: Go and talk to him, Bill. He'll convert you.

SHIRLEY: He'll convert your head into a mashed potato.

BILL (*sullenly*): Aw aint afride of im. Aw aint afride of ennybody. Bat e can lick me. She's dan me. (*He sits down moodily on the edge of the horse-trough*).

SHIRLEY: You aint goin. I thought not. (*He resumes his seat*)

BARBARA (*calling*): Jenny!

JENNY (*appearing at the shelter door with a plaster on the corner of her mouth*): Yes, Major.

BARBARA: Send Rummy Mitchens out to clear away here.

JENNY: I think she's afraid.

BARBARA (*her resemblance to her mother flashing out for a moment*): Nonsense! she must do as she's told.

JENNY (*calling into the shelter*): Rummy: the Major says you must come.

[*JENNY comes to BARBARA, purposely keeping on the side next BILL, lest he should suppose that she shrank from him or bore malice.*]

BARBARA: Poor little Jenny! Are you tired? (*Looking at the wounded cheek*) Does it hurt?

JENNY: No: it's all right now. It was nothing.

BARBARA (*critically*): It was as hard as he could hit, I expect. Poor Bill! You dont feel angry with him, do you?

JENNY: Oh no, no, no: indeed I dont, Major, bless his poor heart! (*BARBARA kisses her; and she runs away merrily into the shelter. BILL writhes with an agonizing return of his new and alarming symptoms, but says nothing. RUMMY MITCHENS comes from the shelter*).

BARBARA (*going to meet RUMMY*): Now Rummy, bustle. Take in those mugs and plates to be washed; and throw the crumbs about for the birds.

[*RUMMY takes the three plates and mugs; but SHIRLEY takes back his mug from her, as there is still some milk left in it.*]

RUMMY: There aint any crumbs. This aint a time to waste good bread on birds.

PRICE (*appearing at the shelter door*): Gentleman come to see the shelter, Major. Says he's your father.

BARBARA: All right. Coming. (*SNOBBY goes back into the shelter, followed by BARBARA*).

RUMMY (*stealing across to BILL and addressing him in a subdued voice, but with intense conviction*): I'd av the lor of you, you flat eared pignosed potwalloper, if she'd let me. Youre no gentleman, to hit a lady in the face. (*BILL, with greater things moving in him, takes no notice*).

SHIRLEY (*following her*): Here! in with you and dont get yourself into more trouble by talking.

RUMMY (*with hauteur*): I aint ad the pleasure o being hintroduced to you, as I can remember. (*She goes into the shelter with the plates*).

SHIRLEY: Thats the—

BILL (*savagely*): Downt you talk to me, d'ye eah? You lea me alown, or Aw'll do you a mischief. Aw'm not dirt under your feet, ennywy.

SHIRLEY (*calmly*): Dont you be afeerd. You aint such prime company that you need expect to be sought after. (*He is about to go into the shelter when BARBARA comes out, with UNDERSHAFT on her right*).

BARBARA: Oh, there you are, Mr Shirley! (*Between them*) This is my father: I told you he was a Secularist, didnt I? Perhaps youll be able to comfort one another.

UNDERSHAFT (*startled*): A Secularist! Not the least in the world: on the contrary, a confirmed mystic.

BARBARA: Sorry, I'm sure. By the way, papa, what is your religion? in case I have to introduce you again.

UNDERSHAFT: My religion? Well, my dear, I am a Millionaire. That is my religion.

BARBARA: Then I'm afraid you and Mr. Shirley wont be able to comfort one another after all. Youre not a Millionaire, are you, Peter?

SHIRLEY: No; and proud of it.

UNDERSHAFT (*gravely*): Poverty, my friend, is not a thing to be proud of.

SHIRLEY (*angrily*): Who made your millions for you? Me and my like. Whats kep us poor? Keepin you rich. I wouldnt have your conscience, not for all your income.

UNDERSHAFT: I wouldnt have your income, not for all your conscience, Mr Shirley. (*He goes to the penthouse and sits down on a form*).

BARBARA (*stopping* SHIRLEY *adroitly as he is about to retort*): You wouldnt think he was my father, would you, Peter? Will you go into the shelter and lend the lasses a hand for a while: we're worked off our feet.

SHIRLEY (*bitterly*): Yes: I'm in their debt for a meal, aint I?

BARBARA: Oh, not because youre in their debt, but for love of them, Peter, for love of them. (*He cannot understand, and is rather scandalized*) There! dont stare at me. In with you; and give that conscience of yours a holiday (*bustling him into the shelter*).

SHIRLEY (*as he goes in*): Ah! it's a pity you never was trained to use your reason, miss. Youd have been a very taking lecturer on Secularism.

[BARBARA *turns to her father.*]

UNDERSHAFT: Never mind me, my dear. Go about your work; and let me watch it for a while.

BARBARA: All right.

UNDERSHAFT: For instance, whats the matter with that out-patient over there?

BARBARA (*looking at* BILL, *whose attitude has never changed, and whose expression of brooding wrath has deepened*): Oh, we shall cure him in no time. Just watch. (*She goes over to* BILL *and waits. He glances up at her and casts his eyes down again, uneasy, but grimmer than ever*). It would be nice to just stamp on Mog Habbijam's face, wouldnt it, Bill?

BILL (*starting up from the trough in consternation*): It's a loy: Aw never said so. (*She shakes her head*). Oo taold you wot was in moy mawnd?

BARBARA: Only your new friend.

BILL: Wot new friend?

BARBARA: The devil, Bill. When he gets round people they get miserable, just like you.

BILL (*with a heartbreaking attempt at devil-may-care cheerfulness*): Aw aint miserable. (*He sits down again, and stretches his legs in an attempt to seem indifferent*).

BARBARA: Well, if youre happy, why dont you look happy, as we do?

BILL (*his legs curling back in spite of him*): Aw'm eppy enaff, Aw tell you. Woy cawnt you lea me alown? Wot ev I dan to you? Aw aint smashed your fice, ev Aw?

BARBARA (*softly: wooing his soul*): It's not me thats getting at you, Bill.

BILL: Oo else is it?

BARBARA: Somebody that doesnt intend you to smash women's faces, I suppose. Somebody or something that wants to make a man of you.

BILL (*blustering*): Mike a menn o me! Aint Aw a menn? eh? Oo sez Aw'm not a menn?

BARBARA: Theres a man in you somewhere, I suppose. But why did he let you hit poor little Jenny Hill? That wasnt very manly of him was it?

BILL (*tormented*): Ev dan wiv it, Aw tell you. Chack it. Aw'm sick o your Jenny Ill and er silly little fice.

BARBARA: Then why do you keep thinking about it? Why does it keep coming up against you in your mind? Youre not getting converted, are you?

BILL (*with conviction*): Not ME. Not lawkly.

BARBARA: Thats right, Bill. Hold out against it. Put out your strength. Dont lets get you cheap. Todger Fairmile said he wrestled for three nights against his salvation harder than he ever wrestled with the Jap at the music hall. He gave in to the Jap when his arm was going to break. But he didnt give in to his salvation until his heart was going to break. Perhaps youll escape that. You havnt any heart, have you?

BILL: Wot d'ye mean? Woy aint Aw got a awt the sime as ennybody else?

BARBARA: A man with a heart wouldnt have bashed poor little Jenny's face, would he?

BILL (*almost crying*): Ow, will you lea me alown? Ev Aw ever offered to meddle with you, that you cam neggin and provowkin me lawk this? (*He writhes convulsively from his eyes to his toes*).

BARBARA (*with a steady soothing hand on his arm and a gentle voice that never lets him go*): It's your soul thats hurting you, Bill, and not me. Weve been through it all ourselves. Come with us, Bill, (*He looks wildly round*). To brave manhood on earth and eternal glory in heaven. (*He is on the point of breaking down*). Come. (*A drum is heard in the shelter; and* BILL, *with a gasp, escapes from the spell as* BARBARA *turns quickly.* ADOLPHUS *enters from the shelter with a big drum*). Oh! there you are, Dolly. Let me introduce a new friend of mine, Mr Bill Walker. This is my bloke, Bill: Mr Cusins. (CUSINS *salutes with his drumstick*).

BILL: Gowin to merry im?

BARBARA: Yes.

BILL (*fervently*): Gawd elp im! Gaw-aw-aw-awd elp im!

BARBARA: Why? Do you think he wont be happy with me?

BILL: Awve aony ed to stend it for a mawnin: e'll ev to stend it for a lawftawm.

CUSINS: That is a frightful reflection, Mr Walker. But I cant tear myself away from her.

BILL: Well, Aw ken. (*To* BARBARA) Eah! do you knaow where Aw'm gowin to, and wot Aw'm gowin to do?

BARBARA: Yes: youre going to heaven; and youre coming back here before the week's out to tell me so.

BILL: You loy. Aw'm gowin to Kennintahn, to spit in Todger Fairmawl's eye. Aw beshed Jenny Ill's fice; an nar Aw'll git me aown fice beshed and cam beck and shaow it to er. Ee'll itt me ardern Aw itt er. Thatll mike us square. (*To* ADOLPHUS) Is thet fair or is it not? Youre a genlmn: you oughter knaow.

BARBARA: Two black eyes wont make one white one, Bill.

BILL: Aw didnt awst you. Cawnt you never keep your mahth shat? Oy awst the genlmn.

CUSINS (*reflectively*): Yes: I think youre right, Mr Walker. Yes: I should do it. It's curious: it's exactly what an ancient Greek would have done.

BARBARA: But what good will it do?

CUSINS: Well, it will give Mr Fairmile some exercise; and it will satisfy Mr Walker's soul.

BILL: Rot! there aint nao sach a thing as a saoul. Ah kin you tell wevver Awve a saoul or not? You never seen it.

BARBARA: Ive seen it hurting you when you went against it.

BILL (*with compressed aggravation*): If you was maw gel and took the word aht o me mahth lawk thet, Aw'd give you sathink youd feel urtin, Aw would. (*To* ADOLPHUS) You tike maw tip, mite. Stop er jawr; or youll doy afoah your tawm. (*With intense expression*) Wore aht: thets wot youll be: wore aht. (*He goes away through the gate*).

CUSINS (*looking after him*): I wonder!

BARBARA: Dolly! (*indignant, in her mother's manner*).

CUSINS: Yes, my dear, it's very wearing to be in love with you. If it lasts, I quite think I shall die young.

BARBARA: Should you mind?

CUSINS: Not at all. (*He is suddenly softened, and kisses her over the drum, evidently not for the first time, as people cannot kiss over a big drum without practice.* UNDERSHAFT *coughs*).

BARBARA: It's all right, papa, weve not forgotten you. Dolly: explain the place to papa: I havnt time. (*She goes busily into the shelter*).

[UNDERSHAFT *and* ADOLPHUS *now have the yard to themselves.,* UNDERSHAFT, *seated on a form, and still keenly attentive, looks hard at* ADOLPHUS. ADOLPHUS *looks hard at him.*]

UNDERSHAFT: I fancy you guess something of what is in my mind, Mr Cusins. (CUSINS *flourishes his drumsticks as if in the act of beating a lively rataplan, but makes no sound*). Exactly so. But suppose Barbara finds you out!

CUSINS: You know, I do not admit that I am imposing on Barbara. I am quite genuinely interested in the views of the Salvation Army. The fact is, I am a sort of collector of religions; and the curious thing is that I find I can believe them all. By the way, have you any religion?

UNDERSHAFT: Yes.

CUSINS: Anything out of the common?

UNDERSHAFT: Only that there are two things necessary to Salvation.

CUSINS (*disappointed, but polite*): Ah, the Church Catechism. Charles Lomax also belongs to the Established Church.

UNDERSHAFT: The two things are—

CUSINS: Baptism and—

UNDERSHAFT: No. Money and gunpowder.

CUSINS (*surprised, but interested*): That is the general opinion of our governing classes. The novelty is in hearing any man confess it.

UNDERSHAFT: Just so.

CUSINS: Excuse me: is there any place in your religion for honor, justice, truth, love, mercy and so forth?

UNDERSHAFT: Yes: they are the graces and luxuries of a rich, strong, and safe life.

CUSINS: Suppose one is forced to choose between them and money or gunpowder?

UNDERSHAFT: Choose money and gunpowder; for without enough of both you cannot afford the others.

CUSINS: That is your religion?

UNDERSHAFT: Yes.

[*The cadence of this reply makes a full close in the conversation.* CUSINS *twists his face dubiously and contemplates* UNDERSHAFT. UNDERSHAFT *contemplates him.*]

CUSINS: Barbara wont stand that. You will have to choose between your religion and Barbara.

UNDERSHAFT: So will you, my friend. She will find out that that drum of yours is hollow.

CUSINS: Father Undershaft: you are mistaken: I am a sincere Salvationist. You do not understand the Salvation Army. It is the army of joy, of love, of courage: it has banished the fear and remorse and despair of the old hell-ridden evangelical sects: it marches to fight the devil with trumpet and drum, with music and dancing, with banner and palm, as becomes a sally from heaven by its happy garrison. It picks the waster out of the public house and makes a man of him: it finds a worm wriggling in a back kitchen, and lo! a woman! Men and women of rank too, sons and daughters of the Highest. It takes the poor professor of Greek, the most artificial and self-suppressed of human creatures, from his meal of roots, and lets loose the rhapsodist in him; reveals the true worship of Dionysos to him; sends him down the public street drumming dithyrambs (*he plays a thundering flourish on the drum*).

UNDERSHAFT: You will alarm the shelter.

CUSINS: Oh, they are accustomed to these sudden ecstasies. However, if the drum worries you—(*he pockets the drumsticks; unhooks the drum; and stands it on the ground opposite the gateway*).

UNDERSHAFT: Thank you.

CUSINS: You remember what Euripides says about your money and gunpowder.

UNDERSHAFT: No.

CUSINS (*declaiming*):

> One and another
> In money and guns may outpass his brother;
> And men in their millions float and flow
> And seethe with a million hopes as leaven;
> And they win their will; or they miss their will;
> And their hopes are dead or are pined for still;
>   But whoe'er can know
>   As the long days go
> That to live is happy, has found his heaven.

My translation: what do you think of it?

UNDERSHAFT: I think, my friend, that if you wish to know, as the long days go, that to live is happy, you must first acquire money enough for a decent life, and power enough to be your own master.

CUSINS: You are damnably discouraging. (*He resumes his declamation*).

> Is it so hard a thing to see
>   That the spirit of God—whate'er it be—
> The Law that abides and changes not, ages long,
> The Eternal and Nature-born: these things be strong?
> What else is Wisdom? What of Man's endeavor,
> Or God's high grace so lovely and so great?
> To stand from fear set free? to breathe and wait?
> To hold a hand uplifted over Fate?
> And shall not Barbara be loved for ever?

UNDERSHAFT: Euripides mentions Barbara, does he?

CUSINS: It is a fair translation. The word means Loveliness.

UNDERSHAFT: May I ask—as Barbara's father—how much a year she is to be loved for ever on?

CUSINS: As Barbara's father, that is more your affair than mine. I can feed her by teaching Greek: that is about all.

UNDERSHAFT: Do you consider it a good match for her?

CUSINS (*with polite obstinacy*): Mr Undershaft: I am in many ways a weak, timid, ineffectual person; and my health is far from satisfactory. But whenever I feel that I must have anything, I get it, sooner or later. I feel that way about Barbara. I dont like marriage: I feel intensely afraid of it; and I dont know what I shall do with Barbara or what she will do with me. But I feel that I and nobody else must marry her. Please regard that as settled.—Not that I wish to be arbitrary; but why should I waste your time in discussing what is inevitable?

UNDERSHAFT: You mean that you will stick at nothing: not even the conversion of the Salvation Army to the worship of Dionysos.

CUSINS: The business of the Salvation Army is to save, not to wrangle about the name of the pathfinder. Dionysos or another: what does it matter?

UNDERSHAFT (*rising and approaching him*): Professor Cusins: you are a young man after my own heart.

CUSINS: Mr Undershaft: you are, as far as I am able to gather, a most infernal old rascal; but you appeal very strongly to my sense of ironic humor.

[Undershaft mutely offers his hand. They shake.]

UNDERSHAFT (*suddenly concentrating himself*): And now to business.

CUSINS: Pardon me. We were discussing religion. Why go back to such an uninteresting and unimportant subject as business?

UNDERSHAFT: Religion is our business at present, because it is through religion alone that we can win Barbara.

CUSINS: Have you, too, fallen in love with Barbara?

UNDERSHAFT: Yes, with a father's love.

CUSINS: A father's love for a grown-up daughter is the most dangerous of all infatuations. I apologize for mentioning my own pale, coy, mistrustful fancy in the same breath with it.

UNDERSHAFT: Keep to the point. We have to win her; and we are neither of us Methodists.

CUSINS: That doesnt matter. The power Barbara wields here—the power that wields Barbara herself—is not Calvinism, not Presbyterianism, not Methodism—

UNDERSHAFT: Not Greek Paganism either, eh?

CUSINS: I admit that. Barbara is quite original in her religion.

UNDERSHAFT (*triumphantly*): Aha! Barbara Undershaft would be. Her inspiration comes from within herself.

CUSINS: How do you suppose it got there?

UNDERSHAFT (*in towering excitement*): It is the Undershaft inheritance. I shall hand on my torch to my daughter. She shall make my converts and preach my gospel—

CUSINS: What! Money and gunpowder!

UNDERSHAFT: Yes, money and gunpowder. Freedom and power. Command of life and command of death.

CUSINS (*urbanely: trying to bring him down to earth*): This is extremely interesting, Mr Undershaft. Of course you know that you are mad.

UNDERSHAFT (*with redoubled force*): And you?

CUSINS: Oh, mad as a hatter. You are welcome to my secret since I have discovered yours. But I am astonished. Can a madman make cannons?

UNDERSHAFT: Would anyone else than a madman make them? And now (*with surging energy*) question for question. Can a sane man translate Euripides?

CUSINS: No.

UNDERSHAFT (*seizing him by the shoulder*): Can a sane woman make a man of a waster or a woman of a worm?

CUSINS (*reeling before the storm*): Father Colossus— Mammoth Millionaire—

UNDERSHAFT (*pressing him*): Are there two mad people or three in this Salvation shelter today?

CUSINS: You mean Barbara is as mad as we are?

UNDERSHAFT: (*pushing him lightly off and resuming his equanimity suddenly and completely*): Pooh, Professor! let us call things by their proper names. I am a millionaire; you are a poet; Barbara is a savior of souls. What have we three to do with the common mob of slaves and idolaters? (*He sits down again with a shrug of contempt for the mob*).

CUSINS: Take care! Barbara is in love with the common people. So am I. Have you never felt the romance of that love?

UNDERSHAFT (*cold and sardonic*): Have you ever been in love with Poverty, like St Francis? Have you ever been in love with Dirt, like St Simeon! Have you ever been in love with disease and suffering, like our nurses and philanthropists? Such passions are not virtues, but the most unnatural of all the vices. This love of the common people may please an earl's granddaughter and a university professor; but I have been a common man and a poor man; and it has no romance for me. Leave it to the poor to pretend that poverty is a blessing: leave it to the coward to make a religion of his cowardice by preaching humility: we know better than that. We three must stand together above the common people: how else can we help their children to climb up beside us? Barbara must belong to us, not to the Salvation Army.

CUSINS: Well, I can only say that if you think you will get her away from the Salvation Army by talking to her as you have been talking to me, you dont know Barbara.

UNDERSHAFT: My friend: I never ask for what I can buy.

CUSINS (*in a white fury*): Do I understand you to imply that you can buy Barbara?

UNDERSHAFT: No; but I can buy the Salvation Army.

CUSINS: Quite impossible.

UNDERSHAFT: You shall see. All religious organizations exist by selling themselves to the rich.

CUSINS: Not the Army. That is the Church of the poor.

UNDERSHAFT: All the more reason for buying it.

CUSINS: I dont think you quite know what the Army does for the poor.

UNDERSHAFT: Oh yes I do. It draws their teeth: that is enough for me as a man of business.

CUSINS: Nonsense! It makes them sober—

UNDERSHAFT: I prefer sober workmen. The profits are larger.

CUSINS: —honest—

UNDERSHAFT: Honest workmen are the most economical.

CUSINS: —attached to their homes—

UNDERSHAFT: So much the better: they will put up with anything sooner than change their shop.

CUSINS: —happy—

UNDERSHAFT: An invaluable safeguard against revolution.

CUSINS: —unselfish—

UNDERSHAFT: Indifferent to their own interests, which suits me exactly.

CUSINS: —with their thoughts on heavenly things—

UNDERSHAFT (*rising*): And not on Trade Unionism nor Socialism. Excellent.

CUSINS (*revolted*): You really are an infernal old rascal.

UNDERSHAFT (*indicating PETER SHIRLEY, who has just come from the shelter and strolled dejectedly down the yard between them*): And this is an honest man!

SHIRLEY: Yes; and what av I got by it? (*He passes on bitterly and sits on the form, in the corner of the penthouse*).

[SNOBBY PRICE, *beaming sanctimoniously, and* JENNY HILL, *with a tambourine full of coppers, come from the shelter and go to the drum, on which* JENNY *begins to count the money.*]

UNDERSHAFT (*replying to* SHIRLEY): Oh, your employers must have got a good deal by it from first to last. (*He sits on the table, with one foot on the side form.* CUSINS, *overwhelmed, sits down on the same form nearer the shelter.* BARBARA *comes from the shelter to the middle of the yard. She is excited and a little overwrought*).

BARBARA: Weve just had a splendid experience meeting at the other gate in Cripps's Lane. Ive hardly ever seen them so much moved as they were by your confession, Mr Price.

PRICE: I could almost be glad of my past wickedness if I could believe that it would elp to keep hathers straight.

BARBARA: So it will, Snobby. How much, Jenny?

JENNY: Four and tenpence, Major.

BARBARA: Oh Snobby, if you had given your poor mother just one more kick, we should have got the whole five shillings!

PRICE: If she heard you say that, miss, she'd be sorry I didnt. But I'm glad. Oh what a joy it will be to her when she hears I'm saved!

UNDERSHAFT: Shall I contribute the odd twopence, Barbara? The millionaire's mite, eh? (*He takes a couple of pennies from his pocket*).

BARBARA: How did you make that twopence?

UNDERSHAFT: As usual. By selling cannons, torpedoes, submarines, and my new patent Grand Duke hand grenade.

BARBARA: Put it back in your pocket. You cant buy your salvation here for twopence: you must work it out.

UNDERSHAFT: Is twopence not enough? I can afford a little more, if you press me.

BARBARA: Two million millions would not be enough. There is bad blood on your hands; and nothing but good blood can cleanse them. Money is no use. Take it away. (*She turns to* CUSINS). Dolly: you must write another letter for me to the papers. (*He makes a wry face*). Yes: I know you dont like it; but it must be done. The starvation this winter is beating us: everybody is unemployed. The General says we must close this shelter if we cant get more money. I force the collections at the meetings until I am ashamed: dont I, Snobby?

PRICE: It's a fair treat to see you work it, miss. The way you got them up from three-and-six to four-and-ten with that hymn, penny by penny and verse by verse, was a caution. Not a Cheap Jack on Mile End Waste could touch you at it.

BARBARA: Yes; but I wish we could do without it. I am getting at last to think more of the collection than of the people's souls. And what are those hatfuls of pence and halfpence? We want thousands! tens of thousands! hundreds of thousands! I want to convert people, not to be always begging for the Army in a way I'd die sooner than beg for myself.

UNDERSHAFT (*in profound irony*): Genuine unselfishness is capable of anything, my dear.

BARBARA (*unsuspectingly, as she turns away to take the money from the drum and put it in a cash bag she carries*): Yes, isnt it? (UNDERSHAFT *looks sardonically at* CUSINS).

CUSINS (*aside to* UNDERSHAFT): Mephistopheles! Machiavelli!

BARBARA (*tears coming into her eyes as she ties the bag and pockets it*): How are we to feed them? I cant talk religion to a man with bodily hunger in his eyes. (*Almost breaking down*) It's frightful.

JENNY (*running to her*): Major, dear—

BARBARA (*rebounding*): No: dont comfort me. It will be all right. We shall get the money.

UNDERSHAFT: How?

JENNY: By praying for it, of course. Mrs Baines says she prayed for it last night; and she has never prayed for it in vain: never once. (*She goes to the gate and looks out into the street*).

BARBARA (*who has dried her eyes and regained her composure*): By the way, dad, Mrs Baines has come to march with us to our big meeting this afternoon; and she is very anxious to meet you, for some reason or other. Perhaps she'll convert you.

UNDERSHAFT: I shall be delighted, my dear.

JENNY (*at the gate: excitedly*): Major! Major! heres that man back again.

BARBARA: What man?

JENNY: The man that hit me. Oh, I hope he's coming back to join us.

[BILL WALKER, *with frost on his jacket, comes through the gate, his hands deep in his pockets and his chin sunk between his shoulders, like a cleaned-out gambler. He halts between* BARBARA *and the drum.*]

BARBARA: Hullo, Bill! Back already!

BILL (*nagging at her*): Bin talkin ever sence, ev you?

BARBARA: Pretty nearly. Well, has Todger paid you out for poor Jenny's jaw?

BILL: Nao e aint.

BARBARA: I thought your jacket looked a bit snowy.

BILL: Sao it is snaowy. You want to knaow where the snaow cam from, downt you?

BARBARA: Yes.

BILL: Well, it cam from orf the grahnd in Pawkinses Corner in Kennintahn. It got rabbed orf be maw shaoulders: see?

BARBARA: Pity you didnt rub some off with your knees, Bill! That would have done you a lot of good.

BILL (*with sour mirthless humor*): Aw was sivin anather menn's knees at the tawm. E was kneelin on moy ed, e was.

JENNY: Who was kneeling on your head?

BILL: Todger was. E was pryin for me: pryin camfortable wiv me as a cawpet. Sow was Mog. Sao was the aol bloomin meetin. Mog she sez "Ow Lawd brike is stabborn sperrit; bat downt urt is dear art." Thet was wot she said. "Downt urt is dear art"! An er blowk—thirteen stun four!—kneelin wiv all is wight on me. Fanny, aint it?

JENNY: Oh no. We're so sorry, Mr Walker.

BARBARA (*enjoying it frankly*): Nonsense! of course it's funny. Served you right, Bill! You must have done something to him first.

BILL (*doggedly*): Aw did wot Aw said Aw'd do. Aw spit in is eye. E looks ap at the skoy and sez, "Ow that Aw should be fahnd worthy to be spit upon for the gospel's sike!" e sez; an Mog sez "Glaory Allelloolier!"; an then e called me Braddher, an dahned me as if Aw was a kid and e was me mather worshin me a Setterda nawt. Aw ednt jast nao shaow wiv im at all. Arf the street pryed; an the tather arf larfed fit to split theirselves. (*To BARBARA*) There! are you settisfawd nah?

BARBARA (*her eyes dancing*): Wish I'd been there, Bill.

BILL: Yus: youd a got in a hextra bit o talk on me, wouldnt you?

JENNY: I'm so sorry, Mr Walker.

BILL (*fiercely*): Downt you gow bein sorry for me: youve no call. Listen eah. Aw browk your jawr.

JENNY: No, it didnt hurt me: indeed it didnt, except for a moment. It was only that I was frightened.

BILL: Aw downt want to be forgive be you, or be ennybody. Wot Aw did Aw'll py for. Aw trawd to gat me aown jawr browk to settisfaw you—

JENNY (*distressed*): Oh no—

BILL (*impatiently*): Tell y' Aw did: cawnt you listen to wots bein taold you? All Aw got be it was bein mide a sawt of in the pablic street for me pines. Well, if Aw cawnt settisfaw you one wy, Aw ken anather. Listen eah! Aw ed two quid sived agen the frost; an Awve a pahnd of it left. A mite o mawn last week ed words with the judy e's gowin to merry. E give er wot-for; an e's bin fawnd fifteen bob. E ed a rawt to itt er cause they was gowin to be merrid; but Aw ednt nao rawt to itt you; sao put anather fawv bob on an call it a pahnd's worth. (*He produces a sovereign*). Eahs the manney. Tike it; and lets ev no more o your forgivin an pryin and your Mijor jawrin me. Let wot Aw dan be dan an pide for; and let there be a end of it.

JENNY: Oh, I couldnt take it, Mr Walker. But if you would give a shilling or two to poor Rummy Mitchens! you really did hurt her; and she's old.

BILL (*contemptuously*): Not lawkly. Aw'd give her anather as soon as look at er. Let her ev the lawr o me as she threatened! She aint forgiven me: not mach. Wot Aw dan to er is not on me mawnd— wot she (*indicating BARBARA*) mawt call on me conscience—no more than stickin a pig. It's this Christian gime o yours that Aw wownt ev plyed agen me: this bloomin forgivin an neggin an jawrin that mikes a menn thet sore that iz lawf's a burdn to im. Aw wownt ev it, Aw tell you; sao tike your manney and stop thraowin your silly beshed fice hap agen me.

JENNY: Major: may I take a little of it for the Army?

BARBARA: No: the Army is not to be bought. We want your soul, Bill; and we'll take nothing less.

BILL (*bitterly*): Aw knaow. Me an maw few shillins is not good enaff for you. Youre a earl's grendorter, you are. Nathink less than a anderd pahnd for you.

UNDERSHAFT: Come, Barbara! you could do a great deal of good with a hundred pounds. If you will set this gentleman's mind at ease by taking his pound, I will give the other ninety-nine.

[*BILL, dazed by such opulence, instinctively touches his cap.*]

BARBARA: Oh, youre too extravagant, papa. Bill offers twenty pieces of silver. All you need offer is the other ten. That will make the standard price to buy anybody who's for sale. I'm not; and the Army's not. (*To BILL*) Youll never have another quiet moment, Bill, until you come round to us. You cant stand out against your salvation.

BILL (*sullenly*): Aw cawnt stend aht agen music awl wrastlers and awtful tangued women. Awve offered to py. Aw can do no more. Tike it or leave it. There it is. (*He throws the sovereign on the drum, and sits down on the horse-trough. The coin fascinates SNOBBY PRICE, who takes an early opportunity of dropping his cap on it*).

[*MRS BAINES comes from the shelter. She is dressed as a Salvation Army Commissioner. She is an earnest looking woman of about 40, with a caressing, urgent voice, and an appealing manner.*]

BARBARA: This is my father, Mrs Baines. (*UNDERSHAFT comes from the table, taking his hat off with marked civility*). Try what you can do with him. He wont listen to me, because he remembers what a fool I was when I was a baby. (*She leaves them together and chats with JENNY*).

MRS BAINES: Have you been shewn over the shelter, Mr Undershaft? You know the work we're doing, of course.

UNDERSHAFT (*very civilly*): The whole nation knows it, Mrs Baines.

MRS BAINES: No, sir: the whole nation does not know it, or we should not be crippled as we are for want of money to carry our work through the length and breadth of the land. Let me tell you that there would have been rioting this winter in London but for us.

UNDERSHAFT: You really think so?

MRS BAINES: I know it. I remember 1886, when you rich gentlemen hardened your hearts against the cry of the poor. They broke the windows of your clubs in Pall Mall.

UNDERSHAFT (*gleaming with approval of their method*): And the Mansion House Fund went up next day from thirty thousand pounds to seventy-nine thousand! I remember quite well.

MRS BAINES: Well, wont you help me to get at the people? They wont break windows then. Come here, Price. Let me shew you to this gentleman

(PRICE *comes to be inspected*). Do you remember the window breaking?

PRICE: My ole father thought it was the revolution, maam.

MRS BAINES: Would you break windows now?

PRICE: Oh no, maam. The windows of eaven av bin opened to me. I know now that the rich man is a sinner like myself.

RUMMY (*appearing above at the loft door*): Snobby Price!

SNOBBY: Wot is it?

RUMMY: Your mother's askin for you at the other gate in Cripps's Lane. She's heard about your confession (PRICE *turns pale*).

MRS BAINES: Go, Mr Price; and pray with her.

JENNY: You can go through the shelter, Snobby.

PRICE (*to* MRS BAINES): I couldnt face her now, maam, with all the weight of my sins fresh on me. Tell her she'll find her son at ome, waitin for her in prayer. (*He skulks off through the gate, incidentally stealing the sovereign on his way out by picking up his cap from the drum*).

MRS BAINES (*with swimming eyes*): You see how we take the anger and the bitterness against you out of their hearts, Mr Undershaft.

UNDERSHAFT: It is certainly most convenient and gratifying to all large employers of labor, Mrs Baines.

MRS BAINES: Barbara: Jenny: I have good news: most wonderful news. (JENNY *runs to her*). My prayers have been answered. I told you they would, Jenny, didnt I?

JENNY: Yes, yes.

BARBARA (*moving nearer to the drum*): Have we got money enough to keep the shelter open?

MRS BAINES: I hope we shall have enough to keep all the shelters open. Lord Saxmundham has promised us five thousand pounds—

BARBARA: Hooray!

JENNY: Glory!

MRS BAINES: —if—

BARBARA: "If!" If what?

MRS BAINES: —if five other gentlemen will give a thousand each to make it up to ten thousand.

BARBARA: Who is Lord Saxmundham? I never heard of him.

UNDERSHAFT (*who has pricked up his ears at the peer's name, and is now watching* BARBARA *curiously*): A new creation, my dear. You have heard of Sir Horace Bodger?

BARBARA: Bodger! Do you mean the distiller? Bodger's whisky!

UNDERSHAFT: That is the man. He is one of the greatest of our public benefactors. He restored the cathedral at Hakington. They made him a baronet for that. He gave half a million to the funds of his party: they made him a baron for that.

SHIRLEY: What will they give him for the five thousand?

UNDERSHAFT: There is nothing left to give him. So the five thousand, I should think, is to save his soul.

MRS BAINES: Heaven grant it may! Oh Mr Undershaft, you have some very rich friends. Cant you help us towards the other five thousand? We are going to hold a great meeting this afternoon at the Assembly Hall in the Mile End Road. If I could only announce that one gentleman had come forward to support Lord Saxmundham, others would follow. Dont you know somebody? couldnt you? wouldnt you? (*her eyes fill with tears*) oh, think of those poor people, Mr Undershaft: think of how much it means to them, and how little to a great man like you.

UNDERSHAFT: (*sardonically gallant*): Mrs Baines: you are irresistible. I cant disappoint you; and I cant deny myself the satisfaction of making Bodger pay up. You shall have your five thousand pounds.

MRS BAINES: Thank God!

UNDERSHAFT: You dont thank me?

MRS BAINES: Oh sir, dont try to be cynical: dont be ashamed of being a good man. The Lord will bless you abundantly; and our prayers will be like a strong fortification round you all the days of your life. (*With a touch of caution*) You will let me have the cheque to shew at the meeting, wont you? Jenny: go in and fetch a pen and ink. (JENNY *runs to the shelter door*).

UNDERSHAFT: Do not disturb Miss Hill: I have a fountain pen (JENNY *halts. He sits at the table and writes the cheque.* CUSINS *rises to make room for him. They all watch him silently*).

BILL (*cynically, aside to* BARBARA, *his voice and accent horribly debased*): Wot prawce selvytion nah?

BARBARA: Stop. (UNDERSHAFT *stops writing: they all turn to her in surprise*). Mrs Baines: are you really going to take this money?

MRS BAINES (*astonished*): Why not, dear?

BARBARA: Why not! Do you know what my father is? Have you forgotten that Lord Saxmundham is Bodger the whisky man? Do you remember how we implored the County Council to stop him from writing Bodger's Whisky in letters of fire against the sky; so that the poor drink-ruined creatures on the Embankment could not wake up from their snatches of sleep without being reminded of their deadly thirst by that wicked sky sign? Do you know that the worst thing I have had to fight here is not the devil, but Bodger, Bodger, Bodger, with his whisky, his distilleries, and his tied houses? Are you going to make our shelter another tied house for him, and ask me to keep it?

BILL: Rotten dranken whisky it is too.

MRS BAINES: Dear Barbara: Lord Saxmundham has a soul to be saved like any of us. If heaven has found the way to make a good use of his money, are we to set ourselves up against the answer to our prayers?

BARBARA: I know he has a soul to be saved. Let him come down here; and I'll do my best to help him to his salvation. But he wants to send his cheque down to buy us, and go on being as wicked as ever.

UNDERSHAFT (*with a reasonableness which* CUSINS *alone perceives to be ironical*): My dear Barbara: alcohol is a very necessary article. It heals the sick—

BARBARA: It does nothing of the sort.

UNDERSHAFT: Well, it assists the doctor: that is perhaps a less questionable way of putting it. It makes life bearable to millions of people who could not endure their existence if they were quite sober. It enables Parliament to do things at eleven at night that no sane person would do at eleven in the morning. Is it Bodger's fault that this inestimable gift is deplorably abused by less than one per cent of the poor? (*He turns again to the table; signs the cheque; and crosses it*).

MRS BAINES: Barbara: will there be less drinking or more if all those poor souls we are saving come tomorrow and find the doors of our shelters shut in their faces? Lord Saxmundham gives us the money to stop drinking—to take his own business from him.

CUSINS [*implishly*]: Pure self-sacrifice on Bodger's part, clearly! Bless dear Bodger! (BARBARA *almost breaks down as* ADOLPHUS, *too, fails her*).

UNDERSHAFT (*tearing out the cheque and pocketing the book as he rises and goes past* CUSINS *to* MRS BAINES): I also, Mrs Baines, may claim a little disinterestedness. Think of my business! think of the widows and orphans! the men and lads torn to pieces with shrapnel and poisoned with lyddite! (MRS BAINES *shrinks; but he goes on remorselessly*) the oceans of blood, not one drop of which is shed in a really just cause! the ravaged crops! the peaceful peasants forced, women and men, to till their fields under the fire of opposing armies on pain of starvation! the bad blood of the fierce little cowards at home who egg on others to fight for the gratification of their national vanity! All this makes money for me: I am never richer, never busier than when the papers are full of it. Well, it is your work to preach peace on earth and goodwill to men. (MRS BAINES's *face lights up again*). Every convert you make is a vote against war. (*Her lips move in prayer*) Yet I give you this money to help you to hasten my own commercial ruin. (*He gives her the cheque*).

CUSINS (*mounting the form in an ecstasy of mischief*): The millennium will be inaugurated by the unselfishness of Undershaft and Bodger. Oh be joyful! (*He takes the drumsticks from his pockets and flourishes them*).

MRS BAINES (*taking the cheque*): The longer I live the more proof I see that there is an Infinite Goodness that turns everything to the work of salvation sooner or later. Who would have thought that any good could have come out of war and drink? And yet their profits are brought today to the feet of salvation to do its blessed work. (*She is affected to tears*).

JENNY (*running to* MRS BAINES *and throwing her arms round her*): Oh dear! how blessed, how glorious it all is!

CUSINS (*in a convulsion of irony*): Let us seize this unspeakable moment. Let us march to the great meeting at once. Excuse me just an instant. (*He rushes into the shelter.* JENNY *takes her tambourine from the drum head*).

MRS BAINES: Mr Undershaft: have you ever seen a thousand people fall on their knees with one impulse and pray? Come with us to the meeting. Barbara shall tell them that the Army is saved, and saved through you.

CUSINS (*returning impetuously from the shelter with a flag and a trombone, and coming between* MRS BAINES *and* UNDERSHAFT): You shall carry the flag down the first street, Mrs Baines (*he gives her the flag*). Mr Undershaft is a gifted trombonist: he shall intone an Olympian diapason to the West Ham Salvation March. (*Aside to* UNDERSHAFT, *as he forces the trombone on him*) Blow, Machiavelli, blow.

UNDERSHAFT (*aside to him, as he takes the trombone*): The trumpet in Zion! (CUSINS *rushes to the drum, which he takes up and puts on.* UNDERSHAFT *continues, aloud*) I will do my best. I could vamp a bass if I knew the tune.

CUSINS: It is a wedding chorus from one of Donizetti's operas; but we have converted it. We convert everything to good here, including Bodger. You remember the chorus. "For thee immense rejoicing—immenso giubilo—immenso giubilo." (*With drum obbligato*) Rum tum ti tum tum, tum tum ti ta—

BARBARA: Dolly: you are breaking my heart.

CUSINS: What is a broken heart more or less here? Dionysos Undershaft has descended. I am possessed.

MRS BAINES: Come, Barbara: I must have my dear Major to carry the flag with me.

JENNY: Yes, yes, Major darling.

CUSINS (*snatches the tambourine out of* JENNY's *hand and mutely offers it to* BARBARA).

BARBARA (*coming forward a little as she puts the offer behind her with a shudder, whilst* CUSINS *recklessly tosses the tambourine back to* JENNY *and goes to the gate*): I cant come.

JENNY: Not come!

MRS BAINES (*with tears in her eyes*): Barbara: do you

think I am wrong to take the money?

BARBARA (*impulsively going to her and kissing her*): No, no: God help you, dear, you must: you are saving the Army. Go; and may you have a great meeting!

JENNY: But arnt you coming?

BARBARA: No. (*She begins taking off the silver S brooch from her collar*).

MRS BAINES: Barbara: what are you doing?

JENNY: Why are you taking your badge off? You cant be going to leave us, Major.

BARBARA (*quietly*): Father: come here.

UNDERSHAFT (*coming to her*): My dear! (*Seeing that she is going to pin a badge on his collar, he retreats to the penthouse in some alarm*).

BARBARA (*following him*): Dont be frightened. (*She pins the badge on and steps back towards the table, shrewing him to the others*) There! It's not much for £5000, is it?

MRS BAINES: Barbara: if you wont come and pray with us, promise me you will pray for us.

BARBARA: I cant pray now. Perhaps I shall never pray again.

MRS BAINES: Barbara!

JENNY: Major!

BARBARA (*almost delirious*): I cant bear any more. Quick march!

CUSINS (*calling to the procession in the street outside*): Off we go. Play up, there! Immenso giubilo. (*He gives the time with his drum; and the band strikes up the march, which rapidly becomes more distant as the procession moves briskly away*).

MRS BAINES: I must go, dear. Youre overworked: you will be all right tomorrow. We'll never lose you. Now Jenny: step out with the old flag. Blood and Fire! (*She marches out through the gate with her flag*).

JENNY: Glory Hallelujah! (*flourishing her tambourine and marching*).

UNDERSHAFT (*to CUSINS, as he marches out past him easing the slide of his trombone*): "My ducats and my daughter"!

CUSINS (*following him out*): Money and gunpowder!

BARBARA: Drunkenness and Murder! My God: why hast thou forsaken me?

[*She sinks on the form with her face buried in her hands. The march passes away into silence. BILL WALKER steals across to her.*]

BILL (*taunting*): Wot prawce selvytion nah?

SHIRLEY: Dont you hither when she's down.

BILL: She itt me wen aw wiz dahn. Waw shouldnt Aw git a bit o me aown beck?

BARBARA (*raising her head*): I didnt take your money, Bill. (*She crosses the yard to the gate and turns her back on the two men to hide her face from them*).

BILL (*sneering after her*): Naow, it warnt enaff for you. (*Turning to the drum, he misses the money*). Ellow! If you aint took it sammun else ez. Weres it gorn? Bly me if Jenny Ill didnt tike it arter all!

RUMMY (*screaming at him from the loft*): You lie, you dirty blackguard! Snobby Price pinched it off the drum when he took up his cap. I was up here all the time an see im do it.

BILL: Wot! stowl maw manney! Waw didnt you call thief on him, you silly aold macker you?

RUMMY: To serve you aht for ittin me acrost the fice. It's cost y'pahnd, that az. (*Raising a pæan of squalid triumph*) I done you. I'm even with you. Ive ad it aht o y— (*BILL snatches up SHIRLEY's mug and hurls it at her. She slams the loft door and vanishes. The mug smashes against the door and falls in fragments*).

BILL (*beginning to chuckle*): Tell us, aol menn, wot o'clock this mawnin was it wen im as they call Snobby Prawce was sived?

BARBARA (*turning to him more composedly, and with unspoiled sweetness*): About half past twelve, Bill. And he pinched your pound at a quarter to two. I know. Well, you cant afford to lose it. I'll send it to you.

BILL (*his voice and accent suddenly improving*): Not if Aw wiz to stawve for it. Aw aint to be bought.

SHIRLEY: Aint you? Youd sell yourself to the devil for a pint o beer; ony there aint no devil to make the offer.

BILL (*unshamed*): Sao Aw would, mite, and often ev, cheerful. But she cawnt baw me. (*Approaching BARBARA*) You wanted maw saoul, did you? Well, you aint got it.

BARBARA: I nearly got it, Bill. But weve sold it back to you for ten thousand pounds.

SHIRLEY: And dear at the money!

BARBARA: No, Peter: it was worth more than money.

BILL (*salvationproof*): It's nao good: you cawnt get rahnd me nah. Aw downt blieve in it; and Awve seen tody that Aw was rawt. (*Going*) Sao long, aol soupkitchener! Ta, ta, Mijor Earl's Grendorter! (*Turning at the gate*) Wot prawce selvytion nah? Snobby Prawce! Ha! ha!

BARBARA (*offering her hand*): Goodbye, Bill.

BILL (*taken aback, half plucks his cap off; then shoves it on again defiantly*): Git aht. (*BARBARA drops her hand, discouraged. He has a twinge of remorse*). But thets aw rawt, you knaow. Nathink pasnl. Naow mellice. Sao long, Judy. (*He goes*).

BARBARA: No malice. So long, Bill.

SHIRLEY (*shaking his head*): You make too much of him, miss, in your innocence.

BARBARA (*going to him*): Peter: I'm like you now. Cleaned out, and lost my job.

SHIRLEY: Youve youth an hope. Thats two better than me.

BARBARA: I'll get you a job, Peter. Thats hope for you: the youth will have to be enough for me. (*She counts her money*). I have just enough left for two teas at Lockharts, a Rowton doss for you, and my tram and bus home. (*He frowns and rises with offended pride. She takes his arm*). Dont be proud, Peter: it's sharing between friends. And promise me youll talk to me and not let me cry. (*She draws him towards the gate*).

SHIRLEY: Well, I'm not accustomed to talk to the like of you—

BARBARA (*urgently*): Yes, yes: you must talk to me. Tell me about Tom Paine's books and Bradlaugh's lectures. Come along.

SHIRLEY: Ah, if you would only read Tom Paine in the proper spirit, miss! (*They go out through the gate together*).

ACT III

Next day after lunch LADY BRITOMART *is writing in the library in Wilton Crescent.* SARAH *is reading in the armchair near the window.* BARBARA, *in ordinary fashionable dress, pale and brooding, is on the settee.* CHARLES LOMAX *enters. He starts on seeing* BARBARA *fashionably attired and in low spirits.*

LOMAX: Youve left off your uniform!

*[*BARBARA *says nothing; but an expression of pain passes over her face.]*

LADY BRITOMART (*warning him in low tones to be careful*): Charles!

LOMAX (*much concerned, coming behind the settee and bending sympathetically over* BARBARA): I'm awfully sorry, Barbara. You know I helped you all I could with the concertina and so forth. (*Momentously*) Still, I have never shut my eyes to the fact that there is a certain amount of tosh about the Salvation Army. Now the claims of the Church of England—

LADY BRITOMART: Thats enough, Charles. Speak of something suited to your mental capacity.

LOMAX: But surely the Church of England is suited to all our capacities.

BARBARA (*pressing his hand*): Thank you for your sympathy, Cholly. Now go and spoon with Sarah.

LOMAX (*dragging a chair from the writing table and seating himself affectionately by* SARAH's *side*): How is my ownest today?

SARAH: I wish you wouldnt tell Cholly to do things, Barbara. He always comes straight and does them. Cholly: we're going to the works this afternoon.

LOMAX: What works?

SARAH: The cannon works.

LOMAX: What! Your governor's shop!

SARAH: Yes.

LOMAX: Oh I say!

*[*CUSINS *enters in poor condition. He also starts visibly when he sees* BARBARA *without her uniform.]*

BARBARA: I expected you this morning, Dolly. Didnt you guess that?

CUSINS (*sitting down beside her*): I'm sorry. I have only just breakfasted.

SARAH: But weve just finished lunch.

BARBARA: Have you had one of your bad nights?

CUSINS: No: I had rather a good night: in fact, one of the most remarkable nights I have ever passed.

BARBARA: The meeting?

CUSINS: No: after the meeting.

LADY BRITOMART: You should have gone to bed after the meeting. What were you doing?

CUSINS: Drinking.

LADY BRITOMART.   ⎤   ⎡ Adolphus!
SARAH: Dolly!
BARBARA: ⎟   ⎟ Dolly!
LOMAX: ⎦   ⎣ Oh I say!

LADY BRITOMART: What were you drinking, may I ask?

CUSINS: A most devilish kind of Spanish burgundy, warranted free from added alcohol: a Temperance burgundy in fact. Its richness in natural alcohol made any addition superfluous.

BARBARA: Are you joking, Dolly?

CUSINS (*patiently*): No. I have been making a night of it with the nominal head of this household: that is all.

LADY BRITOMART: Andrew made you drunk!

CUSINS: No: he only provided the wine. I think it was Dionysos who made me drunk. (*to* BARBARA) I told you I was possessed.

LADY BRITOMART: Youre not sober yet. Go home to bed at once.

CUSINS: I have never before ventured to reproach you, Lady Brit; but how could you marry the Prince of Darkness?

LADY BRITOMART: It was much more excusable to marry him than to get drunk with him. That is a new accomplishment of Andrew's, by the way. He usent to drink.

CUSINS: He doesnt now. He only sat there and completed the wreck of my moral basis, the rout of my convictions, the purchase of my soul. He cares for you, Barbara. That is what makes him so dangerous to me.

BARBARA: That has nothing to do with it, Dolly. There are larger loves and diviner dreams than the fireside ones. You know that, dont you?

CUSINS: Yes: that is our understanding. I know it. I hold to it. Unless he can win me on that holier ground he may amuse me for a while; but he can get no deeper hold, strong as he is.

BARBARA: Keep to that; and the end will be right. Now tell me what happened at the meeting?

CUSINS: It was an amazing meeting. Mrs Baines almost died of emotion. Jenny Hill simply gibbered with hysteria. The Prince of Darkness played his trombone like a madman: its brazen roarings were like the laughter of the damned. 117 conversions took place then and there. They prayed with the most touching sincerity and gratitude for Bodger, and for the anonymous donor of the £5000. Your father would not let his name be given.

LOMAX: That was rather fine of the old man, you know. Most chaps would have wanted the advertisement.

CUSINS: He said all the charitable institutions would be down on him like kites on a battle field if he gave his name.

LADY BRITOMART: Thats Andrew all over. He never does a proper thing without giving an improper reason for it.

CUSINS: He convinced me that I have all my life been doing improper things for proper reasons.

LADY BRITOMART: Adolphus: now that Barbara has left the Salvation Army, you had better leave it too. I will not have you playing that drum in the streets.

CUSINS: Your orders are already obeyed, Lady Brit.

BARBARA: Dolly: were you ever really in earnest about it? Would you have joined if you had never seen me?

CUSINS (*disingenuously*): Well—er—well, possibly, as a collector of religions—

LOMAX (*cunningly*): Not as a drummer, though, you know. You are a very clearheaded brainy chap, Dolly; and it must have been apparent to you that there is a certain amount of tosh about—

LADY BRITOMART: Charles: if you must drivel, drivel like a grown-up man and not like a schoolboy.

LOMAX (*out of countenance*): Well, drivel is drivel, dont you know, whatever a man's age.

LADY BRITOMART: In good society in England, Charles, men drivel at all ages by repeating silly formulas with an air of wisdom. Schoolboys make their own formulas out of slang, like you. When they reach your age, and get political private secretaryships and things of that sort, they drop slang and get their formulas out of The Spectator or The Times. You had better confine yourself to The Times. You will find that there is a certain amount of tosh about The Times; but at least its language is reputable.

LOMAX (*overwhelmed*): You are so awfully strong-minded Lady Brit—

LADY BRITOMART: Rubbish! (*MORRISON comes in*). What is it?

MORRISON: If you please, my lady, Mr Undershaft has just drove up to the door.

LADY BRITOMART: Well, let him in. (*MORRISON hesitates*). Whats the matter with you?

MORRISON: Shall I announce him, my lady; or is he at home here, so to speak, my lady?

LADY BRITOMART: Announce him.

MORRISON: Thank you, my lady. You wont mind my asking, I hope. The occasion is in a manner of speaking new to me.

LADY BRITOMART: Quite right. Go and let him in.

MORRISON: Thank you, my lady. (*He withdraws*).

LADY BRITOMART: Children: go and get ready. (*SARAH and BARBARA go upstairs for their out-of-door wraps*). Charles: go and tell Stephen to come down here in five minutes: you will find him in the drawing room. (*CHARLES goes*). Adolphus: tell them to send round the carriage in about fifteen minutes. (*ADOLPHUS goes*).

MORRISON (*at the door*): Mr Undershaft.

[UNDERSHAFT comes in. MORRISON goes out.]

UNDERSHAFT: Alone! How fortunate!

LADY BRITOMART (*rising*): Dont be sentimental, Andrew. Sit down. (*She sits on the settee: he sits beside her, on her left. She comes to the point before he has time to breathe*). Sarah must have £800 a year until Charles Lomax comes into his property. Barbara will need more, and need it permanently, because Adolphus hasnt any property.

UNDERSHAFT (*resignedly*): Yes, my dear: I will see to it. Anything else? for yourself, for instance?

LADY BRITOMART: I want to talk to you about Stephen.

UNDERSHAFT (*rather wearily*): Dont, my dear. Stephen doesnt interest me.

LADY BRITOMART: He does interest me. He is our son.

UNDERSHAFT: Do you really think so? He has induced us to bring him into the world; but he chose his parents very incongruously, I think. I see nothing of myself in him, and less of you.

LADY BRITOMART: Andrew: Stephen is an excellent son, and a most steady, capable, highminded young man. You are simply trying to find an excuse for disinheriting him.

UNDERSHAFT: My dear Biddy: the Undershaft tradition disinherits him. It would be dishonest of me to leave the cannon foundry to my son.

LADY BRITOMART: It would be most unnatural and improper of you to leave it to anyone else, Andrew. Do you suppose this wicked and immoral tradition can be kept up for ever? Do you pretend that Stephen could not carry on the foundry just as well as all the other sons of the big business houses?

UNDERSHAFT: Yes: he could learn the office routine without understanding the business, like all the other sons; and the firm would go on by its own momentum until the real Undershaft—probably an Italian or a German—would invent a new method and cut him out.

LADY BRITOMART: There is nothing that any Italian or German could do that Stephen could not do. And Stephen at least has breeding.

UNDERSHAFT: The son of a foundling! Nonsense!

LADY BRITOMART: My son, Andrew! And even you may have good blood in your veins for all you know.

UNDERSHAFT: True. Probably I have. That is another argument in favor of a foundling.

LADY BRITOMART: Andrew: dont be aggravating. And dont be wicked. At present you are both.

UNDERSHAFT: This conversation is part of the Undershaft tradition, Biddy. Every Undershaft's wife has treated him to it ever since the house was founded. It is mere waste of breath. If the tradition be ever broken it will be for an abler man than Stephen.

LADY BRITOMART (*pouting*): Then go away.

UNDERSHAFT (*deprecatory*): Go away!

LADY BRITOMART: Yes: go away. If you will do nothing for Stephen, you are not wanted here. Go to your foundling, whoever he is; and look after him.

UNDERSHAFT: The fact is, Biddy—

LADY BRITOMART: Dont call me Biddy. I dont call you Andy.

UNDERSHAFT: I will not call my wife Britomart: it is not good sense. Seriously, my love, the Undershaft tradition has landed me in a difficulty. I am getting on in years; and my partner Lazarus has at last made a stand and insisted that the succession must be settled one way or the other; and of course he is quite right. You see, I havnt found a fit successor yet.

LADY BRITOMART (*obstinately*): There is Stephen.

UNDERSHAFT: Thats just it: all the foundlings I can find are exactly like Stephen.

LADY BRITOMART: Andrew!!

UNDERSHAFT: I want a man with no relations and no schooling: that is, a man who would be out of the running altogether if he were not a strong man. And I cant find him. Every blessed foundling nowadays is snapped up in his infancy by Barnardo homes, or School Board officers, or Boards of Guardians; and if he shews the least ability he is fastened on by schoolmasters; trained to win scholarships like a racehorse; crammed with secondhand ideas; drilled and disciplined in docility and what they call good taste; and lamed for life so that he is fit for nothing but teaching. If you want to keep the foundry in the family, you had better find an eligible foundling and marry him to Barbara.

LADY BRITOMART: Ah! Barbara! Your pet! You would sacrifice Stephen to Barbara.

UNDERSHAFT: Cheerfully. And you, my dear, would boil Barbara to make soup for Stephen.

LADY BRITOMART: Andrew: this is not a question of our likings and dislikings: it is a question of duty. It is your duty to make Stephen your successor.

UNDERSHAFT: Just as much as it is your duty to submit to your husband. Come, Biddy! these tricks of the governing class are of no use with me. I am one of the governing class myself; and it is waste of time giving tracts to a missionary. I have the power in this matter; and I am not to be humbugged into using it for your purposes.

LADY BRITOMART: Andrew: you can talk my head off; but you cant change wrong into right. And your tie is all on one side. Put it straight.

UNDERSHAFT (*disconcerted*): It wont stay unless it's pinned (*he fumbles at it with childish grimaces*)—

[STEPHEN *comes in.*]

STEPHEN (*at the door*): I beg your pardon (*about to retire*).

LADY BRITOMART: No: come in, Stephen. (STEPHEN *comes forward to his mother's writing table*).

UNDERSHAFT (*not very cordially*): Good afternoon.

STEPHEN (*coldly*): Good afternoon.

UNDERSHAFT (*to* LADY BRITOMART): He knows all about the tradition, I suppose?

LADY BRITOMART: Yes. (*To* STEPHEN): It is what I told you last night, Stephen.

UNDERSHAFT (*sulkily*): I understand you want to come into the cannon business.

STEPHEN: *I* go into trade! Certainly not.

UNDERSHAFT (*opening his eyes, greatly eased in mind and manner*): Oh! in that case—

LADY BRITOMART: Cannons are not trade, Stephen. They are enterprise.

STEPHEN: I have no intention of becoming a man of business in any sense. I have no capacity for business and no taste for it. I intend to devote myself to politics.

UNDERSHAFT (*rising*): My dear boy: this is an immense relief to me. And I trust it may prove an equally good thing for the country. I was afraid you would consider yourself disparaged and slighted. (*He moves towards* STEPHEN *as if to shake hands with him*).

LADY BRITOMART (*rising and interposing*): Stephen: I cannot allow you to throw away an enormous property like this.

STEPHEN (*stiffly*): Mother: there must be an end of treating me as a child, if you please. (LADY BRITOMART *recoils, deeply wounded by his tone*). Until last night I did not take your attitude seriously, because I did not think you meant it seriously. But I find now that you left me in the dark as to matters which you should have explained to me years ago. I am extremely hurt and offended. Any further discussion of my intentions had better take place with my father, as between one man and another.

LADY BRITOMART: Stephen! (*She sits down again, her eyes filling with tears*).

UNDERSHAFT (*with grave compassion*): You see, my dear, it is only the big men who can be treated as children.

STEPHEN: I am sorry, mother, that you have forced me—

UNDERSHAFT (*stopping him*): Yes, yes, yes, yes: thats all right, Stephen. She wont interfere with you any more: your independence is achieved: you have won your latchkey. Dont rub it in; and above all, dont apologize. (*He resumes his seat*). Now what about your future, as between one man and another—I beg your pardon, Biddy: as between two men and a woman.

LADY BRITOMART (*who has pulled herself together strongly*): I quite understand, Stephen. By all means go your own way if you feel strong enough. (STEPHEN *sits down magisterially in the chair at the writing table with an air of affirming his majority*).

UNDERSHAFT: It is settled that you do not ask for the succession to the cannon business.

STEPHEN: I hope it is settled that I repudiate the cannon business.

UNDERSHAFT: Come, come! dont be so devilishly sulky: it's boyish. Freedom should be generous. Besides, I owe you a fair start in life in exchange for disinheriting you. You cant become prime minister all at once. Havnt you a turn for something? What about literature, art, and so forth?

STEPHEN: I have nothing of the artist about me, either in faculty or character, thank Heaven!

UNDERSHAFT: A philosopher, perhaps? Eh?

STEPHEN: I make no such ridiculous pretension.

UNDERSHAFT: Just so. Well, there is the army, the navy, the Church, the Bar. The Bar requires some ability. What about the Bar?

STEPHEN: I have not studied law. And I am afraid I have not the necessary push—I believe that is the name barristers give to their vulgarity—for success in pleading.

UNDERSHAFT: Rather, a difficult case, Stephen. Hardly anything left but the stage, is there? (STEPHEN *makes an impatient movement*). Well, come! is there anything you know or care for?

STEPHEN (*rising and looking at him steadily*): I know the difference between right and wrong.

UNDERSHAFT (*hugely tickled*): You dont say so! What! no capacity for business, no knowledge of law, no sympathy with art, no pretension to philosophy; only a simple knowledge of the secret that has puzzled all the philosophers, baffled all the lawyers, muddled all the men of business, and

ruined most of the artists: the secret of right and wrong. Why, man, youre a genius, a master of masters, a god! At twentyfour, too!

STEPHEN (*keeping his temper with difficulty*): You are pleased to be facetious. I pretend to nothing more than any honorable English gentleman claims as his birthright (*he sits down angrily*).

UNDERSHAFT: Oh, thats everybody's birthright. Look at poor little Jenny Hill, the Salvation lassie! she would think you were laughing at her if you asked her to stand up in the street and teach grammar or geography or mathematics or even drawing room dancing; but it never occurs to her to doubt that she can teach morals and religion. You are all alike, you respectable people. You cant tell me the bursting strain of a ten-inch gun, which is a very simple matter; but you all think you can tell me the bursting strain of a man under temptation. You darent handle high explosives; but youre all ready to handle honesty and truth and justice and the whole duty of man, and kill one another at that game. What a country! What a world!

LADY BRITOMART (*uneasily*): What do you think he had better do, Andrew?

UNDERSHAFT: Oh, just what he wants to do. He knows nothing; and he thinks he knows everything. That points clearly to a political career. Get him a private secretaryship to someone who can get him an Under Secretaryship; and then leave him alone. He will find his natural and proper place in the end on the Treasury bench.

STEPHEN (*springing up again*): I am sorry, sir, that you force me to forget the respect due to you as my father. I am an Englishman; and I will not hear the Government of my country insulted. (*He thrusts his hands in his pockets, and walks angrily across to the window*).

UNDERSHAFT (*with a touch of brutality*): The government of your country! *I* am the government of your country: I, and Lazarus. Do you suppose that you and half a dozen amateurs like you, sitting in a row in that foolish gabble shop, can govern Undershaft and Lazarus? No, my friend: you will do what pays us. You will make war when it suits us, and keep peace when it doesnt. You will find out that trade requires certain measures when we have decided on those measures. When I want anything to keep my dividends up, you will discover that my want is a national need. When other people want something to keep my dividends down, you will call out the police and military. And in return you shall have the support and applause of my newspapers, and the delight of imagining that you are a great statesman. Government of your country! Be off with you, my boy, and play with your caucuses and leading articles and historic parties and great leaders and burning questions and the rest of your toys. *I am going back to my countinghouse to pay the piper and call the tune.*

STEPHEN (*actually smiling, and putting his hand on his father's shoulder with indulgent patronage*): Really, my dear father, it is impossible to be angry with you. You dont know how absurd all this sounds to me. You are very properly proud of having been industrious enough to make money; and it is greatly to your credit that you have made so much of it. But it has kept you in circles where you are valued for your money and deferred to for it, instead of in the doubtless very old-fashioned and behind-the-times public school and university where I formed my habits of mind. It is natural for you to think that money governs England; but you must allow me to think I know better.

UNDERSHAFT: And what does govern England, pray?

STEPHEN: Character, father, character.

UNDERSHAFT: Whose character? Yours or mine?

STEPHEN: Neither yours nor mine, father, but the best elements in the English national character.

UNDERSHAFT: Stephen: Ive found your profession for you. Youre a born journalist. I'll start you with a high-toned weekly review. There!

[*Before* STEPHEN *can reply* SARAH, BARBARA, LOMAX, *and* CUSINS *come in ready for walking.* BARBARA *crosses the room to the window and looks out.* CUSINS *drifts amiably to the armchair.* LOMAX *remains near the door, whilst* SARAH *comes to her mother.*

STEPHEN goes to the smaller writing table and busies himself with his letters.]

SARAH: Go and get ready, mamma: the carriage is waiting. (LADY BRITOMART *leaves the room*).

UNDERSHAFT (*to* SARAH): Good day, my dear. Good afternoon, Mr Lomax.

LOMAX (*vaguely*): Ahdedoo.

UNDERSHAFT (*to* CUSINS): Quite well after last night, Euripides, eh?

CUSINS: As well as can be expected.

UNDERSHAFT: Thats right. (*To* BARBARA) So you are coming to see my death and devastation factory, Barbara?

BARBARA (*at the window*): You came yesterday to see my salvation factory. I promised you a return visit.

LOMAX (*coming forward between* SARAH *and* UNDERSHAFT): Youll find it awfully interesting. Ive been through the Woolwich Arsenal; and it gives you a ripping feeling of security, you know, to think of the lot of beggars we could kill if it came to fighting. (*To* UNDERSHAFT, *with sudden solemnity*). Still, it must be rather an awful reflection for

you, from the religious point of view as it were. Youre getting on, you know, and all that.

SARAH: You dont mind Cholly's imbecility, papa, do you?

LOMAX (*much taken aback*): Oh I say!

UNDERSHAFT: Mr. Lomax looks at the matter in a very proper spirit, my dear.

LOMAX: Just so. Thats all I meant, I assure you.

SARAH: Are you coming, Stephen?

STEPHEN: Well, I am rather busy—er— (*Magnanimously*) Oh well, yes: I'll come. That is, if there is room for me.

UNDERSHAFT: I can take two with me in a little motor I am experimenting with for field use. You wont mind its being rather unfashionable. It's not painted yet; but it's bullet proof.

LOMAX (*appalled at the prospect of confronting* WILTON CRESCENT *in an unpainted motor*): Oh I say!

SARAH: The carriage for me, thank you. Barbara doesnt mind what she's seen in.

LOMAX: I say, Dolly, old chap: do you really mind the car being a guy? Because of course if you do I'll go in it. Still—

CUSINS: I prefer it.

LOMAX: Thanks awfully, old man. Come, my ownest. (*He hurries out to secure his seat in the carriage.* SARAH *follows him*).

CUSINS (*moodily walking across to* LADY BRITOMART'S *writing table*): Why are we two coming to this Works Department of Hell? that is what I ask myself.

BARBARA: I have always thought of it as a sort of pit where lost creatures with blackened faces stirred up smoky fires and were driven and tormented by my father? Is it like that, dad?

UNDERSHAFT (*scandalized*): My dear! It is a spotlessly clean and beautiful hillside town.

CUSINS: With a Methodist chapel? Oh do say theres a Methodist chapel.

UNDERSHAFT: There are two: a Primitive one and a sophisticated one. There is even an Ethical Society; but it is not much patronized, as my men are all strongly religious. In the High Explosives Sheds they object to the presence of Agnostics as unsafe.

CUSINS: And yet they dont object to you!

BARBARA: Do they obey all your orders?

UNDERSHAFT: I never give them any orders. When I speak to one of them it is "Well, Jones, is the baby doing well? and has Mrs Jones made a good recovery?" "Nicely, thank you, sir." And thats all.

CUSINS: But Jones has to be kept in order. How do you maintain discipline among your men?

UNDERSHAFT: I dont. They do. You see, the one thing Jones wont stand is any rebellion from the man under him, or any assertion of social equality between the wife of the man with 4 shillings a week less than himself, and Mrs Jones! Of course they all rebel against me, theoretically. Practically, every man of them keeps the man just below him in his place. I never meddle with them. I never bully them. I dont even bully Lazarus. I say that certain things are to be done; but I dont order anybody to do them. I dont say, mind you, that there is no ordering about and snubbing and even bullying. The men snub the boys and order them about; the carmen snub the sweepers; the artisans snub the unskilled laborers; the foremen drive and bully both the laborers and artisans; the assistant engineers find fault with the foremen; the chief engineers drop on the assistants; the departmental managers worry the chiefs; and the clerks have tall hats and hymnbooks and keep up the social tone by refusing to associate on equal terms with anybody. The result is a colossal profit, which comes to me.

CUSINS (*revolted*): You really are a—well, what I was saying yesterday.

BARBARA: What was he saying yesterday?

UNDERSHAFT: Never mind, my dear. He thinks I have made you unhappy. Have I?

BARBARA: Do you think I can be happy in this vulgar silly dress? I! who have worn the uniform. Do you understand what you have done to me? Yesterday I had a man's soul in my hand. I set him in the way of life with his face to salvation. But when we took your money he turned back to drunkenness and derision. (*With intense conviction*) I will never forgive you that. If I had a child, and you destroyed its body with your explosives—if you murdered Dolly with your horrible guns—I could forgive you if my forgiveness would open the gates of heaven to you. But to take a human soul from me, and turn it into the soul of a wolf! that is worse than any murder.

UNDERSHAFT: Does my daughter despair so easily? Can you strike a man to the heart and leave no mark on him?

BARBARA (*her face lighting up*): Oh, you are right: he can never be lost now: where was my faith?

CUSINS: Oh, clever clever devil!

BARBARA: You may be a devil; but God speaks through you sometimes. (*She takes her father's hands and kisses them*). You have given me back my happiness: I feel it deep down now, though my spirit is troubled.

UNDERSHAFT: You have learnt something. That always feels at first as if you had lost something.

BARBARA: Well, take me to the factory of death; and let me learn something more. There must be some truth or other behind all this frightful irony. Come, Dolly. (*She goes out*).

CUSINS: My guardian angel! (*To* UNDERSHAFT) Avaunt! (*He follows* BARBARA).

STEPHEN (*quietly, at the writing table*): You must not mind Cusins, father. He is a very amiable good fellow; but he is a Greek scholar and naturally a little eccentric.

UNDERSHAFT: Ah, quite so. Thank you, Stephen. Thank you. (*He goes out*).

[STEPHEN *smiles patronizingly; buttons his coat responsibly; and crosses the room to the door.* LADY BRITOMART, *dressed for out-of-doors, opens it before he reaches it. She looks round for the others; looks at* STEPHEN; *and turns to go without a word.*]

STEPHEN (*embarrassed*): Mother—

LADY BRITOMART: Dont be apologetic, Stephen. And dont forget that you have outgrown your mother. (*She goes out*).

[*Perivale St Andrews lies between two Middlesex hills, half climbing the northern one. It is an almost smokeless town of white walls, roofs of narrow green slates or red tiles, tall trees, domes, campaniles, and slender chimney shafts, beautifully situated and beautiful in itself. The best view of it is obtained from the crest of a slope about half a mile to the east, where the high explosives are dealt with. The foundry lies hidden in the depths between, the tops of its chimneys sprouting like huge skittles into the middle distance. Across the crest runs an emplacement of concrete, with a firestep, and a parapet which suggests a fortification, because there is a huge cannon of the obsolete Woolwich Infant pattern peering across it at the town. The cannon is mounted on an experimental gun carriage: possibly the original model of the Undershaft disappearing rampart gun alluded to by* STEPHEN. *The firestep, being a convenient place to sit, is furnished here and there with straw disc cushions; and at one place there is the additional luxury of a fur rug.*

Barbara is standing on the firestep, looking over the parapet towards the town. On her right is the cannon; on her left the end of a shed raised on piles, with a ladder of three or four steps up to the door, which opens outwards and has a little wooden landing at the threshold, with a fire bucket in the corner of the landing. Several dummy soldiers, more or less mutilated, with straw protruding from their gashes, have been shoved out of the way under the landing. A few others are nearly upright against the shed; and one has fallen forward and lies, like a grotesque corpse, on the emplacement. The parapet stops short of the shed, leaving a gap which is the beginning of the path down the hill through the foundry to the town. The rug is on the firestep near this gap. Down on the emplacement behind the cannon is a trolley carrying a huge conical bombshell with a red band painted on it. Further to the right is the door of an office, which, like the sheds, is of the lightest possible construction.

[CUSINS arrives by the path from the town.]

BARBARA: Well?

CUSINS: Not a ray of hope. Everything perfect! wonderful! real! It only needs a cathedral to be a heavenly city instead of a hellish one.

BARBARA: Have you found out whether they have done anything for old Peter Shirley?

CUSINS: They have found him a job as gatekeeper and timekeeper. He's frightfully miserable. He calls the timekeeping brainwork, and says he isnt used to it; and his gate lodge is so splendid that he's ashamed to use the rooms, and skulks in the scullery.

BARBARA: Poor Peter!

[STEPHEN arrives from the town. He carries a field-glass.]

STEPHEN (*enthusiastically*): Have you two seen the place? Why did you leave us?

CUSINS: I wanted to see everything I was not intended to see; and Barbara wanted to make the men talk.

STEPHEN: Have you found anything discreditable?

CUSINS: No. They call him Dandy Andy and are proud of his being a cunning old rascal; but it's all horribly, frightfully, immorally, unanswerably perfect.

[SARAH arrives.]

SARAH: Heavens! what a place! (*She crosses to the trolley*). Did you see the nursing home!? (*She sits down on the shell*).

STEPHEN: Did you see the libraries and schools!?

SARAH: Did you see the ball room and the banqueting chamber in the Town Hall!?

STEPHEN: Have you gone into the insurance fund, the pension fund, the building society, the various applications of co-operation!?

[UNDERSHAFT comes from the office, with a sheaf of telegrams in his hand.]

UNDERSHAFT: Well, have you seen everything? I'm sorry I was called away. (*Indicating the telegrams*) Good news from Manchuria.

STEPHEN: Another Japanese victory?

UNDERSHAFT: Oh, I dont know. Which side wins does not concern us here. No: the good news is that the aerial battleship is a tremendous success. At the first trial it has wiped out a fort with three hundred soldiers in it.

CUSINS (*from the platform*): Dummy soldiers?

UNDERSHAFT (*striding across to STEPHEN and kicking the prostrate dummy brutally out of his way*): No: the real thing.

[CUSINS and BARBARA exchange glances. Then CUSINS sits on the step and buries his face in his hands. BARBARA gravely lays her hand on his shoulder. He looks up at her in whimsical desperation.]

UNDERSHAFT: Well, Stephen, what do you think of the place?

STEPHEN: Oh, magnificent. A perfect triumph of modern industry. Frankly, my dear father, I have been a fool: I had no idea of what it all meant: of the wonderful forethought, the power of organization, the administrative capacity, the financial genius, the colossal capital it represents. I have been repeating to myself as I came through your streets "Peace hath her victories no less renowned than War." I have only one misgiving about it all.

UNDERSHAFT: Out with it.

STEPHEN: Well, I cannot help thinking that all this provision for every want of your workmen may sap their independence and weaken their sense of responsibility. And greatly as we enjoyed our tea at that splendid restaurant—how they gave us all that luxury and cake and jam and cream for threepence I really cannot imagine!—still you must remember that restaurants break up home life. Look at the continent, for instance! Are you sure so much pampering is really good for the men's characters?

UNDERSHAFT: Well you see, my dear boy, when you are organizing civilization you have to make up your mind whether trouble and anxiety are good things or not. If you decide that they are, then, I take it, you simply dont organize civilization; and there you are, with trouble and anxiety enough to make us all angels! But if you decide the other way, you may as well go through with it. However, Stephen, our characters are safe here. A sufficient dose of anxiety is always provided by the fact that we may be blown to smithereens at any moment.

SARAH: By the way, papa, where do you make the explosives?

UNDERSHAFT: In separate little sheds, like that one. When one of them blows up, it costs very little; and only the people quite close to it are killed.

[STEPHEN, who is quite close to it, looks at it rather scaredly, and moves away quickly to the cannon. At the same moment the door of the shed is thrown abruptly open; and a foreman in overalls and list slippers comes out on the little landing and holds the door for LOMAX, who appears in the doorway.

LOMAX (*with studied coolness*): My good fellow: you neednt get into a state of nerves. Nothing's going to happen to you; and I suppose it wouldnt be the end of the world if anything did. A little bit of

British pluck is what you want, old chap. (*He descends and strolls across to* SARAH).

UNDERSHAFT (*to the foreman*): Anything wrong, Bilton?

BILTON (*with ironic calm*): Gentleman walked into the high explosives shed and lit a cigaret, sir: thats all.

UNDERSHAFT: Ah, quite so. (*Going over to* LOMAX) Do you happen to remember what you did with the match?

LOMAX: Oh come! I'm not a fool. I took jolly good care to blow it out before I chucked it away.

BILTON: The top of it was red hot inside, sir.

LOMAX: Well, suppose it was! I didn't chuck it into any of your messes.

UNDERSHAFT: Think no more of it, Mr Lomax. By the way, would you mind lending me your matches?

LOMAX (*offering his box*): Certainly.

UNDERSHAFT: Thanks. (*He pockets the matches*).

LOMAX (*lecturing to the company generally*): You know, these high explosives dont go off like gunpowder, except when theyre in a gun. When theyre spread loose, you can put a match to them without the least risk: they just burn quietly like a bit of paper. (*Warming to the scientific interest of the subject*) Did you know that, Undershaft? Have you ever tried?

UNDERSHAFT: Not on a large scale, Mr Lomax. Bilton will give you a sample of gun cotton when you are leaving if you ask him. You can experiment with it at home. (BILTON *looks puzzled*).

SARAH: Bilton will do nothing of the sort, papa. I suppose it's your business to blow up the Russians and Japs; but you might really stop short of blowing up poor Cholly. (BILTON *gives it up and retires into the shed*).

LOMAX: My ownest, there is no danger. (*He sits beside her on the shell*).

[*LADY* BRITOMART *arrives from the town with a bouquet.*]

LADY BRITOMART (*impetuously*): Andrew: you shouldnt have let me see this place.

UNDERSHAFT: Why, my dear?

LADY BRITOMART: Never mind why: you shouldnt have: thats all. To think of all that (*indicating the town*) being yours! and that you have kept it to yourself all these years!

UNDERSHAFT: It does not belong to me. I belong to it. It is the Undershaft inheritance.

LADY BRITOMART: It is not. Your ridiculous cannons and that noisy banging foundry may be the Undershaft inheritance; but all that plate and linen, all that furniture and those houses and orchards and gardens belong to us. They belong to me: they are not a man's business. I wont give them up. You must be out of your senses to throw

them all away; and if you persist in such folly, I will call in a doctor.

UNDERSHAFT (*stooping to smell the bouquet*): Where did you get the flowers, my dear?

LADY BRITOMART: Your men presented them to me in your William Morris Labor Church.

CUSINS: Oh! It needed only that. A Labor Church! (*he mounts the firestep distractedly, and leans with his elbows on the parapet, turning his back to them*).

LADY BRITOMART: Yes, with Morris's words in mosaic letters ten feet high round the dome. NO MAN IS GOOD ENOUGH TO BE ANOTHER MAN'S MASTER. The cynicism of it!

UNDERSHAFT: It shocked the men at first, I am afraid. But now they take no more notice of it than of the ten commandments in church.

LADY BRITOMART: Andrew: you are trying to put me off the subject of the inheritance by profane jokes. Well, you shant. I dont ask it any longer for Stephen: he has inherited far too much of your perversity to be fit for it. But Barbara has rights as well as Stephen. Why should not Adolphus succeed to the inheritance? I could manage the town for him; and he can look after the cannons, if they are really necessary.

UNDERSHAFT: I should ask nothing better if Adolphus were a foundling. He is exactly the sort of new blood that is wanted in English business. But he's not a foundling; and theres an end of it. (*He makes for the office door*).

CUSINS (*turning to them*): Not quite. (*They all turn and stare at him*). I think—Mind! I am not committing myself in any way as to my future course—but I think the foundling difficulty can be got over. (*He jumps down to the emplacement*).

UNDERSHAFT: (*coming back to him*): What do you mean?

CUSINS: Well, I have something to say which is in the nature of a confession.

SARAH:
LADY BRITOMART: } Confession!
BARBARA:
STEPHEN:

LOMAX: Oh I say!

CUSINS: Yes, a confession. Listen, all. Until I met Barbara I thought myself in the main an honorable, truthful man, because I wanted the approval of my conscience more than I wanted anything else. But the moment I saw Barbara, I wanted her far more than the approval of my conscience.

LADY BRITOMART: Adolphus!

CUSINS: It is true. You accused me yourself, Lady Brit, of joining the Army to worship Barbara; and so I did. She bought my soul like a flower at a street corner; but she bought it for herself.

UNDERSHAFT: What! Not for Dionysos or another?

CUSINS: Dionysos and all the others are in herself. I

adored what was divine in her, and was therefore a true worshipper. But I was romantic about her too. I thought she was a woman of the people, and that a marriage with a professor of Greek would be far beyond the wildest social ambitions of her rank.

LADY BRITOMART: Adolphus!!

LOMAX: Oh I say!!!

CUSINS: When I learnt the horrible truth—

LADY BRITOMART: What do you mean by the horrible truth, pray?

CUSINS: That she was enormously rich; that her grandfather was an earl; that her father was the Prince of Darkness—

UNDERSHAFT: Chut!

CUSINS: —and that I was only an adventurer trying to catch a rich wife, then I stooped to deceive her about my birth.

BARBARA (*rising*): Dolly!

LADY BRITOMART: Your birth! Now Adolphus, dont dare to make up a wicked story for the sake of these wretched cannons. Remember: I have seen photographs of your parents; and the Agent General for South Western Australia knows them personally and has assured me that they are most respectable married people.

CUSINS: So they are in Australia; but here they are outcasts. Their marriage is legal in Australia, but not in England. My mother is my father's deceased wife's sister; and in this island I am consequently a foundling. (*Sensation*).

BARBARA: Silly! (*She climbs to the cannon, and leans, listening, in the angle it makes with the parapet*).

CUSINS: Is the subterfuge good enough, Machiavelli?

UNDERSHAFT (*thoughtfully*): Biddy: this may be a way out of the difficulty.

LADY BRITOMART: Stuff! A man cant make cannons any the better for being his own cousin instead of his proper self. (*She sits down on the rug with a bounce that expresses her downright contempt for their casuistry*).

UNDERSHAFT (*to CUSINS*): You are an educated man. That is against the tradition.

CUSINS: Once in ten thousand times it happens that the schoolboy is a born master of what they try to teach him. Greek has not destroyed my mind: it has nourished it. Besides, I did not learn it at an English public school.

UNDERSHAFT: Hm! Well, I cannot afford to be too particular: you have cornered the foundling market. Let it pass. You are eligible, Euripides: you are eligible.

BARBARA: Dolly: yesterday morning, when Stephen told us all about the tradition, you became very silent; and you have been strange and excited ever since. Were you thinking of your birth then?

CUSINS: When the finger of Destiny suddenly points

at a man in the middle of his breakfast, it makes him thoughtful.

UNDERSHAFT: Aha! You have had your eye on the business, my young friend, have you?

CUSINS: Take care! There is an abyss of moral horror between me and your accursed aerial battleships.

UNDERSHAFT: Never mind the abyss for the present. Let us settle the practical details and leave your final decision open. You know that you will have to change your name. Do you object to that?

CUSINS: Would any man named Adolphus—any man called Dolly!—object to be called something else?

UNDERSHAFT: Good. Now, as to money! I propose to treat you handsomely from the beginning. You shall start at a thousand a year.

CUSINS (*with sudden heat, his spectacles twinkling with mischief*): A thousand! You dare offer a miserable thousand to the son-in-law of a millionaire! No, by Heavens, Machiavelli! you shall not cheat me. You cannot do without me; and I can do without you. I must have two thousand five hundred a year for two years. At the end of that time, if I am a failure, I go. But if I am a success, and stay on, you must give me the other five thousand.

UNDERSHAFT: What other five thousand?

CUSINS: To make the two years up to five thousand a year. The two thousand five hundred is only half pay in case I should turn out a failure. The third year I must have ten per cent on the profits.

UNDERSHAFT (*taken aback*): Ten per cent! Why, man, do you know what my profits are?

CUSINS: Enormous, I hope: otherwise I shall require twentyfive per cent.

UNDERSHAFT: But, Mr Cusins, this is a serious matter of business. You are not bringing any capital into the concern.

CUSINS: What! no capital! Is my mastery of Greek no capital? Is my access to the subtlest thought, the loftiest poetry yet attained by humanity, no capital? My character! my intellect! my life! my career! what Barbara calls my soul! are these no capital? Say another word; and I double my salary.

UNDERSHAFT: Be reasonable—

CUSINS (*peremptorily*): Mr Undershaft: you have my terms. Take them or leave them.

UNDERSHAFT (*recovering himself*): Very well. I note your terms; and I offer you half.

CUSINS (*disgusted*): Half!

UNDERSHAFT (*firmly*): Half.

CUSINS: You call yourself a gentleman; and you offer me half!!

UNDERSHAFT: I do not call myself a gentleman; but I offer you half.

CUSINS: This to your future partner! your successor! your son-in-law!

BARBARA: You are selling your own soul, Dolly, not mine. Leave me out of the bargain, please.

UNDERSHAFT: Come! I will go a step further for Barbara's sake. I will give you three fifths; but that is my last word.

CUSINS: Done!

LOMAX: Done in the eye! Why, *I* get only eight hundred, you know.

CUSINS: By the way, Mac, I am a classical scholar, not an arithmetical one. Is three fifths more than half or less?

UNDERSHAFT: More, of course.

CUSINS: I would have taken two hundred and fifty. How you can succeed in business when you are willing to pay all that money to a University don who is obviously not worth a junior clerk's wages!—well! What will Lazarus say?

UNDERSHAFT: Lazarus is a gentle romantic Jew who cares for nothing but string quartets and stalls at fashionable theatres. He will be blamed for your rapacity in money matters, poor fellow! as he has hitherto been blamed for mine. You are a shark of the first order, Euripides. So much the better for the firm!

BARBARA: Is the bargain closed, Dolly? Does your soul belong to him now?

CUSINS: No: the price is settled: that is all. The real tug of war is still to come. What about the moral question?

LADY BRITOMART: There is no moral question in the matter at all, Adolphus. You must simply sell cannons and weapons to people whose cause is right and just, and refuse them to foreigners and criminals.

UNDERSHAFT (*determinedly*): No: none of that. You must keep the true faith of an Armorer, or you dont come in here.

CUSINS: What on earth is the true faith of an Armorer?

UNDERSHAFT: To give arms to all men who offer an honest price for them without respect of persons or principles: to aristocrat and republican, to Nihilist and Tsar, to Capitalist and Socialist, to Protestant and Catholic, to burglar and policeman, to black man white man and yellow man, to all sorts and conditions, all nationalities, all faiths, all follies, all causes and all crimes. The first Undershaft wrote up in his shop IF GOD GAVE THE HAND, LET NOT MAN WITHHOLD THE SWORD. The second wrote up ALL HAVE THE RIGHT TO FIGHT: NONE HAVE THE RIGHT TO JUDGE. The third wrote up TO MAN THE WEAPON: TO HEAVEN THE VICTORY. The fourth had no literary turn; so he did not write up anything; but he sold cannons to Napoleon under the nose of George the Third. The fifth wrote up PEACE SHALL NOT PREVAIL SAVE WITH A SWORD IN HER HAND. The sixth, my master, was the best of all. He wrote up NOTHING IS EVER DONE IN THIS WORLD UNTIL MEN ARE PREPARED TO KILL ONE ANOTHER IF IT IS NOT DONE. After that, there was nothing left for the seventh to say. So he wrote up, simply, UNASHAMED.

CUSINS: My good Machiavelli, I shall certainly write something up on the wall; only, as I shall write it in Greek, you wont be able to read it. But as to your Armorer's faith, if I take my neck out of the noose of my own morality I am not going to put it into the noose of yours. I shall sell cannons to whom I please and refuse them to whom I please. So there!

UNDERSHAFT: From the moment when you become Andrew Undershaft, you will never do as you please again. Dont come here lusting for power, young man.

CUSINS: If power were my aim I should not come here for it. You have no power.

UNDERSHAFT: None of my own, certainly.

CUSINS: I have more power than you, more will. You do not drive this place: it drives you. And what drives the place?

UNDERSHAFT (*enigmatically*): A will of which I am a part.

BARBARA (*startled*): Father! Do you know what you are saying; or are you laying a snare for my soul?

CUSINS: Dont listen to his metaphysics, Barbara. The place is driven by the most rascally part of society, the money hunters, the pleasure hunters, the military promotion hunters; and he is their slave.

UNDERSHAFT: Not necessarily. Remember the Armorer's Faith. I will take an order from a good man as cheerfully as from a bad one. If you good people prefer preaching and shirking to buying my weapons and fighting the rascals, dont blame me. I can make cannons: I cannot make courage and conviction. Bah! you tire me, Euripides, with your morality mongering. Ask Barbara: she understands. (*He suddenly reaches up and takes* BARBARA's *hands, looking powerfully into her eyes*) Tell him, my love, what power really means.

BARBARA (*hypnotized*): Before I joined the Salvation Army, I was in my own power; and the consequence was that I never knew what to do with myself. When I joined it, I had not time enough for all the things I had to do.

UNDERSHAFT (*approvingly*): Just so. And why was that, do you suppose?

BARBARA: Yesterday I should have said, because I was in the power of God. (*She resumes her self-possession, withdrawing her hands from his with a power equal to his own.*) But you came and shewed me that I was in the power of Bodger and Undershaft. Today I feel—oh! how can I put it into words? Sarah: do you remember the earthquake at Cannes, when we were little children?—how little the surprise of the first shock mattered compared to the dread and horror of waiting for the second? That is how I feel in this place today. I stood on the rock I thought eternal; and without a word of warning it reeled and crumbled under me. I was safe with an infinite wisdom watching me, an army marching to Salvation with me; and in a moment, at a stroke of your pen in a cheque book, I stood alone; and the heavens were empty. That was the first shock of the earthquake: I am waiting for the second.

UNDERSHAFT: Come, come, my daughter! dont make too much of your little tinpot tragedy. What do we do here when we spend years of work and thought and thousands of pounds of solid cash on a new gun or an aerial battleship that turns out just a hairsbreadth wrong after all? Scrap it. Scrap it without wasting another hour or another pound on it. Well, you have made for yourself something that you call a morality or a religion or what not. It doesnt fit the facts. Well, scrap it. Scrap it and get one that does fit. That is what is wrong with the world at present. It scraps its obsolete steam engines and dynamos; but it wont scrap its old prejudices and its old moralities and its old religions and its old political constitutions. Whats the result? In machinery it does very well; but in morals and religion and politics it is working at a loss that brings it nearer bankruptcy every year. Dont persist in that folly. If your old religion broke down yesterday, get a newer and a better one for tomorrow.

BARBARA: Oh how gladly I would take a better one to my soul! But you offer me a worse one. (*Turning on him with sudden vehemence*). Justify yourself: shew me some light through the darkness of this dreadful place, with its beautifully clean workshops, and respectable workmen, and model homes.

UNDERSHAFT: Cleanliness and respectability do not need justification, Barbara: they justify themselves. I see no darkness here, no dreadfulness. In your Salvation shelter I saw poverty, misery, cold and hunger. You gave them bread and treacle and dreams of heaven. I give from thirty shillings a week to twelve thousand a year. They find their own dreams; but I look after the drainage.

BARBARA: And their souls?

UNDERSHAFT: I save their souls just as I saved yours.

BARBARA (*revolted*): You saved my soul! What do you mean?

UNDERSHAFT: I fed you and clothed you and housed you. I took care that you should have money enough to live handsomely—more than enough; so that you could be wasteful, careless, generous. That saved your soul from the seven deadly sins.

BARBARA (*bewildered*): The seven deadly sins!

UNDERSHAFT: Yes, the deadly seven. (*Counting on his fingers*) Food, clothing, firing, rent, taxes, respectability and children. Nothing can lift those seven millstones from Man's neck but money; and the spirit cannot soar until the millstones are lifted. I lifted them from your spirit. I enabled Barbara to become Major Barbara; and I saved her from the crime of poverty.

CUSINS: Do you call poverty a crime?

UNDERSHAFT: The worst of crimes. All the other crimes are virtues beside it: all the other dishonors are chivalry itself by comparison. Poverty blights whole cities; spreads horrible pestilences; strikes dead the very souls of all who come within sight, sound, or smell of it. What you call crime is nothing: a murder here and a theft there, a blow now and a curse then: what do they matter? they are only the accidents and illnesses of life: there are not fifty genuine professional criminals in London. But there are millions of poor people, abject people, dirty people, ill fed, ill clothed people. They poison us morally and physically: they kill the happiness of society: they force us to do away with our own liberties and to organize unnatural cruelties for fear they should rise against us and drag us down into their abyss. Only fools fear crime: we all fear poverty. Pah! (*turning on BARBARA*) you talk of your half-saved ruffian in West Ham: you accuse me of dragging his soul back to perdition. Well, bring him to me here; and I will drag his soul back again to salvation for you. Not by words and dreams; but by thirtyeight shillings a week, a sound house in a handsome street, and a permanent job. In three weeks he will have a fancy waistcoat; in three months a tall hat and a chapel sitting; before the end of the year he will shake hands with a duchess at a Primrose League meeting, and join the Conservative Party.

BARBARA: And will he be the better for that?

UNDERSHAFT: You know he will. Dont be a hypocrite, Barbara. He will be better fed, better housed, better clothed, better behaved; and his children will be pounds heavier and bigger. That will be better than an American cloth mattress in a shelter, chopping firewood, eating bread and treacle, and being forced to kneel down from time to time to thank heaven for it: knee drill, I think you call it. It is cheap work converting starving men with a Bible in one hand and a slice of bread in the other. I will undertake to convert West Ham to Mahometanism on the same terms. Try your hand on my men: their souls are hungry because their bodies are full.

BARBARA: And leave the east end to starve?

UNDERSHAFT (*his energetic tone dropping into one of bitter and brooding remembrance*): I was an east ender. I moralized and starved until one day I swore that I would be a full-fed free man at all costs;

that nothing should stop me except a bullet, neither reason nor morals nor the lives of other men. I said "Thou shalt starve ere I starve"; and with that word I became free and great. I was a dangerous man until I had my will: now I am a useful, beneficent, kindly person. That is the history of most self-made millionaires, I fancy. When it is the history of every Englishman we shall have an England worth living in.

LADY BRITOMART: Stop making speeches, Andrew. This is not the place for them.

UNDERSHAFT (*punctured*): My dear: I have no other means of conveying my ideas.

LADY BRITOMART: Your ideas are nonsense. You got on because you were selfish and unscrupulous.

UNDERSHAFT: Not at all. I had the strongest scruples about poverty and starvation. Your moralists are quite unscrupulous about both: they make virtues of them. I had rather be a thief than a pauper. I had rather be a murderer than a slave. I dont want to be either; but if you force the alternative on me, then, by Heaven, I'll choose the braver and more moral one. I hate poverty and slavery worse than any other crimes whatsoever. And let me tell you this. Poverty and slavery have stood up for centuries to your sermons and leading articles: they will not stand up to my machine guns. Dont preach at them: dont reason with them. Kill them.

BARBARA: Killing. Is that your remedy for everything?

UNDERSHAFT: It is the final test of conviction, the only lever strong enough to overturn a social system, the only way of saying Must. Let six hundred and seventy fools loose in the streets; and three policemen can scatter them. But huddle them together in a certain house in Westminster; and let them go through certain ceremonies and call themselves certain names until at last they get the courage to kill; and your six hundred and seventy fools become a government. Your pious mob fills up ballot papers and imagines it is governing its masters; but the ballot paper that really governs is the paper that has a bullet wrapped up in it.

CUSINS: That is perhaps why, like most intelligent people, I never vote.

UNDERSHAFT: Vote! Bah! When you vote, you only change the names of the cabinet. When you shoot, you pull down governments, inaugurate new epochs, abolish old orders and set up new. Is that historically true, Mr Learned man, or is it not?

CUSINS: It is historically true. I loathe having to admit it. I repudiate your sentiments. I abhor your nature. I defy you in every possible way. Still, it is true. But it ought not to be true.

UNDERSHAFT: Ought! ought! ought! ought! ought! Are you going to spend your life saying ought, like the rest of our moralists? Turn your oughts into shalls, man. Come and make explosives with me. Whatever can blow men up can blow society up. The history of the world is the history of those who had courage enough to embrace this truth. Have you the courage to embrace it, Barbara?

LADY BRITOMART: Barbara: I positively forbid you to listen to your father's abominable wickedness. And you, Adolphus, ought to know better than to go about saying that wrong things are true. What does it matter whether they are true if they are wrong?

UNDERSHAFT: What does it matter whether they are wrong if they are true?

LADY BRITOMART (*rising*): Children: come home instantly. Andrew: I am exceedingly sorry I allowed you to call on us. You are wickeder than ever. Come at once.

BARBARA (*shaking her head*): It's no use running away from wicked people, mamma.

LADY BRITOMART: It is every use. It shews your disapprobation of them.

BARBARA: It does not save them.

LADY BRITOMART: I can see that you are going to disobey me. Sarah: are you coming home or are you not?

SARAH: I daresay it's very wicked of papa to make cannons; but I dont think I shall cut him on that account.

LOMAX (*pouring oil on the troubled waters*): The fact is, you know, there is a certain amount of tosh about this notion of wickedness. It doesnt work. You must look at facts. Not that I would say a word in favor of anything wrong; but then, you see, all sorts of chaps are always doing all sorts of things; and we have to fit them in somehow, dont you know. What I mean is that you cant go cutting everybody; and thats about what it comes to. (*Their rapt attention to his eloquence makes him nervous*). Perhaps I dont make myself clear.

LADY BRITOMART: You are lucidity itself, Charles. Because Andrew is successful and has plenty of money to give to Sarah, you will flatter him and encourage him in his wickedness.

LOMAX (*unruffled*): Well, where the carcase is, there will the eagles be gathered, dont you know. (*To Undershaft*) Eh? What?

UNDERSHAFT: Precisely. By the way, may I call you Charles?

LOMAX: Delighted. Cholly is the usual ticket.

UNDERSHAFT (*to* LADY BRITOMART): Biddy—

LADY BRITOMART (*violently*): Dont dare call me Biddy. Charles Lomax: you are a fool. Adolphus Cusins: you are a Jesuit. Stephen: you are a prig. Barbara: you are a lunatic. Andrew: you are a vulgar tradesman. Now you all know my opinion; and my conscience is clear, at all events (*she sits down with a vehemence that the rug fortunately softens).*

UNDERSHAFT: My dear: you are the incarnation of morality. (*She snorts*). Your conscience is clear and your duty done when you have called everybody names. Come, Euripides! it is getting late; and we all want to go home. Make up your mind.

CUSINS: Understand this, you old demon—

LADY BRITOMART: Adolphus!

UNDERSHAFT: Let him alone, Biddy. Proceed, Euripides.

CUSINS: You have me in a horrible dilemma. I want Barbara.

UNDERSHAFT: Like all young men, you greatly exaggerate the difference between one young woman and another.

BARBARA: Quite true, Dolly.

CUSINS: I also want to avoid being a rascal.

UNDERSHAFT (*with biting contempt*): You lust for personal righteousness, for self-approval, for what you call a good conscience, for what Barbara calls salvation, for what I call patronizing people who are not so lucky as yourself.

CUSINS: I do not: all the poet in me recoils from being a good man. But there are things in me that I must reckon with. Pity—

UNDERSHAFT: Pity! The scavenger of misery.

CUSINS: Well, love.

UNDERSHAFT: I know. You love the needy and the outcast: you love the oppressed races, the negro, the Indian ryot, the underdog everywhere. Do you love the Japanese? Do you love the French? Do you love the English?

CUSINS: No. Every true Englishman detests the English. We are the wickedest nation on earth; and our success is a moral horror.

UNDERSHAFT: That is what comes of your gospel of love, is it?

CUSINS: May I not love even my father-in-law?

UNDERSHAFT: Who wants your love, man? By what right do you take the liberty of offering it to me? I will have your due heed and respect, or I will kill you. But your love! Damn your impertinence!

CUSINS (*grinning*): I may not be able to control my affections, Mac.

UNDERSHAFT: You are fencing, Euripides. You are weakening: your grip is slipping. Come! try your last weapon. Pity and love have broken in your hand: forgiveness is still left.

CUSINS: No: forgiveness is a beggar's refuge. I am with you there: we must pay our debts.

UNDERSHAFT: Well said. Come! you will suit me. Remember the words of Plato.

CUSINS (*starting*): Plato! You dare quote Plato to me!

UNDERSHAFT: Plato says, my friend, that society cannot be saved until either the Professors of Greek take to making gunpowder, or else the makers of gunpowder become Professor of Greek.

CUSINS: Oh, tempter, cunning tempter!

UNDERSHAFT: Come! choose, man, choose.

CUSINS: But perhaps Barbara will not marry me if I make the wrong choice.

BARBARA: Perhaps not.

CUSINS (*desperately perplexed*): You hear!

BARBARA: Father: do you love nobody?

UNDERSHAFT: I love my best friend.

LADY BRITOMART: And who is that, pray?

UNDERSHAFT: My bravest enemy. That is the man who keeps me up to the mark.

CUSINS: You know, the creature is really a sort of poet in his way. Suppose he is a great man, after all!

UNDERSHAFT: Suppose you stop talking and make up your mind, my young friend.

CUSINS: But you are driving me against my nature. I hate war.

UNDERSHAFT: Hatred is the coward's revenge for being intimidated. Dare you make war on war? Here are the means: my friend Mr Lomax is sitting on them.

LOMAX (*springing up*): Oh I say! You dont mean that this thing is loaded, do you? My ownest: come off it.

SARAH (*sitting placidly on the shell*): If I am to be blown up, the more thoroughly it is done the better. Dont fuss, Cholly.

LOMAX (*to* UNDERSHAFT, *strongly remonstrant*): Your own daughter, you know!

UNDERSHAFT: So I see. (*To* CUSINS) Well, my friend, may we expect you here at six tomorrow morning?

CUSINS (*firmly*): Not on any account. I will see the whole establishment blown up with its own dynamite before I will get up at five. My hours are healthy, rational hours: eleven to five.

UNDERSHAFT: Come when you please: before a week you will come at six and stay until I turn you out for the sake of your health. (*Calling*) Bilton! (*He turns to* LADY BRITOMART, *who rises*). My dear: let us leave these two young people to themselves for a moment. (BILTON *comes from the shed*). I am going to take you through the gun cotton shed.

BILTON (*barring the way*): You cant take anything explosive in here, sir.

LADY BRITOMART: What do you mean? Are you alluding to me?

BILTON (*unmoved*): No, maam. Mr Undershaft has the other gentleman's matches in his pocket.

LADY BRITOMART (*abruptly*): Oh! I beg your pardon. (*She goes into the shed*).

UNDERSHAFT: Quite right, Bilton, quite right: here you are. (*He gives* BILTON *the box of matches*). Come, Stephen. Come, Charles. Bring Sarah. (*He passes into the shed*).

[Bilton opens the box and deliberately drops the matches into the fire-bucket.]

LOMAX: Oh I say! (BILTON *stolidly hands him the empty box*). Infernal nonsense! Pure scientific ignorance! (*He goes in*).

SARAH: Am I all right, Bilton?

BILTON: Youll have to put on list slippers, miss: thats all. Weve got em inside. (*She goes in*).

STEPHEN (*very seriously to* CUSINS): Dolly, old fellow, think. Think before you decide. Do you feel that you are a sufficiently practical man? It is a huge undertaking, an enormous responsibility. All this mass of business will be Greek to you.

CUSINS: Oh, I think it will be much less difficult than Greek.

STEPHEN: Well, I just want to say this before I leave you to yourselves. Dont let anything I have said about right and wrong prejudice you against this great chance in life. I have satisfied myself that the business is one of the highest character and a credit to our country. (*Emotionally*) I am very proud of my father. I—(*Unable to proceed, he presses* CUSINS' *hand and goes hastily into the shed, followed by* BILTON).

[BARBARA *and* CUSINS, *left alone together, look at one another silently.*]

CUSINS: Barbara: I am going to accept this offer.

BARBARA: I thought you would.

CUSINS: You understand, dont you, that I had to decide without consulting you. If I had thrown the burden of the choice on you, you would sooner or later have despised me for it.

BARBARA: Yes: I did not want you to sell your soul for me any more than for this inheritance.

CUSINS: It is not the sale of my soul that troubles me: I have sold it too often to care about that. I have sold it for a professorship. I have sold it for an income. I have sold it to escape being imprisoned for refusing to pay taxes for hangmen's ropes and unjust wars and things that I abhor. What is all human conduct but the daily and hourly sale of our souls for trifles? What I am now selling it for is neither money nor position nor comfort, but for reality and for power.

BARBARA: You know that you will have no power, and that he has none.

CUSINS: I know. It is not for myself alone. I want to make power for the world.

BARBARA: I want to make power for the world too; but it must be spiritual power.

CUSINS: I think all power is spiritual: these cannons will not go off by themselves. I have tried to make spiritual power by teaching Greek. But the world can never be really touched by a dead language and a dead civilization. The people must have power; and the people cannot have Greek. Now the power that is made here can be wielded by all men.

BARBARA: Power to burn women's houses down and kill their sons and tear their husbands to pieces.

CUSINS: You cannot have power for good without having power for evil too. Even mother's milk nourishes murderers as well as heroes. This power which only tears men's bodies to pieces has never been so horribly abused as the intellectual power, the imaginative power, the poetic, religious power that can enslave men's souls. As a teacher of Greek I gave the intellectual man weapons against the common man. I now want to give the common man weapons against the intellectual man. I love the common people. I want to arm them against the lawyers, the doctors, the priests, the literary men, the professors, the artists, and the politicians, who, once in authority, are more disastrous and tyrannical than all the fools, rascals, and impostors. I want a power simple enough for common men to use, yet strong enough to force the intellectual oligarchy to use its genius for the general good.

BARBARA: Is there no higher power than that (*pointing to the shell*)?

CUSINS: Yes; but that power can destroy the higher powers just as a tiger can destroy a man: therefore Man must master that power first. I admitted this when the Turks and Greeks were last at war. My best pupil went out to fight for Hellas. My parting gift to him was not a copy of Plato's Republic, but a revolver and a hundred Undershaft cartridges. The blood of every Turk he shot—if he shot any—is on my head as well as on Undershaft's. That act committed me to this place for ever. Your father's challenge has beaten me. Dare I make war on war? I dare. I must. I will. And now, is it all over between us?

BARBARA (*touched by his evident dread of her answer*): Silly baby Dolly! How could it be?

CUSINS (*overjoyed*): Then you—you—you—Oh for my drum! (*He flourishes imaginary drumsticks*).

BARBARA (*angered by his levity*): Take care, Dolly, take care. Oh, if only I could get away from you and from father and from it all! if I could have the wings of a dove and fly away to heaven!

CUSINS: And leave me!

BARBARA: Yes, you, and all the other naughty mischievous children of men. But I cant. I was happy in the Salvation Army for a moment. I escaped from the world into a paradise of enthusiasm and prayer and soul saving; but the moment our money ran short, it all came back to Bodger: it was he who saved our people; he, and the Prince of Darkness, my papa. Undershaft and Bodger: their hands stretch everywhere: when we feed a starving fellow creature, it is with their bread, because there is no other bread; when we tend the sick, it is in the hospitals they endow; if we turn from the churches they build, we must kneel on the stones of the streets they pave. As long as that lasts, there is no getting away from them. Turning our backs on Bodger and Undershaft is turning our backs on life.

CUSINS: I thought you were determined to turn your back on the wicked side of life.

BARBARA: There is no wicked side: life is all one. And I never wanted to shirk my share in whatever evil must be endured, whether it be sin or suffering. I wish I could cure you of middle-class ideas, Dolly.

CUSINS (*gasping*): Middle cl—! A snub! A social snub to me! from the daughter of a foundling!

BARBARA: That is why I have no class, Dolly: I come straight out of the heart of the whole people. If I were middle-class I should turn my back on my father's business; and we should both live in an artistic drawing room, with you reading the reviews in one corner, and I in the other at the piano, playing Schumann: both very superior persons, and neither of us a bit of use. Sooner than that, I would sweep out the guncotton shed, or be one of Bodger's barmaids. Do you know what would have happened if you had refused papa's offer?

CUSINS: I wonder!

BARBARA: I should have given you up and married the man who accepted it. After all, my dear old mother has more sense than any of you. I felt like her when I saw this place—felt that I must have it—that never, never, never could I let it go; only she thought it was the houses and the kitchen ranges and the linen and china, when it was really all the human souls to be saved: not weak souls in starved bodies, sobbing with gratitude for a scrap of bread and treacle, but fullfed, quarrelsome, snobbish, uppish creatures, all standing on their little rights and dignities, and thinking that my father ought to be greatly obliged to them for making so much money for him—and so he ought. That is where salvation is really wanted. My father shall never throw it in my teeth again that my converts were bribed with bread. (*She is transfigured*). I have got rid of the bribe of bread. I have got rid of the bribe of heaven. Let God's work be done for its own sake: the work he had to create us to do because it cannot be done

except by living men and women. When I die, let him be in my debt, not I in his; and let me forgive him as becomes a woman of my rank.

CUSINS: Then the way of life lies through the factory of death?

BARBARA: Yes, through the raising of hell to heaven and of man to God, through the unveiling of an eternal light in the Valley of The Shadow. (*Seizing him with both hands*) Oh, did you think my courage would never come back? did you believe that I was a deserter? that I, who have stood in the streets, and taken my people to my heart, and talked of the holiest and greatest things with them, could ever turn back and chatter foolishly to fashionable people about nothing in a drawing room? Never, never, never, never: Major Barbara will die with the colors. Oh! and I have my dear little Dolly boy still; and he has found me my place and my work. Glory Hallelujah! (*She kisses him*).

CUSINS: My dearest: consider my delicate health. I cannot stand as much happiness as you can.

BARBARA: Yes: it is not easy work being in love with me, is it? But it's good for you. (*She runs to the shed, and calls, childlike*) Mamma! Mamma! (BILTON *comes out of the shed, followed by* UNDERSHAFT). I want Mamma.

UNDERSHAFT: She is taking off her list slippers, dear. (*He passes on to* CUSINS). Well? What does she say?

CUSINS: She has gone right up into the skies.

LADY BRITOMART (*coming from the shed and stopping on the steps, obstructing* SARAH, *who follows with* LOMAX. BARBARA *clutches like a baby at her mother's skirt*): Barbara: when will you learn to be independent and to act and think for yourself? I know as well as possible what that cry of "Mamma, Mamma," means. Always running to me!

SARAH (*touching* LADY BRITOMART'S *ribs with her finger tips and imitating a bicycle horn*): Pip! pip!

LADY BRITOMART (*highly indignant*): How dare you say Pip! pip! to me, Sarah? You are both very naughty children. What do you want, Barbara?

BARBARA: I want a house in the village to live in with Dolly. (*Dragging at the skirt*) Come and tell me which one to take.

UNDERSHAFT (*to* CUSINS): Six o'clock tomorrow morning, Euripides.

The End

OSCAR WILDE (1854–1900)

Oscar Wilde was born into a wealthy and well-educated family in Dublin. He was educated at the Portora Royal School, Enniskillen, and attended Trinity College, Dublin, and Magdalen College, Oxford, where he completed his degree with distinction. At Oxford he associated with the famous writer and art critic John Ruskin, with whom he traveled in Europe after graduation. Wilde cultivated and affected a highly aesthetic sensibility throughout his life.

In 1884 Wilde married Constance Lloyd, and the couple had two sons within two years. But by 1891 he had also been involved in several homosexual liaisons, and in that year he met and formed a relationship with Lord Alfred Douglas. The connection ended when Douglas's father, the Marquis of Queensberry, publicly denounced Wilde as a sodomite. In a famous and highly publicized case, Wilde brought suit against Queensberry for libel, but lost; he was convicted of sodomy and sentenced to two years hard labor. The scandal destroyed his family, and on his release from prison in 1897, Wilde went abroad to live in virtual exile in Italy, Sicily, Switzerland, and France. These terrible years for him were memorialized in his autobiographical *De Profundis*. Plagued by financial problems and ill health resulting from his trial and imprisonment, Wilde died in Paris in 1900 at age 46.

Wilde's first novel, *The Picture of Dorian Grey* (1890), concerns a man who remains young-looking while his true self languishes in a closet. The book is eerily prophetic of Wilde's own life—the character's devotion to sensuality destroys him. Although it has since become a classic, initially the novel failed, and Wilde then tried his hand at writing plays. Between 1891 and 1895 he wrote a series of brilliant and remarkably successful plays: *Salome* (1891), which was banned by the Lord Chamberlain in 1892; *Lady Windermere's Fan* (1892); *A Woman of No Importance* (1893); *An Ideal Husband* (1895); and *The Importance of Being Earnest* (1895). All of Wilde's plays offer witty and insightful social commentaries on upper-class British society.

Wilde's career as a playwright lasted only five years before it was cut short by the events in his life. Two months after the opening of *The Importance of Being Earnest*, news of Wilde's conviction of a moral offense effectively undermined his reputation as a playwright, and his work was not performed again until after his death. In one of the many ironies of history, every one of Wilde's plays still entertains, and his plays are often revived, in contrast to most other dramatic work produced during this period in England.

The Importance of Being Earnest

Wilde's play owes much to the construction techniques of the well-made play pioneered by Eugène Scribe and to the devices of melodrama. In melodramas, as in romances, the identity of the hero is often obscured by his apparent low social standing, and the final turn of the plot reveals the hero to be of high social stature, thus providing a solution to all of the characters' (and the play's) problems. In this play, Wilde capitalizes on the conventions of identity and disguise, and on the plot device of giving information in the first act which provides the surprise revelation of the last. Wilde uses these well-made-play conventions brilliantly, turning the play into a parody of the conventions themselves. Many of the devices, characters, and turns of the plot derive from contemporary farces and comedies. As critics have pointed out, for example, the name *Bunbury* comes from *The Godpapa* (1891) and the idea of the child lost with the luggage comes from *The Lost Child* (1863).

In *The Importance of Being Earnest*, Algernon must travel in polite London social circles, and he has developed a means of avoiding tedious social engagements—like Lady Bracknell's dinner parties. He has invented a friend named Bunbury who lives in the country and often needs Algernon's help, so Algernon has a ready excuse whenever he needs one. Meanwhile, Jack, who lives the life of a country gentlemen, has a similar strategy. His imaginary brother Ernest lives in the city. When in the city, Jack pretends to be Ernest, and both Algernon and Gwendolyn know him by that name.

If Wilde was adept at appropriating the conventions of contemporary plays, his satiric handling of them has more affinity with Restoration with than late Victorian humor. The probing into characters' backgrounds to confirm their economic status, family line, and social class before entering into a marriage contract, for example, is the substance of Congreve's *The Way of the World*. Not as cynical about his society as Congreve was, Wilde is nonetheless every bit as witty in exposing its stiffness and pretensions, from Gwendolyn's knowledge of the proper form for marriage proposals to Lady Bracknell's horrified discovery that Jack's "family line" runs to Brighton.

At the request of his producer, Wilde cut the original play from four to three acts, making it much tighter in structure. From the beginning, the public responded to it enthusiastically, and the play was an enormous success when it opened in London in 1895. Its success lasted for only two months, however. Because of the scandal surrounding Wilde's conviction for sodomy, his reputation was ruined for the rest of his life. His work was not staged again or reexamined until after his death; that reexamination is still in progress. Since Wilde's death, however, *The Importance of Being Earnest* has become one of the most popular plays of its era.

Oscar Wilde
The Importance of Being Earnest

CHARACTERS

JOHN WORTHING, J. P.
ALGERNON MONCRIEFF
REV. CANON CHASUBLE, D. D.
MERRIMAN (Butler)
LANE (Manservant)

LADY BRACKNELL
HON. GWENDOLEN FAIRFAX
CECILY CARDEW
MISS PRISM (Governess)

THE SCENES OF THE PLAY

ACT I   Algernon Moncrieff's Flat in Half-Moon Street, W.
ACT II.   The Garden at the Manor House, Woolton.
ACT III. Drawing-Room of the Manor House, Woolton.
Time—The Present.
Place—London.

ACT I

SCENE—Morning-room in ALGERNON's flat in Half Moon Street. The room is luxuriously and artistically furnished. The sound of a piano is heard in the adjoining room.

[LANE is arranging afternoon tea on the table, and after the music has ceased, ALGERNON enters.]

ALGERNON: Did you hear what I was playing, Lane?
LANE: I didn't think it polite to listen, sir.
ALGERNON: I'm sorry for that, for your sake. I don't play accurately—anyone can play accurately—but I play with wonderful expression. As far as the piano is concerned, sentiment is my forte. I keep science for Life.
LANE: Yes, sir.
ALGERNON: And, speaking of the science of Life, have you got the cucumber sandwiches cut for Lady Bracknell?
LANE: Yes, sir. (*Hands them on a salver.*)
ALGERNON (*inspects them, takes two, and sits down on the sofa*): Oh! . . . by the way, Lane, I see from your book that on Thursday night, when Lord Shoreman and Mr. Worthing were dining with me, eight bottles of champagne are entered as having been consumed.
LANE: Yes, sir; eight bottles and a pint.
ALGERNON: Why is it that at a bachelor's establishment the servants invariably drink the champagne? I ask merely for information.
LANE: I attribute it to the superior quality of the wine, sir. I have often observed that in married households the champagne is rarely of a first-rate brand.
ALGERNON: Good Heavens! Is marriage so demoralizing as that?
LANE: I believe it *is* a very pleasant state, sir. I have had very little experience of it myself up to the present. I have only been married once. That was in consequence of a misunderstanding between myself and a young person.
ALGERNON (*languidly*): I don't know that I am much interested in your family life, Lane.
LANE: No, sir; it is not a very interesting subject. I never think of it myself.
ALGERNON: Very natural, I am sure. That will do, Lane, thank you.
LANE: Thank you, sir.

[LANE goes out.]

ALGERNON: Lane's views on marriage seem somewhat lax. Really, if the lower orders don't set us a good example, what on earth is the use of them? They seem, as a class, to have absolutely no sense of moral responsibility.

[Enter LANE.]

LANE: Mr. Ernest Worthing.

[Enter JACK.]

[LANE goes out.]

ALGERNON: How are you, my dear Ernest? What brings you up to town?
JACK: Oh, pleasure, pleasure! What else should bring one anywhere? Eating as usual, I see, Algy!
ALGERNON (*stiffly*): I believe it is customary in good

society to take some slight refreshment at five o'clock. Where have you been since last Thursday?

JACK (*sitting down on the sofa*): In the country.

ALGERNON: What on earth do you do there?

JACK (*pulling off his gloves*): When one is in town one amuses oneself. When one is in the country one amuses other people. It is excessively boring.

ALGERNON: And who are the people you amuse?

JACK (*airily*): Oh, neighbours, neighbours.

ALGERNON: Got nice neighbours in your part of Shropshire?

JACK: Perfectly horrid! Never speak to one of them.

ALGERNON: How immensely you must amuse them! (*Goes over and takes sandwich.*) By the way, Shropshire is your county, is it not?

JACK: Eh? Shropshire? Yes, of course. Hallo! Why all these cups? Why cucumber sandwiches? Why such reckless extravagance in one so young? Who is coming to tea?

ALGERNON: Oh! merely Aunt Augusta and Gwendolen.

JACK: How perfectly delightful!

ALGERNON: Yes, that is all very well; but I am afraid Aunt Augusta won't quite approve of your being here.

JACK: May I ask why?

ALGERNON: My dear fellow, the way you flirt with Gwendolen is perfectly disgraceful. It is almost as bad as the way Gwendolen flirts with you.

JACK: I am in love with Gwendolen. I have come up to town expressly to propose to her.

ALGERNON: I thought you had come up for pleasure? . . . I call that business.

JACK: How utterly unromantic you are!

ALGERNON: I really don't see anything romantic in proposing. It is very romantic to be in love. But there is nothing romantic about a definite proposal. Why, one may be accepted. One usually is, I believe. Then the excitement is all over. The very essence of romance is uncertainty. If ever I get married, I'll certainly try to forget the fact.

JACK: I have no doubt about that, dear Algy. The Divorce Court was specially invented for people whose memories are so curiously constituted.

ALGERNON: Oh! there is no use speculating on that subject. Divorces are made in Heaven—(JACK *puts out his hand to take a sandwich.* ALGERNON *at once interferes.*) Please don't touch the cucumber sandwiches. They are ordered specially for Aunt Augusta. (*Takes one and eats it.*)

JACK: Well, you have been eating them all the time.

ALGERNON: That is quite a different matter. She is my aunt. (*Takes plate from below.*) Have some bread and butter. The bread and butter is for Gwendolen. Gwendolen is devoted to bread and butter.

JACK (*advancing to table and helping himself*): And very good bread and butter it is too.

ALGERNON: Well, my dear fellow, you need not eat as if you were going to eat it all. You behave as if you were married to her already. You are not married to her already, and I don't think you ever will be.

JACK: Why on earth do you say that?

ALGERNON: Well, in the first place girls never marry the men they flirt with. Girls don't think it right.

JACK: Oh, that is nonsense!

ALGERNON: It isn't. It is a great truth. It accounts for the extraordinary number of bachelors that one sees all over the place. In the second place, I don't give my consent.

JACK: Your consent!

ALGERNON: My dear fellow, Gwendolen is my first cousin. And before I allow you to marry her, you will have to clear up the whole question of Cecily. (*Rings bell.*)

JACK: Cecily! What on earth do you mean? What do you mean, Algy, by Cecily? I don't know anyone of the name of Cecily.

[Enter LANE.]

ALGERNON: Bring me that cigarette case Mr. Worthing left in the smoking-room the last time he dined here.

LANE: Yes, sir.

[LANE goes out.]

JACK: Do you mean to say you have had my cigarette case all this time? I wish to goodness you had let me know. I have been writing frantic letters to Scotland Yard about it. I was very nearly offering a large reward.

ALGERNON: Well, I wish you would offer one. I happen to be more than usually hard up.

JACK: There is no good offering a large reward now that the thing is found.

[Enter LANE with the cigarette case on a salver. ALGERNON takes it at once. LANE goes out.]

ALGERNON: I think that is rather mean of you, Ernest, I must say. (*Opens case and examines it.*) However, it makes no matter, for, now that I look at the inscription inside, I find that the thing isn't yours after all.

JACK: Of course it's mine. (*Moving to him.*) You have seen me with it a hundred times, and you have no right whatsoever to read what is written inside. It is a very ungentlemanly thing to read a private cigarette case.

ALGERNON: Oh! it is absurd to have a hard-and-fast rule about what one should read and what one shouldn't. More than half of modern culture depends on what one shouldn't read.

JACK: I am quite aware of the fact, and I don't propose to discuss modern culture. It isn't the sort of thing one should talk of in private. I simply want my cigarette case back.

ALGERNON: Yes; but this isn't your cigarette case. This cigarette case is a present from someone of the name of Cecily, and you said you didn't know anyone of that name.

JACK: Well, if you want to know, Cecily happens to be my aunt.

ALGERNON: Your aunt!

JACK: Yes. Charming old lady she is, too. Lives at Tunbridge Wells. Just give it back to me, Algy.

ALGERNON (*retreating to back of sofa*): But why does she call herself little Cecily if she is your aunt and lives at Tunbridge Wells? (*Reading.*) "From little Cecily with her fondest love."

JACK (*moving to sofa and kneeling upon it*): My dear fellow, what on earth is there in that? Some aunts are tall, some aunts are not tall. That is a matter that surely an aunt may be allowed to decide for herself. You seem to think that every aunt should be exactly like your aunt! That is absurd! For Heaven's sake give me back my cigarette case. (*Follows* ERNEST *round the room.*)

ALGERNON: Yes. But why does your aunt call you her uncle? "From little Cecily, with her fondest love to her dear Uncle Jack." There is no objection, I admit, to an aunt being a small aunt, but why an aunt, no matter what her size may be, should call her own nephew her uncle, I can't quite make out. Besides, your name isn't Jack at all; it is Ernest.

JACK: It isn't Ernest; it's Jack.

ALGERNON: You have always told me it was Ernest. I have introduced you to everyone as Ernest. You answer to the name of Ernest. You look as if your name was Ernest. You are the most earnest looking person I ever saw in my life. It is perfectly absurd your saying that your name isn't Ernest. It's on your cards. Here is one of them. (*Taking it from case.*) "Mr. Ernest Worthing, B 4, The Albany." I'll keep this as a proof your name is Ernest if ever you attempt to deny it to me, or to Gwendolen, or to anyone else. (*Puts the card in his pocket.*)

JACK: Well, my name is Ernest in town and Jack in the country, and the cigarette case was given to me in the country.

ALGERNON: Yes, but that does not account for the fact that your small Aunt Cecily, who lives at Tunbridge Wells, calls you her dear uncle. Come, old boy, you had much better have the thing out at once.

JACK: My dear Algy, you talk exactly as if you were a dentist. It is very vulgar to talk like a dentist when one isn't a dentist. It produces a false impression.

ALGERNON: Well, that is exactly what dentists always do. Now, go on! Tell me the whole thing. I may mention that I have always suspected you of being a confirmed and secret Bunburyist; and I am quite sure of it now.

JACK: Bunburyist? What on earth do you mean by a Bunburyist?

ALGERNON: I'll reveal to you the meaning of that incomparable expression as soon as you are kind enough to inform me why you are Ernest in town and Jack in the country.

JACK: Well, produce my cigarette case first.

ALGERNON: Here it is. (*Hands cigarette case.*) Now produce your explanation, and pray make it improbable. (*Sits on sofa.*)

JACK: My dear fellow, there is nothing improbable about my explanation at all. In fact it's perfectly ordinary. Old Mr. Thomas Cardew, who adopted me when I was a little boy, made me in his will guardian to his grand-daughter, Miss Cecily Cardew. Cecily, who addresses me as her uncle from motives of respect that you could not possibly appreciate, lives at my place in the country under the charge of her admirable governess, Miss Prism.

ALGERNON: Where is that place in the country, by the way?

JACK: That is nothing to you, dear boy. You are not going to be invited. . . . I may tell you candidly that the place is not in Shropshire.

ALGERNON: I suspected that, my dear fellow! I have Bunburyed all over Shropshire on two separate occasions. Now, go on. Why are you Ernest in town and Jack in the country?

JACK: My dear Algy, I don't know whether you will be able to understand my real motives. You are hardly serious enough. When one is placed in the position of guardian, one has to adopt a very high moral tone on all subjects. It's one's duty to do so. And as a high moral tone can hardly be said to conduce very much to either one's health or one's happiness, in order to get up to town I have always pretended to have a younger brother of the name of Ernest, who lives in the Albany, and gets into the most dreadful scrapes. That, my dear Algy, is the whole truth pure and simple.

ALGERNON: The truth is rarely pure and never simple. Modern life would be very tedious if it were either, and modern literature a complete impossibility!

JACK: That wouldn't be at all a bad thing.

ALGERNON: Literary criticism is not your forte, my dear fellow. Don't try it. You should leave that to people who haven't been at a University. They do it so well in the daily papers. What you really are in a Bunburyist. I was quite right in saying you were a Bunburyist. You are one of the most advanced Bunburyists I know.

JACK: What on earth do you mean?

ALGERNON: You have invented a very useful younger brother called Ernest, in order that you may be able to come up to town as often as you like. I have invented an invaluable permanent invalid called Bunbury, in order that I may be able to go down into the country whenever I choose. Bunbury is perfectly invaluable. If it wasn't for Bunbury's extraordinary bad health, for instance, I wouldn't be able to dine with you at Willis's to-night, for I have been really engaged to Aunt Augusta for more than a week.

JACK: I haven't asked you to dine with me anywhere to-night.

ALGERNON: I know. You are absurdly careless about sending out invitations. It is very foolish of you. Nothing annoys people so much as not receiving invitations.

JACK: You had much better dine with your Aunt Augusta.

ALGERNON: I haven't the smallest intention of doing anything of the kind. To begin with, I dined there on Monday, and once a week is quite enough to dine with one's own relations. In the second place, whenever I do dine there I am always treat-ed as a member of the family, and sent down with either no woman at all, or two. In the third place, I know perfectly well whom she will place me next to, to-night. She will place me next Mary Farquhar, who always flirts with her own hus-band across the dinner-table. That is not very pleasant. Indeed, it is not even decent . . . and that sort of thing is enormously on the increase. The amount of women in London who flirt with their own husbands is perfectly scandalous. It looks so bad. It is simply washing one's clean linen in public. Besides, now that I know you to be a con-firmed Bunburyist I naturally want to talk to you about Bunburying. I want to tell you the rules.

JACK: I'm not a Bunburyist at all. If Gwendolen accepts me, I am going to kill my brother, indeed I think I'll kill him in any case. Cecily is a little too much interested in him. It is rather a bore. So I am going to get rid of Ernest. And I strongly advise you to do the same with Mr. . . . with your invalid friend who has the absurd name.

ALGERNON: Nothing will induce me to part with Bunbury, and if you ever get married, which seems to me extremely problematic, you will be very glad to know Bunbury. A man who marries without knowing Bunbury has a very tedious time of it.

JACK: That is nonsense. If I marry a charming girl like Gwendolen, and she is the only girl I ever saw in my life that I would marry, I certainly won't want to know Bunbury.

ALGERNON: Then your wife will. You don't seem to realize, that in married life three is company and two is none.

JACK (*sententiously*): That, my dear young friend, is the theory that the corrupt French Drama has been propounding for the last fifty years.

ALGERNON: Yes; and that the happy English home has proved in half the time.

JACK: For heaven's sake, don't try to be cynical. It's perfectly easy to be cynical.

ALGERNON: My dear fellow, it isn't easy to be any-thing now-a-days. There's such a lot of beastly competition about. (*The sound of an electric bell is heard.*) Ah! that must be Aunt Augusta. Only rela-tives, or creditors, ever ring in that Wagnerian manner. Now, if I get her out of the way for ten minutes, so that you can have an opportunity for proposing to Gwendolen, may I dine with you to-night at Willis's?

JACK: I suppose so, if you want to.

ALGERNON: Yes, but you must be serious about it. I hate people who are not serious about meals. It is so shallow of them.

[*Enter LANE.*]

LANE: Lady Bracknell and Miss Fairfax.

[*ALGERNON goes forward to meet them. Enter LADY BRACKNELL and GWENDOLEN.*]

LADY BRACKNELL: Good afternoon, dear Algernon, I hope you are behaving very well.

ALGERNON: I'm feeling very well, Aunt Augusta.

LADY BRACKNELL: That's not quite the same thing. In fact the two things rarely go together. (*Sees* JACK *and bows to him with icy coldness.*)

ALGERNON (*to* GWENDOLEN): Dear me, you are smart!

GWENDOLEN: I am always smart! Aren't I, Mr. Worthing?

JACK: You're quite perfect, Miss Fairfax.

GWENDOLEN: Oh! I hope I am not that. It would leave no room for developments, and I intend to devel-op in many directions. (GWENDOLEN *and* JACK *sit down together in the corner.*)

LADY BRACKNELL: I'm sorry if we are a little late, Algernon, but I was obliged to call on dear Lady Harbury. I hadn't been there since her poor hus-band's death. I never saw a woman so altered; she looks quite twenty years younger. And now I'll have a cup of tea, and one of those nice cucumber sandwiches you promised me.

ALGERNON: Certainly, Aunt Augusta. (*Goes over to tea-table.*)

LADY BRACKNELL: Won't you come and sit here, Gwendolen?

GWENDOLEN: Thanks, mamma, I'm quite comfortable where I am.

ALGERNON (*picking up empty plate in horror*): Good heavens! Lane! Why are there no cucumber sandwiches? I ordered them specially.

LANE (*gravely*): There were no cucumbers in the market this morning, sir. I went down twice.

ALGERNON: No cucumbers!

LANE: No, sir. Not even for ready money.

ALGERNON: That will do, Lane, thank you.

LANE: Thank you, sir.

[Goes out.]

ALGERNON: I am greatly distressed, Aunt Augusta, about there being no cucumbers, not even for ready money.

LADY BRACKNELL: It really makes no matter, Algernon. I had some crumpets with Lady Harbury, who seems to me to be living entirely for pleasure now.

ALGERNON: I hear her hair has turned quite gold from grief.

LADY BRACKNELL: It certainly has changed its colour. From what cause I, of course, cannot say. (ALGERNON *crosses and hands tea.*) Thank you. I've quite a treat for you to-night, Algernon. I am going to send you down with Mary Farquhar. She is such a nice woman, and so attentive to her husband. It's delightful to watch them.

ALGERNON: I am afraid, Aunt Augusta, I shall have to give up the pleasure of dining with you to-night after all.

LADY BRACKNELL (*frowning*): I hope not, Algernon. It would put my table completely out. Your uncle would have to dine upstairs. Fortunately he is accustomed to that.

ALGERNON: It is a great bore, and, I need hardly say, a terrible disappointment to me, but the fact is I have just had a telegram to say that my poor friend Bunbury is very ill again. (*Exchanges glances with* JACK.) They seem to think I should be with him.

LADY BRACKNELL: It is very strange. This Mr. Bunbury seems to suffer from curiously bad health.

ALGERNON: Yes; poor Bunbury is a dreadful invalid.

LADY BRACKNELL: Well, I must say, Algernon, that I think it is high time that Mr. Bunbury made up his mind whether he was going to live or to die. This shilly-shallying with the question is absurd. Nor do I in any way approve of the modern sympathy with invalids. I consider it morbid. Illness of any kind is hardly a thing to be encouraged in others. Health is the primary duty of life. I am always telling that to your poor uncle, but he never seems to take much notice . . . as far as any improvement in his ailments goes. I should be much obliged if you would ask Mr. Bunbury, from me, to be kind enough not to have a relapse on Saturday, for I rely on you to arrange my music for me. It is my last reception and one wants something that will encourage conversation, particularly at the end of the season when everyone has practically said whatever they had to say, which, in most cases, was probably not much.

ALGERNON: I'll speak to Bunbury, Aunt Augusta, if he is still conscious, and I think I can promise you he'll be all right by Saturday. Of course the music is a great difficulty. You see, if one plays good music, people don't listen, and if one plays bad music people don't talk. But I'll run over the programme I've drawn out, if you will kindly come into the next room for a moment.

LADY BRACKNELL: Thank you, Algernon. It is very thoughtful of you. (*Rising, and following* ALGERNON.) I'm sure the programme will be delightful, after a few expurgations. French songs I cannot possibly allow. People always seem to think that they are improper, and either look shocked, which is vulgar, or laugh, which is worse. But German sounds a thoroughly respectable language, and indeed, I believe is so. Gwendolen, you will accompany me.

GWENDOLEN: Certainly, mamma.

[LADY BRACKNELL and ALGERNON go into the music-room, GWENDOLEN remains behind.]

JACK: Charming day it has been, Miss Fairfax.

GWENDOLEN: Pray don't talk to me about the weather, Mr. Worthing. Whenever people talk to me about the weather, I always feel quite certain that they mean something else. And that makes me so nervous.

JACK: I do mean something else.

GWENDOLEN: I thought so. In fact, I am never wrong.

JACK: And I would like to be allowed to take advantage of Lady Bracknell's temporary absence . . .

GWENDOLEN: I would certainly advise you to do so. Mamma has a way of coming back suddenly into a room that I have often had to speak to her about.

JACK (*nervously*): Miss Fairfax, ever since I met you I have admired you more than any girl . . . I have ever met since . . I met you.

GWENDOLEN: Yes, I am quite aware of the fact. And I often wish that in public, at any rate, you had been more demonstrative. For me you have always had an irresistible fascination. Even before I met you I was far from indifferent to you. (JACK *looks at her in amazement.*) We live, as I hope you know, Mr. Worthing, in an age of ideals. The fact is constantly mentioned in the more expensive monthly magazines, and has reached the provincial pulpits I am told: and my ideal has always been to love some one of the name of Ernest. There is something in that name that inspires absolute confidence. The moment Algernon first mentioned to me that he had a friend called Ernest, I knew I was destined to love you.

JACK: You really love me, Gwendolen?

GWENDOLEN: Passionately!

JACK: Darling! You don't know how happy you've made me.

GWENDOLEN: My own Ernest!

JACK: But you don't really mean to say that you couldn't love me if my name wasn't Ernest?

GWENDOLEN: But your name is Ernest.

JACK: Yes, I know it is. But supposing it was something else? Do you mean to say you couldn't love me then?

GWENDOLEN (*glibly*): Ah! that is clearly a metaphysical speculation, and like most metaphysical speculations has very little reference at all to the actual facts of real life, as we know them.

JACK: Personally, darling, to speak quite candidly, I don't much care about the name of Ernest . . . I don't think the name suits me at all.

GWENDOLEN: It suits you perfectly. It is a divine name. It has a music of its own. It produces vibrations.

JACK: Well, really, Gwendolen, I must say that I think there are lots of other much nicer names. I think Jack, for instance, a charming name.

GWENDOLEN: Jack? . . . No, there is very little music in the name Jack, if any at all, indeed. It does not thrill. It produces absolutely no vibrations. . . . I have known several Jacks, and they all, without exception, were more than usually plain. Besides, Jack is a notorious domesticity for John! And I pity any woman who is married to a man called John. She would probably never be allowed to know the entrancing pleasure of a single moment's solitude. The only really safe name is Ernest.

JACK: Gwendolen, I must get christened at once—I mean we must get married at once. There is no time to be lost.

GWENDOLEN: Married, Mr. Worthing?

JACK (*astounded*): Well . . . surely. You know that I love you, and you led me to believe, Miss Fairfax, that you were not absolutely indifferent to me.

GWENDOLEN: I adore you. But you haven't proposed to me yet. Nothing has been said at all about marriage. The subject has not even been touched on.

JACK: Well . . . may I propose to you now?

GWENDOLEN: I think it would be an admirable opportunity. And to spare you any possible disappointment, Mr. Worthing, I think it only fair to tell you quite frankly beforehand that I am fully determined to accept you.

JACK: Gwendolen!

GWENDOLEN: Yes, Mr. Worthing, what have you got to say to me?

JACK: You know what I have got to say to you.

GWENDOLEN: Yes, but you don't say it.

JACK: Gwendolen, will you marry me? (*Goes on his knees.*)

GWENDOLEN: Of course I will, darling. How long you have been about it! I am afraid you have had very little experience in how to propose.

JACK: My own one, I have never loved anyone in the world but you.

GWENDOLEN: Yes, but men often propose for practice. I know my brother Gerald does. All my girlfriends tell me so. What wonderfully blue eyes you have, Ernest! They are quite, quite, blue. I hope you will always look at me just like that, especially when there are other people present.

[Enter LADY BRACKNELL.]

LADY BRACKNELL: Mr. Worthing! Rise, sir, from this semi-recumbent posture. It is most indecorous.

GWENDOLEN: Mamma! (*He tries to rise; she restrains him.*) I must beg you to retire. This is no place for you. Besides, Mr. Worthing has not quite finished yet.

LADY BRACKNELL: Finished what, may I ask?

GWENDOLEN: I am engaged to Mr. Worthing, mamma. (*They rise together.*)

LADY BRACKNELL: Pardon me, you are not engaged to anyone. When you do become engaged to some one, I, or your father, should his health permit him, will inform you of the fact. An engagement should come on a young girl as a surprise, pleasant or unpleasant, as the case may be. It is hardly a matter that she could be allowed to arrange for herself. . . . And now I have a few questions to put to you, Mr. Worthing. While I am making these inquiries, you, Gwendolen, will wait for me below in the carriage.

GWENDOLEN (*reproachfully*): Mamma!

LADY BRACKNELL: In the carriage, Gwendolen! (GWENDOLEN *goes to the door. She and* JACK *blow kisses to each other behind* LADY BRACKNELL'*s back.* LADY BRACKNELL *looks vaguely about as if she could not understand what the noise was. Finally turns round.*) Gwendolen, the carriage!

GWENDOLEN: Yes, mamma. (*Goes out, looking back at* JACK.)

LADY BRACKNELL (*sitting down*): You can take a seat, Mr. Worthing.

[Looks in her pocket for note-book and pencil.]

JACK: Thank you, Lady Bracknell, I prefer standing.

LADY BRACKNELL (*pencil and note-book in hand*): I feel bound to tell you that you are not down on my list of eligible young men, although I have the same list as the dear Duchess of Bolton has. We work together, in fact. However, I am quite ready to enter your name, should your answers be what a really affectionate mother requires. Do you smoke?

JACK: Well, yes, I must admit I smoke.

LADY BRACKNELL: I am glad to hear it. A man should always have an occupation of some kind. There are far too many idle men in London as it is. How old are you?

JACK: Twenty-nine.

LADY BRACKNELL: A very good age to be married at. I have always been of opinion that a man who desires to get married should know either everything or nothing. Which do you know?

JACK (*after some hesitation*): I know nothing, Lady Bracknell.

LADY BRACKNELL: I am pleased to hear it. I do not approve of anything that tampers with natural ignorance. Ignorance is like a delicate exotic fruit; touch it and the bloom is gone. The whole theory of modern education is radically unsound. Fortunately in England, at any rate, education produces no effect whatsoever. If it did, it would prove a serious danger to the upper classes, and probably lead to acts of violence in Grosvenor Square. What is your income?

JACK: Between seven and eight thousand a year.

LADY BRACKNELL (*makes a note in her book*): In land, or in investments?

JACK: In investments, chiefly.

LADY BRACKNELL: That is satisfactory. What between the duties expected of one during one's lifetime , and the duties exacted from one after one's death, land has ceased to be either a profit or a pleasure. It gives one position, and prevents one from keeping it up. That's all that can be said about land.

JACK: I have a country house with some land, of course, attached to it, about fifteen hundred acres, I believe; but I don't depend on that for my real income. In fact, as far as I can make out, the poachers are the only people who make anything out of it.

LADY BRACKNELL: A country house! How many bedrooms? Well, that point can be cleared up afterwards. You have a town house, I hope? A girl with a simple, unspoiled nature, like Gwendolen, could hardly be expected to reside in the country.

JACK: Well, I own a house in Belgrave Square, but it is let by the year to Lady Bloxham. Of course, I can get it back whenever I like, at six months' notice.

LADY BRACKNELL: Lady Bloxham? I don't know her.

JACK: Oh, she goes about very little. She is a lady considerably advanced in years.

LADY BRACKNELL: Ah, now-a-days that is no guarantee of respectability of character. What number in Belgrave Square?

JACK: 149.

LADY BRACKNELL (*shaking her head*): The unfashionable side. I thought there was something. However, that could easily be altered.

JACK: Do you mean the fashion, or the side?

LADY BRACKNELL (*sternly*): Both, if necessary, I presume. What are you politics?

JACK: Well, I am afraid I really have none. I am a Liberal Unionist.

LADY BRACKNELL: Oh, they count as Tories. They dine with us. Or come in the evening, at any rate. Are your parents living?

JACK: I have lost both my parents.

LADY BRACKNELL: Both? . . . That seems like carelessness. Who was your father? He was evidently a man of some wealth. Was he born in what the Radical papers call the purple of commerce, or did he rise from the ranks of the aristocracy?

JACK: I am afraid I really don't know. The fact is, Lady Bracknell, I said I had lost my parents. It would be nearer the truth to say that my parents seem to have lost me . . . I don't actually know who I am by birth. I was . . . well, I was found.

LADY BRACKNELL: Found!

JACK: The late Mr. Thomas Cardew, an old gentleman of a very charitable and kindly disposition, found me, and gave me the name of Worthing, because he happened to have a first-class ticket for Worthing in his pocket at the time. Worthing is a place in Sussex. It is a seaside resort.

LADY BRACKNELL: Where did the charitable gentleman who had a first-class ticket for this seaside resort find you?

JACK (*gravely*): In a hand-bag.

LADY BRACKNELL: A hand-bag?

JACK (*very seriously*): Yes, Lady Bracknell. I was in a hand-bag—a somewhat large, black leather hand-bag, with handles to it—an ordinary hand-bag in fact.

LADY BRACKNELL: In what locality did this Mr. James, or Thomas, Cardew come across this ordinary hand-bag?

JACK: In the cloak-room at Victoria Station. It was given to him in mistake for his own.

LADY BRACKNELL: The cloak-room at Victoria Station?

JACK: Yes. The Brighton line.

LADY BRACKNELL: The line is immaterial. Mr. Worthing, I confess I feel somewhat bewildered by what you have just told me. To be born, or at any rate bred, in a hand-bag, whether it had handles or not, seems to me to display a contempt for the ordinary decencies of family life that remind one of the worst excesses of the French Revolution. And I presume you know what that unfortunate movement led to? As for the particular locality in which the hand-bag was found, a cloak-room at a railway station might serve to conceal a social indiscretion—has probably, indeed, been used for that purpose before now—but it could hardly be regarded as an assured basis for a recognized position in good society.

JACK: May I ask you then what you would advise me to do? I need hardly say I would do anything in the world to ensure Gwendolen's happiness.

LADY BRACKNELL: I would strongly advise you, Mr. Worthing, to try and acquire some relations as soon as possible, and to make a definite effort to produce at any rate one parent, of either sex, before the season is quite over.

JACK: Well, I don't see how I could possibly manage to do that. I can produce the hand-bag at any moment. It is in my dressing-room at home. I really think that should satisfy you, Lady Bracknell.

LADY BRACKNELL: Me, sir! What has it to do with me? You can hardly imagine that I and Lord Bracknell would dream of allowing our only daughter—a girl brought up with the utmost care—to marry into a cloak-room, and form an alliance with a parcel? Good morning, Mr. Worthing!

[LADY BRACKNELL *sweeps out in majestic indignation.*]

JACK: Good morning! (ALGERNON, *from the other room, strikes up the Wedding March.* JACK *looks perfectly furious, and goes to the door.*) For goodness' sake don't play that ghastly tune, Algy! How idiotic you are!

[*The music stops, and* ALGERNON *enters cheerily.*]

ALGERNON: Didn't it go off all right, old boy? You don't mean to say Gwendolen refused you? I know it is a way she has. She is always refusing people. I think it is most ill-natured of her.

JACK: Oh, Gwendolen is as right as a trivet. As far as she is concerned, we are engaged. Her mother is perfectly unbearable. Never met such a Gorgon . . . I don't really know what a Gorgon is like, but I am quite sure that Lady Bracknell is one. In any case, she is a monster, without being a myth, which is rather unfair. . . . I beg your pardon, Algy, I suppose I shouldn't talk about your own aunt in that way before you.

ALGERNON: My dear boy, I love hearing my relations abused. It is the only thing that makes me put up with them at all. Relations are simply a tedious pack of people, who haven't got the remotest knowledge of how to live, nor the smallest instinct about when to die.

JACK: Oh, that is nonsense!

ALGERNON: It isn't!

JACK: Well, I won't argue about the matter. You always want to argue about things.

ALGERNON: That is exactly what things were originally made for.

JACK: Upon my word, if I thought that, I'd shoot myself . . . (*A pause.*) You don't think there is any chance of Gwendolen becoming like her mother in about a hundred and fifty years, do you Algy?

ALGERNON: All women become like their mothers. That is their tragedy. No man does. That's his.

JACK: Is that clever?

ALGERNON: It is perfectly phrased! and quite as true as any observation in civilized life should be.

JACK: I am sick to death of cleverness. Everybody is clever now-a-days. You can't go anywhere without meeting clever people. The thing has become an absolute public nuisance. I wish to goodness we had a few fools left.

ALGERNON: We have.

JACK: I should extremely like to meet them. What do they talk about?

ALGERNON: The fools? Oh! about the clever people, of course.

JACK: What fools!

ALGERNON: By the way, did you tell Gwendolen the truth about your being Ernest in town, and Jack in the country?

JACK (*in a very patronising manner*): My dear fellow, the truth isn't quite the sort of thing one tells to a nice, sweet, refined girl. What extraordinary ideas you have about the way to behave to a woman!

ALGERNON: The only way to behave to a woman is to make love to her, if she is pretty, and to someone else if she is plain.

JACK: Oh, that is nonsense.

ALGERNON: What about your brother? What about the profligate Ernest?

JACK: Oh, before the end of the week I shall have got rid of him. I'll say he died in Paris of apoplexy. Lots of people die of apoplexy, quite suddenly, don't they?

ALGERNON: Yes, but it's hereditary, my dear fellow. It's a sort of thing that runs in families. You had much better say a severe chill.

JACK: You are sure a severe chill isn't hereditary, or anything of that kind?

ALGERNON: Of course it isn't!

JACK: Very well, then. My poor brother Ernest is carried off suddenly in Paris, by a severe chill. That gets rid of him.

ALGERNON: But I thought you said that . . . Miss Cardew was a little too much interested in your poor brother Ernest? Won't she feel his loss a good deal?

JACK: Oh, that is all right. Cecily is not a silly, romantic girl, I am glad to say. She has got a capital appetite, goes long walks, and pays no attention at all to her lessons.

ALGERNON: I would rather like to see Cecily.

JACK: I will take very good care you never do. She is excessively pretty, and she is only just eighteen.

ALGERNON: Have you told Gwendolen yet that you have an excessively pretty ward who is only just eighteen?

JACK: Oh! one doesn't blurt these things out to people. Cecily and Gwendolen are perfectly certain to be extremely great friends. I'll bet you anything you like that half an hour after they have met, they will be calling each other sister.

ALGERNON: Women only do that when they have called each other a lot of other things first. Now, my dear boy, if we want to get a good table at Willis's, we really must go and dress. Do you know it is nearly seven?

JACK (*irritably*): Oh! it always is nearly seven.

ALGERNON: Well, I'm hungry.

JACK: I never knew you when you weren't. . . .

ALGERNON: What shall we do after dinner? Go to a theatre?

JACK: Oh no! I loathe listening.

ALGERNON: Well, let us go to the Club?

JACK: Oh, no! I hate talking.

ALGERNON: Well, we might trot round to the Empire at ten?

JACK: Oh, no! I can't bear looking at things. It is so silly.

ALGERNON: Well, what shall we do?

JACK: Nothing!

ALGERNON: It is awfully hard work doing nothing. However, I don't mind hard work where there is no definite object of any kind.

[*Enter* LANE.]

LANE: Miss Fairfax.

[*Enter* GWENDOLEN. LANE *goes out.*]

ALGERNON: Gwendolen, upon my word!

GWENDOLEN: Algy, kindly turn your back. I have something very particular to say to Mr. Worthing.

ALGERNON: Really, Gwendolen, I don't think I can allow this at all.

GWENDOLEN: Algy, you always adopt a strictly immoral attitude towards life. You are not quite old enough to do that. (ALGERNON *retires to the fireplace.*)

JACK: My own darling!

GWENDOLEN: Ernest, we may never be married. From the expression on mamma's face I fear we never shall. Few parents now-a-days pay any regard to what their children say to them. The old-fashioned respect for the young is fast dying out.

Whatever influence I ever had over mamma, I lost at the age of three. But although she may prevent us from becoming man and wife, and I may marry someone else, and marry often, nothing that she can possibly do can alter my eternal devotion to you.

JACK: Dear Gwendolen!

GWENDOLEN: The story of your romantic origin, as related to me by mamma, with unpleasing comments, has naturally stirred the deeper fibres of my nature. Your Christian name has an irresistible fascination. The simplicity of your character makes you exquisitely incomprehensible to me. Your town address at the Albany I have. What is your address in the country?

JACK: The Manor House, Woolton, Hertfordshire.

[ALGERNON, *who has been carefully listening, smiles to himself, and writes the address on his shirt-cuff. Then picks up the Railway Guide.*]

GWENDOLEN: There is a good postal service, I suppose? It may be necessary to do something desperate. That, of course, will require serious consideration. I will communicate with you daily.

JACK: My own one!

GWENDOLEN: How long do you remain in town?

JACK: Till Monday.

GWENDOLEN: Good! Algy, you may turn round now.

ALGERNON: Thanks, I've turned round already.

GWENDOLEN: You may also ring the bell.

JACK: You will let me see you to your carriage, my own darling?

GWENDOLEN: Certainly.

JACK (*to* LANE, *who now enters*): I will see Miss Fairfax out.

LANE: Yes, sir.

[JACK *and* GWENDOLEN *go off.*]

[LANE *presents several letters on a salver to* ALGERNON. *It is to be surmised that they are bills, as* ALGERNON *after looking at the envelopes, tears them up.*]

ALGERNON: A glass of sherry, Lane.

LANE: Yes, sir.

ALGERNON: To-morrow, Lane, I'm going Bunburying.

LANE: Yes, sir.

ALGERNON: I shall probably not be back till Monday. You can put up my dress clothes, my smoking jacket, and all the Bunbury suits . . .

LANE: Yes, sir. (*Handing sherry.*)

ALGERNON: I hope to-morrow will be a fine day, Lane.

LANE: It never is, sir.

ALGERNON: Lane, you're a perfect pessimist.

LANE: I do my best to give satisfaction, sir.

[Enter JACK. LANE goes off.]

JACK: There's a sensible, intellectual girl! the only girl I ever cared for in my life. (ALGERNON *is laughing immoderately.*) What on earth are you so amused at?

ALGERNON: Oh, I'm a little anxious about poor Bunbury, that is all.

JACK: If you don't take care, your friend Bunbury will get you into a serious scrape some day.

ALGERNON: I love scrapes. They are the only things that are never serious.

JACK: Oh, that's nonsense, Algy. You never talk anything but nonsense.

ALGERNON: Nobody ever does.

[JACK looks indignantly at him, and leaves the room. ALGERNON lights a cigarette, reads his shirt-cuff, and smiles.]

ACT-DROP.

ACT II

Scene—Garden at the Manor House. A flight of gray stone steps leads up to the house. The garden, an old-fashioned one, full of roses. Time of year, July. Basket chairs, and a table covered with books, are set under a large yew tree.

[MISS PRISM discovered seated at the table. CECILY is at the back watering flowers.]

MISS PRISM (*calling*): Cecily, Cecily! Surely such a utilitarian occupation as the watering of flowers is rather Moulton's duty than yours? Especially at a moment when intellectual pleasures await you. Your German grammar is on the table. Pray open it at page fifteen. We will repeat yesterday's lesson.

CECILY (*coming over very slowly*): But I don't like German. It isn't at all a becoming language. I know perfectly well that I look quite plain after my German lesson.

MISS PRISM: Child, you know how anxious your guardian is that you should improve yourself in every way. He laid particular stress on your German, as he was leaving for town yesterday. Indeed, he always lays stress on your German when he is leaving for town.

CECILY: Dear Uncle Jack is so very serious! Sometimes he is so serious that I think he cannot be quite well.

MISS PRISM (*drawing herself up*): Your guardian enjoys the best of health, and his gravity of demeanour is especially to be commended in one so comparatively young as he is. I know no one who has a higher sense of duty and responsibility.

CECILY: I suppose that is why he often looks a little bored when we three are together.

MISS PRISM: Cecily! I am surprised at you. Mr. Worthing has many troubles in his life. Idle merriment and triviality would be out of place in his conversation. You must remember his constant anxiety about that unfortunate young man, his brother.

CECILY: I wish Uncle Jack would allow that unfortunate young man, his brother, to come down here sometimes. We might have a good influence over him, Miss Prism. I am sure you certainly would. You know German, and geology, and things of that kind influence a man very much. (CECILY *begins to write in her diary.*)

MISS PRISM (*shaking her head*): I do not think that even I could produce any effect on a character that according to his own brother's admission is irretrievably weak and vacillating. Indeed I am not sure that I would desire to reclaim him. I am not in favour of this modern mania for turning bad people into good people at a moment's notice. As a man sows so let him reap. You must put away your diary, Cecily. I really don't see why you should keep a diary at all.

CECILY: I keep a diary in order to enter the wonderful secrets of my life. If I didn't write them down I should probably forget all about them.

MISS PRISM: Memory, my dear Cecily, is the diary that we all carry about with us.

CECILY: Yes, but it usually chronicles the things that have never happened, and couldn't possibly have happened. I believe that Memory is responsible for nearly all the three-volume novels that Mudie sends us.

MISS PRISM: Do not speak slightingly of the three-volume novel, Cecily. I wrote one myself in earlier days.

CECILY: Did you really, Miss Prism? How wonderfully clever you are! I hope it did not end happily? I don't like novels that end happily. They depress me so much.

MISS PRISM: The good ended happily, and the bad unhappily. That is what Fiction means.

CECILY: I suppose so. But it seems very unfair. And was your novel ever published?

MISS PRISM: Alas! no. The manuscript unfortunately was abandoned. I use the word in the sense of lost or mislaid. To your work, child, these speculations are profitless.

CECILY (*smiling*): But I see dear Dr. Chasuble coming up through the garden.

MISS PRISM (*rising and advancing*): Dr. Chasuble! This is indeed a pleasure.

[Enter CANON CHASUBLE.]

CHASUBLE: And how are we this morning? Miss

Prism, you are, I trust, well?

CECILY: Miss Prism has just been complaining of a slight headache. I think it would do her so much good to have a short stroll with you in the Park, Dr. Chasuble.

MISS PRISM: Cecily, I have not mentioned anything about a headache.

CECILY: No, dear Miss Prism, I know that, but I felt instinctively that you had a headache. Indeed I was thinking about that, and not about my German lesson, when the Rector came in.

CHASUBLE: I hope, Cecily, you are not inattentive.

CECILY: Oh, I am afraid I am.

CHASUBLE: That is strange. Were I fortunate enough to be Miss Prism's pupil, I would hang upon her lips. (MISS PRISM *glares*.) I spoke metaphorically.— My metaphor was drawn from bees. Ahem! Mr. Worthing, I suppose, has not returned from town yet?

MISS PRISM: We do not expect him till Monday afternoon.

CHASUBLE: Ah yes, he usually likes to spend his Sunday in London. He is not one of those whose sole aim is enjoyment, as, by all accounts, that unfortunate young man, his brother, seems to be. But I must not disturb Egeria and her pupil any longer.

MISS PRISM: Egeria? My name is Lætitia, Doctor.

CHASUBLE (*bowing*): A classical allusion merely, drawn from the Pagan authors. I shall see you both no doubt at Evensong.

MISS PRISM: I think, dear Doctor, I will have a stroll with you. I find I have a headache after all, and a walk might do it good.

CHASUBLE: With pleasure, Miss Prism, with pleasure. We might go as far as the schools and back.

MISS PRISM: That would be delightful. Cecily, you will read your Political Economy in my absence. The chapter on the Fall of the Rupee you may omit. It is somewhat too sensational. Even these metallic problems have their melodramatic side.

[Goes down the garden with DR. CHASUBLE.]

CECILY (*picks up books and throws them back on table*): Horrid Political Economy! Horrid Geography! Horrid, horrid German!

[Enter MERRIMAN with a card on a salver.]

MERRIMAN: Mr. Ernest Worthing has just driven over from the station. He has brought his luggage with him.

CECILY (*takes the card and reads it*): "Mr. Ernest Worthing, B 4 The Albany, W." Uncle Jack's brother! Did you tell him Mr. Worthing was in town?

MERRIMAN: Yes, Miss. He seemed very much disappointed. I mentioned that you and Miss Prism were in the garden. He said he was anxious to speak to you privately for a moment.

CECILY: Ask Mr. Ernest Worthing to come here. I suppose you had better talk to the housekeeper about a room for him.

MERRIMAN: Yes, Miss.

[MERRIMAN goes off.]

CECILY: I have never met any really wicked person before. I feel rather frightened. I am so afraid he will look just like everyone else.

[Enter ALGERNON, very gay and debonnair.]

He does!

ALGERNON (*raising his hat*): You are my little cousin Cecily, I'm sure.

CECILY: You are under some strange mistake. I am not little. In fact, I believe I am more than usually tall for my age. (ALGERNON *is rather taken aback*.) But I am your cousin Cecily. You, I see from your card, are Uncle Jack's brother, my cousin Ernest, my wicked cousin Ernest.

ALGERNON: Oh! I am not really wicked at all, cousin Cecily. You musn't think that I am wicked.

CECILY: If you are not, then you have certainly been deceiving us all in a very inexcusable manner. I hope you have not been leading a double life, pretending to be wicked and being really good all the time. That would be hypocrisy.

ALGERNON (*looks at her in amazement*): Oh! of course I have been rather reckless.

CECILY: I am glad to hear it.

ALGERNON: In fact, now you mention the subject, I have been very bad in my own small way.

CECILY: I don't think you should be so proud of that, though I am sure it must have been very pleasant.

ALGERNON: It is much pleasanter being here with you.

CECILY: I can't understand how you are here at all. Uncle Jack won't be back till Monday afternoon.

ALGERNON: That is a great disappointment. I am obliged to go up by the first train on Monday morning. I have a business appointment that I am anxious . . . to miss.

CECILY: Couldn't you miss it anywhere but in London?

ALGERNON: No: the appointment is in London.

CECILY: Well, I know, of course, how important it is not to keep a business engagement, if one wants to retain any sense of the beauty of life, but still I think you had better wait till Uncle Jack arrives. I know he wants to speak to you about your emigrating.

ALGERNON: About my what?

CECILY: Your emigrating. He has gone up to buy your outfit.

ALGERNON: I certainly wouldn't let Jack buy my outfit. He has no taste in neckties at all.

CECILY: I don't think you will require neckties. Uncle Jack is sending you to Australia.

ALGERNON: Australia! I'd sooner die.

CECILY: Well, he said at dinner on Wednesday night, that you would have to choose between this world, the next world, and Australia.

ALGERNON: Oh, well! The accounts I have received of Australia and the next world, are not particularly encouraging. This world is good enough for me, cousin Cecily.

CECILY: Yes, but are you good enough for it?

ALGERNON: I'm afraid I'm not that. That is why I want you to reform me. You might make that your mission, if you don't mind, cousin Cecily.

CECILY: I'm afraid I've no time, this afternoon.

ALGERNON: Well, would you mind my reforming myself this afternoon?

CECILY: It is rather Quixotic of you. But I think you should try.

ALGERNON: I will. I feel better already.

CECILY: You are looking a little worse.

ALGERNON: That is because I am hungry.

CECILY: How thoughtless of me. I should have remembered that when one is going to lead an entirely new life, one requires regular and wholesome meals. Won't you come in?

ALGERNON: Thank you. Might I have a buttonhole first? I never have any appetite unless I have a button-hole first.

CECILY: A Maréchal Niel? (*Picks up scissors.*)

ALGERNON: No, I'd sooner have a pink rose.

CECILY: Why? (*Cuts a flower.*)

ALGERNON: Because you are like a pink rose, cousin Cecily.

CECILY: I don't think it can be right for you to talk to me like that. Miss Prism never says such things to me.

ALGERNON: Then Miss Prism is a short-sighted old lady. (CECILY *puts the rose in his button-hole.*) You are the prettiest girl I ever saw.

CECILY: Miss Prism says that all good looks are a snare.

ALGERNON: They are a snare that every sensible man would like to be caught in.

CECILY: Oh! I don't think I would care to catch a sensible man. I shouldn't know what to talk to him about.

[*They pass into the house.* MISS PRISM *and* DR. CHASUBLE *return.*]

MISS PRISM: You are too much alone, dear Dr. Chasuble. You should get married. A misanthrope I can understand—a womanthrope, never!

CHASUBLE (*with a scholar's shudder*): Believe me, I do not deserve so neologistic a phrase. The precept as well as the practice of the Primitive Church was distinctly against matrimony.

MISS PRISM (*sententiously*): That is obviously the reason why the Primitive Church has not lasted up to the present day. And you do not seem to realize, dear Doctor, that by persistently remaining single, a man converts himself into a permanent public temptation. Men should be more careful; this very celibacy leads weaker vessels astray.

CHASUBLE: But is a man not equally attractive when married?

MISS PRISM: No married man is ever attractive except to his wife.

CHASUBLE: And often, I've been told, not even to her.

MISS PRISM: That depends on the intellectual sympathies of the woman. Maturity can always be depended on. Ripeness can be trusted. Young women are green. (DR. CHASUBLE *starts.*) I spoke horticulturally. My metaphor was drawn from fruits. But where is Cecily?

CHASUBLE: Perhaps she followed us to the schools.

[*Enter* JACK *slowly from the back of the garden. He is dressed in the deepest mourning, with crape hat-band and black gloves.*]

MISS PRISM: Mr. Worthing!

CHASUBLE: Mr. Worthing?

MISS PRISM: This is indeed a surprise. We did not look for you till Monday afternoon.

JACK (*shakes* MISS PRISM'S *hand in a tragic manner*): I have returned sooner than I expected. Dr. Chasuble, I hope you are well?

CHASUBLE: Dear Mr. Worthing, I trust this garb of woe does not betoken some terrible calamity?

JACK: My brother.

MISS PRISM: More shameful debts and extravagance?

CHASUBLE: Still leading his life of pleasure?

JACK (*shaking his head*): Dead!

CHASUBLE: Your brother Ernest dead?

JACK: Quite dead.

MISS PRISM: What a lesson for him! I trust he will profit by it.

CHASUBLE: Mr. Worthing, I offer you my sincere condolence. You have at least the consolation of knowing that you were always the most generous and forgiving of brothers.

JACK: Poor Ernest! He had many faults, but it is a sad, sad blow.

CHASUBLE: Very sad indeed. Were you with him at the end?

JACK: No. He died abroad; in Paris, in fact. I had a telegram last night from the manager of the Grand Hotel.

CHASUBLE: Was the cause of death mentioned?

JACK: A severe chill, it seems.

MISS PRISM: As a man sows, so shall he reap.

CHASUBLE (*raising his hand*): Charity, dear Miss Prism, charity! None of us are perfect. I myself am peculiarly susceptible to draughts. Will the interment take place here?

JACK: No. He seemed to have expressed a desire to be buried in Paris.

CHASUBLE: In Paris! (*Shakes his head.*) I fear that hardly points to any very serious state of mind at the last. You would no doubt wish me to make some slight allusion to this tragic domestic affliction next Sunday. (JACK *presses his hand convulsively.*) My sermon on the meaning of the manna in the wilderness can be adapted to almost any occasion, joyful, or, as in the present case, distressing. (*All sigh.*) I have preached it at harvest celebrations, christenings, confirmations, on days of humiliation and festal days. The last time I delivered it was in the Cathedral, as a charity sermon on behalf of the Society for the Prevention of Discontent among the Upper Orders. The Bishop, who was present, was much struck by some of the analogies I drew.

JACK: Ah! that reminds me, you mentioned christenings I think, Dr. Chasuble? I suppose you know how to christen all right? (DR. CHASUBLE *looks astounded.*) I mean, of course, you are continually christening, aren't you?

MISS PRISM: It is, I regret to say, one of the Rector's most constant duties in this parish. I have often spoken to the poorer classes on the subject. But they don't seem to know what thrift is.

CHASUBLE: But is there any particular infant in whom you are interested, Mr. Worthing? Your brother was, I believe, unmarried, was he not?

JACK: Oh, yes.

MISS PRISM (*bitterly*): People who live entirely for pleasure usually are.

JACK: But it is not for any child, dear Doctor. I am very fond of children. No! the fact is, I would like to be christened myself, this afternoon, if you have nothing better to do.

CHASUBLE: But surely, Mr. Worthing, you have been christened already?

JACK: I don't remember anything about it.

CHASUBLE: But have you any grave doubts on the subject?

JACK: I certainly intend to have. Of course, I don't know if the thing would bother you in any way, or if you think I am a little too old now.

CHASUBLE: Not at all. The sprinkling, and, indeed, the immersion of adults is a perfectly canonical practice.

JACK: Immersion!

CHASUBLE: You need have no apprehensions.

Sprinkling is all that is necessary, or indeed I think advisable. Our weather is so changeable. At what hour would you wish the ceremony performed?

JACK: Oh, I might trot round about five if that would suit you.

CHASUBLE: Perfectly, perfectly! In fact I have two similar ceremonies to perform at that time. A case of twins that occurred recently in one of the outlying cottages on your own estate. Poor Jenkins the carter, a most hard-working man.

JACK: Oh! I don't see much fun in being christened along with other babies. It would be childish. Would half-past five do?

CHASUBLE: Admirably! Admirably! (*Takes out watch.*) And now, dear Mr. Worthing, I will not intrude any longer into a house of sorrow. I would merely beg you not to be too much bowed down by grief. What seem to us bitter trials are often blessings in disguise.

MISS PRISM: This seems to me a blessing of an extremely obvious kind.

[*Enter CECILY from the house.*]

CECILY: Uncle Jack! Oh, I am pleased to see you back. But what horrid clothes you have got on! Do go and change them.

MISS PRISM: Cecily!

CHASUBLE: My child! my child! (CECILY *goes towards* JACK; *he kisses her brow in a melancholy manner.*)

CECILY: What is the matter, Uncle Jack? Do look happy! You look as if you had toothache, and I have got such a surprise for you. Who do you think is in the dining-room? Your brother!

JACK: Who?

CECILY: Your brother Ernest. He arrived about half an hour ago.

JACK: What nonsense! I haven't got a brother.

CECILY: Oh, don't say that. However badly he may have behaved to you in the past he is still your brother. You couldn't be so heartless as to disown him. I'll tell him to come out. And you will shake hands with him, won't you, Uncle Jack?

[*Runs back into the house.*]

CHASUBLE: These are very joyful tidings.

MISS PRISM: After we had all been resigned to his loss, his sudden return seems to me peculiarly distressing.

JACK: My brother is in the dining-room? I don't know what it all means. I think it is perfectly absurd.

[*Enter ALGERNON and CECILY hand in hand. They come slowly up to* JACK.]

JACK: Good heavens! (*Motions* ALGERNON *away.*)

ALGERNON: Brother John, I have come down from town to tell you that I am very sorry for all the trouble I have given you, and that I intend to lead a better life in the future. (JACK *glares at him and does not take his hand.*)

CECILY: Uncle Jack, you are not going to refuse your own brother's hand?

JACK: Nothing will induce me to take his hand. I think his coming down here disgraceful. He knows perfectly well why.

CECILY: Uncle Jack, do be nice. There is some good in everyone. Ernest has just been telling me about his poor invalid friend Mr. Bunbury, whom he goes to visit so often. And surely there must be much good in one who is kind to an invalid, and leaves the pleasures of London to sit by a bed of pain.

JACK: Oh! he has been talking about Bunbury, has he?

CECILY: Yes, he has told me all about poor Mr. Bunbury, and his terrible state of health.

JACK: Bunbury! Well, I won't have him talk to you about Bunbury or about anything else. It is enough to drive one perfectly frantic.

ALGERNON: Of course I admit that the faults were all on my side. But I must say that I think that brother John's coldness to me is peculiarly painful. I expected a more enthusiastic welcome, especially considering it is the first time I have come here.

CECILY: Uncle Jack, if you don't shake hands with Ernest I will never forgive you.

JACK: Never forgive me?

CECILY: Never, never, never!

JACK: Well, this is the last time I shall ever do it. (*Shakes hands with* ALGERNON *and glares.*)

CHASUBLE: It's pleasant, is it not, to see so perfect a reconciliation? I think we might leave the two brothers together.

MISS PRISM: Cecily, you will come with us.

CECILY: Certainly, Miss Prism. My little task of reconciliation is over.

CHASUBLE: You have done a beautiful action today, dear child.

MISS PRISM: We must not be premature in our judgments.

CECILY: I feel very happy.

[They all go off.]

JACK: You young scoundrel, Algy, you must get out of this place as soon as possible. I don't allow any Bunburying here.

[Enter MERRIMAN.*]*

MERRIMAN: I have put Mr. Ernest's things in the room next to yours, sir. I suppose that is all right?

JACK: What?

MERRIMAN: Mr. Ernest's luggage, sir. I have unpacked it and put it in the room next to your own.

JACK: His luggage?

MERRIMAN: Yes, sir. Three portmanteaus, a dressing-case, two hat-boxes, and a large luncheon-basket.

ALGERNON: I am afraid I can't stay more than a week this time.

JACK: Merriman, order the dog-cart at once. Mr. Ernest has been suddenly called back to town.

MERRIMAN: Yes, sir.

[Goes back into the house.]

ALGERNON: What a fearful liar you are, Jack. I have not been called back to town at all.

JACK: Yes, you have.

ALGERNON: I haven't heard anyone call me.

JACK: Your duty as a gentlemen calls you back.

ALGERNON: My duty as a gentleman has never interfered with my pleasures in the smallest degree.

JACK: I can quite understand that.

ALGERNON: Well, Cecily is a darling.

JACK: You are not to talk of Miss Cardew like that. I don't like it.

ALGERNON: Well, I don't like your clothes. You look perfectly ridiculous in them. Why on earth don't you go up and change? It is perfectly childish to be in deep mourning for a man who is actually staying for a whole week with you in your house as a guest. I call it grotesque.

JACK: You are certainly not staying with me for a whole week as a guest or anything else. You have got to leave . . . by the four-five train.

ALGERNON: I certainly won't leave you so long as you are in mourning. It would be most unfriendly. If I were in mourning you would stay with me, I suppose. I should think it very unkind if you didn't.

JACK: Well, will you go if I change my clothes?

ALGERNON: Yes, if you are not too long. I never saw anybody take so long to dress, and with such little result.

JACK: Well, at any rate, that is better than being always over-dressed as you are.

ALGERNON: If I am occasionally a little overdressed, I make up for it by being always immensely over-educated.

JACK: Your vanity is ridiculous, your conduct an outrage, and your presence in my garden utterly absurd. However, you have got to catch the four-five, and I hope you will have a pleasant journey back to town. This Bunburying, as you call it, has not been a great success for you.

[Goes into the house.]

ALGERNON: I think it has been a great success. I'm in love with Cecily, and that is everything.

[Enter CECILY at the back of the garden. She picks up the can and begins to water the flowers.]

But I must see her before I go, and make arrangements for another Bunbury. Ah, there she is.

CECILY: Oh, I merely came back to water the roses. I thought you were with Uncle Jack.

ALGERNON: He's gone to order the dog-cart for me.

CECILY: Oh, is he going to take you for a nice drive?

ALGERNON: He's going to send me away.

CECILY: Then have we got to part?

ALGERNON: I am afraid so. It's a very painful parting.

CECILY: It is always painful to part from people whom one has known for a very brief space of time. The absence of old friends one can endure with equanimity. But even a momentary separation from anyone to whom one has just been introduced is almost unbearable.

ALGERNON: Thank you.

[Enter MERRIMAN.]

MERRIMAN: The dog-cart is at the door, sir.
    (ALGERNON *looks appealingly at* CECILY.)

CECILY: It can wait, Merriman . . . for . . . five minutes.

MERRIMAN: Yes, Miss.

[Exit MERRIMAN.]

ALGERNON: I hope, Cecily, I shall not offend you if I state quite frankly and openly that you seem to me to be in every way the visible personification of absolute perfection.

CECILY: I think your frankness does you great credit, Ernest. If you will allow me I will copy your remarks into my diary. (*Goes over to table and begins writing in diary.*)

ALGERNON: Do you really keep a diary? I'd give anything to look at it. May I?

CECILY: Oh, no. (*Puts her hand over it.*) You see, it is simply a very young girl's record of her own thoughts and impressions, and consequently meant for publication. When it appears in volume form I hope you will order a copy. But pray, Ernest, don't stop. I delight in taking down from dictation. I have reached "absolute perfection." You can go on. I am quite ready for more.

ALGERNON (*somewhat taken aback*): Ahem! Ahem!

CECILY: Oh, don't cough, Ernest. When one is dictating one should speak fluently and not cough. Besides, I don't know how to spell a cough. (*Writes as* ALGERNON *speaks.*)

ALGERNON (*speaking very rapidly*): Cecily, ever since I first looked upon your wonderful and incomparable beauty, I have dared to love you wildly, passionately, devotedly, hopelessly.

CECILY: I don't think that you should tell me that you love me wildly, passionately, devotedly, hopelessly. Hopelessly doesn't seem to make much sense, does it?

ALGERNON: Cecily!

[Enter MERRIMAN.]

MERRIMAN: The dog-cart is waiting, sir.

ALGERNON: Tell it to come round next week, at the same hour.

MERRIMAN (*looks at* CECILY, *who makes no sign*): Yes, sir.

[MERRIMAN retires.]

CECILY: Uncle Jack would be very much annoyed if he knew you were staying on till next week, at the same hour.

ALGERNON: Oh, I don't care about Jack. I don't care for anybody in the whole world but you. I love you, Cecily. You will marry me, won't you?

CECILY: You silly boy! Of course. Why, we have been engaged for the last three months.

ALGERNON: For the last three months?

CECILY: Yes, it will be exactly three months on Thursday.

ALGERNON: But how did we become engaged?

CECILY: Well, ever since dear Uncle Jack first confessed to us that he had a younger brother who was very wicked and bad, you of course have formed the chief topic of conversation between myself and Miss Prism. And of course a man who is much talked about is always very attractive. One feels there must be something in him after all. I daresay it was foolish of me, but I fell in love with you, Ernest.

ALGERNON: Darling! And when was the engagement actually settled?

CECILY: On the 14th of February last. Worn out by your entire ignorance of my existence, I determined to end the matter one way or the other, and after a long struggle with myself I accepted you under this dear old tree here. The next day I bought this little ring in your name, and this is the little bangle with the true lovers' knot I promised you always to wear.

ALGERNON: Did I give you this? It's very pretty, isn't it?

CECILY: Yes, you've wonderfully good taste, Ernest. It's the excuse I've always given for your leading such a bad life. And this is the box in which I keep all your dear letters. (*Kneels at table, opens box, and produces letters tied up with blue ribbon.*)

ALGERNON: My letters! But my own sweet Cecily, I have never written you any letters.

CECILY: You need hardly remind me of that, Ernest. I remember only too well that I was forced to write your letters for you. I wrote always three times a week, and sometimes oftener.

ALGERNON: Oh, do let me read them, Cecily?

CECILY: Oh, I couldn't possibly. They would make you far too conceited. (*Replaces box.*) The three you wrote me after I had broken off the engagement are so beautiful, and so badly spelled, that even now I can hardly read them without crying a little.

ALGERNON: But was our engagement ever broken off?

CECILY: Of course it was. On the 22nd of last March. You can see the entry if you like. (*Shows diary.*) "To-day I broke off my engagement with Ernest. I feel it is better to do so. The weather still continues charming."

ALGERNON: But why on earth did you break it off? What had I done? I had done nothing at all. Cecily, I am very much hurt indeed to hear you broke it off. Particularly when the weather was so charming.

CECILY: It would hardly have been a really serious engagement if it hadn't been broken off at least once. But I forgave you before the week was out.

ALGERNON (*crossing to her, and kneeling*): What a perfect angel you are, Cecily.

CECILY: You dear romantic boy. (*He kisses her, she puts her fingers through his hair.*) I hope your hair curls naturally, does it?

ALGERNON: Yes, darling, with a little help from others.

CECILY: I am so glad.

ALGERNON: You'll never break off our engagement again, Cecily?

CECILY: I don't think I could break it off now that I have actually met you. Besides, of course, there is the question of your name.

ALGERNON: Yes, of course. (*Nervously.*)

CECILY: You must not laugh at me, darling, but it had always been a girlish dream of mine to love some one whose name was Ernest. (ALGERNON *rises*, CECILY *also.*) There is something in that name that seems to inspire absolute confidence. I pity any poor married woman whose husband is not called Ernest.

ALGERNON: But, my dear child, do you mean to say you could not love me if I had some other name?

CECILY: But what name?

ALGERNON: Oh, any name you like—Algernon—for instance . . .

CECILY: But I don't like the name of Algernon.

ALGERNON: Well, my own dear, sweet, loving little darling, I really can't see why you should object to the name of Algernon. It is not at all a bad name. In fact, it is rather an aristocratic name. Half of the chaps who get into the Bankruptcy Court are called Algernon. But seriously, Cecily . . (*Moving to her*) . . . if my name was Algy, couldn't

you love me?

CECILY (*rising*): I might respect you, Ernest, I might admire your character, but I fear that I should not be able to give you my undivided attention.

ALGERNON: Ahem! Cecily! (*Picking up hat*). Your Rector here is, I suppose, thoroughly experienced in the practice of all the rites and ceremonials of the Church?

CECILY: Oh yes. Dr. Chasuble is a most learned man. He has never written a single book, so you can imagine how much he knows.

ALGERNON: I must see him at once on a most important christening—I mean on most important business.

CECILY: Oh!

ALGERNON: I shan't be away more than half an hour.

CECILY: Considering that we have been engaged since February the 14th, and that I only met you today for the first time, I think it is rather hard that you should leave me for so long a period as half an hour. Couldn't you make it twenty minutes?

ALGERNON: I'll be back in no time.

[*Kisses her and rushes down the garden.*]

CECILY: What an impetuous boy he is! I like his hair so much. I must enter his proposal in my diary.

[*Enter MERRIMAN.*]

MERRIMAN: A Miss Fairfax has just called to see Mr. Worthing. On very important business Miss Fairfax states.

CECILY: Isn't Mr. Worthing in his library?

MERRIMAN: Mr. Worthing went over in the direction of the Rectory some time ago.

CECILY: Pray ask the lady to come out here; Mr. Worthing is sure to be back soon. And you can bring tea.

MERRIMAN: Yes, Miss.

[*Goes out.*]

CECILY: Miss Fairfax! I suppose one of the many good elderly women who are associated with Uncle Jack in some of his philanthropic work in London. I don't quite like women who are interested in philanthropic work. I think it is so forward of them.

[*Enter MERRIMAN.*]

MERRIMAN: Miss Fairfax.

[*Enter GWENDOLEN.*]

[*Exit MERRIMAN.*]

CECILY (*advancing to meet her*): Pray let me introduce myself to you. My name is Cecily Cardew.

GWENDOLEN: Cecily Cardew? (*Moving to her and shaking hands.*) What a very sweet name! Something tells me that we are going to be great friends. I like you already more than I can say. My first impressions of people are never wrong.

CECILY: How nice of you to like me so much after we have known each other such a comparatively short time. Pray sit down.

GWENDOLEN (*still standing up*): I may call you Cecily, may I not?

CECILY: With pleasure!

GWENDOLEN: And you will always call me Gwendolen, won't you.

CECILY: If you wish.

GWENDOLEN: Then that is all quite settled, is it not?

CECILY: I hope so. (*A pause. They both sit down together.*)

GWENDOLEN: Perhaps this might be a favorable opportunity for my mentioning who I am. My father is Lord Bracknell. You have never heard of papa, I suppose?

CECILY: I don't think so.

GWENDOLEN: Outside the family circle, papa, I am glad to say, is entirely unknown. I think that is quite as it should be. The home seems to me to be the proper sphere for the man. And certainly once a man begins to neglect his domestic duties he becomes painfully effeminate, does he not? And I don't like that. It makes men so very attractive. Cecily, mamma, whose views on education are remarkably strict, has brought me up to be extremely short-sighted; it is part of her system; so do you mind my looking at you through my glasses?

CECILY: Oh! not at all, Gwendolen. I am very fond of being looked at.

GWENDOLEN (*after examining* CECILY *carefully through a lorgnette*): You are here on a short visit I suppose.

CECILY: Oh no! I live here.

GWENDOLEN (*severely*): Really? Your mother, no doubt, or some female relative of advanced years, resides here also?

CECILY: Oh no! I have no mother, nor, in fact, any relations.

GWENDOLEN: Indeed?

CECILY: My dear guardian, with the assistance of Miss Prism, has the arduous task of looking after me.

GWENDOLEN: Your guardian?

CECILY: Yes, I am Mr. Worthing's ward.

GWENDOLEN: Oh! It is strange he never mentioned to me that he had a ward. How secretive of him! He grows more interesting hourly. I am not sure, however, that the news inspires me with feelings of unmixed delight. (*Rising and going to her.*) I am very fond of you, Cecily; I have liked you ever since I met you! But I am bound to state that now that I know that you are Mr. Worthing's ward, I

cannot help expressing a wish you were—well just a little older than you seem to be—and not quite so very alluring in appearance. In fact, if I may speak candidly—

CECILY: Pray do! I think that whenever one has anything unpleasant to say, one should always be quite candid.

GWENDOLEN: Well, to speak with perfect candour, Cecily, I wish that you were fully forty-two, and more than usually plain for your age. Ernest has a strong upright nature. He is the very soul of truth and honour. Disloyalty would be as impossible to him as deception. But even men of the noblest possible moral character are extremely susceptible to the influence of the physical charms of others. Modern, no less than Ancient History, supplies us with many most painful examples of what I refer to. If it were not so, indeed, History would be quite unreadable.

CECILY: I beg your pardon, Gwendolen, did you say Ernest?

GWENDOLEN: Yes.

CECILY: Oh, but it is not Mr. Ernest Worthing who is my guardian. It is his brother—his elder brother.

GWENDOLEN (*sitting down again*): Ernest never mentioned to me that he had a brother.

CECILY: I am sorry to say they have not been on good terms for a long time.

GWENDOLEN: Ah! that accounts for it. And now that I think of it I have never heard any man mention his brother. The subject seems distasteful to most men. Cecily, you have lifted a load from my mind. I was growing almost anxious. It would have been terrible if any cloud had come across a friendship like ours, would it not? Of course you are quite, quite sure that it is not Mr. Ernest Worthing who is your guardian?

CECILY: Quite sure. (*A pause.*) In fact, I am going to be his.

GWENDOLEN (*enquiringly*): I beg your pardon?

CECILY (*rather shy and confidingly*): Dearest Gwendolen, there is no reason why I should make a secret of it to you. Our little county newspaper is sure to chronicle the fact next week. Mr. Ernest Worthing and I are engaged to be married.

GWENDOLEN (*quite politely, rising*): My darling Cecily, I think there must be some slight error. Mr. Ernest Worthing is engaged to me. The announcement will appear in the "Morning Post" on Saturday at the latest.

CECILY (*very politely, rising*): I am afraid you must be under some misconception. Ernest proposed to me exactly ten minutes ago. (*Shows diary.*)

GWENDOLEN (*examines diary through her lorgnette carefully*): It is certainly very curious, for he asked me to be his wife yesterday afternoon at 5.30. If you would care to verify the incident, pray do so.

(*Produces diary of her own.*) I never travel without my diary. One should always have something sensational to read in the train. I am so sorry, dear Cecily, if it is any disappointment to you, but I am afraid *I* have the prior claim.

CECILY: It would distress me more than I can tell you, dear Gwendolen, if it caused you any mental or physical anguish, but I feel bound to point out that since Ernest proposed to you he clearly has changed his mind.

GWENDOLEN (*meditatively*): If the poor fellow has been entrapped into any foolish promise I shall consider it my duty to rescue him at once, and with a firm hand.

CECILY (*thoughtfully and sadly*): Whatever unfortunate entanglement my dear boy may have got into, I will never reproach him with it after we are married.

GWENDOLEN: Do you allude to me, Miss Cardew, as an entanglement? You are presumptuous. On an occasion of this kind it becomes more than a moral duty to speak one's mind. It becomes a pleasure.

CECILY: Do you suggest, Miss Fairfax, that I entrapped Ernest into an engagement? How dare you? This is no time for wearing the shallow mask of manners. When I see a spade I call it a spade.

GWENDOLEN (*satirically*): I am glad to say that I have never seen a spade. It is obvious that our social spheres have been widely different.

[*Enter MERRIMAN, followed by the footman. He carries a salver, table cloth, and plate stand. CECILY is about to retort. The presence of the servants exercises a restraining influence, under which both girls chafe.*]

MERRIMAN: Shall I lay tea here as usual, Miss?

CECILY (*sternly, in a calm voice*): Yes, as usual. (MERRIMAN *begins to clear and lay cloth. A long pause.* CECILY *and* GWENDOLEN *glare at each other.*)

GWENDOLEN: Are there many interesting walks in the vicinity, Miss Cardew?

CECILY: Oh! yes! a great many. From the top of one of the hills quite close one can see five counties.

GWENDOLEN: Five counties! I don't think I should like that. I hate crowds.

CECILY (*sweetly*): I suppose that is why you live in town? (GWENDOLEN *bites her lip, and beats her foot nervously with her parasol.*)

GWENDOLEN (*looking round*): Quite a well-kept garden this is, Miss Cardew.

CECILY: So glad you like it, Miss Fairfax.

GWENDOLEN: I had no idea there were any flowers in the country.

CECILY: Oh, flowers are as common here, Miss Fairfax, as people are in London.

GWENDOLEN: Personally I cannot understand how anybody manages to exist in the country, if anybody who is anybody does. The country always bores me to death.

CECILY: Ah! This is what the newspapers call agricultural depression, is it not? I believe the aristocracy are suffering very much from it just at present. It is almost an epidemic amongst them, I have been told. May I offer you some tea, Miss Fairfax?

GWENDOLEN (*with elaborate politeness*): Thank you. (*Aside.*) Detestable girl! But I require tea!

CECILY (*sweetly*): Sugar?

GWENDOLEN (*superciliously*): No, thank you. Sugar is not fashionable any more. (CECILY *looks angrily at her, takes up the tongs and puts four lumps of sugar into the cup.*)

CECILY (*severely*): Cake or bread and butter?

GWENDOLEN (*In a bored manner*): Bread and butter, please. Cake is rarely seen at the best houses nowadays.

CECILY (*cuts a very large slice of cake, and puts it on the tray*): Hand that to Miss Fairfax.

[MERRIMAN *does so, and goes out with footman.* GWENDOLEN *drinks the tea and makes a grimace. Puts down cup at once, reaches out her hand to the bread and butter, looks at it, and finds it is cake. Rises in indignation.*]

GWENDOLEN: You have filled my tea with lumps of sugar, and though I asked most distinctly for bread and butter, you have given me cake. I am known for the gentleness of my disposition, and the extraordinary sweetness of my nature, but I warn you, Miss Cardew, you may go too far.

CECILY (*rising*): To save my poor, innocent, trusting boy from the machinations of any other girl there are no lengths to which I would not go.

GWENDOLEN: From the moment I saw you I distrusted you. I felt that you were false and deceitful. I am never deceived in such matters. My first impressions of people are invariably right.

CECILY: It seems to me, Miss Fairfax, that I am trespassing on your valuable time. No doubt you have many other calls of a similar character to make in the neighbourhood.

[*Enter JACK.*]

GWENDOLEN (*catching sight of him*): Ernest! My own Ernest!

JACK: Gwendolen! Darling! (*Offers to kiss her.*)

GWENDOLEN (*drawing back*): A moment! May I ask if you are engaged to be married to this young lady? (*Points to* CECILY.)

JACK (*laughing*): To dear little Cecily! Of course not! What could have put such an idea into your pretty little head?

GWENDOLEN: Thank you. You may. (*Offers her cheek.*)

CECILY (*very sweetly*): I knew there must be some misunderstanding, Miss Fairfax. The gentleman whose arm is at present around your waist is my dear guardian, Mr. John Worthing.

GWENDOLEN: I beg your pardon?

CECILY: This is Uncle Jack.

GWENDOLEN (*receding*): Jack! Oh!

[Enter ALGERNON.]

CECILY: Here is Ernest.

ALGERNON (*goes straight over to CECILY without noticing anyone else.*): My own love! (*Offers to kiss her.*)

CECILY (*drawing back*): A moment, Ernest! May I ask you—are you engaged to be married to this young lady?

ALGERNON (*looking round*): To what young lady? Good heavens! Gwendolen!

CECILY: Yes! to good heavens, Gwendolen, I mean to Gwendolen.

ALGERNON (*laughing*): Of course not! What could have put such an idea into your pretty little head?

CECILY: Thank you. (*Presenting her cheek to be kissed.*) You may. (ALGERNON *kisses her.*)

GWENDOLEN: I felt there was some slight error, Miss Cardew. The gentleman who is now embracing you is my cousin, Mr. Algernon Moncrieff.

CECILY (*breaking away from ALGERNON*): Algernon Moncrieff! Oh! (*The two girls move towards each other and put their arms round each other's waist as if for protection.*)

CECILY: Are you called Algernon?

ALGERNON: I cannot deny it.

CECILY: Oh!

GWENDOLEN: Is your name really John?

JACK (*standing rather proudly*): I could deny it if I liked. I could deny anything if I liked. But my name certainly is John. It has been John for years.

CECILY (*to GWENDOLEN*): A gross deception has been practised on both of us.

GWENDOLEN: My poor wounded Cecily!

CECILY: My sweet wronged Gwendolen!

GWENDOLEN (*slowly and seriously*): You will call me sister, will you not? (*They embrace.* JACK *and* ALGERNON *groan and walk up and down.*)

CECILY (*rather brightly*): There is just one question I would like to be allowed to ask my guardian.

GWENDOLEN: An admirable idea! Mr. Worthing, there is just one question I would like to be permitted to put to you. Where is your brother Ernest? We are both engaged to be married to your brother Ernest, so it is a matter of some importance to us to know where your brother Ernest is at present.

JACK (*slowly and hesitatingly*): Gwendolen—Cecily—it is very painful for me to be forced to speak the truth. It is the first time in my life that I have ever been reduced to such a painful position, and I am really quite inexperienced in doing anything of the kind. However I will tell you quite frankly that I have no brother Ernest. I have no brother at all. I never had a brother in my life, and I certainly have not the smallest intention of ever having one in the future.

CECILY (*surprised*): No brother at all?

JACK (*cheerily*): None!

GWENDOLEN (*severely*): Had you never a brother of any kind?

JACK (*pleasantly*): Never. Not even of any kind.

GWENDOLEN: I am afraid it is quite clear, Cecily, that neither of us is engaged to be married to anyone.

CECILY: It is not a very pleasant position for a young girl suddenly to find herself in. Is it?

GWENDOLEN: Let us go into the house. They will hardly venture to come after us there.

CECILY: No, men are so cowardly, aren't they?

[They retire into the house with scornful looks.]

JACK: This ghastly state of things is what you call Bunburying, I suppose?

ALGERNON: Yes, and a perfectly wonderful Bunbury it is. The most wonderful Bunbury I have ever had in my life.

JACK: Well, you've no right whatsoever to Bunbury here.

ALGERNON: That is absurd. One has a right to Bunbury anywhere one chooses. Every serious Bunburyist knows that.

JACK: Serious Bunburyist! Good heavens!

ALGERNON: Well, one must be serious about something, if one wants to have any amusement in life. I happen to be serious about Bunburying. What on earth you are serious about I haven't got the remotest idea. About everything, I should fancy. You have such an absolutely trivial nature.

JACK: Well, the only small satisfaction I have in the whole of this wretched business is that your friend Bunbury is quite exploded. You won't be able to run down to the country quite so often as you used to do, dear Algy. And a very good thing too.

ALGERNON: Your brother is a little off colour, isn't he, dear Jack? You won't be able to disappear to London quite so frequently as your wicked custom was. And not a bad thing either.

JACK: As for your conduct towards Miss Cardew, I must say that your taking in a sweet, simple, innocent girl like that is quite inexcusable. To say nothing of the fact that she is my ward.

ALGERNON: I can see no possible defence at all for your deceiving a brilliant, clever, thoroughly experienced young lady like Miss Fairfax. To say nothing of the fact that she is my cousin.

JACK: I wanted to be engaged to Gwendolen, that is all. I love her.

ALGERNON: Well, I simply wanted to be engaged to Cecily. I adore her.

JACK: There is certainly no chance of your marrying Miss Cardew.

ALGERNON: I don't think there is much likelihood, Jack, of you and Miss Fairfax being united.

JACK: Well, that is no business of yours.

ALGERNON: If it was my business, I wouldn't talk about it. (*Begins to eat muffins.*) It is very vulgar to talk about one's business. Only people like stock-brokers do that, and then merely at dinner parties.

JACK: How can you sit there, calmly eating muffins when we are in this horrible trouble, I can't make out. You seem to me to be perfectly heartless.

ALGERNON: Well, I can't eat muffins in an agitated manner. The butter would probably get on my cuffs. One should always eat muffins quite calmly. It is the only way to eat them.

JACK: I say it's perfectly heartless your eating muffins at all, under the circumstances.

ALGERNON: When I am in trouble, eating is the only thing that consoles me. Indeed, when I am in really great trouble, as anyone who knows me intimately will tell you, I refuse everything except food and drink. At the present moment I am eating muffins because I am unhappy. Besides, I am particularly fond of muffins. (*Rising.*)

JACK (*rising*): Well, that is no reason why you should eat them all in that greedy way. (*Takes muffins from* ALGERNON.)

ALGERNON (*offering tea-cake*): I wish you would have tea-cake instead. I don't like tea-cake.

JACK: Good heavens! I suppose a man may eat his own muffins in his own garden.

ALGERNON: But you have just said it was perfectly heartless to eat muffins.

JACK: I said it was perfectly heartless of you, under the circumstances. That is a very different thing.

ALGERNON: That may be. But the muffins are the same. (*He seizes the muffin-dish from* JACK.)

JACK: Algy, I wish to goodness you would go.

ALGERNON: You can't possibly ask me to go without having some dinner. It's absurd. I never go without my dinner. No one ever does, except vegetarians and people like that. Besides I have just made arrangements with Dr. Chasuble to be christened at a quarter to six under the name of Ernest.

JACK: My dear fellow, the sooner you give up that nonsense the better. I made arrangements this morning with Dr. Chasuble to be christened myself at 5:30, and I naturally will take the name of Ernest. Gwendolen would wish it. We can't both be christened Ernest. It's absurd. Besides, I have a perfect right to be christened if I like. There is no evidence at all that I ever have been christened by anybody. I should think it extremely probable I never was, and so does Dr. Chasuble. It is entirely different in your case. You have been christened already.

ALGERNON: Yes, but I have not been christened for years.

JACK: Yes, but you have been christened. That is the important thing.

ALGERNON: Quite so. So I know my constitution can stand it. If you are not quite sure about your ever having been christened, I must say I think it rather dangerous your venturing on it now. It might make you very unwell. You can hardly have forgotten that someone very closely connected with you was very nearly carried off this week in Paris by a severe chill.

JACK: Yes, but you said yourself that a severe chill was not hereditary.

ALGERNON: It usen't to be, I know—but I daresay it is now. Science is always making wonderful improvements in things.

JACK (*picking up the muffin-dish*): Oh, that is nonsense; you are always talking nonsense.

ALGERNON: Jack, you are at the muffins again! I wish you wouldn't. There are only two left. (*Takes them.*) I told you I was particularly fond of muffins.

JACK: But I hate tea-cake.

ALGERNON: Why on earth then do you allow tea-cake to be served up for your guests? What ideas you have of hospitality!

JACK: Algernon! I have already told you to go. I don't want you here. Why don't you go!

ALGERNON: I haven't quite finished my tea yet! and there is still one muffin left. (JACK *groans, and sinks into a chair.* ALGERNON *still continues eating.*)

ACT-DROP.

ACT III

Scene—Morning-room at the Manor House.

[GWENDOLEN *and* CECILY *are at the window, looking out into the garden.*]

GWENDOLEN: The fact that they did not follow us at once into the house, as anyone else would have done, seems to me to show that they have some sense of shame left.

CECILY: They have been eating muffins. That looks like repentance.

GWENDOLEN (*after a pause*): They don't seem to notice us at all. Couldn't you cough?

CECILY: But I haven't a cough.

GWENDOLEN: They're looking at us. What effrontery!

CECILY: They're approaching. That's very forward of them.

GWENDOLEN: Let us preserve a dignified silence.

CECILY: Certainly. It's the only thing to do now.

[Enter JACK followed by ALGERNON. They whistle some dreadful popular air from a British Opera.]

GWENDOLEN: This dignified silence seems to produce an unpleasant effect.

CECILY: A most distasteful one.

GWENDOLEN: But we will not be the first to speak.

CECILY: Certainly not.

GWENDOLEN: Mr. Worthing, I have something very particular to ask you. Much depends on your reply.

CECILY: Gwendolen, your common sense is invaluable. Mr. Moncrieff, kindly answer me the following question. Why did you pretend to be my guardian's brother?

ALGERNON: In order that I might have an opportunity of meeting you.

CECILY (*to* GWENDOLEN): That certainly seems a satisfactory explanation, does it not?

GWENDOLEN: Yes, dear, if you can believe him.

CECILY: I don't. But that does not affect the wonderful beauty of his answer.

GWENDOLEN: True. In matters of grave importance, style, not sincerity is the vital thing. Mr. Worthing, what explanation can you offer to me for pretending to have a brother? Was it in order that you might have an opportunity of coming up to town to see me as often as possible?

JACK: Can you doubt it, Miss Fairfax?

GWENDOLEN: I have the gravest doubts upon the subject. But I intend to crush them. This is not the moment for German scepticism. (*Moving to* CECILY.) Their explanations appear to be quite satisfactory, especially Mr. Worthing's. That seems to me to have the stamp of truth upon it.

CECILY: I am more than content with what Mr. Moncrieff said. His voice alone inspires one with absolute credulity.

GWENDOLEN: Then you think we should forgive them?

CECILY: Yes. I mean no.

GWENDOLEN: True! I had forgotten. There are principles at stake that one cannot surrender. Which of us should tell them? The task is not a pleasant one.

CECILY: Could we not both speak at the same time?

GWENDOLEN: An excellent idea! I nearly always speak at the same time as other people. Will you take the time from me?

CECILY: Certainly. (GWENDOLEN *beats time with uplifted finger.*)

GWENDOLEN and CECILY (*speaking together*): Your Christian names are still an insuperable barrier. That is all!

JACK and ALGERNON (*speaking together*): Our Christian names! Is that all? But we are going to be christened this afternoon.

GWENDOLEN (*to* JACK): For my sake you are prepared to do this terrible thing?

JACK: I am.

CECILY (*to* ALGERNON): To please me you are ready to face this fearful ordeal?

ALGERNON: I am!

GWENDOLEN: How absurd to talk of the equality of the sexes! Where questions of self-sacrifice are concerned, men are infinitely beyond us.

JACK: We are. (*Clasps hands with* ALGERNON.)

CECILY: They have moments of physical courage of which we women know absolutely nothing.

GWENDOLEN (*to* JACK): Darling!

ALGERNON (*to* CECILY): Darling! (*They fall into each other's arms.*)

[Enter MERRIMAN: When he enters he coughs loudly, seeing the situation.]

MERRIMAN: Ahem! Ahem! Lady Bracknell!

JACK: Good heavens!

[Enter LADY BRACKNELL. The couples separate in alarm. Exit MERRIMAN.]

LADY BRACKNELL: Gwendolen! What does this mean?

GWENDOLEN: Merely that I am engaged to be married to Mr. Worthing, mamma.

LADY BRACKNELL: Come here. Sit down. Sit down immediately. Hesitation of any kind is a sign of mental decay in the young, of physical weakness in the old. (*Turns to* JACK.) Apprised, sir, of my daughter's sudden flight by her trusty maid, whose confidence I purchased by means of a small coin, I followed her at once by a luggage train. Her unhappy father is, I am glad to say, under the impression that she is attending a more than usually lengthy lecture by the University Extension Scheme on the Influence of a permanent income on Thought. I do not propose to undeceive him. Indeed I have never undeceived him on any question. I would consider it wrong. But of course, you will clearly understand that all communication between yourself and my daughter must cease immediately from this moment. On this point, as indeed on all points, I am firm.

JACK: I am engaged to be married to Gwendolen, Lady Bracknell!

LADY BRACKNELL: You are nothing of the kind, sir. And now, as regards Algernon! . . . Algernon!

ALGERNON: Yes, Aunt Augusta.

LADY BRACKNELL: May I ask if it is in this house that your invalid friend Mr. Bunbury resides?

ALGERNON (*stammering*): Oh! No! Bunbury doesn't

live here. Bunbury is somewhere else at present. In fact, Bunbury is dead.

LADY BRACKNELL: Dead! When did Mr. Bunbury die? His death must have been extremely sudden.

ALGERNON (*airly*): Oh! I killed Bunbury this afternoon. I mean poor Bunbury died this afternoon.

LADY BRACKNELL: What did he die of?

ALGERNON: Bunbury? Oh, he was quite exploded.

LADY BRACKNELL: Exploded! Was he the victim of a revolutionary outrage? I was not aware that Mr. Bunbury was interested in social legislation. If so, he is well punished for his morbidity.

ALGERNON: My dear Aunt Augusta, I mean he was found out! The doctors found out that Bunbury could not live, that is what I mean—so Bunbury died.

LADY BRACKNELL: He seems to have had great confidence in the opinion of his physicians. I am glad, however, that he made up his mind at the last to some definite course of action, and acted under proper medical advice. And now that we have finally got rid of this Mr. Bunbury, may I ask, Mr. Worthing, who is that young person whose hand my nephew Algernon is now holding in what seems to me a peculiarly unnecessary manner?

JACK: That lady is Miss Cecily Cardew, my ward.

(LADY BRACKNELL bows coldly to CECILY.)

ALGERNON: I am engaged to be married to Cecily, Aunt Augusta.

LADY BRACKNELL: I beg your pardon?

CECILY: Mr. Moncrieff and I are engaged to be married, Lady Bracknell.

LADY BRACKNELL (*with a shiver, crossing to the sofa and sitting down*): I do not know whether there is anything peculiarly exciting in the air of this particular part of Hertfordshire, but the number of engagements that go on seems to me considerably above the proper average that statistics have laid down for our guidance. I think some preliminary enquiry on my part would not be out of place. Mr. Worthing, is Miss Cardew at all connected with any of the larger railway stations in London? I merely desire information. Until yesterday I had no idea that there were any families or persons whose origin was a Terminus. (JACK *looks perfectly furious, but restrains himself.*)

JACK (*in a clear, cold voice*): Miss Cardew is the granddaughter of the late Mr. Thomas Cardew of 149, Belgrave Square, S.W.; Gervase Park, Dorking, Surrey; and the Sporran, Fifeshire, N.B.

LADY BRACKNELL: That sounds not unsatisfactory. Three addresses always inspire confidence, even in tradesmen. But what proof have I of their authenticity?

JACK: I have carefully preserved the Court Guides of the period. They are open to your inspection, Lady Bracknell.

LADY BRACKNELL (*grimly*): I have known strange errors in that publication.

JACK: Miss Cardew's family solicitors are Messrs. Markby, Markby, and Markby.

LADY BRACKNELL: Markby, Markby, and Markby? A firm of the very highest position in their profession. Indeed I am told that one of the Mr. Markbys is occasionally to be seen at dinner parties. So far I am satisfied.

JACK (*very irritably*): How extremely kind of you, Lady Bracknell! I have also in my possession, you will be pleased to hear, certificates of Miss Cardew's birth, baptism, whooping cough, registration, vaccination, confirmation, and the measles; both the German and the English variety.

LADY BRACKNELL: Ah! A life crowded with incident, I see; though perhaps somewhat too exciting for a young girl. I am not myself in favour of premature experiences. (*Rises, looks at her watch.*) Gwendolen! the time approaches for our departure. We have not a moment to lose. As a matter of form, Mr. Worthing, I had better ask you if Miss Cardew has any little fortune?

JACK: Oh! about a hundred and thirty thousand pounds in the Funds. That is all. Good-bye, Lady Bracknell. So pleased to have seen you.

LADY BRACKNELL (*sitting down again*): A moment, Mr. Worthing. A hundred and thirty thousand pounds! And in the Funds! Miss Cardew seems to me a most attractive young lady, now that I look at her. Few girls of the present day have any really solid qualities, any of the qualities that last, and improve with time. We live, I regret to say, in an age of surfaces. (*To CECILY.*) Come over here, dear. (CECILY *goes across.*) Pretty child! your dress is sadly simple, and your hair seems almost as Nature might have left it. But we can soon alter all that. A thoroughly experienced French maid produces a really marvellous result in a very brief space of time. I remember recommending one to young Lady Lancing, and after three months her own husband did not know her.

JACK (*aside*): And after six months nobody knew her.

LADY BRACKNELL (*glares at JACK for a few moments. Then bends, with a practised smile, to CECILY.*): Kindly turn round, sweet child. (CECILY *turns completely round.*) No, the side view is what I want. (CECILY *presents her profile.*) Yes, quite as I expected. There are distinct social possibilities in your profile. The two weak points in our age are its want of principle and its want of profile. The chin a little higher, dear. Style largely depends on the way the chin is worn. They are worn very high, just at present. Algernon!

ALGERNON: Yes, Aunt Augusta!

LADY BRACKNELL: There are distinct social possibilities in Miss Cardew's profile.

ALGERNON: Cecily is the sweetest, dearest, prettiest girl in the whole world. And I don't care twopence about social possibilities.

LADY BRACKNELL: Never speak disrespectfully of Society, Algernon. Only people who can't get into it do that. (*To* CECILY.) Dear child, of course you know that Algernon has nothing but his debts to depend upon. But I do not approve of mercenary marriages. When I married Lord Bracknell I had no fortune of any kind. But I never dreamed for a moment of allowing that to stand in my way. Well, I suppose I must give my consent.

ALGERNON: Thank you, Aunt Augusta.

LADY BRACKNELL: Cecily, you may kiss me!

CECILY (*kisses her*): Thank you, Lady Bracknell.

LADY BRACKNELL: You may also address me as Aunt Augusta for the future.

CECILY: Thank you, Aunt Augusta.

LADY BRACKNELL: The marriage, I think, had better take place quite soon.

ALGERNON: Thank you, Aunt Augusta.

CECILY: Thank you, Aunt Augusta.

LADY BRACKNELL: To speak frankly, I am not in favour of long engagements. They give people the opportunity of finding out each other's character before marriage, which I think is never advisable.

JACK: I beg your pardon for interrupting you, Lady Bracknell, but this engagement is quite out of the question. I am Miss Cardew's guardian, and she cannot marry without my consent until she comes of age. That consent I absolutely decline to give.

LADY BRACKNELL: Upon what grounds, may I ask? Algernon is an extremely, I may almost say an ostentatiously, eligible young man. He has nothing, but he looks everything. What more can one desire?

JACK: It pains me very much to have to speak frankly to you, Lady Bracknell, about your nephew, but the fact is that I do not approve at all of his moral character. I suspect him of being untruthful. (ALGERNON *and* CECILY *look at him in indignant amazement.*)

LADY BRACKNELL: Untruthful! My nephew Algernon? Impossible! He is an Oxonian.

JACK: I fear there can be no possible doubt about the matter. This afternoon, during my temporary absence in London on an important question of romance, he obtained admission to my house by means of the false pretence of being my brother. Under an assumed name he drank, I've just been informed by my butler, an entire pint bottle of my Perrier-Jouet, Brut, '89; a wine I was specially reserving for myself. Continuing his disgraceful deception, he succeeded in the course of the afternoon in alienating the affections of my only ward.

He subsequently stayed to tea, and devoured every single muffin. And what makes his conduct all the more heartless is, that he was perfectly well aware from the first that I have no brother, that I never had a brother, and that I don't intend to have a brother, not even of any kind. I distinctly told him so myself yesterday afternoon.

LADY BRACKNELL: Ahem! Mr. Worthing, after careful consideration I have decided entirely to overlook my nephew's conduct to you.

JACK: That is very generous of you, Lady Bracknell. My own decision, however, is unalterable. I decline to give my consent.

LADY BRACKNELL (*to* CECILY): Come here, sweet child. (CECILY *goes over.*) How old are you, dear?

CECILY: Well, I am really only eighteen, but I always admit to twenty when I go to evening parties.

LADY BRACKNELL: You are perfectly right in making some slight alteration. Indeed, no woman should ever be quite accurate about her age. It looks so calculating. . . . (*In a meditative manner.*) Eighteen, but admitting to twenty at evening parties. Well, it will not be very long before you are of age and free from the restraints of tutelage. So I don't think your guardian's consent is, after all, a matter of any importance.

JACK: Pray excuse me, Lady Bracknell, for interrupting you again, but it is only fair to tell you that according to the terms of her grandfather's will Miss Cardew does not come legally of age till she is thirty-five.

LADY BRACKNELL: That does not seem to me to be a grave objection. Thirty-five is a very attractive age. London society is full of women of the very highest birth who have, of their own free choice, remained thirty-five for years. Lady Dumbleton is an instance in point. To my own knowledge she has been thirty-five ever since she arrived at the age of forty, which was many years ago now. I see no reason why our dear Cecily should not be even still more attractive at the age you mention that she is at present. There will be a large accumulation of property.

CECILY: Algy, could you wait for me till I was thirty-five?

ALGERNON: Of course I could, Cecily. You know I could.

CECILY: Yes, I felt it instinctively, but I couldn't wait all that time. I hate waiting even five minutes for anybody. It always makes me rather cross. I am not punctual myself, I know, but I do like punctuality in others, and waiting, even to be married, is quite out of the question.

ALGERNON: Then what is to be done, Cecily?

CECILY: I don't know, Mr. Moncrieff.

LADY BRACKNELL: My dear Mr. Worthing, as Miss Cardew states positively that she cannot wait till she is thirty-five—a remark which I am bound to say seems to me to show a somewhat impatient nature—I would beg of you to reconsider your decision.

JACK: But my dear Lady Bracknell, the matter is entirely in your own hands. The moment you consent to my marriage with Gwendolen, I will most gladly allow your nephew to form an alliance with my ward.

LADY BRACKNELL (*rising and drawing herself up*): You must be quite aware that what you propose is out of the question.

JACK: Then a passionate celibacy is all that any of us can look forward to.

LADY BRACKNELL: That is not the destiny I propose for Gwendolen. Algernon, of course, can choose for himself. (*Pulls out her watch.*) Come dear; (GWENDOLEN *rises*) we have already missed five, if not six, trains. To miss any more might expose us to comment on the platform.

[*Enter DR. CHASUBLE.*]

CHASUBLE: Everything is quite ready for the christenings.

LADY BRACKNELL: The christenings, sir! Is not that somewhat premature?

CHASUBLE (*looking rather puzzled, and pointing to* JACK *and* ALGERNON): Both these gentlemen have expressed a desire for immediate baptism.

LADY BRACKNELL: At their age? The idea is grotesque and irreligious! Algernon, I forbid you to be baptised. I will not hear of such excesses. Lord Bracknell would be highly displeased if he learned that that was the way in which you wasted your time and money.

CHASUBLE: Am I to understand then that there are to be no christenings at all this afternoon?

JACK: I don't think that, as things are now, it would be of much practical value to either of us, Dr. Chasuble.

CHASUBLE: I am grieved to hear such sentiments from you, Mr. Worthing. They savour of the heretical views of the Anabaptists, views that I have completely refuted in four of my unpublished sermons. However, as your present mood seems to be one peculiarly secular, I will return to the church at once. Indeed, I have just been informed by the pew-opener that for the last hour and a half Miss Prism has been waiting for me in the vestry.

LADY BRACKNELL (*starting*): Miss Prism! Did I hear you mention a Miss Prism?

CHASUBLE: Yes, Lady Bracknell. I am on my way to join her.

LADY BRACKNELL: Pray allow me to detain you for a moment. This matter may prove to be one of vital importance to Lord Bracknell and myself. Is this Miss Prism a female of repellent aspect, remotely connected with education?

CHASUBLE (*somewhat indignantly*): She is the most cultivated of ladies, and the very picture of respectability.

LADY BRACKNELL: It is obviously the same person. May I ask what position she holds in your household?

CHASUBLE (*severely*): I am a celibate, madam.

JACK (*interposing*): Miss Prism, Lady Bracknell, has been for the last three years Miss Cardew's esteemed governess and valued companion.

LADY BRACKNELL: In spite of what I hear of her, I must see her at once. Let her be sent for.

CHASUBLE (*looking off*): She approaches; she is nigh.

[*Enter MISS PRISM hurriedly.*]

MISS PRISM: I was told you expected me in the vestry, dear Canon. I have been waiting for you there for an hour and three-quarters. (*Catches sight of* LADY BRACKNELL, *who has fixed her with a stony glare.* MISS PRISM *grows pale and quails. She looks anxiously round as if desirous to escape.*)

LADY BRACKNELL (*in a severe, judicial voice*): Prism! (MISS PRISM *bows her head in shame.*) Come here, Prism! (MISS PRISM *approaches in a humble manner.*) Prism! Where is that baby? (*General consternation. The Canon starts back in horror.* ALGERNON *and* JACK *pretend to be anxious to shield* CECILY *and* GWENDOLEN *from hearing the details of a terrible public scandal.*) Twenty-eight years ago, Prism, you left Lord Bracknell's house, Number 104, Upper Grosvenor Street, in charge of a perambulator that contained a baby, of the male sex. You never returned. A few weeks later, through the elaborate investigations of the Metropolitan police, the perambulator was discovered at midnight, standing by itself in a remote corner of Bayswater. It contained the manuscript of a three-volume novel of more than usually revolting sentimentality. (MISS PRISM *starts in involuntary indignation.*) But the baby was not there! (*Everyone looks at* MISS PRISM.) Prism; Where is that baby? (*A pause.*)

MISS PRISM: Lady Bracknell, I admit with shame that I do not know. I only wish I did. The plain facts of the case are these. On the morning of the day you mention, a day that is for ever branded on my memory, I prepared as usual to take the baby out in its perambulator. I had also with me a somewhat old, but capacious hand-bag in which I had intended to place the manuscript of a work of fiction that I had written during my few unoccupied hours. In a moment of mental abstraction, for which I never can forgive myself, I deposited the manuscript in the bassinette, and placed the baby in the hand-bag.

JACK (*who has been listening attentively*): But where did you deposit the hand-bag?

MISS PRISM: Do not ask me, Mr. Worthing.

JACK: Miss Prism, this is a matter of no small importance to me. I insist on knowing where you deposited the hand-bag that contained that infant.

MISS PRISM: I left it in the cloak room of one of the larger railway stations in London.

JACK: What railway station?

MISS PRISM (*quite crushed*): Victoria. The Brighton line. (*Sinks into a chair.*)

JACK: I must retire to my room for a moment. Gwendolen, wait here for me.

GWENDOLEN: If you are not too long, I will wait here for you all my life.

[*Exit JACK in great excitement.*]

CHASUBLE: What do you think this means, Lady Bracknell?

LADY BRACKNELL: I dare not even suspect, Dr. Chasuble. I need hardly tell you that in families of high position strange coincidences are not supposed to occur. They are hardly considered the thing.

[*Noises heard overhead as if someone was throwing trunks about. Everyone looks up.*]

CECILY: Uncle Jack seems strangely agitated.

CHASUBLE: Your guardian has a very emotional nature.

LADY BRACKNELL: This noise is extremely unpleasant. It sounds as if he was having an argument. I dislike arguments of any kind. They are always vulgar, and often convincing.

CHASUBLE (*looking up*): It has stopped now. (*The noise is redoubled.*)

LADY BRACKNELL: I wish he would arrive at some conclusion.

GWENDOLEN: This suspense is terrible. I hope it will last.

[*Enter JACK with a hand-bag of black leather in his hand.*]

JACK (*rushing over to MISS PRISM*): Is this the hand-bag, Miss Prism? Examine it carefully before you speak. The happiness of more than one life depends on your answer.

MISS PRISM (*calmly*): It seems to be mine. Yes, here is the injury it received through the upsetting of a Gower Street omnibus in younger and happier days. Here is the stain on the lining caused by the explosion of a temperance beverage, an incident that occurred at Leamington. And here, on the lock, are my initials. I had forgotten that in an extravagant mood I had had them placed there.

The bag is undoubtedly mine. I am delighted to have it so unexpectedly restored to me. It has been a great inconvenience being without it all these years.

JACK (*in a pathetic voice*): Miss Prism, more is restored to you than this hand-bag. I was the baby you placed in it.

MISS PRISM (*amazed*): You?

JACK (*embracing her*): Yes . . . mother!

MISS PRISM (*recoiling in indignant astonishment*): Mr. Worthing! I am unmarried!

JACK: Unmarried! I do not deny that is a serious blow. But after all, who has the right to cast a stone against one who has suffered? Cannot repentance wipe out an act of folly? Why should there be one law for men, and another for women? Mother, I forgive you. (*Tries to embrace her again.*)

MISS PRISM (*still more indignant*): Mr. Worthing, there is some error. (*Pointing to LADY BRACKNELL.*) There is the lady who can tell you who you really are.

JACK (*after a pause*): Lady Bracknell, I hate to seem inquisitive, but would you kindly inform me who I am?

LADY BRACKNELL: I am afraid that the news I have to give you will not altogether please you. You are the son of my poor sister, Mrs. Moncrieff, and consequently Algernon's elder brother.

JACK: Algy's elder brother! Then I have a brother after all. I knew I had a brother! I always said I had a brother! Cecily,—how could you have ever doubted that I had a brother. (*Seizes hold of ALGERNON.*) Dr. Chasuble, my unfortunate brother. Miss Prism, my unfortunate brother. Gwendolen, my unfortunate brother. Algy, you young scoundrel, you will have to treat me with more respect in the future. You have never behaved to me like a brother in all your life.

ALGERNON: Well, not till to-day, old boy, I admit. I did my best, however, though I was out of practice. (*Shakes hands.*)

GWENDOLEN (*to JACK*): My own! But what own are you? What is your Christian name, now that you have become someone else?

JACK: Good heavens! . . . I had quite forgotten that point. Your decision on the subject of my name is irrevocable, I suppose?

GWENDOLEN: I never change, except in my affections.

CECILY: What a noble nature you have, Gwendolen!

JACK: Then the question had better be cleared up at once. Aunt Augusta, a moment. At the time when Miss Prism left me in the hand-bag, had I been christened already?

LADY BRACKNELL: Every luxury that money could buy, including christening, had been lavished on you by your fond and doting parents.

JACK: Then I was christened! That is settled. Now,

what name was I given? Let me know the worst.

LADY BRACKNELL: Being the eldest son you were naturally christened after your father.

JACK (*irritably*): Yes, but what was my father's Christian name?

LADY BRACKNELL (*meditatively*): I cannot at the present moment recall what the General's christian name was. But I have no doubt he had one. He was eccentric, I admit. But only in later years. And that was the result of the Indian climate, and marriage, and indigestion, and other things of that kind.

JACK: Algy! Can't you recollect what our father's Christian name was?

ALGERNON: My dear boy, we were never even on speaking terms. He died before I was a year old.

JACK: His name would appear in the Army Lists of the period, I suppose, Aunt Augusta?

LADY BRACKNELL: The General was essentially a man of peace, except in his domestic life. But I have no doubt his name would appear in any military directory.

JACK: The Army Lists of the last forty years are here. These delightful records should have been my constant study. (*Rushes to bookcase and tears the books out.*) M. Generals . . . . Mallam, Maxbohm, Magley, what ghastly names they have—Markby, Migsby, Mobbs, Moncrieff! Lieutenant 1840, Captain, Lieutenant-Colonel, Colonel, General

1869, Christian names, Ernest John. (*Puts book very quietly down and speaks quite calmly.*) I always told you, Gwendolen, my name was Ernest, didn't I? Well, it is Ernest after all. I mean it naturally is Ernest.

LADY BRACKNELL: Yes, I remember that the General was called Ernest. I knew I had some particular reason for disliking the name.

GWENDOLEN: Ernest! My own Ernest! I felt from the first that you could have no other name!

JACK: Gwendolen, it is a terrible thing for a man to find out suddenly that all his life he has been speaking nothing but the truth. Can you forgive me?

GWENDOLEN: I can. For I feel that you are sure to change.

JACK: My own one!

CHASUBLE (*to* MISS PRISM): Lætitia! (*Embraces her.*)

MISS PRISM (*enthusiastically*): Frederick! At last!

ALGERNON: Cecily! (*Embraces her.*) At last!

JACK: Gwendolen! (*Embraces her.*) At last!

LADY BRACKNELL: My nephew, you seem to be displaying signs of triviality.

JACK: On the contrary, Aunt Augusta, I've now realized for the first time in my life the vital Importance of Being Earnest.

Tableau.

Curtain.

JOHN MILLINGTON SYNGE
(1871–1909)

W. B. Yeats and Lady Augusta Gregory met Synge in Paris in 1896, where he was studying violin. Impressed by his talent and imagination, they convinced him to return with them to Ireland to write for the Irish National Theatre—soon to become the Abbey Theatre—which they were founding. Established in 1904 in Dublin, the Abbey Theatre became widely known as the most successful of all national theaters. From its opening to the present day, it has produced plays only by Irish writers, many of whom have made a profound impression on twentieth-century theater, including Yeats himself and Lady Gregory, George Bernard Shaw, Synge, Sean O'Casey, and, more recently, Brian Friel. For a while Synge lived in the Aran Islands off the coast of western Ireland, which inspired him to write *Riders to the Sea* (1904). Again it was Yeats who advised Synge to go there, believing that the Aran Islands preserved a distinctive language and culture that could inspire authentic Irish literature.

Within a period of less than ten years, Synge turned out six important plays for the Abbey Theatre: *In the Shadow of the Glen* (1903), *Riders to the Sea* (1904), *The Well of the Saints* (1905), *The Tinker's Wedding* (1907), *The Playboy of the Western World* (1907), and *Deirdre of the Sorrows* (1910). Almost all of his works are still revived periodically there, with one exception: *The Tinker's Wedding*, in which Synge's view of the clergy proved so controversial that it was never produced at the Abbey. Characteristically, his provocative plays present an idealized view of Irish life, occasionally provoking rebellion among audiences who expect better reflections of themselves. In *Playboy of the Western World*, Christy Mahon is made a local hero after he reports that he has killed his father. The subject matter, the language, and the action—Christy actually hits his clearly alive father late in the play—caused riots at the Abbey. And when the play was produced in Boston three years later, more rioting occurred. Synge died relatively young, at age thirty-nine, and his early death prevented him from developing a significant body of work. Nevertheless, even his early work has assured him of a place among the most important dramatists of the century.

Riders to the Sea

Riders to the Sea (1904) is one of the purest and most affecting of Synge's plays. Set in the west of Ireland, it is a one-act, dialect play in which Synge attempts to reproduce the peculiar pronunciation, the expressive rhythms, and words of the

Aran Islanders. Synge modeled the dialogue on actual speech patterns he heard spoken on the islands. The suggestive power of the speech in the world of the play and Synge's faithful portrayal of a local way of life conspire together with a pattern reminiscent of Greek tragedy to create a play of extraordinary power.

Maintaining the unities of time, place, and action, Synge creates a kind of folk tragedy by infusing his characters with a clear sense of fate's unrelenting nature. In the play, Maurya comes to see the inevitability of the death at sea of her last living son. The growing awareness is developed metaphorically in realistic conversations between the daughters, who innocently discuss the number of stitches in the sock that belonged to Michael, now recovered from the sea, and in Bartley's determination to take the horses by sea to the mainland. Maurya's horrifying vision of Michael riding to the sea with Bartley is a premonition of his death. The play ends with the women wailing—keening—for the dead. Maurya is left only to suffer and to face the grim consequences of Michael's death. The short but resonant play compresses the effect of powerful myth about suffering and extraordinary endurance in this harsh environment.

Riders to the Sea

John Millington Synge

CHARACTERS
MAURYA, an old woman
BARTLEY, her son
CATHLEEN, her daughter
NORA, a younger daughter
MEN AND WOMEN

SCENE: *An Island off the West of Ireland.*

[Cottage kitchen, with nets, oil-skins, spinning-wheel, some new boards standing by the wall, etc. Cathleen, a girl of about twenty, finishes kneading cake, and puts it down in the pot-oven° by the fire; then wipes her hands, and begins to spin at the wheel. Nora, a young girl, puts her head in at the door.]

NORA (*in a low voice*): Where is she?
CATHLEEN: She's lying down, God help her, and may be sleeping, if she's able.

[NORA comes in softly, and takes a bundle from under her shawl.]

CATHLEEN (*spinning the wheel rapidly*): What is it you have?
NORA: The young priest is after bringing them. It's a shirt and a plain stocking were got off a drowned man in Donegal.

[CATHLEEN stops her wheel with a sudden movement, and leans out to listen.]

NORA: We're to find out if it's Michael's they are, some time herself will be down looking by the sea.
CATHLEEN: How would they be Michael's, Nora? How would he go the length of that way to the far north?
NORA: The young priest says he's known the like of it. "If it's Michael's they are," says he, "you can tell herself he's got a clean burial by the grace of God, and if they're not his, let no one say a word about them, for she'll be getting her death," says he, "with crying and lamenting."

[The door which NORA half closed is blown open by a gust of wind.]

CATHLEEN (*looking out anxiously*): Did you ask him would he stop Bartley going this day with the horses to the Galway fair?
NORA: "I won't stop him," says he, "but let you not be afraid. Herself does be saying prayers half through the night, and the Almighty God won't

---

¹ **pot-oven** heated iron plate covered by a pot

leave her destitute," says he, "with no son living."

CATHLEEN: Is the sea bad by the white rocks, Nora?

NORA: Middling bad, God help us. There's a great roaring in the west, and it's worse it'll be getting when the tide's turned to the wind. (*She goes over to the table with the bundle.*) Shall I open it now?

CATHLEEN: Maybe she'd wake up on us, and come in before we'd done. (*Coming to the table.*) It's a long time we'll be, and the two of us crying.

NORA (*goes to the inner door and listens*): She's moving about on the bed. She'll be coming in a minute.

CATHLEEN: Give me the ladder, and I'll put them up° in the turf-loft, the way° she won't know of them at all, and maybe when the tide turns she'll be going down to see would he be floating from the east.

[*They put the ladder against the gable of the chimney; CATHLEEN goes up a few steps and hides the bundle in the turf-loft. MAURYA comes from the inner room.*]

MAURYA (*looking up at CATHLEEN and speaking querulously*): Isn't it turf enough you have for this day and evening?

CATHLEEN: There's a cake baking at the fire for a short space (*throwing down the turf*) and Bartley will want it when the tide turns if he goes to Connemara.

[*NORA picks up the turf and puts it round the pot-oven.*]

MAURYA (*sitting down on a stool at the fire*): He won't go this day with the wind rising from the south and west. He won't go this day, for the young priest will stop him surely.

NORA: He'll not stop him, mother, and I heard Eamon Simon and Stephen Pheety and Colum Shawn saying he would go.

MAURYA: Where is he itself?

NORA: He went down to see would there be another boat sailing in the week, and I'm thinking it won't be long till he's here now, for the tide's turning at the green head,° and the hooker's tacking from the east.

CATHLEEN: I hear some one passing the big stones.

NORA (*looking out*): He's coming now, and he in a hurry.

BARTLEY (*comes in and looks round the room. Speaking sadly and quietly*): Where is the bit of new rope, Cathleen, was bought in Connemara?

CATHLEEN (*coming down*): Give it to him, Nora; it's on a nail by the white boards. I hung it up this morning, for the pig with the black feet was eating it.

NORA (*giving him a rope*): Is that it, Bartley?

MAURYA: You'd do right to leave that rope, Bartley, hanging by the board. (*BARTLEY takes the rope.*) It will be wanting in this place, I'm telling you, if Michael is washed up to-morrow morning, or the next morning, or any morning in the week, for it's a deep grave we'll make him by the grace of God.

BARTLEY (*beginning to work with the rope*): I've no halter the way I can ride down on the mare, and I must go now quickly. This is the one boat going for two weeks or beyond it, and the fair will be a good fair for horses I heard them saying below.

MAURYA: It's a hard thing they'll be saying below if the body is washed up and there's no man in it° to make the coffin, and I after giving a big price for the finest white boards you'd find in Connemara. (*She looks round at the boards.*)

BARTLEY: How would it be washed up, and we after looking each day for nine days, and a strong wind blowing a while back from the west and south?

MAURYA: If it wasn't found itself, that wind is raising the sea, and there was a star up against the moon, and it rising in the night. If it was a hundred horses, or a thousand horses you had itself, what is the price of a thousand horses against a son where there is one son only?

BARTLEY (*working at the halter, to CATHLEEN*): Let you go down each day, and see the sheep aren't jumping in on the rye, and if the jobber comes you can sell the pig with the black feet if there is a good price going.

MAURYA: How would the like of her get a good price for a pig?

BARTLEY (*to CATHLEEN*): If the west wind holds with the last bit of the moon let you and Nora get up weed enough for another cock for the kelp.° It's hard set° we'll be from this day with no one in it but one man to work.

MAURYA: It's hard set we'll be surely the day you're drowned'd with the rest. What way will I live and the girls with me, and I an old woman looking for the grave?

[*BARTLEY lays down the halter, takes off his old coat, and puts on a newer one of the same flannel.*]

BARTLEY (*to NORA*): Is she coming to the pier?

NORA (*looking out*): She's passing the green head and letting fall her sails.

---

² **the way** so that ³ **head** headland, promontory

⁴ **in it** there ⁵ **kelp** ash of various seaweeds, used as a source for iodine. Bartley's request means: get seaweed enough to make another pile to be burned to ash. ⁶ **set** put to it

BARTLEY (*getting his purse and tobacco*): I'll have half an hour to go down, and you'll see me coming again in two days, or in three days, or maybe in four if the wind is bad.

MAURYA (*turning round to the fire, and putting her shawl over her head*): Isn't it a hard and cruel man won't hear a word from an old woman, and she holding him from the sea?

CATHLEEN: It's the life of a young man to be going on the sea, and who would listen to an old woman with one thing and she saying it over?

BARTLEY (*taking the halter*): I must go now quickly. I'll ride down on the red mare, and the gray pony'll run behind me. . . . The blessing of God on you.

[He goes out.]

MAURYA (*crying out as he is in the door*): He's gone now, God spare us, and we'll not see him again. He's gone now, and when the black night is falling I'll have no son left in the world.

CATHLEEN: Why wouldn't you give him your blessing and he looking round in the door? Isn't it sorrow enough is on every one in this house without your sending him out with an unlucky word behind him, and a hard word in his ear?

[MAURYA takes up the tongs and begins raking the fire aimlessly without looking round.]

NORA (*turning towards her*): You're taking away the turf from the cake.

CATHLEEN (*crying out*): The Son of God forgive us. Nora, we're after forgetting his bit of bread.

[She comes over to the fire.]

NORA: And it's destroyed he'll be going till dark night, and he after eating nothing since the sun went up.

CATHLEEN (*turning the cake out of the oven*): It's destroyed he'll be, surely. There's no sense left on any person in a house where an old woman will be talking for ever.

[MAURYA sways on her stool.]

CATHLEEN (*cutting off some of the bread and rolling it in a cloth; to* MAURYA): Let you go down now to the spring well and give him this and he passing. You'll see him then and the dark word will be broken, and you can say "God speed you," the way he'll be easy in his mind.

MAURYA (*taking the bread*): Will I be in it as soon as himself?

CATHLEEN: If you go now quickly.

MAURYA (*standing up unsteadily*): It's hard set I am to walk.

CATHLEEN (*looking at her anxiously*): Give her the stick, Nora, or maybe she'll slip on the big stones.

NORA: What stick?

CATHLEEN: The stick Michael brought from Connemara.

MAURYA (*taking a stick* NORA *gives her*): In the big world the old people do be leaving things after them for their sons and children, but in this place it is the young men do be leaving things behind for them that do be old.

[She goes out slowly. NORA *goes over to the ladder.]*

CATHLEEN: Wait, Nora, maybe she'd turn back quickly. She's that sorry,° God help her, you wouldn't know the thing she'd do.

NORA: Is she gone round by the bush?

CATHLEEN (*looking out*): She's gone now. Throw it down quickly, for the Lord knows when she'll be out of it again.

NORA (*getting the bundle from the loft*): The young priest said he'd be passing to-morrow, and we might go down and speak to him below if it's Michael's they are surely.

CATHLEEN (*taking the bundle*): Did he say what way they were found?

NORA (*coming down*): "There were two men," says he, "and they rowing round with poteen before the cocks crowed, and the oar of one of them caught the body, and they passing the black cliffs of the north."

CATHLEEN (*trying to open the bundle*): Give me a knife, Nora, the string's perished° with the salt water, and there's a black knot on it you wouldn't loosen in a week.

NORA (*giving her a knife*): I've heard tell it was a long way to Donegal.

CATHLEEN (*cutting the string*): It is surely. There was a man in here a while ago—the man sold us that knife—and he said if you set off walking from the rocks beyond, it would be seven days you'd be in Donegal.

NORA: And what time would a man take, and he floating?

[CATHLEEN opens the bundle and takes out a bit of stocking. They look at them eagerly.]

CATHLEEN (*in a low voice*): The Lord spare us, Nora! isn't it a queer hard thing to say if it's his they are surely?

NORA: I'll get his shirt off the hook the way we can put the one flannel on the other. (*She looks through some clothes hanging in the corner*). It's not with

---

[7] **sorry** wretched   [8] **perished** stiffened

them, Cathleen, and where will it be?

CATHLEEN: I'm thinking Bartley put it on him in the morning, for his own shirt was heavy with the salt in it. (*Pointing to the corner.*) There's a bit of a sleeve was of the same stuff. Give me that and it will do.

[*NORA brings it to her and they compare the flannel.*]

CATHLEEN: It's the same stuff, Nora; but if it is itself aren't there great rolls of it in the shops of Galway, and isn't it many another man may have a shirt of it as well as Michael himself?

NORA (*who has taken up the stocking and counted the stitches, crying out*): It's Michael, Cathleen, it's Michael; God spare his soul, and what will herself say when she hears this story, and Bartley on the sea?

CATHLEEN (*taking the stocking*): It's a plain stocking.

NORA: It's the second one of the third pair I knitted, and I put up three score stitches, and I dropped four of them.

CATHLEEN (*counts the stitches*): It's that number is in it. (*Crying out.*) Ah, Nora, isn't it a bitter thing to think of him floating that way to the far north, and no one to keen him but the black hags that do be flying on the sea?

NORA (*swinging herself round, and throwing out her arms on the clothes*): And isn't it a pitiful thing when there is nothing left of a man who was a great rower and fisher, but a bit of an old shirt and a plain stocking?

CATHLEEN (*after an instant*): Tell me is herself coming, Nora? I hear a little sound on the path.

NORA (*looking out*): She is, Cathleen. She's coming up to the door.

CATHLEEN: Put these things away before she'll come in. Maybe it's easier she'll be after giving her blessing to Bartley, and we won't let on we've heard anything the time he's on the sea.

NORA (*helping CATHLEEN to close the bundle*): We'll put them here in the corner.

[*They put them into a hole in the chimney corner. CATHLEEN goes back to the spinning-wheel.*]

NORA: Will she see it was crying I was?

CATHLEEN: Keep your back to the door the way the light'll not be on you.

[*NORA sits down at the chimney corner, with her back to the door. MAURYA comes in very slowly, without looking at the girls, and goes over to her stool at the other side of the fire. The cloth with the bread is still in her hand. The girls look at each other, and NORA points to the bundle of bread.*]

CATHLEEN (*after spinning for a moment*): You didn't give him his bit of bread?

[*MAURYA begins to keen softly, without turning round.*]

CATHLEEN: Did you see him riding down?

[*MAURYA goes on keening.*]

CATHLEEN (*a little impatiently*): God forgive you; isn't it a better thing to raise your voice and tell what you seen, than to be making lamentation for a thing that's done? Did you see Bartley, I'm saying to you.

MAURYA (*with a weak voice*): My heart's broken from this day.

CATHLEEN (*as before*): Did you see Bartley?

MAURYA: I seen the fearfulest thing.

CATHLEEN (*leaves her wheel and looks out*): God forgive you; he's riding the mare now over the green head, and the gray pony behind him.

MAURYA (*starts, so that her shawl falls back from her head and shows her white tossed hair. With a frightened voice*): The gray pony behind him.

CATHLEEN (*coming to the fire*): What is it ails you, at all?

MAURYA (*speaking very slowly*): I've seen the fearfulest thing any person has seen, since the day Bride Dara seen the dead man with the child in his arms.

CATHLEEN and NORA: Uah.

[*They crouch down in front of the old woman at the fire.*]

NORA: Tell us what it is you seen.

MAURYA: I went down to the spring well, and I stood there saying a prayer to myself. Then Bartley came along, and he riding on the red mare with the gray pony behind him. (*She puts up her hands, as if to hide something from her eyes.*) The Son of God spare us, Nora!

CATHLEEN: What is it you seen?

MAURYA: I seen Michael himself.

CATHLEEN (*speaking softly*): You did not, mother; it wasn't Michael you seen, for his body is after being found in the far north, and he's got a clean burial by the grace of God.

MAURYA (*a little defiantly*): I'm after seeing him this day, and he riding and galloping. Bartley came first on the red mare; and I tried to say "God speed you," but something choked the words in my throat. He went by quickly; and "the blessing of God on you," says he, and I could say nothing. I looked up then, and I crying, at the gray pony, and there was Michael upon it—with fine clothes on him, and new shoes on his feet.

CATHLEEN (*begins to keen*): It's destroyed we are from this day. It's destroyed, surely.

NORA: Didn't the young priest say the Almight God wouldn't leave her destitute with no son living?

MAURYA (*in a low voice, but clearly*): It's little the like of him knows of the sea. . . . Bartley will be lost now, and let you call in Eamon and make me a good coffin out of the white boards, for I won't live after them. I've had a husband, and a husband's father, and six sons in this house—six fine men, though it was a hard birth I had with every one of them and they coming to the world—and some of them were found and some of them were not found, but they're gone now the lot of them. . . . There were Stephen, and Shawn, were lost in the great wind, and found after in the Bay of Gregory of the Golden Mouth, and carried up the two of them on the one plank, and in by that door.

[*She pauses for a moment, the girls start as if they heard something through the door that is half open behind them.*]

NORA (*in a whisper*): Did you hear that, Cathleen? Did you hear a noise in the northeast?

CATHLEEN (*in a whisper*): There's some one after crying out by the seashore.

MAURYA (*continues without hearing anything*): There was Sheamus and his father, and his own father again, were lost in a dark night, and not a stick or sign was seen of them when the sun went up. There was Patch after was drowned out of a curragh that turned over. I was sitting here with Bartley, and he a baby, lying on my two knees, and I seen two women, and three women, and four women coming in, and they crossing themselves, and not saying a word. I looked out then, and there were men coming after them, and they holding a thing in the half of a red sail, and water dripping out of it—it was a dry day, Nora—and leaving a track to the door.

[*She pauses again with her hand stretched out towards the door. It opens softly and old women begin to come in, crossing themselves on the threshold, and kneeling down in front of the stage with red petticoats over their heads.*]

MAURYA (*half in a dream, to* CATHLEEN): Is it Patch, or Michael, or what is it at all?

CATHLEEN: Michael is after being found in the far north, and when he is found there how could he be here in this place?

MAURYA: There does be a power of young men floating round in the sea, and what way would they know if it was Michael they had, or another man like him, for when a man is nine days in the sea, and the wind blowing, it's hard set his own moth-

er would be to say what man was it.

CATHLEEN: It's Michael, God spare him, for they're after sending us a bit of his clothes from the far north.

[*She reaches out and hands* MAURYA *the clothes that belonged to Michael.* MAURYA *stands up slowly and takes them in her hands.* NORA *looks out.*]

NORA: They're carrying a thing among them and there's water dripping out of it and leaving a track by the big stones.

CATHLEEN (*in a whisper to the women who have come in*): Is it Bartley it is?

ONE OF THE WOMEN: It is surely, God rest his soul.

[*Two younger women come in and pull out the table. Then men carry in the body of Bartley, laid on a plank, with a bit of a sail over it, and lay it on the table.*]

CATHLEEN (*to the women, as they are doing so*): What way was he drowned?

ONE OF THE WOMEN: The gray pony knocked him into the sea, and he was washed out where there is a great surf on the white rocks.

[MAURYA *has gone over and knelt down at the head of the table. The women are keening softly and swaying themselves with a slow movement.* CATHLEEN *and* NORA *kneel at the other end of the table. The men kneel near the door.*]

MAURYA (*raising her head and speaking as if she did not see the people around her*): They're all gone now, and there isn't anything more the sea can do to me. . . . I'll have no call now to be up crying and praying when the wind breaks from the south, and you can hear the surf is in the east, and the surf is in the west, making a great stir with the two noises, and they hitting one on the other. I'll have no call now to be going down and getting Holy Water in the dark nights after Samhain,° and I won't care what way the sea is when the other women will be keening. (*To* NORA.) Give me the Holy Water, Nora, there's a small sup still on the dresser.

[NORA *gives it to her.*]

MAURYA (*drops Michael's clothes across Bartley's feet, and sprinkles the Holy Water over him*): It isn't that I haven't prayed for you, Bartley, to the Almighty

---

9 **Samhain** November 1, the beginning of the Celtic winter half year.

God. It isn't that I haven't said prayers in the dark night till you wouldn't know what I'd be saying; but it's a great rest I'll have now, and it's time surely. It's a great rest I'll have now, and great sleeping in the long nights after Samhain, if it's only a bit of wet flour we do have to eat, and maybe a fish that would be stinking.

[*She kneels down again, crossing herself, and saying prayers under her breath.*]

CATHLEEN (*to an old man*): Maybe yourself and Eamon would make a coffin when the sun rises. We have fine white boards herself bought, God help her, thinking Michael would be found, and I have a new cake you can eat while you'll be working.

THE OLD MAN (*looking at the boards*): Are there nails with them?

CATHLEEN: There are not, Colum; we didn't think of the nails.

ANOTHER MAN: It's a great wonder she wouldn't think of the nails, and all the coffins she's seen made already.

CATHLEEN: It's getting old she is, and broken.

[*MAURYA stands up again very slowly and spreads out the pieces of Michael's clothes beside the body, sprinkling them with the last of the Holy Water.*]

NORA (*in a whisper to* CATHLEEN): She's quiet now and easy; but the day Michael was drowned you could hear her crying out from this to the spring well. It's fonder she was of Michael, and would any one have thought that?

CATHLEEN (*slowly and clearly*): An old woman will be soon tired with anything she will do, and isn't it nine days herself is after crying and keening, and making great sorrow in the house?

MAURYA (*puts the empty cup mouth downwards on the table, and lays her hands together on Bartley's feet*): They're all together this time, and the end is come. May the Almighty God have mercy on Bartley's soul, and on Michael's soul, and on the souls of Sheamus and Patch, and Stephen and Shawn; (*bending her head*) and may He have mercy on my soul, Nora, and on the soul of every one is left living in the world.

[*She pauses, and the keen rises a little more loudly from the women, then sinks away.*]

MAURYA (*continuing*): Michael has a clean burial in the far north, by the grace of the Almighty God. Bartley will have a fine coffin out of the white boards, and a deep grave surely. What more can we want than that? No man at all can be living for ever, and we must be satisfied.

[*She kneels down again and the curtain falls slowly.*]

Contexts and Commentaries

Émile Zola (1840–1902)

During the 1870s, Émile Zola, the French novelist, playwright, and theorist, wrote a series of articles on naturalism in the theater. They were collected and published together in 1878. In this classic statement of the tenets of naturalism, Zola urges the adoption of scientific objectivity in the theater—to treat subjects drawn from life, to portray characters driven by psychological motives, and to use the language of everyday life.

FROM "NATURALISM IN THE THEATRE"

TRANSLATED BY ALBERT BERMEL

Today, then, tragedy and romantic drama are equally old and worn out. And that is hardly to the credit of the latter, it should be said, for in less than half a century it has fallen into the same state of decay as tragedy, which took two centuries to die. There it lies, flattened in its turn, overwhelmed by the same passion it showed on its own battle. Nothing is left. We can only guess at what is to come. Logically all that can grow up on that free ground conquered in 1830 is the formula of naturalism.

It seems impossible that the movement of inquiry and analysis, which is precisely the movement of the nineteenth century, can have revolutionized all the sciences and arts and left dramatic art to one side, as if isolated. The natural sciences date from the end of the last century; chemistry and physics are less than a hundred years old; history and criticism have been renovated, virtually recreated since the Revolution; an entire world has arisen; it has sent us back to the study of documents, to experience, made us realize that to start afresh we must first take things back to the beginning, become familiar with man and nature, verify what is. Thenceforward, the great naturalistic school, which has spread secretly, irrevocably, often making its way in darkness but always advancing, can finally come out triumphantly into the light of day. To trace the history of this movement, with the misunderstandings that might have impeded it and the multiple causes that have thrust it forward or slowed it down, would be to trace the history of the century itself. An irresistible current carries our society towards the study of reality. In the novel Balzac has been the bold and mighty innovator who has replaced the observation of the scholar with the imagination of the poet. But in the theatre the evolution seems slower. No eminent writer has yet formulated the new idea with any clarity.

I certainly do not say that some excellent works have not been produced, with characters in them who are ingeniously examined and bold truths taken right on to the stage. Let me, for instance, cite certain plays by M. Dumas *fils*, whose talent I scarcely admire, and M. Émile Augier, the most humane and powerful of all. Still, they are midgets beside Balzac; they lack the genius to lay down the formula. It must be said that one can never tell quite when a movement is getting under way; generally its source is remote and lost in the earlier movement from which it emerged. In a manner of speaking, the naturalistic current has always existed. It brings with it nothing absolutely novel. But it has finally flowed into a period favourable to it; it is succeeding and expanding because the human mind has attained the necessary maturity. I do not, therefore, deny the past; I affirm the present. The strength of naturalism is precisely that it has deep roots in our national literature which contains plenty of wisdom. It comes from the very entrails of humanity; it is that much the stronger because it has taken longer to grow and is found in a greater number of our masterpieces.

Certain things have come to pass and I point them out. Can we believe that *L'Ami Fritz* would have been applauded at the Comédie-Française twenty years ago? Definitely not! This play, in which people eat all the time and the lover talks in such homely language, would have disgusted both the classicists and the romantics. To explain its success we must concede that as the years have gone by a secret fermentation has been at work. Lifelike paintings, which used to repel the public, today attract them. The majority has been won over and the stage is open to every experiment. This is the only conclusion to draw.

So that is where we stand. To explain my point better—I am not afraid of repeating myself—I will sum up what I have said. Looking closely at the history of our dramatic literature, one can detect several clearly separated periods. First, there was the infancy of the art, farces and the mystery plays of the Middle Ages, the reciting of simple dialogues which developed as part of a naïve convention, with primitive staging and sets. Gradually, the plays became more complex but in a crude fashion. When Corneille appeared he was acclaimed most of all for his status as an innovator, for refining the dramatic formula of the time, and for hallowing it by means of his genius. It would be very interesting to study the pertinent documents and discover how our classical formula came to be created. It corresponded to the social spirit of the period. Nothing is solid that is not built on necessity. Tragedy reigned for two centuries because it satisfied the exact requirements of those centuries. Geniuses of differing temperaments had buttressed it with their masterpieces. And it continued to impose itself long afterwards, even when second-rate talents were producing inferior work. It acquired a momentum. It persisted also as the literary expression of that society, and nothing would have overthrown it if the society had not itself disappeared. After the Revolution, after that profound disturbance that was meant to transform everything and give birth to a new world, tragedy struggled to stay alive for a few more years. Then the formula cracked and romanticism broke through. A new formula asserted itself. We must look back at the first half of the century to understand the meaning of this cry for liberty. The young society was in the tremor of its infancy. The excited, bewildered, violently unleashed people were still racked by a dangerous fever; and in the first flush of their new liberty they yearned for prodigious adventures and superhuman love affairs. They gaped at the stars; some committed suicide, a very curious reaction to the social enfranchisement which had just been declared at the cost of so much blood. Turning specifically to dramatic literature, I maintain that romanticism in the theatre was an uncomplicated revolt, the invasion by a victorious group who took over the stage violently with drums beating and flags flying. In these early moments the combatants dreamed of making their imprint with a new form; to one rhetoric they opposed another: the Middle Ages to Antiquity, the exalting of passion to the exalting of duty. And that was all, for only the scenic conventions were altered. The characters remained marionettes in new clothing. Only the exterior aspect and the language were modified. But for the period that was enough. Romanticism had taken possession of the theatre in the name of literary freedom and it carried out its revolutionary task with incomparable bravura. But who does not see today that its role could extend no farther than that? Does romanticism have anything whatever to say about our present society? Does it meet one of our requirements? Obviously not. It is as outmoded as a jargon we no longer follow. It confidently expected to replace classical literature which had lasted for two centuries because it was based on social conditions. But romanticism was based on nothing but the fantasy of a few poets or, if you will, on the passing malady of minds overwhelmed by historical events; it was bound to disappear with the malady. It provided the occasion for a magnificent flowering of lyricism; that will be its eternal glory. Today, however, with the evolution accomplished, it is plain that romanticism was no more than the necessary link between classicism and naturalism. The struggle is over; now we must found a secure state. Naturalism flows out of classical art, just as our present society has arisen from the wreckage of the old society. Naturalism alone corresponds to our social needs; it alone has deep roots in the spirit of our times; and it alone can provide a living, durable formula for our art, because this formula will express the nature of our contemporary intelligence. There may be fashions and passing fantasies that exist outside naturalism but they will not survive for long. I say again, naturalism is the expression of our century and it will not die until a new upheaval transforms our democratic world.

Only one thing is needed now: men of genius who can fix the naturalistic formula. Balzac has done it for the novel and the novel is established. When will our Corneilles, Molières and Racines appear to establish our new theatre? We must hope and wait.

The period when romantic drama ruled now seems distant. In Paris five or six of its playhouses prospered. The demolition of the old theatres along the Boulevard du Temple was a catastrophe of the first order. The theatres became separated from one another, the public changed, different fashions arose. But the discredit into which the drama has fallen proceeds mostly from the exhaustion of the genre—ridiculous, boring plays have gradually taken over from the potent works of 1830.

To this enfeeblement we must add the absolute lack of new actors who understand and can interpret these kinds of plays, for every dramatic formula that vanishes carries away its interpreters with it. Today the drama, hunted from stage to stage, has only two houses that really belong to it, the Ambigu and the Théâtre-Historique. Even at the Saint-Martin the drama is lucky to win a brief showing for itself, between one great spectacle and the next.

An occasional success may renew its courage. But its decline is inevitable; romantic drama is sliding into oblivion, and if it seems sometimes to check its descent, it does so only to roll even lower afterwards. Naturally, there are loud complaints. The tail-end romanticists are desperately unhappy. They swear that except in the drama—meaning their kind of drama—there is no salvation for dramatic literature. I believe, on the contrary, that we must find a new formula that will transform the drama, just as the writers in the first half of the century transformed tragedy. That is the essence of the matter. Today the battle is between romantic drama and naturalistic drama. By romantic drama I mean every play that mocks truthfulness in its incidents and characterization, that struts about in its puppet-box, stuffed to the belly with noises that flounder, for some idealistic reason or other, in pastiches of Shakespeare and Hugo. Every period has its formula; ours is certainly not that of 1830. We are an age of method, of experimental science; our primary need is for precise analysis. We hardly understand the liberty we have won if we use it only to imprison ourselves in a new tradition. The way is open: we can now return to man and nature.

Finally, there have been great efforts to revive the historical drama. Nothing could be better. A critic cannot roundly condemn the choice of historical subjects, even if his own preferences are entirely for subjects that are modern. It is simply that I am full of distrust. The manager one gives this sort of play to frightens me in advance. It is a question of how history is treated, what unusual characters are presented bearing the names of kings, great captains or great artists, and what awful sauce they are served up in to make the history palatable. As soon as the authors of these concoctions move into the past they think everything is permitted: improbabilities, cardboard dolls, monumental idiocies, the hysterical scribblings that falsely represent local colour. And what strange dialogue—François I talking like a haberdasher straight out of the Rue Saint-Denis, Richelieu using the words of a criminal from the Boulevard du Crime, Charlotte Corday with the weeping sentimentalities of a factory girl.

What astounds me is that our playwrights do not seem to suspect for a moment that the historical genre is unavoidably the least rewarding, the one that calls most strongly for research, integrity, a consummate gift of intuition, a talent for reconstruction. I am all for historical drama when it is in the hands of poets of genius or men of exceptional knowledge who are capable of making the public see an epoch come alive with its special quality, its manners, its civilization. In that case we have a work of prophecy or of profoundly interesting criticism.

But unfortunately I know what it is these partisans of historical drama want to revive: the swaggering and swordplay, the big spectacle with big words, the play of lies that shows off in front of the crowd, the gross exhibition that saddens honest minds. Hence my distrust. I think that all this antiquated business is better left in our museum of dramatic history under a pious layer of dust.

There are, undeniably, great obstacles to original experiments: we run up against the hypocrisies of criticism and the long education in idiocies that has been foisted on the public. This public, which titters at every childishness in melodramas, nevertheless lets itself be carried away by outbursts of fine sentiment. But the public is changing. Shakespeare's public and Molière's are no longer ours. We must reckon with shifts in outlook, with the need for reality which is everywhere getting more insistent. The last few romantics vainly repeat that the public wants this and the public wants that; the day is coming when the public will want the truth.

The old formulas, classical and romantic, were based on the rearrangement and systematic amputation of the truth. They determined on principle that the truth is not good enough; they tried to draw out of it an essence, a `poetry', on the pretext that nature must be expurgated and magnified. Up to the present the different literary schools disputed only over the question of the best way to disguise the truth so that it might not look too brazen to the public. The classicists adopted the toga; the romantics fought a revolution to impose the coat of mail and the doublet. Essentially the change of dress made little difference; the counterfeiting of nature went on. But today the naturalistic thinkers are telling us that the truth does not need clothing; it can walk naked. That, I repeat, is the quarrel.

Writers with any sense understand perfectly that tragedy and romantic drama are dead. The majority, though, are badly troubled when they turn their minds to the as-yet-unclear formula of tomorrow. Does the truth seriously ask them to give up the grandeur, the poetry, the traditional epic effects that their ambition tells them to put into their plays? Does naturalism demand that they shrink their horizons and risk not one flight into fantasy?

I will try to reply. But first we must determine the methods used by the idealists to lift their works into poetry. They begin by placing their chosen subject in a distant time. That provides them with costumes and makes the framework of the story vague enough to give them full scope for lying. Next, they generalize instead of particularizing; their characters are no longer living people but sentiments, arguments, passions that have been induced by reasoning. This false framework calls for heroes of marble or cardboard. A man of flesh and bone with his own originality would jar in such a legendary setting. Moreover, when we see the characters in romantic drama or tragedy walking about they are stiffened into an attitude, one representing duty, another patriotism, a third superstition, a fourth maternal love; thus, all the abstract ideas file by. Never the thorough analysis of an organism, never a character whose muscles and brain function as in nature.

These, then, are the mannerisms that writers with epic inclinations do not want to give up. For them poetry resides in the past and in abstraction, in the idealizing of facts and characters. As soon as one confronts them with daily life, with the people who fill our streets, they blink, they stammer, they are afraid; they no longer see clearly; they find everything ugly and not good enough for art. According to them, a subject must enter the lies of legend, men must harden and turn to stone like statues before the artist can accept them and make them fit the disguises he has prepared.

Now, it is at this point that the naturalistic movement comes along and says squarely that poetry is everywhere, in everything, even more in the present and the real than in the past and the abstract. Each event at each moment has its poetic, superb aspect. We brush up against heroes who are great and powerful in different respects from the puppets of the epic-makers. Not one playwright in this century has brought to life figures as lofty as Baron Hulot, Old Grandet, César Birotteau, and all the other characters of Balzac, who are so individual and so alive. Beside these real, giant creations Greek and Roman heroes quake; the heroes of the Middle Ages fall flat on their faces like lead soldiers.

With the superior works being produced in these times by the naturalistic school—works of high endeavour, pulsing with life—it is ridiculous and false to park our poetry in some antiquated temple and bury it in cobwebs. Poetry flows at its full force through everything that exists; the truer to life, the greater it becomes. And I mean to give the word poetry its widest definition, not to pin it down exclusively to the cadence of two rhymes, nor to bury it in a narrow coterie of dreamers, but to restore its real human significance which concerns the expansion and encouragement of every kind of truth.

Take our present environment, then, and try to make men live in it: you will write great works. It will undoubtedly call for some effort; it means sifting out of the confusion of life the simple formula of naturalism. Therein lies the difficulty: to do great things with the subjects and characters that our eyes, accustomed to the spectacle of the daily round, have come to see as small. I am aware that it is more convenient to present a marionette to the public and name it Charlemagne and puff it up with such tirades that the public believes it is watching a colossus; it is more convenient than taking a bourgeois of our time, a grotesque, unsightly man, and drawing sublime poetry out of him, making him, for example, Père Goriot, the father who gives his guts for his daughters, a figure so gigantic with truth and love that no other literature can offer his equal.

Nothing is as easy as persuading the managers with known formulas; and heroes in the classical or romantic taste cost so little labour that they are manufactured by the dozen, and have become standardized articles that clutter up our literature. But it takes hard work to create a real hero, intelligently analysed, alive and performing. That is probably why naturalism terrifies those authors who are used to fishing up great men from the troubled waters of history. They would have to burrow too deeply into humanity, learn about life, go straight for the greatness of reality and make it function with all their power. And let nobody gainsay this true poetry of humanity; it has been sifted out in the novel and can be in the theatre; only the method of adaptation remains to be found.

I am troubled by a comparison; it has been haunting me and I will now free myself of it. For two long months a play called *Les Danicheff* has been running at the Odéon. It takes place in Russia. It has been very successful here, but is apparently so dishonest, so packed with gross improbabilities, that the author, a Russian, has not even dared to show it in his country. What can you think of this work which is applauded in Paris and would be booed in St. Petersburg? Well, imagine for a moment that the Romans could come back to life and see a performance of *Rome vaincue*. Can you hear their roars of laughter? Do you think the play would complete one performance? It would strike them as a parody; it would sink under the weight of mockery. And is there one historical play that could be performed before the society it claims to portray? A strange theatre, this, which is plausible only among foreigners, is based on the disappearance of the generations it deals with, and is made up of so much misinformation that it is good only for the ignorant!

The future is with naturalism. The formula will be found; it will be proved that there is more poetry in the little apartment of a bourgeois than in all the empty, worm-eaten palaces of history; in the end we will see that everything meets in the real: lovely fantasies that are free of capriciousness and whimsy, and idylls, and comedies, and dramas. Once the soil has been turned over, the task that seems alarming and unfeasible today will become easy.

I am not qualified to pronounce on the form that tomorrow's drama will take; that must be left to the voice of some genius to come. But I will allow myself to indicate the path I consider our theatre will follow.

First, the romantic drama must be abandoned. It would be disastrous for us to take over its outrageous acting, its rhetoric, its inherent thesis of action at the expense of character analysis. The finest models of the genre are, as has been said, mere operas with big effects. I believe, then, that we must go back to tragedy—not, heaven forbid, to borrow more of its rhetoric, its system of confidants, its declaiming, its endless speeches, but to return to its simplicity of action and its unique psychological and physiological study of the characters. Thus understood, the tragic framework is excellent; one deed unwinds in all its reality, and moves the characters to passions and feelings, the exact analysis of which constitutes the sole interest of the play—and in a contemporary environment, with the people who surround us.

My constant concern, my anxious vigil, has made me wonder which of us will have the strength to raise himself to the pitch of genius. If the naturalistic drama must come into being, only a genius can give birth to it. Corneille and Racine made tragedy. Victor Hugo made romantic drama. Where is the as-yet-unknown author who must make the naturalistic drama? In recent years experiments have not been wanting. But either because the public was not ready or because none of the beginners had the necessary staying-power, not one of these attempts has had decisive results.

In battles of this kind, small victories mean nothing; we need triumphs that overwhelm the adversary and win the public to the cause. Audiences would give way before the onslaught of a really strong man. This man would come with the expected word, the solution to the problem, the formula for a real life on stage, combining it with the illusions necessary in the theatre. He would have what the newcomers have as yet lacked: the cleverness or the might to impose himself and to remain so close to truth that his cleverness could not lead him into lies.

And what an immense place this innovator would occupy in our dramatic literature! He would be at the peak. He would build his monument in the middle of the desert of mediocrity that we are crossing, among the jerry-built houses strewn about our most illustrious stages. He would put everything in question and remake everything, scour the boards, create a world whose elements he would lift from life, from outside our traditions. Surely there is no more ambitious dream that a writer of our time could fulfil. The domain of the novel is crowded; the domain of the theatre is free. At this time in France an imperishable glory awaits the man of genius who takes up the work of Molière and finds in the reality of living comedy the full, true drama of modern society.

PHYSIOLOGICAL MAN[1]

. . . In effect, the great naturalistic evolution, which comes down directly from the fifteenth century to ours has everything to do with the gradual substitution of physiological man for metaphysical man. In tragedy metaphysical man, man according to dogma and logic, reigned absolutely. The body did not count; the soul was regarded as the only interesting piece of human machinery; drama took place in the air, in pure mind. Consequently, what use was the tangible world? Why worry about the place where the action was located? Why be surprised at a baroque costume or false declaiming? Why notice that Queen Dido was a boy whose budding beard forced him to wear a mask? None of that mattered; these trifles were not worth stooping to; the play was heard out as if it were a school essay or a law case; it was on a higher plane than man, in the world of ideas, so far away from real man that any intrusion of reality would have spoiled the show.

Such is the point of departure—in Mystery plays, the religious point; the philosophical point in tragedy. And from that beginning natural man, stifling under the rhetoric and dogma, struggled secretly, tried to break free, made lengthy, futile efforts, and in the end asserted himself, limb by limb. The whole history of our theatre is in this conquest by the physiological man, who emerged more clearly in each period from behind the dummy of religious and philosophical idealism. Corneille, Molière, Racine, Voltaire, Beaumarchais and, in our day, Victor Hugo, Émile Augier, Alexandre Dumas *fils*, even Sardou, have had only one task, even when they were not completely aware of it: to increase the reality of our corpus of drama, to progress towards truth, to sift out more and more of the natural man and impose him on the public. And inevitably, the evolution will not end with them. It continues; it will continue forever. Mankind is very young. . . .

COSTUME, STAGE DESIGN, SPEECH

Modern clothes make a poor spectacle. If we depart from bourgeois tragedy, shut in between its four walls, and wish to use the breadth of larger stages for crowd scenes we are embarrassed and constrained by the monotony and the uniformly funereal look of the extras. In this case, I think, we should take advantage of the variety of garb offered by the different classes and occupations. To elaborate: I can imagine an author setting one act in the main marketplace of les Halles in Paris. The setting would be superb, with its bustling life and bold possibilities. In this immense setting we could have a very picturesque ensemble by displaying the porters wearing their large hats, the saleswomen with their white aprons and vividly-coloured scarves, the customers dressed in silk or wool or cotton prints, from the ladies accompanied by their maids to the female beggars

---

[1] What precedes is a complete chapter. Two brief excerpts follow from the chapter on Costume.

on the prowl for anything they can pick up off the street. For inspiration it would be enough to go to les Halles and look about. Nothing is gaudier or more interesting. All of Paris would enjoy seeing this set if it were realized with the necessary accuracy and amplitude.

And how many other settings for popular drama there are for the taking! Inside a factory, the interior of a mine, the gingerbread market, a railway station, flower stalls, a racetrack, and so on. All the activities of modern life can take place in them. It will be said that such sets have already been tried. Unquestionably we have seen factories and railway stations in fantasy plays; but these were fantasy stations and factories. I mean, these sets were thrown together to create an illusion that was at best incomplete. What we need is detailed reproduction: costumes supplied by tradespeople, not sumptuous but adequate for the purposes of truth and for the interest of the scenes. Since everybody mourns the death of the drama our playwrights certainly ought to make a try at this type of popular, contemporary drama. At one stroke they could satisfy the public hunger for spectacle and the need for exact studies which grows more pressing every day. Let us hope, though, that the playwrights will show us real people and not those whining members of the working class who play such strange roles in boulevard melodrama.

As M. Adolphe Jullien has said—and I will never be tired of repeating it— everything is interdependent in the theatre. Lifelike costumes look wrong if the sets, the diction, the plays themselves are not lifelike. They must all march in step along the naturalistic road. When costume becomes more accurate, so do sets; actors free themselves from bombastic declaiming; plays study reality more closely and their characters are more true to life. I could make the same observations about sets I have just made about costume. With them too, we may seem to have reached the highest possible degree of truth, but we still have long strides to take. Most of all we would need to intensify the illusion in reconstructing the environments, less for their picturesque quality than for dramatic utility. The environment must determine the character. When a set is planned so as to give the lively impression of a description by Balzac; when, as the curtain rises, one catches the first glimpse of the characters, their personalities and behaviour, if only to see the actual locale in which they move, the importance of exact reproduction in the decor will be appreciated. Obviously, that is the way we are going. Environment, the study of which has transformed science and literature, will have to take a large role in the theatre. And here I may mention again the question of metaphysical man, the abstraction who had to be satisfied with his three walls in tragedy—whereas the physiological man in our modern works is asking more and more compellingly to be determined by his setting, by the environment that produced him. We see then that the road to progress is still long, for sets as well as costume. We are coming upon the truth but we can hardly stammer it out.

Another very serious matter is diction. True, we have got away from the chanting, the plainsong, of the seventeenth century. But we now have a `theatre voice', a false recitation that is very obtrusive and very annoying. Everything that is wrong with it comes from the fixed traditional code set up by the majority of critics. They found the theatre in a certain state and, instead of looking to the future, and judging the progress we are making and the progress we shall make by the progress we have already made, they stubbornly defend the relics of the old conventions, swearing that these relics must be preserved. Ask them why, make them see how far we have travelled; they will give you no logical reason. They will reply with assertions based on a set of conditions that are disappearing.

In diction the errors come from what the critics call 'theatre language'. Their theory is that on stage you must not speak as you do in everyday life. To support this viewpoint they pick examples from traditional practices, from what was happening yesterday—and is happening still—without taking account of the naturalistic movement. Let us realize that there is no such thing as 'theatre language'. There has been a rhetoric which grew more and more feeble and is now dying out. Those are the facts. If you compare the declaiming of actors under Louis XIV with that of Lekain, and if you compare Lekain's with that of our own artists today, you will clearly distinguish the phases, from tragic chanting down to our search for the natural, precise tone, the cry of truth. It follows that 'theatre language', that language of booming sonority, is vanishing. We are moving towards simplicity, the exact word spoken without emphasis, quite naturally. How many examples I could give if I had unlimited space! Consider the powerful effect that Geoffroy has on the public; all his talent comes from his natural personality. He holds the public because he speaks on stage as he does at home. When a sentence sounds outlandish he cannot pronounce it; the author has to find another one. That is the fundamental criticism of so-called 'theatre language'. Again, follow the diction of a talented actor and at the same time watch the public; the cheers go up, the house is in raptures when a truthful accent gives the words the exact value they must have. All the great successes of the stage are triumphs over convention.

Alas, yes, there is a 'theatre language'. It is the clichés, the resounding platitudes, the hollow words that roll about like empty barrels, all that intolerable rhetoric of our vaudevilles and dramas, which is beginning to make us smile. It would be very interesting to study the style of such talented authors as MM. Augier, Dumas and Sardou. I could find much to criticize, especially in the last two with their conventional language, a language of their own that they put into the mouths of all their characters, men, women, children, old folk, both sexes and all ages. This irritates me, for each character has his own language, and to create living people you must give them to the public not merely in accurate dress and in the environments that have made them what they are, but with their individual ways of thinking and expressing themselves. I repeat that that is the obvious aim of our theatre. There is no theatre language regulated by such a code as 'cadenced sentences' or sonority. There is simply a kind of dialogue that is growing more precise and is following—or rather, leading—sets and costumes towards naturalistic progress. When plays are more truthful, the actors' diction will gain enormously in simplicity and naturalness.

To conclude, I will repeat that the battle of the conventions is far from being finished, and that it will no doubt last forever. Today we are beginning to see clearly where we are going, but our steps are still impeded by the melting slush of rhetoric and metaphysics.

Henrik Ibsen   (1828–1906)

FROM NOTES FOR HEDDA GABLER[1]

TRANSLATED BY EVERT SPRINCHORN

¶This married woman more and more imagines that she is an important personality, and as a consequence feels compelled to create for herself a sensational past—

¶If an interesting female character appears in a new story or in a play, she believes that it is she who is being portrayed.

¶The masculine environment helps to confirm her in this belief.

¶The two lady friends agree to die together. One of them carries out her end of the bargain. But the other one who realizes what lies in store for her loses her courage. This is the reversal—

¶"He has such a disgusting way of walking when one sees him from behind."

¶She hates him because he has a goal, a mission in life. The lady friend has one too, but does not dare to devote herself to it. Her personal life treated in fictional form.

¶In the second act the manuscript that is left behind—

¶"The lost soul" apologizes for the man of culture. The wild horse and the race horse. Drinks—eats paprika. House and clothes. Revolution against the laws of nature—but nothing stupid, not until the position is secure.

¶The pale, apparently cold beauty. Expects great things of life and the joy of life.

The man who has now finally won her, plain and simple in appearance, but an honest and talented, broad-minded scholar.

¶The manuscript that H. L. leaves behind contends that man's mission is: Upward, toward the bearer of light. Life on the present foundations of society is not worth living. Therefore he escapes from it through his imagination. By drinking, etc.—Tesman stands for correct behavior. Hedda for blasé oversophistication. Mrs. R. is the nervous-hysterical modern individual. Brack represents the personal bourgeois point of view.

¶Then H. departs this world. And the two of them are left sitting there with the manuscript they cannot interpret. And the aunt is with them. What an ironic comment on humanity's striving for progress and development.

---

[1] More preliminary notes have been preserved for *Hedda Gabler* than for almost any other play by Ibsen. These notes afford the student of playwriting a rare opportunity to trace the growth of a masterpiece from the first embryonic thoughts through its birth as a full-length draft. Nearly all of these preliminary notes are given here, grouped in seven sets to indicate their different sources.

¶But Holger's double nature intervenes. Only by realizing the basely bourgeois can he win a hearing for his great central idea.

¶Mrs. Rising is afraid that H., although "a model of propriety," is not normal. She can only guess at his way of thinking but cannot understand it. Quotes some of his remarks—

¶One talks about building railways and highways for the cause of progress. But no, no, that is not what is needed. Space must be cleared so that the spirit of man can make its great turnabout. For it has gone astray. The spirit of man has gone astray.

¶*Holger:* I have been out. I have behaved obscenely. That doesn't matter. But the police know about it. That's what counts.

¶H. L.'s despair lies in that he wants to master the world but cannot master himself.

¶Tesman believes that it is he who has in a way seduced H. L. into indulging in excesses again. But that is not so. It is as Hedda has said: that it was *he* she dreamed of when she talked about "the famous man." But she does not dare tell Tesman this.

¶To aid in understanding his own character, L. has made notes in "the manuscript." These are the notes the two of them should interpret, want to interpret, but *cannot* possibly.

¶Brack is inclined to live as a bachelor, and then gain admittance to a good home, become a friend of the family, indispensable—

¶They say it is a law of nature. Very well then, raise an opposition to it. Demand its repeal. Why give way. Why surrender unconditionally—

¶In conversations between T. and L. the latter says that he lives for his studies. The former replies that in that case he can compete with him.—(T. lives *on* his studies) that's the point.

¶L. (Tesman) says: I couldn't step on a worm! "But now I can tell you that I too am seeking the professorship. We are rivals."

¶She has respect for his knowledge, an eye for his noble character, but is embarrassed by his insignificant, ridiculous appearance, makes fun of his conduct and remarks.

¶The aunt asks all sorts of ambiguous questions to find out about those things that arouse her imagination the most.

¶NOTES: One evening as Hedda and Tesman, together with some others, were on their way home from a party, Hedda remarked as they walked by a charming house that was where she would like to live. She meant it, but she said it only to keep the conversation with Tesman going. "He simply cannot carry on a conversation."

The house was actually for rent or sale. Tesman had been pointed out as the coming young man. And later when he proposed, and let slip that he too had dreamed of living there, she accepted.

He too had liked the house very much.

They get married. And they rent the house.[2]

But when Hedda returns as a young wife, with a vague sense of responsibility, the whole thing seems distasteful to her. She conceives a kind of hatred for the house just because it has become her home. She confides this to Brack. She evades the question with Tesman.

¶The play shall deal with "the impossible," that is, to aspire to and strive for something which is against all the conventions, against that which is acceptable to conscious minds—Hedda's included.

¶The episode of the hat makes Aunt Rising lose her composure. She leaves—That it could be taken for the maid's hat—no, that's going too far!

That my hat, which I've had for over nine years, could be taken for the maid's—no, that's really too much!

¶*Hedda:* Yes, once I thought it must be wonderful to live here and own this house.

Brack: But now you are contradicting yourself.

Hedda: That may be so. But that's how it is anyway.

¶*Hedda:* I don't understand these self-sacrificing people. Look at old Miss Rising. She has a paralyzed sister in her house, who has been lying in bed for years. Do you suppose she thinks it is a sacrifice to live for that poor creature, who is a burden even to herself? Far from it! Just the opposite. I don't understand it.

¶*Hedda:* And how greedy they are for married men. Do you know what, Judge Brack? You don't do yourself any good by not getting married.

Brack: Then I can practically consider myself married.

Hedda: Yes, you certainly can—in one way—in many ways even—

Brack: In many ways? What do you mean by that?

Hedda: No thanks. I won't tell you.

¶When Mrs. Elvsted says that the first part of Løvborg's book deals with the historical development of "Sociology," and that another volume will appear later, Tesman looks at her a little startled.

¶Very few true parents are to be found in the world. Most people grow up under the influence of aunts or uncles—either neglected and misunderstood or else spoiled.

¶Hedda rejects him because he does not dare expose himself to temptation. He replies that the same is true of her. The wager! . . . He loses . . . ! Mrs. Elvsted is present. Hedda says: No danger—He loses.

¶Hedda feels herself demoniacally attracted by the tendencies of the times. But she lacks courage. Her thoughts remain theories, ineffective dreams.

---

[2] Both of them, each in his and her own way, have seen in their common love for this house a sign of their mutual understanding. As if they sought and were drawn to a common home. ¶ Then he rents the house. They get married and go abroad. He orders the house bought and his aunt furnishes it at his expense. Now it is their home. It is theirs and yet it is not, because it is not paid for. Everything depends on his getting the professorship. (Ibsen's note.)

¶The feminine imagination is not active and independently creative like the masculine. It needs a bit of reality as a help.

¶Løvborg has had inclinations toward "the bohemian life." Hedda is attracted in the same direction, but she does not dare to take the leap.

¶Buried deep within Hedda there is a level of poetry. But the environment frightens her. Suppose she were to make herself ridiculous!

¶Hedda realizes that she, much more than Thea, has abandoned her husband.

¶The newly wedded couple return home in September—as the summer is dying. In the second act they sit in the garden—but with their coats on.

¶Being frightened by one's own voice. Something strange, foreign.

¶NEWEST PLAN: The festivities in Tesman's garden—Løvborg's defeat—already prepared for in the 1st act. Second act: the party—

¶Hedda energetically refuses to serve as hostess. She will not celebrate their marriage because (in her opinion, it isn't a marriage)

¶*Holger:* Don't you see? I am the cause of your marriage—

¶Hedda is the type of woman in her position and with her character. She marries Tesman but she devotes her imagination to Eilert Løvborg. She leans back in her chair, closes her eyes, and dreams of his adventures. . . . This is the enormous difference: Mrs. Elvsted "works for his moral improvement." But for Hedda he is the object of cowardly, tempting daydreams. In reality she does not have the courage to be a part of anything like that. Then she realizes her condition. Caught! Can't comprehend it. Ridiculous! Ridiculous!

¶The traditional delusion that one man and one woman are made for each other. Hedda has her roots in the conventional. She marries Tesman but she dreams of Eilert Løvborg. . . . She is disgusted by the latter's flight from life. He believes that this has raised him in her estimation. . . . Thea Elvsted is the conventional, sentimental, hysterical Philistine.

¶Those Philistines, Mrs. E. and Tesman, explain my behavior by saying first I drink myself drunk and that the rest is done in insanity. It's a flight from reality which is an absolute necessity to me.

¶*E. L.:* Give me something—a flower—at our parting. Hedda hands him the revolver.

Then Tesman arrives: Has he gone? "Yes." Do you think he will still compete against me? No, I don't think so. You can set your mind at rest.

¶Tesman relates that when they were in Gratz she did not want to visit her relatives—

He misunderstands her real motives.

¶In the last act as Tesman, Mrs. Elvsted, and Miss Rysing are consulting, Hedda plays in the small room at the back. She stops. The conversation continues. She appears in the doorway—Good night—I'm going now. Do you need me for anything? Tesman: No, nothing at all. Good night, my dear! . . . The shot is fired—

¶CONCLUSION: All rush into the back room. Brack sinks as if paralyzed into a chair near the stove: But God have mercy—people don't *do* such things!

¶When Hedda hints at her ideas to Brack, he says: Yes, yes, that's extraordinarily amusing—Ha ha ha! He does not understand that she is quite serious.

¶Hedda is right in this: There is no love on Tesman's part. Nor on the aunt's part. However full of love she may be.

Eilert Løvborg has a double nature. It is a fiction that one loves only *one* person. He loves two—or many—alternately (to put it frivolously). But how can he explain his position? Mrs. Elvsted, who forces him to behave correctly, runs away from her husband. Hedda, who drives him beyond all limits, draws back at the thought of a scandal.

¶Neither he nor Mrs. Elvsted understands the point. Tesman reads in the manuscript that was left behind about "the two ideals." Mrs. Elvsted can't explain to him what E. L. meant. Then comes the burlesque note: both T. and Mrs. E. are going to devote their future lives to interpreting the mystery.

¶Tesman thinks that Hedda hates E. L.

Mrs. Elvsted thinks so too.

Hedda sees their delusion but dares not disabuse them of it. There is something beautiful about having an aim in life. Even if it is a delusion—

She cannot do it. Take part in someone else's.

That is when she shoots herself.

The destroyed manuscript is entitled "The ~~Philosophy~~ Ethics of Future Society."

¶Tesman is on the verge of losing his head. All this work meaningless. New thoughts! New visions! A whole new world! Then the two of them sit there, trying to find the meaning in it. Can't make any sense of it. . . .

¶The greatest misery in this world is that so many have nothing to do but pursue happiness without being able to find it.

¶"From Jochum Tesman there developed a Jørgen Tesman—but it will be a long, long time before this Jørgen gives rise to a George."

¶The simile: The journey of life = the journey on a train.

H.: One doesn't usually jump out of the compartment.

No, not when the train is moving.

Nor stand still when it is stationary. There's always someone on the platform, staring in.

¶*Hedda:* Dream of a scandal—yes, I understand that well enough. But commit one—no, no, no.

¶*Løvborg:* Now I understand. My ideal was an illusion. You aren't a bit better than I. Now I have nothing left to live for. Except pleasure—dissipation—as you call it. . . Wait, here's a present (The pistol)

¶Tesman is nearsighted. Wears glasses. My, what a beautiful rose! Then he stuck his nose in the cactus. Ever since then—!

¶NB: The mutual hatred of women. Women have no influence on external matters of government. Therefore they want to have an influence on souls. And then so many of them have no aim in life (the lack thereof is inherited)—

¶Løvborg and Hedda bent over the photographs at the table.

He: How is it possible? *She:* Why not? *L.:* Tesman! You couldn't find words enough to make fun of him. . . . Then comes the story about the general's "disgrace," dismissal, etc. The worst thing for a lady at a ball is not to be admired for her own sake. . . *L.:* And Tesman? He took you for the sake of your person. That's just as unbearable to think about.

¶Just by marrying Tesman it seems to me I have gotten so unspeakably far away from him.

¶*He:* Look at her. Just look at her! . . . *Hedda:* (stroking her hair) Yes, isn't she beautiful!

¶Men and women don't belong to the same century. . . . What a great prejudice that one should love only *one!*

¶Hedda and Brack talk about traveling to the small university towns. *Hedda:* Now I'm not counting that little trip through the Tyrol—

¶*Brack:* (to Tesman) Are you blind and deaf? Can't you see? Can't you hear—

Tesman: Ah. Take the manuscript. Read to me!

¶The demoniacal element in Hedda is this: She wants to exert her influence on someone—But once she has done so, she despises him. . . . The manuscript?

¶In the third act Hedda questions Mrs. Elvsted. But if he's like that, why is he worth holding on to. . . . Yes, yes, I know—

¶Hedda's discovery that her relations with the maid cannot possibly be proper.

¶In his conversation with Hedda, Løvborg says: Miss H—Miss—You know, I don't believe that you are married.

¶*Hedda:* And now I sit here and talk with these Philistines—And the way we once could talk to each other—No, I won't say any more. . .Talk? How do you mean? Obscenely? Ish. Let us say indecently.

¶NB!! The reversal in the play occurs during the big scene between Hedda and E. L. *He:* What a wretched business it is to conform to the existing morals. It would be ideal if a man of the present could live the life of the future. What a miserable business it is to fight over a professorship!

Hedda—that lovely girl! *H.:* No! *E. L.:* Yes, I'm going to say it. That lovely, cold girl—cold as marble.

I'm not dissipated fundamentally. But the life of reality isn't livable—

¶In the fifth act: *Hedda:* How hugely comic it is that those two harmless people, Tesman and Mrs. E., should try to put the pieces together for a monument to E. L. The man who so deeply despised the whole business—

¶Life becomes for Hedda a ridiculous affair that isn't "worth seeing through to the end."

¶The happiest mission in life is to place the people of today in the conditions of the future.

L.: Never put a child in this world, H.!

¶When Brack speaks of a "triangular affair," Hedda thinks about what is going to happen and refers ambiguously to it. Brack doesn't understand.

¶Brack cannot bear to be in a house where there are small children. "Children shouldn't be allowed to exist until they are fourteen or fifteen. That is, girls. What about boys? Shouldn't be allowed to exist at all—or else they should be raised outside the house."

¶H. admits that children have always been a horror to her too.

¶Hedda is strongly but imprecisely opposed to the idea that one should love "the family." The aunts mean nothing to her.

¶It liberated Hedda's spirit to serve as a confessor to E. L. Her sympathy has secretly been on his side—But it became ugly when the public found out everything. Then she backed out.

¶MAIN POINTS:

1. They are not all made to be mothers.

2. They are passionate but they are afraid of scandal.

3. They perceive that the times are full of missions worth devoting one's life to, but they cannot discover them.

¶And besides Tesman is not exactly a professional, but he is a specialist. The Middle Ages are dead—

¶T.: Now there you see also the great advantages to my studies. I can lose manuscripts and rewrite them—no inspiration needed—

¶Hedda is completely taken up by the child that is to come, but when it is born she dreads what is to follow—

¶Hedda must say somewhere in the play that she did not like to get out of her compartment while on the trip. Why not? I don't like to show my legs. . . . Ah, Mrs. H., but they do indeed show themselves. Nevertheless, I don't.

¶Shot herself! Shot herself!

Brack (collapsing in the easy chair): But great God—people don't *do* such things!

¶NB!! Eilert Løvborg believes that a comradeship must be formed between man and woman out of which the truly spiritual human being can arise. Whatever else the two of them do is of no concern. This is what the people around him do not understand. To them he is dissolute. Inwardly he is not.

¶If a man can have several male friends, why can't he have several lady friends?

¶It is precisely the sensual feelings that are aroused while in the company of his female "friends" or "comrades" that seek release in his excesses.

¶Now I'm going. Don't you have some little remembrance to give me—? You have flowers—and so many other things—(The story of the pistol from before)—But you won't use it anyhow—

¶In the fourth act when Hedda finds out that he has shot himself, she is jubilant. . . . He had courage.

Here is the rest of the manuscript.

¶CONCLUSION: Life isn't tragic. . . . Life is ridiculous. . . . And that's what I can't bear.

¶Do you know what happens in novels? All those who kill themselves— through the head—not in the stomach. . . . How ridiculous—how baroque—

¶In her conversation with Thea in the first act, Hedda remarks that she cannot understand how one can fall in love with an unmarried man—or an unengaged man—or an unloved man—on the other hand—[3]

¶Brack understands well enough that it is Hedda's repression, her hysteria that motivates everything she does.

---

[3] But, my heavens, Tesm. was unmarried. *H.:* Yes, he was *Th.:* But you married him. *H.:* Yes, I did. *Th.:* Then how can you say that . . . Well now— (2) But now he's married. *H.:* Yes, but not to someone else.

¶On her part, Hedda suspects that Brack sees through her without believing that she understands.

¶*H.:* It must be wonderful to take something from someone.

¶When H. talks to B. in the fifth act about those two sitting there trying to piece together the manuscript without the spirit being present, she breaks out in laughter. . . . Then she plays the piano—then—d—

¶Men—in the most indescribable situations how ridiculous they are.

¶NB! She really wants to live a *man's* life wholly. But then she has misgivings. Her inheritance, what is implanted in her.

¶Loving and being loved by aunts . . . Most people who are born of old maids, male and female.

¶This deals with the "underground forces and powers." Woman as a minor. Nihilism. Father and mother belonging to different eras. The female underground revolution in thought. The slave's fear of the outside world.

¶NB!! Why should I conform to social morals that I know won't last more than half a generation. When I run wild, as they call it, it's my escape from the present. Not that I find any joy in my excesses. I'm up to my neck in the established order. . . .

¶What is Tesman working on?

¶*Hedda:* It's a book on the domestic industries of Brabant during the Middle Ages.

¶I have to play the part of an idiot in order to be understood. Pretend that I want to rehabilitate myself in the eyes of the mob—today's mob.

¶When I had finished with my latest book, I conceived the idea for a brilliant new work. You must help me with it. I need women, Hedda—! In the Middle Ages the female conscience was so constituted that if she discovered she had married her nephew, she was filled with rancor—

¶Shouldn't the future strive for the great, the good, and the beautiful as Tesman says it should? Yes! But the great, the good, the beautiful of the future won't be the same as it is for us—

¶*H.:* I remember especially a red-headed girl whom I have seen on the street. *Br.:* I know whom you mean—*H.:* You called her—it was such a pretty name— *Br.:* I know her name too. But how do you know it was pretty? *H.:* Oh, Judge Brack, you are an idiot.

¶The passenger and his trunk at the railway station. P. decides where he is going, buys his ticket. The trunk is attended to—

¶Hedda: Slender figure of average height. Nobly shaped, aristocratic face with fine, wax-colored skin. The eyes have a veiled expression. Hair medium brown. Not especially abundant hair. Dressed in a loose-fitting dressing gown, white with blue trimmings. Composed and relaxed in her manners. The eyes steel-gray, almost lusterless.

¶Mrs. Elvsted: weak build. The eyes round, rather prominent, almost as blue as water. Weak face with soft features. Nervous gestures, frightened expression—

¶See above. E. L.'s idea of comradeship between man and woman. . . . The idea is a life-saver!

¶If society won't let us live morally with them (women), then we'll have to live with them immorally—

¶*Tesman:* The new idea in E. L.'s book is that of progress resulting from the comradeship between man and woman.

¶Hedda's basic demand is: I want to know everything, but keep myself clean.

¶I want to know everything—everything—everything—

H.:— —

H.: If only I could have lived like him!

¶Is there something about Brabant? *B.:* What on earth is that? . . .

¶The wager about the use of both pistols.

¶*Miss T.:* Yes, this is the house of life and health. Now I shall go home to a house of sickness and death. God bless both of you. From now on I'll come out here every day to ask Bertha how things are—

¶In the third act H. tells E. L. that she is not interested in the great questions—nor the great ideas—but in the great freedom of man. . . . But she hasn't the courage.

¶The two ideals! *Tesman:* What in the name of God does he mean by that? What? What do we have to do with ideals?

¶The new book treats of "the two ideals." Thea can give no information.

¶NB! Brack had always thought that Hedda's short engagement to Tesman would come to nothing.

Hedda speaks of how she felt herself set aside, step by step, when her father was no longer in favor, when he retired and died without leaving anything. Then she realized, bitterly, that it was for his sake she had been made much of. And then she was already between twenty-five and twenty-six. In danger of becoming an old maid.

She thinks that in reality Tesman only feels a vain pride in having won her. His solicitude for her is the same as is shown for a thoroughbred horse or a valuable sporting dog. This, however, does not offend her. She merely regards it as a fact.

Hedda says to Brack that she does not think Tesman can be called ridiculous. But in reality she finds him so. Later on she finds him pitiable as well.

Tesman: Could you not call me by my Christian name?

Hedda: No, indeed I couldn't—unless they have given you some other name than the one you have.

Tesman puts Løvborg's manuscript in his pocket so that it may not be lost. Afterward it is Hedda who, by a casual remark, with tentative intention, gives him the idea of keeping it.

Then he reads it. A new line of thought is revealed to him. But the strain of the situation increases. Hedda awakens his jealousy.

¶In the third act one thing after another comes to light about Løvborg's adventures in the course of the night. At last he comes himself, in quiet despair. "Where is the manuscript?" Did I not leave it behind me here?" He does not know that he has done so. But after all, of what use is the manuscript to him now! He is writing of the "moral doctrine of the future"! When he has just been released by the police!

¶ Hedda's despair is that there are doubtless so many chances of happiness in the world, but that she cannot discover them. It is the want of an object in life that torments her.

When Hedda beguiles T. into leading E. L. into ruin, it is done to test T.'s character.

¶It is in Hedda's presence that the irresistible craving for excess always comes over E. L.

Tesman cannot understand that E. L. could wish to base his future on injury to another.

¶*Hedda:* Do I hate T.? No, not at all. I only find him boring.

¶*Brack:* But nobody else thinks so.

Hedda: Neither is there any one but myself who is married to him.

Brack: . . . not at all boring.

Hedda: Heavens, you always want me to express myself so correctly. Very well then, T. is not boring, but I am bored by living with him.

Hedda: . . . had no prospects. Well, perhaps you would have liked to see me in a convent (home for unmarried ladies).

Hedda: . . . then isn't it an honorable thing to profit by one's person? Don't actresses and others turn their advantages into profit. I had no other capital. Marriage—I thought it was like buying an annuity.

Hedda: Remember that I am the child of an old man—and a worn-out man too—or past his prime at any rate—perhaps that has left its mark.

Brack: Upon my word, I believe you have begun to brood over problems.

Hedda: Well, what cannot one take to doing when one has gone and got married.

¶*E. L.:* It's impossible for me to call you Mrs. T. You will always be H. G. to me.

¶Both Miss T. and B. have seen what lies in store for Hedda. . . . T. on the other hand cries out: My God, I had no idea.

Raymond Williams (1921–1988)

Raymond Williams has written several important books on drama and literature, including *Culture and Society* (1958), *Drama from Ibsen to Brecht* (1968), and *The Country and the City* (1973). In the following selection from *Modern Tragedy* (1966) Williams attempts to account for the changes in western tragedy in terms of particular historical and social circumstances.

FROM *MODERN TRAGEDY*: THE MAKING OF LIBERAL TRAGEDY, TO IBSEN AND MILLER

We have seen, in our own time, the climax and the decline of liberal tragedy. To understand its structure of feeling is now a central problem. For we are all to some extent still governed by it, even now when we can see that it is failing to hold.

At the centre of liberal tragedy is a single situation: that of a man at the height of his powers and the limits of his strength, at once aspiring and being defeated, releasing and destroyed by his own energies. The structure is liberal in its emphasis on the surpassing individual, and tragic in its ultimate recognition of defeat or the limits of victory. . . .

. . . What is quite evident, through all the failures of Romantic drama, is a renewal and a renewed assertion of individual energy. The desires of man are again intense and imperative; they reach out and test the universe itself. Society is identified as convention, and convention as the enemy of desire. The individual rebellion is humanist, at a conscious level. Prometheus and Faust, characteristically, are its heroes. But the condition of desire, unconsciously, is that it is always forbidden. What then happens is that the forms of desire become devious and often perverse, and what looks like revolt is more properly a desperate defiance of heaven and hell. There is a related preoccupation with remorse: deep, pervasive, and beyond all its nominal causes. For in Romantic tragedy man is guilty of the ultimate and nameless crime of being himself.

The impossibility of finding a home in the world, the condemnation to a guilty wandering, the dissolution of self and others in a desire that is beyond all relationships: these Romantic themes are an important source of nearly all modern tragedy. Aspiration is absolute, but occurs, paradoxically, within a situation of man on the run from himself. Within this paradox, one dramatist of genius was eventually to work. But also, by the time of Ibsen's maturity, the last source of liberal tragedy had appeared: the increasingly confident identification of a false society as man's real enemy; the naming, in social terms, of the formerly nameless alienation. This body of social thinking had many kinds of influence. In one direction, it led to the denial of tragedy. Man had not only made but could remake himself. The Romantic desire for redemption and regeneration was given, in this tendency, a more or less precise social definition: when man was at the limits which ordinarily produced tragedy he became conscious of their nature and could begin to abolish them. When this abolition was seen as a social process, it did not, at least in the nineteenth century, lead to tragedy at all. The idea of tragedy, indeed, was dismissed as mystification and fatalism: an irony that still haunts us now that collective tragedy, and the tragic society, have been widely and deeply experienced. But this was not, in any case, the liberal path. What emerged there, as a controlling image, was not revolution, but the individual liberator. Acting on his own, and for his own reasons, a single man could change the human limits and transform his world. Looking back to Romantic tragedy, and forward to existentialist tragedy, this conception was still in its purest form in the late nineteenth century. By an act of choice, by an act of will, the individual refused the role of victim and became a new kind of hero. The heroism was not in the nobility of suffering, as the limits were reached. It was now, unambiguously, in the aspiration itself. What was demanded was self-fulfilment, and any such process was a general liberation. The singular man, as a matter of speech, became plural and capital: Man.

Liberal tragedy, at its full development, drew from all the sources that have been named, but in a new form and pressure created a new and specific structure of feeling. It is important, at this stage, not to try to fragment it, when it appears in Ibsen. The humanist exploration of the unknown reaches of life; the bourgeois preoccupation with humanitarianism and with money; the romantic intensities of alienation, remorse and perverted desire; the social recognition of dead institutions and limiting beliefs: all these are present in Ibsen, but in active combination, not as separate influences. To try to resolve his work into one of these lines has been a common practice in criticism: Ibsen the social critic; Ibsen the romantic or existentialist: each has been plausibly presented. But the real interest lies, where the work lies, in the struggle of these forces and in their composition into a particular drama.

Ibsen creates again and again in his plays, with an extraordinary richness of detail, false relationships, a false society, a false condition of man. The marks along this scale are often difficult to discern. The immediate lie is almost always present, but there is great variation in its ultimate reference: sometimes to an alterable condition; sometimes to an absolute condition; often, ambiguously, between these. Yet the generalising reference, in whatever kind, is persistent; the lie is never merely local, for it is seen as a symptom of a general condition. Characteristically, for liberal tragedy, the fight against the lie is individual; a man fights for his own life. Brand's vocation is `All or Nothing', and compromise is personally impossible:

> One thing is yours you may not spend,
> Your very inmost self of all,
> You may not bind it, may not bend,
> Nor stem the river of your call.

Or again:

> *Self completely to fulfil,*
> *That's a valid right of man,*
> *And no more than that I will.*

At the same time, the 'right' is also the 'call':

> *A great one gave me charge.* I must.

The call to wholeness is seen as self-fulfilment, and yet also as necessary. The right and the duty coincide in self-fulfilment, as in the classic liberal statements.

Yet the whole point about self-fulfilment is that it challenges, to the death, the existing compromise order. For here the lie is actual: men are afraid of wholeness and of self-fulfilment. As the Provost argues:

> *The surest way to destroy a man*
> *Is to turn him into an individual.*

Men have settled for a fragmentary life, as the easiest way, but this settlement is the sickness of their own personal lives and of their society. Routine is destructive, but so also are the wild breaks from routine, the simple refusals. What is needed is a new and total assent, for

> *Our time, our generation, that is sick*
> *And must be cured.*

Thus the individual, fulfilling himself absolutely, becomes, or offers himself as, the liberator. This position is reached again and again in Ibsen, but the resolution varies. In *Pillars of Society, A Doll's House, Enemy of the People,* the refusal of compromise is unambiguously carried through, if not to liberation, at least to positive individual defiance. In *Peer Gynt,* what looks like the quest for self-fulfilment is shown in the end to be simple evasion: the self alone, detached from the reality of world and relationships, withers and is wasted, to be redeemed only by return. More commonly, in varying degrees of emphasis, the individual's struggle is seen as both necessary and tragic. The evasion of fulfilment, by compromise, breeds false relationships and a sick society, but the attempt at fulfilment ends again and again in tragedy: the individual is destroyed in his attempt to climb out of his partial world.

This is the crux of liberal tragedy, and it is in many ways difficult to understand. The simple position is that of the heroic liberator opposed and destroyed by a false society: the liberal martyr. It is clear that Ibsen knew this feeling; it finds memorable expression in Stockmann. But it is not in this pattern that Ibsen takes his heroes to their deaths. Stockmann, faced only by this, is stronger and survives:

> The strongest man in the world is he who stands most alone.

Nor is it merely by accident and complication that the hero dies. The tragedy, in fact, is built into the form of the aspiration, in the significant concept of *debt.*

In the action and imagery of the plays, the nature of debt is persistently explored. Just as aspiration cannot be reduced simply to social reform, to a religious calling, or to self-expression, but remains obstinately general—the liberation of human spirit and energy—so debt cannot be reduced to inherited obligations, to a society burdened by compromises, or to original sin. These are often the forms in which aspiration and debt appear, but the actual works are more often explorations of the conflicting forces than definitions of them. Thus while in *Brand* there is a simple fatalism—

> *Blood of children must be spilt*
> *To atone for parents' guilt*

—it is also clear that new debts are contracted in the act of refusal of compromise; it is Brand himself, and not merely Brand the son or the human being, who is eventually guilty. The position would be simpler if this guilt were then condemned, if the voice through the final avalanche—`He is the God of love'—were a verdict. But this is not the case. Brand had to do what he did, and yet had to come to this point. This is not ethical tragedy, where a different choice would have brought safety. The choice and the fate admit no real alternatives.

What happens, again and again in Ibsen, is that the hero defines an opposing world, full of lies and compromises and dead positions, only to find, as he struggles against it, that as a man he belongs to this world, and has its destructive inheritance in himself. Ibsen turned this way and that, looking for a way out of this tragic deadlock, but normally he returned to it, and confessed its terrible power:

> Ghosts! . . . I almost believe we are all ghosts, Pastor Manders. It is not only what we have inherited from our fathers and mothers that walks in us. It is every kind of dead idea, lifeless old beliefs and so on. They are not alive, but they cling to us for all that, and we can never rid ourselves of them. Whenever I read a newspaper I seem to see ghosts stealing between the lines. There must be ghosts the whole country over, as thick as the sands of the sea. And then we are all of us so wretchedly afraid of the light.

This position, so often stated, is not a gloss for surrender to the darkness. The cry for light, the desire to climb out of such a world, is persistent and emphatic:

> *Give me air and the blaze of day . . .*
> *Through darkness to light . . .*
> *A summer night on the uplands . . .*
> *The joy of life . . . always, always the joy of life—light and sunshine*
> *and glorious air . . .*
> *Mother, give me the sun.*

But as the last phrase, the dying cry of Osvald, reminds us, the light is only a breaking aspiration, at the limits of human endurance. The death of Julian the Apostate, not the death of Christ, is the significant ending:

> Beautiful earth, beautiful life . . . O, Helios, Helios, why hast thou betrayed me?

There is no turning away from life to death, no tragic resignation. Ibsen's heroes, characteristically, die fighting and struggling and climbing: the aspiration to light is confirmed, not contradicted, by their deaths. In this sense, they are still heroes, but also they are tragic heroes. The ghosts

> cling to us . . . we can never rid ourselves of them.

Or as the liberal Rosmer puts it:

> We can never escape them, we of this house.

Ibsen seems to depend, as some of his language certainly depends, on a traditional idea of original sin. But the effect of his whole work is in fact a transformation of this. He never gives up the idea of the false society, even when he has realised that its complications eat into the lives of those opposing it. Nor, truly, does he ever mean 'sin' by 'debt'. The debts that count, in bringing his heroes down, are incurred in the struggle for life and light, however wayward this is often shown to be. When we have said 'sin', of Adam's desire, we have discounted human life, in any aspiring sense. But this desire, in Ibsen, is deep and valid. This is most clearly shown in *Emperor and Galilean*, where the false world of power and the false doctrine of resignation are alike rejected, in the struggle for the 'third empire', in which 'the spirit of men shall re-enter on its heritage'. It is the false condition of spirit against flesh that Julian fights, because

> all that is human has become unlawful since the day when the seer of Galilee became ruler of the world. Through him, life has become death.

The desire fails, or is broken, but is never denied. Ibsen's world, from his historical dramas to his domestic plays, is recognisable always by this fact: the struggle of individual desire, in a false and compromising situation, to break free and know itself. This is why we must not render him back to a dramatic tradition which would show the desire as false or unlawful. In the best sense, this is still a liberal world.

It is also, however, the world of liberal tragedy. Implacably, in most of his plays, the affirmed desire is brought to a breaking-point

> —a tight place where you stick fast. There is no going forward or backward—

and the hero, if not the desire itself, is broken. Why should this be so? Why, repeatedly, should so powerful a struggle of human desire fail to break through? It is not any force outside man that breaks him. As Rosmer says, going to his death:

> There is no judge over us, and therefore we must do justice upon ourselves.

But the justice, still, is death. The conviction of guilt, and of necessary retribution, is as strong as ever it was when imposed by an external design.

And this is the heart of liberal tragedy, for we have moved from the heroic position of the individual liberator, the aspiring self against society, to a tragic position, of the self against the self. Guilt, that is to say, has become internal and personal, just as aspiration was internal and personal. The internal and personal fact is the only general fact, in the end. Liberalism, in its heroic phase, begins to pass into its twentieth-century breakdown: the self-enclosed, guilty and isolated world; the time of man his own victim.

We are still in this world, and it is doubtful if we can clearly name all its pressures. A characteristic ideology has presented it as truth and even as science, until argument against it has come to seem hopeless. A structure of feeling as deep as this enacts a world, as well as interpreting it, so that we learn it from experience as well as from ideology. All we can say, reflecting on Ibsen's tragedy, is that the deadlock reached there, the heroic deadlock in which men die still struggling to climb, was indeed necessary. For there is no way out, there is only an inevitable tragic consciousness, while desire is seen as essentially individual. We have to push past Ibsen's undoubted social consciousness to discover, at its roots, this same individual consciousness. Certainly there is to be reform, the 'sick earth' is to be 'made whole', but this is to happen, always, by an individual act: the liberal conscience, *against* society. Change is never to be *with* people; if others come, they can at most be led. But also change, significantly often, is against people; it is against their wills that the liberator is thrown, and disillusion is then rapid. He speaks for human desire, as a general fact, but he knows this only as individual fulfilment. The self then makes its most terrible discovery: that there is not only a world outside it, resisting it, but other selves, capable of similar suffering and desire. It is possible then for fulfilment to be re-defined: a getting away from the world and from others; the loneliness of the high mountains. But desire had included the joy of life: the life of earth, and of men and women, which the hero is still governed by, even while he drives himself to reject it. The conflict is then indeed internal: a desire for relationship when all that is known of relationship is restricting; desire narrowing to an image in the mind, until it is realised that the search for warmth and light has ended in cold and darkness. Every move towards relationship ends in guilt. It is significant that nowhere in Ibsen is there a loving, active, lasting relationship; the image of it, at the end of *Peer Gynt*, is as much a relapse from effort, a return to the mother, as a discovery of a loving equal. More often, the tie to the parent is not even relapse. There is a kind of terror in natural inheritance itself. As later in Freudian psychology, the parent-child relationship is guilty as such, and the revelation of the face or feeling of father and mother, behind the adult self, is in itself horrifying. That inescapable connection haunts, quite literally, the liberal idea of the self. In this sense, to be born is to be guilty, and inheritance is inevitably 'debt'. For the identity of the 'free' self is limited and impugned by the necessary physical inheritance. That connection to others is involuntary, and is in the blood. To the liberal self this is not connection but tainting.

Then, driven by individual desire, which cannot admit any final connection, Ibsen's adult persons simply involve and damage each other, beyond the possibility of fulfilment. Freedom is defined as getting away from this net, or exposing it, in the name of truth. But there is nowhere to get away to, except by renunciation of the individual life and desire which are still active and compelling. Desire, consistently, betrays desire. The most active search to fulfil the self leads away from the persons in whom fulfilment is desired. It was this that Ibsen recognised, in his last plays; most notably in the Dramatic Epilogue:

> *We see the irretrievable only when . . .*
> *When? . . .*
> *When we dead awaken.*
> *What do we really see then?*
> *We see that we have never lived.*

The search for self-fulfilment has ended in the denial of life:

> It was self-murder, a deadly sin against myself. And that sin I can never expiate.

It is the final tragic recognition: that the self, which is all that is known as desire, leads away from fulfilment, and to its own breakdown.

From this recognition, there is no way out, within the liberal consciousness. There is either the movement to common desire, common aspiration, which politically is socialism, or there is the acceptance, reluctant at first but strengthening and darkening, of failure and breakdown as common and inevitable. In one way or the other, a total condition is asserted, and the differentiated self becomes dramatically rare. It is true that Shaw, in *Saint Joan* and elsewhere, could retain the simpler pattern, of the heroic and liberating individual destroyed by a false society. Numerically, many other plays have repeated this, but, at least in European drama, this pattern has commonly failed to include any of the deepest human energies and problems. The heroic individual, as in Shaw, survives only as a romantic portrait, emptied of personality so that the positive role can be played without complications. The act of liberation, correspondingly, is in the narrow sense historical or political; it is not an absolute human demand, but a limited cause here and there. The problem of the frustrated individual is masked by his theatrical transformation into a movement, leaving all the deeper problems, of history and personality, untouched.

The mainstream of tragedy has gone elsewhere: into the self-enclosed, guilty and isolated world of the breakdown of liberalism. We shall need to trace this through its complicated particular phases. But, with Ibsen in mind, it is worth looking briefly at the plays of Arthur Miller, who represents, essentially, a late revival of liberal tragedy, on the edge (but only on the edge) of its transformation into socialism. What distinguishes Miller from the majority contemporary drama of guilt and breakdown is the retained consciousness of a false society, an alterable condition. In *All My Sons* we are in many ways back in the world of Ibsen: a particular lie becomes the demonstration of a general lie. Joe Keller, a small manufacturer, has committed a social crime for which he has escaped responsibility. He acquiesced in the sending of defective parts to the Air Force in wartime, and allowed another man to take the consequences and imprisonment. The action of the play is that the social crime is made personal (by the fact of the death of Keller's own pilot son), and from this realisation made social again, in a new understanding of what society is. This is, in fact, the overcoming of alienation:

> Joe Keller's trouble . . . is not that he cannot tell right from wrong but that his cast of mind cannot admit that he, personally, has any viable connection with his world, his universe, or his society.

This is

> the concept of a man's becoming a function of production or distribution to the point where his personality becomes divorced from the actions it propels.

By seeing a particular case, to which he has a father's connection, he is forced to recognise the general fact of human connection:

> I think to him they were all my sons. And I guess they were, I guess they were.

However, this new positive consciousness cannot go beyond the level of statement; it is a new feeling, of collective responsibility and of collective guilt, personally affirmed, but the tragedy is in the fact that it is retrospective. Keller, and those he has killed, can only be victims.

This sense of the victim is very deep in Miller. *The Crucible* may remind us, dramatically, of *Enemy of the People*, but there is a wholly new sense of the terrible power of collective persecution. Individuals suffer for what they are and naturally desire, rather than for what they try to do, and the innocent are swept up with the guilty, with epidemic force. The social consciousness has now changed, decisively. Society is not merely a false system, which the liberator can challenge. It is actively destructive and evil, claiming its victims merely because they are alive. It is still seen as a false and alterable society, but merely to live in it, now, is enough to become its victim. In *Death of a Salesman* the victim is not the nonconformist, the heroic but defeated liberator; he is, rather, the conformist, the type of the society itself. Willy Loman is a man who from selling things has passed to selling himself, and has become, in effect, a commodity which like other commodities will at a certain point be discarded by the laws of the economy. He brings tragedy down on himself, not by opposing the lie, but by living it. Ironically, the form of his aspiration is again the form of his defeat, but now for no liberating end; simply to get by, to see himself and his sons all right. The connection between parents and children, seen as necessarily contradictory, is again tragically decisive. A new consciousness is then shaped: that of the victim who has no living way out, but who can try, in death, to affirm his lost identity and his lost will.

Proctor, in *The Crucible*, had died as an act of self-preservation: preservation of the truth of himself and of others, in opposition to the lies of the persecuting authority.

> How may I live without my name?

This sense of personal verification by death is the last stage of liberal tragedy. In *The Crucible* it is virtually the position of the liberal martyr, though characteristically complicated by Proctor's personal guilt. But in *Death of a Salesman* and *A View from the Bridge* this wider implication is absent. It is not now the martyr but the victim; the disconnected individual. In Willy Loman's death the disconnection confirmed a general fact about the society; in Eddie Carbone's death, Miller has moved further back, and the death of the victim illustrates a total condition. Here, once again, at the end of a development, is the self against the self. Desire is quickened, releasing energies which destroy. As Eddie moves out of routine and into desire, there is rapid disintegration: the known sexual rhythms break down into their perverse variations, which now alone have energy. He rejects his wife, as his desire transfers to the girl they have brought up. And as his most vital energy drives him towards both incest and homosexuality, guilt becomes so much a part of desire that his identity and his normal connections are simply burned out. In the terror of his complicated jealousies, he betrays the human connection by which he has lived, surrenders immigrants of his wife's kin to the inhuman and alien society. When desire and guilt are thus inextricable, there is no way to live, and he provokes his death shouting `I want my name'.

It is a last tragic cry, in a disintegrating world. Human desire destroys itself, under intolerable pressures, and the figure of the individual hero, who would remake his life and his world, is now quite forgotten, is one of the old stories, while isolated contemporary man, wanting no more than to be himself, fails even in this and transfers significance to his name and his death. To preserve one's life, as things are, is `to settle for half', as Miller puts it at the end of *A View from the Bridge*. And if this is so, in a false society which the individual alone cannot change, then the original liberal impulse, of complete self-fulfilment, becomes inevitably tragic. The self that wills and desires destroys the self that lives, yet the rejection of will and desire is also tragedy: a corroding insignificance, as the self is cut down.

The final step, made clear in *After the Fall*, is the acceptance and generalisation of just this insignificance: the personally urgent yet finally complacent acknowledgement that desire and guilt are inextricable; the identification of the false society—torture, betrayal—as part of one's own desires, so that it can no longer be meaningfully opposed, or even bitterly challenged by death, but has simply to be confirmed, forgiven, and lived with, in our separate and isolated suffering. And then at this point the deadlock is absolute, and we are all victims: aspiration itself is only a disguise for cruelty. But when this has happened, in the mind of a whole culture, liberal tragedy has ended, in its own deadlock.

PART VI

Modern European and American Drama and Theater: Reactions and Modifications

An artist's projection showing the interior arrangement of the Shakespeare Memorial Theatre at Stratford-upon-Avon, England, built in 1932. Despite the forestage, it is typical of early twentieth century theatre design. Its stage is defined by a proscenium arch, its auditorium is fan shaped, and its seats are fixed in place.

© 83, RICHARD LEACROFT.

Even as realism came to dominate theatrical representation, some playwrights and theorists sensed its limitations and began to rebel against it. Realism depicted ordinary people in ordinary situations, costumed in middle- or lower-class clothing, speaking dialogue that reflected everyday conversation, and living out their lives in sets that were photographic likenesses of the world outside the theater. Audiences might easily identify with such characters and situations, but realism focused unrelentingly on the pain and suffering, the happiness and triumph of "real" individuals, and it accepted the world and social values as an unchanging environment. Moreover, realism intensified the distance between audience and performance. Audiences sat silently in darkened auditoriums, watching actors pretend to live in another world, one that by theatrical convention excluded the audience. The resulting aesthetic distance offered a philosophical irony: realistic drama and staging, designed to reflect problems of the "real" world, did so by *separating* the real world from performance, more so than any other theater in history. This division proved a serious limitation. At the same time, findings in psychology, politics, and sociology, along with pressure from technological developments, encouraged many playwrights to experiment with new forms. Within a generation of its triumph in the late nineteenth century, the philosophical principles and aesthetic assumptions underlying the practice of realism in the theater had begun to change.

DRAMA AND SOCIETY

In the twentieth century, massive social, ideological, and technological changes have transformed the sensibilities of Europe and North America, and drama has reflected those changes. In the past hundred years, European colonial empires have broken up, two world wars have been fought, a cold war has been waged, and post–cold war nationalist movements have remapped the entire world several times over. At the same time, electronic communications systems, technological innovation, mass production, new modes of transportation, and global markets have acted to shrink the world. Today, communication with people in geographically remote areas is merely an electronic impulse away. Such technological changes have affected our social lives, too, and the ways we think not only of ourselves but of our relations to family, community, and the rest of the world.

The nineteenth century embraced its material and scientific culture with optimism, and naturalism and realism captured this optimism in the theater in the late part of the century. By the mid-twentieth century, however, experience with the destructive uses of scientific technology had eroded much of that early optimism. The darker side of positivist scientific theories now emerged. If Darwin's *Origin of Species* (1859) suggested that species would continued to evolve in ever more effective directions, it also implied that such evolution was sporadic and accidental. If Marx's early writings on economics and his *Communist Manifesto* declared that the working classes could direct their own destinies, it also suggested that human social organization was itself the result of economic forces that no individual or society could control. If Freud's writing on the unconscious once promised a key to unlocking and treating mental anguish, it also asserted that our behavior is the product of irrational or instinctual drives, that the concept of "character" as something stable or fixed is erroneous. If nuclear energy seemed to offer an unlimited source of cheap power to improve the lives of many, its use as a weapon of indiscriminate mass destruction hovered nightmarishly over the post–World War II period.

As in every other arena, great changes have occurred in drama during the twentieth century. In the late nineteenth century, realist plays had adopted the techniques of the well-made play, with formulaic beginnings, middles, and ends, mapping out a world of predictable cause and effect. But as the twentieth century progressed, faith in this premise became more and more tentative. Dramatists began to explore alternative, less resolvable, and often more disturbing views of individual and social problems, now depicting instability or fluidity of character, now rejecting altogether the idea of plot, now employing conscious distortion in set design, now estranging the audience and mocking human reason itself. The comforts of familiar theatrical conventions and devices were distorted or discarded.

AVANT-GARDE REACTION

Around the turn of the century, avant-garde movements in the arts produced a series of antagonistic reactions to realism and its vision of the world. Symbolism, which regarded realism as altogether inadequate to depict essential experience, proved particularly attractive. The beginning of symbolism in the theater is associated with the work of the Belgian playwright Maurice Maeterlinck (1862–1949), who depicted dramatic worlds of introspection and subjectivity, in which inexplicable forces control and manipulate characters and events. Often written in poetry, symbolist plays were designed to evoke states of mind and emotions in audiences, feelings that corresponded to the playwright's intuitions. Some symbolist plays rely on mythological or imaginative subject matter and dense figurative language or dialect to convey these poetic intuitions, as do some of the plays of W. B. Yeats, Sean O'Casey, John Millington Synge, and Lady Augusta Gregory, who were all connected with the Abbey Theatre in Dublin. In many of these plays, the surface level appears realistic, but on another level symbolist techniques foreground the subjects of Irish myth or peasant life. Symbolism also influenced the theater in the work of emerging theorists such as Adolphe Appia (1862–1928) and Gordon Craig (1872–1966), who emphasized the importance of lighting and music in reflecting shifting moods and emotions. Sometimes symbolist plays were performed behind gauze curtains, or directors used clouds of fog or alternately bright and dark effects to convey an impression of strangeness or poetic mystification. Both Appia and Craig opposed the scenic illusion of realism—and anything resembling photographic reproductions of specific places. Instead, they supported the design of three-dimensional sets within which actors would be regarded as only one element of a group of figures in an integrated set.

Futurism, a movement that first arose in Italy in 1909 with the work of the poet Filippo Marinetti (1876–1944), glorified the technology of the machine age and sought to use it as the basis for art. Practitioners of this movement pioneered innovative techniques in intermingling audience and performers, in using multimedia technology, and in developing multiple focuses in performances. Constructionism, a movement that shared some values of the futurists, had a more direct impact on theater. It is associated with the work of the Russian Vsevolod Meyerhold (1874–1940), who early in his career directed some experimental plays of Stanislavsky's. Meyerhold attempted a theatrical art suitable to a machine age. He developed a technique of acting called biomechanics, training actors in nonrealistic movement. The term *constructivism* refers to Meyerhold's notions of set design. Meyerhold thought the set should not be realistic but rather a nonrepresentational construction, a "machine" suitable for actors to perform in.

Expressionism in the theater relied on dreamlike and often nightmarish visions. Strindberg's work after 1895—particularly *A Dream Play* (1902), in which he adopts the viewpoint of the dreamer to distort time, place, and logical sequence—acted as a forerunner of expressionism. But the movement developed most fully in Germany, where these techniques were used to focus on political and social issues, particularly the possibility of disaster caused by unchecked industrialism and by a depersonalizing modern society that crushed the human spirit. Expressionists explicitly opposed the fundamental tenets of realism, which they felt neglected deeply ingrained social and human issues. Expressionists successfully joined the sensibility and intellect of character with set design and style of performance, and their techniques have been widely adapted to film and theater to modify and enhance realism.

Two other notable artistic movements reacted against realism as well: dada and surrealism. Dada, introduced in Switzerland by Tristan Tzara (1896–1963), interrogated the rational roots of Western culture, which claimed to be founded on logic and reason but had produced the atrocities of world war. The movement advocated producing art that was formless, that cultivated irrationality. The nonsense term *dada* was used to describe this movement, which in performance was restricted mainly to cabarets in Europe, although some of its techniques were later to surface in absurdism. At about the same time as dada was introduced in Switzerland, André Breton (1896–1966) promoted another movement in France, known as surrealism. Following Freud's theories of the subconscious, Breton held that profound works of art would more readily surface when the artist's mind was free of the shackles of the ego's logic and the superego's censorship. Like dada, surrealism had a limited effect on contemporary theatrical practices, but it pioneered a technique of hallucinatory distortion that was widely adapted by later set designers and by absurdist playwrights.

Although this discussion of artistic movements describes in brief the qualities of avant-garde drama and theater, it is nearly impossible to convey how widespread the sense of innovation was in practice. In every region of Europe and America the theater drew inspiration from these artistic movements, often from several of them at a time. Even early realist plays, like Ibsen's *Wild Duck* and Chekhov's *Cherry Orchard*, employed symbolism, for example, and Strindberg's turn to expressionism in *A Dream Play* is anticipated in the development of the action of such a classic realist-naturalist play as *Miss Julie*. Pirandello's *Six Characters in Search of an Author*, written just after World War I, formally begins by challenging the conventions of the well-made play. Clearly, this century has been a time of stress and change and intense artistic experimentation with every kind of theatrical representation.

THEATERS

While avant-garde theaters in Europe and America issued a variety of manifestos and developed a variety of acting styles and production techniques, they shared a common interest in making theater responsive to the issues of contemporary life. Such a program, however, did not always appeal to popular audiences. The production of plays in small independent theaters, pioneered by the realists and continued by avant-garde playwrights, indicates the theater's marginalization during the twentieth century. Pressed by other new popular art forms and representational technologies, including film, radio, and television, theatrical practice tended to define itself as a self-consciously sophisticated art form, exploring its unique powers and cultivating its own audience.

Along with new ideologies and new aesthetics, technological developments did much to transform theater production. Electric lighting, sophisticated audiovisual systems, and the invention of new industrial materials accompanied a shift from the rectangular auditorium with boxes and balconies to the fan-shaped auditorium that emphasized clear sight lines and a perspective view of the stage. Prompted by the avant-garde theater movements, theorists and directors also looked backwards and found inspiration in conventions unexplored since the Middle Ages and the Renaissance. Directors and theater designers experimented with aesthetic distance—that is, with the emotional connection between audience and play. Theater-in-the-round was developed, in which the audience surrounds the stage, and environmental theater, in which action takes place within the audience. These arrangements alter the relationship between audience and actors, and they radically change the way performances are conceived and understood. The development of sophisticated mechanical devices that could raise and lower scenic properties or even alter the shape of the stage itself, along with customized visual projection and audio systems, made new and spectacular effects possible.

BERTOLT BRECHT AND ANTONIN ARTAUD

Like other playwrights of their time, Bertolt Brecht (1898–1956) and Antonin Artaud (1895–1948) reacted against realism in the theater. Brecht, a playwright and director and a prolific theorist of the drama, believed that the primary purpose of theater was social and political education. Attracted by Marxism, he committed himself to a theater of social responsibility. His early work shows the influence of the expressionists; then, influenced by the work of Erwin Piscator and by Meyerhold's constructivism, Brecht developed his ideas of epic theater. Traditional theater, he insisted, strove for illusion, which simply encouraged audiences to identify with characters and situations onstage, a condition that produced "spellbound oblivion." A socially responsible theater, he wrote, ought to work by alternately forcing audiences to identify with and to distance themselves from the action. Such a process—what he called *Verfremdungseffekt*, usually translated as "alienation effect"—would encourage audiences to think about what they saw onstage and motivate them to change their lives and their social conditions.

Brecht realized that an entire range of new ideas about writing, acting, direction, and set design would be required, and he set about accomplishing this task.

Plots, he wrote, could no longer be written on the classical model of tying and untying a knot; rather, "individual events must be tied together in such a way as the knots are visible." In this new theater actors were to distance themselves from their roles, to think of their characters not as people with psychological and real histories but rather as artificial creations, roles that could be demonstrated and evaluated rather than impersonated. Sets were to be built not as reproductions of specific places but rather to remind audiences that they were artificial constructions. Likewise, lighting designers were to expose the mechanical trappings of the theater, reminding audiences that their imaginative experience was constructed. In Brecht's new theater, the elements of production would be juxtaposed: music or costuming, for example, might be used to contradict rather than complement action. Thus, theater would become didactic or "epic," the term Brecht employed to distinguish his work from the drama that he claimed entertains through illusion and fosters complacency.

The second major twentieth-century theorist of the theater was Antonin Artaud. Playwright, actor, director, screenwriter, and poet, he changed and deepened the conception of theater with the publication of *The Theater and Its Double* (1938; translated into English in 1958). His early association with the surrealists helps account for the high value he places on intuition, feeling, and experience and for his distrust of reason. Inspired by a troupe of Balinese dancers at the Colonial Exposition in Paris in 1931, he came to believe that while Western theater had concerned itself with the psychological problems of individuals or the social problems of groups, the most important aspects of experience were located in the unconscious mind. Artaud's theoretical essays thus develop ideas through metaphor and image rather than by argument. In his discussions of theater he uses "double," "cruelty," and "plague" as major metaphors.

Western theater, Artaud asserted, had lost its vitality and intensity. He declared that the text should be displaced because language could not adequately convey meaning; rather, gestures, signs, symbols, rhythms, and sounds could evoke intuitive, primitive, authentic responses. Moving beyond Brecht's social and political program, Artaud contended that the most important function of theater was to move its audiences to powerful spiritual awakenings. Artaud thought theater should make audiences confront their hypocrisies, and so enable people to discard hypocrisies and to move beyond them. The theater of "cruelty" aimed at such a confrontation. He believed the theater could help to expel the causes of division, hatred, and violence and lead to a more harmonious social life. In order to realize its potential, then, the theater had to reject causal plots and rational dialogue; it had to attempt persuasion through intense feeling. Like the "plague," he stated, "the theater has been created to drain abscesses collectively." To stimulate the entire being of his audiences, Artaud experimented with manipulations of light and sound, using abrupt, discordant shifts combined with verbal and visual effects supplied by actors. Clearly, Artaud's innovations flew directly in the face of realism. His theories have proved broadly influential in contemporary theater practice and can even be seen in many films and in such contemporary spectacles as rock concerts.

PERFORMANCE

Just as realism had given rise to a new style of acting, nonrealistic drama required new styles of performance as well. Symbolist theater worked out highly artificial poses for actors who delivered highly charged poetic language. Biomechanics, the performance style developed for Meyerhold's constructivist movement, was intended to render performances more physical, independent of realistic behavior, and certainly unlike the psychological verisimilitude associated with method acting. Likewise, Artaud's notions of nonrepresentational physicality were designed for a theater in revolt against Western realism. Brecht's theories of epic theater, however, spelled out the most radical shift away from realistic acting. He discouraged and subverted any presentation of compelling realistic characters onstage. Distancing themselves from the characters they portrayed, Brechtian actors allowed audiences to participate in understanding the artificiality of theatrical conventions, to see that art was a product of the imagination, not of life.

MODIFICATIONS TO REALISM

Although avant-garde movements in the arts challenged realism, few produced enduring drama; but they modified the assumptions, conventions, and practices of realism, and they broadened the possibilities of twentieth-century theater. Realism remained the dominant mode, but by the end of World War II the avant-garde movements of the early part of the century, along with the growing influence of film, had conditioned audiences to accept simplification, suggestion, and distortion as expected components in art. The theater now depended less on illusion and more on artificiality and theatricality. Scene design came to rely on suggestion rather than representation. Location could be merely indicated and details simplified. The structure of plays depended far less on techniques established by the well-made play. The impulse now was to construct plays in terms of scenes rather than acts and to experiment with a wide range of dramatic techniques.

These modifications to the assumptions and practice of realism accompanied a shift in cultural awareness itself. Science no longer held the key to solving social problems but presented itself as one of the problems. Even worse, scientific accomplishments could now be seen as merely tools that might be used for nationalistic or selfish purposes. While capable of providing rational answers to rational problems, science appeared now as incapable of providing any clear moral guidance. At the same time, results from the developing field of psychoanalysis shook any remaining faith in rational decision making. The "real" was now neither rational nor one-dimensional, and the manner of representation of the real in the theater changed accordingly, incorporating techniques from the "irrational" movements of the early twentieth century.

In the American theater, less sweeping but still noteworthy modifications to realism occurred. Intensely focused playwriting and acting brought American theater to world attention in the 1940s and 1950s. An acting style derived from Stanislavsky's method, emphasizing emotional spontaneity, attention to subtext, and psychological realism, became recognized worldwide as the American style. Exemplified in plays by Arthur Miller (b. 1915), Eugene O'Neill (1888–1953), and

Tennessee Williams (1911–1983), the relationship between the individual psyche of American characters and social issues became important subject matter. American playwrights also modified traditional realism by using nonrealistic devices. In the later plays of O'Neill, for example, and in many of the plays of Miller and Williams can be found symbols, simultaneous staging, representation of memory or imagination, and a fluid sense of time and space.

ABSURDISM

As American theater peaked with the successes of Miller, Williams, and O'Neill in the 1940s and early 1950s, a new kind of nonrealistic drama surfaced in Europe: the theater of the absurd. Absurdism was never a self-declared movement or "school," but the term was applied to several post–World War II playwrights, who were grouped together and identified as such by Martin Esslin in his influential book *The Theater of the Absurd* (1964). The term *absurd* derives from the philosophical movement existentialism, particularly as exemplified in the writings of Albert Camus and Jean-Paul Sartre, who were concerned with the plight of the individual in a world without objective meaning. Esslin noted that in the theater this philosophical premise acted as a catalyst to combine with a variety of techniques derived from early-twentieth-century artistic movements. Like surrealism, absurdism suggests that the prime source of insight into existence is the subconscious. Like dadaism, absurdism suggests that a rational approach to the subconscious is impossible. The existential premise that existence is meaninglessness would best be conveyed by an irrational theater. Such an approach ruled out realism entirely, for there is no shared agreement on what is "real." Instead, absurdist playwrights attempted to communicate experience. The notion of a logical plot, with a beginning, middle, and end, was dismissed, and in its place was substituted a series of apparently unrelated or nonsensical incidents, often suggesting repetition or circularity. Language itself was devalued as a precise or important means of communication, so that in absurdist plays action often contradicts dialogue. Unlike such purely existentialist playwrights as Sartre and Camus, those playwrights labeled as absurdists, such as Eugene Ionesco, Samuel Beckett, Harold Pinter, Edward Albee, and Tom Stoppard, did not write thesis plays to debate the absurdity of life—they simply showed it in action. Beckett modeled Didi and Gogo, the sad pair of clowns in *Waiting for Godot*, on vaudeville comedians and used them to suggest pathetic hopefulness and a curious heroic resignation in a meaningless and absurd world. Absurdist plays often achieve striking theatrical moments by experimenting and by challenging traditional practices of stagecraft, working thematically to derive meaning from meaninglessness itself.

EUGENE O'NEILL (1888–1953)

Eugene O'Neill was born in a New York City hotel, the third son of a successful actor who had become famous for (and trapped in) his rendition of the Count of Monte Cristo. His father, James O'Neill, an Irish immigrant, was a self-made man whose swashbuckling role on stage was wildly popular, and he toured with the play all over the country. The son was thus familiar with the demands and rewards of the theater from an early age. But the household, as we learn from O'Neill's later confessional plays, was troubled. His father's success in fact became a curse: it paid so well as to make the family relatively well-off, but it made any other roles financially risky, while the nightly repetition of the same role year after year was not only monotonous—it spelled professional death for any actor. The constant travels also meant that the family was homeless or split up when the play went on tour. The elder O'Neill eventually took to drink and womanizing, while his wife, who had become addicted to morphine during Eugene's childbirth, slipped into a life of prolonged stupor. Their family life would not by any account seem a likely place to produce the first truly great—and by some lights still the preeminent—American playwright, but it did.

O'Neill attended a Catholic boarding school and high school in New York, which provided him with a deeply ingrained sense of sin and possible redemption—themes that would dominate his late autobiographical plays. In 1906, at age eighteen, he entered Princeton, but he was suspended after a prank during his first year and never returned. He worked at a variety of odd jobs for the next six years: he became a seaman; he went prospecting for gold in Honduras; he worked for his father as an actor and assistant stage manager; he went to work as a reporter for a small-town newspaper in Connecticut. During these years he was briefly married, but this was a disastrous time for him. O'Neill had taken up a dissolute life, and by 1912 he had contracted tuberculosis and was living in a sleazy hotel in New York where he tried to commit suicide.

O'Neill's recovery from his sickness, dissipation, and failed marriage coincided with his turn toward play writing. At a sanitarium, where he received extended treatment for his tuberculosis, O'Neill began to read modern plays, and he was particularly excited by the experiments of Strindberg. He decided to try writing plays and enrolled in a playwriting workshop at Harvard in 1914. By 1915 he had moved to Greenwich Village, where he began to associate with the avant-garde writers who formed the Provincetown Players repertory company, including Susan Glaspell. The association with the Provincetown Players was mutually beneficial: the group staged all of O'Neill's early plays, and largely because of their success became the most influential American company, and internationally famous as well.

The early works of O'Neill included some realistic plays—*Beyond the Horizon* (1920) and *Anna Christie* (1921) both won the Pulitzer Prize—but two expressionistic plays were the ones to bring O'Neill international recognition:

The Emperor Jones (1920) and *The Hairy Ape* (1922), which deal with social issues of tyranny, race, and class, and which offer bleak hope for individuals enmeshed in their workings. In other plays written during the 1920s and early 1930s, O'Neill explored how individual psychology, as understood in Freudian terms, promoted the workings of tragic catastrophe. *Desire Under the Elms* (1924) portrayed the sexual attraction of a son and a young stepmother, and *Strange Interlude* (1928), a very long nine-act play, allowed the characters to speak lengthy asides to express their true feelings. *Strange Interlude* won O'Neill his third Pulitzer Prize. His highly acclaimed trilogy *Mourning Becomes Electra* (1931) depicted the workings of tragic fate over several generations, driven by primal emotions and sexual instinct. Its power and the ongoing inventiveness and flow of his work brought O'Neill the Nobel Prize for literature in 1936.

During this time O'Neill had married for the second time, and then, after a divorce in 1929, he married Carlotta Monterey, with whom he seems to have found a peaceful life. In the late 1930s he began to turn to his own life as a source of drama: *The Iceman Cometh* (1939) features a suicidal alcoholic in a sleazy bar, and *Long Day's Journey Into Night* (1940), perhaps O'Neill's most moving play, portrays his own father and mother and brother as the thinly fictionalized Tyrones, coming to terms with their love and failures. *Long Day's Journey Into Night* won O'Neill his fourth Pulitzer in 1956 after the play's posthumous production. In 1943 he wrote *A Moon for the Misbegotten*, a play based on the life of his alcoholic brother Jamie. In the early 1940s O'Neill was struck by a degenerative disease—probably Parkinson's disease—that made his hands shake so badly he could no longer write. He lived for ten more years, the last two as a recluse in a Boston hotel, and died in 1953.

It would be hard to overestimate the importance and power of O'Neill's plays. They sounded the first full-throated voice of a truly American playwright, one who was unafraid to experiment radically with dramatic forms and theatrical effects. However difficult his life, he was finally able to transform it into art and courageously to avoid the trap of sameness and artistic sterility that had engulfed his father.

The Emperor Jones

The Emperor Jones is a one-act multiscene play that traces the last hours of an ambitious tyrant on a Caribbean island. During the course of the play we learn that Brutus Jones, the protagonist, killed at least one man in the United States, escaped from prison, and had arrived on an island inhabited by superstitious natives. Jones seized the opportunity to make himself Emperor, claiming he could only be killed by a silver bullet, and he has proceeded to exploit the tribes, building up a sizable bank account abroad, a nest egg for his inevitable retirement. He has dominated his ne'er-do-well Cockney confidant in the same way he has ruled the tribes, by bullying, with the difference that Smithers knows the bogus basis of Jones's power and has profited from his protection in crooked trading deals. The play opens in Jones's palace, where he learns that an uprising is imminent, and the main action of the play occurs as he attempts to escape through the jungle.

One of O'Neill's most successful early plays, *The Emperor Jones* introduced two highly original features. It was the first serious play in the mainstream American repertory to have a multiracial cast and an African-American protagonist—whom O'Neill insisted be played by a black actor—and it was the first in which the use of expressionistic sound effects dominate the main character and the audience at the same time. When *The Emperor Jones* was made into a film in the 1930s, it became a main vehicle to fame for actor Paul Robeson. Robeson tempered the dialogue, dropping some of the references Brutus Jones makes to himself as "nigger," and downplaying the dialect that O'Neill had constructed, which in fact was derived from the American minstrel tradition rather than from an accurate observation of spoken dialect. The Cockney dialect of Smithers, equally intrusive, can be seen to serve some of the same purposes as that of Jones: reinforcing a stereotype in order to move beyond it. As Jones strips down during the course of the play's first seven scenes, he loses bit by bit the veneer of political leader and tinpot dictator, to become more and more like the natives whom he has abused and who are determined to hunt him down. He also becomes more human, and the power of his own past comes back literally to haunt him in the jungle.

Brutus Jones's journey into the jungle of his past is accompanied by the insistent beat of drums. Beginning in the first scene, the drumbeat is slow and distant, its tempo the same as the beat of the human heart. O'Neill specifies in the stage directions, scene by scene, how both the tempo and the volume of the drumbeat should be increased, and panic finally overwhelms any semblance of rational thought in Jones. Through the expressionistic drumbeat the audience is forced into a state of apprehension, and thus to an emotional understanding of the trajectory of Brutus Jones's last hours.

When the play was written in 1921, the artistic techniques, the social content, and the productions of the play were distinctly avant-garde. Times change. Our awareness of social stereotyping has changed radically since the 1920s, and the dialogue and stereotyping in *The Emperor Jones* may seem artificial and offensive to contemporary audiences. Still, the sheer theatrical power of the play, with its skillful use of expressionist techniques, has assured it a place in theater history.

The Emperor Jones

Eugene O'Neill

CHARACTERS

BRUTUS JONES, Emperor
HENRY SMITHERS, a Cockney trader
AN OLD NATIVE WOMAN
LEM, A native chief
SOLDIERS, adherents of Lem

THE LITTLE FORMLESS FEARS; JEFF; THE NEGRO
CONVICTS; THE PRISON GUARD; THE PLANTERS; THE
AUCTIONEER; THE SLAVES; THE CONGO WITCH-DOCTOR;
THE CROCODILE GOD

The action of the play takes place on an island in the
West Indies as yet not self-determined by White
Marines. The form of native government is, for the
time being, an Empire.

SCENES

Scene 1, In the palace of the Emperor Jones.
   Afternoon.
Scene 2, The edge of the Great Forest. Dusk.
Scene 3, In the Forest. Night.
Scene 4, In the Forest. Night.
Scene 5, In the Forest. Night.
Scene 6, In the Forest. Night.
Scene 7, In the Forest. Night.
Scene 8, Same as Scene 2–the edge of the Great Forest.
   Dawn.

Scene 1

*The audience chamber in the palace of the Emperor —
a spacious high-ceilinged room with bare, whitewashed walls. The floor is of white tiles. In the rear, to
the left of center, a wide archway giving out on a portico with white pillars. The palace is evidently situated
on high ground for beyond the portico nothing can be
seen but a vista of distant hills, their summits crowned
with thick groves of palm trees. In the right wall, center, a smaller arched doorway leading to the living
quarters of the palace. The room is bare of furniture
with the exception of one huge chair made of uncut
wood which stands at center, its back to rear. This is
very apparently the Emperor's throne. It is painted a
dazzling, eye-smiting scarlet. There is a brilliant
orange cushion on the seat and another smaller one is
placed on the floor to serve as a footstool. Strips of
matting, dyed scarlet, lead from the foot of the throne
to the two entrances.*

*It is late afternoon but the sunlight still blazes yel-
lowly beyond the portico and there is an oppressive
burden of exhausting heat in the air.*

*As the curtain rises, a native negro woman sneaks
in cautiously from the entrance on the right. She is*

*very old, dressed in cheap calico, bare-footed, a red
bandana handkerchief covering all but a few stray
wisps of white hair. A bundle bound in colored cloth is
carried over her shoulder on the end of a stick. She
hesitates beside the doorway, peering back as if in
extreme dread of being discovered. Then she begins to
glide noiselessly, a step at a time, toward the doorway
in the rear. At this moment,* SMITHERS *appears beneath
the portico.*

SMITHERS *is a tall, stoop-shouldered man about
forty. His bald head, perched on a long neck with an
enormous Adam's apple, looks like an egg. The tropics
have tanned his naturally pasty face with its small,
sharp features to a sickly yellow, and native rum has
painted his pointed nose to a startling red. His little,
washy-blue eyes are red-rimmed and dart about him
like a ferret's. His expression is one of unscrupulous
meanness, cowardly and dangerous. He is dressed in
a worn riding suit of dirty white drill, puttees, spurs,
and wears a white cork helmet. A cartridge belt with
an automatic revolver is around his waist. He carries
a riding whip in his hand. He sees the woman and
stops to watch her suspiciously. Then, making up his
mind, he steps quickly on tiptoe into the room. The
woman, looking back over her shoulder continually,
does not see him until it is too late. When she does*
SMITHERS *springs forward and grabs her firmly by the
shoulder. She struggles to get away, fiercely but
silently.*

SMITHERS: (*tightening his grasp—roughly*) Easy! None
   o' that, me birdie. You can't wiggle out, now I
   got me 'ooks on yer.
WOMAN: (*seeing the uselessness of struggling, gives way
   to frantic terror, and sinks to the ground, embracing
   his knees supplicatingly*) No tell him! No tell him,
   Mister!
SMITHERS: (*with great curiosity*) Tell 'im? (*Then scornfully*)
   Oh, you mean 'is bloomin' Majesty. What's the
   gaime, any'ow? What are you sneakin' away
   for? Been stealin' a bit, I s'pose. (*He taps her
   bundle with his riding whip significantly*).

5

10

WOMAN: (*shaking her head vehemently*) No, me no steal.

15 SMITHERS: Bloody liar! But tell me what's up. There's somethin funny goin' on. I smelled it in the air first thing I got up this mornin'. You blacks are up to some devilment. This palace of 'is is like 20 a bleedin' tomb. Where's all the 'ands? (*The WOMAN keeps sullenly silent. SMITHERS raises his whip threateningly*) Ow, yei won't, won't yer? I'll show yer what's what.

WOMAN: (*coweringly*) I tell, Mister. You no hit. They go—all go. (*She makes a sweeping gesture toward 25 the hills in the distance*).

SMITHERS: Run away—to the 'ills?

WOMAN: Yes, Mister. Him Emperor—Great Father (*She touches her forehead to the floor with a quick mechanical jerk*) Him sleep after eat. Then they 30 go—all go. Me old woman. Me left only. Now me go too.

SMITHERS: (*his astonishment giving way to an immense, mean satisfaction*) Ow! So that's the ticket! Well, I know bloody well wot's in the air—when 35 they runs orf to the 'ills. The tom-tom 'll be thumping out there bloomin' soon. (*With extreme vindictiveness*) And I'm bloody glad of it, for one! Serve 'im right! Puttin' on airs, the stinkin' nigger! 'Is Majesty! Gawd blimey! I 40 only 'opes I'm there when they takes 'im out to shoot 'im. (*Suddenly*) 'E's still 'ere all right, ain't 'e?

WOMAN: Him sleep.

SMITHERS: 'E's bound to find out soon as 'e wakes up. 45 'E's cunnin enough to know when 'is time's come. (*He goes to the doorway on right and whistles shrilly with his fingers in his mouth. The old woman springs to her feet and runs out of the doorway, rear. SMITHERS goes after her, reaching for his 50 revolver*) Stop or I'll shoot! (*Then stopping—indifferently*) Pop orf then, if yer like, yer black cow. (*He stands in the doorway, looking after her*).

[JONES *enters from the right. He is a tall, powerfully-built, full-blooded negro of middle age. His features are typically negroid, yet there is something decidedly distinctive about his face—an underlying strength of will, a hardy, self-reliant confidence in himself that inspires respect. His eyes are alive with a keen, cunning intelligence. In manner he is shrewd, suspicious, evasive. He wears a light blue uniform coat, sprayed with brass buttons, heavy gold chevrons on his shoulders, gold braid on the collar, cuffs, etc. His pants are bright red with a light blue stripe down the side. Patent leather laced boots with brass spurs, and a belt with a long-barreled, pearl-handled revolver in a holster complete his make up. Yet there is something not altogether ridiculous about his grandeur. He has a way of carrying it off*].

JONES: (*not seeing anyone—greatly irritated and blinking sleepily—shouts*) Who dare whistle dat way in my palace? Who dare wake up de Emperor? 55 I'll git de hide frayled off some o' you niggers sho'!

SMITHERS: (*showing himself—in a manner half-afraid and half-defiant*) It was me whistled to yer. (*As JONES frowns angrily*) I got news for yer. 60

JONES: (*putting on his suavest manner, which fails to cover up his contempt for the white man*) Oh, it's you, Mister Smithers. (*He sits down on his throne with easy dignity*) What news you got to tell me? 65

SMITHERS: (*coming close to enjoy his discomfiture*) Don't yer notice nothin' funny today?

JONES: (*coldly*) Funny? No. I ain't perceived nothin' of de kind!

SMITHERS: Then yer ain't so foxy as I thought yer 70 was. Where's all your court? (*sarcastically*) the Generals and the Cabinet Ministers and all?

JONES: (*imperturbably*) Where dey mostly runs to minute I closes my eyes—drinkin' rum and talkin' big down in de town. (*Sarcastically*) 75 How come you don't know dat? Ain't you sousin' with 'em most every day?

SMITHERS: (*stung but pretending indifference—with a wink*) That's part of the day's work. I got ter—ain't I—in my business? 80

JONES: (*contemptuously*) Yo' business!

SMITHERS: (*imprudently enraged*) Gawd blimey, you was glad enough for me ter take yer in on it when you landed here first. You didn' 'ave no 'igh and mighty airs in them days! 85

JONES: (*his hand going to his revolver like a flash—menacingly*) Talk polite, white man! Talk polite, you heah me! I'm boss heah now, is you fergettin'? (*The Cockney seems about to challenge this last statement with the facts but something in the 90 other's eyes holds and cows him*).

SMITHERS: (*in a cowardly whine*) No 'arm meant, old top.

JONES: (*condescendingly*) I accepts yo' apology. (*Lets his hand fall from his revolver*) No use'n you 95 rakin' up ole times. What I was den is one thing. What I is now 's another. You didn't let me in on yo' crooked work out o' no kind feelin's dat time. I done do dirty work fo' you—and most o' de brain work, too, fo' dat mat- 100 ter—and I was wu'th money to you, dat's de reason.

SMITHERS: Well, blimey, I give yer a start, didn't I?—when no one else would. I wasn't afraid to 'ire you like the rest was—'count of the story 105 about your breakin' jail back in the States.

JONES: No, you didn't have no s'cuse to look down on me fo' dat. You been in jail you'self more'n once.

110 SMITHERS: (*furiously*) It's a lie! (*Then trying to pass it off by an attempt at scorn*) Garn! Who told yer that fairy tale?

JONES: Dey's some tings I ain't got to be tole. I kin see 'em in folk's eyes. (*Then after a pause—meditatively*) Yes, you sho' give me a start. And it didn't take long from dat time to git dese fool woods' niggers right where I wanted dem. (*With pride*) From stowaway to Emperor in two years! Dat's goin' some!

120 SMITHERS: (*with curiosity*) And I bet you got yer pile o' money 'id safe some place.

JONES: (*with satisfaction*) I sho' has! And it's in a foreign bank where no pusson don't ever git it out but me no matter what come. You didn't s'pose I was holdin' down dis Emperor job for de glory in it, did you? Sho'! De fuss and glory part of it, dat's only to turn de heads o' de low-flung, bush niggers dat's here. Dey wants de big circus show for deir money. I gives it to 'em an' I gits de money. (*With a grin*) De long green, dat's me every time! (*Then rebukingly*) But you ain't got no kick agin me, Smithers. I'se paid you back all you done for me many times. Ain't I pertected you and winked at all de crooked tradin' you been doin' right out in de broad day? Sho' I has—and me makin' laws to stop it at de same time! (*He chuckles*).

SMITHERS: (*grinning*) But, meanin' no 'arm, you been grabbin' right and left yourself, ain't yer? Look at the taxes you've put on 'em! Blimey! You've squeezed 'em dry!

JONES: (*chuckling*) No, dey ain't *all* dry yet. I'se still heah, ain't I?

SMITHERS: (*smiling at his secret thought*) They're dry right now, you'll find out. (*Changing the subject abruptly*) And as for me breakin' laws, you've broke 'em all yerself just as fast as yer made 'em.

JONES: Ain't I de Emperor? De laws don't go for him. (*Judicially*) You heah what I tells you, Smithers. Dere's little stealin' like you does, and dere's big stealin' like I does. For de little stealin' dey gits you in jail soon or late. For de big stealin' dey makes you Emperor and puts you in de Hall o' Fame when you croaks. (*Reminiscently*) If dey's one thing I learns in ten years on de Pullman ca's listenin' to de white quality talk, it's dat same fact. And when I gits a chance to use it I winds up Emperor in two years.

160 SMITHERS: (*unable to repress the genuine admiration of the small fry for the large*) Yes, yer turned the bleedin' trick, all right. Blimey, I never seen a bloke 'as 'ad the bloomin' luck you 'as.

JONES: (*severely*) Luck? What you mean—luck?

165 SMITHERS: I suppose you'll say as that swank about the silver bullet ain't luck—and that was what first got the fool blacks on yer side the time of the revolution, wasn't it?

JONES: (*with a laugh*) Oh, dat silver bullet! Sho' was luck. But I makes dat luck, you heah? I loads de dice! Yessuh! When dat murderin' nigger ole Lem hired to kill me takes aim ten feet away and his gun misses fire and I shoots him dead, what you heah me say?

SMITHERS: You said yer'd got a charm so's no lead bullet'd kill yer. You was so strong only a silver bullet could kill yer, you told 'em. Blimey, wasn't that swank for yer—and plain, fat-'eaded luck?

JONES: (*proudly*) I got brains and I uses 'em quick. Dat ain't luck.

SMITHERS: Yer know they wasn't 'ardly liable to get no silver bullets. And it was luck 'e didn't 'it you that time.

JONES: (*laughing*) And dere all dem fool bush niggers was kneelin' down and bumpin' deir heads on de ground like I was a miracle out o' de Bible. Oh, Lawd, from dat time on I has dem all eatin' out of my hand. I cracks de whip and dey jumps through.

SMITHERS: (*with a sniff*) Yankee bluff done it.

JONES: Ain't a man's talkin' big what makes him big—long as he makes folks believe it? Sho', I talks large when I ain't got nothin' to back it up, but I ain't talkin' wild just de same. I knows I kin fool 'em—I *knows* it—and dat's backin' enough fo' my game. And ain't I got to learn deir lingo and teach some of dem English befo' I kin talk to 'em? Ain't dat wuk? You ain't never learned ary word er it, Smithers, in de ten years you been heah, dough you knows it's money in yo' pocket tradin' wid 'em if you does. But you'se too shiftless to take de trouble.

SMITHERS: (*flushing*) Never mind about me. What's this I've 'eard about yer really 'avin' a silver bullet moulded for yourself?

JONES: It's playin' out my bluff. I has de silver bullet moulded and I tells 'em when de time comes I kills myself wid it. I tells 'em dat's 'cause I'm de on'y man in de world big enuff to git me. No use'n deir tryin'. And dey falls down and bumps deir heads. (*He laughs*) I does dat so's I kin take a walk in peace widout no jealous nigger gunnin' at me from behind de trees.

SMITHERS: (*astonished*) Then you 'ad it made—'onest?

JONES: Sho' did. Heah she be. (*He takes out his revolver, breaks it, and takes the silver bullet out of one chamber*) Five lead an' dis silver baby at de last. Don't she shine pretty? (*He holds it in his hand, looking at it admiringly, as if strangely fascinated*).

SMITHERS: Let me see. (*Reaches out his hand for it*).

225   JONES: (*harshly*) Keep yo' hands whar dey b'long, white man. (*He replaces it in the chamber and puts the revolver back on his hip*).

SMITHERS: (*snarling*) Gawd blimey! Think I'm a bleedin' thief, you would.

230   JONES: No, 'tain't dat. I knows you'se scared to steal from me. On'y I ain't 'lowin' nary body to touch dis baby. She's my rabbit's foot.

SMITHERS: (*sneering*) A bloomin' charm, wot? (*Venomously*) Well, you'll need all the bloody charms you 'as before long, s' 'elp me!

235   JONES: (*judicially*) Oh, I'se good for six months yit 'fore dey gits sick o' my game. Den, when I sees trouble comin', I makes my get-away.

SMITHERS: Ho! You got it all planned, ain't yer?

240   JONES: I ain't no fool. I knows dis Emperor's time is sho't. Dat why I make hay when de sun shine. Was you thinkin' I'se aimin' to hold down dis job for life? No, suh! What good is gittin' money if you stays back in dis raggedy country? I wants action when I spends. And when I

245   sees dese niggers gittin' up deir nerve to tu'n me out, and I'se got all de money in sight, I resigns on de spot and beats it quick.

SMITHERS: Where to?

JONES: None o' yo' business.

250   SMITHERS: Not back to the bloody States, I'll lay my oath.

JONES: (*suspiciously*) Why don't I? (*Then with an easy laugh*) You mean 'count of dat story 'bout me breakin' from jail back dere? Dat's all talk.

255   SMITHERS: (*skeptically*) Ho, yes!

JONES: (*sharply*) You ain't 'sinuatin' I'se a liar, is you?

SMITHERS: (*hastily*) No, Gawd strike me! I was only thinkin' o' the bloody lies you told the blacks 'ere about killin' white men in the States.

260   JONES: (*angered*) How come dey're lies?

SMITHERS: You'd 'ave been in jail if you 'ad, wouldn't yer then? (*With venom*) And from what I've 'eard, it ain't 'ealthy for a black to kill a white man in the States. They burns 'em in oil, don't

265   they?

JONES: (*with cool deadliness*) You mean lynchin' 'd scare me? Well, I tells you, Smithers, maybe I does kill one white man back dere. Maybe I does. And maybe I kills another right heah

270   'fore long if he don't look out.

SMITHERS: (*trying to force a laugh*) I was on'y spoofin' yer. Can't yer take a joke? And you was just sayin' you'd never been in jail.

JONES: (*in the same tone—slightly boastful*) Maybe I

275   goes to jail dere for gettin' in an argument wid razors ovah a crap game. Maybe I gits twenty years when dat colored man die. Maybe I gits in 'nother argument wid de prison guard was overseer ovah us when we're wukin' de road.

280   Maybe he hits me wid a whip and I splits his

head wid a shovel and runs away and files de chain off my leg and gits away safe. Maybe I does all dat an' maybe I don't. It's a story I tells you so's you knows I'se de kind of man dat if you evah repeats one word of it, I ends   285   yo' stealin' on dis yearth mighty damn quick!

SMITHERS: (*terrified*) Think I'd peach on yer? Not me! Ain't I always been yer friend?

JONES: (*suddenly relaxing*) Sho' you has—and you better be.   290

SMITHERS: (*recovering his composure—and with it his malice*) And just to show yer I'm yer friend, I'll tell yer that bit o' news I was goin' to.

JONES: Go ahead! Shoot de piece. Must be bad news from de happy way you look.   295

SMITHERS: (*warningly*) Maybe it's gettin' time for you to resign—with that bloomin' silver bullet, wot? (*He finishes with a mocking grin*).

JONES: (*puzzled*) What's dat you say? Talk plain.

SMITHERS: Ain't noticed any of the guards or servants   300   about the place today, I 'aven't.

JONES: (*carelessly*) Dey're all out in de garden sleepin' under de trees. When I sleeps, dey sneaks a sleep, too, and I pretends I never suspicions it. All I got to do is to ring de bell and dey come   305   flyin', makin' a bluff dey was wukin' all de time.

SMITHERS: (*in the same mocking tone*) Ring the bell now an' you'll bloody well see what I means.

JONES: (*startled to alertness, but preserving the same care-   310   less tone*) Sho' I rings. (*He reaches below the throne and pulls out a big, common dinner bell which is painted the same vivid scarlet as the throne. He rings this vigorously—then stops to listen. Then he goes to both doors, rings again, and   315   looks out*).

SMITHERS: (*watching him with malicious satisfaction, after a pause— mockingly*) The bloody ship is sinkin' an' the bleedin' rats 'as slung their 'ooks.   320

JONES: (*in a sudden fit of anger flings the bell clattering into a corner*) Low-flung, woods' niggers! (*Then catching* SMITHERS' *eye on him, he controls himself and suddenly bursts into a low chuckling laugh*) Reckon I overplays my hand dis once! A man   325   can't take de pot on a bob-tailed flush all de time. Was I sayin' I'd sit in six months mo'? Well, I'se changed my mind den. I cashes in and resigns de job of Emperor right dis minute.   330

SMITHERS: (*with real admiration*) Blimey, but you're a cool bird, and no mistake.

JONES: No use'n fussin'. When I knows de game's up I kisses it good-by widout no long waits. Dey've all run off to de hills, ain't dey?   335

SMITHERS: Yes—every bleedin' man jack of 'em.

JONES: Den de revolution is at de post. And de

Emperor better git his feet smokin' up de trail. (*He starts for the door in rear*).

340 SMITHERS: Goin' out to look for your 'orse? Yer won't find any. They steals the 'orses first thing. Mine was gone when I went for 'im this mornin'. That's wot first give me a suspicion of wot was up.

345 JONES: (*alarmed for a second, scratches his head, then philosophically*) Well, den I hoofs it. Feet, do yo' duty! (*He pulls out a gold watch and looks at it*) Three-thuty. Sundown's at six-thuty or dere-abouts. (*Puts his watch back—with cool confi-*
350 *dence*) I got plenty o' time to make it easy.

SMITHERS: Don't be so bloomin' sure of it. They'll be after you 'ot and 'eavy. Ole Lem is at the bot-tom o' this business an' 'e 'ates you like 'ell. 'E'd rather do for you than eat 'is dinner, 'e
355 would!

JONES: (*scornfully*) Dat fool no-count nigger! Does you think I'se scared o' him? I stands him on his thick head more'n once befo' dis, and I does it again if he comes in my way—(*Fiercely*) And
360 dis time I leave him a dead nigger fo' sho'!

SMITHERS: You'll 'ave to cut through the big forest—an' these blacks 'ere can sniff and follow a trail in the dark like 'ounds. You'd 'ave to 'ustle to get through that forest in twelve hours even if
365 you knew all the bloomin' trails like a native.

JONES: (*with indignant scorn*) Look-a-heah, white man! Does you think I'se a natural bo'n fool? Give me credit fo' havin' some sense, fo' Lawd's sake! Don't you s'pose I'se looked ahead and
370 made sho' of all de chances? I'se gone out in dat big forest, pretendin' to hunt, so many times dat I knows it high an' low like a book. I could go through on dem trails wid my eyes shut. (*With great contempt*) Think dese ign'rent
375 bush niggers dat ain't got brains enuff to know deir own names even can catch Brutus Jones? Huh, I s'pects not! Not on yo' life! Why, man, de white men went after me wid blood-hounds where I come from an' I jes' laughs at
380 'em. It's a shame to fool dese black trash around heah, dey're so easy. You watch me man. I'll make dem look sick, I will. I'll 'cross de plain to de edge of de forest by time dark comes. Once in de woods in de night dey
385 got a swell chance o' findin' dis baby! Dawn tomorrow I'll be out at de oder side and on de coast whar dat French gunboat is stayin'. She picks me up, takes me to Martinique when she go dar, and dere I is safe wid a mighty big
390 bankroll in my jeans. It's easy as rollin' off a log.

SMITHERS: (*maliciously*) But s'posin' somethin' 'appens wrong an' they do nab yer?

JONES: (*decisively*) Dey don't—dat's de answer.

395 SMITHERS: But, just for argyment's sake—what'd you do?

JONES: (*frowning*) I'se got five lead bullets in dis gun good enuff fo' common bush niggers—and after dat I got de silver bullet left to cheat 'em
400 out o' gittin' me.

SMITHERS: (*jeeringly*) Ho, I was fergettin' that silver bullet. You'll bump yourself orf in style, won't yer? Blimey!

JONES: (*gloomily*) You kin bet yo' whole roll on one
405 thing, white man. Dis baby plays out his string to de end and when he quits, he quits wid a bang de way he ought. Silver bullet ain't none too good for him when he go, dat's a fac'! (*Then shaking off his nervousness—with a confi-*
410 *dent laugh*) Sho'! What is I talkin' about? Ain't come to dat yit and I never will—not wid trash niggers like dese yere. (*Boastfully*) Silver bullet bring me luck anyway. I kin outguess, outrun, outfight, an' outplay de whole lot o' dem all
415 ovah de board any time o' de day er night! You watch me! (*From the distant hills comes the faint, steady thump of a tom-tom, low and vibrat-ing. It starts at a rate exactly corresponding to nor-mal pulse beat—72 to the minute—and continues
420 at a gradually accelerating rate from this point uninterruptedly to the very end of the play*).

(JONES *starts at the sound. A strange look of appre-hension creeps into his face for a moment as he listens. Then he asks, with an attempt to regain his most
425 casual manner*) What's dat drum beatin' fo'?

SMITHERS: (*with a mean grin*) For you. That means the bleedin' ceremony 'as started. I've 'eard it before and I knows.

JONES: Cer'mony? What cer'mony?

430 SMITHERS: The blacks is 'oldin' a bloody meetin', 'avin' a war dance, getting their courage worked up b'fore they starts after you.

JONES: Let dem! Dey'll sho' need it!

SMITHERS: And they're there 'oldin' their 'eathen reli-gious service—makin' no end of devil spells
435 and charms to 'elp 'em against your silver bul-let. (*He guffaws loudly*) Blimey, but they're balmy as 'ell!

JONES: (*a tiny bit awed and shaken in spite of himself*) Huh! Takes more'n dat to scare dis chicken!
440

SMITHERS: (*scenting the other's feeling—maliciously*) Ternight when it's pitch black in the forest, they'll 'ave their pet devils and ghosts 'oundin' after you. You'll find yer bloody 'air 'll be standin' on end before termorrow
445 mornin'. (*Seriously*) It's a bleedin' queer place, that stinkin' forest, even in daylight. Yer don't know what might 'appen in there, it's that rot-ten still. Always sends the cold shivers down

450 my back minute I gets in it.

JONES: (*with a contemptuous sniff*) I ain't no chicken-liver like you is. Trees an' me, we'se friends, and dar's a full moon comin' bring me light.

455 And let dem po' niggers make all de fool spells dey'se a min' to. Does yo' s'pect I'se silly enuff to b'lieve in ghosts an' ha'nts an' all dat ole woman's talk? G'long, white man! You ain't talkin' to me. (*With a chuckle*) Doesn't you know dey's got to do wid a man was member

460 in good standin' o' de Baptist Church? Sho' I was dat when I was porter on de Pullmans, befo' I gits into my little trouble. Let dem try deir heathen tricks. De Baptist Church done pertect me and land dem all in hell. (*Then with*

465 *more confident satisfaction*) And I'se got little silver bullet o' my own, don't forget!

SMITHERS: Ho! You 'aven't give much 'eed to your Baptist Church since you been down 'ere. I've 'eard myself you 'ad turned yer coat an' was

470 takin' up with their blarsted witch-doctors, or whatever the 'ell yer calls the swine.

JONES: (*vehemently*) I pretends to! Sho' I pretends! Dat's part o' my game from de fust. If I finds out dem niggers believes dat black is white,

475 den I yells it out louder 'n deir loudest. It don't git me nothin' to do missionary work for de Baptist Church. I'se after de coin, an' I lays my Jesus on de shelf for de time bein'. (*Stops abruptly to look at his watch—alertly*) But I ain't

480 got de time to waste on no more fool talk wid you. I'se gwine away from heah dis secon'. (*He reaches in under the throne and pulls out an expensive Panama hat with a bright multi-colored band and sets it jauntily on his head*) So long, white

485 man! (*With a grin*) See you in jail sometime, maybe!

SMITHERS: Not me, you won't. Well, I wouldn't be in yer bloody boots for no bloomin' money, but 'ere's wishin' yer luck just the same.

490 JONES: (*contemptuously*) You're de frightenedest man evah I see! I tells you I'se safe's 'f I was in New York City. It takes dem niggers from now to dark to git up de nerve to start somethin'. By dat time, I'se got a head start dey never kotch

495 up wid.

SMITHERS: (*maliciously*) Give my regards to any ghosts yer meets up with.

JONES: (*grinning*) If dat ghost got money, I'll tell him never ha'nt you less'n he wants to lose it.

500 SMITHERS: (*flattered*) Garn! (*Then curiously*) Ain't yer takin' no luggage with yer?

JONES: I travels light when I wants to move fast. And I got tinned grub buried on de edge o' de forest. (*Boastfully*) Now say dat I don't look ahead

505 an' use my brains! (*With a wide, liberal gesture*) I will all dat's left in de palace to you—and you better grab all you kin sneak away wid befo' dey gits here.

SMITHERS: (*gratefully*) Righto—and thanks ter yer. (*As JONES walks toward the door in rear—*

510 *cautioningly*) Say! Look 'ere, you ain't goin' out that way, are yer?

JONES: Does you think I'd slink out de back door like a common nigger? I'se Emperor yit, ain't I? And de Emperor Jones leaves de way he

515 comes, and dat black trash don't dare stop him—not yit, leastways (*He stops for a moment in the doorway, listening to the far-off but insistent beat of the tom-tom*) Listen to dat roll-call, will you? Must be mighty big drum carry dat far.

520 (*Then with a laugh*) Well, if dey ain't no whole brass band to see me off, I sho got de drum part of it. So long, white man. (*He puts his hands in his pockets and with studied carelessness, whistling a tune, he saunters out of the doorway*

525 *and off to the left*).

SMITHERS: (*looks after him with a puzzled admiration*) 'E's got 'is bloomin' nerve with 'im, s'elp me! (*Then angrily*) Ho—the bleedin' nigger—puttin' on 'is bloody airs! I 'opes they nabs 'im an'

530 gives 'im what's what!

CURTAIN

Scene 2

The end of the plain where the Great Forest begins. The foreground is sandy, level ground dotted by a few stones and clumps of stunted bushes cowering close against the earth to escape the buffeting of the trade wind. In the rear the forest is a wall of darkness dividing the world. Only when the eye becomes accustomed to the gloom can the outlines of separate trunks of the nearest trees be made out, enormous pillars of deeper blackness. A somber monotone of wind lost in the leaves moans in the air. Yet this sound serves but to intensify the impression of the forest's relentless immobility; to form a background throwing into relief its brooding, implacable silence.

[JONES *enters from the left, walking rapidly. He stops as he nears the edge of the forest, looks around him quickly, peering into the dark as if searching for some familiar landmark. Then, apparently satisfied that he is where he ought to be, he throws himself on the ground, dog-tired*].

Well, heah I is. In de nick o' time, too! Little mo' an' it'd be blacker'n de ace of spades heah-abouts. (*He pulls a bandana handkerchief from his hip pocket and mops off his perspiring face*) 535

Sho'! Gimme air! I'se tuckered out sho' 'nuff.
Dat soft Emperor job ain't no trainin' fo' a long
hike ovah dat plain in de brilin' sun. (*Then with
a chuckle*) Cheer up, nigger, de worst is yet to
540   come. (*He lifts his head and stares at the forest.
His chuckle peters out abruptly. In a tone of awe*)
My goodness, look at dem woods, will you?
Dat no-count Smithers said dey'd be black an'
he sho' called de turn. (*Turning away from them
545   quickly and looking down at his feet, he snatches at
a chance to change the subject—solicitously*) Feet,
you is holdin' up yo' end fine an' I sutinly
hopes you ain't blisterin' none. It's time you
git a rest. (*He takes off his shoes, his eyes studious-
550   ly avoiding the forest. He feels of the soles of his feet
gingerly*) You is still in de pink—on'y a little
mite feverish. Cool yo'selfs. Remember you
done got a long journey yit befo' you. (*He sits
in a weary attitude, listening to the rhythmic beat-
555   ing of the tom-tom. He grumbles in a loud tone to
cover up a growing uneasiness*) Bush niggers!
Wonder dey wouldn't git sick o' beatin' dat
drum. Sound louder, seem like. I wonder if
dey's startin' after me? (*He scrambles to his feet,
560   looking back across the plain*) Couldn't see dem
now, nohow, if dey was hundred feet away.
(*Then shaking himself like a wet dog to get rid of
these depressing thoughts*) Sho', dey's miles an'
miles behind. What you gittin' fidgety about?
565   (*But he sits down and begins to lace up his shoes in
great haste, all the time muttering reassuringly*)
You know what? Yo' belly is empty, dat's
what's de matter wid you. Come time to eat!
Wid nothin' but wind on yo' stumach, o'
570   course you feels jiggedy. Well, we eats right
heah an' now soon's I gits dese pesky shoes
laced up. (*He finishes lacing up his shoes*) Dere!
Now le's see! (*Gets on his hands and knees and
searches the ground around him with his eyes*)
575   White stone, white stone, where is you? (*He
sees the first white stone and crawls to it—with
satisfaction*) Heah you is! I knowed dis was de
right place. Box of grub, come to me. (*He turns
over the stone and feels in under it—in a tone of
580   dismay*) Ain't heah! Gorry, is I in de right place
or isn't I? Dere's 'nother stone. Guess dat's it.
(*He scrambles to the next stone and turns it over*)
Ain't heah, neither! Grub, whar is you? Ain't
heah. Gorry, has I got to go hungry into dem
585   woods—all de night? (*While he is talking he
scrambles from one stone to another, turning them
over in frantic haste. Finally, he jumps to his feet
excitedly*) Is I lost de place? Must have! But
how dat happen when I was followin' de trail
590   across de plain in broad daylight? (*Almost
plaintively*) I'se hungry, I is! I gotta git my feed.
Whar's my strength gonna come from if I

doesn't? Gorry, I gotta find dat grub high an'
low somehow! Why it come dark so quick like   595
dat? Can't see nothin'. (*He scratches a match on
his trousers and peers about him. The rate of the
beat of the far-off tom-tom increases perceptibly as
he does so. He mutters in a bewildered voice*) How
come all dese white stones come heah when I
only remembers one? (*Suddenly, with a fright-   600
ened gasp, he flings the match on the ground and
stamps on it*) Nigger, is you gone crazy mad? Is
you lightin' matches to show dem whar you
is? Fo' Lawd's sake, use yo' haid. Gorry, I'se
got to be careful! (*He stares at the plain behind   605
him apprehensively, his hand on his revolver*) But
how come all dese white stones? And whar's
dat tin box o' grub I hid all wrapped up in oilcloth?

[*While his back is turned, the* LITTLE FORMLESS FEARS
*creep out from the deeper blackness of the forest. They
are black, shapeless, only their glittering little eyes can
be seen. If they have any describable form at all it is
that of a grubworm about the size of a creeping child.
They move noiselessly, but with deliberate, painful
effort, striving to raise themselves on end, failing and
sinking prone again.* JONES *turns about to face the forest. He stares up at the tops of the trees, seeking vainly
to discover his whereabouts by their conformation*].

Can't tell nothin' from dem trees! Gorry, nothin'   610
'round heah looks like I evah seed it befo'. I'se
done lost de place sho' 'nuff! (*With mournful
foreboding*) It's mighty queer! It's mighty queer!
(*With sudden forced defiance—in an angry tone*)
Woods, is you tryin' to put somethin' ovah on   615
me?
(*From the formless creatures on the ground in front of
him comes a tiny gale of low mocking laughter like
a rustling of leaves. They squirm upward toward
him in twisted attitudes.* JONES *looks down, leaps   620
backward with a yell of terror, yanking out his
revolver as he does so—in a quavering voice*)
What's dat? Who's dar? What is you? Git
away from me befo' I shoots you up! You
don't?—   625

[*He fires. There is a flash, a loud report, then silence
broken only by the far-off, quickened throb of the tom-
tom. The formless creatures have scurried back into
the forest.* JONES *remains fixed in his position, listening
intently. The sound of the shot, the reassuring feel of
the revolver in his hand, have somewhat restored his
shaken nerve. He addresses himself with renewed confidence*].

Dey're gone. Dat shot fix 'em. Dey was only little
animals—little wild pigs, I reckon. Dey've

maybe rooted out yo' grub an' eat it. Sho', you fool nigger, what you think dey is—ha'nts? (*Excitedly*) Gorry, you give de game away when you fire dat shot. Dem niggers heah dat fo' su'tin! Time you beat it in de woods widout no long waits. (*He starts for the forest—hesitates before the plunge—then urging himself in with manful resolution*) Git in, nigger! What you skeered at? Ain't nothin' dere but de trees! Git in! (*He plunges boldly into the forest*).

Scene 3

In the forest. The moon has just risen. Its beams, drifting through the canopy of leaves, make a barely perceptible, suffused, eerie glow. A dense low wall of underbrush and creepers is in the nearer foreground, fencing in a small triangular clearing. Beyond this is the massed blackness of the forest like an encompassing barrier. A path is dimly discerned leading down to the clearing from left, rear, and winding away from it again toward the right. As the scene opens nothing can be distinctly made out. Except for the beating of the tom-tom, which is a trifle louder and quicker than at the close of the previous scene, there is silence, broken every few seconds by a queer, clicking sound. Then gradually the figure of the negro, JEFF, *can be discerned crouching on his haunches at the rear of the triangle. He is middle-aged, thin, brown in color, is dressed in a Pullman porter's uniform and cap. He is throwing a pair of dice on the ground before him, picking them up, shaking them, casting them out with the regular, rigid, mechanical movements of an automaton. The heavy, plodding footsteps of someone approaching along the trail from the left are heard and* JONES' *voice, pitched on a slightly higher key and strained in a cheery effort to overcome its own tremors.*

De moon's rizen. Does you heah dat, nigger? You gits more light from dis out. No mo' buttin' yo' fool head agin' de trunks an' scratchin' de hide off yo' legs in de bushes. Now you sees whar yo'se gwine. So cheer up! From now on you has a snap. (*He steps just to the rear of the triangular clearing and mops off his face on his sleeve. He has lost his Panama hat. His face is scratched, his brilliant uniform shows several large rents*) What time's it gittin' to be, I wonder? I dassent light no match to find out. Phoo'. It's wa'm an' dat's a fac'! (*Wearily*) How long I been makin' tracks in dese woods? Must be hours an' hours. Seems like fo'evah! Yit can't be, when de moon's jes' riz. Dis am a long night fo' yo', yo' Majesty! (*With a mournful chuckle*) Majesty! Der ain't much majesty 'bout dis baby now. (*With attempted cheerfulness*) Never min'. It's all part o' de game. Dis night come to an end like everything else. And when you gits dar safe and has dat bankroll in yo' hands you laughs at all dis. (*He starts to whistle but checks himself abruptly*) What yo' whistlin' for, you po' dope? Want all de worl' to heah you? (*He stops talking to listen*) Heah dat ole drum! Sho' gits nearer from de sound. Dey's packin' it along wid 'em. Time fo' me to move. (*He takes a step forward, then stops—worriedly*) What's dat odder queer clickety sound I heah? Dere it is! Sound close! Sound like—sound like—Fo' God sake, sound like some nigger was shootin' crap! (*Frightenedly*) I better beat it quick when I gits dem notions. (*He walks quickly into the clear space—then stands transfixed as he sees* JEFF—*in a terrified gasp*) Who dar? Who dat? Is dat you, Jeff? (*Starting toward the other, forgetful for a moment of his surroundings and really believing it is a living man that he sees—in a tone of happy relief*) Jeff! I'se sho' mighty glad to see you! Dey tol' me you done died from dat razor cut I gives you. (*Stopping suddenly, bewilderedly*) But how you come to be heah, nigger? (*He stares fascinatedly at the other who continues his mechanical play with the dice.* JONES' *eyes begin to roll wildly. He stutters*) Ain't you gwine—look up—can't you speak to me? Is you—is you—a ha'nt? (*He jerks out his revolver in a frenzy of terrified rage*) Nigger, I kills you dead once. Has I got to kill you ag'in? You take it den. (*He fires. When the smoke clears away* JEFF *has disappeared.* JONES *stands trembling—then with a certain reassurance*) He's gone, anyway. Ha'nt or not ha'nt, dat shot fix him. (*The beat of the far-off tom-tom is perceptibly louder and more rapid.* JONES *becomes conscious of it—with a start, looking back over his shoulder*) Dey's gittin' near! Dey's comin' fast! And heah I is shootin' shots to let 'em know jes' whar I is! Oh, Gorry, I'se got to run. (*Forgetting the path he plunges wildly into the underbrush in the rear and disappears in the shadow*).

Scene 4

In the forest. A wide dirt road runs diagonally from right, front, to left, rear. Rising sheer on both sides the forest walls it in. The moon is now up. Under its light the road glimmers ghastly and unreal. It is as if the forest had stood aside momentarily to let the road pass through and accomplish its veiled purpose. This done, the forest will fold in upon itself again and the road will be no more. JONES *stumbles in from the forest on the right. His uniform is ragged and torn. He looks about him with numbed surprise when he sees the road, his eyes blinking in the bright moonlight. He flops down exhaustedly and pants heavily for a while. Then with sudden anger.*

700   I'm meltin' wid heat! Runnin' an' runnin' an' runnin'! Damn dis heah coat! Like a straitjacket! (*He tears off his coat and flings it away from him, revealing himself stripped to the waist*) Dere! Dat's better! Now I kin breathe! (*Looking down at his feet, the spurs catch his eye*) And to hell wid dese
705   high-fangled spurs. Dey're what's been a-trip-pin' me up an' breakin' my neck. (*He unstraps them and flings them away disgustedly*) Dere! I gits rid o' dem frippety Emperor trappin's an' I travels lighter. Lawd! I'se tired! (*After a pause,
710   listening to the insistent beat of the tom-tom in the distance*) I must 'a' put some distance between myself an' dem—runnin' like dat—and yit— dat damn drum sounds jes' de same—nearer, even. Well, I guess I a'most holds my lead any-
715   how. Dey won't never catch up. (*With a sigh*) If on'y my fool legs stands up. Oh, I'se sorry I evah went in for dis. Dat Emperor job is sho' hard to shake. (*He looks around him suspiciously*) How'd dis road evah git heah? Good level
720   road, too. I never remembers seein' it befo' (*Shaking his head apprehensively*) Dese woods is sho' full o' de queerest things at night. (*With a sudden terror*) Lawd God, don't let me see no more o' dem ha'nts! Dey gits my goat! (*Then
725   trying to talk himself into confidence*) Ha'nts! You fool nigger, dey ain't no such things! Don't de Baptist parson tell you dat many time? Is you civilized, or is you like dese ign'rent black nig-gers heah? Sho'! Dat was all in yo' own head.
730   Wasn't nothin' dere. Wasn't no Jeff! Know what? You jus' get seein' dem things 'cause yo' belly's empty and you's sick wid hunger inside. Hunger 'fects yo' head and yo' eyes. Any fool know dat. (*Then pleading fervently*)
735   But bless God, I don't come across no more o' dem, whatever dey is! (*Then cautiously*) Rest! Don't talk! Rest! You needs it. Den you gits on yo' way again. (*Looking at the moon*) Night's half gone a'most. You hits de coast in de
740   mawnin'! Den you's all safe.

[From the right forward a small gang of negroes enter. They are dressed in striped convict suits, their heads are shaven, one leg drags limpingly, shackled to a heavy ball and chain. Some carry picks, the others shovels. They are followed by a white man dressed in the uniform of a prison guard. A Winchester rifle is slung across his shoulders and he carries a heavy whip. At a signal from the GUARD *they stop on the road opposite where* JONES *is sitting.* JONES, *who has*

been staring up at the sky, unmindful of their noiseless approach, suddenly looks down and sees them. His eyes pop out, he tries to get to his feet and fly, but sinks back, too numbed by fright to move. His voice catches in a choking prayer].

Lawd Jesus!

[The PRISON GUARD *cracks his whip—noiselessly—and at that signal all the convicts start to work on the road. They swing their picks, they shovel, but not a sound comes from their labor. Their movements, like those of* JEFF *in the preceding scene, are those of automatons,—rigid, slow, and mechanical. The* PRISON GUARD *points sternly at* JONES *with his whip, motions him to take his place among the other shovelers.* JONES *gets to his feet in a hypnotized stupor. He mumbles subserviently].*

Yes, suh! Yes, suh! I'se comin'.

[As he shuffles, dragging one foot, over to his place, he curses under his breath with rage and hatred].

God damn yo' soul, I gits even wid you yit, some-time.

[As if there were a shovel in his hands he goes through weary, mechanical gestures of digging up dirt, and throwing it to the roadside. Suddenly the GUARD *approaches him angrily, threateningly. He raises his whip and lashes* JONES *viciously across the shoulders with it.* JONES *winces with pain and cowers abjectly. The* GUARD *turns his back on him and walks away contemptuously. Instantly* JONES *straightens up. With arms upraised as if his shovel were a club in his hands he springs murderously at the unsuspecting* GUARD. *In the act of crashing down his shovel on the white man's skull,* JONES *suddenly becomes aware that his hands are empty. He cries despairingly].*

745   Whar's my shovel? Gimme my shovel 'til I splits his damn head! (*Appealing to his fellow convicts*) Gimme a shovel, one o' you, fo' God's sake!

[They stand fixed in motionless attitudes, their eyes on the ground. The GUARD *seems to wait expectantly; his back turned to the attacker.* JONES *bellows with baf-fled, terrified rage, tugging frantically at his revolver].*

I kills you, you white debil, if it's de last thing I evah does! Ghost or debil, I kill you agin!

[He frees the revolver and fires point blank at the GUARD'S *back. Instantly the walls of the forest close in from both sides, the road and the figures of the con-vict gang are blotted out in an enshrouding darkness. The only sounds are a crashing in the underbrush as* JONES *leaps away in mad flight and the throbbing of*

the tom-tom still far distant, but increased in volume of sound and rapidity of beat].

Scene 5

A large circular clearing, enclosed by the serried ranks of gigantic trunks of tall trees whose tops are lost to view. In the center is a big dead stump worn by time into a curious resemblance to an auction block. The moon floods the clearing with a clear light. JONES *forces his way in through the forest on the left. He looks wildly about the clearing with hunted, fearful glances. His pants are in tatters, his shoes cut and misshapen, flapping about his feet. He slinks cautiously to the stump in the center and sits down in a tense position, ready for instant flight. Then he holds his head in his hands and rocks back and forth, moaning to himself miserably.*

750   Oh, Lawd, Lawd! Oh, Lawd, Lawd! (*Suddenly he throws himself on his knees and raises his clasped hands to the sky—in a voice of agonized pleading*) Lawd Jesus, heah my prayer! I'se a po' sinner, a po' sinner! I knows I done wrong, I knows it!
755   When I cotches Jeff cheatin' wid loaded dice my anger overcomes me and I kills him dead! Lawd, I done wrong! When dat guard hits me wid de whip, my anger overcomes me, and I kills him dead. Lawd, I done wrong! And
760   down heah whar dese fool bush niggers raises me up to the seat o' de mighty, I steals all I could grab. Lawd, I done wrong! I knows it! I'se sorry! Forgive me, Lawd! Forgive dis po' sinner! (*Then beseeching terrifiedly*) And keep
765   dem away, Lawd! Keep dem away from me! And stop dat drum soundin' in my ears! Dat begin to sound ha'nted, too. (*He gets to his feet, evidently slightly reassured by his prayer—with attempted confidence*) De Lawd'll preserve me
770   from dem ha'nts after dis. (*Sits down on the stump again*) I ain't skeered o' real men. Let dem come. But dem odders—(*He shudders—then looks down at his feet, working his toes inside the shoes—with a groan*) Oh, my po' feet! Dem
775   shoes ain't no use no more 'ceptin' to hurt. I'se better off widout dem. (*He unlaces them and pulls them off—holds the wrecks of the shoes in his hands and regards them mournfully*) You was real, A-one patin' leather, too. Look at you
780   now. Emperor, you'se gittin' mighty low!

[He sighs dejectedly and remains with bowed shoulders, staring down at the shoes in his hands as if reluctant to throw them away. While his attention is thus occupied, a crowd of figures silently enter the clearing from all sides. All are dressed in Southern costumes of the period of the fifties of the last century. There are middle-aged men who are evidently well-to-do planters. There is one spruce, authoritative individual—the AUCTIONEER. *There is a crowd of curious spectators, chiefly young belles and dandies who have come to the slave-market for diversion. All exchange courtly greetings in dumb show and chat silently together. There is something stiff, rigid, unreal, marionettish about their movements. They group themselves about the stump. Finally a batch of slaves is led in from the left by an attendant—three men of different ages, two women, one with a baby in her arms, nursing. They are placed to the left of the stump, beside* JONES.*

The white planters look them over appraisingly as if they were cattle, and exchange judgments on each. The dandies point with their fingers and make witty remarks. The belles titter bewitchingly. All this in silence save for the ominous throb of the tom-tom. The AUCTIONEER *holds up his hand, taking his place at the stump. The groups strain forward attentively. He touches* JONES *on the shoulder peremptorily, motioning for him to stand on the stump—the auction block.*

JONES *looks up, sees the figures on all sides, looks wildly for some opening to escape, sees none, screams and leaps madly to the top of the stump to get as far away from them as possible. He stands there, cowering, paralyzed with horror. The* AUCTIONEER *begins his silent spiel. He points to* JONES, *appeals to the planters to see for themselves. Here is a good field hand, sound in wind and limb as they can see. Very strong still in spite of his being middle-aged. Look at that back. Look at those shoulders. Look at the muscles in his arms and his sturdy legs. Capable of any amount of hard labor. Moreover, of a good disposition, intelligent and tractable. Will any gentleman start the bidding? The* PLANTERS *raise their fingers, make their bids. They are apparently all eager to possess* JONES. *The bidding is lively, the crowd interested. While this had been going on,* JONES *has been seized by the courage of desperation. He dares to look down and around him. Over his face abject terror gives way to mystification, to gradual realization—stutteringly].*

What you all doin', white folks? What's all dis? What you all lookin' at me fo'? What you doin' wid me, anyhow? (*Suddenly convulsed with raging hatred and fear*) Is dis a auction? Is you sellin' me like dey uster befo' de war? (*Jerking out*   785 *his revolver just as the* AUCTIONEER *knocks him down to one of the planters—glaring from him to the purchaser*) And *you* sells me? And *you* buys

790 me? I shows you I'se a free nigger, damn yo'
souls! (*He fires at the* AUCTIONEER *and at the*
PLANTER *with such rapidity that the two shots
are almost simultaneous. As if this were a signal
the walls of the forest fold in. Only blackness
795 remains and silence broken by* JONES *as he rushes
off, crying with fear—and by the quickened, ever
louder beat of the tom-tom*)

Scene 6

*A cleared space in the forest. The limbs of the trees
meet over it forming a low ceiling about five feet from
the ground. The interlocked ropes of creepers reaching
upward to entwine the tree trunks give an arched
appearance to the sides. The space thus enclosed is
like the dark, noisome hold of some ancient vessel.
The moonlight is almost completely shut out and only
a vague wan light filters through. There is the noise of
someone approaching from the left, stumbling and
crawling through the undergrowth.* JONES' *voice is
heard between chattering moans.*

Oh, Lawd, what I gwine do now? Ain't got no
bullet left on'y de silver one. If mo' o' dem
ha'nts come after me, how I gwine skeer dem
800 away? Oh, Lawd, on'y de silver one left—an' I
gotta save dat fo' luck. If I shoots dat one I'm a
goner sho'! Lawd, it's black heah! Whar's de
moon? Oh, Lawd, don't dis night evah come to
an end! (*By the sounds, he is feeling his way cau-
805 tiously forward*) Dere! Dis feels like a clear
space. I gotta lie down an' rest. I don't care if
dem niggers does cotch me. I gotta rest.

[*He is well forward now where his figure can be dimly
made out. His pants have been so torn away that
what is left of them is no better than a breech cloth.
He flings himself full length, face downward on the
ground, panting with exhaustion. Gradually it seems
to grow lighter in the enclosed space and two rows of
seated figures can be seen behind* JONES. *They are sitting in crumpled, despairing attitudes, hunched, facing one another with their backs touching the forest
walls as if they were shackled to them. All are negroes,
naked save for loin cloths. At first they are silent and
motionless. Then they begin to sway slowly forward
toward each and back again in unison, as if they were
laxly letting themselves follow the long roll of a ship at
sea. At the same time, a low, melancholy murmur rises
among them, increasing gradually by ryhthmic
degrees which seem to be directed and controlled by
the throb of the tom-tom in the distance, to a long,
tremulous wail of despair that reaches a certain pitch,
unbearably acute, then falls by slow gradations of
tone into silence and is taken up again.* JONES *starts,*

*looks up, sees the figures, and throws himself down
again to shut out the sight. A shudder of terror shakes
his whole body as the wail rises up about him again.
But the next time, his voice, as if under some uncanny
compulsion, starts with the others. As their chorus lifts
he rises to a sitting posture similar to the others,
swaying back and forth. His voice reaches the highest
pitch of sorrow, of desolation. The light fades out, the
other voices cease, and only darkness is left.* JONES *can
be heard scrambling to his feet and running off, his
voice sinking down the scale and receding as he moves
farther and farther away in the forest. The tom-tom
beats louder, quicker, with a more insistent, triumphant pulsation*].

Scene 7

*The foot of a gigantic tree by the edge of a great river.
A rough structure of boulders, like an altar, is by the
tree. The raised river bank is in the nearer background. Beyond this the surface of the river spreads
out, brilliant and unruffled in the moonlight, blotted
out and merged into a veil of bluish mist in the distance.* JONES' *voice is heard from the left rising and
falling in the long, despairing wail of the chained
slaves, to the rhythmic beat of the tom-tom. As his
voice sinks into silence, he enters the open space. The
expression of his face is fixed and stony, his eyes have
an obsessed glare, he moves with a strange deliberation like a sleep-walker or one in a trance. He looks
around at the tree, the rough stone altar, the moonlit
surface of the river beyond, and passes his hand over
his head with a vague gesture of puzzled bewilderment. Then, as if in obedience to some obscure
impulse, he sinks into a kneeling, devotional posture
before the altar. Then he seems to come to himself
partly, to have an uncertain realization of what he is
doing, for he straightens up and stares about him hor-
rifiedly—in an incoherent mumble.*

What—what is I doin'? What is—dis place?
Seems like I know dat tree—an' dem stones—
an' de river. I remember—seems like I been   810
heah befo'. (*Tremblingly*) Oh, Gorry, I'se
skeered in dis place! I'se skeered. Oh, Lawd,
pertect dis sinner!

[*Crawling away from the altar, he cowers close to the
ground, his face hidden, his shoulders heaving with
sobs of hysterical fright. From behind the trunk of the
tree, as if he had sprung out of it, the figure of the*
CONGO WITCH-DOCTOR *appears. He is wizened and old,
naked except for the fur of some small animal tied
about his waist, its bushy tail hanging down in front.
His body is stained all over a bright red. Antelope horns*

are on each side of his head, branching upward. In one hand he carries a bone rattle, in the other a charm stick with a bunch of white cockatoo feathers tied to the end. A great number of glass beads and bone ornaments are about his neck, ears, wrists, and ankles. He struts noiselessly with a queer prancing step to a position in the clear ground between JONES *and the altar. Then with a preliminary, summoning stamp of his foot on the earth, he begins to dance and to chant. As if in response to his summons the beating of the tom-tom grows to a fierce, exultant boom whose throbs seem to fill the air with vibrating rhythm.* JONES *looks up, starts to spring to his feet, reaches a half-kneeling, half-squatting position and remains rigidly fixed there, paralyzed with awed fascination by this new apparition. The* WITCH-DOCTOR *sways, stamping with his foot, his bone rattle clicking the time. His voice rises and falls in a weird, monotonous croon, without articulate word divisions. Gradually his dance becomes clearly one of a narrative in pantomime, his croon is an incantation, a charm to allay the fierceness of some implacable deity demanding sacrifice. He flees, he is pursued by devils, he hides, he flees again. Ever wilder and wilder becomes his flight, nearer and nearer draws the pursuing evil, more and more the spirit of terror gains possession of him. His croon, rising to intensity, is punctuated by shrill cries.* JONES *has become completely hypnotized. His voice joins in the incantation, in the cries, he beats time with his hands and sways his body to and fro from the waist. The whole spirit and meaning of the dance has entered into him, has become his spirit. Finally the theme of the pantomime halts on a howl of despair, and is taken up again in a note of savage hope. There is a salvation. The forces of evil demand sacrifice. They must be appeased. The* WITCH-DOCTOR *points with his wand to the sacred tree, to the river beyond, to the altar, and finally to* JONES *with a ferocious command.* JONES *seems to sense the meaning of this. It is he who must offer himself for sacrifice. He beats his forehead abjectly to the ground, moaning hysterically].*

Mercy, Oh, Lawd! Mercy! Mercy on dis po' sinner.

[The WITCH-DOCTOR *springs to the river bank. He stretches out his arms and calls to some God within its depths. Then he starts backward slowly, his arms remaining out. A huge head of a crocodile appears over the bank and its eyes, glittering greenly, fasten upon* JONES. *He stares into them fascinatedly. The* WITCH-DOCTOR *prances up to him, touches him with his wand, motions with hideous command toward the waiting monster.* JONES *squirms on his belly nearer and nearer, moaning continually].*

815 Mercy, Lawd! Mercy!

[The crocodile heaves more of his enormous hulk onto

the land. JONES *squirms toward him. The* WITCH-DOCTOR's *voice shrills out in furious exultation, the tom-tom beats madly.* JONES *cries out in a fierce, exhausted spasm of anguished pleading].*

Lawd, save me! Lawd Jesus, heah my prayer!

[Immediately, in answer to his prayer, comes the thought of the one bullet left him. He snatches at his hip, shouting defiantly].

De silver bullet! You don't git me yit!

[He fires at the green eyes in front of him. The head of the crocodile sinks back behind the river bank, the WITCH-DOCTOR *springs behind the sacred tree and disappears.* JONES *lies with his face to the ground, his arms outstretched, whimpering with fear as the throb of the tom-tom fills the silence about him with a somber pulsation, a baffled but revengeful power].*

Scene 8

Dawn. Same as Scene 2, the dividing line of forest and plain. The nearest tree trunks are dimly revealed but the forest behind them is still a mass of glooming shadow. The tom-tom seems on the very spot, so loud and continuously vibrating are its beats. LEM *enters from the left, followed by a small squad of his soldiers, and by the Cockney trader,* SMITHERS. LEM *is a heavyset, ape-faced old savage of the extreme African type, dressed only in a loin cloth. A revolver and cartridge belt are about his waist. His soldiers are in different degrees of rag-concealed nakedness. All wear broad palmleaf hats. Each one carries a rifle.* SMITHERS *is the same as in Scene One. One of the soldiers, evidently a tracker, is peering about keenly on the ground. He points to the spot where* JONES *entered the forest.* LEM *and* SMITHERS *come to look.*

SMITHERS: *(after a glance, turns away in disgust)* That's where 'e went in right enough. Much good it'll do yer. 'E's miles orf by this an' safe to the 820 Coast, damn 's 'ide! I tole yer yer'd lose im, didn't I?—wastin' the 'ole bloomin' night beatin' yer bloody drum and castin' yer silly spells! Gawd blimey, wot a pack!

LEM: *(gutturally)* We cotch him. *(He makes a motion to* 825 *his soldiers who squat down on their haunches in a semi-circle).*

SMITHERS: *(exasperatedly)* Well, ain't yer goin' in an' 'unt 'im in the woods? What the 'ell's the good of waitin'? 830

LEM: *(imperturbably—squatting down himself)* We cotch him.

SMITHERS: *(turning away from him contemptuously)* Aw!

835   Garn! 'E's a better man than the lot o' you put
together. I 'ates the sight o' 'im but I'll say that
for 'im. (*A sound comes from the forest. The soldiers jump to their feet, cocking their rifles alertly.*
LEM *remains sitting with an imperturbable expression, but listening intently. He makes a quick sig-*
840   *nal with his hand. His followers creep quickly into
the forest, scattering so that each enters at a different spot*).

SMITHERS: You ain't thinkin' that would be 'im, I
'ope?

845 LEM: (*calmly*) We cotch him.

SMITHERS: Blarsted fat 'eads! (*Then after a second's
thought—wonderingly*) Still an' all, it might
'appen. If 'e lost 'is bloody way in these
stinkin' woods 'e'd likely turn in a circle with-
850   out 'is knowin' it.

LEM: (*peremptorily*) Sssh! (*The reports of several rifles
sound from the forest, followed a second later by
savage, exultant yells. The beating of the tom-tom
abruptly ceases.* LEM *looks up at the white man*
855   *with a grin of satisfaction*) We cotch him. Him
dead.

SMITHERS: (*with a snarl*) 'Ow d'yer know it's 'im an'
'ow d'yer know 'e's dead?

LEM: My mens dey got um silver bullets. Lead bullet
860   no kill him. He got um strong charm. I cook
um money, make um silver bullet, make um
strong charm, too.

SMITHERS: (*astonished*) So that's wot you was up to all
night, wot? You was scared to put after 'im till
865   you'd moulded silver bullets, eh?

LEM: (*simply stating a fact*) Yes. Him got strong charm.
Lead no good.

SMITHERS: (*slapping his thigh and guffawing*) Haw-haw!
If yer don't beat all 'ell! (*Then recovering himself—scornfully*) I'll bet yer it ain't 'im they shot
870   at all, yer bleedin' looney!

LEM: (*calmly*) Dey come bring him now. (*The soldiers
come out of the forest, carrying* JONES' *limp body.
He is dead. They carry him to* LEM, *who examines
his body with great satisfaction.* SMITHERS *leans*
875   *over his shoulder—in a tone of frightened awe*)
Well, they did for yer right enough, Jonesey,
me lad! Dead as a 'erring! (*Mockingly*) Where's
yer 'igh an' mighty airs now, yer bloomin'
880   Majesty? (*Then with a grin*) Silver bullets!
Gawd blimey, but yer died in the 'eighth o'
style, any'ow!

CURTAIN

LUIGI PIRANDELLO (1867–1936)

Luigi Pirandello's life, which began with great promise, developed amid turmoil and suffering, which found expression in his plays. The son of the wealthy owner of a sulfur mine, Pirandello grew up on a country estate in southern Sicily. His father pressured him to take over the family businesses, but he soon quit. His real love was literature. He had been writing poetry since he was sixteen, and at eighteen he attended the University of Rome. He earned his doctorate in philology from the University of Bonn in 1891 and settled in Rome, where he was well on his way to becoming a successful writer of poetry and fiction. In 1894 Pirandello married the daughter of his father's business partner in an arrangement made for economic reasons. Seven years later, in 1904, the entire enterprise foundered when both his father's and his father-in-law's sulfur mines were destroyed by floods. This disaster for the family fortunes forced Pirandello to take a job teaching at a girls' school, and his wife began to exhibit signs of emotional instability, finally lapsing into insanity. She was convinced that Pirandello was unfaithful to her, and their married life became a nightmare filled with angry recriminations and violent, jealous rages. Pirandello cared for her for fifteen years, but in 1919 friends and family convinced him to commit her to a mental institution.

Pirandello continued to write. He published several volumes of short stories, novels, collections of poetry, and three short plays. A recurring theme in all his work, in part traceable to his troubled domestic situation, was the uncertainty of identity and a relativistic view of existence. The illusory nature of truth and identity are dramatized most clearly in his early play *Right You Are, If You Think You Are* (1917), which treats the frustrated attempts of a community to discover "the truth" about the identities of a husband and wife and his mother-in-law who have moved into town. The husband and mother-in-law tell completely plausible yet contradictory stories about their situation, and each accuses the other of insanity. At the end of the play, after all their stories, the wife steps forward to declare that "I am the one that each of you thinks I am." It would be fair to say that the truth in Pirandello's works is never one-dimensional.

Pirandello wrote over forty plays, the most important of them elaborating on the complex implications of his earlier relativistic vision, and using metatheatrical metaphors in a completely self-conscious theater, most notably in *Six Characters in Search of an Author* (1921, revised 1925), *Henri IV* (1922), *Each in His Own Way* (1924), and *Tonight We Improvise* (1930). The struggles of his characters to discover and maintain their identities lead them (and the audience) to an awareness that the self itself is a fictional construct. Behavior is essentially acting, and there is no such thing as a real or unchanging self. Some of Pirandello's characters regret the lost sense of a stable and unchanging self—the self portrayed in realistic drama—but for other characters it becomes clear that an unchanging self is a prison. The protagonist of *Henri IV*, for example, discovers exactly that at the end of his play, as does the protagonist of *When One Is Somebody* (1933), who is transformed from a human being into a statue by the adulation of his admirers.

In 1924 Pirandello became director of his own company, the Art Theater of Rome, and the company's tours of Europe and the Americas brought his innovative plays to the attention of a whole generation of playwrights and audiences. Besides his many plays, Pirandello wrote hundreds of stories and critical and scholarly articles during his career. In 1934 he was awarded the Nobel Prize in recognition of his achievements in the modern theater.

Six Characters in Search of an Author

Six Characters in Search of an Author, Pirandello's best-known play, is part of a trilogy that also includes *Each in His Own Way* and *Tonight We Improvise*. All three are concerned with the shifting nature of human identity and role-playing in life and art. *Six Characters in Search of an Author* uses the theater as a metaphor of human existence and of the theater itself, exploring the conflict between one's identity and the multiple roles imposed by society. The six characters of the title begin and end the play probing the difficulty of apprehending what is real.

The six characters—a father, a mother, a stepdaughter, a son, a boy, and a child—show up at the rehearsal for one of Pirandello's other plays, titled *Mixing It Up*, claiming that their author abandoned them as unfinished creations. They are searching for a playwright to complete their stories and for actors to portray them. The conventions of the theater blur with the demands of the world, and Pirandello uses the situation to explore the relationship between audience and actors onstage, between characters and actors and authors, between illusion and reality, and between art and life.

The characters understandably see themselves as experts on their own stories and are contemptuous of the actors' attempts to impersonate them. Because they inhabit a fictive world, the characters take an opposite view of reality from the actors, and an opposing view of the illusion of theater. The characters seem determined to tell the truth, and they rebel against the confining identities imposed on them by their parts in the unfinished melodrama about incest. Their stories, they contend, go beyond the identities they exhibit in the script. The actors, on the other hand, have little concern for the characters' worries about truth. They busy themselves with techniques of presentation and with petty jealousies. The conflict between modes of perception, one representational and the other presentational, deliberately disorients the audience's ordinary understanding of the difference between illusion and reality. The rich and enigmatic meaning of *Six Characters* derives from such continuing confrontations and disagreements, which force attention to the now-vexing problems of representation and presentation.

Six Characters in Search of an Author

Luigi Pirandello

Translated by Edward Storer

CHARACTERS OF THE COMEDY IN THE MAKING:

The Father
The Mother
The Step-Daughter
The Son

The Boy ⎫
The Child ⎭ (*do not speak.*)
Madame Pace

ACTORS OF THE COMPANY

The Manager
Leading Lady
Leading Man
Second Lady
Lead
L'Ingénue
Juvenile Lead

Other Actors and Actresses
Property Man
Prompter
Machinist
Manager's Secretary
Door-Keeper
Scene-Shifters

DAYTIME. THE STAGE OF A THEATRE.

ACT I

N.B. *The Comedy is without acts or scenes. The performance is interrupted once, without the curtain being lowered, when the manager and the chief characters withdraw to arrange the scenario. A second interruption of the action takes place when, by mistake, the stage hands let the curtain down.*

The spectators will find the curtain raised and the stage as it usually is during the day time. It will be half dark, and empty, so that from the beginning the public may have the impression of an impromptu performance.

Prompter's box and a small table and chair for the manager.

Two other small tables and several chairs scattered about as during rehearsals.

The actors and actresses of the company enter from the back of the stage: first one, then another, then two together: nine or ten in all. They are about to rehearse a Pirandello play: Mixing It Up. Some of the company move off towards their dressing rooms. The Prompter *who has the "book" under his arm, is waiting for the manager in order to begin the rehearsal.*

The actors and actresses, some standing, some sitting, chat and smoke. One perhaps reads a paper; another cons his part.

Finally, the Manager *enters and goes to the table prepared for him. His* Secretary *brings him his mail, through which he glances. The* Prompter *takes his seat, turns on a light, and opens the "book."*

The Manager (*throwing a letter down on the table*): I can't see (*to* Property Man). Let's have a little light, please!
Property Man: Yes sir, yes, at once (*a light comes down on to the stage*).
The Manager (*clapping his hands*): Come along! Come along! Second act of "Mixing it Up" (*sits down*).

[*The actors and actresses go from the front of the stage to the wings, all except the three who are to begin the rehearsal*].

The Prompter (*reading the "book"*): "Leo Gala's house. A curious room serving as dining-room and study."

5

10

THE MANAGER (*to* PROPERTY MAN): Fix up the old red room.

PROPERTY MAN (*noting it down*): Red set. All right!

15 THE PROMPTER (*continuing to read from the "book"*): "Table already laid and writing desk with books and papers. Book-shelves. Exit rear to Leo's bedroom. Exit left to kitchen. Principal exit to right."

20 THE MANAGER (*energetically*): Well, you understand: The principal exit over there; here, the kitchen. (*Turning to actor who is to play the part of Socrates*). You make your entrances and exits here. (*To* PROPERTY MAN) The baize doors at the rear, and curtains.

25 PROPERTY MAN (*noting it down*): Right oh!

PROMPTER (*reading as before*): "When the curtain rises, Leo Gala, dressed in cook's cap and apron is busy beating an egg in a cup. Philip, also dressed as a cook, is beating another egg.

30 Guido Venanzi is seated and listening."

LEADING MAN (*to* MANAGER): Excuse me, but must I absolutely wear a cook's cap?

THE MANAGER (*annoyed*): I imagine so. It says so there

35 anyway (*pointing to the "book"*).

LEADING MAN: But it's ridiculous!

THE MANAGER (*jumping up in a rage*): Ridiculous? Ridiculous? Is it my fault if France won't send us any more good comedies, and we are

40 reduced to putting on Pirandello's works, where nobody understands anything, and where the author plays the fool with us all? (*The actors grin. The* MANAGER *goes to* LEADING MAN *and shouts*). Yes sir, you put on the cook's

45 cap and beat eggs. Do you suppose that with all this egg-beating business you are on an ordinary stage? Get that out of your head. You represent the shell of the eggs you are beating! (*Laughter and comments among the actors*).

50 Silence! and listen to my explanations, please! (*To* LEADING MAN): "The empty form of reason without the fullness of instinct, which is blind."—You stand for reason, your wife is instinct. It's a mixing up of the parts, accord-

55 ing to which you who act your own part become the puppet of yourself. Do you understand?

LEADING MAN: I'm hanged if I do.

THE MANAGER: Neither do I. But let's get on with it.

60 It's sure to be a glorious failure anyway. (*Confidentially*): But I say, please face three-quarters. Otherwise, what with the abstruseness of the dialogue, and the public that won't be able to hear you, the whole thing will go to

65 hell. Come on! come on!

PROMPTER: Pardon sir, may I get into my box? There's a bit of a draught.

THE MANAGER: Yes, yes, of course!

[*At this point, the* DOOR-KEEPER *has entered from the stage door and advances towards the* MANAGER's *table, taking off his braided cap. During this manoeuvre, the* SIX CHARACTERS *enter, and stop by the door at back of stage, so that when the* DOOR-KEEPER *is about to announce their coming to the* MANAGER, *they are already on the stage. A tenuous light surrounds them, almost as if irradiated by them—the faint breath of their fantastic reality.*

This light will disappear when they come forward towards the actors. They preserve, however, something of the dream lightness in which they seem almost suspended; but this does not detract from the essential reality of their forms and expressions.

He who is known as THE FATHER *is a man of about 50: hair, reddish in colour, thin at the temples; he is not bald, however; thick moustaches, falling over his still fresh mouth, which often opens in an empty and uncertain smile. He is fattish, pale; with an especially wide forehead. He has blue, oval-shaped eyes, very clear and piercing. Wears light trousers and a dark jacket. He is alternatively mellifluous and violent in his manner.*

THE MOTHER *seems crushed and terrified as if by an intolerable weight of shame and abasement. She is dressed in modest black and wears a thick widow's veil of crêpe. When she lifts this, she reveals a wax-like face. She always keeps her eyes downcast.*

THE STEP-DAUGHTER, *is dashing, almost impudent, beautiful. She wears mourning too, but with great elegance. She shows contempt for the timid half-frightened manner of the wretched* BOY (*14 years old, and also dressed in black*); *on the other hand, she displays a lively tenderness for her little sister, THE CHILD (about four), who is dressed in white, with a black silk sash at the waist.*

THE SON (*22*) *tall, severe in his attitude of contempt for* THE FATHER, *supercilious and indifferent to the* MOTHER. *He looks as if he had come on the stage against his will.*]

DOOR-KEEPER (*cap in hand*): Excuse me, sir . . .

THE MANAGER (*rudely*): Eh? What is it?   70

DOOR-KEEPER (*timidly*): These people are asking for you, sir.

THE MANAGER (*furious*): I am rehearsing, and you know perfectly well no one's allowed to come in during rehearsals! (*Turning to the*   75 CHARACTERS): Who are you, please? What do you want?

THE FATHER (*coming forward a little, followed by the others who seem embarrassed*): As a matter of fact... we have come here in search of an author . . .   80

THE MANAGER (*half angry, half amazed*): An author? What author?

THE FATHER: Any author, sir.

THE MANAGER: But there's no author here. We are not

85   rehearsing a new piece.

THE STEP-DAUGHTER (*vivaciously*): So much the better, so much the better! We can be your new piece.

AN ACTOR (*coming forward from the others*): Oh, do you hear that?

90 THE FATHER (*to* STEP-DAUGHTER): Yes, but if the author isn't here . . . (*To* MANAGER) . . . unless you would be willing . . .

THE MANAGER: You are trying to be funny.

THE FATHER: No, for Heaven's sake, what are you

95   saying? We bring you a drama, sir.

THE STEP-DAUGHTER: We may be your fortune.

THE MANAGER: Will you oblige me by going away? We haven't time to waste with mad people.

THE FATHER (*mellifluously*): Oh sir, you know well

100   that life is full of infinite absurdities, which, strangely enough, do not even need to appear plausible, since they are true.

THE MANAGER: What the devil is he talking about?

THE FATHER: I say that to reverse the ordinary

105   process may well be considered a madness: that is, to create credible situations, in order that they may appear true. But permit me to observe that if this be madness, it is the sole *raison d'être* of your profession, gentlemen. (*The*

110   *actors look hurt and perplexed*).

THE MANAGER (*getting up and looking at him*): So our profession seems to you one worthy of madmen then?

THE FATHER: Well, to make seem true that which isn't

115   true . . . without any need . . . for a joke as it were . . . Isn't that your mission, gentlemen: to give life to fantastic characters on the stage?

THE MANAGER (*interpreting the rising anger of the Company*): But I would beg you to believe, my

120   dear sir, that the profession of the comedian is a noble one. If today, as things go, the playwrights give us stupid comedies to play and puppets to represent instead of men, remember we are proud to have given life to immor-

125   tal works here on these very boards! (*The actors, satisfied, applaud their* MANAGER).

THE FATHER (*interrupting furiously*): Exactly, perfectly, to living beings more alive than those who breathe and wear clothes: beings less real per-

130   haps, but truer! I agree with you entirely. (*The actors look at one another in amazement*).

THE MANAGER: But what do you mean? Before, you said . . .

THE FATHER: No, excuse me, I meant it for you, sir,

135   who were crying out that you had no time to lose with madmen, while no one better than yourself knows that nature uses the instrument of human fantasy in order to pursue her high creative purpose.

140 THE MANAGER: Very well,—but where does all this take us?

THE FATHER: Nowhere! It is merely to show you that one is born to life in many forms, in many shapes, as tree, or as stone, as water, as butter- 145 fly, or as woman. So one may also be born a character in a play.

THE MANAGER (*with feigned comic dismay*): So you and these other friends of yours have been born characters?

THE FATHER: Exactly, and alive as you see! (MANAGER 150 *and actors burst out laughing*).

THE FATHER (*hurt*): I am sorry you laugh, because we carry in us a drama, as you can guess from this woman here veiled in black.

THE MANAGER (*losing patience at last and almost indig-* 155 *nant*): Oh, chuck it! Get away please! Clear out of here! (*to* Property Man). For Heaven's sake, turn them out!

THE FATHER (*resisting*): No, no, look here, we . . .

THE MANAGER (*roaring*): We come here to work, you 160 know.

LEADING ACTOR: One cannot let oneself be made such a fool of.

THE FATHER (*determined, coming forward*): I marvel at your incredulity, gentlemen. Are you not 165 accustomed to see the characters created by an author spring to life in yourselves and face each other? Just because there is no "book" (*pointing to the* PROMPTER'*s box*) which contains us, you refuse to believe . . . 170

THE STEP-DAUGHTER (*advances towards* MANAGER, *smiling and coquettish*): Believe me, we are really six most interesting characters, sir; side-tracked however.

THE FATHER: Yes, that is the word! (*To* MANAGER *all at* 175 *once*): In the sense, that is, that the author who created us alive no longer wished, or was no longer able, materially to put us into a work of art. And this was a real crime, sir; because he who has had the luck to be born a character 180 can laugh even at death. He cannot die. The man, the writer, the instrument of the creation will die, but his creation does not die. And to live for ever, it does not need to have extraordinary gifts or to be able to work wonders. 185 Who was Sancho Panza? Who was Don Abbondio? Yet they live eternally because— live germs as they were—they had the fortune to find a fecundating matrix, a fantasy which could raise and nourish them: make them live 190 for ever!

THE MANAGER: That is quite all right. But what do you want here, all of you?

THE FATHER: We want to live.

THE MANAGER (*ironically*): For Eternity? 195

THE FATHER: No, sir, only for a moment . . . in you.

AN ACTOR: Just listen to him!

LEADING LADY: They want to live, in us . . . !

JUVENILE LEAD (*pointing to the* STEP-DAUGHTER): I've no objection, as far as that one is concerned!

THE FATHER: Look here! look here! The comedy has to be made. (*To the* MANAGER): But if you and your actors are willing, we can soon concert it among ourselves.

THE MANAGER (*annoyed*): But what do you want to concert? We don't go in for concerts here. Here we play dramas and comedies!

THE FATHER: Exactly! That is just why we have come to you.

THE MANAGER: And where is the "book"?

THE FATHER: It is in us! (*The actors laugh*). The drama is in us, and we are the drama. We are impatient to play it. Our inner passion drives us on to this.

THE STEP-DAUGHTER (*disdainful, alluring, treacherous, full of impudence*): My passion, sir! Ah, if you only knew! My passion for him! (*Points to the* FATHER *and makes a pretence of embracing him. Then she breaks out into a loud laugh*).

THE FATHER (*angrily*): Behave yourself! And please don't laugh in that fashion.

THE STEP-DAUGHTER: With your permission, gentlemen, I, who am a two months' orphan, will show you how I can dance and sing.

[*Sings and then dances* Prenez garde à Tchou-Thin-Tchou].

Les chinois sont un peuple malin,
De Shangaî à Pekin,
Ils ont mis des écriteux partout:
Prenez garde à Tchou-Thin-Tchou.

ACTORS and ACTRESSES: Bravo! Well done! Tip-top!

THE MANAGER: Silence! This isn't a café concert, you know! (*Turning to the* FATHER *in consternation*): Is she mad?

THE FATHER: Mad? No, she's worse than mad.

THE STEP-DAUGHTER (*to* MANAGER): Worse? Worse? Listen! Stage this drama for us at once! Then you will see that at a certain moment I . . . when this little darling here . . . (*Takes the* CHILD *by the hand and leads her to the* MANAGER): Isn't she a dear? (*Takes her up and kisses her*). Darling! Darling! (*Puts her down again and adds feelingly*): Well, when God suddenly takes this dear little child away from that poor mother there; and this imbecile here (*seizing hold of the* BOY *roughly and pushing him forward*) does the stupidest things, like the fool he is, you will see me run away. Yes, gentleman, I shall be off. But the moment hasn't arrived yet. After what has taken place between him and me (*indicates the* FATHER *with a horrible wink*), I can't remain any longer in this society, to have to witness the anguish of this mother here for that fool... (*indicates the* SON). Look at him! Look at him! See how indifferent, how frigid he is, because he is the legitimate son. He despises me, despises him (*pointing to the* BOY), despises this baby here; because . . . we are bastards (*goes to the* MOTHER *and embraces her*). And he doesn't want to recognize her as his mother—she who is the common mother of us all. He looks down upon her as if she were only the mother of us three bastards. Wretch! (*She says all this very rapidly, excitedly. At the word "bastards" she raises her voice, and almost spits out the final "Wretch!"*).

THE MOTHER (*to the* MANAGER, *in anguish*): In the name of these two little children, I beg you . . . (*She grows faint and is about to fall*). Oh God!

THE FATHER (*coming forward to support her as do some of the actors*): Quick a chair, a chair for this poor widow!

THE ACTORS: Is it true? Has she really fainted?

THE MANAGER: Quick, a chair! Here!

[*One of the actors brings a chair, the others proffer assistance. The* MOTHER *tries to prevent the* FATHER *from lifting the veil which covers her face*].

THE FATHER: Look at her! Look at her!

THE MOTHER: No, no; stop it please!

THE FATHER (*raising her veil*): Let them see you!

THE MOTHER (*rising and covering her face with her hands, in desperation*): I beg you, sir, to prevent this man from carrying out his plan which is loathsome to me.

THE MANAGER (*dumbfounded*): I don't understand at all. What is the situation? Is this lady your wife? (*to the* FATHER).

THE FATHER: Yes, gentlemen: my wife!

THE MANAGER: But how can she be a widow if you are alive? (*The actors find relief for their astonishment in a loud laugh*).

THE FATHER: Don't laugh! Don't laugh like that, for Heaven's sake. Her drama lies just here in this: she has had a lover, a man who ought to be here.

THE MOTHER (*with a cry*): No! No!

THE STEP-DAUGHTER: Fortunately for her, he is dead. Two months ago as I said. We are in mourning, as you see.

THE FATHER: He isn't here you see, not because he is dead. He isn't here—look at her a moment and you will understand—because her drama isn't a drama of the love of two men for whom she was incapable of feeling anything except possibly a little gratitude—gratitude not for me but for the other. She isn't a woman, she is a moth-

er, and her drama—powerful sir, I assure
you—lies, as a matter of fact, all in these four
children she has had by two men.

305 THE MOTHER: I had them? Have you got the courage
to say that I wanted them? (*To the company*). It
was his doing. It was he who gave me that
other man, who forced me to go away with
him.

310 THE STEP-DAUGHTER: It isn't true.
THE MOTHER (*startled*): Not true, isn't it?
THE STEP-DAUGHTER: No, it isn't true, it just isn't true.
THE MOTHER: And what can you know about it?
THE STEP-DAUGHTER: It isn't true. Don't believe it. (*To*
315 MANAGER). Do you know why she says so? For
that fellow there (*indicates the* SON). She tortures herself, destroys herself on account of the
neglect of that son there; and she wants him to
believe that if she abandoned him when he
320 was only two years old, it was because he
(*indicates the* FATHER) made her do so.
THE MOTHER (*vigorously*): He forced me to it, and I
call God to witness it (*to the* MANAGER). Ask
him (*indicates husband*) if it isn't true. Let him
325 speak. You (*to daughter*) are not in a position to
know anything about it.
THE STEP-DAUGHTER: I know you lived in peace and
happiness with my father while he lived. Can
you deny it?
330 THE MOTHER: No, I don't deny it . . .
THE STEP-DAUGHTER: He was always full of affection
and kindness for you (*to the* BOY, *angrily*). It's
true, isn't it? Tell them! Why don't you speak,
you little fool?
335 THE MOTHER: Leave the poor boy alone. Why do you
want to make me appear ungrateful, daughter? I don't want to offend your father. I have
answered him that I didn't abandon my house
and my son through any fault of mine, nor
340 from any wilful passion.
THE FATHER: It is true. It was my doing.
LEADING MAN (*to the* COMPANY): What a spectacle!
LEADING LADY: We are the audience this time.
JUVENILE LEAD: For once, in a way.
345 THE MANAGER (*beginning to get really interested*): Let's
hear them out. Listen!
THE SON: Oh yes, you're going to hear a fine bit now.
He will talk to you of the Demon of
Experiment.
350 THE FATHER: You are a cynical imbecile. I've told you
so already a hundred times (*to the* MANAGER).
He tries to make fun of me on account of this
expression which I have found to excuse
myself with.
355 THE SON (*with disgust*): Yes, phrases! phrases!
THE FATHER: Phrases! Isn't everyone consoled when
faced with a trouble or fact he doesn't understand, by a word, some simple word, which

tells us nothing and yet calms us?
THE STEP-DAUGHTER: Even in the case of remorse. In 360
fact, especially then.
THE FATHER: Remorse? No, that isn't true. I've done
more than use words to quieten the remorse in
me.
THE STEP-DAUGHTER: Yes, there was a bit of money 365
too. Yes, yes, a bit of money. There were the
hundred lire he was about to offer me in payment, gentlemen . . . (*sensation of horror among
the actors*).
THE SON (*to the* STEP-DAUGHTER): This is vile. 370
THE STEP-DAUGHTER: Vile? There they were in a pale
blue envelope on a little mahogany table in the
back of Madame Pace's shop. You know
Madame Pace—one of those ladies who attract
poor girls of good family into their ateliers, 375
under the pretext of their selling *robes et man-
teaux.*
THE SON: And he thinks he has bought the right to
tyrannise over us all with those hundred lire
he was going to pay; but which, fortunately— 380
note this, gentlemen—he had no chance of
paying.
THE STEP-DAUGHTER: It was a near thing, though, you
know! (*laughs ironically*).
THE MOTHER (*protesting*): Shame, my daughter, 385
shame!
THE STEP-DAUGHTER: Shame indeed! This is my
revenge! I am dying to live that scene . . . The
room . . . I see it . . . Here is the window with
the mantles exposed, there the divan, the look- 390
ing-glass, a screen, there in front of the window the little mahogany table with the blue
envelope containing one hundred lire. I see it. I
see it. I could take hold of it . . . But you, gentlemen, you ought to turn your backs now: I 395
am almost nude, you know. But I don't blush: I
leave that to him (*indicating* FATHER).
THE MANAGER: I don't understand this at all.
THE FATHER: Naturally enough. I would ask you, sir,
to exercise your authority a little here, and let 400
me speak before you believe all she is trying to
blame me with. Let me explain.
THE STEP-DAUGHTER: Ah yes, explain it in your own
way.
THE FATHER: But don't you see that the whole trouble 405
lies here. In words, words. Each one of us has
within him a whole world of things, each man
of us his own special world. And how can we
ever come to an understanding if I put in the
words I utter the sense and value of things as I 410
see them; while you who listen to me must
inevitably translate them according to the conception of things each one of you has within
himself. We think we understand each other,
but we never really do. Look here! This 415

woman (*indicating the* MOTHER) takes all my
pity for her as a specially ferocious form of
cruelty.

THE MOTHER: But you drove me away.

420 THE FATHER: Do you hear her? I drove her away! She
believes I really sent her away.

THE MOTHER: You know how to talk, and I don't; but,
believe me sir, (*to* MANAGER) after he had married me . . . who knows why? . . . I was a poor

425 insignificant woman . . .

THE FATHER: But, good Heavens! it was just for your
humility that I married you. I loved this simplicity in you. (*He stops when he sees she makes
signs to contradict him, opens his arms wide in
430 sign of desperation, seeing how hopeless it is to
make himself understood*). You see she denies it.
Her mental deafness, believe me, is phenome-
nal, the limit (*touches his forehead*): deaf, deaf,
mentally deaf! She has plenty of feeling. Oh
435 yes, a good heart for the children; but the
brain—deaf, to the point of desperation—!

THE STEP-DAUGHTER: Yes, but ask him how his intelligence has helped us.

THE FATHER: If we could see all the evil that may
440 spring from good, what should we do? (*At this
point the* LEADING LADY *who is biting her lips
with rage at seeing the* LEADING MAN *flirting with
the* STEP-DAUGHTER, *comes forward and says to the*
MANAGER).

445 LEADING LADY: Excuse me, but are we going to
rehearse today?

MANAGER: Of course, of course; but let's hear them
out.

JUVENILE LEAD: This is something quite new.

450 L'INGÉNUE: Most interesting!

LEADING LADY: Yes, for the people who like that kind
of thing (*casts a glance at* LEADING MAN).

THE MANAGER (*to* FATHER): You must please explain
yourself quite clearly (*sits down*).

455 THE FATHER: Very well then: listen! I had in my service a poor man, a clerk, a secretary of mine,
full of devotion, who became friends with her
(*indicating the* MOTHER). They understood one
another, were kindred souls in fact, without,
460 however, the least suspicion of any evil existing. They were incapable even of thinking of
it.

THE STEP-DAUGHTER: So he thought of it—for them!

THE FATHER: That's not true. I meant to do good to
465 them—and to myself, I confess, at the same
time. Things had come to the point that I could
not say a word to either of them without their
making a mute appeal, one to the other, with
their eyes. I could see them silently asking
470 each other how I was to be kept in countenance, how I was to be kept quiet. And this,
believe me, was just about enough of itself to

keep me in a constant rage, to exasperate me
beyond measure.

THE MANAGER: And why didn't you send him away   475
then—this secretary of yours?

THE FATHER: Precisely what I did, sir. And then I had
to watch this poor woman drifting forlornly
about the house like an animal without a master, like an animal one has taken in out of pity.   480

THE MOTHER: Ah yes . . . !

THE FATHER (*suddenly turning to the* MOTHER): It's true
about the son anyway, isn't it?

THE MOTHER: He took my son away from me first of
all.   485

THE FATHER: But not from cruelty. I did it so that he
should grow up healthy and strong by living
in the country.

THE STEP-DAUGHTER (*pointing to him ironically*): As
one can see.   490

THE FATHER (*quickly*): Is it my fault if he has grown
up like this? I sent him to a wet nurse in the
country, a peasant, as *she* did not seem to me
strong enough, though she is of humble origin.
That was, anyway, the reason I married her.   495
Unpleasant all this maybe, but how can it be
helped? My mistake possibly, but there we are!
All my life I have had these confounded aspirations towards a certain moral sanity. (*At this
point the* STEP-DAUGHTER *bursts out into a noisy   500
laugh*). Oh, stop, it! Stop it! I can't stand it.

THE MANAGER: Yes, please stop it, for Heaven's sake.

THE STEP-DAUGHTER: But imagine moral sanity from
him, if you please—the client of certain ateliers
like that of Madame Pace!   505

THE FATHER: Fool! That is the proof that I am a man!
This seeming contradiction, gentlemen, is the
strongest proof that I stand here a live man
before you. Why, it is just for this very incon-
gruity in my nature that I have had to suffer   510
what I have. I could not live by the side of that
woman (*indicating the* MOTHER) any longer; but
not so much for the boredom she inspired me
with as for the pity I felt for her.

THE MOTHER: And so he turned me out—.   515

THE FATHER: —well provided for! Yes, I sent her to
that man, gentlemen . . . to let her go free of
me.

THE MOTHER: And to free himself.

THE FATHER: Yes, I admit it. It was also a liberation   520
for me. But great evil has come of it. I meant
well when I did it; and I did it more for her
sake than mine. I swear it (*crosses his arms on
his chest; then turns suddenly to the* MOTHER).
Did I ever lose sight of you until that other   525
man carried you off to another town, like the
angry fool he was? And on account of my pure
interest in you . . . my pure interest, I repeat,
that had no base motive in it . . . I watched

530   with the tenderest concern the new family that
grew up around her. She can bear witness to
this (*points to the* STEP-DAUGHTER).

THE STEP-DAUGHTER: Oh yes, that's true enough.
535   When I was a kiddie, so so high, you know,
with plaits over my shoulders and knickers
longer than my skirts, I used to see him waiting outside the school for me to come out. He
came to see how I was growing up.

THE FATHER: This is infamous, shameful!

540   THE STEP-DAUGHTER: No, Why?

THE FATHER: Infamous! infamous! (*Then excitedly to*
MANAGER *explaining*). After she (*indicating*
MOTHER) went away, my house seemed suddenly empty. She was my incubus, but she
545   filled my house. I was like a dazed fly alone in
the empty rooms. This boy here (*indicating the*
SON) was educated away from home, and
when he came back, he seemed to me to be no
more mine. With no mother to stand between
550   him and me, he grew up entirely for himself,
on his own, apart, with no tie of intellect or
affection binding him to me. And then—
strange but true—I was driven, by curiosity at
first and then by some tender sentiment,
555   towards her family, which had come into being
through my will. The thought of her began
gradually to fill up the emptiness I felt all
around me. I wanted to know if she were
happy in living out the simple daily duties of
560   life. I wanted to think of her as fortunate and
happy because far away from the complicated
torments of my spirit. And so, to have proof of
this, I used to watch that child coming out of
school.

565   THE STEP-DAUGHTER: Yes, yes. True. He used to follow me in the street and smiled at me, waved
his hand, like this. I would look at him with
interest, wondering who he might be. I told
my mother, who guessed at once (*the* MOTHER
570   *agrees with a nod*). Then she didn't want to send
me to school for some days; and when I finally
went back, there he was again—looking so
ridiculous—with a paper parcel in his hands.
He came close to me, caressed me, and drew
575   out a fine straw hat from the parcel, with a
bouquet of flowers—all for me!

THE MANAGER: A bit discursive this, you know!

THE SON (*contemptuously*): Literature! Literature!

THE FATHER: Literature indeed! This is life, this is
580   passion!

THE MANAGER: It may be, but it won't act.

THE FATHER: I agree. This is only the part leading up.
I don't suggest this should be staged. She
(*pointing to the* STEP-DAUGHTER), as you see, is
585   no longer the flapper with plaits down her
back—.

THE STEP-DAUGHTER: —and the knickers showing
below the skirt!

THE FATHER: The drama is coming now, sir; something new, complex, most interesting.   590

THE STEP-DAUGHTER: As soon as my father died . . .

THE FATHER: —there was absolute misery for them.
They came back here, unknown to me.
Through her stupidity (*pointing to the* MOTHER)!
It is true she can barely write her own name;   595
but she could anyhow have got her daughter
to write to me that they were in need . . .

THE MOTHER: And how was I to divine all this sentiment in him?

THE FATHER: That is exactly your mistake, never to   600
have guessed any of my sentiments.

THE MOTHER: After so many years apart, and all that
had happened . . .

THE FATHER: Was it my fault if that fellow carried
you away? It happened quite suddenly; for   605
after he had obtained some job or other, I
could find no trace of them; and so, not unnaturally, my interest in them dwindled. But the
drama culminated unforeseen and violent on
their return, when I was impelled by my mis-   610
erable flesh that still lives . . . Ah! what misery,
what wretchedness is that of the man who is
alone and disdains debasing *liaisons!* Not old
enough to do without women, and not young
enough to go and look for one without shame.   615
Misery? It's worse than misery; it's a horror;
for no woman can any longer give him love;
and when a man feels this . . . One ought to do
without, you say? Yes, yes, I know. Each of us
when he appears before his fellows is clothed   620
in a certain dignity. But every man knows
what unconfessable things pass within the
secrecy of his own heart. One gives way to the
temptation, only to rise from it again, afterwards, with a great eagerness to reestablish   625
one's dignity, as if it were a tombstone to place
on the grave of one's shame, and a monument
to hide and sign the memory of our weaknesses. Everybody's in the same case. Some folks
haven't the courage to say certain things, that's   630
all!

THE STEP-DAUGHTER: All appear to have the courage
to do them though.

THE FATHER: Yes, but in secret. Therefore, you want
more courage to say these things. Let a man   635
but speak these things out, and folks at once
label him a cynic. But it isn't true. He is like all
the others, better indeed, because he isn't
afraid to reveal with the light of the intelligence the red shame of human bestiality on   640
which most men close their eyes so as not to
see it.

Woman—for example, look at her case! She turns

THE STEP-DAUGHTER: Sometimes she can close them no more: when she no longer feels the need of hiding her shame to herself, but dry-eyed and dispassionately, sees only that of the man who has blinded himself without love. Oh, all these intellectual complications make me sick, disgust me—all this philosophy that uncovers the beast in man, and then seeks to save him, excuse him . . . I can't stand it, sir. When a man seeks to "simplify" life bestially, throwing aside every relic of humanity, every chaste aspiration, every pure feeling, all sense of ideality, duty, modesty, shame . . . then nothing is more revolting and nauseous than a certain kind of remorse—crocodiles' tears, that's what it is.

THE MANAGER: Let's come to the point. This is only discussion.

THE FATHER: Very good, sir! But a fact is like a sack which won't stand up when it is empty. In order that it may stand up, one has to put into it the reason and sentiment which have caused it to exist. I couldn't possibly know that after the death of that man, they had decided to return here, that they were in misery, and that she (*pointing to the* MOTHER) had gone to work as a modiste, and at a shop of the type of that of Madame Pace.

THE STEP-DAUGHTER: A real high-class modiste, you must know, gentlemen. In appearance, she works for the leaders of the best society; but she arranges matters so that these elegant ladies serve her purpose . . . without prejudice to other ladies who are . . . well . . . only so so.

THE MOTHER: You will believe me, gentlemen, that it never entered my mind that the old hag offered me work because she had her eye on my daughter.

THE STEP-DAUGHTER: Poor mamma! Do you know, sir, what that woman did when I brought her back the work my mother had finished? She would point out to me that I had torn one of my frocks, and she would give it back to my mother to mend. It was I who paid for it, always I; while this poor creature here believed she was sacrificing herself for me and these two children here, sitting up at night sewing Madame Pace's robes.

THE MANAGER: And one day you met there . . .

THE STEP-DAUGHTER: Him, him. Yes sir, an old client. There's a scene for you to play! Superb!

THE FATHER: She, the Mother arrived just then . . .

THE STEP-DAUGHTER (*treacherously*): Almost in time!

THE FATHER (*crying out*): No, in time! in time! Fortunately I recognized her . . . in time. And I took them back home with me to my house. You can imagine now her position and mine: she, as you see her; and I who cannot look her in the face.

THE STEP-DAUGHTER: Absurd! How can I possibly be expected—after that—to be a modest young miss, a fit person to go with his confounded aspirations for "a solid moral sanity"?

THE FATHER: For the drama lies all in this—in the conscience that I have, that each one of us has. We believe this conscience to be a single thing, but it is many-sided. There is one for this person, and another for that. Diverse consciences. So we have this illusion of being one person for all, of having a personality that is unique in all our acts. But it isn't true. We perceive this when, tragically perhaps, in something we do, we are as it were, suspended, caught up in the air on a kind of hook. Then we perceive that all of us was not in that act, and that it would be an atrocious injustice to judge us by that action alone, as if all our existence were summed up in that one deed. Now do you understand the perfidy of this girl? She surprised me in a place, where she ought not to have known me, just as I could not exist for her; and she now seeks to attach to me a reality such as I could never suppose I should have to assume for her in a shameful and fleeting moment of my life. I feel this above all else. And the drama, you will see, acquires a tremendous value from this point. Then there is the position of the others . . . his . . . (*indicating the* SON).

THE SON (*shrugging his shoulders scornfully*): Leave me alone! I don't come into this.

THE FATHER: What? You don't come into this?

THE SON: I've got nothing to do with it, and don't want to have; because you know well enough I wasn't made to be mixed up in all this with the rest of you.

THE STEP-DAUGHTER: We are only vulgar folk! He is the fine gentleman. You may have noticed, Mr. Manager, that I fix him now and again with a look of scorn while he lowers his eyes—for he knows the evil he has done me.

THE SON (*scarcely looking at her*): I?

THE STEP-DAUGHTER: You! you! I owe my life on the streets to you. Did you or did you not deny us, with your behaviour, I won't say the intimacy of home, but even that mere hospitality which makes guests feel at their ease? We were intruders who had come to disturb the kingdom of your legitimacy. I should like to have

you witness, Mr. Manager, certain scenes
between him and me. He says I have tyran-
760 nized over everyone. But it was just his behaviour which made me insist on the reason for
which I had come into the house,—this reason
he calls "vile"—into his house, with my mother who is his mother too. And I came as mis-
765 tress of the house.

THE SON: It's easy for them to put me always in the
wrong. But imagine, gentlemen, the position of
a son, whose fate it is to see arrive one day at
his home a young woman of impudent bear-
770 ing, a young woman who inquires for his
father, with whom who knows what business
she has. This young man has then to witness
her return bolder than ever, accompanied by
that child there. He is obliged to watch her
775 treat his father in an equivocal and confidential manner. She asks money of him in a way
that lets one suppose he must give it her, *must*,
do you understand, because he has every
obligation to do so.

780 THE FATHER: But I have, as a matter of fact, this obligation. I owe it to your mother.

THE SON: How should I know? When had I ever seen
or heard of her? One day there arrive with her
(*indicating* STEP-DAUGHTER) that lad and this
785 baby here. I am told: "This is *your* mother too,
you know." I divine from her manner (*indicating* STEP-DAUGHTER *again*) why it is they have
come home. I had rather not say what I feel
and think about it. I shouldn't even care to
790 confess to myself. No action can therefore be
hoped for from me in this affair. Believe me,
Mr. Manager, I am an "unrealized" character,
dramatically speaking; and I find myself not at
all at ease in their company. Leave me out of it,
795 I beg you.

THE FATHER: What? It is just because you are so
that...

THE SON: How do you know what I am like? When
did you ever bother your head about me?

800 THE FATHER: I admit it. I admit it. But isn't that a situation in itself? This aloofness of yours which is
so cruel to me and to your mother, who
returns home and sees you almost for the first
time grown up, who doesn't recognize you but
805 knows you are her son . . . (*pointing out the*
MOTHER *to the* MANAGER). See, she's crying!

THE STEP-DAUGHTER (*angrily, stamping her foot*): Like a
fool!

THE FATHER (*indicating* STEP-DAUGHTER): She can't
810 stand him you know. (*Then referring again to the*
SON): He says he doesn't come into the affair,
whereas he is really the hinge of the whole
action. Look at that lad who is always clinging
to his mother, frightened and humiliated. It is

on account of this fellow here. Possibly his sit- 815
uation is the most painful of all. He feels himself a stranger more than the others. The poor
little chap feels mortified, humiliated at being
brought into a home out of charity as it were.
(*In confidence*)—: He is the image of his father. 820
Hardly talks at all. Humble and quiet.

THE MANAGER: Oh, we'll cut him out. You've no
notion what a nuisance boys are on the stage...

THE FATHER: He disappears soon, you know. And the
baby too. She is the first to vanish from the 825
scene. The drama consists finally in this: when
that mother re-enters my house, her family
born outside of it, and shall we say superim-
posed on the original, ends with the death of
the little girl, the tragedy of the boy and the 830
flight of the elder daughter. It cannot go on,
because it is foreign to its surroundings. So
after much torment, we three remain: I, the
mother, that son. Then, owing to the disappearance of that extraneous family, we too find 835
ourselves strange to one another. We find we
are living in an atmosphere of mortal desolation which is the revenge, as he (*indicating*
SON) scornfully said of the Demon of
Experiment, that unfortunately hides in me. 840
Thus, sir, you see when faith is lacking, it
becomes impossible to create certain states of
happiness, for we lack the necessary humility.
Vaingloriously, we try to substitute ourselves
for this faith, creating thus for the rest of the 845
world a reality which we believe after their
fashion, while, actually, it doesn't exist. For
each one of us has his own reality to be
respected before God, even when it is harmful
to one's very self. 850

THE MANAGER: There is something in what you say. I
assure you all this interests me very much. I
begin to think there's the stuff for a drama in
all this, and not a bad drama either.

THE STEP-DAUGHTER (*coming forward*): When you've 855
got a character like me.

THE FATHER (*shutting her up, all excited to learn the
decision of the* MANAGER): You be quiet!

THE MANAGER (*reflecting, heedless of interruption*): It's
new ... hem ... yes ... 860

THE FATHER: Absolutely new!

THE MANAGER: You've got a nerve though, I must
say, to come here and fling it at me like this ...

THE FATHER: You will understand, sir, born as we are
for the stage ... 865

THE MANAGER: Are you amateur actors then?

THE FATHER: No. I say born for the stage, because ...

THE MANAGER: Oh, nonsense. You're an old hand,
you know.

THE FATHER: No sir, no. We act that rôle for which we 870
have been cast, that rôle which we are given in

life. And in my own case, passion itself, as usually happens, becomes a trifle theatrical when it is exalted.

875 THE MANAGER: Well, well, that will do. But you see, without an author . . . I could give you the address of an author if you like . . .

THE FATHER: No, no. Look here! You must be the author.

THE MANAGER: I? What are you talking about?

880 THE FATHER: Yes, you, you! Why not?

THE MANAGER: Because I have never been an author: that's why.

THE FATHER: Then why not turn author now? Everybody does it. You don't want any special 885 qualities. Your task is made much easier by the fact that we are all here alive before you . . .

THE MANAGER: It won't do.

THE FATHER: What? When you see us live our drama…

890 THE MANAGER: Yes, that's all right. But you want someone to write it.

THE FATHER: No, no. Someone to take it down, possibly, while we play it, scene by scene! It will be enough to sketch it out at first, and then try it 895 over.

THE MANAGER: Well . . . I am almost tempted. It's a bit of an idea. One might have a shot at it.

THE FATHER: Of course. You'll see what scenes will come out of it. I can give you one, at once . . .

900 THE MANAGER: By Jove, it tempts me. I'd like to have a go at it. Let's try it out. Come with me to my office (*turning to the* ACTORS). You are at liberty for a bit, but don't stop out of the theatre for long. In a quarter of an hour, twenty minutes, 905 all back here again! (*To the* FATHER): We'll see what can be done. Who knows if we don't get something really extraordinary out of it?

THE FATHER: There's no doubt about it. They (*indicating the* CHARACTERS) had better come with us 910 too, hadn't they?

THE MANAGER: Yes, yes. Come on! come on! (*Moves away and then turning to the actors*): Be punctual, please! (MANAGER *and the* SIX CHARACTERS *cross the stage and go off. The other actors remain,* 915 *looking at one another in astonishment*).

LEADING MAN: Is he serious? What the devil does he want to do?

JUVENILE LEAD: This is rank madness.

THIRD ACTOR: Does he expect to knock up a drama in 920 five minutes?

JUVENILE LEAD: Like the improvisers!

LEADING LADY: If he thinks I'm going to take part in a joke like this . . .

JUVENILE LEAD: I'm out of it anyway.

925 FOURTH ACTOR: I should like to know who they are (*alludes to* CHARACTERS).

THIRD ACTOR: What do you suppose? Madmen or rascals!

JUVENILE LEAD: And he takes them seriously!

L'INGÉNUE: Vanity! He fancies himself as an author now. 930

LEADING MAN: It's absolutely unheard of. If the stage has come to this . . . well I'm . . .

FIFTH ACTOR: It's rather a joke.

THIRD ACTOR: Well, we'll see what's going to happen next. 935

[*Thus talking, the actors leave the stage; some going out by the little door at the back; others retiring to their dressing-rooms.*

The curtain remains up.

The action of the play is suspended for twenty minutes.]

ACT II

The stage call-bells ring to warn the company that the play is about to begin again.

THE STEP-DAUGHTER *comes out of the* MANAGER's *office along with* THE CHILD *and* THE BOY. *As she comes out of the office, she cries:—*

Nonsense! nonsense! Do it yourselves! I'm not going to mix myself up in this mess. (*Turning to the* CHILD *and coming quickly with her on to the stage*): Come on, Rosetta, let's run!

[THE BOY *follows them slowly, remaining a little behind and seeming perplexed*].

THE STEP-DAUGHTER: (*Stops, bends over the* CHILD *and* 940 *takes the latter's face between her hands*). My little darling! You're frightened, aren't you? You don't know where we are, do you? (*Pretending to reply to a question of the* CHILD): What is the stage? It's a place, baby, you know, where 945 people play at being serious, a place where they act comedies. We've got to act a comedy now, dead serious, you know; and you're in it also, little one. (*Embraces her, pressing the little head to her breast, and rocking the* CHILD *for a* 950 *moment*). Oh darling, darling, what a horrid comedy you've got to play! What a wretched part they've found for you! A garden . . . a fountain . . . look . . . just suppose, kiddie, it's here. Where, you say? Why, right here in the 955 middle. It's all pretence you know. That's the trouble, my pet: it's all make-believe here. It's better to imagine it though, because if they fix it up for you, it'll only be painted cardboard, painted cardboard for the rockery, the water, 960 the plants . . . Ah, but I think a baby like this one would sooner have a make-believe fountain than a real one, so she could play with it.

965 What a joke it'll be for the others! But for you, alas! not quite such a joke: you who are real, baby dear, and really play by a real fountain that is big and green and beautiful, with ever so many bamboos around it that are reflected in the water, and a whole lot of little ducks

970 swimming about . . . No, Rosetta, no, your mother doesn't bother about you on account of that wretch of a son there. I'm in the devil of a temper, and as for that lad . . . (*Seizes* BOY *by the arm to force him to take one of his hands out of*

975 *his pockets*). What have you got there? What are you hiding? (*Pulls his hand out of his pocket, looks into it and catches the glint of a revolver*). Ah! where did you get this?

[THE BOY, *very pale in the face, looks at her, but does not answer*].

Idiot! If I'd been in your place, instead of killing
980 myself, I'd have shot one of those two, or both of them: father and son.

[THE FATHER *enters from the office, all excited from his work*. THE MANAGER *follows him*].

THE FATHER: Come on, come on dear! Come here for a minute! We've arranged everything. It's all fixed up.
985 THE MANAGER (*also excited*): If you please, young lady, there are one or two points to settle still. Will you come along?
THE STEP-DAUGHTER (*following him towards the office*): Ouff! what's the good, if you've arranged
990 everything.

[THE FATHER, MANAGER *and* STEP-DAUGHTER *go back into the office again (off) for a moment. At the same time*, THE SON *followed by* THE MOTHER, *comes out*].

THE SON (*looking at the three entering office*): Oh this is fine, fine! And to think I can't even get away!

[THE MOTHER *attempts to look at him, but lowers her eyes immediately when he turns away from her. She then sits down. The* BOY *and The* CHILD *approach her. She casts a glance again at the Son, and speaks with humble tones trying to draw him into conversation*].

THE MOTHER: And isn't my punishment the worst of all? (*Then seeing from the* SON's *manner that he*
995 *will not bother himself about her*). My God! Why are you so cruel? Isn't it enough for one person to support all this torment? Must you then insist on others seeing it also?
THE SON (*half to himself, meaning the* MOTHER *to hear*
1000 *however*): And they want to put it on the stage!

If there was at least a reason for it! He thinks he has got at the meaning of it all. Just as if each one of us in every circumstance of life couldn't find his own explanation of it! (*Pauses*). He complains he was discovered in a 1005
place where he ought not to have been seen, in a moment of his life which ought to have remained hidden and kept out of the reach of that convention which he has to maintain for other people. And what about my case? 1010
Haven't I had to reveal what no son ought ever to reveal: how father and mother live and are man and wife for themselves quite apart from that idea of father and mother which we give them? When this idea is revealed, our life 1015
is then linked at one point only to that man and that woman; and as such it should shame them, shouldn't it?

[The MOTHER *hides her face in her hands. From the dressing-rooms and the little door at the back of the stage the actors and* STAGE MANAGER *return, followed by the* PROPERTY MAN, *and the* PROMPTER. *At the same moment, The* MANAGER *comes out of his office, accompanied by the* FATHER *and the* STEP-DAUGHTER].

THE MANAGER: Come on, come on, ladies and gentlemen! Heh! you there, machinist? 1020
MACHINIST: Yes sir?
THE MANAGER: Fix up the white parlor with the floral decorations. Two wings and a drop with a door will do. Hurry up!

[The MACHINIST *runs off at once to prepare the scene, and arranges it while* THE MANAGER *talks with the* STAGE MANAGER, *the* PROPERTY MAN, *and the* PROMPTER *on matters of detail*].

THE MANAGER (*to Property Man*): Just have a look, 1025
and see if thre isn't a sofa or divan in the wardrobe . . .
PROPERTY MAN: There's the green one.
The STEP-DAUGHTER: No no! Green won't do. It was yellow, ornamented with flowers—very large! 1030
and most comfortable!
PROPERTY MAN: There isn't one like that.
THE MANAGER: It doesn't matter. Use the one we've got.
THE STEP-DAUGHTER: Doesn't matter? It's most 1035
important!
THE MANAGER: We're only trying it now. Please don't interfere. (*To* PROPERTY MAN): See if we've got a shop window-long and narrowish.
THE STEP-DAUGHTER: And the little table! The little 1040
mahogany table for the pale blue envelope!
PROPERTY MAN: (*To* MANAGER): There's that little gilt one.

THE MANAGER: That'll do fine.

1045 THE FATHER: A mirror.

THE STEP-DAUGHTER: And the screen! We must have a screen. Otherwise how can I manage?

PROPERTY MAN: That's all right, Miss. We've got any amount of them.

1050 THE MANAGER: (to the STEP-DAUGHTER): We want some clothes pegs too, don't we?

THE STEP-DAUGHTER: Yes, several, several!

THE MANAGER: See how many we've got and bring them all.

1055 PROPERTY MAN: All right!

[The PROPERTY MAN *hurries off to obey his orders. While he is putting the things in their places, the* MANAGER *talks to the* PROMPTER *and then with the* CHARACTERS *and the* ACTORS*].*

THE MANAGER (*to* PROMPTER): Take your seat. Look here: this is the outline of the scenes, act by act (*hands him some sheets of paper*). And now I'm going to ask you to do something out of the
1060 ordinary.

PROMPTER: Take it down in shorthand?

THE MANAGER (*pleasantly surprised*): Exactly! Can you do shorthand?

PROMPTER: Yes, a little.

1065 MANAGER: Good! (*Turning to a stage hand*): Go and get some paper from my office, plenty, as much as you can find.

(The stage hand goes off, and soon returns with a handful of paper which he gives to the PROMPTER*).*

THE MANAGER (*To* PROMPTER): You follow the scenes as we play them, and try and get the points
1070 down, at any rate the most important ones. (*Then addressing the* ACTORS): Clear the stage, ladies and gentlemen! Come over here (*pointing to the left*) and listen attentively.

LEADING LADY: But, excuse me, we . . .

1075 THE MANAGER (*guessing her thought*): Don't worry! You won't have to improvise.

LEADING MAN: What have we to do then?

THE MANAGER: Nothing. For the moment you just watch and listen. Everybody will get his part
1080 written out afterwards. At present we're going to try the thing as best we can. They're going to act now.

THE FATHER (*as if fallen from the clouds into the confusion of the stage*): We? What do you mean, if
1085 you please, by a rehearsal?

THE MANAGER: A rehearsal for them (*points to the* ACTORS).

THE FATHER: But since we are the characters . . .

THE MANAGER: All right: "characters" then, if you
1090 insist on calling yourselves such. But here, my

dear sir, the characters don't act. Here the actors do the acting. The characters are there, in the "book" (*pointing towards* PROMPTER'S *box*)—when there is a "book"!

THE FATHER: I won't contradict you; but excuse me, 1095
the actors aren't the characters. They want to be, they pretend to be, don't they? Now if these gentlemen here are fortunate enough to have us alive before them . . .

THE MANAGER: Oh this is grand! You want to come 1100
before the public yourselves then?

THE FATHER: As we are . . .

THE MANAGER: I can assure you it would be a magnificent spectacle!

LEADING MAN: What's the use of us here anyway 1105
then?

THE MANAGER: You're not going to pretend that you can act? It makes me laugh! (*The* ACTORS *laugh*). There, you see, they are laughing at the notion. But, by the way, I must cast the parts. That 1110
won't be difficult. They cast themselves. (*To the* SECOND LADY LEAD): You play the Mother. (*To the* FATHER): We must find her a name.

THE FATHER: Amalia, sir.

THE MANAGER: But that is the real name of your wife. 1115
We don't want to call her by her real name.

THE FATHER: Why ever not, if it is her name? . . . Still, perhaps, if that lady must . . . (*makes a slight motion of the hand to indicate the* SECOND LADY Lead). I see this woman here (*means the* MOTHER) 1120
as Amalia. But do as you like (*gets more and more confused*). I don't know what to say to you. Already, I begin to hear my own words ring false, as if they had another sound . . .

THE MANAGER: Don't you worry about it. It'll be our 1125
job to find the right tones. And as for her name, if you want her Amalia, Amalia it shall be; and if you don't like it, we'll find another! For the moment though, we'll call the characters in this way: (*to* JUVENILE LEAD) You are the 1130
Son; (*to the* LEADING LADY) You naturally are the Step-Daughter . . .

THE STEP-DAUGHTER: What? what? I, that woman there? (*Bursts out laughing*).

THE MANAGER (*angry*): What is there to laugh at? 1135

LEADING LADY (*indignant*): Nobody has ever dared to laugh at me. I insist on being treated with respect; otherwise I go away.

THE STEP-DAUGHTER: No, no, excuse me . . . I am not laughing at you . . . 1140

THE MANAGER (*to* STEP-DAUGHTER): You ought to feel honoured to be played by . . .

LEADING LADY (*at once, contemptuously*): "That woman there" . . .

THE STEP-DAUGHTER: But I wasn't speaking of you, you 1145
know. I was speaking of myself—whom I can't see at all in you! That is all. I don't know . . . but

. . . you . . . aren't in the least like me . . .

THE FATHER: True. Here's the point. Look here, sir,
1150   our temperaments, our souls . . .

THE MANAGER: Temperament, soul, be hanged! Do
you suppose the spirit of the piece is in you?
Nothing of the kind!

THE FATHER: What, haven't we our own tempera-
1155   ments, our own souls?

THE MANAGER: Not at all. Your soul or whatever you
like to call it takes shape here. The actors give
body and form to it, voice and gesture. And
my actors—I may tell you—have given expres-
1160   sion to much more lofty material than this little drama of yours, which may or may not
hold up on the stage. But if it does, the merit
of it, believe me, will be due to my actors.

THE FATHER: I don't dare contradict you, sir; but,
1165   believe me, it is a terrible suffering for us who
are as we are, with these bodies of ours, these
features to see . . .

THE MANAGER (*cutting him short and out of patience*):
Good heavens! The make-up will remedy all
1170   that, man, the make-up . . .

THE FATHER: Maybe. But the voice, the gestures . . .

THE MANAGER: Now, look here! On the stage, you as
yourself, cannot exist. The actor here acts you,
and that's an end to it!

1175 THE FATHER: I understand. And now I think I see why
our author who conceived us as we are, all
alive, didn't want to put us on the stage after
all. I haven't the least desire to offend your
actors. Far from it! But when I think that I am
1180   to be acted by . . . I don't know by whom . . .

LEADING MAN (*on his dignity*): By me, if you've no
objection!

THE FATHER (*humbly, mellifluously*): Honoured, I assure
you, sir. (*Bows*). Still, I must say that try as this
1185   gentleman may, with all his good will and
wonderful art, to absorb me into himself . . .

LEADING MAN: Oh chuck it! "Wonderful art!"
Withdraw that, please!

THE FATHER: The performance he will give, even
1190   doing his best with make-up to look like me . . .

LEADING MAN: It will certainly be a bit difficult! (*The
ACTORS laugh*.)

THE FATHER: Exactly! It will be difficult to act me as I
really am. The effect will be rather—apart from
1195   the make-up—according as to how he suppos-
es I am, as he senses me—if he does sense
me—and not as I inside of myself feel myself
to be. It seems to me then that account should
be taken of this by everyone whose duty it
1200   may become to criticize us . . .

THE MANAGER: Heavens! The man's starting to think
about the critics now! Let them say what they
like. It's up to us to put on the play if we can
(*looking around*). Come on! come on! Is the

stage set? (*To the* ACTORS *and* CHARACTERS):   1205
Stand back—stand back! Let me see, and don't
let's lose any more time! (*To the* STEP-
DAUGHTER): Is it all right as it is now?

THE STEP-DAUGHTER: Well, to tell the truth, I don't
recognize the scene.   1210

THE MANAGER: My dear lady, you can't possibly suppose that we can construct that shop of
Madame Pace piece by piece here? (*To the*
FATHER): You said a white room with flowered
wall paper, didn't you?   1215

THE FATHER: Yes.

THE MANAGER: Well then. We've got the furniture
right more or less. Bring that little table a bit
further forward. (*The stage hands obey the order.
To* PROPERTY MAN): You go and find an enve-   1220
lope, if possible, a pale blue one; and give it to
that gentleman (*indicates* FATHER).

PROPERTY MAN: An ordinary envelope?

MANAGER *and* FATHER: Yes, yes, an ordinary envelope.

PROPERTY MAN: At once, sir (*exit*).   1225

THE MANAGER: Ready, everyone! First scene—the
Young Lady. (*The* LEADING LADY *comes forward*).
No, no, you must wait. I meant her (*indicating
the* STEP-DAUGHTER). You just watch—

THE STEP-DAUGHTER (*adding at once*): How I shall play   1230
it, how I shall live it! . . .

LEADING LADY (*offended*): I shall live it also, you may
be sure, as soon as I begin!

THE MANAGER (*with his hands to his head*): Ladies and
gentlemen, if you please! No more useless dis-   1235
cussions! Scene I: the young lady with
Madame Pace: Oh! (*looks around as if lost*). And
this Madame Pace, where is she?

THE FATHER: She isn't with us, sir.

THE MANAGER: Then what the devil's to be done!   1240

THE FATHER: But she is alive too.

THE MANAGER: Yes, but where is she?

THE FATHER: One minute. Let me speak! (*turning to
the* ACTRESSES). If these ladies would be so
good as to give me their hats for a moment . . .   1245

THE ACTRESSES (*half surprised, half laughing, in chorus*):
What?
Why?
Our hats?
What does he say?   1250

THE MANAGER: What are you going to do with the
ladies' hats? (*The* ACTORS *laugh*.)

THE FATHER: Oh nothing. I just want to put them on
these pegs for a moment. And one of the ladies
will be so kind as to take off her mantle . . .   1255

THE ACTORS: Oh, what d'you think of that?
Only the mantle?
He must be mad.

SOME ACTRESSES: But why?
Mantles as well?   1260

THE FATHER: To hang them up here for a moment.

Please be so kind, will you?

THE ACTRESSES (*taking off their hats, one or two also their cloaks, and going to hang them on the racks*): After
1265   all, why not?

There you are!

This is really funny.

We've got to put them on show.

THE FATHER: Exactly; just like that, on show.

1270 THE MANAGER: May we know why?

THE FATHER: I'll tell you. Who knows if, by arranging
the stage for her, she does not come here herself, attracted by the very articles of her trade?
(*Inviting the* ACTORS *to look towards the exit at*
1275   *back of stage*): Look! Look!

[*The door at the back of stage opens and* MADAME
PACE *enters and takes a few steps forward. She is a
fat, oldish woman with puffy oxygenated hair. She is
rouged and powdered, dressed with a comical elegance in black silk. Round her waist is a long silver
chain from which hangs a pair of scissors. The* STEP-
DAUGHTER *runs over to her at once amid the stupor of
the actors*].

THE STEP-DAUGHTER (*turning towards her*): There she
is! There she is!

THE FATHER (*radiant*): It's she! I said so, didn't I?
There she is!

1280 THE MANAGER (*conquering his surprise, and then becoming indignant*): What sort of a trick is this?

LEADING MAN (*almost at the same time*): What's going
to happen next?

JUVENILE LEAD: Where does *she* come from?

1285 L'INGENUE: They've been holding her in reserve, I
guess.

LEADING LADY: A vulgar trick!

THE FATHER (*dominating the protests*): Excuse me, all of
you! Why are you so anxious to destroy in the
1290   name of a vulgar, commonplace sense of truth,
this reality which comes to birth attracted and
formed by the magic of the stage itself, which
has indeed more right to live here than you,
since it is much truer than you—if you don't
1295   mind my saying so? Which is the actress
among you who is to play Madame Pace?
Well, here is Madame Pace herself. And, you
will allow, I fancy, that the actress who acts her
will be less true than this woman here, who is
1300   herself in person. You see my daughter recognized her and went over to her at once. Now
you're going to witness the scene!

[*But the scene between the* STEP-DAUGHTER *and*
MADAME PACE *has already begun despite the protest of
the actors and the reply of* THE FATHER. *It has begun
quietly, naturally, in a manner impossible for the
stage. So when the actors, called to attention by* THE

FATHER, *turn round and see* MADAME PACE, *who has
placed one hand under the* THE STEP-DAUGHTER'S *chin
to raise her head, they observe her at first with great
attention, but hearing her speak in an unintelligible
manner their interest begins to wane*].

THE MANAGER: Well? well?

LEADING MAN: What does she say?

LEADING LADY: One can't hear a word.   1305

JUVENILE LEAD: Louder! Louder please!

THE STEP-DAUGHTER (*leaving* MADAME PACE, *who
smiles a Sphinx-like smile, and advancing towards
the actors*): Louder? Louder? What are you talking about? These aren't matters which can be 1310
shouted at the top of one's voice. If I have spoken them out loud, it was to shame him and
have my revenge (*indicates* FATHER). But for
Madame it's quite a different matter.

THE MANAGER: Indeed? indeed? But here, you know, 1315
people have got to make themselves heard, my
dear. Even we who are on the stage can't hear
you. What will it be when the public's in the
theatre? And anyway, you can very well speak
up now among yourselves, since we shan't be 1320
present to listen you as we are now. You've got
to pretend to be alone in a room at the back of
a shop where no one can hear you.

(THE STEP-DAUGHTER *coquettishly and with a touch of
malice makes a sign of disagreement two or three
times with her finger*).

THE MANAGER: What do you mean by no?

THE STEP-DAUGHTER (*sotto voce, mysteriously*): There's 1325
someone who will hear us if she (*indicating*
MADAME PACE) speaks out loud.

THE MANAGER (*in consternation*): What? Have you got
someone else to spring on us now? (*The*
ACTORS *burst out laughing*).   1330

THE FATHER: No, no sir. She is alluding to me. I've
got to be here—there behind that door, in waiting; and Madame Pace knows it. In fact, if you
will allow me, I'll go there at once, so I can be
quite ready. (*Moves away*).   1335

THE MANAGER (*stopping him*): No! Wait! wait! We
must observe the conventions of the theatre.
Before you are ready . . .

THE STEP-DAUGHTER (*interrupting him*): No, get on
with it at once! I'm just dying, I tell you, to act 1340
this scene. If he's ready, I'm more than ready.

THE MANAGER (*shouting*): But, my dear young lady,
first of all, we must have the scene between
you and this lady . . . (*indicates* MADAME PACE).
Do you understand? . . .   1345

THE STEP-DAUGHTER: Good Heavens! She's been
telling me what you know already; that
mamma's work is badly done again, that the

1350   material's ruined; and that if I want her to continue to help us in our misery I must be patient . . .

MADAME PACE (*coming forward with an air of great importance*): Yes indeed, sir, I no wanta take advantage of her, I no wanta be hard . . .

1355   [*Note.* MADAME PACE *is supposed to talk in a jargon half Italian, half Spanish*].

THE MANAGER (*alarmed*): What? What? She talks like that? (*The actors burst out laughing again*).

THE STEP-DAUGHTER (*also laughing*): Yes yes, that's the

1360   way she talks, half English, half Italian! Most comical it is!

MADAME PACE: Itta seem not verra polite gentlemen laugha atta me eef I trya best speaka English.

THE MANAGER: *Diamine!* Of course! Of course! Let

1365   her talk like that! Just what we want. Talk just like that, Madam, if you please! The effect will be certain. Exactly what was wanted to put a little comic relief into the crudity of the situation. Of course she talks like that! Magnificent!

1370   THE STEP-DAUGHTER: Magnificent? Certainly! When certain suggestions are made to one in language of that kind, the effect is certain, since it seems almost a joke. One feels inclined to laugh when one hears her talk about an "old

1375   signore" "who wanta talka nicely with you." Nice old signore, eh, Madame?

MADAME PACE: Not so old my dear, not so old! And even if you no lika him, he won't make any scandal!

1380   THE MOTHER (*jumping up amid the amazement and consternation of the* ACTORS *who had not been noticing her. They move to restrain her*): You old devil! You murderess!

THE STEP-DAUGHTER (*running over to calm her*

1385   MOTHER): Calm yourself, mother, calm yourself! Please don't . . .

THE FATHER (*going to her also at the same time*): Calm yourself! Don't get excited! Sit down now!

THE MOTHER: Well, then, take that woman away out

1390   of my sight!

THE STEP-DAUGHTER (*to* MANAGER): It is impossible for my mother remain here.

THE FATHER (*to* MANAGER): They can't be here together. And for this reason, you see: that woman

1395   there was not with us when we came . . . If they are on together, the whole thing is given away inevitably, as you see.

THE MANAGER: It doesn't matter. This is only a first rough sketch—just to get an idea of the vari-

1400   ous points of the scene, even confusedly . . . (*Turning to the* MOTHER *and leading her to her chair*): Come along, my dear lady, sit down now, and let's get on with the scene . . .

[*Meanwhile, the* STEP-DAUGHTER, *coming forward again,*

1405   *turns to* MADAME PACE].

THE STEP-DAUGHTER: Come on, Madame, come on!

MADAME PACE (*offended*): No, no, *grazie*. I not do anything witha your mother present.

THE STEP-DAUGHTER: Nonsense! Introduce this "old

1410   signore" who wants to talk nicely to me (*addressing the company imperiously*). We've got to do this scene one way or another, haven't we? Come on! (*to* MADAME PACE): You can go!

MADAME PACE: Ah yes! I go'way! I go'way!

1415   Certainly! (*Exits furious*).

THE STEP-DAUGHTER (*to the* FATHER): Now you make your entry. No, you needn't go over here. Come here. Let's suppose you've already come in. Like that, yes! I'm here with bowed head,

1420   modest like. Come on! Out with your voice! Say "Good morning, Miss" in that peculiar tone, that special tone . . .

THE MANAGER: Excuse me, but are you the Manager, or am I? (*To the* FATHER, *who looks undecided and*

1425   *perplexed*): Get on with it, man! Go down there to the back of the stage. You needn't go off. Then come right forward here.

[THE FATHER *does as he is told, looking troubled and perplexed at first. But as soon as he begins to move, the reality of the action affects him, and he begins to smile and to be more natural. The* ACTORS *watch intently*].

THE MANAGER (*sotto voce, quickly to the* PROMPTER *in his box*): Ready! ready? Get ready to write now.

THE FATHER (*coming forward and speaking in a different*

1430   *tone*): Good afternoon, Miss!

THE STEP-DAUGHTER (*head bowed down slightly, with restrained disgust*): Good afternoon!

THE FATHER (*looks under her hat which partly covers her face. Perceiving she is very young, he makes an*

1435   *exclamation, partly of surprise, partly of fear lest he compromise himself in a risky adventure*): Ah . . . but . . . ah . . . I say . . . this is not the first time that you have come here, is it?

THE STEP-DAUGHTER (*modestly*): No, sir.

1440

THE FATHER: You've been here before, eh? (*Then seeing her nod agreement*): More than once? (*Waits for her to answer, looks under her hat, smiles, and then says*): Well then, there's no need to be so shy, is there? May I take off your hat?

1445

THE STEP-DAUGHTER (*anticipating him and with veiled disgust*): No sir . . . I'll do it myself. (*Takes it off quickly*).

[THE MOTHER, *who watches the progress of the scene with* THE SON *and the other two children who cling to her, is on thorns; and follows with varying expressions of sorrow, indignation, anxiety, and horror the words and actions of the other two. From time to time she hides her face in her hands and sobs*].

THE MOTHER: Oh, my God, my God!

1450 THE FATHER: (*playing his part with a touch of gallantry*). Give it to me! I'll put it down (*takes hat from her hands*). But a dear little head like yours ought to have a smarter hat. Come and help me choose one from the stock, won't you?

1455 L'INGENUE (*interrupting*): I say . . . those are our hats you know.

THE MANAGER (*furious*): Silence! silence! Don't try and be funny, if you please . . . We're playing the scene now I'd have you notice. (*To the* STEP-

1460 DAUGHTER). Begin again, please!

THE STEP-DAUGHTER (*continuing*): No thank you, sir.

THE FATHER: Oh, come now. Don't talk like that. You must take it. I shall be upset if you don't. There are some lovely little hats here; and

1465 then—Madame will be pleased. She expects it, anyway, you know.

THE STEP-DAUGHTER: No, no! I couldn't wear it!

THE FATHER: Oh, you're thinking about what they'd say at home if they saw you come in with a

1470 new hat? My dear girl, there's always a way round these little matters, you know.

THE STEP-DAUGHTER (*all keyed up*): No, it's not that. I couldn't wear it because I am . . . as you see . . . you might have noticed . . . (*showing her black

1475 dress*).

THE FATHER: . . . in mourning! Of course: I beg your pardon: I'm frightfully sorry . . .

THE STEP-DAUGHTER (*forcing herself to conquer her indignation and nausea*): Stop! Stop! It's I who

1480 must thank you. There's no need for you to feel mortified or specially sorry. Don't think any more of what I've said. (*Tries to smile*). I must forget that I am dressed so . . .

THE MANAGER (*interrupting and turning to the

1485 PROMPTER): Stop a minute! Stop! Don't write that down. Cut out that last bit. (*Then to the* FATHER *and* STEP-DAUGHTER). Fine! it's going fine! (*To the* FATHER *only*). And now you can go on as we arranged. (*To the* ACTORS). Pretty good

1490 that scene, where he offers her the hat, eh?

THE STEP-DAUGHTER: The best's coming now. Why can't we go on?

THE MANAGER: Have a little patience! (*To the* ACTORS): Of course, it must be treated rather lightly.

1495 LEADING MAN: Still, with a bit of go in it!

LEADING LADY: Of course! It's easy enough! (*To* LEADING MAN): Shall you and I try it now?

LEADING MAN: Why, yes! I'll prepare my entrance. (*Exit in order to make his entrance*).

1500 THE MANAGER (*to* LEADING LADY): See here! The scene between you and Madame Pace is finished. I'll have it written out properly after. You remain here . . . oh, where are you going?

LEADING LADY: One minute. I want to put my hat on

1505 again (*goes over to hat-rack and puts her hat on her head*).

THE MANAGER: Good! You stay here with your head bowed down a bit.

THE STEP-DAUGHTER: But she isn't dressed in black.

LEADING LADY: But I shall be, and much more effec- 1510 tively than you.

THE MANAGER (*to* STEP-DAUGHTER): Be quiet please, and watch! You'll be able to learn something. (*Clapping his hands*) Come on! come on! Entrance, please! 1515

[*The door at rear of stage opens, and the* LEADING MAN *enters with the lively manner of an old gallant. The rendering of the scene by the actors from the very first words is seen to be quite a different thing, though it has not in any way the air of a parody. Naturally, the* STEP-DAUGHTER *and the* FATHER, *not being able to recognize themselves in the* LEADING LADY *and the* LEADING MAN, *who deliver their words in different tones and with a different psychology, express, sometimes with smiles, sometimes with gestures, the impression they receive*].

LEADING MAN: Good afternoon, Miss . . .

THE FATHER (*at once unable to contain himself*): No! no!

(THE STEP-DAUGHTER *noticing the way the* LEADING MAN *enters, bursts out laughingf*).

THE MANAGER (*furious*): Silence! And you please just stop that laughing. If we go on like this, we shall never finish. 1520

THE STEP-DAUGHTER: Forgive me, sir, but it's natural enough. This lady (*indicating* LEADING LADY) stands there still; but if she is supposed to be me, I can assure you that if I heard anyone say "Good afternoon" in that manner and in that 1525 tone, I should burst out laughing as I did.

THE FATHER: Yes, yes, the manner, the tone . . .

THE MANAGER: Nonsense! Rubbish! Stand aside and let me see the action.

LEADING MAN: If I've got to represent an old fellow 1530 who's coming into a house of an equivocal character . . .

THE MANAGER: Don't listen to them, for Heaven's sake! Do it again! It goes fine. (*Waiting for the* ACTORS *to begin again*): Well? 1535

LEADING MAN: Good afternoon, Miss.

LEADING LADY: Good afternoon.

LEADING MAN (*imitating the gesture of the* FATHER *when he looked under the hat, and then expressing quite clearly first satisfaction and then fear*): Ah, but . . . 1540 I say . . . this is not the first time that you have come here, is it?

THE MANAGER: Good, but not quite so heavily. Like this (*acts himself*): "This isn't the first time that you have come here" . . . (*To* LEADING LADY) 1545

And you say: "No, sir."

LEADING LADY: No, sir.

LEADING MAN: You've been here before, more than once.

1550 THE MANAGER: No, no stop! Let her nod "yes" first. "You've been here before, eh?" (*The* LEADING LADY *lifts up her head slightly and closes her eyes as though in disgust. Then she inclines her head twice*).

1555 THE STEP-DAUGHTER (*unable to contain herself*): Oh my God! (*Puts a hand to her mouth to prevent herself from laughing*).

THE MANAGER (*turning round*): What's the matter?

THE STEP-DAUGHTER: Nothing, nothing!

1560 THE MANAGER (*to Leading Man*): Go on!

LEADING MAN: You've been here before, eh? Well then, there's no need to be so shy, is there? May I take off your hat?

[THE LEADING MAN *says this last speech in such a tone and with such gestures that the* STEP-DAUGHTER, *though she has her hand to her mouth, cannot keep from laughing*].

LEADING LADY (*indignant*): I'm not going to stop her
1565 to be made a fool of by that woman there.

LEADING MAN: Neither am I! I'm through with it!

THE MANAGER (*shouting to* STEP-DAUGHTER): Silence! for once and all, I tell you!

THE STEP-DAUGHTER: Forgive me! forgive me!

1570 THE MANAGER: You haven't any manners: that's what it is! You go too far.

THE FATHER (*endeavoring to intervene*): Yes, it's true, but excuse her . . .

THE MANAGER: Excuse what? It's absolutely disgust-
1575 ing.

THE FATHER: Yes, sir, but believe me, it has such a strange effect when . . .

THE MANAGER: Strange? Why strange? Where is it strange?

1580 THE FATHER: No, sir; I admire your actors—this gentleman here, this lady; but they are certainly not us!

THE MANAGER: I should hope not. Evidently they cannot be you, if they are actors.

1585 THE FATHER: Just so: actors! Both of them act our parts exceedingly well. But, believe me, it produces quite a different effect on us. They want to be us, but they aren't, all the same.

THE MANAGER: What is it then anyway?

1590 THE FATHER: Something that is . . . that is theirs—and no longer ours . . .

THE MANAGER: But naturally, inevitably. I've told you so already.

THE FATHER: Yes, I understand . . . I understand . . .

1595 THE MANAGER: Well then, let's have no more of it! (*Turning to the* ACTORS): We'll have the

rehearsals by ourselves, afterwards, in the ordinary way. I never could stand rehearsing with the author present. He's never satisfied! (*Turning to* FATHER *and* STEP-DAUGHTER): Come 1600 on! Let's get on with it again; and try and see if you can't keep from laughing.

THE STEP-DAUGHTER: Oh, I shan't laugh any more. There's a nice little bit coming for me now: you'll see. 1605

THE MANAGER: Well then: when she says "Don't think any more of what I've said. I must forget, etc.," you (*addressing the* FATHER) come in sharp with "I understand, I understand"; and then you ask her . . . 1610

THE STEP-DAUGHTER (*interrupting*): What?

THE MANAGER: Why she is in mourning.

THE STEP-DAUGHTER: Not at all! See here: when I told him that it was useless for me to be thinking about my wearing mourning, do you know 1615 how he answered me? "Ah well," he said, "then let's take off this little frock."

THE MANAGER: Great! Just what we want, to make a riot in the theatre!

THE STEP-DAUGHTER: But it's the truth! 1620

THE MANAGER: What does that matter? Acting is our business here. Truth up to a certain point, but no further.

THE STEP-DAUGHTER: What do you want to do then?

THE MANAGER: You'll see, you'll see! Leave it to me. 1625

THE STEP-DAUGHTER: No sir! What you want to do is to piece together a little romantic sentimental scene out of my disgust, out of all the reasons, each more cruel and viler than the other, why I am what I am. He is to ask me why I'm in 1630 mourning; and I'm to answer with tears in my eyes, that it is just two months since papa died. No sir, no! He's got to say to me; as he did say: "Well, let's take off this little dress at once." And I; with my two months' mourning 1635 in my heart, went there behind that screen, and with these fingers tingling with shame . . .

THE MANAGER (*running his hands through his hair*): For Heaven's sake! What are you saying?

THE STEP-DAUGHTER (*crying out excitedly*): The truth! 1640 The truth!

THE MANAGER: It may be. I don't deny it, and I can understand all your horror; but you must surely see that you can't have this kind of thing on the stage. It won't go. 1645

THE STEP-DAUGHTER: Not possible, eh? Very well! I'm much obliged to you—but I'm off!

THE MANAGER: Now be reasonable! Don't lose your temper!

THE STEP-DAUGHTER: I won't stop here! I won't! I can 1650 see you've fixed it all up with him in your office. All this talk about what is possible for the stage . . . I understand! He wants to get at

his complicated "cerebral drama," to have his
famous remorses and torments acted; but I
want to act my part, *my part!*

THE MANAGER (*annoyed, shaking his shoulders*): Ah!
Just *your* part! But, if you will pardon me,
there are other parts than yours: His (*indicating
the* FATHER) and hers (*indicating the* MOTHER)!
On the stage you can't have a character becoming too prominent and overshadowing all the
others. The thing is to pack them all into a neat
little framework and then act what is actable. I
am aware of the fact that everyone has his own
interior life which he wants very much to put
forward. But the difficulty lies in this fact: to
set out just so much as is necessary for the
stage, taking the other characters into consideration, and at the same time hint at the unrevealed interior life of each. I am willing to
admit, my dear young lady, that from your
point of view it would be a fine idea if each
character could tell the public all his troubles
in a nice monologue or a regular one hour lecture (*good humoredly*). You must restrain yourself, my dear, and in your own interest, too;
because this fury of yours, this exaggerated
disgust you show, may make a bad impression, you know. After you have confessed to
me that there were others before him at
Madame Pace's and more than once . . .

THE STEP-DAUGHTER (*bowing her head, impressed*): It's
true. But remember those others mean him for
me all the same.

THE MANAGER (*not understanding*): What? The others?
What do you mean?

THE STEP-DAUGHTER: For one who has gone wrong,
sir, he who was responsible for the first fault is
responsible for all that follow. He is responsible for my faults, was, even before I was born.
Look at him, and see if it isn't true!

THE MANAGER: Well, well! and does the weight of so
much responsibility seem nothing to you?
Give him a chance to act it, to get it over!

THE STEP-DAUGHTER: How? How can he act all his
"noble remorses" all his "moral torments," if
you want to spare him the horror of being discovered one day—after he had asked her what
he did ask her—in the arms of her, that already
fallen woman, that child, sir, that child he used
to watch come out of school? (*She is moved*).

[THE MOTHER *at this point is overcome with emotion,
and breaks out into a fit of crying. All are touched. A
long pause*].

THE STEP-DAUGHTER (*as soon as the* MOTHER *becomes a
little quieter, adds resolutely and gravely*): At present, we are unknown to the public.

Tomorrow, you will act us as you wish, treating us in your own manner. But do you really
want to see drama, do you want to see it flash
out as it really did?

THE MANAGER: Of course! That's just what I do want,
so I can use as much of it as is possible.

THE STEP-DAUGHTER: Well then, ask that Mother there
to leave us.

THE MOTHER (*changing her low plaint into a sharp cry*):
No! No! Don't permit it, sir, don't permit it!

THE MANAGER: But it's only to try it.

THE MOTHER: I can't bear it. I can't.

THE MANAGER: But since it has happened already . . .
I don't understand!

THE MOTHER: It's taking place now. It happens all the
time. My torment isn't a pretended one. I live
and feel every minute of my torture. Those
two children there—have you heard them
speak? They can't speak any more. They cling
to me to keep my torment actual and vivid for
me. But for themselves, they do not exist, they
aren't any more. And she (*indicating* STEP-
DAUGHTER) has run away, she has left me, and
is lost. If I now see her here before me, it is
only to renew for me the tortures I have suffered for her too.

THE FATHER: The eternal moment! She (*indicating the*
STEP-DAUGHTER) is here to catch me, fix me,
and hold me eternally in the stocks for that
one fleeting and shameful moment of my life.
She can't give it up! And you sir, cannot either
fairly spare me it.

THE MANAGER: I never said I didn't want to act it. It
will form, as a matter of fact, the nucleus of
the whole first act right up to her surprise
(*indicates the* MOTHER).

THE FATHER: Just so! This is my punishment: the passion in all of us that must culminate in her
final cry.

THE STEP-DAUGHTER: I can hear it still in my ears. It's
driven me mad, that cry!—You can put me on
as you like; it doesn't matter. Fully dressed, if
you like-provided I have at least the arm bare;
because, standing like this (*she goes close to the
FATHER and leans her head on his breast*) with my
hand so, and my arms round his neck, I saw a
vein pulsing in my arm here; and then, as if
that live vein had awakened disgust in me, I
closed my eyes like this, and let my head sink
on his breast. (*Turning to the* MOTHER): Cry out
mother! Cry out! (*Buries head in* FATHER's *breast,
and with her shoulders raised as if to prevent her
hearing the cry, adds in tones of intense emotion*):
Cry out as you did then!

THE MOTHER (*coming forward to separate them*): No!
My daughter, my daughter! (*And after having
pulled her away from him*): You brute! you brute!

She is my daughter! Don't you see she's my
daughter?

1765 THE MANAGER (*walking backwards towards footlights*):
Fine! fine! Damned good! And then, of course-
curtain!

THE FATHER (*going towards him excitedly*): Yes, of
course, because that's the way it really hap-
1770   pened.

THE MANAGER (*convinced and pleased*): Oh, yes, no
doubt about it. Curtain here, curtain!

[*At the reiterated cry of* THE MANAGER, THE MACHINIST
lets the curtain down, leaving THE MANAGER *and* THE
FATHER *in front of it before the footlights*].

THE MANAGER: The darned idiot! I said "curtain" to
show the act should end there, and he goes
1775   and lets it down in earnest (*to the* FATHER, *while
he pulls the curtain back to go on to the stage
again*): Yes, yes, it's all right. Effect certain!
That's the right ending. I'll guarantee the first
act at any rate.

ACT III

*When the curtain goes up again, it is seen that the
stage hands have shifted the bit of scenery used in the
last part, and have rigged up instead at the back of
the stage a drop, with some trees, and one or two
wings. A portion of a fountain basin is visible. The
MOTHER is sitting on the right with the two children by
her side. The SON is on the same side, but away from
the others. He seems bored, angry, and full of shame.
The FATHER and The STEP-DAUGHTER are also seated
towards the right front. On the other side (left) are the
actors, much in the positions they occupied before the
curtain was lowered. Only the MANAGER is standing up
in the middle of the stage, with his hand closed over
his mouth in the act of meditating.*

1780 THE MANAGER (*shaking his shoulders after a brief pause*):
Ah yes: the second act! Leave it to me, leave it
all to me as we arranged, and you'll see! It'll
go fine!

THE STEP-DAUGHTER: Our entry into his house (*indicates
1785   FATHER) in spite of him (*indicates the* SON) . . .

THE MANAGER (*out of patience*): Leave it to me, I tell
you!

THE STEP-DAUGHTER: Do let it be clear, at any rate,
that it is in spite of my wishes.

1790 THE MOTHER (*from her corner, shaking her head*): For all
the good that's come of it . . .

THE STEP-DAUGHTER (*turning towards her quickly*): It
doesn't matter. The more harm done us, the
more remorse for him.

1795 THE MANAGER (*impatiently*): I understand! Good

Heavens! I understand! I'm taking it into
account.

THE MOTHER (*supplicatingly*): I beg you, sir, to let it
appear quite plain that for conscience sake I
did try in every way . . .   1800

THE STEP-DAUGHTER (*interrupting indignantly and continuing for the* MOTHER): . . . to pacify me, to
dissuade me from spiting him. (*To* MANAGER):
Do as she wants: satisfy her, because it is true!
I enjoy it immensely. Anyhow, as you can see,   1805
the meeker she is, the more she tries to get at
his heart, the more distant and aloof does he
become.

THE MANAGER: Are we going to begin this second act
or not?   1810

THE STEP-DAUGHTER: I'm not going to talk any more
now. But I must tell you this: you can't have
the whole action take place in the garden, as
you suggest. It isn't possible!

THE MANAGER: Why not?   1815

THE STEP-DAUGHTER: Because he (*indicates the* SON
again) is always shut up alone in his room.
And then there's all the part of that poor
dazed-looking boy there which takes place
indoors.   1820

THE MANAGER: Maybe! On the other hand, you will
understand—we can't change scenes three or
four times in one act.

THE LEADING MAN: They used to once.

THE MANAGER: Yes, when the public was up to the   1825
level of that child there.

THE LEADING LADY:It makes the illusion easier.

THE FATHER (*irritated*): The illusion! For Heaven's
sake, don't say illusion. Please don't use that
word, which is particularly painful for us.   1830

THE MANAGER (*astounded*): And why, if you please?

THE FATHER: It's painful, cruel, really cruel; and you
ought to understand that.

THE MANAGER: But why? What ought we to say
then? The illusion, I tell you, sir, which we've   1835
got to create for the audience . . .

THE LEADING MAN: With our acting.

THE MANAGER: The illusion of a reality.

THE FATHER: I understand; but you, perhaps, do not
understand us. Forgive me! You see . . . here   1840
for you and your actors, the thing is only—and
rightly so . . . a kind of game . . .

THE LEADING LADY (*interrupting indignantly*): A game!
We're not children here, if you please! We are
serious actors.   1845

THE FATHER: I don't deny it. What I mean is the
game, or play, of your art, which has to give,
as the gentleman, says a perfect illusion of
reality.

THE MANAGER: Precisely—!   1850

THE FATHER: Now, if you consider the fact that we
(*indicates himself and the other five* CHARACTERS),

as we are, have no other reality outside of this illusion . . .

1855 THE MANAGER (*astonished, looking at his actors, who are also amazed*): And what does that mean?

THE FATHER (*after watching them for a moment with a wan smile*): As I say, sir, that which is a game of art for you is our sole reality. (*Brief pause. He
1860 goes a step or two nearer the* MANAGER *and adds*): But not only for us, you know, by the way. Just you think it over well. (*Looks him in the eyes*). Can you tell me who you are?

THE MANAGER (*perplexed, half smiling*): What? Who
1865 am I? I am myself.

THE FATHER: And if I were to tell you that that isn't true, because you are I . . . ?

THE MANAGER: I should say you were mad—! (*The* ACTORS *laugh*).

1870 THE FATHER: You're quite right to laugh: because we are all making believe here (*to* MANAGER). And you can therefore object that it's only for a joke that that gentleman there (*indicates the* LEADING MAN), who naturally is himself, has to be me,
1875 who am on the contrary myself—this thing you see here. You see I've caught you in a trap! (*The* ACTORS *laugh*).

THE MANAGER (*annoyed*): But we've had all this over once before. Do you want to begin again?

1880 THE FATHER: No, no! That wasn't my meaning! In fact, I should like to request you to abandon this game of art (*looking at the* LEADING LADY *as if anticipating her*) which you are accustomed to play here with your actors, and to ask you
1885 seriously once again: who are you?

THE MANAGER (*astonished and irritated, turning to his actors*): If this fellow here hasn't got a nerve! A man who calls himself a character comes and asks me who I am!

1890 THE FATHER (*with dignity, but not offended*): A character, sir, may always ask a man who he is. Because a character has really a life of his own, marked with his especial characteristics; for which reason he is always "somebody." But a
1895 man—I'm not speaking of you now—may very well be "nobody."

THE MANAGER: Yes, but you are asking these questions of me, the boss, the manager! Do you understand?

1900 THE FATHER: But only in order to know if you, as you really are now, see yourself as you once were with all the illusions that were yours then, with all the things both inside and outside of you as they seemed to you—as they were then
1905 indeed for you. Well, sir, if you think of all those illusions that mean nothing to you now, of all those things which don't even *seem* to you to exist any more, while once they *were* for you, don't you feel that—I won't say these

boards—but the very earth under your feet is
1910 sinking away from you when you reflect that in the same way this *you* as you feel it today— all this present reality of yours—is fated to seem a mere illusion to you tomorrow?

THE MANAGER (*without having understood much, but
1915 astonished by the specious argument*): Well, well! And where does all this take us anyway?

THE FATHER: Oh, nowhere! It's only to show you that if we (*indicating the* CHARACTERS) have no other reality beyond the illusion, you too must not
1920 count overmuch on your reality as you feel it today, since, like that of yesterday, it may prove an illusion for you tomorrow.

THE MANAGER (*determining to make fun of him*): Ah, excellent! Then you'll be saying next that you,
1925 with this comedy of yours that you brought here to act, are truer and more real than I am.

THE FATHER (*with the greatest seriousness*): But of course; without doubt!

THE MANAGER: Ah, really?
1930
THE FATHER: Why, I thought you'd understand that from the beginning.

THE MANAGER: More real than I?

THE FATHER: If your reality can change from one day
1935 to another . . .

THE MANAGER: But everyone knows it can change. It is always changing, the same as anyone else's.

THE FATHER (*with a cry*): No, sir, not ours! Look here! That is the very difference! Our reality doesn't
1940 change: it can't change! It can't be other than what it is, because it is already fixed for ever. It's terrible. Ours is an immutable reality which should make you shudder when you approach us if you are really conscious of the
1945 fact that your reality is a mere transitory and fleeting illusion, taking this form today and that tomorrow, according to the conditions, according to your will, your sentiments, which in turn, are controlled by an intellect that
1950 shows them to you today in one manner and tomorrow . . . who knows how? . . . Illusions of reality represented in this fatuous comedy of life that never ends, nor can ever end! Because if tomorrow it were to end . . . then why, all
1955 would be finished.

THE MANAGER: Oh for God's sake, will you *at least* finish with this philosophizing and let us try and shape this comedy which you yourself have brought me here? You argue and philoso-
1960 phize a bit too much, my dear sir. You know you seem to me almost, almost . . . (*Stops and looks him over from head to foot*). Ah, by the way, I think you introduced yourself to me as a— what shall . . . we say—a "character," created
1965 by an author who did not afterward care to make a drama of his own creations.

THE FATHER: It is the simple truth, sir.

THE MANAGER: Nonsense! Cut that out, please! None of us believes it, because it isn't a thing, as you must recognize yourself, which one can believe seriously. If you want to know, it seems to me you are trying to imitate the manner of a certain author whom I heartily detest—I warn you—although I have unfortunately bound myself to put on one of his works. As a matter of fact, I was just starting to rehearse it, when you arrived. (*Turning to the* ACTORS): And this is what we've gained—out of the frying-pain into the fire!

THE FATHER: I don't know to what author you may be alluding, but believe me I feel what I think; and I seem to be philosophizing only for those who do not think what they feel, because they blind themselves with their own sentiment. I know that for many people this self-blinding seems much more "human"; but the contrary is really true. For man never reasons so much and becomes so introspective as when he suffers; since he is anxious to get at the cause of his sufferings, to learn who has produced them, and whether it is just or unjust that he should have to bear them. On the other hand, when he is happy, he takes his happiness as it comes and doesn't analyze it, just as if happiness were his right. The animals suffer without reasoning about their sufferings. But take the case of a man who suffers and begins to reason about it. Oh no! it can't be allowed! Let him suffer like an animal, and then—ah yes, he is "human!"

THE MANAGER: Look here! Look here! You're off again, philosophizing worse than ever.

THE FATHER: Because I suffer, sir! I'm not philosophizing: I'm crying aloud the reason of my sufferings.

THE MANAGER (*makes brusque movement as he is taken with a new idea*): I should like to know if anyone has ever heard of a character who gets right out of his part and perorates and speechifies as you do. Have you ever heard of a case? I haven't.

THE FATHER: You have never met such a case, sir, because authors, as a rule, hide the labour of their creations. When the characters are really alive before their author, the latter does nothing but follow them in their action, in their words, in the situations which they suggest to him; and he has to will them the way they will themselves—for there's trouble if he doesn't. When a character is born, he acquires at once such an independence, even of his own author, that he can be imagined by everybody even in many other situations where the author never dreamed of placing him; and so he acquires for himself a meaning which the author never thought of giving him.

THE MANAGER: Yes, yes, I know this.

THE FATHER: What is there then to marvel at in us? Imagine such a misfortune for characters as I have described to you: to be born of an *author's fantasy*, and be denied life by him; and then answer me if these characters left alive, and yet without life, weren't right in doing what they did, do and are doing now, after they have attempted everything in their power to persuade him to give them their stage life. We've all tried him in turn, I, she (*indicating the* STEP-DAUGHTER) and she (*indicating the* MOTHER).

THE STEP-DAUGHTER: It's true. I too have sought to tempt him, many, many times, when he has been sitting at his writing table, feeling a bit melancholy, at the twilight hour. He would sit in his armchair too lazy to switch on the light, and all the shadows that crept into his room were full of our presence coming to tempt him. (*As if she saw herself still there by the writing table, and was annoyed by the presence of the actors*): Oh, if you would only go away, go away and leave us alone—mother here with that son of hers—I with that Child—that Boy there always alone—and then I with him (*just hints at the* FATHER)—and then I alone, alone . . . in those shadows! (*Makes a sudden movement as if in the vision she has of herself illuminating those shadows she wanted to seize hold of herself*). Ah! my life! my life! Oh, what scenes we proposed to him-and I tempted him more than any of the others!

THE FATHER: Maybe. But perhaps it was your fault that he refused to give us life: because you were too insistent, too troublesome.

THE STEP-DAUGHTER: Nonsense! Didn't he make me so himself? (*Goes close to the* MANAGER *to tell him as if in confidence*). In my opinion he abandoned us in a fit of depression, of disgust for the ordinary theatre as the public knows it and likes it.

THE SON: Exactly what it was, sir; exactly that!

THE FATHER: Not at all! Don't believe it for a minute. Listen to me! You'll be doing quite right to modify, as you suggest, the excesses both of this girl here, who wants to do too much, and of this young man, who won't do anything at all.

THE SON: No, nothing!

THE MANAGER: You too get over the mark occasionally, my dear sir, if I may say so.

THE FATHER: I? When? Where?

THE MANAGER: Always! Continuously! Then there's this insistence of yours in trying to make us

believe you are a character. And then too, you
must really argue and philosophize less, you
know, much less.

2085 THE FATHER: Well, if you want to take away from me
the possibility of representing the torment of
my spirit which never gives me peace, you
will be suppressing me: that's all. Every true
man, sir, who is a little above the level of the
2090 beasts and plants does not live for the sake of
living, without knowing how to live; but he
lives so as to give a meaning and a value of his
own life. For me this is *everything.* I cannot
give up this, just to represent a mere fact as
she (*indicating the* STEP-DAUGHTER) wants. It's
2095 all very well for her, since her "vendetta" lies
in the "fact." I'm not going to do it. It destroys
my *raison d'etre.*

THE MANAGER: Your *raison d'etre!* Oh, we're going
ahead fine! First she starts off, and then you
2100 jump in. At this rate, we'll never finish.

THE FATHER: Now, don't be offended! Have it your
own way—provided, however, that within the
limits of the parts you assign us each one's
sacrifice isn't too great.

2105 THE MANAGER: You've got to understand that you
can't go on arguing at your own pleasure.
Drama is action, sir, action and not confounded philosophy.

THE FATHER: All right. I'll do just as much arguing
2110 and philosophizing as everybody does when
he is considering his own torments.

THE MANAGER: If the drama permits! But for
Heaven's sake, man, let's get along and come
to the scene.

2115 THE STEP-DAUGHTER: It seems to me we've got too
much action with our coming into his house
(*indicating* FATHER). You said, before, you
couldn't change the scene every five minutes.

THE MANAGER: Of course not. What we've got to do
2120 is to combine and group up all the facts in one
simultaneous, close-knit, action. We can't have
it as you want, with your little brother wandering like a ghost from room to room, hiding
behind doors and meditating a project
2125 which—what did you say it did to him?

THE STEP-DAUGHTER: Consumes him, sir, wastes him
away!

THE MANAGER: Well, it may be. And then at the same
time, you want the little girl there to be play-
2130 ing the garden . . . one in the house, and the
other in the garden: isn't that it?

THE STEP-DAUGHTER: Yes, in the sun, in the sun! That
is my only pleasure: to see her happy and careless in the garden after the misery and squalor
2135 of the horrible room where we all all four slept
together. And I had to sleep with he——I, do
you understand?—with my vile contaminated

body next to hers; with her folding me fast in
her loving little arms. In the garden, whenever
she spied me, she would run to take me by the 2140
hand. She didn't care for the big flowers, only
the little ones; and she loved to show me them
and pet me.

THE MANAGER: Well then, we'll have it in the garden.
Everything shall happen in the garden; and 2145
we'll group the other scenes there. (*Calls a stage
hand*). Here, a backcloth with trees and something to do as a fountain basin. (*Turning round
to look at the back of the stage*). Ah, you've fixed
it up. Good! (*To* STEP-DAUGHTER). This is just to 2150
give an idea, of course. The Boy, instead of
hiding behind the doors, will wander about
here in the garden, hiding behind the trees. But
it's going to be rather difficult to find a child to
do that scene with you where she shows you 2155
the flowers. (*Turning to the* YOUTH). Come forward a little, will you please? Let's try it now!
Come along! come along! (*Then seeing him come
shyly forward, full of fear and looking lost*). It's a
nice business, this lad here. What's the matter 2160
with him? We'll have to give him a word or
two to say. (*Goes close to him, puts a hand on his
shoulders, and leads him behind one of the trees*).
Come on! come on! Let me see you a little!
Hide here . . . yes, like that. Try and show your 2165
head just a little as if you were looking for
someone . . . (*Goes back to observe the effect, when
the* BOY *at once goes through the action*).
Excellent! fine! (*Turning to* STEP-DAUGHTER).
Suppose the little girl there were to surprise 2170
him as he looks round, and run over to him, so
we could give him a word or two to say?

THE STEP-DAUGHTER: It's useless to hope he will
speak, as long as that fellow there is here . . .
(*Indicates the* SON). You must send him away 2175
first.

THE SON (*jumping up*): Delighted! delighted! I don't
ask for anything better. (*Begins to move away*).

THE MANAGER (*at once stopping him*): No! No! Where
are you going? Wait a bit? 2180

[*The* MOTHER *gets up alarmed and terrified at the
thought that he is really about to go away.
Instinctively she lifts her arms to prevent him, without,
however, leaving her seat*].

THE SON (*to* MANAGER *who stops him*): I've got nothing to do with this affair. Let me go please! Let
me go!

THE MANAGER: What do you mean by saying you've
got nothing to do with this? 2185

THE STEP-DAUGHTER (*calmly, with irony*): Don't bother
to stop him: he won't go away.

THE FATHER: He has to act the terrible scene in the

garden with his mother.

2190 THE SON (*suddenly resolute and with dignity*): I shall act nothing at all. I've said so from the very beginning (*to the* MANAGER). Let me go!

THE STEP-DAUGHTER (*going over to the* MANAGER): Allow me? (*Puts down the* MANAGER'S *arm*
2195 *which is restraining the* SON). Well, go away then, if you want to! (*The* SON *looks at her with contempt and hatred. She laughs and says*): You see, he can't, he can't go away! He is obliged to stay here, indissolubly bound to the chain. If
2200 I, who fly off when that happens which has to happen, because I can't bear him—if I am still here and support that face and expression of his, you can well imagine that he is unable to move. He has to remain here, has to stop with
2205 that nice father of his, and that mother whose only son he is. (*Turning to the* MOTHER). Come on, mother, come along! (*Turning to* MANAGER *to indicate her*). You see, she was getting up to keep him back. (*To the* MOTHER, *beckoning her*
2210 *with her hand*). Come on! come on! (*Then to* MANAGER). You can imagine how little she wants to show these actors of yours what she really feels; but so eager is she to get near him that . . . There, you see? She is willing to act
2215 her part. (*And in fact, the* MOTHER *approaches him; and as soon as the* STEP-DAUGHTER *has finished speaking, opens her arms to signify that she consents*).

THE SON (*suddenly*): No! no! If I can't go away, then
2220 I'll stop here; but I repeat: I act nothing!

THE FATHER (*to* MANAGER *excitedly*): You can force him, sir.

THE SON: Nobody can force me.

THE FATHER: I can.

2225 THE STEP-DAUGHTER: Wait a minute, wait . . . First of all, the baby has to go to the fountain . . . (*Runs to take the* CHILD *and leads her to the fountain*).

THE MANAGER: Yes, yes of course; that's it. Both at the same time.

[The second LADY LEAD *and the* JUVENILE LEAD *at this point separate themselves from the group of actors. One watches the* MOTHER *attentively; the other moves about studying the movements and manner of the* SON *whom he will have to act].*

2230 THE SON (*to* MANAGER): What do you mean by both at the same time? It isn't right. There was no scene between me and her. (*Indicates the* MOTHER). Ask her how it was!

THE MANAGER: Yes, it's true. I had come into his
2235 room . . .

THE SON: Into my room, do you understand? Nothing to do with the garden.

THE MANAGER: It doesn't matter. Haven't I told you

we've got to group the action?

THE SON (*observing the* JUVENILE LEAD *studying him*): 2240 What do you want?

THE JUVENILE LEAD: Nothing! I was just looking at you.

THE SON (*turning towards the second* LADY LEAD): Ah! she's at it too: to re-act her part (*indicating the* MOTHER)! 2245

THE MANAGER: Exactly! And it seems to me that you ought to be grateful to them for their interest.

THE SON: Yes, but haven't you yet perceived that it isn't possible to live in front of a mirror which not only freezes us with the image of ourselves, but throws our likeness back at us with 2250 a horrible grimace?

THE FATHER: That is true, absolutely true. You must see that.

THE MANAGER (*to second* LADY LEAD *and* JUVENILE 2255 LEAD): He's right! Move away from them!

THE SON: Do as you like. I'm out of this!

THE MANAGER: Be quiet, you, will you? And let me hear your mother! (*To* MOTHER): You were saying you had entered . . . 2260

THE MOTHER: Yes, into his room, because I couldn't stand it any longer. I went to empty my heart to him of all the anguish that tortures me . . . But as soon as he saw me come in . . .

THE SON: Nothing happened! There was no scene. I 2265 went away, that's all! I don't care for scenes!

THE MOTHER: It's true, true. That's how it was.

THE MANAGER: Well now, we've got to do this bit between you and him. It's indispensable.

THE MOTHER: I'm ready . . . when you are ready. If 2270 you could only find a chance for me to tell him what I feel here in my heart.

THE FATHER (*going to* SON *in a great rage*): You'll do this for your mother, for your mother, do you understand? 2275

THE SON (*quite determined*): I do nothing!

THE FATHER (*taking hold of him and shaking him*): For God's sake, do as I tell you! Don't you hear your mother asking you for a favour? Haven't you even got the guts to be a son? 2280

THE SON (*taking hold of the* FATHER): No! No! And for God's sake stop it, or else . . . (*General agitation. The* MOTHER, *frightened, tries to separate them*).

THE MOTHER (*pleading*): Please! please!

THE FATHER (*not leaving hold of the* SON): You've got to 2285 obey, do you hear?

THE SON (*almost crying from rage*): What does it mean, this madness you've got? (*They separate*). Have you no decency, that you insist on showing everyone our shame? I won't do it! I won't! 2290 And I stand for the will of our author in this. He didn't want to put us on the stage, after all!

THE MANAGER: Man alive! You came here . . .

THE SON (*indicating* FATHER): He did! I didn't!

THE MANAGER: Aren't you here now? 2295

THE SON: It was his wish, and he dragged us along with him. He's told you not only the things that did happen, but also things that have never happened at all.

2300 THE MANAGER: Well, tell me then what did happen. You went out of your room without saying a word?

THE SON: Without a word, so as to avoid a scene!

THE MANAGER: And then what did you do?

2305 THE SON: Nothing . . . walking in the garden . . . (*hesitates for a moment with expression of gloom*).

THE MANAGER (*coming closer to him, interested by his extraordinary reserve*): Well, well . . . walking in the garden . . .

2310 THE SON (*exasperated*): Why on earth do you insist? It's horrible! (*The* MOTHER *trembles, sobs, and looks towards the fountain*).

THE MANAGER (*slowly observing the glance and turning towards the* SON *with increasing apprehension*):

2315 The baby?

THE SON: There in the fountain . . .

THE FATHER (*pointing with tender pity to the* MOTHER): She was following him at the moment . . .

THE MANAGER (*to the Son anxiously*): And then you . . .

2320 THE SON: I ran over to her; I was jumping in to drag her out when I saw something that froze my blood . . . the boy there standing stock still, with eyes like a madman's, watching his little drowned sister, in the fountain! (*The* STEP-

2325 DAUGHTER *bends over the fountain to hide the* CHILD. *She sobs*). Then . . . (*A revolver shot rings out behind the trees where the* BOY *is hidden*).

THE MOTHER (*With a cry of terror runs over in that direction together with several of the actors amid*

2330 *general confusion*).

My son! My son! (*Then amid the cries and exclamations one hears her voice*): Help! Help!

THE MANAGER (*pushing the actors aside while they life up the* BOY *and carry him off*): Is he really

2335 wounded?

SOME ACTORS: He's dead! dead!

OTHER ACTORS: No, no, it's only make believe, it's only pretence!

THE FATHER (*with a terrible cry*): Pretence? Reality, sir,

2340 reality!

THE MANAGER: Pretence? Reality? To hell with it all! Never in my life has such a thing happened to me. I've lost a whole day over these people, a whole day!

Curtain.

BERTOLT BRECHT (1898–1956)

Born into a wealthy family in Augsburg, Germany, Bertolt Brecht began studying the natural sciences at Munich University in 1917, but he was already working as a drama critic, and he soon began to write plays himself. His earliest play, *Baal* (1917), met with some success, but the following year he was drafted into the army and spent the duration of the war working in a military hospital. After the war he moved to Berlin, where he became associated with Erwin Piscator and Max Reinhardt, two of Germany's most influential theatrical innovators. Brecht owed many of his later ideas about theater to the influence of these men, especially Piscator. By the early 1930s Brecht had achieved a reputation for his satirical plays—*Drums in the Night* (1922), *In the Jungle of Cities* (1921), *Man is Man* (1927)—and for the musicals he wrote with Kurt Weill—*The Threepenny Opera* (1928) and *The Rise and Fall of the Town of Mahagonny* (1929).

It was at this time, during the years of disenchantment between the wars, that Brecht became a serious student of Marxism and developed radical ideas about the role of theater in society. He despised realism, convinced that while it appeared to be an objective and detached view of social issues, in fact it was an ideologically charged and reactionary mode, presenting a view of the world uncritically determined by history and evolution and, worst of all, incapable of change. Brecht adapted the Marxist concept of alienation to the theater, adopting every means he could to discourage empathetic identification. His plays cut across the grain of realism and are designed to convince the audience that realistic theater embodies a political vision and ideological view of the world and that it is produced in the interest of profit. In contrast to the conventions and devices of realism, Brecht's theater worked to alienate or estrange the audience from the realities of ordinary life, which they had come to accept as natural and inevitable. Brecht called his new concept epic theater; he wanted to expose the process by which theatrical illusion is produced in the work of the actors and in the machinery of the stage and setting. He wanted his audience to recognize that realism in the theater, like the social reality outside of the theater, is created and changed by everyone involved in its production. Brecht's name for the deliberate estrangement of the audience is *Verfremdungseffekt* (usually translated into English as "alienation effect" or A-effect).

Brecht wrote episodic plays and produced them in ways that made specific demands on audiences. He refused to interpret the action in his plays, instead requiring the audience to come to their own understanding of how events are connected and what they might mean. Generally, Brecht preferred a bare stage and exposed machinery and lighting in his productions to discourage audiences from succumbing to the illusion, the mood, and the atmosphere of the theater. Brecht urged his actors not to empathize with the characters they played, but rather to view the characters from several perspectives. He wanted his plays to develop critical sophistication in his audiences which might carry over into their social lives.

During the leftist purges of 1933 Brecht was forced to flee Germany, and he spent most of the rest of his life in exile in Sweden, Finland, and California, where he worked as a screenwriter. He produced some of his most important work during this period: *The Life of Galileo* (1938), *The Good Woman of Sezuan* (1939), *Mother Courage and Her Children* (1939), *The Caucasian Chalk Circle* (1944). He also wrote his most important theoretical essays then. His ideas and his plays of these years owed much to the work of the women in his life, particularly his actress wife and theoretical collaborator, Helene Weigel. In 1947 he was summoned before the House Un-American Activities Committee as a suspected communist. Although he was not officially charged, he left the United States and settled in East Berlin, where he established the Berliner Ensemble theater company. In the Eastern Bloc countries of this period, however, his antirealism was regarded with suspicion by communist authorities, in part because it conflicted with the social realism officially promoted by the party.

Brecht changed the course of European theater and influenced theatrical practices around the world. He was a playwright who produced a remarkable body of plays, a theoretician who inspired sweeping innovation and change in the way we conceive of theater, and director of the Berliner Ensemble, considered by many to be the most important theater company in postwar Europe.

Mother Courage and Her Children: A Chronicle of the Thirty Years' War

Mother Courage and Her Children employs virtually all of the techniques of Brecht's epic theater, posing questions rather than giving answers. Is Mother Courage a heroine or a villain? Is the play concerned with war or with business? If war is business, is business war? Is Mother Courage's survival to be applauded or deplored? There are no easy answers to any of these questions—in fact, there may not be "right" answers at all. *Mother Courage* centers on contradictions and dramatic situations in which Brecht encourages his audience to question assumptions about social relationships, about the connections between business, war, morality, personal responsibility, and history itself.

Brecht certainly believed that war, like many other social evils, was an extension of the business mentality of capitalistic societies. The means of production in capitalism, he felt, required that money substitute for more fundamentally satisfying human interrelations. Mother Courage's wagon is the central stage property in the play: it serves as her family home; it serves as her place of business; and it serves the interests of the army. It reflects Brecht's notion of the economic and social base of Mother Courage's society as well as her own fortunes.

In a realistic treatment of this subject Mother Courage might be portrayed as a heroine, but Brecht's play, as epic theater, takes a more complicated perspective. In keeping with his ideas of a socially responsible theater, Brecht questions the idea of heroism and even the fact of Mother Courage's survival. He does so by calling attention to the economic and social forces that victimize his characters. Mother Courage is forced to develop appropriate values and strategies of survival that finally render our ordinary notions about heroism, and even about survival, repellent. Brecht suggests the inevitability of victimization under capitalism through the lack of "progress" or development in the play's action. Mother Courage enters singing a song, and in this first scene her wagon is loaded with goods, pulled by her sons. She sings the same song at the end of the play, but now she pulls an empty wagon by herself as she follows the army into history.

Mother Courage and Her Children

BERTOLT BRECHT

TRANSLATED BY RALPH MANHEIM

CHARACTERS

MOTHER COURAGE	A CLERK
KATTRIN, her mute daughter	A YOUNG SOLDIER
EILIF, her elder son	AN OLDER SOLDIER
SWISS CHEESE, her younger son	A PEASANT
THE RECRUITER	THE PEASANT'S WIFE
THE SERGEANT	THE YOUNG MAN
THE COOK	THE OLD WOMAN
THE GENERAL	ANOTHER PEASANT
THE CHAPLAIN	THE PEASANT WOMAN
THE ORDNANCE OFFICER	A YOUNG PEASANT
YVETTE POTTIER	THE LIEUTENANT
THE MAN WITH THE PATCH OVER HIS EYE	SOLDIERS
THE OTHER SERGEANT	A VOICE
THE OLD COLONEL	

ACT 1

SPRING, 1624. General Oxenstjerna recruits troops in Dalarna for the Polish campaign. The canteen woman, Anna Fierling, known as Mother Courage, loses a son.

Highway near a city.

A SERGEANT *and a* RECRUITER *stand shivering.*

THE RECRUITER: How can anybody get a company together in a place like this? Sergeant, some-times I feel like committing suicide. The general wants me to recruit four platoons by the twelfth, and the people around here are so depraved I can't sleep at night. I finally get hold of a man, I close my eyes and pretend not to see that he's chicken-breasted and he's got

5

varicose veins, I get him good and drunk and
10 he signs up. While I'm paying for the drinks,
he steps out, I follow him to the door because I
smell a rat: Sure enough, he's gone, like a fart
out of a goose. A man's word doesn't mean a
thing, there's no honor, no loyalty. This place
15 has undermined my faith in humanity,
sergeant.

THE SERGEANT: It's easy to see these people have
gone too long without a war. How can you
have morality without a war, I ask you? Peace
20 is a mess, it takes a war to put things in order.
In peacetime the human race goes to the dogs.
Man and beast are treated like so much dirt.
Everybody eats what they like, a big piece of
cheese on white bread, with a slice of meat on
25 top of the cheese. Nobody knows how many
young men or good horses there are in that
town up ahead, they've never been counted.
I've been in places where they hadn't had a
war in as much as seventy years, the people
30 had no names, they didn't even know who
they were. It takes a war before you get decent
lists and records; then your boots are done up
in bales and your grain in sacks, man and
beast are properly counted and marched away,
35 because people realize that without order they
can't have a war.

THE RECRUITER: How right you are!

THE SERGEANT: Like all good things, a war is hard to
get started. But once it takes root, it's vigorous;
40 then people are as scared of peace as dice players are of laying off, because they'll have to
reckon up their losses. But at first they're
scared of war. It's the novelty.

THE RECRUITER: Say, there comes a wagon. Two
45 women and two young fellows. Keep the old
woman busy, sergeant. If this is another flop,
you won't catch me standing out in this April
wind any more.

*[A Jew's harp is heard. Drawn by two young men, a
covered wagon approaches. In the wagon sit* MOTHER
COURAGE *and her mute daughter* KATTRIN]

MOTHER COURAGE: Good morning, sergeant.
50 SERGEANT (*barring the way*): Good morning, friends.
Who are you?

MOTHER COURAGE: Business people. (*Sings*)

*Hey, Captains, make the drum stop drumming
And let your soldiers take a seat.*
55 *Here's Mother Courage, with boots she's coming
To help along their aching feet.
How can they march off to the slaughter
With baggage, cannon, lice and fleas
Across the rocks and through the water*

60 *Unless their boots are in one piece?
The spring is come. Christian, revive!
The snowdrifts melt. The dead lie dead.
And if by chance you're still alive
It's time to rise and shake a leg.*

65 *O Captains, don't expect to send them
To death with nothing in their crops.
First you must let Mother Courage mend them
In mind and body with her schnapps.
On empty bellies it's distressing
70 To stand up under shot and shell.
But once they're full, you have my blessing
To lead them to the jaws of hell.
The spring is come. Christian, revive!
The snowdrifts melt, the dead lie dead.
75 And if by chance you're still alive
It's time to rise and shake a leg.*

THE SERGEANT: Halt, you scum. Where do you
belong?

THE ELDER SON: Second Finnish Regiment.

THE SERGEANT: Where are your papers?
80 MOTHER COURAGE: Papers?

THE YOUNGER SON: But she's Mother Courage!

THE SERGEANT: Never heard of her. Why Courage?

MOTHER COURAGE: They call me Courage, sergeant,
because when I saw ruin staring me in the face I
85 drove out of Riga through cannon fire with fifty
loaves of bread in my wagon. They were getting moldy, it was high time, I had no choice.

THE SERGEANT: No wisecracks. Where are your
papers?
90 MOTHER COURAGE (*fishing a pile of papers out of a tin
box and climbing down*): Here are my papers,
sergeant. There's a whole missal, picked it up
in Alt-Ötting to wrap cucumbers in, and a map
of Moravia, God knows if I'll ever get there, if
95 I don't it's a total loss. And this here certifies
that my horse hasn't got foot-and-mouth disease, too bad, he croaked on us, he cost fifteen
guilders, but not out of my pocket, glory be. Is
that enough paper?
100 THE SERGEANT: Are you trying to pull my leg? I'll
teach you to get smart. You know you need a
license.

MOTHER COURAGE: You mind your manners and
don't go telling my innocent children that I'd
105 go anywhere near your leg, it's indecent. I
want no truck with you. My license in the
Second Regiment is my honest face, and if you
can't read it, that's not my fault. I'm not letting
anybody put his seal on it.
110 THE RECRUITER: Sergeant, I detect a spirit of insubor-
dination in this woman. In our camp we need
respect for authority.

MOTHER COURAGE: Wouldn't sausage be better?

115 THE SERGEANT: Name.

MOTHER COURAGE: Anna Fierling.

THE SERGEANT: Then you're all Fierlings?

MOTHER COURAGE: What do you mean? Fierling is my name. Not theirs.

120 THE SERGEANT: Aren't they all your children?

MOTHER COURAGE: That they are, but why should they all have the same name? (*Pointing at the elder son*) This one, for instance. His name is Eilif Nojocki. How come? Because his father

125 always claimed to be called Kojocki or Mojocki. The boy remembers him well, except the one he remembers was somebody else, a Frenchman with a goatee. But aside from that, he inherited his father's intelligence; that man

130 could strip the pants off a peasant's ass without his knowing it. So, you see, we've each got our own name.

THE SERGEANT: Each different, you mean?

MOTHER COURAGE: Don't act so innocent.

135 THE SERGEANT: I suppose that one's a Chinaman? (*Indicating the younger son*)

MOTHER COURAGE: Wrong. He's Swiss.

THE SERGEANT: After the Frenchman?

MOTHER COURAGE: What Frenchman? I never heard

140 of any Frenchman. Don't get everything balled up or we'll be here all day. He's Swiss, but his name is Fejos, the name has nothing to do with his father. He had an entirely different name, he was an engineer, built fortifications, but he

145 drank.

[SWISS CHEESE *nods, beaming; the mute* KATTRIN *is also tickled*]

THE SERGEANT: Then how can his name be Fejos?

MOTHER COURAGE: I wouldn't want to offend you, but you haven't got much imagination. Naturally his name is Fejos because when he

150 came I was with a Hungarian, it was all the same to him, he was dying of kidney trouble though he never touched a drop, a very decent man. The boy takes after him.

THE SERGEANT: But you said he wasn't his father?

155 MOTHER COURAGE: He takes after him all the same. I call him Swiss Cheese, how come, because he's good at pulling the wagon. (*Pointing at her daughter*) Her name is Kattrin Haupt, she's half German.

160 THE SERGEANT: A fine family, I must say.

MOTHER COURAGE: Yes, I've been all over the world with my wagon.

THE SERGEANT: It's all being taken down. (*He takes it down*) You're from Bamberg, Bavaria. What

165 brings you here?

MOTHER COURAGE: I couldn't wait for the war to kindly come to Bamberg.

THE RECRUITER: You wagon pullers ought to be called Jacob Ox and Esau Ox. Do you ever get out of harness?

170

EILIF: Mother, can I clout him one on the kisser? I'd like to.

MOTHER COURAGE: And I forbid you. You stay put. And now, gentlemen, wouldn't you need a nice pistol, or a belt buckle, yours is all worn

175 out, sergeant.

THE SERGEANT: I need something else. I'm not blind. Those young fellows are built like tree trunks, big broad chests, sturdy legs. Why aren't they in the army? That's what I'd like to know.

180

MOTHER COURAGE (*quickly*): Nothing doing, sergeant. My children aren't cut out for soldiers.

THE RECRUITER: Why not? There's profit in it, and glory. Peddling shoes is woman's work. (*To* EILIF) Step up; let's feel if you've got muscles

185 or if you're a sissy.

MOTHER COURAGE: He's a sissy. Give him a mean look and he'll fall flat on his face.

THE RECRUITER: And kill a calf if it happens to be standing in the way. (*Tries to lead him away*)

190

MOTHER COURAGE: Leave him alone. He's not for you.

THE RECRUITER: He insulted me. He referred to my face as a kisser. Him and me will now step out in the field and discuss this thing as man to man.

195

EILIF: Don't worry, mother. I'll take care of him.

MOTHER COURAGE: You stay put. You no-good! I know you, always fighting. He's got a knife in his boot, he's a knifer.

THE RECRUITER: I'll pull it out of him like a milk

200 tooth. Come on, boy.

MOTHER COURAGE: Sergeant, I'll report you to the colonel. He'll throw you in the lock-up. The lieutenant is courting my daughter.

THE SERGEANT: No rough stuff, brother. (*To* MOTHER

205 COURAGE) What have you got against the army? Wasn't his father a soldier? Didn't he die fair and square? You said so yourself.

MOTHER COURAGE: He's only a child. You want to lead him off to slaughter, I know you. You'll

210 get five guilders for him.

THE RECRUITER: He'll get a beautiful cap and top boots.

EILIF: Not from you.

MOTHER COURAGE: Oh, won't you come fishing with

215 me? said the fisherman to the worm. (*To* SWISS CHEESE) Run and yell that they're trying to steal your brother. (*She pulls a knife*) Just try and steal him. I'll cut you down, you dogs. I'll teach you to put him in your war! We do an

220 honest business in ham and shirts, we're peaceful folk.

THE SERGEANT: I can see by the knife how peaceful

225 you are. You ought to be ashamed of yourself, put that knife away, you bitch. A minute ago you admitted you lived off war, how else would you live, on what? How can you have a war without soldiers?

MOTHER COURAGE: It doesn't have to be my children.

230 THE SERGEANT: I see. You'd like the war to eat the core and spit out the apple. You want your brood to batten on war, taxfree. The war can look out for itself, is that it? You call yourself Courage, eh? And you're afraid of the war that
235 feeds you. Your sons aren't afraid of it, I can see that.

EILIF: I'm not afraid of any war.

THE SERGEANT: Why should you be? Look at me: Has the soldier's life disagreed with me? I was sev-
240 enteen when I joined up.

MOTHER COURAGE: You're not seventy yet.

THE SERGEANT: I can wait.

MOTHER COURAGE: Sure. Under ground.

THE SERGEANT: Are you trying to insult me? Telling
245 me I'm going to die?

MOTHER COURAGE: But suppose it's the truth? I can see the mark on you. You look like a corpse on leave.

SWISS CHEESE: She's got second sight. Everybody says
250 so. She can tell the future.

THE RECRUITER: Then tell the sergeant his future. It might amuse him.

THE SERGEANT: I don't believe in that stuff.

MOTHER COURAGE: Give me your helmet. (*He gives it*
255 *to her*)

THE SERGEANT: It doesn't mean any more than taking a shit in the grass. But go ahead for the laugh.

MOTHER COURAGE (*takes a sheet of parchment and tears it in two*): Eilif, Swiss Cheese, Kattrin: That's
260 how we'd all be torn apart if we got mixed up too deep in the war. (*To the* SERGEANT) Seeing it's you, I'll do it for nothing. I make a black cross on this piece. Black is death.

SWISS CHEESE: She leaves the other one blank. Get it?

265 MOTHER COURAGE: Now I fold them, and now I shake them up together. Same as we're all mixed up together from the cradle to the grave. And now you draw, and you'll know the answer. (*The* SERGEANT *hesitates*)

270 THE RECRUITER (*to* EILIF): I don't take everybody, I'm known to be picky and choosy, but you've got spirit, I like that.

THE SERGEANT (*fishing in the helmet*): Damn foolishness! Hocus-pocus!

275 SWISS CHEESE: He's pulled a black cross. He's through.

THE RECRUITER: Don't let them scare you, there's not enough bullets for everybody.

THE SERGEANT (*hoarsely*): You've fouled me up.

280 MOTHER COURAGE: You fouled yourself up the day you joined the army. And now we'll be going, there isn't a war every day, I've got to take advantage.

THE SERGEANT: Hell and damnation! Don't try to hornswoggle me. We're taking your bastard to be a soldier.   285

EILIF: I'd like to be a soldier, mother.

MOTHER COURAGE: You shut your trap, you Finnish devil.

EILIF: Swiss Cheese wants to be a soldier too.

MOTHER COURAGE: That's news to me. I'd better let   290 you draw too, all three of you. (*She goes to the rear to mark crosses on slips of parchment*)

THE RECRUITER (*to* EILIF): It's been said to our discredit that a lot of religion goes on in the Swedish camp, but that's slander to blacken our reputa-   295 tion. Hymn singing only on Sunday, one verse! And only if you've got a voice.

MOTHER COURAGE (*comes back with the slips in the sergeant's helmet*): Want to sneak away from their mother, the devils, and run off to war like   300 calves to a salt lick. But we'll draw lots on it, then they'll see that the world is no vale of smiles with a "Come along, son, we're short on generals." Sergeant, I'm very much afraid they won't come through the war. They've got   305 terrible characters, all three of them. (*She holds out the helmet to* EILIF) There. Pick a slip. (*He picks one and unfolds it. She snatches it away from him*) There you have it. A cross! Oh, unhappy mother that I am, oh, mother of sorrows. Has   310 he got to die? Doomed to perish in the springtime of his life? If he joins the army, he'll bite the dust, that's sure. He's too brave, just like his father. If he's not smart, he'll go the way of all flesh, the slip proves it. (*She roars at him*)   315 Are you going to be smart?

EILIF: Why not?

MOTHER COURAGE: The smart thing to do is to stay with your mother, and if they make fun of you and call you a sissy, just laugh.   320

THE RECRUITER: If you're shitting in your pants, we'll take your brother.

MOTHER COURAGE: I told you to laugh. Laugh! And now you pick, Swiss Cheese. I'm not so worried about you, you're honest. (*He picks a slip*)   325 Oh! Why, have you got that strange look? It's got to be blank. There can't be a cross on it. No, I can't lose you. (*She takes the slip*) A cross? Him too? Maybe it's because he's so stupid. Oh, Swiss Cheese, you'll die too, unless you're very   330 honest the whole time, the way I've taught you since you were a baby, always bringing back the change when I sent you to buy bread. That's the only way you can save yourself. Look, sergeant, isn't that a black cross?   335

THE SERGEANT: It's a cross all right. I don't see how I could have pulled one. I always stay in the rear. (*To the* RECRUITER) It's on the up and up. Her own get it too.

340 SWISS CHEESE: I get it too. But I can take a hint.

MOTHER COURAGE: (*to* KATTRIN): Now you're the only one I'm sure of, you're a cross yourself because you've got a good heart. (*She holds up the hel-*

345 *met to* KATTRIN *in the wagon, but she herself takes out the slip*) It's driving me to despair. It can't be right, maybe I mixed them wrong. Don't be too good-natured, Kattrin, don't, there's a cross on your path too. Always keep very quiet, that ought to be easy seeing you're

350 dumb. Well, now you know. Be careful, all of you, you'll need to be. And now we'll climb up and drive on. (*She returns the* SERGEANT'S *helmet and climbs up into the wagon*)

THE RECRUITER (*to the* SERGEANT): Do something!

355 THE SERGEANT: I'm not feeling so good.

THE RECRUITER: Maybe you caught cold when you took your helmet off in the wind. Tell her you want to buy something. Keep her busy. (*Aloud*) You could at least take a look at that buckle,

360 sergeant. After all, selling things is these good people's living. Hey, you, the sergeant wants to buy that belt buckle.

MOTHER COURAGE: Half a guilder. A buckle like that is worth two guilders. (*She climbs down*)

365 THE SERGEANT: It's not new. This wind! I can't exam-ine it here. Let's go where it's quiet. (*He goes behind the wagon with the buckle*)

MOTHER COURAGE: I haven't noticed any wind.

THE SERGEANT: Maybe it is worth half a guilder. It's

370 silver.

MOTHER COURAGE (*joins him behind the wagon*): Six solid ounces.

THE RECRUITER (*to* EILIF): And then we'll have a drink, just you and me. I've got your enlistment

375 bonus right here. Come on.

[EILIF *stands undecided*]

MOTHER COURAGE: All right. Half a guilder.

THE SERGEANT: I don't get it. I always stay in the rear. There's no safer place for a sergeant. You can send the men up forward to win glory. You've

380 spoiled my dinner. It won't go down, I know it, not a bite.

MOTHER COURAGE: Don't take it to heart. Don't let it spoil your appetite. Just keep behind the lines. Here, take a drink of schnapps, man. (*She*

385 *hands him the bottle*)

THE RECRUITER (*has taken* EILIF'S *arm and is pulling him away toward the rear*): A bonus of ten guilders, and you'll be a brave man and you'll fight for the king, and the women will tear each other's hair out over you. And you can clout me one

390 on the kisser for insulting you. (*Both go out*)

[*Mute* KATTRIN *jumps down from the wagon and emits raucous sounds*]

MOTHER COURAGE: Just a minute, Kattrin, just a minute. The sergeant's paying up. (*Bites the half guilder*) I'm always suspicious of money. I'm a burnt child, sergeant. But your coin is 395 good. And now we'll be going. Where's Eilif?

SWISS CHEESE: He's gone with the recruiter.

MOTHER COURAGE (*stands motionless, then*): You sim-ple soul. (*To* KATTRIN) I know. You can't talk, you couldn't help it. 400

THE SERGEANT: You could do with a drink yourself, mother. That's the way it goes. Soldiering isn't the worst thing in the world. You want to live off the war, but you want to keep you and yours out of it. Is that it? 405

MOTHER COURAGE: Now you'll have to pull with your brother, Kattrin.

[*Brother and sister harness themselves to the wagon and start pulling.* MOTHER COURAGE *walks beside them. The wagon rolls off*]

THE SERGEANT (*looking after them*):
   If you want the war to work for you
   You've got to give the war its due. 410

ACT 2

In 1625 and 1626 MOTHER COURAGE *crosses Poland in the train of the Swedish armies. Outside the fortress of Wallhof she meets her son again.—A capon is success-fully sold, the brave son's fortunes are at their zenith.*
   The GENERAL'S *tent.*
   Beside it the kitchen. The thunder of cannon. The cook is arguing with MOTHER COURAGE, *who is trying to sell him a capon.*

THE COOK: Sixty hellers for that pathetic bird?

MOTHER COURAGE: Pathetic bird? You mean this plump beauty? Are you trying to tell me that a general who's the biggest eater for miles around—God help you if you haven't got any-thing for his dinner—can't afford a measly 415 sixty hellers?

THE COOK: I can get a dozen like it for ten hellers right around the corner.

MOTHER COURAGE: What, you'll find a capon like this right around the corner? With a siege on and 420 everybody so starved you can see right through them. Maybe you'll scare up a rat, maybe, I say, 'cause they've all been eaten, I've seen five men chasing a starved rat for hours. Fifty hellers for a giant capon in the middle of 425 a siege.

THE COOK: We're not besieged; they are. We're the

430 besiegers, can't you get that through your head?

MOTHER COURAGE: But we haven't got anything to eat either, in fact we've got less than the people in the city. They've hauled it all inside. I hear their life is one big orgy. And look at us.

435 I've been around to the peasants, they haven't got a thing.

THE COOK: They've got plenty. They hide it.

MOTHER COURAGE (*triumphantly*): Oh, no! They're ruined, that's what they are. They're starving.

440 I've seen them. They're so hungry they're digging up roots. They lick their fingers when they've eaten a boiled strap. That's the situation. And here I've got a capon and I'm supposed to let it go for forty hellers.

445 THE COOK: Thirty, not forty. Thirty, I said.

MOTHER COURAGE: It's no common capon. They tell me this bird was so talented that he wouldn't eat unless they played music, he had his own favorite march. He could add and subtract,

450 that's how intelligent he was. And you're trying to tell me forty hellers is too much. The general will bite your head off if there's nothing to eat.

THE COOK: You know what I'm going to do? (*He takes

455 a piece of beef and sets his knife to it*) Here I've got a piece of beef. I'll roast it. Think it over. This is your last chance.

MOTHER COURAGE: Roast and be damned. It's a year old.

460 THE COOK: A day old. That ox was running around only yesterday afternoon, I saw him with my own eyes.

MOTHER COURAGE: Then he must have stunk on the hoof.

465 THE COOK: I'll cook it five hours if I have to. We'll see if it's still tough. (*He cuts into it*)

MOTHER COURAGE: Use plenty of pepper, maybe the general won't notice the stink.

[*The* GENERAL, *a* CHAPLAIN *and* EILIF *enter the tent*]

THE GENERAL (*slapping* EILIF *on the back*): All right,

470 son, into your general's tent you go, you'll sit at my right hand. You've done a heroic deed and you're a pious trooper, because this is a war of religion and what you did was done for God, that's what counts with me. I'll reward

475 you with a gold bracelet when I take the city. We come here to save their souls and what do those filthy, shameless peasants do? They drive their cattle away. And they stuff their priests with meat, front and back. But you

480 taught them a lesson. Here's a tankard of red wine for you. (*He pours*) We'll down it in one gulp. (*They do so*) None for the chaplain, he's

got his religion. What would you like for dinner, sweetheart?

EILIF: A scrap of meat. Why not? 485

THE GENERAL: Cook! Meat!

THE COOK: And now he brings company when there's nothing to eat.

[*Wanting to listen,* MOTHER COURAGE *makes him stop talking*]

EILIF: Cutting down peasants whets the appetite.

MOTHER COURAGE: God, it's my Eilif. 490

THE COOK: Who?

MOTHER COURAGE: My eldest. I haven't seen hide nor hair of him in two years, he was stolen from me on the highway. He must be in good if the general invites him to dinner, and what have 495 you got to offer? Nothing. Did you hear what the general's guest wants for dinner? Meat! Take my advice, snap up this capon. The price is one guilder.

THE GENERAL (*has sat down with* EILIF. *Bellows*): Food, 500 Lamb, you lousy, no-good cook, or I'll kill you.

THE COOK: All right, hand it over. This is extortion.

MOTHER COURAGE: I thought it was a pathetic bird.

THE COOK: Pathetic is the word. Hand it over. Fifty hellers! It's highway robbery. 505

MOTHER COURAGE: One guilder, I say. For my eldest son, the general's honored guest, I spare no expense.

THE COOK (*gives her the money*): Then pluck it at least while I make the fire. 510

MOTHER COURAGE (*sits down to pluck the capon*): Won't he be glad to see me! He's my brave, intelligent son. I've got a stupid one too, but he's honest. The girl's a total loss. But at least she doesn't talk, that's something. 515

THE GENERAL: Take another drink, son, it's my best Falerno, I've only got another barrel or two at the most, but it's worth it to see that there's still some true faith in my army. The good shepherd here just looks on, all he knows how 520 to do is preach. Can he do anything? No. And now, Eilif my son, tell us all about it, how cleverly you hoodwinked those peasants and captured those twenty head of cattle. I hope they'll be here soon. 525

EILIF: Tomorrow. Maybe the day after.

MOTHER COURAGE: Isn't my Eilif considerate, not bringing those oxen in until tomorrow, or you wouldn't have even said hello to my capon.

EILIF: Well, it was like this: I heard the peasants were 530 secretly—mostly at night—rounding up the oxen they'd hidden in a certain forest. The city people had arranged to come and get them. I let them round the oxen up, I figured they'd find them easier than I would. I made my men 535

ravenous for meat, put them on short rations
for two days until their mouths watered if they
even heard a word beginning with *me* . . . like
measles.

540 THE GENERAL: That was clever of you.
EILIF: Maybe. The rest was a pushover. Except the
peasants had clubs and there were three times
more of them and they fell on us like bloody
murder. Four of them drove me into a clump
545 of bushes, they knocked my sword out of my
hand and yelled: Surrender! Now what'll I do,
I says to myself, they'll make hash out of me.
THE GENERAL: What did you do?
EILIF: I laughed.
550 THE GENERAL: You laughed?
EILIF: I laughed. Which led to a conversation. The
first thing you know, I'm bargaining. Twenty
guilders is too much for that ox, I say, how
about fifteen? Like I'm meaning to pay. They're
555 flummoxed, they scratch their heads. Quick, I
reach for my sword and mow them down.
Necessity knows no law. See what I mean?
THE GENERAL: What do you say to that, shepherd?
CHAPLAIN: Strictly speaking, that maxim is not in the
560 Bible. But our Lord was able to turn five
loaves into five hundred. So there was no
question of poverty; he could tell people to
love their neighbors because their bellies were
full. Nowadays it's different.
565 THE GENERAL (*laughs*): Very different. All right, you
Pharisee, take a swig. (*To* EILIF) You mowed
them down, splendid, so my fine troops could
have a decent bite to eat. Doesn't the Good
Book say: "Whatsoever thou doest for the least
570 of my brethren, thou doest for me"? And what
have you done for them? You've got them a
good chunk of beef for their dinner. They're
not used to moldy crusts; in the old days they
had a helmetful of white bread and wine
575 before they went out to fight for God.
EILIF: Yes, I reached for my sword and I mowed them
down.
THE GENERAL: You're a young Caesar. You deserve to
see the king.
580 EILIF: I have, in the distance. He shines like a light.
He's my ideal.
THE GENERAL: You're something like him already,
Eilif. I know the worth of a brave soldier like
you. When I find one, I treat him like my own
585 son. (*He leads him to the map*) Take a look at the
situation, Eilif; we've still got a long way to go.
MOTHER COURAGE (*who has been listening starts plucking
her capon furiously*): He must be a rotten general.
THE COOK: Eats like a pig, but why rotten?
590 MOTHER COURAGE: Because he needs brave soldiers,
that's why. If he planned his campaigns right,
what would he need brave soldiers for? The

run-of-the-mill would do. Take it from me,
whenever you find a lot of virtues, it shows
that something's wrong. 595
THE COOK: I'd say it proves that something is all right.
MOTHER COURAGE: No, that something's wrong. See,
when a general or a king is real stupid and
leads his men up shit creek, his troops need
courage, that's a virtue. If he's stingy and 600
doesn't hire enough soldiers, they've all got to
be Herculeses. And if he's a slob and lets
everything go to pot, they've got to be as sly as
serpents or they're done for. And if he's
always expecting too much of them, they need 605
an extra dose of loyalty. A country that's run
right, or a good king or a good general, does-
n't need any of these virtues. You don't need
virtues in a decent country, the people can all
be perfectly ordinary, medium-bright, and 610
cowards too for my money.
THE GENERAL: I bet your father was a soldier.
EILIF: A great soldier, I'm told. My mother warned
me about it. Makes me think of a song.
THE GENERAL: Sing it! (*Bellowing*) Where's that food! 615
EILIF: It's called: The Song of the Old Wife and the
Soldier.

[He sings, doing a war dance with his saber]

A gun or a pike, they can kill who they like
And the torrent will swallow a wader
You had better think twice before battling with ice 620
Said the old wife to the soldier.
Cocking his rifle he leapt to his feet
Laughing for joy as he heard the drum beat
The wars cannot hurt me, he told her.
He shouldered his gun and he picked up his knife 625
To see the wide world. That's the soldier's life.
Those were the words of the soldier.

Ah, deep will they lie who wise counsel defy
Learn wisdom from those that are older
Oh, don't venture too high or you'll fall from the sky 630
Said the old wife to the soldier.
But the young soldier with knife and with gun
Only laughed a cold laugh and stepped into the run.
The water can't hurt me, he told her.
And when the moon on the rooftop shines white 635
We'll be coming back. You can pray for that night.
Those were the words of the soldier.

MOTHER COURAGE (*in the kitchen, continues the song,
beating a pot with a spoon*):

Like the smoke you'll be gone and no warmth linger on 640
And your deeds only leave me the colder!

Oh, see the smoke race. Oh, dear God keep him safe!
That's what she said of the soldier.

EILIF: What's that?

645 MOTHER COURAGE (*goes on singing*):

And the young soldier with knife and with gun
Was swept from his feet till he sank in the run
And the torrent swallowed the waders.
Cold shone the moon on the rooftop white
650 *But the soldier was carried away with the ice*
And what was it she heard from the soldiers?

Like the smoke he was gone and no warmth lingered on
And his deeds only left her the colder.
Ah, deep will they lie who wise counsel defy!
655 *That's what she said to the soldiers.*

THE GENERAL: What do they think they're doing in
    my kitchen?

EILIF (*has gone into the kitchen. He embraces his mother*):
    Mother! It's you! Where are the others?

660 MOTHER COURAGE (*in his arms*): Snug as a bug in a
    rug. Swiss Cheese is paymaster of the Second
    Regiment; at least he won't be fighting. I
    couldn't keep him out altogether.

EILIF: And how about your feet?

665 MOTHER COURAGE: Well, it's hard getting my shoes
    on in the morning.

THE GENERAL (*has joined them*): Ah, so you're his
    mother. I hope you've got more sons for me
    like this fellow here.

670 EILIF: Am I lucky! There you're sitting in the kitchen
    hearing your son being praised.

MOTHER COURAGE: I heard it all right! (*She gives him a
    slap in the face*)

EILIF (*holding his cheek*): For capturing the oxen?

675 MOTHER COURAGE: No. For not surrendering when
    the four of them were threatening to make
    hash out of you! Didn't I teach you to take care
    of yourself? You Finnish devil!

[*The GENERAL and the CHAPLAIN laugh*]

ACT 3

Three years later MOTHER COURAGE *and parts of a
Finnish regiment are taken prisoner. She is able to
save her daughter and her wagon, but her honest son
dies.*
    Army camp.
    Afternoon. On a pole the regimental flag. MOTHER
COURAGE *has stretched a clothesline between her
wagon, on which all sorts of merchandise is hung in
display; and a large cannon. She and* KATTRIN *are fold-*

*ing washing and piling it on the cannon. At the same
time she is negotiating with an* ORDNANCE OFFICER *over
a sack of bullets.* SWISS CHEESE, *now in the uniform of a
paymaster, is looking on. A pretty woman,* YVETTE
POTTIER, *is sitting with a glass of brandy in front of her,
sewing a gaudy-colored hat. She is in her stocking feet,
her red high-heeled shoes are on the ground beside her.*

THE ORDNANCE OFFICER: I'll let you have these bullets
    for two guilders. It's cheap, I need the money,   680
    because the colonel's been drinking with the
    officers for two days and we're out of liquor.

MOTHER COURAGE: That's ammunition for the troops.
    If it's found here, I'll be court-martialed. You
    punks sell their bullets and the men have   685
    nothing to shoot at the enemy.

THE ORDNANCE OFFICER: Don't be hard-hearted, you
    scratch my back, I'll scratch yours.

MOTHER COURAGE: I'm not taking any army property.
    Not at that price.   690

THE ORDNANCE OFFICER: You can sell it for five
    guilders, maybe eight, to the ordnance officer
    of the Fourth before the day is out, if you're
    quiet about it and give him a receipt for
    twelve. He hasn't an ounce of ammunition left.   695

MOTHER COURAGE: Why don't you do it yourself?

THE ORDNANCE OFFICER: Because I don't trust him,
    he's a friend of mine.

MOTHER COURAGE (*takes the sack*): Hand it over. (*To*
    KATTRIN) Take it back there and pay him one   700
    and a half guilders. (*In response to the* ORDNANCE
    OFFICER's *protest*) One and a half guilders, I say.
    (KATTRIN *drags the sack behind the wagon, the ord-
    nance officer follows her.* MOTHER COURAGE *to*
    SWISS CHEESE) Here's your underdrawers, take   705
    good care of them, this is October, might be
    coming on fall, I don't say it will be, because
    I've learned that nothing is sure to happen the
    way we think, not even the seasons. But what-
    ever happens, your regimental funds have to   710
    be in order. Are your funds in order?

SWISS CHEESE: Yes, mother.

MOTHER COURAGE: Never forget that they made you
    paymaster because you're honest and not
    brave like your brother, and especially because   715
    you're too simple-minded to get the idea of
    making off with the money. That's a comfort to
    me. And don't go mislaying your drawers.

SWISS CHEESE: No, mother. I'll put them under my
    mattress. (*Starts to go*)   720

ORDNANCE OFFICER: I'll go with you, paymaster.

MOTHER COURAGE: Just don't teach him any of your
    tricks.

[*Without saying good-bye the* ORDNANCE OFFICER *goes
out with* SWISS CHEESE]

YVETTE (*waves her hand after the* ORDNANCE OFFICER):
725   You might say good-bye, officer.
MOTHER COURAGE (*to Yvette*): I don't like to see those
         two together. He's not the right kind of compa-
         ny for my Swiss Cheese. But the war's getting
730   along pretty well. More countries are joining in
         all the time, it can go on for another four, five
         years, easy. With a little planning ahead, I can
         do good business if I'm careful. Don't you
         know you shouldn't drink in the morning with
         your sickness?
735 YVETTE: Who says I'm sick, it's slander.
MOTHER COURAGE: Everybody says so.
YVETTE: Because they're all liars. Mother Courage,
         I'm desperate. They all keep out of my way
         like I'm a rotten fish on account of those lies.
740   What's the good of fixing my hat? (*She throws
         it down*) That's why I drink in the morning, I
         never used to, I'm getting crow's-feet, but it
         doesn't matter now. In the Second Finnish
         Regiment they all know me. I should have
745   stayed home when my first love walked out
         on me. Pride isn't for the likes of us. If we
         can't put up with shit, we're through.
MOTHER COURAGE: Just don't start in on your Pieter
         and how it all happened in front of my inno-
750   cent daughter.
YVETTE: She's just the one to hear it, it'll harden her
         against love.
MOTHER COURAGE: Nothing can harden them.
YVETTE: Then I'll talk about it because it makes me
755   feel better. It begins with my growing up in
         fair Flanders, because if I hadn't I'd never have
         laid eyes on him and I wouldn't be here in
         Poland now, because he was an army cook,
         blond, a Dutchman, but skinny. Kattrin, watch
760   out for the skinny ones, but I didn't know that
         then, and another thing I didn't know is that
         he had another girl even then, and they all
         called him Pete the Pipe, because he didn't
         even take his pipe out of his mouth when he
765   was doing it, that's all it meant to him. (*She
         sings the Song of Fraternization*)

When I was only sixteen
The foe came into our land.
He laid aside his sabre
770 And with a smile he took my hand.
     After the May parade
     The May light starts to fade.
     The regiment dressed by the right
     Then drums were beaten, that's the drill.
775 The foe took us behind the hill
     And fraternized all night.

There were so many foes came

And mine worked in the mess.
I loathed him in the daytime.
At night I loved him none the less.   780
     After the May parade
     The May light starts to fade.
     The regiment dressed by the right
     Then drums were beaten, that's the drill.
     The foe took us behind the hill   785
     And fraternized all night.

The love which came upon me
Was wished on me by fate.
My friends could never grasp why
I found it hard to share their hate.   790
     The fields were wet with dew
     When sorrow first I knew.
     The regiment dressed by the right
     Then drums were beaten, that's the drill
     And then the foe, my lover still   795
     Went marching from our sight.

Well, I followed him, but I never found him. That
         was five years ago. (*She goes behind the wagon
         with an unsteady gait*)
MOTHER COURAGE: You've left your hat.   800
YVETTE: Anybody that wants it can have it.
MOTHER COURAGE: Let that be a lesson to you,
         Kattrin. Have no truck with soldiers. It's love
         that makes the world go round, so you'd bet-
         ter watch out. Even with a civilian it's no pic-   805
         nic. He says he'd kiss the ground you put your
         little feet on, talking of feet, did you wash
         yours yesterday, and then you're his slave. Be
         glad you're dumb, that way you'll never con-
         tradict yourself or want to bite your tongue off 810
         because you've told the truth, it's a gift of God
         to be dumb. Here comes the general's cook, I
         wonder what he wants.

[*The* COOK *and the* CHAPLAIN *enter*]

THE CHAPLAIN: I've got a message for you from your
         son Eilif. The cook here thought he'd come   815
         along, he's taken a shine to you.
THE COOK: I only came to get a breath of air.
MOTHER COURAGE: You can always do that here if
         you behave, and if you don't, I can handle
         you. Well, what does he want? I've got no   820
         money to spare.
THE CHAPLAIN: Actually he wanted me to see his
         brother, the paymaster.
MOTHER COURAGE: He's not here any more, or any-
         where else either. He's not his brother's pay-   825
         master. I don't want him leading him into
         temptation and being smart at his expense.
         (*Gives him money from the bag slung around her*

waist) Give him this, it's a sin, he's speculating on mother love and he ought to be ashamed.

830 THE COOK: He won't do it much longer, then he'll be marching off with his regiment, maybe to his death, you never can tell. Better make it a little more, you'll be sorry later. You women are
835 hard-hearted, but afterwards you're sorry. A drop of brandy wouldn't have cost much when it was wanted, but it wasn't given, and later, for all you know, he'll be lying in the cold ground and you can't dig him up again.

840 THE CHAPLAIN: Don't be sentimental, cook. There's nothing wrong with dying in battle, it's a blessing, and I'll tell you why. This is a war of religion. Not a common war, but a war for the faith, and therefore pleasing to God.

845 THE COOK: That's a fact. In a way you could call it a war, because of the extortion and killing and looting, not to mention a bit of rape, but it's a war of religion, which makes it different from all other wars, that's obvious. But it makes a man
850 thirsty all the same, you've got to admit that.

THE CHAPLAIN (*to* MOTHER COURAGE, *pointing at the* COOK): I tried to discourage him, but he says you've turned his head, he sees you in his dreams.

855 THE COOK (*lights a short-stemmed pipe*): All I want is a glass of brandy from your fair hand, nothing more sinful. I'm already so shocked by the jokes the chaplain's been telling me, I bet I'm still red in the face.

860 MOTHER COURAGE: And him a clergyman! I'd better give you fellows something to drink or you'll be making me immoral propositions just to pass the time.

THE CHAPLAIN: This is temptation, said the deacon,
865 and succumbed to it. (*Turning toward* KATTRIN *as he leaves*) And who is this delightful young lady?

MOTHER COURAGE: She's not delightful, she's a respectable young lady.

[*The* CHAPLAIN *and the* COOK *go behind the wagon with* MOTHER COURAGE. KATTRIN *looks after them, then she walks away from the washing and approaches the hat. She picks it up, sits down and puts on the red shoes. From the rear* MOTHER COURAGE *is heard talking politics with the* CHAPLAIN *and the* COOK]

870 MOTHER COURAGE: The Poles here in Poland shouldn't have butted in. All right, our king marched his army into their country. But instead of keeping the peace, the Poles start butting into their own affairs and attack the king while he's
875 marching quietly through the landscape. That was a breach of the peace and the blood is on their head.

THE CHAPLAIN: Our king had only one thing in mind: freedom. The emperor had everybody under his yoke, the Poles as much as the Germans;
880 the king had to set them free.

THE COOK: I see it this way, your brandy's first-rate, I can see why I liked your face, but we were talking about the king. This freedom he was trying to introduce into Germany cost him a
885 fortune, he had to levy a salt tax in Sweden, which, as I said, cost the poor people a fortune. Then he had to put the Germans in jail and break them on the rack because they liked being the emperor's slaves. Oh yes, the king
890 made short shrift of anybody that didn't want to be free. In the beginning he only wanted to protect Poland against wicked people, especially the emperor, but the more he ate the more he wanted, and pretty soon he was protecting all
895 of Germany. But the Germans didn't take it lying down and the king got nothing but trouble for all his kindness and expense, which he naturally had to defray from taxes, which made for bad blood, but that didn't discourage
900 him. He had one thing in his favor, the word of God, which was lucky, because otherwise people would have said he was doing it all for himself and what he hoped to get out of it. As it was, he always had a clear conscience and
905 that was all he really cared about.

MOTHER COURAGE: It's easy to see you're not a Swede, or you wouldn't talk like that about the Hero-King.

THE CHAPLAIN: You're eating his bread, aren't you? 910

THE COOK: I don't eat his bread, I bake it.

MOTHER COURAGE: He can't be defeated because his men believe in him. (*Earnestly*) When you listen to the big wheels talk, they're making war for reasons of piety, in the name of everything 915 that's fine and noble. But when you take another look, you see that they're not so dumb; they're making war for profit. If they weren't, the small fry like me wouldn't have anything to do with it. 920

THE COOK: That's a fact.

THE CHAPLAIN: And it wouldn't hurt you as a Dutchman to take a look at that flag up there before you express opinions in Poland.

MOTHER COURAGE: We're all good Protestants here! 925 Prosit! (KATTRIN *has started strutting about with* YVETTE's *hat on, imitating Yvette's gait.*)

[*Suddenly cannon fire and shots are heard. Drums.* MOTHER COURAGE, *the* COOK *and the* CHAPLAIN *run out from behind the wagon, the two men still with glasses in hand. The* ORDNANCE OFFICER *and a* SOLDIER *rush up to the cannon and try to push it away*]

MOTHER COURAGE: What's going on? Let me get my washing first, you lugs. (*She tries to rescue her washing*)

THE ORDNANCE OFFICER: The Catholics. They're attacking. I don't know as we'll get away. (*To the SOLDIER*) Get rid of the gun! (*Runs off*)

THE COOK: Christ, I've got to find the general. Courage, I'll be back for a little chat in a day or two. (*Rushes out*)

MOTHER COURAGE: Stop, you've forgotten your pipe.

THE COOK (*from the distance*): Keep it for me! I'll need it.

MOTHER COURAGE: Just when we were making a little money!

THE CHAPLAIN: Well, I guess I'll be going too. It might be dangerous though, with the enemy so close. Blessed are the peaceful is the best motto in wartime. If only I had a cloak to cover up with.

MOTHER COURAGE: I'm not lending any cloaks, not on your life. I've had bitter experience in that line.

THE CHAPLAIN: But my religion puts me in special danger.

MOTHER COURAGE (*bringing him a cloak*): It's against my better conscience. And now run along.

THE CHAPLAIN: Thank you kindly, you've got a good heart. But maybe I'd better sit here a while. The enemy might get suspicious if they see me running.

MOTHER COURAGE (*to the SOLDIER*): Leave it lay, you fool, you won't get paid extra. I'll take care of it for you, you'd only get killed.

THE SOLDIER (*running away*): I tried. You're my witness.

MOTHER COURAGE: I'll swear it on the Bible. (*Sees her daughter with the hat*) What are you doing with that floozy hat? Take it off, have you gone out of your mind? Now of all times, with the enemy on top of us? (*She tears the hat off KATTRIN's head*) You want them to find you and make a whore out of you? And those shoes! Take them off, you woman of Babylon! (*She tries to pull them off*) Jesus Christ, chaplain, make her take those shoes off! I'll be right back. (*She runs to the wagon*)

YVETTE (*enters, powdering her face*): What's this I hear? The Catholics are coming? Where's my hat? Who's been stamping on it? I can't be seen like this if the Catholics are coming. What'll they think of me? I haven't even got a mirror. (*To the CHAPLAIN*) How do I look? Too much powder?

THE CHAPLAIN: Just right.

YVETTE: And where are my red shoes? (*She doesn't see them because KATTRIN hides her feet under her skirt*) I left them here. I've got to get back to my tent. In my bare feet. It's disgraceful! (*Goes out*)

[SWISS CHEESE *runs in carrying a small box*]

MOTHER COURAGE (*Comes out with her hands full of ashes. To KATTRIN*): Ashes. (*To SWISS CHEESE*) What you got there?

SWISS CHEESE: The regimental funds.

MOTHER COURAGE: Throw it away! No more paymastering for you.

SWISS CHEESE: I'm responsible for it. (*He goes rear*)

MOTHER COURAGE (*to the CHAPLAIN*): Take your clergyman's coat off, chaplain, or they'll recognize you, cloak or no cloak. (*She rubs KATTRIN's face with ashes*) Hold still! There. With a little dirt you'll be safe. What a mess! The sentries were drunk. Hide your light under a bushel, as the Good Book says. When a soldier, especially a Catholic, sees a clean face, she's a whore before she knows it. Nobody feeds them for weeks. When they finally loot some provisions, the next thing they want is women. That'll do it. Let me look at you. Not bad. Like you'd been wallowing in a pigsty. Stop shaking. You're safe now. (*To SWISS CHEESE*) What did you do with the cashbox?

SWISS CHEESE: I thought I'd put it in the wagon.

MOTHER COURAGE (*horrified*): What! In my wagon? Of all the sinful stupidity! If my back is turned for half a second! They'll hang us all!

SWISS CHEESE: Then I'll put it somewhere else, or I'll run away with it.

MOTHER COURAGE: You'll stay right here. It's too late.

THE CHAPLAIN (*still changing, comes forward*): Heavens, the flag!

MOTHER COURAGE (*takes down the regimental flag*): Bozhe moi! I'm so used to it I don't see it. Twenty-five years I've had it.

[*The cannon fire grows louder*]

[*Morning, three days later. The cannon is gone.* MOTHER COURAGE, KATTRIN, *the* CHAPLAIN *and* SWISS CHEESE *are sitting dejectedly over a meal*]

SWISS CHEESE: This is the third day I've been sitting here doing nothing; the sergeant has always been easy on me, but now he must be starting to wonder: where can Swiss Cheese be with the cashbox?

MOTHER COURAGE: Be glad they haven't tracked you down.

THE CHAPLAIN: What about me? I can't hold a service here either. The Good Book says: "Whosoever hath a full heart, his tongue runneth over." Heaven help me if mine runneth over.

MOTHER COURAGE: That's the way it is. Look what I've got on my hands: one with a religion and one with a cashbox. I don't know which is worse.

THE CHAPLAIN: Tell yourself that we're in the hands of God.

MOTHER COURAGE: I don't think we're that bad off, but all the same I can't sleep at night. If it weren't for you, Swiss Cheese, it'd be easier. I think I've put myself in the clear. I told them I was against the antichrist; he's a Swede with horns, I told them, and I'd noticed the left horn was kind of worn down. I interrupted the questioning to ask where I could buy holy candles cheap. I knew what to say because Swiss Cheese's father was a Catholic and he used to make jokes about it. They didn't really believe me, but their regiment had no provisioner, so they looked the other way. Maybe we stand to gain. We're prisoners, but so are lice on a dog.

THE CHAPLAIN: This milk is good. Though there's not very much of it or of anything else. Maybe we'll have to cut down on our Swedish appetites. But such is the lot of the vanquished.

MOTHER COURAGE: Who's vanquished? Victory and defeat don't always mean the same thing to the big wheels up top and the small fry underneath. Not by a long shot. In some cases defeat is a blessing to the small fry. Honor's lost, but nothing else. One time in Livonia our general got such a shellacking from the enemy that in the confusion I laid hands on a beautiful white horse from the baggage train. That horse pulled my wagon for seven months, until we had a victory and they checked up. On the whole, you can say that victory and defeat cost us plain people plenty. The best thing for us is when politics gets bogged down. (*To* SWISS CHEESE) Eat!

SWISS CHEESE: I've lost my appetite. How's the sergeant going to pay the men?

MOTHER COURAGE: Troops never get paid when they're running away.

SWISS CHEESE: But they've got it coming to them. If they're not paid, they don't need to run. Not a step.

MOTHER COURAGE: Swiss Cheese, you're too conscientious, it almost frightens me. I brought you up to be honest, because you're not bright, but somewhere it's got to stop. And now me and the chaplain are going to buy a Catholic flag and some meat. Nobody can buy meat like the chaplain, he goes into a trance and heads straight for the best piece, I guess it makes his mouth water and that shows him the way. At least they let me carry on my business. Nobody cares about a shopkeeper's religion, all they want to know is the price. Protestant pants are as warm as any other kind.

THE CHAPLAIN: Like the friar said when somebody told him the Lutherans were going to stand the whole country on its head. They'll always need beggars, he says. (MOTHER COURAGE *disappears into the wagon*) But she's worried about that cashbox. They've taken no notice of us so far, they think we're all part of the wagon, but how long can that go on?

SWISS CHEESE: I can take it away.

THE CHAPLAIN: That would be almost more dangerous. What if somebody sees you? They've got spies. Yesterday morning, just as I'm relieving myself, one of them jumps out of the ditch. I was so scared I almost let out a prayer. That would have given me away. I suppose they think they can tell a Protestant by the smell of his shit. He was a little runt with a patch over one eye.

MOTHER COURAGE (*climbing down from the wagon with a basket*): Look what I've found. You shameless slut! (*She holds up the red shoes triumphantly*) Yvette's red shoes! She's swiped them in cold blood. It's your fault. Who told her she was a delightful young lady? (*She puts them into the basket*) I'm giving them back. Stealing Yvette's shoes! She ruins herself for money, that I can understand. But you'd like to do it free of charge, for pleasure. I've told you, you'll have to wait for peace. No soldiers! Just wait for peace with your worldly ways.

THE CHAPLAIN: She doesn't seem very worldly to me.

MOTHER COURAGE: Too worldly for me. In Dalarna she was like a stone, which is all they've got around there. The people used to say: We don't see the cripple. That's the way I like it. That way she's safe. (*To* SWISS CHEESE) You leave that box where it is, hear? And keep an eye on your sister, she needs it. The two of you will be the death of me. I'd sooner take care of a bag of fleas. (*She goes off with the* CHAPLAIN. KATTRIN *starts clearing away the dishes*)

SWISS CHEESE: Won't be many more days when I can sit in the sun in my shirtsleeves. (KATTRIN *points to a tree*) Yes, the leaves are all yellow. (KATTRIN *asks him, by means of gestures, whether he wants a drink*) Not now. I'm thinking. (*Pause*) She says she can't sleep. I'd better get the cashbox out of here, I've found a hiding place. All right, get me a drink. (KATTRIN *goes behind the wagon*) I'll hide it in the rabbit hole down by the river until I can take it away. Maybe late tonight. I'll go get it and take it to the regiment. I wonder how far they've run in three days? Won't the sergeant be surprised! Well, Swiss Cheese, this is a pleasant disappointment, that's what he'll say. I trust you with the regimental cashbox and you bring it back.

[*As* KATTRIN *comes out from behind the wagon with a glass of brandy, she comes face to face with two men.*

One is a SERGEANT. *The other removes his hat and swings it through the air in a ceremonious greeting. He has a patch over one eye]*

THE MAN WITH THE PATCH: Good morning, my dear.
1145   Have you by any chance seen a man from the headquarters of the Second Finnish Regiment?

[Scared out of her wits, KATTRIN *runs front, spilling the brandy. The two exchange looks and withdraw after seeing* SWISS CHEESE *sitting there]*

SWISS CHEESE (*starting up from his thoughts*): You've spilled half of it. What's the fuss about? Poke yourself in the eye? I don't understand you. I'm
1150   getting out of here, I've made up my mind, it's best. (*He stands up. She does everything she can think of to call his attention to the danger. He only evades her*) I wish I could understand you. Poor thing, I know you're trying to tell me some-
1155   thing, you just can't say it. Don't worry about spilling the brandy, I'll be drinking plenty more. What's one glass? (*He takes the cashbox out of the wagon and hides it under his jacket*) I'll be right back. Let me go, you're making me angry. I
1160   know you mean well. If only you could talk.

[When she tries to hold him back, he kisses her and tears himself away. He goes out. She is desperate, she races back and forth, uttering short inarticulate sounds. The CHAPLAIN *and* MOTHER COURAGE *come back.* KATTRIN *gesticulates wildly at her mother)*

MOTHER COURAGE: What's the matter? You're all upset. Has somebody hurt you? Where's Swiss Cheese? Tell it to me in order, Kattrin. Your mother understands you. What, the nogood's
1165   taken the cashbox? I'll hit him over the head with it, the sneak. Take your time, don't talk nonsense, use your hands, I don't like it when you howl like a dog, what will the chaplain think? It gives me the creeps. A one-eyed man?
1170   THE CHAPLAIN: The one-eyed man is a spy. Did they arrest Swiss Cheese? (KATTRIN *shakes her head and shrugs her shoulders*) We're done for.
MOTHER COURAGE (*takes a Catholic flag out of her basket. The* CHAPLAIN *fastens it to the flagpole*): Hoist
1175   the new flag!
THE CHAPLAIN (*bitterly*): All good Catholics here.

(Voices are heard from the rear. The two men bring in SWISS CHEESE)

SWISS CHEESE: Let me go, I haven't got anything. Stop twisting my shoulder, I'm innocent.
THE SERGEANT: He belongs here. You know each other.
1180   MOTHER COURAGE: What makes you think that?

SWISS CHEESE: I don't know them. I don't even know who they are. I had a meal here, it cost me ten hellers. Maybe you saw me sitting here, it was too salty.
THE SERGEANT: Who are you anyway?   1185
MOTHER COURAGE: We're respectable people. And it's true. He had a meal here. He said it was too salty.
THE SERGEANT: Are you trying to tell me you don't know each other?   1190
MOTHER COURAGE: Why should I know him? I don't know everybody. I don't ask people what their name is or if they're heathens; if they pay, they're not heathens. Are you a heathen?
SWISS CHEESE: Of course not.   1195
THE CHAPLAIN: He ate his meal and he behaved himself. He didn't open his mouth except when he was eating. Then you have to.
THE SERGEANT: And who are you?
MOTHER COURAGE: He's only my bartender. You gen- 1200
tlemen must be thirsty, I'll get you a drink of brandy, you must be hot and tired.
THE SERGEANT: We don't drink on duty. (*To* SWISS CHEESE) You were carrying something. You must have hidden it by the river. You had   1205
something under your jacket when you left here.
MOTHER COURAGE: Was it really him?
SWISS CHEESE: I think you must have seen somebody else. I saw a man running with something   1210
under his jacket. You've got the wrong man.
MOTHER COURAGE: That's what I think too, it's a misunderstanding. These things happen. I'm a good judge of people, I'm Mother Courage, you've heard of me, everybody knows me.   1215
Take it from me, this man has an honest face.
THE SERGEANT: We're looking for the cashbox of the Second Finnish Regiment. We know what the man in charge of it looks like. We've been after him for two days. You're him.   1220
SWISS CHEESE: I'm not.
THE SERGEANT: Hand it over. If you don't you're a goner, you know that. Where is it?
MOTHER COURAGE (*with urgency*): He'd hand it over, wouldn't he, knowing he was a goner if he did- 1225
n't? I've got it, he'd say, take it, you're stronger. He's not that stupid. Speak up, you stupid idiot, the sergeant's giving you a chance.
SWISS CHEESE: But I haven't got it.
THE SERGEANT: In that case come along. We'll get it 1230
out of you.

[They lead him away]

MOTHER COURAGE (*shouts after them*): He'd tell you. He's not that stupid. And don't twist his shoulder off! (*Runs after them*)

[The same evening. The CHAPLAIN *and mute* KATTRIN *are washing dishes and scouring knives]*

1235　THE CHAPLAIN: That boy's in trouble. There are cases like that in the Bible. Take the Passion of our Lord and Saviour. There's an old song about it. (*He sings the Song of the Hours*)

1240
In the first hour Jesus mild
Who had prayed since even
Was betrayed and led before
Pontius the heathen.

Pilate found him innocent
Free from fault and error.
1245　Therefore, having washed his hands
Sent him to King Herod.

In the third hour he was scourged
Stripped and clad in scarlet
And a plaited crown of thorns
1250　Set upon his forehead.

On the Son of Man they spat
Mocked him and made merry.
Then the cross of death was brought
Given him to carry.

1255　At the sixth hour with two thieves
To the cross they nailed him
And the people and the thieves
Mocked him and reviled him.

This is Jesus King of Jews
1260　Cried they in derision
Till the sun withdrew its light
From that awful vision.

At the ninth hour Jesus wailed
Why hast thou me forsaken?
1265　Soldiers brought him vinegar
Which he left untaken.

Then he yielded up the ghost
And the earth was shaken.
Rended was the temple's veil
1270　And the saints were wakened.

Soldiers broke the two thieves' legs
As the night descended
Thrust a spear in Jesus' side
When his life had ended.

Still they mocked, as from his wound　1275
Flowed the blood and water
Thus blasphemed the Son of Man
With their cruel laughter.

MOTHER COURAGE (*enters in a state of agitation*): His life's at stake. But they say the sergeant will　1280 listen to reason. Only it mustn't come out that he's our Swiss Cheese, or they'll say we've been giving him aid and comfort. All they want is money. But where will we get the money? Hasn't Yvette been here? I met her just　1285 now, she's latched onto a colonel, he's thinking of buying her a provisioner's business.

THE CHAPLAIN: Are you really thinking of selling?

MOTHER COURAGE: How else can I get the money for the sergeant?　1290

THE CHAPLAIN: But what will you live on?

MOTHER COURAGE: That's the hitch.

*[*YVETTE POTTIER *comes in with a doddering* COLONEL*]*

YVETTE (*embracing* MOTHER COURAGE): My dear Mother Courage. Here we are again! (*Whispering*) He's willing. (*Aloud*) This is my dear friend who　1295 advises me on business matters. I just chanced to hear that you wish to sell your wagon, due to circumstances. I might be interested.

MOTHER COURAGE: Mortgage it, not sell it, let's not be hasty. It's not so easy to buy a wagon like this　1300 in wartime.

YVETTE (*disappointed*): Only mortgage it? I thought you wanted to sell it. In that case, I don't know if I'm interested. (*To the* COLONEL) What do you think?　1305

THE COLONEL: Just as you say, my dear.

MOTHER COURAGE: It's only being mortgaged.

YVETTE: I thought you needed money.

MOTHER COURAGE (*firmly*): I need the money, but I'd rather run myself ragged looking for an offer　1310 than sell now. The wagon is our livelihood. It's an opportunity for you, Yvette, God knows when you'll find another like it and have such a good friend to advise you. See what I mean?

YVETTE: My friend thinks I should snap it up, but I　1315 don't know. If it's only being mortgaged . . . Don't you agree that we ought to buy?

THE COLONEL: Yes, my dear.

MOTHER COURAGE: Then you'll have to look for something that's for sale, maybe you'll find　1320 something if you take your time and your friend goes around with you. Maybe in a week or two you'll find the right thing.

YVETTE: Then we'll go looking, I love to go looking for things, and I love to go around with you,　1325 Poldi, it's a real pleasure. Even if it takes two weeks. When would you pay the money back if you get it?

MOTHER COURAGE: I can pay it back in two weeks, maybe one. 1330

YVETTE: I can't make up my mind, Poldi, chéri, tell me what to do. (*She takes the* COLONEL *aside*) I know she's got to sell, that's definite. The lieutenant, you know who I mean, the blond one, he'd be glad to lend me the money. He's mad about me, he says I remind him of somebody. What do you think? 1335

THE COLONEL: Keep away from that lieutenant. He's no good. He'll take advantage. Haven't I told you I'd buy you something, pussykins? 1340

YVETTE: I can't accept it from you. But then if you think the lieutenant might take advantage . . . Poldi, I'll accept it from you.

THE COLONEL: I hope so.

YVETTE: Your advice is to take it? 1345

THE COLONEL: That's my advice.

YVETTE (*goes back to* MOTHER COURAGE): My friend advises me to do it. Write me out a receipt, say the wagon belongs to me complete with stock and furnishings when the two weeks are up. We'll take inventory right now, then I'll bring you the two hundred guilders. (*To the* COLONEL) You go back to camp, I'll join you in a little while, I've got to take inventory, I don't want anything missing from my wagon. (*She kisses him. He leaves. She climbs up in the wagon*) I don't see very many boots. 1350 / 1355

MOTHER COURAGE: Yvette. This is no time to inspect your wagon if it is yours. You promised to see the sergeant about my Swiss Cheese, you've got to hurry. They say he's to be court-martialed in an hour. 1360

YVETTE: Just let me count the shirts.

MOTHER COURAGE (*pulls her down by the skirt*): You hyena, it's Swiss Cheese, his life's at stake. And don't tell anybody where the offer comes from, in heaven's name say it's your gentleman friend, or we'll all get it, they'll say we helped him. 1365

YVETTE: I've arranged to meet One-Eye in the woods, he must be there already. 1370

THE CHAPLAIN: And there's no need to start out with the whole two hundred, offer a hundred and fifty, that's plenty.

MOTHER COURAGE: Is it your money? You just keep out of this. Don't worry, you'll get your bread and soup. Go on now and don't haggle. It's his life. (*She gives* YVETTE *a push to start her on her way*) 1375

THE CHAPLAIN: I didn't mean to butt in, but what are we going to live on? You've got an unemployable daughter on your hands. 1380

MOTHER COURAGE: You muddlehead, I'm counting on the regimental cashbox. They'll allow for his expenses, won't they?

THE CHAPLAIN: But will she handle it right? 1385

MOTHER COURAGE: It's in her own interest. If I spend her two hundred, she gets the wagon. She's mighty keen on it, how long can she expect to hold on to her colonel? Kattrin, you scour the knives, use pumice. And you, don't stand around like Jesus on the Mount of Olives, bestir yourself, wash those glasses, we're expecting at least fifty for dinner, and then it'll be the same old story: "Oh my feet, I'm not used to running around, I don't run around in the pulpit." I think they'll set him free. Thank God they're open to bribery. They're not wolves, they're human and out for money. Bribe-taking in humans is the same as mercy in God. It's our only hope. As long as people take bribes, you'll have mild sentences and even the innocent will get off once in a while. 1390 / 1395 / 1400

YVETTE (*comes in panting*): They want two hundred. And we've got to be quick. Or it'll be out of their hands. I'd better take One-Eye to see my colonel right away. He confessed that he'd had the cashbox, they put the thumb screws on him. But he threw it in the river when he saw they were after him. The box is gone. Should I run and get the money from my colonel? 1405 / 1410

MOTHER COURAGE: The box is gone? How will I get my two hundred back?

YVETTE: Ah, so you thought you could take it out of the cashbox? You thought you'd put one over on me. Forget it. If you want to save Swiss Cheese, you'll just have to pay, or maybe you'd like me to drop the whole thing and let you keep your wagon? 1415

MOTHER COURAGE: This is something I hadn't reckoned with. But don't rush me, you'll get the wagon, I know it's down the drain, I've had it for seventeen years. Just let me think a second, it's all so sudden. What'll I do, I can't give them two hundred, I guess you should have bargained. If I haven't got a few guilders to fall back on, I'll be at the mercy of the first Tom, Dick, or Harry. Say I'll give them a hundred and twenty, I'll lose my wagon anyway. 1420 / 1425

YVETTE: They won't go along. One-Eye's in a hurry, he's so keyed-up he keeps looking behind him. Hadn't I better give them the whole two hundred? 1430

MOTHER COURAGE (*in despair*): I can't do it. Thirty years I've worked. She's twenty-five and no husband. I've got her to keep too. Don't needle me, I know what I'm doing. Say a hundred and twenty or nothing doing. 1435

YVETTE: It's up to you. (*Goes out quickly*)

[MOTHER COURAGE *looks neither at the* CHAPLAIN *nor at her daughter. She sits down to help* KATTRIN *scour the knives*]

MOTHER COURAGE: Don't break the glasses. They're not ours any more. Watch what you're doing, you'll cut yourself. Swiss Cheese will be back, I'll pay two hundred if I have to. You'll have your brother. With eighty guilders we can buy a peddler's pack and start all over. Worse things have happened.

THE CHAPLAIN: The Lord will provide.

MOTHER COURAGE: Rub them dry. (*They scour the knives in silence. Suddenly* KATTRIN *runs sobbing behind the wagon*)

YVETTE (*comes running*): They won't go along. I warned you. One-Eye wanted to run out on me, he said it was no use. He said we'd hear the drums any minute, meaning he'd been sentenced. I offered a hundred and fifty. He didn't even bother to shrug his shoulders. When I begged and pleaded, he promised to wait till I'd spoken to you again.

MOTHER COURAGE: Say I'll give him the two hundred. Run. (YVETTE *runs off. They sit in silence. The* CHAPLAIN *has stopped washing the glasses*) Maybe I bargained too long. (*Drums are heard in the distance. The* CHAPLAIN *stands up and goes to the rear.* MOTHER COURAGE *remains seated. It grows dark. The drums stop. It grows light again.* MOTHER COURAGE *has not moved*)

YVETTE (*enters, very pale*): Now you've done it with your haggling and wanting to keep your wagon. Eleven bullets he got, that's all. I don't know why I bother with you any more, you don't deserve it. But I've picked up a little information. They don't believe the cashbox is really in the river. They suspect it's here and they think you were connected with him. They're going to bring him here, they think maybe you'll give yourself away when you see him. I'm warning you: You don't know him, or you're all dead ducks. I may as well tell you, they're right behind me. Should I keep Kattrin out of the way? (MOTHER COURAGE *shakes her head*) Does she know? Maybe she didn't hear the drums or maybe she didn't understand.

MOTHER COURAGE: She knows. Get her.

[YVETTE *brings* KATTRIN, *who goes to her mother and stands beside her.* MOTHER COURAGE *takes her by the hand. Two soldiers come in with a stretcher on which something is lying under a sheet. The* SERGEANT *walks beside them. They set the stretcher down*]

THE SERGEANT: We've got a man here and we don't know his name. We need it for the records. He had a meal with you. Take a look, see if you know him. (*He removes the sheet*) Do you know him? (MOTHER COURAGE *shakes her head*) What? You'd never seen him before he came here for a meal? (MOTHER COURAGE *shakes her head*) Pick him up. Throw him on the dump. Nobody knows him. (*They carry him away*)

ACT 4

MOTHER COURAGE *sings the Song of the Great Capitulation.*
   Outside an officer's tent.
   MOTHER COURAGE *is waiting. A* CLERK *looks out of the tent.*

THE CLERK: I know you. You had a Protestant paymaster at your place, he was hiding. I wouldn't put in any complaints if I were you.

MOTHER COURAGE: I'm putting in a complaint. I'm innocent. If I take this lying down, it'll look as if I had a guilty conscience. First they ripped up my whole wagon with their sabers, then they wanted me to pay a fine of five talers for no reason at all.

THE CLERK: I'm advising you for your own good: Keep your trap shut. We haven't got many provisioners and we'll let you keep on with your business, especially if you've got a guilty conscience and pay a fine now and then.

MOTHER COURAGE: I'm putting in a complaint.

THE CLERK: Have it your way. But you'll have to wait till the captain can see you. (*Disappears into the tent*)

A YOUNG SOLDIER (*enters in a rage*): Bouque la Madonne! Where's that stinking captain? He embezzled my reward and now he's drinking it up with his whores. I'm going to get him!

AN OLDER SOLDIER (*comes running after him*): Shut up. They'll put you in the stocks!

THE YOUNG SOLDIER: Come on out, you crook! I'll make chops out of you. Embezzling my reward! Who jumps in the river? Not another man in the whole squad, only me. And I can't even buy myself a beer. I won't stand for it. Come on out and let me cut you to pieces!

THE OLDER SOLDIER: Holy Mary! He'll ruin himself.

MOTHER COURAGE: They didn't give him a reward?

THE YOUNG SOLDIER: Let me go. I'll run you through too, the more the merrier.

THE OLDER SOLDIER: He saved the colonel's horse and they didn't give him a reward. He's young, he hasn't been around long.

MOTHER COURAGE: Let him go, he's not a dog, you don't have to tie him up. Wanting a reward is perfectly reasonable. Why else would he distinguish himself?

THE YOUNG SOLDIER: And him drinking in there! You're all a lot of yellowbellies. I distinguished myself and I want my reward.

1535 MOTHER COURAGE: Young man, don't shout at me. I've got my own worries and besides, go easy on your voice, you may need it. You'll be hoarse when the captain comes out, you won't
1540 be able to say boo and he won't be able to put you in the stocks till you're blue in the face. People that yell like that don't last long, maybe half an hour, then they're so exhausted you have to sing them to sleep.
THE YOUNG SOLDIER: I'm not exhausted and who
1545 wants to sleep? I'm hungry. They make our bread out of acorns and hemp seed, and they skimp on that. He's whoring away my reward and I'm hungry. I'll murder him.
MOTHER COURAGE: I see. You're hungry. Last year
1550 your general made you cut across the fields to trample down the grain. I could have sold a pair of boots for ten guilders if anybody'd had ten guilders and if I'd had any boots. He thought he'd be someplace else this year, but
1555 now he's still here and everybody's starving. I can see that you might be good and mad.
THE YOUNG SOLDIER: He can't do this to me, save your breath, I won't put up with injustice.
MOTHER COURAGE: You're right, but for how long?
1560 How long won't you put up with injustice? An hour? Two hours? You see, you never thought of that, though it's very important, because it's miserable in the stocks when it suddenly dawns on you that you *can* put up with injustice.
1565 THE YOUNG SOLDIER: I don't know why I listen to you. Bouque la Madonne! Where's the captain?
MOTHER COURAGE: You listen to me because I'm not telling you anything new. You know your temper has gone up in smoke, it was a short tem-
1570 per and you need a long one, but that's a hard thing to come by.
THE YOUNG SOLDIER: Are you trying to say I've no right to claim my reward?
MOTHER COURAGE: Not at all. I'm only saying your
1575 temper isn't long enough, it won't get you anywhere. Too bad. If you had a long temper, I'd even egg you on. Chop the bastard up, that's what I'd say, but suppose you don't chop him up, because your tail's drooping and
1580 you know it. I'm left standing there like a fool and the captain takes it out on me.
THE OLDER SOLDIER: You're right. He's only blowing off steam.
THE YOUNG SOLDIER: We'll see about that. I'll cut him
1585 to pieces. (*He draws his sword*) When he comes out, I'll cut him to pieces.
THE CLERK (*looks out*): The captain will be here in a moment. Sit down.

(*The* YOUNG SOLDIER *sits down*)

MOTHER COURAGE: There he sits. What did I tell you? Sitting, aren't you? Oh, they know us like a 1590 book, they know how to handle us. Sit down! And down we sit. You can't start a riot sitting down. Better not stand up again, you won't be able to stand the way you were standing before. Don't be embarrassed on my account, 1595 I'm no better, not a bit of it. We were full of piss and vinegar, but they've bought it off. Look at me. No back talk, it's bad for business. Let me tell you about the great capitulation. (*She sings the Song of the Great Capitulation*) 1600

When I was young, no more than a spring chicken
I too thought that I was really quite the cheese
(No common peddler's daughter, not I with my looks and
*   my talent and striving for higher things!)*
One little hair in the soup would make me sicken 1605
And at me no man would dare to sneeze.
(It's all or nothing, no second best for me. I've got what
*   it takes, the rules are for somebody else!)*

But a chickadee
Sang wait and see! 1610
*   And you go marching with the show*
*   In step, however fast or slow*
*   And rattle off your little song:*
*   It won't be long.*
*   And then the whole thing slides.* 1615
*   You think God provides—*
*   But you've got it wrong.*

And before one single year had wasted
I had learned to swallow down the bitter brew
(Two kids on my hands and the price of bread and who 1620
*   do they take me for anyway!)*
Man, the double-edged shellacking that I tasted
On my ass and knees I was when they were through.
(You've got to get along with people, one good turn
*   deserves another, no use trying to ram your head* 1625
*   through the wall!)*
And the chickadee
Sang wait and see!
*   And she goes marching with the show*
*   In step, however fast or slow* 1630
*   And rattles off her little song:*
*   It won't be long.*
*   And then the whole thing slides*
*   You think God provides—*
*   But you've got it wrong.* 1635

I've seen many fired by high ambition
No star's big or high enough to reach out for.
(It's ability that counts, where there's a will there's a
*   way, one way or another we'll swing it!)*
Then while moving mountains they get a suspicion 1640

That to wear a straw hat is too big a chore.
(No use being too big for your britches!)
And the chickadee
Sings wait and see!
1645   And they go marching with the show
In step, however fast or slow
And rattle off their little song:
It won't be long.
And then the whole thing slides!
1650   You think God provides—
But you've got it wrong!

MOTHER COURAGE (to the YOUNG SOLDIER): So here's
    what I think: Stay here with your sword if
    your anger's big enough, I know you have
1655   good reason, but if it's a short quick anger, bet-
    ter make tracks!
THE YOUNG SOLDIER: Kiss my ass! (He staggers off, the
    OLDER SOLDIER after him)
THE CLERK (sticking his head out): The captain is here.
1660   You can put in your complaint now.
MOTHER COURAGE: I've changed my mind. No com-
    plaint. (She goes out)

ACT 5

Two years have passed. The war has spread far and
wide. With scarcely a pause MOTHER COURAGE's little
wagon rolls through Poland, Moravia, Bavaria, Italy,
and back again to Bavaria. 1631. Tilly's victory at
Magdeburg costs MOTHER COURAGE four officers'
shirts.
    MOTHER COURAGE's wagon has stopped in a devas-
tated village.
    Thin military music is heard from the distance.
Two soldiers at the bar are being waited on by
KATTRIN and MOTHER COURAGE. One of them is wearing a lady's fur coat over his shoulders.

MOTHER COURAGE: What's that? You can't pay? No
    money, no schnapps. Plenty of victory marches
1665   for the Lord but no pay for the men.
THE SOLDIER: I want my schnapps. I came too late for
    the looting. The general skunked us: permission
    to loot the city for exactly one hour. Says he's
    not a monster; the mayor must have paid him.
1670 THE CHAPLAIN (staggers in): There's still some
    wounded in the house. The peasant and his
    family. Help me, somebody, I need linen.

[The SECOND SOLDIER goes out with him. KATTRIN gets
very excited and tries to persuade her mother to hand
out linen]

MOTHER COURAGE: I haven't got any. The regiment's

bought up all my bandages. You think I'm
going to rip up my officers' shirts for the likes 1675
of them?
THE CHAPLAIN (calling back): I need linen, I tell you.
MOTHER COURAGE (sitting down on the wagon steps to
    keep KATTRIN out): Nothing doing. They don't
    pay, they got nothing to pay with. 1680
THE CHAPLAIN (bending over a woman whom he has car-
    ried out): Why did you stay here in all that
    gunfire?
THE PEASANT WOMAN (feebly): Farm.
MOTHER COURAGE: You won't catch them leaving 1685
    their property. And I'm expected to foot the
    bill. I won't do it.
THE FIRST SOLDIER: They're Protestants. Why do they
    have to be Protestants?
MOTHER COURAGE: Religion is the least of their wor- 1690
    ries. They've lost their farm.
THE SECOND SOLDIER: They're no Protestants. They're
    Catholics like us.
THE FIRST SOLDIER: How do we know who we're
    shooting at? 1695
A PEASANT (whom the CHAPLAIN brings in): They got
    my arm.
THE CHAPLAIN: Where's the linen?

[All look at MOTHER COURAGE, who does not move]

MOTHER COURAGE: I can't give you a thing. What with
    all my taxes, duties, fees and bribes! (Making 1700
    guttural sounds, KATTRIN picks up a board and
    threatens her mother with it) Are you crazy? Put
    that board down, you slut, or I'll smack you. I'm
    not giving anything, you can't make me, I've got
    to think of myself. (The CHAPLAIN picks her up 1705
    from the step and puts her down on the ground. Then
    he fishes out some shirts and tears them into strips)
    My shirts! Half a guilder apiece! I'm ruined!

[The anguished cry of a baby is heard from the house]

THE PEASANT: The baby's still in there! 1710

[KATTRIN runs in]

THE CHAPLAIN (to the woman): Don't move. They're
    bringing him out.
MOTHER COURAGE: Get her out of there. The roof'll
    cave in.
THE CHAPLAIN: I'm not going in there again. 1715
MOTHER COURAGE (torn): Don't run hog-wild with
    my expensive linen.

[KATTRIN emerges from the ruins carrying an infant]

MOTHER COURAGE: Oh, so you've found another baby
    to carry around with you? Give that baby back

1720 to its mother this minute, or it'll take me all day to get it away from you. Do you hear me? (*To the second soldier*) Don't stand there gaping, go back and tell them to stop that music, I can see right here that they've won a victory. Your 1725 victory's costing me a pretty penny.

[KATTRIN *rocks the baby in her arms, humming a lullaby*]

MOTHER COURAGE: There she sits, happy in all this misery; give it back this minute, the mother's coming to. (*She pounces on the* FIRST SOLDIER *who has been helping himself to the drinks and is now* 1730 *making off with the bottle*) Pshagreff! Beast! Haven't you had enough victories for today? Pay up.
FIRST SOLDIER: I'm broke.
MOTHER COURAGE (*tears the fur coat off him*): Then 1735 leave the coat here, it's stolen anyway.
THE CHAPLAIN: There's still somebody in there.

ACT 6

Outside Ingolstadt in Bavaria MOTHER COURAGE *attends the funeral of Tilly, the imperial field marshal. Conversations about heroes and the longevity of the war. The* CHAPLAIN *deplores the waste of his talents. Mute* KATTRIN *gets the red shoes. 1632.*
    Inside MOTHER COURAGE's *tent.*
    A bar open to the rear. Rain. In the distance drum rolls and funeral music. The CHAPLAIN *and the regimental* CLERK *are playing a board game.* MOTHER COURAGE *and her daughter are taking inventory.*

THE CHAPLAIN: The procession's starting.
MOTHER COURAGE: It's a shame about the general—socks: twenty-two pairs—I hear he was killed 1740 by accident. On account of the fog in the fields. He's up front encouraging the troops. "Fight to the death, boys," he sings out. Then he rides back, but he gets lost in the fog and rides back forward. Before you know it he's in the middle 1745 of the battle and stops a bullet—lanterns: we're down to four. (*A whistle from the rear. She goes to the bar*) You men ought to be ashamed, running out on your late general's funeral! (*She pours drinks*)
1750 THE CLERK: They shouldn't have been paid before the funeral. Now they're getting drunk instead.
THE CHAPLAIN (*to the clerk*): Shouldn't you be at the funeral?
THE CLERK: In this rain?
1755 MOTHER COURAGE: With you it's different, the rain might spoil your uniform. It seems they wanted to ring the bells, naturally, but it turned out

the churches had all been shot to pieces by his orders, so the poor general won't hear any bells when they lower him into his grave. 1760 They're going to fire a three-gun salute instead, so it won't be too dull—seventeen sword belts.
CRIES (*from the bar*): Hey! Brandy!
MOTHER COURAGE: Money first! No, you can't come 1765 into my tent with your muddy boots! You can drink outside, rain or no rain. (*To the* CLERK) I'm only letting officers in. It seems the general had been having his troubles. Mutiny in the Second Regiment because he hadn't paid 1770 them. It's a war of religion, he says, should they profit by their faith?

[*Funeral march. All look to the rear*]

THE CHAPLAIN: Now they're marching past the body.
MOTHER COURAGE: I feel sorry when a general or an emperor passes away like this, maybe he 1775 thought he'd do something big, that posterity would still be talking about and maybe put up a statue in his honor, conquer the world, for instance, that's a nice ambition for a general, he doesn't know any better. So he knocks him- 1780 self out, and then the common people come and spoil it all, because what do they care about greatness, all they care about is a mug of beer and maybe a little company. The most beautiful plans have been wrecked by the 1785 smallness of the people that are supposed to carry them out. Even an emperor can't do anything by himself, he needs the support of his soldiers and his people. Am I right?
THE CHAPLAIN (*laughing*): Courage, you're right, 1790 except about the soldiers. They do their best. With those fellows out there, for instance, drinking their brandy in the rain, I'll undertake to carry on one war after another for a hundred years, two at once if I have to, and 1795 I'm not a general by trade.
MOTHER COURAGE: Then you don't think the war might stop?
THE CHAPLAIN: Because the general's dead? Don't be childish. They grow by the dozen, there'll 1800 always be plenty of heroes.
MOTHER COURAGE: Look here, I'm not asking you for the hell of it. I've been wondering whether to lay in supplies while they're cheap, but if the war stops, I can throw them out the window. 1805
THE CHAPLAIN: I understand. You want a serious answer. There have always been people who say: "The war will be over some day." I say there's no guarantee the war will ever be over. Naturally a brief intermission is conceivable. 1810 Maybe the war needs a breather, a war can

even break its neck, so to speak. There's always a chance of that, nothing is perfect here below. Maybe there never will be a perfect war, one that lives up to all our expectations. Suddenly, for some unforeseen reason, a war can bog down, you can't think of everything. Some little oversight and your war's in trouble. And then you've got to pull it out of the mud. But the kings and emperors, not to mention the pope, will always come to its help in adversity. On the whole, I'd say this war has very little to worry about, it'll live to a ripe old age.

A SOLDIER (*sings at the bar*):

> A drink, and don't be slow!
> A soldier's got to go
> And fight for his religion.

Make it double, this is a holiday.

MOTHER COURAGE: If I could only be sure . . .

THE CHAPLAIN: Figure it out for yourself. What's to stop the war?

THE SOLDIER (*sings*):

> Your breasts, girl, don't be slow!
> A soldier's got to go
> And ride away to Pilsen.

THE CLERK (*suddenly*): But why can't we have peace? I'm from Bohemia, I'd like to go home when the time comes.

THE CHAPLAIN: Oh, you'd like to go home? Ah, peace! What becomes of the hole when the cheese has been eaten?

THE SOLDIER (*sings*):

> Play cards, friends, don't be slow!
> A soldier's got to go
> No matter if it's Sunday.

> A prayer, priest, don't be slow!
> A soldier's got to go
> And die for king and country.

THE CLERK: In the long run nobody can live without peace.

THE CHAPLAIN: The way I see it, war gives you plenty of peace. It has its peaceful moments. War meets every need, including the peaceful ones, everything's taken care of, or your war couldn't hold its own. In a war you can shit the same as in the dead of peace, you can stop for a beer between battles, and even on the march you can always lie down on your elbows and take a little nap by the roadside. You can't play cards when you're fighting; but then you can't when you're plowing in the dead of peace either, but after a victory the sky's the limit. Maybe you've had a leg shot off, at first you raise a howl, you make a big thing of it. But then you calm down or they give you schnapps, and in the end you're hopping around again and the war's no worse off than before. And what's to prevent you from multiplying in the thick of the slaughter, behind a barn or someplace, in the long run how can they stop you, and then the war has your progeny to help it along. Take it from me, the war will always find an answer. Why would it have to stop?

[KATTRIN *has stopped working and is staring at the* CHAPLAIN]

MOTHER COURAGE: Then I'll buy the merchandise. You've convinced me. (KATTRIN *suddenly throws down a basket full of bottles and runs out*) Kattrin! (*Laughs*) My goodness, the poor thing's been hoping for peace. I promised her she'd get a husband when peace comes. (*She runs after her*)

THE CLERK (*getting up*): I win, you've been too busy talking. Pay up.

MOTHER COURAGE (*comes back with* KATTRIN): Be reasonable, the war'll go on a little longer and we'll make a little more money, then peace will be even better. Run along to town now, it won't take you ten minutes, and get the stuff from the Golden Lion, only the expensive things, we'll pick up the rest in the wagon later, it's all arranged, the regimental clerk here will go with you. They've almost all gone to the general's funeral, nothing can happen to you. Look sharp, don't let them take anything away from you, think of your dowry.

[KATTRIN *puts a kerchief over her head and goes with the* CLERK]

THE CHAPLAIN: Is it all right letting her go with the clerk?

MOTHER COURAGE: Who'd want to ruin her? She's not pretty enough.

THE CHAPLAIN: I've come to admire the way you handle your business and pull through every time. I can see why they call you Mother Courage.

MOTHER COURAGE: Poor people need courage. Why? Because they're sunk. In their situation it takes gumption just to get up in the morning. Or to

1910

1915

plow a field in the middle of a war. They even show courage by bringing children into the world, because look at the prospects. The way they butcher and execute each other, think of the courage they need to look each other in the face. And putting up with an emperor and a pope takes a whale of a lot of courage, because those two are the death of the poor. (*She sits down, takes a small pipe from her pocket and smokes*) You could be making some kindling.

THE CHAPLAIN (*reluctantly takes his jacket off and prepares to chop*): Chopping wood isn't really my trade, you know, I'm a shepherd of souls.

1920 MOTHER COURAGE: Sure. But I have no soul and I need firewood.

THE CHAPLAIN: What's that pipe?

MOTHER COURAGE: Just a pipe.

THE CHAPLAIN: No, it's not "just a pipe," it's a very

1925 particular pipe.

MOTHER COURAGE: Really?

THE CHAPLAIN: It's the cook's pipe from the Oxenstjerna regiment.

MOTHER COURAGE: If you know it all, why the mealy-

1930 mouthed questions?

THE CHAPLAIN: I didn't know if *you* knew. You could have been rummaging through your belongings and laid hands on some pipe and picked it up without thinking.

1935 MOTHER COURAGE: Yes. Maybe that's how it was.

THE CHAPLAIN: Except it wasn't. You knew who that pipe belongs to.

MOTHER COURAGE: What of it?

THE CHAPLAIN: Courage, I'm warning you. It's my

1940 duty. I doubt if you ever lay eyes on the man again, but that's no calamity, in fact you're lucky. If you ask me, he wasn't steady. Not at all.

MOTHER COURAGE: What makes you say that? He was a nice man.

1945 THE CHAPLAIN: Oh, you think he was nice? I differ. Far be it from me to wish him any harm, but I can't say he was nice. I'd say he was a scheming Don Juan. If you don't believe me, take a look at his pipe. You'll have to admit that it

1950 shows up his character.

MOTHER COURAGE: I don't see anything. It's beat up.

THE CHAPLAIN: It's half bitten through. A violent man. That is the pipe of a ruthless, violent man, you must see that if you've still got an

1955 ounce of good sense.

MOTHER COURAGE: Don't wreck my chopping block.

THE CHAPLAIN: I've told you I wasn't trained to chop wood. I studied theology. My gifts and abilities are being wasted on muscular effort. The talents that God gave me are lying fallow. That's

1960 a sin. You've never heard me preach. With one sermon I can whip a regiment into such a state that they take the enemy for a flock of sheep.

Then men care no more about their lives than they would about a smelly old sock that they're ready to throw away in hopes of final victory. God has made me eloquent. You'll swoon when you hear me preach.

1965

MOTHER COURAGE: I don't want to swoon. What good would that do me?

1970

THE CHAPLAIN: Courage, I've often wondered if maybe you didn't conceal a warm heart under that hard-bitten talk of yours. You too are human, you need warmth.

MOTHER COURAGE: The best way to keep this tent warm is with plenty of firewood.

1975

THE CHAPLAIN: Don't try to put me off. Seriously, Courage, I sometimes wonder if we couldn't make our relationship a little closer. I mean, seeing that the whirlwind of war has whirled us so strangely together.

1980

MOTHER COURAGE: Seems to me it's close enough. I cook your meals and you do chores, such as chopping wood, for instance.

THE CHAPLAIN (*goes toward her*): You know what I mean by "closer"; it has nothing to do with meals and chopping wood and such mundane needs. Don't harden your heart, let it speak.

1985

MOTHER COURAGE: Don't come at me with that ax. That's too close a relationship.

1990

THE CHAPLAIN: Don't turn it to ridicule. I'm serious, I've given it careful thought.

MOTHER COURAGE: Chaplain, don't be silly. I like you, I don't want to have to scold you. My aim in life is to get through, me and my children and my wagon. I don't think of it as mine and besides I'm not in the mood for private affairs. Right now I'm taking a big risk, buying up merchandise with the general dead and everybody talking peace. What'll you do if I'm ruined? See? You don't know. Chop that wood, then we'll be warm in the evening, which is a good thing in times like these. Now what? (*She stands up*)

1995

2000

[*Enter* KATTRIN *out of breath, with a wound across her forehead and over one eye. She is carrying all sorts of things, packages, leather goods, a drum, etc.*]

MOTHER COURAGE: What's that? Assaulted? On the way back? She was assaulted on the way back. Must have been that soldier that got drunk here! I shouldn't have let you go! Throw the stuff down! It's not bad, only a flesh wound. I'll bandage it, it'll heal in a week. They're worse than wild beasts. (*She bandages the wound*)

2005

2010

THE CHAPLAIN: I can't find fault with them. At home they never raped anybody. I blame the people that start wars, they're the ones that dredge up man's lowest instincts.

MOTHER COURAGE: Didn't the clerk bring you back?

2015

That's because you're respectable, they don't give a damn. It's not a deep wound, it won't leave a mark. There, all bandaged. Don't fret, I've got something for you. I've been keeping it for you on the sly, it'll be a surprise. (*She fishes* YVETTE'S *red shoes out of a sack*) See? You've always wanted them. Now you've got them. Put them on quick before I regret it. It won't leave a mark, though I wouldn't mind if it did. The girls that attract them get the worst of it. They drag them around till there's nothing left of them. If you don't appeal to them, they won't harm you. I've seen girls with pretty faces, a few years later they'd have given a wolf the creeps. They can't step behind a bush without fearing the worst. It's like trees. The straight tall ones get chopped down for ridgepoles, the crooked ones enjoy life. In other words, it's a lucky break. The shoes are still in good condition, I've kept them nicely polished.

[KATTRIN *leaves the shoes where they are and crawls into the wagon*]

THE CHAPLAIN: I hope she won't be disfigured.
MOTHER COURAGE: There'll be a scar. She can stop waiting for peace.
THE CHAPLAIN: She didn't let them take anything.
MOTHER COURAGE: Maybe I shouldn't have drummed it into her. If I only knew what went on in her head. One night she stayed out, the only time in all these years. Afterwards she traipsed around as usual, except she worked harder. I never could find out what happened. I racked my brains for quite some time. (*She picks up the articles brought by* KATTRIN *and sorts them angrily*) That's war for you! A fine way to make a living! (*Cannon salutes are heard*)
THE CHAPLAIN: Now they're burying the general. This is a historic moment.
MOTHER COURAGE: To me it's a historic moment when they hit my daughter over the eye. She's a wreck, she'll never get a husband now, and she's so crazy about children. It's the war that made her dumb too, a soldier stuffed something in her mouth when she was little. I'll never see Swiss Cheese again and where Eilif is, God knows. God damn the war.

ACT 7

MOTHER COURAGE *at the height of her business career.*
  Highway.
  The CHAPLAIN, MOTHER COURAGE *and her daughter* KATTRIN *are pulling the wagon. New wares are hanging on it.* MOTHER COURAGE *is wearing a necklace of silver talers.*

MOTHER COURAGE: Stop running down the war. I won't have it. I know it destroys the weak, but the weak haven't a chance in peacetime either. And war is a better provider. (*Sings*)

*If you're not strong enough to take it
The victory will find you dead.
A war is only what you make it.
It's business, not with cheese but lead.*

  And what good is it staying in one place? The stay-at-homes are the first to get it. (*Sings*)

*Some people think they'd like to ride out
The war, leave danger to the brave
And dig themselves a cozy hideout—
They'll dig themselves an early grave.
I've seen them running from the thunder
To find a refuge from the war
But once they're resting six feet under
They wonder what they hurried for.*

[*They plod on*]

ACT 8

In the same year Gustavus Adolphus, King of Sweden, is killed at the battle of Lützen. Peace threatens to ruin MOTHER COURAGE'*s business. Her brave son performs one heroic deed too many and dies an ignominious death.*
  A camp.
  A summer morning. An OLD WOMAN *and her son are standing by the wagon. The son is carrying a large sack of bedding.*

MOTHER COURAGE'S VOICE (*from the wagon*): Does it have to be at this unearthly hour?
THE YOUNG MAN: We've walked all night, twenty miles, and we've got to go back today.
MOTHER COURAGE'S VOICE: What can I do with bedding? The people haven't any houses.
THE YOUNG MAN: Wait till you've seen it.
THE OLD WOMAN: She won't take it either. Come on.
THE YOUNG MAN: They'll sell the roof from over our heads for taxes. Maybe she'll give us three guilders if you throw in the cross. (*Bells start ringing*) Listen, mother!
VOICES (*from the rear*): Peace! The king of Sweden is dead!
MOTHER COURAGE (*sticks her head out of the wagon. She*

has not yet done her hair): Why are the bells ringing in the middle of the week?

2095   THE CHAPLAIN (*crawls out from under the wagon*): What are they shouting?

MOTHER COURAGE: Don't tell me peace has broken out when I've just taken in more supplies.

THE CHAPLAIN (*shouting toward the rear*): Is it true?
2100   Peace?

VOICE: Three weeks ago, they say. But we just found out.

THE CHAPLAIN (*to* MOTHER COURAGE): What else would they ring the bells for?

2105   VOICE: There's a whole crowd of Lutherans, they've driven their carts into town. They brought the news.

THE YOUNG MAN: Mother, it's peace. What's the matter?

[The OLD WOMAN *has collapsed]*

2110   MOTHER COURAGE (*going back into the wagon*): Heavenly saints! Kattrin, peace! Put your black dress on! We're going to church. We owe it to Swiss Cheese. Can it be true?

THE YOUNG MAN: The people here say the same
2115   thing. They've made peace. Can you get up? (*The* OLD WOMAN *stands up, still stunned*) I'll get the saddle shop started again. I promise. Everything will be all right. Father will get his bed back. Can you walk? (*To the* CHAPLAIN) She
2120   fainted. It was the news. She thought peace would never come again. Father said it would. We'll go straight home. (*Both go out*)

MOTHER COURAGE'S VOICE: Give her some brandy.

THE CHAPLAIN: They're gone.

2125   MOTHER COURAGE'S VOICE: What's going on in camp?

THE CHAPLAIN: A big crowd. I'll go see. Shouldn't I put on my clericals?

MOTHER COURAGE'S VOICE: Better make sure before you step out in your antichrist costume. I'm
2130   glad to see peace, even if I'm ruined. At least I've brought two of my children through the war. Now I'll see my Eilif again.

THE CHAPLAIN: Look who's coming down the road. If it isn't the general's cook!

2135   THE COOK (*rather bedraggled, carrying a bundle*): Can I believe my eyes? The chaplain!

THE CHAPLAIN: Courage! A visitor!

[MOTHER COURAGE climbs down]

THE COOK: Didn't I promise to come over for a little chat as soon as I had time? I've never forgotten
2140   your brandy, Mrs. Fierling.

MOTHER COURAGE: Mercy, the general's cook! After all these years! Where's Eilif, my eldest?

THE COOK: Isn't he here yet? He left ahead of me, he

was coming to see you too.

THE CHAPLAIN: I'll put on my clericals, wait for me.   2145 (*Goes out behind the wagon*)

MOTHER COURAGE: Then he'll be here any minute. (*Calls into the wagon*) Kattrin, Eilif's coming! Bring the cook a glass of brandy! (KATTRIN *does not appear*) Put a lock of hair over it, and forget   2150 it! Mr. Lamb is no stranger. (*Gets the brandy herself*) She won't come out. Peace doesn't mean a thing to her, it's come too late. They hit her over the eye, there's hardly any mark, but she thinks people are staring at her.   2155

THE COOK: Ech, war! (*He and* MOTHER COURAGE *sit down*)

MOTHER COURAGE: Cook, you find me in trouble. I'm ruined.

THE COOK: What? Say, that's a shame.

MOTHER COURAGE: Peace has done me in. Only the   2160 other day I stocked up. The chaplain's advice. And now they'll all demobilize and leave me sitting on my merchandise.

THE COOK: How could you listen to the chaplain? If I'd had time, I'd have warned you against him,   2165 but the Catholics came too soon. He's a fly-by-night. So now he's the boss here?

MOTHER COURAGE: He washed my dishes and helped me pull the wagon.

THE COOK: Him? Pulling? I guess he's told you a few   2170 of his jokes too, I wouldn't put it past him, he has an unsavory attitude toward women, I tried to reform him, it was hopeless. He's not steady.

MOTHER COURAGE: Are you steady?   2175

THE COOK: If nothing else, I'm steady. Prosit!

MOTHER COURAGE: Steady is no good. I've only lived with one steady man, thank the Lord. I never had to work so hard, he sold the children's blankets when spring came, and he thought   2180 my harmonica was unchristian. In my opinion you're not doing yourself any good by admitting you're steady.

THE COOK: You've still got your old bite, but I respect you for it.   2185

MOTHER COURAGE: Don't tell me you've been dreaming about my old bite.

THE COOK: Well, here we sit, with the bells of peace and your world-famous brandy, that hasn't its equal.   2190

MOTHER COURAGE: The bells of peace don't strike my fancy right now. I don't see them paying the men, they're behind-hand already. Where does that leave me with my famous brandy? Have you been paid?   2195

THE COOK (*hesitantly*): Not really. That's why we demobilized ourselves. Under the circumstances, I says to myself, why should I stay on? I'll go see my friends in the meantime. So here we are.   2200

MOTHER COURAGE: You mean you're out of funds?

THE COOK: If only they'd stop those damn bells! I'd be glad to go into some kind of business. I'm sick of being a cook. They give me roots and shoe leather to work with, and then they throw the hot soup in my face. A cook's got a dog's life these days. I'd rather be in combat, but now we've got peace. (*The* CHAPLAIN *appears in his original dress*). We'll discuss it later.

THE CHAPLAIN: It's still in good condition. There were only a few moths in it.

THE COOK: I don't see why you bother. They won't take you back. Who are you going to inspire now to be an honest soldier and earn his pay at the risk of his life? Besides, I've got a bone to pick with you. Advising this lady to buy useless merchandise on the ground that the war would last forever.

THE CHAPLAIN (*heatedly*):And why, I'd like to know, is it any of your business?

THE COOK: Because it's unscrupulous. How can you meddle in other people's business and give unsolicited advice?

THE CHAPLAIN: Who's meddling? (*To* MOTHER COURAGE) I didn't know you were accountable to this gentleman, I didn't know you were so intimate with him.

MOTHER COURAGE: Don't get excited, the cook is only giving his private opinion. And you can't deny that your war was a dud.

THE CHAPLAIN: Courage, don't blaspheme against peace. You're a battlefield hyena.

MOTHER COURAGE: What am I?

THE COOK: If you insult this lady, you'll hear from me.

THE CHAPLAIN: I'm not talking to you. Your intentions are too obvious. (*To* MOTHER COURAGE) But when I see you picking up peace with thumb and forefinger like a snotty handkerchief, it revolts my humanity; you don't want peace, you want war, because you profit by it, but don't forget the old saying: "He hath need of a long spoon that eateth with the devil."

MOTHER COURAGE: I've no use for war and war hasn't much use for me. Anyway, I'm not letting anybody call me a hyena, you and me are through.

THE CHAPLAIN: How can you complain about peace when it's such a relief to everybody else? On account of the old rags in your wagon?

MOTHER COURAGE: My merchandise isn't old rags, it's what I live off, and so did you.

THE CHAPLAIN: Off war, you mean. Aha!

THE COOK (*to the* CHAPLAIN): You're a grown man, you ought to know there's no sense in giving advice. (*To* MOTHER COURAGE) The best thing you can do now is to sell off certain articles quick, before the prices hit the floor. Dress yourself and get started, there's no time to lose.

MOTHER COURAGE: That's very sensible advice. I think I'll do it.

THE CHAPLAIN: Because the cook says so!

MOTHER COURAGE: Why didn't *you* say so? He's right, I'd better run over to the market. (*She goes into the wagon*)

THE COOK: My round, chaplain. No presence of mind. Here's what you should have said: me give you advice? All I ever did was talk politics! Don't try to take me on. Cockfighting is undignified in a clergyman.

THE CHAPLAIN: If you don't shut up, I'll murder you, undignified or not.

THE COOK (*taking off his shoe and unwinding the wrappings from his feet*): If the war hadn't made a godless bum out of you, you could easily come by a parsonage now that peace is here. They won't need cooks, there's nothing to cook, but people still do a lot of believing, that hasn't changed.

THE CHAPLAIN: See here, Mr. Lamb. Don't try to squeeze me out. Being a bum has made me a better man. I couldn't preach to them any more.

[YVETTE POTTIER *enters, elaborately dressed in black, with a cane. She is much older and fatter and heavily powdered. Behind her a servant*]

YVETTE: Hello there! Is this the residence of Mother Courage?

CHAPLAIN: Right you are. With whom have we the pleasure?

YVETTE: The Countess Starhemberg, my good people. Where is Mother Courage?

THE CHAPLAIN (*calls into the wagon*): Countess Starhemberg wishes to speak to you!

MOTHER COURAGE: I'm coming.

YVETTE: It's Yvette!

MOTHER COURAGE'S VOICE: My goodness! It's Yvette!

YVETTE: Just dropped in to see how you're doing. (*The* COOK *has turned around in horror*) Pieter!

THE COOK: Yvette!

YVETTE: Blow me down! How did you get here?

THE COOK: In a cart.

THE CHAPLAIN: Oh, you know each other? Intimately?

YVETTE: I should think so. (*She looks the* COOK *over*) Fat!

THE COOK: You're not exactly willowy yourself.

YVETTE: All the same I'm glad I ran into you, you bum. Now I can tell you what I think of you.

THE CHAPLAIN: Go right ahead, spare no details, but

2310   wait until Courage comes out.

MOTHER COURAGE (*comes out with all sorts of merchandise*): Yvette! (*They embrace*) But what are you in mourning for?

YVETTE: Isn't it becoming? My husband the colonel

2315   died a few years ago.

MOTHER COURAGE: The old geezer that almost bought my wagon?

YVETTE: His elder brother.

MOTHER COURAGE: You must be pretty well fixed. It's

2320   nice to find somebody that's made a good thing out of the war.

YVETTE: Oh well, it's been up and down and back up again.

MOTHER COURAGE: Let's not say anything bad about

2325   colonels. They make money by the bushel.

THE CHAPLAIN: If I were you, I'd put my shoes back on again. (*To* YVETTE) Countess Starhemberg, you promised to tell us what you think of this gentleman.

2330 THE COOK: Don't make a scene here.

MOTHER COURAGE: He's a friend of mine, Yvette.

YVETTE: He's Pete the Pipe, that's who he is.

THE COOK: Forget the nicknames, my name is Lamb.

MOTHER COURAGE (*laughs*): Pete the Pipe! That drove

2335   the women crazy! Say, I've saved your pipe.

THE CHAPLAIN: And smoked it.

YVETTE: It's lucky I'm here to warn you. He's the worst rotter that ever infested the coast of Flanders. He ruined more girls than he's got

2340   fingers.

THE COOK: That was a long time ago. I've changed.

YVETTE: Stand up when a lady draws you into a conversation! How I loved this man! And all the while he was seeing a little bandylegged

2345   brunette, ruined her too, naturally.

THE COOK: Seems to me I started you off on a prosperous career.

YVETTE: Shut up, you depressing wreck! Watch your step with him, his kind are dangerous even

2350   when they've gone to seed.

MOTHER COURAGE (*to* YVETTE): Come along, I've got to sell my stuff before the prices drop. Maybe you can help me, with your army connections. (*Calls into the wagon*) Kattrin, forget about

2355   church, I'm running over to the market. When Eilif comes, give him a drink. (*Goes out with* YVETTE)

YVETTE (*in leaving*): To think that such a man could lead me astray! I can thank my lucky stars that

2360   I was able to rise in the world after that. I've put a spoke in your wheel, Pete the Pipe, and they'll give me credit for it in heaven when my time comes.

THE CHAPLAIN: Our conversation seems to illustrate

2365   the old adage: The mills of God grind slowly. What do you think of my jokes now?

THE COOK: I'm just unlucky. I'll come clean: I was hoping for a hot meal. I'm starving. And now they're talking about me, and she'll get the wrong idea. I think I'll beat it before she comes 2370 back.

THE CHAPLAIN: I think so too.

THE COOK: Chaplain, I'm fed up on peace already. Men are sinners from the cradle, fire and sword are their natural lot. I wish I were cook- 2375 ing for the general again, God knows where he is, I'd roast a fine fat capon, with mustard sauce and a few carrots.

THE CHAPLAIN: Red cabbage. Red cabbage with capon. 2380

THE COOK: That's right, but he wanted carrots.

THE CHAPLAIN: He was ignorant.

THE COOK: That didn't prevent you from gorging yourself.

THE CHAPLAIN: With repugnance. 2385

THE COOK: Anyway you'll have to admit those were good times.

THE CHAPLAIN: I might admit that.

THE COOK: Now you've called her a hyena, your good times here are over. What are you staring 2390 at?

THE CHAPLAIN: Eilif! (EILIF *enters, followed by soldiers with pikes. His hands are fettered. He is deathly pale*) What's wrong?

EILIF: Where's mother? 2395

THE CHAPLAIN: Gone to town.

EILIF: I heard she was here. They let me come and see her.

THE COOK (*to the* SOLDIERS): Where are you taking him? 2400

A SOLDIER: No good place.

THE CHAPLAIN: What has he done?

THE SOLDIER: Broke into a farm. The peasant's wife is dead.

THE CHAPLAIN: How could you do such a thing? 2405

EILIF: It's what I've been doing all along.

THE COOK: But in peacetime!

EILIF: Shut your trap. Can I sit down till she comes?

THE SOLDIER: We haven't time.

THE CHAPLAIN: During the war they honored him for 2410 it, he sat at the general's right hand. Then it was bravery. Couldn't we speak to the officer?

THE SOLDIER: No use. What's brave about taking a peasant's cattle?

THE COOK: It was stupid. 2415

EILIF: If I'd been stupid, I'd have starved, wise guy.

THE COOK: And for being smart your head comes off.

THE CHAPLAIN: Let's get Kattrin at least.

EILIF: Leave her be. Get me a drink of schnapps.

THE SOLDIER: No time. Let's go! 2420

THE CHAPLAIN: And what should we tell your mother?

EILIF: Tell her it wasn't any different, tell her it was the same. Or don't tell her anything.

[The SOLDIERS *drive him away*]

THE CHAPLAIN: I'll go with you on your hard journey.
2425 EILIF: I don't need any sky pilot.
THE CHAPLAIN: You don't know yet. (*He follows him*)
THE COOK (*calls after them*): I'll have to tell her, she'll
    want to see him.
THE CHAPLAIN: Better not tell her anything. Or say he
2430   was here and he'll come again, maybe tomor-
    row. I'll break it to her when I get back.
    (*Hurries out*)

[The COOK *looks after them, shaking his head, then he
walks anxiously about. Finally he approaches the
wagon*]

THE COOK: Hey! Come on out! I can see why you'd
    hide from peace. I wish I could do it myself.
2435   I'm the general's cook, remember? Wouldn't
    you have a bite to eat, to do me till your moth-
    er gets back? A slice of ham or just a piece of
    bread while I'm waiting. (*He looks in*) She's
    buried her head in a blanket. (*The sound of gun-
2440   fire in the rear*)
MOTHER COURAGE (*runs in. She is out of breath and still
    has her merchandise*): Cook, the peace is over,
    the war started up again three days ago. I had-
    n't sold my stuff yet when I found out. Heaven
2445   be praised! They're shooting each other up in
    town, the Catholics and Lutherans. We've got
    to get out of here. Kattrin, start packing. What
    have *you* got such a long face about? What's
    wrong?
2450 THE COOK: Nothing.
MOTHER COURAGE: Something's wrong. I can tell by
    your expression.
THE COOK: Maybe it's the war starting up again.
    Now I probably won't get anything hot to eat
2455   before tomorrow night.
MOTHER COURAGE: That's a lie, cook.
THE COOK: Eilif was here. He couldn't stay.
MOTHER COURAGE: He was here? Then we'll see him
    on the march. I'm going with our troops this
2460   time. How does he look?
THE COOK: The same.
MOTHER COURAGE: He'll never change. The war
    couldn't take him away from me. He's smart.
    Could you help me pack? (*She starts packing*)
2465   Did he tell you anything? Is he good with
    the general? Did he say anything about his
    heroic deeds?
THE COOK (*gloomily*): They say he's been at one of
    them again.
2470 MOTHER COURAGE:Tell me later, we've got to be
    going. (KATTRIN *emerges*) Kattrin, peace is over.
    We're moving. (*To the* COOK) What's the matter
    with you?

THE COOK: I'm going to enlist.
MOTHER COURAGE: I've got a suggestion. Why don't 2475
    . . . ? Where's the chaplain?
THE COOK: Gone to town with Eilif.
MOTHER COURAGE: Then come a little way with me,
    Lamb. I need help.
THE COOK: That incident with Yvette . . . 2480
MOTHER COURAGE: It hasn't lowered you in my esti-
    mation. Far from it. Where there's smoke
    there's fire. Coming?
THE COOK: I won't say no.
MOTHER COURAGE: The Twelfth Regiment has shoved 2485
    off. Take the shaft. Here's a chunk of bread.
    We'll have to circle around to meet the
    Lutherans. Maybe I'll see Eilif tonight. He's
    my favorite. It's been a short peace. And we're
    on the move again. 2490

[*She sings, while the* COOK *and* KATTRIN *harness themselves to the wagon*]

From Ulm to Metz, from Metz to Pilsen
Courage is right there in the van.
The war both in and out of season
With shot and shell will feed its man.
But lead alone is not sufficient 2495
The war needs soldiers to subsist!
Its diet elseways is deficient.
The war is hungry! So enlist!

ACT 9

*The great war of religion has been going on for six-
teen years. Germany has lost more than half its population. Those whom the slaughter has spared have
been laid low by epidemics. Once-flourishing country-
sides are ravaged by famine. Wolves prowl through the
charred ruins of the cities. In the fall of 1634 we find*
MOTHER COURAGE *in Germany, in the Fichtelgebirge,
at some distance from the road followed by the
Swedish armies. Winter comes early and is exceptionally severe. Business is bad, begging is the only resort.
The* COOK *receives a letter from Utrecht and is dismissed.*
    Outside a half-demolished presbytery.
    Gray morning in early winter. Gusts of wind.
MOTHER COURAGE *and the* COOK *in shabby sheepskins
by the wagon.*

THE COOK: No light. Nobody's up yet.
MOTHER COURAGE: But it's a priest. He'll have to 2500
    crawl out of bed to ring the bells. Then he'll
    get himself a nice bowl of hot soup.
THE COOK: Go on, you saw the village, everything's
    been burned to a crisp.

2505   MOTHER COURAGE: But somebody's here, I heard a
dog bark.

THE COOK: If the priest's got anything, he won't give
it away.

MOTHER COURAGE: Maybe if we sing . . .

2510   THE COOK: I've had it up to here. (*Suddenly*) I got a
letter from Utrecht. My mother's died of
cholera and the tavern belongs to me. Here's
the letter if you don't believe me. It's no business of yours what my aunt says about my evil
2515   ways, but never mind, read it.

MOTHER COURAGE (*reads the letter*): Lamb, I'm sick of
roaming around, myself. I feel like a butcher's
dog that pulls the meat cart but doesn't get
any for himself. I've nothing left to sell and the
2520   people have no money to pay for it. In Saxony
a man in rags tried to foist a cord of books on
me for two eggs, and in Württemberg they'd
have let their plow go for a little bag of salt.
What's the good of plowing? Nothing grows
2525   but brambles. In Pomerania they say the villagers have eaten up all the babies, and that
nuns have been caught at highway robbery.

THE COOK: It's the end of the world.

MOTHER COURAGE: Sometimes I have visions of
2530   myself driving through hell, selling sulphur
and brimstone, or through heaven peddling
refreshments to the roaming souls. If me and
the children I've got left could find a place
where there's no shooting, I wouldn't mind a
2535   few years of peace and quiet.

THE COOK: We could open up the tavern again.
Think it over, Anna. I made up my mind last
night; with or without you, I'm going back to
Utrecht. In fact I'm leaving today.

2540   MOTHER COURAGE: I'll have to talk to Kattrin. It's
kind of sudden, and I don't like to make decisions in the cold with nothing in my stomach.
Kattrin! (KATTRIN *climbs out of the wagon*)
Kattrin, I've got something to tell you. The
2545   cook and me are thinking of going to Utrecht.
They've left him a tavern there. You'd be living
in one place, you'd meet people. A lot of men
would be glad to get a nice, well-behaved girl,
looks aren't everything. I'm all for it. I get
2550   along fine with the cook. I've got to hand it to
him: He's got a head for business. We'd eat
regular meals, wouldn't that be nice? And
you'd have your own bed, wouldn't you like
that? It's no life on the road, year in year out.
2555   You'll go to rack and ruin. You're crawling
with lice already. We've got to decide, you see,
we could go north with the Swedes, they must
be over there. (*She points to the left*) I think we'll
do it, Kattrin.

2560   THE COOK: Anna, could I have a word with you alone?

MOTHER COURAGE: Get back in the wagon, Kattrin.

[KATTRIN *climbs back in*]

THE COOK: I interrupted you because I see there's
been a misunderstanding. I thought it was too
obvious to need saying. But if it isn't, I'll just
have to say it. You can't take her, it's out of the   2565
question. Is that plain enough for you?

[KATTRIN *sticks her head out of the wagon and listens*]

MOTHER COURAGE: You want me to leave Kattrin?

THE COOK: Look at it this way. There's no room in
the tavern. It's not one of those places with
three taprooms. If the two of us put our shoul-   2570
der to the wheel, we can make a living, but not
three, it can't be done. Kattrin can keep the
wagon.

MOTHER COURAGE: I'd been thinking she could find a
husband in Utrecht.   2575

THE COOK: Don't make me laugh! How's she going
to find a husband? At her age? And dumb!
And with that scar!

MOTHER COURAGE: Not so loud.

THE COOK: Shout or whisper, the truth's the truth.   2580
And that's another reason why I can't have her
in the tavern. The customers won't want a
sight like that staring them in the face. Can
you blame them?

MOTHER COURAGE: Shut up. Not so loud, I say.   2585

THE COOK: There's a light in the presbytery. Let's sing.

MOTHER COURAGE: How could she pull the wagon by
herself? She's afraid of the war. She couldn't
stand it. The dreams she must have! I hear her
groaning at night. Especially after battles.   2590
What she sees in her dreams, God knows. It's
pity that makes her suffer so. The other day
the wagon hit a hedgehog, I found it hidden in
her blanket.

THE COOK: The tavern's too small. (*He calls*) Worthy   2595
gentleman and members of the household! We
shall now sing the Song of Solomon, Julius
Caesar, and other great men, whose greatness
didn't help them any. Just to show you that
we're God-fearing people ourselves, which   2600
makes it hard for us, especially in the winter.
(*They sing*)

You saw the wise King Solomon
You know what came of him.
To him all hidden things were plain.   2605
He cursed the hour gave birth to him
And saw that everything was vain.
How great and wise was Solomon!
Now think about his case. Alas
A useful lesson can be won.   2610
It's wisdom that had brought him to that pass!
How happy is the man with none!

Our beautiful song proves that virtues are dangerous things, better steer clear of them, enjoy
2615   life, eat a good breakfast, a bowl of hot soup, for instance. Take me, I haven't got any soup and wish I had, I'm a soldier, but what has my bravery in all those battles got me, nothing, I'm starving, I'd be better off if I'd stayed
2620   home like a yellowbelly. And I'll tell you why.

You saw the daring Caesar next
You know what he became.
They deified him in his life
But then they killed him just the same.
2625   *And as they raised the fatal knife*
How loud he cried: "You too, my son!"
Now think about his case. Alas
A useful lesson can be won.
It's daring that had brought him to that pass!
2630   *How happy is the man with none!*

(*In an undertone*) They're not even looking out. Worthy gentleman and members of the household! Maybe you'll say, all right, if bravery won't keep body and soul together, try hon-
2635   esty. That may fill your belly or at least get you a drop to drink. Let's look into it.

You've heard of honest Socrates
Who never told a lie.
They weren't so grateful as you'd think
2640   *Instead they sentenced him to die*
And handed him the poisoned drink.
How honest was the people's noble son!
Now think about his case. Alas
A useful lesson can be won.
2645   *His honesty had brought him to that pass.*
How happy is the man with none!

Yes, they tell us to be charitable and to share what we have, but what if we haven't got anything? Maybe philanthropists have a rough time of it
2650   too, it stands to reason, they need a little something for themselves. Yes, charity is a rare virtue, because it doesn't pay.

St. Martin couldn't bear to see
His fellows in distress.
2655   *He saw a poor man in the snow.*
"Take half my cloak!" He did, and lo!
They both of them froze none the less.
He thought his heavenly reward was won.
Now think about his case. Alas
2660   *A useful lesson can be won.*
Unselfishness had brought him to that pass.
How happy is the man with none!

That's our situation. We're God-fearing folk, we stick together, we don't steal, we don't murder,
2665   we don't set fire to anything! You could say that we set an example which bears out the song, we sink lower and lower, we seldom see any soup, but if we were different, if we were thieves and murderers, maybe our bellies
2670   would be full. Because virtue isn't rewarded, only wickedness, the world needn't be like this, but it is.

And here you see God-fearing folk
Observing God's ten laws.
2675   *So far He hasn't taken heed.*
You people sitting warm indoors
Help to relieve our bitter need!
Our virtue can be counted on.
Now think about our case. Alas
2680   *A useful lesson can be won.*
The fear of God has brought us to this pass.
How happy is the man with none!

VOICE (*from above*): Hey, down there! Come on up! We've got some good thick soup.
MOTHER COURAGE: Lamb, I couldn't get anything 2685
   down. I know what you say makes sense, but is it your last word? We've always been good friends.
THE COOK: My last word. Think it over.
MOTHER COURAGE: I don't need to think it over. I 2690
   won't leave her.
THE COOK: It wouldn't be wise, but there's nothing I can do. I'm not inhuman, but it's a small tavern. We'd better go in now, or there won't be anything left, we'll have been singing in the 2695
   cold for nothing.
MOTHER COURAGE: I'll get Kattrin.
THE COOK: Better bring it down for her. They'll get a fright if the three of us barge in. (*They go out*)

[KATTRIN *climbs out of the wagon. She is carrying a bundle. She looks around to make sure the others are gone. Then she spreads out an old pair of the* COOK*'s trousers and a skirt belonging to her mother side by side on a wheel of the wagon so they can easily be seen. She is about to leave with her bundle when* MOTHER COURAGE *comes out of the house*]

MOTHER COURAGE (*with a dish of soup*): Kattrin! Stop! 2700
   Kattrin! Where do you think you're going with that bundle? Have you taken leave of your wits? (*She examines the bundle*) She's packed her things. Were you listening? I've told him it's no go with Utrecht and his lousy tavern, what 2705
   would we do there? A tavern's no place for you and me. The war still has a thing or two up its sleeve for us. (*She sees the trousers and skirt*) You're stupid. Suppose I'd seen that and

2710 you'd been gone? (KATTRIN *tries to leave,*
MOTHER COURAGE *holds her back*) And don't go
thinking I've given him the gate on your
account. It's the wagon. I won't part with the
wagon, I'm used to it, it's not you, it's the
2715 wagon. We'll go in the other direction, we'll
put the cook's stuff out here where he'll find it,
the fool. (*She climbs up and throws down a few
odds and ends to join the trousers*) There. Now
we're shut of him, you won't see me taking
2720 anyone else into the business. From now on
it's you and me. This winter will go by like all
the rest. Harness up, it looks like snow. (*They
harness themselves to the wagon, turn it around
and pull it away. When the* COOK *comes out he*
2725 *sees his things and stands dumbfounded*)

ACT 10

Throughout 1635 MOTHER COURAGE *and her daughter*
KATTRIN *pull the wagon over the roads of central
Germany in the wake of the increasingly bedraggled
armies.*
    Highway.
    MOTHER COURAGE *and* KATTRIN *are pulling the
wagon. They come to a peasant's house. A voice is
heard singing from within.*

THE VOICE:

 *The rose bush in our garden
 Rejoiced our hearts in spring
 It bore such lovely flowers.*
2730 *We planted it last season
 Before the April showers.
 A garden is a blessèd thing
 It bore such lovely flowers.*

 *When winter comes a-stalking
2735 *And gales great snow storms bring
 They trouble us but little.
 We've lately finished caulking
 The roof with moss and wattle.
 A sheltering roof's a blessèd thing
2740 *When winter comes a-stalking.*

[MOTHER COURAGE *and* KATTRIN *have stopped to listen.
Then they move on*]

ACT 11

*January 1636. The imperial troops threaten the
Protestant city of Halle. The stone speaks.* MOTHER
COURAGE *loses her daughter and goes on alone. The
end of the war is not in sight.*

    *The wagon, much the worse for wear, is standing
beside a peasant house with an enormous thatch roof.
The house is built against the side of a stony hill. Night.*
    A LIEUTENANT *and three* SOLDIERS *in heavy armor
step out of the woods.*

THE LIEUTENANT: I don't want any noise. If anybody
    yells, run him through with your pikes.
FIRST SOLDIER: But we need a guide. We'll have to
    knock if we want them to come out.
THE LIEUTENANT: Knocking sounds natural. It could   2745
    be a cow bumping against the barn wall.

[*The* SOLDIERS *knock on the door. A* PEASANT WOMAN
*opens. They hold their hands over her mouth. Two sol-
diers go in*]

A MAN'S VOICE (*inside*): Who's there?

[*The soldiers bring out a peasant and his son*]

THE LIEUTENANT (*points to the wagon, in which* KATTRIN
    has appeared): There's another one. (*A soldier
    pulls her out*) Anybody else live here?   2750
THE PEASANT COUPLE: This is our son.—That's a
    dumb girl.—Her mother's gone into the town
    on business.—Buying up people's belongings,
    they're selling cheap because they're getting
    out.—They're provisioners.   2755
THE LIEUTENANT: I'm warning you to keep quiet, one
    squawk and you'll get a pike over the head.
    All right. I need somebody who can show us
    the path into the city. (*Points to the* YOUNG
    PEASANT) You. Come here!   2760
THE YOUNG PEASANT: I don't know no path.
THE SECOND SOLDIER (*grinning*): He don't know no
    path.
THE YOUNG PEASANT: I'm not helping the Catholics.
THE LIEUTENANT (*to the* SECOND SOLDIER): Give him a   2765
    feel of your pike!
THE YOUNG PEASANT (*forced down on his knees and
    threatened with the pike*): You can kill me. I
    won't do it.
THE FIRST SOLDIER: I know what'll make him think   2770
    twice. (*He goes over to the barn*) Two cows and
    an ox. Get this: If you don't help us, I'll cut
    them down.
THE YOUNG PEASANT: Not the animals!
THE PEASANT WOMAN (*in tears*): Captain, spare our   2775
    animals or we'll starve.
THE LIEUTENANT: If he insists on being stubborn,
    they're done for.
THE FIRST SOLDIER: I'll start with the ox.
THE YOUNG PEASANT (*to the old man*): Do I have to?   2780
    (*The old woman nods*) I'll do it.
THE PEASANT WOMAN: And thank you kindly for your
    forbearance, Captain, for ever and ever, amen.

[The PEASANT *stops her from giving further thanks]*

THE FIRST SOLDIER: Didn't I tell you? With them it's
2785   the animals that come first.

[Led by the YOUNG PEASANT, *the* LIEUTENANT *and the*
SOLDIERS *continue on their way]*

THE PEASANT: I wish I knew what they're up to.
          Nothing good.
THE PEASANT WOMAN: Maybe they're only scouts.—
          What are you doing?
2790   THE PEASANT (*putting a ladder against the roof and*
          climbing up): See if they're alone. (*On the roof*)
          Men moving in the woods. All the way to the
          quarry. Armor in the clearing. And a cannon.
          It's more than a regiment. God have mercy on
2795   the city and everybody in it.
THE PEASANT WOMAN: See any light in the city?
THE PEASANT: No. They're all asleep. (*He climbs down*)
          If they get in, they'll kill everybody.
THE PEASANT WOMAN: The sentry will see them in
2800   time.
THE PEASANT: They must have killed the sentry in the
          tower on the hill, or he'd have blown his horn.
THE PEASANT WOMAN: If there were more of us . . .
THE PEASANT: All by ourselves up here with a cripple
2805   . . .
THE PEASANT WOMAN: We can't do a thing. Do you
          think . . .
THE PEASANT: Not a thing.
THE PEASANT WOMAN: We couldn't get down there in
2810   the dark.
THE PEASANT: The whole hillside is full of them. We
          can't even give a signal.
THE PEASANT WOMAN: They'd kill us.
THE PEASANT: No, we can't do a thing.
2815   THE PEASANT WOMAN (*to* KATTRIN): Pray, poor thing,
          pray! We can't stop the bloodshed. If you can't
          talk, at least you can pray. He'll hear you if
          nobody else does. I'll help you. (*All kneel,*
          KATTRIN *behind the peasants*) Our Father which
2820   art in heaven, hear our prayer. Don't let the
          town perish with everybody in it, all asleep
          and unsuspecting. Wake them, make them get
          up and climb the walls and see the enemy
          coming through the night with cannon and
2825   pikes, through the fields and down the hill-
          side. (*Back to* KATTRIN) Protect our mother and
          don't let the watchman sleep, wake him before
          it's too late. And succor our brother-in-law,
          he's in there with his four children, let them
2830   not perish, they're innocent and don't know a
          thing. (*To* KATTRIN, *who groans*) The littlest is
          less than two, the oldest is seven. (*Horrified,*
          KATTRIN *stands up*) Our Father, hear us, for
          Thou alone canst help, we'll all be killed, we're

weak, we haven't any pikes or anything, we   2835
are powerless and in Thine hands, we and our
animals and the whole farm, and the city too,
it's in Thine hands, and the enemy is under the
walls with great might.

*[*KATTRIN *has crept unnoticed to the wagon, taken*
something out of it, put it under her apron and
climbed up the ladder to the roof of the barn]

THE PEASANT WOMAN: Think upon the children in   2840
          peril, especially the babes in arms and the old
          people that can't help themselves and all
          God's creatures.
THE PEASANT: And forgive us our trespasses as we
          forgive them that trespass against us. Amen.   2845

*[*KATTRIN, *sitting on the roof, starts beating the drum*
that she has taken out from under her apron]

THE PEASANT WOMAN: Jesus! What's she doing?
THE PEASANT: She's gone crazy.
THE PEASANT WOMAN: Get her down, quick!

[The PEASANT *runs toward the ladder, but* KATTRIN
pulls it up on the roof]

THE PEASANT WOMAN: She'll be the death of us all.
THE PEASANT: Stop that, you cripple!   2850
THE PEASANT WOMAN: She'll have the Catholics
          down on us.
THE PEASANT (*looking around for stones*): I'll throw
          rocks at you.
THE PEASANT WOMAN: Have you no pity? Have you   2855
          no heart? We're dead if they find out it's us!
          They'll run us through!

*[*KATTRIN *stares in the direction of the city, and goes*
on drumming]

THE PEASANT WOMAN (*to the* PEASANT): I told you not
          to let those tramps stop here. What do they
          care if the soldiers drive our last animals   2860
          away?
THE LIEUTENANT (*rushes in with his* SOLDIERS *and the*
          YOUNG PEASANT): I'll cut you to pieces!
THE PEASANT WOMAN: We're innocent, captain. We
          couldn't help it. She sneaked up there. We   2865
          don't know her.
THE LIEUTENANT: Where's the ladder?
THE PEASANT: Up top.
THE LIEUTENANT (*to* KATTRIN): Throw down that
          drum. It's an order!   2870

*[*KATTRIN *goes on drumming]*

THE LIEUTENANT: You're all in this together! This'll be

the end of you!

THE PEASANT: They've felled some pine trees in the
woods over there. We could get one and knock
her down . . .

2875

THE FIRST SOLDIER (*to the* LIEUTENANT): Request permission to make a suggestion. (*He whispers something in the* LIEUTENANT'S *ear. He nods*) Listen.
We've got a friendly proposition. Come down,
we'll take you into town with us. Show us your
mother and we won't touch a hair of her head.

2880

[KATTRIN *goes on drumming*]

THE LIEUTENANT (*pushes him roughly aside*): Shes does-
n't trust you. No wonder with your mug. (*He
calls up*) If I give you my word? I'm an officer,
you can trust my word of honor.

2885

[*She drums still louder*]

THE LIEUTENANT: Nothing is sacred to her.

THE YOUNG PEASANT: It's not just her mother, lieutenant!

THE FIRST SOLDIER: We can't let this go on. They'll
hear it in the city.

2890

THE LIEUTENANT: We'll have to make some kind of
noise that's louder than the drums. What
could we make noise with?

THE FIRST SOLDIER: But we're not supposed to make
noise.

2895

THE LIEUTENANT: An innocent noise, stupid. A peace-
able noise.

THE PEASANT: I could chop wood.

THE LIEUTENANT: That's it, chop! (*The* PEASANT *gets an
ax and chops at a log*) Harder! Harder! You're
chopping for your life.

2900

[*Listening,* KATTRIN *has been drumming more softly.
Now she looks anxiously around and goes on drumming as before*]

THE LIEUTENANT (*to the* PEASANT): Not loud enough.
(*To the* FIRST SOLDIER) You chop too.

THE PEASANT: There's only one ax. (*Stops chopping*)

THE LIEUTENANT: We'll have to set the house on fire.
Smoke her out.

2905

THE PEASANT: That won't do any good, captain. If the
city people see fire up here, they'll know
what's afoot.

[*Still drumming,* KATTRIN *has been listening again.
Now she laughs*]

THE LIEUTENANT: Look, she's laughing at us. I'll shoot
her down, regardless. Get the musket!

2910

[*Two* SOLDIERS *run out.* KATTRIN *goes on drumming*]

THE PEASANT WOMAN: I've got it, captain. That's their
wagon over there. If we start smashing it up,
she'll stop. The wagon's all they've got.

THE LIEUTENANT (*to the* YOUNG PEASANT): Smash
away. (*To* KATTRIN) We'll smash your wagon if
you don't stop.

2915

[*The* YOUNG PEASANT *strikes a few feeble blows at the
wagon*]

THE PEASANT WOMAN: Stop it, you beast!

[KATTRIN *stares despairingly at the wagon and emits
pitiful sounds. But she goes on drumming*]

THE LIEUTENANT: Where are those stinkers with the
musket?

THE FIRST SOLDIER: They haven't heard anything in
the city yet, or we'd hear their guns.

2920

THE LIEUTENANT (*to* KATTRIN): They don't hear you.
And now we're going to shoot you down. For
the last time: Drop that drum!

THE YOUNG PEASANT (*suddenly throws the plank away*):
Keep on drumming! Or they'll all be killed!
Keep on drumming, keep on drumming . . .

2925

[*The* SOLDIERS *throws him down and hits him with his
pike.* KATTRIN *starts crying, but goes on drumming*]

THE PEASANT WOMAN: Don't hit him in the back! My
God, you're killing him.

[*The* SOLDIERS *run in with the musket*]

THE SECOND SOLDIER: The colonel's foaming at the
mouth. We'll be court-martialed.

2930

THE LIEUTENANT: Set it up! Set it up! (*To* KATTRIN,
while the musket is being set up on its stand) For
the last time: Stop that drumming! (KATTRIN *in
tears drums as loud as she can*) Fire!

2935

[*The* SOLDIERS *fire.* KATTRIN *is hit. She beats the drum
a few times more and then slowly collapses*]

THE LIEUTENANT: Now we'll have some quiet.

[*But* KATTRIN'S *last drumbeats are answered by the
city's cannon. A confused hubbub of alarm bells and
cannon is heard in the distance*]

FIRST SOLDIER: She's done it.

ACT 12

Night, toward morning. The fifes and drums of troops

marching away.
   Outside the wagon MOTHER COURAGE *sits huddled over her daughter. The peasant couple are standing beside them.*

THE PEASANT (*hostile*): You'll have to be going, woman. There's only one more regiment to come. You can't go alone.
2940

MOTHER COURAGE: Maybe I can get her to sleep. (*She sings*)

Lullaby baby
What stirs in the hay?
2945 The neighbor brats whimper
Mine are happy and gay.
They go in tatters
And you in silk down
Cut from an angel's
2950 Best party gown.

They've nothing to munch on
And you will have pie
Just tell your mother
In case it's too dry.
2955 Lullaby baby
What stirs in the hay?
The one lies in Poland
The other—who can say?

Now she's asleep. You shouldn't have told her
2960 about your brother-in-law's children.
THE PEASANT: Maybe it wouldn't have happened if you hadn't gone to town to swindle people.
MOTHER COURAGE: I'm glad she's sleeping now.
THE PEASANT WOMAN: She's not sleeping, you'll have
2965 to face it, she's dead.
THE PEASANT: And it's time you got started. There are wolves around here, and what's worse, marauders.
MOTHER COURAGE: Yes. (*She goes to the wagon and
2970 takes out a sheet of canvas to cover the body with*)
THE PEASANT WOMAN: Haven't you anybody else? Somebody you can go to?
MOTHER COURAGE: Yes, there's one of them left. Eilif.
THE PEASANT (*while* MOTHER COURAGE *covers the body*):
2975 Go find him. We'll attend to this one, give her a decent burial. Set your mind at rest.
MOTHER COURAGE: Here's money for your expenses. (*She gives the* PEASANT *money*)

[*The* PEASANT *and his son shake hands with her and carry* KATTRIN *away*]

THE PEASANT WOMAN (*on the way out*): Hurry up!
2980 MOTHER COURAGE (*harnesses herself to the wagon*): I hope I can pull the wagon alone. I'll manage,

there isn't much in it. I've got to get back in business.

[*Another regiment marches by with fifes and drums in the rear*]

MOTHER COURAGE: Hey, take me with you! (*She starts to pull*) 2985

[*Singing is heard in the rear:*]

With all the killing and recruiting
The war will worry on a while.
In ninety years they'll still be shooting.
It's hardest on the rank-and-file.
Our food is swill, our pants all patches 2990
The higher-ups steal half our pay
And still we dream of God-sent riches.
Tomorrow is another day!

The spring is come! Christian, revive!
The snowdrifts melt, the dead lie dead! 2995
And if by chance you're still alive
It's time to rise and shake a leg.

ARTHUR MILLER (B. 1915)

A rthur Miller was born in Manhattan, the son of Jewish immigrants, and raised in Brooklyn. Miller received his early education in New York public schools, graduating during the Depression. He worked to save the tuition money to attend the University of Michigan, where an admissions officer was willing to bet that Miller's undistinguished academic background was not an indication of his true abilities. While still in college he began to write plays that received university awards. After taking his B.A. in 1938 at age twenty-three, he returned to New York to work with the Federal Theater Project, a division of the Works Progress Administration (WPA)—one of the Depression programs designed to put Americans back to work. Between 1938 and 1947 Miller wrote radio plays for CBS and NBC, screenplays, articles, stories, and a novel. His first Broadway production, *The Man Who Had All the Luck* (1944), did not succeed, but it anticipated the concern with guilt and moral responsibility that would shortly become the themes of his great plays.

Despite his initial lack of commercial success, Miller had received a number of prizes: two Hopewood awards, the Bureau of New Plays Prize, and two Theater Guild National Awards. Then, between 1947 and 1953 he wrote three extraordinary and powerful plays that earned him the reputation as the most eminent American playwright of the postwar period: *All My Sons* (1947), *Death of a Salesman* (1949), and *The Crucible* (1953). In *All My Sons*, Joe Keller produces defective airplane parts during the war, blaming the resulting crashes on his partner, who goes to prison. Joe's son, Chris, discovers the truth and rejects his father. Joe commits suicide, but not before he recognizes that his own criminal behavior has led to the loss of his son, and that the army pilots who died in his planes were also, in an important sense, his sons. Miller's *Death of a Salesman* is perhaps the most famous American play ever written. In it Miller explores the ethics and morality and values of American business practices, which come to have fatal consequences. The play depicts the illusions of an ordinary man, Willy Loman, who is crushed by the American dream, which has failed him. The play has continued to stir debates on the nature of modern tragedy and whether tragedy is possible for a common man. For these two plays and *The Crucible*, Miller was showered with awards at home and abroad, and they have been produced in translation throughout the world for two generations.

Miller's work ranges widely, inspired by memories of his family life, by the political and economic issues of the Depression and the postwar period, and by the forces of anti-Semitism. His plays, along with those of Tennessee Williams and Eugene O'Neill, represent a high point of American theater in the mid-twentieth century. Written in the 1940s and early 1950s, at a time when America commanded center stage as a superpower in a war-ravaged world, these gritty plays modified the style of realism and received worldwide attention.

The Crucible

The Crucible is set in seventeenth-century New England, but it is by design a modern play. It concerns witch-hunting, and Miller draws clear parallels to the anticommunist "witch-hunts" by the House Un-American Activities Committee (HUAC) in the late 1940s and early 1950s, spearheaded by Senator Joseph McCarthy. By 1953 John Proctor's prosecution-persecution in the play had a number of obvious contemporary parallels. HUAC had been charged to investigate Soviet spying and subversion in the United States at a time when more than half the world's population was formally under communist governments with aggressive foreign policies. All circumstances conspired to create a hysterical domestic climate in the United States. During these years HUAC subpoenaed suspected individuals and questioned them about past activities in left-wing political organizations. The list of those summoned included government officials, prominent entertainers, and intellectuals, who were pressured to implicate or testify against friends, relatives, and associates. Many people broke under the public browbeating and threats, and many careers and lives were ruined. Others refused to cooperate with the committee and as a result were "blacklisted," a technique whereby HUAC brought political pressure to bear on employers to keep uncooperative witnesses out of work.

Miller ran afoul of HUAC, in part for the implications of *The Crucible*, which expresses his concern that in the United States conscience had become "no longer a private matter but one of state administration." He was denied a passport in 1954 on the grounds that he was believed to support the communist movement, and in 1956 he was summoned before HUAC. He admitted attending Communist Party meetings during the 1930s, as many people had who were concerned with the desperate economic conditions of the Depression and with the threat of fascism in Europe. His refusal to name anyone else led to a citation for contempt by a federal grand jury. His conviction was reversed two years later by the United States Court of Appeals for the District of Columbia, but his writing suffered during this period. His later plays and screenplays—*A View from the Bridge* (1955); *After the Fall* (1964), based on the failure of his marriage to Marilyn Monroe; *Incident at Vichy* (1964), about Nazi persecution of Jews during World War II; *The Misfits* (1961); and *Playing for Time* (1981)—have not received the kind of acclaim that his earlier work did.

In *The Crucible*, Abigail Williams creates hysteria in a New England village by playing on the citizens' fear of witchcraft and the supernatural. The fear and the harm it does are furthered by some very down-to-earth motives. Abigail acts out of love for John Proctor, who has returned to his wife after an affair with Abigail, and she manages to manipulate Proctor into a position in which he must confess to adultery and witchcraft to save his wife. All he has to do to save the people he loves is to perjure himself, but Proctor refuses to compromise his principles and condemns himself to a death he now feels he deserves for his betrayal of his wife. Proctor's decision to take responsibility for his own actions lies at the heart of Miller's tragedy.

The Crucible

Arthur Miller

A Note on the Historical Accuracy of This Play

This play is not history in the sense in which the word is used by the academic historian. Dramatic purposes have sometimes required many characters to be fused into one; the number of girls involved in the "crying-out" has been reduced; Abigail's age has been raised; while there were several judges of almost equal authority, I have symbolized them all in Hathorne and Danforth. However, I believe that the reader will discover here the essential nature of one of the strangest and most awful chapters in human history. The fate of each character is exactly that of his historical model, and there is no one in the drama who did not play a similar—and in some cases exactly the same—role in history.

As for the characters of the persons, little is known about most of them excepting what may be surmised from a few letters, the trial record, certain broadsides written at the time, and references to their conduct in sources of varying reliability. They may therefore be taken as creations of my own, drawn to the best of my ability in conformity with their known behavior, except as indicated in the commentary I have written for this text.

ACT I

(AN OVERTURE)

A small upper bedroom in the home of Reverend Samuel Parris, Salem, Massachusetts, in the spring of the year 1692.

There is a narrow window at the left. Through its leaded panes the morning sunlight streams. A candle still burns near the bed, which is at the right. A chest, a chair, and a small table are the other furnishings. At the back a door opens on the landing of the stairway to the ground floor. The room gives off an air of clean spareness. The roof rafters are exposed, and the wood colors are raw and unmellowed.

As the curtain rises, Reverend Parris is discovered kneeling beside the bed, evidently in prayer. His daughter, Betty Parris, aged ten, is lying on the bed, inert.

At the time of these events Parris was in his middle forties. In history he cut a villainous path, and there is very little good to be said for him. He believed he was being persecuted wherever he went, despite his best efforts to win people and God to his side. In meeting, he felt insulted if someone rose to shut the door without first asking his permission. He was a widower with no interest in children, or talent with them. He regarded them as young adults, and until this strange crisis he, like the rest of Salem, never conceived that the children were anything but thankful for being permitted to walk straight, eyes slightly lowered, arms at the sides, and mouths shut until bidden to speak.

His house stood in the "town"—but we today would hardly call it a village. The meeting house was nearby, and from this point outward—toward the bay or inland—there were a few small-windowed, dark houses snuggling against the raw Massachusetts winter. Salem had been established hardly forty years before. To the European world the whole province was a barbaric frontier inhabited by a sect of fanatics who, nevertheless, were shipping out products of slowly increasing quantity and value.

No one can really know what their lives were like. They had no novelists—and would not have permitted anyone to read a novel if one were handy. Their creed forbade anything resembling a theater or "vain enjoyment." They did not celebrate Christmas, and a holiday from work meant only that they must concentrate even more upon prayer.

Which is not to say that nothing broke into this strict and somber way of life. When a new farmhouse was built, friends assembled to "raise the roof," and there would be special foods cooked and probably some potent cider passed around. There was a good supply of ne'er-do-wells in Salem, who dallied at the shovelboard in Bridget Bishop's tavern. Probably more than the creed, hard work kept the morals of the place from spoiling, for the people were forced to fight the land like heroes for every grain of corn, and no man had very much time for fooling around.

That there were some jokers, however, is indicated by the practice of appointing a two-man patrol whose duty was to "walk forth in the time of God's worship to take notice of such as either lye about the meeting house, without attending to the word and ordinances, or that lye at home or in the fields without giving good account thereof, and to take the names of such persons, and to present them to the magistrates, whereby they may be accordingly proceeded against." This predilection for minding other people's business was time-honored among the people of Salem, and it undoubtedly created many of the suspicions which were to feed the coming madness. It *was also, in my opinion, one of the things that a John Proctor would rebel against, for the time of the armed camp had almost passed, and since the country was reasonably—although not wholly—safe, the old disciplines were beginning to rankle. But, as in all such matters, the issue was not clear-cut, for danger was still a possibility, and in unity still lay the best promise of safety.*

The edge of the wilderness was close by. The American continent stretched endlessly west, and it was full of mystery for them. It stood, dark and threatening, over their shoulders night and day, for out of it Indian tribes marauded from time to time, and Reverend Parris had parishioners who had lost relatives to these heathen.

The parochial snobbery of these people was partly responsible for their failure to convert the Indians. Probably they also preferred to take land from heathens rather than from fellow Christians. At any rate, very few Indians were converted, and the Salem folk believed that the virgin forest was the Devil's last preserve, his home base and the citadel of his final stand. To the best of their knowledge the American forest was the last place on earth that was not paying homage to God.

For these reasons, among others, they carried about an air of innate resistance, even of persecution. Their fathers had, of course, been persecuted in England. So now they and their church found it necessary to deny any other sect its freedom, lest their New Jerusalem be defiled and corrupted by wrong ways and deceitful ideas.

They believed, in short, that they held in their steady hands the candle that would light the world. We have inherited this belief, and it has helped and hurt us. It helped them with the discipline it gave them. They were a dedicated folk, by and large, and they had to be to survive the life they had chosen or been born into in this country.

The proof of their belief's value to them may be taken from the opposite character of the first Jamestown settlement, farther south, in Virginia. The Englishmen who landed there were motivated mainly by a hunt for profit. They had thought to pick off the wealth of the new country and then return rich to England. They were a band of individualists, and a much more ingratiating group than the Massachusetts men. But Virginia destroyed them. Massachusetts tried to kill off the Puritans, but they combined; they set up a communal society which, in the beginning, was little more than an armed camp with an autocratic and very devoted leadership. It was, however, an autocracy by consent, for they were united from top to bottom by a commonly held ideology whose perpetuation was the reason and justification for all their sufferings. So their self-denial, their purposefulness, their suspicion of all vain pursuits, their hard-handed justice, were

altogether perfect instruments for the conquest of this space so antagonistic to man.

But the people of Salem in 1692 were not quite the dedicated folk that arrived on the Mayflower. A vast differentiation had taken place, and in their own time a revolution had unseated the royal government and substituted a junta which was at this moment in power. The times, to their eyes, must have been out of joint, and to the common folk must have seemed as insoluble and complicated as do ours today. It is not hard to see how easily many could have been led to believe that the time of confusion had been brought upon them by deep and darkling forces. No hint of such speculation appears on the court record, but social disorder in any age breeds such mystical suspicions, and when, as in Salem, wonders are brought forth from below the social surface, it is too much to expect people to hold back very long from laying on the victims with all the force of their frustrations.

The Salem tragedy, which is about to begin in these pages, developed from a paradox. It is a paradox in whose grip we still live, and there is no prospect yet that we will discover its resolution. Simply, it was this: for good purposes, even high purposes, the people of Salem developed a theocracy, a combine of state and religious power whose function was to keep the community together, and to prevent any kind of disunity that might open it to destruction by material or ideological enemies. It was forged for a necessary purpose and accomplished that purpose. But all organization is and must be grounded on the idea of exclusion and prohibition, just as two objects cannot occupy the same space. Evidently the time came in New England when the repressions of order were heavier than seemed warranted by the dangers against which the order was organized. The witch-hunt was a perverse manifestation of the panic which set in among all classes when the balance began to turn toward greater individual freedom.

When one rises above the individual villainy displayed, one can only pity them all, just as we shall be pitied someday. It is still impossible for man to organize his social life without repressions, and the balance has yet to be struck between order and freedom.

The witch-hunt was not, however, a mere repression. It was also, and as importantly, a long overdue opportunity for everyone so inclined to express publicly his guilt and sins, under the cover of accusations against the victims. It suddenly became possible—and patriotic and holy—for a man to say that Martha Corey had come into his bedroom at night, and that, while his wife was sleeping at his side, Martha laid herself down on his chest and "nearly suffocated him." Of course it was her spirit only, but his satisfaction at confessing himself was no lighter than if it had been Martha herself. One could not ordinarily speak such things in public.

Long-held hatreds of neighbors could now be openly expressed, and vengeance taken, despite the Bible's charitable injunctions. Land-lust which had been expressed before by constant bickering over boundaries and deeds, could now be elevated to the arena of morality; one could cry witch against one's neighbor and feel perfectly justified in the bargain. Old scores could be settled on a plane of heavenly combat between Lucifer and the Lord; suspicions and the envy of the miserable toward the happy could and did burst out in the general revenge.

REVEREND PARRIS is praying now, and, though we cannot hear his words, a sense of his confusion hangs about him. He mumbles, then seems about to weep; then he weeps, then prays again; but his daughter does not stir on the bed.

The door opens, and his Negro slave enters. TITUBA is in her forties. PARRIS brought her with him from Barbados, where he spent some years as a merchant before entering the ministry. She enters as one does who can no longer bear to be barred from the sight of her beloved, but she is also very frightened because her slave sense has warned her that, as always, trouble in this house eventually lands on her back.

TITUBA (*already taking a step backward*): My Betty be hearty soon?
PARRIS: Out of here!
TITUBA (*backing to the door*): My Betty not goin' die...
5   PARRIS (*scrambling to his feet in a fury*): Out of my sight! (*She is gone.*) Out of my—(*He is overcome with sobs. He clamps his teeth against them and closes the door and leans against it, exhausted.*) Oh, my God! God help me! (*Quaking with fear,*
10   *mumbling to himself through his sobs, he goes to the bed and gently takes* BETTY's *hand.*) Betty. Child. Dear child. Will you wake, will you open up your eyes! Betty, little one . . .

[*He is bending to kneel again when his niece,* ABIGAIL WILLIAMS, *seventeen, enters—a strikingly beautiful girl, an orphan, with an endless capacity for dissembling. Now she is all worry and apprehension and propriety.*]

ABIGAIL: Uncle? (*He looks to her.*) Susanna Walcott's
15   here from Doctor Griggs.
PARRIS: Oh? Let her come, let her come.
ABIGAIL (*leaning out the door to call to* SUSANNA, *who is down the hall a few steps*): Come in, Susanna.

[SUSANNA WALCOTT, *a little younger than* ABIGAIL, *a nervous, hurried girl, enters.*]

PARRIS (*eagerly*): What does the doctor say, child?
20   SUSANNA (*craning around* PARRIS *to get a look at* BETTY): He bid me come and tell you, reverend sir, that

he cannot discover no medicine for it in his books.
PARRIS: Then he must search on.
SUSANNA: Aye, sir, he have been searchin' his books   25
since he left you, sir. But he bid me tell you, that you might look to unnatural things for the cause of it.
PARRIS (*his eyes going wide*): No—no. There be no unnatural cause here. Tell him I have sent for   30
Reverend Hale of Beverly, and Mr. Hale will surely confirm that. Let him look to medicine and put out all thought of unnatural causes here. There be none.
SUSANNA: Aye, sir. He bid me tell you. (*She turns to go.*)   35
ABIGAIL: Speak nothin' of it in the village, Susanna.
PARRIS: Go directly home and speak nothing of unnatural causes.
SUSANNA: Aye, sir. I pray for her. (*She goes out.*)
ABIGAIL: Uncle, the rumor of witchcraft is all about; I   40
think you'd best go down and deny it yourself. The parlor's packed with people, sir. I'll sit with her.
PARRIS (*pressed, turns on her*): And what shall I say to them? That my daughter and my niece I dis-   45
covered dancing like heathen in the forest?
ABIGAIL: Uncle, we did dance; let you tell them I confessed it—and I'll be whipped if I must be. But they're speakin' of witchcraft. Betty's not witched.   50
PARRIS: Abigail, I cannot go before the congregation when I know you have not opened with me. What did you do with her in the forest?
ABIGAIL: We did dance, uncle, and when you leaped out of the bush so suddenly, Betty was fright-   55
ened and then she fainted. And there's the whole of it.
PARRIS: Child. Sit you down.
ABIGAIL (*quavering, as she sits*): I would never hurt Betty. I love her dearly.   60
PARRIS: Now look you, child, your punishment will come in its time. But if you trafficked with spirits in the forest I must know it now, for surely my enemies will, and they will ruin me with it.   65
ABIGAIL: But we never conjured spirits.
PARRIS: Then why can she not move herself since midnight? This child is desperate! (ABIGAIL *lowers her eyes.*) It must come out—my enemies will bring it out. Let me know what you done   70
there. Abigail, do you understand that I have many enemies?
ABIGAIL: I have heard of it, uncle.
PARRIS: There is a faction that is sworn to drive me from my pulpit. Do you understand that?   75
ABIGAIL: I think so, sir.
PARRIS: Now then, in the midst of such disruption, my own household is discovered to be the

very center of some obscene practice.
80   Abominations are done in the forest—
ABIGAIL: It were sport, uncle!
PARRIS (*pointing at* BETTY): You call this sport? (*She
      lowers her eyes. He pleads:*) Abigail, if you know
      something that may help the doctor, for God's
85   sake tell it to me. (*She is silent.*) I saw Tituba
      waving her arms over the fire when I came on
      you. Why was she doing that? And I heard a
      screeching and gibberish coming from her
      mouth. She were swaying like a dumb beast
90   over that fire!
ABIGAIL: She always sings her Barbados songs, and
      we dance.
PARRIS: I cannot blink what I saw, Abigail, for my
      enemies will not blink it. I saw a dress lying on
95   the grass.
ABIGAIL (*innocently*): A dress?
PARRIS—(*it is very hard to say*): Aye, a dress. And I
      thought I saw—someone naked running
      through the trees!
100   ABIGAIL (*in terror*): No one was naked! You mistake
      yourself, uncle!
PARRIS (*with anger*): I saw it! (*He moves from her. Then,
      resolved.*) Now tell me true, Abigail. And I pray
      you feel the weight of truth upon you, for now
105   my ministry's at stake, my ministry and per-
      haps your cousin's life. Whatever abomination
      you have done, give me all of it now, for I dare
      not be taken unaware when I go before them
      down there.
110   ABIGAIL: There is nothin' more. I swear it, uncle!
PARRIS (*studies her, then nods, half convinced*): Abigail, I
      have fought here three long years to bend
      these stiff-necked people to me, and now, just
      now when some good respect is rising for me
115   in the parish, you compromise my very char-
      acter. I have given you a home, child, I have
      put clothes upon your back—now give me
      upright answer. Your name in the town—it is
      entirely white, is it not?
120   ABIGAIL (*with an edge of resentment*): Why, I am sure it
      is, sir. There be no blush about my name.
PARRIS (*to the point*): Abigail, is there any other cause
      than you have told me, for your being dis-
      charged from Goody Proctor's service? I have
125   heard it said, and I tell you as I heard it, that
      she comes so rarely to the church this year for
      she will not sit so close to something soiled.
      What signified that remark?
ABIGAIL: She hates me, uncle, she must, for I would
130   not be her slave. It's a bitter woman, a lying,
      cold, sniveling woman, and I will not work for
      such a woman!
PARRIS: She may be. And yet it has troubled me that
      you are now seven month out of their house,
135   and in all this time no other family has ever

called for your service.
ABIGAIL: They want slaves, not such as I. Let them
      send to Barbados for that. I will not black my
      face for any of them! (*With ill-concealed resent-
      ment at him:*) Do you begrudge my bed, uncle?   140
PARRIS: No—no.
ABIGAIL (*in a temper*): My name is good in the village!
      I will not have it said my name is soiled!
      Goody Proctor is a gossiping liar!

[*Enter* MRS. ANN PUTNAM. *She is a twisted soul of forty-
five, a death-ridden woman, haunted by dreams.*]

PARRIS (*as soon as the door begins to open*): No—no, I   145
      cannot have anyone. (*He sees her, and a certain
      deference springs into him, although his worry
      remains.*) Why, Goody Putnam, come in.
MRS. PUTNAM (*full of breath, shiny-eyed*): It is a marvel.
      It is surely a stroke of hell upon you.   150
PARRIS: No, Goody Putnam, it is—
MRS. PUTNAM (*glancing at* BETTY): How high did she
      fly, how high?
PARRIS: No, no, she never flew—
MRS. PUTNAM (*very pleased with it*): Why, it's sure she   155
      did. Mr. Collins saw her goin' over Ingersoll's
      barn, and come down light as bird, he says!
PARRIS: Now, look you, Goody Putnam, she never—
      (*Enter* THOMAS PUTNAM, *a well-to-do, hard-hand-
      ed landowner, near fifty.*) Oh, good morning, Mr.   160
      Putnam.
PUTNAM: It is a providence the thing is out now! It is
      a providence. (*He goes directly to the bed.*)
PARRIS: What's out, sir, what's—?

[MRS. PUTNAM *goes to the bed.*]

PUTNAM (*looking down at* BETTY): Why, *her* eyes is   165
      closed! Look you, Ann.
MRS. PUTNAM: Why, that's strange. (*To* PARRIS:) Ours
      is open.
PARRIS (*shocked*): Your Ruth is sick?
MRS. PUTNAM (*with vicious certainty*): I'd not call it   170
      sick; the Devil's touch is heavier than sick. It's
      death, y'know, it's death drivin' into them,
      forked and hoofed.
PARRIS: Oh, pray not! Why, how does Ruth ail?
MRS. PUTNAM: She ails as she must—she never   175
      waked this morning, but her eyes open and
      she walks, and hears naught, sees naught, and
      cannot eat. Her soul is taken, surely.

[PARRIS *is struck.*]

PUTNAM (*as though for further details*): They say you've
      sent for Reverend Hale of Beverly?   180
PARRIS (*with dwindling conviction now*): A precaution
      only. He has much experience in all demonic

arts, and I—

MRS. PUTNAM: He has indeed; and found a witch in
185   Beverly last year, and let you remember that.

PARRIS: Now, Goody Ann, they only thought that
were a witch, and I am certain there be no element of witchcraft here.

PUTNAM: No witchcraft! Now look you, Mr. Parris—

190   PARRIS: Thomas, Thomas, I pray you, leap not to
witchcraft. I know that you—you least of all,
Thomas, would ever wish so disastrous a
charge laid upon me. We cannot leap to witchcraft. They will howl me out of Salem for such
195   corruption in my house.

*A word about Thomas Putnam. He was a man with
many grievances, at least one of which appears justified. Some time before, his wife's brother-in-law, James
Bayley, had been turned down as minister of Salem.
Bayley had all the qualifications, and a two-thirds
vote into the bargain, but a faction stopped his acceptance, for reasons that are not clear.*

*Thomas Putnam was the eldest son of the rich-
est man in the village. He had fought the Indians at
Narragansett, and was deeply interested in parish
affairs. He undoubtedly felt it poor payment that the
village should so blatantly disregard his candidate for
one of its most important offices, especially since he
regarded himself as the intellectual superior of most of
the people around him.*

*His vindictive nature was demonstrated long
before the witchcraft began. Another former Salem
minister, George Burroughs, had had to borrow money
to pay for his wife's funeral, and, since the parish was
remiss in his salary, he was soon bankrupt. Thomas
and his brother John had Burroughs jailed for debts
the man did not owe. The incident is important only
in that Burroughs succeeded in becoming minister
where Bayley, Thomas Putnam's brother-in-law, had
been rejected; the motif of resentment is clear here.
Thomas Putnam felt that his own name and the honor
of his family had been smirched by the village, and he
meant to right matters however he could.*

*Another reason to believe him a deeply embit-
tered man was his attempt to break his father's will,
which left a disproportionate amount to a stepbrother.
As with every other public cause in which he tried to
force his way, he failed in this.*

*So it is not surprising to find that so many
accusations against people are in the handwriting of
Thomas Putnam, or that his name is so often found as
a witness corroborating the supernatural testimony, or
that his daughter led the crying-out at the most
opportune junctures of the trials, especially when—
But we'll speak of that when we come to it.*

PUTNAM—(*at the moment he is intent upon getting*
PARRIS, *for whom he has only contempt, to move*

toward the abyss): Mr. Parris, I have taken your
part in all contention here, and I would continue; but I cannot if you hold back in this. There   200
are hurtful, vengeful spirits layin' hands on
these children.

PARRIS: But, Thomas, you cannot—

PUTNAM: Ann! Tell Mr. Parris what you have done.

MRS. PUTNAM: Reverend Parris, I have laid seven   205
babies unbaptized in the earth. Believe me, sir,
you never saw more hearty babies born. And
yet, each would wither in my arms the very
night of their birth. I have spoke nothin', but
my heart has clamored intimations. And now,   210
this year, my Ruth, my only—I see her turning
strange. A secret child she has become this
year, and shrivels like a sucking mouth were
pullin' on her life too. And so I thought to
send her to your Tituba—   215

PARRIS: To Tituba! What may Tituba—?

MRS. PUTNAM: Tituba knows how to speak to the
dead, Mr. Parris.

PARRIS: Goody Ann, it is a formidable sin to conjure
up the dead!   220

MRS. PUTNAM: I take it on my soul, but who else may
surely tell us what person murdered my
babies?

PARRIS (*horrified*): Woman!

MRS. PUTNAM: They were murdered, Mr. Parris! And   225
mark this proof! Mark it! Last night my Ruth
were ever so close to their little spirits; I know
it, sir. For how else is she struck dumb now
except some power of darkness would stop
her mouth? It is a marvelous sign, Mr. Parris!   230

PUTNAM: Don't you understand it, sir? There is a
murdering witch among us, bound to keep
herself in the dark. (PARRIS *turns to* BETTY, *a
frantic terror rising in him.*) Let your enemies
make of it what they will, you cannot blink it   235
more.

PARRIS (*to* ABIGAIL): Then you were conjuring spirits
last night.

ABIGAIL (*whispering*): Not I, sir—Tituba and Ruth.

PARRIS (*turns now, with new fear, and goes to* BETTY,   240
looks down at her, and then, gazing off): Oh,
Abigail, what proper payment for my charity!
Now I am undone.

PUTNAM: You are not undone! Let you take hold here.
Wait for no one to charge you—declare it your-   245
self. You have discovered witchcraft—

PARRIS: In my house? In my house, Thomas? They will
topple me with this! They will make of it a—

[*Enter* MERCY LEWIS, *the* PUTNAMs' *servant, a fat, sly,
merciless girl of eighteen.*]

MERCY: Your pardons. I only thought to see how
Betty is.   250

PUTNAM: Why aren't you home? Who's with Ruth?

MERCY: Her grandma come. She's improved a little, I think—she give a powerful sneeze before.

MRS. PUTNAM: Ah, there's a sign of life!

255 MERCY: I'd fear no more, Goody Putnam. It were a grand sneeze; another like it will shake her wits together, I'm sure. (*She goes to the bed to look.*)

PARRIS: Will you leave me now, Thomas? I would
260 pray a while alone.

ABIGAIL: Uncle, you've prayed since midnight. Why do you not go down and—

PARRIS: No—no. (*To* PUTNAM:) I have no answer for that crowd. I'll wait till Mr. Hale arrives. (*To*
265 *get* MRS. PUTNAM *to leave:*) If you will, Goody Ann . . .

PUTNAM: Now look you, sir. Let you strike out against the Devil, and the village will bless you for it! Come down, speak to them—pray
270 with them. They're thirsting for your word, Mister! Surely you'll pray with them.

PARRIS (*swayed*): I'll lead them in a psalm, but let you say nothing of witchcraft yet. I will not discuss it. The cause is yet unknown. I have had enough
275 contention since I came; I want no more.

MRS. PUTNAM: Mercy, you go home to Ruth, d'y'hear?

MERCY: Aye, mum.

*[*MRS. PUTNAM *goes out.]*

PARRIS (*to* ABIGAIL): If she starts for the window, cry for me at once.

280 ABIGAIL: I will, uncle.

PARRIS (*to* PUTNAM): There is a terrible power in her arms today. (*He goes out with* PUTNAM.)

ABIGAIL (*with hushed trepidation*): How is Ruth sick?

MERCY: It's weirdish, I know not—she seems to walk
285 like a dead one since last night.

ABIGAIL (*turns at once and goes to* BETTY, *and now, with fear in her voice*): Betty? (BETTY *doesn't move. She shakes her.*) Now stop this! Betty! Sit up now!

*[*BETTY *doesn't stir.* MERCY *comes over.]*

MERCY: Have you tried beatin' her? I gave Ruth a
290 good one and it waked her for a minute. Here, let me have her.

ABIGAIL (*holding* MERCY *back*): No, he'll be comin' up. Listen, now; if they be questioning us, tell them we danced—I told him as much already.

295 MERCY: Aye. And what more?

ABIGAIL: He knows Tituba conjured Ruth's sisters to come out of the grave.

MERCY: And what more?

ABIGAIL: He saw you naked.

300 MERCY (*clapping her hands together with a frightened laugh*): Oh, Jesus!

[Enter MARY WARREN, *breathless. She is seventeen, a subservient, naive, lonely girl.]*

MARY WARREN: What'll we do? The village is out! I just come from the farm; the whole country's talkin' witchcraft! They'll be callin' us witches,
305 Abby!

MERCY (*pointing and looking at* MARY WARREN): She means to tell, I know it.

MARY WARREN: Abby, we've got to tell. Witchery's a hangin' error, a hangin' like they done in
310 Boston two years ago! We must tell the truth, Abby! You'll only be whipped for dancin', and the other things!

ABIGAIL: Oh, *we'll* be whipped!

MARY WARREN: I never done none of it, Abby. I only
315 looked!

MERCY (*moving menacingly toward* MARY): Oh, you're a great one for lookin', aren't you, Mary Warren? What a grand peeping courage you have!

*[*BETTY, *on the bed, whimpers.* ABIGAIL *turns to her at once.]*

ABIGAIL: Betty? (*She goes to* BETTY.) Now, Betty,
320 dear, wake up now. It's Abigail. (*She sits* BETTY *up and furiously shakes her.*) I'll beat you, Betty! (BETTY *whimpers.*) My, you seem improving. I talked to your papa and I told him everything. So there's nothing to—
325

BETTY (*darts off the bed, frightened of* ABIGAIL, *and flattens herself against the wall*): I want my mama!

ABIGAIL (*with alarm, as she cautiously approaches* BETTY): What ails you, Betty? Your mama's dead and buried.
330

BETTY: I'll fly to Mama. Let me fly! (*She raises her arms as though to fly, and streaks for the window, gets one leg out.*)

ABIGAIL (*pulling her away from the window*): I told him everything; he knows now, he knows every-
335 thing we—

BETTY: You drank blood, Abby! You didn't tell him that!

ABIGAIL: Betty, you never say that again! You will never—
340

BETTY: You did, you did! You drank a charm to kill John Proctor's wife! You drank a charm to kill Goody Proctor!

ABIGAIL (*smashes her across the face*): Shut it! Now shut it!
345

BETTY (*collapsing on the bed*): Mama, Mama! (*She dissolves into sobs.*)

ABIGAIL: Now look you. All of you. We danced. And Tituba conjured Ruth Putnam's dead sisters. And that is all. And mark this. Let either of
350 you breathe a word, or the edge of a word,

355 about the other things, and I will come to you in the black of some terrible night and I will bring a pointy reckoning that will shudder you. And you know I can do it; I saw Indians smash my dear parents' heads on the pillow next to mine, and I have seen some reddish work done at night, and I can make you wish

360 you had never seen the sun go down! (*She goes to* BETTY *and roughly sits her up.*)Now, you—sit up and stop this!

[*But* BETTY *collapses in her hands and lies inert on the bed.*]

MARY WARREN (*with hysterical fright*): What's got her? (ABIGAIL *stares in fright at* BETTY.) Abby, she's going to die! It's a sin to conjure, and we—

365 ABIGAIL (*starting for* MARY): I say shut it, Mary Warren!

[*Enter* JOHN PROCTOR. *On seeing him,* MARY WARREN *leaps in fright.*]

Proctor was a farmer in his middle thirties. He need not have been a partisan of any faction in the town, but there is evidence to suggest that he had a sharp and biting way with hypocrites. He was the kind of man—powerful of body, even-tempered, and not easily led—who cannot refuse support to partisans without drawing their deepest resentment. In Proctor's presence a fool felt his foolishness instantly—and a Proctor is always marked for calumny therefore.

But as we shall see, the steady manner he displays does not spring from an untroubled soul. He is a sinner, a sinner not only against the moral fashion of the time, but against his own vision of decent conduct. These people had no ritual for the washing away of sins. It is another trait we inherited from them, and it has helped to discipline us as well as to breed hypocrisy among us. Proctor, respected and even feared in Salem, has come to regard himself as a kind of fraud. But no hint of this has yet appeared on the surface, and as he enters from the crowded parlor below it is a man in his prime we see, with a quiet confidence and an unexpressed, hidden force. Mary Warren, his servant, can barely speak for embarrassment and fear.

MARY WARREN: Oh! I'm just going home, Mr. Proctor.
PROCTOR: Be you foolish, Mary Warren? Be you deaf? I forbid you leave the house, did I not? Why

370 shall I pay you? I am looking for you more often than my cows!
MARY WARREN: I only come to see the great doings in the world.
PROCTOR: I'll show you a great doin' on your arse

375 one of these days. Now get you home; my wife

is waitin' with your work! (*Trying to retain a shred of dignity, she goes slowly out.*)
MERCY LEWIS (*both afraid of him and strangely titillated*): I'd best be off. I have my Ruth to watch. Good morning, Mr. Proctor.   380

[MERCY *sidles out. Since* PROCTOR's *entrance,* ABIGAIL *has stood as though on tiptoe, absorbing his presence, wide-eyed. He glances at her, then goes to* BETTY *on the bed.*]

ABIGAIL: Gah! I'd almost forgot how strong you are, John Proctor!
PROCTOR (*looking at* ABIGAIL *now, the faintest suggestion of a knowing smile on his face*): What's this mischief here?   385
ABIGAIL (*with a nervous laugh*): Oh, she's only gone silly somehow.
PROCTOR: The road past my house is a pilgrimage to Salem all morning. The town's mumbling witchcraft.   390
ABIGAIL: Oh, posh! (*Winningly she comes a little closer, with a confidential, wicked air.*) We were dancin' in the woods last night, and my uncle leaped in on us. She took fright, is all.
PROCTOR (*his smile widening*): Ah, you're wicked yet,   395
aren't y'! (*A trill of expectant laughter escapes her, and she dares come closer, feverishly looking into his eyes.*) You'll be clapped in the stocks before you're twenty.

[*He takes a step to go, and she springs into his path.*]

ABIGAIL: Give me a word, John. A soft word. (*Her   400
concentrated desire destroys his smile.*)
PROCTOR: No, no, Abby. That's done with.
ABIGAIL (*tauntingly*): You come five mile to see a silly girl fly? I know you better.
PROCTOR (*setting her firmly out of his path*): I come to   405
see what mischief your uncle's brewin' now. (*With final emphasis:*) Put it out of mind, Abby.
ABIGAIL (*grasping his hand before he can release her*): John—I am waitin' for you every night.
PROCTOR: Abby, I never give you hope to wait for me.   410
ABIGAIL (*now beginning to anger—she can't believe it*): I have something better than hope, I think!
PROCTOR: Abby, you'll put it out of mind. I'll not be comin' for you more.
ABIGAIL: You're surely sportin' with me.   415
PROCTOR: You know me better.
ABIGAIL: I know how you clutched my back behind your house and sweated like a stallion whenever I come near! Or did I dream that? It's she put me out, you cannot pretend it were you. I   420
saw your face when she put me out, and you loved me then and you do now!
PROCTOR: Abby, that's a wild thing to say—

425 ABIGAIL: A wild thing may say wild things. But not so wild, I think. I have seen you since she put me out; I have seen you nights.

PROCTOR: I have hardly stepped off my farm this sevenmonth.

430 ABIGAIL: I have a sense for heat, John, and yours has drawn me to my window, and I have seen you looking up, burning in your loneliness. Do you tell me you've never looked up at my window?

PROCTOR: I may have looked up.

435 ABIGAIL (*now softening*): And you must. You are no wintry man. I know you, John. I *know* you. (*She is weeping.*) I cannot sleep for dreamin'; I cannot dream but I wake and walk about the house as though I'd find you comin' through some door. (*She clutches him desperately.*)

440 PROCTOR (*gently pressing her from him, with great sympathy but firmly*): Child—

ABIGAIL (*with a flash of anger*): How do you call me child!

PROCTOR: Abby, I may think of you softly from time
445 to time. But I will cut off my hand before I'll ever reach for you again. Wipe it out of mind. We never touched, Abby.

ABIGAIL: Aye, but we did.

PROCTOR: Aye, but we did not.

450 ABIGAIL (*with a bitter anger*): Oh, I marvel how such a strong man may let such a sickly wife be—

PROCTOR (*angered—at himself as well*): You'll speak nothin' of Elizabeth!

ABIGAIL: She is blackening my name in the village!
455 She is telling lies about me! She is a cold, sniveling woman, and you bend to her! Let her turn you like a—

PROCTOR (*Shaking her*): Do you look for whippin'?

[*A psalm is heard being sung below.*]

ABIGAIL (*in tears*): I look for John Proctor that took
460 me from my sleep and put knowledge in my heart! I never knew what pretense Salem was, I never knew the lying lessons I was taught by all these Christian women and their covenanted men! And now you bid me tear the light
465 out of my eyes? I will not, I cannot! You loved me, John Proctor, and whatever sin it is, you love me yet! (*He turns abruptly to go out. She rushes to him.*) John, pity me, pity me!

[*The words "going up to Jesus" are heard in the psalm, and* BETTY *claps her ears suddenly and whines loudly.*]

ABIGAIL: Betty? (*She hurries to* BETTY, *who is now sit-*
470 *ting up and screaming.* PROCTOR *goes to* BETTY *as* ABIGAIL *is trying to pull her hands down, calling* "BETTY!")

PROCTOR (*growing unnerved*): What's she doing? Girl, what ails you? Stop that wailing!

[*The singing has stopped in the midst of this, and now* PARRIS *rushes in.*]

475 PARRIS: What happened? What are you doing to her? Betty! (*He rushes to the bed, crying, "BETTY, BETTY!"* MRS. PUTNAM *enters, feverish with curiosity, and with her* THOMAS PUTNAM *and* MERCY LEWIS. PARRIS, *at the bed, keeps lightly*
480 *slapping* BETTY'S *face, while she moans and tries to get up.*)

ABIGAIL: She heard you singin' and suddenly she's up and screamin'.

MRS. PUTNAM: The psalm! The psalm! She cannot bear to hear the Lord's name!
485

PARRIS: No, God forbid. Mercy, run to the doctor! Tell him what's happened here! (MERCY LEWIS *rushes out.*)

MRS. PUTNAM: Mark it for a sign, mark it!

[REBECCA NURSE, *seventy-two, enters. She is white-haired, leaning upon her walking-stick.*]

PUTNAM (*pointing at the whimpering* BETTY): That is a
490 notorious sign of witchcraft afoot. Goody Nurse, a prodigious sign!

MRS. PUTNAM: My mother told me that! When they cannot bear to hear the name of—

PARRIS (*trembling*): Rebecca, Rebecca, go to her, we're
495 lost. She suddenly cannot bear to hear the Lord's—

[GILES COREY, *eighty-three, enters. He is knotted with muscle, canny, inquisitive, and still powerful.*]

REBECCA: There is hard sickness here, Giles Corey, so please to keep the quiet.

GILES: I've not said a word. No one here can testify
500 I've said a word. Is she going to fly again? I hear she flies.

PUTNAM: Man, be quiet now!

[*Everything is quiet.* REBECCA *walks across the room to the bed. Gentleness exudes from her.* BETTY *is quietly whimpering, eyes shut.* REBECCA *simply stands over the child, who gradually quiets.*]

And while they are so absorbed, we may put a word in for Rebecca. Rebecca was the wife of Francis Nurse, who, from all accounts, was one of those men for whom both sides of the argument had to have respect. He was called upon to arbitrate disputes as though he were an unofficial judge, and Rebecca also enjoyed the high opinion most people had for him. By the time of the delusion, they had three hundred acres, and their children were settled in separate homesteads within the same estate. However, Francis had originally rented the land, and one theory has it that, as he gradually paid for it and raised his social status, there were those who resented his rise.

Another suggestion to explain the systematic campaign against Rebecca, and inferentially against Francis, is the land war he fought with his neighbors, one of whom was a Putnam. This squabble grew to the proportions of a battle in the woods between partisans of both sides, and it is said to have lasted for two days. As for Rebecca herself, the general opinion of her character was so high that to explain how anyone dared cry her out for a witch—and more, how adults could bring themselves to lay hands on her—we must look to the fields and boundaries of that time.

As we have seen, Thomas Putnam's man for the Salem ministry was Bayley. The Nurse clan had been in the faction that prevented Bayley's taking office. In addition, certain families allied to the Nurses by blood or friendship, and whose farms were contiguous with the Nurse farm or close to it, combined to break away from the Salem town authority and set up Topsfield, a new and independent entity whose existence was resented by old Salemites.

That the guiding hand behind the outcry was Putnam's is indicated by the fact that, as soon as it began, this Topsfield-Nurse faction absented themselves from church in protest and disbelief. It was Edward and Jonathan Putnam who signed the first complaint against Rebecca; and Thomas Putnam's little daughter was the one who fell into a fit at the hearing and pointed to Rebecca as her attacker. To top it all, Mrs. Putnam—who is now staring at the bewitched child on the bed—soon accused Rebecca's spirit of "temping her to iniquity," a charge that had more truth in it than Mrs. Putnam could know.

MRS. PUTNAM (*astonished*): What have you done?

[REBECCA, *in thought, now leaves the bedside and sits.*]

505 PARRIS (*wondrous and relieved*): What do you make of it, Rebecca?

PUTNAM (*eagerly*): Goody Nurse, will you go to my Ruth and see if you can wake her?

REBECCA (*sitting*): I think she'll wake in time. Pray
510 calm yourselves. I have eleven children, and I am twenty-six times a grandma, and I have seen them all through their silly seasons, and when it come on them they will run the Devil bowlegged keeping up with their mischief. I
515 think she'll wake when she tires of it. A child's spirit is like a child, you can never catch it by running after it; you must stand still, and, for love, it will soon itself come back.

PROCTOR: Aye, that's the truth of it, Rebecca.
520 MRS. PUTNAM: This is no silly season, Rebecca. My

Ruth is bewildered, Rebecca; she cannot eat.
REBECCA: Perhaps she is not hungered yet. (*To* PARRIS:) I hope you are not decided to go in search of loose spirits, Mr. Parris. I've heard promise of that outside. 525
PARRIS: A wide opinion's running in the parish that the Devil may be among us, and I would satisfy them that they are wrong.
PROCTOR: Then let you come out and call them wrong. Did you consult the wardens before 530 you called this minister to look for devils?
PARRIS: He is not coming to look for devils!
PROCTOR: Then what's he coming for?
PUTNAM: There be children dyin' in the village, Mister! 535
PROCTOR: I seen none dyin'. This society will not be a bag to swing around your head, Mr. Putnam. (*To* PARRIS:) Did you call a meeting before you—?
PUTNAM: I am sick of meetings; cannot the man turn 540 his head without he have a meeting?
PROCTOR: He may turn his head, but not to Hell!
REBECCA: Pray, John, be calm. (*Pause. He defers to her.*) Mr. Parris, I think you'd best send Reverend Hale back as soon as he come. This will set us 545 all to arguin' again in the society, and we thought to have peace this year. I think we ought rely on the doctor now, and good prayer.
MRS. PUTNAM: Rebecca, the doctor's baffled! 550
REBECCA: If so he is, then let us go to God for the cause of it. There is prodigious danger in the seeking of loose spirits. I fear it, I fear it. Let us rather blame ourselves and—
PUTNAM: How may we blame ourselves? I am one of 555 nine sons; the Putnam seed have peopled this province. And yet I have but one child left of eight—and now she shrivels!
REBECCA: I cannot fathom that.
MRS. PUTNAM (*with a growing edge of sarcasm*): But I 560 must! You think it God's work you should never lose a child, nor grandchild either, and I bury all but one? There are wheels within wheels in this village, and fires within fires!
PUTNAM (*to* PARRIS): When Reverend Hale comes, 565 you will proceed to look for signs of witchcraft here.
PROCTOR (*to* PUTNAM): You cannot command Mr. Parris. We vote by name in this society, not by acreage. 570
PUTNAM: I never heard you worried so on this society, Mr. Proctor. I do not think I saw you at Sabbath meeting since snow flew.
PROCTOR: I have trouble enough without I come five mile to hear him preach only hellfire and 575 bloody damnation. Take it to heart, Mr. Parris. There are many others who stay away from

church these days because you hardly ever mention God any more.

580   PARRIS (*now aroused*): Why, that's a drastic charge!

REBECCA: It's somewhat true; there are many that quail to bring their children—

PARRIS: I do not preach for children, Rebecca. It is not the children who are unmindful of their oblig-

585   ations toward this ministry.

REBECCA: Are there really those unmindful?

PARRIS: I should say the better half of Salem village—

PUTNAM: And more than that!

PARRIS: Where is my wood? My contract provides I

590   be supplied with all my firewood. I am wait- ing since November for a stick, and even in November I had to show my frostbitten hands like some London beggar!

GILES: You are allowed six pound a year to buy your

595   wood, Mr. Parris.

PARRIS: I regard that six pound as part of my salary. I am paid little enough without I spend six pound on firewood.

PROCTOR: Sixty, plus six for firewood—

600   PARRIS: The salary is sixty-six pound, Mr. Proctor! I am not some preaching farmer with a book under my arm; I am a graduate of Harvard College.

GILES: Aye, and well instructed in arithmetic!

605   PARRIS: Mr. Corey, you will look far for a man of my kind at sixty pound a year! I am not used to this poverty; I left a thrifty business in the Barbados to serve the Lord. I do not fathom it, why am I persecuted here? I cannot offer one

610   proposition but there be a howling riot of argument. I have often wondered if the Devil be in it somewhere; I cannot understand you people otherwise.

PROCTOR: Mr. Parris, you are the first minister ever

615   did demand the deed to this house—

PARRIS: Man! Don't a minister deserve a house to live in?

PROCTOR: To live in, yes. But to ask ownership is like you shall own the meeting house itself; the last

620   meeting I were at you spoke so long on deeds and mortgages I thought it were an auction.

PARRIS: I want a mark of confidence, is all! I am your third preacher in seven years. I do not wish to be put out like the cat whenever some majority

625   feels the whim. You people seem not to com- prehend that a minister is the Lord's man in the parish; a minister is not to be so lightly crossed and contradicted—

PUTNAM: Aye!

630   PARRIS: There is either obedience or the church will burn like Hell is burning!

PROCTOR: Can you speak one minute without we land in Hell again? I am sick of Hell!

PARRIS: It is not for you to say what is good for you

to hear!   635

PROCTOR: I may speak my heart, I think!

PARRIS (*in a fury*): What, are we Quakers? We are not Quakers here yet, Mr. Proctor. And you may tell that to your followers!

PROCTOR: My followers!   640

PARRIS—(*now he's out with it*): There is a party in this church. I am not blind; there is a faction and a party.

PROCTOR: Against you?

PUTNAM: Against him and all authority!   645

PROCTOR: Why, then I must find it and join it.

[There is shock among the others.]

REBECCA: He does not mean that.

PUTNAM: He confessed it now!

PROCTOR: I mean it solemnly, Rebecca; I like not the smell of this "authority."   650

REBECCA: No, you cannot break charity with your minister. You are another kind, John. Clasp his hand, make your peace.

PROCTOR: I have a crop to sow and lumber to drag home. (*He goes angrily to the door and turns to*   655
  COREY *with a smile.*) What say you, Giles, let's find the party. He says there's a party.

GILES: I've changed my opinion of this man, John. Mr. Parris, I beg your pardon. I never thought you had so much iron in you.   660

PARRIS (*surprised*): Why, thank you, Giles!

GILES: It suggests to the mind what the trouble be among us all these years. (*To all:*) Think on it. Wherefore is everybody suing everybody else? Think on it now, it's a deep thing, and dark as   665
  a pit. I have been six time in court this year—

PROCTOR (*familiarly, with warmth, although he knows he is approaching the edge of* GILES' *tolerance with this*): Is it the Devil's fault that a man cannot say you good morning without you clap him   670
  for defamation? You're old, Giles, and you're not hearin' so well as you did.

GILES—(*he cannot be crossed*): John Proctor, I have only last month collected four pound damages for you publicly sayin' I burned the roof off   675
  your house, and I—

PROCTOR (*laughing*): I never said no such thing, but I've paid you for it, so I hope I can call you deaf without charge. Now come along, Giles, and help me drag my lumber home.   680

PUTNAM: A moment, Mr. Proctor. What lumber is that you're draggin', if I may ask you?

PROCTOR: My lumber. From out my forest by the riverside.

PUTNAM: Why, we are surely gone wild this year.   685
  What anarchy is this? That tract is in my bounds, it's in my bounds, Mr. Proctor.

PROCTOR: In your bounds! (*Indicating* REBECCA:) I

690   bought that tract from Goody Nurse's husband
        five months ago.
PUTNAM: He had no right to sell it. It stands clear in
        my grandfather's will that all the land
        between the river and—
PROCTOR: Your grandfather had a habit of willing land
695   that never belonged to him, if I may say it plain.
GILES: That's God's truth; he nearly willed away my
        north pasture but he knew I'd break his fingers
        before he'd set his name to it. Let's get your
        lumber home, John. I feel a sudden will to
700   work coming on.
PUTNAM: You load one oak of mine and you'll fight
        to drag it home!
GILES: Aye, and we'll win too, Putnam—this fool and
        I. Come on! (*He turns to* PROCTOR *and starts out.*)
705   PUTNAM: I'll have my men on you, Corey! I'll clap a
        writ on you!

[*Enter* REVEREND JOHN HALE *of Beverly.*]

*Mr. Hale is nearing forty, a tight-skinned, eager-eyed
intellectual. This is a beloved errand for him; on being
called here to ascertain witchcraft he felt the pride of
the specialist whose unique knowledge has at last
been publicly called for. Like almost all men of learning, he spent a good deal of his time pondering the
invisible world, especially since he had himself
encountered a witch in his parish not long before.
That woman, however, turned into a mere pest under
his searching scrutiny, and the child she had allegedly
been afflicting recovered her normal behavior after
Hale had given her his kindness and a few days of rest
in his own house. However, that experience never
raised a doubt in his mind as to the reality of the
underworld or the existence of Lucifer's many-faced
lieutenants. And his belief is not to his discredit. Better
minds than Hale's were—and still are—convinced that
there is a society of spirits beyond our ken. One cannot help noting that one of his lines has never yet
raised a laugh in any audience that has seen this
play; it is his assurance that "We cannot look to
superstition in this. The Devil is precise." Evidently we
are not quite certain even now whether diabolism is
holy and not to be scoffed at. And it is no accident
that we should be so bemused.*

*Like Reverend Hale and the others on this stage,
we conceive the Devil as a necessary part of a
respectable view of cosmology. Ours is a divided
empire in which certain ideas and emotions and
actions are of God, and their opposites are of Lucifer.
It is as impossible for most men to conceive of a morality without sin as of an earth without "sky." Since
1692 a great but superficial change has wiped out
God's beard and the Devil's horns, but the world is
still gripped between two diametrically opposed
absolutes. The concept of unity, in which positive and*

*negative are attributes of the same force, in which
good and evil are relative, ever-changing, and always
joined to the same phenomenon—such a concept is
still reserved to the physical sciences and to the few
who have grasped the history of ideas. When it is
recalled that until the Christian era the underworld
was never regarded as a hostile area, that all gods
were useful and essentially friendly to man despite
occasional lapses; when we see the steady and
methodical inculcation into humanity of the idea of
man's worthlessness—until redeemed—the necessity of
the Devil may become evident as a weapon, a weapon
designed and used time and time again in every age to
whip men into a surrender to a particular church or
church-state.*

*Our difficulty in believing the—for want of a
better word—political inspiration of the Devil is due in
great part to the fact that he is called up and damned
not only by our social antagonists but by our own
side, whatever it may be. The Catholic Church,
through its Inquisition, is famous for cultivating
Lucifer as the arch-fiend, but the Church's enemies
relied no less upon the Old Boy to keep the human
mind enthralled. Luther was himself accused of
alliance with Hell, and he in turn accused his enemies.
To complicate matters further, he believed that he had
had contact with the Devil and had argued theology
with him. I am not surprised at this, for at my own
university a professor of history—a Lutheran, by the
way—used to assemble his graduate students, draw
the shades, and commune in the classroom with
Erasmus. He was never, to my knowledge, officially
scoffed at for this, the reason being that the university
officials, like most of us, are the children of a history
which still sucks at the Devil's teats. At this writing,
only England has held back before the temptations of
contemporary diabolism. In the countries of the
Communist ideology, all resistance of any import is
linked to the totally malign capitalist succubi, and in
America any man who is not reactionary in his views
is open to the charge of alliance with the Red hell.
Political opposition, thereby, is given an inhumane
overlay which then justifies the abrogation of all normally applied customs of civilized intercourse. A political policy is equated with moral right, and opposition
to it with diabolical malevolence. Once such an equation is effectively made, society becomes a congerie of
plots and counterplots, and the main role of government changes from that of the arbiter to that of the
scourge of God.*

*The results of this process are no different now
from what they ever were, except sometimes in the
degree of cruelty inflicted, and not always even in that
department. Normally the actions and deeds of a man
were all that society felt comfortable in judging. The
secret intent of an action was left to the ministers,
priests, and rabbis to deal with. When diabolism rises,*

however, actions are the least important manifests of the true nature of a man. The Devil, as Reverend Hale said, is a wily one, and, until an hour before he fell, even God thought him beautiful in Heaven.

The analogy, however, seems to falter when one considers that, while there were no witches then, there are Communists and capitalists now, and in each camp there is certain proof that spies of each side are at work undermining the other. But this is a snobbish objection and not at all warranted by the facts. I have no doubt that people were communing with, and even worshiping, the Devil in Salem, and if the whole truth could be known in this case, as it is in others, we should discover a regular and conventionalized propitiation of the dark spirit. One certain evidence of this is the confession of Tituba, the slave of Reverend Parris, and another is the behavior of the children who were known to have indulged in sorceries with her.

There are accounts of similar klatches in Europe, where the daughters of the towns would assemble at night and, sometimes with fetishes, sometimes with a selected young man, give themselves to love, with some bastardly results. The Church, sharp-eyed as it must be when gods long dead are brought to life, condemned these orgies as witchcraft and interpreted them, rightly, as a resurgence of the Dionysiac forces it had crushed long before. Sex, sin, and the Devil were early linked, and so they continued to be in Salem, and are today. From all accounts there are no more puritanical mores in the world than those enforced by the Communists in Russia, where women's fashions, for instance, are as prudent and all-covering as any American Baptist would desire. The divorce laws lay a tremendous responsibility on the father for the care of his children. Even the laxity of divorce regulations in the early years of the revolution was undoubtedly a revulsion from the nineteenth-century Victorian immobility of marriage and the consequent hypocrisy that developed from it. If for no other reasons, a state so powerful, so jealous of the uniformity of its citizens, cannot long tolerate the atomization of the family. And yet, in American eyes at least, there remains the conviction that the Russian attitude toward women is lascivious. It is the Devil working again, just as he is working within the Slav who is shocked at the very idea of a woman's disrobing herself in a burlesque show. Our opposites are always robed in sexual sin, and it is from this unconscious conviction that demonology gains both its attractive sensuality and its capacity to infuriate and frighten.

Coming into Salem now, Reverend Hale conceives of himself much as a young doctor on his first call. His painfully acquired armory of symptoms, catchwords, and diagnostic procedures are now to be put to use at last. The road from Beverly is unusually busy this morning, and he has passed a hundred

rumors that make him smile at the ignorance of the yeomanry in this most precise science. He feels himself allied with the best minds of Europe—kings, philosophers, scientists, and ecclesiasts of all churches. His goal is light, goodness and its preservation, and he knows the exaltation of the blessed whose intelligence, sharpened by minute examinations of enormous tracts, is finally called upon to face what may be a bloody fight with the Fiend himself.

[He appears loaded down with half a dozen heavy books.]

HALE: Pray you, someone take these!

PARRIS (*delighted*): Mr. Hale! Oh! it's good to see you again! (*Taking some books:*) My, they're heavy!

HALE (*setting down his books*): They must be; they are weighted with authority.   710

PARRIS (*a little scared*): Well, you do come prepared!

HALE: We shall need hard study if it comes to tracking down the Old Boy. (*Noticing* REBECCA:) You cannot be Rebecca Nurse?   715

REBECCA: I am, sir. Do you know me?

HALE: It's strange how I knew you, but I suppose you look as such a good soul should. We have all heard of your great charities in Beverly.

PARRIS: Do you know this gentleman? Mr. Thomas   720
Putnam. And his good wife Ann.

HALE: Putnam! I had not expected such distinguished company, sir.

PUTNAM (*pleased*): It does not seem to help us today, Mr. Hale. We look to you to come to our house   725
and save our child.

HALE: Your child ails too?

MRS. PUTNAM: Her soul, her soul seems flown away. She sleeps and yet she walks . . .

PUTNAM: She cannot eat.   730

HALE: Cannot eat! (*Thinks on it. Then, to* PROCTOR *and* GILES COREY:) Do you men have afflicted children?

PARRIS: No, no, these are farmers. John Proctor—

GILES COREY: He don't believe in witches.   735

PROCTOR (*to* HALE): I never spoke on witches one way or the other. Will you come, Giles?

GILES: No—no, John, I think not. I have some few queer questions of my own to ask this fellow.

PROCTOR: I've heard you to be a sensible man, Mr.   740
Hale. I hope you'll leave some of it in Salem.

*[*PROCTOR *goes.* HALE *stands embarrassed for an instant.]*

PARRIS (*quickly*): Will you look at my daughter, sir? (*Leads* HALE *to the bed.*) She has tried to leap out the window; we discovered her this morning on the highroad, waving her arms as   745
though she'd fly.

HALE (*narrowing his eyes*): Tries to fly.

PUTNAM: She cannot bear to hear the Lord's name, Mr. Hale; that's a sure sign of witchcraft afloat.

750 HALE (*holding up his hands*): No, no. Now let me instruct you. We cannot look to superstition in this. The Devil is precise; the marks of his presence are definite as stone, and I must tell you all that I shall not proceed unless you are
755 prepared to believe me if I should find no bruise of hell upon her.

PARRIS: It is agreed, sir—it is agreed—we will abide by your judgment.

HALE: Good then. (*He goes to the bed, looks down at*
760 BETTY. *To* PARRIS:) Now, sir, what were your first warning of this strangeness?

PARRIS: Why, sir—I discovered her—(*indicating* ABIGAIL)—and my niece and ten or twelve of the other girls, dancing in the forest last night.

765 HALE (*surprised*): You permit dancing?

PARRIS: No, no, it were secret—

MRS. PUTNAM (*unable to wait*): Mr. Parris's slave has knowledge of conjurin', sir.

PARRIS (*to* MRS. PUTNAM): We cannot be sure of that,
770 Goody Ann—

MRS. PUTNAM (*frightened, very softly*): I know it, sir. I sent my child—she should learn from Tituba who murdered her sisters.

REBECCA (*horrified*): Goody Ann! You sent a child to
775 conjure up the dead?

MRS. PUTNAM: Let God blame me, not you, not you, Rebecca! I'll not have you judging me any more! (*To* HALE:) Is it a natural work to lose seven children before they live a day?

780 PARRIS: Sssh!

[REBECCA, *with great pain, turns her face away. There is a pause.*]

HALE: Seven dead in childbirth.

MRS. PUTNAM (*softly*): Aye. (*Her voice breaks; she looks up at him. Silence.* HALE *is impressed.* PARRIS *looks to him. He goes to his books, opens one, turns*
785 *pages, then reads. All wait, avidly.*)

PARRIS (*hushed*): What book is that?

MRS. PUTNAM: What's there, sir?

HALE (*with a tasty love of intellectual pursuit*): Here is all the invisible world, caught, defined, and calcu-
790 lated. In these books the Devil stands stripped of all his brute disguises. Here are all your familiar spirits—your incubi and succubi; your witches that go by land, by air, and by sea; your wizards of the night and of the day. Have no
795 fear now—we shall find him out if he has come among us, and I mean to crush him utterly if he has shown his face! (*He starts for the bed.*)

REBECCA: Will it hurt the child, sir?

HALE: I cannot tell. If she is truly in the Devil's grip we may have to rip and tear to get her free. 800

REBECCA: I think I'll go, then. I am too old for this. (*She rises.*)

PARRIS (*striving for conviction*): Why, Rebecca, we may open up the boil of all our troubles today!

REBECCA: Let us hope for that. I go to God for you, sir. 805

PARRIS (*with trepidation—and resentment*): I hope you do not mean we go to Satan here! (*Slight pause.*)

REBECCA: I wish I knew. (*She goes out; they feel resentful of her note of moral superiority.*) 810

PUTNAM (*abruptly*): Come, Mr. Hale, let's get on. Sit you here.

GILES: Mr. Hale, I have always wanted to ask a learned man—what signifies the readin' of strange books? 815

HALE: What books?

GILES: I cannot tell; she hides them.

HALE: Who does this?

GILES: Martha, my wife. I have waked at night many a time and found her in a corner, readin' of a 820 book. Now what do you make of that?

HALE: Why, that's not necessarily—

GILES: It discomfits me! Last night—mark this—I tried and tried and could not say my prayers. And then she close her book and walks out of 825 the house, and suddenly—mark this—I could pray again!

Old Giles must be spoken for, if only because his fate was to be so remarkable and so different from that of all the others. He was in his early eighties at this time, and was the most comical hero in the history. No man has ever been blamed for so much. If a cow was missed, the first thought was to look for her around Corey's house; a fire blazing up at night brought suspicion of arson to his door. He didn't give a hoot for public opinion, and only in his last years—after he had married Martha—did he bother much with the church. That she stopped his prayer is very probable, but he forgot to say that he'd only recently learned any prayers and it didn't take much to make him stumble over them. He was a crank and a nuisance, but withal a deeply innocent and brave man. In court once, he was asked if it were true that he had been frightened by the strange behavior of a hog and had then said he knew it to be the Devil in an animal's shape. "What frighted you?" he was asked. He forgot everything but the word "frighted," and instantly replied, "I do not know that I ever spoke that word in my life."

HALE: Ah! The stoppage of prayer—that is strange. I'll speak further on that with you.

GILES: I'm not sayin' she's touched the Devil, now, 830 but I'd admire to know what books she reads and why she hides them. She'll not answer me, y' see.

HALE: Aye, we'll discuss it. (*To all:*) Now mark me, if
835   the Devil is in her you will witness some fright-
    ful wonders in this room, so please to keep
    your wits about you. Mr. Putnam, stand close
    in case she flies. Now, Betty, dear, will you sit
    up? (PUTNAM *comes in closer, ready-handed.* HALE
840   *sits* BETTY *up, but she hangs limp in his hands.*)
    Hmmm. (*He observes her carefully. The others
    watch breathlessly.*) Can you hear me? I am John
    Hale, minister of Beverly. I have come to help
    you, dear. Do you remember my two little girls
845   in Beverly? (*She does not stir in his hands.*)
PARRIS (*in fright*): How can it be the Devil? Why
    would he choose my house to strike? We have
    all manner of licentious people in the village!
HALE: What victory would the Devil have to win a
850   soul already bad? It is the best the Devil
    wants, and who is better than the minister?
GILES: That's deep, Mr. Parris, deep, deep!
PARRIS (*with resolution now*): Betty! Answer Mr. Hale!
    Betty!
855 HALE: Does someone afflict you, child? It need not be
    a woman, mind you, or a man. Perhaps some
    bird invisible to others comes to you—perhaps
    a pig, a mouse, or any beast at all. Is there some
    figure bids you fly? (*The child remains limp in his
860   hands. In silence he lays her back on the pillow.
    Now, holding out his hands toward her, he intones:*)
    In nomine Domini Sabaoth sui filiique ite ad
    infernos. (*She does not stir. He turns to* ABIGAIL,
    his eyes narrowing.) Abigail, what sort of dancing
865   were you doing with her in the forest?
ABIGAIL: Why—common dancing is all.
PARRIS: I think I ought to say that I—I saw a kettle in
    the grass where they were dancing.
ABIGAIL: That were only soup.
870 HALE: What sort of soup were in this kettle, Abigail?
ABIGAIL: Why, it were beans—and lentils, I think,
    and—
HALE: Mr. Parris, you did not notice, did you, any
    living thing in the kettle? A mouse, perhaps, a
875   spider, a frog—?
PARRIS (*fearfully*): I—do believe there were some
    movement—in the soup.
ABIGAIL: That jumped in, we never put it in!
HALE (*quickly*): What jumped in?
880 ABIGAIL: Why, a very little frog jumped—
PARRIS: A frog, Abby!
HALE (*grasping* ABIGAIL): Abigail, it may be your cousin
    is dying. Did you call the Devil last night?
ABIGAIL: I never called him! Tituba, Tituba . . .
885 PARRIS (*blanched*): She called the Devil?
HALE: I should like to speak with Tituba.
PARRIS: Goody Ann, will you bring her up? (MRS.
    PUTNAM *exits.*)
HALE: How did she call him?
890 ABIGAIL: I know not—she spoke Barbados.

HALE: Did you feel any strangeness when she called
    him? A sudden cold wind, perhaps? A trem-
    bling below the ground?
ABIGAIL: I didn't see no Devil! (*Shaking* BETTY:) Betty,
    wake up. Betty! Betty!   895
HALE: You cannot evade me, Abigail. Did your
    cousin drink any of the brew in that kettle?
ABIGAIL: She never drank it!
HALE: Did you drink it?
ABIGAIL: No, sir!   900
HALE: Did Tituba ask you to drink it?
ABIGAIL: She tried, but I refused.
HALE: Why are you concealing? Have you sold your-
    self to Lucifer?
ABIGAIL: I never sold myself! I'm a good girl! I'm a   905
    proper girl!

[MRS. PUTNAM *enters with* TITUBA, *and instantly*
ABIGAIL *points at* TITUBA.]

ABIGAIL: She made me do it! She made Betty do it!
TITUBA (*shocked and angry*): Abby!
ABIGAIL: She makes me drink blood!
PARRIS: Blood!!   910
MRS. PUTNAM: My baby's blood?
TITUBA: No, no, chicken blood. I give she chicken
    blood!
HALE: Woman, have you enlisted these children for
    the Devil?   915
TITUBA: No, no, sir. I don't truck with no Devil!
HALE: Why can she not wake? Are you silencing this
    child?
TITUBA: I love me Betty!
HALE: You have sent your spirit out upon this child,   920
    have you not? Are you gathering souls for the
    Devil?
ABIGAIL: She sends her spirit on me in church; she
    makes me laugh at prayer!
PARRIS: She have often laughed at prayer!   925
ABIGAIL: She comes to me every night to go and
    drink blood!
TITUBA: You beg *me* to conjure! She beg *me* make
    charm—
ABIGAIL: Don't lie! (*To* HALE:) She comes to me while   930
    I sleep; she's always making me dream corrup-
    tions!
TITUBA: Why you say that, Abby?
ABIGAIL: Sometimes I wake and find myself standing
    in the open doorway and not a stitch on my   935
    body! I always hear her laughing in my sleep.
    I hear her singing her Barbados songs and
    tempting me with—
TITUBA: Mister Reverend, I never—
HALE (*resolved now*): Tituba, I want you to wake this   940
    child.
TITUBA: I have no power on this child, sir.
HALE: You most certainly do, and you will free her

945 from it now! When did you compact with the Devil?

TITUBA: I don't compact with no Devil!

PARRIS: You will confess yourself or I will take you out and whip you to your death, Tituba!

950 PUTNAM: This woman must be hanged! She must be taken and hanged!

TITUBA (*terrified, falls to her knees*): No, no, don't hang Tituba! I tell him I don't desire to work for him, sir.

PARRIS: The Devil?

955 HALE: Then you saw him! (TITUBA *weeps.*) Now Tituba, I know that when we bind ourselves to Hell it is very hard to break with it. We are going to help you tear yourself free—

TITUBA (*frightened by the coming process*): Mister

960 Reverend, I do believe somebody else be witchin' these children.

HALE: Who?

TITUBA: I don't know, sir, but the Devil got him numerous witches.

965 HALE: Does he! (*It is a clue.*) Tituba, look into my eyes. Come, look into me. (*She raises her eyes to his fearfully.*) You would be a good Christian woman, would you not, Tituba?

TITUBA: Aye, sir, a good Christian woman.

970 HALE: And you love these little children?

TITUBA: Oh, yes, sir, I don't desire to hurt little children.

HALE: And you love God, Tituba?

TITUBA: I love God with all my bein'.

HALE: Now, in God's holy name—

975 TITUBA: Bless Him. Bless Him. (*She is rocking on her knees, sobbing in terror.*)

HALE: And to His glory—

TITUBA: Eternal glory. Bless Him—bless God . . .

HALE: Open yourself, Tituba—open yourself and let

980 God's holy light shine on you.

TITUBA: Oh, bless the Lord.

HALE: When the Devil comes to you does he ever come—with another person? (*She stares up into his face.*) Perhaps another person in the village?

985 Someone you know.

PARRIS: Who came with him?

PUTNAM: Sarah Good? Did you ever see Sarah Good with him? Or Osburn?

PARRIS: Was it man or woman came with him?

990 TITUBA: Man or woman. Was—was woman.

PARRIS: What woman? A woman, you said. What woman?

TITUBA: It was black dark, and I—

PARRIS: You could see him, why could you not see her?

995 TITUBA: Well, they was always talking; they was always runnin' round and carryin' on—

PARRIS: You mean out of Salem? Salem witches?

TITUBA: I believe so, yes, sir.

[*Now* HALE *takes her hand. She is surprised.*]

HALE: Tituba. You must have no fear to tell us who they are, do you understand? We will protect 1000 you. The Devil can never overcome a minister. You know that, do you not?

TITUBA (*kisses* HALE'S *hand*): Aye, sir, oh, I do.

HALE: You have confessed yourself to witchcraft, and that speaks a wish to come to Heaven's side. 1005 And we will bless you, Tituba.

TITUBA (*deeply relieved*): Oh, God bless you, Mr. Hale!

HALE (*with rising exaltation*): You are God's instrument put in our hands to discover the Devil's agents among us. You are selected, Tituba, you 1010 are chosen to help us cleanse our village. So speak utterly, Tituba, turn your back on him and face God—face God, Tituba, and God will protect you.

TITUBA (*joining with him*): Oh, God, protect Tituba! 1015

HALE (*kindly*): Who came to you with the Devil? Two? Three? Four? How many?

[TITUBA *pants, and begins rocking back and forth again, staring ahead.*]

TITUBA: There was four. There was four.

PARRIS (*pressing in on her*): Who? Who? Their names, their names! 1020

TITUBA (*suddenly bursting out*): Oh, how many times he bid me kill you, Mr. Parris!

PARRIS: Kill me!

TITUBA (*in a fury*): He say Mr. Parris must be kill! Mr. Parris no goodly man, Mr. Parris mean man 1025 and no gentle man, and he bid me rise out of my bed and cut your throat! (*They gasp.*) But I tell him "No! I don't hate that man. I don't want kill that man." But he say, "You work for me, Tituba, and I make you free! I give you 1030 pretty dress to wear, and put you way high up in the air, and you gone fly back to Barbados!" And I say, "You lie, Devil, you lie!" And then he come one stormy night to me, and he say, "Look! I have *white* people belong to me." And 1035 I look—and there was Goody Good.

PARRIS: Sarah Good!

TITUBA (*rocking and weeping*): Aye, sir, and Goody Osburn.

MRS. PUTNAM: I knew it! Goody Osburn were mid- 1040 wife to me three times. I begged you, Thomas, did I not? I begged him not to call Osburn because I feared her. My babies always shriv- eled in her hands!

HALE: Take courage, you must give us all their 1045 names. How can you bear to see this child suf- fering? Look at her, Tituba. (*He is indicating* BETTY *on the bed.*) Look at her God-given inno- cence; her soul is so tender; we must protect her, Tituba; the Devil is out and preying on her 1050 like a beast upon the flesh of the pure lamb.

God will bless you for your help.

[ABIGAIL *rises, staring as though inspired, and cries out.*]

ABIGAIL: I want to open myself! (*They turn to her, startled. She is enraptured, as though in a pearly light.*)
1055   I want the light of God, I want the sweet love of Jesus! I danced for the Devil; I saw him; I wrote in his book; I go back to Jesus; I kiss His hand. I saw Sarah Good with the Devil! I saw Goody Osburn with the Devil! I saw Bridget
1060   Bishop with the Devil!

[*As she is speaking,* BETTY *is rising from the bed, a fever in her eyes, and picks up the chant.*]

BETTY (*staring too*): I saw George Jacobs with the Devil! I saw Goody Howe with the Devil!
PARRIS: She speaks! (*He rushes to embrace* BETTY.) She speaks!
1065   HALE: Glory to God! It is broken, they are free!
BETTY (*calling out hysterically and with great relief*): I saw Martha Bellows with the Devil!
ABIGAIL: I saw Goody Sibber with the Devil! (*It is rising to a great glee.*)
1070   PUTNAM: The marshal, I'll call the marshal!

[PARRIS *is shouting a prayer of thanksgiving.*]

BETTY: I saw Alice Barrow with the Devil!

[*The curtain begins to fall.*]

HALE (*as* PUTNAM *goes out*): Let the marshal bring irons!
ABIGAIL: I saw Goody Hawkins with the Devil!
BETTY: I saw Goody Bibber with the Devil!
1075   ABIGAIL: I saw Goody Booth with the Devil!

[*On their ecstatic cries, the curtain falls*]

ACT II

The common room of PROCTOR'*s house, eight days later.*
       At the right is a door opening on the fields outside. A fireplace is at the left, and behind it a stairway leading upstairs. It is the low, dark, and rather long living room of the time. As the curtain rises, the room is empty. From above, ELIZABETH *is heard softly singing to the children. Presently the door opens and* JOHN PROCTOR *enters, carrying his gun. He glances about the room as he comes toward the fireplace, then halts for an instant as he hears her singing. He continues on to the fireplace, leans the gun against the wall as he swings a pot out of the fire and smells it. Then he lifts out the ladle and tastes. He is not quite pleased. He reaches to a cupboard, takes a pinch of*

salt, and drops it into the pot. As he is tasting again, her footsteps are heard on the stair. He swings the pot into the fireplace and goes to a basin and washes his hands and face. ELIZABETH *enters.*

ELIZABETH: What keeps you so late? It's almost dark.
PROCTOR: I were planting far out to the forest edge.
ELIZABETH: Oh, you're done then.
PROCTOR: Aye, the farm is seeded. The boys asleep?
ELIZABETH: They will be soon. (*And she goes to the fire- 1080
       place, proceeds to ladle up stew in a dish.*)
PROCTOR: Pray now for a fair summer.
ELIZABETH: Aye.
PROCTOR: Are you well today?
ELIZABETH: I am. (*She brings the plate to the table, and,* 1085
       indicating the food:) It is a rabbit.
PROCTOR (*going to the table:*): Oh, is it! In Jonathan's trap?
ELIZABETH: No, she walked into the house this afternoon; I found her sittin' in the corner like she 1090
       come to visit.
PROCTOR: Oh, that's a good sign walkin' in.
ELIZABETH: Pray God. It hurt my heart to strip her, poor rabbit. (*She sits and watches him taste it.*)
PROCTOR: It's well seasoned. 1095
ELIZABETH (*blushing with pleasure*): I took great care. She's tender?
PROCTOR: Aye. (*He eats. She watches him.*) I think we'll see green fields soon. It's warm as blood beneath the clods. 1100
ELIZABETH: That's well.

[PROCTOR *eats, then looks up.*]

PROCTOR: If the crop is good I'll buy George Jacob's heifer. How would that please you?
ELIZABETH: Aye, it would.
PROCTOR (*with a grin*): I mean to please you, 1105
       Elizabeth.
ELIZABETH (*it is hard to say*): I know it, John.

[*He gets up, goes to her, kisses her. She receives it. With a certain disappointment, he returns to the table.*]

PROCTOR (*as gently as he can*): Cider?
ELIZABETH (*with a sense of reprimanding herself for having forgot*): Aye! (*She gets up and goes and pours a 1110
       glass for him. He now arches his back.*)
PROCTOR: This farm's a continent when you go foot by foot droppin' seeds in it.
ELIZABETH (*coming with the cider*): It must be.
PROCTOR (*drinks a long draught, then, putting the glass 1115
       down*): You ought to bring some flowers in the house.
ELIZABETH: Oh! I forgot! I will tomorrow.
PROCTOR: It's winter in here yet. On Sunday let you

1120   come with me, and we'll walk the farm together; I never see such a load of flowers on the
earth. (*With good feeling he goes and looks up at
the sky through the open doorway.*) Lilacs have a
purple smell. Lilac is the smell of nightfall, I
1125   think. Massachusetts is a beauty in the spring!
ELIZABETH: Aye, it is.

[*There is a pause. She is watching him from the table
as he stands there absorbing the night. It is as though
she would speak but cannot. Instead, now, she takes
up his plate and glass and fork and goes with them to
the basin. Her back is turned to him. He turns to her
and watches her. A sense of their separation rises.*]

PROCTOR: I think you're sad again. Are you?
ELIZABETH—(*she doesn't want friction, and yet she
must*): You come so late I thought you'd gone
1130   to Salem this afternoon.
PROCTOR: Why? I have no business in Salem.
ELIZABETH: You did speak of going, earlier this week.
PROCTOR—(*he knows what she means*): I thought better
of it since.
1135   ELIZABETH: Mary Warren's there today.
PROCTOR: Why'd you let her? You heard me forbid
her go to Salem any more!
ELIZABETH: I couldn't stop her.
PROCTOR (*holding back a full condemnation of her*): It is a
1140   fault, it is a fault, Elizabeth—you're the mis-
tress here, not Mary Warren.
ELIZABETH: She frightened all my strength away.
PROCTOR: How may that mouse frighten you,
Elizabeth? You—
1145   ELIZABETH: It is a mouse no more. I forbid her go,
and she raises up her chin like the daughter of
a prince and says to me, "I must go to Salem,
Goody Proctor; I am an official of the court!"
PROCTOR: Court! What court?
1150   ELIZABETH: Aye, it is a proper court they have now.
They've sent four judges out of Boston, she
says, weighty magistrates of the General
Court, and at the head sits the Deputy
Governor of the Province.
1155   PROCTOR (*astonished*): Why, she's mad.
ELIZABETH: I would to God she were. There be fourteen people in the jail now, she says. (PROCTOR
simply looks at her, unable to grasp it.) And
they'll be tried, and the court have power to
1160   hang them too, she says.
PROCTOR (*scoffing, but without conviction*): Ah, they'd
never hang—
ELIZABETH: The Deputy Governor promise hangin' if
they'll not confess, John. The town's gone wild,
I think. She speak of Abigail, and I thought she
1165   were a saint, to hear her. Abigail brings the
other girls into the court, and where she walks
the crowd will part like the sea for Israel. And

folks are brought before them, and if they
scream and howl and fall to the floor—the per-   1170
son's clapped in the jail for bewitchin' them.
PROCTOR (*wide-eyed*): Oh, it is a black mischief.
ELIZABETH: I think you must go to Salem, John. (*He
turns to her.*) I think so. You must tell them it is
a fraud.   1175
PROCTOR (*thinking beyond this*): Aye, it is, it is surely.
ELIZABETH: Let you go to Ezekiel Cheever—he knows
you well. And tell him what she said to you
last week in her uncle's house. She said it had
naught to do with witchcraft, did she not?   1180
PROCTOR (*in thought*): Aye, she did, she did. (*Now, a
pause.*)
ELIZABETH (*quietly, fearing to anger him by prodding*):
God forbid you keep that from the court, John.
I think they must be told.   1185
PROCTOR (*quietly, struggling with his thought*): Aye,
they must, they must. It is a wonder they do
believe her.
ELIZABETH: I would go to Salem now, John—let you
go tonight.   1190
PROCTOR: I'll think on it.
ELIZABETH (*with her courage now*): You cannot keep it,
John.
PROCTOR (*angering*): I know I cannot keep it. I say I
will think on it!   1195
ELIZABETH (*hurt, and very coldly*): Good, then, let you
think on it. (*She stands and starts to walk out of
the room.*)
PROCTOR: I am only wondering how I may prove
what she told me, Elizabeth. If the girl's a saint   1200
now, I think it is not easy to prove she's fraud,
and the town gone so silly. She told it to me in
a room alone—I have no proof for it.
ELIZABETH: You were alone with her?
PROCTOR (*stubbornly*): For a moment alone, aye.   1205
ELIZABETH: Why, then, it is not as you told me.
PROCTOR (*his anger rising*): For a moment, I say. The
others come in soon after.
ELIZABETH (*quietly—she has suddenly lost all faith in
him*): Do as you wish, then. (*She starts to turn.*)   1210
PROCTOR: Woman. (*She turns to him.*) I'll not have
your suspicion any more.
ELIZABETH (*a little loftily*): I have no—
PROCTOR: I'll not have it!
ELIZABETH: Then let you not earn it.   1215
PROCTOR (*with a violent undertone*): You doubt me yet?
ELIZABETH (*with a smile, to keep her dignity*): John, if it
were not Abigail that you must go to hurt,
would you falter now? I think not.
PROCTOR: Now look you—   1220
ELIZABETH: I see what I see, John.
PROCTOR (*with solemn warning*): You will not judge
me more, Elizabeth. I have good reason to
think before I charge fraud on Abigail, and I
will think on it. Let you look to your own   1225

improvement before you go to judge your husband any more. I have forgot Abigail, and—

ELIZABETH: And I.

PROCTOR: Spare me! You forget nothin' and forgive nothin'. Learn charity, woman. I have gone tiptoe in this house all seven month since she is gone. I have not moved from there to there without I think to please you, and still an everlasting funeral marches round your heart. I cannot speak but I am doubted, every moment judged for lies, as though I come into a court when I come into this house!

ELIZABETH: John, you are not open with me. You saw her with a crowd, you said. Now you—

PROCTOR: I'll plead my honesty no more, Elizabeth.

ELIZABETH—(now she would justify herself): John, I am only—

PROCTOR: No more! I should have roared you down when first you told me your suspicion. But I wilted, and, like a Christian, I confessed. Confessed! Some dream I had must have mistaken you for God that day. But you're not, you're not, and let you remember it! Let you look sometimes for the goodness in me, and judge me not.

ELIZABETH: I do not judge you. The magistrate sits in your heart that judges you. I never thought you but a good man, John—(with a smile)—only somewhat bewildered.

PROCTOR (laughing bitterly): Oh, Elizabeth, your justice would freeze beer! (He turns suddenly toward a sound outside. He starts for the door as MARY WARREN enters. As soon as he sees her, he goes directly to her and grabs her by her cloak, furious.) How do you go to Salem when I forbid it? Do you mock me? (Shaking her.) I'll whip you if you dare leave this house again!

[Strangely, she doesn't resist him, but hangs limply by his grip.]

MARY WARREN: I am sick, I am sick, Mr. Proctor. Pray, pray, hurt me not. (Her strangeness throws him off, and her evident pallor and weakness. He frees her.) My insides are all shuddery; I am in the proceedings all day, sir.

PROCTOR (with draining anger—his curiosity is draining it): And what of these proceedings here? When will you proceed to keep this house, as you are paid nine pound a year to do—and my wife not wholly well?

[As though to compensate, MARY WARREN goes to ELIZABETH with a small rag doll.]

MARY WARREN: I made a gift for you today, Goody Proctor. I had to sit long hours in a chair, and passed the time with sewing.

ELIZABETH (perplexed, looking at the doll): Why, thank you, it's a fair poppet.

MARY WARREN (with a trembling, decayed voice): We must all love each other now, Goody Proctor.

ELIZABETH (amazed at her strangeness): Aye, indeed we must.

MARY WARREN (glancing at the room): I'll get up early in the morning and clean the house. I must sleep now. (She turns and starts off.)

PROCTOR: Mary. (She halts.) Is it true? There be fourteen women arrested?

MARY WARREN: No, sir. There be thirty-nine now— (She suddenly breaks off and sobs and sits down, exhausted.)

ELIZABETH: Why, she's weepin'! What ails you, child?

MARY WARREN: Goody Osburn—will hang!

[There is a shocked pause, while she sobs.]

PROCTOR: Hang! (He calls into her face.) Hang, y'say?

MARY WARREN (through her weeping): Aye.

PROCTOR: The Deputy Governor will permit it?

MARY WARREN: He sentenced her. He must. (To ameliorate it:) But not Sarah Good. For Sarah Good confessed, y'see.

PROCTOR: Confessed! To what?

MARY WARREN: That she—(in horror at the memory)—she sometimes made a compact with Lucifer, and wrote her name in his black book—with her blood—and bound herself to torment Christians till God's thrown down—and we all must worship Hell forevermore.

[Pause.]

PROCTOR: But—surely you know what a jabberer she is. Did you tell them that?

MARY WARREN: Mr. Proctor, in open court she near to choked us all to death.

PROCTOR: How, choked you?

MARY WARREN: She sent her spirit out.

ELIZABETH: Oh, Mary, Mary, surely you—

MARY WARREN (with an indignant edge): She tried to kill me many times, Goody Proctor!

ELIZABETH: Why, I never heard you mention that before.

MARY WARREN: I never knew it before. I never knew anything before. When she come into the court I say to myself, I must not accuse this woman, for she sleep in ditches, and so very old and poor. But then—then she sit there, denying and denying, and I feel a misty coldness climbin' up my back, and the skin on my skull begin to creep, and I feel a clamp around my neck and I cannot breathe air; and then—(entranced)—I hear a voice, a screamin' voice, and it were my voice—and all at once I remembered everything she done to me!

PROCTOR: Why? What did she do to you?

MARY WARREN (*like one awakened to a marvelous secret insight*): So many time, Mr. Proctor, she come to this very door, beggin' bread and a cup of cider—and mark this: whenever I turned her away empty, she *mumbled*.

ELIZABETH: Mumbled! She may mumble if she's hungry.

MARY WARREN: But *what* does she mumble? You must remember, Goody Proctor. Last month— a Monday, I think—she walked away, and I thought my guts would burst for two days after. Do you remember it?

ELIZABETH: Why—I do, I think, but—

MARY WARREN: And so I told that to Judge Hathorne, and he asks her so. "Sarah Good," says he, "what curse do you mumble that this girl must fall sick after turning you away?" And then she replies—(*mimicking an old crone*)—"Why, your excellence, no curse at all. I only say my commandments; I hope I may say my commandments," says she!

ELIZABETH: And that's an upright answer.

MARY WARREN: Aye, but then Judge Hathorne say, "Recite for us your commandments!"—(*leaning avidly toward them*)—and of all the ten she could not say a single one. She never knew no commandments, and they had her in a flat lie!

PROCTOR: And so condemned her?

MARY WARREN (*now a little strained, seeing his stubborn doubt*): Why, they must when she condemned herself.

PROCTOR: But the proof, the proof!

MARY WARREN (*with greater impatience with him*): I told you the proof. It's hard proof, hard as rock, the judges said.

PROCTOR (*pauses an instant, then*): You will not go to court again, Mary Warren.

MARY WARREN: I must tell you, sir, I will be gone every day now. I am amazed you do not see what weighty work we do.

PROCTOR: What work you do! It's strange work for a Christian girl to hang old women!

MARY WARREN: But, Mr. Proctor, they will not hang them if they confess. Sarah Good will only sit in jail some time—(*recalling*)—and here's a wonder for you; think on this. Goody Good is pregnant!

ELIZABETH: Pregnant! Are they mad? The woman's near to sixty!

MARY WARREN: They had Doctor Griggs examine her, and she's full to the brim. And smokin' a pipe all these years, and no husband either! But she's safe, thank God, for they'll not hurt the innocent child. But be that not a marvel? You must see it, sir, it's God's work we do. So I'll be gone every day for some time. I'm—I am an official of the court, they say, and I—(*She has been edging toward offstage.*)

PROCTOR: I'll official you! (*He strides to the mantel, takes down the whip hanging there.*)

MARY WARREN (*terrified, but coming erect, striving for her authority*): I'll not stand whipping any more!

ELIZABETH (*hurriedly, as PROCTOR approaches*): Mary, promise now you'll stay at home—

MARY WARREN (*backing from him, but keeping her erect posture, striving, striving for her way*): The Devil's loose in Salem, Mr. Proctor; we must discover where he's hiding!

PROCTOR: I'll whip the Devil out of you! (*With whip raised he reaches out for her, and she streaks away and yells.*)

MARY WARREN (*pointing at ELIZABETH*): I saved her life today!

[*Silence. His whip comes down.*]

ELIZABETH (*softly*): I am accused?

MARY WARREN (*quaking*): Somewhat mentioned. But I said I never see no sign you ever sent your spirit out to hurt no one, and seeing I do live so closely with you, they dismissed it.

ELIZABETH: Who accused me?

MARY WARREN: I am bound by law, I cannot tell it. (*To PROCTOR:*) I only hope you'll not be so sarcastical no more. Four judges and the King's deputy sat to dinner with us but an hour ago. I—I would have you speak civilly to me, from this out.

PROCTOR (*in horror, muttering in disgust at her*): Go to bed.

MARY WARREN (*with a stamp of her foot*): I'll not be ordered to bed no more, Mr. Proctor! I am eighteen and a woman, however single!

PROCTOR: Do you wish to sit up? Then sit up.

MARY WARREN: I wish to go to bed!

PROCTOR (*in anger*): Good night, then!

MARY WARREN: Good night. (*Dissatisfied, uncertain of herself, she goes out. Wide-eyed, both, PROCTOR and ELIZABETH stand staring.*)

ELIZABETH (*quietly*): Oh, the noose, the noose is up!

PROCTOR: There'll be no noose.

ELIZABETH: She wants me dead. I knew all week it would come to this!

PROCTOR (*without conviction*): They dismissed it. You heard her say—

ELIZABETH: And what of tomorrow? She will cry me out until they take me!

PROCTOR: Sit you down.

ELIZABETH: She wants me dead, John, you know it!

PROCTOR: I say sit down! (*She sits, trembling. He speaks quietly, trying to keep his wits.*) Now we must be wise, Elizabeth.

ELIZABETH (*with sarcasm, and a sense of being lost*): Oh, indeed, indeed!

PROCTOR: Fear nothing. I'll find Ezekiel Cheever. I'll
1440   tell him she said it were all sport.

ELIZABETH: John, with so many in the jail, more than Cheever's help is needed now, I think. Would you favor me with this? Go to Abigail.

PROCTOR (*his soul hardening as he senses . . .*): What
1445   have I to say to Abigail?

ELIZABETH (*delicately*): John—grant me this. You have a faulty understanding of young girls. There is a promise made in any bed—

PROCTOR (*striving against his anger*): What promise!

1450 ELIZABETH: Spoke or silent, a promise is surely made. And she may dote on it now—I am sure she does—and thinks to kill me, then to take my place.

[PROCTOR's *anger is rising; he cannot speak.*]

ELIZABETH: It is her dearest hope, John, I know it.
1455   There be a thousand names; why does she call mine? There be a certain danger in calling such a name—I am no Goody Good that sleeps in ditches, nor Osburn, drunk and half-witted. She'd dare not call out such a farmer's wife
1460   but there be monstrous profit in it. She thinks to take my place, John.

PROCTOR: She cannot think it! (*He knows it is true.*)

ELIZABETH (*"reasonably"*): John, have you ever shown her somewhat of contempt? She cannot pass
1465   you in the church but you will blush—

PROCTOR: I may blush for my sin.

ELIZABETH: I think she sees another meaning in that blush.

PROCTOR: And what see you? What see you,
1470   Elizabeth?

ELIZABETH (*"conceding"*): I think you be somewhat ashamed, for I am there, and she so close.

PROCTOR: When will you know me, woman? Were I stone I would have cracked for shame this
1475   seven month!

ELIZABETH: Then go and tell her she's a whore. Whatever promise she may sense—break it, John, break it.

PROCTOR (*between his teeth*): Good, then. I'll go. (*He
1480   starts for his rifle.*)

ELIZABETH (*trembling, fearfully*): Oh, how unwillingly!

PROCTOR (*turning on her, rifle in hand*): I will curse her hotter than the oldest cinder in hell. But pray, begrudge me not my anger!

1485 ELIZABETH: Your anger! I only ask you—

PROCTOR: Woman, am I so base? Do you truly think me base?

ELIZABETH: I never called you base.

PROCTOR: Then how do you charge me with such a
1490   promise? The promise that a stallion gives a

mare I gave that girl!

ELIZABETH: Then why do you anger with me when I bid you break it?

PROCTOR: Because it speaks deceit, and I am honest! But I'll plead no more! I see now your spirit   1495
twists around the single error of my life, and I will never tear it free!

ELIZABETH (*crying out*): You'll tear it free—when you come to know that I will be your only wife, or no wife at all! She has an arrow in you yet,   1500
John Proctor, and you know it well!

[*Quite suddenly, as though from the air, a figure appears in the doorway. They start slightly. It is* MR. HALE. *He is different now—drawn a little, and there is a quality of deference, even of guilt, about his manner now.*]

HALE: Good evening.

PROCTOR (*still in his shock*): Why, Mr. Hale! Good evening to you, sir. Come in, come in.

HALE (*to Elizabeth*): I hope I do not startle you.   1505

ELIZABETH: No, no, it's only that I heard no horse—

HALE: You are Goodwife Proctor.

PROCTOR: Aye; Elizabeth.

HALE (*nods, then*): I hope you're not off to bed yet.

PROCTOR (*setting down his gun*): No, no. (HALE *comes*   1510
further into the room. And PROCTOR, *to explain his nervousness:*) We are not used to visitors after dark, but you're welcome here. Will you sit you down, sir?

HALE: I will. (*He sits.*) Let you sit, Goodwife Proctor.   1515

[*She does, never letting him out of her sight. There is a pause as* HALE *looks about the room.*]

PROCTOR (*to break the silence*): Will you drink cider, Mr. Hale?

HALE: No, it rebels my stomach; I have some further traveling yet tonight. Sit you down, sir. (PROCTOR *sits.*) I will not keep you long, but I   1520
have some business with you.

PROCTOR: Business of the court?

HALE: No—no, I come of my own, without the court's authority. Hear me. (*He wets his lips.*) I know not if you are aware, but your wife's   1525
name is—mentioned in the court.

PROCTOR: We know it, sir. Our Mary Warren told us. We are entirely amazed.

HALE: I am a stranger here, as you know. And in my ignorance I find it hard to draw a clear opinion   1530
of them that come accused before the court. And so this afternoon, and now tonight, I go from house to house—I come now from Rebecca Nurse's house and—

ELIZABETH (*shocked*): Rebecca's charged!   1535

HALE: God forbid such a one be charged. She is,

however—mentioned somewhat.

ELIZABETH (*with an attempt at a laugh*): You will never believe, I hope, that Rebecca trafficked with the Devil.

HALE: Woman, it is possible.

PROCTOR (*taken aback*): Surely you cannot think so.

HALE: This is a strange time, Mister. No man may longer doubt the powers of the dark are gathered in monstrous attack upon this village. There is too much evidence now to deny it. You will agree, sir?

PROCTOR (*evading*): I—have no knowledge in that line. But it's hard to think so pious a woman be secretly a Devil's bitch after seventy year of such good prayer.

HALE: Aye. But the Devil is a wily one, you cannot deny it. However, she is far from accused, and I know she will not be. (*Pause*). I thought, sir, to put some questions as to the Christian character of this house, if you'll permit me.

PROCTOR (*coldly, resentful*): Why, we—have no fear of questions, sir.

HALE: Good, then. (*He makes himself more comfortable.*) In the book of record that Mr. Parris keeps, I note that you are rarely in the church on Sabbath Day.

PROCTOR: No, sir, you are mistaken.

HALE: Twenty-six time in seventeen month, sir. I must call that rare. Will you tell me why you are so absent?

PROCTOR: Mr. Hale, I never knew I must account to that man for I come to church or stay at home. My wife were sick this winter.

HALE: So I am told. But you, Mister, why could you not come alone?

PROCTOR: I surely did come when I could, and when I could not I prayed in this house.

HALE: Mr. Proctor, your house is not a church; your theology must tell you that.

PROCTOR: It does, sir, it does; and it tells me that a minister may pray to God without he have golden candlesticks upon the altar.

HALE: What golden candlesticks?

PROCTOR: Since we built the church there were pewter candlesticks upon the altar; Francis Nurse made them, y'know, and a sweeter hand never touched the metal. But Parris came, and for twenty week he preach nothin' but golden candlesticks until he had them. I labor the earth from dawn of day to blink of night, and I tell you true, when I look to heaven and see my money glaring at his elbows—it hurt my prayer, sir, it hurt my prayer. I think, sometimes, the man dreams cathedrals, not clapboard meetin' houses.

HALE (*thinks, then*): And yet, Mister, a Christian on Sabbath Day must be in church. (*Pause.*) Tell me—you have three children?

PROCTOR: Aye. Boys.

HALE: How comes it that only two are baptized?

PROCTOR (*starts to speak, then stops, then, as though unable to restrain this*): I like it not that Mr. Parris should lay his hand upon my baby. I see no light of God in that man. I'll not conceal it.

HALE: I must say it, Mr. Proctor; that is not for you to decide. The man's ordained, therefore the light of God is in him.

PROCTOR (*flushed with resentment but trying to smile*): What's your suspicion, Mr. Hale?

HALE: No, no, I have no—

PROCTOR: I nailed the roof upon the church, I hung the door—

HALE: Oh, did you! That's a good sign, then.

PROCTOR: It may be I have been too quick to bring the man to book, but you cannot think we ever desired the destruction of religion. I think that's in your mind, is it not?

HALE (*not altogether giving way*): I—have—there is a softness in your record, sir, a softness.

ELIZABETH: I think, maybe, we have been too hard with Mr. Parris. I think so. But sure we never loved the Devil here.

HALE (*nods, deliberating this. Then, with the voice of one administering a secret test*): Do you know your Commandments, Elizabeth?

ELIZABETH (*without hesitation, even eagerly*): I surely do. There be no mark of blame upon my life, Mr. Hale. I am a covenanted Christian woman.

HALE: And you, Mister?

PROCTOR (*a trifle unsteadily*): I—am sure I do, sir.

HALE (*glances at her open face, then at* JOHN, *then*): Let you repeat them, if you will.

PROCTOR: The Commandments.

HALE: Aye.

PROCTOR (*looking off, beginning to sweat*): Thou shalt not kill.

HALE: Aye.

PROCTOR (*counting on his fingers*): Thou shalt not steal. Thou shalt not covet they neighbor's goods, nor make unto thee any graven image. Thou shalt not take the name of the Lord in vain; thou shalt not have no other gods before me. (*With some hesitation:*) Thou shalt remember the Sabbath Day and keep it holy. (*Pause. Then:*) Thou shalt honor thy father and mother. Thou shalt not bear false witness. (*He is stuck. He counts back on his fingers, knowing one is missing.*) Thou shalt not make unto thee any graven image.

HALE: You have said that twice, sir.

PROCTOR (*lost*): Aye. (*He is flailing for it.*)

ELIZABETH (*delicately*): Adultery, John.

PROCTOR (*as though a secret arrow had pained his heart*): Aye. (*Trying to grin it away—to* HALE): You see, sir, between the two of us we do know them all. (HALE *only looks at* PROCTOR, *deep in his attempt to define this man.* PROCTOR *grows more uneasy.*) I think it be a small fault.

1655   HALE: Theology, sir, is a fortress; no crack in a fortress may be accounted small. (*He rises; he seems worried now. He paces a little, in deep thought.*)

PROCTOR: There be no love for Satan in this house, 1660   Mister.

HALE: I pray it, I pray it dearly. (*He looks to both of them, an attempt at a smile on his face, but his misgivings are clear.*) Well, then—I'll bid you good night.

ELIZABETH (*unable to restrain herself*): Mr. Hale. (*He* 1665   *turns.*) I do think you are suspecting me somewhat? Are you not?

HALE (*obviously disturbed—and evasive*): Goody Proctor, I do not judge you. My duty is to add what I may to the godly wisdom of the court. I 1670   pray you both good health and good fortune. (*To* JOHN:) Good night, sir. (*He starts out.*)

ELIZABETH (*with a note of desperation*): I think you must tell him, John.

HALE: What's that?

1675   ELIZABETH (*restraining a call*): Will you tell him?

[Slight pause. HALE *looks questioningly at* JOHN*].*

PROCTOR (*with difficulty*): I—I have no witness and cannot prove it, except my word be taken. But I know the children's sickness had naught to do with witchcraft.

1680   HALE (*stopped, struck*): Naught to do—?

PROCTOR: Mr. Parris discovered them sportin' in the woods. They were startled and took sick.

[Pause.]

HALE: Who told you this?

PROCTOR (*hesitates, then*): Abigail Williams.

1685   HALE: Abigail!

PROCTOR: Aye.

HALE (*his eyes wide*): Abigail Williams told you it had naught to do with witchcraft!

PROCTOR: She told me the day you came, sir.

1690   HALE (*suspiciously*): Why—why did you keep this?

PROCTOR: I never knew until tonight that the world is gone daft with this nonsense.

HALE: Nonsense! Mister, I have myself examined Tituba, Sarah Good, and numerous others that 1695   have confessed to dealing with the Devil. They have *confessed* it.

PROCTOR: And why not, if they must hang for denyin' it? There are them that will swear to anything before they'll hang; have you never 1700   thought of that?

HALE: I have. I—I have indeed. (*It is his own suspi-*

cion, but he resists it. He glances at ELIZABETH, *then at* JOHN.*)* And you—would you testify to this in court?

PROCTOR: I—had not reckoned with goin' into court. 1705 But if I must I will.

HALE: Do you falter here?

PROCTOR: I falter nothing, but I may wonder if my story will be credited in such a court. I do wonder on it, when such a steady-minded 1710 minister as you will suspicion such a woman that never lied, and cannot, and the world knows she cannot! I may falter somewhat, Mister; I am no fool.

HALE (*quietly—it has impressed him*): Proctor, let you 1715 open with me now, for I have a rumor that troubles me. It's said you hold no belief that there may even be witches in the world. Is that true, sir?

PROCTOR—(*he knows this is critical, and is striving* 1720 *against his disgust with* HALE *and with himself for even answering*): I know not what I have said, I may have said it. I have wondered if there be witches in the world—although I cannot believe they come among us now. 1725

HALE: Then you do not believe—

PROCTOR: I have no knowledge of it; the Bible speaks of witches, and I will not deny them.

HALE: And you, woman?

ELIZABETH: I—I cannot believe it. 1730

HALE (*shocked*): You cannot!

PROCTOR: Elizabeth, you bewilder him!

ELIZABETH (*to* HALE): I cannot think the Devil may own a woman's soul, Mr. Hale, when she keeps an upright way, as I have. I am a good 1735 woman, I know it; and if you believe I may do only good work in the world, and yet be secretly bound to Satan, then I must tell you, sir, I do not believe it.

HALE: But, woman, you do believe there are witches 1740 in—

ELIZABETH: If you think that I am one, then I say there are none.

HALE: You surely do not fly against the Gospel, the Gospel— 1745

PROCTOR: She believe in the Gospel, every word!

ELIZABETH: Question Abigail Williams about the Gospel, not myself!

*[*HALE *stares at her.]*

PROCTOR: She do not mean to doubt the Gospel, sir, you cannot think it. This be a Christian house, 1750 sir, a Christian house.

HALE: God keep you both; let the third child be quickly baptized, and go you without fail each Sunday in to Sabbath prayer; and keep a solemn, quiet way among you. I think— 1755

[GILES COREY appears in doorway.]

GILES: John!
PROCTOR: Giles! What's the matter?
GILES: They take my wife.

[FRANCIS NURSE enters.]

GILES: And his Rebecca!
1760 PROCTOR (*to* FRANCIS): Rebecca's in the *jail*!
FRANCIS: Aye, Cheever come and take her in his
        wagon. We've only now come from the jail,
        and they'll not even let us in to see them.
ELIZABETH: They've surely gone wild now, Mr. Hale!
1765 FRANCIS (*going to* HALE): Reverend Hale! Can you not
        speak to the Deputy Governor? I'm sure he
        mistakes these people—
HALE: Pray calm yourself, Mr. Nurse.
FRANCIS: My wife is the very brick and mortar of the
1770   church, Mr. Hale—(*indicating* GILES)—and
        Martha Corey, there cannot be a woman closer
        yet to God than Martha.
HALE: How is Rebecca charged, Mr. Nurse?
FRANCIS (*with a mocking, half-hearted laugh*): For mur-
1775   der, she's charged! (*Mockingly quoting the war-
        rant:*) "For the marvelous and supernatural
        murder of Goody Putnam's babies." What am
        I to do, Mr. Hale?
HALE (*turns from* FRANCIS, *deeply troubled, then*):
1780   Believe me, Mr. Nurse, if Rebecca Nurse be
        tainted, then nothing's left to stop the whole
        green world from burning. Let you rest upon
        the justice of the court; the court will send her
        home, I know it.
1785 FRANCIS: You cannot mean she will be tried in court!
HALE (*pleading*): Nurse, though our hearts break, we
        cannot flinch; these are new times, sir. There is
        a misty plot afoot so subtle we should be crim-
        inal to cling to old respects and ancient friend-
1790   ships. I have seen too many frightful proofs in
        court—the Devil is alive in Salem, and we dare
        not quail to follow wherever the accusing fin-
        ger points!
PROCTOR (*angered*): How may such a woman murder
1795   children?
HALE (*in great pain*): Man, remember, until an hour
        before the Devil fell, God thought him beauti-
        ful in Heaven.
GILES: I never said my wife were a witch, Mr. Hale; I
1800   only said she were reading books!
HALE: Mr. Corey, exactly what complaint were made
        on your wife?
GILES: That bloody mongrel Walcott charge her. Y'see,
        he buy a pig of my wife four or five year ago,
1805   and the pig died soon after. So he come dancin'
        in for his money back. So my Martha, she says
        to him, "Walcott, if you haven't the wit to feed

a pig properly, you'll not live to own many,"
she says. Now he goes to court and claims that
from that day to this he cannot keep a pig alive   1810
for more than four weeks because my Martha
bewitch them with her books!

[Enter EZEKIEL CHEEVER. A shocked silence.]

CHEEVER: Good evening to you, Proctor.
PROCTOR: Why, Mr. Cheever. Good evening.
CHEEVER: Good evening, all. Good evening, Mr. Hale.   1815
PROCTOR: I hope you come not on business of the court.
CHEEVER: I do, Proctor, aye. I am clerk of the court
        now, y'know.

*[Enter MARSHAL HERRICK, a man in his early thirties,
who is somewhat shamefaced at the moment.]*

GILES: It's a pity, Ezekiel, that an honest tailor might
        have gone to Heaven must burn in Hell. You'll   1820
        burn for this, do you know it?
CHEEVER: You know yourself I must do as I'm told.
        You surely know that, Giles. And I'd as lief
        you'd not be sending me to Hell. I like not the
        sound of it, I tell you; I like not the sound of it.   1825
        (*He fears* PROCTOR, *but starts to reach inside his
        coat.*) Now believe me, Proctor, how heavy be
        the law, all its tonnage I do carry on my back
        tonight. (*He takes out a warrant.*) I have a war-
        rant for your wife.   1830
PROCTOR (*to* HALE): You said she were not charged!
HALE: I know nothin' of it. (*To* CHEEVER:) When were
        she charged?
CHEEVER: I am given sixteen warrant tonight, sir, and
        she is one.   1835
PROCTOR: Who charged her?
CHEEVER: Why, Abigail Williams charge her.
PROCTOR: On what proof, what proof?
CHEEVER (*looking about the room*): Mr. Proctor, I have
        little time. The court bid me search your   1840
        house, but I like not to search a house. So will
        you hand me any poppets that your wife may
        keep here?
PROCTOR: Poppets?
ELIZABETH: I never kept no poppets, not since I were   1845
        a girl.
CHEEVER (*embarrassed, glancing toward the mantel where
        sits* MARY WARREN's *poppet*): I spy a poppet,
        Goody Proctor.
ELIZABETH: Oh! (*Going for it:*) Why, this is Mary's.   1850
CHEEVER (*shyly*): Would you please to give it to me?
ELIZABETH (*handing it to him, asks* HALE): Has the
        court discovered a text in poppets now?
CHEEVER (*carefully holding the poppet*): Do you keep
        any others in this house?   1855
PROCTOR: No, nor this one either till tonight. What
        signifies a poppet?

CHEEVER: Why, a poppet—(*he gingerly turns the poppet over*)—a poppet may signify—Now, woman, will you please to come with me?

1860

PROCTOR: She will not! (*To* ELIZABETH:) Fetch Mary here.

CHEEVER (*ineptly reaching toward* ELIZABETH:) No, no, I am forbid to leave her from my sight.

PROCTOR (*pushing his arm away*): You'll leave her out of sight and out of mind, Mister. Fetch Mary, Elizabeth. (ELIZABETH *goes upstairs.*)

1865

HALE: What signifies a poppet, Mr. Cheever?

CHEEVER (*turning the poppet over in his hands*): Why, they say it may signify that she—(*He has lifted the poppet's skirt, and his eyes widen in astonished fear.*) Why, this, this—

1870

PROCTOR (*reaching for the poppet*): What's there?

CHEEVER: Why—(*He draws out a long needle from the poppet*)—it is a needle! Herrick, Herrick, it is a needle!

1875

[HERRICK *comes toward him.*]

PROCTOR (*angrily, bewildered*): And what signifies a needle!

CHEEVER (*his hands shaking*): Why, this go hard with her, Proctor, this—I had my doubts, Proctor, I had my doubts, but here's calamity. (*To* HALE, *showing the needle:*) You see it, sir, it is a needle!

1880

HALE: Why? What meanin' has it?

CHEEVER (*wide-eyed, trembling*): The girl, the Williams girl, Abigail Williams, sir. She sat to dinner in Reverend Parris's house tonight, and without word nor warnin' she falls to the floor. Like a struck beast, he says, and screamed a scream that a bull would weep to hear. And he goes to save her, and, stuck two inches in the flesh of her belly, he draw a needle out. And demandin' of her how she come to be so stabbed, she—(*to* PROCTOR *now*)—testify it were your wife's familiar spirit pushed it in.

1885

1890

PROCTOR: Why, she done it herself! (*To* HALE:) I hope you're not takin' this for proof, Mister!

1895

[HALE, *struck by the proof, is silent.*]

CHEEVER: 'Tis hard proof! (*To* HALE:) I find here a poppet Goody Proctor keeps. I have found it, sir. And in the belly of the poppet a needle's stuck. I tell you true, Proctor, I never warranted to see such proof of Hell, and I bid you obstruct me not, for I—

1900

[*Enter* ELIZABETH *with* MARY WARREN. PROCTOR, *seeing* MARY WARREN, *draws her by the arm to* HALE.]

PROCTOR: Here now! Mary, how did this poppet come into my house?

MARY WARREN (*frightened for herself, her voice very small*): What poppet's that, sir?

1905

PROCTOR (*impatiently, pointing at the doll in* CHEEVER's *hand*): This poppet, this poppet.

MARY WARREN (*evasively, looking at it*): Why, I—I think it is mine.

PROCTOR: It is your poppet, is it not?

1910

MARY WARREN (*not understanding the direction of this*): It—is, sir.

PROCTOR: And how did it come into this house?

MARY WARREN (*glancing about at the avid faces*): Why—I made it in the court, sir, and—give it to Goody Proctor tonight.

1915

PROCTOR (*to* HALE): Now, sir—do you have it?

HALE: Mary Warren, a needle have been found inside this poppet.

MARY WARREN (*bewildered*): Why, I meant no harm by it, sir.

1920

PROCTOR (*quickly*): You stuck that needle in yourself?

MARY WARREN: I—I believe I did, sir, I—

PROCTOR (*to* HALE): What say you now?

HALE (*watching* MARY WARREN *closely*): Child, you are certain this be your natural memory? May it be, perhaps, that someone conjures you even now to say this?

1925

MARY WARREN: Conjures me? Why, no, sir, I am entirely myself, I think. Let you ask Susanna Walcott—she saw me sewin' it in court. (*Or better still:*) Ask Abby, Abby sat beside me when I made it.

1930

PROCTOR (*to* HALE, *of* CHEEVER): Bid him begone. Your mind is surely settled now. Bid him out, Mr. Hale.

1935

ELIZABETH: What signifies a needle?

HALE: Mary—you charge a cold and cruel murder on Abigail.

MARY WARREN: Murder! I charge no—

1940

HALE: Abigail were stabbed tonight; a needle were found stuck into her belly—

ELIZABETH: And she charges me?

HALE: Aye.

ELIZABETH (*her breath knocked out*): Why—! The girl is murder! She must be ripped out of the world!

1945

CHEEVER (*pointing at* ELIZABETH): You've heard that, sir! Ripped out of the world! Herrick, you heard it!

PROCTOR (*suddenly snatching the warrant out of* CHEEVER's *hands*): Out with you.

1950

CHEEVER: Proctor, you dare not touch the warrant.

PROCTOR (*ripping the warrant:*) Out with you!

CHEEVER: You've ripped the Deputy Governor's warrant, man!

1955

PROCTOR: Damn the Deputy Governor! Out of my house!

HALE: Now, Proctor, Proctor!

PROCTOR: Get y'gone with them! You are a broken minister.

1960

HALE: Proctor, if she is innocent, the court—

PROCTOR: If *she* is innocent! Why do you never wonder if Parris be innocent, or Abigail? Is the accuser always holy now? Were they born this morning as clean as God's fingers? I'll tell you what's walking Salem—vengeance is walking Salem. We are what we always were in Salem, but now the little crazy children are jangling the keys of the kingdom, and common vengeance writes the law! This warrant's vengeance! I'll not give my wife to vengeance!

ELIZABETH: I'll go, John—

PROCTOR: You will not go!

HERRICK: I have nine men outside. You cannot keep her. The law binds me, John, I cannot budge.

PROCTOR (*to* HALE, *ready to break him*): Will you see her taken?

HALE: Proctor, the court is just—

PROCTOR: Pontius Pilate! God will not let you wash your hands of this!

ELIZABETH: John—I think I must go with them. (*He cannot bear to look at her.*) Mary, there is bread enough for the morning; you will bake, in the afternoon. Help Mr. Proctor as you were his daughter—you owe me that, and much more. (*She is fighting her weeping. To* PROCTOR:) When the children wake, speak nothing of witchcraft—it will frighten them. (*She cannot go on.*)

PROCTOR: I will bring you home. I will bring you soon.

ELIZABETH: Oh, John, bring me soon!

PROCTOR: I will fall like an ocean on that court! Fear nothing, Elizabeth.

ELIZABETH (*with great fear*): I will fear nothing. (*She looks about the room, as though to fix it in her mind.*) Tell the children I have gone to visit someone sick.

[*She walks out the door,* HERRICK *and* CHEEVER *behind her. For a moment,* PROCTOR *watches from the doorway. The clank of chain is heard.*]

PROCTOR: Herrick! Herrick, don't chain her! (*He rushes out the door. From outside:*) Damn you, man, you will not chain her! Off with them! I'll not have it! I will not have her chained!

[*There are other men's voices against his.* HALE, *in a fever of guilt and uncertainty, turns from the door to avoid the sight;* MARY WARREN *bursts into tears and sits weeping.* GILES COREY *calls to* HALE.]

GILES: And yet silent, minister? It is fraud, you know it is fraud! What keeps you, man?

[PROCTOR *is half braced, half pushed into the room by two deputies and* HERRICK.]

PROCTOR: I'll pay you, Herrick, I will surely pay you!

HERRICK (*panting*): In God's name, John, I cannot help myself. I must chain them all. Now let you keep inside this house till I am gone! (*He goes out with his deputies.*)

[PROCTOR *stands there, gulping air. Horses and a wagon creaking are heard.*]

HALE (*in great uncertainty*): Mr. Proctor—

PROCTOR: Out of my sight!

HALE: Charity, Proctor, charity. What I have heard in her favor, I will not fear to testify in court. God help me, I cannot judge her guilty or innocent—I know not. Only this consider: the world goes mad, and it profit nothing you should lay the cause to the vengeance of a little girl.

PROCTOR: You are a coward! Though you be ordained in God's own tears, you are a coward now!

HALE: Proctor, I cannot think God be provoked so grandly by such a petty cause. The jails are packed—our greatest judges sit in Salem now—and hangin's promised. Man, we must look to cause proportionate. Were there murder done, perhaps, and never brought to light? Abomination? Some secret blasphemy that stinks to Heaven? Think on cause, man, and let you help me to discover it. For there's your way, believe it, there is your only way, when such confusion strikes upon the world. (*He goes to* GILES *and* FRANCIS.) Let you counsel among yourselves; think on your village and what may have drawn from heaven such thundering wrath upon you all. I shall pray God open up our eyes.

[HALE *goes out.*]

FRANCIS (*struck by* HALE's *mood*): I never heard no murder done in Salem.

PROCTOR (*he has been reached by* HALE's *words*): Leave me, Francis, leave me.

GILES (*shaken*): John—tell me, are we lost?

PROCTOR: Go home now, Giles. We'll speak on it tomorrow.

GILES: Let you think on it. We'll come early, eh?

PROCTOR: Aye. Go now, Giles.

GILES: Good night, then.

[GILES COREY *goes out. After a moment:*]

MARY WARREN (*in a fearful squeak of a voice*): Mr. Proctor, very likely they'll let her come home once they're given proper evidence.

PROCTOR: You're coming to the court with me, Mary. You will tell it in the court.

MARY WARREN: I cannot charge murder on Abigail.

PROCTOR (*moving menacingly toward her*): You will tell

the court how that poppet come here and who
stuck the needle in.
MARY WARREN: She'll kill me for sayin' that!
(PROCTOR *continues toward her.*) Abby'll charge
2055   lechery on you, Mr. Proctor!
PROCTOR (*halting*): She's told you!
MARY WARREN: I have known it, sir. She'll ruin you
with it, I know she will.
PROCTOR (*hesitating, and with deep hatred of himself*):
2060   Good. Then her saintliness is done with. (MARY
backs from him.) We will slide together into our
pit; you will tell the court what you know.
MARY WARREN (*in terror*): I cannot, they'll turn on me—

[PROCTOR *strides and catches her, and she is repeating, "I cannot, I cannot!"*]

PROCTOR: My wife will never die for me! I will bring
2065   your guts into your mouth but that goodness
will not die for me!
MARY WARREN (*struggling to escape him:*) I cannot do
it, I cannot!
PROCTOR (*grasping her by the throat as though he would
2070   strangle her*): Make your peace with it! Now
Hell and Heaven grapple on our backs, and all
our old pretense is ripped away—make your
peace! (*He throws her to the floor, where she sobs,
"I cannot, I cannot . . ." And now, half to himself,
2075   staring, and turning to the open door:*) Peace. It is
a providence, and no great change; we are
only what we always were, but naked now.
(*He walks as though toward a great horror, facing
the open sky.*) Aye, naked! And the wind, God's
2080   icy wind, will blow!

[*And she is over and over again sobbing, "I cannot, I
cannot, I cannot," as the curtain falls*]

ACT III

*The vestry room of the Salem Meeting House, now
serving as the anteroom of the General Court.*

    *As the curtain rises, the room is empty, but for sun-
light pouring through two high windows in the back
wall. The room is solemn, even forbidding. Heavy
beams jut out, boards of random widths make up the
walls. At the right are two doors leading into the
meeting house proper, where the court is being held.
At the left another door leads outside.*

    *There is a plain bench at the left, and another at
the right. In the center a rather long meeting table,
with stools and a considerable armchair snugged up
to it.*

    *Through the partitioning wall at the right we hear
a prosecutor's voice, JUDGE HATHORNE's, asking a question; then a woman's voice, MARTHA COREY's, replying.*

HATHORNE'S VOICE: Now, Martha Corey, there is
abundant evidence in our hands to show that
you have given yourself to the reading of for-
tunes. Do you deny it?
MARTHA COREY'S VOICE: I am innocent to a witch. I   2085
know not what a witch is.
HATHORNE'S VOICE: How do you know, then, that
you are not a witch?
MARTHA COREY'S VOICE: If I were, I would know it.
HATHORNE'S VOICE: Why do you hurt these children?   2090
MARTHA COREY'S VOICE: I do not hurt them. I scorn it!
GILES'S VOICE (*roaring*): I have evidence for the court!

[*Voices of townspeople rise in excitement.*]

DANFORTH'S VOICE: You will keep your seat!
GILES' VOICE: Thomas Putnam is reaching out for
land!   2095
DANFORTH'S VOICE: Remove that man, Marshal!
GILES' VOICE: You're hearing lies, lies!

[*A roaring goes up from the people.*]

HATHORNE'S VOICE: Arrest him, excellency!
GILES' VOICE: I have evidence. Why will you not hear
my evidence?   2100

[*The door opens and* GILES *is half carried into the
vestry room by* HERRICK.]

GILES: Hands off, damn you, let me go!
HERRICK: Giles, Giles!
GILES: Out of my way, Herrick! I bring evidence—
HERRICK: You cannot go in there, Giles; it's a court!

[*Enter* HALE *from the court.*]

HALE: Pray be calm a moment.   2105
GILES: You, Mr. Hale, go in there and demand I speak.
HALE: A moment, sir, a moment.
GILES: They'll be hangin' my wife!

[*JUDGE HATHORNE enters. He is in his sixties, a bitter,
remorseless Salem judge.*]

HATHORNE: How do you dare come roarin' into this
court! Are you gone daft, Corey?   2110
GILES: You're not a Boston judge yet, Hathorne.
You'll not call me daft!

[*Enter Deputy Governor* DANFORTH *and, behind him,*
EZEKIEL CHEEVER *and* PARRIS. *On his appearance,
silence falls.* DANFORTH *is a grave man in his sixties, of
some humor and sophistication that does not, however, interfere with an exact loyalty to his position and
his cause. He comes down to* GILES, *who awaits his
wrath.*]

DANFORTH (*looking directly at Giles*): Who is this man?

PARRIS: Giles Corey, sir, and a more contentious—

2115 GILES (*to* PARRIS): I am asked the question, and I am old enough to answer it! (*To* DANFORTH, *who impresses him and to whom he smiles through his strain:*) My name is Corey, sir, Giles Corey. I have six hundred acres, and timber in addi-

2120 tion. It is my wife you be condemning now. (*He indicates the courtroom.*)

DANFORTH: And how do you imagine to help her cause with such contemptuous riot? Now be gone. Your old age alone keeps you out of jail

2125 for this.

GILES (*beginning to plead*): They be tellin' lies about my wife, sir, I—

DANFORTH: Do you take it upon yourself to determine what this court shall believe and what it

2130 shall set aside?

GILES: Your Excellency, we mean no disrespect for—

DANFORTH: Disrespect indeed! It is disruption, Mister. This is the highest court of the supreme government of this province, do you know it?

2135 GILES (*beginning to weep*): Your Excellency, I only said she were readin' books, sir, and they come and take her out of my house for—

DANFORTH (*mystified*): Books! What books?

GILES (*through helpless sobs*): It is my third wife, sir; I

2140 never had no wife that be so taken with books, and I thought to find the cause of it, d'y'see, but it were no witch I blamed her for. (*He is openly weeping.*) I have broke charity with the woman, I have broke charity with her. (*He covers his face,

2145 ashamed. Danforth is respectfully silent.*)

HALE: Excellency, he claims hard evidence for his wife's defense. I think that in all justice you must—

DANFORTH: Then let him submit his evidence in

2150 proper affidavit. You are certainly aware of our procedure here, Mr. Hale. (*To* HERRICK:) Clear this room.

HERRICK: Come now, Giles. (*He gently pushes* COREY *out.*)

2155 FRANCIS: We are desperate, sir; we come here three days now and cannot be heard.

DANFORTH: Who is this man?

FRANCIS: Francis Nurse, Your Excellency.

HALE: His wife's Rebecca that were condemned this

2160 morning.

DANFORTH: Indeed! I am amazed to find you in such uproar. I have only good report of your character, Mr. Nurse.

HATHORNE: I think they must both be arrested in con-

2165 tempt, sir.

DANFORTH (*to* FRANCIS): Let you write your plea, and in due time I will—

FRANCIS: Excellency, we have proof for your eyes; God forbid you shut them to it. The girls, sir,

the girls are frauds.   2170

DANFORTH: What's that?

FRANCIS: We have proof of it, sir. They are all deceiving you.

[DANFORTH *is shocked, but studying* FRANCIS.]

HATHORNE: This is contempt, sir, contempt!

DANFORTH: Peace, Judge Hathorne. Do you know   2175
who I am, Mr. Nurse?

FRANCIS: I surely do, sir, and I think you must be a wise judge to be what you are.

DANFORTH: And do you know that near to four hundred are in the jails from Marblehead to Lynn,   2180
and upon my signature?

FRANCIS: I—

DANFORTH: And seventy-two condemned to hang by that signature?

FRANCIS: Excellency, I never thought to say it to such   2185
a weighty judge, but you are deceived.

[*Enter* GILES COREY *from left. All turn to see as he beckons in* MARY WARREN *with* PROCTOR. MARY *is keeping her eyes to the ground;* PROCTOR *has her elbow as though she were near collapse.*]

PARRIS (*on seeing her, in shock*): Mary Warren! (*He goes directly to bend close to her face.*) What are you about here?

PROCTOR (*pressing* PARRIS *away from her with a gentle   2190
but firm motion of protectiveness*): She would speak with the Deputy Governor.

DANFORTH (*shocked by this, turns to* HERRICK): Did you not tell me Mary Warren were sick in bed?

HERRICK: She were, Your Honor. When I go to fetch   2195
her to the court last week, she said she were sick.

GILES: She has been strivin' with her soul all week, Your Honor; she comes now to tell the truth of this to you.   2200

DANFORTH: Who is this?

PROCTOR: John Proctor, sir. Elizabeth Proctor is my wife.

PARRIS: Beware this man, Your Excellency, this man is mischief.   2205

HALE (*excitedly*): I think you must hear the girl, sir, she—

DANFORTH (*who has become very interested in* MARY WARREN *and only raises a hand toward* HALE): Peace. What would you tell us, Mary Warren?   2210

[PROCTOR *looks at her, but she cannot speak.*]

PROCTOR: She never saw no spirits, sir.

DANFORTH (*with great alarm and surprise, to* MARY): Never saw no spirits!

GILES (*eagerly:*) Never.

2215 PROCTOR (*reaching into his jacket*): She has signed a
          deposition, sir—
      DANFORTH (*instantly*): No, no, I accept no deposi-
          tions. (*He is rapidly calculating this; he turns from
          her to* PROCTOR.) Tell me, Mr. Proctor, have you
2220   given out this story in the village?
      PROCTOR: We have not.
      PARRIS: They've come to overthrow the court, sir!
          This man is—
      DANFORTH: I pray you, Mr. Parris. Do you know, Mr.
2225   Proctor, that the entire contention of the state
          in these trials is that the voice of Heaven is
          speaking through the children?
      PROCTOR: I know that, sir.
      DANFORTH (*thinks, staring at* PROCTOR, *then turns to*
2230   MARY WARREN): And you, Mary Warren, how
          came you to cry out people for sending their
          spirits against you?
      MARY WARREN: It were pretense, sir.
      DANFORTH: I cannot hear you.
2235 PROCTOR: It were pretense, she says.
      DANFORTH: Ah? And the other girls? Susanna Walcott,
          and—the others? They are also pretending?
      MARY WARREN: Aye, sir.
      DANFORTH (*wide-eyed*): Indeed. (*Pause. He is baffled by
2240   this. He turns to study* PROCTOR's *face.*)
      PARRIS (*in a sweat*): Excellency, you surely cannot
          think to let so vile a lie be spread in open court!
      DANFORTH: Indeed not, but it strike hard upon me
          that she will dare come here with such a tale.
2245   Now, Mr. Proctor, before I decide whether I
          shall hear you or not, it is my duty to tell you
          this. We burn a hot fire here; it melts down all
          concealment.
      PROCTOR: I know that, sir.
2250 DANFORTH: Let me continue. I understand well, a
          husband's tenderness may drive him to
          extravagance in defense of a wife. Are you cer-
          tain in your conscience, Mister, that your evi-
          dence is the truth?
2255 PROCTOR: It is. And you will surely know it.
      DANFORTH: And you thought to declare this revela-
          tion in the open court before the public?
      PROCTOR: I thought I would, aye—with your permis-
          sion.
2260 DANFORTH (*his eyes narrowing*): Now, sir, what is your
          purpose in so doing?
      PROCTOR: Why, I—I would free my wife, sir.
      DANFORTH: There lurks nowhere in your heart, nor
          hidden in your spirit, any desire to undermine
2265   this court?
      PROCTOR (*with the faintest faltering*): Why, no, sir.
      CHEEVER (*clears his throat, awakening*): I—Your
          Excellency.
      DANFORTH: Mr. Cheever.
2270 CHEEVER: I think it be my duty, sir—(*Kindly, to*
          PROCTOR:) You'll not deny it, John. (*To*

          DANFORTH:) When we come to take his wife, he
          damned the court and ripped your warrant.
      PARRIS: Now you have it!
      DANFORTH: He did that, Mr. Hale?   2275
      HALE (*takes a breath:*) Aye, he did.
      PROCTOR: It were a temper, sir. I knew not what I did.
      DANFORTH (*studying him*): Mr. Proctor.
      PROCTOR: Aye, sir.
      DANFORTH (*straight into his eyes*): Have you ever seen 2280
          the Devil?
      PROCTOR: No, sir.
      DANFORTH: You are in all respects a Gospel
          Christian?
      PROCTOR: I am, sir.   2285
      PARRIS: Such a Christian that will not come to church
          but once in a month!
      DANFORTH (*restrained—he is curious*): Not come to
          church?
      PROCTOR: I—I have no love for Mr. Parris. It is no   2290
          secret. But God I surely love.
      CHEEVER: He plow on Sunday, sir.
      DANFORTH: Plow on Sunday!
      CHEEVER (*apologetically*): I think it be evidence, John. I
          am an official of the court, I cannot keep it.   2295
      PROCTOR: I—I have once or twice plowed on Sunday.
          I have three children, sir, and until last year
          my land give little.
      GILES: You'll find other Christians that do plow on
          Sunday if the truth be known.   2300
      HALE: Your Honor, I cannot think you may judge the
          man on such evidence.
      DANFORTH: I judge nothing. (*Pause. He keeps watching*
          PROCTOR, *who tries to meet his gaze.*) I tell you
          straight, Mister—I have seen marvels in this   2305
          court. I have seen people choked before my
          eyes by spirits; I have seen them stuck by pins
          and slashed by daggers. I have until this
          moment not the slightest reason to suspect that
          the children may be deceiving me. Do you   2310
          understand my meaning?
      PROCTOR: Excellency, does it not strike upon you that
          so many of these women have lived so long
          with such upright reputation, and—
      PARRIS: Do you read the Gospel, Mr. Proctor?   2315
      PROCTOR: I read the Gospel.
      PARRIS: I think not, or you should surely know that
          Cain were an upright man, and yet he did kill
          Abel.
      PROCTOR: Aye, God tells us that. (*To* DANFORTH:) But 2320
          who tells us Rebecca Nurse murdered seven
          babies by sending out her spirit on them? It is
          the children only, and this one will swear she
          lied to you.

      [DANFORTH *considers, then beckons* HATHORNE *to him.*
      HATHORNE *leans in, and he speaks in his ear.*
      HATHORNE *nods.*]

2325 HATHORNE: Aye, she's the one.

DANFORTH: Mr. Proctor, this morning, your wife send me a claim in which she states that she is pregnant now.

PROCTOR: My wife pregnant!

2330 DANFORTH: There be no sign of it—we have examined her body.

PROCTOR: But if she say she is pregnant, then she must be! That woman will never lie, Mr. Danforth.

DANFORTH: She will not?

2335 PROCTOR: Never, sir, never.

DANFORTH: We have thought it too convenient to be credited. However, if I should tell you now that I will let her be kept another month; and if she begin to show her natural signs, you shall 2340 have her living yet another year until she is delivered—what say you to that? (JOHN PROCTOR *is struck silent.*) Come now. You say your only purpose is to save your wife. Good, then, she is saved at least this year, and a year 2345 is long. What say you, sir? It is done now. (*In conflict,* PROCTOR *glances at* FRANCIS *and* GILES.) Will you drop this charge?

PROCTOR: I—I think I cannot.

DANFORTH (*now an almost imperceptible hardness in his* 2350 *voice*): Then your purpose is somewhat larger.

PARRIS: He's come to overthrow this court, Your Honor!

PROCTOR: These are my friends. Their wives are also accused—

2355 DANFORTH (*with a sudden briskness of manner*): I judge you not, sir. I am ready to hear your evidence.

PROCTOR: I come not to hurt the court; I only—

DANFORTH (*cutting him off*): Marshal, go into the court and bid Judge Stoughton and Judge Sewall 2360 declare recess for one hour. And let them go to the tavern, if they will. All witnesses and prisoners are to be kept in the building.

HERRICK: Aye, sir. (*Very deferentially:*) If I may say it, sir, I know this man all my life. It is a good 2365 man, sir.

DANFORTH (*it is the reflection on himself he resents*): I am sure of it, Marshal. (HERRICK *nods, then goes out.*) Now, what deposition do you have for us, Mr. Proctor? And I beg you be clear, open as 2370 the sky, and honest.

PROCTOR (*as he takes out several papers*): I am no lawyer, so I'll—

DANFORTH: The pure in heart need no lawyers. Proceed as you will.

2375 PROCTOR (*handing* DANFORTH *a paper*): Will you read this first, sir? It's a sort of testament. The people signing it declare their good opinion of Rebecca, and my wife, and Martha Corey. (DANFORTH *looks down at the paper.*)

2380 PARRIS (*to enlist* DANFORTH's *sarcasm*): Their good opinion! (*But* DANFORTH *goes on reading, and*

PROCTOR *is heartened.*)

PROCTOR: These are all landholding farmers, members of the church. (*Delicately, trying to point out a paragraph:*) If you'll notice, sir—they've 2385 known the women many years and never saw no sign they had dealings with the Devil.

[PARRIS *nervously moves over and reads over* DANFORTH's *shoulder.*]

DANFORTH (*glancing down a long list*): How many names are here?

FRANCIS: Ninety-one, Your Excellency. 2390

PARRIS (*sweating*): These people should be summoned. (DANFORTH *looks up at him questioningly.*) For questioning.

FRANCIS (*trembling with anger*): Mr. Danforth, I gave them all my word no harm would come to 2395 them for signing this.

PARRIS: This is a clear attack upon the court!

HALE (*to* PARRIS, *trying to contain himself*): Is every defense an attack upon the court? Can no one—?

PARRIS: All innocent and Christian people are happy 2400 for the courts in Salem! These people are gloomy for it. (*To* DANFORTH *directly:*) And I think you will want to know, from each and every one of them, what discontents them with you! 2405

HATHORNE: I think they ought to be examined, sir.

DANFORTH: It is not necessarily an attack, I think. Yet—

FRANCIS: These are all covenanted Christians, sir.

DANFORTH: Then I am sure they may have nothing to fear. (*Hands* CHEEVER *the paper.*) Mr. Cheever, 2410 have warrants drawn for all of these—arrest for examination. (*To* PROCTOR:) Now, Mister, what other information do you have for us? (FRANCIS *is still standing, horrified.*) You may sit, Mr. Nurse. 2415

FRANCIS: I have brought trouble on these people; I have—

DANFORTH: No, old man, you have not hurt these people if they are of good conscience. But you must understand, sir, that a person is either 2420 with this court or he must be counted against it, there be no road between. This is a sharp time, now, a precise time—we live no longer in the dusky afternoon when evil mixed itself with good and befuddled the world. Now, by 2425 God's grace, the shining sun is up, and them that fear not light will surely praise it. I hope you will be one of those. (MARY WARREN *suddenly sobs.*) She's not hearty, I see.

PROCTOR: No, she's not, sir. (*To* MARY, *bending to her,* 2430 *holding her hand, quietly:*) Now remember what the angel Raphael said to the boy Tobias. Remember it.

MARY WARREN (*hardly audible*): Aye.

2435 PROCTOR: "Do that which is good, and no harm shall
          come to thee."
      MARY WARREN: Aye.
      DANFORTH: Come, man, we wait you.

      [MARSHAL HERRICK *returns, and takes his post at the
      door.*]

      GILES: John, my deposition, give him mine.
2440 PROCTOR: Aye. (*He hands* DANFORTH *another paper.*)
          This is Mr. Corey's deposition.
      DANFORTH: Oh? (*He looks down at it. Now* HATHORNE
          comes behind him and reads with him.)
      HATHORNE (*suspiciously*): What lawyer drew this,
2445   Corey?
      GILES: You know I never hired a lawyer in my life,
          Hathorne.
      DANFORTH (*finishing the reading*): It is very well
          phrased. My compliments. Mr. Parris, if Mr.
2450   Putnam is in the court, will you bring him in?
          (HATHORNE *takes the deposition, and walks to the
          window with it.* PARRIS *goes into the court.*) You
          have no legal training, Mr. Corey?
      GILES (*very pleased*): I have the best, sir—I am thirty-
2455   three time in court in my life. And always
          plaintiff, too.
      DANFORTH: Oh, then you're much put-upon.
      GILES: I am never put-upon; I know my rights, sir,
          and I will have them. You know, your father
2460   tried a case of mine—might be thirty-five year
          ago, I think.
      DANFORTH: Indeed.
      GILES: He never spoke to you of it?
      DANFORTH: No, I cannot recall it.
2465 GILES: That's strange, he give me nine pound dam-
          ages. He were a fair judge, your father. Y'see, I
          had a white mare that time, and this fellow
          come to borrow the mare—(*Enter* PARRIS *with
          THOMAS PUTNAM. When he sees* PUTNAM, GILES'
2470   ease goes; he is hard.*) Aye, there he is.
      DANFORTH: Mr. Putnam, I have here an accusation by
          Mr. Corey against you. He states that you cold-
          ly prompted your daughter to cry witchery
          upon George Jacobs that is now in jail.
2475 PUTNAM: It is a lie.
      DANFORTH (*turning to* GILES): Mr. Putnam states your
          charge is a lie. What say you to that?
      GILES (*furious, his fists clenched*): A fart on Thomas
          Putnam, that is what I say to that!
2480 DANFORTH: What proof do you submit for your
          charge, sir?
      GILES: My proof is there! (*Pointing to the paper.*) If
          Jacobs hangs for a witch he forfeit up his prop-
          erty—that's law! And there is none but
2485   Putnam with the coin to buy so great a piece.
          This man is killing his neighbors for their land!
      DANFORTH: But proof, sir, proof.

      GILES (*pointing at his deposition*): The proof is there! I
          have it from an honest man who heard Putnam
          say it! The day his daughter cried out on Jacobs, 2490
          he said she'd given him a fair gift of land.
      HATHORNE: And the name of this man?
      GILES (*taken aback*): What name?
      HATHORNE: The man that give you this information.
      GILES (*hesitates, then*): Why, I—I cannot give you his 2495
          name.
      HATHORNE: And why not?
      GILES (*hesitates, then bursts out*): You know well why
          not! He'll lay in jail if I give his name!
      HATHORNE: This is contempt of the court, Mr.   2500
          Danforth!
      DANFORTH (*to avoid that*): You will surely tell us the
          name.
      GILES: I will not give you no name. I mentioned my
          wife's name once and I'll burn in hell long   2505
          enough for that. I stand mute.
      DANFORTH: In that case, I have no choice but to arrest
          you for contempt of this court, do you know
          that?
      GILES: This is a hearing; you cannot clap me for con- 2510
          tempt of a hearing.
      DANFORTH: Oh, it is a proper lawyer! Do you wish
          me to declare the court in full session here? Or
          will you give me good reply?
      GILES (*faltering*): I cannot give you no name, sir, I can- 2515
          not.
      DANFORTH: You are a foolish old man. Mr. Cheever,
          begin the record. The court is now in session. I
          ask you, Mr. Corey—
      PROCTOR (*breaking in*): Your Honor—he has the story 2520
          in confidence, sir, and he—
      PARRIS: The Devil lives on such confidences! (*To
          DANFORTH:*) Without confidences there could
          be no conspiracy, Your Honor!
      HATHORNE: I think it must be broken, sir.   2525
      DANFORTH (*to* GILES): Old man, if your informant tells
          the truth let him come here openly like a
          decent man. But if he hide in anonymity I
          must know why. Now sir, the government and
          central church demand of you the name of him 2530
          who reported Mr. Thomas Putnam a common
          murderer.
      HALE: Excellency—
      DANFORTH: Mr. Hale.
      HALE: We cannot blink it more. There is a prodigious 2535
          fear of this court in the country—
      DANFORTH: Then there is a prodigious guilt in the
          country. Are *you* afraid to be questioned here?
      HALE: I may only fear the Lord, sir, but there is fear
          in the country nevertheless.   2540
      DANFORTH (*angered now*): Reproach me not with the
          fear in the country; there is fear in the country
          because there is a moving plot to topple Christ
          in the country!

2545   HALE: But it does not follow that everyone accused is part of it.

DANFORTH: No uncorrupted man may fear this court, Mr. Hale! None! (*To* GILES:) You are under arrest in contempt of this court. Now sit you

2550   down and take counsel with yourself, or you will be set in the jail until you decide to answer all questions.

[GILES COREY *makes a rush for* PUTNAM. PROCTOR *lunges and holds him.*]

PROCTOR: No, Giles!

GILES (*over* PROCTOR's *shoulder at* PUTNAM): I'll cut

2555   your throat, Putnam, I'll kill you yet!

PROCTOR (*forcing him into a chair*): Peace, Giles, peace. (*Releasing him.*) We'll prove ourselves. Now we will. (*He starts to turn to* DANFORTH.)

GILES: Say nothin' more, John. (*Pointing at*

2560   DANFORTH:) He's only playin' you! He means to hang us all!

[MARY WARREN *bursts into sobs.*]

DANFORTH: This is a court of law, Mister. I'll have no effrontery here!

PROCTOR: Forgive him, sir, for his old age. Peace,

2565   Giles, we'll prove it all now. (*He lifts up* MARY's *chin.*) You cannot weep, Mary. Remember the angel, what he say to the boy. Hold to it, now; there is your rock. (MARY *quiets. He takes out a paper, and turns to* DANFORTH.) This is Mary

2570   Warren's deposition. I—I would ask you remember, sir, while you read it, that until two week ago she were no different than the other children are today. (*He is speaking reasonably, restraining all his fears, his anger, his anxiety.*) You

2575   saw her scream, she howled, she swore familiar spirits choked her; she even testified that Satan, in the form of women now in jail, tried to win her soul away, and then when she refused—

DANFORTH: We know all this.

2580   PROCTOR: Aye, sir. She swears now that she never saw Satan; nor any spirit, vague or clear, that Satan may have sent to hurt her. And she declares her friends are lying now.

[PROCTOR *starts to hand* DANFORTH *the deposition, and* HALE *comes up to* DANFORTH *in a trembling state.*]

HALE: Excellency, a moment. I think this goes to the

2585   heart of the matter.

DANFORTH (*with deep misgivings*): It surely does.

HALE: I cannot say he is an honest man; I know him little. But in all justice, sir, a claim so weighty cannot be argued by a farmer. In God's name,

2590   sir, stop here; send him home and let him come again with a lawyer—

DANFORTH (*patiently*): Now look you, Mr. Hale—

HALE: Excellency, I have signed seventy-two death warrants; I am a minister of the Lord, and I dare not take a life without there be a proof so   2595 immaculate no slightest qualm of conscience may doubt it.

DANFORTH: Mr. Hale, you surely do not doubt my justice.

HALE: I have this morning signed away the soul of   2600 Rebecca Nurse, Your Honor. I'll not conceal it, my hand shakes yet as with a wound! I pray you, sir, *this* argument let lawyers present to you.

DANFORTH: Mr. Hale, believe me; for a man of such   2605 terrible learning you are most bewildered—I hope you will forgive me. I have been thirty-two year at the bar, sir, and I should be confounded were I called upon to defend these people. Let you consider, now—(*To* PROCTOR   2610 *and the others:*) And I bid you all do likewise. In an ordinary crime, how does one defend the accused? One calls up witnesses to prove his innocence. But witchcraft is *ipso facto*, on its face and by its nature, an invisible crime, is it   2615 not? Therefore, who may possibly be witness to it? The witch and the victim. None other. Now we cannot hope the witch will accuse herself; granted? Therefore, we must rely upon her victims—and they do testify, the children certainly   2620 do testify. As for the witches, none will deny that we are most eager for all their confessions. Therefore, what is left for a lawyer to bring out? I think I have made my point. Have I not?

HALE: But this child claims the girls are not truthful,   2625 and if they are not—

DANFORTH: That is precisely what I am about to consider, sir. What more may you ask of me? Unless you doubt my probity?

HALE (*defeated*): I surely do not, sir. Let you consider   2630 it, then.

DANFORTH: And let you put your heart to rest. Her deposition, Mr. Proctor.

[PROCTOR *hands it to him.* HATHORNE *rises, goes beside* DANFORTH, *and starts reading.* PARRIS *comes to his other side.* DANFORTH *looks at* JOHN PROCTOR, *then proceeds to read.* HALE *gets up, finds position near the judge, reads too.* PROCTOR *glances at* GILES. FRANCIS *prays silently; hands pressed together.* CHEEVER *waits placidly; the sublime official, dutiful.* MARY WARREN *sobs once.* JOHN PROCTOR *touches her head reassuringly. Presently* DANFORTH *lifts his eyes, stands up, takes out a kerchief and blows his nose. The others stand aside as he moves in thought toward the window.*]

PARRIS (*hardly able to contain his anger and fear*): I

2635 should like to question—

DANFORTH (*his first real outburst, in which his contempt for* PARRIS *is clear*): Mr. Parris, I bid you be silent! (*He stands in silence, looking out the window. Now, having established that he will set the gait:*) Mr. Cheever, will you go into the court and bring the children here? (CHEEVER *gets up and goes out upstage.* DANFORTH *now turns to* MARY.) Mary Warren, how came you to this turnabout? Has Mr. Proctor threatened you for this deposition?

MARY WARREN: No, sir.

DANFORTH: Has he ever threatened you?

MARY WARREN (*weaker*): No, sir.

DANFORTH (*sensing a weakening*): Has he threatened you?

2650 MARY WARREN: No, sir.

DANFORTH: Then you tell me that you sat in my court, callously lying, when you knew that people would hang by your evidence? (*She does not answer.*) Answer me!

2655 MARY WARREN (*almost inaudibly*): I did, sir.

DANFORTH: How were you instructed in your life? Do you not know that God damns all liars? (*She cannot speak.*) Or is it now that you lie?

MARY WARREN: No, sir—I am with God now.

2660 DANFORTH: You are with God now.

MARY WARREN: Aye, sir.

DANFORTH (*containing himself*): I will tell you this— you are either lying now, or you were lying in the court, and in either case you have committed perjury and you will go to jail for it. You cannot lightly say you lied, Mary. Do you know that?

MARY WARREN: I cannot lie no more. I am with God, I am with God.

[*But she breaks into sobs at the thought of it, and the right door opens, and enter* SUSANNA WALCOTT, MERCY LEWIS, BETTY PARRIS, *and finally* ABIGAIL. CHEEVER *comes to* DANFORTH.]

2670 CHEEVER: Ruth Putnam's not in the court, sir, nor the other children.

DANFORTH: These will be sufficient. Sit you down, children. (*Silently they sit.*) Your friend, Mary Warren, has given us a deposition. In which she swears that she never saw familiar spirits, apparitions, nor any manifest of the Devil. She claims as well that none of you have seen these things either. (*Slight pause.*) Now, children, this is a court of law. The law, based upon the Bible, and the Bible, writ by Almighty God, forbid the practice of witchcraft, and describe death as the penalty thereof. But likewise, children, the law and Bible damn all bearers of false witness. (*Slight pause.*) Now then. It does not escape me that this

deposition may be devised to blind us; it may well be that Mary Warren has been conquered by Satan, who sends her here to distract our sacred purpose. If so, her neck will break for it. But if she speak true, I bid you now drop your guile and confess your pretense, for a quick confession will go easier with you. (*Pause.*) Abigail Williams, rise. (ABIGAIL *slowly rises.*) Is there any truth in this?

2695 ABIGAIL: No, sir.

DANFORTH (*thinks, glances at* MARY, *then back to* ABIGAIL): Children, a very augur bit will now be turned into your souls until your honesty is proved. Will either of you change your positions now, or do you force me to hard questioning?

2700

ABIGAIL: I have naught to change, sir. She lies.

DANFORTH (*to* MARY): You would still go on with this?

MARY WARREN (*faintly*): Aye, sir.

DANFORTH (*turning to* ABIGAIL): A poppet were discovered in Mr. Proctor's house, stabbed by a needle. Mary Warren claims that you sat beside her in the court when she made it, and that you saw her make it and witnessed how she herself stuck her needle into it for safekeeping. What say you to that?

2705

2710

ABIGAIL (*with a slight note of indignation*): It is a lie, sir.

DANFORTH (*after a slight pause*): While you worked for Mr. Proctor, did you see poppets in that house?

ABIGAIL: Goody Proctor always kept poppets.

PROCTOR: Your Honor, my wife never kept no poppets. Mary Warren confesses it was her poppet.

2715

CHEEVER: Your Excellency.

DANFORTH: Mr. Cheever.

CHEEVER: When I spoke with Goody Proctor in that house, she said she never kept no poppets. But she said she did keep poppets when she were a girl.

2720

PROCTOR: She has not been a girl these fifteen years, Your Honor.

HATHORNE: But a poppet will keep fifteen years, will it not?

2725

PROCTOR: It will keep if it is kept, but Mary Warren swears she never saw no poppets in my house, nor anyone else.

PARRIS: Why could there not have been poppets hid where no one ever saw them?

2730

PROCTOR (*furious*): There might also be a dragon with five legs in my house, but no one has ever seen it.

PARRIS: We are here, Your Honor, precisely to discover what no one has ever seen.

2735

PROCTOR: Mr. Danforth, what profit this girl to turn herself about? What may Mary Warren gain but hard questioning and worse?

DANFORTH: You are charging Abigail Williams with a marvelous cool plot to murder, do you understand that?

2740

PROCTOR: I do, sir. I believe she means to murder.

2745 DANFORTH (*pointing at* ABIGAIL, *incredulously*): This child would murder your wife?

PROCTOR: It is not a child. Now hear me, sir. In the sight of the congregation she were twice this year put out of this meetin' house for laughter during prayer.

2750 DANFORTH (*shocked, turning to* ABIGAIL): What's this? Laughter during—!

PARRIS: Excellency, she were under Tituba's power at that time, but she is solemn now.

GILES: Aye, now she is solemn and goes to hang peo-
2755 ple!

DANFORTH: Quiet, man.

HATHORNE: Surely it have no bearing on the question, sir. He charges contemplation of murder.

DANFORTH: Aye. (*He studies* ABIGAIL *for a moment,*
2760 *then:*) Continue, Mr. Proctor.

PROCTOR: Mary. Now tell the Governor how you danced in the woods.

PARRIS (*instantly*): Excellency, since I come to Salem this man is blackening my name. He—

2765 DANFORTH: In a moment, sir. (*To* MARY WARREN, *sternly, and surprised:*) What is this dancing?

MARY WARREN: I—(*She glances at* ABIGAIL, *who is staring down at her remorselessly. Then, appealing to* PROCTOR:) Mr. Proctor—

2770 PROCTOR (*taking it right up*): Abigail leads the girls to the woods, Your Honor, and they have danced there naked—

PARRIS: Your Honor, this—

PROCTOR (*at once*): Mr. Parris discovered them him-
2775 self in the dead of night! There's the "child" she is!

DANFORTH—(*it is growing into a nightmare, and he turns, astonished, to* PARRIS): Mr. Parris—

PARRIS: I can only say, sir, that I never found any of
2780 them naked, and this man is—

DANFORTH: But you discovered them dancing in the woods? (*Eyes on* PARRIS, *he points at* ABIGAIL.) Abigail?

HALE: Excellency, when I first arrived from Beverly,
2785 Mr. Parris told me that.

DANFORTH: Do you deny it, Mr. Parris?

PARRIS: I do not, sir, but I never saw any of them naked.

DANFORTH: But she have *danced*?

2790 PARRIS (*unwillingly*): Aye, sir.

[DANFORTH, *as though with new eyes, looks at* ABIGAIL.]

HATHORNE: Excellency, will you permit me? (*He points at* MARY WARREN.)

DANFORTH (*with great worry*): Pray, proceed.

HATHORNE: You say you never saw no spirits, Mary,
2795 were never threatened or afflicted by any manifest of the Devil or the Devil's agents.

MARY WARREN (*very faintly*): No, sir.

HATHORNE (*with a gleam of victory*): And yet, when people accused of witchery confronted you in court, you would faint, saying their spirits   2800 came out of their bodies and choked you—

MARY WARREN: That were pretense, sir.

DANFORTH: I cannot hear you.

MARY WARREN: Pretense, sir.

PARRIS: But you did turn cold, did you not? I myself   2805 picked you up many times, and your skin were icy. Mr. Danforth, you—

DANFORTH: I saw that many times.

PROCTOR: She only pretended to faint, Your Excellency. They're all marvelous pretenders.   2810

HATHORNE: Then can she pretend to faint now?

PROCTOR: Now?

PARRIS: Why not? Now there are no spirits attacking her, for none in this room is accused of witchcraft. So let her turn herself cold now, let her   2815 pretend she is attacked now, let her faint. (*He turns to* MARY WARREN.) Faint!

MARY WARREN: Faint?

PARRIS: Aye, faint. Prove to us how you pretended in the court so many times.   2820

MARY WARREN (*looking to* PROCTOR): I—cannot faint now, sir.

PROCTOR (*alarmed, quietly*): Can you not pretend it?

MARY WARREN: I—(*She looks about as though searching for the passion to faint.*) I—have no *sense* of it   2825 now, I—

DANFORTH: Why? What is lacking now?

MARY WARREN: I—cannot tell, sir, I—

DANFORTH: Might it be that here we have no afflicting spirit loose, but in the court there were some?   2830

MARY WARREN: I never saw no spirits.

PARRIS: Then see no spirits now, and prove to us that you can faint by your own will, as you claim.

MARY WARREN (*stares, searching for the emotion of it, and then shakes her head*): I—cannot do it.   2835

PARRIS: Then you will confess, will you not? It were attacking spirits made you faint!

MARY WARREN: No, sir, I—

PARRIS: Your Excellency, this is a trick to blind the court!   2840

MARY WARREN: It's not a trick! (*She stands.*) I—I used to faint because I—I thought I saw spirits.

DANFORTH: *Thought* you saw them!

MARY WARREN: But I did not, Your Honor.

HATHORNE: How could you think you saw them   2845 unless you saw them?

MARY WARREN: I—I cannot tell how, but I did. I—I heard the other girls screaming, and you, Your Honor, you seemed to believe them, and I—It were only sport in the beginning, sir, but then   2850 the whole world cried spirits, spirits, and I—I promise you, Mr. Danforth, I only thought I saw them but I did not.

[DANFORTH peers at her.]

PARRIS (*smiling, but nervous because* DANFORTH *seems to*
2855   *be struck by* MARY WARREN'*s story*): Surely Your
       Excellency is not taken by this simple lie.
DANFORTH (*turning worriedly to* ABIGAIL): Abigail. I bid
       you now search your heart and tell me this—
       and beware of it, child, to God every soul is pre-
2860   cious and His vengeance is terrible on them that
       take life without cause. Is it possible, child, that
       the spirits you have seen are illusion only, some
       deception that may cross your mind when—
ABIGAIL: Why, this—this—is a base question, sir.
2865 DANFORTH: Child, I would have you consider it—
ABIGAIL: I have been hurt, Mr. Danforth; I have seen
       my blood runnin' out! I have been near to
       murdered every day because I done my duty
       pointing out the Devil's people—and this is
2870   my reward? To be mistrusted, denied, ques-
       tioned like a—
DANFORTH (*weakening*): Child, I do not mistrust you—
ABIGAIL (*in an open threat*): Let *you* beware, Mr.
       Danforth. Think you to be so mighty that the
2875   power of Hell may not turn *your* wits? Beware
       of it! There is—(*Suddenly, from an accusatory
       attitude, her face turns, looking into the air
       above—it is truly frightened.*)
DANFORTH (*apprehensively*): What is it, child?
2880 ABIGAIL (*looking about in the air, clasping her arms about
       her as though cold*): I—I know not. A wind, a cold
       wind, has come. (*Her eyes fall on* MARY WARREN.)
MARY WARREN (*terrified, pleading*): Abby!
MERCY LEWIS (*shivering*): Your Honor, I freeze!
2885 PROCTOR: They're pretending!
HATHORNE (*touching* ABIGAIL'*s hand*): She is cold, Your
       Honor, touch her!
MERCY LEWIS (*through chattering teeth*): Mary, do you
       send this shadow on me?
2890 MARY WARREN: Lord, save me!
SUSANNA WALCOTT: I freeze, I freeze!
ABIGAIL (*shivering visibly*): It is a wind, a wind!
MARY WARREN: Abby, don't do that!
DANFORTH (*himself engaged and entered by* ABIGAIL):
2895   Mary Warren, do you witch her? I say to you,
       do you send your spirit out?

[With a hysterical cry MARY WARREN *starts to run.*
PROCTOR *catches her.]*

MARY WARREN (*almost collapsing*): Let me go, Mr.
       Proctor, I cannot, I cannot—
ABIGAIL (*crying to Heaven*): Oh, Heavenly Father, take
2900   away this shadow!

[Without warning or hesitation, PROCTOR *leaps at*
ABIGAIL *and, grabbing her by the hair, pulls her to her
feet. She screams in pain.* DANFORTH, *astonished, cries,*

"*What are you about?*" *and* HATHORNE *and* PARRIS
call, "*Take your hands off her!*" *and out of it all comes*
PROCTOR'*s roaring voice.]*

PROCTOR: How do you call Heaven! Whore! Whore!

*[*HERRICK *breaks* PROCTOR *from her.]*

HERRICK: John!
DANFORTH: Man! Man, what do you—
PROCTOR (*breathless and in agony*): It is a whore!
DANFORTH (*dumfounded*): You charge—?   2905
ABIGAIL: Mr. Danforth, he is lying!
PROCTOR: Mark her! Now she'll suck a scream to stab
       me with, but—
DANFORTH: You will prove this! This will not pass!
PROCTOR (*trembling, his life collapsing about him*): I   2910
       have known her, sir. I have known her.
DANFORTH: You—you are a lecher?
FRANCIS (*horrified*): John, you cannot say such a—
PROCTOR: Oh, Francis, I wish you had some evil in
       you that you might know me! (*To* DANFORTH:)   2915
       A man will not cast away his good name. You
       surely know that.
DANFORTH (*dumfounded*): In—in what time? In what
       place?
PROCTOR (*his voice about to break, and his shame great*):   2920
       In the proper place—where my beasts are bed-
       ded. On the last night of my joy, some eight
       months past. She used to serve me in my
       house, sir. (*He has to clamp his jaw to keep from
       weeping.*) A man may think God sleeps, but   2925
       God sees everything, I know it now. I beg you,
       sir, I beg you—see her what she is. My wife,
       my dear good wife, took this girl soon after,
       sir, and put her out on the highroad. And
       being what she is, a lump of vanity, sir—(*He is*   2930
       being overcome.) Excellency, forgive me, forgive
       me. (*Angrily against himself, he turns away from
       the Governor for a moment. Then, as though to cry
       out is his only means of speech left:*) She thinks to
       dance with me on my wife's grave! And well   2935
       she might, for I thought of her softly. God help
       me, I lusted, and there *is* a promise in such
       sweat. But it is a whore's vengeance, and you
       must see it; I set myself entirely in your hands.
       I know you must see it now.   2940
DANFORTH (*blanched, in horror, turning to* ABIGAIL):
       You deny every scrap and tittle of this?
ABIGAIL: If I must answer that, I will leave and I will
       not come back again!

*[*DANFORTH *seems unsteady.]*

PROCTOR: I have made a bell of my honor! I have   2945
       rung the doom of my good name—you will
       believe me, Mr. Danforth! My wife is innocent,

except she knew a whore when she saw one!

2950 ABIGAIL (*stepping up to* DANFORTH): What look do you give me? (DANFORTH *cannot speak.*) I'll not have such looks! (*She turns and starts for the door.*)

DANFORTH: You will remain where you are! (HERRICK *steps into her path. She comes up short, fire in her eyes.*) Mr. Parris, go into the court and bring

2955 Goodwife Proctor out.

PARRIS (*objecting*): Your Honor, this is all a—

DANFORTH (*sharply to* PARRIS): Bring her out! And tell her not one word of what's been spoken here. And let you knock before you enter. (PARRIS

2960 *goes out.*) Now we shall touch the bottom of this swamp. (*To* PROCTOR:) Your wife, you say, is an honest woman.

PROCTOR: In her life, sir, she have never lied. There are them that cannot sing, and them that can-

2965 not weep—my wife cannot lie. I have paid much to learn it, sir.

DANFORTH: And when she put this girl out of your house, she put her out for a harlot?

PROCTOR: Aye, sir.

2970 DANFORTH: And knew her for a harlot?

PROCTOR: Aye, sir, she knew her for a harlot.

DANFORTH: Good then. (*To* ABIGAIL:) And if she tell me, child, it were for harlotry, may God spread His mercy on you! (*There is a knock. He calls to

2975 the door.*) Hold! (*To* ABIGAIL:) Turn your back. Turn your back. (*To* PROCTOR:) Do likewise. (*Both turn their backs—*ABIGAIL *with indignant slowness.*) Now let neither of you turn to face Goody Proctor. No one in this room is to speak

2980 one word, or raise a gesture aye or nay. (*He turns toward the door, calls:*) Enter! (*The door opens.* ELIZABETH *enters with* PARRIS. PARRIS *leaves her. She stands alone, her eyes looking for* PROCTOR.) Mr. Cheever, report this testimony

2985 in all exactness. Are you ready?

CHEEVER: Ready, sir.

DANFORTH: Come here, woman. (ELIZABETH *comes to him, glancing at* PROCTOR'S *back.*) Look at me only, not at your husband. In my eyes only.

2990 ELIZABETH (*faintly*): Good, sir.

DANFORTH: We are given to understand that at one time you dismissed your servant, Abigail Williams.

ELIZABETH: That is true, sir.

DANFORTH: For what cause did you dismiss her?

2995 (*Slight pause. Then* ELIZABETH *tries to glance at* PROCTOR.) You will look in my eyes only and not at your husband. The answer is in your memory and you need no help to give it to me. Why did you dismiss Abigail Williams?

3000 ELIZABETH (*not knowing what to say, sensing a situation, wetting her lips to stall for time*): She—dissatisfied me. (*Pause.*) And my husband.

DANFORTH: In what way dissatisfied you?

ELIZABETH: She were—(*She glances at* PROCTOR *for a cue.*)

DANFORTH: Woman, look at me! (ELIZABETH *does.*) 3005 Were she slovenly? Lazy? What disturbance did she cause?

ELIZABETH: Your Honor, I—in that time I were sick. And I—My husband is a good and righteous man. He is never drunk as some are, nor 3010 wastin' his time at the shovelboard, but always at his work. But in my sickness—you see, sir, I were a long time sick after my last baby, and I thought I saw my husband somewhat turning from me. And this girl—(*She turns to* ABIGAIL.) 3015

DANFORTH: Look at me.

ELIZABETH: Aye, sir. Abigail Williams—(*She breaks off.*)

DANFORTH: What of Abigail Williams?

ELIZABETH: I came to think he fancied her. And so one night I lost my wits, I think, and put her 3020 out on the highroad.

DANFORTH: Your husband—did he indeed turn from you?

ELIZABETH (*in agony*): My husband—is a goodly man, sir. 3025

DANFORTH: Then he did not turn from you.

ELIZABETH (*starting to glance at* PROCTOR): He—

DANFORTH (*reaches out and holds her face, then*): Look at me! To your own knowledge, has John Proctor ever committed the crime of lechery? (*In a crisis* 3030 *of indecision she cannot speak.*) Answer my question! Is your husband a lecher!

ELIZABETH (*faintly*): No, sir.

DANFORTH: Remove her, Marshal.

PROCTOR: Elizabeth, tell the truth! 3035

DANFORTH: She has spoken. Remove her!

PROCTOR (*crying out*): Elizabeth, I have confessed it!

ELIZABETH: Oh, God! (*The door closes behind her.*)

PROCTOR: She only thought to save my name!

HALE: Excellency, it is a natural lie to tell; I beg you, 3040 stop now before another is condemned! I may shut my conscience to it no more—private vengeance is working through this testimony! From the beginning this man has struck me true. By my oath to Heaven, I believe him now, 3045 and I pray you call back his wife before we—

DANFORTH: She spoke nothing of lechery, and this man has lied!

HALE: I believe him! (*Pointing at* ABIGAIL:) This girl has always struck me false! She has— 3050

[ABIGAIL, *with a weird, wild, chilling cry, screams up to the ceiling.*]

ABIGAIL: You will not! Begone! Begone, I say!

DANFORTH: What is it, child? (*But* ABIGAIL, *pointing with fear, is now raising up her frightened eyes, her awed face, toward the ceiling—the girls are doing the same—and now* HATHORNE, HALE, 3055 PUTNAM, CHEEVER, HERRICK, *and* DANFORTH *do the same.*) What's there? (*He lowers his eyes from*

*the ceiling, and now he is frightened; there is real
tension in his voice.*) Child! (*She is transfixed—
with all the girls, she is whimpering open-mouthed,
agape at the ceiling.*) Girls! Why do you—?

3060

MERCY LEWIS (*pointing*): It's on the beam! Behind the
rafter!

DANFORTH (*looking up*): Where!

3065 ABIGAIL: Why—? (*She gulps.*) Why do you come, yellow bird?

PROCTOR: Where's a bird? I see no bird!

ABIGAIL (*to the ceiling*): My face? My face?

PROCTOR: Mr. Hale—

3070 DANFORTH: Be quiet!

PROCTOR (*to* HALE): Do you see a bird?

DANFORTH: Be quiet!

ABIGAIL (*to the ceiling, in a genuine conversation with the
"bird," as though trying to talk it out of attacking
her*): But God made my face; you cannot want
to tear my face. Envy is a deadly sin, Mary.

3075

MARY WARREN (*on her feet with a spring, and horrified,
pleading*): Abby!

ABIGAIL (*unperturbed, continuing to the "bird"*): Oh,
Mary, this is a black art to change your shape.
No, I cannot, I cannot stop my mouth; it's
God's work I do.

3080

MARY WARREN: Abby, I'm *here*!

PROCTOR (*frantically*): They're pretending, Mr. Danforth!

3085 ABIGAIL (*now she takes a backward step, as though in fear
the bird will swoop down momentarily*): Oh,
please, Mary! Don't come down.

SUSANNA WALCOTT: Her claws, she's stretching her
claws!

3090 PROCTOR: Lies, lies.

ABIGAIL (*backing further, eyes still fixed above*): Mary,
please don't hurt me!

MARY WARREN (*to* DANFORTH): I'm not hurting her!

DANFORTH (*to* MARY WARREN): Why does she see this
vision?

3095

MARY WARREN: She sees nothin'!

ABIGAIL (*now staring full front as though hypnotized,
and mimicking the exact tone of* MARY WARREN's
cry*): She sees nothin'!

3100 MARY WARREN (*pleading*): Abby, you mustn't!

ABIGAIL AND ALL THE GIRLS (*all transfixed*): Abby, you
mustn't!

MARY WARREN (*to all the girls*): I'm here, I'm here!

GIRLS: I'm here, I'm here!

3105 DANFORTH (*horrified*): Mary Warren! Draw back your
spirit out of them!

MARY WARREN: Mr. Danforth!

GIRLS (*cutting her off*): Mr. Danforth!

DANFORTH: Have you compacted with the Devil?
Have you?

3110

MARY WARREN: Never, never!

GIRLS: Never, never!

DANFORTH (*growing hysterical*): Why can they only
repeat you?

PROCTOR: Give me a whip—I'll stop it!   3115

MARY WARREN: They're sporting. They—!

GIRLS: They're sporting!

MARY WARREN (*turning on them all hysterically and
stamping her feet*): Abby, stop it!

GIRLS (*stamping their feet*): Abby, stop it!   3120

MARY WARREN: Stop it!

GIRLS: Stop it!

MARY WARREN (*screaming it out at the top of her lungs,
and raising her fists*): Stop it!!

GIRLS (*raising their fists*): Stop it!!   3125

[MARY WARREN, *utterly confounded, and becoming overwhelmed by* ABIGAIL's—*and the girls'—utter conviction,
starts to whimper, hands half raised, powerless, and all
the girls begin whimpering exactly as she does.*]

DANFORTH: A little while ago you were afflicted.
Now it seems you afflict others; where did you
find this power?

MARY WARREN (*staring at* ABIGAIL): I—have no power.

GIRLS: I have no power.   3130

PROCTOR: They're gulling you, Mister!

DANFORTH: Why did you turn about this past two
weeks? You have seen the Devil, have you not?

HALE (*indicating* ABIGAIL *and the girls*): You cannot
believe them!   3135

MARY WARREN: I—

PROCTOR (*sensing her weakening*): Mary, God damns
all liars!

DANFORTH (*pounding it into her*): You have seen the
Devil, you have made compact with Lucifer,   3140
have you not?

PROCTOR: God damns liars, Mary!

[MARY *utters something unintelligible, staring at*
ABIGAIL, *who keeps watching the "bird" above.*]

DANFORTH: I cannot hear you. What do you say?
(MARY *utters again unintelligibly.*) You will confess yourself or you will hang! (*He turns her*   3145
roughly to face him.) Do you know who I am? I
say you will hang if you do not open with me!

PROCTOR: Mary, remember the angel Raphael—do
that which is good and—

ABIGAIL (*pointing upward*): The wings! Her wings are   3150
spreading! Mary, please, don't, don't—!

HALE: I see nothing, Your Honor!

DANFORTH: Do you confess this power! (*He is an inch
from her face.*) Speak!

ABIGAIL: She's going to come down! She's walking   3155
the beam!

DANFORTH: Will you speak!

MARY WARREN (*staring in horror*): I cannot!

GIRLS: I cannot!

PARRIS: Cast the Devil out! Look him in the face!   3160
Trample him! We'll save you, Mary, only stand

fast against him and—
ABIGAIL (*looking up*): Look out! She's coming down!

[*She and all the girls run to one wall, shielding their eyes. And now, as though cornered, they let out a gigantic scream, and* MARY, *as though infected, opens her mouth and screams with them. Gradually* ABIGAIL *and the girls leave off, until only* MARY *is left there, staring up at the "bird," screaming madly. All watch her, horrified by this evident fit.* PROCTOR *strides to her.*]

PROCTOR: Mary, tell the Governor what they—(*He has*
3165 *hardly got a word out, when, seeing him coming for her, she rushes out of his reach, screaming in horror.*)
MARY WARREN: Don't touch me—don't touch me! (*At which the girls halt at the door.*)
PROCTOR (*astonished*): Mary!
3170 MARY WARREN (*pointing at* PROCTOR): You're the Devil's man!

[*He is stopped in his tracks.*]

PARRIS: Praise God!
GIRLS: Praise God!
PROCTOR (*numbed*): Mary, how—?
3175 MARY WARREN: I'll not hang with you! I love God, I love God.
DANFORTH (*to* MARY): He bid you do the Devil's work?
MARY WARREN (*hysterically, indicating* PROCTOR): He come at me by night and every day to sign, to
3180 sign, to—
DANFORTH: Sign what?
PARRIS: The Devil's book? He come with a book?
MARY WARREN (*hysterically, pointing at* PROCTOR, *fearful of him*): My name, he want my name. "I'll
3185 murder you," he says, "if my wife hangs! We must go and overthrow the court," he says!

[DANFORTH'*s head jerks toward* PROCTOR, *shock and horror in his face.*]

PROCTOR (*turning, appealing to* HALE): Mr. Hale!
MARY WARREN (*her sobs beginning*): He wake me every night, his eyes were like coals and his
3190 fingers claw my neck, and I sign, I sign . . .
HALE: Excellency, this child's gone wild!
PROCTOR (*as* DANFORTH'*s wide eyes pour on him*): Mary, Mary!
MARY WARREN (*screaming at him*): No, I love God; I
3195 go your way no more. I love God, I bless God. (*Sobbing, she rushes to* ABIGAIL.) Abby, Abby, I'll never hurt you more! (*They all watch, as* ABIGAIL, *out of her infinite charity, reaches out and draws the sobbing* MARY *to her, and then looks up* DANFORTH.)
(to PROCTOR): What are you? (PROCTOR *is speech in his anger.*) You are combined with

anti-Christ, are you not? I have seen your power; you will not deny it! What say you, Mister?
HALE: Excellency— 3205
DANFORTH: I will have nothing from you, Mr. Hale! (*To* PROCTOR:) Will you confess yourself befouled with Hell, or do you keep that black allegiance yet? What say you?
PROCTOR (*his mind wild, breathless*): I say—I say—God 3210
is dead!
PARRIS: Hear it, hear it!
PROCTOR (*laughs insanely, then*): A fire, a fire is burning! I hear the boot of Lucifer, I see his filthy face! And it is my face, and yours, Danforth! 3215
For them that quail to bring men out of ignorance, as I have quailed, and as you quail now when you know in all your black hearts that this be fraud—God damns our kind especially, and we will burn, we will burn together! 3220
DANFORTH: Marshal! Take him and Corey with him to the jail!
HALE (*starting across to the door*): I denounce these proceedings!
PROCTOR: You are pulling Heaven down and raising 3225
up a whore!
HALE: I denounce these proceedings, I quit this court! (*He slams the door to the outside behind him.*)
DANFORTH (*calling to him in a fury*): Mr. Hale! Mr. Hale!

[*The curtain falls*]

ACT IV

A Cell in Salem jail, that fall.
At the back is a high barred window; near it, a great, heavy door. Along the walls are two benches.
The place is in darkness but for the moonlight seeping through the bars. It appears empty. Presently footsteps are heard coming down a corridor beyond the wall, keys rattle, and the door swings open.
Marshal HERRICK *enters with a lantern.*
He is nearly drunk, and heavy-footed. He goes to a bench and nudges a bundle of rags lying on it.

HERRICK: Sarah, wake up! Sarah Good! (*He then crosses* 3230
es to the other bench.)
SARAH GOOD (*rising in her rags*): Oh, Majesty! Comin', comin'! Tituba, he's here, His Majesty's come!
HERRICK: Go to the north cell; this place is wanted now. (*He hangs his lantern on the wall.* TITUBA *sits up.*) 3235
TITUBA: That don't look to me like His Majesty; look to me like the marshal.
HERRICK (*taking out a flask*): Get along with you now, clear this place. (*He drinks, and* SARAH GOOD *comes and peers up into his face.*) 3240
SARAH GOOD: Oh, is it you, Marshal! I thought sure

you be the devil comin' for us. Could I have a
sip of cider for me goin'-away?

3245 HERRICK (*handing her the flask*): And where are you off
to, Sarah?

TITUBA (*as* SARAH *drinks*): We goin' to Barbados, soon
the Devil gits here with the feathers and the
wings.

HERRICK: Oh? A happy voyage to you.

3250 SARAH GOOD: A pair of bluebirds wingin' southerly,
the two of us! Oh, it be a grand transformation, Marshal! (*She raises the flask to drink again.*)

HERRICK (*taking the flask from her lips*): You'd best give
me that or you'll never rise off the ground.

3255 Come along now.

TITUBA: I'll speak to him for you, if you desires to
come along, Marshal.

HERRICK: I'd not refuse it, Tituba; it's the proper
morning to fly into Hell.

3260 TITUBA: Oh, it be no Hell in Barbados. Devil, him be
pleasure-man in Barbados, him be singin' and
dancin' in Barbados. It's you folks—you riles
him up' round here; it be too cold 'round here
for that Old Boy. He freeze his soul in

3265 Massachusetts, but in Barbados he just as
sweet and—(*A bellowing cow is heard, and*
TITUBA *leaps up and calls to the window:*) Aye, sir!
That's him, Sarah!

SARAH GOOD: I'm here, Majesty! (*They hurriedly pick*

3270 *up their rags as* HOPKINS, *a guard, enters.*)

HOPKINS: The Deputy Governor's arrived.

HERRICK (*grabbing* TITUBA): Come along, come along.

TITUBA (*resisting him*): No, he comin' for me. I goin'
home!

3275 HERRICK (*pulling her to the door*): That's not Satan, just
a poor old cow with a hatful of milk. Come
along now, out with you!

TITUBA (*calling to the window*): Take me home, Devil!
Take me home!

3280 SARAH GOOD (*following the shouting* TITUBA *out*): Tell
him I'm goin', Tituba! Now you tell him Sarah
Good is goin' too!

[*In the corridor outside* TITUBA *calls on—"Take me
home, Devil; Devil take me home!" and* HOPKINS' *voice
orders her to move on.* HERRICK *returns and begins to
push old rags and straw into a corner. Hearing footsteps, he turns, and enter* DANFORTH *and* JUDGE
HATHORNE. *They are in greatcoats and wear hats
against the bitter cold. They are followed in by*
CHEEVER, *who carries a dispatch case and a flat
wooden box containing his writing materials.*]

HERRICK: Good morning, Excellency.

DANFORTH: Where is Mr. Parris?

3285 HERRICK: I'll fetch him. (*He starts for the door.*)

DANFORTH: Marshal. (HERRICK *stops.*) When did
Reverend Hale arrive?

HERRICK: It were toward midnight, I think.

DANFORTH (*suspiciously*): What is he about here?

3290 HERRICK: He goes among them that will hang, sir.
And he prays with them. He sits with Goody
Nurse now. And Mr. Parris with him.

DANFORTH: Indeed. That man have no authority to
enter here, Marshal. Why have you let him in?

3295 HERRICK: Why, Mr. Parris command me, sir. I cannot
deny him.

DANFORTH: Are you drunk, Marshal?

HERRICK: No, sir; it is a bitter night, and I have no
fire here.

DANFORTH (*containing his anger*): Fetch Mr. Parris. 3300

HERRICK: Aye, sir.

DANFORTH: There is a prodigious stench in this place.

HERRICK: I have only now cleared the people out for
you.

DANFORTH: Beware hard drink, Marshal. 3305

HERRICK: Aye, sir. (*He waits an instant for further
orders. But* DANFORTH, *in dissatisfaction, turns his
back on him, and* HERRICK *goes out. There is a
pause.* DANFORTH *stands in thought.*)

HATHORNE: Let you question Hale, Excellency; I 3310
should not be surprised he have been preaching in Andover lately.

DANFORTH: We'll come to that; speak nothing of
Andover. Parris prays with him. That's
strange. (*He blows on his hands, moves toward the* 3315
window, and looks out.)

HATHORNE: Excellency, I wonder if it be wise to let
Mr. Parris so continuously with the prisoners.
(DANFORTH *turns to him, interested.*) I think,
sometimes, the man has a mad look these days. 3320

DANFORTH: Mad?

HATHORNE: I met him yesterday coming out of his
house, and I bid him good morning—and he
wept and went his way. I think it is not well
the village sees him so unsteady. 3325

DANFORTH: Perhaps he have some sorrow.

CHEEVER (*stamping his feet against the cold*): I think it
be the cows, sir.

DANFORTH: Cows?

CHEEVER: There be so many cows wanderin' the high- 3330
roads, now their masters are in the jails, and
much disagreement who they will belong to
now. I know Mr. Parris be arguin' with farmers
all yesterday—there is great contention, sir,
about the cows. Contention make him weep, 3335
sir; it were always a man that weep for contention. (*He turns, as do* HATHORNE *and*
DANFORTH, *hearing someone coming up the corridor.* DANFORTH *raises his head as* PARRIS *enters*
is gaunt, frightened, and sweating in his gr

PARRIS (*to* DANFORTH, *instantly*): Oh, good
sir, thank you for coming, I beg
wakin' you so early. Good
Hathorne.

3345 DANFORTH: Reverend Hale have no right to enter this—

PARRIS: Excellency, a moment. (*He hurries back and shuts the door.*)

HATHORNE: Do you leave him alone with the prisoners?

3350 DANFORTH: What's his business here?

PARRIS (*prayerfully holding up his hands*): Excellency, hear me. It is a providence. Reverend Hale has returned to bring Rebecca Nurse to God.

DANFORTH (*surprised*): He bids her confess?

3355 PARRIS (*sitting*): Hear me. Rebecca have not given me a word this three month since she came. Now she sits with him, and her sister and Martha Corey and two or three others, and he pleads with them, confess their crimes and save their lives.

3360 DANFORTH: Why—this is indeed a providence. And they soften, they soften?

PARRIS: Not yet, not yet. But I thought to summon you, sir, that we might think on whether it be not wise, to—(*He dares not say it.*) I had thought

3365 to put a question, sir, and I hope you will not—

DANFORTH: Mr. Parris, be plain, what troubles you?

PARRIS: There is news, sir, that the court—the court must reckon with. My niece, sir, my niece—I believe she has vanished.

3370 DANFORTH: Vanished!

PARRIS: I had thought to advise you of it earlier in the week, but—

DANFORTH: Why? How long is she gone?

PARRIS: This be the third night. You see, sir, she told

3375 me she would stay a night with Mercy Lewis. And next day, when she does not return, I send to Mr. Lewis to inquire. Mercy told him she would sleep in *my* house for a night.

DANFORTH: They are both gone?!

3380 PARRIS (*in fear of him*): They are, sir.

DANFORTH (*alarmed*): I will send a party for them. Where may they be?

PARRIS: Excellency, I think they be aboard a ship. (*DANFORTH stands agape.*) My daughter tells me

3385 how she heard them speaking of ships last week, and tonight I discover my—my strong-box is broke into. (*He presses his fingers against his eyes ... back tears.*)

HATHO...ed): She have robbed you?

3390 P... ound is gone. I am penniless.
... e and sobs.)
... you are a brainless man! (*He ... eply worried.*)
... it nothing you should
... hink they would run off
... ep in Salem any more.
... t, sir, Abigail had close
... and since the news of
... ?—
... d. The court returns
... sume examinations.

PARRIS: I am sure of it, sir. But the rumor here speaks rebellion in Andover, and it—

DANFORTH: There is no rebellion in Andover!

3405 PARRIS: I tell you what is said here, sir. Andover have thrown out the court, they say, and will have no part of witchcraft. There be a faction here, feeding on that news, and I tell you true, sir, I fear there will be riot here.

3410 HATHORNE: Riot! Why at every execution I have seen naught but high satisfaction in the town.

PARRIS: Judge Hathorne—it were another sort that hanged till now. Rebecca Nurse is no Bridget that lived three year with Bishop before she

3415 married him. John Proctor is not Isaac Ward that drank his family to ruin. (*To* DANFORTH:) I would to God it were not so, Excellency, but these people have great weight yet in the town. Let Rebecca stand upon the gibbet and

3420 send up some righteous prayer, and I fear she'll wake a vengeance on you.

HATHORNE: Excellency, she is condemned a witch. The court have—

DANFORTH (*in deep concern, raising a hand to* HATHORNE): Pray you. (*To* PARRIS:) How do you

3425 propose, then?

PARRIS: Excellency, I would postpone these hangin's for a time.

DANFORTH: There will be no postponement.

3430 PARRIS: Now Mr. Hale's returned, there is hope, I think—for if he bring even one of these to God, that confession surely damns the others in the public eye, and none may doubt more that they are all linked to Hell. This way, unconfessed

3435 and claiming innocence, doubts are multiplied, many honest people will weep for them, and our good purpose is lost in their tears.

DANFORTH (*after thinking a moment, then going to* CHEEVER): Give me the list.

[CHEEVER *opens the dispatch case, searches.*]

3440 PARRIS: It cannot be forgot, sir, that when I summoned the congregation for John Proctor's excommunication there were hardly thirty people come to hear it. That speak a discontent, I think, and—

3445 DANFORTH (*studying the list*): There will be no postponement.

PARRIS: Excellency—

DANFORTH: Now, sir—which of these in your opinion may be brought to God? I will myself strive with him till dawn. (*He hands the list to* PARRIS,

3450 *who merely glances at it.*)

PARRIS: There is not sufficient time till dawn.

DANFORTH: I shall do my utmost. Which of them do you have hope for?

3455 PARRIS (*not even glancing at the list now, and in a qua-*

vering voice, quietly): Excellency—a dagger—
(*He chokes up.*)

DANFORTH: What do you say?

PARRIS: Tonight, when I open my door to leave my
3460   house—a dagger clattered to the ground.
(*Silence.* DANFORTH *absorbs this. Now* PARRIS *cries
out:*) You cannot hang this sort. There is danger
for me. I dare not step outside at night!

[*REVEREND HALE enters. They look at him for an
instant in silence. He is steeped in sorrow, exhausted,
and more direct than he ever was.*]

DANFORTH: Accept my congratulations, Reverend
3465   Hale; we are gladdened to see you returned to
your good work.

HALE (*coming to* DANFORTH *now*): You must pardon
them. They will not budge.

[HERRICK *enters, waits.*]

DANFORTH (*conciliatory*): You misunderstand, sir; I
3470   cannot pardon these when twelve are already
hanged for the same crime. It is not just.

PARRIS (*with failing heart*): Rebecca will not confess?

HALE: The sun will rise in a few minutes. Excellency,
I must have more time.

3475   DANFORTH: Now hear me, and beguile yourselves no
more. I will not receive a single plea for pardon
or postponement. Them that will not confess
will hang. Twelve are already executed; the
names of these seven are given out, and the vil-
3480   lage expects to see them die this morning.
Postponement now speaks a floundering on
my part; reprieve or pardon must cast doubt
upon the guilt of them that died till now. While
I speak God's law, I will not crack its voice
3485   with whimpering. If retaliation is your fear,
know this—I should hang ten thousand that
dared to rise against the law, and an ocean of
salt tears could not melt the resolution of the
statutes. Now draw yourselves up like men
3490   and help me, as you are bound by Heaven to
do. Have you spoken with them all, Mr. Hale?

HALE: All but Proctor. He is in the dungeon.

DANFORTH (*to* HERRICK): What's Proctor's way now?

HERRICK: He sits like some great bird; you'd not
3495   know he lived except he will take food from
time to time.

DANFORTH (*after thinking a moment*): His wife—his
wife must be well on with child now.

HERRICK: She is, sir.

3500   DANFORTH: What think you, Mr. Parris? You have
closer knowledge of this man; might her presence soften him?

PARRIS: It is possible, sir. He have not laid eyes on
her these three months. I should summon her.

DANFORTH (*to* HERRICK): Is he yet adamant? Has he   3505
struck at you again?

HERRICK: He cannot, sir, he is chained to the wall now.

DANFORTH (*after thinking on it*): Fetch Goody Proctor
to me. Then let you bring him up.

HERRICK: Aye, sir. (HERRICK *goes. There is silence.*)   3510

HALE: Excellency, if you postpone a week and publish to the town that you are striving for their
confessions, that speak mercy on your part,
not faltering.

DANFORTH: Mr. Hale, as God have not empowered   3515
me like Joshua to stop this sun from rising, so I
cannot withhold from them the perfection of
their punishment.

HALE (*harder now*): If you think God wills you to raise
rebellion, Mr. Danforth, you are mistaken!   3520

DANFORTH (*instantly*): You have heard rebellion spoken in the town?

HALE: Excellency, there are orphans wandering from
house to house; abandoned cattle bellow on
the highroads, the stink of rotting crops hangs   3525
everywhere, and no man knows when the harlots' cry will end his life—and you wonder yet
if rebellion's spoke? Better you should marvel
how they do not burn your province!

DANFORTH: Mr. Hale, have you preached in Andover   3530
this month?

HALE: Thank God they have no need of me in
Andover.

DANFORTH: You baffle me, sir. Why have you
returned here?   3535

HALE: Why, it is all simple. I come to do the Devil's
work. I come to counsel Christians they should
belie themselves. (*His sarcasm collapses.*) There
is blood on my head! Can you not see the
blood on my head!!   3540

PARRIS: Hush! (*For he has heard footsteps. They all face
the door.* HERRICK *enters with* ELIZABETH. *Her
wrists are linked by heavy chain, which* HERRICK
*now removes. Her clothes are dirty; her face is pale
and gaunt.* HERRICK *goes out.*)   3545

DANFORTH (*very politely*): Goody Proctor. (*She is
silent.*) I hope you are hearty?

ELIZABETH (*as a warning reminder*): I am yet six month
before my time.

DANFORTH: Pray be at your ease, we come not for   3550
your life. We—(*uncertain how to plead, for he is
not accustomed to it:*) Mr. Hale, will you speak
with the woman?

HALE: Goody Proctor, your husband is marked to
hang this morning.

[*Pause.*]

ELIZABETH (*quietly*): I have heard it.

HALE: You know, do you not, th
tion with the court? (*S

884   PART VI   Modern European and American Drama and Theater: Reactions and Modifications

3560 come of my own, Goody Proctor. I would save
your husband's life, for if he is taken I count
myself his murderer. Do you understand me?

ELIZABETH: What do you want of me?

HALE: Goody Proctor, I have gone this three month
3565 like our Lord into the wilderness. I have
sought a Christian way, for damnation's doubled on a minister who counsels men to lie.

HATHORNE: It is no lie, you cannot speak of lies.

HALE: It is a lie! They are innocent!

DANFORTH: I'll hear no more of that!

3570 HALE (*continuing to* ELIZABETH): Let you not mistake
your duty as I mistook my own. I came into
this village like a bridegroom to his beloved,
bearing gifts of high religion; the very crowns
of holy law I brought, and what I touched with
3575 my bright confidence, it died; and where I
turned the eye of my great faith, blood flowed
up. Beware, Goody Proctor—cleave to no faith
when faith brings blood. It is mistaken law
that leads you to sacrifice. Life, woman, life is
3580 God's most precious gift; no principle, however glorious, may justify the taking of it. I beg
you, woman, prevail upon your husband to
confess. Let him give his lie. Quail not before
God's judgment in this, for it may well be God
3585 damns a liar less than he that throws his life
away for pride. Will you plead with him? I
cannot think he will listen to another.

ELIZABETH (*quietly*): I think that be the Devil's argument.

HALE (*with a climactic desperation*): Woman, before the
3590 laws of God we are as swine! We cannot read
His will!

ELIZABETH: I cannot dispute with you, sir; I lack
learning for it.

DANFORTH (*going to her*): Goody Proctor, you are not
3595 summoned here for disputation. Be there no
wifely tenderness within you? He will die with
the sunrise. Your husband. Do you understand
it? (*She only looks at him.*) What say you? Will
you contend with him? (*She is silent.*) Are you
3600 stone? I tell you true, woman, had I no other
proof of ⸻ nnatural life, your dry eyes now
w⸻ nt evidence that you delivered
⸻ ell! A very ape would weep
⸻ Have the devil dried up any
⸻ (*She is silent.*) Take her out.
⸻ should speak to him!
⸻ speak with him,

⸻ with him? (*She hesitates.*)
⸻ his confession or will

⸻ et me speak with him.

⸻ g feet on stone.
⸻ with JOHN

3555

⸻ at I have no connec-
⸻ I have no doubt it.) I
⸻ he seems to doubt it.)

PROCTOR. *His wrists are chained. He is another man,
bearded, filthy, his eyes misty as though webs had
overgrown them. He halts inside the doorway, his eye
caught by the sight of* ELIZABETH. *The emotion flowing
between them prevents anyone from speaking for an
instant. Now* HALE, *visibly affected, goes to* DANFORTH
and speaks quietly.]

HALE: Pray, leave them, Excellency.

DANFORTH (*pressing* HALE *impatiently aside*): Mr. Proctor,
you have been notified, have you not? (PROCTOR   3615
is silent, staring at ELIZABETH.) I see light in the
sky, Mister; let you counsel with your wife, and
may God help you turn your back on Hell.
(PROCTOR *is silent, staring at* ELIZABETH.)

HALE (*quietly*): Excellency, let—   3620

[DANFORTH *brushes past* HALE *and walks out.* HALE *follows.* CHEEVER *stands and follows,* HATHORNE *behind.*
HERRICK *goes.* PARRIS, *from a safe distance, offers:*]

PARRIS: If you desire a cup of cider, Mr. Proctor, I am
sure I—(PROCTOR *turns an icy stare at him, and
he breaks off.* PARRIS *raises his palms toward*
PROCTOR.) God lead you now. (PARRIS *goes out.*)

[*Alone.* PROCTOR *walks to her, halts. It is as though they
stood in a spinning world. It is beyond sorrow, above it.
He reaches out his hand as though toward an embodiment not quite real, and as he touches her, a strange
soft sound, half laughter, half amazement, comes from
his throat. He pats her hand. She covers his hand with
hers. And then, weak, he sits. Then she sits, facing him.*]

PROCTOR: The child?   3625

ELIZABETH: It grows.

PROCTOR: There is no word of the boys?

ELIZABETH: They're well. Rebecca's Samuel keeps them.

PROCTOR: You have not seen them?

ELIZABETH: I have not. (*She catches a weakening in her-*   3630
self and downs it.)

PROCTOR: You are a—marvel, Elizabeth.

ELIZABETH: You—have been tortured?

PROCTOR: Aye. (*Pause. She will not let herself be drowned
in the sea that threatens her.*) They come for my   3635
life now.

ELIZABETH: I know it.

[*Pause.*]

PROCTOR: None—have yet confessed?

ELIZABETH: There be many confessed.

PROCTOR: Who are they?   3640

ELIZABETH: There be a hundred or more, they say.
Goody Ballard is one; Isaiah Goodkind is one.
There be many.

PROCTOR: Rebecca?

3645 ELIZABETH: Not Rebecca. She is one foot in Heaven
            now; naught may hurt her more.
      PROCTOR: And Giles?
      ELIZABETH: You have not heard of it?
      PROCTOR: I hear nothin', where I am kept.
3650 ELIZABETH: Giles is dead.

[He looks at her incredulously.]

      PROCTOR: When were he hanged?
      ELIZABETH (*quietly, factually*): He were not hanged. He
            would not answer aye or nay to his indict-
            ment; for if he denied the charge they'd hang
3655   him surely, and auction out his property. So he
            stand mute, and died Christian under the law.
            And so his sons will have his farm. It is the
            law, for he could not be condemned a wizard
            without he answer the indictment, aye or nay.
3660 PROCTOR: Then how does he die?
      ELIZABETH (*gently*): They press him, John.
      PROCTOR: Press?
      ELIZABETH: Great stones they lay upon his chest until
            he plead aye or nay. (*With a tender smile for the
3665   old man:*) They say he give them but two
            words. "More weight," he says. And died.
      PROCTOR (*numbed—a thread to weave into his agony*):
            "More weight."
      ELIZABETH: Aye. It were a fearsome man, Giles Corey.

[Pause.]

3670 PROCTOR (*with great force of will, but not quite looking at
            her*): I have been thinking I would confess to
            them, Elizabeth. (*She shows nothing.*) What say
            you? If I give them that?
      ELIZABETH: I cannot judge you, John.

[Pause.]

3675 PROCTOR (*simply—a pure question*): What would you
            have me do?
      ELIZABETH: As you will, I would have it. (*Slight
            pause:*) I want you living, John. That's sure.
      PROCTOR (*pauses, then with a flailing of hope*): Giles'
3680   wife? Have she confessed?
      ELIZABETH: She will not.

[Pause.]

      PROCTOR: It is a pretense, Elizabeth.
      ELIZABETH: What is?
      PROCTOR: I cannot mount the gibbet like a saint. It is
3685   a fraud. I am not that man. (*She is silent.*) My
            honesty is broke, Elizabeth; I am no good man.
            Nothing's spoiled by giving them this lie that
            were not rotten long before.
      ELIZABETH: And yet you've not confessed till now.

            That speak goodness in you.   3690
      PROCTOR: Spite only keeps me silent. It is hard to
            give a lie to dogs. (*Pause, for the first time he
            turns directly to her.*) I would have your forgive-
            ness, Elizabeth.
      ELIZABETH: It is not for me to give, John, I am—   3695
      PROCTOR: I'd have you see some honesty in it. Let
            them that never lied die now to keep their
            souls. It is pretense for me, a vanity that will
            not blind God nor keep my children out of the
            wind. (*Pause.*) What say you?   3700
      ELIZABETH (*upon a heaving sob that always threatens*):
            John, it come to naught that I should forgive
            you, if you'll not forgive yourself. (*Now he turns
            away a little, in great agony.*) It is not my soul,
            John, it is yours. (*He stands, as though in physical 3705
            pain, slowly rising to his feet with a great immortal
            longing to find his answer. It is difficult to say, and
            she is on the verge of tears.*) Only be sure of this,
            for I know it now: Whatever you will do, it is a
            good man does it. (*He turns his doubting, search- 3710
            ing gaze upon her.*) I have read my heart this three
            month, John. (*Pause.*) I have sins of my own to
            count. It needs a cold wife to prompt lechery.
      PROCTOR (*in great pain*): Enough, enough—
      ELIZABETH (*now pouring out her heart*): Better you   3715
            should know me!
      PROCTOR: I will not hear it! I know you!
      ELIZABETH: You take my sins upon you, John—
      PROCTOR (*in agony*): No, I take my own, my own!
      ELIZABETH: John, I counted myself so plain, so poorly   3720
            made, no honest love could come to me!
            Suspicion kissed you when I did; I never knew
            how I should say my love. It were a cold house I
            kept! (*In fright, she swerves, as* HATHORNE *enters.*)
      HATHORNE: What say you, Proctor? The sun is soon up. 3725

*[*PROCTOR, *his chest heaving, stares, turns to*
ELIZABETH. *She comes to him as though to plead, her
voice quaking.]*

      ELIZABETH: Do what you will. But let none be your
            judge. There be no higher judge under Heaven
            than Proctor is! Forgive me, forgive me, John—
            I never knew such goodness in the world! (*She
            covers her face, weeping.*)   3730

*[*PROCTOR *turns from her to* HATHORNE; *he is off the
earth, his voice hollow.]*

      PROCTOR: I want my life.
      HATHORNE (*electrified, surprised*): You'll confess yourself?
      PROCTOR: I will have my life.
      HATHORNE (*with a mystical tone*): God be praised! It is
            a providence! (*He rushes out the door, and his   3735
            voice is heard calling down the corridor:*) He will
            confess! Proctor will confess!

PROCTOR (*with a cry, as he strides to the door*): Why do you cry it? (*In great pain he turns back to her.*) It
3740   is evil, is it not? It is evil.

ELIZABETH (*in terror, weeping*): I cannot judge you, John, I cannot!

PROCTOR: Then who will judge me? (*Suddenly clasping his hands:*) God in Heaven, what is John Proctor,
3745   what is John Proctor? (*He moves as an animal, and a fury is riding in him, a tantalized search.*) I think it is honest, I think so; I am no saint. (*As though she had denied this he calls angrily at her:*) Let Rebecca go like a saint; for me it is fraud!

[*Voices are heard in the hall, speaking together in suppressed excitement.*]

3750   ELIZABETH: I am not your judge, I cannot be. (*As though giving him release:*) Do as you will, do as you will!

PROCTOR: Would you give them such a lie? Say it. Would you ever give them this? (*She cannot
3755   answer.*) You would not; if tongs of fire were singeing you you would not! It is evil. Good, then—it is evil, and I do it!

[HATHORNE *enters with* DANFORTH, *and, with them,* CHEEVER, PARRIS, *and* HALE. *It is a businesslike, rapid entrance, as though the ice had been broken.*]

DANFORTH (*with great relief and gratitude*): Praise to God, man, praise to God; you shall be blessed
3760   in Heaven for this. (CHEEVER *has hurried to the bench with pen, ink, and paper.* PROCTOR *watches him.*) Now then, let us have it. Are you ready, Mr. Cheever?

PROCTOR (*with a cold, cold horror at their efficiency*):
3765   Why must it be written?

DANFORTH: Why, for the good instruction of the village, Mister; this we shall post upon the church door! (*To* PARRIS, *urgently:*) Where is the marshal?

PARRIS (*runs to the door and calls down the corridor*):
3770   Marshal! Hurry!

DANFORTH: Now, then, Mister, will you speak slowly, and directly to the point, for Mr. Cheever's sake. (*He is on record now, and is really dictating to* CHEEVER, *who writes.*) Mr. Proctor, have you
3775   seen the Devil in your life? (PROCTOR'S *jaws lock.*) Come, man, there is light in the sky; the town waits at the scaffold; I would give out this news. Did you see the Devil?

PROCTOR: I did.

3780   PARRIS: Praise God!

DANFORTH: And when he come to you, what were his demand? (PROCTOR *is silent.* DANFORTH *helps.*) Did he bid you to do his work upon the earth?

PROCTOR: He did.

3785   DANFORTH: And you bound yourself to his service?

(DANFORTH *turns, as* REBECCA NURSE *enters, with* HERRICK *helping to support her. She is barely able to walk.*) Come in, come in, woman!

REBECCA (*brightening as she sees* PROCTOR): Ah, John! You are well, then, eh?   3790

[PROCTOR *turns his face to the wall.*]

DANFORTH: Courage, man, courage—let her witness your good example that she may come to God herself. Now hear it, Goody Nurse! Say on, Mr. Proctor. Did you bind yourself to the Devil's service?   3795

REBECCA (*astonished*): Why, John!

PROCTOR (*through his teeth, his face turned from* REBECCA): I did.

DANFORTH: Now, woman, you surely see it profit nothin' to keep this conspiracy any further.   3800
Will you confess yourself with him?

REBECCA: Oh, John—God send his mercy on you!

DANFORTH: I say, will you confess yourself, Goody Nurse?

REBECCA: Why, it is a lie, it is a lie; how may I damn   3805
myself? I cannot, I cannot.

DANFORTH: Mr. Proctor. When the Devil came to you did you see Rebecca Nurse in his company? (PROCTOR *is silent.*) Come, man, take courage—did you ever see her with the Devil?   3810

PROCTOR (*almost inaudibly*): No.

[DANFORTH, *now sensing trouble, glances at* JOHN *and goes to the table, and picks up a sheet—the list of condemned.*]

DANFORTH: Did you ever see her sister, Mary Easty, with the Devil?

PROCTOR: No, I did not.

DANFORTH (*his eyes narrow on* PROCTOR): Did you ever   3815
see Martha Corey with the Devil?

PROCTOR: I did not.

DANFORTH (*realizing, slowly putting the sheet down*): Did you ever see anyone with the Devil?

PROCTOR: I did not.   3820

DANFORTH: Proctor, you mistake me. I am not empowered to trade your life for a lie. You have most certainly seen some person with the Devil. (PROCTOR *is silent.*) Mr. Proctor, a score of people have already testified they saw this   3825
woman with the Devil.

PROCTOR: Then it is proved. Why must I say it?

DANFORTH: Why "must" you say it! Why, you should rejoice to say it if your soul is truly purged of any love for Hell!   3830

PROCTOR: They think to go like saints. I like not to spoil their names.

DANFORTH (*inquiring, incredulous*): Mr. Proctor, do you think they go like saints?

3835   PROCTOR (*evading*): This woman never thought she done the Devil's work.

DANFORTH: Look you, sir. I think you mistake your duty here. It matters nothing what she thought—she is convicted of the unnatural
3840   murder of children, and you for sending your spirit out upon Mary Warren. Your soul alone is the issue here, Mister, and you will prove its whiteness or you cannot live in a Christian country. Will you tell me now what persons
3845   conspired with you in the Devil's company? (PROCTOR *is silent.*) To your knowledge was Rebecca Nurse ever—

PROCTOR: I speak my own sins; I cannot judge another. (*Crying out, with hatred:*) I have no tongue for it.

3850   HALE (*quickly to* DANFORTH): Excellency, it is enough he confess himself. Let him sign it, let him sign it.

PARRIS (*feverishly*): It is a great service, sir. It is a weighty name; it will strike the village that Proctor confess. I beg you, let him sign it. The
3855   sun is up, Excellency!

DANFORTH (*considers; then with dissatisfaction*): Come, then, sign your testimony. (*To* CHEEVER:) Give it to him. (CHEEVER *goes to* PROCTOR, *the confession and a pen in hand.* PROCTOR *does not look at it.*)
3860   Come, man, sign it.

PROCTOR (*after glancing at the confession*): You have all witnessed it—it is enough.

DANFORTH: You will not sign it?

PROCTOR: You have all witnessed it; what more is
3865   needed?

DANFORTH: Do you sport with me? You will sign your name or it is no confession, Mister! (*His breast heaving with agonized breathing,* PROCTOR *now lays the paper down and signs his name.*)

3870   PARRIS: Praise be to the Lord!

[PROCTOR *has just finished signing when* DANFORTH *reaches for the paper. But* PROCTOR *snatches it up, and now a wild terror is rising in him, and a boundless anger.*]

DANFORTH (*perplexed, but politely extending his hand*): If you please, sir.

PROCTOR: No.

DANFORTH (*as though* PROCTOR *did not understand*): Mr.
3875   Proctor, I must have—

PROCTOR: No, no. I have signed it. You have seen me. It is done! You have no need for this.

PARRIS: Proctor, the village must have proof that—

PROCTOR: Damn the village! I confess to God, and
3880   God has seen my name on this! It is enough!

DANFORTH: No, sir, it is—

PROCTOR: You came to save my soul, did you not? Here! I have confessed myself; it is enough!

DANFORTH: You have not con—

3885   PROCTOR: I have confessed myself! Is there no good

penitence but it be public? God does not need my name nailed upon the church! God sees my name; God knows how black my sins are! It is enough!

DANFORTH: Mr. Proctor—   3890

PROCTOR: You will not use me! I am no Sarah Good or Tituba, I am John Proctor! You will not use me! It is no part of salvation that you should use me!

DANFORTH: I do not wish to—

PROCTOR: I have three children—how may I teach   3895
them to walk like men in the world, and I sold my friends?

DANFORTH: You have not sold your friends—

PROCTOR: Beguile me not! I blacken all of them when this is nailed to the church the very day they   3900
hang for silence!

DANFORTH: Mr. Proctor, I must have good and legal proof that you—

PROCTOR: You are the high court, your word is good enough! Tell them I confessed myself; say   3905
Proctor broke his knees and wept like a woman; say what you will, but my name cannot—

DANFORTH (*with suspicion*): It is the same, is it not? If I report it or you sign to it?

PROCTOR—(*he knows it is insane*): No, it is not the   3910
same! What others say and what I sign to is not the same!

DANFORTH: Why? Do you mean to deny this confession when you are free?

PROCTOR: I mean to deny nothing!   3915

DANFORTH: Then explain to me, Mr. Proctor, why you will not let—

PROCTOR (*with a cry of his whole soul*): Because it is my name! Because I cannot have another in my life! Because I lie and sign myself to lies! Because I   3920
am not worth the dust on the feet of them that hang! How may I live without my name? I have given you my soul; leave me my name!

DANFORTH (*pointing at the confession in* PROCTOR'S *hand*): Is that document a lie? If it is a lie I will   3925
not accept it! What say you? I will not deal in lies, Mister! (PROCTOR *is motionless.*) You will give me your honest confession in my hand, or I cannot keep you from the rope. (PROCTOR *does not reply.*) Which way do you go, Mister?   3930

[*His breast heaving, his eyes staring,* PROCTOR *tears the paper and crumples it, and he is weeping in fury, but erect.*]

DANFORTH: Marshal!

PARRIS (*hysterically, as though the tearing paper were his life*): Proctor, Proctor!

HALE: Man, you will hang! You cannot!

PROCTOR (*his eyes full of tears*): I can. And there's your   3935
first marvel, that I can. You have made your magic now, for now I do think I see some

shred of goodness in John Proctor. Not enough
to weave a banner with, but white enough to
3940   keep it from such dogs. (ELIZABETH, *in a burst of*
terror, rushes to him and weeps against his hand.)
Give them no tear! Tears pleasure them! Show
honor now, show a stony heart and sink them
with it! (*He has lifted her, and kisses her now with*
3945   *great passion.*)

REBECCA: Let you fear nothing! Another judgment
waits us all!

DANFORTH: Hang them high over the town! Who
weeps for these, weeps for corruption! (*He*
3950   *sweeps out past them.* HERRICK *starts to lead*
REBECCA, *who almost collapses, but* PROCTOR *catch-*
es her, and she glances up at him apologetically.)

REBECCA: I've had no breakfast.

HERRICK: Come, man.

[HERRICK *escorts them out,* HATHORNE *and* CHEEVER
behind them. ELIZABETH *stands staring at the empty*
doorway.]

3955   PARRIS (*in deadly fear, to* ELIZABETH): Go to him,
Goody Proctor! There is yet time!

[*From outside a drumroll strikes the air.* PARRIS *is star-*
tled. ELIZABETH *jerks about toward the window.*]

PARRIS: Go to him! (*He rushes out the door, as though to*
hold back his fate.) Proctor! Proctor!

[*Again, a short burst of drums.*]

HALE: Woman, plead with him! (*He starts to rush out*
3960   *the door, and then goes back to her.*) Woman! It is
pride, it is vanity. (*She avoids his eyes, and moves*
to the window. He drops to his knees.) Be his
helper!—What profit him to bleed? Shall the
dust praise him? Shall the worms declare his
3965   truth? Go to him, take his shame away!

ELIZABETH (*supporting herself against collapse, grips the*
bars of the window, and with a cry): He have his
goodness now. God forbid I take it from him!

[*The final drumroll crashes, then heightens violently.*
HALE *weeps in frantic prayer, and the new sun is*
pouring in upon her face, and the drums rattle like
bones in the morning air.]

The Curtain Falls

TENNESSEE WILLIAMS

(1911–1983)

Thomas Lanier ("Tennessee") Williams was born in Columbus, Mississippi, but raised in a tenement in St. Louis. He contracted diphtheria as a child, and the disease left him paralyzed and homebound for a period of time during which he read extensively and began to write. A brief stint at the University of Missouri was cut short by his ill health; then he attended Washington University in St. Louis for a while and finally went to the University of Iowa, where he received his degree in playwriting in 1938. Williams had a powerful relationship with his beloved sister, Rose. Subject to serious and chronic depression, she underwent a lobotomy, and the operation left her incapacitated. Rose became the model for some of Williams's most striking women characters—like Laura in *The Glass Menagerie*—women whose inner beauty is too fragile for the brutal world they inhabit, and who are plagued by sexual frustration. In some sense, this was his own story as well. He kept his homosexuality a secret until the 1970s, and in his later life he was institutionalized for alcoholism on several occasions.

Many of the themes of Williams's great plays can be traced to the personal and economic problems of his early life and to his attraction to the faded splendor of his place of birth—the Old South. His first great play, *The Glass Menagerie* (1944), won the coveted New York Drama Critics' Circle Award, establishing his reputation. This was followed by a string of successes that propelled him into the front ranks of American dramatists in this period: *Summer and Smoke* (1947); *A Streetcar Named Desire* (1947), which won a Pulitzer Prize; *The Rose Tatoo* (1951); *Camino Real* (1953); *Cat on a Hot Tin Roof* (1955), another Pulitzer Prize–winning play; *Suddenly, Last Summer* (1958); *Sweet Bird of Youth* (1959); and *The Night of the Iguana* (1961). All are marked with William's special talent for characterization, particularly his characterization of sensitive individuals who are driven by inner passions and are unable to cope in an insensitive world.

Cat on a Hot Tin Roof

Cat on a Hot Tin Roof was Williams's favorite play. He remarked in his memoirs that he managed to give Big Daddy the kind of crude eloquence that he could not give any of his other characters. It is also a very tightly constructed play. According to Williams's notes, the action takes place in a bed-sitting-room along an upstairs gallery once shared by the former owners, two old bachelors whose relationship "involved a tenderness which was uncommon," a relationship that informs Brick's difficulties in the play. The occasion is a family gathering for Big Daddy's sixty-fifth birthday. He is dying of cancer, and the action concerns who is fittest to inherit his fortune.

Big Daddy's sons are disappointments. Gooper, a lawyer who has produced five children to please his father, is dominated by his ambitious wife. Big Daddy's favorite is Brick, a former football star who lost himself in alcohol after the death of his dear friend Skipper, and who now has no apparent ambition—or passion for his wife, Maggie the Cat. Maggie wants to inherit Big Daddy's money, but the only way she can get it is to produce a child. During the play Brick is confined to his room with a broken ankle that he suffered in a drunken competition at the high school track. Maggie tries to rehabilitate Brick, whose latent but unmistakable homosexuality has been compounded by his guilt over Skipper. This real impasse is the center of conflict in the play.

Elia Kazan directed the play in its award-winning expressionistic New York production of 1955, but when Williams first approached him with the idea, Kazan had reservations about the script. He felt that Big Daddy was too brilliant a character to disappear after the second act, and he wanted Brick to change significantly after his interview with Big Daddy in that act. Finally, he wanted Maggie to be a more sympathetic character. Williams made all of the changes, although he personally agreed only with the third, claiming that Maggie the Cat had "become steadily more charming" to him as he worked on her character. When Williams published the play in 1955, he included both versions of Act III. Williams did not want Big Daddy back in Act III, and he felt that Brick's moral paralysis was "a root thing in his tragedy, and to show a dramatic progression would obscure the meaning of that tragedy in him." Further, he did not believe that a conversation, no matter how revelatory, could effect such an immediate change of heart or conduct in a character like Brick.

Cat on a Hot Tin Roof

TENNESSEE WILLIAMS

CHARACTERS

MARGARET
BRICK
MAE, sometimes called Sister Woman
BIG MAMA
DIXIE, a little girl
BIG DADDY

REVEREND TOOKER
GOOPER, sometimes called Brother Man
DOCTOR BAUGH, pronounced "Baw"
LACEY, a Negro servant
SOOKEY, another
CHILDREN

Notes for the Designer

The set is the bed-sitting-room of a plantation home in the Mississippi Delta. It is along an upstairs gallery which probably runs around the entire house; it has two pairs of very wide doors opening onto the gallery, showing white balustrades against a fair summer sky that fades into dusk and night during the course of the play, which occupies precisely the time of its performance, excepting, of course, the fifteen minutes of intermission.

Perhaps the style of the room is not what you would expect in the home of the Delta's biggest cotton-planter. It is Victorian with a touch of the Far East. It hasn't changed much since it was occupied by the original owners of the place, Jack Straw and Peter Ochello, a pair of old bachelors who shared this room all their lives together. In other words, the room must evoke some ghosts; it is gently and poetically haunted by a relationship that must have involved a tenderness which was uncommon. This may be irrelevant or unnecessary, but I once saw a reproduction of a faded photograph of the verandah of Robert Louis Stevenson's home on that Samoan Island where he spent his last years, and there was a quality of tender light on weathered wood, such as porch furniture made of bamboo and wicker, exposed to tropical suns and tropical rains, which came to mind when I thought about the set for this play, bringing also to mind the grace and comfort of light, the reassurance it gives, on a late and fair afternoon in summer, the way that no matter what, even dread of death, is gently touched and soothed by it. For the set is the background for a play that deals with human extremities of emotion, and it needs that softness behind it.

The bathroom door, showing only pale-blue tile and silver towel racks, is in one side wall; the hall door in the opposite wall. Two articles of furniture need mention: a big double bed which staging should make a functional part of the set as often as suitable, the surface of which should be slightly raked to make figures on it seen more easily; and against the wall space between the two huge double doors upstage: a monumental monstrosity peculiar to our times, a *huge* console combination of radio-phonograph (hi-fi with three speakers) TV set *and* liquor cabinet, bearing and containing many glasses and bottles, all in one piece, which is a composition of muted silver tones, and the opalescent tones of reflecting glass, a chromatic link, this thing, between the sepia (tawny gold) tones of the interior and the cool (white and blue) tones of the gallery and sky. This piece of furniture (?!), this monument, is a very complete and compact little shrine to virtually all the comforts and illusions behind which we hide from such things as the characters in the play are faced with. . . .

The set should be far less realistic than I have so far implied in this description of it. I think the walls below the ceiling should dissolve mysteriously into air; the set should be roofed by the sky; stars and moon suggested by traces of milky pallor, as if they were observed through a telescope lens out of focus.

Anything else I can think of? Oh, yes, fanlights (transoms shaped like an open glass fan) above all the doors in the set, with panes of blue and amber, and above all, the designer should take as many pains to give the actors room to move about freely (to show their restlessness, their passion for breaking out) as if it were a set for a ballet.

An evening in summer. The action is continuous, with two intermissions.

ACT I

At the rise of the curtain someone is taking a shower in the bathroom, the door of which is half open. A pretty young woman, with anxious lines in her face, enters the bedroom and crosses to the bathroom door.

MARGARET (*shouting above roar of water*): One of those no-neck monsters hit me with a hot buttered biscuit so I have t' change!

*[*MARGARET*'s voice is both rapid and drawling. In her long speeches she has the vocal tricks of a priest delivering a liturgical chant, the lines are almost sung, always continuing a little beyond her breath so she has to gasp for another. Sometimes she intersperses the lines with a little wordless singing, such as "Da-da-daaaa!"*

Water turns off and BRICK *calls out to her, but is still unseen. A tone of politely feigned interest, masking indifference, or worse, is characteristic of his speech with* MARGARET.*]*

5   BRICK: Wha'd you say, Maggie? Water was on s' loud I couldn't hearya. . . .
MARGARET: Well, I!—just remarked that!—one of th' no-neck monsters messed up m' lovely lace dress so I got t'—cha-a-ange. . . .

[She opens and kicks shut drawers of the dresser.]

10   BRICK: Why d'ya call Gooper's kiddies no-neck monsters?
MARGARET: Because they've got no necks! Isn't that a good enough reason?
BRICK: Don't they have any necks?
MARGARET: None visible. Their fat little heads are set
15   on their fat little bodies without a bit of connection.
BRICK: That's too bad.
MARGARET: Yes, it's too bad because you can't wring their necks if they've got no necks to wring!
20   Isn't that right, honey?

[She steps out of her dress, stands in a slip of ivory satin and lace.]

Yep, they're no-neck monsters, all no-neck people are monsters . . .

[Children shriek downstairs.]

Hear them? Hear them screaming? I don't know where their voice boxes are located since they
25   don't have necks. I tell you I got so nervous at that table tonight I thought I would throw back my head and utter a scream you could

hear across the Arkansas border an' parts of Louisiana an' Tennessee. I said to your charming sister-in-law, Mae, honey, couldn't you   30
feed those precious little things at a separate table with an oilcloth cover? They make such a mess an' the lace cloth looks *so* pretty! She made enormous eyes at me and said, "Ohhh, noooooo! On Big Daddy's birthday? Why, he   35
would never forgive me!" Well, I want you to know, Big Daddy hadn't been at the table two minutes with those five no-neck monsters slobbering and drooling over their food before he threw down his fork an' shouted, "Fo'   40
God's sake, Gooper, why don't you put them pigs at a trough in th' kitchen?"—Well, I swear, I simply could have di-ieed!
Think of it, Brick, they've got five of them and number six is coming. They've brought the   45
whole bunch down here like animals to dis-play at a county fair. Why, they have those children doin' tricks all the time! "Junior, show Big Daddy how you do this, show Big Daddy how you do that, say your little piece fo' Big   50
Daddy, Sister. Show your dimples, Sugar. Brother, show Big Daddy how you stand on your head!"—It goes on all the time, along with constant little remarks and innuendos about the fact that you and I have not pro-   55
duced any children, are totally childless and therefore totally useless!—Of course it's comi-cal but it's also disgusting since it's so obvious what they're up to!
BRICK (*without interest*): What are they up to, Maggie?   60
MARGARET: Why, you know what they're up to!
BRICK (*appearing*): No, I don't know what they're up to.

[He stands there in the bathroom doorway drying his hair with a towel and hanging onto the towel rack because one ankle is broken, plastered and bound. He is still slim and firm as a boy. His liquor hasn't started tearing him down outside. He has the additional charm of that cool air of detachment that people have who have given up the struggle. But now and then, when disturbed, something flashes behind it, like light-ning in a fair sky, which shows that at some deeper level he is far from peaceful. Perhaps in a stronger light he would show some signs of deliquescence, but the fading, still warm, light from the gallery treats him gently.]

MARGARET: I'll tell you what they're up to, boy of mine!—They're up to cutting you out of your father's estate, and—   65

[She freezes momentarily before her next remark. Her voice drops as if it were somehow a personally embarrassing admission.]

—Now we know that Big Daddy's dyin' of—
 cancer. . . .

[*There are voices on the lawn below: long-drawn calls across distance.* MARGARET *raises her lovely bare arms and powders her armpits with a light sigh.*

She adjusts the angle of a magnifying mirror to straighten an eyelash, then rises fretfully saying:*]

There's so much light in the room it—
BRICK (*softly but sharply*): Do we?
70 MARGARET: Do we what?
BRICK: Know Big Daddy's dyin' of cancer?
MARGARET: Got the report today.
BRICK: Oh. . .
MARGARET (*letting down bamboo blinds which cast long,*
75 *gold-fretted shadows over the room*): Yep, got th'
 report just now. . . it didn't surprise me,
 Baby. . . .

[*Her voice has range, and music; sometimes it drops low as a boy's and you have a sudden image of her playing boy's games as a child.*]

 I recognized the symptoms soon's we got here
 last spring and I'm willin' to bet you that
80 Brother Man and his wife were pretty sure of
 it, too. That more than likely explains why
 their usual summer migration to the coolness
 of the Great Smokies was passed up this summer in favor of—hustlin' down here ev'ry
85 whipstitch with their whole screamin' tribe!
 And why so many allusions have been made
 to Rainbow Hill lately. You know what
 Rainbow Hill is? Place that's famous for
 treatin' alcoholics an dope fiends in the
90 movies!
BRICK: I'm not in the movies.
MARGARET: No, and you don't take dope. Otherwise
 you're a perfect candidate for Rainbow Hill,
 Baby, and that's where they aim to ship you—
95 over my dead body! Yep, over my dead body
 they'll ship you there, but nothing would
 please them better. Then Brother Man could get
 a-hold of the purse strings and dole out remittances to us, maybe get power of attorney and
100 sign checks for us and cut off our credit wherever, whenever he wanted! Son-of-a-bitch!—
 How'd you like that, Baby?—Well, you've been
 doin' just about ev'rything in your power to
 bring it about, you've just been doin' ev'ry-
105 thing you can think of to aid and abet them in
 this scheme of theirs! Quittin' work, devoting
 yourself to the occupation of drinkin'!—
 Breakin' your ankle last night on the high
 school athletic field: doin' what? Jumpin' hur-

dles? At two or three in the morning? Just fan- 110
tastic! Got in the paper. *Clarksdale Register* carried a nice little item about it, human interest
story about a well-known former athlete stagin'
a one-man track meet on the Glorious Hill
High School athletic field last night, but was 115
slightly out of condition and didn't clear the
first hurdle! Brother Man Gooper claims he
exercised his influence t' keep it from goin' out
over AP or UP or every goddam "P."
But, Brick? You still have one big advantage! 120

[*During the above swift flood of words,* BRICK *has reclined with contrapuntal leisure on the snowy sur-face of the bed and has rolled over carefully on his side or belly.*]

BRICK (*wryly*): Did you *say* something, Maggie?
MARGARET: Big Daddy dotes on you, honey. And he
 can't stand Brother Man and Brother Man's
 wife, that monster of fertility, Mae. Know how
 I know? By little expressions that flicker over 125
 his face when that woman is holding fo'th on
 one of her choice topics such as—how she
 refused twilight sleep!—when the twins were
 delivered! Because she feels motherhood's an
 experience that a woman ought to experience 130
 fully!—in order to fully appreciate the wonder
 and beauty of it! HAH!—and how she made
 Brother Man come in an' stand beside her in
 the delivery room so he would not miss out on
 the "wonder and beauty" of it either!—pro- 135
 ducin' those no-neck monsters. . . .

[*A speech of this kind would be antipathetic from almost anybody but* MARGARET; *she makes it oddly funny, because her eyes constantly twinkle and her voice shakes with laughter which is basically indulgent.*]

 —Big Daddy shares my attitude toward those
 two! As for me, well—I give him a laugh now
 and then and he tolerates me. In fact!—I sometimes suspect that Big Daddy harbors a little 140
 unconscious "lech" fo' me. . . .
BRICK: What makes you think that Big Daddy has a
 lech for you, Maggie?
MARGARET: Way he always drops his eyes down my
 body when I'm talkin' to him, drops his eyes 145
 to my boobs an' licks his old chops! Ha ha!
BRICK: That kind of talk is disgusting.
MARGARET: Did anyone ever tell you that you're an
 ass-aching Puritan, Brick?
 I think it's mighty fine that that ole fellow, on the 150
 doorstep of death, still takes in my shape with
 what I think is deserved appreciation!
 And you wanta know something else? Big Daddy
 didn't know how many little Maes and

155 Goopers had been produced! "How many kids have you got?" he asked at the table, just like Brother Man and his wife were new acquaintances to him! Big Mama said he was jokin', but that ole boy wasn't jokin', Lord, no!

160 And when they infawmed him that they had five already and were turning out number six!—the news seemed to come as a sort of unpleasant surprise. . .

[Children yell below.]

Scream, monsters!

[Turns to BRICK *with a sudden, gay, charming smile which fades as she notices that he is not looking at her but into fading gold space with a troubled expression.*

It is constant rejection that makes her humor "bitchy."]

165 Yes, you should of been at that supper-table, Baby.

[Whenever she calls him "baby" the word is a soft caress.]

Y'know, Big Daddy, bless his ole sweet soul, he's the dearest ole thing in the world, but he does hunch over his food as if he preferred not to notice anything else. Well, Mae an' Gooper
170 were side by side at the table, directly across from Big Daddy, watchin' his face like hawks while they jawed an' jabbered about the cuteness an' brillance of th' no-neck monsters!

[She giggles with a hand fluttering at her throat and her breast and her long throat arched.

She comes downstage and recreates the scene with voice and gesture.]

And the no-neck monsters were ranged around the
175 table, some in high chairs and some on th' *Books of Knowledge,* all in fancy little paper caps in honor of Big Daddy's birthday, and all through dinner, well, I want you to know that Brother Man an' his partner never once, for one
180 moment, stopped exchanging pokes an' pinches an' kicks an' signs an' signals!—Why, they were like a couple of cardsharps fleecing a sucker.—Even Big Mama, bless her ole sweet soul, she isn't th' quickest an' brightest thing in the
185 world, she finally noticed, at last, an' said to Gooper, "Gooper, what are you an' Mae makin' all these signs at each other about?"—I swear t' goodness, I nearly choked on my chicken!

*[*MARGARET, *back at the dressing table, still doesn't see* BRICK. *He is watching her with a look that is not quite*

definable—*Amused? shocked? contemptuous?*—*part of those and part of something else.]*

Y'know—your brother Gooper still cherishes the illusion he took a giant step up on the social 190 ladder when he married Miss Mae Flynn of the Memphis Flynns.
But I have a piece of Spanish news for Gooper. The Flynns never had a thing in this world but money and they lost that, they were nothing at 195 all but fairly successful climbers. Of course, Mae Flynn came out in Memphis eight years before I made my debut in Nashville, but I had friends at Ward-Belmont who came from Memphis and they used to come to see me and I used to go to 200 see them for Christmas and spring vacations, and so I know who rates an' who doesn't rate in Memphis society. Why, y'know ole Papa Flynn, he barely escaped doing time in the Federal pen for shady manipulations on th' stock market 205 when his chain stores crashed, and as for Mae having been a cotton carnival queen, as they remind us so often, lest we forget, well, that's one honor that I don't envy her for!—Sit on a brass throne on a tacky float an' ride down Main 210 Street, smilin', bowin', and blowin' kisses to all the trash on the street—

[She picks out a pair of jeweled sandals and rushes to the dressing table.]

Why, year before last, when Susan McPheeters was singled out fo' that honor, y' know what happened to her? Y'know what happened to 215 poor little Susie McPheeters?

BRICK *(absently)*: No. What happened to little Susie McPheeters?

MARGARET: Somebody spit tobacco juice in her face.

BRICK *(dreamily)*: Somebody spit tobacco juice in her 220 face?

MARGARET: That's right, some old drunk leaned out of a window in the Hotel Gayoso and yelled, "Hey, Queen, hey, hey, there, Queenie!" Poor Susie looked up and flashed him a radiant 225 smile and he shot out a squirt of tobacco juice right in poor Susie's face.

BRICK: Well, what d'you know about that.

MARGARET *(gaily)*: What do I know about it? I was there, I saw it! 230

BRICK *(absently)*: Must have been kind of funny.

MARGARET: Susie didn't think so. Had hysterics. Screamed like a banshee. They had to stop th' parade an' remove her from her throne an' go on with— 235

[She catches sight of him in the mirror, gasps slightly, wheels about to face him. Count ten.]

—Why are you looking at me like that?

240 BRICK (*whistling softly, now*): Like what, Maggie?

MARGARET (*intensely, fearfully*): The way y' were lookin' at me just now, befo' I caught your eye in the mirror and you started t' whistle! I don't know how t' describe it but it froze my

245 blood!—I've caught you lookin' at me like that so often lately. What are you thinkin' of when you look at me like that?

BRICK: I wasn't conscious of lookin' at you, Maggie.

MARGARET: Well, I was conscious of it! What were

250 you thinkin'?

BRICK: I don't remember thinking of anything, Maggie.

MARGARET: Don't you think I know that—? Don't you—?—Think I know that—?

BRICK (*coolly*): Know *what*, Maggie?

255 MARGARET (*struggling for expression*): That I've gone through this—*hideous!*—transformation, become—*hard! Frantic!*

[*Then she adds, almost tenderly:*]

—*cruel!!*

That's what you've been observing in me lately.

260 How could y' help but observe it? That's all right. I'm not—thin-skinned any more, can't afford t' be thin-skinned any more.

[*She is now recovering her power.*]

—But Brick? Brick?

BRICK: Did you say something?

265 MARGARET: I was *goin'* t' say something: that I get— lonely. Very!

BRICK: Ev'rybody gets that. . .

MARGARET: Living with someone you love can be lonelier—than living entirely *alone!*—if the one

270 that y' love doesn't love you. . . .

[*There is a pause.* BRICK *hobbles downstage and asks, without looking at her:*]

BRICK: Would you like to live alone, Maggie?

[*Another pause: then—after she has caught a quick, hurt breath:*]

MARGARET: *No!—God!—God!—I wouldn't!*

[*Another gasping breath. She forcibly controls what must have been an impulse to cry out. We see her deliberately, very forcibly, going all the way back to the world in which you can talk about ordinary matters.*]

Did you have a nice shower?

BRICK: Uh-huh.

275 MARGARET: Was the water cool?

BRICK: No.

MARGARET: But it made y' feel fresh, huh?

BRICK: Fresher. . . .

MARGARET: I know something would make y' feel *much* fresher! 280

BRICK: What?

MARGARET: An alcohol rub. Or cologne, a rub with cologne!

BRICK: That's good after a workout but I haven't been workin' out, Maggie. 285

MARGARET: You've kept in good shape, though.

BRICK (*indifferently*): You think so, Maggie?

MARGARET: I always thought drinkin' men lost their looks, but I was plainly mistaken.

BRICK (*wryly*): Why, thanks, Maggie. 290

MARGARET: You're the only drinkin' man I know that it never seems t' put fat on.

BRICK: I'm gettin' softer, Maggie.

MARGARET: Well, sooner or later it's bound to soften you up. It was just beginning to soften up 295 Skipper when—

[*She stops short.*]

I'm sorry. I never could keep my fingers off a sore—I wish you *would* lose your looks. If you did it would make the martyrdom of Saint Maggie a little more bearable. But no such 300 goddam luck. I actually believe you've gotten better looking since you've gone on the bottle. Yeah, a person who didn't know you would think you'd never had a tense nerve in your body or a strained muscle. 305

[*There are sounds of croquet on the lawn below: the click of mallets, light voices, near and distant.*]

Of course, you always had that detached quality as if you were playing a game without much concern over whether you won or lost, and now that you've lost the game, not lost but just quit playing, you have that rare sort of charm 310 that usually only happens in very old or hope-lessly sick people, the charm of the defeated.— You look so cool, so cool, so enviably cool.

REVEREND TOOKER (*off stage right*): Now looka here, boy, lemme show you how to get outa that! 315

MARGARET: They're playing croquet. The moon has appeared and it's white, just beginning to turn a little bit yellow. . . .

You were a wonderful lover. . . .

Such a wonderful person to go to bed with, and I 320 think mostly because you were really indiffer-ent to it. Isn't that right? Never had any anxi-ety about it, did it naturally, easily, slowly, with absolute confidence and perfect calm, more like opening a door for a lady or seating 325 her at a table than giving expression to any longing for her. Your indifference made you wonderful at lovemaking—*strange?*—but true.

. . .

330   REVEREND TOOKER: Oh! That's a beauty.

DOCTOR BAUGH: Yeah. I got you boxed.

MARGARET: You know, if I thought you would never, never, *never*, make love to me again—I would go downstairs to the kitchen and pick out the

335   longest and sharpest knife I could find and stick it straight into my heart, I swear that I would!

REVEREND TOOKER: Watch out, you're gonna miss it.

DOCTOR BAUGH: You just don't know me, boy!

MARGARET: But one thing I don't have is the charm

340   of the defeated, my hat is still in the ring, and I am determined to win!

[There is the sound of croquet mallets hitting croquet balls.]

REVEREND TOOKER: Mmm—You're too slippery for me.

MARGARET: —What is the victory of a cat on a hot tin roof?—I wish I knew. . . .

345   Just staying on it, I guess, as long as she can. . . .

DOCTOR BAUGH: Jus' like an eel, boy, jus' like an eel!

[More croquet sounds.]

MARGARET: Later tonight I'm going to tell you I love you an' maybe by that time you'll be drunk enough to believe me. Yes, they're playing cro-

350   quet. . . .

Big Daddy is dying of cancer. . . .

What were you thinking of when I caught you looking at me like that? Were you thinking of Skipper?

[BRICK takes up his crutch, rises.]

355   Oh, excuse me, forgive me, but laws of silence don't work! No, laws of silence don't work. . . .

[BRICK crosses to the bar, takes a quick drink, and rubs his head with a towel.]

Laws of silence don't work. . . .

When something is festering in your memory or your imagination, laws of silence don't work, it's

360   just like shutting a door and locking it on a house on fire in hope of forgetting that the house is burning. But not facing a fire doesn't put it out. Silence about a thing just magnifies it. It grows and festers in silence, becomes malignant. . . .

[He drops his crutch.]

365   BRICK: Give me my crutch.

[He has stopped rubbing his hair dry but still stands hanging onto the towel rack in a white towel-cloth robe.]

MARGARET: Lean on me.

BRICK: No, just give me my crutch.

MARGARET: Lean on my shoulder.

BRICK: *I don't want to lean on your shoulder, I want my crutch!*   370

[This is spoken like sudden lightning.]

Are you going to give me my crutch or do I have to get down on my knees on the floor and—

MARGARET: *Here, here, take it, take it!*

[She has thrust the crutch at him.]

BRICK (*hobbling out*): Thanks. . . .

MARGARET: We mustn't scream at each other, the   375 walls in this house have ears. . . .

[He hobbles directly to liquor cabinet to get a new drink.]

—but that's the first time I've heard you raise your voice in a long time, Brick. A crack in the wall?—Of composure?

—I think that's a good sign. . . .   380

A sign of nerves in a player on the defensive!

[BRICK turns and smiles at her coolly over his fresh drink.]

BRICK: It just hasn't happened yet, Maggie.

MARGARET: What?

BRICK: The click I get in my head when I've had enough of this stuff to make me peaceful. . . .   385

Will you do me a favor?

MARGARET: Maybe I will. What favor?

BRICK: Just, just keep your voice down!

MARGARET (*in a hoarse whisper*): I'll do you that favor, I'll speak in a whisper, if not shut up complete-   390 ly, if *you* will do *me* a favor and make that drink your last one till after the party.

BRICK: What party?

MARGARET: Big Daddy's birthday party.

BRICK: Is this Big Daddy's birthday?   395

MARGARET: You know this is Big Daddy's birthday!

BRICK: No, I don't, I forgot it.

MARGARET: Well, I remembered it for you. . . .

[They are both speaking as breathlessly as a pair of kids after a fight, drawing deep exhausted breaths and looking at each other with faraway eyes, shaking and panting together as if they had broken apart from a violent struggle.]

BRICK: Good for you, Maggie.

400 MARGARET: You just have to scribble a few lines on
        this card.
      BRICK: You scribble something, Maggie.
      MARGARET: It's got to be your handwriting; it's your
        present, I've given him my present; it's got to
405   be your handwriting!

[*The tension between them is building again, the voices becoming shrill once more.*]

      BRICK: I didn't get him a present.
      MARGARET: I got one for you.
      BRICK: All right. You write the card, then.
      MARGARET: And have him know you didn't remem-
410   ber his birthday?
      BRICK: I didn't remember his birthday.
      MARGARET: You don't have to prove you didn't!
      BRICK: I don't want to fool him about it.
      MARGARET: Just write "Love, Brick!" for God's—
415 BRICK: No.
      MARGARET: You've *got* to!
      BRICK: I don't have to do anything I don't want to
        do. You keep forgetting the conditions on
        which I agreed to stay on living with you.
420 MARGARET (*out before she knows it*): I'm not living with
        you. We occupy the same cage.
      BRICK: You've got to remember the conditions agreed on.
      SONNY (*off stage*): Mommy, give it to me. I had it first.
      MAE: Hush.
425 MARGARET: They're impossible conditions!
      BRICK: Then why don't you—?
      SONNY: I want it, I want it!
      MAE: Get away!
      MARGARET: HUSH! Who is out there? Is somebody at
430   the door?

[*There are footsteps in hall.*]

      MAE (*outside*): May I enter a moment?
      MARGARET: Oh, *you*! Sure. Come in, Mae.

[MAE *enters bearing aloft the bow of a young lady's archery set.*]

      MAE: Brick, is this thing yours?
      MARGARET: Why, Sister Woman—that's my Diana
435   Trophy. Won it at the intercollegiate archery
        contest on the Ole Miss campus.
      MAE: It's a mighty dangerous thing to leave exposed
        round a house full of nawmal rid-blooded chil-
        dren attracted t'weapons.
440 MARGARET: "Nawmal rid-blooded children attracted
        t'weapons" ought t'be taught to keep their
        hands off things that don't belong to them.
      MAE: Maggie, honey, if you had children of your own
        you'd know how funny that is. Will you please
445   lock this up and put the key out of reach?

      MARGARET: Sister Woman, nobody is plotting the
        destruction of your kiddies.—Brick and I still
        have our special archers' license. We're goin'
        deer-huntin' on Moon Lake as soon as the sea-
        son starts. I love to run with dogs through   450
        chilly woods, run, run leap over obstructions—

[*She goes into the closet carrying the bow.*]

      MAE: How's the injured ankle, Brick?
      BRICK: Doesn't hurt. Just itches.
      MAE: Oh, my! Brick—Brick, you should've been
        downstairs after supper! Kiddies put on a   455
        show. Polly played the piano, Buster an' Sonny
        drums, an' then they turned out the lights an'
        Dixie an' Trixie puhfawmed a toe dance in
        fairy costume with *spahkluhs*! Big Daddy just
        beamed! He just beamed!   460
      MARGARET (*from the closet with a sharp laugh*): Oh, I
        bet. It breaks my heart that we missed it!

[*She reenters.*]

      But Mae? Why did y'give dawgs' names to all
        your kiddies?
      MAE: *Dogs'* names?   465
      MARGARET (*sweetly*): Dixie, Trixie, Buster, Sonny,
        Polly!—Sounds like four dogs and a parrot . . .
      MAE: Maggie?

[MARGARET *turns with a smile.*]

      Why are you so catty?
      MARGARET: Cause I'm a cat! But why can't *you* take a   470
        joke, Sister Woman?
      MAE: Nothin' pleases me more than a joke that's
        funny. You know the real names of our kid-
        dies. Buster's real name is Robert. Sonny's real
        name is Saunders. Trixie's real name is   475
        Marlene and Dixie's—

[GOOPER *downstairs calls for her.* "Hey, Mae! Sister Woman, intermission is over!"—*She rushes to door, saying:*]

      Intermission is over! See ya later!
      MARGARET: I wonder what Dixie's real name is?
      BRICK: Maggie, being catty doesn't help things any. . .
      MARGARET: I know! WHY!—Am I so catty?—Cause   480
        I'm consumed with envy an' eaten up with
        longing?—Brick, I'm going to lay out your
        beautiful Shantung silk suit from Rome and
        one of your monogrammed silk shirts. I'll put
        your cuff links in it, those lovely star sapphires   485
        I get you to wear so rarely. . . .
      BRICK: I can't get trousers on over this plaster cast.
      MARGARET: Yes, you can, I'll help you.

BRICK: I'm not going to get dressed, Maggie.

490 MARGARET: Will you just put on a pair of white silk pajamas?

BRICK: Yes, I'll do that, Maggie.

MARGARET: *Thank* you, thank you so *much!*

BRICK: Don't mention it.

495 MARGARET: *Oh, Brick!* How long does it have t' go on? This punishment? Haven't I done time enough, haven't I served my term, can't I apply for a—pardon?

BRICK: Maggie, you're spoiling my liquor. Lately 500 your voice always sounds like you'd been running upstairs to warn somebody that the house was on fire!

MARGARET: Well, no wonder, no wonder. Y'know what I feel like, Brick?

505 *I feel all the time like a cat on a hot tin roof!*

BRICK: Then jump off the roof, jump off it, cats can jump off roofs and land on their four feet uninjured!

MARGARET: Oh, yes!

510 BRICK: Do it!—fo' God's sake, do it . . .

MARGARET: Do what?

BRICK: Take a lover!

MARGARET: I can't see a man but you! Even with my eyes closed, I just see you! Why don't you get 515 ugly, Brick, why don't you please get fat or ugly or something so I could stand it?

[She rushes to hall door, opens it, listens.]

The concert is still going on! Bravo, no-necks, bravo!

[She slams and locks door fiercely.]

BRICK: What did you lock the door for?

520 MARGARET: To give us a little privacy for a while.

BRICK: You know better, Maggie.

MARGARET: No, I don't know better. . . .

[She rushes to gallery doors, draws the rose-silk drapes across them.]

BRICK: Don't make a fool of yourself.

MARGARET: I don't mind makin' a fool of myself over 525 you!

BRICK: I mind, Maggie. I feel embarrassed for you.

MARGARET: Feel embarrassed! But don't continue my torture. I can't live on and on under these circumstances.

530 BRICK: You agreed to—

MARGARET: I know but—

BRICK: —Accept that condition!

MARGARET: I CAN'T! CAN'T! CAN'T!

[She seizes his shoulder.]

BRICK: Let go!

[He breaks away from her and seizes the small boudoir chair and raises it like a lion-tamer facing a big circus cat.

Count five. She stares at him with her fist pressed to her mouth, then bursts into shrill, almost hysterical laughter. He remains grave for a moment, then grins and puts the chair down.]

[BIG MAMA calls through closed door.]

BIG MAMA: Son? Son? Son? 535

BRICK: What is it, Big Mama?

BIG MAMA (*outside*): Oh, son! We got the most wonderful news about Big Daddy. I just had t' run up an' tell you right this—

[She rattles the knob.]

—What's this door doin', locked, faw? You all 540 think there's robbers in the house?

MARGARET: Big Mama, Brick is dressin', he's not dressed yet.

BIG MAMA: That's all right, it won't be the first time I've seen Brick not dressed. Come on, open 545 this door!

[MARGARET, with a grimace, goes to unlock and open the hall door, as BRICK hobbles rapidly to the bathroom and kicks the door shut. BIG MAMA has disappeared from the hall.]

MARGARET: Big Mama?

[BIG MAMA appears through the opposite gallery doors behind MARGARET, huffing and puffing like an old bulldog. She is a short, stout woman; her sixty years and 170 pounds have left her somewhat breathless most of the time; she's always tensed like a boxer, or rather, a Japanese wrestler. Her "family" was maybe a little superior to BIG DADDY's, but not much. She wears a black or silver lace dress and at least half a million in flashy gems. She is very sincere.]

BIG MAMA (*loudly, startling* MARGARET): Here—I come through Gooper's and Mae's gall'ry door. Where's Brick? *Brick*—Hurry on out of there, 550 son, I just have a second and want to give you the news about Big Daddy.—I hate locked doors in a house. . . .

MARGARET (*with affected lightness*): I've noticed you do, Big Mama, but people have got to have 555 *some* moments of privacy, don't they?

BIG MAMA: No, ma'am, not in *my* house. (*without pause*) Whacha took off you' dress faw? I thought that little lace dress was so sweet on

560   yuh, honey.
      MARGARET: I thought it looked sweet on me, too, but
            one of m' cute little table-partners used it for a
            napkin so—!
      BIG MAMA (*picking up stockings on floor*): What?
565   MARGARET: You know, Big Mama, Mae and Gooper's
            so touchy about those children—thanks, Big
            Mama . . .

*[BIG MAMA has thrust the picked-up stockings in
MARGARET's hand with a grunt.]*

      —that you just don't dare to suggest there's any
            room for improvement in their—
570   BIG MAMA: Brick, hurry out!—Shoot, Maggie, you
            just don't like children.
      MARGARET: I DO SO like children! Adore them!—well
            brought up!
      BIG MAMA (*gentle—loving*): Well, why don't you have
575   some and bring them up well, then, instead of
            all the time pickin' on Gooper's an' Mae's?
      GOOPER (*shouting up the stairs*): Hey, hey, Big Mama,
            Betsy an' Hugh got to go, waitin' t' tell yuh g'by!
      BIG MAMA: Tell 'em to hold their hawses, I'll be right
580   down in a jiffy!
      GOOPER: Yes ma'am!

[She turns to the bathroom door and calls out.]

      BIG MAMA: Son? Can you hear me in there?

[There is a muffled answer.]

      We just got the full report from the laboratory at
            the Ochsner Clinic, completely negative, son,
585   ev'rything negative, right on down the line!
            Nothin' a-tall's wrong with him but some little
            functional thing called a spastic colon. Can
            you hear me, son?
      MARGARET: He can hear you, Big Mama.
590   BIG MAMA: Then why don't he say something? God
            Almighty, a piece of news like that should
            make him shout. It made *me* shout, I can tell
            you. I shouted and sobbed and fell right down
            on my knees!—Look!

[She pulls up her skirt.]

595   See the bruises where I hit my kneecaps? Took
            both doctors to haul me back on my feet!

[She laughs—she always laughs like hell at herself.]

      Big Daddy was furious with me! But ain't that
            wonderful news?

[Facing bathroom again, she continues:]

After all the anxiety we been through to git a
      report like that on Big Daddy's birthday? Big
      Daddy tried to hide how much of a load that
      news took off his mind, but didn't fool *me*. He
      was mighty close to crying about it *himself!*   600

*[Goodbyes are shouted downstairs, and she rushes to
door.]*

GOOPER: Big Mama!
BIG MAMA: *Hold those people down there, don't let them*   605
      go!—Now, git dressed, we're all comin' up to
      this room fo' Big Daddy's birthday party
      because of your ankle.—How's his ankle,
      Maggie?
MARGARET: Well, he broke it, Big Mama.   610
BIG MAMA: I know he broke it.

*[A phone is ringing in hall. A Negro voice answers:
"Mistuh Polly's res'dence."]*

I mean does it hurt him much still.
MARGARET: I'm afraid I can't give you that informa-
      tion, Big Mama. You'll have to ask Brick if it
      hurts much still or not.   615
SOOKEY (*in the hall*): It's Memphis, Mizz Polly, it's
      Miss Sally in Memphis.
BIG MAMA: Awright, Sookey.

*[BIG MAMA rushes into the hall and is heard shouting
on the phone:]*

Hello, Miss Sally. How are you, Miss Sally?—Yes,
      well, I was just gonna call you about it.   620
      Shoot!—
MARGARET: Brick, don't!

[BIG MAMA raises her voice to a bellow.]

BIG MAMA: *Miss Sally? Don't ever call me from the*
      Gayoso Lobby, too much talk goes on in that hotel
      lobby, no wonder you can't hear me! Now listen,   625
      Miss Sally. They's nothin' serious wrong with
      Big Daddy. We got the report just now, they's
      nothin' wrong but a thing called a—spastic!
      SPASTIC!—colon . . .

[She appears at the hall door and calls to MARGARET.]

—Maggie, come out here and talk to that fool on   630
      the phone. I'm shouted breathless!
MARGARET (*goes out and is heard sweetly at phone*):
      Miss Sally? This is Brick's wife, Maggie. So
      nice to hear your voice. Can you hear *mine?*
      Well, *good!*—Big Mama just wanted you to   635
      know that they've got the report from the
      Ochsner Clinic and what Big Daddy has is a

spastic colon. Yes. Spastic colon, Miss Sally.
  That's right, spastic colon. *G'bye, Miss Sally,*
  640 *hope I'll see you real soon!*

[*Hangs up a little before* MISS SALLY *was probably
ready to terminate the talk. She returns through the
hall door.*]

She heard me perfectly. I've discovered with deaf
  people the thing to do is not shout at them but
  just enunciate clearly. My rich old Aunt
  Cornelia was deaf as the dead but I could make
  645 her hear me just by sayin' each word slowly,
  distinctly, close to her ear. I read her the
  Commercial Appeal ev'ry night, read her the
  classified ads in it, even, she never missed a
  word of it. But was she a mean ole thing! Know
  650 what I got when she died? Her unexpired subscriptions to five magazines and the Book-of-
  the-Month Club and a LIBRARY full of ev'ry dull
  book ever written! All else went to her hellcat
  of a sister . . . meaner than she was, even!

[BIG MAMA *has been straightening things up in the
room during this speech.*]

655 BIG MAMA (*closing closet door on discarded clothes*):
  Miss Sally sure is a case! Big Daddy says she's
  always got her hand out fo' something. He's
  not mistaken. That poor ole thing always has
  her hand out fo' somethin'. I don't think Big
  660 Daddy gives her as much as he should.
  GOOPER: Big Mama! Come on now! Betsy and Hugh
  can't wait no longer!
  BIG MAMA (*shouting*): I'm comin'!

[*She starts out. At the hall door, turns and jerks a forefinger, first toward the bathroom door, then toward the
liquor cabinet, meaning: "Has Brick been drinking?"*
MARGARET *pretends not to understand, cocks her head
and raises her brows as if the pantomimic performance
was completely mystifying to her.*]

BIG MAMA *rushes back to* MARGARET:]

Shoot! Stop playin' so dumb!—I mean has he been
  665 drinkin' that stuff much yet?
  MARGARET (*with a little laugh*): Oh! I think he had a
  highball after supper.
  BIG MAMA: Don't laugh about it!—Some single men
  stop drinkin' when they git married and others
  670 start! Brick never touched liquor before he—!
  MARGARET (*crying out*): THAT'S NOT FAIR!
  BIG MAMA: Fair or not fair I want to ask you a question,
  one question: D'you make Brick happy in bed?
  MARGARET: Why don't you ask if he makes *me* happy
  675 in bed?

BIG MAMA: Because I know that—
  MARGARET: *It works both ways!*
  BIG MAMA: Something's not right! You're childless
  and my son drinks!
  GOOPER: Come on, Big Mama!   680

[GOOPER *has called her downstairs and she has rushed
to the door on the line above. She turns at the door
and points at the bed.*]

—When a marriage goes on the rocks, the rocks
  are *there*, right *there!*
  MARGARET: *That's*—

[BIG MAMA *has swept out of the room and slammed the
door.*]

—not—*fair* . . .

[MARGARET *is alone, completely alone, and she feels it.
She draws in, hunches her shoulders, raises her arms
with fists clenched, shuts her eyes tight as a child
about to be stabbed with a vaccination needle. When
she opens her eyes again, what she sees is the long
oval mirror and she rushes straight to it, stares into it
with a grimace and says: "Who are you?"—Then she
crouches a little and answers herself in a different
voice which is high, thin, mocking: "I am Maggie the
Cat!"—Straightens quickly as bathroom door opens a
little and* BRICK *calls out to her.*]

BRICK: Has Big Mama gone?   685
  MARGARET: She's gone.

[*He opens the bathroom door and hobbles out, with
his liquor glass now empty, straight to the liquor cabinet. He is whistling softly.* MARGARET*'s head pivots on
her long, slender throat to watch him.*

*She raises a hand uncertainly to the base of her throat,
as if it was difficult for her to swallow, before she speaks:*]

You know, our sex life didn't just peter out in the
  usual way, it was cut off short, long before the
  natural time for it to, and it's going to revive
  again, just as sudden as that. I'm confident of it.   690
  That's what I'm keeping myself attractive for. For
  the time when you'll see me again like other men
  see me. Yes, like other men see me. They still see
  me, Brick, and they like what they see. Uh-huh.
  Some of them would give their—Look, Brick!   695

[*She stands before the long oval mirror, touches her
breast and then her hips with her two hands.*]

How high my body stays on me!—Nothing has
  fallen on me—not a fraction. . . .

[Her voice is soft and trembling: a pleading child's. At this moment as he turns to glance at her—a look which is like a player passing a ball to another player, third down and goal to go—she has to capture the audience in a grip so tight that she can hold it till the first intermission without any lapse of attention.]

700 Other men still want me. My face looks strained, sometimes, but I've kept my figure as well as you've kept yours, and men admire it. I still turn heads on the street. Why, last week in Memphis everywhere that I went men's eyes burned holes in my clothes, at the country club and in restaurants and department stores,
705 there wasn't a man I met or walked by that didn't just eat me up with his eyes and turn around when I passed him and look back at me. Why, at Alice's party for her New York cousins, the best-lookin' man in the crowd—
710 followed me upstairs and tried to force his way in the powder room with me, followed me to the door and tried to force his way in!
BRICK: Why didn't you let him, Maggie?
MARGARET: Because I'm not that common, for one
715 thing. Not that I wasn't almost tempted to. You like to know who it was? It was Sonny Boy Maxwell, that's who!
BRICK: Oh, yeah, Sonny Boy Maxwell, he was a good end-runner but had a little injury to his back
720 and had to quit.
MARGARET: He has no injury now and has no wife and still has a lech for me!
BRICK: I see no reason to lock him out of a powder room in that case.
725 MARGARET: And have someone catch me at it? I'm not that stupid. Oh, I might sometime cheat on you with someone, since you're so insultingly eager to have me do it!—But if I do, you can be damned sure it will be in a place and a time
730 where no one but me and the man could possibly know. Because I'm not going to give you any excuse to divorce me for being unfaithful or anything else. . . .
BRICK: Maggie, I wouldn't divorce you for being
735 unfaithful or anything else. Don't you know that? Hell. I'd be relieved to know that you'd found yourself a lover.
MARGARET: Well, I'm taking no chances. No, I'd rather stay on this hot tin roof.
740 BRICK: A hot tin roof's 'n uncomfo'table place t' stay on. . . .

[He starts to whistle softly.]

MARGARET *(through his whistle)*: Yeah, but I can stay on it just as long as I have to.
BRICK: You could leave me, Maggie.

[He resumes whistle. She wheels about to glare at him.]

745 MARGARET: *Don't want to and will not!* Besides if I did, you don't have a cent to pay for it but what you get from Big Daddy and he's dying of cancer!

[For the first time a realization of BIG DADDY's *doom seems to penetrate to* BRICK's *consciousness, visibly, and he looks at* MARGARET.]*

BRICK: Big Mama just said he *wasn't*, that the report
750 was okay.
MARGARET: That's what she thinks because she got the same story that they gave Big Daddy. And was just as taken in by it as he was, poor ole things. . . .
755 But tonight they're going to tell her the truth about it. When Big Daddy goes to bed, they're going to tell her that he is dying of cancer.

[She slams the dresser drawer.]

—It's malignant and it's terminal.
BRICK: Does Big Daddy know it?
760 MARGARET: Hell, do they *ever* know it? Nobody says, "You're dying." You have to fool them. They have to fool *themselves.*
BRICK: Why?
MARGARET: *Why?* Because human beings dream of
765 life everlasting, that's the reason! But most of them want it on earth and not in heaven.

[He gives a short, hard laugh at her touch of humor.]

Well. . . . *(She touches up her mascara.)* That's how it is, anyhow. . . . *(She looks about.)* Where did I put down my cigarette? Don't want to burn up
770 the home-place, at least not with Mae and Gooper and their five monsters in it!

[She has found it and sucks at it greedily. Blows out smoke and continues:]

So this is Big Daddy's last birthday. And Mae and Gooper, they know it, oh, *they* know it, all right. They got the first information from the
775 Ochsner Clinic. That's why they rushed down here with their no-neck monsters. Because. Do you know something? Big Daddy's made no will? Big Daddy's never made out any will in his life, and so this campaign's afoot to
780 impress him, forcibly as possible, with the fact that you drink and I've borne no children!

[He continues to stare at her a moment, then mutters something sharp but not audible and hobbles rather

rapidly out onto the long gallery in the fading, much faded, gold light.]

MARGARET (*continuing her liturgical chant*): Y'know, I'm *fond* of Big Daddy, I am genuinely fond of that old man, I really *am*, you know. . . .

785   BRICK (*faintly, vaguely*): Yes, I know you are. . . .

MARGARET: I've always sort of admired him in spite of his coarseness, his four-letter words and so forth. Because Big Daddy *is* what he *is,* and he makes no bones about it. He hasn't turned
790   gentleman farmer, he's still a Mississippi redneck, as much of a redneck as he must have been when he was just overseer here on the old Jack Straw and Peter Ochello place. But he got hold of it an' built it into th' biggest an'
795   finest plantation in the Delta.—I've always *liked* Big Daddy. . . .

[She crosses to the proscenium.]

Well, this is Big Daddy's last birthday. I'm sorry about it. But I'm facing the facts. It takes money to take care of a drinker and that's the
800   office that I've been elected to lately.

BRICK: You don't have to take care of me.

MARGARET: Yes, I do. Two people in the same boat have got to take care of each other. At least you want money to buy more Echo Spring
805   when this supply is exhausted, or will you be satisfied with a ten-cent beer?

Mae an' Gooper are plannin' to freeze us out of Big Daddy's estate because you drink and I'm childless. But we can defeat that plan. We're
810   *going* to defeat that plan!

Brick, y'know, I've been so God damn disgustingly poor all my life!—That's the *truth,* Brick!

BRICK: I'm not sayin' it isn't.

MARGARET: Always had to suck up to people I could-
815   n't stand because they had money and I was poor as Job's turkey. You don't know what that's like. Well, I'll tell you, it's like you would feel a thousand miles away from Echo Spring!—And had to get back to it on that bro-
820   ken ankle . . . without a crutch!

That's how it feels to be as poor as Job's turkey and have to suck up to relatives that you hated because they had money and all you had was a bunch of hand-me-down clothes and a few
825   old moldly three-per-cent government bonds. My daddy loved his liquor, he fell in love with his liquor the way you've fallen in love with Echo Spring!—And my poor Mama, having to maintain some semblance of social position, to
830   keep appearances up, on an income of one hundred and fifty dollars a month on those old government bonds!

When I came out, the year that I made my debut, I had just two evening dresses! One Mother made me from a pattern in *Vogue,* the other a   835
hand-me-down from a snotty rich cousin I hated!

—The dress that I married you in was my grandmother's weddin' gown. . . .

So that's why I'm like a cat on a hot tin roof!   840

[BRICK is still on the gallery. Someone below calls up to him in a warm Negro voice, "Hiya, Mistuh Brick, how yuh feelin'?" BRICK raises his liquor glass as if that answered the question.]

MARGARET: You can be young without money, but you can't be old without it. You've got to be old *with* money because to be old without it is just too awful, you've got to be one or the other, either *young* or *with money,* you can't be   845
old and *without* it.—That's the *truth,* Brick. . . .

[BRICK whistles softly, vaguely.]

Well, now I'm dressed, I'm all dressed, there's nothing else for me to do.

[Forlornly, almost fearfully.]

I'm dressed, all dressed, nothing else for me to do. . . .   850

[She moves about restlessly, aimlessly, and speaks, as if to herself.]

What am I—? Oh!—my bracelets. . . .

[She starts working a collection of bracelets over her hands onto her wrists, about six on each, as she talks.]

I've thought a whole lot about it and now I know when I made my mistake. Yes, I made my mistake when I told you the truth about that thing with Skipper. Never should have confessed it,   855
a fatal error, tellin' you about that thing with Skipper.

BRICK: Maggie, shut up about Skipper. I mean it, Maggie; you got to shut up about Skipper.

MARGARET: You ought to understand that Skipper   860
and I—

BRICK: You don't think I'm serious, Maggie? You're fooled by the fact that I am saying this quiet? Look, Maggie. What you're doing is a dangerous thing to do. You're—you're—you're—   865
foolin' with something that—nobody ought to fool with.

MARGARET: This time I'm going to finish what I have to say to you. Skipper and I made love, if love

870 you could call it, because it made both of us
feel a little bit closer to you. You see, you son of
a bitch, you asked too much of people, of me,
of him, of all the unlucky poor damned sons of
875 bitches that happen to love you, and there was
a whole pack of them, yes, there was a pack of
them besides me and Skipper, you asked too
goddam much of people that loved you, you—
superior creature!—you godlike being!—And
so we made love to each other to dream it was
880 you, both of us! Yes, yes, yes! Truth, truth!
What's so awful about it? I like it, I think the
truth is—yeah! I shouldn't have told you. . . .
BRICK (*holding his head unnaturally still and uptilted a
bit*): It was Skipper that told me about it. Not
885 you, Maggie.
MARGARET: I told you!
BRICK: After he told me!
MARGARET: What does it matter who—?
DIXIE: I got your mallet, I got your mallet.
890 TRIXIE: Give it to me, give it to me. It's mine.

[BRICK *turns suddenly out upon the gallery and calls:*]

BRICK: Little girl! Hey, little girl!
LITTLE GIRL (*at a distance*): What, Uncle Brick?
BRICK: Tell the folks to come up!—Bring everybody
upstairs!
895 TRIXIE: It's mine, it's mine.
MARGARET: I can't stop myself! I'd go on telling you
this in front of them all, if I had to!
BRICK: Little girl! Go on, go on, will you? Do what I
told you, call them!
900 DIXIE: Okay.
MARGARET: Because it's got to be told and you,
you!—you never let me!

[She sobs, then controls herself, and continues almost
calmly.]

It was one of those beautiful, ideal things they tell
about in the Greek legends, it couldn't be any-
905 thing else, you being you, and that's what
made it so sad, that's what made it so awful,
because it was love that never could be carried
through to anything satisfying or even talked
about plainly.
910 BRICK: Maggie, you gotta stop this.
MARGARET: Brick, I tell you, you got to believe me,
Brick, I *do* understand all about it! I—I think it
was—*noble!* Can't you tell I'm sincere when I
say I respect it? My only point, the only point
915 that I'm making, is life has got to be allowed to
continue even after the *dream* of life is—all—
over. . . .

[BRICK *is without his crutch. Leaning on furniture, he*

*crosses to pick it up as she continues as if possessed by
a will outside herself:*]

Why I remember when we double-dated at college, Gladys Fitzgerald and I and you and
Skipper, it was more like a date between you 920
and Skipper. Gladys and I were just sort of
tagging along as if it was necessary to chaper-
one you!—to make a good public impression—
BRICK (*turns to face her, half lifting his crutch*): Maggie,
you want me to hit you with this crutch? Don't 925
you know I could kill you with this crutch?
MARGARET: Good Lord, man, d'you think I'd care if
you did?
BRICK: One man has one great good true thing in his
life. One great good thing which is true!—I 930
had friendship with Skipper.—You are naming
it dirty!
MARGARET: I'm not naming it dirty! I am naming it
clean.
BRICK: Not love with you, Maggie, but friendship 935
with Skipper was that one great true thing,
and you are naming it dirty!
MARGARET: Then you haven't been listenin', not
understood what I'm saying! I'm naming it so
damn clean that it killed poor Skipper!—You 940
two had something that had to be kept on ice,
yes, incorruptible, yes!—and death was the
only icebox where you could keep it. . . .
BRICK: I married you, Maggie. Why would I marry
you, Maggie, if I was—? 945
MARGARET: Brick, let me finish!—I know, believe me
I know, that it was only Skipper that harbored
even any *unconscious* desire for anything not
perfectly pure between you two!—Now let me
skip a little. You married me early that sum- 950
mer we graduated out of Ole Miss, and we
were happy, weren't we, we were blissful, yes,
hit heaven together ev'ry time that we loved!
But that fall you an' Skipper turned down
wonderful offers of jobs in order to keep on 955
bein' football heroes—pro-football heroes. You
organized the Dixie Stars that fall, so you
could keep on bein' teammates forever! But
somethin' was not right with it!—*Me
included!*—between you. Skipper began hittin' 960
the bottle . . . you got a spinal injury—couldn't
play the Thanksgivin' game in Chicago,
watched it on TV from a traction bed in
Toledo. I joined Skipper. The Dixie Stars lost
because poor Skipper was drunk. We drank 965
together that night all night in the bar of the
Blackstone and when cold day was comin' up
over the Lake an' we were comin' out drunk to
take a dizzy look at it, I said, "*SKIPPER! STOP
LOVIN' MY HUSBAND OR TELL HIM HE'S GOT TO LET* 970
YOU ADMIT IT TO HIM!"—one way or another!

He slapped me hard on the mouth!—then turned
and ran without stopping once, I am sure, all
the way back into his room at the Blackstone
. . . .

975

—When I came to his room that night, with a little scratch like a shy little mouse at his door,
he made that pitiful, ineffectual little attempt
to prove that what I had said wasn't true. . . .

*[Brick strikes at her with crutch, a blow that shatters
the gemlike lamp on the table.]*

980

—In this way, I destroyed him, by telling him
truth that he and his world which he was born
and raised in, yours and his world, had told
him could not be told?

—From then on Skipper was nothing at all but a
receptacle for liquor and drugs. . . .

985

—*Who shot cock robin? I with my*—

[She throws back her head with tight shut eyes.]

—*merciful arrow!*

[Brick strikes at her; misses.]

Missed me!—Sorry,—I'm not tryin' to whitewash
my behavior, Christ, no! Brick, I'm not good. I
don't know why people have to pretend to be
good, nobody's good. The rich or the well-to-
do can afford to respect moral patterns, conventional moral patterns, but I could never
afford to, yeah, but—I'm honest! Give me credit for just that, will you *please?*—Born poor,
raised poor, expect to die poor unless I manage
to get us something out of what Big Daddy
leaves when he dies of cancer! But Brick?!—
Skipper is dead! I'm alive! Maggie the cat is—

990

995

*[Brick hops awkwardly forward and strikes at her
again with his crutch.]*

1000

—*alive! I am alive, alive! I am . . .*

*[He hurls the crutch at her, across the bed she took
refuge behind, and pitches forward on the floor as she
completes her speech.]*

—*alive!*

*[A little girl, Dixie, bursts into the room, wearing an
Indian war bonnet and firing a cap pistol at Margaret
and shouting: "Bang, bang, bang!"]*

*Laughter downstairs floats through the open hall door.
Margaret had crouched gasping to bed at child's
entrance. She now rises and says with cool fury:]*

Little girl, your mother or someone should teach
you—(*gasping*)—to knock at a door before you
come into a room. Otherwise people might
think that you—lack—good breeding. . . .

1005

Dixie: Yanh, yanh, yanh, what is Uncle Brick doin' on
th' floor?

Brick: I tried to kill your Aunt Maggie, but I failed—
and I fell. Little girl, give me my crutch so I
can get up off th' floor.

1010

Margaret: Yes, give your uncle his crutch, he's a cripple, honey, he broke his ankle last night jumping hurdles on the high school athletic field!

Dixie: What were you jumping hurdles for, Uncle
Brick?

1015

Brick: Because I used to jump them, and people like
to do what they used to do, even after they've
stopped being able to do it. . . .

Margaret: That's right, that's your answer, now go
away, little girl.

1020

[Dixie fires cap pistol at Margaret three times.]

Stop, you stop that, monster! You little no-neck monster!

*[She seizes the cap pistol and hurls it through gallery
doors.]*

Dixie (*with a precocious instinct for the cruelest thing*):
You're *jealous!*—You're just jealous because
you can't have babies!

*[She sticks out her tongue at Margaret as she sashays
past her with her stomach stuck out, to the gallery.
Margaret slams the gallery doors and leans panting
against them. There is a pause. Brick has replaced his
spilt drink and sits, faraway, on the great four-poster bed.]*

Margaret: You see?—they gloat over us being childless, even in front of their five little no-neck
monsters!

1025

[Pause. Voices approach on the stairs.]

Brick?—I've been to a doctor in Memphis, a—a
gynecologist. . . .

I've been completely examined, and there is no
reason why we can't have a child whenever
we want one. And this is my time by the calendar to conceive. Are you listening to me? Are
you? Are you LISTENING TO ME!

1030

Brick: Yes. I hear you, Maggie.

1035

[His attention returns to her inflamed face.]

—But how in hell on earth do you imagine—that
you're going to have a child by a man that
can't stand you?

MARGARET: That's a problem that I will have to work
1040   out.

[She wheels about to face the hall door.]

MAE (off stage left): Come on, Big Daddy. We're all
goin' up to Brick's room.

[From off stage left, voices: REVEREND TOOKER, DOCTOR
BAUGH, MAE.]

MARGARET: Here they come!

[The lights dim.]

CURTAIN

ACT II

There is no lapse of time. MARGARET and BRICK are in
the same positions they held at the end of Act I.

MARGARET (at door): Here they come!

[BIG DADDY appears first, a tall man with a fierce,
anxious look, moving carefully not to betray his weakness even, or especially, to himself.]

1045   GOOPER: I read in the Register that you're getting a
new memorial window.

[Some of the people are approaching through the hall,
others along the gallery: voices from both directions.
GOOPER and REVEREND TOOKER become visible outside
gallery doors, and their voices come in clearly.

They pause outside as GOOPER lights a cigar.]

REVEREND TOOKER (vivaciously): Oh, but St. Paul's in
Grenada has three memorial windows, and the
latest one is a Tiffany stained-glass window
1050   that cost twenty-five hundred dollars, a picture
of Christ the Good Shepherd with a Lamb in
His arms.
MARGARET: Big Daddy.
BIG DADDY: Well, Brick.
1055   BRICK: Hello Big Daddy.—Congratulations!
BIG DADDY: —Crap. . . .
GOOPER: Who give that window, Preach?
REVEREND TOOKER: Clyde Fletcher's widow. Also presented St. Paul's with a baptismal font.
1060   GOOPER: Y'know what somebody ought t' give your
church is a coolin' system, Preach.
MAE (almost religiously): —Let's see now, they've had
their tyyy-phoid shots, and their tetanus shots,
their diphtheria shots and their hepatitis shots

and their polio shots, they got those shots every   1065
month from May through September, and—
Gooper? Hey! Gooper!—What all have the kiddies been shot faw?
REVEREND TOOKER: Yes, siree, Bob! And y'know what
Gus Hamma's family gave in his memory to   1070
the church at Two Rivers? A complete new
stone parish-house with a basketball court in
the basement and a—
BIG DADDY (uttering a loud barking laugh which is far
from truly mirthful): Hey, Preach! What's all this   1075
talk about memorials, Preach? Y' think somebody's about t' kick off around here? 'S that it?

[Startled by this interjection, REVEREND TOOKER decides
to laugh at the question almost as loud as he can.

How he would answer the question we'll never know,
as he's spared that embarrassment by the voice of
GOOPER's wife, MAE, rising high and clear as she
appears with "DOC" BAUGH, the family doctor, through
the hall door.]

MARGARET (overlapping a bit): Turn on the hi-fi, Brick!
Let's have some music t' start off th' party with!
BRICK: You turn it on, Maggie.   1080

[The talk becomes so general that the room sounds
like a great aviary of chattering birds. Only BRICK
remains unengaged, leaning upon the liquor cabinet
with his faraway smile, an ice cube in a paper napkin
with which he now and then rubs his forehead. He
doesn't respond to MARGARET's command. She bounds
forward and stoops over the instrument panel of the
console.]

GOOPER: We gave 'em that thing for a third anniver-
sary present, got three speakers in it.

[The room is suddenly blasted by the climax of a
Wagnerian opera or a Beethoven symphony.]

BIG DADDY: Turn that dam thing off!

[Almost instant silence, almost instantly broken by the
shouting charge of BIG MAMA, entering through hall
door like a charging rhino.]

BIG MAMA: Wha's my Brick, wha's mah precious baby!!
BIG DADDY: Sorry! Turn it back on!   1085

[Everyone laughs very loud. BIG DADDY is famous for
his jokes at BIG MAMA's expense, and nobody laughs
louder at these jokes than BIG MAMA herself, though
sometimes they're pretty cruel and BIG MAMA has to
pick up or fuss with something to cover the hurt that
the loud laugh doesn't quite cover.]

On this occasion, a happy occasion because the dread in her heart has also been lifted by the false report on BIG DADDY's condition, she giggles, grotesquely, coyly, in BIG DADDY's direction and bears down upon BRICK, all very quick and alive.]

BIG MAMA: Here he is, here's my precious baby! What's that you've got in your hand? You put that liquor down, son, your hand was made fo' holdin' somethin' better than that!

1090   GOOPER: Look at Brick put it down!

[BRICK has obeyed BIG MAMA by draining the glass and handing it to her. Again everyone laughs, some high, some low.]

BIG MAMA: Oh, you bad boy, you, you're my bad lit-
    tle boy. Give Big Mama a kiss, you bad boy,
    you!—Look at him shy away, will you? Brick
    never liked bein' kissed or made a fuss over, I
1095   guess because he's always had too much of it!
    Son, you turn that thing off!

[BRICK has switched on the TV set.]

I can't stand TV, radio was bad enough but TV
    has gone it one better, I mean—*(plops wheezing
    in chair)*—one worse, ha ha! Now what'm I sit-
1100   tin' down here faw? I want t' sit next to my
    sweetheart on the sofa, hold hands with him
    and love him up a little!

[BIG MAMA has on a black and white figured chiffon. The large irregular patterns, like the markings of some massive animal, the luster of her great diamonds and many pearls, the brilliants set in the silver frames of her glasses, her riotous voice, booming laugh, have dominated the room since she entered. BIG DADDY has been regarding her with a steady grimace of chronic annoyance.]

BIG MAMA *(still louder)*: Preacher, Preacher, hey,
    Preach! Give me you' hand an' help me up
1105   from this chair!
REVEREND TOOKER: None of your tricks, Big Mama!
BIG MAMA: What tricks? You give me you' hand so I
    can get up an'—

[REVEREND TOOKER extends her his hand. She grabs it and pulls him into her lap with a shrill laugh that spans an octave in two notes.]

Ever seen a preacher in a fat lady's lap? Hey, hey,
1110   folks! Ever seen a preacher in a fat lady's lap?

[BIG MAMA is notorious throughout the Delta for this sort of inelegant horseplay. MARGARET looks on with indulgent humor, sipping Dubonnet "on the rocks"

and watching BRICK, but MAE and GOOPER exchange signs of humorless anxiety over these antics, the sort of behavior which MAE thinks may account for their failure to quite get in with the smartest young married set in Memphis, despite all. One of the Negroes, LACY or SOOKEY, peeks in, cackling. They are waiting for a sign to bring in the cake and champagne. But BIG DADDY's not amused. He doesn't understand why, in spite of the infinite mental relief he's received from the doctor's report, he still has these same old fox teeth in his guts. "This spastic condition is something else," he says to himself, but aloud he roars at BIG MAMA:]

BIG DADDY: BIG MAMA, WILL YOU QUIT HORSIN'?—
    You're too old an' too fat fo' that sort of crazy
    kid stuff an' besides a woman with your blood
    pressure—she had two hundred last spring!—
    is riskin' a stroke when you mess around like   1115
    that. . . .

[MAE blows on a pitch pipe.]

BIG MAMA: *Here comes Big Daddy's birthday!*

[Negroes in white jackets enter with an enormous birth-day cake ablaze with candles and carrying buckets of champagne with satin ribbons about the bottle necks.

MAE and GOOPER strike up song, and everybody, including the NEGROES and CHILDREN, joins in. Only BRICK remains aloof.]

EVERYONE:
    Happy birthday to you.
    Happy birthday to you.
    Happy birthday, Big Daddy—   1120

[Some sing: "Dear, Big Daddy!"]

    Happy birthday to you.

[Some sing: "How old are you?"]

MAE *has come down center and is organizing her chil-dren like a chorus. She gives them a barely audible: "One, two, three!" and they are off in the new tune.]*

CHILDREN:
    Skinamarinka—dinka—dink
    Skinamarinka—do
    We love you.   1125
    Skinamarinka—dinka—dink
    Skinamarinka—do.

[All together, they turn to BIG DADDY.]

    Big Daddy, you!

[They turn back front, like a musical comedy chorus.]

1130   *We love you in the morning;*
    We love you in the night.
    We love you when we're with you,
    And we love you out of sight.
    Skinamarinka—dinka—dink
1135   *Skinamarinka—do.*

[Mae turns to Big Mama.]

    Big Mama, too!

[Big Mama bursts into tears. The Negroes leave.]

Big Daddy: Now Ida, what the hell is the matter
    with you?
Mae: She's just so happy.
1140   Big Mama: I'm just so happy, Big Daddy, I have to
    cry or something.

[Sudden and loud in the hush:]

    Brick, do you know the wonderful news that Doc
    Baugh got from the clinic about Big Daddy?
    Big Daddy's one hundred per cent!
1145   Margaret: Isn't that wonderful?
Big Mama: He's just one hundred per cent. Passed
    the examination with flying colors. Now that
    we know there's nothing wrong with Big
    Daddy but a spastic colon, I can tell you some-
1150   thing. I was worried sick, half out of my mind,
    for fear that Big Daddy might have a thing
    like—

*[Margaret cuts through this speech, jumping up and
exclaiming shrilly:]*

Margaret: Brick, honey, aren't you going to give Big
    Daddy his birthday present?

[Passing by him, she snatches his liquor glass from him.

She picks up a fancily wrapped package.]

1155   Here it is, Big Daddy, this is from Brick!
Big Mama: This is the biggest birthday Big Daddy's
    ever had, a hundred presents and bushels of
    telegrams from—
Mae (*at same time*): What is it, Brick?
1160   Gooper: I bet 500 to 50 that Brick don't *know* what it is.
Big Mama: The fun of presents is not knowing what
    they are till you open the package. Open your
    present, Big Daddy.
Big Daddy: Open it you'self. I want to ask Brick
1165   somethin! Come here, Brick.
Margaret: Big Daddy's callin' you, Brick.

[She is opening the package.]

Brick: Tell Big Daddy I'm crippled.
Big Daddy: I see you're crippled. I want to know
    how you got crippled.
Margaret (*making diversionary tactics*): Oh, look, oh,   1170
    look, why, it's a cashmere robe!

[She holds the robe up for all to see.]

Mae: You sound surprised, Maggie.
Margaret: I never saw one before.
Mae: That's funny.—*Hah!*
Margaret (*turning on her fiercely, with a brilliant*   1175
    smile): Why is it funny? All my family ever had
    was family—and luxuries such as cashmere
    robes still surprise me!
Big Daddy (*ominously*): Quiet!
Mae (*heedless in her fury*): I don't see how you could   1180
    be so surprised when you bought it yourself at
    Loewenstein's in Memphis last Saturday. You
    know how I know?
Big Daddy: I said, Quiet!
Mae: —I know because the salesgirl that sold it to   1185
    you waited on me and said, Oh, Mrs. Pollitt,
    your sister-in-law just bought a cashmere robe
    for your husband's father!
Margaret: Sister Woman! Your talents are wasted as
    a housewife and mother, you really ought to   1190
    be with the FBI or—
Big Daddy: Quiet!

*[Reverend Tooker's reflexes are slower than the oth-
ers'. He finishes a sentence after the bellow.]*

Reverend Tooker (*to Doc Baugh*): —the Stork and
    the Reaper are running neck and neck!

*[He starts to laugh gaily when he notices the silence
and Big Daddy's glare. His laugh dies falsely.]*

Big Daddy: Preacher, I hope I'm not butting in on   1195
    more talk about memorial stained-glass win-
    dows, am I, Preacher?

*[Reverend Tooker laughs feebly, then coughs dryly in
the embarrassed silence.]*

    Preacher?
Big Mama: Now, Big Daddy, don't you pick on
    Preacher!   1200
Big Daddy (*raising his voice*): You ever hear that
    expression all hawk and no spit? You bring
    that expression to mind with that little dry
    cough of yours, all hawk an' no spit. . . .

[The pause is broken only by a short startled laugh

from MARGARET, *the only one there who is conscious of and amused by the grotesque.*]

1205   MAE (*raising her arms and jangling her bracelets*): I wonder if the mosquitoes are active tonight?

BIG DADDY: What's that, Little Mama? Did you make some remark?

MAE: Yes, I said I wondered if the mosquitoes would
1210   eat us alive if we went out on the gallery for a while.

BIG DADDY: Well, if they do, I'll have your bones pulverized for fertilizer!

BIG MAMA (*quickly*): Last week we had an airplane
1215   spraying the place and I think it done some good, at least I haven't had a—

BIG DADDY (*cutting her speech*): Brick, they tell me, if what they tell me is true, that you done some jumping last night on the high school athletic
1220   field?

BIG MAMA: Brick, Big Daddy is talking to you, son.

BRICK (*smiling vaguely over his drink*): What was that, Big Daddy?

BIG DADDY: They said you done some jumping on
1225   the high school track field last night.

BRICK: That's what they told me, too.

BIG DADDY: Was it jumping or humping that you were doing out there? What were doing out there at three A.M., layin' a woman on that cin-
1230   der track?

BIG MAMA: Big Daddy, you are off the sick-list, now, and I'm not going to excuse you for talkin' so—

BIG DADDY: Quiet!

1235   BIG MAMA: —*nasty* in front of Preacher and—

BIG DADDY: QUIET!—I ast you, Brick, if you was cuttin' you'self a piece o' poon-tang last night on that cinder track? I thought maybe you were chasin' poon-tang on that track an' tripped over some-
1240   thing in the heat of the chase—'sthat it?

[GOOPER *laughs, loud and false, others nervously following suit.* BIG MAMA *stamps her foot, and purses her lips, crossing to* MAE *and whispering something to her as* BRICK *meets his father's hard, intent, grinning stare with a slow, vague smile that he offers all situations from behind the screen of his liquor.*]

BRICK: No, sir, I don't think so. . . .

MAE (*at the same time, sweetly*): Reverend Tooker, let's you and I take a stroll on the widow's walk.

[*She and the preacher go out on the gallery as* BIG DADDY *says:*]

BIG DADDY: Then what the hell were you doing out
1245   there at three o'clock in the morning?

BRICK: Jumping the hurdles, Big Daddy, runnin' and

jumpin' the hurdles, but those high hurdles have gotten too high for me, now.

BIG DADDY: Cause you was drunk?

BRICK (*his vague smile fading a little*): Sober I wouldn't   1250
have tried to jump the *low* ones. . . .

BIG MAMA (*quickly*): Big Daddy, blow out the candles on your birthday cake!

MARGARET (*at the same time*): I want to propose a toast to Big Daddy Pollitt on his sixty-fifth   1255
birthday, the biggest cotton planter in—

BIG DADDY (*bellowing with fury and disgust*): I told you to stop it, now stop it, quit this—!

BIG MAMA (*coming in front of* BIG DADDY *with the cake*): Big Daddy, I will not allow you to talk that   1260
way, not even on your birthday, I—

BIG DADDY: I'll talk like I want to on my birthday, Ida, or any other goddam day of the year and anybody here that don't like it knows what they can do!   1265

BIG MAMA: You don't mean that!

BIG DADDY: What makes you think I don't mean it?

[*Meanwhile various discreet signals have been exchanged and* GOOPER *has also gone out on the gallery.*]

BIG MAMA: I just know you don't mean it.

BIG DADDY: You don't know a goddam thing and you never did!   1270

BIG MAMA: Big Daddy, you don't mean that.

BIG DADDY: Oh, yes, I do, oh, yes, I do, I mean it! I put up with a whole lot of crap around here because I thought I was dying. And you thought I was dying and you started taking   1275
over, well, you can stop taking over now, Ida, because I'm not gonna die, you can just stop now this business of taking over because you're not taking over because I'm not dying, I went through the laboratory and the goddam   1280
exploratory operation and there's nothing wrong with me but a spastic colon. And I'm not dying of cancer which you thought I was dying of. Ain't that so? Didn't you think that I was dying of cancer, Ida?   1285

[*Almost everybody is out on the gallery but the two old people glaring at each other across the blazing cake.*

BIG MAMA's *chest heaves and she presses a fat fist to her mouth.*

BIG DADDY *continues, hoarsely:*]

Ain't that so, Ida? Didn't you have an idea I was dying of cancer and now you could take control of this place and everything on it? I got that impression, I seemed to get that impres-

1290   sion. Your loud voice everywhere, your fat old
       body butting in here and there!
BIG MAMA: Hush! The Preacher!
BIG DADDY: Fuck the goddam preacher!

*[BIG MAMA gasps loudly and sits down on the sofa
which is almost too small for her.]*

       Did you hear what I said? I said fuck the goddam
1295   preacher!

*[Somebody closes the gallery doors from outside just
as there is a burst of fireworks and excited cries from
the children.]*

BIG MAMA: I never seen you act like this before and I
       can't think what's got in you!
BIG DADDY: I went through all that laboratory and
       operation and all just so I would know if you
1300   or me was boss here! Well, now it turns out
       that I am and you ain't—and that's my birth-
       day present—and my cake and champagne!—
       because for three years now you been gradual-
       ly taking over. Bossing. Talking. Sashaying
1305   your fat old body around the place I made! I
       made this place! I was overseer on it! I was the
       overseer on the old Straw and Ochello planta-
       tion. I quit school at ten! I quit school at ten
       years old and went to work like a nigger in the
1310   fields. And I rose to be overseer of the Straw
       and Ochello plantation. And old Straw died
       and I was Ochello's partner and the place got
       bigger and bigger and bigger and bigger and
       bigger! I did all that myself with no goddam
1315   help from you, and now you think you're just
       about to take over. Well, I am just about to tell
       you that you are not just about to take over,
       you are not just about to take over a God
       damn thing. Is that clear to you, Ida? Is that
1320   very plain to you, now? Is that understood
       completely? I been through the laboratory
       from A to Z. I've had the goddam exploratory
       operation, and nothing is wrong with me but a
       spastic colon—made spastic, I guess, by *dis-*
1325   *gust!* By all the goddam lies and liars that I
       have had to put up with, and all the goddam
       hypocrisy that I lived with all these forty years
       that we been livin' together!
       Hey! Ida!! Blow out the candles on the birthday
1330   cake! Purse up your lips and draw a deep breath
       and blow out the goddam candles on the cake!
BIG MAMA: Oh, Big Daddy, oh, oh, oh, Big Daddy!
BIG DADDY: What's the matter with you?
BIG MAMA: *In all these years you never believed that I*
1335   *loved you??*
BIG DADDY: Huh?
BIG MAMA: *And I did, I did so much, I did love you!—I*

       even loved your hate and your hardness, Big
       Daddy!

[She sobs and rushes awkwardly out onto the gallery.]

BIG DADDY (*to himself*): *Wouldn't it be funny if that was*   1340
       true. . . .

*[A pause is followed by a burst of light in the sky from
the fireworks.]*

       BRICK! HEY, BRICK!

[He stands over his blazing birthday cake.

*After some moments, BRICK hobbles in on his crutch,
holding his glass.*

MARGARET *follows him with a bright, anxious smile.]*

       I didn't call you, Maggie. I called Brick.
MARGARET: I'm just delivering him to you.

*[She kisses BRICK on the mouth which he immediately
wipes with the back of his hand. She flies girlishly
back out. BRICK and his father are alone.]*

BIG DADDY: Why did you do that?   1345
BRICK: Do what, Big Daddy?
BIG DADDY: Wipe her kiss off your mouth like she'd
       spit on you.
BRICK: I don't know. I wasn't conscious of it.
BIG DADDY: That woman of yours has a better shape   1350
       on her than Gooper's but somehow or other
       they got the same look about them.
BRICK: What sort of look is that, Big Daddy?
BIG DADDY: I don't know how to describe it but it's
       the same look.   1355
BRICK: They don't look peaceful, do they?
BIG DADDY: No, they sure in hell don't.
BRICK: They look nervous as cats?
BIG DADDY: That's right, they look nervous as cats.
BRICK: Nervous as a couple of cats on a hot tin roof?   1360
BIG DADDY: That's right, boy, they look like a couple
       of cats on a hot tin roof. It's funny that you
       and Gooper being so different would pick out
       the same type of woman.
BRICK: Both of us married into society, Big Daddy.   1365
BIG DADDY: Crap . . . I wonder what gives them both
       that look?
BRICK: Well. They're sittin' in the middle of a big
       piece of land, Big Daddy, twenty-eight thou-
       sand acres is a pretty big piece of land and so   1370
       they're squaring off on it, each determined to
       knock off a bigger piece of it than the other
       whenever you let it go.
BIG DADDY: I got a surprise for those women. I'm not

1375 gonna let it go for a long time yet if that's what
they're waiting for.
BRICK: That's right, Big Daddy. You just sit tight and
let them scratch each other's eyes out. . . .
BIG DADDY: You bet your life I'm going to sit tight on
1380 it and let those sons of bitches scratch their
eyes out, ha ha ha. . . .
But Gooper's wife's a good breeder, you got to
admit she's fertile. Hell, at supper tonight she
had them all at the table and they had to put a
1385 couple of extra leafs in the table to make room
for them, she's got five head of them, now, and
another one's comin'.
BRICK: Yep, number six is comin'. . . .
BIG DADDY: Six hell, she'll probably drop a litter next
1390 time. Brick, you know, I swear to God, I don't
know the way it happens?
BRICK: The way what happens, Big Daddy?
BIG DADDY: You git you a piece of land, by hook or
crook, an' things start growin' on it, things accu-
1395 mulate on it, and the first thing you know it's
completely out of hand, completely out of hand!
BRICK: Well, they say nature hates a vacuum, Big
Daddy.
BIG DADDY: That's what they say, but sometimes I
1400 think that a vacuum is a hell of a lot better than
some of the stuff that nature replaces it with.
Is someone out there by that door?
GOOPER: Hey Mae.
BRICK: Yep.
1405 BIG DADDY: Who?

[He has lowered his voice.]

BRICK: Someone int'rested in what we say to each other.
BIG DADDY: Gooper?—*GOOPER!*

[After a discreet pause, MAE appears in the gallery door.]

MAE: Did you call Gooper, Big Daddy?
BIG DADDY: Aw, it was you.
1410 MAE: Do you want Gooper, Big Daddy?
BIG DADDY: No, and I don't want you. I want some
privacy here, while I'm having a confidential
talk with my son Brick. Now it's too hot in
here to close them doors, but if I have to close
1415 those fuckin' doors in order to have a private
talk with my son Brick, just let me know and
I'll close 'em. Because I hate eavesdroppers, I
don't like any kind of sneakin' an' spyin'.
MAE: Why, Big Daddy—
1420 BIG DADDY: You stood on the wrong side of the
moon, it threw your shadow!
MAE: I was just—
BIG DADDY: You was just nothing but *spyin'* an' you
know it!
1425 MAE (*begins to sniff and sob*): Oh, Big Daddy, you're so

unkind for some reason to those that really
love you!
BIG DADDY: Shut up, shut up, shut up! I'm going to
move you and Gooper out of that room next to
this! It's none of your goddam business what   1430
goes on in here at night between Brick an'
Maggie. You listen at night like a couple of rut-
ten peekhole spies and go and give a report on
what you hear to Big Mama an' she comes to
me and says they say such and such and so   1435
and so about what they heard goin' on
between Brick an' Maggie, and Jesus, it makes
me sick. I'm goin' to move you an' Gooper out
of that room, I can't stand sneakin' an' spyin',
it makes me puke. . . .   1440

*[MAE throws back her head and rolls her eyes heaven-
ward and extends her arms as if invoking God's pity
for this unjust martyrdom; then she presses a handkerchief to her nose and flies from the room with a loud
swish of skirts.]*

BRICK (*now at the liquor cabinet*): They listen, do they?
BIG DADDY: Yeah. They listen and give reports to Big
Mama on what goes on in here between you
and Maggie. They say that—

[He stops as if embarrassed.]

—You won't sleep with her, that you sleep on the   1445
sofa. Is that true or not true? If you don't like
Maggie, get rid of Maggie!—What are you
doin' there now?
BRICK: Fresh'nin' up my drink.
BIG DADDY: Son, you know you got a real liquor   1450
problem?
BRICK: Yes, sir, yes, I know.
BIG DADDY: Is that why you quit sports-announcing,
because of this liquor problem?
BRICK: Yes, sir, yes, sir, I guess so.   1455

*[He smiles vaguely and amiably at his father across
his replenished drink.]*

BIG DADDY: Son, don't guess about it, it's too important.
BRICK (*vaguely*): Yes, sir.
BIG DADDY: And listen to me, don't look at the damn
chandelier. . . .

[Pause. BIG DADDY's voice is husky.]

—Somethin' else we picked up at th' big fire sale   1460
in Europe.

[Another pause.]

Life is important. There's nothing else to hold

1465 onto. A man that drinks is throwing his life away. Don't do it, hold onto your life. There's nothing else to hold onto. . . .

Sit down over here so we don't have to raise our voices, the walls have ears in this place.

BRICK (*hobbling over to sit on the sofa beside him*): All right, Big Daddy.

1470 BIG DADDY: Quit!—how'd that come about? Some disappointment?

BRICK: I don't know. Do you?

BIG DADDY: I'm askin' you, God damn it! How in hell would I know if you don't?

1475 BRICK: I just got out there and found that I had a mouth full of cotton. I was always two or three beats behind what was goin' on on the field and so I—

BIG DADDY: Quit!

1480 BRICK (*amiably*): Yes, quit.

BIG DADDY: Son?

BRICK: Huh?

BIG DADDY (*inhales loudly and deeply from his cigar; then bends suddenly a little forward, exhaling loud-*
1485 *ly and raising a hand to his forehead*): —Whew!— ha ha!—I took in too much smoke, it made me a little lightheaded. . . .

[*The mantel clock chimes.*]

Why is it so damn hard for people to talk?

BRICK: Yeah. . . .

[*The clock goes on sweetly chiming till it has complet- ed the stroke of ten.*]

1490 —Nice peaceful-soundin' clock, I like to hear it all night. . . .

[*He slides low and comfortable on the sofa; BIG DADDY sits up straight and rigid with some unspoken anxiety. All his gestures are tense and jerky as he talks. He wheezes and pants and sniffs through his nervous speech, glancing quickly, shyly, from time to time, at his son.*]

BIG DADDY: We got that clock the summer we wint to Europe, me an' Big Mama on that damn Cook's Tour, never had such an awful time in
1495 my life, I'm tellin' you, son, those gooks over there, they gouge your eyeballs out in their grand hotels. And Big Mama bought more stuff than you could haul in a couple of box- cars, that's no crap. Everywhere she wint on
1500 this whirlwind tour, she bought, bought, bought. Why, half that stuff she bought is still crated up in the cellar, under water last spring!

[*He laughs.*]

That Europe is nothin' on earth but a great big auction, that's all it is, that bunch of old worn- out places, it's just a big fire sale, the whole 1505 fuckin' thing, an' Big Mama wint wild in it, why, you couldn't hold that woman with a mule's harness! Bought, bought, bought!— lucky I'm a rich man, yes siree, Bob, an' half that stuff is mildewin' in th' basement. It's 1510 lucky I'm a rich man, it sure is lucky, well, I'm a rich man, Brick, yep, I'm a mighty rich man.

[*His eyes light up for a moment.*]

Y'know how much I'm worth? Guess, Brick! Guess how much I'm worth!

[BRICK *smiles vaguely over his drink.*]

Close on ten million in cash an' blue-chip stocks, 1515 outside, mind you, of twenty-eight thousand acres of the richest land this side of the valley Nile!

But a man can't buy his life with it, he can't buy back his life with it when his life has been 1520 spent, that's one thing not offered in the Europe fire-sale or in the American markets or any markets on earth, a man can't buy his life with it, he can't buy back his life when his life is finished. . . . 1525

That's a sobering thought, a very sobering thought, and that's a thought that I was turn- ing over in my head, over and over and over— until today. . . .

I'm wiser and sadder, Brick, for this experience 1530 which I just gone through. They's one thing else that I remember in Europe.

BRICK: What is that, Big Daddy?

BIG DADDY: The hills around Barcelona in the coun- try of Spain and the children running over 1535 those bare hills in their bare skins beggin' like starvin' dogs with howls and screeches, and how fat the priests are on the streets of Barcelona, so many of them and so fat and so pleasant, ha ha!—Y'know I could feed that 1540 country? I got money enough to feed that god- dam country, but the human animal is a selfish beast and I don't reckon the money I passed out there to those howling children in the hills around Barcelona would more than upholster 1545 the chairs in this room, I mean pay to put a new cover on this chair!

Hell, I threw them money like you'd scatter feed corn for chickens, I threw money at them just to get rid of them long enough to climb back 1550 into th' car and—drive away. . . .

And then in Morocco, them Arabs, why, I remem- ber one day in Marrakech, that old walled

1555 Arab city, I set on a broken-down wall to have a cigar, it was fearful hot there and this Arab woman stood in the road and looked at me till I was embarrassed, she stood stock still in the dusty hot road and looked at me till I was embarrassed. But listen to this. She had a

1560 naked child with her, a little naked girl with her, barely able to toddle, and after a while she set this child on the ground and give her a push and whispered something to her.

This child come toward me, barely able t' walk,
1565 come toddling up to me and—

Jesus, it makes you sick t' remember a thing like this!

It stuck out its hand and tried to unbutton my trousers!

1570 That child was not yet five! Can you believe me? Or do you think that I am making this up? I wint back to the hotel and said to Big Mama, Git packed! We're clearing out of this country. . . .

BRICK: Big Daddy, you're on a talkin' jag tonight.
1575 BIG DADDY (*ignoring this remark*): Yes, sir, that's how it is, the human animal is a beast that dies but the fact that he's dying don't give him pity for others, no, sir, it—

—Did you say something?
1580 BRICK: Yes.
BIG DADDY: What?
BRICK: Hand me over that crutch so I can get up.
BIG DADDY: Where you goin'?
BRICK: I'm takin' a little short trip to Echo Spring.
1585 BIG DADDY: To where?
BRICK: Liquor cabinet. . . .
BIG DADDY: Yes, sir, boy—

[*He hands* BRICK *the crutch.*]

—the human animal is a beast that dies and if he's got money he buys and buys and buys
1590 and I think the reason he buys everything he can buy is that in the back of his mind he has the crazy hope that one of his purchases will be life everlasting!—Which it never can be. . . . The human animal is a beast that—
1595 BRICK (*at the liquor cabinet*): Big Daddy, you sure are shootin' th' breeze here tonight.

[*There is a pause and voices are heard outside.*]

BIG DADDY: I been quiet here lately, spoke not a word, just sat and stared into space. I had something heavy weighing on my mind but
1600 tonight that load was took off me. That's why I'm talking.—The sky looks diff'rent to me. . . .
BRICK: You know what I like to hear most?
BIG DADDY: What?
BRICK: Solid quiet. Perfect unbroken quiet.

BIG DADDY: Why?   1605
BRICK: Because it's more peaceful.
BIG DADDY: Man, you'll hear a lot of that in the grave.

[*He chuckles agreeably.*]

BRICK: Are you through talkin' to me?
BIG DADDY: Why are you so anxious to shut me up?   1610
BRICK: Well, sir, ever so often you say to me, Brick, I want to have a talk with you, but when we talk, it never materializes. Nothing is said. You sit in a chair and gas about this and that and I look like I listen. I try to look like I listen, but I   1615 don't listen, not much. Communication is— awful hard between people an'—somehow between you and me, it just don't—happen.
BIG DADDY: Have you ever been scared? I mean have you ever felt downright terror of something?   1620

[*He gets up.*]

Just one moment.

[*He looks off as if he were going to tell an important secret.*]

BIG DADDY: Brick?
BRICK: What?
BIG DADDY: Son, I thought I had it!
BRICK: Had what? Had what, Big Daddy?   1625
BIG DADDY: Cancer!
BRICK: Oh . . .
BIG DADDY: I thought the old man made out of bones had laid his cold and heavy hand on my shoulder!   1630
BRICK: Well, Big Daddy, you kept a tight mouth about it.
BIG DADDY: A pig squeals. A man keeps a tight mouth about it, in spite of a man not having a pig's advantage.   1635
BRICK: What advantage is that?
BIG DADDY: Ignorance—of mortality—is a comfort. A man don't have that comfort, he's the only living thing that conceives of death, that knows what it is. The others go without knowing   1640 which is the way that anything living should go, go without knowing, without any knowledge of it, and yet a pig squeals, but a man sometimes, he can keep a tight mouth about it. Sometimes he—   1645

[*There is a deep, smoldering ferocity in the old man.*]

—can keep a tight mouth about it. I wonder if—
BRICK: What, Big Daddy?
BIG DADDY: A whiskey highball would injure this

spastic condition?
1650 BRICK: No, sir, it might do it good.
BIG DADDY (*grins suddenly, wolfishly*): Jesus, I can't tell
    you! The sky is open! Christ, it's open again! It's
    open, boy, it's open!

[BRICK looks down at his drink.]

BRICK: You feel better, Big Daddy?
1655 BIG DADDY: Better? Hell! I can breathe!—All of my
    life I been like a doubled up fist. . . .

[He pours a drink.]

—Poundin', smashin', drivin'!—now I'm going to
loosen these doubled-up hands and touch
things *easy* with them. . . .

[He spreads his hands as if caressing the air.]

1660 You know what I'm contemplating?
BRICK (*vaguely*): No, sir. What are you contemplating?
BIG DADDY: Ha ha!—*Pleasure!*—pleasure with *women!*

[BRICK's smile fades a little but lingers.]

—Yes, boy. I'll tell you something that you might
not guess. I still have desire for women and
1665 this is my sixty-fifth birthday.
BRICK: I think that's mighty remarkable, Big Daddy.
BIG DADDY: Remarkable?
BRICK: *Admirable*, Big Daddy.
BIG DADDY: You're damn right it is, remarkable and
1670 admirable both. I realize now that I never had
me enough. I let many chances slip by because
of scruples about it, scruples, convention—crap.
. . . All that stuff is bull, bull, bull!—It took the
shadow of death to make me see it. Now that
1675 shadow's lifted, I'm going to cut loose and
have, what is it they call it, have me a—ball!
BRICK: A ball, huh?
BIG DADDY: That's right, a ball, a ball! Hell!—I slept
with Big Mama till, let's see, five years ago, till
1680 I was sixty and she was fifty-eight, and never
even liked her, never did!

*[The phone has been ringing down the hall. BIG MAMA
enters, exclaiming:]*

BIG MAMA: Don't you men hear that phone ring? I
heard it way out on the gall'ry.
BIG DADDY: There's five rooms off this front gall'ry
1685 that you could go through. Why do you go
through this one?

*[BIG MAMA makes a playful face as she bustles out the
hall door.]*

Hunh!—Why, when Big Mama goes out of a room,
I can't remember what that woman looks like—
BIG MAMA: Hello.
BIG DADDY: —But when Big Mama comes back into 1690
the room, boy, then I see what she looks like,
and I wish I didn't!

*[Bends over laughing at this joke till it hurts his guts
and he straightens with a grimace. The laugh subsides
to a chuckle as he puts the liquor glass a little dis-
trustfully down the table.]*

BIG MAMA: Hello, Miss Sally.

[BRICK has risen and hobbled to the gallery doors.]

BIG DADDY: Hey! Where you goin'?
BRICK: Out for a breather. 1695
BIG DADDY: Not yet you ain't. Stay here till this talk
is finished, young fellow.
BRICK: I thought it was finished, Big Daddy.
BIG DADDY: It ain't even begun.
BRICK: My mistake. Excuse me. I just wanted to feel 1700
that river breeze.
BIG DADDY: Set back down in that chair.

[BIG MAMA's voice rises, carrying down the hall.]

BIG MAMA: Miss Sally, you're a case! You're a cau-
tion, Miss Sally.
BIG DADDY: Jesus, she's talking to my old maid sister 1705
again.
BIG MAMA: Why didn't you give me a chance to
explain it to you?
BIG DADDY: Brick, this stuff burns me.
BIG MAMA: Well, goodbye, now, Miss Sally. You come 1710
down real soon. Big Daddy's dying to see you.
BIG DADDY: Crap!
BIG MAMA: Yaiss, goodbye, Miss Sally. . . .

*[She hangs up and bellows with mirth. BIG DADDY
groans and covers his ears as she approaches.*

Bursting in:]

Big Daddy, that was Miss Sally callin' from
Memphis again! You know what she done, Big 1715
Daddy? She called her doctor in Memphis to
git him to tell her what that spastic thing is!
Ha-HAAAA!—! And called back to tell me how
relieved she was that—Hey! Let me in!

*[BIG DADDY has been holding the door half closed
against her.]*

BIG DADDY: Naw I ain't. I told you not to come and 1720
go through this room. You just back out and go

through those five other rooms.

BIG MAMA: Big Daddy? Big Daddy? Oh, big Daddy!—You didn't mean those things you said to me, did you?

1725

[He shuts door firmly against her but she still calls.]

Sweetheart? Sweetheart? Big Daddy? You didn't mean those awful things you said to me?—I know you didn't. I know you didn't mean those things in your heart. . . .

[The childlike voice fades with a sob and her heavy footsteps retreat down the hall. BRICK has risen once more on his crutches and starts for the gallery again.]

1730 BIG DADDY: All I ask of that woman is that she leave me alone. But she can't admit to herself that she makes me sick. That comes of having slept with her too many years. Should of quit much sooner but that old woman she never got
1735 enough of it—and I was good in bed . . . I never should of wasted so much of it on her. . . . They say you got just so many and each one is numbered. Well, I got a few left in me, a few, and I'm going to pick me a good one to spend
1740 'em on! I'm going to pick me a choice one, I don't care how much she costs, I'll smother her in—minks! Ha ha! I'll strip her naked and smother her in minks and choke her with diamonds! Ha ha! I'll strip her naked and choke
1745 her with diamonds and smother her with minks and hump her from hell to breakfast. *Ha aha ha ha ha!*

MAE *(gaily at door)*: Who's that laughin' in there?

GOOPER: Is Big Daddy laughin' in there?

1750 BIG DADDY: Crap!—them two—*drips.* . . .

[He goes over and touches BRICK's shoulder.]

Yes, son. Brick, boy.—I'm—*happy!* I'm happy, son, I'm happy!

[He chokes a little and bites his under lip, pressing his head quickly, shyly against his son's head and then, coughing with embarrassment, goes uncertainly back to the table where he set down the glass. He drinks and makes a grimace as it burns his guts. BRICK sighs and rises with effort.]

What makes you so restless? Have you got ants in your britches?

1755 BRICK: Yes, sir . . .

BIG DADDY: Why?

BRICK: —Something—hasn't—happened. . . .

BIG DADDY: Yeah? What is that!

BRICK *(sadly)*: —the click. . . .

BIG DADDY: Did you say click? 1760

BRICK: Yes, click.

BIG DADDY: What click?

BRICK: A click that I get in my head that makes me peaceful.

BIG DADDY: I sure in hell don't know what you're 1765 talking about, but it disturbs me.

BRICK: It's just a mechanical thing.

BIG DADDY: What is a mechanical thing?

BRICK: This click that I get in my head that makes me peaceful. I got to drink till I get it. It's just a 1770 mechanical thing, something like a—like a—like a—

BIG DADDY: Like a—

BRICK: Switch clicking off in my head, turning the hot light off and the cool night on and— 1775

[He looks up, smiling sadly.]

—all of a sudden there's—peace!

BIG DADDY *(whistles long and soft with astonishment; he goes back to Brick and clasps his son's two shoulders)*: Jesus! I didn't know it had gotten that bad with you. Why, boy, you're—*alcoholic!* 1780

BRICK: That's the truth, Big Daddy. I'm alcoholic.

BIG DADDY: This shows how I—let things go!

BRICK: I have to hear that little click in my head that makes me peaceful. Usually I hear it sooner than this, sometimes as early as—noon, but— 1785

—Today it's—dilatory. . . .

—I just haven't got the right level of alcohol in my bloodstream yet!

[This last statement is made with energy as he freshens his drink.]

BIG DADDY: Uh—huh. Expecting death made me blind. I didn't have no idea that a son of mine 1790 was turning into a drunkard under my nose.

BRICK *(gently)*: Well, now you do, Big Daddy, the news has penetrated.

BIG DADDY: Uh-huh, yes, now I do, the news has—penetrated. . . . 1795

BRICK: And so if you'll excuse me—

BIG DADDY: No, I won't excuse you.

BRICK: —I'd better sit by myself till I hear that click in my head, it's just a mechanical thing but it don't happen except when I'm alone or talking 1800 to no one. . . .

BIG DADDY: You got a long, long time to sit still, boy, and talk to no one, but now you're talkin' to me. At least I'm talking to you. And you set there and listen until I tell you the conversa- 1805 tion is over!

BRICK: But this talk is like all the others we've ever had together in our lives! It's nowhere, nowhere!—it's—it's *painful*, Big Daddy. . . .

1810   BIG DADDY: All right, then let it be painful, but don't
       you move from that chair!—I'm going to
       remove that crutch. . . .

[He seizes the crutch and tosses it across room.]

BRICK: I can hop on one foot, and if I fall, I can crawl!
BIG DADDY: If you ain't careful you're gonna crawl
1815   off this plantation and then, by Jesus, you'll
       have to hustle your drinks along Skid Row!
BRICK: That'll come, Big Daddy.
BIG DADDY: Naw, it won't. You're my son and I'm going
       to straighten you out; now that *I'm* straightened
1820   out, I'm going to straighten out you!
BRICK: Yeah?
BIG DADDY: Today the report come in from Ochsner
       Clinic. Y'know what they told me?

[His face glows with triumph.]

       The only thing that they could detect with all the
1825   instruments of science in that great hospital is
       a little spastic condition of the colon! And
       nerves torn to pieces by all that worry about it.

*[A little girl bursts into room with a sparkler clutched
in each fist, hops and shrieks like a monkey gone mad
and rushes back out again as BIG DADDY strikes at her.*

*Silence. The two men stare at each other. A woman
laughs gaily outside.]*

       I want you to know I breathed a sigh of relief
       almost as powerful as the Vicksburg tornado!

*[There is laughter outside, running footsteps, the soft,
plushy sound and light of exploding rockets.*

*BRICK stares at him soberly for a long moment; then
makes a sort of startled sound in his nostrils and
springs up on one foot and hops across the room to
grab his crutch, swinging on the furniture for support.
He gets the crutch and flees as if in horror for the
gallery. His father seizes him by the sleeve of his white
silk pajamas.]*

1830   Stay here, you son of a bitch!—till I say go!
BRICK: I can't.
BIG DADDY: You sure in hell will, God damn it.
BRICK: No, I can't. We talk, you talk, in—circles! We
       get no where, no where! It's always the same,
1835   you say you want to talk to me and don't have
       a fuckin' thing to say to me!
BIG DADDY: Nothin' to say when I'm tellin' you I'm
       going to live when I thought I was dying?!
BRICK: Oh—*that!*—Is that what you have to say to me?
1840   BIG DADDY: Why, you son of a bitch! Ain't that, ain't

that—*important?!*
BRICK: Well, you said, that, that's said, and now I—
BIG DADDY: Now you set back down.
BRICK: You're all balled up, you—
BIG DADDY: I ain't balled up!   1845
BRICK: You are, you're all balled up!
BIG DADDY: Don't tell me what I am, you drunken
       whelp! I'm going to tear this coat sleeve off if
       you don't set down!
BRICK: Big Daddy—   1850
BIG DADDY: Do what I tell you! I'm the boss here,
       now! I want you to know I'm back in the dri-
       ver's seat now!

[BIG MAMA rushes in, clutching her great heaving bosom.]

BIG MAMA: Big Daddy!
BIG DADDY: What in hell do you want in here, Big   1855
       Mama?
BIG MAMA: Oh, Big Daddy! Why are you shouting
       like that? I just cain't *stainnnnnnnd*—it. . . .
BIG DADDY *(raising the back of his hand above his head):*
       GIT!—outa here.   1860

[She rushes back out, sobbing.]

BRICK *(softly, sadly):* Christ. . . .
BIG DADDY *(fiercely):* Yeah! Christ!—is right . . .

[BRICK breaks loose and hobbles toward the gallery.

*BIG DADDY jerks his crutch from under BRICK so he
steps with the injured ankle. He utters a hissing cry of
anguish, clutches a chair and pulls it over on top of
him on the floor.]*

       Son of a—tub of—hog fat. . . .
BRICK: Big Daddy! Give me my crutch.

[BIG DADDY throws the crutch out of reach.]

       Give me that crutch, Big Daddy.   1865
BIG DADDY: Why do you drink?
BRICK: Don't know, give me my crutch!
BIG DADDY: You better think why you drink or give
       up drinking!
BRICK: Will you please give me my crutch so I can   1870
       get up off this floor?
BIG DADDY: First you answer my question. Why do
       you drink? Why are you throwing your life
       away, boy, like somethin' disgusting you
       picked up on the street?   1875
BRICK *(getting onto his knees):* Big Daddy, I'm in pain,
       I stepped on that foot.
BIG DADDY: Good! I'm glad you're not too numb
       with the liquor in you to feel some pain!
BRICK: You—spilled my—drink . . .   1880

BIG DADDY: I'll make a bargain with you. You tell me why you drink and I'll hand you one. I'll pour you the liquor myself and hand it to you.

BRICK: Why do I drink?

1885 BIG DADDY: Yea! Why?

BRICK: Give me a drink and I'll tell you.

BIG DADDY: Tell me first!

BRICK: I'll tell you in one word.

BIG DADDY: What word?

1890 BRICK: DISGUST!

[The clock chimes softly, sweetly. BIG DADDY gives it a short, outraged glance.]

Now how about that drink?

BIG DADDY: What are you disgusted with? You got to tell me that, first. Otherwise being disgusted don't make no sense!

1895 BRICK: Give me my crutch.

BIG DADDY: You heard me, you got to tell me what I asked you first.

BRICK: I told you, I said to kill my disgust!

BIG DADDY: DISGUST WITH WHAT!

1900 BRICK: You strike a hard bargain.

BIG DADDY: What are you disgusted with?—an' I'll pass you the liquor.

BRICK: I can hop on one foot, and if I fall, I can crawl.

BIG DADDY: You want liquor that bad?

1905 BRICK (*dragging himself up, clinging to bedstead*): Yeah, I want it that bad.

BIG DADDY: If I give you a drink, will you tell me what it is you're disgusted with, Brick?

BRICK: Yes, sir, I will try to.

[The old man pours him a drink and solemnly passes it to him.

There is silence as BRICK drinks.]

1910 Have you ever heard the word "mendacity"?

BIG DADDY: Sure. Mendacity is one of them five dollar words that cheap politicians throw back and forth at each other.

BRICK: You know what it means?

1915 BIG DADDY: Don't it mean lying and liars?

BRICK: Yes, sir, lying and liars.

BIG DADDY: Has someone been lying to you?

CHILDREN (*chanting in chorus offstage*):

We want Big Dad-dee!

1920 We want Big Dad-dee!

[GOOPER appears in the gallery door.]

GOOPER: Big Daddy, the kiddies are shouting for you out there.

BIG DADDY (*fiercely*): Keep out, Gooper!

GOOPER: 'Scuse me!

[BIG DADDY slams the doors after GOOPER.]

BIG DADDY: Who's been lying to you, has Margaret   1925 been lying to you, has your wife been lying to you about something, Brick?

BRICK: Not her. That wouldn't matter.

BIG DADDY: Then who's been lying to you, and what about?   1930

BRICK: No one single person and no one lie. . . .

BIG DADDY: Then what, what then, for Christ's sake?

BRICK: —The whole, the whole—thing. . . .

BIG DADDY: Why are you rubbing your head? You got a headache?   1935

BRICK: No, I'm tryin' to—

BIG DADDY: —Concentrate, but you can't because your brain's all soaked with liquor, is that the trouble? Wet brain!

[He snatches the glass from BRICK's hand.]

What do you know about this mendacity thing?   1940 Hell! I could write a book on it! Don't you know that? I could write a book on it and still not cover the subject? Well, I could, I could write a goddam book on it and still not cover the subject anywhere near enough!!—Think of all the   1945 lies I got to put up with!—Pretenses! Ain't that mendacity? Having to pretend stuff you don't think or feel or have any idea of? Having for instance to act like I care for Big Mama!—I haven't been able to stand the sight, sound, or   1950 smell of that woman for forty years now!—even when I *laid* her!—regular as a piston. . . .

Pretend to love that son of a bitch of a Gooper and his wife Mae and those five same screechers out there like parrots in a jungle? Jesus!   1955 Can't stand to look at 'em!

Church!—it bores the bejesus out of me but I go!—I go an' sit there and listen to the fool preacher!

Clubs!—Elks! Masons! Rotary!—*crap!*   1960

[A spasm of pain makes him clutch his belly. He sinks into a chair and his voice is softer and hoarser.]

You I *do* like for some reason, did always have some kind of real feeling for—affection—respect—yes, always. . . .

You and being a success as a planter is all I ever had any devotion to in my whole life!—and   1965 that's the truth. . . .

I don't know why, but it is!

I've lived with mendacity!—Why can't *you* live with it? Hell, you *got* to live with it, there's

1970 nothing *else* to *live* with except mendacity, is
there?
BRICK: Yes, sir. Yes, sir there is something else that
you can live with!
BIG DADDY: What?
1975 BRICK (*lifting his glass*): This!—Liquor. . . .
BIG DADDY: That's not living, that's dodging away
from life.
BRICK: I want to dodge away from it.
BIG DADDY: Then why don't you kill yourself, man?
1980 BRICK: I like to drink. . . .
BIG DADDY: Oh, God, I can't talk to you. . . .
BRICK: I'm sorry, Big Daddy.
BIG DADDY: Not as sorry as I am. I'll tell you some-
thing. A little while back when I thought my
1985 number was up—

[This speech should have torrential pace and fury.]

—before I found out it was just this—spastic—
colon. I thought about you. Should I or should I
not, if the jig was up, give you this place when I
go—since I hate Gooper an' Mae an' know that
1990 they hate me, and since all five same monkeys
are little Maes an' Goopers.—And I thought,
No!—Then I thought, Yes!—I couldn't make up
my mind. I hate Gooper and his five same monkeys and that bitch Mae! Why should I turn
1995 over twenty-eight thousand acres of the richest
land this side of the valley Nile to not my
kind?—But why in hell, on the other hand,
Brick—should I subsidize a goddam fool on the
bottle?—Liked or not liked, well, maybe even—
2000 *loved!*—Why should I do that?—Subsidize
worthless behavior? Rot? Corruption?
BRICK (*smiling*): I understand.
BIG DADDY: Well, if you do, you're smarter than I am,
God damn it, because I don't understand. And
2005 this I will tell you frankly. I didn't make up my
mind at all on that question and still to this day
I ain't made out no will!—Well, now I don't
have to. The pressure is gone. I can just wait and
see if you pull yourself together or if you don't.
2010 BRICK: That's right, Big Daddy.
BIG DADDY: You sound like you thought I was kidding.
BRICK (*rising*): No, sir, I know you're not kidding.
BIG DADDY: But you don't care—?
BRICK (*hobbling toward the gallery door*): No, sir, I don't
2015 care. . . .

*[He stands in the gallery doorway as the night sky turns
pink and green and gold with successive flashes of light.]*

BIG DADDY: *WAIT!*—Brick. . . .

*[His voice drops. Suddenly there is something shy,
almost tender, in his restraining gesture.]*

Don't let's—leave it like this, like them other talks
we've had, we've always—talked around
things, we've—just talked around things for
some fuckin' reason, I don't know what, it's 2020
always like something was left not spoken,
something avoided because neither of us was
honest enough with the—other. . . .
BRICK: I never lied to you, Big Daddy.
BIG DADDY: Did I ever to *you?* 2025
BRICK: No, sir. . . .
BIG DADDY: Then there is at least two people that
never lied to each other.
BRICK: But we've never *talked* to each other.
BIG DADDY: We can *now.* 2030
BRICK: Big Daddy, there don't seem to be anything
much to say.
BIG DADDY: You say that you drink to kill your dis-
gust with lying.
BRICK: You said to give you a reason. 2035
BIG DADDY: Is liquor the only thing that'll kill this
disgust?
BRICK: Now. Yes.
BIG DADDY: But not once, huh?
BRICK: Not when I was still young an' believing. A 2040
drinking man's someone who wants to forget
he isn't still young an' believing.
BIG DADDY: Believing what?
BRICK: Believing. . . .
BIG DADDY: Believing *what?* 2045
BRICK (*stubbornly evasive*): Believing. . . .
BIG DADDY: I don't know what the hell you mean by
believing and I don't think you know what you
mean by believing, but if you still got sports in
your blood, go back to sports announcing and— 2050
BRICK: Sit in a glass box watching games I can't play?
Describing what I can't do while players do it?
Sweating out their disgust and confusion in
contests I'm not fit for? Drinkin' a coke, half
bourbon, so I can stand it? That's no goddam 2055
good any more, no help—time just outran me,
Big Daddy—got there first. . .
BIG DADDY: I think you're passing the buck.
BRICK: You know many drinkin' men?
BIG DADDY (*with a slight, charming smile*): I have 2060
known a fair number of that species.
BRICK: Could any of them tell you why he drank?
BIG DADDY: Yep, you're passin' the buck to things
like time and disgust with "mendacity" and—
crap!—if you got to use that kind of language 2065
about a thing, it's ninety-proof bull, and I'm
not buying any.
BRICK: I had to give you a reason to get a drink!
BIG DADDY: You started drinkin' when your friend
Skipper died. 2070

*[Silence for five beats. Then BRICK makes a startled
movement, reaching for his crutch.]*

BRICK: What are you suggesting?
BIG DADDY: I'm suggesting nothing.

[The shuffle and clop of BRICK'S *rapid hobble away from his father's steady, grave attention.]*

—But Gopper an' Mae suggested that there was something not right exactly in your—

2075   BRICK (*stopping short downstage as if backed to a wall*): "Not right"?

BIG DADDY: Not, well, exactly *normal* in your friendship with—

BRICK: They suggested that, too? I thought that was
2080   Maggie's suggestion.

*[*BRICK'S *detachment is at last broken through. His heart is accelerated; his forehead sweat-beaded; his breath becomes more rapid and his voice hoarse. The thing they're discussing, timidly and painfully on the side of* BIG DADDY, *fiercely, violently on* BRICK'S *side, is the inadmissible thing that* SKIPPER *died to disavow between them. The fact that if it existed it had to be disavowed to "keep face" in the world they lived in, may be at the heart of the "mendacity" that* BRICK *drinks to kill his disgust with. It may be the root of his collapse. Or maybe it is only a single manifestation of it, not even the most important. The bird that I hope to catch in the net of this play is not the solution of one man's psychological problem. I'm trying to catch the true quality of experience in a group of people, that cloudy, flickering, evanescent—fiercely charged!—interplay of live human beings in the thundercloud of a common crisis. Some mystery should be left in the revelation of character in a play, just as a great deal of mystery is always left in the revelation of character in life, even in one's own character to himself. This does not absolve the playwright of his duty to observe and probe as clearly and deeply as he legitimately can: but it should steer him away from "pat" conclusions, facile definitions which make a play just a play, not a snare for the truth of human experience.*

The following scene should be played with great concentration, with most of the power leashed but palpable in what is left unspoken.]

Who else's suggestion is it, is it *yours*? How many others thought that Skipper and I were—

BIG DADDY (*gently*): Now, hold on, hold on a minute, son.—I knocked around in my time.

2085   BRICK: What's that got to do with—

BIG DADDY: I said "Hold on!"—I bummed, I bummed this country till I was—

BRICK: Whose suggestion, who else's suggestion is it?

BIG DADDY: Slept in hobo jungles and railroad Y's and flophouses in all cities before I—

2090   BRICK: Oh, *you* think so, too, you call me your son

and a queer. Oh! Maybe that's why you put Maggie and me in this room that was Jack Straw's and Peter Ochello's, in which that pair of old sisters slept in a double bed where both   2095
of 'em died!

BIG DADDY: *Now just don't go throwing rocks at—*

[Suddenly REVEREND TOOKER *appears in the gallery doors, his head slightly, playfully, fatuously cocked, with a practised clergyman's smile, sincere as a bird call blown on a hunter's whistle, the living embodiment of the pious, conventional lie.*

BIG DADDY *gasps a little at this perfectly timed, but incongruous, apparition.]*

—What're you lookin' for, Preacher?

REVEREND TOOKER: The gentleman's lavatory, ha ha!—heh, heh . . .   2100

BIG DADDY (*with strained courtesy*): —Go back out and walk down to the other end of the gallery, Reverend Tooker, and use the bathroom connected with my bedroom, and if you can't find it, ask them where it is!   2105

REVEREND TOOKER: Ah, thanks.

[He goes out with a deprecatory chuckle.]

BIG DADDY: It's hard to talk in this place . . .

BRICK: Son of a—!

BIG DADDY (*leaving a lot unspoken*): —I seen all things and understood a lot of them, till 1910. Christ,   2110
the year that—I had worn my shoes through, hocked my—I hopped off a yellow dog freight car half a mile down the road, slept in a wagon of cotton outside the gin—Jack Straw an' Peter Ochello took me in. Hired me to manage this   2115
place which grew into this one.—When Jack Straw died—why, old Peter Ochello quit eatin' like a dog does when its master's dead, and died, too!

BRICK: Christ!   2120

BIG DADDY: I'm just saying I understand such—

BRICK (*violently*): Skipper is dead. I have not quit eating!

BIG DADDY: No, but you started drinking.

*[*BRICK *wheels on his crutch and hurls his glass across the room shouting.]*

BRICK: YOU THINK SO, TOO?

[Footsteps run on the gallery. There are women's calls.

BIG DADDY *goes toward the door.*   2125

BRICK *is transformed, as if a quiet mountain blew suddenly up in volcanic flame.]*

BRICK: You think so, too? You think so, too? You
    think me an' Skipper did, did, did!—*sodomy!*—
    together?
BIG DADDY: Hold—!
2130 BRICK: That what you—
BIG DADDY: —ON—a minute!
BRICK: You think we did dirty things between us,
    Skipper an'—
BIG DADDY: Why are you shouting like that? Why are
2135   you—
BRICK: —Me, is that what you think of Skipper, is
    that—
BIG DADDY: —so excited? I don't think nothing. I don't
    know nothing. I'm simply telling you what—
2140 BRICK: You think that Skipper and me were a pair of
    dirty old men?
BIG DADDY: Now that's—
BRICK: Straw? Ochello? A couple of—
BIG DADDY: Now just—
2145 BRICK: —fucking sissies? Queers? Is that what you—
BIG DADDY: Shhh.
BRICK: —think?

[*He loses his balance and pitches to his knees without
noticing the pain. He grabs the bed and drags himself
up.*]

BIG DADDY: Jesus!—Whew. . . . Grab my hand!
BRICK: Naw, I don't want your hand. . . .
2150 BIG DADDY: Well, I want yours. Git up!

[*He draws him up, keeps an arm about him with concern and affection.*]

    You broken out in a sweat! You're panting like
      you'd run a race with—
BRICK (*freeing himself from his father's hold*): Big Daddy,
    you shock me, Big Daddy, you, you—*shock* me!
2155   Talkin' so—

[*He turns away from his father.*]

    —casually!—about a—thing like that . . .
    —Don't you know how people *feel* about things
      like that? How, how *disgusted* they are by
      things like that? Why, at Ole Miss when it was
2160   discovered a pledge to our fraternity, Skipper's
      and mine, did a, *attempted* to do a, unnatural
      thing with—
    We not only dropped him like a hot rock!—We
      told him to git off the campus, and he did, he
2165   got!—All the way to—

[*He halts, breathless.*]

BIG DADDY: —Where?
BRICK: —North Africa, last I heard!

BIG DADDY: Well, I have come back from further away
    than that, I have just now returned from the
    other side of the moon, death's country, son,   2170
    and I'm not easy to shock by anything here.

[*He comes downstage and faces out.*]

    Always, anyhow, lived with too much space
      around me to be infected by ideas of other peo-
      ple. One thing you can grow on a big place more
      important than cotton!—is *tolerance!*—I grown it. 2175

[*He returns toward* BRICK.]

BRICK: Why can't exceptional friendship, *real, real,
    deep, deep friendship!* between two men be
    respected as something clean and decent with-
    out being thought of as—
BIG DADDY: It can, it is, for God's sake.   2180
BRICK: —Fairies. . . .

[*In his utterance of this word, we gauge the wide and
profound reach of the conventional mores he got from
the world that crowned him with early laurel.*]

BIG DADDY: I told Mae an' Gooper—
BRICK: Frig Mae and Gopper, frig all dirty lies and
    liars!—Skipper and me had a clean, true thing
    between us!—had a clean friendship, practical- 2185
    ly all our lives, till Maggie got the idea you're
    talking about. Normal? No!—It was too rare to
    be normal, any true thing between two people
    is too rare to be normal. Oh, once in a while he
    put his hand on my shoulder or I'd put mine 2190
    on his, oh, maybe even, when we were touring
    the country in pro-football an' shared hotel-
    rooms we'd reach across the space between the
    two beds and shake hands to say goodnight,
    yeah, one or two times we—   2195
BIG DADDY: Brick, nobody thinks that that's not normal!
BRICK: Well, they're mistaken, it was! It was a pure
    an' true thing an' that's not normal.
MAE (*off stage*): Big Daddy, they're startin' the fire-
    works.   2200

[*They both stare straight at each other for a long moment.
The tension breaks and both turn away as if tired.*]

BIG DADDY: Yeah, it's—hard t'—talk. . . .
BRICK: All right, then, let's—let it go. . . .
BIG DADDY: Why did Skipper crack up? Why have you?

[BRICK *looks back at his father again. He has already
decided, without knowing that he has made this decision, that he is going to tell his father that he is dying
of cancer. Only this could even the score between
them: one inadmissible thing in return for another.*]

BRICK (*ominously*): All right. You're asking for it, Big Daddy. We're finally going to have that real true talk you wanted. It's too late to stop it, now, we got to carry it through and cover every subject.

[*He hobbles back to the liquor cabinet.*]

Uh-huh.

[*He opens the ice bucket and picks up the silver tongs with slow admiration of their frosty brightness.*]

Maggie declares that Skipper and I went into pro-football after we left "Ole Miss" because we were scared to grow up . . .

[*He moves downstage with the shuffle and clop of a cripple on a crutch. As* MARGARET *did when her speech became "recitative," he looks out into the house, commanding its attention by his direct, concentrated gaze—a broken, "tragically elegant" figure telling simply as much as he knows of "the Truth":*]

—Wanted to—keep on tossing—those long, long!—high, high!—passes that—couldn't be intercepted except by time, the aerial attack that made us famous! And so we did, we did, we kept it up for one season, that aerial attack, we held it high!—Yeah, but—
—that summer, Maggie, she laid the law down to me, said, Now or never, and so I married Maggie. . . .
BIG DADDY: How was Maggie in bed?
BRICK (*wryly*): Great! the greatest!

[BIG DADDY *nods as if he thought so.*]

She went on the road that fall with the Dixie Stars. Oh, she made a great show of being the world's best sport. She wore a—wore a—tall bearskin cap! A shako, they call it, a dyed moleskin coat, a moleskin coat dyed red!—Cut up crazy! Rented hotel ballrooms for victory celebrations, wouldn't cancel them when it—turned out—defeat. . . .
MAGGIE THE CAT! Ha ha!

[BIG DADDY *nods.*]

—But Skipper, he had some fever which came back on him which doctors couldn't explain and I got that injury—turned out to be just a shadow on the X-ray plate—and a touch of bursitis. . . .
I lay in a hospital bed, watched our games on TV, saw Maggie on the bench next to Skipper when he was hauled out of a game for stum-bles, fumbles!—Burned me up the way she hung on his arm!—Y'know, I think that Maggie had always felt sort of left out because she and me never got any closer together than two people just get in bed, which is not much closer than two cats on a—fence humping. . . .
So! She took this time to work on poor dumb Skipper. He was a less than average student at Ole Miss, you know that, don't you?!—Poured in his mind the dirty, false idea that what we were, him and me, was a frustrated case of that ole pair of sisters that lived in this room, Jack Straw and Peter Ochello!—He, poor Skipper, went to bed with Maggie to prove it wasn't true, and when it didn't work out, he thought it *was* true!—Skipper broke in two like a rotten stick—nobody ever turned so fast to a lush—or died of it so quick. . . .
—Now are you satisfied?

[BIG DADDY *has listened to this story, dividing the grain from the chaff. Now he looks at his son.*]

BIG DADDY: Are *you* satisfied?
BRICK: With what?
BIG DADDY: That half-ass story!
BRICK: What's half-ass about it?
BIG DADDY: Something's left out of that story. What did you leave out?

[*The phone has started ringing in the hall.*]

GOOPER (*off stage*): Hello.

[*As if it reminded him of something,* BRICK *glances suddenly toward the sound and says:*]

BRICK: Yes!—I left out a long-distance call which I had from Skipper—
GOOPER: Speaking, go ahead.
BRICK: —In which he made a drunken confession to me and on which I hung up!
GOOPER: No.
BRICK: —Last time we spoke to each other in our lives . . .
GOOPER: No, sir.
BIG DADDY: You musta said something to him before you hung up.
BRICK: What could I say to him?
BIG DADDY: Anything. Something.
BRICK: Nothing.
BIG DADDY: Just hung up?
BRICK: Just hung up.
BIG DADDY: Uh-huh. Anyhow now!—we have tracked down the lie with which you're disgusted and which you are drinking to kill your disgust with, Brick. You been passing the buck. This

disgust with mendacity is disgust with yourself. *You!*—dug the grave of your friend and kicked him in it!—before you'd face truth with him!

BRICK: *His* truth, not *mine!*

2290 BIG DADDY: His truth, okay! But you wouldn't face it with him!

BRICK: Who *can* face truth? Can *you?*

BIG DADDY: Now don't start passin' the rotten buck again, boy!

2295 BRICK: How about these birthday congratulations, these many, many happy returns of the day, when ev'rybody knows there won't be any except you!

[GOOPER, *who has answered the hall phone, lets out a high, shrill laugh; the voice becomes audible saying:* "No, no, you got it all wrong! Upside down! Are you crazy?"]

BRICK *suddenly catches his breath as he realized that he has made a shocking disclosure. He hobbles a few paces, then freezes, and without looking at his father's shocked face, says:]*

2300 Let's, let's—go out, now, and—watch the fireworks. Come on, Big Daddy.

[BIG DADDY *moves suddenly forward and grabs hold of the boy's crutch like it was a weapon for which they were fighting for possession.]*

BIG DADDY: Oh, no, no! No one's going out! What did you start to say?

BRICK: I don't remember.

BIG DADDY: "Many happy returns when they know
2305 there won't be any"?

BRICK: Aw, hell, Big Daddy, forget it. Come on out on the gallery and look at the fireworks they're shooting off for your birthday. . . .

BIG DADDY: First you finish that remark you were
2310 makin' before you cut off. "Many happy returns when they know there won't be any"?—Ain't that what you just said?

BRICK: Look, now. I can get around without that crutch if I have to but it would be a lot easier
2315 on the furniture an' glassware if I didn' have to go swinging along like Tarzan of th'—

BIG DADDY: FINISH! WHAT YOU WAS SAYIN'!

[*An eerie green glow shows in sky behind him.]*

BRICK (*sucking the ice in his glass, speech becoming thick*): Leave th' place to Gooper and Mae an'
2320 their five little same little monkeys. All I want is—

BIG DADDY: "LEAVE TH' PLACE," did you say?

BRICK (*vaguely*): All twenty-eight thousand acres of the richest land this side of the valley Nile.

BIG DADDY: Who said I was "leaving the place" to 2325 Gooper or anybody? This is my sixty-fifth birthday! I got fifteen years or twenty years left in me! I'll outlive *you!* I'll bury you an' have to pay for your coffin!

BRICK: Sure. Many happy returns. Now let's go 2330 watch the fireworks, come on, let's—

BIG DADDY: Lying, have they been lying? About the report from th'—clinic? Did they, did they— find something?—*Cancer.* Maybe?

BRICK: Mendacity is a system that we live in. Liquor 2335 is one way out an' death's the other. . . .

[*He takes the crutch from* BIG DADDY's *loose grip and swings out on the gallery leaving the doors open.*

A song, "Pick a Bale of Cotton," is heard.]

MAE (*appearing in door*): Oh, Big Daddy, the field hands are singin' fo' you!

BRICK: I'm sorry, Big Daddy. My head don't work any more and it's hard for me to understand 2340 how anybody could care if he lived or died or was dying or cared about anything but whether or not there was liquor left in the bottle and so I said what I said without thinking. In some ways I'm no better than the others, in 2345 some ways worse because I'm less alive. Maybe it's being alive that makes them lie, and being almost *not* alive makes me sort of accidentally truthful—I don't know but—any- way—we've been friends. . . 2350 —And being friends is telling each other the truth. . . .

[*There is a pause.]*

You told *me!* I told *you!*

BIG DADDY (*slowly and passionately*): CHRIST—DAMN—
GOOPER (*off stage*): Let her go!   2355

[*Fireworks off stage right.]*

BIG DADDY: —ALL—LYING SONS OF—LYING BITCHES!

[*He straightens at last and crosses to the inside door. At the door he turns and looks back as if he had some desperate question he couldn't put into words. Then he nods reflectively and says in a hoarse voice:]*

Yes, all liars, all liars, all lying dying liars!

[*This is said slowly, slowly, with a fierce revulsion. He goes on out.]*

—Lying! Dying! Liars!

[BRICK remains motionless as the lights dim out and the curtain falls.]

Curtain

ACT III

There is no lapse of time. BIG DADDY is seen leaving as at the end of Act II.

BIG DADDY: ALL LYIN'—DYIN'!—LIARS! LIARS!—LIARS!

[MARGARET enters.]

2360 MARGARET: Brick, what in the name of God was goin' on in this room?

[DIXIE and TRIXIE enter through the doors and circle around MARGARET shouting. MAE enters from the lower gallery window.]

MAE: Dixie, Trixie, you quit that!

[GOOPER enters through the doors.]

Gooper, will y' please get these kiddies to bed right now!

2365 GOOPER: Mae, you seen Big Mama?
MAE: Not yet.

[GOOPER and kids exit through the doors. REVEREND TOOKER enters through the windows.]

REVEREND TOOKER: Those kiddies are so full of vitali-ty. I think I'll have to be starting back to town.
MAE: Not yet, Preacher. You know we regard you as
2370 a member of this family, one of our closest an' dearest, so you just got t' be with us when Doc Baugh gives Big Mama th' actual truth about th' report from the clinic.
MARGARET: Where do you think you're going?
2375 BRICK: Out for some air.
MARGARET: Why'd Big Daddy shout "Liars"?
MAE: Has Big Daddy gone to bed, Brick?
GOOPER (*entering*): Now where is that old lady?
REVEREND TOOKER: I'll look for her.

[He exits to the gallery.]

2380 MAE: Cain'tcha find her, Gooper?
GOOPER: She's avoidin' this talk.
MAE: I think she senses somethin'.
MARGARET (*going out on the gallery to BRICK*): Brick, they're goin' to tell Big Mama the truth about
2385 Big Daddy and she's goin' to need you.

DOCTOR BAUGH: This is going to be painful.
MAE: Painful things caint always be avoided.
REVEREND TOOKER: I see Big Mama.
GOOPER: Hey, Big Mama, come here.
MAE: Hush, Gooper, don't holler. 2390
BIG MAMA (*entering*): Too much smell of burnt fire-works makes me feel a little bit sick at my stomach.—Where is Big Daddy?
MAE: That's what I want to know, where has Big Daddy gone? 2395
BIG MAMA: He must have turned in, I reckon he went to baid. . .
GOOPER: Well, then, now we can talk.
BIG MAMA: What *is* this talk, *what* talk?

[MARGARET appears on the gallery, talking to DOCTOR BAUGH.]

MARGARET (*musically*): My family freed their slaves ten 2400
years before abolition. My great-great-grandfa-ther gave his slaves their freedom five years before the War between the States started!
MAE: Oh, for God's sake! Maggie's climbed back up in her family tree! 2405
MARGARET (*sweetly*): What, Mae?

[The pace must be very quick: great Southern anima-tion.]

BIG MAMA (*addressing them all*): I think Big Daddy was just worn out. He loves his family, he loves to have them around him, but it's a strain on his nerves. He wasn't himself 2410
tonight, Big Daddy wasn't himself, I could tell he was all worked up.
REVEREND TOOKER: I think he's remarkable.
BIG MAMA: Yaisss! Just remarkable. Did you all notice the food he ate at that table? Did you all 2415
notice the supper he put away? Why he ate like a hawss!
GOOPER: I hope he doesn't regret it.
BIG MAMA: What? Why that man—ate a huge piece of cawn bread with molasses on it! Helped 2420
himself twice to hoppin' John.
MARGARET: Big Daddy loves hoppin' John.—We had a real country dinner.
BIG MAMA (*overlapping MARGARET*): Yaiss, he simply adores it! an' candied yams? Son? That man 2425
put away enough food at that table to stuff a *field* hand!
GOOPER (*with grim relish*): I hope he don't have to pay for it later on . . .
BIG MAMA (*fiercely*): What's *that*, Gooper? 2430
MAE: Gooper says he hopes Big Daddy doesn't suffer tonight.
BIG MAMA: Oh, shoot, Gooper says, Gooper says! Why should Big Daddy suffer for satisfying a

2435　normal appetite? There's nothin' wrong with
　　　that man but nerves, he's sound as a dollar!
　　　And now he knows he is an' that's why he ate
　　　such a supper. He had a big load off his mind,
　　　knowin' he wasn't doomed t'—what he
2440　thought he was doomed to . . .
　　MARGARET (*sadly and sweetly*): Bless his old sweet soul. . .
　　BIG MAMA (*vaguely*): Yais, bless his heart, where's Brick?
　　MAE: Outside.
　　GOOPER: —Drinkin' . . .
2445　BIG MAMA: I know he's drinkin'. Cain't I see he's
　　　drinkin' without you continually tellin' me
　　　that boy's drinkin'?
　　MARGARET: Good for you, Big Mama!

[She applauds.]

　　BIG MAMA: Other people *drink* and *have* drunk an'
2450　will *drink*, as long as they make that stuff an'
　　　put it in bottles.
　　MARGARET: That's the truth. I never trusted a man
　　　that didn't drink.
　　BIG MAMA: Brick? Brick!
2455　MARGARET: He's still on the gall'ry. I'll go bring him
　　　in so we can talk.
　　BIG MAMA (*worriedly*): I don't know what this myste-
　　　rious family conference is about.

*[Awkward silence. BIG MAMA looks from face to face,
then belches slightly and mutters, "Excuse me . . ."
She opens an ornamental fan suspended about her
throat. A black lace fan to go with her black lace
gown, and fans her wilting corsage, sniffing nervously
and looking from face to face in the uncomfortable
silence as MARGARET calls "Brick?" and BRICK sings to
the moon on the gallery.]*

　　MARGARET: Brick, they're gonna tell Big Mama the
2460　truth an' she's gonna need you.
　　BIG MAMA: I don't know what's wrong here, you all
　　　have such long faces! Open that door on the
　　　hall and let some air circulate through here,
　　　will you please, Gooper?
2465　MAE: I think we'd better leave that door closed, Big
　　　Mama, till after the talk.
　　MARGARET: Brick!
　　BIG MAMA: Reveren' Tooker, will *you* please open
　　　that door?
2470　REVEREND TOOKER: I sure will, Big Mama.
　　MAE: I just didn't think we ought t' take any chance
　　　of Big Daddy hearin' a word of this discussion.
　　BIG MAMA: *I swan!* Nothing's going to be said in Big
　　　Daddy's house that he caint hear if he want to!
2475　GOOPER: Well, Big Mama, it's—

*[MAE gives him a quick, hard poke to shut him up. He
glares at her fiercely as she circles before him like a*

*burlesque ballerina, raising her skinny bare arms over
her head, jangling her bracelets, exclaiming:]*

　　MAE: A breeze! A breeze!
　　REVEREND TOOKER: I think this house is the coolest
　　　house in the Delta.—Did you all know that
　　　Halsey Banks's widow put air-conditioning
　　　units in the church and rectory at Friar's Point　2480
　　　in memory of Halsey?

*[General conversation has resumed; everybody is chat-
ting so that the stage sounds like a bird cage.]*

　　GOOPER: Too bad nobody cools your church off for
　　　you. I bet you sweat in that pulpit these hot
　　　Sundays, Reverend Tooker.
　　REVEREND TOOKER: Yes, my vestments are drenched.　2485
　　　Last Sunday the gold in my chasuble faded
　　　into the purple.
　　GOOPER: Reveren', you musta been preachin' hell's
　　　fire last Sunday.
　　MAE (*at the same time to* DOCTOR BAUGH): You reckon　2490
　　　those vitamin B12 injections are what they're
　　　cracked up t' be, Doc Baugh?
　　DOCTOR BAUGH: Well, if you want to be stuck with
　　　something I guess they're as good to be stuck
　　　with as anything else.　　　　　　　　　　　　2495
　　BIG MAMA (*at the gallery door*): Maggie, Maggie, aren't
　　　you comin' with Brick?
　　MAE (*suddenly and loudly, creating a silence*): I have a
　　　strange feeling, I have a peculiar feeling!
　　BIG MAMA (*turning from the gallery*): What feeling?　2500
　　MAE: That Brick said somethin' he shouldn't of said
　　　t' Big Daddy.
　　BIG MAMA: Now what on earth could Brick of said t'
　　　Big Daddy that he shouldn't say?
　　GOOPER: Big Mama, there's somethin'—　　　　　　2505
　　MAE: Now, WAIT!

*[She rushes up to BIG MAMA and gives her a quick hug
and kiss. BIG MAMA pushes her impatiently off.]*

　　DOCTOR BAUGH: In my day they had what they call
　　　the Keeley cure for heavy drinkers.
　　BIG MAMA: Shoot!
　　DOCTOR BAUGH: But now I understand they just take　2510
　　　some kind of tablets.
　　GOOPER: They call them "Annie Bust" tablets.
　　BIG MAMA: *Brick* don't need to take *nothin'*.

*[BRICK and MARGARET appear in gallery doors, BIG
MAMA unaware of his presence behind her.]*

　　That boy is just broken up over Skipper's death.
　　　You know how poor Skipper died. They gave　2515
　　　him a big, big dose of that sodium amytal stuff
　　　at his home and then they called the ambu-

2520 lance and give him another big, big dose of it
at the hospital and that and all of the alcohol
in his system fo' months an' months just
proved too much for his heart . . . I'm scared of
needles! I'm more scared of a needle than the
knife . . . I think more people have been nee-
dled out of this world than—

[She stops short and wheels about.]

2525   Oh—here's Brick! My precious baby—

[She turns upon BRICK *with short, fat arms extended, at
the same time uttering a loud, short sob, which is both
comic and touching.* BRICK *smiles and bows slightly,
making a burlesque gesture of gallantry for* MARGARET
*to pass before him into the room. Then he hobbles on
his crutch directly to the liquor cabinet and there is
absolute silence, with everybody looking at* BRICK *as
everybody has always looked at* BRICK *when he spoke or
moved or appeared. One by one he drops ice cubes in
his glass, then suddenly, but not quickly, looks back
over his shoulder with a wry, charming smile, and says:]*

BRICK: I'm sorry! Anyone else?
BIG MAMA (*sadly*): No, son. I *wish* you wouldn't!
BRICK: I wish I didn't have to, Big Mama, but I'm still
    waiting for that click in my head which makes
2530   it all smooth out!
BIG MAMA: Ow, Brick, you—BREAK MY HEART!
MARGARET (*at same time*): Brick, go sit with Big Mama!
BIG MAMA: I just cain't staiiiiiii-nnnnnnnnd-it . . .

[She sobs.]

MAE: Now that we're all assembled—
2535 GOOPER: We kin talk . . .
BIG MAMA: Breaks my heart . . .
MARGARET: Sit with Big Mama, Brick, and hold her hand.

*[BIG MAMA *sniffs very loudly three times, almost like
three drumbeats in the pocket of silence.]*

BRICK: You do that, Maggie. I'm a restless cripple. I
    got to stay on my crutch.

*[BRICK *hobbles to the gallery door; leans there as if
waiting.*

MAE *sits beside* BIG MAMA, *while* GOOPER *moves in front
and sits on the end of the couch, facing her.* REVEREND
TOOKER *moves nervously into the space between them; on
the other side,* DOCTOR BAUGH *stands looking at nothing
in particular and lights a cigar.* MARGARET *turns away.]*

2540 BIG MAMA: Why're you all *surroundin'* me—like this?
    Why're you all starin' at me like this an'

makin' signs at each other?

*[REVEREND TOOKER *steps back startled.]*

MAE: Calm yourself, Big Mama.
BIG MAMA: Calm you'self, *you'self*, Sister Woman.
    How could I calm myself with everyone starin'   2545
    at me as if big drops of blood had broken out
    on m'face? What's this all about, annh! What?

*[GOOPER *coughs and takes a center position.]*

GOOPER: Now, Doc Baugh.
MAE: Doc Baugh?
GOOPER: Big Mama wants to know the complete truth   2550
    about the report we got from the Ochsner Clinic.
MAE (*eagerly*): —on Big Daddy's condition!
GOOPER: Yais, on Big Daddy's condition, we got to
    face it.
DOCTOR BAUGH: Well . . .   2555
BIG MAMA (*terrified, rising*): Is there? Something?
    Something that I? Don't—know?

*[In these few words, this startled, very soft, question,
BIG MAMA *reviews the history of her forty-five years
with* BIG DADDY, *her great, almost embarrassingly
true-hearted and simple-minded devotion to* BIG
DADDY, *who must have had something* BRICK *has, who
made himself loved so much by the "simple expedient"
of not loving enough to disturb his charming detachment, also once coupled, like* BRICK, *with virile beauty.*

BIG MAMA *has a dignity at this moment; she almost
stops being fat.]*

DOCTOR BAUGH (*after a pause, uncomfortably*): Yes?—
    Well—
BIG MAMA: I!!!—want to—*knowwwwww* . . .   2560

*[Immediately she thrusts her fist to her mouth as if to
deny that statement. Then for some curious reason, she
snatches the withered corsage from her breast and hurls
it on the floor and steps on it with her short, fat feet.]*

    Somebody must be lyin'!—I want to know!
MAE: Sit down, Big Mama, sit down on this sofa.
MARGARET: Brick, go sit with Big Mama.
BIG MAMA: *What is it, what is it?*
DOCTOR BAUGH: I never have seen a more thorough   2565
    examination than Big Daddy Pollitt was given
    in all my experience with the Ochsner Clinic.
GOOPER: It's one of the best in the country.
MAE: It's THE best in the country—bar *none!*

[For some reason she gives GOOPER *a violent poke as
she goes past him. He slaps at her hand without
removing his eyes from his mother's face.]*

2570   DOCTOR BAUGH: Of course they were ninety-nine and
            nine-tenths per cent sure before they even
            started.
       BIG MAMA: Sure of what, sure of what, sure of—
            what?—what?

*[She catches her breath in a startled sob. MAE kisses
her quickly. She thrusts MAE fiercely away from her,
staring at the DOCTOR.]*

2575   MAE: Mommy, be a brave girl!
       BRICK (*in the doorway, softly*): "By the light, by the
            light, Of the sil-ve-ry mo-oo-n . . ."
       GOOPER: Shut up!—Brick.
       BRICK: Sorry . . .

[He wanders out on the gallery.]

2580   DOCTOR BAUGH: But now, you see, Big Mama, they
            cut a piece off this growth, a specimen of the
            tissue and—
       BIG MAMA: Growth? You told Big Daddy—
       DOCTOR BAUGH: Now wait.
2585   BIG MAMA (*fiercely*): You told me and Big Daddy
            there wasn't a thing wrong with him but—
       MAE: Big Mama, they always—
       GOOPER: Let Doc Baugh talk, will yuh?
       BIG MAMA: —little spastic condition of—

[Her breath gives out in a sob.]

2590   DOCTOR BAUGH: Yes, that's what we told Big Daddy.
            But we had this bit of tissue run through the
            laboratory and I'm sorry to say the test was
            positive on it. It's—well—malignant . . .

[Pause]

       BIG MAMA: —Cancer?! Cancer?!

*[DOCTOR BAUGH nods gravely. BIG MAMA gives a long
gasping cry.]*

2595   MAE AND GOOPER: Now, now, now, Big Mama, you
            had to know . . .
       BIG MAMA: WHY DIDN'T THEY CUT IT OUT OF HIM?
            HANH? HANH?
       DOCTOR BAUGH: Involved too much, Big Mama, too
2600   many organs affected.
       MAE: Big Mama, the liver's affected and so's the kid-
            neys, both! It's gone way past what they call a—
       GOOPER: A surgical risk.
       MAE: —Uh-huh . . .

[BIG MAMA draws a breath like a dying gasp.]

2605   REVEREND TOOKER: Tch, tch, tch, tch, tch!

DOCTOR BAUGH: Yes it's gone past the knife.
MAE: *That's why he's turned yellow, Mommy!*
BIG MAMA: *Git away from me, git away from me, Mae!*

[She rises abruptly.]

    I want Brick! Where's Brick? Where is my only son?
MAE: Mama! Did she say "*only* son"?   2610
GOOPER: What does that make *me*?
MAE: A sober responsible man with five precious
        children!—Six!
BIG MAMA: I want Brick to tell me! Brick! Brick!
MARGARET (*rising from her reflections in a corner*): Brick   2615
        was so upset he went back out.
BIG MAMA: *Brick!*
MARGARET: Mama, let *me* tell you!
BIG MAMA: No, no, leave me alone, you're not my
        blood!   2620
GOOPER: *Mama, I'm your son!* Listen to me!
MAE: Gooper's your son, he's your first-born!
BIG MAMA: Gooper never liked Daddy.
MAE (*as if terribly shocked*): That's not TRUE!

[There is a pause. The minister coughs and rises.]

REVEREND TOOKER (to MAE): I think I'd better slip   2625
        away at this point.

[Discreetly]

    Good night, good night, everybody, and God
        bless you all . . . on this place . . .

[He slips out.]

MAE *coughs and points at* BIG MAMA.*]*

GOOPER: Well, Big Mama . . .

[He sighs.]

BIG MAMA: It's all a mistake, I know it's just a bad   2630
        dream.
DOCTOR BAUGH: We're gonna keep Big Daddy as
        comfortable as we can.
BIG MAMA: Yes, it's just a bad dream, that's all it is,
        it's just an awful dream.   2635
GOOPER: In my opinion Big Daddy is having some
        pain but won't admit he has it.
BIG MAMA: Just a dream, a bad dream.
DOCTOR BAUGH: That's what lots of them do, they
        think if they don't admit they're having the   2640
        pain they can sort of escape the fact of it.
GOOPER (*with relish*): Yes, they get sly about it, they
        get real sly about it.
MAE: Gooper and I think—
GOOPER: Shut up, Mae! Big Mama, I think—Big   2645

Daddy ought to be started on morphine.
BIG MAMA: Nobody's going to give Big Daddy morphine.
DOCTOR BAUGH: Now, Big Mama, when that pain
2650   strikes it's going to strike mighty hard and Big
Daddy's going to need the needle to bear it.
BIG MAMA: I tell you, nobody's going to give him
morphine.
MAE: Big Mama, you don't want to see Big Daddy
2655   suffer, you know you—

[GOOPER, *standing beside her, gives her a savage poke.*]

DOCTOR BAUGH (*placing a package on the table*): I'm
leaving this stuff here, so if there's a sudden
attack you all won't have to send out for it.
MAE: I know how to give a hypo.
2660   BIG MAMA: Nobody's gonna give Big Daddy morphine.
GOOPER: Mae took a course in nursing during the war.
MARGARET: Somehow I don't think Big Daddy would
want Mae to give him a hypo.
MAE: You think he'd want *you* to do it?
2665   DOCTOR BAUGH: Well . . .

[DOCTOR BAUGH *rises.*]

GOOPER: Doctor Baugh is goin'.
DOCTOR BAUGH: Yes, I got to be goin'. Well, keep
your chin up, Big Mama.
GOOPER (*with jocularity*): She's gonna keep *both* chins
2670   up, aren't you, Big Mama?

[BIG MAMA *sobs.*]

Now stop that, Big Mama.
GOOPER (*at the door with DOCTOR BAUGH*): Well, Doc,
we sure do appreciate all you done. I'm telling
you, we're surely obligated to you for—

[DOCTOR BAUGH *has gone out without a glance at him.*]

2675   —I guess that doctor has got a lot on his mind but it
wouldn't hurt him to act a little more human . . .

[BIG MAMA *sobs.*]

Now be a brave girl, Mommy.
BIG MAMA: It's not true, I know that it's just not true!
GOOPER: Mama, those tests are infallible!
2680   BIG MAMA: Why are you so determined to see your
father daid?
MAE: Big Mama!
MARGARET (*gently*): I know what Big Mama means.
MAE (*fiercely*): Oh, do you?
2685   MARGARET (*quietly and very sadly*): Yes, I think I do.
MAE: For a newcomer in the family you sure do
show a lot of understanding.

MARGARET: Understanding is needed on this place.
MAE: I guess you must have needed a lot of it in
your family, Maggie, with your father's liquor   2690
problem and now you've got Brick with his!
MARGARET: Brick does not have a liquor problem at
all. Brick is devoted to Big Daddy. This thing is
a terrible strain on him.
BIG MAMA: Brick is Big Daddy's boy, but he drinks too   2695
much and it worries me and Big Daddy, and,
Margaret, you've got to co-operate with us,
you've got to co-operate with Big Daddy and
me in getting Brick straightened out. Because it
will break Big Daddy's heart if Brick don't pull   2700
himself together and take hold of things.
MAE: Take hold of *what* things, Big Mama?
BIG MAMA: The place.

[There is a quick violent look between MAE and GOOPER.]

GOOPER: Big Mama, you've had a shock.
MAE: Yais, we've all had a shock, but . . .   2705
GOOPER: Let's be realistic—
MAE: —Big Daddy would never, would *never*, be
foolish enough to—
GOOPER: —put this place in irresponsible hands!
BIG MAMA: Big Daddy ain't going to leave the place in   2710
anybody's hands; Big Daddy is *not* going to die.
I want you to get that in your heads, all of you!
MAE: Mommy, Mommy, Big Mama, we're just as hopeful an' optimistic as you are about Big Daddy's
prospects, we have faith in *prayer*—but never-   2715
theless there are certain matters that have to be discussed an' dealt with, because otherwise—
GOOPER: Eventualities have to be considered and
now's the time . . . Mae, will you please get my
brief case out of our room?   2720
MAE: Yes, honey.

[She rises and goes out through the hall door.]

GOOPER (*standing over BIG MAMA*): Now, Big Mom.
What you said just now was not at all true and
you know it. I've always loved Big Daddy in
my own quiet way. I never made a show of it,   2725
and I know that Big Daddy has always been
fond of me in a quiet way, too, and he never
made a show of it neither.

[MAE *returns with GOOPER's brief case.*]

MAE: Here's your brief case, Gooper, honey.
GOOPER (*handing the brief case back to her*): Thank you   2730
. . . Of cou'se, my relationship with Big Daddy
is different from Brick's.
MAE: You're eight years older'n Brick an' always had
t' carry a bigger load of th' responsibilities
than Brick ever had t' carry. He never carried a   2735

thing in his life but a football or a highball.

GOOPER: Mae, will y' let me talk, please?

MAE: Yes, honey.

GOOPER: Now, a twenty-eight-thousand-acre planta-
2740   tion's a mighty big thing t' run.

MAE: Almost singlehanded.

[MARGARET *has gone out onto the gallery and can be
heard calling softly to* BRICK.]

BIG MAMA: You never had to run this place! What are
you talking about? As if Big Daddy was dead
and in his grave, you had to run it? Why, you
2745   just helped him out with a few business details
and had your law practice at the same time in
Memphis!

MAE: Oh, Mommy, Mommy, Big Mommy! Let's be fair!

MARGARET: Brick!

2750 MAE: Why, Gooper has given himself body and soul
to keeping this place up for the past five years
since Big Daddy's health started failing.

MARGARET: Brick!

MAE: Gooper won't say it, Gooper never thought of
2755   it as a duty, he just did it. And what did Brick
do? Brick kept living in his past glory at college! Still a football player at twenty-seven!

MARGARET (*returning alone*): Who are you talking
about now? Brick? A football player? He isn't a
2760   football player and you know it. Brick is a
sports announcer on T.V. and one of the best-
known ones in the country!

MAE: I'm talking about what he was.

MARGARET: Well, I wish you would just stop talking
2765   about my husband.

GOOPER: I've got a right to discuss my brother with
other members of MY OWN family, which don't
include *you*. Why don't you go out there and
drink with Brick?

2770 MARGARET: I've never seen such malice toward a
brother.

GOOPER: How about his for me? Why, he can't stand
to be in the same room with me!

MARGARET: This is a deliberate campaign of vilifica-
2775   tion for the most disgusting and sordid reason
on earth, and I know what it is! It's *avarice,
avarice, greed, greed!*

BIG MAMA: Oh, I'll scream! I will scream in a moment
unless this stops!

[GOOPER *has stalked up to* MARGARET *with clenched
fists at his sides as if he would strike her.* MAE *distorts
her face again into a hideous grimace behind*
MARGARET's *back.*]

2780 BIG MAMA (*sobs*): Margaret. Child. Come here. Sit
next to Big Mama.

MARGARET: Precious Mommy. I'm sorry, I'm sorry, I—!

[She bends her long graceful neck to press her forehead
to BIG MAMA's bulging shoulder under its black chiffon.]

MAE: How beautiful, how touching, this display of
devotion! Do you know why she's childless?
She's childless because that big beautiful ath-   2785
lete husband of hers won't go to bed with her!

GOOPER: You jest won't let me do this in a nice way,
will yah? Aw right—I don't give a goddam if
Big Daddy likes me or don't like me or did or
never did or will or will never! I'm just appeal-   2790
ing to a sense of common decency and fair play.
I'll tell you the truth. I've resented Big Daddy's
partiality to Brick ever since Brick was born,
and the way I've been treated like I was just
barely good enough to spit on and sometimes   2795
not even good enough for that. Big Daddy is
dying of cancer, and it's spread all through him
and it's attacked all his vital organs including
the kidneys and right now he is sinking into
uremia, and you all know what uremia is, it's   2800
poisoning of the whole system due to the failure of the body to eliminate its poisons.

MARGARET (*to herself, downstage, hissingly*): *Poisons,
poisons! Venomous thoughts and words! In hearts
and minds!—That's poisons!*   2805

GOOPER (*overlapping her*): I am asking for a square
deal, and, by God, I expect to get one. But if I
don't get one, if there's any peculiar shenani-
gans going on around here behind my back,
well, I'm not a corporation lawyer for nothing,   2810
I know how to protect my own interests.

[BRICK *enters from the gallery with a tranquil, blurred
smile, carrying an empty glass with him.*]

BRICK: Storm coming up.

GOOPER: Oh! A late arrival!

MAE: Behold the conquering hero comes!

GOOPER: The fabulous Brick Pollitt! Remember   2815
him?—Who could forget him!

MAE: He looks like he's been injured in a game!

GOOPER: Yep, I'm afraid you'll have to warm the
bench at the Sugar Bowl this year, Brick!

[MAE *laughs shrilly.*]

Or was it the Rose Bowl that he made that   2820
famous run in?—

[Thunder]

MAE: The punch bowl, honey. It was in the punch
bowl, the cut-glass punch bowl!

GOOPER: Oh, that's right, I'm getting the bowls
mixed up!   2825

MARGARET: Why don't you stop venting your malice

and envy on a sick boy?

BIG MAMA: *Now you two hush, I mean it, hush, all of you, hush!*

2830   DAISY, SOOKEY: Storm! Storm comin'! Storm! Storm!

LACEY: Brightie, close them shutters.

GOOPER: Lacey, put the top up on my Cadillac, will yuh?

LACEY: Yes, suh, Mistah Pollitt!

2835   GOOPER (*at the same time*): Big Mama, you know it's necessary for me t' go back to Memphis in th' mornin' t' represent the Parker estate in a lawsuit.

[MAE *sits on the bed and arranges papers she has taken from the brief case.*]

BIG MAMA: Is it, Gooper?

2840   MAE: Yaiss.

GOOPER: That's why I'm forced to—to bring up a problem that—

MAE: Somethin' that's too important t' be put off!

GOOPER: If Brick was sober, he ought to be in on this.

2845   MARGARET: Brick is present; we're present.

GOOPER: Well, good. I will now give you this outline my partner, Tom Bullitt, an' me have drawn up—a sort of dummy—trusteeship.

MARGARET: Oh, that's it! You'll be in charge an' dole

2850   out remittances, will you?

GOOPER: This we did as soon as we got the report on Big Daddy from th' Ochsner Laboratories. We did this thing, I mean we drew up this dummy outline with the advice and assistance of the

2855   Chairman of the Boa'd of Directors of th' Southern Plantahs Bank and Trust Company in Memphis, C. C. Bellowes, a man who handles estates for all th' prominent fam'lies in West Tennessee and th' Delta.

2860   BIG MAMA: Gooper?

GOOPER (*crouching in front of* BIG MAMA): Now this is not—not final, or anything like it. This is just a preliminary outline. But it does provide a basis—a design—a—possible, feasible—*plan!*

2865   MARGARET: Yes, I'll bet it's a plan.

[*Thunder*]

MAE: It's a plan to protect the biggest estate in the Delta from irresponsibility an'—

BIG MAMA: Now you listen to me, all of you, you listen here! They's not goin' to be any more catty

2870   talk in my house! And Gooper, you put that away before I grab it out of your hand and tear it right up! I don't know what the hell's in it, and I don't want to know what the hell's in it. I'm talkin' in Big Daddy's language now; I'm

2875   his *wife*, not his *widow*, I'm still his *wife!* And I'm talkin' to you in his language an'—

GOOPER: Big Mama, what I have here is—

MAE (*at the same time*): Gooper explained that it's just a plan . . .

BIG MAMA: I don't care what you got there. Just put   2880   it back where it came from, an' don't let me see it again, not even the outside of the envelope of it! Is that understood? Basis! Plan! Preliminary! Design! I say—what is it Big Daddy always says when he's disgusted?   2885

BRICK (*from the bar*): Big Daddy says "crap" when he's disgusted.

BIG MAMA (*rising*): That's right—CRAP! I say CRAP too, like Big Daddy!

[*Thunder*]

MAE: Coarse language doesn't seem called for in   2890   this—

GOOPER: Somethin' in me is *deeply outraged* by hearin' you talk like this.

BIG MAMA: *Nobody's goin' to take nothin'!*—till Big Daddy lets go of it—maybe, just possibly,   2895   not—not even then! No, not even then!

[*Thunder*]

MAE: Sookey, hurry up an' git that po'ch furniture covahed; want th' paint to come off?

GOOPER: Lacey, put mah car away!

LACEY: Caint, Mistah Pollitt, you got the keys!   2900

GOOPER: Naw, you got 'em, man. Where th' keys to th' car, honey?

MAE: You got 'em in your pocket!

BRICK: "You can always hear me singin' this song, Show me the way to go home."   2905

[*Thunder distantly*]

BIG MAMA: Brick! Come here, Brick, I need you. Tonight Brick looks like he used to look when he was a little boy, just like he did when he played wild games and used to come home when I hollered myself hoarse for him, all   2910   sweaty and pink cheeked and sleepy, with his—red curls shining . . .

[BRICK *draws aside as he does from all physical contact and continues the song in a whisper, opening the ice bucket and dropping in the ice cubes one by one as if he were mixing some important chemical formula.*

Distant thunder.]

Times goes by so fast. Nothin' can outrun it. Death commences too early—almost before you're half acquainted with life—you meet the other . . .   2915   Oh, you know we just got to love each other an' stay together, all of us, just as close as we can, especially now that such a *black* thing has come and moved into this place without invitation.

[Awkwardly embracing BRICK, *she presses her head to his shoulder.*

A dog howls off stage.]

2920   Oh, Brick, son of Big Daddy, Big Daddy does so love you. Y'know what would be his fondest dream come true? If before he passed on, if Big Daddy has to pass on . . .

[A dog howls.]

    . . . you give him a child of yours, a grandson as
2925   much like his son as his son is like Big Daddy . . .
MARGARET: I know that's Big Daddy's dream.
BIG MAMA: That's his dream.
MAE: Such a pity that Maggie and Brick can't oblige.
BIG DADDY (*off down stage right on the gallery*): Looks
2930   like the wind was takin' liberties with this place.
SERVANT (*off stage*): Yes, sir, Mr. Pollitt.
MARGARET (*crossing to the right door*): Big Daddy's on the gall'ry.

*[*BIG MAMA *has turned toward the hall door at the sound of* BIG DADDY's *voice on the gallery.]*

BIG MAMA: I can't stay here. He'll see somethin' in
2935   my eyes.

*[*BIG DADDY *enters the room from up stage right.]*

BIG DADDY: Can I come in?

[He puts his cigar in an ash tray.]

MARGARET: Did the storm wake you up, Big Daddy?
BIG DADDY: Which stawm are you talkin' about—th' one outside or th' hullballoo in here?

*[*GOOPER *squeezes past* BIG DADDY.]*

2940 GOOPER: 'Scuse me:

*[*MAE *tries to squeeze past* BIG DADDY *to join* GOOPER, *but* BIG DADDY *puts his arm firmly around her.]*

BIG DADDY: I heard some mighty loud talk. Sounded like somethin' important was bein' discussed. What was the powwow about?
MAE (*flustered*): Why—nothin', Big Daddy . . .
2945 BIG DADDY (*crossing to extreme left center, taking* MAE *with him*): What is that pregnant-lookin' envelope you're puttin' back in your brief case,

Gooper?
GOOPER (*at the foot of the bed, caught, as he stuffs papers into envelope*): That? Nothin,' suh—nothin'   2950
    much of anythin' at all . . .
BIG DADDY: Nothin'? It looks like a whole lot of nothin'!

[He turns up stage to the group.]

    You all know th' story about th' young married couple—
GOOPER: Yes, sir!   2955
BIG DADDY: Hello, Brick—
BRICK: Hello, Big Daddy.

[The group is arranged in a semicircle above BIG DADDY, MARGARET *at the extreme right, then* MAE *and* GOOPER, *then* BIG MAMA, *with* BRICK *at the left.]*

BIG DADDY: Young married couple took Junior out to th' zoo one Sunday, inspected all of God's creatures in their cages, with satisfaction.   2960
GOOPER: Satisfaction.
BIG DADDY (*crossing to up stage center, facing front*): This afternoon was a warm afternoon in spring an' that ole elephant had somethin' else on his mind which was bigger'n peanuts. You know   2965
    this story, Brick?

*[*GOOPER *nods.]*

BRICK: No, sir, I don't know it.
BIG DADDY: Y'see, in th' cage adjoinin' they was a young female elephant in heat!
BIG MAMA (*at* BIG DADDY's *shoulder*): Oh, Big Daddy!   2970
BIG DADDY: What's the matter, preacher's gone, ain't he? All right. That female elephant in the next cage was permeatin' the atmosphere about her with a powerful and excitin' odor of female fertility! Huh! Ain't that a nice way to put it, Brick?   2975
BRICK: Yes, sir, nothin' wrong with it.
BIG DADDY: Brick says th's nothin' wrong with it!
BIG MAMA: Oh, Big Daddy!
BIG DADDY (*crossing to down stage center*): So this ole bull elephant still had a couple of fornications left in him. He reared back his trunk an' got a whiff of that elephant lady next door!—began to paw at the dirt in his cage an' butt his head against the separatin' partition and, first thing y'know, there was a conspicuous change in his   2985
    profile—very *conspicuous!* Ain't I tellin' this story in decent language, Brick?
BRICK: Yes, sir, too fuckin' decent!
BIG DADDY: So, the little boy pointed at it and said, "What's that?" His mama said, "Oh, that's—   2990
    nothin'!"—His papa said, "She's spoiled!"

*[*BIG DADDY *crosses to* BRICK *at left.]*

You didn't laugh at that story, Brick.

[BIG MAMA crosses to down stage right crying. MARGARET goes to her. MAE and GOOPER hold up stage right center.]

BRICK: No, sir, I didn't laugh at that story.

BIG DADDY: What is the smell in this room? Don't you
2995   notice it, Brick? Don't you notice a powerful
and obnoxious odor of mendacity in this room?

BRICK: Yes, sir, I think I do, sir.

GOOPER: Mae, Mae . . .

BIG DADDY: There is nothing more powerful. Is there,
3000   Brick?

BRICK: No, sir. No, sir, there isn't, an' nothin' more
obnoxious.

BIG DADDY: Brick agrees with me. The odor of mendacity is a powerful and obnoxious odor an'
3005   the stawm hasn't blown it away from this
room yet. You notice it, Gooper?

GOOPER: What, sir?

BIG DADDY: How about you, Sister Woman? You notice
the unpleasant odor of mendacity in this room?

3010 MAE: Why, Big Daddy, I don't even know what that is.

BIG DADDY: You can smell it. Hell it smells like death!

[BIG MAMA sobs. BIG DADDY looks toward her.]

What's wrong with that fat woman over there,
loaded with diamonds? Hey, what's-you-
name, what's the matter with you?

3015 MARGARET *(crossing toward BIG DADDY)*: She had a
slight dizzy spell, Big Daddy.

BIG DADDY: You better watch that, Big Mama. A
stroke is a bad way to go.

MARGARET *(crossing to BIG DADDY at center)*: Oh,
3020   Brick, Big Daddy has on your birthday present
to him, Brick, he has on your cashmere robe,
the softest material I have ever felt.

BIG DADDY: Yeah, this is my soft birthday, Maggie . . .
Not my gold or my silver birthday, but my soft
3025   birthday, everything's got to be soft for Big
Daddy on this soft birthday.

[MAGGIE kneels before BIG DADDY at center.]

MARGARET: Big Daddy's got on his Chinese slippers
that I gave him, Brick. Big Daddy, I haven't
given you my big present yet, but now I will,
3030   now's the time for me to present it to you! I
have an announcement to make!

MAE: What? What kind of announcement?

GOOPER: A sports announcement, Maggie?

MARGARET: Announcement of life beginning! A child
3035   is coming, sired by Brick, and out of Maggie
the Cat! I have Brick's child in my body, an'
that's my birthday present to Big Daddy on
this birthday!

[BIG DADDY looks at BRICK who crosses behind BIG DADDY to down stage portal, left.]

BIG DADDY: Get up, girl, get up off your knees, girl.

[BIG DADDY helps MARGARET to rise. He crosses above her, to her right, bites of the end of a fresh cigar, taken from his bathrobe pocket, as he studies MARGARET.]

Uh-huh, this girl has life in her body, that's no lie!   3040

BIG MAMA: BIG DADDY'S DREAM COME TRUE!

BRICK: Jesus!

BIG DADDY *(crossing right below wicker stand)*: Gooper,
I want my lawyer in the mornin'.

BRICK: Where are you goin', Big Daddy?   3045

BIG DADDY: Son, I'm goin' up on the roof, to the
belvedere on th' roof to look over my kingdom
before I give up my kingdom—twenty-eight
thousand acres of th' richest land this side of
the valley Nile!   3050

[He exits through right doors, and down right on the gallery.]

BIG MAMA *(following)*: Sweetheart, sweetheart, sweetheart—can I come with you?

[She exits down stage right.

MARGARET *is down stage center in the mirror area. MAE has joined GOOPER and she gives him a fierce poke, making a low hissing sound and a grimace of fury.]*

GOOPER *(pushing her aside)*: Brick, could you possibly
spare me one small shot of that liquor?

BRICK: Why, help yourself, Gooper boy.   3055

GOOPER: I will.

MAE *(shrilly)*: Of course we know that this is—a lie.

GOOPER: Be still, Mae.

MAE: I won't be still! I know she's made this up!

GOOPER: Goddam it, I said shut up!   3060

MARGARET: Gracious! I didn't know that my little
announcement was going to provoke such a
storm!

MAE: *That* woman isn't *pregnant!*

GOOPER: Who said she was?   3065

MAE: *She* did.

GOOPER: The doctor didn't. Doc Baugh didn't.

MARGARET: I haven't gone to Doc Baugh.

GOOPER: Then who'd you go to, Maggie?

MARGARET: One of the best gynecologists in the South.   3070

GOOPER: Uh huh, uh huh!—I see . . .

[He takes out a pencil and notebook.]

—May we have his name, please?

MARGARET: No, you may not, Mister Prosecuting

Attorney!

3075   MAE: He doesn't have any name, he doesn't exist!

MARGARET: Oh, he exists all right, and so does my
        child, Brick's baby!

MAE: You can't conceive a child by a man that won't
        sleep with you unless you think you're—

*[BRICK has turned on the phonograph. A scat song
cuts MAE's speech.]*

3080   GOOPER: *Turn that off!*

MAE: We know it's a lie because we hear you in here;
        he won't sleep with you, we hear you! So
        don't imagine you're going to put a trick over
        on us, to fool a dying man with a—

*[A long drawn cry of agony and rage fills the house.
MARGARET turns the phonograph down to a whisper.
The cry is repeated.]*

3085   MAE: Did you hear that, Gooper, did you hear that?

GOOPER: Sounds like the pain has struck.

GOOPER: Come along and leave these lovebirds
        together in their nest!

*[He goes out first. MAE follows but turns at the door,
contorting her face and hissing at MARGARET.]*

MAE: *Liar!*

[She slams the door.

*MARGARET exhales with relief and moves a little
unsteadily to catch hold of BRICK's arm.]*

3090   MARGARET: Thank you for—keeping still . . .

BRICK: O.K., Maggie.

MARGARET: It was gallant of you to save my face!

*[He now pours down three shots in quick succession
and stands waiting, silent. All at once he turns with a
smile and says:]*

BRICK: *There!*

MARGARET: What?

3095   BRICK: The *click* . . .

*[His gratitude seems almost infinite as he hobbles out
on the gallery with a drink. We hear his crutch as he
swings out of sight. Then, at some distance, he begins
singing to himself a peaceful song. MARGARET holds the
big pillow forlornly as if it were her only companion,
for a few moments, then throws it on the bed. She
rushes to the liquor cabinet, gathers all the bottles in
her arms, turns about undecidedly, then runs out of
the room with them, leaving the door ajar on the dim
yellow hall. BRICK is heard hobbling back along the*

*gallery, singing his peaceful song. He comes back in,
sees the pillow on the bed, laughs lightly, sadly, picks
it up. He has it under his arm as MARGARET returns to
the room. MARGARET softly shuts the door and leans
against it, smiling softly at BRICK.]*

MARGARET: Brick, I used to think that you were
        stronger than me and I didn't want to be over-
        powered by you. But now, since you've taken
        to liquor—you know what?—I guess it's bad,
        but now I'm stronger than you and I can love   3100
        you more truly! Don't move that pillow. I'll
        move it right back if you do!—Brick?

*[She turns out all the lamps but a single rose-silk-
shaded one by the bed.]*

I really have been to a doctor and I know what to
        do and—Brick?—this is my time by the calen-
        dar to conceive?   3105

BRICK: Yes, I understand, Maggie. But how are you
        going to conceive a child by a man in love
        with his liquor?

MARGARET: By locking his liquor up and making him
        satisfy my desire before I unlock it!   3110

BRICK: Is that what you've done, Maggie?

MARGARET: Look and see. That cabinet's mighty
        empty compared to before!

BRICK: Well, I'll be a son of a—

*[He reaches for his crutch but she beats him to it and
rushes out on the gallery, hurls the crutch over the rail
and comes back in, panting.]*

MARGARET: And so tonight we're going to make the   3115
        lie true, and when that's done, I'll bring the
        liquor back here and we'll get drunk together,
        here, tonight, in this place that death has come
        into . . . —What do you say?

BRICK: I don't say anything. I guess there's nothing to 3120
        say.

MARGARET: Oh, you weak people, you weak, beauti-
        ful people!—who give up with such grace.
        What you want is someone to—

[She turns out the rose-silk lamp.]

—take hold of you.—Gently, gently with love   3125
        hand your life back to you, like somethin' gold
        you let go of. I *do* love you, Brick, I *do!*

BRICK *[smiling with charming sadness]*: Wouldn't it be
        funny if that was true?

THE END

SAMUEL BECKETT (1906–1989)

Samuel Beckett was born near Dublin, Ireland, into an upper-middle-class Protestant family. He was given a first-rate education at Portora Royal School and then at Trinity College, Dublin, where he studied modern languages. In 1928 he received an appointment as lecturer at l'École Normale Supérieure in Paris where he met and became friends with James Joyce, whose radical fiction inspired Beckett to experiment with avant-garde styles of writing. During the late 1920s and 1930s Beckett was associated with various avant-garde movements; he wrote a work on Joyce's *Finnegans Wake* and a prize-winning series of poems entitled "Whoroscope"; a study of Proust; a volume of short stories; and a novel, *Murphy* (1938), which earned him a reputation in literary circles. During World War II his service in the French Resistance earned Beckett the Croix de Guerre and Médaille de la Resistance. Discovered by the Nazis in 1942, he was forced to flee to unoccupied France, where he worked as a farmhand and completed his novel *Watt*, published in 1953. After the war he began to write only in French and published a trilogy of novels—*Molloy* (1951), *Malone Dies* (1951), and *The Unnamable* (1953)—and a play, *En attendant Godot* (1953; translated as *Waiting for Godot*, 1954).

Although Beckett had experimented with drama in the 1930s and 1940s, he had no real success until *Waiting for Godot* was produced in Paris in 1953, in London in 1955, and in Miami in 1956. Almost from the beginning, the play was recognized as a major postwar statement. Beckett has since become internationally recognized as the most revolutionary and influential postwar European dramatist. He continued to write fiction, but his plays have garnered most attention, especially those written in the 1950s and 1960s: *All That Fall* (1957), *Endgame* (1957; Engl. trans. 1958), *Krapp's Last Tape* (1958), *Happy Days* (1961), and *Play* (1964). In 1969 he won the Nobel Prize for literature in recognition of his diverse and extraordinarily influential work.

Beckett's plays exhibit the influence of the French existentialist philosophers Albert Camus and Jean-Paul Sartre. Simply put, existentialism holds that human beings are not essentially good or bad; they simply exist, and they are essentially what they choose to believe and what they make of themselves. While Beckett's work sometimes seems pessimistic, the search for values and beliefs is central to much of it. His influence on the contemporary theater would be almost impossible to overestimate. His minimalism challenges virtually every tenet of conventional theater; he experiments with the use of stage space, the use of dialogue, the relationship between actor and audience, and the relationship between theater and reality. Beckett's plays opened up new possibilities for the stage in their exploration of the nature and limitations of theater and their exploration of the limitations of language. Seeking to push the limits of drama, Beckett stripped away virtually all of the traditional elements of theater by employing spare settings, few actors, and nothing in the way of conventional action. The number of characters in his plays decreased from five in *Waiting for Godot* to one in *Krapp's Last Tape*. Even the spare language of the early plays disappears entirely in the mimes *Act Without Words I* (1957) and *Act Without Words II* (1960). *Breath* (1970), just sixty seconds long, contains only the sounds of breathing and cries. Action in his plays has progressed (or regressed) to inaction. If the characters in *Waiting for Godot* are capable of moving across the stage, in *Not I* (1972) the only action is the mouth of a woman speaking. Beckett pushed his minimalist theater to the extreme and, paradoxically, the spareness of the conception takes on a haunting beauty.

Endgame

Beckett's plays are among the most intriguing in modern theater, in part because they rebel against virtually every accepted tenet of playwriting and theatrical production. He has been described as a minimalist because of his preference for spare settings and very few stage properties; he also uses very few actors, and he constructs almost no action in the conventional sense. Out of the spareness of setting, characterization, and action Beckett has managed to create the most suggestive plays in the modern theater. *Endgame*, for example, is a play about stasis, a subject far removed from topics usually found in conventional drama.

 Endgame was first produced in 1957, at a time when world politics was deeply divided between the Western powers led by the United States and the so-called Iron Curtain countries led by the Soviet Union. These superpowers were locked in cold war, and the threat of a global thermonuclear holocaust hung over the world. The landscape of *Endgame*, at least what Clov can see from his window, is one in which some kind of disaster has struck. When Hamm wants Clov to report what he sees, Clov says, "Zero," and some time later, "Corpsed." The sense of a post-holocaust world is so strong in the play that when JoAnn Akalaitis mounted a production in 1984 at the American Repertory Theater in Cambridge, Massachusetts, she set it in a half-destroyed subway tunnel and had minimalist composer Philip Glass supply a complementary musical score. The production was criticized for ignoring Beckett's characteristic spareness of conception. However strongly it may suggest the aftermath of a holocaust, there are other aspects of the play, such as its chess and theatrical images and its humor, that also deserve attention.

 Beckett once described the character Hamm as "a king in a chess game lost from the start." The title of the play, *Endgame*, refers to the third and final stage of a chess game. Endgame strategies in chess center on the protection of the king, who is always in danger of being checked and who can move only one space at a time. Few pieces are left on the board at that stage of the game, the moves are restricted and repetitive, and stalemate is a very real possibility. In Beckett's *Endgame* Hamm is like the king in an endgame. He cannot move or stand by himself without the help of Clov, who throughout the play is a relative-

ly powerle   at cannot sit down to rest. Hamm's
parents, N;   trash bins and cannot move at all.

In add.....   trical allusions abound in the play,
including allusions to anu   kespeare's plays. Hamm parodies
Richard III's last lines, for example, calling out, "'My kingdom for a nightman;"
he quotes Prospero's line from *The Tempest*, "Our revels now are ended"; and he
throws away his gaff, just as Prospero throws away his staff at the end of that
play. These and other allusions to Shakespeare, along with self-conscious references to theater and to playing, complement the chess imagery. Hamm's opening line announces that he is playing: "Me—(*he yawns*)—to play." The motif continues as Clov looks toward the audience and says, "I see . . . a multitude . . . in
transports . . . of joy." The characters remind the spectators that they are in a theater watching a play which, like a game of chess, has its own rules and movements. The seemingly arbitrary movements that Clov helps Hamm make, a little
to the left and then a little to the right, appear to have no meaning. But they do
mean something to the characters, and the movements are meaningful within
the context of the play, just as the moves in chess may seem arbitrary but are
meaningful within the context of the game.

Beckett approaches comedy in the same way he approaches his other dramatic materials; he is a minimalist who uses humor very differently than it
would be used in conventional comedy. Nell seems to get to the heart of his idea
of humor when she says, "Nothing is funnier than unhappiness, I grant you
that." From unhappiness Beckett derives humor that gives his characters not
only their absurd but also their pathetic—and perhaps even heroic—stature. He
is fond of interweaving fragments of comic routines from vaudeville acts. Clov
and Hamm and Nag and Nell play out some of these comic routines. When Clov
thinks he has discovered a flea, Hamm fears that "humanity might start from
there all over again," an observation that leads Clov to pour insecticide into his
own trousers. Nagg insists that at least their hearing has not failed them, only to
have Nell ask "Our what?"

In *Endgame* Beckett reduces the realistic theater and the world it represents
to bare essentials, using them to evoke a sense of the absurdity of a play and a
world in a state of stasis, yet emotionally full of conflict, loss, and laughter.

Endgame

SAMUEL BECKETT

TRANSLATED BY SAMUEL BECKETT

CHARACTERS:

NAGG
NELL

HAMM
CLOV

Bare interior.
Grey light.
Left and right back, high up, two small windows,
*   curtains drawn.*
Front right, a door. Hanging near door, its face to
*   wall, a picture.*
Front left, touching each other, covered with an old
*   sheet, two ashbins.*
Center, in an armchair on castors, covered with an old
*   sheet, HAMM. Motionless by the door, his eyes fixed*
*   on HAMM, CLOV. Very red face.*

Brief tableau.

[CLOV goes and stands under window left. Stiff, stag-
gering walk. He looks up at window left. He turns and
looks at window right. He goes and stands under win-
dow right. He looks up at window right. He turns and
looks at window left. He goes out, comes back immedi-
ately with a small step-ladder, carries it over and sets
it down under window left, gets up on it, draws back
curtain. He gets down, takes six steps (for example)
towards window right, goes back for ladder, carries it
over and sets it down under window right, gets up on
it, draws back curtain. He gets down, takes three steps
towards window left, goes back for ladder, carries it
over and sets it down under window left, gets up on it,
looks out of window. Brief laugh. He gets down, takes
one step towards window right, goes back for ladder,
carries it over and sets it down under window right,
gets up on it, looks out of window. Brief laugh. He gets
down, goes with ladder towards ashbins, halts, turns,
carries back ladder and sets it down under window
right, goes to ashbins, removes sheet covering them,
folds it over his arm. He raises one lid, stoops and
looks into bin. Brief laugh. He closes lid. Same with
other bin. He goes to HAMM, removes sheet covering
him, folds it over his arm. In a dressing-gown, a stiff
toque on his head, a large blood-stained handkerchief
over his face, a whistle hanging from his neck, a rug
over his knees, thick socks on his feet, HAMM seems to
be asleep. CLOV looks him over. Brief laugh. He goes to
door, halts, turns towards auditorium.]

CLOV (*fixed gaze, tonelessly*): Finished, it's finished,
   nearly finished, it must be nearly finished.

[Pause.]

   Grain upon grain, one by one, and one day,
      suddenly, there's a heap, a little heap, the
      impossible heap.   5

[Pause.]

   I can't be punished any more.

[Pause.]

   I'll go now to my kitchen, ten feet by ten feet by
      ten feet, and wait for him to whistle me.

[Pause.]

   Nice dimensions, nice proportions, I'll lean on the
      table, and look at the wall, and wait for him to   10
      whistle me.

[He remains a moment motionless, then goes out. He
comes back immediately, goes to window right, takes
up the ladder and carries it out. Pause. HAMM stirs. He
yawns under the handkerchief. He removes the hand-
kerchief from his face. Very red face. Black glasses.]

HAMM: Me—(*he yawns*)—to play.

[He holds the handkerchief spread out before him.]

   Old stancher!

[He takes off his glasses, wipes his eyes, his face, the
glasses, puts them on again, folds the handkerchief and
puts it back neatly in the breast-pocket of his dressing-
gown. He clears his throat, joins the tips of his fingers.]

   Can there be misery—(*he yawns*)—loftier than
      mine? No doubt. Formerly. But now?

[Pause.]

   My father?   15

[Pause.]

   My mother?

[Pause.]

My . . . dog?

[Pause.]

Oh I am willing to believe they suffer as much as such creatures can suffer. But does that mean
20   their sufferings equal mine? No doubt.

[Pause.]

No, all is a—(*he yawns*)—bsolute, (*proudly*) the bigger a man is the fuller he is.

[Pause. Gloomily.]

And the emptier.

[He sniffs.]

Clov!

[Pause.]

25   No, alone.

[Pause.]

What dreams! Those forests!

[Pause.]

Enough, it's time it ended, in the shelter too.

[Pause.]

And yet I hesitate, I hesitate to . . . to end. Yes, there it is, it's time it ended and yet I hesitate
30   to—(*he yawns*)—to end. (*Yawns.*) God, I'm tired, I'd be better off in bed.

[He whistles. Enter CLOV *immediately. He halts beside the chair.]*

You pollute the air!

[Pause.]

Get me ready, I'm going to bed.
CLOV: I've just got you up.
35   HAMM: And what of it?
CLOV: I can't be getting you up and putting you to bed every five minutes, I have things to do.

[Pause.]

HAMM: Did you ever see my eyes?
CLOV: No.
40   HAMM: Did you never have the curiosity, while I was sleeping, to take off my glasses and look at my

eyes?
CLOV: Pulling back the lids?

[Pause.]

No.
HAMM: One of these days I'll show them to you.   45

[Pause.]

It seems they've gone all white.

[Pause.]

What time is it?
CLOV: The same as usual.
HAMM (*gesture towards window right*): Have you looked?   50
CLOV: Yes.
HAMM: Well?
CLOV: Zero.
HAMM: It'd need to rain.
CLOV: It won't rain.   55

[Pause.]

HAMM: Apart from that, how do you feel?
CLOV: I don't complain.
HAMM: You feel normal?
CLOV (*irritably*): I tell you I don't complain.
HAMM: I feel a little queer.   60

[Pause.]

Clov!
CLOV: Yes.
HAMM: Have you not had enough?
CLOV: Yes!

[Pause.]

Of what?   65
HAMM: Of this . . . this . . . thing.
CLOV: I always had.

[Pause.]

Not you?
HAMM (*gloomily*): Then there's no reason for it to change.   70
CLOV: It may end.

[Pause.]

All life long the same questions, the same answers.
HAMM: Get me ready.

*[*CLOV *does not move.]*

Go and get the sheet.

[Clov does not move.]

75   Clov!
CLOV: Yes.
HAMM: I'll give you nothing more to eat.
CLOV: Then we'll die.
HAMM: I'll give you just enough to keep you from
80   dying. You'll be hungry all the time.
CLOV: Then we won't die.

[Pause.]

I'll go and get the sheet.

[He goes towards the door.]

HAMM: No!

[Clov halts.]

I'll give you one biscuit per day.

[Pause.]

85   One and a half.

[Pause.]

Why do you stay with me?
CLOV: Why do you keep me?
HAMM: There's no one else.
CLOV: There's nowhere else.

[Pause.]

90 HAMM: You're leaving me all the same.
CLOV: I'm trying.
HAMM: You don't love me.
CLOV: No.
HAMM: You loved me once.
95 CLOV: Once!
HAMM: I've made you suffer too much.

[Pause.]

Haven't I?
CLOV: It's not that.
HAMM (*shocked*): I haven't made you suffer too
100   much?
CLOV: Yes!
HAMM (*relieved*): Ah you gave me a fright!

[Pause. Coldly.]

Forgive me.

[Pause. Louder.]

I said, Forgive me.
CLOV: I heard you.   105

[Pause.]

Have you bled?
HAMM: Less.

[Pause.]

Is it not time for my pain-killer?
CLOV: No.

[Pause.]

HAMM: How are your eyes?   110
CLOV: Bad.
HAMM: How are your legs?
CLOV: Bad.
HAMM: But you can move.
CLOV: Yes.   115
HAMM (*violently*): Then move!

*[Clov goes to back wall, leans against it with his fore-
head and hands.]*

Where are you?
CLOV: Here.
HAMM: Come back!

[Clov returns to his place beside the chair.]

Where are you?   120
CLOV: Here.
HAMM: Why don't you kill me?
CLOV: I don't know the combination of the cupboard.

[Pause.]

HAMM: Go and get two bicycle-wheels.
CLOV: There are no more bicycle-wheels.   125
HAMM: What have you done with your bicycle?
CLOV: I never had a bicycle.
HAMM: The thing is impossible.
CLOV: When there were still bicycles I wept to have
        one. I crawled at your feet. You told me to go   130
        to hell. Now there are none.
HAMM: And your rounds? When you inspected my
        paupers. Always on foot?
CLOV: Sometimes on horse.

*[The lid of one of the bins lifts and the hands of NAGG
appear, gripping the rim. Then his head emerges.
Nightcap. Very white face. NAGG yawns, then listens.]*

I'll leave you, I have things to do.   135
HAMM: In your kitchen?

CLOV: Yes.

HAMM: Outside of here it's death.

[Pause.]

All right, be off.

[Exit CLOV. Pause.]

140   We're getting on.

NAGG: Me pap!

HAMM: Accursed progenitor!

NAGG: Me pap!

HAMM: The old folks at home! No decency left!

145   Guzzle, guzzle, that's all they think of.

[He whistles. Enter CLOV. He halts beside the chair.]

Well! I thought you were leaving me.

CLOV: Oh not just yet, not just yet.

NAGG: Me pap!

HAMM: Give him his pap.

150   CLOV: There's no more pap.

HAMM (to NAGG): Do you hear that? There's no more
pap. You'll never get any more pap.

NAGG: I want me pap!

HAMM: Give him a biscuit.

[Exit CLOV.]

155   Accursed fornicator! How are your stumps?

NAGG: Never mind me stumps.

[Enter CLOV with biscuit.]

CLOV: I'm back again, with the biscuit.

[He gives biscuit to NAGG who fingers it, sniffs it.]

NAGG (plaintively): What is it?

CLOV: Spratt's medium.

160   NAGG (as before): It's hard! I can't!

HAMM: Bottle him!

[CLOV pushes NAGG back into the bin, closes the lid.]

CLOV (returning to his place beside the chair): If age but
knew!

HAMM: Sit on him!

165   CLOV: I can't sit.

HAMM: True. And I can't stand.

CLOV: So it is.

HAMM: Every man his speciality.

[Pause.]

No phone calls?

[Pause.]

Don't we laugh?   170

CLOV (after reflection): I don't feel like it.

HAMM (after reflection): Nor I.

[Pause.]

Clov!

CLOV: Yes.

HAMM: Nature has forgotten us.   175

CLOV: There's no more nature.

HAMM: No more nature! You exaggerate.

CLOV: In the vicinity.

HAMM: But we breathe, we change! We lose our hair,
our teeth! Our bloom! Our ideals!   180

CLOV: Then she hasn't forgotten us.

HAMM: But you say there is none.

CLOV (sadly): No one that ever lived ever thought so
crooked as we.

HAMM: We do what we can.   185

CLOV: We shouldn't.

[Pause.]

HAMM: You're a bit of all right, aren't you?

CLOV: A smithereen.

[Pause.]

HAMM: This is slow work.

[Pause.]

Is it not time for my pain-killer?   190

CLOV: No.

[Pause.]

I'll leave you, I have things to do.

HAMM: In your kitchen?

CLOV: Yes.

HAMM: What, I'd like to know.   195

CLOV: I look at the wall.

HAMM: The wall! And what do you see on your
wall? Mene, mene? Naked bodies?

CLOV: I see my light dying.

HAMM: Your light dying! Listen to that! Well, it can   200
die just as well here, your light. Take a look at
me and then come back and tell me what you
think of your light.

[Pause.]

CLOV: You shouldn't speak to me like that.

[Pause.]

205 HAMM (*coldly*): Forgive me.

[*Pause. Louder.*]

    I said, Forgive me.
CLOV: I heard you.

[*The lid of* NAGG's *bin lifts. His hands appear, gripping the rim. Then his head emerges. In his mouth the biscuit. He listens.*]

HAMM: Did your seeds come up?
CLOV: No.
210 HAMM: Did you scratch round them to see if they
    had sprouted?
CLOV: They haven't sprouted.
HAMM: Perhaps it's still too early.
CLOV: If they were going to sprout they would have
215   sprouted.

[*Violently.*]

    They'll never sprout!

[*Pause.* NAGG *takes biscuit in his hand.*]

HAMM: This is not much fun.

[*Pause.*]

    But that's always the way at the end of the day,
    isn't it, Clov?
220 CLOV: Always.
HAMM: It's the end of the day like any other day,
    isn't it, Clov?
CLOV: Looks like it.

[*Pause.*]

HAMM (*anguished*): What's happening, what's hap-
225   pening?
CLOV: Something is taking its course.

[*Pause.*]

HAMM: All right, be off.

[*He leans back in his chair, remains motionless.* CLOV *does not move, heaves a great groaning sigh.* HAMM *sits up.*]

    I thought I told you to be off.
CLOV: I'm trying.

[*He goes to door, halts.*]

230   Ever since I was whelped.

[*Exit* CLOV.]

HAMM: We're getting on.

[*He leans back in his chair, remains motionless.* NAGG *knocks on the lid of the other bin. Pause. He knocks harder. The lid lifts and the hands of* NELL *appear, gripping the rim. Then her head emerges. Lace cap. Very white face.*]

NELL: What is it, my pet?

[*Pause.*]

    Time for love?
NAGG: Were you asleep?
NELL: Oh no! 235
NAGG: Kiss me.
NELL: We can't.
NAGG: Try.

[*Their heads strain towards each other, fail to meet, fall apart again.*]

NELL: Why this farce, day after day?

[*Pause.*]

NAGG: I've lost me tooth. 240
NELL: When?
NAGG: I had it yesterday.
NELL (*elegiac*): Ah yesterday!

[*They turn painfully towards each other.*]

NAGG: Can you see me?
NELL: Hardly. And you? 245
NAGG: What?
NELL: Can you see me?
NAGG: Hardly.
NELL: So much the better, so much the better.
NAGG: Don't say that. 250

[*Pause.*]

    Our sight has failed.
NELL: Yes.

[*Pause. They turn away from each other.*]

NAGG: Can you hear me?
NELL: Yes. And you?
NAGG: Yes. 255

[*Pause.*]

    Our hearing hasn't failed.

NELL: Our what?
NAGG: Our hearing.
NELL: No.

[Pause.]

260   Have you anything else to say to me?
NAGG: Do you remember—
NELL: No.
NAGG: When we crashed on our tandem and lost our shanks.

[They laugh heartily.]

265   NELL: It was in the Ardennes.

[They laugh less heartily.]

NAGG: On the road to Sedan.

[They laugh still less heartily.]

Are you cold?
NELL: Yes, perished. And you?
NAGG:

[Pause.]

270   I'm freezing.

[Pause.]

Do you want to go in?
NELL: Yes.
NAGG: Then go in.

[NELL does not move.]

Why don't you go in?
275   NELL: I don't know.

[Pause.]

NAGG: Has he changed your sawdust?
NELL: It isn't sawdust.

[Pause. Wearily.]

Can you not be a little accurate, Nagg?
NAGG: Your sand then. It's not important.
280   NELL: It is important.

[Pause.]

NAGG: It was sawdust once.
NELL: Once!
NAGG: And now it's sand.

[Pause.]

From the shore.

[Pause. Impatiently.]

Now it's sand he fetches from the shore.   285
NELL: Now it's sand.
NAGG: Has he changed yours?
NELL: No.
NAGG: Nor mine.

[Pause.]

I won't have it!   290

[Pause. Holding up the biscuit.]

Do you want a bit?
NELL: No.

[Pause.]

Of what?
NAGG: Biscuit. I've kept you half.

[He looks at the biscuit. Proudly.]

Three quarters. For you. Here.   295

[He proffers the biscuit.]

No?

[Pause.]

Do you not feel well?
HAMM (*wearily*): Quiet, quiet, you're keeping me awake.

[Pause.]

Talk softer.   300

[Pause.]

If I could sleep I might make love. I'd go into the woods. My eyes would see . . . the sky, the earth. I'd run, run, they wouldn't catch me.

[Pause.]

Nature!

[Pause.]

There's something dripping in my head.   305

[Pause.]

A heart, a heart in my head.

[Pause.]

NAGG (*soft*): Do you hear him? A heart in his head!

[He chuckles cautiously.]

NELL: One mustn't laugh at those things, Nagg. Why must you always laugh at them?
310 NAGG: No so loud!
NELL (*without lowering her voice*): Nothing is funnier than unhappiness, I grant you that. But—
NAGG (*shocked*): Oh!
NELL: Yes, yes, it's the most comical thing in the
315 world. And we laugh, we laugh, with a will, in the beginning. But it's always the same thing. Yes, it's like the funny story we have heard too often, we still find it funny, but we don't laugh any more.

[Pause.]

320 Have you anything else to say to me?
NAGG: No.
NELL: Are you quite sure?

[Pause.]

Then I'll leave you.
NAGG: Do you not want your biscuit?

[Pause.]

325 I'll keep it for you.

[Pause.]

I thought you were going to leave me.
NELL: I am going to leave you.
NAGG: Could you give me a scratch before you go?
NELL: No.

[Pause.]

330 Where?
NAGG: In the back.
NELL: No.

[Pause.]

Rub yourself against the rim.
NAGG: It's lower down. In the hollow.
335 NELL: What hollow?
NAGG: The hollow!

[Pause.]

Could you not?

[Pause.]

Yesterday you scratched me there.
NELL (*elegiac*): Ah yesterday!
NAGG: Could you not?   340

[Pause.]

Would you like me to scratch you?

[Pause.]

Are you crying again?
NELL: I was trying.

[Pause.]

HAMM: Perhaps it's a little vein.

[Pause.]

NAGG: What was that he said?   345
NELL: Perhaps it's a little vein.
NAGG: What does that mean?

[Pause.]

That means nothing.

[Pause.]

Will I tell you the story of the tailor?
NELL: No.   350

[Pause.]

What for?
NAGG: To cheer you up.
NELL: It's not funny.
NAGG: It always made you laugh.

[Pause.]

The first time I thought you'd die.   355
NELL: It was on Lake Como.

[Pause.]

One April afternoon.

[Pause.]

Can you believe it?

NAGG: What?

360 NELL: That we once went out rowing on Lake Como.

[Pause.]

One April afternoon.

NAGG: We had got engaged the day before.

NELL: Engaged!

NAGG: You were in such fits that we capsized. By
365   rights we should have been drowned.

NELL: It was because I felt happy.

NAGG (*indignant*): It was not, it was not, it was my
        story and nothing else. Happy! Don't you
        laugh at it still? Every time I tell it. Happy!

370 NELL: It was deep, deep. And you could see down to
        the bottom. So white. So clean.

NAGG: Let me tell it again.

[Raconteur's voice.]

An Englishman, needing a pair of striped trousers
      in a hurry for the New Year festivities, goes to
375   his tailor who takes his measurements.

[Tailor's voice.]

"That's the lot, come back in four days, I'll have it
      ready." Good. Four days later.

[Tailor's voice.]

"So sorry, come back in a week, I've made a mess
      of the seat." Good, that's all right, a neat seat
380   can be very ticklish. A week later.

[Tailor's voice.]

"Frightfully sorry, come back in ten days, I've
      made a hash of the crotch." Good, can't be
      helped, a snug crotch is always a teaser. Ten
      days later.

[Tailor's voice.]

385 "Dreadfully sorry, come back in a fortnight, I've
      made a balls of the fly." Good, at a pinch, a
      smart fly is a stiff proposition.

[Pause. Normal voice.]

I never told it worse.

[Pause. Gloomy.]

I tell this story worse and worse.

[Pause. Raconteur's voice.]

Well, to make it short, the bluebells are blowing   390
      and he ballockses the buttonholes.

[Customer's voice.]

"God damn you to hell, Sir, no, it's indecent, there
      are limits! In six days, do you hear me, six days,
      God made the world. Yes Sir, no less Sir, the
      WORLD! And you are not bloody well capable of   395
      making me a pair of trousers in three months!"

[Tailor's voice, scandalized.]

"But my dear Sir, my dear Sir, look—(*disdainful
      gesture, disgustedly*)—at the world—(*pause*) and
      look—(*loving gesture, proudly*)—at my TROUSERS!"

*[Pause. He looks at NELL who has remained impas-
sive, her eyes unseeing, breaks into a high forced
laugh, cuts it short, pokes his head towards NELL,
launches his laugh again.]*

HAMM: Silence!   400

[NAGG starts, cuts short his laugh.]

NELL: You could see down to the bottom.

HAMM (*exasperated*): Have you not finished? Will you
      never finish?

[With sudden fury.]

Will this never finish?

*[NAGG disappears into his bin, closes the lid behind
him. NELL does not move. Frenziedly.]*

My kingdom for a nightman!   405

[He whistles. Enter CLOV.]

Clear away this muck! Chuck it in the sea!

[CLOV goes to bins, halts.]

NELL: So white.

HAMM: What? What's she blathering about?

[CLOV stoops, takes NELL's hand, feels her pulse.]

NELL (*to* CLOV): Desert!

*[CLOV lets go her hand, pushes her back in the bin,
closes the lid.]*

CLOV (*returning to his place beside the chair*): She has   410
      no pulse.

HAMM: What was she drivelling about?
CLOV: She told me to go away, into the desert.
HAMM: Damn busybody! Is that all?
415 CLOV: No.
HAMM: What else?
CLOV: I didn't understand.
HAMM: Have you bottled her?
CLOV: Yes.
420 HAMM: Are they both bottled?
CLOV: Yes.
HAMM: Screw down the lids.

[CLOV goes towards door.]

   Time enough.

[CLOV halts.]

   My anger subsides, I'd like to pee.
425 CLOV (*with alacrity*): I'll go and get the catheter.

[He goes towards door.]

HAMM: Time enough.

[CLOV halts.]

   Give me my pain-killer.
CLOV: It's too soon.

[Pause.]

   It's too soon on top of your tonic, it wouldn't act.
430 HAMM: In the morning they brace you up and in the
      evening they calm you down. Unless it's the
      other way round.

[Pause.]

   That old doctor, he's dead naturally?
CLOV: He wasn't old.
435 HAMM: But he's dead?
CLOV: Naturally.

[Pause.]

   You ask *me* that?

[Pause.]

HAMM: Take me for a little turn.

[CLOV goes behind the chair and pushes it forward.]

   Not too fast!

[CLOV pushes chair.]

Right round the world!   440

[CLOV pushes chair.]

Hug the walls, then back to the center again.

[CLOV pushes chair.]

   I was right in the center, wasn't I?
CLOV (*pushing*): Yes.
HAMM: We'd need a proper wheel-chair. With big
      wheels. Bicycle wheels!   445

[Pause.]

   Are you hugging?
CLOV (*pushing*): Yes.
HAMM (*groping for wall*): It's a lie! Why do you lie to me?
CLOV (*bearing closer to wall*): There! There!
HAMM: Stop!   450

*[CLOV stops chair close to back wall. HAMM lays his
hand against wall.]*

   Old wall!

[Pause.]

   Beyond is the . . . other hell.

[Pause. Violently.]

   Closer! Closer! Up against!
CLOV: Take away your hand.

*[HAMM withdraws his hand. CLOV rams chair against
wall.]*

   There!   455

[HAMM leans towards wall, applies his ear to it.]

HAMM: Do you hear?

[He strikes the wall with his knuckles.]

   Do you hear? Hollow bricks!

[He strikes again.]

   All that's hollow!

[Pause. He straightens up. Violently.]

   That's enough. Back!
CLOV: We haven't done the round.   460
HAMM: Back to my place!

[CLOV pushes chair back to center.]

Is that my place?
CLOV: Yes, that's your place.
HAMM: Am I right in the center?
465   CLOV: I'll measure it.
HAMM: More or less! More or less!
CLOV *(moving chair slightly)*: There!
HAMM: I'm more or less in the center?
CLOV: I'd say so.
470   HAMM: You'd say so! Put me right in the center!
CLOV: I'll go and get the tape.
HAMM: Roughly! Roughly!

[CLOV moves chair slightly.]

Bang in the center!
CLOV: There!

[Pause.]

475   HAMM: I feel a little too far to the left.

[CLOV moves chair slightly.]

Now I feel a little too far to the right.

[CLOV moves chair slightly.]

I feel a little too far forward.

[CLOV moves chair slightly.]

Now I feel a little too far back.

[CLOV moves chair slightly.]

Don't stay there *(i.e. behind the chair)*, you give me
480   the shivers.

[CLOV returns to his place beside the chair.]

CLOV: If I could kill him I'd die happy.

[Pause.]

HAMM: What's the weather like?
CLOV: As usual.
HAMM: Look at the earth.
485   CLOV: I've looked.
HAMM: With the glass?
CLOV: No need of the glass.
HAMM: Look at it with the glass.
CLOV: I'll go and get the glass.

[Exit CLOV.]

HAMM: No need of the glass!   490

[Enter CLOV with telescope.]

CLOV: I'm back again, with the glass.

[He goes to window right, looks up at it.]

I need the steps.
HAMM: Why? Have you shrunk?

[Exit CLOV with telescope.]

I don't like that, I don't like that.

[Enter CLOV with ladder, but without telescope.]

CLOV: I'm back again, with the steps.   495

*[He sets down ladder under window right, gets up on
it, realizes he has not the telescope, gets down.]*

I need the glass.

[He goes towards door.]

HAMM *(violently)*: But you have the glass!
CLOV *(halting, violently)*: No, I haven't the glass!

[Exit CLOV.]

HAMM: This is deadly.

[Enter CLOV with telescope. He goes towards ladder.]

CLOV: Things are livening up.   500

[He gets up on ladder, raises the telescope, lets it fall.]

I did it on purpose.

*[He gets down, picks up the telescope, turns it on
auditorium.]*

I see . . . a multitude . . . in transports . . . of joy.

[Pause.]

That's what I call a magnifier.

[He lowers the telescope, turns towards HAMM.]

Well? Don't we laugh?
HAMM *(after reflection)*: I don't.   505
CLOV *(after reflection)*: Nor I.

[He gets up on ladder, turns the telescope on the without.]

Let's see.

[He looks, moving the telescope.]

Zero . . .

[he looks]

. . . zero . . .

[he looks]

510 . . . and zero.
HAMM: Nothing stirs. All is—
CLOV: Zer—
HAMM (*violently*): Wait till you're spoken to!

[Normal voice.]

All is . . . all is . . . all is what?

[Violently.]

515 All is what?
CLOV: What all is? In a word? Is that what you want
to know? Just a moment.

*[He turns the telescope on the without, looks, lowers
the telescope, turns towards HAMM.]*

Corpsed.

[Pause.]

Well? Content?
520 HAMM: Look at the sea.
CLOV: It's the same.
HAMM: Look at the ocean!

*[CLOV gets down, takes a few steps towards window left,
goes back for ladder, carries it over and sets it down
under window left, gets up on it, turns the telescope on
the without, looks at length. He starts, lowers the telescope, examines it, turns it again on the without.]*

CLOV: Never seen anything like that!
HAMM (*anxious*): What? A sail? A fin? Smoke?
525 CLOV (*looking*): The light is sunk.
HAMM (*relieved*): Pah! We all knew that.
CLOV (*looking*): There was a bit left.
HAMM: The base.
CLOV (*looking*): Yes.
530 HAMM: And now?
CLOV (*looking*): All gone.
HAMM: No gulls?
CLOV (*looking*): Gulls!
HAMM: And the horizon? Nothing on the horizon?

535 CLOV (*lowering the telescope, turning towards* HAMM,
exasperated): What in God's name could there
be on the horizon?

[Pause.]

HAMM: The waves, how are the waves?
CLOV: The waves?

[He turns the telescope on the waves.]

540 Lead.
HAMM: And the sun?
CLOV (*looking*): Zero.
HAMM: But it should be sinking. Look again.
CLOV (*looking*): Damn the sun.
545 HAMM: Is it night already then?
CLOV (*looking*): No.
HAMM: Then what is it?
CLOV (*looking*): Gray.

[Lowering the telescope, turning towards HAMM, *louder.]*

Gray!

[Pause. Still louder.]

550 GRRAY!

[Pause. He gets down, approaches HAMM *from behind,
whispers in his ear.]*

HAMM (*starting*): Gray! Did I hear you say gray?
CLOV: Light black. From pole to pole.
HAMM: You exaggerate.

[Pause.]

Don't stay there, you give me the shivers.

[CLOV returns to his place beside the chair.]

555 CLOV: Why this farce, day after day?
HAMM: Routine. One never knows.

[Pause.]

Last night I saw inside my breast. There was a big
sore.
CLOV: Pah! You saw your heart.
560 HAMM: No, it was living.

[Pause. Anguished.]

Clov!
CLOV: Yes.
HAMM: What's happening?

CLOV: Something is taking its course.

[Pause.]

565   HAMM: Clov!
CLOV (*impatiently*): What is it?
HAMM: We're not beginning to . . . to . . . mean some-
      thing?
CLOV: Mean something! You and I, mean something!

[Brief laugh.]

570   Ah that's a good one!
HAMM: I wonder.

[Pause.]

      Imagine if a rational being came back to earth,
          wouldn't he be liable to get ideas into his head
          if he observed us long enough.

[Voice of rational being.]

575   Ah, good, now I see what it is, yes, now I under-
          stand what they're at!

*[CLOV starts, drops the telescope and begins to scratch
his belly with both hands. Normal voice.]*

      And without going so far as that, we ourselves . . .
          (*with emotion*) . . . we ourselves . . . at certain
          moments . . . (*Vehemently*) To think perhaps it
580   won't all have been for nothing!
CLOV (*anguished, scratching himself*): I have a flea!
HAMM: A flea! Are there still fleas?
CLOV: On me there's one.

[Scratching.]

      Unless it's a crablouse.
585   HAMM (*very perturbed*): But humanity might start
          from there all over again! Catch him, for the
          love of God!
CLOV: I'll go and get the powder.

[Exit CLOV.]

HAMM: A flea! This is awful! What a day!

[Enter CLOV with a sprinkling-tin.]

590   CLOV: I'm back again, with the insecticide.
HAMM: Let him have it!

*[CLOV loosens the top of his trousers, pulls it forward
and shakes powder into the aperture. He stoops, looks,
waits, starts, frenziedly shakes more powder, stoops,*
looks, waits.]*

CLOV: The bastard!
HAMM: Did you get him?
CLOV: Looks like it.

[He drops the tin and adjusts his trousers.]

      Unless he's laying doggo.   595
HAMM: Laying! Lying you mean. Unless he's *lying*
          doggo.
CLOV: Ah? One says lying? One doesn't say laying?
HAMM: Use your head, can't you. If he was laying
          we'd be bitched.   600
CLOV: Ah.

[Pause.]

      What about that pee?
HAMM: I'm having it.
CLOV: Ah that's the spirit, that's the spirit!

[Pause.]

HAMM (*with ardour*): Let's go from here, the two of   605
          us! South! You can make a raft and the cur-
          rents will carry us away, far away, to other . . .
          mammals!
CLOV: God forbid!
HAMM: Alone, I'll embark alone! Get working on that   610
          raft immediately. Tomorrow I'll be gone for
          ever.
CLOV (*hastening towards door*): I'll start straight away.
HAMM: Wait!

[CLOV halts.]

      Will there be sharks, do you think?   615
CLOV: Sharks? I don't know. If there are there will be.

[He goes towards door.]

HAMM: Wait!

[CLOV halts.]

      Is it not yet time for my pain-killer?
CLOV (*violently*): No!

[He goes towards door.]

HAMM: Wait!   620

[CLOV halts.]

      How are your eyes?
CLOV: Bad.

HAMM: But you can see.
CLOV: All I want.
625 HAMM: How are your legs?
CLOV: Bad.
HAMM: But you can walk.
CLOV: I come . . . and go.
HAMM: In my house.

[Pause. With prophetic relish.]

630 One day you'll be blind, like me. You'll be sitting
there, a speck in the void, in the dark, for ever,
like me.

[Pause.]

One day you'll say to yourself, I'm tired, I'll sit
down, and you'll go and sit down. Then you'll
635 say, I'm hungry, I'll get up and get something
to eat. But you won't get up. You'll say, I
shouldn't have sat down, but since I have I'll
sit on a little longer, then I'll get up and get
something to eat. But you won't get up and
640 you won't get anything to eat.

[Pause.]

You'll look at the wall a while, then you'll say, I'll
close my eyes, perhaps have a little sleep, after
that I'll feel better, and you'll close them. And
when you open them again there'll be no wall
645 any more.

[Pause.]

Infinite emptiness will be all around you, all the
resurrected dead of all the ages wouldn't fill it,
and there you'll be like a little bit of grit in the
middle of the steppe.

[Pause.]

650 Yes, one day you'll know what it is, you'll be like
me, except that you won't have anyone with
you, because you won't have had pity on anyone and because there won't be anyone left to
have pity on.

[Pause.]

655 CLOV: It's not certain.

[Pause.]

And there's one thing you forget.
HAMM: Ah?
CLOV: I can't sit down.

HAMM *(impatiently)*: Well you'll lie down then, what
the hell! Or you'll come to a standstill, simply 660
stop and stand still, the way you are now. One
day you'll say, I'm tired, I'll stop. What does
the attitude matter?

[Pause.]

CLOV: So you all want me to leave you.
HAMM: Naturally. 665
CLOV: Then I'll leave you.
HAMM: You can't leave us.
CLOV: Then I won't leave you.

[Pause.]

HAMM: Why don't you finish us?

[Pause.]

I'll tell you the combination of the cupboard if 670
you promise to finish me.
CLOV: I couldn't finish you.
HAMM: Then you won't finish me.

[Pause.]

CLOV: I'll leave you, I have things to do.
HAMM: Do you remember when you came here? 675
CLOV: No. Too small, you told me.
HAMM: Do you remember your father.
CLOV *(wearily)*: Same answer.

[Pause.]

You've asked me these questions millions of times.
HAMM: I love the old questions. 680

[With fervour.]

Ah the old questions, the old answers, there's
nothing like them!

[Pause.]

It was I was a father to you.
CLOV: Yes.

[He looks at HAMM fixedly.]

You were that to me. 685
HAMM: My house a home for you.
CLOV: Yes.

[He looks about him.]

This was that for me.

HAMM (*proudly*): But for me, (*gesture towards himself*) no father. But for Hamm, (*gesture towards surroundings*) no home.

[Pause.]

CLOV: I'll leave you.
HAMM: Did you ever think of one thing?
CLOV: Never.
HAMM: That here we're down in a hole.

[Pause.]

But beyond the hills? Eh? Perhaps it's still green. Eh?

[Pause.]

Flora! Pomona! (*Ecstatically.*) Ceres!

[Pause.]

Perhaps you won't need to go very far.
CLOV: I can't go very far.

[Pause.]

I'll leave you.
HAMM: Is my dog ready?
CLOV: He lacks a leg.
HAMM: Is he silky?
CLOV: He's a kind of Pomeranian.
HAMM: Go and get him.
CLOV: He lacks a leg.
HAMM: Go and get him!

[Exit CLOV.]

We're getting on.

[Enter CLOV holding by one of its three legs a black toy dog.]

CLOV: Your dogs are here.

[He hands the dog to HAMM who feels it, fondles it.]

HAMM: He's white, isn't he?
CLOV: Nearly.
HAMM: What do you mean, nearly? Is he white or isn't he?
CLOV: He isn't.

[Pause.]

HAMM: You've forgotten the sex.
CLOV (*vexed*): But he isn't finished. The sex goes on at the end.

[Pause.]

HAMM: You haven't put on his ribbon.
CLOV (*angrily*): But he isn't finished, I tell you! First you finish your dog and then you put on his ribbon!

[Pause.]

HAMM: Can he stand?
CLOV: I don't know.
HAMM: Try.

[He hands the dog to CLOV who places it on the ground.]

Well?
CLOV: Wait!

[He squats down and tries to get the dog to stand on its three legs, fails, lets it go. The dog falls on its side.]

HAMM (*impatiently*): Well?
CLOV: He's standing.
HAMM (*groping for the dog*): Where? Where is he?

[CLOV holds up the dog in a standing position.]

CLOV: There.

[He takes HAMM's hand and guides it towards the dog's head.]

HAMM (*his hand on the dog's head*): Is he gazing at me?
CLOV: Yes.
HAMM (*proudly*): As if he were asking me to take him for a walk?
CLOV: If you like.
HAMM (*as before*): Or as if he were begging me for a bone.

[He withdraws his hand.]

Leave him like that, standing there imploring me.

[CLOV straightens up. The dog falls on its side.]

CLOV: I'll leave you.
HAMM: Have you had your visions?
CLOV: Less.
HAMM: Is Mother Pegg's light on?
CLOV: Light! How could anyone's light be on?
HAMM: Extinguished!
CLOV: Naturally it's extinguished. If it's not on it's extinguished.
HAMM: No, I mean Mother Pegg.
CLOV: But naturally she's extinguished!

[Pause.]

What's the matter with you today?

750 HAMM: I'm taking my course.

[Pause.]

Is she buried?

CLOV: Buried! Who would have buried her?

HAMM: You.

CLOV: Me! Haven't I enough to do without burying

755 people?

HAMM: But you'll bury me.

CLOV: No I won't bury you.

[Pause.]

HAMM: She was bonny once, like a flower of the field.

[With reminiscent leer.]

And a great one for the men!

760 CLOV: We too were bonny—once. It's a rare thing not
to have been bonny—once.

[Pause.]

HAMM: Go and get the gaff.

[CLOV goes to door, halts.]

CLOV: Do this, do that, and I do it. I never refuse.
Why?

765 HAMM: You're not able to.

CLOV: Soon I won't do it any more.

HAMM: You won't be able to any more.

[Exit CLOV.]

Ah the creatures, the creatures, everything has to
be explained to them.

[Enter CLOV with gaff.]

770 CLOV: Here's your gaff. Stick it up.

*[He gives the gaff to HAMM who, wielding it like a
puntpole, tries to move his chair.]*

HAMM: Did I move?

CLOV: No.

[HAMM throws down the gaff.]

HAMM: Go and get the oilcan.

CLOV: What for?

775 HAMM: To oil the castors.

CLOV: I oiled them yesterday.

HAMM: Yesterday! What does that mean? Yesterday!

CLOV *(violently)*: That means that bloody awful day,
long ago, before this bloody awful day. I use
the words you taught me. If they don't mean 780
anything any more, teach me others. Or let me
be silent.

[Pause.]

HAMM: I once knew a madman who thought the end
of the world had come. He was a painter—and
engraver. I had a great fondness for him. I 785
used to go and see him, in the asylum. I'd take
him by the hand and drag him to the window.
Look! There! All that rising corn! And there!
Look! The sails of the herring fleet! All that
loveliness! 790

[Pause.]

He'd snatch away his hand and go back into his
corner. Appalled. All he had seen was ashes.

[Pause.]

He alone had been spared.

[Pause.]

Forgotten.

[Pause.]

It appears the case is . . . was not so . . . so unusual. 795

CLOV: A madman? When was that?

HAMM: Oh way back, way back, you weren't in the
land of the living.

CLOV: God be with the days!

[Pause. HAMM raises his toque.]

HAMM: I had a great fondness for him. 800

[Pause. He puts on his toque again.]

He was a painter—and engraver.

CLOV: There are so many terrible things.

HAMM: No, no, there are not so many now.

[Pause.]

Clov!

CLOV: Yes. 805

HAMM: Do you not think this has gone on long
enough?

CLOV: Yes!

[Pause.]

What?

810 HAMM: This . . . this . . . thing.
CLOV: I've always thought so.

[Pause.]

You not?
HAMM (*gloomily*): Then it's a day like any other day.
CLOV: As long as it lasts.

[Pause.]

815   All life long the same inanities.
HAMM: I can't leave you.
CLOV: I know. And you can't follow me.

[Pause.]

HAMM: If you leave me how shall I know?
CLOV (*briskly*): Well you simply whistle me and if I
820   don't come running it means I've left you.

[Pause.]

HAMM: You won't come and kiss me goodbye?
CLOV: Oh I shouldn't think so.

[Pause.]

HAMM: But you might be merely dead in your
        kitchen.
825 CLOV: The result would be the same.
HAMM: Yes, but how would I know, if you were
        merely dead in your kitchen?
CLOV: Well . . . sooner or later I'd start to stink.
HAMM: You stink already. The whole place stinks of
830   corpses.
CLOV: The whole universe.
HAMM (*angrily*): To hell with the universe.

[Pause.]

      Think of something.
CLOV: What?
835 HAMM: An idea, have an idea.

[Angrily.]

      A bright idea!
CLOV: Ah good.

*[He starts pacing to and fro, his eyes fixed on the
ground, his hands behind his back. He halts.]*

      The pains in my legs! It's unbelievable! Soon I

won't be able to think any more.
HAMM: You won't be able to leave me.   840

[CLOV resumes his pacing.]

      What are you doing?
CLOV: Having an idea.

[He paces.]

      Ah!

[He halts.]

HAMM: What a brain!

[Pause.]

      Well?   845
CLOV: Wait!

[He meditates. Not very convinced.]

      Yes . . .

[Pause. More convinced.]

      Yes!

[He raises his head.]

      I have it! I set the alarm.

[Pause.]

HAMM: This is perhaps not one of my bright days,   850
        but frankly—
CLOV: You whistle me. I don't come. The alarm rings.
        I'm gone. It doesn't ring. I'm dead.

[Pause.]

HAMM: Is it working?

[Pause. Impatiently.]

      The alarm, is it working?   855
CLOV: Why wouldn't it be working?
HAMM: Because it's worked too much.
CLOV: But it's hardly worked at all.
HAMM (*angrily*): Then because it's worked too little!
CLOV: I'll go and see.   860

*[Exit CLOV. Brief ring of alarm off. Enter CLOV with
alarm-clock. He holds it against HAMM's ear and
releases alarm. They listen to it ringing to the end.
Pause.]*

Fit to wake the dead! Did you hear it?
HAMM: Vaguely.
CLOV: The end is terrific!
HAMM: I prefer the middle.

[Pause.]

865   Is it not time for my pain-killer?
CLOV: No!

[He goes to door, turns.]

I'll leave you.
HAMM: It's time for my story. Do you want to listen
    to my story.
870 CLOV: No.
HAMM: Ask my father if he wants to listen to my story.

*[CLOV goes to bins, raises the lid of NAGG's, stoops,
looks into it. Pause. He straightens up.]*

CLOV: He's asleep.
HAMM: Wake him.

*[CLOV stoops, wakes NAGG with the alarm.
Unintelligible words. CLOV straightens up.]*

CLOV: He doesn't want to listen to your story.
875 HAMM: I'll give him a bon-bon.

[CLOV stoops. As before.]

CLOV: He wants a sugar-plum.
HAMM: He'll get a sugar-plum.

[CLOV stoops. As before.]

CLOV: It's a deal.

*[He goes towards door. NAGG's hands appear, gripping the
rim. Then the head emerges. CLOV reaches door, turns.]*

Do you believe in the life to come?
880 HAMM: Mine was always that.

[Exit CLOV.]

Got him that time!
NAGG: I'm listening.
HAMM: Scoundrel! Why did you engender me?
NAGG: I didn't know.
885 HAMM: What? What didn't you know?
NAGG: That it'd be you.

[Pause]

You'll give me a sugar-plum?

HAMM: After the audition.
NAGG: You swear?
HAMM: Yes.   890
NAGG: On what?
HAMM: My honor.

[Pause. They laugh heartily.]

NAGG: Two.
HAMM: One.
NAGG: One for me and one for—   895
HAMM: One! Silence!

[Pause]

Where was I?

[Pause. Gloomily.]

It's finished, we're finished.

[Pause]

Nearly finished.

[Pause]

There'll be no more speech.   900

[Pause]

Something dripping in my head, ever since the
    fontanelles.

[Stifled hilarity of NAGG.]

Splash, splash, always on the same spot.

[Pause]

Perhaps it's a little vein.

[Pause]

A little artery.   905

[Pause. More animated.]

Enough of that, it's story time, where was I?

[Pause. Narrative tone.]

The man came crawling towards me, on his belly.
    Pale, wonderfully pale and thin, he seemed on
    the point of—

[Pause. Normal tone.]

910   No, I've done that bit.

[*Pause. Narrative tone.*]

   I calmly filled my pipe—the meerschaum, lit it with
   . . . let us say a vesta, drew a few puffs. Aah!

[*Pause*]

   Well, what is it *you* want?

[*Pause*]

   It was an extra-ordinarily bitter day, I remember,
915   zero by the thermometer. But considering it
   was Christmas Eve there was nothing . . .
   extra-ordinary about that. Seasonable weather,
   for once in a way.

[*Pause*]

   Well, what ill wind blows you my way? He raised
920   his face to me, black with mingled dirt and
   tears.

[*Pause. Normal tone.*]

   That should do it.

[*Narrative tone.*]

   No no, don't look at me, don't look at me. He
   dropped his eyes and mumbled something,
925   apologies I presume.

[*Pause*]

   I'm a busy man, you know, the final touches,
   before the festivities, you know what it is.

[*Pause. Forcibly.*]

   Come on now, what is the object of this invasion?

[*Pause*]

   It was a glorious bright day, I remember, fifty by
930   the heliometer, but already the sun was sinking down into the . . . down among the dead.

[*Normal tone.*]

   Nicely put, that.

[*Narrative tone.*]

   Come on now, come on, present your petition and

let me resume my labors.

[*Pause. Normal tone.*]

   There's English for you. Ah well . . .   935

[*Narrative tone.*]

   It was then he took the plunge. It's my little one,
   he said. Tsstss, a little one, that's bad. My little
   boy, he said, as if the sex mattered. Where did
   he come from? He named the hole. A good
   half-day, on horse. What are you insinuating?   940
   That the place is still inhabited? No no, not a
   soul, except himself and the child—assuming
   he existed. Good. I enquired about the situation at Kov, beyond the gulf. Not a sinner.
   Good. And you expect me to believe you have   945
   left your little one back there, all alone, and
   alive into the bargain? Come now!

[*Pause*]

   It was a howling wild day, I remember, a hundred
   by the anenometer. The wind was tearing up
   the dead pines and sweeping them . . . away.   950

[*Pause. Normal tone.*]

   A bit feeble, that.

[*Narrative tone.*]

   Come on, man, speak up, what is you want from
   me, I have to put up my holly.

[*Pause*]

   Well to make it short it finally transpired that
   what he wanted from me was . . . bread for his   955
   brat? Bread? But I have no bread, it doesn't
   agree with me. Good. Then perhaps a little
   corn?

[*Pause. Normal tone.*]

   That should do it.

[*Narrative tone.*]

   Corn, yes, I have corn, it's true, in my granaries.   960
   But use your head. I give you some corn, a
   pound, a pound and a half, you bring it back
   to your child and you make him—if he's still
   alive—a nice pot of porridge,

[NAGG *reacts*]

965 a nice pot and a half of porridge, full of nourish-
ment. Good. The colors come back into his little cheeks—perhaps. And then?

[Pause]

I lost patience.

[Violently.]

970 Use your head, can't you, use your head, you're
on earth, there's no cure for that!

[Pause]

It was an exceedingly dry day, I remember, zero
by the hygrometer. Ideal weather, for my lum-
bago.

[Pause. Violently.]

975 But what in God's name do you imagine? That
the earth will awake in spring? That the rivers
and seas will run with fish again? That there's
manna in heaven still for imbeciles like you?

[Pause]

Gradually I cooled down, sufficiently at least to
ask him how long he had taken on the way.
980 Three whole days. Good. In what condition he
had left the child. Deep in sleep.

[Forcibly.]

But deep in what sleep, deep in what sleep
already?

[Pause]

Well to make it short I finally offered to take him
985 into my service. He had touched a chord. And
then I imagined already that I wasn't much
longer for this world.

[He laughs. Pause.]

Well?

[Pause]

Well? Here if you were careful you might die a
990 nice natural death, in peace and comfort.

[Pause]

Well?

[Pause]

In the end he asked me would I consent to take in
the child as well—if he were still alive.

[Pause]

It was the moment I was waiting for.

[Pause]

Would I consent to take in the child . . .   995

[Pause]

I can see him still, down on his knees, his hands
flat on the ground, glaring at me with his mad
eyes, in defiance of my wishes.

[Pause. Normal tone.]

I'll soon have finished with this story.

[Pause]

Unless I bring in other characters.   1000

[Pause]

But where would I find them?

[Pause]

Where would I look for them?

[Pause. He whistles. Enter CLOV.]

Let us pray to God.
NAGG: Me sugar-plum!
CLOV: There's a rat in the kitchen!   1005
HAMM: A rat! Are there still rats?
CLOV: In the kitchen there's one.
HAMM: And you haven't exterminated him?
CLOV: Half. You disturbed us.
HAMM: He can't get away?   1010
CLOV: No.
HAMM: You'll finish him later. Let us pray to God.
CLOV: Again!
NAGG: Me sugar-plum!
HAMM: God first!   1015

[Pause]

Are you right?
CLOV (*resigned*): Off we go.
HAMM (*to* NAGG): And you?
NAGG (*clasping his hands, closing his eyes, in a gabble*):

1020   Our Father which art—
HAMM: Silence! In silence! Where are your manners?

[Pause]

Off we go.

[Attitudes of prayer. Silence. Abandoning his attitude, discouraged.]

Well?
CLOV (*abandoning his attitude*): What a hope! And
1025   you?
HAMM: Sweet damn all!

[To NAGG.]

And you?
NAGG: Wait!

[Pause. Abandoning his attitude.]

Nothing doing!
1030   HAMM: The bastard! He doesn't exist!
CLOV: Not yet.
NAGG: Me sugar-plum!
HAMM: There are no more sugar-plums!

[Pause]

NAGG: It's natural. After all I'm your father. It's true
1035   if it hadn't been me it would have been someone else. But that's no excuse.

[Pause]

Turkish Delight, for example, which no longer
exists, we all know that, there is nothing in the
world I love more. And one day I'll ask you
1040   for some, in return for a kindness, and you'll
promise it to me. One must live with the times.

[Pause]

Whom did you call when you were a tiny boy,
and were frightened, in the dark? Your mother?
No. Me. We let you cry. Then we moved you
1045   out of earshot, so that we might sleep in peace.

[Pause]

I was asleep, as happy as a king, and you woke
me up to have me listen to you. It wasn't
indispensable, you didn't really need to have
me listen to you.

[Pause]

I hope the day will come when you'll really need   1050
to have me listen to you, and need to hear my
voice, any voice.

[Pause]

Yes, I hope I'll live till then, to hear you calling
me like when you were a tiny boy, and were
frightened, in the dark, and I was your only   1055
hope.

[Pause. NAGG knocks on lid of NELL's bin. Pause.]

Nell!

[Pause. He knocks louder. Pause. Louder.]

Nell!

[Pause. NAGG sinks back into his bin, closes the lid behind him. Pause.]

HAMM: Our revels now are ended.

[He gropes for the dog.]

The dog's gone.   1060
CLOV: He's not a real dog, he can't go.
HAMM (*groping*): He's not there.
CLOV: He's lain down.
HAMM: Give him up to me.

[CLOV picks up the dog and gives it to HAMM. HAMM holds it in his arms. Pause. HAMM throws away the dog.]

Dirty brute!   1065

[CLOV begins to pick up the objects lying on the ground.]

What are you doing?
CLOV: Putting things in order.

[He straightens up. Fervently.]

I'm going to clear everything away!

[He starts picking up again.]

HAMM: Order!
CLOV (*straightening up*): I love order. It's my dream. A   1070
world where all would be silent and still and
each thing in its last place, under the last dust.

[He starts picking up again.]

HAMM (*exasperated*): What in God's name do you

think you are doing?

1075 CLOV (*straightening up*): I'm doing my best to create a
        little order.
    HAMM: Drop it!

[CLOV drops the objects he has picked up.]

CLOV: After all, there or elsewhere.

[He goes towards door.]

    HAMM (*irritably*): What's wrong with your feet?
1080 CLOV: My feet?
    HAMM: Tramp! Tramp!
    CLOV: I must have put on my boots.
    HAMM: Your slippers were hurting you?

[Pause]

    CLOV: I'll leave you.
1085 HAMM: No!
    CLOV: What is there to keep me here?
    HAMM: The dialogue.

[Pause]

    I've got on with my story.

[Pause]

    I've got on with it well.

[Pause. Irritably.]

1090   Ask me where I've got to.
    CLOV: Oh, by the way, your story?
    HAMM (*surprised*): What story?
    CLOV: The one you've been telling yourself all your
        days.
1095 HAMM: Ah you mean my chronicle?
    CLOV: That's the one.

[Pause]

    HAMM (*angrily*): Keep going, can't you, keep going!
    CLOV: You've got on with it, I hope.
    HAMM (*modestly*): Oh not very far, not very far.

[He sighs.]

1100   There are days like that, one isn't inspired.

[Pause]

    Nothing you can do about it, just wait for it to come.

[Pause]

No forcing, no forcing, it's fatal.

[Pause]

I've got on with it a little all the same.

[Pause]

Technique, you know.

[Pause. Irritably.]

    I say I've got on with it a little all the same.   1105
CLOV (*admiringly*): Well I never! In spite of every-
        thing you were able to get on with it!
HAMM (*modestly*): Oh not very far, you know, not
        very far, but nevertheless, better than nothing.
CLOV: Better than nothing! Is it possible?   1110
HAMM: I'll tell you how it goes. He comes crawling
        on his belly—
CLOV: Who?
HAMM: What?
CLOV: Who do you mean, he?   1115
HAMM: Who do I mean! Yet another.
CLOV: Ah him! I wasn't sure.
HAMM: Crawling on his belly, whining for bread for
        his brat. He's offered a job as gardener. Before—

[CLOV bursts out laughing.]

    What is there so funny about that?   1120
CLOV: A job as gardener!
HAMM: Is that what tickles you?
CLOV: It must be that.
HAMM: It wouldn't be the bread?
CLOV: Or the brat.   1125

[Pause]

HAMM: The whole thing is comical, I grant you that.
        What about having a good guffaw the two of
        us together?
CLOV (*after reflection*): I couldn't guffaw again today.
HAMM (*after reflection*): Nor I.   1130

[Pause]

    I continue then. Before accepting with gratitude
        he asks if he may have his little boy with him.
CLOV: What age?
HAMM: Oh tiny.
CLOV: He would have climbed the trees.   1135
HAMM: All the little odd jobs.
CLOV: And then he would have grown up.
HAMM: Very likely.

[Pause]

CLOV: Keep going, can't you, keep going!
1140 HAMM: That's all. I stopped there.

[Pause]

CLOV: Do you see how it goes on.
HAMM: More or less.
CLOV: Will it not soon be the end?
HAMM: I'm afraid it will.
1145 CLOV: Pah! You'll make up another.
HAMM: I don't know.

[Pause]

I feel rather drained.

[Pause]

The prolonged creative effort.

[Pause]

If I could drag myself down to the sea! I'd make a
1150 pillow of sand for my head and the tide would
come.
CLOV: There's no more tide.

[Pause]

HAMM: Go and see is she dead.

*[*CLOV *goes to bins, raises the lid of* NELL's, *stoops,
looks into it. Pause.]*

CLOV: Looks like it.

[He closes the lid, straightens up. HAMM *raises his
toque. Pause. He puts it on again.]*

1155 HAMM (*with his hand to his toque*): And Nagg?

*[*CLOV *raises lid of* NAGG's *bin, stoops, looks into it.
Pause.]*

CLOV: Doesn't look like it.

[He closes the lid, straightens up.]

HAMM (*letting go his toque*): What's he doing?

*[*CLOV *raises lid of* NAGG's *bin, stoops, looks into it. Pause.]*

CLOV: He's crying.

[He closes lid, straightens up.]

HAMM: Then he's living.

[Pause]

Did you ever have an instant of happiness? 1160
CLOV: Not to my knowledge.

[Pause]

HAMM: Bring me under the window.

*[*CLOV *goes towards chair.]*

I want to feel the light on my face.

*[*CLOV *pushes chair.]*

Do you remember, in the beginning, when you
took me for a turn? You used to hold the chair 1165
too high. At every step you nearly tipped me
out.

[With senile quaver.]

Ah great fun, we had, the two of us, great fun.

[Gloomily.]

And then we got into the way of it.

*[*CLOV *stops the chair under window right.]*

There already? 1170

[Pause. He tilts back his head.]

Is it light?
CLOV: It isn't dark.
HAMM (*angrily*): I'm asking you is it light.
CLOV: Yes.

[Pause]

HAMM: The curtain isn't closed? 1175
CLOV: No.
HAMM: What window is it?
CLOV: The earth.
HAMM: I knew it!

[Angrily.]

But there's no light there! The other! 1180

*[*CLOV *pushes chair towards window left.]*

The earth!

*[*CLOV *stops the chair under window left.* HAMM *tilts
back his head.]*

That's what I call light!

[Pause]

Feels like a ray of sunshine.

[Pause]

No?
1185 CLOV: No.
HAMM: It isn't a ray of sunshine I feel on my face?
CLOV: No.

[Pause]

HAMM: Am I very white?

[Pause. Angrily.]

I'm asking you am I very white!
1190 CLOV: Not more so than usual.

[Pause]

HAMM: Open the window.
CLOV: What for?
HAMM: I want to hear the sea.
CLOV: You wouldn't hear it.
1195 HAMM: Even if you opened the window?
CLOV: No.
HAMM: Then it's not worth while opening it?
CLOV: No.
HAMM (*violently*): Then open it!

[CLOV gets up on the ladder, opens the window. Pause.]

1200 Have you opened it?
CLOV: Yes.

[Pause]

HAMM: You swear you've opened it?
CLOV: Yes.

[Pause]

HAMM: Well . . . !

[Pause]

1205 It must be very calm.

[Pause. Violently.]

I'm asking you is it very calm!
CLOV: Yes.
HAMM: It's because there are no more navigators.

[Pause]

You haven't much conversation all of a sudden.
  Do you not feel well?   1210
CLOV: I'm cold.
HAMM: What month are we?

[Pause]

Close the window, we're going back.

*[CLOV closes the window, gets down, pushes the chair
back to its place, remains standing behind it, head
bowed.]*

Don't stay there, you give me the shivers!

[CLOV returns to his place beside the chair.]

Father!   1215

[Pause. Louder.]

Father!

[Pause]

Go and see did he hear me.

*[CLOV goes to NAGG's bin, raises the lid, stoops.
Unintelligible words. CLOV straightens up.]*

CLOV: Yes.
HAMM: Both times?

[CLOV stoops. As before.]

CLOV: Once only.   1220
HAMM: The first time or the second?

[CLOV stoops. As before.]

CLOV: He doesn't know.
HAMM: It must have been the second.
CLOV: We'll never know.

[He closes lid.]

HAMM: Is he still crying?   1225
CLOV: No.
HAMM: The dead go fast.

[Pause]

What's he doing?
CLOV: Sucking his biscuit.
HAMM: Life goes on.   1230

[CLOV *returns to his place beside the chair.*]

Give me a rug, I'm freezing.
CLOV: There are no more rugs.

[*Pause*]

HAMM: Kiss me.

[*Pause*]

Will you not kiss me?
1235 CLOV: No.
HAMM: On the forehead.
CLOV: I won't kiss you anywhere.

[*Pause*]

HAMM (*holding out his hand*): Give me your hand at
    least.

[*Pause*]

1240 Will you not give me your hand?
CLOV: I won't touch you.

[*Pause*]

HAMM: Give me the dog.

[CLOV *looks round for the dog.*]

No!
CLOV: Do you not want your dog?
1245 HAMM: No.
CLOV: Then I'll leave you.
HAMM (*head bowed, absently*): That's right.

[CLOV *goes to door, turns.*]

CLOV: If I don't kill that rat he'll die.
HAMM (*as before*): That's right.

[*Exit* CLOV. *Pause.*]

1250 Me to play.

[*He takes out his handkerchief, unfolds it, holds it
spread out before him.*]

We're getting on.

[*Pause*]

You weep, and weep, for nothing, so as not to
    laugh, and little by little . . . you begin to grieve.

[*He folds the handkerchief, puts it back in his pocket,
raises his head.*]

All those I might have helped.

[*Pause*]

Helped!   1255

[*Pause*]

Saved.

[*Pause*]

Saved!

[*Pause*]

The place was crawling with them!

[*Pause. Violently.*]

Use your head, can't you, use your head, you're
    on earth, there's no cure for that!   1260

[*Pause*]

Get out of here and love one another! Lick your
    neighbor as yourself!

[*Pause. Calmer.*]

When it wasn't bread they wanted it was crumpets.

[*Pause. Violently.*]

Out of my sight and back to your petting parties!

[*Pause*]

All that, all that!   1265

[*Pause*]

Not even a real dog!

[*Calmer.*]

The end is in the beginning and yet you go on.

[*Pause*]

Perhaps I could go on with my story, end it and
    begin another.

[*Pause*]

1270   Perhaps I could throw myself out on the floor.

[*He pushes himself painfully off his seat, falls back again.*]

Dig my nails into the cracks and drag myself for-
    ward with my fingers.

[*Pause*]

It will be the end and there I'll be, wondering
    what can have brought it on and wondering
1275   what can have . . . (*he hesitates*) . . . why it was
    so long coming.

[*Pause*]

There I'll be, in the old shelter, alone against the
    silence and . . . (*he hesitates*) . . . the stillness. If I
    can hold my peace, and sit quiet, it will be all
1280   over with sound, and motion, all over and
    done with.

[*Pause*]

I'll have called my father and I'll have called
    my . . . (*he hesitates*) . . . my son. And even
    twice, or three times, in case they shouldn't
1285   have heard me, the first time, or the second.

[*Pause*]

I'll say to myself, He'll come back.

[*Pause*]

And then?

[*Pause*]

And then?

[*Pause*]

He couldn't, he has gone too far.

[*Pause*]

1290   And then?

[*Pause. Very agitated.*]

All kinds of fantasies! That I'm being watched! A
    rat! Steps! Breath held and then . . .

[*He breathes out.*]

Then babble, babble, words, like the solitary child

who turns himself into children, two, three, so as
to be together, and whisper together, in the dark. 1295

[*Pause*]

Moment upon moment, pattering down, like the
    millet grains of . . . (*he hesitates*) . . . that old
    Greek, and all life long you wait for that to
    mount up to a life.

[*Pause. He opens his mouth to continue, renounces.*]

Ah let's get it over!   1300

[*He whistles. Enter* CLOV *with alarm-clock. He halts
beside the chair.*]

What? Neither gone nor dead?
CLOV: In spirit only.
HAMM: Which?
CLOV: Both.
HAMM: Gone from me you'd be dead.   1305
CLOV: And vice versa.
HAMM: Outside of here it's death!

[*Pause*]

And the rat?
CLOV: He's got away.
HAMM: He can't go far.   1310

[*Pause. Anxious.*]

Eh?
CLOV: He doesn't need to go far.

[*Pause*]

HAMM: Is it not time for my pain-killer?
CLOV: Yes.
HAMM: Ah! At last! Give it to me! Quick!   1315

[*Pause*]

CLOV: There's no more pain-killer.

[*Pause*]

HAMM (*appalled*): Good . . . !

[*Pause*]

No more pain-killer!
CLOV: No more pain-killer. You'll never get any more
    pain-killer.   1320

[*Pause*]

HAMM: But the little round box. It was full!
CLOV: Yes. But now it's empty.

[Pause. CLOV starts to move about the room. He is looking for a place to put down the alarm-clock.]

HAMM (soft): What'll I do?

[Pause. In a scream.]

What'll I do?

[CLOV sees the picture, takes it down, stands it on the floor with its face to the wall, hangs up the alarm-clock in its place.]

1325 What are you doing?
CLOV: Winding up.
HAMM: Look at the earth.
CLOV: Again!
HAMM: Since it's calling to you.
1330 CLOV: Is your throat sore?

[Pause]

Would you like a lozenge?

[Pause]

No.

[Pause]

Pity.

[CLOV goes, humming, towards window right, halts before it, looks up at it.]

HAMM: Don't sing.
1335 CLOV (turning towards HAMM): One hasn't the right to sing any more?
HAMM: No.
CLOV: Then how can it end?
HAMM: You want it to end?
1340 CLOV: I want to sing.
HAMM: I can't prevent you.

[Pause. CLOV turns towards window right.]

CLOV: What did I do with that steps?

[He looks around for ladder.]

You didn't see that steps?

[He sees it.]

Ah, about time.

[He goes towards window left.]

Sometimes I wonder if I'm in my right mind.   1345
Then it passes over and I'm as lucid as before.

[He gets up on ladder, looks out of window.]

Christ, she's under water!

[He looks.]

How can that be?

[He pokes forward his head, his hand above his eyes.]

It hasn't rained.

[He wipes the pane, looks. Pause.]

Ah what a fool I am! I'm on the wrong side!   1350

[He gets down, takes a few steps towards window right.]

Under water!

[He goes back for ladder.]

What a fool I am!

[He carries ladder towards window right.]

Sometimes I wonder if I'm in my right senses.
Then it passes off and I'm as intelligent as ever.

[He sets down ladder under window right, gets up on it, looks out of window. He turns towards HAMM.]

Any particular sector you fancy? Or merely the   1355
whole thing?
HAMM: Whole thing.
CLOV: The general effect? Just a moment.

[He looks out of window. Pause.]

HAMM: Clov.
CLOV (absorbed): Mmm.   1360
HAMM: Do you know what it is?
CLOV (as before): Mmm.
HAMM: I was never there.

[Pause]

Clov!
CLOV (turning towards HAMM, exasperated): What is it?   1365
HAMM: I was never there.

CLOV: Lucky for you.

[*He looks out of window.*]

HAMM: Absent, always. It all happened without me. I
    don't know what's happened.

[*Pause*]

1370   Do you know what's happened?

[*Pause*]

    Clov!
CLOV (*turning towards* HAMM, *exasperated*): Do you
    want me to look at this muckheap, yes or no?
HAMM: Answer me first.
1375 CLOV: What?
HAMM: Do you know what's happened?
CLOV: When? Where?
HAMM (*violently*): When! What's happened? Use your
    head, can't you! What has happened?
1380 CLOV: What for Christ's sake does it matter?

[*He looks out of window.*]

HAMM: I don't know.

[*Pause.* CLOV *turns towards* HAMM.]

CLOV (*harshly*): When old Mother Pegg asked you for
    oil for her lamp and you told her to get out to
    hell, you knew what was happening then, no?

[*Pause*]

1385   You know what she died of, Mother Pegg? Of
    darkness.
HAMM (*feebly*): I hadn't any.
CLOV (*as before*): Yes, you had.

[*Pause*]

HAMM: Have you the glass?
1390 CLOV: No, it's clear enough as it is.
HAMM: Go and get it.

[*Pause.* CLOV *casts up his eyes, brandishes his fists.
He loses balance, clutches on to the ladder. He starts
to get down, halts.*]

CLOV: There's one thing I'll never understand.

[*He gets down.*]

    Why I always obey you. Can you explain that to me?
HAMM: No . . . Perhaps it's compassion.

[*Pause*]

    A kind of great compassion.   1395

[*Pause*]

    Oh you won't find it easy, you won't find it easy.

[*Pause.* CLOV *begins to move about the room in search
of the telescope.*]

CLOV: I'm tired of our goings on, very tired.

[*He searches.*]

    You're not sitting on it?

[*He moves the chair, looks at the place where it stood,
resumes his search.*]

HAMM (*anguished*): Don't leave me there!

[*Angrily* CLOV *restores the chair to its place.*]

    Am I right in the center?   1400
CLOV: You'd need a microscope to find this—

[*He sees the telescope.*]

    Ah, about time.

[*He picks up the telescope, gets up on the ladder,
turns the telescope on the without.*]

HAMM: Give me the dog.
CLOV (*looking*): Quiet!
HAMM (*angrily*): Give me the dog!   1405

[CLOV *drops the telescope, clasps his hands to his
head. Pause. He gets down precipitately, looks for the
dog, sees it, picks it up, hastens towards* HAMM *and
strikes him violently on the head with the dog.*]

CLOV: There's your dog for you!

[*The dog falls to the ground. Pause.*]

HAMM: He hit me!
CLOV: You drive me mad, I'm mad!
HAMM: If you must hit me, hit me with the axe.

[*Pause*]

    Or with the gaff, hit me with the gaff. Not with   1410
    the dog. With the gaff. Or with the axe.

[CLOV *picks up the dog and gives it to* HAMM *who*

takes it in his arms.]

CLOV (*imploringly*): Let's stop playing!
HAMM: Never!

[Pause]

    Put me in my coffin.
1415 CLOV: There are no more coffins.
HAMM: Then let it end!

*[*CLOV *goes towards ladder.]*

    With a bang!

*[*CLOV *gets up on ladder, gets down again, looks for telescope, sees it, picks it up, gets up ladder, raises telescope.]*

    Of darkness! And me? Did anyone ever have pity on me?
1420 CLOV (*lowering the telescope, turning towards* HAMM):
    What?

[Pause]

    Is it me you're referring to?
HAMM (*angrily*): An aside, ape! Did you never hear an aside before?

[Pause]

1425   I'm warming up for my last soliloquy.
CLOV: I warn you. I'm going to look at this filth since it's an order. But it's the last time.

[He turns the telescope on the without.]

    Let's see.

[He moves the telescope.]

    Nothing . . . nothing . . . good . . . good . . .
1430   nothing . . . goo—

[He starts, lowers the telescope, examines it, turns it again on the without. Pause.]

    Bad luck to it!
HAMM: More complications!

*[*CLOV *gets down.]*

    Not an underplot, I trust.

*[*CLOV *moves ladder nearer window, gets up on it, turns telescope on the without.]*

CLOV (*dismayed*): Looks like a small boy!
HAMM (*sarcastic*): A small . . . boy!   1435
CLOV: I'll go and see.

[He gets down, drops the telescope, goes towards door, turns.]

    I'll take the gaff.

[He looks for the gaff, sees it, picks it up, hastens towards door.]

HAMM: No!

*[*CLOV *halts.]*

CLOV: No? A potential procreator?
HAMM: If he exists he'll die there or he'll come here.   1440
    And if he doesn't . . .

[Pause]

CLOV: You don't believe me? You think I'm inventing?

[Pause]

HAMM: It's the end, Clov, we've come to the end. I
    don't need you any more.

[Pause]

CLOV: Lucky for you.   1445

[He goes towards door.]

HAMM: Leave me the gaff.

*[*CLOV *gives him the gaff, goes towards door, halts, looks at alarm-clock, takes it down, looks round for a better place to put it, goes to bins, puts it on lid of* NAGG's *bin. Pause.]*

CLOV: I'll leave you.

[He goes towards door.]

HAMM: Before you go . . .

*[*CLOV *halts near door.]*

    . . . say something.
CLOV: There is nothing to say.   1450
HAMM: A few words . . . to ponder . . . in my heart.
CLOV: Your heart!
HAMM: Yes.

[Pause. Forcibly.]

Yes!

[Pause]

1455 With the rest, in the end, the shadows, the murmurs, all the trouble, to end up with.

[Pause]

Clov. . . . He never spoke to me. Then, in the end, before he went, without my having asked him, he spoke to me. He said . . .

1460 CLOV *(despairingly)*: Ah. . . !
HAMM: Something . . . from your heart.
CLOV: My heart!
HAMM: A few words . . . from your heart.

[Pause]

CLOV *(fixed gaze, tonelessly, towards auditorium)*: They
1465 said to me, That's love, yes, yes, not a doubt, now you see how—
HAMM: Articulate!
CLOV *(as before)*: How easy it is. They said to me. That's friendship, yes, yes, no question, you've
1470 found it. They said to me, Here's the place, stop, raise your head and look at all that beauty. That order! They said to me, Come now, you're not a brute beast, think upon these things and you'll see how all becomes clear. And simple!
1475 They said to me, What skilled attention they get, all these dying of their wounds.
HAMM: Enough!
CLOV *(as before)*: I say to myself—sometimes, Clov, you must learn to suffer better than that if you
1480 want them to weary of punishing you—one day. I say to myself—sometimes, Clov, you must be there better than that if you want them to let you go—one day. But I feel too old, and too far, to form new habits. Good, it'll
1485 never end, I'll never go.

[Pause]

Then one day, suddenly, it ends, it changes, I don't understand, it dies, or it's me, I don't understand, that either. I ask the words that remain—sleeping, waking, morning, evening.
1490 They have nothing to say.

[Pause]

I open the door of the cell and go. I am so bowed I only see my feet, if I open my eyes, and between my legs a little trail of black dust. I say to myself that the earth is extinguished,
1495 though I never saw it lit.

[Pause]

It's easy going.

[Pause]

When I fall I'll weep for happiness.

[Pause. He goes towards door.]

HAMM: Clov!

[CLOV halts, without turning.]

Nothing.

[CLOV moves on.]

Clov! 1500

[CLOV halts, without turning.]

CLOV: This is what we call making an exit.
HAMM: I'm obliged to you, Clov. For your services.
CLOV *(turning, sharply)*: Ah pardon, it's I am obliged to you.
HAMM: It's we are obliged to each other. 1505

[Pause. CLOV goes towards door.]

One thing more.

[CLOV halts.]

A last favor.

[Exit CLOV.]

Cover me with the sheet.

[Long pause.]

No? Good.

[Pause]

Me to play. 1510

[Pause. Wearily.]

Old endgame lost of old, play and lose and have done with losing.

[Pause. More animated.]

Let me see.

[Pause]

Ah yes!

[He tries to move the chair, using the gaff as before. Enter CLOV, *dressed for the road. Panama hat, tweed coat, raincoat over his arm, umbrella, bag. He halts by the door and stands there, impassive and motionless, his eyes fixed on* HAMM, *till the end.* HAMM *gives up.]*

1515   Good.

[Pause]

Discard.

[He throws away the gaff, makes to throw away the dog, thinks better of it.]

Take it easy.

[Pause]

And now?

[Pause]

Raise hat.

[He raises his toque.]

1520   Peace to our . . . arses.

[Pause]

And put on again.

[He puts on his toque.]

Deuce.

[Pause. He takes off his glasses.]

Wipe.

[He takes out his handkerchief and, without unfolding it, wipes his glasses.]

And put on again.

[He puts on his glasses, puts back the handkerchief in his pocket.]

1525   We're coming. A few more squirms like that and I'll call.

[Pause]

A little poetry.

[Pause]

You prayed—

[Pause. He corrects himself.]

You CRIED for night; it comes—

[Pause. He corrects himself.]

It FALLS: now cry in darkness.

[He repeats, chanting.]

You cried for night; it falls: now cry in darkness.   1530

[Pause]

Nicely put, that.

[Pause]

And now?

[Pause]

Moments for nothing, now as always, time was never and time is over, reckoning closed and story ended.   1535

[Pause. Narrative tone.]

If he could have his child with him . . . .

[Pause]

It was the moment I was waiting for.

[Pause]

You don't want to abandon him? You want him to bloom while you are withering? Be there to solace your last million last moments?   1540

[Pause]

He doesn't realize, all he knows is hunger, and cold, and death to crown it all. But you! You ought to know what the earth is like, nowadays. Oh I put him before his responsibilities!

[Pause. Normal tone.]

1545   Well, there we are, there I am, that's enough.

[He raises the whistle to his lips, hesitates, drops it. Pause.]

   Yes, truly!

[He whistles. Pause. Louder. Pause.]

   Good.

[Pause]

   Father!

[Pause. Louder.]

   Father!

[Pause]

   Good.

1550
[Pause]

   We're coming.

[Pause]

   And to end up with?

[Pause]

   Discard.

[He throws away the dog. He tears the whistle from his neck.]

   With my compliments.

[He throws whistle towards auditorium. Pause. He sniffs. Soft.]

   Clov!

1555
[Long pause.]

   No? Good.

[He takes out the handkerchief.]

   Since that's the way we're playing it . . . (*he
      unfolds handkerchief*) . . . let's play it that way . . .
      (*he unfolds*) . . . and speak no more about it . . .
      (*he finishes unfolding*) . . . speak no more.

1560
[He holds handkerchief spread out before him.]

   Old stancher!

[Pause]

   You . . . remain.

[Pause. He covers his face with handkerchief, lowers his arms to armrests, remains motionless.]

[Brief tableau.]

CURTAIN

LORRAINE HANSBERRY

(1930–1965)

Lorraine Hansberry grew up in Chicago in the 1930s. Her father, a successful entrepreneur in real estate, also founded a bank for African Americans. Hansberry, clearly a gifted student, attended a number of schools in Chicago, including the Art Institute. In the 1950s she moved to New York where she met and married playwright Robert Nemiroff. She began writing plays herself, and in 1959 her first play, *A Raisin in the Sun*, was staged with seed money raised by her friends. The success of the play brought Hansberry national attention and brought notoriety to director Lloyd Richardson and to actor Sidney Poitier, who played the role of Walter Lee Younger. At twenty-nine years of age Hansberry had become the first black woman to have a play produced on Broadway and the first African American to win the New York Drama Critics Circle Award. *A Raisin in the Sun* was voted best play of 1959; two years later it was made into a film (1961), and (posthumously) into a musical (1973).

Hansberry completed only one more play, *The Sign in Sidney Brustein's Window* (1964), which concerns a Jewish intellectual who believes that the radical activism of the 1930s and the commitment to personal involvement and political action has been lost in the decade of the 1950s. Hansberry's untimely death from cancer in January of 1965 occurred shortly after this play finished its Broadway run, depriving America of one of its most promising playwrights. When she died Hansberry was working on *Les Blancs*, which was adapted and produced after her death by Nemiroff on Broadway in 1970. The play concerns the struggle of a black African intellectual to come to terms with both European and African cultures; it is one of the first major plays to register a self-consciousness of and within black culture. In 1971 Nemiroff put together another posthumous work by Hansberry, *To Be Young, Gifted and Black*, compiled from her papers. In all her writings Hansberry brings an intense concern with the black struggle that is committed but not militant, expressing personal investment in a political vision. Embedded in the 1960s, her work easily transcends its own times.

A Raisin in the Sun

Lorraine Hansberry's *A Raisin in the Sun* is now regarded as a classic of post–World War II American realism. It opened in New York in 1959, at the beginning of the rise of African-American consciousness that has in turn so affected the social consciousness and social fabric of America. The use of the word *negro* in the play firmly dates it in the 1950s; in the late 1960s the word came to a signal a kind of benign social oppression and was replaced by the word *black*.

Hansberry took her title for *A Raisin in the Sun* from a poem by Langston Hughes which begins with the line "What happens to a dream deferred?" The poem suggests the social volatility of a situation in which an entire class of people is denied the opportunity to participate in the dreams that sustain the rest of the society. The basic plot of *A Raisin in the Sun* is an exploration of the implications of a family matriarch's decision to use the $10,000 from her late husband's life insurance policy to purchase a home in a white neighborhood. The play is about the personal, familial, and social difficulties facing black people who insist on participating in the American dream—the dream that through hard work, thrift, and ownership all people in America can give their lives meaning and dignity. After the play appeared in 1959 *Life* magazine reported that *A Raisin in the Sun* transcended the particulars of individual experience to create a universal play because of Hansberry's ability to create characters who were "human beings rather than social problem cases." Critics continue to agree. Richard Sharine has suggested that *A Raisin in the Sun* is the best protest play ever written because of its ability to turn an audience's perception of "them" into a mutual "we." The play has been revived many times since its first production in 1959, and virtually every time critics have been in agreement that the issues the play treats are still relevant.

Some of the critical reaction to the character of Lena Younger dismayed Hansberry, and she tried to correct what she thought were misconceptions. To some critics Lena appeared to be a typical black American matriarch. To Hansberry Lena was much more than that. Lena is a hardworking domestic servant who never loses her faith in herself and in her family, but for Hansberry she also symbolizes the "will to transcendence." Lena objects to Walter Lee's plan to buy into a liquor store because it would dishonor the memory of her husband and would have an adverse effect on the community. Lena's dream is not merely one of ownership but of a better life for herself, her family, and her community.

Walter Lee's weaknesses and gullibility are plainly apparent. Very late in the play, his change in character is brought about by his recognition of his family's heritage and his responsibility to their future. His mother reminds him of the five generations of ancestors who were slaves and sharecroppers but never let anyone tell them they were unfit to walk the earth. Prompted by that reminder and by the presence of his ten-year-old son, Travis, Walter Lee rejects the offer of the Clybourne Park Improvement Association to buy back their home: "We called you over here to tell you we are very proud and that this is—this is my son, who makes the sixth generation of our family in this country, and that we have all thought about your offer and we have decided to move into our house because my father—my father—he earned it."

A Raisin in the Sun

Lorraine Hansberry

CHARACTERS

RUTH YOUNGER
TRAVIS YOUNGER
WALTER LEE YOUNGER (BROTHER)
BENEATHA YOUNGER
LENA YOUNGER (MAMA)

JOSEPH ASAGAI
GEORGE MURCHISON
KARL LINDNER
BOBO
MOVING MEN

The action of the play is set in Chicago's Southside, sometime between World War II and the present.

What happens to a dream deferred?
Does it dry up
Like a raisin in the sun?
Or fester like a sore—
And then run?
Does it stink like rotten meat?
Or crust and sugar over—
Like a syrupy sweet?

Maybe it just sags
Like a heavy load.

Or does it explode?

—Langston Hughes

ACT I

SCENE 1. Friday morning.

SCENE 2. The following morning.

ACT II

SCENE 1. Later, the same day.

SCENE 2. Friday night, a few weeks later.

SCENE 3. Moving day, one week later.

ACT III

An hour later.

ACT I

Scene 1

The YOUNGER *living room would be a comfortable and well-ordered room if it were not for a number of inde-structible contradictions to this state of being. Its furnishings are typical and undistinguished and their primary feature now is that they have clearly had to accommodate the living of too many people for too many years—and they are tired. Still, we can see that at some time, a time probably no longer remembered by the family (except perhaps for* MAMA*), the furnishings of this room were actually selected with care and love and even hope—and brought to this apartment and arranged with taste and pride.*

That was a long time ago. Now the once loved pattern of the couch upholstery has to fight to show itself from under acres of crocheted doilies and couch covers which have themselves finally come to be more important than the upholstery. And here a table or a chair has been moved to disguise the worn places in the carpet; but the carpet has fought back by showing its weariness, with depressing uniformity, elsewhere on its surface.

Weariness has, in fact, won in this room. Everything has been polished, washed, sat on, used, scrubbed too often. All pretenses but living itself have long since vanished from the very atmosphere of this room.

Moreover, a section of this room, for it is not really a room unto itself, though the landlord's lease would make it seem so, slopes backward to provide a small kitchen area, where the family prepares the meals that are eaten in the living room proper, which must also serve as dining room. The single window that has been provided for these "two" rooms is located in this kitchen area. The sole natural light the family may enjoy in the course of a day is only that which fights its way through this little window.

At left, a door leads to a bedroom which is shared by MAMA *and her daughter,* BENEATHA. *At right, opposite, is a second room (which in the beginning of the life of this apartment was probably a breakfast room) which serves as a bedroom for* WALTER *and his wife,* RUTH.

Time: Sometime between World War II and the present.

Place: Chicago's Southside.

At Rise: It is morning dark in the living room. TRAVIS *is asleep on the make-down bed at center. An alarm clock sounds from within the bedroom at right, and presently* RUTH *enters from that room and closes the door behind her. She crosses sleepily toward the window. As she passes her sleeping son she reaches down and shakes him a little. At the window she raises the shade and a dusky Southside morning light comes in feebly. She fills a pot with water and puts it on to boil. She calls to the boy, between yawns, in a slightly muffled voice.*

RUTH is about thirty. We can see that she was a pretty girl, even exceptionally so, but now it is apparent that life has been little that she expected, and disappointment has already begun to hang in her face. In a few years, before thirty-five even, she will be known among her people as a "settled woman."

She crosses to her son and gives him a good, final, rousing shake.

RUTH: Come on now, boy, it's seven thirty! (*Her son sits up at last, in a stupor of sleepiness*) I say hurry up, Travis! You ain't the only person in the world got to use a bathroom! (*The child, a stur-*
5 *dy, handsome little boy of ten or eleven, drags himself out of the bed and almost blindly takes his towels and "today's clothes" from drawers and a closet and goes out to the bathroom, which is in an outside hall and which is shared by another family or fami-*
10 *lies on the same floor.* RUTH *crosses to the bedroom door at right and opens it and calls in to her husband*) Walter Lee! . . . It's after seven thirty! Lemme see you do some waking up in there now! (*She waits*) You better get up from there,
15 man! It's after seven thirty I tell you. (*She waits again*) All right, you just go ahead and lay there and next thing you know Travis be finished and Mr. Johnson'll be in there and you'll be fussing and cussing round here like a mad
20 man! And be late too! (*She waits, at the end of patience*) Walter Lee—it's time for you to get up!

[*She waits another second and then starts to go into the bedroom, but is apparently satisfied that her husband has begun to get up. She stops, pulls the door to, and returns to the kitchen area. She wipes her face with a moist cloth and runs her fingers through her sleep-disheveled hair in a vain effort and ties an apron around her housecoat. The bedroom door at right opens*

and her husband stands in the doorway in his pajamas, which are rumpled and mismated. He is a lean, intense young man in his middle thirties, inclined to quick nervous movements and erratic speech habits—and always in his voice there is a quality of indictment]

WALTER: Is he out yet?

RUTH: What you mean *out*? He ain't hardly got in there good yet.

WALTER (*Wandering in, still more oriented to sleep than   25
to a new day*): Well, what was you doing all that yelling for if I can't even get in there yet? (*Stopping and thinking*) Check coming today?

RUTH: They *said* Saturday and this is just Friday and I hopes to God you ain't going to get up here   30
first thing this morning and start talking to me 'bout no money—'cause I 'bout don't want to hear it.

WALTER: Something the matter with you this morning?

RUTH: No—I'm just sleepy as the devil. What kind of   35
eggs you want?

WALTER: Not scrambled. (RUTH *starts to scramble eggs*) Paper come? (RUTH *points impatiently to the rolled up Tribune on the table, and he gets it and spreads it out and vaguely reads the front page*) Set   40
off another bomb yesterday.

RUTH (*Maximum indifference*): Did they?

WALTER (*Looking up*): What's the matter with you?

RUTH: Ain't nothing the matter with me. And don't keep asking me that this morning.   45

WALTER: Ain't nobody bothering you. (*Reading the news of the day absently again*) Say Colonel McCormick is sick.

RUTH (*Affecting tea-party interest*): Is he now? Poor thing.   50

WALTER (*Sighing and looking at his watch*): Oh, me. (*He waits*) Now what is that boy doing in that bathroom all this time? He just going to have to start getting up earlier. I can't be being late to work on account of him fooling around in   55
there.

RUTH (*Turning on him*): Oh, no he ain't going to be getting up no earlier no such thing! It ain't his fault that he can't get to bed no earlier nights 'cause he got a bunch of crazy good-for-noth-   60
ing clowns sitting up running their mouths in what is supposed to be his bedroom after ten o'clock at night . . .

WALTER: That's what you mad about, ain't it? The things I want to talk about with my friends just   65
couldn't be important in your mind, could they?

[*He rises and finds a cigarette in her handbag on the table and crosses to the little window and looks out, smoking and deeply enjoying this first one]*

RUTH (*Almost matter of factly, a complaint too automatic*

to deserve emphasis): Why you always got to
smoke before you eat in the morning?

70 WALTER (*At the window*): Just look at 'em down there
. . . Running and racing to work . . . (*He turns
and faces his wife and watches her a moment at the
stove, and then, suddenly*) You look young this
morning, baby.

75 RUTH (*Indifferently*): Yeah?

WALTER: Just for a second—stirring them eggs. It's
gone now—just for a second it was—you
looked real young again. (*Then, drily*) It's gone
now—you look like yourself again.

80 RUTH: Man, if you don't shut up and leave me alone.

WALTER (*Looking out to the street again*): First thing a
man ought to learn in life is not to make love
to no colored woman first thing in the morning. You all some evil people at eight o'clock in

85 the morning.

[TRAVIS *appears in the hall doorway, almost fully
dressed and quite wide awake now, his towels and
pajamas across his shoulders. He opens the door and
signals for his father to make the bathroom in a hurry*]

TRAVIS (*Watching the bathroom*): Daddy, come on!

[WALTER *gets his bathroom utensils and flies out to the
bathroom*]

RUTH: Sit down and have your breakfast, Travis.

TRAVIS: Mama, this is Friday. (*Gleefully*) Check coming tomorrow, huh?

90 RUTH: You get your mind off money and eat your
breakfast.

TRAVIS (*Eating*): This is the morning we supposed to
bring the fifty cents to school.

RUTH: Well, I ain't got no fifty cents this morning.

95 TRAVIS: Teacher say we have to.

RUTH: I don't care what teacher say. I ain't got it. Eat
your breakfast, Travis.

TRAVIS: I *am* eating.

RUTH: Hush up now and just eat!

[*The boy gives her an exasperated look for her lack of
understanding, and eats grudgingly*]

100 TRAVIS: You think Grandmama would have it?

RUTH: No! And I want you to stop asking your
grandmother for money, you hear me?

TRAVIS (*Outraged*): Gaaaleee! I don't ask her, she just
gimme it sometimes!

105 RUTH: Travis Willard Younger—I got too much on
me this morning to be—

TRAVIS: Maybe Daddy—

RUTH: Travis!

[*The boy hushes abruptly. They are both quiet and*

tense for several seconds]

TRAVIS (*Presently*): Could I maybe go carry some groceries in front of the supermarket for a little   110
while after school then?

RUTH: Just hush, I said. (TRAVIS *jabs his spoon into his
cereal bowl viciously, and rests his head in anger
upon his fists*) If you through eating, you can
get over there and make up your bed.   115

[*The boy obeys stiffly and crosses the room, almost
mechanically, to the bed and more or less carefully
folds the covering. He carries the bedding into his
mother's room and returns with his books and cap*]

TRAVIS (*Sulking and standing apart from her unnaturally*):
I'm gone.

RUTH (*Looking up from the stove to inspect him automatically*): Come here. (*He crosses to her and she
studies his head*) If you don't take this comb and   120
fix this here head, you better! (TRAVIS *puts down
his books with a great sigh of oppression, and crosses to the mirror. His mother mutters under her
breath about his "slubbornness"*) 'Bout to march
out of here with that head looking just like   125
chickens slept in it! I just don't know where
you get your slubborn ways . . . And get your
jacket, too. Looks chilly out this morning.

TRAVIS (*With conspicuously brushed hair and jacket*): I'm
gone.   130

RUTH: Get carfare and milk money—(*Waving one finger*)—and not a single penny for no caps, you
hear me?

TRAVIS (*With sullen politeness*): Yes'm.

[*He turns in outrage to leave. His mother watches
after him as in his frustration he approaches the door
almost comically. When she speaks to him, her voice
has become a very gentle tease*]

RUTH (*Mocking; as she thinks he would say it*): Oh,   135
Mama makes me so mad sometimes, I don't
know what to do! (*She waits and continues to his
back as he stands stock-still in front of the door*) I
wouldn't kiss that woman good-bye for noth-
ing in this world this morning! (*The boy finally*   140
*turns around and rolls his eyes at her, knowing the
mood has changed and he is vindicated; he does not,
however, move toward her yet*) Not for nothing in
this world! (*She finally laughs aloud at him and
holds out her arms to him and we see that it is a*   145
*way between them, very old and practiced. He
crosses to her and allows her to embrace him warmly but keeps his face fixed with masculine rigidity.
She holds him back from her presently and looks at
him and runs her fingers over the features of his*   150
face. With utter gentleness—) Now—whose little

old angry man are you?

TRAVIS (*The masculinity and gruffness start to fade at last*): Aw gaalee—Mama . . .

155 RUTH (*Mimicking*): Aw—gaaaaalleeeee, Mama! (*She pushes him, with rough playfulness and finality, toward the door*) Get on out of here or you going to be late.

TRAVIS (*In the face of love, new aggressiveness*): Mama,
160 could I *please* go carry groceries?

RUTH: Honey, it's starting to get so cold evenings.

WALTER (*Coming in from the bathroom and drawing a make-believe gun from a make-believe holster and shooting at his son*): What is it he wants to do?

165 RUTH: Go carry groceries after school at the super-market.

WALTER: Well, let him go . . .

TRAVIS (*Quickly, to the ally*): I *have* to—she won't gimme the fifty cents . . .

170 WALTER (*To his wife only*): Why not?

RUTH (*Simply, and with flavor*): 'Cause we don't have it.

WALTER (*To* RUTH *only*): What you tell the boy things like that for? (*Reaching down into his pants with a rather important gesture*) Here, son—

[He hands the boy the coin, but his eyes are directed to his wife's. TRAVIS *takes the money happily]*

175 TRAVIS: Thanks, Daddy.

[He starts out. RUTH *watches both of them with murder in her eyes.* WALTER *stands and stares back at her with defiance, and suddenly reaches into his pocket again on an afterthought]*

WALTER (*Without even looking at his son, still staring hard at his wife*): In fact, here's another fifty cents . . . Buy yourself some fruit today—or take a taxi cab to school or something!

180 TRAVIS: Whoopee—

[He leaps up and clasps his father around the middle with his legs, and they face each other in mutual appreciation; slowly WALTER LEE *peeks around the boy to catch the violent rays from his wife's eyes and draws his head back as if shot]*

WALTER: You better get down now—and get to school, man.

TRAVIS (*At the door*): O.K. Good-bye.

[He exits]

WALTER (*After him, pointing with pride*): That's *my* boy.
185 (*She looks at him in disgust and turns back to her work*) You know what I was thinking 'bout in the bathroom this morning?

RUTH: No.

WALTER: How come you always try to be so pleasant!

RUTH: What is there to be pleasant 'bout!   190

WALTER: You want to know what I was thinking 'bout in the bathroom or not!

RUTH: I know what you was thinking 'bout.

WALTER (*Ignoring her*): 'Bout what me and Willy Harris was talking about last night.   195

RUTH (*Immediately—a refrain*): Willy Harris is a good-for-nothing loud mouth.

WALTER: Anybody who talks to me has got to be a good-for-nothing loud mouth, ain't he? And what you know about who is just a good-for-   200
nothing loud mouth? Charlie Atkins was just a "good-for-nothing loud mouth" too, wasn't he! When he wanted me to go in the dry-cleaning business with him. And now—he's grossing a hundred thousand a year. A hundred thousand   205
dollars a year! You still call *him* a loud mouth!

RUTH (*Bitterly*): Oh, Walter Lee . . .

[She folds her head on her arms over on the table]

WALTER (*Rising and coming to her and standing over her*): You tired, ain't you? Tired of everything. Me, the boy, the way we live—this beat-up hole—   210
everything. Ain't you? (*She doesn't look up, doesn't answer*) So tired—moaning and groaning all the time, but you wouldn't do nothing to help, would you? You couldn't be on my side that long for nothing, could you?   215

RUTH: Walter, please leave me alone.

WALTER: A man needs for a woman to back him up . . .

RUTH: Walter—

WALTER: Mama would listen to you. You know she listen to you more than she do me and Bennie.   220
She think more of you. All you have to do is just sit down with her when you drinking your coffee one morning and talking 'bout things like you do and—(*He sits down beside her and demonstrates graphically what he thinks her   225
methods and tone should be*)—you just sip your coffee, see, and say easy like that you been thinking 'bout that deal Walter Lee is so inter-ested in, 'bout the store and all, and sip some more coffee, like what you saying ain't really   230
that important to you—And the next thing you know, she be listening good and asking you questions and when I come home—I can tell her the details. This ain't no fly-by-night proposition, baby. I mean we figured it out, me   235
and Willy and Bobo.

RUTH (*With a frown*): Bobo?

WALTER: Yeah. You see, this little liquor store we got in mind cost seventy-five thousand and we figured the initial investment on the place be   240
'bout thirty thousand, see. That be ten thou-sand each. Course, there's a couple of hundred

you got to pay so's you don't spend your life
just waiting for them clowns to let your license
245   get approved—

RUTH: You mean graft?

WALTER (*Frowning impatiently*): Don't call it that. See
there, that just goes to show you what women
understand about the world. Baby, don't *noth-*
250   *ing* happen for you in this world 'less you pay
somebody off!

RUTH: Walter, leave me alone! (*She raises her head and
stares at him vigorously—then says, more quietly*)
Eat your eggs, they gonna be cold.

255   WALTER (*Straightening up from her and looking off*):
That's it. There you are. Man say to his
woman: I got me a dream. His woman say: Eat
your eggs. (*Sadly, but gaining in power*) Man
say: I got to take hold of this here world, baby!
260   And a woman will say: Eat your eggs and go
to work. (*Passionately now*) Man say: I got to
change my life, I'm choking to death, baby!
And his woman say—(*In utter anguish as he
brings his fists down on his thighs*)—Your eggs is
265   getting cold!

RUTH (*Softly*): Walter, that ain't none of our money.

WALTER (*Not listening at all or even looking at her*): This
morning, I was lookin' in the mirror and thinking about it . . . I'm thirty-five years old; I been
270   married eleven years and I got a boy who
sleeps in the living room—(*Very, very quietly*)—
and all I got to give him is stories about how
rich white people live . . .

RUTH: Eat your eggs, Walter.

275   WALTER: *Damn my eggs . . . damn all the eggs that ever was!*

RUTH: Then go to work.

WALTER (*Looking up at her*): See—I'm trying to talk to
you 'bout myself—(*Shaking his head with the
repetition*)—and all you can say is eat them
280   eggs and go to work.

RUTH (*Wearily*): Honey, you never say nothing new. I
listen to you every day, every night and every
morning, and you never say nothing new.
(*Shrugging*) So you would rather *be* Mr. Arnold
285   than be his chauffeur. So—I would *rather* be
living in Buckingham Palace.

WALTER: That is just what is wrong with the colored
woman in this world . . . Don't understand
about building their men up and making 'em
290   feel like they somebody. Like they can do
something.

RUTH (*Drily, but to hurt*): There *are* colored men who
do things.

WALTER: No thanks to the colored woman.

295   RUTH: Well, being a colored woman, I guess I can't
help myself none.

[*She rises and gets the ironing board and sets it up
and attacks a huge pile of rough-dried clothes, sprin-*

*kling them in preparation for the ironing and then
rolling them into tight fat balls*]

WALTER (*Mumbling*): We one group of men tied to a
race of women with small minds.

[*His sister BENEATHA enters. She is about twenty, as
slim and intense as her brother. She is not as pretty as
her sister-in-law, but her lean, almost intellectual face
has a handsomeness of its own. She wears a bright-red
flannel nightie, and her thick hair stands wildly about
her head. Her speech is a mixture of many things; it is
different from the rest of the family's insofar as education has permeated her sense of English—and perhaps
the Midwest rather than the South has finally—at
last—won out in her inflection; but not altogether,
because over all of it is a soft slurring and transformed
use of vowels which is the decided influence of the
Southside. She passes through the room without looking at either RUTH or WALTER and goes to the outside
door and looks, a little blindly, out to the bathroom.
She sees that it has been lost to the Johnsons. She closes the door with a sleepy vengeance and crosses to the
table and sits down a little defeated*]

BENEATHA: I am going to start timing those people.

WALTER: You should get up earlier.   300

BENEATHA (*Her face in her hands. She is still fighting the
urge to go back to bed*): Really—would you suggest dawn? Where's the paper?

WALTER (*Pushing the paper across the table to her as he
studies her almost clinically, as though he has   305
never seen her before*): You a horrible-looking
chick at this hour.

BENEATHA (*Drily*): Good morning, everybody.

WALTER (*Senselessly*): How is school coming?

BENEATHA (*In the same spirit*): Lovely. Lovely. And   310
you know, biology is the greatest. (*Looking up
at him*) I dissected something that looked just
like you yesterday.

WALTER: I just wondered if you've made up your
mind and everything.   315

BENEATHA (*Gaining in sharpness and impatience*): And
what did I answer yesterday morning—and
the day before that?

RUTH (*From the ironing board, like someone disinterested
and old*): Don't be so nasty, Bennie.   320

BENEATHA (*Still to her brother*): And the day before
that and the day before that!

WALTER (*Defensively*): I'm interested in you.
Something wrong with that? Ain't many girls
who decide—   325

WALTER *and* BENEATHA (*In unison*): —"to be a doctor."

[*Silence*]

WALTER: Have we figured out yet just exactly how

much medical school is going to cost?

RUTH: Walter Lee, why don't you leave that girl
    alone and get out of here to work?

BENEATHA (*Exits to the bathroom and bangs on the door*):
    Come on out of there, please!

[She comes back into the room]

WALTER (*Looking at his sister intently*): You know the
    check is coming tomorrow.

BENEATHA (*Turning on him with a sharpness all her
    own*): That money belongs to Mama, Walter,
    and it's for her to decide how she wants to use
    it. I don't care if she wants to buy a house or a
    rocket ship or just nail it up somewhere and
    look at it. It's hers. Not ours—*hers*.

WALTER (*Bitterly*): Now ain't that fine! You just got
    your mother's interest at heart, ain't you, girl?
    You such a nice girl—but if Mama got that
    money she can always take a few thousand
    and help you through school too—can't she?

BENEATHA: I have never asked anyone around here to
    do anything for me!

WALTER: No! And the line between asking and just
    accepting when the time comes is big and
    wide—ain't it!

BENEATHA (*With fury*): What do you want from me,
    Brother—that I quit school or just drop dead,
    which!

WALTER: I don't want nothing but for you to stop act-
    ing holy 'round here. Me and Ruth done made
    some sacrifices for you—why can't you do
    something for the family?

RUTH: Walter, don't be dragging me in it.

WALTER: You are in it—Don't you get up and go
    work in somebody's kitchen for the last three
    years to help put clothes on her back?

RUTH: Oh, Walter—that's not fair . . .

WALTER: It ain't that nobody expects you to get on
    your knees and say thank you, Brother; thank
    you, Ruth; thank you, Mama—and thank you,
    Travis, for wearing the same pair of shoes for
    two semesters—

BENEATHA (*Dropping to her knees*): Well—I *do*—all
    right?—thank everybody . . . and forgive me
    for ever wanting to be anything at all . . . for-
    give me, forgive me!

RUTH: Please stop it! Your mama'll hear you.

WALTER: Who the hell told you you had to be a doc-
    tor? If you so crazy 'bout messing 'round with
    sick people—then go be a nurse like other
    women—or just get married and be quiet . . .

BENEATHA: Well—you finally got it said . . . It took you
    three years but you finally got it said. Walter,
    give up; leave me alone—it's Mama's money.

WALTER: *He was my father, too!*

BENEATHA: So what? He was mine, too—and Travis'

grandfather—but the insurance money belongs
    to Mama. Picking on me is not going to make
    her give it to you to invest in any liquor
    stores—(*Underbreath, dropping into a chair*)—
    and I for one say, God bless Mama for that!

WALTER (*To* RUTH): See—did you hear? Did you hear!

RUTH: Honey, please go to work.

WALTER: Nobody in this house is ever going to
    understand me.

BENEATHA: Because you're a nut.

WALTER: Who's a nut?

BENEATHA: You—you are a nut. Thee is mad, boy.

WALTER (*Looking at his wife and his sister from the door,
    very sadly*): The world's most backward race of
    people, and that's a fact.

BENEATHA (*Turning slowly in her chair*): And then
    there are all those prophets who would lead us
    out of the wilderness—(WALTER *slams out of the
    house*)—into the swamps!

RUTH: Bennie, why you always gotta be pickin' on
    your brother? Can't you be a little sweeter
    sometimes? (*Door opens.* WALTER *walks in*)

WALTER (*To* RUTH): I need some money for carfare.

RUTH (*Looks at him, then warms; teasing, but tenderly*):
    Fifty cents? (*She goes to her bag and gets money*)
    Here, take a taxi.

*[*WALTER *exits.* MAMA *enters. She is a woman in her
early sixties, full-bodied and strong. She is one of
those women of a certain grace and beauty who wear
it so unobstrusively that it takes a while to notice. Her
dark-brown face is surrounded by the total whiteness
of her hair, and, being a woman who has adjusted to
many things in life and overcome many more, her face
is full of strength. She has, we can see, wit and faith of
a kind that keep her eyes lit and full of interest and
expectancy. She is, in a word, a beautiful woman. Her
bearing is perhaps most like the noble bearing of the
women of the Hereros of Southwest Africa—rather as
if she imagines that as she walks she still bears a basket or a vessel upon her head. Her speech, on the
other hand, is as careless as her carriage is precise—
she is inclined to slur everything—but her voice is perhaps not so much quiet as simply soft]*

MAMA: Who that 'round here slamming doors at this
    hour?

*[She crosses through the room, goes to the window,
opens it, and brings in a feeble little plant growing
doggedly in a small pot on the window sill. She feels
the dirt and puts it back out]*

RUTH: That was Walter Lee. He and Bennie was at it
    again.

MAMA: My children and they tempers. Lord, if this
    little old plant don't get more sun than it's been

415 getting it ain't never going to see spring again. (*She turns from the window*) What's the matter with you this morning, Ruth? You looks right peaked. You aiming to iron all them things? Leave some for me. I'll get to 'em this after-
420 noon. Bennie honey, it's too drafty for you to be sitting 'round half dressed. Where's your robe?

BENEATHA: In the cleaners.

MAMA: Well, go get mine and put it on.

BENEATHA: I'm not cold, Mama, honest.

MAMA: I know—but you so thin . . .

425 BENEATHA (*Irritably*): Mama, I'm not cold.

MAMA (*Seeing the make-down bed as* TRAVIS *has left it*): Lord have mercy, look at that poor bed. Bless his heart—he tries, don't he?

[*She moves to the bed* TRAVIS *has sloppily made up*]

RUTH: No—he don't half try at all 'cause he knows
430 you going to come along behind him and fix everything. That's just how come he don't know how to do nothing right now—you done spoiled that boy so.

MAMA: Well—he's a little boy. Ain't supposed to
435 know 'bout housekeeping. My baby, that's what he is. What you fix for his breakfast this morning?

RUTH (*Angrily*): I feed my son, Lena!

MAMA: I ain't meddling—(*Underbreath; busy-bodyish*)
440 I just noticed all last week he had cold cereal, and when it starts getting this chilly in the fall a child ought to have some hot grits or something when he goes out in the cold—

RUTH (*Furious*): I gave him hot oats—is that all right!

445 MAMA: I ain't meddling. (*Pause*) Put a lot of nice butter on it? (RUTH *shoots her an angry look and does not reply*) He likes lots of butter.

RUTH (*Exasperated*): Lena—

MAMA (*To* BENEATHA. MAMA *is inclined to wander con-*
450 *versationally sometimes*): What was you and your brother fussing 'bout this morning?

BENEATHA: It's not important, Mama.

[*She gets up and goes to look out at the bathroom, which is apparently free, and she picks up her towels and rushes out*]

MAMA: What was they fighting about?

RUTH: Now you know as well as I do.

455 MAMA (*Shaking her head*): Brother still worrying his-self sick about that money?

RUTH: You know he is.

MAMA: You had breakfast?

RUTH: Some coffee.

460 MAMA: Girl, you better start eating and looking after yourself better. You almost thin as Travis.

RUTH: Lena—

MAMA: Un-hunh?

RUTH: What are you going to do with it?

MAMA: Now don't you start, child. It's too early in
465 the morning to be talking about money. It ain't Christian.

RUTH: It's just that he got his heart set on that store—

MAMA: You mean that liquor store that Willy Harris
470 want him to invest in?

RUTH: Yes—

MAMA: We ain't no business people, Ruth. We just plain working folks.

RUTH: Ain't nobody business people till they go into
475 business. Walter Lee say colored people ain't never going to start getting ahead till they start gambling on some different kinds of things in the world—investments and things.

MAMA: What done got into you, girl? Walter Lee
480 done finally sold you on investing.

RUTH: No. Mama, something is happening between Walter and me. I don't know what it is—but he needs something—something I can't give him any more. He needs this chance, Lena.

485 MAMA (*Frowning deeply*): But liquor, honey—

RUTH: Well—like Walter say—I spec people going to always be drinking themselves some liquor.

MAMA: Well—whether they drinks it or not ain't none of my business. But whether I go into business
490 selling it to 'em *is*, and I don't want that on my ledger this late in life. (*Stopping suddenly and studying her daughter-in-law*) Ruth Younger, what's the matter with you today? You look like you could fall over right there.

495 RUTH: I'm tired.

MAMA: Then you better stay home from work today.

RUTH: I can't stay home. She'd be calling up the agency and screaming at them, "My girl didn't come in today—send me somebody! My girl
500 didn't come in!" Oh, she just have a fit . . .

MAMA: Well, let her have it. I'll just call her up and say you got the flu—

RUTH (*Laughing*): Why the flu?

MAMA: 'Cause it sounds respectable to 'em.
505 Something white people get, too. They know 'bout the flu. Otherwise they think you been cut up or something when you tell 'em you sick.

RUTH: I got to go in. We need the money.

MAMA: Somebody would of thought my children
510 done all but starved to death the way they talk about money here late. Child, we got a great big old check coming tomorrow.

RUTH (*Sincerely, but also self-righteously*): Now that's your money. It ain't got nothing to do with me.
515 We all feel like that—Walter and Bennie and me—even Travis.

MAMA (*Thoughtfully, and suddenly very far away*): Ten thousand dollars—

RUTH: Sure is wonderful.

520　MAMA: Ten thousand dollars.
　　　RUTH: You know what you should do, Miss Lena? You should take yourself a trip somewhere. To Europe or South America or someplace—
　　　MAMA (*Throwing up her hands at the thought*): Oh, child!
525　RUTH: I'm serious. Just pack up and leave! Go on away and enjoy yourself some. Forget about the family and have yourself a ball for once in your life.
　　　MAMA (*Drily*): You sound like I'm just about ready to
530　die. Who'd go with me? What I look like wandering 'round Europe by myself?
　　　RUTH: Shoot—these here rich white women do it all the time. They don't think nothing of packing up they suitcases and piling on one of them big
535　steamships and—swoosh!—they gone, child.
　　　MAMA: Something always told me I wasn't no rich white woman.
　　　RUTH: Well—what are you going to do with it then?
　　　MAMA: I ain't rightly decided. (*Thinking. She speaks*
540　*now with emphasis*) Some of it got to be put away for Beneatha and her schoolin'—and ain't nothing going to touch that part of it. Nothing. (*She waits several seconds, trying to make up her mind about something, and looks at*
545　RUTH *a little tentatively before going on*) Been thinking that we maybe could meet the notes on a little old two-story somewhere, with a yard where Travis could play in the summertime, if we use part of the insurance for a
550　down payment and everybody kind of pitch in. I could maybe take on a little day work again, few days a week—
　　　RUTH (*Studying her mother-in-law furtively and concentrating on her ironing, anxious to encourage without*
555　*seeming to*): Well, Lord knows, we've put enough rent into this here rat trap to pay for four houses by now . . .
　　　MAMA (*Looking up at the words "rat trap" and then looking around and leaning back and sighing—in a*
560　*suddenly reflective mood—*): "Rat trap"—yes, that's all it is. (*Smiling*) I remember just as well the day me and Big Walter moved in here. Hadn't been married but two weeks and wasn't planning on living here no more than a
565　year. (*She shakes her head at the dissolved dream*) We was going to set away, little by little, don't you know, and buy a little place out in Morgan Park. We had even picked out the house. (*Chuckling a little*) Looks right dumpy today.
570　But Lord, child, you should know all the dreams I had 'bout buying that house and fixing it up and making me a little garden in the back—(*She waits and stops smiling*) And didn't none of it happen.

　　　[*Dropping her hands in a futile gesture*]

575　RUTH (*Keeps her head down, ironing*): Yes, life can be a barrel of disappointments, sometimes.
　　　MAMA: Honey, Big Walter would come in here some nights back then and slump down on that couch there and just look at the rug, and look
580　at me and look at the rug and then back at me—and I'd know he was down then . . . really down. (*After a second very long and thoughtful pause; she is seeing back to times that only she can see*) And then, Lord, when I lost that baby—lit-
585　tle Claude—I almost thought I was going to lose Big Walter too. Oh, that man grieved hisself! He was one man to love his children.
　　　RUTH: Ain't nothin' can tear at you like losin' your baby.
　　　MAMA: I guess that's how come that man finally
590　worked hisself to death like he done. Like he was fighting his own war with this here world that took his baby from him.
　　　RUTH: He sure was a fine man, all right. I always liked Mr. Younger.
　　　MAMA: Crazy 'bout his children! God knows there
595　was plenty wrong with Walter Younger—hardheaded, mean, kind of wild with women—plenty wrong with him. But he sure loved his children. Always wanted them to have something—be something. That's where Brother
600　gets all these notions, I reckon. Big Walter used to say, he'd get right wet in the eyes sometimes, lean his head back with the water standing in his eyes and say, "Seem like God didn't
605　see fit to give the black man nothing but dreams—but He did give us children to make them dreams seem worth while." (*She smiles*) He could talk like that, don't you know.
　　　RUTH: Yes, he sure could. He was a good man, Mr.
610　Younger.
　　　MAMA: Yes, a fine man—just couldn't never catch up with his dreams, that's all.

　　　[BENEATHA *comes in, brushing her hair and looking up to the ceiling, where the sound of a vacuum cleaner has started up*]

　　　BENEATHA: What could be so dirty on that woman's rugs that she has to vacuum them every single
615　day?
　　　RUTH: I wish certain young women 'round here who I could name would take inspiration about certain rugs in a certain apartment I could also mention.
620　BENEATHA (*Shrugging*): How much cleaning can a house need, for Christ's sakes.
　　　MAMA (*Not liking the Lord's name used thus*): Bennie!
　　　RUTH: Just listen to her—just listen!
　　　BENEATHA: Oh, God!
625　MAMA: If you use the Lord's name just one more time—
　　　BENEATHA (*A bit of a whine*): Oh, Mama—

RUTH: Fresh—just fresh as salt, this girl!

BENEATHA (*Drily*): Well—if the salt loses its savor—

MAMA: Now that will do. I just ain't going to have
630   you 'round here reciting the scriptures in
vain—you hear me?

BENEATHA: How did I manage to get on everybody's
wrong side by just walking into a room?

RUTH: If you weren't so fresh—

635 BENEATHA: Ruth, I'm twenty years old.

MAMA: What time you be home from school today?

BENEATHA: Kind of late. (*With enthusiasm*) Madeline is
going to start my guitar lessons today.

[MAMA *and* RUTH *look up with the same expression*]

MAMA: Your *what* kind of lessons?

640 BENEATHA: Guitar.

RUTH: Oh, Father!

MAMA: How come you done taken it in your mind to
learn to play the guitar?

BENEATHA: I just want to, that's all.

645 MAMA (*Smiling*): Lord, child, don't you know what
to do with yourself? How long it going to be
before you get tired of this now—like you got
tired of that little play-acting group you joined
last year? (*Looking at* RUTH) And what was it
650   the year before that?

RUTH: The horseback-riding club for which she
bought that fifty-five-dollar riding habit that's
been hanging in the closet ever since!

MAMA (*To* BENEATHA): Why you got to flit so from
655   one thing to another, baby?

BENEATHA (*Sharply*): I just want to learn to play the
guitar. Is there anything wrong with that?

MAMA: Ain't nobody trying to stop you. I just wonders sometimes why you has to flit so from
660   one thing to another all the time. You ain't
never done nothing with all that camera
equipment you brought home—

BENEATHA: I don't flit! I—I experiment with different
forms of expression—

665 RUTH: Like riding a horse?

BENEATHA: —People have to express themselves one
way or another.

MAMA: What is it you want to express?

BENEATHA (*Angrily*): Me! (MAMA *and* RUTH *look at*
670   *each other and burst into raucous laughter*)
Don't worry—I don't expect you to understand.

MAMA (*To change the subject*): Who you going out
with tomorrow night?

BENEATHA (*With displeasure*): George Murchison
675   again.

MAMA (*Pleased*): Oh—you getting a little sweet on him?

RUTH: You ask me, this child ain't sweet on nobody
but herself—(*Underbreath*) Express herself!

[*They laugh*]

BENEATHA: Oh—I like George all right, Mama. I mean
I like him enough to go out with him and stuff,   680
but—

RUTH (*For devilment*): What does *and stuff* mean?

BENEATHA: Mind your own business.

MAMA: Stop picking at her now, Ruth. (*A thoughtful
pause, and then a suspicious sudden look at her*   685
daughter as she turns in her chair for emphasis)
What *does* it mean?

BENEATHA (*Wearily*): Oh, I just mean I couldn't ever
really be serious about George. He's—he's so
shallow.   690

RUTH: Shallow—what do you mean he's shallow?
He's *Rich!*

MAMA: Hush, Ruth.

BENEATHA: I know he's rich. He knows he's rich, too.

RUTH: Well—what other qualities a man got to have   695
to satisfy you, little girl?

BENEATHA: You wouldn't even begin to understand.
Anybody who married Walter could not possibly understand.

MAMA (*Outraged*): What kind of way is that to talk   700
about your brother?

BENEATHA: Brother is a flip—let's face it.

MAMA (*To* RUTH, *helplessly*): What's a flip?

RUTH (*Glad to add kindling*): She's saying he's crazy.

BENEATHA: Not crazy. Brother isn't really crazy yet—   705
he—he's an elaborate neurotic.

MAMA: Hush your mouth!

BENEATHA: As for George. Well. George looks good—
he's got a beautiful car and he takes me to nice
places and, as my sister-in-law says, he is prob-   710
ably the richest boy I will ever get to know and
I even like him sometimes—but if the Youngers
are sitting around waiting to see if their little
Bennie is going to tie up the family with the
Murchisons, they are wasting their time.   715

RUTH: You mean you wouldn't marry George
Murchison if he asked you someday? That pretty, rich thing? Honey, I knew you was odd—

BENEATHA: No I would not marry him if all I felt for
him was what I feel now. Besides, George's   720
family wouldn't really like it.

MAMA: Why not?

BENEATHA: Oh, Mama—the Murchisons are honest-
to-God-real-*live*-rich colored people, and the
only people in the world who are more snob-   725
bish than rich white people are rich colored
people. I thought everybody knew that. I've
met Mrs. Murchison. She's a scene!

MAMA: You must not dislike people 'cause they well
off, honey.   730

BENEATHA: Why not? It makes just as much sense as
disliking people 'cause they are poor, and lots
of people do that.

RUTH (*A wisdom-of-the-ages manner. To* MAMA): Well,
she'll get over some of this—   735

BENEATHA: Get over it? What are you talking about, Ruth? Listen, I'm going to be a doctor. I'm not worried about who I'm going to marry yet—if I ever get married.

740   MAMA and RUTH: *If!*

MAMA: Now, Bennie—

BENEATHA: Oh, I probably will . . . but first I'm going to be a doctor, and George, for one, still thinks that's pretty funny. I couldn't be bothered with

745   that. I am going to be a doctor and everybody around here better understand that!

MAMA (*Kindly*): 'Course you going to be a doctor, honey, God willing.

BENEATHA (*Drily*): God hasn't got a thing to do with it.

750   MAMA: Beneatha—that just wasn't necessary.

BENEATHA: Well—neither is God. I get sick of hearing about God.

MAMA: Beneatha!

BENEATHA: I mean it! I'm just tired of hearing about

755   God all the time. What has He got to do with anything? Does he pay tuition?

MAMA: You 'bout to get your fresh little jaw slapped!

RUTH: That's just what she needs, all right!

BENEATHA: Why? Why can't I say what I want to

760   around here, like everybody else?

MAMA: It don't sound nice for a young girl to say things like that—you wasn't brought up that way. Me and your father went to trouble to get you and Brother to church every Sunday.

765   BENEATHA: Mama, you don't understand. It's all a matter of ideas, and God is just one idea I don't accept. It's not important. I am not going out and be immoral or commit crimes because I don't believe in God. I don't even think about

770   it. It's just that I get tired of Him getting credit for all the things the human race achieves through its own stubborn effort. There simply is no blasted God—there is only man and it is he who makes miracles!

[MAMA *absorbs this speech, studies her daughter and rises slowly and crosses to* BENEATHA *and slaps her powerfully across the face. After, there is only silence and the daughter drops her eyes from her mother's face, and* MAMA *is very tall before her*]

775   MAMA: Now—you say after me, in my mother's house there is still God. (*There is a long pause and* BENEATHA *stares at the floor wordlessly.* MAMA *repeats the phrase with precision and cool emotion*) In my mother's house there is still

780   God.

BENEATHA: In my mother's house there is still God.

[A long pause]

MAMA (*Walking away from* BENEATHA, *too disturbed for*

triumphant posture. Stopping and turning back to her daughter): There are some ideas we ain't going to have in this house. Not long as I am   785 at the head of this family.

BENEATHA: Yes, ma'am.

[MAMA *walks out of the room*]

RUTH (*Almost gently, with profound understanding*): You think you a woman, Bennie—but you still a little girl. What you did was childish—so   790 you got treated like a child.

BENEATHA: I see. (*Quietly*) I also see that everybody thinks it's all right for Mama to be a tyrant. But all the tyranny in the world will never put a God in the heavens!   795

[She picks up her books and goes out]

RUTH (*Goes to* MAMA's *door*): She said she was sorry.

MAMA (*Coming out, going to her plant*): They frightens me, Ruth. My children.

RUTH: You got good children, Lena. They just a little off sometimes—but they're good.   800

MAMA: No—there's something come down between me and them that don't let us understand each other and I don't know what it is. One done almost lost his mind thinking 'bout money all the time and the other done commence to talk about things I   805 can't seem to understand in no form or fashion. What is it that's changing, Ruth?

RUTH (*Soothingly, older than her years*): Now . . . you taking it all too seriously. You just got strong-willed children and it takes a strong woman   810 like you to keep 'em in hand.

MAMA (*Looking at her plant and sprinkling a little water on it*): They spirited all right, my children. Got to admit they got spirit—Bennie and Walter. Like this little old plant that ain't never had enough   815 sunshine or nothing—and look at it . . .

[She has her back to RUTH, *who has had to stop ironing and lean against something and put the back of her hand to her forehead*]

RUTH (*Trying to keep* MAMA *from noticing*): You . . . sure . . . loves that little old thing, don't you? . . .

MAMA: Well, I always wanted me a garden like I used to see sometimes at the back of the hous-   820 es down home. This plant is close as I ever got to having one. (*She looks out of the window as she replaces the plant*) Lord, ain't nothing as dreary as the view from this window on a dreary day, is there? Why ain't you singing this morning,   825 Ruth? Sing that "No Ways Tired." That song always lifts me up so—(*She turns at last to see that* RUTH *has slipped quietly into a chair, in a*

830 *state of semiconsciousness*) Ruth! Ruth honey—what's the matter with you . . . Ruth!

CURTAIN

Scene 2

It is the following morning; a Saturday morning, and house cleaning is in progress at the YOUNGERS. *Furniture has been shoved hither and yon and* MAMA *is giving the kitchen-area walls a washing down.* BENEATHA, *in dungarees, with a handkerchief tied around her face, is spraying insecticide into the cracks in the walls. As they work, the radio is on and a Southside diskjockey program is inappropriately filling the house with a rather exotic saxophone blues.* TRAVIS, *the sole idle one, is leaning on his arms, looking out of the window.*

TRAVIS: Grandmama, that stuff Bennie is using smells awful. Can I go downstairs, please?

MAMA: Did you get all them chores done already? I ain't seen you doing much.

835 TRAVIS: Yes'm—finished early. Where did Mama go this morning?

MAMA (*Looking at* BENEATHA): She had to go on a little errand.

TRAVIS: Where?

840 MAMA: To tend to her business.

TRAVIS: Can I go outside then?

MAMA: Oh, I guess so. You better stay right in front of the house, though . . . and keep a good lookout for the postman.

845 TRAVIS: Yes'm. (*He starts out and decides to give his* AUNT BENEATHA *a good swat on the legs as he passes her*) Leave them poor little old cockroaches alone, they ain't bothering you none.

[He runs as she swings the spray gun at him both viciously and playfully. WALTER *enters from the bedroom and goes to the phone]*

MAMA: Look out there, girl, before you be spilling
850   some of that stuff on that child!

TRAVIS (*Teasing*): That's right—look out now!

[He exits]

BENEATHA (*Drily*): I can't imagine that it would hurt him—it has never hurt the roaches.

MAMA: Well, little boys' hides ain't as tough as
855   Southside roaches.

WALTER (*Into phone*): Hello—Let me talk to Willy Harris.

MAMA: You better get over there behind the bureau. I seen one marching out of there like Napoleon
860   yesterday.

WALTER: Hello, Willy? It ain't come yet. It'll be here in a few minutes. Did the lawyer give you the papers?

BENEATHA: There's really only one way to get rid of them, Mama—   865

MAMA: How?

BENEATHA: Set fire to this building.

WALTER: Good. Good. I'll be right over.

BENEATHA: Where did Ruth go, Walter?

WALTER: I don't know.   870

[He exits abruptly]

BENEATHA: Mama, where did Ruth go?

MAMA (*Looking at her with meaning*): To the doctor, I think.

BENEATHA: The doctor? What's the matter? (*They exchange glances*) You don't think—   875

MAMA (*With her sense of drama*): Now I ain't saying what I think. But I ain't never been wrong 'bout a woman neither.

[The phone rings]

BENEATHA (*At the phone*): Hay-lo . . . (*Pause, and a moment of recognition*) Well—when did you get   880
back! . . . And how was it? . . . Of course I've missed you—in my way . . . This morning? No . . . house cleaning and all that and Mama hates it if I let people come over when the house is like this . . . You *have*? Well, that's dif-   885
ferent . . . What is it—Oh, what the hell, come on over . . . Right, see you then.

[She hangs up]

MAMA (*Who has listened vigorously, as is her habit*): Who is that you inviting over here with this house looking like this? You ain't got the pride   890
you was born with!

BENEATHA: Asagai doesn't care how houses look, Mama—he's an intellectual.

MAMA: *Who?*

BENEATHA: Asagai—Joseph Asagai. He's an African   895
boy I met on campus. He's been studying in Canada all summer.

MAMA: What's his name?

BENEATHA: Asagai, Joseph. Ah-sah-guy . . . He's from Nigeria.   900

MAMA: Oh, that's the little country that was founded by slaves way back . . .

BENEATHA: No, Mama—that's Liberia.

MAMA: I don't think I never met no African before.

BENEATHA: Well, do me a favor and don't ask him a   905
whole lot of ignorant questions about Africans. I mean, do they wear clothes and all that—

MAMA: Well, now, I guess if you think we so igno-

910 rant 'round here maybe you shouldn't bring
your friends here—
BENEATHA: It's just that people ask such crazy things.
All anyone seems to know about when it
comes to Africa is Tarzan—
915 MAMA (*Indignantly*): Why should I know anything
about Africa?
BENEATHA: Why do you give money at church for the
missionary work?
MAMA: Well, that's to help save people.
BENEATHA: You mean save them from *heathenism*—
920 MAMA (*Innocently*): Yes.
BENEATHA: I'm afraid they need more salvation from
the British and the French.

[RUTH *comes in forlornly and pulls off her coat with
dejection. They both turn to look at her*]

RUTH (*Dispiritedly*): Well, I guess from all the happy
faces—everybody knows.
925 BENEATHA: You pregnant?
MAMA: Lord have mercy, I sure hope it's a little old
girl. Travis ought to have a sister.

[BENEATHA *and* RUTH *give her a hopeless look for this
grandmotherly enthusiasm*]

BENEATHA: How far along are you?
RUTH: Two months.
930 BENEATHA: Did you mean to? I mean did you plan it
or was it an accident?
MAMA: What do you know about planning or not
planning?
BENEATHA: Oh, Mama.
935 RUTH (*Wearily*): She's twenty years old, Lena.
BENEATHA: Did you plan it, Ruth?
RUTH: Mind your own business.
BENEATHA: It is my business—where is he going to live,
on the *roof*? (*There is silence following the remark as
940 the three women react to the sense of it*) Gee—I did-
n't mean that, Ruth, honest. Gee, I don't feel like
that at all. I—I think it is wonderful.
RUTH (*Dully*): Wonderful.
BENEATHA: Yes—really.
945 MAMA (*Looking at* RUTH, *worried*): Doctor say everything going to be all right?
RUTH (*Far away*): Yes—she says everything is going
to be fine . . .
MAMA (*Immediately suspicious*): "She"—What doctor
950 you went to?

[RUTH *folds over, near hysteria*]

MAMA (*Worriedly hovering over* RUTH): Ruth honey—
what's the matter with you—you sick?

[RUTH *has her fists clenched on her thighs and is*

*fighting hard to suppress a scream that seems to be
rising in her*)

BENEATHA: What's the matter with her, Mama?
MAMA (*Working her fingers in* RUTH's *shoulder to relax
her*): She be all right. Women gets right   955
depressed sometimes when they get her way.
(*Speaking softly, expertly, rapidly*) Now you just
relax. That's right . . . just lean back, don't
think 'bout nothing at all . . . nothing at all—
RUTH: I'm all right . . .   960

[*The glassy-eyed look melts and then she collapses
into a fit of heavy sobbing. The bell rings*]

BENEATHA: Oh, my God—that must be Asagai.
MAMA (*To* RUTH): Come on now, honey. You need to
lie down and rest awhile . . . then have some
nice hot food.

[*They exit,* RUTH's *weight on her mother-in-law.*
BENEATHA, *herself profoundly disturbed, opens the
door to admit a rather dramatic-looking young man
with a large package*]

ASAGAI: Hello, Alaiyo—   965
BENEATHA (*Holding the door open and regarding him
with pleasure*): Hello . . . (*Long pause*) Well—
come in. And please excuse everything. My
mother was very upset about my letting anyone come here with the place like this.   970
ASAGAI (*Coming into the room*): You look disturbed
too . . . Is something wrong?
BENEATHA (*Still at the door, absently*): Yes . . . we've all
got acute ghetto-itus. (*She smiles and comes
toward him, finding a cigarette and sitting*) So— 975
sit down! How was Canada?
ASAGAI (*A sophisticate*): Canadian.
BENEATHA (*Looking at him*): I'm very glad you are back.
ASAGAI (*Looking back at her in turn*): Are you really?
BENEATHA: Yes—very.   980
ASAGAI: Why—you were quite glad when I went
away. What happened?
BENEATHA: You went away.
ASAGAI: Ahhhhhhhh.
BENEATHA: Before—you wanted to be so serious   985
before there was time.
ASAGAI: How much time must there be before one
knows what one feels?
BENEATHA (*Stalling this particular conversation. Her
hands pressed together, in a deliberately childish
gesture*): What did you bring me?   990
ASAGAI (*Handing her the package*): Open it and see.
BENEATHA (*Eagerly opening the package and drawing out
some records and the colorful robes of a Nigerian
woman*): Oh, Asagai! . . . You got them for me!   995
. . . How beautiful . . . and the records too! (*She

lifts out the robes and runs to the mirror with them and holds the drapery up in front of herself)

1000 ASAGAI (*Coming to her at the mirror*): I shall have to teach you how to drape it properly. (*He flings the material about her for the moment and stands back to look at her*) Ah—*Oh-pay-gay-day, oh-gbah-mu-shay* (*A Yoruba exclamation for admiration*) You wear it well . . . very well . . . mutilated
1005 hair and all.

BENEATHA (*Turning suddenly*): My hair—what's wrong with my hair?

ASAGAI (*Shrugging*): Were you born with it like that?

BENEATHA (*Reaching up to touch it*): No . . . of course
1010 not.

[She looks back to the mirror, disturbed]

ASAGAI (*Smiling*): How then?

BENEATHA: You know perfectly well how . . . as crinkly as yours . . . that's how.

ASAGAI: And it is ugly to you that way?

1015 BENEATHA (*Quickly*): Oh, no—not ugly . . . (*More slowly, apologetically*) But it's so hard to manage when it's, well—raw.

ASAGAI: And so to accommodate that—you mutilate it every week?

1020 BENEATHA: It's not mutilation!

ASAGAI (*Laughing aloud at her seriousness*): Oh . . . please! I am only teasing you because you are so very serious about these things. (*He stands back from her and folds his arms across his chest as
1025 he watches her pulling at her hair and frowning in the mirror*) Do you remember the first time you met me at school? . . . (*He laughs*) You came up to me and you said—and I thought you were the most serious little thing I had ever seen—
1030 you said: (*He imitates her*) "Mr. Asagai—I want very much to talk with you. About Africa. You see, Mr. Asagai, I am looking for my *identity!*"

[He laughs]

BENEATHA (*Turning to him, not laughing*): Yes—

[Her face is quizzical, profoundly disturbed]

1035 ASAGAI (*Still teasing and reaching out and taking her face in his hands and turning her profile to him*): Well . . . it is true that this is not so much a profile of a Hollywood queen as perhaps a queen of the Nile—(*A mock dismissal of the importance of the question*) But what does it mat-
1040 ter? Assimilationism is so popular in your country.

BENEATHA (*Wheeling, passionately, sharply*): I am not an assimilationist!

ASAGAI (*The protest hangs in the room for a moment and

ASAGAI *studies her, his laughter fading*): Such a   1045
serious one. (*There is a pause*) So—you like the robes? You must take excellent care of them—they are from my sister's personal wardrobe.

BENEATHA (*With incredulity*): You—you sent all the way home—for me?   1050

ASAGAI (*With charm*): For you—I would do much more . . . Well, that is what I came for. I must go.

BENEATHA: Will you call me Monday?

ASAGAI: Yes . . . We have a great deal to talk about. I mean about identity and time and all that.   1055

BENEATHA: Time?

ASAGAI: Yes. About how much time one needs to know what one feels.

BENEATHA: You never understood that there is more than one kind of feeling which can exist   1060
between a man and a woman—or, at least, there should be.

ASAGAI (*Shaking his head negatively but gently*): No. Between a man and a woman there need be only one kind of feeling. I have that for you . . .   1065
Now even . . . right this moment . . .

BENEATHA: I know—and by itself—it won't do. I can find that anywhere.

ASAGAI: For a woman it should be enough.

BENEATHA: I know—because that's what it says in all   1070
the novels that men write. But it isn't. Go ahead and laugh—but I'm not interested in being someone's little episode in America or—(*With feminine vengeance*)—one of them! (*ASAGAI has burst into laughter again*) That's   1075
funny as hell, huh!

ASAGAI: It's just that every American girl I have known has said that to me. White—black—in this you are all the same. And the same speech, too!   1080

BENEATHA (*Angrily*): Yuk, yuk, yuk!

ASAGAI: It's how you can be sure that the world's most liberated women are not liberated at all. You all talk about it too much!

*[*MAMA *enters and is immediately all social charm because of the presence of a guest]*

BENEATHA: Oh—Mama—this is Mr. Asagai.   1085

MAMA: How do you do?

ASAGAI (*Total politeness to an elder*): How do you do, Mrs. Younger. Please forgive me for coming at such an outrageous hour on a Saturday.

MAMA: Well, you are quite welcome. I just hope you   1090
understand that our house don't always look like this. (*Chatterish*) You must come again. I would love to hear all about—(*Not sure of the name*)—your country. I think it's so sad the way our American Negroes don't know noth-   1095
ing about Africa 'cept Tarzan and all that. And all that money they pour into these churches

when they ought to be helping you people
over there drive out them French and
1100   Englishmen done taken away your land.

[*The mother flashes a slightly superior look at her
daughter upon completion of the recitation*]

ASAGAI (*Taken aback by this sudden and acutely unrelated expression of sympathy*): Yes . . . yes . . .
MAMA (*Smiling at him suddenly and relaxing and looking him over*): How many miles is it from here
1105   to where you come from?
ASAGAI: Many thousands.
MAMA (*Looking at him as she would* WALTER): I bet you
don't half look after yourself, being away from
your mama either. I spec you better come
1110   'round here from time to time and get yourself
some decent home-cooked meals . . .
ASAGAI (*Moved*): Thank you. Thank you very much.
(*They are all quiet, then—*) Well . . . I must go. I
will call you Monday, Alaiyo.
1115   MAMA: What's that he call you?
ASAGAI: Oh—"Alaiyo." I hope you don't mind. It is
what you would call a nickname, I think. It is a
Yoruba word. I am a Yoruba.
MAMA (*Looking at* BENEATHA): I—I thought he was
1120   from—
ASAGAI (*Understanding*): Nigeria is my country.
Yoruba is my tribal origin—
BENEATHA: You didn't tell us what Alaiyo means . . .
for all I know, you might be calling me Little
1125   Idiot or something . . .
ASAGAI: Well . . . let me see . . . I do not know how
just to explain it . . . The sense of a thing can be
so different when it changes languages.
BENEATHA: You're evading.
1130   ASAGAI: No—really it is difficult . . . (*Thinking*) It
means . . . it means One for Whom Bread—
Food—Is Not Enough. (*He looks at her*) Is that
all right?
BENEATHA (*Understanding, softly*): Thank you.
1135   MAMA (*Looking from one to the other and not understanding any of it*): Well . . . that's
nice . . . You must come see us again—Mr.—
ASAGAI: Ah-sah-guy . . .
MAMA: Yes . . . Do come again.
1140   ASAGAI: Good-bye.

[*He exits*]

MAMA (*After him*): Lord, that's a pretty thing just
went out here! (*Insinuatingly, to her daughter*)
Yes, I guess I see why we done commence to
get so interested in Africa 'round here.
1145   Missionaries my aunt Jenny!

[*She exits*]

BENEATHA: Oh, Mama! . . .

[*She picks up the Nigerian dress and holds it up to her
in front of the mirror again. She sets the headdress on
haphazardly and then notices her hair again and
clutches at it and then replaces the headdress and
frowns at herself. Then she starts to wriggle in front of
the mirror as she thinks a Nigerian woman might.*
TRAVIS *enters and regards her*]

TRAVIS: You cracking up?
BENEATHA: Shut up.

[*She pulls the headdress off and looks at herself in the
mirror and clutches at her hair again and squinches
her eyes as if trying to imagine something. Then, suddenly, she gets her raincoat and kerchief and hurriedly prepares for going out*]

MAMA (*Coming back into the room*): She's resting now.
Travis, baby, run next door and ask Miss   1150
Johnson to please let me have a little kitchen
cleanser. This here can is empty as Jacob's kettle.
TRAVIS: I just came in.
MAMA: Do as you told. (*He exits and she looks at her
daughter*) Where you going?   1155
BENEATHA (*Halting at the door*): To become a queen of
the Nile!

[*She exits in a breathless blaze of glory.* RUTH *appears
in the bedroom doorway*]

MAMA: Who told you to get up?
RUTH: Ain't nothing wrong with me to be lying in no
bed for. Where did Bennie go?   1160
MAMA (*Drumming her fingers*): Far as I could make
out—to Egypt. (RUTH *just looks at her*) What
time is it getting to?
RUTH: Ten twenty. And the mailman going to ring
that bell this morning just like he done every   1165
morning for the last umpteen years.

[TRAVIS *comes in with the cleanser can*]

TRAVIS: She say to tell you that she don't have much.
MAMA (*Angrily*): Lord, some people I could name
sure is tight-fisted! (*Directing her grandson*)
Mark two cans of cleanser down on the list   1170
there. If she that hard up for kitchen cleanser, I
sure don't want to forget to get her none!
RUTH: Lena—maybe the woman is just short on
cleanser—
MAMA (*Not listening*): —Much baking powder as she   1175
done borrowed from me all these years, she
could of done gone into the baking business!

[*The bell sounds suddenly and sharply and all three*

are stunned—serious and silent—mid-speech. In spite of all the other conversations and distractions of the morning, this is what they have been waiting for, even TRAVIS, *who looks helplessly from his mother to his grandmother.* RUTH *is the first to come to life again]*

RUTH (*To* TRAVIS): Get down them steps, boy!

*[*TRAVIS *snaps to life and flies out to get the mail]*

MAMA (*Her eyes wide, her hand to her breast*): You
1180   mean it done really come?
RUTH (*Excited*): Oh, Miss Lena!
MAMA (*Collecting herself*): Well . . . I don't know what we all so excited about 'round here for. We known it was coming for months.
1185   RUTH: That's a whole lot different from having it come and being able to hold it in your hands . . . a piece of paper worth ten thousand dollars . . . (TRAVIS *bursts back into the room. He holds the envelope high above his head, like a little*
1190   *dancer, his face is radiant and he is breathless. He moves to his grandmother with sudden slow ceremony and puts the envelope into her hands. She accepts it, and then merely holds it and looks at it)* Come on! Open it . . . Lord have mercy, I wish
1195   Walter Lee was here!
TRAVIS: Open it, Grandmama!
MAMA (*Staring at it*): Now you all be quiet. It's just a check.
RUTH: Open it . . .
1200   MAMA (*Still staring at it*): Now don't act silly . . . We ain't never been no people to act silly 'bout no money—
RUTH (*Swiftly*): We ain't never had none before— open it!

*[*MAMA *finally makes a good strong tear and pulls out the thin blue slice of paper and inspects it closely. The boy and his mother study it raptly over* MAMA*'s shoulders]*

1205   MAMA: *Travis!* (*She is counting off with doubt*) Is that the right number of zeros.
TRAVIS: Yes'm . . . ten thousand dollars. Gaalee, Grandmama, you rich.
MAMA (*She holds the check away from her, still looking at*
1210   *it. Slowly her face sobers into a mask of unhappiness*): Ten thousand dollars. (*She hands it to* RUTH) Put it away somewhere, Ruth. (*She does not look at* RUTH; *her eyes seem to be seeing something somewhere very far off*) Ten thousand dol-
1215   lars they give you. Ten thousand dollars.
TRAVIS (*To his mother, sincerely*): What's the matter with Grandmama—don't she want to be rich?
RUTH (*Distractedly*): You go on out and play now, baby. (TRAVIS *exits.* MAMA *starts wiping dishes*
1220   *absently, humming intently to herself.* RUTH *turns*

to her, with kind exasperation) You've gone and got yourself upset.
MAMA (*Not looking at her*): I spec if it wasn't for you all . . . I would just put that money away or give it to the church or something.   1225
RUTH: Now what kind of talk is that. Mr. Younger would just be plain mad if he could hear you talking foolish like that.
MAMA (*Stopping and staring off*): Yes . . . he sure would. (*Sighing*) We got enough to do with   1230
that money, all right. (*She halts then, and turns and looks at her daughter-in-law hard;* RUTH *avoids her eyes and* MAMA *wipes her hands with finality and starts to speak firmly to* RUTH) Where did you go today, girl?   1235
RUTH: To the doctor.
MAMA (*Impatiently*): Now, Ruth . . . you know better than that. Old Doctor Jones is strange enough in his way but there ain't nothing 'bout him make somebody slip and call him "she"—like   1240
you done this morning.
RUTH: Well, that's what happened—my tongue slipped.
MAMA: You went to see that woman, didn't you?
RUTH (*Defensively, giving herself away*): What woman   1245
you talking about?
MAMA (*Angrily*): That woman who—

*[*WALTER *enters in great excitement]*

WALTER: Did it come?
MAMA (*Quietly*): Can't you give people a Christian greeting before you start asking about money?   1250
WALTER (*To* RUTH): Did it come? (RUTH *unfolds the check and lays it quietly before him, watching him intently with thoughts of her own.* WALTER *sits down and grasps it close and counts off the zeros*) Ten thousand dollars—(*He turns suddenly, fran-*   1255
tically to his mother and draws some papers out of his breast pocket) Mama—look. Old Willy Harris put everything on paper—
MAMA: Son—I think you ought to talk to your wife . . . I'll go on out and leave you alone if you want—   1260
WALTER: I can talk to her later—Mama, look—
MAMA: Son—
WALTER: WILL SOMEBODY PLEASE LISTEN TO ME TODAY!
MAMA (*Quietly*): I don't 'low no yellin' in this house, Walter Lee, and you know it—(WALTER *stares*   1265
at them in frustration and starts to speak several times) And there ain't going to be no investing in no liquor stores. I don't aim to have to speak on that again.

[A long pause]

WALTER: Oh—so you don't aim to have to speak on   1270
that again? So *you* have decided . . . (*Crumpling*

his papers) Well, *you* tell that to my boy tonight when you put him to sleep on the living-room couch . . . (*Turning to* MAMA *and speaking direct-ly to her*) Yeah—and tell it to my wife, Mama, tomorrow when she has to go out of here to look after somebody else's kids. And tell it to *me*, Mama, every time we need a new pair of curtains and I have to watch *you* go out and work in somebody's kitchen. Yeah, you tell me then!

[WALTER *starts out*]

RUTH: Where you going?
WALTER: I'm going out!
RUTH: Where?
WALTER: Just out of this house somewhere—
RUTH (*Getting her coat*): I'll come too.
WALTER: I don't want you to come!
RUTH: I got something to talk to you about, Walter.
WALTER: That's too bad.
MAMA (*Still quietly*): Walter Lee—(*She waits and he finally turns and looks at her*) Sit down.
WALTER: I'm a grown man, Mama.
MAMA: Ain't nobody said you wasn't grown. But you still in my house and my presence. And as long as you are—you'll talk to your wife civil. Now sit down.
RUTH (*Suddenly*): Oh, let him go on out and drink himself to death! He makes me sick to my stomach! (*She flings her coat against him*)
WALTER (*Violently*): And you turn mine too, baby! (RUTH *goes into their bedroom and slams the door behind her*) That was my greatest mistake—
MAMA (*Still quietly*): Walter, what is the matter with you?
WALTER: Matter with me? Ain't nothing the matter with *me*!
MAMA: Yes there is. Something eating you up like a crazy man. Something more than me not giv-ing you this money. The past few years I been watching it happen to you. You get all nervous acting and kind of wild in the eyes—(WALTER *jumps up impatiently at her words*) I said sit there now, I'm talking to you!
WALTER: Mama—I don't need no nagging at me today.
MAMA: Seem like you getting to a place where you always tied up in some kind of knot about something. But if anybody ask you 'bout it you just yell at 'em and bust out the house and go out and drink somewhere. Walter Lee, people can't live with that. Ruth's a good, patient girl in her way—but you getting to be too much. Boy, don't make the mistake of driving that girl away from you.
WALTER: Why—what she do for me?
MAMA: She loves you.

WALTER: Mama—I'm going out. I want to go off somewhere and be by myself for a while.
MAMA: I'm sorry 'bout your liquor store, son. It just wasn't the thing for us to do. That's what I want to tell you about—
WALTER: I got to go out, Mama—

[*He rises*]

MAMA: It's dangerous, son.
WALTER: What's dangerous?
MAMA: When a man goes outside his home to look for peace.
WALTER (*Beseechingly*): Then why can't there never be no peace in this house then?
MAMA: You done found it in some other house?
WALTER: No—there ain't no woman! Why do women always think there's a woman somewhere when a man gets restless. (*Coming to her*) Mama—Mama—I want so many things . . .
MAMA: Yes, son—
WALTER: I want so many things that they are driving me kind of crazy . . . Mama—look at me.
MAMA: I'm looking at you. You a good-looking boy. You got a job, a nice wife, a fine boy and—
WALTER: A job. (*Looks at her*) Mama, a job? I open and close car doors all day long. I drive a man around in his limousine and I say, "Yes, sir; no, sir; very good, sir; shall I take the Drive, sir?" Mama, that ain't no kind of job . . . that ain't nothing at all. (*Very quietly*) Mama, I don't know if I can make you understand.
MAMA: Understand what, baby?
WALTER (*Quietly*): Sometimes it's like I can see the future stretched out in front of me—just plain as day. The future, Mama. Hanging over there at the edge of my days. Just waiting for me—a big, looming blank space—full of *nothing*. Just waiting for *me*. (*Pause*) Mama—sometimes when I'm downtown and I pass them cool, quiet-looking restaurants where them white boys are sitting back and talking 'bout things . . . sitting there turning deals worth millions of dollars . . . sometimes I see guys don't look much older than me—
MAMA: Son—how come you talk so much 'bout money?
WALTER (*With immense passion*): Because it is life, Mama!
MAMA (*Quietly*): Oh—(*Very quietly*) So now it's life. Money is life. Once upon a time freedom used to be life—now it's money. I guess the world really do change . . .
WALTER: No—it was always money, Mama. We just didn't know about it.
MAMA: No . . . something has changed. (*She looks at him*) You something new, boy. In my time we

1380 was worried about not being lynched and getting to the North if we could and how to stay
alive and still have a pinch of dignity too . . .
Now here come you and Beneatha—talking
'bout things we ain't never even thought about
1385 hardly, me and your daddy. You ain't satisfied
or proud of nothing we done. I mean that you
had a home; that we kept you out of trouble
till you was grown; that you don't have to ride
to work on the back of nobody's streetcar—
1390 You my children—but how different we done
become.

WALTER: You just don't understand, Mama, you just
don't understand.

MAMA: Son—do you know your wife is expecting
1395 another baby? (WALTER *stands, stunned, and
absorbs what his mother has said*) That's what she
wanted to talk to you about. (WALTER *sinks
down into a chair*) This ain't for me to be
telling—but you ought to know. (*She waits*) I
1400 think Ruth is thinking 'bout getting rid of that
child.

WALTER (*Slowly understanding*): No—no—Ruth
wouldn't do that.

MAMA: When the world gets ugly enough—a
1405 woman will do anything for her family. *The
part that's already living.*

WALTER: You don't know Ruth, Mama, if you think
she would do that.

[RUTH *opens the bedroom door and stands there a little limp*]

RUTH (*Beaten*): Yes I would too, Walter. (*Pause*) I gave
1410 her a five-dollar down payment.

[*There is total silence as the man stares at his wife
and the mother stares at her son*]

MAMA (*Presently*): Well—(*Tightly*) Well—son, I'm waiting to hear you say something . . . I'm waiting
to hear how you be your father's son. Be the
man he was . . . (*Pause*) Your wife say she going
1415 to destroy your child. And I'm waiting to hear
you talk like him and say we a people who give
children life, not who destroys them—(*She rises*)
I'm waiting to see you stand up and look like
your daddy and say we done give up one baby
1420 to poverty and that we ain't going to give up
nary another one . . . I'm waiting.

WALTER: Ruth—

MAMA: If you a son of mine, tell her! (WALTER *turns,
looks at her and can say nothing. She continues,
bitterly*) You . . . you are a disgrace to your
1425 father's memory. Somebody get me my hat.

CURTAIN

ACT II

Scene 1

Time: Later the same day.

At rise: RUTH *is ironing again. She has the radio
going. Presently* BENEATHA'*s bedroom door opens and*
RUTH'*s mouth falls and she puts down the iron in fascination.*

RUTH: What have we got on tonight!

BENEATHA (*Emerging grandly from the doorway so that
we can see her thoroughly robed in the costume
Asagai brought*): You are looking at what a well- 1430
dressed Nigerian woman wears—(*She parades
for* RUTH, *her hair completely hidden by the headdress; she is coquettishly fanning herself with an
ornate oriental fan, mistakenly more like Butterfly
than any Nigerian that ever was*) Isn't it beauti- 1435
ful? (*She promenades to the radio and, with an
arrogant flourish, turns off the good loud blues that
is playing*) Enough of this assimilationist junk!
(RUTH *follows her with her eyes as she goes to the
phonograph and puts on a record and turns and* 1440
*waits ceremoniously for the music to come up.
Then, with a shout—*) OCOMOGOSIAY!

[RUTH *jumps. The music comes up, a lovely Nigerian
melody.* BENEATHA *listens, enraptured, her eyes far
away—"back to the past." She begins to dance.* RUTH
is dumfounded]

RUTH: What kind of dance is that?

BENEATHA: A folk dance.

RUTH (*Pearl Bailey*): What kind of folks do that, 1445
honey?

BENEATHA: It's from Nigeria. It's a dance of welcome.

RUTH: Who you welcoming?

BENEATHA: The men back to the village.

RUTH: Where they been? 1450

BENEATHA: How should I know—out hunting or
something. Anyway, they are coming back
now . . .

RUTH: Well, that's good.

BENEATHA (*With the record*): 1455

Alundi, alundi
Alundi alunya
Jop pu a jeepua
Ang gu sooooooooooo

Ai yai yae . . . 1460
Ayehaye—alundi . . .

[WALTER *comes in during this performance; he has
obviously been drinking. He leans against the door*

heavily and watches his sister, at first with distaste.
1465 *Then his eyes look off—"back to the past"—as he lifts*
both his fists to the roof, screaming]

WALTER: YEAH . . . AND ETHIOPIA STRETCH FORTH HER
HANDS AGAIN! . . .

RUTH (*Drily, looking at him*): Yes—and Africa sure is
1470 claiming her own tonight. (*She gives them both
up and starts ironing again*)

WALTER (*All in a drunken, dramatic shout*): Shut up! . . .
I'm digging them drums . . . them drums move
me! . . . (*He makes his weaving way to his wife's face*
1475 *and leans in close to her*) In my heart of hearts—(*He
thumps his chest*)—I am much warrior!

RUTH (*Without even looking up*): In your heart of
hearts you are much drunkard.

WALTER (*Coming away from her and starting to wander*
1480 *around the room, shouting*): Me and Jomo . . .
(*Intently, in his sister's face. She has stopped dancing to watch him in this unknown mood*) That's
my man, Kenyatta. (*Shouting and thumping his
chest*) FLAMING SPEAR! HOT DAMN! (*He is suddenly*
1485 *in possession of an imaginary spear and actively
spearing enemies all over the room*) OCOMOGOSIAY
. . . THE LION IS WALKING . . . OWIMOWEH! (*He pulls
his shirt open and leaps up on a table and gestures
with his spear. The bell rings. RUTH goes to answer*)
1490 BENEATHA (*To encourage WALTER, thoroughly caught up
with this side of him*): OCOMOGOSIAY, FLAMING
SPEAR!

WALTER (*On the table, very far gone, his eyes pure glass
sheets. He sees what we cannot, that he is a leader*
1495 *of his people, a great chief, a descendant of Chaka,
and that the hour to march has come*): Listen, my
black brothers—

BENEATHA: OCOMOGOSIAY!

WALTER: —Do you hear the waters rushing against
1500 the shores of the coastlands—

BENEATHA: OCOMOGOSIAY!

WALTER: —Do you hear the screeching of the cocks
in yonder hills beyond where the chiefs meet
in council for the coming of the mighty war—
1505 BENEATHA: OCOMOGOSIAY!

WALTER: —Do you hear the beating of the wings of
the birds flying low over the mountains and
the low places of our land—

[RUTH opens the door. GEORGE MURCHISON enters]

BENEATHA: OCOMOGOSIAY!
1510 WALTER: —Do you hear the singing of the women,
singing the war songs of our fathers to the
babies in the great houses . . . singing the
sweet war songs? OH, DO YOU HEAR, MY BLACK
BROTHERS!
1515 BENEATHA (*Completely gone*): We hear you, Flaming
Spear—

WALTER: Telling us to prepare for the greatness of the
time—(*To* GEORGE) Black Brother!

[He extends his hand for the fraternal clasp]

GEORGE: Black Brother, hell!

RUTH (*Having had enough, and embarrassed for the*   1520
family): Beneatha, you got company—what's the
matter with you? Walter Lee Younger, get down
off that table and stop acting like a fool . . .

*[WALTER comes down off the table suddenly and
makes a quick exit to the bathroom]*

RUTH: He's had a little to drink . . . I don't know
what her excuse is.   1525

GEORGE (*To* BENEATHA): Look honey, we're going *to*
the theatre—we're not going to be *in* it . . . so
go change, huh?

RUTH: You expect this boy to go out with you looking like that?   1530

BENEATHA (*Looking at* GEORGE): That's up to George.
If he's ashamed of his heritage—

GEORGE: Oh, don't be so proud of yourself, Bennie—
just because you look eccentric.

BENEATHA: How can something that's natural be   1535
eccentric?

GEORGE: That's what being eccentric means—being
natural. Get dressed.

BENEATHA: I don't like that, George.

RUTH: Why must you and your brother make an   1540
argument out of everything people say?

BENEATHA: Because I hate assimilationist Negroes!

RUTH: Will somebody please tell me what assimila-
whoever means!

GEORGE: Oh, it's just a college girl's way of calling   1545
people Uncle Toms—but that isn't what it
means at all.

RUTH: Well, what does it mean?

BENEATHA (*Cutting* GEORGE *off and staring at him as she
replies to* RUTH): It means someone who is will-   1550
ing to give up his own culture and submerge
himself completely in the dominant, and in
this case, *oppressive* culture!

GEORGE: Oh, dear, dear, dear! Here we go! A lecture
on the African past! On our Great West African   1555
Heritage! In one second we will hear all about
the great Ashanti empires; the great Songhay
civilizations; and the great sculpture of
Bénin—and then some poetry in the Bantu—
and the whole monologue will end with the   1560
word *heritage!* (*Nastily*) Let's face it, baby, your
heritage is nothing but a bunch of raggedy-
assed spirituals and some grass huts!

BENEATHA: *Grass huts!* (RUTH *crosses to her and forcibly
pushes her toward the bedroom*) See there . . . you   1565
are standing there in your splendid ignorance

talking about people who were the first to smelt iron on the face of the earth! (RUTH *is pushing her through the door*) The Ashanti were performing surgical operations when the English—(RUTH *pulls the door to, with* BENEATHA *on the other side, and smiles graciously at* GEORGE. BENEATHA *opens the door and shouts the end of the sentence defiantly at* GEORGE)—were still tatooing themselves with blue dragons . . . (*She goes back inside*)

RUTH: Have a seat, George. (*They both sit.* RUTH *folds her hands rather primly on her lap, determined to demonstrate the civilization of the family*) Warm, ain't it? I mean for September. (*Pause*) Just like they always say about Chicago weather: If it's too hot or cold for you, just wait a minute and it'll change. (*She smiles happily at this cliché of clichés*) Everybody say it's got to do with them bombs and things they keep setting off. (*Pause*) Would you like a nice cold beer?

GEORGE: No, thank you. I don't care for beer. (*He looks at his watch*) I hope she hurries up.

RUTH: What time is the show?

GEORGE: It's an eight-thirty curtain. That's just Chicago, though. In New York standard curtain time is eight forty.

[*He is rather proud of this knowledge*]

RUTH (*Properly appreciating it*): You get to New York a lot?

GEORGE (*Offhand*): Few times a year.

RUTH: Oh—that's nice. I've never been to New York.

[WALTER *enters. We feel he has relieved himself, but the edge of unreality is still with him*]

WALTER: New York ain't got nothing Chicago ain't. Just a bunch of hustling people all squeezed up together—being "Eastern."

[*He turns his face into a screw of displeasure*]

GEORGE: Oh—you've been?

WALTER: Plenty of times.

RUTH (*Shocked at the lie*): Walter Lee Younger!

WALTER (*Staring her down*): Plenty! (*Pause*) What we got to drink in this house? Why don't you offer this man some refreshment. (*To* GEORGE) They don't know how to entertain people in this house, man.

GEORGE: Thank you—I don't really care for anything.

WALTER (*Feeling his head; sobriety coming*): Where's Mama?

RUTH: She ain't come back yet.

WALTER (*Looking* MURCHISON *over from head to toe, scrutinizing his carefully casual tweed sports jacket*

over cashmere V-neck sweater over soft eyelet shirt and tie, and soft slacks, finished off with white buckskin shoes*): Why all you college boys wear them fairyish-looking white shoes?

RUTH: Walter Lee!

[GEORGE MURCHISON *ignores the remark*]

WALTER (*To* RUTH): Well, they look crazy as hell—white shoes, cold as it is.

RUTH (*Crushed*): You have to excuse him—

WALTER: No he don't! Excuse me for what? What you always excusing me for! I'll excuse myself when I needs to be excused! (*A pause*) They look as funny as them black knee socks Beneatha wears out of here all the time.

RUTH: It's the college *style*, Walter.

WALTER: Style, hell. She looks like she got burnt legs or something!

RUTH: Oh, Walter—

WALTER (*An irritable mimic*): Oh, Walter! Oh, Walter! (*To* MURCHISON) How's your old man making out? I understand you all going to buy that big hotel on the Drive? (*He finds a beer in the refrigerator, wanders over to* MURCHISON, *sipping and wiping his lips with the back of his hand, and straddling a chair backwards to talk to the other man*) Shrewd move. Your old man is all right, man. (*Tapping his head and half winking for emphasis*) I mean he knows how to operate. I mean he thinks *big*, you know what I mean, I mean for a *home*, you know? But I think he's kind of running out of ideas now. I'd like to talk to him. Listen, man, I got some plans that could turn this city upside down. I mean I think like he does. *Big*. Invest big, gamble big, hell, lose *big* if you have to, you know what I mean. It's hard to find a man on this whole Southside who understands my kind of thinking—you dig? (*He scrutinizes* MURCHISON *again, drinks his beer, squints his eyes and leans in close, confidential, man to man*) Me and you ought to sit down and talk sometimes, man. Man, I got me some ideas . . .

MURCHISON (*With boredom*): Yeah—sometimes we'll have to do that, Walter.

WALTER (*Understanding the indifference, and offended*): Yeah—well, when you get the time, man. I know you a busy little boy.

RUTH: Walter, please—

WALTER (*Bitterly, hurt*): I know ain't nothing in this world as busy as you colored college boys with your fraternity pins and white shoes . . .

RUTH (*Covering her face with humiliation*): Oh, Walter Lee—

WALTER: I see you all all the time—with the books tucked under your arms—going to your

(*British A—a mimic*) "clahsses." And for what! What the hell you learning over there! Filling up your heads—(*Counting off on his fingers*)—with the sociology and the psychology—but they teaching you how to be a man? How to take over and run the world? They teaching you how to run a rubber plantation or a steel mill? Naw—just to talk proper and read books and wear white shoes . . .

GEORGE (*Looking at him with distaste, a little above it all*): You're all wacked up with bitterness, man.

WALTER (*Intently, almost quietly, between the teeth, glaring at the boy*): And you—ain't you bitter, man? Ain't you just about had it yet? Don't you see no stars gleaming that you can't reach out and grab? You happy?—you contented son-of-a-bitch—you happy? You got it made? Bitter? Man, I'm a volcano. Bitter? Here I am a giant—surrounded by ants! Ants who can't even understand what it is the giant is talking about.

RUTH (*Passionately and suddenly*): Oh, Walter—ain't you with nobody!

WALTER (*Violently*): No! 'Cause ain't nobody with me! Not even my own mother!

RUTH: Walter, that's a terrible thing to say!

[BENEATHA *enters, dressed for the evening in a cocktail dress and earrings*]

GEORGE: Well—hey, you look great.

BENEATHA: Let's go, George. See you all later.

RUTH: Have a nice time.

GEORGE: Thanks. Good night. (*To* WALTER, *sarcastically*) Good night, *Prometheus*.

[BENEATHA *and* GEORGE *exit*]

WALTER (*To* RUTH): Who is Prometheus?

RUTH: I don't know. Don't worry about it.

WALTER (*In fury, pointing after* GEORGE): See there—they get to a point where they can't insult you man to man—they got to go talk about something ain't nobody never heard of!

RUTH: How you know it was an insult? (*To humor him*) Maybe Prometheus is a nice fellow.

WALTER: Prometheus! I bet there ain't even no such thing! I bet that simple-minded clown—

RUTH: Walter—

[*She stops what she is doing and looks at him*]

WALTER (*Yelling*): Don't start!

RUTH: Start what?

WALTER: Your nagging! Where was I? Who was I with? How much money did I spend?

RUTH (*Plaintively*): Walter Lee—why don't we just try to talk about it . . .

WALTER (*Not listening*): I been out talking with people who understand me. People who care about the things I got on my mind.

RUTH (*Wearily*): I guess that means people like Willy Harris.

WALTER: Yes, people like Willy Harris.

RUTH (*With a sudden flash of impatience*): Why don't you all just hurry up and go into the banking business and stop talking about it!

WALTER: Why? You want to know why? 'Cause we all tied up in a race of people that don't know how to do nothing but moan, pray and have babies!

[*The line is too bitter even for him and he looks at her and sits down*]

RUTH: Oh, Walter . . . (*Softly*) Honey, why can't you stop fighting me?

WALTER (*Without thinking*): Who's fighting you? Who even cares about you?

[*This line begins the retardation of his mood*]

RUTH: Well—(*She waits a long time, and then with resignation starts to put away her things*) I guess I might as well go on to bed . . . (*More or less to herself*) I don't know where we lost it . . . but we have . . . (*Then, to him*) I—I'm sorry about this new baby, Walter. I guess maybe I better go on and do what I started . . . I guess I just didn't realize how bad things was with us . . . I guess I just didn't really realize—(*She starts out to the bedroom and stops*) You want some hot milk?

WALTER: Hot milk?

RUTH: Yes—hot milk.

WALTER: Why hot milk?

RUTH: 'Cause after all that liquor you come home with you ought to have something hot in your stomach.

WALTER: I don't want no milk.

RUTH: You want some coffee then?

WALTER: No, I don't want no coffee. I don't want nothing hot to drink. (*Almost plaintively*) Why you always trying to give me something to eat?

RUTH (*Standing and looking at him helplessly*): What else can I give you, Walter Lee Younger?

[*She stands and looks at him and presently turns to go out again. He lifts his head and watches her going away from him in a new mood which began to emerge when he asked her "Who cares about you?"*]

WALTER: It's been rough, ain't it, baby? (*She hears and stops but does not turn around and he continues to*

1760 *her back*) I guess between two people there
ain't never as much understood as folks generally thinks there is. I mean like between me
and you—(*She turns to face him*) How we gets
to the place where we scared to talk softness to
1765 each other. (*He waits, thinking hard himself*) Why
you think it got to be like that? (*He is thoughtful, almost as a child would be*) Ruth, what is it
gets into people ought to be close?

RUTH: I don't know, honey. I think about it a lot.

WALTER: On account of you and me, you mean? The
1770 way things are with us. The way something
done come down between us.

RUTH: There ain't so much between us, Walter . . .
Not when you come to me and try to talk to
me. Try to be with me . . . a little even.

1775 WALTER (*Total honesty*): Sometimes . . . sometimes
. . . I don't even know how to try.

RUTH: Walter—

WALTER: Yes?

RUTH (*Coming to him, gently and with misgiving, but
1780 coming to him*): Honey . . . life don't have to be
like this. I mean sometimes people can do
things so that things are better . . . You remember how we used to talk when Travis was born
. . . about the way we were going to live . . .
1785 the kind of house . . . (*She is stroking his head*)
Well, it's all starting to slip away from us . . .

[MAMA *enters, and* WALTER *jumps up and shouts at her*]

WALTER: Mama, where have you been?

MAMA: My—them steps is longer than they used to
be. Whew! (*She sits down and ignores him*) How
1790 you feeling this evening, Ruth?

[RUTH *shrugs, disturbed some at having been prematurely interrupted and watching her husband knowingly*]

WALTER: Mama, where have you been all day?

MAMA (*Still ignoring him and leaning on the table and
changing to more comfortable shoes*): Where's
Travis?

1795 RUTH: I let him go out earlier and he ain't come back
yet. Boy, is he going to get it!

WALTER: Mama!

MAMA (*As if she has heard him for the first time*): Yes,
son?

1800 WALTER: Where did you go this afternoon?

MAMA: I went down town to tend to some business
that I had to tend to.

WALTER: What kind of business?

MAMA: You know better than to question me like a
1805 child, Brother.

WALTER (*Rising and bending over the table*): Where
were you, Mama? (*Bringing his fists down and
shouting*) Mama, you didn't go do something

with that insurance money, something crazy?

[*The front door opens slowly, interrupting him, and*
TRAVIS *peeks his head in, less than hopefully*]

TRAVIS (*To his mother*): Mama, I—   1810
RUTH: "Mama I" nothing! You're going to get it, boy!
Get on in that bedroom and get yourself ready!

TRAVIS: But I—

MAMA: Why don't you all never let the child explain
hisself.   1815

RUTH: Keep out of it now, Lena.

[MAMA *clamps her lips together, and* RUTH *advances
toward her son menacingly*]

RUTH: A thousand times I have told you not to go off
like that—

MAMA (*Holding out her arms to her grandson*): Well—at
least let me tell him something. I want him to   1820
be the first one to hear . . . Come here, Travis.
(*The boy obeys, gladly*) Travis—(*She takes him by
the shoulders and looks into his face*)—you know
that money we got in the mail this morning?

TRAVIS: Yes'm   1825

MAMA: Well—what you think your grandmama gone
and done with that money?

TRAVIS: I don't know, Grandmama.

MAMA (*Putting her finger on his nose for emphasis*): She
went out and she bought you a house! (*The*   1830
explosion comes from WALTER *at the end of the revelation and he jumps up and turns away from all of
them in a fury.* MAMA *continues, to* TRAVIS) You
glad about the house? It's going to be yours
when you get to be a man.   1835

TRAVIS: Yeah—I always wanted to live in a house.

MAMA: All right, gimme some sugar then—(TRAVIS
*puts his arms around her neck as she watches her
son over the boy's shoulder. Then, to* TRAVIS, *after
the embrace*) Now when you say your prayers   1840
tonight, you thank God and your grandfather—'cause it was him who give you the
house—in his way.

RUTH (*Taking the boy from* MAMA *and pushing him
toward the bedroom*): Now you get out of here   1845
and get ready for your beating.

TRAVIS: Aw, Mama—

RUTH: Get on in there—(*Closing the door behind him
and turning radiantly to her mother-in-law*) So
you went and did it!   1850

MAMA (*Quietly, looking at her son with pain*): Yes, I did.

RUTH (*Raising both arms classically*): *Praise God!* (*Looks
at* WALTER *a moment, who says nothing. She crosses rapidly to her husband*) Please, honey—let me
be glad . . . you be glad too. (*She has laid her   1855
hands on his shoulders, but he shakes himself free of
her roughly, without turning to face her*) Oh,

Walter . . . a home . . . *a home. (She comes back to* MAMA) Well—where is it? How big is it? How much it going to cost?

MAMA: Well—

RUTH: When we moving?

MAMA (*Smiling at her*): First of the month.

RUTH (*Throwing back her head with jubilance*): Praise God!

MAMA (*Tentatively, still looking at her son's back turned against her and* RUTH): It's—it's a nice house too . . . (*She cannot help speaking directly to him. An imploring quality in her voice, her manner, makes her almost like a girl now*) Three bedrooms—nice big one for you and Ruth. . . . Me and Beneatha still have to share our room, but Travis have one of his own—and—(*With difficulty*) I figures if the—new baby—is a boy, we could get one of them double-decker outfits . . . And there's a yard with a little patch of dirt where I could maybe get to grow me a few flowers . . . And a nice big basement . . .

RUTH: Walter honey, be glad—

MAMA (*Still to his back, fingering things on the table*): 'Course I don't want to make it sound fancier than it is . . . It's just a plain little old house—but it's made good and solid—and it will be *ours.* Walter Lee—it makes a difference in a man when he can walk on floors that belong to *him* . . .

RUTH: Where is it?

MAMA (*Frightened at this telling*): Well—well—it's out there in Clybourne Park—

[RUTH's *radiance fades abruptly, and* WALTER *finally turns slowly to face his mother with incredulity and hostility*]

RUTH: Where?

MAMA (*Matter-of-factly*): Four o six Clybourne Street, Clybourne Park.

RUTH: Clybourne Park? Mama, there ain't no colored people living in Clybourne Park.

MAMA (*Almost idiotically*): Well, I guess there's going to be some now.

WALTER (*Bitterly*): So that's the peace and comfort you went out and bought for us today!

MAMA (*Raising her eyes to meet his finally*): Son—I just tried to find the nicest place for the least amount of money for my family.

RUTH (*Trying to recover from the shock*): Well—well—'course I ain't one never been 'fraid of no crackers, mind you—but—well, wasn't there no other houses nowhere?

MAMA: Them houses they put up for colored in them areas way out all seem to cost twice as much as other houses. I did the best I could.

RUTH (*Struck senseless with the news, in its various degrees of goodness and trouble, she sits a moment, her fists propping her chin in thought, and then she starts to rise, bringing her fists down with vigor, the radiance spreading from cheek to cheek again*): Well—well!—All I can say is—if this is my time in life—my time—to say good-bye—(*And she builds with momentum as she starts to circle the room with an exuberant, almost tearfully happy release*)—to these Goddamned cracking walls!—(*She pounds the walls*)—and these marching roaches!—(*She wipes at an imaginary army of marching roaches*)—and this cramped little closet which ain't now or never was no kitchen! . . . then I say it loud and good, Hallelujah! and good-bye misery . . . I don't never want to see your ugly face again! (*She laughs joyously, having practically destroyed the apartment, and flings her arms up and lets them come down happily, slowly, reflectively, over her abdomen, aware for the first time perhaps that the life therein pulses with happiness and not despair*) Lena?

MAMA (*Moved, watching her happiness*): Yes, honey?

RUTH (*Looking off*): Is there—is there a whole lot of sunlight?

MAMA (*Understanding*): Yes, child, there's a whole lot of sunlight.

[*Long pause*]

RUTH (*Collecting herself and going to the door of the room* TRAVIS *is in*): Well—I guess I better see 'bout Travis. (*To* MAMA) Lord, I sure don't feel like whipping nobody today!

[*She exits*]

MAMA (*The mother and son are left alone now and the mother waits a long time, considering deeply, before she speaks*): Son—you—you understand what I done, don't you? (WALTER *is silent and sullen*) I—I just seen my family falling apart today . . . just falling to pieces in front of my eyes . . . We couldn't of gone on like we was today. We was going backwards 'stead of forwards—talking 'bout killing babies and wishing each other was dead . . . When it gets like that in life—you just got to do something different, push on out and do something bigger . . . (*She waits*) I wish you say something, son . . . I wish you'd say how deep inside you you think I done the right thing—

WALTER (*Crossing slowly to his bedroom door and finally turning there and speaking measuredly*): What you need me to say you done right for? *You* the head of this family. You run our lives like you want. It was your money and you did what you wanted with it. So what you need for me to say it was all right for? (*Bitterly, to hurt her as deeply as he knows is possible)* So you butchered up a dream of mine—you—who always talking 'bout your children's dreams . . .

MAMA: Walter Lee—

[He just closes the door behind him. MAMA sits alone, thinking heavily]

CURTAIN

Scene 2

Time: Friday night. A few weeks later.

At rise: Packing crates mark the intention of the family to move. BENEATHA and GEORGE come in, presumably from an evening out again.

1965   GEORGE: O.K. . . . O.K., whatever you say . . . (*They both sit on the couch. He tries to kiss her. She moves away)* Look, we've had a nice evening; let's not spoil it, huh? . . .

[He again turns her head and tries to nuzzle in and she turns away from him, not with distaste but with momentary lack of interest; in a mood to pursue what they were talking about]

BENEATHA: I'm *trying* to talk to you.

1970   GEORGE: We always talk.

BENEATHA: Yes—and I love to talk.

GEORGE (*Exasperated; rising*): I know it and I don't mind it sometimes . . . I want you to cut it out, see—The moody stuff, I mean. I don't like it.

1975   You're a nice-looking girl . . . all over. That's all you need, honey, forget the atmosphere. Guys aren't going to go for the atmosphere—they're going to go for what they see. Be glad for that. Drop the Garbo routine. It doesn't go with

1980   you. As for myself, I want a nice—(*Groping*)—simple—(*Thoughtfully*)—sophisticated girl . . . not a poet—O.K.?

[She rebuffs him again and he starts to leave]

BENEATHA: Why are you angry?

GEORGE: Because this is stupid! I don't go out with

1985   you to discuss the nature of "quiet desperation" or to hear all about your thoughts—because the world will go on thinking what it thinks regardless—

BENEATHA: Then why read books? Why go to school?

1990   GEORGE (*With artificial patience, counting on his fingers*): It's simple. You read books—to learn facts—to get grades—to pass the course—to get a degree.

That's all—it has nothing to do with thoughts.

[A long pause]

BENEATHA: I see. (*A longer pause as she looks at him*) Good night, George.　　　　1995

[GEORGE looks at her a little oddly, and starts to exit. He meets MAMA coming in]

GEORGE: Oh—hello, Mrs. Younger.

MAMA: Hello, George, how you feeling?

GEORGE: Fine—fine, how are you?

MAMA: Oh, a little tired. You know them steps can get you after a day's work. You all have a nice　2000 time tonight?

GEORGE: Yes—a fine time. Well, good night.

MAMA: Good night. (*He exits. MAMA closes the door behind her)* Hello, honey. What you sitting like that for?　　　　2005

BENEATHA: I'm just sitting.

MAMA: Didn't you have a nice time?

BENEATHA: No.

MAMA: No? What's the matter?

BENEATHA: Mama, George is a fool—honest. (*She rises)*　2010

MAMA (*Hustling around unloading the packages she has entered with. She stops*): Is he, baby?

BENEATHA: Yes.

[BENEATHA makes up TRAVIS' bed as she talks]

MAMA: You sure?

BENEATHA: Yes.

MAMA: Well—I guess you better not waste your time　2015 with no fools.

[BENEATHA looks up at her mother, watching her put groceries in the refrigerator. Finally she gathers up her things and starts into the bedroom. At the door she stops and looks back at her mother]

BENEATHA: Mama—

MAMA: Yes, baby—

BENEATHA: Thank you.　　　　2020

MAMA: For what?

BENEATHA: For understanding me this time.

[She exits quickly and the mother stands, smiling a little, looking at the place where BENEATHA just stood. RUTH enters]

RUTH: Now don't you fool with any of this stuff, Lena—

MAMA: Oh, I just thought I'd sort a few things out.

[The phone rings. RUTH answers]

RUTH (*At the phone*): Hello—Just a minute. (*Goes to*　2025

door) Walter, it's Mrs. Arnold. (*Waits. Goes back to the phone. Tense*) Hello. Yes, this is his wife speaking . . . He's lying down now. Yes . . . well, he'll be in tomorrow. He's been very sick. Yes—
2030   I know we should have called, but we were so sure he'd be able to come in today. Yes—yes, I'm very sorry. Yes . . . Thank you very much. (*She hangs up.* WALTER *is standing in the doorway of the bedroom behind her*) That was Mrs. Arnold.
2035   WALTER (*Indifferently*): Was it?
RUTH: She said if you don't come in tomorrow that they are getting a new man . . .
WALTER: Ain't that sad—ain't that crying sad.
RUTH: She said Mr. Arnold has had to take a cab for
2040   three days . . . Walter, you ain't been to work for three days! (*This is a revelation to her*) Where you been, Walter Lee Younger? (WALTER *looks at her and starts to laugh*) You're going to lose your job.
WALTER: That's right . . .
2045   RUTH: Oh, Walter, and with your mother working like a dog every day—
WALTER: That's sad too—Everything is sad.
MAMA: What you been doing for these three days, son?
WALTER: Mama—you don't know all the things a
2050   man what got leisure can find to do in this city . . . What's this—Friday night? Well—Wednesday I borrowed Willy Harris' car and I went for a drive . . . just me and myself and I drove and drove . . . Way out . . . way past
2055   South Chicago, and I parked the car and I sat and looked at the steel mills all day long. I just sat in the car and looked at them big black chimneys for hours. Then I drove back and I went to the Green Hat. (*Pause*) And
2060   Thursday—Thursday I borrowed the car again and I got in it and I pointed it the other way and I drove the other way—for hours—way, way up to Wisconsin, and I looked at the farms. I just drove and looked at the farms.
2065   Then I drove back and I went to the Green Hat. (*Pause*) And today—today I didn't get the car. Today I just walked. All over the Southside. And I looked at the Negroes and they looked at me and finally I just sat down
2070   on the curb at Thirty-ninth and South Parkway and I just sat there and watched the Negroes go by. And then I went to the Green Hat. You all sad? You all depressed? And you know where I am going right now—

[RUTH *goes out quietly*]

2075   MAMA: Oh, Big Walter, is this the harvest of our days?
WALTER: You know what I like about the Green Hat? (*He turns the radio on and a steamy, deep blues pours into the room*) I like this little cat they got there who blows a sax . . . He blows. He talks

to me. He ain't but 'bout five feet tall and he's   2080
got a conked head and his eyes is always
closed and he's all music—
MAMA (*Rising and getting some papers out of her hand-bag*): Walter—
WALTER: And there's this other guy who plays the   2085
piano . . . and they got a sound. I mean they can
work on some music . . . They got the best little
combo in the world in the Green Hat . . . You
can just sit there and drink and listen to them
three men play and you realize that don't noth-   2090
ing matter worth a damn, but just being there—
MAMA: I've helped do it to you, haven't I, son?
Walter, I been wrong.
WALTER: Naw—you ain't never been wrong about
nothing, Mama.   2095
MAMA: Listen to me, now. I say I been wrong, son.
That I been doing to you what the rest of the
world been doing to you. (*She stops and he looks
up slowly at her and she meets his eyes pleadingly*)
Walter—what you ain't never understood is   2100
that I ain't got nothing, don't own nothing,
ain't never really wanted nothing that wasn't
for you. There ain't nothing as precious to me
. . . There ain't nothing worth holding on to,
money, dreams, nothing else—if it means—if it   2105
means it's going to destroy my boy. (*She puts
her papers in front of him and he watches her without speaking or moving*) I paid the man thirty-
five hundred dollars down on the house. That
leaves sixty-five hundred dollars. Monday   2110
morning I want you to take this money and
take three thousand dollars and put it in a savings account for Beneatha's medical schooling.
The rest you put in a checking account—with
your name on it. And from now on any penny   2115
that come out of it or that go in it is for you to
look after. For you to decide. (*She drops her
hands a little helplessly*) It ain't much, but it's all
I got in the world and I'm putting in your
hands. I'm telling you to be the head of this   2120
family from now on like you supposed to be.
WALTER (*Stares at the money*): You trust me like that,
Mama?
MAMA: I ain't never stop trusting you. Like I ain't
never stop loving you.   2125

[*She goes out, and* WALTER *sits looking at the money
on the table as the music continues in its idiom, pulsing in the room. Finally, in a decisive gesture, he gets
up and, in a furious action, flings the bedclothes wildly from his son's makeshift bed to all over the floor—
with a cry of desperation. Then he picks up the money
and goes out in a hurry*]

CURTAIN

Scene 3

Time: Saturday, moving day, one week later.

Before the curtain rises, Ruth's *voice, a strident, dramatic church alto, cuts through the silence.*

It is, in the darkness, a triumphant surge, a penetrating statement of expectation: "Oh, Lord, I don't feel no ways tired! Children, oh, glory hallelujah!"

As the curtain rises we see that Ruth *is alone in the living room, finishing up the family's packing. It is moving day. She is nailing crates and tying cartons.* Beneatha *enters, carrying a guitar case, and watches her exuberant sister-in-law.*

Ruth: Hey!

Beneatha (*Putting away the case*): Hi.

Ruth (*Pointing at a package*): Honey—look in that
2130   package there and see what I found on sale
this morning at the South Center. (Ruth *gets up and moves to the package and draws out some curtains*) Lookahere—hand-turned hems!

Beneatha: How do you know the window size out
2135   there?

Ruth (*Who hadn't thought of that*): Oh—Well, they
bound to fit something in the whole house.
Anyhow, they was too good a bargain to pass
us. (Ruth *slaps her head, suddenly remembering something*) Oh, Bennie—I meant to put a spe-
2140   cial note on that carton over there. That's your
mama's good china and she wants 'em to be
very careful with it.

Beneatha: I'll do it.

[Beneatha *finds a piece of paper and starts to draw large letters on it*]

Ruth: You know what I'm going to do soon as I get
2145   in that new house?

Beneatha: What?

Ruth: Honey—I'm going to run me a tub of water
up to here . . . (*With her fingers practically up to her nostrils*) And I'm going to get in it—and I
2150   am going to sit . . . and sit . . . and sit in that
hot water and the first person who knocks to
tell *me* to hurry up and come-out—

Beneatha: Gets shot at sunrise.

Ruth (*Laughing happily*): You said it, sister! (*Noticing*
2155   *how large* Beneatha *is absent-mindedly making the note*) Honey, they ain't going to read that
from no airplane.

Beneatha (*Laughing herself*): I guess I always think
things have more emphasis if they are big,
2160   somehow.

Ruth (*Looking up at her and smiling*): You and your
brother seem to have that as a philosophy of

life. Lord, that man—done changed so 'round
here. You know—you know what we did last
night? Me and Walter Lee?   2165

Beneatha: What?

Ruth (*Smiling to herself*): We went to the movies.
(*Looking at* Beneatha *to see if she understands*)
We went to the movies. You know the last time
me and Walter went to the movies together? 2170

Beneatha: No.

Ruth: Me neither. That's how long it been. (*Smiling again*) But we went last night. The picture was-
n't much good, but that didn't seem to matter.
We went—and we held hands.   2175

Beneatha: Oh, Lord!

Ruth: We held hands—and you know what?

Beneatha: What?

Ruth: When we come out of the show it was late and
dark and all the stores and things was closed   2180
up . . . and it was kind of chilly and there was-
n't many people on the streets . . . and we was
still holding hands, me and Walter.

Beneatha: You're killing me.

[Walter *enters with a large package. His happiness is deep in him; he cannot keep still with his new-found exuberance. He is singing and wiggling and snapping his fingers. He puts his package in a corner and puts a phonograph record, which he has brought in with him, on the record player. As the music comes up he dances over to* Ruth *and tries to get her to dance with him. She gives in at last to his raunchiness and in a fit of giggling allows herself to be drawn into his mood and together they deliberately burlesque an old social dance of their youth*]

Beneatha (*Regarding them a long time as they dance,*   2185
then drawing in her breath for a deeply exaggerated comment which she does not particularly mean):
Talk about—olddddddddddd-fashioned-
dddddd—Negroes!

Walter (*Stopping momentarily*): What kind of   2190
Negroes?

[*He says this in fun. He is not angry with her today, nor with anyone. He starts to dance with his wife again*]

Beneatha: Old-fashioned.

Walter (*As he dances with* Ruth): You know, when
these *New Negroes* have their convention—
(*Pointing at his sister*)—that is going to be the
chairman of the Committee on Unending   2195
Agitation. (*He goes on dancing, then stops*) Race,
race, race! . . . Girl, I do believe you are the
first person in the history of the entire human
race to successfully brainwash yourself.   2200
(Beneatha *breaks up and he goes on dancing. He stops again, enjoying his tease*) Damn, even the N
double A C P takes a holiday sometimes!

(BENEATHA *and* RUTH *laugh. He dances with* RUTH *some more and starts to laugh and stops and pantomimes someone over an operating table*) I can just see that chick someday looking down at some poor cat on an operating table before she starts to slice him, saying . . . (*Pulling his sleeves back maliciously*) "By the way, what are your views on civil rights down there? . . ."

[*He laughs at her again and starts to dance happily. The bell sounds*]

BENEATHA: Sticks and stones may break my bones but . . . words will never hurt me!

[BENEATHA *goes to the door and opens it as* WALTER *and* RUTH *go on with the clowning.* BENEATHA *is somewhat surprised to see a quiet-looking middle-aged white man in a business suit holding his hat and a briefcase in his hand and consulting a small piece of paper*]

MAN: Uh—how do you do, miss. I am looking for a Mrs.—(*He looks at the slip of paper*) Mrs. Lena Younger?

BENEATHA (*Smoothing her hair with slight embarrassment*): Oh—yes, that's my mother. Excuse me. (*She closes the door and turns to quiet the other two*) Ruth! Brother! Somebody's here. (*Then she opens the door. The man casts a curious quick glance at all of them*) Uh—come in please.

MAN (*Coming in*): Thank you.

BENEATHA: My mother isn't here just now. Is it business?

MAN: Yes . . . well, of a sort.

WALTER (*Freely, the Man of the House*): Have a seat. I'm Mrs. Younger's son. I look after most of her business matters.

[RUTH *and* BENEATHA *exchange amused glances*]

MAN (*Regarding* WALTER, *and sitting*): Well—My name is Karl Lindner . . .

WALTER (*Stretching out his hand*): Walter Younger. This is my wife—(RUTH *nods politely*)—and my sister.

LINDNER: How do you do.

WALTER (*Amiably, as he sits himself easily on a chair, leaning with interest forward on his knees and looking expectantly into the newcomer's face*): What can we do for you, Mr. Lindner!

LINDNER (*Some minor shuffling of the hat and briefcase on his knees*): Well—I am a representative of the Clybourne Park Improvement Association—

WALTER (*Pointing*): Why don't you sit your things on the floor?

LINDNER: Oh—yes. Thank you. (*He slides the briefcase and hat under the chair*): And as I was saying—I am from the Clybourne Park Improvement

Association and we have had it brought to our attention at the last meeting that you people— or at least your mother—has bought a piece of residential property at—(*He digs for the slip of paper again*)—four o six Clybourne Street . . .

WALTER: That's right. Care for something to drink? Ruth, get Mr. Lindner a beer.

LINDNER (*Upset for some reason*): Oh—no, really. I mean thank you very much, but no thank you.

RUTH (*Innocently*): Some coffee?

LINDNER: Thank you, nothing at all.

[BENEATHA *is watching the man carefully*]

LINDNER: Well, I don't know how much you folks know about our organization. (*He is a gentle man; thoughtful and somewhat labored in his manner*) It is one of these community organizations set up to look after—oh, you know, things like block upkeep and special projects and we also have what we call our New Neighbors Orientation Committee . . .

BENEATHA (*Drily*): Yes—and what do they do?

LINDNER (*Turning a little to her and then returning the main force to* WALTER): Well—it's what you might call a sort of welcoming committee, I guess. I mean they, we, I'm the chairman of the committee—go around and see the new people who move into the neighborhood and sort of give them the lowdown on the way we do things out in Clybourne Park.

BENEATHA (*With appreciation of the two meanings, which escape* RUTH *and* WALTER): Un-huh.

LINDNER: And we also have the category of what the association calls—(*He looks elsewhere*)—uh— special community problems . . .

BENEATHA: Yes—and what are some of those?

WALTER: Girl, let the man talk.

LINDNER (*With understated relief*): Thank you. I would sort of like to explain this thing in my own way. I mean I want to explain to you in a certain way.

WALTER: Go ahead.

LINDNER: Yes. Well. I'm going to try to get right to the point. I'm sure we'll all appreciate that in the long run.

BENEATHA: Yes.

WALTER: Be still now!

LINDNER: Well—

RUTH (*Still innocently*): Would you like another chair—you don't look comfortable.

LINDNER (*More frustrated than annoyed*): No, thank you very much. Please. Well—to get right to the point I—(*A great breath, and he is off at last*) I am sure you people must be aware of some of the incidents which have happened in various parts of the city when colored people have moved into certain areas—(BENEATHA *exhales*

2300 *heavily and starts tossing a piece of fruit up and down in the air*) Well—because we have what I think is going to be a unique type of organization in American community life—not only do we deplore that kind of thing—but we are try-
2305 ing to do something about it. (BENEATHA *stops tossing and turns with a new and quizzical interest to the man*) We feel—(*gaining confidence in his mission because of the interest in the faces of the people he is talking to*)—we feel that most of the
2310 trouble in this world, when you come right down to it—(*He hits his knee for emphasis*)—most of the trouble exists because people just don't sit down and talk to each other.

RUTH (*Nodding as she might in church, pleased with the*
2315 *remark*): You can say that again, mister.

LINDNER (*More encouraged by such affirmation*): That we don't try hard enough in this world to understand the other fellow's problem. The other guy's point of view.

2320 RUTH: Now that's right.

[BENEATHA *and* WALTER *merely watch and listen with genuine interest*]

LINDNER: Yes—that's the way we feel out in Clybourne Park. And that's why I was elected to come here this afternoon and talk to you people. Friendly like, you know, the way peo-
2325 ple should talk to each other and see if we couldn't find some way to work this thing out. As I say, the whole business is a matter of *caring* about the other fellow. Anybody can see that you are a nice family of folks, hard work-
2330 ing and honest I'm sure. (BENEATHA *frowns slightly, quizzically, her head tilted regarding him*) Today everybody knows what it means to be on the outside of *something*. And of course, there is always somebody who is out to take
2335 the advantage of people who don't always understand.

WALTER: What do you mean?

LINDNER: Well—you see our community is made up of people who've worked hard as the dickens
2340 for years to build up that little community. They're not rich and fancy people; just hard-working, honest people who don't really have much but those little homes and a dream of the kind of community they want to raise their
2345 children in. Now, I don't say we are perfect and there is a lot wrong in some of the things they want. But you've got to admit that a man, right or wrong, has the right to want to have the neighborhood he lives in a certain kind of way.
2350 And at the moment the overwhelming majority of our people out there feel that people get along better, take more of a common interest in

the life of the community, when they share a common background. I want you to believe me when I tell you that race prejudice simply does- 2355 n't enter into it. It is a matter of the people of Clybourne Park believing, rightly or wrongly, as I say, that for the happiness of all concerned that our Negro families are happier when they live in their *own* communities. 2360

BENEATHA (*With a grand and bitter gesture*): This, friends, is the Welcoming Committee!

WALTER (*Dumfounded, looking at* LINDNER): Is this what you came marching all the way over here to tell us? 2365

LINDNER: Well, now we've been having a fine conversation. I hope you'll hear me all the way through.

WALTER (*Tightly*): Go ahead, man.

LINDNER: You see—in the face of all things I have said, we are prepared to make your family a 2370 very generous offer . . .

BENEATHA: Thirty pieces and not a coin less!

WALTER: Yeah?

LINDNER (*Putting on his glasses and drawing a form out of the briefcase*): Our association is prepared, 2375 through the collective effort of our people, to buy the house from you at a financial gain to your family.

RUTH: Lord have mercy, ain't this the living gall!

WALTER: All right, you through? 2380

LINDNER: Well, I want to give you the exact terms of the financial arrangement—

WALTER: We don't want to hear no exact terms of no arrangements. I want to know if you got any more to tell us 'bout getting together? 2385

LINDNER (*Taking off his glasses*): Well—I don't suppose that you feel . . .

WALTER: Never mind how I feel—you got any more to say 'bout how people ought to sit down and talk to each other? . . . Get out of my house, man. 2390

[*He turns his back and walks to the door*]

LINDNER (*Looking around at the hostile faces and reaching and assembling his hat and briefcase*): Well—I don't understand why you people are reacting this way. What do you think you are going to gain by moving into a neighborhood where you just 2395 aren't wanted and where some elements— well—people can get awful worked up when they feel that their whole way of life and every-thing they've ever worked for is threatened.

WALTER: Get out. 2400

LINDNER (*At the door, holding a small card*): Well—I'm sorry it went like this.

WALTER: Get out.

LINDNER (*Almost sadly regarding* WALTER): You just can't force people to change their hearts, son. 2405

[*He turns and puts his card on a table and exits.* WALTER *pushes the door to with stinging hatred, and stands looking at it.* RUTH *just sits and* BENEATHA *just stands. They say nothing.* MAMA *and* TRAVIS *enter*]

MAMA: Well—this all the packing got done since I left out of here this morning. I testify before God that my children got all the energy of the

2410   dead. What time the moving men due?
BENEATHA: Four o'clock. You had a caller, Mama.

[*She is smiling, teasingly*]

MAMA: Sure enough—who?
BENEATHA (*Her arms folded saucily*): The Welcoming Committee.

[WALTER *and* RUTH *giggle*]

2415 MAMA (*Innocently*): Who?
BENEATHA: The Welcoming Committee. They said they're sure going to be glad to see you when you get there.
WALTER (*Devilishly*): Yeah, they said they can't hardly
2420   wait to see your face.

[*Laughter*]

MAMA (*Sensing their facetiousness*): What's the matter with you all?
WALTER: Ain't nothing the matter with us. We just telling you 'bout the gentleman who came to
2425   see you this afternoon. From the Clybourne Park Improvement Association.
MAMA: What he want?
RUTH (*In the same mood as* BENEATHA *and* WALTER): To welcome you, honey.
2430 WALTER: He said they can't hardly wait. He said the one thing they don't have, that they just *dying* to have out there is a fine family of colored people! (*To* RUTH *and* BENEATHA) Ain't that right!
2435 RUTH *and* BENEATHA (*Mockingly*): Yeah! He left his card in case—

[*They indicate the card, and* MAMA *picks it up and throws it on the floor—understanding and looking off as she draws her chair up to the table on which she has put her plant and some sticks and some cord*]

MAMA: Father, give us strength. (*Knowingly—and without fun*) Did he threaten us?
BENEATHA: Oh—Mama—they don't do it like that
2440   any more. He talked Brotherhood. He said everybody ought learn how to sit down and hate each other with good Christian fellowship.

[*She and* WALTER *shake hands to ridicule the remark*]

MAMA (*Sadly*): Lord, protect us . . .
RUTH: You should hear the money those folks raised   2445
to buy the house from us. All we paid and then some.
BENEATHA: What they think we going to do—eat 'em?
RUTH: No, honey, marry 'em.
MAMA (*Shaking her head*): Lord, Lord, Lord . . .   2450
RUTH: Well—that's the way the crackers crumble. Joke.
BENEATHA (*Laughingly noticing what her mother is doing*): Mama, what are you doing?
MAMA: Fixing my plant so it won't get hurt none on the way . . .   2455
BENEATHA: Mama, you going to take *that* to the new house?
MAMA: Un-huh—
BENEATHA: That raggedy-looking old thing?
MAMA (*Stopping and looking at her*): It expresses *me*.   2460
RUTH (*With delight, to* BENEATHA): So there, Miss Thing!

[WALTER *comes to* MAMA *suddenly and bends down behind her and squeezes her in his arms with all his strength. She is overwhelmed by the suddenness of it and, though delighted, her manner is like that of* RUTH *with* TRAVIS]

MAMA: Look out now, boy! You make me mess up my thing here!
WALTER (*His face lit, he slips down on his knees beside   2465
her, his arms still about her*): Mama . . . you know what it means to climb up in the chariot?
MAMA (*Gruffly, very happy*): Get on away from me now . . .
RUTH (*Near the gift-wrapped package, trying to catch   2470
WALTER's eye*): Psst—
WALTER: What the old song say, Mama . . .
RUTH: Walter—Now?

[*She is pointing at the package*]

WALTER (*Speaking the lines, sweetly, playfully, in his   2475
mother's face*):

I got wings . . . you got wings . . .
All God's children got wings . . .

MAMA: Boy—get out of my face and do some work . . .
WALTER:

When I get to heaven gonna put on my wings,   2480
Gonna fly all over God's heaven . . .

BENEATHA (*Teasingly, from across the room*): Everybody talking 'bout heaven ain't going there!

WALTER (*To* RUTH, *who is carrying the box across to them*): I don't know, you think we ought to give her that . . . Seems to me she ain't been very appreciative around here.

MAMA (*Eying the box, which is obviously a gift*): What is that?

WALTER (*Taking it from* RUTH *and putting it on the table in front of* MAMA): Well—what you all think. Should we give it to her?

RUTH: Oh—she was pretty good today.

MAMA: I'll good you—

[*She turns her eyes to the box again*]

BENEATHA: Open it, Mama.

[*She stands up, looks at it, turns and looks at all of them, and then presses her hands together and does not open the package*]

WALTER (*Sweetly*): Open it, Mama. It's for you. (MAMA *looks in his eyes. It is the first present in her life without its being Christmas. Slowly she opens her package and lifts out, one by one, a brand-new sparkling set of gardening tools.* WALTER *continues, prodding*) Ruth made up the note—read it . . .

MAMA (*Picking up the card and adjusting her glasses*): "To our own Mrs. Miniver—Love from Brother, Ruth and Beneatha." Ain't that lovely . . .

TRAVIS (*Tugging at his father's sleeve*): Daddy, can I give her mine now?

WALTER: All right, son. (TRAVIS *flies to get his gift*) Travis didn't want to go in with the rest of us, Mama. He got his own. (*Somewhat amused*) We don't know what it is . . .

TRAVIS (*Racing back in the room with a large hatbox and putting it in front of his grandmother*): Here!

MAMA: Lord have mercy, baby. You done gone and bought your grandmother a hat?

TRAVIS (*Very proud*): Open it!

[*She does and lifts out an elaborate, but very elaborate, wide gardening hat, and all the adults break up at the sight of it*]

RUTH: Travis, honey, what is that?

TRAVIS (*Who thinks it is beautiful and appropriate*): It's a gardening hat! Like the ladies always have on in the magazines when they work in their gardens.

BENEATHA (*Giggling fiercely*): Travis—we were trying to make Mama Mrs. Miniver—not Scarlett O'Hara!

MAMA (*Indignantly*): What's the matter with you all! This here is a beautiful hat! (*Absurdly*) I always wanted me one just like it!

[*She pops it on her head to prove it to her grandson, and the hat is ludicrous and considerably oversized*]

RUTH: Hot dog! Go, Mama!

WALTER (*Doubled over with laughter*): I'm sorry, Mama—but you look like you ready to go out and chop you some cotton sure enough!

[*They all laugh except* MAMA, *out of deference to* TRAVIS' *feelings*]

MAMA (*Gathering the boy up to her*): Bless your heart—this is the prettiest hat I ever owned— (WALTER, RUTH, *and* BENEATHA *chime in—noisily, festively and insincerely congratulating* TRAVIS *on his gift*) What are we all standing around here for? We ain't finished packin' yet. Bennie, you ain't packed one book.

[*The bell rings*]

BENEATHA: That couldn't be the movers . . . it's not hardly two good yet—

[BENEATHA *goes into her room.* MAMA *starts for door*]

WALTER (*Turning, stiffening*):Wait—wait—I'll get it.

[*He stands and looks at the door*]

MAMA: You expecting company, son?

WALTER (*Just looking at the door*): Yeah—yeah . . .

[MAMA *looks at* RUTH, *and they exchange innocent and unfrightened glances*]

MAMA (*Not understanding*): Well, let them in, son.

BENEATHA (*From her room*): We need some more string.

MAMA: Travis—you run to the hardware and get me some string cord.

[MAMA *goes out and* WALTER *turns and looks at* RUTH. TRAVIS *goes to a dish for money*]

RUTH: Why don't you answer the door, man?

WALTER (*Suddenly bounding across the floor to her*): 'Cause sometimes it hard to let the future begin! (*Stooping down in her face*)

I got wings! You got wings!
All God's children got wings!

[*He crosses to the door and throws it open. Standing there is a very slight little man in a not too prosperous business suit and with haunted frightened eyes and a hat pulled down tightly, brim up, around his forehead.*]

TRAVIS *passes between the men and exits.* WALTER *leans deep in the man's face, still in his jubilance]*

2555   *When I get to heaven gonna put on my wings,*
    Gonna fly all over God's heaven . . .

    [The little man just stares at him]

    Heaven—

        (Suddenly he stops and looks past the little man into the empty hallway) Where's Willy, man?
2560 BOBO: He ain't with me.
    WALTER *(Not disturbed):* Oh—come on in. You know my wife.
    BOBO *(Dumbly, taking off his hat):* Yes—h'you, Miss Ruth.
2565 RUTH *(Quietly, a mood apart from her husband already, seeing* BOBO): Hello, Bobo.
    WALTER: You right on time today . . . Right on time. That's the way! *(He slaps* BOBO *on his back)* Sit down . . . lemme hear.

*[*RUTH *stands stiffly and quietly in back of them, as though somehow she senses death, her eyes fixed on her husband]*

2570 BOBO *(His frightened eyes on the floor, his hat in his hands):* Could I please get a drink a water, before I tell you about it, Walter Lee?

*[*WALTER *does not take his eyes off the man.* RUTH *goes blindly to the tap and gets a glass of water and brings it to* BOBO]

    WALTER: There ain't nothing wrong, is there?
    BOBO: Lemme tell you—
2575 WALTER: Man—didn't nothing go wrong?
    BOBO: Lemme tell you—Walter Lee. *(Looking at* RUTH *and talking to her more than to* WALTER) You know how it was. I got to tell you how it was. I mean first I got to tell you how it was all the way . . . I
2580 mean about the money I put in Walter Lee . . .
    WALTER *(With taut agitation now):* What about the money you put in?
    BOBO: Well—it wasn't much as we told you—me and Willy— *(He stops)* I'm sorry, Walter. I got a bad
2585 feeling about it. I got a real bad feeling about it . . .
    WALTER: Man, what you telling me about all this for? . . . Tell me what happened in Springfield . . .
    BOBO: Springfield.
2590 RUTH *(Like a dead woman):* What was supposed to happen in Springfield?
    BOBO *(To her):* This deal that me and Walter went into with Willy—Me and Willy was going to go down to Springfield and spread some money

'round so's we wouldn't have to wait so long 2595 for the liquor license . . . That's what we were going to do. Everybody said that was the way you had to do, you understand, Miss Ruth?
WALTER: Man—what happened down there?
BOBO *(A pitiful man, near tears):* I'm trying to tell you, 2600 Walter.
WALTER *(Screaming at him suddenly):* THEN TELL ME, GODDAMNIT . . .WHAT'S THE MATTER WITH YOU?
BOBO: Man . . . I didn't go to no Springfield, yesterday.
WALTER *(Halted, life hanging in the moment):* Why not? 2605
BOBO *(The long way, the hard way to tell):* 'Cause I didn't have no reasons to . . .
WALTER: Man, what are you talking about!
BOBO: I'm talking about the fact that when I got to the train station yesterday morning—eight 2610 o'clock like we planned . . . Man—*Willy didn't never show up.*
WALTER: Why . . . where was he . . . where is he?
BOBO: That's what I'm trying to tell you . . . I don't know . . . I waited six hours . . . I called his 2615 house . . . and I waited . . . six hours . . . I waited in that train station six hours . . . *(Breaking into tears)* That was all the extra money I had in the world . . . *(Looking up at* WALTER *with the tears running down his face)* Man, *Willy is gone.* 2620
WALTER: Gone, what you mean Willy is gone? Gone where? You mean he went by himself. You mean he went off to Springfield by himself—to take care of getting the license—*(Turns and looks anxiously at* RUTH) You mean maybe he 2625 didn't want too many people in on the business down there? *(Looks to* RUTH *again, as before)* You know Willy got his own ways. *(Looks back to* BOBO) Maybe you was late yesterday and he just went on down there with- 2630 out you. Maybe—maybe—he's been callin' you at home tryin' to tell you what happened or something. Maybe—maybe—he just got sick. He's somewhere—he's got to be some-where. We just got to find him—me and you 2635 got to find him. *(Grabs* BOBO *senselessly by the collar and starts to shake him)* We got to!
BOBO *(In sudden angry, frightened agony):* What's the matter with you, Walter! *When a cat take off with your money he don't leave you no maps!* 2640
WALTER *(Turning madly, as though he is looking for* WILLY *in the very room):* Willy! . . . Willy . . . don't do it . . . Please don't do it . . . Man, not with that money . . . Man, please, not with that money . . . Oh, God . . . Don't let it be true . . . 2645 *(He is wandering around, crying out for* WILLY *and looking for him or perhaps for help from God)* Man . . . I trusted you . . . Man, I put my life in your hands . . . *(He starts to crumple down on the floor as* RUTH *just covers her face in horror.* MAMA 2650 *opens the door and comes into the room, with*

BENEATHA behind her) Man . . . (He starts to pound the floor with his fists, sobbing wildly) That money is made out of my father's flesh . . .

2655 BOBO (Standing over him helplessly): I'm sorry, Walter . . . (Only WALTER's sobs reply. BOBO puts on his hat) I had my life staked on this deal, too . . .

[He exits]

MAMA (To WALTER): Son—(She goes to him, bends down to him, talks to his bent head) Son . . . Is
2660 it gone? Son, I gave you sixty-five hundred dollars. Is it gone? All of it? Beneatha's money too?
WALTER (Lifting his head slowly): Mama . . . I never . . . went to the bank at all . . .
MAMA (Not wanting to believe him): You mean . . .
2665 your sister's school money . . . you used that too . . . Walter? . . .
WALTER: Yessss! . . . All of it . . . It's all gone . . .

[There is total silence. RUTH stands with her face covered with her hands; BENEATHA leans forlornly against a wall, fingering a piece of red ribbon from the mother's gift. MAMA stops and looks at her son without recognition and then, quite without thinking about it, starts to beat him senselessly in the face. BENEATHA goes to them and stops it]

BENEATHA: Mama!

[MAMA stops and looks at both of her children and rises slowly and wanders vaguely, aimlessly away from them]

MAMA: I seen . . . him . . . night after night . . . come
2670 in . . . and look at that rug . . . and then look at me . . . the red showing in his eyes . . . the veins moving in his head . . . I seen him grow thin and old before he was forty . . . working and working and working like somebody's old
2675 horse . . . killing himself . . . and you—you give it all away in a day . . .
BENEATHA: Mama—
MAMA: Oh, God . . . (She looks up to Him) Look down here—and show me the strength.
2680 BENEATHA: Mama—
MAMA (Folding over): Strength . . .
BENEATHA (Plaintively): Mama . . .
MAMA: Strength!

CURTAIN

ACT III

An hour later.

At curtain, there is a sullen light of gloom in the living room, gray light not unlike that which began

the first scene of Act I. At left we can see WALTER within his room, alone with himself. He is stretched out on the bed, his shirt out and open, his arms under his head. He does not smoke, he does not cry out, he merely lies there, looking up at the ceiling, much as if he were alone in the world.

In the living room BENEATHA sits at the table, still surrounded by the now almost ominous packing crates. She sits looking off. We feel that this is a mood struck perhaps an hour before, and it lingers now, full of the empty sound of profound disappointment. We see on a line from her brother's bedroom the sameness of their attitudes. Presently the bell rings and BENEATHA rises without ambition or interest in answering. It is ASAGAI, smiling broadly, striding into the room with energy and happy expectation and conversation.

ASAGAI: I came over . . . I had some free time. I
2685 thought I might help with the packing. Ah, I like the look of packing crates! A household in preparation for a journey! It depresses some people . . . but for me . . . it is another feeling. Something full of the flow of life, do you
2690 understand? Movement, progress . . . It makes me think of Africa.
BENEATHA: Africa!
ASAGAI: What kind of a mood is this? Have I told you how deeply you move me?
2695 BENEATHA: He gave away the money, Asagai . . .
ASAGAI: Who gave away what money?
BENEATHA: The insurance money. My brother gave it away.
ASAGAI: Gave it away?
2700 BENEATHA: He made an investment! With a man even Travis wouldn't have trusted.
ASAGAI: And it's gone?
BENEATHA: Gone!
ASAGAI: I'm very sorry . . . And you, now?
2705 BENEATHA: Me? . . . Me? . . . Me I'm nothing . . . Me. When I was very small . . . we used to take our sleds out in the wintertime and the only hills we had were the ice-covered stone steps of some houses down the street. And we used to
2710 fill them in with snow and make them smooth and slide down them all day . . . and it was very dangerous you know . . . far too steep . . . and sure enough one day a kid named Rufus came down too fast and hit the sidewalk . . .
2715 and we saw his face just split open right there in front of us . . . And I remember standing there looking at his bloody open face thinking that was the end of Rufus. But the ambulance came and they took him to the hospital and
2720 they fixed the broken bones and they sewed it all up . . . and the next time I saw Rufus he just had a little line down the middle of his face . . . I never got over that . . .

ASAGAI: What?

2725 BENEATHA: That that was what one person could do for another, fix him up—sew up the problem, make him all right again. That was the most marvelous thing in the world . . . I wanted to do
2730 that. I always thought it was the one concrete thing in the world that a human being could do. Fix up the sick, you know—and make them whole again. This was truly being God . . .

ASAGAI: You wanted to be God?

2735 BENEATHA: No—I wanted to cure. It used to be so important to me. I wanted to cure. It used to matter. I used to care. I mean about people and how their bodies hurt . . .

ASAGAI: And you've stopped caring?

BENEATHA: Yes—I think so.

2740 ASAGAI: Why?

BENEATHA: Because it doesn't seem deep enough, close enough to the truth.

ASAGAI: Truth? Why is it that you despairing ones always think that only you have the truth? I
2745 never thought to see *you* like that. You! Your brother made a stupid, childish mistake—and you are grateful to him. So that now you can give up the ailing human race on account of it. You talk about what good is struggle; what
2750 good is anything? Where are we all going? And why are we bothering?

BENEATHA: *And you cannot answer it!* All your talk and dreams about Africa and Independence. Independence and then what? What about all
2755 the crooks and petty thieves and just plain idiots who will come into power to steal and plunder the same as before—only now they will be black and do it in the name of the new Independence—You cannot answer that.

2760 ASAGAI (*Shouting over her*): I live the answer! (*Pause*) In my village at home it is the exceptional man who can even read a newspaper . . . or who ever *sees* a book at all. I will go home and much of what I will have to say will seem
2765 strange to the people of my village . . . But I will teach and work and things will happen, slowly and swiftly. At times it will seem that nothing changes at all . . . and then again . . . the sudden dramatic events which make histo-
2770 ry leap into the future. And then quiet again. Retrogression even. Guns, murder, revolution. And I even will have moments when I wonder if the quiet was not better than all that death and hatred. But I will look about my village at
2775 the illiteracy and disease and ignorance and I will not wonder long. And perhaps . . . perhaps I will be a great man . . . I mean perhaps I will hold on to the substance of truth and find my way always with the right course . . . and
2780 perhaps for it I will be butchered in my bed

some night by the servants of empire . . .

BENEATHA: *The martyr!*

ASAGAI: . . . or perhaps I shall live to be a very old man respected and esteemed in my new nation
2785 . . . And perhaps I shall hold office and this is what I'm trying to tell you, Alaiyo; perhaps the things I believe now for my country will be wrong and outmoded, and I will not under- stand and do terrible things to have things my
2790 way or merely to keep my power. Don't you see that there will be young men and women, not British soldiers then, but my own black coun- trymen . . . to step out of the shadows some evening and slit my then useless throat? Don't
2795 you see they have always been there . . . that they always will be. And that such a thing as my own death will be an advance? They who might kill me even . . . actually replenish me!

BENEATHA: Oh, Asagai, I know all that.

2800 ASAGAI: Good! Then stop moaning and groaning and tell me what you plan to do.

BENEATHA: Do?

ASAGAI: I have a bit of a suggestion.

BENEATHA: What?

2805 ASAGAI (*Rather quietly for him*): That when it is all over—that you come home with me—

BENEATHA (*Slapping herself on the forehead with exasper- ation born of misunderstanding*): Oh—Asagai—at this moment you decide to be romantic!

2810 ASAGAI (*Quickly understanding the misunderstanding*): My dear, young creature of the New World—I do not mean across the city—I mean across the ocean; home—to Africa.

BENEATHA (*Slowly understanding and turning to him with murmured amazement*): To—to Nigeria?

2815

ASAGAI: Yes! . . . (*Smiling and lifting his arms playfully*) Three hundred years later the African Prince rose up out of the seas and swept the maiden back across the middle passage over which her ancestors had come—

2820

BENEATHA (*Unable to play*): Nigeria?

ASAGAI: Nigeria. Home. (*Coming to her with genuine romantic flippancy*) I will show you our moun- tains and our stars; and give you cool drinks from gourds and teach you the old songs and
2825 the ways of our people—and, in time, we will pretend that—(*Very softly*)—you have only been away for a day—

[*She turns her back to him, thinking. He swings her around and takes her full in his arms in a long embrace which proceeds to passion*]

BENEATHA (*Pulling away*): You're getting me all mixed up—
2830

ASAGAI: Why?

BENEATHA: Too many things—too many things have

happened today. I must sit down and think. I don't know what I feel about anything right this minute.

[*She promptly sits down and props her chin on her fist*]

ASAGAI (*Charmed*): All right, I shall leave you. No—don't get up. (*Touching her, gently, sweetly*) Just sit awhile and think . . . Never be afraid to sit awhile and think. (*He goes to door and looks at her*) How often I have looked at you and said, "Ah—so this is what the New World hath finally wrought . . ."

[*He exits.* BENEATHA *sits on alone. Presently* WALTER *enters from his room and starts to rummage through things, feverishly looking for something. She looks up and turns in her seat*]

BENEATHA (*Hissingly*): Yes—just look at what the New World hath wrought! . . . Just look! (*She gestures with bitter disgust*) There he is! Monsieur le petit bourgeois noir—himself! There he is—Symbol of a Rising Class! Entrepreneur! Titan of the system! (WALTER *ignores her completely and continues frantically and destructively looking for something and hurling things to floor and tearing things out of their place in his search.* BENEATHA *ignores the eccentricity of his actions and goes on with the monologue of insult*) Did you dream of yachts on Lake Michigan, Brother? Did you see yourself on that Great Day sitting down at the Conference Table, surrounded by all the mighty bald-headed men in America? All halted, waiting, breathless, waiting for your pronouncements on industry? Waiting for you—Chairman of the Board? (WALTER *finds what he is looking for—a small piece of white paper—and pushes it in his pocket and puts on his coat and rushes out without ever having looked at her. She shouts after him*) I look at you and I see the final triumph of stupidity in the world!

[*The door slams and she returns to just sitting again.* RUTH *comes quickly out of* MAMA'S *room*]

RUTH: Who was that?
BENEATHA: Your husband.
RUTH: Where did he go?
BENEATHA: Who knows—maybe he has an appointment at U.S. Steel.
RUTH (*Anxiously, with frightened eyes*): You didn't say nothing bad to him, did you?
BENEATHA: Bad? Say anything bad to him? No—I told him he was a sweet boy and full of dreams and everything is strictly peachy keen, as the ofay kids say!

[MAMA *enters from her bedroom. She is lost, vague, trying to catch hold, to make some sense of her former command of the world, but it still eludes her. A sense of waste overwhelms her gait; a measure of apology rides on her shoulders. She goes to her plant, which has remained on the table, looks at it, picks it up and takes it to the window sill and sits it outside, and she stands and looks at it a long moment. Then she closes the window, straightens her body with effort and turns around to her children*]

MAMA: Well—ain't it a mess in here, though? (*A false cheerfulness, a beginning of something*) I guess we all better stop moping around and get some work done. All this unpacking and everything we got to do. (RUTH *raises her head slowly in response to the sense of the line; and* BENEATHA *in similar manner turns very slowly to look at her mother*) One of you all better call the moving people and tell 'em not to come.
RUTH: Tell 'em not to come?
MAMA: Of course, baby. Ain't no need in 'em coming all the way here and having to go back. They charges for that too. (*She sits down, fingers to her brow, thinking*) Lord, ever since I was a little girl, I always remembers people saying, "Lena—Lena Eggleston, you aims too high all the time. You needs to slow down and see life a little more like it is. Just slow down some." That's what they always used to say down home—"Lord, that Lena Eggleston is a high-minded thing. She'll get her due one day!"
RUTH: No, Lena . . .
MAMA: Me and Big Walter just didn't never learn right.
RUTH: Lena, no! We gotta go. Bennie—tell her . . . (*She rises and crosses to* BENEATHA *with her arms outstretched.* BENEATHA *doesn't respond*) Tell her we can still move . . . the notes ain't but a hundred and twenty five a month. We got four grown people in this house—we can work . . .
MAMA (*To herself*): Just aimed too high all the time—
RUTH (*Turning and going to* MAMA *fast—the words pouring out with urgency and desperation*): Lena—I'll work . . . I'll work twenty hours a day in all the kitchens in Chicago . . . I'll strap my baby on my back if I have to and scrub all the floors in America and wash all the sheets in America if I have to—but we got to move . . . We got to get out of here . . .

[MAMA *reaches out absently and pats* RUTH'S *hand*]

MAMA: No—I sees things differently now. Been thinking 'bout some of the things we could do to fix this place up some. I seen a second-hand bureau over on Maxwell Street just the other day that could fit right there. (*She points to where*

2920 *the new furniture might go.* RUTH *wanders away from her*) Would need some new handles on it and then a little varnish and then it look like something brand-new. And—we can put up
2925 them new curtains in the kitchen . . . Why this place be looking fine. Cheer us all up so that we forget trouble ever came . . . (*To* RUTH) And you could get some nice screens to put up in your room round the baby's basinet . . . (She looks at both of them, pleadingly) Sometimes you just
2930 got to know when to give up some things . . . and hold on to what you got.

[WALTER *enters from the outside, looking spent and leaning against the door, his coat hanging from him*]

MAMA: Where you been, son?
WALTER (*Breathing hard*): Made a call.
MAMA: To who, son?
2935 WALTER: To The Man.
MAMA: What man, baby?
WALTER: The Man, Mama. Don't you know who The Man is?
RUTH: Walter Lee?
2940 WALTER: *The Man.* Like the guys in the streets say—The Man. Captain Boss—Mistuh Charley . . . Old Captain Please Mr. Bossman . . .
BENEATHA (*Suddenly*): Lindner!
WALTER: That's right! That's good. I told him to come
2945 right over.
BENEATHA (*Fiercely, understanding*): For what? What do you want to see him for!
WALTER (*Looking at his sister*): We going to do business with him.
2950 MAMA: What you talking 'bout, son?
WALTER: Talking 'bout life, Mama. You all always telling me to see life like it is. Well—I laid in there on my back today . . . and I figured it out. Life just like it is. Who gets and who don't get.
2955 (*He sits down with his coat on and laughs*) Mama, you know it's all divided up. Life is. Sure enough. Between the takers and the "tooken." (*He laughs*) I've figured it out finally. (He looks around at them) Yeah. Some of us always get-
2960 ting "tooken." (*He laughs*). People like Willy Harris, they don't never get "tooken." And you know why the rest of us do? 'Cause we all mixed up. Mixed up bad. We get to looking 'round for the right and the wrong; and we
2965 worry about it and cry about it and stay up nights trying to figure out 'bout the wrong and the right of things all the time . . . And all the time, man, them takers is out there operating, just taking and taking. Willy Harris? Shoot—
2970 Willy Harris don't even count. He don't even count in the big scheme of things. But I'll say one thing for old Willy Harris . . . he's taught me something. He's taught me to keep my eye on what counts in this world. Yeah—(*Shouting out a little*) Thanks, Willy!
2975 RUTH: What did you call that man for, Walter Lee?
WALTER: Called him to tell him to come on over to the show. Gonna put on a show for the man. Just what he wants to see. You see, Mama, the man came here today and he told us that them
2980 people out there where you want us to move—well they so upset they willing to pay us not to move out there. (*He laughs again*) And—and oh, Mama—you would of been proud of the way me and Ruth and Bennie acted. We told
2985 him to get out . . . Lord have mercy! We told the man to get out. Oh, we was some proud folks this afternoon, yeah. (*He lights a cigarette*) We were still full of that old-time stuff . . .
RUTH (*Coming toward him slowly*): You talking 'bout
2990 taking them people's money to keep us from moving in that house?
WALTER: I ain't just talking 'bout it, baby—I'm telling you that's what's going to happen.
BENEATHA: Oh, God! Where is the bottom! Where is
2995 the real honest-to-God bottom so he can't go any farther!
WALTER: See—that's the old stuff. You and that boy that was here today. You all want everybody to carry a flag and a spear and sing some march-
3000 ing songs, huh? You wanna spend your life looking into things and trying to find the right and the wrong part, huh? Yeah. You know what's going to happen to that boy someday—he'll find himself sitting in a dungeon, locked
3005 in forever—and the takers will have the key! Forget it, baby! There ain't no causes—there ain't nothing but taking in this world, and he who takes most is smartest—and it don't make a damn bit of difference *how*.
3010 MAMA: You making something inside me cry, son. Some awful pain inside me.
WALTER: Don't cry, Mama. Understand. That white man is going to walk in that door able to write checks for more money than we ever had. It's
3015 important to him and I'm going to help him . . . I'm going to put on the show, Mama.
MAMA: Son—I come from five generations of people who was slaves and sharecroppers—but ain't nobody in my family never let nobody pay
3020 'em no money that was a way of telling us we wasn't fit to walk the earth. We ain't never been that poor. (*Raising her eyes and looking at him*) We ain't never been that dead inside.
BENEATHA: Well—we are dead now. All the talk about
3025 dreams and sunlight that goes on in this house. All dead.
WALTER: What's the matter with you all! I didn't make this world! It was give to me this way!

3030 Hell, yes, I want me some yachts someday! Yes, I want to hang some real pearls 'round my wife's neck. Ain't she supposed to wear no pearls? Somebody tell me—tell me, who decides which women is suppose to wear 3035 pearls in this world. I tell you I am a *man*—and I think my wife should wear some pearls in this world!

[This last line hangs a good while and WALTER *begins to move about the room. The word "Man" has penetrated his consciousness; he mumbles it to himself repeatedly between strange agitated pauses as he moves about]*

MAMA: Baby, how you going to feel on the inside?
WALTER: Fine! . . . Going to feel fine . . . a man . . .
3040 MAMA: You won't have nothing left then, Walter Lee.
WALTER (*Coming to her*): I'm going to feel fine, Mama. I'm going to look that son-of-a-bitch in the eyes and say—(*He falters*)—and say, "All right, Mr. Lindner—(*He falters even more*)—that's 3045 your neighborhood out there. You got the right to keep it like you want. You got the right to have it like you want. Just write the check and—the house is yours." And, and I am going to say—(*His voice almost breaks*) And 3050 you—you people just put the money in my hand and you won't have to live next to this bunch of stinking niggers! . . . (*He straightens up and moves away from his mother, walking around the room*) Maybe—maybe I'll just get 3055 down on my black knees . . . (*He does so;* RUTH *and* BENNIE *and* MAMA *watch him in frozen horror*) Captain, Mistuh, Bossman. (*He starts crying*) A-hee-hee-hee! (*Wringing his hands in profoundly anguished imitation*) Yasssssuh! Great 3060 White Father, just gi' ussen de money, fo' God's sake, and we's ain't gwine come out deh and dirty up yo' white folks neighborhood . . .

[He breaks down completely, then gets up and goes into the bedroom]

BENEATHA: That is not a man. That is nothing but a toothless rat.
3065 MAMA: Yes—death done come in this here house. (*She is nodding, slowly, reflectively*) Done come walking in my house. On the lips of my children. You what supposed to be my beginning again. You—what supposed to be my harvest. (*To* 3070 BENEATHA) You—you mourning your brother?
BENEATHA: He's no brother of mine.
MAMA: What you say?
BENEATHA: I said that that individual in that room is no brother of mine.
3075 MAMA: That's what I thought you said. You feeling like you better than he is today? (BENEATHA *does not answer*) Yes? What you tell him a minute ago? That he wasn't a man? Yes? You give him up for me? You done wrote his epi-taph too—like the rest of the world? Well, who 3080 give you the privilege?
BENEATHA: Be on my side for once! You saw what he just did, Mama! You saw him—down on his knees. Wasn't it you who taught me—to despise any man who would do that. Do what 3085 he's going to do.
MAMA: Yes—I taught you that. Me and your daddy. But I thought I taught you something else too . . . I thought I taught you to love him.
BENEATHA: Love him? There is nothing left to love. 3090
MAMA: There is always something left to love. And if you ain't learned that, you ain't learned noth-ing. (*Looking at her*) Have you cried for that boy today? I don't mean for yourself and for the family 'cause we lost the money. I mean for 3095 him; what he been through and what it done to him. Child, when do you think is the time to love somebody the most; when they done good and made things easy for everybody? Well then, you ain't through learning—because 3100 that ain't the time at all. It's when he's at his lowest and can't believe in hisself 'cause the world done whipped him so. When you starts measuring somebody, measure him right, child, measure him right. Make sure you done 3105 taken into account what hills and valleys he come through before he got to wherever he is.

*[*TRAVIS *bursts into the room at the end of the speech, leaving the door open]*

TRAVIS: Grandmama—the moving men are down-stairs! The truck just pulled up.
MAMA (*Turning and looking at him*): Are they, baby? 3110 They downstairs?

[She sighs and sits. LINDNER *appears in the doorway. He peers in and knocks lightly, to gain attention, and comes in. All turn to look at him]*

LINDNER (*Hat and briefcase in hand*): Uh—hello . . .

*[*RUTH *crosses mechanically to the bedroom door and opens it and lets it swing open freely and slowly as the lights come up on* WALTER *within, still in his coat, sit-ting at the far corner of the room. He looks up and out through the room to* LINDNER]*

RUTH: He's here.

[A long minute passes and WALTER *slowly gets up]*

LINDNER (*Coming to the table with efficiency, putting his*

3115   *briefcase on the table and starting to unfold papers
        and unscrew fountain pens*): Well, I certainly was
        glad to hear from you people. (WALTER *has
        begun the trek out of the room, slowly and awk-
        wardly, rather like a small boy, passing the back of
3120   his sleeve across his mouth from time to time*) Life
        can really be so much simpler than people let
        it be most of the time. Well—with whom do I
        negotiate? You, Mrs. Younger, or your son
        here? (MAMA *sits with her hands folded on her lap
3125   and her eyes closed as* WALTER *advances.* TRAVIS
        goes close to LINDNER *and looks at the papers curi-
        ously*) Just some official papers, sonny.
RUTH: Travis, you go downstairs.
MAMA (*Opening her eyes and looking into* WALTER's):
3130   No. Travis, you stay right here. And you make
        him understand what you doing, Walter Lee.
        You teach him good. Like Willy Harris taught
        you. You show where our five generations
        done come to. Go ahead, son—
3135 WALTER (*Looks down into his boy's eyes.* TRAVIS *grins at
        him merrily and* WALTER *draws him beside him
        with his arm lightly around his shoulder*): Well,
        Mr. Lindner. (BENEATHA *turns away*) We called
        you—(*There is a profound, simple groping quality
3140   in his speech*)—because, well, me and my fami-
        ly (*He looks around and shifts from one foot to the
        other*) Well—we are very plain people . . .
LINDNER: Yes—
WALTER: I mean—I have worked as a chauffeur most
3145   of my life—and my wife here, she does domes-
        tic work in people's kitchens. So does my
        mother. I mean—we are plain people . . .
LINDNER: Yes, Mr. Younger—
WALTER (*Really like a small boy, looking down at his
3150   shoes and then up at the man*): And—uh—well,
        my father, well, he was a laborer most of his
        life.
LINDNER (*Absolutely confused*): Uh, yes—
WALTER (*Looking down at his toes once again*): My
3155   father almost beat a man to death once
        because this man called him a bad name or
        something, you know what I mean?
LINDNER: No, I'm afraid I don't.
WALTER (*Finally straightening up*): Well, what I mean
3160   is that we come from people who had a lot of
        pride. I mean—we are very proud people. And
        that's my sister over there and she's going to
        be a doctor—and we are very proud—
LINDNER: Well—I am sure that is very nice, but—
3165 WALTER (*Starting to cry and facing the man eye to eye*):
        What I am telling you is that we called you
        over here to tell you that we are very proud
        and that this is—this is my son, who makes
        the sixth generation of our family in this coun-
3170   try, and that we have all thought about your
        offer and we have decided to move into our

house because my father—my father—he
earned it. (MAMA *has her eyes closed and is rocking back and forth as though she were in church,
with her head nodding the amen yes*) We don't   3175
want to make no trouble for nobody or fight
no causes—but we will try to be good neighbors. That's all we got to say. (*He looks the man
absolutely in the eyes*) We don't want your
money.   3180

[*He turns and walks away from the man*]

LINDNER (*Looking around at all of them*): I take it then
        that you have decided to occupy.
BENEATHA: That's what the man said.
LINDNER (*To* MAMA *in her reverie*): Then I would like
        to appeal to you, Mrs. Younger. You are older   3185
        and wiser and understand things better I am
        sure . . .
MAMA (*Rising*): I am afraid you don't understand.
        My son said we was going to move and there
        ain't nothing left for me to say. (*Shaking her   3190
        head with double meaning*) You know how these
        young folks is nowadays, mister. Can't do a
        thing with 'em. Good-bye.
LINDNER (*Folding up his materials*): Well—if you are
        that final about it . . . There is nothing left for   3195
        me to say. (*He finishes. He is almost ignored by
        the family, who are concentrating on* WALTER LEE.
        At the door LINDNER *halts and looks around*) I
        sure hope you people know what you're
        doing.   3200

[*He shakes his head and exits*]

RUTH (*Looking around and coming to life*): Well, for
        God's sake—if the moving men are here—LET'S
        GET THE HELL OUT OF HERE!
MAMA (*Into action*): Ain't it the truth! Look at all this
        here mess. Ruth put Travis' good jacket on him   3205
        . . . Walter Lee, fix your tie and tuck your shirt
        in, you look just like somebody's hoodlum.
        Lord have mercy, where is my plant? (*She flies
        to get it amid the general bustling of the family,
        who are deliberately trying to ignore the nobility of   3210
        the past moment*) You all start on down . . .
        Travis child, don't go empty-handed . . . .
        Ruth, where did I put that box with my skillets
        in it? I want to be in charge of it myself . . . I'm
        going to make us the biggest dinner we ever   3215
        ate tonight . . . Beneatha, what's the matter
        with them stockings? Pull them things up,
        girl . . .

[*The family starts to file out as two moving men
appear and begin to carry out the heavier pieces of
furniture, bumping into the family as they move about*]

BENEATHA: Mama, Asagai—asked me to marry him today and go to Africa—

MAMA (*In the middle of her getting-ready activity*): He did? You ain't old enough to marry nobody— (*Seeing the moving men lifting one of her chairs precariously*) Darling, that ain't no bale of cotton, please handle it so we can sit in it again. I had that chair twenty-five years . . .

[*The movers sigh with exasperation and go on with their work*]

BENEATHA (*Girlishly and unreasonably trying to pursue the conversation*): To go to Africa, Mama—be a doctor in Africa . . .

MAMA (*Distracted*): Yes, baby—

WALTER: Africa! What he want you to go to Africa for?

BENEATHA: To practice there . . .

WALTER: Girl, if you don't get all them silly ideas out your head! You better marry yourself a man with some loot . . .

BENEATHA (*Angrily, precisely as in the first scene of the play*): What have you got to do with who I marry!

WALTER: Plenty. Now I think George Murchison—

[*He and BENEATHA go out yelling at each other vigorously; BENEATHA is heard saying that she would not marry GEORGE MURCHISON if he were Adam and she were Eve, etc. The anger is loud and real till their voices diminish. RUTH stands at the door and turns to MAMA and smiles knowingly*]

MAMA (*Fixing her hat at last*): Yeah—they something all right, my children . . .

RUTH: Yeah—they're something. Let's go, Lena.

MAMA (*Stalling, starting to look around at the house*): Yes—I'm coming. Ruth—

RUTH: Yes?

MAMA (*Quietly, woman to woman*): He finally come into his manhood today, didn't he? Kind of like a rainbow after the rain . . .

RUTH (*Biting her lip lest her own pride explode in front of MAMA*): Yes, Lena.

[*WALTER's voice calls for them raucously*]

MAMA (*Waving RUTH out vaguely*): All right, honey— go on down. I be down directly.

[*RUTH hesitates, then exits. MAMA stands, at last alone in the living room, her plant on the table before her as the lights start to come down. She looks around at all the walls and ceilings and suddenly, despite herself, while the children call below, a great heaving thing rises in her and she puts her fist to her mouth, takes a*

final desperate look, pulls her coat about her, pats her hat and goes out. The lights dim down. The door opens and she comes back in, grabs her plant, and goes out for the last time]

CURTAIN

Contexts and Commentaries

Bertolt Brecht (1898–1956)

Bertolt Brecht objected to a theater of illusion that left audiences spellbound. He argued against realism and for a theater that teaches and empowers the audience, which he calls epic theatre. In the first selection, from "The Modern Theatre is the Epic Theatre," Brecht supplies a chart to distinguish the characteristics of traditional theater from epic theater. In the second, "Theatre for Pleasure or Theatre for Instruction," he attacks the idea of a separation between entertainment and instruction in the theater.

From "The Modern Theatre Is the Epic Theatre"

The modern theatre is the epic theatre. The following table° shows certain changes of emphasis as between the dramatic and the epic theatre:

DRAMATIC THEATRE	EPIC THEATRE
plot	narrative
implicates the spectator in a stage situation	turns the spectator into an observer, but
wears down his capacity for action	arouses his capacity for action
provides him with sensations	forces him to take decisions
experience	picture of the world
the spectator is involved in something	he is made to face something
suggestion	argument
instinctive feelings are preserved	brought to the point of recognition
the spectator is in the thick of it, shares the experience	the spectator stands outside, studies
the human being is taken for granted	the human being is the object of the inquiry

---

° This table does not show absolute antitheses but mere shifts of accent. In a communication of fact, for instance, we may choose whether to stress the element of emotional suggestion or that of plain rational argument.

he is unalterable	he is alterable and able to alter
eyes on the finish	eyes on the course
one scene makes another	each scene for itself
growth	montage
linear development	in curves
evolutionary determinism	jumps
man as a fixed point	man as a process
thought determines being	social being determines thought
feeling	reason

Theatre for Pleasure or Theatre for Instruction°

Translated by John Willett

A few years back, anybody talking about the modern theatre meant the theatre in Moscow, New York and Berlin. He might have thrown in a mention of one of Jouvet's productions in Paris or Cochran's in London, or *The Dybbuk* as given by the Habima (which is to all intents and purposes part of the Russian theatre, since Vakhtangov was its director). But broadly speaking there were only three capitals so far as modern theatre was concerned.

Russian, American and German theatres differed widely from one another, but were alike in being modern, that is to say in introducing technical and artistic innovations. In a sense they even achieved a certain stylistic resemblance, probably because technology is international (not just that part which is directly applied to the stage but also that which influences it, the film for instance), and because large progressive cities in large industrial countries are involved. Among the older capitalist countries it is the Berlin theatre that seemed of late to be in the lead. For a period all that is common to the modern theatre received its strongest and (so far) maturest expression there.

The Berlin theatre's last phase was the so-called epic theatre, and it showed the modern theatre's trend of development in its purest form. Whatever was labelled '*Zeitstück*' or '*Piscatorbühne*' or '*Lehrstück*' belongs to the epic theatre.

The Epic Theatre

Many people imagine that the term 'epic theatre' is self-contradictory, as the epic and dramatic ways of narrating a story are held, following Aristotle, to be basically distinct. The difference between the two forms was never thought simply to lie in the fact that the one is performed by living beings while the other operates via the written word; epic works such as those of Homer and the medieval singers were at the same time theatrical performances, while dramas like

---

° Note: This essay was unpublished in Brecht's lifetime, and its exact date and purpose are unknown.

Goethe's *Faust* and Byron's *Manfred* are agreed to have been more effective as books. Thus even by Aristotle's definition the difference between the dramatic and epic forms was attributed to their different methods of construction, whose laws were dealt with by two different branches of aesthetics. The method of construction depended on the different way of presenting the work to the public, sometimes via the stage, sometimes through a book; and independently of that there was the 'dramatic element' in epic works and the 'epic element' in dramatic. The bourgeois novel in the last century developed much that was 'dramatic', by which was meant the strong centralization of the story, a momentum that drew the separate parts into a common relationship. A particular passion of utterance, a certain emphasis on the clash of forces are hallmarks of the 'dramatic'. The epic writer Döblin provided an excellent criterion when he said that with an epic work, as opposed to a dramatic, one can as it were take a pair of scissors and cut it into individual pieces, which remain fully capable of life.

This is no place to explain how the opposition of epic and dramatic lost its rigidity after having long been held to be irreconcilable. Let us just point out that the technical advances alone were enough to permit the stage to incorporate an element of narrative in its dramatic productions. The possibility of projections, the greater adaptability of the stage due to mechanization, the film, all completed the theatre's equipment, and did so at a point where the most important transactions between people could no longer be shown simply by personifying the motive forces or subjecting the characters to invisible metaphysical powers.

To make these transactions intelligible the environment in which the people lived had to be brought to bear in a big and 'significant' way.

This environment had of course been shown in the existing drama, but only as seen from the central figure's point of view, and not as an independent element. It was defined by the hero's reactions to it. It was seen as a storm can be seen when one sees the ships on a sheet of water unfolding their sails, and the sails filling out. In the epic theatre it was to appear standing on its own.

The stage began to tell a story. The narrator was no longer missing, along with the fourth wall. Not only did the background adopt an attitude to the events on the stage—by big screens recalling other simultaneous events elsewhere, by projecting documents which confirmed or contradicted what the characters said, by concrete and intelligible figures to accompany abstract conversations, by figures and sentences to support mimed transactions whose sense was unclear—but the actors too refrained from going over wholly into their role, remaining detached from the character they were playing and clearly inviting criticism of him.

The spectator was no longer in any way allowed to submit to an experience uncritically (and without practical consequences) by means of simple empathy with the characters in a play. The production took the subject-matter and the incidents shown and put them through a process of alienation: the alienation that is necessary to all understanding. When something seems 'the most obvious thing in the world' it means that any attempt to understand the world has been given up.

What is 'natural' must have the force of what is startling. This is the only way to expose the laws of cause and effect. People's activity must simultaneously be so and be capable of being different.

It was all a great change.

The dramatic theatre's spectator says: Yes, I have felt like that too—Just like me—It's only natural—It'll never change—The sufferings of this man appal me, because they are inescapable—That's great art; it all seems the most obvious thing in the world—I weep when they weep, I laugh when they laugh.

The epic theatre's spectator says: I'd never have thought it—That's not the way—That's extraordinary, hardly believable—It's got to stop—The sufferings of this man appal me, because they are unnecessary—That's great art: nothing obvious in it—I laugh when they weep, I weep when they laugh.

THE INSTRUCTIVE THEATRE

The stage began to be instructive.

Oil, inflation, war, social struggles, the family, religion, wheat, the meat market, all became subjects for theatrical representation. Choruses enlightened the spectator about facts unknown to him. Films showed a montage of events from all over the world. Projections added statistical material. And as the 'background' came to the front of the stage so people's activity was subjected to criticism. Right and wrong courses of action were shown. People were shown who knew what they were doing, and others who did not. The theatre became an affair for philosophers, but only for such philosophers as wished not just to explain the world but also to change it. So we had philosophy, and we had instruction. And where was the amusement in all that? Were they sending us back to school, teaching us to read and write? Were we supposed to pass exams, work for diplomas?

Generally there is felt to be a very sharp distinction between learning and amusing oneself. The first may be useful, but only the second is pleasant. So we have to defend the epic theatre against the suspicion that it is a highly disagreeable, humourless, indeed strenuous affair.

Well: all that can be said is that the contrast between learning and amusing oneself is not laid down by divine rule; it is not one that has always been and must continue to be.

Undoubtedly there is much that is tedious about the kind of learning familiar to us from school, from our professional training, etc. But it must be remembered under what conditions and to what end that takes place.

It is really a commercial transaction. Knowledge is just a commodity. It is acquired in order to be resold. All those who have grown out of going to school have to do their learning virtually in secret, for anyone who admits that he still has something to learn devalues himself as a man whose knowledge is inadequate. Moreover the usefulness of learning is very much limited by factors outside the learner's control. There is unemployment, for instance, against which no knowledge can protect one. There is the division of labour, which makes generalized knowledge unnecessary and impossible. Learning is often among the concerns of those whom no amount of concern will get any forwarder. There is not much knowledge that leads to power, but plenty of knowledge to which only power can lead.

Learning has a very different function for different social strata. There are strata who cannot imagine any improvement in conditions: they find the conditions good enough for them. Whatever happens to oil they will benefit from it. And: they feel the years beginning to tell. There can't be all that many years more. What is the point of learning a lot now? They have said their final word: a grunt. But there are also strata 'waiting their turn' who are discontented with conditions, have a vast interest in the practical side of learning, want at all costs to find out where they stand, and know that they are lost without learning; these are the best and keenest learners. Similar differences apply to countries and peoples. Thus the pleasure of learning depends on all sorts of things; but none the less there is such a thing as pleasurable learning, cheerful and militant learning.

If there were not such amusement to be had from learning the theatre's whole structure would unfit it for teaching.

Theatre remains theatre even when it is instructive theatre, and in so far as it is good theatre it will amuse.

THEATRE AND KNOWLEDGE

But what has knowledge got to do with art? We know that knowledge can be amusing, but not everything that is amusing belongs in the theatre.

I have often been told, when pointing out the invaluable services that modern knowledge and science, if properly applied, can perform for art and specially for the theatre, that art and knowledge are two estimable but wholly distinct fields of human activity. This is a fearful truism, of course, and it is as well to agree quickly that, like most truisms, it is perfectly true. Art and science work in quite different ways: agreed. But, bad as it may sound, I have to admit that I cannot get along as an artist without the use of one or two sciences. This may well arouse serious doubts as to my artistic capacities. People are used to seeing poets as unique and slightly unnatural beings who reveal with a truly godlike assurance things that other people can only recognize after much sweat and toil. It is naturally distasteful to have to admit that one does not belong to this select band. All the same, it must be admitted. It must at the same time be made clear that the scientific occupations just confessed to are not pardonable side interests, pursued on days off after a good week's work. We all know how Goethe was interested in natural history, Schiller in history: as a kind of hobby, it is charitable to assume. I have no wish promptly to accuse these two of having needed these sciences for their poetic activity; I am not trying to shelter behind them; but I must say that I do need the sciences. I have to admit, however, that I look askance at all sorts of people who I know do not operate on the level of scientific understanding: that is to say, who sing as the birds sing, or as people imagine the birds to sing. I don't mean by that that I would reject a charming poem about the taste of fried fish or the delights of a boating party just because the writer had not studied gastronomy or navigation. But in my view the great and complicated things that go on in the world cannot be adequately recognized by people who do not use every possible aid to understanding.

Let us suppose that great passions or great events have to be shown which influence the fate of nations. The lust for power is nowadays held to be such a passion. Given that a poet 'feels' this lust and wants to have someone strive for power, how is he to show the exceedingly complicated machinery within which the struggle for power nowadays takes place? If his hero is a politician, how do politics work? If he is a business man, how does business work? And yet there are writers who find business and politics nothing like so passionately interesting as the individual's lust for power. How are they to acquire the necessary knowledge? They are scarcely likely to learn enough by going round and keeping their eyes open, though even then it is more than they would get by just rolling their eyes in an exalted frenzy. The foundation of a paper like the *Völkischer Beobachter* or a business like Standard Oil is a pretty complicated affair, and such things cannot be conveyed just like that. One important field for the playwright is psychology. It is taken for granted that a poet, if not an ordinary man, must be able without further instruction to discover the motives that lead a man to commit murder; he must be able to give a picture of a murderer's mental state 'from within himself'. It is taken for granted that one only has to look inside oneself in such a case; and then there's always one's imagination. . . . There are various reasons why I can no longer surrender to this agreeable hope of getting a result quite so simply. I can no longer find in myself all those motives which the press or scientific reports show to have been observed in people. Like the average judge when pronouncing sentence, I cannot without further ado conjure up an adequate picture of a murderer's mental state. Modern psychology, from psychoanalysis to behaviourism, acquaints me with facts that lead me to judge the case quite differently, especially if I bear in mind the findings of sociology and do not overlook economics and history. You will say: but that's getting complicated. I have to answer that it *is* complicated. Even if you let yourself be convinced, and agree with me that a large slice of literature is exceedingly primitive, you may still ask with profound concern: won't an evening in such a theatre be a most alarming affair? The answer to that is: no.

Whatever knowledge is embodied in a piece of poetic writing has to be wholly transmuted into poetry. Its utilization fulfils the very pleasure that the poetic element provokes. If it does not at the same time fulfil that which is fulfilled by the scientific element, none the less in an age of great discoveries and inventions one must have a certain inclination to penetrate deeper into things—a desire to make the world controllable—if one is to be sure of enjoying its poetry.

IS THE EPIC THEATRE SOME KIND OF 'MORAL INSTITUTION'?

According to Friedrich Schiller the theatre is supposed to be a moral institution. In making this demand it hardly occurred to Schiller that by moralizing from the stage he might drive the audience out of the theatre. Audiences had no objection to moralizing in his day. It was only later that Friedrich Nietzsche attacked him for blowing a moral trumpet. To Nietzsche any concern with morality was a depressing affair; to Schiller it seemed thoroughly enjoyable. He knew of nothing that could give greater amusement and satisfaction than the propagation of ideas. The bourgeoisie was setting about forming the ideas of the nation.

Putting one's house in order, patting oneself on the back, submitting one's account, is something highly agreeable. But describing the collapse of one's house, having pains in the back, paying one's account, is indeed a depressing affair, and that was how Friedrich Nietzsche saw things a century later. He was poorly disposed towards morality, and thus towards the previous Friedrich too.

The epic theatre was likewise often objected to as moralizing too much. Yet in the epic theatre moral arguments only took second place. Its aim was less to moralize than to observe. That is to say it observed, and then the thick end of the wedge followed: the story's moral. Of course we cannot pretend that we started our observations out of a pure passion for observing and without any more practical motive, only to be completely staggered by their results. Undoubtedly there were some painful discrepancies in our environment, circumstances that were barely tolerable, and this not merely on account of moral considerations. It is not only moral considerations that make hunger, cold and oppression hard to bear. Similarly the object of our inquiries was not just to arouse moral objections to such circumstances (even though they could easily be felt—though not by all the audience alike; such objections were seldom for instance felt by those who profited by the circumstances in question) but to discover means for their elimination. We were not in fact speaking in the name of morality but in that of the victims. These truly are two distinct matters, for the victims are often told that they ought to be contented with their lot, for moral reasons. Moralists of this sort see man as existing for morality, not morality for man. At least it should be possible to gather from the above to what degree and in what sense the epic theatre is a moral institution.

CAN EPIC THEATRE BE PLAYED ANYWHERE?

Stylistically speaking, there is nothing all that new about the epic theatre. Its expository character and its emphasis on virtuosity bring it close to the old Asiatic theatre. Didactic tendencies are to be found in the medieval mystery plays and the classical Spanish theatre, and also in the theatre of the Jesuits.

These theatrical forms corresponded to particular trends of their time, and vanished with them. Similarly the modern epic theatre is linked with certain trends. It cannot by any means be practised universally. Most of the great nations today are not disposed to use the theatre for ventilating their problems. London, Paris, Tokyo and Rome maintain their theatres for quite different purposes. Up to now favourable circumstances for an epic and didactic theatre have only been found in a few places and for a short period of time. In Berlin Fascism put a very definite stop to the development of such a theatre.

It demands not only a certain technological level but a powerful movement in society which is interested to see vital questions freely aired with a view to their solution, and can defend this interest against every contrary trend.

The epic theatre is the broadest and most far-reaching attempt at large-scale modern theatre, and it has all those immense difficulties to overcome that always confront the vital forces in the sphere of politics, philosophy, science and art.

Eric Bentley (B. 1916)

Distinguished critic, director, author, and Professor of Dramatic Literature at Columbia University, Eric Bentley here provides a reading of *Mother Courage* originally written for the program at the National Theater in London in 1965.

WHO IS MOTHER COURAGE?

The role is hard to play and is always being miscast. Why? "Because middle-aged actresses are such ladies and lack earthiness." But who has succeeded in the role? Outstandingly, Helene Weigel. Is she very earthy, is she notably prole-tarian? On the contrary—there is nothing proletarian about her except her opin-ions. Then what is it those other ladies lack that Helene Weigel has? Among other things, I would suggest: an appreciation of the role, an understanding of what is in it, and above all the ability to portray contradictions. For whenever anyone says, "Mother Courage is essentially X" it is equally reasonable for someone to retort: "Mother Courage is essentially the exact opposite of X."

Mother Courage is essentially courageous. That is well-known, isn't it? Mr. Tennessee Williams has written of the final moment of Brecht's play as one of the inspiring moments in all theatre—inspiring because of the woman's indomitability. On she marches with her wagon after all that has happened, a symbol of the way humanity itself goes on its way after all that has happened, *if* it can find the courage. And after all we don't have to wait for the final scene to learn that we have to deal with a woman of considerable toughness and resilience. This is not the first time she has shown that she can pick up the pieces and continue. One might even find courage in the very first scene where we learn that she has not been content to cower in some corner of Bamberg but has boldly come to meet the war. A trouble-shooter, we might say on first meeting the lady, but the reverse of a coward.

Yet it is impossible to continue on this tack for long without requiring an: *On the other hand.* Beginning with the reason why she is nicknamed "Courage" in the first place.

> They call me Mother Courage because I was afraid I'd be ruined, so I drove
> through the bombardment of Riga like a madwoman with fifty loaves of bread
> in my cart. They were going moldy, what else could I do?

Did those who gave her the name intend a joke against an obvious cow-ard? Or did they think she was driven by heroic valor when in fact she was impelled by sheer necessity? Either way her act is utterly devoid of the moral quality imputed. Whether in cowardice or in down-to-earth realism, her stance is Falstaffian. What is courage? A word.

Somewhere hovering over this play is the image of a pre-eminently coura-geous mother who courageously tries to hold on to her young. More than one actress, offering herself for the role, has seen this image and nothing else. Yet valor is conspicuously absent at those times when Mother Courage (however unwittingly) seals the fate of her children. At moments when, in heroic melodrama, the protagonist would be riding to the rescue, come hell or high water, Mother Courage is in the back room concluding a little deal. For her, it is emphatically not "a time for greatness." *She is essentially cowardly.*

A basic contradiction, then, which the actress in the role must play both sides of, or the play will become the flat and simple thing which not a few journalistic commentators have declared it to be. An actress may be said to be beginning to play Mother Courage when she is putting both courage and cowardice into the role with equal conviction and equal effect. She is still only beginning to play it, though; for, as she proceeds with her interpretation, she will find that, in this play, courage and cowardice are not inherent and invariable qualities but by-products.

Of what? We can hunt for the answer by looking further into particular sequences of action. It is not really from cowardice that Mother Courage is in the back room concluding a little deal when her children are claimed by the war. It is from preoccupation with "business." Although *Mother Courage* is spoken of as a war play, it is actually a business play, in the sense that the incidents in it, one and all, are business transactions—from the deal with the belt in Scene One, through the deal with the capon in Scene Two, the deal with the wagon in Scene Three, the deals with bullets and shirts in Scene Five, through to the economical funeral arrangements of the final scene. And since these transactions (except for the last) are what Courage supports her children by, they are "necessary." Those who condemn her have to face the question: what alternative had she? Of what use would it have been to save the life of Swiss Cheese if she lacked the wherewithal to *keep* him alive? The severe judge will answer that she could take a chance on this, provided she does save his life. But this is exactly Mother Courage's own position. She is fully prepared to take the chance if she has to. It is in determining whether she has to that her boy's life slips through her fingers: life or death is a matter of timing.

To say that Swiss Cheese is a victim of circumstances, not of Courage's character, will not, however, be of much use to the actress interpreting this character. If cowardice is *less* important here than at first appears, what is *more* important? Surely it is a failure in understanding, rather than in virtue. Let me elaborate.

Though only one of Brecht's completed plays is about anyone that a university would recognize as a philosopher, several of his plays present what one might call philosophers in disguise, such as Schweyk, the philosopher of a pub in Prague, and Azdak, the philosopher of a Georgian village. To my mind, *Mother Courage is above all a philosopher*, defining the philosopher along Socratic lines as a person who likes to talk all the time and explain everything to everybody. (A simple trait in itself, one would think, yet there have been actresses and directors who wish to have all Courage's speeches shortened into mere remarks. But your philosopher never makes remarks; he always speechifies; hence such abridgement enforces a radical misinterpretation of character.) I do not mean at all that Courage is an idle or armchair philosopher whose teachings make no contact with life. On the contrary, her ideas are nothing if not a scheme of life by which, she hopes, her family is to do pretty well in a world which is doing pretty badly.

Here one sees the danger of thinking of Mother Courage as the average person. Rather, she resembles the thoughtfully ambitious modern mother of the lower-middle or better-paid working class who wants her children to win scholarships and end up in the Labour Cabinet. (Minister of Education: Kattrin. Chancellor of the Exchequer: Swiss Cheese. Minister of War: Eilif.) Has it escaped attention that if one of her children turns out a cutthroat, this is blamed on circumstances ("Otherwise, I'd have starved, smarty"), while *the other two are outright heroes?* Anyone who considers this an average family takes a far higher view of the average than is implicit in the works of Bertolt Brecht.

What is the philosophy of this philosopher? Reduced to a single proposition, it is that if you concede defeat on the larger issue, you can achieve some nice victories in smaller ways. The larger issue is whether the world can be changed. It can't. But brandy is still drunk, and can be sold. One can survive, and one can help one's children to survive by teaching each to make appropriate use of the qualities God gave him. The proposition I have just mentioned will apply to this upbringing. A child endowed with a particular talent or virtue should not pursue it to its logical end: defeat on such projects should be conceded at the outset. The child should cunningly exploit his characteristic talent for its incidental uses along the way. In this fashion the unselfishness of a Swiss Cheese or a Kattrin can be harnessed to selfishness. The result, if the philosophy works, is that while the world may shoot itself to blazes, the little Courage family, one and all, will live out its days in moderate wealth and moderate happiness. The scheme is not utopian. Just the opposite: the hope is to make optimism rational by reducing human demands to size.

The main reason it doesn't work is that the little world which Mother Courage's wisdom tries to regulate is dependent upon the big world which she has given up as a bad job. Small business is part of the big war which is part of the big business of ownership of *all* the means of production and distribution. No more than the small businessman can live in a separate economic system from the big, can the small philosopher live in a separate philosophic system from the big. *Mother Courage*, one can conclude, exposes the perennial illusions of the petit bourgeois scheme of things. This has of course often been done before in modern literature. But usually only the idealism has been exposed. Mother Courage, on the other hand, could claim to be a cynic. She has the theatre audience laughing most of the time on the score of this cynicism—by which *she* deflates illusions. Cynicism is nothing, after all, if not "realistic." What a cynical remark lays bare *has* to be the truth. Brecht makes the truth of his play the more poignant through the fact that the cynicism in it ultimately favors illusion. Mother Courage had gone to all lengths to trim her sails to the wind but even then the ship wouldn't move. So there is irony within irony (as, in Brecht's work, there usually is). Courage's cynicism can cut down the windy moralizing of the Chaplain easily enough, but only to be itself cut down by a world that cannot be comprehended even by this drastically skeptical kind of thinking.

What alternative did Mother Courage have? The only alternatives shown in the play are, on the one hand, the total brutalization of men like the Swedish Commander (and, for that matter, her own son Eilif) and, on the other hand, the martyrdom achieved by Swiss Cheese and Kattrin. Presumably, to the degree that the playwright criticizes her, he is pushing her toward the second alternative. Yet, not only would such a destiny be completely out of character, within the terms of the play itself it is not shown to be really preferable. Rather, the fruitlessness of both deaths is underlined. Why add a third?

Given her character, Mother Courage had no alternative to what she thought—or, for that matter, to the various "bad" things she did. In this case, can she be condemned? Logically, obviously not; but was Brecht logical? The printed editions of the play indicate that he made changes in his script to render Mother Courage less sympathetic. In other words, after having made her thoroughly sympathetic in his first version, Brecht later wanted her less so. One can see the sense of the changes in polemical terms: he did not wish to seem to condone behavior which is to be deplored. But to make this point, is it necessary to make Mother Courage a less good person? Personally I would think not, and I should like to see *Courage* played sometime in the Urtext of 1940 and without the later "improvements." But one should not minimize the complexity of the problem. Like many other playwrights, Brecht wanted to show a kind of inevitability combined with a degree of free will, and if it doesn't matter whether Courage is less good or more, because she is trapped by circumstances, then the play is fatalistic. I tend to think it *is* fatalistic as far as the movement of history is concerned, and that the element of hope in its springs only from Brecht's rendering of human character. Brecht himself is not satisfied with this and made changes in the hope of suggesting that things might have been different had Mother Courage acted otherwise. (What would she have done? Established Socialism in seventeenth-century Germany? One must not ask.)

Brecht has stressed, in his Notes, that Mother Courage never sees the light, never realizes what has happened, is incapable of learning. As usual, Brecht's opinions, as stated in outside comments, are more doctrinaire than those to be found embodied in the plays. It may be true that Mother Courage never sees that "small business" is a hopeless case, though to prove even this Brecht had to manufacture the evidence by inserting, later, the line at the end: "I must get back into business." She does see through her own philosophy of education. The "Song of Solomon" in Scene Nine concedes that the program announced in Scene One has failed. The manipulation of the virtues has not worked: "a man is better off without." The song is perhaps more symbolic, as well as more schematic, than most Brechtians wish Brecht to be, for there is a verse about each of her children under the form of famous men (Eilif is Caesar, Swiss Cheese is Socrates, Kattrin is St. Martin) but more important is that this is the "Song of Solomon" (from *Threepenny Opera*) and that Solomon is Courage herself:

> King Solomon was very wise
> So what's his history?
> He came to view this world with scorn
> Yes, he came to regret he ever had been born
> Declaring: all is vanity.
> King Solomon was very wise

But long before the day was out
The consequence was clear, alas:
It was his wisdom brought him to this pass.
A man is better off without.

I have heard the question asked whether this conclusion was not already reached in the "Song of the Great Capitulation" in Scene Four. Both songs are songs of defeat (Brecht's great subject) but of two different defeats. The second is defeat total and final: Courage has staked everything on wisdom, and wisdom has ruined her and her family. The first is the setback of "capitulation," that is of disenchantment. When Yvette was only seventeen she was in love, and love was heaven. Soon afterward she had learned to "fraternize behind the trees"; she had capitulated. It is perhaps hard to imagine Courage as a younger and different person from the woman we meet in the play, but in the "Song of the Great Capitulation" we are definitely invited to imagine her as a young woman who thought she could storm the heavens, whose faith seemed able to move mountains.

Scene Four is one of several in this play which one can regard as the whole play in miniature. For Brecht is not finished when he has set forth the character of Mother Courage as one who has passed from youthful idealism to cynical realism. For many a playwright, that would no doubt be that, but Courage's exchange with the angry young soldier leads to other things. We discover that Mother Courage is not a happy Machiavellian, boasting of her realism as an achievement. We find that she is deeply ashamed. And in finding this, we discover in Courage the mother of those two roaring idealists (not to say again: martyrs) Swiss Cheese and Kattrin. "Kiss my arse," says the soldier, and why? His bad language had not hitherto been directed at her. But she has been kind to him only to be cruel. If she has not broken his spirit, she has done something equally galling: she has made clear to him how easily his spirit can be broken. When you convert a person to the philosophy of You Can't Win, you can hardly expect to earn his gratitude at the same time.

In the way Courage puts matters to the soldier we see how close she came to being a truly wise woman. We also discover in this scene that, despite the confident tone of her cynical lingo, Courage is not really sure of herself and her little philosophy. She teaches the soldier that it is futile to protest, but she apparently does not know this herself until she reminds herself of it, for she has come here precisely to protest. Here we learn to recognize in Courage not only contradiction but conflict. She knows what she has thought. She is not sure what to think.

And this is communicated by Brecht in a very bold—or, if you prefer, just poetic—manner. For while Courage does not give herself to despair until the end (and not even then for those who can take at face value her: "I must get back into business"), she had correctly foreseen the end from the beginning: the despair she gives herself to had been there from the moment of capitulation. At times it would strike her between the eyes: she is very responsive and, for example, has worked out the Marxist interpretation of religion for herself. Scene Two contains a song she had taught Eilif as a boy: it accurately predicts the manner

of his death. In Scene One she predicts doom for the whole family in her elaborate pantomine of fortune telling. And it could be said that everything is there
from the start, for the first thing Mother Courage does is to try and sell things by
announcing an early death for her prospective customers. The famous "Song of
Mother Courage" is the most extraordinary parody of the kind of song any real
vivandière might try to attract customers with. Mother Courage's Come and buy!
is nothing other than: Come and die! In that respect, her fortunetelling is on the
level, and her wisdom is valid.

Scene Four, I have been saying, is one of several in this play which one can
regard as the whole play in miniature. The main purpose of the play, for Brecht,
was, I think, to generate anger over what it shows. Yet Brecht realizes how
pointless angry plays have been—and angry speeches outside the drama. It is
said that Clifford Odets' *Waiting for Lefty* made millionaires angry for as long as
it took them to get from their seats to where their chauffeurs tactfully waited for
them at the end of the block. Such is the anger of the social drama in general.

There is the anger of a sudden fit, which boils up and over and is gone.
And there is the anger which informs the work of long years of change. *Why*
can't the world be changed? For Mother Courage, it is not from any inherent
unchangeability in the world. It is because our wish to change it is not strong
enough. Nor is this weakness innate. It is simply that our objection to the present world isn't as strong as it once was. What is outrageous does not outrage us
as it once did. Today, it only arouses the "short rage" of Brecht's soldier—and of
Courage herself—not the long one that is required. Because we—they—have
capitulated.

Capitulation is not just an idea but a feeling, an agony in fact, and is located not just in the scene of the Great Capitulation but in the whole play of *Mother
Courage*. Everything that happens is related to it, above all the things that are
furthest away from it: namely, the deaths of Swiss Cheese and Kattrin. And if
these children are what their mother made them, then their refusal to capitulate
stems from her, is her own youth, her own original nature.

The ultimate achievement of an actress playing this role would be that she
made us sense to what an extent Courage's children are truly hers.

Antonin Artaud (1896–1948)

Antonin Artaud, initially involved in the surrealist movement, became well known during the 1930s as an avant-garde actor, playwright, and theorist. In his most influential book, *The Theater and Its Double* (1938), Artaud attacks traditional theatrical representation and argues for a theater willing to experiment with the relationship between performers and audience. His name for this new theater, the theater of cruelty, refers to its attempt to engage and challenge audiences. Artaud was committed to a mental hospital in 1937, where he remained until his death in 1948 at fifty-two years of age. His innovative theories are some of the most influential in contemporary theater.

THE THEATER AND ITS DOUBLE

TRANSLATED BY MARY CAROLINE RICHARDS

NO MORE MASTERPIECES

One of the reasons for the asphyxiating atmosphere in which we live without possible escape or remedy—and in which we all share, even the most revolutionary among us—is our respect for what has been written, formulated, or painted, what has been given form, as if all expression were not at last exhausted, were not at a point where things must break apart if they are to start anew and begin fresh.

We must have done with this idea of masterpieces reserved for a self-styled elite and not understood by the general public; the mind has no such restricted districts as those so often used for clandestine sexual encounters.

Masterpieces of the past are good for the past: they are not good for us. We have the right to say what has been said and even what has not been said in a way that belongs to us, a way that is immediate and direct, corresponding to present modes of feeling, and understandable to everyone.

It is idiotic to reproach the masses for having no sense of the sublime, when the sublime is confused with one or another of its formal manifestations, which are moreover always defunct manifestations. And if for example a contemporary public does not understand *Oedipus Rex*, I shall make bold to say that it is the fault of *Oedipus Rex* and not of the public.

In *Oedipus Rex* there is the theme of incest and the idea that nature mocks at morality and that there are certain unspecified powers at large which we would do well to beware of, call them *destiny* or anything you choose.

There is in addition the presence of a plague epidemic which is a physical incarnation of these powers. But the whole in a manner and language that have lost all touch with the rude and epileptic rhythm of our time. Sophocles speaks grandly perhaps, but in a style that is no longer timely. His language is too refined for this age, it is as if he were speaking beside the point.

However, a public that shudders at train wrecks, that is familiar with earthquakes, plagues, revolutions, wars; that is sensitive to the disordered anguish of love, can be affected by all these grand notions and asks only to become aware of them, but on condition that it is addressed in its own language, and that its knowledge of these things does not come to it through adulterated trappings and speech that belong to extinct eras which will never live again.

Today as yesterday, the public is greedy for mystery: it asks only to become aware of the laws according to which destiny manifests itself, and to divine perhaps the secret of its apparitions.

Let us leave textual criticism to graduate students, formal criticism to esthetes, and recognize that what has been said is not still to be said; that an expression does not have the same value twice, does not live two lives; that all words, once spoken, are dead and function only at the moment when they are uttered, that a form, once it has served, cannot be used again and asks only to be replaced by another, and that the theater is the only place in the world where a gesture, once made, can never be made the same way twice.

If the public does not frequent our literary masterpieces, it is because those masterpieces are literary, that is to say, fixed; and fixed in forms that no longer respond to the needs of the time.

Far from blaming the public, we ought to blame the formal screen we interpose between ourselves and the public, and this new form of idolatry, the idolatry of fixed masterpieces which is one of the aspects of bourgeois conformism.

This conformism makes us confuse sublimity, ideas, and things with the forms they have taken in time and in our minds—in our snobbish, precious, aesthetic mentalities which the public does not understand.

How pointless in such matters to accuse the public of bad taste because it relishes insanities, so long as the public is not shown a valid spectacle; and I defy anyone to show me *here* a spectacle valid—valid in the supreme sense of the theater—since the last great romantic melodramas, i.e., since a hundred years ago.

The public, which takes the false for the true, has the sense of the true and always responds to it when it is manifested. However it is not upon the stage that the true is to be sought nowadays, but in the street; and if the crowd in the street is offered an occasion to show its human dignity, it will always do so.

If people are out of the habit of going to the theater, if we have all finally come to think of theater as an inferior art, a means of popular distraction, and to use it as an outlet for our worst instincts, it is because we have learned too well what the theater has been, namely, falsehood and illusion. It is because we have been accustomed for four hundred years, that is since the Renaissance, to a purely descriptive and narrative theater—storytelling psychology; it is because every possible ingenuity has been exerted in bringing to life on the stage plausible but detached beings, with the spectacle on one side, the public on the other—and because the public is no longer shown anything but the mirror of itself.

Shakespeare himself is responsible for this aberration and decline, this disinterested idea of the theater which wishes a theatrical performance to leave the public intact, without setting off one image that will shake the organism to its foundations and leave an ineffaceable scar.

If, in Shakespeare, a man is sometimes preoccupied with what transcends him, it is always in order to determine the ultimate consequences of this preoccupation within him, i.e., psychology.

Psychology, which works relentlessly to reduce the unknown to the known, to the quotidian and the ordinary, is the cause of the theater's abasement and its fearful loss of energy, which seems to me to have reached its lowest point. And I think both the theater and we ourselves have had enough of psychology.

I believe furthermore that we can all agree on this matter sufficiently so that there is no need to descend to the repugnant level of the modern and French theater to condemn the theater of psychology.

Stories about money, worry over money, social careerism, the pangs of love unspoiled by altruism, sexuality sugar-coated with an eroticism that has lost its mystery have nothing to do with the theater, even if they do belong to psychology. These torments, seductions, and lusts before which we are nothing but Peeping Toms gratifying our cravings, tend to go bad, and their rot turns to revolution: we must take this into account.

But this is not our most serious concern.

If Shakespeare and his imitators have gradually insinuated the idea of art for art's sake, with art on one side and life on the other, we can rest on this feeble and lazy idea only as long as the life outside endures. But there are too many signs that everything that used to sustain our lives no longer does so, that we are all mad, desperate, and sick. And I call for *us* to react.

This idea of a detached art, of poetry as a charm which exists only to distract our leisure, is a decadent idea and an unmistakable symptom of our power to castrate.

Our literary admiration for Rimbaud, Jarry, Lautréamont, and a few others, which has driven two men to suicide, but turned into café gossip for the rest, belongs to this idea of literary poetry, of detached art, of neutral spiritual activity which creates nothing and produces nothing; and I can bear witness that at the very moment when that kind of personal poetry which involves only the man who creates it and only at the moment he creates it broke out in its most abusive fashion, the theater was scorned more than ever before by poets who have never had the sense of direct and concerted action, nor of efficacity, nor of danger.

We must get rid of our superstitious valuation of texts and *written* poetry. Written poetry is worth reading once, and then should be destroyed. Let the dead poets make way for others. Then we might even come to see that it is our veneration for what has already been created, however beautiful and valid it may be, that petrifies us, deadens our responses, and prevents us from making contact with that underlying power, call it thought-energy, the life force, the determinism of change, lunar menses, or anything you like. Beneath the poetry of the texts, there is the actual poetry, without form and without text. And just as the efficacity of masks in the magic practices of certain tribes is exhausted—and these masks are no longer good for anything except museums—so the poetic efficacity of a text is exhausted; yet the poetry and the efficacity of the theater are exhausted least quickly of all, since they permit the *action* of what is gesticulated and pronounced, and which is never made the same way twice.

It is a question of knowing what we want. If we are prepared for war, plague, famine, and slaughter we do not even need to say so, we have only to continue as we are; continue behaving like snobs, rushing en masse to hear such and such a singer, to see such and such an admirable performance which never transcends the realm of art (and even the Russian ballet at the height of its splendor never transcended the realm of art), to marvel at such and such an exhibition of painting in which exciting shapes explode here and there but at random and without any genuine consciousness of the forces they could rouse.

This empiricism, randomness, individualism, and anarchy must cease.

Enough of personal poems, benefitting those who create them much more than those who read them.

Once and for all, enough of this closed, egoistic, and personal art.

Our spiritual anarchy and intellectual disorder is a function of the anarchy of everything else—or rather, everything else is a function of this anarchy.

I am not one of those who believe that civilization has to change in order for the theater to change; but I do believe that the theater, utilized in the highest and most difficult sense possible, has the power to influence the aspect and formation of things: and the encounter upon the stage of two passionate manifestations, two living centers, two nervous magnetisms is something as entire, true, even decisive, as, in life, the encounter of one epidermis with another in a timeless debauchery.

That is why I propose a theater of cruelty.—With this mania we all have for depreciating everything, as soon as I have said "cruelty," everybody will at once take it to mean "blood." But *"theater of cruelty"* means a theater difficult and cruel for myself first of all. And, on the level of performance, it is not the cruelty we can exercise upon each other by hacking at each other's bodies, carving up our personal anatomies, or, like Assyrian emperors, sending parcels of human ears, noses, or neatly detached nostrils through the mail, but the much more terrible and necessary cruelty which things can exercise against us. We are not free. And the sky can still fall on our heads. And the theater has been created to teach us that first of all.

Either we will be capable of returning by present-day means to this superior idea of poetry and poetry-through-theater which underlies the Myths told by the great ancient tragedians, capable once more of entertaining a religious idea of the theater (without meditation, useless contemplation, and vague dreams), capable of attaining awareness and a possession of certain dominant forces, of certain notions that control all others, and (since ideas, when they are effective, carry their energy with them) capable of recovering within ourselves those energies which ultimately create order and increase the value of life, or else we might as well abandon ourselves now, without protest, and recognize that we are no longer good for anything but disorder, famine, blood, war, and epidemics.

Either we restore all the arts to a central attitude and necessity, finding an analogy between a gesture made in painting or the theater, and a gesture made by lava in a volcanic explosion, or we must stop painting, babbling, writing, or doing whatever it is we do.

I propose to bring back into the theater this elementary magical idea, taken up by modern psychoanalysis, which consists in effecting a patient's cure by making him assume the apparent and exterior attitudes of the desired condition.

I propose to renounce our empiricism of imagery, in which the unconscious furnishes images at random, and which the poet arranges at random too, calling them poetic and hence hermetic images, as if the kind of trance that poetry provides did not have its reverberations throughout the whole sensibility, in every nerve, and as if poetry were some vague force whose movements were invariable.

I propose to return through the theater to an idea of the physical knowledge of images and the means of inducing trances, as in Chinese medicine which knows, over the entire extent of the human anatomy, at what points to puncture in order to regulate the subtlest functions.

Those who have forgotten the communicative power and magical mimesis of a gesture, the theater can reinstruct, because a gesture carries its energy with it, and there are still human beings in the theater to manifest the force of the gesture made.

To create art is to deprive a gesture of its reverberation in the organism, whereas this reverberation, if the gesture is made in the conditions and with the force required, incites the organism and, through it, the entire individuality, to take attitudes in harmony with the gesture.

The theater is the only place in the world, the last general means we still possess of directly affecting the organism and, in periods of neurosis and petty sensuality like the one in which we are immersed, of attacking this sensuality by physical means it cannot withstand.

If music affects snakes, it is not on account of the spiritual notions it offers them, but because snakes are long and coil their length upon the earth, because their bodies touch the earth at almost every point; and because the musical vibrations which are communicated to the earth affect them like a very subtle, very long massage; and I propose to treat the spectators like the snakecharmer's subjects and conduct them *by means of their organisms* to an apprehension of the subtlest notions.

At first by crude means, which will gradually be refined. These immediate crude means will hold their attention at the start.

That is why in the "theater of cruelty" the spectator is in the center and the spectacle surrounds him.

In this spectacle the sonorisation is constant: sounds, noises, cries are chosen first for their vibratory quality, then for what they represent.

Among these gradually refined means light is interposed in its turn. Light which is not created merely to add color or to brighten, and which brings its power, influence, suggestions with it. And the light of a green cavern does not sensually dispose the organism like the light of a windy day.

After sound and light there is action, and the dynamism of action: here the theater, far from copying life, puts itself whenever possible in communication with pure forces. And whether you accept or deny them, there is nevertheless a way of speaking which gives the name of "forces" to whatever brings to birth images of energy in the unconscious, and gratuitous crime on the surface.

A violent and concentrated action is a kind of lyricism: it summons up supernatural images, a bloodstream of images, a bleeding spurt of images in the poet's head and in the spectator's as well.

Whatever the conflicts that haunt the mind of a given period, I defy any spectator to whom such violent scenes will have transferred their blood, who will have felt in himself the transit of a superior action, who will have seen the extraordinary and essential movements of his thought illuminated in extraordinary deeds—the violence of blood having been placed at the service of the violence of the thought—I defy that spectator to give himself up, once outside the theater, to ideas of war, riot, and blatant murder.

So expressed, this idea seems dangerous and sophomoric. It will be claimed that example breeds example, that if the attitude of cure induces cure, the attitude of murder will induce murder. Everything depends upon the manner and the purity with which the thing is done. There is a risk. But let it not be forgotten that though a theatrical gesture is violent, it is disinterested; and that the theater teaches precisely the uselessness of the action which, once done, is not to be done, and the superior use of the state unused by the action and which, *restored*, produces a purification.

I propose then a theater in which violent physical images crush and hypnotize the sensibility of the spectator seized by the theater as by a whirlwind of higher forces.

A theater which, "abandoning psychology," recounts the extraordinary, stages natural conflicts, natural and subtle forces, and presents itself first of all as an exceptional power of redirection. A theater that induces trance, as the dances of Dervishes induce trance, and that addresses itself to the organism by precise instruments, by the same means as those of certain tribal music cures which we admire on records but are incapable of originating among ourselves.

There is a risk involved, but in the present circumstances I believe it is a risk worth running. I do not believe we have managed to revitalize the world we live in, and I do not believe it is worth the trouble of clinging to; but I do propose something to get us out of our marasmus, instead of continuing to complain about it, and about the boredom, inertia, and stupidity of everything . . . .

THE THEATER AND CRUELTY

An idea of the theater has been lost. And as long as the theater limits itself to showing us intimate scenes from the lives of a few puppets, transforming the public into Peeping Toms, it is no wonder the elite abandon it and the great public looks to the movies, the music hall or the circus for violent satisfactions, whose intentions do not deceive them.

At the point of deterioration which our sensibility has reached, it is certain that we need above all a theater that wakes us up: nerves and heart.

The misdeeds of the psychological theater descended from Racine have unaccustomed us to that immediate and violent action which the theater should possess. Movies in their turn, murdering us with second-hand reproductions which, filtered through machines, cannot *unite with* our sensibility, have maintained us for ten years in an ineffectual torpor, in which all our faculties appear to be foundering.

In the anguished, catastrophic period we live in, we feel an urgent need for a theater which events do not exceed, whose resonance is deep within us, dominating the instability of the times.

Our long habit of seeking diversion has made us forget the idea of a serious theater, which, overturning all our preconceptions, inspires us with the fiery magnetism of its images and acts upon us like a spiritual therapeutics whose touch can never be forgotten.

Everything that acts is a cruelty. It is upon this idea of extreme action, pushed beyond all limits, that theater must be rebuilt.

Imbued with the idea that the public thinks first of all with its senses and that to address oneself first to its understanding as the ordinary psychological theater does is absurd, the Theater of Cruelty proposes to resort to a mass spectacle; to seek in the agitation of tremendous masses, convulsed and hurled against each other, a little of that poetry of festivals and crowds when, all too rarely nowadays, the people pour out into the streets.

The theater must give us everything that is in crime, love, war, or madness, if it wants to recover its necessity.

Everyday love, personal ambition, struggles for status, all have value only in proportion to their relation to the terrible lyricism of the Myths to which the great mass of men have assented.

This is why we shall try to concentrate, around famous personages, atrocious crimes, superhuman devotions, a drama which, without resorting to the defunct images of the old Myths, shows that it can extract the forces which struggle within them.

In a word, we believe that there are living forces in what is called poetry and that the image of a crime presented in the requisite theatrical conditions is something infinitely more terrible for the spirit than that same crime when actually committed.

We want to make out of the theater a believable reality which gives the heart and the senses that kind of concrete bite which all true sensation requires. In the same way that our dreams have an effect upon us and reality has an effect upon our dreams, so we believe that the images of thought can be identified with a dream which will be efficacious to the degree that it can be projected with the necessary violence. And the public will believe in the theater's dreams on condition that it take them for true dreams and not for a servile copy of reality; on condition that they allow the public to liberate within itself the magical liberties of dreams which it can only recognize when they are imprinted with terror and cruelty.

Hence this appeal to cruelty and terror, though on a vast scale, whose range probes our entire vitality, confronts us with all our possibilities.

It is in order to attack the spectator's sensibility on all sides that we advocate a revolving spectacle which, instead of making the stage and auditorium two closed worlds, without possible communication, spreads its visual and sonorous outbursts over the entire mass of the spectators.

Also, departing from the sphere of analyzable passions, we intend to make use of the actor's lyric qualities to manifest external forces, and by this means to cause the whole of nature to re-enter the theater in its restored form.

However vast this program may be, it does not exceed the theater itself, which appears to us, all in all, to identify itself with the forces of ancient magic.

Practically speaking, we want to resuscitate an idea of total spectacle by which the theater would recover from the cinema, the music hall, the circus, and from life itself what has always belonged to it. The separation between the analytic theater and the plastic world seems to us a stupidity. One does not separate the mind from the body nor the senses from the intelligence, especially in a domain where the endlessly renewed fatigue of the organs requires intense and sudden shocks to revive our understanding.

Thus, on the one hand, the mass and extent of a spectacle addressed to the entire organism; on the other, an intensive mobilization of objects, gestures, and signs, used in a new spirit. The reduced role given to the understanding leads to an energetic compression of the text; the active role given to obscure poetic emotion necessitates concrete signs. Words say little to the mind; extent and objects speak; new images speak, even new images made with words. But space thundering with images and crammed with sounds speaks too, if one knows how to intersperse from time to time a sufficient extent of space stocked with silence and immobility.

On this principle we envisage producing a spectacle where these means of direct action are used in their totality; a spectacle unafraid of going as far as necessary in the exploration of our nervous sensibility, of which the rhythms, sounds, words, resonances, and twitterings, and their united quality and surprising mixtures belong to a technique which must not be divulged.

The images in certain paintings by Grunewald or Hieronymus Bosch tell enough about what a spectacle can be in which, as in the brain of some saint, the objects of external nature will appear as temptations.

It is in this spectacle of a temptation from which life has everything to lose and the mind everything to gain that the theater must recover its true signification.

Elsewhere we have given a program which will allow the means of pure staging, found on the spot, to be organized around historic or cosmic themes, familiar to all.

And we insist on the fact that the first spectacle of the Theater of Cruelty will turn upon the preoccupations of the great mass of men, preoccupations much more pressing and disquieting than those of any individual whatsoever.

It is a matter of knowing whether now, in Paris, before the cataclysms which are at our door descend upon us, sufficient means of production, financial or otherwise, can be found to permit such a theater to be brought to life—it is bound to in any case, because it is the future. Or whether a little real blood will be needed, right away, in order to manifest this cruelty . . . .

THE THEATER OF CRUELTY (FIRST MANIFESTO)

We cannot go on prostituting the idea of theater whose only value is in its excruciating, magical relation to reality and danger.

Put in this way, the question of the theater ought to arouse general attention, the implication being that theater, through its physical aspect, since it requires *expression in space* (the only real expression, in fact), allows the magical means of art and speech to be exercised organically and altogether, like renewed exorcisms. The upshot of all this is that theater will not be given its specific powers of action until it is given its language.

That is to say: instead of continuing to rely upon texts considered definitive and sacred, it is essential to put an end to the subjugation of the theater to the text, and to recover the notion of a kind of unique language half-way between gesture and thought.

This language cannot be defined except by its possibilities for dynamic expression in space as opposed to the expressive possibilities of spoken dialogue. And what the theater can still take over from speech are its possibilities for extension beyond words, for development in space, for dissociative and vibratory action upon the sensibility. This is the hour of intonations, of a word's particular pronunciation. Here too intervenes (besides the auditory language of sounds) the visual language of objects, movements, attitudes, and gestures, but on condition that their meanings, their physiognomies, their combinations be carried to the point of becoming signs, making a kind of alphabet out of these signs. Once aware of this language in space, language of sounds, cries, lights, onomatopoeia, the theater must organize it into veritable hieroglyphs, with the help of characters and objects, and make use of their symbolism and interconnections in relation to all organs and on all levels.

The question, then, for the theater, is to create a metaphysics of speech, gesture, and expression, in order to rescue it from its servitude to psychology and "human interest." But all this can be of no use unless behind such an effort there is some kind of real metaphysical inclination, an appeal to certain unhabitual ideas, which by their very nature cannot be limited or even formally depicted. These ideas which touch on Creation, Becoming, and Chaos, are all of a cosmic order and furnish a primary notion of a domain from which the theater is now entirely alien. They are able to create a kind of passionate equation between Man, Society, Nature, and Objects.

It is not, moreover, a question of bringing metaphysical ideas directly onto the stage, but of creating what you might call temptations, indraughts of air around these ideas. And humor with its anarchy, poetry with its symbolism and its images, furnish a basic notion of ways to channel the temptation of these ideas.

We must speak now about the uniquely material side of this language—that is, about all the ways and means it has of acting upon the sensibility.

It would be meaningless to say that it includes music, dance, pantomime, or mimicry. Obviously it uses movement, harmonies, rhythms, but only to the point that they can concur in a sort of central expression without advantage for any one particular art. This does not at all mean that it does not use ordinary actions, ordinary passions, but like a springboard uses them in the same way that HUMOR AS DESTRUCTION can serve to reconcile the corrosive nature of laughter to the habits of reason.

But by an altogether Oriental means of expression, this objective and concrete language of the theater can fascinate and ensnare the organs. It flows into the sensibility. Abandoning Occidental usages of speech, it turns words into incantations. It extends the voice. It utilizes the vibrations and qualities of the voice. It wildly tramples rhythms underfoot. It pile-drives sounds. It seeks to exalt, to benumb, to charm, to arrest the sensibility. It liberates a new lyricism of gesture which, by its precipitation or its amplitude in the air, ends by surpassing the lyricism of words. It ultimately breaks away from the intellectual subjugation of the language, by conveying the sense of a new and deeper intellectuality which hides itself beneath the gestures and signs, raised to the dignity of particular exorcisms.

For all this magnetism, all this poetry, and all these direct means of spellbinding would be nothing if they were not used to put the spirit physically on the track of something else, if the true theater could not give us the sense of a creation of which we possess only one face, but which is completed on other levels.

And it is of little importance whether these other levels are really conquered by the mind or not, i.e., by the intelligence; it would diminish them, and that has neither interest nor sense. What is important is that, by positive means, the sensitivity is put in a state of deepened and keener perception, and this is the very object of the magic and the rites of which the theater is only a reflection.

It is a question then of making the theater, in the proper sense of the word, a function; something as localized and as precise as the circulation of the blood in the arteries or the apparently chaotic development of dream images in the brain, and this is to be accomplished by a thorough involvement, a genuine enslavement of the attention.

The theater will never find itself again—i.e., constitute a means of true illusion—except by furnishing the spectator with the truthful precipitates of dreams, in which his taste for crime, his erotic obsessions, his savagery, his chimeras, his utopian sense of life and matter, even his cannibalism, pour out, on a level not counterfeit and illusory, but interior.

In other terms, the theater must pursue by all its means a reassertion not only of all the aspects of the objective and descriptive external world, but of the internal world, that is, of man considered metaphysically. It is only thus, we believe, that we shall be able to speak again in the theater about the rights of the imagination. Neither humor, nor poetry, nor imagination means anything unless, by an anarchistic destruction generating a prodigious flight of forms which will constitute the whole spectacle, they succeed in organically reinvolving man, his ideas about reality, and his poetic place in reality.

To consider the theater as a second-hand psychological or moral function, and to believe that dreams themselves have only a substitute function, is to diminish the profound poetic bearing of dreams as well as of the theater. If the theater, like dreams, is bloody and inhuman, it is, more than just that, to manifest and unforgettably root within us the idea of a perpetual conflict, a spasm in which life is continually lacerated, in which everything in creation rises up and exerts itself against our appointed rank; it is in order to perpetuate in a concrete and immediate way the metaphysical ideas of certain Fables whose very atrocity and energy suffice to show their origin and continuity in essential principles.

This being so, one sees that, by its proximity to principles which transfer their energy to it poetically, this naked language of the theater (not a virtual but a real language) must permit, by its use of man's nervous magnetism, the transgression of the ordinary limits of art and speech, in order to realize actively, that is to say magically, *in real terms*, a kind of total creation in which man must reassume his place between dream and events.

THE THEMES

It is not a matter of boring the public to death with transcendent cosmic preoccupations. That there may be profound keys to thought and action with which to interpret the whole spectacle, does not in general concern the spectator, who is simply not interested. But still they must be there; and that concerns us.

THE SPECTACLE: Every spectacle will contain a physical and objective element, perceptible to all. Cries, groans, apparitions, surprises, theatricalities of all kinds, magic beauty of costumes taken from certain ritual models; resplendent lighting, incantational beauty of voices, the charms of harmony, rare notes of music, colors of objects, physical rhythm of movements whose crescendo and decrescendo will accord exactly with the pulsation of movements familiar to everyone, concrete appearances of new and surprising objects, masks, effigies yards high, sudden changes of light, the physical action of light which arouses sensations of heat and cold, etc.

THE MISE EN SCENE: The typical language of the theater will be constituted around the mise en scène considered not simply as the degree of refraction of a text upon the stage, but as the point of departure for all theatrical creation. And it is in the use and handling of this language that the old duality between author and director will be dissolved, replaced by a sort of unique Creator upon whom will devolve the double responsibility of the spectacle and the plot.

THE LANGUAGE OF THE STAGE: It is not a question of suppressing the spoken language, but of giving words approximately the importance they have in dreams.

Meanwhile new means of recording this language must be found, whether these means belong to musical transcription or to some kind of code.

As for ordinary objects, or even the human body, raised to the dignity of signs, it is evident that one can draw one's inspiration from hieroglyphic characters, not only in order to record these signs in a readable fashion which permits them to be reproduced at will, but in order to compose on the stage precise and immediately readable symbols.

On the other hand, this code language and musical transcription will be valuable as a means of transcribing voices.

Since it is fundamental to this language to make a particular use of intonations, these intonations will constitute a kind of harmonic balance, a secondary deformation of speech which must be reproducible at will.

Similarly the ten thousand and one expressions of the face caught in the form of masks can be labeled and catalogued, so they may eventually participate directly and symbolically in this concrete language of the stage, independently of their particular psychological use.

Moreover, these symbolical gestures, masks, and attitudes, these individual or group movements whose innumerable meanings constitute an important part of the concrete language of the theater, evocative gestures, emotive or arbitrary attitudes, excited pounding out of rhythms and sounds, will be doubled, will be multiplied by reflections, as it were, of the gestures and attitudes consisting of the mass of all the impulsive gestures, all the abortive attitudes, all the lapses of mind and tongue, by which are revealed what might be called the impotences of speech, and in which is a prodigious wealth of expressions, to which we shall not fail to have recourse on occasion.

There is, besides, a concrete idea of music in which the sounds make their entrance like characters, where harmonies are coupled together and lose themselves in the precise entrances of words.

From one means of expression to another, correspondences and levels of development are created—even light can have a precise intellectual meaning.

MUSICAL INSTRUMENTS: They will be treated as objects and as part of the set.

Also, the need to act directly and profoundly upon the sensibility through the organs invites research, from the point of view of sound, into qualities and vibrations of absolutely new sounds, qualities which present-day musical instruments do not possess and which require the revival of ancient and forgotten instruments or the invention of new ones. Research is also required, apart from music, into instruments and appliances which, based upon special combinations or new alloys of metal, can attain a new range and compass, producing sounds or noises that are unbearably piercing.

LIGHTS, LIGHTING: The lighting equipment now in use in theaters is no longer adequate. The particular action of light upon the mind, the effects of all kinds of luminous vibration must be investigated, along with new ways of spreading the light in waves, in sheets, in fusillades of fiery arrows. The color gamut of the equipment now in use is to be revised from beginning to end. In order to produce the qualities of particular musical tones, light must recover an element of thinness, density, and opaqueness, with a view to producing the sensations of heat, cold, anger, fear, etc.

COSTUMES: Where costumes are concerned, modern dress will be avoided as much as possible without at the same time assuming a uniform theatrical costuming that would be the same for every play—not from a fetishist and superstitious reverence for the past, but because it seems absolutely evident that certain age-old costumes, of ritual intent, though they existed at a given moment of time, preserve a beauty and a revelational appearance from their closeness to the traditions that gave them birth.

THE STAGE—THE AUDITORIUM: We abolish the stage and the auditorium and replace them by a single site, without partition or barrier of any kind, which will become the theater of the action. A direct communication will be re-established between the spectator and the spectacle, between the actor and the spectator, from the fact that the spectator, placed in the middle of the action, is engulfed and physically affected by it. This envelopment results, in part, from the very configuration of the room itself.

Thus, abandoning the architecture of present-day theaters, we shall take some hangar or barn, which we shall have reconstructed according to processes which have culminated in the architecture of certain churches or holy places, and of certain temples in Tibet.

In the interior of this construction special proportions of height and depth will prevail. The hall will be enclosed by four walls, without any kind of ornament, and the public will be seated in the middle of the room, on the ground floor, on mobile chairs which will allow them to follow the spectacle which will take place all around them. In effect, the absence of a stage in the usual sense of the word will provide for the deployment of the action in the four corners of the room. Particular positions will be reserved for actors and action at the four cardinal points of the room. The scenes will be played in front of whitewashed wall-backgrounds designed to absorb the light. In addition, galleries overhead will run around the periphery of the hall as in certain primitive paintings. These galleries will permit the actors, whenever the action makes it necessary, to be pursued from one point in the room to another, and the action to be deployed on all levels and in all perspectives of height and depth. A cry uttered at one end of the room can be transmitted from mouth to mouth with amplifications and successive modulations all the way to the other. The action will unfold, will extend its trajectory from level to level, point to point; paroxysms will suddenly burst forth, will flare up like fires in different spots. And to speak of the spectacle's character as true illusion or of the direct and immediate influence of the action on the spectator will not be hollow words. For this diffusion of action over an immense space will oblige the lighting of a scene and the varied lighting of a performance to fall upon the public as much as upon the actors—and to the several simultaneous actions or several phases of an identical action in which the characters, swarming over each other like bees, will endure all the onslaughts of the situations and the external assaults of the tempestuous elements, will correspond the physical means of lighting, of producing thunder or wind, whose repercussions the spectator will undergo.

However, a central position will be reserved which, without serving, properly speaking, as a stage, will permit the bulk of the action to be concentrated and brought to a climax whenever necessary.

OBJECTS—MASKS—ACCESSORIES: Manikins, enormous masks, objects of strange proportions will appear with the same sanction as verbal images, will enforce the concrete aspect of every image and every expression—with the corollary that all objects requiring a stereotyped physical representation will be discarded or disguised.

THE SET: There will not be any set. This function will be sufficiently undertaken by hieroglyphic characters, ritual costumes, manikins ten feet high representing the beard of King Lear in the storm, musical instruments tall as men, objects of unknown shape and purpose.

IMMEDIACY: But, people will say, a theater so divorced from life, from facts, from immediate interests. . . . From the present and its events, yes! From whatever preoccupations have any of that profundity which is the prerogative of some men, no! In the *Zohar*, the story of Rabbi Simeon who burns like fire is as immediate as fire itself.

WORKS: We shall not act a written play, but we shall make attempts at direct staging, around themes, facts, or known works. The very nature and disposition of the room suggest this treatment, and there is no theme, however vast, that can be denied us.

SPECTACLE: There is an idea of integral spectacles which must be regenerated. The problem is to make space speak, to feed and furnish it; like mines laid in a wall of rock which all of a sudden turns into geysers and bouquets of stone.

THE ACTOR: The actor is both an element of first importance, since it is upon the effectiveness of his work that the success of the spectacle depends, and a kind of passive and neutral element, since he is rigorously denied all personal initiative. It is a domain in which there is no precise rule; and between the actor of whom is required the mere quality of a sob and the actor who must deliver an oration with all his personal qualities of persuasiveness, there is the whole margin which separates a man from an instrument.

THE INTERPRETATION: The spectacle will be calculated from one end to the other, like a code (*un langage*). Thus there will be no lost movements, all movements will obey a rhythm; and each character being merely a type, his gesticulation, physiognomy, and costume will appear like so many rays of light.

THE CINEMA: To the crude visualization of what is, the theater through poetry opposes images of what is not. However, from the point of view of action, one cannot compare a cinematic image which, however poetic it may be, is limited by the film, to a theatrical image which obeys all the exigencies of life.

CRUELTY: Without an element of cruelty at the root of every spectacle, the theater is not possible. In our present state of degeneration it is through the skin that metaphysics must be made to re-enter our minds

Arthur Miller (B. 1915)

Arthur Miller published this controversial essay in the *New York Times* after the opening of *Death of a Salesman* in 1949. In his argument for a new conception of tragedy suited to modern sensibilities, Miller modifies Aristotle's notions of the tragic protagonist and of tragic action.

TRAGEDY AND THE COMMON MAN

In this age few tragedies are written. It has often been held that the lack is due to a paucity of heroes among us, or else that modern man has had the blood drawn out of his organs of belief by the skepticism of science, and the heroic attack on life cannot feed on an attitude of reserve and circumspection. For one reason or another, we are often held to be below tragedy—or tragedy above us. The inevitable conclusion is, of course, that the tragic mode is archaic, fit only for the very highly placed, the kings or the kingly, and where this admission is not made in so many words it is most often implied.

I believe that the common man is as apt a subject for tragedy in its highest sense as kings were. On the face of it this ought to be obvious in the light of modern psychiatry, which bases its analysis upon classic formulations, such as the Oedipus and Orestes complexes, for instances, which were enacted by royal beings, but which apply to everyone in similar emotional situations.

More simply, when the question of tragedy in art is not at issue, we never hesitate to attribute to the well-placed and the exalted the very same mental processes as the lowly. And finally, if the exaltation of tragic action were truly a property of the high-bred character alone, it is inconceivable that the mass of mankind should cherish tragedy above all other forms, let alone be capable of understanding it.

As a general rule, to which there may be exceptions unknown to me, I think the tragic feeling is evoked in us when we are in the presence of a character who is ready to lay down his life, if need be, to secure one thing—his sense of personal dignity. From Orestes to Hamlet, Medea to Macbeth, the underlying struggle is that of the individual attempting to gain his "rightful" position in his society.

Sometimes he is one who has been displaced from it, sometimes one who seeks to attain it for the first time, but the fateful wound from which the inevitable events spiral is the wound of indignity, and its dominant force is indignation. Tragedy, then, is the consequence of a man's total compulsion to evaluate himself justly.

In the sense of having been initiated by the hero himself, the tale always reveals what has been called his "tragic flaw," a failing that is not peculiar to grand or elevated characters. Nor is it necessarily a weakness. The flaw, or crack in the character, is really nothing—and need be nothing—but his inherent unwillingness to remain passive in the face of what he conceives to be a challenge to his dignity, his image of his rightful status. Only the passive, only those who accept their lot without active retaliation, are "flawless." Most of us are in that category.

But there are among us today, as there always have been, those who act against the scheme of things that degrades them, and in the process of action everything we have accepted out of fear or insensitivity or ignorance is shaken before us and examined, and from this total onslaught by an individual against the seemingly stable cosmos surrounding us—from this total examination of the "unchangeable" environment—comes the terror and the fear that is classically associated with tragedy.

More important, from this total questioning of what has previously been unquestioned, we learn. And such a process is not beyond the common man. In revolutions around the world, these past thirty years, he has demonstrated again and again this inner dynamic of all tragedy.

Insistence upon the rank of the tragic hero, or the so-called nobility of his character, is really but a clinging to the outward forms of tragedy. If rank or nobility of character was indispensable, then it would follow that the problems of those with rank were the particular problems of tragedy. But surely the right of one monarch to capture the domain from another no longer raises our passions, nor are our concepts of justice what they were to the mind of an Elizabethan king.

The quality in such plays that does shake us, however, derives from the underlying fear of being displaced, the disaster inherent in being torn away from our chosen image of what and who we are in this world. Among us today this fear is as strong, and perhaps stronger, than it ever was. In fact, it is the common man who knows this fear best.

Now, if it is true that tragedy is the consequence of a man's total compulsion to evaluate himself justly, his destruction in the attempt posits a wrong or an evil in his environment. And this is precisely the morality of tragedy and its lesson. The discovery of the moral law, which is what the enlightenment of tragedy consists of, is not the discovery of some abstract or metaphysical quantity.

The tragic right is a condition of life, a condition in which the human personality is able to flower and realize itself. The wrong is the condition which suppresses man, perverts the flowing out of his love and creative instinct. Tragedy enlightens—and it must, in that it points the heroic finger at the enemy of man's freedom. The thrust for freedom is the quality in tragedy which exalts. The revolutionary questioning of the stable environment is what terrifies. In no way is the common man debarred from such thoughts or such actions.

Seen in this light, our lack of tragedy may be partially accounted for by the turn which modern literature has taken toward the purely psychiatric view of life, or the purely sociological. If all our miseries, our indignities, are born and bred within our minds, then all action, let alone the heroic action, is obviously impossible.

And if society alone is responsible for the cramping of our lives, then the protagonist must needs be so pure and faultless as to force us to deny his validity as a character. From neither of these views can tragedy derive, simply because neither represents a balanced concept of life. Above all else, tragedy requires the finest appreciation by the writer of cause and effect.

No tragedy can therefore come about when its author fears to question absolutely everything, when he regards any institution, habit or custom as being either everlasting, immutable or inevitable. In the tragic view the need of man to wholly realize himself is the only fixed star, and whatever it is that hedges his nature and lowers it is ripe for attack and examination. Which is not to say that tragedy must preach revolution.

The Greeks could probe the very heavenly origin of their ways and return to confirm the rightness of laws. And Job could face God in anger, demanding his right and end in submission. But for a moment everything is in suspension, nothing is accepted, and in this stretching and tearing apart of the cosmos, in the very action of so doing, the character gains "size," the tragic stature which is spuriously attached to the royal or the highborn in our minds. The commonest of men may take on that stature to the extent of his willingness to throw all he has into the contest, the battle to secure his rightful place in his world.

There is a misconception of tragedy with which I have been struck in review after review, and in many conversations with writers and readers alike. It is the idea that tragedy is of necessity allied to pessimism. Even the dictionary says nothing more about the word than that it means a story with a sad or unhappy ending. This impression is so firmly fixed that I almost hesitate to claim that in truth tragedy implies more optimism in its author than does comedy, and that its final result ought to be the reinforcement of the onlooker's brightest opinions of the human animal.

For, if it is true to say that in essence the tragic hero is intent upon claiming his whole due as a personality, and if this struggle must be total and without reservation, then it automatically demonstrates the indestructible will of man to achieve his humanity.

The possibility of victory must be there in tragedy. Where pathos rules, where pathos is finally derived, a character has fought a battle he could not possibly have won. The pathetic is achieved when the protagonist is, by virtue of his witlessness, his insensitivity or the very air he gives off, incapable of grappling with a much superior force.

Pathos truly is the mode for the pessimist. But tragedy requires a nicer balance between what is possible and what is impossible. And it is curious, although edifying, that the plays we revere, century after century, are the tragedies. In them, and in them alone, lies the belief—optimistic, if you will, in the perfectibility of man.

It is time, I think, that we who are without kings, took up this bright thread of our history and followed it to the only place it can possibly lead in our time—the heart and spirit of the average man.

Martin Esslin (B. 1918)

Drama critic Martin Esslin is author of several influential books on contemporary drama and theater, including *Brecht: A Choice of Evils* (1959), *Pinter: A Study of His Plays* (1976), and *Anatomy of Drama* (1976). In his pioneering study of Beckett, Pinter, Ionesco, and other contemporary playwrights he coined the term "theater of the absurd" to describe the disorienting quality of their plays.

from THE THEATRE OF THE ABSURD

THE ABSURDITY OF THE ABSURD

On 19 November 1957, a group of worried actors were preparing to face their audience. The actors were members of the company of the San Francisco Actors' Workshop. The audience consisted of fourteen hundred convicts at the San Quentin penitentiary. No live play had been performed at San Quentin since Sarah Bernhardt appeared there in 1913. Now, forty-four years later, the play that had been chosen, largely because no woman appeared in it, was Samuel Beckett's *Waiting for Godot*.

No wonder the actors and Herbert Blau, the director, were apprehensive. How were they to face one of the toughest audiences in the world with a highly obscure, intellectual play that had produced near riots among a good many highly sophisticated audiences in Western Europe? Herbert Blau decided to prepare the San Quentin audience for what was to come. He stepped on to the stage and addressed the packed, darkened North Dining Hall—a sea of flickering matches that the convicts tossed over their shoulders after lighting their cigarettes. Blau compared the play to a piece of jazz music 'to which one must listen for whatever one may find in it'. In the same way, he hoped, there would be some meaning, some personal significance for each member of the audience in *Waiting for Godot*.

The curtain parted. The play began. And what had bewildered the sophisticated audiences of Paris, London, and New York was immediately grasped by an audience of convicts. As the writer of 'Memos of a first-nighter' put it in the columns of the prison paper, the *San Quentin News*:

> The trio of muscle-men, biceps overflowing . . . parked all 642 lbs on the aisle and waited for the girls and funny stuff. When this didn't appear they audibly fumed and audibly decided to wait until the house lights dimmed before escaping. They made one error. They listened and looked two minutes too long—and stayed. Left at the end. All shook . . .

Or as the writer of the lead story of the same paper reported, under the headline, 'San Francisco Group Leaves S.Q. Audience Waiting for Godot':

> From the moment Robin Wagner's thoughtful and limbo-like set was dressed with light, until the last futile and expectant handclasp was hesitantly activated between the two searching vagrants, the San Francisco company had its audience of captives in its collective hand. . . . Those that had felt a less controversial vehicle should be attempted as a first play here had their fears allayed a short five minutes after the Samuel Beckett piece began to unfold.

A reporter from the San Francisco *Chronicle* who was present noted that the convicts did not find it difficult to understand the play. One prisoner told him, 'Godot is society.' Said another: 'He's the outside.' A teacher at the prison was quoted as saying, 'They know what is meant by waiting . . . and they knew if Godot finally came, he would only be a disappointment.' The leading article of the prison paper showed how clearly the writers had understood the meaning of the play:

> It was an expression, symbolic in order to avoid all personal error, by an author who expected each member of his audience to draw his own conclusions, make his own errors. It asked nothing in point, it forced no dramatized moral on the viewer, it held out no specific hope. . . . We're still waiting for Godot, and shall continue to wait. When the scenery gets too drab and the action too slow, we'll call each other names and swear to part forever—but then, there's no place to go!

It is said that Godot himself, as well as turns of phrase and characters from the play, has since become a permanent part of the private language, the institutional mythology of San Quentin.

Why did a play of the supposedly esoteric avant-garde make so immediate and so deep an impact on an audience of convicts? Because it confronted them with a situation in some ways analogous to their own? Perhaps. Or perhaps because they were unsophisticated enough to come to the theatre without any preconceived notions and ready-made expectations, so that they avoided the mistake that trapped so many established critics who condemned the play for its lack of plot, development, characterization, suspense, or plain common sense. Certainly the prisoners of San Quentin could not be suspected of the sin of intellectual snobbery, for which a sizeable proportion of the audiences of *Waiting for Godot* have often been reproached; of pretending to like a play they did not even begin to understand, just to appear in the know.

The reception of *Waiting for Godot* at San Quentin, and the wide acclaim given to plays by Ionesco, Adamov, Pinter, and others, testify that these plays, which are so often superciliously dismissed as nonsense or mystification, *have* something to say and *can* be understood. Most of the incomprehension with which plays of this type are still being received by critics and theatrical reviewers, most of the bewilderment they have caused and to which they still give rise, come from the fact that they are part of a new and still developing stage convention that has not yet been generally understood and has hardly ever been defined. Inevitably, plays written in this new convention will, when judged by the standards and criteria of another, be regarded as impertinent and outrageous impostures. If a good play must have a cleverly constructed story, these have no story or plot to speak of; if a good play is judged by subtlety of characterization and motivation, these are often without recognizable characters and present the audience with almost mechanical puppets; if a good play has to have a fully explained theme, which is neatly exposed and finally solved, these often have neither a beginning nor an end; if a good play is to hold the mirror up to nature and portray the manners and mannerisms of the age in finely observed sketches, these seem often to be reflections of dreams and nightmares; if a good play relies on witty repartee and pointed dialogue, these often consist of incoherent babblings.

But the plays we are concerned with here pursue ends quite different from those of the conventional play and therefore use quite different methods. They can be judged only by the standards of the Theatre of the Absurd, which it is the purpose of this book to define and clarify.

It must be stressed, however, that the dramatists whose work is here discussed do not form part of any self-proclaimed or self-conscious school or movement. On the contrary, each of the writers in question is an individual who regards himself as a lone outsider, cut off and isolated in his private world. Each has his own personal approach to both subject-matter and form; his own roots, sources, and background. If they also, very clearly and in spite of themselves, have a good deal in common, it is because their work most sensitively mirrors and reflects the preoccupations and anxieties, the emotions and thinking of many of their contemporaries in the Western world.

This is not to say that their works are representative of mass attitudes. It is an oversimplification to assume that any age presents a homogeneous pattern. Ours being, more than most others, an age of transition, it displays a bewilderingly stratified picture: medieval beliefs still held and overlaid by eighteenth-century rationalism and mid-nineteenth-century Marxism, rocked by sudden volcanic eruptions of prehistoric fanaticisms and primitive tribal cults. Each of these components of the cultural pattern of the age finds its own artistic expression. The Theatre of the Absurd, however, can be seen as the reflection of what seems to be the attitude most genuinely representative of our own time.

The hallmark of this attitude is its sense that the certitudes and unshakable basic assumptions of former ages have been swept away, that they have been tested and found wanting, that they have been discredited as cheap and somewhat childish illusions. The decline of religious faith was masked until the end of the Second World War by the substitute religions of faith in progress, nationalism, and various totalitarian fallacies. All this was shattered by the war. By 1942, Albert Camus was calmly putting the question why, since life had lost all meaning, man should not seek escape in suicide. In one of the great, seminal heart-searchings of our time, *The Myth of Sisyphus*, Camus tried to diagnose the human situation in a world of shattered beliefs:

> A world that can be explained by reasoning, however faulty, is a familiar world. But in a universe that is suddenly deprived of illusions and of light, man feels a stranger. His is an irremediable exile, because he is deprived of memories of a lost homeland as much as he lacks the hope of a promised land to come. This

divorce between man and his life, the actor and his setting, truly constitutes the feeling of Absurdity.

'Absurd' originally means 'out of harmony', in a musical context. Hence its dictionary definition: 'out of harmony with reason or propriety; incongruous, unreasonable, illogical'. In common usage, 'absurd' may simply mean 'ridiculous', but this is not the sense in which Camus uses the word, and in which it is used when we speak of the Theatre of the Absurd. In an essay on Kafka, Ionesco defined his understanding of the term as follows: 'Absurd is that which is devoid of purpose. . . . Cut off from his religious, metaphysical, and transcendental roots, man is lost; all his actions become senseless, absurd, useless.'

This sense of metaphysical anguish at the absurdity of the human condition is, broadly speaking, the theme of the plays of Beckett, Adamov, Ionesco, Genet, and the other writers discussed in this book. But it is not merely the subject-matter that defines what is here called the Theatre of the Absurd. A similar sense of the senselessness of life, of the inevitable devaluation of ideals, purity, and purpose, is also the theme of much of the work of dramatists like Giraudoux, Anouilh, Salacrou, Sartre, and Camus himself. Yet these writers differ from the dramatists of the Absurd in an important respect (they present their sense of the irrationality of the human condition in the form of highly lucid and logically constructed reasoning, while the Theatre of the Absurd strives to express its sense of the senselessness of the human condition and the inadequacy of the rational approach by the open abandonment of rational devices and discursive thought.) While Sartre or Camus express the new content in the old convention, the Theatre of the Absurd goes a step further in trying to achieve a unity between its basic assumptions and the form in which these are expressed. In some senses, the *theatre* of Sartre and Camus is less adequate as an expression of the *philosophy* of Sartre and Camus—in artistic, as distinct from philosophic, terms—than the Theatre of the Absurd.

If Camus argued that in our disillusioned age the world has ceased to make sense, he did so in the elegantly rationalistic and discursive style of an eighteenth-century moralist, in well-constructed and polished plays. If Sartre argues that existence comes before essence and that human personality can be reduced to pure potentiality and the freedom to choose itself anew at any moment, he presents his ideas in plays based on brilliantly drawn characters who remain wholly consistent and thus reflect the old convention that each human being has a core of immutable, unchanging essence—in fact, an immortal soul. And the beautiful phrasing and argumentative brilliance of both Sartre and Camus in their relentless probing still, by implication, proclaim a tacit conviction that logical discourse can offer valid solutions, that the analysis of language will lead to the uncovering of basic concepts—Platonic ideas.

This is an inner contradiction that the dramatists of the Absurd are trying, by instinct and intuition rather than by conscious effort, to overcome and resolve. The Theatre of the Absurd has renounced arguing *about* the absurdity of the human condition; it merely *presents* it in being—that is, in terms of concrete stage images. This is the difference between the approach of the philosopher and that of the poet; the difference, to take an example from another sphere, between the *idea* of God in the works of Thomas Aquinas or Spinoza and the *intuition* of

God in those of St John of the Cross or Meister Eckhart—the difference between theory and experience.

It is this striving for an integration between the subject-matter and the form in which it is expressed that separates the Theatre of the Absurd from the Existentialist theatre.

It must also be distinguished from another important, and parallel, trend in the contemporary French theatre, which is equally preoccupied with the absurdity and uncertainty of the human condition: the 'poetic avant-garde' theatre of dramatists like Michel de Ghelderode, Jacques Audiberti, Georges Neveux, and, in the younger generation, Georges Schehadé, Henri Pichette, and Jean Vauthier, to name only some of its most important exponents. This is an even more difficult dividing line to draw, for the two approaches overlap a good deal. The 'poetic avant-garde' relies on fantasy and dream reality as much as the Theatre of the Absurd does; it also disregards such traditional axioms as that of the basic unity and consistency of each character or the need for a plot. Yet basically the 'poetic avant-garde' represents a different mood; it is more lyrical, and far less violent and grotesque. Even more important is its different attitude toward language: the 'poetic avant-garde' relies to a far greater extent on consciously 'poetic' speech; it aspires to plays that are in effect poems, images composed of a rich web of verbal associations.

The Theatre of the Absurd, on the other hand, tends toward a radical devaluation of language, toward a poetry that is to emerge from the concrete and objectified images of the stage itself. The element of language still plays an important part in this conception, but what *happens* on the stage transcends, and often contradicts, the *words* spoken by the characters. In Ionesco's *The Chairs*, for example, the poetic content of a powerfully poetic play does not lie in the banal words that are uttered but in the fact that they are spoken to an ever-growing number of empty chairs.

The Theatre of the Absurd is thus part of the 'anti-literary' movement of our time, which has found its expression in abstract painting, with its rejection of 'literary' elements in pictures; or in the 'new novel' in France, with its reliance on the description of objects and its rejection of empathy and anthropomorphism.

PART VII

Contemporary Drama and Theater

An example of a late twentieth century playing space: The thrust stage at the Tyrone Guthrie theater in Minneapolis.

With the development of the independent theater movement in the late nineteenth century, drama and theater divided into two channels: a commercial mainstream, catering to audiences primarily seeking entertainment, and a more experimental fringe, catering to audiences interested in the avant-garde. The separation between mainstream and avant-garde is not absolute, however. A number of avant-garde dramatists have also been successful in mainstream venues, and many of the techniques pioneered in avant-garde drama and theater have influenced mainstream productions.

Drama, Theater, and Society

The counterculture that developed in the 1960s and 1970s produced a wide range of experiments in drama and theater. Some saw drama and theater as a weapon in the struggle for social reform, for revolution, or for generating alternative visions for political action. Groups took plays into streets and parks and workplaces. "Street theater" grew up. El Teatro Campesino (1965–1970), which staged short plays in Spanish and English in the fields of Southern California, attempted to help organize migrant workers. The Living Theater, founded in 1947, was reorganized in the 1960s as a theatrical commune dedicated to producing plays that promoted revolution. The San Francisco Mime Troupe, founded in 1959, was also reorganized in the 1960s as a collective dedicated to using theater to promote social change. Other groups of experimenters saw the need not so much to use drama and theater as a revolutionary tool as to revitalize the theater, to make it once again the center of artistic life in communities. These groups, inspired by the theories of Brecht and Artaud, experimented with different relations between actors and audience, script and performance, and they rethought the relationship between theater and society. None of these groups aspired to succeed in the commercial mainstream; indeed, many viewed such success as a betrayal of their principles.

Women playwrights have written successfully for the stage since the time of Aphra Behn in the late seventeenth century, and there were many successful women playwrights in the United States in the nineteenth century. By the 1960s, the women's theater movement began to promote the goals of feminism and the careers of women artists. Such prominent feminist dramatists as Megan Terry, Maria Irene Fornes, Adrienne Kennedy, and Rochelle Owens were all writing and being produced at this time. Feminist drama was originally oriented toward a specific audience. Some women's groups saw drama and theater as revolutionary tools, like street theater, in the struggle to promote feminist goals. Some rejected the idea of acceptance by the male-dominated mainstream; others attempted to give women artists better odds to succeed in the mainstream. Over the past twenty years women's theater has changed along with the goals of feminism, and feminist playwrights have succeeded in commercial theaters since the early 1980s. Tina Howe, considered so radically feminist that she had difficulty getting her earlier works staged, won an Obie award in 1983 for *Painting Churches*. While less obviously feminist in orientation, Beth Henley received a Pulitzer Prize in 1981 for *Crimes of the Heart*, and Marsha Norman received a Pulitzer Prize in 1983 for *'night, Mother*. Few highly experimental women playwrights have achieved commercial success, however, with the notable exception of British playwright Caryl

The theater-in-the-round arrangement of the Penthouse Theater at the University of Washington, Seattle.

Churchill. Churchill integrated many feminist concepts into the avant-garde tradition of British theater with such plays as *Top Girls*, *Cloud 9*, and *Serious Money*. In general, the women's theater movement has succeeded remarkably in making the ways in which society and theater construct gender a subject of interest in many contemporary plays.

African-American theatrical companies had been firmly established in the United States by the late nineteenth century. Musicals rather than serious plays were preferred in mainstream venues because they were considered exotic and entertaining. Some African Americans were successful with more substantial plays. Willis Richardson's *The Chip Woman's Fortune* was produced on Broadway as early as 1923, but it was not until Lorraine Hansberry won the New York Drama Critics Circle Award for her play about African-American family life, *A Raisin in the Sun* (1959), that serious plays by African Americans began to be produced more often in mainstream commercial theaters. Since that time several African-American playwrights have risen to prominence in the mainstream theater. Ntozake Shange's experimental plays, the best-known of them *For Colored Girls Who Have Considered Suicide/When the Rainbow is Enuf* (1976), were originally produced in women's bars. *For Colored Girls* eventually moved to Broadway, where it won a Tony award. The first four of August Wilson's series of plays about

African Americans pursuing the American dream, including *Fences* (Tony 1986; Pulitzer 1987) and *The Piano Lesson* (Pulitzer 1990), have won major awards. Today serious plays by African-American dramatists are produced in mainstream theaters in the United States and in the repertories of many regional theaters throughout the country.

The combined effect of this plurality of groups and movements from the late 1950s to the 1990s has been to open up previously excluded subjects. Plays about racism, about exploitation, about homosexuality, and about gender are now produced regularly in mainstream commercial theaters. Predictably, language and costuming have been affected, and profanity and nudity are not uncommon on the contemporary stage. Casts of plays now include actors and actresses of diverse racial, ethnic, and religious backgrounds. Finally, the plurality has produced a willingness to experiment in integrating theater with the other arts.

CONTEMPORARY VENUES

The major centers for commercial mainstream theater are Broadway in New York and the West End in London. Commercial theater exists to make a profit. To do so requires reducing costs, attracting affluent financial backers, and appealing to a large, relatively prosperous clientele. These considerations often determine the kind of drama produced in mainstream theaters. Productions are expensive to mount, so the long-run possibilities of a single play loom as an important factor. Attracting affluent theatergoers to pay high ticket prices involves catering to conservative tastes and casting well-known actors and actresses in leading parts. Not surprisingly, most of the financially successful productions on Broadway and the West End over the past thirty years have been musicals, followed in popularity by comedies, which have made up a good portion of the repertory. Occasionally serious plays are produced, but usually only after they have been tested in other markets and the potential for profit is evident.

Other markets where plays are tested are the so-called off-Broadway theaters in New York and the off–West End theaters in London. The names derive from their location on the edges of mainstream theater districts. The goals of these theaters once differed from those of Broadway and London's West End, and they were originally places where new artists could work, where new plays could find production, and where established artists might experiment. The pressure from rising costs, however, both in England and the United States, have driven some of these theaters to become more concerned with box office receipts, turning them into simply less elaborate versions of the West End or Broadway. Some serve mainly as rehearsal spaces for Broadway and West End productions, while others try to pursue their initial, more idealistic goals. One of the most famous off–West End theaters, the Royal Court in Sloane Square, is still dedicated to producing new plays and offering established artists the opportunity to experiment, and occasionally such experiments do transfer to the West End. In recent years, David Mamet's *Oleanna* moved from the Royal Court, where it was directed by Harold Pinter, to a successful run in the West End, as did Ariel Dorfman's *Death and the Maiden* before it was made into a film directed by Roman Polanski.

"Fringe" theater in London and off-off-Broadway theater in New York have arisen in the shadow of their profit-driven relatives. In alternative theaters, designers, playwrights, directors, and actors work together in a noncommercial environment. These theaters grew up in the 1960s and 1970s in New York and London as part of the counterculture movement, dedicated to exploring new possibilities of theatrical representation. Often the plays and productions in these theaters are socially, politically, and artistically alien to the values of those who patronize commercial mainstream theaters. The venues are coffeehouses, pubs, bars, cellars, churches, and small theaters, some far from the centers of New York and London. Fringe and off-off-Broadway theaters have become the main venues for experimental and political theater.

Meanwhile, regional and festival theaters have cropped up throughout Great Britain and the United States and Canada, and Great Britain is fortunate enough to have a national theater. In contrast to the commercial mainstream, most of these theaters are nonprofit organizations, so they can be adventurous in play selections. Many are repertory companies, which means that they offer several different plays either at the same time or in short runs over the course of a season. Well-known theater classics alternate with contemporary plays, comedies, and musicals. Instead of playing a single role every night, as in the commercial mainstream, actors get to play a variety of parts. At the National Theatre of Great Britain, for example, a leading actor or actress in one play might perform three or four minor parts in others in the repertory. Some regional and festival theaters have achieved distinguished reputations. The Guthrie Theater in Minneapolis, for instance, is well known for its classical revivals. The Royal Shakespeare Company (RSC) at Stratford-upon-Avon specializes primarily in Shakespeare's plays, but the company also includes many other kinds of plays in its repertory, and some go on to productions in the commercial mainstream. The RSC's production of *Les Misérables*, for example, continued to play in London for years and was licensed to touring companies throughout the world. While new drama may come from London or New York to play in the regional theaters, it is now common for regional theaters themselves to produce plays that eventually move to Broadway or the West End.

Success in the commercial mainstream is measured in box office receipts. Much more difficult to measure is the success of experimental plays that push drama and theater beyond their current limits and that express the dreams and anxieties of our own time. Both popular and fringe theater reflect and help to create the values of the culture that produces them, and great plays have always captured the essence of an age while posing serious questions about its most pressing issues. As in the past, contemporary drama and theater may not be able to resolve our problems, but theater can help audiences to face many of the pressing social questions of our own time—world health, population growth, conservation of natural resources, technological interference in biological processes, the right to death with dignity, social justice—which elude most of the ethical and moral frameworks we have in place. And it can do this as only theater can, by entertaining us and challenging us at the same time.

HAROLD PINTER (b. 1930)

Harold Pinter has enjoyed a long and varied career as an actor, director, and playwright, in addition to writing for the stage and for radio, television, and film. Pinter grew up in Hackney in predominantly Jewish East London and was sent off to a boarding school in Cornwall for a time during World War II, but he returned to London in 1944 in time to experience the German air raids. At an early age he was already writing stories and poems for magazines, and he took part in school theatrical productions. After graduating from Hackney Downs grammar school, Pinter received a grant to attend the Royal Academy of Dramatic Art, although he suffered a nervous breakdown before completing his studies. During his twenties he began a career as a radio and stage actor, and he toured Ireland as a member of an acting company. On returning to England he continued to act in London and in regional theaters under the stage name David Baron until he wrote his first play, *The Room*, in 1957. Even this early one-act play displays Pinter's characteristic sense of theatrical menace: in it an old couple is suddenly and inexplicably harassed by threatening visits and messages. In his first full-length play, *The Birthday Party*, also written in 1957, the protagonist is subjected to inexplicable harassment, to verbal and physical abuse that renders him incoherent, at which point he is abducted by his abusers. Pinter admits to being influenced by Beckett, but Pinter develops a much more realistic kind of play. In contrast to Beckett, Pinter uses seemingly recognizable characters and locales, although in the end he often frustrates the audience's expectations about the characters and the worlds they inhabit. Pinter's spare and oblique dialogue makes the characters' motives and intentions difficult to comprehend and suggests an undefinable danger and violence lurking just below the surface.

Three of Pinter's early plays—*The Room, The Birthday Party*, and *The Dumb Waiter*—were first produced by the drama department at Bristol University in 1957. The latter two plays went into commercial production in 1958 and 1960, bringing complaints from reviewers about the opaque language, the seemingly aimless dialogue filled with non sequiturs, and the absurdist qualities. In these early plays Pinter pioneered his distinct use of language, character, and situation, anticipating the implied violence and quietly menacing atmosphere that have become the hallmarks of his work. *The Birthday Party* closed after a week, but six years later it was revived in a successful production by the Royal Shakespeare Company, directed by Pinter himself. By this time Pinter had achieved popular success with *The Caretaker* (1960), a play about the owner of a house, his brain-damaged brother, and a tramp who befriends the brother. By the mid-1960s he also had begun to receive wide acclaim and distinguished awards for his television scripts and screenplays. In 1965 *The Homecoming* opened in London in a successful production by the Royal Shakespeare Company. In the following year Pinter was invested as Commander of the Order of the British Empire by Queen Elizabeth II.

All of Pinter's major plays have been produced in London and New York and in regional theaters throughout Great Britain and the United States and Canada, and the plays are no longer considered as incomprehensible as they seemed in the late 1950s. Pinter's work, like that of his predecessors who have been grouped together in the theater of the absurd—Jean Genet, Eugène Ionesco, and Samuel Beckett—shows a trend in contemporary theater away from clearly motivated characters with histories, away from coherent plots, and away from rational dialogue. In Pinter's plays, characters who do not offer convincing information to explain their experience or behavior or aspirations or motives are as legitimate as those who do. His characterization suggests that the more acute the experience, the less articulately it can be expressed. Pinter communicates this inarticulateness in meaningful silences and in banal speech, which simply masks an underlying fear. His work is thus linked not only to the absurdists but also to Chekhov, who long before had employed inarticulateness and silences and torrents of words to communicate psychological states of mind.

Pinter continues to write plays. One of his better-known works is *Betrayal* (1978). He has also written screenplays, including *Turtle Diary*, *The Trial*, and *The French Lieutenant's Woman*, and he continues to direct. He recently directed a production of David Mamet's *Oleanna* for the Royal Court Theatre, and the play went on to a commercial run at the Albery Theatre in the West End.

The Dumb Waiter

Most of Pinter's characters seem realistic, as do his settings and dialogue. But what happens in his plays is often strange and disturbing. Pinter himself claims, "I'd say my plays were realistic, but what I'm doing is not realism."

In *The Dumb Waiter* (1957) Ben and Gus—two hit men, apparently—are waiting for instructions in a cramped basement room. They receive strange messages and clothing from somewhere above by means of a dumbwaiter, which is operated by someone whose identity remains unknown. The title of the play refers both to this machine and to Ben and Gus themselves, who have a relationship that never rises above banality and aimless conversation about trivial subjects. The vaguely threatening dialogue and the silences play off audience expectations for significance. As the audience strains to find meaning in the relationship between Ben and Gus, a deeper suggestive quality emerges from the dialogue, along with a growing sense of menace. The only apparent conflict in the play is the series of petty disagreements between Ben and Gus, and all would seem inconsequential were it not for the mysterious dumbwaiter, which keeps sending down messages directing their action. The characters of Ben and Gus, reminiscent of Didi and Gogo in Beckett's *Waiting for Godot*, add a darker element and a brutal mood to the play. At the same time the play builds on and parodies American gangster films, bringing to the stage the unmistakable resonance of cinematic dialogue, character type, and stylized realism.

The Dumb Waiter

Harold Pinter

CHARACTERS
BEN
Gus

SCENE. A basement room. Two beds, flat against the back wall. A serving hatch, closed, between the beds. A door to the kitchen and lavatory, left. A door to a passage, right.

[*BEN is lying on a bed, left, reading a paper. GUS is sitting on a bed, right, tying his shoelaces, with difficulty. Both are dressed in shirts, trousers and braces.*
    Silence.
    GUS ties his laces, rises, yawns and begins to walk slowly to the door, left. He stops, looks down, and shakes his foot.
    BEN lowers his paper and watches him. GUS kneels and unties his shoe-lace and slowly takes off the shoe. He looks inside it and brings out a flattened match-box. He shakes it and examines it. Their eyes meet. BEN rattles his paper and reads. GUS puts the match-box in his pocket and bends down to put on his shoe. He ties his lace, with difficulty. BEN lowers his paper and watches him. GUS walks to the door, left, stops, and shakes the other foot. He kneels, unties his shoe-lace, and slowly takes off the shoe. He looks inside it and brings out a flattened cigarette packet. He shakes it and examines it. Their eyes meet. BEN rattles his paper and reads. GUS puts the packet in his pocket, bends down, puts on his shoe and ties the lace.
    He wanders off, left.
    BEN slams the paper down on the bed and glares after him. He picks up the paper and lies on his back, reading.
    Silence.
    A lavatory chain is pulled twice off, left, but the lavatory does not flush.
    Silence.
    GUS re-enters, left, and halts at the door, scratching his head.
    BEN slams down the paper.]

BEN: Kaw!

[*He picks up the paper.*]

What about this? Listen to this!

[*He refers to the paper.*]

A man of eighty-seven wanted to cross the road. But there was a lot of traffic, see? He couldn't see how he was going to squeeze through. So he crawled under a lorry.
GUS: He what?
BEN: He crawled under a lorry. A stationary lorry.
GUS: No?
BEN: The lorry started and ran over him.
GUS: Go on!
BEN: That's what it says here.
GUS: Get away.
BEN: It's enough to make you want to puke, isn't it?
GUS: Who advised him to do a thing like that?
BEN: A man of eighty-seven crawling under a lorry!
GUS: It's unbelievable.
BEN: It's down here in black and white.
GUS: Incredible.

[*Silence.*
    GUS shakes his head and exits. BEN lies back and reads.
    The lavatory chain is pulled once off left, but the lavatory does not flush.
    BEN whistles at an item in the paper.
    GUS re-enters.]

I want to ask you something.
BEN: What are you doing out there?
GUS: Well, I was just—
BEN: What about the tea?
GUS: I'm just going to make it.
BEN: Well, go on, make it.
GUS: Yes, I will. (*He sits in a chair. Ruminatively.*) He's laid on some very nice crockery this time, I'll say that. It's sort of striped. There's a white stripe.

[*BEN reads.*]

It's very nice. I'll say that.

[*BEN turns the page.*]

You know, sort of round the cup. Round the rim. All the rest of it's black, you see. Then the saucer's black, except for right in the middle, where the cup goes, where it's white.

[BEN reads.]

Then the plates are the same, you see. Only they've got a black stripe—the plates—right across the middle. Yes, I'm quite taken with the crockery.

BEN: (*still reading*): What do you want plates for? You're not going to eat.

GUS: I've brought a few biscuits.

BEN: Well, you'd better eat them quick.

GUS: I always bring a few biscuits. Or a pie. You know I can't drink tea without anything to eat.

BEN: Well, make the tea then, will you? Time's getting on.

[GUS brings out the flattened cigarette packet and examines it.]

GUS: You got any cigarettes? I think I've run out.

[He throws the packet high up and leans forward to catch it.]

I hope it won't be a long job, this one.

[Aiming carefully, he flips the packet under his bed.]

Oh, I wanted to ask you something.

BEN (*slamming his paper down*): Kaw!

GUS: What's that?

BEN: A child of eight killed a cat!

GUS: Get away.

BEN: It's a fact. What about that, eh? A child of eight killing a cat!

GUS: How did he do it?

BEN: It was a girl.

GUS: How did she do it?

BEN: She—

[He picks up the paper and studies it.]

It doesn't say.

GUS: Why not?

BEN: Wait a minute. It just says—Her brother, aged eleven, viewed the incident from the toolshed.

GUS: Go on!

BEN: That's bloody ridiculous.

[Pause.]

GUS: I bet he did it.

BEN: Who?

GUS: The brother.

BEN: I think you're right.

[Pause.]

(*Slamming down the paper.*) What about that, eh? A kid of eleven killing a cat and blaming it on his little sister of eight! It's enough to—

[He breaks off in disgust and seizes the paper. GUS rises.]

GUS: What time is he getting in touch?

[BEN reads.]

What time is he getting in touch?

BEN: What's the matter with you? It could be any time. Any time.

GUS (*moves to the foot of BEN's bed*): Well, I was going to ask you something.

BEN: What?

GUS: Have you noticed the time that tank takes to fill?

BEN: What tank?

GUS: In the lavatory.

BEN: No. Does it?

GUS: Terrible.

BEN: Well, what about it?

GUS: What do you think's the matter with it?

BEN: Nothing.

GUS: Nothing?

BEN: It's got a deficient ballcock, that's all.

GUS: A deficient what?

BEN: Ballcock.

GUS: No? Really?

BEN: That's what I should say.

GUS: Go on! That didn't occur to me.

[GUS wanders to his bed and presses the mattress.]

I didn't have a very restful sleep today, did you? It's not much of a bed. I could have done with another blanket too. (*He catches sight of a picture on the wall.*) Hello, what's this? (*Peering at it.*) "The First Eleven." Cricketers. You seen this, Ben?

BEN (*reading*): What?

GUS: The first eleven.

BEN: What?

GUS: There's a photo here of the first eleven.

BEN: What first eleven?

GUS (*studying the photo*): It doesn't say.

BEN: What about that tea?

GUS: They all look a bit old to me.

[GUS wanders downstage, looks out front, then all about the room.]

I wouldn't like to live in this dump. I wouldn't mind if you had a window, you could see what it looked like outside.

BEN: What do you want a window for?

GUS: Well, I like to have a bit of a view, Ben. It whiles away the time.

[He walks about the room.]

I mean, you come into a place when it's still dark, you come into a room you've never seen before, you sleep all day, you do your job, and then you go away in the night again.

[Pause.]

I like to get a look at the scenery. You never get the chance in this job.

BEN: You get your holidays, don't you?

GUS: Only a fortnight.

BEN *(lowering the paper)*: You kill me. Anyone would think you're working every day. How often do we do a job? Once a week? What are you complaining about?

GUS: Yes, but we've got to be on tap though, haven't we? You can't move out of the house in case a call comes.

BEN: You know what your trouble is?

GUS: What?

BEN: You haven't got any interests.

GUS: I've got interests.

BEN: What? Tell me one of your interests.

[Pause.]

GUS: I've got interests.

BEN: Look at me. What have I got?

GUS: I don't know. What?

BEN: I've got my woodwork. I've got my model boats. Have you ever seen me idle? I'm never idle. I know how to occupy my time, to its best advantage. Then when a call comes, I'm ready.

GUS: Don't you ever get a bit fed up?

BEN: Fed up? What with?

[Silence.]

[BEN reads. GUS feels in the pocket of his jacket, which hangs on the bed.]

GUS: You got any cigarettes? I've run out.

[The lavatory flushes off left.]

There she goes.

[GUS sits on his bed.]

No, I mean, I say the crockery's good. It is. It's very nice. But that's about all I can say for this place. It's worse than the last one. Remember that last place we were in? Last time, where was it? At least there was a wireless there. No,

honest. He doesn't seem to bother much about our comfort these days.

BEN: When are you going to stop jabbering?

GUS: You'd get rheumatism in a place like this, if you stay long.

BEN: We're not staying long. Make the tea, will you? We'll be on the job in a minute.

[GUS picks up a small bag by his bed and brings out a packet of tea. He examines it and looks up.]

GUS: Eh, I've been meaning to ask you.

BEN: What the hell is it now?

GUS: Why did you stop the car this morning, in the middle of that road?

BEN *(lowering the paper)*: I thought you were asleep.

GUS: I was, but I woke up when you stopped. You did stop, didn't you?

[Pause.]

In the middle of that road. It was still dark, don't you remember? I looked out. It was all misty. I thought perhaps you wanted to kip, but you were sitting up dead straight, like you were waiting for something.

BEN: I wasn't waiting for anything.

GUS: I must have fallen asleep again. What was all that about then? Why did you stop?

BEN *(picking up the paper)*: We were too early.

GUS: Early? *(He rises.)* What do you mean? We got the call, didn't we, saying we were to start right away. We did. We shoved out on the dot. So how could we be too early?

BEN *(quietly)*: Who took the call, me or you?

GUS: You.

BEN: We were too early.

GUS: Too early for what?

[Pause.]

You mean someone had to get out before we got in?

[He examines the bedclothes.]

I thought these sheets didn't look too bright. I thought they ponged a bit. I was too tired to notice when I got in this morning. Eh, that's taking a bit of a liberty, isn't it? I don't want to share my bed-sheets. I told you things were going down the drain. I mean, we've always had clean sheets laid on up till now. I've noticed it.

BEN: How do you know those sheets weren't clean?

GUS: What do you mean?

BEN: How do you know they weren't clean? You've spent the whole day in them, haven't you?

GUS: What, you mean it might be my pong? *(He sniffs*

sheets.) Yes. (*He sits slowly on bed.*) It could be my pong, I suppose. It's difficult to tell. I don't really know what I pong like, that's the trouble.

BEN (*referring to the paper*): Kaw!

GUS: Eh, Ben.

BEN: Kaw!

GUS: Ben.

BEN: What?

GUS: What town are we in? I've forgotten.

BEN: I've told you. Birmingham.

GUS: Go on!

[*He looks with interest about the room.*]

That's in the Midlands. The second biggest city in Great Britain. I'd never have guessed.

[*He snaps his fingers.*]

Eh, it's Friday today, isn't it? It'll be Saturday tomorrow.

BEN: What about it?

GUS (*excited*): We could go and watch the Villa.

BEN: They're playing away.

GUS: No, are they? Caarr! What a pity.

BEN: Anyway, there's no time. We've got to get straight back.

GUS: Well, we have done in the past, haven't we? Stayed over and watched a game, haven't we? For a bit of relaxation.

BEN: Things have tightened up, mate. They've tightened up.

[*GUS chuckles to himself.*]

GUS: I saw the Villa get beat in a cup tie once. Who was it against now? White shirts. It was one-all at half-time. I'll never forget it. Their opponents won by a penalty. Talk about drama. Yes, it was a disputed penalty. Disputed. They got beat two–one, anyway, because of it. You were there yourself.

BEN: Not me.

GUS: Yes, you were there. Don't you remember that disputed penalty?

BEN: No.

GUS: He went down just inside the area. Then they said he was just acting. I didn't think the other bloke touched him myself. But the referee had the ball on the spot.

BEN: Didn't touch him! What are you talking about? He laid him out flat!

GUS: Not the Villa. The Villa don't play that sort of game.

BEN: Get out of it.

[*Pause.*]

GUS: Eh, that must have been here, in Birmingham.

BEN: What must?

GUS: The Villa. That must have been here.

BEN: They were playing away.

GUS: Because you know who the other team was? It was the Spurs. It was Tottenham Hotspur.

BEN: Well, what about it?

GUS: We've never done a job in Tottenham.

BEN: How do you know?

GUS: I'd remember Tottenham.

[*BEN turns on his bed to look at him.*]

BEN: Don't make me laugh, will you?

[*BEN turns back and reads. GUS yawns and speaks through his yawn.*]

GUS: When's he going to get in touch?

[*Pause.*]

Yes, I'd like to see another football match. I've always been an ardent football fan. Here, what about coming to see the Spurs tomorrow?

BEN (*tonelessly*): They're playing away.

GUS: Who are?

BEN: The Spurs.

GUS: Then they might be playing here.

BEN: Don't be silly.

GUS: If they're playing away they might be playing here. They might be playing the Villa.

BEN (*tonelessly*): But the Villa are playing away.

[*Pause. An envelope slides under the door, right. GUS sees it. He stands, looking at it.*]

GUS: Ben.

BEN: Away. They're all playing away.

GUS: Ben, look here.

BEN: What?

GUS: Look.

[*BEN turns his head and sees the envelope. He stands.*]

BEN: What's that?

GUS: I don't know.

BEN: Where did it come from?

GUS: Under the door.

BEN: Well, what is it?

GUS: I don't know.

[*They stare at it.*]

BEN: Pick it up.

GUS: What do you mean?

BEN: Pick it up!

[*GUS slowly moves towards it, bends and picks it up.*]

What is it?
GUS: An envelope.
BEN: Is there anything on it?
GUS: No.
BEN: Is it sealed?
GUS: Yes.
BEN: Open it.
GUS: What?
BEN: Open it!

[GUS *opens it and looks inside.*]

What's in it?

[GUS *empties twelve matches into his hand.*]

GUS: Matches.
BEN: Matches?
GUS: Yes.
BEN: Show it to me.

[GUS *passes the envelope.* BEN *examines it.*]

Nothing on it. Not a word.
GUS: That's funny, isn't it?
BEN: It came under the door?
GUS: Must have done.
BEN: Well, go on.
GUS: Go on where?
BEN: Open the door and see if you can catch anyone
     outside.
GUS: Who, me?
BEN: Go on!

[GUS *stares at him, puts the matches in his pocket,
goes to his bed and brings a revolver from under the
pillow. He goes to the door, opens it, looks out and
shuts it.*]

GUS: No one.

[*He replaces the revolver.*]

BEN: What did you see?
GUS: Nothing.
BEN: They must have been pretty quick.

[GUS *takes the matches from pocket and looks at them.*]

GUS: Well, they'll come in handy.
BEN: Yes.
GUS: Won't they?
BEN: Yes, you're always running out, aren't you?
GUS: All the time.
BEN: Well, they'll come in handy then.
GUS: Yes.
BEN: Won't they?
GUS: Yes, I could do with them. I could do with them
     too.

BEN: You could, eh?
GUS: Yes.
BEN: Why?
GUS: We haven't got any.
BEN: Well, you've got some now, haven't you?
GUS: I can light the kettle now.
BEN: Yes, you're always cadging matches. How
     many have you got there?
GUS: About a dozen.
BEN: Well, don't lose them. Red too. You don't even
     need a box.

[GUS *probes his ear with a match.*]

(*Slapping his hand*). Don't waste them! Go on,
     go and light it.
GUS: Eh?
BEN: Go and light it.
GUS: Light what?
BEN:The kettle.
GUS:You mean the gas.
BEN: Who does?
GUS: You do.
BEN (*his eyes narrowing*): What do you mean, I mean
     the gas?
GUS: Well, that's what you mean, don't you? The gas.
BEN (*powerfully*): If I say go and light the kettle I
     mean go and light the kettle.
GUS: How can you light a kettle?
BEN: It's a figure of speech! Light the kettle. It's a fig-
     ure of speech!
GUS: I've never heard it.
BEN: Light the kettle! It's common usage!
GUS: I think you've got it wrong.
BEN (*menacing*): What do you mean?
GUS: They say put on the kettle.
BEN (*taut*): Who says?

[*They stare at each other, breathing hard.*]

(*Deliberately.*) I have never in all my life heard
     anyone say put on the kettle.
GUS: I bet my mother used to say it.
BEN: Your mother? When did you last see your
     mother?
GUS: I don't know, about—
BEN: Well, what are you talking about your mother
     for?

[*They stare.*]

Gus, I'm not trying to be unreasonable. I'm just try-
     ing to point out something to you.
GUS: Yes, but—
BEN: Who's the senior partner here, me or you?
GUS: You.
BEN: I'm only looking after your interests, Gus.
     You've got to learn, mate.

Gus: Yes, but I've never heard—
Ben (*vehemently*): Nobody says light the gas! What does the gas light?
Gus: What does the gas—?
Ben (*grabbing him with two hands by the throat, at arm's length*): THE KETTLE, YOU FOOL!

[*Gus takes the hands from his throat.*]

Gus: All right, all right.

[*Pause.*]

Ben: Well, what are you waiting for?
Gus: I want to see if they light.
Ben: What?
Gus: The matches.

[*He takes out the flattened box and tries to strike.*]

No.

[*He throws the box under the bed.
Ben stares at him.
Gus raises his foot.*]

Shall I try it on here?

[*Ben stares. Gus strikes a match on his shoe. It lights.*]

Here we are.
Ben (*wearily*): Put on the bloody kettle, for Christ's sake.

[*Ben goes to his bed, but, realising what he has said, stops and half turns. They look at each other. Gus slowly exits, left. Ben slams his paper down on the bed and sits on it, head in hands.*]

Gus (*entering*): It's going.
Ben: What?
Gus: The stove.

[*Gus goes to his bed and sits.*]

I wonder who it'll be tonight.

[*Silence.*]

Eh, I've been wanting to ask you something.
Ben (*putting his legs on the bed*): Oh, for Christ's sake.
Gus: No. I was going to ask you something.

[*He rises and sits on Ben's bed.*]

Ben: What are you sitting on my bed for?

[*Gus sits.*]

What's the matter with you? You're always asking me questions. What's the matter with you?

Gus: Nothing.
Ben: You never used to ask me so many damn questions. What's come over you?
Gus: No, I was just wondering.
Ben: Stop wondering. You've got a job to do. Why don't you just do it and shut up?
Gus: That's what I was wondering about.
Ben: What?
Gus: The job.
Ben: What job?
Gus (*tentatively*): I thought perhaps you might know something.

[*Ben looks at him.*]

I thought perhaps you—I mean—have you got any idea—who it's going to be tonight?
Ben: Who what's going to be?

[*They look at each other.*]

Gus (*at length*): Who it's going to be.

[*Silence.*]

Ben: Are you feeling all right?
Gus: Sure.
Ben: Go and make the tea.
Gus: Yes, sure.

[*Gus exits, left, Ben looks after him. He then takes his revolver from under the pillow and checks it for ammunition. Gus re-enters.*]

The gas has gone out.
Ben: Well, what about it?
Gus: There's a meter.
Ben: I haven't got any money.
Gus: Nor have I.
Ben: You'll have to wait.
Gus: What for?
Ben: For Wilson.
Gus: He might not come. He might just send a message. He doesn't always come.
Ben: Well, you'll have to do without it, won't you?
Gus: Blimey.
Ben: You'll have a cup of tea afterwards. What's the matter with you?
Gus: I like to have one before.

[*Ben holds the revolver up to the light and polishes it.*]

Ben: You'd better get ready anyway.
Gus: Well, I don't know, that's a bit much, you know, for my money.

[*He picks up a packet of tea from the bed and throws it into the bag.*]

I hope he's got a shilling, anyway, if he comes. He's entitled to have. After all, it's his place, he could have seen there was enough gas for a cup of tea.

BEN: What do you mean, it's his place?

GUS: Well, isn't it?

BEN: He's probably only rented it. It doesn't have to be his place.

GUS: I know it's his place. I bet the whole house is. He's not even laying on any gas now either.

[GUS sits on his bed.]

It's his place all right. Look at all the other places. You go to this address, there's a key there, there's a teapot, there's never a soul in sight—(*He pauses.*) Eh, nobody ever hears a thing, have you ever thought of that? We never get any complaints, do we, too much noise or anything like that? You never see a soul, do you?—except the bloke who comes. You ever noticed that? I wonder if the walls are sound-proof. (*He touches the wall above his bed.*) Can't tell. All you do is wait, eh? Half the time he doesn't even bother to put in an appearance, Wilson.

BEN: Why should he? He's a busy man.

GUS (*thoughtfully*): I find him hard to talk to, Wilson. Do you know that, Ben?

BEN: Scrub round it, will you?

[Pause.]

GUS: There are a number of things I want to ask him. But I can never get round to it, when I see him.

[Pause.]

I've been thinking about the last one.

BEN: What last one?

GUS: That girl.

[BEN grabs the paper, which he reads.]

(*Rising, looking down at* BEN): How many times have you read that paper?

[BEN slams the paper down and rises.]

BEN (*angrily*): What do you mean?

GUS: I was just wondering how many times you'd—

BEN: What are you doing, criticising me?

GUS: No, I was just—

BEN: You'll get a swipe round your earhole if you don't watch your step.

GUS: Now look here, Ben—

BEN: I'm not looking anywhere! (*He addresses the room.*) How many times have I—! A bloody liberty!

GUS: I didn't mean that.

BEN: You just get on with it, mate. Get on with it, that's all.

[BEN gets back on the bed.]

GUS: I was just thinking about that girl, that's all.

[GUS sits on his bed.]

She wasn't much to look at, I know, but still. It was a mess though, wasn't it? What a mess. Honest, I can't remember a mess like that one. They don't seem to hold together like men, women. A looser texture, like. Didn't she spread, eh? She didn't half spread. Kaw! But I've been meaning to ask you.

[BEN sits up and clenches his eyes.]

Who clears up after we've gone? I'm curious about that. Who does the clearing up? Maybe they don't clear up. Maybe they just leave them there, eh? What do you think? How many jobs have we done? Blimey, I can't count them. What if they never clear anything up after we've gone.

BEN (*pityingly*): You mutt. Do you think we're the only branch of this organisation? Have a bit of common. They got departments for every-thing.

GUS: What cleaners and all?

BEN: You birk!

GUS: No, it was that girl made me start to think—

[There is a loud clatter and racket in the bulge of wall between the beds, of something descending. They grab their revolvers, jump up and face the wall. The noise comes to a stop. Silence. They look at each other. BEN gestures sharply towards the wall. GUS approaches the wall slowly. He bangs it with his revolver. It is hollow. BEN moves to the head of his bed, his revolver cocked. GUS puts his revolver on his bed and pats along the bottom of the centre panel. He finds a rim. He lifts the panel. Disclosed is a serving-hatch, a "dumb waiter". A wide box is held by pulleys. GUS peers into the box. He brings out a piece of paper.]

BEN: What is it?

GUS: You have a look at it.

BEN: Read it.

GUS (*reading*): Two braised steak and chips. Two sago puddings. Two teas without sugar.

BEN: Let me see that. (*He takes the paper.*)

GUS (*to himself*): Two teas without sugar.

BEN: Mmnn.

GUS: What do you think of that?

BEN: Well—

[The box goes up. BEN levels his revolver.]

GUS: Give us a chance! They're in a hurry, aren't they?

[BEN re-reads the note. GUS looks over his shoulder.]

That's a bit—that's a bit funny, isn't it?

BEN (*quickly*): No. It's not funny. It probably used to be a café here, that's all. Upstairs. These places change hands very quickly.

GUS: A café?

BEN: Yes.

GUS: What, you mean this was the kitchen, down here?

BEN: Yes, they change hands overnight, these places. Go into liquidation. The people who run it, you know, they don't find it a going concern, they move out.

GUS: You mean the people who ran this place didn't find it a going concern and moved out?

BEN: Sure.

GUS: WELL, WHO'S GOT IT NOW?

[Silence.]

BEN: What do you mean, who's got it now?

GUS: Who's got it now? If they moved out, who moved in?

BEN: Well, that all depends—

[The box descends with a clatter and bang. BEN levels his revolver. GUS goes to the box and brings out a piece of paper.]

GUS (*reading*): Soup of the day. Liver and onions. Jam tart.

[A pause. GUS looks at BEN. BEN takes the note and reads it. He walks slowly to the hatch. GUS follows. BEN looks into the hatch but not up it. GUS puts his hand on BEN's shoulder. BEN throws it off. GUS puts his finger to his mouth. He leans on the hatch and swiftly looks up it. BEN flings him away in alarm. BEN looks at the note. He throws his revolver on the bed and speaks with decision.]

BEN: We'd better send something up.

GUS: Eh?

BEN: We'd better send something up.

GUS: Oh! Yes. Yes. Maybe you're right.

[They are both relieved at the decision.]

BEN (*purposefully*): Quick! What have you got in that bag?

GUS: Not much.

[GUS goes to the hatch and shouts up it.]

Wait a minute!

BEN: Don't do that!

[GUS examines the contents of the bag and brings them out, one by one.]

GUS: Biscuits. A bar of chocolate. Half a pint of milk.

BEN: That all?

GUS: Packet of tea.

BEN: Good.

GUS: We can't send the tea. That's all the tea we've got.

BEN: Well, there's no gas. You can't do anything with it, can you?

GUS: Maybe they can send us down a bob.

BEN: What else is there?

GUS (*reaching into bag*): One Eccles cake.

BEN: One Eccles cake?

GUS: Yes.

BEN: You never told me you had an Eccles cake.

GUS: Didn't I?

BEN: Why only one? Didn't you bring one for me?

GUS: I didn't think you'd be keen.

BEN: Well, you can't send up one Eccles cake, anyway.

GUS: Why not?

BEN: Fetch one of those plates.

GUS: All right.

[GUS goes towards the door, left, and stops.]

Do you mean I can keep the Eccles cake then?

BEN: Keep it?

GUS: Well, they don't know we've got it, do they?

BEN: That's not the point.

GUS: Can't I keep it?

BEN: No, you can't. Get the plate.

[GUS exits, left. BEN looks in the bag. He brings out a packet of crisps. Enter GUS with a plate.]

(*Accusingly, holding up the crisps*): Where did these come from?

GUS: What?

BEN: Where did these crisps come from?

GUS: Where did you find them?

BEN (*hitting him on the shoulder*): You're playing a dirty game, my lad!

GUS: I only eat those with beer!

BEN: Well, where were you going to get the beer?

GUS: I was saving them till I did.

BEN: I'll remember this. Put everything on the plate.

[They pile everything on to the plate. The box goes up without the plate.]

Wait a minute!

[They stand.]

GUS: It's gone up.
BEN: It's all your stupid fault, playing about!
GUS: What do we do now?
BEN: We'll have to wait till it comes down.

[BEN puts the plate on the bed, puts on his shoulder holster, and starts to put on his tie.]

You'd better get ready.

[GUS goes to his bed, puts on his tie, and starts to fix his holster.]

GUS: Hey, Ben.
BEN: What?
GUS: What's going on here?

[Pause.]

BEN: What do you mean?
GUS: How can this be a café?
BEN: It used to be a café.
GUS: Have you seen the gas stove?
BEN: What about it?
GUS: It's only got three rings.
BEN: So what?
GUS: Well, you couldn't cook much on three rings, not for a busy place like this.
BEN *(irritably)*: That's why the service is slow!

[BEN puts on his waistcoat.]

GUS: Yes, but what happens when we're not here? What do they do then? All these menus coming down and nothing going up. It might have been going on like this for years.

[BEN brushes his jacket.]

What happens when we go?

[BEN puts on his jacket.]

They can't do much business.

[The box descends. They turn about. GUS goes to the hatch and brings out a note.]

GUS *(reading)*: Macaroni Pastitsio. Ormitha Macarounada.
BEN: What was that?
GUS: Macaroni Pastitsio. Ormitha Macarounada.
BEN: Greek dishes.
GUS: No.
BEN: That's right.
GUS: That's pretty high class.
BEN: Quick before it goes up.

[GUS puts the plate in the box.]

GUS *(calling up the hatch)*: Three McVitie and Price! One Lyons Red Label! One Smith's Crisps! One Eccles cake! One Fruit and Nut!
BEN: Cadbury's.
GUS *(up the hatch)*: Cadbury's!
BEN *(handing the milk)*: One bottle of milk.
GUS *(up the hatch)*: One bottle of milk! Half a pint! *(He looks at the label.)* Express Dairy! *(He puts the bottle in the box.)*

[The box goes up.]

Just did it.
BEN: You shouldn't shout like that.
GUS: Why not?
BEN: It isn't done.

[BEN goes to his bed.]

Well, that should be all right, anyway, for the time being.
GUS: You think so, eh?
BEN: Get dressed, will you? It'll be any minute now.

[GUS puts on his waistcoat. BEN lies down and looks up at the ceiling.]

GUS: This is some place. No tea and no biscuits.
BEN: Eating makes you lazy, mate. You're getting lazy, you know that? You don't want to get slack on your job.
GUS: Who me?
BEN: Slack, mate, slack.
GUS: Who me? Slack?
BEN: Have you checked your gun? You haven't even checked your gun. It looks disgraceful, anyway. Why don't you ever polish it?

[GUS rubs his revolver on the sheet. BEN takes out a pocket mirror and straightens his tie.]

GUS: I wonder where the cook is. They must have had a few, to cope with that. Maybe they had a few more gas stoves. Eh! Maybe there's another kitchen along the passage.
BEN: Of course there is! Do you know what it takes to make an Ormitha Macarounada?
GUS: No, what?
BEN: An Ormitha—! Buck your ideas up, will you?
GUS: Takes a few cooks, eh?

[GUS puts his revolver in its holster.]

The sooner we're out of this place the better.

[He puts on his jacket.]

Why doesn't he get in touch? I feel like I've been here years. (*He takes his revolver out of its holster to check the ammunition.*) We've never let him down though, have we? We've never let him down. I was thinking only the other day, Ben. We're reliable, aren't we?

[*He puts his revolver back in its holster.*]

Still, I'll be glad when it's over tonight.

[*He brushes his jacket.*]

I hope the bloke's not going to get excited tonight, or anything. I'm feeling a bit off. I've got a splitting headache.

[*Silence.*]

[*The box descends. BEN jumps up. GUS collects the note.*]

(*Reading.*) One Bamboo Shoots, Water Chestnuts and Chicken. One Char Siu and Beansprouts.
BEN: Beansprouts?
GUS: Yes.
BEN: Blimey.
GUS: I wouldn't know where to begin.

[*He looks back at the box. The packet of tea is inside it. He picks it up.*]

They've sent back the tea.
BEN (*anxious*): What'd they do that for?
GUS: Maybe it isn't tea-time.

[*The box goes up. Silence.*]

BEN (*throwing the tea on the bed, and speaking urgently*): Look here. We'd better tell them.
GUS: Tell them what?
BEN: That we can't do it, we haven't got it.
GUS: All right then.
BEN: Lend us your pencil. We'll write a note.

[*GUS, turning for a pencil, suddenly discovers the speaking-tube, which hangs on the right wall of the hatch facing his bed.*]

GUS: What's this?
BEN: What?
GUS: This.
BEN (*examining it*): This? It's a speaking-tube.
GUS: How long has that been there?
BEN: Just the job. We should have used it before, instead of shouting up there.
GUS: Funny I never noticed it before.
BEN: Well, come on.

GUS: What do you do?
BEN: See that? That's a whistle.
GUS: What, this?
BEN: Yes, take it out. Pull it out.

[*GUS does so.*]

That's it.
GUS: What do we do now?
BEN: Blow into it.
GUS: Blow?
BEN: It whistles up there if you blow. Then they know you want to speak. Blow.

[*GUS blows. Silence.*]

GUS (*tube at mouth*): I can't hear a thing.
BEN: Now you speak! Speak into it!

[*GUS looks at BEN, then speaks into the tube.*]

GUS: The larder's bare!
BEN: Give me that!

[*He grabs the tube and puts it to his mouth.*]

(*Speaking with great deference.*) Good evening. I'm sorry to—bother you, but we just thought we'd better let you know that we haven't got anything left. We sent up all we had. There's no more food down here.

[*He brings the tube slowly to his ear.*]

What?

[*To mouth.*]

What?

[*To ear. He listens. To mouth.*]

No, all we had we sent up.

[*To ear. He listens. To mouth.*]

Oh, I'm very sorry to hear that.

[*To ear. He listens. To GUS.*]

The Eccles cake was stale.

[*He listens. To GUS.*]

The chocolate was melted.

[*He listens. To GUS.*]

The milk was sour.
GUS: What about the crisps?
BEN (*listening*): The biscuits were mouldy.

[He glares at GUS. Tube to mouth.]

Well, we're very sorry about that.

[Tube to ear.]

What?

[To mouth.]

What?

[To ear.]

Yes. Yes.

[To mouth.]

Yes certainly. Certainly. Right away.

[To ear. The voice has ceased. He hangs up the tube.]

(*Excitedly*). Did you hear that?

GUS: What?

BEN: You know what he said? Light the kettle! Not put on the kettle! Not light the gas! But light the kettle!

GUS: How can we light the kettle?

BEN: What do you mean?

GUS: There's no gas.

BEN (*clapping hand to head*): Now what do we do?

GUS: What did he want us to light the kettle for?

BEN: For tea. He wanted a cup of tea.

GUS: *He* wanted a cup of tea! What about me? I've been wanting a cup of tea all night!

BEN (*despairingly*): What do we do now?

GUS: What are we supposed to drink?

[BEN sits on his bed, staring.]

What about us?

[BEN sits.]

I'm thirsty too. I'm starving. And he wants a cup of tea. That beats the band, that does.

[BEN lets his head sink on to his chest.]

I could do with a bit of sustenance myself. What about you? You look as if you could do with something too.

[GUS sits on his bed.]

We send him up all we've got and he's not satisfied. No, honest, it's enough to make the cat laugh. Why did you send him up all that stuff? (*Thoughtfully.*) Why did I send it up?

[Pause.]

Who knows what he's got upstairs? He's probably got a salad bowl. They must have something up there. They won't get much from down here. You notice they didn't ask for any salads? They've probably got a salad bowl up there. Cold meat, radishes, cucumbers. Watercress. Roll mops.

[Pause.]

Hardboiled eggs.

[Pause.]

The lot. They've probably got a crate of beer too. Probably eating my crisps with a pint of beer now. Didn't have anything to say about those crisps, did he? They do all right, don't worry about that. You don't think they're just going to sit there and wait for stuff to come up from down here, do you? That'll get them nowhere.

[Pause.]

They do all right.

[Pause.]

And he wants a cup of tea.

[Pause.]

That's past a joke, in my opinion.

[He looks over at BEN, rises, and goes to him.]

What's the matter with you? You don't look too bright. I feel like an Alka-Seltzer myself.

[BEN sits up.]

BEN (*in a low voice*): Time's getting on.

GUS: I know. I don't like doing a job on an empty stomach.

BEN (*wearily*): Be quiet a minute. Let me give you your instructions.

GUS: What for? We always do it the same way, don't we?

BEN: Let me give you your instructions.

[GUS sighs and sits next to BEN on the bed. The instructions are stated and repeated automatically.]

When we get the call, you go over and stand behind the door.

GUS: Stand behind the door.

BEN: If there's a knock on the door you don't answer it.

GUS: If there's a knock on the door I don't answer it.

BEN: But there won't be a knock on the door.

GUS: So I won't answer it.
BEN: When the bloke comes in—
GUS: When the bloke comes in—
BEN: Shut the door behind him.
GUS: Shut the door behind him.
BEN: Without divulging your presence.
GUS: Without divulging my presence.
BEN: He'll see me and come towards me.
GUS: He'll see you and come towards you.
BEN: He won't see you.
GUS (*absently*): Eh?
BEN: He won't see you.
GUS: He won't see me.
BEN: But he'll see me.
GUS: He'll see you.
BEN: He won't know you're there.
GUS: He won't know you're there.
BEN: He won't know *you're* there.
GUS: He won't know I'm there.
BEN: I take out my gun.
GUS: You take out your gun.
BEN: He stops in his tracks.
GUS: He stops in his tracks.
BEN: If he turns round—
GUS: If he turns round—
BEN: You're there.
GUS: I'm here.

[*BEN frowns and presses his forehead.*]

You've missed something out.
BEN: I know. What?
GUS: I haven't taken my gun out, according to you.
BEN: You take your gun out—
GUS: After I've closed the door.
BEN: After you've closed the door.
GUS: You've never missed that out before, you know that?
BEN: When he sees you behind him—
GUS: Me behind him—
BEN: And me in front of him—
GUS: And you in front of him—
BEN: He'll feel uncertain—
GUS: Uneasy.
BEN: He won't know what to do.
GUS: So what will he do?
BEN: He'll look at me and he'll look at you.
GUS: We won't say a word.
BEN: We'll look at him.
GUS: He won't say a word.
BEN: He'll look at us.
GUS: And we'll look at him.
BEN: Nobody says a word.

[*Pause.*]

GUS: What do we do if it's a girl?

BEN: We do the same.
GUS: Exactly the same?
BEN: Exactly.

[*Pause.*]

GUS: We don't do anything different?
BEN: We do exactly the same.
GUS: Oh.

[*GUS rises, and shivers.*]

Excuse me.

[*He exits through the door on the left. BEN remains sitting on the bed, still.*
The lavatory chain is pulled once off left, but the lavatory does not flush.
Silence.
GUS re-enters and stops inside the door, deep in thought. He looks at BEN, then walks slowly across to his own bed. He is troubled. He stands, thinking. He turns and looks at BEN. He moves a few paces towards him.]

(*Slowly in a low, tense voice.*) Why did he send us matches if he knew there was no gas?

[*Silence.*
BEN stares in front of him. GUS crosses to the left side of BEN, to the foot of his bed, to get to his other ear.]

Ben. Why did he send us matches if he knew there was no gas?

[*BEN looks up.*]

Why did he do that?
BEN: Who?
GUS: Who sent us those matches?
BEN: What are you talking about?

[*GUS stares down at him.*]

GUS (*thickly*): Who is it upstairs?
BEN (*nervously*): What's one thing to do with another?
GUS: Who is it, though?
BEN: What's one thing to do with another?

[*BEN fumbles for his paper on the bed.*]

GUS: I asked you a question.
BEN: Enough!
GUS (*with growing agitation*): I asked you before. Who moved in? I asked you. You said the people who had it before moved out. Well, who moved in?

BEN (*hunched*): Shut up.
GUS: I told you, didn't I?
BEN (*standing*): Shut up!
GUS (*feverishly*): I told you before who owned this place, didn't I? I told you.

[*BEN hits him viciously on the shoulder.*]

I told you who ran this place, didn't I?

[*BEN hits him viciously on the shoulder.*]

(*Violently.*) Well, what's he playing all these games for? That's what I want to know. What's he doing it for?
BEN: What games?
GUS (*passionately, advancing*): What's he doing it for? We've been through our tests, haven't we? We got right through our tests, years ago, didn't we? We took them together, don't you remember, didn't we? We've proved ourselves before now, haven't we? We've always done our job. What's he doing all this for? What's the idea? What's he playing these games for?

[*The box in the shaft comes down behind them. The noise is this time accompanied by a shrill whistle, as it falls. GUS rushes to the hatch and seizes the note.*]

(*Reading.*) Scampi!

[*He crumples the note, picks up the tube, takes out the whistle, blows and speaks.*]

WE'VE GOT NOTHING LEFT! NOTHING! DO YOU UNDERSTAND?

[*BEN seizes the tube and flings GUS away. He follows GUS and slaps him hard, back-handed, across the chest.*]

BEN: Stop it! You maniac!
GUS: But you heard!
BEN (*savagely*): That's enough! I'm warning you!

[*Silence.
  BEN hangs the tube. He goes to his bed and lies down. He picks up his paper and reads.
  Silence.
  The box goes up.
  They turn quickly, their eyes meet. BEN turns to his paper.
  Slowly GUS goes back to his bed, and sits.
  Silence.
  The hatch falls back into place.
  They turn quickly, their eyes meet. BEN turns back to his paper.
  Silence.
  BEN throws his paper down.*]

BEN: Kaw!

[*He picks up the paper and looks at it.*]

Listen to this!

[*Pause.*]

What about that, eh?

[*Pause.*]

Kaw!

[*Pause.*]

Have you ever heard such a thing?
GUS (*dully*): Go on!
BEN: It's true.
GUS: Get away.
BEN: It's down here in black and white.
GUS (*very low*): Is that a fact?
BEN: Can you imagine it.
GUS: It's unbelievable.
BEN: It's enough to make you want to puke, isn't it?
GUS (*almost inaudible*): Incredible.

[*BEN shakes his head. He puts the paper down and rises. He fixes the revolver in his holster.
  GUS stands up. He goes towards the door on the left.*]

BEN: Where are you going?
GUS: I'm going to have a glass of water.

[*He exits. BEN brushes dust off his clothes and shoes. The whistle in the speaking-tube blows. He goes to it, takes the whistle out and puts the tube to his ear. He listens. He puts it to his mouth.*]

BEN: Yes.

[*To ear. He listens. To mouth.*]

Straight away. Right.

[*To ear. He listens. To mouth.*]

Sure we're ready.

[*To ear. He listens. To mouth.*]

Understood. Repeat. He has arrived and will be coming in straight away. The normal method to be employed. Understood.

[*To ear. He listens. To mouth.*]

Sure we're ready.

[*To ear. He listens. To mouth.*]

Right.

[He hangs the tube up.]

Gus!

[He takes out a comb and combs his hair, adjusts his jacket to diminish the bulge of the revolver. The lavatory flushes off left. BEN goes quickly to the door, left.]

Gus!

[The door right opens sharply. BEN turns, his revolver levelled at the door.
GUS stumbles in.
He is stripped of his jacket, waistcoat, tie, holster and revolver.
He stops, body stooping, his arms at his sides.
He raises his head and looks at BEN.
A long silence.
They stare at each other.]

Curtain

WOLE SOYINKA (b. 1934)

Wole Soyinka is the most celebrated African author writing in English, and the first African to receive the Nobel Prize for literature. His literary output includes poetry and novels, but as Soyinka himself admits, his Nobel Prize in 1986 was principally for his work in the theater. He was educated at the University of Ibadan and then took his bachelor's degree in English (1957) at the University of Leeds. He worked as play reader for the Royal Court Theatre in London, and when he returned to Nigeria in 1959, where he taught first at the University of Ife and later at the University of Ibadan, he produced his first plays, *The Swamp Dwellers* (1958) and *The Lion and the Jewel*, the former about superstition and the latter about colonial values. Throughout the next decade Soyinka developed a reputation as an actor, poet, and playwright with *The Trials of Brother Jero* (1960), *The Strong Breed* (1962), *Kongi's Harvest* (1964), and *The Road* (1965). He also founded his own company, the 1960 Masks, which produced *A Dance of the Forests* in October 1960 to celebrate Nigerian independence.

Because much of his work is critical of government policies, Soyinka was imprisoned from 1967 to 1969 during Nigeria's civil war, and his account of the experience, *The Man Died*, was published in 1972. His verse includes *Idanre and Other Poems* (1967) and *A Shuttle in the Crypt* (1972). During the 1970s Soyinka's work in the theater included an adaptation of Euripides' *The Bacchae* (1973) to a tribal and ritualistic setting and plays on contemporary African politics. His *Play of the Giants* (1984) is an attack on the abuse of political power by some African leaders.

Soyinka has been criticized by other African writers for writing in English rather than his native Yoruba and for being too concerned with European forms. Although Soyinka has written poetry in his native language, the majority of his work is in English by choice. Soyinka has opposed himself to cultural parochialism and consciously rejects what he regards as an insular view of African experience. Several of Soyinka's plays are about the commonalities among European and Yoruba tradition. *The Strong Breed* (1962), for example, examines a Yoruba sacrificial renewal ritual, and in so doing evokes strong echoes of similar rituals in European tradition.

The Strong Breed

In *The Strong Breed*, the village elders Jaguna and Oroge search for a "carrier" capable of bearing the burden of the community's guilt. By tradition the carrier must be an outsider. They settle on Ifada, an idiot, but his terrified protests bring an offer from Eman to become the carrier in Ifada's place. Eman demonstrates that he is one of "the strong breed," a man capable of undertaking the annual sacrifice needed to rejuvenate the community. Eman's sacrifice resembles that of Christ in Christian tradition. Like Christ, Eman is a teacher and a healer who champions the cause of the weak and oppressed. He willingly sacrifices himself for the community.

The Strong Breed reflects Soyinka's interest in Greek tragedy as well as in Christian sacrifice. In *The Bacchae* (1973) of Euripides and *Death and the King's Horsemen* (1976) Soyinka explores Greek notions of fate and inevitability, echoing his earlier work in this play. As in many of the Greek tragedies, the qualities of "the strong breed" in Eman are passed from father to son, from one generation to the next. In some ways like Oedipus, Eman leaves home after he has been identified as one of the strong breed by his father, but he unknowingly goes to another village where he fulfills the destiny he was born to.

Despite the Greek and Christian echoes, Soyinka's play is firmly rooted in native Yoruba tradition. Its plot turns on Yoruba ideas about heredity, about the individual's relationship to community, and about sacrifice. Soyinka seems determined to bring about an awareness that everything in the present is determined by the past, just as Eman's sacrifice is determined by his being his father's son—born to be one of the strong breed. At the end of the play Soyinka leaves his audiences wondering about Eman's sacrifice. Was this community worth dying for? Will Eman's sacrifice help any of the characters? Is Eman heroic in saving Ifada, courageous in his willingness to become the substitute, or is he simply a victim fated to fulfill the role of sacrifice?

The Strong Breed

Wole Soyinka

CHARACTERS

EMAN, a stranger
SUNMA, Jaguna's daughter
IFADA, an idiot
A GIRL
JAGUNA
OROGE

ATTENDANT STALWARTS, The villagers from
    Eman's past—
OLD MAN, his father
OMAE, his betrothed
TUTOR
PRIEST
ATTENDANTS, The villagers

The scenes are described briefly, but very often a darkened stage with lit areas will not only suffice but is necessary. Except for the one indicated place, there can be no break in the action. A distracting scene-change would be ruinous.

A mud house, with space in front of it. EMAN, in light buba and trousers stands at the window, looking out. Inside, SUNMA is clearing the table of what looks like a modest clinic, putting the things away in a cupboard. Another rough table in the room is piled with exercise books, two or three worn text-books, etc. SUNMA appears agitated. Outside, just below the window crouches IFADA. He looks up with a shy smile from time to time, waiting for EMAN to notice him.

SUNMA (*hesitant.*): You will have to make up your mind soon Eman. The lorry leaves very shortly.

[As EMAN does not answer, SUNMA continues her work, more nervously. Two villagers, obvious travellers, pass hurriedly in front of the house, the man has a small raffia sack, the woman a cloth-covered basket, the man enters first, turns and urges the woman who is just emerging to hurry.]

SUNMA (*seeing them, her tone is more intense.*): Eman, are we going or aren't we? You will leave it till too late.

EMAN (*quietly.*): There is still time—if you want to go.

SUNMA: If I want to go . . . and you?

[EMAN makes no reply.]

SUNMA (*bitterly.*): You don't really want to leave here. You never want to go away—even for a minute.

[IFADA continues his antics. EMAN eventually pats him on the head and the boy grins happily. Leaps up suddenly and returns with a basket of oranges which he offers to EMAN.]

EMAN: My gift for today's festival enh?

[IFADA nods, grinning.]

EMAN: They look ripe—that's a change.

SUNMA (*she has gone inside the room. Looks round the door.*): Did you call me?

EMAN: No. (*She goes back.*) And what will you do tonight Ifada? Will you take part in the dancing? Or perhaps you will mount your own masquerade?

[IFADA shakes his head, regretfully.]

EMAN: You won't? So you haven't any? But you would like to own one.

[IFADA nods eagerly.]

EMAN: Then why don't you make your own?

[IFADA stares, puzzled by this idea.]

EMAN: Sunma will let you have some cloth you know. And bits of wool . . .

SUNMA (*coming out.*): Who are you talking to Eman?

EMAN: Ifada. I am trying to persuade him to join the young maskers.

SUNMA (*losing control.*): What does he want here? Why is he hanging round us?

EMAN (*amazed.*): What . . . ? I said Ifada. Ifada.

SUNMA: Just tell him to go away. Let him go and play somewhere else!

EMAN: What is this? Hasn't he always played here?

SUNMA: I don't want him here. (*Rushes to the window.*) Get away idiot. Don't bring your foolish face here any more, do you hear? Go on, go away from here . . .

EMAN (*restraining her.*): Control yourself Sunma. What on earth has got into you?

[IFADA, hurt and bewildered, backs slowly away.]

SUNMA: He comes crawling round here like some horrible insect. I never want to lay my eyes on him again.

EMAN: I don't understand. It *is* Ifada you know. Ifada! The unfortunate one who runs errands for you and doesn't hurt a soul.

SUNMA: I cannot bear the sight of him.

EMAN: You can't do what? It can't be two days since he last fetched water for you.

SUNMA: What else can he do except that? He is useless. Just because we have been kind to him . . . Others would have put him in an asylum.

EMAN: You are not making sense. He is not a madman, he is just a little more unlucky than other children. (*Looks keenly at her.*) But what is the matter?

SUNMA: It's nothing. I only wish we had sent him off to one of those places for creatures like him.

EMAN: He is quite happy here. He doesn't bother anyone and he makes himself useful.

SUNMA: Useful! Is that one of any use to anybody? Boys of his age are already earning a living but all he can do is hang around and drool at the mouth.

EMAN: But he does work. You know he does a lot for you.

SUNMA: Does he? And what about the farm you started for him! Does he ever work on it? Or have you forgotten that it was really for Ifada you cleared that bush. Now you have to go and work it yourself. You spend all your time on it and you have no room for anything else.

EMAN: That wasn't his fault. I should first have asked him if he was fond of farming.

SUNMA: Oh, so he can choose? As if he shouldn't be thankful for being allowed to live.

EMAN: Sunma!

SUNMA: He does not like farming but he knows how to feast his dumb mouth on the fruits.

EMAN: But I want him to. I encourage him.

SUNMA: Well keep him. I don't want to see him any more.

EMAN (*after some moments.*): But why? You cannot be telling all the truth. What has he done?

SUNMA: The sight of him fills me with revulsion.

EMAN (*goes to her and holds her.*): What really is it? (SUNMA *avoids his eyes.*) It is almost as if you are forcing yourself to hate him. Why?

SUNMA: That is not true. Why should I?

EMAN: Then what is the secret? You've even played with him before.

SUNMA: I have always merely tolerated him. But I cannot any more. Suddenly my disgust won't take him any more. Perhaps . . . perhaps it is the new year. Yes, yes, it must be the new year.

EMAN: I don't believe that.

SUNMA: It must be. I am a woman, and these things matter. I don't want a mis-shape near me. Surely for one day inthe in the year, I may demand some wholesomeness.

EMAN: I do not understand you.

[SUNMA is silent.]

It was cruel of you. And to Ifada who is so helpless and alone. We are the only friends he has.

SUNMA: No, just you. I have told you, with me it has always been only an act of kindness. And now I haven't any pity left for him.

EMAN: No. He is not a wholesome being.

[He turns back to looking through the window.]

SUNMA (*half-pleading.*): Ifada can rouse your pity. And yet if anything, I need more kindness from you. Every time my weakness betrays me, you close your mind against me . . . Eman . . . Eman . . .

[A GIRL comes in view, dragging an effigy by a rope attached to one of its legs. She stands for a while gazing at EMAN. IFADA, who has crept back shyly to his accustomed position, becomes somewhat excited when he sees the effigy. The GIRL is unsmiling. She possesses in fact, a kind of inscrutability which does not make her hard but is unsettling.]

GIRL: Is the teacher in?

Eman (*smiling.*): No.

GIRL: Where is he gone?

EMAN: I don't really know. Shall I ask?

GIRL: Yes, do.

Eman (*turning slightly.*): Sunma, a girl outside wants to know . . .

[SUNMA turns away, goes into the inside room.]

EMAN: Oh. (*Returns to the GIRL, but his slight gaiety is lost.*) There is no one at home who can tell me.

GIRL: Why are you not in?

EMAN: I don't really know. Maybe I went some-where.

GIRL: All right. I will wait until you get back.

[She pulls the effigy to her, sits down.]

Eman (*slowly regaining his amusement.*): So you are all ready for the new year.

GIRL (*without turning round.*): I am not going to the festival.

EMAN: Then why have you got that?

GIRL: Do you mean my carrier? I am unwell you know. My mother says it will take away my sickness with the old year.

EMAN: Won't you share the carrier with your play-mates?

GIRL: Oh, no. Don't you know I play alone? The other children won't come near me. Their mothers would beat them.

EMAN: But I have never seen you here. Why don't you come to the clinic?

GIRL: My mother said No.

[Gets up, begins to move off.]

EMAN: You are not going away?

GIRL: I must not stay talking to you. If my mother caught me . . .

EMAN: All right, tell me what you want before you go.

GIRL (*stops. For some moments she remains silent.*): I must have some clothers clothes for my carrier.

EMAN: Is that all? You wait a moment.

[SUNMA comes out as he takes down a buba from the wall. She goes to the window and glares almost with hatred at the GIRL. The GIRL retreats hastily, still impassive.]

By the way Sunma, do you know who that girl is?

SUNMA: I hope you don't really mean to give her that.

EMAN: Why not? I hardly ever use it.

SUNMA: Just the same don't give it to her. She is not a child. She is as evil as the rest of them.

EMAN: What has got into you today?

SUNMA: All right, all right. Do what you wish.

[She withdraws. Baffled, EMAN returns to the window.]

EMAN: Here . . . will this do? Come and look at it.

GIRL: Throw it.

EMAN: What is the matter? I am not going to eat you.

GIRL: No one lets me come near them.

EMAN: But I am not afraid of catching your disease.

GIRL: Throw it.

[EMAN shrugs and tosses the buba. She takes it without a word and slips it on the effigy, completely absorbed in the task. EMAN watches for a while, then joins SUNMA in the inner room.]

GIRL *(after a long, cool survey of* IFADA.*)*: You have a head like a spider's egg, and your mouth dribbles like a roof. But there is no one else. Would you like to play?

[IFADA nods eagerly, quite excited.]

GIRL: You will have to get a stick.

[IFADA rushes around, finds a big stick and whirls it aloft, bearing down on the carrier.]

GIRL: Wait. I don't want you to spoil it. If it gets gts torn I shall drive you away. Now, let me see how you are going to beat it.

[IFADA hits it gently.]

GIRL: You may hit harder than that. As long as there is something left to hand hang at the end.

[She appraises him up and down.]

You are not very tall . . . will you be able to hang it from a tree?

[IFADA nods, grinning happily.]

GIRL: You will hang it up and I will set fire to it. *(Then, with surprising venom.)* But just because you are helping me, don't think it is going to cure you. I am the one who will get well at midnight, do you understand? It is my carrier and it is for me alone.

[She pulls at the rope to make sure that it is well attached to the leg.]

Well don't stand there drooling. Let's go.

[She begins to walk off, dragging the effigy in the dust. IFADA remains where he is for some moments, seemingly puzzled. Then his face breaks into a large grin and he leaps after the procession, belabouring the effigy with all his strength. The stage remains empty for some moments. Then the horn of a lorry is sounded and SUNMA rushes out. The hooting continues for some time with a rhythmic pattern. EMAN comes out.]

EMAN: I am going to the village . . . I shan't be back before nightfall.

SUNMA *(blankly.)*: Yes.

EMAN *(hesitates.)*: Well what do you want me to do?

SUNMA: The lorry was hooting just now.

EMAN: I didn't hear it.

SUNMA: It will leave in a few minutes. And you did promise we could go away.

EMAN: I promised nothing. Will you go home by yourself or shall I come back for you?

SUNMA: You don't even want me here?

EMAN: But you have to go home haven't you?

SUNMA: I had hoped we would watch the new year together—in some other place.

EMAN: Why do you continue to distress yourself?

SUNMA: Because you will not listen to me. Why do you continue to stay where nobody wants you?

EMAN: That is not true.

SUNMA: It is. You are wasting your life on people who really want you out of their way.

EMAN: You don't know what you are saying.

SUNMA: You think they love you? Do you think they care at all for what you—or I—do for them?

EMAN: *Them?* These are your own people. Sometimes you talk as if you were a stranger too.

SUNMA: I wonder if I really sprang from here. I know they are evil and I am not. From the oldest to the smallest child, they are nourished in evil and unwholesomeness in which I have no part.

EMAN: You knew this when you returned?

SUNMA: You reproach me then for trying at all?

EMAN: I reproach you with nothing. But you must leave me out of your plans. I can have no part in them.

SUNMA *(nearly pleading.)*: Once I could have run away. I would have gone and never looked back.

EMAN: I cannot listen when you talk like that.

SUNMA: I swear to you, I do not mind what happens afterwards. But you must help me tear myself away from here. I can no longer do it by myself . . . It is only a little thing. And we have worked so hard this past year . . . surely we can go away for a week . . . even a few days would be enough.

EMAN: I have told you Sunma . . .

SUNMA *(desperately.)*: Two days Eman. Only two days.

EMAN *(distressed.)*: But I tell you I have no now wish to go.

SUNMA *(suddenly angry.)*: Are you so afraid then?

EMAN: Me? Afraid of what?

SUNMA: You think you will not want to come back.

EMAN *(pitying.)*: You cannot dare me that way.

SUNMA: Then why won't you leave here, even for an hour? If you are so sure that your life is settled here, why are you afraid to do this thing for me? What is so wrong that you will not go into the next town for a day or two?

EMAN: I don't want to. I do not have to persuade you, or myself about anything. I simply have no desire to go away.

SUNMA (*his quiet confidence appears to incense her.*): You are afraid. You accuse me of losing my sense of mission, but you are afraid to put yours to the test.

EMAN: You are wrong Sunma. I have no sense of mission. But I have found peace here and I am content with that.

SUNMA: I haven't. For a while I thought that too, but I found there could be no peace in the midst of so much cruelty. Eman, tonight at least, the last night of the old year . . .

EMAN: No Sunma. I find this too distressing; you should go home now.

SUNMA: It is the time for making changes in one's life Eman. Let's breathe in the new year away from here.

EMAN: You are hurting yourself.

SUNMA: Tonight. Only tonight. We will come back tomorrow, as early as you like. But let us go away for this one night. Don't let another year break on me in this place . . . you don't know how important it is to me, but I will tell you, I will tell you on the way . . . but we must not be here today, Eman, do this one thing for me.

EMAN (*sadly.*): I cannot.

SUNMA (*suddenly calm.*): I was a fool to think it would be otherwise. The whole village may use you as they will but for me there is nothing. Sometimes I think you believe that doing anything for me makes you unfaithful to some part of your life. If it was a woman then I pity her for what she must have suffered.

[*EMAN winces and hardens slowly. SUNMA notices nothing.*]

Keeping faith with so much is slowly making you inhuman. (*Seeing the change in* EMAN.) Eman. Eman. What is it?

[*As she goes towards him, EMAN goes into the house.*]

SUNMA (*apprehensive, follows him.*): What did I say? Eman, forgive me, forgive me please.

[*EMAN remains facing into the slow darkness of the room. SUNMA, distressed, cannot decide what to do.*]

I swear I didn't know . . . I would not have said it for all the world.

[*A lorry is heard taking off somewhere nearby. The sound comes up and slowly fades away into the distance. SUNMA starts visibly goes slowly to the window.*]

SUNMA (*as the sound dies off, to herself.*): What happens now?

EMAN (*joining her at the window.*): What did you say?

SUNMA: Nothing.

EMAN: Was that not the lorry going off?

SUNMA: It was.

EMAN: I am sorry I couldn't help you.

[*SUNMA, about to speak, changes her mind.*]

EMAN: I think you ought to go home now.

SUNMA: No, don't send me away. It's the least you can do for me. Let me stay here until all the noise is over.

EMAN: But are you not needed at home? You have a part in the festival.

SUNMA: I have renounced it; I am Jaguna's eldest daughter only in name.

EMAN: Renouncing one's self is not so easy—surely you know that.

SUNMA: I don't want to talk about it. Will you at least let us be together tonight?

EMAN: But . . .

SUNMA: Unless you are afraid my father will accuse you of harbouring me.

EMAN: All right, we will go out together.

SUNMA: Go out? I want us to stay here.

EMAN: When there is so much going on outside?

SUNMA: Some day you will wish that you went away when I tried to make you.

EMAN: Are we going back to that?

SUNMA: No. I promise you I will not recall it again. But you must know that it was also for your sake that I tried to get us away.

EMAN: For me? How?

SUNMA: By yourself you can do nothing here. Have you not noticed how tightly we shut out strangers? Even if you lived here for a lifetime, you would remain a stranger.

EMAN: Perhaps that is what I like. There is peace in being a stranger.

SUNMA: For a while perhaps. But they would reject you in the end. I tell you it is only I who stand between you and contempt. And because of this you have earned their hatred. I don't know why I say this now, except that somehow, I feel that it no longer matters. It is only I who have stood between you and much humiliation.

EMAN: Think carefully before you say any more. I am incapable of feeling indebted to you. This will make no difference at all.

SUNMA: I ask for nothing. But you must know it all the same. It is true I hadn't the strength to go by myself. And I must confess this now, if you had come with me, I would have done everything to keep you from returning.

EMAN: I know that.

SUNMA: You see, I bare myself to you. For days I had thought it over, this was to be a new beginning for us. And I placed my fate wholly in your hands. Now the thought will not leave me, I have a feeling which will not be shaken off, that in some way, you have tonight totally destroyed my life.

EMAN: You are depressed, you don't know what you are saying.

SUNMA: Don't think I am accusing you. I say all this only because I cannot help it.

EMAN: We must not remain shut up here. Let us go and be part of the living.

SUNMA: No. Leave them alone.

EMAN: Surely you don't want to stay indoors when the whole town is alive with rejoicing.

SUNMA: Rejoicing! Is that what it is seems to you? No, let us remain here. Whatever happens I must not go out until all this is over.

[There is silence. It has grown much darker.]

EMAN: I shall light the lamp.

SUNMA (*eager to do something.*): No, let me do it.

[She goes into the inner room.

EMAN paces the room, stops by a shelf and toys with the seeds in an 'ayo' board, takes down the whole board and places it on a table, playing by himself.

The GIRL is now seen coming back, still dragging her 'carrier'.

IFADA brings up the rear as before. As he comes round the corner of the house two men emerge from the shadows. A sack is thrown over IFADA's head, the rope is pulled tight rendering him instantly helpless. The GIRL has reached the front of the house before she turns round at the sound of scuffle. She is in time to see IFADA thrown over the shoulders and borne away. Her face betraying no emotion at all, the GIRL backs slowly away, turns and flees, leaving the 'carrier' behind.

SUNMA enters, carrying two kerosene lamps. She hangs one up from the wall.]

EMAN: One is enough.

SUNMA: I want to leave one outside.

[She goes out, hangs the lamp from a nail just above the door. As she turns she sees the effigy and gasps. EMAN rushes out.]

EMAN: What is it? Oh, is that what frightened you?

SUNMA: I thought . . . I didn't really see it properly.

[EMAN goes towards the object, stoops to pick it up.]

EMAN: It must belong to that sick girl.

SUNMA: Don't touch it.

EMAN: Let's keep it for her.

SUNMA: Leave it alone. Don't touch it Eman.

EMAN (*shrugs and goes back.*): You are very nervous.

SUNMA: Let's go in.

EMAN: Wait. (*He detains her by the door, under the lamp.*) I know there is something more than you've told me. What are you afraid of tonight?

SUNMA: I was only scared by that thing. There is nothing else.

EMAN: I am not blind Sunma. It is true I would not run away when you wanted me to, but that doesn't mean I do not feel things. What does tonight really mean that it makes you so helpless?

SUNMA: It is only a mood. And your indifference to me . . . let's go in.

[EMAN moves aside and she enters; he remains there for a moment and then follows.

She fiddles with the lamp, looks vaguely round the room, then goes and shuts the door, bolting it. When she turns, it is to meet EMAN's eyes, questioning.]

SUNMA: There is a cold wind coming in.

[EMAN keeps his gaze on her.]

SUNMA: It *was* getting cold.

[She moves guiltily to the table and stands by the 'ayo' board, rearranging the seeds. EMAN remains where he is a few moments, then brings a stool and sits opposite her. She sits down also and they begin to play in silence.]

SUNMA: What brought you here at all, Eman? And what makes you stay?

[There is another silence.]

SUNMA: I am not trying to share your life. I know you too well by now. But at least we have worked together since you came. Is there nothing at all I deserve to know?

EMAN: Let me continue a stranger—especially to you. Those who have much to give fulfil themselves only in total loneliness.

SUNMA: Then there is no love in what you do.

EMAN: There is. Love comes to me more easily with strangers.

SUNMA: That is unnatural.

EMAN: Not for me. I know I find consummation only when I have spent myself for a total stranger.

SUNMA: It seems unnatural to me. But then I am a woman. I have a woman's longings and weaknesses. And the ties of blood are very strong in me.

EMAN (*smiling.*): You think I have cut loose from all these—ties of blood.

SUNMA: Sometimes you are so inhuman.

EMAN: I don't know what that means. But I am very much my father's son.

[*They play in silence. Suddenly* EMAN *pauses listening.*]

EMAN: Did you hear that?

SUNMA (*quickly.*): I heard nothing . . . it's your turn.

EMAN: Perhaps some of the mummers are coming this way.

[EMAN *about to play, leaps up suddenly.*]

SUNMA: What is it? Don't you want to play any more?

[EMAN *moves to the door.*]

SUNMA: No. Don't don't go out Eman.

EMAN: If it's the dancers I want to ask them to stay. At least we won't have to miss everything.

SUNMA: No, no. Don't open the door. Let us keep out everyone tonight.

[*A terrified and disordered figure bursts suddenly round the corner, past the window and begins hammering at the door. It is* IFADA. *Desperate with terror, he pounds madly at the door, dumb-moaning all the while.*]

EMAN: Isn't that Ifada?

SUNMA: They are only fooling about. Don't pay any attention.

EMAN (*looks round the window.*): That is Ifada. (*Begins to unbolt the door.*)

SUNMA (*pulling at his hands.*): It is only a trick they are playing on you. Don't take any notice Eman.

EMAN: What are you saying? The boy is out of his senses with fear.

SUNMA: No, no. Don't interfere Eman. For God's sake don't interfere.

EMAN: Do you know something of this then?

SUNMA: You are a stranger here Eman. Just leave us alone and go your own way. There is nothing you can do.

EMAN (*he tries to push her out of the way but she clings fiercely to him.*): Have you gone mad? I tell you the boy must come in.

SUNMA: Why won't you listen to me Eman? I tell you it's none of your business. For your own sake do as I say.

[EMAN *pushes her off, unbolts the door.* IFADA *rushes in, clasps* EMAN *round the knees, dumb-moaning against his legs.*]

EMAN (*manages to re-bolt the door.*): What is it Ifada?

What is the matter?

[*Shouts and voices are heard coming nearer the house.*]

SUNMA: Before it's too late, let him go. For once Eman, believe what I tell you. Don't harbour him or you will regret it all your life.

[EMAN *tries to calm* IFADA *who becomes more and more abject as the outside voices get nearer.*]

EMAN: What have they done to him? At least tell me that. What is going on Sunma?

SUNMA: (*with sudden venom.*) Monster! Could you not take yourself somewhere else?

EMAN: Stop talking like that.

SUNMA: He could have run into the bush couldn't he? Toad! Why must he follow us with his own disasters!

VOICES OUTSIDE: It's here . . . Round the back . . . Spread, spread . . . this way . . . no, head him off . . . use the bush path and head him off . . . get some more lights . . .

[EMAN *listens. Lifts* IFADA *bodily and carries him into the inner room. Returns at once, shutting the door behind him.*]

SUNMA (*slumps into a chair, resigned.*): You always follow your own way.

JAGUNA (*comes round the corner followed by* OROGE *and three men, one bearing a torch.*): I knew he would come here.

OROGE: I hope our friend won't make trouble.

JAGUNA: He had better not. You, recall all the men and tell them to surround the house.

OROGE: But he may not be in the house after all.

JAGUNA: I know he is here . . . (*to the men.*) . . . go on, do as I say.

[*He bangs on the door.*]

Teacher, open your door . . . you two stay by the door. If I need you I will call you.

[EMAN *opens the door.*]

JAGUNA (*speaks as he enters.*): We know he is here.

EMAN: Who?

JAGUNA: Don't let us waste time. We are grown men, teacher. You understand me and I understand you. But we must take back the boy.

EMAN: This is my house.

JAGUNA: Daughter, you'd better tell your friend. I don't think he quite knows our ways. Tell him why he must give up the boy.

SUNMA: Father, I . . .

JAGUNA: Are you going to tell him or aren't you?

SUNMA: Father, I beg you, leave us alone tonight . . .

JAGUNA: I thought you might be a hindrance. Go home then if you will not use your sense.

SUNMA: But there are other ways . . .

JAGUNA (turning to the men.): See that she gets home. I no longer trust her. If she gives trouble carry her. And see that the women stay with her until all this is over.

[SUMNA departs, accompanied by one of the men.]

JAGUNA: Now, teacher . . .

OROGE (restrains him.): You see, Mister Eman, it is like this. Right now, nobody knows that Ifada has taken refuge here. No one except us and our men—and they know how to keep their mouths shut. We don't want to have to burn down the house you see, but if the word gets around, we would have no choice.

JAGUNA: In fact, it may be too late already. A carrier should end up in the bush, not in a house. Anyone who doesn't guard his door when the carrier goes by has himself to blame. A contaminated house should be burnt down.

OROGE: But we are willing to let it pass. Only, you must bring him out quickly.

EMAN: All right. But at least you will let me ask you something.

JAGUNA: What is there to ask? Don't you understand what we have told you?

EMAN: Yes. But why did you pick on a helpless boy. Obviously he is not willing.

JAGUNA: What is the man talking about? Ifada is a godsend. Does he have to be willing?

EMAN: In my home, we believe that a man should be willing.

OROGE: Mister Eman, I don't think you quite understand. This is not a simple matter at all. I don't know what you do, but here, it is not a cheap task for anybody. No one in his senses would do such a job. Why do you think we give refuge to idiots like him? We don't know where he came from. One morning, he is simply there, just like that. From nowhere at all. You see, there is a purpose in that.

JAGUNA: We only waste time.

OROGE: Jaguna, be patient. After all, the man has been with us for some time now and deserves to know. The evil of the old year is no light thing to load on any man's head.

EMAN: I know something about that.

OROGE: You do? (Turns to JAGUNA who snorts impatiently.) You see, I told you so didn't I? From the moment you came I saw you were one of the knowing ones.

JAGUNA: Then let him behave like a man and give back the boy.

EMAN: It is you who are not behaving like men.

JAGUNA (advances aggressively.): That is a quick mouth you have . . .

OROGE: Patience Jaguna . . . if you want the new year to cushion the land there must be no deeds of anger. What did you mean my friend?

EMAN: It is a simple thing. A village which cannot produce its own carrier contains no men.

JAGUNA: Enough. Let there be no more talk or this business will be ruined by some rashness. You . . . come inside. Bring the boy out, he must be in the room there.

EMAN: Wait.

[The men hestitate.]

JAGUNA (hitting the nearer one and propelling him forward.): Go on. Have you changed masters now that you listen to what he says?

OROGE (sadly.): I am sorry you would not understand Mister Eman. But you ought to know that no carrier may return to the village. If he does, the people will stone him to death. It has happened before. Surely it is too much to ask a man to give up his own soil.

EMAN: I know others who have done more.

[IFADA is brought out, abjectly dumb-moaning.]

EMAN: You can see him with your own eyes. Does it really have meaning to use one as unwilling as that.

OROGE (smiling.): He shall be willing. Not only willing but actually joyous. I am the one who prepares them all, and I have seen worse. This one escaped before I began to prepare him for the event. But you will see him later tonight, the most joyous creature in the festival. Then perhaps you will understand.

EMAN: Then it is only a deceit. Do you believe the spirit of a new year is so easily fooled?

JAGUNA: Take him out. (The men carry out IFADA.) You see, it is so easy to talk. You say there are no men in this village because they cannot provide a willing carrier. And yet I heard Oroge tell you we only use strangers. There is only one other stranger in the village, but I have not heard him offer himself (spits.) It is so easy to talk is it not?

[He turns his back on him.
They go off, taking IFADA with them, limp and silent. The only sign of life is that he strains his neck to keep his eyes on EMAN till the very moment that he disappears from sight. EMAN remains where they left him, staring after the group.]

[A black-out lasting no more than a minute. The lights come up slowly and IFADA is seen returning to the house. He stops at the window and looks in. Seeing no one, he bangs on the sill.

Appears surprised that there is no response. He slithers down on his favourite spot, then sees the effigy still lying where the GIRL had dropped it in her flight. After some hesitation, he goes towards it, begins to strip it of the clothing. Just then the GIRL comes in.]

GIRL: Hey, leave that alone. You know it's mine.

[IFADA pauses, then speeds up his action.]

GIRL: I said it is mine. Leave it where you found it.

[She rushes at him and begins to struggle for possession of the carrier.]

GIRL: Thief! Thief! Let it go, it is mine. Let it go. You
    animal, just because I let you play with it.
    Idiot! Idiot!

[The struggle becomes quite violent. The GIRL is hanging to the effigy and IFADA lifts her with it, flinging her all about. The GIRL hangs on grimly.]

GIRL: You are spoiling it . . . why don't you get your
    own? Thief! Let it go you thief!

[SUNMA comes in walking very fast, throwing apprehensive glances over her shoulder. Seeing the two children, she becomes immediately angry. Advances on them.]

SUNMA: So you've made this place your playground.
    Get away you untrained pigs. Get out of here.

[IFADA flees at once, the GIRL retreats also, retaining possession of the 'carrier'.

SUNMA goes to the door. She has her hand on the door when the significance of IFADA's presence strikes her for the first time. She stands rooted to the spot, then turns slowly round.]

SUNMA: Ifada! What are you doing here?

[IFADA is bewildered. SUNMA turns suddenly and rushes into the house, flying into the inner room and out again.]

    Eman! Eman! Eman!

[She rushes outside.]

    Where did he go? Where did they take him?

[IFADA distressed, points. SUNMA seizes him by the arm, drags him off.]

Take me there at once. God help you if we are
    too late. You loathsome thing, if you have let
    him suffer . . .

[Her voice fades into other shouts, running footsteps, banged tins, bells, dogs, etc., rising in volume.]

[It is a narrow passage-way between two mud-houses. At the far end one man after another is seen running across the entry, the noise dying off gradually.

About half-way down the passage, EMAN is crouching against the wall, tense with apprehension. As the noise dies off, he seems to relax, but the alert hunted look is still in his eyes which are ringed in a reddish colour. The rest of his body has been whitened with a floury substance. He is naked down to the waist, wears a baggy pair of trousers, calf-length, and around both feet are bangles.]

EMAN: I will simply stay here till dawn. I have done
    enough.

[A window is thrown open and a woman empties some slop from a pail. With a startled cry EMAN leaps aside to avoid it and the woman puts out her head.]

WOMAN: Oh, my head. What have I done! Forgive
    me neighbour. . . . Eh, it's the carrier!

[Very rapidly she clears her throat and spits on him, flings the pail at him and runs off, shouting.]

    He's here. The carrier is hiding in the passage.
    Quickly, I have found the carrier!

[The cry is taken up and EMAN flees down the passage. Shortly afterwards his pursuers come pouring down the passage in full cry. After the last of them come JAGUNA and OROGE.]

OROGE: Wait, wait. I cannot go so fast.

JAJUNA: We will rest a little then. We can do nothing
    anyway.

OROGE: If only he had let me prepare him.

JAGUNA: They are the ones who break first, these
    fools who think they were born to carry suffer-
    ing like a hat. What are we to do now?

OROGE: When they catch him I must prepare him.

JAGUNA: He? It will be impossible now. There can be
    no joy left in that one.

OROGE: Still, it took him by surprise. He was not
    expecting what he met.

JAGUNA: Why then did he refuse to listen? Did he
    think he was coming to sit down to a feast. He
    had not even gone through one compound
    before he bolted. Did he think he was taken
    round the people to be blessed? A woman, that
    is all he is.

OROGE: No, no. He took the beating well enough. I think he is the kind who would let himself be beaten from night till dawn and not utter a sound. He would let himself be stoned until he dropped dead.

JAGUNA: Then what made him run like a coward?

OROGE: I don't know. I don't really know. It is a night of curses Jaguna. It is not many unprepared minds will remain unhinged under the load.

JAGUNA: We must find him. It is a poor beginning for a year when our own curses remain hovering over our homes because the carrier refused to take them.

[They go. The scene changes. EMAN is crouching beside some shrubs, torn and bleeding.]

EMAN: They are even guarding my house . . . as if I would go there, but I need water . . . they could at least grant me that . . . I can be thirsty too . . . (*he pricks his ears.*) . . . there must be a stream nearby . . . (*as he looks round him, his eyes widen at a scene he encounters.*)

[An OLD MAN, short and vigorous looking is seated on a stool. He also is wearing calf-length baggy trousers, white. On his head, a white cap. An ATTENDANT is engaged in rubbing his body with oil. Round his eyes, two white rings have already been marked.]

OLD MAN: Have they prepared the boat?

ATTENDANT: They are making the last sacrifice.

OLD MAN: Good. Did you send for my son?

ATTENDANT: He's on his way.

OLD MAN: I have never met the carrying of the boat with such a heavy heart. I hope nothing comes of it.

ATTENDANT: The gods will not desert us on that account.

OLD MAN: A man should be at his strongest when he takes the boat my friend. To be weighed down inside and out is not a wise thing. I hope when the moment comes I shall have found my strength.

[Enter EMAN, a wrapper round his waist and a 'dans-ki' over it.]

OLD MAN: I meant to wait until after my journey to the river, but my mind is so burdened with my own grief and yours I could not delay it. You know I must have all my strength. But I sit here, feeling it all eat slowly away by my unspoken grief. It helps to say it out. It even helps to cry sometimes.

[He signals to the ATTENDANT to leave them.]

Come nearer . . . we will never meet again son. Not on this side of the flesh. What I do not know is whether you will return to take my place.

EMAN: I will never come back.

OLD MAN: Do you know what you are saying? Ours is a strong breed my son. It is only a strong breed that can take this boat to the river year after year and wax stronger on it. I have taken down each year's evils for over twenty years. I hoped you would follow me.

EMAN: My life here died with Omae.

OLD MAN: Omae died giving birth to your child and you think the world is ended. Eman, my pain did not begin when Omae died. Since you sent her to stay with me son, I lived with the burden of knowing that this child would die bearing your son.

EMAN: Father . . .

OLD MAN: Don't you know it was the same with you? And me? No woman survives the bearing of the strong ones. Son, it is not the mouth of the boaster that says he belongs to the strong breed. It is the tongue that is red with pain and black with sorrow. Twelve years you were away my son, and for those twelve years I knew the love of an old man for his daughter and the pain of a man helplessly awaiting his loss.

EMAN: I wish I had stayed away. I wish I never came back to meet her.

OLD MAN: It had to be. But you know now what slowly ate away my strength. I awaited your return with love and fear. Forgive me then if I say that your grief is light. It will pass. This grief may drive you now from home. But you must return.

EMAN: You do not understand. It is not grief alone.

OLD MAN: What is it then? Tell me, I can still learn.

EMAN: I was away twelve years. I changed much in that time.

OLD MAN: I am listening.

EMAN: I am unfitted for your work father. I wish to say no more. But I am totally unfitted for your call.

OLD MAN: It is only time you need son. Stay longer and you will answer the urge of your blood.

EMAN: That I stayed at all was because of Omae. I did not expect to find her waiting. I would have taken her away, but hard as you claim to be, it would have killed you. And I was a tired man. I needed peace. Because Omae was peace, I stayed. Now nothing holds me here.

OLD MAN: Other men would rot and die doing this task year after year. It is strong medicine which only we can take. Our blood is strong like no other. Anything you do in life must be less than this, son.

EMAN: That is not true father.

OLD MAN: I tell you it is true. Your own blood will betray you son, because you cannot hold it back. If you make it do less than this, it will rush to your head and burst it open. I say what I know my son.

EMAN: There are other tasks in life father. This one is not for me. There are even greater things you know nothing of.

OLD MAN: I am very sad. You only go to give to others what rightly belongs to us. You will use your strength among thieves. They are thieves because they take what is ours, they have no claim of blood to it. They will even lack the knowledge to use it wisely. Truth is my companion at this moment my son. I know everything I say will surely bring the sadness of truth.

EMAN: I am going father.

OLD MAN: Call my attendant. And be with me in your strength for this last journey. A-ah, did you hear that? It came out without my knowing it; this is indeed my last journey. But I am not afraid.

[EMAN goes out. A few moments later, the ATTENDANT enters.]

ATTENDANT: The boat is ready.

OLD MAN: So am I.

[He sits perfectly still for several moments. Drumming begins somewhere in the distance, and the OLD MAN sways his head almost imperceptibly. Two men come in bearing a miniature boat, containing an indefinable mound. They rush it in and set it briskly down near the OLD MAN, and stand well back. The OLD MAN gets up slowly; the ATTENDANT watching him keenly. He signs to the men, who lift the boat quickly onto the OLD MAN's head. As soon as it touches his head, he holds it down with both hands and runs off, the men give him a start, then follow at a trot.

As the last man disappears OROGE limps in and comes face to face with EMAN—as carrier—who is now seen still standing beside the shrubs, staring into the scene he has just witnessed. OROGE, struck by the look on EMAN's face, looks anxiously behind him to see what has engaged EMAN's attention. EMAN notices him then, and the pair stare at each other. JAGUNA enters, sees him and shouts, 'Here he is', rushes at EMAN who is whipped back to the immediate and flees, JAGUNA in pursuit. Three or four others enter and follow them. OROGE remains where he is, thoughtful.]

JAGUNA (*re-enters.*): They have closed in on him now, we'll get him this time.

OROGE: It is nearly midnight.

JAGUNA: You were standing there looking at him as if he was some strange spirit. Why didn't you shout?

OROGE: You shouted didn't you? Did that catch him?

JAGUNA: Don't worry. We have him now. But things have taken a bad turn. It is no longer enough to drive him past every house. There is too much contamination about already.

OROGE (*not listening.*): He saw something. Why may I not know what it was?

JAGUNA: What are you talking about?

OROGE: Hm. What is it?

JAGUNA: I said there is too much harm done already. The year will demand more from this carrier than we thought.

OROGE: What do you mean?

JAGUNA: Do we have to talk with the full mouth?

OROGE: S-sh . . . look!

[JAGUNA turns just in time to see SUNMA fly at him, clawing at his face like a crazed tigress.]

SUNMA: Murderer! What are you doing to him. Murderer! Murderer!

[JAGUNA finds himself struggling really hard to keep off his daughter, he succeeds in pushing her off and striking her so hard on the face that she falls to her knees. He moves on her to hit her again.]

OROGE (*comes between.*): Think what you are doing Jaguna, she is your daughter.

JAGUNA: My daughter! Does this one look like my daughter? Let me cripple the harlot for life.

OROGE: That is a wicked thought Jaguna.

JAGUNA: Don't come between me and her.

OROGE: Nothing in anger—do you forget what tonight is?

JAGUNA: Can you blame me for forgetting?

[Draws his hand across his cheek—it is covered with blood.]

OROGE: This is an unhappy night for us all. I fear what is to come of it.

JAGUNA: Let's go. I cannot restrain myself in this creature's presence. My own daughter . . . and for a stranger . . .

[They go off. IFADA, who came in with SUNMA and had stood apart, horror-stricken, comes shyly forward. He helps SUNMA up. They go off, he holding SUNMA bent and sobbing.]

[Enter EMAN—as carrier. He is physically present in the bounds of this next scene, a side of a round

thatched hut. A young girl, about fourteen runs in, stops beside the hut. She looks carefully to see that she is not observed, puts her mouth to a little hole in the wall.]

OMAE: Eman . . . Eman . . .

[EMAN—as carrier—responds, as he does throughout the scene, but they are unaware of him.]

EMAN (*from inside.*): Who is it?
OMAE: It is me, Omae.
EMAN: How dare you come here!

[Two hands appear at the hole and pushing outwards, create a much larger hole through which EMAN puts out his head. It is EMAN as a boy, the same age as the girl.]

Go away at once. Are you trying to get me into trouble?
OMAE: What is the matter?
EMAN: You. Go away.
OMAE: But I came to see you.
EMAN: Are you deaf? I say I don't want to see you. Now go before my tutor catches you.
OMAE: All right. Come out.
EMAN: Do what!
OMAE: Come out.
EMAN: You must be mad.
OMAE (*sits on the ground.*): All right, if you don't come out I shall simply stay here until your tutor arrives.
EMAN (*about to explode, thinks better of it and the head disappears. A moment later he emerges from behind the hut.*): What sort of a devil has got into you?
OMAE: None. I just wanted to see you.
EMAN (*his mimicry is nearly hysterical.*): 'None. I just wanted to see you.' Do you think this place is the stream where you can go and molest innocent people?
OMAE (*coyly.*): Aren't you glad to see me?
EMAN: I am not.
OMAE: Why?
EMAN: Why? Do you really ask me why? Because you are a woman and a most troublesome woman. Don't you know anything about this at all. We are not meant to see any woman. So go away before more harm is done.
OMAE (*flirtatious.*): What is so secret about it anyway? What do they teach you?
EMAN: Nothing any woman can understand.
OMAE: Ha ha. You think we don't know eh? You've all come to be circumcised.
EMAN: Shut up. You don't know anything.
OMAE: Just think, all this time you haven't been circumcised, and you dared make eyes at us women.

EMAN: Thank you—woman. Now go.
OMAE: Do they give you enough to eat?
EMAN (*testily.*): No. We are so hungry that when silly girls like you turn up, we eat them.
OMAE (*feigning tears.*): Oh, oh, oh, now he's abusing me. He's abusing me.
EMAN (*alarmed.*): Don't try that here. Go quickly if you are going to cry.
OMAE: All right, I won't cry.
EMAN: Cry or no cry, go away and leave me alone. What do you think will happen if my tutor turns up now.
OMAE: He won't.
EMAN (*mimicking.*): 'He won't.' I suppose you are his wife and he tells you where he goes. In fact this is just the time he comes round to our huts. He could be at the next hut this very moment.
OMAE: Ha-ha. You're lying. I left him by the stream, pinching the girls' bottoms. Is that the sort of thing he teaches you?
EMAN: Don't say anything against him or I shall beat you. Isn't it you loose girls who tease him, wiggling your bottoms under his nose?
OMAE (*going tearful again.*): A-ah, so I am one of the loose girls eh?
EMAN: Now don't start accusing me of things I didn't say.
OMAE: But you said it. You said it.
EMAN: I didn't. Look Omae, someone will hear you and I'll be in disgrace. Why don't you go before anything happens.
OMAE: It's all right. My friends have promised to hold your old rascal tutor till I get back.
EMAN: Then you go back right now. I have work to do. (*Going in.*)
OMAE (*runs after and tries to hold him. EMAN leaps back, genuinely scared.*): What is the matter? I was not going to bite you.
EMAN: Do you know what you nearly did? You almost touched me!
OMAE: Well?
EMAN: Well! Isn't it enough that you let me set my eyes on you? Must you now totally pollute me with your touch? Don't you understand anything?
OMAE: Oh, that.
EMAN (*nearly screaming.*): It is not 'oh that.' Do you think this is only a joke or a little visit like spending the night with your grandmother? This is an important period of my life. Look, these huts, we built them with our own hands. Every boy builds his own. We learn things, do you understand? And we spend much time just thinking. At least, I do. It is the first time I have had nothing to do except think. Don't you see, I am becoming a man. For the first

time, I understand that I have a life to fulfil. Has that thought ever worried you?

OMAE: You are frightening me.

EMAN: There. That is all you can say. And what use will that be when a man finds himself alone— like that? (*Points to the hut.*) A man must go on his own, go where no one can help him, and test his strength. Because he may find himself one day sitting alone in a wall as round as that. In there, my mind could hold no other thought. I may never have such moments again to myself. Don't dare to come and steal any more of it.

OMAE (*this time, genuinely tearful.*): Oh, I know you hate me. You only want to drive me away.

EMAN (*impatiently.*): Yes, yes, I know I hate you—but go.

OMAE (*going, all tears. Wipes her eyes, suddenly all mischief.*): Eman.

EMAN: What now?

OMAE: I only want to ask one thing . . . do you promise to tell me?

EMAN: Well, what is it?

OMAE (*gleefully.*): Does it hurt?

[*She turns instantly and flees, landing straight into the arms of the returning tutor.*]

TUTOR: Te-he-he . . . what have we here? What little mouse leaps straight into the beak of the wise old owl eh?

[*OMAE struggles to free herself, flies to the opposite side, grimacing with distaste.*]

TUTOR: I suppose you merely came to pick some fruits eh? You did not sneak here to see any of my children.

OMAE: Yes, I came to steal your fruits.

TUTOR: Te-he-he . . . I thought so. And that dutiful son of mine over there. He saw you and came to chase you off my fruit trees didn't he? Te-he-he . . . I'm sure he did, isn't that so my young Eman?

EMAN: I was talking to her.

TUTOR: Indeed you were. Now be good enough to go into your hut until I decide your punishment. (EMAN *withdraws.*) Te-he-he . . . now now my little daughter, you need not be afraid of me.

OMAE (*spiritedly.*): I am not.

TUTOR: Good. Very good. We ought to be friendly. (*His voice becomes leering.*) Now this is nothing to worry you my daughter . . . a very small thing indeed. Although of course if I were to let it slip that your young Eman had broken a strong taboo, it might go hard on him you know. I am sure you would not like that to

happen, would you?

OMAE: No.

TUTOR: Good. You are sensible my girl. Can you wash clothes?

OMAE: Yes.

TUTOR: Good. If you will come with me now to my hut, I shall give you some clothes to wash, and then we will forget all about this matter eh? Well, come on.

OMAE: I shall wait here. You go and bring the clothes.

TUTOR: Eh? What is that? Now now, don't make me angry. You should know better than to talk back at your elders. Come now.

[*He takes her by the arm, and tries to drag her off.*]

OMAE: No no, I won't come to your hut. Leave me. Leave me alone you shameless old man.

TUTOR: If you don't come I shall disgrace the whole family of Eman, and yours too.

[*EMAN re-enters with a small bundle.*]

EMAN: Leave her alone. Let us go Omae.

TUTOR: And where do you think you are going?

EMAN: Home.

TUTOR: Te-he-he . . . As easy as that eh? You think you can leave here any time you please? Get right back inside that hut!

[*EMAN takes OMAE by the arm and begins to walk off.*]

TUTOR: Come back at once.

[*He goes after him and raises his stick. EMAN catches it, wrenches it from him and throws it away.*]

OMAE (*hopping delightedly.*): Kill him. Beat him to death.

TUTOR: Help! Help! He is killing me! Help!

[*Alarmed, EMAN clamps his hand over his mouth.*]

EMAN: Old tutor, I don't mean you any harm, but you mustn't try to harm me either. (*He removes his hand.*)

TUTOR: You think you can get away with your crime. My report shall reach the elders before you ever get into town.

EMAN: You are afraid of what I will say about you? Don't worry. Only if you try to shame me, then I will speak. I am not going back to the village anyway. Just tell them I have gone, no more. If you say one word more than that I shall hear of it the same day and I shall come back.

TUTOR: You are telling me what to do? But don't think to come back next year because I will drive you away. Don't think to come back here

even ten years from now. And don't send your
children.

[Goes off with threatening gestures.]

EMAN: I won't come back.
OMAE: Smoked vulture! But Eman, he says you can-
not return next year. What will you do?
EMAN: It is a small thing one can do in the big towns.
OMAE: I thought you were going to beat him that
time. Why didn't you crack his dirty hide?
EMAN: Listen carefully Omae . . . I am going on a
journey.
OMAE: Come on. Tell me about it on the way.
EMAN: No, I go that way. I cannot return to the vil-
lage.
OMAE: Because of that wretched man? Anyway you
will first talk to your father.
EMAN: Go and see him for me. Tell him I have gone
away for some time. I think he will know.
OMAE: But Eman . . .
EMAN: I haven't finished. You will go and live with
him till I get back. I have spoken to him about
you. Look after him!
OMAE: But what is this journey? When will you come
back?
EMAN: I don't know. But this is a good moment to
go. Nothing ties me down.
OMAE: But Eman, you want to leave me.
EMAN: Don't forget all I said. I don't know how long
I will be. Stay in my father's house as long as
you remember me. When you become tired of
waiting, you must do as you please. You
understand? You must do as you please.
OMAE: I cannot understand anything Eman. I don't
know where you are going or why. Suppose
you never came back! Don't go Eman. Don't
leave me by myself.
EMAN: I must go. Now let me see you on your way.
OMAE: I shall come with you.
EMAN: Come with me! And who will look after you?
Me? You will only be in my way, you know
that! You will hold me back and I shall desert
you in a strange place. Go home and do as I
say. Take care of my father and let him take
care of you.

[He starts going but OMAE clings to him.]

OMAE: But Eman, stay the night at least. You will
only lose your way. Your father Eman, what
will he say? I won't remember what you said
. . . come back to the village . . . I cannot return
alone Eman . . . come with me as far as the
crossroads.

*[His face set, EMAN strides off and OMAE loses balance
as he increases his pace. Falling, she quickly wraps*

*her arms around his ankle, but EMAN continues
unchecked, dragging her along.]*

OMAE: Don't go Eman . . . Eman, don't leave me,
don't leave me . . . don't leave your Omae . . .
don't go Eman . . . don't leave your Omae . . .

*[EMAN—as carrier—makes a nervous move as if he
intends to go after the vanished pair. He stops but
continues to stare at the point where he last saw them.
There is stillness for a while. Then the GIRL enters
from the same place and remains looking at EMAN.
Startled, EMAN looks apprehensively round him. The
GIRL goes nearer but keeps beyond arm's length.]*

GIRL: Are you the carrier?
EMAN: Yes. I am Eman.
GIRL: Why are you hiding?
EMAN: I really came for a drink of water . . . er . . . is
there anyone in front of the house?
GIRL: No.
EMAN: But there might be people in the house. Did
you hear voices?
GIRL: There is no one there.
EMAN: Good. Thank you. (*He is about to go, stops sud-
denly.*) Er . . . would you . . . you will find a
cup on the table. Could you bring me the
water out here? The water-pot is in a corner.

*[The GIRL goes. She enters the house, then, watching
EMAN carefully, slips out and runs off.]*

EMAN (*sitting.*): Perhaps they have all gone home. It
will be good to rest. (*He hears voices and listens
hard.*) Too late. (*Moves cautiously nearer the
house.*) Quickly girl, I can hear people coming.
Hurry up. (*Looks through the window.*) Where
are you? Where is she? (*The truth dawns on him
suddenly and he moves off, sadly.*)

[Enter JAGUNA and OROGE, led by the GIRL.]

GIRL (*pointing.*): He was there.
JAGUNA: Ay, he's gone now. He is a sly one is your
friend. But it won't save him for ever.
OROGE: What was he doing when you saw him?
GIRL: He asked me for a drink of water.
JAGUNA:
OROGE: }Ah! [*They look at each other.*]
OROGE: We should have thought of that.
JAGUNA: He is surely finished now. If only we had
thought of it earlier.
OROGE: It is not too late. There is still an hour before
midnight.
JAGUNA: We must call back all the men. Now we
need only wait for him—in the right place.
OROGE: Everyone must be told. We don't want any-
one heading him off again.

JAGUNA: And it works so well. This is surely the help of the gods themselves Oroge. Don't you know at once what is on the path to the stream?

OROGE: The sacred trees.

JAGUNA: I tell you it is the very hand of the gods. Let us go.

[An overgrown part of the village. EMAN wanders in, aimlessly, seemingly uncaring of discovery. Beyond him, an area lights up, revealing a group of people clustered round a spot, all the heads are bowed. One figure stands away and separate from them.

Even as EMAN looks, the group break up and the people disperse, coming down and past him. Only three people are left, a man (EMAN) whose back is turned, the village PRIEST and the isolated one.

They stand on opposite sides of the grave, the man on the mound of earth.

The PRIEST walks round to the man's side and lays a hand on his shoulder.]

PRIEST: Come.

EMAN: I will. Give me a few moments here alone.

PRIEST: Be comforted.

[They fall silent.]

EMAN: I was gone twelve years but she waited. She whom I thought had too much of the laughing child in her. Twelve years I was a pilgrim, seeking the vain shrine of secret strength. And all the time, strange knowledge, this silent strength of my child-woman.

PRIEST: We all saw it. It was a lesson to us; we did not know that such goodness could be found among us.

EMAN: Then why? Why the wasted years if she had to perish giving birth to my child? (*They are both silent.*) I do not really know for what great meaning I searched. When I returned, I could not be certain I had found it. Until I reached my home and I found her a full-grown woman, still a child at heart. When I grew to believe it, I thought, this, after all, is what I sought. It was here all the time. And I threw away my new-gained knowledge. I buried the part of me that was formed in strange places. I made a home in my birthplace.

PRIEST: That was as it should be.

EMAN: Any truth of that was killed in the cruelty of her brief happiness.

PRIEST (*looks up and sees the figure standing away from them, the child in his arms. He is totally still.*): Your father—he is over there.

EMAN: I knew he would come. Has he my son with him?

PRIEST: Yes.

EMAN: He will let no one take the child. Go and comfort him priest. He loved Omae like a daughter, and you all know how well she looked after him. You see how strong we really are. In his heart of hearts the old man's love really awaited a daughter. Go and comfort him. His grief is more than mine.

[The PRIEST goes. The OLD MAN has stood well away from the burial group. His face is hard and his gaze unswerving from the grave. The PRIEST goes to him, pauses, but sees that he can make no dent in the man's grief. Bowed, he goes on his way.]

[EMAN, as carrier, walking towards the graveside, the other EMAN having gone. His feet sink into the mound and he breaks slowly on to his knees, scooping up the sand in his hands and pouring it on to his head. The scene blacks out slowly.]

[Enter JAGUNA and OROGE.]

OROGE: We have only a little time.

JAGUNA: He will come. All the wells are guarded. There is only the stream left him. The animal must come to drink.

OROGE: You are sure it will not fail—the trap I mean.

JAGUNA: When Jaguna sets the trap, even elephants pay homage—their trunks downwards and one leg up in the sky. When the carrier steps on the fallen twigs, it is up in the sacred trees with him.

OROGE: I shall breathe again when this long night is over.

[They go out.]

[Enter EMAN—as carrier—from the same direction as the last two entered. In front of him is a still figure, the OLD MAN as he was, carrying the dwarf boat.]

EMAN (*joyfully.*): Father.

[The figure does not turn round.]

EMAN: It is your son. Eman. (*He moves nearer.*) Don't you want to look at me? It is I, Eman. (*He moves nearer still.*)

OLD MAN: You are coming too close. Don't you know what I carry on my head?

EMAN: But Father, I am your son.

OLD MAN: Then go back. We cannot give the two of us.

EMAN: Tell me first where you are going.

OLD MAN: Do *you* ask that? Where else but to the river?

EMAN (*visibly relieved.*): I only wanted to be sure. My throat is burning. I have been looking for the stream all night.

OLD MAN: It is the other way.

EMAN: But you said . . .

OLD MAN: I take the longer way, you know how I must do this. It is quicker if you take the other way. Go now.

EMAN: No, I will only get lost again. I shall go with you.

OLD MAN: Go back my son. Go back.

EMAN: Why? Won't you even look at me?

OLD MAN: Listen to your father. Go back.

EMAN: But father!

[He makes to hold him. Instantly the OLD MAN breaks into a rapid trot. EMAN hesitates, then follows, his strength nearly gone.]

EMAN: Wait father. I am coming with you . . . wait . . . wait for me father . . .

[There is a sound of twigs breaking, of a sudden trembling in the branches. Then silence.]

[The front of EMAN's house. The effigy is hanging from the sheaves. Enter SUNMA, still supported by IFADA, she stands transfixed as she sees the hanging figure. IFADA appears to go mad, rushes at the object and tears it down. SUNMA, her last bit of will gone, crumbles against the wall. Some distance away from them, partly hidden, stands the GIRL, impassively watching. IFADA hugs the effigy to him, stands above SUNMA. The GIRL remains where she is, observing.

Almost at once, the villagers begin to return, subdued and guilty. They walk across the front, skirting the house as widely as they can. No word is exchanged. JAGUNA and OROGE eventually appear.

JAGUNA who is leading, sees SUNMA as soon as he comes in view.

He stops at once, retreating slightly.]

OROGE (*almost whispering.*): What is it?

JAJUNA: The viper.

[OROGE looks cautiously at the woman.]

OROGE: I don't think she will even see you.

JAGUNA: Are you sure? I am in no frame of mind for another meeting with her.

OROGE: Let's go home.

JAGUNA: I am sick to the heart of the cowardice I have seen tonight.

OROGE: That is the nature of men.

JAGUNA: Then it is a sorry world to live in. We did it for them. It was all for their own common good. What did it benefit me whether the man lived or died. But did you see them? One and all they looked up at the man and words died in their throats.

OROGE: It was no common sight.

JAGUNA: Women could not have behaved so shamefully. One by one they crept off like sick dogs. Not one could raise a curse.

OROGE: It was not only him they fled. Do you see how unattended we are?

JAGUNA: There are those who will pay for this night's work!

OROGE: Ay, let us go home.

[They go off. SUNMA, IFADA, and the GIRL remain as they are, the light fading slowly on them.]

THE END

TOM STOPPARD (b. 1937)

Thomas Stoppard was born Thomas Straussler in Zlin (modern Gottwaldov), Czechoslovakia, in 1937. When the German army invaded the country during the early stages of World War II, the family fled to Singapore, which was then itself threatened by the Japanese. Stoppard's mother set off with her two sons to India, where she managed a shoe store in Darjeeling while his father remained in Singapore. There he was killed under mysterious circumstances. In Darjeeling Stoppard attended a multiracial American school where he learned English. Meanwhile, his widowed mother married an officer in the British army, Kenneth Stoppard, who moved with his new family back to England in 1946, taking up a career as a machine-tool salesman. From this point on Tom Stoppard received a traditional middle-class education: he attended a preparatory boarding school in Nottinghamshire and then a public school in Yorkshire. In 1954, at age seventeen, rather than going on to a university, Stoppard took a job as a reporter for the *Western Daily Press* in Bristol, where his family had finally settled. By 1960 he had begun to write film and theater criticism, and it was during this period that he began writing plays, initially influenced by John Osborn and other "angry young men."

From 1960 to 1966 Stoppard wrote fiction, plays, and criticism in Bristol and in London, paying his rent by writing radio and television scripts. His first play, a one-act piece called *The Gamblers*, was written in 1960; Stoppard later described it as *Waiting for Godot* in a death cell. His first full-length play was *A Walk on Water*, later retitled *Enter a Free Man* (1968). The main character, George Riley, deludes himself into thinking he can achieve independence and make his fortune as an inventor. Riley depends entirely on his wife and daughter for food, shelter, and money, and they are wearily aware that his fantasies about self-sufficiency are just that.

Aside from these plays Stoppard had few theatrical successes before the production of *Rosencrantz and Guildenstern Are Dead* at the 1966 Edinburgh festival. The play caught the immediate attention of reviewers and was performed within a year at the National Theatre. This play, Stoppard's most famous, was followed by a string of major theatrical successes: *The Real Inspector Hound* (1968), a broad parody of Agatha Christie mysteries; *Jumpers* (1972); *Travesties* (1974); *Dirty Linen* (1976), a farce about sexual misconduct in the House of Commons; *Dogg's Hamlet* and *Cahoot's Macbeth* (1979); and *The Real Thing* (1982). In addition to his full-length plays, Stoppard continued to write short plays, including *Teeth* (1967) and *After Magritte* (1970), television plays, including *Professional Foul* (1977) and *Squaring the Circle* (1984); and radio plays, including *Albert's Bridge* (1967), *Where Are They Now?* (1969), *Artist Descending a Staircase* (1972), and *The Dog It Was That Died* (1982).

Every Good Boy Deserves Favour (1977) marked Stoppard's entry into the area of political theater. The play concerns the use of pseudopsychiatry to brainwash political dissenters in Soviet mental hospitals. Some months before its opening, the Eastern European playwright and later president of the Czech Republic, Vaclav Havel, whom Stoppard much admired, was arrested in Prague. Havel had attempted to deliver a petition urging the then-communist Czech government to guarantee freedom of expression. Stoppard made a brief trip to the Soviet Union as a member of Amnesty International and to the former Czechosolvakia, focusing much of his attention during the late 1970s on politics and freedom of expression in Eastern Europe.

Stoppard's work has provoked widely divergent responses—more so than any other modern playwright. *Rosencrantz and Guildenstern Are Dead*, for example, brought high praise from Charles Marowitz, who felt that Stoppard's transformation of Shakespearean and absurdist materials into something new was brilliant. By contrast, the critic Robert Brustein believed that the play depended too heavily on existentialist and absurdist thought and that Stoppard had achieved his success by offering a form of "Beckett without tears." Although his work had never encouraged lukewarm responses, no critics have doubted Stoppard's ear for dialogue, his flair for crafting surprising twists of plot, or his ability to compose plays that push the limits of self-conscious theater.

Rosencrantz and Guildenstern Are Dead

Rosencrantz and Guildenstern Are Dead was first performed by the Oxford Theater Group as part of the 1966 Edinburgh festival, and the circumstances of performance seemed far from promising. It was put on in a church hall on a flat floor, which meant that the audience could barely see what was going on. There was no scenery, and only a dozen actors could be found for the performance instead of the thirty-five required by the play. The director failed to show up altogether, so Stoppard himself spent nearly thirty-six hours advising the actors on the production. Still, the reviewer for the *Observer* was impressed and praised *Rosencrantz and Guildenstern Are Dead* as an erudite comedy by a brilliant young playwright. Within a week the National Theatre acquired the rights to the play, and the theater launched its London production in April 1967. The play was an overnight success, though it was subject to all sorts of critical interpretation. Criticism of Stoppard's plays has run the entire range. He has been criticized for using theatrical tricks that masquerade as important ideas and also for trivializing his important ideas with theatrical tricks.

The inspiration for *Rosencrantz and Guildenstern Are Dead* occurred to Stoppard during a conversation with a friend in 1964 about which king of England—Lear or Cymbeline—would have received Claudius's letter to execute

Hamlet. The conflation of play worlds sparked Stoppard's imagination, and shortly afterward, while in West Berlin on a Ford Foundation grant, Stoppard developed the idea into a one-act comedy. Back in England Stoppard returned to work on the play. His chief interest, he claimed, was "to exploit a situation which seemed to me to have enormous dramatic and comic potential—of these two guys who in Shakespeare's context don't really know what they're doing. The little they are told is mainly lies, and there's no reason to suppose that they ever find out why they are killed. And, probably more in the early 1960s than at any other time, that would strike a young playwright as being a pretty good thing to explore."

Stoppard explored the situation as a metatheatrical game in which actors are dimly aware of their existence as actors but are unable to puzzle out the implications of such an existence. The master rule book for the game is Shakespeare's *Hamlet*, which everyone knows except Ros and Guil. All they know is that they have been summoned. When we first meet them they are on the road to Elsinore in the middle of a game of their own, tossing coins. The game gives an apparent, though momentary, sense of purpose. As it turns out, the game defies reason, logic, and probability theory itself—all the rules by which Ros and Guil expected to play. The coin comes up heads several dozen times in a row. At Elsinore, they have to play a different game, but its rules are just as mysterious. Ros and Guil know how to play their parts; they respond to all the cues for their lines in the play; but the nature of the game—the play itself—eludes them.

For Ros and Guil, like Becket's Didi and Gogo, one thing obstinately refuses to lead to the next. But unlike Didi and Gogo, Ros and Guil are articulate and sympathetic characters who try to fill their time meaningfully. The ugly truth is that their identities and destinies have been established elsewhere. In *Hamlet*, Rosencrantz and Guildenstern are shallow henchmen who eagerly and fawningly accept Claudius's invitation to spy on their old childhood friend. Shakespeare's Hamlet has no sympathy and no regrets when he sends them to their deaths. Indeed, they are so expendable that they have been omitted from some *Hamlet* productions, so bland as to have become bywords of anonymity. In Stoppard's play, however, Rosencrantz and Guildenstern take center stage, drawing our sympathy, amusing us with their droll dialogue, and amazing us with their bewildered innocence.

What carries through and beyond *Rosencrantz and Guildenstern Are Dead* is the band of players, who operate so spiritedly in this most self-conscious play. Originally playing in the play-within-a-play in *Hamlet*, the players cross theatrical boundaries in Stoppard's play, capable of any action, at home in any world. Ros and Guil first meet them on the road; they appear together at Elsinore; and they show up again in the fateful voyage to England. At the end of this play, as in *Hamlet*, Rosencrantz and Guildenstern are dead, but the players live on to play again. Stoppard seems to imply that this is an appropriate metaphor for modern humanity—we are adrift, yet contained by a script about which we have no knowledge, and how well we play our parts has little bearing on the outcome.

Rosencrantz and Guildenstern Are Dead

TOM STOPPARD

CHARACTERS

ROSENCRANTZ
GUILDENSTERN
THE PLAYER
ALFRED
TRAGEDIANS
MUSICIANS
HAMLET
OPHELIA
CLAUDIUS

GERTRUDE
LAERTES
POLONIUS
HORATIO
FORTINBRAS
AMBASSADOR
SOLDIER
COURTIERS AND ATTENDANTS

ACT I

Two ELIZABETHANS passing the time in a place without any visible character.

They are well dressed—hats, cloaks, sticks and all.
Each of them has a large leather money bag.
GUILDENSTERN's bag is nearly empty.
ROSENCRANTZ's bag is nearly full.
The reason being: they are betting on the toss of a coin, in the following manner: GUILDENSTERN (hereafter "GUIL") takes a coin out of his bag, spins it, letting it fall. ROSENCRANTZ (hereafter "ROS") studies it, announces it as "heads" (as it happens) and puts it into his own bag. Then they repeat the process. They have apparently been doing this for some time.
The run of "heads" is impossible, yet ROS betrays no surprise at all—he feels none. However, he is nice enough to feel a little embarrassed at taking so much money off his friend. Let that be his character note.
GUIL is well alive to the oddity of it. He is not worried about the money, but he is worried by the implications; aware but not going to panic about it—his character note.
GUIL sits. ROS stands (he does the moving, retrieving coins).
GUIL spins. ROS studies coin.

ROS: Heads.

[He picks it up and puts it in his bag. The process is repeated.]

Heads.

[Again.]

Heads.

[Again.]

Heads.

[Again.]

Heads.

GUIL *(flipping a coin)*: There is an art to the building up of suspense.
ROS: Heads.
GUIL *(flipping another)*: Though it can be done by luck alone.
ROS: Heads.
GUIL: If that's the word I'm after.
ROS *(raises his head at GUIL)*: Seventy-six—love.

[GUIL gets up but has nowhere to go. He spins another coin over his shoulder without looking at it, his attention being directed at his environment or lack of it.]

Heads.
GUIL: A weaker man might be moved to re-examine his faith, if in nothing else at least in the law of probability. *(He slips a coin over his shoulder as he goes to look upstage.)*
ROS: Heads.

[GUIL, examining the confines of the stage, flips over two more coins as he does so, one by one of course. ROS announces each of them as "heads."]

GUIL *(musing)*: The law of probability, it has been oddly asserted, is something to do with the proposition that if six monkeys *(he has surprised himself)* . . . if six monkeys were . . .

Ros: Game?

Guil: Were they?

Ros: Are you?

Guil (*understanding*): Game. (*Flips a coin.*) The law of averages, if I have got this right, means that if six monkeys were thrown up in the air for long enough they would land on their tails about as often as they would land on their——

Ros: Heads. (*He picks up the coin.*)

Guil: Which even at first glance does not strike one as a particularly rewarding speculation, in either sense, even without the monkeys. I mean you wouldn't *bet* on it. I mean *I* would, but *you* wouldn't. . . . (*As he flips a coin.*)

Ros: Heads.

Guil: Would you? (*Flips a coin.*)

Ros: Heads.

[*Repeat.*]

Heads. (*He looks up at* Guil—*embarrassed laugh.*) Getting a bit of a bore, isn't it?

Guil (*coldly*): A bore?

Ros: Well . . .

Guil: What about the suspense?

Ros (*innocently*): What suspense?

[*Small pause.*]

Guil: It must be the law of diminishing returns. . . . I feel the spell about to be broken. (*Energizing himself somewhat. He takes out a coin, spins it high, catches it, turns it over on to the back of his other hand, studies the coin—and tosses it to* Ros. *His energy deflates and he sits.*) Well, it was an even chance . . . if my calculations are correct.

Ros: Eighty-five in a row—beaten the record!

Guil: Don't be absurd.

Ros: Easily!

Guil (*angry*): Is that *it*, then? Is that all?

Ros: What?

Guil: A new record? Is that as far as you are prepared to go?

Ros: Well . . .

Guil: No questions? Not even a pause?

Ros: You spun them yourself.

Guil: Not a flicker of doubt?

Ros (*aggrieved, aggressive*): Well, I won—didn't I?

Guil (*approaches him—quieter*): And if you'd lost? If they'd come down against you, eighty-five times, one after another, just like that?

Ros (*dumbly*): Eighty-five in a row? *Tails*?

Guil: Yes! What would you think?

Ros (*doubtfully*): Well. . . . (*Jocularly.*) Well, I'd have a

good look at your coins for a start!

Guil (*retiring*): I'm relieved. At least we can still count on self-interest as a predictable factor. . . . I suppose it's the last to go. Your capacity for trust made me wonder if perhaps . . . you, alone . . . (*He turns on him suddenly, reaches out a hand.*) Touch.

[Ros *clasps his hand.* Guil *pulls him up to him.*]

Guil (*more intensely*): We have been spinning coins together since——(*He releases him almost as violently.*) This is not the first time we have spun coins!

Ros: Oh no—we've been spinning coins for as long as I remember.

Guil: How long is that?

Ros: I forget. Mind you—eighty-five times!

Guil: Yes?

Ros: It'll take some beating, I imagine.

Guil: Is *that* what you imagine? Is that it? No *fear*?

Ros: Fear?

Guil (*in fury—flings a coin on the ground*):Fear! The crack that might flood your brain with light!

Ros: Heads. . . .(*He puts it in his bag.*)

[Guil *sits despondently. He takes a coin, spins it, lets it fall between his feet. He looks at it, picks it up, throws it to* Ros, *who puts it in his bag.*

Guil takes another coin, spins it, catches it, turns it over on to his other hand, looks at it, and throws it to Ros, *who puts it in his bag.*

Guil takes a third coin, spins it, catches it in his right hand, turns it over onto his left wrist, lobs it in the air, catches it with his left hand, raises his left leg, throws the coin up under it, catches it and turns it over on the top of his head, where it sits. Ros *comes, looks at it, puts it in his bag.*]

Ros: I'm afraid——

Guil: So am I.

Ros: I'm afraid it isn't your day.

Guil: I'm afraid it is.

[*Small pause.*]

Ros: Eighty-nine.

Guil: It must be indicative of something, besides the redistribution of wealth. (*He muses.*) List of possible explanations. One: I'm willing it. Inside where nothing shows, I am the essence of a man spinning double-headed coins, and betting against himself in private atonement for an unremembered past. (*He spins a coin at* Ros.)

Ros: Heads.

Guil: Two: time has stopped dead, and the single experience of one coin being spun once has been repeated ninety times. . . . (*He flips a coin, looks at it, tosses it to* Ros.) On the whole, doubtful. Three: divine intervention, that is to say, a good turn from above concerning him, cf. children of Israel, or retribution from above concerning me, cf. Lot's wife. Four: a spectacular vindication of the principle that each individual coin spun individually (*he spins one*) is as likely to come down heads as tails and therefore should cause no surprise each individual time it does. (*It does. He tosses it to* Ros.)

Ros: I've never known anything like it!

Guil: And a syllogism: One, he has never known anything like it. Two, he has never known anything to write home about. Three, it is nothing to write home about. . . . Home . . . What's the first thing you remember?

Ros: Oh, let's see. . . . The first thing that comes into my head, you mean?

Guil: No—the first thing you remember.

Ros: Ah. (*Pause.*) No, it's no good, it's gone. It was a long time ago.

Guil (*patient but edged*): You don't get my meaning. What is the first thing after all the things you've forgotten?

Ros: Oh I see. (*Pause.*) I've forgotten the question.

[Guil leaps up and paces.]

Guil: Are you happy?

Ros: What?

Guil: Content? At ease?

Ros: I suppose so.

Guil: What are you going to do now?

Ros: I don't know. What do you want to do?

Guil: I have no desires. None. (*He stops pacing dead.*) There was a messenger . . . that's right. We were sent for. (*He wheels at* Ros *and raps out:*) Syllogism the second: One, probability is a factor which operates within natural forces. Two, probability is not operating as a factor. Three, we are now within un-, sub- or supernatural forces. Discuss. (Ros *is suitably startled. Acidly.*) Not too heatedly.

Ros: I'm sorry I—What's the matter with you?

Guil: The scientific approach to the examination of phenomena is a defence against the pure emotion of fear. Keep tight hold and continue while there's time. Now—counter to the previous syllogism: tricky one, follow me carefully, it may prove a comfort. If we postulate, and we just have, that within un-, sub- or supernatural forces *the probability is* that the law of probability will not operate as a factor, then we

must accept that the probability of the *first* part will not operate as a factor, in which case the law of probability *will* operate as a factor within un-, sub- or supernatural forces. And since it obviously hasn't been doing so, we can take it that we are not held within un-, sub- or supernatural forces after all; in all probability, that is. Which is a great relief to me personally. (*Small pause.*) Which is all very well, except that——(*He continues with tight hysteria, under control.*) We have been spinning coins together since I don't know when, and in all that time (if it *is* all that time) I don't suppose either of us was more than a couple of gold pieces up or down. I hope that doesn't sound surprising because its very unsurprisingness is something I am trying to keep hold of. The equanimity of your average tosser of coins depends upon a law, or rather a tendency, or let us say a probability, or at any rate a mathematically calculable chance, which ensures that he will not upset himself by losing too much nor upset his opponent by winning too often. This made for a kind of harmony and a kind of confidence. It related the fortuitous and the ordained into a reassuring union which we recognized as nature. The sun came up about as often as it went down, in the long run, and a coin showed heads about as often as it showed tails. Then a messenger arrived. We had been sent for. Nothing else happened. Ninety-two coins spun consecutively have come down heads ninety-two consecutive times . . . and for the last three minutes on the wind of a windless day I have heard the sound of drums and flute. . . .

Ros (*cutting his fingernails*): Another curious scientific phenomenon is the fact that the fingernails grow after death, as does the beard.

Guil: What?

Ros (*loud*): Beard!

Guil: But you're not dead.

Ros (*irritated*): I didn't say they *started* to grow after death! (*Pause, calmer.*) The fingernails also grow before birth, though *not* the beard.

Guil: What?

Ros (*shouts*): Beard! What's the matter with you? (*Reflectively.*) The toenails, on the other hand, never grow at all.

Guil (*bemused*): The toenails never grow at all?

Ros: Do they? It's a funny thing—I cut my fingernails all the time, and every time I think to cut them, they need cutting. Now, for instance. And yet, I never, to the best of my knowledge, cut my toenails. They ought to be curled under my feet by now, but it doesn't happen. I never think about them. Perhaps I cut them absent-mindedly, when I'm thinking of something else.

GUIL (*tensed up by this rambling*): Do you remember the first thing that happened today?

ROS (*promptly*): I woke up, I suppose. (*Triggered.*) Oh—I've got it now—that man, a foreigner, he woke us up——

GUIL: A messenger. (*He relaxes, sits.*)

ROS: That's it—pale sky before dawn, a man standing on his saddle to bang on the shutters—shouts—What's all the row about?! Clear off!—But then he called our names. You remember that—this man woke us up.

GUIL: Yes.

ROS: We were sent for.

GUIL: Yes.

ROS: That's why we're here. (*He looks round, seems doubtful, then the explanation.*) Travelling.

GUIL: Yes.

ROS (*dramatically*): It was urgent—a matter of extreme urgency, a royal summons, his very words: official business and no questions asked—lights in the stable-yard, saddle up and off headlong and hotfoot across the land, our guides outstripped in breakneck pursuit of our duty! Fearful lest we come too late!!

[*Small pause.*]

GUIL: Too late for what?

ROS: How do I know? We haven't got there yet.

GUIL: Then what are we doing here, I ask myself.

ROS: You might well ask.

GUIL: We better get on.

ROS: You might well think.

GUIL: We better get on.

ROS (*actively*): Right! (*Pause.*) On where?

GUIL: Forward.

ROS (*forward to footlights*): Ah. (*Hesitates.*) Which way do we——(*He turns round.*) Which way did we——?

GUIL: Practically starting from scratch. . . . An awakening, a man standing on his saddle to bang on the shutters, our names shouted in a certain dawn, a message, a summons . . . A new record for heads and tails. We have not been . . . picked out . . . simply to be abandoned . . . set loose to find our own way. . . . We are entitled to some direction. . . . I would have thought.

ROS (*alert, listening*): I say——! I say——

GUIL: Yes?

ROS: I can hear—I thought I heard—music.

[*GUIL raises himself.*]

GUIL: Yes?

ROS: Like a band. (*He looks around, laughs embarrassedly, expiating himself.*) It sounded like—a band.

Drums.

GUIL: Yes.

ROS (*relaxes*): It couldn't have been real.

GUIL: "The colours red, blue and green are real. The colour yellow is a mystical experience shared by everybody"—demolish.

ROS (*at edge of stage*): It must have been thunder. Like drums . . .

[*By the end of the next speech, the band is faintly audible.*]

GUIL: A man breaking his journey between one place and another at a third place of no name, character, population or significance, sees a unicorn cross his path and disappear. That in itself is startling, but there are precedents for mystical encounters of various kinds, or to be less extreme, a choice of persuasions to put it down to fancy; until—"My God," says a second man, "I must be dreaming, I thought I saw a unicorn." At which point, a dimension is added that makes the experience as alarming as it will ever be. A third witness, you understand, adds no further dimension but only spreads it thinner, and a fourth thinner still, and the more witnesses there are the thinner it gets and the more reasonable it becomes until it is as thin as reality, the name we give to the common experience. . . . "Look, look!" recites the crowd. "A horse with an arrow in its forehead! It must have been mistaken for a deer."

ROS (*eagerly*): I knew all along it was a band.

GUIL (*tiredly*): He knew all along it was a band.

ROS: Here they come!

GUIL (*at the last moment before they enter—wistfully*): I'm sorry it wasn't a unicorn. It would have been nice to have unicorns.

[*The TRAGEDIANS are six in number, including a small BOY (ALFRED). Two pull and push a cart piled with props and belongings. There is also a DRUMMER, a HORN-PLAYER and a FLAUTIST. The SPOKESMAN ("the PLAYER") has no instrument. He brings up the rear and is the first to notice them.*]

PLAYER: Halt!

[*The group turns and halts.*]

(*Joyously.*) An audience!

[*ROS and GUIL half rise.*]

Don't move!

[*They sink back. He regards them fondly.*]

Perfect! A lucky thing we came along.

ROS: For us?

PLAYER: Let us hope so. But to meet two gentlemen on the road—we would not hope to meet them off it.

ROS: No?

PLAYER: Well met, in fact, and just in time.

ROS: Why's that?

PLAYER: Why, we grow rusty and you catch us at the very point of decadence—by this time tomorrow we might have forgotten everything we ever knew. That's a thought, isn't it? (*He laughs generously.*) We'd be back where we started—improvising.

ROS: Tumblers, are you?

PLAYER: We can give you a tumble if that's your taste, and times being what they are.... Otherwise, for a jingle of coin we can do you a selection of gory romances, full of fine cadence and corpses, pirated from the Italian; and it doesn't take much to make a jingle—even a single coin has music in it.

[They all flourish and bow, raggedly.]

Tragedians, at your command.

[ROS and GUIL have got to their feet.]

ROS: My name is Guildenstern, and this is Rosencrantz.

[GUIL confers briefly with him.]

(*Without embarrassment.*) I'm sorry—*his* name's Guildenstern, and *I'm* Rosencrantz.

PLAYER: A pleasure. We've played to bigger, of course, but quality counts for something. I recognized you at once——

ROS: And who are we?

PLAYER: —as fellow artists.

ROS: I thought we were gentlemen.

PLAYER: For some of us it is performance, for others, patronage. They are two sides of the same coin, or, let us say, being as there are so many of us, the same side of two coins. (*Bows again.*) Don't clap too loudly—it's a very old world.

ROS: What is your line?

PLAYER: Tragedy, sir. Deaths and disclosures, universal and particular, denouements both unexpected and inexorable, transvestite melodrama on all levels including the suggestive. We transport you into a world of intrigue and illusion ... clowns, if you like, murderers—we can do you ghosts and battles, on the skirmish level, heroes, villains, tormented lovers—set pieces in the poetic vein; we can do you rapiers or rape or both, by all means, faithless wives and ravished virgins—*flagrante delicto* at

a price, but that comes under realism for which there are special terms. Getting warm, am I?

ROS (*doubtfully*): Well, I don't know....

PLAYER: It costs little to watch, and little more if you happen to get caught up in the action, if that's your taste and times being what they are.

ROS: What are they?

PLAYER: Indifferent.

ROS: Bad?

PLAYER: Wicked. Now what precisely is your pleasure? (*He turns to the* TRAGEDIANS.) Gentlemen, disport yourselves.

[The TRAGEDIANS *shuffle into some kind of line.]*

There! See anything you like?

ROS (*doubtful, innocent*): What do they do?

PLAYER: Let your imagination run riot. They are beyond surprise.

ROS: And how much?

PLAYER: To take part?

ROS: To watch.

PLAYER: Watch what?

ROS: A private performance.

PLAYER: How private?

ROS: Well, there are only two of us. Is that enough?

PLAYER: For an audience, disappointing. For voyeurs, about average.

ROS: What's the difference?

PLAYER: Ten guilders.

ROS (*horrified*): Ten *guilders*!

PLAYER: I mean eight.

ROS: Together?

PLAYER: Each. I don't think you understand—

ROS: What are you *saying*?

PLAYER: What am I saying—seven.

ROS: Where have you *been*?

PLAYER: Roundabout. A nest of children carries the custom of the town. Juvenile companies, they are the fashion. But they cannot match our repertoire ... we'll stoop to anything if that's your bent. ...

[He regards ROS *meaningfully but* ROS *returns the stare blankly.]*

ROS: They'll grow up.

PLAYER (*giving up*): There's one born every minute. (*To* TRAGEDIANS:) On-ward!

[The TRAGEDIANS *start to resume their burdens and their journey.* GUIL *stirs himself at last.]*

GUIL: Where are you going?

PLAYER: Ha-alt!

[They halt and turn.]

Home, sir.
GUIL: Where from?
PLAYER: Home. We're travelling people. We take our chances where we find them.
GUIL: It was chance, then?
PLAYER: Chance?
GUIL: You found us.
PLAYER: Oh yes.
GUIL: You were looking?
PLAYER: Oh no.
GUIL: Chance, then.
PLAYER: Or fate.
GUIL: Yours or ours?
PLAYER: It could hardly be one without the other.
GUIL: Fate, then.
PLAYER: Oh yes. We have no control. Tonight we play to the court. Or the night after. Or to the tavern. Or not.
GUIL: Perhaps I can use my influence.
PLAYER: At the tavern?
GUIL: At the court. I would say I have some influence.
PLAYER: Would you say so?
GUIL: I have influence yet.
PLAYER: Yet what?

[GUIL seizes the PLAYER violently.]

GUIL: I have influence!

[The PLAYER does not resist. GUIL loosens his hold.]

(More calmly.) You said something—about getting caught up in the action——
PLAYER (gaily freeing himself): I did!—I did!—You're quicker than your friend. . . . (Confidingly.) Now for a handful of guilders I happen to have a private and uncut performance of The Rape of the Sabine Women—or rather woman, or rather Alfred——(Over his shoulder.) Get your skirt on, Alfred——

[The BOY starts struggling into a female robe.]

. . . and for eight you can participate.

[GUIL backs, PLAYER follows.]

. . . taking either part.

[GUIL backs.]

. . . or both for ten.

[GUIL tries to turn away, PLAYER holds his sleeve.]

. . . with encores——

[GUIL smashes the PLAYER across the face. The PLAYER

recoils. GUIL stands trembling.]

(Resigned and quiet). Get your skirt off, Alfred. . . .

[ALFRED struggles out of his half-on robe.]

GUIL (shaking with rage and fright): It could have been—it didn't have to be obscene. . . . It could have been—a bird out of season, dropping bright-feathered on my shoulder. . . . It could have been a tongueless dwarf standing by the road to point the way. . . . I was prepared. But it's this, is it? No enigma, no dignity, nothing classical, portentous, only this—a comic pornographer and a rabble of prostitutes. . . .
PLAYER (acknowledging the description with a sweep of his hat, bowing; sadly): You should have caught us in better times. We were purists then. (Straightens up.) On-ward.

[The PLAYERS make to leave.]

ROS (his voice has changed: he has caught on): Excuse me!
PLAYER: Ha-alt!

[They halt.]

A-al-l-fred!

[ALFRED resumes the struggle. The PLAYER comes forward.]

ROS: You're not—ah—exclusively players, then?
PLAYER: We're inclusively players, sir.
ROS: So you give—exhibitions?
PLAYER: Performances, sir.
ROS: Yes, of course. There's more money in that, is there?
PLAYER: There's more trade, sir.
ROS: Times being what they are.
PLAYER: Yes.
ROS: Indifferent.
PLAYER: Completely.
ROS: You know I'd no idea——
PLAYER: No——
ROS: I mean, I've heard of—but I've never actually—
PLAYER: No.
ROS: I mean, what exactly do you do?
PLAYER: We keep to our usual stuff, more or less, only inside out. We do on stage the things that are supposed to happen off. Which is a kind of integrity, if you look on every exit being an entrance somewhere else.
ROS (nervy, loud): Well, I'm not really the type of man who—no, but don't hurry off—sit down and tell us about some of the things people ask you to do——

[The PLAYER turns away.]

PLAYER: On-ward!
ROS: Just a minute!

[They turn and look at him without expression.]

>   Well, all right—I wouldn't mind seeing—just an idea of the kind of—(*Bravely.*) What will you do for that? (*And tosses a single coin on the ground between them.*)

[The PLAYER spits at the coin, from where he stands. The TRAGEDIANS demur, trying to get at the coin. He kicks and cuffs them back.]
>   On!

[ALFRED is still half in and out of his robe. The PLAYER cuffs him.]

>   (*To* ALFRED:) What are you playing at?

[ROS is shamed into fury.]

ROS: Filth! Disgusting—I'll report you to the authorities—*perverts*! I know your game all right, it's all filth!

[The PLAYERS are about to leave. GUIL has remained detached.]

GUIL (*casually*): Do you like a bet?

[The TRAGEDIANS turn and look interested. The PLAYER comes forward.]

PLAYER: What kind of bet did you have in mind?

[GUIL walks half the distance towards the PLAYER, stops with his foot over the coin.]

GUIL: Double or quits.
PLAYER: Well . . . heads.

[GUIL raises his foot. The PLAYER bends. The TRAGEDIANS crowd round. Relief and congratulations. The PLAYER picks up the coin. GUIL throws him a second coin.]

GUIL: Again?

[Some of the TRAGEDIANS are for it, others against.]

GUIL: Evens.

[The PLAYER nods and tosses the coin.]

GUIL: Heads.

[It is. He picks it up.]

Again.

[GUIL spins coin.]

PLAYER: Heads.

[It is. PLAYER picks up coin. He has two coins again. He spins one.]

GUIL: Heads.

[It is. GUIL picks it up. Then tosses it immediately.]

PLAYER (*fractional hesitation*): Tails.

[But it's heads. GUIL picks it up. PLAYER tosses down his last coin by way of paying up, and turns away. GUIL doesn't pick it up; he puts his foot on it.]

GUIL: Heads.
PLAYER: No!

[Pause. The TRAGEDIANS are against this.]

>   (*Apologetically.*) They don't like the odds.
GUIL (*lifts his foot, squats; picks up the coin still squatting; looks up*): You were right—heads. (*Spins it, slaps his hand on it, on the floor.*) Heads I win.
PLAYER: No.
GUIL (*uncovers coin*): Right again. (*Repeat.*) Heads I win.
PLAYER: No.
GUIL (*uncovers coin*): And right again. (*Repeat.*) Heads I win.
PLAYER: *No!*

[He turns away, the TRAGEDIANS with him. GUIL stands up, comes close.]

GUIL: Would you believe it? (*Stands back, relaxes, smiles.*) Bet me the year of my birth doubled is an odd number.
PLAYER: *Your* birth——!
GUIL: If you don't trust me don't bet with me.
PLAYER: Would you trust *me*?
GUIL: *Bet* me then.
PLAYER: My birth?
GUIL: Odd numbers you win.
PLAYER: You're on——

[The TRAGEDIANS have come forward, wide awake.]

GUIL: Good. Year of your birth. Double it. Even numbers I win, odd numbers I lose.

[Silence. An awful sigh as the TRAGEDIANS realize that any number doubled is even. Then a terrible row as they object. Then a terrible silence.]

PLAYER: We have no money.

[GUIL turns to him.]

GUIL: Ah. Then what *have* you got?

[The PLAYER silently brings ALFRED forward. GUIL regards ALFRED sadly.]

Was it for this?

PLAYER: It's the best we've got.

GUIL (*looking up and around*): Then the times are bad indeed.

[The PLAYER starts to speak, protestation, but GUIL turns on him viciously.]

The very *air* stinks.

[The PLAYER moves back. GUIL moves down to the footlights and turns.]

Come here, Alfred.

[ALFRED moves down and stands, frightened and small.]

(*Gently.*) Do you lose often?

ALFRED: Yes, sir.

GUIL: Then what could you have left to lose?

ALFRED: Nothing, sir.

[Pause. GUIL regards him.]

GUIL: Do you like being . . . an actor?

ALFRED: No, sir.

[GUIL looks around, at the audience.]

GUIL: You and I, Alfred—we could create a dramatic precedent here.

[And ALFRED, who has been near tears, starts to sniffle.]

Come, come, Alfred, this is no way to fill the theatres of Europe.

[The PLAYER has moved down, to remonstrate with ALFRED. GUIL cuts him off again.]

(*Viciously.*) Do you know any good plays?

PLAYER: Plays?

ROS (*coming forward, faltering shyly*): Exhibitions. . . .

GUIL: I thought you said you were actors.

PLAYER (*dawning*): Oh. Oh well, we *are*. We are. But there hasn't been much call——

GUIL: You lost. Well then—one of the Greeks, perhaps? You're familiar with the tragedies of antiquity, are you? The great homicidal classics? Matri, patri, fratri, sorrori, uxori and it goes without saying——

ROS: Saucy——

GUIL: —Suicidal—hm? Maidens aspiring to godheads——

ROS: And vice versa——

GUIL: Your kind of thing, is it?

PLAYER: Well, no, I can't say it is, really. We're more of the blood, love and rhetoric school.

GUIL: Well, I'll leave the choice to you, if there is anything to choose between them.

PLAYER: They're hardly divisible, sir—well, I can do you blood and love without the rhetoric, and I can do you blood and rhetoric without the love, and I can do you all three concurrent or consecutive, but I can't do you love and rhetoric without the blood. Blood is compulsory—they're all blood, you see.

GUIL: Is that what people want?

PLAYER: It's what we do. (*Small pause. He turns away.*)

[GUIL touches ALFRED on the shoulder.]

GUIL (*wry, gentle*): Thank you; we'll let you know.

[The PLAYER has moved upstage. ALFRED follows.]

PLAYER (*to* TRAGEDIANS): Thirty-eight!

ROS (*moving across, fascinated and hopeful*): Position?

PLAYER: Sir?

ROS: One of your—tableaux?

PLAYER: No, sir.

ROS: Oh.

PLAYER (*to the* TRAGEDIANS, *now departing with their cart, already taking various props off it*): Entrances there and there (*indicating upstage*).

[The PLAYER has not moved his position for his last four lines. He does not move now. GUIL waits.]

GUIL: Well . . . aren't you going to change into your costume?

PLAYER: I never change out of it, sir.

GUIL: Always in character.

PLAYER: That's it.

[Pause.]

GUIL: Aren't you going to—come *on*?

PLAYER: I *am* on.

GUIL: But if you *are* on, you can't *come* on. Can you?

PLAYER: I *start* on.

GUIL: But it hasn't *started*. Go on. We'll look out for you.

PLAYER: I'll give you a wave.

[He does not move. His immobility is now pointed, and getting awkward. Pause. ROS walks up to him till they are face to face.]

ROS: Excuse me.

[Pause. The PLAYER *lifts his downstage foot. It was covering* GUIL's *coin.* ROS *puts his foot on the coin. Smiles.]*

Thank you.

[The PLAYER *turns and goes.* ROS *has bent for the coin.]*

GUIL *(moving out)*: Come on.
ROS: I say—that was lucky.
GUIL *(turning)*: What?
ROS: It was tails.

[He tosses the coin to GUIL *who catches it. Simultaneously—a lighting change sufficient to alter the exterior mood into interior, but nothing violent.*

And OPHELIA *runs on in some alarm, holding up her skirts—followed by* HAMLET.

OPHELIA *has been sewing and she holds the garment. They are both mute.* HAMLET, *with his doublet all unbraced, no hat upon his head, his stockings fouled, ungartered and down-gyved to his ankle, pale as his shirt, his knees knocking each other . . . and with a look so piteous, he takes her by the wrist and holds her hard, then he goes to the length of his arm, and with his other hand over his brow, falls to such perusal of her face as he would draw it. . . . At last, with a little shaking of his arm, and thrice his head waving up and down, he raises a sigh so piteous and profound that it does seem to shatter all his bulk and end his being. That done he lets her go, and with his head over his shoulder turned, he goes out backwards without taking his eyes off her . . . she runs off in the opposite direction.*

ROS *and* GUIL *have frozen.* GUIL *unfreezes first. He jumps at* ROS.]

GUIL: Come on!

[But a flourish—enter CLAUDIUS *and* GERTRUDE, *attended.]*

CLAUDIUS: Welcome, dear Rosencrantz . . . *(he raises a hand at* GUIL *while* ROS *bows—*GUIL *bows late and hurriedly) . . . and Guildenstern.*

[He raises a hand at ROS *while* GUIL *bows to him—*ROS *is still straightening up from his previous bow and halfway up he bows down again. With his head down, he twists to look at* GUIL, *who is on the way up.]*

Moreover that we did much long to see you,
The need we have to use you did provoke
Our hasty sending.

*[*ROS *and* GUIL *still adjusting their clothing for* CLAUDIUS's *presence.]*

Something have you heard

Of Hamlet's transformation, so call it,
Sith nor th'exterior nor the inward man
Resembles that it was. What it should be,
More than his father's death, that thus hath
   put him,
So much from th'understanding of himself,
I cannot dream of. I entreat you both
That, being of so young days brought up with
   him
And sith so neighboured to his youth and
   haviour
That you vouchsafe your rest here in our court
Some little time, so by your companies
To draw him on to pleasures, and to gather
So much as from occasion you may glean,
Whether aught to us unknown afflicts him
   thus,
That opened lies within our remedy.
GERTRUDE: Good *(fractional suspense)* gentlemen . . .

[They both bow.]

He hath much talked of you,
And sure I am, two men there is not living
To whom he more adheres. If it will please you
To show us so much gentry and goodwill
As to expand your time with us awhile
For the supply and profit of our hope,
Your visitation shall receive such thanks
As fits a king's remembrance.
ROS: Both your majesties
Might, by the sovereign power you have of us,
Put your dread pleasures more into command
Than to entreaty.
GUIL: But we both obey,
And here give up ourselves in the full bent
To lay our service freely at your feet,
To be commanded.
CLAUDIUS: Thanks, Rosencrantz *(turning to* ROS *who is caught unprepared, while* GUIL *bows)* and gentle Guildenstern *(turning to* GUIL *who is bent double).*
GERTRUDE *(correcting)*: Thanks Guildenstern *(turning to* ROS, *who bows as* GUIL *checks upward movement to bow too—both bent double, squinting at each other) . . . and gentle Rosencrantz (turning to* GUIL, *both straightening up—*GUIL *checks again and bows again).*
And I beseech you instantly to visit
My too much changed son. Go, some of you,
And bring these gentlemen where Hamlet is.

[Two ATTENDANTS *exit backwards, indicating that* ROS *and* GUIL *should follow.]*

GUIL: Heaven make our presence and our practices
Pleasant and helpful to him.

GERTRUDE: Ay, amen!

[ROS and GUIL move towards a downstage wing. Before they get there, POLONIUS enters. They stop and bow to him. He nods and hurries upstage to CLAUDIUS. They turn to look at him.]

POLONIUS: The ambassadors from Norway, my good lord, are joyfully returned.

CLAUDIUS: Thou still hast been the father of good news.

POLONIUS: Have I, my lord? Assure you, my good liege,
I hold my duty as I hold my soul,
Both to my God and to my gracious King;
And I do think, or else this brain of mine
Hunts not the trail of policy so sure
As it hath used to do, that I have found
The very cause of Hamlet's lunacy. . . .

[Exeunt—leaving ROS and GUIL.]

ROS: I want to go home.

GUIL: Don't let them confuse you.

ROS: I'm out of my step here——

GUIL: We'll soon be home and high—dry and home—I'll——

ROS: It's all over my *depth*——

GUIL: —I'll hie you home and——

ROS: —out of my head——

GUIL: —dry you high and——

ROS *(cracking, high)*: —over my step over my head body!—I tell you it's all stopping to a death, it's boding to a depth, stepping to a head, it's all heading to a dead stop——

GUIL *(the nursemaid)*: There! . . . and we'll soon be home and dry . . . and *high* and dry. . . . *(Rapidly.)* Has it ever happened to you that all of a sudden and for no reason at all you haven't the faintest idea how to spell the word—"wife"—or "house"—because when you write it down you just can't remember ever having seen those letters in that order before . . . ?

ROS: I remember——

GUIL: Yes?

ROS: I remember when there were no questions.

GUIL: There were always questions. To exchange one set for another is no great matter.

ROS: Answers, yes. There were answers to everything.

GUIL: You've forgotten.

ROS *(flaring)*: I haven't forgotten—how I used to remember my own name—and yours, oh *yes!* There were answers everywhere you *looked*. There was no question about it—people knew who I was and if they didn't they asked and I

told them.

GUIL: You did, the trouble is, each of them is . . . plausible, without being instinctive. All your life you live so close to truth, it becomes a permanent blur in the corner of your eye, and when something nudges it into outline it is like being ambushed by a grotesque. A man standing in his saddle in the half-lit half-alive dawn banged on the shutters and called two names. He was just a hat and a cloak levitating in the grey plume of his own breath, but when he called we came. That much is certain—we came.

ROS: Well I can tell you I'm sick to death of it. I don't care one way or another, so why don't you make up your mind.

GUIL: We can't afford anything quite so arbitrary. Nor did we come all this way for a christening. All *that*—preceded us. But we are comparatively fortunate; we might have been left to sift the whole field of human nomenclature, like two blind men looting a bazaar for their own portraits. . . . At least we are presented with alternatives.

ROS: Well as from now——

GUIL: —But not choice.

ROS: You made me look ridiculous in there.

GUIL: I looked just as ridiculous as you did.

ROS *(an anguished cry)*: Consistency is all I ask!

GUIL *(low, wry rhetoric)*: Give us this day our daily mask.

ROS *(a dying fall)*: I want to go home. *(Moves.)* Which way did we come in? I've lost my sense of direction.

GUIL: The only beginning is birth and the only end is death—if you can't count on that, what can you count on?

[They connect again.]

ROS: We don't owe anything to anyone.

GUIL: We've been caught up. Your smallest action sets off another somewhere else, and is set off by it. Keep an eye open, an ear cocked. Tread warily, follow instructions. We'll be all right.

ROS: For how long?

GUIL: Till events have played themselves out. There's a logic at work—it's all done for you, don't worry. Enjoy it. Relax. To be taken in hand and led, like being a child again, even without the innocence, a child—it's like being given a prize, an extra slice of childhood when you least expect it, as a prize for being good, or compensation for never having had one. . . . Do I contradict myself?

ROS: I can't remember. . . . What have we got to go on?

GUIL: We have been briefed. Hamlet's transformation. What do you recollect?

ROS: Well, he's changed, hasn't he? The exterior and inward man fails to resemble——

GUIL: Draw him on to pleasures—glean what afflicts him.

ROS: Something more than his father's death——

GUIL: He's always talking about us—there aren't two people living whom he dotes on more than us.

ROS: We cheer him up—find out what's the matter——

GUIL: Exactly, it's a matter of asking the right questions and giving away as little as we can. It's a game.

ROS: And then we can go?

GUIL: And receive such thanks as fits a king's remembrance.

ROS: I like the sound of that. What do you think he means by remembrance?

GUIL: He doesn't forget his friends.

ROS: Would you care to estimate?

GUIL: Difficult to say, really—some kings tend to be amnesiac, others I suppose—the opposite, whatever that is. . . .

ROS: Yes—but——

GUIL: Elephantine . . . ?

ROS: Not how long—how much?

GUIL: *Retentive*—he's a very retentive king, a royal retainer. . . .

ROS: What are you playing at?

GUIL: Words, words. They're all we have to go on.

[*Pause.*]

ROS: Shouldn't we be doing something—constructive?

GUIL: What did you have in mind? . . . A short, blunt human pyramid . . . ?

ROS: We could go.

GUIL: Where?

ROS: After him.

GUIL: Why? They've got us placed now—if we start moving around, we'll all be chasing each other all night.

[*Hiatus.*]

ROS (*at footlights*): How very intriguing! (*Turns.*) I feel like a spectator—an appalling business. The only thing that makes it bearable is the irrational belief that somebody interesting will come on in a minute. . . .

GUIL: See anyone?

ROS: No. You?

GUIL: No. (*At footlights.*) What a fine persecution—to be kept intrigued without ever quite being enlightened. . . . (*Pause.*) We've had no practice.

ROS: We could play at questions.

GUIL: What good would that do?

ROS: Practice!

GUIL: Statement! One—love.

ROS: Cheating!

GUIL: How?

ROS: I hadn't started yet.

GUIL: Statement. Two—love.

ROS: Are you counting that?

GUIL: What?

ROS: Are you counting that?

GUIL: Foul! No repetitions. Three—love. First game to . . .

ROS: I'm not going to play if you're going to be like that.

GUIL: Whose serve?

ROS: Hah?

GUIL: Foul! No grunts. Love—one.

ROS: Whose go?

GUIL: Why?

ROS: Why not?

GUIL: What for?

ROS: Foul! No synonyms! One—all.

GUIL: What in God's name is going on?

ROS: Foul! No rhetoric. Two—one.

GUIL: What does it all add up to?

ROS: Can't you guess?

GUIL: Were you addressing me?

ROS: Is there anyone else?

GUIL: Who?

ROS: How would I know?

GUIL: Why do you ask?

ROS: Are you serious?

GUIL: Was that rhetoric?

ROS: No.

GUIL: Statement! Two—all. Game point.

ROS: What's the matter with you today?

GUIL: When?

ROS: What?

GUIL: Are you deaf?

ROS: Am I dead?

GUIL: Yes or no?

ROS: Is there a choice?

GUIL: Is there a God?

ROS: Foul! No *non sequiturs*, three—two, one game all.

GUIL (*seriously*): What's your name?

ROS: What's yours?

GUIL: I asked you first.

ROS: Statement. One—love.

GUIL: What's your name when you're at home?

ROS: What's yours?

GUIL: When I'm at home?

ROS: Is it different at home?

GUIL: What home?

ROS: Haven't you got one?

GUIL: Why do you ask?

Ros: What are you driving at?

Guil (*with emphasis*): What's your name?!

Ros: Repetition. Two—love. Match point to me.

Guil (*seizing him violently*): WHO DO YOU THINK YOU ARE?

Ros: Rhetoric! Game and match! (*Pause.*) Where's it going to end?

Guil: That's the question.

Ros: It's *all* questions.

Guil: Do you think it matters?

Ros: Doesn't it matter to you?

Guil: Why should it matter?

Ros: What does it matter why?

Guil (*teasing gently*): Doesn't it *matter* why it matters?

Ros (*rounding on him*): What's the *matter* with you?

[*Pause.*]

Guil: It doesn't matter.

Ros (*voice in the wilderness*): . . . What's the game?

Guil: What are the rules?

[*Enter HAMLET behind, crossing the stage, reading a book—as he is about to disappear GUIL notices him.*]

Guil (*sharply*): Rosencrantz!

Ros (*jumps*): What!

[*HAMLET goes. Triumph dawns on them, they smile.*]

Guil: There! How was that?

Ros: Clever!

Guil: Natural?

Ros: Instinctive.

Guil: Got it in your head?

Ros: I take my hat off to you.

Guil: Shake hands.

[*They do.*]

Ros: Now I'll try you—Guil—!

Guil: —Not yet—catch me unawares.

Ros: Right.

[*They separate. Pause. Aside to GUIL.*]

Ready?

Guil (*explodes*): Don't be stupid.

Ros: Sorry.

[*Pause.*]

Guil (*snaps*): Guildenstern!

Ros (*jumps*): What?

[*He is immediately crestfallen, GUIL is disgusted.*]

Guil: Consistency is all I ask!

Ros (*quietly*): Immortality is all I seek. . . .

Guil (*dying fall*): Give us this day our daily week. . . .

[*Beat.*]

Ros: Who was that?

Guil: Didn't you know him?

Ros: He didn't know me.

Guil: He didn't see you.

Ros: I didn't see him.

Guil: We shall see. I *hardly* knew him, he's changed.

Ros: You could see that?

Guil: Transformed.

Ros: How do you know?

Guil: Inside and out.

Ros: I see.

Guil: He's not himself.

Ros: He's changed.

Guil: I could see that.

[*Beat.*]

Glean what afflicts him.

Ros: Me?

Guil: Him.

Ros: How?

Guil: Question and answer. Old ways are the best ways.

Ros: He's afflicted.

Guil: You question, I'll answer.

Ros: He's not himself, you know.

Guil: I'm him, you see.

[*Beat.*]

Ros: Who am I then?

Guil: You're yourself.

Ros: And he's you?

Guil: Not a bit of it.

Ros: Are you afflicted?

Guil: That's the idea. Are you ready?

Ros: Let's go back a bit.

Guil: I'm afflicted.

Ros: I see.

Guil: Glean what afflicts me.

Ros: Right.

Guil: Question and answer.

Ros: How should I begin?

Guil: Address me.

Ros: My dear Guildenstern!

Guil (*quietly*): You've forgotten—haven't you?

Ros: My dear Rosencrantz!

Guil (*great control*): I don't think you quite understand. What we are attempting is a hypothesis in which *I* answer for *him*, while *you* ask me questions.

Ros: Ah! Ready?

Guil: You know what to do?

Ros: What?

Guil: Are you stupid?

Ros: Pardon?

Guil: Are you deaf?

Ros: Did you speak?

Guil (*admonishing*): Not now——

Ros: Statement.

Guil (*shouts*): Not now! (*Pause.*) If I had any doubts, or rather hopes, they are dispelled. What could we possibly have in common except our situation? (*They separate and sit.*) Perhaps he'll come back this way.

Ros: Should we go?

Guil: Why?

[*Pause.*]

Ros (*starts up. Snaps fingers*): Oh! You mean—you pretend to be *him*, and *I* ask you questions!

Guil (*dry*): Very good.

Ros: You had me confused.

Guil: I could see I had.

Ros: How should I begin?

Guil: Address me.

[*They stand and face each other, posing.*]

Ros: My honoured Lord!

Guil: My dear Rosencrantz!

[*Pause.*]

Ros: Am I pretending to be you, then?

Guil: Certainly not. If you like. Shall we continue?

Ros: Question and answer.

Guil: Right.

Ros: Right. My honoured lord!

Guil: My dear fellow!

Ros: How are you?

Guil: Afflicted!

Ros: Really? In what way?

Guil: Transformed.

Ros: Inside or out?

Guil: Both.

Ros: I see. (*Pause.*) Not much new there.

Guil: Go into details. *Delve.* Probe the background, establish the situation.

Ros: So—so your uncle is the king of Denmark?!

Guil: And my father before him.

Ros: His father before him?

Guil: No, my father before him.

Ros: But surely——

Guil: You might well ask.

Ros: Let me get it straight. Your father was king. You were his only son. Your father dies. You are of age. Your uncle becomes king.

Guil: Yes.

Ros: Unorthodox.

Guil: Undid me.

Ros: Undeniable. Where were you?

Guil: In Germany.

Ros: Usurpation, then.

Guil: He slipped in.

Ros: Which reminds me.

Guil: Well, it would.

Ros: I don't want to be personal.

Guil: It's common knowledge.

Ros: Your mother's marriage.

Guil: He slipped in.

[*Beat.*]

Ros (*lugubriously*): His body was still warm.

Guil: So was hers.

Ros: Extraordinary.

Guil: Indecent.

Ros: Hasty.

Guil: Suspicious.

Ros: It makes you think.

Guil: Don't think I haven't thought of it.

Ros: And with her husband's brother.

Guil: They were close.

Ros: She went to him——

Guil: —Too close——

Ros: —for comfort.

Guil: It looks bad.

Ros: It adds up.

Guil: Incest to adultery.

Ros: Would you go so far?

Guil: Never.

Ros: To sum up: your father, whom you love, dies, you are his heir, you come back to find that hardly was the corpse cold before his young brother popped onto his throne and into his sheets, thereby offending both legal and natural practice. Now why exactly are you behaving in this extraordinary manner?

Guil: I can't imagine! (*Pause.*) But all that is well known, common property. Yet he sent for us. And we did come.

Ros (*alert, ear cocked*): I say! I heard music——

Guil: We're here.

Ros: —Like a band—I thought I heard a band.

Guil: Rosencrantz . . .

Ros (*absently, still listening*): What?

[*Pause, short.*]

Guil (*gently wry*): Guildenstern . . .

Ros (*irritated by the repetition*): What?

Guil: Don't you discriminate at all?

Ros (*turning dumbly*): Wha'?

[*Pause.*]

Guil: Go and see if he's there.

ROS: Who?
GUIL: There.

[ROS goes to an upstage wing, looks, returns, formally making his report.]

ROS: Yes.
GUIL: What is he doing?

[ROS repeats movement.]

ROS: Talking.
GUIL: To himself?

[ROS starts to move. GUIL cuts in impatiently.]

Is he alone?
ROS: No.
GUIL: Then he's not talking to himself, is he?
ROS: Not *by* himself. . . . Coming this way, I think. (*Shiftily.*) Should we go?
GUIL: Why? We're marked now.

[HAMLET enters, backwards, talking, followed by POLONIUS, upstage. ROS and GUIL occupy the two downstage corners looking upstage.]

HAMLET: . . . for you yourself, sir, should be as old as I am if like a crab you could go backward.
POLONIUS (*aside*): Though this be madness, yet there is method in it. Will you walk out of the air, my lord?
HAMLET: Into my grave.
POLONIUS: Indeed, that's out of the air.

[HAMLET crosses to upstage exit, POLONIUS asiding unintelligibly until——]

My lord, I will take my leave of you.
HAMLET: You cannot take from me anything that I will more willingly part withal—except my life, except my life, except my life. . . .
POLONIUS (*crossing downstage*): Fare you well, my lord. (*To* ROS:) You go to seek Lord Hamlet? There he is.
ROS (*to* POLONIUS): God save you sir.

[POLONIUS goes.]

GUIL (*calls upstage to* HAMLET): My honoured lord!
ROS: My most dear lord!

[HAMLET centred upstage, turns to them.]

HAMLET: My excellent good friends! How dost thou Guildenstern? (*Coming downstage with an arm raised to* ROS, GUIL *meanwhile bowing to no greeting.* HAMLET *corrects himself. Still to* ROS:) Ah Rosencrantz!

[They laugh good-naturedly at the mistake. They all meet midstage, turn upstage to walk, HAMLET in the middle, arm over each shoulder.]

HAMLET: Good lads how do you both?

BLACKOUT

ACT II

HAMLET, ROS and GUIL talking, the continuation of the previous scene. Their conversation, on the move, is indecipherable at first. The first intelligible line is HAMLET's, coming at the end of a short speech—see Shakespeare Act II, scene 2.

HAMLET: S'blood, there is something in this more than natural, if philosophy could find it out.

[A flourish from the TRAGEDIANS' *band.]*

GUIL: There are the players.
HAMLET: Gentlemen, you are welcome to Elsinore. Your hands, come then. (*He takes their hands.*) The appurtenance of welcome is fashion and ceremony. Let me comply with you in this garb, lest my extent to the players (which I tell you must show fairly outwards) should more appear like entertainment than yours. You are welcome. (*About to leave.*) But my uncle-father and aunt-mother are deceived.
GUIL: In what, my dear lord?
HAMLET: I am but mad north north-west; when the wind is southerly I know a hawk from a hand-saw.

[POLONIUS enters as GUIL turns away.]

POLONIUS: Well be with you gentlemen.
HAMLET (*to* ROS): Mark you, Guildenstern (*uncertainly to* GUIL) and you too; at each ear a hearer. That great baby you see there is not yet out of his swaddling clouts. . . . (*He takes* ROS *upstage with him, talking together.*)
POLONIUS: My Lord! I have news to tell you.
HAMLET (*releasing* ROS *and mimicking*): My lord, I have news to tell you. . . . When Roscius was an actor in Rome . . .

[ROS comes downstage to rejoin GUIL.]

POLONIUS (*as he follows* HAMLET *out*): The actors are come hither my lord.
HAMLET: Buzz, buzz.

*[Exeunt HAMLET and POLONIUS.
ROS and GUIL ponder. Each reluctant to speak first.]*

GUIL: Hm?
ROS: Yes?
GUIL: What?
ROS: I thought you . . .
GUIL: No.
ROS: Ah.

[Pause.]

GUIL: I think we can say we made some headway.
ROS: You think so?
GUIL: I think we can say that.
ROS: I think we can say he made us look ridiculous.
GUIL: We played it close to the chest of course.
ROS (*derisively*): "Question and answer. Old ways are the best ways!" He was scoring off us all down the line.
GUIL: He caught us on the wrong foot once or twice, perhaps, but I thought we gained some ground.
ROS (*simply*): He murdered us.
GUIL: He might have had the edge.
ROS (*roused*): Twenty-seven—three, and you think he might have had the edge?! He *murdered* us.
GUIL: What about our evasions?
ROS: Oh, our evasions were lovely. "Were you sent for?" he says. "My lord, we were sent for. . . ." I didn't know where to put myself.
GUIL: He had six rhetoricals——
ROS: It was question and answer, all right. Twenty-seven questions he got out in ten minutes, and answered three. I was waiting for you to *delve*. "When is he going to start *delving*?" I asked myself.
GUIL:—And two repetitions.
ROS: Hardly a leading question between us.
GUIL: We got his *symptoms*, didn't we?
ROS: Half of what he said meant something else, and the other half didn't mean anything at all.
GUIL: Thwarted ambition—a sense of grievance, that's my diagnosis.
ROS: Six rhetorical and two repetition, leaving nineteen, of which we answered fifteen. And what did we get in return? He's depressed! . . . Denmark's a prison and he'd rather live in a nutshell; some shadow-play about the nature of ambition, which never got down to cases, and finally one direct question which might have led somewhere, and led in fact to his illuminating claim to tell a hawk from a handsaw.

[Pause.]

GUIL: When the wind is southerly.
ROS: And the weather's clear.
GUIL: And when it isn't he can't.
ROS: He's at the mercy of the elements. (*Licks his fin-ger and holds it up—facing audience.*) Is that southerly?

[They stare at audience.]

GUIL: It doesn't *look* southerly. What made you think so?
ROS: I didn't *say* I think so. It could be northerly for all I know.
GUIL: I wouldn't have thought so.
ROS: Well, if you're going to be dogmatic.
GUIL: Wait a minute—we came from roughly south according to a rough map.
ROS: I see. Well, which way did we come in? (GUIL *looks round vaguely.*) Roughly.
GUIL (*clears his throat*): In the morning the sun would be easterly. I think we can assume that.
ROS: That it's morning?
GUIL: If it is, and the sun is over *there* (*his right as he faces the audience*) for instance, *that* (*front*) would be northerly. On the other hand, if it is not morning and the sun is over *there* (*his left*) . . . *that* . . . (*lamely*) would *still* be northerly. (*Picking up.*) To put it another way, if we came from down there (*front*) and it is morning, the sun would be up there (*his left*), and if it is actually over *there* (*his right*) and it's still morning, we must have come from up *there* (*behind him*), and if *that* is southerly (*his left*) and the sun is really over *there* (*front*), then it's the afternoon. However, if none of these is the case——
ROS: Why don't you go and have a look?
GUIL: Pragmatism?!—is that all you have to offer? You seem to have no conception of where we stand! You won't find the answer written down for you in the bowl of a compass—I can tell you that. (*Pause.*) Besides, you can never tell this far north—it's probably dark out there.
ROS: I merely suggest that the position of the sun, if it is out, would give you a rough idea of the time; alternatively, the clock, if it is going, would give you a rough idea of the position of the sun. I forget which you're trying to establish.
GUIL: I'm trying to establish the direction of the wind.
ROS: There isn't any wind. *Draught*, yes.
GUIL: In that case, the origin. Trace it to its source and it might give us a rough idea of the way we came in—which might give us a rough idea of south, for further reference.
ROS: It's coming up through the floor. (*He studies the floor.*) That can't be south, can it?
GUIL: That's not a direction. Lick your toe and wave it around a bit.

[ROS considers the distance of his foot.]

Ros: No, I think you'd have to lick it for me.

[Pause.]

Guil: I'm prepared to let the whole matter drop.
Ros: Or I could lick yours, of course.
Guil: No thank you.
Ros: I'll even wave it around for you.
Guil (*down* Ros's *throat*): What in God's name is the matter with you?
Ros: Just being friendly.
Guil (*retiring*): Somebody might come in. It's what we're counting on, after all. Ultimately.

[Good pause.]

Ros: Perhaps they've all trampled each other to death in the rush. . . . Give them a shout. Something provocative. *Intrigue* them.
Guil: Wheels have been set in motion, and they have their own pace, to which we are . . . condemned. Each move is dictated by the previous one—that is the meaning of order. If we start being arbitrary it'll just be a shambles: at least, let us hope so. Because if we happened, just happened to discover, or even suspect, that our spontaneity was part of their order, we'd know that we were lost. (*He sits.*) A Chinaman of the T'ang Dynasty—and, by which definition, a philosopher—dreamed he was a butterfly, and from that moment he was never quite sure that he was not a butterfly dreaming it was a Chinese philosopher. Envy him; in his two-fold security.

[A good pause. Ros leaps up and bellows at the audience.]

Ros: Fire!

[Guil jumps up.]

Guil: Where?
Ros: It's all right—I'm demonstrating the misuse of free speech. To prove that it exists. (*He regards the audience, that is the direction, with contempt—and other directions, then front again.*) Not a move. They should burn to death in their shoes. (*He takes out one of his coins. Spins it. Catches it. Looks at it. Replaces it.*)
Guil: What was it?
Ros: What?
Guil: Heads or tails?
Ros: Oh. I didn't look.
Guil: Yes you did.
Ros: Oh, did I? (*He takes out a coin, studies it.*) Quite right—it rings a bell.
Guil: What's the last thing you remember?

Ros: I don't wish to be reminded of it.
Guil: We cross our bridges when we come to them and burn them behind us, with nothing to show for our progress except a memory of the smell of smoke, and a presumption that once our eyes watered.

[Ros approaches him brightly, holding a coin between finger and thumb. He covers it with his other hand, draws his fists apart and holds them for Guil. Guil considers them. Indicates the left hand, Ros opens it to show it empty.]

Ros: No.

[Repeat process. Guil indicates left hand again. Ros shows it empty.]

Double bluff!

[Repeat process—Guil taps one hand, then the other hand, quickly. Ros inadvertently shows that both are empty. Ros laughs as Guil turns upstage. Ros stops laughing, looks around his feet, pats his clothes, puzzled.]

    Polonius breaks that up by entering upstage followed by the Tragedians and Hamlet.]
Polonius (*entering*): Come sirs.
Hamlet: Follow him, friends. We'll hear a play tomorrow. (*Aside to the* Player, *who is the last of the* Tragedians:) Dost thou hear me, old friend? Can you play *The Murder of Gonzago*?
Player: Ay, my lord.
Hamlet: We'll ha't tomorrow night. You could for a need study a speech of some dozen or sixteen lines which I would set down and insert in't, could you not?
Player: Ay, my lord.
Hamlet: Very well. Follow that lord, and look you mock him not.

[The Player crossing downstage, notes Ros and Guil. Stops. Hamlet crossing downstage addresses them without pause.]

Hamlet: My good friends, I'll leave you till tonight. You are welcome to Elsinore.
Ros: Good, my lord.

[Hamlet goes.]

Guil: So you've caught up.
Player (*coldly*): Not yet, sir.
Guil: Now mind your tongue, or we'll have it out and throw the rest of you away, like a nightingale at a Roman feast.
Ros: Took the very words out of my mouth.
Guil: You'd be *lost* for words.

ROS: You'd be tongue-tied.
GUIL: Like a mute in a monologue.
ROS: Like a nightingale at a Roman feast.
GUIL: Your diction will go to pieces.
ROS: Your lines will be cut.
GUIL: To dumbshows.
ROS: And dramatic pauses.
GUIL: You'll never *find* your tongue.
ROS: Lick your lips.
GUIL: Taste your tears.
ROS: Your breakfast.
GUIL: You won't know the difference.
ROS: There won't be any.
GUIL: We'll take the very words out of your mouth.
ROS: So you've caught on.
GUIL: So you've caught up.
PLAYER (*tops*): Not yet! (*Bitterly.*) You left us.
GUIL: Ah! I'd forgotten—you performed a dramatic spectacle on the way. Yes, I'm sorry we had to miss it.
PLAYER (*bursts out*): We can't look each other in the face! (*Pause, more in control.*) You don't understand the humiliation of it—to be tricked out of the single assumption which makes our existence viable—that somebody is *watching*. . . . The plot was two corpses gone before we caught sight of ourselves, stripped naked in the middle of nowhere and pouring ourselves down a bottomless well.
ROS: Is *that* thirty-eight?
PLAYER (*lost*): There we were—demented children mincing about in clothes that no one ever wore, speaking as no man ever spoke, swearing love in wigs and rhymed couplets, killing each other with wooden swords, hollow protestations of faith hurled after empty promises of vengeance—and every gesture, every pose, vanishing into the thin unpopulated air. We ransomed our dignity to the clouds, and the uncomprehending birds listened. (*He rounds on them.*) Don't you see?! We're *actors*—we're the opposite of people! (*They recoil nonplussed, his voice calms.*) Think, in your head, *now*, think of the most . . . *private* . . . *secret* . . . intimate thing you have ever done secure in the knowledge of its privacy. . . . (*He gives them—and the audience—a good pause. Ros takes on a shifty look.*) Are you thinking of it? (*He strikes with his voice and his head.*) Well, I saw you do it!

[*Ros leaps up, dissembling madly.*]

ROS: You never! It's a lie! (*He catches himself with a giggle in a vacuum and sits down again.*)
PLAYER: We're actors. . . . We pledged our identities, secure in the conventions of our trade, that someone would be watching. And then, grad-

ually, no one was. We were caught, high and dry. It was not until the murderer's long soliloquy that we were able to look around, frozen as we were in profile, our eyes searched you out, first confidently, then hesitantly, then desperately as each patch of turf, each log, every exposed corner in every direction proved uninhabited, and all the while the murderous King addressed the horizon with his dreary interminable guilt. . . . Our heads began to move, wary as lizards, the corpse of unsullied Rosalinda peeped through his fingers, and the King faltered. Even then, habit and a stubborn trust that our audience spied upon us from behind the nearest bush, forced our bodies to blunder on long after they had emptied of meaning, until like runaway carts they dragged to a halt. No one came forward. No one shouted at us. The silence was unbreakable, it imposed itself upon us; it was obscene. We took off our crowns and swords and cloth of gold and moved silent on the road to Elsinore.

[*Silence. Then GUIL claps solo with slow measured irony.*]

GUIL: Brilliantly re-created—if these eyes could weep! . . . Rather strong on metaphor, mind you. No criticism—only a matter of taste. And so here you are—with a vengeance. That's a figure of speech . . . isn't it? Well let's say we've made up for it, for you may have no doubt whom to thank for your performance at the court.
ROS: We are counting on you to take him out of himself. You are the pleasures which we draw him on to—(*he escapes a fractional giggle but recovers immediately*) and by that I don't mean your usual filth; you can't treat royalty like people with normal perverted desires. They know nothing of that and you know nothing of them, to your mutual survival. So give him a good clean show suitable for all the family, or you can rest assured you'll be playing the tavern tonight.
GUIL: Or the night after.
ROS: Or not.
PLAYER: We already have an entry here. And always have had.
GUIL: You've played for him before?
PLAYER: Yes, sir.
ROS: And what's *his* bent?
PLAYER: Classical.
ROS: Saucy!
GUIL: What will you play?
PLAYER: *The Murder of Gonzago.*

GUIL: Full of fine cadence and corpses.
PLAYER: Pirated from the Italian. . . .
ROS: What is it about?
PLAYER: It's about a King and Queen. . . .
GUIL: Escapism! What else? ✖
PLAYER: Blood——
GUIL:—Love and rhetoric.
PLAYER: Yes. (*Going.*)
GUIL: Where are you going?
PLAYER: I can come and go as I please.
GUIL: You're evidently a man who knows his way around.
PLAYER: I've been here before.
GUIL: We're still finding our feet.
PLAYER: I should concentrate on not losing your heads.
GUIL: Do you speak from knowledge?
PLAYER: Precedent.
GUIL: You've been here before.
PLAYER: And I know which way the wind is blowing.
GUIL: Operating on two levels, are we?! How clever! I expect it comes naturally to you, being in the business so to speak.

[The PLAYER's grave face does not change. He makes to move off again. GUIL for the second time cuts him off.]

The truth is, we value your company, for want of any other. We have been left so much to our own devices—after a while one welcomes the uncertainty of being left to other people's.
PLAYER: Uncertainty is the normal state. You're nobody special.

[He makes to leave again. GUIL loses his cool.]

GUIL: But for God's sake what are we supposed to *do*?!
PLAYER: Relax. Respond. That's what people do. You can't go through life questioning your situation at every turn.
GUIL: But we don't know what's going on, or what to do with ourselves. We don't know how to *act*.
PLAYER: Act natural. You know why you're here at least.
GUIL: We only know what we're told, and that's little enough. And for all we know it isn't even true.
PLAYER: For all anyone knows, nothing is. Everything has to be taken on trust; truth is only that which is taken to be true. It's the currency of living. There may be nothing behind it, but it doesn't make any difference so long as it is honoured. One acts on assumptions. What do you assume?
ROS: Hamlet is not himself, outside or in. We have to glean what afflicts him.

GUIL: He doesn't give much away.
PLAYER: Who does, nowadays?
GUIL: He's—melancholy.
PLAYER: Melancholy?
ROS: Mad.
PLAYER: How is he mad?
ROS: Ah. (*To* GUIL:) How is he mad?
GUIL: More morose than mad, perhaps.
PLAYER: Melancholy.
GUIL: Moody.
ROS: He has moods.
PLAYER: Of moroseness?
GUIL: Madness. And yet.
ROS: Quite.
GUIL: For instance.
ROS: He talks to himself, which might be madness.
GUIL: If he didn't talk sense, which he does.
ROS: Which suggests the opposite.
PLAYER: Of what?

[Small pause.]

GUIL: I think I have it. A man talking sense to himself is no madder than a man talking nonsense not to himself.
ROS: Or just as mad.
GUIL: Or just as mad.
ROS: And he does both.
GUIL: So there you are.
ROS: Stark raving sane.

[Pause.]

PLAYER: Why?
GUIL: Ah. (*To* ROS:) Why?
ROS: Exactly.
GUIL: Exactly what?
ROS: Exactly why.
GUIL: Exactly why *what*?
ROS: What?
GUIL:*Why*?
ROS: Why what, exactly?
GUIL: Why is he mad?!
ROS: *I* don't know!

[Beat.]

PLAYER: The old man thinks he's in love with his daughter.
ROS (*appalled*): Good God! We're out of our depth here.
PLAYER: No, no, no—*he* hasn't got a daughter—the old man thinks he's in love with *his* daughter.
ROS: The old man is?
PLAYER: Hamlet, in love with the old man's daughter, the old man thinks.
ROS: Ha! It's beginning to make sense! Unrequited passion!

[The PLAYER moves.]

GUIL (*Fascist.*): Nobody leaves this room! (*Pause, lamely.*) Without a *very* good reason.
PLAYER: Why not?
GUIL: All this strolling about is getting too arbitrary by half—I'm rapidly losing my grip. From now on reason will prevail.
PLAYER: I have lines to learn.
GUIL: Pass!

[The PLAYER passes into one of the wings. ROS cups his hands and shouts into the opposite one.]

ROS: Next!

[But no one comes.]

GUIL: What did you expect?
ROS: Something . . . someone . . . nothing.

[They sit facing front.]

Are you hungry?
GUIL: No, are you?
ROS (*thinks*): No. You remember that coin?
GUIL: No.
ROS: I think I lost it.
GUIL: What coin?
ROS: I don't remember exactly.

[Pause.]

GUIL: Oh, that coin . . . clever.
ROS: I can't remember how I did it.
GUIL: It probably comes natural to you.
ROS: Yes, I've got a show-stopper there.
GUIL: Do it again.

[Slight pause.]

ROS: We can't afford it.
GUIL: Yes, one must think of the future.
ROS: It's the normal thing.
GUIL: To have one. One is, after all, having it all the time . . . now . . . and now . . . and now. . . .
ROS: It could go on for ever. Well, not for *ever*, I suppose. (*Pause.*) Do you ever think of yourself as actually *dead*, lying in a box with a lid on it?
GUIL: No.
ROS: Nor do I, really. . . . It's silly to be depressed by it. I mean one thinks of it like being *alive* in a box, one keeps forgetting to take into account the fact that one is *dead* . . . which should make all the difference . . . shouldn't it? I mean, you'd never *know* you were in a box, would you? It would be just like being *asleep* in a box. Not that I'd like to sleep in a box, mind you, not without any air—you'd wake up dead, for

a start, and then where would you be? Apart from inside a box. That's the bit I don't like, frankly. That's why I don't think of it. . . .

[GUIL stirs restlessly, pulling his cloak round him.]

Because you'd be helpless, wouldn't you? Stuffed in a box like that, I mean you'd be in there for ever. Even taking into account the fact that you're dead, it isn't a pleasant thought. *Especially* if you're dead, really . . . *ask* yourself, if I asked you straight off—I'm going to stuff you in this box now, would you rather be alive or dead? Naturally, you'd prefer to be alive. Life in a box is better than no life at all. I expect. You'd have a chance at least. You could lie there thinking—well, at least I'm not dead! In a minute someone's going to bang on the lid and tell me to come out. (*Banging the floor with his fists.*) "Hey you, whatsyername! Come out of there!"
GUIL (*jumps up savagely*): You don't have to flog it to death!

[Pause.]

ROS: I wouldn't think about it, if I were you. You'd only get depressed. (*Pause.*) Eternity is a terrible thought. I mean, where's it going to end? (*Pause, then brightly.*) Two early Christians chanced to meet in Heaven. "Saul of Tarsus yet!" cried one. "What are *you* doing here?!" . . . "Tarsus-Schmarsus," replied the other, "I'm Paul already." (*He stands up restlessly and flaps his arms.*) They don't care. We count for nothing. We could remain silent till we're green in the face, they wouldn't come.
GUIL: Blue, red.
ROS: A Christian, a Moslem and a Jew chanced to meet in a closed carriage. . . . "Silverstein!" cried the Jew. "Who's your friend?" . . . "His name's Abdullah," replied the Moslem, "but he's no friend of mine since he became a convert." (*He leaps up again, stamps his foot and shouts into the wings.*) All right, we know you're in there! Come out talking! (*Pause.*) We have no control. None at all . . . (*He paces.*) Whatever became of the moment when one first knew about death? There must have been one, a moment, in childhood when it first occurred to you that you don't go on for ever. It must have been shattering—stamped into one's memory. And yet I can't remember it. It never occurred to me at all. What does one make of that? We must be born with an intuition of mortality. Before we know the words for it, before we know that there are words,

out we come, bloodied and squalling with the knowledge that for all the compasses in the world, there's only one direction, and time is its only measure. (*He reflects, getting more desperate and rapid.*) A Hindu, a Buddhist and a lion-tamer chanced to meet, in a circus on the Indo-Chinese border. (*He breaks out.*) They're taking us for granted! Well, I won't stand for it! In future, notice will be taken. (*He wheels again to face into the wings.*) Keep out, then! I forbid anyone to enter! (*No one comes. Breathing heavily.*) That's better. . . .

[*Immediately, behind him a grand procession enters, principally* CLAUDIUS, GERTRUDE, POLONIUS *and* OPHELIA. CLAUDIUS *takes Ros's elbow as he passes and is immediately deep in conversation: the context is Shakespeare Act III, scene 1.* GUIL *still faces front as* CLAUDIUS, ROS, *etc., pass upstage and turn.*]

GUIL: Death followed by eternity . . . the worst of both worlds. It *is* a terrible thought.

[*He turns upstage in time to take over the conversation with* CLAUDIUS. GERTRUDE *and* ROS *head downstage.*]

GERTRUDE: Did he receive you well?
ROS: Most like a gentleman.
GUIL (*returning in time to take it up*): But with much forcing of his disposition.
ROS (*a flat lie and he knows it and shows it, perhaps catching* GUIL's *eye*): Niggard of question, but of our demands most free in his reply.
GERTRUDE: Did you assay him to any pastime?
ROS: Madam, it so fell out that certain players
    We o'erraught on the way: of these we told
        him
    And there did seem in him a kind of joy
    To hear of it. They are here about the court,
    And, as I think, they have already order
    This night to play before him.
POLONIUS: 'Tis most true
    And he beseeched me to entreat your Majesties
    To hear and see the matter.
CLAUDIUS: With all my heart, and it doth content me
    To hear him so inclined.
    Good gentlemen, give him a further edge
    And drive his purpose into these delights.
ROS: We shall, my lord.
CLAUDIUS (*leading out procession*):
    Sweet Gertrude, leave us, too,
    For we have closely sent for Hamlet hither,
    That he, as t'were by accident, may here
    Affront Ophelia. . . .

[*Exeunt* CLAUDIUS *and* GERTRUDE.]

ROS (*peevish*): Never a moment's peace! In and out, on and off, they're coming at us from all sides.
GUIL: You're never satisfied.
ROS: Catching us on the trot. . . . Why can't *we* go by them?
GUIL: What's the difference?
ROS: I'm going.

[ROS *pulls his cloak round him.* GUIL *ignores him. Without confidence* ROS *heads upstage. He looks out and comes back quickly.*]

He's coming.
GUIL: What's he doing?
ROS: Nothing.
GUIL: He must be doing something.
ROS: Walking.
GUIL: On his hands?
ROS: No, on his feet.
GUIL: Stark naked?
ROS: Fully dressed.
GUIL: Selling toffee apples?
ROS: Not that I noticed.
GUIL: You could be wrong?
ROS: I don't think so.

[*Pause.*]

GUIL: I can't for the life of me see how we're going to get into conversation.

[HAMLET *enters upstage, and pauses, weighing up the pros and cons of making his quietus.*

ROS *and* GUIL *watch him.*]

ROS: Nevertheless, I suppose one might say that this was a chance. . . . One might well . . . accost him. . . . Yes, it definitely looks like a chance to me. . . . Something on the lines of a direct informal approach . . . man to man . . . straight from the shoulder. . . . Now look here, what's it all about . . . sort of thing. Yes. Yes, this looks like one to be grabbed with both hands, I should say . . . if I were asked. . . . No point in looking at a gift horse till you see the whites of its eyes, etcetera. (*He has moved towards* HAMLET *but his nerve fails. He returns.*) We're overawed, that's our trouble. When it comes to the point we succumb to their personality. . . .

[OPHELIA *enters, with prayerbook, a religious procession of one.*]

HAMLET: Nymph, in thy orisons be all my sins remembered.

[*At his voice she has stopped for him, he catches her up.*]

OPHELIA: Good my lord, how does your honour for
    this many a day?
HAMLET: I humbly thank you—well, well, well.

[They disappear talking into the wing.]

ROS: It's like living in a public park!
GUIL: Very impressive. Yes, I thought your direct infor-
    mal approach was going to stop this thing dead
    in its tracks there. If I might make a suggestion—
    shut up and sit down. Stop being perverse.
ROS (*near tears*): I'm not going to stand for it!

*[A FEMALE FIGURE, ostensibly the QUEEN, enters. ROS
marches up behind her, puts his hands over her eyes
and says with a desperate frivolity.]*

ROS: Guess who?!
PLAYER (*having appeared in a downstage corner*): Alfred!

*[ROS lets go, spins around. He has been holding ALFRED,
in his robe and blond wig. PLAYER is in the downstage
corner still. ROS comes down to that exit. The PLAYER
does not budge. He and ROS stand toe to toe.]*

ROS: Excuse me.

*[The PLAYER lifts his downstage foot. ROS bends to put
his hand on the floor. The PLAYER lowers his foot. ROS
screams and leaps away.]*

PLAYER (*gravely*): I beg your pardon.
GUIL (*to ROS*): What did he do?
PLAYER: I put my foot down.
ROS: My hand was on the floor!
GUIL: You put your hand under his foot?
ROS: I——
GUIL: What for?
ROS: I thought——(*Grabs GUIL.*) Don't leave me!

*[He makes a break for an exit. A TRAGEDIAN dressed as
a KING enters. ROS recoils, breaks for the opposite
wing. Two cloaked TRAGEDIANS enter. ROS tries again
but another TRAGEDIAN enters, and ROS retires to midstage. The PLAYER claps his hands matter-of-factly.]*

PLAYER: Right! We haven't got much time.
GUIL: What are you doing?
PLAYER: Dress rehearsal. Now if you two wouldn't
    mind just moving back . . . there . . . good. . . .
    (*To TRAGEDIANS.*) Everyone ready? And for
    goodness' sake, remember what we're doing.
    (*To ROS and GUIL:*) We always use the same cos-
    tumes more or less, and they forget what they
    are supposed to be *in* you see. . . . Stop picking
    your nose, Alfred. When Queens have to they
    do it by a cerebral process passed down in the
    blood. . . . Good. Silence! Off we go!

PLAYER-KING: Full thirty times hath Phoebus' cart——

[PLAYER jumps up angrily.]

PLAYER: No, no, no! Dumbshow first, your confound-
    ed majesty! (*To ROS and GUIL:*) They're a bit out
    of practice, but they always pick up wonder-
    fully for the deaths—it brings out the poetry in
    them.
GUIL: How nice.
PLAYER: There's nothing more unconvincing than an
    unconvincing death.
GUIL: I'm sure.

[PLAYER claps his hands.]

PLAYER: Act One—moves now.

*[The mime. Soft music from a recorder. PLAYER-KING
and PLAYER-QUEEN embrace. She kneels and makes a
show of protestation to him. He takes her up, declining his head upon her neck. He lies down. She, seeing
him asleep, leaves him.]*

GUIL: What is the dumbshow for?
PLAYER: Well, it's a device, really—it makes the action
    that follows more or less comprehensible; you
    understand, we are tied down to a language
    which makes up in obscurity what it lacks in
    style.

*[The mime (continued)—enter another. He takes off the
SLEEPER's crown, kisses it. He has brought in a small bottle of liquid. He pours the poison in the SLEEPER's ear,
and leaves him. The SLEEPER convulses heroically, dying.]*

ROS: Who was that?
PLAYER: The King's brother and uncle to the Prince.
GUIL: Not exactly fraternal.
PLAYER: Not exactly avuncular, as time goes on.

*[The QUEEN returns, makes passionate action, finding the
KING dead. The POISONER comes in again, attended by two
others (the two in cloaks). The POISONER seems to console
with her. The dead body is carried away. The POISONER
woos the QUEEN with gifts. She seems harsh awhile but in
the end accepts his love. End of mime, at which point, the
wail of a woman in torment and OPHELIA appears, wailing, closely followed by HAMLET in a hysterical state,
shouting at her, circling her, both midstage.]*

HAMLET: Go to, I'll no more on't; it hath made me mad!

[She falls on her knees weeping.]

I say we will have no more marriage! (*His voice
drops to include the TRAGEDIANS, who have
frozen.*) Those that are married already (*he leans

close to the PLAYER-QUEEN *and* POISONER, *speaking with quiet edge)* all but one shall live. (*He smiles briefly at them without mirth, and starts to back out, his parting shot rising again.*) The rest shall keep as they are. (*As he leaves,* OPHELIA *tottering upstage, he speaks into her ear a quick clipped sentence.*) To a nunnery, go.

[He goes out. OPHELIA *falls on to her knees upstage, her sobs barely audible. A slight silence.]*

PLAYER-KING: Full thirty times hath Phoebus' cart——

*[*CLAUDIUS *enters with* POLONIUS *and goes over to* OPHELIA *and lifts her to her feet. The* TRAGEDIANS *jump back with heads inclined.]*

CLAUDIUS: Love? His affections do not that way tend,
    Or what he spake, though it lacked form a
        little,
    Was not like madness. There's something
    In his soul o'er which his melancholy sits on
    Brood, and I do doubt the hatch and the
    Disclose will be some danger; which for to
    Prevent I have in quick determination thus set
    It down: he shall with speed to England . . .

*[Which carries the three of them—*CLAUDIUS, POLONIUS, OPHELIA*—out of sight. The* PLAYER *moves, clapping his hands for attention.]*

PLAYER: Gentlemen! (*They look at him.*) It doesn't seem to be coming. We are not getting it at all. (*To* GUIL:) What did you think?
GUIL: What was I supposed to think?
PLAYER (*to* TRAGEDIANS): You're not getting across!

*[*ROS *had gone halfway up to* OPHELIA; *he returns.]*

ROS: That didn't look like love to me.
GUIL: Starting from scratch again . . .
PLAYER (*to* TRAGEDIANS): It was a *mess.*
ROS (*to* GUIL): It's going to be chaos on the night.
GUIL: Keep back—we're spectators.
PLAYER: Act Two! Positions!
GUIL: Wasn't that the end?
PLAYER: Do you call that an ending?—with practically everyone on his feet? My goodness no— over your dead body.
GUIL: How am I supposed to take that?
PLAYER: Lying down. (*He laughs briefly and in a second has never laughed in his life.*) There's a design at work in all art—surely you know that? Events must play themselves out to aesthetic, moral and logical conclusion.
GUIL: And what's that, in this case?
PLAYER: It never varies—we aim at the point where everyone who is marked for death dies.

GUIL: Marked?
PLAYER: Between "just desserts" and "tragic irony" we are given quite a lot of scope for our particular talent. Generally speaking, things have gone about as far as they can possibly go when things have got about as bad as they reasonably get. (*He switches on a smile.*)
GUIL: Who decides?
PLAYER (*switching off his smile*):Decides? It is *written.*

[He turns away. GUIL *grabs him and spins him back violently.]*

    (*Unflustered.*) Now if you're going to be subtle, we'll miss each other in the dark. I'm referring to oral tradition. So to speak.

*[*GUIL *releases him.]*

    We're tragedians, you see. We follow directions—there is no *choice* involved. The bad end unhappily, the good unluckily. That is what tragedy means. (*Calling.*) Positions!

[The TRAGEDIANS *have taken up positions for the continuation of the mime: which in this case means a love scene, sexual and passionate, between the* QUEEN *and the* POISONER/KING.]*

PLAYER: Go!

[The lovers begin. The PLAYER *contributes a breathless commentary for* ROS *and* GUIL.]*

    Having murdered his brother and wooed the widow—the poisoner mounts the throne! Here we see him and his queen give rein to their unbridled passion! She little knowing that the man she holds in her arms——!
ROS: Oh, I say—here—really! You can't do that!
PLAYER: Why not?
ROS: Well, really—I mean, people want to be *entertained*—they don't come expecting sordid and gratuitous filth.
PLAYER: You're wrong—they do! Murder, seduction and incest—what do you want—*jokes*?
ROS: I want a good story, with a beginning, middle and end.
PLAYER (*to* GUIL): And you?
GUIL: I'd prefer art to mirror life, if it's all the same to you.
PLAYER: It's all the same to me, sir. (*To the grappling* LOVERS:) All right, no need to indulge yourselves. (*They get up. To* GUIL:) I come on in a minute. Lucianus, nephew to the king! (*Turns his attention to the* TRAGEDIANS.) Next!

[They disport themselves to accommodate the next piece

of mime, which consists of the PLAYER *himself exhibiting an excitable anguish (choreographed, stylized) leading to an impassioned scene with the* QUEEN *(cf. "The Closet Scene," Shakespeare Act III, scene 4) and a very stylized reconstruction of a* POLONIUS *figure being stabbed behind the arras (the murdered* KING *to stand in for* POLONIUS*) while the* PLAYER *himself continues his breathless commentary for the benefit of* ROS *and* GUIL.]

PLAYER: Lucianus, nephew to the king . . . usurped by his uncle and shattered by his mother's incestuous marriage . . . loses his reason . . . throwing the court into turmoil and disarray as he alternates between bitter melancholy and unrestricted lunacy . . . staggering from the suicidal (*a pose*) to the homicidal (*here he kills "*POLONIUS*"*) . . . he at last confronts his mother and in a scene of provocative ambiguity—(*a somewhat oedipal embrace*) begs her to repent and recant——(*He springs up, still talking.*) The King—(*he pushes forward the* POISONER/KING*)* tormented by guilt—haunted by fear—decides to despatch his nephew to England—and entrusts this undertaking to two smiling accomplices—friends—courtiers—to two spies——

[He has swung round to bring together the POISONER/KING *and the two cloaked* TRAGEDIANS; *the latter kneel and accept a scroll from the* KING.]

—giving them a letter to present to the English court——! And so they depart—on board ship——

[The two SPIES *position themselves on either side of the* PLAYER, *and the three of them sway gently in unison, the motion of a boat; and then the* PLAYER *detaches himself.]*

—and they arrive——

[One SPY *shades his eyes at the horizon.]*

—and disembark—and present themselves before the English king——(*He wheels round.*) The English king——

[An exchange of headgear creates the ENGLISH KING *from the remaining player—that is, the* PLAYER *who played the original murdered king.*

But where is the Prince? Where indeed? The plot has thickened—a twist of fate and cunning has put into their hands a letter that seals their deaths!

[The two SPIES *present their letter; the* ENGLISH KING *reads it and orders their deaths. They stand up as the* PLAYER *whips off their cloaks preparatory to execution.]*

Traitors hoist by their own petard?—or victims of the gods?—we shall never know!

[The whole mime has been fluid and continuous but now ROS *moves forward and brings it to a pause. What brings* ROS *forward is the fact that under their cloaks the two* SPIES *are wearing coats identical to those worn by* ROS *and* GUIL, *whose coats are now covered by their cloaks.* ROS *approaches "his"* SPY *doubtfully. He does not quite understand why the coats are familiar.* ROS *stands close, touches the coat, thoughtfully. . . .]*

ROS: Well, if it isn't——! No, wait a minute, don't tell me—it's a long time since—where was it? Ah, this is taking me back to—when was it? I know you, don't I? I never forget a face—(*he looks into the* SPY*'s face*) . . . not that I know yours, that is. For a moment I thought—no, I don't know you, do I? Yes, I'm afraid you're quite wrong. You must have mistaken me for someone else.

*[*GUIL *meanwhile has approached the other* SPY, *brow creased in thought.]*

PLAYER (*to* GUIL): Are you familiar with this play?
GUIL: No.
PLAYER: A slaughterhouse—eight corpses all told. It brings out the best in us.
GUIL (*tense, progressively rattled during the whole mime and commentary*): You!—What do *you* know about *death*?
PLAYER: It's what the actors do best. They have to exploit whatever talent is given to them, and their talent is dying. They can die heroically, comically, ironically, slowly, suddenly, disgustingly, charmingly, or from a great height. My own talent is more general. I extract significance from melodrama, a significance which it does not in fact contain; but occasionally, from out of this matter, there escapes a thin beam of light that, seen at the right angle, can crack the shell of mortality.
ROS: Is that all they can do—die?
PLAYER: No, no—they kill beautifully. In fact some of them kill even better than they die. The rest die better than they kill. They're a team.
ROS: Which ones are which?
PLAYER: There's not much in it.
GUIL (*fear, derision*): Actors! The mechanics of cheap melodrama! That isn't *death*! (*More quietly.*) You scream and choke and sink to your knees, but it doesn't bring death home to anyone—it doesn't catch them unawares and start the whisper in their skulls that says—"One day you are going to die." (*He straightens up.*) You die so many times; how can you expect them

to believe in your death?

PLAYER: On the contrary, it's the only kind they do believe. They're conditioned to it. I had an actor once who was condemned to hang for stealing a sheep—or a lamb, I forget which—so I got permission to have him hanged in the middle of a play—had to change the plot a bit but I thought it would be effective, you know—and you wouldn't believe it, he just *wasn't* convincing! It was impossible to suspend one's disbelief—and what with the audience jeering and throwing peanuts, the whole thing was a *disaster!*—he did nothing but cry all the time—right out of character—just stood there and cried. . . . Never again.

[In good humour he has already turned back to the mime: the two SPIES awaiting execution at the hands of the PLAYER, who takes his dagger out of his belt.]

Audiences know what to expect, and that is all that they are prepared to believe in. (*To the* SPIES:) Show!

[The SPIES die at some length, rather well.
The light has begun to go, and it fades as they die, and as GUIL speaks.]

GUIL: No, no, no . . . you've got it all wrong . . . you can't act death. The *fact* of it is nothing to do with seeing it happen—it's not gasps and blood and falling about—that isn't what makes it death. It's just a man failing to reappear, that's all—now you see him, now you see him, now you don't, that's the only thing that's real: here one minute and gone the next and never coming back—an exit, unobtrusive and unannounced, a disappearance gathering weight as it goes on, until, finally, it is heavy with death.

[The two SPIES lie still, barely visible. The PLAYER comes forward and throws the SPIES' cloaks over their bodies. ROS starts to clap, slowly.]

[A second of silence, then much noise. Shouts . . . "The King rises!" . . . "Give o'er the play!" . . . and cries for "Lights, lights, lights!"
When the light comes, after a few seconds, it comes as a sunrise.
The stage is empty save for two cloaked figures sprawled on the ground in the approximate positions last held by the dead SPIES. As the light grows, they are seen to be ROS and GUIL, and to be resting quite comfortably. ROS raises himself on his elbows and shades his eyes as he stares into the auditorium. Finally:]

ROS: That must be east, then. I think we can assume that.

GUIL: I'm assuming nothing.

ROS: No, it's all right. That's the sun. East.

GUIL (*looks up*): Where?

ROS: I watched it come up.

GUIL: No . . . it was light all the time, you see, and you opened your eyes very, very slowly. If you'd been facing back there you'd be swearing *that* was east.

ROS (*standing up*): You're a mass of prejudice.

GUIL: I've been taken in before.

ROS (*looks out over the audience*): Rings a bell.

GUIL: They're waiting to see what we're going to do.

ROS: Good old east.

GUIL: As soon as we make a move they'll come pouring in from every side, shouting obscure instructions, confusing us with ridiculous remarks, messing us about from here to breakfast and getting our names wrong.

[ROS starts to protest but he has hardly opened his mouth before:]

CLAUDIUS (*off stage—with urgency*): Ho, Guildenstern!

[GUIL is still prone. Small pause.]

ROS AND GUIL: You're wanted. . . .

[GUIL furiously leaps to his feet as CLAUDIUS and GERTRUDE enter. They are in some desperation.]

CLAUDIUS: Friends both, go join you with some further aid: Hamlet in madness hath Polonius slain, and from his mother's closet hath he dragged him. Go seek him out; speak fair and bring the body into the chapel. I pray you haste in this. (*As he and* GERTRUDE *are hurrying out.*) Come Gertrude, we'll call up our wisest friends and let them know both what we mean to do. . . .

[They've gone. ROS and GUIL remain quite still.]

GUIL: Well . . .

ROS: Quite . . .

GUIL: Well, well.

ROS: Quite, quite. (*Nods with spurious confidence.*) Seek him out. (*Pause.*) Etcetera.

GUIL: Quite.

ROS: Well. (*Small pause.*) Well, that's a step in the right direction.

GUIL: You didn't like him?

ROS: Who?

GUIL: Good God, I hope more tears are shed for *us!* . . .

ROS: Well, it's *progress*, isn't it? Something positive. Seek him out. (*Looks round without moving his feet.*) Where does one begin . . . ? (*Takes one step towards the wings and halts.*)

GUIL: Well, that's a step in the right direction.

ROS: You think so? He could be anywhere.

GUIL: All right—you go that way, I'll go this way.

ROS: Right.

[They walk towards opposite wings. Ros halts.]

    No.

[GUIL halts.]

    You go this way—I'll go that way.

GUIL: All right.

[They march towards each other, cross. Ros halts.]

ROS: Wait a minute.

[GUIL halts.]

    I think we should stick together. He might be violent.

GUIL: Good point. I'll come with you.

[GUIL marches across to Ros. They turn to leave. Ros halts.]

ROS: No, I'll come with *you.*

GUIL: Right.

[They turn, march across to the opposite wing. Ros halts. GUIL halts.]

ROS: I'll come with *you, my* way.

GUIL: All right.

[They turn again and march across. Ros halts. GUIL halts.]

ROS: I've just thought. If we both go, he could come *here.* That would be stupid, wouldn't it?

GUIL: All right—I'll stay, you go.

ROS: Right.

[GUIL marches to midstage.]

    I say.

[GUIL wheels and carries on marching back towards Ros, who starts marching downstage. They cross. Ros halts.]

    I've just thought.

[GUIL halts.]

    We ought to stick together; he might be violent.

GUIL: Good point.

[GUIL marches down to join Ros. They stand still for a moment in their original positions.]

    Well, at last we're getting somewhere.

[Pause.]

    Of course, he might not come.

ROS (*airily*): Oh, he'll come.

GUIL: We'd have some explaining to do.

ROS: He'll come. (*Airily wanders upstage.*) Don't worry—take my word for it—(*Looks out—is appalled.*) He's coming!

GUIL: What's he doing?

ROS: Walking.

GUIL: Alone?

ROS: No.

GUIL: Not walking?

ROS: No.

GUIL: Who's with him?

ROS: The old man.

GUIL: Walking?

ROS: No.

GUIL: Ah. That's an opening if ever there was one. (*And is suddenly galvanized into action.*) Let him walk into the trap!

ROS: What trap?

GUIL: You stand there! Don't let him pass!

[He positions Ros with his back to one wing, facing HAMLET's entrance.

    GUIL positions himself next to Ros, a few feet away, so that they are covering one side of the stage, facing the opposite side. GUIL unfastens his belt. Ros does the same. They join the two belts, and hold them taut between them. Ros's trousers slide slowly down.

    HAMLET enters opposite, slowly, dragging POLONIUS's body. He enters upstage, makes a small arc and leaves by the same side, a few feet downstage.

    Ros and GUIL, holding the belts taut, stare at him in some bewilderment.

    HAMLET leaves, dragging the body. They relax the strain on the belts.]

ROS: That was close.

GUIL: There's a limit to what two people can do.

[They undo the belts: Ros pulls up his trousers.]

ROS (*worriedly—he walks a few paces towards HAMLET's exit*): He *was* dead.

GUIL: Of course he's dead!

ROS (*turns to GUIL*): Properly.

GUIL (*angrily*): Death's death, isn't it?

[Ros falls silent. Pause.]

    Perhaps he'll come back this way.

[ROS starts to take off his belt.]

No, no, no!—if we can't learn by experience, what else have we got?

[ROS desists.]

[Pause.]

ROS: Give him a shout.
GUIL: I thought we'd been into all that.
ROS *(shouts)*: Hamlet!
GUIL: Don't be absurd.
ROS *(shouts)*: Lord Hamlet!

[HAMLET enters. ROS is a little dismayed.]

What have you done, my lord, with the dead body?
HAMLET: Compounded it with dust, whereto 'tis kin.
ROS: Tell us where 'tis, that we may take it thence and bear it to the chapel.
HAMLET: Do not believe it.
ROS: Believe what?
HAMLET: That I can keep your counsel and not mine own. Besides, to be demanded of a sponge, what replication should be made by the son of a king?
ROS: Take you me for a sponge, my lord?
HAMLET: Ay, sir, that soaks up the King's countenance, his rewards, his authorities. But such officers do the King best service in the end. He keeps them, like an ape, in the corner of his jaw, first mouthed, to be last swallowed. When he needs what you have gleaned, it is but squeezing you and, sponge, you shall be dry again.
ROS: I understand you not, my lord.
HAMLET: I am glad of it: a knavish speech sleeps in a foolish ear.
ROS: My lord, you must tell us where the body is and go with us to the King.
HAMLET: The body is with the King, but the King is not with the body. The King is a thing——
GUIL: A thing, my lord——?
HAMLET: Of nothing. Bring me to him.

[HAMLET moves resolutely towards one wing. They move with him, shepherding. Just before they reach the exit, HAMLET, apparently seeing CLAUDIUS approaching from off stage, bends low in a sweeping bow. ROS and GUIL, cued by HAMLET, also bow deeply—a sweeping ceremonial bow with their cloaks swept round them. HAMLET, however, continues the movement into an about-turn and walks off in the opposite direction. ROS and GUIL, with their heads low, do not notice.

No one comes on. ROS and GUIL squint upwards and find that they are bowing to nothing.]

[CLAUDIUS enters behind them. At first words they leap up and do a double-take.]

CLAUDIUS: How now? What hath befallen?
ROS: Where the body is bestowed, my lord, we cannot get from him.
CLAUDIUS: But where is he?
ROS *(fractional hesitation)*: Without, my lord; guarded to know your pleasure.
CLAUDIUS *(moves)*: Bring him before us.

[This hits ROS between the eyes but only his eyes show it. Again his hesitation is fractional. And then with great deliberation he turns to GUIL.]

ROS: Ho! Bring in the lord.

[Again there is a fractional moment in which ROS is smug, GUIL is trapped and betrayed. GUIL opens his mouth and closes it.

The situation is saved: HAMLET, escorted, is marched in just as CLAUDIUS leaves. HAMLET and his ESCORT cross the stage and go out, following CLAUDIUS.

Lighting changes to Exterior.]

ROS *(moves to go)*: All right, then?
GUIL *(does not move; thoughtfully)*: And yet it doesn't seem enough; to have breathed such significance. Can that be all? And why us?—anybody would have done. And we have contributed nothing.
ROS: It was a trying episode while it lasted, but they've done with us now.
GUIL: Done what?
ROS: I don't pretend to have understood. Frankly, I'm not very interested. If they won't tell us, that's their affair. *(He wanders upstage towards the exit.)* For my part, I'm only glad that that's the last we've seen of him—*(And he glances off stage and turns front, his face betraying the fact that HAMLET is there.)*
GUIL: I knew it wasn't the end. . . .
ROS *(high)*: What else?!
GUIL: We're taking him to England. What's he doing?

[ROS goes upstage and returns.]

ROS: Talking.
GUIL: To himself?

[ROS makes to go, GUIL cuts him off.]

Is he alone?
ROS: No, he's with a soldier.
GUIL: Then he's not talking to himself, is he?
ROS: Not *by* himself . . . Should we go?
GUIL: Where?
ROS: Anywhere.
GUIL: Why?

[ROS *puts up his head listening.*]

ROS: There it is again. (*In anguish.*) All I ask is a change of ground!
GUIL (*coda*): Give us this day our daily round. . . .

[HAMLET *enters behind them, talking with a soldier in arms.* ROS *and* GUIL *don't look round.*]

ROS: They'll have us hanging about till we're dead. At least. And the weather will change. (*Looks up.*) The spring can't last for ever.
HAMLET: Good sir, whose powers are these?
SOLDIER: They are of Norway, sir.
HAMLET: How purposed, sir, I pray you?
SOLDIER: Against some part of Poland.
HAMLET: Who commands them, sir?
SOLDIER: The nephew to old Norway, Fortinbras.
ROS: We'll be cold. The summer won't last.
GUIL: It's autumnal.
ROS (*examining the ground*): No leaves.
GUIL: Autumnal—nothing to do with leaves. It is to do with a certain brownness at the edges of the day. . . . Brown is creeping up on us, take my word for it. . . . Russets and tangerine shades of old gold flushing the very outside edge of the senses . . . deep shining ochres, burnt umber and parchments of baked earth— reflecting on itself and through itself, filtering the light. At such times, perhaps, coincidentally, the leaves might fall, somewhere, by repute. Yesterday was blue, like smoke.
ROS (*head up, listening*): I got it again then.

[*They listen—faintest sound of* TRAGEDIANS' *band.*]

HAMLET: I humbly thank you, sir.
SOLDIER: God by you, sir. (*Exit.*)

[ROS *gets up quickly and goes to* HAMLET.]

ROS: Will it please you go, my lord?
HAMLET: I'll be with you straight. Go you a little before.

[HAMLET *turns to face upstage.* ROS *returns down.* GUIL *faces front, doesn't turn.*]

GUIL: Is he there?
ROS: Yes.
GUIL: What's he doing?

[ROS *looks over his shoulder.*]

ROS: Talking.
GUIL: To himself?
ROS: Yes.

[*Pause.* ROS *makes to leave.*]

ROS: He *said* we can go. Cross my heart.
GUIL: I like to know where I am. Even if I don't know where I am, I like to know *that.* If we go there's no knowing.
ROS: No knowing what?
GUIL: If we'll ever come back.
ROS: We don't want to come back.
GUIL: That may very well be true, but do we want to go?
ROS: We'll be free.
GUIL: I don't know. It's the same sky.
ROS: We've come this far.

[*He moves towards exit.* GUIL *follows him.*]

And besides, anything could happen yet.

[*They go.*]

BLACKOUT

ACT III

Opens in pitch darkness.
    Soft sea sounds.
    After several seconds of nothing, a voice from the dark . . .

GUIL: Are you there?
ROS: Where?
GUIL (*bitterly*): A flying start. . . .

[*Pause.*]

ROS: Is that you?
GUIL: Yes.
ROS: How do you know?
GUIL (*explosion*): Oh-for-God's-sake!
ROS: We're not finished, then?
GUIL: Well, we're here, aren't we?
ROS: Are we? I can't see a thing.
GUIL: You can still *think,* can't you?
ROS: I think so.
GUIL: You can still *talk.*
ROS: What should I say?
GUIL: Don't bother. You can *feel,* can't you?
ROS: Ah! There's life in me yet!
GUIL: What are you feeling?
ROS: A leg. Yes, it feels like my leg.
GUIL: How does it feel?
ROS: Dead.
GUIL: Dead?
ROS (*panic*): I can't feel a thing!
GUIL: Give it a pinch! (*Immediately he yelps.*)
ROS: Sorry.
GUIL: Well, that's cleared that up.

[Longer pause: the sound builds a little and identifies itself—the sea. Ship timbers, wind in the rigging, and then shouts of sailors calling obscure but inescapably nautical instructions from all directions, far and near: A short list:]

> Hard a larboard!
> Let go the stays!
> Reef down me hearties!
> Is that you, cox'n?
> Hel-llo! Is that you?
> Hard a port!
> Easy as she goes!
> Keep her steady on the lee!
> Haul away, lads!
> (Snatches of sea shanty maybe.)
> Fly the jib!
> Tops'l up, me maties!

[When the point has been well made and more so.]

Ros: We're on a boat. (*Pause.*) Dark, isn't it?
Guil: Not for night.
Ros: No, not for *night*.
Guil: Dark for day.

[Pause.]

Ros: Oh yes, it's dark for *day*.
Guil: We must have gone north, of course.
Ros: Off course?
Guil: Land of the midnight sun, that is.
Ros: Of course.

[Some sailor sounds.
A lantern is lit upstage—in fact by HAMLET.
The stage lightens disproportionately—
Enough to see:
Ros and Guil *sitting downstage.*
Vague shapes of rigging, etc., behind.]

I think it's getting light.
Guil: Not for night.
Ros: This far north.
Guil: Unless we're off course.
Ros (*small pause*): Of course.

[A better light—Lantern? Moon? . . . Light.
Revealing, among other things, three large man-sized casks on deck, upended, with lids. Spaced but in line. Behind and above—a gaudy striped umbrella, on a pole stuck into the deck, tilted so that we do not see behind it—one of those huge six-foot-diameter jobs. Still dim upstage. Ros and Guil *still facing front.]*

Ros: Yes, it's lighter than it was. It'll be night soon. This far north. (*Dolefully.*) I suppose we'll have to go to sleep. (*He yawns and stretches.*)

Guil: Tired?
Ros: No . . . I don't think I'd take to it. Sleep all night, can't see a thing all day. . . . Those eskimos must have a quiet life.
Guil: Where?
Ros: What?
Guil: I thought you——(*Relapses.*) I've lost all capacity for disbelief. I'm not sure that I could even rise to a little gentle scepticism.

[Pause.]

Ros: Well, shall we stretch our legs?
Guil: I don't feel like stretching my legs.
Ros: I'll stretch them for you, if you like.
Guil: No.
Ros: We could stretch each other's. That way we wouldn't have to go anywhere.
Guil (*pause*): No, somebody might come in.
Ros: In where?
Guil: Out here.
Ros: In out here?
Guil: On deck.

[Ros considers the floor: slaps it.]

Ros: Nice bit of planking, that.
Guil: Yes, I'm very fond of boats myself. I like the way they're—contained. You don't have to worry about which way to go, or whether to go at all—the question doesn't arise, because you're on a *boat*, aren't you? Boats are safe areas in the game of tag . . . the players will hold their positions until the music starts. . . . I think I'll spend most of my life on boats.
Ros: Very healthy.

[Ros inhales with expectation, exhales with boredom. Guil stands up and looks over the audience.]

Guil: One is free on a boat. For a time. Relatively.
Ros: What's it like?
Guil: Rough.

[Ros joins him. They look out over the audience.]

Ros: I think I'm going to be sick.

[Guil licks a finger, holds it up experimentally.]

Guil: Other side, I think.

[Ros goes upstage: Ideally a sort of upper deck joined to the downstage lower deck by short steps. The umbrella being on the upper deck. Ros pauses by the umbrella and looks behind it. Guil meanwhile has been resuming his own theme—looking out over the audience——]

Free to move, speak, extemporise, and yet. We

have not been cut loose. Our truancy is
defined by one fixed star, and our drift represents merely a slight change of angle to it: we
may seize the moment, toss it around while
the moments pass, a short dash here, an exploration there, but we are brought round full circle to face again the single immutable fact—
that we, Rosencrantz and Guildenstern, bearing a letter from one king to another, are taking Hamlet to England.

*[By which time, Ros has returned, tiptoeing with great
import, teeth clenched for secrecy, gets to Guil, points
surreptitiously behind him—and a tight whisper:]*

Ros: I say—*he's there!*
Guil (*unsurprised*): What's he doing?
Ros: Sleeping.
Guil: It's all right for him.
Ros: What is?
Guil: He can sleep.
Ros: It's all right for him.
Guil: He's got us now.
Ros: He can sleep.
Guil: It's all done for him.
Ros: He's got us.
Guil: And we've got nothing. (*A cry.*) All I ask is our
      common due!
Ros: For those in peril on the sea. . . .
Guil: Give us this day our daily cue.

[Beat, pause. Sit. Long pause.]

Ros (*after shifting, looking around*): What now?
Guil: What do you mean?
Ros: Well, nothing is happening.
Guil: We're on a boat.
Ros: I'm aware of that.
Guil (*angrily*): Then what do you expect? (*Unhappily.*)
      We act on scraps of information . . . sifting half-
      remembered directions that we can hardly sep-
      arate from instinct.

*[Ros puts a hand into his purse, then both hands
behind his back, then holds his fists out.*
      Guil taps one fist.
      Ros opens it to show a coin.
      He gives it to Guil.
      *He puts his hand back into his purse. Then both
hands behind his back, then holds his fists out.*
      Guil taps one.
      Ros opens it to show a coin. He gives it to Guil.
      Repeat.
      Repeat.
      Guil getting tense. Desperate to lose.
      Repeat.
      *Guil taps a hand, changes his mind, taps the
other, and Ros inadvertently reveals that he has a coin*

in both fists.]

Guil: You had money in both hands.
Ros (*embarrassed*): Yes.
Guil: Every time?
Ros: Yes.
Guil: What's the point of that?
Ros (*pathetic*): I wanted to make you happy.

[Beat.]

Guil: How much did he give you?
Ros: Who?
Guil: The King. He gave us some money.
Ros: How much did he give you?
Guil: I asked you first.
Ros: I got the same as you.
Guil: He wouldn't discriminate between us.
Ros: How much did you get?
Guil: The same.
Ros: How do you know?
Guil: You just told me—how do *you* know?
Ros: He wouldn't discriminate between us.
Guil: Even if he could.
Ros: Which he never could.
Guil: He couldn't even be sure of mixing us up.
Ros: Without mixing us up.
Guil (*turning on him furiously*): Why don't you say
      something original! No wonder the whole thing
      is so stagnant! You don't take me up on any-
      thing—you just repeat it in a different order.
Ros: I can't think of anything original. I'm only good
      in support.
Guil: I'm sick of making the running.
Ros (*humbly*): It must be your dominant personality.
      (*Almost in tears.*) Oh, what's going to become
      of us!

[And Guil comforts him, all harshness gone.]

Guil: Don't cry . . . it's all right . . . there . . . there, I'll
      see we're all right.
Ros: But we've got nothing to go on, we're out on
      our own.
Guil: We're on our way to England—we're taking
      Hamlet there.
Ros: What for?
Guil: What for? Where have you been?
Ros: When? (*Pause.*) We won't know what to do
      when we get there.
Guil: We take him to the King.
Ros: Will *he* be there?
Guil: No—the king of England.
Ros: He's expecting us?
Guil: No.
Ros: He won't know what we're playing at. What
      are we going to *say*?
Guil: We've got a letter. You remember the letter.

Ros: Do I?

Guil: Everything is explained in the letter. We count
    on that.

Ros: Is that it, then?

Guil: What?

Ros: We take Hamlet to the English king, we hand
    over the letter—what then?

Guil: There may be something in the letter to keep
    us going a bit.

Ros: And if not?

Guil: Then that's it—we're finished.

Ros: At a loose end?

Guil: Yes.

[Pause.]

Ros: Are there likely to be loose ends? (*Pause.*) Who
    is the English king?

Guil: That depends on when we get there.

Ros: What do you think it says?

Guil: Oh . . . greetings. Expressions of loyalty.
    Asking of favours, calling in of debts. Obscure
    promises balanced by vague threats. . . .
    Diplomacy. Regards to the family.

Ros: And about Hamlet?

Guil: Oh yes.

Ros: And us—the full background?

Guil: I should say so.

[Pause.]

Ros: So we've got a letter which explains everything.

Guil: You've got it.

[Ros takes that literally. He starts to pat his pockets, etc.]

What's the matter?

Ros: The letter.

Guil: Have you got it?

Ros (*rising fear*): Have I? (*Searches frantically.*) Where
    would I have put it?

Guil: You can't have lost it.

Ros: I must have!

Guil: That's odd—I thought he gave it to me.

[Ros looks at him hopefully.]

Ros: Perhaps he did.

Guil: But you seemed so sure it was *you* who hadn't
    got it.

Ros (*high*): It *was* me who hadn't got it!

Guil: But if he gave it to me there's no reason why
    you should have had it in the first place, in
    which case I don't see what all the fuss is
    about you *not* having it.

Ros (*pause*): I admit it's confusing.

Guil: This is all getting rather undisciplined. . . . The
    boat, the night, the sense of isolation and

y
ca
pock
ter) . . .
other.*)* We

[Pause. Ros takes the

Ros: Now that we have f
    ing for it?

Guil (*thinks*): We thought it wa

Ros: Something else?

Guil: No.

[Deflation.]

Ros: Now we've lost the tension.

Guil: What tension?

Ros: What was the last thing I said before we wan
    dered off?

Guil: When was that?

Ros (*helplessly*): I can't remember.

Guil (*leaping up*): What a shambles! We're just not
    getting anywhere.

Ros (*mournfully*): Not even England. I don't believe
    in it anyway.

Guil: What?

Ros: England.

Guil: Just a conspiracy of cartographers, you mean?

Ros: I mean I don't believe it! (*Calmer.*) I have no
    image. I try to picture us arriving, a little har-
    bour perhaps . . . roads . . . inhabitants to point
    the way . . . horses on the road . . . riding for a
    day or a fortnight and then a palace and the
    English king. . . . That would be the logical
    kind of thing. . . . But my mind remains a
    blank. No. We're slipping off the map.

Guil: Yes . . . yes. . . . (*Rallying.*) But you don't
    believe anything till it happens. And it *has* all
    happened. Hasn't it?

Ros: We drift down time, clutching at straws. But
    what good's a brick to a drowning man?

Guil: Don't give up, we can't be long now.

Ros: We might as well be dead. Do you think death
    could possibly be a boat?

Guil: No, no, no . . . Death is . . . not. Death isn't. You
    take my meaning. Death is the ultimate nega-
    tive. Not-being. You can't not-be on a boat.

Ros: I've frequently not been on boats.

Guil: No, no, no—what you've been is not on boats.

Ros: I wish I was dead. (*Considers the drop.*) I could
    jump over the side. That would put a spoke in

uncertainty . . . all these induce a loosening of the concentration. We must not lose control. Tighten up. Now. Either you have lost the letter or you didn't have it to lose in the first place, in which case the King never gave it to you, in which case he gave it to me, in which case I would have put it into my inside top ...et, in which case (*calmly producing the let-* ...it will be . . . here. (*They smile at each* ...mustn't drop off like that again.

...*letter gently from him.*]

...und it, why were we look-

...s lost.

...g days brought up with him. ...ot their word for it. ...t we depend on. ...then again no. (*Airily.*) Let us ... proportion. Assume, if you like, ...ing to kill him. Well, he is a ...rtal, death comes to us all, ...consequently he would have died ...er or later. Or to look at it from ...t of view—he's just one man ...the loss would be well within ...nvenience. And then again, what ...bout death? As Socrates so philo- ...it, since we don't know what ...logical to fear it. It might be . . . ...ainly it is a release from the bur- ...l, for the godly, a haven and a ...ook at it another way—we are ...don't know the ins and outs of ...e are wheels within wheels, ...uld be presumptuous of us to ...he designs of fate or even of ..., I think we'd be well advised ...one. Tie up the letter—there— ...t. —They won't notice the bro- ...ing you were in character. ...oint? ...ic.

GUIL: But——

ROS: You march in here without so much as a by-your-leave and expect me to take in every lunatic you try to pass off with a lot of unsubstantiated——

GUIL: We've got a letter——

[*ROS snatches it and tears it open.*]

ROS (*efficiently*): I see . . . I see . . . well, this seems to support your story such as it is—it is an exact command from the king of Denmark, for several different reasons, importing Denmark's health and England's too, that on the reading of this letter, without delay, I should have Hamlet's head cut off——!

[*GUIL snatches the letter. ROS, double-taking, snatches it back. GUIL snatches it half back. They read it together, and separate.*
    Pause.
    They are well downstage looking front.]

ROS: The sun's going down. It will be dark soon.

GUIL: Do you think so?

ROS: I was just making conversation. (*Pause.*) We're his *friends*.

GUIL: How do you know?

...e's done nothing to us.

GUIL: Or justice.

ROS: It's awful.

GUIL: But it could have been worse. I was beginning to think it was. (*And his relief comes out in a laugh.*)

[*Behind them HAMLET appears from behind the umbrella. The light has been going. Slightly. HAMLET is going to the lantern.*]

ROS: The position as I see it, then. We, Rosencrantz and Guildenstern, from our young days brought up with him, awakened by a man standing on his saddle, are summoned, and arrive, and are instructed to glean what afflicts him and draw him on to pleasures, such as a play, which unfortunately, as it turns out, is abandoned in some confusion owing to certain nuances outside our appreciation—which, among other causes, results in, among other effects, a high, not to say, homicidal, excitement in Hamlet, whom we, in consequence, are escorting, for his own good, to England. Good. We're on top of it now.

[*HAMLET blows out the lantern. The stage goes pitch black. The black resolves itself to moonlight, by which HAMLET approaches the sleeping ROS and GUIL. He extracts the letter and takes it behind his umbrella;*

the light of his lantern shines through the fabric,
HAMLET *emerges again with a letter, and replaces it,*
and retires, blowing out his lantern.

Morning comes.
      ROS *watches it coming—from the auditorium.*
Behind him is a gay sight. Beneath the re-tilted
umbrella, reclining in a deck-chair, wrapped in a rug,
reading a book, possibly smoking, sits HAMLET.
      ROS *watches the morning come, and brighten to*
high noon.]

ROS: I'm assuming nothing. (*He stands up.* GUIL *wakes.*)
     The position as I see it, then. That's west unless
     we're off course, in which case it's night; the
     King gave me the same as you, the King gave
     you the same as me; the King never gave me
     the letter, the King gave you the letter, we don't
     know what's in the letter; we take Hamlet to
     the English king, it depending on when we get
     there who he is, and we hand over the letter,
     which may or may not have something in it to
     keep us going, and if not, we are finished and at
     a loose end, if they have loose ends. We could
     have done worse. I don't think we missed any
     chances. . . . Not that we're getting much help.
     (*He sits down again. They lie down—prone.*) If we
     stopped breathing we'd vanish.

[*The muffled sound of a recorder. They sit up with dis-*
proportionate interest.]

GUIL: Here we go.
ROS: Yes, but what?

[*They listen to the music.*]

GUIL (*excitedly*): Out of the void, finally, a sound;
     while on a boat (admittedly) outside the action
     (admittedly) the perfect and absolute silence of
     the wet lazy slap of water against water and
     the rolling creak of timber—breaks; giving rise
     at once to the speculation or the assumption or
     the hope that something is about to happen; a
     pipe is heard. One of the sailors has pursed his
     lips against a woodwind, his fingers and
     thumb governing, shall we say, the ventages,
     whereupon, giving it breath, let us say, with
     his mouth, it, the pipe, discourses, as the say-
     ing goes, most eloquent music. A thing like
     that, it could change the course of events.
     (*Pause.*) Go and see what it is.
ROS: It's someone playing on a pipe.
GUIL: Go and find him.
ROS: And then what?
GUIL: I don't know—request a tune.
ROS: What for?
GUIL: Quick—before we lose our momentum.

ROS: Why!—something is happening. It had quite
     escaped my attention!

[*He listens: Makes a stab at an exit. Listens more*
carefully: Changes direction.
      GUIL *takes no notice.*
      ROS *wanders about trying to decide where the music*
comes from. Finally he tracks it down—unwillingly—to
the middle barrel. There is no getting away from it. He
turns to GUIL *who takes no notice.* ROS, *during this*
whole business, never quite breaks into articulate
speech. His face and his hands indicate his incredulity.
He stands gazing at the middle barrel. The pipe plays
on within. He kicks the barrel. The pipe stops. He
leaps back towards GUIL. *The pipe starts up again. He*
approaches the barrel cautiously. He lifts the lid. The
music is louder. He slams down the lid. The music is
softer. He goes back towards GUIL. *But a drum starts,*
muffled. He freezes. He turns. Considers the left-hand
barrel. The drumming goes on within, in time to the
flute. He walks back to GUIL. *He opens his mouth to*
speak. Doesn't make it. A lute is heard. He spins round
at the third barrel. More instruments join in. Until it is
quite inescapable that inside the three barrels, distrib-
uted, playing together a familiar tune which has been
heard three times before, are the TRAGEDIANS.
      They play on.
      ROS *sits beside* GUIL. *They stare ahead.*
      The tune comes to an end.]
      [*Pause.*]

ROS: I thought I heard a band. (*In anguish.*)
     Plausibility is all I presume!
GUIL (*coda*): Call us this day our daily tune. . . .

[*The lid of the middle barrel flies open and the*
PLAYER'S *head pops out.*]

PLAYER: Aha! All in the same boat, then! (*He climbs*
     out. He goes round banging on the barrels.)
     Everybody out!

[*Impossibly, the* TRAGEDIANS *climb out of the barrels.*
With their instruments, but not their cart. A few bun-
dles. Except ALFRED. *The* PLAYER *is cheerful.*]

(*To* ROS:) Where are we?
ROS: Travelling.
PLAYER: Of course, we haven't got there yet.
ROS: Are we all right for England?
PLAYER: You look all right to me. I don't think they're
     very particular in England. Al-l-fred!

[ALFRED *emerges from the* PLAYER'S *barrel.*]

GUIL: What are you doing here?
PLAYER: Travelling. (*To* TRAGEDIANS:) Right—blend

into the background!

[The Tragedians are in costume (from the mime): A King with crown, Alfred as Queen, Poisoner and the two cloaked figures.
They blend.]

(*To* Guil:) Pleased to see us? (*Pause.*) You've come out of it very well, so far.
Guil: And you?
Player: In disfavour. Our play offended the King.
Guil: Yes.
Player: Well, he's a second husband himself. Tactless, really.
Ros: It was quite a good play nevertheless.
Player: We never really got going—it was getting quite interesting when they stopped it.

[Looks up at Hamlet.]

That's the way to travel. . . .
Guil: What were you doing in there?
Player: Hiding. (*Indicating costumes.*) We had to run for it just as we were.
Ros: Stowaways.
Player: Naturally—we didn't get paid, owing to circumstances ever so slightly beyond our control, and all the money we had we lost betting on certainties. Life is a gamble, at terrible odds—if it was a bet you wouldn't take it. Did you know that any number doubled is even?
Ros: Is it?
Player: We learn something every day, to our cost. But we troupers just go on and on. Do you know what happens to old actors?
Ros: What?
Player: Nothing. They're still acting. Surprised, then?
Guil: What?
Player: Surprised to see us?
Guil: I knew it wasn't the end.
Player: With practically everyone on his feet. What do you make of it, so far?
Guil: We haven't got much to go on.
Player: You speak to him?
Ros: It's possible.
Guil: But it wouldn't make any difference.
Ros: But it's possible.
Guil: Pointless.
Ros: It's allowed.
Guil: Allowed, yes. We are not restricted. No boundaries have been defined, no inhibitions imposed. We have, for the while, secured, or blundered into, our release, for the while. Spontaneity and whim are the order of the day. Other wheels are turning but they are not our concern. We can breathe. We can relax. We

can do what we like and say what we like to whomever we like, without restriction.
Ros: Within limits, of course.
Guil: Certainly within limits.

[Hamlet comes down to footlights and regards the audience. The others watch but don't speak. Hamlet clears his throat noisily and spits into the audience. A split second later he claps his hand to his eye and wipes himself. He goes back upstage.]

Ros: A compulsion towards philosophical introspection is his chief characteristic, if I may put it like that. It does not mean he is mad. It does not mean he isn't. Very often, it does not mean anything at all. Which may or may not be a kind of madness.
Guil: It really boils down to symptoms. Pregnant replies, mystic allusions, mistaken identities, arguing his father is his mother, that sort of thing; intimations of suicide, forgoing of exercise, loss of mirth, hints of claustrophobia not to say delusions of imprisonment; invocations of camels, chameleons, capons, whales, weasels, hawks, handsaws—riddles, quibbles and evasions; amnesia, paranoia, myopia; day-dreaming, hallucinations; stabbing his elders, abusing his parents, insulting his lover, and appearing hatless in public—knock-kneed, droop-stockinged and sighing like a love-sick schoolboy, which at his age is coming on a bit strong.
Ros: And talking to himself.
Guil: And talking to himself.

[Ros and Guil move apart together.]

Well, where has that got us?
Ros: He's the Player.
Guil: His play offended the King——
Ros: —offended the King——
Guil: —who orders his arrest——
Ros: —orders his arrest——
Guil: —so he escapes to England——
Ros: On the boat to which he meets——
Guil: Guildenstern and Rosencrantz taking Hamlet——
Ros:—who also offended the King——
Guil:—and killed Polonius——
Ros: —offended the King in a variety of ways——
Guil:—to England. (*Pause.*) That seems to be it.

[Ros jumps up.]

Ros: Incidents! All we get is incidents! Dear God, is it too much to expect a little sustained action?!

[And on the word, the Pirates attack. That is to say:

Noise and shouts and rushing about. "Pirates."

    Everyone visible goes frantic. HAMLET draws his sword and rushes downstage. GUIL, ROS and PLAYER draw swords and rush upstage. Collision. HAMLET turns back up. They turn back down. Collision. By which time there is general panic right upstage. All four charge upstage with ROS, GUIL and PLAYER shouting:]

> At last!
> To arms!
> Pirates!
> Up there!
> Down there!
> To my sword's length!
> Action!

[All four reach the top, see something they don't like, waver, run for their lives downstage:

    HAMLET, in the lead, leaps into the left barrel. PLAYER leaps into the right barrel. ROS and GUIL leap into the middle barrel. All closing the lids after them.

    The lights dim to nothing while the sound of fighting continues. The sound fades to nothing. The lights come up. The middle barrel (ROS's and GUIL's) is missing.

    The lid of the right-hand barrel is raised cautiously, the heads of ROS and GUIL appear.

    The lid of the other barrel (HAMLET's) is raised. The head of the PLAYER appears.

    All catch sight of each other and slam down lids. Pause.

    Lids raised cautiously.]

ROS (*relief*): They've gone. (*He starts to climb out.*)
    That was close. I've never thought quicker.

[They are all three out of barrels. GUIL is wary and nervous. ROS is light-headed. The PLAYER is phlegmatic. They note the missing barrel.

    ROS looks round.]

ROS: Where's——?

[The PLAYER takes off his hat in mourning.]

PLAYER: Once more, alone—on our own resources.
GUIL (*worried*): What do you mean? Where is he?
PLAYER: Gone.
GUIL: Gone where?
PLAYER: Yes, we were dead lucky there. If that's the word I'm after.
ROS (*not a pick up*): Dead?
PLAYER: Lucky.
ROS (*he means*): Is he dead?
PLAYER: Who knows?
GUIL (*rattled*): He's not coming back?
PLAYER: Hardly.
ROS: He's dead then. He's dead as far as we're concerned.

PLAYER: Or we are as far as he is. (*He goes and sits on the floor to one side.*) Not too bad, is it?
GUIL (*rattled*): But he can't—we're supposed to be—we've got a *letter*—we're going to England with a letter for the King——
PLAYER: Yes, that much seems certain. I congratulate you on the unambiguity of your situation.
GUIL: But you don't understand—it contains—we've had our instructions——the whole thing's pointless without him.
PLAYER: Pirates could happen to anyone. Just deliver the letter. They'll send ambassadors from England to explain. . . .
GUIL (*worked up*): Can't you see—the pirates left us home and high—dry and home—drome—— (*Furiously.*) The pirates left us high and dry!
PLAYER (*comforting*): There . . .
GUIL (*near tears*): Nothing will be resolved without him. . . .
PLAYER: There . . . !
GUIL: We need Hamlet for our release!
PLAYER: There!
GUIL: What are we supposed to do?
PLAYER: This.

[He turns away, lies down if he likes. ROS and GUIL apart.]

ROS: Saved again.
GUIL: Saved for what?

[ROS sighs.]

ROS: The sun's going down. (*Pause.*) It'll be night soon. (*Pause.*) If that's west. (*Pause.*) Unless we've——
GUIL (*shouts*): Shut up! I'm sick of it! Do you think conversation is going to help us now?
ROS (*hurt, desperately ingratiating*): I—I bet you all the money I've got the year of my birth doubled is an odd number.
GUIL (*moan*): No-o.
ROS: *Your* birth!

[GUIL smashes him down.]

GUIL (*broken*): We've travelled too far, and our momentum has taken over; we move idly towards eternity, without possibility of reprieve or hope of explanation.
ROS: Be happy—if you're not even *happy* what's so good about surviving? (*He picks himself up.*) We'll be all right. I suppose we just go on.
GUIL: Go where?
ROS: To England.
GUIL: England! *That's* a dead end. I never believed in it anyway.
ROS: All we've got to do is make our report and

that'll be that. Surely.

GUIL: I don't *believe* it—a shore, a harbour, say—and we get off and we stop someone and say—Where's the King?—And he says, Oh, you follow that road there and take the first left and—— (*Furiously.*) I don't believe any of it!

ROS: It doesn't sound very plausible.

GUIL: And even if we came face to face, what do we say?

ROS: We say—We've arrived!

GUIL (*kingly*): And who are you?

ROS: We are Guildenstern and Rosencrantz.

GUIL: Which is which?

ROS: Well, I'm—You're——

GUIL: What's it all about?——

ROS: Well, we were bringing Hamlet—but then some pirates——

GUIL: I don't begin to understand. Who are all these people, what's it got to do with me? You turn up out of the blue with some cock and bull story——

ROS (*with letter*): We have a letter——

GUIL (*snatches it, opens it*): A letter—yes—that's true. That's something . . . a letter . . . (*Reads.*) "As England is Denmark's faithful tributary . . . as love between them like the palm might flourish, etcetera . . . that on the knowing of this contents, without delay of any kind, should those bearers, Rosencrantz and Guildenstern, put to sudden death——"

[He double-takes. ROS snatches the letter. GUIL snatches it back. ROS snatches it half back. They read it again and look up.

The PLAYER gets to his feet and walks over to his barrel and kicks it and shouts into it.]

PLAYER: They've gone! It's all over!

[One by one the PLAYERS emerge, impossibly, from the barrel, and form a casually menacing circle round ROS and GUIL, who are still appalled and mesmerised.]

GUIL (*quietly*): Where we went wrong was getting on a boat. We can move, of course, change direction, rattle about, but our movement is contained within a larger one that carries us along as inexorably as the wind and current. . . .

ROS: They had it in for us, didn't they? Right from the beginning. Who'd have thought that we were so important?

GUIL: But why? Was it all for this? Who are we that so much should converge on our little deaths? (*In anguish to the* PLAYER:) Who are *we*?

PLAYER: You are Rosencrantz and Guildenstern. That's enough.

GUIL: No—it is not enough. To be told so little—to

such an end—and still, finally, to be denied an explanation——

PLAYER: In our experience, most things end in death.

GUIL (*fear, vengeance, scorn*): Your experience!—Actors!

[He snatches a dagger from the PLAYER's belt and holds the point at the PLAYER's throat: the PLAYER backs and GUIL advances, speaking more quietly.]

I'm talking about death—and you've never experienced *that*. And you cannot *act* it. You die a thousand casual deaths—with none of that intensity which squeezes out life . . . and no blood runs cold anywhere. Because even as you die you know that you will come back in a different hat. But no one gets up after *death*—there is no applause—there is only silence and some second-hand clothes, and that's—*death*——

[And he pushes the blade in up to the hilt. The PLAYER stands with huge, terrible eyes, clutches at the wound as the blade withdraws: he makes small weeping sounds and falls to his knees, and then right down.

While he is dying, GUIL, nervous, high, almost hysterical, wheels on the TRAGEDIANS—]

If we have a destiny, then so had he—and if this is ours, then that was his—and if there are no explanations for us, then let there be none for him——

[The TRAGEDIANS watch the PLAYER die: they watch with some interest. The PLAYER finally lies still. A short moment of silence. Then the TRAGEDIANS start to applaud with genuine admiration. The PLAYER stands up, brushing himself down.]

PLAYER (*modestly*): Oh, come, come, gentlemen—no flattery—it was merely competent——

[The TRAGEDIANS are still congratulating him. The PLAYER approaches GUIL, who stands rooted, holding the dagger.]

PLAYER: What did you think? (*Pause.*) You see, it *is* the kind they do believe in—it's what is expected.

[He holds his hand out for the dagger. GUIL slowly puts the point of the dagger on to the PLAYER's hand, and pushes . . . the blade slides back into the handle. The PLAYER smiles, reclaims the dagger.]

For a moment you thought I'd—cheated.

[ROS relieves his own tension with loud nervy laughter.]

ROS: Oh, very good! *Very* good! Took me in completely—didn't he take you in completely—

(*claps his hands*). Encore! Encore!

PLAYER (*activated, arms spread, the professional*): Deaths for all ages and occasions! Deaths by suspension, convulsion, consumption, incision, execution, asphyxiation and malnutrition—! Climactic carnage, by poison and by steel—! Double deaths by duel—! Show!—

[*ALFRED, still in his Queen's costume, dies by poison: the PLAYER, with rapier, kills the "KING" and duels with a fourth TRAGEDIAN, inflicting and receiving a wound. The two remaining TRAGEDIANS, the two "SPIES" dressed in the same coats as ROS and GUIL, are stabbed, as before. And the light is fading over the deaths which take place right upstage.*]

(*Dying amid the dying—tragically; romantically.*) So there's an end to that—it's commonplace: light goes with life, and in the winter of your years the dark comes early. . . .

GUIL (*tired, drained, but still an edge of impatience; over the mime*): No . . . no . . . not for *us*, no like that. Dying is not romantic, and death is not a game which will soon be over . . . Death is not anything . . . death is not . . . It's the absence of presence, nothing more . . . the endless time of never coming back . . . a gap you can't see, and when the wind blows through it, it makes no sound. . . .

[*The light has gone upstage. Only GUIL and ROS are visible as ROS's clapping falters to silence.*]
[*Small pause.*]

ROS: That's it, then, is it?

[*No answer. He looks out front.*]

The sun's going down. Or the earth's coming up, as the fashionable theory has it.

[*Small pause.*]

Not that it makes any difference.

[*Pause.*]

What was it all about? When did it begin?

[*Pause. No answer.*]

Couldn't we just stay put? I mean no one is going to come on and drag us off. . . . They'll just have to wait. We're still young . . . fit . . . we've got years. . . .

[*Pause. No answer.*]

(*A cry.*) We've done nothing wrong! We didn't harm anyone. Did we?

GUIL: I can't remember.

[*ROS pulls himself together.*]

ROS: All right, then. I don't care. I've had enough. To tell you the truth, I'm relieved.

[*And he disappears from view. GUIL does not notice.*]

GUIL: Our names shouted in a certain dawn . . . a message . . . a summons . . . There must have been a moment, at the beginning, where we could have said—no. But somehow we missed it. (*He looks round and sees he is alone.*) Rosen—? Guil—?

[*He gathers himself.*]

Well, we'll know better next time. Now you see me, now you—(*and disappears*).

[*Immediately the whole stage is lit up, revealing, upstage, arranged in the approximate positions last held by the dead TRAGEDIANS, the tableau of court and corpses which is the last scene of Hamlet.*
That is: The KING, QUEEN, LAERTES and HAMLET all dead. HORATIO holds HAMLET. FORTINBRAS is there.
So are two AMBASSADORS from England.]

AMBASSADOR: The sight is dismal;
  and our affairs from England come too late.
  The ears are senseless that should give us hearing
  to tell him his commandment is fulfilled,
  that Rosencrantz and Guildenstern are dead.
  Where should we have our thanks?

HORATIO: Not from his mouth,
  had it the ability of life to thank you:
  He never gave commandment for their death.
  But since, so jump upon this bloody question,
  you from the Polack wars, and you from England,
  are here arrived, give order that these bodies
  high on a stage be placed to the view;
  and let me speak to the yet unknowing world
  how these things came about: so shall you hear
  of carnal, bloody and unnatural acts,
  of accidental judgments, casual slaughters,
  of deaths put on by cunning and forced cause,
  and, in this upshot, purposes mistook
  fallen on the inventors' heads: all this can I
  truly deliver.

[*But during the above speech, the play fades out, overtaken by dark and music.*]

THE END

CLARE BOOTHE LUCE

(1903–1987)

Clare Boothe Luce, politician, diplomat, editor, journalist, and author, was born in 1903 in New York to William Franklin, a violinist, and Anna Clare Boothe. She attended private schools in New York before beginning her career in journalism in 1930, as editor first of *Vogue* and later of *Vanity Fair*. In 1935 she married the publishing magnate Henry Robinson Luce (d. 1967). She was war correspondent for *Life* in 1940 and a correspondent for *Life*, *Time*, and *Fortune* from 1941 to 1942. Active in politics, Luce served two terms as Republican congresswoman from Connecticut (1943–1947), and President Eisenhower appointed her United States ambassador to Italy from 1953 to 1957. She was the first woman ever to serve in such a major diplomatic post, and she later served as ambassador to Brazil. Luce was popular as a consultant and served on the boards of directors of many foundations and institutes. In recognition of her high accomplishments Luce received a number of honorary doctorates from American universities. She was also dubbed Knight of the Grand Cross of the Order of Merit of the Italian Republic and Dame of Malta.

While Luce wrote widely on politics and society, she is best known for her plays: *Abide with Me* (1935), *Kiss the Boys Goodbye* (1938; film, 1941), *Margin for Error* (1940; film, 1943), *Child of the Morning* (1950), and *Slam the Door Softly* (1970). Her best-known play, *The Women* (1936; film, 1939), a satire, was enormously successful on Broadway. Later adapted into a 1949 film *Come to the Stable*, it received a nomination for an Academy Award.

Slam the Door Softly

Slam the Door Softly, we learn from its Foreword, originally appeared in *Life* magazine in late 1970, entitled *A Doll's House, 1970*. In it, Luce updates the feminist vision of Henrik Ibsen's play *A Doll's House* (1879). Ibsen's play depicts the relationship between Torvald Helmer, a protective, dominant man, and his wife Nora, a submissive, childlike woman. Torvald displays middle-class attitudes of the late nineteenth century toward women: they are basically ornaments whose main jobs are to buttress their husbands' reputations, keep house, and keep their men amused. As Ibsen's play progresses, the stable bourgeois world that Torvald's household and marriage represents is shown to be a deception.

Marriage, respectability, and even justice are exposed as fictions created by the powerful to serve their own purposes. At the end of the play Nora leaves Torvald and their three children, determined to find her own individuality at any cost. The sound of the Helmer's private door slamming behind Nora, however shocking to nineteenth-century sensibilities, is widely considered to have opened up the public door of feminist discourse. Indeed, in its day the subject matter was considered so explosive that both a German actress in 1880 and an English actress in 1889 refused to play the part of Nora for fear their fans would think that they endorsed such behavior. *A Doll's House* upset audiences everywhere it played, but by the turn of the twentieth century the play had become a rallying point for the international women's movement, which sought the vote and other legal rights for women.

In the late nineteenth century Torvald was a much more sympathetic character, and Nora a much less sympathetic character, than they seem today. Luce's counterparts, Thaw and Nora Wald, are in any case far better versed in their positions, and the issues go well beyond those of legal rights and voting. The classic conflict between work and home, the responsibilities to self and to others, the nature and convenience of love and marriage, all are revisited and re-articulated by Luce. The soft closing of the Wald door behind Nora, with which Luce's play ends, demonstrates how complicated these matters have become in the late twentieth century.

Slam the Door Softly

Clare Boothe Luce

CHARACTERS
THAW WALD, about 35
NORA WALD, his wife, about 32

The scene is the Thaw Walds' cheerfully furnished middle-class living room in New York's suburbia. There are a front door and hall, a door to the kitchen area, and a staircase to the bedroom floor. Two easy chairs and two low hassocks with toys on them, grouped around a television, indicate a family of four. Drinks are on a bar cart at one end of a comfortable sofa, and an end table at the other. There are slightly more than the average number of bookshelves. The lamps are on, but as we don't hear the children, we know it is the Parents' Hour.

As the curtain rises, Thaw Wald, a good-looking fellow, about 35, is sitting in one of the easy chairs, smoking and watching TV. His back is to the sofa and staircase, so he does not see his wife coming down the stairs. Nora Wald is a rather pretty woman of about 32. She is carrying a suitcase, handbag and an armful of books.

Thaw switches channels, and lands in the middle of a panel show. During the TV dialogue that follows Nora somewhat furtively deposits her suitcase in the hall, takes her coat out of the hall closet, and comes back to the sofa carrying coat, purse and books. She lays her coat on the sofa, and the books on the end table. The books are full of little paper slips—bookmarkers. All of the above actions are unobserved by Thaw. We cannot see the TV screen, but we hear the voices of four women, all talking excitedly at once.

THAW (*To the screen and the world in general.*): God, these Liberation gals! Still at it.

MALE MODERATOR'S VOICE (*Full of paternal patience wearing a bit thin.*): Ladies! Lay-deez! Can't we switch now from the question of the sex-typing of jobs to what the Women's Liberation Movement thinks about—

OLDER WOMAN'S VOICE: May I finish! In the Soviet Union 83% of the dentists, 75% of the doctors and 37% of the lawyers are women. In Poland and Denmark—

MODERATOR: I think you have already amply made your point, Mrs. Epstein—anything men can do, women can do better!

YOUNG WOMAN'S VOICE (*Angrily.*): That was *not* her point—and you know it! What she said was, there are very few professional jobs men are doing that women couldn't do, if only—

THAW: Well, for God's sake then, shuddup, and go do 'em—

BLACK WOMAN'S VOICE: What she's been saying, what we've all been saying, and you men just don't want to hear us, is—things are the same for women as they are for us black people. We try to get up, you just sit down on us, like a big elephant sits down on a bunch of poor little mice.

MODERATOR: Well, sometimes moderators have to play the elephant, and sit down on one subject in order to develop another. As I was about to say, ladies, there is *one thing* a woman can do, no man can do—(*In his best holy-night-all-is-bright voice.*) give birth to a *child.*

YOUNG WOMAN'S VOICE: So what else is new?

THAW: One gets up ten, she's a Lesbo—

MODERATOR (*Forcefully.*): And *that* brings us to marriage! Now, if *I* may be permitted to get in just *one* statistic, edgewise: two thirds of all adult American females are married women. And now! (*At last he's got them where he wants them.*) What *is* the Women's Lib view of Woman's No. 1 job—Occupation Housewife?

THAW: Ha! That's the one none of 'em can handle—

YOUNG WOMAN'S VOICE (*Loud and clear.*): Marriage, as an institution, is as thoroughly corrupt as prostitution. It is, in fact, legalized and romanticized prostitution. A woman who marries is

selling her sexual services and domestic services for permanent bed and board—

BLACK WOMAN'S VOICE: There's no human being a man can buy anymore—except a woman—

THAW (*Snapping off the TV.*): Crrr-ap! Boy, what a bunch of battle-axes! (*He goes back to studying his TV listings.*)

NORA (*Raising her voice.*): Thaw! I'd like to say something about what they just said about marriage—

THAW (*In a warning voice.*): Uh-uh, Nora! We both agreed months ago, you'd lay off the feminist bit, if I'd lay off watching Saturday football—

NORA: And do something with the children . . . But Thaw, there's something maybe, I ought to try to tell you myself—(*Thaw is not listening. Nora makes a "what's the use" gesture, then opens her purse, takes out three envelopes, carefully inserts two of them under the covers of the top two books.*)

THAW: Like to hear Senators Smithers, Smethers and Smothers on "How Fast Can We Get Out of Vietnam?"

NORA (*Cool mockery.*): That bunch of pot-bellied, bald-headed old goats! Not one of them could get a woman—well, yes, maybe for two dollars.

THAW: You don't look at Senators, Nora. You listen to them.

NORA (*Nodding.*): Women are only to look at. Men are to listen to. Got it. (*Thaw snaps off the TV. He is now neither looking at her nor listening to her, as he methodically turns pages of the magazine he has picked up.*)

THAW: Finished reading to the kids?

NORA: I haven't been reading to the children. I've been reading to myself—and talking to myself—for a long time now.

THAW: That's good. (*She passes him, carrying the third envelope, and goes into kitchen. Then, unenthusiastically.*) Want some help with the dishes?

NORA'S VOICE: I'm not doing the dishes.

THAW (*Enthusiastically.*): Say, Nora, this is quite an ad we've got in LIFE for Stone Mountain Life Insurance.

NORA'S VOICE: Yes, I saw it. Great. (*She comes back and goes to sofa.*)

THAW: It's the kind of ad that grabs you. This sad-faced, nice-looking woman of 50, sitting on a bench with a lot of discouraged old biddies, in an employment agency. Great caption— (*Reading.*)

NORA AND THAW (*Together.*): "Could this happen to your wife?"

NORA: I'll let you know the answer very shortly. (*A pause.*) You really don't hear me anymore, do you? (*He really doesn't. She buttons herself into her coat, pulls on her gloves.*) Well, there are enough groceries for a week. All the telephone numbers you'll need and menus for the children are in the envelope on the spindle. A girl will come in to take care of them after school— until your mother gets here.

THAW: Uh-huh. . . .

NORA (*Looks around sadly.*): Well, goodby dear little doll house. Goodby dear husband. You've had the best ten years of my life. (*She goes to the staircase, blows two deep kisses upstairs, just as Thaw glances up briefly at her, but returns automatically to his magazine. Nora picks up suitcase, opens the door, goes out, closing it quietly.*)

THAW (*Like a man suddenly snapping out of a hypnotic trance.*): Nora? Nora? NOR-ra! (*He is out of the door in two seconds.*)

THAW'S AND NORA'S VOICES: Nora, where're you going?—I'll miss my train—I don't understand—it's all in my letter—let me go!—You come back—(*They return. He is pulling her by the arm. He yanks the suitcase away from her, drops it in the hall.*)

NORA: Ouch! You're hurting me!

THAW: Now what is this all about? (*He shoves her into the room, then stands between her and door.*) Why the hell . . . What're you sneaking out of the house . . . What's that suitcase for?

NORA: I wasn't sneaking. I told you. But you weren't listening.

THAW: I was listening . . . it just didn't register. You said you were reading to yourself. Then you started yakking about the kids and the groceries and the doll house mother sent . . . (*Flabbergasted.*) Goodby?! What do you mean, goodby?!

NORA: Just that. I'm leaving you. (*Pointing to books.*) My letter will explain everything—

THAW: Have you blown your mind?

NORA: Thaw, I've got to scoot, or I'll miss the eight-o-nine.

THAW: You'll miss it. (*He backs her to the sofa, pushes her onto it, goes and slams the door and strides back.*) Now, my girl, explain this—

NORA: You mean what's just happened now?

THAW: Yes. What's happened now.

NORA: Oh, that's easy. Muscle. You're made with the muscle—like a typical male. The heavier mus-

culature of the male is a secondary sexual characteristic. Although that's not certain. It could be just the result of selective breeding. In primitive times, of course, the heavier musculature of the male was necessary to protect the pregnant female and the immobile young—

THAW (*His anger evaporates.*): Nora, are you sick?

NORA: But what's just happened now shows that nothing has changed—I mean, fundamentally changed—in centuries, in the relations between the sexes. *You* still Tarzan, *me* still Jane.

THAW (*Sits on sofa beside her, feels her head.*): I've noticed you've been . . . well . . . acting funny lately. . . .

NORA: Funny?

THAW: Like there was something on your mind. . . . Tell me , what's wrong, sweetheart? Where does it hurt?

NORA: It hurts (*Taps head.*) here. Isn't that where thinking hurts *you*? No. You're used to it. I was, too, when I was at Wellesley. But I sort of stopped when I left. It's really hard to think of anything else when you're having babies.

THAW: Nora, isn't it about time for your period?

NORA: But if God had wanted us to think just with our wombs, why did He give us a brain? No matter what men say, Thaw, the female brain is not a vestigial organ, like a vermiform appendix.

THAW: Nora . . .

NORA: Thaw, I can just about make my train. I'll leave the car and keys in the usual place at the station. Now, I have a very important appointment in the morning. (*She starts to rise.*)

THAW: Appointment? (*Grabs her shoulders.*) Nora, look at me! You weren't sneaking out of the house to . . . get an abortion?

NORA: When a man can't explain a woman's actions, the first thing he thinks about is the condition of her uterus. Thaw, if you were leaving me and I didn't know why, would I ask, first thing, if you were having prostate trouble?

THAW: Don't try to throw me off the track, sweetie! Now, if you want another baby . . .

NORA: Thaw, don't you remember, we both agreed about the overpopulation problem—

THAW: To hell with the overpopulation problem. Let Nixon solve that. Nora, I can swing another baby—

NORA: Maybe you can. I can't. For me there are no more splendid, new truths to be learned from scanning the contents of babies' diapers. Thaw, I *am* pregnant. But not in a feminine way. In the way only men are supposed to get pregnant.

THAW: Men, pregnant?

NORA (*Nodding.*): With ideas. Pregnancies there (*Taps his head.*) are masculine. And a very superior form of labor. Pregnancies here (*Taps her tummy.*) are feminine—a very inferior form of labor. That's an example of male linguistic chauvinism. Mary Ellmann is *great* on that. You'll enjoy her *Thinking about Women*. . . .

THAW (*Going to telephone near bookshelf.*): I'm getting the doctor. (*Nora makes a dash for the door, he drops the phone.*) Oh, no, you don't! (*He reaches for her as she passes, misses. Grabs her ponytail and hauls her back by it, and shoves her into the easy chair.*)

NORA: Brother, Millett sure had you taped.

THAW: Milly *who*? (*A new thought comes to him.*) Has one of your goddamgossipyfemale friends been trying to break up our marriage? (*He suddenly checks his conscience. It is not altogether pure.*) What did she tell you? That she saw me having lunch, uh, dinner, with some girl?

NORA (*Nodding to herself.*): Right on the button!

THAW: Now, Nora, I can explain about that girl—

NORA: You don't have to. Let's face it. Monogamy is not natural to the male—

THAW: You know I'm not in love with anybody but you—

NORA: Monogamy is not natural to the female, either. Making women think it is, is the man's most successful form of brainwashing the female—

THAW: Nora I swear, that girl means nothing to me—

NORA: And you probably mean nothing to her. So whose skin is off whose nose?

THAW (*Relieved, but puzzled.*): Well, uh, I'm glad you feel that way about—uh—things.

NORA: Oh, it's not the way I *feel*. It's the way things really are. What with the general collapse of the mores, and now the Pill, women are becoming as promiscuous as men. It figures. We're educated from birth to think of ourselves just as man-traps. Of course, in my mother's day, good women thought of themselves as private man-traps. Only bad women were public man-traps. Now we've all gone public. (*Looks at watch.*) I'll have to take the eight-forty. (*She gets out of her coat, lays it, ready to slip into, on back of sofa.*)

THAW (*A gathering suspicion.*): Nora, are you trying to tell me . . . that *you*—

NORA: Of course, a lot of it, today, is the fault of the advertising industry. Making women think they're failures in life if they don't make like sex-pots around the clock. We're even supposed to wear false eyelashes when we're vacuuming. Betty Friedan's great on that. She says many lonely suburban housewives, unable to identify their real problem, think more sex is the answer. So they sleep with the milkman, or the delivery boy. If I felt like sleeping with anybody like that, I'd pick the plumber. When you need *him*, boy you *need* him!

THAW (*The unpleasant thought he has been wrestling with has now jelled.*): Nora . . . are you . . . trying to tell me you are leaving me—for someone else?

NORA: Why, Thaw Wald! How could you even *think* such a thing? (*To herself.*) Now, how naïve can I be? What else do men think about, in connection with women, *but* sex? He is saying to himself, she's not having her period, she's not pregnant, she's not jealous: it's *got* to be another man.

THAW: Stop muttering to yourself, and answer my question.

NORA: I forgot what it was. Oh, yes. *No.*

THAW: No what?

NORA: No, I'm not in love with anybody else. I was a virgin when I married you. And intacta. And that wasn't par for the course—even at Wellesley. And I've never slept with anybody else, partly because I never wanted to. And partly because, I suppose, of our family's Presbyterian hangup. So, now that all the vital statistics are out of the way, I'll just drive around until— (*Begins to slip her arms into coat. He grabs coat, throws it on easy chair.*)

THAW: You're not leaving until you tell me *why*.

NORA: But it's all in my letter. (*Points.*) The fat one sticking out of Simone de Beauvoir's *Second Sex*—

THAW: If you have a bill of particulars against me, I want it—straight. From you.

NORA: Oh, darling, I have no bill of particulars. By all the standards of our present-day society, you are a very good husband. And, mark me, you'll be president of Stone Mountain Life Insurance Company before you're 50. The point is, what will I be when I'm 50—

THAW: You'll be my wife, if I have anything to say. Okay. So you're not leaving me because I'm a bad husband, or because my financial future is dim.

NORA: No. Oh, Thaw, you just wouldn't understand.

THAW (*Patiently.*): I might, if you would try, for just one minute, to talk logically—

NORA: Thaw, women aren't trained to talk logically. Men don't like women who talk logically. They find them unfeminine—aggressive—

THAW: Dammit, Nora, will you talk sense . . .

NORA: But boy! does a man get sore when a woman won't talk logically when *he* wants her to, and (*Snaps fingers.*) like that! And *that* isn't illogical? What women men are! Now, if you will step aside—

THAW (*Grabbing her and shaking her.*): You're going to

tell me why you're walking out on me, if I have to *sock* you!

NORA: Thaw, eyeball to eyeball, *I am leaving you—* and not for a man. For reasons of my own I just don't think you *can* understand. And if you mean to stop me, you'll have to beat me to a pulp. But I'm black and blue already.

THAW (*Seizes her tenderly in his arms, kisses her.*): Nora, sweetheart! You know I couldn't really hurt you. (*Kisses, kisses.*) Baaaby, what do you say we call it a night? (*Scoops her up in his arms.*) You can tell me *all* about it in bed . . .

NORA: The classical male one-two. Sock 'em and screw 'em.

THAW (*Dumping her on sofa.*): Well, it's been known to work on a lot of occasions. Something tells me this isn't one of them. (*Pours a drink.*)

NORA: I guess I need one, too. (*He mixes them.*) Thaw?

THAW: Yes.

NORA: I couldn't help being a *little* pleased when you made like a caveman. It shows you really do value my sexual services.

THAW: Geez!

NORA: Well, it can't be my domestic services—you don't realize, yet, what they're worth. (*Drinks.*) Thaw, you do have a problem with me. But you can't solve it with force. And *I* do have a problem. But I can't solve it with sex.

THAW: Could you, would you, *try* to tell me what my-you-our problem is?

NORA: Friedan's *Feminine Mystique* is very good on The Problem. I've marked all the relevant passages. And I've personalized them in my letter—(*He goes to book. Yanks out letter, starts to tear it up. Nora groans. He changes his mind, and stuffs it in his pocket.*)

THAW: Look, Nora, there's one thing I've always said about you. For a woman, you're pretty damn honest. Don't you think you owe it to me to level and give me a chance to defend myself?

NORA: The trouble is, *you* would have to listen to *me*. And that's hard for you. I *understand why*. Not listening to women is a habit that's been passed on from father to son for generations. You could almost say, tuning out on women is another secondary sexual male characteristic.

THAW: So our problem is that *I* don't listen?

NORA: Thaw, you always go on talking, no matter how hard I'm interrupting.

THAW: Okay. You have the floor.

NORA: Well, let's begin where this started tonight. When you oppressed me, and treated me as an inferior—

THAW: I oppressed . . . (*Hesitates.*) Lay on, MacDuff.

NORA: You honestly don't think that yanking me around by my hair and threatening to sock me

are not the oppressive gestures of a superior male toward an inferior female?

THAW: For Chrissake, Nora, a man isn't going to let the woman he loves leave him, if he can stop her!

NORA: Exactly. Domination of the insubordinate female is an almost instinctive male reflex. *In extremis,* Thaw, it is rape. Now, would I like it if you should say you were going to leave me? No. But could I drag you back—

THAW: You'd just have to crook your little finger.

NORA: Flattery will get you nowhere this evening. So, where was I?

THAW: I am a born rapist.

NORA: Wasn't that what you had in mind when you tried to adjourn this to our bedroom? But that's just your primitive side. There's your civilized side too. You are a patriarchal *paterfamilias.*

THAW: What am I now?

NORA: Thaw, you do realize we all live in a patriarchy, where men govern women by playing sexual politics?

THAW: Look, you're not still sore because I talked you into voting for Nixon? (*She gives him a withering look.*) Okay. So we all live in a patriarchy . . .

NORA: Our little family, the Walds, are just one nuclear patriarchal unit among the millions in our patriarchal male-dominated civilization, which is worldwide. It's all in that book—

THAW: Look Nora, I promise I'll read the damn book—but . . .

NORA: So who's interrupting? Well, Thaw, all history shows that the hand that cradles the *rock* has ruled the world, *not* the hand that rocks the cradle! Do you know what brutal things men have done to women? Bought and sold them like cattle. Bound their feet at birth to deform them—so they couldn't run away—like in China. Made widows throw themselves on the funeral pyres of their husbands, like in India. And men who committed adultery were almost never punished. But women were always brutally punished. Why, in many countries unfaithful wives were *stoned* to death—

THAW: This is America, 1970, Nora. And here, when wives are unfaithful, *husbands* get stoned. (*Drinks.*) Mind if *I* do?

NORA: Be your guest. Oh, there's no doubt that relations between the sexes have been greatly ameliorated . . .

THAW: Now, about *our* relations, Nora. You're not holding it against *me* that men, the dirty bastards, have done a lot of foul things to women in the past?

NORA (*Indignant.*): What do you mean, in the *past?*

THAW (*Determined to be patient.*): Past, present, future—what has what other men have done to other women got to do with us?

NORA: Quite a lot. We *are* a male and a female—

THAW: That's the supposition I've always gone on. But Nora, we are a *particular* male and a *particular* female: Thaw Wald and his wife, Nora—

NORA: Yes. That's why it's so shattering when you find out you are such a typical husband and—

THAW (*A new effort to take command.*): Nora, how many men do you know who are still in love with their wives after ten years?

NORA: Not many. And, Thaw, listen, maybe the reason is—

THAW: So you agree that's not typical? Okay. Now, do I ever grumble about paying the bills? So that's not typical. I liked my mother-in-law, even when she was alive. And God knows that's not typical. And don't I do every damn thing I can to keep *my* mother off your back? And that's not typical. I'm even thoughtful about the little things. You said so yourself, remember, when I bought you that black see-through nightgown for Mother's Day. That I went out and chose myself. And which *you* never wear.

NORA: I had to return it. It was too small. And do you know what the saleswoman said? She said, "Men who buy their wives things in this department are in love with them. But why do they all seem to think they are married to midgets?" That's it, Thaw, that's *it!* Men "think little"—like "thinking thin"—even about women they love. They don't think at all about women they don't love or want to sleep with. Now, I can't help it if you think of me as a midget. But don't you see, I've got to stop thinking of myself as one. Thaw, *listen* . . .

THAW: Why the devil should *you* think of yourself as a midget? *I* think you're a great woman. A *real* woman! Why, you're the dearest, sweetest, most understanding little wife—most of the time—a man ever had. And the most intelligent and wonderful little mother! Dammit, those kids are the smartest, best-behaved, most self-reliant little kids . . .

NORA: Oh, I've been pretty good at Occupation Housewife, if I do say so myself. But, Thaw, *listen.* Can't you even imagine that there might be something *more* a woman needs and wants—

THAW: My God, Nora, what more can a woman want than a nice home, fine children and a husband who adores her?

NORA (*Discouraged.*): You sound like old Dr. Freud, in person.

THAW: I sound like Freud? I wish I were. Then I'd know why you're so uptight.

NORA: Oh, no you wouldn't. Know what Freud wrote in his diary, when he was 77? "What do women want? My God, what do they want?" Fifty years this giant brain spends analyzing women. And he still can't find out what they want. So this makes him the world's greatest expert on feminine psychology? (*She starts to look at her watch.*) To think I bought him, in college.

THAW: You've got plenty of time. You were saying about Freud—(*He lights a cigarette, hands it to her, determined to stick with it to the end.*)

NORA: History is full of ironies! Freud was the foremost exponent of the theory of the natural inferiority of women. You know, "Anatomy is destiny"?

THAW: I was in the School of Business, remember?

NORA: Well, old Freud died in 1939. He didn't live to see what happened when Hitler adopted his theory that "anatomy is destiny." Six millions of his own people went to the gas chambers. One reason, Hitler said, that the Jews were *naturally* inferior was because they were effeminate people, with a slave mentality. He said they were full of those vices which men always identify with women—when they're feeling hostile: You know, sneakiness and deception, scheming and wheedling, whining and pushiness, oh, and materialism, sensuousness and sexuality. Thaw, what's *your* favorite feminine vice?

THAW: At this moment, feminine monologues.

NORA: I didn't think you'd have the nerve to say sneakiness. I saw you sneak a look at your watch, and egg me on to talk about Freud, hoping I'll miss my train. I won't.

THAW: So nothing I've said—what little I've had a chance to say . . . (*She shakes her head.*)—you still intend to divorce me?

NORA: Oh, I never said I was divorcing you. I'm deserting you. So you can divorce me.

THAW: You do realize, Nora, that if a wife deserts her husband he doesn't have to pay her alimony?

NORA: I don't want alimony. But I do want severance pay. (*Points to books.*) There's my bill, rendered for 10 years of domestic services—the thing sticking in *Woman's Place*, by Cynthia Fuchs Epstein. I figured it at the going agency rates for a full-time cook, cleaning woman, handyman, laundress, seamstress, and part-time gardener and chauffeur. I've worked an average ten-hour day. So I've charged for overtime. Of course, you've paid my rent, taxes, clothing, medical expenses and food. So I've deducted those. Even though as a housewife, I've had no fringe benefits. Just the same, the bill . . . well,

I'm afraid you're going to be staggered. I was. It comes to over $53,000. I'd like to be paid in 10 installments.

THAW (*He is staggered.*): Mathematics isn't really your bag, Nora.

NORA: I did it on that little calculating machine you gave me at Christmas. If you think it's not really fair, I'll be glad to negotiate. And, please notice, I haven't charged anything for sleeping with you!

THAW: Wow! (*He is really punch drunk.*)

NORA: I'm not a prostitute. And *this* is what I wanted to say about the Lib girls. They're right about women who marry *just* for money. But they're wrong about women who marry for love. It's love makes all the difference—

THAW (*Dispirited.*): Well, *vive la différence.*

NORA: And, of course, I haven't charged anything for being a nurse. I've adored taking care of the children, especially when they were babies. I'm going to miss them—*awfully.*

THAW (*On his feet, with outrage.*): You're deserting the children, too? My God, Nora, what kind of woman *are* you? You're going to leave those poor little kids alone in this house—

NORA: You're here. And I told you, your mother is coming. I wired her that her son needed her. She'll be happy again—and be needed again—for the first time in years—

THAW (*This is a real blow.*): My *mother!* Oh, migod, you *can't,* Nora. You know how she—*swarms* over me! She thinks I'm still 12 years old . . . (*His head is now in his hands.*) You know she drives me out of my cotton-picking mind.

NORA: Yes. But you never said so before.

THAW: I love my mother. She's been a good mother, and wife. But, Nora, she's a *very* limited woman! Yak, yak—food, shopping, the kids . . .

NORA: Thaw, the children love this house, and I don't want to take them out of school. And I can't give them another home. Women, you know, can't borrow money to buy a house. Besides, legally this house and everything in it, except my mother's few things and my wedding presents, are yours. All the worldly goods with which thou didst me endow seem to be in that suitcase.

THAW: Nora, you know damn well that all my life insurance is in your name. If I died tomorrow—and I'll probably blow my brains out tonight—everything would go to you and the kids.

NORA: Widowhood is one of the few fringe benefits of marriage. But, today, all the money I have is what I've saved in the past year out of my clothes allowance—$260.33. But I hope you will give me my severance pay—

THAW: And if I don't—you know legally I don't have to—how do you propose to support yourself?

NORA: Well, if I can't get a job right away—sell my engagement ring. That's why they say diamonds are a gal's best friend. What else do most women *have* they can turn into ready cash—except their bodies?

THAW: What kind of job do you figure on getting?

NORA: Well, I do have a master's in English. So I'm going to try for a spot in TIME Research. That's the intellectual harem kept by the Time Inc. editors. The starting pay is good.

THAW: How do you know that?

NORA: From your own research assistant, Molly Peapack. We're both Wellesley, you know. She's a friend of the chief researcher at TIME, Marylois Vega. Also, Molly says, computer programming is a field that may open to women—

THAW (*Indignant.*): You told Peapack you were leaving me? Before you even told *me?* How do you like *that* for treating a mate like an inferior!

NORA: Thaw, I've told you at least three times a week for the last year that with the kids both in school, I'd like to get a job. You always laughed at me. You said I was too old to be a Playboy Bunny, and that the only job an inexperienced woman my age could get would be as a saleswoman—

THAW: Okay. Where are you going to live?

NORA: Peapack's offered to let me stay with her until I find something—

THAW: I'm going to have a word with Miss Molly Peapack tomorrow. She's been too damned aggressive lately, anyway—

NORA: She's going to have a word with you, too. *She's* leaving.

THAW: Peapack is leaving? Leaving *me?*

NORA: When you got her from Prudential, you promised her, remember, you'd recommend her for promotion to office manager. So, last week you took on a man. A new man. Now she's got a job offer where she's sure she's got a 40–60 chance for advancement to management. So you've lost your home wife and your office wife, too.

THAW: And *this* is a male-dominated world?

NORA: Thaw, I've got just five minutes—

THAW: You've still not told me *why*—

NORA: Oh, Thaw darling! You poor—*man.* I have told you why: I'm leaving because I want a job. I want to do some share, however small, of the world's work, and be paid for it. Isn't the work you do in the world—and the salary *you* get— what makes you respect yourself, and other men respect *you?* Women have begun to want to respect themselves a little, too—

THAW: You mean, the real reason you are leaving is that you want a *paying* job?

NORA: Yes.

THAW: God, Nora, why didn't you say that in the beginning? All right, go get a job, if it's that important to you. But that doesn't mean you have to leave me and the kids.

NORA: I'm afraid it does. Otherwise, I'd have to do two jobs. Out there. And here.

THAW: Look, Nora, I heard some of the Lib gals say there are millions of working wives and mothers who are doing two jobs. Housework can't be all that rough—

NORA: Scrubbing floors, walls. Cleaning pots, pans, windows, ovens. Messes—dog messes, toilet messes, children's messes. Garbage. Laundry. Shopping for pounds of stuff. Loading them into the car, out of the car—(*A pause.*) Not all of it hard. But all of it routine. All of it *boring*.

THAW: Listen, Nora, what say, you work, I work. And we split the housework? How's that for a deal?

NORA: It's a deal you are not quite free to make, Thaw. You sometimes *can't* get home until very late. And you have to travel a lot, you know. Oh, it might work for a little while. But not for long. After 10 years, you still won't empty an ashtray, or pick up after yourself in the bathroom. No. I don't have the physical or moral strength to swing two jobs. So I've got to choose the one, before it's too late, that's most important for me—oh, not for me just now, but for when *I'm* 50—

THAW: When you're 50, Nora, if you don't leave me, you'll be the wife of the president of Stone Mountain Life Insurance Company. Sharing my wealth, sharing whatever status I have in the community. And with servants of your own. Now you listen to *me*, Nora. It's a man's world out there. It's a man's world where there are a lot of women working. I see them every day. What are most of them really

doing? Marking time, and looking, always looking, for a man who will offer them a woman's world . . . the world you have here. Marriage is still the best deal that the world has to offer women. And most women know it. It's always been like that. And it's going to be like that for a long, long time.

NORA: Just now I feel that the best deal I, Nora Wald, can hope to get out of life is to learn to esteem myself as a person . . . to stop feeling that every day a little bit more of my mind—and heart—is being washed down the drain with the soapsuds. . . . Thaw—listen. If I don't stop shrinking, I'll end up secretly hating you, and trying to cut you—and *your* son—down to my size. The way your swarmy mommie does you and your Dad. And you'll become like your father, the typical henpecked husband. Thinking of his old wife as the Ball and Chain. You know he has a mistress? (*Thaw knows. He belts down a stiff drink.*) A smart gal who owns her own shop . . . a woman who doesn't bore him.

THAW: Well, Nora . . . (*Pours another drink.*) One for the road?

NORA: Right. For the road.

THAW: Nora . . . I'll wait. But I don't know how long—

NORA: I've thought of that, too . . . that you might remarry . . . that girl, maybe, who means nothing—

THAW: Dammit, a man needs a woman of his own—

NORA (*Nodding.*): I know. A sleep-in, sleep-with body servant of his very own. Well, that's your problem. Just now, I have to wrestle with my problem . . . (*Goes to door, picks up suitcase.*) I'm not bursting with self-confidence, Thaw. I do love you. And I also need . . . a man. So I'm not slamming the door. I'm closing it . . . very . . . softly.

Exits. Curtain falls.

Sam Shepard (b. 1943)

Samuel Shepard Rogers VII was born in Fort Sheridan, Illinois while his father was serving in the military. The family moved from base to base until his father retired and settled in Southern California. Shepard left college and toured with the Bishop's Company Repertory Players before landing in New York in 1963, where he worked as a busboy in the Village Gate jazz club. There he wrote his first plays for off-Broadway theaters, including *Cowboys* (1964), *Red Cross* (1966), *La Turista* (1966), *The Unseen Hand* (1971), *Cowboy Mouth* (1971), and *of The Tooth Crime* (1972). In these early plays Shepard pioneered what were to become sustaining themes in his work: the destructiveness of family life and loneliness, longing, and loss, often focused on the search for the American West of myth.

Shepard is one of America's best-known contemporary playwrights and has been showered with awards for his work. He received ten Obie awards for off-Broadway plays before 1979, a Pulitzer Prize for *Buried Child* in 1979, another Obie for sustained achievement in 1980, and the New York's Drama Critics Circle Award for *A Lie of the Mind* (which he also directed) in 1985. His plays have most often been produced in off-Broadway venues and regional theaters rather than in the commercial mainstream. Because of his tendency to work with theater companies known for their artistic integrity rather than their capacity to attract large audiences, Shepard has earned a reputation as an avant-garde play-wright. At the same time, he has also managed to achieve a reputation as a screenwriter and a popular actor in the commercial film business. He played the role of Chuck Yeager in *The Right Stuff* (1983), he appeared in various parts in his own *Fool for Love* (1983; film, 1985), in *Country* (1984), and *Crimes of the Heart* (1986), and he wrote the screenplay for *Paris, Texas* (1983).

True West

True West (1980) is Shepard's most spare and elemental play, one that focuses on the issues of cultural and individual identity. Its protagonists are two brothers recalling the jealousies of Cain and Abel and the fortunes of the prince and the pauper. Austin is a screenwriter and Lee, his older brother, a drifter and petty thief who spends much of his time in the desert. Lee envies the more successful Austin, but over the course of the play they exchange roles and identities. Lee manages to interest a producer in his screenplay for a western film, one drawn from his own experience. Meanwhile, Austin appears to lose his interest in writing and steals toasters from the neighbors to prove himself to his brother. Their struggle shifts ground until Austin, to refute Lee's claim that his idea for a western reveals the true West, declares that "there's no such thing as the West anymore," asserting that the myths are all used up. Ironically, Shepard's play itself is a contemporary western of sorts. Although Lee and Austin are not frontier farmers or cattle herders competing for the same land, they are struggling for control of something larger: the myths of the American West upon which their own identities depend.

TRUE WEST

Sam Shepard

CHARACTERS

AUSTIN, early thirties, light blue sports shirt, light tan cardigan sweater, clean blue jeans, white tennis shoes
LEE, his older brother, early forties, filthy white t-shirt, tattered brown overcoat covered with dust, dark blue baggy suit pants from the Salvation Army, pink suede belt, pointed black forties dress shoes scuffed up, holes in the soles, no socks, no hat, long pronounced sideburns, "Gene Vincent" hairdo, two days' growth of beard, bad teeth.

SAUL KIMMER, late forties, Hollywood producer, pink and white flower print sports shirt, white sports coat with matching polyester slacks, black and white loafers.
MOM, early sixties, mother of the brothers, small woman, conservative white skirt and matching jacket, red shoulder bag, two pieces of matching red luggage.

SCENE: All nine scenes take place on the same set; a kitchen and adjoining alcove of an older home in a Southern California suburb, about 40 miles east of Los Angeles. The kitchen takes up most of the playing area to stage left. The kitchen consists of a sink, upstage center, surrounded by counter space, a wall telephone, cupboards, and a small window just above it bordered by neat yellow curtains. Stage left of sink is a stove. Stage right, a refrigerator. The alcove adjoins the kitchen to stage right. There is no wall division or door to the alcove. It is open and easily accessible from the kitchen and defined only by the objects in it: a small round glass breakfast table mounted on white iron legs, two matching white iron chairs set across from each other. The two exterior walls of the alcove which prescribe a corner in the upstage right are composed of many small windows, beginning from a solid wall about three feet high and extending to the ceiling. The windows look out to bushes and citrus trees. The alcove is filled with all sorts of house plants in various pots, mostly Boston ferns hanging in planters at different levels. The floor of the alcove is composed of green synthetic grass.

All entrances and exits are made stage left from the kitchen. There is no door. The actors simply go off and come onto the playing area.

NOTE ON SET AND COSTUME: The set should be constructed realistically with no attempt to distort its dimensions, shapes, objects, or colors. No objects should be introduced which might draw special attention to themselves other than the props demanded by the script. If a stylistic "concept" is grafted onto the set design it will only serve to confuse the evolution of the characters' situation, which is the most important focus of the play.

Likewise, the costumes should be exactly representative of who the characters are and not added onto for the sake of making a point to the audience.

NOTE ON SOUND: The Coyote of Southern California has a distinct yapping, dog-like bark, similar to a Hyena. This yapping grows more intense and maniacal as the pack grows in numbers, which is usually the case when they lure and kill pets from suburban yards. The sense of growing frenzy in the pack should be felt in the background, particularly in Scenes 7 and 8. In any case, these Coyotes never make the long, mournful, solitary howl of the Hollywood stereotype.

The sound of Crickets can speak for itself.

These sounds should also be treated realistically even though they sometimes grow in volume and numbers.

ACT I

Scene 1

Night. Sound of crickets in dark. Candlelight appears in alcove, illuminating AUSTIN, seated at glass table hunched over a writing notebook, pen in hand, cigarette burning in ashtray, cup of coffee, typewriter on table, stacks of paper, candle burning on table.

Soft moonlight fills kitchen illuminating LEE, beer in hand, six-pack on counter behind him. He's leaning against the sink, mildly drunk; takes a slug of beer.

LEE: So, Mom took off for Alaska, huh?

AUSTIN: Yeah.

LEE: Sorta' left you in charge.

AUSTIN: Well, she knew I was coming down here so she offered me the place.

LEE: You keepin' the plants watered?

AUSTIN: Yeah.

LEE: Keepin' the sink clean? She don't like even a single tea leaf in the sink ya' know.

AUSTIN (*trying to concentrate on writing*): Yeah, I know.

[*pause*]

LEE: She gonna' be up there a long time?

AUSTIN: I don't know.

LEE: Kinda' nice for you, huh? Whole place to yourself.

AUSTIN: Yeah, it's great.

LEE: Ya' got crickets anyway. Tons a' crickets out there. (*looks around kitchen*) Ya' got groceries? Coffee?

AUSTIN (*looking up from writing*): What?

LEE: You got coffee?

AUSTIN: Yeah.

LEE: At's good. (*short pause*) Real coffee? From the bean?

AUSTIN: Yeah. You want some?

LEE: Naw. I brought some uh—(*motions to beer*)

AUSTIN: Help yourself to whatever's—(*motions to refrigerator*)

LEE: I will. Don't worry about me. I'm not the one to worry about. I mean I can uh—(*pause*) You always work by candlelight?

AUSTIN: No—uh—Not always.

LEE: Just sometimes?

AUSTIN (*puts pen down, rubs his eyes*): Yeah. Sometimes it's soothing.

LEE: Isn't that what the old guys did?

AUSTIN: What old guys?

LEE: The Forefathers. You know.

AUSTIN: Forefathers?

LEE: Isn't that what they did? Candlelight burning into the night? Cabins in the wilderness.

AUSTIN (*rubs hand through his hair*): I suppose.

LEE: I'm not botherin' you am I? I mean I don't wanna break into yer uh—concentration or nothin'.

AUSTIN: No, it's all right.

LEE: That's good. I mean I realize that yer line a' work demands a lota' concentration.

AUSTIN: It's okay.

LEE: You probably think that I'm not fully able to comprehend somethin' like that, huh?

AUSTIN: Like what?

LEE: That stuff yer doin'. That art. You know. Whatever you call it.

AUSTIN: It's just a little research.

LEE: You may not know it but I did a little art myself once.

AUSTIN: You did?

LEE: Yeah! I did some a' that. I fooled around with it. No future in it.

AUSTIN: What'd you do?

LEE: Never mind what I did! Just never mind about that. (*pause*) It was ahead of its time.

[pause]

AUSTIN: So, you went out to see the old man, huh?

LEE: Yeah, I seen him.

AUSTIN: How's he doing?

LEE: Same. He's doin' just about the same.

AUSTIN: I was down there too, you know.

LEE: What d'ya' want, an award? You want some kinda' medal? You were down there. He told me all about you.

AUSTIN: What'd he say?

LEE: He told me. Don't worry.

[pause]

AUSTIN: Well—

LEE: You don't have to say nothin'.

AUSTIN: I wasn't.

LEE: Yeah, you were gonna' make somethin' up. Somethin' brilliant.

[pause]

AUSTIN: You going to be down here very long, Lee?

LEE: Might be. Depends on a few things.

AUSTIN: You got some friends down here?

LEE (*laughs*): I know a few people. Yeah.

AUSTIN: Well, you can stay here as long as I'm here.

LEE: I don't need your permission do I?

AUSTIN: No.

LEE: I mean she's my mother too, right?

AUSTIN: Right.

LEE: She might've just as easily asked me to take care of her place as you.

AUSTIN: That's right.

LEE: I mean I know how to water plants.

[long pause]

AUSTIN: So you don't know how long you'll be staying then?

LEE: Depends mostly on houses, ya' know.

AUSTIN: Houses?

LEE: Yeah. Houses. Electric devices. Stuff like that. I gotta' make a little tour first.

[short pause]

AUSTIN: Lee, why don't you just try another neighborhood, all right?

LEE (*laughs*): What'sa' matter with this neighborhood? This is a great neighborhood. Lush. Good class a' people. Not many dogs.

AUSTIN: Well, our uh—Our mother just happens to live here. That's all.

LEE: Nobody's gonna' know. All they know is somethin's missing. That's all. She'll never even hear about it. Nobody's gonna know.

AUSTIN: You're going to get picked up if you start walking around here at night.

LEE: Me? I'm gonna' git picked up? What about you? You stick out like a sore thumb. Look at you. You think yer regular lookin'?

AUSTIN: I've got too much to deal with here to be worrying about—

LEE: Yer not gonna' have to worry about me! I've been doin' all right without you. I haven't been anywhere near you for five years! Now isn't that true?

AUSTIN: Yeah.

LEE: So you don't have to worry about me. I'm a free agent.

AUSTIN: All right.

LEE: Now all I wanna' do is borrow yer car.

AUSTIN: No!

LEE: Just fer a day. One day.

AUSTIN: No!

LEE: I won't take it outside a twenty mile radius. I promise ya'. You can check the speedometer.

AUSTIN: You're not borrowing my car! That's all there is to it.

[pause]

LEE: Then I'll just take the damn thing.

AUSTIN: Lee, look—I don't want any trouble, all right?

LEE: That's a dumb line. That is a dumb fuckin' line. You git paid fer dreamin' up a line like that?

AUSTIN: Look, I can give you some money if you need money.

[LEE suddenly lunges at AUSTIN, grabs him violently by the shirt and shakes him with tremendous power]

LEE: Don't you say that to me! Don't you ever say that to me! (*just as suddenly he turns him loose, pushes him away and backs off*) You may be able to git away with that with the Old Man. Git him tanked up for a week! Buy him off with yer Hollywood blood money, but not me! I can git my own money my own way. Big money!

AUSTIN: I was just making an offer.

LEE: Yeah, well keep it to yourself!

[long pause]

Those are the most monotonous fuckin' crickets I ever heard in my life.

AUSTIN: I kinda' like the sound.

LEE: Yeah. Supposed to be able to tell the temperature by the number a' pulses. You believe that?

AUSTIN: The temperature?

LEE: Yeah. The air. How hot it is.

AUSTIN: How do you do that?

LEE: I don't know. Some woman told me that. She was a Botanist. So I believed her.

AUSTIN: Where'd you meet her?

LEE: What?

AUSTIN: The woman Botanist?

LEE: I met her on the desert. I been spendin' a lota' time on the desert.

AUSTIN: What were you doing out there?

LEE (*pause, stares in space*): I forgit. Had me a Pit Bull there for a while but I lost him.

AUSTIN: Pit Bull?

LEE: Fightin' dog. Damn I made some good money off that little dog. Real good money.

[pause]

AUSTIN: You could come up north with me, you know.

LEE: What's up there?

AUSTIN: My family.

LEE: Oh, that's right, you got the wife and kiddies now don't ya'. The house, the car, the whole slam. That's right.

AUSTIN: You could spend a couple days. See how you like it. I've got an extra room.

LEE: Too cold up there.

[pause]

AUSTIN: You want to sleep for a while?

LEE (*pause, stares at* AUSTIN): I don't sleep.

[lights to black]

Scene 2

Morning. AUSTIN is watering plants with a vaporizer, LEE sits at glass table in alcove drinking beer.

LEE: I never realized the old lady was so security-minded.

AUSTIN: How do you mean?

LEE: Made a little tour this morning. She's got locks on everything. Locks and double-locks and chain locks and—What's she got that's so valuable?

AUSTIN: Antiques I guess. I don't know.

LEE: Antiques? Brought everything with her from the old place, huh. Just the same crap we always had around. Plates and spoons.

AUSTIN: I guess they have personal value to her.

LEE: Personal value. Yeah. Just a lota' junk. Most of it's phony anyway. Idaho decals. Now who in the hell wants to eat offa plate with the State of Idaho starin' ya' in the face. Every time ya' take a bite ya' get to see a little bit more.

AUSTIN: Well it must mean something to her or she wouldn't save it.

LEE: Yeah, well personally I don't wann' be invaded by Idaho when I'm eatin'. When I'm eatin' I'm home. Ya' know what I'm sayin'? I'm not driftin', I'm home. I don't need my thoughts swept off to Idaho. I don't need that!

[pause]

AUSTIN: Did you go out last night?

LEE: Why?

AUSTIN: I thought I heard you go out.

LEE: Yeah, I went out. What about it?

AUSTIN: Just wondered.

LEE: Damn coyotes kept me awake.

AUSTIN: Oh yeah, I heard them. They must've killed somebody's dog or something.

LEE: Yappin' their fool heads off. They don't yap like that on the desert. They howl. These are city coyotes here.

AUSTIN: Well, you don't sleep anyway do you?

[pause, LEE stares at him]

LEE: You're pretty smart aren't ya?

AUSTIN: How do you mean?

LEE: I mean you never had any more on the ball than I did. But here you are gettin' invited into prominent people's houses. Sittin' around talkin' like you know somethin'.

AUSTIN: They're not so prominent.

LEE: They're a helluva' lot more prominent than the houses I get invited into.

AUSTIN: Well you invite yourself.

LEE: That's right. I do. In fact I probably got a wider range a' choices than you do, come to think of it.

AUSTIN: I wouldn't doubt it.

LEE: In fact I been inside some pretty classy places in my time. And I never even went to an Ivy League school either.

AUSTIN: You want some breakfast or something?

LEE: Breakfast?

AUSTIN: Yeah. Don't you eat breakfast?

LEE: Look, don't worry about me pal. I can take care a' myself. You just go ahead as though I wasn't even here, all right?

[AUSTIN goes into kitchen, makes coffee]

AUSTIN: Where'd you walk to last night?

[pause]

LEE: I went up in the foothills there. Up in the San Gabriels. Heat was drivin' me crazy.

AUSTIN: Well, wasn't it hot out on the desert?

LEE: Different kinda' heat. Out there it's clean. Cools off at night. There's a nice little breeze.

AUSTIN: Where were you, the Mojave?

LEE: Yeah. The Mojave. That's right.

AUSTIN: I haven't been out there in years.

LEE: Out past Needles there.

AUSTIN: Oh yeah.

LEE: Up here it's different. This country's real different.

AUSTIN: Well, it's been built up.

LEE: Built up? Wiped out is more like it. I don't even hardly recognize it.

AUSTIN: Yeah. Foothills are the same though, aren't they?

LEE: Pretty much. It's funny goin' up in there. The smells and everything. Used to catch snakes up there, remember?

AUSTIN: You caught snakes.

LEE: Yeah. And you'd pretend you were Geronimo or some damn thing. You used to go right out to lunch.

AUSTIN: I enjoyed my imagination.

LEE: That what you call it? Looks like yer still enjoyin' it.

AUSTIN: So you just wandered around up there, huh?

LEE: Yeah. With a purpose.

AUSTIN: See any houses?

[pause]

LEE: Couple. Couple a' real nice ones. One of 'em didn't even have a dog. Walked right up and stuck my head in the window. Not a peep. Just a sweet kinda' surburban silence.

AUSTIN: What kind of a place was it?

LEE: Like a paradise. Kinda' place that sorta' kills ya' inside. Warm yellow lights. Mexican tile all around. Copper pots hangin' over the stove. Ya' know like they got in the magazines. Blonde people movin' in and outa' the rooms, talkin' to each other. *(pause)* Kinda' place you wish you sorta' grew up in, ya' know.

AUSTIN: That's the kind of place you wish you'd grown up in?

LEE: Yeah, why not?

AUSTIN: I thought you hated that kind of stuff.

LEE: Yeah, well you never knew too much about me did ya'?

[pause]

AUSTIN: Why'd you go out to the desert in the first place?

LEE: I was on my way to see the old man.

AUSTIN: You mean you just passed through there?

LEE: Yeah. That's right. Three months of passin' through.

AUSTIN: Three months?

LEE: Somethin' like that. Maybe more. Why?

AUSTIN: You lived on the Mojave for three months?

LEE: Yeah. What'sa' matter with that?

AUSTIN: By yourself?

LEE: Mostly. Had a couple a' visitors. Had that dog for a while.

AUSTIN: Didn't you miss people?

LEE *(laughs)*: People?

AUSTIN: Yeah. I mean I go crazy if I have to spend three nights in a motel by myself.

LEE: Yer not in a motel now.

AUSTIN: No, I know. But sometimes I have to stay in motels.

LEE: Well, they got people in motels don't they?

AUSTIN: Strangers.

LEE: Yer friendly aren't ya'? Aren't you the friendly type?

[pause]

AUSTIN: I'm going to have somebody coming by here later, Lee.

LEE: Ah! Lady friend?

AUSTIN: No, a producer.

LEE: Aha! What's he produce?

AUSTIN: Film. Movies. You know.

LEE: Oh, movies. Motion Pictures! A Big Wig huh?

AUSTIN: Yeah.

LEE: What's he comin' by here for?

AUSTIN: We have to talk about a project.

LEE: Whadya' mean, "a project"? What's "a project"?

AUSTIN: A script.

LEE: Oh. That's what yer doin' with all these papers?

AUSTIN: Yeah.

LEE: Well, what's the project about?

AUSTIN: We're uh—it's a period piece.

LEE: What's "a period piece"?

AUSTIN: Look, it doesn't matter. The main thing is we need to discuss this alone. I mean—

LEE: Oh, I get it. You want me outa' the picture.

AUSTIN: Not exactly. I just need to be alone with him

for a couple of hours. So we can talk.

LEE: Yer afraid I'll embarrass ya' huh?

AUSTIN: I'm not afraid you'll embarrass me!

LEE: Well, I tell ya' what—Why don't you just gimme the keys to yer car and I'll be back here around six o'clock or so. That give ya' enough time?

AUSTIN: I'm not loaning you my car, Lee.

LEE: You want me to just git lost huh? Take a hike? Is that it? Pound the pavement for a few hours while you bullshit yer way into a million bucks.

AUSTIN: Look, it's going to be hard enough for me to face this character on my own without—

LEE: You don't know this guy?

AUSTIN: No I don't know—He's a producer. I mean I've been meeting with him for months but you never get to know a producer.

LEE: Yer tryin' to hustle him? Is that it?

AUSTIN: I'm not trying to hustle him! I'm trying to work out a deal! It's not easy.

LEE: What kinda' deal?

AUSTIN: Convince him it's a worthwhile story.

LEE: He's not convinced? How come he's comin' over here if he's not convinced? I'll convince him for ya'.

AUSTIN: You don't understand the way things work down here.

LEE: How do things work down here?

[pause]

AUSTIN: Look, if I loan you my car will you have it back here by six?

LEE: On the button. With a full tank a' gas.

AUSTIN (*digging in his pocket for keys*): Forget about the gas.

LEE: Hey, these days gas is gold, old buddy.

[AUSTIN hands the keys to LEE]

You remember that car I used to loan you?

AUSTIN: Yeah.

LEE: Forty Ford. Flathead.

AUSTIN: Yeah.

LEE: Sucker hauled ass didn't it?

AUSTIN: Lee, it's not that I don't want to loan you my car—

LEE: You are loanin' me yer car.

[LEE gives AUSTIN a pat on the shoulder, pause]

AUSTIN: I know. I just wish—

LEE: What? You wish what?

AUSTIN: I don't know. I wish I wasn't—I wish I didn't have to be doing business down here. I'd like to just spend some time with you.

LEE: I thought it was "Art" you were doin'.

[LEE moves across kitchen toward exit, tosses keys in his hand]

AUSTIN: Try to get it back here by six, okay?

LEE: No sweat. Hey, ya' know, if that uh—story of yours doesn't go over with the guy—tell him I got a couple a' "projects" he might be interested in. Real commercial. Full a' suspense. True-to-life stuff.

[LEE exits, AUSTIN stares after LEE then turns, goes to papers at table, leafs through pages, lights fade to black]

Scene 3

Afternoon. Alcove, SAUL KIMMER and AUSTIN seated across from each other at table.

SAUL: Well, to tell you the truth Austin, I have never felt so confident about a project in quite a long time.

AUSTIN: Well, that's good to hear, Saul.

SAUL: I am absolutely convinced we can get this thing off the ground. I mean we'll have to make a sale to television and that means getting a major star. Somebody bankable. But I think we can do it. I really do.

AUSTIN: Don't you think we need a first draft before we approach a star?

SAUL: No, no, not at all. I don't think it's necessary. Maybe a brief synopsis. I don't want you to touch the typewriter until we have some seed money.

AUSTIN: That's fine with me.

SAUL: I mean it's a great story. Just the story alone. You've really managed to capture something this time.

AUSTIN: I'm glad you like it, Saul.

[LEE enters abruptly into kitchen carrying a stolen television set, short pause]

LEE: Aw shit, I'm sorry about that. I am really sorry Austin.

AUSTIN (*standing*): That's all right.

LEE (*moving toward them*): I mean I thought it was way past six already. You said to have it back here by six.

AUSTIN: We were just finishing up. (*to Saul*) This is my, uh—brother, Lee.

SAUL (*standing*): Oh, I'm very happy to meet you.

[LEE sets T.V. on sink counter, shakes hands with SAUL]

LEE: I can't tell ya' how happy I am to meet you sir.

SAUL: Saul Kimmer.

LEE: Mr. Kipper.

SAUL: Kimmer.

AUSTIN: Lee's been living out on the desert and he just uh—

SAUL: Oh, that's terrific! (*to* LEE) Palm Springs?

LEE: Yeah. Yeah, right. Right around in that area. Near uh—Bob Hope Drive there.

SAUL: Oh I love it out there. I just love it. The air is wonderful.

LEE: Yeah. Sure is. Healthy.

SAUL: And the golf. I don't know if you play golf, but the golf is just about the best.

LEE: I play a lota' golf.

SAUL: Is that right?

LEE: Yeah. In fact I was hoping I'd run into somebody out here who played a little golf. I've been lookin' for a partner.

SAUL: Well, I uh—

AUSTIN: Lee's just down for a visit while our mother's in Alaska.

SAUL: Oh, your mother's in Alaska?

AUSTIN: Yes. She went up there on a little vacation. This is her place.

SAUL: I see. Well isn't that something. Alaska.

LEE: What kinda' handicap do ya' have, Mr. Kimmer?

SAUL: Oh I'm just a Sunday duffer really. You know.

LEE: That's good 'cause I haven't swung a club in months.

SAUL: Well we ought to get together sometime and have a little game. Austin, do you play?

[*SAUL mimes a Johnny Carson golf swing for* AUSTIN]

AUSTIN: No. I don't uh—I've watched it on T.V.

LEE (*to* SAUL): How 'bout tomorrow morning? Bright and early. We could get out there and put in eighteen holes before breakfast.

SAUL: Well. I've got uh—I have several appointments—

LEE: No, I mean real early. Crack a'dawn. While the dew's still thick on the fairway.

SAUL: Sounds really great.

LEE: Austin could be our caddie.

SAUL: Now that's an idea. (*laughs*)

AUSTIN: I don't know the first thing about golf.

LEE: There's nothin' to it. Isn't that right, Saul? He'd pick it up in fifteen minutes.

SAUL: Sure. Doesn't take long. 'Course you have to play for years to find your true form. (*chuckles*)

LEE (*to* AUSTIN): We'll give ya' a quick run-down on the club faces. The irons, the woods. Show ya' a couple pointers on the basic swing. Might even let ya' hit the ball a couple times. Whadya' think, Saul?

SAUL: Why not. I think it'd be great. I haven't had any exercise in weeks.

LEE: 'At's the spirit! We'll have a little orange juice right afterwards.

[*pause*]

SAUL: Orange juice?

LEE: Yeah! Vitamin C! Nothin' like a shot a' orange juice after a round a' golf. Hot shower. Snappin' towels at each others' privates. Real sense a' fraternity.

SAUL (*smiles at* AUSTIN): Well, you make it sound very inviting, I must say. It really does sound great.

LEE: Then it's a date.

SAUL: Well, I'll call the country club and see if I can arrange something.

LEE: Great! Boy, I sure am sorry that I busted in on ya' all in the middle of yer meeting.

SAUL: Oh that's quite all right. We were just about finished anyway.

LEE: I can wait out in the other room if you want.

SAUL: No really—

LEE: Just got Austin's color T.V. back from the shop. I can watch a little amateur boxing now.

[*LEE and AUSTIN exchange looks*]

SAUL: Oh—Yes.

LEE: You don't fool around in Television, do you Saul?

SAUL: Uh—I have in the past. Produced some T.V. Specials. Network stuff. But it's mainly features now.

LEE: That's where the big money is, huh?

SAUL: Yes. That's right.

AUSTIN: Why don't I call you tomorrow, Saul and we'll get together. We can have lunch or something.

SAUL: That'd be terrific.

LEE: Right after the golf.

[*pause*]

SAUL: What?

LEE: You can have lunch right after the golf.

SAUL: Oh, right.

LEE: Austin was tellin' me that yer interested in stories.

SAUL: Well, we develop certain projects that we feel have commercial potential.

LEE: What kinda' stuff do ya' go in for?

SAUL: Oh, the usual. You know. Good love interest. Lots of action. (*chuckles at* AUSTIN)

LEE: Westerns?

SAUL: Sometimes.

AUSTIN: I'll give you a ring, Saul.

[*AUSTIN tries to move* SAUL *across the kitchen but* LEE *blocks their way*]

LEE: I got a Western that'd knock yer lights out.

SAUL: Oh really?

LEE: Yeah. Contemporary Western. Based on a true story. 'Course I'm not a writer like my brother here. I'm not a man of the pen.
SAUL: Well—
LEE: I mean I can tell ya' a story off the tongue but I can't put it down on paper. That don't make any difference though does it?
SAUL: No, not really.
LEE: I mean I got plenty a' guys have stories don't they? True-life stories. Musta' been a lota' movies made from real life.
SAUL: Yes. I suppose so.
LEE: I haven't seen a good Western since "Lonely Are the Brave." You remember that movie?
SAUL: No, I'm afraid I—
LEE: Kirk Douglas. Helluva' movie. You remember that movie, Austin?
AUSTIN: Yes.
LEE (to SAUL): The man dies for the love of a horse.
SAUL: Is that right.
LEE: Yeah. Ya' hear the horse screamin' at the end of it. Rain's comin' down. Horse is screamin'. Then there's a shot. BLAM! Just a single shot like that. Then nothin' but the sound of rain. And Kirk Douglas is ridin' in the ambulance. Ridin' away from the scene of the accident. And when he hears that shot he knows that his horse has died. He knows. And you see his eyes. And his eyes die. Right inside his face. And then his eyes close. And you know that he's died too. You know that Kirk Douglas has died from the death of his horse.
SAUL (eyes AUSTIN nervously): Well, it sounds like a great movie. I'm sorry I missed it.
LEE: Yeah, you shouldn't a' missed that one.
SAUL: I'll have to try to catch it some time. Arrange a screening or something. Well, Austin, I'll have to hit the freeway before rush hour.
AUSTIN (ushers him toward exit): It's good seeing you, Saul.

[AUSTIN and SAUL shake hands]

LEE: So ya' think there's room for a real Western these days? A true-to-life Western?
SAUL: Well, I don't see why not. Why don't you uh— tell the story to Austin and have him write a little outline.
LEE: You'd take a look at it then?
SAUL: Yes. Sure. I'll give it a read-through. Always eager for new material. (smiles at AUSTIN)
LEE: That's great! You'd really read it then huh?
SAUL: It would just be my opinion of course.
LEE: That's all I want. Just an opinion. I happen to think it has a lota' possibilities.
SAUL: Well, it was great meeting you and I'll—

[SAUL and LEE shake]

LEE: I'll call you tomorrow about the golf.
SAUL: Oh. Yes, right.
LEE: Austin's got your number, right?
SAUL: Yes.
LEE: So long Saul. (gives SAUL a pat on the back)

[SAUL exits, AUSTIN turns to LEE, looks at T.V. then back to LEE]

AUSTIN: Give me the keys.

[AUSTIN extends his hand toward LEE, LEE doesn't move, just stares at AUSTIN, smiles, lights to black]

Scene 4

Night. Coyotes in distance, fade, sound of typewriter in dark, crickets, candlelight in alcove, dim light in kitchen, lights reveal AUSTIN at glass table typing, LEE sits across from him, foot on table, drinking beer and whiskey, the T.V. is still on sink counter, AUSTIN types for a while, then stops.

LEE: All right, now read it back to me.
AUSTIN: I'm not reading it back to you, Lee. You can read it when we're finished. I can't spend all night on this.
LEE: You got better things to do?
AUSTIN: Let's just go ahead. Now what happens when he leaves Texas?
LEE: Is he ready to leave Texas yet? I didn't know we were that far along. He's not ready to leave Texas.
AUSTIN: He's right at the border.
LEE (sitting up): No, see this is one a' the crucial parts. Right here. (taps paper with beer can) We can't rush through this. He's not right at the border. He's a good fifty miles from the border. A lot can happen in fifty miles.
AUSTIN: It's only an outline. We're not writing an entire script now.
LEE: Well ya' can't leave things out even if it is an outline. It's one a' the most important parts. Ya' can't go leavin' it out.
AUSTIN: Okay, okay. Let's just—get it done.
LEE: All right. Now. He's in the truck and he's got his horse trailer and his horse.
AUSTIN: We've already established that.
LEE: And he sees this other guy comin' up behind him in another truck. And that truck is pullin' a gooseneck.
AUSTIN: What's a gooseneck?
LEE: Cattle trailer. You know the kind with a goose-neck, goes right down in the bed a' the pick-up.

AUSTIN: Oh. All right. (*types*)
LEE: It's important.
AUSTIN: Okay. I got it.
LEE: All these details are important.

[*AUSTIN types as they talk*]

AUSTIN: I've got it.
LEE: And this other guy's got his horse all saddled up in the back a' the gooseneck.
AUSTIN: Right.
LEE: So both these guys have got their horses right along with 'em, see.
AUSTIN: I understand.
LEE: Then this first guy suddenly realizes two things.
AUSTIN: The guy in front?
LEE: Right. The guy in front realizes two things almost at the same time. Simultaneous.
AUSTIN: What were the two things?
LEE: Number one, he realizes that the guy behind him is the husband of the woman he's been—

[*LEE makes gesture of screwing by pumping his arm*]

AUSTIN (*sees LEE's gesture*): Oh. Yeah.
LEE: And number two, he realizes he's in the middle of Tornado Country.
AUSTIN: What's "Tornado Country"?
LEE: Panhandle.
AUSTIN: Panhandle?
LEE: Sweetwater. Around in that area. Nothin'. Nowhere. And number three—
AUSTIN: I thought there was only two.
LEE: There's three. There's a third unforeseen realization.
AUSTIN: And what's that?
LEE: That he's runnin' outa' gas.
AUSTIN (*stops typing*): Come on, Lee.

[*AUSTIN gets up, moves to kitchen, gets a glass of water*]

LEE: Whadya' mean, "come on"? That's what it is. Write it down! He's runnin' outa' gas.
AUSTIN: It's too—
LEE: What? It's too what? It's too real! That's what ya' mean isn't it? It's too much like real life!
AUSTIN: It's not like real life! It's not enough like real life. Things don't happen like that.
LEE: What! Men don't fuck other men's women?
AUSTIN: Yes. But they don't end up chasing each other across the Panhandle. Through "Tornado Country."
LEE: They do in this movie!
AUSTIN: And they don't have horses conveniently along with them when they run out of gas! And they don't run out of gas either!
LEE: These guys run outa' gas! This is my story and

one a' these guys runs outa' gas!
AUSTIN: It's just a dumb excuse to get them into a chase scene. It's contrived.
LEE: It is a chase scene! It's already a chase scene. They been chasin' each other fer days.
AUSTIN: So now they're supposed to abandon their trucks, climb on their horses and chase each other into the mountains?
LEE (*standing suddenly*): There aren't any mountains in the Panhandle! It's flat!

[*LEE turns violently toward windows in alcove and throws beer can at them*]

LEE: Goddamn these crickets! (*yells at crickets*) Shut up out there! (*pause, turns back toward table*) This place is like a fuckin' rest home here. How're you supposed to think!
AUSTIN: You wanna' take a break?
LEE: No, I don't wanna' take a break! I wanna' get this done! This is my last chance to get this done.
AUSTIN (*moves back into alcove*): All right. Take it easy.
LEE: I'm gonna' be leavin' this area. I don't have time to mess around here.
AUSTIN: Where are you going?
LEE: Never mind where I'm goin'! That's got nothin' to do with you. I just gotta' get this done. I'm not like you. Hangin' around bein' a parasite offa' other fools. I gotta' do this thing and get out.

[*pause*]

AUSTIN: A parasite? Me?
LEE: Yeah, you!
AUSTIN: After you break into people's houses and take their televisions?
LEE: They don't need their televisions! I'm doin' them a service.
AUSTIN: Give me back my keys, Lee.
LEE: Not until you write this thing! You're gonna' write this outline thing for me or that car's gonna' wind up in Arizona with a different paint job.
AUSTIN: You think you can force me to write this? I was doing you a favor.
LEE: Git off yer high horse will ya'! Favor! Big favor. Handin' down favors from the mountain top.
AUSTIN: Let's just write it, okay? Let's sit down and not get upset and see if we can just get through this.

[*AUSTIN sits at typewriter*]

[*long pause*]

LEE: Yer not gonna' even show it to him, are ya'?

AUSTIN: What?

LEE: This outline. You got no intention of showin' it to him. Yer just doin' this 'cause yer afraid a' me.

AUSTIN: You can show it to him yourself.

LEE: I will, boy! I'm gonna' read it to him on the golf course.

AUSTIN: And I'm not afraid of you either.

LEE: Then how come yer doin' it?

AUSTIN (*pause*): So I can get my keys back.

[*pause as LEE takes keys out of his pocket slowly and throws them on table, long pause, AUSTIN stares at keys*]

LEE: There. Now you got yer keys back.

[*AUSTIN looks up at LEE but doesn't take keys*]

LEE: Go ahead. There's yer keys.

[*AUSTIN slowly takes keys off table and puts them back in his own pocket*]

Now what're you gonna' do? Kick me out?

AUSTIN: I'm not going to kick you out, Lee.

LEE: You couldn't kick me out, boy.

AUSTIN: I know.

LEE: So you can't even consider that one. (*pause*) You could call the police. That'd be the obvious thing.

AUSTIN: You're my brother.

LEE: That don't mean a thing. You go down to the L.A. Police Department there and ask them what kinda' people kill each other the most. What do you think they'd say?

AUSTIN: Who said anything about killing?

LEE: Family people. Brothers. Brothers-in-law. Cousins. Real American-type people. They kill each other in the heat mostly. In the Smog-Alerts. In the Brush Fire Season. Right about this time a' year.

AUSTIN: This isn't the same.

LEE: Oh no? What makes it different?

AUSTIN: We're not insane. We're not driven to acts of violence like that. Not over a dumb movie script. Now sit down.

[*long pause, LEE considers which way to go with it.*]

LEE: Maybe not. (*he sits back down at table across from AUSTIN*) Maybe you're right. Maybe we're too intelligent, huh? (*pause*) We got our heads on our shoulders. One of us has even got an Ivy League diploma. Now that means somethin' don't it? Doesn't that mean somethin'?

AUSTIN: Look, I'll write this thing for you, Lee. I don't mind writing it. I just don't want to get

all worked up about it. It's not worth it. Now, come on. Let's just get through it, okay?

LEE: Nah. I think there's easier money. Lotsa' places I could pick up thousands. Maybe millions. I don't need this shit. I could go up to Sacramento Valley and steal me a diesel. Ten thousand a week dismantling one a' those suckers. Ten thousand a week!

[*LEE opens another beer, puts his foot back up on table*]

AUSTIN: No, really, look, I'll write it out for you. I think it's a great idea.

LEE: Nah, you got yer own work to do. I don't wanna' interfere with yer life.

AUSTIN: I mean it'd be really fantastic if you could sell this. Turn it into a movie. I mean it.

[*pause*]

LEE: Ya' think so huh?

AUSTIN: Absolutely. You could really turn your life around, you know. Change things.

LEE: I could get me a house maybe.

AUSTIN: Sure you could get a house. You could get a whole ranch if you wanted to.

LEE (*laughs*): A ranch? I could get a ranch?

AUSTIN: 'Course you could. You know what a screen-play sells for these days?

LEE: No. What's it sell for?

AUSTIN: A lot. A whole lot of money.

LEE: Thousands?

AUSTIN: Yeah. Thousands.

LEE: Millions?

AUSTIN: Well—

LEE: We could get the old man outa' hock then.

AUSTIN: Maybe.

LEE: Maybe? Whadya' mean, maybe?

AUSTIN: I mean it might take more than money.

LEE: You were just tellin' me it'd change my whole life around. Why wouldn't it change his?

AUSTIN: He's different.

LEE: Oh, he's of a different ilk huh?

AUSTIN: He's not gonna' change. Let's leave the old man out of it.

LEE: That's right. He's not gonna' change but I will. I'll just turn myself right inside out. I could be just like you then, huh? Sittin' around dreamin' stuff up. Gettin' paid to dream. Ridin' back and forth on the freeway just dreamin' my fool head off.

AUSTIN: It's not all that easy.

LEE: It's not, huh?

AUSTIN: No. There's a lot of work involved.

LEE: What's the toughest part? Deciding whether to jog or play tennis?

[long pause]

AUSTIN: Well, look. You can stay here—do whatever you want to. Borrow the car. Come in and out. Doesn't matter to me. It's not my house. I'll help you write this thing or—not. Just let me know what you want. You tell me.

LEE: Oh. So now suddenly you're at my service. Is that it?

AUSTIN: What do you want to do Lee?

[long pause, LEE stares at him then turns and dreams at windows]

LEE: I tell ya' what I'd do if I still had that dog. Ya' wanna' know what I'd do?

AUSTIN: What?

LEE: Head out to Ventura. Cook up a little match. God that little dog could bear down. Lota' money in dog fightin'. Big money.

[pause]

AUSTIN: Why don't we try to see this through, Lee. Just for the hell of it. Maybe you've really got something here. What do you think?

[pause, LEE considers]

LEE: Maybe so. No harm in tryin' I guess. You think it's such a hot idea. Besides, I always wondered what'd be like to be you.

AUSTIN: You did?

LEE: Yeah, sure. I used to picture you walkin' around some campus with yer arms fulla' books. Blondes chasin' after ya'.

AUSTIN: Blondes? That's funny.

LEE: What's funny about it?

AUSTIN: Because I always used to picture you somewhere.

LEE: Where'd you picture me?

AUSTIN: Oh, I don't know. Different places. Adventures. You were always on some adventure.

LEE: Yeah.

AUSTIN: And I used to say to myself, "Lee's got the right idea. He's out there in the world and here I am. What am I doing?"

LEE: Well you were settin' yourself up for somethin'.

AUSTIN: I guess.

LEE: We better get started on this thing then.

AUSTIN: Okay.

[AUSTIN sits up at typewriter, puts new paper in]

LEE: Oh. Can I get the keys back before I forget?

[AUSTIN hesitates]

You said I could borrow the car if I wanted, right? Isn't that what you said?

AUSTIN: Yeah. Right.

[AUSTIN takes keys out of his pocket, sets them on table, LEE takes keys slowly, plays with them in his hand]

LEE: I could get a ranch, huh?

AUSTIN: Yeah. We have to write it first though.

LEE: Okay. Let's write it.

[lights start dimming slowly to end of scene as AUSTIN types, LEE speaks]

So they take off after each other straight into an endless black prairie. The sun is just comin' down and they can feel the night on their backs. What they don't know is that each one of 'em is afraid, see. Each one separately thinks that he's the only one that's afraid. And they keep ridin' like that straight into the night. Not knowing. And the one who's chasin' doesn't know where the other one is taking him. And the one who's being chased doesn't know where he's going.

[lights to black, typing stops in the dark, crickets fade]

ACT II

Scene 5

Morning. LEE at the table in alcove with a set of golf clubs in a fancy leather bag, AUSTIN at sink washing a few dishes.

AUSTIN: He really liked it, huh?

LEE: He wouldn't a' gave me these clubs if he didn't like it.

AUSTIN: He gave you the clubs?

LEE: Yeah. I told ya' he gave me the clubs. The bag too.

AUSTIN: I thought he just loaned them to you.

LEE: He said it was part a' the advance. A little gift like. Gesture of his good faith.

AUSTIN: He's giving you an advance?

LEE: Now what's so amazing about that? I told ya' it was a good story. You even said it was a good story.

AUSTIN: Well that is really incredible Lee. You know how many guys spend their whole lives down here trying to break into this business? Just trying to get in the door?

LEE *(pulling clubs out of bag, testing them)*: I got no idea. How many?

[pause]

AUSTIN: How much of an advance is he giving you?
LEE: Plenty. We were talkin' big money out there.
  Ninth hole is where I sealed the deal.
AUSTIN: He made a firm commitment?
LEE: Absolutely.
AUSTIN: Well, I know Saul and he doesn't fool
  around when he says he likes something.
LEE: I thought you said you didn't know him.
AUSTIN: Well, I'm familiar with his tastes.
LEE: I let him get two up on me goin' into the back
  nine. He was sure he had me cold. You shoul-
  da' seen his face when I pulled out the old
  pitching wedge and plopped it pin-high, two
  feet from the cup. He 'bout shit his pants.
  "Where'd a guy like you ever learn how to
  play golf like that?" he says.

[LEE laughs, AUSTIN stares at him]

AUSTIN: 'Course there's no contract yet. Nothing's
  final until it's on paper.
LEE: It's final, all right. There's no way he's gonna'
  back out of it now. We gambled for it.
AUSTIN: Saul, gambled?
LEE: Yeah, sure. I mean he liked the outline already
  so he wasn't risking that much. I just guaranteed it with my short game.

[pause]

AUSTIN: Well, we should celebrate or something. I
  think Mom left a bottle of champagne in the
  refrigerator. We should have a little toast.

*[AUSTIN gets glasses from cupboard, goes to refrigera-
tor, pulls out bottle of champagne]*

LEE: You shouldn't oughta' take her champagne,
  Austin. She's gonna' miss that.
AUSTIN: Oh, she's not going to mind. She'd be glad
  we put it to good use. I'll get her another bottle. Besides, it's perfect for the occasion.

[pause]

LEE: Yer gonna' get a nice fee fer writin' the script a'
  course. Straight fee.

*[AUSTIN stops, stares at LEE, puts glasses and bottle on
table, pause]*

AUSTIN: I'm writing the script?
LEE: That's what he said. Said we couldn't hire a better screenwriter in the whole town.
AUSTIN: But I'm already working on a script. I've got
  my own project. I don't have time to write two
  scripts.

LEE: No, he said he was gonna' drop that other one.

[pause]

AUSTIN: What? You mean mine? He's going to drop
  mine and do yours instead?
LEE (*smiles*): Now look, Austin, it's jest beginner's
  luck ya' know. I mean I sank a fifty foot putt
  for this deal. No hard feelings.

[AUSTIN goes to phone on wall, grabs it, starts dialing]

He's not gonna' be in, Austin. Told me he wouldn't
  be in 'till late this afternoon.
AUSTIN (*stays on phone, dialing, listens*): I can't believe
  this. I just can't believe it. Are you sure he said
  that? Why would he drop mine?
LEE: That's what he told me.
AUSTIN: He can't do that without telling me first.
  Without talking to me at least. He wouldn't
  just make a decision like that without talking
  to me!
LEE: Well I was kinda' surprised myself. But he was
  real enthusiastic about my story.

[AUSTIN hangs up phone violently, paces]

AUSTIN: What'd he say! Tell me everything he said!
LEE: I been tellin' ya'! He said he liked the story a
  whole lot. It was the first authentic Western to
  come along in a decade.
AUSTIN: He liked that story! Your story?
LEE: Yeah! What's so surprisin' about that?
AUSTIN: It's stupid! It's the dumbest story I ever
  heard in my life.
LEE: Hey, hold on! That's my story yer talkin' about!
AUSTIN: It's a bullshit story! It's idiotic. Two lame-
  brains chasing each other across Texas! Are
  you kidding? Who do you think's going to go
  see a film like that?
LEE: It's not a film! It's a movie. There's a big differ-
  ence. That's somethin' Saul told me.
AUSTIN: Oh he did, huh?
LEE: Yeah, he said, "In this business we make
  movies, American movies. Leave the films to
  the French."
AUSTIN: So you got real intimate with old Saul huh?
  He started pouring forth his vast knowledge of
  Cinema.
LEE: I think he liked me a lot, to tell ya' the truth. I
  think he felt I was somebody he could confide
  in.
AUSTIN: What'd you do, beat him up or something?
LEE (*stands fast*): Hey, I've about had it with the
  insults buddy! You think yer the only one in
  the brain department here? Yer the only one
  that can sit around and cook things up?
  There's other people got ideas too, ya' know!

AUSTIN: You must've done something. Threatened him or something. Now what'd you do Lee?

LEE: I convinced him!

[LEE makes sudden menacing lunge toward AUSTIN, wielding golf club above his head, stops himself, frozen moment, long pause, LEE lowers club]

AUSTIN: Oh, Jesus. You didn't hurt him did you?

[long silence, LEE sits back down at table]

Lee! Did you hurt him?

LEE: I didn't do nothin' to him! He liked my story. Pure and simple. He said it was the best story he's come across in a long, long time.

AUSTIN: That's what he told me about my story! That's the same thing he said to me.

LEE: Well, he musta' been lyin'. He musta' been lyin' to one of us anyway.

AUSTIN: You can't come into this town and start pushing people around. They're gonna' put you away!

LEE: I never pushed anybody around! I beat him fair and square. (*pause*) They can't touch me anyway. They can't put a finger on me. I'm gone. I can come in through the window and go out through the door. They never knew what hit 'em. You, yer stuck. Yer the one that's stuck. Not me. So don't be warnin' me what to do in this town.

[pause. AUSTIN crosses to table, sits at typewriter, rests]

AUSTIN: Lee, come on, level with me will you? It doesn't make any sense that suddenly he'd throw my idea out the window. I've been talking to him for months. I've got too much at stake. Everything's riding on this project.

LEE: What's yer idea?

AUSTIN: It's just a simple love story.

LEE: What kinda' love story?

AUSTIN (*stands, crosses into kitchen*): I'm not telling you!

LEE: Ha! 'Fraid I'll steal it huh? Competition's gettin' kinda' close to home isn't it?

AUSTIN: Where did Saul say he was going?

LEE: He was gonna' take my story to a couple studios.

AUSTIN: That's *my* outline you know! I wrote that outline! You've got no right to be peddling it around.

LEE: You weren't ready to take credit for it last night.

AUSTIN: Give me my keys!

LEE: What?

AUSTIN: The keys! I want my keys back!

LEE: Where you goin'?

AUSTIN: Just give me my keys! I gotta' take a drive. I gotta' get out of here for a while.

LEE: Where you gonna' go, Austin?

AUSTIN: (*pause*) I might just drive out to the desert for a while.

LEE: You can think here just as good. This is the perfect setup for thinkin'. We got some writin' to do here, boy. Now let's just have us a little toast. Relax. We're partners now.

[LEE pops the cork of the champagne bottle, pours two drinks as the lights fade to black]

Scene 6

Afternoon. LEE and SAUL in kitchen, AUSTIN in alcove

LEE: Now you tell him. You tell him, Mr. Kipper.

SAUL: Kimmer.

LEE: Kimmer. You tell him what you told me. He don't believe me.

AUSTIN: I don't want to hear it.

SAUL: It's really not a big issue, Austin. I was simply amazed by your brother's story and—

AUSTIN: Amazed? You lost a bet! You gambled with my material!

SAUL: That's really beside the point, Austin. I'm ready to go all the way with your brother's story. I think it has a great deal of merit.

AUSTIN: I don't want to hear about it, okay? Go tell it to the executives! Tell it to somebody who's going to turn it into a package deal or something. A T.V. series. Don't tell it to me.

SAUL: But I want to continue with your project too, Austin. It's not as though we can't do both. We're big enough for that aren't we?

AUSTIN: "We"? *I* can't do both! I don't know about "we."

LEE (*to SAUL*): See, what'd I tell ya'. He's totally unsympathetic.

SAUL: Austin, there's no point in our going to another screenwriter for this. It just doesn't make sense. You're brothers. You know each other. There's a familiarity with the material that just wouldn't be possible otherwise.

AUSTIN: There's no familiarity with the material! None! I don't know what "Tornado Country" is. I don't know what a "gooseneck" is. And I don't want to know! (*pointing to LEE*) He's a hustler! He's a bigger hustler than you are! If you can't see that, then—

LEE (*to AUSTIN*): Hey, now hold on. I didn't have to bring this bone back to you, boy. I persuaded Saul here that you were the right man for the job. You don't have to go throwin' up favors in my face.

AUSTIN: Favors! I'm the one who wrote the fuckin'

outline! You can't even spell.

SAUL (*to* AUSTIN): Your brother told me about the situation with your father.

[pause]

AUSTIN: What? (*looks at* LEE)

SAUL: That's right. Now we have a clear-cut deal here, Austin. We have big studio money standing behind this thing. Just on the basis of your outline.

AUSTIN (*to* SAUL): What'd he tell you about my father?

SAUL: Well—that he's destitute. He needs money.

LEE: That's right. He does.

[AUSTIN shakes his head, stares at them both]

AUSTIN (*to* LEE): And this little assignment is supposed to go toward the old man? A charity project? Is that what this is? Did you cook this up on the ninth green too?

SAUL: It's a big slice, Austin.

AUSTIN (*to* LEE): I gave him money! I already gave him money. You know that. He drank it all up!

LEE: This is a different deal here.

SAUL: We can set up a trust for your father. A large sum of money. It can be doled out to him in parcels so he can't misuse it.

AUSTIN: Yeah, and who's doing the doling?

SAUL: Your brother volunteered.

[AUSTIN laughs]

LEE: That's right. I'll make sure he uses it for groceries.

AUSTIN (*to* SAUL): I'm not doing this script! I'm not writing this crap for you or anybody else. You can't blackmail me into it. You can't threaten me into it. There's no way I'm doing it. So just give it up. Both of you.

[long pause]

SAUL: Well, that's it then. I mean this is an easy three hundred grand. Just for a first draft. It's incredible, Austin. We've got three different studios all trying to cut each other's throats to get this material. In one morning. That's how hot it is.

AUSTIN: Yeah, well you can afford to give me a percentage on the outline then. And you better get the genius here an agent before he gets burned.

LEE: Saul's gonna' be my agent. Isn't that right, Saul?

SAUL: That's right. (*to* AUSTIN) Your brother has really got something, Austin. I've been around too long not to recognize it. Raw talent.

AUSTIN: He's got a lota' balls is what he's got. He's taking you right down the river.

SAUL: Three hundred thousand, Austin. Just for a first draft. Now you've never been offered that kind of money before.

AUSTIN: I'm not writing it.

[pause]

SAUL: I see. Well—

LEE: We'll just go to another writer then. Right, Saul? Just hire us somebody with some enthusiasm. Somebody who can recognize the value of a good story.

SAUL: I'm sorry about this, Austin.

AUSTIN: Yeah.

SAUL: I mean I was hoping we could continue both things but now I don't see how it's possible.

AUSTIN: So you're dropping my idea altogether. Is that it? Just trade horses in midstream? After all these months of meetings.

SAUL: I wish there was another way.

AUSTIN: I've got everything riding on this, Saul. You know that. It's my only shot. If this falls through—

SAUL: I have to go with what my instincts tell me—

AUSTIN: Your instincts!

SAUL: My gut reaction.

AUSTIN: You lost! That's your gut reaction. You lost a gamble. Now you're trying to tell me you like his story? How could you possibly fall for that story? It's as phony as Hoppalong Cassidy. What do you see in it? I'm curious.

SAUL: It has the ring of truth, Austin.

AUSTIN (*laughs*): Truth?

LEE: It is true.

SAUL: Something about the real West.

AUSTIN: Why? Because it's got horses? Because it's got grown men acting like little boys?

SAUL: Something about the land. Your brother is speaking from experience.

AUSTIN: So am I!

SAUL: But nobody's interested in love these days, Austin. Let's face it.

LEE: That's right.

AUSTIN (*to* SAUL): He's been camped out on the desert for three months. Talking to cactus. What's he know about what people wanna' see on the screen! I drive on the freeway every day. I swallow the smog. I watch the news in color. I shop in the Safeway. I'm the one who's in touch! Not him!

SAUL: I have to go now, Austin.

[SAUL starts to leave]

AUSTIN: There's no such thing as the West anymore!

It's a dead issue! It's dried up, Saul, and so are you.

[SAUL *stops and turns to* AUSTIN]

SAUL: Maybe you're right. But I have to take the gamble, don't I?
AUSTIN: You're a fool to do this, Saul.
SAUL: I've always gone on my hunches. Always. And I've never been wrong. (*to* LEE) I'll talk to you tomorrow, Lee.
LEE: All right, Mr. Kimmer.
SAUL: Maybe we could have some lunch.
LEE: Fine with me. (*smiles at* AUSTIN)
SAUL: I'll give you a ring.

[SAUL *exits, lights to black as brothers look at each other from a distance*]

Scene 7

Night. Coyotes, crickets, sound of typewriter in dark, candlelight up on LEE *at typewriter struggling to type with one finger system,* AUSTIN *sits sprawled out on kitchen floor with whiskey bottle, drunk.*

AUSTIN (*singing, from floor*):

"Red sails in the sunset
Way out on the blue
Please carry my loved one
Home safely to me

Red sails in the sunset—"

LEE (*slams fist on table*): Hey! Knock it off will ya'! I'm tryin' to concentrate here.
AUSTIN (*laughs*): You're tryin' to concentrate?
LEE: Yeah. That's right.
AUSTIN: Now you're tryin' to concentrate.
LEE: Between you, the coyotes and the crickets a thought don't have much of a chance.
AUSTIN: "Between me, the coyotes and the crickets." What a great title.
LEE: I don't need a title! I need a thought.
AUSTIN (*laughs*): A thought! Here's a thought for ya'—
LEE: I'm not askin' fer yer thoughts! I got my own. I can do this thing on my own.
AUSTIN: You're going to write an entire script on your own?
LEE: That's right.

[*pause*]

AUSTIN: Here's a thought. Saul Kimmer—
LEE: Shut up will ya'!

AUSTIN: He thinks we're the same person.
LEE: Don't get cute.
AUSTIN: He does! He's lost his mind. Poor old Saul. (*giggles*) Thinks we're one and the same.
LEE: Why don't you ease up on that champagne.
AUSTIN (*holding up bottle*): This isn't champagne anymore. We went through the champagne a long time ago. This is serious stuff. The days of champagne are long gone.
LEE: Well, go outside and drink it.
AUSTIN: I'm enjoying your company, Lee. For the first time since your arrival I am finally enjoying your company. And now you want me to go outside and drink alone?
LEE: That's right.

[LEE *reads through paper in typewriter, makes an erasure*]

AUSTIN: You think you'll make more progress if you're alone? You might drive yourself crazy.
LEE: I could have this thing done in a night if I had a little silence.
AUSTIN: Well you'd still have the crickets to contend with. The coyotes. The sounds of the Police Helicopters prowling above the neighborhood. Slashing their searchlights down through the streets. Hunting for the likes of you.
LEE: I'm a screenwriter now! I'm legitimate.
AUSTIN (*laughing*): A screenwriter!
LEE: That's right. I'm on salary. That's more'n I can say for you. I got an advance coming.
AUSTIN: This is true. This is very true. An advance. (*pause*) Well, maybe I oughta' go out and try my hand at your trade. Since you're doing so good at mine.
LEE: Ha!

[LEE *attempts to type some more but gets the ribbon tangled up, starts trying to re-thread it as they continue talking*]

AUSTIN: Well why not? You don't think I've got what it takes to sneak into people's houses and steal their T.V.s?
LEE: You couldn't steal a toaster without losin' yer lunch.

[AUSTIN *stands with a struggle, supports himself by the sink*]

AUSTIN: You don't think I could sneak into somebody's house and steal a toaster?
LEE: Go take a shower or somethin' will ya!

[LEE *gets more tangled up with the typewriter ribbon, pulling it out of the machine as though it was fishing line*]

AUSTIN: You really don't think I could steal a crumby toaster? How much you wanna' bet I can't steal a toaster! How much? Go ahead! You're a gambler aren't you? Tell me how much yer willing to put on the line. Some part of your big advance? Oh, you haven't got that yet have you. I forgot.

LEE: All right. I'll bet you your car that you can't steal a toaster without gettin' busted.

AUSTIN: You already got my car!

LEE: Okay, your house then.

AUSTIN: What're you gonna' give me! I'm not talkin' about my house and my car, I'm talkin' about what are you gonna' give me. You don't have nothin' to give me.

LEE: I'll give you—shared screen credit. How 'bout that? I'll have it put in the contract that this was written by the both of us.

AUSTIN: I don't want my name on that piece of shit! I want something of value. You got anything of value? You got any tidbits from the desert? Any Rattlesnake bones? I'm not a greedy man. Any little personal treasure will suffice.

LEE: I'm gonna' just kick yer ass out in a minute.

AUSTIN: Oh, so now you're gonna' kick me out! Now I'm the intruder. I'm the one who's invading your precious privacy.

LEE: I'm trying to do some screenwriting here!!

[LEE stands, picks up typewriter, slams it down hard on table, pause, silence except for crickets]

AUSTIN: Well, you got everything you need. You got plenty a' coffee? Groceries. You got a car. A contract. (*pause*) Might need a new typewriter ribbon but other than that you're pretty well fixed. I'll just leave ya' alone for a while.

[AUSTIN tries to steady himself to leave, LEE makes a move toward him]

LEE: Where you goin'?

AUSTIN: Don't worry about me. I'm not the one to worry about.

[AUSTIN weaves toward exit, stops]

LEE: What're you gonna' do? Just go wander out into the night?

AUSTIN: I'm gonna' make a little tour.

LEE: Why don't ya' just go to bed for Christ's sake. Yer makin' me sick.

AUSTIN: I can take care a' myself. Don't worry about me.

[AUSTIN weaves badly in another attempt to exit, he crashes to the floor, LEE goes to him but remains standing]

LEE: You want me to call your wife for ya' or something?

AUSTIN (*from floor*): My wife?

LEE: Yeah. I mean maybe she can help ya' out. Talk to ya' or somethin'.

AUSTIN (*struggles to stand again*): She's five hundred miles away. North. North of here. Up in the North country where things are calm. I don't need any help. I'm gonna' go outside and I'm gonna' steal a toaster. I'm gonna' steal some other stuff too. I might even commit bigger crimes. Bigger than you ever dreamed of. Crimes beyond the imagination!

[AUSTIN manages to get himself vertical, tries to head for exit again]

LEE: Just hang on a minute, Austin.

AUSTIN: Why? What for? You don't need my help, right? You got a handle on the project. Besides, I'm lookin' forward to the smell of the night. The bushes. Orange blossoms. Dust in the driveways. Rain bird sprinklers. Lights in people's houses. You're right about the lights, Lee. Everybody else is livin' the life. Indoors. Safe. This is a Paradise down here. You know that? We're livin' in a Paradise. We've forgotten about that.

LEE: You sound just like the old man now.

AUSTIN: Yeah, well we all sound alike when we're sloshed. We just sorta' echo each other.

LEE: Maybe if we could work on this together we could bring him back out here. Get him settled down some place.

[AUSTIN turns violently toward LEE, takes a swing at him, misses and crashes to the floor again, LEE stays standing]

AUSTIN: I don't want him out here! I've had it with him! I went all the way out there! I went out of my way. I gave him money and all he did was play Al Jolson records and spit at me! I gave him money!

[pause]

LEE: Just help me a little with the characters, all right? You know how to do it, Austin.

AUSTIN (*on floor, laughs*): The characters!

LEE: Yeah. You know. The way they talk and stuff. I can hear it in my head but I can't get it down on paper.

AUSTIN: What characters?

LEE: The guys. The guys in the story.

AUSTIN: Those aren't characters.

LEE: Whatever you call 'em then. I need to write somethin' out.

AUSTIN: Those are illusions of characters.

LEE: I don't give a damn what ya' call 'em! You know what I'm talkin' about!

AUSTIN: Those are fantasies of a long lost boyhood.

LEE: I gotta' write somethin' out on paper!!

[pause]

AUSTIN: What for? Saul's gonna' get you a fancy screenwriter isn't he?

LEE: I wanna' do it myself!

AUSTIN: Then do it! Yer on your own now, old buddy. You bulldogged yer way into contention. Now you gotta' carry it through.

LEE: I will but I need some advice. Just a couple a' things. Come on, Austin. Just help me get 'em talkin' right. It won't take much.

AUSTIN: Oh, now you're having a little doubt huh? What happened? The pressure's on, boy. This is it. You gotta' come up with it now. You don't come up with a winner on your first time out they just cut your head off. They don't give you a second chance ya' know.

LEE: I got a good story! I know it's a good story. I just need a little help is all.

AUSTIN: Not from me. Not from yer little old brother. I'm retired.

LEE: You could save this thing for me, Austin. I'd give ya' half the money. I would. I only need half anyway. With this kinda' money I could be a long time down the road. I'd never bother ya' again. I promise. You'd never even see me again.

AUSTIN (*still on floor*): You'd disappear?

LEE: I would for sure.

AUSTIN: Where would you disappear to?

LEE: That don't matter. I got plenty a' places.

AUSTIN: Nobody can disappear. The old man tried that. Look where it got him. He lost his teeth.

LEE: He never had any money.

AUSTIN: I don't mean that. I mean his teeth! His real teeth. First he lost his real teeth, then he lost his false teeth. You never knew that did ya'? He never confided in you.

LEE: Nah, I never knew that.

AUSTIN: You wanna' drink?

[AUSTIN offers bottle to LEE, LEE takes it, sits down on kitchen floor with AUSTIN, they share the bottle]

Yeah, he lost his real teeth one at a time. Woke up every morning with another tooth lying on the mattress. Finally, he decides he's gotta' get 'em all pulled out but he doesn't have any money. Middle of Arizona with no money and no insurance and every morning another tooth is lying on the mattress. (*takes a drink*) So what does he do?

LEE: I dunno'. I never knew about that.

AUSTIN: He begs the government. G.I. Bill or some damn thing. Some pension plan he remembers in the back of his head. And they send him out the money.

LEE: They did?

[they keep trading the bottle between them, taking drinks]

AUSTIN: Yeah. They send him the money but it's not enough money. Costs a lot to have all yer teeth yanked. They charge by the individual tooth, ya' know. I mean one tooth isn't equal to another tooth. Some are more expensive. Like the big ones in the back—

LEE: So what happened?

AUSTIN: So he locates a Mexican dentist in Juarez who'll do the whole thing for a song. And he takes off hitchhiking to the border.

LEE: Hitchhiking?

AUSTIN: Yeah. So how long you think it takes him to get to the border? A man his age.

LEE: I dunno.

AUSTIN: Eight days it takes him. Eight days in the rain and the sun and every day he's droppin' teeth on the blacktop and nobody'll pick him up 'cause his mouth's full a' blood.

[pause, they drink]

So finally he stumbles into the dentist. Dentist takes all his money and all his teeth. And there he is, in Mexico, with his gums sewed up and his pockets empty.

[long silence, AUSTIN drinks]

LEE: That's it?

AUSTIN: Then I go out to see him, see. I go out there and I take him out for a nice Chinese dinner. But he doesn't eat. All he wants to do is drink Martinis outa' plastic cups. And he takes his teeth out and lays 'em on the table 'cause he can't stand the feel of 'em. And we ask the waitress for one a' those doggie bags to take the Chop Suey home in. So he drops his teeth in the doggie bag along with the Chop Suey. And then we go out to hit all the bars up and down the highway. Says he wants to introduce me to all his buddies. And in one a' those bars, in one a' those bars up and down the highway, he left that doggie bag with his teeth laying in the Chop Suey.

LEE: You never found it?

AUSTIN: We went back but we never did find it. (*pause*) Now that's a true story. True to life.

[they drink as lights fade to black]

Scene 8

Very early morning, between night and day. No crickets, coyotes yapping feverishly in distance before light comes up, a small fire blazes up in the dark from alcove area, sound of LEE *smashing typewriter with a golf club, lights coming up,* LEE *seen smashing typewriter methodically then dropping pages of his script into a burning bowl set on the floor of alcove, flames leap up,* AUSTIN *has a whole bunch of stolen toasters lined up on the sink counter along with* LEE's *stolen T.V., the toasters are of a wide variety of models, mostly chrome,* AUSTIN *goes up and down the line of toasters, breathing on them and polishing them with a dish towel, both men are drunk, empty whiskey bottles and beer cans litter floor of kitchen, they share a half empty bottle on one of the chairs in the alcove,* LEE *keeps periodically taking deliberate ax-chops at the typewriter using a nine-iron as* AUSTIN *speaks, all of their mother's house plants are dead and drooping.*

AUSTIN (*polishing toasters*): There's gonna' be a general lack of toast in the neighborhood this morning. Many, many unhappy, bewildered breakfast faces. I guess it's best not to even think of the victims. Not to even entertain it. Is that the right psychology?

LEE (*pauses*): What?

AUSTIN: Is that the correct criminal psychology? Not to think of the victims?

LEE: What victims?

[LEE takes another swipe at typewriter with nine-iron, adds pages to the fire]

AUSTIN: The victims of crime. Of breaking and entering. I mean is it a prerequisite for a criminal not to have a conscience?

LEE: Ask a criminal.

[pause, LEE stares at AUSTIN]

What're you gonna' do with all those toasters? That's the dumbest thing I ever saw in my life.

AUSTIN: I've got hundreds of dollars worth of household appliances here. You may not realize that.

LEE: Yeah, and how many hundreds of dollars did you walk right past?

AUSTIN: It was toasters you challenged me to. Only toasters. I ignored every other temptation.

LEE: I never challenged you! That's no challenge. Anybody can steal a toaster.

[LEE smashes typewriter again]

AUSTIN: You don't have to take it out on my type-

writer ya' know. It's not the machine's fault that you can't write. It's a sin to do that to a good machine.

LEE: A sin?

AUSTIN: When you consider all the writers who never even had a machine. Who would have given an eyeball for a good typewriter. Any typewriter.

[LEE smashes typewriter again]

AUSTIN (*polishing toasters*): All the ones who wrote on matchbook covers. Paper bags. Toilet paper. Who had their writing destroyed by their jailers. Who persisted beyond all odds. Those writers would find it hard to understand your actions.

[LEE comes down on typewriter with one final crushing blow of the nine-iron then collapses in one of the chairs, takes a drink from bottle, pause]

AUSTIN (*after pause*): Not to mention demolishing a perfectly good golf club. What about all the struggling golfers? What about Lee Trevino? What do you think he would've said when he was batting balls around with broomsticks at the age of nine. Impoverished.

[pause]

LEE: What time is it anyway?

AUSTIN: No idea. Time stands still when you're havin' fun.

LEE: Is it too late to call a woman? You know any women?

AUSTIN: I'm a married man.

LEE: I mean a local woman.

[AUSTIN looks out at light through window above sink]

AUSTIN: It's either too late or too early. You're the nature enthusiast. Can't you tell the time by the light in the sky? Orient yourself around the North Star or something?

LEE: I can't tell anything.

AUSTIN: Maybe you need a little breakfast. Some toast! How 'bout some toast?

[AUSTIN goes to cupboard, pulls out loaf of bread and starts dropping slices into every toaster, LEE stays sitting, drinks, watches AUSTIN]

LEE: I don't need toast. I need a woman.

AUSTIN: A woman isn't the answer. Never was.

LEE: I'm not talkin' about permanent. I'm talkin' about temporary.

AUSTIN (*putting toast in toasters*): We'll just test the

merits of these little demons. See which brands have a tendency to burn. See which one can produce a perfectly golden piece of fluffy toast.

LEE: How much gas you got in yer car?

AUSTIN: I haven't driven my car for days now. So I haven't had an opportunity to look at the gas gauge.

LEE: Take a guess. You think there's enough to get me to Bakersfield?

AUSTIN: Bakersfield? What's in Bakersfield?

LEE: Just never mind what's in Bakersfield! You think there's enough goddamn gas in the car!

AUSTIN: Sure.

LEE: Sure. You could care less, right. Let me run outa' gas on the Grapevine. You could give a shit.

AUSTIN: I'd say there was enough gas to get you just about anywhere, Lee. With your determination and guts.

LEE: What the hell time is it anyway?

[LEE pulls out his wallet, starts going through dozens of small pieces of paper with phone numbers written on them, drops some on the floor, drops others in the fire]

AUSTIN: Very early. This is the time of morning when the coyotes kill people's cocker spaniels. Did you hear them? That's what they were doing out there. Luring innocent pets away from their homes.

LEE (*searching through his papers*): What's the area code for Bakersfield? You know?

AUSTIN: You could always call the operator.

LEE: I can't stand that voice they give ya'.

AUSTIN: What voice?

LEE: That voice that warns you that if you'd only tried harder to find the number in the phone book you wouldn't have to be calling the operator to begin with.

[LEE gets up, holding a slip of paper from his wallet, stumbles toward phone on wall, yanks receiver, starts dialing]

AUSTIN: Well I don't understand why you'd want to talk to anybody else anyway. I mean you can talk to me. I'm your brother.

LEE (*dialing*): I wanna' talk to a woman. I haven't heard a woman's voice in a long time.

AUSTIN: Not since the Botanist?

LEE: What?

AUSTIN: Nothing. (*starts singing as he tends toast*)

"Red sails in the sunset
Way out on the blue
Please carry my loved one
Home safely to me"

LEE: Hey, knock it off will ya'! This is long distance here.

AUSTIN: Bakersfield?

LEE: Yeah, Bakersfield. It's Kern County.

AUSTIN: Well, what County are *we* in?

LEE: You better get yourself a 7-Up, boy.

AUSTIN: One County's as good as another.

[AUSTIN hums "Red Sails" softly as LEE talks on phone]

LEE (*to phone*): Yeah, operator look—first off I wanna' know the area code for Bakersfield. Right. Bakersfield! Okay. Good. Now I wanna' know if you can help me track somebody down. (*pause*) No, no I mean a phone number. Just a phone number. Okay. (*holds a piece of paper up and reads it*) Okay, the name is Melly Ferguson. Melly. (*pause*) I dunno'. Melly. Maybe. Yeah. Maybe Melanie. Yeah. Melanie Ferguson. Okay. (*pause*) What? I can't hear ya' so good. Sounds like yer under the ocean. (*pause*) You got ten Melanie Fergusons? How could that be? Ten Melanie Fergusons in Bakersfield? Well gimme all of 'em then. (*pause*) What d'ya' mean? Gimmie all ten Melanie Fergusons! That's right. Just a second. (*to* AUSTIN) Gimme a pen.

AUSTIN: I don't have a pen.

LEE: Gimme a pencil then!

AUSTIN: I don't have a pencil.

LEE (*to phone*): Just a second, operator. (*to* AUSTIN) Yer a writer and ya' don't have a pen or a pencil!

AUSTIN: I'm not a writer. You're a writer.

LEE: I'm on the phone here! Get me a pen or a pencil.

AUSTIN: I gotta' watch the toast.

LEE (*to phone*): Hang on a second, operator.

[LEE lets the phone drop then starts pulling all the drawers in the kitchen out on the floor and dumping the contents, searching for a pencil, AUSTIN watches him casually]

LEE (*crashing through drawers, throwing contents around kitchen*): This is the last time I try to live with people, boy! I can't believe it. Here I am! Here I am again in a desperate situation! This would never happen out on the desert. I would never be in this kinda' situation out on the desert. Isn't there a pen or a pencil in this house! Who lives in this house anyway!

AUSTIN: Our mother.

LEE: How come she don't have a pen or a pencil! She's a social person isn't she? Doesn't she have to make shopping lists? She's gotta' have a pencil. (*finds a pencil*) Aaha! (*he rushes back to phone, picks up receiver*) All right operator. Operator? Hey! Operator! Goddamnit!

[LEE rips the phone off the wall and throws it down, goes back to chair and falls into it, drinks, long pause]

AUSTIN: She hung up?
LEE: Yeah, she hung up. I knew she was gonna' hang up. I could hear it in her voice.

[LEE starts going through his slips of paper again]

AUSTIN: Well, you're probably better off staying here with me anyway. I'll take care of you.
LEE: I don't need takin' care of! Not by you anyway.
AUSTIN: Toast is almost ready.

[AUSTIN starts buttering all the toast as it pops up]

LEE: I don't want any toast!

[long pause]

AUSTIN: You gotta' eat something. Can't just drink. How long have we been drinking, anyway?
LEE *(looking through slips of paper)*: Maybe it was Fresno. What's the area code for Fresno? How could I have lost that number! She was beautiful.

[pause]

AUSTIN: Why don't you just forget about that, Lee. Forget about the woman.
LEE: She had green eyes. You know what green eyes do to me?
AUSTIN: I know but you're not gonna' get it on with her now anyway. It's dawn already. She's in Bakersfield for Christ's sake.

[long pause, LEE considers the situation]

LEE: Yeah. *(looks at windows)* It's dawn?
AUSTIN: Let's just have some toast and—
LEE: What is this bullshit with the toast anyway! You make it sound like salvation or something. I don't want any goddamn toast! How many times I gotta' tell ya'! *(LEE gets up, crosses upstage to windows in alcove, looks out, AUSTIN butters toast))*
AUSTIN: Well it is like salvation sort of. I mean the smell. I love the smell of toast. And the sun's coming up. It makes me feel like anything's possible. Ya' know?
LEE *(back to AUSTIN, facing windows upstage)*: So go to church why don't ya'.
AUSTIN: Like a beginning. I love beginnings.
LEE: Oh yeah. I've always been kinda' partial to endings myself.
AUSTIN: What if I come with you, Lee?
LEE *(pause as LEE turns toward AUSTIN)*: What?
AUSTIN: What if I come with you out to the desert?

LEE: Are you kiddin'?
AUSTIN: No. I'd just like to see what it's like.
LEE: You wouldn't last a day out there pal.
AUSTIN: That's what you said about the toasters. You said I couldn't steal a toaster either.
LEE: A toaster's got nothin' to do with the desert.
AUSTIN: I could make it, Lee. I'm not that helpless. I can cook.
LEE: Cook?
AUSTIN: I can.
LEE: So what! You can cook. Toast.
AUSTIN: I can make fires. I know how to get fresh water from condensation.

[AUSTIN stacks buttered toast up in a tall stack on plate]
[LEE slams table]

LEE: It's not somethin' you learn out of a Boy Scout handbook!
AUSTIN: Well how do you learn it then! How're you supposed to learn it!

[pause]

LEE: Ya' just learn it, that's all. Ya' learn it 'cause ya' have to learn it. You don't *have* to learn it.
AUSTIN: You could teach me.
LEE *(stands)*: What're you, crazy or somethin'? You went to college. Here, you are down here, rollin' in bucks. Floatin' up and down in elevators. And you wanna' learn how to live on the desert!
AUSTIN: I do, Lee. I really do. There's nothin' down here for me. There never was. When we were kids here it was different. There was a life here then. But now—I keep comin' down here thinkin' it's the fifties or somethin'. I keep finding myself getting off the freeway at familiar landmarks that turn out to be unfamiliar. On the way to appointments. Wandering down streets I thought I recognized that turn out to be replicas of streets I remember. Streets I misremember. Streets I can't tell if I lived on or saw in a postcard. Fields that don't even exist anymore.
LEE: There's no point cryin' about that now.
AUSTIN: There's nothin' real down here, Lee! Least of all me!
LEE: Well I can't save you from that!
AUSTIN: You can let me come with you.
LEE: No dice, pal.
AUSTIN: You could let me come with you, Lee!
LEE: Hey, do you actually think I chose to live out in the middle a' nowhere? Do ya'? Ya' think it's some kinda' philosophical decision I took or somethin'? I'm livin' out there 'cause I can't

make it here! And yer bitchin' to me about all yer success!

AUSTIN: I'd cash it all in in a second. That's the truth.

LEE (*pause, shakes his head*): I can't believe this.

AUSTIN: Let me go with you.

LEE: Stop sayin' that will ya'! Yer worse than a dog.

[*AUSTIN offers out the plate of neatly stacked toast to LEE*]

AUSTIN: You want some toast?

[*LEE suddenly explodes and knocks the plate out of AUSTIN's hand, toast goes flying, long frozen moment where it appears LEE might go all the way this time when AUSTIN breaks it by slowly lowering himself to his knees and begins gathering the scattered toast from the floor and stacking it back on the plate. LEE begins to circle AUSTIN in a slow, predatory way, crushing pieces of toast in his wake, no words for a while, AUSTIN keeps gathering toast, even the crushed pieces*]

LEE: Tell ya' what I'll do, little brother. I might just consider makin' you a deal. Little trade. (AUSTIN *continues gathering toast as* LEE *circles him through this*) You write me up this screenplay thing just like I tell ya'. I mean you can use all yer usual tricks and stuff. Yer fancy language. Yer artistic hocus pocus. But ya' gotta' write everything like I say. Every move. Every time they run outa' gas, they run outa' gas. Every time they wanna' jump on a horse, they do just that. If they wanna' stay in Texas, by God they'll stay in Texas! (*Keeps circling*) And you finish the whole thing up for me. Top to bottom. And you put my name on it. And I own all the rights. And every dime goes in my pocket. You do that and I'll sure enough take ya' with me to the desert. (LEE *stops, pause, looks down at* AUSTIN) How's that sound?

[*pause as AUSTIN stands slowly holding plate of demolished toast, their faces are very close, pause*]

AUSTIN: It's a deal.

[*LEE stares straight into AUSTIN's eyes, then he slowly takes a piece of toast off the plate, raises it to his mouth and takes a huge crushing bite never taking his eyes off AUSTIN's, as LEE crunches into the toast the lights black out*]

Scene 9

Mid-day. No sound, blazing heat, the stage is ravaged; bottles, toasters, smashed typewriter, ripped out telephone, etc. All the debris from previous scene is now starkly visible in intense yellow light, the effect should be like a desert junkyard at high noon, the coolness of the preceding scenes is totally obliterated. AUSTIN is seated at table in alcove, shirt open, pouring with sweat, hunched over a writing notebook, scribbling notes desperately with a ballpoint pen. LEE with no shirt, beer in hand, sweat pouring down his chest, is walking a slow circle around the table, picking his way through the objects, sometimes kicking them aside.

LEE (*as he walks*): All right, read it back to me. Read it back to me!

AUSTIN (*scribbling at top speed*): Just a second.

LEE: Come on, come on! Just read what ya' got.

AUSTIN: I can't keep up! It's not the same as if I had a typewriter.

LEE: Just read what we got so far. Forget about the rest.

AUSTIN: All right. Let's see—okay—(*wipes sweat from his face, reads as* LEE *circles*) Luke says uh—

LEE: Luke?

AUSTIN: Yeah.

LEE: His name's Luke? All right, all right—we can change the names later. What's he say? Come on, come on.

AUSTIN: He says uh—(*reading*) "I told ya' you were a fool to follow me in here. I know this prairie like the back a' my hand."

LEE: No, no, no! That's not what I said. I never said that.

AUSTIN: That's what I wrote.

LEE: It's not what I said. I never said "like the back a' my hand." That's stupid. That's one a' those—whadya' call it? Whadya' call that?

AUSTIN: What?

LEE: Whadya' call it when somethin's been said a thousand times before. Whadya' call that?

AUSTIN: Um—a cliché?

LEE: Yeah. That's right. Cliché. That's what that is. A cliché. "The back a' my hand." That's stupid.

AUSTIN: That's what you said.

LEE: I never said that! And even if I did, that's where yer supposed to come in. That's where yer supposed to change it to somethin' better.

AUSTIN: Well how am I supposed to do that and write down what you say at the same time?

LEE: Ya' just do, that's all! You hear a stupid line you change it. That's yer job.

AUSTIN: All right. (*makes more notes*)

LEE: What're you changin' it to?

AUSTIN: I'm not changing it. I'm just trying to catch up.

LEE: Well change it! We gotta' change that, we can't leave that in there like that. ". . . the back a' my hand." That's dumb.

AUSTIN (*stops writing, sits back*): All right.

LEE (*pacing*): So what'll we change it to?

AUSTIN: Um—How 'bout—"I'm on intimate terms with this prairie."

LEE (*to himself considering line as he walks*): "I'm on intimate terms with this prairie." Intimate terms, intimate terms. Intimate—that means like uh—sexual right?

AUSTIN: Well—yeah—or—

LEE: He's on sexual terms with the prairie? How dya' figure that?

AUSTIN: Well it doesn't necessarily have to mean sexual.

LEE: What's it mean then?

AUSTIN: It means uh—close—personal—

LEE: All right. How's it sound? Put it into the uh—the line there. Read it back. Let's see how it sounds. (*to himself*) "Intimate terms."

AUSTIN (*scribbles in notebook*): Okay. It'd go something like this: (*reads*) "I told ya' you were a fool to follow me in here. I'm on intimate terms with this prairie."

LEE: That's good. I like that. That's real good.

AUSTIN: You do?

LEE: Yeah. Don't you?

AUSTIN: Sure.

LEE: Sounds original now. "Intimate terms." That's good. Okay. Now we're cookin! That has a real ring to it.

[*AUSTIN makes more notes, LEE walks around, pours beer on his arms and rubs it over his chest feeling good about the new progress, as he does this MOM enters unobtrusively down left with her luggage, she stops and stares at the scene still holding luggage as the two men continue, unaware of her presence, AUSTIN absorbed in his writing, LEE cooling himself off with beer*]

LEE (*continues*): "He's on intimate terms with this prairie." Sounds real mysterious and kinda' threatening at the same time.

AUSTIN (*writing rapidly*): Good.

LEE: Now—(LEE *turns and suddenly sees* MOM, *he stares at her for a while, she stares back,* AUSTIN *keeps writing feverishly, not noticing.* LEE *walks slowly over to* MOM *and takes a closer look, long pause*)

LEE: Mom?

[*AUSTIN looks up suddenly from his writing, sees MOM, stands quickly, long pause, MOM surveys the damage*]

AUSTIN: Mom. What're you doing back?

MOM: I'm back.

LEE: Here, lemme take those for ya.

[*LEE sets beer on counter then takes both her bags but doesn't know where to set them down in the sea of junk so he just keeps holding them*]

AUSTIN: I wasn't expecting you back so soon. I thought uh—How was Alaska?

MOM: Fine.

LEE: See any igloos?

MOM: No. Just glaciers.

AUSTIN: Cold huh?

MOM: What?

AUSTIN: It must've been cold up there?

MOM: Not really.

LEE: Musta' been colder than this here. I mean we're havin' a real scorcher here.

MOM: Oh? (*she looks at damage*)

LEE: Yeah. Must be in the hundreds.

AUSTIN: You wanna' take your coat off, Mom?

MOM: No. (*pause, she surveys space*) What happened in here?

AUSTIN: Oh um—Me and Lee were just sort of celebrating and uh—

MOM: Celebrating?

AUSTIN: Yeah. Uh—Lee sold a screenplay. A story, I mean.

MOM: Lee did?

AUSTIN: Yeah.

MOM: Not you?

AUSTIN: No. Him.

MOM (*to* LEE): You sold a screenplay?

LEE: Yeah. That's right. We're just sorta' finishing it up right now. That's what we're doing here.

AUSTIN: Me and Lee are going out to the desert to live.

MOM: You and Lee?

AUSTIN: Yeah. I'm taking off with Lee.

MOM (*she looks back and forth at each of them, pause*): You gonna go live with your father?

AUSTIN: No. We're going to a different desert Mom.

MOM: I see. Well, you'll probably wind up on the same desert sooner or later. What're all these toasters doing here?

AUSTIN: Well—we had kind of a contest.

MOM: Contest?

LEE: Yeah.

AUSTIN: Lee won.

MOM: Did you win a lot of money, Lee?

LEE: Well not yet. It's comin' in any day now.

MOM: (*to* LEE) What happened to your shirt?

LEE: Oh. I was sweatin' like a pig and I took it off.

[*AUSTIN grabs LEE's shirt off the table and tosses it to him, LEE sets down suitcases and puts his shirt on*]

MOM: Well it's one hell of a mess in here isn't it?

AUSTIN: Yeah, I'll clean it up for you, Mom. I just didn't know you were coming back so soon.

MOM: I didn't either.

AUSTIN: What happened?

MOM: Nothing. I just started missing all my plants.

[she notices dead plants]

AUSTIN: Oh.

MOM: Oh, they're all dead aren't they. (*she crosses toward them, examines them closely*) You didn't get a chance to water I guess.

AUSTIN: I was doing it and then Lee came and—

LEE: Yeah I just distracted him a whole lot here, Mom. It's not his fault.

[pause, as MOM stares at plants]

MOM: Oh well, one less thing to take care of I guess. (*turns toward brothers*) Oh, that reminds me—You boys will probably never guess who's in town. Try and guess.

[long pause, brothers stare at her]

AUSTIN: Whadya' mean, Mom?

MOM: Take a guess. Somebody very important has come to town. I read it, coming down on the Greyhound.

LEE: Somebody very important?

MOM: See if you can guess. You'll never guess.

AUSTIN: Mom—we're trying to uh—(*points to writing pad*)

MOM: Picasso. (*pause*) Picasso's in town. Isn't that incredible. Right now.

[pause]

AUSTIN: Picasso's dead, Mom.

MOM: No, he's not dead. He's visiting the museum. I read it on the bus. We have to go down there and see him.

AUSTIN: Mom—

MOM: This is the chance of a lifetime. Can you imagine? We could all go down and meet him. All three of us.

LEE: Uh—I don't think I'm really up fer meetin' anybody right now. I'm uh—What's his name?

MOM: Picasso! Picasso! You've never heard of Picasso? Austin, you've heard of Picasso.

AUSTIN: Mom, we're not going to have time.

MOM: It won't take long. We'll just hop in the car and go down there. An opportunity like this doesn't come along every day.

AUSTIN: We're gonna' be leavin' here, Mom!

[pause]

MOM: Oh.

LEE: Yeah.

[pause]

MOM: You're both leaving?

LEE (*looks at* AUSTIN): Well we were thinkin' about

that before but now I—

AUSTIN: No, we are! We're both leaving. We've got it all planned.

MOM (*to* AUSTIN): Well you can't leave. You have a family.

AUSTIN: I'm leaving. I'm getting out of here.

LEE (*to* MOM): I don't really think Austin's cut out for the desert do you?

MOM: No. He's not.

AUSTIN: I'm going with you, Lee!

MOM: He's too thin.

LEE: Yeah, he'd just burn up out there.

AUSTIN (*to* LEE): We just gotta' finish this screenplay and then we're gonna' take off. That's the plan. That's what you said. Come on, let's get back to work, Lee.

LEE: I can't work under these conditions here. It's too hot.

AUSTIN: Then we'll do it on the desert.

LEE: Don't be tellin' me what we're gonna' do!

MOM: Don't shout in the house.

LEE: We're just gonna' have to postpone the whole deal.

AUSTIN: I can't postpone it! It's gone past postponing! I'm doing everything you said. I'm writing down exactly what you tell me.

LEE: Yeah, but you were right all along see. It is a dumb story. "Two lamebrains chasin' each other across Texas." That's what you said, right?

AUSTIN: I never said that.

[LEE sneers in AUSTIN'S *face then turns to* MOM]*

LEE: I'm gonna' just borrow some a' your antiques, Mom. You don't mind do ya'? Just a few plates and things. Silverware.

[LEE starts going through all the cupboards in kitchen pulling out plates and stacking them on counter as MOM *and* AUSTIN *watch]*

MOM: You don't have any utensils on the desert?

LEE: Nah, I'm fresh out.

AUSTIN (*to* LEE): What're you doing?

MOM: Well some of those are very old. Bone China.

LEE: I'm tired of eatin' outa' my bare hands, ya' know. It's not civilized.

AUSTIN (*to* LEE): What're you doing? We made a deal!

MOM: Couldn't you borrow the plastic ones instead? I have plenty of plastic ones.

LEE (*as he stacks plates*): It's not the same. Plastic's not the same at all. What I need is somethin' authentic. Somethin' to keep me in touch. It's easy to get outa' touch out there. Don't worry I'll get em' back to ya'.

[AUSTIN rushes up to LEE, grabs him by shoulders]

AUSTIN: You can't just drop the whole thing, Lee!

[LEE turns, pushes AUSTIN in the chest knocking him backwards into the alcove, MOM watches numbly, LEE returns to collecting the plates, silverware, etc.]

MOM: You boys shouldn't fight in the house. Go out-
　　side and fight.
LEE: I'm not fightin'. I'm leavin'.
MOM: There's been enough damage done already.
LEE (*his back to* AUSTIN *and* MOM, *stacking dishes on
　　counter*): I'm clearin' outa' here once and for
　　all. All this town does is drive a man insane.
　　Look what it's done to Austin there. I'm not
　　lettin' that happen to me. Sell myself down the
　　river. No sir. I'd rather be a hundred miles
　　from nowhere than let that happen to me.

[during this AUSTIN has picked up the ripped-out phone from the floor and wrapped the cord tightly around both his hands, he lunges at LEE whose back is still to him, wraps the cord around LEE's neck, plants a foot in LEE's back and pulls back on the cord, tightening it, LEE chokes desperately, can't speak and can't reach AUSTIN with his arms, AUSTIN keeps applying pressure on LEE's back with his foot, bending him into the sink, MOM watches)

AUSTIN (*tightening cord*): You're not goin' anywhere!
　　You're not takin' anything with you. You're
　　not takin' my car! You're not takin' the dishes!
　　You're not takin' anything! You're stayin' right
　　here!
MOM: You'll have to stop fighting in the house.
　　There's plenty of room outside to fight. You've
　　got the whole outdoors to fight in.

[LEE tries to tear himself away, he crashes across the stage like an enraged bull dragging AUSTIN with him, he snorts and bellows but AUSTIN hangs on and manages to keep clear of LEE's attempts to grab him, they crash into the table, to the floor, LEE is face down thrashing wildly and choking, AUSTIN pulls cord tighter, stands with one foot planted on LEE's back and the cord stretched taut]

AUSTIN (*holding cord*): Gimme back my keys, Lee!
　　Take the keys out! Take 'em out!

[LEE desperately tries to dig in his pockets, searching for the car keys, MOM moves closer]

MOM (*calmly to* AUSTIN): You're not killing him are
　　you?
AUSTIN: I don't know. I don't know if I'm killing him.
　　I'm stopping him. That's all. I'm just stopping
　　him.

[LEE thrashes but AUSTIN is relentless]

MOM: You oughta' let him breathe a little bit.
AUSTIN: Throw the keys out, Lee!

[LEE finally gets keys out and throws them on floor but out of AUSTIN's reach, AUSTIN keeps pressure on cord, pulling LEE's neck back, LEE gets one hand to the cord but can't relieve the pressure]

Reach me those keys would ya', Mom.
MOM (*not moving*): Why are you doing this to him?
AUSTIN: Reach me the keys!
MOM: Not until you stop choking him.
AUSTIN: I can't stop choking him! He'll kill me if I
　　stop choking him!
MOM: He won't kill you. He's your brother.
AUSTIN: Just get me the keys would ya'!

[pause. MOM picks keys up off floor, hands them to AUSTIN]

AUSTIN (*to* MOM): Thanks.
MOM: Will you let him go now?
AUSTIN: I don't know. He's not gonna' let me get
　　outa' here.
MOM: Well you can't kill him.
AUSTIN: I can kill him! I can easily kill him. Right
　　now. Right here. All I gotta' do is just tighten
　　up. See? (*he tightens cord,* LEE *thrashes wildly,*
　　AUSTIN *releases pressure a little, maintaining con-
　　trol*) Ya' see that?
MOM: That's a savage thing to do.
AUSTIN: Yeah well don't tell me I can't kill him
　　because I can. I can just twist. I can just keep
　　twisting. (AUSTIN *twists the cord tighter,* LEE
　　weakens, his breathing changes to a short rasp)
MOM: Austin!

[AUSTIN relieves pressure, LEE breathes easier but AUSTIN keeps him under control]

AUSTIN (*eyes on* LEE, *holding cord*): I'm goin' to the
　　desert. There's nothing stopping me. I'm going
　　by myself to the desert.

[MOM moving toward her luggage]

MOM: Well, I'm going to go check into a motel. I
　　can't stand this anymore.
AUSTIN: Don't go yet!

[MOM pauses]

MOM: I can't stay here. This is worse than being
　　homeless.
AUSTIN: I'll get everything fixed up for you, Mom. I
　　promise. Just stay for a while.
MOM (*picking up luggage*): You're going to the desert.

AUSTIN: Just wait!

[LEE thrashes, AUSTIN subdues him, MOM watches holding luggage, pause]

MOM: It was the worst feeling being up there. In Alaska. Staring out a window. I never felt so desperate before. That's why when I saw that article on Picasso I thought—

AUSTIN: Stay here, Mom. This is where you live.

[she looks around the stage]

MOM: I don't recognize it at all.

[she exits with luggage, AUSTIN makes a move toward her but LEE starts to struggle and AUSTIN subdues him again with cord, pause]

AUSTIN (*holding cord*): Lee? I'll make ya' a deal. You let me get outa' here. Just let me get to my car. All right, Lee? Gimme a little headstart and I'll turn you loose. Just gimme a little headstart. All right?

[LEE makes no response, AUSTIN slowly releases tension cord, still nothing from LEE]

AUSTIN: Lee?

[LEE is motionless, AUSTIN very slowly begins to stand, still keeping a tenuous hold on the cord and his eyes riveted to LEE for any sign of movement, AUSTIN slowly drops the cord and stands, he stares down at LEE who appears to be dead]

AUSTIN (*whispers*): Lee?

[pause, AUSTIN considers, looks toward exit, back to LEE, then makes a small movement as if to leave. Instantly LEE is on his feet and moves toward exit, blocking AUSTIN's escape. They square off to each other, keeping a distance between them. Pause, a single coyote heard in distance, lights fade softly into moonlight, the figures of the brothers now appear to be caught in a vast desert-like landscape, they are very still but watchful for the next move, lights go slowly to black as the after-image of the brothers pulses in the dark, coyote fades]

THE END

MARSHA NORMAN (b. 1947)

Marsha Norman (neé Williams) was born and raised in Louisville, Kentucky, where she was apparently brought up under strict conditions by her mother. Norman remembers her mother as a domineering woman who refused on religious grounds to allow a television in her house, who never let the radio be turned on, who forbade her daughter to go to movies or to play with neighborhood children, and who permitted no raising of the voice in anger or conflict. Perhaps, then, it is no wonder that in Norman's work as a dramatist she touches on recurrent themes of confinement, repression, and both a yearning for and distrust of freedom. Her mother did allow young Marsha to read, to write stories, to play the piano, and to attend children's productions of the Actors Theater of Louisville, one of the most active regional theaters in the country at the time. After high school, Norman attended Agnes Scott College in Decatur, Georgia, where she majored in philosophy, graduating in 1969. Afterward, she returned to Louisville, eventually marrying her high school English teacher, the first of three marriages. Norman continued her studies, receiving an M.A. from the University of Louisville in 1971, and then went to work at Kentucky Central State Hospital for two years as a teacher of disturbed teenagers. One vicious young woman she taught there proved so violent that the experience gave her nightmares and eventually suggested the central focus of her first play.

Norman went on to work at a school for gifted children, where she taught humanities and performing arts, including filmmaking, from 1973 to 1976. During this time she began to write children's television scripts and musicals, and she was encouraged by Jon Jory, the artistic director of the Actors Theater, to write a play—which he promised to produce. Jory suggested that she focus on a moment in her life when she was really frightened. Norman remembered the vicious thirteen-year-old at the mental hospital and wrote *Getting Out* (1977), which portrays two personas of a woman who has recently been released from an eight-year prison term: an older, mature character, Arlene, who is moving into her new apartment; and the younger, nastier Arlie, who appears as a living memory to engage her older self and other figures from the past in vivid interchanges. The play was an instant success, and by 1978 productions had been mounted not only at the Actors Theater in Louisville but in Los Angeles and New York to enthusiastic acclaim. That year it won the award for the best new play by an American playwright. Norman became playwright-in-residence for the Actors Theater in 1978, and within a year she had completed two successful one-acts, *Third & Oak: The Laundromat* and *Third & Oak: The Pool Hall*. Both of these plays deal with ordinary—even banal—people whose experiences—and clarity of vision about their experiences—make them extraordinary.

In 1983, now living in New York and devoting herself full time to playwriting, Norman wrote *'night, Mother*, which premiered at the American Repertory Theater in Cambridge, Massachusetts, and then opened on Broadway. The play won a number of prizes, including the Pulitzer, and it has been frequently revived. Its depiction of a woman intent on committing suicide as a means of "getting out" of her constricted life with her mother has continued to produce controversy; and whatever the conclusions an audience might make about the subject, the play faces the issue squarely and powerfully.

After *'night, Mother*, Norman's most successful play to date has been *The Secret Garden* (1990), which was adapted from the Frances Hodgson Burnett novel. It was produced on the New York stage in 1991 and won a Tony Award.

'night, Mother

One of the most chilling features of *'night, Mother* is its logic and the sense of inevitability as Jessie, the protagonist, moves to embrace her death. Indeed, the play traces how thoroughly Jessie has arranged for all eventualities; she has prepared for her suicide meticulously and with a cool, clear mind. The climax of the play is not the action of an emotionally distraught or hysterical figure, but rather the action of one who has apparently reasoned out the most effective strategy, one who acts deliberately and decisively. The conflict and the tension in the play arise from the increasing desperation of Jessie's mother, Thelma, whose every attempt to remonstrate with Jessie or to thwart her plan seems already to have been taken into account. Thelma, whom Jessie has had to care for, is cast both as a reason for Jessie's wanting to commit suicide and, at the same time, as the one who must articulate the reasons Jessie should live. In the end her arguments are insufficient, and her own compromises, evasions, and illusions are revealed and stripped away. The two characters are quite literally battling for life.

Although strictly speaking *'night, Mother* is a one-act play, it divides naturally into three parts, or movements, as Norman herself has pointed out. The first movement ends with the elaborate stage direction as Mama looks for a pan to make cocoa, and the second begins with Jessie's "You talk to Agnes today?" The second movement ends after Mama begs, "Don't leave me, Jessie!" with the stage directions having Jessie going to get the box of presents. At the same time, the play follows the classical pattern for tragedy closely and intentionally. Its frame employs the unities of time, place, and action, and it closes off all avenues of hope one by one. In the course of the play both personal decision and fate conspire to push the protagonist closer to doom. Ironically, the alternatives offered by Jessie's mother lead to further revelations and reversals of intention, simply reinforcing Jessie's decision. After Mama reveals her early hiding of Jessie's epileptic seizures, for example, she reveals that Jessie's beloved father had also suffered from them and had passed them down to her. Significantly, he had ended his life in silence, refusing to speak to Mama: "It was his last chance not to talk to me and he took full advantage of it." During this evening of homey chatter, behind which lurks Jessie's grim suicidal determination and Mama's equally grim determination to wheedle, badger, or blackmail her daughter into living (and taking care of her), Jessie discovers the truth about her life in a number of ways, and each discovery edges her closer toward her death. The truth allows her to own her life at last, to control it, and to whisper "'Night Mother" and end it.

'night, Mother trades on realism in a number of ways: in its amazingly accurate surface of colloquial dialogue, in its familiar mother-daughter conflicts and comforts, and in its living-room-and-kitchen set with the door to Jessie's bedroom looming more and more ominously in the background. Norman's stage directions stress realism as well, insisting, for example, that "Under no circumstances should the set and its dressing make a judgment about the intelligence or taste of Jessie and Mama. It should simply indicate that they are very specific real people who happen to live in a particular part of the country." Yet this very particularity, which steers clear of class issues or explicit arguments about gender, gives the play a universal appeal. The kitchen is at once localized and ordinary, while the characters' common chatter in fact is bent on the intensely serious questions of owning one's life and of suicide, questions common to all.

Norman never lets the audience lose sight of where the play is heading, either. Some of the most touching interchanges take place, for instance, at the same time as Jessie is cleaning her father's gun, making sure the pistol is fully operational for the final event. Like *Hedda Gabler*, the play ends with the protagonist deliberately leaving the parlor for the unseen room where the anticipated—and dreaded—shot will ring out, and in both plays suicide is a means of escaping intolerable confinement. But 'night, Mother suggests that the final gunshot is not a sound that signifies desperate failure or pathetic trauma, but rather the sound of triumph, self-assertion, and ultimate self-determination.

'night Mother

Marsha Norman

CHARACTERS

JESSIE CATES, in her late thirties or early forties, is pale and vaguely unsteady physically. It is only in the last year that Jessie has gained control of her mind and body, and tonight she is determined to hold on to that control. She wears pants and a long black sweater with deep pockets, which contain scraps of paper, and there may be a pencil behind her ear or a pen clipped to one of the pockets of the sweater.

As a rule, Jessie doesn't feel much like talking. Other people have rarely found her quirky sense of humor amusing. She has a peaceful energy on this night, a sense of purpose, but is clearly aware of the time passing moment by moment. Oddly enough, Jessie has never been as communicative or as enjoyable as she is on this evening, but we must know she has not always been this way. There is a familiarity between these two women that comes from having lived together for a long time. There is a shorthand to the talk and a sense of routine comfort in the way they relate to each other physically. Naturally, there are also routine aggravations.

THELMA CATES, "Mama," is Jessie's mother, in her late fifties or early sixties. She has begun to feel her age and so takes it easy when she can, or when it serves her purpose to let someone help her. But she speaks quickly and enjoys talking. She believes that things *are* what she says they are. Her sturdiness is more a mental quality than a physical one, finally. She is chatty and nosy, and this is *her* house.

The play takes place in a relatively new house built way out on a country road, with a living room and connecting kitchen, and a center hall that leads off to the bedrooms. A pull cord in the hall ceiling releases a ladder which leads to the attic. One of these bedrooms opens directly onto the hall, and its entry should be visible to everyone in the audience. It should be, in fact, the focal point of the entire set, and the lighting should make it disappear completely at times and draw the entire set into it at others. It is a point of both threat and promise. It is an ordinary door that opens onto absolute nothingness. That door is the point of all the action, and the utmost care should be given to its design and construction.

The living room is cluttered with magazines and needlework catalogues, ashtrays and candy dishes. Examples of Mama's needlework are everywhere—pillows, afghans, and quilts, doilies and rugs, and they are quite nice examples. The house is more comfortable than messy, but there is quite a lot to keep in place here. It is more personal than charming. It is not quaint. Under no circumstances should the set and its dressing make a judgment about the intelligence or taste of Jessie and Mama. It should simply indicate that they are very specific real people who happen to live in a particular part of the country. Heavy accents, which would further distance the audience from Jessie and Mama, are also wrong.

The time is the present, with the action beginning about 8:15. Clocks onstage in the kitchen and on a table in the living room should run throughout the performance and be visible to the audience.

There will be no intermission.

[MAMA *stretches to reach the cupcakes in a cabinet in the kitchen. She can't see them, but she can feel around for them, and she's eager to have one, so she's working pretty hard at it. This may be the most serious exercise* MAMA *ever gets. She finds a cupcake, the coconut-covered, raspberry-and-marshmallow-filled kind known as a snowball, but sees that there's one missing from the package. She calles to* JESSIE, *who is apparently somewhere else in the house.*]

MAMA (*Unwrapping the cupcake*): Jessie, it's the last snowball, sugar. Put it on the list, O.K.? And we're out of Hershey bars, and where's that peanut brittle? I think maybe Dawson's been in it again. I ought to put a big mirror on the refrigerator door. That'll keep him out of my treats, won't it? You hear me, honey? (*Then more to herself*) I hate it when the coconut falls off. Why does the coconut fall off?

[JESSIE *enters from her bedroom, carrying a stack of newspapers*]

JESSIE: We got any old towels?

MAMA: There you are!

JESSIE (*Holding a towel that was on the stack of newspapers*): Towels you don't want anymore. (*Picking up* MAMA's *snowball wrapper*) How about this swimming towel Loretta gave us? Beach towel, that's the name of it. You want it? (MAMA *shakes her head no*)

MAMA: What have you been doing in there?

JESSIE: And a big piece of plastic like a rubber sheet or something. Garbage bags would do if there's enough.

MAMA: Don't go making a big mess, Jessie. It's eight o'clock already.

JESSIE: Maybe an old blanket or towels we got in a soap box sometime?

MAMA: I said don't make a mess. Your hair is black enough, hon.

JESSIE (*Continuing to search the kitchen cabinets, finding two or three more towels to add to her stack*): It's not for my hair, Mama. What about some old pillows anywhere, or a foam cushion out of a yard chair would be real good.

MAMA: You haven't forgot what night it is, have you? (*Holding up her fingernails*) They're all chipped, see? I've been waiting all week, Jess. It's Saturday night, sugar.

JESSIE: I know. I got it on the schedule.

MAMA (*Crossing to the living room*): You want me to wash 'em now or are you making your mess first? (*Looking at the snowball*) We're out of these. Did I say that already?

JESSIE: There's more coming tomorrow. I ordered you a whole case.

MAMA (*Checking the* TV Guide): A whole case will go stale, Jessie.

JESSIE: They can go in the freezer till you're ready for them. Where's Daddy's gun?

MAMA: In the attic.

JESSIE: Where in the attic? I looked your whole nap and couldn't find it anywhere.

MAMA: One of his shoeboxes, I think.

JESSIE: Full of shoes. I looked already.

MAMA: Well, you didn't look good enough, then. There's that box from the ones he wore to the hospital. When he died, they told me I could have them back, but I never did like those shoes.

JESSIE (*Pulling them out of her pocket*): I found the bullets. They were in an old milk can.

MAMA (*As* JESSIE *starts for the hall*): Dawson took the shotgun, didn't he? Hand me that basket, hon.

JESSIE (*Getting the basket for her*): Dawson better not've taken that pistol.

MAMA (*Stopping her again*): Now my glasses, please. (JESSIE *returns to get the glasses*) I told him to take those rubber boots, too, but he said they were for fishing. I told him to take up fishing.

(JESSIE *reaches for the cleaning spray, and cleans* MAMA's *glasses for her*)

JESSIE: He's just too lazy to climb up there, Mama. Or maybe he's just being smart. That floor's not very steady.

MAMA (*Getting out a piece of knitting*): It's not a floor at all, hon, it's a board now and then. Measure this for me. I need six inches.

JESSIE (*As she measures*): Dawson could probably use some of those clothes up there. Somebody should have them. You ought to call the Salvation Army before the whole thing falls in on you. Six inches exactly.

MAMA: It's plenty safe! As long as you don't go up there.

JESSIE (*Turning to go again*): I'm careful.

MAMA: What do you want the gun for, Jess?

JESSIE (*Not returning this time. Opening the ladder in the hall*): Protection. (*She steadies the ladder as* MAMA *talks*)

MAMA: You take the TV way too serious, hon. I've never seen a criminal in my life. This is way too far to come for what's out here to steal. Never seen a one.

JESSIE (*Taking her first step up*): Except for Ricky.

MAMA: Ricky is mixed up. That's not a crime.

JESSIE: Get your hands washed. I'll be right back. And get 'em real dry. You dry your hands till I get back or it's no go, all right?

MAMA: I thought Dawson told you not to go up those stairs.

JESSIE (*Going up*): He did.

MAMA: I don't like the idea of a gun, Jess.

JESSIE (*Calling down from the attic*): Which shoebox, do you remember?

MAMA: Black.

JESSIE: The box was black?

MAMA: The shoes were black.

JESSIE: That doesn't help much, Mother.

MAMA: I'm not trying to help, sugar. (*No answer*) We don't have anything anybody'd want, Jessie. I mean, I don't even want what we got, Jessie.

JESSIE: Neither do I. Wash your hands. (MAMA *gets up and crosses to stand under the ladder*)

MAMA: You come down from there before you have a fit. I can't come up and get you, you know.

JESSIE: I know.

MAMA: We'll just hand it over to them when they come, how's that? Whatever they want, the criminals.

JESSIE: That's a good idea, Mama.

MAMA: Ricky will grow out of this and be a real fine boy, Jess. But I have to tell you, I wouldn't want Ricky to know we had a gun in the house.

JESSIE: Here it is. I found it.

MAMA: It's just something Ricky's going through. Maybe he's in with some bad people. He just needs some time, sugar. He'll get back in school or get a job or one day you'll get a call and he'll say he's sorry for all the trouble he's caused and invite you out for supper some-place dress-up.

JESSIE (*Coming back down the steps*): Don't worry. It's not for him, it's for me.

MAMA: I didn't think you would shoot your own boy, Jessie. I know you've felt like it, well, we've all felt like shooting somebody, but we don't do it. I just don't think we need . . .

JESSIE (*Interrupting*): Your hands aren't washed. Do you want a manicure or not?

MAMA: Yes, I do, but . . .

JESSIE (*Crossing to the chair*): Then wash your hands

and don't talk to me any more about Ricky. Those two rings he took were the last valuable things *I* had, so now he's started in on other people, door to door. I hope they put him away sometime. I'd turn him in myself if I knew where he was.

MAMA: You don't mean that.

JESSIE: Every word. Wash your hands and that's the last time I'm telling you.

[*JESSIE sits down with the gun and starts cleaning it, pushing the cylinder out, checking to see that the chambers and barrel are empty, then putting some oil on a small patch of cloth and pushing it through the barrel with the push rod that was in the box. MAMA goes to the kitchen and washes her hands, as instructed, trying not to show her concern about the gun*]

MAMA: I shoulda got you to bring down that milk can. Agnes Fletcher sold hers to somebody with a flea market for forty dollars apiece.

JESSIE: I'll go back and get it in a minute. There's a wagon wheel up there, too. There's even a churn. I'll get it all if you want.

MAMA(*Coming over, now, taking over now*): What are you doing?

JESSIE: The barrel has to be clean, Mama. Old powder, dust gets in it . . .

MAMA: What for?

JESSIE: I told you.

MAMA (*Reaching for the gun*): And I told you, we don't get criminals out here.

JESSIE (*Quickly pulling it to her*): And I told you . . . (*Then trying to be calm*) The gun is for me.

MAMA: Well, you can have it if you want. When I die, you'll get it all, anyway.

JESSIE: I'm going to kill myself, Mama.

MAMA (*Returning to the sofa*): Very funny. Very funny.

JESSIE: I am.

MAMA: You are not! Don't even say such a thing, Jessie.

JESSIE: How would you know if I didn't say it? You want it to be a surprise? You're lying there in your bed or maybe you're just brushing your teeth and you hear this . . . noise down the hall?

MAMA: Kill yourself.

JESSIE: Shoot myself. In a couple of hours.

MAMA: It must be time for your medicine.

JESSIE: Took it already.

MAMA: What's the matter with you?

JESSIE: Not a thing. Feel fine.

MAMA: You feel fine. You're just going to kill yourself.

JESSIE: Waited until I felt good enough, in fact.

MAMA: Don't make jokes, Jessie. I'm too old for jokes.

JESSIE: It's not a joke, Mama.

[*MAMA watches for a moment in silence*]

MAMA: That gun's no good, you know. He broke it right before he died. He dropped it in the mud one day.

JESSIE: Seems O.K. (*She spins the chamber, cocks the pistol, and pulls the trigger. The gun is not yet loaded, so all we hear is the click, but it will definitely work. It's also obvious that JESSIE knows her way around a gun. MAMA cannot speak*) I had Cecil's all ready in there, just in case I couldn't find this one, but I'd rather use Daddy's.

MAMA: Those bullets are at least fifteen years old.

JESSIE (*Pulling out another box*): These are from last week.

MAMA: Where did you get those?

JESSIE: Feed store Dawson told me about.

MAMA: Dawson!

JESSIE: I told him I was worried about prowlers. He said he thought it was a good idea. He told me what kind to ask for.

MAMA: If he had any idea . . .

JESSIE: He took it as a compliment. He thought I might be taking an interest in things. He got through telling me all about the bullets and then he said we ought to talk like this more often.

MAMA: And where was I while this was going on?

JESSIE: On the phone with Agnes. About the milk can, I guess. Anyway, I asked Dawson if he thought they'd send me some bullets and he said he'd just call for me, because he knew they'd send them if he told them to. And he was absolutely right. Here they are.

MAMA: How could he do that?

JESSIE: Just trying to help, Mama.

MAMA: And then I told you where the gun was.

JESSIE (*Smiling, enjoying this joke*): See? Everybody's doing what they can.

MAMA: You told me it was for protection!

JESSIE: It *is*! I'm still doing your nails, though. Want to try that new Chinaberry color?

MAMA: Well, I'm calling Dawson right now. We'll just see what he has to say about this little stunt.

JESSIE: Dawson doesn't have any more to do with this.

MAMA: He's your brother.

JESSIE: And that's all.

MAMA (*Stands up, moves toward the phone*): Dawson will put a stop to this. Yes he will. He'll take the gun away.

JESSIE: If you call him, I'll just have to do it before he gets here. Soon as you hang up the phone, I'll just walk in the bedroom and lock the door.

Dawson will get here just in time to help you clean up. Go ahead, call him. Then call the police. Then call the funeral home. Then call Loretta and see if *she'll* do your nails.

MAMA: You will not! This is crazy talk, Jessie!

[MAMA *goes directly to the telephone and starts to dial, but* JESSIE *is fast, coming up behind her and taking the receiver out of her hand, putting it back down*]

JESSIE (*Firm and quiet*): I said no. This is private. Dawson is not invited.

MAMA: Just me.

JESSIE: I don't want anybody else over here. Just you and me. If Dawson comes over, it'll make me feel stupid for not doing it ten years ago.

MAMA: I think we better call the doctor. Or how about the ambulance. You like that one driver, I know. What's his name, Timmy? Get you somebody to talk to.

JESSIE (*Going back to her chair*): I'm through talking, Mama. You're it. No more.

MAMA: We're just going to sit around like every other night in the world and then you're going to kill yourself? (JESSIE *doesn't answer*) You'll miss. (*Again there is no response*) You'll just wind up a vegetable. How would you like that? Shoot your ear off? You know what the doctor said about getting excited. You'll cock the pistol and have a fit.

JESSIE: I think I can kill myself, Mama.

MAMA: You're not going to kill yourself, Jessie. You're not even upset! (JESSIE *smiles, or laughs quietly, and* MAMA *tries a different approach*) People don't really kill themselves, Jessie. No, mam, doesn't make sense, unless you're retarded or deranged, and you're as normal as they come, Jessie, for the most part. We're all *afraid* to die.

JESSIE: I'm not, Mama. I'm cold all the time, anyway.

MAMA: That's ridiculous.

JESSIE: It's exactly what I want. It's dark and quiet.

MAMA: So is the back yard, Jessie! Close your eyes. Stuff cotton in your ears. Take a nap! It's quiet in your room. I'll leave the TV off all night.

JESSIE: So quiet I don't know it's quiet. So nobody can get me.

MAMA: You don't know what dead is like. It might not be quiet at all. What if it's like an alarm clock and you can't wake up so you can't shut it off. Ever.

JESSIE: Dead is everybody and everything I ever knew, gone. Dead is dead quiet.

MAMA: It's a sin. You'll go to hell.

JESSIE: Uh-huh.

MAMA: You will!

JESSIE: Jesus was a suicide, if you ask me.

MAMA: You'll go to hell just for saying that. Jessie!

JESSIE (*With genuine surprise*): I didn't know I thought that.

MAMA: Jessie!

[JESSIE *doesn't answer. She puts the now-loaded gun back in the box and crosses to the kitchen. But* MAMA *is afraid she's headed for the bedroom*]

MAMA (*In a panic*): You can't use my towels! They're my towels. I've had them for a long time. I like my towels.

JESSIE: I asked you if you wanted that swimming towel and you said you didn't.

MAMA: And you can't use your father's gun, either. It's mine now, too. And you can't do it in my house.

JESSIE: Oh, come on.

MAMA: No. You can't do it. I won't let you. The house is in my name.

JESSIE: I have to go in the bedroom and lock the door behind me so they won't arrest you for killing me. They'll probably test your hands for gunpowder, anyway, but you'll pass.

MAMA: Not in my house!

JESSIE: If I'd known you were going to act like this, I wouldn't have told you.

MAMA: How am I supposed to act? Tell you to go ahead? O.K. by me, sugar? Might try it myself. What took you so long?

JESSIE: There's just no point in fighting me over it, that's all. Want some coffee?

MAMA: Your birthday's coming up, Jessie. Don't you want to know what we got you?

JESSIE: You got me dusting powder, Loretta got me a new housecoat, pink probably, and Dawson got me new slippers, too small, but they go with the robe, he'll say. (MAMA *cannot speak*) Right? (*Apparently* JESSIE *is right*) Be back in a minute.

[JESSIE *takes the gun box, puts it on top of the stack of towels and garbage bags, and takes them into her bedroom.* MAMA, *alone for a moment, goes to the phone, picks up the receiver, looks toward the bedroom, starts to dial, and then replaces the receiver in its cradle as* JESSIE *walks back into the room.* JESSIE *wonders, silently. They have lived together for so long there is very rarely any reason for one to ask what the other was about to do*]

MAMA: I started to, but I didn't. I didn't call him.

JESSIE: Good. Thank you.

MAMA (*Starting over, a new approach*): What's this all about, Jessie?

JESSIE: About?

[JESSIE *now begins the next task she had "on the*

schedule," which is refilling all the candy jars, taking *the empty papers out of the boxes of chocolates, etc.* MAMA *generally snitches when* JESSIE *does this. Not tonight, though. Nevertheless,* JESSIE *offers]*

MAMA: What did I do?

JESSIE: Nothing. Want a caramel?

MAMA (*Ignoring the candy*): You're mad at me.

JESSIE: Not a bit. I am worried about you, but I'm going to do what I can before I go. We're not just going to sit around tonight. I made a list of things.

MAMA: What things?

JESSIE: How the washer works. Things like that.

MAMA: I know how the washer works. You put the clothes in. You put the soap in. You turn it on. You wait.

JESSIE: You do something else. You don't just wait.

MAMA: Whatever else you find to do, you're still mainly waiting. The waiting's the worst part of it. The waiting's what you pay somebody else to do, if you can.

JESSIE (*Nodding*): O.K. Where do we keep the soap?

MAMA: I could find it.

JESSIE: See?

MAMA: If you're mad about doing the wash, we can get Loretta to do it.

JESSIE: Oh now, that might be worth staying to see.

MAMA: She'd never in her life, would she?

JESSIE: Nope.

MAMA: What's the matter with her?

JESSIE: She thinks she's better than we are. She's not.

MAMA: Maybe if she didn't wear that yellow all the time.

JESSIE: The washer repair number is on a little card taped to the side of the machine.

MAMA: Loretta doesn't ever have to come over here again. Dawson can just leave her at home when he comes. And we don't ever have to see Dawson either if he bothers you. Does he bother you?

JESSIE: Sure he does. Be sure you clean out the lint tray every time you use the dryer. But don't ever put your house shoes in, it'll melt the soles.

MAMA: What does Dawson do, that bothers you?

JESSIE: He just calls me Jess like he knows who he's talking to. He's always wondering what I do all day. I mean, I wonder that myself, but it's my day, so it's mine to wonder about, not his.

MAMA: Family is just accident, Jessie. It's nothing personal, hon. They don't mean to get on your nerves. They don't even mean to be your family, they just are.

JESSIE: They know too much.

MAMA: About what?

JESSIE: They know things about you, and they learned it before you had a chance to say whether you wanted them to know it or not. They were there when it happened and it don't belong to them, it belongs to you, only they got it. Like my mail-order bra got delivered to their house.

MAMA: By accident!

JESSIE: All the same . . . they opened it. They saw the little rosebuds on it. (*Offering her another candy*) Chewy mint?

MAMA (*Shaking her head no*): What do they know about you? I'll tell them never to talk about it again. Is it Ricky or Cecil or your fits or your hair is falling out or you drink too much coffee or you never go out of the house or what?

JESSIE: I just don't like their talk. The account at the grocery is in Dawson's name when you call. The number's on a whole list of numbers on the back cover of the phone book.

MAMA: Well! Now we're getting somewhere. They're none of them ever setting foot in this house again.

JESSIE: It's not them, Mother. I wouldn't kill myself just to get away from them.

MAMA: You leave the room when they come over, anyway.

JESSIE: I stay as long as I can. Besides, it's you they come to see.

MAMA: That's because I stay in the room when they come.

JESSIE: It's not them.

MAMA: Then what is it?

JESSIE (*Checking the list on her note pad*): The grocery won't deliver on Saturday anymore. And if you want your order the same day, you have to call before ten. And they won't deliver less than fifteen dollars' worth. What I do is tell them what we need and tell them to add on cigarettes until it gets to fifteen dollars.

MAMA: It's Ricky. You're trying to get through to him.

JESSIE: If I thought I could do that, I would stay.

MAMA: Make him sorry he hurt you, then. That's it, isn't it?

JESSIE: He's hurt me, I've hurt him. We're about even.

MAMA: You'll be telling him killing is O.K. with you, you know. Want him to start killing next? Nothing wrong with it. Mom did it.

JESSIE: Only a matter of time, anyway, Mama. When the call comes, you let Dawson handle it.

MAMA: Honey, nothing says those calls are always going to be some new trouble he's into. You could get one that he's got a job, that he's getting married, or how about he's joined the army, wouldn't that be nice?

JESSIE: If you call the Sweet Tooth before you call the grocery, that Susie will take your fudge next door to the grocery and it'll all come out together. Be sure you talk to Susie, though. She won't let them put it in the bottom of a sack like that one time, remember?

MAMA: Ricky could come over, you know. What if he calls us?

JESSIE: It's not Ricky, Mama.

MAMA: Or anybody could call us, Jessie.

JESSIE: Not on Saturday night, Mama.

MAMA: Then what is it? Are you sick? If your gums are swelling again, we can get you to the dentist in the morning.

JESSIE: No. Can you order your medicine or do you want Dawson to? I've got a note to him. I'll add that to it if you want.

MAMA: Your eyes don't look right. I thought so yesterday.

JESSIE: That was just the ragweed. I'm not sick.

MAMA: Epilepsy is sick, Jessie.

JESSIE: It won't kill me. (*A pause*) If it would, I wouldn't have to.

MAMA: You don't *have* to.

JESSIE: No, I don't. That's what I like about it.

MAMA: Well, I won't let you!

JESSIE: It's not up to you.

MAMA: Jessie!

JESSIE: I want to hang a big sign around my neck, like Daddy's on the barn. GONE FISHING.

MAMA: You don't like it here.

JESSIE (*Smiling*): Exactly.

MAMA: I meant here in my house.

JESSIE: I know you did.

MAMA: You never should have moved back in here with me. If you'd kept your little house or found another place when Cecil left you, you'd have made some new friends at least. Had a life to lead. Had your own things around you. Give Ricky a place to come see you. You never should've come here.

JESSIE: Maybe.

MAMA: But I didn't force you, did I?

JESSIE: If it was a mistake, we made it together. You took me in. I appreciate that.

MAMA: You didn't have any business being by yourself right then, but I can see how you might want a place of your own. A grown woman should . . .

JESSIE: Mama . . . I'm just not having a very good time and I don't have any reason to think it'll get anything but worse. I'm tired. I'm hurt. I'm sad. I feel used.

MAMA: Tired of what?

JESSIE: It all.

MAMA: What does that mean?

JESSIE: I can't say it any better.

MAMA: Well, you'll have to say it better because I'm not letting you alone till you do. What were

those other things? Hurt . . . (*Before* JESSIE *can answer*) You had this all ready to say to me, didn't you? Did you write this down? How long have you been thinking about this?

JESSIE: Off and on, ten years. On all the time, since Christmas.

MAMA: What happened at Christmas?

JESSIE: Nothing.

MAMA: So why Christmas?

JESSIE: That's it. On the nose.

[A pause. MAMA *knows exactly what* JESSIE *means. She was there, too, after all]*

JESSIE (*Putting the candy sacks away*): See where all this is? Red hots up front, sour balls and horehound mixed together in this one sack. New packages of toffee and licorice right in back there.

MAMA: Go back to your list. You're hurt by what?

JESSIE (MAMA *knows perfectly well*): Mama . . .

MAMA: O.K. Sad about what? There's nothing real sad going on right now. If it was after your divorce or something, that would make sense.

JESSIE (*Looking at her list, then opening the drawer*): Now, this drawer has everything in it that there's no better place for. Extension cords, batteries for the radio, extra lighters, sandpaper, masking tape, Elmer's glue, thumbtacks, that kind of stuff. The mousetraps are under the sink, but you call Dawson if you've got one and let him do it.

MAMA: Sad about what?

JESSIE: The way things are.

MAMA: Not good enough. What things?

JESSIE: Oh, everything from you and me to Red China.

MAMA: I think we can leave the Chinese out of this.

JESSIE (*Crosses back into the living room*): There's extra light bulbs in a box in the hall closet. And we've got a couple of packages of fuses in the fuse box. There's candles and matches in the top of the broom closet, but if the lights go out, just call Dawson and sit tight. But don't open the refrigerator door. Things will stay cool in there as long as you keep the door shut.

MAMA: I asked you a question.

JESSIE: I read the paper. I don't like how things are. And they're not any better out there than they are in here.

MAMA: If you're doing this because of the newspapers, I can sure fix that!

JESSIE: There's just more of it on TV.

MAMA (*Kicking the television set*): Take it out, then!

JESSIE: You wouldn't do that.

MAMA: Watch me.

JESSIE: What would you do all day?

MAMA (*Desperately*): Sing. (JESSIE *laughs*) I would, too. You want to watch? I'll sing till morning to keep you alive, Jessie, please!

JESSIE: No. (*Then affectionately*) It's a funny idea, though. What do you sing?

MAMA (*Has no idea how to answer this*): We've got a good life here!

JESSIE (*Going back into the kitchen*): I called this morning and canceled the papers, except for Sunday, for your puzzles; you'll still get that one.

MAMA: Let's get another dog, Jessie! You liked a big dog, now, didn't you? That King dog, didn't you?

JESSIE (*Washing her hands*): I did like that King dog, yes.

MAMA: I'm so dumb. He's the one run under the tractor.

JESSIE: That makes him dumb, not you.

MAMA: For bringing it up.

JESSIE: It's O.K. Handi-Wipes and sponges under the sink.

MAMA: We could get a new dog and keep him in the house. Dogs are cheap!

JESSIE (*Getting big pill jars out of the cabinet*): No.

MAMA: Something for you to take care of.

JESSIE: I've had you, Mama.

MAMA (*Frantically starting to fill pill bottles*): You do too much for me. I can fill pill bottles all day, Jessie, and change the shelf paper and wash the floor when I get through. You just watch me. You don't have to do another thing in this house if you don't want to. You don't have to take care of me, Jessie.

JESSIE: I know that. You've just been letting me do it so I'll have something to do, haven't you?

MAMA (*Realizing this was a mistake*): I don't do it as well as you. I just meant if it tires you out or makes you feel used . . .

JESSIE: Mama, I know you used to ride the bus. Riding the bus and it's hot and bumpy and crowded and too noisy and more than anything in the world you want to get off and the only reason in the world you don't get off is it's still fifty blocks from where you're going? Well, I can get off right now if I want to, because even if I ride fifty more years and get off then, it's the same place when I step down to it. Whenever I feel like it, I can get off. As soon as I've had enough, it's my stop. I've had enough.

MAMA: You're feeling sorry for yourself!

JESSIE: The plumber's helper is under the sink, too.

MAMA: You're not having a good time! Whoever promised you a good time? Do you think I've had a good time?

JESSIE: I think you're pretty happy, yeah. You have

things you like to do.

MAMA: Like what?

JESSIE: Like crochet.

MAMA: I'll teach you to crochet.

JESSIE: I can't do any of that nice work, Mama.

MAMA: Good time don't come looking for you, Jessie. You could work some puzzles or put in a garden or go to the store. Let's call a taxi and go to the A&P!

JESSIE: I shopped you up for about two weeks already. You're not going to need toilet paper till Thanksgiving.

MAMA (*Interrupting*): You're acting like some little brat, Jessie. You're mad and everybody's boring and you don't have anything to do and you don't like me and you don't like going out and you don't like staying in and you never talk on the phone and you don't watch TV and you're miserable and it's your own sweet fault.

JESSIE: And it's time I did something about it.

MAMA: Not something like killing yourself. Something like . . . buying us all new dishes! I'd like that. Or maybe the doctor would let you get a driver's license now, or I know what let's do right this minute, let's rearrange the furniture.

JESSIE: I'll do that. If you want. I always thought if the TV was somewhere else, you wouldn't get such a glare on it during the day. I'll do whatever you want before I go.

MAMA (*Badly frightened by those words*): You could get a job!

JESSIE: I took that telephone sales job and I didn't even make enough money to pay the phone bill, and I tried to work at the gift shop at the hospital and they said I made people real uncomfortable smiling at them the way I did.

MAMA: You could keep books. You kept your dad's books.

JESSIE: But nobody ever checked them.

MAMA: When he died, they checked them.

JESSIE: And that's when they took the books away from me.

MAMA: That's because without him there wasn't any business, Jessie!

JESSIE (*Putting the pill bottles away*): You know I couldn't work. I can't do anything. I've never been around people my whole life except when I went to the hospital. I could have a seizure any time. What good would a job do? The kind of job I could get would make me feel worse.

MAMA: Jessie!

JESSIE: It's true!

MAMA: It's what you think is true!

JESSIE (*Struck by the clarity of that*): That's right. It's what I think is true.

MAMA (*Hysterically*): But I can't do anything about
that!

JESSIE (*Quietly*): No. You can't. (MAMA *slumps, if not
physically, at least emotionally*) And I can't do
anything either, about my life, to change it,
make it better, make me feel better about it.
Like it better, make it work. But I can stop it.
Shut it down, turn it off like the radio when
there's nothing on I want to listen to. It's all I
really have that belongs to me and I'm going
to say what happens to it. And it's going to
stop. And I'm going to stop it. So. Let's just
have a good time.

MAMA: Have a good time.

JESSIE: We can't go on fussing all night. I mean, I
could ask you things I always wanted to know
and you could make me some hot chocolate.
The old way.

MAMA (*In despair*): It takes cocoa, Jessie.

JESSIE (*Gets it out of the cabinet*): I bought cocoa,
Mama. And I'd like to have a caramel apple
and do your nails.

MAMA: You didn't eat a bite of supper.

JESSIE: Does that mean I can't have a caramel apple?

MAMA: Of course not. I mean . . . (*Smiling a little*) Of
course you can have a caramel apple.

JESSIE: I thought I could.

MAMA: I make the best caramel apples in the world.

JESSIE: I know you do.

MAMA: Or used to. And you don't get cocoa like
mine anywhere anymore.

JESSIE: It takes time, I know, but . . .

MAMA: The salt is the trick.

JESSIE: Trouble and everything.

MAMA (*Backing away toward the stove*): It's no trouble.
What trouble? You put it in the pan and stir it
up. All right. Fine. Caramel apples. Cocoa.
O.K.

[*JESSIE walks to the counter to retrieve her cigarettes
as MAMA looks for the right pan. There are brief near-
smiles, and maybe MAMA clears her throat. We have a
truce, for the moment. A genuine but nevertheless
uneasy one. JESSIE, who has been in constant motion
since the beginning, now seems content to sit.*

*MAMA starts looking for a pan to make the
cocoa, getting out all the pans in the cabinets in the
process. It looks like she's making a mess on purpose
to JESSIE will have to put them all away again. MAMA
is buying time, or trying to, and entertaining*]

JESSIE: You talk to Agnes today?

MAMA: She's calling me from a pay phone this week.
God only knows why. She has a perfectly good
Trimline at home.

JESSIE (*Laughing*): Well, how is she?

MAMA: How is she every day, Jessie? Nuts.

JESSIE: Is she really crazy or just silly?

MAMA: No, she's really crazy. She was probably
using the pay phone because she had another
little fire problem at home.

JESSIE: Mother . . .

MAMA: I'm serious! Agnes Fletcher's burned down
every house she ever lived in. Eight fires, and
she's due for a new one any day now.

JESSIE (*Laughing*): No!

MAMA: Wouldn't surprise me a bit.

JESSIE (*Laughing*): Why didn't you tell me this before?
Why isn't she locked up somewhere?

MAMA: 'Cause nobody ever got hurt, I guess. Agnes
woke everybody up to watch the fires as soon
as she set 'em. One time she set out porch
chairs and served lemonade.

JESSIE (*Shaking her head*): Real lemonade?

MAMA: The houses they lived in, you knew they
were going to fall down anyway, so why wait
for it, is all I could ever make out about it.
Agnes likes a feeling of accomplishment.

JESSIE: Good for her.

MAMA (*Finding the pan she wants*): Why are you asking about Agnes? One cup or two?

JESSIE: One. She's your friend. No marshmallows.

MAMA (*Getting the milk, etc.*): You have to have
marshmallows. That's the old way, Jess. Two
or three? Three is better.

JESSIE: Three, then. Her whole house burns up? Her
clothes and pillows and everything? I'm not
sure I believe this.

MAMA: When she was a girl, Jess, not now. Long
time ago. But she's still got it in her, I'm sure
of it.

JESSIE: She wouldn't burn her house down now.
Where would she go? She can't get Buster to
build her a new one, he's dead. How could she
burn it up?

MAMA: Be exciting, though, if she did. You never
know.

JESSIE: You do too know, Mama. She wouldn't do it.

MAMA (*Forced to admit, but reluctant*): I guess not.

JESSIE: What else? Why does she wear all those whistles around her neck?

MAMA: Why does she have a house full of birds?

JESSIE: I didn't know she had a house full of birds!

MAMA: Well, she does. And she says they just follow
her home. Well, I know for a fact she's still
paying on the last parrot she bought. You gotta
keep your life filled up, she says. She says a lot
of stupid things. (JESSIE *laughs*, MAMA *continues,
convinced she's getting somewhere*) It's all that
okra she eats. You can't just willy-nilly eat okra
two meals a day and expect to get away with
it. Made her crazy.

JESSIE: She really eats okra twice a day? Where does
she get it in the winter?

MAMA: Well, she eats it a lot. Maybe not two meals, but . . .

JESSIE: More than the average person.

MAMA (*Beginning to get irritated*): I don't know how much okra the average person eats.

JESSIE: Do you know how much okra Agnes eats?

MAMA: No.

JESSIE: How many birds does she have?

MAMA: Two.

JESSIE: Then what are the whistles for?

MAMA: They're not real whistles. Just little plastic ones on a necklace she won playing Bingo, and I only told you about it because I thought I might get a laugh out of you for once even if it wasn't the truth, Jessie. Things don't have to be true to talk about 'em, you know.

JESSIE: Why won't she come over here?

[MAMA is suddenly quiet, but the cocoa and milk are in the pan now, so she lights the stove and starts stirring]

MAMA: Well now, what a good idea. We should've had more cocoa. Cocoa is perfect.

JESSIE: Except you don't like milk.

MAMA (*Another attempt, but not as energetic*): I hate milk. Coats your throat as bad as okra. Something just downright disgusting about it.

JESSIE: It's because of me, isn't it?

MAMA: No, Jess.

JESSIE: Yes, Mama.

MAMA: O.K. Yes, then, but she's crazy. She's as crazy as they come. She's a lunatic.

JESSIE: What is it exactly? Did I say something, sometime? Or did she see me have a fit and's afraid I might have another one if she came over, or what?

MAMA: I guess.

JESSIE: You guess what? What's she ever said? She must've given you some reason.

MAMA: Your hands are cold.

JESSIE: What difference does that make?

MAMA: "Like a corpse," she says, "and I'm gonna be one soon enough as it is."

JESSIE: That's crazy.

MAMA: That's Agnes. "Jessie's shook the hand of death and I can't take the chance it's catching, Thelma, so I ain't comin' over, and you can understand or not, but I ain't comin'. I'll come up the driveway, but that's as far as I go."

JESSIE (*Laughing, relieved*): I thought she didn't like me! She's scared of me! How about that! Scared of me.

MAMA: I could make her come over here, Jessie. I could call her up right now and she could bring the birds and come visit. I didn't know you ever thought about her at all. I'll tell her she just has to come and she'll come, all right.

She owes me one.

JESSIE: No, that's all right. I just wondered about it. When I'm in the hospital, does she come over here?

MAMA: Her kitchen is just a tiny thing. When she comes over here, she feels like . . . (*Toning it down a little*) Well, we all like a change of scene, don't we?

JESSIE (*Playing along*): Sure we do. Plus there's no birds diving around.

MAMA: I hate those birds. She says I don't understand them. What's there to understand about birds?

JESSIE: Why Agnes likes them, for one thing. Why they stay with her when they could be outside with the other birds. What their singing means. How they fly. What they think Agnes is.

MAMA: Why do you have to know so much about things, Jessie? There's just not that much *to* things that I could ever see.

JESSIE: That you could ever *tell*, you mean. You didn't have to lie to me about Agnes.

MAMA: I didn't lie. You never asked before!

JESSIE: You lied about setting fire to all those houses and about how many birds she has and how much okra she eats and why she won't come over here. If I have to keep dragging the truth out of you, this is going to take all night.

MAMA: That's fine with me. I'm not a bit sleepy.

JESSIE: Mama . . .

MAMA: All right. Ask me whatever you want. Here.

[They come to an awkward stop, as the cocoa is ready and MAMA pours it into the cups JESSIE has set on the table]

JESSIE (*As MAMA takes her first sip*): Did you love Daddy?

MAMA: No.

JESSIE (*Pleased that MAMA understands the rules better now*): I didn't think so. Were you really fifteen when you married him?

MAMA: The way he told it? I'm sitting in the mud, he comes along, drags me in the kitchen, "She's been there ever since"?

JESSIE: Yes.

MAMA: No. It was a big fat lie, the whole thing. He just thought it was funnier that way. God, this milk in here.

JESSIE: The cocoa helps.

MAMA (*Pleased that they agree on this, at least*): Not enough, though, does it? You can still taste it, can't you?

JESSIE: Yeah, it's pretty bad. I thought it was my memory that was bad, but it's not. It's the milk, all right.

MAMA: It's a real waste of chocolate. You don't have to finish it.

JESSIE (*Putting her cup down*): Thanks, though.

MAMA: I should've known not to make it. I knew you wouldn't like it. You never did like it.

JESSIE: You didn't ever love him, or he did something and you stopped loving him, or what?

MAMA: He felt sorry for me. He wanted a plain country woman and that's what he married, and then he held it against me the rest of my life like I was supposed to change and surprise him somehow. Like I remember this one day he was standing on the porch and I told him to get a shirt on and he went in and got one and then he said, real peaceful, but to the point, "You're right, Thelma. If God had meant for people to go around without any clothes on, they'd have been born that way."

JESSIE (*Sees* MAMA's *hurt*): He didn't mean anything by that, Mama.

MAMA: He never said a word he didn't have to, Jessie. That was probably all he'd said to me all day, Jessie. So if he said it, there was something to it, but I never did figure that one out. What did that mean?

JESSIE: I don't know. I liked him better than you did, but I didn't know him any better.

MAMA: How could I love him, Jessie. I didn't have a thing he wanted. (JESSIE *doesn't answer*) He got his share, though. You loved him enough for both of us. You followed him around like some . . . Jessie, all the man ever did was farm and sit . . . and try to think of somebody to sell the farm to.

JESSIE: Or make me a boyfriend out of pipe cleaners and sit back and smile like the stick man was about to dance and wasn't I going to get a kick out of that. Or sit up with a sick cow all night and leave me a chain of sleepy stick elephants on my bed in the morning.

MAMA: Or just sit.

JESSIE: I liked him sitting. Big old faded blue man in the chair. Quiet.

MAMA: Agnes gets more talk out of her birds than I got from the two of you. He could've had that GONE FISHING sign around his neck in that chair. I saw him stare off at the water. I saw him look at the weather rolling in. I got where I could practically see the boat myself. But you, you knew what he was thinking about and you're going to tell me.

JESSIE: I don't know, Mama! His life, I guess. His corn. His boots. Us. Things. You know.

MAMA: No, I don't know, Jessie! You had those quiet little conversations after supper every night. What were you whispering about?

JESSIE: We weren't whispering, you were just across the room.

MAMA: What did you talk about?

JESSIE: We talked about why black socks are warmer than blue socks. Is that something to go tell Mother? You were just jealous because I'd rather talk to him than wash the dishes with you.

MAMA: I was jealous because you'd rather talk to him than anything! (JESSIE *reaches across the table for the small clock and starts to wind it*) If I had died instead of him, he wouldn't have taken you in like I did.

JESSIE: I wouldn't have expected him to.

MAMA: Then what would you have done?

JESSIE: Come visit.

MAMA: Oh, I see. He died and left you stuck with me and you're mad about it.

JESSIE (*Getting up from the table*): Not anymore. He didn't mean to. I didn't have to come here. We've been through this.

MAMA: He felt sorry for you, too, Jessie, don't kid yourself about that. He said you were a runt and he said it from the day you were born and he said you didn't have a chance.

JESSIE (*Getting the canister of sugar and starting to refill the sugar bowl*): I know he loved me.

MAMA: What if he did? It didn't change anything.

JESSIE: It didn't have to. I miss him.

MAMA: He never really went fishing, you know. Never once. His tackle box was full of chewing tobacco and all he ever did was drive out to the lake and sit in his car. Dawson told me. And Bennie at the bait shop, he told Dawson. They all laughed about it. And he'd come back from fishing and all he'd have to show for it was . . . a whole pipe-cleaner *family*—chickens, pigs, a dog with a bad leg—it was creepy strange. It made me sick to look at them and I hid his pipe cleaners a couple of times but he always had more somewhere.

JESSIE: I thought it might be better for you after he died. You'd get interested in things. Breathe better. Change somehow.

MAMA: Into what? The Queen? A clerk in a shoe store? Why should I? Because he said to? Because you said to? (JESSIE *shakes her head*) Well I wasn't here for his entertainment and I'm not here for yours either, Jessie. I don't know what I'm here for, but then I don't think about it. (*Realizing what all this means*) But I bet you wouldn't be killing yourself if he were still alive. That's a fine thing to figure out, isn't it?

JESSIE (*Filling the honey jar now*): That's not true.

MAMA: Oh no? Then what were you asking about him for? Why did you want to know if I loved him?

JESSIE: I didn't think you did, that's all.

MAMA: Fine then. You were right. Do you feel better now?

JESSIE (*Cleaning the honey jar carefully*): It feels good to be right about it.

MAMA: It didn't matter whether I loved him. It didn't matter to me and it didn't matter to him. And it didn't mean we didn't get along. It wasn't important. We didn't talk about it. (*Sweeping the pots off the cabinet*) Take all these pots out to the porch!

JESSIE: What for?

MAMA: Just leave me this one pan. (*She jerks the silverware drawer open*) Get me one knife, one fork, one big spoon, and the can opener, and put them out where I can get them. (*Starts throwing knives and forks in one of the pans*)

JESSIE: Don't do that! I just straightened that drawer!

MAMA (*Throwing the pan in the sink*): And throw out all the plates and cups. I'll use paper. Loretta can have what she wants and Dawson can sell the rest.

JESSIE (*Calmly*): What are you doing?

MAMA: I'm not going to cook. I never liked it, anyway. I like candy. Wrapped in plastic or coming in sacks. And tuna. I like tuna. I'll eat tuna, thank you.

JESSIE (*Taking the pan out of the sink*): What if you want to make apple butter? You can't make apple butter in that little pan. What if you leave carrots on cooking and burn up that pan?

MAMA: I don't like carrots.

JESSIE: What if the strawberries are good this year and you want to go picking with Agnes.

MAMA: I'll tell her to bring a pan. You said you would do whatever I wanted! I don't want a bunch of pans cluttering up my cabinets I can't get down to, anyway. Throw them out. Every last one.

JESSIE (*Gathering up the pots*): I'm putting them all back in. I'm not taking them to the porch. If you want them, they'll be here. You'll bend down and get them, like you got the one for the cocoa. And if somebody else comes over here to cook, they'll have something to cook in, and that's the end of it!

MAMA: Who's going to come cook here?

JESSIE: Agnes.

MAMA: In my pots. Not on your life.

JESSIE: There's no reason why the two of you couldn't just live here together. Be cheaper for both of you and somebody to talk to. And if the birds bothered you, well, one day when Agnes is out getting her hair done, you could take them all for a walk!

MAMA (*As* JESSIE *straightens the silverware*): So that's why you're pestering me about Agnes. You think you can rest easy if you get me a new

babysitter? Well, I don't want to live with Agnes. I barely want to talk with Agnes. She's just around. We go back, that's all. I'm not letting Agnes near this place. You don't get off as easy as that, child.

JESSIE: O.K., then. It's just something to think about.

MAMA: I don't like things to think about. I like things to go on.

JESSIE (*Closing the silverware drawer*): I want to know what Daddy said to you the night he died. You came storming out of his room and said I could wait it out with him if I wanted to, but you were going to watch *Gunsmoke*. What did he say to you?

MAMA: He didn't have *anything* to say to me, Jessie. That's why I left. He didn't say a thing. It was his last chance not to talk to me and he took full advantage of it.

JESSIE (*After a moment*): I'm sorry you didn't love him. Sorry for you, I mean. He seemed like a nice man.

MAMA (*As* JESSIE *walks to the refrigerator*): Ready for your apple now?

JESSIE: Soon as I'm through here, Mama.

MAMA: You won't like the apple, either. It'll be just like the cocoa. You never liked eating at all, did you? Any of it! What have you been living on all these years, toothpaste?

JESSIE (*As she starts to clean out the refrigerator*): Now, you know the milkman comes on Wednesdays and Saturdays, and he leaves the order blank in an egg box, and you give the bills to Dawson once a month.

MAMA: Do they still make that orangeade?

JESSIE: It's not orangeade, it's just orange.

MAMA: I'm going to get some. I thought they stopped making it. You just stopped ordering it.

JESSIE: You should drink milk.

MAMA: Not anymore, I'm not. That hot chocolate was the last. Hooray.

JESSIE (*Getting the garbage can from under the sink*): I told them to keep delivering a quart a week no matter what you said. I told them you'd run out of Cokes and you'd have to drink it. I told them I knew you wouldn't pour it on the ground . . .

MAMA (*Finishing her sentence*): And you told them you weren't going to be ordering anymore?

JESSIE: I told them I was taking a little holiday and to look after you.

MAMA: And they didn't think something was funny about that? You who doesn't go to the front steps? You, who only sees the driveway looking down from a stretcher passed out cold?

JESSIE (*Enjoying this, but not laughing*): They said it was about time, but why didn't I take you with me? And I said I didn't think you'd want to go, and they said, "Yeah, everybody's got their own idea of vacation."

MAMA: I guess you think that's funny.

JESSIE (*Pulling jars out of the refrigerator*): You know there never was any reason to call the ambulance for me. All they ever did for me in the emergency room was let me wake up. I could've done that here. Now, I'll just call them out and you say yes or no. I know you like pickles. Ketchup?

MAMA: Keep it.

JESSIE: We've had this since last Fourth of July.

MAMA: Keep the ketchup. Keep it all.

JESSIE: Are you going to drink ketchup from the bottle or what? How can you want your food and not want your pots to cook it in? This stuff will all spoil in here, Mother.

MAMA: Nothing I ever did was good enough for you and I want to know why.

JESSIE: That's not true.

MAMA: And I want to know why you've lived here this long feeling the way you do.

JESSIE: You have no earthly idea how I feel.

MAMA: Well, how could I? You're real far back there, Jessie.

JESSIE: Back where?

MAMA: What's it like over there, where you are? Do people always say the right thing or get whatever they want, or what?

JESSIE: What are you talking about?

MAMA: Why do you read the newspaper? Why don't you wear that sweater I made for you? Do you remember how I used to look, or am I just any old woman now? When you have a fit, do you see stars or what? How did you fall off the horse, really? Why did Cecil leave you? Where did you put my old glasses?

JESSIE (*Stunned by* MAMA's *intensity*): They're in the bottom drawer of your dresser in an old Milk of Magnesia box. Cecil left me because he made me choose between him and smoking.

MAMA: Jessie, I know he wasn't that dumb.

JESSIE: I never understood why he hated it so much when it's so good. Smoking is the only thing I know that's always just what you think it's going to be. Just like it was the last time, right there when you want it and real quiet.

MAMA: Your fits made him sick and you know it.

JESSIE: Say seizures, not fits. Seizures.

MAMA: It's the same thing. A seizure in the hospital is a fit at home.

JESSIE: They didn't bother him at all. Except he did feel responsible for it. It *was* his idea to go horseback riding that day. It was his idea I could do *anything* if I just made up my mind to. I fell off the horse because I didn't know

how to hold on. Cecil left for pretty much the same reason.

MAMA: He had a girl, Jessie. I walked right in on them in the toolshed.

JESSIE (*After a moment*): O.K. That's fair. (*Lighting another cigarette*) Was she very pretty?

MAMA: She was Agnes's girl, Carlene. Judge for yourself.

JESSIE (*As she walks to the living room*): I guess you and Agnes had a good talk about that, huh?

MAMA: I never thought he was good enough for you. They moved here from Tennessee, you know.

JESSIE: What are you talking about? You liked him better than I did. You flirted him out here to build your porch or I'd never even met him at all. You thought maybe he'd help you out around the place, come in and get some coffee and talk to you. God knows what you thought. All that curly hair.

MAMA: He's the best carpenter I ever saw. That little house of yours will still be standing at the end of the world, Jessie.

JESSIE: You didn't need a porch, Mama.

MAMA: All right! I wanted you to have a husband.

JESSIE: And I couldn't get one on my own, of course.

MAMA: How were you going to get husband never opening your mouth to a living soul?

JESSIE: So I was quiet about it, so what?

MAMA: So I should have let you just sit here? Sit like your daddy? Sit here?

JESSIE: Maybe.

MAMA: Well, I didn't think so.

JESSIE: Well, what did you know?

MAMA: I never said I knew much. How was I supposed to learn anything living out here? I didn't know enough to do half the things I did in my life. Things happen. You do what you can about them and you see what happens next. I married you off to the wrong man, I admit that. So I took you in when he left. I'm sorry.

JESSIE: He wasn't the wrong man.

MAMA: He didn't love you, Jessie, or he wouldn't have left.

JESSIE: He wasn't the wrong man, Mama. I loved Cecil so much. And I tried to get more exercise and I tried to stay awake. I tried to learn to ride a horse. And I tried to stay outside with him, but he always knew I was trying, so it didn't work.

MAMA: He was a selfish man. He told me once he hated to see people move into his houses after he built them. He knew they'd mess them up.

JESSIE: I loved that bridge he built over the creek in back of the house. It didn't have to be anything special, a couple of boards would have been just fine, but he used that yellow pine and rubbed it so smooth . . .

MAMA: He had responsibilities here. He had a wife and son here and he failed you.

JESSIE: Or that baby bed he built for Ricky. I told him he didn't have to spend so much time on it, but he said it had to last, and the thing ended up weighing two hundred pounds and I couldn't move it. I said, "How long does a baby bed have to last, anyway?" But maybe he thought if it was strong enough, it might keep Ricky a baby.

MAMA: Ricky is too much like Cecil.

JESSIE: He is not. Ricky is as much like me as it's possible for any human to be. We even wear the same size pants. These are his, I think.

MAMA: That's just the same size. That's not you're the same person.

JESSIE: I see it on his face. I hear it when he talks. We look out at the world and we see the same thing: Not Fair. And the only difference between us is Ricky's out there trying to get even. And he knows not to trust anybody and he got it straight from me. And he knows not to try to get work, and guess where he got that. He walks around like there's loose boards in the floor, and you know who laid that floor, I did.

MAMA: Ricky isn't through yet. You don't know how he'll turn out!

JESSIE (*Going back to the kitchen*): Yes I do and so did Cecil. Ricky is the two of us together for all time in too small a space. And we're tearing each other apart, like always, inside that boy, and if you don't see it, then you're just blind.

MAMA: Give him time, Jess.

JESSIE: Oh, he'll have plenty of that. Five years for forgery, ten years for armed assault . . .

MAMA (*Furious*): Stop that! (*Then pleading*) Jessie, Cecil might be ready to try it again, honey, that happens sometimes. Go downtown. Find him. Talk to him. He didn't know what he had in you. Maybe he sees things different now, but you're not going to know that till you go see him. Or call him up! Right now! He might be home.

JESSIE: And say what? Nothing's changed, Cecil, I'd just like to look at you, if you don't mind? No. He loved me, Mama. He just didn't know how things fall down around me like they do. I think he did the right thing. He gave himself another chance, that's all. But I did beg him to take me with him. I did tell him I would leave Ricky and you and everything I loved out here if only he would take me with him, but he couldn't and I understood that. (*Pause*) I wrote that note I showed you. I wrote it. Not Cecil. I said "I'm sorry, Jessie, I can't fix it all for you." I said I'd always love me, not Cecil. But that's

how he felt.

MAMA: Then he should've taken you with him!

JESSIE (*Picking up the garbage bag she has filled*): Mama, you don't pack your garbage when you move.

MAMA: You will not call yourself garbage, Jessie.

JESSIE (*Taking the bag to the big garbage can near the back door*): Just a way of saying it, Mama. Thinking about my list, that's all. (*Opening the can, putting the garbage in, then securing the lid*) Well, a little more than that. I was trying to say it's all right that Cecil left. It was . . . a relief in a way. I never was what he wanted to see, so it was better when he wasn't looking at me all the time.

MAMA: I'll make your apple now.

JESSIE: No thanks. You get the manicure stuff and I'll be right there.

[*JESSIE ties up the big garbage bag in the can and replaces the small garbage bag under the sink, all the time trying desperately to regain her calm. MAMA watches, from a distance, her hand reaching unconsciously for the phone. Then she has a better idea. Or rather she thinks of the only other thing left and is willing to try it. Maybe she is even convinced it will work*]

MAMA: Jessie, I think your daddy had little . . .

JESSIE (*Interrupting her*): Garbage night is Tuesday. Put it out as late as you can. The Davis's dogs get in it if you don't. (*Replacing the garbage bag in the can under the sink*) And keep ordering the heavy black bags. It doesn't pay to buy the cheap ones. And I've got all the ties here with the hammers and all. Take them out of the box as soon as you open a new one and put them in this drawer. They'll get lost if you don't, and rubber bands or something else won't work.

MAMA: I think your daddy had fits, too. I think he sat in his chair and had little fits. I read this a long time ago in a magazine, how little fits go, just little blackouts where maybe their eyes don't even close and people just call them "thinking spells."

JESSIE (*Getting the slipcover out of the laundry basket*): I don't think you want this manicure we've been looking forward to. I washed this cover for the sofa, but it'll take both of us to get it back on.

MAMA: I watched his eyes. I know that's what it was. The magazine said some people don't even know they've had one.

JESSIE: Daddy would've known if he'd had fits, Mama.

MAMA: The lady in this story had kept track of hers and she'd had eighty thousand of them in the last eleven years.

JESSIE: Next time you wash this cover, it'll dry better if you put it on wet.

MAMA: Jessie, listen to what I'm telling you. This lady had anywhere between five and five hundred fits a day and they lasted maybe fifteen seconds apiece, so that out of her life, she'd only lost about two weeks altogether, and she had a full-time secretary job and an IQ of 120.

JESSIE (*Amused by* MAMA's *approach*): You want to talk about fits, is that it?

MAMA: Yes. I do. I want to say . . .

JESSIE (*Interrupting*): Most of the time I wouldn't even know I'd had one, except I wake up with different clothes on, feeling like I've been run over. Sometimes I feel my head start to turn around or hear myself scream. And sometimes there *is* this dizzy stupid feeling a little before it, but if the TV's on, well, it's easy to miss.

[*As* JESSIE *and* MAMA *replace the slipcover on the sofa and the afghan on the chair, the physical struggle somehow mirrors the emotional one in the conversation*]

MAMA: I can tell when you're about to have one. Your eyes get this big! But, Jessie, you haven't . . .

JESSIE (*Taking charge of this*): What do they look like? The seizures.

MAMA (*Reluctant*): Different each time, Jess.

JESSIE: O.K. Pick one, then. A good one. I think I want to know now.

MAMA: There's not much to tell. You just . . . crumple, in a heap, like a puppet and somebody cut the strings all at once, or like the firing squad in some Mexican movie, you just slide down the wall, you know. You don't know what happens? How can you not know what happens?

JESSIE: I'm busy.

MAMA: That's not funny.

JESSIE: I'm not laughing. My head turns around and I fall down and then what?

MAMA: Well, your chest squeezes in and out, and you sound like you're gagging, sucking air in and out like you can't breathe.

JESSIE: Do it for me. Make the sound for me.

MAMA: I will not. It's awful-sounding.

JESSIE: Yeah. It felt like it might be. What's next?

MAMA: Your mouth bites down and I have to get your tongue out of the way fast, so you don't bite yourself.

JESSIE: Or you. I bite you, too, don't I?

MAMA: You got me once real good. I had to get a tetanus! But I know what to watch for now. And then you turn blue and the jerks start up. Like I'm standing there poking you with a cattle prod or you're sticking your finger in a

light socket as fast as you can . . .

JESSIE: Foaming like a mad dog the whole time.

MAMA: It's bubbling, Jess, not foam like the washer overflowed, for God's sake; it's bubbling like a baby spitting up. I go get a wet washcloth, that's all. And then the jerks slow down and you wet yourself and it's over. Two minutes tops.

JESSIE: How do I get to the bed?

MAMA: How do you think?

JESSIE: I'm too heavy for you now. How do you do it?

MAMA: I call Dawson. But I get you cleaned up before he gets here and I make him leave before you wake up.

JESSIE: You could just leave me on the floor.

MAMA: I want you to wake up someplace nice, O.K.? (*Then making a real effort*) But, Jessie, and this is the reason I even brought this up! You haven't had a seizure for a solid year. A whole year, do you realize that?

JESSIE: Yeah, the phenobarb's about right now, I guess.

MAMA: You bet it is. You might never have another one, ever! You might be through with it for all time!

JESSIE: Could be.

MAMA: You are. I know you are!

JESSIE: I sure am feeling good. I really am. The double vision's gone and my gums aren't swelling. No rashes or anything. I'm feeling as good as I ever felt in my life. I'm even feeling like worrying or getting mad and I'm not afraid it will start a fit if I do, I just go ahead.

MAMA: Of course you do! You can even scream at me, if you want to. I can take it. You don't have to act like you're just visiting here, Jessie. This is your house, too.

JESSIE: The best part is, my memory's back.

MAMA: Your memory's always been good. When couldn't you remember things? You're always reminding me what . . .

JESSIE: Because I've made lists for everything. But now I remember what things mean on my lists. I see "dish towels," and I used to wonder whether I was supposed to wash them, buy them, or look for them because I wouldn't remember where I put them after I washed them, but now I know it means wrap them up, they're a present for Loretta's birthday.

MAMA (*Finished with the sofa now*): You used to go looking for your lists, too, I've noticed that. You always know where they are now! (*Then suddenly worried*) Loretta's birthday isn't coming up, is it?

JESSIE: I made a list of all the birthdays for you. I even put yours on it. (*A small smile*) So you can call Loretta and remind her.

MAMA: Let's take Loretta to Howard Johnson's and have those fried clams. I *know* you love that clam roll.

JESSIE (*Slight pause*): I won't be here, Mama.

MAMA: What have we just been talking about? You'll be here. You're well, Jessie. You're starting all over. You said it yourself. You're remembering things and . . .

JESSIE: I won't be here. If I'd ever had a year like this, to think straight and all before now, I'd be gone already.

MAMA (*Not pleading, commanding*): No, Jessie.

JESSIE (*Folding the rest of the laundry*): Yes, Mama. Once I started remembering, I could see what it all added up to.

MAMA: The fits are over!

JESSIE: It's not the fits, Mama.

MAMA: Then it's me for giving them to you, but I didn't do it!

JESSIE: It's not the fits! You said it yourself, the medicine takes care of the fits.

MAMA (*Interrupting*): Your daddy gave you those fits, Jessie. He passed it down to you like your green eyes and your straight hair. It's not my fault!

JESSIE: So what if he had little fits? It's not inherited. I fell off the horse. It was an accident.

MAMA: The horse wasn't the first time, Jessie. You had a fit when you were five years old.

JESSIE: I did not.

MAMA: You did! You were eating a popsicle and down you went. He gave it to you. It's *his* fault, not mine.

JESSIE: Well, you took your time telling me.

MAMA: How do you tell that to a five-year-old?

JESSIE: What did the doctor say?

MAMA: He said kids have them all the time. He said there wasn't anything to do but wait for another one.

JESSIE: But I didn't have another one.

[*Now there is a real silence*]

JESSIE: You mean to tell me I had fits all the time as a kid and you just told me I fell down or something and it wasn't till I had the fit when Cecil was looking that anybody bothered to find out what was the matter with me?

MAMA: It wasn't *all the time*, Jessie. And they changed when you started to school. More like your daddy's. Oh, that was some swell time, sitting here with the two of you turning off and on like light bulbs some nights.

JESSIE: How many fits did I have?

MAMA: You never hurt yourself. I never let you out of my sight. I caught you every time.

JESSIE: But you didn't tell anybody.

MAMA: It was none of their business.

JESSIE: You were ashamed.

MAMA: I didn't want anybody to know. Least of all you.

JESSIE: Least of all me. Oh, right. That was mine to know, Mama, not yours. Did Daddy know?

MAMA: He thought you were . . . you fell down a lot. That's what he thought. You were careless. Or maybe he thought I beat you. I don't know what he thought. He didn't think about it.

JESSIE: Because you didn't tell him!

MAMA: If I told him about you, I'd have to tell him about him!

JESSIE: I don't like this. I don't like this one bit.

MAMA: I didn't think you'd like it. That's why I didn't tell you.

JESSIE: If I'd known I was an epileptic, Mama, I wouldn't have ridden any horses.

MAMA: Make you feel like a freak, is that what I should have done?

JESSIE: Just get the manicure tray and sit down!

MAMA (*Throwing it to the floor*): I don't want a manicure!

JESSIE: Doesn't look like you do, no.

MAMA: Maybe I did drop you, you don't know.

JESSIE: If you say you didn't, you didn't.

MAMA (*Beginning to break down*): Maybe I fed you the wrong thing. Maybe you had a fever sometime and I didn't know it soon enough. Maybe it's a punishment.

JESSIE: For what?

MAMA: I don't know. Because of how I felt about your father. Because I didn't want any more children. Because I smoked too much or didn't eat right when I was carrying you. It has to be something I did.

JESSIE: It does not. It's just a sickness, not a curse. Epilepsy doesn't mean anything. It just is.

MAMA: I'm not talking about the fits here, Jessie! I'm talking about this killing yourself. It has to be me that's the matter here. You wouldn't be doing this if it wasn't. I didn't tell you things or I married you off to the wrong man or I took you in and let your life get away from you or all of it put together. I don't know what I did, but I did it, I know. This is all my fault, Jessie, but I don't know what to do about it now!

JESSIE (*Exasperated at having to say this again*): It doesn't have anything to do with you!

MAMA: Everything you do has to do with me, Jessie. You can't do *anything*, wash your face or cut your finger, without doing it to me. That's right! You might as well kill me as you, Jessie, it's the same thing. This has to do with me, Jessie.

JESSIE: Then what if it does! What if it has everything

to do with you! What if you are all I have and you're not enough? What if I could take all the rest of it if only I didn't have you here? What if the only way I can get away from you for good is to kill myself? What if it is? I can *still* do it!

MAMA (*In desperate tears*): Don't leave me, Jessie! (JESSIE *stands for a moment, then turns for the bedroom*) No! (*She grabs* JESSIE's *arm*)

JESSIE (*Carefully taking her arm away*): I have a box of things I want people to have. I'm just going to go get it for you. You . . . just rest a minute.

[JESSIE *is gone.* MAMA *heads for the telephone, but she can't even pick up the receiver this time and, instead, stoops to clean up the bottles that have spilled out of the manicure tray*

JESSIE returns, carrying a box that groceries were delivered in. It probably says Hershey Kisses or Starkist Tuna. MAMA *is still down on the floor cleaning up, hoping that maybe if she just makes it look nice enough,* JESSIE *will stay*]

MAMA: Jessie, how can I live here without you? I need you! You're supposed to tell me to stand up straight and say how nice I look in my pink dress, and drink my milk. You're supposed to go around and lock up so I know we're safe for the night, and when I wake up, you're supposed to be out there making the coffee and watching me get older every day, and you're supposed to help me die when the time comes. I can't do that by myself, Jessie. I'm not like you, Jessie. I hate the quiet and I don't want to die and I don't want you to go, Jessie. How can I . . . (*Has to stop a moment*) How can I get up every day knowing you had to kill yourself to make it stop hurting and I was here all the time and I never even saw it. And then you gave me this chance to make it better, convince you to stay alive, and I couldn't do it. How can I live with myself after this, Jessie?

JESSIE: I only told you so I could explain it, so you wouldn't blame yourself, so you wouldn't feel bad. There wasn't anything you could say to change my mind. I didn't want you to save me. I just wanted you to know.

MAMA: Stay with me just a little longer. Just a few more years. I don't have that many more to go, Jessie. And as soon as I'm dead, you can do whatever you want. Maybe with me gone, you'll have all the quiet you want, right here in the house. And maybe one day you'll put in some begonias up the walk and get just the right rain for them all summer. And Ricky will be married by then and he'll bring your grandbabies over and you can sneak them a piece of candy when their daddy's not looking and

then be real glad when they've gone home and left you to your quiet again.

JESSIE: Don't you see, Mama, everything I do winds up like this. How could I think you would understand? How could I think you would want a manicure? We could hold hands for an hour and then I could go shoot myself? I'm sorry about tonight, Mama, but it's exactly why I'm doing it.

MAMA: If you've got the guts to kill yourself, Jessie, you've got the guts to stay alive.

JESSIE: I know that. So it's really just a matter of where I'd rather be.

MAMA: Look, maybe I can't think of what you should do, but that doesn't mean there isn't something that would help. *You* find it. *You* think of it. You can keep trying. You can get brave and try some more. You don't have to give up!

JESSIE: I'm *not* giving up! This *is* the other thing I'm trying. And I'm sure there are some other things that might work, but *might* work isn't good enough anymore. I need something that *will* work. *This* will work. That's why I picked it.

MAMA: But something might happen. Something that could change everything. Who knows what it might be, but it might be worth waiting for! (JESSIE *doesn't respond*) Try it for two more weeks. We could have more talks like tonight.

JESSIE: No, Mama.

MAMA: I'll pay more attention to you. Tell the truth when you ask me. Let you have your say.

JESSIE: No, Mama! We wouldn't have more talks like tonight, because it's this next part that's made this last part so good, Mama. No, Mama. *This* is how I have my say. This is how I say what I thought about it *all* and I say no. To Dawson and Loretta and the Red Chinese and epilepsy and Ricky and Cecil and you. And me. And hope. I say no! (*Then going to* MAMA *on the sofa*) Just let me go easy, Mama.

MAMA: How can I let you go?

JESSIE: You can because you have to. It's what you've always done.

MAMA: You are my child!

JESSIE: I am what became of your child. (MAMA *cannot answer*) I found an old baby picture of me. And it was somebody else, not me. It was somebody pink and fat who never heard of sick or lonely, somebody who cried and got fed, and reached up and got held and kicked but didn't hurt anybody, and slept whenever she wanted to, just by closing her eyes. Somebody who mainly just laid there and laughed at the colors waving around over her head and chewed on a polka-dot whale and woke up knowing some new trick nearly every day, and rolled over and drooled on the sheet and felt your hand pulling my quilt back up over me. That's who I started out and this is who is left. (*There is no self-pity here*) That's what this is about. It's somebody I lost, all right, it's my own self. Who I never was. Or who I tried to be and never got there. Somebody I waited for who never came. And never will. So, see, it doesn't much matter what else happens in the world or in this house, even. I'm what was worth waiting for and I didn't make it. Me . . . who might have made a difference to me . . . I'm not going to show up, so there's no reason to stay, except to keep you company, and that's . . . not reason enough because I'm not . . . very good company. (*Pause*) Am I.

MAMA (*Knowing she must tell the truth*): No. And neither am I.

JESSIE: I had this strange little thought, well, maybe it's not so strange. Anyway, after Christmas, after I decided to do this, I would wonder, sometimes, what might keep me here, what might be worth staying for, and you know what it was? It was maybe if there was something I really liked, like maybe if I really liked rice pudding or cornflakes for breakfast or something, that might be enough.

MAMA: Rice pudding is good.

JESSIE: Not to me.

MAMA: And you're not afraid?

JESSIE: Afraid of what?

MAMA: I'm afraid of it, for me, I mean. When my time comes. I know it's coming, but . . .

JESSIE: You don't know when. Like in a scary movie.

MAMA: Yeah, sneaking up on me like some killer on the loose, hiding out in the back yard just waiting for me to have my hands full someday and how am I supposed to protect myself anyhow when I don't know what he looks like and I don't know how he sounds coming up behind me like that or if it will hurt or take very long or what I don't get done before it happens.

JESSIE: You've got plenty of time left.

MAMA: I forget what for, right now.

JESSIE: For whatever happens, I don't know. For the rest of your life. For Agnes burning down one more house or Dawson losing his hair or . . .

MAMA (*Quickly*): Jessie. I can't just sit here and say O.K., kill yourself if you want to.

JESSIE: Sure you can. You just did. Say it again.

MAMA (*Really startled*): Jessie! (*Quiet horror*) How dare you! (*Furious*) How dare you! You think you can just leave whenever you want, like you're watching television here? No, you can't, Jessie. You make me feel like a fool for being

alive, child, and you are so wrong! I like it here, and I will stay here until they make me go, until they drag me screaming and I mean screeching into my grave, and you're real smart to get away before then because, I mean, honey, you've never heard noise like that in your life. (JESSIE *turns away*) Who am I talking to? You're gone already, aren't you? I'm looking right through you! I can't stop you because you're already gone! I guess you think they'll all have to talk about you now! I guess you think this will really confuse them. Oh yes, ever since Christmas you've been laughing to yourself and thinking, "Boy, are they all in for a surprise." Well, nobody's going to be a bit surprised, sweetheart. This is just like you. Do it the hard way, that's my girl, all right. (JESSIE *gets up and goes into the kitchen, but* MAMA *follows her*) You know who they're going to feel sorry for? Me! How about that! Not you, me! They're going to be *ashamed* of you. Yes. *Ashamed!* If somebody asks Dawson about it, he'll change the subject as fast as he can. He'll talk about how much he has to pay to park his car these days.

JESSIE: Leave me alone.

MAMA: It's the truth!

JESSIE: I should've just left you a note!

MAMA (*Screaming*): Yes! (*Then suddenly understanding what she has said, nearly paralyzed by the thought of it, she turns slowly to face* JESSIE, *nearly whispering*) No. No. I . . . might not have thought of all the things you've said.

JESSIE: It's O.K., Mama.

[MAMA *is nearly unconscious from the emotional devastation of these last few moments. She sits down at the kitchen table, hurt and angry and desperately afraid. But she looks almost numb. She is so far beyond what is known as pain that she is virtually unreachable and* JESSIE *knows this, and talks quietly, watching for signs of recovery*]

JESSIE (*Washes her hands in the sink*): I remember you liked that preacher who did Daddy's, so if you want to ask him to do the service, that's O.K. with me.

MAMA (*Not an answer, just a word*): What.

JESSIE (*Putting on hand lotion as she talks*). And pick some songs you like or let Agnes pick, she'll know exactly which ones. Oh, and I had your dress cleaned that you wore to Daddy's. You looked real good in that.

MAMA: I don't remember, hon.

JESSIE: And it won't be so bad once your friends start coming to the funeral home. You'll probably see people you haven't seen for years, but I thought about what you should say to get you over that nervous part when they first come in.

MAMA (*Simply repeating*): Come in.

JESSIE: Take them up to see their flowers, they'd like that. And when they say, "I'm so sorry, Thelma," you just say, "I appreciate your coming, Connie." And then ask how their garden was this summer or what they're doing for Thanksgiving or how their children . . .

MAMA: I don't think I should ask about their children. I'll talk about what they have on, that's always good. And I'll have some crochet work with me.

JESSIE: And Agnes will be there, so you might not have to talk at all.

MAMA: Maybe if Connie Richards does come, I can get her to tell me where she gets that Irish yarn, she calls it. I know it doesn't come from Ireland. I think it just comes with a green wrapper.

JESSIE: And be sure to invite enough people home afterward so you get enough food to feed them all and have some left for you. But don't let anybody take anything home, especially Loretta.

MAMA: Loretta will get all the food set up, honey. It's only fair to let her have some macaroni or something.

JESSIE: No, Mama. You have to be more selfish from now on. (*Sitting at the table with* MAMA) Now, somebody's bound to ask you why I did it and you just say you don't know. That you loved me and you know I loved you and we just sat around tonight like every other night of our lives, and then I came over and kissed you and said, "'Night, Mother," and you heard me close my bedroom door and the next thing you heard was the shot. And whatever reason I had, well, you guess I just took them with me.

MAMA (*Quietly*): It was something personal.

JESSIE: Good. That's good, Mama.

MAMA: That's what I'll say, then.

JESSIE: Personal. Yeah.

MAMA: Is that what I tell Dawson and Loretta, too? We sat around, you kissed me, "'Night, Mother"? They'll want to know more, Jessie. They won't believe it.

JESSIE: Well, then, tell them what we did. I filled up the candy jars. I cleaned out the refrigerator. We made some hot chocolate and put the cover back on the sofa. You had no idea. All right? I really think it's better that way. If they know we talked about it, they really won't understand how you let me go.

MAMA: I guess not.

JESSIE: It's private. Tonight is private, yours and mine, and I don't want anybody else to have

any of it.

MAMA: O.K., then.

JESSIE (*Standing behind* MAMA *now, holding her shoulders*): Now, when you hear the shot, I don't want you to come in. First of all, you won't be able to get in by yourself, but I don't want you trying. Call Dawson, then call the police, and then call Agnes. And then you'll need something to do till somebody gets here, so wash the hot-chocolate pan. You wash that pan till you hear the doorbell ring and I don't care if it's an hour, you keep washing that pan.

MAMA: I'll make my calls and then I'll just sit. I won't need something to do. What will the police say?

JESSIE: They'll do that gunpowder test, I guess, and ask you what happened, and by that time, the ambulance will be here and they'll come in and get me and you know how that goes. You stay out here with Dawson and Loretta. You keep Dawson out here. I want the police in the room first, not Dawson, O.K.?

MAMA: What if Dawson and Loretta want me to go home with them?

JESSIE (*Returning to the living room*): That's up to you.

MAMA: I think I'll stay here. All they've got is Sanka.

JESSIE: Maybe Agnes could come stay with you for a few days.

MAMA (*Standing up, looking into the living room*): I'd rather be by myself, I think. (*Walking toward the box* JESSIE *brought in earlier*) You want me to give people those things?

JESSIE (*They sit down on the sofa,* JESSIE *holding the box on her lap*): I want Loretta to have my little calculator. Dawson bought it for himself, you know, but then he saw one he liked better and he couldn't bring both of them home with Loretta counting every penny the way she does, so he gave the first one to me. Be funny for her to have it now, don't you think? And all my house slippers are in a sack for her in my closet. Tell her I know they'll fit and I've never worn any of them, and make sure Dawson hears you tell her that. I'm glad he loves Loretta so much, but I wish he knew not everybody has her size feet.

MAMA (*Taking the calculator*): O.K.

JESSIE (*Reaching into the box again*): This letter is for Dawson, but it's mostly about you, so read it if you want. There's a list of presents for you for at least twenty more Christmases and birthdays, so if you want anything special you better add it to this list before you give it to him. Or if you want to be surprised, just don't read that page. This Christmas, you're getting mostly stuff for the house, like a new rug in your bathroom and needlework, but next

Christmas, you're really going to cost him next Christmas. I think you'll like it a lot and you'd never think of it.

MAMA: And you think he'll go for it?

JESSIE: I think he'll feel like a real jerk if he doesn't. Me telling him to, like this and all. Now, this number's where you call Cecil. I called it last week and he answered, so I know he still lives there.

MAMA: What do you want me to tell him?

JESSIE: Tell him we talked about him and I only had good things to say about him, but mainly tell him to find Ricky and tell him what I did, and tell Ricky you have something for him, out here, from me, and to come get it. (*Pulls a sack out of the box*)

MAMA (*The sack feels empty*): What is it?

JESSIE (*Taking it off*):My watch. (*Putting it in the sack and taking a ribbon out of the sack to tie around the top of it*)

MAMA: He'll sell it!

JESSIE: That's the idea. I appreciate him not stealing it already. I'd like to buy him a good meal.

MAMA: He'll buy dope with it!

JESSIE: Well, then, I hope he gets some good dope with it, Mama. And the rest of this is for you. (*Handing* MAMA *the box now.* MAMA *picks up the things and looks at them*)

MAMA (*Surprised and pleased*): When did you do all this? During my naps, I guess.

JESSIE: I guess. I tried to be quiet about it. (*As* MAMA *is puzzled by the presents*) Those are just little presents. For whenever you need one. They're not bought presents, just things I thought you might like to look at, pictures or things you think you've lost. Things you didn't know you had, even. You'll see.

MAMA: I'm not sure I want them. They'll make me think of you.

JESSIE: No they won't. They're just things, like a free tube of toothpaste I found hanging on the door one day.

MAMA: Oh. All right, then.

JESSIE: Well, maybe there's one nice present in there somewhere. It's Granny's ring she gave me and I thought you might like to have it, but I didn't think you'd wear it if I gave it to you right now.

MAMA (*Taking the box to a table nearby*): No. Probably not. (*Turning back to face her*) I'm ready for my manicure, I guess. Want me to wash my hands again?

JESSIE (*Standing up*): It's time for me to go, Mama.

MAMA (*Starting for her*): No, Jessie, you've got all night!

JESSIE (*As* MAMA *grabs her*): No, Mama.

MAMA: It's not even ten o'clock.

JESSIE (*Very calm*): Let me go, Mama.

MAMA: I can't. You can't go. You can't do this. You didn't say it would be so soon, Jessie. I'm scared. I love you.

JESSIE (*Takes her hands away*): Let go of me, Mama. I've said everything I had to say.

MAMA (*Standing still a minute*): You said you wanted to do my nails.

JESSIE (*Taking a small step backward*): I can't. It's too late.

MAMA: It's not too late!

JESSIE: I don't want you to wake Dawson and Loretta when you call. I want them to still be up and dressed so they can get right over.

MAMA (*As* JESSIE *backs up,* MAMA *moves in on her, but carefully*): They wake up fast, Jessie, if they have to. They don't matter here, Jessie. You do. I do. We're not through yet. We've got a lot of things to take care of here. I don't know where my prescriptions are and you didn't tell me what to tell Dr. Davis when he calls or how much you want me to tell Ricky or who I call to rake the leaves or . . .

JESSIE: Don't try and stop me, Mama, you can't do it.

MAMA (*Grabbing her again, this time hard*): I can too! I'll stand in front of this hall and you can't get past me. (*They struggle*) You'll have to knock me down to get away from me, Jessie. I'm not about to let you . . .

[MAMA *struggles with* JESSIE *at the door and in the struggle* JESSIE *gets away from her and—*

JESSIE (*Almost a whisper*): 'Night, Mother. (*She vanishes into her bedroom and we hear the door lock just as* MAMA *gets to it*)

MAMA (*Screams*): Jessie! (*Pounding on the door*) Jessie, you let me in there. Don't you do this, Jessie. I'm not going to stop screaming until you open this door, Jessie. Jessie! Jessie! What if I don't do any of the things you told me to do! I'll tell Cecil what a miserable man he was to make you feel the way he did and I'll give Ricky's watch to Dawson if I feel like it and the only way you can make sure I do what you want is you come out here and make me, Jessie! (*Pounding again*) Jessie! Stop this! I didn't know! I was here with you all the time. How could I know you were so alone?

[And MAMA *stops for a moment, breathless and frantic, putting her ear to the door, and when she doesn't hear anything, she stands up straight again and screams once more*)

Jessie! Please!

[And we hear the shot, and it sounds like an answer, it sounds like No.

MAMA collapses against the door, tears streaming down her face, but not screaming anymore. In shock now]

Jessie, Jessie, child . . . Forgive me. (*Pause*) I thought you were mine.

[And she leaves the door and makes her way through the living room, around the furniture, as though she didn't know where it was, not knowing what to do. Finally, she goes to the stove in the kitchen and picks up the hot-chocolate pan and carries it with her to the telephone, and holds on to it while she dials the number. She looks down at the pan, holding it tight like her life depended on it. She hears Loretta answer]

MAMA: Loretta, let me talk to Dawson, honey.

TINA HOWE (b. 1937)

Tina Howe grew up in New York City and attended private schools there before moving to Urbana, Illinois, where her father was a professor of journalism at the University of Illinois. She attended Sarah Lawrence College, where she discovered playwriting and graduated in 1959. Howe began her active career as a playwright some years later, in the early 1970s, with two absurdist comedies about women: *The Nest* (1970), on the subject of courtship ritual and the savagery between women when they battle one another for husbands; and *Birth and After Birth* (1973), an absurdist look at woman's roles as wife, mother, and child bearer. These satires were regarded as so radically feminist that Howe had difficulty getting her works staged. *The Nest* was successful in Provincetown, Massachusetts, but it closed after only one performance in its off-Broadway production, and Howe's agent dropped her. *Birth and After Birth* in fact has never been produced. Howe withdrew professionally for a while, reshaping her work into a surrealistic style that is still feminist, absurdist, and comic. Her comedies juxtapose the familiar with the outrageous and so provoke a revisioning of reality. *Museum* (1976), which parodies art criticism, is the first of a series of plays preoccupied with the centrality of women as creators and artists. The series continues with *The Art of Dining* (1979), *Painting Churches* (1983), and *Coastal Disturbances* (1986). In these plays Howe poses probing metatheatrical questions about the relationship between fiction and reality. *Approaching Zanzibar* (1989) and *One Shoe Off* (1993) use the intimate settings of a long car trip and a dinner table to explore how poignancy and humor counterbalance crisis and neurosis. Howe has taught drama since 1990 at Hunter College and New York University.

Painting Churches

Howe felt that her feminist and aesthetic voices fused at last in *Painting Churches,* a play that brings together the metatheatrical and thematic concerns of her earlier plays. The critics agreed wholeheartedly, and Howe won the Obie award in 1983. The title *Painting Churches* is a pun. Its principal character is Mags Church, an anorexic painter who returns to her home in Boston to paint for her first one-woman show a portrait of her eccentric parents—the senile Gardner and the flamboyant Fanny Church. Mags's anorexia as well as her artistic talent are traceable to her childhood defiance of parental control. In a probing study of character, Howe examines a child's need for parental approval and the coexisting need to find confidence and self-expression that will distinguish her from her parents. Howe also explores debilitation in the aging process and the terrors of facing death, as Fanny cares for her ailing husband Gardner during the last years of their lives. Mags has returned home on her own terms with recognized talent, and Howe uses the event to explore the artist's struggle to repair the ravages of time.

In her metatheatrical structure, Howe has Mags painting the portrait of her parents within a play, and at the end Howe merges the painting with the play as Fanny and Gardner see the portrait for the first time. It reminds them of a Renoir painting of a couple dancing, and when Fanny and Gardner dance together they are transformed into the artist's vision in the painting. The play is presented as Mags's memory of this incident, which occurred "several years ago." Fanny and Gardner's dance is the last we see of them; their real life has faded into this memory that Mags has of them. The artist has given her parents a kind of immortality which redeems the pain she felt as a child. Just as the portrait captures this for her, the play does so for us. When asked in an interview if the play was autobiographical, Howe replied, "All of the events are true, but none of them happened."

Painting Churches

TINA HOWE

Why on earth does a person become a playwright? In my case it was because I was so tall and goofy-looking as a child, and because of Aunt Helen, my father's hilarious sister, who was a monologist on the order of Ruth Draper. She performed at the White House, the Blue Angel, and at ladies' clubs all across the country. Helen Howe and I had the exact same face. I mean, *identical*—the same wide mouth and the same deep-set blue eyes. It was spooky—except she was 4 foot 11 inches and I was almost 6 feet tall. Well, you can imagine, here I was, this enormous ungainly girl yearning to be accepted, and here was my tiny twin Aunt Helen cracking them up from coast to coast. So I decided to become a mimic like her. It's the ultimate defense: Get them to laugh *with* you before they laugh *at* you. So all through school and college I was the class clown. In fact, I almost signed up to study with the great mime Etienne Decroux. But his students were all beautiful dancers, not baggy clowns, so I retreated in panic.

What turned me around was writing a little one-act play my senior year at Sarah Lawrence. If I was too awkward to get up on stage, I'd have others do it in my stead. When the audience burst into applause at the end of the show and started yelling, "Author, author," I was hooked.

People often ask me where my characters come from. This is a pathetic confession, but they're simply all the voices I yearn to perform if only I had the talent.

TINA HOWE
1990

CHARACTERS

FANNY SEDGWICK CHURCH, a Bostonian from a fine old family, in her sixties.

GARDNER CHURCH, her husband, an eminent New England poet from a finer family, in his seventies.

MARGARET CHURCH (MAGS), their daughter, a painter, in her early thirties.

TIME: Several years ago.

PLACE: Boston, Massachusetts.

ACT I

Scene 1

The living room of the Churches' townhouse on Beacon Hill one week before everything will be moved to Cape Cod. Empty packing cartons line the room and all the furniture has been tagged with brightly colored markers. At first glance it looks like any discreet Boston interior, but on closer scrutiny one notices a certain flamboyance. Oddities from secondhand stores are mixed in with the fine old furniture, and exotic handmade curios vie with tasteful family objets d'art. What makes the room remarkable, though, is the play of light that pours through three soaring arched windows. At one hour it's hard edged and brilliant; the next, it's dappled and yielding. It transforms whatever it touches, giving the room a distinct feeling of unreality. It's several years ago, a bright spring morning.

FANNY is sitting on the sofa, wrapping a valuable old silver coffee service. She's wearing a worn bathrobe and fashionable hat. As she works, she makes a list of everything on a yellow legal pad. GARDNER can be heard typing in his study down the hall.

FANNY (*Picks up a coffee pot*): God, this is good-looking! I'd forgotten how handsome Mama's old silver was! It's probably worth a fortune. It certainly weighs enough! (*Calling*) GAR-RRRRRRRRRRRRRRRRRDNERRRRRRRRRRRR? . . . Well, it should bring us a pretty penny, that's for sure: (*Wraps it, places it in a carton, and then picks up the tray that goes with it. She holds it up like a mirror and adjusts her hat. Louder in another register*) OH, GARRRRRRRRRRRRRRRRDNERRRRR? (GARDNER *continues typing. She then reaches for a small box and opens it with reverence*) Grandma's Paul Revere teaspoons! . . . (*She takes out several and fondles them*) I don't care how desperate things get, these will never go! One has to maintain some standards! (*She writes on her list*) Grandma's Paul Revere teaspoons, Cotuit! WASN'T IT THE AMERICAN WING OF THE METROPOLITAN MUSEUM OF ART THAT WANTED GRANDMA'S PAUL REVERE TEASPOONS SO BADLY? . . . (*She looks at her reflection in the tray again*) This is a very good-looking hat, if I do say so. I was awfully smart to grab it up. (*Silence*) DON'T YOU REMEMBER A DISTINGUISHED-LOOKING MAN COMING TO THE HOUSE AND OFFERING US FIFTY THOUSAND DOLLARS FOR GRANDMA'S PAUL REVERE TEASPOONS? . . . HE HAD ON THESE MARVELOUS SHOES! THEY WERE SO POINTED AT THE ENDS WE COULDN'T IMAGINE HOW HE EVER GOT THEM ON AND THEY WERE SHINED TO WITHIN AN INCH OF THEIR LIVES AND I REMEMBER HIM SAYING HE CAME FROM THE . . . AMERICAN WING OF THE METROPOLITAN MUSEUM OF ART! . . . HELLO? . . . GARDNER? . . . ARE YOU THERE! (*The typing stops*) YOO-HOOOOOOO . . . (*Like a foghorn*) GAR-RRRRRRRRRRDNERRRRRRR?

GARDNER (*Offstage; from his study*): YES, DEAR . . . IS THAT YOU?

FANNY: OF COURSE IT'S ME! WHO ELSE COULD IT POSSIBLY BE? . . . DARLING, PLEASE COME HERE FOR A MINUTE. (*The typing resumes*) FOR GOD'S SAKE, WILL YOU STOP THAT DREADFUL TYPING BEFORE YOU SEND ME STRAIGHT TO THE NUT HOUSE? . . . (*In a new register*) GARRRRRRRRRRRRRRRDNERRRRRR?

[*He stops.*]

GARDNER (*Offstage*): WHAT'S THAT? MAGS IS BACK FROM THE NUT HOUSE?

FANNY: I SAID . . . Lord, I hate this yelling. . . . PLEASE . . . COME . . . HERE!

[*Brief silence.*]

GARDNER (*Offstage*): I'LL BE WITH YOU IN A MOMENT, I DIDN'T HEAR HER RING. (*Starts singing*) "Nothing could be finer than to be in Carolina."

FANNY: It's a wonder I'm not in a straight-jacket already. Actually, it might be rather nice for a change . . . peaceful. DARLING . . . I WANT TO SHOW YOU MY NEW HAT!

[*Silence. GARDNER enters, still singing. He's wearing mismatched tweeds and is holding a stack of papers which keep drifting to the floor.*]

GARDNER: Oh, don't you look nice! Very attractive, very attractive!

FANNY: But I'm still in my bathrobe.

GARDNER (*Looking around the room, leaking more papers*): Well, where's Mags?

FANNY: Darling, you're dropping your papers all over the floor.

GARDNER (*Spies the silver tray*): I remember this! Aunt Alice gave it to us, didn't she? (*He picks it up*) Good Lord, it's heavy. What's it made of? Lead?!

FANNY: No, Aunt Alice did *not* give it to us. It was Mama's.

GARDNER: Oh, yes . . . (*He starts to exit with it*)

FANNY: Could I have it back, please?

GARDNER (*Hands it to her, dropping more papers*): Oh, sure thing. . . . Where's Mags? I thought you said she was here.

FANNY: I didn't say Mags was here, I asked *you* to come here.

GARDNER (*Papers spilling*): Damned papers keep falling . . .

FANNY: I wanted to show you my new hat. I bought it in honor of Mags' visit. Isn't it marvelous?

GARDNER (*Picking up the papers as more drop*): Yes, yes, very nice . . .

FANNY: Gardner, you're not even looking at it!

GARDNER: Very becoming . . .

FANNY: You don't think it's too bright, do you? I don't want to look like a traffic light. Guess how much it cost?

GARDNER (*A whole sheaf of papers slides to the floor; he dives for them*): OH, SHIT!

FANNY (*Gets to them first*): It's all right, I've got them, I've got them. (*She hands them to him*)

GARDNER: You'd think they had wings on them . . .

FANNY: Here you go . . .   GARDNER: . . . damned things won't hold still!

FANNY: Gar . . . ?

GARDNER (*Engrossed in one of the pages*): Mmmmm?

FANNY: HELLO?

GARDNER (*Startled*): What's that?

FANNY (*In a whisper*): My hat. Guess how much it cost.

GARDNER: Oh, yes. Let's see . . . ten dollars?

FANNY: Ten dollars . . . IS THAT ALL?

GARDNER: Twenty?

FANNY: GARDNER, THIS HAPPENS TO BE A DESIGNER HAT! DESIGNER HATS START AT FIFTY DOLLARS . . . SEVENTY-FIVE!

GARDNER (*Jumps*): Was that the door bell?

FANNY: No, it wasn't the door bell. Though it's high time Mags were here. She was probably in a train wreck!

GARDNER (*Looking through his papers*): I'm beginning

to get fond of Wallace Stevens again.

FANNY: This damned move is going to kill me! Send me straight to my grave!

GARDNER (*Reading from a page*):

> "The mules that angels ride come slowly down
> The blazing passes, from beyond the sun.
> Descensions of their tinkling bells arrive.
> These muleteers are dainty of their way . . ."

(*Pause*) Don't you love that! "These muleteers are *dainty* of their way"!?

FANNY: Gar, the hat. How much? (GARDNER *sighs*) Darling . . . ?

GARDNER: Oh, yes. Let's see . . . fifty dollars? Seventy-five?

FANNY: It's French.

GARDNER: Three hundred!

FANNY (*Triumphant*): No, eighty-five cents.

GARDNER: Eighty-five cents! . . . I thought you said . . .

FANNY: That's right . . . eighty . . . five . . . *cents!*

GARDNER: Well, you sure had me fooled!

FANNY: I found it at the thrift shop.

GARDNER: I thought it cost at least fifty dollars or seventy-five. You know, designer hats are very expensive!

FANNY: It was on the markdown table. (*She takes it off and shows him the label*) See that? Lily Daché! When I saw that label, I nearly keeled over right into the fur coats!

GARDNER (*Handling it*): Well, what do you know, that's the same label that's in my bathrobe.

FANNY: Darling, Lily Daché designed hats, not men's bathrobes!

GARDNER: Yup . . . Lily Daché . . . same name . . .

FANNY: If you look again, I'm sure you'll see . . .

GARDNER: . . . same script, same color, same size. I'll show you. (*He exits*)

FANNY: Poor lamb can't keep anything straight anymore. (*Looks at herself in the tray again*) God, this is a good-looking hat!

GARDNER (*Returns with a nondescript plaid bathrobe. He points to the label*): See that? . . . What does it say?

FANNY (*Refusing to look at it*): Lily Daché was a *hat* designer! She designed ladies' *hats!*

GARDNER: What . . . does . . . it . . . say?

FANNY: Gardner, you're being ridiculous.

GARDNER (*Forcing it on her*): Read . . . the label!

FANNY: Lily Daché did *not* design this bathrobe, I don't care what the label says!

GARDNER: READ! (FANNY *reads it*) ALL RIGHT, NOW WHAT DOES IT SAY?

FANNY (*Chagrined*): Lily Daché.

GARDNER: I told you!

FANNY: Wait a minute, let me look at that again. (*She*

does; then throws the robe at him in disgust) Gar, Lily Daché never designed a bathrobe in her life! Someone obviously ripped the label off one of her hats and then sewed it into the robe.

GARDNER (*Puts it on over his jacket*): It's damned good-looking. I've always loved this robe. I think you gave it to me. . . . Well, I've got to get back to work. (*He abruptly exits*)

FANNY: Where did you get that robe anyway? . . . I didn't give it to you, did I . . . ?

[*Silence.* GARDNER *resumes typing.*]

FANNY (*Holding the tray up again and admiring herself*): You know, I think I *did* give it to him. I remember how excited I was when I found it at the thrift shop . . . fifty cents and never worn! *I* couldn't have sewn that label in to impress him, could I? . . . I can't be that far gone! . . . The poor lamb wouldn't even notice it, let alone understand its cachet. . . . Uuuuuuh, this damned tray is even heavier than the coffee pot. They must have been amazons in the old days! (*Writes on her pad*) "Empire tray, Parke-Bernet Galleries," and good riddance! (*She wraps it and drops it into the carton with the coffee pot*) Where *is* that wretched Mags? It would be just like her to get into a train wreck! She was supposed to be here hours ago. Well, if she doesn't show up soon, I'm going to drop dead of exhaustion. God, wouldn't that be wonderful? . . . Then they could just cart me off into storage with all the old chandeliers and china . . .

[*The doorbell rings.*]

FANNY: It's Mags, it's Mags! (*A pause. Dashing out of the room, colliding into* GARDNER) Good god, look at me! I'm still in my bathrobe!

GARDNER (*Offstage*): Coming, coming . . . I've got it . . . coming! (*Dashing into the room, colliding into* FANNY) I've got it . . . hold on . . . coming . . . coming . . .

FANNY (*Offstage*): mags is here! it's mags. . . she's finally here!

[GARDNER *exits to open the front door.* MAGS *comes staggering in carrying a suitcase and an enormous duffel bag. She wears wonderfully distinctive clothes and has very much her own look. She's extremely out of breath and too wrought up to drop her heavy bags.*]

MAGS: I'm sorry. . . . I'm sorry I'm so late. . . . Everything went wrong! A passenger had a heart attack outside of New London and we had to stop. . . . It was terrifying! All these medics and policemen came swarming onto the train and the conductor kept running up and down the aisles telling everyone not to leave their seats under any circumstances. . . . Then the New London fire department came screeching down to the tracks, sirens blaring, lights whirling, and all these men in black rubber suits started pouring through the doors. . . . *That* took two hours . . .

FANNY (*Offstage*): Darling . . . darling . . . where are you?

MAGS: *Then,* I couldn't get a cab at the station. There just weren't any! I must have circled the block fifteen times. Finally I just stepped out into the traffic with my thumb out, but no one would pick me up . . . so I walked . . .

FANNY (*Offstage*): Damned zipper's stuck . . .

GARDNER: You walked all the way from the South Station?

MAGS: Well actually, I ran . . .

GARDNER: You had poor Mum scared to death.

MAGS (*Finally puts the bags down with a deep sigh*): I'm sorry. . . . I'm really sorry. It was a nightmare.

[FANNY *reenters the room, her dress over her head. The zipper's stuck; she staggers around blindly.*]

FANNY: Damned zipper! Gar, will you please help me with this?

MAGS: I sprinted all the way up Beacon Hill.

GARDNER (*Opening his arms wide*): Well come here and let's get a look at you. (*He hugs her*) Mags!

MAGS (*Squeezing him tight*): Oh, Daddy . . . Daddy!

GARDNER: My Mags!

MAGS: I never thought I'd get here! . . . Oh, you look wonderful!

GARDNER: Well, you don't look so bad yourself!

MAGS: I love your hair. It's gotten so . . . white!

FANNY (*Still lost in her dress, struggling with the zipper*): This is *so* typical . . . just as Mags arrives, my zipper has to break! (*She grunts and struggles*)

MAGS (*Waves at her*): Hi, Mum . . .

FANNY: Just a minute, dear, my zipper's . . .

GARDNER (*Picks up* MAGS' *bags*): Well, sit down and take a load off your feet . . .

MAGS: I was so afraid I'd never make it . . .

GARDNER (*Staggering under the weight of the bags*): What have you got in here? Lead weights?

MAGS: I can't believe you're finally letting me do you.

[FANNY *flings her arms around* MAGS, *practically knocking her over.*]

FANNY: Oh, darling . . . my precious Mags, you're here at last.

GARDNER (*Lurching around in circles*): Now let's see . . . where should I put these . . . ?

FANNY: I was sure your train had derailed and you were lying dead in some ditch!

MAGS (*Pulls away from* FANNY *to come to* GARDNER's *rescue*): Daddy, please, let me . . . these are much too heavy.

FANNY (*Finally noticing* MAGS): GOOD LORD, WHAT HAVE YOU DONE TO YOUR HAIR?!

MAGS (*Struggling to take the bags from* GARDNER): Come on, give them to me . . . please? (*She sets them down by the sofa*)

FANNY (*As her dress starts to slide off one shoulder*): Oh, not again! . . . Gar, would you give me a hand and see what's wrong with this zipper. One minute it's stuck, the next it's falling to pieces.

*[*GARDNER *goes to her and starts fussing with it.]*

MAGS (*Pacing*): I don't know, it's been crazy all week. Monday, I forgot to keep an appointment I'd made with a new model. . . . Tuesday, I overslept and stood up my advanced painting students. . . . Wednesday, the day of my meeting with Max Zoll, I forgot to put on my underpants . . .

FANNY: GODDAMMIT, GAR, CAN'T YOU DO ANYTHING ABOUT THIS ZIPPER?!

MAGS: I mean, there I was, racing down Broome Street in this gauzy Tibetan skirt when I tripped and fell right at his feet . . . SPLATTT! My skirt goes flying over my head and there I am . . . everything staring him in the face . . .

FANNY: COME ON GAR, USE A LITTLE MUSCLE!

MAGS (*Laughing*): Oh, well, all that matters is that I finally got here. . . . I mean . . . there you are . . .

GARDNER (*Struggling with the zipper*): I can't see it, it's too small!

FANNY (*Whirls away from* GARDNER, *pulling her dress off altogether*): OH, FORGET IT! JUST FORGET IT! The trolley's probably missing half its teeth, just like someone else I know. (*To* MAGS) I grind my teeth in my sleep now, I've worn them all down to stubs. Look at that! (*She flings open her mouth and points*) Nothing left but the gums!

GARDNER: I never hear you grind your teeth . . .

FANNY: That's because I'm snoring so loud. How could you hear anything through all that racket? It even wakes me up. It's no wonder poor Daddy has to sleep downstairs.

MAGS (*Looking around*): Jeez, look at the place! So, you're finally doing it . . . selling the house and moving to Cotuit year round. I don't believe it.

I just don't believe it!

GARDNER: Well, how about a drink to celebrate Mags' arrival?

MAGS: You've been here so long. Why move now?

FANNY: Gardner, what are you wearing that bathrobe for?

MAGS: You can't move. I won't let you!

FANNY (*Softly to* GARDNER): Really, darling, you ought to pay more attention to your appearance.

MAGS: You love this house. *I* love this house . . . the room . . . the light.

GARDNER: So, Mags, how about a little . . . (*He drinks from an imaginary glass*) to wet your whistle?

FANNY: We can't start drinking now, it isn't even noon yet!

MAGS: I'm starving. I've got to get something to eat before I collapse! (*She exits towards the kitchen*)

FANNY: What *have* you done to your hair, dear? The color's so queer and all your nice curl is gone.

GARDNER: It looks to me as if she dyed it.

FANNY: Yes, that's it. You're absolutely right! It's a completely different color. She dyed it bright red!

*[*MAGS *can be heard thumping and thudding through the icebox.]*

FANNY: NOW, MAGS, I DON'T WANT YOU FILLING UP ON SNACKS. . . . I'VE MADE A PERFECTLY BEAUTIFUL LEG OF LAMB FOR LUNCH! . . . HELLO? . . . DO YOU HEAR ME? . . . (*To* GARDNER) No one in our family has *ever* had red hair, it's so common looking.

GARDNER: I like it. It brings out her eyes.

FANNY: WHY ON EARTH DID YOU DYE YOUR HAIR *RED*, OF ALL COLORS?!

MAGS (*Returns, eating Saltines out of the box*): I didn't dye my hair, I just added some highlight.

FANNY: I suppose that's what your arty friends in New York do . . . dye their hair all the colors of the rainbow!

GARDNER: Well, it's damned attractive if you asked me . . . damned attractive!

*[*MAGS *unzips her duffel bag and rummages around in it while eating the Saltines.]*

FANNY: Darling, I told you not to bring a lot of stuff with you. We're trying to get rid of things.

MAGS (*Pulls out a folding easel and starts setting it up*): AAAAAHHHHHH, here it is. Isn't it a beauty? I bought it just for you!

FANNY: Please don't get crumbs all over the floor. Crystal was just here yesterday. It was her last time before we move.

MAGS (*At her easel*): God, I can hardly wait! I can't believe you're finally letting me do you.

FANNY: Do *us*? . . . What *are* you talking about?

GARDNER (*Reaching for the Saltines*): Hey, Mags, could I have a couple of those?

MAGS (*Tosses him the box*): Sure! (*To* FANNY) Your portrait.

GARDNER: Thanks. (*He starts munching on a handful*)

FANNY: You're planning to paint our portrait now? While we're trying to move . . . ?

GARDNER (*Sputtering Saltines*): Mmmmm, I'd forgotten just how delicious Saltines are!

MAGS: It's a perfect opportunity. There'll be no distractions; you'll be completely at my mercy. Also, you promised.

FANNY: I did?

MAGS: Yes, you did.

FANNY: Well, I must have been off my rocker.

MAGS: No, you said, "You can paint us, you can dip us in concrete, you can do anything you want with us just so long as you help us get out of here!"

GARDNER (*Offering the box of Saltines to* FANNY): You really ought to try some of these, Fan, they're absolutely delicious!

FANNY (*Taking a few*): Why, thank you.

MAGS: I figure we'll pack in the morning and you'll pose in the afternoons. It'll be a nice diversion.

FANNY: These *are* good!

GARDNER: Here, dig in . . . take some more.

MAGS: I have some wonderful news . . . amazing news! I wanted to wait till I got here to tell you.

[GARDNER *and* FANNY *eat their Saltines, passing the box back and forth as* MAGS *speaks.*]

MAGS: You'll die! Just fall over into the packing cartons and die! Are you ready? . . . BRACE YOURSELVES . . . OKAY, HERE GOES. . . . I'm being given a one-woman show at one of the most important galleries in New York this fall. Me, Margaret Church, exhibited at Castelli's, 420 West Broadway. . . . Can you believe it?! . . . MY PORTRAITS HANGING IN THE SAME ROOMS THAT HAVE SHOWN RAUSCHENBERG, JOHNS, WARHOL, KELLY, LICHTENSTEIN, STELLA, SERRA, ALL THE HEAVIES. . . . It's incredible, beyond belief . . . I mean, at my age. . . . Do you know how good you have to be to get in there? It's a miracle . . . an honest-to-God, star-spangled miracle!

[Pause.]

FANNY (*Mouth full*): Oh, darling, that's wonderful. We're so happy for you!

GARDNER (*Mouth full*): No one deserves it more, no one deserves it more!

MAGS: Through some fluke, some of Castelli's people showed up at our last faculty show at Pratt

and were knocked out . . .

FANNY (*Reaching for the box of Saltines*): More, more . . .

MAGS: They said they hadn't seen anyone handle light like me since the French Impressionists. They said I was this weird blend of Pierre Bonnard, Mary Cassatt and David Hockney . . .

GARDNER (*Swallowing his mouthful*): I told you they were good.

MAGS: Also, no one's doing portraits these days. They're considered passé. I'm so out of it, I'm in.

GARDNER: Well, you're loaded with talent and always have been.

FANNY: She gets it all from Mama, you know. Her miniature of Henry James is still one of the main attractions at the Atheneum. Of course no woman of breeding could be a professional artist in her day. It simply wasn't done. But talk about talent . . . that woman had talent to burn!

MAGS: I want to do one of you for the show.

FANNY: Oh, do Daddy, he's the famous one.

MAGS: No, I want to do you both. I've always wanted to do you and now I've finally got a good excuse.

FANNY: It's high time somebody painted Daddy again! I'm sick to death of that dreadful portrait of him in the National Gallery they keep reproducing. He looks like an undertaker!

GARDNER: Well, I think you should just do Mum. She's never looked handsomer.

FANNY: Oh, come on, I'm a perfect fright and you know it.

MAGS: I want to do you both. Side by side. In this room. Something really classy. You look so great. Mum with her crazy hats and everything and you with that face. If I could just get you to hold still long enough and actually pose.

GARDNER (*Walking around, distracted*): Where are those papers I just had? Goddammit, Fanny . . .

MAGS: I have the feeling it's either now or never.

GARDNER: I can't hold on to anything around here. (*He exits to his study*)

MAGS: I've always wanted to do you. It would be such a challenge.

FANNY (*Pulling* MAGS *onto the sofa next to her*): I'm so glad you're finally here, Mags. I'm very worried about Daddy.

MAGS: Mummy, please. I just got here.

FANNY: He's getting quite gaga.

MAGS: Mummy . . . !

FANNY: You haven't seen him in almost a year. Two weeks ago he walked through the front door of the Codman's house, kissed Emily on the cheek and settled down in the maid's room, thinking he was home!

MAGS: Oh, come on, you're exaggerating.

FANNY: He's as mad as a hatter and getting worse every day! It's this damned new book of his. He works on it around the clock. I've read some of it, and it doesn't make one word of sense, it's all at sixes and sevens . . .

GARDNER (*Pokes his head back in the room, spies some of his papers on a table and grabs them*): Ahhh, here they are. (*He exits*)

FANNY (*Voice lowered*): Ever since this dry spell with his poetry, he's been frantic, absolutely . . . frantic!

MAGS: I hate it when you do this.

FANNY: I'm just trying to get you to face the facts around here.

MAGS: There's nothing wrong with him! He's just as sane as the next man. Even saner, if you ask me.

FANNY: You know what he's doing now? You couldn't guess in a million years! . . . He's writing criticism! Daddy! (*She laughs*) Can you believe it? The man doesn't have one analytic bone in his body. His mind is a complete jumble and always has been!

[*There's a loud crash from GARDNER's study.*]

GARDNER (*Offstage*): SHIT!

MAGS: He's abstracted. . . . That's the way he is.

FANNY: He doesn't spend any time with me anymore. He just holes up in that filthy study with Toots. God, I hate that bird! Though actually they're quite cunning together. Daddy's teaching him Gray's *Elegy*. You ought to see them in there, Toots perched on top of Daddy's head, spouting out verse after verse . . . Daddy, tap-tap-tapping away on his typewriter. They're quite a pair.

GARDNER (*Pokes his head back in*): Have you seen that Stevens' poem I was reading before?

FANNY (*Long-suffering*): NO, I HAVEN'T SEEN THAT STEVENS' POEM YOU WERE READING BEFORE! . . . Things are getting very tight around here, in case you haven't noticed. Daddy's last Pulitzer didn't even cover our real estate tax, and now that he's too doddery to give readings anymore, that income is gone . . . (*Suddenly handing MAGS the sugar bowl she'd been wrapping*) Mags, *do* take this sugar bowl. You can use it to serve tea to your students at that wretched art school of yours . . .

MAGS: It's called Pratt! The Pratt Institute.

FANNY: Pratt, Splatt, whatever . . .

MAGS: And I don't serve tea to my students, I teach them how to paint.

FANNY: Well, I'm sure none of them has ever seen a sugar bowl as handsome as this before.

GARDNER (*Reappearing again*): You're sure you haven't seen it?

FANNY (*Loud and angry*): YES, I'M SURE I HAVEN'T SEEN IT! I JUST TOLD YOU I HAVEN'T SEEN IT!

GARDNER (*Retreating*): Right you are, right you are. (*He exits*)

FANNY: God!

[*Silence.*]

MAGS: What do you have to yell at him like that for?

FANNY: Because the poor thing's as deaf as an adder!

[*MAGS sighs deeply; silence. FANNY, suddenly exuberant, leads her over to a lamp.*]

FANNY: Come, I want to show you something.

MAGS (*Looking at it*): What is it?

FANNY: Something I made. (*MAGS is about to turn it on*) WAIT, DON'T TURN IT ON YET! It's got to be dark to get the full effect. (*She rushes to the windows and pulls down the shades*)

MAGS: What *are* you doing?

FANNY: Hold your horses a minute. You'll see . . . (*As the room gets darker and darker*) Poor me, you wouldn't believe the lengths I go to to amuse myself these days . . .

MAGS (*Touching the lampshade*): What is this? It looks like a scene of some sort.

FANNY: It's an invention I made . . . a kind of magic lantern.

MAGS: Gee . . . it's amazing . . .

FANNY: What I did was buy an old engraving of the Grand Canal . . .

MAGS: You *made* this?

FANNY: . . . and then color it in with crayons. Next, I got out my sewing scissors and cut out all the street lamps and windows . . . anything that light would shine through. Then I pasted it over a plain lampshade, put the shade on this old horror of a lamp, turned on the switch and . . . (*She turns it on*) VOILA . . . VENICE TWINKLING AT DUSK! It's quite effective, don't you think . . . ?

MAGS (*Walking around it*): Jeez . . .

FANNY: And see, I poked out all the little lights on the gondolas with a straight pin.

MAGS: Where on earth did you get the idea?

FANNY: Well you know, idle minds . . . (*She spins the shade, making the lights whirl*)

MAGS: It's really amazing. I mean, you could sell this in a store!

GARDNER (*Enters*): Here it is. it was right on top of my desk the whole time. (*He crashes into a table*) OOOOOWWWWW!

FANNY: LOOK OUT, LOOK OUT!

MAGS (*Rushes over to* GARDNER): Oh, Daddy, are you all right?

FANNY: Watch where you're going, watch where you're going!

GARDNER (*Hopping up and down on one leg*): GOD-DAMMIT! . . . I HIT MY SHIN.

FANNY: I was just showing Mags my lamp . . .

GARDNER (*Limping over to it*): Oh, yes, isn't that something? Mum is awfully clever with that kind of thing. . . . It was all her idea. Buying the engraving, coloring it in, cutting out all those little dots.

FANNY: Not "dots" . . . lights and windows, lights and windows!

GARDNER: Right, right . . . lights and windows.

FANNY: Well, we'd better get some light back in here before someone breaks their neck. (*She zaps the shades back up*)

GARDNER (*Puts his arm around* MAGS): Gee, it's good to have you back.

MAGS: It's good to be back.

GARDNER: And I like that new red hair of yours. It's very becoming.

MAGS: But I told you, I hardly touched it . . .

GARDNER: Well, something's different. You've got a glow. So . . . how do you want us to pose for this grand portrait of yours . . . ? (*He poses self-consciously*)

MAGS: Oh, Daddy, setting up a portrait takes a lot of time and thought. You've got to figure out the background, the lighting, what to wear, the sort of mood you want to—

FANNY: OOOOH, LET'S DRESS UP, LET'S DRESS UP! (*She grabs a packing blanket, drapes it around herself and links arms with* GARDNER, *striking an elegant pose*) This *is* going to be fun. She was absolutely right! Come on, Gar, look distinguished!

MAGS: Mummy, please, it's not a game!

FANNY (*More and more excited*): You still have your tuxedo, don't you? And I'll wear my marvelous long black dress that makes me look like that fascinating woman in the Sargent painting! (*She strikes the famous profile pose*)

MAGS: MUMMY?!

FANNY: I'm sorry, we'll behave, just tell us what to do.

[*FANNY and GARDNER settle down next to each other.*]

GARDNER: That's right, you're the boss.

FANNY: Yes, you're the boss.

MAGS: But I'm not ready yet; I haven't set anything up.

FANNY: Relax, darling, we just want to get the hang of it . . .

[*FANNY and GARDNER stare straight ahead, trying to*

look like suitable subjects, but they can't hold still. They keep making faces, lifting an eyebrow, wriggling a nose, twitching a lip. Nothing big and grotesque, just flickering changes; a half-smile here, a self-important frown there. They steal glances at each other every so often.]

GARDNER: How am I doing, Fan?

FANNY: Brilliantly, absolutely brilliantly!

MAGS: But you're making faces.

FANNY: *I'm* not making faces. (*Turning to* GARDNER *and making a face*) Are *you* making faces, Gar?

GARDNER (*Instantly making one*): Certainly not! I'm the picture of restraint!

[*Without meaning to,* FANNY *and* GARDNER *get sillier and sillier. They start giggling, then laughing.*]

MAGS (*Can't help but join in*): You two are impossible . . . completely impossible! I was crazy to think I could ever pull this off! (*Laughing away*) Look at you . . . just . . . look at you!

[*Blackout.*]

Scene 2

Two days later, around five in the afternoon. Half of the Church household has been dragged into the living room for packing. Overflowing cartons are everywhere. They're filled with pots and pans, dishes and glasses, and the entire contents of two linen closets. MAGS *has placed a stepladder under one of the windows. A pile of tablecloths and curtains is flung beneath it. Two side chairs are in readiness for the eventual pose.*

MAGS has just pulled a large crimson tablecloth out of a carton. She unfurls it with one shimmering toss.

MAGS: PERFECT . . . PERFECT!

FANNY (*Seated on the sofa, clutches an old pair of galoshes to her chest*): Look at these old horrors; half the rubber is rotted away and the fasteners are falling to pieces. . . . GARDNER? . . . OH, GAR-RRRRRRRRRDNERRRRR?

MAGS (*Rippling out the tablecloth with shorter snapping motions*): Have you ever seen such a color?

FANNY: I've found your old sledding galoshes in with the pots and pans. Do you still want them?

MAGS: It's like something out of a Rubens!

[*MAGS slings the tablecloth over a chair and then sits on a footstool to finish the Sara Lee banana cake she started. As she eats, she looks at the tablecloth, making happy grunting sounds.* FANNY *lovingly puts the galoshes on over her shoes and wiggles her feet.*]

FANNY: God, these bring back memories! There were

real snowstorms in the old days. Not these pathetic little two-inch droppings we have now. After a particularly heavy one, Daddy and I used to go sledding on the Common. This was way before you were born. . . . God, it was a hundred years ago! . . . Daddy would stop writing early, put on these galoshes and come looking for me, jingling the fasteners like castanets. It was a kind of mating call, almost . . . (*She jingles them*) The Common was always deserted after a storm; we had the whole place to ourselves. It was so romantic. . . . We'd haul the sled up Beacon Street, stop under the State House, and aim it straight down to the Park Street Church, which was much further away in those days. . . . Then Daddy would lie down on the sled, I'd lower myself on top of him, we'd rock back and forth a few times to gain momentum and then . . . WHOOOOOOOOOSSSSSSSHHHHH . . . down we'd plunge like a pair of eagles locked in a spasm of lovemaking. God, it was wonderful! . . . The city whizzing past us at ninety miles an hour . . . the cold . . . the darkness . . . Daddy's hair in my mouth . . . GAR . . . REMEMBER HOW WE USED TO GO SLEDDING IN THE OLD DAYS? . . . Sometimes he'd lie on top of me. That was fun. I liked that even more. (*In her foghorn voice*) GARRRRRRRRRDNERRRRR?

MAGS: Didn't he say he was going out this afternoon?

FANNY: Why, so he did! I completely forgot. (*She takes off the galoshes*) I'm getting just as bad as him. (*She drops them into a different carton—wistful*) Gar's galoshes, Cotuit.

[*A pause. MAGS picks up the tablecloth again, holds it high over her head.*]

MAGS: Isn't this fabulous? . . . (*She then wraps FANNY in it*) It's the perfect backdrop. Look what it does to your skin.

FANNY: Mags, what *are* you doing?

MAGS: It makes you glow like a pomegranate . . . (*She whips it off her*) Now all I need is a hammer and nails . . . (*She finds them*) YES! (*She climbs up the stepladder and starts hammering a corner of the cloth into the molding of one of the windows*) This is going to look so great! . . . I've never seen such color!

FANNY: Darling, what is going on . . . ?

MAGS: Rembrandt, eat your heart out! You seventeenth-century Dutch has-been, you. (*She hammers more furiously*)

FANNY: MARGARET, THIS IS NOT A CONSTRUCTION SITE. . . . PLEASE . . . STOP IT . . . YOO-HOOOOO . . . DO YOU HEAR ME?

[*GARDNER suddenly appears, dressed in a raincoat.*]

GARDNER: yes, dear, here i am. i just stepped out for a walk down chestnut street. beautiful afternoon, absolutely beautiful! . . . why, that looks very nice, mags, very nice indeed . . .

FANNY (*To Mags*): You're going to ruin the walls to say nothing of mama's best tablecloth. . . . Mags, do you hear me? . . . yoo-hoo! . . . darling, I must insist you stop that dreadful . . .

MAGS (*Steps down; stands back and looks at the tablecloth*): That's it. That's IT!

FANNY (*To GARDNER, worried*): Where have *you* been?

[*MAGS kisses her fingers at the backdrop and settles back into her banana cake.*]

GARDNER (*To FANNY*): You'll never guess who I ran into on Chestnut Street . . . Pate Baldwin!

[*GARDNER takes his coat off and drops it on the floor. He sits in one of the posing chairs.*]

MAGS (*Mouth full of cake*): Oh, Daddy, I'm nowhere near ready for you yet.

FANNY (*Picks up GARDNER's coat and hands it to him*): Darling, coats do *not* go on the floor.

GARDNER (*Rises, but forgets where he's supposed to go*): He was in terrible shape. I hardly recognized him. Well, it's the Parkinson's disease . . .

FANNY: You mean, Hodgkin's disease . . .

GARDNER: Hodgkin's disease . . . ?

MAGS (*Leaves her cake and returns to the tablecloth*): Now to figure out exactly how to use this gorgeous light . . .

FANNY: Yes, Pate has Hodgkin's disease, not Parkinson's disease. Sammy Bishop has Parkinson's disease. In the closet . . . your coat goes . . . in the closet!

GARDNER: You're absolutely right! Pate has Hodgkin's disease. (*He stands motionless, the coat over his arm*)

FANNY: And Goat Davis has Addison's disease.

GARDNER: I always get them confused.

FANNY (*Pointing towards the closet*): That way . . .

[*GARDNER exits to the closet; FANNY calls after him.*]

FANNY: Grace Phelps has it too, I think. Or, it might be Hodgkin's, like Pate. I can't remember.

GARDNER (*Returns with a hanger*): Doesn't The Goat have Parkinson's disease?

FANNY: No, that's Sammy Bishop.

GARDNER: God, I haven't seen The Goat in ages! (*The*

coat still over his arm, he hands FANNY *the hanger)*

FANNY: He hasn't been well.

GARDNER: Didn't Heppy . . . *die?!*

FANNY: What are you giving me this for? . . . Oh, Heppy's been dead for years. She died on the same day as Luster Bright, don't you remember?

GARDNER: I always liked her.

FANNY (*Gives* GARDNER *back the hanger*): Here, I don't want this.

GARDNER: She was awfully attractive.

FANNY: Who?

GARDNER: Heppy!

FANNY: Oh, yes, Heppy had real charm.

MAGS (*Keeps adjusting the tablecloth*): Better . . . better . . .

GARDNER: Which is something The Goat is short on, if you ask me. He has Hodgkin's disease, doesn't he? (*Puts his raincoat back on and sits down*)

FANNY: Darling, what *are* you doing? I thought you wanted to hang up your coat!

GARDNER (*After a pause*): OH, YES, THAT'S RIGHT!

[GARDNER *goes back to the closet; a pause.*]

FANNY: Where were we?

GARDNER (*Returns with yet another hanger*): Let's see . . .

FANNY (*Takes both hangers from him*): FOR GOD'S SAKE, GAR, PAY ATTENTION!

GARDNER: It was something about The Goat . . .

FANNY (*Takes the coat from* GARDNER): HERE, LET ME DO IT! . . . (*Under her breath to* MAGS) See what I mean about him? You don't know the half of it!

[FANNY *hangs the raincoat up in the closet.*]

FANNY: Not the half.

MAGS (*Still tinkering with the backdrop*): Almost . . . almost . . .

GARDNER (*Sitting back down in one of the posing chairs*): Oh, Fan, did I tell you, I ran into Pate Baldwin just now. I'm afraid he's not long for this world.

FANNY (*Returning*): Well, it's that Hodgkin's disease . . . (*She sits on the posing chair next to him*)

GARDNER: God, I'd hate to see him go. He's one of the great editors of our times. I couldn't have done it without him. He gave me everything, everything!

MAGS (*Makes a final adjustment*): Yes, that's it! (*She stands back and gazes at them*) You look wonderful!

FANNY: Isn't it getting to be . . . (*She taps at an imaginary watch on her wrist and drains an imaginary glass*) cocktail time?!

GARDNER (*Looks at his watch*): On the button, on the button! (*He rises*)

FANNY: I'll have the usual, please. Do join us, Mags! Daddy bought some Dubonnet especially for you!

MAGS: Hey. I was just getting some ideas.

GARDNER (*To* MAGS, *as he exists for the bar*): How about a little . . . Dubonnet to wet your whistle?

FANNY: Oh, Mags, it's like old times having you back with us like this!

GARDNER (*Offstage*): THE USUAL FOR YOU, FAN?

FANNY: I wish we saw more of you . . . . PLEASE! . . . Isn't he darling? Have you ever known anyone more darling than Daddy?

GARDNER (*Offstage; hums Jolson's "You Made Me Love You"*): MAGS, HOW ABOUT YOU? . . . A LITTLE . . . DUBONNET?

FANNY: Oh, *do* join us!   MAGS (*To* GARDNER): No, nothing, thanks.

FANNY: Well, what do you think of your aged parents picking up and moving to Cotuit year round? Pretty crazy, eh what? . . . Nothing but the gulls, oysters and us!

GARDNER (*Returns with* FANNY's *drink*): Here you go . . .

FANNY: Why thank you, Gar. (*To* MAGS) You sure you won't join us?

GARDNER (*Lifts his glass towards* FANNY *and* MAGS): Cheers!

[GARDNER *and* FANNY *take that first lifesaving gulp.*]

FANNY: Aaaaahhhhh!   GARDNER: Hits the spot, hits the spot!

MAGS: Well, I certainly can't do you like that!

FANNY: Why not? I think we look very . . . *comme il faut!*

[FANNY *slouches into a rummy pose;* GARDNER *joins her.*]

FANNY: WAIT . . . I'VE GOT IT! I'VE GOT IT! (*She whispers excitedly to* GARDNER)

MAGS: Come on, let's not start this again!

GARDNER: What's that? . . . Oh, yes . . . yes, yes . . . I know the one you mean. Yes, right, right . . . of course.

[*A pause.*]

FANNY: How's . . . *this?!*

[FANNY *grabs a large serving fork and she and* GARDNER *fly into an imitation of Grant Wood's* American Gothic.]

MAGS: And I wonder why it's taken me all these years to get you to pose for me. You just don't take me seriously! Poor old Mags and her ridiculous portraits . . .

FANNY: Oh, darling, your portraits aren't *ridiculous!* They may not be all that one *hopes* for, but they're certainly not—

MAGS: Remember how you behaved at my first group show in Soho? . . . Oh, come on, you remember. It was a real circus! Think back. . . . It was about six years ago. . . . Daddy had just been awarded some presidential medal of achievement and you insisted he wear it around his neck on a bright red ribbon, and you wore this . . . *huge* feathered hat to match! I'll never forget it! It was the size of a giant pizza with twenty-inch red turkey feathers shooting straight up into the air. . . . Oh, come on, you remember, don't you?

FANNY (*Leaping to her feet*): HOLD EVERYTHING! THIS IS IT! THIS IS REALLY IT! Forgive me for interrupting, Mags darling, it'll just take a minute. (*She whispers excitedly to* GARDNER)

MAGS: I had about eight portraits in the show, mostly of friends of mine, except for this old one I'd done of Mrs. Crowninshield.

GARDNER: All right, all right . . . let's give it a whirl.

[A pause; then they mime Michelangelo's Pietà *with* GARDNER *lying across Fanny's lap as the dead Christ.]*

MAGS (*Depressed*): The *Pietà.* Terrific!

FANNY (*Jabbing* GARDNER *in the ribs*): Hey, we're getting good at this.

GARDNER: Of course it would help if we didn't have all these modern clothes on.

MAGS: AS I WAS SAYING . . .

FANNY: Sorry, Mags . . . sorry . . .

[Huffing and creaking with the physical exertion of it all, FANNY *and* GARDNER *return to their seats.*

MAGS: As soon as you stepped foot in the gallery you spotted it and cried out, "MY GOD, WHAT'S MILLICENT CROWNINSHIELD DOING HERE?" Everyone looked up, what with Daddy's clanking medal and your amazing hat which I was sure would take off and start flying around the room. A crowd gathered. . . . Through some utter fluke, you latched on to *the* most important critic in the city, I mean . . . Mr. Modern Art himself, and you hauled him over to the painting, trumpeting out for all to hear, "THAT'S MILLICENT CROWNINSHIELD! I GREW UP WITH HER. SHE LIVES RIGHT DOWN THE STREET FROM US IN BOSTON. BUT IT'S A VERY POOR LIKE-NESS, IF YOU ASK ME! HER NOSE ISN'T NEARLY THAT LARGE AND SHE DOESN'T HAVE SOMETHING QUEER GROWING OUT OF HER CHIN! THE CROWNINSHIELDS ARE REALLY QUITE GOOD-LOOKING, STUFFY, BUT GOOD-LOOKING NONETHELESS!"

GARDNER (*Suddenly jumps up, ablaze*): WAIT, WAIT . . . IF IT'S MICHELANGELO YOU WANT . . . I'm sorry, Mags. . . . One more . . . just one more . . . please?

MAGS: Sure, why not? Be my guest.

GARDNER: FANNY, *prepare yourself!*

[More whispering.]

FANNY: But I think *you* should be God.

GARDNER: Me? . . . Really?

FANNY: Yes, it's much more appropriate.

GARDNER: Well, if you say so . . .

[FANNY and GARDNER ease down to the floor with some difficulty and lie on their sides, FANNY *as Adam,* GARDNER *as God, their fingers inching closer and closer in the attitude of Michelangelo's The Creation. Finally they touch. MAGS cheers, whistles, applauds.]*

MAGS: THREE CHEERS . . . VERY GOOD . . . NICELY DONE, NICELY DONE!

[FANNY and GARDNER hold the pose a moment more, flushed with pleasure; then rise, dust themselves off and grope back to their chairs.]

MAGS: So, there we were . . .

FANNY: Yes, *do* go on!

MAGS: . . . huddled around Millicent Crowninshield, when you whipped into your pocketbook and suddenly announced, "HOLD EVERYTHING! I'VE GOT A PHOTOGRAPH OF HER RIGHT HERE, THEN YOU CAN SEE WHAT SHE REALLY LOOKS LIKE!" . . . You then proceeded to crouch down to the floor and dump everything out of your bag, and I mean . . . *everything!* . . . leaking packets of sequins and gummed stars, seashells, odd pieces of fur, crochet hooks, a monarch butter-fly embedded in plastic, dental floss, antique glass buttons, small jingling bells, lace . . . I thought I'd die! Just sink to the floor and qui-etly die! . . . You couldn't find it, you see. I mean, you spent the rest of the afternoon on your hands and knees crawling through this ocean of junk, muttering, "It's *got* to be here somewhere; I know I had it with me!" . . . Then Daddy pulled me into the thick of it all and said, "By the way, have you met our daughter Mags yet? She's the one who did all these pictures . . . paintings . . . portraits . . . whatever you call them." (*She drops to her hands and knees and begins crawling out of the room*) By this time, Mum had somehow crawled out of the gallery and was lost on another floor. She began calling for me . . .

"YOO-HOO, MAGS . . . WHERE ARE YOU? . . . OH, MAGS, DARLING . . . HELLO? . . . ARE YOU THERE?" (*She reenters and faces them*) This was at my *first* show.

[*Blackout.*]

Scene 3

Twenty-four hours later. The impact of the impending move has struck with hurricane force. FANNY has lugged all their clothing into the room and dumped it in various cartons. There are coats, jackets, shoes, skirts, suits, hats, sweaters, dresses, the works. She and GARDNER are seated on the sofa, going through it all. FANNY, wearing a different hat and dress, holds up a ratty overcoat.

FANNY: What about this gruesome old thing?

[*GARDNER is wearing several sweaters and vests, a Hawaiian holiday shirt, and a variety of scarves and ties around his neck. He holds up pair of shoes.*]

GARDNER: God . . . remember these shoes? Pound gave them to me when he came back from Italy. I remember it vividly.
FANNY: *Do* let me give it to the thrift shop! (*She stuffs the coat into the appropriate carton*)
GARDNER: He bought them for me in Rome. Said he couldn't resist; bought himself a pair too since we both wore the same size. God, I miss him! (*Pause*) HEY, WHAT ARE YOU DOING WITH MY OVER-COAT?!
FANNY: Darling, it's threadbare!
GARDNER: But that's my overcoat! (*He grabs it out of the carton*) I've been wearing it every day for the past thirty-five years!
FANNY: That's just my point: it's had it.
GARDNER (*Puts it on over everything else*): There's nothing wrong with this coat!
FANNY: I trust you remember that the cottage is an eighth the size of this place and you simply won't have room for half this stuff! (*She holds up a sports jacket*) This dreary old jacket, for instance. You've had it since Hector was a pup!
GARDNER (*Grabs the jacket and puts it on over his coat*): Oh, no, you don't . . .
FANNY: And this God-awful hat . . .
GARDNER: Let me see that.

[*GARDNER stands next to FANNY and they fall into a lovely tableau. MAGS suddenly pops out from behind a wardrobe carton with a flash camera and takes a picture of them.*]

MAGS: PERFECT!

FANNY (*Hands flying to her face*): GOOD GOD, WHAT WAS THAT . . . ?

Gardner (*Hands flying to his heart*): JESUS CHRIST, I'VE BEEN SHOT!

MAGS (*Walks to the center of the room, advancing the film*): That was terrific. See if you can do it again.
FANNY: What *are* you doing . . . ?
GARDNER (*Feeling his chest*): Is there blood?
FANNY: I see lace everywhere . . .
MAGS: It's all right, I was just taking a picture of you. I often use a Polaroid at this stage.
FANNY (*Rubbing her eyes*): Really, Mags, you might have given us some warning!
MAGS: But that's the whole point: to catch you unawares!
GARDNER (*Rubbing his eyes*): It's the damndest thing . . . I see lace everywhere.
FANNY: Yes, so do I . . .
GARDNER: It's rather nice, actually. It looks as if you're wearing a veil.
FANNY: I *am* wearing a veil!

[*The camera spits out the photograph.*]

MAGS: OH GOODY, HERE COMES THE PICTURE!
FANNY (*Grabs the partially developed print out of her hands*): Let me see, let me see . . .
GARDNER: Yes, let's have a look.

[*GARDNER and FANNY have another quiet moment together looking at the photograph. MAGS tiptoes away from them and takes another picture.*]

MAGS: YES!

FANNY: NOT AGAIN! PLEASE, DARLING!

GARDNER: WHAT WAS THAT? . . . WHAT HAPPENED?

[*FANNY and GARDNER stagger towards each other.*]

MAGS: I'm sorry, I just couldn't resist. You looked so—
FANNY: WHAT ARE YOU TRYING TO DO . . . *BLIND* US?!
GARDNER: Really, Mags, enough is enough . . .

[*GARDNER and FANNY keep stumbling about kiddingly.*]

FANNY: Are you still there, Gar?
GARDNER: Right as rain, right as rain!
MAGS: I'm sorry; I didn't mean to scare you. It's just a photograph can show you things you weren't aware of. Here, have a look. (*She gives them to FANNY*) Well, I'm going out to the kitchen to get something to eat. Anybody want anything? (*She exits*)
FANNY (*Looking at the photos, half-amused, half-*

horrified): Oh, Gardner, have you ever . . . ?

GARDNER (*Looks at the photos and laughs*): Good grief . . .

MAGS (*Offstage; from the kitchen*): IS IT ALL RIGHT IF I TAKE THE REST OF THIS TAPIOCA FROM LAST NIGHT?

FANNY: IT'S ALL RIGHT WITH ME. How about you, Gar?

GARDNER: Sure, go right ahead. I've never been that crazy about tapioca.

FANNY: What are you talking about, tapioca is one of your favorites.

MAGS (*Enters, slurping from a large bowl*): Mmmmmmmm . . .

FANNY: Really, Mags, I've never seen anyone eat as much as you.

MAGS (*Takes the photos back*): It's strange. I only do this when I come home.

FANNY: What's the matter, don't I feed you enough?

GARDNER: Gee, it's hot in here! (*Starts taking off his coat*)

FANNY: God knows, you didn't eat anything as a child! I've never seen such a fussy eater. Gar, what *are* you doing?

GARDNER (*Shedding clothes to the floor*): Taking off some of these clothes. It's hotter than Tophet in here!

MAGS (*Looking at her photos*): Yes, I like you looking at each other like that . . .

FANNY (*To* GARDNER): Please watch where you're dropping things; I'm trying to keep some order around here.

GARDNER (*Picks up what he dropped, dropping even more in the process*): Right, right . . .

MAGS: Now all I've got to do is figure out what you should wear.

FANNY: Well, I'm going to wear my long black dress, and you'd be a fool not to do Daddy in his tuxedo. He looks so distinguished in it, just like a banker!

MAGS: I haven't really decided yet.

FANNY: Just because you walk around looking like something the cat dragged in, doesn't mean Daddy and I want to, do we Gar?

[*GARDNER is making a worse and worse tangle of his clothes.*]

FANNY: HELLO . . . ?

GARDNER (*Looks up at* FANNY): Oh, yes, awfully attractive, awfully attractive!

FANNY (*To* MAGS): If you don't mind me saying so, I've never seen you looking so forlorn. You'll never catch a husband looking that way. Those peculiar clothes, that God-awful hair . . . really, Mags, it's very distressing!

MAGS: I don't think my hair's so bad, not that it's terrific or anything . . .

FANNY: Well, I don't see other girls walking around like you. I mean, girls from your background.

What would Lyman Wigglesworth think if he saw you in the street?

MAGS: Lyman Wigglesworth?! . . . Uuuuuuughhhhhhh! (*She shudders*)

FANNY: All right then, that brilliant Cabot boy . . . what *is* his name?

GARDNER: Sammy.

FANNY: No, not Sammy . . .

GARDNER: Stephen . . . Stanley . . . Stuart . . . Sheldon . . . Sherlock . . . Sherlock! It's *Sherlock!*

MAGS: Spence!

FANNY: SPENCE, THAT'S IT! HIS NAME IS SPENCE!	GARDNER: THAT'S IT . . . SPENCE! SPENCE CABOT!

FANNY: Spence Cabot was first in his class at Harvard.

MAGS: Mum, he has no facial hair.

FANNY: He has his own law firm on Arlington Street.

MAGS: Spence Cabot has six fingers on his right hand!

FANNY: So, he isn't the best-looking thing in the world. Looks isn't everything. He can't help it if he has extra fingers. Have a little sympathy!

MAGS: But the extra one has this weird nail on it that looks like a talon. . . . It's long and black and . . . (*She shudders*)

FANNY: No one's perfect, darling. He has lovely handwriting and an absolutely saintly mother. Also, he's as rich as Croesus! He's a lot more promising than some of those creatures you've dragged home. What was the name of that dreadful Frenchman who smelled like sweaty socks? . . . Jean Duke of Scripto?

MAGS: (*Laughing*): Jean-Luc Zichot!

FANNY: And that peculiar little Oriental fellow with all the teeth! Really, Mags, he could have been put on display at the circus!

MAGS: Oh, yes, Tsu Chin. He was strange, but very sexy . . .

FANNY: (*Shudders*): He had such tiny . . . feet! Really, Mags, you've got to bear down. You're not getting any younger. Before you know it, all the nice young men will be taken and then where will you be? . . . All by yourself in that grim little apartment of yours with those peculiar clothes and that bright red hair . . .

MAGS: MY HAIR IS NOT BRIGHT RED!

FANNY: I only want what's best for you, you know that. You seem to go out of your way to look wanting. I don't understand it. . . . Gar, what *are* you putting your coat on for? . . . You look like some derelict out on the street. We don't wear coats in the house. (*She helps him out of it*) That's the way. . . . I'll just put this in the carton along with everything else . . . (*She drops it into the carton, then pauses*) Isn't it about time

for . . . *cocktails!*
GARDNER: What's that?

[*FANNY taps her wrist and mimes drinking.*]

GARDNER (*Looks at his watch*): Right you are, right you are! (*Exits to the bar*) THE USUAL . . . ?
FANNY: *Please!*
GARDNER (*Offstage*): HOW ABOUT SOMETHING FOR YOU MAGS?
MAGS: SURE, WHY NOT? . . . LET'ER RIP!
GARDNER (*Offstage*): WHAT'S THAT . . . ?
FANNY: SHE SAID YES. SHE   MAGS: I'LL HAVE SOME
  SAID YES!   DUBONNET! YES!

GARDNER (*Poking his head back in*): How about a little Dubonnet?
FANNY: That's just what she said. . . . She'd like some . . . Dubonnet!
GARDNER (*Goes back to the bar and hums another Jolson tune*): GEE, IT'S GREAT HAVING YOU BACK LIKE THIS, MAGS . . . IT'S JUST GREAT! (*More singing*)
FANNY (*Leaning closer to MAGS*): You have such *potential,* darling! It breaks my heart to see how you've let yourself go. If Lyman Wigglesworth . . .
MAGS: Amazing as it may seem, I don't *care* about Lyman Wigglesworth!
FANNY: From what I've heard, he's quite a lady killer!
MAGS: But with whom? . . . Don't think I haven't heard about his fling with . . . Hopie Stonewall!
FANNY (*Begins to laugh*): Oh, God, let's not get started on Hopie Stonewall again . . . ten feet tall with spots on her neck . . . (*To GARDNER*) OH, DAR-LING, DO HURRY BACK! WE'RE TALKING ABOUT PATHETIC HOPIE STONEWALL!
MAGS: It's not so much her incredible height and spotted skin; it's those tiny pointed teeth and the size eleven shoes!
FANNY: I love it when you're like this!

[*MAGS starts clomping around the room making tiny pointed-teeth nibbling sounds*]

FANNY: GARDNER . . . YOU'RE MISSING EVERYTHING! (*Still laughing*) Why is it Boston girls are always so . . . tall?
MAGS: Hopie Stonewall isn't a Boston girl; she's a giraffe. (*She prances around the room with an imaginary dwarf-sized Lyman*) She's perfect for Lyman Wigglesworth!
GARDNER (*Returns with FANNY's drink, which he hands her*): Now, where were we . . . ?
FANNY (*Trying not to laugh*): HOPIE STONEWALL . . . !
GARDNER: Oh, yes, she's the very tall one, isn't she?

[*FANNY and MAGS burst into gales*]

MAGS: The only hope for us . . . "Boston girls" is to get as far away from our kind as possible.
FANNY: She always asks after you, darling. She's very fond of you, you know.
MAGS: Please, I don't want to hear!
FANNY: Your old friends are *always* asking after you.
MAGS: It's not so much how creepy they all are, as how much they remind me of myself!
FANNY: But you're not "creepy," darling . . . just . . . shabby!
MAGS: I mean, give me a few more inches and some brown splotches here and there, and Hopie and I could be sisters!
FANNY (*In a whisper to GARDNER*): Don't you love it when Mags is like this? I could listen to her forever!
MAGS: I mean . . . look at me!
FANNY (*Gasping*): Don't stop, don't stop!
MAGS: Awkward . . . plain . . . I don't know how to dress, I don't know how to talk. When people find out Daddy's my father, they're always amazed. . . . "Gardner Church is YOUR father?! Aw, come on, you're kidding?!"
FANNY (*In a whisper*): Isn't she divine . . . ?
MAGS: Sometimes I don't even tell them. I pretend I grew up in the Midwest somewhere . . . farm-ing people . . . we work with our hands.
GARDNER (*To MAGS*): Well, how about a little refill . . . ?
MAGS: No, no more thanks.

[*Pause.*]

FANNY: What did you have to go and interrupt her for? She was just getting up a head of steam . . .
MAGS (*Walking over to her easel*): The great thing about being a portrait painter, you see, is it's the *other* guy that's exposed; you're safely hid-den behind the canvas and easel. (*Standing behind it*) You can be as plain as a pitchfork, as inarticulate as mud, but it doesn't matter because you're completely concealed: your body, your face, your intentions. Just as you make your most intimate move, throw open your soul . . . they stretch and yawn, remem-bering the dog has to be let out at five. . . . To be so invisible while so enthralled . . . it takes your breath away!
GARDNER: Well put, Mags. Awfully well put!
MAGS: That's why I've always wanted to paint you, to see if I'm up to it. It's quite a risk. Remember what I went through as a child with my great masterpiece . . . ?
FANNY: You painted a masterpiece when you were a child . . . ?

MAGS: Well, it was a masterpiece to me.

FANNY: I had no idea you were precocious as a child. Gardner, do you remember Mags painting a masterpiece as a child?

MAGS: I didn't paint it. It was something I made!

FANNY: Well, this is all news to me! Gar, *do* get me another drink! I haven't had this much fun in years! (*She hands him her glass and reaches for* MAGS'S) Come on, darling, join me . . .

MAGS: No, no more, thanks. I don't really like the taste.

FANNY: Oh, come on, kick up your heels for once!

MAGS: No, nothing . . . really.

FANNY: Please? Pretty please? . . . To keep me company?!

MAGS (*Hands* GARDNER *her glass*): Oh, all right, what the hell . . .

FANNY: That's a good girl!

GARDNER (*Existing*): Coming right up, coming right up!

FANNY (*Yelling after* GARDNER): DON'T GIVE ME TOO MUCH NOW. THE LAST ONE WAS AWFULLY STRONG . . . AND HURRY BACK SO YOU DON'T MISS ANYTHING! . . . Daddy's so cunning, I don't know what I'd do without him. If anything should happen to him, I'd just . . .

MAGS: Mummy, nothing's going to happen to him . . . !

FANNY: Well, wait till you're our age, it's no garden party. Now . . . where were we . . . ?

MAGS: My first masterpiece . . .

FANNY: Oh, yes, but *do* wait till Daddy gets back so he can hear it too. . . . YOO-HOO . . . GARRRRRRDNERRRRRR? . . . ARE YOU COMING? (*Silence*) Go and check on him will you?

[GARDNER *enters with both drinks. He's very shaken.*]

GARDNER: I couldn't find the ice.

FANNY: Well, *finally!*

GARDNER: It just up and disappeared . . . (*Hands* FANNY *her drink*) There you go. (FANNY *kisses her fingers and takes a hefty swig*) Mags. (*He hands* MAGS *her drink*)

MAGS: Thanks, Daddy.

GARDNER: Sorry about the ice.

MAGS: No problem, no problem.

[GARDNER *sits down; silence.*]

FANNY (*To* MAGS): Well, drink up, drink up! (MAGS *downs it in one gulp*) GOOD-GIRL! . . . Now, what's all this about a masterpiece . . . ?

MAGS: I did it during that winter you sent me away from the dinner table. I was about nine years old.

FANNY: We sent you from the dinner table?

MAGS: I was banished for six months.

FANNY: You *were?* . . . How extraordinary!

MAGS: Yes, it *was* rather extraordinary!

FANNY: But why?

MAGS: Because I played with my food.

FANNY: You did?

MAGS: I used to squirt it out between my front teeth.

FANNY: Oh, I remember that! God, it used to drive me crazy, absolutely . . . crazy! (*Pause*) "MARGARET, STOP THAT OOZING RIGHT THIS MINUTE, YOU ARE NOT A TUBE OF TOOTHPASTE!"

GARDNER: Oh, yes . . .

FANNY: It was perfectly disgusting!

GARDNER: I remember. She used to lean over her plate and squirt it out in long runny ribbons . . .

FANNY: That's enough, dear.

GARDNER: They were quite colorful, actually; decorative almost. She made the most intricate designs. They looked rather like small, moist Oriental rugs . . .

FANNY (*To* MAGS): But why, darling? What on earth possessed you to do it?

MAGS: I couldn't swallow anything. My throat just closed up. I don't know, I must have been afraid of choking or something.

GARDNER: I remember one in particular. We'd had chicken fricassee and spinach. . . . She made the most extraordinary—

FANNY (*To* GARDNER): WILL YOU PLEASE SHUT UP?! (*Pause*) Mags, what *are* you talking about? You never choked in your entire life! This is the most distressing conversation I've ever had. Don't you think it's distressing, Gar?

GARDNER: Well, that's not quite the word I'd use.

FANNY: What word *would* you use, then?

GARDNER: I don't know right off the bat, I'd have to think about it.

FANNY: THEN, THINK ABOUT IT!

[*Silence.*]

MAGS: I guess I was afraid of making a mess. I don't know; you were awfully strict about table manners. I was always afraid of losing control. What if I started to choke and began spitting up over everything . . . ?

FANNY: All right, dear, that's enough.

MAGS: No, I was really terrified about making a mess; you always got so mad whenever I spilled. If I just got rid of everything in neat little curlicues beforehand, you see . . .

FANNY: I SAID: THAT'S ENOUGH!

[*Silence.*]

MAGS: *I* thought it was quite ingenious, but you didn't see it that way. You finally sent me from the table with, "When you're ready to eat like a human being, you can come back and join us!" . . . So, it was off to my room with a tray. But I couldn't seem to eat there either. I mean, it was so strange settling down to dinner in my *bed-room*. . . . So I just flushed everything down the toilet and sat on my bed listening to you: clinkity-clink, clatter clatter, slurp, slurp . . . but that got pretty boring after a while, so I looked around for something to do. It was wintertime, because I noticed I'd left some crayons on top of my radiator and they'd melted down into these beautiful shimmering globs, like spilled jello, trembling and pulsing . . .

GARDNER (*Overlapping; eyes closed*):
"This luscious and impeccable fruit of life
Falls, it appears, of its own weight to earth . . ."

MAGS: Naturally, I wanted to try it myself, so I grabbed a red one and pressed it down against the hissing lid. It oozed and bubbled like raspberry jam!

GARDNER:
"When you were Eve, its acrid juice was sweet,
Untasted, in its heavenly, orchard air . . ."

MAGS: I mean, that radiator was really hot! It took incredible will power not to let go, but I held on, whispering, "Mags, if you let go of this crayon, you'll be run over by a truck on Newberry Street, so help you God!" . . . So I pressed down harder, my fingers steaming and blistering . . .

FANNY: I had no idea about any of this, did you, Gar?

MAGS: Once I'd melted one, I was hooked! I finished off my entire supply in one night, mixing color over color until my head swam! . . . The heat, the smell, the brilliance that sank and rose . . . I'd never felt such exhilaration! . . . Every week I spent my allowance on crayons. I must have cleared out every box of Crayolas in the city!

GARDNER (*Gazing at MAGS*): You know, I don't think I've ever seen you looking prettier! You're awfully attractive when you get going!

FANNY: Why, what a lovely thing to say.

MAGS: AFTER THREE MONTHS THAT RADIATOR WAS . . . SPECTACULAR! I MEAN, IT LOOKED LIKE SOME COLOSSAL FRUITCAKE, FIVE FEET TALL . . . !

FANNY: It sounds perfectly hideous.

MAGS: It was a knockout; shimmering with pinks and blues, lavenders, and maroons, turquoise and golds, oranges and creams. . . . For every color, I imagined a taste . . . YELLOW: lemon curls dipped in sugar . . . RED: glazed cherries laced with rum . . . GREEN: tiny peppermint leaves veined with chocolate . . . PURPLE:—

FANNY : That's quite enough!

MAGS: And then the frosting . . . ahhhh, the frosting! A satiny mix of white and silver . . . I kept it hidden under blankets during the day. . . . My huge . . . (*She starts laughing*) looming . . . teetering sweet—

FANNY: I ASKED YOU TO STOP! GARDNER, WILL YOU PLEASE GET HER TO STOP!

GARDNER: See here, Mags, Mum asked you to—

MAGS: I was so . . . *hungry* . . . losing weight every week. I looked like a scarecrow what with the bags under my eyes and bits of crayon wrapper leaking out of my clothes. It's a wonder you didn't notice. But finally you came to my rescue . . . if you could call what happened rescue. It was more like a rout!

FANNY: Darling . . . *please!*   GARDNER: Now, look, young lady—

MAGS: The winter was almost over . . . It was very late at night. . . . I must have been having a nightmare because suddenly you and Daddy were at my bed, shaking me. . . . I quickly glanced towards the radiator to see if it was covered. . . . *It wasn't!* It glittered and towered in the moonlight like some . . . gigantic Viennese pastry! You followed my gaze and saw it. Mummy screamed . . . "WHAT HAVE YOU GOT IN HERE? . . . MAGS, WHAT HAVE YOU BEEN DOING?" . . . She crept forward and touched it, and then jumped back. "IT'S FOOD!" she cried . . . "IT'S ALL THE FOOD SHE'S BEEN SPITTING OUT! OH, GARDNER, ITS A MOUNTAIN OF ROTTING GARBAGE!"

FANNY (*Softly*): Yes . . . it's coming back . . . it's coming back . . .

MAGS: Daddy exited as usual; left the premises. He fainted, just keeled over onto the floor . . .

GARDNER: Gosh, I don't remember any of this . . .

MAGS: My heart stopped! I mean, I knew it was all over. My lovely creation didn't have a chance. Sure enough . . . out came the blowtorch. Well, it couldn't have *really* been a blowtorch, I mean, where would you have ever gotten a blowtorch? . . . I just have this very strong memory of you standing over my bed, your hair streaming around your face, aiming this . . . flamethrower at my confection . . . my cake . . . my tart . . . my strudel. . . . "IT'S GOT TO BE DESTROYED IMMEDIATELY! THE THING'S ALIVE WITH VERMIN! . . . JUST LOOK AT IT! . . . IT'S PRACTICALLY CRAWLING ACROSS THE ROOM!" . . . Of course in a sense you were right. It *was* a monument of my castoff dinners, only I hadn't built it with food. . . . I found my own materials. I was languishing with hunger, but oh, dear Mother . . . I FOUND MY OWN MATERIALS . . . !

FANNY: Darling . . . *please?!*

MAGS: I tried to stop you, but you wouldn't listen. . . .

OUT SHOT THE FLAME! . . . I remember these waves of wax rolling across the room and Daddy coming to, wondering what on earth was going on. . . . Well, what did you know about my abilities? . . . You see, I had . . . I mean, I *have* abilities . . . (*Struggling to say it*) I have abilities. I have . . . strong abilities. I have . . . very strong abilities. They are very strong . . . very, very strong . . .

[*MAGS rises and runs out of the room overcome as FANNY and GARDNER watch, speechless. The curtain falls.*]

ACT II

Scene 1

Three days later. Miracles have been accomplished. Almost all of the Churches' furniture has been moved out, and the cartons of dishes and clothing are gone. All that remains are odds and ends. MAGS'S tableau looms, impregnable. FANNY and GARDNER are dressed in their formal evening clothes, frozen in their pose. They hold absolutely still. MAGS stands at her easel, her hands covering her eyes.

FANNY: All right, you can look now.
MAGS (*Removes her hands*): Yes! . . . I told you you could trust me on the pose.
FANNY: Well, thank God you let us dress up. It makes all the difference. Now we really look like something.
MAGS (*Starts to sketch them*): I'll say . . .

[*A silence as she sketches.*]

GARDNER (*Recites Yeats's "The Song of Wandering Aengus" in a wonderfully resonant voice as they pose*):

"I went out to the hazel wood,
Because a fire was in my head,
And cut and peeled a hazel wand,
And hooked a berry to a thread,
And when white moths were on the wing,
And moth-like stars were flickering out,
I dropped the berry in a stream
And caught a little silver trout.

When I had laid it on the floor
I went to blow the fire a-flame,

But something rustled on the floor,
And someone called me by my name:
It had become a glimmering girl
With apple blossoms in her hair
Who called me by my name and ran
And faded through the brightening air.

Though I am old with wandering
Through hollow lands and hilly lands,
I will find out where she has gone,
And kiss her lips and take her hands;
And walk among long dappled grass,
And pluck till time and times are done,
The silver apples of the moon,
The golden apples of the sun."

FANNY: That's lovely, dear. Just lovely. Is it one of yours?
GARDNER: No, no, it's Yeats. I'm using it in my book.
FANNY: Well, you recited it beautifully, but then you've always recited beautifully. That's how you wooed me, in case you've forgotten. . . . You must have memorized every love poem in the English language! There was no stopping you when you got going . . . your Shakespeare, Byron, and Shelley . . . you were shameless . . . shameless!
GARDNER (*Eyes closed*):

"I will find out where she has gone,
And kiss her lips and take her hands . . ."

FANNY: And then there was your own poetry to do battle with; your sonnets and quatrains. When you got going with them, there was nothing left of me! You could have had your pick of any girl in Boston! Why you chose me, I'll never understand. I had no looks to speak of and nothing much in the brains department. . . . Well, what did you know about women and the world? . . . What did any of us know . . . ?

[*Silence.*]

FANNY: GOD, MAGS, HOW LONG ARE WE SUPPOSED TO SIT LIKE THIS? . . . IT'S AGONY!
MAGS (*Working away*): You're doing fine . . . just fine . . .
FANNY (*Breaking her pose*): It's so . . . boring!
MAGS: Come on, don't move. You can have a break soon.
FANNY: I had no idea it would be so boring!
GARDNER: Gee, I'm enjoying it.
FANNY: You would . . . !

[*A pause.*]

GARDNER (*Begins reciting more Yeats, almost singing it*):

> "He stood among a crowd at Drumahair;
> His heart hung all upon a silken dress,
> And he had known at last some tenderness,
> Before earth made of him her sleepy care;
> But when a man poured fish into a pile,
> It seemed they raised their little silver
>   heads . . ."

FANNY: Gar . . . PLEASE! (*She lurches out of her seat*) God, I can't take this anymore!

MAGS (*Keeps sketching GARDNER*): I know it's tedious at first, but it gets easier . . .

FANNY: It's like a Chinese water torture! (*Crosses to MAGS and looks at GARDNER posing*) Oh, darling, you look marvelous, absolutely marvelous! Why don't you just do Daddy!?

MAGS: Because you look marvelous too. I want to do you both!

FANNY: Please! . . . I have one foot in the grave and you know it! Also, we're way behind in our packing. There's still one room left which everyone seems to have forgotten about!

GARDNER: Which one is that?

FANNY: You know perfectly well which one it is!

GARDNER: I do . . . ?

FANNY: Yes, you do!

GARDNER: Well, it's news to me.

FANNY: I'll give you a hint. It's in . . . *that* direction. (*She points*)

GARDNER: The dining room?

FANNY: No.

GARDNER: The bedroom?

FANNY: No.

GARDNER: Mags' room?

FANNY: No.

GARDNER: The kitchen?

FANNY: *Gar?!*

GARDNER: The guest room?

FANNY: Your God-awful study!

GARDNER: Oh, shit!

FANNY: That's right, "Oh, shit!" It's books and papers up to the ceiling! If you ask me, we should just forget it's there and quietly tiptoe away . . .

GARDNER: My study . . . !

FANNY: Let the new owners dispose of everything . . .

GARDNER (*Gets out of his posing chair*): Now, just one minute . . .

FANNY: You never look at half the stuff in there!

GARDNER: I don't want you touching those books! They're mine!

FANNY: Darling, we're moving to a cottage the size of a handkerchief! Where, pray tell, is there room for all your books?

GARDNER: I don't know. We'll just have to make

room!

MAGS (*Sketching away*): RATS!

FANNY: I don't know what we're doing fooling around with Mags like this when there's still so much to do . . .

GARDNER (*Sits back down, overwhelmed*): My study . . . !

FANNY: You can stay with her if you'd like, but one of us has got to tackle those books! (*She exits to his study*)

GARDNER: I'm not up to this.

MAGS: Oh, good, you're staying!

GARDNER: There's a lifetime of work in there . . .

MAGS: Don't worry, I'll help. Mum and I will be able to pack everything up in no time.

GARDNER: God . . .

MAGS: It won't be so bad . . .

GARDNER: I'm just not up to it.

MAGS: We'll all pitch in . . .

[*GARDNER sighs, speechless. A silence as FANNY comes staggering in with an armload of books, which she drops to the floor with a crash.*]

GARDNER: WHAT WAS   MAGS: GOOD GRIEF!
    THAT?!

FANNY (*Sheepish*): Sorry, sorry . . . (*She exits for more*)

GARDNER: I don't know if I can take this . . .

MAGS: Moving is awful . . . I know . . .

GARDNER (*Settling back into his pose*): Ever since Mum began tearing the house apart, I've been having these dreams. . . . I'm a child again back at 16 Louisberg Square . . . and this stream of moving men is carrying furniture into our house . . . van after van of tables and chairs, sofas and love seats, desks and bureaus . . . rugs, bathtubs, mirrors, chiming clocks, pianos, iceboxes, china cabinets . . . but what's amazing is that all of it is familiar . . .

[*FANNY comes in with another load, which she drops on the floor. She exits for more.*]

GARDNER: No matter how many items appear, I've seen every one of them before. Since my mother is standing in the midst of it directing traffic, I ask her where it's all coming from, but she doesn't hear me because of the racket . . . so finally I just scream out . . . "WHERE IS ALL THIS FURNITURE COMING FROM?" . . . Just as a moving man is carrying Toots into the room, she looks at me and says, "Why, from the land of Skye!" . . . The next thing I know, *people* are being carried in along with it . . .

[*FANNY enters with her next load; drops it and exits.*]

GARDNER: People I've never seen before are sitting

around our dining-room table. A group of foreigners is going through my books, chattering
in a language I've never heard before. A man
is playing a Chopin polonaise on Aunt Alice's
piano. Several children are taking baths in our
tubs from Cotuit . . .

MAGS: It sounds marvelous.

GARDNER: Well, it isn't marvelous at all because all of
these perfect strangers have taken over our
things . . .

[FANNY enters, hurls down another load and exits.]

MAGS: How odd . . .

GARDNER: Well, it *is* odd, but then something even
odder happens . . .

MAGS (*Sketching away*): Tell me, tell me!

GARDNER: Well, our beds are carried in. They're all
made up with sheets and everything, but
instead of all these strange people in them,
we're in them . . . !

MAGS: What's so odd about that?

GARDNER: Well, you and Mum are brought in, both
sleeping like angels . . . Mum snoring away to
beat the band . . .

MAGS: Yes . . .

[FANNY enters with another load, lets it fall.]

GARDNER: But there's no one in mine. It's completely
empty, never even been slept in! It's as if I
were dead or had never even existed . . .

[FANNY exits.]

GARDNER: "HEY . . . WAIT UP!" I yell to the moving
men . . . "THAT'S MY BED YOU'VE GOT THERE!" But
they don't stop; they don't even acknowledge
me. . . . "HEY, COME BACK HERE . . . I WANT TO GET
INTO MY BED!" I cry again and I start running
after them . . . down the hall, through the dining room, past the library. . . . Finally I catch
up to them and hurl myself right into the center of the pillow. Just as I'm about to land, the
bed suddenly vanishes and I go crashing
down to the floor like some insect that's been
hit by a fly swatter!

[FANNY staggers in with her final load; she drops it
with a crash and then collapses in her posing chair.]

FANNY: THAT'S IT FOR ME! I'M DEAD!

[Silence.]

FANNY: Come on, Mags, how about you doing a little
work around here.

MAGS: That's all I've been doing! This is the first free

moment you've given me!

FANNY: You should see all the books in there . . . and
papers! There are enough loose papers to sink
a ship!

GARDNER: Why is it we're moving, again . . . ?

FANNY: Because life is getting too complicated here.

GARDNER: (*Remembering*): Oh, yes . . .

FANNY: And we can't afford it anymore.

GARDNER: That's right, that's right . . .

FANNY: We don't have the . . . *income* we used to!

GARDNER: Oh, yes . . . *income!*

FANNY (*Assuming her pose again*): Of course, we have
our savings and various trust funds, but I
wouldn't dream of touching those!

GARDNER: No, no, you must never dip into capital!

FANNY: I told Daddy I'd be perfectly happy to buy a
gun and put a bullet through our heads so we
could avoid all this, but he wouldn't hear of it!

MAGS (*Sketching away*): No, I shouldn't think so.

[Pause.]

FANNY: I've always admired people who kill themselves when they get to our stage of life. Well,
no one can touch my Uncle Edmond in that
department . . .

MAGS: I know, I know . . .

FANNY: The day before his seventieth birthday he
climbed to the top of the Old North Church
and hurled himself face down into Salem
Street! They had to scrape him up with a spat-
ula! God, he was a remarkable man . . . state
senator, president of Harvard . . .

GARDNER (*Rises and wanders over to his books*): Well, I
guess I'm going to have to do something about
all of these . . .

FANNY: Come on Mags, help Daddy! Why don't you
start bringing in his papers . . .

[GARDNER sits on the floor; he picks up a book and
soon is engrossed in it. MAGS keeps sketching, obliv-
ious. Silence.]

FANNY (*To* MAGS): Darling? . . . HELLO? . . . God, you
two are impossible! Just look at you . . . heads
in the clouds! No one would ever know we've
got to be out of here in two days. If it weren't
for me, nothing would get done around here . . .
(*She starts stacking* GARDNER'S *books into piles*)
There! That's all the maroon ones!

GARDNER (*Looks up*): What do you mean, *maroon*
ones?!

FANNY: All your books that are maroon are in *this*
pile . . . and your books that are green in *that*
pile! . . . I'm trying to bring some order into
your life for once. This will make unpacking so
much easier.

GARDNER: But, my dear Fanny, it's not the color of a book that distinguishes it, but what's *inside* it!

FANNY: This will be a great help, you'll see. Now what about this awful striped thing? (*She picks up a slim, aged volume*) Can't it go . . . ?

GARDNER: No!

FANNY: But it's as queer as Dick's hatband! There are no others like it.

GARDNER: Open it and read. Go on . . . open it!

FANNY: We'll get nowhere at this rate.

GARDNER: I said . . . READ!

FANNY: Really, Gar, I—

GARDNER: Read the dedication!

FANNY (*Opens and reads*): "To Gardner Church, you led the way. With gratitude and affection, Robert Frost." (*She closes it and hands it to him*)

GARDNER: It was published the same year as my *Salem Gardens*.

FANNY (*Picking up a very worn book*): Well, what about this dreadful thing? It's filthy. (*She blows off a cloud of dust*)

GARDNER: Please . . . *please?!*

FANNY (*Looking through it*): It's all in French.

GARDNER (*Snatching it away from her*): André Malraux gave me that . . . !

FANNY: I'm just trying to help.

GARDNER: It's a first edition of Baudelaire's *Fleurs du mal.*

FANNY (*Giving it back*): Well, pardon me for living!

GARDNER: Why do you have to drag everything in here in the first place . . . ?

FANNY: Because there's no room in your study. You ought to see the mess in there! . . . WAKE UP, MAGS, ARE YOU GOING TO PITCH IN OR NOT?!

GARDNER: I'm not up to this.

FANNY: Well, you'd better be unless you want to be left behind!

MAGS: (*Stops her sketching*): All right, all right . . . I just hope you'll give me some more time later this evening.

FANNY: (*To MAGS*): Since you're young and in the best shape, why don't you bring in the books and I'll cope with the papers. (*She exits to the study*)

GARDNER: Now just a minute . . .

FANNY (*Offstage*): WE NEED A STEAM SHOVEL FOR THIS!

MAGS: Okay, what do you want me to do?

GARDNER: Look, I don't want you messing around with my—

[*FANNY enters with an armful of papers, which she drops into an empty carton.*]

GARDNER: HEY, WHAT'S GOING ON HERE?!

FANNY: I'm packing up your papers. COME ON, MAGS, LET'S GET CRACKING! (*She exits for more papers*)

GARDNER (*Plucks several papers out of the carton*): What

is this . . . ?

MAGS (*Exits into his study*): GOOD LORD, WHAT HAVE YOU DONE IN HERE?!

GARDNER (*Reading*): This is my manuscript.

[*FANNY enters with another batch, which she tosses on top of the others.*]

GARDNER: What *are* you doing?!

FANNY: Packing, darling . . . PACKING! (*She exits for more*)

GARDNER: SEE HERE, YOU CAN'T MANHANDLE MY THINGS THIS WAY!

[*MAGS enters, staggering under a load of books, which she sets down on the floor.*]

GARDNER: *I* PACK MY MANUSCRIPT! I KNOW WHERE EVERYTHING IS!

FANNY (*Offstage*): IF IT WERE UP TO YOU, WE'D NEVER GET OUT OF HERE! WE'RE UNDER A TIME LIMIT, GARDNER. KITTY'S PICKING US UP IN TWO DAYS . . . TWO . . . DAYS! (*She enters with a larger batch of papers and heads for the carton*)

GARDNER (*Grabbing FANNY's wrist*): NOW, HOLD IT! . . . JUST . . . HOLD IT RIGHT THERE!

FANNY: OOOOOWWWWWWWW!

GARDNER: *I* PACK MY THINGS!

FANNY: LET GO, YOU'RE HURTING ME!

GARDNER: THAT'S MY MANUSCRIPT! GIVE IT TO ME!

FANNY (*Lifting the papers high over her head*): I'M IN CHARGE OF THIS MOVE, GARDNER! WE'VE GOT TO GET CRACKING!

GARDNER: I said . . . GIVE IT TO ME!

MAGS: Come on, Mum, let him have it.

[*FANNY and GARDNER struggle.*]

GARDNER (*Finally wrenches the pages from FANNY*): LET . . . ME . . . HAVE IT! . . . THAT'S MORE LIKE IT!

FANNY (*Soft and weepy*): You see what he's like? . . . I try and help with his packing and what does he do . . . ?

GARDNER (*Rescues the rest of his papers from the carton*): YOU DON'T JUST THROW EVERYTHING INTO A BOX LIKE A PILE OF GARBAGE! THIS IS A BOOK, FANNY. SOMETHING I'VE BEEN WORKING ON FOR TWO YEARS! (*Trying to assemble his papers, but only making things worse, dropping them all over the place*) You show a little respect for my things. . . . You don't just throw them around every which way. . . . It's tricky trying to make sense of poetry; it's much easier to write the stuff . . . that is, if you've still got it in you . . .

MAGS: Here, let me help . . . (*Taking some of the papers*)

GARDNER: Criticism is tough sledding. You can't just dash off a few images here, a few rhymes there . . .

MAGS: Do you have these pages numbered in any way?

FANNY (*Returning to her posing chair*): HA!

GARDNER: This is just the introduction.

MAGS: I don't see any numbers on these.

GARDNER (*Exiting to his study*): The important stuff is in my study . . .

FANNY (*To* MAGS): You don't know the half of it . . . not the half . . . !

GARDNER (*Offstage; thumping around*): HAVE YOU SEEN THOSE YEATS POEMS I JUST HAD . . . ?

MAGS (*Reading over several pages*): What is this? . . . It doesn't make sense. It's just fragments . . . pieces of poems.

FANNY: That's it, honey! That's his book. His great critical study! Now that he can't write his own poetry, he's trying to explain other people's. The only problem is, he can't get beyond typing them out. The poor lamb doesn't have the stamina to get beyond the opening stanzas, let alone trying to make sense of them.

GARDNER (*Thundering back with more papers, which keep falling*): GODDAMMIT, FANNY, WHAT DID YOU DO IN THERE? I CAN'T FIND ANYTHING!

FANNY: I just took the papers that were on your desk.

GARDNER: Well, the entire beginning is gone. (*He exits*)

FANNY: I'M TRYING TO HELP YOU, DARLING!

GARDNER (*Returns with another armload*): SEE THAT? . . . NO SIGN OF CHAPTER ONE OR TWO . . . (*He flings it all down to the floor*)

FANNY: Gardner . . . PLEASE?!

GARDNER (*Kicking through the mess*): I TURN MY BACK FOR ONE MINUTE AND WHAT HAPPENS? . . . MY ENTIRE STUDY IS TORN APART! (*He exits*)

MAGS: Oh, Daddy . . . don't . . . please . . . Daddy . . . please?!

GARDNER (*Returns with a new batch of papers, which he tosses up into the air*): THROWN OUT! . . . THE BEST PART IS THROWN OUT! . . . lost . . . (*He starts to exit again*)

MAGS (*Reads one of the fragments to steady herself*):

> "I have known the inexorable sadness of
>   pencils,
> Neat in their boxes, dolor of pad and
>   paperweight,
> All the misery of manila folders and
>   mucilage . . ."

They're beautiful . . . just beautiful.

GARDNER (*Stops*): Hey, what's that you've got there?

FANNY: It's your manuscript, darling. You see, it's right where you left it.

GARDNER (*To* MAGS): Read that again.

MAGS:

> "I have known the inexorable sadness of
>   pencils,
> Neat in their boxes, dolor of pad and
>   paperweight,
> All the misery of manila folders and
>   mucilage . . ."

GARDNER: Well, well, what do you know . . .

FANNY (*Hands him several random papers*): You see . . . no one lost anything. Everything's here, still intact.

GARDNER (*Reads*):

> "I knew a woman, lovely in her bones,
> When small birds sighed, she would sigh
>   back at them;
> Ah, when she moved, she moved more ways
>   than one:
> The shapes a bright container can contain! . . ."

FANNY (*Hands him another*): And . . .

GARDNER (*Reads*): Ahh . . . Frost . . .

> "Some say the world will end in fire,
> Some say in ice.
> From what I've tasted of desire
> I hold with those who favor fire."

FANNY (*Under her breath to* MAGS): He can't give up the words. It's the best he can do. (*Handing him another*) Here you go, here's more.

GARDNER:

> "Farm boys wild to couple
> With anything   with soft-wooded trees
> With mounds of earth   mounds
> Of pinestraw   will keep themselves off
> Animals by legends of their own . . ."

MAGS (*Eyes shut*): Oh, Daddy, I can't bear it . . . I . . .

FANNY: Of course no one will ever publish this.

GARDNER: Oh, here's a marvelous one. Listen to this!

> "There came a Wind like a Bugle—
> It quivered through the Grass
> And a Green Chill upon the Heat
> So ominous did pass
> We barred the Windows and the Doors
> As from an Emerald Ghost—
> The Doom's electric Moccasin . . ."

SHIT, WHERE DID THE REST OF IT GO . . . ?

FANNY: Well, don't ask *me*.

GARDNER: It just stopped in mid-air!

FANNY: Then go look for the original.

GARDNER: Good idea, good idea! (*He exits to his study*)

FANNY (*To* MAGS): He's incontinent now, too. He wets his pants, in case you haven't noticed. (*She starts laughing*) You're not laughing. Don't you think it's funny? Daddy needs diapers. . . . I don't know about you, but I could use a drink! GAR . . . WILL YOU GET ME A SPLASH WHILE YOU'RE OUT THERE . . . ?

MAGS: STOP IT!

FANNY: It means we can't go out anymore. I mean, what would people say . . . ?

MAGS: Stop it. Just stop it.

FANNY: My poet laureate can't hold it in! (*She laughs harder*)

MAGS: That's enough . . . STOP IT . . . Mummy . . . I beg of you . . . *please stop it!*

[GARDNER *enters with a book and indeed a large stain has blossomed on his trousers. He plucks it away from his leg.*]

GARDNER: Here we go . . . I found it . . .

FANNY (*Pointing at it*): See that? See? . . . He just did it again! (*Goes off into a shower of laughter*)

MAGS: (*Looks, turns away*): SHUT . . . UP! . . . (*Building to a howl*) WILL YOU PLEASE JUST . . . SHUT . . . UP!

FANNY (*To* GARDNER): Hey, what about that drink?

FANNY: Never mind, I'll get it, I'll get it.

[FANNY *exits, convulsed. Silence.*]

GARDNER: Well, where were we?

MAGS (*Near tears*): Your poem.

GARDNER: Oh yes . . . the Dickinson. (*He shuts his eyes, reciting from memory, holding the book against his chest*)

> "There came a Wind like a Bugle—
> It quivered through the Grass
> And a Green Chill upon the Heat
> So ominous did pass
> We barred the Windows and the Doors
> As from an Emerald Ghost—"

(*Opens the book and starts riffling through it*) Let's see now, where's the rest? . . . (*He finally finds it*) Ahhh, here we go . . . !

FANNY (*Reenters, drink in hand*): I'm back! (*Takes one look at* GARDNER *and bursts out laughing again*)

MAGS: I don't believe you! How you can laugh at him?!

[*They all speak simultaneously as* MAGS *gets angrier and angrier.*]

FANNY: I'm sorry, I wish I could stop, but there's really nothing else to do. Look at him . . . just . . . look at him . . . !

MAGS: It's so cruel. . . . You're so . . . incredibly cruel to him. . . . I mean, YOUR DISDAIN REALLY TAKES MY BREATH AWAY! YOU'RE IN A CLASS BY YOURSELF WHEN IT COMES TO HUMILIATION!

GARDNER (*Reading*):

> "The Doom's electric Moccasin
> That very instant passed—
> On a strange Mob of panting Trees
> And Fences fled away
> And Rivers where the Houses ran
> Those looked that lived—that Day—
> The Bell within the steeple wild
> The flying tidings told—
> How much can come
> And much can go,
> And yet abide the World!"

(*He shuts the book with a bang, pauses and looks around the room, confused*) Now, where was I . . . ?

FANNY: Safe and sound in the middle of the living room with Mags and me.

GARDNER: But I was looking for something, wasn't I . . . ?

FANNY: Your manuscript.

GARDNER: THAT'S RIGHT! MY MANUSCRIPT! My manuscript!

FANNY: And here it is all over the floor. See, you're standing on it.

GARDNER (*Picks up a few pages and looks at them*): Why, so I am . . .

FANNY: Now all we have to do is get it up off the floor and packed neatly into these cartons!

GARDNER: Yes, yes, that's right. Into the cartons.

FANNY (*Kicks a carton over to him*): Here, you use this one and I'll start over here . . . (*She starts dropping papers into a carton nearby*) BOMBS AWAY! . . . Hey . . . this is fun!

GARDNER (*Picks up his own pile, lifts it high over his head and flings it down into the carton*): BOMBS AWAY . . . This *is* fun!

FANNY: I told you! The whole thing is to figure out a system!

GARDNER: I don't know what I'd do without you, Fan. I thought I'd lost everything.

FANNY (*Makes dive-bomber noises and machine-gun explosions as she wheels more and more papers into the carton*): TAKE THAT AND THAT AND THAT!

GARDNER (*Joins in the fun, outdoing her with dips, dives, and blastings of his own*): BLAM BLAM BLAM BLAM! . . . ZZZZZZZZRAAAAAA FOOM! . . . BLATTY-DE-BLAT-TY-DE-BLATTY-DE-KABOOOOOOOOOM! . . . WHAAAAAAA . . . DA-DAT-DAT-DAT-DAT-DAT . . .

WHEEEEEEEE AAAAAAAAAAAAA . . . FOOOOOO . . .

[They get louder and louder as papers fly every which way.]

FANNY (*Mimes getting hit with a bomb*): AEEEEEEEIIIIIIIII-III! YOU GOT ME RIGHT IN THE GIZZARD! (*She collapses on the floor and starts going through death throes, having an absolute ball*)

GARDNER: TAKE THAT AND THAT AND THAT AND THAT . . . (*A series of explosions follow*)

MAGS (*Furious*): This is how you help him? . . . THIS IS HOW YOU PACK HIS THINGS?

FANNY: I keep him company. I get involved . . . which is a hell of a lot more than you do!

MAGS (*Wild with rage*): BUT YOU'RE MAKING A MOCKERY OF HIM. . . . YOU TREAT HIM LIKE A CHILD OR SOME DIMWITTED SERVING BOY. HE'S JUST AN AMUSEMENT TO YOU!

FANNY (*Fatigue has finally overtaken her. She's calm, almost serene*): And to you who see him once a year, if that . . . what is he to *you*? . . . I mean, what do you give him from yourself that costs you something? . . . Hmmmmmm? . . . (*Imitating* MAGS) "Oh, hi Daddy, it's great to see you again. How have you been? . . . Gee, I love your hair. It's gotten so . . . *white!*" . . . What color do you expect it to get when he's this age? . . . I mean, if you care so much how he looks, why don't you come and see him once in a while? . . . But oh, no . . . you have your paintings to do and your shows to put on. You just come and see us when the whim strikes. (*Imitating* MAGS) "Hey, you know what would be really great? . . . To do a portrait of you! I've always wanted to paint you, you're such great subjects!" . . . *Paint* us?! . . . What about opening your eyes and really *seeing* us? . . . Noticing what's going on around here for a change! It's all over for Daddy and me. This is it! "Finita la commedia!" . . . All I'm trying to do is exit with a little flourish; have some fun. . . . What's so terrible about that? . . . It can get pretty grim around here, in case you haven't noticed . . . Daddy, tap-tap-tapping out his nonsense all day; me traipsing around to the thrift shops trying to amuse myself. . . . He never keeps me company anymore; never takes me out anywhere. . . . I'd put a bullet through my head in a minute, but then who'd look after him? . . . What do you think we're moving to the cottage for? . . . So I can watch him like a hawk and make sure he doesn't get lost. Do you think that's anything to look forward to? . . . Being Daddy's nursemaid out in the middle of nowhere? I'd much rather stay here in Boston with the few friends I have left, but you can't always do what you want in this world! "L'homme propose, Dieu dispose!" . . . If you want to paint us so badly, you ought to paint us as we really are. There's your picture."

[FANNY points to GARDNER, who's quietly playing with a paper glider.]

FANNY: Daddy spread out on the floor with all his toys and me hovering over him to make sure he doesn't hurt himself! (*She goes over to him*) YOO-HOO . . . GAR? . . . HELLO?

GARDNER (*Looks up at her*): Oh, hi there, Fan. What's up?

FANNY: How's the packing coming . . . ?

GARDNER: Packing . . . ?

FANNY: Yes, you were packing your manuscript, remember? (*She lifts up a page and lets it fall into a carton*)

GARDNER: Oh, yes . . .

FANNY: Here's your picture, Mags. Face over this way . . . turn your easel over here . . . (*She lets a few more papers fall*) Up, up . . . and away . . .

[Blackout.]

Scene 2

The last day. All the books and boxes are gone. The room is completely empty except for MAGS's backdrop. Late afternoon light dapples the walls; it changes from pale peach to deeper violet. The finished portrait sits on the easel, covered with a cloth. MAGS is taking down the backdrop.

FANNY (*Offstage to* GARDNER): DON'T FORGET TOOTS!

GARDNER (*Offstage; from another part of the house*): WHAT'S THAT?

FANNY (*Offstage*): I SAID: DON'T FORGET TOOTS! HIS CAGE IS SITTING IN THE MIDDLE OF YOUR STUDY!

[Silence.]

FANNY (*Offstage*): HELLO? . . . ARE YOU THERE?   GARDNER (*Offstage*): I'LL BE RIGHT WITH YOU; I'M JUST GETTING TOOTS!

GARDNER (*Offstage*): WHAT'S THAT? I CAN'T HEAR YOU?

FANNY (*Offstage*): I'M GOING THROUGH THE ROOMS ONE MORE TIME TO MAKE SURE WE DIDN'T FORGET ANYTHING . . . KITTY'S PICKING US UP IN FIFTEEN MINUTES, SO PLEASE BE READY. . . . SHE'S DROPPING MAGS OFF AT THE STATION AND THEN IT'S OUT TO ROUTE 3 AND THE CAPE HIGHWAY . . .

GARDNER (*Enters, carrying* TOOTS *in his cage*): Well, this is it. The big moment has finally come, eh what, Toots? (*He see* MAGS) Oh, hi there, Mags, I didn't see you . . .

MAGS: Oh, hi, Daddy, I'm just taking this down . . . (*She does and walks over to* TOOTS) Oh, Toots, I'll miss you. (*She makes little chattering noises into his cage*)

GARDNER: Come on, recite a little Gray's *Elegy* for Mags before we go.

MAGS: Yes, Mum said he was really good at it now.

GARDNER: Well, the whole thing is to keep at it every day. (*Slowly to* TOOTS)

> "The curfew tolls the knell of parting day,
> The lowing herd wind slowly o'er the lea . . ."

Come on, show Mags your stuff! (*Slower*)

> "The curfew tolls the knell of parting day,
> The lowing herd wind slowly o'er the lea . . ."

[*Silence;* GARDNER *makes little chattering sounds.*]

GARDNER: Come on, Toots, old boy . . .

MAGS: How does it go?

GARDNER (*To* MAGS):

> "The curfew tolls the knell of parting day,
> The lowing herd wind slowly o'er the lea . . ."

MAGS (*Slowly to* TOOTS):

> The curfew tolls for you and me,
> As quietly the herd winds down . . .

GARDNER: No, no, it's "The curfew tolls the knell of parting *day* . . ."!

MAGS (*Repeating after him*): "The curfew tolls the knell of parting day . . ."

GARDNER: "The lowing herd wind slowly o'er the lea . . ."

MAGS (*With a deep breath*):

> The curfew tolls at parting day,
> The herd low slowly down the lea . . . no, *knell*!
> They come winding down the *knell*!

GARDNER: Listen, Mags . . . *listen*!

[*A pause.*]

TOOTS (*Loud and clear with* GARDNER's *inflection*):

> "The curfew tolls the knell of parting day,

> The lowing herd wind slowly o'er the lea,
> The ploughman homeward plods his weary way,
> And leaves the world to darkness and to me."

MAGS: HE SAID IT. . . . HE SAID IT! . . . AND IN YOUR VOICE . . . OH, DADDY, THAT'S AMAZING!

GARDNER: Well, Toots is very smart, which is more than I can say for a lot of people I know . . .

MAGS (*To* TOOTS): Polly want a cracker? Polly want a cracker?

GARDNER: You can teach a parakeet to say anything; all you need is patience . . .

MAGS: But *poetry* . . . that's so hard . . .

[FANNY *enters carrying a suitcase and* GARDNER's *typewriter in its case. She's dressed in her traveling suit, wearing a hat to match.*]

FANNY: WELL, THERE YOU ARE! I I THOUGHT YOU'D DIED!

MAGS (*To* FANNY): HE SAID IT! I FINALLY HEARD TOOTS RECITE GRAY'S ELEGY. (*She makes silly clucking sounds into the cage*)

FANNY: Isn't it uncanny how much he sounds like Daddy? Sometimes when I'm alone here with him, I've actually thought he *was* Daddy and started talking to him. Oh, yes, Toots and I have had quite a few meaty conversations together!

[FANNY *wolf-whistles into the cage; then draws back.* GARDNER *covers the cage with a traveling cloth. Silence.*]

FANNY (*Looking around the room*): God, the place looks so bare.

MAGS: I still can't believe it . . . Cotuit, year round. I wonder if there'll be any phosphorus when you get there?

FANNY: What on earth are you talking about? (*She carries the discarded backdrop out into the hall*)

MAGS: Remember that summer when the ocean was full of phosphorus?

GARDNER (*Taking* TOOTS *out into the hall*): Oh, yes . . .

MAGS: It was a great mystery where it came from or why it settled in Cotuit. But one evening when Daddy and I were taking a swim, suddenly it was there!

GARDNER (*Returns*): I remember.

MAGS: I don't know where Mum was . . .

FANNY (*Reentering*): Probably doing the dishes!

MAGS (*To* GARDNER): As you dove into the water, this shower of silvery green sparks erupted all around you. It was incredible! I thought you were turning into a saint or something; but then you told me to jump in too and the same thing happened to me . . .

GARDNER: Oh, yes, I remember that . . . the water smelled all queer.

MAGS: What *is* phosphorus, anyway?

GARDNER: Chemicals, chemicals . . .

FANNY: No, it isn't. Phosphorus is a green liquid inside insects. Fireflies have it. When you see sparks in the water it means insects are swimming around . . .

GARDNER: Where on earth did you get that idea . . . ?

FANNY: If you're bitten by one of them, it's fatal!

MAGS: And the next morning it was still there . . .

GARDNER: It was the damndest stuff to get off! We'd have to stay in the shower a good ten minutes. It comes from chemical waste, you see . . .

MAGS: Our bodies looked like mercury as we swam around . . .

GARDNER: It stained all the towels a strange yellow green.

MAGS: I was in heaven, and so were you for that matter. You'd finished your day's poetry and would turn somersaults like some happy dolphin . . .

FANNY: Damned dishes . . . why didn't I see any of this?!

MAGS: I remember one night in particular. . . . We sensed the phosphorus was about to desert us; blow off to another town. We were chasing each other under water. At one point I lost you, the brilliance was so intense . . . but finally your foot appeared . . . then your leg. I grabbed it! . . . I remember wishing the moment would hold forever; that we could just be fixed there, laughing and iridescent. . . . Then I began to get panicky because I knew it would pass; it was passing already. You were slipping from my grasp. The summer was almost over. I'd be going back to art school; you'd be going back to Boston. . . . Even as I was reaching for you, you were gone. We'd never be like that again.

[*Silence.* FANNY *spies* MAGS'S *portrait covered on the easel.*]

FANNY: What's that over there? Don't tell me we forgot something!

MAGS: It's your portrait. I finished it.

FANNY: You finished it? How on earth did you manage that?

MAGS: I stayed up all night.

FANNY: You did? . . . *I* didn't hear you, did you hear her, Gar . . . ?

GARDNER: Not a peep, not a peep!

MAGS: Well, I wanted to get it done before you left. You know, see what you thought. It's not bad, considering . . . I mean, I did it almost completely from memory. The light was terrible and I was trying to be quiet so I wouldn't wake you. It was hardly an ideal situation. . . . I mean, you weren't the most cooperative models . . . (*She suddenly panics and snatches the painting off the easel. She hugs it to her chest and starts dancing around the room with it*) Oh, God, you're going to hate it! You're going to hate it! How did I ever get into this? . . . Listen, you don't really want to see it . . . it's nothing . . . just a few dabs here and there. . . . It was awfully late when I finished it. The light was really impossible and my eyes were hurting like crazy. . . . Look, why don't we just go out to the sidewalk and wait for Kitty so she doesn't have to honk—

GARDNER (*Snatches the painting out from under her grasp*): WOULD YOU JUST SHUT UP A MINUTE AND LET US SEE IT?

MAGS (*Laughing and crying*): But it's nothing, Daddy . . . *really!* . . . I've done better with my eyes closed! It was so late I could hardly see anything and then I spilled a whole bottle of thinner into my palette . . .

GARDNER (*Sets the portrait down on the easel and stands back to look at it*): THERE!

MAGS: (*Dancing around them in a panic*): Listen, it's just a quick sketch. . . . It's still wet. . . . I didn't have enough time. . . . It takes at least forty hours to do a decent portrait . . .

[*Suddenly it's very quiet as* FANNY *and* GARDNER *stand back to look at the painting. More and more beside herself,* MAGS *keeps leaping around the room wrapping her arms around herself, making little whimpering sounds.*]

MAGS: Please don't . . . no . . . don't . . . oh, please! . . . Come on, don't look. . . . Oh, God, don't . . . please . . .

[*An eternity passes as* FANNY *and* GARDNER *gaze at their portrait.*]

GARDNER: Well . . .

FANNY: Well . . .

[*More silence.*]

FANNY: I think it's perfectly dreadful!	GARDNER: Awfully clever, awfully clever!

FANNY: What on earth did you do to my face . . . ?

GARDNER: I particularly like Mum!

FANNY: Since when do I have purple skin?!

MAGS: I told you it was nothing, just a silly—

GARDNER: She looks like a million dollars!

FANNY: AND WILL YOU LOOK AT MY HAIR . . . IT'S BRIGHT

ORANGE!

GARDNER (*Views the painting from another angle*): It's really very good!

FANNY (*Pointing*): That doesn't look anything like me!

GARDNER: First-rate!

FANNY: Since when do I have purple skin and bright orange hair?

MAGS (*Trying to snatch the painting off the easel*): Listen, you don't have to worry about my feelings . . . really . . . I—

GARDNER (*Blocking her way*): NOT SO FAST . . .

FANNY: And look at how I'm sitting! I've never sat like that in my life!

GARDNER (*Moving closer to the painting*): Yes, yes, it's awfully clever . . .

FANNY: I HAVE NO FEET!

GARDNER: The whole thing is quite remarkable!

FANNY: And what happened to my legs, pray tell? . . . They just vanish below the knees! . . . At least my dress is presentable. I've always loved that dress.

GARDNER: It sparkles somehow . . .

FANNY (*To GARDNER*): Don't you think it's becoming?

GARDNER: Yes, very becoming, awfully becoming . . .

FANNY (*Examining it at closer range*): Yes, she got the dress very well, how it shows off what's left of my figure . . . My smile is nice too.

GARDNER: Good and wide . . .

FANNY: I love how the corners of my mouth turn up . . .

Gardner: It's very clever . . .

FANNY: They're almost quivering . . .

GARDNER: Good lighting effects!

FANNY: Actually, I look quite . . . *young*, don't you think?

GARDNER (*To MAGS*): You're awfully good with those highlights.

FANNY (*Looking at it from different angles*): And *you* look darling . . . !

GARDNER: Well, I don't know about that . . .

FANNY: No, you look absolutely darling. Good enough to eat.

MAGS (*In a whisper*): They like it. . . . They like it!

[*A silence as FANNY and GARDNER keep gazing at their portrait.*]

FANNY: You know what it is? The wispy brush stroke makes us look like a couple in a French Impressionist painting.

GARDNER: Yes, I see what you mean . . .

FANNY: A Manet or Renoir . . .

GARDNER: It's very evocative.

FANNY: There's something about the light . . .

[*They back up to survey the picture from a distance.*]

FANNY: You know those Renoir café scenes . . . ?

GARDNER: She doesn't lay on the paint with a trowel; it's just touches here and there . . .

MAGS: They *like* it . . . !

FANNY: You know the one with the couple dancing? . . . Not that we're dancing. There's just something similar in the mood . . . a kind of gaiety, almost. . . . The man has his back to you and he's swinging the woman around. . . . OH, GAR, YOU'VE SEEN IT A MILLION TIMES! IT'S HANGING IN THE MUSEUM OF FINE ARTS! . . . They're dancing like this . . .

[*FANNY goes up to GARDNER and puts an arm on his shoulders.*]

MAGS: They like it. . . . They like it!

FANNY: She's got on this wonderful flowered dress with ruffles at the neck and he's holding her like this. . . . That's right . . . and she's got the most rhapsodic expression on her face . . .

[*Getting into the spirit of it, GARDNER takes FANNY in his arms and slowly begins to dance around the room.*]

GARDNER: Oh, yes . . . I know the one you mean. . . . They're in a sort of haze . . . and isn't there a little band playing off to one side . . . ?

FANNY: Yes, that's it!

[*KITTY's horn honks outside. MAGS is the only one who hears it.*]

MAGS: There's Kitty! (*She's torn and keeps looking towards the door, but finally gives in to their stolen moment*)

FANNY: And there's a man in a dark suit playing the violin and someone's conducting, I think. . . . And aren't Japanese lanterns strung up . . . ?

[*FANNY and GARDNER pick up speed, dipping and whirling around the room. Strains of a faraway Chopin waltz are heard.*]

GARDNER: Oh, yes! There are all these little lights twinkling in the trees . . .

FANNY: And doesn't the woman have a hat on? . . . A big red hat . . . ?

GARDNER: . . . and lights all over the dancers, too. Everything shimmers with this marvelous glow. Yes, yes . . . I can see it perfectly! The whole thing is absolutely extraordinary!

[*The lights become dreamy and dappled as FANNY and GARDNER dance around the room. MAGS watches them, moved to tears as slowly the curtain falls.*]

END

MANUEL PUIG (1932–1990)

anuel Puig was born in rural Argentina in the town of General Villegas but attended private boarding schools in Buenos Aires for his education. In 1950 he began studying architecture at the University of Buenos Aires, switching to the study of philosophy before taking his degree in 1955. He left Argentina shortly afterward and spent a number of years living abroad in Europe, mainly in Rome, where he held a scholarship, and in London, where he gave lessons in Spanish and Italian. In 1960 Puig returned to Argentina to work as an assistant director on films, and in 1963 he moved to New York, where he began writing his first novel, *Betrayed by Rita Hayworth* (1968, Engl. trans. 1971). In all Puig wrote eight novels and two plays. The best known titles include *Heartbreak Tango* (1969), *The Buenos Aires Affair* (1973, Engl. trans. 1976), and *Kiss of the Spider Woman* (1976, Engl. trans. 1979). Puig's play based on the latter novel was first produced in Spain and South America in the early 1980s before its production in London in 1985. Also in 1985 the film version of *Kiss of the Spider Woman* was released, with the screenplay written by Leonard Schrader and directed by Hector Babenco. Puig died of a heart attack following surgery in Cuernavaca, Mexico, in 1990 and was buried in his hometown. He remains one of the most popular contemporary Latin American writers.

Kiss of the Spider Woman

Kiss of the Spider Woman (1976) dramatizes the brutality of Latin American military dictatorships, particularly the Argentine dictatorship of the 1970s, when thousands of citizens suspected of political dissidence were arrested and tortured or killed. Puig's play begins in a prison and centers on the developing relationship between two inmates: Valentin, a political prisoner, the leader of a resistance movement, and his cellmate Molina, a jailed homosexual. In his novel Puig uses a variety of devices, such as police reports and popular music, as narrative frames for the action. In the play these layers are also important. Molina entertains Valentin with stories, narrations of films, to gain his confidence. Because he has agreed to betray Valentin to earn his own release, Molina becomes the "spider woman" who devours her partner after mating. Each segment of the story Molina tells Valentin is a strand of the web designed to weaken Valentin's resistance, to entrap him into revealing the identity of his fellows in the resistance movement. But their interactions become more complex as their relationship develops into one that includes introspection, respect, and love. Molina seduces Valentin but also falls in love with him, and so Molina himself is caught in the web he has woven. He ultimately sacrifices his life in order to pass information to Valentin's revolutionaries, becoming a hero in spite of himself. *Kiss of the Spider Woman* goes far beyond a condemnation of the Argentine government's repressive practices in the 1970s, pursuing a subtle investigation into the politics of political and sexual identity, the snares and triumphs of love.

Kiss of the Spider Woman

Manuel Puig

Translated by Alan Barker

ACT I

Scene 1

A small cell in the Villa Devoto prison in Buenos Aires. The stage is in total darkness. Suddenly two overhead white spots light up the heads of the two men. They are sitting down, looking in opposite directions.

MOLINA: You can see there's something special about her, that she's not any ordinary woman. Quite young . . . and her face more round than oval, with a little pointy chin like a cat's.

VALENTIN: And her eyes?

MOLINA: Most probably green. She looks up at the model, the black panther lying down in its cage in the zoo. But she scratches her pencil against the sketch pad, and the panther sees her.

VALENTIN: How come it didn't smell her before?

MOLINA (*deliberately not answering*): But who's that behind her? Someone trying to light a cigarette, but the wind blows out the match.

VALENTIN: Who is it?

MOLINA: Hold on. She flusters. He's no matinée idol, but he's nice-looking, in a hat with a low brim. He touches the brim like he's saluting and says the drawing is terrific. She fiddles with the curls of her fringe.

VALENTIN: Go on.

MOLINA: He can tell she's a foreigner by her accent. She tells him that she came to New York when the war broke out. He asks her if she's homesick. And then it's like a cloud passes across her eyes and she tells him she comes from the mountains, some place not far from Transylvania.

VALENTIN: Where Dracula comes from.

MOLINA: The next day he's in his office with some colleagues—he's an architect—and this girl, another architect he works with—and when the clock strikes three he just wants to drop everything and go to the zoo. It's right across the street. And the architect girls asks him why he's so happy. Deep down, she's really in love with him, no use her pretending otherwise.

VALENTIN: Is she a dog?

MOLINA: No, nothing out of this world: chestnut hair, but pleasant enough. But the other one, the one at the zoo, Irene—no, Irina—has disappeared. As time goes by he just can't get her out of his mind until one day he's walking down this fashionable avenue and he notices something in the window of an art gallery. They're pictures by an artist who only paints . . . panthers. The guy goes in, and there's Irina being congratulated by all the guests. And I don't remember what comes next.

VALENTIN: Try to remember.

MOLINA: Hold on a sec . . . Okay . . . then the architect goes up and congratulates her too. She drops the critics and walks off with him. He tells her that he just happened to be passing by, really he was on his way to buy a present.

VALENTIN: For the girl architect.

MOLINA: Now he's wondering if he's got enough money with him to buy two presents. And he stops outside a shop, and she gets a really funny feeling when she sees what kind of a shop it is. There are all different kinds of birds in little cages, sipping fresh water from their bowls.

VALENTIN: Excuse me . . . is there any water in the bottle?

MOLINA: Yes, I filled it up when they let us out to the lavatory.

[The white light which up till now has lit just their heads widens to fully light both actors: we see the cell for the first time.]

VALENTIN: That's okay then.

MOLINA: Do you want some? It's nice and cool.

VALENTIN: No, or we won't have enough for tea in the morning.

MOLINA: Don't exaggerate. We've got enough to last all day.

VALENTIN: Don't spoil me. I forgot to fetch some when they let us out to shower. If it wasn't for you, we wouldn't have any.

MOLINA: Look, there's plenty . . . Anyway, when they go inside that shop it's like—I don't know what—it's like the devil just came in. The birds, blind with fear, hurl themselves against the wire mesh and hurt their wings. She grabs his hand and drags him outside. Straight away the birds calm down. She asks him to let her go home. When he comes back into the shop, the birds are chirruping and singing just like normal and he buys one for the other girl's birthday. And then . . . it's no good, I can't remember what happens next, I'm pooped.

VALENTIN: Just a little more.

MOLINA: When I'm sleepy, my memory goes. I'll carry on with the morning tea.

VALENTIN: No, it's better at night. During the day I don't want to bother with this trivia. There are more important things . . .

[MOLINA says nothing.]

If I'm not reading and I'm keeping quiet, it's because I'm thinking. But don't take it wrong.

[MOLINA is upset by VALENTIN's remark.]

MOLINA (*with almost concealed irony*): I shan't bother you. You can count on that!

VALENTIN: I see you understand. See you in the morning.

[He settles down to sleep.]

MOLINA: Till tomorrow. Pleasant dreams of Irina.

[MOLINA settles down too, but he is troubled by something.]

VALENTIN: I prefer the architect girl.

MOLINA: I'd already sussed that.

Scene 2

MOLINA and VALENTIN are sitting in different positions. They do not look at one another. Only their heads are

lit; seconds later the night light comes on.

MOLINA: So they go on seeing each other and they fall in love. She pampers him, cuddles up in his arms, but when he wants to hold her tight and kiss her she slips away from him. She asks him not to kiss her but to let her kiss him with her full lips, but she keeps her mouth shut tight.

[VALENTIN is about to interrupt, but MOLINA forges ahead.]

So, on their next date they go to this quaint restaurant. He tells her she's prettier than ever in her shimmering black blouse. But she's lost her appetite, she can't manage a thing, and they leave. It's snowing gently. The noise of the city is muffled, but far away you can just hear the growling of wild animals. The zoo's close, that's why. Barely in a whisper she says she's afraid to return to her house and spend the night alone. He hails a taxi, and they go to his house. It's a huge place, all *fin-de-siècle* decor; it used to be his mother's.

VALENTIN: And what does he do?

MOLINA: Nothing. He lights up his pipe and looks over at her. You always guessed he had a kind heart.

VALENTIN: I'd like to ask you something: how do you picture his mother?

MOLINA: So you can make fun of her?

VALENTIN: I swear I won't.

MOLINA: I don't know . . . someone really charming. She made her husband happy and her children too. She's always well groomed.

VALENTIN: And do you picture her scrubbing floors?

MOLINA: No, she's always impeccable. The high-necked dress hides the wrinkles round her throat.

VALENTIN: Always impeccable. With servants. People with no other choice than to fetch and carry for her. And, of course, she was happy with her husband who also exploited her in his turn, kept her locked up in the house like a slave, waiting for him . . .

MOLINA: . . . listen . . .

VALENTIN: . . . waiting for him to come home every night from his chambers or his surgery. And she condoned the system, fed all this crap to her son, and now he trips over the panther-woman. Serves him right.

MOLINA (*irritated*): Why did you have to bring up all that . . . ? I'd forgotten all about this dump while I was telling you the movie.

VALENTIN: I'd forgotten about it too.

MOLINA: Well, then . . . why d'you have to go and

break the spell?

VALENTIN: I dont' know what you want me to say.

MOLINA: That I have your permission to escape from reality . . . Why should I make myself more depressed than I am already? What's the point in making myself more unhappy . . . ? Otherwise, I'll just go crazy, like Charlotte of Mexico. Though I'd rather be Christina of Sweden, since at least that way I'll end up a queen.

VALENTIN: No, be serious, you're right, being in here can drive you crazy, and not just because it gets you down . . . but because you can alienate yourself just the way you do. This habit of yours, only thinking about the nice things as you call it, that has its own dangers.

MOLINA: That's nonsense . . . How?

VALENTIN: Escaping from reality all the time the way you do becomes a vice, like taking drugs or something. Because, listen to me, reality, *your* reality, isn't only this cell. I mean, if you're reading or studying something, you can transcend whatever cell you're in, do you understand me? That's why I read, that's why I study every day.

MOLINA: Politics . . . I don't know what's become of the world, look where it's got us . . . you and all those politicians . . .

VALENTIN: Stop wingeing like a nineteenth-century housewife . . . You're not a housewife, and this isn't the nineteenth century. Tell me a little more of the movie, have we much more to go?

MOLINA: Yes, lots . . . Why did I get lumbered with you and not the panther-woman's boyfriend?

VALENTIN: That's another story and one that doesn't interest me.

MOLINA: Frightened to talk about it?

VALENTIN: It bores me. I know all about it—even though you've never said a word.

MOLINA: Fine. I told you I was put away for gross indecency. There's nothing more to add. So don't come the psychologist with me.

VALENTIN (*shielding himself behind humour*): Admit that you like him because he smokes a pipe.

MOLINA: No, it's not that, it's because he's gentle and understanding.

VALENTIN: His mother castrated him, that's all.

MOLINA: I like him and that's that. And you like the architect girl—she's not exactly manning the barricades.

VALENTIN: I prefer her to the panther-woman, that's for sure. But the guy with the pipe won't suit you.

MOLINA: Why not?

VALENTIN: Your intentions aren't exactly chaste, are they?

MOLINA: Certainly not.

VALENTIN: Exactly. He likes Irina because she's frigid and he doesn't have to pounce on her, and that's why he takes her to the house where his mother is still present even if she is dead.

MOLINA (*getting angrier and angrier*): Continue.

VALENTIN: If he's still kept all his mother's things, it's because he wants to remain a child. He doesn't bring home a woman but a child to play with.

MOLINA: That's all in your head. I don't even know if the place is his mother's—I said that because I liked the place, and since I saw antiques in there, I told you it belonged to his mother. For all I know, he rents it furnished.

VALENTIN: So you're making up half the movie?

MOLINA: I'm not, I swear. But—you know—there are some things I add to fill it out for you. The house, for example. And, in any case, don't forget I'm a window-dresser, and that's almost like being an interior designer . . . Anyway . . . she begins to tell him her story, and I don't remember all the details, but I do remember that in her village, a long time ago, there used to be panther-women. And these tales frightened her a lot when she was a little girl.

VALENTIN: And the birds . . . ? Why were they afraid of her?

MOLINA: That's what the architect asks her. And what does she say? She doesn't say anything! And the scene ends with him in pyjamas and a dressing-gown, good quality, no pattern, something serviceable—and he looks at her sleeping on the sofa from his bedroom door, and he lights up his pipe and stands there, all thoughtful.

VALENTIN: Do you know what I like about it? That it's like an allegory of women's fear of submitting to the male, because when it comes to sex, the animal part takes over. You see?

[MOLINA doesn't approve of VALENTIN's comments.]

MOLINA: Irina wakes up, it's morning already.

VALENTIN: She wakes up because of the cold, like us.

MOLINA (*irritated*): I knew you were going to say that . . . She wakes up because there's a canary singing in its cage. At first she's afraid to go near it, but the little bird is chirpy so she dares to move a little closer. She heaves a sigh of relief because the bird isn't frightened of her. And then she makes breakfast . . . toast and cereals and pancakes . . .

VALENTIN: Don't mention food.

MOLINA: . . . and pancakes . . .

VALENTIN: I'm serious. Neither food nor women.

MOLINA: She wakes him up and he's all happy to see her settling in, and so he asks her to stay there forever and be his wife. And she says, yes, from the bottom of her heart, and she looks around and the curtains look so beautiful to her, they're made of thick dark velvet. (*aggressively*) And now you can fully appreciate the *fin-de-siècle* decor. Then Irina asks him if he truly wants her to be his wife to give her just a little more time, just long enough for her to get over her fears.

VALENTIN: You can see what's going on with her, can't you?

MOLINA: Hold on. He agrees and they get married. And on their wedding night she sleeps in the bed and he sleeps on the couch.

VALENTIN: Looking at his mother's ornaments. Admit it, it's your ideal home, isn't it?

MOLINA: Of course it is! Now you're going to tell me what they all say.

VALENTIN: What d'you mean? What do they all say?

MOLINA: They're all the same, they all tell me the same thing.

VALENTIN: What?

MOLINA: That I was fussed over as a kid and that's why I'm like I am now, that I was clinging to my mother's skirts, but it's never too late to straighten out, and all I need is a good woman because there's nothing better than a good woman.

VALENTIN: And that's what they all tell you?

MOLINA: And this is what I tell them . . . You're dead right . . . ! And since there's nothing better than a good woman . . . I want to be one! So spare me the advice please, because I know what I feel like, and it's all as clear as day to me.

VALENTIN: I don't see it as clear—at least, not the way you've just put it.

MOLINA: I don't need you telling me what's what—if you want I'll go on with the picture, if not, ciao . . . I'll just whisper it to myself, and arrivederci, Sparafucile!

VALENTIN: Who's Sparafucile?

MOLINA: You don't have a clue about opera. He's the hatchet-man in *Rigoletto* . . . Where were we?

VALENTIN: The wedding night. He hasn't laid a finger on her.

MOLINA: And I forgot to tell you that they'd agreed she'd go and see a psychoanalyst.

VALENTIN: Excuse me again . . . don't get upset.

MOLINA: What is it?

VALENTIN (*less communicative than ever, sombre*): I can't keep my mind on the story.

MOLINA: Is it boring you?

VALENTIN: No, it's not that. It's . . . My head is in a state.

[*He talks more to himself than to* MOLINA.]

I just want to be quiet for a while. I don't know if this has ever happened to you, that you're just about to understand something, you've got the end of the thread and if you don't yank it now . . . you'll lose it.

MOLINA: Why do you like the architect girl?

VALENTIN: It has to come out some way or other . . . (*self-contemptuous*) Weakness, I mean . . .

MOLINA: Ttt . . . it's not weakness.

VALENTIN (*bitter, impersonally*): Funny how you just can't avoid getting attached to something. It's . . . it's as if the mind just oozed sentiment constantly.

MOLINA: Is that what you believe?

VALENTIN: Like a leaky tap. Drips falling over anything.

MOLINA: Anything?

VALENTIN: You can't stop the drips.

MOLINA: And you don't want to be reminded of your girlfriend, is that it?

VALENTIN (*mistrustful*): How do you know whether I have a girlfriend?

MOLINA: It's only natural.

VALENTIN: I can't help it . . . I get attached to anything that reminds me of her. Anyway, I'd do better to get my mind on what I ought to, right?

MOLINA: Yank the thread.

VALENTIN: Exactly.

MOLINA: And if you get it all in a tangle, Missy Valentina, you'll flunk needlework.

VALENTIN: Don't worry on my account.

MOLINA: Okay, I won't say another word.

VALENTIN: And don't call me Valentina. I'm not a woman.

MOLINA: How should I know?

VALENTIN: I'm sorry, Molina, but I don't give demonstrations.

MOLINA: I wasn't asking for one.

Scene 3

Night. The prison light is on. MOLINA *and* VALENTIN *are sitting on the floor eating.*

VALENTIN (*speaking as soon as he finishes his last mouthful*): You're a good cook.

MOLINA: Thank you, Valentin.

VALENTIN: It could cause problems later on. I'm getting spoiled.

MOLINA: You're crazy. Live for today!

VALENTIN: I don't believe in that live for today crap. We haven't earned that paradise yet.

MOLINA: Do you believe in heaven and hell?

VALENTIN: Hold on a minute. If we're going to have a discussion, then we need a framework. Otherwise you'll just ramble on.

MOLINA: I'm not going to ramble.

VALENTIN: Okay, I'll state an opening proposition. Let me put it to you like this.

MOLINA: Put it any way you like.

VALENTIN: I can't live just for today. All I do is determined by the ongoing political struggle, d'you get me? Everything that I endure here, which is bad enough . . . is nothing if you compare it to torture . . . but you don't know what that's like.

MOLINA: I can imagine.

VALENTIN: No, Molina, you can't imagine what it's like . . . Well, anyway, I can put up with all this because there's a blueprint. The essential thing is the social revolution, and the pleasures of the senses come second. The greatest pleasure, well, it's knowing that I'm part of the most noble cause . . . my ideas, for instance . . .

[*The prison lights go out. The blue nighttime light stays on.*]

It's eight . . .

MOLINA: What do you mean, "your ideas"?

VALENTIN: My ideals. Marxism. And that good feeling is one I can experience anywhere, even here in this cell, and even in torture. And that's my strength.

MOLINA: And what about your girlfriend?

VALENTIN: That has to be second too. And I'm second for her. Because she also knows what's most important.

[*MOLINA remains silent.*]

You don't look convinced.

MOLINA: Don't mind me. I'm going to turn in soon.

VALENTIN: You're mad. What about the panther-woman?

MOLINA: Tomorrow.

VALENTIN: What's up?

MOLINA: Look, Valentin, that's me. I get hurt easy. I cooked that food for you, with my supplies, and worse still I give you half my avocado—which is my favorite and could have eaten tomorrow . . . Result? You throw it in my face that I'm spoiling you . . .

VALENTIN: Don't be so soft! It's just like a . . .

MOLINA: Say it!

VALENTIN: Say what?

MOLINA: I know what you were going to say, Valentin.

VALENTIN: Cut it out.

MOLINA: "It's just like a woman." That's what you were going to say.

VALENTIN: Yes.

MOLINA: And what's wrong with being soft like a woman? Why can't a man—or whatever—a dog, or a fairy—why can't he be sensitive if he feels like it?

VALENTIN: In excess, it can get in a man's way.

MOLINA: In the way of what? Of torturing someone?

VALENTIN: No, of getting rid of the torturers.

MOLINA: But if all men were like women, then there'd be no torturers.

VALENTIN: And what would you do without men?

MOLINA: You're right. They're brutes, but I need them.

VALENTIN: Molina . . . you just said that if all men were like women, there'd be no torturers. You've got a point there; kind of weird, but a point at least.

MOLINA: The way you say things. (*imitating* VALENTIN) "A point at least."

VALENTIN: I'm sorry I upset you.

MOLINA: I'm not upset.

VALENTIN: Well, cheer up then. Don't sulk, man.

MOLINA: Man? What man? Where . . . ? Tell me so he won't get away . . . ! Do you want me to go on with the picture?

VALENTIN (*trying to hide he finds this funny*): Start.

MOLINA: Irina goes along to the psychoanalyst who's a ladykiller, real handsome.

VALENTIN: Tell me what you mean by real handsome. I'd like to know.

MOLINA: Well, if you're really interested, he isn't my type at all.

VALENTIN: Who's the actor?

MOLINA: I don't remember. Too skinny for my taste. With a pencil moustache. But there's something about him, so full of himself, he just puts you off. And he puts off Irina. She skips the next appointment, she lies to her husband, and instead of going to the doctor's she puts on that black fleecy coat and goes along to the zoo, to look at the panther. The keeper comes along, opens the cage, throws in the meat and closes the door again. But he's absent-minded and leaves the key in the lock. Irina sneaks up to the door and puts her hand on the key. And she just stands there, musing, rapt in her thoughts.

VALENTIN: What does she do then?

MOLINA: That's all for tonight. I'll continue tomorrow.

VALENTIN: At least, let me ask you something.

MOLINA: What?

VALENTIN: Who do you identify with? Irina or the architect girl?

MOLINA: With Irina—who do you think? *Moi*—always with the leading lady.

VALENTIN: Continue.

MOLINA: What about you? I guess you're stuck because the guy is such a wimp.

VALENTIN: Don't laugh—with the psychoanalyst. But

I didn't say anything about your choice, so don't mock mine . . . You know something? I'm finding it hard to keep my mind on it.

MOLINA: What's the problem?

VALENTIN: Nothing.

MOLINA: Come on, open up a little.

VALENTIN: When you said the girl was there in front of the cage, I imagined it was my girl who was in danger.

MOLINA: I understand.

VALENTIN: I shouldn't be telling you this, Molina. But I guess you've figured it all out for yourself anyhow. My girl is in the organization too.

MOLINA: So what?

VALENTIN: It's only that I don't want to burden you with information it's better you don't know.

MOLINA: With me, it's not a woman, a girlfriend, I mean. It's my mother. She's got blood pressure and a weak heart.

VALENTIN: People can live for years with that.

MOLINA: Sure, but they don't need more aggravation, Valentin. Imagine the shame of having a son inside—and why.

VALENTIN: Look, the worst has already happened, hasn't it?

MOLINA: Yes, but the risk is ever-present inside her. It's that dodgy heart.

VALENTIN: She's waiting for you. Eight years'll fly by, what with remission and all that . . .

MOLINA (*a little contrived*): Tell me about your girlfriend if you like . . .

VALENTIN: I'd give anything to hold her in my arms right now.

MOLINA: It won't be long. You're not in for life.

VALENTIN: Something might happen to her.

MOLINA: Write to her, tell her not to take chances, that you need her.

VALENTIN: Never. Impossible. If you think like that, you'll never change anything in the world.

MOLINA (*not realizing he's mocking* VALENTIN): And you think you're going to change the world?

VALENTIN: Yes, and I don't care that you laugh. It makes people laugh to hear this, but what I have to do before anything is to change the world.

MOLINA: Sure, but you can't do it all at once, *and* on your own.

VALENTIN: But I'm not on my own—that's it! I'm with her and all those other people who think like we do. That's the end of the thread that slips through my fingers . . . I'm not apart from my comrades—I'm with them, right now . . . ! It doesn't matter whether I can see them or not.

MOLINA (*with a slight drawl, sceptically*): If that makes you feel good, terrific!

VALENTIN: Christ, what a moron!

MOLINA: Sticks and stones . . .

VALENTIN: Don't provoke me, then. I'm not some loudmouth who just spouts off about politics in a bar. The proof is that I'm in here.

MOLINA: I'm sorry.

VALENTIN: It's okay . . .

MOLINA (*pretending not to pry*): You were going to tell me something . . . about your girlfriend.

VALENTIN: We'd better drop that.

MOLINA: As you like.

VALENTIN: Why it gets me so upset, I can't fathom.

MOLINA: Better not, then, if it upsets you . . .

VALENTIN: The one thing I shouldn't tell you is her name.

MOLINA: What sort of girl is she?

VALENTIN: She's twenty-four, two years younger than me.

MOLINA: Thirteen years younger than me . . . No, I tell a lie, sixteen.

VALENTIN: She was always politically conscious. First it was . . . well, I needn't be shy with you, at first it was because of the sexual revolution.

MOLINA (*bracing himself for some saucy tidbit*): I mustn't miss this bit.

VALENTIN: She comes from a bourgeois family, not really wealthy, but comfortably off. But as a kid and all through her adolescence she had to watch her parents destroy each other. Her father cheating her mother, you know what I mean?

MOLINA: No, I don't.

VALENTIN: Cheating her by not telling her he needed other relationships. I don't hold with monogamy.

MOLINA: But it's beautiful when a couple love each other for ever and ever.

VALENTIN: Is that what you'd like?

MOLINA: It's my dream.

VALENTIN: Why do you like men, then?

MOLINA: What's that got to do with it? I want to marry a man—to love and to cherish, for ever and ever.

VALENTIN: So, basically, you're just a bourgeois man?

MOLINA: A bourgeois lady, please.

VALENTIN: If you were a woman, you'd think otherwise.

MOLINA: The only thing I want is to live forever with a wonderful man.

VALENTIN: And that's impossible because . . . well, if he's a man, he wants a woman . . . you'll always be living in a fool's paradise.

MOLINA: Go on about your girlfriend. I don't want to talk about me.

VALENTIN: She was brought up to be the lady of the house. Piano lessons, French, drawing . . . I'll tell you the rest tomorrow, Molina . . . I want to think about something I was studying today.

MOLINA: Now you're getting your own back.
VALENTIN: No, silly. I'm tired, too.
MOLINA: I'm not sleepy at all.

Scene 4

Night. The prison lights are on. VALENTIN is engrossed in a book. MOLINA restless, is flicking through a magazine he already knows backwards.

VALENTIN (*lifting his head from the book*): Why are they late with dinner? Next door had it ages ago.
MOLINA (*ironic*): Is *that* all you're studying tonight? I'm not hungry, thank goodness.
VALENTIN: That's unusual. Don't you feel well?
MOLINA: No, it's just my nerves.
VALENTIN: Listen . . . I think they're coming.
MOLINA: Better hide the magazines or else they'll pinch them.
VALENTIN: I'm famished.
MOLINA: Please, Valentin, promise me you won't make a scene with the guards.
VALENTIN: No.

[Through the grille in the other door come two plates of porridge—one visibly more loaded than the other. MOLINA looks at VALENTIN.]

　　Porridge.
MOLINA: Yes.

[MOLINA looks at the two plates which VALENTIN has collected from the hatch.]

(*exchanging an enigmatic glance with the invisible guard*) Thank you.
VALENTIN (*to the guard*): What about this one? Why's it got less? (*to MOLINA*) I didn't say anything for your sake. Otherwise I'd have thrown it in his face, this bloody glue.
MOLINA: What's the use of complaining?
VALENTIN: One plate's only got half as much as the other. That bastard guard, he's out of his fucking mind.
MOLINA: It's okay, Valentin, I'll take the small portion.
VALENTIN (*serving MOLINA the larger one*): No, you like porridge, you always lap it up.
MOLINA: Skip the chivalry. You have it.
VALENTIN: I told you no.
MOLINA: Why should I have the big one?
VALENTIN: Because I know you like porridge.
MOLINA: But I'm not hungry.
VALENTIN: Eat it, it'll do you good.

[VALENTIN starts eating from the small plate.]

MOLINA: No.

VALENTIN: It's not too bad today.
MOLINA: I don't want it.
VALENTIN: Afraid of putting on weight?
MOLINA: No.
VALENTIN: Get stuck in then. This porridge à la glue isn't so bad today. This small plate is plenty for me.

[MOLINA starts eating.]

MOLINA (*overcoming his resistance: his voice nostalgic now*): Thursday. Ladies' day. The cinema in my neighborhood used to show a romantic triple feature on Thursdays. Years ago now.
VALENTIN: Is that where you saw the panther-woman?
MOLINA: No, that was in a smart little cinema in that German neighborhood where all those posh houses with gardens are. My house was near there, but in the run-down part. Every Monday they'd show a German-language feature. Even during the war. They still do.
VALENTIN: Nazi propaganda films.
MOLINA: But the musical numbers were fabulous!
VALENTIN: You're touched.

[He finishes his dinner.]

　　They'll be turning off the lights soon, that's it for studying today. (*unconsciously authoritarian*) You can go on with the film now—Irina's hand was on the key in the lock.
MOLINA (*picking at his porridge*): She takes the key out of the lock and gives it back to the keeper. The old fellow thanks her, and she goes back home to wait for her husband. She's all out to kiss him, on the mouth this time.
VALENTIN (*absorbed*): Mmmm . . .
MOLINA: Irina calls him up at his office, it's getting late, and the girl architect answers. Irina slams down the phone. She's eaten up with jealousy. She paces up and down the apartment like a caged beast, and when she walks by the canary she notices it's frenetically flapping its wings. She can't control herself, and she opens the little door and puts her hand right inside the cage. The little bird drops stone dead before she even touches it. Irina panics and flees from the house, looking for her husband, but, of course, she has to go past the bar on the corner and she sees them both inside. And she just wants to tear the other woman to shreds. Irina only wears black clothes, but she's never again worn that blouse he liked so much, the one in the restaurant scene, the one with all the rhinestones.
VALENTIN: What are they?

MOLINA (*shocked*): Rhinestones! I don't believe this! You don't know . . . ?

VALENTIN: Not a clue.

MOLINA: They're like diamonds only worthless; little pieces of glass that shine.

[*At this moment the cell light goes out.*]

VALENTIN: I'm going to turn in early tonight. I've had enough of all this drivel.

MOLINA (*overreacting, but deeply hurt*): Thank goodness there's no light so I don't have to see your face. Don't ever speak another word to me!

[*Note: The production must establish that when the blue light is on—meaning nighttime—MOLINA and VALENTIN cannot see each other, and so are free to express themselves as they like in gestures and body language.*]

VALENTIN: I'm sorry . . .

[*MOLINA stays silent.*]

Really, I'm sorry, I didn't think you'd get so upset.

MOLINA: You upset me because it's one of my favorite movies, you can't know . . .

[*He starts to cry.*]

. . . you didn't see it.

VALENTIN: Are you crazy? It's nothing to cry about.

MOLINA: I'll . . . I'll cry if I feel like it.

VALENTIN: Suit yourself . . . I'm very sorry.

MOLINA: And don't get the idea you've made me cry. It's because today's my mother's birthday and I'm dying to be with her . . . and not with you. (*Pause.*) Ay . . . ! Ay . . . ! I don't feel well.

VALENTIN: What's wrong?

MOLINA: Ay . . . ! Ay . . . !

VALENTIN: What is it? What's the matter?

MOLINA: The girl's fucked!

VALENTIN: Which girl?

MOLINA: Me, dummy. It's my stomach.

VALENTIN: Do you want to throw up?

MOLINA: The pain's lower down. It's in my guts.

VALENTIN: I'll call the guard, okay?

MOLINA: No, it'll pass, Valentin.

VALENTIN: The food didn't do any harm to me.

MOLINA: I bet it's my nerves. I've been on edge all day. I think it's letting up now.

VALENTIN: Try to relax. Relax your arms and legs, let them go loose.

MOLINA: Yes, that's better. I think it's going.

VALENTIN: Do you want to go to sleep?

MOLINA: I don' know . . . Ugh! It's awful . . .

VALENTIN: Maybe it'd be better if you talk, it'll take your mind off the pain.

MOLINA: You mean the movie?

VALENTIN: Where had we got to?

MOLINA: Afraid I'm going to croak before we get to the end?

VALENTIN: This is for your benefit. We broke off when they were in the bar on the corner.

MOLINA: Okay . . . The two of them get up together to leave, and Irina takes cover behind a tree. The architect girl decides to take the shortcut home through the park. He told her everything while they were in the bar, that Irina doesn't make love to him, that she has nightmares about panther-women and all. The other girl, who'd just got used to the idea that she'd lost him, now begins to think maybe she has a chance again. So she's walking along, and then you hear heels clicking behind her. She turns round and sees the silhouette of a woman. And then the clicking gets faster and now, right, the girl begins to get frightened, because you know what it's like when you've been talking about scary things . . . But she's right in the middle of the park, and if she starts to run she'll be in even worse trouble . . . and, then, suddenly, you can't bear the human footsteps any more . . . Ay . . . ! Ay . . . ! It's still hurting me.

Scene 5

Day. VALENTIN is lying down, doubled-up with stomach pains. MOLINA stands looking on at him.

VALENTIN: You can't imagine how much it hurts. Like a stabbing pain.

MOLINA: Just what I had two days ago.

VALENTIN: And each time it gets worse, Molina.

MOLINA: You should go to the clinic.

VALENTIN: Don't be thick, I already told you I don't want to go.

MOLINA: They'll only give you a little Seconol. It can't harm you.

VALENTIN: Of course it can; you can get hooked on it. You don't have a clue.

MOLINA: About what?

VALENTIN: Nothing.

MOLINA: Go on, tell me. Don't be like that.

VALENTIN: It happened to one of my comrades once. They got him hooked, his will-power just went. A political prisoner can't afford to end up in prison hospital. You follow me? Never. Once you're in there they come along and interrogate you and you have no resistance . . . Ay . . . ! Ay . . . ! It feels like my guts are splitting open. Aaargh!

MOLINA: I told you not to gobble down your food

like that.

VALENTIN (*raising himself with difficulty*): You were right. I'm ready to burst.

MOLINA: Stretch out a little.

VALENTIN: No, I don't want to sleep, I had nightmares all last night and this morning.

MOLINA (*relenting, like a middle-class housewife*): I swore I wouldn't tell you another film. I'll probably go to hell for breaking my word.

VALENTIN: Ay . . . ! Oh, fucking hell . . . !

[*MOLINA hesitates.*]

You carry on. Pay no attention if I groan.

MOLINA: I'll tell you another movie, one for tummy-ache. Now, you seemed keen on those German movies, am I right?

VALENTIN: In their propaganda machine . . . but, listen, go on with the panther-woman. We left off where the architect girl stopped hearing the human footsteps behind her in the park.

MOLINA: Well . . . she's shaking with fear, she won't dare turn around in case she sees the panther. She stops for a second to see if she still can't hear the woman's footsteps, but there's nothing, absolute silence, and then suddenly she begins to notice this rustling noise coming from the bushes being stirred by the wind . . . or maybe by something else . . .

[*MOLINA imitates the actions he describes.*]

And she turns round with a start.

VALENTIN: I think I want to go to the toilet again.

MOLINA: Shall I call them to open up?

VALENTIN: They'll catch on that I'm ill.

MOLINA: They're not going to whip you into hospital for a dose of the runs.

VALENTIN: It'll go away, carry on with the story.

MOLINA: Okay . . . (*repeating the same actions*) . . . she turns around with a start . . .

VALENTIN: Ay . . . ! Ay . . . ! The pain . . .

MOLINA (*suddenly*): Tell me something: you never told me why your mother doesn't bring you any food.

VALENTIN: She's a difficult woman. That's why I don't talk about her. She could never stand my ideas—she believes she's entitled to everything she's got, her family's got a certain position to keep up.

MOLINA: The family name.

VALENTIN: Only second league, but a name all the same.

MOLINA: Let her know that she can bring you a week's supplies at a time. You're only spiting yourself.

VALENTIN: If I'm in here it's because I brought it on myself, it's got nothing to do with her.

MOLINA: My mother didn't visit lately 'cos she's ill, did I tell you?

VALENTIN: You never mentioned it.

MOLINA: She thinks she's going to recover from one minute to the next. She won't let anyone but her bring me food, so I'm in a pickle.

VALENTIN: If you could get out of this hole, she'd improve, right?

MOLINA: You're a mind-reader . . . Okay, let's get on with it. (*repeating the same actions as before*) She turns round with a start.

VALENTIN: Ay . . . ! Ay . . . ! What have I gone and done? I'm sorry.

MOLINA: No, no . . . hold still, don't clean yourself with the sheet, wait a second.

VALENTIN: No, not your shirt . . .

MOLINA: Here, take it, wipe yourself with it. You'll need the sheet to keep warm.

VALENTIN: No, you haven't got a change of shirt.

MOLINA: Wait . . . get up, that way it won't go through . . . like this . . . mind it doesn't soil the sheet.

VALENTIN: Did it go through?

MOLINA: Your underpants held it in. Here, take them off . . .

VALENTIN: I'm embarrassed . . .

MOLINA: Didn't you say you have to be a man . . . ? So what's all this about being embarrassed?

VALENTIN: Wrap my underpants up well, Molina, so they don't smell.

MOLINA: I know how to handle this. You see . . . all wrapped up in the shirt. It'll be easier to wash than the sheet. Take the toilet paper.

VALENTIN: No, not yours. You'll have none left.

MOLINA: You never had any. So cut it out.

VALENTIN: Thank you.

[*He takes the tissue and wipes himself and hands the roll back to* MOLINA.]

MOLINA: You're welcome. Relax a little, you're shaking.

VALENTIN: It's with rage. I could cry . . . I'm furious for letting myself get caught.

MOLINA: Calm down. Pull yourself together.

[*VALENTIN watches* MOLINA *wrap the shirt and soiled tissue in a newspaper.*]

VALENTIN: Good idea . . . so it won't smell, eh?

MOLINA: Clever, isn't it?

VALENTIN: I'm freezing.

[*MOLINA is meanwhile lighting the stove and putting water on to boil.*]

MOLINA: I'm just making some tea. We're down to

the last little bag. It's camomile, good for the nerves.

VALENTIN: No, leave it, it'll go away now.

MOLINA: Don't be silly.

VALENTIN: You're crazy—you're using up all your supplies.

MOLINA: I'll be getting more soon.

VALENTIN: But your mother's sick and can't come.

MOLINA: I'll continue. (*with irony, repeating the same gestures as before but without the same élan*) She turns round with a start. The rustling noise gets nearer, and she lets rip with a desperate scream, when . . . whack! The door of the bus opens in front of her. The driver saw her standing there and stopped for her . . . The tea's almost ready.

[MOLINA pours the hot water.]

VALENTIN: Thanks. I mean that sincerely. And I want to apologize . . . sometimes I get too rough and hurt people without thinking.

MOLINA: Don't talk nonsense.

VALENTIN: Instead of a film, I want to tell you something real. About me. I lied to you when I told you about my girlfriend. I was talking about another one, someone I loved very much. I didn't tell you the truth about my real girlfriend, you'd like her a lot, she's just a sweet and simple kid, but really courageous.

MOLINA: Please don't tell me anything about her. I don't want to know anything about your political business.

VALENTIN: Don't be dumb. Who's going to question you about me?

MOLINA: They might interrogate me.

VALENTIN (*finishing his tea; much improved*): You trust me, don't you?

MOLINA: Yes . . .

VALENTIN: Well, then . . . Inside here it's got to be share and share alike.

MOLINA: It's not that . . .

[VALENTIN lies down on the pillow, relaxing.]

VALENTIN: There's nothing worse than feeling bad about having hurt someone. And I hurt her, I forced her to join the organization when she wasn't ready for it; she's very . . . unsophisticated.

MOLINA: But don't tell me any more now. I'm doing the telling for the moment. Where were we? Where did we stop . . . ?

[Hearing no response, MOLINA looks at VALENTIN, who has fallen asleep.]

How did it continue? What comes next?

[MOLINA feels proud of having helped his fellow cell-mate.]

Scene 6

Daylight. Both MOLINA and VALENTIN are stretched out on their beds, lost in a private sorrow. In the distance we hear a bolero tune.

MOLINA is singing softly.

MOLINA:

> "My love, I write to you again
> The night brings an urge to inquire
> If you, too, dear, recall the tender pain
> And the sad dreams our love would inspire."

VALENTIN: What's that you're singing?

MOLINA: A bolero. "My letter."

VALENTIN: Only you would go for that stuff.

MOLINA: What's wrong with it?

VALENTIN: It's romantic eyewash, that's what. You're daft.

MOLINA: I'm sorry. I think I've put my foot in it.

VALENTIN: In what?

MOLINA: Well, after you got that letter, you were really down in the dumps, and here I am singing about sad love letters.

VALENTIN: It was some bad news. You can read it if you like.

MOLINA: Better not.

VALENTIN: Don't start all that again; no one's going to ask you anything. Besides, they read it through before I did.

[He unfolds the letter and reads it as he talks.]

MOLINA: The handwriting's like hens' tracks.

VALENTIN: She didn't have much education . . . One of the comrades was killed, and now she's leader of the group. It's all written in code.

MOLINA: Ah . . .

VALENTIN: And she writes that she's having relations with another of the lads, just like I told her.

MOLINA: What relations?

VALENTIN: She was missing me too much. In the organization we take an oath not to get too involved with someone because it can paralyze you when you go into action.

MOLINA: Into action?

VALENTIN: Direct action. Risking your life . . . We can't afford to worry about someone who wants us to go on living because it makes you scared of dying. Well, maybe not scared exactly, but you hate the suffering it'll cause others. And that's why she's having a relationship with another comrade.

MOLINA: You said that your girlfriend wasn't really the one you told me about.

VALENTIN: Damn, staring at this letter has made me dizzy again.

MOLINA: You're still weak.

VALENTIN: I'm shivering and I feel queasy.

[He covers himself with the sheet.]

MOLINA: I told you not to start taking food again.

VALENTIN: But I was famished.

[MOLINA helps VALENTIN wrap up well.]

MOLINA: You were getting better yesterday, and then you went and ate and got sick again. And today it's the same story. Promise me you won't touch a thing tomorrow.

VALENTIN: The girl I told you about, the bourgeois one, she joined the organization with me, but she dropped out and tried to persuade me to split with her.

MOLINA: Why?

VALENTIN: She loved life too much and she was happy just to be with me, that's all she wanted. So we had to break up.

MOLINA: Because you loved each other too much.

VALENTIN: You make it sound like one of your boleros.

MOLINA: Listen, tough guy, haven't you cottoned on yet? Those songs are full of really deep truths, and that's why I like them. The truth is you mock them because they're too close to home. You laugh to keep from crying. . . . As a tango says.

VALENTIN: I was lying low for a while in that guy's flat, the one they killed. With his wife and kid. I even used to change the kid's nappies . . . And do you want to know what the worst of it is? I can't write to a single one of them without blowing them to the police.

MOLINA: Not even your girlfriend?

VALENTIN (*struggling to hold back his tears*): Oh, God . . . ! What a mess . . . ! It's all so sad! Give me your hand, Molina. Squeeze hard . . .

MOLINA: Hold it tight.

VALENTIN: There's something else. It's wrecking me. It's shameful, awful . . .

MOLINA: Tell me, get it off your chest.

VALENTIN: It's . . . the girl I want to hear from, the one I want to have next to me right now and hug and kiss . . . it's not the one in the movement, but the other one . . . Marta, that's her name . . .

MOLINA: If that's what you feel deep down . . . Oh, I forgot, if your stomach feels real empty, there's a few digestives I'd forgotten all about.

[Without taking his hand from VALENTIN's he reaches for the packet of digestives.]

VALENTIN: For all I shoot my mouth off about progress . . . when it comes to women, what I really like is a woman with class, and I'm just like all the reactionary sons-of-bitches that killed my comrade . . . The same, exactly the same . . .

MOLINA: That's not true . . .

VALENTIN: And sometimes I think maybe I don't even love Marta because of who she is but because she's got . . . class . . . I'm just like all the other class-conscious sons-of-bitches . . . in the world.

GUARD'S VOICE: Luis Alberto Molina! To the visiting room!

[VALENTIN and MOLINA let go of each other's hand as if caught in a shameful act. The cell door opens and MOLINA exits, but not before he's managed to slip the biscuits under VALENTIN's blanket. Hereafter, the dialogue is on prerecorded tape. Meanwhile, VALENTIN remains onstage and takes the biscuits from under his covers, manages to find just three at the bottom of the large packet and begins to eat them, one at a time, savoring each one.]

WARDEN'S VOICE: Stop shaking, man, no one's going to do anything to you.

MOLINA'S VOICE: I had a bad stomachache before, sir, but I'm fine now.

WARDEN'S VOICE: You've got nothing to be afraid of. We've made it look like you've had a visitor. The other one won't suspect a thing.

MOLINA'S VOICE: No, he won't suspect anything.

WARDEN'S VOICE: At home last night I had dinner with your benefactor, and he had some good news for you. Your mother is on the road to recovery . . . It seems the chance of your pardon is doing her good . . .

MOLINA'S VOICE: Are you sure?

WARDEN'S VOICE: What's the matter with you? Why are you trembling . . . ? You should be jubilant . . . Well, have you got any news for me yet? Has he told you anything? Is he opening up to you yet?

MOLINA'S VOICE: No, sir, not so far. You have to take these things a step at a time.

WARDEN'S VOICE: Didn't it help at all when we weakened him physically?

MOLINA'S VOICE: I had to eat the first plate of fixed food myself.

WARDEN'S VOICE: You shouldn't have done that.

MOLINA'S VOICE: The truth is he doesn't like porridge, and since one portion was bigger than the other . . . he insisted I ate it. If I'd refused, he might have got suspicious. You told me, sir, that the doctored food would be on the newest plate, but they made a mistake piling it high like that.

WARDEN'S VOICE: Ah, well, in that case, I'm obliged to you, Molina. I'm sorry about the mistake.

MOLINA'S VOICE: Now you should let him get some of his strength back.

WARDEN'S VOICE (*irritated*): That's for us to decide. We know what we're doing. And when you get back to your cell, say you had a visit from your mother. That'll explain why you're so excited.

MOLINA'S VOICE: No, I couldn't say that, she always brings me a food parcel.

WARDEN'S VOICE: Okay, we'll send out for some groceries. Think of it as a reward for the trouble with the porridge. Poor Molina!

MOLINA'S VOICE: Thank you, Warden.

WARDEN'S VOICE: Reel off a list of what she usually brings. (*Pause.*) Now!

MOLINA'S VOICE: To you?

WARDEN'S VOICE: Yes, and be quick about it, I've got work to catch up with.

MOLINA'S VOICE (*as the curtain falls*): Condensed milk, a can of peaches . . . two roast chickens . . . a big bag of sugar . . . two packs of tea, one breakfast, one camomile . . . powdered milk, a bar of soap—bathsize—oh, let me think a second, my mind's a complete blank . . .

END OF ACT ONE

ACT II

Scene 1

Lighting as in the previous scene. The cell door opens, and MOLINA *enters with a shopping bag.*

MOLINA: Look what I've got!

VALENTIN: No! Your mother's been!

MOLINA: Yes!

VALENTIN: So she's better now?

MOLINA: A little better . . . and look what she brought me. Oops! Sorry, brought us!

VALENTIN (*secretly flattered*): No, it's for you. Cut the nonsense.

MOLINA: Shut it, you're the invalid. The chickens are for you, they'll get you back on your feet.

VALENTIN: No, I won't let you do this.

MOLINA: It's no sacrifice. I can go without the chicken if it means I don't have to put up with your pong . . . No, listen, I'm being serious now, you've got to stop eating this pig-swill they serve in here. At least for a day or two.

VALENTIN: You think so?

MOLINA: And then when you're better . . . Close your eyes.

*[*VALENTIN *closes his eyes, and* MOLINA *places a large tin in one of his hands.]*

    Three guesses . . .

VALENTIN: Ahem . . . er . . . er . . .

[Enjoying the game, MOLINA *places an identical tin in* VALENTIN'S *other hand.]*

MOLINA: The weight ought to help you . . .

VALENTIN: Heavy all right . . . I give up.

MOLINA: Open your eyes.

VALENTIN: Condensed milk!

MOLINA: But you can't have it yet, not until you're better. And this is for both of us.

VALENTIN: Marvelous.

MOLINA: First . . . we'll have a cup of camomile tea because my nerves are shot, and you can have a drumstick, no, better not, it's only five . . . Anyway, we can have tea and some biscuits, they're even lighter than those digestives.

VALENTIN: Please, can't I have one right away?

MOLINA: Why not! But just with a little marmalade . . . ! Luckily, everything she brought is easy to get down so it won't give you any trouble. Except for the condensed milk, for the time being.

VALENTIN: Oh, Molina, I'm wilting with hunger. Why won't you let me have that chicken leg now?

*[*MOLINA *hesitates a moment.]*

MOLINA: Here . . .

VALENTIN (*wolfing down the chicken*): Honest, I really was beginning to feel bad . . .

[He devours the chicken]

    Thanks . . .

MOLINA: You're welcome.

VALENTIN (*with his mouth full*): But there's just one thing missing to round off the picnic.

MOLINA: Tut, and I thought I was supposed to be the pervert here.

VALENTIN: Stop fooling around! What we need is a movie . . .

MOLINA: Ah! Well, never mind . . . Now there's a scene where Irina has a completely new hairstyle.

VALENTIN: Oh, I'm sorry, I don't feel too good, it's that dizziness again.

MOLINA: Are you positive?

VALENTIN: Yes, it's been threatening all night.

MOLINA: But it can't be the chicken. Maybe you're imagining it.

VALENTIN: I felt full up all of a sudden.

MOLINA: That's because you wolfed it down without even chewing.

VALENTIN: And this itching is driving me wild. I don't know when I last had a bath.

MOLINA: Don't even think about that. That freezing water in your present state! (*Pause.*) Anyway, she looks stunning here, you can see her reflection in a window pane; it's drizzling and all the drops are running down the glass. She's got raven black hair and it's all scooped up in a bun. Let me describe it to you . . .

VALENTIN: It's all scooped up, okay, never mind the silly details . . .

MOLINA: Silly, my foot! And she's got a rhinestone flower in her hair.

VALENTIN (*very agitated now because of his itch*): I know what rhinestones are, so you can save your breath!

MOLINA: My, you are touchy today!

VALENTIN: Can I ask you something?

MOLINA: Go ahead.

VALENTIN: I feel all screwed up—and confused. If it's not too much trouble, I'd like to dictate a letter to her. Would you mind taking it down . . . ? I get dizzy if I try to focus my eyes too hard.

MOLINA: Let me get a pencil.

VALENTIN: You're very kind to me.

MOLINA: We'll do a rough draft first on a bit of paper.

VALENTIN: Here, take my pen-case.

MOLINA: Wait till I sharpen this pencil.

VALENTIN (*short-tempered*): I told you! Use one of mine!

MOLINA: Okay, don't blow your top!

VALENTIN: I'm sorry, it's just that everything is going black.

MOLINA: Okay, ready, shoot . . .

VALENTIN (*very sad*): Dear Marta . . . you don't expect this letter . . . In your case, it won't endanger you . . . I'm feeling . . . lonely, I need you, I want to be . . . near you . . . I want you to give me . . . a word of encouragement.

MOLINA: . . . "of encouragement" . . .

VALENTIN: . . . in this moment I couldn't face my comrades, I'd be ashamed of being so weak . . . I have sores all over inside, I need somebody to pour some honey . . . over my wounds . . . And only you could understand . . . because you too were brought up in a nice clean house to enjoy life to the full . . . I can't accept becoming a martyr, it makes me angry to be one . . . or, it isn't that, I see it clearer now . . . I'm afraid because I'm sick, horribly afraid of dying . . . that it may just end here, that my life has amounted to nothing more than this, I never exploited anyone . . . and ever since I had any sense, I've been struggling against the exploitation of my fellow man . . .

MOLINA: Go on.

VALENTIN: Where was I?

MOLINA: "My fellow man" . . .

VALENTIN: . . . because I want to go out into the street one day and not die. And sometimes I get this idea that never ever again will I be able to touch a woman, and I can't accept it, and when I think of women I only see you, and what a relief it would be to believe that right until I finish writing this letter you'll be thinking of me . . . and that you'll be running your hands over your body I so well remember . . .

MOLINA: Hold on, don't go so fast.

VALENTIN: . . . over your body I so well remember, and you'll be thinking that it's my hand . . . it would be as if I were touching you, darling . . . because there's still something of me inside you, isn't that so? Just as your own scent has stayed in my nose . . . beneath my fingertips lies a sort of memory of your skin, do you understand me? Although it's not a matter of understanding . . . it's a matter of believing, and sometimes I'm convinced that I took something of you with me . . . and that I haven't lost it, and then sometimes not, I feel there's just me all alone in this cell . . .

[*Pause.*]

MOLINA: Yes . . . "all alone in this cell" . . . Go on.

VALENTIN: . . . because nothing leaves any trace, and my luck in having had such happiness with you, of spending those nights and afternoons and mornings of sheer enjoyment, none of this is any use now, just the opposite, it all turns against me, because I miss you madly, and all I can feel is the torture of my loneliness, and in my nose there is only the stench of this cell, and of myself . . . and I can't have a wash because I'm ill, really weak, and the cold water would give me pneumonia, and beneath my fingertips what I feel is the chill of my fear of death, I can feel it in my joints . . . what a terrible thing to lose hope, and that's what's happened to me . . .

MOLINA: I'm sorry for butting in . . .

VALENTIN: What is it?

MOLINA: When you finish dictating the letter, there's something I want to say.

VALENTIN (*wound up*): What?

MOLINA: Because if you take one of those freezing showers, it'll kill you.

VALENTIN (*almost hysterical*): And . . . ? So what? Tell me, for Christ's sake.

MOLINA: I could help you to get cleaned up. You see, we've got the hot water we were going to use

to boil the potatoes and we've got two towels,
so we lather one of them and you do your
front and I'll do the back and then you can dry
yourself with the other towel.

VALENTIN: And then I'd stop itching?

MOLINA: Sure. And we'd clean up a bit at a time so
you won't catch cold.

VALENTIN: And you'll help me?

MOLINA: Of course I will.

VALENTIN: When?

MOLINA: Now, if you like. The water's boiling, we
can mix it with a little cold water.

*[MOLINA starts to do this. VALENTIN can't believe in
such happiness.]*

VALENTIN: And I'd be able to get to sleep without
scratching?

MOLINA: Take your shirt off. I'll put some more
water on.

[He mixes the hot and cold water.]

VALENTIN: But you're using up all your paraffin.

MOLINA: I don't mind.

VALENTIN: Give me the letter, Molina.

MOLINA: What for?

VALENTIN: Just hand it over.

MOLINA: Here.

*[MOLINA gives VALENTIN the letter. VALENTIN starts to
tear it up.]*

What are you doing?

VALENTIN: This.

[He tears the letter into quarters.]

Let's not mention it again.

MOLINA: As you like . . .

VALENTIN: It's wrong to get carried away like that by
despair.

MOLINA: But it's good to get it into the open. You
said so yourself.

VALENTIN: But it's bad for me. I have to learn to
restrain myself. (*Pause.*) Listen, I mean it, one
day I'll thank you properly for all this.

[MOLINA puts more water on the stove.]

Are you going to waste all that water?

MOLINA: Yes . . . and don't be daft, there's no need to
thank me.

[MOLINA signals to VALENTIN to turn around.]

VALENTIN: Tell me, how does the movie end? Just the
last scene.

MOLINA (*scrubbing VALENTIN's back*): It's either all or

nothing.

VALENTIN: Why?

MOLINA: Because of the details. Her hairdo is very
important, it's the style that women wear, or
used to wear, when they wanted to show that
this was a crucial moment in their lives,
because the hair all scooped up in a bun,
which left the neck bare, gave the woman's
face a certain nobility.

*[VALENTIN, despite the tensions and turmoil of this dif-
ficult day, changes his expression and smiles.]*

Why have you got that mocking little grin on
your face? I don't see anything to laugh at.

VALENTIN: Because my back doesn't itch any more!

Scene 2

*Day. MOLINA is tidying up his belongings with extreme
care so as not to wake VALENTIN. VALENTIN, nevertheless, wakes up. Both of them are charged with
renewed energy, and the dialogue begins at its normal
pace but accelerates rapidly into tenseness.*

VALENTIN: Good morning.

MOLINA: Good morning.

VALENTIN: What's the time?

MOLINA: Ten past ten. I call my mother "ten past
ten," the poor dear, because of the way her feet
stick out when she walks.

VALENTIN: It's late.

MOLINA: When they brought the tea round, you just
turned over and carried on sleeping.

VALENTIN: What were you saying about your old
lady?

MOLINA: Look who's still sleeping. Nothing. Sleep
well?

VALENTIN: I feel a lot better.

MOLINA: You don't feel dizzy?

VALENTIN: Lying in bed, no.

MOLINA: Great—why don't you try to walk a little?

VALENTIN: No, you'll laugh.

MOLINA: At what?

VALENTIN: Something that happens to a normal
healthy man when he wakes up in the morning with too much energy.

MOLINA: You've got a hard-on? Well, God bless . . .

VALENTIN: But look away, please. I get embarrassed . . .

*[He gets up to wash his face with water from the jug.
MOLINA puts his hand over his eyes and looks away.]*

MOLINA: My eyes are shut tight.

VALENTIN: It's all thanks to your food. My legs are a
bit shaky still, but I don't feel queasy. You can
look now.

[He gets back into bed.]

> I'll lie down a bit more now.

MOLINA (*overprotective and smothering*): I'll put the water on for tea.

VALENTIN: No, just reheat the crap they brought us this morning.

MOLINA: I threw it out when I went to the loo. You must look after yourself properly if you want to get better.

VALENTIN: It embarrasses me to use up your things. I'm better now.

MOLINA: Button it.

VALENTIN: No, listen . . .

MOLINA: Listen nothing. My mother's bringing stuff again.

VALENTIN: Okay, thanks, but just for today.

[He collects his books together.]

MOLINA: And no reading. Rest . . . ! I'll start another film while I'm making tea.

VALENTIN: I'd better try and study, if I can, now that I'm on form.

[He starts to read.]

MOLINA: Won't it be too tiring?

VALENTIN: I'll give it a go.

MOLINA: You're a real fanatic.

VALENTIN (*throwing the book to the ground as his tenseness increases*): I can't . . . the words are jumping around.

MOLINA: I told you so. Are you feeling dizzy?

VALENTIN: Only when I try to read.

MOLINA: You know what it is? It's probably just a temporary weakness—if you have a ham sandwich you'll be right as rain.

VALENTIN: Do you think so?

MOLINA: Sure, and then later, after you've had lunch and another little snooze, you'll feel up to studying again.

VALENTIN: I feel lazy as hell. I'll just lie down.

MOLINA (*schoolmistressy*): No, lying in bed only weakens the constitution; you'd be better standing or at least sitting up.

[MOLINA hands VALENTIN his tea.]

VALENTIN: This is the last day I'm taking any more of this.

MOLINA (*mistress of the situation*): Ha! Ha! I already told the guard not to bring you any more tea in the morning.

VALENTIN: Listen, you decide what you want for yourself, but I want them to bring me the tea even if it is horse's piss.

MOLINA: You don't know the first thing about a healthy diet.

VALENTIN (*trying to control himself*): I'm not joking, Molina, I don't like other people controlling my life.

MOLINA (*counting on his fingers*): Today is Wednesday . . . everything will hang on what happens on Monday. That's what my lawyer says. I don't believe in appeals and all that, but if there's someone who can pull a few strings, maybe there's a chance.

VALENTIN: I hope so.

MOLINA (*with concealed cunning, as he makes more tea*): If they let me out . . . who knows who you'll get as a cell-mate?

VALENTIN: Haven't you had breakfast yet?

MOLINA: I didn't want to disturb you. You were sleeping.

[He takes VALENTIN's cup to refill it.]

> Will you join me in another cup?

VALENTIN: No, thanks.

[MOLINA opens a new packet, not letting VALENTIN see.]

MOLINA: Tell me, what are you going to study later on?

VALENTIN: What are you doing?

MOLINA: A surprise. Tell me what you're reading.

VALENTIN: Nothing . . .

MOLINA: Cat got your tongue . . . ? And now . . . we untie the mystery parcel . . . which I had hidden about my person . . . and, what have we got here . . . ? something that goes a treat with tea . . . a cherry madeira!

VALENTIN: No, thanks.

MOLINA: What d'you mean "no" . . . ? The kettle's on . . . Oh, I know why not—you want to go to the loo. Ask them to open up, and then fly back here.

VALENTIN: For Christ's sake, don't tell me what to do!

[MOLINA squeezes VALENTIN's chin.]

MOLINA: Oh, come on, let me pamper you a little.

VALENTIN: That's enough . . . you prick!

MOLINA: Are you crazy . . . ? What's the matter with you?

[VALENTIN hurls the teacup and the cake against the wall.]

VALENTIN: Shut your fucking trap!

MOLINA: The cake . . .

[VALENTIN is silent.]

> Look what you've done . . . If the stove's

broke, we're done for . . . (*Pause.*) . . . and the saucer . . . (*Pause.*) . . . and the tea . . .

VALENTIN: I'm sorry . . .

[*MOLINA is silent now.*]

I lost control . . . I'm really sorry.

[*MOLINA remains silent.*]

The stove is okay; but the paraffin spilled.

[*MOLINA still doesn't answer.*]

. . . I'm sorry I got carried away, forgive me . . .

MOLINA (*deeply wounded*): There's nothing to forgive.

VALENTIN: There is. A lot.

MOLINA: Forget it. Nothing happened.

VALENTIN: It did, I'm dying with shame.

[*MOLINA says nothing.*]

. . . I behaved like an animal . . . Look, I'll call the guard and fill up the bottle while I'm at it. We're almost out of water . . . Molina, please look at me. Raise your head.

[*MOLINA remains silent.*]

GUARD'S VOICE: Luis Alberto Molina. To the visiting room!

[*The door opens and MOLINA exits. The recorded dialogue begins as soon as MOLINA moves towards the door. MOLINA returns with the provisions to find VALENTIN picking up the things he has just thrown on the floor. MOLINA starts to unpack the shopping bag. The recorded dialogue is heard while the action takes place onstage.*]

WARDEN'S VOICE: Today's Monday, Molina, what have you got for me?

MOLINA'S VOICE: Nothing, I'm afraid, sir.

WARDEN'S VOICE: Indeed.

MOLINA'S VOICE: But he's taking me more into his confidence.

WARDEN'S VOICE: The problem is they're putting pressure on me, Molina. From the top: from the President's private office. You understand what I'm saying to you, Molina? They want to try interrogation again. Less carrot, more stick.

MOLINA'S VOICE: Not that, sir. It'd be even worse if you lost him in interrogation.

WARDEN'S VOICE: That's what I tell them, but they won't listen.

MOLINA'S VOICE: Just one more week, sir. Please. I have an idea . . .

WARDEN'S VOICE: What?

MOLINA'S VOICE: He's a hard nut, but he has an emo-

tional side.

WARDEN'S VOICE: So?

MOLINA'S VOICE: Well, if the guard were to come and say they're moving me to another block in a week's time because of the appeal, that might really soften him up.

WARDEN'S VOICE: What are you driving at?

MOLINA'S VOICE: Nothing, I swear. It's just a hunch. If he thinks I'm leaving soon, he'll feel like opening up even more with me. Prisoners are like that, sir . . . when one of their pals is leaving, they feel more defenseless than ever.

[*At this moment MOLINA is back in the cell, and he takes out the food as the WARDEN'S VOICE mentions each item. VALENTIN looks at MOLINA.*]

WARDEN'S VOICE: Guard, take this down: two roast chickens, four baked apples, one carton of coleslaw, one pound of bacon, one pound of cooked ham, four French loaves, four pieces of crystalized fruit . . .

[*The recorded voice begins to fade out.*]

. . . a carton of orange juice, two cherry madeiras . . .

[*MOLINA is very calm and sad; he is still upset by VALENTIN's remarks.*]

MOLINA: This is the bacon and this one's the ham. I'm going to make a sandwich while the bread's fresh. You fix yourself whatever you want.

VALENTIN (*deeply ashamed*): Thank you.

MOLINA: (*reserved and calm*) I'm going to cut this roll in half and spread it with butter and have a sandwich. And a baked apple.

VALENTIN: Sounds delicious.

MOLINA: If you'd like some of the chicken while it's still warm, go ahead. Feel free.

VALENTIN: Thank you, Molina.

MOLINA: We'll each fend for ourselves. Then I won't get on your nerves.

VALENTIN: If that's what you prefer.

MOLINA: There's some crystalized fruit, too. All I ask is that you leave me the pumpkin. Otherwise, take what you want.

VALENTIN (*finding it hard to apologize*): I'm still embarrassed . . . because of that tantrum.

MOLINA: Don't be silly.

VALENTIN: If I got annoyed with you . . . it was because you were kind to me . . . and I didn't want . . . to treat you the same way.

MOLINA: Look, I've been thinking too, and I remembered something you once said, right . . . ? That when you're involved in a struggle like that, well, it's not too convenient to get fond of someone. Well, fond is maybe going too far . . . or, why not? Fond as a friend.

VALENTIN: That's a very noble way of looking at it.

MOLINA: You see, sometimes I do understand what you tell me.

VALENTIN: But are we so fettered by the world outside that we can't act like human beings just for a minute . . . ?

MOLINA: I don't follow.

VALENTIN: Our persecutors are on the outside, not inside this cell . . . The problem is I'm so brainwashed that it freaks me out when someone is nice to me without asking anything in return.

MOLINA: I don't know about that . . .

VALENTIN: About what?

MOLINA: Don't get me wrong, but if I'm nice to you, well, it's because I want you to be my friend . . . and why not admit it? I want your affection. Just like I treat my mother well because she's a good person and I want her to love me. And you're a good person too, and unselfish because you're risking your life for an ideal . . . that I don't understand but, all the same, it's not just for yourself . . . Don't look away like that, are you embarrassed?

VALENTIN: A bit.

[He looks MOLINA in the face.]

MOLINA: And that's why I respect you and have warm feelings toward you . . . and why I want you to like me . . . because, you see, my mother's love is the only good thing I've felt in my life, because she likes me . . . just the way I am.

VALENTIN (*pointing to the loaf MOLINA put aside*): Can I cut the loaf for you?

MOLINA: Of course . . .

VALENTIN (*cutting the loaf*): And did you never have good friends that meant a lot to you?

MOLINA: My friends were all . . . screaming queens, like me, we never really count on each other because . . . how can I express it?—because we know we're so easily frightened off. We're always looking, you know, for friendship, or whatever, with somebody more serious, with a man, you see? And that just doesn't happen, right? Because what a man wants is a woman.

VALENTIN (*taking a slice of ham for MOLINA's sandwich*): And are all homosexuals like that?

MOLINA: Oh no, there are some who fall in love with each other. But me and my friends, we're women. One hundred percent. We don't go in for those little games. We're normal women; *we* only go to bed with men.

VALENTIN (*too absorbed to see the funny side of this*): Butter?

MOLINA: Yes, thanks. There's something I have to tell you.

VALENTIN: Of course, the movie . . .

MOLINA (*with cunning, but nervous all the same*): My lawyer said things were looking up.

VALENTIN: What a creep I am! I didn't ask you.

MOLINA: And when there's an appeal pending, the prisoner gets moved to another block in the prison. They'll probably shift me within a week or so.

VALENTIN (*upset by this but dissimulating*): That's terrific . . . You ought to be pleased.

MOLINA: I don't want to dwell on it too much, build my hopes . . . Have some coleslaw.

VALENTIN: Should I?

MOLINA: It's very good.

VALENTIN: Your news made me lose my appetite.

[He gets up.]

MOLINA: Pretend I didn't say anything, nothing's settled yet.

VALENTIN: No, it all looks good for you, we should be happy.

MOLINA: Have some salad.

VALENTIN: I don't know what's wrong, but all of a sudden I don't feel too good.

MOLINA: Is your stomach hurting?

VALENTIN: No . . . it's my head. I'm all confused.

MOLINA: About what?

VALENTIN: Let me rest for a while.

[VALENTIN sits down again, resting his head in his palms. The light changes to indicate a shift to a different time—the two characters stay where they are: there is a special tension, a hypersensitivity in the air.]

MOLINA: The guy is all muddled up, he doesn't know how to handle this freaky wife of his. She comes in, sees that he's dead serious and goes to the bathroom to put away her shoes, all dirty with mud. He says he went to the doctor's to look for her and found out that she didn't go anymore. Then she breaks into tears and tells him that she's just what she always feared, a madwoman with hallucinations or even worse, a panther-woman. Then he gives in and takes her in his arms, and you were right, she's really just a little girl for him, because when he sees her so defenseless and lost, he feels again he loves her with all his heart and tells her that everything will sort itself out . . .

[MOLINA sighs deeply.]

Ahhh . . . !

VALENTIN: What a sigh!

MOLINA: Life is so difficult . . .
VALENTIN: What's the matter?
MOLINA: I don't know, I'm afraid of building up my
    hopes of getting out of here . . . and that I'll get
    put in some other cell and spend my life there
    with God knows what sort of creep.
VALENTIN: Don't lose sight of this. Your mother's
    health is the most precious thing to you, right?
MOLINA: Yes . . .
VALENTIN: Think about her recovery. Period!

[MOLINA laughs involuntarily in his distress.]

MOLINA: I don't want to think about it.
VALENTIN: What's wrong?
MOLINA: Nothing!
VALENTIN: Don't bury your head in the pillow . . .
    Are you hiding something from me?
MOLINA: It's . . .
VALENTIN: It's what . . . ? Look, when you get out of
    here, you're going to be a free man. You can
    join a political organization if you like.
MOLINA: You're crazy! They won't trust a fag.
VALENTIN: But I can tell you who to speak to . . .
MOLINA (*suddenly forceful, raising his head from the pil-
    low*): Promise me on whatever you hold most
    dear, never, never, you understand, never tell
    me anything about your comrades.
VALENTIN: But who would ever think you're seeing
    them?
MOLINA: They could interrogate me, whatever, but if
    I know nothing, I say nothing.
VALENTIN: In any case, there are all kinds of groups,
    of political action; there are even some who
    just sit and talk. When you get out, things'll be
    different.
MOLINA: Things *won't* be different. That's the worst
    of it.
VALENTIN: How many times have I seen you cry?
    Come on, you annoy me with your snivelling.
MOLINA: It's just that I can't take any more . . . I've
    had nothing but bad luck . . . always.

[The prison light goes out.]

VALENTIN: Lights out already . . . ? In the first place,
    you must join a group, avoid being alone.
MOLINA: I don't understand any of that . . . (*suddenly
    grave*) . . . and I don't believe in it much either.
VALENTIN (*tough*): Then like it or lump it.
MOLINA (*still crying a little*): Let's . . . skip it.
VALENTIN (*conciliatory*): Come on, don't be like that . . .

[He pats MOLINA on the back affectionately.]

MOLINA: I'm asking you . . . please don't touch me.
VALENTIN: Can't a friend pat you on the back?
MOLINA: It makes it worse . . .

VALENTIN: Why . . . ? Tell me what's troubling you . . .
MOLINA (*with deep, deep feeling*): I'm so tired, Valentin
    . . . I'm tired of suffering. I hurt all over inside.
VALENTIN: Where does it hurt you?
MOLINA: Inside my chest and my throat . . . Why
    does sadness always get you there? It's chok-
    ing me, like a knot . . .
VALENTIN: It's true, that's where people always feel
    it.

[MOLINA is quiet.]

    Is it hurting you a lot, this knot?
MOLINA: Yes.
VALENTIN: Is it here?
MOLINA: Yes.
VALENTIN: Want me to stroke it . . . here?
MOLINA: Yes.

[Short pause.]

VALENTIN: This is relaxing . . .
MOLINA: Why relaxing, Valentin?
VALENTIN: Not to think about myself for a while.
    Thinking about you, that you need me, and I
    can be of some use to you.
MOLINA: You're always looking for explanations . . .
    You're crazy.
VALENTIN: I don't want events to get the better of me.
    I want to know why they happen.
MOLINA: Can I touch you?
VALENTIN: Yes . . .
MOLINA: I want to touch that mole—the little round
    one over your eye.

[MOLINA touches the mole.]

    You're very kind.
VALENTIN: No, you're the one who's kind.
MOLINA: If you like, you can do what you want with
    me . . . because I want it too . . . If it won't dis-
    gust you . . .
VALENTIN: Don't say that—let's not say anything.

[VALENTIN goes under MOLINA's top sheet.]

    Shift a bit closer to the wall . . . (*Pause.*) You
    can't see a thing, it's so dark.
MOLINA: Gently . . . (*Pause.*) No, it hurts too much
    like that. (*Pause.*) Slowly please . . . (*Pause.*)
    That's it . . . (*Pause.*) . . . thanks . . .
VALENTIN: Thank you, too. Are you feeling better?
MOLINA: Yes. And what about you, Valentin?
VALENTIN: Don't ask me . . . I don't know anything
    anymore . . .
MOLINA: Oh . . . it's beautiful . . .
VALENTIN: Don't say anything . . . not for now . . .
MOLINA: It's just that I feel . . . such strange things . . .

Without thinking, I just lifted my hand to my eye, looking for that mole.

VALENTIN: What mole . . . ? I'm the one with the mole, not you.

MOLINA: I know, but I just lifted up my hand . . . to touch the mole . . . I don't have.

VALENTIN: Ssh, try and keep quiet for a while . . .

MOLINA: And do you know what else I felt, but only for a minute, no longer . . . ?

VALENTIN: Tell me, but keep still, like that . . .

MOLINA: For just a minute, it felt like I wasn't here . . . not in here, nor anywhere else . . . (*Pause.*) It felt like I wasn't here, there was just you . . . Or that I wasn't me any more. As if I was . . . you.

Scene 3

Day. MOLINA *and* VALENTIN *are in their beds.*

VALENTIN: Good morning.

[*He is reinvigorated, happy.* MOLINA *is also highly charged.*]

MOLINA: Good morning, Valentin.

VALENTIN: Did you sleep well?

MOLINA: Yes. (*calmly, not insisting*) Would you like tea or coffee?

VALENTIN: Coffee. To wake me up well—and study. Try to get back into the swing of things . . . What about you? Is the gloom over? Or not?

MOLINA: Yes it is, but I feel groggy. I can't think . . . my mind's blank.

VALENTIN: I don't want to think about anything either, so I'm going to read. That'll keep my mind off things.

MOLINA: Off what? Feeling guilty about what happened?

VALENTIN: I'm more and more convinced that sex is innocence itself.

MOLINA: Can I ask you a favor . . . ? Can we not analyze anything, just for today.

VALENTIN: Whatever you like.

MOLINA: I feel . . . fine and I don't want anything to rob me of that feeling. I haven't felt so good since I was a kid. Since my mother bought me some toy.

VALENTIN: Do you remember what toy you liked most?

MOLINA: A doll.

VALENTIN: Ay!

[*He starts to laugh.*]

MOLINA: What's funny about that?

VALENTIN: As a psychologist I would starve.

MOLINA: Why?

VALENTIN: Nothing . . . I was just wondering if there was any link between your favorite toy and . . . me.

MOLINA (*playing along*): It was your own fault for asking.

VALENTIN: Are you sure it wasn't a boy doll?

MOLINA: Absolutely. She had blonde braids and a little Tyrolese folk dress.

[*They laugh together, unselfconsciously.*]

VALENTIN: One question . . . Physically, you're as much a man as I am.

MOLINA: Ummm . . .

VALENTIN: Why then don't you behave like a man . . . ? I don't mean with women if you're not attracted to them, but with another man?

MOLINA: It's not me. I only enjoy myself like that.

VALENTIN: Well, if you like being a woman . . . you shouldn't feel diminished because of that.

[MOLINA *doesn't answer.*]

I mean you shouldn't feel you owe anyone, or feel obliged to them because that's what you happen to feel like . . . You shouldn't yield . . .

MOLINA: But if a man is . . . my husband, he has to be boss to feel good. That's only natural.

VALENTIN: No, the man and the woman should be equal partners inside the home. Otherwise, it's exploitation. Don't you see?

MOLINA: But there's no thrill like that.

VALENTIN: What?

MOLINA: Since you want to know about it . . . the thrill is that when a man embraces you, you're a little bit afraid.

VALENTIN: Who put that idea into your head? That's all crap.

MOLINA: But it's what I feel.

VALENTIN: No, it's not what you feel, it's what you've been taught to feel. Being a woman doesn't make you . . . how shall I say . . . ? A martyr. And if I didn't think it would hurt like hell, I'd ask you to do it to me, to show you that all this business about being macho doesn't give anyone rights over another person.

MOLINA (*now disturbed*): This is getting us nowhere.

VALENTIN: On the contrary, I want to talk about it.

MOLINA: Well, I don't, so that's it. I'm begging you, no more, please.

VALENTIN: As you like.

MOLINA: There is something I want to tell you, though . . . When you were here it was like I wasn't myself, it was such a relief. And then later, when you were back in your bed . . . I still wasn't me, it's so strange, I can't explain.

VALENTIN: Tell me . . . try . . .

MOLINA: Don't rush me, I have to concentrate . . . Yes . . . when I was alone in my bed, and I was no longer you, I still felt like I was somebody else, neither male nor female . . . what I felt was . . .

VALENTIN: . . . out of danger . . .

MOLINA: Yes! That's it, exactly. How did you know?

VALENTIN: Because it's just what I felt too.

MOLINA: Valentin, why should we feel like that?

VALENTIN: I don't know . . .

MOLINA: Valentin . . .

VALENTIN: Mmm . . .

MOLINA: I'm going to tell you something, but promise me you won't laugh.

VALENTIN: Tell me.

MOLINA: When you come to my bed, afterwards . . . I hope I'll never wake up anymore once I've fallen asleep. I'd be sorry for my mother, sure, because she'd be on her own . . . but if it was just me, then I wouldn't want to wake ever again. And this isn't just some half-baked notion that I've just dreamed up either, no, it's the honest truth . . .

VALENTIN: But first you have to finish the movie.

GUARD'S VOICE: Prisoner Luis Alberto Molina! To the visiting room!

WARDEN'S VOICE: Put me through to your boss, please . . . How's it going? Nothing this end. Yes, that's why I called. He's on his way here now . . . Yes, they need the information, I'm aware of that . . . and if Molina still hasn't found out anything, what should I do with him . . . ? Are you sure . . . ? Let him out . . . But why . . . ? Yes, of course, there's no time to lose. Quite, and if the other one gives him a message, Molina will lead us straight to the group . . . I've got it, yes, we'll give him just enough time for the other to pass on the message . . . The tricky thing will be if Molina catches on that he's under surveillance . . . It's hard to anticipate the reactions of someone like Molina: a pervert after all.

[The cell door opens and MOLINA *comes back in totally deflated.]*

MOLINA: Poor Valentin, you're looking at my hands.

VALENTIN: I didn't mean to.

MOLINA: Your eyes gave you away, poor love . . .

VALENTIN: Such language . . .

MOLINA: I didn't get a parcel. You'll have to forgive me . . . Ay! Valentin . . .

VALENTIN: What's wrong.

MOLINA: Ay, you can't imagine . . .

VALENTIN: What's up. Tell me.

MOLINA: I'm going.

VALENTIN: To another cell . . .

MOLINA: No, they're releasing me.

VALENTIN: No.

MOLINA: I'm out on parole.

VALENTIN (*exploding with unexpected happiness*): But that's incredible~!

*[*MOLINA *is confused by the way* VALENTIN *is taking this.]*

MOLINA: You're very kind to be so pleased for me.

VALENTIN: I'm happy for you too, of course . . . but, it's terrific! And I guarantee there's not the slightest risk.

MOLINA: What are you saying?

VALENTIN: Listen . . . I had to get urgent information out to my people, and I was dying with frustration because I couldn't do anything about it. I was racking my brains trying to find a way . . . And you come and serve it to me on a plate.

MOLINA (*as if he'd just had an electric shock*): I can't do that, you're out of your head.

VALENTIN: You'll memorize it in a minute. That's how easy it is. All you have to do is tell them that Number Three Command has been knocked out and they have to go to Corrientes for new orders.

MOLINA: No, I'm on parole, they can lock me up again for anything.

VALENTIN: I give you my word there's no risk.

MOLINA: I'm pleading with you. I don't want to hear another word. Not who they are or where they are. Nothing.

VALENTIN: Don't you want me to get out one day too?

MOLINA: Of here?

VALENTIN: Yes, to be free.

MOLINA: There's nothing I want more. But listen to me, I'm telling you this for your own good . . . I'm not good at this sort of thing, if they catch me, I'll spill everything.

VALENTIN: I'll answer for my comrades. You just have to wait a few days and then call from a public telephone, and make an appointment with someone in some bogus place.

MOLINA: What do you mean "a bogus place"?

VALENTIN: You just give them a name in code, let's say the Ritz cinema, and that means a certain bench in a particular square.

MOLINA: I'm frightened.

VALENTIN: You won't be when I explain the procedure to you.

MOLINA: But if the phone's tapped, I'll get in trouble.

VALENTIN: Not from a public call-box and if you disguise your voice. It's the easiest thing in the world, I'll show you how to do it. There are millions of ways—a sweet in your mouth, or a toothpick under your tongue . . .

MOLINA: No.

VALENTIN: We'll discuss it later.
MOLINA: No!
VALENTIN: Whatever you say.

[MOLINA *flops on the bed, all done in, and buries his face in the pillow.*]

Look at me please.
MOLINA (*not looking at* VALENTIN): I made a promise, I don't know who to, maybe God, even though I don't much believe in that.
VALENTIN: Yes . . .
MOLINA: I swore that I'd sacrifice anything if I could only get out of here and look after my mother. And my wish has come true.
VALENTIN: It was very generous of you to put someone else first.
MOLINA: But where's the justice in it? I always get left with nothing . . .
VALENTIN: You have your mother and she needs you. You have to assume that responsibility.
MOLINA: Listen, my mother's already had her life, she's lived, been married, had a child . . . She's old now, and her life is almost finished . . .
VALENTIN: But she's still alive . . .
MOLINA: And so am I . . . But when is my life going to begin . . . ? When is it my turn for something good to happen? To have something for myself?
VALENTIN: You can start a new life outside . . .
MOLINA: All I want is to stay with you . . .

[VALENTIN *doesn't say anything.*]

Doesn't that embarrass you?
VALENTIN: No . . . er, well, yes . . .
MOLINA: Yes what?
VALENTIN: That . . . it makes me a little embarrassed . . . Molina, try to understand this. Everything in a man's life, which may be short or long, is only temporary. Nothing lasts forever.
MOLINA: Maybe . . . but why can't it last a little longer, just that at least . . . ? If I can relay the information, will you get out sooner?
VALENTIN: It's a way of helping the cause.
MOLINA: But you won't get out sooner. You just think it'll bring the revolution a bit closer.
VALENTIN: Yes, it . . . Don't dwell on it, we'll discuss it later.
MOLINA: There's no time left to discuss.
VALENTIN: Besides, you have to finish the panther movie.
MOLINA: It's a sad ending.
VALENTIN: How?
MOLINA: She's a flawed woman . . . (*with his usual irony*) All we flawed women come to a sad ending.

VALENTIN (*laughing*): And the psychoanalyst? Does he get her in the end?
MOLINA: She gets him! And good! No, it's not so terrible, she just tears him to pieces.
VALENTIN: Does she kill him?
MOLINA: In the movie, yes. In real life, no.
VALENTIN: Tell me.
MOLINA: Let's see. Irina goes from bad to worse, she's insanely jealous of the other girl and tries to kill her. But the other one's lucky like hell, and she gets away. Then one day the husband, who's at his wits' end now, arranges to meet the psychoanalyst at their house while she's out. But things get all muddled up, and when the psychoanalyst arrives, she's there on her own. He tries to take advantage of the situation and throws himself at her and kisses her. And right there she turns into a panther. By the time the husband gets home, the guy's bled to death. Meanwhile, Irina has made it to the zoo, and she sidles up to the panther's cage. She's all alone, in the night. That afternoon she got the key when the keeper left it in the lock. It's like Irina's in another world. The husband is on his way with the cops at top speed. Irina opens the panther's cage, and it pounces on her and mortally wounds her with the first blow. The animal is scared away by the police siren, it dashes out into the street, a car runs over it and kills it.
VALENTIN: I'm going to miss you, Molinita.
MOLINA: The movies, at least.
VALENTIN: At least.
MOLINA: I want to ask you for a going-away present. Something that we never did, although we got up to worse.
VALENTIN: What?
MOLINA: A kiss.
VALENTIN: It's true. We never did.
MOLINA: But right at the end, just as I'm leaving.
VALENTIN: Okay.
MOLINA: I'm curious . . . Did the idea of kissing me disgust you?
VALENTIN: Ummm . . . Maybe I was afraid you'd turn into a panther.
MOLINA: I'm not the panther-woman.
VALENTIN: I know.
MOLINA: It's not fun to be a panther-woman, no one can kiss you. Or anything else.
VALENTIN: You're the spider woman who traps men in her web.
MOLINA (*flattered*): How sweet! I like that!
VALENTIN: And now it's your turn to promise me something: that you'll make people respect you, that you won't let anybody take advantage of you . . . Promise me you won't let anybody degrade you.

GUARD'S VOICE: Prisoner Luis Alberto Molina, be
     ready with your belongings!
MOLINA: Valentin . . .
VALENTIN: What?
MOLINA: Nothing, it doesn't matter . . . (*Pause.*)
     Valentin . . .
VALENTIN: What is it?
MOLINA: Rubbish, skip it.
VALENTIN: Do you want . . . ?
MOLINA: What?
VALENTIN: The kiss.
MOLINA: No, it was something else.
VALENTIN: Don't you want your kiss now?
MOLINA: Yes, if it won't disgust you.
VALENTIN: Don't get me mad.

[He walks over to MOLINA *and timidly gives him a kiss
on the mouth.]*

MOLINA: Thank you.
VALENTIN: Thank you.

[Long pause.]

MOLINA: And now give me the number of your com-
     rades.
VALENTIN: If you want.
MOLINA: I'll get the message to them.
VALENTIN: Okay . . . Is that what you wanted to ask?
MOLINA: Yes.

*[*VALENTIN *kisses* MOLINA *one more time.]*

VALENTIN: You don't know how happy you've made
     me. It's 323–1025.

[Bolero music starts playing: it chokes VALENTIN's *voice
as he gives his instructions.* MOLINA *and* VALENTIN *separate slowly.* MOLINA *puts all his belongings into a
duffel bag. They are now openly broken-hearted:*
MOLINA *can hardly keep his mind on what he's doing.*
VALENTIN *looks at him in total helplessness. Their
taped voices are heard as all this action takes place
onstage.]*

MOLINA'S VOICE: What happened to me, Valentin,
     when I got out of here?
VALENTIN'S VOICE: The police kept you under con-
     stant surveillance, listened in on your phone,
     everything. The first call you got was from an
     uncle, your godfather; he told you not to dally
     with minors again. You told him what he
     deserved, that he should go to hell, because in
     jail you'd learned what dignity was. Your

friends telephoned and you called each other
Greta and Marlene and Marilyn, and the police
thought maybe it was a secret code. You got a
job as a window dresser, and then finally one
day you called my comrades. You took your
mother to the movies and bought her some
fashion magazines. And one day you went to
meet my friends, but the police were shadowing you and they arrested you. My friends
opened fire and killed you from their getaway
car as you'd asked them to if the police caught
you. And that was all . . . And what about me,
Molina, what happened to me?
MOLINA'S VOICE: They tortured you a lot . . . and then
     your wounds turned septic. A nurse took pity
     on you and secretly he gave you some mor-
     phine, and you had a dream.
VALENTIN'S VOICE: About what?
MOLINA'S VOICE: You dreamed that inside you, in
     your chest, you were carrying Marta and that
     you'd never ever be apart from one another.
     And she asked you if you regretted what hap-
     pened to me, my death, which she said was
     your fault.
VALENTIN'S VOICE: And what did I answer her?
MOLINA'S VOICE: You replied that I had died for a
     noble and selfless ideal. And she said that was-
     n't true, she said that I had sacrificed myself
     just so I could die like the heroine in a movie.
     And you said that only I knew the answer.
     And you dreamed you were very hungry
     when you escaped from prison and that you
     ended up on a savage island, and in the mid-
     dle of the jungle you met a spider woman who
     gave you food to eat. And she was so lonely
     there in the jungle, but you had to carry on
     with your struggle and go back to join your
     comrades, and your strength was restored by
     the food the spider woman gave you.
VALENTIN'S VOICE: And, at the end, did I get away
     from the police, or did they catch up with me?
MOLINA'S VOICE: No, at the end you left the island,
     you were glad to be reunited with your com-
     rades in the struggle, because it was a short
     dream, but a pleasant one . . .

[The door opens: MOLINA *and* VALENTIN *embrace one
another with infinite sadness.* MOLINA *exits. The door
closes behind him.]*

CURTAIN

AUGUST WILSON (b. 1945)

Augustus Wilson is one of the most successful contemporary American playwrights. His plays on the African-American experience have opened at
the prestigious Yale Repertory Theater and have been moved to
Broadway, where they have won numerous awards. Wilson has planned to write
a series of ten plays on this subject, one for each decade of the century. Several of
them have already been completed: *Ma Rainey's Black Bottom* (1984), *Fences*
(1985), and *Joe Turner's Come and Gone* (1986), all of which have won the New
York Drama Critics Circle Award; *The Piano Lesson* (1989), which won a Pulitzer
prize; and *Two Trains Running* (1990).

Wilson's plays harken back to his own experience of growing up in
Pittsburgh. He was raised in a two-room apartment there by his mother, after
she had been abandoned by the white father of her six children. Wilson kept the
name of his natural father even though he was raised during his teenage years
by his stepfather, David Bedford. Wilson and Bedford clashed over Wilson's
decision to drop out of school and off the football team at age fifteen. The tensions in the relationship between them are reflected in *Fences*, a play about Troy
Maxson, an African-American garbage collector in Pittsburgh. Proud of his
accomplishment in providing for his family, he nevertheless wrestles with a history of social oppression and personal compromises which surface in the difficult relationship he has with his son.

After leaving school, Wilson read African-American authors at the public
library and determined that someday his books would be on the shelf along
with them. In the 1960s and 1970s Wilson was involved in the civil rights movement and the Black Power movement. The latter taught him about the power of
the theater to raise consciousness, and he co-founded the Black Horizons
Theater Company on the Hill in Pittsburgh, where his first plays were staged.

Wilson moved from Pittsburgh to St. Paul, where he became involved with
the Playwright's Center of Minneapolis. Here in the late 1970s and early 1980s he
discovered the dramatic potential in the rich language, music, and culture of the
African-American ghetto, and he began to write plays that attempted a realistic
evocation of African-American life. *Ma Rainey's Black Bottom* was his first commercial and critical success. The play is about an African-American blues singer and
the accommodations she and her band make in becoming complicit in their
exploitation by white managers and executives. *Joe Turner's Come and Gone*, a play
set in 1911, examines the lives of the children of former slaves who came to
Pittsburgh to find work. *The Piano Lesson* treats African-Americans' attitudes
toward their cultural heritage. How one lives with or without a heritage and a
past is a recurrent theme in Wilson's work. *Two Trains Running*, set in the tumul-
tuous events of 1969 with its protests, riots, and assassinations, examines the indif-

ferent attitudes of characters in Memphis Lee's Diner to the two metaphorical trains for African Americans—one running to Africa and one to the Old South.

The Piano Lesson

In some of Wilson's earlier plays, the migration of African Americans to the north is a major theme. In *The Piano Lesson*, which is set in Pittsburgh in the 1930s, Lymon represents the hopes of these characters. Lymon will use his share of the sale of the load of watermelons to help start a new life in urban Pittsburgh, and the suit that he buys from Wining Boy expresses his optimism and enthusiasm. But Wining Boy is heading back south, and essentially *The Piano Lesson* is a play about return. The difficult issues surrounding it are reflected in the opposition between Boy Willie, who wishes to sell the family piano, and his sister, Berniece, who wants to keep it. The opposition raises questions about cultural identity, culminating in an attempt to exorcise the ghost that has haunted the Charles family.

The central dilemma of *The Piano Lesson* is symbolized by the piano itself. If African Americans cling to their past and traditions as a separate people, they become isolated from mainstream development. If they choose to integrate into the mainstream, they compromise their identity. The dilemma is embodied in the piano, a product of European technology and formerly owned by the white Sutter household. The piano is the instrument through which African Americans have preserved in artistic form the music of their ancestors through the period of slavery, reaching back to their roots in Africa. This particular piano also symbolizes their struggle for freedom. The African sculptures carved into the piano record generations of the Charles family history.

For Berniece, the piano is a painful connection to a tragic past, yet one she wants to preserve. Her father, Boy Charles, was burned to death in an incident involving the piano, and her husband, Crawley, was killed during a shoot-out with deputies over some firewood. While actually playing the piano raises too many painful feelings for her, she still wants to keep it as a link to her ancestors. Meanwhile, Boy Willie wants to realize his dream of owning land in the South, and to do so he must sell the piano. He too feels a kinship with the past, but it is to the daring act of Boy Charles, who took the piano from the Sutter household, that he now compares his own daring act of selling the piano.

The presence of Sutter's ghost, which has roamed freely in the Charles household, intensifies as Boy Willie arrives to demand the piano. Getting rid of the terrible presence of the ghost takes the courage and determination of Boy Willie, who tackles it head-on, and the inner strength of Berniece, who plays the piano for the first time since her mother's death. She plays an African-American spiritual and invokes the names of her ancestors. Together Boy Willie and Berniece exorcise the ghost, and the play concludes with a meeting of minds. Boy Willie agrees not to sell the piano if Maretha, his young niece, will be allowed to play it.

The Piano Lesson

AUGUST WILSON

THE SETTING. The action of the play takes place in the kitchen and parlor of the house where DOAKER CHARLES lives with his niece, BERNIECE, and her eleven-year-old daughter, MARETHA. The house is sparsely furnished, and although there is evidence of a woman's touch, there is a lack of warmth and vigor. BERNIECE and MARETHA occupy the upstairs rooms. DOAKER's room is prominent and opens onto the kitchen. Dominating the parlor is an old upright piano. On the legs of the piano, carved in the manner of African sculpture, are mask-like figures resembling totems. The carvings are rendered with a grace and power of invention that lifts them out of the realm of craftsmanship and into the realm of art. At left is a staircase leading to the upstairs.

ACT I

Scene 1

[The lights come up on the Charles household. It is five o'clock in the morning. The dawn is beginning to announce itself, but there is something in the air that belongs to the night. A stillness that is a portent, a gathering, a coming together of something akin to a storm. There is a loud knock at the door.]

BOY WILLIE (*Off stage, calling.*): Hey, Doaker . . . Doaker!

[He knocks again and calls.]

   Hey, Doaker! Hey, Berniece! Berniece!

[DOAKER enters from his room. He is a tall, thin man of forty-seven, with severe features, who has for all intents and purposes retired from the world though he works full-time as a railroad cook.]

DOAKER: Who is it?
BOY WILLIE: Open the door, nigger! It's me . . . Boy Willie!
DOAKER: Who?
BOY WILLIE: Boy Willie! Open the door!

[DOAKER opens the door and BOY WILLIE and LYMON enter. BOY WILLIE is thirty years old. He has an infectious grin and a boyishness that is apt for his name. He is brash and impulsive, talkative and somewhat crude in speech and manner. LYMON is twenty-nine. BOY WILLIE's partner, he talks little, and then with a straightforwardness that is often disarming.]

DOAKER: What you doing up here?
BOY WILLIE: I told you, Lymon. Lymon talking about you might be sleep. This is Lymon. You remember Lymon Jackson from down home? This my Uncle Doaker.
DOAKER: What you doing up here? I couldn't figure out who that was. I thought you was still down in Mississippi.
BOY WILLIE: Me and Lymon selling watermelons. We got a truck out there. Got a whole truckload of watermelons. We brought them up here to sell. Where's Berniece?

[Calls.]

   Hey, Berniece!
DOAKER: Berniece up there sleep.
BOY WILLIE: Well, let her get up.

[Calls.]

   Hey, Berniece!
DOAKER: She got to go to work in the morning.
BOY WILLIE: Well she can get up and say hi. It's been three years since I seen her.

[Calls.]

   Hey, Berniece! It's me . . . Boy Willie.

DOAKER: Berniece don't like all that hollering now. She got to work in the morning.

BOY WILLIE: She can go on back to bed. Me and Lymon been riding two days in that truck . . . the least she can do is get up and say hi.

DOAKER (*Looking out the window.*): Where you all get that truck from?

BOY WILLIE: It's Lymon's. I told him let's get a load of watermelons and bring them up here.

LYMON: Boy Willie say he going back, but I'm gonna stay. See what it's like up here.

BOY WILLIE: You gonna carry me down there first.

LYMON: I told you I ain't going back down there and take a chance on that truck breaking down again. You can take the train. Hey, tell him Doaker, he can take the train back. After we sell them watermelons he have enough money he can buy him a whole railroad car.

DOAKER: You got all them watermelons stacked up there no wonder the truck broke down. I'm surprised you made it this far with a load like that. Where you break down at?

BOY WILLIE: We broke down three times! It took us two and a half days to get here. It's a good thing we picked them watermelons fresh.

LYMON: We broke down twice in West Virginia. The first time was just as soon as we got out of Sunflower. About forty miles out she broke down. We got it going and got all the way to West Virginia before she broke down again.

BOY WILLIE: We had to walk about five miles for some water.

LYMON: It got a hole in the radiator but it runs pretty good. You have to pump the brakes sometime before they catch. Boy Willie have his door open and be ready to jump when that happens.

BOY WILLIE: Lymon think that's funny. I told the nigger I give him ten dollars to get the brakes fixed. But he thinks that funny.

LYMON: They don't need fixing. All you got to do is pump them till they catch.

[BERNIECE *enters on the stairs. Thirty-five years old, with an eleven-year-old daughter, she is still in mourning for her husband after three years.*]

BERNIECE: What you doing all that hollering for?

BOY WILLIE: Hey, Berniece. Doaker said you was sleep. I said at least you could get up and say hi.

BERNIECE: It's five o'clock in the morning and you come in here with all this noise. You can't come like normal folks. You got to bring all that noise with you.

BOY WILLIE: Hell, I ain't done nothing but come in and say hi. I ain't got in the house good.

BERNIECE: That's what I'm talking about. You start all that hollering and carry on as soon as you hit the door.

BOY WILLIE: Aw hell, woman, I was glad to see Doaker. You ain't had to come down if you didn't want to. I come eighteen hundred miles to see my sister I figure she might want to get up and say hi. Other than that you can go back upstairs. What you got, Doaker? Where your bottle? Me and Lymon want a drink.

[*To* BERNIECE.]

This is Lymon. You remember Lymon Jackson from down home.

LYMON: How you doing, Berniece. You look just like I thought you looked.

BERNIECE: Why you all got to come in hollering and carrying on? Waking the neighbors with all that noise.

BOY WILLIE: They can come over and join the party. We fixing to have a party. Doaker, where your bottle? Me and Lymon celebrating. The Ghosts of the Yellow Dog got Sutter.

BERNIECE: Say what?

BOY WILLIE: Ask Lymon, they found him the next morning. Say he drowned in his well.

DOAKER: When this happen, Boy Willie?

BOY WILLIE: About three weeks ago. Me and Lymon was over in Stoner County when we heard about it. We laughed. We thought it was funny. A great big old three-hundred-and-forty-pound man gonna fall down his well.

LYMON: It remind me of Humpty Dumpty.

BOY WILLIE: Everybody say the Ghosts of the Yellow Dog pushed him.

BERNIECE: I don't want to hear that nonsense. Somebody down there pushing them people in their wells.

DOAKER: What was you and Lymon doing over in Stoner County?

BOY WILLIE: We was down there working. Lymon got some people down there.

LYMON: My cousin got some land down there. We was helping him.

BOY WILLIE: Got near about a hundred acres. He got it set up real nice. Me and Lymon was down there chopping down trees. We was using Lymon's truck to haul the wood. Me and Lymon used to haul wood all around them parts.

[*To* BERNIECE.]

Me and Lymon got a truckload of watermelons out there.

[BERNIECE *crosses to the window to the parlor.*]

Doaker, where your bottle? I know you got a bottle stuck up in your room. Come on, me and Lymon want a drink.

[DOAKER exits into his room.]

BERNIECE: Where you all get that truck from?

BOY WILLIE: I told you it's Lymon's.

BERNIECE: Where you get the truck from, Lymon?

LYMON: I bought it.

BERNIECE: Where he get that truck from, Boy Willie?

BOY WILLIE: He told you he bought it. Bought it for a hundred and twenty dollars. I can't say where he got that hundred and twenty dollars from . . . but he bought that old piece of truck from Henry Porter. (*To* LYMON.) Where you get that hundred and twenty dollars from, nigger?

LYMON: I got it like you get yours. I know how to take care of money.

[DOAKER brings a bottle and sets it on the table.]

BOY WILLIE: Aw hell, Doaker got some of that good whiskey. Don't give Lymon none of that. He ain't used to good whiskey. He liable to get sick.

LYMON: I done had good whiskey before.

BOY WILLIE: Lymon bought that truck so he have him a place to sleep. He down there wasn't doing no work or nothing. Sheriff looking for him. He bought that truck to keep away from the sheriff. Got Stovall looking for him too. He down there sleeping in that truck ducking and dodging both of them. I told him come on let's go up and see my sister.

BERNIECE: What the sheriff looking for you for, Lymon?

BOY WILLIE: The man don't want you to know all his business. He's my company. He ain't asking you no questions.

LYMON: It wasn't nothing. It was just a misunderstanding.

BERNIECE: He in my house. You say the sheriff looking for him, I wanna know what he looking for him for. Otherwise you all can go back out there and be where nobody don't have to ask you nothing.

LYMON: It was just a misunderstanding. Sometimes me and the sheriff we don't think alike. So we just got crossed on each other.

BERNIECE: Might be looking for him about that truck. He might have stole that truck.

BOY WILLIE: We ain't stole no truck, woman. I told you Lymon bought it.

DOAKER: Boy Willie and Lymon got more sense than to ride all the way up here in a stolen truck with a load of watermelons. Now they might have stole them watermelons, but I don't believe they stole that truck.

BOY WILLIE: You don't even know the man good and you calling him a thief. And we ain't stole them watermelons either. Them old man Pitterford's watermelons. He give me and Lymon all we could load for ten dollars.

DOAKER: No wonder you got them stacked up out there. You must have five hundred watermelons stacked up out there.

BERNIECE: Boy Willie, when you and Lymon planning on going back?

BOY WILLIE: Lymon say he staying. As soon as we sell them watermelons I'm going on back.

BERNIECE (Starts to exit up the stairs.): That's what you need to do. And you need to do it quick. Come in here disrupting the house. I don't want all that loud carrying on around here. I'm surprised you ain't woke Maretha up.

BOY WILLIE: I was fixing to get her now.

[Calls.]

  Hey, Maretha!

DOAKER: Berniece don't like all that hollering now.

BERNIECE: Don't you wake that child up!

BOY WILLIE: You going up there . . . wake her up and tell her her uncle's here. I ain't seen her in three years. Wake her up and send her down here. She can go back to bed.

BERNIECE: I ain't waking that child up . . . and don't you be making all that noise. You and Lymon need to sell them watermelons and go on back.

[BERNIECE exits up the stairs.]

BOY WILLIE: I see Berniece still try to be stuck up.

DOAKER: Berniece alright. She don't want you making all that noise. Maretha up there sleep. Let her sleep until she get up. She can see you then.

BOY WILLIE: I ain't thinking about Berniece. You hear from Wining Boy? You know Cleotha died?

DOAKER: Yeah, I heard that. He come by here about a year ago. Had a whole sack of money. He stayed here about two weeks. Ain't offered nothing. Berniece asked him for three dollars to buy some food and he got mad and left.

LYMON: Who's Wining Boy?

BOY WILLIE: That's my uncle. That's Doaker's brother. You heard me talk about Wining Boy. He play piano. He done made some records and everything. He still doing that, Doaker?

DOAKER: He made one or two records a long time ago. That's the only ones I ever known him to make. If you let him tell it he a big recording star.

BOY WILLIE: He stopped down home about two years ago. That's what I hear. I don't know. Me and Lymon was up on Parchman Farm doing them three years.

DOAKER: He don't never stay in one place. Now, he been here about eight months ago. Back in the winter. Now, you subject not to see him for another two years. It's liable to be that long before he stop by.

BOY WILLIE: If he had a whole sack of money you liable never to see him. You ain't gonna see him until he get broke. Just as soon as that sack of money is gone you look up and he be on your doorstep.

LYMON (Noticing the piano.): Is that the piano?

BOY WILLIE: Yeah . . . look here, Lymon. See how it got all those carvings on it. See, that's what I was talking about. See how it's carved up real nice and polished and everything? You never find you another piano like that.

LYMON: Yeah, that look real nice.

BOY WILLIE: I told you. See how it's polished? My mama used to polish it every day. See all them pictures carved on it? That's what I was talking about. You can get a nice price for that piano.

LYMON: That's all Boy Willie talked about the whole trip up here. I got tired of hearing him talk about the piano.

BOY WILLIE: All you want to talk about is women. You ought to hear this nigger, Doaker. Talking about all the women he gonna get when he get up here. He ain't had none down there but he gonna get a hundred when he get up here.

DOAKER: How your people doing down there, Lymon?

LYMON: They alright. They still there. I come up here to see what it's like up here. Boy Willie trying to get me to go back and farm with him.

BOY WILLIE: Sutter's brother selling the land. He say he gonna sell it to me. That's why I come up here. I got one part of it. Sell them watermelons and get me another part. Get Berniece to sell that piano and I'll have the third part.

DOAKER: Berniece ain't gonna sell that piano.

BOY WILLIE: I'm gonna talk to her. When she see I got a chance to get Sutter's land she'll come around.

DOAKER: You can put that thought out your mind. Berniece ain't gonna sell that piano.

BOY WILLIE: I'm gonna talk to her. She been playing on it?

DOAKER: You know she won't touch that piano. I ain't never known her to touch it since Mama Ola died. That's over seven years now. She say it got blood on it. She got Maretha playing on it though. Say Maretha can go on and do everything she can't do. Got her in an extra school down at the Irene Kaufman Settlement House. She want Maretha to grow up and be a schoolteacher. Say she good enough she can teach on the piano.

BOY WILLIE: Maretha don't need to be playing on no piano. She can play on the guitar.

DOAKER: How much land Sutter got left?

BOY WILLIE: Got a hundred acres. Good land. He done sold it piece by piece, he kept the good part for himself. Now he got to give that up. His brother come down from Chicago for the funeral . . . he up there in Chicago got some kind of business with soda fountain equipment. He anxious to sell the land, Doaker. He don't want to be bothered with it. He called me to him and said cause of how long our families done known each other and how we been good friends and all, say he wanted to sell the land to me. Say he'd rather see me with it than Jim Stovall. Told me he'd let me have it for two thousand dollars cash money. He don't know I found out the most Stovall would give him for it was fifteen hundred dollars. He trying to get that extra five hundred out of me telling me he doing me a favor. I thanked him just as nice. Told him what a good man Sutter was and how he had my sympathy and all. Told him to give me two weeks. He said he'd wait on me. That's why I come up here. Sell them watermelons. Get Berniece to sell that piano. Put them two parts with the part I done saved. Walk in there. Tip my hat. Lay my money down on the table. Get my deed and walk on out. This time I get to keep all the cotton. Hire me some men to work it for me. Gin my cotton. Get my seed. And I'll see you again next year. Might even plant some tobacco or some oats.

DOAKER: You gonna have a hard time trying to get Berniece to sell that piano. You know Avery Brown from down there don't you? He up here now. He followed Berniece up here trying to get her to marry him after Crawley got killed. He been up here about two years. He call himself a preacher now.

BOY WILLIE: I know Avery. I know him from when he used to work on the Willshaw place. Lymon know him too.

DOAKER: He after Berniece to marry him. She keep telling him no but he won't give up. He keep pressing her on it.

BOY WILLIE: Avery think all white men is bigshots. He don't know there some white men ain't got as much as he got.

DOAKER: He supposed to come past here this morning. Berniece going down to the bank with him to see if he can get a loan to start his church. That's why I know Berniece ain't gonna sell that piano. He tried to get her to sell it to help him start his church. Sent the man around and everything.

BOY WILLIE: What man?

DOAKER: Some white fellow was going around to all the colored people's houses looking to buy up musical instruments. He'd buy anything. Drums. Guitars. Harmonicas. Pianos. Avery sent him past here. He looked at the piano and got excited. Offered her a nice price. She turned him down and got on Avery for sending him past. The man kept on her about two weeks. He seen where she wasn't gonna sell it, he gave her his number and told her if she ever wanted to sell it to call him first. Say he'd go one better than what anybody else would give her for it.

BOY WILLIE: How much he offer her for it?

DOAKER: Now you know me. She didn't say and I didn't ask. I just know it was a nice price.

LYMON: All you got to do is find out who he is and tell him somebody else wanna buy it from you. Tell him you can't make up your mind who to sell it to, and if he like Doaker say, he'll give you anything you want for it.

BOY WILLIE: That's what I'm gonna do. I'm gonna find out who he is from Avery.

DOAKER: It ain't gonna do you no good. Berniece ain't gonna sell that piano.

BOY WILLIE: She ain't got to sell it. I'm gonna sell it. I own just as much of it as she does.

BERNIECE (*Offstage, hollers.*): Doaker! Go on get away. Doaker!

DOAKER (*Calling*): Berniece?

[*DOAKER and BOY WILLIE rush to the stairs, BOY WILLIE runs up the stairs, passing BERNIECE as she enters, running.*]

DOAKER: Berniece, what's the matter? You alright? What's the matter?

[*BERNIECE tries to catch her breath. She is unable to speak.*]

DOAKER: That's alright. Take your time. You alright. What's the matter?

[*He calls.*]

Hey, Boy Willie?

BOY WILLIE (*Offstage.*): Ain't nobody up here.

BERNIECE: Sutter . . . Sutter's standing at the top of the steps.

DOAKER (*Calls.*): Boy Willie!

[*LYMON crosses to the stairs and looks up. BOY WILLIE enters from the stairs.*]

BOY WILLIE: Hey Doaker, what's wrong with her? Berniece, what's wrong? Who was you talking to?

DOAKER: She say she seen Sutter's ghost standing at the top of the stairs.

BOY WILLIE: Seen what? Sutter? She ain't seen no Sutter.

BERNIECE: He was standing right up there.

BOY WILLIE (*Entering on the stairs.*): That's all in Berniece's head. Ain't nobody up there. Go on up there, Doaker.

DOAKER: I'll take your word for it. Berniece talking about what she seen. She say Sutter's ghost standing at the top of the steps. She ain't just make all that up.

BOY WILLIE: She up there dreaming. She ain't seen no ghost.

LYMON: You want a glass of water, Berniece? Get her a glass of water, Boy Willie.

BOY WILLIE: She don't need no water. She ain't seen nothing. Go on up there and look. Ain't nobody up there but Maretha.

DOAKER: Let Berniece tell it.

BOY WILLIE: I ain't stopping her from telling it.

DOAKER: What happened, Berniece?

BERNIECE: I come out my room to come back down here and Sutter was standing there in the hall.

BOY WILLIE: What he look like?

BERNIECE: He look like Sutter. He look like he always look.

BOY WILLIE: Sutter couldn't find his way from Big Sandy to Little Sandy. How he gonna find his way all the way up here to Pittsburgh? Sutter ain't never even heard of Pittsburgh.

DOAKER: Go on, Berniece.

BERNIECE: Just standing there with the blue suit on.

BOY WILLIE: The man ain't never left Marlin County when he was living . . . and he's gonna come all the way up here now that he's dead?

DOAKER: Let her finish. I want to hear what she got to say.

BOY WILLIE: I'll tell you this. If Berniece had seen him like she think she seen him she'd still be running.

DOAKER: Go on, Berniece. Don't pay Boy Willie no mind.

BERNIECE: He was standing there . . . had his hand on top of his head. Look like he might have thought if he took his hand down his head might have fallen off.

LYMON: Did he have on a hat?

BERNIECE: Just had on that blue suit . . . I told him to go away and he just stood there looking at me . . . calling Boy Willie's name.

BOY WILLIE: What he calling my name for?

BERNIECE: I believe you pushed him in the well.

BOY WILLIE: Now what kind of sense that make? You telling me I'm gonna go out there and hide in the weeds with all them dogs and things he got around there . . . I'm gonna hide and wait till I catch him looking down his well just right . . . then I'm gonna run over and push him in. A great big old three-hundred-and-forty-pound man.

BERNIECE: Well, what he calling your name for?

BOY WILLIE: He bending over looking down his well, woman . . . how he know who pushed him? It could have been anybody. Where was you when Sutter fell in his well? Where was Doaker? Me and Lymon was over in Stoner County. Tell her, Lymon. The Ghosts of the Yellow Dog got Sutter. That's what happened to him.

BERNIECE: You can talk all that Ghosts of the Yellow Dog stuff if you want. I know better.

LYMON: The Ghosts of the Yellow Dog pushed him. That's what the people say. They found him in his well and all the people say it must be the Ghosts of the Yellow Dog. Just like all them other men.

BOY WILLIE: Come talking about he looking for me. What he come all the way up here for? If he looking for me all he got to do is wait. He could have saved himself a trip if he looking for me. That ain't nothing but in Berniece's head. Ain't no telling what she liable to come up with next.

BERNIECE: Boy Willie, I want you and Lymon to go ahead and leave my house. Just go on somewhere. You don't do nothing but bring trouble with you everywhere you go. If it wasn't for you Crawley would still be alive.

BOY WILLIE: Crawley what? I ain't had nothing to do with Crawley getting killed. Crawley three time seven. He had his own mind.

BERNIECE: Just go on and leave. Let Sutter go somewhere else looking for you.

BOY WILLIE: I'm leaving. Soon as we sell them watermelons. Other than that I ain't going nowhere. Hell, I just got here. Talking about Sutter looking for me. Sutter was looking for that piano. That's what he was looking for. He had to die to find out where that piano was at . . . If I was you I'd get rid of it. That's the way to get rid of Sutter's ghost. Get rid of that piano.

BERNIECE: I want you and Lymon to go on and take all this confusion out of my house!

BOY WILLIE: Hey, tell her, Doaker. What kind of sense that make? I told you, Lymon, as soon as Berniece see me she was gonna start something. Didn't I tell you that? Now she done

made up that story about Sutter just so she could tell me to leave her house. Well, hell, I ain't going nowhere till I sell them watermelons.

BERNIECE: Well why don't you go out there and sell them! Sell them and go on back!

BOY WILLIE: We waiting till the people get up.

LYMON: Boy Willie say if you get out there too early and wake the people up they get mad at you and won't buy nothing from you.

DOAKER: You won't be waiting long. You done let the sun catch up with you. This the time everybody be getting up around here.

BERNIECE: Come on, Doaker, walk up here with me. Let me get Maretha up and get her started. I got to get ready myself. Boy Willie, just go on out there and sell them watermelons and you and Lymon leave my house.

[BERNIECE and DOAKER exit up the stairs.]

BOY WILLIE (*Calling after them.*): If you see Sutter up there . . . tell him I'm down here waiting on him.

LYMON: What if she see him again?

BOY WILLIE: That's all in her head. There ain't no ghost up there.

[Calls.]

Hey, Doaker . . . I told you ain't nothing up there.

LYMON: I'm glad he didn't say he was looking for me.

BOY WILLIE: I wish I would see Sutter's ghost. Give me a chance to put a whupping on him.

LYMON: You ought to stay up here with me. You be down there working his land . . . he might come looking for you all the time.

BOY WILLIE: I ain't thinking about Sutter. And I ain't thinking about staying up here. You stay up here. I'm going back and get Sutter's land. You think you ain't got to work up here. You think this the land of milk and honey. But I ain't scared of work. I'm going back and farm every acre of that land.

[DOAKER enters from the stairs.]

I told you there ain't nothing up there, Doaker. Berniece dreaming all that.

DOAKER: I believe Berniece seen something. Berniece level-headed. She ain't just made all that up. She say Sutter had on a suit. I don't believe she ever seen Sutter in a suit. I believe that's what he was buried in, and that's what Berniece saw.

BOY WILLIE: Well, let her keep on seeing him then. As

long as he don't mess with me.

[DOAKER starts to cook his breakfast.]

I heard about you, Doaker. They say you got all the women looking out for you down home. They be looking to see you coming. Say you got a different one every two weeks. Say they be fighting one another for you to stay with them.

[To LYMON.]

Look at him, Lymon. He know it's true.

DOAKER: I ain't thinking about no women. They never get me tied up with them. After Coreen I ain't got no use for them. I stay up on Jack Slattery's place when I be down there. All them women want is somebody with a steady payday.

BOY WILLIE: That ain't what I hear. I hear every two weeks the women all put on their dresses and line up at the railroad station.

DOAKER: I don't get down there but once a month. I used to go down there every two weeks but they keep switching me around. They keep switching all the fellows around.

BOY WILLIE: Doaker can't turn that railroad loose. He was working the railroad when I was walking around crying for sugartit. My mama used to brag on him.

DOAKER: I'm cooking now, but I used to line track. I pieced together the Yellow Dog stitch by stitch. Rail by rail. Line track all up around there. I lined track all up around Sunflower and Clarksdale. Wining Boy worked with me. He helped put in some of that track. He'd work it for six months and quit. Go back to playing piano and gambling.

BOY WILLIE: How long you been with the railroad now?

DOAKER: Twenty-seven years. Now, I'll tell you something about the railroad. What I done learned after twenty-seven years. See, you got North. You got West. You look over here you got South. Over there you got East. Now, you can start from anywhere. Don't care where you at. You got to go one of them four ways. And whichever way you decide to go they got a railroad that will take you there. Now, that's something simple. You think anybody would be able to understand that. But you'd be surprised how many people trying to go North get on a train going West. They think the train's supposed to go where they going rather than where it's going.

Now, why people going? Their sister's sick.

They leaving before they kill somebody . . . and they sitting across from somebody who's leaving to keep from getting killed. They leaving cause they can't get satisfied. They going to meet someone. I wish I had a dollar for every time that someone wasn't at the station to meet them. I done seen that a lot. In between the time they sent the telegram and the time the person get there . . . they done forgot all about them.

They got so many trains out there they have a hard time keeping them from running into each other. Got trains going every whichaway. Got people on all of them. Somebody going where somebody just left. If everybody stay in one place I believe this would be a better world. Now what I done learned after twenty-seven years of railroading is this . . . if the train stays on the track . . . it's going to get where it's going. It might not be where you going. If it ain't, then all you got to do is sit and wait cause the train's coming back to get you. The train don't never stop. It'll come back every time. Now I'll tell you another thing . . .

BOY WILLIE: What you cooking over there, Doaker? Me and Lymon's hungry.

DOAKER: Go on down there to Wylie and Kirkpatrick to Eddie's restaurant. Coffee cost a nickel and you can get two eggs, sausage, and grits for fifteen cents. He even give you a biscuit with it.

BOY WILLIE: That look good what you got. Give me a little piece of that grilled bread.

DOAKER: Here . . . go on take the whole piece.

BOY WILLIE: Here you go, Lymon . . . you want a piece?

[He gives LYMON a piece of toast. MARETHA enters from the stairs.]

BOY WILLIE: Hey, sugar. Come here and give me a hug. Come on give Uncle Boy Willie a hug. Don't be shy. Look at her, Doaker. She done got bigger. Ain't she got big?

DOAKER: Yeah, she getting up there.

BOY WILLIE: How you doing, sugar?

MARETHA: Fine.

BOY WILLIE: You was just a little old thing last time I seen you. You remember me, don't you? This your Uncle Boy Willie from down South. That there's Lymon. He my friend. We come up here to sell watermelons. You like watermelons?

[MARETHA nods.]

We got a whole truckload out front. You can

have as many as you want. What you been
doing?

MARETHA: Nothing.

BOY WILLIE: Don't be shy now. Look at you getting
all big. How old is you?

MARETHA: Eleven. I'm gonna be twelve soon.

BOY WILLIE: You like it up here? You like the North?

MARETHA: It's alright.

BOY WILLIE: That there's Lymon. Did you say hi to
Lymon?

MARETHA: Hi.

LYMON: How you doing? You look just like your
mama. I remember you when you was wearing diapers.

BOY WILLIE: You gonna come down South and see
me? Uncle Boy Willie gonna get him a farm.
Gonna get a great big old farm. Come down
there and I'll teach you how to ride a mule.
Teach you how to kill a chicken, too.

MARETHA: I seen my mama do that.

BOY WILLIE: Ain't nothing to it. You just grab him by
his neck and twist it. Get you a real good grip
and then you just wring his neck and throw
him in the pot. Cook him up. Then you got
some good eating. What you like to eat? What
kind of food you like?

MARETHA: I like everything . . . except I don't like no
black-eyed peas.

BOY WILLIE: Uncle Doaker tell me your mama got
you playing that piano. Come on play something for me.

[BOY WILLIE crosses over to the piano followed by
MARETHA.]

Show me what you can do. Come on now.
Here . . . Uncle Boy Willie give you a dime . . .
show me what you can do. Don't be bashful
now. That dime say you can't be bashful.

[MARETHA plays. It is something any beginner first
learns.]

Here, let me show you something.

[BOY WILLIE sits and plays a simple boogie-woogie.]

See that? See what I'm doing? That's what you
call the boogie-woogie. See now . . . you can
get up and dance to that. That's how good it
sound. It sound like you wanna dance. You
can dance to that. It'll hold you up. Whatever
kind of dance you wanna do you can dance to
that right there. See that? See how it go? Ain't
nothing to it. Go on you do it.

MARETHA: I got to read it on the paper.

BOY WILLIE: You don't need no paper. Go on. Do just
like that there.

BERNIECE: Maretha! You get up here and get ready to
go so you be on time. Ain't no need you trying
to take advantage of company.

MARETHA: I got to go.

BOY WILLIE: Uncle Boy Willie gonna get you a guitar.
Let Uncle Doaker teach you how to play that.
You don't need to read no paper to play the
guitar. Your mama told you about that piano?
You know how them pictures got on there?

MARETHA: She say it just always been like that since
she got it.

BOY WILLIE: You hear that, Doaker? And you sitting
up here in the house with Berniece.

DOAKER: I ain't got nothing to do with that. I don't
get in the way of Berniece's raising her.

BOY WILLIE: You tell your mama to tell you about
that piano. You ask her how them pictures got
on there. If she don't tell you I'll tell you.

BERNIECE: Maretha!

MARETHA: I got to get ready to go.

BOY WILLIE: She getting big, Doaker. You remember
her, Lymon?

LYMON: She used to be real little.

[There is a knock on the door. DOAKER goes to answer
it. AVERY enters. Thirty-eight years old, honest and
ambitious, he has taken to the city like a fish to water,
finding in it opportunities for growth and advancement that did not exist for him in the rural South. He
is dressed in a suit and tie with a gold cross around
his neck. He carries a small Bible.]

DOAKER: Hey, Avery, come on in. Berniece upstairs.

BOY WILLIE: Look at him . . . look at him . . . he don't
know what to say. He wasn't expecting to see
me.

AVERY: Hey, Boy Willie. What you doing up here?

BOY WILLIE: Look at him, Lymon.

AVERY: Is that Lymon? Lymon Jackson?

BOY WILLIE: Yeah, you know Lymon.

DOAKER: Berniece be ready in a minute, Avery.

BOY WILLIE: Doaker say you a preacher now. What . . .
we supposed to call you Reverend? You used to
be plain old Avery. When you get to be a
preacher, nigger?

LYMON: Avery say he gonna be a preacher so he
don't have to work.

BOY WILLIE: I remember when you was down there
on the Willshaw place planting cotton. You
wasn't thinking about no Reverend then.

AVERY: That must be your truck out there. I saw that
truck with them watermelons, I was trying to
figure out what it was doing in front of the
house.

BOY WILLIE: Yeah, me and Lymon selling watermelons. That's Lymon's truck.

DOAKER: Berniece say you all going down to the

bank.

AVERY: Yeah, they give me a half day off work. I got an appointment to talk to the bank about getting a loan to start my church.

BOY WILLIE: Lymon say preachers don't have to work. Where you working at, nigger?

DOAKER: Avery got him one of them good jobs. He working at one of them skyscrapers downtown.

AVERY: I'm working down there at the Gulf Building running an elevator. Got a pension and everything. They even give you a turkey on Thanksgiving.

LYMON: How you know the rope ain't gonna break? Ain't you scared the rope's gonna break?

AVERY: That's steel. They got steel cables hold it up. It take a whole lot of breaking to break that steel. Naw, I ain't worried about nothing like that. It ain't nothing but a little old elevator. Now, I wouldn't get in none of them airplanes. You couldn't pay me to do nothing like that.

LYMON: That be fun. I'd rather do that than ride in one of them elevators.

BOY WILLIE: How many of them watermelons you wanna buy?

AVERY: I thought you was gonna give me one seeing as how you got a whole truck full.

BOY WILLIE: You can get one, get two. I'll give you two for a dollar.

AVERY: I can't eat but one. How much are they?

BOY WILLIE: Aw, nigger, you know I'll give you a watermelon. Go on, take as many as you want. Just leave some for me and Lymon to sell.

AVERY: I don't want but one.

BOY WILLIE: How you get to be a preacher, Avery? I might want to be a preacher one day. Have everybody call me Reverend Boy Willie.

AVERY: It come to me in a dream. God called me and told me he wanted me to be a shepherd for his flock. That's what I'm gonna call my church . . . The Good Shepherd Church of God in Christ.

DOAKER: Tell him what you told me. Tell him about the three hobos.

AVERY: Boy Willie don't want to hear all that.

LYMON: I do. Lots a people say your dreams can come true.

AVERY: Naw. You don't want to hear all that.

DOAKER: Go on. I told him you was a preacher. He didn't want to believe me. Tell him about the three hobos.

AVERY: Well, it come to me in a dream. See . . . I was sitting out in this railroad yard watching the trains go by. The train stopped and these three hobos got off. They told me they had come from Nazareth and was on their way to Jerusalem. They had three candles. They gave me one and told me to light it . . . but to be careful that it didn't go out. Next thing I knew I was standing in front of this house. Something told me to go knock on the door. This old woman opened the door and said they had been waiting on me. Then she led me into this room. It was a big room and it was full of all kinds of different people. They looked like anybody else except they all had sheep heads and was making noise like sheep make. I heard somebody call my name. I looked around and there was these same three hobos. They told me to take off my clothes and they give me a blue robe with gold thread. They washed my feet and combed my hair. Then they showed me these three doors and told me to pick one.

I went through one of them doors and that flame leapt off that candle and it seemed like my whole head caught fire. I looked around and there was four or five other men standing there with these same blue robes on. Then we heard a voice tell us to look out across this valley. We looked out and saw the valley was full of wolves. The voice told us that these sheep people that I had seen in the other room had to go over to the other side of this valley and somebody had to take them. Then I heard another voice say, "Who shall I send?" Next thing I knew I said, "Here I am. Send me." That's when I met Jesus. He say, "If you go, I'll go with you." Something told me to say, "Come on. Let's go." That's when I woke up. My head still felt like it was on fire . . . but I had a peace about myself that was hard to explain. I knew right then that I had been filled with the Holy Ghost and called to be a servant of the Lord. It took me a while before I could accept that. But then a lot of little ways God showed me that it was true. So I became a preacher.

LYMON: I see why you gonna call it the Good Shepherd Church. You dreaming about them sheep people. I can see that easy.

BOY WILLIE: Doaker say you sent some white man past the house to look at that piano. Say he was going around to all the colored people's houses looking to buy up musical instruments.

AVERY: Yeah, but Berniece didn't want to sell that piano. After she told me about it . . . I could see why she didn't want to sell it.

BOY WILLIE: What's this man's name?

AVERY: Oh, that's a while back now. I done forgot his name. He give Berniece a card with his name and telephone number on it, but I believe she throwed it away.

[BERNIECE and MARETHA enter from the stairs.]

BERNIECE: Maretha, run back upstairs and get my pocketbook. And wipe that hair grease off your forehead. Go ahead, hurry up.

[MARETHA exits up the stairs.]

How you doing, Avery? You done got all dressed up. You look nice. Boy Willie, I thought you and Lymon was going to sell them watermelons.

BOY WILLIE: Lymon done got sleepy. We liable to get some sleep first.

LYMON: I ain't sleepy.

DOAKER: As many watermelons as you got stacked up on that truck out there, you ought to have been gone.

BOY WILLIE: We gonna go in a minute. We going.

BERNIECE: Doaker. I'm gonna stop down there on Logan Street. You want anything?

DOAKER: You can pick up some ham hocks if you going down there. See if you can get the smoked ones. If they ain't got that get the fresh ones. Don't get the ones that got all that fat under the skin. Look for the long ones. They nice and lean.

[He gives her a dollar.]

Don't get the short ones lessen they smoked. If you got to get the fresh ones make sure that they the long ones. If they ain't got them smoked then go ahead and get the short ones.

[Pause.]

You may as well get some turnip greens while you down there. I got some buttermilk . . . if you pick up some cornmeal I'll make me some cornbread and cook up them turnip greens.

[MARETHA enters from the stairs.]

MARETHA: We gonna take the streetcar?

BERNIECE: Me and Avery gonna drop you off at the settlement house. You mind them people down there. Don't be going down there showing your color. Boy Willie, I done told you what to do. I'll see you later, Doaker.

AVERY: I'll be seeing you again, Boy Willie.

BOY WILLIE: Hey, Berniece . . . what's the name of that man Avery sent past say he want to buy the piano?

BERNIECE: I knew it. I knew it when I first seen you. I knew you was up to something.

BOY WILLIE: Sutter's brother say he selling the land to me. He waiting on me now. Told me he'd give me two weeks. I got one part. Sell them watermelons get me another part. Then we can sell that piano and I'll have the third part.

BERNIECE: I ain't selling that piano, Boy Willie. If that's why you come up here you can just forget about it.

[To DOAKER.]

Doaker, I'll see you later. Boy Willie ain't nothing but a whole lot of mouth. I ain't paying him no mind. If he come up here thinking he gonna sell that piano then he done come up here for nothing.

[BERNIECE, AVERY, and MARETHA exit the front door.]

BOY WILLIE: Hey, Lymon! You ready to go sell these watermelons.

[BOY WILLIE and LYMON start to exit. At the door BOY WILLIE turns to DOAKER.]

Hey, Doaker . . . if Berniece don't want to sell that piano . . . I'm gonna cut it in half and go on and sell my half.

[BOY WILLIE and LYMON exit.]

[The lights go down on the scene.]

Scene 2

[The lights come up on the kitchen. It is three days later. WINING BOY sits at the kitchen table. There is a half-empty pint bottle on the table. DOAKER busies himself washing pots. WINING BOY is fifty-six years old. DOAKER's older brother, he tries to present the image of a successful musician and gambler, but his music, his clothes, and even his manner of presentation are old. He is a man who looking back over his life continues to live it with an odd mixture of zest and sorrow.]

WINING BOY: So the Ghosts of the Yellow Dog got Sutter. That just go to show you I believe I always lived right. They say every dog gonna have his day and time it go around it sure come back to you. I done seen that a thousand times. I know the truth of that. But I'll tell you outright . . . if I see Sutter's ghost I'll be on the first thing I find that got wheels on it.

[DOAKER enters from his room.]

DOAKER: Wining Boy!

WINING BOY: And I'll tell you another thing . . . Berniece ain't gonna sell that piano.

DOAKER: That's what she told him. He say he gonna cut it in half and go on and sell his half. They been around here three days trying to sell them watermelons. They trying to get out to where the white folks live but the truck keep breaking down. They go a block or two and it break down again. They trying to get out to Squirrel Hill and can't get around the corner. He say soon as he can get that truck empty to where he can set the piano up in there he gonna take it out of here and go sell it.

WINING BOY: What about them boys Sutter got? How come they ain't farming that land?

DOAKER: One of them going to school. He left down there and come North to school. The other one ain't got as much sense as that frying pan over yonder. That is the dumbest white man I ever seen. He'd stand in the river and watch it rise till it drown him.

WINING BOY: Other than seeing Sutter's ghost how's Berniece doing?

DOAKER: She doing alright. She still got Crawley on her mind. He been dead three years but she still holding on to him. She need to go out here and let one of these fellows grab a whole handful of whatever she got. She act like it done got precious.

WINING BOY: They always told me any fish will bite if you got good bait.

DOAKER: She stuck up on it. She think it's better than she is. I believe she messing around with Avery. They got something going. He a preacher now. If you let him tell it the Holy Ghost sat on his head and heaven opened up with thunder and lightning and God was calling his name. Told him to go out and preach and tend to his flock. That's what he gonna call his church. The Good Shepherd Church.

WINING BOY: They had that joker down in Spear walking around talking about he Jesus Christ. He gonna live the life of Christ. Went through the Last Supper and everything. Rented him a mule on Palm Sunday and rode through the town. Did everything . . . talking about he Christ. He did everything until they got up to that crucifixion part. Got up to that part and told everybody to go home and quit pretending. He got up to the crucifixion part and changed his mind. Had a whole bunch of folks come down there to see him get nailed to the cross. I don't know who's the worse fool. Him or them. Had all them folks come down there . . . even carried the cross up this little hill. People standing around waiting to see him get nailed to the cross and he stop everything and preach a little sermon and told everybody to go home. Had enough nerve to tell them to come to church on Easter Sunday to celebrate his resurrection.

DOAKER: I'm surprised Avery ain't thought about

that. He trying every little thing to get him a congregation together. They meeting over at his house till he get him a church.

WINING BOY: Ain't nothing wrong with being a preacher. You got the preacher on one hand and the gambler on the other. Sometimes there ain't too much difference in them.

DOAKER: How long you been in Kansas City?

WINING BOY: Since I left here. I got tied up with some old gal down there.

[Pause.]

You know Cleotha died.

DOAKER: Yeah, I heard that last time I was down there. I was sorry to hear that.

WINING BOY: One of her friends wrote and told me. I got the letter right here.

[He takes the letter out of his pocket.]

I was down in Kansas City and she wrote and told me Cleotha had died. Name of Willa Bryant. She say she know cousin Rupert.

[He opens the letter and reads.]

Dear Wining Boy: I am writing this letter to let you know Miss Cleotha Holman passed on Saturday the first of May she departed this world in the loving arms of her sister Miss Alberta Samuels. I know you would want to know this and am writing as a friend of Cleotha. There have been many hardships since last you seen her but she survived them all and to the end was a good woman whom I hope have God's grace and is in His Paradise. Your cousin Rupert Bates is my friend also and he give me your address and I pray this reaches you about Cleotha. Miss Willa Bryant. A friend.

[He folds the letter and returns it to his pocket.]

They was nailing her coffin shut by the time I heard about it. I never knew she was sick. I believe it was that yellow jaundice. That's what killed her mama.

DOAKER: Cleotha wasn't but forty-some.

WINING BOY: She was forty-six. I got ten years on her. I met her when she was sixteen. You remember I used to run around there. Couldn't nothing keep me still. Much as I loved Cleotha I loved to ramble. Couldn't nothing keep me still. We got married and we used to fight about it all the time. Then one day she asked me to leave. Told me she loved me before I left. Told me, Wining Boy, you got a home as long as I got

mine.
And I believe in my heart I always felt that
and that kept me safe.

DOAKER: Cleotha always did have a nice way about
her.

WINING BOY: Man that woman was something. I
used to thank the Lord. Many a night I sat up
and looked out over my life. Said, well, I had
Cleotha. When it didn't look like there was
nothing else for me, I said, thank God, at least
I had that. If ever I go anywhere in this life I
done known a good woman. And that used to
hold me till the next morning.

[Pause.]

What you got? Give me a little nip. I know you
got something stuck up in your room.

DOAKER: I ain't seen you walk in here and put nothing on the table. You done sat there and drank
up your whiskey. Now you talking about what
you got.

WINING BOY: I got plenty money. Give me a little nip.

[DOAKER carries a glass into his room and returns with
it half-filled. He sets it on the table in front of WINING
BOY.]

WINING BOY: You hear from Coreen?

DOAKER: She up in New York. I let her go from my
mind.

WINING BOY: She was something back then. She was-
n't too pretty but she had a way of looking at
you made you know there was a whole lot of
woman there. You got married and snatched
her out from under us and we all got mad at
you.

DOAKER: She up in New York City. That's what I
hear.

[The door opens and BOY WILLIE and LYMON enter.]

BOY WILLIE: Aw hell . . . look here! We was just talking about you. Doaker say you left out of here
with a whole sack of money. I told him we
wasn't going see you till you got broke.

WINING BOY: What you mean broke? I got a whole
pocketful of money.

DOAKER: Did you all get that truck fixed?

BOY WILLIE: We got it running and got halfway out
there on Centre and it broke down again.
Lymon went out there and messed it up some
more. Fellow told us we got to wait till tomorrow to get it fixed. Say he have it running like
new. Lymon going back down there and sleep
in the truck so the people don't take the watermelons.

LYMON: Lymon nothing. You go down there and

sleep in it.

BOY WILLIE: You was sleeping in it down home, nigger! I don't know nothing about sleeping in no
truck.

LYMON: I ain't sleeping in no truck.

BOY WILLIE: They can take all the watermelons. I
don't care. Wining Boy, where you coming
from? Where you been?

WINING BOY: I been down in Kansas City.

BOY WILLIE: You remember Lymon? Lymon Jackson.

WINING BOY: Yeah, I used to know his daddy.

BOY WILLIE: Doaker say you don't never leave no
address with nobody. Say he got to depend on
your whim. See when it strike you to pay a
visit.

WINING BOY: I got four or five addresses.

BOY WILLIE: Doaker say Berniece asked you for three
dollars and you got mad and left.

WINING BOY: Berniece try and rule over you too
much for me. That's why I left. It wasn't about
no three dollars.

BOY WILLIE: Where you getting all these sacks of
money from? I need to be with you. Doaker
say you had a whole sack of money . . . turn
some of it loose.

WINING BOY: I was just fixing to ask you for five dollars.

BOY WILLIE: I ain't got no money. I'm trying to get
some. Doaker tell you about Sutter? The
Ghosts of the Yellow Dog got him about three
weeks ago. Berniece done seen his ghost and
everything. He right upstairs.

[Calls.]

Hey Sutter! Wining Boy's here. Come on, get a
drink!

WINING BOY: How many that make the Ghosts of the
Yellow Dog done got?

BOY WILLIE: Must be about nine or ten, eleven or
twelve. I don't know.

DOAKER: You got Ed Saunders. Howard Peterson.
Charlie Webb.

WINING BOY: Robert Smith. That fellow that
shot Becky's boy . . . say he was stealing
peaches . . .

DOAKER: You talking about Bob Mallory.

BOY WILLIE: Berniece say she don't believe all that
about the Ghosts of the Yellow Dog.

WINING BOY: She ain't got to believe. You go ask
them white folks in Sunflower County if they
believe. You go ask Sutter if he believe. I don't
care if Berniece believe or not. I done been to
where the Southern cross the Yellow Dog and
called out their names. They talk back to you,
too.

LYMON: What they sound like? The wind or something?

BOY WILLIE: You done been there for real, Wining Boy?

WINING BOY: Nineteen thirty. July of nineteen thirty I stood right there on that spot. It didn't look like nothing was going right in my life. I said everything can't go wrong all the time . . . let me go down there and call on the Ghosts of the Yellow Dog, see if they can help me. I went down there and right there where them two railroads cross each other . . . I stood right there on that spot and called out their names. They talk back to you, too.

LYMON: People say you can ask them questions. They talk to you like that?

WINING BOY: A lot of things you got to find out on your own. I can't say how they talked to nobody else. But to me it just filled me up in a strange sort of way to be standing there on that spot. I didn't want to leave. It felt like the longer I stood there the bigger I got. I seen the train coming and it seem like I was bigger than the train. I started not to move. But something told me to go ahead and get on out the way. The train passed and I started to go back up there and stand some more. But something told me not to do it. I walked away from there feeling like a king. Went on and had a stroke of luck that run on for three years. So I don't care if Berniece believe or not. Berniece ain't got to believe. I know cause I been there. Now Doaker'll tell you about the Ghosts of the Yellow Dog.

DOAKER: I don't try and talk that stuff with Berniece. Avery got her all tied up in that church. She just think it's a whole lot of nonsense.

BOY WILLIE: Berniece don't believe in nothing. She just think she believe. She believe in anything if it's convenient for her to believe. But when that convenience run out then she ain't got nothing to stand on.

WINING BOY: Let's not get on Berniece now. Doaker tell me you talking about selling that piano.

BOY WILLIE: Yeah . . . hey, Doaker, I got the name of that man Avery was talking about. The man what's fixing the truck gave me his name. Everybody know him. Say he buy up anything you can make music with. I got his name and his telephone number. Hey, Wining Boy, Sutter's brother say he selling the land to me. I got one part. Sell them watermelons get me the second part. Then . . . soon as I get them watermelons out that truck I'm gonna take and sell that piano and get the third part.

DOAKER: That land ain't worth nothing no more. The smart white man's up here in these cities. He cut the land loose and step back and watch you and the dumb white man argue over it.

WINING BOY: How you know Sutter's brother ain't sold it already? You talking about selling the piano and the man's liable to sold the land two or three times.

BOY WILLIE: He say he waiting on me. He say he give me two weeks. That's two weeks from Friday. Say if I ain't back by then he might gonna sell it to somebody else. He say he wanna see me with it.

WINING BOY: You know as well as I know the man gonna sell the land to the first one walk up and hand him the money.

BOY WILLIE: That's just who I'm gonna be. Look, you ain't gotta know he waiting on me. I know. Okay. I know what the man told me. Stovall already done tried to buy the land from him and he told him no. The man say he waiting on me . . . he waiting on me. Hey, Doaker . . . give me a drink. I see Wining Boy got his glass.

[DOAKER exits into his room.]

Wining Boy, what you doing in Kansas City? What they got down there?

LYMON: I hear they got some nice-looking women in Kansas City. I sure like to go down there and find out.

WINING BOY: Man, the women down there is something else.

[DOAKER enters with a bottle of whiskey. He sets it on the table with some glasses.]

DOAKER: You wanna sit up here and drink up my whiskey, leave a dollar on the table when you get up.

BOY WILLIE: You ain't doing nothing but showing your hospitality. I know we ain't got to pay for your hospitality.

WINING BOY: Doaker say they had you and Lymon down on the Parchman Farm. Had you on my old stomping grounds.

BOY WILLIE: Me and Lymon was down there hauling wood for Jim Miller and keeping us a little bit to sell. Some white fellows tried to run us off of it. That's when Crawley got killed. They put me and Lymon in the penitentiary.

LYMON: They ambushed us right there where that road dip down and around that bend in the creek. Crawley tried to fight them. Me and Boy Willie got away but the sheriff got us. Say we was stealing wood. They shot me in my stomach.

BOY WILLIE: They looking for Lymon down there now. They rounded him up and put him in jail for not working.

LYMON: Fined me a hundred dollars. Mr. Stovall come and paid my hundred dollars and the judge say I got to work for him to pay him back his hundred dollars. I told them I'd rather take my thirty days but they wouldn't let me do that.

BOY WILLIE: As soon as Stovall turned his back, Lymon was gone. He down there living in that truck dodging the sheriff and Stovall. He got both of them looking for him. So I brought him up here.

LYMON: I told Boy Willie I'm gonna stay up here. I ain't going back with him.

BOY WILLIE: Ain't nobody twisting your arm to make you go back. You can do what you want to do.

WINING BOY: I'll go back with you. I'm on my way down there. You gonna take the train? I'm gonna take the train.

LYMON: They treat you better up here.

BOY WILLIE: I ain't worried about nobody mistreating me. They treat you like you let them treat you. They mistreat me I mistreat them right back. Ain't no difference in me and the white man.

WINING BOY: Ain't no difference as far as how somebody supposed to treat you. I agree with that. But I'll tell you the difference between the colored man and the white man. Alright. Now you take and eat some berries. They taste real good to you. So you say I'm gonna go out and get me a whole pot of these berries and cook them up to make a pie or whatever. But you ain't looked to see them berries is sitting in the white fellow's yard. Ain't got no fence around them. You figure anybody want something they'd fence it in. Alright. Now the white man come along and say that's my land. Therefore everything that grow on it belong to me. He tell the sheriff, "I want you to put this nigger in jail as a warning to all the other niggers. Otherwise first thing you know these niggers have everything that belong to us."

BOY WILLIE: I'd come back at night and haul off his whole patch while he was sleep.

WINING BOY: Alright. Now Mr. So and So, he sell the land to you. And he come to you and say, "John, you own the land. It's all yours now. But them is my berries. And come time to pick them I'm gonna send my boys over. You got the land . . . but them berries, I'm gonna keep them. They mine." And he go and fix it with the law that them is his berries. Now that's the difference between the colored man and the white man. The colored man can't fix nothing with the law.

BOY WILLIE: I don't go by what the law say. The law's liable to say anything. I go by if it's right or not. It don't matter to me what the law say. I

take and look at it for myself.

LYMON: That's why you gonna end up back down there on the Parchman Farm.

BOY WILLIE: I ain't thinking about no Parchman Farm. You liable to go back before me.

LYMON: They work you too hard down there. All that weeding and hoeing and chopping down trees. I didn't like all that.

WINING BOY: You ain't got to like your job on Parchman. Hey, tell him, Doaker, the only one got to like his job is the waterboy.

DOAKER: If he don't like his job he need to set that bucket down.

BOY WILLIE: That's what they told Lymon. They had Lymon on water and everybody got mad at him cause he was lazy.

LYMON: That water was heavy.

BOY WILLIE: They had Lymon down there singing: (Sings.)

O Lord Berta Berta O Lord gal oh-ah
O Lord Berta Berta O Lord gal well

[LYMON and WINING BOY join in.]

Go 'head marry don't you wait on me oh-ah
Go 'head marry don't you wait on me well
Might not want you when I go free oh-ah
Might not want you when I go free well

BOY WILLIE: Come on, Doaker. Doaker know this one.

[As DOAKER joins in the men stamp and clap to keep time. They sing in harmony with great fervor and style.]

O Lord Berta Berta O Lord gal oh-ah
O Lord Berta Berta O Lord gal well

Raise them up higher, let them drop on down oh-ah
Raise them up higher, let them drop on down well
Don't know the difference when the sun go down oh-ah
Don't know the difference when the sun go down well

Berta in Meridan and she living at ease oh-ah
Berta in Meridan and she living at ease well
I'm on old Parchman, got to work or leave oh-ah
I'm on old Parchman, got to work or leave well

O Alberta, Berta, O Lord gal oh-ah
O Alberta, Berta, O Lord gal well

When you marry, don't marry no farming
    man oh-ah
When you marry, don't marry no farming
    man well
Everyday Monday, hoe handle in your hand
    oh-ah
Everyday Monday, hoe handle in your hand
    well

When you marry, marry a railroad man, oh-ah
When you marry, marry a railroad man, well
Everyday Sunday, dollar in your hand oh-ah
Everyday Sunday, dollar in your hand well

O Alberta, Berta, O Lord gal oh-ah
O Alberta, Berta, O Lord gal well

BOY WILLIE: Doaker like that part. He like that rail-
    road part.
LYMON: Doaker sound like Tangleye. He can't sing a
    lick.
BOY WILLIE: Hey, Doaker, they still talk about you
    down on Parchman. They ask me, "You
    Doaker Boy's nephew?" I say, "Yeah, me and
    him is family." They treated me alright soon as
    I told them that. Say, "Yeah, he my uncle."
DOAKER: I don't never want to see none of them nig-
    gers no more.
BOY WILLIE: I don't want to see them either. Hey,
    Wining Boy, come on play some piano. You a
    piano player, play some piano. Lymon wanna
    hear you.
WINING BOY: I give that piano up. That was the best
    thing that ever happened to me, getting rid of
    that piano. That piano got so big and I'm car-
    rying it around on my back. I don't wish that
    on nobody. See, you think it's all fun being a
    recording star. Got to carrying that piano
    around and man did I get slow. Got just like
    molasses. The world just slipping by me and
    I'm walking around with that piano. Alright.
    Now, there ain't but so many places you can
    go. Only so many road wide enough for you
    and that piano. And that piano get heavier and
    heavier. Go to a place and they find out you
    play piano, the first thing they want to do is
    give you a drink, find you a piano, and sit you
    right down. And that's where you gonna be
    for the next eight hours. They ain't gonna let
    you get up! Now, the first three or four years
    of that is fun. You can't get enough whiskey
    and you can't get enough women and you

don't never get tired of playing that piano. But
that only last so long. You look up one day
and you hate the whiskey, and you hate the
women, and you hate the piano. But that's all
you got. You can't do nothing else. All you
know how to do is play that piano. Now, who
am I? Am I me? Or am I the piano player?
Sometime it seem like the only thing to do is
shoot the piano player cause he the cause of all
the trouble I'm having.
DOAKER: What you gonna do when your troubles get
    like mine?
LYMON: If I knew how to play it, I'd play it. That's a
    nice piano.
BOY WILLIE: Whoever playing better play quick.
    Sutter's brother say he waiting on me. I sell
    them watermelons. Get Berniece to sell that
    piano. Put them two parts with the part I done
    saved . . .
WINING BOY: Berniece ain't gonna sell that piano. I
    don't see why you don't know that.
BOY WILLIE: What she gonna do with it? She ain't
    doing nothing but letting it sit up there and
    rot. That piano ain't doing nobody no good.
LYMON: That's a nice piano. If I had it I'd sell it.
    Unless I knew how to play like Wining Boy.
    You can get a nice price for that piano.
DOAKER: Now I'm gonna tell you something, Lymon
    don't know this . . . but I'm gonna tell you
    why me and Wining Boy say Berniece ain't
    gonna sell that piano.
BOY WILLIE: She ain't got to sell it! I'm gonna sell it!
    Berniece ain't got no more rights to that piano
    than I do.
DOAKER: I'm talking to the man . . . let me talk to the
    man. See, now . . . to understand why we say
    that . . . to understand about that piano . . .
    you got to go back to slavery time. See, our
    family was owned by a fellow named Robert
    Sutter. That was Sutter's grandfather. Alright.
    The piano was owned by a fellow named Joel
    Nolander. He was one of the Nolander broth-
    ers from down in Georgia. It was coming up
    on Sutter's wedding anniversary and he was
    looking to buy his wife . . . Miss Ophelia was
    her name . . . he was looking to buy her an
    anniversary present. Only thing with him . . .
    he ain't had no money. But he had some nig-
    gers. So he asked Mr. Nolander to see if maybe
    he could trade off some of his niggers for that
    piano. Told him he would give him one and a
    half niggers for it. That's the way he told him.
    Say he could have one full grown and one half
    grown. Mr. Nolander agreed only he say he
    had to pick them. He didn't want Sutter to
    give him just any old nigger. He say he want-
    ed to have the pick of the litter. So Sutter lined

up his niggers and Mr. Nolander looked them over and out of the whole bunch he picked my grandmother . . . her name was Berniece . . . same like Berniece . . . and he picked my daddy when he wasn't nothing but a little boy nine years old. They made the trade off and Miss Ophelia was so happy with that piano that it got to be just about all she would do was play on that piano.

WINING BOY: Just get up in the morning, get all dressed up and sit down and play on that piano.

DOAKER: Alright. Time go along. Time go along. Miss Ophelia got to missing my grandmother . . . the way she would cook and clean the house and talk to her and what not. And she missed having my daddy around the house to fetch things for her. So she asked to see if maybe she could trade back that piano and get her niggers back. Mr. Nolander said no. Said a deal was a deal. Him and Sutter had a big falling out about it and Miss Ophelia took sick to the bed. Wouldn't get out of the bed in the morning. She just lay there. The doctor said she was wasting away.

WINING BOY: That's when Sutter called our grand-daddy up to the house.

DOAKER: Now, our granddaddy's name was Boy Willie. That's who Boy Willie's named after . . . only they called him Willie Boy. Now, he was a worker of wood. He could make you anything you wanted out of wood. He'd make you a desk. A table. A lamp. Anything you wanted. Them white fellows around there used to come up to Mr. Sutter and get him to make all kinds of things for them. Then they'd pay Mr. Sutter a nice price. See, everything my granddaddy made Mr. Sutter owned cause he owned him. That's why when Mr. Nolander offered to buy him to keep the family together Mr. Sutter wouldn't sell him. Told Mr. Nolander he didn't have enough money to buy him. Now . . . am I telling it right, Wining Boy?

WINING BOY: You telling it.

DOAKER: Sutter called him up to the house and told him to carve my grandmother and my daddy's picture on the piano for Miss Ophelia. And he took and carved this . . .

[DOAKER crosses over to the piano.]

See that right there? That's my grandmother, Berniece. She looked just like that. And he put a picture of my daddy when he wasn't nothing but a little boy the way he remembered him. He made them up out of his memory. Only thing . . . he didn't stop there. He carved all

this. He got a picture of his mama . . . Mama Esther . . . and his daddy, Boy Charles.

WINING BOY: That was the first Boy Charles.

DOAKER: Then he put on the side here all kinds of things. See that? That's when him and Mama Berniece got married. They called it jumping the broom. That's how you got married in them days. Then he got here when my daddy was born . . . and here he got Mama Esther's funeral . . . and down here he got Mr. Nolander taking Mama Berniece and my daddy away down to his place in Georgia. He got all kinds of things what happened with our family. When Mr. Sutter seen the piano with all them carvings on it he got mad. He didn't ask for all that. But see . . . there wasn't nothing he could do about it. When Miss Ophelia seen it . . . she got excited. Now she had her piano and her niggers too. She took back to playing it and played on it right up till the day she died. Alright . . . now see, our brother Boy Charles . . . that's Berniece and Boy Willie's daddy . . . he was the oldest of us three boys. He's dead now. But he would have been fifty-seven if he had lived. He died in 1911 when he was thirty-one years old. Boy Charles used to talk about that piano all the time. He never could get it off his mind. Two or three months go by and he be talking about it again. He be talking about taking it out of Sutter's house. Say it was the story of our whole family and as long as Sutter had it . . . he had us. Say we was still in slavery. Me and Wining Boy tried to talk him out of it but it wouldn't do any good. Soon as he quiet down about it he'd start up again. We seen where he wasn't gonna get it off his mind . . . so, on the Fourth of July, 1911 . . . when Sutter was at the picnic what the county give every year . . . me and Wining Boy went on down there with him and took that piano out of Sutter's house. We put it on a wagon and me and Wining Boy carried it over into the next county with Mama Ola's people. Boy Charles decided to stay around there and wait until Sutter got home to make it look like business as usual.

Now, I don't know what happened when Sutter came home and found that piano gone. But somebody went up to Boy Charles's house and set it on fire. But he wasn't in there. He must have seen them coming cause he went down and caught the 3:57 Yellow Dog. He didn't know they was gonna come down and stop the train. Stopped the train and found Boy Charles in the boxcar with four of them hobos. Must have got mad when they couldn't find the piano cause they set the boxcar afire and killed everybody. Now, nobody know who done that. Some people say it was Sutter cause it was his piano. Some people say it was Sheriff Carter. Some people say it was Robert Smith and Ed Saunders. But don't nobody know for sure. It was about two months after that that Ed Saunders fell down his well. Just upped and fell down his well for no reason. People say it was the ghost of them men who burned up in the boxcar that pushed him in his well. They started calling them the Ghosts of the Yellow Dog. Now, that's how all that got started and that why we say Berniece ain't gonna sell that piano. Cause her daddy died over it.

BOY WILLIE: All that's in the past. If my daddy had seen where he could have traded that piano in for some land of his own, it wouldn't be sitting up here now. He spent his whole life farming on somebody else's land. I ain't gonna do that. See, he couldn't do no better. When he come along he ain't had nothing he could build on. His daddy ain't had nothing to give him. The only thing my daddy had to give me was that piano. And he died over giving me that. I ain't gonna let it sit up there and rot without trying to do something with it. If Berniece can't see that, then I'm gonna go ahead and sell my half. And you and Wining Boy know I'm right.

DOAKER: Ain't nobody said nothing about who's right and who's wrong. I was just telling the man about the piano. I was telling him why we say Berniece ain't gonna sell it.

LYMON: Yeah, I can see why you say that now. I told Boy Willie he ought to stay up here with me.

BOY WILLIE: You stay! I'm going back! That's what I'm gonna do with my life! Why I got to come up here and learn to do something I don't know how to do when I already know how to farm? You stay up here and make your own way if that's what you want to do. I'm going back and live my life the way I want to live it.

[WINING BOY gets up and crosses to the piano.]

WINING BOY: Let's see what we got here. I ain't played on this thing for a while.

DOAKER: You can stop telling that. You was playing on it the last time you was through here. We couldn't get you off of it. Go on and play something.

[WINING BOY sits down at the piano and plays and sings. The song is one which has put many dimes and quarters in his pocket, long ago, in dimly remembered towns and way stations. He plays badly, without hesitation, and sings in a forceful voice.]

WINING BOY *(Singing.)*:

I am a rambling gambling man
I gambled in many towns
I rambled this wide world over
I rambled this world around
I had my ups and downs in life
And bitter times I saw
But I never knew what misery was
Till I lit on old Arkansas.

I started out one morning
to meet that early train
He said, "You better work for me
I have some land to drain.
I'll give you fifty cents a day,
Your washing, board and all
And you shall be a different man
In the state of Arkansas."

I worked six months for the rascal
Joe Herrin was his name
He fed me old corn dodgers
They was hard as any rock
My tooth is all got loosened
And my knees begin to knock
That was the kind of hash I got
In the state of Arkansas.

Traveling man
I've traveled all around this world
Traveling man
I've traveled from land to land
Traveling man
I've traveled all around this world
Well it ain't no use
writing no news
I'm a traveling man.

[The door opens and BERNIECE enters with MARETHA.]

BERNIECE: Is that . . . Lord, I know that ain't Wining Boy sitting there.

WINING BOY: Hey, Berniece.

BERNIECE: You all had this planned. You and Boy Willie had this planned.

WINING BOY: I didn't know he was gonna be here. I'm on my way down home. I stopped by to see you and Doaker first.

DOAKER: I told the nigger he left out of here with that sack of money, we thought we might never see him again. Boy Willie say he wasn't gonna see him till he got broke. I looked up and seen him sitting on the doorstep asking for two dollars. Look at him laughing. He know it's the truth.

BERNIECE: Boy Willie, I didn't see that truck out there. I thought you was out selling watermelons.

BOY WILLIE: We done sold them all. Sold the truck too.

BERNIECE: I don't want to go through none of your stuff. I done told you to go back where you belong.

BOY WILLIE: I was just teasing you, woman. You can't take no teasing?

BERNIECE: Wining Boy, when you get here?

WINING BOY: A little while ago. I took the train from Kansas City.

BERNIECE: Let me go upstairs and change and then I'll cook you something to eat.

BOY WILLIE: You ain't cooked me nothing when I come.

BERNIECE: Boy Willie, go on and leave me alone. Come on, Maretha, get up here and change your clothes before you get them dirty.

[BERNIECE exits up the stairs, followed by MARETHA.]

WINING BOY: Maretha sure getting big, ain't she, Doaker. And just as pretty as she want to be. I didn't know Crawley had it in him.

[BOY WILLIE crosses to the piano.]

BOY WILLIE: Hey, Lymon . . . get up on the other side of this piano and let me see something.

WINING BOY: Boy Willie, what is you doing?

BOY WILLIE: I'm seeing how heavy this piano is. Get up over there, Lymon.

WINING BOY: Go on and leave that piano alone. You ain't taking that piano out of here and selling it.

BOY WILLIE: Just as soon as I get them watermelons out that truck.

WINING BOY: Well, I got something to say about that.

BOY WILLIE: This my daddy's piano.

WINING BOY: He ain't took it by himself. Me and Doaker helped him.

BOY WILLIE: He died by himself. Where was you and Doaker at then? Don't come telling me nothing about this piano. This is me and Berniece's piano. Am I right, Doaker?

DOAKER: Yeah, you right.

BOY WILLIE: Let's see if we can lift it up, Lymon. Get a good grip on it and pick it up on your end. Ready? Lift!

[As they start to move the piano, the sound of SUTTER's GHOST is heard. DOAKER is the only one to hear it. With difficulty they move the piano a little bit so it is out of place.]

BOY WILLIE: What you think?

LYMON: It's heavy . . . but you can move it. Only it ain't gonna be easy.

BOY WILLIE: It wasn't that heavy to me. Okay, let's put it back.

[The sound of SUTTER's GHOST is heard again. They all hear it as BERNIECE enters on the stairs.]

BERNIECE: Boy Willie . . . you gonna play around with me one too many times. And then God's gonna bless you and West is gonna dress you. Now set that piano back over there. I done told you a hundred times I ain't selling that piano.

BOY WILLIE: I'm trying to get me some land, woman. I need that piano to get me some money so I can buy Sutter's land.

BERNIECE: Money can't buy what that piano cost. You can't sell your soul for money. It won't go with the buyer. It'll shrivel and shrink to know that you ain't taken on to it. But it won't go with the buyer.

BOY WILLIE: I ain't talking about all that, woman. I ain't talking about selling my soul. I'm talking about trading that piece of wood for some land. Get something under your feet. Land the only thing God ain't making no more of. You can always get you another piano. I'm talking about some land. What you get something out the ground from. That's what I'm talking about. You can't do nothing with that piano but sit up there and look at it.

BERNIECE: That's just what I'm gonna do. Wining Boy, you want me to fry you some pork chops?

BOY WILLIE: Now, I'm gonna tell you the way I see it. The only thing that make that piano worth something is them carvings Papa Willie Boy put on there. That's what make it worth something. That was my great-granddaddy. Papa Boy Charles brought that piano into the house. Now, I'm supposed to build on what they left me. You can't do nothing with that piano sitting up here in the house. That's just like if I let them watermelons sit out there and rot. I'd be a fool. Alright now, if you say to me, Boy Willie, I'm using that piano. I give out lessons on it and that help me make my rent or whatever. Then that be something else. I'd have to go on and say, well, Berniece using that piano. She building on it. Let her go on and use it. I got to find another way to get Sutter's land. But Doaker say you ain't touched that piano the whole time it's been up here. So why you wanna stand in my way? See, you just looking at the sentimental value. See, that's good. That's alright. I take my hat off whenever somebody say my daddy's name. But I ain't gonna be no fool about no sentimental value.

You can sit up here and look at the piano for the next hundred years and it's just gonna be a piano. You can't make more than that. Now I want to get Sutter's land with that piano. I get Sutter's land and I can go down and cash in the crop and get my seed. As long as I got the land and the seed then I'm alright. I can always get me a little something else. Cause that land give back to you. I can make me another crop and cash that in. I still got the land and the seed. But that piano don't put out nothing else. You ain't got nothing working for you. Now, the kind of man my daddy was he would have understood that. I'm sorry you can't see it that way. But that's why I'm gonna take that piano out of here and sell it.

BERNIECE: You ain't taking that piano out of my house.

[She crosses to the piano.]

Look at this piano. Look at it. Mama Ola polished this piano with her tears for seventeen years. For seventeen years she rubbed on it till her hands bled. Then she rubbed the blood in . . . mixed it up with the rest of the blood on it. Every day that God breathed life into her body she rubbed and cleaned and polished and prayed over it. "Play something for me, Berniece. Play something for me, Berniece." Every day. "I cleaned it up for you, play something for me, Berniece." You always talking about your daddy but you ain't never stopped to look at what his foolishness cost your mama. Seventeen years' worth of cold nights and an empty bed. For what? For a piano? For a piece of wood? To get even with somebody? I look at you and you're all the same. You, Papa Boy Charles, Wining Boy, Doaker, Crawley . . . you're all alike. All this thieving and killing and thieving and killing. And what it ever lead to? More killing and more thieving. I ain't never seen it come to nothing. People getting burned up. People getting shot. People falling down their wells. It don't never stop.

DOAKER: Come on now, Berniece, ain't no need in getting upset.

BOY WILLIE: I done a little bit of stealing here and there, but I ain't never killed nobody. I can't be speaking for nobody else. You all got to speak for yourself, but I ain't never killed nobody.

BERNIECE: You killed Crawley just as sure as if you pulled the trigger.

BOY WILLIE: See, that's ignorant. That's downright foolish for you to say something like that. You ain't doing nothing but showing your ignorance. If the nigger was here I'd whup his ass for getting me and Lymon shot at.

BERNIECE: Crawley ain't knew about the wood.

BOY WILLIE: We told the man about the wood. Ask Lymon. He knew all about the wood. He seen we was sneaking it. Why else we gonna be out there at night? Don't come telling me Crawley ain't knew about the wood. Them fellows come up on us and Crawley tried to bully them. Me and Lymon seen the sheriff with them and give in. Wasn't no sense in getting killed over fifty dollars' worth of wood.

BERNIECE: Crawley ain't knew you stole that wood.

BOY WILLIE: We ain't stole no wood. Me and Lymon was hauling wood for Jim Miller and keeping us a little bit on the side. We dumped our little bit down there by the creek till we had enough to make a load. Some fellows seen us and we figured we better get it before they did. We come up there and got Crawley to help us load it. Figured we'd cut him in. Crawley trying to keep the wolf from his door . . . we was trying to help him.

LYMON: Me and Boy Willie told him about the wood. We told him some fellows might be trying to beat us to it. He say let me go back and get my thirty-eight. That's what caused all the trouble.

BOY WILLIE: If Crawley ain't had the gun he'd be alive today.

LYMON: We had it about half loaded when they come up on us. We seen the sheriff with them and we tried to get away. We ducked around near the bend in the creek . . . but they was down there too. Boy Willie say let's give in. But Crawley pulled out his gun and started shooting. That's when they started shooting back.

BERNIECE: All I know is Crawley would be alive if you hadn't come up there and got him.

BOY WILLIE: I ain't had nothing to do with Crawley getting killed. That was his own fault.

BERNIECE: Crawley's dead and in the ground and you still walking around here eating. That's all I know. He went off to load some wood with you and ain't never come back.

BOY WILLIE: I told you, woman . . . I ain't had nothing to do with . . .

BERNIECE: He ain't here, is he? He ain't here!

[BERNIECE hits BOY WILLIE.]

I said he ain't here. Is he?

[BERNIECE continues to hit BOY WILLIE, who doesn't move to defend himself, other than back up and turning his head so that most of the blows fall on his chest and arms.]

DOAKER *(Grabbing BERNIECE.)*: Come on, Berniece . . .

let it go, it ain't his fault.

BERNIECE: He ain't here, is he? Is he?

BOY WILLIE: I told you I ain't responsible for Crawley.

BERNIECE: He ain't here.

BOY WILLIE: Come on now, Berniece . . . don't do this now. Doaker get her. I ain't had nothing to do with Crawley . . .

BERNIECE: You come up there and got him!

BOY WILLIE: I done told you now. Doaker, get her. I ain't playing.

DOAKER: Come on. Berniece.

[MARETHA *is heard screaming upstairs. It is a scream of stark terror.*]

MARETHA: Mama! . . . Mama!

[*The lights go down to black. End of Act I.*]

ACT II

Scene 1

[*The lights come up on the kitchen. It is the following morning.* DOAKER *is ironing the pants to his uniform. He has a pot cooking on the stove at the same time. He is singing a song. The song provides him with the rhythm for his work and he moves about the kitchen with the ease born of many years as a railroad cook.*]

DOAKER:

> Gonna leave Jackson Mississippi
> and go to Memphis
> and double back to Jackson
> Come on down to Hattiesburg
> Change cars on the Y.D.
> coming through the territory to Meridian
> and Meridian to Greenville
> and Greenville to Memphis
> I'm on my way and I know where
>
> Change cars on the Katy
> Leaving Jackson
> and going through Clarksdale
> Hello Winona!
> Courtland!
> Bateville!
> Como!
> Senitobia!
> Lewisberg!
> Sunflower!
> Glendora!
> Sharkey!

> And double back to Jackson
> Hello Greenwood
> I'm on my way Memphis
> Clarksdale
> Moorhead
> Indianola
> Can a highball pass through?
> Highball on through sir
> Grand Carson!
> Thirty First Street Depot
> Fourth Street Depot
> Memphis!

[WINING BOY *enters carrying a suit of clothes.*]

DOAKER: I thought you took that suit to the pawnshop?

WINING BOY: I went down there and the man tell me the suit is too old. Look at this suit. This is one hundred percent silk! How a silk suit gonna get too old? I know what it was he just didn't want to give me five dollars for it. Best he wanna give me is three dollars. I figure a silk suit is worth five dollars all over the world. I wasn't gonna part with it for no three dollars so I brought it back.

DOAKER: They got another pawnshop up on Wylie.

WINING BOY: I carried it up there. He say he don't take no clothes. Only thing he take is guns and radios. Maybe a guitar or two. Where's Berniece?

DOAKER: Berniece still at work. Boy Willie went down there to meet Lymon this morning. I guess they got that truck fixed, they been out there all day and ain't come back yet. Maretha scared to sleep up there now. Berniece don't know, but I seen Sutter before she did.

WINING BOY: Say what?

DOAKER: About three weeks ago. I had just come back from down there. Sutter couldn't have been dead more than three days. He was sitting over there at the piano. I come out to go to work . . . and he was sitting right there. Had his hand on top of his head just like Berniece said. I believe he broke his neck when he fell in the well. I kept quiet about it. I didn't see no reason to upset Berniece.

WINING BOY: Did he say anything? Did he say he was looking for Boy Willie?

DOAKER: He was just sitting there. He ain't said nothing. I went on out the door and left him sitting there. I figure as long as he was on the other side of the room everything be alright. I don't know what I would have done if he had started walking toward me.

WINING BOY: Berniece say he was calling Boy Willie's name.

DOAKER: I ain't heard him say nothing. He was just sitting there when I seen him. But I don't believe Boy Willie pushed him in the well. Sutter here cause of that piano. I heard him playing on it one time. I thought it was Berniece but then she don't play that kind of music. I come out here and ain't seen nobody, but them piano keys was moving a mile a minute. Berniece need to go on and get rid of it. It ain't done nothing but cause trouble.

WINING BOY: I agree with Berniece. Boy Charles ain't took it to give it back. He took it cause he figure he had more right to it than Sutter did. If Sutter can't understand that . . . then that's just the way that go. Sutter dead and in the ground . . . don't care where his ghost is. He can hover around and play on the piano all he want. I want to see him carry it out the house. That's what I want to see. What time Berniece get home? I don't see how I let her get away from me this morning.

DOAKER: You up there sleep. Berniece leave out of here early in the morning. She out there in Squirrel Hill cleaning house for some bigshot down there at the steel mill. They don't like you to come late. You come late they won't give you your carfare. What kind of business you got with Berniece?

WINING BOY: My business. I ain't asked you what kind of business you got.

DOAKER: Berniece ain't got no money. If that's why you was trying to catch her. She having a hard enough time trying to get by as it is. If she go ahead and marry Avery . . . he working every day . . . she go ahead and marry him they could do alright for themselves. But as it stands she ain't got no money.

WINING BOY: Well, let me have five dollars.

DOAKER: I just give you a dollar before you left out of here. You ain't gonna take my five dollars out there and gamble and drink it up.

WINING BOY: Aw, nigger, give me five dollars. I'll give it back to you.

DOAKER: You wasn't looking to give me five dollars when you had that sack of money. You wasn't looking to throw nothing my way. Now you wanna come in here and borrow five dollars. If you going back with Boy Willie you need to be trying to figure out how you gonna get train fare.

WINING BOY: That's why I need the five dollars. If I had five dollars I could get me some money.

[DOAKER goes into his pocket.]

Make it seven.

DOAKER: You take this five dollars . . . and you bring my money back here too.

[BOY WILLIE and LYMON enter. They are happy and excited. They have money in all of their pockets and are anxious to count it.]

DOAKER: How'd you do out there?

BOY WILLIE: They was lining up for them.

LYMON: Me and Boy Willie couldn't sell them fast enough. Time we got one sold we'd sell another.

BOY WILLIE: I seen what was happening and told Lymon to up the price on them.

LYMON: Boy Willie say charge them a quarter more. They didn't care. A couple of people give me a dollar and told me to keep the change.

BOY WILLIE: One fellow bought five. I say now what he gonna do with five watermelons? He can't eat them all. I sold him the five and asked him did he want to buy five more.

LYMON: I ain't never seen nobody snatch a dollar fast as Boy Willie.

BOY WILLIE: One lady asked me say, "Is they sweet?" I told her say, "Lady, where we grow these watermelons we put sugar in the ground." You know, she believed me. Talking about she had never heard of that before. Lymon was laughing his head off. I told her, "Oh, yeah, we put the sugar right in the ground with the seed." She say, "Well, give me another one." Them white folks is something else . . . ain't they, Lymon?

LYMON: Soon as you holler watermelons they come right out their door. Then they go and get their neighbors. Look like they having a contest to see who can buy the most.

WINING BOY: I got something for Lymon.

[WINING BOY goes to get his suit. BOY WILLIE and LYMON continue to count their money.]

BOY WILLIE: I know you got more than that. You ain't sold all them watermelons for that little bit of money.

LYMON: I'm still looking. That ain't all you got either. Where's all them quarters?

BOY WILLIE: You let me worry about the quarters. Just put the money on the table.

WINING BOY *(Entering with his suit.):* Look here, Lymon . . . see this? Look at his eyes getting big. He ain't never seen a suit like this. This is one hundred percent silk. Go ahead . . . put it on. See if it fit you.

[LYMON tries the suit coat on.]

Look at that. Feel it. That's one hundred percent genuine silk. I got that in Chicago. You can't get clothes like that nowhere but New York and Chicago. You can't get clothes like that in Pittsburgh. These folks in Pittsburgh ain't never seen clothes like that.

LYMON: This is nice, feel real nice and smooth.

WINING BOY: That's a fifty-five-dollar suit. That's the kind of suit the bigshots wear. You need a pistol and a pocketful of money to wear that suit. I'll let you have it for three dollars. The women will fall out their windows they see you in a suit like that. Give me three dollars and go on and wear it down the street and get you a woman.

BOY WILLIE: That looks nice, Lymon. Put the pants on. Let me see it with the pants.

[LYMON begins to try on the pants.]

WINING BOY: Look at that . . . see how it fits you? Give me three dollars and go on and take it. Look at that, Doaker . . . don't he look nice?

DOAKER: Yeah . . . that's a nice suit.

WINING BOY: Got a shirt to go with it. Cost you an extra dollar. Four dollars you got the whole deal.

LYMON: How this look, Boy Willie?

BOY WILLIE: That look nice . . . if you like that kind of thing. I don't like them dress-up kind of clothes. If you like it, look real nice.

WINING BOY: That's the kind of suit you need for up here in the North.

LYMON: Four dollars for everything? The suit and the shirt?

WINING BOY: That's cheap. I should be charging you twenty dollars. I give you a break cause you a homeboy. That's the only way I let you have it for four dollars.

LYMON *(Going into his pocket.):* Okay . . . here go the four dollars.

WINING BOY: You got some shoes? What size you wear?

LYMON: Size nine.

WINING BOY: That's what size I got! Size nine. I let you have them for three dollars.

LYMON: Where they at? Let me see them.

WINING BOY: They real nice shoes, too. Got a nice tip to them. Got pointy toe just like you want.

[WINING BOY goes to get his shoes.]

LYMON: Come on, Boy Willie, let's go out tonight. I wanna see what it looks like up here. Maybe we go to a picture show. Hey, Doaker, they got picture shows up here?

DOAKER: The Rhumba Theater. Right down there on Fullerton Street. Can't miss it. Got the speakers outside on the sidewalk. You can hear it a

block away. Boy Willie know where it's at.

[DOAKER exits into his room.]

LYMON: Let's go to the picture show, Boy Willie. Let's go find some women.

BOY WILLIE: Hey, Lymon, how many of them watermelons would you say we got left? We got just under a half a load . . . right?

LYMON: About that much. Maybe a little more.

BOY WILLIE: You think that piano will fit up in there?

LYMON: If we stack them watermelons you can sit it up in the front there.

BOY WILLIE: I'm gonna call that man tomorrow.

WINING BOY *(Returns with his shoes.):* Here you go . . . size nine. Put them on. Cost you three dollars. That's a Florsheim shoe. That's the kind Staggerlee wore.

LYMON *(Trying on the shoes.):* You sure these size nine?

WINING BOY: You can look at my feet and see we wear the same size. Man, you put on that suit and them shoes and you got something there. You ready for whatever's out there. But is they ready for you? With them shoes on you be the King of the Walk. Have everybody stop to look at your shoes. Wishing they had a pair. I'll give you a break. Go on and take them for two dollars.

[LYMON pays WINING BOY two dollars.]

LYMON: Come on, Boy Willie . . . let's go find some women. I'm gonna go upstairs and get ready. I'll be ready to go in a minute. Ain't you gonna get dressed?

BOY WILLIE: I'm gonna wear what I got on. I ain't dressing up for these city niggers.

[LYMON exits up the stairs.]

That's all Lymon think about is women.

WINING BOY: His daddy was the same way. I used to run around with him. I know his mama too. Two strokes back and I would have been his daddy! His daddy's dead now . . . but I got the nigger out of jail one time. They was fixing to name him Daniel and walk him through the Lion's Den. He got in a tussle with one of them white fellows and the sheriff lit on him like white on rice. That's how the whole thing come about between me and Lymon's mama. She knew me and his daddy used to run together and he got in jail and she went down there and took the sheriff a hundred dollars. Don't get me to lying about where she got it from. I don't know. The sheriff looked at that hundred dollars and turned his nose up. Told her, say, "That ain't gonna do him no good.

You got to put another hundred on top of that." She come up there and got me where I was playing at this saloon . . . said she had all but fifty dollars and asked me if I could help. Now the way I figured it . . . without that fifty dollars the sheriff was gonna turn him over to Parchman. The sheriff turn him over to Parchman it be three years before anybody see him again. Now I'm gonna say it right . . . I will give anybody fifty dollars to keep them out of jail for three years. I give her the fifty dollars and she told me to come over to the house. I ain't asked her. I figure if she was nice enough to invite me I ought to go. I ain't had to say a word. She invited me over just as nice. Say, "Why don't you come over to the house?" She ain't had to say nothing else. Them words rolled off her tongue just as nice. I went on down there and sat about three hours. Started to leave and changed my mind. She grabbed hold to me and say, "Baby, it's all night long." That was one of the shortest nights I have ever spent on this earth! I could have used another eight hours. Lymon's daddy didn't even say nothing to me when he got out. He just looked at me funny. He had a good notion something had happened between me an' her. L. D. Jackson. That was one bad-luck nigger. Got killed at some dance. Fellow walked in and shot him thinking he was somebody else.

[DOAKER enters from his room.]

Hey, Doaker, you remember L. D. Jackson?
DOAKER: That's Lymon's daddy. That was one bad-luck nigger.
BOY WILLIE: Look like you ready to railroad some.
DOAKER: Yeah, I got to make that run.

[LYMON enters from the stairs. He is dressed in his new suit and shoes, to which he has added a cheap straw hat.]

LYMON: How I look?
WINING BOY: You look like a million dollars. Don't he look good, Doaker? Come on, let's play some cards. You wanna play some cards?
BOY WILLIE: We ain't gonna play no cards with you. Me and Lymon gonna find some women. Hey, Lymon, don't play no cards with Wining Boy. He'll take all your money.
WINING BOY *(To LYMON.)*: You got a magic suit there. You can get you a woman easy with that suit . . . but you got to know the magic words. You know the magic words to get you a woman?
LYMON: I just talk to them to see if I like them and they like me.

WINING BOY: You just walk right up to them and say, "If you got the harbor I got the ship." If that don't work ask them if you can put them in your pocket. The first thing they gonna say is, "It's too small." That's when you look them dead in the eye and say, "Baby, ain't nothing small about me." If that don't work then you move on to another one. Am I telling him right, Doaker?
DOAKER: That man don't need you to tell him nothing about no women. These women these days ain't gonna fall for that kind of stuff. You got to buy them a present. That's what they looking for these days.
BOY WILLIE: Come on, I'm ready. You ready, Lymon? Come on, let's go find some women.
WINING BOY: Here, let me walk out with you. I wanna see the women fall out their window when they see Lymon.

[They all exit and the lights go down on the scene.]

Scene 2

[The lights come up on the kitchen. It is late evening of the same day. BERNIECE has set a tub for her bath in the kitchen. She is heating up water on the stove. There is a knock at the door.]

BERNIECE: Who is it?
AVERY: It's me, Avery.

[BERNIECE opens the door and lets him in.]

BERNIECE: Avery, come on in. I was just fixing to take my bath.
AVERY: Where Boy Willie? I see that truck out there almost empty. They done sold almost all them watermelons.
BERNIECE: They was gone when I come home. I don't know where they went off to. Boy Willie around here about to drive me crazy.
AVERY: They sell them watermelons . . . he'll be gone soon.
BERNIECE: What Mr. Cohen say about letting you have the place?
AVERY: He say he'll let me have it for thirty dollars a month. I talked him out of thirty-five and he say he'll let me have it for thirty.
BERNIECE: That's a nice spot next to Benny Diamond's store.
AVERY: Berniece . . . I be at home and I get to thinking you up here an' I'm down there. I get to thinking how that look to have a preacher that ain't married. It makes for a better congregation if the preacher was settled down and mar-

ried.

BERNIECE: Avery . . . not now. I was fixing to take my bath.

AVERY: You know how I feel about you, Berniece. Now . . . I done got the place from Mr. Cohen. I get the money from the bank and I can fix it up real nice. They give me a ten cents a hour raise down there on the job . . . now Berniece, I ain't got much in the way of comforts. I got a hole in my pockets near about as far as money is concerned. I ain't never found no way through life to a woman I care about like I care about you. I need that. I need somebody on my bond side. I need a woman that fits in my hand.

BERNIECE: Avery, I ain't ready to get married now.

AVERY: You too young a woman to close up, Berniece.

BERNIECE: I ain't said nothing about closing up. I got a lot of woman left in me.

AVERY: Where's it at? When's the last time you looked at it?

BERNIECE (*Stunned by his remark.*): That's a nasty thing to say. And you call yourself a preacher.

AVERY: Anytime I get anywhere near you . . . you push me away.

BERNIECE: I got enough on my hands with Maretha. I got enough people to love and take care of.

AVERY: Who you got to love you? Can't nobody get close enough to you. Doaker can't half say nothing to you. You jump all over Boy Willie. Who you got to love you, Berniece?

BERNIECE: You trying to tell me a woman can't be nothing without a man. But you alright, huh? You can just walk out of here without me—without a woman—and still be a man. That's alright. Ain't nobody gonna ask you, "Avery, who you got to love you?" That's alright for you. But everybody gonna be worried about Berniece. "How Berniece gonna take care of herself? How she gonna raise that child without a man? Wonder what she do with herself. How she gonna live like that?" Everybody got all kinds of questions for Berniece. Everybody telling me I can't be a woman unless I got a man. Well, you tell me, Avery—you know—how much woman am I?

AVERY: It wasn't me, Berniece. You can't blame me for nobody else. I'll own up to my own shortcomings. But you can't blame me for Crawley or nobody else.

BERNIECE: I ain't blaming nobody for nothing. I'm just stating the facts.

AVERY: How long you gonna carry Crawley with you, Berniece? It's been over three years. At some point you got to let go and go on. Life's got all kinds of twists and turns. That don't

mean you stop living. That don't mean you cut yourself off from life. You can't go through life carrying Crawley's ghost with you. Crawley's been dead three years. Three years, Berniece.

BERNIECE: I know how long Crawley's been dead. You ain't got to tell me that. I just ain't ready to get married right now.

AVERY: What is you ready for, Berniece? You just gonna drift along from day to day. Life is more than making it from one day to another. You gonna look up one day and it's all gonna be past you. Life's gonna be gone out of your hands—there won't be enough to make nothing with. I'm standing here now, Berniece—but I don't know how much longer I'm gonna be standing here waiting on you.

BERNIECE: Avery, I told you . . . when you get your church we'll sit down and talk about this. I got too many other things to deal with right now. Boy Willie and the piano . . . and Sutter's ghost. I thought I might have been seeing things, but Maretha done seen Sutter's ghost, too.

AVERY: When this happen, Berniece?

BERNIECE: Right after I came home yesterday. Me and Boy Willie was arguing about the piano and Sutter's ghost was standing at the top of the stairs. Maretha scared to sleep up there now. Maybe if you bless the house he'll go away.

AVERY: I don't know, Berniece. I don't know if I should fool around with something like that.

BERNIECE: I can't have Maretha scared to go to sleep up there. Seem like if you bless the house he would go away.

AVERY: You might have to be a special kind of preacher to do something like that.

BERNIECE: I keep telling myself when Boy Willie leave he'll go on and leave with him. I believe Boy Willie pushed him in the well.

AVERY: That's been going on down there a long time. The Ghosts of the Yellow Dog been pushing people in their wells long before Boy Willie got grown.

BERNIECE: Somebody down there pushing them people in their wells. They ain't just upped and fell. Ain't no wind pushed nobody in their well.

AVERY: Oh, I don't know. God works in mysterious ways.

BERNIECE: He ain't pushed nobody in their wells.

AVERY: He caused it to happen. God is the Great Causer. He can do anything. He parted the Red Sea. He say I will smite my enemies. Reverend Thompson used to preach on the Ghosts of the Yellow Dog as the hand of God.

BERNIECE: I don't care who preached what. Somebody down there pushing them people in their wells. Somebody like Boy Willie. I can see him doing something like that. You ain't gonna tell me that Sutter just upped and fell in his well. I believe Boy Willie pushed him so he could get his land.

AVERY: What Doaker say about Boy Willie selling the piano?

BERNIECE: Doaker don't want no part of that piano. He ain't never wanted no part of it. He blames himself for not staying behind with Papa Boy Charles. He washed his hands of that piano a long time ago. He didn't want me to bring it up here—but I wasn't gonna leave it down there.

AVERY: Well, it seems to me somebody ought to be able to talk to Boy Willie.

BERNIECE: You can't talk to Boy Willie. He been that way all his life. Mama Ola had her hands full trying to talk to him. He don't listen to nobody. He just like my daddy. He get his mind fixed on something and can't nobody turn him from it.

AVERY: You ought to start a choir at the church. Maybe if he seen you was doing something with it—if you told him you was gonna put it in my church—maybe he'd see it different. You ought to put it down in the church and start a choir. The Bible say "Make a joyful noise unto the Lord." Maybe if Boy Willie see you was doing something with it he'd see it different.

BERNIECE: I done told you I don't play on that piano. Ain't no need in you to keep talking this choir stuff. When my mama died I shut the top on that piano and I ain't never opened it since. I was only playing it for her. When my daddy died seem like all her life went into that piano. She used to have me playing on it . . . had Miss Eula come in and teach me . . . say when I played it she could hear my daddy talking to her. I used to think them pictures came alive and walked through the house. Sometime late at night I could hear my mama talking to them. I said that wasn't gonna happen to me. I don't play that piano cause I don't want to wake them spirits. They never be walking around in this house.

AVERY: You got to put all that behind you, Berniece.

BERNIECE: I got Maretha playing on it. She don't know nothing about it. Let her go on and be a schoolteacher or something. She don't have to carry all of that with her. She got a chance I didn't have. I ain't gonna burden her with that piano.

AVERY: You got to put all of that behind you, Berniece. That's the same thing like Crawley. Everybody got stones in their passway. You got to step over them or walk around them.

You picking them up and carrying them with you. All you got to do is set them down by the side of the road. You ain't got to carry them with you. You can walk over there right now and play that piano. You can walk over there right now and God will walk over there with you. Right now you can set that sack of stones down by the side of the road and walk away from it. You don't have to carry it with you. You can do it right now.

[AVERY crosses over to the piano and raises the lid.]

Come on, Berniece . . . set it down and walk away from it. Come on, play "Old Ship of Zion." Walk over here and claim it as an instrument of the Lord. You can walk over here right now and make it into a celebration.

[BERNIECE moves toward the piano.]

BERNIECE: Avery . . . I done told you I don't want to play that piano. Now or no other time.

AVERY: The Bible say, "The Lord is my refuge . . . and my strength!" With the strength of God you can put the past behind you, Berniece. With the strength of God you can do anything! God got a bright tomorrow. God don't ask what you done . . . God ask what you gonna do. The strength of God can move mountains! God's got a bright tomorrow for you . . . all you got to do is walk over here and claim it.

BERNIECE: Avery, just go on and let me finish my bath. I'll see you tomorrow.

AVERY: Okay, Berniece. I'm gonna go home. I'm gonna go home and read up on my Bible. And tomorrow . . . if the good Lord give me strength tomorrow . . . I'm gonna come by and bless the house . . . and show you the power of the Lord.

[AVERY crosses to the door.]

It's gonna be alright, Berniece. God say he will soothe the troubled waters. I'll come by tomorrow and bless the house.

[The lights go down to black.]

Scene 3

[Several hours later. The house is dark. BERNIECE has retired for the night. BOY WILLIE enters the darkened house with GRACE.]

BOY WILLIE: Come on in. This my sister's house. My sister live here. Come on, I ain't gonna bite you.

GRACE: Put some light on. I can't see.

BOY WILLIE: You don't need to see nothing, baby. This here is all you need to see. All you need to do is see me. If you can't see me you can feel me in the dark. How's that, sugar?

[He attempts to kiss her.]

GRACE: Go on now . . . wait!

BOY WILLIE: Just give me one little old kiss.

GRACE (*Pushing him away.*): Come on, now. Where I'm gonna sleep at?

BOY WILLIE: We got to sleep out here on the couch. Come on, my sister don't mind. Lymon come back he just got to sleep on the floor. He run off with Dolly somewhere he better stay there. Come on, sugar.

GRACE: Wait now . . . you ain't told me nothing about no couch. I thought you had a bed. Both of us can't sleep on that little old couch.

BOY WILLIE: It don't make no difference. We can sleep on the floor. Let Lymon sleep on the couch.

GRACE: You ain't told me nothing about no couch.

BOY WILLIE: What difference it make? You just wanna be with me.

GRACE: I don't want to be with you on no couch. Ain't you got no bed?

BOY WILLIE: You don't need no bed, woman. My granddaddy used to take women on the backs of horses. What you need a bed for? You just want to be with me.

GRACE: You sure is country. I didn't know you was this country.

BOY WILLIE: There's a lot of things you don't know about me. Come on, let me show you what this country boy can do.

GRACE: Let's go to my place. I got a room with a bed if Leroy don't come back there.

BOY WILLIE: Who's Leroy? You ain't said nothing about no Leroy.

GRACE: He used to be my man. He ain't coming back. He gone off with some other gal.

BOY WILLIE: You let him have your key?

GRACE: He ain't coming back.

BOY WILLIE: Did you let him have your key?

GRACE: He got a key but he ain't coming back. He took off with some other gal.

BOY WILLIE: I don't wanna go nowhere he might come. Let's stay here. Come on, sugar.

[He pulls her over to the couch.]

Let me heist your hood and check your oil. See if your battery needs charged.

[He pulls her to him. They kiss and tug at each other's

clothing. In their anxiety they knock over a lamp.]*

BERNIECE: Who's that . . . Wining Boy?

BOY WILLIE: It's me . . . Boy Willie. Go on back to sleep. Everything's alright.

[To GRACE.]

That's my sister. Everything's alright, Berniece. Go on back to sleep.

BERNIECE: What you doing down there? What you done knocked over?

BOY WILLIE: It wasn't nothing. Everything's alright. Go on back to sleep.

[To GRACE.]

That's my sister. We alright. She gone back to sleep.

[They begin to kiss. BERNIECE enters from the stairs dressed in a nightgown. She cuts on the light.]

BERNIECE: Boy Willie, what you doing down here?

BOY WILLIE: It was just that there lamp. It ain't broke. It's okay. Everything's alright. Go on back to bed.

BERNIECE: Boy Willie, I don't allow that in my house. You gonna have to take your company some-place else.

BOY WILLIE: It's alright. We ain't doing nothing. We just sitting here talking. This here is Grace. That's my sister Berniece.

BERNIECE: You know I don't allow that kind of stuff in my house.

BOY WILLIE: Allow what? We just sitting here talking.

BERNIECE: Well, your company gonna have to leave. Come back and talk in the morning.

BOY WILLIE: Go on back upstairs now.

BERNIECE: I got an eleven-year-old girl upstairs. I can't allow that around here.

BOY WILLIE: Ain't nobody said nothing about that. I told you we just talking.

GRACE: Come on . . . let's go to my place. Ain't nobody got to tell me to leave but once.

BOY WILLIE: You ain't got to be like that, Berniece.

BERNIECE: I'm sorry, Miss. But he know I don't allow that in here.

GRACE: You ain't got to tell me but once. I don't stay nowhere I ain't wanted.

BOY WILLIE: I don't know why you want to embarrass me in front of my company.

GRACE: Come on, take me home.

BERNIECE: Go on, Boy Willie. Just go on with your company.

[BOY WILLIE and GRACE exit. BERNIECE puts the light on in the kitchen and puts on the teakettle. Presently

there is a knock at the door. BERNIECE *goes to answer it.* BERNIECE *opens the door.* LYMON *enters.*]

LYMON: How you doing, Berniece? I thought you'd be asleep. Boy Willie been back here?

BERNIECE: He just left out of here a minute ago.

LYMON: I went out to see a picture show and never got there. We always end up doing something else. I was with this woman she just wanted to drink up all my money. So I left her there and came back looking for Boy Willie.

BERNIECE: You just missed him. He just left out of here.

LYMON: They got some nice-looking women in this city. I'm gonna like it up here real good. I like seeing them with their dresses on. Got them high heels. I like that. Make them look like they real precious. Boy Willie met a real nice one today. I wish I had met her before he did.

BERNIECE: He come by here with some woman a little while ago. I told him to go on and take all that out of my house.

LYMON: What she look like, the woman he was with? Was she a brown-skinned woman about this high? Nice and healthy? Got nice hips on her?

BERNIECE: She had on a red dress.

LYMON: That's her! That's Grace. She real nice. Laugh a lot. Lot of fun to be with. She don't be trying to put on. Some of these woman act like they the Queen of Sheba. I don't like them kind. Grace ain't like that. She real nice with herself.

BERNIECE: I don't know what she was like. He come in here all drunk knocking over the lamp, and making all kind of noise. I told them to take that somewhere else. I can't really say what she was like.

LYMON: She real nice. I seen her before he did. I was trying not to act like I seen her. I wanted to look at her a while before I said something. She seen me when I come into the saloon. I tried to act like I didn't see her. Time I looked around Boy Willie was talking to her. She was talking to him kept looking at me. That's when her friend Dolly came. I asked her if she wanted to go to the picture show. She told me to buy her a drink while she thought about it. Next thing I knew she done had three drinks talking about she too tired to go. I bought her another drink, then I left. Boy Willie was gone and I thought he might have come back here. Doaker gone, huh? He say he had to make a trip.

BERNIECE: Yeah, he gone on his trip. This is when I can usually get me some peace and quiet, Maretha asleep.

LYMON: She look just like you. Got them big eyes. I remember her when she was in diapers.

BERNIECE: Time just keep on. It go on with or without you. She going on twelve.

LYMON: She sure is pretty. I like kids.

BERNIECE: Boy Willie say you staying . . . what you gonna do up here in this big city? You thought about that?

LYMON: They never get me back down there. The sheriff looking for me. All because they gonna try and make me work for somebody when I don't want to. They gonna try and make me work for Stovall when he don't pay nothing. It ain't like that up here. Up here you more or less do what you want to. I figure I find me a job and try to get set up and then see what the year brings. I tried to do that two or three times down there . . . but it never would work out. I was always in the wrong place.

BERNIECE: This ain't a bad city once you get to know your way around.

LYMON: Up here is different. I'm gonna get me a job unloading boxcars or something. One fellow told me say he know a place. I'm gonna go over there with him next week. Me and Boy Willie finish selling them watermelons I'll have enough money to hold me for a while. But I'm gonna go over there and see what kind of jobs they have.

BERNIECE: You shouldn't have too much trouble finding a job. It's all in how you present yourself. See now, Boy Willie couldn't get no job up here. Somebody hire him they got a pack of trouble on their hands. Soon as they find that out they fire him. He don't want to do nothing unless he do it his way.

LYMON: I know. I told him let's go to the picture show first and see if there was any women down there. They might get tired of sitting at home and walk down to the picture show. He say he wanna look around first. We never did get down there. We tried a couple of places and then we went to this saloon where he met Grace. I tried to meet her before he did but he beat me to her. We left Wining Boy sitting down there running his mouth. He told me if I wear this suit I'd find me a woman. He was almost right.

BERNIECE: You don't need to be out there in them saloons. Ain't no telling what you liable to run into out there. This one liable to cut you as quick as that one shoot you. You don't need to be out there. You start out that fast life you can't keep it up. It makes you old quick. I don't know what them women out there be thinking about.

LYMON: Mostly they be lonely and looking for somebody to spend the night with them. Sometimes it matters who it is and sometimes it don't. I used to be the same way. Now it got to matter. That's why I'm here now. Dolly liable not to even recognize me if she sees me again. I don't like women like that. I like my women to be with me in a nice and easy way. That way we can both enjoy ourselves. The way I see it we the only two people like us in the world. We got to see how we fit together. A woman that don't want to take the time to do that I don't bother with. Used to. Used to bother with all of them. Then I woke up one time with this woman and I didn't know who she was. She was the prettiest woman I had ever seen in my life. I spent the whole night with her and didn't even know it. I had never taken the time to look at her. I guess she kinda knew I ain't never really looked at her. She must have known that cause she ain't wanted to see me no more. If she had wanted to see me I believe we might have got married. How come you ain't married? It seem like to me you would be married. I remember Avery from down home. I used to call him plain old Avery. Now he Reverend Avery. That's kinda funny about him becoming a preacher. I like when he told about how that come to him in a dream about them sheep people and them hobos. Nothing ever come to me in a dream like that. I just dream about women. Can't never seem to find the right one.

BERNIECE: She out there somewhere. You just got to get yourself ready to meet her. That's what I'm trying to do. Avery's alright. I ain't really got nobody in mind.

LYMON: I get me a job and a little place and get set up to where I can make a woman comfortable I might get married. Avery's nice. You ought to go ahead and get married. You be a preacher's wife you won't have to work. I hate living by myself. I didn't want to be no strain on my mama so I left home when I was about sixteen. Everything I tried seem like it just didn't work out. Now I'm trying this.

BERNIECE: You keep trying it'll work out for you.

LYMON: You ever go down there to the picture show?

BERNIECE: I don't go in for all that.

LYMON: Ain't nothing wrong with it. It ain't like gambling and sinning. I went to one down in Jackson once. It was fun.

BERNIECE: I just stay home most of the time. Take care of Maretha.

LYMON: It's getting kind of late. I don't know where Boy Willie went off to. He's liable not to come back. I'm gonna take off these shoes. My feet hurt. Was you in bed? I don't mean to be keeping you up.

BERNIECE: You ain't keeping me up. I couldn't sleep after that Boy Willie woke me up.

LYMON: You got on that nightgown. I likes women when they wear them fancy nightclothes and all. It makes their skin look real pretty.

BERNIECE: I got this at the five-and-ten-cents store. It ain't so fancy.

LYMON: I don't too often get to see a woman dressed like that.

[There is a long pause. LYMON takes off his suit coat.]

Well, I'm gonna sleep here on the couch. I'm supposed to sleep on the floor but I don't reckon Boy Willie's coming back tonight. Wining Boy sold me this suit. Told me it was a magic suit. I'm gonna put it on again tomorrow. Maybe it bring me a woman like he say.

[He goes into his coat pocket and takes out a small bottle of perfume.]

I almost forgot I had this. Some man sold me this for a dollar. Say it come from Paris. This is the same kind of perfume the Queen of France wear. That's what he told me. I don't know if it's true or not. I smelled it. It smelled good to me. Here . . . smell it see if you like it. I was gonna give it to Dolly. But I didn't like her too much.

BERNIECE (Takes the bottle.): It smells nice.

LYMON: I was gonna give it to Dolly if she had went to the picture with me. Go on, you take it.

BERNIECE: I can't take it. Here . . . go on you keep it. You'll find somebody to give it to.

LYMON: I wanna give it to you. Make you smell nice.

[He takes the bottle and puts perfume behind BERNIECE's ear.]

They tell me you supposed to put it right here behind your ear. Say if you put it there you smell nice all day.

[BERNIECE stiffens at his touch. LYMON bends down to smell her.]

There . . . you smell real good now.

[He kisses her neck.]

You smell real good for Lymon.

[He kisses her again. BERNIECE returns the kiss, then breaks the embrace and crosses to the stairs. She turns and they look silently at each other. LYMON hands her the bottle of perfume. BERNIECE exits up the stairs. LYMON picks up his suit coat and strokes it lovingly, with the full knowledge that it is indeed a magic suit. The lights go down on the scene.]

Scene 4

[It is late the next morning. The lights come up on the parlor. LYMON is asleep on the sofa. BOY WILLIE enters the front door.]

BOY WILLIE: Hey, Lymon! Lymon, come on get up.

LYMON: Leave me alone.

BOY WILLIE: Come on, get up, nigger! Wake up, Lymon.

LYMON: What you want?

BOY WILLIE: Come on, let's go. I done called the man about the piano.

LYMON: What piano?

BOY WILLIE (*Dumps LYMON on the floor.*): Come on, get up!

LYMON: Why you leave, I looked around and you was gone.

BOY WILLIE: I come back here with Grace, then I went looking for you. I figured you'd be with Dolly.

LYMON: She just want to drink and spend up your money. I come on back here looking for you to see if you wanted to go to the picture show.

BOY WILLIE: I been up at Grace's house. Some nigger named Leroy come by but I had a chair up against the door. He got mad when he couldn't get in. He went off somewhere and I got out of there before he could come back. Berniece got mad when we came here.

LYMON: She say you was knocking over the lamp busting up the place.

BOY WILLIE: That was Grace doing all that.

LYMON: Wining Boy seen Sutter's ghost last night.

BOY WILLIE: Wining Boy's liable to see anything. I'm surprised he found the right house. Come on, I done called the man about the piano.

LYMON: What he say?

BOY WILLIE: He say to bring it on out. I told him I was calling for my sister, Miss Berniece Charles. I told him some man wanted to buy it for eleven hundred dollars and asked him if he would go any better. He said yeah, he would give me eleven hundred and fifty dollars for it if it was the same piano. I described it to him and he told me to bring it out.

LYMON: Why didn't you tell him to come and pick it up?

BOY WILLIE: I didn't want to have no problem with Berniece. This way we just take it on out there and it be out the way. He want to charge twenty-five dollars to pick it up.

LYMON: You should have told him the man was gonna give you twelve hundred for it.

BOY WILLIE: I figure I was taking a chance with that eleven hundred. If I had told him twelve hundred he might have run off. Now I wish I had told him twelve-fifty. It's hard to figure out white folks sometimes.

LYMON: You might have been able to tell him anything. White folks got a lot of money.

BOY WILLIE: Come on, let's get it loaded before Berniece come back. Get that end over there. All you got to do is pick it up on that side. Don't worry about this side. You wanna stretch you' back for a minute?

LYMON: I'm ready.

BOY WILLIE: Get a real good grip on it now.

[The sound of SUTTER'S GHOST is heard. They do not hear it.]

LYMON: I got this end. You get that end.

BOY WILLIE: Wait till I say ready now. Alright. You got it good? You got a grip on it?

LYMON: Yeah, I got it. You lift up on that end.

BOY WILLIE: Ready? Lift!

[The piano will not budge.]

LYMON: Man, this piano is heavy! It's gonna take more than me and you to move this piano.

BOY WILLIE: We can do it. Come on—we did it before.

LYMON: Nigger—you crazy! That piano weighs five hundred pounds!

BOY WILLIE: I got three hundred pounds of it! I know you can carry two hundred pounds! You be lifting them cotton sacks! Come on lift this piano!

[They try to move the piano again without success.]

LYMON: It's stuck. Something holding it.

BOY WILLIE: How the piano gonna be stuck? We just moved it. Slide you' end out.

LYMON: Naw—we gonna need two or three more people. How this big old piano get in the house?

BOY WILLIE: I don't know how it got in the house. I know how it's going out though! You get on this end. I'll carry three hundred and fifty pounds of it. All you got to do is slide your end out. Ready?

[They switch sides and try again without success. DOAKER enters from his room as they try to push and shove it.]

LYMON: Hey, Doaker . . . how this piano get in the house?

DOAKER: Boy Willie, what you doing?

BOY WILLIE: I'm carrying this piano out the house. What it look like I'm doing? Come on, Lymon, let's try again.

DOAKER: Go on let the piano sit there till Berniece come home.

BOY WILLIE: You ain't got nothing to do with this, Doaker. This my business.

DOAKER: This is my house, nigger! I ain't gonna let you or nobody else carry nothing out of it. You ain't gonna carry nothing out of here without my permission!

BOY WILLIE: This is my piano. I don't need your permission to carry my belongings out of your house. This is mine. This ain't got nothing to do with you.

DOAKER: I say leave it over there till Berniece come home. She got part of it too. Leave it set there till you see what she say.

BOY WILLIE: I don't care what Berniece say. Come on, Lymon. I got this side.

DOAKER: Go on and cut it half in two if you want to. Just leave Berniece's half sitting over there. I can't tell you what to do with your piano. But I can't let you take her half out of here.

BOY WILLIE: Go on, Doaker. You ain't got nothing to do with this. I don't want you starting nothing now. Just go on and leave me alone. Come on, Lymon. I got this end.

[DOAKER goes into his room. BOY WILLIE and LYMON prepare to move the piano.]

LYMON: How we gonna get it in the truck?

BOY WILLIE: Don't worry about how we gonna get it on the truck. You got to get it out the house first.

LYMON: It's gonna take more than me and you to move this piano.

BOY WILLIE: Just lift up on that end, nigger!

[DOAKER comes to the doorway of his room and stands.]

DOAKER (*Quietly with authority.*): Leave that piano set over there till Berniece come back. I don't care what you do with it then. But you gonna leave it sit over there right now.

BOY WILLIE: Alright . . . I'm gonna tell you this, Doaker. I'm going out of here . . . I'm gonna get me some rope . . . find me a plank and some wheels . . . and I'm coming back. Then I'm gonna carry that piano out of here . . . sell it and give Berniece half the money. See . . . now that's what I'm gonna do. And you . . . or nobody else is gonna stop me. Come on, Lymon . . . let's go get some rope and stuff. I'll be back, Doaker.

[BOY WILLIE and LYMON exit. The lights go down on the scene.]

Scene 5

[The lights come up. BOY WILLIE sits on the sofa, screwing casters on a wooden plank. MARETHA is sitting on the piano stool. DOAKER sits at the table playing solitaire.]

BOY WILLIE (*To MARETHA.*): Then after that them white folks down around there started falling down their wells. You ever seen a well? A well got a wall around it. It's hard to fall down a well. You got to be leaning way over. Couldn't nobody figure out too much what was making these fellows fall down their well . . . so everybody says the Ghosts of the Yellow Dog must have pushed them. That's what everybody called them four men what got burned up in the boxcar.

MARETHA: Why they call them that?

BOY WILLIE: Cause the Yazoo Delta railroad got yellow boxcars. Sometime the way the whistle blow sound like an old dog howling so the people call it the Yellow Dog.

MARETHA: Anybody ever see the Ghosts?

BOY WILLIE: I told you they like the wind. Can you see the wind?

MARETHA: No.

BOY WILLIE: They like the wind you can't see them. But sometimes you be in trouble they might be around to help you. They say if you go where the Southern cross the Yellow Dog . . . you go to where them two railroads cross each other . . . and call out their names . . . they say they talk back to you. I don't know, I ain't never done that. But Uncle Wining Boy he say he been down there and talked to them. You have to ask him about that part.

[BERNIECE has entered from the front door.]

BERNIECE: Maretha, you go on and get ready for me to do your hair.

[MARETHA crosses to the steps.]

     Boy Willie, I done told you to leave my house.

[To MARETHA.]

     Go on, Maretha.

[MARETHA is hesitant about going up the stairs.]

BOY WILLIE: Don't be scared. Here, I'll go up there with you. If we see Sutter's ghost I'll put a whupping on him. Come on, Uncle Boy Willie going with you.

[BOY WILLIE and MARETHA exit up the stairs.]

BERNIECE: Doaker—what is going on here?

DOAKER: I come home and him and Lymon was moving the piano. I told them to leave it over there till you got home. He went out and got that board and them wheels. He say he gonna take that piano out of here and ain't nobody gonna stop him.

BERNIECE: I ain't playing with Boy Willie. I got Crawley's gun upstairs. He don't know but I'm through with it. Where Lymon go?

DOAKER: Boy Willie sent him for some rope just before you come in.

BERNIECE: I ain't studying Boy Willie or Lymon—or the rope. Boy Willie ain't taking that piano out this house. That's all there is to it.

[BOY WILLIE and MARETHA enter on the stairs. MARETHA carries a hot comb and a can of hair grease. BOY WILLIE crosses over and continues to screw the wheels on the board.]

MARETHA: Mama, all the hair grease is gone. There ain't but this little bit left.

BERNIECE (*Gives her a dollar.*): Here . . . run across the street and get another can. You come straight back, too. Don't you be playing around out there. And watch the cars. Be careful when you cross the street.

[MARETHA exits out the front door.]

Boy Willie, I done told you to leave my house.

BOY WILLIE: I ain't in you' house. I'm in Doaker's house. If he ask me to leave then I'll go on and leave. But consider me done left your part.

BERNIECE: Doaker, tell him to leave. Tell him to go on.

DOAKER: Boy Willie ain't done nothing for me to put him out of the house. I told you if you can't get along just go on and don't have nothing to do with each other.

BOY WILLIE: I ain't thinking about Berniece.

[He gets up and draws a line across the floor with his foot.]

There! Now I'm out of your part of the house. Consider me done left your part. Soon as Lymon come back with that rope. I'm gonna take that piano out of here and sell it.

BERNIECE: You ain't gonna touch that piano.

BOY WILLIE: Carry it out of here just as big and bold. Do like my daddy would have done come time to get Sutter's land.

BERNIECE: I got something to make you leave it over there.

BOY WILLIE: It's got to come better than this thirty-two-twenty.

DOAKER: Why don't you stop all that! Boy Willie, go on and leave her alone. You know how Berniece get. Why you wanna sit there and pick with her?

BOY WILLIE: I ain't picking with her. I told her the truth. She the one talking about what she got. I just told her what she better have.

BERNIECE: That's alright, Doaker. Leave him alone.

BOY WILLIE: She trying to scare me. Hell, I ain't scared of dying. I look around and see people dying every day. You got to die to make room for somebody else. I had a dog that died. Wasn't nothing but a puppy. I picked it up and put it in a bag and carried it up there to Reverend C. L. Thompson's church. I carried it up there and prayed and asked Jesus to make it live like he did the man in the Bible. I prayed real hard. Knelt down and everything. Say ask in Jesus' name. Well, I must have called Jesus' name two hundred times. I called his name till my mouth got sore. I got up and looked in the bag and the dog still dead. It ain't moved a muscle! I say, "Well, ain't nothing precious." And then I went out and killed me a cat. That's when I discovered the power of death. See, a nigger that ain't afraid to die is the worse kind of nigger for the white man. He can't hold that power over you. That's what I learned when I killed that cat. I got the power of death too. I can command him. I can call him up. The white man don't like to see that. He don't like for you to stand up and look him square in the eye and say, "I got it too." Then he got to deal with you square up.

BERNIECE: That's why I don't talk to him, Doaker. You try and talk to him and that's the only kind of stuff that comes out his mouth.

DOAKER: You say Avery went home to get his Bible?

BOY WILLIE: What Avery gonna do? Avery can't do nothing with me. I wish Avery would say something to me about this piano.

DOAKER: Berniece ain't said about that. Avery went home to get his Bible. He coming by to bless the house see if he can get rid of Sutter's ghost.

BOY WILLIE: Ain't nothing but a house full of ghosts down there at the church. What Avery look like chasing away somebody's ghost?

[MARETHA enters the front door.]

BERNIECE: Light that stove and set that comb over there to get hot. Get something to put around your shoulders.

BOY WILLIE: The Bible say an eye for an eye, a tooth for a tooth, and a life for a life. Tit for tat. But you and Avery don't want to believe that. You gonna pass up that part and pretend it ain't in there. Everything else you gonna agree with. But if you gonna agree with part of it you got to agree with all of it. You can't do nothing halfway. You gonna go at the Bible halfway. You gonna act like that part ain't in there. But you pull out the Bible and open it and see what it say. Ask Avery. He a preacher. He'll tell you it's in there. He the Good Shepherd. Unless he gonna shepherd you to heaven with half the Bible.

BERNIECE: Maretha, bring me that comb. Make sure it's hot.

[MARETHA brings the comb. BERNIECE begins to do her hair.]

BOY WILLIE: I will say this for Avery. He done figured out a path to go through life. I don't agree with it. But he done fixed it so he can go right through it real smooth. Hell, he liable to end up with a million dollars that he done got from selling bread and wine.

MARETHA: OWWWWWW!

BERNIECE: Be still, Maretha. If you was a boy I wouldn't be going through this.

BOY WILLIE: Don't you tell that girl that. Why you wanna tell her that?

BERNIECE: You ain't got nothing to do with this child.

BOY WILLIE: Telling her you wished she was a boy. How's that gonna make her feel?

BERNIECE: Boy Willie, go on and leave me alone.

DOAKER: Why don't you leave her alone? What you got to pick with her for? Why don't you go on out and see what's out there in the streets? Have something to tell the fellows down home.

BOY WILLIE: I'm waiting on Lymon to get back with that truck. Why don't you go on out and see what's out there in the streets? You ain't got to work tomorrow. Talking about me . . . why don't you go out there? It's Friday night.

DOAKER: I got to stay around here and keep you all from killing one another.

BOY WILLIE: You ain't got to worry about me. I'm gonna be here just as long as it takes Lymon to get back here with that truck. You ought to be talking to Berniece. Sitting up there telling Maretha she wished she was a boy. What kind of thing is that to tell a child? If you want to tell her something tell her about that piano. You ain't even told her about that piano. Like that's something to be ashamed of. Like she supposed to go off and hide somewhere about that piano. You ought to mark down on the calendar the day that Papa Boy Charles brought that piano into the house. You ought to mark that day down and draw a circle around it . . . and every year when it come up throw a party. Have a celebration. If you did that she wouldn't have no problem in life. She could walk around here with her head held high. I'm talking about a big party! Invite everybody! Mark that day down with a special meaning. That way she know where she at in the world. You got her going out here thinking she wrong in the world. Like there ain't no part of it belong to her.

BERNIECE: Let me take care of my child. When you get one of your own then you can teach it what you want to teach it.

[DOAKER exits into his room.]

BOY WILLIE: What I want to bring a child into this world for? Why I wanna bring somebody else into all this for? I'll tell you this . . . If I was Rockefeller I'd have forty or fifty. I'd make one every day. Cause they gonna start out in life with all the advantages. I ain't got no advantages to offer nobody. Many is the time I looked at my daddy and seen him staring off at his hands. I got a little older I know what he was thinking. He sitting there saying, "I got these big old hands but what I'm gonna do with them? Best I can do is make a fifty-acre crop for Mr. Stovall. Got these big old hands capable of doing anything. I can take and build something with these hands. But where's the tools? All I got is these hands. Unless I go out here and kill me somebody and take what they got . . . it's a long row to hoe for me to get something of my own. So what I'm gonna do with these big old hands? What would you do?"

See now . . . if he had his own land he wouldn't have felt that way. If he had something under his feet that belonged to him he could stand up taller. That's what I'm talking about. Hell, the land is there for everybody. All you got to do is figure out how to get you a piece. Ain't no mystery to life. You just got to go out and meet it square on. If you got a piece of land you'll find everything else fall right into place. You can stand right up next to the white man and talk about the price of cotton . . . the weather, and anything else you want to talk about. If you teach that girl that she living at the bottom of life, she's gonna grow up and hate you.

BERNIECE: I'm gonna teach her the truth. That's just where she living. Only she ain't got to stay there.

[To MARETHA.]

Turn you' head over to the other side.
BOY WILLIE: This might be your bottom but it ain't
mine. I'm living at the top of life. I ain't gonna
just take my life and throw it away at the bottom. I'm in the world like everybody else. The
way I see it everybody else got to come up a
little taste to be where I am.
BERNIECE: You right at the bottom with the rest of us.
BOY WILLIE: I'll tell you this . . . and ain't a living
soul can put a come back on it. If you believe
that's where you at then you gonna act that
way. If you act that way then that's where you
gonna be. It's as simple as that. Ain't no mystery to life. I don't know how you come to
believe that stuff. Crawley didn't think like
that. He wasn't living at the bottom of life.
Papa Boy Charles and Mama Ola wasn't living
at the bottom of life. You ain't never heard
them say nothing like that. They would have
taken a strap to you if they heard you say
something like that.

[DOAKER enters from his room.]

Hey, Doaker . . . Berniece say the colored folks
is living at the bottom of life. I tried to tell her
if she think that . . . that's where she gonna be.
You think you living at the bottom of life? Is
that how you see yourself?
DOAKER: I'm just living the best way I know how. I
ain't thinking about no top or no bottom.
BOY WILLIE: That's what I tried to tell Berniece. I
don't know where she got that from. That
sound like something Avery would say. Avery
think cause the white man give him a turkey
for Thanksgiving that makes him better than
everybody else. That's gonna raise him out of
the bottom of life. I don't need nobody to give
me a turkey. I can get my own turkey. All you
have to do is get out my way. I'll get me two
or three turkeys.
BERNIECE: You can't even get a chicken let alone two
or three turkeys. Talking about get out your
way. Ain't nobody in your way.

[To MARETHA.]

Straighten your head, Maretha! Don't be bending down like that. Hold your head up!

[To BOY WILLIE.]

All you got going for you is talk. You' whole
life that's all you ever had going for you.
BOY WILLIE: See now . . . I'll tell you something about
me. I done strung along and strung along.

Going this way and that. Whatever way would
lead me to a moment of peace. That's all I
want. To be as easy with everything. But I
wasn't born to that. I was born to a time of
fire.

The world ain't wanted no part of me. I
could see that since I was about seven. The
world say it's better off without me. See,
Berniece accept that. She trying to come up to
where she can prove something to the world.
Hell, the world a better place cause of me. I
don't see it like Berniece. I got a heart that
beats here and it beats just as loud as the next
fellow's. Don't care if he black or white.
Sometime it beats louder. When it beats louder,
then everybody can hear it. Some people get
scared of that. Like Berniece. Some people get
scared to hear a nigger's heart beating. They
think you ought to lay low with that heart.
Make it beat quiet and go along with everything the way it is. But my mama ain't birthed
me for nothing. So what I got to do? I got to
mark my passing on the road. Just like you
write on a tree, "Boy Willie was here."

That's all I'm trying to do with that piano.
Trying to put my mark on the road. Like my
daddy done. My heart say for me to sell that
piano and get me some land so I can make a
life for myself to live in my own way. Other
than that I ain't thinking about nothing
Berniece got to say.

*[There is a knock at the door. BOY WILLIE crosses to it
and yanks it open thinking it is LYMON. AVERY enters.
He carries a Bible.]*

BOY WILLIE: Where you been, nigger? Aw . . . I
thought you was Lymon. Hey, Berniece, look
who's here.
BERNIECE: Come on in, Avery. Don't you pay Boy
Willie no mind.
BOY WILLIE: Hey . . . Hey, Avery . . . tell me this . . .
can you get to heaven with half the Bible?
BERNIECE: Boy Willie . . . I done told you to leave me
alone.
BOY WILLIE: I just ask the man a question. He can
answer. He don't need you to speak for him.
Avery . . . if you only believe on half the Bible
and don't want to accept the other half . . . you
think God let you in heaven? Or do you got to
have the whole Bible? Tell Berniece . . . if you
only believe in part of it . . . when you see God
he gonna ask you why you ain't believed in
the other part . . . then he gonna send you
straight to Hell.
AVERY: You got to be born again. Jesus say unless a
man be born again he cannot come unto the

Father and who so ever heareth my words and believeth them not shall be cast into a fiery pit.

BOY WILLIE: That's what I was trying to tell Berniece. You got to believe in it all. You can't go at nothing halfway. She think she going to heaven with half the Bible.

[To BERNIECE.]

You hear that . . . Jesus say you got to believe in it all.

BERNIECE: You keep messing with me.

BOY WILLIE: I ain't thinking about you.

DOAKER: Come on in, Avery, and have a seat. Don't pay neither one of them no mind. They been arguing all day.

BERNIECE: Come on in, Avery.

AVERY: How's everybody in here?

BERNIECE: Here, set this comb back over there on that stove.

[To AVERY.]

Don't pay Boy Willie no mind. He been around here bothering me since I come home from work.

BOY WILLIE: Boy Willie ain't bothering you. Boy Willie ain't bothering nobody. I'm just waiting on Lymon to get back. I ain't thinking about you. You heard the man say I was right and you still don't want to believe it. You just wanna go and make up anythin'. Well there's Avery . . . there's the preacher . . . go on and ask him.

AVERY: Berniece believe in the Bible. She been baptized.

BOY WILLIE: What about that part that say an eye for an eye a tooth for a tooth and a life for a life? Ain't that in there?

DOAKER: What they say down there at the bank, Avery?

AVERY: Oh, they talked to me real nice. I told Berniece . . . they say maybe they let me borrow the money. They done talked to my boss down at work and everything.

DOAKER: That's what I told Berniece. You working every day you ought to be able to borrow some money.

AVERY: I'm getting more people in my congregation every day. Berniece says she gonna be the Deaconess. I get me my church I can get married and settled down. That's what I told Berniece.

DOAKER: That be nice. You all ought to go ahead and get married. Berniece don't need to be by herself. I tell her that all the time.

BERNIECE: I ain't said nothing about getting married.

I said I was thinking about it.

DOAKER: Avery get him his church you all can make it nice.

[To AVERY.]

Berniece said you was coming by to bless the house.

AVERY: Yeah, I done read up on my Bible. She asked me to come by and see if I can get rid of Sutter's ghost.

BOY WILLIE: Ain't no ghost in this house. That's all in Berniece's head. Go on up there and see if you see him. I'll give you a hundred dollars if you see him. That's all in her imagination.

DOAKER: Well, let her find that out then. If Avery blessing the house is gonna make her feel better . . . what you got to do with it?

AVERY: Berniece say Maretha seen him too. I don't know, but I found a part in the Bible to bless the house. If he is here then that ought to make him go.

BOY WILLIE: You worse than Berniece believing all that stuff. Talking about . . . if he here. Go on up there and find out. I been up there I ain't seen him. If you reading from that Bible gonna make him leave out of Berniece imagination, well, you might be right. But if you talking about . . .

DOAKER: Boy Willie, why don't you just be quiet? Getting all up in the man's business. This ain't got nothing to do with you. Let him go ahead and do what he gonna do.

BOY WILLIE: I ain't stopping him. Avery ain't got no power to do nothing.

AVERY: Oh, I ain't got no power. God got the power! God got power over everything in His creation. God can do anything. God say, "As I commandeth so it shall be." God said, "Let there be light," and there was light. He made the world in six days and rested on the seventh. God's got a wonderful power. He got power over life and death. Jesus raised Lazareth from the dead. They was getting ready to bury him and Jesus told him say, "Rise up and walk." He got up and walked and the people made great rejoicing at the power of God. I ain't worried about him chasing away a little old ghost!

[There is a knock at the door. BOY WILLIE goes to answer it. LYMON enters carrying a coil of rope.]

BOY WILLIE: Where you been? I been waiting on you and you run off somewhere.

LYMON: I ran into Grace. I stopped and bought her drink. She say she gonna go to the picture show with me.

BOY WILLIE: I ain't thinking about no Grace nothing.

LYMON: Hi, Berniece.

BOY WILLIE: Give me that rope and get up on this side of the piano.

DOAKER: Boy Willie, don't start nothing now. Leave the piano alone.

BOY WILLIE: Get that board there, Lymon. Stay out of this, Doaker.

[BERNIECE exits up the stairs.]

DOAKER: You just can't take the piano. How you gonna take the piano? Berniece ain't said nothing about selling that piano.

BOY WILLIE: She ain't got to say nothing. Come on, Lymon. We got to lift one end at a time up on the board. You got to watch so that the board don't slide up under there.

LYMON: What we gonna do with the rope?

BOY WILLIE: Let me worry about the rope. You just get up on this side over here with me.

[BERNIECE enters from the stairs. She has her hand in her pocket where she has Crawley's gun.]

AVERY: Boy Willie . . . Berniece . . . why don't you all sit down and talk this out now?

BERNIECE: Ain't nothing to talk out.

BOY WILLIE: I'm through talking to Berniece. You can talk to Berniece till you get blue in the face, and it don't make no difference. Get up on that side, Lymon. Throw that rope around there and tie it to the leg.

LYMON: Wait a minute . . . wait a minute, Boy Willie. Berniece got to say. Hey, Berniece . . . did you tell Boy Willie he could take this piano?

BERNIECE: Boy Willie ain't taking nothing out of my house but himself. Now you let him go ahead and try.

BOY WILLIE: Come on, Lymon, get up on this side with me.

[LYMON stands undecided.]

Come on, nigger! What you standing there for?

LYMON: Maybe Berniece is right, Boy Willie. Maybe you shouldn't sell it.

AVERY: You all ought to sit down and talk it out. See if you can come to an agreement.

DOAKER: That's what I been trying to tell them. Seem like one of them ought to respect the other one's wishes.

BERNIECE: I wish Boy Willie would go on and leave my house. That's what I wish. Now, he can respect that. Cause he's leaving here one way or another.

BOY WILLIE: What you mean one way or another?

What's that supposed to mean? I ain't scared of no gun.

DOAKER: Come on, Berniece, leave him alone with that.

BOY WILLIE: I don't care what Berniece say. I'm selling my half. I can't help it if her half got to go along with it. It ain't like I'm trying to cheat her out of her half. Come on, Lymon.

LYMON: Berniece . . . I got to do this . . . Boy Willie say he gonna give you half of the money . . . say he want to get Sutter's land.

BERNIECE: Go on, Lymon. Just go on . . . I done told Boy Willie what to do.

BOY WILLIE: Here, Lymon . . . put that rope up over there.

LYMON: Boy Willie, you sure you want to do this? The way I figure it . . . I might be wrong . . . but I figure she gonna shoot you first.

BOY WILLIE: She just gonna have to shoot me.

BERNIECE: Maretha, get on out the way. Get her out the way, Doaker.

DOAKER: Go on, do what your mama told you.

BERNIECE: Put her in your room.

[MARETHA exits to Doaker's room. BOY WILLIE and LYMON try to lift the piano. The door opens and WINING BOY enters. He has been drinking.]

WINING BOY: Man, these niggers around here! I stopped down there at Seefus. . . . These folks standing around talking about Patchneck Red's coming. They jumping back and getting off the sidewalk talking about Patchneck Red this and Patchneck Red that. Come to find out . . . you know who they was talking about? Old John D. from up around Tyler! Used to run around with Otis Smith. He got everybody scared of him. Calling him Patchneck Red. They don't know I whupped the nigger's head in one time.

BOY WILLIE: Just make sure that board don't slide, Lymon.

LYMON: I got this side. You watch that side.

WINING BOY: Hey, Boy Willie, what you got? I know you got a pint stuck up in your coat.

BOY WILLIE: Wining Boy, get out the way!

WINING BOY: Hey, Doaker. What you got? Gimme a drink. I want a drink.

DOAKER: It look like you had enough of whatever it was. Come talking about "What you got?" You ought to be trying to find somewhere to lay down.

WINING BOY: I ain't worried about no place to lay down. I can always find me a place to lay down in Berniece's house. Ain't that right, Berniece?

BERNIECE: Wining Boy, sit down somewhere. You

been out there drinking all day. Come in here smelling like an old polecat. Sit on down there, you don't need nothing to drink.

DOAKER: You know Berniece don't like all that drinking.

WINING BOY: I ain't disrespecting Berniece. Berniece, am I disrespecting you? I'm just trying to be nice. I been with strangers all day and they treated me like family. I come in here to family and you treat me like a stranger. I don't need your whiskey. I can buy my own. I wanted your company, not your whiskey.

DOAKER: Nigger, why don't you go upstairs and lay down? You don't need nothing to drink.

WINING BOY: I ain't thinking about no laying down. Me and Boy Willie fixing to party. Ain't that right, Boy Willie? Tell him. I'm fixing to play me some piano. Watch this.

[WINING BOY sits down at the piano.]

BOY WILLIE: Come on, Wining Boy! Me and Lymon fixing to move the piano.

WINING BOY: Wait a minute . . . wait a minute. This a song I wrote for Cleotha. I wrote this song in memory of Cleotha.

(He begins to play and sing.)

> Hey little woman what's the matter with you now
> Had a storm last night and blowed the line all down
> Tell me how long
> Is I got to wait
> Can I get it now
> Or must I hesitate
>
> It takes a hesitating stocking in her hesitating shoe
> It takes a hesitating woman wanna sing the blues
>
> Tell me how long
> Is I got to wait
> Can I kiss you now
> Or must I hesitate.

BOY WILLIE: Come on, Wining Boy, get up! Get up, Wining Boy! Me and Lymon's fixing to move the piano.

WINING BOY: Naw . . . Naw . . . you ain't gonna move this piano!

BOY WILLIE: Get out the way, Wining Boy.

[WINING BOY, his back to the piano, spreads his arms out over the piano.]

WINING BOY: You ain't taking this piano out the house. You got to take me with it!

BOY WILLIE: Get on out the way, Wining Boy! Doaker get him!

[There is a knock on the door.]

BERNIECE: I got him, Doaker. Come on, Wining Boy. I done told Boy Willie he ain't taking the piano.

[BERNIECE tries to take WINING BOY away from the piano.]

WINING BOY: He got to take me with it!

[DOAKER goes to answer the door. GRACE enters.]

GRACE: Is Lymon here?

DOAKER: Lymon.

WINING BOY: He ain't taking that piano.

BERNIECE: I ain't gonna let him take it.

GRACE: I thought you was coming back. I ain't gonna sit in that truck all day.

LYMON: I told you I was coming back.

GRACE (*Sees* BOY WILLIE.): Oh, hi, Boy Willie. Lymon told me you was gone back down South.

LYMON: I said he was going back. I didn't say he had left already.

GRACE: That's what you told me.

BERNIECE: Lymon, you got to take your company someplace else.

LYMON: Berniece, this is Grace. That there is Berniece. That's Boy Willie's sister.

GRACE: Nice to meet you.

[To LYMON.]

I ain't gonna sit out in that truck all day. You told me you was gonna take me to the movie.

LYMON: I told you I had something to do first. You supposed to wait on me.

BERNIECE: Lymon, just go on and leave. Take Grace or whoever with you. Just go on get out my house.

BOY WILLIE: You gonna help me move this piano first, nigger!

LYMON (*To* GRACE.): I got to help Boy Willie move the piano first.

[Everybody but GRACE suddenly senses SUTTER's presence.]

GRACE: I ain't waiting on you. Told me you was coming right back. Now you got to move a piano. You just like all the other men.

[GRACE now senses something.]

Something ain't right here. I knew I shouldn't have come back up in this house.

[GRACE exits.]

LYMON: Hey, Grace! I'll be right back, Boy Willie.

BOY WILLIE: Where you going, nigger?

LYMON: I'll be back. I got to take Grace home.

BOY WILLIE: Come on, let's move the piano first!

LYMON: I got to take Grace home. I told you I'll be back.

[LYMON exits. BOY WILLIE exits and calls after him.]

BOY WILLIE: Come on, Lymon! Hey . . . Lymon! Lymon . . . come on!

[Again, the presence of SUTTER is felt.]

WINING BOY: Hey, Doaker, did you feel that? Hey, Berniece . . . did you get cold? Hey, Doaker . . .

DOAKER: What you calling me for?

WINING BOY: I believe that's Sutter.

DOAKER: Well, let him stay up there. As long as he don't mess with me.

BERNIECE: Avery, go on and bless the house.

DOAKER: You need to bless that piano. That's what you need to bless. It ain't done nothing but cause trouble. If you gonna bless anything go on and bless that.

WINING BOY: Hey, Doaker, if he gonna bless something let him bless everything. The kitchen . . . the upstairs. Go on and bless it all.

BOY WILLIE: Ain't no ghost in this house. He need to bless Berniece's head. That's what he need to bless.

AVERY: Seem like that piano's causing all the trouble. I can bless that. Berniece, put me some water in that bottle.

[AVERY takes a small bottle from his pocket and hands it to BERNIECE, who goes into the kitchen to get water. AVERY takes a candle from his pocket and lights it. He gives it to BERNIECE as she gives him the water.]

Hold this candle. Whatever you do make sure it don't go out.

O Holy Father we gather here this evening in the Holy Name to cast out the spirit of one James Sutter. May this vial of water be empowered with thy spirit. May each drop of it be a weapon and a shield against the presence of all evil and may it be a cleansing and blessing of this humble abode.

Just as Our Father taught us how to pray so He say, "I will prepare a table for you in the midst of mine enemies," and in His hands we place ourselves to come unto his presence. Where there is Good so shall it cause Evil to scatter to the Four Winds.

[He throws water at the piano at each commandment.]

AVERY: Get thee behind me, Satan! Get thee behind the face of Righteousness as we Glorify His Holy Name! Get thee behind the Hammer of Truth that breaketh down the Wall of Falsehood! Father. Father. Praise. Praise. We ask in Jesus' name and call forth the power of the Holy Spirit as it is written. . . .

[He opens the Bible and reads from it.]

I will sprinkle clean water upon thee and ye shall be clean.

BOY WILLIE: All this old preaching stuff. Hell, just tell him to leave.

[AVERY continues reading throughout BOY WILLIE's outburst.]

AVERY: I will sprinkle clean water upon you and you shall be clean: from all your uncleanliness, and from all your idols, will I cleanse you. A new heart also will I give you, and a new spirit will I put within you: and I will take out of your flesh the heart of stone, and I will give you a heart of flesh. And I will put my spirit within you, and cause you to walk in my statutes, and ye shall keep my judgments, and do them.

[BOY WILLIE grabs a pot of water from the stove and begins to fling it around the room.]

BOY WILLIE: Hey Sutter! Sutter! Get your ass out this house! Sutter! Come on and get some of this water! You done drowned in the well, come on and get some more of this water!

[BOY WILLIE is working himself into a frenzy as he runs around the room throwing water and calling SUTTER's name. AVERY continues reading.]

BOY WILLIE: Come on, Sutter!

[He starts up the stairs.]

Come on, get some water! Come on, Sutter!

[The sound of SUTTER's GHOST is heard. As BOY WILLIE approaches the steps he is suddenly thrown back by the unseen force, which is choking him. As he struggles he frees himself, then dashes up the stairs.]

BOY WILLIE: Come on, Sutter!

AVERY: (Continuing.) A new heart also will I give you and a new spirit will I put within you: and I will take out of your flesh the heart of stone, and I will give you a heart of flesh. And I will put my spirit within you, and cause you to walk in my statutes, and ye shall keep my judgments, and do them.

*[There are loud sounds heard from upstairs as BOY
WILLIE begins to wrestle with SUTTER's GHOST. It is a
life-and-death struggle fraught with perils and faultless terror. BOY WILLIE is thrown down the stairs. AVERY
is stunned into silence. BOY WILLIE picks himself up
and dashes back upstairs.]*

AVERY: Berniece, I can't do it.

*[There are more sounds heard from upstairs. DOAKER
and WINING BOY stare at one another in stunned disbelief. It is in this moment, from somewhere old, that
BERNIECE realizes what she must do. She crosses to the
piano. She begins to play. The song is found piece by
piece. It is an old urge to song that is both a commandment and a plea. With each repetition it gains in
strength. It is intended as an exorcism and a dressing
for battle. A rustle of wind blowing across two continents.]*

BERNIECE (*Singing.*):

   I want you to help me
   I want you to help me
   I want you to help me
   I want you to help me
   I want you to help me
   I want you to help me
   Mama Berniece
   I want you to help me
   Mama Esther
   I want you to help me
   Papa Boy Charles
   I want you to help me
   Mama Ola
   I want you to help me

   I want you to help me
   I want you to help me

   I want you to help me
   I want you to help me
   I want you to help me
   I want you to help me
   I want you to help me
   I want you to help me

*[The sound of a train approaching is heard. The noise
upstairs subsides.]*

BOY WILLIE: Come on, Sutter! Come back, Sutter!

[BERNIECE begins to chant:]

BERNIECE:
   Thank you.
   Thank you.
   Thank you.

*[A calm comes over the house. MARETHA enters from
DOAKER's room. BOY WILLIE enters on the stairs. He
pauses a moment to watch BERNIECE at the piano.]*

BERNIECE:
   Thank you.
   Thank you.
BOY WILLIE: Wining Boy, you ready to go back down
    home? Hey, Doaker, what time the train leave?
DOAKER: You still got time to make it.

[MARETHA crosses and embraces BOY WILLIE.]

BOY WILLIE: Hey Berniece . . . if you and Maretha
    don't keep playing on that piano . . . ain't no
    telling . . . me and Sutter both liable to be back.

[He exits.]

BERNIECE: Thank you.

[The lights go down to black.]

DAVID MAMET (b. 1947)

Widely considered to be one of the finest living American playwrights, David Mamet was born in Chicago in 1947. He was brought up on the South Side, attending Francis Parker High School and then going away to school at Goddard College in Plainfield, Vermont, where he graduated in 1969. While still a teenager he had begun to work backstage at Hull House Theater in Chicago, and during his junior year in college he studied acting at New York's Neighborhood Playhouse under Sanford Meisner. While at Goddard he also finished the first drafts of the first two plays that were to bring him critical notice: *The Duck Variations* and *Sexual Perversity in Chicago*. During two years spent as artist-in-residence at Goddard (1971–1973), Mamet founded and became artistic director of the St. Nicholas Theater Company. He eventually moved the company to Chicago, where his plays were widely performed. In 1975 *American Buffalo* premiered in Chicago to critical acclaim, and in 1976 it opened in New York. That year Mamet received an Obie for Distinguished Playwriting, and in 1977 he received the New York Drama Critics Circle Award for *American Buffalo*. He was thirty years old.

In the 1980s Mamet began working on screenplays as well as dramas; his first, *The Postman Always Rings Twice*, premiered in 1981, starring Jack Nicholson and Jessica Lange. His second, *The Verdict*, was nominated for an Academy Award for Best Adapted Screenplay in 1982. During the next few years he wrote a number of screenplays, including *The Untouchables* (1985), *House of Games* (1987), *Things Change* (with Shel Silverstein, 1988), *We're No Angels* (1989), *Homicide* (1990), *Ace in the Hole* (1990), and *The Deerslayer* (1990). His screenplays have been nominated for or have received many awards, including the Golden Globe and Writers Guild Awards.

During this same time Mamet's output of plays has continued, including *Edmond* (1982) and *Glengarry Glen Ross*, which opened in London at the National Theatre in 1983. In 1984 *Glengarry Glen Ross* won both the Pulitzer Prize and the Drama Critics Award for Best American Play, and it has since been made into a film (1993). Its depiction of four real-estate salesmen offers a scathing indictment of American business practices. In *Speed-the-Plow* (1988) the dirty underside of the film industry is savagely revealed, while in "Bobby Gould in Hell" in *Oh, Hell* (1989) the afterlife of one of these Hollywood antiheroes is described. *Oleanna*, one of Mamet's most controversial plays, was first performed in 1992 and was made into a film two years later.

Besides his substantial outpouring of plays and screenplays, Mamet has adapted Chekhov's *Cherry Orchard*, *Uncle Vanya*, and *Three Sisters*; he has written radio plays, four books of essays, and, quite recently, a novel, *The Village* (1994). Mamet is widely recognized as one of the most prolific and powerful voices in contemporary American theater. His precise social observation, his sensitivity to language and his extraordinary ear for ordinary speech, his theatrical imagination, and his complex depiction of betrayal and loss and entrapment all contribute to this reputation.

Oleanna

Mamet's plays sometimes explore the relationship between a teaching figure and an acolyte, a master and a disciple. They depict hard lessons that each must learn, frequently switching their roles. But no earlier play carries the ideological and sexual/political charge as powerfully as *Oleanna*. The play has only two characters in it: John, an English professor who is up for tenure, and Carol, a female student who is having difficulty in one of his classes. The tenure process will determine whether John will continue to have a position in his department; John has anticipated a positive outcome and is negotiating to buy a new house. In the first act, Carol seems to have a self-esteem problem that is undermining her attempts to learn. What seems to be at stake for her is her grade in the class and perhaps her future career. Throughout the play the phone on John's desk acts as a substitute for two other characters whom the audience never sees: John's wife, Grace, and his lawyer, Jerry, who call during his conversation with Carol to tell him about an apparent crisis in the house negotiations. Tension rises as John, a kind of intellectual bully, offers a despairing Carol the possibility of private tutoring, with some indication that he might well take advantage of her.

Carol's demeanor in the second act, which takes place a month later, shows an entirely different side from her earlier whining insecurity: now assertive, sometimes hectoring, she has brought sexual harassment charges against John with the help of her "group," and his tenure committee has made their report. Their decision is foregone, given her complaint. She presses her advantage and he loses his temper. In the final act, the two characters meet once more; Carol attempts to blackmail John with the threat of rape charges, and their intensity dissolves into violence.

At the center of *Oleanna* lies sexual politics. John's intellectual bluster and professional status give him a position of power in the first act, so he can make the rules while Carol remains entirely passive and uncomprehending. The telephone interruptions step up the pace and give a sense of impending crisis as John's solicitude of Carol turns to physical comforting. His is a world of expected privilege, of condescension, and it is clear from the start that he is intellectually fraudulent. But when he puts his arm around Carol, the game changes. In the next act John is made to understand that the rules of his game have been made part of another game in which intellectual issues take a back seat to the politics of gender. It is now Carol's turn to "teach" John, to exercise the brutal power that her accusations carry in the world outside John's classroom and office. Words seem to have as many consequences as the actions they figure forth, perhaps more in the world of hiring and firing and the law courts. The conflict between these two characters illustrates how our codes of behavior are mirrored in language, but by the end of the play words have failed altogether, and the chasm of deliberate hostility and mutual misunderstanding between John and Carol has become unbridgeable.

Mamet's compression of language and his sense of verbal implication in *Oleanna* are brilliantly deployed. The play begins with a one-sided telephone conversation and moves to half-finished sentences, but the audience is never lost. Indeed, the dialogue throughout the play is absolutely spare, and the unfinished or interrupted dialogue allows the audience to complete thought processes signaled by very few words. As in Pinter's plays, pauses and silences are significant, and the unspoken often carries as much power as the spoken. The intentions of the characters are telegraphed by their language, which, it turns out, can be put to several purposes. In *Oleanna* Mamet has crafted a play that presents two sides of a political war between the sexes; it is not clear which side wins, or should win.

Oleanna

DAVID MAMET

The want of fresh air does not seem much to affect the happiness of children in a London alley: the greater part of them sing and play as though they were on a moor in Scotland. So the absence of a genial mental atmosphere is not commonly recognized by children who have never known it. Young people have a marvelous faculty of either dying or adapting themselves to circumstances. Even if they are unhappy—very unhappy—it is astonishing how easily they can be prevented from finding it out, or at any rate from attributing it to any other cause than their own sinfulness.

The Way of All Flesh
Samuel Butler

"Oh, to be in Oleanna,
That's where I would rather be.
Than be bound in Norway
And drag the chains of slavery."
   —folk song

CHARACTERS

CAROL, A woman of twenty
JOHN, A man in his forties

The play takes place in John's office.

ACT I

[JOHN is talking on the phone. CAROL is seated across the desk from him.]

JOHN (*on phone*): And what about the land. (*Pause*) The land. And what about the land? (*Pause*) What about it? (*Pause*) No. I don't understand. Well, yes, I'm I'm . . . no, I'm *sure* it's signif . . . I'm sure it's significant. (*Pause*) Because it's

significant to mmmmmm . . . did you call
Jerry? (*Pause*) Because . . . no, no, no, no, no.
What did they say . . . ? Did you speak to the
real estate . . . where *is* she . . . ? Well, well, all
right. Where are her notes? Where are the
notes we took with her. (*Pause*) I thought you
were? No. No, I'm sorry, I didn't mean that, I
just thought that I saw you, when we were
there . . . what . . . ? I thought I saw you with a
pencil. WHY NOW? is what I'm say . . . well,
that's why I say "call Jerry." Well, I can't right
now, be . . . no, I *didn't* schedule any . . . Grace:
I *didn't* . . . I'm well aware . . . Look: Look. Did
you call Jerry? Will you call Jerry . . . ? Because
I can't now. I'll be there, I'm sure I'll be there
in fifteen, in twenty. I intend to. No, we aren't
going to lose the, we aren't *going* to lose the
house. Look: Look, I'm not minimizing it. The
"easement." Did she say "easement"? (*Pause*)
What did she *say; is* it a "term of art," are we
bound by it . . . I'm sorry . . . (*Pause*) are: we:
yes. *Bound* by . . . Look: (*He checks his watch.*)
before the other side *goes home*, all right? "a
term of art." Because: that's right (*Pause*) The
yard for the boy. Well, that's the whole . . .
Look: I'm going to meet you there . . . (*He
checks his watch.*) Is the realtor there? All right,
tell her to show you the basement again. Look
at the *this* because . . . Bec . . . I'm leaving in,
I'm leaving in ten or fifteen . . . Yes. No, no, I'll
meet you at the new . . . That's a good. If he
thinks it's necc . . . you tell Jerry to meet . . . All
right? We *aren't* going to lose the deposit. All
right? I'm sure it's going to be . . . (*Pause*) I
hope so. (*Pause*) I love you, too. (*Pause*) I love
you, too. As soon as . . . I will.

 (*He hangs up.*) (*He bends over the desk and
makes a note.*) (*He looks up.*) (*To* CAROL:) I'm
sorry . . .
CAROL: (*Pause*) What is a "term of art"?
JOHN: (*Pause*) I'm sorry . . . ?
CAROL: (*Pause*) What is a "term of art"?
JOHN: Is that what you want to talk about?
CAROL: . . . to talk about . . . ?
JOHN: Let's take the mysticism out of it, shall we?
 Carol? (*Pause*) Don't you think? I'll tell you:
 when you have some "thing." Which must be
 broached. (*Pause*) Don't you think . . . ? (*Pause*)
CAROL: . . . don't I think . . . ?
JOHN: Mmm?
CAROL: . . . did I . . . ?
JOHN: . . . what?
CAROL: Did . . . did I . . . did I say something wr . . .
JOHN: (*Pause*) No. I'm sorry. No. You're right. I'm
 very sorry. I'm somewhat rushed. As you see.
 I'm sorry. You're right. (*Pause*) What is a "term
 of art"? It seems to mean a *term*, which has

come, through its use, to mean something *more
specific* than the words would, to someone *not
acquainted* with them . . . indicate. That, I
believe, is what a "term of art," would mean.
(*Pause*)
CAROL: You don't know what it means . . . ?
JOHN: I'm not sure that I know what it means. It's
 one of those things, perhaps you've had them,
 that, you look them up, or have someone
 explain them to you, and you say "aha," and,
 you immediately *forget* what . . .
CAROL: You don't do that.
JOHN: . . . I . . . ?
CAROL: You don't do . . .
JOHN: . . . I don't what . . . ?
CAROL: . . . for . . .
JOHN: . . . I don't for . . .
CAROL: . . . no . . .
JOHN: . . . forget things? Everybody does that.
CAROL: No, they don't.
JOHN: They don't . . .
CAROL: No.
JOHN: (*Pause*) No. Everybody does that.
CAROL: Why would they do that . . . ?
JOHN: Because. I don't know. Because it doesn't inter-
 est them.
CAROL: No.
JOHN: I think so, though. (*Pause*) I'm sorry that I was
 distracted.
CAROL: You don't have to say that to me.
JOHN: You paid me the compliment, or the "obei-
 sance"—all right—of coming in here . . . All
 right. *Carol*. I find that I am at a *standstill*. I find
 that I . . .
CAROL: . . . what . . .
JOHN: . . . one moment. In regard to your . . . to your . . .
CAROL: Oh, oh. You're buying a new house!
JOHN: No, let's get on with it.
CAROL: "get on"? (*Pause*)
JOHN: I know how . . . *believe* me. I know how . . .
 potentially *humiliating* these . . . I have no
 desire to . . . I have no desire other than to help
 you. But: (*He picks up some papers on his desk.*) I
 won't even say "but." I'll say that as I go back
 over the . . .
CAROL: I'm just, I'm just trying to . . .
JOHN: . . . no, it will not do.
CAROL: . . . what? What will . . . ?
JOHN: No. I see, I see what you, it . . . (*He gestures to
 the papers.*) but your work . . .
CAROL: I'm just: I sit in class I . . . (*She holds up her
 notebook.*) I take notes . . .
JOHN (*simultaneously with* "notes"): Yes. I understand.
 What I am trying to *tell* you is that some, some
 basic . . .
CAROL: . . . I . . .
JOHN: . . . one moment: some basic missed communi . . .

CAROL: I'm doing what I'm told. I bought your book, I read your . . .

JOHN: No, I'm sure you . . .

CAROL: No, no, no. I'm doing what I'm told. It's *difficult* for me. It's *difficult* . . .

JOHN: . . . but . . .

CAROL: I don't . . . lots of the *language* . . .

JOHN: . . . please . . .

CAROL: The *language*, the "things" that you say . . .

JOHN: I'm sorry. No. I don't think that that's true.

CAROL: It *is* true. I . . .

JOHN: I think . . .

CAROL: It *is* true.

JOHN: . . . I . . .

CAROL: Why would I . . . ?

JOHN: I'll tell you why: you're an incredibly bright girl.

CAROL: . . . I . . .

JOHN: You're an incredibly . . . you have no problem with the . . . Who's kidding who?

CAROL: . . . I . . .

JOHN: No. No. I'll tell you why. I'll tell . . . I think you're *angry*, I . . .

CAROL: . . . why would I . . .

JOHN: . . . wait one moment. I . . .

CAROL: It *is* true. I have *problems* . . .

JOHN: . . . every . . .

CAROL: . . . I come from a different *social* . . .

JOHN: . . . ev . . .

CAROL: a different economic . . .

JOHN: . . . Look:

CAROL: No. I: when I *came* to this school:

JOHN: Yes. Quite . . . (*Pause*)

CAROL: . . . does that mean nothing . . . ?

JOHN: . . . but look: look . . .

CAROL: . . . I . . .

JOHN (*Picks up paper.*): Here: Please: Sit down. (*Pause*) Sit down. (*Reads from her paper.*) "I think that the ideas contained in this work express the author's feelings in a way that he intended, based on his results." What can that mean? Do you see? What . . .

CAROL: I, the best that I . . .

JOHN: I'm saying, that perhaps this course . . .

CAROL: No, no, no, you can't, you can't . . . I have to . . .

JOHN: . . . how . . .

CAROL: . . . I have to pass it . . .

JOHN: Carol, I:

CAROL: I *have* to pass this course, I . . .

JOHN: Well.

CAROL: . . . don't you . . .

JOHN: Either the . . .

CAROL: . . . I . . .

JOHN: . . . either the, I . . . either the *criteria* for judging progress in the class are . . .

CAROL: No, no, no, no, I have to pass it.

JOHN: Now, look: I'm a human being, I . . .

CAROL: I did what you told me. I did, I did everything that, I read your *book*, you told me to buy your book and read it. Everything you *say* I . . . (*She gestures to her notebook.*) (*The phone rings.*) I do. . . . Ev . . .

JOHN: . . . look:

CAROL: . . . everything I'm told . . .

JOHN: Look. Look. I'm not your *father*. (*Pause*)

CAROL: What?

JOHN: I'm.

CAROL: Did I say you were my father?

JOHN: . . . no . . .

CAROL: Why did you say that . . . ?

JOHN: I . . .

CAROL: . . . why . . . ?

JOHN: . . . in class I . . . (*He picks up the phone.*) (*Into phone:*) Hello. I can't talk now. Jerry? Yes? I underst . . . I can't talk now. I know . . . I know . . . Jerry. I can't *talk* now. Yes, I. Call me back in . . . Thank you. (*He hangs up.*) (*To* CAROL:) What do you want me to do? We are two people, all right? Both of whom have subscribed to . . .

CAROL: No, no . . .

JOHN: . . . certain arbitrary . . .

CAROL: No. You have to help me.

JOHN: Certain institutional . . . you tell me what you want me to do. . . . You tell me what you want me to . . .

CAROL: How can I go back and tell them the *grades* that I . . .

JOHN: . . . what can I do . . . ?

CAROL: *Teach* me. *Teach* me.

JOHN: . . . I'm trying to teach you.

CAROL: I read your book. I read it. I don't under . . .

JOHN: . . . you don't understand it.

CAROL: No.

JOHN: Well, perhaps it's not well *written* . . .

CAROL (*simultaneously with* "written"): No. No. No. I want to *understand* it.

JOHN: What don't you understand? (*Pause*)

CAROL: *Any* of it. What you're trying to say. When you talk about . . .

JOHN: . . . yes . . . ? (*She consults her notes.*)

CAROL: "Virtual warehousing of the young" . . .

JOHN: "Virtual warehousing of the young." If we artificially prolong adolescence . . .

CAROL: . . . and about "The Curse of Modern Education."

JOHN: . . . well . . .

CAROL: I don't . . .

JOHN: Look. It's just a *course*, it's just a *book*, it's just a . . .

CAROL: No. No. There are *people* out there. People who came *here*. To know something they didn't *know*. Who *came* here. To be *helped*. To be *helped*. So someone would *help* them. To *do* something. To *know* something. To get, what do they say? "To get on in the world." How can I do that if I don't, if I fail? But I don't *understand.* I don't *understand.* I don't understand what anything means . . . and I walk around. From morning 'til night: with this one thought in my head. I'm *stupid.*

JOHN: No one thinks you're stupid.

CAROL: No? What am I . . . ?

JOHN: I . . .

CAROL: . . . what am I, then?

JOHN: I think you're angry. Many people are. I have a *telephone* call that I have to make. And an *appointment,* which is rather *pressing;* though I sympathize with your concerns, and though I wish I had the time, this was not a previously scheduled meeting and I . . .

CAROL: . . . you think I'm nothing . . .

JOHN: . . . have an appointment with a *realtor,* and with my wife and . . .

CAROL: You think that I'm stupid.

JOHN: No. I certainly don't.

CAROL: You said it.

JOHN: No. I did not.

CAROL: You did.

JOHN: When?

CAROL: . . . you . . .

JOHN: No. I never did, or never would say that to a student, and . . .

CAROL: You said, "What can that mean?" (*Pause*) "What can that mean?" . . . (*Pause*)

JOHN: . . . and what did that mean to you . . . ?

CAROL: That meant I'm stupid. And I'll never learn. That's what that meant. And you're right.

JOHN: . . . I . . .

CAROL: But then. But then, what am I doing here . . . ?

JOHN: . . . if you thought that I . . .

CAROL: . . . when nobody wants me, and . . .

JOHN: . . . if you interpreted . . .

CAROL: Nobody *tells* me anything. And I *sit* there . . . in the *corner.* In the *back.* And everybody's talking about "this" all the time. And "concepts," and "precepts" and, and, and, and, and, WHAT IN THE WORLD ARE YOU TALKING ABOUT? And I read your book. And they said, "Fine, go in that class." Because you talked about responsibility to the young. I DON'T KNOW WHAT IT MEANS AND I'M FAILING . . .

JOHN: May . . .

CAROL: No, you're right. "Oh, hell." I failed. Flunk me out of it. It's garbage. Everything I do. "The ideas contained in this work express the author's feelings." That's right. That's right. I know I'm stupid. I know what I am. (*Pause*) I know what I am, Professor. You don't have to tell me. (*Pause*) It's pathetic. Isn't it?

JOHN: . . . Aha . . . (*Pause*) Sit down. Sit down. Please.

(*Pause*) Please sit down.

CAROL: Why?

JOHN: I want to talk to you.

CAROL: Why?

JOHN: Just sit down. (*Pause*) Please. Sit down. Will you, please . . . ? (*Pause. She does so.*) Thank you.

CAROL: What?

JOHN: I want to tell you something.

CAROL: (*Pause*) What?

JOHN: Well, I know what you're talking about.

CAROL: No. You don't.

JOHN: I think I do. (*Pause*)

CAROL: How can you?

JOHN: I'll tell you a story about myself. (*Pause*) Do you mind? (*Pause*) I was raised to think myself stupid. That's what I want to tell you. (*Pause*)

CAROL: What do you mean?

JOHN: Just what I said. I was brought up, and my earliest, and most persistent memories are of being told that I was stupid. "You have such *intelligence.* Why must you behave so *stupidly?*" Or, "Can't you *understand?* Can't you *understand?*" And I could *not* understand. I could *not* understand.

CAROL: What?

JOHN: The simplest problem. Was beyond me. It was a mystery.

CAROL: What was a mystery?

JOHN: How people learn. How *I* could learn. Which is what I've been speaking of in class. And of *course* you can't hear it. Carol. Of *course* you can't. (*Pause*) I used to speak of "real people," and wonder what the *real* people did. The *real* people. Who were they? *They* were the people other than myself. The *good* people. The *capable* people. The people who could do the things, *I* could not do: learn, study, retain . . . all that *garbage*—which is what I have been talking of in class, and that's *exactly* what I have been talking of—If you are told. . . . Listen to this. If the young child is told he cannot understand. Then he takes it as a *description* of himself. What am I? I am *that which can not understand.* And I saw you out there, when we were speaking of the concepts of . . .

CAROL: I can't understand any of them.

JOHN: Well, then, that's *my* fault. That's not your fault. And that is not verbiage. That's what I firmly hold to be the truth. And I am sorry, and I owe you an apology.

CAROL: Why?

JOHN: And I suppose that I have had some *things* on my mind. . . . We're buying a *house,* and . . .

CAROL: People said that you were stupid . . . ?

JOHN: Yes.

CAROL: When?

JOHN: I'll tell you when. Through my life. In my childhood; and, perhaps, they stopped. But I heard them continue.

CAROL: And what did they say?

JOHN: They said I was incompetent. Do you see? And when I'm tested the, the, the *feelings* of my youth about the *very subject of learning* come up. And I . . . I become, I feel "unworthy," and "unprepared." . . .

CAROL: . . . yes.

JOHN: . . . eh?

CAROL: . . . yes.

JOHN: And I feel that I must fail. (*Pause*)

CAROL: . . . but then you *do* fail. (*Pause*) You have to. (*Pause*) Don't you?

JOHN: A *pilot*. Flying a plane. The pilot is flying the plane. He thinks: Oh, my *God*, my mind's been drifting! Oh, my God! What kind of a cursed imbecile am I, that I, with this so precious cargo of *Life* in my charge, would allow my attention to wander. Why was I born? How deluded are those who put their trust in me, . . . et cetera, so on, and he crashes the plane.

CAROL: (*Pause*) He could just . . .

JOHN: That's right.

CAROL: He could say:

JOHN: My attention *wandered* for a moment . . .

CAROL: . . . uh huh . . .

JOHN: I had a *thought* I did not like . . . but now:

CAROL: . . . but now it's . . .

JOHN: That's what I'm telling you. It's time to put my attention . . . see: it is not: this is what I learned. It is Not Magic. Yes. Yes. *You.* You are going to be frightened. When faced with what may or may not be but which you are going to perceive as a test. You will become frightened. And you will say: "I am incapable of . . ." and everything *in* you will think these two things. "I must. But I can't." And you will think: Why was I born to be the laughingstock of a world in which everyone is better than I? In which I am entitled to nothing. Where I can not learn.

[*Pause*]

CAROL: Is that . . . (*Pause*) Is that what I have . . . ?

JOHN: Well. I don't know if I'd put it that way. Listen: I'm talking to you as I'd talk to my son. Because that's what I'd like him to have that I never had. I'm talking to you the way I wish that someone had talked to me. I don't know how to do it, other than to be *personal*, . . . but . . .

CAROL: Why would you want to be personal with me?

JOHN: Well, you see? That's what I'm saying. We can only interpret the behavior of others through the screen we . . . (*The phone rings.*) Through . . .

(*To phone:*) Hello . . . ? (*To* CAROL:) Through the screen we create. (*To phone:*) Hello. (*To* CAROL:) Excuse me a moment. (*To phone:*) Hello? No, I can't talk nnn . . . I know I did. In a few . . . I'm . . . is he coming to the . . . yes. I talked to him. We'll meet you at the No, because I'm with a *student.* It's going to be fff . . . This is important, too. I'm with a *student,* Jerry's going to . . . Listen: the sooner I get off, the sooner I'll be down, all right. I love you. Listen, listen, I said "I love you," it's going to work *out* with the, because I feel that it is, I'll be right down. All right? Well, then it's going to take as long as it takes. (*He hangs up.*) (*To* CAROL:) I'm sorry.

CAROL: What was that?

JOHN: There are some problems, as there usually are, about the final agreements for the new house.

CAROL: You're buying a new house.

JOHN: That's right.

CAROL: Because of your promotion.

JOHN: Well, I suppose that that's right.

CAROL: Why did you stay here with me?

JOHN: Stay here.

CAROL: Yes. When you should have gone.

JOHN: Because I like you.

CAROL: You like me.

JOHN: Yes.

CAROL: Why?

JOHN: Why? Well? Perhaps we're similar. (*Pause*) Yes. (*Pause*)

CAROL: You said "everyone has problems."

JOHN: Everyone has problems.

CAROL: Do they?

JOHN: Certainly.

CAROL: You do?

JOHN: Yes.

CAROL: What are they?

JOHN: Well. (*Pause*) Well, you're perfectly right. (*Pause*) If we're going to take off the Artificial *Stricture,* of "Teacher," and "Student," why should *my* problems be any more a mystery than your own? Of *course* I have problems. As you saw.

CAROL: . . . with what?

JOHN: With my *wife* . . . with *work* . . .

CAROL: With work?

JOHN: Yes. And, and, perhaps my problems are, do you see? *Similar* to yours.

CAROL: Would you tell me?

JOHN: All right. (*Pause*) I came *late* to teaching. And I found it Artificial. The notion of "I know and you do not"; and I saw an *exploitation* in the education process. I told you. I hated school, I hated teachers. I hated everyone who was in the position of a "boss" because I *knew*—I didn't *think*, mind you, I *knew* I was going to fail. Because I was a fuckup. I was just no god-

damned good. When I . . . late in life . . .
(*Pause*) When I *got out from under* . . . when I
worked my way out of the need to fail. When I
. . .

CAROL: How do you do that? (*Pause*)

JOHN: You have to look at what you are, and what
you feel, and how you act. And, finally, you
have to look at how you act. And say: If that's
what I *did*, that must be how I think of myself.

CAROL: I don't understand.

JOHN: If I fail all the time, it must be that I think of
myself as a failure. If I do not want to think of
myself as a failure, perhaps I should begin by
succeeding now and again. Look. The tests, you
see, which you encounter, in school, in college,
in life, were designed, in the most part, for
idiots. *By* idiots. There is no need to fail at
them. They are not a test of your worth. They
are a test of your ability to retain and spout
back misinformation. Of *course* you fail them.
They're *nonsense*. And I . . .

CAROL: . . . no . . .

JOHN: Yes. They're *garbage*. They're a *joke*. Look at
me. Look at me. The Tenure Committee. The
Tenure Committee. Come to judge me. The
Bad Tenure Committee.

The "Test." Do you see? They put me to the
test. Why, they had people voting on me I
wouldn't employ to wax my car. And yet, I go
before the Great Tenure Committee, and I have
an urge, to *vomit*, to, to, to puke my *badness* on
the table, to show them: "I'm no good. Why
would you pick *me*?"

CAROL: They granted you tenure.

JOHN: Oh no, they announced it, but they haven't
signed. Do you see? "At any moment . . ."

CAROL: . . . mmm . . .

JOHN: "They might not *sign*" . . . I might not . . . the
house might not go through . . . Eh? Eh? They'll
find out my "dark secret." (*Pause*)

CAROL: . . . what is it . . . ?

JOHN: There *isn't* one. But *they* will find an index of
my badness . . .

CAROL: Index?

JOHN: A ". . . pointer." A "Pointer." You see? Do you
see? I *understand* you. I. Know. That. Feeling.
Am I entitled to my job, and my nice *home*,
and my *wife*, and my *family*, and so on. This is
what I'm saying: That theory of education
which, that *theory*:

CAROL: I . . . I . . . (*Pause*)

JOHN: What?

CAROL: I . . .

JOHN: What?

CAROL: I want to know about my grade. (*Long pause*)

JOHN: Of course you do.

CAROL: Is that bad?

JOHN: No.

CAROL: Is it bad that I asked you that?

JOHN: No.

CAROL: Did I upset you?

JOHN: No. And I apologize. Of *course* you want to
know about your grade. And, of course, you
can't concentrate on anyth . . . (*The telephone
starts to ring*.) Wait a moment.

CAROL: I should go.

JOHN: I'll make you a deal.

CAROL: No, you have to . . .

JOHN: Let it ring. I'll make you a deal. You stay here.
We'll start the whole course over. I'm going to
say it was not you, it was I who was not pay-
ing attention. We'll start the whole course over.
Your grade is an "A." Your final grade is an
"A." (*The phone stops ringing*.)

CAROL: But the class is only half over . . .

JOHN (*simultaneously with "over"*): Your grade for the
whole term is an "A." If you will come back
and meet with me. A few more times. Your
grade's an "A." Forget about the paper. You
didn't like it, you didn't like writing it. It's not
important. What's important is that I awake
your interest, if I can, and that I answer your
questions. Let's start over. (*Pause*)

CAROL: Over. With what?

JOHN: Say this is the beginning.

CAROL: The beginning.

JOHN: Yes.

CAROL: Of what?

JOHN: Of the class.

CAROL: But we can't start over.

JOHN: I say we can. (*Pause*) I say we can.

CAROL: But I don't believe it.

JOHN: Yes, I know that. But it's true. What is The
Class but you and me? (*Pause*)

CAROL: There are rules.

JOHN: Well. We'll break them.

CAROL: How can we?

JOHN: We won't tell anybody.

CAROL: Is that all right?

JOHN: I say that it's fine.

CAROL: Why would you do this for me?

JOHN: I like you. Is that so difficult for you to . . .

CAROL: Um . . .

JOHN: There's no one here but you and me. (*Pause*)

CAROL: All right. I did not understand. When you
referred . . .

JOHN: All right, yes?

CAROL: When you referred to hazing.

JOHN: Hazing.

CAROL: You wrote, in your book. About the comparative . . . the comparative . . . (*She checks her
notes.*)

JOHN: Are you checking your notes . . . ?

CAROL: Yes.

JOHN: Tell me in your own . . .

CAROL: I want to make sure that I have it right.

JOHN: No. Of course. You want to be exact.

CAROL: I want to know everything that went on.

JOHN: . . . that's good.

CAROL: . . . so I . . .

JOHN: That's very good. But I was suggesting, many times, that that which we wish to retain is retained oftentimes, I think, *better* with less expenditure of effort.

CAROL (*Of notes*): Here it is: you wrote of *hazing*.

JOHN: . . . that's correct. Now: I said " hazing." It means ritualized annoyance. We shove this book at you, we say read it. Now, you say you've read it? I think that you're *lying*. I'll *grill* you, and when I find you've lied, you'll be disgraced, and your life will be ruined. It's a sick game. Why do we do it? Does it educate? In no sense. Well, then, what is higher education? It is something-other-than-useful.

CAROL: What is "something-other-than-useful?"

JOHN: It has become a ritual, it has become an article of faith. That all must be subjected to, or to put it differently, that all are entitled to Higher Education. And my point . . .

CAROL: You disagree with that?

JOHN: Well, let's address that. What do you think?

CAROL: I don't know.

JOHN: What do you think, though? (*Pause*)

CAROL: I don't know.

JOHN: I spoke of it in class. Do you remember my example?

CAROL: Justice.

JOHN: Yes. Can you repeat it to me? (*She looks down at her notebook.*) Without your notes? I ask you as a favor to me, so that I can see if my idea was interesting.

CAROL: You said "justice" . . .

JOHN: Yes?

CAROL: . . . that all are entitled . . . (*Pause*) I . . . I . . . I . . .

JOHN: Yes. To a speedy trial. To a fair trial. But they needn't be given a trial *at all* unless they stand accused. Eh? Justice is their right, should they choose to avail themselves of it, they should have a fair trial. It does not follow, of necessity, a person's life is incomplete without a trial in it. Do you see?

My point is a confusion between equity and *utility* arose. So we confound the *usefulness* of higher education with our, granted, right to equal access to the same. We, in effect, create a *prejudice* toward it, completely independent of . . .

CAROL: . . . that it is prejudice that we should go to school?

JOHN: Exactly. (*Pause*)

CAROL: How can you say that? How . . .

JOHN: Good. Good. *Good*. That's right! Speak up! What is a prejudice? An unreasoned belief. We are all subject to it. None of us is not. When it is threatened, or opposed, we feel anger, and feel, do we not? As you do now. Do you not? Good.

CAROL: . . . but how can you . . .

JOHN: . . . let us examine. Good.

CAROL: How . . .

JOHN: Good. Good. When . . .

CAROL: I'M SPEAKING . . . (*Pause*)

JOHN: I'm sorry.

CAROL: How can you . . .

JOHN: . . . I beg your pardon.

CAROL: That's all right.

JOHN: I beg your pardon.

CAROL: That's all right.

JOHN: I'm sorry I interrupted you.

CAROL: That's all right.

JOHN: You were saying?

CAROL: I was saying . . . I was saying . . . (*She checks her notes.*) How can you say in a class. Say in a college class, that college education is prejudice?

JOHN: I said that our predilection for it . . .

CAROL: Predilection . . .

JOHN: . . . you know what that means.

CAROL: Does it mean "liking"?

JOHN: Yes.

CAROL: But how can you say that? That College . . .

JOHN: . . . that's my *job*, don't you know.

CAROL: What is?

JOHN: To provoke you.

CAROL: No.

JOHN: Oh. Yes, though.

CAROL: To provoke me?

JOHN: That's right.

CAROL: To make me mad?

JOHN: That's right. To force you . . .

CAROL: . . . to make me mad is your job?

JOHN: To force you to . . . listen: (*Pause*) Ah. (*Pause*) When I was young somebody told me, are you ready, the rich copulate less often than the poor. But when they do, they take more of their clothes off. Years. Years, mind you, I would compare experiences of my own to this dictum, saying, aha, this fits the norm, or ah, this is a variation from it. What did it mean? Nothing. It was some jerk thing, some school kid told me that took up room inside my head. (*Pause*) Somebody told *you*, and you hold it as an article of faith, that higher education is an unassailable good. This notion is so dear to you that when I question it you become angry. Good. Good, I say. Are not those the very things which we should question? I say college education, since the war, has become so a matter of course, and such a fashionable necessity, for those either of or aspiring *to* to the new vast middle class, that we *espouse* it, as a matter of right, and have ceased to ask, "What is it good for?" (*Pause*)

What might be some reasons for pursuit of higher education?

One: A love of learning.

Two: The wish for mastery of a skill.

Three: For economic betterment.

[*Stops. Makes a note.*]

CAROL: I'm keeping you.

JOHN: One moment. I have to make a note . . .

CAROL: It's something that I said?

JOHN: No, we're buying a house.

CAROL: You're buying the new house.

JOHN: To go with the tenure. That's right. Nice *house*, close to the *private school* . . . (*He continues making his note.*) . . . We were talking of economic betterment (CAROL *writes in her notebook.*) . . . I was thinking of the School Tax. (*He continues writing.*) (*To himself:*) . . . *where is it written* that I have to send my child to public school. . . . Is it a law that I have to improve the City Schools at the expense of my own interest? And, is this not simply *The White Man's Burden?* Good. And (*Looks up to* CAROL) . . . does this interest you?

CAROL: No. I'm taking notes . . .

JOHN: You don't have to take notes, you know, you can just listen.

CAROL: I want to make sure I remember it. (*Pause*)

JOHN: I'm not lecturing you, I'm just trying to tell you some things I think.

CAROL: What do you think?

JOHN: Should all kids go to college? *Why* . . .

CAROL: (*Pause*) To learn.

JOHN: But if he does not learn.

CAROL: If the child does not learn?

JOHN: Then why is he in college? Because he was told it was his "right"?

CAROL: Some might find college instructive.

JOHN: I would hope so.

CAROL: But how do they feel? Being told they are wasting their time?

JOHN: I don't think I'm telling them that.

CAROL: You said that education was "prolonged and systematic hazing."

JOHN: Yes. It can be so.

CAROL: . . . if education is so *bad*, why do you do it?

JOHN: I do it because I love it. (*Pause*) Let's. . . . I suggest you look at the demographics, wage-earning capacity, college- and non-college-educated men and women, 1855 to 1980, and let's see if we can wring some worth from the statistics. Eh? And . . .

CAROL: No.

JOHN: What?

CAROL: I can't understand them.

JOHN: . . . you . . . ?

CAROL: . . . the "charts." The *Concepts*, the . . .

JOHN: "Charts" are simply . . .

CAROL: When I leave here . . .

JOHN: Charts, do you see . . .

CAROL: No, I can't . . .

JOHN: You can, though.

CAROL: No, NO—I DON'T UNDERSTAND. DO YOU SEE??? I DON'T UNDERSTAND . . .

JOHN: What?

CAROL: *Any* of it. *Any* of it. I'm *smiling* in class, I'm *smiling*, the whole time. What are you *talking* about? What is everyone *talking* about? I don't *understand*. I don't know what it *means*. I don't know what it means to *be* here . . . you tell me I'm intelligent, and then you tell me I should not be *here*, what do you *want* with me? What does it *mean*? Who should I *listen* to . . . I . . .

[*He goes over to her and puts his arm around her shoulder.*]

NO! (*She walks away from him.*)

JOHN: Sshhhh.

CAROL: No, I don't under . . .

JOHN: Sshhhhh.

CAROL: I don't know what you're *saying* . . .

JOHN: Sshhhhh. It's all right.

CAROL: . . . I have no . . .

JOHN: Sshhhhh. Sshhhhh. Let it go a moment. (*Pause*) Sshhhhh . . . let it go. (*Pause*) Just let it go. (*Pause*) Just let it go. It's all right. (*Pause*) Sshhhhh. (*Pause*) I understand . . . (*Pause*) What do you feel?

CAROL: I feel bad.

JOHN: I know. It's all right.

CAROL: I . . . (*Pause*)

JOHN: What?

CAROL: I . . .

JOHN: What? Tell me.

CAROL: I don't understand you.

JOHN: I know. It's all right.

CAROL: I . . .

JOHN: What? (*Pause*) What? *Tell* me.

CAROL: I can't tell you.

JOHN: No, you must.

CAROL: I can't.

JOHN: No. Tell me. (*Pause*)

CAROL: I'm bad. (*Pause*) Oh, God. (*Pause*)

JOHN: It's all right.

CAROL: I'm . . .

JOHN: It's all right.

CAROL: I can't talk about this.

JOHN: It's all right. Tell me.

CAROL: Why do you want to know this?

JOHN: I don't want to know. I want to know whatever you . . .

CAROL: I always . . .

JOHN: . . . good . . .

CAROL: I always . . . all my life . . . I have never told anyone this . . .

JOHN: Yes. Go on. (*Pause*) Go on.

CAROL: All of my life . . . (*The phone rings.*) (*Pause. JOHN goes to the phone and picks it up.*)

JOHN (*into phone*): I can't talk now. (*Pause*) What? (*Pause*) Hmm. (*Pause*) All right, I . . . I. Can't. Talk. Now. No, no, no, I *Know* I did, but. . . . What? Hello. What? She *what*? She *can't*, she said the agreement is void? How, how is the agreement *void? That's our House.*

I have the *paper*; when we come down, next week, with the payment, and the paper, that house is . . . wait, wait, wait, wait, wait, wait, wait: Did Jerry . . . is Jerry there? (*Pause*) Is *she* there . . . ? Does she have a *lawyer* . . . ? How the *hell*, how the *Hell*. That is . . . it's a question, you said, of the *easement.* I don't underst . . . it's not the *whole agreement.* It's just the *easement*, why would she? Put, put, put, *Jerry* on. (*Pause*) Jer, Jerry: What the *Hell* . . . that's my *house.* That's . . . Well, I'm, no, no, no, I'm *not* coming ddd . . . List, *Listen, screw* her. You *tell* her. You, listen: I want you to take *Grace*, you take Grace, and get out of that house. You *leave* her there. Her and her lawyer, and you *tell* them, we'll see them in court next . . . no. No. Leave her there, leave her to *stew* in it: You tell her, we're *getting* that house, and we are going to . . . No. I'm *not* coming down. I'll be damned if I'll sit in the same rrr . . . the next, you tell her the next time I *see* her is in court . . . I . . . (*Pause*) What? (*Pause*) What? I don't understand. (*Pause*) Well, what about the house? (*Pause*) There isn't any problem with the hhh . . . (*Pause*) No, no, no, that's all right. All ri . . . All right . . . (*Pause*) Of course. Tha . . . Thank you. No, I will. Right away. (*He hangs up.*) (*Pause*)

CAROL: What is it? (*Pause*)

JOHN: It's a surprise party.

CAROL: It is.

JOHN: Yes.

CAROL: A party for you.

JOHN: Yes.

CAROL: Is it your birthday?

JOHN: No.

CAROL: What is it?

JOHN: The tenure announcement.

CAROL: The tenure announcement.

JOHN: They're throwing a party for us in our new house.

CAROL: Your new house.

JOHN: The house that we're buying.

CAROL: You have to go.

JOHN: It seems that I do.

CAROL: (*Pause*) They're proud of you.

JOHN: Well, there are those who would say it's a form of aggression.

CAROL: What is?

JOHN: A surprise.

ACT II

[*JOHN and CAROL seated across the desk from each other.*]

JOHN: You see, (*pause*) I love to teach. And flatter myself I am *skilled* at it. And I love the, the aspect of *performance.* I think I must confess that.

When I found I loved to teach I swore that I would not become that cold, rigid automation of an instructor which I had encountered as a child.

Now, I was not unconscious that it was given me to err upon the other side. And, so, I asked and *ask* myself if I engaged in heterodoxy, I will not say "gratuitously" for I do not care to posit orthodoxy as a given good—but, "to the detriment of, of my students." (*Pause*)

As I said. When the possibility of tenure opened, and, of course, I'd long pursued it, I was, of course *happy*, and *covetous* of it.

I asked myself if I was wrong to covet it. And thought about it long, and, I hope, truthfully, and saw in myself several things in, I think, no particular order. (*Pause*)

That I *would* pursue it. That I *desired* it, that I was not pure of longing for security, and that that, perhaps, was not reprehensible in me. That I had duties *beyond* the school, and that my duty to my home, for instance, was, or should be, if it were not, of an equal weight. That tenure, and security, and yes, and *comfort*, were not, of themselves, to be scorned; and were even worthy of honorable pursuit. And that it was given me. Here, in this place, which I enjoy, and in which I find comfort, to assure myself of—as far as it rests in The Material—a continuation of that joy and comfort. In exchange for what? Teaching. Which I love. What was the price of this security? To obtain *tenure.* Which tenure the committee is in the process of granting me. And on the basis of which I contracted to purchase a house. Now, as you don't have your own family, at this point, you may not know what that means. But to me it is important. A home. A Good Home. To raise my family. Now: The Tenure Committee will meet. This is the process, and a *good* process. Under which the school has functioned for quite a long time. They will meet, and hear your complaint—which you have the right to make; and they will dismiss it. They will *dismiss* your complaint; and, in the intervening period, I will lose my house. I will not be able to close on my house. I will lose my *deposit*, and the home I'd picked out for my wife and son will go by the boards. Now: I see I have angered you. I understand your anger at teachers. I was angry with mine. I felt hurt and humiliated by them. Which is one of the reasons that I went into education.

CAROL: What do you want of me?

JOHN: (*Pause*) I was hurt. When I received the report. Of the tenure committee. I was shocked. And I was hurt. No, I don't mean to subject you to my weak sensibilities. All right. Finally, I didn't understand. Then I thought: is it not always at those points at which we reckon ourselves unassailable that we are most vulnerable and . . . (*Pause*) Yes. All right. You find me pedantic. Yes. I am. By nature, by *birth*, by profession, I don't know . . . I'm always looking for a *paradigm* for . . .

CAROL: I don't know what a paradigm is.

JOHN: It's a model.

CAROL: Then why can't you use that word? (*Pause*)

JOHN: If it is important to you. Yes, all right. I was looking for a model. To continue: I feel that one point . . .

CAROL: I . . .

JOHN: One second . . . upon which I am unassailable is my unflinching concern for my students' dignity. I asked you here to . . . in the spirit of *investigation*, to ask you . . . to ask . . . (*Pause*) What have I done to you? (*Pause*) And, and, I suppose, how I can make amends. Can we not settle this now? It's pointless, really, and I want to know.

CAROL: What you can do to force me to retract?

JOHN: That is not what I meant at all.

CAROL: To bribe me, to convince me . . .

JOHN: . . . No.

CAROL: To retract . . .

JOHN: That is not what I meant at all. I think that you know it is not.

CAROL: That is not what I know. I *wish* I . . .

JOHN: I do not want to . . . you wish what?

CAROL: No, you said what amends can you make. To force me to retract.

JOHN: That is not what I said.

CAROL: I have my notes.

JOHN: Look. Look. The Stoics say . . .

CAROL: The Stoics?

JOHN: The Stoical Philosophers say if you remove the phrase "I have been injured," you have removed the injury. Now: Think: I know that you're upset. Just tell me. Literally. Literally: what wrong have I done you?

CAROL: Whatever you have done to me—to the extent that you've done it to *me*, do you know, rather than to me as a *student*, and, so, to the student body, is contained in my report. To the tenure committee.

JOHN: Well, all right. (*Pause*) Let's see. (*He reads.*) I find that I am sexist. That I am *elitist*. I'm not sure I know what that means, other than it's a derogatory word, meaning "bad." That I . . . That I insist on wasting time, in nonprescribed, in self-aggrandizing and theatrical *diversions* from the prescribed *text* . . . that these have taken both sexist and pornographic forms . . . here we find listed . . . (*Pause*) Here we find listed . . . instances ". . . closeted with a student" . . . "Told a rambling, sexually explicit story, in which the frequency and attitudes of fornication of the poor and rich are, it would seem, the central point . . . moved to *embrace* said student and . . . all part of a pattern . . ." (*Pause*)

(*He reads.*) That I used the phrase "The White Man's Burden" . . . that I told you how I'd asked you to my room because I quote like you. (*Pause*)

(*He reads.*) "'He' said he 'liked' me. That he 'liked being with me.' He'd let me write my examination paper over, if I could come back oftener to see him in his office." (*Pause*) (*To* CAROL:) It's *ludicrous*. Don't you know that? It's not *necessary*. It's going to *humiliate* you, and it's going to cost me my *house*, and . . .

CAROL: It's "ludicrous . . ."?

[JOHN *picks up the report and reads again.*]

JOHN: "He told me he had problems with his wife; and that he wanted to take off the artificial stricture of Teacher and Student. He put his arm around me . . ."

CAROL: Do you deny it? Can you deny it . . . ? Do you see? (*Pause*) Don't you see? You don't see, do you?

JOHN: I don't see . . .

CAROL: You think, you think you can deny that these things happened; or, if they *did*, if they *did*, that they meant what you *said* they meant. Don't you see? You drag me in here, you drag us, to listen to you "go on"; and "go on" about this, or that, or we don't "express" ourselves very well. We don't say what we mean. Don't we? Don't we? We *do* say what we mean. And you say that "I don't understand you . . .": Then *you* . . . (*Points.*)

JOHN: "Consult the Report"?

CAROL: . . . that's right.

JOHN: You see. You see. Can't you. . . . You see what I'm saying? Can't you tell me in your own words?

CAROL: Those are my own words. (*Pause*)

JOHN (*He reads.*): "He told me that if I would stay alone with him in his office, he would change my grade to an A." (*To* CAROL:) What have I done to you? Oh. My God, are you so hurt?

CAROL: What I "feel" is irrelevant. (*Pause*)

JOHN: Do you know that I tried to help you?

CAROL: What I know I have reported.

JOHN: I would like to help you now. I would. Before this escalates.

CAROL (*simultaneously with "escalates"*): You see. I don't think that I need your help. I don't think I need anything you have.

JOHN: I feel . . .

CAROL: I don't *care* what you feel. Do you see? Do YOU SEE? You can't *do* that anymore. You. Do. Not. Have. The. Power. Did you misuse it? *Someone* did. Are you part of that group? *Yes. Yes.* You Are. You've *done* these things. And to say, and to say, "Oh. Let me help you with your problem . . ."

JOHN: Yes. I understand. I understand. You're *hurt*. You're *angry*. Yes. I think your *anger* is *betraying* you. Down a path which helps no one.

CAROL: I don't *care* what you think.

JOHN: You don't? (*Pause*) But you talk of *rights*. Don't you see? *I* have rights too. Do you see? I have a *house* . . . part of the *real* world; and The Tenure Committee, Good Men and True . . .

CAROL: . . . Professor . . .

JOHN: . . . Please: *Also* part of that world: you understand? This is my *life*. I'm not a *bogeyman*. I don't "stand" for something, I . . .

CAROL: . . . Professor . . .

JOHN: . . . I . . .

CAROL: Professor. I came here as a *favor*. At your personal request. Perhaps I should not have done so. But I did. On my behalf, and on behalf of my group. And you speak of the tenure committee, one of whose members is a woman, as you know. And though you might call it Good Fun, or An Historical Phrase, or An Oversight, or, All of the Above, to refer to the committee as Good Men and True, it is a demeaning remark. It is a sexist remark, and to overlook it is to countenance continuation of that method

of thought. It's a remark . . .

JOHN: OH COME ON. Come on. . . . Sufficient to deprive a family of . . .

CAROL: Sufficient? Sufficient? Sufficient? Yes. It is a *fact* . . . and that story, which I quote, is *vile* and *classist*, and *manipulative* and *pornographic*. It . . .

JOHN: . . . it's pornographic . . . ?

CAROL: What gives you the *right*. Yes. To speak to a *woman* in your private . . . Yes. Yes. I'm sorry. I'm sorry. You feel yourself empowered . . . you say so yourself. To *strut*. To *posture*. To "perform." To "Call me in here . . ." Eh? You say that higher education is a joke. And treat it as such, you *treat* it as such. And *confess* to a taste to play the *Patriarch* in your class. To grant *this*. To deny *that*. To embrace your students.

JOHN: How can you assert. How can you stand there and . . .

CAROL: How can you *deny* it. You did it to me. *Here.* You *did* . . . . You *confess*. You love the Power. To *deviate*. To *invent*, to transgress . . . to *transgress* whatever norms have been established for us. And you think it's charming to "question" in yourself this taste to mock and destroy. But you should question it. Professor. And you pick those things which you feel *advance* you: publication, *tenure*, and the steps to get them you call "harmless rituals." And you perform those steps. Although you say it is hypocrisy. But to the aspirations of your students. Of *hardworking students*, who come here, who *slave* to come here—you have no idea what it cost me to come to this school—you *mock* us. You call education "hazing," and from your so-protected, so-elitist seat you hold our confusion as a *joke*, and our hopes and efforts with it. Then you sit there and say "what have I done?" And ask me to understand that *you* have aspirations too. But I tell you. I tell you. That you are vile. And that you are exploitative. And if you possess one ounce of that inner honesty you describe in your book, you can look in yourself and see those things that I see. And you can find revulsion equal to my own. Good day. (*She prepares to leave the room.*)

JOHN: Wait a second, will you, just one moment. (*Pause*) Nice day today.

CAROL: What?

JOHN: You said "Good day." I think that it is a nice day today.

CAROL: *Is* it?

JOHN: Yes, I think it is.

CAROL: And why is that important?

JOHN: Because it is the essence of all human communication. I say something conventional, you respond, and the information we exchange is not about the "weather," but that we both agree to converse. In effect, we agree that we are both human. (*Pause*)

I'm not a . . . "exploiter," and you're not a . . . "deranged," what? *Revolutionary* . . . that we may, that we may have . . . positions, and that we may have . . . desires, which are in *conflict,* but that we're just human. (*Pause*) That means that sometimes we're *imperfect.* (*Pause*) Often we're in conflict . . . (*Pause*) *Much* of what we do, you're right, in the name of "principles" is *self-serving* . . . much of what we do is *conventional.* (*Pause*) You're right. (*Pause*) You said you came in the class because you wanted to learn about *education.* I don't know that I can teach you about education. But I know that I can tell you what I *think* about education, and then *you* decide. And you don't have to fight with me. *I'm* not the subject. (*Pause*) And where I'm *wrong* . . . perhaps it's not your job to "fix" me. I don't want to fix *you.* I would like to tell you what I *think,* because that *is* my job, conventional as it is, and flawed as I may be. And then, if you can show me some better *form,* then we can proceed from there. But, just like "nice day, isn't it . . . ?" I don't think we can proceed until we accept that each of us is human. (*Pause*) And we still can have difficulties. We *will* have them . . . that's all right too. (*Pause*) Now:

CAROL: . . . wait . . .

JOHN: Yes. I want to hear it.

CAROL: . . . the . . .

JOHN: Yes. Tell me frankly.

CAROL: . . . my position . . .

JOHN: I want to hear it. In your own words. What you want. And what you feel.

CAROL: . . . I . . .

JOHN: . . . yes . . .

CAROL: My Group.

JOHN: Your "Group" . . . ? (*Pause*)

CAROL: The people I've been talking to . . .

JOHN: There's no shame in that. Everybody needs advisers. Everyone needs to expose themselves. To various points of view. It's not wrong. It's essential. Good. Good. Now: You and I . . . (*The phone rings.*) You and I . . .

(*He hesitates for a moment, and then picks it up.*) (*Into phone*) Hello. (*Pause*) Um . . . no, I know they do. (*Pause*) I know she does. Tell her that I . . . can I call you back? . . . Then tell her that I think it's going to be fine. (*Pause*) Tell her just, just hold on, I'll . . . can I get back to you? . . . Well . . . no, no, no, we're *taking* the house . . . we're . . . no, no, nn . . . no, she will nnn, it's

not a *question* of refunding the dep . . . no . . . it's not a *question* of the deposit . . . will you call Jerry? Babe, baby, will you just call Jerry? Tell him, nnn . . . tell him they, well, they're to keep the deposit, because the deal, be . . . because the deal is going to go *through* . . . because I know . . . be . . . will you please? Just *trust* me. Be . . . well, I'm dealing with the complaint. Yes. Right *Now.* Which is why I . . . yes, no, no, it's really, I can't *talk* about it now. Call Jerry, and I can't talk now. Ff . . . fine. Gg . . . good-bye. (*Hangs up.*) (*Pause*) I'm sorry we were interrupted.

CAROL: No . . .

JOHN: I . . . I was saying:

CAROL: You said that we should agree to talk about my complaint.

JOHN: That's correct.

CAROL: But we *are* talking about it.

JOHN: Well, that's correct too. You see? This is the *gist* of education.

CAROL: No, no. I mean, we're talking about it at the Tenure Committee Hearing. (*Pause*)

JOHN: Yes, but I'm saying: we can talk about it *now,* as easily as . . .

CAROL: No. I think that we should stick to the process . . .

JOHN: . . . wait a . . .

CAROL: . . . the "conventional" process. As you said. (*She gets up.*) And you're right, I'm sorry if I was, um, if I was "discourteous" to you. You're right.

JOHN: Wait, wait a . . .

CAROL: I really should go.

JOHN: Now, look, granted. I have an interest. In the status quo. All right? Everyone does. But what I'm saying is that the *committee* . . .

CAROL: Professor, you're right. Just don't impinge on me. We'll take our differences, and . . .

JOHN: You're going to make a . . . look, look, look, you're going to . . .

CAROL: I shouldn't have come here. They told me . . .

JOHN: One moment. No. No. There are *norms,* here, and there's no reason. Look: I'm trying to *save* you . . .

CAROL: No one *asked* you to . . . you're trying to save *me*? Do me the courtesy to . . .

JOHN: I *am* doing you the courtesy. I'm talking *straight* to you. We can settle this *now.* And I want you to sit *down* and . . .

CAROL: You must excuse me . . . (*She starts to leave the room.*)

JOHN: Sit down, it seems we each have a. . . . Wait one moment. Wait one moment . . . just do me the courtesy to . . .

[*He restrains her from leaving.*]

CAROL: LET ME GO.

JOHN: I have no desire to *hold* you, I just want to *talk* to you . . .

CAROL: LET ME GO. LET ME GO. WOULD SOMEBODY *HELP* ME? WOULD SOMEBODY *HELP* ME PLEASE . . . ?

ACT III

[At rise, CAROL and JOHN are seated.]

JOHN: I have asked you here. (*Pause*) I have asked you here against, against my . . .

CAROL: I was most surprised you asked me.

JOHN: . . . against my better *judgment*, against . . .

CAROL: I was most surprised . . .

JOHN: . . . against the . . . yes. I'm sure.

CAROL: . . . If you would like me to leave, I'll leave. I'll go right now . . . (*She rises.*)

JOHN: Let us begin *correctly*, may we? I feel . . .

CAROL: That is what I wished to do. That's why I came here, but now . . .

JOHN: . . . I feel . . .

CAROL: But now perhaps you'd like me to leave . . .

JOHN: I don't want you to leave. I asked you to come . . .

CAROL: I didn't have to come here.

JOHN: No. (*Pause*) Thank you.

CAROL: All right. (*Pause*) (*She sits down.*)

JOHN: Although I feel that it *profits*, it would *profit* you something, to . . .

CAROL: . . . what I . . .

JOHN: If you would hear me out, if you would hear me out.

CAROL: I came here to, the court officers told me not to come.

JOHN: . . . the "court" officers . . . ?

CAROL: I was shocked that you asked.

JOHN: . . . wait . . .

CAROL: Yes. But I did *not* come here to hear what it "profits" me.

JOHN: The "court" officers . . .

CAROL: . . . no, no, perhaps I should leave . . . (*She gets up.*)

JOHN: Wait.

CAROL: No. I shouldn't have . . .

JOHN: . . . wait. Wait. Wait a moment.

CAROL: Yes? What is it you want? (*Pause*) What is it you want?

JOHN: I'd like you to stay.

CAROL: You want me to stay.

JOHN: Yes.

CAROL: You do.

JOHN: Yes. (*Pause*) Yes. I would like to have you hear me out. If you would. (*Pause*) Would you please? If you would do that I would be in your debt. (*Pause*) (*She sits.*) Thank You. (*Pause*)

CAROL: What is it you wish to tell me?

JOHN: All right. I cannot . . . (*Pause*) I cannot help but feel you are owed an apology. (*Pause*) (*Of papers in his hands*) I have read. (*Pause*) And reread these accusations.

CAROL: What "accusations"?

JOHN: The, the tenure comm . . . what other accusations . . . ?

CAROL: The tenure committee . . . ?

JOHN: Yes.

CAROL: Excuse me, but those are not accusations. They have been *proved*. They are facts.

JOHN: . . . I . . .

CAROL: No. Those are not "accusations."

JOHN: . . . those?

CAROL: . . . the committee (*The phone starts to ring.*) the committee has . . .

JOHN: . . . All right . . .

CAROL: . . . those are not accusations. The Tenure Committee.

JOHN: ALL RIGHT. ALL RIGHT. ALL RIGHT. (*He picks up the phone.*) Hello. Yes. No. I'm here. Tell Mister . . . No, I can't talk to him now . . . I'm sure he has, but I'm fff . . . I know . . . No, I have no time t. . . tell Mister . . . tell Jerry that I'm *fine* and that I'll call him right aw . . . (*Pause*) My wife . . . Yes. I'm sure she has. Yes, thank you. Yes, I'll call her too. I cannot talk to you now. (*He hangs up.*) (*Pause*) All right. It was good of you to come. Thank you. I have studied. I have spent some time studying the indictment.

CAROL: You will have to explain that word to me.

JOHN: An "indictment" . . .

CAROL: Yes.

JOHN: Is a "bill of particulars." A . . .

CAROL: All right. Yes.

JOHN: In which is alleged . . .

CAROL: No. I cannot allow that. I cannot allow that. Nothing is alleged. Everything is proved . . .

JOHN: Please, wait a sec . . .

CAROL: I cannot *come* to allow . . .

JOHN: If I may . . . If I may, from whatever you feel is "established," by . . .

CAROL: The issue here is not what I "feel." It is not my "feelings," but the feelings of women. And men. Your superiors, who've been "polled," do you see? To whom *evidence* has been presented, who have *ruled*, do you see? Who have weighed the testimony and the evidence, and have *ruled*, do you see? That you are *negligent*. That you are *guilty*, that you are found *wanting*, and in *error*; and are *not*, for the reasons so-told, to be given tenure. That you are to be disciplined. For facts. For *facts*. Not "alleged," what is the word? But *proved*. Do you see? *By your own actions.*

That is what the tenure committee has said. That is what my lawyer said. For what you did in class. For what you did *in this office*.

JOHN: They're going to discharge me.

CAROL: As full well they should. You don't understand? You're angry? What has *led* you to this place? Not your sex. Not your race. Not your class. YOUR OWN ACTIONS. And you're *angry*. You *ask* me here. What *do* you want? You want to "charm" me. You want to "convince" me. You want me to recant. I will *not* recant. Why should I . . . ? What I say is right. You tell me, you are going to tell me that you have a wife and child. You are going to say that you have a career and that you've worked for twenty years for this. Do you know what you've *worked* for? *Power*. For *power*. Do you understand? And you sit there, and you tell me *stories*. About your *house*, about all the private *schools*, and about *privilege*, and how you are entitled. To *buy*, to *spend*, to *mock*, to *summon*. All your stories. All your silly weak *guilt*, it's all about *privilege*; and you won't know it. Don't you see? You worked twenty years for the right to *insult* me. And you feel entitled to be *paid* for it. Your Home. Your Wife . . . Your sweet "deposit" on your house . . .

JOHN: Don't you have feelings?

CAROL: That's my point. You see? Don't you have feelings? Your final argument. What is it that has no feelings. *Animals*. I don't take your side, you question if I'm Human.

JOHN: Don't you have feelings?

CAROL: I have a responsibility. I . . .

JOHN: . . . to . . . ?

CAROL: To? This institution. To the *students*. To my group.

JOHN: . . . your "group." . . .

CAROL: Because I speak, yes, not for myself. But for the group; for those who suffer what I suffer. On behalf of whom, even if I, were, inclined, to what, forgive? Forget? What? Overlook your . . .

JOHN: . . . my behavior?

CAROL: . . . it would be wrong.

JOHN: Even if you were inclined to "forgive" me.

CAROL: It would be wrong.

JOHN: And what would transpire.

CAROL: Transpire?

JOHN: Yes.

CAROL: "Happen?"

JOHN: Yes.

CAROL: Then *say* it. For Christ's sake. Who the *hell* do you think that you are? You want a post. You want unlimited power. To do and to say what you want. As it pleases you—Testing, Questioning, Flirting . . .

JOHN: I never . . .

CAROL: Excuse me, one moment, will you?

[She reads from her notes.]

The twelfth: "Have a good day, dear."
The fifteenth: "Now, don't *you* look fetching . . ."
April seventeenth: "If you girls would come over here . . ." I saw you. I saw you, Professor. For two semesters sit there, stand there and exploit our, as you thought, "paternal prerogative," and what is that but rape; I swear to God. You asked me in here to explain something to me, as a child, that I did not understand. But I came to explain something to you. You Are Not God. You ask me why I came? I came here to instruct you.

[She produces his book.]

And your book? You think you're going to show me some "light"? You "maverick." Outside of tradition. No, no, (*She reads from the book's liner notes.*) "of that fine tradition of inquiry. Of Polite *skepticism*" . . . and you say you believe in free intellectual discourse. YOU BELIEVE IN NOTHING. YOU BELIEVE IN NOTHING AT ALL.

JOHN: I believe in freedom of thought.

CAROL: Isn't that fine. *Do* you?

JOHN: Yes. I do.

CAROL: Then why do you question, for one moment, the committee's decision refusing your tenure? Why do you question your suspension? You believe in what *you call* freedom of thought. Then, fine. *You* believe in freedom-of-thought *and* a home, and, *and* prerogatives for your kid, *and* tenure. And I'm going to tell you. You believe *not* in "freedom of thought," but in an elitist, in, in a protected hierarchy which rewards you. And for whom you are the clown. And you mock and exploit the system which pays your rent. You're wrong. I'm not wrong. You're wrong. You think that I'm full of hatred. I know what you think I am.

JOHN: Do you?

CAROL: You think I'm a, of course I do. You think I am a frightened, repressed, confused, I don't know, abandoned young thing of some doubtful sexuality, who wants, power and revenge. (*Pause*) *Don't* you? (*Pause*)

JOHN: Yes. I do. (*Pause*)

CAROL: Isn't that better? And I feel that that is the first moment which you've treated me with respect. For you told me the truth. (*Pause*) I did not come here, as you are assured, to gloat. Why would I want to gloat? I've profited nothing from your, your, as you say, your "misfortune." I came here, as you did me the honor to *ask* me here, I came here to *tell* you something. (*Pause*) That I think . . . that I think you've been wrong. That I think you've been terribly wrong. Do you hate me now? (*Pause*)

JOHN: Yes.

CAROL: Why do you hate me? Because you think me wrong? No. Because I have, you think, *power* over you. Listen to me. Listen to me, Professor. (*Pause*) It is the power that you hate. So deeply that, that any atmosphere of free discussion is impossible. It's not "unlikely." It's *impossible.* Isn't it?

JOHN: Yes.

CAROL: Isn't it . . . ?

JOHN: Yes. I suppose.

CAROL: Now. The thing which you find so cruel is the selfsame process of selection I, and my group, go through *every day of our lives.* In admittance to school. In our tests, in our class rankings. . . . Is it unfair? I can't tell you. But, if it is fair. Or even if it is "unfortunate but necessary" for us, then, by God, so must it be for you. (*Pause*) You write of your "responsibility to the young." Treat us with respect, and that will *show* you your responsibility. You write that education is just hazing. (*Pause*) But we worked to get to this school. (*Pause*) And some of us. (*Pause*) Overcame prejudices. Economic, sexual, you cannot begin to imagine. And endured humiliations I *pray* that you and those you love never will encounter. (*Pause*) To gain admittance here. To pursue that same dream of security *you* pursue. We, who, who are, at any moment, in danger of being deprived of it. By . . .

JOHN: . . . by . . . ?

CAROL: By the administration. By the teachers. By *you.* By, say, one low grade, that keeps us out of graduate school; by one, say, one capricious or inventive answer on our parts, which, perhaps, you don't find amusing. Now you *know,* do you see? What it is to be subject to that power. (*Pause*)

JOHN: I don't understand. (*Pause*)

CAROL: My charges are not trivial. You see that in the haste, I think, with which they were accepted. A *joke* you have told, with a sexist tinge. The language you use, a verbal or physical caress, yes, yes, I know, you say that it is meaningless. I understand. I differ from you. To lay a hand on someone's shoulder.

JOHN: It was devoid of sexual content.

CAROL: I say it was not. I SAY IT WAS NOT. Don't you begin to *see* . . . ? Don't you begin to understand? IT'S NOT FOR YOU TO SAY.

JOHN: I take your point, and I see there is much good

in what you refer to.

CAROL: . . . do you think so . . . ?

JOHN: . . . but, and this is not to say that I cannot change, in those things in which I am deficient . . . But, the . . .

CAROL: Do you hold yourself harmless from the charge of sexual exploitativeness . . . ? (*Pause*)

JOHN: Well, I . . . I . . . I . . . You know I, as I said. I . . . think I am not too old to *learn,* and I *can* learn, I . . .

CAROL: Do you hold yourself innocent of the charge of . . .

JOHN: . . . wait, wait, wait . . . All right, let's go back to . . .

CAROL: YOU FOOL. Who do you think I am? To come here and be taken in by a *smile.* You little yapping fool. You think I want "revenge." I don't want revenge. I WANT UNDERSTANDING.

JOHN: . . . *do* you?

CAROL: I do. (*Pause*)

JOHN: What's the use. It's over.

CAROL: Is it? What is?

JOHN: My job.

CAROL: Oh. Your job. That's what you want to talk about. (*Pause*) (*She starts to leave the room. She steps and turns back to him.*) All right. (*Pause*) What if it were possible that my Group withdraws its complaint. (*Pause*)

JOHN: What?

CAROL: That's right. (*Pause*)

JOHN: Why.

CAROL: Well, let's say as an act of friendship.

JOHN: An act of friendship.

CAROL: Yes. (*Pause*)

JOHN: In exchange for what.

CAROL: Yes. But I don't think, "exchange." Not "in exchange." For what do we derive from it? (*Pause*)

JOHN: "Derive."

CAROL: Yes.

JOHN: (*Pause*) Nothing. (*Pause*)

CAROL: That's right. We derive nothing. (*Pause*) Do you see that?

JOHN: Yes.

CAROL: That is a little word, Professor. "Yes." "I see that." But you will.

JOHN: And you might speak to the committee . . . ?

CAROL: To the committee?

JOHN: Yes.

CAROL: Well. Of course. That's on your mind. We might.

JOHN: "If" what?

CAROL: "Given" what. Perhaps. I think that that is more friendly.

JOHN: GIVEN WHAT?

CAROL: And, believe me, I understand your rage. It is not that I don't feel it. But I do not see that it is deserved, so I do not resent it. . . . All right. I have a list.

JOHN: . . . a list.

CAROL: Here is a list of books, which we . . .

JOHN: . . . a list of books . . . ?

CAROL: That's right. Which we find questionable.

JOHN: What?

CAROL: Is this so bizarre . . . ?

JOHN: I can't believe . . .

CAROL: It's not necessary you believe it.

JOHN: Academic freedom . . .

CAROL: Someone chooses the books. If you can choose them, others can. What are you, "God"?

JOHN: . . . no, no, the "dangerous." . . .

CAROL: You have an agenda, we have an agenda. I am not interested in your feelings or your motivation, but your actions. If you would like me to speak to the Tenure Committee, here is my list. You are a Free Person, you decide. (*Pause*)

JOHN: Give me the list. (*She does so. He reads.*)

CAROL: I think you'll find . . .

JOHN: I'm capable of reading it. Thank you.

CAROL: We have a number of *texts* we need re . . .

JOHN: I see that.

CAROL: We're amenable to . . .

JOHN: Aha. Well, let me look over the . . . (*He reads.*)

CAROL: I think that . . .

JOHN: LOOK. I'm reading your demands. All right?! (*He reads*) (*Pause*) You want to ban my book?

CAROL: We do not . . .

JOHN (*Of list*): It says here . . .

CAROL: . . . We want it removed from inclusion as a representative example of the university.

JOHN: Get out of here.

CAROL: If you put aside the issues of personalities.

JOHN: Get the fuck out of my office.

CAROL: No, I think I would reconsider.

JOHN: . . . you think you can.

CAROL: We can and we *will*. Do you want our support? That is the only quest . . .

JOHN: . . . to ban my *book* . . . ?

CAROL: . . . that is correct . . .

JOHN: . . . this . . . this is a *university* . . . we . . .

CAROL: . . . and we have a statement . . . which we need you to . . . (*She hands him a sheet of paper.*)

JOHN: No, no. It's out of the question. I'm sorry. I don't know what I was thinking of. I want to tell you something. I'm a teacher. I am a teacher. Eh? It's my *name* on the door, and *I* teach the class, and that's what I do. I've got a book with my name on it. And my son will *see* that *book* someday. And I have a respon . . . No, I'm sorry I have a *responsibility* . . . to *myself*, to my *son*, to my *profession*. . . . I haven't been *home* for two days, do you know that?

Thinking this out.

CAROL: . . . you haven't?

JOHN: I've been, no. If it's of interest to you. I've been in a *hotel*. Thinking. (*The phone starts ringing.*) *Thinking* . . .

CAROL: . . . you haven't been home?

JOHN: . . . *thinking*, do you see.

CAROL: Oh.

JOHN: And, and, I owe you a debt, I see that now. (*Pause*) You're *dangerous*, you're *wrong* and it's my *job* . . . to say no to you. That's my job. You are absolutely right. You want to ban my book? Go to *hell*, and they can do whatever they want to me.

CAROL: . . . you haven't been home in two days . . .

JOHN: I think I told you that.

CAROL: . . . you'd better get that phone. (*Pause*) I think that you should pick up the phone. (*Pause*)

[JOHN *picks up the phone.*]

JOHN (*on phone*): Yes. (*Pause*) Yes. Wh . . . I. I. I had to be away. All ri . . . did they wor . . . did they worry ab . . . No. I'm all right, now, Jerry. I'm f . . . I got a little turned *around*, but I'm *sitting* here and . . . I've got it figured out. I'm fine. I'm fine don't worry about me. I got a little bit mixed up. But I am not sure that it's not a blessing. It cost me my job? Fine. Then the job was not worth having. Tell Grace that I'm coming home and everything is fff . . . (*Pause*) What? (*Pause*) What? (*Pause*) What do you *mean*? WHAT? Jerry . . . Jerry. They . . . Who, who, what can they do . . . ? (*Pause*) NO. (*Pause*) NO. They can't do th . . . What do you mean? (*Pause*) But how . . . (*Pause*) She's, she's, she's *here* with me. To . . . Jerry. I don't underst . . . (*Pause*) (*He hangs up.*) (*To* CAROL:) What does this mean?

CAROL: I thought you knew.

JOHN: What. (*Pause*) What does it mean. (*Pause*)

CAROL: You tried to rape me. (*Pause*) According to the law. (*Pause*)

JOHN: . . . what . . . ?

CAROL: You tried to rape me. I was leaving this office, you "pressed" yourself into me. You "pressed" your body into me.

JOHN: . . . I . . .

CAROL: My Group has told your lawyer that we may pursue criminal charges.

JOHN: . . . no . . .

CAROL: . . . under the statute. I am told. It was battery.

JOHN: . . . no . . .

CAROL: Yes. And attempted rape. That's right. (*Pause*)

JOHN: I think that you should go.

CAROL: Of course. I thought you knew.
JOHN: I have to talk to my lawyer.
CAROL: Yes. Perhaps you should.

[The phone rings again.] [Pause]

JOHN (*Picks up phone. Into phone*): Hello? I . . . Hello . . . ? I . . . Yes, he just called. No . . . I. I can't talk to you now, Baby. (*To* CAROL:) Get out.
CAROL: . . . your wife . . . ?
JOHN: . . . who it is is no concern of yours. Get out. (*To phone:*) No, no, it's going to be all right. I. I can't talk now, Baby. (*To* CAROL:) Get out of here.
CAROL: I'm going.
JOHN: Good.
CAROL (*exiting*): . . . and don't call your wife "baby."
JOHN: What?
CAROL: Don't call your wife baby. You heard what I said.

*[*CAROL *starts to leave the room.* JOHN *grabs her and begins to beat her.]*

JOHN: You vicious little bitch. You think you can come in here with your political correctness and destroy my life?

[He knocks her to the floor.]

After how I treated you . . . ? You should be . . . *Rape you* . . . ? Are you kidding me . . . ?

[He picks up a chair, raises it above his head, and advances on her.]

I wouldn't touch you with a ten-foot pole. You little *cunt* . . .

[She cowers on the floor below him. Pause. He looks down at her. He lowers the chair. He moves to his desk, and arranges the papers on it. Pause. He looks over at her.]

. . . well . . .

[Pause. She looks at him.]

CAROL: Yes. That's right.
(*She looks away from him, and lowers her head. To herself:*) . . . yes. That's right.

END

EDWARD ALBEE (b. 1928)

Edward Franklin Albee, born in Washington , D.C. in 1928, is regarded as one of America's most important playwrights. He was adopted as an infant by Reed and Frances Albee and named after his adopted grandfather, who was part owner of a chain of vaudeville theaters. The family lived a prosperous life in Westchester, New York, and Albee grew up in the company of entertainers and celebrities. He was educated in private boarding and military schools before attending Trinity College in Hartford, Connecticut, which he left without taking a degree. He settled in Greenwich Village, working at a number of odd jobs for nearly a decade before writing his first successful play, *Zoo Story*. This short, two character play, about how the failure of communication leads to violence, was first produced in Berlin in 1959 on the same bill with Beckett's *Krapp's Last Tape*. It moved to an off-Broadway venue in New York the following year. The production of *Zoo Story* initiated a string of successes. *The Sandbox* (1960) and *The American Dream* (1961) parody family life and the American dream of success, while *The Death of Bessie Smith* (1960) comments on racial prejudice and cruelty. Albee first attained popular as well as critical success with *Who's Afraid of Virginia Woolf?* (1962; film, 1966), a play about two couples who engage in a painful verbal and psychological battle that strips away their illusions. The play received both the Tony and the Drama Critics Circle awards. Albee thus became established as the most prominent American representative of the theater of the absurd, and he continued his experiments through the 1960s and 1970s. Three of his works won Pulitzer Prizes: *A Delicate Balance* (1966), *Seascape* (1975), and *Three Tall Women* (1994), and Albee received an Obie award for sustained achievement in theater. He continues to direct his own and other plays, on and off Broadway and at theaters across the country and in Europe.

Three Tall Women

After nearly twenty years when his plays fell into disregard, Albee's *Three Tall Women* (1991) won the 1994 Pulitzer Prize for drama, the Drama Critics Circle, Lucille Lortel, and Outer Critics Circle awards for best play. It opened at Vienna's English Theatre with Albee as the director, and its New York premiere was at the Vineyard Theater. New York critic Clive Barnes described it as the best and most forceful play Albee has yet written.

The first act of the play is a recounting of the life of a 92-year-old woman during the hour preceding her final stroke. The character named A, the elderly woman, and B, her middle-aged companion, are assisted by C, a young lawyer, to get A's papers in order. As the three get on each other's nerves we learn perhaps more than we might want to about A. Her body is deteriorating and frequently humiliates her. She has an injured arm disintegrating around the pins that hold it in place, and along with the physical breakdown she has lost the psychological ability to restrain her meanspiritedness. A's story, told as A fades in and out of senility, and contested by the others, is the tale of a tall, beautiful woman undermined by her desire to succeed in a society in which women are superfluous; by the contrast between the poverty of her own upbringing and the wealth she married; by the envy she has of her prettier sister; by frustration with her wealthy, penguin-shaped husband and her family; by her sexual excesses; and finally by old age and illness. Act I ends as A falls into a coma.

In Act II, the three women, A, B, and C, become one character, representing three stages in the life of the same woman. The lawyer is now A at 26 years old; the secretary is A at 52 years old; and A is herself at 92. Youth is insecure and fearful, middle age is optimistic, and old age is serene. Out of this situation, triangulated in time, space, and character Albee creates a memorable trinity of women figures caught in a moving and darkly amusing play.

Three Tall Women

Edward Albee

INTRODUCTION

People often ask me how long it takes me to write a play, and I tell them "all of my life." I know that's not the answer they're after—what they really want is some sense of the time between the first glimmer of the play in my mind and the writing down, and perhaps the duration of the writing down—but "all of my life" is the truest answer I can give, for it is the only one which is exact, since the thinking about the play and the putting it to paper vary so from play to play.

Few sensible authors are happy discussing the creative process—it is, after all, black magic, and may lose its power if we look that particular gift horse too closely in the mouth, or anywhere else, for that matter; further, since the creative process cannot be taught or learned, but only described, of what use is the discussion? Still, along with "where do your ideas come from?", the question is greatly on the mind of that tiny group of civilians who bother to worry it at all.

With *Three Tall Women* I can pinpoint the instant I began writing it, for it coincides with my first awareness of consciousness. I was in a group of four who were on a knoll (I could even now show you the exact spot, the exact knoll) observing the completion of a new house, the scaffolding still on it. There were three adults and tiny me—my adoptive mother, my adoptive father, my nanny (Nanny Church) and, in Nanny Church's arms—what? three-month-old Edward, certainly no older. My memory of the incident is wholly visual—the scaffolding, the people; and while I have no deep affection for it, it *is* my first awareness of being aware, and so I suppose I treasure it.

I have the kind of mind that does not retain much consciously—I experience, absorb, consider, banish into the deeps. Oh, should someone remind me of a significant event, its sights and sounds will come flooding back, but free of emotional baggage—that dealt with at the time of the incident, or catalogued elsewhere. And I know that my present self is shaped by as much self-deception as anyone else's, that my objectivities are guided by the maps I myself have drawn, and that nothing is really ever forgotten, merely filed away as inconvenient or insupportable.

So, when I decided to write what became *Three Tall Women*, I was more aware of what I did *not* want to do than exactly what I did want to accomplish. I knew my subject— my adoptive mother, whom I knew from my infancy (that knoll!) until her death over sixty years later, and who, perhaps, knew me as well. Perhaps.

I knew I did not want to write a revenge piece—could not honestly do so, for I felt no need for revenge. We had managed to make each other very unhappy over the years, but I was past all that, though I think she was not. I harbor no ill-will toward her; it is true I did not like her much, could not abide her prejudices, her loathings, her paranoias, but I did admire her pride, her sense of self. As she moved toward ninety, began rapidly failing both physically and mentally, I was touched by the survivor, the figure clinging to the wreckage only partly of her own making, refusing to go under.

No, it was not a revenge piece I was after, and I was not interested in "coming to terms" with my feelings toward her. I knew my feelings, I thought they were pretty much on the mark, and knew that I would not move much beyond the grudging respect I'd slowly developed for her. I was not seeking self-catharsis, in other words.

I realized then that what I wanted to do was write as objective a play as I could about a fictional character who resembled in every way, in every event, someone I had known very, very well. And it was only when I invented, when I translated fact intact into fiction, that I was aware I would be able to be accurate without prejudice, objective without the distortive folly of "interpretation."

I did not cry and gnash my teeth as I put this woman down on paper. I cannot recall suffering either *with* her or because of her as I wrote her. I recall being very interested in what I was doing—fascinated by the horror and sadness I was (re)creating.

Writers have the schizophrenic ability to both participate in their lives and, at the same time, observe themselves participating in their lives. Well . . . some of us have this ability, and I suspect it was this (frightening?) talent that allowed me to write *Three Tall Women* without prejudice, if you will.

I know that I "got her out of my system" by writing this play, but then again I get *all* the characters in *all* of my plays out of my system by writing about them.

Finally, when I based the character "Grandma" (*The American Dream, The Sandbox*) on my own (adoptive) maternal grandmother, I noticed that while I liked the lady a lot—we were in alliance against those folk in the middle—the character I created was both funnier and more interesting than the model. Have I done that here? Is the woman I wrote in *Three Tall Women* more human, more multifaceted than its source? Very few people who met my adoptive mother in the last twenty years of her life could abide her, while many people who have seen my play find her fascinating. Heavens, what have I done?!

Edward Albee
Montauk, NY
1994

CHARACTERS

A, a very old woman; thin, autocratic, proud, as
together as the ravages of time will allow. Nails
scarlet, hair nicely done, wears makeup. Lovely
nightgown and dressing gown.

B, looks rather as A would have at 52; plainly
dressed.

C, looks rather as B would have at 26.

THE BOY, 23 or so; preppy dress (jacket, tie, shirt,
jeans, loafers, etc.)

*THE SETTING. The play is set in a "wealthy" bed-
room, French in feeling. Pastels, with blue predominant. A bed upstage center, with a small bench at its
foot. Lacy pillows, a lovely spread. Nineteenth century
French paintings. Two light armchairs, beautifully
covered in silk. If there is a window, silk swags. Pastel
carpeted floor. Two doors, one to left, one to right.
Archways for both.*

*Note: Act Two has the same set as Act One, except for
medical stuff to be decided.*

ACT I

*At rise, A is in the stage left armchair, B in the stage
right one, C on the bed foot bench.*

It is afternoon.

[Some silence.]

A (*An announcement from nowhere; to no one in particu-
lar.*): I'm ninety-one.
B (*Pause.*): Is that so?
A (*Pause.*): Yes.
C (*Small smile.*): You're ninety-*two.*
A (*Longer pause; none too pleasant.*): Be that as it *may.*
B (*To C.*): Is that so?
C (*Shrugs; indicates papers.*): Says so here.
B (*Pause; stretching.*): Well . . . what does it matter?
C: Vanity is amazing.
B: So's forgetting.
A (*General.*): I'm ninety-one.
B (*Accepting sigh.*): OK.
C (*Smaller smile.*): You're ninety-*two.*
B (*Unconcerned.*): Oh . . . let it alone.
C: No! It's important. Getting things . . .
B: It doesn't matter!
C (*Sotto voce.*): It does to *me.*
A (*Pause.*): I know because he says, "You're exactly
thirty years older than I am; I know how old I
am because I know how old *you* are, and if
you ever forget how old you are ask me how
old *I* am, and then you'll know."(*Pause.*) Oh,
he's said that a lot.
C: What if he's wrong?
A (*From a distance; curiously lighter, higher voice.*):
What?

B: Let it *be.*
C (*Still to A.*): What if he's wrong? What if he's not
thirty years younger than you?
A (*Oddly loud, tough.*): You'd think he'd know how
old he is!
C: No, I mean . . . what if he's wrong about how old
you are.
A (*Pause.*): Don't be silly. How couldn't he be thirty
years younger than me when I'm thirty years
older than he is? He's said it over and over.
(*Pause.*) Every time he comes to see me. What
is today?
B: It's (*whatever day it is in reality*).
A: You see?!
C (*A bit as if to a child.*): Well, one of you might be
wrong, and it might not be him.
B (*Small sneer.*): He.
C (*Quick smile.*): Yes; I know.
A: don't be stupid. *What* is it? *What day* is it?
B: It's (*ibid.*)
A (*Shakes her head.*): No.
C (*Interested.*): No what?
A: No it *isn't.*
B: OK.
C (*To A.*): What day do you *think* it is?
A (*Confusion.*): What day is it? What day do I . . . ?
(*Eyes narrowing.*) Why, it's today, of course.
What day do you *think* it is?! (*Turns to B; cack-
les.*)
B: Right on, girl!
C (*Scoffs.*): What an answer! What a dumb . . .
A: Don't you talk to me that way!
C (*Offended.*): Well! I'm sorry!
A: I pay you, don't I? You can't talk to me that way.
C: In a way.
A (*A daring tone.*): What?!

C: Indirectly. You pay someone who pays me, some-
   one who . . .
A: Well; there; you see? You can't talk to me that
   way.
B: She isn't talking to you that way.
A: What?
B: She isn't *talking* to you that way.
A (*Dismissive laugh.*): I don't know what you're talk-
   ing about. (*Pause.*) Besides.

[*Silence; then she cries. They let her. It begins in self-
pity, proceeds to crying for crying's sake, and concludes with rage and self-loathing at having to cry. It
takes quite a while.*]

B (*When it's over.*): There. Feel better?
C (*Under her breath.*): Honestly.
B (*To A.*): A good cry lets it all out.
A (*Laughs; sly.*): What does a *bad* one do? (*Laughs
   again; B joins her.*)
C (*Shakes her head in admiration.*): Sometimes you're
   so . . .
A (*Ugly; suddenly.*): What?!
C (*Tiny pause.*): Never mind. I was going to say some-
   thing *nice*. Never *mind*.
A (*To B.*): What did she say?! She mumbles all the
   time.
C: I don't mumble! (*Annoyance at herself.*) Never
   mind!
A: How is anybody expected to hear what she says?!
B (*Placating.*): She didn't finish her sentence. It doesn't
   matter.
A (*Small, smug triumph.*): I'll *bet* it doesn't.
C (*Dogged, but not unpleasant.*): What I meant was
   you may have been incorrect about your age
   for so long—may have made up the fiction so
   many years ago, though why anyone would
   lie about one year . . .
B (*Weary.*): Let her alone; let her have it if she wants
   to.
C: I will *not*.
A: Have what?!
C: Why you would lie about one *year*? I can imagine
   taking off ten—or *trying* to. Though more
   probably seven, or five—good and tricky—but
   one?! Taking off *one year*? What kind of vanity
   is *that*?
B (*Clucks.*): How you go *on*.
A (*Imitation.*): How you go *on*.
C (*Purrs.*): How I go *on*. So, I can understand ten, or
   five, or seven, but not one.
B: How you *do*.
A (*To C.*): How you do. (*To B.*) How *what*?!
B: How she goes on.
A (*Cheerful.*): Yes! How you go *on*!
C (*Smiles.*): Yes; I do.
A (*Suddenly, but not urgently.*): I want to go.

C: On?
A (*More urgently.*): I want to go. I want to go.
B: You want to go? (*Rises.*) You want the pan? Is it
   number one? Do you want the pan?
A (*Embarrassed to discuss it.*): No . . . Noooo!
B: Ah. (*Moves to A.*) All right. Can you walk?
A (*Weepy.*): I don't know!
B: Well, we'll try you. OK? (*Indicates walker.*) You
   want the walker?
A (*Near tears.*): I want to walk! I don't know!
   Anything! I have to *go*! (*Starts to fret-weep.*)
B: All right! (*She moves A to a standing position. We dis-
   cover A's left arm is in a sling, useless.*)
A: You're hurting me!! You're hurting me!!
B: All right; I'm being careful!
A: No, you're *not*!!
B: Yes, I am!
A: No, you're *not*!!!
B (*Angry.*): Yes, I am.
A: No, you're *not*! (*On her feet, weeping, shuffling with
   B's help, off.*) You're trying to hurt me; you
   know how I hurt!!
B (*To C, as they exit.*): Hold the fort.
C: I will. I will hold the fort. (*Muffled exchanges off-
   stage. C looks toward them, shakes her head, looks
   back down.*)
   (*Both to herself and to be heard.*) I suppose one
   could lie about one year—some kind of one-
   upmanship, a private vengeance, perhaps,
   some tiny victory, maybe. (*Shrugs.*) I don't
   know, maybe these things get important. Why
   can't I be nice?
B (*Reenters.*): Made it that time. (*Sighs.*) And so it
   goes.
C: Not always, eh?
B: In the morning, when she wakes up she wets—a
   kind of greeting to the day, I suppose: the
   sphincter and the cortex not in sync. Never
   during the *night*, but *as* she wakes.
C: Good morning to the morning, eh?
B: Something to something.
C: Put a diaper on her.
B (*Shakes her head.*): She won't have it. I'm working
   on it, but she won't have it.
C: Rubber sheet?
B: Won't have it. Get her up, put her in the chair and
   she does the other. Give her a cup of coffee . . .
C: Black.
B (*Chuckles.*): Half cream and all that sugar! Three
   spoons! How has she lived this long? Give her
   a cup of coffee, put her in her chair, give her a
   cup of coffee, and place your bets.
C (*Looks at the chair she is in.*): What chair?! *This*
   chair?!
B (*Laughs.*): You got it. Don't worry.
C: It must be awful.
B (*Deprecating.*): For whom?

C (*Rising to it.*): For her! You're paid. It's probably awful for you, too, but you're paid.

B: As she never ceases to inform me . . . *and* you.

C: To begin to lose it, I mean—the control, the loss of dignity, the . . .

B: Oh, stop it! It's downhill from sixteen on! For all of us!

C: Yes, but . . .

B: What *are* you, *twenty* something? Haven't you figured it out yet? (*Demonstrates.*) You take the breath in . . . you let it out. The first one you take in you're upside down and they slap you into it. The last one . . . well, the last one you let it all out . . . and that's it. You start . . . and then you stop. Don't be so soft. I'd like to see children learn it—have a six-year-old say, I'm dying and know what it means.

C: You're horrible!

B: Start in young; make 'em aware they've got only a little time. Make 'em aware they're dying from the minute they're alive.

C: Awful!

B: Grow up! Do *you* know it? Do *you* know you're dying?

C: Well, of course, but . . .

B (*Ending it.*): Grow up.

A (*Wobbling, shuffling in.*): A person could die in there and nobody'd care.

B (*Bright.*): Done already!

A: A person could die! A person could fall down and break something! A person could die! Nobody would care!

B (*Going to her.*): Let me help you.

A (*Good arm flailing.*): Get your *hands* off me! A person could die for all anybody'd care.

C (*To herself, but to be overheard.*): Who is this . . . person? A person could do this, a person could do . . .

B: It's a figure of speech.

C (*Mildly sarcastic.*): No. Really?

B (*Not rising to it.*): So they tell me.

A (*Flailing about.*): Hold *on* to me! Do you want me to fall?! You want me to *fall*!

B: Yes, I want you to fall; I want you to fall and shatter in . . . ten pieces.

C: Or five, or seven.

A: Where's my chair? (*Sees it perfectly well.*) Where's my chair gone to?

B (*Playing the game.*): Goodness, where's her chair *gone* to?! Somebody's taken her *chair*!

C (*Realizing.*): What?!

A (*Does she know? Probably.*): Who's got my chair?

C (*High horse.*): I'm sorry! (*Gets up quickly; moves away.*) Your majesty!

B (*Placating.*): There's your chair. Do you want your pillow? Shall I get you your pillow? (*To C.*) Fetch her pillow.

A: I want to sit *down*.

B: Yes, yes. Here we go. (*Gently lowers A into the vacated armchair.*)

C (*At bed.*): Which *pillow*?

B (*To A.*): Are you comfortable? Do you want your pillow?

A (*Petulant.*): Of course I'm not comfortable; of *course* I want my pillow.

C (*At the bed still; to B.*): I don't know which one!

B (*Moving to the bed.*): It's two, actually, one for the back (*Takes it.*) and this one for the arm. (*Takes it; moves toward A.*) Here we are; lean forward. (*Positions back pillow.*) That's a girl.

A: My arm! My arm! Where's the pillow?!

B: Here we go. (*Arranges arm pillow.*) All comfy? (*Silence.*) All comfy?

A: What?

B: Nothing. (*A knowing smile to C.*)

C: And so it goes?

B: Uh-huh.

C: What a production.

B: You haven't seen anything.

C: I bet!

A (*To B.*): You can't just leave me in there like that. What if I fell? What if I died?

B (*Considers it; calm.*): Well . . . if you fell I'd either hear you or you'd raise a racket, and if you died what would it matter?

A (*Pause; then she laughs; true enjoyment.*): You can say that again! (*Is amused at seeing C not amused.*) What's the matter with you?

C (*Small silence, until she realizes she's being talked to.*): Who?! Me?!

A: Yes. You.

C: What's the *matter* with me?

B (*Amused.*): That's what she *said*.

A: That's what I *said*.

C (*Panicking a little.*): What are you all doing—ganging up on me?

B (*To A.*): Is that what we're doing?

A (*Enjoying it greatly.*): Maybe!

C (*To defend herself.*): There's *nothing* the matter with me.

B (*Sour smile.*): Well . . . you just *wait*.

A: What did she say?

B: She says there's nothing the matter with her— Miss Perfect over there.

C: I didn't *say* that; that's not what I . . . !!

A (*To B; sincere.*): Why is she *yelling* at me?!

B: She's *not*.

C: I'm *not*!

B: *Now* you are.

A: You see?! (*Confused.*) What day is it?

B: It's (*whatever day it is in reality.*)

A: Will he come today? Is today the day he comes?

B: No; not today.

A (*Whining.*): Why not?!

B (*Making nothing of it.*): Oh, he probably has something else to do; he probably has a full schedule.

A (*Teary.*): He never comes to see me, and when he does he never stays. (*A sudden shift in tone to hatred.*) I'll fix him; I'll fix all of 'em. They all think they can treat me like this. You all think you can get away with anything. I'll fix you all.

C (*To B, an aside.*): Is it always like this?

B (*Overly patient.*): No . . . it's often very pleasant.

C: Huh!

A (*Muttering now.*): You all want something; there's nobody doesn't want something. My mother taught me that; be careful, she said; they all want something; she taught me what to expect, me and my sister. She prepared us and somebody had to. I mean, we were girls and that was way back then, and it was different then. We didn't have a lot, and being a girl wasn't easy. We knew we'd have to make our own way, and being a girl back then . . . why am I talking about this?!

B: Because you want to.

A: That's right. She tried to prepare us . . . for going out in the world, for men, for making our own way. Sis couldn't do it; that's too bad. *I* could; *I* did. I met him at a party, and he said he'd seen me before. He'd been married twice—the first one was a whore, the second one was a drunk. He was funny! He said, Let's go riding in the park, and I said all right . . . scared to death. I lied; I said I rode. *He* didn't care; he wanted me; I could tell that. It only took six weeks.

B: Good girl!

A: We had horses when we were married; we had a stable; we had saddle horses; we rode.

C (*Mildly.*): Hoity-toity.

A: I learned to ride and I was very good.

B (*Encouraging.*): I'm sure!

C (*Mildly contemptuous.*): *How* are you sure?!

B: Shhhhhhh.

A (*Childlike enthusiasm.*): I rode sidesaddle and I rode astride, and I drove ponies—hackneys—and I loved it all. He would go with me and we would ride every morning, and the dalmation would go with us—what was her name . . . Suzie? No. We had good horses and we showed them and we won all the ribbons, and we kept them in a big case down in the . . . no, that was the other house. We kept them. (*Pause; reinvigorating herself.*) And cups. All the silver cups we won, and bowls, and platters. We knew all the judges but that's not why we would win: we won because we were the best.

C (*Under her breath.*): Of course.

B (*Sotto voce.*): Be decent.

A (*Dismissive.*): Oh, she'll learn. (*Back to the memory.*) We had horses! I knew all the judges, and I'd go in the ring when we were in the championships, and I'd sit there and I'd watch the horses—I never rode when we were in the championships; Earl did that; he was our rider. I would sit there and watch with the judges. They all knew me; we were famous; we had a famous stable, and when the judging was done they'd tell me if we'd won, and we almost always did, and if they told me, and they almost always did, I'd signal. I'd take my hat off and I'd touch my hair (*Does it: touches hair.*) and that way they'd know we'd won.

C (*To B; whispers.*): Who?!

[*B shrugs, keeps her eyes on A.*]

A (*Very rational; explaining.*): Everyone in our box. (*Childish again.*) Oh, I used to love it, riding in the morning, going to the stable in the station wagon in my coat and jodhpurs and my derby, and petting . . . what was her name?, the dalmation—Suzie, I think . . . no—and mounting and riding off. Sometimes he came with me and sometimes he didn't. Sometimes I went off alone.

C (*To B.*): Who?

B: Her husband, most likely. (*To A.*) Did you ride when you were little?

A (*A little, deprecating laugh.*): No. We were poor.

C (*To A.*): Poor? Really . . . poor?

A: Well, no; not really poor; my father was an architect; he designed furniture; he made it.

C: That's not an architect, that's . . .

B: Let it be.

A: He made such beautiful furniture; he was an architect. Strict, but fair. No, my *mother* was strict. No, they were *both* strict. *And* fair. (*This confuses her; she cries.*)

B: Now, now.

A: I don't know what I'm saying! What am I *saying*?

B (*Comforting.*): You're talking about horses; you were talking about riding, and we asked: when you were a little girl . . .

A (*Rational; tough.*): We never rode; the neighbors had a horse but we never rode it. I don't think my sister ever rode. But I can't swim. (*Conspiratorial whisper.*) She drank.

C: When she was a little girl?

B: Oh, please!

A (*Truly innocent.*): What? What are we talking about?

B: Horses. You didn't ride when you were a little girl.

A: You rode if you were a farmer or if you were ...

C (*Mildly mocking.*): Or if you were a rich farme...

B: Shhhhhhh.

A (*Of C, to B.*): She'll learn. (*To C; ominous.*) *Won't* you.

C (*Flustered laugh.*): Well, I dare *say.*

A (*Story again.*): I wasn't rich until I got married, and I wasn't really right then 'til later. It all adds up. We had saddle horses; we rode. I learned to ride and I was very good. I rode sidesaddle and I rode astride, and I drove ponies—hackneys . . .

C: . . . and you loved it all.

B: Shhhhhhh.

A: And I what?

C: You loved it all.

B: You loved it all.

A: I did?

B: So you say.

A (*Laughs.*): Well, then, it must be true. I didn't like sex much, but I had an affair.

C (*Interested.*): Oh?

A (*Suddenly suspicious.*): What?! What do you want!?

B: *She* doesn't want anything.

A (*Off again.*): We used to ride. *He* would go with me—not all the time. Sometimes I would go off alone, or with the dog, part way, never too far from the stable; she had a cat she was in love with. She'd go back, but I'd go on. I had my jodhpurs and my coat and my switch and my derby hat. I always rode in all my costume. Never go out except you're properly dressed, I always say. I'd drive the station wagon from the house—I loved to drive. I was good at it. I was good at everything; I *had* to be; *he* wasn't. I'd drive in the station wagon to the stable, and Earl would be there, or . . . or one of the stable boys: Tom . . . or Bradley. (*Long pause.*) Am I doing in my panties?! (*Starts to cry.*)

B (*Leisurely.*): Well . . . let's see. (*Goes to A.*) Upseedaisy! (*Raises her; she whimpers; cries more. B feels under A.*) Nope, but I bet you're going to. Off you go. (*Helps A off.*)

C: Hold the fort?

(*Goes to window; looks out; looks at bed; goes to it; smooths the covers. B reenters.*) Why am I doing this?

B: Because it's unnecessary? Because I've already done it?

C: The princess and the pea, maybe? What's wrong with her arm?

B: She fell and broke it. It didn't heal. Mostly they don't at that age. They put pins in it, metal pins; the bone disintegrates around the pins and the arm just hangs there. They want to take it off.

Vhat?!

'atter of fact.*): The arm; they want to take the *arm* off.

C (*Protest.*): No!

B (*Shrugs.*): It hurts.

C: Still!

B: She won't *let* them.

C: I shouldn't *think* so.

B: What do *you* know? She makes us go into the city once a week—to see the surgeon, the one who set it, the one who wants to take it off. God, he's almost as old as she is! She trusts him, she says. She goes in once a week, and she makes them x-ray it, and *look* at it, and each time the pins are looser, and the bone is gone more, and she tells the old guy—the surgeon—it's so much better, and she wants him to agree, and he waffles, and he looks at me and I'm no help, and she makes him promise that he'll never take the arm off, and won't let anyone *else* do it either, and he promises—assuming she'll forget? Probably; but she won't. There are some things she never forgets. He promised me; you were there; you heard him. I think she says that every other day: He promised me; you were there; you heard him.

(*A crack of glass from offstage.*)

Oh, God!

(*She exits.. From offstage now.*) Now, why did you do that?! You naughty, naughty girl! Bad, bad girl! (*A hoots and cackles offstage.*) What do I have to do—take everything away from you? Huh?!

[*A appears onstage again, hooting and giggling, followed by B.*]

A (*Drifting, hobbling; very happy; to C.*): I broke the glass! I took the glass and I threw it down in the sink! I broke the glass and now she has to clean it up!

[*B has reentered.*]

B: Bad girl!

A: I broke the glass! I broke the glass! (*Giggles; suddenly her face collapses and she cries; then:*) I have to sit down! I can't sit down by my*self*! Why won't somebody help me?!

B (*Helping her.*): Now, now; here we go.

A: Ow! Ow!

B: *All* right, now.

C (*Under her breath.*): Jesus!

B (*To C; settling A.*): You're a big help.

C (*Cold.*): I didn't know I was supposed to be.

B (*Sneers.*): Just here from the lawyer, eh?

C: Yes; just here from the lawyer.

A (*Suddenly suspiciously alert.*): What? What did you say?

B (*Matter of fact.*) I said—well, what I implied was,

since she's here from the lawyer, why should
she behave like a human being; why should
she be any help; why should she . . .

A (*To C; happy.*): You're from Harry?

C: No; Harry's dead; Harry's been dead for years.

A (*Tears again.*): Harry's *dead*? When did *Harry* die?

C (*Loud.*): Thirty years ago!

A (*Tiny pause; tears off.*): Well, I knew *that*. What are
you talking about *Harry* for?

C: You asked if I'd come from Harry; you asked . . .

A: I wouldn't do anything that *stupid*.

B (*Amused; to* C.): And so it goes.

A (*Clarifying it for the world.*): Harry *used* to be my
lawyer, but that was *years* ago. Harry died—
what? Thirty years ago?—Harry died. Now his
son's the lawyer. I go to *him*; well, he comes to
me; *some*times I go to him.

C: Yes; you do. *And* yes he does.

A: Why are *you* here?

C (*Sighs.*): Some things have been . . . misplaced;
aren't being done. Some things . . .

A (*Panic.*): Somebody's stealing things?!

C: No no no no. We send you papers to sign and you
don't sign them; we call you and you don't call
back; we send you checks to sign and you
don't sign them; things like that.

A: I don't know what you're talking about.

C: Well . . .

A: None of it's true! You're lying! Get Harry on the
phone!

C: Harry is . . .

B (*To* A.): Excuse me? The "I'll get to it" pile?

A (*Suspicious of* B *now.*) What?!

B (*Calm.*): The "I'll get to it" pile?

A: I don't know *what* you're talking about.

C (*To* B.): Papers? Checks?

B (*Broad.*): Oh . . . lots of stuff.

A (*Adamant.*): There's *nothing*!

C (*To* B.): What *is* there? What *is* it?

B (*To* A; *patiently.*): You have a drawer full; the bills
come and you look at them, and some of them
you send on and they get paid, and some of
them you say you can't remember and so you
don't send them, and . . .

A (*Defiant.*): Why would I send in a bill for something I never ordered?

B (*Shuts eyes briefly.*): And they send you your
checks—to sign? To pay bills? And some of
them you sign because you remember what
they were for, but some of them—some of the
checks—you can't remember?

A: I *what*?!

B (*Smiles tolerantly.*): . . . you don't remember what
they're for and so you don't sign them and
you put them in the drawer.

A: So?

B (*Shrugs.*): These things pile up.

C: I *see*; I *see.*

A: Everybody out there's ready to rob me blind. I'm
not made of money, you know.

B (*Laughs.*): Yes, you *are.* (*To* C.) Isn't she?

C (*Smiles.*): More or less.

A (*Conspiratorially.*): They'd steal you blind if you
didn't pay attention: the help, the stores, the
markets, that little Jew makes my furs—what's
her name? She's nice. They all rob you blind if
you so much as turn your back on them. All of
them!

C: We've asked you: let all your bills come to us;
we'll know what to do; let me *bring* you your
checks every month; I'll stay here while you
sign them. Whatever you like.

A (*A superior smile, but hesitant around the edges.*):
None of you think I can handle my own
affairs? I've done it for . . . when he was so sick
I did it all; I did all the bills; I did all the
checks; I did everything.

C (*Gentle.*): But now you don't *have* to.

A (*Proud.*): I didn't have to then: I *wanted* to. I wanted everything to be *right*; and I do now; I still
do!

C: Well, of *course* you do.

B: Of *course* you do.

A (*Ending it; superior.*): And so I'll handle my own
affairs, thank you.

C (*Defeated; shrugs.*): Well; certainly.

B: And *I'll* watch you *pretend* to handle them.

A: And I watch you, every one of you. I used to love
horses.

B: It's just people you don't like.

A (*Noncommittal.*): Oh? Is that it? We rode western
saddle, too. It was when he almost died—the
first time, the first time I was with him. He
had a blood infection. He was hunting, they
were all hunting, and a gun went off and it hit
him in the arm, the shoulder.

(*Touches hers; realizes the parallel; smiles
sadly.*) My God! (*Pause.*) They shot him in the
shoulder, and they didn't get all the bullet out,
and it got infected and his arm swelled up like
a balloon and they lanced it and it burst and
there was pus all over . . .

C: Stop!

B (*Cold.*): Why? What's it to you?

[*C shudders.*]

A: . . . and they put drains in it and there weren't
any medicines then . . .

B: No antibiotics, you mean.

A: What?

B: No antibiotics.

A: Yes, and it wouldn't go away and it would get
worse, and everybody said he was going to

die, but I wouldn't let him! I said, No! he is not going to die! I told that to the doctors, and I told him that, too, and he said all right, he would try, if I would sleep with him, if I wouldn't leave him alone at night, be next to him, and I did and it smelled so awful—the pus, the rot, the . . .

C: Don't! Please!

A: . . . and they said take him to the desert, bake his arm in the hot sun, and so we went there—we went to Arizona—and he sat in the baking sun all day—his arm oozing, and stinking, and splitting and . . . and in six months it went away and the arm went down in size and there was no more pus and he was saved—except for the scars, all the scars, and I learned to ride western saddle.

B: My, my.

A: And it was outside of Phoenix—Camelback Mountain; we used to ride out into the desert. And the movie star was there—the one who married the young fellow who ran the studio; she had eyes of a different color.

C (*Small pause.*): She had *what?*

A: She had eyes of a different color: one eye was blue, or something, and the other one was green, I think.

C (*To B.*): Who *was* this?

[*B shrugs.*]

A: Oh, she was a big star; she was tiny and she had a very big head. I think *she* drank too.

B: You think *everyone* drinks. Merle Oberon?

A: No; of course not! *You* know!

B (*Enjoying this a little.*): How long ago *was* this? Claire Trevor?

A: Oh . . . when I was there; when we were there. She was tiny! She had two eyes!

B: In the thirties?

A: Probably. She had a son; she cooked an egg on the sidewalk; it was so hot. He *told* me.

C (*Lost.*): Her . . . son . . . told you?

A: No! Ours! He was a little boy, too; he played with all the other children: the chewing gum twins; *that* one.

B: That must have been before the *war.*

C: Which one?!

B: Civil.

A (*Triumphant.*): Thalberg! *That's* who she married. Arnold Thalberg; he was a real smart little Jew.

B (*To C; ironic.*): All smart Jews are *little.* Have you noticed? (*To A.*) Irving; *Irving* Thalberg.

C (*Cold.*): I'm a Democrat; I notice a lot of things.

B: Most of us *are;* most of us *do.* But still, it's fascinating, isn't it—grisly, but fascinating. She doesn't *mean* anything by it—or if she did, once, she

doesn't now. It just falls out.

A (*Joyous.*): Norma Shearer!

B: Of course!

C: Who?

A (*Laughs.*): What's the matter with all you people?!

C (*Explaining.*): We're Democrats.

A: What?

C: Well, you asked what the matter was.

A: Don't you get fresh!

B: My God! I haven't heard that in a long time. (*Imitates.*) Don't you get fresh!

A: My mother would say that to me all the time: Don't you get fresh! To Sis and me. She made us eat everything she put before us, and wash the dishes; she made us know what being a grown-up was. She was strict but fair. No, that was our father; no, that was both of them. (*A little girl whine.*) They're dead; Sis, they're dead!

C: A smart little Jew?

B: At least she didn't say kike.

A (*Back to her memory.*): She would make us write thank-you notes, and take little gifts whenever we went somewhere, and made us wash everything we wore the night we wore it, by hand, before we went to bed. Sometimes Sis wouldn't and I had to do hers, too. She made us be proper young ladies.

C: And go to church twice a day? And pray a lot?

A: What? Oh, yes, we went to church but we didn't talk about it very much. We took it for granted, I suppose. (*To B.*) How much did you *steal?*

B (*Not rising to it.*): When?

A: Whenever.

B (*Drawling.*): Well, I waited until you were asleep . . .

A: I never sleep.

B: . . . until you were pretending to be asleep, and then I went into the silver closet and took down all the big silver bowls, and I stuck them up under my skirt, and I waddled out into the hall . . .

A: Joke about it if you want to. (*A sudden fit of giggles.*) You must have looked *funny!*

B (*Playing along.*): Well, I suppose.

A: Waddling out like that; you probably clanked, too.

B: Yes; I'm sure I did. Clank, clank.

A (*Hoots.*): Clank, clank!
(*Notices C isn't amused; tough.*) You don't think anything's funny, do you?

C: Oh, yes; I'm just trying to decide what I think's really the most hilarious—unpaid bills, anti-Semitism, senility, or . . .

B: Now, now. Play in your own league, huh?

C (*Miffed.*): Well! I'm *sorry!*

A (*Looks right at C.*): I'll have to talk to Harry about you.

B (*Ibid.*): Harry's dead; Harry's been dead for years.

A (*With increasing self-absorption.*): I know; so's everybody. I don't have any friends anymore; most of them are dead, and the ones aren't dead are dying, and the ones aren't dying have moved away or I don't see anymore.

B (*Comforting.*): Well, what does it matter? You don't like any of them anymore anyway.

A (*Uncomplicated agreement.*): That's true. But you're supposed to like them, to have them with you. Isn't it a contract? You take people as friends and you spend time at it, you put effort in, and it doesn't matter if you don't like them anymore—who likes anybody anymore?—you've put in all that time, and what right do they have to . . . to . . .

C (*Incredulous.*): To die?!

A: What?!

C: What right do they have to die?

A: No! To not be what they were.

C: To change, you mean?

B (*Gently.*): Let her alone.

A: No! No right! You count on them! And they change. The Bradleys! The Phippses! They die; they go away. And family dies; family goes away. Nobody should *do* this! Look at Sis!

B: What about her?

A: My sister was a drunk. (*Not friendly.*) She was smarter than me . . . no: brighter, two years younger.

C (*Smiles.*): Or five, or seven.

A: What?!

C: Nothing.

A: She always got better grades, had more beaux—when we were growing up. Only then; she missed more boats than you can shake a stick at.

C (*Examining her nails.*): I've never shook a stick at a boat.

B (*Dry.*): Well, maybe you should give it a try. Shaken; not shook.

A: We came to the city together, after she finished school, and we had a tiny little apartment, and our mother and our father came to see it, to be sure it was all right, not dangerous, I suppose. It was furnished, but he didn't like it, so he gave us some of theirs, some from the garage. He made the most beautiful furniture: he was an architect. We went out all the time—looking for jobs, jobs that a young lady could accept—being escorted out at night. We were the same size, so we could wear each other's clothes; *that* saved money. We had a little allowance, but a very little one, nothing to spoil us. She was a little shorter, but not much. We kept a list so the boys—the young men, the men—who took us out—we went out with them together a lot—wouldn't know we were wearing each other's. Is that what I mean?

B: Yes; I think so; most probably.

C: Keep awake.

A: "No, no, I wore that at the Plaza; don't you remember? You'd better wear the beads." We had a regular list. We had big feet. (*A silence.*)

B (*About the non sequitur.*): What?!

C: They had big *feet*.

A: We had big feet. I still do . . . I guess. (*To B.*) Do I still have big feet?

B: Yes; yes, you do.

A: Well, I'd never know. I think we liked each other. We used to confide a lot, and laugh, and . . . Mother made us write twice a week—or call, later. We tried sending letters together—one letter together—but she'd make us send two—each of us one. They had to be newsy, and long, and she'd send them back to us with things like That's not true, or Don't abbreviate, or Your sister said the same thing, if she didn't like them. Or spelling. Sis couldn't spell. She drank.

C (*Incredulous.*): Your mother?!

A: What?! No, of course not. My *sister*!

B: Of course.

C: Even then?

A: When?

C: When you . . . when you first came to the city.

A: No, of course not! Later. Well, we'd have champagne when we went out—before the speakeasies. We would drink champagne and nibble on candied orange rind. *He* brings me some, sometimes, when he comes. Or flowers—freesia, when they're in season. It's the least he can do. And he *knows* it!

C (*To B; and aside.*): Who? Who *is* this?

B (*Absorbed with A.*) Shhhhhhh. Her son.

A: We'd go out, but we didn't take each other's boyfriends. She was prim; I liked . . . wilder men, I suppose.

C: Tsk, tsk, tsk.

B (*To C; amused.*): Why? Don't you?

A: We never liked the same boys . . . men. I don't think she liked men very much. Well, I *know* she didn't—sex, anyway. We had to make her get married, when she was almost forty—*get* someone for her. I don't think she wanted him; he was a wop.

C (*Shakes her head.*): I don't believe it sometimes.

B (*Sharp, as A tries to adjust herself in her chair.*): Why not? Wop, nigger, kike? I told you: It doesn't *mean* anything. It's the way she learned things.

C: From these strict but fair parents. (B *shrugs.*)

A (*She has heard.*): I have Jewish friends, and I have Irish friends, and I have South American friends—I *did*. Not Puerto Rican, or like that, but Venezuelan, and Cuban. Oh, we loved to go to Havana.

C (*To B, more or less.*): Another world, eh?

B: Uh-huh.

A: I've never known any colored—well, *help*, yes. In Pinehurst they had colored help and we used to visit them there. They knew their place; they were polite, and well behaved; none of those uppity niggers, the city ones.

C (*Dismay.*): Oh, Jesus Christ!

A: He keeps telling me I can't say these things. I don't know what things he means. He said once he wouldn't come to see me anymore if I said those things. I don't know what things he means. What did he mean?

B: Don't worry yourself. Your sister married an *Italian.*

A (*Confused.*): She did . . . what? Oh, that was later. I always had my eye out for the right man.

C: And she didn't?

A: No; she always thought everything would fall right into her lap. And it *did*; a *lot*. I had to work for *everything*; nothing came my way. I was tall and handsome; she was tall and pretty, tall but shorter, not as tall as I am . . . was. (*Weeps.*) I've shrunk! I'm not tall! I used to be so tall! Why have I shrunk?!

B (*To A; patient.*): It happens with time: we get shorter. It happens every day, too: we're taller in the morning than we are at night.

A (*Still weeping.*): How?!

B: The spine compresses as the day goes on.

A (*Even weepier.*): I don't *have* one. I used to have a spine; I don't have one anymore!

C (*To B; sotto voce.*): What does she mean?

B: She means osteoporosis.

A (*To C; ugly; weeping down to sniveling.*): It hasn't happened to you yet? You wait!

B: . . . the spine collapses; you can fracture it by walking, turning around . . . whatever.

A (*Weepy again.*): I used to be *tall*! I've shrunk!

C: I know.

[*B smiles.*]

A (*Off again.*): He was *short*. A lot of my beaux were tall, but he was short.

C (*Sotto voce; to B.*): Who *is* this?

B (*Sotto voce, too.*): Her husband, I think.

C: Oh; that's a long time ago.

A: Oh, I knew such tall boys, such dancers. Sis and I would dance all night with all the tall boys. Some of them were showboys—they were fairies—but some of them were regular. We would dance the night away; and sometimes I'd go off.

B (*Smiling.*): Naughty girl!

A: I was the wild one. Sis would say to me, How can you *do* that?! and I'd laugh and I'd say, Oh, come on! I liked to have a good time, but I had my eye out. I always had my eye out. (*A shift of tone toward bitter.*) If I don't have my eye out, who will? I've always had to be on my toes, them sneaking around, stealing and . . . conniving. If I didn't keep my eye out we wouldn't have had *anything*. His *sister*! That one she married? The first one! The dumpy little . . . dentist was he? What did *he* know about running an office? What did *he* know about handling money? Enough to steal! Enough to line his *own* pockets. And of course the old man kept his head turned the other way because the—what's his name, the dentist—was married to his precious daughter! Oh *that* one! Whining and finagling, wrapping him around her little finger! I had to stay one step ahead of *all* of them. I fixed 'em.

B (*Proud of her.*): *Did* you?

A (*Confused.*): What?!

B: *Did* you fix them?

A (*Panicking.*): Who?! Who are you talking about?!

B: The ones you fixed.

A: How do *I* know? I don't know what you're talking about! Fix who?!

B: I don't *know.*

C (*To help.*): The ones who were robbing you blind.

B (*To A.*): Yes: those.

A (*Grim.*): *Every*body's robbing me—right and left. Everybody steals. Everybody steals *something.*

B (*Without comment.*): Including me? Do *I* steal?

A (*Nervous laugh.*): I don't know. How would I know? He says I should have more money.

B (*To C.*): Doesn't your office . . . ?

C: We deal with what comes *in*. There's more than one handles her money. There's plenty of chance, if anyone *wanted* to.

A: Sis used to envy me after I married. She never *did* well. I always had my eye out.

C: You use all your income as far as *I* can see.

A: Well, why not? It's mine.

C: Well, just don't complain. If you wanted an increase in principal, you'd have to . . .

A: I don't complain: I *never* complain. I have you, and I have her (*points to B*), and I have the chauffeur, and I have this place here, and I have to look pretty, and sometimes I have the nurses—though they're black. Why *is* that?—and I have all those things . . . I have the cook, I have the . . .

C: I know; I know.

A: They all steal; every one of them.

B (*After a pause, a sigh.*): Ah, well.

A: Sis didn't have her eye out; not like I did. I married him. He was short; he had one eye; one was glass; a golf ball hit him there; they took it out; he had a glass one.

C: Which eye?

B (*To C; chiding.*): Oh, *come* on!

C (*Amused.*): No, I want to know. (*To A.*) Which eye? Which eye was glass?

A: Which eye was . . . ? Well, I don't . . . (*becomes weepy*) I can't remember! I don't know which eye was the glass one! (*Full weep.*) I . . . can't . . . remember. I . . . can't . . . remember!

B (*Moves to A, to comfort.*): Now, now; now, now.

A: I can't remember! (*Sudden venom.*) Get your *hands* off me! How *dare* you!

B (*Retreating.*): Sorry; sorry.

A (*To B; tearful again.*): Why can't I remember anything?

B: I think you remember everything; I think you just can't bring it to mind all the time.

A (*Quieting.*): Yes? Is that it?

B: Of course!

A: I remember everything?

B: Somewhere in there.

A (*Laughs.*): My gracious! (*To C.*) I remember everything!

C: Gracious. That must be a burden.

B: *Be* nice.

C: Isn't salvation in forgetting? Lethe, and all?

A: Who?

B: No one.

C: Lethe.

A: I don't *know* her. Well, maybe I do, I just don't have it right now. (*To B.*) Is that right?

B: That's *right*.

A: I *loved* my husband. (*Silly, remembering smile.*)

B: I bet you *did*.

A: He gave me pretty things; he gave me jewelry.

B: *Them's* pretty.

A: My God, he said, you're so big, so tall, you'll cost me a fortune! I can't give you little things. And he *couldn't*. I liked pearls and diamonds best.

C: No kidding!

B (*Amused.*): Oh, hush!

A: I had my pearls, and I had some bracelets, and he wanted me to have another—he'd found one without telling me. We wore wide bracelets back then—diamond ones—wide, *this* wide. (*She demonstrates: two inches, or so.*) Flat and wide, the stones in designs, very . . . what? Very what?

B: Ornate.

A: Yes, ornate . . . and wide. We had been out—I'll never forget it, I'll never forget this—we'd been to a party, and we'd had champagne, and we were . . . what? Tipsy? A little I suppose. And we came home and we were on the way to bed. We had our big bedroom, and it had its separate dressing rooms, and—you know—its

separate bathrooms—and we were undressing; we were getting ready for bed. I was at my table, and I'd taken off my clothes—my shoes, my dress, and my underthings—and I was sitting there at my dressing table (*She really enjoys telling this: laughs, giggles, etc.*), and I was . . . well, I was naked; I didn't have a stitch, except I had on all my jewelry. I hadn't taken off my jewelry.

B: How wonderful!

A: Yes! And there I was, all naked with my pearls—my necklace—and my bracelets, my diamond bracelets . . . two, no: three! Three! And in he walked, naked as a jaybird—he was funny when he wanted to be—we were naked a lot, early on, pretty early on. All that stopped. (*Pause.*) Where am I?

B: In your story?

A: What?

B: In your story. Where are you in your story?

A: Yes; of course.

C: You're naked at your dresser, and *he* walks in, and *he's* naked, too.

A: . . . as a jaybird; yes! Oh, I shouldn't *tell* this!

B: Yes! Yes, you should!

C: Yes!

A: Yes? Oh . . . well, there I was, and I had my big powder puff, and I was powdering myself, and I was paying attention to *that*. I knew he was there, but I wasn't paying attention. I *have* something for you, he said, I *have* something for you. And I was sitting there, and I raised my eyes and looked in the mirror and . . . no! I can't tell this!

B & C (*Silly schoolgirls.*): Yes, yes; tell, tell. Tell us! Yes! Tell us! (*This ad lib.*)

A: And I looked and there he was, and his . . . his peepee was all hard, and . . . and hanging on it was a new bracelet.

C (*Awe.*): Oh, my God!

[B smiles.]

A: And it was on his pee-pee, and he came close and it was the most beautiful bracelet I'd ever seen; it was diamonds, and it was wide, so wide and . . . I thought you might like this, he said. Oh, my goodness, it's so beautiful, I said. Do you want it? he said. Yes, yes! I said, Oh, goodness, yes! (*Mood shifts a little toward darkness.*) And he came closer, and his pee-pee touched my shoulder—he was short, and I was tall, or something. Do you want it? he said, and he poked me with it, with his pee-pee, and I turned, and he had a little pee-pee. Oh, I shouldn't say that; that's terrible to say, but I *know*. He had a little . . . *you* know . . . and there was the bracelet on it, and he moved closer, to my face, and Do you want it? I thought you might like it. And I said, No! I can't *do* that! You *know* I can't *do* that! and I couldn't; I could *never* do that, and I said, No! I can't do that! And he stood there for . . . well, I don't know . . . and his pee-pee got . . . well, it started to go soft, and the bracelet slid off, and it fell into my lap. I was naked; deep into my lap. Keep it, he said, and he turned and he walked out of my dressing room.

[Long silence; finally she weeps, slowly, conclusively.]

B (*Eventually.*): It's all right; it's all right.

[Goes and comforts A.]

C (*Kindly.*): The wild one.

B (*Still comforting.*): It's all right; it's all right.

A (*Little child.*): Take me to bed; take me to bed.

B: Sure. (*To* C.) Help me.

[They ease her up from her chair and to the bed during the following.]

A (*Screams.*): My arm! My arm!

C (*Terrified.*): I'm sorry!

A: Bed! I wanna go to bed!

B: All right now; we're almost there. (*At bed.*) OK. Here we are.

A (*Full baby.*): I wanna go to bed! (*It hurts!*) Oh! Oh! Oh!

B: All right, now. (A *is now on the bed, under covers, sitting up part way.*) There. Comfy?

C (*To* B.): I'm sorry; I didn't mean to . . .

B (*To* C.): It's all right. (*To* A.) Comfy?

A (*Tiny voice.*): Yes. Thank you.

B (*As she moves downstage.*): You're welcome.

C: I'm not good at . . . all that.

B: You'll get there.

C: I can't project.

B (*Comforting.*): Well, think of it this way: if you live long enough you won't have to; you'll be there.

C: Thanks.

B: And since it's the far past we're supposed to recall best—if we *get* to the future—you'll remember not being able to project.

C: As I said: thanks.

B (*Pause; sighs.*): A-ha.

C (*Pause.*): What happens now?

B (*Eyes closed.*): You tell *me*.

C: *You're* the one works here.

B (*Smiles; eyes still closed.*): As I said: *you* tell *me*. (*Silence.*)

A (*Propped up; eyes opening and closing from time to time, eyes wandering; very stream of conscious-ness.*): The things we're able to do and the things we're *not*. What we remember doing and what we're not sure. What do I re*mem*ber? I remember being *tall.* I remember first it mak-ing me unhappy, being taller in my class, taller than the boys. I remember, and it comes and goes. I think they're all robbing me. I *know* they are, but I can't prove it. I think I know, and then I can't remember what I know. (*Cries a little.*) He never comes to see me.

B (*Mildly.*): *Yes,* he does.

A: When he has to; now and then.

B: More than most; he's a good son.

A (*Tough.*): Well, I don't know about that. (*Softer.*) He brings me things; he brings me flowers— orchids, freesia, those big violets . . . ?

B: African.

A: Yes. He brings me those, and he brings me choco-lates—orange rind in chocolate, that dark chocolate I like; he does *that.* But he doesn't love me.

B: Oh, now.

A: He doesn't! He loves his . . . he loves his boys, those boys he has. You don't know! He doesn't love me and I don't know if I love him. I can't *remember*!

B: *He* loves you.

A (*Near tears.*): I can't remember; I can't remember what I can't remember. (*Suddenly alert and self-mocking.*) Isn't *that* something!

B (*Nicely.*): It certainly *is.*

A (*Rambling again.*): There's so much: holding on; fighting for everything; *he* wouldn't do it; *I* had to do *every*thing; tell him how handsome he was, clean up his blood. Everything came on *me:* Sis being that way, hiding her bottles in her night things where she thought I wouldn't find them when she came to stay with me for a little; falling . . . falling down the way she did. Mother coming to stay, to live with us; he *said* she could; where else could she go? Did we like each other even? At the end? Not at the end, not when she hated me. I'm helpless, she . . . she screamed; I hate you! She stank; her room stank; she stank; I hate you, she screamed at me. I think they all hated me, because I was strong, because I *had* to be. Sis hated me; Ma hated me; all those others, *they* hated me; *he* left home; he ran away. Because I was strong. I was tall and I was strong. *Somebody* had to be. If I wasn't, then . . . (*Silence;* A *still, eyes open. Has she shuddered a little before her silence?*)

[After a bit B and C look at one another. B rises, goes to the bed, leans over, gazes at A, feels her pulse.]

C (*Looks over after a little.*): Is she . . . oh, my God, is she dead?

B (*After a little.*): No. She's alive. I think she's had a stroke.

C: Oh, my God!

B: You better call her son. I'll call the doctor.

[*C rises, exits right, looking at A as she exits; B strokes A's head, exits left.*]

[*A alone; still; silence.*]

END OF ACT ONE

ACT II

"*A*" *is propped up in bed. (Actually a life mask of the actress playing A—wearing exact, same costume as on A in Act I. We must believe it to be A—a breathing mask over the nose and mouth helps this.)*

When A appears she is dressed in a lovely, lavender dress.

[*Some silence. B and C enter, opposite from their exits at the end of Act I. They—and A, when she enters— are dressed differently from the way they were at the end of Act I, except that the dummy of A is dressed as A was at the end of Act I. C seats herself. B goes to the bed, looks at "A."*]

B (*General.*): No change.

C (*Wistful.*): No?

B: That's the way it goes.

C (*Shudders.*): Yes?

B (*Grim.*): Something to look forward to. (*No response from C.*) No?

C (*Hard.*): I don't want to *talk* about it; I don't want to *think* about it. Let me alone.

B (*Sharp.*): It's worth thinking about—even at *your* age.

C: Let me *alone!*

B (*Wandering about; touching things.*): It's got to be *some* way . . . stroke, cancer or, as the lady said, heading into a mountain with a jet. No? (*No response.*) Or . . . walking off a curb into a sixty-mile-an-hour wall . . .

C: *Stop* it!

B: Or . . . even worse; *think* about this . . . home alone in the evening, servants off, him out, at the club, sitting home alone, the window jimmied, *they* get in, little cat feet and all, *find* you, sitting there in the upstairs sitting room . . .

C: I said: *stop* it!

B (*Smiles.*): . . . find me sitting there in the upstairs sitting room, going over invitations, or whatever . . . bills; come up behind me, slit my

throat, me thinking, Oh, my God, my throat's being slit, *if* that, if there's *time* for that.

C (*Animal growl of protest.*): Arghhhhhhhhhhh!

B (*Tranquil.*): I'm almost done. Or I hear them . . . you hear them turn around, see them—how many? Two? Three?—fall apart, start screaming, so they have to slit your throat, my throat, though they may not have planned it that way. All that blood on the Chinese rug. My, my.

C (*Pause; curious.*): Chinese rug?

B (*Very natural.*): Yes, beige, with rose embroidery all around the edges. We get it at auction.

C: I wouldn't know.

B (*Momentary surprise.*): No; of course not; you *wouldn't*. You will, though—the rug, I mean. Clearly nobody slits your throat, or mine, for that matter. (*Considers it.*) Might be better.

C (*Rue and helplessness.*): You have things to tell me, I suppose.

B: Oh, I certainly do. But, then again, I don't know everything either, *do* I. (*Gestures towards A.*)

C (*She looks, too.*): I'll do a will; I'll do some paper that won't let me go on if I get like that.

B: There *aren't* any . . . *weren't* any then, I tried. You can't get your way in this world.

[*A enters during this next speech, from stage left.*]

C: There *must* be one. You have your way in everything and then you can't at the last? There *must* be!

A: There *must* be what?

[*She is thoroughly rational during this act; B and C are not surprised to see her.*]

C: A living will.

A (*Observing "A."*): I was going to, but then I forgot, or it slipped my mind, or something. He kept saying, Make one! He has one for himself, he says. I meant to; nothing much to do about it now. Any change?

B: No, we're . . . just as we were; no change.

A: I wonder how long *this'll* go on. I hope it's quick. What's-her-name took six years; not a move, not a blink, hooked up, breathed for, pissed for.

B: Do I know her?

A: No; after your time, so to speak.

B: A-*ha*.

A: A lot of money—a *lot*. The kids—hah! Fifty the youngest—the "kids" disagreed. They wanted to see the will first, the lawyer wouldn't *show* it to 'em, they came down on both sides—*kill* her off! keep her going! Not pretty.

C (*Really beside herself.*): Stop it! Stop it!

A (*To a naughty child.*): Grow . . . up.

B (*Smiles.*): She will; she does.

A: Well; yes; of course. And so do *you.*

C (*Rage.*): I will not become . . . *that!* (*Points to* "A.")

A (*Come off it.*): Oh, *really.*

B (*Oh, really!*): Come *off* it.

C: I *won't.*

B (*Smiles.*): What do you plan to *do* about it?

A (*Amused.*): Yes; *that's* interesting.

C (*To A; pointing to B.*): Nor will I become *this.*

B (*A hoot.*): Hah!

C (*To the audience, unless otherwise indicated; she comes down front. A and B relax, comment from time to time, react with each other, etc.*): I won't. I *know* I won't—*that's* what I mean. That . . . (*points to* "A") . . . *thing* there? I'll never be like that. (B *hoots; A shakes her head, chuckles.*) *Nobody* could. I'm twenty-six; I'm a *good* girl; my mother was strict but fair—she still *is;* she *loves* me; she loves me and Sis, and she wants the very best for us. We have a *nice* little apartment, Sis and I, and at night we go out with our beaux, and I *do* have my eye out for . . . for what—the man of my dreams? And so does Sis, I *guess.* I don't think I've been in love, but I've been loved—by a couple of them, but they weren't the right ones.

B (*Rue; to herself.*): They never *are.*

A (*Purring.*): Hmmmm.

C: Mother taught us what the right one would be. We have fun with the others—dancing, staying out late, seeing the sun up sometimes. Things get a little . . . involved now and again, and that's fun too, though Sis doesn't think so as much as I do. They get involved, but they never get very . . . *serious.* I have my eye out, and we do have our *jobs.* We're mannequins: the fanciest shop in town!

B: I don't want that *known!*

A (*To B; pleasantly chiding.*): Oh, stop; it was fun.

C: We go into work and we put on these lovely frocks, and we walk elegantly around the store (*imitates*), among the ladies shopping, sometimes with their men, sometimes not, and we stop, and they touch our dresses—the silk, the fabric—and they ask us questions, and then we pass on to another group, to another section. We twirl, we . . . sashay. (*Does so; B imitates; A, too, but sitting.*) (*To A and B.*): We *do!*

B: Oh, I *know.*

A: Yes, we *know;* do *we* know.

C (*To the audience again.*): Don't look at them; don't . . . listen to them. (A *and* B laugh a little.) We wear our beautiful evening gowns, and we parade about, and we know there are people looking at us, studying us, and we smile, and we . . . well, I suppose we flirt a little with the men who are doing it—the husbands, or whatever.

B (*To A; mock astonishment.*): Flirt?! You?!

A: Me?! Flirt?!

B (*Sashays; twirls.*): Wheeeee!

A (*Claps with one hand; her knee, probably.*): Brava! Brava!

B (*Twirls.*): Wheeeee!

C: Stop it! *Stay* out of my life!

B: Oh! My dear!

A (*To C.*): I remember it differently, little one. I remember more . . . design. I remember a little calculation.

B: Oh, yes; a little calculation; a little design.

C (*To audience.*): Don't listen to them. Design? What are they talking about?

B (*Cheerful.*): Never mind.

C (*To audience.*): They don't *know* me!

B (*Looking at A; mocking.*): Noooooooooooo!

C: *Remember* me!

A (*Ibid.*): Noooooooooooo! (C *claps her hands over her ears, shuts her eyes.*) Oh, all right, dear; go on. (C *can't hear; louder.*) I said, go on!

B (*Loud.*): She says go *on!* Honestly.

C: I am a . . . good . . . girl.

B (*To A.*): Well, yes; I suppose so.

A: And not dumb.

C: I'm a good girl. I know how to attract *men.* I'm *tall;* I'm striking; *I* know how to do it. Sis slouches and caves her front in; I stand tall, breasts out, chin up, hands . . . just so. I walk between the aisles and they know there's somebody coming, that there's somebody *there.* But, I'm a *good* girl. I'm not a virgin, but I'm a good girl. The boy who took me was a good boy.

[C *does not necessarily hear—or, at least, notice—the asides to come.*]

B: Oh, yes he *was.*

A: Yes? Was he?

B: *You* remember.

A (*Laughs.*): Well, it *was* a *while* ago.

B: But you *do* remember.

A: *Oh* yes, I remember him. He was . . .

C: . . . sweet and handsome; no, not handsome: beautiful. He was beautiful!

A (*To B.*): He was; yes.

B (*To A and herself.*): Yes.

C: He has coal black hair and violet eyes and such a smile!

A: Ah!

B: Yes!

C: His body was . . . well, it was thin, but *hard;* all sinew and muscle; he fenced, he told me, and he was the one with the megaphone on the crew. When I held him when we danced, there was only sinew and muscle. We dated a lot; I liked him; I didn't tell Mother, but I liked him a lot. I like him, Sis, I said; I really like him. Have you told mother? No, and don't *you*; I like him a lot, but I don't *know*. Has he? . . . *you* know. No, I said, no, he hasn't. But then he did. We were dancing—slowly—late, the end of the evening, and we danced so close, all . . . pressed, and . . . we were pressed, and I could feel that he was hard, *that* muscle and sinew, pressed against me while we danced. We were the same height and he looked into my eyes as we danced, slowly, and I felt the pressure up against me, and he tensed it and I felt it move against me.

B (*Dreamy.*): Whatever is *that*? I said.

A: Hmmmmmmmmm.

C: Whatever is *that*? I said. I *knew*, but Whatever is that, I said, and he smiled, and his eyes shone, and, It's me in love with you, he said. You have an interesting way of showing it, I said. Appropriate, he said, and I felt the muscle move again, and . . . well, I knew it was time; I knew I was ready, and I knew I wanted him— whatever that *meant*—that I wanted *him*, that I wanted *it*.

B (*Looking back; agreeing.*): Yes; oh, yes.

A: Hmmmmmmmmmm.

C: Remember, don't give it away, Mother said; don't give it away like it was nothing.

B (*Remembering.*): They won't respect you for it and you'll get known as a loose girl. *Then* who will you marry?

A (*To B.*): Is that what she said? I can't remember.

B (*Laughs.*): *Yes* you can.

C: They won't respect you for it and you'll get known as a loose girl. *Then* who will you marry? But he was pressed against me, exactly against where he wanted to be—we were the same height—and he was *so* beautiful, and his eyes shone, and he smiled at me and he moved his hips as we danced, so slowly, as we danced, and he breathed on my neck and he said, You don't want me to embarrass myself right here on the dance floor, do you?

B (*Remembering.*): No, no; of course not.

C: I said, No, no; of course not. Let's go to my place, he said, and I heard myself saying (*incredulous*), I'm not that kind of girl? I mean, as soon as I said it I blushed: it was so . . . stupid, so . . . expected. Yes, you are, he said; *you're* that kind of girl.

B: And I was, and my God it was wonderful.

A: It hurt! (*Afterthought: to* B.) Didn't it?

B (*Admonishing.*): Oh . . . well, a little.

C: You're that kind of girl, and I guess I was. We did it a lot. (*Shy.*) I know it's trite to say your first time is your best, but he was wonderful, and I

know I'm only twenty-six now and there've been a few others, and I imagine I'll marry, and I'll be very happy.

B (*Grudging.*): Well . . .

A: We'll talk about happy sometime.

C: I *know* I'll be very happy, but will I ever *not* think about him? He was long and thick and knew what I wanted, what I needed, and while I couldn't do . . . you know: the thing he wanted . . . I just *couldn't: I can't.*

B (*Stretches.*): Nope; never could.

A (*Sort of dreamy.*): I wonder why.

C (*Very agitated; upset.*): I tried! I wanted to do what . . . but I choked, and I . . . (*whispered*) I threw up. I just . . . couldn't.

A (*To C.*): Don't worry about it; don't worry about what can't be helped.

B: And . . . there's more than one way to skin a cat.

A (*Puzzles that.*): Why?

B: Hm?

A: *Why* is there more than one way to skin a *cat*?

B (*Puzzles that.*): Why not?

A: Who needs it?! Isn't one way *enough*?

C (*To the audience; still; simply.*): I just want you to know that I'm a good girl, that I was a good girl.

B (*To C.*): You meet him in two years.

C (*Self-absorbed.*): What? Who?

B (*Pleasant.*): Your husband. We're what—twenty-six? We'll meet him in two years.

C (*Making light of it.*): The man of my dreams?

B: Well, a man you'll *dream* about.

A: For a long, long time.

C: Like the boy I was . . . ?

A: Well, yes, he was wonderful, but then there's life.

B (*To A.*): *How* long?

A: Hm?

B: How *long*?

A: *Long* enough. (*To* B.) You're . . . what?

B: Fifty-two.

A (*Calculating.*): I marry when I'm twenty-eight; you're sixty-six when he dies. (*To* C; *smiles.*) We have him a good long time.

B (*Musing.*): Another fourteen years.

A: Yes, but the last *six* aren't much fun.

C: That's almost forty years with one man.

B (*To* C; *chuckles.*): Well, more or less: more or less one man. (*To* A.) No? Not much fun?

A: Not much.

C: How *is* he? Have I *met* him?

B: The one-eyed man? The little one; the little one-eyed man?

A (*Chuckles.*): Oh, now.

C (*Confused.*): What?

B: The one we meet at the party—Sis and me. Sis is with him, but I see him looking over at me.

A (*Recalled with pleasure.*): Yes!

B: Sis doesn't much care, I don't think.

C: More or less? What is this more or less?

A: Hm?

B (*Mildly annoyed.*): I beg your pardon?

C: I said almost forty years with one man; you said, more or less; more or less one man.

B: Oh? Ah! Well, what are you expecting? Monogamy or something?

C: Yes! If I care: yes!

B (*To A.*): Remember monogamy?

A (*Pretends to puzzle it.*): No. (*New tone; to B.*) *You* can talk about monogamy, if you like—pro and con, if you like. Leave me out of *that* one.

B (*General, then to A.*): Infidelity is a matter of spirit—isn't that what they say? Aside from bad taste, disease, confusion as to where you live, having to lie all the time—*and* remember the lies! God, remember the lies!

A: Hmmmm. Well, there wasn't much, not *too* much.

B: Except for the groom, eh?

A: Oh, my! The groom.

C: Why do I marry him?

B: Who—the groom? (*A and B laugh.*)

C: The one-eyed man! I marry the one-eyed man!

B: Yes, you do.

C: Why?!

B (*To C.*): Why do I *marry* him? Why did I *marry* him? (*To A.*)

A (*To B.*): Why did I?

B: Hmmmmmmmmmm.

C: *Tell* me!

B: Because he makes me *laugh*. Because he's little and he's funny looking—and a little like a penguin.

A (*Has she thought this before?*): Yes! Quite a bit like one.

B (*Generous.*): Well . . . especially in his bib and tucker.

C (*Some panic.*): Why would I marry him if I'm going to cheat on *him*?!

A (*Smiles.*): Why would you marry him if he's going to cheat on *you*?

C: I don't *know*!

B: Calm down; adjust; settle in. Men cheat; men cheat a *lot*. We cheat *less*, and we cheat because we're lonely; men cheat because they're men.

A: No. We cheat because we're bored, sometimes. We cheat to get back; we cheat because we don't know any better; we cheat because we're whores. *We* cheat for *lots* of reasons. Men cheat for only one—as you say, because they're men.

C: *Tell* me about him!

A: Don't you want to be surprised?

C: No!

B: You've seen him, or . . . he's seen *you*. I don't think you've met him. He's something of what they call a playboy—at least in *my* time, not yours. He's rich—or his father is—and he's divorcing

his second wife; she's just plain bad; the first one drank; still does.

A: That one dies eventually—eighty, or something: pickled; preserved.

C (*Timid again.*): What's he like?

B (*Expansive.*): Well . . . he's short, and he has one eye, and he's a great dancer—'cept he keeps running into things, the eye, you know—and he sings like a dream! A lovely tenor—and he's funny! God, he's funny!

A (*Wistful.*): Yes; yes, he was.

B (*Pleased.*): And he likes tall women!

A (*Wistful.*): Yes; yes, he did.

C (*Uncertain.*): I *have seen* him?

B: He tells me—I think I remember—he tells me he saw me with Sis before he dated her, that I was taller, that he had—you'll forgive the joke—his eye on me. (*To A.*) Didn't he tell you that—that he had his eye on us?

A: I can't remember. He was going with that comedienne did the splits, the eight-foot one.

B: Well, you put a stop to that soon enough.

A: Once you got your claws into him you mean?

C (*Puzzling.*): Why did I *like* him? Is funny enough? Is having a voice, is dancing enough?

B: Don't forget one eye.

A: Oh, he was *nice*; we liked him a lot.

C: *Liked*? *Liked* him a lot.

B (*Looking right at C.*): Oh, stop it! You're twenty-six years old, which is not a tot; there *is* the future to look out for . . .

A: . . . and he *is* rich, or is going to be: rich family.

C: I don't *believe* this.

A (*Sharp.*): Our father *dies*.

B (*About her father.*): I *loved* him.

C: No! He doesn't!

B: *Every*body does.

A (*To herself.*): Except me, maybe.

B (*To C.*): Except *us*.

C: I *love* him!

B: Well, that should be enough to keep the old heart going: Jesus, she loves me; how can I go and die on her?

C: Is it . . . quick?

A (*Pensive.*): I don't remember.

B: Not bad: heart *failure*, fluid in the lungs, some bad breathing; oh, God, the terror in the eyes! (*C begins to weep; B notices.*) We did that, yes. We cried when Dad died. I cried; Sis cried; Mom went out on the porch and did it there.

A (*Loss.*): I don't remember.

C: What happens to Ma?

B: She holds out; she stays on alone for almost twenty years, and then she moves in with us. (*To A.*) How does it go?

A (*Toneless.*): What? She becomes an enemy. She dies when she's eighty-four—seventeen years of it, of staying up in her room in the big house with us. The colitis, the cigarettes, the six or seven Pekingese she goes through. I stopped liking her.

C: I *couldn't!*

A (*Shrugs.*): She becomes an enemy.

B (*Interested, but not too much.*): How?

A (*Sighs.*): She comes to resent me; she starts to resent getting old, getting . . . helpless—the eyes, the spine, the mind. She starts to resent that I have—*we* have—so much, and that I'm being generous—*we're* being generous. She snaps at everything; she sides with Sis; she criticizes me.

B (*Some awe.*): She wasn't *like* that.

C: No! She *couldn't* be.

A: I don't care. Forget I told you. She never moved in; she's still alive up there in the country, in the same house; she's a hundred and thirty-seven now, does her own baking, jogs three times a week . . .

B: *All* right; *all* right.

A (*To B.*): There's more. You want to hear it? (B *shakes her head to C.*) Of course *you* don't. (C *shakes her head.*) No, of course not. Anyhow, you marry him.

C (*Getting it straight.*): I do.

A: Yes; he's fun, and he's nice.

B: He sings . . .

A: He dances . . .

B: . . . and he's rich, or going to be . . .

A: . . . and he loves tall women.

B: And you suddenly realize you love short men.

A: Penguins. (A *and* B *both giggle.*)

B (*Still to C.*): *And* it goes all right. His mother doesn't *like* me—doesn't *like* you—at all, but the old *man* does.

A: He certainly does! You're tall; I bet you're hot stuff.

B (*To C.*): You win him over. (*To A.*) You know, I think the old buzzard had letch for us?

A: Yes; *I* think so.

B: And, boy did he want a *grand*son.

A: Oh, that made him happy.

C (*Wonder.*): I have children?

B (*None too pleasant.*): We have one; we have a boy.

A (*Same.*): Yes, we do. I have a son.

[He appears in the stage right archway, stands stock still, stares at "A" on the bed.]

B (*Seeing him; sneering.*): Well, fancy seeing you again. (*Sudden, and enraged, into his face.*) Get out of my house! (*He doesn't react.*)

C (*Rising.*): Stop it! (*Moves toward him.*) Is . . . is that him?

B: I said, get out of my house!

A (*To B.*): Do be quiet. (*To C.*) Let him alone; he's come to see me. (*He goes to "A", sits on the bed stage right of her, either on the bed or on a chair, takes her right arm; shoulders shake, puts his forehead to her arm, or it to his forehead, becomes still. Does not react to anything about him until indicated.*) That's it; do your duty.

C: He's . . . my goodness. How nice; how handsome, how very . . .

B: You wouldn't say that if you knew!

A: Shhhhhhh.

B (*To A.*): She wouldn't! (*To him.*) Filthy little . . .

A: Shhhhh. Shhhhh. I don't want to think about *that.* He came back; he never loved me, he never loved us, but he came back. Let him alone.

C: He's so young.

A: Yes . . . well. This is how he looked when he went away, took his life and one bag and went off. (*To B.*) No?

B (*To his back; less venom, but mixed with hurt.*): You wore that coat the day you left. I thought I told you to get your hair cut!

A: Yes; yes, he did; he wore that coat. I'm leaving, he said, and he took one bag. (*Pause.*) And his life.

C (*Bewildered.*): He went away from me? Why?

B (*Bitter.*): Maybe you changed; they say you changed; I haven't noticed. (*To A.*) He comes back? He comes back to me—to me? I let him?

A: Sure. We have a heart attack; they tell him; he comes back. Twenty plus years? That's a long enough sulk—on both sides. He didn't come back when his father died.

B (*Scathing.*): Of course not!

A: But he came to me. They call me up and they tell me he's coming to see me; they say he's going to call. He calls. I hear his voice and it all floods back, but I'm formal. Well, hello there, I say. Hello there to you, he says. Nothing about this shouldn't have happened. Nothing about I've missed you, not even that little lie. Sis is visiting; she's lying drunk and passed out upstairs and not even that little lie. I thought I'd come over. Yes, you do that. He comes; we look at each other and we both hold in whatever we've been holding in since that day he went away. You're looking well, he says; and, You, too, I say. And there are no apologies, no recriminations, no tears, no hugs; dry lips on my dry cheeks; yes that. And we never discuss it? Never go into why? Never go beyond where we are? We're strangers; we're curious about each other; we leave it at that.

B: I'll *never* forgive him.

A (*Wistful, sad.*): No; I never do. But we play the game. We dine; he takes me places—mother, son going to formal places. We never . . . reminisce. Eventually he lets me talk about when he was a little boy, but he never has an opinion on that; he doesn't seem to have an opinion on much of anything that has to do with us, with me.

B (*Clenched teeth.*): Never!

A (*To B.*): Or with *you*. (*To C; and sad smile.*) Or *you*.

C: Did we . . . did we drive him away? Did I change so?

B (*Rage.*): He left!! He packed up his attitudes and he *left*! !And I never want to see him again. (*To him.*) Go away!! (*Angry, humiliated, tears.*)

A (*Very calm; sad smile.*): Well, yes you *do*, you see. You *do* want to see him again. *Wait* twenty years. Be alone except for her upstairs passed out on the floor, and the piano top with the photos in the silver frames, and the butler, and . . . be all alone; you *do* want to see him again, but the terms are too hard. We never forgive him. We let him come, but we never forgive him. (*To him.*) I bet you don't know *that* . . . do you!

C (*To A.*): How did we change? (*To him.*) How did I change? (*He strokes "A's" face, shudders a little.*)

B: Don't bother yourself. He *never* belonged.

C (*Enraged.*): I don't believe it!

B (*Furious.*): Let it *alone*!

C: No! How did I *change*?! What *happened* to me?!

A (*Sighs.*): Oh, God.

C (*Determined.*): How did I *change*?!

B (*Sarcasm; to the audience.*): She wants to know how she *changed*. She wants to know how she turned into *me*. Next she'll want to know how I turned into *her*. (*Indicates* A.) No; I'll want to know *that; maybe* I'll want to know that.

A: Hahh!

B: *Maybe*. (*To C.*) You want to know how I changed?

C (*Very alone.*): I don't know. Do I?

B: Twenty-six to fifty-two? Double it? Double your pleasure, double your fun? Try *this*. Try *this* on for size. They *lie* to you. You're growing up and they go out of their way to hedge, to qualify, to . . . to evade; to avoid—to lie. Never tell it how it is—how it's *going* to be—when a half-truth can be got in there. Never give the alternatives to the "pleasing prospects," the "what you have to look forward to." God, if they did the streets'd be littered with adolescent corpses! Maybe it's better they don't.

A (*Mild ridicule.*): They? *They?*

B: Parents, teachers, all the others. You *lie* to us. You don't tell us things change—that Prince Charming has the morals of a sewer rat, that you're supposed to *live* with that . . . *and* like it, or give the ap*pea*rance of liking it. Chasing the chambermaid into closets, the kitchen maid into the root cellar, and God knows *what* goes

on at the stag at the club! They probably nail the whores to the billiard tables for easy access. Nobody *tells* you any of this.

A (*Lay it on.*): Poor, poor you.

C: The root cellar?

B (*To A and C.*): Hush. No wonder one day we come back from riding, the horse all slathered, snorting, and he takes the reins, the groom does, and he helps us dismount, the groom does, his hand touching the back of our thigh, and we notice, and he notices we notice, and we remember that we've noticed him before, most especially bare chested that day heaving the straw, those arms, that butt. And no wonder we smile in that way he understands so quickly, and no wonder he leads us into a further stall—into the fucking *hay*, for God's sake!—and down we go, and it's revenge and self-pity we're doing it for until we notice it turning into pleasure for its own sake, for *our* own sake, and we're dripping wet and he rides us like we've seen in the pornos and we actually scream, and then we lie there in the straw—which probably has shit on it—cooling down, and he tells us he's wanted us a lot, that he likes big women, but he didn't dare, and will he get fired now? And I say, No, no, of course you won't and for a month more of it I don't, but then I do; I do have him fired, because it's dangerous not to, because it's a good deal I've got with the penguin, a long-term deal in spite of the crap he pulls, and you'd better keep your nose clean—or polished, anyway—for the *real* battles—for the penguin's *other* lady folk, the *real* ones—the mother who "just doesn't like you" for no good reason except her daughter hates you, fears you and hates you— *envies* and therefore hates you—dumpy, stupid, whining little bitch! Just *doesn't* like you— maybe in part because she senses the old man's got the letch for you and besides, no girl's good enough for the penguin, not *her* penguin; the first two sure weren't and this one's not going to be either. Try to keep on the good side of the whole wretched family, stand up for your husband when he won't do it for himself, watch out for all the intrigue; start *really* worrying about your sister who's really stopped worrying about herself—about *anything*, watch your own mother begin to change even more than you're aware *you* are, and then try to raise that?! (*Points to him.*) That?!—gets himself thrown out of every school he can find, even one or two we haven't sent him to, sense he hates you, catch him doing it with your niece-in-law *and* your nephew-in-law the same week?! Start reading the letters he's getting from—how do they call it—older friends?—telling him how to outwit *you*, how to survive living with his awful family; tell him you'll brain him with the fucking crystal ashtray if he doesn't stop getting letters, doesn't stop saying anything, doesn't stop . . . just . . . doesn't . . . stop? And he sneers, and he says very quietly that he can have me put in jail for opening his mail. Not while you're a minor, I tell him; you just wait, I tell him, you just wait; I'll have you thrown out of this house so quick it'll make your head spin. *You're* going to fire me, he says, quietly, smiling; you going to *fire* me too? Just like you fired *him*? He's good in bed, *isn't* he! Of course, *you* wouldn't know about *bed*, he says. He gets up, stops by me, touches my hair. I thought I saw some straw, he says; sorry. And he walks out of the solarium, out of the house, out of our lives. He doesn't say good-bye to either of us. He says good-bye to Mother, upstairs; he says good-bye to the Pekingese, too, I imagine. He packs one bag, and he leaves. (*To him; range.*) Get out of my house!! (*Pause; to* C.) Does that tell you a little something about change? Does that tell you what you want to know?

C (*Pause; softly.*): Yes. Thank you.

[*Silence.*]

A (*Curious.*): You want some more?

C: No, thank you.

B: I shouldn't *think* so.

A: Yes, you *do*; you *want* more.

C (*Trying to stay polite.*): I said, no, thank you.

A: *That* doesn't cut any ice around here. (*Points to* B.) How you got to *her* is one thing; how you got to me is another. How do you put it . . . that *thing* there? (*Points to* "A.")

C: *I'm* sorry.

A: Well . . . maybe.

B: Yeah, I've got a few doubts about *that* route myself.

A: You!

B: *Yeah*; well. I'm not so bad. There's been shit, but there've been *good* times, too. Some of the best.

A (*Oddly bright.*): Of course; there are always good times: like when we broke our back. (*To* C.) You break your back.

B (*Laughs a little.*): Yeah; you sure *do*.

C (*Scared of this.*): I do?

B: Snap!

A (*Smiles.*): Well, not exactly. Snap! Really!

B: I should *know*; it was *only* ten years ago, and . . .

A: Riding, yes; jumping. We never liked jumping—hunters. Saddle horses, yes, hunters, no. Brutes, every one of them, brutes or hysterics;

but hunters it was *that* day, entertaining some damn fools. Brisk, burned leaves in the air, smell of burning, just dawn; mist on the ground, dawn all green and yellow. We didn't like our *mount*, did we. (*This last to* B.)

B: No.

A: No, I didn't *like* her; she was hysteric *and* a brute.

C: When do I learn to ride? I mean really *ride*.

B: It goes with the marriage.

A: Yes, I didn't trust her; I'd ridden her earlier that fall; she was stupid and cantankerous, shied at a moving shadow. (*To* C.) I said to him, You go on, I'll stay; you go on.

B: Yes.

A: But he looked so hurt I said, Oh, all right, and off we went, into the wood, the green, the gold, the mist knee high to a . . . to your knees! Stupid *cow* of a horse! Couldn't she see the fence in the mist? Did she come on it too fast and shy like that? Over we *went*!

B: Over we *went*.

C: Oh, no!

A (*To* B.): Could have broken my *neck*, I suppose. Lucky.

B: Well, yes, there *is* that.

A (*To* B.): We never mounted a hunter again, did we?

B: Nope.

A: Damned cast weighed a ton! And you know what I thought about most?

B (*Remembering.*): Who he's doing it with; who's he got cornered in what corner, what hallway, who he's poking his little dick into.

A: That he might leave us, that he might decide to get one isn't broken.

C (*Awe.*): What kind of man *is* this?!

A (*To* C.): Man-man.

B (*To* C.): Man-man.

C: How was this happy time? Good times, you said?

B (*To* C.): Oh, well, we proved we were human. (*To* A.) No?

A (*To* B.): Of course. (*To* C.) We were fallible. Once you fall—whether you get up or not—once you fall, and they see it, they know you can be pushed. Whether you're made of crockery and smash into pieces, or you're bronze and you clang when you topple, it makes no never mind; it's the plinth is important.

B (*To* C.): To translate . . .

C: Thank you.

A (*Sweet smile.*): Thank you.

B: To translate . . . you can go around fixing the *world*, patching everything up—*everyone*—and they're *grateful* to you—grudgingly, but grateful—but once you fall yourself, prove you're not quite as *much* better than they are than they thought, then they'll *let* you go right on doing everything for them, fixing the world et cetera, but they won't hate you quite so much . . . because you're not perfect.

A (*Very bright.*): And so everything's *better*. Nice and better. Doesn't that make it a good time? He *doesn't* leave you for something else; he's sweet and gives you a big diamond ring, and you don't have to get back up on a hunter anymore. Doesn't that make it a happy time?

C: Do I get to shoot the horse?

B (*Laughs.*): I *beg* your pardon?!

A (*Whoops!*): Whoooo! Never occurred to me!

[*A and B laugh together.*]

C (*Grit.*): I'll never become you—either of you.

B (*Looks at C.*): Oh, stop! (*To A.*) And the great ring—the big diamond? You don't wear it anymore?

A (*Suddenly sober.*): Gone.

B (*Sobered too.*): Oh?

A: I *sold* it.

B: Oh?

A (*A little bitter.*): I've sold *everything*. Well, not everything . . . but most. Money doesn't go as far these days? Money doesn't go *anywhere*! I have no money. I have *money*, but I eat into it . . . every year; every year it's less.

B: We should cut back; we should . . .

A: Don't talk to me about cutting back! It's all paste! It's fake! All the jewelry sitting in the vault, in the bank? It's all fake!

C: Why is it there? Why do you . . . why do we *bother*?

A (*Contempt.*): Huh!

B (*To C, then to A.*): Because we take it out and we wear it? Because the fake look as good as the real, even feels the same, and why should anybody know our business? (*Specifically to A.*): No?

C: Appearances?

B: Appearances? That which appears to be?

C: I mean, who are we trying to impress?

A: Ourselves. You'll learn. I took the big diamond in. When we bought it—when he brought it in for me, he said . . .

B: This is a perfect stone; I've never seen a better one. You ever want to sell this you bring it back to me I'll give you better than you paid for it. He patted my hand. Pat-pat.

A: Pat-pat. And so I took it back—after he died after the cancer and all, after all that. They looked at it; they said it was deeply flawed, or it was cloudy . . . or something.

B: Sons of bitches!

A: They offered me a third of what he paid for it, and the dollar wasn't worth half of what it had been?

C (*To A.*): Didn't you sue? (*To B.*) I mean, what can

we do? We just can't . . .

A (*Accepting.*): What can you *do*? There's nothing you can *do*. You go *on*; you . . . eat *into* yourself. Starving people absorb their own bodies. The money's there—the investments are there, except less each year; it absorbs itself. It's all you've planned to *count* on *isn't*; the extras?

B (*To A.*): The big diamond, eh?

A: The big diamond . . . *and* most of the rest. Well, what does it matter? It's all glitter.

C (*Protest.*): No! It's more than that! It's tangible proof . . . that we're valuable . . . (*embarrassed*) . . . that we're valued.

A (*Shrugs.*): Well, it's gone; all the glitter's gone.

B (*Rue.*): Yup. (*Waves.*) Bye.

C: Are there any *other* surprises?

B (*Grating laugh.*): Oh, yeah; lots!

A: Oh, my dear; you just wait. (*Over toward the bed.*) She hides the money. Whatever she gets for the jewelry she keeps in cash, and spends a little whenever there isn't enough of the regular. There's a lot; she can't spend it all—without people knowing what she's doing, I mean. She hides it, and then eventually she can't remember where she hid it, and she can't find it . . . ever. And she can't tell anybody.

[*Silence.*]

B (*A little shy.*): Is the cancer bad?

A: When is it good?

C: *How* bad?

A (*Mocking.*) Fill me *in*; fill me in! (*To C.*) Pretty terrible! (*To B; softer tone.*) Six years; I told you that; it takes him six years from when he knows it—when they tell him he has it—to when he goes. Prostate—spreads to the bladder, spreads to the bone, spreads to the brain, and to the liver, of course; everything does—the *ancients* knew something. It's all right at first—except for the depression, *and* the fear—it's all right at first, but then the pain comes, slowly, growing, and then the day he screams in the bathroom, and I rush in; I expect to see him lying there, but no, he's standing at the toilet, and his face is filled with horror and he points to the bowl, and I look, and it's all pink in there, that the blood is coming with the urine now. And it's all downhill from there: the pink becomes red, and then there's blood in the bed, at night, as I'm lying with him, holding him; and then there's . . . no! Why go on with it?! (*To C; ugly.*) It's terrible! And there's nothing you can do to prepare yourself! I don't like you; you deserve it!

C (*So softly.*): Thank you.

A (*Quietly dismissive.*): You're welcome.

C: I don't like you either.

B (*Pause.*): And so it goes. (*A silence. A moves to the bed, sits on it, opposite from him.*)

A (*Speaks directly to him; now he can hear her, can respond.*): I had a premonition. I know you say there's no such thing, but I *had* one. It was I died. (*His hand up.*) Oh, stop it! You don't think I'm going to? You can hardly—wait! Just you wait! I died, you see, and when I did it—when I died—I was all alone . . . no one there in the room with me—the hospital room: I was back in that awful hospital! (*Suddenly weepy.*) Why didn't you take me *out* of there?! Why did you leave me in that . . . (*He tries to touch her, to comfort her.*) Don't you touch me!! There I was, and I was in a coma, in and out, in and out. Sometimes I'd wake up and wonder who I was, and *where* I was, and who were all those people looking at me? Sometimes I wouldn't wake up . . . not all the way, and I'd half try, and then I wouldn't. You brought me flowers, you brought freesia. You know I love freesia; that's why you bring them to me, because I *love* them! Why do you do that?! You hate me; why do you do that?! What do you want?! You *want* something. Well, you just wait. You'll get what's coming to you. In my premonition I knew I was dead, and it didn't seem to matter any, and I was all alone. There was no one there with me and I was *dead*! No one! Just the chauffeur and the maid. I was there an hour, and I was *dead*, and then *you* came in, and you had your flowers, your freesia. You came into the room, and they were there, and I was dead, and you stopped at the door of the room, and you knew right away, and you stopped and you . . . *thought*! (*Loathing.*) I *watched* you *think*! And your face didn't change. (*Wistful.*) Why didn't your face ever change? And there you were, and you thought, and you decided, and you walked over to the bed, and you touched my hand, and you bent down, and you kissed me on the forehead . . . for them! They were there and they were watching and you kissed me for *them*! (*Softer.*) And then you stood up, still holding on to my hand, as if . . . what? You didn't know what to do with it? You held on to my hand, and my hand wasn't warm anymore, was it? My hand was cold, *wasn't* it? (*Pause.*) *Wasn't* it?

[He looks at her once more, shudders, weeps, looks back at " A." A moves away from the bed.]

B (*Softly.*): And so it goes.

C (*To A; slowly, with great emphasis, but no anger.*): I . . . will . . . not . . . become . . . you. I will *not*. I . . . I deny *you*.

A (*Mildly amused.*): Oh? Yes? You *deny* me? (*To them all.*) Yes? You all deny me? (*To C.*) You deny me? (*To B.*) I suppose you do too. (B *lowers her gaze.*) Yes; of course. (*To him.*) And, of course, *you* deny me. (*He looks at her.*) (*General.*) Well, that's all right: I deny you too; I deny you all. (*To C.*) I deny *you*, (*to B*) and I deny *you*, (*to him*) and, of course, I deny *you*. (*General.*) I'm *here*, and I deny you *all*; I deny every *one* of you.

C: *Is* it like this? What about the happy times . . . the *happiest* moments? *I haven't* had them yet, have I? All done at twenty-six? I can't imagine that. I had *some*, of course, some of what probably will *be* the happiest even when I get to the point I can begin to think about looking back without feeling silly, though God knows when *that* will be!—not feeling silly—if *ever*. Confirmation, for example, that wonderful time: the white dress Mother made, Sis all jealous and excited, jumping up and down and sulking at the same time. But even now, you see, I'm remembering, and what I'm remembering doesn't have to do with what I *felt*, but what I remember. They say you can't remember pain. Well, maybe you can't remember pleasure, either—in the same way, I mean, in the way you can't remember pain. Maybe all you can remember is the memory of it . . . remembering, remembering it. I *know* my best times—what is it? happiest?—haven't happened yet. They're to *come*. Aren't they? Please? And . . . and whatever evil comes, whatever loss and taking away comes, won't it all be balanced out? Please? I'm not a fool, but there *is* a lot of happiness along the way. *Isn't* there?! And isn't it always ahead? Aren't I *right*? Aren't I? I mean . . . all along the way? No? Please?

B (*Comes downstage to where C is not—either right or left, leaving center free for A later. Shakes her head to C, not unkindly.*): Silly, silly girl; silly baby. The happiest time? Now; now . . . always. This must be the happiest time: half of being adult done, the rest ahead of me. Old enough to be a *little* wise, past being *really* dumb . . . (*An aside to C.*) No offense.

C (*Looking forward: tight smile.*): None taken.

B: Enough shit gone through to have a sense of the shit that's ahead, but way past sitting and *play-ing* in it. This *has* to be the happiest time—in theory, anyway. Things nibble away, of course; your job is to know *that*, too. The wood *may* be rotten under your feet—your nicely spread legs—and you'll be up to your ass in sawdust and dry rot before you know it, before you know it, before you can say, This is the happiest time. Well, I can *live* with that, *die* with that. I mean, these things happen, but what I like most about being where I am—and fifty *is* a peak, in the sense of a mountain.

C (*An aside.*): Fifty-two.

B: Yes, I know, thank you. What I like most about being where I am is that there's a lot I don't have to go through anymore, and that doesn't mean closing down—for *me*, at any rate. It opens up whole vistas—of decline, of obsolescence, peculiarity, but really *interesting*! Standing up here right on top of the middle of it *has* to be the happiest time. I mean, it's the only time you get a three-hundred-and-sixty-degree view—see in all directions. Wow! What a view!

[*A moves downstage center, B and C stay where they are.*]

A (*Shakes her head; chuckles; to* B *and* C.): You're both such children. The happiest moment of all? Really? The happiest moment? (*To the audience now.*) Coming to the end of it, I think, when all the waves cause the greatest woes to subside, leaving breathing space, time to concentrate on the greatest woe of all—that blessed one—the end of it. Going through the whole thing and coming out . . . not out *beyond* it, of course, but sort of to . . . one side. None of that "further shore" nonsense, but to the point where you *can* think about yourself in the third person without being crazy. I've waked up in the morning, and I've thought, well, now, she's waking up, and now she's going to see what works—the eyes, for example. Can she *see*? She *can*? Well, good, I suppose; so much for that. Now she's going to test all the other stuff—the

joints, the inside of the mouth, and now she's going to have to pee. What's she going to do—go for the walker? Lurch from chair to chair—pillar to post? Is she going to call for somebody—anybody . . . the tiniest thought there might be nobody there, that she's not making a sound, that maybe she's not alive—so's anybody'd notice, that is? *I* can do that. I can think about myself that way, which means, I suppose, that that's the way I'm *living*—beside myself, to one side. Is that what they mean by that?—I'm beside myself? I don't think so. I think they're talking about *another* kind of joy. There's a difference between knowing you're going to *die* and *knowing* you're going to die. The second is better; it moves away from the theoretical. I'm rambling, aren't I?

B (*Gently; face forward.*): A little.

A (*To* B.): Well, we *do* that at ninety, or whatever I'm supposed to be. I mean, give a girl a break! (*To the audience again now.*) Sometimes when I wake up and start thinking about myself like that—like I was watching—I really get the feeling that I *am dead*, but going on at the same time, and I wonder if she can talk and fear and . . . and then I wonder which has died—me, or the one I think about. It's a fairly confusing business. I'm rambling. (*A gesture to stop* B.) Yes; I know! (*To the audience.*) I was talking about . . . what: coming to the end of it, yes. So. There it is. You asked after all. That's the happiest moment. (*A looks to C and B, puts her hand out, takes theirs.*) When it's all done. When we stop. When we can stop.

END

HOWARD BARKER (b. 1946)

Howard Barker was born in Dulwich, in the south part of metropolitan London, and attended Battersea grammar school. After graduating from Sussex University he began his writing career, and in 1970 his first play, *Cheek*, was produced at the Royal Court's Theatre Upstairs, the main venue since the 1970s for London's avant-garde plays. Since then, Barker has become a prolific writer, with many plays to his credit. The more well-known plays include *Victory* (1983), *The Castle* (1984), *The Power of the Dog: Moments in History and Anti-History* (1985), *Scenes from an Execution* (1985), *Women Beware Women* (1986), an adaptation of Thomas Middleton's play of that name, and *The Bite of the Night* (1988). In addition he has written film scripts, television and radio plays as well as several volumes of poetry and a volume of dramatic theory.

Barker's plays routinely baffle critics, who praise his verbal bravura, his structural extravagance, and the energy and excitement his plays generate in performance. Yet they have often wondered where it all goes, what it all "means." In his theoretical statements on the subject of what he calls his theater of catastrophe, Barker insists that his plays do not convey just a single meaning, which would insult the intelligence of his audience and set himself up as the arbiter of truth. Rather, his plays are intended to provoke thought and discussion on a range of subjects. Some have suggested that his theater attempts to fulfill Artaud's call for a theater of drastic action pushed to its limits. Artaud urged the pursuit of metaphysical principles and trance-like states through combinations of sound, light, movement, and stagecraft. Barker tries to achieve his effects through impassioned and convulsive language in which not a syllable is wasted, with all the words moving to create a compelling rhythm. In Barker's drama, actors do not create characters; the author creates them through his distinctive use of language.

This quality led to the founding of the Wrestling School theater company in 1988 by a group of actors, musicians, designers, and directors, all of whom shared an enthusiasm for Barker's plays and who dedicated themselves to producing and performing them. The best-known member of the Wrestling School is Ian McDiarmid, director of the Almeida Theatre, with a wealth of experience in the theater and in films. The complexity of Barker's texts and his refusal to admit to a single interpretation (a stance that continues to baffle and irritate critics), together with the linguistic and imagistic density of his language, required a new style of acting suitable to their presentation. This new style is characterized by an emphasis on language, music, and extreme theatricality. The Wrestling School, in conjunction with the Royal Court Theater has produced six of Barker's works: *The Last Supper* (1989), *Seven Lears* (1990), *Golgo* (1991), *Victory* (1992), *The Europeans* (1993), and *Hated Nightfall* (1994).

Hated Nightfall

Barker's plays are often concerned with political and with metaphysical inquiry. His Brechtian characters move through a world in which catastrophe has struck. Barker is fascinated with periods in history between regimes when social and political order is dissolved and anything is possible. Here are fit subjects for characters in the theater of catastrophe. Like Dancer in *Hated Nightfall*, Barker's characters attempt to negotiate a world in which society's laws have broken down, in the hope of discovering something more fundamental. Barker's savage comedy, which often provokes dissociation between thought and expression, is grounded in the belief that all social and political organizations, even the cosmos itself, are flawed and degrading mechanisms. His characters do not respond to this awareness by believing that life is absurd, however, but rather by believing that all things are fluid and that humans describe themselves in such moments.

The remains of two unidentified human beings, discovered together with those of the Russian imperial family some seventy years after their execution, inspired *Hated Nightfall*. In the play Barker allows his imagination to roam freely on the question of how the royal family met their deaths at the hands of the revolutionaries, and the result is an unobjective, emotional, and poetic treatment of the charged subject. The material goals of the Bolshevik Revolution do not entirely square with the all-too-human act which initiated it—the execution of the royal family. The protagonist, Dancer, former tutor to the royal children, is catapulted into a position of power by the revolution, but he has designs that only tangentially coincide with official revolutionary ideology. Dancer is plagued by the awareness that he is a transient phenomenon, a tool of history in its transition from one form of political repression to another. He alternates between cruelty and pity, and with comic abandon he murders all those members of the revolutionary party who get in the way of realizing his ambition—to make the murder of the family his personal work of art. His own sacrificial death is, Barker claims, "a profound gesture of refusal," an artistic insight into a century that will be filled with atrocities—an apotheosis of a sensibility which has seen through the deceptions of political organization. Dancer's death is an act of self-description, and it earns something of the audience's admiration.

Howard Barker has compared Dancer to a saint. Like a saint, Dancer finds the world inadequate, and like a saint he conveys the profundity of his disappointment in the horrible means by which he rejects the world. For the saint there is no worthwhile earthly object suitable to his passion; human love is wholly inadequate. Dancer thus rejects the Empress's offer for them to become lovers and move to Paris. He desires instead a gesture to repudiate the inadequacy of the world and to validate the purity of his aspirations. The more horrible and bizarre this gesture, the more noteworthy. Like a saint at last, Dancer becomes an artist who creates with his own death a profound work of art.

Hated Nightfall

HOWARD BARKER

The Tutor of The Romanoffs
His Exemplification of Desire and Subsequent Martyrdom in the
Schoolroom at Ekaterinburg
16th July, 1918

Seventy years after the murder of the Russian Imperial family by
Revolutionaries, their remains were discovered. Alongside them lay
two as yet unidentified human beings.

CHARACTERS

DANCER, A Tutor
ROMANOFF, An Emperor
CAROLINE, An Empress
CHRISTOPHE ⎫
HELEN   ⎬ Their Children
GRISELDA   ⎭
JANE, A Servant

FITCH   ⎫
ARRANT   ⎪
DISBANNER ⎬ Officials of the Revolution
DENADIR   ⎪
ALBEIT   ⎭
A CHORUS
(To include the above)

PART I

*[A substantial interior space, barren. A single upright
chair on which a* WOMAN *sits asleep. It is the sleep of
exhaustion, manifested in her posture. The silence is
ruptured by the intrusion of orchestral music, which
ceases. In the restored silence, a* CHILD *passes, dragging a pillow. A* MAN *enters. He goes to the sleeping*
WOMAN *and places his hands kindly on her shoulders.]*

ROMANOFF: I'm sorry
    I'm sorry
    I'm so sorry
    So sorry
    So sorry (*The* WOMAN *is not awakened. He
goes out. A* SECOND MAN *enters. He stares at the*
WOMAN.)

DANCER (*pause*): This will not be my decision the
    decision comes from elsewhere rather far away
    by telephone no not by telephone (*Pause*)
    By telegram and this decision is irrevocable
    so please don't entertain hopes of reprieve no
    messenger will arrive no stained rider on a
    lathering horse etcetera no and further more I
    am the one who (*Pause*)
    I volunteered (*Pause*)
    No one persuaded me or appealed to high-
    er principles (*Pause*)
    I think with a rifle (*Pause*)

    No a knife (*Pause*)
    A rifle or a knife (*Pause*)
    I have a knife whereas a rifle I should need
to borrow so what I can borrow it (*Pause*)
    It is perhaps important the executioner
regards himself as a professional his actions
unimpaired by enthusiasm or reluctance in
this case however (*Pause*)
    I confess to very real desire I am immensely
(*Pause*)
    Drawn to the task (*Pause*)
    My only fear believe me being that another
might offer his services and the thing degenerate into a competition short and long straws
the tossing of a coin etcetera no when the decision is announced over the telephone it will be
I and no other I alone who (*Pause*)
    Or telegraph I think however the existence
of the order its material existence (*Pause*)
    Incriminating bits of paper (*Pause*)
    Caroline (*Pause*)
    Most likely therefore to be the telephone by
which (*He stops, aware he is being observed by a*
WOMAN *holding a broom and bucket. Pause.*)

JANE: Let her sleep.
DANCER: I'm not stopping her.
JANE (*cleaning the floor*): You're pestering her.
DANCER: Not in the least.
JANE: Muttering and so on.

DANCER: Be quiet you are a servant.

JANE: I am a servant and so are you.

DANCER: A servant and no one cares for your opinions.

JANE: No one cares for them but they still exist.

DANCER: Let them exist but unarticulated.

JANE: Shut up.

DANCER: You shut up.

JANE: No.

DANCER: Do as you are told.

JANE: Of course I won't.

DANCER: Look, her knees have drifted open with that abolition of all consciousness that comes with sleep and if I—(*He cranes.*)
Stoop or—(*and kneels.*)
Kneel—
The shadows fall between her thighs and—
What's there
What's there (*He squirms.* JANE *looks at him. He gets up, brushes his knees.*)
No one will ever understand my attitude to women. Never. (JANE *goes out.*)
So what.
I am never to be understood.
So what.
Let them bury me beneath a tree
An insubstantial tree
Never mind the oaks the urns the obelisks
And when the tree blows down
So what
So what (*He covers his face with his hands. The overture is revived, clamorous. The* CHILD *passes with a pillow.* ROMANOFF *appears. Silence.*)

ROMANOFF: If we are guilty of anything it is an excess of love.

DANCER (*recovering*): Excellent!
Preposterous!
And excellent!
I do so love the apologia of kings!
Hilarity!
Impertinence.
Presumption.
I'm not conducting the trial, someone else is.

ROMANOFF: Love of one another. Consuming love which blinded me to circumstances beyond the wall.

DANCER: Wall? What wall?

ROMANOFF: The wall of love.

DANCER: Is love a wall, then?

ROMANOFF: A wall behind which the most tender flowers of affection, intimacy and—

DANCER: Push her knees together, you are her husband. (*Pause.* ROMANOFF *glares at him.*)
Her knees. (*Pause*)
Have come apart. (*Pause*)
A wall, is it? I am wholly ignorant of love but that is possibly only a reflection of my dissi-

dence, a characteristic of my revolutionary nature which cannot subscribe to platitudes. Perhaps I know more about love even than you, but love of a different kind. Perhaps at this stage I am obliged to be strictly theoretical about this love, but with the changing circumstances of our time, I might—

[ROMANOFF *seizes* DANCER *by the throat. Comic music accompanies his attempt to throttle him. They move to and fro in a terrible embrace. A* CHORUS *of shadowy figures laughs as an accompaniment. The music stops, and the* CHORUS *is silent. Only* DANCER'S *laugh is heard, as he adjusts his collar.* ROMANOFF, *exhausted, hangs his head. The* CHILD *is discovered, watching, holding his pillow by its corner.* DANCER *goes to the* CHILD.]

DANCER: Your father cannot forgive me, cannot, no matter how he tries, and he is Christian, he is devout! (*He looks at* ROMANOFF.) As to whether I am able to forgive him, that hardly enters into it—

ROMANOFF: Forgive for what?

DANCER: No, no—

ROMANOFF: For what?

DANCER: You see, he cannot even conceive of his offence—

ROMANOFF: For what, I said—

DANCER: What am I, after all, a tutor, a servant, a domestic animal—

ROMANOFF: Please—

DANCER: Which whilst possessing the propensity for craven gratitude—

ROMANOFF: Stop this—

DANCER: Is incapable of registering resentment—

ROMANOFF: Stop , I beg you—

DANCER: **Hatred or contempt** (*The* CHILD *shudders.* DANCER *holds him tight.*) It's all right, it's all right, don't be frightened, what does it matter, after all, I am a transient phenomenon whose own extinction is already written in the Book of Circumstance, yes, a transient phenomenon, can you say that? (*The* CHILD *opens his mouth.*) Yes, quite so, that's what I am, remember that and the firing squad, that also is, look boldly in the barrels of the guns, transient phenomenon, shout . . . ! (*He pushes the* CHILD *violently towards* ROMANOFF.)

CHORUS: **Dancer**
Dancer
We think it possible you are a fraud

DANCER: I never rule it out, gentlemen!

CHORUS: **And we will pay a price to follow you**

DANCER: Yes, why shouldn't you? Pay the price and be damned!

CHORUS: **Dancer**

What kind of tutor were you?
DANCER: Not nice, obviously.
CHORUS: **All your certificates were forged**
DANCER: Yes, I am without qualifications! On the other hand, I am blessed with this extraordinary facility for speech. Words tumble. Words froth. And in the proper order! Now, stop pestering me, I am expecting a communication of the highest significance. (*He turns.*)
CHORUS: **Dancer**
DANCER: What!
CHORUS: **If you were a liar under one regime**
   How can we tell
   You will not lie under another? (*Pause. DANCER is patient.*)
DANCER: Listen, the words are moribund. The words are wasted with disease. They haunt old libraries as sick men creep the corridors of sanitoria. (*He smiles.*)
   New words, please . . . (*He goes to leave, turns swiftly.*)
   You want me to confess!
   Confession is your solitary need. (*Pause*)
   I do not confess. The instinct is missing in me . . . (*He looks at them, provocatively.*)
   I leapt into the fireplace as a baby, from my mother's arms, which is why I have this scar on me. Why, I wonder? Did I think no flame could scorch me? (*Pause*)
   I'll perish, obviously, and in a ghastly way. Take comfort from the fact that I shall suffer. The world abhors me. It writhes to know I walk upon its surfaces . . . (*He is suddenly possessed.*)
   I jump on it (*He jumps, stops, laughs.*)
   Oh, the pathos of the man who cannot assent, for assent he must . . . eventually . . . (*The CHORUS turns to leave.*)
   Stay with me . . .!
   Oh, stay . . .!
CHORUS: **Dancer**
   Circumstances elevate unlikely men
   The wave that lifted you
   Will swallow you again (*They leave. DANCER turns.*)
DANCER: Thirty years a tutor! And I was handsome, yes, I had the looks, I had the acumen, and so many learned from me, what could I not teach? For example
   The ambiguities of parental love
   I saw it all
   The tortures of domestic bliss
   I've seen the instruments
   Oh, the terrible ordeal of infants
   Especially the rich
   Pity the rich
   I do (*He turns to ROMANOFF.*)

I am best qualified to govern you, believe me, I have your interests at heart. (*He sits, dismissing ROMANOFF with a slight gesture.*) Go now, but leave your wife. (*ROMANOFF takes his son by the shoulder.*) How appallingly she sleeps. Disaster she interprets as a sickness, which can be healed by diet or a period of rest . . .
ROMANOFF: She is depressed.
DANCER: Yes.
ROMANOFF: She deserved nothing but love.
DANCER: Mm.
ROMANOFF: Gratitude.
DANCER: Mm.
ROMANOFF: And loyalty.
DANCER: Indeed.
ROMANOFF: A perfect mother. A perfect wife.
DANCER: Why are you rehearsing this?
ROMANOFF: **Because our misery is incomprehensible to me.** (*Pause. He shrugs.*) Not entirely. I am the guilty one. And I have brought these innocents to the brink of murder. (*Pause. He turns to go.*) Don't kill my son. (*Pause*)
DANCER: Why not? (*A slow, pitiful shrug arises from ROMANOFF's shoulders. He leads the CHILD away.*)
   Innocents? (*DANCER gets up.*)
   Innocents?
   Thank God I am not young, oh, the words of the young, the ponderous vocabulary of youth, their phrases dip like over-laden freighters, morality and rectitude strapped to the decks
   Innocent of what? (*A wind whispers round the room. DANCER looks at the sleeping WOMAN.*)
   I am innocent if anybody is . . . (*Two young WOMEN appear, pensive, anxious, they wait for his attention. He detects them, looks up.*)
HELEN: Are you in charge now, Citizen?
DANCER: Me, yes.
HELEN: Ridiculous!
DANCER: Isn't it?
HELEN: Only a week ago we were studying the Gallic Wars. The tribes. The topography.
DANCER: So we were . . .
HELEN: It's all so incomprehensible to us . . .
DANCER: Is it? So your father says. And yet it is so lucid to me.
GRISELDA: And I hate calling people Citizen!
DANCER: Do you? Say it more often, and it will cease to offend you.
HELEN: What we find particularly hard to understand is why—
DANCER: Please, do not inflict me with the poverty of your understanding. I am no longer a teacher. Your ignorance is no longer a concern of mine. (*GRISELDA weeps. Her SISTER clasps her.*) Oh, how I long to make you weep . . . how gratifying the spectacle of a young girl's tears!
HELEN: You are vile and—

DANCER: **All things cowardly and reprehensible I know.** (*Pause. He smiles.*)
And once you trusted me.

HELEN: No. Not entirely.

DANCER: Yes.

HELEN: Not entirely, I said—

DANCER: **You trusted me.** (*Pause*)
Why pretend to insights you could not possibly possess? None of you has the slightest subtlety of mind—

HELEN: That isn't true!

DANCER: Helen, I know your mediocrity . . . (*She turns away, bitterly.*) You trusted me, and now you are ashamed. You are ashamed of your own disingenuousness . . . (*He shrugs.*) What does it matter? We are all dead now . . .

HELEN: I hate you Citizen . . .

DANCER: Very well, I am hated . . . and yet the sun still shines . . .

HELEN (*turning on him*): **It is dead matter, that is why. Volatile, but lifeless** . . . (*He stares at her.*) Shall we be killed?

DANCER: I think so, yes.

HELEN: Save my little sister—

DANCER: She is not little, she has merely failed to mature—

HELEN: Oh, stop this fatuous and futile—

DANCER (*rising to his feet*): **I can't help it, I can't help it** . . .! (*He pushes them.*) Get outside, now, get outside, find a corner and wait to be killed . . .! (*They stare. He shudders. Pause.*) I am fifty. My chance has come. **Fifty and absolute.** (*Pause*)

GRISELDA: You are not really bad, Citizen . . .

DANCER: I am—

GRISELDA: No, not really, really bad—

DANCER: I am
I am that bad (*Pause*)
Believe me.
You merely cannot bear to contemplate it. (*He touches* GRISELDA *weakly on the shoulder.*)
Go away now. I am capable of such artificial sentiments, things that make my own flesh crawl . . . (*Suddenly* GRISELDA *seizes his hand and kisses it. He withdraws it.*)
You see . . .! You see how colonized we are by other people's gestures! On the rim of the grave even you are insincere! Too many novels, Miss! Too many plays! (*GRISELDA bursts into tears and hurries out.* HELEN *boldly keeps her ground.*)

HELEN: I pity you, Citizen.

DANCER: Oh, don't bother . . .!

HELEN: Pity, I said—

DANCER: **I mock your pity. I repudiate your pity. Take your pity to death's ditch with you.**
(HELEN *stares in disbelief, then goes out. He watches her departure. A* MAN *has entered, with a sheaf of papers. He looks at* DANCER, *bemused.*)

FITCH: You'll hurt yourself.

DANCER: Hurt myself? How?

FITCH: All this effort to be vile.

DANCER: No effort, I assure you.

FITCH: It's not required. (DANCER *turns to him at last.*) No one suspects you of disloyalty.

DANCER: Don't they? I suspect myself of it.

FITCH: Well, that is consistent with the earnestness with which you have adopted the revolutionary cause, Citizen, and wholly laudable, but—

DANCER: I do hate that (*Pause*)
Forgive me
I do hate that—confectionery—of words I tell you a truth and you offer me these impeccably I am talking for example of
These immaculately
My sexuality
Its lethal nature
Coiffured words
We must be careful, mustn't we, not to smother things in words?
This woman has not woken yet
No, that helps nobody. (*Pause.* FITCH *stares at him.*)

FITCH: I have to go . . .

DANCER: What are these papers? I receive so many papers and quite frankly they are not always read . . . (*Pause*)
Their appearance is detrimental . . .
And what are they? The usual exhortations to solidarity . . . quotations from the works of dead economists and completely biased news, no one places the slightest credence in them, you would need to be the most diseased fanatic to even (*He stops.*)

FITCH: Please, put your criticisms on paper and I will forward them to the appropriate committee.

DANCER: Yes, I will. (FITCH *turn to go.* DANCER *hurries to him and stabs him.* FITCH *cries out in disbelief.*)
Oh . . .!
Oh . . .! (*The* CHORUS *appears, with* JANE. *A frantic, anxious cascade of music.*)
You see, if they don't listen to me, what occurs!

CHORUS: **Dancer**
We can forgive the revolutionary death but this

DANCER: I've killed!

CHORUS: **This**

DANCER: It's easy! I'm amazed!

CHORUS: **This**

JANE: He isn't dead . . .

DANCER: I've killed, I said!

CHORUS: **The tutor is a murderer**

DANCER (*turning on them*): **The educator always is.**
(*Pause.* FITCH *stirs on the ground.*)

JANE: Not dead I said. (*Pause. Silence but for a thin*

wind blowing.)

DANCER: I'll try again.

JANE: You'll have to. (*Pause.* FITCH *moans.* DANCER *offers* JANE *the knife.*)

DANCER: You do it. (*The* CHORUS *laughs.*)
  Why shouldn't she? (*Pause.* JANE *has not taken the knife.*)
  All right . . . I will . . . (*He goes to* FITCH, *who sees him.*)

FITCH: I'm hurt. . .

DANCER: Yes, you are . . . so badly hurt you can't come back . . . it's . . . a matter of—(*He hacks the throat brutally, his eyes shut.*)

CHORUS: **Dancer**
  Dancer
  You are insane

DANCER (*swiftly rising to his feet.*): You would say that! How necessary you should think I am insane! Think so if it relieves you! (*With a gesture of contempt he tosses the knife away.*)

JANE: He's still not dead . . .

DANCER (*turning on her now*): **If you know so much about it, do it.** (*She is adamantly still.*)
  He is in pain there, and really, I am an amateur . . . (*She stares.*)
  Haven't you killed cattle, sheep and things? (*Pause*)
  So what if he's in pain. He was an idiot. (*To* CHORUS.)
  That is an authentic idiot,
  Not me . . .

CHORUS: **Dancer**
  You have stabbed the agent of the Revolution
  He was on your side!

DANCER: *My* side?
  Do I have a side? (*They are aghast.*)
  Oh, how horrified you are to find me pure . . .
  Yes . . .
  Rinsed of all belief . . .
  You'd prefer any old catechism to the echo of the unbeliever
  Lies
  Filth
  Encrusted ideology

[*DANCER walks coolly to the dying* MAN *and slits his throat, this time effectively and in a routine manner. As he moves away he senses he is watched and turns to see* CHRISTOPHE, *in a corner of the stage. The* CHILD *tilts his toy watering-can. A dark fluid trickles out . . . * DANCER *turns back to the* CHORUS.]

DANCER: Humans really are enslaved by books
  I'll give you a book
  Oh, I intend to write one
  I am as narcissistic as the next man (*He wipes the blade of the knife this time and pockets it.*)

I say a book
  I must warn you, I mean a shelf (*He laughs.*)
  Yes!
  And you will memorize it, oh, whole paragraphs word-perfectly . . . (*He looks at the* CHORUS. *They drift away.* JANE *looks at* DANCER.)
  Swab away the blood.

JANE: Swab it yourself.

DANCER: Jane, you are a servant

JANE: I am a servant, and so are you.

DANCER: Must we go through this every hour? I tell you for the first and last time, I am a law unto myself.

JANE: You're Billy the tutor with the balding bonce as far as I'm concerned.

DANCER: Oh, your rustic charm . . .! Swab it, I said.

JANE: No. (*Pause. He takes the bucket and broom away from her and begins to wash the floor.*)

DANCER: 'Make my criticisms on paper and forward them to the Committee . . .!' What does he think I am, a suicide?

JANE: He asked for it.

DANCER: I'm nobody's fool.

JANE: That's true, Citizen. But perhaps it's no bad thing to be a fool . . .?

DANCER (*stopping, appearing to think*): The ramifications of such an opinion stretch even my imagination to breaking point . . . (*He lays down the broom, goes to move the body.*) I so detest the wisdom of the people . . . you take this arm.

JANE: Nope.

DANCER: Oh, come on . . .

JANE: No I said. (*Pause.* DANCER *tries to drag the body by its arms. It scarcely moves.*)

DANCER: The bulk of humanity suspends its entire existence from three or four bucolic and inane proverbs. This enables it to—(*He heaves.*) tolerate its own annihilation, even . . . (*He drops the arms and goes to the legs, and pulls.*) Jane . . . (*She ignores him. He pulls again.*) The lyrics of some whimpering ballad can compensate them for the most appalling blows of fate **I can't move this by myself.** (*She watches, still.*)
  You will remember this moment. My apparent helplessness. My apparent foolishness. You will recollect it. The nadir, possibly, of my existence. I hope you will not rue the day . . .

[JANE *goes out.* DANCER *is still for a long time. A light, pastoral music, he stares at the sleeping* WOMAN. *He goes to her, and leaning close to her ear, whispers. He looks to assure himself he is alone, then proceeds to whisper in her other ear. He tears himself away in a paroxysm of ecstasy.*]

DANCER: I wonder
  I wonder if

This
Passion
Is
Sincere
The distinction between an honest and dishon-
est passion being what precisely
Well
I essay
I tentatively
And
Humbly
Propose (*He laughs, shaking his head.*)
Typical tutor
Typical philosophe
Nothing is experienced but needs to be
explained! (*He reflects. He makes an effort to
achieve perfect expression.*)
Princesses sleep a thousand years and Queens
perish on the block
We so adore
We so adore to (*He whispers torrentially into the
WOMAN's ear, and turns away abruptly.*)
And I am after all a modern man
Yes
Nothing quaint or archaic clings to me
They also require me to die
Humiliation
Is
Their
Apotheosis . . . (*He looks at her, half-pityingly.
ROMANOFF enters. DANCER senses him.*)
I am pitying her death . . .
ROMANOFF: And what of yours?
DANCER: Mine?
I expect it hourly, and from any source but
don't come near me I have a knife which I
have just employed in an almost but not quite
arbitrary manner
There is the man of the future throat cut
Typical future
Short-lived and banal
Promises and inexorable laws of
Engineer of human souls etcetera
Dead now
Never mind
So keep your distance
Would you kindly help me move him I was
rather too spontaneous and he fell right in the
door
Next time
Plan it better obviously (*Pause. ROMANOFF
shakes his head.*)
What are you, a saint? (*ROMANOFF looks away.*)
Some say you are but I keep an open mind
**Drag the corpse away or I will do some cruel
thing to those you love.** (*ROMANOFF thinks
briefly.*)

ROMANOFF: Drag him where?
DANCER: Anywhere, you choose. (*ROMANOFF goes to
the dead man, looks.*) I fear my own death for
one reason only, that it would render me inca-
pable of experiencing the particular act of love
I know myself to be supremely capable of . . .
ROMANOFF: You . . .?
DANCER: Yes. (*ROMANOFF studiedly declines to reply. He
leans to the corpse. His hand falters.*)
ROMANOFF: I have never touched a dead man . . .
DANCER: This act of love may not at first be recogniz-
able as such. I think it will be misrepresented.
The subtlest minds may be required to identify
and elaborate it. (*Pause*)
ROMANOFF: **And that is why we failed . . .!**
DANCER: Please, you are forever analyzing this thing
you call your failure, who cares about your
failure, already it is of negligible importance,
the preposterous fantasy of academics, and
nostalgic picture books—
ROMANOFF: **The prince must touch . . .** (*Pause*)
DANCER: Yes . . . (*He shrugs.*)
But the princess, what of her . . .? (*ROMANOFF
stands away.*)
ROMANOFF: I decline to do your dirty work for you!
Punish as you will. But spare my children—
DANCER: Shhh—
ROMANOFF: Inflict your malice where you will but—
DANCER: Please, you are so—extreme, indulgent—
ROMANOFF: **Me?**
DANCER: You, yes—indulgent with your fear—
ROMANOFF: **You threatened me.**
DANCER: Did I? I forget . . . (*He shrugs.*) I threaten
everybody . . . (*He gets up.*)
Come on, help me conceal him or I shall be
discovered and consequently you will find
yourself in the hands of someone for whom no
ties of sentiment restrain his violence . . . (*He
smiles.*)
Oh, believe me, I entertain obscure feelings of
devotion for you all! Yes! Now, take his legs!
(*ROMANOFF hesitates, returns to the body, stoops.
DANCER does not move, but watches, and then
laughs.*)
Yes . . . (*ROMANOFF looks up.*)
It is so—(*He selects the word.*)
Necessary—
The Prince should be porter to a lout.
(*ROMANOFF is patient.*)
I am the lout. (*He goes to the arms. Together they
hoist the corpse. DANCER does not move.*)
I am not presumptious, am I? I do not call
myself History. The Agent of Destiny. Justice.
The People's Will. I don't drape myself.

[*DANCER nods his head. ROMANOFF staggers. They go
out with the body. An effect of sound and light. A cry.*

The CHILD passes dragging its pillow. The cry again. The sleeping WOMAN is aroused, shocked from her state. She speaks as if resuming a diatribe suspended by a spell.]

CAROLINE: Logic . . .! The contemptible and thread-bare thing how dare you bring it near me its smell offends me! (*Pause. She perceives her situation, looking side to side, almost surreptitiously. A wind rattles.*)
That's what I'll say. (*Pause*)
Because a princess cannot possibly negotiate the nature of her privilege. Conceding even, that it could be argued would be a profound mistake **I am not in the same domain of law let alone language**
No
Royalty has no defence
Shoot me
Silence is most eloquent and I shan't utter one syllable of expiation
I am not culpable
God is the sole judge of all monarchy
They know that
They want to drag us through their courts
They want to smear us with their language
I want a priest, please! (*Silence. She is still. She smiles.*)
I thought I was modern. I read modern books, but one must be careful of these things, keeping abreast of course but not permitting one-self to be
Penetrated
Spiked
Some specimen of etymology pinned to the board
Darling, come here! (*The CHILD is discovered standing forlornly. She opens her arms.*)
I was asleep! I do sleep such sleeps, don't I, deeper than cats certainly, more like a toad! They sleep whole winters!
Come here! (*The CHILD approaches her, slowly. She kneels.*)
Who knows why I sleep so? Or what wakes me? (*She bites her lip. She caresses him.*)
Things are so very out of order . . .! But what is certain is that order reasserts itself.
It must
That is a law
Do you know what a law is?
A law is what cannot be disputed
So
All this
Inconvenience
Will last for such and such a time
A week perhaps!
But not longer

Promise you
Promise
Promise (*She suddenly crushes him.*)
Little Monarch
How they hate you . . .!
But don't hate them because it would demean you
Their hatred is the proof we are elect! (*She suddenly repulses him.*)
Quick now, find your sisters! Find Helen! (*He starts to go.*)
Listen . . .! (*He stops.*)
When you are the monarch, remember this! To suffer also is the privilege of princes! (*The CHILD goes out, as ROMANOFF returns. She sees his state.*)
You are covered in mud!
ROMANOFF: Yes . . .
CAROLINE: Why?
ROMANOFF: Dancer asked me to assist him with a—
CAROLINE: Dancer asked—
ROMANOFF: Not asked exactly—
CAROLINE: Dancer—
ROMANOFF: **Ordered me**—
CAROLINE: **Dancer is a tutor**—
ROMANOFF: **Ordered me I said.** (*Pause*)
CAROLINE: You see, I am awake. (*She shrugs.*)
I wake, and it is arbitrary, just as it is arbitrary when I go to sleep. Something is preparing me for death. (*She shrugs again.*)
I say death . . . (*She looks at him.*)
The death of something . . . obviously . . .
ROMANOFF: Everything is my fault.
CAROLINE: Yes.
ROMANOFF (*horrified*): Do yo believe that, Caroline?
CAROLINE: Yes.
ROMANOFF: And in what may be our final hours you are prepared to burden me with the entire responsibility for what's—
CAROLINE: Absolutely, yes. (*ROMANOFF looks at her, distraught. She experiences a surge of pity.*) Oh, come here, little mouse . . .
ROMANOFF (*fixed to the spot*): My son—my innocent and inoffensive son—
CAROLINE: Come here, I said . . . (*ROMANOFF silently chokes tears.*) Always we called one another little mouse . . . (*ROMANOFF does not take her hand. It falters.*)
ROMANOFF: I am without sin. Blameless and without sin.
CAROLINE: Yes.
But I require another life. (*ROMANOFF looks at her, bewildered*).)
The one about to close I . . . do not feel, on reflection, fulfilled my needs . . . (*His mouth hangs open with incredulity. The DAUGHTERS enter.*)

HELEN: Mother!

CAROLINE: Shh! (*She gestures them impatiently with a hand. They stop, also puzzled.* CAROLINE *walks.*)

> I do not want to die. (*She looks, one to the other.*)

HELEN: We neither! And we are frightened, Mother!

CAROLINE: Yes.

> But whereas I think I possess the means of my deliverance, I am not certain either of you do . . . (*Pause. They follow her movements.*)
>
> In my sleep, I hear voices. These voices urge me to—(*She laughs.*)
>
> Oh, all sorts of things, both poetry and the most obscence—

ROMANOFF: Caroline—

CAROLINE: Preposterous and

ROMANOFF: Caroline—

CAROLINE (*turning to him*): Degenerate things . . . (*Pause*)

ROMANOFF: These sleeps are sickness, Caroline . . .

CAROLINE: Yes, and like all sickness, they originate in God . . . (*She turns to the* GIRLS.)

> I tell you this because—in the most unkind way—oh, such a very unkind way—I never felt a greater distance existed between myself and you . . . (*They look to their* FATHER.)
>
> When you would think, under such circumstances—

ROMANOFF: Christophe, Helen, Griselda—

CAROLINE: A mother would manifest the opposite tendency, if anything, an excess of intimacy—

ROMANOFF: Christophe, Helen, Griselda—

CAROLINE: A tidal wave of all those maternal instincts which impending murder—

ROMANOFF: **Christophe**

> **Helen**
>
> **Griselda** (*He shudders.* CAROLINE *is by contrast, icy.*)

CAROLINE: Licenses . . . (*Pause*)

> There is no priest, is there? They killed him in the hospital. (*She laughs.*)
>
> All the buildings are misused . . .! The hospital became a slaughterhouse, and as for the schoolroom . . . (*She gestures to the room they are in.*)
>
> Who knows what we shall learn in here?

HELEN: Frankly Mother, I preferred it when you slept all the time—

ROMANOFF: Helen—

HELEN: I did! When she slept, it was possible to invent her, whereas awake she is—

> **Not nice, is she?** (*She looks boldly at* CAROLINE.)
>
> Not that it matters, if you are being killed, what—(*She falters.*)
>
> Memory is . . .! (ROMANOFF *goes to console her. She pulls away from him.*)
>
> No! (CAROLINE *laughs.*)
>
> We are forever—grasping one another—I don't

wish to be grasped . . .!

ROMANOFF: It is not *grasping* . . .

HELEN: It feels like it . . .

ROMANOFF: Always we were intimate . . . what has happened here? Always we embraced . . . and you call it grasping . . .

HELEN: It's suffocating . . .!

GRISELDA (*suddenly*): Where is Christophe?

ROMANOFF: We kissed, always, and on the mouth, we were not reserved, God knows—

HELEN: That was happiness, kissing from happiness somehow is different from this—

GRISELDA: Christophe isn't here . . .!

HELEN: **Perpetual comforting!** I do it myself! (*She turns to* GRISELDA.)

> Don't I? I am the first!

GRISELDA: Christophe isn't here! (*She turns to go and look for the* CHILD. *As she does so,* DANCER *enters, the* CHILD *on his shoulders. Instinctively, they crowd together.*)

DANCER: **He is not critical**

> **He is not ethical**
>
> **He can't discriminate**
>
> **Where is his guilt, therefore?** (*He turns about, amusing the* CHILD.)
>
> **He does not arbitrate**
>
> **He cannot calculate**
>
> **No one could like him more**
>
> **Than**
>
> **Me** . . . (*Pause*)
>
> Paradox . . . (*Pause*)
>
> The executioner's affection for his victim . . . Paradoxical! (*To the* CHILD.) Do you know that word?
>
> No?
>
> I paid too little attention to vocabulary, that's obvious, and far too much to grammar! (*He lifts the* CHILD *off his shoulders.*)
>
> I found him staring at me! There I was, spade in hand, ankle-deep in grave-making, and I sensed these melancholy eyes upon me. At once I ceased my labours, which were in any case, too strenuous for me. I was obliged to find another solution to the trivial problem I had set myself. I am in his debt, I might have put my back out . . .

GRISELDA (*extending a hand to the* CHILD *who has been staring at* DANCER): Christophe . . .! (*The* CHILD *does not react.*)

CAROLINE: He hardly speaks now . . . it is as if he knew the dynasty concludes with him . . . (*A single resonant sound announces the presence of the* CHORUS, *who have entered unobserved.* DANCER *advances on them.*)

DANCER: Patience . . .!

> Patience . . .! (*He claps his hands at them, they inch back.*)

CHORUS: **Dancer**
Dancer
DANCER: I promise you nothing will occur without your acquiescence!
CHORUS: **You are a calculating and unfathomable man**
DANCER: And would you have me otherwise? Are our enemies not calculating? Do you want me fathomed by the likes of them? This family is steeped in treachery! (*He shrugs.*)
Sophisticated treachery. Educated treachery. I am a transient phenomenon, but these . . .!
Four hundred years of . . .! (*He shakes his head. The* CHORUS *goes, warily.*)
They have the curiosity of cattle . . . the comic and yet faintly menacing curiosity of cattle . . .

[*The piercing sound of a telephone. It transfixes everyone.* DANCER *is swaying with anticipation, yet quite unable to move. Apprehension has seized the entire* FAMILY. *At last,* JANE *appears.*]

JANE: Are you answering that? (DANCER *cannot find a voice. It rings on, with increasing violence.*)
Are you or not? (DANCER *doesn't speak. It stops.*)
DANCER: Oh . . . (*Pause. His body relaxes.*)
They'll ring back, no doubt. (*It rings again.*)
They have rung back. (*He goes out, slowly. It stops.*)
JANE: I'm in favour. (*Pause*)
HELEN: In favour of what?
JANE: Goodness.
HELEN: Are you? Then tell the world what is happening to us!.
JANE: I will do.
ROMANOFF: No, go now!
JANE: I can't go now, I've got so much to do—
HELEN: Please, now!
JANE: I promise, when everything is over, I will tell, I won't miss out a single bit of it—
ROMANOFF: No, that's too late, you must go now and—
CAROLINE: **You are making idiots of yourselves.**
(*Pause*)
JANE: If you've jewellery . . . watches or anything . . . (*They are silent. She shrugs.*)
I'm not unkind.
I believe in God.
Also, I believe in monarchy.
I believe in all things that are natural.
Like God.
Like monarchy.
And Mr Dancer, I'm sorry to say, is also natural.
Everything that happens, I will tell.
Honestly. (*She goes out. Pause.*)
HELEN: Is that evil? (*Pause*)

Is that the absolute in evil?
ROMANOFF: If I had a gun, I would kill. I, who have never killed, would kill and kill . . .!
CAROLINE: Shut up . . .
ROMANOFF: A man with such a placid disposition must always look absurd when driven to making threats, but—
CAROLINE: If you had a gun you would not use it—
ROMANOFF: **I would, I would, I would . . .!**
GRISELDA: Please, don't quarrel—
ROMANOFF: During the last offensive of the war it was I who gave the order to advance, I alone accept responsibility, no, **I claim it, I claim the thirty thousand dead!**
CAROLINE: You are hardly placid at all . . .
ROMANOFF: I am not placid, no—
GRISELDA: This is ridiculous!
ROMANOFF: I wish I had another life! I wish! I wish!

[DANCER *enters. A fall of silence. He is simultaneously apprehensive and vulgar, arrogant, tender. He walks, feeling their eyes upon him. He gestures, in a Roman manner, to himself . . .*]

DANCER: The Doorman of our Century . . . (*A stillness. The wind in the boards.*) Me . . . (*He shakes his head. He laughs. He stops.*)
Great moments of human endeavour stimulate a sort of poetry . . . the mundane minds of lawyers are shaken from the attic to the basements . . .
Earthquakes of phraseology . . . the sudden discovery of
The
Style
Of
Rome (*He laughs, bending, shaking his head.*)
He was— you could feel it through the crackling of the telephone, through snow and hail and regiments of rocket launchers, saboteurs, air raids, you name it, it was conspiring to spoil the moment but he was not thrown, he knew this message called for poise and the ponderous delivery of never-to-be-forgotten syllables, a compromise between electrification and the oratorial manner of the late Republic, Cato, Mirabeau, oh, the competition, but he persevered, and it was excellent in many ways, I don't criticize
Yes
He
Says (*The wind again. He stares.*)
And I, the transient phenomenon, will open the door to a new—(*He shakes his head, wearily, then recovers.*)
I like the new
The new what

The new anything
The New itself
It conceals my transience from me! (*He looks at them.*)
And your extermination is the threshold . . . (*He grins.*)
I say extermination because death apparently is inadequate, there has to be **obliteration** or someone, some superstitious, crippled-with-religion, infantile, irrational—you know the sort of idiot—will excavate and find a bone, a glove or something and there will be
A cult of monarchy
Yes
The Citizen at the far end of the telephone has studied History he reads he spent five years in an English library eyes down too, no looking up for passing skirt or knicker he was pellucid on the subject affirmative and absolute that not a shred of any one of you should persist . . . (*Pause*)
A problem in itself (*Pause*)
He left that to me, of course
Mere detail
Couldn't expect him to
What with his responsibilities
I had this staggering compliment
What more could I
Might have made him angry
The Doorman of the Century surely knows a thing or two about (*Pause*)
Acid, presumably . . . (*Pause. ROMANOFF looks at him, shaking his head in disbelief.*)
ROMANOFF: You do not want to do this thing . . . I do not believe you honestly wish to do this thing, Mr Dancer . . .
DANCER: Honestly . . . I wonder if I hear you right . . . did you say honestly . . . ?
HELEN: **You know very well he said honestly.**
DANCER (*turning on her*): It's such a quaint word! Such an exotic notion, picturesque, obscure!
ROMANOFF: **Examine yourself and—**
DANCER: Oh, please—
ROMANOFF: **Confront your conscience—**
DANCER: **Examine the labyrinth . . . !** Hands and knees . . . ! Magnifying glass . . . ! (*CAROLINE laughs, ROMANOFF, losing control, slaps her.*)
Stop that
Detestable
Brutality
Stop that
GRISELDA: Daddy . . . !
CAROLINE: Yes, restrain your father if you can, everything he says is calculated to aggravate the situation—
DANCER: The resort to violence is the very hallmark of domesticity . . . (*He turns away.*)

How I shuddered . . .
Something in this family made me recoil, as if I'd touched a loathsome thing which lay hidden under foliage . . .
HELEN: It is you who is the loathsome thing, and it is you who lay hidden under foliage . . . ! (*He looks at her. Pause.*)
DANCER: The toad was once a prince . . . and the prince . . . he bears the character of the toad . . . (*He smiles.*)
Go now, and walk together in the grounds, hand in hand, with that slow pace which always seemed to me not so much a demonstration of assurance, power, continuity, but the restraint of madness . . . a measured defiance of decline . . . (*They look to ROMANOFF. He leads them out.*) Take coats . . . ! (*They stop.*) You might take cold . . . (*Pause. ROMANOFF looks at the floor.*)
ROMANOFF: This is a pleasure to you . . . (*He shakes his head, uncomprehending. They go out. DANCER watches, then claps his hands swiftly. The CHORUS enter, bearing a large table, covered in immaculate white linen and dressed with vases, candelabra, crockery. They stagger it to the middle of the room, go out, and return with chairs. DANCER, in a sort of ecstasy, fusses.*)
DANCER: And all I want is love . . . ! (*The CHORUS laughs, staccato, in unison.*)
It's true!
I think of nothing else, it is the single and obsessive object of my life! (*And again*)
You laugh! (*And again*)
You laugh because the poverty of your imagination blinds you to the possibility! The circumstances seem to abolish it! I assure you, the most comely children are the product of the most squalid copulations, it's the comedy of nature! (*They laugh.*)
Laugh, it's obligatory! (*They stop. They are suddenly dark.*)
CHORUS: **Dancer**
The circumstances which created you are
DANCER: Shhh!
CHORUS: **The flood which carried you this far will certainly**
DANCER: I am not naive . . .
CHORUS: **Recede**
DANCER: I know it all . . .
CHORUS: **Leaving your body hanging in the trees . . .** (*DANCER shrugs, eloquently.*)
DANCER: What you describe as a rebuke to me, is no more or less than my desire . . . (*He nods as if in gratitude. The CHORUS goes out. A FIGURE is discovered observing DANCER. He wears an overcoat, glasses. There is a quality of authority in him. DANCER catches him in the corner of his eye.*)

Citizen Fitch . . .! Have you seen him? He is sa regular as clockwork, and I must confess, his pile of documents becomes almost an addiction to me—we rely on such people to deliver, don't we, in all weathers . . .?

Perhaps the terrorists got him. I do hope not. (The FIGURE *just looks.*)

Or are you his substitute? (*And looks.*)

People come and go . . .

ARRANT (*going to a seat, and sitting*): They say you are learned, Citizen . . .

DANCER: Do they? Well, they are correct for once.

ARRANT: Are they not always so?

DANCER: Sometimes their innate correctness is distorted by the falsifications of perspective induced by crisis. I compare the wisdom of the people to a figure wandering in a hall of mirrors. Always the individual recognizes himself, but in grotesque forms. This nightmare of perceptions does not preclude the existence of a proper mirror, which, the more outrageous the reflections, the more certain he becomes in his faith that it does exist, must exist, and above all, will exist, so long as he does not give up hope. (*Pause*)

Hope is the problem, given that for most of us, it is not a bottomless well. (*Pause*)

I am mixing my metaphors . . .!

Mirrors . . . wells . . . (*Pause*)

Yes, of course I'm learned, what about you? (*Pause*)

ARRANT: Faith . . . (*Pause*)

DANCER: Yes.

ARRANT: In the future . . .

DANCER: Yes.

ARRANT: Our children's children . . .

DANCER: Them especially . . . (*Suddenly*) I don't have any children . . .! (*Pause. He laughs.*) So what? Other people do . . . (ARRANT *stares at* DANCER.) You stare a great deal. I've noticed, since the Revolution, a vast increase in staring. Fitch used to do it! (*Pause*) Still does do it, I expect . . . are you staying, or . . . I've things to do . . . (*Pause*) This staring is supposed to wreck the nerves, a sort of permanent interrogation . . . I don't mind it myself . . . (*He laughs.*) Of course I mind it, for one thing I think it's rude . . . (*Pause*)

ARRANT: Rudeness?

DANCER: Yes, staring and conversations in which one party confines himself to single words must be construed as rudeness . . . (*Pause*) Under the old regime . . .! (*He laughs.*)

I know all the proper answers, Citizen! (*He walks boldly to the table, adjusts a glass or two.*)

ARRANT: Let's talk about faith . . .

DANCER: Faith? Any time! But you begin. After all, you initiated this discussion and I haven't the least idea who you are nor whether you possess the authority to be here, whether you are a charlatan, a counter-revolutionary or simply a man who has stolen a decent overcoat and wandered off the street . . .! Things are like that now, it is a paradise for imposters, but I don't criticize, I take you at face value, and if you are an imposter, so what, the people have the right to engage their masters in discussion at a moment's notice!

I agree with it! (*He grins.*)

I said masters! You flinched! (*He laughs.*)

Do take your coat off. (ARRANT *looks.*)

There you go! Staring again! At least undo the neck. (*Pause*)

Citizen. (*Long pause. A wind blows.*)

ARRANT: What distinguishes the rebel from the revolutionary is faith.

DANCER: Yes . . .

ARRANT: The rebel has none.

DANCER: He has no point of reference but himself.

ARRANT: Consequently he cannot be relied upon.

DANCER: Not relied upon, no. But used, perhaps? How can you sit buttoned up like that? This room is sweltering. Are you about to leave?

ARRANT: I discomfort you, Citizen.

DANCER (*shrugging*): I am discomforted by the spectacle of a man with too much clothing on.

ARRANT: Or too little?

DANCER: That also would offend me! I think it must be the remnants of some decadent belief in hospitality. The taking of coats, and so on, a servile instinct I have not entirely erased from my reconstructed soul, but then, **the Doorman of the Century** is after all, a menial post . . . (ARRANT *looks at him.* DANCER *smiles.*) I got the order. (*He jerks his head to indicate a room.*)

Down the telephone . . . (*Pause.* ARRANT *unbuttons his neck, opens his coat.*)

ARRANT: What matters to you, Citizen? (*Pause.* DANCER's *eyes are fixed on* ARRANT's *throat.*)

I said—

DANCER: Love! (*Pause*) So much murder . . . torture . . . the squalor of blighted lives . . . requires some perfect apotheosis . . . to be justified . . .

ARRANT: Justified?

DANCER: Yes, oh yes, you see,

The Doorman is a moralist (*He laughs, stops.*) No, some impeccable, some—immaculate moment of love—brief as the metamorphosis which brings to birth the butterfly, perfect, trembling on damp wings and frail as the dew which shakes on the stem—(*He has contrived to place himself behind* ARRANT.)

New in form, and possibly, unobserved—

Only one such needs occur (*He grabs* ARRANT

by the head, forcing it back.)
For
Us
To
Say (ARRANT *struggles,* DANCER *slashes his throat.*)
The sacrifice was perfect (*They struggle.* ARRANT *chokes.*)
The sacrifice was more than necessary
We
Craved
It!
Faith!
Faith! (ARRANT *lies back in the chair.*)
Jane!
Where are you!
Jane! (*He runs around in a fit of uncontrollable excitement.*)
I'm changing! I'm altering! I'm undergoing something **that was far from spontaneous** (JANE *appears with a bucket.*)
JANE: What!
DANCER: **I plotted every move** (ARRANT *is dying, but noisily.*)
Shut up!
JANE: You're mad!
DANCER: (*kicking* ARRANT): Shut up, shut up!
JANE: **Mad**
  Utterly
  Mad
DANCER: Faith he said (*He jeers at the dying man.*)
  Faith in me!
  Finish him off, I can't
JANE: No—
DANCER: **Do it I said**—
JANE: Absolutely not—
DANCER (*going to her, taking her roughly*): You know your trouble—
JANE: Nope—
DANCER: I'll tell you what your trouble is—
JANE: Don't wanna know—
DANCER: **You have no loyalty!**
JANE: Nope—
DANCER: Neither to the past nor to the future, I find that **contemptible**
  Do it or I'll have you shot
JANE: Rubbish
  That horrible noise
DANCER: Well, cover him up! (*They stare at each other like a quarrelling husband and wife. Pause.*) All right, I will! (*He goes to throw* ARRANT's *coat over him, but senses the presence of* CHRISTOPHE. CHRISTOPHE *pours fluid from his little can.* DANCER *pauses, throws the coat over* ARRANT. *The sound is muffled.*)
I knew him at once
The way they

Swaggering about as if
And staring
I don't stare, do I? Tell me if I do I hate it
And just arrive!
No introductions
Good morning would be nice
I'm too subtle
For my own good, possibly . . . (*The grunting stops. He looks, shakes his head.*)
And he called **me** the doorman . . .
How little they know of our rareness, and our beauty . . .
JANE: Beauty? You?
DANCER: Yes . . . Me . . . (*She turns to go out.*)
Jane . . .
I don't know what to do with these . . .!

[JANE *shrugs, goes out, leaving* DANCER *alone. The wind makes the boards creak. He hurries to the body and picks up an arm, but the body is if anything, heavier than the last. As he pulls, and falters, he becomes aware of* CAROLINE, *who has returned alone, watching him. Pause. He allows the arm to fall with a feigned indifference. Music, percussive, brief.*]

PART II

[CAROLINE, *alone.* ROMANOFF *is revealed, staring at her . . .*]

ROMANOFF: Your shoes are covered in mud . . .
  (*Pause*)
  Not just your shoes . . . (*Pause*)
  Your legs . . . (*Pause*)
  Your legs are covered in—(*The* CHILDREN *enter.*)
GRISELDA (*seeing the laid table*): What's this . . .!
HELEN: This is the old service from the summer house!
ROMANOFF (*to* CAROLINE): I hate to see you spoiled in any way—
CAROLINE: I'm not spoiled—
ROMANOFF (*hurrying to her, kneeling with a handkerchief*): Horrible—
CAROLINE: Not spoiled, I said—
HELEN: Laid for six . . .
GRISELDA: And the high chair, though Christophe doesn't use it any more . . .!
ROMANOFF: All right, I won't attempt to clean your legs, what does it matter if we are clean or dirty?
HELEN (*to* CHRISTOPHE *who has wandered near the table*): **Don't touch the food . . .**
ROMANOFF (*applying spittle to his handkerchief*): No, I think it does matter, actually . . . (*He wipes* CAROLINE's *legs desperately.*) I think it is

supremely important . . .

GRISELDA (*staring at the banquet*): What is this for? If they are going to murder us, what is this for?

HELEN: I think they want to make us foolish. I think it is grotesque and horrible and—

GRISELDA: The food *is* poisoned, I suppose . . .?

HELEN: **Altogether typical of Mr Dancer.** (ROMANOFF *is working with a passion.*)
I can see exactly what they want. They want us to sit here in a parody of plenty and then possibly on film, certainly with photographs, to suffer an agonizing death, falling across the table, choking on the silverware—(GRISELDA *bursts out laughing.*) No, it isn't funny, it is the way they think, it is the very essence of their mentality and—

CAROLINE (*who has not moved*): **It's a wedding.** (*Pause. They look at the table.*)

GRISELDA: Yes . . .! There's a cake . . .!

[Pause. They look at CAROLINE. Music. DANCER enters. He stops. It is as if he suffers an embarrassment, and chooses not to speak the thing he had intended. He goes to the chair at the bottom of the table and sits in it, thoughtfully. No one else moves. The wind and creaking woodwork. At last he looks up.]

DANCER: A transient phenomenon . . .
Celebrates . . . (*He jumps up, clumsily.*)
Well, that's what we're supposed to do, isn't it? Celebrate! (*He stares at them.*) Revolution has become associated with austerity, we can't have that. The fall of dynasties has forfeited its glamour and become a sordid and obscure transaction occurring in a cellar
The committee lacks imagination
I have always said so
I would go so far as to say it defines the thing . . .! (*Pause*)
One would think we were ashamed . . . (*Pause*)
So . . . (*Pause*)
I am so frightened my greatness may go unremarked . . . (*He gestures for them to sit. They do not respond.*)

CHORUS: **Dancer**
They will humiliate you

DANCER: Obviously, they'll try . . .

CHORUS: **Four hundred years of power**
Do you think they'll play with you
They'd rather die

DANCER: They're decadent. Even the boy.

CHORUS: **Drag them outside**
One volley and forget

DANCER: That is precisely what I wish to avoid! That is precisely the mundane practice of all revolutions and I think it fails to grasp
The

Symbolism
Of
The
Sacrifice (*He looks at* ROMANOFF.)
Please . . .

ROMANOFF: You are asking me to sit at my own table.

DANCER: Yes.

ROMANOFF: To eat off my own plates.

DANCER: Yes.

ROMANOFF: With cutlery that bears my own initials.

DANCER: Yes. (*Pause*)

ROMANOFF: You are a man of such mean sensibilities I do not think you even comprehend the gravity of your own offence . . .

HELEN: He does . . .

ROMANOFF: Does he . . .! Then he also understands why I will not concede to him the right to extend me such an invitation!

HELEN (*turning away*): I'm sure he does . . .

ROMANOFF: **The servant offers dinner to his master . . .!**

CAROLINE: Yes!

ROMANOFF: **The mutinous tutor invites the prince to eat off his own crockery!** (*Suddenly he sits at a chair.*)
I am as subtle as you, Mr Dancer!
Wretch!
Animal!
Simian deformity!
What's the hors d'œuvre?
It had better be good you cur
Not that you'd know cuisine from the stable floor
Insect
Parasite
I can play this game
Any game
Better than you
Lout
Rodent
Did you think me trapped in regal postures?
Stiff and fragile?
Morally obtuse?
A Fabergé of manners and conventions?
Inflexible?
Absurd?
No
No
No
The laugh's on you (*He gestures to his family.*)
Do sit
Do sit (*He spontaneously flings a plate to the floor.*)
Oh, dear, the family crest . . .! (*He leans across the table violently.*)
Monarchy is not material, citizen!

[Pause. DANCER is taken off-guard by this tirade. He

stares at ROMANOFF, as do the entire family. The CHILD goes silently to his father and takes his hand. Pause. Tears come into ROMANOFF's eyes. Without further instruction, the CHILDREN and CAROLINE take their places at the table. Pause. JANE appears at the door in an apron.]

JANE: Do you want it, now? (DANCER *does not reply.*) Look, Dancer, I am not sweating to pieces in the kitchen while you—

DANCER: Shh!

JANE: Make up your mind what time you might or might not—

DANCER: **Shh I said . . .**

JANE: I've got a home to go to! (*She goes out with a cross shrug.*)

ROMANOFF: Servant problem? (*The briefest pause. He does not look up from the table.*) Listen, if you get us out of here I will pay you one hundred and fifty thousand American dollars . . . (*Pause*)

DANCER: (*as if abstracted*): Mmm?

ROMANOFF: I said if you—

DANCER: That's nothing to you—

ROMANOFF: No, but a great deal to you—

DANCER: The merest trickle from the great lake of your estate—

ROMANOFF: Very well, five hundred thousand American dollars—

DANCER: Really, this is embarrassing—

ROMANOFF: It doesn't embarrass me—

DANCER: It should do—

ROMANOFF: I have children and a wife to—

DANCER: Precisely, and to save them you are prepared to dispense—

ROMANOFF: Double that figure—

DANCER: To dispense the merest fraction of one part of your annual income—

ROMANOFF: Triple it—

DANCER: The microscopic portion of your wealth you deem appropriate to ransom your so-called loved ones **some love this**—

ROMANOFF: **I deemed it adequate to corrupt a worm like you.**

DANCER (*shouting off*): **We'll have it now!** (*Pause.* JANE *appears.*)

JANE: Are you trying to be funny, Citizen?

DANCER: I do not have to try. Apparently I bring it out in others
     Do you seriously believe my passion has a price . . .? (*Pause*)

ROMANOFF: Passion? (*The wind. A single note, discordant.* JANE *goes out.*)

GRISELDA: Father . . . I can't eat . . .

HELEN: Me neither . . .

ROMANOFF: Stay in your places.

HELEN: I want to go to a priest . . .!

ROMANOFF: There is no priest, stay in your places . . .

HELEN: And all this is trickery!

ROMANOFF: Of course it is trickery, but we are not humiliated by the antics of others, History will record how—(JANE *appears with a large tureen. She stands in the doorway. Pause.*) In our ordeal we—

GRISELDA: I am not interested in History—

ROMANOFF: We ignore it at our peril—

GRISELDA: I want a child . . . (*Pause*)
     So what if I'm fifteen? (*She stands.*)
     Mr Dancer
     I think the sins of royalty cannot be extended to the children of the children of
     Etcetera
     My body has no politics and
     You can be the father if you wish

[A great silence, in which the sound of the snoring of CAROLINE is audible. They look at her, for the first time aware she has fallen asleep. DANCER is deeply moved, not by GRISELDA, but by CAROLINE . . .]

DANCER: She snores . . .! (*He looks to* ROMANOFF, *in amazement.*)
     Oh, God . . .! She snores . . .! (*He half-laughs, half-snorts.*)
     Impossible . . .!

JANE: Do you want it or not?

DANCER: Jane! She snores . . .!

JANE: So do I—

DANCER: Yes, but—

JANE: Shall I serve it up or—

DANCER: **Shh shh philistine shh . . .!** (*Pause. The sound of sleep.*)
     She dreams . . .

GRISELDA: You're not listening to me . . . (*Pause*)
     Nobody is . . .!

ROMANOFF: Sit still, please . . .

GRISELDA: I can't, I want a child . . .!

ROMANOFF: You will have a child, I promise you—

GRISELDA: How!

ROMANOFF: I don't know yet, sit still . . .

GRISELDA: **Mr Dancer I am prepared to make children for the Revolution**
     Kindly
     Make
     Me
     Pregnant
     Or
     Anybody
     Please . . . (*Pause. She sits, humiliated. Pause.*)
     I cannot understand how your ideas can interfere with the functions of my body
     I am so healthy
     I am so fertile
     My womb is not guilty, is it?

HELEN: He is not listening, Griselda. . . .

GRISELDA: No? What is he doing then?
   I am a princess how can he resist me? (*She laughs derisively.*)
   What's in the tureen? Some ghastly thing, no doubt, no, it's peculiar, this desire to live, do you have it?
HELEN: Yes . . . (*She looks at her sister.*)
GRISELDA: **What's in the tureen, something to make us sick**
ROMANOFF: Shh . . .
GRISELDA: Daddy . . .
ROMANOFF: Shh . . .
GRISELDA: Daddy . . . (*The tureen is placed on the table at a signal from* DANCER. *Pause. He stands.*)
DANCER: I'd like to serve you . . . (*He goes to the tureen and picks up a silver ladle.* JANE *reappears.*)
JANE: Psst! (DANCER *is irritated by the interruption to a rite.*)
   Psst!
DANCER: What?
JANE: There's another one of those Citizens . . .
DANCER: What!
JANE: Outside.
DANCER: Can't be . . .!
JANE: Came by car . . .
DANCER: **Car** . . .! (*The brutal interruption of the telephone.* DANCER *closes his eyes. It rings again and again.*)
JANE: Shall I get it?
DANCER (*shaking his head*): It's funny, isn't it, you would think, in the chaos of a revolution and a civil war, the complete disintegration of the transport system, the telegraphic networks and the rest of it, such a resolute supervision of the minor executives of the People's Will would be impossible, but no, the contrary is the case, a profusion of messengers, a plethora of orders emanating from every corner, and the paperwork . . .!
   I'll see to this. (JANE *goes out. He goes to follow, stops.*)
   You'd think I couldn't be trusted. (*He leaves. The* FAMILY *remains at the table. The phone ceases.* CAROLINE *snores.* DANCER *returns, stops in the doorway.*)
   They're dead I said. (*Pause.*)
   He thanked me. (*Pause. He shrugs.*)
   A few minutes either side . . . what difference does it make?
JANE (*coming in again*): I'm wrong, there's two of them.
DANCER (*shaken*): Two?
JANE: Two Citizens. High ups.
DANCER: **Two.**
JANE: That's what I said—(ROMANOFF *laughs.*)
HELEN: Be quiet!
DANCER: **Two** . . .

CHORUS: **Dancer . . .!**
DANCER: Yes, I'm here . . .
CHORUS: **Dancer**
   What are you
   Are you a liar?
DANCER: A liar, yes. . .! And infinitely resourceful . . .!
CHORUS: **Dancer**
   Your lies will bring you to the ditch
DANCER: I'm too good a rider, sorry . . .
CHORUS: **History will**
DANCER: **I know all about history, thank you . . .!**
   (*Pause*)
   And as for lies, mine are so thoroughbred they leap the brooks and hedges of your mediocrity. Give me a great lie, and I will be its jockey . . . (*Two* MEN *Enter.* DANCER *turns to face them.*)
   Where *is* Citizen Fitch? And not only Citizen Fitch, but Arrant, where is he? I try to cope but all I have is a flock of bleating peasants. (*They look.*)
   No disrespect, but we know their limitations, don't we? (*Pause*)
   All right, not bleating. Unenlightened. (*He smiles.*)
   Are you my assistants, or am I yours? (*They laugh.*)
   Yes! That is how it is here, one does not know! One greets in pure ignorance God knows what rank of official! It's as well we have abolished all the old formality!
DENADIR (*looking at the table*): Has one abolished it, Citizen?
DANCER: Oh yes, one has most certainly.
DENADIR: Tablecloths, napkins, silverware . . . one seems to have a soft spot for those, notwithstanding . . .
DANCER (*through his teeth*): One has however, an entirely different attitude to objects which once bore particular significance, commanded particular responses, and so on. It is crucial, Citizens, that we address ourselves not simply to the material, albeit we call ourselves materialists, but to the meanings with which the material is endowed. (*He smiles.*)
DISBANNER: Yer love nice stuff . . .
DANCER: **Don't tilt with me I am an ideologist** (*They stare, puzzled.*)
   The Doorman, me . . . (*Pause*)
   The title has no meaning for you? I promise you it will. (*He goes to the table.*)
   Are you on your way somewhere or—
DISBANNER: Who are these? (*Pause.* DANCER *hesitates, marshals his resources, smiles, in the space of a second.*)
DANCER: Chaos.
   I like it. (*They look at him.*)
   Chaos.

How it suits me. (*Pause*)

It's my medium. (*Pause*)

But you . . .! (*He walks to the chair where the* CHILD *is seated.*)

Gentlemen, I can see from your expressions you are gardeners at heart . . . (*He suddenly seizes the* CHILD *in his arms and holds his head in a fixed grip as if he were demonstrating the qualities of a calf.*)

Who's this . . .! (*He laughs.* ROMANOFF *jumps to his feet, shuddering, tense.*)

Who's this, he says . . .!

Look . . .! (*The* MEN *stare.*)

Look, then! (DISBANNER *looks at* DENADIR, *who nods, to authorize him.* DISBANNER *stares at the* CHILD.)

No . . .

I don't call that looking . . . (*He drags the* CHILD *nearer.*)

Stare into his eyes . . . (DISBANNER, *hands on knees, stoops.*)

Do you not know the eyes? (*Pause*)

The shape of them?

The colour?

Oh, Citizen, are you such an ethereal scholar you never stooped to pick up the magazines? (DISBANNER's *eyes meet* DANCER's.)

Not once?

In the dentist's waiting room?

Many a passion has been kindled there . . .! (*Pause. Something dawns on* DISBANNER.)

Yes . . .

This peculiar and distinctive physiognomy is all we loathe . . . (*He shakes his head.*)

Whose humiliation and disfigurement can never satisfy our rage . . . (*He propels the* CHILD *bodily into* DISBANNER's *arms.*)

Kiss him. (DISBANNER *smiles, kisses the* CHILD. DANCER *turns to* DENADIR.)

Here are my papers, where are yours? (*He thrusts his documents into* DENADIR's *face.*)

DENADIR: In the car.

DANCER: Get them. (DENADIR *pointedly declines to examine* DANCER's *authority.*)

When I said kiss him—(*He looks to* DISBANNER.) I meant once . . .

DISBANNER (*to the family, in a spasm of savage delight*):

I'm treading in your brains you!

I'm wiping my boots on your wombs!

And kicking your eyeballs high into the branches! (*He stops, turns to* DANCER.)

It is them . . .?

Is it? (*He returns.*)

And when I walk away I'll drag your entrails through the gardens . . . wiping bits on twigs as if I'd trod in shit . . . kidneys . . .! Lung clinging to my ankle!

HELEN: Shut up . . . (DISBANNER *grins.*)

DISBANNER: It is them, isn't it . . .? (DENADIR *goes to* DISBANNER *and mutters in his ear. He leaves smartly, stops in his tracks.*)

DENADIR: Did I hear a telephone, Citizen?

DANCER: In the hallway, Citizen. You dial seven, for the Central Committee . . .

[DENADIR *goes out.* DANCER *knifes* DISBANNER, *thrusting his hand over his mouth. Instant music. The* FAMILY *variously rise to their feet, cover their mouths, gasp.* CHRISTOPHE *holds out his can . . . The music ceases as abruptly. A peculiar silence.* DANCER *holds* DISBANNER *in a fatal embrace. In this silence,* CAROLINE *can be heard snoring.* DANCER *listens to this. Then he lowers* DISBANNER *to the ground. The wind, the creaking of boards. The* FAMILY *do nothing but watch. One by one, they sit again.* JANE *enters.*]

JANE (*pointing*): He's on the telephone!

DANCER: Help me move—

JANE: No—

DANCER: Please—

JANE: I can't—

DANCER: Jane—

JANE: **Don't want anything to do with History!** (*Pause*)

DANCER: This is not History. This is the opposite of History.

JANE: **Won't help a murderer.** (*She stares at* DANCER. *He appears disconcerted.*)

DANCER: Murderer . . .?

JANE: You! (DANCER *releases a slow, tentative shrug of the shoulders. He looks to* ROMANOFF.)

DANCER: Get his legs.

ROMANOFF: No, and nor will anybody else. (DANCER *looks at* ROMANOFF.)

DANCER: You think the transient phenomenon has run out of luck . . . how little you understand me . . . and how correct it is I am obliged to do everything myself . . . to be suspected by every one . . . and trusted by nobody . . . how splendid I have slipped from human knowledge like a playing card lying beneath a desk . . .

JANE: He's coming . . .! (*She hurries out.* DANCER *goes to a chair and sits, extending and crossing his ankles, and joining his fingers as if contemplatively.* DENADIR *enters, see the body.*)

DANCER: He died. (*Pause*)

His contribution to the future was significant, but brief . . . (*Pause.* DENADIR *looks, coolly.*)

I knew when I saw you, that man was a priest . . .

I knew it, I could smell the clinging odour of the seminary which no rebellion of the will or cleansing of the intellect can ever shift.

Throw open the windows of the soul! Let the

winds of civil disorder and the rhetoric of
lawyers whirl the pages of the antique books,
sheets in the gutter, splintering crucifixes
underneath your boots but still—(*Pause*)
No, it's painted on your eyes, some profound
antipathy to logic . . . (*Pause*)
Help me kill this lot . . . (*Pause.* DENADIR *stares.*)
The Doorman cannot lift the latch . . . (*The tension is too great for* ROMANOFF, *who stands suddenly.*)

ROMANOFF: We love . . .!
We love each other . . .! (DENADIR *stares at him.*)
Pity us . . .

CHORUS (*quietly, intimately*):
Dancer
Can you corrupt the so-corrupted
Dancer
Is it possible
You've met your match? (*Pause*)

DENADIR: Pity . . .? (*Pause. He walks, stops.*)
We are replacing that by organization.

CHORUS: **Dancer**
He is not susceptible

DANCER: We don't know yet . . .!

CHORUS: **Dancer**
He fathoms you

DANCER: We know nothing yet!

GRISELDA: I think you have such a nice face. (*Pause*)
Such a nice face and you ought to look after it,
it's the face of an angel. (DENADIR *looks at her.*)
I think if you were capable of murder it would
show in your face. (*Pause*)
Perhaps you don't like to have the face of an
angel, perhaps it's a burden to you and you
think by doing ugly deeds your face will
change. (*Pause*)
No doubt angels have a lot to put up with and
would happily conceal it. (*Pause*)
But it's fate. The weak will always come to
you. The weak and the destitute. Obviously,
you'll hate them for it. You will squirm at their
dependence and their whimpering, you will be
enraged to know that your own liberty is
trampled on by their persistence but . . .
(*Pause*)
The perfect are unlucky . . . have you not
heard the angels complain . . .? They do! They
groan . . .! (*She looks down at her plate.*)
They grasp at anything which will suffocate
the pity that consumes them . . . (*Pause.*
DENADIR *is staring at her. The wind and the
boards.*)

DENADIR: It's true I have wings under my overcoat I
hide them obviously I fold them occasionally a
single feather drifts to the ground what's that
they say what's that white thing. (*He bursts out
laughing.*)

You parade your sensibility
The blood of thousands oozes from beneath
your fingernails (*Suddenly he throws down a set
of motor car keys. They lie on the floor, the subject
of everyone's gaze. A long pause.*)
There is a car
It's parked by the lodge
A full tank of benzine
Maps and (*Suddenly he suffers a paroxysm of
mental pain that doubles him. They watch. He
sobs.*)

DANCER: None of them drives, unfortunately . . . (*He
goes to* DENADIR, *and with a gentleness, runs his
hands along the man's arms.* DENADIR *weeps on*
DANCER's *shoulder.* DANCER *kills him with the
knife in this embrace. A cry.*)
It's better . . .! (*A cry again.*)
No, this is better . . .! (*And again*)
The torments of a pure soul!
I couldn't bear to witness it! (*He staggers, lowers
him.*)
Martyr!
Martyr to an instinct which all life abhors! (*He
looks at the dying man, then turns to* GRISELDA.)
Console him . . . (*She is staring in fixed horror.*)
Console him, then . . .! (*She goes unsteadily,
kneels, weeps.*)

ROMANOFF: He would have saved us . . .

DANCER: Yes . . .

ROMANOFF: **He would have got us out of here!**

DANCER: Of course he would! I saw it in his eyes!

ROMANOFF: **Then what—**

DANCER: Do you think we have had a revolution in
order that idealistic priests masquerading as
policemen could indulge an appetite for gestures by liberating oppressors such as you?
What do you think the revolution is, a stage?

ROMANOFF: Yes, what else is it? (*Pause.* DANCER
shrugs.)

DANCER: Yes, and this performance, however predictable, threatened to overshadow me . . . (*He
calls.*)

HELEN: You kill people. You just keep killing them

DANCER: Yes, it's so much easier than I thought—

GRISELDA (*holding up a tiny crucifix*): Look! He wore
this round his neck . . .!

JANE (*entering*): **What.**

DANCER (*to* GRISELDA): Wear it yourself . . . your eloquence entitles you to some reward. . . .

JANE: **Christ you've gone and—**

DANCER: Both of them, yes—

GRISELDA (*through a sob*): **I caused his death . . .!**

ROMANOFF: Nonsense! All you said was true and
beautiful and nothing caused his death but
this monster and his delinquency!

DANCER: Excellent. Unfortunately, she is too sophisticated for your platitudes. (*To* JANE.)

Help me move these to the—
ROMANOFF: **I detest you,** Dancer. **I curse you.** (*Pause*)
JANE: You keep asking me to shift these bodies—
DANCER: I know, and you keep refusing, but—
JANE: **I'm innocent and that's how I'm staying.**
DANCER: Do you think I want to kill these people?
They keep turning up, one after another, it's like hacking the limbs off a centipede . . .! (*He shudders.*)
Horrible . . .
And their banality . . . their philistine instincts, glamorized by philosophical quotation, their cruelty, legitimized by slogans, they don't know what cruelty is . . .! It's pure savagery to them . . .! Indulgence . . .! (*He shakes his head.*)
It is such a difficult time to love . . . to surpass oneself . . . to triumph over the servile characteristics of a rebellious character like mine . . . and love . . . difficult . . . oh, difficult . . .
CHORUS: **Dancer**
Dancer
Some lapse some complication
Makes us distrust you
We crave their execution and you give them
Dinner
DANCER: It's no more than a ritual, I assure you . . .
CHORUS: **We demand their deaths**
DANCER: Yes . . .
Yes . . . and the people must be gratified, of course. I feel your breath, hot on my neck . . . not very sweet breath, but sweet breath is almost certainly evidence of degeneracy . . . (*He leans over the sleeping* CAROLINE, *so her breath falls on his face. Silence. A note played. He is ecstatic. Suddenly, he turns and sweeps the car keys off the floor.*)
How fortunate I am I do not need a chauffeur!
ROMANOFF (*standing*): Take us. Drive us to the frontier. Redeem your stunted life by a single act of perfect charity. (*Pause.* DANCER *laughs quietly, shaking his head.*)
DANCER: Do you think I have not thought of that? From the very first day of the uprising, do you not think I anticipated that? Whilst you were scarcely troubled by reports of riots, whilst the disintegration of the army cost you hardly any sleep, I was rehearsing the very moment of your passion, and the role I'd play in it . . .
ROMANOFF: Yes, I believe you.
DANCER: Most men would, of course. The gratification, the celebration, the reputation the everything heroic and magnanimous, who could refuse? (*Pause*)
Only me. (*Pause*)
Unfortunately, I am cursed with subtlety. (*He makes a tremendous throw, sending the keys far into the night. A wind.*)

I have to guard against myself. We all long to evade our destiny . . .
ROMANOFF (*to* HELEN): Come here . . .! Come here . . .! (*She goes to her father, weeps in his arms.*)
Griselda . . .!
GRISELDA (*not unkindly*): No . . .
ROMANOFF: Christophe . . .! (*The* CHILD *goes to him. The group rock, tearfully, in each other's arms.* DANCER *watches. Then, to rupture the tension, bursts out.*)
DANCER: Firstly, I mastered the vocabulary. Less than one hundred words, I promise you, is adequate, two hundred makes you an expert, entitling you, to a limited extent, to innovate! Yes, I am a most convincing exponent of the theory of revolution whilst at the same time disciplining myself against the temptation—always present in a man of real intelligence—to intervene in the higher levels of debate—a fatal error because it renders you—(*Pause*) Please stop that—(HELEN *wails.*) It renders you an object of suspicion to the—(GRISELDA *cannot help herself, and wails also.*) Please . . .! (*Pause*)
The very individuals you most hoped to—(JANE *now shakes with grief.* DANCER *watches with a peculiar disbelief.*) satisfy . . .

[*The sound fills the stage,* ROMANOFF *himself grieving loudly. In this orchestration,* DANCER *moves, like a fascinated child in a museum of anguish. His delicate steps take him round the table, to where* CAROLINE *still sleeps. He takes her head between his hands and kisses her, deeply, lengthily. Through their grief, the others are slowly made aware of this. They cease, their horrified gaze falling on the spectacle.* ROMANOFF, *repressing an urge to attack* DANCER, *moves away thoughtful . . . watches from a distance*]

CAROLINE (*as* DANCER *withdraws his lips*): I sleep—I can't describe the clinical reasons—I sleep to isolate myself—as if like some insect I might undergo a change of such proportions I would not, on waking, recognize myself . . . (*Pause*) I do recognize myself . . . (*Pause*) And the sleep's hell. Perhaps it is for butterflies. Perhaps there is a price to be paid for such brief apotheosis. (*Suddenly*)
I keep dreaming I'm on trial . . .!
ROMANOFF: I think, this time, there will be no trial . . .
CAROLINE: Pity. I would have conducted myself very well, if the dream is anything to go by. I would not be acquitted, but they would suffer the humiliation of committing a judicial murder. The public would know this, and . . . (*She shrugs.*)
How romantic . . .! As if the public cared . . .!
HELEN: Mother . . .

CAROLINE: Yes . . . (*She looks to* DANCER.)

JANE: **Let 'em go . . .! Let 'em go, Dancer . . .!**

DANCER: Jane . . .

JANE: **I can't bear this . . .!**

DANCER: It's difficult . . .

JANE: **Bodies, more bodies . . .!**

DANCER: I know . . .

JANE: I try to be historical, I try to be—(*Pause*) to be—what's it—

DANCER: Objective—

JANE: That's it, I do and—

DANCER: You've done splendidly—

JANE: **Children . . .!** (*Pause.* DANCER *looks at her.*)

DANCER: Yes. (*Pause*)

ROMANOFF: Citizen Dancer has a personal interest in this . . . (*He goes to* JANE, *touches her lightly on the shoulder.*)

Which, even were the ground not thoroughly patrolled . . . would render your pleas meaningless . . . (JANE *wipes her eyes with her sleeve.*) Help me move these dead men out . . . who . . . for all their cruelty . . . were simple . . . raging but possibly also . . . kind . . . (*Pause, then* JANE *assists him to drag away the two dead men.* CAROLINE *goes to* DANCER, *boldly.*)

CAROLINE: You won't escape the consequences of this, Mr Dancer—

DANCER: No—

CAROLINE: On the contrary, you will be the next to be eliminated—

DANCER: Yes—

CAROLINE: The shame of this will oblige them to destroy every piece of evidence, including the witnesses—

DANCER: Yes—

CAROLINE: You and the man who murders you and him who murders him, they all—

DANCER: **I understand that very well—**

CAROLINE: **My life is perfect, look at me.** (*Pause*)

HELEN: Mother . . .

CAROLINE: Shhh—

HELEN: Mother, we are all—

CAROLINE: **I am fighting for my life and you should fight for yours** (*A cold wind, she shrugs.*) Or if you prefer not to, don't . . . (ROMANOFF *watches her, having returned from moving the bodies.*) If you would rather acquiesce . . . with dignity and so on . . . do . . . I don't criticize . . . (*Pause*) I am not a good mother, am I? I plead for myself, and my humiliation, if it is humiliation, embarrasses you.

HELEN: You shouldn't stoop to such a—

GRISELDA: Oh, let her, let her stoop . . .!

HELEN: **Such a horrible and—**

GRISELDA: I stooped! Stoop yourself!

HELEN: **Never**

GRISELDA: It would do you good to stoop for once—

HELEN: Shut up!

GRISELDA: No, it would do . . .!

HELEN: You'd take your clothes off for this monster, you just said so, what kind of family lets a child—(CAROLINE *laughs bitterly.*) **What kind of family.** (*Pause. Slowly,* JANE *goes out.*)

We have offended her . . .

CAROLINE: Yes. The poor cannot bear their masters to be human. *They* can be human, but not us . . . (GRISELDA *grasps* HELEN *in her arms.*)

DANCER: The beautiful exists . . . but only because the hideous exists . . . I am the hideous, and the agent of the hideous . . . I have never concealed it from myself.

CAROLINE: I don't find you hideous, Mr Dancer . . .

DANCER: Please . . .

CAROLINE: I am perfectly serious, I don't find you—

DANCER: **Time's very short**

Too short

For transparent compliments

And the arrière pensée, madame! (*He laughs, shakes his head.*)

I find . . .

How infuriating . . .

I find . . .

So few who are in any sense worthy of great sacrifice, so few, and possibly—one must grasp the nettle—such individuals do not exist, but this does not diminish in the least, the will to sacrifice, misery of miseries, it possibly enhances it . . . (*Pause. He looks at* CAROLINE.)

I adore you . . .

And you are—spiritually—poor . . . (*Pause*)

CAROLINE: I resent that, Citizen.

DANCER: Of course you do . . .

CAROLINE: I am beautiful, a princess of royal blood, and you—

DANCER: I am an ugly and mutinous tutor, yes . . . (*Pause*)

There is a cake there, but where is my bride? (*Pause*)

CAROLINE: I'm here—(*Pause. She looks to her* HUSBAND. *He makes a slight move of his head, encouraging her.* DANCER *puts his hands to his cheeks.*)

DANCER: The innocence of me . . .!

Even these—(*He indicates the* CHILDREN.)

Are more—

Sophisticated! (*Pause.* ROMANOFF *steps forward.*)

ROMANOFF: I'll give the bride away . . . (DANCER *is puzzled. The telephone rings. He is still. It rings and rings.*)

Shall I?

Wouldn't you like that? (*Ignoring him,* DANCER *walks out of the room. Pause. They speak at once.*)

It's all right, I know what I'm doing—

HELEN: Don't quarrel with him—

ROMANOFF: I know his type—

HELEN: Whatever he says, do it—

ROMANOFF: Humour him—

HELEN: Things that horrify or possibly disgust you, still—

ROMANOFF: Grit your teeth and—

HELEN: Crawl, Mother—

ROMANOFF: I never thought I'd say this but—

HELEN: Creep, Mother—

ROMANOFF: The lives of our children depend on the denial of our feelings—

HELEN: Submit—

ROMANOFF: Caroline—

HELEN: Submit—

ROMANOFF: Caroline . . .! (*He stretches out an imploring hand.*) I shall suffer every second of your degradation . . .!

　Every second . . .! (*His hand, extended over the table, is ignored by her. It remains.*)

HELEN: We so admire you . . .! (*Pause.* DANCER *enters, slowly. He walks as if in deep thought, ignoring them. He stops. He turns at last.*)

DANCER: I have been ordered to place myself under arrest. (*Pause*)

　I've done so, obviously. (*Pause*)

　The higher wisdom of the Committee, the exigencies of the Terror, who could quarrel with it? Not me. (*He looks at them.*)

　A Transient Phenomenon expects nothing less than to be crushed beneath the wheels of Progress. I don't hesitate. I fling myself headlong. (*Pause*)

　Privacy.

　Idiosyncrasy.

　Call it what you like.

　Must be extinguished like a cigarette.

　His words, not mine. (*Pause*)

　The personality is no longer the exotic garden of indulgence but the park of the people. (*Pause*)

　His words, not mine. (*Pause*)

　Gates down. Walls down. The squeals of dirty infants in the summer house . . . (*Pause*)

　My words, not his . . . (*Pause*)

　Really, he has a fine mind, the Citizen at the terminus of all the telephones. And not bereft of sensibility, no . . .!

[*Pause. It is darker, the evening closes in. The wind blows in the silence. Suddenly, as if in horrible anticipation,* CHRISTOPHE *runs from his* FATHER's *arms to his* MOTHER. *She clasps him . . .*]

CAROLINE: Shh . . . (*She strokes his hair.*)

DANCER (*looking into the night*):

　Hated nightfall

　As long as there was day

I sensed the power to distinguish

Will from appetite

What thrilled me in the sun

Is threatening by night

Hated nightfall

I'll lie awake all hours

Plotting injury to those I love

And you will pass an unclean hand

Over the eyes of malcontents

The senile dissidents

And those

Who find a recompense in cruelty . . .

[*Pause.* CAROLINE, *steering her* SON *into the direction of his* SISTERS, *goes towards* DANCER, *who gazes into the evening.*]

CAROLINE: Save yourself . . . (DANCER *turns to her.*)

　Yourself and me . . . (*He examines her, not without suspicion.*)

　You because you believe in nothing.

　And me, because I represent everything.

　The cynic.

　The symbol.

　Lucidity.

　And illusion.

　Take me to a foreign city and we can live as poor as beggars in a room . . .

　I will be a mystery to you.

　Naked.

　On a mattress

　Poverty

　Exile

　And

　Desire . . . (DANCER *looks at her . . .*)

　My body is not perfect—

DANCER: I've seen it—

CAROLINE: Three children leave their mark—

DANCER: Seen it I said—

CAROLINE: But an empress is an empress and— (*Pause*)

　Seen it, how? (DANCER *shrugs . . .*)

DANCER: All night on a balcony . . . nothing to me . . . soaked to the skin and clinging to a creeper . . . nothing to me . . . (GRISELDA *laughs, stops.*)

ROMANOFF: Wretch . . .! Monkey and wretch . . .! (GRISELDA *forces her hand into her mouth.*)

DANCER: Underneath the curtain an inch of light. . . . adequate for me!

ROMANOFF: Pitiful and melancholy dwarf!

DANCER (*staring at* CAROLINE): And the underwear . . .! (GRISELDA *bursts out again.*)

　Yes!

　Absurd! (*He looks to* GRISELDA.)

　She knows! The tutor scrambling in the laundry, there's religion for you . . .!

CAROLINE (*measured*): If ever a man needed to sleep

with an empress, that man is you. . . .

DANCER: Sleep with. . . .? Sleep with, she says . . . as if that mundane act could compass the terrible extent of my devotion . . . how little you know of love, Caroline.

CAROLINE: Instruct me, then . . .

DANCER: How shallow you are . . . as I always knew . . . so shallow it wounds me where I am most pervious to pain . . .

CAROLINE: Teach me . . .

DANCER: I preferred you sleeping . . . then at least I was deceived—

CAROLINE: **Teach me I said.** (DANCER *falters.*) Night after night. Noon upon noon. Teach me. I have had a life of poverty. Drag me to a room and we will pulp our misery in the pursuit of some smothering ecstasy **drag me** (DANCER *stares, moved by her vehemence. She tears her dress from the shoulder.*) This is my flesh and it is dead. Unlit as Arctic winter. Breathe on me.

DANCER (*struggling against her*): Fifteen nights in Paris . . . belly to belly underneath the roof—

CAROLINE: Yes—

DANCER: Venice . . . Deauville . . . Longchamps . . . Nice . . .

CAROLINE: Yes—

DANCER: The thrashing of limbs and dreams in mouldering resorts—

CAROLINE: Yes! Yes! Why not! Or on some lonely lookout tower clinging to the cliff where we will caress each other under changing skies with the intense devotion of the archivist . . . (*She stares at* DANCER.) I've not been entered. . . . believe me . . . I'm unrevealed . . . (DANCER *is in acute pain . . . He sways.*)

DANCER: It'll only—it'll simply—

GRISELDA: Do go, Citizen . . . (DANCER *turns, shocked at her encouragement.*) I thought I was unhappy but how small my unhappiness is compared to yours . . . leave us, do . . . Oh, my poor mother! What she says is true! (ROMANOFF *covers his face in grief.*)

DANCER: Yes . . . and the way she says it . . . is the proof . . . (CAROLINE *flings herself on* DANCER, *sliding down to his knees.* DANCER, *profoundly moved, looks at* ROMANOFF.)

ROMANOFF: It isn't too late, Dancer . . . you can go . . .

DANCER (*as if lost*): Go . . .?

ROMANOFF: **Love her and go.**

[DANCER *yearns towards* CAROLINE, *but a movement catches his eye.* CHRISTOPHE, *with his watering can, climbs onto the table and proceeds to pour the contents over the cake.* DANCER *watches with fascination. The spell is broken. A low laugh comes from him . . .]*

DANCER: That was not the love I had in mind . . . I would lie with the silence of a spent lover and grieve under the seagulls for the apotheosis I had shirked . . . (*He looks to* CAROLINE.) Madame, you—

[*With a percussive shock, an arm, holding a rifle extended, is thrust through the floor. The rifle is flung down with a clatter. The arm remains fixed in the air.* CAROLINE *falls forward onto her hands, sobbing.* ROMANOFF *goes to dash to her.*]

ROMANOFF: Oh, Caroline—(*He is stopped by the appearance of a second rifle thrust through and flung down as before. He takes account of it, then goes to* CAROLINE *and places his hands on her shoulders.*) I'm sorry
I'm so sorry
I'm so sorry
So sorry
So sorry

CHORUS: **Dancer**
Forgive us we
Suspected you of
Ambiguity
Lukewarm in your devotion
To the future
And inclined to
Clemency . . .

DANCER: Clemency . . .? But History doesn't know the word. . . .

[DANCER *seizes the tiered wedding cake in his arms . . . He staggers under the weight . . . A pipe plays a dance off-key.* CAROLINE *goes to a chair, sits, sleeps.* DANCER *revolves with the cake as the* CHORUS *laugh. His dance takes him past the figure of* CAROLINE.]

CHORUS: **Mock her**
Mock her
The bitch's garments are woven from our poverty
Humiliate her
She fucked with priests

DANCER (*revolving*): She did, did she. . . .? (*Some laugh in staccato contempt. Others excite themselves in chanting.*)

CHORUS: **Monarchy**
Monarchy
Another word for depravity

DANCER: You know everything. . . .!

CHORUS: **And the husband was anyway**
Completely
Impotent! (*They laugh derisively.*)

DANCER: I never knew. . . .!

[DANCER *falls at* CAROLINE's *feet, clutching the cake. A silence. A wind blows.* GRISELDA *sings a psalm.* JANE *enters, clutching a saucepan.* Griselda *stops.*]

JANE: There's a woman outside says—

DANCER: A woman . . . ?

JANE: A woman yes and—(DANCER *takes the knife from his pocket again.* JANE *is horrified.*)
Dancer . . . (*She swallows with apprehension.*)
Dancer, you can't—(DANCER *plunges the knife into the cake. He looks at* JANE, *then at the others.*)

DANCER: My bride's arrived . . . (JANE *stares.*)
Do share my cake . . . (*He extends a slice.* JANE *is motionless.*)
You are afraid . . .
The consequences of partaking of my wedding cake . . . appall you. . . . (*He tosses the slice. It strikes* JANE *on her apron, falls. . . .*)

JANE: Dancer . . . you are a stupid, stupid man . . .

DANCER (*hacking another slice*): **Let them eat cake!** (*He tosses it wildly over his shoulder.*) She was not cruel . . . she was struggling with incomprehension, Marie Antoinette . . . (*He flings another. Into the silence, a* WOMAN OFFICIAL *of the Revolution. It is as if they all knew her and expected her.* JANE, *desperate, turns to her.*)

JANE: Can I go now?
I did nothing except when I was forced and even then my soul revolted
Can I?
At all times my inclination was to say no thank you
Thank you I would rather not
Another time
Etcetera
God knows my innocence
God I love him God (*She closes her eyes. She goes to move.*)
I'm wiping up, I—

ALBEIT: Stay where you are.

[*A musical effect.* ALBEIT *goes among the family, touching them lightly on the shoulder one by one and indicating they should move to the back of the room. She touches* CAROLINE *last. She does not move.*]

DANCER: She sleeps . . . the Empress . . . (ALBEIT *indicates to the* CHORUS *with a movement of her head. They come and lift* CAROLINE *in the chair.* CHRISTOPHE *goes to his mother.*)
She sleeps because she cannot tolerate a world whose poverty of spirit includes even her . . .

JANE: **I want to wipe up, please!**

DANCER: Oh, let her wipe up. She is a servant, and they deteriorate without their servitude I've noticed—

ALBEIT (*to the* CHORUS): Arrest this man. (JANE *drops the saucepan with a clatter.*) And her.

DANCER: Oh, Jane, and you did nothing!

JANE: **Done nothing, no!**

CHORUS (*as they jerk* DANCER *and* JANE *into chairs*):
Dancer
Some misunderstanding obviously
Some temporary
Some
Some
Ideological
Complexity

ALBEIT: Where are the Citizens named Fitch and Arrant, Disbanner and Denadir?

ROMANOFF: Dead! They're dead!

ALBEIT (*to* DANCER): Where are the citizens, I said—

ROMANOFF: He killed them
He tortured them
He slit their throats before our eyes
Abominable monstrosity
No loyalty to anything exists in that
deformed and poisoned soul

HELEN: Father!

ROMANOFF: The world revolves and dynasties can come and go but that diabolical and cynical parcel of depravity—

GRISELDA: **Shut up**

ROMANOFF: **Shut up?**
Never will I
Cease in my indictment of—(*Pause*)
Citizen, look in the soup tureen. They were feeding us human remains.

HELEN (*incredulous*): What . . . ?

ROMANOFF: Yes, oh, yes, he was up to all sorts of—

JANE: **Human remains?**

ROMANOFF: The heads, yes, hacked them off and boiled them, arms and legs—

HELEN: What. . . . !

ROMANOFF: In the soup . . . !

HELEN: Father!

ROMANOFF (*to* ALBEIT): The ones you mentioned, I don't know their names—

HELEN: Father, please . . . !

ROMANOFF (*to* ALBEIT): **Cleanse the world, Madame!**
(ALBEIT *hesitates* . . .)

JANE: What heads . . . ? I spent hours finding mushrooms for that soup—(ALBEIT *strikes* JANE *across the face.*)

ROMANOFF: Good . . . ! Good . . . !

CHORUS: **Dancer**
Dancer
The vegetables will testify against you
The banquet will rise up and point
An
Incriminating
Finger . . . (*Pause, then* ALBEIT *goes to the soup tureen.*)

HELEN: It's impossible . . . !

ROMANOFF: Shut up.

HELEN: Impossible—

ROMANOFF: Shut up you idiotic child nobody requires your interventions!

HELEN (*aghast*): Idiotic child . . . ?

ROMANOFF (*whose gaze is fixed on the table*): That's what I said . . . !

HELEN: I forgive you . . how hard it is but I forgive you . . .

ROMANOFF (*staring madly at* ALBEIT): Good! (ALBEIT *removes the lid of the tureen. She looks in. She calculates. She replaces the lid.*)

JANE: There you are, now you can see what's what I'd like permission to—(ALBEIT *silences* JANE, *taking her face between the fingers of one hand menacingly and twisting her.* JANE *is still. Her head hangs.* ALBEIT *walks up and down.*)

ALBEIT: Chaos . . . (*Pause*)

How it licenses depravity . . . (*Pause*)

And we, constructing on the ruins of the past a new society, encounter in the strangest places exotic delinquencies . . . (*She looks at* DANCER.)

Cannibals

Perverts

Amoralists

ROMANOFF: **Abandoned by God and reviled by man . . . !**

JANE: Cannibals?

ALBEIT: Old and rotting systems whose debauched relations bring to birth in their senility transient phenomena such as this . . .

ROMANOFF: **Cleanse, Madame . . . !**

JANE: What cannibals . . . ?

ROMANOFF: **Cleanse . . . !**

DANCER: Oh, how they hate me, Jane . . . in this, these arch-opponents are of one accord . . . for I am the antithesis of History, which has manacled their souls . . . (ALBEIT *seizes him by his hair and forces back his head. At once, the* CHORUS *flock to observe his ordeal.*)

CHORUS: **Dancer**

Dancer

We feared you would display this (*He lets out a cry.*)

Arrogant

And

Petulant (*He cries again.*)

Disharmony . . . !

JANE (*horrified*): Leave him . . . leave him . . . ! (*He cries again. The* GIRLS *cover their mouths.*)

ROMANOFF (*in a rambling, disconnected tone*): We were tired, obviously we were tired, but it was not just tiredness—

HELEN: Don't die . . . ! Don't die, Dancer!

ROMANOFF: No, I think one must acknowledge tiredness such as ours owed something to the greater lassitude of God, I think God Himself was tired—(DANCER *concealed behind the gathered* CHORUS, *lets out a profound groan* . . .)

I think His silence was the withdrawal of His love which possibly we had ceased to value . . . and in consequence He turned—not far—the slightest averting of His face is after all, sufficient for the eclipsing of all happiness—

GRISELDA: Shh!

ROMANOFF (*mildly now*): Shh . . . why?

[*The* CHORUS, ALBEIT, *stand back from* DANCER. CHRISTOPHE, *irresistibly drawn to* DANCER, *slips off his* MOTHER's *lap and silently peers at him.* JANE *extends her hand to hold* DANCER's . . .]

JANE: Dancer . . . Oh, Dancer. . . . that woman's blinded you . . .

GRISELDA: We love you . . . We love you. . . . !

HELEN: Yes, oh, yes . . . !

DANCER (*croaking*): Yes. . . . I know you do. . . .

ROMANOFF: Oh, Dancer, what are you . . . **What are you . . . !**

DANCER: Afraid . . .

ROMANOFF: Afraid . . . ?

DANCER: Afraid death even . . . will be poorer than my imagination predicted. . . .

ROMANOFF: **Our souls will meet in paradise!**

GRISELDA: Yes! Yes! And Mr Dancer will be—oh, will be—

HELEN: Content!

GRISELDA: Content at last!

JANE: It's all right, Dancer . . . it is . . . even if it seems. . . . not right. . . . at all . . .

ROMANOFF: **I take him in my arms!**

GRISELDA: We all do! We all do! (DANCER *is aware of* CHRISTOPHE's *proximity. His head turns to him* . . .)

DANCER: Listen. . . .

Listen. . . .

[*The wind blows. The sound of* CAROLINE's *snore.* CHRISTOPHE *lifts his watering can and pours the contents over* DANCER's *uptilted face* . . .]

CONTEXTS AND COMMENTARIES

Eldred Durosimi Jones (b. 1925)

Eldred Jones is professor of English at the University of Sierra Leone in West Africa. In his discussion of The Strong Breed *Professor Jones calls attention to the parallels Soyinka explores between Yoruba and Christian ideas of sacrifice.*

THE STRONG BREED

The Strong Breed is an extraordinarily compact play. In spite of its comparative brevity it is one of Soyinka's most significant works in which one of the play-wright's constant preoccupations—the need for sacrifice—is dramatized. It is also one of Soyinka's most symbolic plays. (*Camwood on the Leaves*, a radio play, is more obviously symbolic but lacks the subtlety of this play.) It avoids clutter-ing detail, and thus succeeds in presenting its themes in an archetypal form. Evil, for example, about which the play is so concerned, the evil of the village which has to be expiated is never defined although it hovers over the whole play like a pall. The effect of this avoidance of definition is to give the play a generality of application. Sacrifice too, which Eman represents, is treated sym-bolically. The 'carrier' obviously in the case of the effigy, but also in the case of Eman-as-carrier is a symbol for the moral force required to save the society.

Eman's sacrifice is modelled on the sacrifice of Christ, whose death is recalled by a number of subtle references. Like Christ, Eman is both teacher and healer. This is economically dramatized before even the first words of the play are spoken. (Soyinka's stage directions are almost always significant, but the opening ones particularly so, for they often have symbolic significance.) When the play opens, '*Sunma is clearing the table of what looks like a modest clinic . . . Another rough table in the room is piled with exercise-books, two or three worn text-books etc.*' The suggestions of this opening tableau are dramatized later in Eman's painful efforts at helping in the rehabilitation of the helpless idiot Ifada, as well as in his kindness to the inscrutable girl who, Judas-like, betrays him. Eman eventually goes on to carry the evil of the village on his own head. The parallel with Christ continues in that Eman works among people who neither understand nor really want him. As Sunma complains, 'You are wasting your life on people who really want you out of their way.' Other analogies with Christ are Eman's conscious sacrifice of himself for an ungrateful people, his supreme sacrifice taking the form of his being hanged on a sacred tree. Towards the climax of the physical sacrifice, his body flinches, and he needs water. Eman's pathetic appeal to the girl who betrays him parallels Christ's agonized cry 'I thirst'. Eman's death, like Christ's, stuns the people in whose name it had been demanded, and leaves a remarkable impression on some unlikely minds. There is no dramatic parallel to the dying thief, but one of the elders of the village, Oroge, suddenly pauses at a crucial stage of the pursuit of Eman, because he has caught a reflection of something in the victim's face which impresses him: 'He saw something. Why may I not know what it was?' This influence at his death is also reflected in the inability of the villagers 'to raise a curse'—the traditional curse with which each man is expected to empty his evil on the victim. The analogies with Christ also link Eman with Soyinka's crucified figure in his poem 'The Dreamer. . . .' Eman, then, within the play is the saviour.

In consonance with the archetypal nature of the play, the evil against which he works is not treated in detail. It is nevertheless potently symbolized. It is an opposite force to what Eman himself represents. He is sensitive to human need regardless of kinship, while in the tradition of the village, outsiders are fair game. It is easy to see here a symbolic treatment of that ethnic exclusiveness, tribalism, which so bedevils life in modern Africa, but the applications are even wider. Eman represents a responsiveness to human need wherever it arises. He himself is a 'stranger' in a village where the plight of the stranger, particularly on the eve of the New Year, is a fearful one. An early tableau dramatizes this: '*Two villagers, obvious travellers, pass hurriedly in front of the house . . . the man enters first, turns and urges the woman who is just emerging to hurry.*' The reason for the anxiety of the travellers to escape from the hostile village becomes clear as the play develops. Sunma, an insider who has become disgusted with the village and seeks to escape from it refers to the tribal exclusiveness in one of her appeals to Eman to leave: 'Have you not noticed how tightly we shut out strangers? Even if you lived here for a lifetime, you remain a stranger.' But the attitude of the village to strangers goes further. A stranger is required to bear the evils of the village, a task none of the villagers has the moral strength to undertake. Their seeming kindness to outsiders like the helpless Ifada is shown to be a mere device for recruiting victims:

> OROGE: No one in his senses would do such a job. Why do you think
> we give refuge to idiots like him? We don't know where he came
> from. One morning, he is simply there, just like that. From
> nowhere at all. You see, there is a purpose in that.

Ifada thus becomes a prime candidate for the ordeal of 'carrier'. To Eman this is appalling—'But why do you pick on a helpless boy? Obviously he is not willing.' He has been brought up in a different tradition: 'In my home, we believe that a man should be willing.' There is a confrontation of values here which leads directly to Eman's substitution of himself for Ifada, and his assumption of the role of the willing carrier of the evils of the village, a decision which leads to his martyrdom. Eman's humanity is in contrast to the brutal callousness of the village. He is a moral force without which the village would remain unregenerate in spite of the ritual of an annual sacrifice.

If Eman is the symbol of a human response to need, the inscrutable girl symbolizes the attitudes of the village. She is curiously detached and is totally unaffected by human need. The stage directions make the following requirements of the actress: *'The girl is unsmiling. She possesses in fact, a kind of inscrutability which does not make her hard but is unsettling.'* Her sickness also isolates her from the rest of the village—a fact she states without much discomposure: 'I am unwell you know . . . Don't you know I play alone? The other children won't come near me. Their mothers would beat them.' Typically in the play the precise nature of her illness is not stated. It merely isolates her and, in her mother's hope, will disappear, borne away by her carrier with the old year. It is significant that she does not seek medical help for the illness, and refuses to go near Eman who runs a free clinic. Her sickness seems to be another symbol for archetypal evil. To Sunma, 'She is not a child. She is as evil as the rest of them.' All her actions confirm her as cold-blooded and selfish, characteristics she shares with the rest of the village.

In the symbolism of the play, her carrier also represents Eman; this effigy is tortured and eventually hanged to represent his fate. Given the child's identification with the village, this use of her carrier is most appropriate, and saves the play from a distracting concern with the details of Eman's agony which could have reduced tragedy to melodrama. The girl of course proves to be a Judas and callously betrays Eman when at the end of the play he asks her for water, and instead of giving it to him she reveals his hiding-place to his pursuers.

Her callousness is manifested particularly in her relations with Ifada whom she merely uses because he is all that is available. Ifada is the play's symbol of need, a need which makes no more impression on the girl than it does on the village she represents. To her Ifada is a despicable object for which, however, because of her isolation she has some need. (This reflects exactly the boy's position in the village as a whole.) The girl's invitation to play comes at the end of a callous inventory:

[after a long, cool survey of IFADA*]*

You have a head like a spider's egg, and your mouth dribbles like a roof. But there is no one else. Would you like to play?

Sunma is a member of the village, but one who moves in the play from consciousness of the evil of the village and a desire to escape from it, to an open renunciation of its evil, a renunciation which totally isolates her from the protection of the village, and thus puts her in line for a path which might, like Eman's, lead to a life of further sacrifice.

Sunma's concern for most of the play is that she and Eman should escape from a village that had come to revolt her. Obviously she has come under his influence and is inclined to his way of life. It is she who is seen clearing away the tools of Eman's trade in the opening tableau. What she lacks is Eman's extraordinary strength which enables him to keep his composure in the face of evil. She has to get away from it:

I wonder if I really sprang from here. I know they are evil and I am not. From the oldest to the smallest child, they are nourished in evil and unwholesomeness in which I have no part.

But you must help me tear myself away from here.

In her consciousness of evil and her instinctive desire to run away from something she has come to hate, Sunma is a good, humane person, but unlike Eman, an *ordinarily* good, humane person. She lacks the strength of an *exceptionally* good, humane, person such as Eman is. (Eman is after all one of the Strong Breed—an exceptional breed as the play makes clear.) She had in fact run away once before, but had bravely returned to help Eman in his work. Eman is thus a prop to her weak humanity. Without her strong attachment to him, she would have left the village and its needs for ever. At the opening of the play she is poised once again on a moment of decision: 'Eman, are we going or aren't we? You will leave it till too late.' And again: 'It is the time for making changes in one's life.' Eman will not leave and, as the sounds of the departing lorry symbolize, the moment of decision passes, and she stays on with Eman in his battle with evil. She is thus forced to remain and continue to face the evil of the village. Already in her heart she had renounced this evil, but her open renunciation was to come later in the confrontation with her father.

Sunma's attempts at escape are of a piece with her sudden fierce hostility towards Ifada at the beginning of the play. This too is an attempt at escape. She after all had seemed to be as responsive to Ifada's need as Eman who is consequently surprised at her sudden outbursts against the boy. After one of her expressions of disgust—'horrible insect'—Eman cannot conceal his surprise: 'I don't understand. It is *Ifada* you know. Ifada! the unfortunate one who runs errands for you and doesn't hurt a soul.' Sunma's frustration at Eman's refusal to leave finds an outlet in the symbol of the need which keeps him tied to the village. Indeed as Eman points out, 'It is almost as if you are forcing yourself to hate him. Why?' Sunma is trying another break from her responsibility; she is trying to escape into hatred from love—the responsibilities of love make much greater demands than those of hate. Her decision to stay by Eman has committed her to a path the full consequences of which appear later. She reinforces her mental renunciation of the evil of the village with a physical confrontation with her father in which the antipathy of their conflicting attitudes is externally dramatized. Sunma attacks her father savagely, drawing blood. The symbolic struggle is brief but intense:

[JAGUNA turns just in time to see SUNMA fly at him, clawing at his face like a crazed tigress.]

SUNMA: Murderer! What are you doing to him. Murderer! Murderer!

[JAGUNA finds himself struggling really hard to keep off his daughter, he succeeds in pushing her off and striking her so hard on the face that she falls to her knees. He moves on her to hit her again.]

OROGE (*comes between*): Think what you are doing, Jaguna, she is your daughter.

JAGUNA: My daughter! Does this one look like my daughter? Let me cripple the harlot for life . . .

[*Draws his hand across his cheek—it is covered with blood.*]

This is Sunma's final break with the society. It is true that this open confrontation is stimulated by her personal concern for the fate of Eman who at this point is being pursued as the victim, but it is no less of a conscious break with evil for all that. It is an evil which she had mentally renounced much earlier anyway. Whatever the reasons, her actions had now made her an outsider.

Her position in this regard is dramatized by her new relationship with Ifada. She had tried earlier to reject him, identifying him with the cause of her frustration. Now, after the break with Jaguna, she accepts him as rescuer, comforter and friend. The tableau required by the stage directions after the fight between father and daughter dramatizes the new relationship:

[. . . IFADA, who came in with SUNMA and had stood apart, horror-stricken, comes shyly forward. He helps SUNMA up. They go off, he holding SUNMA bent and sobbing.]

Later too they are united by their common feelings at the sight of the hanging effigy which represents the martyred Eman. Their feelings are in contrast to the reactions of the girl who stands 'impassively watching', as detached from any contact with the human situation as she has always been.

The role of Eman has been incidentally demonstrated in the examination of other characters, since he is central to the play. He represents a moral force which transcends social boundaries. His is the broad humanity which the world both needs and rejects at the same time, while individuals and individual societies relentlessly pursue their particular concerns. But Eman is also a man. As a son and a pupil, he has relations with a father and his tutor. As a lover and husband he suffers the agony of losing his wife. He is human enough to prefer a quiet life to a life of self-sacrifice, but eventually an inner urge which he is unable to resist drives him on to accept the burden of sacrifice. He cannot escape this role because he is of the Strong Breed.

Through the concept of the Strong Breed Soyinka makes the point that the quality of personal leadership through suffering is not a common characteristic. It is rare. This is well symbolized in the notion of the carrier. The role carries with it a tremendous moral burden at which strong men flinch. It involves a moral preparedness which is implied in these words of Eman's father as he prepares to carry the evils of his own village:

A man should be at his strongest when he takes the boat, my friend. To be weighed down inside and out is not a wise thing. I hope when the moment comes I shall have found my strength!

Such is the weight of the burden, that the men of Jaguna's village have to foist the role on an unwilling outsider trapped for the purpose. For them, in the words of Oroge, 'No one in his senses would do such a job.' Such then is the burden—its weight but not its detail is defined—which Eman assumes on behalf of strangers. The martyr is often a man who in the eyes of the world is out of his mind. His conduct is inexplicable in terms of a selfish rat race in which each man fends for himself. But as Soyinka reiterates in his work, without this type of self-sacrificing man society cannot be saved (even temporarily) from itself.

Eman's path is essentially a lonely one from the start. The main value for him of the traditional period of initiation is the opportunity it gives for individual labour and solitary contemplation. As for the specific ritual 'It is a small thing one can do in the big towns.' He points out the significance of the period for him to Omae in one of the flashbacks to his earlier life:

> This is an important period of my life. Look, These huts, we built them with our own hands. Every boy built his own. We learn things, do you understand? And we spend much time just thinking. At least I do, it is the first time I have had nothing to do except think. Don't you see, I am becoming a man. For the first time, I understand that I have a life to fulfil.

And a little later, 'A man must go on his own, go where no one can help him, and test his strength.' This is the lonely road of the man of genius, whose renewing influence society sorely needs.

When Eman discovers the hollowness of his tutor—the latter is one of Soyinka's many false prophets and leaders—he suddenly leaves the place of initiation—he has got all he wants out of it—and goes on a lonely pilgrimage. Once he has made up his mind, nothing can stop him. Omae's pathetic attempts to hold him back—he actually drags her along as she clings to him—are paralleled by the fruitlessness of Sunma's attempts to make him leave her village and its evil. All the essential decisions for Eman are personal ones made after a lonely internal struggle. In this lies the uniqueness of this type of character; from it also arises his seeming callousness to the normal human ties—of love for example. The pilgrim (another favourite figure for the type—see 'Idanre' for another example) has to leave all, and follow his chosen life—'Nothing ties me down'.

Eman's sacrifice really ends the play. The possible effects on society are only faintly suggested. His effect on Sunma is clear; she will never be the same again after having met and worked with him, but she is an ordinary individual, without Eman's strength. (His death and her very isolation might possibly produce the necessary strength.) Oroge's momentary glimpse of something in Eman's face at the height of the chase has been noticed earlier. (Will anything come of it?) The most general effect is seen in the horrified reaction of the villagers at the sight of him hanging on the tree. In the words of Jaguna himself who is totally unmoved by the sacrifice, 'One and all they looked up at the man and words died in their throats.' They should have poured their curses on the helpless victim but the sight of their selfless benefactor hanging dead penetrated to a sensitive vein. They 'fled' their leaders. That is all the reaction. How far will this experience take them? How effectively will the already threatened reprisals of Jaguna kill the incipient reaction? We do not know. It is apparently enough that the sacrifice has been made and noticed. The silent set tableau on which the lights fade at the end of the play represents a society still in need of salvation.

[... SUNMA, *her last bit of will gone, crumbles against the wall. Some distance away from them, partly hidden, stands the* GIRL, *impassively watching.* IFADA *hugs the effigy to him, stands above* SUNMA. *The* GIRL *remains where she is, observing . . .*]

What price salvation?

Soyinka's use of scrambled chronology—a feature of *The Interpreters*—is noteworthy here. The flashback which gives us a glimpse of the past as a fill-in on the present is a favourite device of the playwright. Faintly suggested in *The Swamp-Dwellers* (Makuri's narration of their wedding night's escapade in the marsh) the technique is more elaborately exploited in *The Lion and the Jewel*. In *The Strong Breed* we have the backward flashes into Eman's past, some of which he watches from his position in the present of the play, thus giving an uncanny feeling of a suspension of the dimension of time. This effect is further heightened in the pageant at the end as Eman disappears from the play to his death behind the scenes, symbolically following the path of his father in what must be taken as his mental evocation of his father's last journey as carrier. Soyinka externalizes Eman's thoughts as he must have remembered his earlier attempts to renounce his inherited role, and the words of his father: 'Your own blood will betray you, son, because you cannot hold it back. If you make it do less than this, it will rush to your head and burst it open.' He has now offered himself as a victim—a role he had declared himself unfitted for—but his body has flinched, and he is now running away from the ordeal. The sight of his father (in his mind, for the father had been long dead) revives his will, and he accepts his role to follow in his father's footsteps (the metaphor is made flesh). 'Wait, father. I am coming with you . . . wait . . . wait for me, father.' It is the father's turn to flinch, and to try in his paternal concern to divert his son from the path of martyrdom by pointing in the opposite direction. But Eman, with the words just quoted, follows his father to the symbolic river and to the real trap: '[*There is a sound of twigs breaking, of a sudden trembling in the branches. Then silence.*]' Eman has made the supreme sacrifice.

Soyinka has used a fairly common scapegoat ritual as the vehicle for a tremendous moral statement which once again transcends its setting. One of the playwright's greatest strengths is his ability to manipulate symbols. This is as true of his plays as of his poetry. *The Strong Breed* succeeds in a way that *Camwood on the Leaves* does not. In the radio play both the symbols and what they represent retain their separate entities and operate independently. In *The Strong Breed* there is a complete fusion of object and symbol and a resulting greater suggestiveness.

Joan Fishman (b. 1945)

Motion picture producer Joan Fishman, whose credits include The Prince of Pennsylvania *and* Age Isn't Everything, *has written a dissertation and has published articles on August Wilson's work. In this selection Fishman examines the influence of painter Romare Bearden on Wilson's plays.*

ROMARE BEARDEN, AUGUST WILSON, AND THE TRADITIONS OF AFRICAN PERFORMANCE

A painter and a playwright. Romare Bearden and August Wilson. Perhaps with nothing in common. Romare Bearden grew up among the elite, acquainted with Duke Ellington and Eleanor Roosevelt. August Wilson grew up on the street. Bearden is schooled. Wilson is self-taught, a high school dropout. When Bearden began his work, he had studied classical forms and painting history for years. When Wilson began, he had not read Shakespeare, or Molière, or Williams, or O'Neill.

And yet, as if they stood side by side peering through the same window on life, Romare Bearden and August Wilson created art that similarly presents the human condition: art that simultaneously captures the energy of the African American experience and releases it back into the world, art that speaks clearly to African Americans and is heard clearly by all audiences, and art that speaks for a generation and to a generation.

What brings these two artists together is the incorporation into their art of the elements that define traditional African performance forms. In the selection of their themes and the portrayals of their characters, they incorporate the true-to-life and the familiar into ritualistic drama recognizable and influential to their audiences. They present a rainbow of the life cycle incorporating the past and the present, the dead and the yet-to-be-born, offering images and inspirations intended to heal the community. They offer conflict and struggle not within what Wole Soyinka identifies as the traditional Western context, which sees "human anguish as viable only within strictly temporal capsules," but rather within the African context, "whose tragic understanding transcends the causes of individual disjunction and recognizes them as reflections of a far greater disharmony in the communal psyche." . . .

The two Wilson plays directly influenced by Bearden, *Joe Turner's Come and Gone* and *The Piano Lesson,* are his most spiritual plays, having moved away from traditional Western forms and including non-naturalistic elements. In Bearden's most innovative collages, the artist finds a place for African spiritualism; for example, the presence of the conjure woman in the several paintings which bear this title.

In these spiritual elements combined with the everyday ritualistic actions of their characters, Wilson and Bearden capture a strong sense of continuity which speaks to the mysterious connection between the past and present. And, in order to emphasize the linkage between generations, both Bearden and Wilson bring traditional African elements into contemporary African American culture. Bearden combines African masks with African American faces cut out from magazines; Wilson's characters in *Joe Turner* perform the African juba dance after Sunday dinner.

Common to African performance is an exploration of the reconciliation of old and new ways. Traditional values vs. modern methods is a recurring theme. Many works carry the same clear message: For life to continue, each of the traditional and modern ways must moderate itself in the face of the other.

Wilson and Bearden similarly portray African Americans trying to find their place in time, to meld past and future. This requires an acceptance of what African culture provides to all African Americans and a reconciliation of this with their contemporary culture. "In a world dominated by white culture," Wilson explains, "the black must be strong enough not only to survive but to re-establish his own identity and heritage which flows unbroken from an African fountainhead."

The issues of baggage or treasure from the past and their integration into contemporary life are the backbone of Wilson's fourth play, *The Piano Lesson*, inspired by Bearden's painting of the same name. When Wilson saw Bearden's painting in an art gallery, he turned to a friend and said, "This is my next play."

The Piano Lesson focuses on a struggle between brother, Boy Willie, and sister, Berniece, over whether to sell an heirloom piano. The piano was previously owned by the Sutter family, who held Boy Willie and Berniece's family enslaved. The slaveowner acquired the piano in a trade —he traded Berniece and Boy Willie's grandmother and their father for it. Berniece and Boy Willie's grandfather carved portraits of his family into the piano legs in memory of the loss of his wife and son.

Boy Willie wants to sell the piano to buy a piece of the property where his family served as slaves. His eye is only to the future. Berniece refuses to part with the instrument. She is unable to play the piano that she insists on retaining because she fears that to do so is to raise the spirits embodied within it. Berniece cannot reconcile her past with her present. At the end of *The Piano Lesson*, however, when Boy Willie is struggling for life against Sutter's ghost, Berniece finally understands that the only way to save him is to call upon her heritage, thereby empowering herself with its strength. Her Christian faith alone is not enough; Berniece plays the piano and in a ritual chant calling on her ancestors, defeats the evil spirit.

In *Joe Turner's Come and Gone*, Wilson has brought to life another Bearden creation in the character of Bertha (*Miss Bertha and Mr. Seth*, 1978). In contrast to Berniece, Bertha serves as a positive example of reconciling old and new. She brings with her the remedies of the past and combines them with a practical approach to the future.

When her husband, Seth, bothers Bertha about her daily activities, about "all that heebie-jeebie stuff . . . sprinkling salt all over the place . . . pennies lined up across the threshold," Bertha responds, "It don't hurt none. I can't say if it help . . . but it don't hurt none." For Bertha, there is no contradiction between attending church and maintaining the more ritualistic traditions of the past.

This theme of conflict between cultures is still strong in contemporary African performance. For example, in the Ethiopian play *The Coffin Dealer and the Grave Digger*, the central character has a comical nightmare which inverts Christian ideals of heaven and hell as they have been unsuccessfully laid onto African culture. The juxtaposition of African and Western ideas about death appears in many plays.

Both Wilson and Bearden address the juxtaposition between African and Christian religious tradition, revealing parallels and contrasts. Bearden weaves together aligned cultural rituals. His *Baptism* is linked to John the Baptist, which leads back to ancient purification rites in Africa. Bearden says, "I feel this continuation of ritual gives a dimension to the works so that the works are something other than mere designs." Bearden's painting titled *The Prevalence of Ritual: Conjur Woman* also connects two worlds.

Wilson's and Bearden's works serve the same function as the traditional performers. As Soyinka notes, the principal function of these performers "is to reinforce by observances, rituals, and mytho-historical recitals the existing consciousness or cosmic entanglement in the community, and to arbitrate in the sometimes difficult application of such truths to domestic and community undertakings."

Traditional African performance shares many characteristics with traditional forms of other cultures. Thus, Wilson's and Bearden's use of these elements promotes a universal applicability of their art. Wilson and Bearden have addressed what Wole Soyinka describes as the "deep-seated need of creative man to recover this archetypal consciousness," and their art, which shares many characteristics, shares most of all its ability to speak across racial and cultural lines.

Wilson and Bearden thus understand a theory which underlies the tragedy in traditional performance in which the sickness of one individual, according to Soyinka, "is a sign of, or may portend, the sickness of the world around him. Something has occurred to disrupt the natural rhythms and the cosmic balances of the total community."

In African performances history is thus often repeated for moral or educational purposes. Both Wilson and Bearden understand the power of revisiting the past and undertake the African view of art as what Soyinka calls "retrieval vehicles for, or assertive links with a lost sense of origin."

Bearden's paintings therefore speak through centuries of history, and, as Campbell writes, "what makes Bearden's art particularly difficult to grasp . . . is that even as his art points to the future, it also wholeheartedly embraces the past."

Wilson intends to write a play for every decade of this century. He, like Bearden, has brought to contemporary audiences a powerful chronicle of African American history. And yet, neither Wilson's nor Bearden's works stands merely as historical reflections. Rather they carry great relevance to contemporary life, and they promote promise for tomorrow. Wilson says, "Without knowing your past, you don't know your present—and you certainly can't plot your future."

Improving prospects for the future is at the center of traditional performances whose goal is the harmonious resolution of issues and an improvement in the well-being of the community. Wilson's characters are examples meant to help heal. Wilson hopes his work may "indicate some directions toward which we might possibly move." He speaks to all people when he addresses our need to make a connection with the past as we move toward the future. In *Two Trains Running*, Memphis is advised by Aunt Ester: "If you drop the ball you got to go back and pick it up. Ain't no need in keeping running cause if you get to the end zone, it ain't gonna be a touchdown."

Wilson's plays and Bearden's paintings, like traditional performances, rarely guide toward external solution. Instead, they focus on the greatest magic, the magic of the individual to become part of the community and thus to heal himself and the community. African performance doesn't offer resolution; the final outcome will be determined by the learning the performance has hopefully inspired in its audience. The performances rise out of their communities, reflect social and political upheaval within their communities, and they hold the potential for harmonious resolution not within the confines of the actual drama but within the workings of the community.

August Wilson and Romare Bearden challenge women and men to respect and believe in who they are on their own and as part of a larger population. They challenge every heart to search for truth and every individual to sing his own song loudly for survival, strength, and growth. It is a powerful and valuable message.

Wilson offered to send a limousine to bring Bearden to a performance of his play *Fences*. Bearden chose instead to travel by bus with a senior citizens group. In the end, he decided not to make the trip at all. Later Bearden was scheduled to attend the opening of Wilson's *Joe Turner's Come and Gone* but sadly died two weeks before the event.

Wilson writes:

> I never had the privilege of meeting Romare Bearden. Once I stood outside 357 Canal Street [New York] in silent homage, daring myself to knock on his door. I am sorry I didn't, for I have never looked back from that moment when I first encountered his art.
>
> I have often thought of what I would have said to him that day if I had knocked on his door and he had answered. I probably would just have looked at him. I would have looked, and if I were wearing a hat, I would have taken it off in tribute.

Romare Bearden never saw an August Wilson play performed, the men never met, and they never spoke. But these two artists drank from the same well and carry to contemporary audiences art created from age-old elements.

On their separate roads, these two artists offer images of a people, indeed of all people, in defeat and triumph, joy and despair. In the smallest details of day-to-day existence, Wilson and Bearden find the energy of life, and through their art, they send it out to each of us.

David Mamet (b. 1947)

In the following selection from his book Writing in Restaurants, *playwright David Mamet explores the concept of realism in theatrical production.*

REALISM

Most American theatrical workers are in thrall to the idea of *realism*. A very real urge to be truthful, to be *true*, constrains them to judge their efforts and actions against an inchoate, which is to say against an *unspecified* standard of reality.

That the standard is unspecified is important, as it thus becomes the explanation and excuse for any action or effort the artist feels disinclined to make. It becomes a peremptory challenge.

A necessary response to the artist who says "It's not *true*" must be "True to what?"

Stanislavsky and, more notably, Vakhtangov suggested that—that to which the artist must be *true* is the aesthetic integrity of the play.

This places a huge responsibility on the artist. He or she faced with this charge—to care for the *scenic truth*—can no longer take refuge in a blanket dismissal or *endorsement* of anything on the grounds of its being not realistic.

In general, each facet of every production must be weighed and understood solely on the basis of its interrelationship to the other elements; on its service or lack of service to the meaning, the *action* of the play.

A chair is not *per se* truthful or untruthful. That one may say, "Yes, but it is a chair, an actual chair, people sit on it and I found it in a cafeteria, therefore it belongs in this play about a cafeteria," is beside the point. Why was that *particular* chair chosen? Just as that particular chair said something about the cafeteria *in* the cafeteria (its concern for looks over comfort, for economy over durability, etc.), so that chair, on stage, will say something *about the play*; so the question is: What do you, the theatrical director, wish to say *about the play*?

What does the chair mean *in the play*? Does it symbolize power? Then have *that* chair. Abasement? Possession, and so on. Choose the correspondingly appropriate chair. One might say, "Give it up, *it's just a chair. . . .*" But, again, someone is going to *choose* it; shouldn't that someone *recognize* that he is consciously or unconsciously making a choice, and make the choice consciously, and in favor of an idea more specific to the play than the idea of "reality."

A conscious devotion to the *Idea* of a play is a concern for what Stanislavsky called the Scenic Truth, which is to say, the truth *in this particular scene*. The important difference between realism and truth, Scenic Truth, is the difference between acceptability and necessity, which is the difference between entertainment and Art.

So what if the play is set in a cafeteria? A cafeteria has no objective reality, as far as we artists are concerned. Our question is *why* is the play set in a cafeteria, what does it mean that the play is set in a cafeteria, and what *aspect* of this cafeteria is important *to the meaning of the play*. Having determined that, we may discard immediately all other aspects of the cafeteria and concentrate *only* on that which puts forward the meaning of the play. E.g.: if, in our particular play, the cafeteria means a place where the hero is always open to surveillance, the designer can build a set which reflects the idea: inability to hide. If the meaning of the cafeteria is a place where reflection and rest are possible, the designer's work can reflect *these* ideas. In neither case is the designer's first question: "What does a cafeteria look like?" His first question is: "What does it mean *in this instance*?" This is a concern for Scenic Truth.

In devotion to this Scenic Truth the artist gives him- or herself a choice. In discarding the armor of realism he or she accepts the responsibility of making every choice in light of specific *meaning*—of making every choice assertive rather than protective. For, in this age, to make a "realistic" choice, to assert that such and such a choice was made because it is, in fact, *as it is in life* is to say no more than that the choice was made in such a way as to avoid any potential criticism.

Everything which does not put forward the meaning of the play impedes the meaning of the play. To do too much or too little is to mitigate and weaken the meaning. The acting, the design, the direction should all consist only of that bare minimum necessary to put forward the action. Anything else is embellishment.

The problem of realism in design and its deleterious effects should be studied as a guide to the similar problem in acting. Actors for the last thirty years have been hiding in a ludicrously incorrect understanding of the Stanislavsky System and employing incorrectly understood jargon as an excuse for not acting.

Almost *never* are the teachings of Stanislavsky employed as an incitement; they are offered as an excuse—a substitute for action. The purpose of the system was, and is, to *free* the actor from extraneous considerations and permit him or her to turn all of his or her concentration to the objective, which is not "this performance," but the *meaning* of the play.

The notions of objective, activity, moment, beat, and so on are all devoted toward reducing the scene to a specific action which is true to the author's intention, and physically capable of being performed. The purpose of these concepts is to incite the actor to act. They all prod the actor to answer the one question which is capable of freeing him from self-consciousness and permitting him or her to become an artist: "What am I doing?"

The purpose of the Stanislavsky System of thought was to permit the actor to freely give the truth, the highest truth, of him- or herself, to the ideas, to the words of the playwright. The system teaches specificity as a tool of release rather than constraint. To make the transition from realism to truth, from self-consciousness to creativity, the artist must learn how to be specific to *something greater than him- or herself* on different levels of abstraction: the meaning of the scene, the intention of the author, the thrust of the play. But never "reality," or "truth," in general.

That to which one must learn to be true is not one's vision of reality, which, by its very nature, will make the actor more self-conscious and less able to act, but to the *aspirations* central to the meaning of the play and expressed in the objectives of the characters.

All theater is about aspirations—it is about longing and the desire for answers—small theater concerns itself with small questions, and great theater with great. In any case, the question at stake is never the *comfort* of the artist.

To have this never-ceasing concern with one's personal comfort, with the "naturalness" of the script, the blocking, the direction, the other actors, is to reduce every play to the *same* play—to a play about "That which I am not prepared to do" or "Those choices I will not make, and which I cannot be *forced* to make."

And so what?

Let us cast aside concerns of comfortability on stage. Why should one be comfortable acting Othello or St. Joan? The study of all theatrical artists should be action. *Movement.* A first test of all elements should be not "Do I feel comfortable (i.e., *immobile*) when considering it?" but "Do I feel *impelled*? Do I start to *move*? Does it make me want to *do* something?"

Actors are many times afraid of feeling foolish. We should teach each other to feel *power* rather than fear when faced with the necessity of choice, to seek out and enjoy, to feel the life-giving pleasure of the power of artistic choice.

Howard Barker (b. 1947)

Playwright Howard Barker has described his ideas for a theater of catastrophe in a number of essays which have been collected together in his book, Arguments for a Theatre. *In the first selection printed here, "The Consolations of Catastrophe," Barker explains the role of the audience in the theatrical experience. Brecht had drawn a comparison between the effects of his own epic theater and what he called dramatic theater. Likewise in the second selection presented here, "The Humanist Theatre" and "The Catastrophic Theatre" Barker draws a comparison between the effects of what he calls "humanist" theater and his own theater of catastrophe. In the third selection, "The Idea of Promiscuity in the Theatre of Catastrophe," Barker discusses in more detail the relationship between playwright, theatrical experience, and audience.*

THE CONSOLATIONS OF CATASTROPHE

'Once, when I saw men with miserable faces staring at the ground, I nutted them. In streets in Attica where I ran yobbish prior to the war, I said cheer up you cunt and if they did not grin to order rammed my forehead through their gristle. This was instinct but now I see it also must be politics.'

The Bite of the Night, Act I

For some years I have been attempting to create a theatre which lent its audience rights of interpretation. To do this has involved transgressing in the two sacred groves of contemporary theatre—Clarity and Realism. The text or production which is lauded for its clarity is inevitably the one which allows the least ambiguity, the least contradiction, and the least room for evading the smothering sense that someone is giving you a meaning to take away with you. It is a form of oppression masquerading as enlightenment. Similarly, the emphasis on Realism, now a term almost defunct but still plucked like the last string of a battered guitar, presupposes a moral weakness in the audience, which must be presented with positive landmarks, like posts in an estuary, if it is not to be dangerously lost in the wastes of imagination. These dominating critical categories are, however, potent only so long as there is common ethical ground among artist, actor and audience. As long as the moral landscape in which theatre operated was morally coherent, whether Christian or Bourgeois-Humanist, the artist's right to exhort, elucidate and educate was unquestioned. The last decade has indicated such a deterioration of the moral consensus that it is now reasonable to ask whether even the most cherished statements of moral rectitude command a genuine assent. For example, the voluntarist statement 'It is self-evident that all men are created equal' does not, after a decade of Thatcherism and the international retreat from Official Communism, carry the same aura of authority that it once did. It requires examination, it requires to be reborn, and to be reborn, requires to be rediscovered. The function of a theatre in this climate, whose laissez-faire coolness among men points to further fractures in social morality in spite of all propaganda to the contrary, must be to return the responsibility for moral argument to the audience itself. I believe this offers the artist new opportunities but also demands of him new practices.

I have suggested that in certain states of society it is better to take nothing for granted, and a crisis in public morality provides an aperture for a new kind of theatre which I believe must locate its creative tension not between characters and arguments on the stage but between the audience and the stage itself. This theatre intervenes at an earlier point in human relations than that at which it has done heretofore. The usual focus of contemporary theatre is how we live with one another on given moral predicates ('it is bad to hurt people', 'the unfortunate should induce feelings of pity', etc.), but clearly there is now a problem with the predicates themselves. A braver theatre asks the audience to test the validity of the categories it believes it lives by. In other words, it is not about life as it is lived at all, but about life as it might be lived, about the thought which is not licensed, and about the abolished unconscious. Sympathy, and the sudden liquidation of sympathy, the permanent disruption of character, the instability of motive, are some of the means available to this project. The abolition of routine distinctions between good and bad actions, the sense that good and evil co-exist within the same psyche, that freedom and kindness may not be compatible, that pity is both a poison and an erotic stimulant, that laughter might be as often oppressive as it is rarely liberating, all these constitute the territory of a new theatrical practice, which lends its audience the potential of a personal re-assessment in the light of dramatic action. The consequence of this is a modern form of tragedy which I would call Catastrophism.

The fallacy most warmly embraced by the entertainment industry in times of moral uncertainty is the one which insists depressed peoples hunger for song and oblivion. But as many hunger for the problem to be embraced as hunger for its abolition. A theatre of Catastrophe, like the tragic theatre, insists on the limits of tolerance as its territory. It inhabits the area of maximum risk, both to the imagination and invention of its author, and to the comfort of its audience. It commands the loyalty and attention of those for whom the raucous repetition of social platitudes of both left and right appear as aridities. But the conflict experienced between the audience and what it witnesses, its exposure to the unbidden thought, creates pain and even resentment. It is distinctly not an experience associated with entertainment, and consequently an audience needs to be both prepared and, as is the case with all new theatre, educated in its own freedom. Not being conducted either by fetishisms of Clarity or Realism, it must be liberated from its fear of obscurity and encouraged to welcome its moments of loss. These moments of loss involve the breaking of the narrative thread, the sudden suspension of the story, the interruption of the obliquely related interlude, and a number of devices designed to complicate and to overwhelm the audience's habitual method of seeing. The panic which can seize an audience, oppressed by years of trained obeisance, at 'losing the thread' (as if life were a thread), whether the author's (who since Brecht has been given the status of a deity in modern theatre, the one who knows all and is permanently in command of his thoughts) or the director's (who must impose coherence at all costs) must be replaced by a sense of security in not knowing, and welcoming the same risks the author himself took in charting unknown territory, and the actors took in making the journey with maps. As Adorno wrote of the great nineteenth-century novels, whose ambition the theatre must imitate if it is not to be made yet more tolerable and yet more brief, it derives its meaning precisely from the dissolution of coherent meaning.

The aim of a theatre of catastrophe in overwhelming the normal barriers of tolerance in its audience opens it to the complaint most frequently levelled at my work—the charge of pessimism. But pain and apparent defeat are not synonymous with pessimism, which is a narrow concept dear to the totalitarian mind and outlawed by the totalitarian state, where the idea of 'the depressing thought' as a threat to public morale has maimed literature and art. The nauseating cheerfulness of socialist realist literature, with its exhortations and beckonings to an impossible future, forced its practitioners to exercise their depression in private and contributed to the high suicide rate among 'progressive' artists. A similar imperative to enlighten, amuse, and stimulate good thoughts of a collective nature (family, nation, party, community) clings to the carnival mania of the left and the moral crusade of the right. But the banging of the drum is hollow and the rhetoric shallow. It is simply not credible. It is not the sum of experience. The catastrophe is also the property of the people, and it is the spectacle of human pain, of charismatic defeat, that constitutes the fascination and strength of tragedy. My own theatre has never aimed for solidarity, but to address the soul where it feels its difference. It is intended to plunge beneath the ground of common belief and to test the ground of first principles. The exhaustion felt by the audience in a theatre of this nature is not enervating, but the imagination is stimulated and the structures of morality are tested, even if only to be affirmed. But it is the audience who must calibrate and assess. Traditional tragedy was a restatement of public morality over the corpse of the transgressing protagonist—thus Brecht saw catharsis as essentially passive. But in a theatre of Catastrophe there is no restoration of certitudes, and in a sense more compelling and less manipulated than in the Epic theatre, it is the audience which is freed into authority. In a culture now so rampantly populist that the cultural distinctions of right and left have evaporated, the public have a right of access to a theatre which is neither brief nor relentlessly uplifting, but which insists on complexity and pain, and the beauty that can only be created from the spectacle of pain. In Catastrophe, whose imaginative ambition exposes the reactionary content in the miserabilism of everyday life, lies the possibility of reconstruction.

THE HUMANIST THEATRE

We all really agree.
When we laugh we are together.
Art must be understood.
Wit greases the message.
The actor is a man/woman not
unlike the author.
The production must be clear.
We celebrate our unity.
The critic is already
on our side.
The message is important.
The audience is educated
and goes home
happy
or
fortified.

THE CATASTROPHIC THEATRE

We only sometimes agree.
Laughter conceals fear.
Art is a problem of understanding.
There is no message.
The actor is different in kind.

The audience cannot grasp
everything; nor did the author.
We quarrel to love.
The critic must suffer like
everyone else.
The play is important.
The audience is divided
and goes home
disturbed
or
amazed.

THE IDEA OF PROMISCUITY IN THE THEATRE OF CATASTROPHE

The Critical Theatre, which for the sake of argument I shall take to be that of Brecht, Shaw and the bulk of our contemporaries, is essentially a theatre of clear objectives. It is predicated on the idea of 'saying'. In the Critical Theatre the play 'says' something to the audience, and the elucidation of this 'saying' is the function of the production, the aim of the director and actors alike. The contemporary audience is now thoroughly versed in this method, and a party to it, by training and experience. So much so, in fact, that it brings with it the demand that the play should 'say' unambiguously—a demand which, if unsatisfied, leaves this audience with the nagging sense that the dramatist and the actors are guilty of an act of collective bad faith. Consequently, the Critical Theatre moves inexorably towards an art of anodyne humanism, in which the actors and the audience tacitly collaborate in an act of 'saying' and the theatre diminishes itself in pursuit of the limited objective of communicating an idea, albeit in the form of a narrative. Behind this lies the notion of the author as a 'good' man or woman, whose trade is principally the dispensing of wisdom and whose vocation is the creation of harmony.

In this collective deception, where the audience is traditionally ranked above the stage like benches of judges for receiving and validating the idea, and where clarity becomes a fetish, falsely democratic in its elimination of ambiguity, what the play 'says' becomes merely the pretext for debate—the play is a means, not an end. What occurs therefore, when the play says nothing? What chaos ensues when the text refuses to admit an objective and evades clarity? What nightmare awaits an audience when the time-honoured Brechtian/Stanislavskian contract is denied, the contract which has as its main clause the obligation to communicate the idea? This is breakdown, of course, in the essentially polite social relations of the contemporary theatre, leading to a suspicion that the dramatist has no morals and the actors are being misused. Under these circumstances, the theatre becomes not a locus for the restatement of collectively-approved positions—hostility to war, hatred of exploitation, the rights of women—not a place in other words, for the rehearsal of humanist platitudes—but a site, or a landscape, for a morally promiscuous journey in which—since there is no objective—the detours are likely to be as significant as the route itself. The single most important consequence of such a mutiny against governing principles is the overthrow of the audience.

The notion of the audience as an indivisible authority with rights of judgement over works of imagination is central to the Critical Theatre, but it is an authority only so long as the dramatist regards himself as tutor, enlightener, truth-teller. If he or she refuses to plead an argument, and offers instead the spectacle of a free imagination disciplined not by morality but by an aesthetic of language and vision the audience is obliged to approach the work with neither power nor contempt—it is not under these circumstances anything strictly 'truthful' that is on show, there is no criterion from politics or consensus against which it can be judged. The net effect of this is that the stage acquires an authority over the audience, and in symbolic space this would entail the audience sitting on an inferior plane to the actor, who is no longer the didactic agent of clarity but something dangerously unreliable, something altogether more hypnotic and unlicensed. This is a theatre which abolishes debate, in which the play is a substitute for debate, and without obligation to notions of entertainment or enlightenment, neither 'delightful' nor instructive, it resolves nothing—on the contrary, resolution is anathema: it is tragedy without catharsis, tragedy in which the audience is implicated in the acts of cruelty it witnesses, and from which there is no relief or refuge in the reiteration of the utilitarian concept of the public good. It is, consequently, a theatre of silence and contemplation.

Given that dissension in mass society is almost an obligation, a theatre of promiscuity requires no special justification—indeed to talk of art requiring justification at all is one of the melancholy consequences of humanist culture—but its particular interest lies in its refutation of the *solution* as a moral category, for just as the Critical Theatre *says* the *idea*, it implies necessarily the idea of the *solution*, which is, broadly speaking, the elimination of pain as the universal objective of human effort. The humanist theatre, along with its Marxist and Christian allies, poses painlessness, the elimination of tensions, as ideals against which the drama is judged; conflict exists only to be resolved. Art does not simply exist—it is annexed as part of the armoury in the struggle for human perfection. The narrating of facts in the researched play, the description of conflict or poverty of communication in the domestic play, the retailing of injustices in the play of issues, comedies of misunderstandings, are all essentially demonstrations of the possibility of the Solution for which the audience hankers, and which it pathetically believes it can discover in the mind of the dramatist. It seems to me there is a profound sadness in the relationship between the Reconciler—the dramatist—and the Seekers after Harmony—the audience—in the humanist theatre, a Utopian pathos which affects both Chekhov's appalling gift for renunciation and Brecht's hammering insistence that we can discover the Truth if we look hard enough. Even an idea as seemingly innocuous as Harmony hides within it the shadow of the torture chamber.

If the Theatre of Catastrophe willingly divests the dramatist of his divine status as dispenser of truth or harmony, and the audience of its absurd status as monolithic critic, what is it that constitutes the substance of the transaction between them? What is the theatre that has no Saying? Its method can only be the erosion of narrative, because narrative is itself the first element in the construction of moral meaning. What occurs in the form of consecutive scenes, or in real time played on the stage, inevitably implies a moral perspective unless the seductive effect of the stage is subverted, as I attempted in *Victory*—a highly narrative play but one in which intense imaginative efforts are made—by me in the first instance—to prevent the audience wandering into a state of dreamy sympathy with a preordained morality, the sort of Christian–humanist ethic that says all victims are good. Susan Bradshaw is relentlessly bad, even if she is a victim of political pendulums.

In later works of Catastrophic Theatre, I have attempted to deny narrative its authority by resorting to digression—certainly in *The Bite of the Night*, where time itself is also dethroned from its eminence, and in my most recent play, *Rome*, where the existence of one narrative is continually displaced by the eruption of others which only tangentially relate to it in terms of theme. I might also mention in this regard *The Last Supper*, the first play of The Wrestling School, which parallels one familiar narrative with parables of a completely amoral, and possibly incomprehensible, nature—or indeed, *The Possibilities*, ten related plays, which are simply scenes, on the theme of making terrible but necessary mistakes, the very idea of the Necessary Mistake being wholly inappropriate to the Theatre of Saying or a Theatre of Solutions. Apart from this disruption of narrative discipline, a second means of dislocation—and dislocation is the function of art in a time of smothering consensus—is the employment of the Chorus, which stands outside, and interferes with, the working of the Realist narrative, often in a form which refuses the audience the opportunity to take its statements for granted—I am thinking here of the wholly unreliable chorus in *Golgo*—but which also permits the restoration of poetry to the stage, thereby insisting on the distinction between the stage and common life. If the humanist theatre is essentially unpoetic, because it can only assert the collective language, the Catastrophic Theatre insists on the distinction between stage and street, and on the peculiarities of the dramatist's voice; it will not renounce its licence to speculate both on how things are done, and also on how things are said.

The question so often raised about all forms of artistic practice—'how does this help us?', the anxious cry of the alienated in mass society—is best countered by refuting its very formulation, which threatens to diminish art and to render it as utilitarian as any other kind of manufacture. The Catastrophic Theatre cannot satisfy this mechanistic demand because its ecstatic possibility lies in its denial of the possibility of Solution. As a form of theatre it is so overloaded, so apparently excessive in language, metaphor, event, diversity of form and image, so promiscuous in its speculation, it denies the very concept of the ordered life even as an ideal. It is a non-Utopian art which pits cruelty against pity and recognizes their coexistence in the guilty and the innocent alike. Who could take sides when the court of Charles II exposes the spectacle of Scrope, maimed, in a wedding cake? The merciless humour of Charles II draws the audience into a conspiracy of his wit rather than into indignation at the fate of a decent man. It is indeed difficult to state whether any character in a Catastrophic play commits a bad act, so complex is the state of emotion which surrounds it. I have often said that the audience for this kind of theatre needs to re-fashion itself, since what it brings from conventional theatre merely excludes it from the experience—there needs to be a surrender of the critical habit, the value-assessment of the Brechtian school, the posture of offence, and, instead, a wilful abnegation of loyalties. So much contemporary theatre consists of the statement of loyalties, to gender, to ideology, to concepts of the progressive, even to melancholy, whilst the Catastrophic Theatre replaces loyalty with an aesthetic of will to experience—it discovers light in the unlikeliest places and air where it seemed at first impossible to breathe. It is my contention that the twin disciplines of entertainment and enlightenment have relegated theatre to a position of philosophical impotence, and that its much-vaunted ability to 'respond' to issues, its journalistic flirtations with research, have merely rendered it down to a classifiable commodity, a suitable product for the morality of a national theatre. In a promiscuous theatre, nothing is given or predicated, neither rebellion nor abnegation, and its aims are not to console but to stimulate a restlessness which is not—as in the classic tragic formula—discharged, but carried away by the individuals of the audience whose contrasting reactions to what they have witnessed divides them against themselves. I repeat that no one is educated by a play of this sort—no information, useful or otherwise, is communicated, nor is communication the essence. The actor is elevated, through language and through the extent of the pain he embodies, to a dominant status, one which obviates pity or judgement. The effect of this is that debate—the stimulation of which is the purpose of the Critical play—is abolished, the grounds for it subsumed *in* the production, rather than the production providing dramatized material to stimulate argument. The promiscuity of the imagination in the Catastrophic play, its unapologetic intimacy with the forbidden—indeed, the rupturing of the forbidden as a category—evacuates the territory of values. The production must become, in essence, a poem, and, like a poem, not reducible to a series of statements in other forms. In these terms, the experience of pain, which is the most significant emotion, is not viewed as a subject for amelioration, or abolition, nor made material for a moral argument, a pretext for Utopian aspirations, but is affirmed in itself, and for itself. The liberating of pain from its social subjects, and from its so-called objective conditions, is possible only in a theatre which is essentially promiscuous in moral terms, and, far from becoming what is inevitably described as 'pessimistic', affirms the individual's right to chaos, extremity and self-description.

Howard Barker, "Saintliness, Death and the Perfect Family"

In the following comment on Hated Nightfall *Howard Barker compares the aspirations of his main character, Dancer, to those of a saint.*

Saintliness, Death and the Perfect Family

If the sign of the saint is sacrifice, it is a sign illuminated by the vehemence with which he or she repudiates the world. For the saint finds the world lacking, and his desire is focused on what can never be satisfied. His passion can discover no worthwhile object, and the more searching is his gaze, the more contamination is revealed. For Dancer, all is transparent, and this transparency is appalling pain, for we require to be deceived, it is the condition of social existence. Without deception there is perhaps no hope. Dancer possesses desire, and this desire lends him terrible insights. Also, it impales him on a spike of solitude. For the saint is lured by human love only to discover its inadequacy. Evidence of abjection piles against his door, producing in him on immaculate desire for the single purity nothing can besmirch—his own death, a moment of ecstasy which the violence of others can only enhance, and which stands as enduring testimony that even in death there is a *hierarchy* of excellence . . .

The failure of the saint is therefore mandatory, the path strewn with the wreckage of a shattered sensibility a necessary way to the cross. It requires only the application of faith to the wounds of the traumatized ego for the sacrifice to become a sign of love . . .

Dancer is poised on the threshold of an age which the more desperately it announced its total novelty, the more sinisterly came the echoes of the past. For all its philosophy of materiality, the Bolshevik Revolution opened with a symbolic murder as antique as massacre itself, and shortly afterwards its unsentimental architect was embalmed with the hysterical palaver of an Egyptian god. Dancer's private inclinations until this cataclysm have been concentrated in the servant's erotic congress with his master's wife, a sexual mutiny enshrined in tradition, but Catastrophe is also opportunity, and Revolution's seductive fallacy has always been the promise of absolute licence. Three centuries of revolution, to speak only of the modern age, remind us of the speed at which the ruptured reins of one social order are fashioned into the garrotte of the next, but in the exhilaration of the vortex the ordered life dissolves and what beckons through chaos is *permission*. Here, one who aspires to sainthood might rinse his personality in the foaming hydrants of a collapsed authority, wring himself out in a new shape and discover performances of self which however insubstantial their foundations, are incandescent with *invention* . . .

Dancer luxuriates in revenge until revenge is seen to be, while necessary, all the same inadequate, unsubtle and above all, not a work of art, for the saint is first and foremost his own work of art, exhibited primarily to himself. But neither saints nor works of art are socially desired, for they are disruptive to the bourgeois and the collectivist alike. Dancer knows that whilst his immaculate temper might be *used*, it can never be legitimized. He is the *Transient Phenomenon*, use-value epitomized, function in the grinding mechanisms of History that substitutes new pain for old. Why not therefore, make of this transience a perfect epiphany? Since revolution is unforgivable except by reference to its alibi—the future, and since reaction is grotesque with sham dignities, it is the brief life of the present which is the refuge of imagination, an inebriating atmosphere where both saint and artist perform their seductive dance and encourage a similar motion in others. All obstacles to this brief ecstasy are literally destroyed until the closing down of night—the inevitable imperative of History—reminds the saint that sacrifice is both his apotheosis and his destiny . . .

Dancer's wilful martyrdom in the bosom of History's Most Perfect Family is a profound gesture of refusal, an insight into a future which shudders and booms with massacre and negation. It is a final act of self-description by one whose passionate gesture earns him—as befits a saint—the half-reluctant pity of his erstwhile enemies . . .

Howard Barker

Writing About Drama and Theater

Writing about drama and theater is both the same and yet different from writing about the genres of poetry or prose. It is the same in that certain conventions need to be learned, along with some basic concepts and terms that have specific meaning within the field. The glossary in Appendix 2 is designed to help you in this regard, and you will probably want to consult it regularly. To write about drama and theater, for example, you have to know the difference between plot and action, between antagonist and protagonist, between aside and soliloquy. You need to be able to recognize that many characters fit into time-honored patterns or types, allowing certain expectations to adhere to them. Such is the case, for example, with braggart soldiers, shrewish wives, and vengeful ghosts in plays from classical to neoclassical times, and with dowager widows, young virgins, and courageous heroes from the nineteenth-century well-made-play tradition to the present.

More central to the process of writing about drama is to realize that the text on the page constitutes much less of the story than it does in a work of fiction, and that one way a play achieves meaning depends greatly on its performance. What a character may say or do must be considered in light of how the lines are delivered or the action is acted, and the apparently unadorned text is thus somewhat more difficult to understand than it might be in a prose story written only to be read. A play text can still draw on much of the verbal and emotional power that fuels poetry and prose fiction, developing complex images and spinning out a theme or a motif, as Shakespeare does, for example, with the images of rotting and disease in *Hamlet*. The study of plays as both literature and theater over the course of time will develop your dramatic imagination, your ability to see and hear the details of performance in your own head, and this imagining of plays not only offers the greatest pleasure but also feeds into writing about them.

The long-term goal of writing about drama and theater is a more complete understanding of what plays, or a certain play, may be capable of accomplishing, both onstage and in your own imagination. Beyond that, because plays are social artifacts, they can offer windows into current or distant cultures and behaviors, and much, much more. Given that plays share a certain verbal complexity with poetry (and with many works of fiction), and that this complexity is further complicated by their physical representation on the stage, current and past, it may seem that to write well about a play's literary or theatrical aspects is a daunting task. In many ways it is, but there are some basic rules to follow, and there are some fruitful ways of thinking about plays that will make the task of writing easier and more enjoyable.

To begin with, you should know well the play you have chosen to write about. This may sound like stating the obvious, but it is not. Even if you are working on only one scene or section of a play, you need to know how the particular situation arose, what stake each character has in the scene, what the conflict is about, and how this part of the play contributes toward the ultimate resolution of that conflict. Practice visualizing and hearing the dramatic moments of the play, annotating the text as you read it. Pay particular attention to moments when you find yourself moved, excited, or especially interested in the outcome of the immediate action, and to speeches or exchanges of dialogue that seem charged. Also pay attention to the places where you feel bored, determining what, if anything, the playwright used to hold the interest of an audience watching this part of the play. Make notes on the text every time you read it.

Many plays in this anthology are available on videotape, but you should keep in mind the problems associated with seeing only one acted version of a play. You may always be tempted to see it this way in your mind's eye, and your preconceptions may hamper your ability to envision alternative ways of construing the lines or acting the script, thus limiting both your grasp of the play and your ability to push beyond what has already been thought and said about the play by the actors or the director. One way of treating this potential problem is to see one version with a group of other students and then to discuss the production as an interpretation of the text. Another way is to see more than one version of the play and to form your own opinion about which elements in each version seemed most successful. In any case you should try to imagine alternative ways of performing the play, thinking about how these alternatives may highlight some of its different strengths.

It may help to think about a play's action as being experienced in two quite different ways. One is as a text that you read as if it were any literary text. You can reread it. You can connect disparate parts with one another, in or out of the order of their occurrence in the play; you can leave out intervening parts, jump from the beginning to the ending, or focus on similar actions or on events that occur only in the middle of the play. Thinking about the play in this way, you can treat the written text as if it were a puzzle, noting similarities and differences among various pieces, seeing how the play *as a text* works toward a certain organic unity. To use the example of *Hamlet* again, you might note that Hamlet's first and last lines are self-characterizing puns, and then follow up this observation by examining other examples of dialogue in which Hamlet and perhaps other characters pun or refer to themselves in self-conscious literary ways. You would thus be subjecting the play to a kind of literary analysis, and because it is a verbal structure it will readily respond to your examination. But the lines that you have singled out are in fact spoken as dialogue, acted, and clearly, some important aspects of the play are necessarily left out in a purely literary analysis.

A second way to think about a play is as an experience in the theater, where the first line of text is followed by the second line, the second by the third, and so on, the beginning by the middle and the middle by the end, in that order and only in that order. Your theatrical experience is in this regard a *linear* one, subject to the immediate configuration of actor, stage, and any other important performative elements, such as song or spectacle. The kinds of observations you might make from this starting point would be very different from those of a purely literary analysis. Far more emphasis would fall on the elements of staging that help produce a state of tension, anticipation, suspense, surprise, humor, or horror in the spectator. Beginning *Hamlet*, for example, with a bell tolling at midnight would have enormous emotional consequences from this point of view: it would help set the expectations of the audience, perhaps sending a chill of recognition through the spectators and literally sounding a graveyard theme, suggesting the haunting of ghosts and the grim specter of death hovering nearby. All these ominous elements, of course, are introduced in the course of the play, but in some important ways they are all there from the start, planted by a theatrical beginning. While remaining peripheral to the dialogue, the play's theatrical opening arguably constitutes one of the most important features of the entire first part. In other plays as well, theatrical spectacle, including scenic splendor, violent or suggestive action, background sounds, meaningful gestures, and even singing, often provides potent counterparts to verbal and literary qualities. These effects are worth noting and worth writing about, since they are intimately bound up in the ways a play can be understood. Writing about a play's theatrical power as well its verbal richness can help illuminate the fullness of a play's potential.

One useful method of getting started on a writing topic is to consider one or more of Aristotle's six elements of drama (discussed in the General Introduction) as starting points for further examination. The elements are plot, character, diction or language, thought or theme, melody or music, and spectacle. Aristotle's categories describe the basic qualities of almost any play: the first four relate to literary composition, the last two to performance. They are useful in criticism precisely because they provide a focus for the possibilities of interpretation. What does the arrangement of the plot allow? How does the plot relate to the story? How does the plot develop key themes? How do characters define themselves in this play? How does this playwright's particular use of language affect our understanding of the play? How do music and spectacle enhance our understanding and appreciation of the play's deepest concerns? These questions about a play's basic operations can easily lead to other, larger questions about the social and material functions of plays in society, about the psychological truths inherent in their productions, and about the cultural power that drama and theater continue to exercise over our collective imagination. Since at least the time of Aristotle, writing about drama has offered the opportunity to explore a form crucial to representing our world both in conflict and at peace, and to representing ourselves.

SOME PRACTICAL MATTERS OF FORM

Some conventions of writing about drama and theater may be useful to remember. First, when writing about a play, always refer to the action as occurring in the present ("Hamlet tells Rosencrantz and Guildenstern that they will never understand the heart of his mystery"); refer to the author's writing of the play in the past ("Shakespeare completed *Hamlet* by 1600"), but refer to literary and dramatic strategies in the present ("Over and over again in his plays, Shakespeare uses the pattern of a brother betraying a brother") and refer to your viewing or other consideration of the play as occurring in the present ("A second wave of action is brought on by the ghost of Hamlet's father").

When you quote a speech from a play, the conventional practice is to refer to it by act and scene and line number immediately following the quotation: "There are more things in heaven and earth, Horatio / Than are dreamt of in your philosophy" (1.5.166–67). An alternative practice is to use Roman numerals for the act and scene: (I.v.166–67). Note that in excerpts from plays written in verse (as in the preceding example from Shakespeare's *Hamlet*), the lines are separated by a virgule (/); otherwise the lines are understood to run on. If the play is not broken into acts and scenes, or if the copy you quote form has only line numbering running through the play, simply use the standard abbreviation for "lines": (ll. 459–460). The reference to a stage direction is abbreviated *s.d.* and keyed to the line it follows: "*Re-enter* PLAYERS *with recorders*" (3.2.359 s.d.). Remember that you should use quotations to prove a point or build an argument—never string together lines from the play and consider them self-explanatory. One of your most important jobs is to discuss what the lines say and what they mean; you can be sure that the meaning you find will not always be evident to your reader.

Secondary readings often help to clarify issues found in plays, and a good number of excerpts from critical writings have been included in this book for that purpose. You may want to seek out the articles themselves to provide a larger context for these excerpts, or you may want to consult Appendix 3 for our suggestions for further reading. It lists many useful leads to other resources. In any case, a word needs to be said here about quotation etiquette as it relates to the serious issue of plagiarism. Plagiarism is taking a quotation or an important concept (even a paraphrase) from someone else's writing and using it as your own, without giving credit to the original source. The rule of thumb is always to err on the conservative side: if in doubt, give the source.

There are two standard ways of referring to your sources: footnotes and endnotes. A footnote appears at the bottom of the page on which the quotation appears, including all the relevant data about the source: author, title, place of publication, date, and page number. Endnotes include the same information, but they appear at the end of the paper. A third way of presenting source information is to cite the sources parenthetically in the text of the paper, usually with the name of the author and the page number of the quotation, and provide a list of works cited with full bibliographical information at the end of the paper. In this system, footnotes are used to discuss matters relating to the text. Whatever method of citation you decide upon or are required to use, treat your sources fully and consistently to ensure that your own abilities are clear to the reader and that your references can be tracked down for more details.

Glossary

absurd, theater of the A type of late-twentieth-century theater and drama characterized by abstract settings and by arbitrary action which often contradicts dialogue. Absurdism regards the human condition much as the existentialists did. The term was coined by Martin Esslin; an example of the genre is Samuel Beckett's *Endgame*.

act A division of the action of a play. Ancient Greek drama was not formally divided into acts, but the Roman poet Horace suggested a five-act structure, and this pattern was adopted by such seventeenth-century French neoclassical dramatists as Jean Racine. A three-act structure is common in twentieth-century drama.

action According to Aristotle, the causally linked sequence of events in a play, consisting of a beginning, middle, and end. More generally, the human process that a play imitates.

aesthetics The study of the nature of beauty.

alienation effect The usual translation of Brecht's *Verfremdungseffekt*, a technique developed to make characters and action seem unusual to audiences in order to force a confrontation with the social and political implications of a play.

allegory A literary or dramatic technique that uses characters, places, and action to represent more abstract political, moral, historical, or religious ideas.

amphitheater A semicircular theater in which the playing space is faced by rising tiers of seats.

allusion An implicit reference to people, events, or literary works that the author assumes the audience will recognize.

anachronism Using people, places, or things that are out of chronological order with the rest of the fictive world or narrative.

antagonist The character or force that opposes the protagonist.

antiphony Alternate or responsive singing between individuals or groups, as in the antiphonal singing of tropes.

apron The part of a stage that extends in front of the proscenium arch.

avant-garde "Advance group," a term that refers to innovative or experimental work, usually in the nineteenth and twentieth centuries.

archetype A term derived from the psychological theories of Carl Jung, who posited the existence of a collective unconscious containing images that are recognized by all people.

aside A remark, inaudible to the other characters, made by a dramatic character directly to the audience. Like the soliloquy, the aside is a convention that allows direct disclosure of a character's inner thoughts.

balcony In theaters from the seventeenth through twentieth century, the ascending rows of bench seats located opposite the stage and above the orchestra.

biomechanics Both the concept and the complex of techniques developed by Vsevolod Meyerhold for the physical training of actors, including acrobatic and choreographic training.

blank verse An English verse form consisting of unrhymed iambic pentameter lines.

border Short curtains (sometimes flats) suspended at intervals behind the proscenium arch to conceal overhead lights and machinery about the stage.

box seating Small structures arranged around the sides of the stage and auditorium; beginning in the late seventeenth century, the most expensive type of seating.

cabaret A restaurant serving food and drink; site for innovative performances in twentieth-century avant-garde drama.

canon An accepted or authorized body of texts associated with a writer or genre.

catastrophe The moment in a drama (particularly in a classical tragedy) that ends the major conflict in the plot, for example, the death of the protagonist.

catharsis "Purging" of the emotions of pity and fear experienced by the audience. According to Aristotle, catharsis is the effect of tragedy. Although the meaning of the term is disputed, it is often thought to imply that tragedy produces an emotionally therapeutic effect.

character A fictional person appearing in a play or other literary work and having particular motives and distinctive speech and action.

chorus A group of costumed and masked men who sang and danced as a group in Greek tragedy and comedy.

City Dionysia An annual spring festival in Athens honoring the god Dionysus. The festival included dramatic competitions.

classical drama Specifically, the drama produced in Greece between 534 B.C. and 336 B.C.; more generally, Greek and Roman drama.

climax See *crisis*.

closet drama Plays meant to be read rather than performed.

comedy of manners Usually late seventeenth-century and eighteenth-century comedies dealing with the manners or social behavior of upper-class characters.

commedia dell'arte Italian comedy of the fifteenth through seventeenth centuries performed by itinerant troupes and featuring improvised plots and stock characters.

confidante A character to whom another character gives private information.

conflict The struggle between the protagonist and antagonist that drives the rising action of the plot and that is ended in the catastrophe and resolved in the denouement.

constructivism A nonrealistic style of set design associated with the work of Vsevolod Meyerhold, who held that sets ought to be machines for acting rather than representations of particular places.

convention A manner of presentation of drama understood by audiences and actors.

Corpus Christi A spring festival established in the fourteenth century in honor of the Eucharist. Cycle plays were often performed at Corpus Christi.

crisis The turning point in a play's action; it is preceded by the rising action and followed by the falling action.

cross-dressing Cross-gendered casting in which men in women's costumes play female characters or women in men's costumes play male characters.

cycle plays Series of plays dramatizing Christian history from the Creation to the Last Judgment. Also called mystery plays.

dada A nonsense term applied to an avant-garde movement in Europe in the 1920s which celebrated the irrational.

decorum The neoclassical idea that the subject matter, action, language, and moral purpose of a play should be stylistically integrated, and more specifically, that a character's behavior must be in keeping with his or her class.

denouement The part of a plot that follows the crisis and includes the resolution.

deus ex machina "God from the machine," referring to a deity who descended to ensure a proper conclusion in some Greek tragedies; more generally, a contrived ending.

dialogue Exchange of words between characters in drama or fiction.

discovery According to Aristotle, a character's movement from ignorance to knowledge.

doubling The practice of having an actor perform more than one part in a play.

drama A literary composition in dialogue or verse which concerns the actions of fictional characters.

dramatic irony The effect that occurs when the audience is apprised of facts hidden from a character, or when a character's words or acts have an implication of which he or she is unaware.

environmental theater Performance in which there is no distinction between playing space and audience space.

epic theater A type of performance influenced by Erwin Piscator and popularized by Brecht, in which various techniques of playwriting, set design, and acting are used to stimulate the audience to view a play objectively rather than subjectively.

episode A dramatic scene in Greek tragedy distinct from the choral odes; more generally, any incident or event in a play.

exodos The final scene and exit of the characters and chorus in a Greek play.

existentialism A philosophy that underlies absurdism; its chief principles are the absence of transcendental values, the isolation of human beings, and the lack of causality in the universe.

exposition Introductory material that, in a play or narrative, introduces setting, characters, and other facts essential to understanding the work.

expressionism An early-twentieth-century movement that reacted to realism through the use of symbolic presentation of meaning and the attempt to present emotions directly.

facade stage A nonrepresentational, permanent background for action.

farce Literally, "stuffed" with laughs; a short comic play that relies on misunderstandings, mix-ups, mistaken identities, and physical humor.

flat A structure of canvas stretched over a wooden frame, on which scenery is painted.

fourth wall realism A realistic style of setting in which the stage is set as a room with one wall missing.

fringe theater Small, nontraditional theaters in pubs, warehouses, and so on, with limited and nontraditional seating, catering to specialized audiences, and located considerably off the West End in London. See *off off Broadway*.

gallery In sixteenth-century theaters in England, a covered platform for spectators; more generally, the highest and cheapest seating in seventeenth-century through nineteenth-century theaters. Galleries were placed one above another and surrounding the thrust stage. See *balcony*.

genre "Kind" or "type"; generally, any type or kind of literature or drama, such as comedy or tragedy.

hamartia   A term used by Aristotle to describe the tragic protagonist's decisive mistake or error that precipitates the tragedy.

iambic pentameter   The iamb is a "foot" or measure consisting of two syllables, in which the nominal stress falls on the second syllable; pentameter, or "five measure," refers to five feet or measures in a line.

liturgical drama   Plays associated with the liturgy of the Church, performed inside churches and monasteries by the clergy and chanted or sung in Latin.

mansion   A small scenic structure used in medieval theater.

masque   A sixteenth- or seventeenth-century performance, usually by aristocrats, including music, song, dance, costuming, visual spectacle, and dialogue.

melodrama   A type of nineteenth-century popular play that used music to underscore action; more generally, any play with a simplified moral framework, episodic action, and one-dimensional characters.

method acting   A technique pioneered by Stanislavsky, in which actors employ their own emotions and memories to communicate the emotions of a character realistically and persuasively to an audience.

monopoly   Legal right to exclusive production of drama.

morality play   A late medieval or early Renaissance allegorical play, originally intended to depict moral and ethical problems of Christian life and later adapted to secular subjects.

mystery plays   See *cycle plays.*

myth   A story with magical or religious roots, with a hero or heroine who embodies the most important traits of a culture.

naturalism   A late-nineteenth-century movement that adapted scientific method to theater and literature, emphasizing the role of history, society, and heredity in determining the actions of characters.

neoclassicism   A pan–Western European movement from the sixteenth century through the eighteenth century which attempted to revive classical form and style; based loosely on the theories of Aristotle and Horace.

New Comedy   A form of Greek comedy from the fourth and third centuries B.C., centering on the relationship between a young man and young woman. New Comedy influenced the practice of Roman comedy.

ode   In Greek drama, a song the chorus performed while dancing.

off Broadway   Small, originally experimental theaters located outside the Times Square and Broadway areas in New York City. See *off West End.*

off off Broadway   Small, nontraditional theaters located in warehouses, churches, coffee houses, and so on, with limited, nontraditional seating, and catering to specialized audiences. See *fringe theater.*

off West End   Small, originally experimental theaters located outside the West End in London. See *off Broadway.*

Old Comedy   Satiric social comedy produced in Athens in the fifth century B.C., of which Aristophanes' plays are the only surviving examples.

orchestra   "Dancing place," the circular area before the skene where the chorus performed in the ancient Greek theater; the area of theater formerly called the pit, located on the ground level in front of the stage; the area of a theater in front of the stage used by musicians in opera, ballet, and musical comedies. See *pit.*

pageant wagon   A wagon used as a movable stage, carrying sets for medieval cycle plays and on which the plays were performed, principally in England and parts of Spain.

parabasis   A speech in ancient Greek comedy in which the chorus comments on issues raised in the episodes.

parodos   A song sung at the entry of the chorus in a Greek tragedy.

patent A license given by the Crown which permitted an acting company to perform. See *monopoly.*

peripeteia A term used by Aristotle to describe a reversal in the action of a tragedy.

pit In theaters of the sixteenth through eighteenth centuries, an area located immediately in front of the stage. See *orchestra.*

plot The most important of the six parts of a play, according to Aristotle; the pattern of events in a play or any literature, which differs from story and which encompasses earlier events, having a particular causal structure and a unity of purpose or theme.

political theater Theater committed to political and social as opposed to artistic goals.

private theater A term used to describe indoor hall theaters, such as the Blackfriars, in late-sixteenth- and early-seventeenth-century England.

postmodernism A critical approach advocating open acknowledgment of socially constructed meaning as opposed to objective meaning.

prologue In Greek drama, the introductory scene preceding the entrance of the chorus; more generally, an introductory speech or scene that introduces the main play but is not an integral part of it.

proscenium An arch over the front part of the stage; first used in Italian neoclassical revivals of the sixteenth century.

protagonist In ancient Greek theater, the first or primary actor; more generally, the lead character in any play.

public theaters Large outdoor amphitheaters of late-sixteenth- and early-seventeenth-century London, consisting of three-story galleries surrounding an open pit and a thrust stage.

raked stage A stage slanted upward from front to back to enhance perspective.

realism A nineteenth-century movement in theater and literature; allied to naturalism, it attempted to reproduce the details of everyday life.

regional theater Theater outside New York in the United States and Canada and outside London in Great Britain.

repertory A company that performs several plays in rotation throughout a season; also, a group of plays to be performed by a company.

resolution The untangling of the plot's complication. See *denouement.*

Restoration A period in English history beginning in 1660, the year in which Charles II was "restored" to the throne.

romantic comedy See *New Comedy.*

romanticism A theatrical style, dating from about 1790 to 1850, which reacted to neoclassicism and was characterized by an interest in the exotic, the subjective, the emotional, the individual.

satyr play A short rustic play performed by men costumed as satyrs on mythological subjects after the trilogy of tragedies at City Dionysia.

scene The smallest subdivision of a play or its setting.

script The text of a play.

setting The details of place and time relating to a play's environment.

sharers Actors in Renaissance playing companies who "shared" the company's debts and profits.

skene In Greek theater, a low building behind the orchestra and facing the audience.

soliloquy A device by which a dramatic character, alone on the stage, delivers a speech expressing his or her thoughts, emotions, and intentions to the audience.

spectacle One of Aristotle's six parts of a play, which distinguishes drama from narrative and epic; more generally, the visual aspects of a production.

subplot A subsidiary action in a play or a narrative that accompanies the main plot in a contrasting or contradictory relationship.

subtext   According to Stanislavsky, the unspoken motive for a line or speech.

surrealism   An artistic movement of the 1920s in which attempts were made to represent subconscious experience directly.

symbolism   A late-nineteenth- and early-twentieth-century movement that dramatized subjectivity and spirituality through symbol, myth, and mood.

text   The written form of a play.

theater-in-the-round   A theater in which the playing space is surrounded by the audience.

theater of cruelty   A term used by Antonin Artaud to describe a complex of techniques in nonrepresentational theater designed to evoke strong emotional responses from the audience.

theme   The consistent meaning held by critics in a particular historical period to be asserted by a work of art.

thrust stage   A stage surrounded on three sides by the audience; originally used in the Elizabethan period and revived in the twentieth century.

tragedy   According to Aristotle, a worthy action conveyed in elevated language, in which a protagonist falls from prosperity to misery and evokes pity and fear in the audience; more generally, any serious play with an unhappy ending.

tragicomedy   In Renaissance England, a play that embodied the characteristics of both comedy and tragedy but that ended happily; in the twentieth century, a play that ironically embraces the visions of both comedy and tragedy.

trope   An interpolation into or expansion of a medieval liturgical text with song and dramatic action. An example of the genre is the *Quem Quaeritis* trope.

unities   Classical requirements for a play as described by Aristotle, who believed that tragedy should have a single action, should take place within a short period of time, and should be confined to one location. Some Neoclassical critics interpreted Aristotle strictly to mean that tragedy should observe the unities of action, time, and place—that all tragedies should have a single action and should take place within a single day and in one location.

verisimilitude   A central concept in neoclassicism, which insisted that plays reflect the truth as defined by theorists—i.e., normative truth; more generally, any play or set that copies the appearance of life offstage.

well-made play   A popular form of nineteenth-century drama, associated principally with the work of Eugene Scribe, in which the plot is carefully constructed; more generally in the twentieth century, a term of derision.

wings   Flats placed in parallel at the sides of the stage to create a scene of perspective; also, the working area of the stage beyond the scenery and not visible to the audience.

Suggestions for Further Reading

PART I: GREEK DRAMA AND THEATER

Beare, William. *The Roman Stage*. 3rd ed. London: Metheun, 1969.

Bieber, Margaret. *The History of the Greek and Roman Theater*. 2nd ed. Princeton, NJ: Princeton University Press, 1961.

Hamilton, Edith. *The Greek Way*. New York: Norton, 1983.

Knox, Bernard M. *Word and Action: Essays on the Ancient Theater*. Baltimore: Johns Hopkins University Press, 1979.

Konstan, David. *Roman Comedy*. Ithaca, NY: Cornell University Press, 1983.

Pickard-Cambridge, Arthur W. *Dramatic Festivals of Athens*. 2nd ed. Rev. John Gould and D. M. Lewis. Oxford: Clarendon Press, 1962.

Taplin, Oliver. *Greek Tragedy in Action*. Berkeley: University of California Press, 1978.

Walcot, Peter. *Greek Drama in Its Theatrical and Social Context*. Cardiff: University of Wales Press, 1976.

Walton, Michael J. *Living Greek Theater: A Handbook of Classical Performance and Modern Production*. New York: Greenwood, 1987.

Winkler, John J., and Froma I. Zeitlin, eds. *Nothing to Do with Dionysus? Athenian Drama in Its Social Context*. Princeton, NJ: Princeton University Press, 1990.

AESCHYLUS, *Agamemnon*

Gagarin, Michael. *Aeschylean Drama*. Berkeley: University of California Press, 1976.

Lloyd-Jones, Hugh. "The Guilt of Agamemnon." *Greek Tragedy: Modern Essays in Criticism*. Ed. Erich Segal. New York: Harper & Row, 1983.

McCall, Marsh, ed. *Aeschylus, A Collection of Critical Essays*. Englewood Cliffs, NJ: Prentice Hall, 1972.

Podlecki, Anthony J. *The Political Background of Aeschylean Tragedy*. Ann Arbor: University of Michigan Press, 1966.

Rosenmeyer, Thomas G. *The Art of Aeschylus*. Berkeley: University of California Press, 1982.

Taplin, Oliver. *The Stagecraft of Aeschylus*. Oxford: Oxford University Press, 1977.

SOPHOCLES, *Oedipus Rex*

Bloom, Harold, ed. *Sophocles*. New York: Chelsea, 1990.

Fergusson, Francis. *The Idea of a Theater*. Princeton, NJ: Princeton University Press, 1949.

Knox, Bernard M. W. *Oedipus at Thebes: Sophocles' Tragic Hero and His Time*. New York: Norton, 1971.

O'Brien, M. J., ed. *Twentieth-Century Interpretations of Oedipus Rex*. Englewood Cliffs, NJ: Prentice Hall, 1968.

Segal, Charles. *Tragedy and Civilization: An Interpretation of Sophocles*. Cambridge, MA: Harvard University Press, 1981.

Segal, Charles. *Oedipus Tyrannus: Tragic Heroism and the Limits of Knowledge*. New York: Twayne, 1993.

Winnington-Ingram, R. P. *Sophocles: An Interpretation*. New York: Cambridge University Press, 1980.

EURIPIDES, *Medea*

Burian, Peter, ed. *Directions in Euripidean Criticism:*

1365

A Collection of Essays. Durham, NC: Duke University Press, 1985.

Burnett, Anne. *Catastrophe Survived: Euripides' Plays of Mixed Reversal.* Oxford: Clarendon Press, 1971; reprint 1985.

Collard, Christopher. *Euripides.* New York: Oxford University Press, 1981.

Halleran, M. R. *The Stagecraft in Euripides.* Totowa, NJ: Barnes, 1985.

Segal, Erich, ed. *Euripides: A Collection of Critical Essays.* Englewood Cliffs, NJ: Prentice Hall, 1968.

Whitman, Cedric. *Euripides and the Full Circle of Myth.* Cambridge, MA: Harvard University Press, 1974.

ARISTOPHANES, *Lysistrata*

Deardon, C. W. *The State of Aristophanes.* London: Athlone, 1976.

Dover, K. J. *Aristophanic Comedy.* Berkeley: University of California Press, 1972.

Harriott, Rosemary. *Aristophanes: Poet and Dramatist.* Baltimore: Johns Hopkins University Press, 1986.

Henderson, Jeffrey. *Aristophanes' Lysistrata.* New York: Oxford University Press, 1980.

McLeish, Kenneth. *The Theater of Aristophanes.* New York: Taplinger, 1980.

Reckford, Kenneth J. *Aristophanes, Old-and-New Comedy.* Chapel Hill: University of North Carolina Press, 1987.

Ussher, Robert Glenn. *Aristophanes.* New York: Oxford University Press, 1979.

PART II: MEDIEVAL DRAMA AND THEATER IN ENGLAND

Axton, Richard. *European Drama of the Early Middle Ages.* London: Hutchinson, 1974.

Beadle, Richard. *The Cambridge Companion to Medieval English Theatre.* Cambridge: Cambridge University Press, 1994.

Bevington, David, ed. *Medieval Drama.* Boston: Houghton Mifflin, 1975.

Briscoe, Marian, and John Coldewey. *Contexts for Early English Drama.* Bloomington: Indiana University Press, 1989.

Coldewey, John C., ed. *Early English Drama: An Anthology.* New York: Garland, 1993.

Craig, Hardin. *English Religious Drama of the Middle Ages.* Westport, CT: Greenwood, 1978.

Davidson, Clifford, C. J. Gianakaris, and John H. Stroupe, eds. *Drama in the Middle Ages: Comparative and Critical Essays.* New York: AMS, 1982.

Dutka, JoAnna. *Music in the English Mystery Plays.* Kalamazoo: Western Michigan University Press, 1980.

Gibson, Gail MacMurray. *The Theater of Devotion.* Chicago: University of Chicago Press, 1989.

Hardison, O. B., Jr. *Christian Rite and Christian Drama in the Middle Ages: Essays on the Origin and Early History of Modern Drama.* Baltimore: Johns Hopkins University Press, 1965.

Kahrl, Stanley J. *Traditions of Medieval English Drama.* Pittsburgh, PA: University of Pittsburgh Press, 1974.

Kolve, V. A. *The Play Called Corpus Christi.* Palo Alto, CA: Stanford University Press, 1966.

Prosser, Eleanor. *Drama and Religion in the English Mystery Plays.* Palo Alto, CA: Stanford University Press, 1961.

Woolf, Rosemary. *The English Mystery Plays.* Berkeley: University of California Press, 1972.

THE WAKEFIELD MASTER, *The Second Shepherd's Play*

Fiondella, Maris G. "Derrida, Typology, and *The Second Shepherd's Play*: The Theatrical Production of Christian Metaphysics." *Exemplaria*, 6 (1994): 429–58.

Mack, Maynard. "*The Second Shepherd's Play*: A Reconsideration." *Publications of the Modern Language Association of America*, 93 (1978): 78–85.

Ross, Lawrence J. "Symbol and Structure in *Secunda Pastorum*." *Comparative Drama*, 1 (1967): 122–149.

Vaughan, Micael F. "The Three Advents in the *Secunda Pastorum*." *Speculum*, 55 (1980): 484–504.

EVERYMAN

Bevington, David. *From "Mankind" to Marlowe.* Cambridge, MA: Harvard University Press, 1962.

Garner, Stanton B. "Theatricality in *Mankind* and *Everyman*." *Studies in Philology*, 84 (1987): 272–85.

Gilman, Donald, ed. *Everyman and Company: Essays on the Theme and Structure of the European Moral Play.* New York: AMS Press, 1988.

Potter, Robert. *The English Morality Play: Origin, History, and Influence of a Dramatic Tradition.* London: Routledge Kegan Paul, 1975.

PART III: RENAISSANCE DRAMA AND THEATER

Bentley, Gerald Eades. *The Jacobean and Caroline Stage.* 7 vols. Oxford: Oxford University Press, 1941–56.

Bentley, Gerald Eades. *The Profession of Dramatist in Shakespeare's Time, 1590–1642.* Princeton, NJ: Princeton University Press, 1971.

Bentley, Gerald Eades. *The Profession of Player in Shakespeare's Time, 1590–1642.* Princeton, NJ: Princeton University Press, 1984.

Bevington, David. *From "Mankind" to Marlowe: Growth and Structure in the Popular Drama of Tudor England.* Cambridge, MA: Harvard University Press, 1962.

Bowers, Fredson T. *Elizabethan Revenge Tragedy, 1587–1642.* Princeton, NJ: Princeton University Press, 1940.

Boyce, Charles, and David White. *Shakespeare A to Z: The Essential Reference to His Plays, His Poems, His Life and Times, and More.* New York: Facts on File, 1990.

Braunmuller, A. R., and Michael Hattaway. *The Cambridge Companion to Renaissance Drama.* New York: Cambridge University Press, 1990.

Briggs, Julia. *This Stage-Play World: English Literature and Its Background.* Oxford: Oxford University Press, 1983.

Campbell, Lily B. *Scenes and Machines on the English Stage During the Renaissance.* Cambridge: Cambridge University Press, 1923.

Chambers, E. K. *The Elizabethan Stage.* 4 vols. Oxford: Clarendon Press, 1923.

Greenblatt, Stephen, ed. *Representing the Renaissance.* Berkeley: University of California Press, 1988.

Gurr, Andrew. *The Shakespearean Stage, 1574–1642.* 3rd ed. Cambridge: Cambridge University Press, 1991.

Gurr, Andrew, and John Orrell. *Rebuilding Shakespeare's Globe.* London, 1989.

Loomba, Ania. *Gender, Race, and Renaissance Drama.* Manchester: Manchester University Press, 1989.

Orgel, Stephen. *The Illusion of Power: Political Theatre in the English Renaissance.* Berkeley: University of California Press, 1975.

Wickham, Glynne. *Early English Stages, 1300–1660.* 3 vols. London: Routledge & Kegan Paul, 1959–1972.

CHRISTOPHER MARLOWE, *Dr. Faustus*

Bevington, David. *From "Mankind" to Marlowe.* Cambridge, MA: Harvard University Press, 1962.

Cole, Douglas. *Suffering and Evil in the Plays of Christopher Marlowe.* Princeton, NJ: Princeton University Press, 1962; reprint 1971.

Dollimore, Jonathan. *Radical Tragedy: Religion, Ideology, and Power in the Drama of Shakespeare and His Contemporaries.* 2nd ed. London: Harvester Wheatsheaf, 1989.

Godshalk, William L. *The Marlovian World-Picture.* The Hague: Mouton, 1974.

Leech, Clifford, ed. *Marlowe: A Collection of Critical Essays.* Englewood Cliffs, NJ: Prentice Hall, 1964.

Levin, Harry. *The Overreacher: A Study of Christopher Marlowe.* Boston: Beacon, 1964.

WILLIAM SHAKESPEARE, *A Midsummer Night's Dream*

Barber, C. L. *Shakespeare's Festive Comedy.* Princeton, NJ: Princeton University Press, 1959.

Garber, Marjorie. *Dream in Shakespeare: From Metaphor to Metamorphosis.* New Haven, CT: Yale University Press, 1974.

Girard, René. "Myth and Ritual in Shakespeare: *A Midsummer Night's Dream.*" *Textual Strategies: Perspectives in Post-Structuralist Criticism.* Ed. Josue V. Harari. Ithaca, NY: Cornell University Press, 1979.

Legatt, Alexander. *A Midsummer Night's Dream: Shakespeare's Comedy of Love.* London: Methuen, 1974.

Montrose, Louis. "'Shaping Fantasies': Figures of Gender and Power in Elizabethan Culture." *Representations,* 1 (1983): 61–94.

Shelbourne, David. *The Making of* A Midsummer Night's Dream. London: Methuen, 1982.

Schoenbaum, Samuel. *William Shakespeare: A Documentary Life.* Oxford: Clarendon Press, 1975.

WILLIAM SHAKESPEARE, *Hamlet*

Bamber, Linda. *Comic Women, Tragic Men: A Study of Gender and Genre in Shakespeare.* Palo Alto, CA: Stanford University Press, 1982.

Bloom, Harold, ed. *William Shakespeare's* Hamlet. New York: Chelsea, 1986.

Bradley, A. C. *Shakespearean Tragedy.* New York: Meridian, 1955.

Calderwood, James. *To Be and Not to Be: Negation and Metadrama in* Hamlet. New York: Columbia University Press, 1983.

Dollimore, Jonathan, and Alan Sinfield, eds. *Political Shakespeare: New Essays in Cultural Materialism.* 2nd ed. Manchester: Manchester University Press, 1994.

Drakakis, John, ed. *Alternative Shakespeares.* New York: Methuen, 1985.

Frye, Northrop. *Fools of Time: Studies in Shakespearean Tragedy.* Buffalo, NY: University of Toronto Press, 1973.

Greenblatt, Stephen. *Shakespearean Negotiations.* Berkeley: University of California Press, 1988.

Jones, Ernest. *Hamlet and Oedipus.* New York: Norton, 1976.

Lacan, Jacques. "Desire and the Interpretation of Desire in *Hamlet.*" *Literature and Psychoanalysis: The Question of Reading Otherwise.* Ed. Soshana Felman. Baltimore: Johns Hopkins University Press, 1982.

Mack, Maynard. "The World of *Hamlet.*" *Yale Review,* 41 (1952): 502–23.

Showalter, Elaine. "Representing Ophelia: Women, Madness, and the Responsibilities of Feminist Criticism." *Shakespeare and the Question of Theory.* Eds. Patricia Parker and Geoffrey Hartman. New York: Methuen, 1985.

Wofford, Suzanne L., ed. *Case Studies in Contemporary Criticism: William Shakespeare,* Hamlet. Boston: Bedford Books, 1994.

BEN JONSON, *Volpone*

Barish, Jonas A. *Ben Jonson and the Language of Prose Comedy.* New York: Norton, 1970.

Barish, Jonas A., ed. *Ben Jonson: A Collection of Critical Essays.* Englewood Cliffs, NJ: Prentice Hall, 1963.

Craig, D. H., ed. *Ben Jonson: The Critical Heritage, 1599–1798.* New York: Routledge, 1990.

Miles, Rosalind. *Ben Jonson: His Craft and Art.* London: Routledge, 1990.

Miles, Rosalind. *Ben Jonson: His Life and Work.* New York: Routledge & Kegan Paul, 1986.

Orgel, Stephen. *The Jonsonian Masque.* Cambridge, MA: Harvard University Press, 1967; reprint Columbia, 1981.

PART IV: FRENCH NEOCLASSICAL AND ENGLISH RESTORATION DRAMA AND THEATER

Holland, Norman N. *The First Modern Comedies: The Significance of Etherege, Wycherly, and Congreve.* Cambridge, MA: Harvard University Press, 1959.

Lancaster, H. C. *A History of French Dramatic Literature in the Seventeenth Century.* 5 vols. Baltimore: Johns Hopkins University Press, 1929–42.

Loftis, John. *The Politics of Drama in Augustan England.* New York: Oxford University Press, 1963.

Nicoll, Allardyce. *A History of Restoration Drama, 1600–1700.* New York: Cambridge University Press, 1923.

Powell, Jocelyn. *Restoration Theatre Production.* Boston: Routledge, 1984.

Styan, J. L. *Restoration Comedy in Performance.* Cambridge: Cambridge University Press, 1986.

Turnell, Martin. *The Classical Movement: Studies in Corneille, Molière, and Racine.* New York: New Directions, 1948.

Wiley, W. L. *The Early Public Theatre in France.* Cambridge, MA: Harvard University Press, 1920.

MOLIÈRE, *The Misanthrope*

Bermel, Albert. *Molière's Theatrical Bounty: A New View of the Plays.* Carbondale: Southern Illinois University Press, 1990.

Gaines, James F. *Molière's Theater.* Columbus: Ohio State University Press, 1984.

Gross, Nathan. *From Gesture to Idea: Esthetics and Ethics in Molière's Comedy.* New York: Columbia University Press, 1982.

Guicharnaud, Jacques, ed. *Molière: A Collection of Critical Essays.* Englewood Cliffs, NJ: Prentice Hall, 1964.

Knutson, Harold C. *the Triumph of Wit: Molière and Restoration Comedy.* Columbus: Ohio State University Press, 1988.

JEAN RACINE, *Phaedra*

Barthes, Roland. *On Racine.* Trans. Richard Howard. New York: Hill and Wang, 1964.

Brereton, Geoffrey. *Jean Racine: A Critical Biography.* 2d ed. New York: Barnes, 1973.

Cook, A. S. *French Tragedy: The Power of Enactment.* Chicago: University of Chicago Press, 1980.

Knight, Roy Clement, ed. *Racine: Modern Judgements.* London: Methuen, 1969.

Maskell, D. *Racine: A Theatrical Reading.* Oxford: Clarendon Press, 1991.

WILLIAM CONGREVE, *The Way of the World*

Dobree, Bonamy. *Congreve.* London: British Council, 1963.

Hodges, John C. *Congreve the Man: A Biography.* London: Oxford University Press, 1941.

Markley, Robert. *Two-Edged Weapons: Style and Ideology in the Comedies of Etherege, Wycherly, and Congreve.* New York: Oxford University Press, 1988.

Morris, Brian, ed. *Congreve: A Collection of Critical Essays.* London: Benn, 1972.

Meuschke, Paul, and Carol Meuschke. *A New View of Congreve's* Way of the World. Ann Arbor: University of Michigan Press, 1958.

Williams, Aubrey Lake. *An Approach to Congreve.* New Haven, CT: Yale University Press, 1979.

PART V: MODERN EUROPEAN DRAMA: BACKGROUNDS AND BEGINNINGS

Antoine, André. *Memories of the Théâtre Libre*. Trans. Marvin Carlson. Coral Gables, FL: University of Miami Press, 1964.

Bennett, Benjamin. *Theater as Problem: Modern Drama and Its Place in Literature*. Ithaca, NY: Cornell University Press, 1990.

Bentley, Eric. *The Playwright as Thinker: A Study of Drama in Modern Times*. New York: Harcourt, 1967.

Braun, Edward. *Meyerhold on Theatre*. New York: Hill and Wang, 1969.

Brockett, Oscar G., and Robert R. Findlay. *Century of Innovation: A History of European and American Theatre and Drama Since 1870*. Englewood Cliffs, NJ: Prentice Hall, 1973.

Brustein, Robert. *The Theatre of Revolt*. Boston: Little, Brown, 1964.

Cole, Toby, ed. *Playwrights on Playwriting: The Meaning and Making of Modern Drama from Ibsen to Ionesco*. New York: Hill and Wang, 1960.

Finney, Gail. *Women in Modern Drama: Freud; Feminism, and European Theater at the Turn of the Century*. Ithaca, NY: Cornell University Press, 1989.

Gilman, Richard. *The Making of Modern Drama*. New York: Farrar, Straus & Giroux, 1974.

Quigley, Austin. *The Modern Stage and Other Worlds*. London: Methuen, 1985.

Stanislavsky, Konstantin. *An Actor Prepares*. Trans. Elizabeth R. Hapgood. New York: Theatre Arts, 1949.

Stanislavsky, Konstantin. *Creating a Role*. Trans. Elizabeth R. Hapgood. New York: Theatre Arts, 1961.

Stanislavsky, Konstantin. *My Life in Art*. Trans. J. J. Robbins. Boston: Little, Brown, 1924.

Styan, J. L. *Modern Drama in Theory and Practice*. 3 vols. Cambridge: Cambridge University Press, 1980.

Worthen, W. B. *Modern Drama and the Rhetoric of the Theater*. Berkeley: University of California Press, 1992.

HENRIK IBSEN, *Hedda Gabler*

Ackley, Katherine Anne. "A Rage to Live: The Violent Life and Death of Hedda Gabler." *Women and Violence in Literature: An Essay Collection*. Ed. Katherine Anne Ackley. New York: Garland, 1990.

Braunmuller, A. R. "Hedda Gabler and the Sources of Symbolism." *Drama and Symbolism*. Ed. James Redmond. New York: Cambridge University Press, 1982.

Egan, Michael, ed. *Ibsen: The Critical Heritage*. London: Routledge & Kegan Paul, 1985.

Lyons, Charles R. *Henrik Ibsen: The Divided Consciousness*. Carbondale: Southern Illinois University Press, 1972.

Lyons, Charles. Hedda Gabler: *Gender, Role, and World*. Boston: Twayne, 1991.

Suzman, Janet. "*Hedda Gabler*: The Play in Performance." *Ibsen and the Theatre*. Ed. Errol Durbach. New York: New York University Press, 1980.

Fjelde, Rolf, ed. *Ibsen: A Collection of Critical Essays*. Englewood Cliffs, NJ: Prentice Hall, 1965.

Shaw, George Bernard. *The Quintessence of Ibsenism*. New York: Hill and Wang, 1957.

AUGUST STRINDBERG, *Miss Julie*

Carlson, Henry. *Strindberg and the Poetry of Myth*. Berkeley: University of California Press, 1982.

Lucas, F. L. *The Drama of Ibsen and Strindberg*. London: Cassell, 1962.

Reinert, Otto, ed. *Strindberg: A Collection of Critical Essays*. Englewood Cliffs, NJ: Prentice Hall, 1971.

Sprinchorn, Evert. *Stringberg as Dramatist*. New Haven, CT: Yale University Press, 1982.

Steene, Birgitta. *The Greatest Fire: A Study of August Strindberg*. Carbondale: Southern Illinois University Press, 1973.

Stockenstrom, Goran, ed. *Strindberg's Dramaturgy*. Minneapolis: University of Minnesota Press, 1988.

ANTON CHEKHOV, *The Cherry Orchard*

Baricelli, Jean-Pierre, ed. *Chekhov's Great Plays: A Critical Anthology*. New York: New York University Press, 1981.

Ekman, Thomas A., ed. *Critical Essays on Anton Chekhov*. Boston: Hall, 1989.

Emeljianow, Victor. *Chekhov: The Critical Heritage*. Boston: Routledge, 1981.

Hingley, Ronald. *Chekhov: A Biographical and Critical Study*. New York: Barnes, 1966.

Jackson, Robert Louis. *Chekhov: A Collection of Critical Essays*. Englewood Cliffs, NJ: Prentice Hall, 1967.

Karlinsky, Simon, and Michael Heim, eds. *Anton Chekhov's Life and Thought: Selected Letters and Commentary*. Berkeley: University of California Press, 1975.

Meister, Charles. *Chekhov Criticism, 1880 Through 1986*. New York: McFarland, 1988.

Peace, Richard. *Chekhov: A Study of the Four Major Plays*. New Haven, CT: Yale University Press, 1983.

GEORGE BERNARD SHAW, *Major Barbara*

Bentley, Eric. *Bernard Shaw*. New York: Norton, 1976.

Berst, Charles A. *Bernard Shaw and the Art of Drama*. Urbana: University of Illinois Press, 1973.

Evans, T. F., ed. *Shaw: The Critical Heritage*. London: Routledge, 1976.

Ganz, Arthur F. *George Bernard Shaw*. New York: Grove Press, 1983.

Kaufman, R. J., ed. *G. B. Shaw: A Collection of Critical Essays*. Englewood Cliffs, NJ: Prentice Hall, 1965.

Meisel, Martin. *Shaw and the Nineteenth-Century Theater*. Princeton, NJ: Princeton University Press, 1963.

Zimbardo, Rose, ed. *Twentieth Century Interpretations of Major Barbara*. Englewood Cliffs, NJ: Prentice Hall, 1970.

OSCAR WILDE, *The Importance of Being Earnest*

Bloom, Harold. *Oscar Wilde's* The Importance of Being Earnest. New York: Chelsea, 1988.

Cohen, Philip K. *The Moral Vision of Oscar Wilde*. Rutherford, NJ: Fairleigh Dickinson University Press, 1978.

Ellman, Richard. *Oscar Wilde*. New York: Knopf, 1988.

Ellman, Richard, ed. *Oscar Wilde: A Collection of Critical Essays*. Englewood Cliffs, NJ: Prentice Hall, 1969.

Erikson, Donald. *Oscar Wilde*. Boston: Twayne, 1977.

Miller, Robert Keith. *Oscar Wilde*. New York: Ungar, 1982.

San Juan, Epifiano. *The Art of Oscar Wilde*. Princeton, NJ: Princeton University Press, , 1967.

JOHN MILLINGTON SYNGE, *Riders to the Sea*

Benson, Eugene. *J. M. Synge*. New York: Grove, 1983.

Gerstenberger, Donna. *John Millington Synge*. Rev. ed. Boston: Twayne, 1990.

Greene, David H., and Edward M. Stephens. *John Millington Synge, 1871–1909*. Rev. ed. New York: New York University Press, 1989.

King, Mary C. *The Drama of J. M. Synge*. Syracuse, NY: Syracuse University Press, 1985.

Kopper, Edward A. *A John Millington Synge Literary Companion*. New York: Greenwood, 1988.

PART VI: MODERN EUROPEAN AND AMERICAN DRAMA: REACTIONS AND MODIFICATIONS

Artaud, Antonin. *The Theatre and Its Double*. Trans. Mary C. Richards. New York: Grove Press, 1958.

Bentley, Eric. *The Theatre of Commitment and Other Essays on Drama in Our Society*. New York: Atheneum, 1967.

Bentley, Eric. *Theatre of War*. New York: Viking, 1972.

Berkowitz, Gerald M. *American Drama of the Twentieth Century*. London: Longman, 1992.

Bigsby, C. W. E. *A Critical Introduction to Twentieth-Century American Drama*. 3 vols. Cambridge: Cambridge University Press, 1982–85.

Blau, Herbert. *The Impossible Theatre: A Manifesto*. New York: Macmillan, 1964.

Bogard, Travis, and William I. Oliver. *Modern Drama: Essays in Criticism*. New York: Oxford University Press, 1965.

Brater, Enoch, and Ruby Cohn, eds. *Around the Absurd: Essays in Modern and Postmodern Drama*. Ann Arbor: University of Michigan Press, 1990.

Brook, Peter. *The Empty Space*. New York: Avon, 1968.

Cohn, Ruby. *From Desire to Godot: Pocket Theater of Postwar Paris*. Berkeley: University of California Press, 1987.

Downer, Alan S., ed. *American Drama and Its Critics*. Chicago: University of Chicago Press, 1965.

Esslin, Martin. *The Theatre of the Absurd*. Woodstock, NY: Overlook, 1973.

Gassner, John. *Theatre at the Crossroads*. New York: Holt, 1960.

Grotowski, Jerzy. *Towards a Poor Theatre*. New York: Simon & Schuster, 1968.

Piscator, Erwin. *The Political Theatre: A History, 1914–1929*. Trans. Hugh Rorrison. London: Methuen, 1980.

Schechner, Richard. *Environmental Theater*. New York: Hawthorn, 1973.

Steiner, George. *The Death of Tragedy*. New York: Oxford University Press, 1980.

Szliassy, Zolt N. *American Theater of the 1960s*. Carbondale: Southern Illinois University Press, 1986.

Taylor, John Russell. *Anger and After*. London: Methuen, 1969.

Wellworth, George E. *The Theater of Protest and Paradox*. New York: New York University Press, 1971.

Williams, Raymond. *Modern Tragedy*. Palo Alto, CA: Stanford University Press, 1966.

Williams, Raymond. *Drama from Ibsen to Brecht*. London: Hogarth, 1986.

EUGENE O'NEILL, *The Emperor Jones*

Bogard, Travis. *Contour in Time: The Plays of Eugene O'Neill*. New York: Oxford University Press, 1988.

Cargill, Oscar, N. Bryllion Fagin, and William J. Fisher, eds. *O'Neill and His Plays: Four Decades of Criticism*. New York: New York University Press, 1961.

Chothia, Jean. *Forging a Language: A Study of the Plays of Eugene O'Neill*. Cambridge: Cambridge University Press, 1979.

Gassner, John, ed. *O'Neill: A Collection of Critical Essays*. Englewood Cliffs, NJ: Prentice Hall, 1964.

Gelb, Arthur, and Barbara Gelb. *O'Neill*. New York: Harper & Row, 1973.

Wainscott, Ronald H. *Staging O'Neill: The Experimental Years, 1920–1934*. New Haven, CT: Yale University Press, 1988.

LUIGI PIRANDELLO, *Six Characters in Search of an Author*

Bassnet, Susan. *File on Pirandello*. London: Methuen, 1989.

Bassnet-McGuire, Susan. *Luigi Pirandello*. New York: Grove, 1983.

Bentley, Eric. *The Pirandello Commentaries*. Evanston, IL: Northwestern University Press, 1986.

Cambon, Glauco, ed. *Pirandello: A Collection of Critical Essays*. Englewood Cliffs, NJ: Prentice Hall, 1967.

Caputi, Anthony. *Pirandello and the Crisis of Modern Consciousness*. Urbana: University of Illinois Press, 1988.

Guidice, Gaspar. *Pirandello: A Biography*. Trans. Alastair Hamilton. New York: Oxford University Press, 1975.

Oliver, Roger. *Dreams of Passion: The Theater of Luigi Pirandello*. New York: New York University Press, 1979.

Paolucci, Anne. *Pirandello's Theater*. Carbondale: Southern Illinois University Press, 1974.

BERTOLT BRECHT, *Mother Courage*

Bentley, Eric. *The Brecht Commentaries, 1943–1980*. New York: Grove, 1981.

Brecht, Bertolt. *Brecht on Theatre: The Development of an Aesthetic*. Ed. and trans. John Willett. New York: Hill and Wang, 1964.

Demetz, Peter, ed. *Brecht: A Collection of Critical Essays*. Englewood Cliffs, NJ: Prentice Hall, 1962.

Esslin, Martin. *Brecht: The Man and His Work*. Garden City, NY: Doubleday, 1971.

Ewen, Frederick. *Bertolt Brecht: His Life, His Art and His Times*. New York: Citadel, 1967.

Fuegi, John. *Bertolt Brecht: Chaos According to Plan*. New York: Cambridge University Press, 1987.

Willett, John. *Brecht in Context: Contemporary Approaches*. London: Methuen, 1984.

Wright, Elizabeth. *Postmodern Brecht: A Re-Presentation*. London: Routledge, 1989.

ARTHUR MILLER, *The Crucible*

Carson, Neil. *Arthur Miller*. New York: Grove Press, 1982.

Corrigan, Robert W., ed. *Arthur Miller: A Collection of Critical Essays*. Englewood Cliffs, NJ: Prentice Hall, 1969.

Martin, Robert A., ed. *Arthur Miller: New Perspectives*. Englewood Cliffs, NJ: Prentice Hall, 1982.

Miller, Arthur. *The Theater Essays of Arthur Miller*. Ed. Robert Martin. New York: Viking, 1978.

Miller, Arthur. *Timebends: A Life*. New York: Grove Press, 1987.

TENNESSEE WILLIAMS, *Cat on a Hot Tin Roof*

Boxill, Roger. *Tennessee Williams*. New York: St. Martin's, 1987.

Devlin, Albert J., ed. *Conversations with Tennessee Williams*. Jackson: University of Mississippi Press, 1986.

Griffin, Alice. *Understanding Tennessee Williams*. Columbia: University of South Carolina Press, 1995.

Huzzard, Jere. "Williams' *Cat on a Hot Tin Roof*." *Explicator*, 43 (1985); 46–47.

Leavitt, Richard Freeman, ed. *The World of Tennessee Williams*. New York: Putnam, 1978.

Stanton, Stephen, ed. *Tennessee Williams: A Collection of Critical Essays*. Englewood Cliffs, NJ: Prentice Hall, 1977.

Thompson, Judith. *Tennessee Williams' Plays: Memory, Myth, and Symbol*. New York: Lang, 1987.

SAMUEL BECKETT, *Endgame*

Bloom, Harold. *Samuel Beckett's Endgame*. New York: Chelsea, 1988.

Brater, Enoch. *Beyond Minimalism: Beckett's Later Style in the Theater*. Oxford: Oxford University Press, 1987.

Chevigny, Bell Gale, ed. *Twentieth Century Interpretations of Endgame*. Englewood Cliffs, NJ: Prentice Hall, 1969.

Cohn, Ruby. *Just Play: Beckett's Theater*. Princeton, NJ: Princeton University Press, 1980.

Gontarski, S. E. *On Beckett: Essays and Criticism*. New York: Grove Press, 1986.

Noguchi, Rei. "Style and Strategy in *Endgame*." *Journal of Beckett Studies*, 9 (1984): 101–11.

LORRAINE HANSBERRY, *A Raisin in the Sun*

Carter, Steven R. *Hansberry's Drama: Commitment and Complexity*. Urbana: University of Illinois Press, 1991.

Freedman, Morris. *American Drama in Social Context*. Carbondale, IL: Southern Illinois University Press, 1971.

Nemiroff, Howard. *To be Young, Gifted, and Black: A Portrait of Lorraine Hansberry*. Englewood Cliffs, NJ: Prentice Hall, 1969.

Scheader, Catherine. *They Found a Way: Lorraine Hansberry*. Chicago: Children's, 1978.

Washington, J. Charles. "*A Raisin in the Sun* Revisited." *Black American Literature Forum*, 22 (1988): 109–24.

PART VII: CONTEMPORARY DRAMA AND THEATER

Barker, Howard. *Arguments for a Theater*. 2nd ed. Manchester: Manchester University Press, 1993.

Betsko, Kathleen, and Rachel Koenig, eds. *Interviews with Contemporary Women Playwrights*. New York: Beech Tree, 1987.

Blau, Herbert. *Eye of the Prey: Subversions of the Postmodern*. Bloomington: Indiana University Press, 1987.

Brater, Enoch, ed. *Feminine Focus: The New Woman Playwrights*. New York: Oxford University Press, 1989.

Dolan, Jill. *The Feminist Spectator as Critic*. Ann Arbor, MI: UMI Research Press, 1988.

Hart, Lynda, ed. *Making a Spectacle: Feminist Essays on Contemporary Women's Theatre*. Ann Arbor: University of Michigan Press, 1989.

Hayman, Ronald. *Theatre and Anti-Theatre: New Movements Since Beckett*. New York: Oxford University Press, 1979.

Hill, Errol, ed. *The Theatre of Black Americans*. 2 vols. Englewood Cliffs, NJ: Prentice Hall, 1980.

Inverso, Mary Beth. *The Gothic Impulse in Contemporary Drama*. Ann Arbor: University of Michigan Press, 1990.

Marranca, Bonnie, ed. *The Theatre of Images*. New York: Drama Books Specialists, 1977.

Orr, John. *Tragicomedy and Contemporary Culture: Play and Performance from Beckett to Shepard*. Ann Arbor: University of Michigan Press, 1990.

Savran, David. *In Their Own Words: Contemporary American Playwrights*. New York: Theatre Communications Group, 1988.

HAROLD PINTER, *The Dumb Waiter*

Diamond, Elin. *Pinter's Comic Play*. Lewisburg, PA: Buckne University Press, 1985.

Esslin, Martin. *Pinter*. New York: Norton, 1976.

Gale, Stephen H., ed. *Critical Essays on Harold Pinter*. Boston: Hall, 1990.

Gale, Stephen H. *Harold Pinter: Critical Approaches*. Rutherford, NJ: Fairleigh Dickinson University Press, 1986.

Ganz, Arthur, ed. *Pinter: A Collection of Critical Essays*. Englewood Cliffs, NJ: Prentice Hall, 1979.

Quigley, Austin E. *The Pinter Problem*. Princeton, NJ: Princeton University Press, 1975.

WOLE SOYINKA, *The Strong Breed*

Gibbs, James. *Wole Soyinka*. London: Macmillan, 1986.

Gibbs, James, ed. *Critical Perspectives on Wole Soyinka*. Washington, DC: Three Continents, 1980.

Gibbs, James, Ketu H. Katrak, and Henry Louis Gates, Jr., eds. *Wole Soyinka: A Bibliography of Primary and Secondary Sources*. Westport, CT: Greenwood, 1986.

Jones, Eldred D. *The Writings of Wole Soyinka*. Portsmouth, NH: Heinemann, 1988.

Katrak, Ketu H. *Wole Soyinka and Modern Tragedy: A Study of Dramatic Theory and Practice*. Westport, CT: Greenwood, 1986.

TOM STOPPARD, *Rosencrantz and Guildenstern Are Dead*

Babula, William. "The Play-Life Metaphor in Shakespeare and Stoppard." *Modern Drama*, 15 (1972): 279–81.

Bareham, T., ed. *Tom Stoppard: Rosencrantz and Guildenstern Are Dead, Jumpers, Travesties: A Casebook*. New York: Macmillan, 1990.

Bratt, David. *Tom Stoppard: A Reference Guide*. Boston: Hall, 1982.

Jenkins, Anthony. *The Theatre of Tom Stoppard*. Cambridge: Cambridge University Press, 1987.

Page, Malcolm. *File on Stoppard*. London: Methuen, 1986.

Sales, Roger. *Tom Stoppard, Rosencrantz and Guildenstern Are Dead*. London: Penguin, 1988.

Tynan, Kenneth. "Withdrawing in Style from the Chaos: Tom Stoppard." *Show People: Profiles in Entertainment*. New York: Weidenfeld and Nicolson, 1980.

Whitaker, Thomas. *Tom Stoppard*. New York: Grove Press, 1983.

CLARE BOOTHE LUCE, *Slam the Door Softly*

Hatch, Alden. *Ambassador Extraordinary Clare Boothe Luce*. New York: Holt, 1956.

Martin, Ralph G. *Henry and Clare: An Intimate Portrait of the Luces*. New York: Putnam and Sons, 1991.

Sheed, Wilfrid. *Clare Boothe Luce*. New York: Dutton, 1982.

SAM SHEPARD, *True West*

Hart, Lynda. *Sam Shepard's Metaphorical Stages*. Westport, CT: Greenwood, 1987.

King, Kimball. *Sam Shepard: A Casebook*. New York: Garland, 1988.

Marranca, Bonnie, ed. *American Dreams: The Imagination of Sam Shepard*. New York: Performing Arts Journal Publications, 1981.

Mottram, Ron. *Inner Landscapes: The Theater of Sam Shepard*. Columbia, MO: University of Missouri Press, 1984.

Oumano, Ellen. *Sam Shepard: The Life and Work of an American Dreamer*. New York: St. Martin's, 1986.

MARSHA NORMAN, 'night, Mother

Browder, Sally. "'I thought you were mine': Marsha Norman's 'night, Mother." *Mothers and Daughters in Contemporary American Literature.* Ed. Mickey Pearlman. Westport, CT: Greenwood, 1989.

Burkman, Katherine H. "The Demeter Myth and Doubling in Marsha Norman's 'night, Mother." *Modern American Drama: The Female Canon.* Ed. June Schlueter. Rutherford, NJ: Fairleigh Dickinson University Press, 1990.

Grieff, Louis K. "Fathers, Daughters, and Spiritual Sisters: Marsha Norman's 'night, Mother and Tennessee Williams's *The Glass Menagerie.*" *Text and Performance Quarterly*, 9 (1989): 224–28.

Hart, Lynda. "Doing Time: Hunger for Power in Marsha Norman's Plays." *Southern Quarterly*, 25 (1987): 67–69.

Kane, Leslie. "The Way Out, the Way In: Paths to Self in the Plays of Marsha Norman." *Feminine Focus: The New Women Playwrights.* Ed. Enoch Brater. Oxford: Oxford University Press, 1989.

Spenser, Jenny S. "Norman's 'night, Mother: Psychodrama of Female Identity." *Modern Drama*, 30 (1987): 364–375.

TINA HOWE, Painting Churches

Backes, Nancy. "Body Art: Hunger and Satiation in the Plays of Tina Howe." *Making a Spectacle: Feminist Essays on Contemporary Women's Theatre.* Ed. Lynda Hart. Ann Arbor: University of Michigan Press, 1989.

Lamonte, Rosette C. "Tina Howe's Secret Surrealism; Walking a Tightrope." *Modern Drama*, 36 (1993): 27–37.

McLaughlin, Buzz. "Conversations with Tina Howe." *The Dramatists Guild Quarterly*, 31 (1994): 2–9.

Painting Churches. New York Theatre Critics' Reviews, 44 (1983): 74–77.

MANUEL PUIG, Kiss of the Spider Woman

Kerr, Lucille. *Suspended Fictions: A Reading of Novels by Manuel Puig.* Urbana: University of Illinois Press, 1987.

Gallagher, D. P. *Modern Latin American Literature.* Oxford: Oxford University Press, 1973.

MacAdam, Alfred J. *Modern Latin American Narratives: The Dream of Reason.* Chicago: University of Chicago Press, 1977.

Tittler, Jonathan. *Narrative Irony in the Contemporary Spanish-American Novel.* Ithaca, NY: Cornell University Press, 1984.

AUGUST WILSON, The Piano Lesson

Elkins, Marilyn, ed. *August Wilson: A Casebook.* New York: Garland, 1994.

Nadel, Alan, ed. *May All Your Fences Have Gates, Essays on the Drama of August Wilson.* Iowa City: University of Iowa Press, 1994.

Pereia, Kim. *August Wilson and the African American Odyssey.* Urbana: University of Illinois Press, 1995.

Shannon, Sandra. *The Dramatic Vision of August Wilson.* Baltimore: Howard University Press, 1995.

DAVID MAMET, Oleanna

Berkowitz, Gerald M. "David Mamet." *American Drama of the Twentieth Century.* London: Longman, 1992.

Bigsby, C. W. E. "David Mamet." *Modern American Drama, 1945–1990.* Cambridge: Cambridge University Press, 1992.

Cohn, Ruby. "Phrasal Energies: Harold Pinter and David Mamet." *Anglo-American Interplay in Recent Drama.* Cambridge: Cambridge University Press, 1995.

Carroll, Dennis. *David Mamet.* New York: St. Martin's, 1987.

Dean, Anne. *David Mamet: Language as Dramatic Action.* Rutherford, NJ: Fairleigh Dickinson University Press, 1990.

Jones, Nesta Wyn. *File on Mamet.* London: Methuen, 1991.

Kane, Leslie. *David Mamet: A Casebook.* New York: Garland, 1992.

EDWARD ALBEE, Three Tall Women

Bigsby, C. W. E. *Edward Albee: A Collection of Critical Essays.* Englewood Cliffs, NJ: Prentice-Hall, 1975.

Kolin, Philip C. *Critical Essays on Edward Albee.* Boston: Hall, 1986.

McCarthy, Gerry. *Edward Albee.* New York: St. Martin's, 1987.

Roudane, Matthew Charles. *Understanding Edward Albee.* Columbia: University of South Carolina Press, 1987.

Three Tall Women. New York Theatre Critics' Reviews, 55 (1994): 37–44.

HOWARD BARKER, Hated Nightfall

Barker, Howard. "Saintliness, Death and the Perfect Family." *Hated Nightfall, Wounds to the Face.* London: Calder Publications, Riverrun Press, 1994.

Cohn, Ruby. "Digging the Greeks: New Versions of Old Classics." *Contemporary British Theatre.* Ed. Theodore Shank. New York: St. Martin's, 1994.

Klotz, Gunther. "Howard Barker: Paradigm of Postmodernism." *New Theatre Quarterly*, 25 (1991): 20–26.

Rylance, Rick. "Forms of Dissent in Contemporary Drama and Contemporary Theory." *The Death of the Playwright? Modern British Drama and*

Literary Theory. Ed. Adrian Page. Basingstoke: Macmillan, 1992.

Thomas, Alan. "Howard Barker: Modern Allegorist." *Modern Drama*, 35 (1992): 433–443.

Wilcher, Robert. "Honouring the Audience: The Theatre of Howard Barker." *British and Irish Drama Since 1960.* Ed. James Acheson. New York: St. Martin's, 1993.

Selected List of Film and Video Productions

PART I: GREEK DRAMA AND THEATER

Aeschylus, *Agamemnon* (1983), 90 min. National Theater of Great Britain company, directed by Peter Hall. Distributed by Films for the Humanities and Sciences.

Sophocles, *Oedipus the King* (1987), 120 min. With Michael Pennington, Sir John Gielgud, and Claire Bloom. Distributed by Films for the Humanities and Sciences.

Sophocles, *Oedipus the King* (1957), 90 min. Stratford, Ontario, Players, directed by Sir Tyrone Guthrie, with Yeats's translation and masks. Distributed by Insight Media.

Sophocles, *Oedipus the King* (1967), 97 min. Directed by Philip Saville. With Orson Welles, Christopher Plummer, and Donald Sutherland. Distributed by Crossroads Video.

Sophocles, *Oedipus the King* (1975). With Anthony Quayle, James Mason, Claire Bloom, and Ian Richardson. Distributed by Films for the Humanities and Sciences.

Euripides, *Medea* (1959), 107 min. Color. With Judith Anderson and Colleen Dewhurst. Distributed by Filmic Archives.

Euripides, *Medea* (1979), 110 min. With Maria Callas. In Italian with English subtitles. Distributed by DVC, Inc.

Euripides, *Medea* (1982), 90 min. With Zoe Caldwell and Judith Anderson. A Kennedy Center production based on Robinson Jeffers's version. Distributed by Films for the Humanities and Sciences.

Aristophanes, *Lysistrata* (1987), 97 min. Contemporary adaptation shot on location. Greek with English subtitles. Distributed by Insight Media.

PART II: MEDIEVAL DRAMA AND THEATER IN ENGLAND

Anonymous, *Everyman* (1991), 53 min. Produced in conjunction with Howard Schless of Columbia University. Distributed by Insight Media.

Wakefield Master, *The Second Shepherd's Play* (1988), 55 min. With Quem Quaeritis and Abraham and Isaac. Distributed by Films for the Humanities and Sciences.

(All VHS unless otherwise noted)

PART III: RENAISSANCE DRAMA AND THEATER IN ENGLAND

Christopher Marlowe, *Dr. Faustus* (1968), 93 min. Directed by Richard Burton and Nevill Coghill. With Richard Burton and Elizabeth Taylor. Distributed by RCA/Columbia Pictures Home Video and Filmic Archives.

William Shakespeare, *Hamlet* (1990), 135 min. Directed by Franco Zeffirelli. With Mel Gibson, Glenn Close, Alan Bates, and Paul Scofield. Distributed by DVC, Inc.; Facets Multimedia; and Filmic Archives.

William Shakespeare, *Hamlet* (1969), 114 min. Directed by Tony Richardson. With Nicol Williamson, Anthony Hopkins, Gordon Jackson, Judy Parfitt, and Marianne Faithfull. Distributed by DVC, Inc.; Facets Multimedia; and Filmic Archives.

William Shakespeare, *Hamlet* (1948), 153 min. Directed by Laurence Olivier. With Laurence Olivier. Distributed by DVC, Inc., and Paramount Home Video.

William Shakespeare, *A Midsummer Night's Dream* (1983), 165 min. Directed by Joseph Papp. With William Hurt and Michelle Shay. Distributed by Films for the Humanities and Sciences.

William Shakespeare, *A Midsummer Night's Dream* (1968), 124 min. Royal Shakespeare Company, directed by Peter Hall. With Helen Mirren, Diana Rigg, David Warner, Ian Richardson, Judy Dench, Ian Holm, and Peter McEnery. Distributed by Facets Multimedia and Drama Classics Video.

William Shakespeare, *A Midsummer Night's Dream* (1935), 35 min. Directed by Max Reinhardt. With Olivia de Havilland, Dick Powell, James Cagney, Mickey Rooney, and Joe E. Brown; music by Mendelssohn and choreography by Nijinska and Got. Distributed by Key Video.

Ben Johnson, *Volpone* (1967), 90 min. 16 mm film. BBC production with Clive Revell and Eric Thompson. Sir Politic Would-be subplot cut. Distributed by BBC and Time-Life Film and Video.

PART IV: FRENCH NEOCLASSICAL AND ENGLISH RESTORATION DRAMA AND THEATER

Molière, *Le Misanthrope* (1986), 106 min. French with English subtitles. Distributed by Films for the Humanities and Sciences.

Comedy of Manners: Molière, *The Misanthrope* (1986), 52 min. Richard Wilbur's translation, with Edward Petherbridge. Distributed by Films for the Humanities and Sciences.

Jean Racine, *Phaedre* (1968), 93 min. With Marie Bell as Phaedre. In French with English subtitles. Distributed by Insight Media.

William Congreve, *The Way of the World* (1978), 59 min. Distributed by Films Inc.

PART V: MODERN DRAMA AND THEATER: BACKGROUNDS AND BEGINNINGS

Henrik Ibsen, *Hedda Gabler* (1980), 80 min. BBC production adapted by John Osborne. With Diana Rigg. Distributed by Films for the Humanities.

Henrik Ibsen, *Hedda Gabler* (1975), 102 min. Directed by Trevor Nunn. With Glenda Jackson and Timothy West. Distributed by Fox Video.

August Strindberg, *Miss Julie* (1990), 102 min. Royal Shakespeare Company. Distributed by Filmic Archives.

August Strindberg, *Miss Julie* (1951), 90 min. Directed by Alf Sjoberg. With Max von Sydow and Anita Bjork. In Swedish with English subtitles. Distributed by Nelson Entertainment.

Oscar Wilde, *The Importance of Being Earnest* (1952), 95 min. Directed by Anthony Asquith. With Michael Redgrave and Edith Evans. Distributed by DVC, Inc., and Paramount Home Video.

Oscar Wilde, *The Importance of Being Earnest* (1980), 99 min. BBC production. Distributed by Time-Life Film and Video.

George Bernard Shaw, *Major Barbara* (1941), 131 min. Directed by Gabriel Pascal. With Wendy Hiller, Rex Harrison and Robert Morley. Distributed by Learning Corporation of America and Filmic Archives.

Anton Chekhov, *The Cherry Orchard, Part I: Chekhov, Innovator of Modern Drama*, (1968) 21 min., and *Part II: Comedy or Tragedy?* (1967), 21 min. Key scenes with discussion by Norris Houghton of subtext and Chekhov's dramatization of interior action. Distributed by Britannica Films and Insight Media.

J. M. Synge, *Riders to the Sea* (1989), 47 min. Directed by Ronan O'Leary. With Geraldine Page, Amanda Plummer, and Barry McGovern. Distributed by Films for the Humanities and Sciences.

PART VI: MODERN EUROPEAN AND AMERICAN DRAMA AND THEATER: REACTIONS AND MODIFICATIONS

Arthur Miller, *The Crucible* (1996), 150 min. With Daniel Day-Lewis, Winona Ryder, and Joan Allen. Distributed by Insight Media.

Samuel Beckett (1989), 80 min. Uses Beckett's work to provide a biography of his life. Distributed by Films for the Humanities and Sciences.

Lorrainne Hansberry, *A Raisin in the Sun* (1961), 128 min. Directed by Daniel Petrie. With Sidney Poitier, Claudia McNeil, and Ruby Dee. Distributed by RCA/Columbia Pictures Home Video.

Lorrainne Hansberry, *A Raisin in the Sun* (1989), 171 min. Directed by Bill Duke. With Danny Glover, Esther Rolle, and Starletta duPois. Distributed by Fries Home Video.

Luigi Pirandello, *Six Characters in Search of an Author* (1978), 52 min. Distributed by Films Inc.

Luigi Pirandello, *Six Characters in Search of an Author* (1977), 60 min. BBC production with a condensed version of Act I. Distributed by Insight Media.

Bertolt Brecht (1989), 55 min. A biographical portrait of Brecht through his works. Distributed by Films for the Humanities and Sciences.

Gisela May: Reflections on the Theater of Brecht (1979), 30 min. Gisela May of the Berliner Ensemble performs excerpts from Brecht's plays. Distributed by the New York State Education Department.

Eugene O'Neill, *The Emperor Jones* (1933), 72 min. With Paul Robeson, Duddly Digges, Fredi Washington, and Moms Mabley.

Arthur Miller, *The Crucible* (1957), 108 min. Directed by Raymond Rouleau. With Simone Signoret and Yves Montand. Distributed by Hen's Tooth Video.

Tennessee Williams, *Cat on a Hot Tin Roof* (1958), 108 min. Directed by Richard Brooks. With Paul Newman, Elizabeth Taylor, and Burl Ives. Distributed by Filmic Archives and MGM/UA Home Video.

Tennessee Williams, *Cat on a Hot Tin Roof* (1984), 148 min. Directed by Jack Hofsiss. With Jessica Lange, Tommy Lee Jones, and Rip Torn. Distributed by Vestron Video.

PART VII: CONTEMPORARY DRAMA AND THEATER

Harold Pinter, *The Dumb Waiter* (1987), 60 min. Directed by Robert Altman. With John Travolta and Tom Conti. Distributed by Prism Entertainment.

Wole Soyinka (1985), 50 min. Interview with Soyinka, who discusses political and cultural life in Africa and the United States. Distributed by the Roland Collection.

Tom Stoppard, *Rosencrantz and Guildenstern Are Dead* (1991), 117 min. With Gary Oldman, Tim Roth, and Richard Dreyfuss. Distributed by Buena Vista Home Video.

Sam Shepard, *True West* (1984), 110 min. Directed by Allan Goldstein. With John Malkovitch and Gary Sinise. Distributed by Academy Entertainment.

Marsha Norman, *'night, Mother* (1986), 97 min. Directed by Tom Moore. With Sissy Spacek and Anne Bancroft. Dist. by MCA/Universal Home Video.

Tina Howe, *Painting Churches* (1985), 89 min. Distributed by Turber Home Entertainment.

Manuel Puig, *Kiss of the Spider Woman* (1985), 119 min. Directed by Hector Babenco. With William Hurt, Raul Julia, and Sonia Braga. Distributed by Facets.

August Wilson, *The Piano Lesson* (1992), 99 min. Distributed by Facets.

August Wilson (1994), 50 min. Interview with Bill Moyers about Wilson's plays as expressions of the African-American experience. Distributed by Films for the Humanities.

David Mamet, *Oleanna* (1995), 89 min. With William H. Macy and Debra Eisenstadt. Distributed by Hallmark Home Entertainment.

Credits

PLAYS

INTRODUCTION

Susan Glaspell, *Trifles,* Copyright 1916 by Susan Glaspell. Reprinted with the permission of the Estate of Susan Glaspell.

PART I: GREEK DRAMA AND THEATER

Aeschylus, *Agamemnon,* trans. Hugh Lloyd-Jones (New York: Prentice Hall, Copyright © 1970). Reprinted with the permission of the publishers.

Aristophanes, *Lysistrata,* trans. Dudley Fitts (New York: Harcourt Brace Jovanovich, Copyright © 1954 by Harcourt Brace & World. Renewed © 1982 by Cornelia Fitts, Daniel H. Fitts, and Deborah W. Fitts). Reprinted with the permission of the publishers.

Euripides, *Medea,* from *Three Plays of Euripides: Alcestis, Medea, The Bacchae,* trans. Paul Roche (New York: Norton, Copyright © 1974 by Paul Roche). Reprinted with the permission of the publishers. All rights reserved.

Sophocles, *Oedipus Rex,* trans. Dudley Fitts and Robert Fitzgerald (New York: Harcourt Brace Jovanovich, 1949). Copyright 1949 by Harcourt Brace & World and renewed © 1977 by Cornelia Fitts and Robert Fitzgerald. Reprinted with the permission of the publishers.

PART II: MEDIEVAL DRAMA AND THEATER IN ENGLAND

Quem Quaeritis Trope, from J. Q. Adams, *Chief Pre-Shakespearean Dramas* (New York: Houghton-Mifflin, 1924).

The Wakefield Master, *The Second Shepherds' Play,* from John C. Coldewey, ed., *Early English Drama, An Anthology* (New York: Garland Publishing, 1993).

Anonymous, *Everyman,* from John C. Coldewey, ed., *Early English Drama, An Anthology* (New York: Garland Publishing, 1993).

PART III: RENAISSANCE DRAMA AND THEATER IN ENGLAND

Christopher Marlowe, *Dr. Faustus,* from Russell A. Fraser and Norman Rabkin, eds., *English Drama of the Renaissance, I: The Tudor Period* (New York: Macmillan, Copyright © 1976 by Macmillan Publishing Company). Reprinted with the permission of the publishers.

William Shakespeare, *A Midsummer Night's Dream,* from Oscar Campbell, ed., *The Living Shakespeare* (New York: Macmillan, Copyright © 1949 by Macmillan Publishing Company, renewed © 1975 by Robert F. Campbell, Eunice C. Goodale, and Emily F. C. Meyer). Reprinted with the permission of the publishers.

William Shakespeare, *Hamlet,* from Oscar Campbell, ed., *The Living Shakespeare* (New York: Macmillan, Copyright © 1949 by Macmillan Publishing Company, renewed © 1975 by Robert F. Campbell, Eunice C. Goodale, and Emily F. C. Meyer). Reprinted with the permission of the publishers.

Ben Johnson, *Volpone,* from Russell A. Fraser and Norman Rabkin, eds., *English Drama of the Renaissance, II: The Stuart Period* (New York: Macmillan, Copyright © 1976 by Macmillan Publishing Company). Reprinted with the permission of the publishers.

PART IV: FRENCH NEOCLASSICAL AND ENGLISH RESTORATION DRAMA AND THEATER

Molière, *The Misanthrope,* trans. Richard Wilbur (New York: Harcourt, Brace, Copyright © 1954, and renewed by Richard Wilbur). Reprinted with the permission of the publishers.

Jean Racine, *Preface to Phaedra* and *Phaedra,* trans. R. C. Knight (Edinburgh: Edinburgh University Press,

Copyright © 1971 by R. C. Knight). Reprinted with the permission of the publishers.

William Congreve, *The Way of the World,* from Louis Kronenberger, ed., *Cavalcade of Comedy* (New York: Simon & Schuster, 1953). Reprinted with the permission of the Estate of Louis Kronenberger.

PART V: MODERN EUROPEAN DRAMA: BACKGROUNDS AND BEGINNINGS

Henrik Ibsen, *Hedda Gabler,* from Otto Reinert; trans. and ed., *Drama: An Introductory Anthology* (Boston: Little Brown, 1961 with changes by the translator (1995). Copyright © 1961, 1995 by Otto Reinert. Reprinted with the permission of the translator.

August Strindberg, *Miss Julie,* trans. Harry Carlson (Berkeley: University of California Press, Copyright © 1983). Reprinted with the permission of the publishers.

Anton Chekhov, *The Cherry Orchard,* trans. Constance Garnett (London: Chatto & Windus, Copyright © 1925). Reprinted with the permission of the publishers.

George Bernard Shaw, *Preface to Major Barbara* and *Major Barbara,* from *Plays* (New York: W. H. Wise & Co., 1930), vol. XI, by permission of The Public Trustees as Executor for George Bernard Shaw. Reprinted with the permission of the publishers.

PART VI: MODERN EUROPEAN AND AMERICAN DRAMA: REACTIONS AND MODIFICATIONS

Luigi Pirandello, *Six Characters in Search of an Author,* trans. Edward Storer, from *Plays* (New York: E. P. Dutton, Copyright © 1922 by E. P. Dutton, renewed 1950 by Stefano, Fausto, and Lietta Pirandello). Reprinted with the permission of the publishers.

Bertolt Brecht, *Mother Courage and Her Children,* trans. Ralph Manheim, from John Willett and Ralph Manheim, eds., *Bertolt Brecht, Collected Plays* (New York: Vintage Books, 1972), vol. 5.

Arthur Miller, *The Crucible* (New York: Viking-Penguin, 1976). Copyright 1952, 1953, 1954, and renewed © 1980 by Arthur Miller. Reprinted with the permission of the publishers.

Tennessee Williams, *Cat on a Hot Tin Roof* (New York: New Directions, 1955). Copyright 1954, 1955, 1971, 1975 by Tennessee Williams. Reprinted with the permission of the publishers.

Samuel Beckett, *Endgame* (New York: Grove Press, 1958). Copyright © 1958 by Grove Press, renewed 1986 by Samuel Beckett. Reprinted with the permission of the publishers.

Lorraine Hansberry, *A Raisin in the Sun* (New York: Random House, 1959). Copyright © 1959, 1966, 1984 by Robert Nemiroff. Reprinted with the permission of the publishers.

PART VII: CONTEMPORARY DRAMA AND THEATER

Harold Pinter, *The Dumb Waiter* (New York: Grove Press, Copyright © 1960). Renewed 1980 by Harold Pinter. Reprinted with the permission of the publishers.

Wole Soyinka, *The Strong Breed,* from *Wole Soyinka: Five Plays* (London: Oxford University Press, Copyright © 1964). Reprinted with the permission of the publishers.

Tom Stoppard, *Rozencrantz and Guildenstern Are Dead* (New York: Grove Press, 1967).

Clare Boothe Luce, *Slam the Door Softly* (New York: Dramatists Play Services, Copyright © 1971). Reprinted with the permission of the publishers.

Sam Shepard, *True West,* from *Sam Shepard, Seven*

Plays (New York: Bantam, Copyright © 1981). Reprinted with the permission of the publishers.

Marsha Norman, *'night, Mother* (New York: Farrar, Straus & Giroux, Copyright © 1983). Reprinted with the permission of the publishers.

Tina Howe, *Painting Churches,* from Emilie S. Kilgore, ed., *Contemporary Plays by Women* (New York: Prentice Hall, Copyright © 1991). Reprinted with the permission of the publishers.

Manuel Puig, *Kiss of the Spider Woman,* from *Kiss of the Spider Woman and Two Other Plays* (New York: Norton, 1994). Reprinted with the permission of the publishers.

CONTEXTS AND COMMENTARIES

PART I: GREEK DRAMA AND THEATER

PART II: MEDIEVAL DRAMA AND THEATER IN ENGLAND

PART III: RENAISSANCE DRAMA AND THEATER IN ENGLAND

PART IV FRENCH NEOCLASSICAL AND ENGLISH RESTORATION DRAMA AND THEATER

PART V: MODERN EUROPEAN DRAMA AND THEATER: BACKGROUNDS AND BEGINNINGS

PART VI: MODERN EUROPEAN AND AMERICAN DRAMA AND THEATER: REACTIONS AND MODIFICATIONS

PART VII: CONTEMPORARY DRAMA AND THEATER

ILLUSTRATIONS
PART I: GREEK DRAMA AND THEATER

Theater of Dionysus, phase III, from Richard and Helen Leacroft, *Theatre and Playhouse* (London: Methuen, 1984), p. 14, fig. 28.

PART II: MEDIEVAL DRAMA AND THEATER IN ENGLAND

Reconstruction of the stage for *The Castle of*

sion of Houghton Mifflin Company.

The Martyrdom of St. Appolonia, ca. 1452–1456 by Jean Fouquet.

Perseverance, from Richard Southern. Adams, Joseph Quincy. *Chief Pre-Shakespearean Dramas*, Copyright© 1924 by Joseph Quincy Adams. Copyright renewed 1952 by Helen Banks Adams. Reprinted with permis-

PART III: RENAISSANCE DRAMA AND THEATER IN ENGLAND

Johannes de Witt's drawing of the Swan Theater (ca.

1596). Courtesy of Bibliotheek dei Rijksuniversiteit, Utrecht, Netherlands.

Photograph of a reconstruction of an unidentified theater designed by Inigo Jones, from Richard and Helen Leacroft, *Theatre and Playhouse* (London: Methuen, 1984), p. 65, fig. 108.

PART IV: FRENCH NEOCLASSICAL AND ENGLISH RESTORATION DRAMA AND THEATER

Interior and exterior of Davennant's The Duke's Theater in Lincoln's Inn Fields, from Robert Wilkinson,

Londina Illustrata (London, 1819). Courtesy of the Folger Shakespeare Library.

Comedie Francaise, Paris, 1689, from Richard and

Helen Leacroft, *Theatre and Playhouse* (London: Methuen, 1984), p. 69, fig. 113.

PART V: MODERN EUROPEAN DRAMA AND THEATER: BACKGROUNDS AND BEGINNINGS

Interior of the English Opera House from Robert Wilkinson, *Londina Illustrata* (London, 1819). Courtesy of the Folger Shakespeare Library.

The Little Theater, New York, from Richard and Helen Leacroft, *Theatre and Playhouse* (London: Methuen, 1984), p. 138, fig. 209.

PART VI: MODERN EUROPEAN AND AMERICAN DRAMA AND THEATER: REACTIONS AND MODIFICATIONS

Shakespeare Memorial Theatre, Stratford-upon-

Avon, from Richard and Helen Leacroft, *Theatre and Playhouse* (London: Methuen, 1984), p. 157, fig. 229.